BENEATH THE HARVEST MOON

The National Library of Poetry

Diana Zeiger, Editor

BENEATH THE HARVEST MOON

Beneath the Harvest Moon

Library of Congress
Cataloging in Publication Data

ISBN 1-57553-063-5

Proudly manufactured in The United States of America by
Watermark Press
One Poetry Plaza
11419 Cronridge Dr., Suite 10
Owings Mills, MD 21117

Editor's Note

Infinite. Endless. Unlimited. These words rarely fail to capture the imagination; indeed, they are its very essence. Throughout the ages, philosophers, mathematicians, scientists, and artists of all types have attempted to characterize infinity, a concept which can never be truly represented, simply because a representation in itself must be finite. But as long as people can ever dream or create, the notion of infinity will continue to challenge our imaginations.

The popularity of science fiction, and especially science fiction whose subject is space travel, is evidence of just how fascinated we are by the limitless possibilities of the universe. In fact, *Star Trek*, a science fiction favorite the world over for decades, has created a race of characters, the Vulcans, whose very credo is "Infinite diversity in infinite combinations." This motto counsels tolerance of others' differences, be they physical, mental, political, or cultural; in addition, it is a reminder of the existence of these differences.

Although we have yet to make contact with beings from outer space, there is enough variety here on Earth to make such a reminder relevant, even necessary. In the case of Art, especially, the theory of "infinite diversity in infinite combinations" is paramount — it is the very wellspring of creativity. And it is just this notion which makes an anthology such as *Beneath the Harvest Moon* such a joy to produce as well as to read: each poet's 'take' on a particular subject is as unique as the sum of his or her own personal experiences, beliefs, and opinions.

For example, there is John Kelso's "Speculations on a Martian Desert" (p. 1) This poem explores the idea of human imagination, as well as the (often futile) attempts to make real the products of imagination. In the poem, Kelso reflects upon the mysteries of Mars. Even though Mars is closer to the Earth than any other planet, we still know relatively little about it, and consequently have devised many theories to explain its secrets. Giovanni Virginio Schiaparelli (1835-1910), who is referred to in line 12 of the poem, discovered the canals on the surface of Mars, which were later revealed to be optical illusions; these 'canals' have often been thought to be remnants of the work of an advanced civilization. Some have proposed that an ancient human civilization, perhaps Atlantis, may have been responsible — they suggest that this long-gone society had developed the means for space travel and perhaps journeyed to Mars. Kelso muses upon this possibility in the following lines:

Perhaps our pale long shadows descended
once here, commanding some grandiose ark
whose memory in Egyptian ash ended
in Napoleon's maze of rubied conquest.

His use of the word "Egyptian" is also an allusion to the theory that the ancient Egyptians may have been aliens or had alien contacts. Offered by those who believe that it would have been impossible to build the pyramids given the technology of the time, this rationale suggests that ancient Egyptian society had some otherworldly aid in erecting those structures. Perhaps these same aliens landed on the surface of Mars as well, so the theory supposes, and left behind similar evidence of their presence:

We think rubber scalps and nickel bellies
brought their hand and zeal to their very best, . . .

The "rubber scalps and nickel bellies" are indicative of the traditonal representation of aliens as bald creatures with either metallic skin or metallic clothing.

Still, despite the relentless hypothesizing and the numerous attempts to prove that these suppositions are true, we have yet to find credible evidence to back them up:

Yet ninety years and thirty Schiaparellis
found no seed of trace, canals nor fortress. . . .

Try as we might, reality cannot put a damper on the tendency of the human mind to indulge in fanciful speculation.

With "Speculations on a Martian Desert," John Kelso has demonstrated an ability to express truly profound thoughts, combined with a clear mastery of poetic technique — note the vividness of the images, the careful choice of words, and the completely unforced rhyme scheme. The judges of the contest held in connection with *Beneath the Harvest Moon* took all of these attributes into consideration, and awarded this poem the Grand Prize.

Returning to more earthly matters, Jeff Fret's "A Tributary To You" (p.430) uses water imagery to illustrate the mercurial nature of thought and personality. Even the overall shape of the poem is fluid, with its curves reminiscent of the flow of a river, or perhaps the trail of a teardrop. According to the poem, it is only possible to capture but a small and random portion of whatever others present to us:

How to capture
a meandering
thought —
cup a draught
of understanding
from the spattering
of whatever drops?. . .

The persona ponders how best to accomplish this, and along the way, Fret achieves many graceful and clever turns of phrase; for example, the use of the word "arraigning, " (a play on 'rain,'), and the alliterative potency of "transient transparency." When read aloud, the verbal flow of the poem also mimics the flow of a body of water: in the beginning, the language is slower, without a distinct rhythm; but in the second verse, the staccato feel of the words and the more precise rhymes propel the poem faster, almost in the manner of a river's rapids. Even the title of the poem is a play on words that neatly represents its clever nature.

In a more serious vein, Bonnie Miranda's "Quickening" (p. 346) deals with what appears to be the termination of a pregnancy and its effects upon a relationship. Violent, terrifying images ("Voiceless, blind, the spastic fish retracts. . . .", "slamming into oxygen,. . .", "Draining onto metal, it claims its Ziploc home. . . .") convey the horror of the experience. Its nightmare quality is enhanced in that the remaining two characters

. . .wake to their bodies alone,
twisting feline out of the bedclothes, lost.

Although there was only one literal death in this case ("the parasite bastard will die as the dove"), each player in this drama loses something which can never be recovered: one will forget that there was ever any pleasure in this relationship, while the other will deny that there was a relationship at all. It seems, also, that the survivors grieve for different reasons: the one mourns for both the lost child and for what " 'should have been,' "; while the other grieves only for herself and for what has already happened.

The title of the poem has a twofold meaning: literally, "quickening" is the moment at which fetal movement becomes perceptible, but, in an ironic twist, it can also mean "a restoration of life." After reading this poem, one wonders to what sort of life the two survivors have been restored.

Another poem which contemplates the aftermath of a death is Gregory Lauck's

"Thoughts From The Third Rail," (p. 35) though the death in this case is the death of a relationship, not that of a person. The persona who narrates this poem is a mass of conflicting feelings:

> *I awoke in a chokehold from the sorrow of premature goodbyes*
> *to a woman who was giving me space to get to know someone I'd already*
> *begun to hate.*

He wants the relationship to end, yet he doesn't; he loves her, yet he hates her. After the persona meditates on the history of the romance, he reaches a conclusion about how best to deal with the situation: he decides to cut himself off from all feelings in order to elude pain. He decides to "avoid the message/behind green m and m's and Barry White, and do everything 'iced.' " He hopes that in numbing himself, he will never be forced to confront his pain; the loss of pleasure is a small price to pay if he can just stop hurting.

There are many other exceptional poems in *Beneath the Harvest Moon,* including: Phyllis Grover's "The Dream Maker" (p. 252), Jim Head's "A Song For Enzo" (p. 167), Jane Huntzicker's "X" (p. 377), Nancy G. Oxman's "In This Corner" (p. 230), Bob Russell's "Robin Ascending" (p. 452), Violeta San Juan's "The Hands That Knit" (p. 292), and L. M. Young's "South End Optimism" (p. 525). Please be certain to take special note of these poems as you read through this anthology.

Every poem published in *Beneath the Harvest Moon* is worthy of commendation. I wish that time and space permitted a detailed examination of each and every work. However, as this is not possible, I can only salute and thank all of you who took the time to put pen to paper and to share your creativity with us.

I would also like to thank the staff at The National Library of Poetry. This anthology is the culmination of the efforts of numerous individuals whose contributions were vital to the production of *Beneath the Harvest Moon.* I am profoundly grateful to all the editors, judges, graphic and layout artists, customer service and data entry operators, and office administrators who participated in the production of this publication.

Congratulations to all those featured in *Beneath the Harvest Moon.* I hope you will enjoy reading it as much as I have enjoyed editing it.

Diana Zeiger, Editor

Cover Art: Tracy Hetzel

iv

Grand Prize Winner

John Kelso/Schwetzingen, Germany

Second Prize

Jeff Fret/Toronto, Ontario
Phyllis Grover/Santa Fe, NM
Jim Head/East York, Ontario
Jane Huntzicker/Ann Arbor, MI
Gregory Lauck/Oak Park, IL

Bonnie Miranda/Taneytown, MD
Nancy Oxman/Havertown, PA
Bob Russell/Easthampton, MA
Violeta San Juan/Hamilton, Ontario
L. M. Young/Saint John, New Brunswick

Third Prize

L. Lee Abelard/New York, NY
Baloian/Half Moon Bay, CA
E. C. Barton/Vancouver, British Columbia
Rachel Bennett/Rock Island, IL
Rebecca Bernemann/Clear Lake, IA
Sonia Bodnar/Edmonton, Alberta
Brenda Bottas/Regina, Saskatchewan
Audrey Botz/Oshkosh, WI
Julie Bowring/Irving, TX
Carey Buczwinski/Appleton, WI
Katherine Carlton/Mechanicsville, VA
Jane Cass/Bayside, NY
William Champion/Oxford, MS
Dragos Chima/Saint Laurent, Quebec
David Clair/Pittsburgh, PA
Ann Cosh/Fort Saskatchewan, Alberta
Krzystof Dabrowiecki/Byron, CA
Michael DeMicco/Westminster, CO
Richard Eichman/Union Bridge, MD
Heather Fortinberry/Los Angeles, CA
Karl Gordon/Nepean, Ontario
Malise Graham/Shawnee Msn KS
Frederick Hanna/Baltimore, MD
Bruce Irvine/Middleburg, FL
Andrew Jasie/Rochester, NY
Marko Kiansten/Victoria, British Columbia
Merle Kinne/Long Beach, CA
Itala Langmar/Kenilworth, IL
Lois MacDonald/Etobicoke, Ontario
Janis Matuga/San Antonio, TX

Ev McTaggart/Niagara-on-the-Lake, Ontario
Tatiana Mudrak/Park Ridge, IL
Edith Murray/Texarkana, TX
Jeannette Okamura/Kaneohe, HI
Mary-Frazier Paul/Fort Pierce, FL
Maya Payne/Lawrence, KS
Patrick Penland/Bellingham, WA
Howard Peterson/Bothell, WA
Lela Peterson, Phoenix, AZ
Clare Petrany/New Westminster, British Columbia
Marian Prochnik/Fairfax, VA
Tony Ravelo/Miami, FL
Susan Rowland/Cincinnati, OH
Paul Sandison/Bath, England
Marion Sargeant/Key Largo, FL
Ruth Shireman/Dubuque, IA
Thomas Shoemake/Commerce, TX
Anita Shumake/Parkersburg, WV
Karen Sigl/Green Bay, WI
Gerald Somers/Green Bay, WI
Taryn Stewart/Little Rock, AR
Teri Strain/Omemee, Ontario
Marsha Strawser/Sacramento, CA
Ruth Strong/Redding, CA
W. Turner/Santa Fe Springs, CA
Larry Vandervert/Spokane, WA
John Vaught/Springfield, VA
Victoria Vu/Durham, CT
Sarah Walters/Seattle, WA

Congratulations also to our Editor's Choice Winners!

Speculations On A Martian Desert

There is deathless humor about these winds
without air which only pink crystal sand
can inhale. The thought of life makes us wince
at sixty histories of threats unmanned,
doomed before the fire that they cannot spark.
Perhaps our pale long shadows descended
once here, commanding some grandiose ark
whose memory in Egyptian ash ended
in Napoleon's maze of rubied conquest.
We think rubber scalps and nickel bellies
brought their hand and zeal to their very best,
yet ninety years and thirty Schiaparellis
found no seed of trace, canals nor fortress.
But the turtle sands still slip their ancient
undertow, burying the frozen mistress
Mars in bed, her infertile womb translucent.

John Kelso

Grand Prize
Winner

My Little One

My little one - don't hurry so.
You've lots of time in which to grow.
Don't race so madly up that hill -
You'll get there too - by standing still.
My little one don't rush the years -
You'll know too soon the taste of tears.
Don't strain your little legs to climb -
You'll stand alone a long long time.
Ah! Little one do this for me -
Be young as you were meant to be.
Don't strain against your childhood bars -
Just be the child I never was!

Evelyn J. Blackstone

Just You And I

A Beauty such as
yours should never be ignored
but instead be adored, like
winds of ancient times a love
like yours could never be unkind.
As I watch the sunset between
two sea's I think to myself no one
is as lucky as me.
No one is so lucky to see such
beauty in thee as me. From your long
silky brown hair, to your sweet and gentle
voice that reminds me of an angel playing
a harp in mid-air, floating to the North.
Now as the sight and smell
of fire and brim-stone fill the night
air, I notice the outline of the sky,
I think of a time when there was just you and I.
Thinking of how our love has lasted these years,
and knowing in a few short tears that we will meet
in the sky, and it will be just you and I.

John Walter Tackett II

"My Goodnight Prayer"

You're the queen of my heart,
You're the love of my soul.
You're the keeper of my feelings,
As you well know;
Your face is imprinted in my mind to keep,
As I lay my head on my pillow,
Each night to sleep.

Bill Noble

You're Free, You're Free

You're free to spread your wings and fly...
Your wings are like no others, they are strong and wide
They will take you to heights to which you've never known
Like a Phoenix out of the ashes of ruin, you'll fly high
As high as your dreams will go.
YOU'RE FREE YOU'RE FREE
You're free to spread your wings and soar.
As you fly above the nest, you'll experience the best
As you soar through the clouds, you'll have no regrets
You'll have no fear of new places,
Only sadness when leaving old faces
Faces that wish you well,
Standing below with support and admiration.
YOU'RE FREE YOU'RE FREE
You're free to spread your wings and go!

Jeannie King

Honey, Let's Have A Family

Honey, it's so nice, just to know we belongs together.
Your love is mine, my love is yours,
Honey, it will be yours forever,
Honey, if that's true, then honey, let's have a family,
   yes honey, I give my love to you,
You give your love to me, let's give our love
   to a sweet little family.

Honey, lets have a family.

How nice to know, my dream lover.
My Secret treasure, will be my only pleasure,
Now and forever, please honey, let's have a sweet,
   little family, just a nice, little family,
Makes my dream come true, makes my dream
So sweet, so,—complete.
Please honey, let's have a sweet, nice, little family.

Evon Clarke

When...

Life seems hard in times like these
Your health has gone all wrong
But understand that I'm still here
To help you stand up strong
So many friends you thought you had
Wined and dined them; you always paid
But now they no longer come around
Since they learned that you have AIDS
Often as I watch you I feel so helpless too
So this poem to you I bring
Thought you had many friends living far and near
But now your telephone won't ring
When you feel that you can't go on
When you feel that all hope is gone
When you feel that your life is through
God and I care, we will always be there for you
Life seems hard in times like these
Your health has gone all wrong
I'm not afraid my friend, understand
God and I are here, take my hand.

Adonis V. Sharpe

In Darkness Left Again

I wait for your knock,
Your footsteps in the dark.
I imagine your journey, rushing, cold and tired.
You hoping I will be as you remember, smiling and warm.
Too many hours apart,
Too far away to be peaceful.
I see you shiver in the night.
I delve into your thoughts,
A clear mind yet anxious to end the journey.
Not forever though,
You will leave asking me to wonder more about thoughts,
Making the journey once again.

KNOCK,
You startled me.
Rest and prepare your journey home.

Erin Elizabeth Robinson

Love?

"Love, what is it really?
Your first crush on the boy next door?
Or the love for that certain someone,
That can't be touched...?
Love, is it the feelings of friends, maybe
Even more than friends, that can't
be expressed into words or actions?
No one can describe their feelings of love;
Until that day comes.
A girl and boy, both friends forever until
a love comes between them and they have
to choose.
Will it be their friendship, or will a new
relationship of love, blossom like a rose
in spring?
Love, what is it really?
Love's a feeling that can't be expressed
or shared without the one you love..."

Andrea Scalfani

The King Of Surf Land

As you walk the sandy beach,
Your every dream's within your reach.
You know your body is brown with tan,
You'll hit the beach whenever you can.
Your hair so blond, so wavy too,
You know the girls look up to you.
And when the pounding surf you ride,
You'll have your favorite by your side.
And we all know when you're filled with joy,
It's when you're surfing young surfer boy.

Jerry F. Pollock

Remembrance

Cascading through the kaleidoscope of my reflections
you will always be there.
Entwined into the fabric of my thoughts
So as the sweet bird sings his mindless chatter,
in the shimmering light of summer, in the early
morn, or the fallen leaves rustle and crunch
underfoot, you are there.
As the snow falls in its heavy silence whistling and
whirling you are in its mist in the shrouds and eaves
of my memory forever.

Gay M. Lingar

Hide

Why do you hide your feelings inside
You should be proud about the love we found

My love for you is real, nothing to kill
I never lied so why do you hide

Why do you hide your fear down inside
Don't be afraid, I'm always the same

Don't ever fear I'm always here
My love is true, only for you

Please don't hide the things in your life
I really care, so please don't be scared

The things you should learn from this little rhyme
is just never hide anything inside

So don't ever hide the things in your head
'Cause you might end up dead with your thoughts never said

Harry Graham

"I Didn't Know You"

I didn't know you Precious One,
You were taken so quickly, you were so young.

Ahead in your future, no telling what you would be!
A president, a preacher, or even a part of my family.

Your Mom and your Dad, for you, had such a great plan,
Only to be destroyed by the evil of man.

God didn't want to make us sad or blue,
He only saw how much Heaven needed you.

The world He made in His perfect way,
Has only become more wicked with each passing day.

He knew that by taking you,
It would show us what we are to do.

To have more love and more compassion,
Just the way His world was fashioned.

Yes! My Dear One, I'm sorry that we never met,
But one thing is certain and you can bet.

It changed more hearts, all over this Earth,
To show us the value, that friends and families are worth.

So thank you dear Precious one, for your life so shortly ended,
I'll meet you in heaven , where all broken hearts will be mended.

Brenda S. Fears

Inseparable

As I read it, I could feel my eyes.
You were open, and honest.
When I thought about it, it hurt like a wound.
You wrote of confusion, and pain.
I felt helpless. Useless. Man impotente.
I knew there was nothing I could do.
I knew your words were not
   going to magically change.
I read your sorrow, and felt its loneliness.
I hurt knowing where I could not be.
Why I could not help.
My thoughts continued. Unconcentrated.
I had no desire to move.
There I faded; alone; with your letter.
There I ached; wanting to have been
   wrong. Misled. Unastute.
And there I realized the utter truth.
Bare. Honest. Untouchable.
Nothing could ever come
   between us.

Amy L. Monastero

The Bridge

Goodbye, old friend dear bridge. You've been there a long time
You were built near a century ago. Oh how your span did shine.
My grandmother was there when you first opened. Oh what a wonder
you were. Time took her as it has done you too, but this
somehow I think we always knew could happen to you.
For years you carried us on your back as we crossed the great
St. Johns. Safely you guided us high up from the darkness below.
Never asking in what direction we were wanting to go.
We took you for granted, because you were always there. We
Traveled on you, back and forth without ever a care. Somehow I guess
we thought that you would always be there. In time your paint
would peel and rust would attack your steel, but your foundation
stood fast. We thought we could make you last. Now it seems
that time has caught up with you old friend. Your time is at its end.
I will miss your manly beauty and the strength that you have
given. Goodbye old friend dear bridge your memory will not
be forgotten and your death shall not be forgiven.

Charles Thomas Sams Jr.

4

Unconditional Love

(Dedicated to L. McIntosh)
I could never ask for anyone more devoted,
You were always there for me.
Through it all you bore my pain
You were my eyes, my ears, my very soul.
I could not tell you how much it hurt
To see the sorrow in your eyes.
I silently prayed that peace would come
To end the burden you bore.

I wanted to say good-bye
But you knew it was only so long...
Thank you for being there!

God knows, you did your best
I could not have asked for more
There will be many a star in your crown
When you sit on our Father's throne.

Blossom R. Latty

A Dream

Unexpectedly you appear in my dream.
You smile at me, and this makes me glad.
I run across the field to touch you,
But you vanish, and this makes me sad.

Breathless and trembling I awake with a start.
In the quiet room I look for visions
from my dream.
But what I see flirting on the wall
Is a single, brilliant moonbeam.

I sit and think of you, and I feel safe and strong.
I wonder why we are separated by death,
And I wonder why I could not touch you,
Though I was close enough to feel
your warm breath.

Carmela VanMeter

To My Mom

When I was little,
You showed me the way,
And made me what I am today.
For all your guidance, caring and love,
I thank my lucky stars above.
I caused you problems years ago,
For that I am sorry, I hope you know.
You taught me how to stand on my own.
If only then, I wish I'd known.
There would be times when I was mad at you,
For little things you made me do.
But you were always there for me,
Yet let me be what I wanted to be.
I love you more than words can say.
And learn new things from you each day.
You're someone on whom I can depend,
You're not only my mother, you're my friend.
And I hope that someday I will be,
As a good mother as you are to me.

Carole Ashley

"Salt Water Dreams"

I day dream of sunny days, peaceful oceans, sandy shores
Where whispers glisten in the waves
Where my eyes are squinted from the suns rays
Where life amounts to lazy days
I couldn't ask for more
Sand castles fill my head
Nothing heard, nothing said
Softwoven beaches, blue skies, and me
Salt water dreams till eternity

Joy Canaday

Vahid

The demons were closing in; life growing darker and darker.
You saw no possibility of hope-
  you never even looked.
The warmth of love you could not feel,
  yet you were surrounded by our embrace.
Help was beyond your reach, but lying at your fingertips.

So you took care of the despair;
You thought you were eliminating the problem.
Now there is no hope,
        no love,
        no help,
And the demons are multiplying.
Maybe not for you, perhaps God has forgiven.
But for those who remain, the demons,
                the questions,
                the tears,
Face us in your memory each day.

As time passes we will accept the way you left
And remember only you.
Until then our hearts will break,
        our minds will rage,
        our throats will choke,
On the imagery of your departure.
But regardless of the time, you will always be loved.

Jennifer L. C. McDowell

Hold My Hand

"Hold my hand"
  You said with the single sparkle that remained in your eyes
Your voice had long failed and no longer could I hear it calling my name

I held your limp hand as tight as I could...
  willing my own strength to pull you back to life...

While I sat there in the midst of now silent monitors and IV's
  I was swept back...
    back to the days you were so full of life

You'd stay up all night just to see the sun rise
We'd talk for hours...
  about nothing...
    about everything...

As long as we were together....

These last few months have been the hardest
You were the strong one
Since you entered this hole of electronics and doctors who
  "hold the keys to life"
I am left to be strong

Amy Bartlett

Father

Throughout the years you've led us with a gentle guiding hand
You never questioned what we did, but always tried to understand.
You gave us all strong values, you taught us to be proud
With each of our accomplishments you applauded strong and loud.
What a wonderful father you were to all of us in each and every way
You lived your life to the fullest and encouraged us to do the same.
Your spirit will be with each one of us every moment of our lives
And when something has gone amiss with us we'll look into the skies.
When we see the bright sunshine lighting up each gorgeous day, we know
you have knelt down with us and reminded us to pray.
We love you dad with all of our heart and can't wait to meet once more.
Thank you for all you have given us
Forever we are yours.

Diane Lellock

"A New Beginning"

You called me the other day saying
you missed me.
It's been a year since we were last
together.
I couldn't help but be surprised to
hear from you.
Because I never knew I could have a
second chance with you.
The things I done in the past to hurt
you so.
Never knowing you really loved me
I guess I was unsure at the time.
How can I be so blind to let you go the way
I did,
at the time it never mattered but I
realize now through the worst it
brought us back together, like a
new beginning, a new beginning
with you.

Jenny Razo

Great-Grandfather

Standing on the old porch
you look down into the yard.
The autumn wind bending the bare branches.
Yet again, the nest is empty.

The third summer is over.
The swallows have just left.
Once again the winter is coming.
Always heavier than the previous one.

Turning, you walk away.
Spring will come again,
the swallows will return,
and build yet another nest.
Different, yet so very much the same
but you will not witness it.

Walking away, a tear runs down a path,
and mingles with a smile.

Adamandia Dimopoulos

To A Dreamer

You live in a dream world
You live in a world that cannot be

You live in a dream world
Yet you don't change the things you see

Work towards one goal undivided
Then you might not get chided

But stop this dreaming else it stops you
And you die like grass, fade like dew

You'll always be one step behind
If you don't stop in time

Keep your mind turning
Keep the cobwebs out; don't stop learning

You only have less than a life to live
So give what's worth it all you can give

Heidi Bockus

Nuclear Destruction

I have travelled many miles. I have no face. I pity no one.
You know me, some of you love me, some hate me.
I brought sorrow to many. I leave destruction where-ever I go.
I'm on this world because you created me.
Destroying everything in my path.
I am the power of your impetuous creation.

Gladys Taylor

My Michael!

Dear Michael,
   You know I miss you, so why did you have to go.
You know you are so true to me, and that I love you so.
When you hurt me it seemed as if you did not care, I want you
back in my life the way you were before. Michael where did you
go, who did you run to because I sure know it was not me. Now
nothing really matters anymore. Michael I really love you and
I wanted you to know that and I wanted you to know that you
hurt me in a way no one has before.
   My Michael, my dearest Michael, how much I love you no one
will ever know but you and me.

P.S.

   I hope if you find a girl that you fall in love, she will
hurt you the way you hurt me. And that will make you remember
the way I felt when I was hurt.
So remember that if that does ever happen you will always have
a shoulder to cry on.

Cheyanna Davis

My Son

Your Dad and I divorced. You hurt.
You hurt more than we did
   And we told you that this
      Had nothing to do with you.
We just had to move on.

You hurt and there was nothing
   You could do to ease your pain.
Nothing to make it OK.
You just had to deal with it.

Now, you are doing this to me.
Your leaving has nothing to do with me.
I cannot make it right.
I have only to cry and deal with it.

Is this KARMA?
Do I have to experience the pain I caused?
Better now than in my next life
   When I have no idea
      Where the pain originated.
I will miss you, my son.

Bonnie J. Clark

Thankfulness

   We are thankful Father, for this day,
you have given us to seek your face.
Without you, in this life we live,
there would be, no way to feel.
You are there, when we need a helping hand.
You help us through life's troubled lands.
When we're in pain you hear our prayers and with your hands,
you take our cares. We rest in you with our heart content
and believe in your word that you have lent.
We wait on you day and night,
for your returning to make things right.
We're thankful for the forgiveness of our sins,
for without it our lives would end.
Amen

Deena Bryant

Dear Brother

The days of summer are nearby over, but
you found a way to make them last forever.
Each night beside you, from this moment on,
will be the warmth of the sun and a
reminder of a day in August.
She may not have watched you grow from childhood,
but she has been blessed with who you have become.
An Irish luck is with you both.
The Golden Dome has brought on a golden ring
and golden vows
and has given me another sister.
She is beautiful my brother.
I will miss you.
With Love,
Your Sister.

Bernadette Donovan

Untitled

If you could see you through my own eyes
You could drink of the beauty untamed, so alive

It burns from within you
So softly, so bright,
Warming my spirit
A delicious delight

It glows from without you
Unbridled, running free
With a life of its own
It reaches out, soothing me

Your heart always would quest
For this wonderful prize
If you could see you through my own eyes.

John C. Taylor

The End Of A Season Beginning Of Another

The snow is falling on the ground.
You cannot hear; it makes no sound.
Just like a mass of feathers snowy white.
Drifting, drifting, into the night.
Under the moon light soft and low,
The snow flakes fall; the north winds blow.
Always seeming to whisper near,
Fall is gone; winter is here.

Anne Carlson

My World Of Dreams

Dream on my world, as I would have
you be,
Full of love long past eternity.
The cares and woes of reality
Live in our lives endlessly.
O why are there tears and troubles galore,
In order to get the heaven's door?
To try to do right is so hard to do,
When others descend and devour you.
Tears of joy are very few, just about
a thimble full.
While tears of sorrow flood one's life,
And cry in the blanket of the night.
Dream on in a land of "Let's Pretend,"
Where the love we're seeking
has no end.

James S. Lamb

Because I Feel It In My Heart

Ever time I think of you
You are near but yet so far
I'm here for you because
I feel it in my heart
Each time we walk away
We feel sad in a special way
We know what is real
That's the times we share and feel
We've grown closer day by day
As the time slips away
We foresee what life's about
And that's the feelings we talk about
There is only one that I know
Who could understand and not ignore
For the love I have for you because I feel it in my heart

James Craig Henning

My Love, My Life

You my love
You are my life
You brought me flowers
and we talked till the wee hours
You my love
You are my life
You taught me to dance
and together we pranced
You my love
You are my life
You gave me a kiss
and we would forever caress
You my love
You are my life
You were with me for the good times and strife
You my love
You are my life, and now my love
You have left this life
but forever
You will be the love of my life

Donna L. Hadley

Sometimes

Sometimes I've just got to say, exactly how I feel and tell
You all to go to hell, and walk on up my hill.
You've told me what to say and do and even told me how,
I've scrapped and bowed and kissed your ass and still you
push me down.
Why can't you ever understand, I think all by myself, I
walk, I talk, and even laugh, but only by myself.
My life's become so lonely that I don't know what to do,
I think up dreams and re-live the past and pray that I get through.
I never thought I'd asked so much and though you never
know, love and understanding is very hard to show.

Carolyn Sue Allen

The Outsider

Do you know what it's like to be on the outside looking in;
Yet always thinking of what might have been?
This all began when I was only a child,
But through the years things seemed to run wild.
As I grew up there was a lot of hurt and pain
No matter what I did, no ground did I gain.
Having a family should be lots of good times to share:
For me it only brings more pain to bear.
I guess I'll go to my grave with my family unable to see
The real person that lives inside of me.

Janet Perez

"Lost Love"

As I soar above the explosions of clouds, like thousands of atom bombs
...yet with great serenity, I leave you behind my love. Because I
love you, I let you go.

As we climb higher... the depth of the earth almost disappears before
my eyes. Still higher, and higher... It appears as a city under water.
Have I found Atlantis? No, it's only a day dream...

I pass above this silver object in the sky... It is going from where
I came. It makes my heart weak to know that our journey may be complete.

We should have known, it was only a stepping stone. Two lonely
people thrown together by one of life's most difficult paths. Now
I leave you to go as you wish... to stand alone.

No more tears, no more fears, for I loved you with all my heart. As
I soar above the clouds, farther and farther away... Yes, I have
found Atlantis on that cloudy, dreary, day.

For the heavens are shining as I fly into eternity... into the blue majestic sky.

My darling, be happy, find love, as I soar through the clouds above...
To love you is to set you free.

                    Happiness and love always,
        Joann M. Dohler

One Little Flower

One little flower really isn't so much.
Yet, it can have a Midas touch,
Bringing cheer on a lonely day,
Or chasing someone's blues away.
A single blossom, like a friendly smile,
Can spread good cheer for at least a while;
And sometimes, in its own small way,
A flower can help a person to say
A thousand words that cannot be verbalized.
A million dreams can be thus realized.

A flower is such a friendly thing.
As graceful as ever a bird on the wing,
As soft as down, or the breeze, or the snow.
As lovely a creature as ever did grow.
Cultivated or wild, growing indoors or out,
Arranged in a pattern, or just scattered about,
Their pistils and petals and stamen and stems
Have been moulded by nature to form living gems.
But with all of their beauty and wonder and such,
It remains that a flower really isn't so much.

        Brian Jaybush

Yellow

Yellow is painful, like the sting of honey bees.
Yellow is sweet and tasty, like the taste of a twinkie.

Yellow is wild and free, like a tall giraffe.
Yellow is sometimes sour, like lemon juice coming in a carafe.

Yellow is struggling like the bus that takes me to Short Pump Middle.
Yellow is the wood that people like to whittle.

Yellow is the box that holds the traffic light.
Yellow is the smiley face that makes me feel all right.

Yellow is yucky and gritty, like when you fall into sand.
Yellow is fairly smooth, like Bart Simpson's hand.

Yellow is the locker that holds all my books.
Yellow is the police badge, complex in its looks.

Yellow is sweet and chewy like a gumball.
Yellow glides so well, like a leaf in the fall.

Yellow is the paper I use when passing post-it notes.
Yellow is warm, like an Eggo, going down my throat.

Yellow is bright, like the light of flash light.
Yellow is the color that makes me feel all right.

        David Duvigneaud

Who Are You? What's Your Name?

Who are you? What's your name?
Years fled ere (untouchable) you came.

I had prayed my Lord most wistfully
For someone to walk with through all Eternity.

One day you said if you were free—
Away we would go most joyfully!

But, Lord, I need someone to whom I could say,
"Remember when on that special day—?"

We would smile, laugh and love again
In that wondrous place where Love alone can reign.

Still, I'm glad you came.
I know you. I know your name.

        Doris Penrod

Time

   Time is a predator and we are its prey, it devours our youth,
wrinkles our skin and turns our hair gray. Time is an entity unique
in itself, it is not a wristwatch or a clock on the shelf. Time is
just time it can neither speed up or slow down, it is the events
within time that cause us to smile or to frown. Much like the wind
time cannot be seen, it has no color or odor but it surrounds each
and every being. It is the effects of time and the wind that are
visible to us, like the changing of seasons and leaves dancing on
branches, making such a terrible fuss. Time makes no enemies nor
does it make friends, nobody knows where it begins or it ends. Time
really does nothing it moves at its own pace, it is people who try
to put time into a space.

   Time is also a victim that we eagerly abuse, it is in many of the
excuses that we so commonly use. So many times we have heard people
say, "I ran out of time" or, "I have no time today." You know we all
do this with a clear conscience and no shame, for our lack of planning
it is time that we blame. Each day is so busy with not a minute to
spare but time doesn't worry and time doesn't care. Time would be
laughing if it had a face, for time knows there is no way we will ever
win this race. So who's chasing who can you tell me? The answer my
friends is not so easy to see. If you look all around you, you will
recognize each sign, what you see is the remains of the presence of time.

        David Hedberg

I Found It!

I am the man on the corner without a dream
Wrapped up in problems with low self-esteem.
Dropped out of school because it didn't meet my needs
Joined the "In Crowd" with motivation aimed to please.

Got caught up in the midst of self-destruction
No mind to listen or contribute to positive production.
Who cares what I do, who cares about me!
All people want these days are the "big bucks", you see.
Talk is cheap-peer pressure is steep
Can't find a role model that isn't a creep.

I have no place to go for a helping hand
No job possibilities, no education training or
guidelines to become a man.
But today, I can't use these accusations as a crutch
For I have all the opportunities I need in a
community that loves me so much!

        Ann M. Austin

If You Had Someone Special...

If you had someone special
Would you hide them in a box
And throw away the key
So that it never unlocks?

Would you show them to the world,
All their beauty that you treasure,
Reveal all their secrets,
Release every bit of pleasure?

Would you put them in a closet
Where there would be no light,
Or would you remove them from the darkness
And let them shine so bright?

Would you raise them on a pedestal
That was miles high
Where they'll touch the heavens
Where the angels fly?

If you had someone special,
Who do you wish it would be?
I pray to the Lord above,
I hope that you pick me.

Elizabeth M. Jesson

Pick Your Dream

If you could pick a dream, what would it be?
Would you be a Captain of a ship in the sea?
Or would you choose to meet a teddy bear?
Or maybe to be at a circus or fair?
It's your dream so you can choose,
To either win or to loose
But don't let your dream pass you by,
You can even learn to fly!
And when your dream's over,
Don't be blue,
'Cause there's good kids out there,
Who get good dreams like you!

Ashley Interlandi

Untitled

How do you explain the loss of a son
Words go unsaid things go undone
In his life he gave us such joy
In his death such pain.
And now he's gone our baby boy
We'll never see him again
What we wouldn't give if just once more
We could see him coming in or going
Out the door
To see his face his funny smile saying don't
worry folks I'll be back in awhile

So if there is anyone please
Tell me how do you explain the loss of a son

Daniel P. Sullivan

Untitled

Looking to the sky
With vision blurred by tears,
Watching my beloved dove.
I found no joy in her freedom and her flight
In spite of its beauty and delight,
If she does not return some day soon,
My mind will take wings
And in search of her will fly,
Leaving me here insane.
Looking to the skies.

Frederick A. Ashman

A Man's Prayer

He folds his hands in a silent prayer
wondering and hoping that God would forgive him
He knows in life he was very dim
He looks up as a tear escapes his eye
Sometimes I wonder why people lie
He sees a flash of light
His spirits are suddenly bright
"My son I forgive all." The Lord spoke
the man got to his feet and bowed his head
The Lord took his hand
The Lord led him to a far off land
"Remember son I created you and I love you."
The Lord's words were solemn and true
The man looked up at the Lord's face and
he suddenly felt what it was like to be alive.
"Go my son be happy." He whispered
The man knew then the meaning of life.

Christie Laird

Hate Turned Cold

The stone turned cold,
Without a notion of belief.
As he who drinks the dragons blood drinks without grief.
Those who may see do not see yet the truth,
That lies in the soul of the man with the child.
With no hope for the ones who will die in denial.
The stone turned cold.
The petal wilts as slow as the hour stays long,
To go alone and to not belong.
Simply forced with no words and to walk with no face,
The essence of hate may exist in the race.
With no true reason just doubt,
The stone turned cold.

Helen Allen

"My Baby Boy"

My baby boy with hair so light, how you bring me such delight!
With your skin so soft and eyes so dark and a smile that could
melt the coldest of hearts.

I look at you and see - the world through different eyes.
Everything is peaceful, innocent, and kind.

I look at you and see - all my hopes and dreams come true.
You're the baby I've always wished for, so precious and brand new!

I look at you and hope - the best will always come your way.
I hope the good morals that are passed on stay with you every day.

I'm sure you'll have your faults, like all of us do. But believe
in God and love and doing what is right will come naturally to you.

As I hold you in my arms and whisper wonderful things that will
be - you smell so sweet and feel so warm and already have a personality!

We'll have such fun every day! We'll read, laugh, and play!
And I'll always be here to help make the tears go away.

You've blessed my life in so many ways and brought me such
great joy! I love you so very much - my beautiful, sweet baby boy.

Jill M. Howard

O Love

'Tis you I will love with each given day.
With you I will stay for love will not stray.
By your side, I will never leave;
My heart with yours dares not deceive.

'Tis you, O Love, I will love with life,
Till time ceases, till wrong is right.
And when the future is a distant past,
Still near is my love for you to grasp.

For you, forever, I will love and care.
My love with yours is yours to share.
But if you find my love no longer a need,
I will stand aside and alone you will proceed.

Then at the end, life leaves each heart;
Only death will make us part.
Tho' still at death's beginning, we will love as before,
For our souls will grow and maybe - love more.

Emily Susan McFaddin

Why Did He Die?

Who can know the hearts of men?
With wars and rumors there is no end.
But the thing I cannot understand
Is why they killed the Son of Man.
From two rough poles the cross was made
On which our Savior's form was laid
With bruised back so cruelly beat
And nails driven through His hands and feet.
But from those lips not one moan or sob
Could be heard by that motley mob
Whose blood thirsty shouts of "crucify"
Doomed millions yet unborn to die.
For this He was to die, not for the things that He had done
But because He claimed to be God's son.
All mankind was changed that day, our Savior paid the price
Those cruel stripes He took for us, O what a sacrifice.
Dear Lord, forgive our sins, we pray; help us forever to be kind.
For when You were on that cruel cross, we were on Your mind.

Asa A. Cree

The Southern Desert

Mid-Summer solstice wishes away the night,
  with trembling, desert beauty smiles;
Distant mountain's lavender haze,
  reaches bluest of blue skies;
Summertide sound of reaching trees,
  showering white blossoms down;
A sultry sun blesses man and vine,
  bearing sweet fruit for the taking;
Twilight reposes in purple and orange,
  painting mountain shadows of rose;
Daytime wilts from the sun's heat,
  as it drowns in the Southern night;
Wild wind blows a fury near and far,
  shaking the twinkling stars;
Suddenly Heaven and Earth become one,
  welded by lightning and rumbles of thunder;
Summertime's thirst, now, quenched and washed,
  sleeps serenely in slumber 'til dawn.

Joan M. McCarthy

Moonlight

Have you awakened from your dreams in the late, late night
With the house invaded by a pale silver light?
Oh soft and pearly it fills the room
Putting you and the night gently in tune.
While out of the window the silver gold light
Has stilled and calmed the hunters of the night.
A soft gold light so glimmering that hence
The hunters of the day would not dare to commence.
With the night beautiful, gentle, serene;
How untempting the bed with its muddled dreams.
I sit by my window enjoying the sight,
And commune with the maker, Lord of day and night.

Josephine H. Kale

Black Lace On Blue Velvet

She stretches long slender bare arms
With the grace of a dancer's alluring charms.
Sometimes she stands in a motionless state,
But usually sways with a rhythmic gait.

So few will notice as they hasten by,
But against the blue velvet of a winter's sky
She continues to sway with such dignity—
This black lace silhouette of a slender tree.

Doris W. Wells

Why.......

Is there any wonder why man can live so long
  With so much Anger and Hatred inside.
Not willing to say hello or good-bye.
No wave, no smile, just frowns.

Is there any wonder why some lead Great lives
  And others Meaningless lives.
Always cheerful or Always depressed with thoughts of suicide.

My, oh my, one wonders and almost cries.
If only we realize our chances for Success and Happiness
  Lies in the Almighty one.
Are you Surprised?

I Wonder Why!

Angela Thomaston

That Old Oak Tree

Out there my friend now can't you see,
  with plenty of shade, that old oak tree.
Now there's the place you ought to be,
  out in that shade, believe you me.

Now don't you fret, and don't you whine,
  mark my word it's not a pine,
but it's the place for you to unwind,
  to throw your cares, old friend of mine.

But not in the fall when acorns come down,
  for they'll hit your head with a hurtin' pound.
So avoid that time so you won't frown
  'cause them acorns will fall all around.

But it ain't fall to my delight,
  so come with me to my favorite site.
Don't be afraid, it'll treat you right,
  under that oak tree, the breeze of delight.

Diane Plugge

A Fisherman's Dream

A fisherman's dream is a river or lake...
With musical waters and lures that's fake...
Freedom from noise indescribable pleasure...
Natures great gift a sportsman treasure...

Peaceful echoes of the waters rippling sound...
Smiling when you see fish jumping 'round...
You cast you line then wait for a bite...
At the first nibble you're ready to fight...

You may be seen in the news, no doubt.
Or they'll take a picture of you and that trout.
Remember the time the big one got away.
Well! Look out fish I'll get you today...

Suddenly! Your line gives a big jerk.
You and that fish almost went berserk.
The delightful feeling. You've hooked a whale.
Makes you hold on tighter to that fish's tail...

(The Rest Of The Story)

My feet went up my head stuck in mud. I soaked up a gallon of that
river's crud. They dragged my body to the edge of the lake...
Through power of survival I began to awake...

I opened my eyes to see my reviver...
The fish I caught "WAS A LADY SCUBA DIVER!!"

Evelyn A. Hood

"Family Quilt"

This quilt I took the time to sew
With many memories you should know
Each block is very old
A flour sack turned to gold
A little girl's dress for school
Gram's apron from all as a rule
She'd put trim on a pillow slip
Or a pretty patch to cover a rip
Gram could make any piece do
Now I've found the scraps to quilt for you
Each block is from the family dress
Aunt Mickey - preferred brown and yellow to press
Aunt Kath - liked tan and green
It always looked neat and clean
Aunt Marg - liked checks in blue
Aunt Trudy - liked stripes and checks too
My Mom - liked mostly bright red, she wore
As for me, I wore lavender and pink by the score.

Dorothy I. Brown

Bikers

I once knew, the crusty few men of iron will,
With leather bands and golden tans,
Upon their wings of steel.

Their steeds of power, roar for hours,
Ore desert hot lands.
Through mountain streams,
And paradise dreams,
Controlled by their gloved hands.

Their damsels fair, with jet black hair,
Wrapped around their sides.
With language brass, that cuts like glass,
Free as the wind to ride.

Charlene Teed

My Place

A grassy spot in our Gupton Hills
With its green grass,
A big buck deer, and
A warm breeze.
Smells of clean air,
Sweat from my horse, and
All the animals on our land.
Reminds me of a place
In the mountains
With air that's never been breathed before.

Jory Colt Bulkley

Changes

The tall oak trees
with giant trunks.
Limbs like arms
beckon to me.
Your shiny green leaves
have turned to gold.
What beauty to behold.

Now they dance on their way
saying, "turn to the right,
turn to the left, we'll dance on the green,
to the first fall of snow."
Ah, Spring, then Summer, you know.

Ina Headlee

Broken Promises

From beginning of time growing up has been hard to do,
with all the broken promises and hardships we go through.

What's the point of life with all that we see and hear.
It seems everything is out of focus, everything so unclear.

What do we do with promises that are broken and never kept?
For a child a promise is a promise, and a broken one is hard to accept.

A parent's promise is so important when it has been said.
But can break a child's heart when they have been misled.

A broken promise can have an array of meaning in this life of ours.
Maybe a friendship that we cherished then suddenly sours.

But what ever broken promise that has hurt us inside,
there is help and hope in God, who is not man that he should lie.

The Word of God is a forever extended promise,
in which we can trust.
With the continuing help of our Father,
we can learn to adjust.

All the hurts will gradually begin to fall away.
As our Lord brings more and more trust, into our hearts each day.

So our hope of a healed heart, can only lie with him.
Thank God for kept promises, never to be broken again.

Debra Conner

Never Again

Never again in my dreams
Will I ever be with you.
Never again will I think about
The things we used to do.
Never again will the sound of your name
Be music to my ear,
And never again will saying "Good-bye"
Produce in my eye a tear.
Never again will I speak of your absence
And punctuate it with sighs.
Never again could there ever be equalled
Such utterly ridiculous lies!

Jay E. Boyd

Flannel Underware

They sit in their corner booths
With aesthetical countenances
Languidly sipping their black espressos,
And envisioning future works of art.
Their lithe fingers
Wrapped around various pens and pencils
Immaculately marking anything
In their path.
The future is in their ubiquitous minds
Screaming to be unleashed on the world.
It's in these minds that intriguing
Mysteries still remain in these times.
They are the sorcerers of illusion, in which
Love and Death stand in the center of their
Devious plot.
They are the spirit of the Diamond Stars in the sky.

Anda Scafaru

Someday

Someday the rivers and lake will be crystal clear
With abundant fish swimming without care
Where skies will be blue with cumulus clouds
Where eagles fly free in fresh clean air
Where green forests stretch from coast to coast
Where there are no smog nor acid rain
Where there are no garbage dumps nor toxic waste
Where the ozone once again protects nature's domain
Someday this will all come to pass
When man no longer walks this fragile earth
For it has been given back to mother earth

John Hybridge

The Tree And Me

There once was a tree who lived with me.
With a very very big crown.
It was a crown like a king's except it was brown.
One day I said: Why with me?
Why not like a tree?
Brown on the ground with leaves.
I don't know?
Said the tree to me,
if you wish, I'll leave!

Cassie Eacker

A Heartfelt Prayer

My Lord and my Saviour I come to Thee
With a heartfelt prayer on bended knee
I hurt inside for the things I have done
Knowing who to blame, I'm the only one
I've hurt my family and friends, and this I know
I ask for forgiveness to save my soul
I pray to You Lord to show me Your way
To make things better for my family and friends each and every day
I know I've done wrong but now my earnest desire
Is to live for you with my heart on fire
To give you the Glory and Honor you deserve
With a pure heart I'm here to serve
I pray that my family and friends will one day forgive me
And in my life your light they will see
Please give me the chance to make things right
This is my heartfelt prayer every night
To my family and friends and the Good Lord above
This poem I wrote with all my love.

Charles Edward Lee

The River And The Boat

I see a river, calm and still
with a boat a float, hitching a ride.
The river moves at nature's will
as the parasite tumbles with the tide.

The large volume, a breathtaking blue,
bears a small body of metal and wood.
The large volume could break it in two,
but does not, even thought it could.

The mass calleth, so sharp and profound.
The little toy does as the river commands.
The mass makes a beautiful sound,
as the toy is led by the river's hand.

Oh no! The river went from a good to bad!
It has taken my boat unsung.
You horrible liquid, have you gone mad?
Do you see what you have done?

You have calmed down now, like nothing has happened,
leaving my little boat without a life.
Damn you river, now I have to been saddened,
because my little boat too had its rights.

Anthony Arthur Young

"Dreams"

Timeless wanderings; distant cries
Wishful daydreams; sunny skies.
So many doors; which one to choose?
So many dreams; no one can lose.

Though many people can never see.
A young person's face when he dreams!
His eyes will shine with endless limits,
His face will glow with an awaiting infinity.

In his heart, there dwells a love; for to accomplish his
dream - he looks above;
The skies will dance, the wind will sing - the voices
of glory in his ears will ring.

Dreams enlighten with the scent of heaven
valiantly fly with eagle's wings
And when there caught in a young person's heart
The bells of enrichment proudly ring.

Dreams an encouragement to try with might; to succeed with
a finish line in sight.
To make life's journey an endless road; to lessen the
burdens and the load.

Jennifer Thomas

A Wall Became An Altar

The old church wall at Mt. Hebron Cemetery
Winchester Va.
Mt. Hebron claims the old church wall for those within her keep
A tribute to the living as well as those who sleep.
Once a church called Grace, four walls complete to steeple.
Rang out its bells across the land to welcome in her people.
A mighty Lutheran chorus came, for worship and to pray.
So God would grant them mercy and guidance in that day.
This building just a structure, to save all from the storm.
The church is all Gods People, in Christ its faith and form.
When once a fire transformed this wall, into a mighty altar.
No longer they would be outside, though sin was still their falter.
Indeed here Christians gather still, upon this hallowed ground.
The light of Christ renewing hope, as distant church bells sound.
The sins of all have been forgiven, that stone is rolled away.
Now all can come to praise their God, it's Easter every Day.

John Kinser Hall

Autumn Captive

How lovely, so very lovely, the autumn.
　Winter is hiding in the shadows,
　　The persimmons are falling,
　　　All of nature is moving about,
　Each leaf begs to cling to the tree just one more day.

How alluring, so very alluring, the autumn.
　Colors subdued, entreat the eye, the mind,
　　Breezes soft, brush the face, the hair,
　　　All of nature whispers the summons.
　Each wave of grain knows the harvester is coming.

How captivating, so very captivating, the autumn.
　Beauty is radiated at every scene,
　　Music is made by every living thing,
　　　All of nature entangles the witness,
　Each scene of artistry in its final act.

How fleeting, so very fleeting, the autumn.
　Azure skies, empty of clouds, long to be touched,
　　Vacant pastures are laden with ironweed,
　　　All of nature hauntingly dances away,
　Each wondrous day is filled with fields of dreams...
　　　Silas Farmer

Pyramid Of Straw

The rusty binder scythed the ripened oats,
winnowing threads of braided gold.
Four neatly-tied bundles awaited the
calloused farmer's hands to be shocked.

Myriads of shocks dried in the scorching
heat of the piercing August sun,
Amidst jumping grasshoppers,
Chewing bloately on rich kernels.

Trudging through the brilliant stubbles,
the tethered horse drew the weathered
wooden wagon, as Minnesota's rural
yeoman loaded each foursome of grain.

The revved up engine of the tottering John Deere
spun the wheel, which turned the long conveyor belt,
setting the rattling thresh machine in rhythmic
revolutions to chew and swallow the crunchy shock.

The rhapsodic thresher sifted grain from chaff,
while spitting and belching chunks of straw
upon a soft stack, whose peak offered rest
and nest to the swallows alighting upon it.
　　　Darrell M. Schmidt

Little Bird Flying High

Little bird up in the sky
　why is it that you fly so high?
Your wings flutter and you're so free
　is there someplace you would rather be?

Birds come in such brilliant colors,
　oranges, blues and even yellows.

Have you ever watched a bird go by
　with a look of freedom in his eye?
Clean and graceful, soaring down
　just long enough to touch the ground.

Off and flying once again
　I wonder just where you have been.
Little bird in a sky of blue
　I wish I could fly away with you!
　　　CoLetta M. O'Neill

Why?

WHY-is there so much killing so much stealing?

WHY-do people like to abuse the people they love?
WHY-do they like to misuse the people they need?

WHY-can't we just love each other?
For if we'd love more, we'd hate less,
society wouldn't be in such a mess,
sexism, favoritism, racism would be a thing of the past.

WHY-aren't married couples forever together?
WHY-do we change like the weather? WHY-so much confusion?

WHY-aren't married couples forever together?
WHY-do we change like the weather? WHY-so much confusion?

WHY-can't this world be a better place?
WHY-can't we live together?
WHY-don't we care for each other?

WHY-don't we eat right?
WHY-do we argue, fuss and fight?

Magic may come raining down and sprinkle us with joy, kindness, and love.
Maybe then all the wrong things in our lives won't have
to have the question, WHY? Why we'll all have a better life.
Why these answers aren't difficult at all, are they? If so, WHY?
　　　Darryl D. Lassiter

Only One Lifetime?

Where do the days go, Lord...
Why do the hours speed by...
October rains are flooding the streets
Were not crocuses just appearing?

Has time sped up as New Agers say?
Is Earth really spinning faster?
If only I could stop the clock
Give the world another 24 hours...

So many books are going unread
Concerts performed without me
So many beautiful places not seen,
More lifetimes than this one are needed.

How else can one smell all the flowers blooming
Visit deserts, mountains and seas...
A few short years that fly by so fast
Please stop — there's too much to see!

I, for one, want to come back
For a chance to do all that I couldn't
For time relentlessly moves ever faster
Lord, please a little bit slower!
　　　Evelyn P. Googe

Talking To Coffee

YOU WICKED BLACK BREW!
Why do I adore your bitterness?
Old china cups cannot be bleached
Of your sordid stains.
This stomach complains with your acids -
These hands tremble like a drunkard's
After tippling your muddied waters.
Caffeine!
A drug! That's what it is!
Addictive — Seductive —
Luring me back - every day back for more.
What Merlin concocted such a potion
To make me fall victim to this spell?
YOU WICKED BLACK BREW!
　　　Joyce Irene Pipes

Big And Brown

Noose him... loose him,
Why did you choose him?
He's big, he's brown - he was strutting around...
His big strong hoof was pawing the ground!
His nostrils flaring, those men are daring
To take his freedom away.
His front feet raring, his eyes are glaring
At the men who stand in his way.
"With greatest pride, I take the ride."
His bronco busters say...
"You dudes may think you're tough,
But this guy is rough,
This is definitely not your day!"
Throwing his head, he charges at Ned...
Poor man, we had to dig his grave.
Red dirt is flying...
Cowboys are dying...
"Bill, come put this horse away."

Esha Lee Shutts

Beauty

Beauty on beauty, world of beauty.
Why can't we keep the world on duty.
To be aware of sure beauty to the world
we live is not of beauty.
People fight, day and night.
Drugs kill young kids on sight.
Trees die from smog in the air.
Water is green, but does anybody care.
People grow old and lose their beauty.
Do the young people care about their duty?
To help someone old and tell them
that they have beauty.
But all they get are hopeless fears.
I am so scared, nobody cares.
Young kids all over the world die from hunger.
That gives me anger.
I care, but what can I do?
I have beauty, what about you!

Joab Skott Morano

Depression

How can the world be so cold
why can't anyone seem to really understand how I feel
All I can do is let my anger rise
so high, so high I think I might burst
What can I do to let it all out
How can I express myself
to the full extend of myself
Sometimes I think I should just cry
But I can't
I'm forever stuck in a feeling like no other
A feeling of hopelessness, of fear and sorrow depression
I am full of empty spaces I'm afraid will never be filled
When my dying day finally comes
I'll be sure of what's happening
My burden will be lifted
from me as well as others
And I will be gone, in more ways
than one.

Amber Strampp

My Inca

Wide is the face of my Inca
Whose visions of conquest match cheekbones
Bursting with the pride of ancient bloodlines.
Crowned with thick, black plumage
He peers out over jungle, sierra, then coast
Scanning his heritage through almond eyes
And molded by the wisdom of Tupac.

My Inca endures,
Heedless of defeat and destiny's scourge
For gleaming bronze and noble,
He has mastered the master's whip
Writhing in nature's dance
He supplants their seed with his
While intoning the mantra of the God's.

Helen Draher

Things That Matter Most

The gentle breath of sleeping babes,
   whose smiles could light the sky,
   a teddy bear, a cradle warm,
   a mother's lullaby.
A father's heart so filled with pride,
   it almost makes him cry.
These are the things that matter most,
   as life goes quickly by.

A moonlit night, a tender kiss,
   two hearts that beat as one,
   the vows once made and treasured still,
   the love that makes a home.
The twilight of each passing day,
   God's love for you and I.
These are the things that matter most,
   as life goes quickly by.

   And shadows chase the setting sun,
   As life goes quickly by.

John A. McIntosh Jr.

If Only I Could Say

Like a flower I adore.
Whose gentle touch I would love to know more.
Whose beauty is wondrous, to me unmatched.
Like a butterfly in reach yet hard to catch.
But if I could for just one day
Catch that beauty, then I would say:
Your beauty is as lovely as the morning sunrise.
Even more so within your eyes.
For one kiss, and to hold you in my arms;
Or to share your company and your lovely charm.
I would chase the butterfly from dawn to dawn.
For I do adore you, more than you know.
If only I could tell you; if only I could show.
But since I cannot tell you face to face,
Within this poem I plead my case.
For you are that flower I do adore.
Yes, you are that gentle touch
I would love to know more.

Ivory Hinton

"Good Grief"

She is the gauche misfit who "proves herself" by diminishing that self
who affirms that the great guest of a woman's life is not to use her
given talents, to have a direct relationship with life, but to seize
and dishonor those talents in order to find fulfillment with Mr. Right
To the careful of conquest and surrender.

I am the clearest, brightest star, seen by all wise men near and far,
over the highways, over the street, sparkling lights along the
pathway dim...like an angel on fly unseen.

Deborah Sue Adams

Who's Afraid Of Lowki?

Who's afraid of the cannibal man in the woods?
Who's afraid of the beast that follows you in the dark?
Who's afraid of that ole' myth that lingers in our minds?
The myth of the young Indian who changes into a wolf and runs
through the woods at night?
Who's afraid of Lowki?
You are. We are. We all are. We have seen him. He has seen us as well.
We are brothers now. Now I am the cannibal man in the woods.
The beast that follows you in the dark. I am now the Indian who
changes into a wolf and preys on you. Who hunts you.
For I am Lowki, spirit of the man wolf. The one who howls at the full moon.
Yes, I am the one who brings the chill up your spine.
And when you come out tonight you might see me.
Raging under the blood red moon.
But don't worry, I'm not real. Only a myth.
That is what I first thought as well.
Join me brother, come join me.
Running, running, running, swiftly through the deep, dark woods.
For I am Lowki, King of the wolf pack.
Long live the King.

Andrew J. Arrasmith

To A Professor

Our lady is a tapestry
who weaves her riches of knowledge
around and through us.

Patterns of fragmented sunlight
she mixes and molds and strings
along a framework
of impressionable minds,
tapping lightly like butterflies lighting,
her glorious radiance blinding us
as she pricks our hearts.

Our lady is a tapestry, a weaver —
whose threads of pulsation
tap softly at our brains, tug gently at our heartstrings,
and we — toppled —
ever love the weaver,
ever desire the mystic threads of her web
on fire with the sun.

Julia A. Horner

Press On Living

In days of my youth, I remember a man
   who lived a simple life.
In a small house, on the edge of a meadow,
   he lived with his kids and wife.

The house was heated with coal and wood,
   and the wood stove baked great bread.
I remember sleeping under 5 or 6 quilts,
   and a fireplace roared by the bed.

Although he had very little,
   he loved with all of his might.
When he spoke soft words, we all listened;
   because it was filled with wisdom of life.

I still see the porch, with rustic chairs,
   where on evenings he played guitar.
And songs that he played: some were happy,
   some praise, and some longed for a place afar.

These memories I keep, as the man grows old,
   I will forever hold close to my heart.
When I close my eyes I hear music,
   and see a man who made simple an art.

Donald W. Parks

"Daddy's Little Girl"

Who has been beside me each step of each new day
Who is there to pick me up from all the mistakes I've made
Who wipes away the tears that silently run down my cheek
Who knows the words I have to say before I ever speak
Who taught me how different are "right" and "wrong"
Who is left beside me when everyone else is gone
Who has let me learn things the hard way
When it was much easier to do than say
Someone went through a lot of pain to bring me where I stand
Someone loved me an awful lot, to let me be who I am
Taking on a responsibility that was intended for someone else
When no one wanted to claim me you took me in yourself
Now take it from a mother who's the only one for her son
It means much more to be someone's choice of want
Now I know very little of what was my life before you adopted me
I'm perfectly content with the parent I have seen
Even if it be forever, I rather care not to know
I was given a chance to be the one's father loves her so
All the things you mean to me get harder to say
Most of all I want to be "Daddy's little girl" still today

Andrea Shannon Ford

My Identity Is Me

During the conception of me, my parents did not know who I was or
who I was going to be. All my mother knew was that a PERSON was
growing inside of her. So now you know, I am a PERSON; first with
feelings, ideas, and dreams just like you.

When I was born the doctor looked at me and said to my mother, "You
have a wonderful baby girl." My mother new the day would come
when I would be a beautiful young WOMAN. So now you know, I am a
WOMAN; second with feelings, ideas, and dreams just like you.

Then the nurse typed up my birth certificate and she came to the
line for the race. I was BLACK. I am BLACK, and I will be BLACK,
Last but never overlooked. I am BLACK with feelings, ideas, and
dreams just like you.

So when you look at me, let it be known I am a PERSON with
feelings, ideas, and dreams just like you. A WOMAN standing with
a group that has given birth to this nation. A BLACK so proud I am
to be, because you see it still started with me.

Crystal Marce Jones

Future Of Hope?

The putrid stench of death fills the air,
while sunken, sullen eyes betray humanity's despair.

Different races wallowing in bitter distrust of each other,
give birth to the seeds of contempt for their human
   sister and brother.

Religious doctrines, like opium, mesmerize the human mind,
while sacred symbols, like banners in the wind,
   galvanize us against our own kind.

This century of death, like a vast cemetery, in its lapidary
   way, records time's dreadful deeds,
as our culture of death, in a miasmical mode,
   already sows the future's deadly seeds.

The macabre dance continues - rooted in poverty, disease,
   hatred and nature's fury,
as with each shovel of intolerance, ignorance and indifference,
we slowly love's gentle soul bury!

Frank J. Bober

15

The Outdoors

Some people can see the overwhelming beauty of the outdoors
While others go about their business doing their everyday chores

The outdoors is a place to look and see
It's made up of every kind of beautiful tree

The wildlife is a breathless wonder of the mind
Its gracefulness and authentic nature is one of a kind

The sky and the rolling plains are a sight to enjoy and take in
The awe-inspiring sunset will make you look again and again

The wind and rain always have something to say
They replenish the wilderness so it can survive another day

When you sit outdoors your senses are unlatched
The smell, sight, and sound you encounter is unmatched

But the outdoors are being polluted with unnatural makings of man
We need to realize the harshness and danger of this devastating plan

We need to keep the outdoors fresh and free from invasion
It's a necessity for the upbringing of the next generation
It's sometimes impossible to unravel some aspects of the great outside
This is why some people are so interested and inspired by
    this amazing nature ride

To me the outdoors is a beautiful realm of harmony and peace at its best
So remember, take advantage of this gripping scene of wonder
    while it's at its crest
        Donald C. Aker

Pilgrim Mother I Give You My Greatest Praise

For Examples You Set In So Many Ways

I was thinking of all of my comforts
    While I lounged in my nice home tonight
And then of you, my dear Pilgrim Mother,
    Without a house, without warmth, without light.
By campfires you did all of your cooking
    Yet your love for this land of the free
Made you cleanse the bare soil with your teardrops
    In the dreams you were building for me.
You sang songs to Our Father in Heaven—
    Indians joined your group on that day.
You deserve our broadcasts of devotion;
    With blessings you prepared for our way.
So many years you lived as a Pilgrim
    With no stores to buy food or a treat
Only wilds in the Colony of Plymouth,
    Not a Chapel or even a street.
We thank you our brave Pilgrim Mother;
    Your courage as a beacon will shine.
Our lives in this land you blessed and lightened,
    Your example you set is divine.
        Emma T. W. S. Fuller

Nicolette

Sleep opens the doorway into he realm of dreams
where she smiles
caressing my body in completeness
a rival to the warmth,
of mother's fiery eye
her skin, so soft
petals of a flower in bloom
offering me her nectar,
I drink with hungry eyes
my angel
carrying me on her wings
to heaven
as my joy surpasses the stars
the rushing wind forever whispers her name
Nicolette
        Dathon A. Helsel

Where Shall We Meet?

I wonder on what part of the earth are your feet treading.
Which path is slowly directing you towards me?
We are both moving, circling the solar plexus of the earth in search of purity.

Meaning exists within one's heart and mind.
Meaning the uncarved stone.
Our experience shapes it and provides a true realization of the stones composition.
I roll, tumble, drift toward you, today it does not seem fast enough.
We are not ready to congeal.
I imagine I'm prepared for our union, the moment assures me I'm not.

I breathe deep and part in my lips in such a way as to show my chagrin.
The beautiful line which acts as a crescent moon to the sides of my lips has proven my journey has not been in vain.
When we meet, you will touch the line slowly with one hand and move down towards my chin and embrace me as if it's the last time.
I will kiss your finger and hold it near my breath.

The south has called upon you for pleasure, the north has detained me for wisdom.

Where shall we meet?
        Gail Emily Arriola

"Nuggets"

There are rare times in our lives
Which our minds eye sets aside
In a category reserved for the uncommon.
These are times spent and shared with
    a person whom we have loved and lost.
Oh, how lucky to have a file of such
    rare moments.
Reachable at a time of reflection -
To bolster our efforts to perhaps again
    reach that plateau.
We now know, at least, to be attainable,
Yet oh how illusive.
        John E. Hibbs Jr.

Soul In Isolation

I believe in substance and not a facade of shame,
where time serves only as an abstract void of human pain.

An evolution of thought coupled with the body of change,
leads the mannequin to an existence rather than a mindless identity.

With an altitude of dissention comes the disarray of belief.
Inside awaits a biome of crass pessimistic thought based on the absolute value of gold and the resurrection of a falsely idoltric God.

Can fear be the grounds of moral indecision or the impotence of humanistic thought?
Brash destruction and a cavalier attitude do not make revolution, only aimless rebellion void of thought.

Change, a vision from deep within penetrating the social conscious, breaks the vicious cycle of deception employed by a constitution of venomous self-importance.

Far from the cauldron of lifeless identity lies the culmination of societal failure, an existence of altruistic human desire necessitated by the realm of isolation.

Viewed from the window of an immoral majority a sentence comes forth, one of abandonment and critical resentment.

Isolation shields these blows from the transcendence of meaning to a moral place as yet untouched.
From the capacity to endure without compromise comes a strength of indestructible proportion.

Is this youth of mind or perhaps thoughts purged of the urban filth of political mind control an monetary worship?
Introspection yields a return to innocence necessitated in faith, not of religion but rather of self.
        Craig R. Brandon

16

The Valley

Love is found in the valley
Where the mountains stand so tall
Where the mighty Hudson flows so freely
Through spring summer and the fall.

Its appearance changes to crystal
As the wrath of winter comes to call
The scene is rather unique and logical
For God's hand truly created it all.

I love the softness found in the valley
Where God chose to speak to me
The gospel truth of His sons Lord Jesus
It was here in the valley that I was set free

Chip Copeland

"Beyond Revelation"

There lies a place, with the malignant stench of inflammation,
Where sinners lie, no hope for salvation,
At the hand of Satan- at the hand of Death,
Among the forsaken, those without breath,

In this abyss, which harbors transgressors,
Is the school of death, of which Satan is professor,
In every dismal corner, death appears,
And no matter how hard the afflicted may try, darkness perseveres,

As Satan makes his manifestation, of his everlasting reign,
Not even humble supplications, can stop the consternation, that proceeds in his domain,
And when he bestows incessant lashes, upon the body's of the impure,
The whip will leave profound traces, that they must endure,

Those who dwell with insubordination,
Satan will see no discrimination,
Thrown into the pit, where pain and torture go hand in hand,
The reminisces of civilizations damned.

Dustin Lee

O, Love Of Mine

O, love of mine
   where might you be
   secluded so far away from me.

I've searched the mountains, valleys so low
   to seek out my soul from which you flow.
   I know not where you hide.

The days are dark and so very slow
   while in vain I search to let you know
   that life is a vacuum suspended in time.

Until you return and claim your prize
   of desire of which only you can light the fire
   seize these moments so quickly mired.

And free my spirit which is encased in a veil
   of suspenseful longing and who can tell
   when we will meet as fate may decide.

To unleash the tide of love
   and join us once again
   I can no longer wait, my love, my friend.

Elena Diamond Randolph

"Stuck"

I sit alone in the mind of darkness
Trying to find my way to the light of day
Hoping my sorrow will someday fly away
High above to a place it's never been before
But the light of day is hard to gain
In my heart there's always pain

Amber Simerly Balogh

Where Little Children Laugh And Play

There is a place tucked safe away,
Where little children laugh and play.

Where dark clouds never hide the day,
Where blue skies and dreams are always real.

Butterflies still give a thrill,
In fields of flowers that dance in the wind.

In a day of love that has no end.

So, come with me, let time stand still,
Share the joy of love that's real.

In this place tucked safe-away
Where little children laugh and play.

John M. McKinney Sr.

Christina's World

In a sea of rolling grain,
where homes are like ships
sits Christina.
Her best friend is the field mouse.
They have their tea at noon.
Her enemy is an empty house,
lonely as the moon.
Her pleasure is to run barefoot through the fields.
Tumbling she falls out of sight and mind
into another.
Now, she is a queen, or a star on a once seen magazine.
Cotton transforms to silk while jewels pour from above
garmenting the bare.
Swirling and twirling her colors fly
dancing with wings up out of the sky.
Then a sound is carried over acres of barren wheat
shattering all...
"Christina! Come home."

Charla Mealer

Farmer's Enigma

Scorching heat, day by day, without a drop of rain...

In States of the plains, the country's heart,
Where farmers in fall and early spring,
Bet their hopes and means and brawn
And plow and sow and watch it grow,
Do pray and hope this year for more
To balance the sheet for better score
Than year just passed and years before.

The power of hope on top of hope
Keeps them working and help them cope.
Not a provider more blessed on Earth,
Then farmers who feed and keep us from hurt.
Reward is due and God would know,
Then why should they suffer more and some more...

Scorching heat, day by day, without a drop of rain?!....

Geza Tomosy

"Come To Me"

Come to me!
When the sun rises and birds start singing.
Come to me!
When the air is cool and sun is setting.
Come to me!
Before memory fades,
Powerful, shared ecstasy, so strong,
Like the strains of a symphonic song.
And if you don't,
I will ever wonder what went wrong.

Elaine C. Barton

Teresa

¿Adonde estàs, Teresa?
Where are you, Teresa?
Near your heart and inside your soul, Mommy.

¿Quien eres, Teresa?
Who are you, Teresa?
A unique, special person, Mama.

¿Adonde vas, Teresa?
Where are you going, Teresa?
I'm going to explore my world, Mother.

¿Qué te pasa, Teresa?
What is the matter, Teresa?
I am a mother—abandoned.

Teresa, estòy aqui!
Teresa, I am here!
Lean on me, take my strength.

¿Còmo estàs, Teresa?
How are you, Teresa?
I am growing strong, Mom.

Te amo, Teresa.
I love you too, Mamà.

Helene Bigler

"Finding Myself"

Sometimes I ask myself,
Where are you?
Why are you the way you are?
When did you loose yourself?

I look back at the happiness I once gave,
the love that once burst out of me,
the patience and caring I used to have.
To what I am now, a soul that doesn't want to see.

So many things have come and gone.
So many people that have left their foot prints.
My children who now seem all alone,
the dreams we shared fading away into a blur of tints.

What have I done with myself?
The woman who could handle anything,
protector, counselor, mother, lover, always willing to help.
Where has she gone, why has she forgotten the important things?

Jonna S. Tritt

Your Head Or Your Heart

So what do you listen to, your head or your heart?
When you're in a bad relationship and feel that you should part?

Your head says to leave, end it all real fast, but your
heart says "no" and you hope it will last.

Do you really win, no matter what you do?
Leave the one you love and say "that we are through."

If you leave what do you gain?
What we have today can all be gone tomorrow.

The things that brought you pleasure can also bring you sorrow.
So what do you listen to, your head or your heart.
Should we stay together or should we break apart?

Dianna Feece

Valerie

The lifters vie and nightly strain
To trim the extra from their frame;
While Val from birth did naught to gain
Her tautly muscled bod, their aim.

Donald G. MacEachern

"Isn't It Funny?"

Isn't it funny how the time goes by
when you're all alone touching the sunshine?
Hiding secrets and tales from long ago
Wondering how long in the currents will flow
Laughing at shadows in the corner of the room
Watching the sunrise and the flowers bloom
Erasing memories that only brought sadness
Hoping someday you'll snap out of this madness
Days come and go like the Dragon you used to know
Wings spread majestically as the wild wind blows
Knowledge flows with neverending conclusions
while haunting thoughts of you return in quiet illusions
It seems lately you've rejected my desires
To walk on coals of brilliant fire
To fulfill that one final destiny
of confirming secret meetings through eternity
Hoping someday that the dance will never end
but still retreating from the sunshine you send -
and isn't it funny how the time goes by
when you're all alone touching the sky?

Brian A. Felion

How Can I

How can I get you to see
  When your eyes look dimly at the light

How can I get you to laugh
  When your smile only curls the corners of your lips

How can I get you to sparkle
  When the sun shines on you, yet you shiver

How can I get you to believe
  When you hear only the roar, not the whisper

How can I get you to sing
  When you can not feel the melody of the rain dropping softly

How can I get you to love
  When the child in you does not play

How can I. How can I.

Joyce Turner

Who Can We Blame?

Who can we blame when the world is in pain,
When we lose all the meaning of gain?
When nations fight nations, and brothers kill brothers,
And children are scared of even their mothers?
When toys are now weapons and snacks are now drugs,
And there's now no such thing as valuable hugs?

Who can we blame when the world is in pain,
And it's almost the end and we lost all the gain?
Who else, but it's us, again and again
With nothing to do, but cause all that pain again.
But that will be the day to ask for forgiveness and learn to say,

"Oh Father up high, help us live day by day."
With love, and share and even shame,
But please let us change this awful blame.
Who can we blame when the world is in pain?
Oh no! Not again, now we have tried to
Change pain for gain!

Carolina Herrera

What A Beautiful, Beautiful Morning

Good morning, Good Morning.
When time will be no more.
And all God children will be dressed in white
around the great white throne

What a wonderful time we will have
there will be laughing every where.
And what fun we will have as we walk the
golden stairs

The choir will be singing a brand new song
and the angels we read about
will be gathered around Jesus. As he sits on
the golden throne. Oh! I can't hardly wait
so let us be faithful and true

Jesus keep telling us he is coming
real, real, soon.

Jeannetta Powers

Tornado Warning

Fearing I would come to harm
when the sirens blew alarm
I hid in the closet
my hands over head
and prayed that after the storm
I would not be dead.

It was then I recalled the disciples at sea
fighting the waves, and what they thought they could see
They swore with no hope what they saw was a ghost
though it was Christ, the almighty host.

He protected his own from an untimely fate
for they had a mission so death had to wait
It was not their time
nor was it mine
But I continued to pray
with my life on the line.

Praise the Son for what he has done!
The clouds dissolves as I resolved
never to doubt my faith in prayer
and to do it even without a scare.

Bill W. Miller

The Mystery Horse

It was a dark and gloomy night
When suddenly appeared a horse of a great pale white.

His head held high, tail and all,
As he let out a ferocious call.

Yelling to anyone who could here,
As I looked into his eyes, I saw no fear.

Listening for an answer, His ears kept cropped.
After realizing no one would, the challenging stopped.

Then the strangest thing came to.
The horse reared up and up he flew.

After lifting himself high in the air,
He looked over the town with bunches of care.

Turning his head right and then left,
A careful eye on the city was all he kept.

He reared as if to say something to me.
Then I realized he was saying he was happy.

His eyes were happier and full of cheer.
Minutes later he had disappeared.
For this a guardian angel, a guiding light.
This pale white beast protected us that night.

Betty Coyle

Happiness

When winter brushes 'gainst the trees,
When spring spreads its gentle breeze,
When summer's humid air is here,
When autumn's days are cold and drear,
Inside the houses near the hearth,
The home is filled with joy and warmth,
Until tomorrow's time is spread,
You never know what lies ahead.
You have to face the world outside,
So there's no hope if you just hide,
You know the house is safe and silent,
But if you never leave, you'll never show
Your talent,
So go and enjoy your time on this earth,
And show this planet what you're worth.
If you live life to its fullest,
You'll be more wealthy than any of us.

Brandon Lee Holzhueter

Turmoil And Strife

Working in this time in life,
When society is threatened with turmoil and strife.

You get married, have a family,
Economy demands a second salary.
That's not bad enough, loyalty they expect,
You lose your job; who are you to get respect?

Fighting, frustration, the burden to share,
Do it in a conforming way or no one will care.

Maintain a job, show aggression,
Then watch out when you get too much attention.

I've never really wanted to take what belongs to another.
I just wanted to be recognized along with the others.

With a brain that has been given,
Logic, and common sense of mankind,
I want to stand up and be counted from time to time.

If that is asking too much,
Then maybe I'm not living in the right land,
As I was taught this country gives
Equality to every woman and man.

Joyce A. McCartin

Love

God's love is like a small fragile seed
When planted in an empty heart:
If cherished, it will grow
And send forth a rare, tender bud
To reach up and search for
Its first sunrise.

As the delicate petals gently unfold
Showing their beauty to the world,
They glisten in the freshness of the day.
The blossom opens its heart wide
To the heavens above and calls to God:
He reaches down and holds it in his hands—
It will bloom forever.

Dorothy A. Thompson

To My Granddaughter

Cierra, you make me smile
When my day seems longer than a mile

Your smiling face stares back at me
And makes me realize how great it is to see

I see so many troubles and problems and so
Your smile makes them all go

They go to other places in my mind
And help me get out of that bind

So, little one who is so precious to all of us
Now, you know why we fuss

We fuss cause we can't see you when we should
But we wish that we could

I hope some day you'll see these lines
And be able to remember good times

Times of memories great and small
Times that were important to all
  Joan Cuppett

"Claire"

A seal pup in need as they find her alone,
When mom seal disappeared from causes unknown.

As the people gathered at a beach on Resurrection Bay,
They noticed a bald eagle eating what looked like a lump of clay.

But no! It was a seal, so small, weak and wet,
This baby was soon to be a story we will never forget.

She was driven to Anchorage where a medical team awaits,
Preparing for her arrival and calling everywhere for herring bait.

She'll need to be fed by many volunteers,
To fatten her up which brought us many cheers.

Then as you know it would soon be time,
To release her back to the wild; keeping her would be a crime.

So please be thankful there is some rehab in sight,
How Alaska is lacking and maybe we might
 see programs get a boost by political endeavor,
Before Alaska's wildlife disappears forever!
  Janice Marksberry

Angel Wings

Do you remember on a hot summer's day,
When in a field of daises you would play,
Then all at once, a breeze came and kissed your face?
It was angel wings, gently, cooling the place.

Do you remember a day when school was hard,
And tears came easily, as you took that test?
Then suddenly, in the background, you thought you heard,
The whisper of angel wings...and you understood.

Do you remember your first school dance,
The first time you drove, or your first romance,
Those times when your knees shook, and you felt unsure?
Then the presence of angel wings bolstered you through.

How do I know about these special times,
And the presence of angels, with gossamer wings?
It just might be, that God answered my prayer,
And it was your guardian angel you felt and heard there.

As you continue to grow, through life's ups and downs,
As you fulfill your dreams, climbing mountains steep,
Remember to listen, for whispers that sing,
And feel the gentle breeze from angel wings.
  Carolyn J. McNeel

Best Friends

You were a friend
When I wanted my life to end.
You were a friend
When life took its bend.

We've had our fights
Which wasn't always right.
We've had our ups and downs
But we've always stuck around.

You've helped me through
Some rough time in my career
It's times like this I wish you were here.

You've been with me through broken hearts
And as a friend you did your part.
You told me it would hurt for awhile
And you would be there: All I had to do was dial.

You said our friendship would never end
So we'll remain the best of friends.
  Carlos P. Aguinaga

"To A Friend"

If ignorance is bliss is there something I missed
When I long to be give in the night by her lips, her hips,
The tips of her fingers that up's a scar in my mind,
My soul, my world?
You know I don't think I can remember a time
When I felt this world was mine.
You are much too young to understand all of this
To grow something wrong, to feel insanities kiss
You're ahead of your time
And your knowledge is vast,
Kick hack and relax, greet it all in the past
With the sun in the last and the horizon a haze
Believe in this in days through time and I think
You'll find that the heart will conquer the mind everything
  Christopher C. Grant

My Tears

My tears are falling like the rain
when I let go of my tears, I let
go of my pain.
My heart is crying out to you.
I'm going through hell, what can I do?
Tears are rolling down my face.
There's no one on earth who can
take your place.
You always meant so much to me.
I just hate the fact that you broke free.
All the love we had is down the drain.
That's why my tears are falling like the rain.
  Hannah Friedel

Broken Barrier

Welcome, child, man, artist, poet, dreamer
Welcome to the realm, where dreams are made
Come forward you, child, and set foot upon Eden's forbidden earth
Come into the world where the spirit soars on unclipped wings,
And the mind is free to expand to unlimited dimensions
Greetings to you, who have started the journey past the minds barriers
You the first to see this land, where Orion pursues Taurus, and the
master cradles his blessed child, wrapped in infinite, black void
Welcome you, the first to look upon the master's face,
And touched his star-spattered cloak and robe.
Welcome, youth, adult, explorer, adventurer,
and....the...dreamer
  Joshua LeSuer

"God's Creation"

God sure did know what He was doing
When He created me,
For without His creation
Lord knows, where I would be;

He gave me my own special look and style
Of which I am very pleased,
You see....No one can copy it
Because He created it, just for me;

When I look at myself each day
I wonder what will come next,
Will I still have that great spirit?
And know, I won't turn back?

Or will it be another day
Filled with His wonderful Blessings,
Feeling complete and wholesome
Knowing He's there; just for the asking

So I'm thankful for God's creation
Thankful as I can be,
Because if we didn't have "God"
Then there surely, wouldn't be "me"

Gwynneth White

The Blame Game

It's hard for men to ponder that there was once a day
When harmony existed in games that people play.
But something dreadful happened that brought a weight of shame
When people started playing another kind of game.

Eve started it by blaming the devil for her sin,
Then eve was blamed by Adam, her very next of kin.
Succeeding generations caught on to this new game,
And soon each erring person found someone else to blame.

The black man blames the white man, the white man blames the black,
As if a person's color is reason to attack.
The person from the ghetto soon blames his neighborhood
For no one from that setting can ever turn out good.

Republicans will argue that they are not to blame
For all our nation's problems, its politics of shame.
The democrats will argue that this is not their fault
Then flay their adversaries and rub their wounds with salt.

I sometimes pause to wonder, how very nice 'twould be
If I quit blaming others, and they quit blaming me.
This would will be much better when we can say "I'm wrong,"
Start praying for each other, and learn to get along.

Bill Murphy

Wishing

Oh to be a child again
    when dreams were fresh and hopes were high,
    and an ice cream cone satisfied -
To fly a kite and reach the sky,
    to stumble and fall and not care why.

Oh to be a child again
    when Mother's arms calmed the fears
    and her love dried the tears
To fall asleep without a care,
    and always know that Mother's there.

Oh take me back where I belong
    to days gone by where there was song
    and sweet dreams lasted all night long,
Where mother made all hurt go away
    and Dad was there to help me play.

Please take me back
For I am sad and my heart cries
    when I remember fireflies.

Ellen Augustynowicz

A Friend's Importance

What remains when friends forsake?
When good times pass and memories bake?
What reads the rending of some soul
by once companions now gone foul?

There was a while when weather was fair
Mates were abundant and sisters were there
Sweet songs heard and harried hearts lulled
In fraternal forge was mettle not dulled

But soon skies sprayed when casting clouds formed
'Twas unforeseen yet some had warned
Those soothing spirits and spicing souls
now no more angels than granting ghouls

Distance, quite some convenient excuse,
becomes a damned, cursed noose
around the neck of trestled trust
and choking, faithfulness fades to dust

Paths diverge as the stream digs deep
A roar, a trickle, an unquenching weep
Can, through rushing rapids, eye of Source
be our belay as we run our course?

Bill T. Craig

Anthony My Angel Boy

How my heart filled with joy and love
When God sent you to me from above
I remember still your sweet smile
You made my life on earth special for awhile
I remember the day you turned one
I love you so much my son.

You filled my days with laughter and joy
Anthony my special little boy
Then you turned two the ninth of May
In two short weeks God would call you away
How could I know you would leave earth so soon
You went to join God's angels the third of June.

The pain and grief it was so hard to bear
But God wanted another angel with Him there
It was so hard to let you go
I cried out in pain and let my tears flow
It took along time, but now I understand,
And I'll be ready when Jesus takes my hand.

Frances J. Hammons

"Our Flag"

'Twas the seventh of December, 'forty-one,
When all through the U.S. was frolic and fun.
Then over the world there came like a flash,
The roar of shells with a screaming crash.
While at the same moment in Washington, D.C.,
A Japanese Ambassador our President came to see.
Begging and pleading like a holy written prayer,
For time and consideration for his homeland fare.
While across the ocean so deep and blue,
With vengeance and death the Japanese flew.
While planning and scheming against the U.S.A.,
to bomb her and burn her in a cruel way.
The U.S. wasn't ready with munitions and feed,
For Great Britain they had helped when they were in need.
But let us get started, then watch our colors fly,
The Red, White and Blue of "Our Flag" will float high!

Jean McDowell Bjordahl

"Hey Dude"

Hey Dude!
What's all this crying?
I didn't die, I am in the glory, I am playing Pro.

Hey Dude!
I am the sweat that drips from your forehead.
I am the basket's rim.
I am the basket ball that bounces on the court.

Hey Dude!
Look I may not be here.
So, who's going to bounce that ball?

Hey Dude!
No need to cry.
I am in peace, I am a Pro.
I am at the top.
So shoot that ball and remember me,
LEE WILLIAMS, the Pro, who loved basketball.

Hey Dude!
What's all this crying?
I didn't die, I am only waiting for
you on the other side of the court.

Ermelinda Maria Noriega Moyers

Life At Sixty

One of a life's mysteries as age takes its toll
What will my body be able to do when I am old?

Will I have teeth to chew my food
Or a nurse to feed me and keep me cool?

Will I have hair or be bald as stone
Travel without glasses and still find my way home?

Will I be able to walk without a cane
Shoot 110 and still love the game?

Can I run a 10K or take a long hike
Swim across the river or ride a big bike?

Can I shoot some baskets or hit a home run
Dance the twist and really have some fun?

Can I have sex as often as I wish
Or maybe I had rather just catch a fish?

Will I cut the grass or plow a field
Without it being such a big deal?

Can I drink three martinis and eat red meat
Without my body having to pay for the treat?

I should be content with all I have done
Because one year from now, I will be sixty-one.

Don R. Burkhalter

The Third Family Reunion "At The Drink"

August fifth again with familiarity
We're all together as a family
To have a beer is what is required
To all those who relate to Dad as an inspire.

Not a single person can deny the truth
That none of us will keep our youth
With Uncle Walt turning seventy-one
He had surgery and still he won.

So now I raise my beer to all
May our name live forever that name being Hall
And as we're here about to drink
For Uncle Walt and Dad let's stop and think.

Jim Hall

"The Time By Your Watch"

Is your watch correct?
What time is it by your watch?
"Well I never think about what time it is now..."

I never worry about time.
I'm enjoying in a day.
I'm living every moment, but...
I really never think about what time it is now!

The watch said to me,
"Time to go back to the real world"
What is the real world?

The watch said to me,
"Time to wake up from the dream"
What is the dream?

The real world is a dream, Dreams are real world.

What time is it now?
"Well, my watch stopped a very very long time ago"

Where am I? Who am I?
The time by your watch.

Junko Shimada

Cherished Things

What things do you cherish and keep?
What things do you remember and reap?
  Whether it's your father or brother,
  Your sister or mother.
  Your gerbil or kitten,
  And that red, lucky mitten.
  Your schoolwork or sports,
  Your tee shirt and shorts.
  Cozy fires and family times,
  Favorite songs, plays, music, and rhymes.
To find the things you cherish most,
Here's a start: Just look within your heart.

Ashlee Pruett

"A Cure"

Lying in bed, gazing outside,
What I am thinking is all in my mind,
My mother says I'll be okay,
But I know that's all she say.

These bleach-white walls have become my home,
Oh how I'd love to go out and roam,
There's doctors here, nurses are there,
What I am feeling no-one can share.

Angrily tearing at my inside,
The disease that I bear I cannot hide,
The friends that I had are nowhere to be found,
I get so sick of just sitting around.

My dark hair is gone, a bald head to prove,
I feel so weak I cannot move,
I used to play alive and so free,
Needles and testing that's all for me.

My life is draining, draining away,
The cancer is worsening everyday.
I go to chemo, to therapy and more,
But it is not helping please God send a cure.

Christin Sauers, age 13

Destiny

When all is said and done, when time has made its closure,
what fate will await my soul. The warm, open arms of the
immaculate being in the blue above? The burning retched claws of
the baneful in the crimson below? Have I been good enough to be
swept up into the extravagant light which illuminates above us
all or am I deserving of an eternity suppressed in a fiery,
hateful, torturous realm below. All will spend their after lives
in one. Some will know sooner than others. Some have already
received their fate. It is all dependent on our present existence
and how we choose to live our lives. This is what will decide our destiny.

Jeanette Giorsos

Walk In The Hall

What is it about you that is so special
What ever it is it's definitely delightful.

I get weak in the knees, my throat dries,
My hope to talk to you, quickly dies.

Your confidence blows me away, I'm in awe
With nowhere to hide my stride keeps me near.

We pass each other now concentrating on smiling
I wonder if you'll look at me, if I'll respond

Nope, I'm now past you, disappointed again
Nevertheless, I'll see you in the hall
    tomorrow.

Jade Cody

My Family Tree

While writing out my family tree.
What a wonderful thing it came to be.
MOM and DAD were our branches on the trunk.
They never grew a rotten stump.
We were planted in good family soil.
Some leaf's from the family tree are gone.
But their beauty still lives on.
This old tree has taken a lot of blows.
But we are growing strong and tall.
With young spouts popping up here below.
We are holding our limps high.
For one of these days.
The wind will carry us to join the others.
In the heavens blue sky.

Bobbie Lovell

The Brighter Side

Just sitting here a thinkin'
What a nice world this would be
If some folks weren't so stinkin'.

The day will always be sunny
Somewhere in this big ole world
And hopefully some things will be funny.

Now I don't want to see a frown
For things sometimes could be worse
So turn that frown upside down.

Some folks always look on the bad side
Come on people don't be so pessimistic
Look for the good, don't let it hide.

Good always comes for those who wait
Or at least that's how the saying goes
So just be patient and ready to open the gate.

Elizabeth H. Eder

Madman

Understanding you is hard today,
We've stopped hearing the words we say.
Confusion results and the price is paid,
Hidden tears burn, keeping our broken hearts caged.

Where are you when I stumble?
I don't recognize us any longer as our marriage crumbles.
I long for a word and a touch to show you care,
Receiving instead your cold stare.

Mind blocks lie hidden beneath the surface,
Weighing me down in spite of my curses.
Why can't you understand!!? I scream in red rage.
I watch your reflection echoing me as I stop dazed.

I want to tear the veils that hide us asunder.
Their substance elusive as distant thunder.
My motions become more spastic as I begin to foam,
Madman at last, trying to hold our melting home.

Glenn L. Barton

Kroger

Kroger is the store that you've grown to love;
We try to give quality a step above.
We are here to help you,
To serve you - as you wish.
When it comes to our customers,
For you seafood, we will fish;
Our produce is fresh,
Our deli is so fine,
Come and get our fresh meat,
To cook it is divine.
And then there is our ideas
Our flowers and our wine.
And if you're feeling ailing,
Our pharmacy will make you fine.
So come and see us often,
We'll meet you with a smile
And if you can't come to us
We'll deliver, you just dial

Etta Wisdom

Untitled

As we fall into greed
We softly slip into blindness
The darker our vision becomes
The quicker we are to sow the seed
And as my symptoms grow
I try to iron out the folds of my brain
To find something I know
I listen to everything except what is said
And I know I can cure my blindness w/a whore's spittle
Or so says the author of whom I have read
The heat from my pondering makes me sweat
I am the most dangerous man I have never meet
It's over quite quickly
The solution was soft
On one hand I'm happy
The other I cut off.

John Greco

Why

My heart so lonely and solemn, why must it turn out this way?
We promised to hold on forever, but I lost you this morbid day.

My heart is lost in emptiness, my soul in blasphemy.
Why can I not get past this, you promised love for eternity?
I know in my heart we were meant to be,
But something's wrong, God just disagreed.

How can I explain these tears that fall inside,
Will you hear me when I scream my silent cries?
I turn to hold you in my arms, all I find is empty charms.
I long to embrace you and feel your loving kiss,
Yet what I feel in my heart is cold and loneliness.

When I think of the sparkle in your eye,
The gleam of your smile, it makes me cry.
The tears fall down my cheek
As I think of the distance between us.

I can't understand, I demand to know why,
God chose to separate me from you, the only true love of mine.

Jason P. Baker

The Righteous Way

I want to, I need to, know who you are
We meet, we speak, no more from afar
I never imagined you and I here
Talking, embracing, a friendship we share
The scent of my perfume, linger in the air
Whispering visions of me, I dance in your head
Representing joy, honesty, peace, and love
For I possess these things, my gifts from above
No influencing your decision, like Adam and Eve
No apple to bite from, just those four seeds
Together we must water them, with tender loving care
If we do not, no growth can we share
For I am rare, precious beyond your belief
I'm one of your ribs
Halt! No more shall you seek
Defying all others, righteously you speak
We're given a chance, a gift placed at our feet
Letting nothing, no obstacle, stand in our way
We are heirs to his throne, in the most righteous way

Denise Fenner

Life

What's life all about pray tell.
We marry, raise children, work and live in hell.
We fear for our family, our jobs our life.
What happen to the American rights.
To enjoy God given things! The air, trees and flowers he brings.
All he ask is to become one of his to enjoy the
abundant life he gives.

"For the whole duty of man is to fear God and
keep his commandments."

When this life is all said and done! We have
only just begun, for now the judgement we must
go through. Wishing you well I hope to see you.

Cynthia McMiller

We Live On Patch Road

Come visit us, old relatives, lost friends.
We live on Patch Road.
The sun is bright, the air is warm.
We long for visitors. There can be no harm.
The last time someone came it was 1954.
Can't you find us?
We live on Patch Road.
Please come; bring your friends, children.
Flowers would be nice too.
You see, we'll be here a long, long time.
If you can't find us, look for the gravestones marked:
Jacob. Harriet. Mary Ann. Lewis Amos. Jane. Harriet
Belle. Our house numbers are: 1861. 1849. 1849. 1896.
1870. 1954.
We live on Patch Road.

Joyce A. Fox

The Best Of Friends

I have a slew of sisters, we are the best of friends
We laugh together, we cry together and tell a joke or two
For we are the very best of friends and that's what sisters do

We know when one is happy, we know when one is blue
We are always there for one another, and that's what sisters do

We've shared together through times of loss and celebrated too
For we are the very best of friends and that's what sisters do

We can tell when one is hurting and even feel the pain
We can tell when one has prospered and even shared the gain
We can even fuss and argue and give our separative views
For we are the very best of friends and that's what sisters do

Bonnie Dues

Music

Music is the beauty among all arts.
We express all our emotions and our thoughts wish music,
We create artistic scenes with the sounds and with rhythm.

Music is the almighty art of all arts.
Music can conquer all hearts of man without aggress,
Music can reach out to people everywhere on the Earth.

Music is the great art among all arts.
Music is close to man all his life from birth to his death,
From berceuse and wedding march to funeral and fare-well.

Music is the finest art among all arts.
Our hearts and souls improve so much with the sounds of music,
Our lives are filled with more pleasure when there is good music.

Music is the endless art of all arts.
Music is the sum of all men's hearts and all his senses,
The mathematicians of the soul and all his being.

Music is the one immortal true sound...
Music genius always lives by their great compositions
Music is the symphony of life all over the world.

Ferdinand Suhodobnik

Untitled

When I see the setting sun
    Upon the western horizon
I feel that all my hopes and dreams
    have come to an end
Yet, when I awaken and see
    the golden glow of the sun
Over the eastern horizon
    I know that all my hopes and dreams
That I hold so dear to my heart
    have yet another day in which to come true.

Bobby J. Miller

24

Once Upon A Dream

Once we thought we would last forever
We couldn't see beyond our dream
Our love clouded the vision to see
That one day we would be a part
But our love would continue in our hearts
We have our joys and happy times
To help our hearts mend with time
Is it wrong to think beyond
The time we have together
To be the one to dream a dream
Knowing it's not forever
It seems it wasn't meant to be
But can we start again
Once upon a dream.

Carol Markland

The Pains Of Life

Some of us sing our sorrows away.
　　We become singers.
Some of us joke our sorrows away.
　　We become comedians.
Some of us write our sorrows away.
　　We become writers.
Some of us think our sorrows away.
　　We are called thinkers.
Sometimes we cry our sorrows away...
　　We are all children.
Always learning, but never all knowing.
Always teaching, but someone is never taught.
Always dying, but something never dies.

Girard Armstead

"We Are Here"

We are mortals of the past, hear our cry "We are here.
We are human kind you speak of, so long past,
See our language scrawled on ancient walls at last.
"Look here," our skulls and bones so neatly laid rest.
See our brave warrior sword against his breast.
Over there, our plundered cites scarred by wars of old,
Our hidden history of secrets, do unfold.
Hear our chanting language, will you ever know,
We maids sing our song in the temple of Apollo.
On the Earth our Mummies laying where their lives were spent,
A mockery of life gone by, wonder where they went.
Decades and decades of our crumbling life,
Our long stories now tell of our struggles and strife.
Yet in Eternal slumber so far away, yet so near,
We send our messages of the past, "We are here" "We are here"

June D. Ferrier

Medicine Man

Accepted, respected apart from all others.
Truths, fears, soft spoken lies
with fervent eyes and medicine man sees through.

Calculating, analyzing, more than you see.
Strong truths reflect medicine man's sooth.

He above all others understands.
The one who listens is often not heard over
he who babbles.
The medicine man travels alone.

Inside insecurity, jealousy, pain and turbulence.
Necessary elements for achievement
of self-fulfilling appeasement.
Medicine man devoid of sanity protects those full
of vanity.

Amy Lynn Smith

Reminders

Hurtling down the highway, "hell-bent for election",
we are given reminders, that alter our direction.

A big bird feet up, a deer on the shoulder,
each a reminder, that we are getting older.

The remains of a squirrel, which made it half-way,
a reminder of the brevity of our very own stay.

A procession of cars inconveniences us,
the hearse, a reminder: "Why all the fuss?"

Life's too short - no matter how long!
Tomorrow we may sing our farewell song.

Stalks of corn, orchards full grown,
fields of grain results of seeds sown.

Spring gives birth and Summer growth spells,
the Fall prepares for Winter's farewells.

The sun sets in the distance and colorfully waves "bye",
a daily reminder that we, too, shall die.

At tomorrow's dawn, it shall again rise,
a reminder to us, that our spirit never dies.

Hurtling down the highway, we can't miss the reminders;
unless, of course, we are wearing blinders!

Charles J. Scherer

"Reflection"

In this world of strife and terror
We all need to reflect anew
Stop! Take time and look in your mirror
Are you among the very few
Who will try and make a change
In the way you think and talk
To this great effort we must not balk
For the youth, the old need encouragement
Lest we all descend to derangement
Take that step to help your brother
Put this planet back in order

Barbara C. DiFonzo

"Stones"

As I reminisce, reflecting back on winding roads of stones
Way beyond where the early morning meets the earth,
I know someday under this ground I will lay my bones
As millions have done so before me and just as life gives birth,

And then tests us to where we no longer feel we walk on solid ground.
I'll share the pain and suffering you'll feel when those you love
In time just die, leaving life as others past, but I'll stand sound
Holding my own knowing I must someday rise above these clouds above.

Beyond the mountains I surpass yet conquer my own fear of the unknown,
I search for love within my blood which does thin out is passing time.
I've walked in heavy rains and freezing nights and, now grown,
I carry my own blood of stones deep in my heart knowing they are mine.

So as I follow my own trail of life filled with memories still to come
I realize laughter does bring tears in time as life hardens my soul,
And as I reach the summit of my life, looking back I hear a drum
Pounding in my heart "These stones are lives and love's your goal".

So, I forward my pace into the valley that's at the end of life
With these brotherhood of stones in hand and tears from my heart.
This burden is mine inherited until I die, therefore, I'll strive
To someday die and know my life of stones and I, never did depart.

Jose Luis Gonzalez

An Indo-American Prayer

Preacher my friend is the wind or the air
Water the father so very dear
Earth is the mother she holds us stable
So very powerful so very capable
The day and the night they nurse us together
They don't discriminate the weak or the better
God's judge watches from above
Eventually we get what we really deserve
Pray to him so very gently
You are saved and a lot more instantly

Ajit Kaur Chadha

Loving Memories

The most precious thing I've seen in awhile,
Was my mothers warm and beautiful smile.
With her strength and will, she fought so long,
This mother of mine was very strong.

The suffering she did, the toil, the pain,
Gave us relief when the end came.
That horrible disease took her you see,
But with the Lord, she'll forever be.

If your mothers alive, treat her well and kind,
Cause mother like her you'll never find.
You just never know how strong the bond,
Until it's to late and there gone.

I miss her more than words can say,
But I hope to see her mother day.
The time spent with her I'll never regret,
Deepest warm memories, I'll never forget.

If I stay with God close to me,
My mother again, I will see.
What a glorious day that will be,
My Jesus, My God, My Mother, and me....

Darlynn Tolman

Anticipation

And he said to me:

The trees are tall here in Atlanta. Very green and very calm.

The cool misty air of the fall drifts in. I'm torn between a
warm bowl of spicy "Ambush" chili or a cup of hot apple cider.
My thoughts flow on the cool air, spelunking in the caves, and
the right sweater. The din of traffic rumbles in the distance.
I listen...

"Look at the people around you - so busy in the game of Life.
Do they know? Do they see?"

He takes me on a placid walk through a forlorn cemetery.
The sun is hiding behind the clouds.
The worn headstones bring reality crashing into present time.

"Is this the end result? Is this where a frantic society is heading?"

A huge oak tree stands solid in the center of the field.
Remnants of the civil war lay scattered, all but forgotten.

Where is Rome?

"Learn...from the mistakes we have made. That's why we are here."
"That's why we are here," his voice fades into my mind.

I decide on the "Ambush". Where is Rome?

Chili it is...

Daniel Robert Rezac

The Future Me

Young ladies twirling around in a sphere,
Waltzes and flowers permeating the air,
As a little girl so fragile and small,
I admired the ladies at the Debutante's Ball.
Spinning 'round and 'round so fancy and free,
That's how I see the future me.

Gallant young men full of vigor and charm,
Leading the ladies with a tuxedoed arm,
Proud moms and dads wiping away tears,
Reflecting on their daughter's childhood years.
Pretty white gowns as far as you can see,
That's how I see the future me.

Barbara A. Brice

Reality

Life begins at 5:00 in the morning,
Waking up more than bills.
The kids need lunch money and more.
Tuesday morning the car won't start,
I've had better days.

Two weeks of beans and cornbread.
The water and gas are way over due.
Final notice comes three days before pay,
But still we find ways to postpone.

Adults and kids are sleeping in the streets.
Guns and rockets are trivial points in life,
Food and clothes mean much more.

For it's so cold!
"The world can be so cruel"
It's still so cold.

Dusty Gene Rhodes Sr.

You're Worth Waiting For

She sits there all alone
waiting for her name to be called.
She feels like she doesn't belong,
like she's not welcome there at all.

To her they say not a word,
yet their hearts are filled with sorrow,
as they see this young girl
throw away her chance for tomorrow.

As she sits in that downtown clinic,
this young girl of age sixteen,
she already knows she's pregnant,
for the evidence can already be seen.

She knows that she made a mistake,
so she asked God for forgiveness.
And her fear she prays God will take,
for she knows that what she's doing is best.

So please remember this story
and know that, for your own sake,
when it comes down to your body,
it's always best to wait.

Carmen Lyles

Hunger Vs. Love

A hungry cat sat beneath a tree
Very still! Very still!
As still as still can be.

Perched on the branch of the tree above
Was a bird who sang to his lady love.
With gusts! With gusto!
Their goals were different, let me relate

The cat wanted dinner— the bird, a mate!

Eileen Pentecost

As I Rapidly Go Through Life

As I rapidly go through Life, my God, help me to continue
valuing all the beauty that you have created, such as a rose that
fills the air with its sweet aroma as it blooms towards the bright
sun, the animals, the blue sky, and so many other innumerable creations.
As I rapidly go through Life, my God, help me to continue
valuing the diverse talents that you have given Man in order to
create artistic, literary, and musical works, for through them we
are able to learn about the world in which we live in.
As I rapidly go through Life, my God, help me to continue
valuing my parents, my other family members and friends, for through
them I can find happiness and motivation in life in order to
continue developing as a self-fulfilled person.
As I rapidly go through Life, my God, help me to remember
that the most beautiful and everlasting thing that exists in this
World is the Love that You offer us each day, for through It we
can overcome the obstacles that interfere with our journey towards
Your paradise, being this the height of human existence.

Giselle Maria Crespo

Footprint

The silence wafted from the forest floor, like incense being coaxed
upward by a hazy sun.
Somewhere a footfall shatters virgin leaves, crushed under a presence
alien to this foliage.
What uninvited guest transgresses here?
What intruder peals this cacophony of obscene decibel on tenderground?
He trudges on, seemingly oblivious to the horror of his action, caring
not to pause, nor contemplate his ruinous trek, he marches on.
Many years hence, as the last tree is felled, the last trickle falls
over the rocks, and the last blade of grass withers and dries in the
torrid sun, there will be no one in this place to remember that first footprint.
That first invasion did onset a trek to destruction.
Seeming eons are but a twinkle on natures plain, and the stars remind
us of promises unkept. No forgiveness.

Jeff Harless

A Gentle Friend

You cannot know Tim
unless you've read his roguish letters
sloshed with him through marshes
knee-deep in Martinis
with joy's broken compass in the tumbler.

If you have a moment
he will sling you through a Texas back road
strapped in his white diesel time machine
to talk to a cow.

You may see him on the podium
perched like an egret
waiting for a mackerel
and then the downbeat dart
of his spiraling baton
spearing a tempo
flying with it, wings beating.

You cannot know this gentle friend
and not be touched
by the Van Gogh depth
of simple human kindness.

Jim Price

Tomorrow

Wonder and ponder for however long you will
Those soft yesterdays do still, in their turn
move across the landscape,
in shades of blue and green
Borrowed yesterdays
Rented tomorrows
For life does move on
On and on

Anthony Imes

Building A Being

Shaped within the realms of our parents' past
unknowingly grasping and accepting their claylike form

Lives impaled with ones' history building
character into another flailing being searching for love

Shadows constantly appearing lest we forget
mistakes borne upon a sinless creature now growing old

Those childless remain blameless and free of the
responsibility for societies immeasurable improprieties

Future dreams impregnated by footprints
deeply rooted in young souls through precious upbringing

'Tis not their fault yet possibly their fate
a family tree revealed within the framework of two lives

Yesterday we were young and received the
teachings of two transpiring their ghosts and conscience

Today our children prepare for the future
anxious to build upon the foundation and support we created

Let's pray each can survive our hands-on mold
believe in themselves and achieve beyond our expectations

Without carrying the burden of our phantoms or
reliving our past mistakes embedded at birth upon our souls

Garthalene Chrzan

The Beauty In The Bubbles

In a marble emerald green sunken tub,
Two-thirty in the morning,
A popped cork makes a simple thud.
One small oil lantern is burning.

Warmth under the bubbles and water is found,
Bubbles crackling and popping ever so lightly,
A million little convex domes round,
Reflecting the one lamp brightly.

Turning over your hand,
Every little orb winks,
Your complexion seems brilliantly tan.
A champagne glass sinks.

Movements causes multiple explosions,
Bubbles disappearing to reveal others,
Your face is in motion,
In the bubbles and their brothers.

The bubbles have an inner beauty,
Your face and your smile,
Your reflection is their duty,
They serve until they die.

Anthony G. Carey

"Lush Lands"

Warm, moist air filled the entire rainforest
Triple layer canopy preventing strong lights entrance
A misty vapor engulfed the jungle constantly
A rich diversity of life welled up from the earthly jungle body
Rotten masses of plant remains await their return to the fertile earth
Lush green plants sprouting from the productive soils
Strikingly beautiful orange - red birds crossed the extremely forested sky
dissipated water vapor
Loss of leafy layers
Animals slaughtered all about
Fertile soils leached, a barren land plot to remain
gaseous fumes displace plentiful oxygen
colorless horror awaits all destructors
Life's ultimate armageddon

Jason Galetka

27

Echo In The Wind

The lighting strikes and the thunder that pursues is deafening as two hearts tear apart. The love they once shared is in shambles, with no hope of ever binding them as one again.

Understanding has departed these two lives as one walks alone in the sands. A pair of footprints where there once was a set, has drifted away in the tides of loneliness, never again to return. Anguish fills the void left behind, and isolation sets them apart from the world.

The pleading of one's soul to another is but an echo in the wind. Pride builds the obstacle so high that even the wisdom to over come is demolished before it tries.
As somber as the thunderset skies, so is there perspective on continuing on together. Tarnished is the memories that once sparkled, and illuminated each other eyes.

Honesty to confess one's wrong doings is turned to blame. Fatal is the mistake to accept the status of this struggle of wills.
This decision is made, and each chose their sides, for unto these two lives results in the failure of the other.
Can two hearts mend the severed ties and set to flight again?

The uncertainties of this sets one soul into rage, and a skeptic emerges to seal the fate of two fallen hearts.

Joi Ellen Luce

Black Sheep

Nineteen years have they been wed; seven mouths in all that need be fed. Two decades now the eldest child stands; three brothers younger yield not demands. One sister makes the total five; seven so far the contrive.

In the numbers holds the key; to find the one who black sheep be.

At birth there was no banter played; the name would go to he who stayed. The one who left by choice it's told; will now not see the babe grow old. At the start a gift he left; to leave a mark from fruit he theft.

One was righteous, one was rude; the black sheep now can you extrude.

A gesture made that was quiet thoughtful; papers signed to keep it lawful. A mouth to feed and bills not paid; is well his mind that one who stayed? A pact was made on bended knee; sealed with band on digit three.

We and licensed, iron clad; black sheep now shall call him dad.

Review the lines of questions linger; the answer like with index finger. Youngsters five for you to choose; answer right and yet you lose. To know the one these lines reveal; a sorrow shared with no appeal.

Answer not if heart be torn; the black sheep still shall be forlorn.

John Shanline

Reality

In my dream I run down a hall,
Turn many corners and try not to fall,
Don't know where I am,
Don't know where I've been,
Trying to figure out, what tunnel I'm in,
Then I come to a big bright light,
And take in my breath at the sickening sight,
The air is so thick with a foul smell,
From exhaust and smoke, I can't really tell,
Garbage everywhere, gangs on the street,
And people who don't have shoes for their feet,
I hear a gunshot, and a frightened child cry,
And some that wish that they would just die,
    I slap myself to try and wake,
From this horrible nightmare, I just couldn't shake,
    As it started getting hazy to see,
        I realized this was no dream,
            But reality

Jeanine Audette Koszalka

Judgement Day

Justice is blind, she cannot see.
Truth is elusive, where might it be?
Is it in the evidence that is shown?
Or in the witness and the words they own.
The facts, just the facts will be told.
Can the truth be bought, can it be sold?

Will the lawyers present the truth
To the twelve sitting in the booth?
Will the jury be fair in the end?
Only time will tell, my friend.
And on the day when the verdict is read,
What are the words that shall be said?

Guilty, not guilty, what will it be?
Justice is blind, she cannot see.
The victims are gone, but can they tell
If the decision is just at the final bell?
Truth and justice, it's the American way
Shall we believe it on judgement day?

Jimmy R. Davis

The Hill

Ominous eyes watched his burdened steps, traveling slow.
Troubled by unknowing on lookers,
eyes shaded by branches of hate - ignorance.

Red sweat washed his torn eyes and a vision filled his mind,
a vision of a better world, an after world, a life after life.

His utopia was broken
as his knees crashed to the graveled surface.
A whipped and beaten shell now, trickled
blood from a new wound, staining a stained journey.

Relief - gained for a moment.
A burden lightened,
but demons drew comfort as he stumbled on.

A head, raised,
hung low,
shamed, no longer looking upward for comfort.
Spit and sweat thinned the blood that teared his face,
but no hate, no blame shone from his sunken eyes.

He slowed
then stood still - and raised his paled face.
Waiting was the hill.

Frank A. Applin

Autumn

Mornings are colder, sun less bright
Trees turn to golden hues.
Autumn is coming, so said the news.
Frost at dawn, so thick and white
Lay upon lawns from a cold cold night
Chased away by the light of the rising sun
It's sure to return when day is done.
Air was cold and crisp when I awoke
Now mingles with the scent of smoke.
Birds and their songs will soon disappear
No longer to linger upon ones ears.
Tinted sunsets in the evening sky
Welcome the autumn, as do you and I.
It is again that time of year
When colorful flowers will appear
Autumn is near and it's coming soon
We often can tell by the looks of the moon.
Yes, autumn is coming...autumn is here.

Dorothea Pogue

Brush With A Stranger

Strolling on a lonely street
Total strangers chance to meet.
They bid "hello," share a smile—
Strange lives touching for a while.

The gent who opens wide the door
To help a lady out the store
May never see again the one
For whom this service he has done.

A doctor treats a strangers pain;
A shared umbrella shields the rain;
A man stands up to give his seat—
Strangers for a moment meet!

Happiness each one derives
From gently touching other lives.
The more lives touched, more smiles we see,
The richer our own lives will be!

Betty Valle Gegg

"Child Abuse"

Battles we have to win; why does everyone know such sin
Tortured from a child; said you were "too wild"
Cried out loud each night; just once you wished to win the fight
Seeping, deepening, endless coldness
Just needed warm someday to hold
The shadowed stillness, gave you no will,
Living such fear, afraid to cry a single tear
Came only at night; knew you could not fight
Afraid, alone, speechless; never did reach this;
Desperate, independent, always alone
Terrified of his connection, the phone
Fifteen, sixteen, twenty....life goes by...
Able to see the anger inside, always in his raging eyes...
The shadowed stillness, he haunts your dreams
At night, often, you still wake up and scream
For open arms to greet you warm....
You never have...they're never there...your tears come down...
like a panicked storm....once again...you reach out, into open air,
You're still alone....you never deserved this; you never wanted.
But it's your despair...it was never theirs...EDG

Erin Green

Lost Values

Buttons, pencils, pans and pins,
Torn up clothes, old rusty tins.
Day after day, day in and out,
The people come and look about.
They look at each other, to watch and see,
And ask themselves, "Who's better than me?"
Their memories left to no one knows,
While yesterday comes, and then it goes.
Torn up clothes, old rusty tins,
Buttons, pencils, pans and pains.

Doreen Mussetter

The Remedy

I look at you and see the marks
too smart for others to see.
Judged by your appearance, job, skin.
What happened to goodness, a goodness within
others can't touch you. Can't they see? Life
is not just about you of he.
What happened to goodness, a goodness within.
Power it feeds them, it seethes within.
You fight, you fight, drugs, disease.
Whose to listen not the birds and the bees.
What happened to goodness, a goodness within.

Dawn Ilacqua

The Talking Wind

I've missed you again,
Too many times you've passed me by
Howling through the fingers of my open hand
Like all the lifetimes you've known.

I gaze into the wonderful chaos of a reflection pool
Loved by you—in a circle
A thousand times over.

To the beautiful epochs played out by your hand
Joining the ancestry,
Scattering the sorrow to a city
Where ages are born.

Ben Edward Mickelberry

Idle Chatter

Idle chatter
Tongues that hurt, tears that fall, fall
Ah Fall! It lifts me from my fallen wall
Warm reds, oranges, yellows, golds, flutter in the wind
Wind, the sound of long ago; it is told.
Stirs what from my soul?
Frees my spirit from that wall.
To shout and feel so glad and tall!
Idle chatter...you don't matter anymore!

Annou Drabier Heric

Today

Today is all that I have. I will not waste time worrying about
     tomorrow or dwelling on yesterday.
With every moment I live, each of my feelings and actions will
     determine my past and become memories I will one day reflect upon.
With every breath I take I will act, think, dream and live to the
     fullest of my ability, for there is no time to waste.
No one person's attitude will get my spirits down.
No one's actions will deter my faith.
The more I live, the more I am.
With the inevitable passing of time, I become stronger and wiser in
     every dimension.
I will be all that I am capable of being.
Others around me will take my energy, motivation and love into their
     own being and pass it to others, and so on.
If my smiles are contagious, so is my attitude.
I will put an abundance of power into everything I do everyday, and
     live each day to the fullest...as if it were my last.

Analisa Felix

Ode To Love

Based on gross and most particular care
Told by the nether brain with tongue in cheek
A something, nothing, held against despair:
That need finds apt the pliant eyes frame fair.
As beavers build a dam across a creek
Whose waters rise and calm and cover well
That secret that the lurking mink would seek,
We rig our purchased rainbows here to quell
The gathered drabness of this, our Hell
Where all is bulwark against death to come,
Where all our music comes to one poor drum,
One savage roll, one neighing of the steed,
One hope for us or any wasting weed
That holds its tendrils to the wind: TO BREED.

Benjamin Miller

Three Faces

Yesterday I saw a rose in all its beauty, haunting,
Today I feel its prickly thorns and ache from sudden hurting.
Tomorrow I will see its death and smell its fragrance leaving.
    Why so different every day?

Yesterday the voice was here, filled with strength and license.
Today it weakens ever slightly, hinting of a silence.
Tomorrow only echoes cold from whispering like ice.
    Why so different every day?

Yesterday the sky was fair, the sun was glory, dazzling.
Today the heaven's storming rain with skies above still threatening.
Tomorrow's just a hazy mist, but promises bright gleaming.
    Why so different every day?

Helen M. Martin

Trying To Write A Poem

Trying to become inspired and trying
to write a poem;
while the rain falls light and slow.
My soul is longing for the quiet voice
of silence;
while the gap between joy and sadness
becomes wider.
All I hear is people laughing and talking
in the street.
I hear the engines of cars in a race against
time.
As the Sunday goes by, I am still trying to
write a poem;
trying to become inspired and longing for
what I left behind.

Ana Santana

Blue Is Just A Color

Blue is just a color
to those who watch the sky and sea roll by
without a thought of how they came to be
or why,
it means much more to me...

Blue is a baby's eyes
clear, liquid pools of hope and trust
without disgust, untruth or lust...

Blue is a lone small flower
rising above a field of thorny grass
that grabs at ankles like slivers of polished glass...

Blue is a sharp-cornered memory
of love that had two paths
one built with trust and hope and faith
...where blue is clear and calm
and made of all life's "best"
one strewn with fragments of life, deceit, and wrath
...where blue is a pale, soft blanket
in which a tiny fragile form
will be laid to rest...

Deanna Hines

Knowing Me

Before I can appreciate you - I have to value me...
To not relish myself is impiety against my spirituality...
It is sacrilege against the blessed words I speak

To declass, demote, and depress my
distinctiveness is a despondent practice
that needs to be addressed
in the essence of my very soul.

And to say "I know you" in the least - is
contradictory to any emotion I will ever feel.

Jorja Angela Porter

Walt And The Dancer

He was youthful seventy and saying goodbye
To the hundred and fifty who were there.
They dressed him in a white hat and big bow tie
To accentuate the loving personality we'd come to share.

Laughter abounded with the lighthearted roast,
But the mood turned when the question was asked.
What motivates this man to always give and never boast
Of his personal accomplishments of the past?

Then the beautiful, haunting melody began to flow
And the singer's glorious voice filled our emotions
As the dancer began the heartwarming lyrics to show
Through elegance of form and sensitivity of expression.

Across the floor she glided with beauty and grace,
Sharing warm feelings of love as she flowed;
For the dancer's inner love permeated her limbs and face,
Extolling the virtues of this man with the giving of a rose.

Jim Lisk

Rolling Hills

From the rolling hills of North Carolina
To the beautiful sandy shore
To the roaring Atlantic Ocean
And the never ending folklore

You can smell the white gardenias
As they bloom along the way
Their aroma is so pungent
You just can't resist a small bouquet

The sandy hills are the highest
You will find anywhere
You only have to climb to the top
To see the scenery in the distance there

You may take a dip in the ocean
Feel the cold water against your skin
You'll come out so refreshed
And feel a certain peace from within

The home folks are so friendly
A stranger you will never be
They will take you to their bosom
And you'll be just like family

Anne Winnan

Memory

It had become the old man's mode,
To tell his story for any one to hear,
So he hastened across the road,
To seek my listening ear,

"You remember Barnie," he'd start.
Barnie was long since laid to rest.
"Now Barnie, for a cat, sure was smart."
"He'd be waiting for me back at the crest."

"I'd get off at the mill,"
"Catch me a ride home, you see,"
"And there'd be old Barnie at the top of the hill,"
"Just ah waiting there for me."

"Barnie didn't know I worked at the plant,"
"But he knew I was ah coming home."
So on and on he would rant,
Down old paths his thoughts would rome.

Till even ponderance over a love deceased,
Could become, I have supposed,
A sorrow tenderly released,
A memory sweetly reposed.

David O. Logan Jr.

Is Anyone Listening?

I try with all that is in me
To struggle against the undertow,
I strive to gain a little ground...
Make a friend, feel the sun on my face,
Share my inner self.
Then...
Betrayal again!
Frantic to keep my head above water
I cry out with silent screams,
No one hears... no one cares...
I'm drowning.
The voice inside me says, "I have something to say I count!"
I will not be sucked under the murky depths of obedient conformity.
This time they almost did it,
Almost extinguished that inner me...
But... I am stronger than I seem
I swear, if I am dragged down, I'll be re-surface,
I'll beat the tide...
And when I speak, ... with a quiet voice, I'll be heard.

Dawn Virginia Kuykendall

Peace

I would sometimes like the chance
    to spread my wings and fly
To soar above these daily problems
    that make me question why

To reason out the ways and means
    we use to hurt each other
When love and tolerance are simple needs
    and our neighbors are our brothers

Ignorance is the spark that flames
    the fire of fear and doubt
An open mind and an open heart
    are the means to stamp it out

Let's lift our faces heavenward
    and pray for strength and courage
to know the peace and serenity
    our God intended for us

Deborah Abbott Rose

Unanswered Prayer

Oh how I've prayed to the LORD above
to someday soon find my true LOVE
No matter how much I pray
I have no reason to believe,
that someone could actually care deeply for me
just when I've found someone new
GOD always points out to me
it's too good to be true
There's times when I just
break down and cry
I don't understand is God punishing me?
If so why?
My heart has been broken so many times
I don't think I'll ever have
someone to call mine
Many times I've had feelings for someone
that they couldn't return
You'd think by now that I'd have learned
I ask myself is there someone out there just for me?
No one knows but GOD he knows my DESTINY

Jennifer L. Perkins

Unrequited Love

Sometimes it takes a while
To see the love you feel is not returned.
No matter how much you love
Doesn't mean you won't be burned.
It's hard to know, which feelings should be revealed
Because when you are hurt,
It takes so long, before your heart is healed.
I'm trying to learn to love from afar
And not pin my hopes, on a shooting star
I keep my wishes and dreams inside of me,
And pray someday, you will set them free.

Anna U. Hebert

My Taunting Spirit

The taunting spirit,
To see it is to hear it.
Creep along on it chains of gold.
Is it a child or full grown, male or female.
To not find out, would be to fail.
This taunting spirit within me,
This spirit would then make three.
Good or bad this spirit in my soul.
Is it what does make me whole.
What ever it is, it is part of me.
And I'll make the best of it just we three.

Jennifer Bennett

Good-bye

They asked me not to see you
    To remember you from before.
I wish they only knew,
    That moment my heart fell to the floor.
They said it would be better this way,
    How would they know what's better?!
Why should I be the one who has to pay?!
    I shouldn't have to say good-bye in a letter.
I need to see you the way you are,
    I'll never be able to forget the past.
I know that the end is not far,
    I just want to make this time last.
There must be some closure for me.
    I just can't turn my back.
I'll never let something like this be,
    Something in my heart I would lack.
I'd never relieve the guilt in my heart,
    If I just let you die.
I know it would just tear me apart,
    If I never said good-bye.

Bobbi Ristain

Can I Make You Understand?

In the hierarchy of dreams the first one is this:
    To love and be loved, to me this is bliss.
All other dreams come from this one
    Without you in my world, there is no sun.

You inspire me, desire me, make me tremble at your touch.
    I've never known a man a like - I didn't know I could want so much.
For so long now I've looked for love, and then it took me by surprise.
    When you held me close, I felt no fear, and then I looked into your eyes.

I knew at once I could get lost in depths of blue so clear,
    And then my body turned to fire whenever you came near.
Now I'm at my greatest peril 'cos I'm helpless to control
    The power of my love for you - you're now a part of my soul.

Cindy Clifford

Jehovah Is God

The Alpha and Omega is the name that's given
to our God that dwells in the eternal heaven.

Jehovah-Jireh, "The Lord Will Provide"
yes, He is always at our side.

Jehovah-Shammah, "The Lord Is There"
He will answer our every prayer.

Jehovah-M'Kaddech changes our lives
he is "The Lord Who Sanctifies".

Jehovah-Nissi is what I say
He's "The Lord My Banner" this very day.

If you are sick and so badly you feel
ask of Jehovah-Rophe, "The Lord Heals".

Jehovah-Tsiudkenu came to bless
he is "The Lord Our Righteousness".

When King David called on Jehovah-Rohi,
"The Lord Our Shepherd" was at his side.

If you call on Jehovah with your request
Then God will answer the way He knows best.

I've found Him, The Answer, as my heart cried.
Ask in His will, 'twill not be denied.

Ivan E. Cousins

A Friend

The loveliest thing in the world is a friend,
To one you can talk when at your wit's end.
Or maybe you're just in the mood to chat,
With a good old friend, you can't beat that.

A friend in your life is so good to see,
Make sure I'm the same when they're looking at me.
When I am the friend or you turn it about,
Are you true to the end without even a doubt?

A friend is a person to cherish so dear,
A friend is one who sees us so clear.
A friend takes us completely, just as we are.
They love us today and also tomorrow.

Bill Young

The Dance

How do we know when to dance the dance of love?
To move to the rhythms of the music...
To lift up our hearts to Him and accept this beat as the one we sway
to... To not question or deny or fear what has been put before us.
How do we let go of the past to drift towards a future that is waiting...

Rhythmically, we move to the beat as visions of failure dance in our heads.
Do we not listen to our hearts... from what comes failure?
Do we fear the growth, the expansions of our hearts as the music
continues to play?

Patiently and lovingly He lifts us out of despair... only by our asking.
He puts before us a new song...a new partner...our inner child, our
spiritual being so that we may move to the rhythms of our own soul.

So we look to Him and to the child within as our companion... We
decorate our own souls, we plant our own garden... We dance the
dance of love...
We move to the rhythms so peacefully... knowing He has given us
the wisdom to step to the beat of our own hearts...

Giving us the wisdom to know that a broken heart is an expanded
heart... A heart that is overflowing with love and acceptance of SELF...
We pick up a new beat... a new rhythm and we Dance the Dance of LIFE.

Judy Harper

Just A House

It's interesting, what you have to do
To make your every dream come true
Sometimes I wonder, is it worth it all?
Why did I have to build to tall?

The years it's taken, the money spent
I guess that's where my youth went
and now I wonder—after 100 years
who will care about all my tears?

What difference will it make to my grandchild
if the floors had rugs or if they were tiled?
The important thing is that I love
with the power given from God above

Carole L. Lever

This Is The Escape...

This is the escape for a natural poet.
To look at the stars and be able to see, what no one
but you is able to see.
There is no place you can't touch
No place you can't be.
For your imagination can reach farther than
any state of being.
It is a mystery to those who do not know it.
This is the escape for a natural poet.
You are not here, you are not there.
You are not anywhere, but yet everywhere.
You are never bored, lonely, but at times
very scared.
I say to those who do not understand
take a breath, look around, and try to see what I have found
Do not try to learn it, it is not to be taught,
because on its own it will bond.
It is a world only YOU can touch
It is the world only as YOU know it.
This is the escape for a natural poet.

Debbie Rachel Arreola

On Dying Young

Sometimes I think perhaps it would be much better
  to leave this world before the hurt sets in—
Before all the innocence is gone
    Before the heart is worn with battle-scars
      from half-forgotten love affairs
We should all be spared in the sweetness of childhood
  to die happy and free with no haunting wishes
      of what might have been
Let's not ever grieve for those who leave us in
    the first soft bloom of youth
For they have known happiness and contentment
      as God meant it to be
  I had that happiness once long ago
      but that was before you
      Before you made me love you and then
        so coldly went away
Now I shall die old in heart if not in body
  and I'm all too sure that my soul
      is far too empty
          for even heaven to accept—

Glenna S. White

32

Desert Storm

A maniac's uncertainty orders death squads certainly
to kill his own who dare to question his wavering authority.
No course he takes is questioned and never spoke aloud.
A cooling breeze, a tall cold drink—"My kingdom for a cloud!"

Anxiety is building as the clock continues ticking.
The quiet yells its revelry and the heat is somewhat sickening.
No voices swear, no screams are heard—just silence, oh so loud!
A cooling breeze, a tall cold drink—"My kingdom for a cloud!"

The battle ends so quickly, the people are so sickly, from famine
brought upon the land by this demon in charge so quickly.
Environmental disaster by this hypocritical master—we must feed
the starving crowds.
A cooling breeze, a tall cold drink—"My kingdom for a cloud!"

When will mankind have the day, to live together in a better way,
to teach the weak not make them pay?
I hope not when destruction's won and havoc becomes destruction's
son, so I'll speak up bold and loud.
It's when a cooling breeze will be ore the earth, when peace
resounds from our birth and a tall cold drink is shared by all —
When we live in the kingdom in the clouds.

Connie B. Rodgers

My Daughter

My daughter killed herself again today, from what began as fun
to impress her friends five long years ago.
"Just for us" they said, "It's cool, it's fun,
we wouldn't lie to you, you know us we're your friends."

The cool—the fun became a need that never went away.
Pills—caps—needles—smoke, whatever was ok.
Grades—morals, old friends went, family was forgotten.
Her only thing was where to score, and dealers won't give credit.

Cures were tried, the steps, and groups, we bared our souls our pocketbooks.
"Just one more chance, just one—I'll change", but we both knew the score.
A man is there, bony hand held out
and the specter won't give credit.

I saw the change, knew well the cause,
but denied it out of pride and fear.
So I'm guilty too of my daughter's death,
who killed herself again today.

Anthony Pendleton

A New Day

A guardian angel is what you need,
To help you through this time indeed.

The ins and outs the ups and downs,
The tears and laughter the smiles and frowns.

When the road is rocky and seems all up hill,
The Lord will give you the strength and will,

To keep moving forward through all thick and thin,
To conquer this sadness that's wallowing within.

Strength you are gaining with each passing day,
To put it behind you and go on your way.

It will all come together just wait and see,
A beginning an end and a time to be free.

Free from the pain the hurt and the sorrow,
Free to be Sandy today and tomorrow.

Debra Ann Johnston

Alone

I am alone no mother here
To help me with my pain
My pain of loss, my pain of fear, my pain of being one.
My mother was my soul, my peace, my inner strength,
Without her in my world; my days are lonely spent.
Why did my God, my savior, take away my soul,
Take away my only link to happiness, that I could ever hold
As I watch the light of life dim in her beautiful brown eyes
I looked into the heavens above and damned the bluish skies
Now I am alone and dealing with my grief
Think of me as that little tree that has just lost its leaf
It only had one, and one it lost
But at what price, and how high a cost.
Mother of Earth, and Mother of Sky
I will love you forever until the day I die.

Ava Bounds

Pieces Of The Heart

You,   Another

A first love,   A lost love
To give,   To take
To share my heart with you,   To keep my heart from you

To have a nearness,   To be separated
  To be the center of your life,   To be on the perimeter

To learn of love's balancing act

To know you're there,   To imagine you "out there"

To have you as a reality,   To have you as a memory

To know that you have   To know that I
  gone on to other loves,   have gone on to
                                              other loves too.

I now stand with
a branch of bittersweet
in my hands.

Carol M. Damon

"A Last Plea Before The End"

Your many faces torment me in my sleepless dreams...
To even touch you would be the ultimate scheme.

My heart pounds out a cry for whispers of your love....
Your killing eyes are as gentle as a dove.

My aching loins long to die in your arms....
Your persuasive smile is a part of your crafted charms.

This weak existence fails to withstand your every move...
SCREAM, whisper, Cry, SPEAK! What can I do to prove?

If I can't have one vague precious sign from you....
Then I'll make my final peace, and be damned, eternally blue.

Jennifer Jonea Furner

To See Thy Face

If Gods be bribed with them would I arrange,
To be this sheet thou holds and take its place;
A lovestruck sum therefore would I exchange,
To occupy thy hands and see thy face.
For when to thee sweet poems I send unsigned,
And picture thee alone that verse to read,
O'ercome by envy for my rhymes I find,
Myself and wish at once their life to lead.
With a kiss wouldst I ask thee grace this sheet,
As I have done to send to thy embrace,
So our lips may with this same paper meet,
To join if not in time at least in place.
Would that I were this poem that thee unfolds,
Doth bless with thy sweet gaze and gently holds.

Bruce Hendricks

A Yearning Heart

Thoughts of truth is her spiritual renewal
To emerge from bitterness and fear...
It's time to erase marital tension,
And overcome suffering and pain.

Her need is to be loved with affection...
With an intensity she cannot describe
She must take a correct view of this situation
To see a brightness that radiates light.

To begin with a new sense of reasoning..
There are important decisions to make,
To cope with life's startling moments,
So she can live in a carefree world.

She is yearning to hear sounds of laughter...
Release anxiety and oppose the hurts,
So she can glimpse into a future
And find herself in a world where she belongs.

Now that she is progressively weaker,
She writes this poem that shall endure,
To relate about something not yet in existence...
But optimistically convinced with blessing from G-D.

Eva Widawski

Parent's True Love

It's so lonely when children have left you
    To climb their ladders alone.
They seem to forget for a moment
    That their ladders were fashioned at home.

We painted the braces with sunshine
    And hung a star at the top.
Each rung we drove with a prayer
And secured it with love, for a stop.

So while you are climbing your ladders,
    Don't falter and don't be afraid,
We'll steady it and help you go higher.
    The extension is already made!!!

So fill up your pockets with sunshine
    And grab a hat full of dreams,
Scribble a note in the stardust,
    Hasten it home on a ray of moonbeams.

We will gather the message you send us
    Like the sun draws the dew from the rose.
We hope it will be a note of love and forgiveness
    And pray that your love only grows.

Frances M. Loscher

A Soldier's Farewell And Prayer

As I stand before you
To bid you a fond farewell
I consider an honor and privilege
To have served with you for many years

As long as our flag flies over us
We know that we are free
Old Glory is a mighty symbol
For all the world to see

I have served my God and country
With the best from within me
And if I have made mistakes, along the way
I pray that God will forgive me
When I am called away

Edgar H. Kleckley

The Stagecoach

Another stop at a wayside inn
    To change the horses and sup a bit.
The lumbering coach's creaky din
    Is stilled, though our ears yet ring of it.

We've traveled long and shall travel more
    As long as the coach holds together.
We'll finish the trip we're destined for
    No matter the perils or weather.

All such journeys, whether long or short,
    Are set at a gallop at the start,
Yet danger and fear are set at naught.
    Youth's bold expectation plays the part.

Mishaps, indeed, there will be enough;
    From misfortune no journey is free.
The cowards stop when the way gets rough,
    The faithful go on, whatever be!

The coach awaits. Our driver paces.
    Ahead, are dreams to be discovered.
We'll nestle in our well worn places
    And travel on, we two, beloved!

Humphrey J. Darling

Here, A Morning Pick Me Up

Time, gathered together
to be shared by all
As steam from the top
For the breeze to move about
Around the room
For all to enjoy like friendship
Steam from the brew
The relationship
To be as one has intended
The small amount of taste you thirst for
In a small cup of brew
All in all a warm cup of brew
And piece of mind moving over the room
Steam and vapor to happiness
Even if you can't see it doesn't mean it isn't there
Nevertheless it's there
The invisible sense
The knowing for a few

Alan G. Swanson

The Mask

Hide your thoughts and hide your actions
to be a part of the popular factions.
"Do as I say, not as I do"
You'd be surprised if you only knew.
Those that are held in awe
If found out would make you guffaw.
They are just as false as can be.
Their hedges are all you can see
Immoral, corrupt, and unjust,
yet they frown on us with disgust.

The "High" are abashed to admit to their past.
Their present and future appear with no suture
to seal the wound and silence the boon
to keep it from weeping and the truth from seeping
out from behind their mask

Ian Michael Magonigal

34

Reflection

My aging brain can be compared,
To an old and much used dwelling,
Where cluttered memories fill its space,
As closets crammed to swelling.

Many things are hard to find,
Confusing to remember.
Some thoughts held in this old mind,
Are like a wound that's tender.

Years pour out, fast and jumbled,
Into well worn halls,
And reflect in speech, over which I stumble,
Causing embarrassing falls.

I take each item and dust it off,
Exposing the fine grained wood.
Some of them I dearly love,
Others are not so good.

I examine each detail, quite minutely,
And every flaw it holds.
Then, I discover, more astutely,
Beneath each fault, there's gold.

Dawn A. Ek

A Sincere Plea For Help

Please, Dear God, please let me try,
To abide by your Divine Will, as time goes by,
Please, oh, please help me understand,
That if I ask in prayer you will lend a helping hand,
No matter how difficult the task will be,
I will have your guiding hand if I just ask of thee,
Please, oh, please help me not to cry,
As I part with all my loved ones when I must say goodbye,
Please let me try to always mend,
Each broken heart when misfortune has no end,
Let me forever try to do,
Whatever you plan and want me to,
God, oh, God, please hear my prayer,
And keep me always in your tender loving care.
Please, oh, please God hear my plea,
Let me always aspire to be close to thee,
As I end this special plea and prayer to you,
I know in my heart you will see me through in all I do,
For no one in this whole wide world could ever possess,
Without sincere prayer your guidance and eternal happiness.

Georgia E. Hamil

Thoughts From The Third Rail

I awoke in a chokehold from the sorrow of premature goodbyes
to a woman who was giving me space to get to know someone I'd already
begin to hate.
Hers was a passage from sunlit thoughts while she licked my half-dead
flames with collective aspirations and plans that always included
somebody I thought I should want to be for her.
Now a rehearsed, stale social distance has every intention of
replacing the feeling of her hands on me. Freshly squeezed spite
and laughter under words take the place of a warm waterfall I knew
while swimming, eyes open through the layers of darkness... always
consummated in an embrace. We had journeyed through anger and
resentment, negotiated through stubborn and complacent boundaries,
and fallen asleep in laughter only to find the travel had been a
circle, punctuated by some fierce hold of the hollow safety that
isolation provides... to what end? My phone is too close, my regrets
too fresh, my pain too apparent; I sit with my principles, take down
the pictures, listen in on other's conversations, avoid the message
behind green m and m's and Barry White, and do everything "iced."
Life's little movement, reluctantly entitled "repression."

Gregory J. Lauck

Naked

See through my shell
'Tis only a barrier, concealing my identity.
Little do you know of who I really am;
obstacles I surpass everyday.

I am as a paragraph, unsporadically perused.
You read only what is there, yet I am the message,
between the lines.

The cotton attire of my choice,
the label you have given.
Vigilant as I enter intimated with my knowledge.

Belittled, discredited, an interminable lecture,
steeped with comparing pestered by authorities
badgered like a misguided orphan.

Look past my cotton lining
rid of all pretext
Do away with the violent thoughts
expected that I commit.

I make these clothes.
These clothes do not
make me.

Juan Hernandez

Galway Bay Of My Dreams

Stereotype:
Tireless, I am not.
Motionless on a must-stained
Forest green blanket,
Generations blown in from the froth,
Not speaking, just blowing, blowing.
The smell could remind you of something...
Tennyson's God that blew strange smells, perhaps.
That's it!
Archaic, toothy, smiles.
Archaic smells run rampant through them.
No one greets you.
Words sift through their teeth,
But fall, lifeless and tired, on the floor.
I gather them to tell my life story,
My impassioned, exhausted life story.
Finished, I wrap them in a new blanket
And throw them into the bay of my dreams.

Ben Medley

Dreaming With Open Eyes

Sitting down on the ground under a tree
tired and a smooth breeze swallowing
with the fragrance of just cut lawn free
in an ideal world I began dreaming!

It was my most exciting experience
occurred like a retarded knockout
the best dream in my existence
a former boxer knows what he talks about!

Not asleep nor awake, with a stroke
and not being as I'm now, so old
I was walking in clear cloud of perfumed smoke
and found my self in a very different world!

There were no crimes, racial slurs,
wars or personal conflicts at all
nobody rich nobody poor
everything in perennial Fall

Then, back to reality
has been hard to believe
the world of cruelty
in which we humans live !

Henrique De Paula

The Golden Rule

We each have times of sadness and joy
  times for every girl and boy.

We must get through the bad and the good
  and live together in brotherhood.

Sisters, brothers all are we
  fighting for peace and unity.

Gifts of love we give to you
  even when you're sad and blue

Honesty, integrity
  Where can we find these qualities?

You're not judged by money and wealth
  but by just being yourself.

Love each person everyday
  Care for someone in a special way.

Abigail M. Didyoung

Houses

Who needs a house? Or shelter, says I,
'Til a wolf came along with a hungry eye.
She gobbled me up in a wink and a blink,
But left me alive, I think.

So I built a house — the best that I could
All out of straw; I should have used wood.
The wolves tore it down as quick as can be
And made a light snack out of me.

I'll have to build out of sterner stuff
Which no huff and no puff
Can destroy. Sticks should suffice,
And for building they're nice.

But the wolves don't care
'Cause they see me in there.
Down goes the house made of sticks;
Next time, I'll build my heart out of bricks.

Ben Lingenfelter

"The Scream Of Terror"

The shell burst in the night
Throwing a ray of fire and light
On the murderous crying
As the brave and faithful dying

You can hear the crack of guns
From large battle wagon cannon
To down the missile or plane
What cause this great terror

You can see the blood of an arm and part of a head
Who has cause no harm
No not when the time will come
To be with the screaming ones

Now this crucial war is over
But only part of brave men have returned
To stop this sorrowful horror
For the young men of tomorrow

Ernest Noles

The Painstaker

Give me your sorrow and hand over your pain
Throw me the sadness and anger in vain.
Things in your head lay heavy on heart
Cast them aside and begin a new start.
Yet here I shall stand with words and warm smiles
With comforting hands, easing pain of the miles.
Here is my shoulder...use it and weep
Humming slow tunes, the kindness does creep.
Life often goes wrong and who says what is right?
So many battles and losing the fight.
I know what you feel 'cuz I've been there too
The anguish and loss fills up inside you.
Here is your chance to let it all out
Understanding ears know what it's about.
I beg you to see I'm filled with concern
Your sadness and pain I'm willing to learn.
I just want to help...a pain it may be
Remember it's not as bad as it seems.
I'm here for you friend...all of this while
And no reward needed except for your smile.

Ami Sheffield

The Meadow Of Life

My endless journey continues
through the meadow of life..
no paths ahead of me -
only my footsteps behind me -
and my ever-lasting ambition to guide me -
through the open field
of tangled roots
sweet odors
bumble bees
wild roses and their thorns...
And "which way?" is my decision
and mine alone...
And I know to follow the rising sun at dawn...
which becomes more distant
with every rose I approach....
but my limitless journey continues -
I love the scent of every petal
and the prick of each thorn -
because they grow in
my meadow

Jordan Slutsky

Yesterdays Life; Todays Lost Dream

The smell of rain
Through the majestic mountain trees
The chill of the air
From a late night autumn breeze

The cattle roaming
Through the fields and streams
The rooster crowing
Before I finished my dreams

The waste and population
Forced a young man from his life
The only way to earn a living
Is in a strange world flooded with lights

My grandfathers farm
Taken back by the bank
Subdivisions and men in suits
Are whom I have to thank

Hard work and heritage
Doesn't seem to matter
As long as the suits
Continue getting fatter

Jeff Williams

Time After Time

Time after time, alas, destined to repeat
Through the endless space continuum our love bittersweet
What, when, afore, again
The circumstances I wish, yet D'nae Ken

We wander about each but half a soul
Pining for thine other to make us each whole
But like wrong faced magnets doth deflect
We come so close yet can nae connect

Once our station, once our age
Next race or mayhap someone unsage
Pride, innocence, insecurities aside
They were but excuses to keep us off stride

Mayhap this curse 'tis but fear
For our love we held too dear
We, once found, should be rooted like tree
Yet run away from that which would set us free

But joy! Our destiny so shall we yet meet
And e'ermore shall our love be complete
Me thinks this so, for abed last night
The circumstances I dreamt, an end to our plight

John C. O'Keefe

Immortal Thirst

Whose soft kisses of passion you give me, blood thirsty am I.
Through darkness you invoke me leading me into your desired shadows.
But when light prevails, it is I who can run with the sun while you
    are trapped by the moon.
So with metaphors, you savor your wit of countless ages gone past.
Like chaos, you grip tragedy with a fetal clutch, iron claws
    gripping steel.
To know death and its pleasures, you stand among the world
    something to account about.
But it is I, King Humanity, that still listens with ignorant ears.
So by what night do you wish to take me, immortal I must know.

Joey Pyatt

Nature Study

The turbulent wind whips outside my window,
threatening all in its path;
unsettling me.

Though safe within my walls,
I witness the violence waged against a weeping willow;
shaking me.

A whistling wails slips beneath blinds closed to the pane,
giving vent to fear in the darkness;
intimidating me.

Sounds of the wind bully my senses,
stimulating thoughts of destruction;
terrifying me.

I will not move from my window,
as raised blinds shed light on the weeping willow;
inspiring me.

So it is in the wake of a raging bluster,
I hold my ground to discover deep roots;
strengthening me.

Cathy Coon

A Soldier's Tribute

Into Vietnam by transport plane,
Thousands on thousands of GI's came,
Tag 'em and bag 'em are the words they heard,
Men going home in bags on this big bird.

These soldiers came from cities and farms,
To the thickness of jungle that only harms,
A bandolier of arms strapped across their chest,
For this platoon, there will be no rest.

On night patrol, paralyzed with fear,
I hope this night God will be near,
For there is the booby trapped underbrush,
The end of the tunnel for some of us.

Running head on in witless fright,
We're in the thick of a firefight.
Foxtrot Ridge they call this hell,
A place where lots of buddies fell.

In our capital of Washington, D.C.,
They built a wall for all to see,
With names of all the men who fell,
Remember them America and honor them well.

Jean Karcher

"Listening"

Mighty soaring winds may rattle our world,
Thoughts and feelings may boggle our minds.
Demands of life may take away our attentions,
    but if I become still, and listen,
    I can hear the small voice of my Lord!
For after the wind comes a peaceful world,
    and when I listen there some peace of mind,
    and when I relax to life's demands,
    a joy fills my attentions, because I
    listened, and let God's will be done!
    Not mine!
I became still long enough to listen,
    and not think of me!
Gentle Lord of everyone's being, help others,
    and me to always "Listen To Thee"!
Not "We"!

Angela J. Hicks

Friendship

Friendship is a state of mind
    Thoughtful, merciful and very kind
It is not measured by the hour
    Rather by its staying power

Friendship to us is never free
    Most often bought down on your knee
Tho you have money, you cannot buy
    There is no need for you to try

Friendship, my kind is tried and true
    Give me a chance I'll share it with you
Hard work will always make it pay
    Giving of yourself day after day

Friendship is good and always right
    It doesn't matter if you're black or white
It's not an order that you can heed
    It's not a word or offered deed

Friendship, you say, it cannot be,
    We are different colors, don't you see
God our creator, I'm sure he knows
    We are created equal in different clothes

George C. Parker

"Unforgettable Dream"

Though the weather outside is cold, you warm me
Though the world is frightening you, protect me

Your smile is bright like a May morn
You touch is soft like the April rain

The way you look entices me
The way you kiss engulfs me

When you hold me there is no tomorrow
When you love me time stands still

There could never be another, my unforgettable dream
John Carter

Decided Destiny

I am not a part of this world
Though my feet walk in the dust
That rises around me, calling to mind
That from dust I came and dust I will
return someday

My hand reaches out to the rain bringing
quite to the turmoil of mankind,
My face lifts to the warmth of the sun and
Follows as its journey travels the path
of a well known way

My eyes seek the heavens and as the
evening star brings on the night the sky
Becomes a crown upon my very being,
The wind is a flight of passion that carries
My breath beyond earth's bounds

I am not a part of this world,
I am only a moment remembered a time
in waiting, I touch others and become
as one, until I am a memory
No longer found
Faith A. Pierson

She Doesn't Know I Write For Sanity In The Midst Of

Ethnic Strife

I stare at the paper my supervisor handed me at work. "Did you see this? You should enter, with your talent," she gushed. Based on two poems she now owns from me, she thinks I'm worthy of acclaim. Poetry Contest the headline read. "Sanity Contest would be better," I think.

I don't tell her why I write poetry. I don't tell her that I can't vocalize when I feel. My tongue ties and my voice chokes and embarrassment overcomes me. "Not done," said thinking Father's German family. Mother's French heart passed to me could never learn that lesson well. It left me a hybrid oddity.

She doesn't know that I mail my poems or leave them on desks rather than face those to whom they are intended, to escape embarrassing thank yous they evoke. She doesn't know that I feel because on the outside I'm so careful, so controlled. She doesn't know that without poems, throughout my life I would have disappeared, the suffocating words and screams choking me inside my chest.

My sister, with her German heart, cooks and cleans and sews to perfection, cool, calm, rational, the perfect daughter, no tumultuous feelings interfering.

She doesn't know that writing keeps me sane. I don't do it because of talent. She just knows that I love to write because that's what I tell her. She doesn't know I have to write. Otherwise I would be entirely mute. My Father's German heredity would still my French heart forever. *My sister inherited the perfection. I, the soul. Writing calms the ethnic strife.*
Jeanne C. Rosenbohm

Living Life

Life persists but do we engage upon...?
This wonderful world offers so much to look forward to.
The shortness of life should haunt your every thought.
Excepting life shows no mind.
Shows no imagination;
Shows no creativity;
Or shows your limitations.

Are we ever in the present...?
Ever notice living in the past or future?
Or living in the past to protect the future.
Unleash your mind and live.
Let go and do whatever can be done.

IT'S YOUR TURN TO LIVE NOW!
Jason Clay Schroder

Lets Go Under The Waterfall

Lets go under the waterfall
This will rid you of the pain that you are use to
She says boy I know your going place somewhere somehow
Your not moving too fast

When the stream of life
Sends you down the river of doubt
Let the water rock you gently and move you
Hold on

Boy if someone comes along to hurt you my friend
I will take you in my arms and remove them
Lets talk

Hear the voice you have heard a thousand times before
Listen to what I am trying to tell you
Open your heart
Then close down your mind
This will relieve you of your state of confusion

Lets go under the waterfall
This will rid you of the pain that you are use to
She says boy I know your going place somewhere somehow
Your not moving to fast
Catherine Valdez

This Little Girl

I watched her cross the river bridge slowly.
   This little girl, crippled, bent and lowly.
I asked God in some way to bless
   So that she could withstand life's stress
And all the extra pain she would have to bear,
   Help her have hope and never despair.

Her hair in penciled tresses hangs,
   She is barefoot, snaggled tooth, with shaggy bangs,
Her bent and dwarfed body causes her no concern
   She is too young troubles to discern.

Love has been given her without stint
   From a poverty stricken father who is also bent,
Her mother is a simple soul who lends content
   To the dirty hovel and all the children sent.
Surrounded by a small world all her own
   Just a few acres and a stream is all she's known.

When father and mother are gone and family torn apart,
   Will there be anyone to take this child into their heart?
When life becomes more serious than playing by the way,
   Dear God, please provide against that day.
Diecy G. Brennemann

"Separation"

This last year, of feeling Depression.
This last year, of having no expression
This last year, of knowing not, how to cope
This last fear, of giving up, all hope.
The one I loved, left my sight,
Leaving me alone, like the still of night.
Bearing all this great, pain and sorrow.
Grasping for the promise of a new tomorrow.
Like a bird held captive, then faring flight.
I'm finally releasing her, with all my might.
By asking for help, from the lord above.
He answered, giving me, someone else to love.

John J. Madera

"Beginning To End"

First there is a kick, then there is a scream
This is the sound in every girl's dream.
A baby is born, a mother is proud,
And every new father rides high on the clouds.

The mother is tired, she has been through a storm
Yet she holds her child, all cuddly and warm.
From her breast of life, the child she will feed
Giving love and nurturing the baby will need.

Her baby will grow, her baby will cry,
And she will love her baby until she dies.
She will watch him crawl, then watch him walk
And she will teach her baby the right way to talk.

Her child will stumble and her child will fall
But mother will be there, to help him stand tall.
She will teach him good, and she will show him bad
Watching for the day, her child will grow to a man.

He will leave her home but remain in her heart
For her once little baby, she has given a start.
The world is his to conquer and win
But her child he will be, from beginning to end.

Gene Muren

Forever Yours

Dear Anita and Tom,
This is a glorious day for both of you
With the promise of a bright future, and many fun things left to do
It's interesting to see how our lives unfold
So many ups and downs-then it suddenly turns to gold
The very day we meet that special person to love
It is a gift made in heaven by our dear Lord above
Today you celebrate 25, but oh, so quickly, 50 will arrive
Because you are God's children, you are held very dear
And with his continuous blessing, your love will grow year by year
How comforting to have your chosen mate by you side
To share problems, joys, successes - a truly triumphant ride!
Continue to love one another with all your heart
Because then, and only then, can you truly re-affirm
 "'till death do us part".

Frances A. Hines

Lifespan

I'm just passing through
This world that is yours and mine
Leaving my footprints in the sands of time
Only to be erased by gentle winds
Never to be seen again
For only through the lives
We have touched with love
and understand can be hope
to obtain immortality.

Juanita C. Arnicone

This Lonely Western

Oh, what a wondrous story
This awesome land could tell.
How close it would be to heaven
But some might think it hell.

If it could talk and relate
All the hardship and happiness, too
It would say you will never leave here
This land was meant for you.

You can grow your own food and raise cattle,
You can even raise a family here
I can't say it will be easy
But lights from the city don't fear.

'Cause there's nothing but glorious wonder
And the stars and the moon in the sky
If the Indians and settlers can live here
Then I wonder why can't I?

Well, I guess I'll quit my dreaming
And go back to my job at hand
Of writing this lovely story
Of our lonely western land.

Ed Eads

Corrected Indecision

To and fro, alacrity, irresolution
Thirst only to settle my mind
Blundering to a question like water to speech
Distinction of loss gained
and ever lost again
Question Indecisive?
Invariably Incorrected?
More marked, more meaningful?
Particularly plausible babbling brook
Thirst to create one
Only of making one
But,
can't decide how
How!
    How!
        How?
Look, there's one ——————————. Ha!

Curtis Callahan

Stars Above

Sitting here looking at the stars above
Thinking about true love
Knowing that if you wish on them your dreams will come true
Because that is how I found you
On one warm spring night
I wished with all my might
To find someone like you
And out of the blue
You came
And now nothing is the same
Just as the stars brighten the sky above
You brighten my life with your love
And as the darkness first welcomed the stars to give it light
I'm glad I welcomed your love that one warm May night

Dawn Wheeler

Child

A child is like a shooting star, that shines so bright.
They work real hard, with all their might.
Then when they think, their work is done.
They always try, to have a little fun.
But, there's always one thing an adult would say.
When kids get older, they can't play.
They think a child is just something for people to see.
But, a child is a child just like me.

Jamie Anne Bonura

Power Of Dreams

A friend is hard to come by, in your lowest struggle of life.
They will turn their backs against you vanish through the night.
A true friend will stick beside you, no matter thick or thin,
Never point a finger, or be judgmental within.
People can take our possessions, they will even take our pride.
But they can never take our faith in God, for we cherish it deep down inside.
You have the strength and the ability to go far in life.
Do not let anyone tell you different, they will fill your days with strife.
My Grandma taught me a lot before she passed away,
I would like to share it with you "Only if I may!"
Remember within our reach lies the path we dream of taking.
Within our power lies the step we may dream of making.
Within our range lies every joy we ever dream of seeing.
Within ourselves lies everything we ever dream of being.

Debbie Richmeier

Grandfather's Hands

My Grandfather's hands weren't large, but they held my world.
They weren't soft, but could speak the softest words and gently
wipe away my tears.

They weren't pretty but they could paint a pretty picture.
They weren't educated but full of wisdom
They weren't skilled but could build a great tree house.
They weren't violent hands but had fought in a war.

They knew the Bible and they knew how to bait a hook, they knew
how to tie a knot in a rope so you could swing on it.

They could tan your hide and were great for hugs and you could
always find a dime in those hands.

They had seen their better days, they were old and rough, but they
were full of love and kindness. You know, the really good stuff.

DeAnna Sigrest Bridges

Our Gems

   Mothers are like precious gems,
They sparkle like diamonds,
Like the beautiful rubies too.
   They enjoy giving you the best of care,
When needed, Mom's help is always there.
   They're happy when you hug them tight,
And kiss them good night.
   But she knows some day you will break her heart,
That day came and you played the part.
   At the reception when the bride and groom departed,
Mom was left down hearted.
   But she smiled through her tears,
And looked back at the happy years
When she was his only sweetheart dear.
   Now mom is happy and gay,
Because her grandson was born today.

Jeannette V. Steiner

An Autumn Day

Did you ever rise at break of day and watch the cloudlets at their play
They skirmish with each autumn breeze as harmlessly the sun they tease

And then you take that first chilled breath that starts your senses churning
It's filled with dewy aftermath of dried leaves left still burning

Did you ever stand at high noontide and listen to the trees that signed
And clapped their yellow, withered hands in tune with autumn lyrics grand

What happiness they find to share they've fulfilled natures duty
They'll stand in silent darkness there till spring restores their beauty

Did you ever sit at the close of day and watch the red sun stillfully sway
Beyond some far-off wooded crest before it finally comes to rest

Then to your thought cold winter steals and daydreams cloud all reason
When sudden consciousness reveals 'tis only autumns season

Elmer Sperry

Tell Me What's Right

Now a days the world is wound so tight,
They say nothing is wrong but tell me
what's right,
Kids killing first for fun,
leaves the rest of the world on the run,
So I think before it's too late,
let's push love in and pull out hate,
it seems nothing is fun any more either
your rich or your poor,
No one wants to give to those who need,
watch them drawn in all of their greed,
So far once, listen to what I say,
let's help this world not tomorrow, for we
need it today.

Clarence Russell Gunnoe

Caterpillar — Butterfly (Two Chances Of A Lifetime)

Crawling steadfastly to the other side,
They hurry to store themselves inside.
Knowing one day we will see you and I,
The biggest, the brightest, the butterfly.

Carie L. Paro

Childhood

Childhood is the kingdom where children dream
They have fun in the woods or by a stream.
If you look around they are all at play,
Whether it's a rainy or sunny day.
They all admire someone, someone very dear.
Their admiration grows with every passing year.
They enjoy pretending they are grown-up, it is a change for which they
    cannot wait.
If only they would let it fall upon the shoulders of fate.
They are so young they believe whatever they are told.
Their love for you will never grow old.
They love to go out, out to explore.
They are always wondering if there could be more.
One day they will find out there is more than the thought and ask why
They will be told stories they will not buy
They will try to hold on to dreams which have faded over they years.
They will be shedding a lot of unexplainable tears.
The time will come when they are forced to continue up the mountain of life
Then there will be a time when they search for a friend.
It is then and there that their childhood will end.

Anna Wilson

Gossip And Lies Kills Love Heals

I am so tired of people gossiping and lying on me,
They go from one person to another bearing false
Witness you see.
They lie on me, they lie on each other, they
Keep telling lies one after the other.

They tell lies about the preacher, and tell lies
About his wife,
When they can't find enough to gossip about, they
Start telling lies on his child.

Some people use any excuse to gossip, and any old subject will do
They seem to thrive on lying, rather than
Telling the truth.

You had better stop spreading lies people and start
Spreading love,
Don't you know God is watching you from heaven
Above

Finally I say to you my brothers, and my sisters too
Stop living your lives on gossip and lies,
Start focusing on telling the truth.

Imogene Adkins Gaffney

Belated Thanks

Thank you, God, for Betty and Joe,
They gave me a home when I had nowhere to go,
Had they not come along and taken me in,
I shudder to think what life could have been.

The day they came for me it began to snow,
They started early 'cause it was a long way to go,
They arrived at the home very nearly on time,
When I got in their car, my life was sublime.

As my new life began in this small rural town,
Where times were simple and friendships were found,
No one will every know what their love meant to me,
Nor the years in the future that came to be.

When my children were born, their love had grown,
Like all grandparents, they accepted mine as their own,
As for my husband, they really like my choice,
If they felt differently, an opinion they'd voice.

Dora C. Morrison

The Couple

In the minutes preceding the alarm
They find a peaceful existence in each others arms

The soft press of flesh on flesh
The connection of souls
The absence of lust
The purity of love

All is at once clear and content
The love of and for a spouse
Flowing from one to the other

Engraved on the rings
Is truth
My friend, my lover, my soulmate, my spouse

For all of eternity
The rings shall declare
The love of this woman and this man.

Julie L. Harris

Angels

There are angels in the blue heavens above
They cry for you in the wind
But you can't hear them
They call for you during each night
Still, you can't hear them
They come to you during each time of day
But you can't see them
They come to you again when it's your turn
But until then..
They visit you.

Carolyn Prigmore

Mother And Daughter

Their connection is special their bond is true
They can't be separated by time, by distance, by me or you
There's a sort of magic in what mother and daughter share
There's no need or problem without each others care
Heavy burdens. Run!! When mothers and daughter are there
There is no weight that's to heavy to hold
Like mother. Like daughter. She'll lighten the load
When one needs the other. Here is what occurs
Mother is her strength and daughter is mothers'

When mother and daughter can not be together
The days in between must be like forever
And when time finds them separated by years
Warmth, love and security will overflow when they are near
Absence makes the heart grow fonder. That's no cliche'
It defines mothers and daughter who are far away
As mother and daughter get on in years
They travel common ground that makes them closer still
So when all is said and all is done
Mother and daughter are truly one

Johnnie M. Bennett

Georgian Bay Pines

Such delicate goldish green
They are when young
And so slimly balanced
In dark trunk, limb and needle cluster!
The wonder is how any seed
Can suck from lean Precambrian granite fissure
Life for one day
And one day join her towering sisters
To lean away from insistent westerlies,
Soughing from the agony of being
Twisted into a Chinese ideograph.

James H. Blackwood

Sorrow

When sorrow filled my mind,
there was always "Someone" to find.
But when this "Someone" died,
I sat down and cried.

My "Someone" was there to talk to.
While I talked, he listened, as time flew.
Although he never said a word,
I know he understood what he heard.

When I became very upset,
he was by my side to pet.
He would greet me when I came home,
where I went he would roam.

I miss this "Someone" so dear,
for the others I feel fear.
This poem I dedicate to my dog,
Snuffles, to whom I will always love.

Amanda Jones

Friendship

My friends are an adventure—
   They all expand my mind
In one way or another.
   They are of every kind,
Color, shape, description.
   I hold them in my heart
From life through life through life to life-
   Of me, they are a part.

We laugh, we share, we cry, we care,
   We always find each other
For growth experience routine or rare
   As relative, enemy, friend or lover!
Through secrets dark and lessons fun
   Our lives entwine once more,
And part—yet keep entwining
   Till we reach the final shore.

Our Creator gives us every chance
   To become a perfect soul.
Until we attain that perfection,
   Friendship will console.

Constance C. Pettigrew

To My Son Jonathan

These days fly by, these banner days,
These days of sun and sand and swims;
These summer days so full of fun
With high school concerts, proms and trips to places you have never been.
Oh glorious days, these summer days of life, of school, of time.
How sweet the tastes, how clear the sounds and beauty, to the eyes, abounds.
Savor them now, my handsome son, for sooner than a blink they're gone.

Live to the full these banner days, these summer days of life.
Keep energy and spirit high,
Don't let this moment pass you by, but live it to its full!

Be careful, though, to savor what is good, for too,
Satan, in fancy dress, abounds to capture you.
He's all around in pretty package, bottle, face.
You may not even see a trace; but, be aware that he is there
To grab you every time he can before your youth becomes a man.

So, live to the full these banner days, these summer days of life;
And grow into a man, my son, who God in Heaven smiles upon;
with memories not lost, but won.

Joyce Lunn

Untitled

A thought, a touch, a hug, a kiss,
these are the things I would like from you.
To talk, to laugh, to smile, to play,
these are the things I would like with you.
To share, to care, to listen, to grow,
these are the things I want from you.
Happiness, joyfulness, prayerfulness, and togetherness.
These are the things I want to share with you.

Although we've known each other for a long time,
there's so much more to learn. So many possibilities
in the future to come.
My friend, my companion, my confident, my lover,
these are things I need from you.

Time, patience, communication and prayer,
these are the things we'll do together.
Respect, concern, support and trust,
These are all the things I'll give to you.
I only ask the same in return.

Felecia A. Norris

My Friendship Star

This poem was inspired by the Rosenthal Star, a gift to me when I retired from the university in 1982. One day as I worked at my desk, the sun struck my star and a blaze of color resulted. It was a joyous experience. Thus: this poem.

There's the Star Spangled Banner.
There's the star of the sea.
There's the star of Bethlehem.
And a friendship star for me.

Stars are made of paper.
Stars are made of glass.
There's the Rosenthal Star
Designed with dignity and class.

Stars fell on Alabama.
Stars top a Christmas tree.
Stars are in the movies,
But a love star came to me.

My star will go in a high place
For the sun to shine through.
The heart of my love star
Ties friendship to you!!!

Charlotte Palmer

Simple Treasures

When the ironies of my life, do twist and turn,
There's a constant within, that teaches me to learn.
On wings so soft, it comes to each and all
That still small voice, making that still, quiet call.
Be still and listen for My voice.

Family and home, do I hold so dear,
With love abounding, nothing to fear.
For all the gold and silver, weigh as I might,
Never would I trade, for that voice in the night.
Be still and listen for My voice.

A hug, a kiss, or a gentle touch I crave,
With all that is love, my life's effort to save.
It is all these moments of simple pleasures,
That for all my life, become simple treasures.
Be still and listen for My voice.

Moments to remember are wondrous and fine,
Memories to carry me, throughout all time.
Reminding me often, it is always my choice,
Treasures from within, that causes me to rejoice.
Be still and listen of My voice.

Joseph E. Schild Jr.

Up On The Mountain

Up on the Mountain where I usually play,
   There's a cat and a dog and three blue jays
      That howl in the night and scream in the day.

The sun shines in my face,
   With a golden raindrop in its place.

The dog and the cat came to play,
   With the bugs and the bees that ran away,
      from the dog and the cat that just wanted to play.

I played with the dog, and ran through the bog,
   then I heard a voice say,
      Come on dear Micay, and I ran away.

Anna E. Trees

Untitled

I don't know....I feel so confused about you!
There so many things I want to tell you...but...I don't think I should.
How come I can't think of a damn thing to do?
I know I should leave but I just don't think I could!

You put the sun in my mornings and a smile on my face!
We are so far apart....distant in our lives.
You're everything to me that I couldn't possibly replace.
But it's the truth, not the dream that I need to realize!

I've fallen in love with the idea of being in love
And you're everything I want love to be....
Look at me! It's you I can't stop thinking of!
You have no idea what you do to me...

How can someone feel this way about someone they don't know?
I have feelings for you that I don't understand!
If I try to move on my heart refuses to go...
I never knew someone could feel this way...but I guess I can!

Cheryl Ann Slaughter

Time

As time travels onward down the endless road beyond
There seems to be a mystery in the way it travels on
There is no start no ending, there's just an in-between.
We live today, this hour, this minute, tomorrow's never seen

And as we travel onward down this one-way road of life,
We encounter all the emotions of happiness to strife.
From the cross roads of decision to the side roads of regret.
Our lives entwined with places and people we have met.

There is no stopping place on this road which we're upon
Forever forward into the future we must go on and on.
We sometime linger with our memories, realizing that which we may lack.
Yet we must go forever forward for there is no turning back.

Alfred C. Sumner

The Kingdom

The world to me is a misguided place,
There is so much hatred on everyone's face.

Everyone is a ruler with a Kingdom to find,
To twist and corrupt each others minds.

To control and take over each other's souls,
And destroy the part that keeps them whole.

If love and kindness is all we had,
It would destroy the thoughts that make us bad.

We all would rule the Kingdom with grace,
And the earth we walk on, would be a much better place.

Diane Goy

Thank You Sincerely

As my birthdays rush by more frequently, it seems
There is nothing so pleasing among my silent dreams
As the notes from my friends both near and far
That arrive in my mailbox from the mailman's car.

It is really a treat to have each of you remember
That I am no longer a person so young and tender
But have accumulated eighty three years of age and grace
So I wonder if you would recognize me face to face.

Your thoughts and greetings fill my heart with deepest joy
And I savor them so much better than a complicated toy.
As I think of you as a precious friend you remind me
Of times we spent together and things I've left behind me.

So with this poem I send to you my sincere love
With best wishes and my prayers to our God above
That He will assist you personally in all of your needs
As I thank you from my heart for your gracious deeds.

Frank F. Farley

"Almost Halloween"

Down in the woods, below our house,
there is a creepy hollow,
and walking down the path,
not even the moon will follow.
The rustle of the leaves in the wind,
the bats, twitter in the night,
and a noise, of a broken twig,
makes the heart race, from fright.

Down in the hollow, they come along,
real fast, they are the goblins and,
ghosts, of Halloweens past.

So I broke into a run, I came out of
that hollow, even the moon was there, too,
around the barn, and to the house, I flew,
I glanced back to see, there was probably
three or four, I reached the house,
went in and closed the door.
So when you start to hear,
the things unseen, then almost,
it's Halloween.

Geraldine McDonough

The Rose

With this rose I thee give, all my love as long as I live.
There are times we are distressed some days,
but please don't doubt, my love is here to stay.
We have been through trying times together
and I would do it again, forever and ever.
You are my life, love and the world to me;
I have no cheating heart, I want you to believe.
The vows we took were, "'til death do us part,"
so just remember I love you with all my heart.
You have given me so much love and devotion
and I take this serious with every breath and emotion.
This single rose symbolizes my love for only you,
and the expression of my love is so very true.
If you ever have doubts about my love as
long as we both live,
Remember this rose, I thee give.

Jodi Tripp

In Reality

In Reality,
There are gangs and fights,
Suicidal thoughts night after night.
In Reality,
There is pressure and stress,
Some kids life are a total mess.
In Reality,
There are pregnant teens,
And none of them know what responsibility means.
In Reality,
There are moms and dads,
Who help you through your goods and bad.
In Reality,
There are teachers and friends,
That help you through your odds and ends.

So the next time that your feeling bad,
Take a good look at reality and maybe you'll be glad.
For every thing you have.

Crystal Hamm

Lost Her Heart

The nights are so long when we are apart
Then the time finally comes and I can feel my heart
You're in my arms and my cares go away
Our moments together make my day.
If only our world's weren't so far apart
I'm afraid some day I will lose her heart.
So lay your head on my chest and hold so close
Tonight is forever let's make it the most.

Arthur Cormier

Again

I was happy? I was content? I was, then.
Then, I felt you.
Next, I saw you.
My heart recognized you first.
It was an explosion.
One born of Love, Trust, and Lust.
It hammered away at my soul, knowing in that instant it was,
You.
How long did I look?
When did I stop?
Can you feel me? Can you see me?
I will wait.
It can't be too long, for I have waited for so long.
When we first kiss,
You will already know the taste of my lips,
The pulsing of my heart.
Then,
You will know me,
Again.

Dawn M. Dinsmore

Autumn

The giant oaks are not crowding the firmament any longer.
Their withered leaves have departed
the height of their slenderest fingers.
The autumn moon is filled with gratitude.
Her face lights up the depth of the night,
making shadows of even the spirits
that dwell on the branches.
The breeze betrays the stillness of the cool air
with its whispers that travel among the swaying twigs
whose tips bear the last of the late summer fragrance.
The queen of the night reigns,
her luminescent smile exposing the silent earth
cushioned now with thickening layers of leaves
whose presence is as light as feathers of geese.

Anna Maria Siti Kawuryan

Snowflakes

There are those who love the snowflakes as they fall onto the ground
   Their eyes twinkle with excitement at the wintry scene around.
They are thinking only good thoughts of the fun that snow provides
   Snowball throwing, skiing, sledding ... and exciting four wheel drives.
How they marvel at the beauty of the ice upon the trees
   And their pleasure only heightens as the snow reaches their knees.

Other see those falling snowflakes and their thoughts are full of fears
   Can they stand up without falling? Can they drive as darkness nears?
They can feel their knees are shaking as they slide out of control
   And those cars and trucks in ditches only make their panic grow.
Will they catch a cold and be sick after scraping off the ice?
   Will another storm be coming ... and will their woodpiles suffice?

Over simple things like snowflakes ... people often disagree
   I suspect those who enjoy them are the luckiest, you see!

Barbara Lou Neblett

Reason

Some people have very long illness
Their death drags over a long period of time
While for some life is snuffed out immediately
Many times the answer for this seems hard to find

There is a reason for the way things happen
God has his plans all worked out
He knows what is best for the whole world
About this there could never be a doubt

It doesn't matter what length span our life covers
as long as we have Gods will in our life
Through us He performs many miracles
as He leads us through this world of trouble and strife

To us some things might seen small and useless
There is a purpose for all good things in Gods plan
In the end when these things all fit together
It will be easier for man to understand

When God makes His plans he has a king size view
He can see inside and out all the way through
While our view is very Limited
To the things man can see and do

Claude Carter

Earthquake - 18th Of 10

Why do I sit so passively, while only a mile away,
The world is crumbling, crumbling, and a million people pray?
And a mile away a shuttle goes, to investigate our stars,
But while I sit, I wish I wish I wish, I were on Mars!!
Society says I have my own, tall tale of blues,
But nothing I've experienced, can begin to be the news!
I have faced the "A" disease, the drugs and all of that.
But still a mile away, it doesn't matter about that!
What matters now, on the 18th of 10, can we be willing to begin again?
Begin to love, to be and to share, and not to sit so passively,
and begin to really care!

Julie Kerschion

Just A Poem

A poem is words to express how you feel
the words themselves are no big deal.
You take up your pen and make stroke after stroke
and sometimes you come up with a great big joke.
But other times a river runs through
with a lifetime of accomplishments made by you
who says you can't write whatever you please?
Your story in words flies by like a breeze
and soon comes the end to the tale you have told
So give it to others to have and to hold.

Ina Fleetwood

"The Senses I Need"

Lord, give me eyes so that I may see
   The wonderful works you have done for me;
Lord, give me ears so that I may hear
   The joyous sounds of song you have made so clear;
Lord, give me a nose so that I may smell
   The beautiful flowers you have painted so well;
Lord, give me a tongue so that I may speak
   To others who are too somber and meek.

Lord, give me hands so that I may touch
   The hands of the ones I love so much;
Lord, give me a brain so that I can tell
   And give testimony of how you can never fail.
Lord, give me a prayer that I can pray
   To lead me and guide me from day to day;
Lord, please give me a heart so that I can love
   And appreciate all of the wonders above.

Ethelene B. Williams

Amelia

It should have rained the day she died
The wind should have blown the clouds through the sky
But it didn't, the sun shined.

It should have stormed the day she died
The thunder should have roared until men cried
But it didn't, birds sang at sunrise.

It should have rained the day she died
The lighting should have blinded the sight from my eyes
But it didn't, the tears the sun dried.

Oh Lord!
What a foolish son am I
She wasn't rain
She was Sunshine.

James Kubala

Lake Louise's Breezes

Whate'er the course I want to race
The wind is always in my face—
Then disappears without a trace
And leaves me sitting on my ace. Lake Louise's breezes!

Louise's breezes are capricious
But even worse, they are malicious,
They never will obey my wicious
And sometimes serve me to the ficious. Lake Louise's breezes!

The wind wheezes and it sneezes
'Round the houses and the trees-es,
Bringing sailors to their knees-es.
It won't blow steady 'til Hell freezes. Lake Louise's breezes!

They test this sailor's aptitude
And give me a bad attitude.
I'd sure be filled with gratitude
If they'd find some other latitude. Lake Louise's breezes!

And just when I'm about to win
A calm is sure to come again
And leave me wailing with chagrin
While someone else slides past the pin. Lake Louise's breezes!

John T. Dempsey

The Weekend

Saturday and Sunday are my favorite days of the week.
The weekend—no more work for two whole days.
I wait, I wait, to be at my peak.

Only forty-eight hours—no need to be meek,
We'll have fun shopping, sightseeing, attending plays;
Saturday and Sunday are my favorite days of the week.

They come and go so fast sometimes I feel weak.
Movies, errands, concerts, how many ways,
I wait, I wait, to be at my peak.

It is on Saturday that I run 'til my knees creak.
On Sunday we like breakfast in bed on trays.
Saturday and Sunday are my favorite days of the week.

Monday, Tuesday, Wednesday, and Thursday I'm bleak.
Friday, the weekend is near—on my mind it stays.
I wait, I wait, to be at my peak.

I know every day is a gift I should seek.
And although I'll try to give the other days their praise.
Saturday and Sunday are my favorite days of the week.
I wait, I wait, to be at my peak.

Antoinette Cleveland

Welcome Fall

Listen very carefully - you can hear it in the trees.
The very subtle rustling of a cooling autumn breeze.

A time of change is drawing neigh.
As Summer whispers her last goodbye.

But Summer as she goes to bed.
Invites in Autumn with hues of red.

And green and yellow and rust and gold.
As nature's grandest show unfolds.

Hills and valleys - mountains and streams.
Each more beautiful or so it seems.

God's gift to us one and all.
Welcome, welcome, welcome fall.

DonnaJo Lindstrom

To Walk

The journey of life is long and narrow,
The valley of hope is the sight of a sparrow,
The sound of love is a thundering fall...
That bubbles like a whippoorwill call,
The bounty of peace is as fragrant as spring
Sweet but elusive as the brush of the wind,
Happiness is but the chill in the air
That catches you still..., unaware,
Curiosity is as expansive as stars
Shining brightly aloft and afar,
Yet only peace of the heart can be found
By knowing ourselves, and learning how
To listen to the voice from within,
Giving thanks up above,
And walking with him.

Cynthia L. Feroce

Jay's Song

I sense your fear
The urge to run
And, hide within yourself
That frightened, fragile, little boy
You're sure no one could love

You must have reached out, once or twice
To only find rejection
The pain so great, you hid away
Your heart for its own protection

How lonely you must be, my friend
All locked up, safe and sound
No one could ever hurt you
But, then why?
This depression so profound!

You've so skillfully erected
Your barriers of pride
But, that same small boy keeps crying
"Please love me and let yourself inside."

"C.J." (Carol J. Guagliardo)

At Night

Sometimes at night when I'm asleep, I can hear the drizzle of the rain. It's so peaceful to hear the breeze of the wind and the leaves gently hitting my window pane. To hear the chirping of the crickets gives me visions of Heaven. But sometimes it's hard to see through all the crime, the injustice, the no reason or rhyme. But if you try as hard as you can maybe you can feel the soft calmness of every creature, every person, everything.

Laura Peebles

Hymn

I looked around and saw the sky,
the trees, flowers,
all the beauty around me,
and I saw Him.

Along the beach I walked, the sound of waves on the shore;
wind gently moving through grasses.
The birds called out above,
and I heard Him.

Surely there must be more.
I looked again;
there you were, and in your eyes
I saw Him.

Somehow it was not complete.
I searched again so I could fully see,
and there was the answer,
I found Him in me.

Bett Wallace

The Littlest Light

You there with the telescope, see me, here I am,
The teeny one, just to your left, I'm shining best I can,
No! You've moved too far, I guess that's not your fault,
I know I'm rather hard to see, I'm nothing to exult.

I've been up here ten thousand years, maybe three or two,
I'll bet you never noticed me, but I cannot blame you,
My light wasn't bright enough to lead the wise men's way,
When they journeyed to Bethlehem, that Holy, Holy Day.

I tried, I shone as best I could, I did my very most,
But who'd see such a little light among the heaven's host?
He did, He saw my glow, He saw my teeny ray,
I know 'cause when He came back up, He kissed me on the way.

George J. Luther

The Awakening

And as we turn with unconscious purpose, remembering,
The sudden sweetness overwhelms us:
And together, our spirits stir and begin
Awakening.

The silent glide of hands between our bodies surely
Echoes last night's soft, murmuring warmth.
Our eyes seeking, opening, smiling...
We slowly awake.

So, quietly moving, sliding into and around
The soft and subtle hills and valleys,
We reach into each other's warmth;
Waking, still waking.

As arms slide gently round
To gather warmly waiting bodies,
Our mouths move into fitted patterns naturally:
Awake! Awake! Awake!

Our lips move, warm-wet, together, divine pressures;
Softly rubbing, they silently nibble
At our consciousness, now uncontrollably
Awakened.

Frank T. Kerby

My Reply

Snow falls like pieces of cotton,
The tears of someone that feels forgotten.
It hits the ground, as it falls around,
In hopes of love lost will be found.
You can hold it for a moment, but it melts in your fist,
so you face the sky, feels great to be kissed,
it's my reply, someone's love hasn't missed.

Steve Bacon

Emotions

Life is filled with emotions
The strongest are the hardest to see.
They come and go every now and then
But they are there in reality.
Love is one of the emotions
It's there all of the time.
It's there for you when you're feeling sad
Or even when your glad
It comforts you with the warmth it holds
Makes you feel strong in the best
or worst times.
Love may come from a family or friend
That is the best love that you can
ever intend
On keeping till the end.

Beoulah R. McIntyre

Stormy Mission

The winches roar, the booms swing o'er
    the stevedores are loading
Each hatch they fill with careful skill
    against stormy seas aboding
Roll high' roll low' as along we go
    in a turbulent sea of spray
With our hatches full, and job to do
    we're merrily on our way
It's a sight to see, believe you me
    and one that will thrill you through
To see a convoy of a hundred ships
    Majestically cut the "blue"
So blow you winds and roll you waves
    But our course we'll never alter
For we are the men of the Merchant Marine
    And our mission must not falter.

Bradford W. Gregory

Going Home

Entering without a word, a shutter, or hesitation,
the spirit slips into the body like a hand into a glove —
gracefully, beautifully, and for comfort and warmth

It fills the being and the body with meaning, purpose,
but also life. Without it, we are all one with nothing,
yet we are all individuals with something special

How can the spirit both define us and distinguish us?

The spirit is born as part of a mystical creator of
undeniable realm. Not defined with letters, but all
knowing, granting each a unique characteristic with
which to share with others

Leaving without a sound or fear, just how it entered,
the spirit sets off from the body. The hand releases
itself from the glove, free to go beyond imaginable
realms, beyond set boundaries, beyond life itself

Danielle Swiger

Untitled

There are many things we take for granted:
the sun's warmth upon our skin,
the tender touch of another person,
a pleasant conversation among friends or family,
the natural aroma of flowers in a park or pine in a forest,
children laughing and playing with dogs,
birds whistling everywhere,
the beautiful mist and rushing sound of an unpolluted stream,
that just right breeze that covers your body with serenity,
snow sparkling in the sun and
an incredible world to live on with life to spend on it.

Ronald P. Farrell

"Starting Over"

A cold winter's night, I'm alone
the spark of life so often shown.
I dream to walk under a sky of snow
I'd like to ask and finally know.
The day will break, so bright, so gold
and life's little mysteries would soon be told.
What we are and why we fight
often to end without a kiss tonight.
In a world of never ending dreams
the hearing turn deaf to your silent screams.
Let all truths be free and bygones bail
Look to the wind to tell its tale,
a million miles away
Lost and alone we search for the day
Searching for something that isn't real
Grasping for someone to touch, to feel.
It will not help to run away
find yourself here and start a new day.

Jennifer Dean

Early Morning Song

The gentle breeze blows in the window.
The soft howl of the tall pine trees.
The moon has every shadow moving in the paths.
The night is warm cuddly.
The soft wrestling of the leaves is soothing.
The crickets sing undisturbed.
The oh so quiet night.
The signal of the passing of Indian Summer.
The quite before the days of the storms.
The roar of a plane off in a distance,
Does not effect the calming effect this night
Has on ones self being.
The coyote howls in an echo as the moon glares
Its rays on everything.
We are blessed with to few of these nights, so
We have to enjoy the tranquil it so much deserves.

Corriene Schendel

A Winter Storm

A winter storm - snow is in the air.
The sky is gray, and silence abounds.
All sounds muted - all is still.
Finally, the storm descends with cold winds and swirling snow.
Darkness comes early, but the snow finds its way over trees and fields
Covering them with a soft white blanket.
In the morning, the trees stand like stately soldiers at attention,
Majestic in their uniforms of snow.
Glistening like diamonds in the brilliant sunlight.
Touched by the sun, but not by its warmth.
Moving when the wind forces them,
And then gracefully bending and swaying,
They whisper a lullaby to those who would listen.
While they patiently wait for winter to pass,
And the spring sun and warm breezes unlock the stillness
And breathe life back into their branches.

Elizabeth J. Fulmer

Being There

You've been there for me since birth,
Through all the pain and the rage
That burned within my soul.

No matter what I've done,
You were the one who cared.
You were the one who always helped me make it through.

Shawn M. Dial

Blue Into Black

The waves are weak,
The sea is calm,
A gentle ebb and flow...
Beyond the horizon lies a blue, peaceful sky,
Watching and waiting...

The soft blue becomes a darker hue,
And the gentle waves become restless,
As a light breeze begins,
To slap across my face,
Dark blue, dark gray, then black.

The sea swells in blackness,
And rain erases the horizon,
The angry waves pounce upon the shoreline,
As fierce, powerful rain rips
At me and my clothes.

The waves swallow the land,
And the thunder echoes a warning,

"Go home, go home!—This is a storm!"

Daniel Pantano

A New Idea

The waves roll in, then run back to sea.
The rain falls down, then soaks into the earth.
The sun rises east, then falls to the west.
We see these things happening,
    but do not take heed,
    these wonders of the earth are
    special in themselves.
I see with new eyes the beauty of my life.
I can make a difference in this world
    full of hate and anger.
I can be the key to open every door.
    To smile upon someone's hatred
and challenge their burning anger
is only the beginning to a life
soon lived in happiness.

Sarah Orvis

The Rain Forest

The babble of a brook,
the rustling of the trees,
the whisper of the wind,
the buzzing of the bees.
Familiar sounds, now lost.

We needed wood, and what was the cost?
Forest and nature,
Once living, gone,
no longer giving.

We took for granted,
the flowers and the trees,
vegetation to cure a disease.

Our Earth has commodities,
mountains, deserts, oceans and forests.
But if the forest is forsaken, all that's left?
A wasteland, barren and dead.

Contemplate the future,
where will the forest be?
Continued destruction,
and no forest for us to see.

Melissa Jean Eckl

The Chameleon

There's a light somewhere in the distance,
the rays peak through and shine on with persistence.

I see the stars shine brightly in the sky,
one stares back and urges me to try.

I move forward, then back, staggering through each day,
as the minutes creep by, I pray time will carve the way.

Searching for the next step, it's so very hard to find,
until I realize...I've not a choice, but to leave the old one far behind.

The light gets closer, but I keep it at arm's length,
I must build a new beginning, and find a whole new strength.

The chameleon changes colors before it sheds its skin,
looking back one last time... then forward, to the new life it will begin.

Kathleen J. Schippers

"The Wanderer"

The ground was soft from yesterday's rain, the air was cool and damp.
The road was long and stony too, so hard for me to tramp.
Still the sun was warm and friendly, playing peek-a-boo with clouds
 of gray
as if he found it difficult to shine some light my way.
The day was filled with promise, this morning showed signs of spring
and I was pleased to hear at dawn a hungry little bird sing.
I watched his mother bring breakfast, 'twas more than I had...for sure
and then I walked into the day, what would it hold in store?
I tighten my belt and head held high swept a tear from my weary eye.
Not a tear of loneliness though I was truly alone,
nor a tear of sadness, such thoughts I do not own.
....but a simple tear of gratitude which filled my heart with glee.
I thanked the God who was so kind to give this day to me.

Lee Raymond

Cloud Jumping

There are no words to describe,
The sadness we all feel.
Your passing came far too early.
It somehow doesn't seem real.

I'm sitting here the morn after your passing
Watching the dawn of the new day.
How can we get through this?
I don't even know if I can pray.

Happiness, energy, and laughter
Of all these things you were made.
You were so very young
How could the Lord take you away.

I know that you're in Heaven
Running and singing with glee
Jumping from cloud to cloud
Happy and carefree.

Nothing will be the same without you
You're hugs and sweet little face
I try to remember you're cloud jumping
In a far better place.

Nancy D. Melcher

Untitled

Arise sweet child; forget your mothers shame.
The world rotates below your toes; you have entered the realm of fame.
Your sacred beginnings with the waters touch desecrated and
contradicted your secular rush.
You go through life without a backwards glance,
your body spells heave and your eyes flame hell, there is no fate only chance
The weeks past in a surreal way; drugs, alcohol a moonlight fight,
the best things happen in the dead of night.
So forget your mother as her tears run dry,
fore you have felt your lips against the immaculate sky.

Matt Klingforth

The Palace

As I sit I feel as a queen
The seat of my throne
is earthen, cushioned pleasantly with grass
The back of my throne is a tree trunk

My palace is scented with sage and pine
A beautiful lake is life giving to my castle
My castle uses the most exquisite
colors, shapes, and forms
My friends, escorts, and jinxes
are the lady bug in the sage
the ant on my shoe
as for musicians
crickets fiddle well too
come visit my palace
but mind you, never leave trash
for that's the golden rule.

Kimberly Brökling

Love

Life is very complex and things always seem so blurred.
The secret is to be tenacious for your dreams and from mistakes
to have learned.
You stroll into many totally different situations, which help
you to know your one true destination.
To find the rainbow which at the end holds the pot of gold;
where you search for the treasure only to realize your heart
has already been sold.
For you can't help but stop and think of her for a while, and
every time you do the same result; an invigorating smile.
So it seems your journey is over since you've reached your final endeavor.
For once is enough; if it is forever.

Michael Todfield

The Message

On a cold, crisp winter's night, I stop to look about.
 The sky, a dark blanket, is covered with many
 stars, reminding me of my friends.

I cannot help but think of the manager babe; His message
 of love pierces my night, as I gaze at each star shining
 so bright. At once are thoughts of each friend I've known
 through the years...my eyes well up with tears.

The MESSAGE of CHRISTMAS I can see —
 CHRISTMAS LOVE IN YOU AND ME.

The stars, like diamonds twinkle on.
 Forever there, they are never gone.
 JUST LIKE CHRISTMAS LOVE.

True friends, they are just the same,
 A twinkling star by another name.
Forever there, they are never gone.
 Like the stars, they twinkle on.
 JUST LIKE CHRISTMAS LOVE.

For if God is love — then I have found
 The Christmas message in you... MY FRIEND.

Susan Murray Majerus

Eyes

Just open your eyes and see
They are cutting down the beautiful trees
The world was better without cars
If they didn't make the sky so foggy we'd
know more about the stars

We've got to find a solution
We've got to stop the pollution
We've got to save our earth
Just open your eyes and see before we run out of time!

Sara Smith

48

The Day That The Birds Left The Bay

It was a sunny day in May by the bay.
The sky was blue that day.
Birds were flying in the sky.
Why do they cry up there is the sky?
Where do they go when they are sad?
Do they go up on the mountains so far away?
Will they go into the waters below?
Why do they go so far away?
Will they return another day?
Will they come back to the bay, or are they gone to stay?
Have they found another bay so very far away?
Where will they stay so far away?
Will they come back home to my bay?
If they do, will they return to stay?
Will they go again another day?
It is getting lonely here on the bay,
Since the birds left that day in May.

Seth Thomas McKinney

What A Day

The morning sky was a dark and gray
The sky was clouded ready to rain
The sun was hidden as the day slowly changed
The air so damp it clouded the window pane
It was not a great day to go out and play

Each day demands decisions while you are living
Make use of the time the Lord has given
Clear up the problems that were forgotten
Don't start projects that you can't do
Check what you have accomplished when you are through

Live those dreams you had in your mind
Just enjoy life while you have the time
Say a pray of thanks for what you have been given
A beautiful day is one to enjoy and you are livin'
This time given, on the dice of life you have a seven

Don't waste time on projects that are not accepted
Love and say thanks, it's more than I expected
Many have nothing in their life but total rejection
Poverty and disease is not a respecter
Thanks the Lord that you are an exception

W. Drury Clark

The Old Man And His Pup

Each day rain or shine, into
The snow and cold they always
go: The big man who is old, and
His happy Little Pup.
   Hers: A playful, peppy, puppy
Prance, zigzagging into a circling dance.
   His: A slow, sliding, shuffling step;
   A walk exerted, a stride uneven,
   A path off-center and off-step.
   Her's: A carefree, bounding bounce, and run,
Dragging the old one into having some fun!
   His tired old legs no match for
   Her tireless energy.
   Her's: Puppy Pandemonium at its best!
   His: Now no time for peaceful poetry or rest.
How do they manage to get along so well?
   So opposite......So mismatched a pair.
      Yet wonderf'ly
Love and friendship they surely share.

Salvatore T. Badamo

Breathless Is The Earth

The soles of my feet touch the bare earth

I feel
the spirit of my ancestors and
   hear the rattles of their turtle shells;
the words of my unseen grandmother that
   speaks in volumes of her wisdom;
the hissing from the ground as it releases
   tongues that do not speak in forkness;
the eagles soar in the blue sky
   voicing with feathers their gift to us;
the trees sway to the forces,
   singing in a whisper, turning into a roar;
the animals of warning, hidden from sight,
   howling the coming of the enemy;
the earth become silent, and
   screams come from our death;

I feel
the arrows as they cease to cross the land,
   fallen with our dead.

Ronda R. Garrah

The Morning Meadow

The moon gracefully drifts behind your rising hills.
The stars casually dance away.
The sun appears, the dew drops glisten on your sea of grass.
And out of the dense forest,
Deer emerge from its shadows,
Seeking the acorns from your trees.
The birds flutter about, sing their peaceful songs.
The day wears on and the morning is gone.
The animals retreat, to the safety of their forest home.
And the your meadow floor is once again left alone,
Waiting for the next morning to come.

Paul Pugsley

A Brand New Day

The gray mist of dawn rises over the sleepy mountainside:
The stillness of the morning is awakened
   by rambling waters.
Sunshine peeping through billowed clouds,
   penetrates the coolness of the morning.
Dancing rays catch a ride with the water
   and travel with it to the sea.
A brand new day has begun.

Warren W. Holdren

The Blink

Cruising,
the sun glared down the front of the hood.
My eyes squint as I dream a daydream far away.
I blink as the signs roll past. STOP
Sirens wailing in the dark of my night.
   One one-thousand
   Two one-thousand
   Three one-thousand
   Four one-thousand
   Five one-thousand
      Breathe!
My eyes flutter to see nameless faces.
Then all of a sudden I am alone,
being entrapped in the belly of a steel bird,
it spits me out.
I am surrounded by green suits,
being wheeled around until I lose my way.
I awake minutes later to find years gone by.
All I own has been taken by a single ray of light.

Kathy Olp

Just A Thought

The customers are gone and the racks are empty
The sun sets and the eyes get misty

The memories and experiences of voices gone by
The times were good, let me dry my eye

My wife my children and all of my life
I say thank you Lord through the good times and strife

The Lord was my shepherd, I never wanted
Through the tests of life I was never daunted

As I finish this chapter and begin a new book
I'm sad but I'm happy for another time and outlook

I'll miss my wrench and my screwdriver too
But life's a mystery and I'm still not through

I have closed the doors and eaten all my cake
But the memories, oh the memories, no one can ever take

So as I ponder the past and wonder the future
Be happy with me, I have the unknown to nurture

When I first heard the news that it was time to go
I cried then I stopped and thought, what do they know

For my world is my family and life goes on
Even long after the station is gone

Richard D. McGough

Where I Belong

The golden sun was heading west
The time of day I like the best
I sighed a wistful, soulful sigh
I felt nature was so very nigh.
The moon came up so lovely and bright
To shed its glow of beautiful light
And I sat there all alone not really knowing where I belong.
The moon is now a yellow glow,
I think of things I would like to know.
Will the sun come up in the east?
Will I starve or will I feast?
I'll set here all alone and nod,
Just me, the moon and God.

Nana Lane

A Whisper Of Life

We live. We die and go to dust.
The use of it is unknown except to God.
Someday we will see what the purpose, the
whole idea, and the birth of life means for
it to have been created. It's all in all, over
and over again. You're born, you love, you
die and leave the loved behind. As
generations pass and love chains come and
go, we keep on living that life that knows
no one. You are a soul living a forgotten
life in a big piece of flesh controlled by
an unmovable soul gasping for air and
not wanting to be there. Finally at the time
of death the soul is relieved at the freedom
it has once again staring down at the
lifeless body it at one time had been
embraced.

William E. Gunnett

The Beach

The ocean waves the rocky beach
The vast green land it might reach
The grainy sand fills with many shells
That hold secrets they perhaps might tell
The sun rises, the sea gull screeches
On these sunny exotic beaches
The strange fragrance fill the air
It reaches up to the mysterious lair
The blue whales floats on the breeze
The great shark hunts it prey with ease
The small minnows swim,
The crab reaches the beach pails rim
The vident waves crash
The water goes splash, splash,
Splash, splash, splash, splash, splash
Molly Stowe

My Hero

The bandits erased a life he once knew.
The village was burned leaving him orphaned.
Little Aaron was alone with just a drum.
The drum, a memory of a life that had been destroyed.
My heart beats to this drum.

Little Aaron the Drummer Boy.
The world treated him like a toy.
The world tore him down, down to the core.
But something built him up.

The world moved against him.
Pushing on him stronger than any hurricane wind.
But little Aaron still moved forward.

Oh, the world was dark, darker than the color black,
But somewhere in the blackness,
The Drummer Boy noticed there was some light.
With light, came a search.

He found hope while others all around him fell into despair.
He found love when so many around were filled with hate.
Oh, little orphan boy, you're my hero.
The only hero I'll ever need.
Thomas Berntsen

"Sweet Memories"

Gently cradled, lullabies hummed,
the white wicker rocks a reluctant child to sleep
as the summer breeze, with noisy bees
and well-fed birds promise her safe to keep
in a glorious trance of contentment.

These dreams of a child, too indulged
and cocooned in the fuzzy warmth and love
of your patient voice and capable arms,
are nudged by the familiar scent from a stove
as age-old receipts promise tasting.

And when awake, time whiles away
since scraps of lace and silky ribbon is found,
with frilly doilies and old satin slips,
carefully saved, such treasures abound
in a drawer just for her to create with.

Your ancient wisdom diminishes now
from the weariness of a century of living.
Though passage of time dulls our precious riches,
the child lives forever with the love that keeps giving
in the sweet memories of her cherished grandmother.
Marion R. Sargeant

Untitled

Break free-those chains won't hold much longer,
The will to survive has got to be stronger.
You need to take complete control of your life,
In order to combat any troubles or strife.
Desires are many when one's down and out,
I know how it feels, what it's all about.
The dreams don't die - they just seem far-fetched,
Don't ever lose sight; in your mind keep them sketched.
People will be people, so you've got to be you,
Don't pace yourself or judge by what they might do.
The pleasures in life will be all yours one day,
You'll see things change and everything go your way.
The feeling will be one of great relief,
Just remember that when you feel disbelief.
Sweet and pleasurable will be your emotions,
Keep that in mind when you get negative notions.
Don't let go of your dreams for anyone,
Don't quit the chase before it's done.
You will defeat all of your fears and fulfill all of your dreams,
Live up to the challenge of life's little schemes.

Robin K. Pinkerman

I Stand Alone

I stand alone mid stones and mounds of clay,
The wind blowing cold around me — whispering.
I speak your name, a teardrop falls upon the
Withered flowers
That lay upon your mound of clay.

You rest in peace apart from pain
Beneath this mound of clay.
Yes, you go first and I remain
To stand alone to bear this pain, and wait —

Until that day when I will lay beneath my mound of clay,
Beside you I will rest in peace to join you in that land above.
Together we will be again.
Until that time — I stand alone.

E. Jean Henry

The Storm

As the clouds grew dark so did our hearts,
The winds blew as our tears swelled,
Thunder crashed as our screams cried out,
The rain fell like tears,
Lightning ripped through the sky like dreams flashing
  before our eyes,
But as dawn came,
Our hearts were filled with a new horizon,
The tears we shed have made new life,
Our screams are now the beautiful music of the Blue Jay
  outside our windows,
And new dreams are brought by the morning sun.

Sandi R. Dunkelberger

Untitled

At last I am at the water's edge
This night being extra special
My last evening in the safe corner I created
Tomorrow I venture out
But tonight, inhaling is even sweeter
As I take in the smells that have become
So familiar and so comforting
This mixture of salt air and vanilla
I can take the vanilla with me when I leave
With hope that I will start anew
In an old place called home.

Marilyn M. Highland

A Woman's Prayer

God give me the courage to become...
The woman you know I can be

God give me the wisdom to walk
with thee...In divine purity

God make me whole and fill my soul...
with holy inspiration

God help me find the righteous path...
To walk with total dedication

God grant me love of all mankind...
That I can make daylight brighter

God help me help the gentle child...
That I can make burdens lighter

God carry me through the toughest times...
So I can walk with thee

God grant me the courage to become...
The woman you know that I can be

Saundra Scott Brower

From Dreams To Reality

Columbus had a dream.
The world is round.
He sailed across the sea.
Found America, this land of the free.

Abraham Lincoln had a dream.
Freedom for you and for me.
He fought a war for this great cause.
He died for America, this land of the free.

Martin Luther King had a dream
Freedom, justice, and peace for you and me.
He marched and died, but not in vain,
With his dying lips, he did proclaim.

"March on! March on!
Keep the peace! keep the peace!
Do right for rights!
For Americans, in this land of the free"

Martha Thompson

My World In Time

I came into this world
The world of Glitz and Charleston
The world of bootlegging and depression
The world of CCC - WPA - Survival.

I moved into this world
This world of tension and war
This world of blackouts and rationing
This world of conflict, strife and death.

I moved into this world
This world of selfishness and greed
This world of segregation and hate
Family destruction, hippies and addiction

I moved into this world
This world of runaways and latch key kids
This world of distrust and corruption
This world of floundering and seeking solutions

As I move further into this world
I wonder, will families survive, values return
Will the children return, will we become strong
Will people walk proudly side by side? For this world I truly pray!

M. B. Bickett

A Poem For My Mother

I sit here and think - It breaks my heart
The years have gone by - we've drifted apart

You were my best friend - year after year
I know that now - my head is clear

I remember seeing Hank Williams with you and sis
So many good times through the years I did miss

I think of you working out in the yard
I know I had hurt you - these years have been hard

We would turn on TV - watch monsters all night
With Mom by my side - I was all right

You were always there through my years of softball
You were my biggest fan - you gave it your all

With a strong mother like you - how did I get weak
Wish I could go back and earn what I seek

The years have been rough - I got off track
But I want my life and my mother back

It will be like riding in that old Chevy car
I'll be with my mom - I'll feel like a star

I'll try to make things how they should have been
Put a smile on your face make you proud again
Melanie Stringer

Soaring To New Heights

The days are short
the years seem long
some things are right, some things seem wrong
I try to succeed and do my best
now good things come to me and I can rest
some friendship are lost, some last till the end
once in a while you'll find a true friend
sometimes you are a winner
sometimes you end up last
make good choices for your future
you can never change the past
trying to fit in, trying to be me
we slowly make our way on the path to destiny
enjoy all that you have and every day you live
instead of always taking, take the time to give
everyday I choose between the wrongs and rights
but succeeding in the world means soaring to new heights
Megan R. Bills & Laura Schlesenberg

Destiny

The green has turned to yellow,
the yellow changed to brown,
As the dry, crisp, leaves of autumn,
come tumbling to the ground.

A final bid to summer,
when they spread their welcome shade,
And lived in splendid glory,
their life-span now must fade.

An old man shuffles through the leaves,
with faulty steps and failing sight.
Recalls a season now gone by,
when life was good and hopes soared bright.

Remembers a time long gone by,
when life was young and hope reached high.
Had known his neighbors high esteem,
ambition climbed into the sky.

The leaves will sleep, man must go,
to reap his choice of seeds now grown.
Ready for harvest in the vast unknown,
labor is over, what has he sown?
Marjorie Blankenbaker

Dancing Angels At Limantour Beach

I watch my children
Their bodies outlined against the shimmering background of sea and sky
Untrained athletes, they are slender, strong and graceful

They tease the waves, enormous crashing waves
These children buoyant with human spirit
In their element

Her long hair flying, Kirsten twirls with outstretched arms
David sprints across the sand and turns on a dime
She digs with her feet for sandcrabs
He collects treasures large and small

I reflect on their exuberance, their joyous freedom
Founded in wonder, delight, movement, spontaneity
And nature's magnificent offerings

"Can we swim in our underwear?" they had asked
"Yes, my loves," I allowed
Swim in your underwear, get wet in the rain,
Mud on your shoes, sand in your hair

And when we return from the salt air and the cold sea
I'll be sure that you're warm and cozy

My beloved dancing angels
Yvonne Marie Arcus

Emeralds In The Pale Moonlight

In the pale moonlight, he held her hand as they walked and shared
   their dreams.
Oh, they were young, but so much in love the future was theirs, it seems.
She could marry first, then finish school. She was sure he was her man,
As he walked her home in the pale moonlight he always held her hand

A lovely bride, and a handsome groom, some said they were much too young.
But they made their vows on Christian Love, happiness was sure to come.
He built their house, then the children came and filled it with delight.
In sorrow too, he would hold her hand as they sat in the pale moonlight

They both found joy in the work they did, raised a family, then retired.
Growing flowers became her passion, while he volunteered to help
   fight fires.
For 55 years they've been in love Oh sure, they've argued some,
It's not easy for two individuals to try live as one.

Long years ago they made their vows, but ask, and they will say,
"When you marry the one you really love it seems just like yesterday!"
On this Emerald wedding anniversary with their family here tonight,
They'll recall those times they held each other, with love, in the
   pale moonlight.
Stanley Christian

Violent Strikes

   A child lies motionless in the street. A family kneels,
then cries at her feet.

   Violence has struck again. Her life had just begun.
Her body and soul sleep for an eternity. How many
smiles will be missed by her community?

   A child lies motionless in the street. A town kneels,
then cries at her feet.

   What could she have grown-up to be? What talents did
she have to share with you and me?

   A child lies motionless in the street. A nation kneels,
then cries at her feet.

   What knowledge did she possess? World peace may have
been a success.

   A child lies motionless in the street. A world kneels,
then cries at her feet.

   Violence has struck again. Her life had just begun.
Can we learn from his tragedy and stop this atrocity?
Nancy Adams

Of Man

Like a great canyon, is the mind of man.
There are secrets and memories hidden away.
And caves of darkness dwelling within.
On the surface you seem to figure it out.
Unprepared for the challenge ahead.
Like a giant mountain, is the heart of man.
Temptations and troubles may tug and pull,
But the land of the heart remains the same.
The struggle between desire and duty, may confuse at times,
But the rhythm of the heart always leads the way.
Like the vast sky, is the soul of man.
With endless beauties and treasures above.
The wind will blow you into the clouds,
It will send you into a mode of flight.
Peace and purity enable the soul to soar.
Regardless of the challenges the mind may encounter,
Or the aches that the heart may feel,
If the soul is kept pure of unpleasant things,
In you, happiness will dwell...

Wendy A. Boothe

The Rose

With this rose I thee give, all my love as long as I live.
There are times we are distressed some days,
but please don't doubt, my love is here to stay.
We have been through trying times together
and I would do it again, forever and ever.
You are my life, love and the world to me;
I have no cheating heart, I want you to believe.
The vows we took were, "'til death do us part,"
so just remember I love you with all my heart.
You have given me so much love and devotion
and I take this serious with every breath and emotion.
This single rose symbolizes my love for only you,
and the expression of my love is so very true.
If you ever have doubts about my love as
long as we both live,
Remember this rose, I thee give.

Jodi Tripp

Great Day Ahead

When I awake in the morning
There is a great day ahead
I think why waste a minute
So I quickly bound out of bed.

I never question what God has planned
For me to do today
I pray, Dear Lord, please show me,
I want to go your way.

Please guide me to those that need me,
And in some small way,
To brighten up someone's life
At least just for today.

As you lead me down life's path Dear Lord,
Hold tightly to my hand,
So that I do not miss one,
That needs to understand.

Your way of life is a happy one,
That your Love is all around.
We only have to obey your word,
Your strength will greatly abound.

Ruby Anna Winton

There Is A Time

There is a time for birth, a time for joy,
There is a time for pride, a time to be coy,
There is a time for praise, a time to boast,
There is a time to party, a time to host.

There is a time for growth, a time to learn,
There is a time for love, a time to yearn,
There is a time to choose, a time to commit,
There is a time to acknowledge, a time to submit.

There is a time to relate, a time to adjust,
There is a time to build, a time to lust,
There is a time for family, a time for hope,
There is a time to celebrate, a time to cope.

There is a time to age, a time to reject,
There is a time for pain, a time to reflect,
There is a time for prayer, a time for dismay,
There is a time for death, a time to pay.

Sidney Silberman

Faith

Although the sun doesn't always shine,
There lingers a brightness so delicate and fine...
Dreams encountered, visions scorned,
I beg of you, let faith be born.
Within the heart our creation thrives,
Sometimes misplaced; yet with a will survives.
Sanctioned for the self and others,
Seeking love with trusting wonder.
Possessed, entangled, evident pain to bear;
Praying in hopes, by twilights end,
May all be fair.
Our conception of times is unlike the Lord's...
It's as if the heart is pierced by a sword.
Witness, testify and live on;
Believe... for all things awaken with each new dawn...

Stephanie Vita Salerno

Oh But What Is Life

To see the beauty all around you, yes and see the cruelness there may be.
To smell the sweetness of the air, and some of the sourness there may be.
To taste the sweetness of the fruit of the earth, along with
the bitterness there may be.
To reach out and touch the softness there may be, and feel the
hardness all around.
To walk in the sun, felling the cool fresh air troth the
wood of life, when some times the hard dry earth crack's beneath
your feet and the hot dry air is all around you.
To sleep and dream of all the good thing in life, lease we not
forget the nightmares there shell be.
To hear the birds sing the song of happiness, to hear the cry
of the Hawk as he comes in for his kill.
To see life as it is, or to see life as you may wish it to
be, for life is not too sweet nor too cruel but just life.

Warren N. Whitworth

Gina

Dearest Gina, so precious, like a diamond in the rough
To know you, to see you, is just not enough.
One must love you and squeeze you, and hold you so tight
Only then comes the feeling that all is all right.
Your name is Virginia, like my mother's so dear
But Grandpa could not love her, for she was not here.
I thank my dear God, and pray each night
To protect my dear Gina, and keep her all right.
For Grandpa does love you, as Grandma does too.
And the world is so much nicer, cause God gave us you.

Wilfrid J. Smith

The End Of Time

The memories that I hold within are a treasured part of my soul,
There the only part of me that I haven't had to let go...
Selling this house and moving away is something that I wanted to do,
Only because there is nothing here for me, nothing without you...

Time stood still for me when we said our final goodbye's,
I was filled with emptiness and our children with tear stained eye's..
The shock of your passing was a mountain that I could not climb,
My whole world came tumbling down around me like the end of time...

Your smile I see in our daughter and your laughter in our son's
Their growing up with your talent's and their full of your wacky fun..
Through their eye's I see the love that you gave so true,
And in their heart's I feel their sadness of missing you...

Moving back home to all my family and friend's.
Bring's me back to my childhood secret's and old fashioned trend's...
But I must move on as I leave some thing's behind,
But in my soul I'll carry you with me, until the end of time...

Sandra L. Rogers

Summer Breeze

The silence was broken, crickets chirping through night,
there was a breeze through the window, with only the moon as my light.
My body was chilled, and the sheets felt so cold,
in his bed that we lay in, without his body to hold.
As we lay there together, I felt so alone,
the darkness surrounding, once a loneliness unknown.
As I turned toward his body; in silence he lay,
his cheek I touch gently, without a word I could say.
The bed seemed so large, like I was lost dark at sea,
his touched became foreign, he's become so distant from me.
The silence grew louder, yet his heartbeat grew clear,
I felt his breath on my neck, as his body seemed near.
He reached out his arm, and his hand touched my chest,
so quiet and calm, it become a night without rest.
His touch was so tender, on night that was cold,
with beauty came passion, as the night would unfold.
His hand became soft, and his strength became weak,
we were only shadows at night, from the curtains light leaked.
The silence was broken, and the darkness grew light,
two bodies created warmth, as we became the summer breeze through
  the night.

Sarah R. Merrill

"Coffee"

The lights dimmed from bright to not quite dark
There was a quiet awe as the performer
  placed himself on the stage
And then as the dying artist is woken by his masterpiece;
  the spotlight burst onto the passioned face

Meanwhile, in the back of the coffee house,
  the waitresses talked back and forth, exchanging
  non-essential meaningless
They had seen the show no less than 12 times
  and wished not to show respect again

As the performer took hold of the microphone,
  mystic revelations floated off his tortured tongue
And hurriedly, the waitresses served more
  black, cold, unsweetened coffee

The attendants were forced to take one last drink
Then they sadly filed out never to return

Lucas Klotzbach

How Old Is Santa

When I was little long ago,
there was something I didn't know,
with present for me, little sister and brother,
Santa was really, my father or mother
The presents of the future, present and past
Tell a little white lie.
So Santa Clause will never die.
With friends and family all around.
Even the one's from out of town,
You open the gifts, you eat and drink,
about the cost you do not think.
Such fun, such fun,
  But it will not last.
One week from now.
It's part of the past.

Mary Weiser

The Championship Game

I can almost Jam
Therefore I am.
We are down by two
I got the ball,
I really hope I don't fall.
Watch out for the Gump down low
He throws elbows
Once I took a blow.
Four ticks left,
Championship game
There goes the try
Twisting, Turning, Spinning. Silence,
Among the jam of people as they watch the sphere soar high
The people all gaze..............SWOOOOSH!!!
It's a three from the cove,
The school fight song plays
The applauding chiefs cheer
The crowd cheers, the team cheers as we
Won the Championship Game.

Matthew D'John

Just A Bud Among His Roses

God called her home to be a bud among His roses
There's no thorns among God's Roses
Her light out shown, her beauty revealed
God's bud among His roses
Her love was shown by the people there
No Thorns among God's Roses
Her peace was shown and her beauty revealed
God's Bud among His roses
Children don't despair, someday you will see her there
You too will be a bud among God's Roses
Husband, her love will always be there
Don't be discouraged, you too will be a bud
Among God's Roses
Friends, family look what she left you
Love, joy, friendship
All those who knew her can say
She is truly God's Bud among His roses
This is God's special day,
His bud just bloomed into a beautiful rose

Maxine Phillips

54

My Pain

Losing your parents is the worst pain a child could ever endure
There's not a day that goes by you're crying behind closed doors.
Calling out and wishing they were here,
So that they could help me to see clear
Each day you grow stronger - praying the pain will ease away.
Knowing in your heart you'll never hear "I love you" anymore,
Or get a loving hug when you walk out the door.
Asking why did they have to go - only God can answer - I'll never know
I was only seven when this began and nine when the Lord was done.
Now I'll be thirty-two and with God's help he'll see me through.
Growing up without the two that teach you every thing
Can drive a person crazy mentally.
Some children fight and say cruel things to their parents
But if they could walk in my shoes for just one day,
They would be sorry for all the things they say.
I only wish I could do things all over again,
Instead I never let my pain end.
So Mommie and Daddy I can't bring myself to say "Good-bye",
Only that I will see you when God feels it's my time.

Nancy Campana

What Are Angels

What are angels? Well let me tell you what I think.
They are God's blessings and his glorious love link.
A friend, a heavenly protector, by God's own design.
A guardian to always be there, our crooked road align.

Times when something that could be devastating occurs.
A feeling of fright, despair and vision of hope blurs.
Seemingly a miracle takes place and everything is okay.
A warmth of peace comes sending our life on its way.

We belong to God, always in need of his love and touch.
His guardian angels show that he does love us very much.
We travel through life having many problems to endure.
Know God and his angels will protect us, we are secure.

Life certainly has its ups and downs, overs and under.
Realize God sends the sunshine, lightening and thunder.
Storms of life help make us strong and on God to depend.
God is life; believe, know the great love he does send.

What a very wonderful gift, having God's warmth and love.
With him all things are possible, guiding us from above.
Angels are heaven sent, they are part of the army of God.
Watchman, caretaker, friend, guided by the shepherd's rod.

Maxine Jones

Untitled

My eyes are wide, I hear it.
They are the hard tears of an angry sky.
This is traffic of the mind,
the rain is my sunrise.

I awaken, thoughts are not reality.
My brain is a taxi to transport emotions.
I feel nothing,
where are the birds to greet my unhappiness.

Goodbye!
Is there anything else to say?
Life so incomplete,
I am like money, a traded thought.

No one really cares, another masquerade ball.
It is a front.
Morning is a new beginning. Not for me,
the rain is my sunrise.

Sara A. Shank

Tears Are Never Far From The Surface

Tears are wonderful tools.
They come to my rescue, when I'm not sure what to do.
They come in happy times, in times of sadness,
In times of loneliness and distress.
When I am overcome with emotion,
My tears pour forth their healing lotion.

She began as a small butterfly touch:
I never knew I could love anything so much.
She was caring in all her ways
And her friends were more numerous than her days.
To her smile, the sun did not compare.
Her voice was like laughter dancing on air.

So I'll cry tears of remembrance, tears of pain,
But from tears of loneliness I shall try to refrain.
I will not dwell on the negative- the evil she fought;
I will remember the good times-all the joy she brought.
Although I accept God's divine purpose,
Tears are never far from the surface.

Tammy Harper

Case A88-61

Just a number to a case is all you were to them.
They did their job of diagnosing; they followed the protocol.
They visually inspected and histologically reported what you were.

To me you were life; my friend; my lover; the father of my children;
my mentor—now you're gone—my life is gone.
Where did you go? Why did you go?

Did the Agent Orange you unknowingly bathed in take you? Did the
cigarette smoke you infused throughout your body do it? Was it the
environmental poisons your body could no longer fight off?

Your defenses lowered they x-rayed you; they surgically manipulated
you. Yet never once did they say the word terminal. We never planned
what would be, how to deal with the outcome.

Your life has ended and so has part of mine. That little transitional
cell carcinoma has taken you from us. A husband for sixteen years,
a father for thirteen and now—case A88-61 forever.

Rebecca Brittain

Untitled

The heart of an Aunt is enormous.
They do things like shape and conform us.

Wise black female,
Share your story with me tonight.
Tell of your travels and share your light.
This light, it shines on dreary day.
Please come with me so we can play.

Let's listen to the sounds of your time.
Then with you I will share some of mine.

Many pictures on t.v. are not reality,
But they do mold part of my personality.
Help teach me the way that I ought to be.
So that I can be proud to show the real me.

From the dream world in my head I did plummet
But you and others helped bring me back from it.
And since you too possess power and might,
I know now that not all angels are white.

Terrance Lee Dobyns

I Told My Love

Once I saw the viking ships sail across a lake -
They had no sails, nor even a crew, but sail they did my mate.

In total uniformity magnificent ships did glide -
In autumn haze across the lake to find the other side.

I sat alone upon a swing and watched these ships sail past -
I thought how very much I hurt for my love had gone, alas.

Many a season has come and gone since first I saw them sail -
And how my life has changed since then would make a fancy tale.

I told my new love the other night of viking ships I saw
And how they sailed across the lake to find another shore.

The ending to my story I'll softly tell you now -
'Twas only autumn leaves that fell from some great Oak trees bough -
To sail across the hazy lake to reach the other side.

Nancy Langley-Bishop

The 7th Cavalry

The 7th Cavalry was gallant, brave and strong,
They had pride, determination and song.
Well disciplined and fine soldiers one and all,
It was hard to find one with a flaw.

Gen. George A. Custer was the 7th Calvary's glorious leader,
He was a good kind man who stood firm like a cedar.
Custer never drank liquor and he liked to read,
He was noble in both thought and deed.

The 7th Cavalry was an awesome fighting force, hard to beat,
They found the Sioux and Cheyenne foe and didn't retreat.
The rifles were roaring, the arrows did fly,
Outnumbered ten to one, a time to die.

On June 25, 1876 about 260 soldiers perished in Indian war,
Into heaven, their battle scarred souls did mightily soar.
Custer's two brothers Tom and Boston were killed in the battle,
No longer will these fine men ride upon their saddle.

When most of the 260 soldiers were butchered and slain,
The dust settled again on the hot Montana sun baked plains.
The savage battle of the Little Big Horn cost them their lives,
Leaving grieving friends, children and wives.

Terry Pieszchala

Dogs, We Love Them

Dogs like to play in the sun.
They like to have fun in the sun, sun, sun.
Dogs are big. Dogs are small.
Most of all they smell.
They eat all of their food,
they love our's but no,
no, no it's not good for their power.
It's fun to play with them.
They never bite, well sometimes.
Dogs love you to pet them.
They have a fit when you don't.
Dogs rule. They're so cool, they drool.
Dogs never stay little.
They always get big sooner or later.
But you'll still love them any ways.

Renee Fortin

Gaze upon an ocean grey.

I see the ocean blue a grey
Upon its surface not a stray
The flapping birds, the dead sea worms
The sky's asunder the trees that sway
I look to the sky, upon the nigh
Its reflective silence, it's blue and gray.

Mariam Wharton-Ali

Brave

The war calls—my duty is to help my fellow man
They say I am dedicated
They say I am fearless
They say I am an Angel of Mercy
They say I am brave

My hands are warm with their blood
My heart races with fear
My tears fall in their open wounds
I want to run away and never look back
My hands ease their pain and comfort their death
I am dying with each drop of their spilled blood

They say I am brave
I say, I am a nurse

Rhonda Kiracofe

A Tribute To Samuel A. Mudd

There was a time long long ago, when our country was just young. They talked about extending equal rights to everyone, but the rich landowners just did not agree. One man Abraham Lincoln wanted all slaves to be free. So with pen in hand and great expectations he sat down and composed the Emancipation Proclamation The Government hierarchy weren't very pleased, they thought it was dangerous for slaves to be freed. They tried to silence Mr. Lincoln but could not succeed. One fiery Southerner with great hatred for the North, went to Fords Theater and killed Lincoln. The fervent cry went up Mr. Lincoln died. They set out to search the Maryland countryside. There lived a Doctor Samuel Mudd where Booth had spent the night. He did not recognize the man for he was in disguise, he fixed his leg and left him rest till morning did rise. When the Army came to Samuel's farm it was a great surprise, He did not know of Lincoln's death. He said I did nothing wrong. I followed my Hippocratic Oath. They said they did not believe him, at trial he must stand. He was found guilty any how. He was innocent man. He helped to cure the Yellow Fever in the Dry Tortugas. He was pardoned by Andrew Johnson and then he was set free, but they refuse to clear his name to this very day. I'm sorry Uncle Samuel they've hurt you this way.

Nora Lane Mudd

Heart Of Love

When I am no longer here,
Think of me with laughter in your heart
And a smile upon your lips.

Remember the silly things I would do.
The way I looked at the world
And the love I had in my heart.

Feel my strength when faced with problems.
Feel my forgiveness when hurt.
Feel my love when you think you're alone.
Look around and know I'm right there.

Talk to each other and hear my words.
Look at the babies and see my soul.
Remember the good I found in each person.
Share the love I gave freely.

Use my patience when you deal with others.
Use my heart when you deal with each other.

To you I leave - beauty in your soul.
Love in your heart and strength in your spirit.

Yvonne B. Kane

Heard In Heaven 4:30 A.M.

Oh, rescue the feet of the babies from hell, we've cut them off,
  thinking the dragons won't tell
but they're chewing on toes and they're asking for more, as the blind
  ones are causing a fleshy downpour
of more and still more of the small feet and shoes, in a tumbledown
  perfectly desperate move
to appease the fat monsters who are barring the door, in terror we
  frantically give them some more
Hoping to make them move out of the way, so the door will be open
  again soon some day.
We trust they won't blame us for what we've all done, maiming
  the babies and pretending it's fun.
The dragons they clamor and pace as they must, for they feed on
  discarded faith, honor and trust.
And the more that we feed them, the more they will eat of the naive
  and happy and joyful small feet.

Please, rescue the feet of the babies from hell, they're crying and
  don't understand why they fell,
they're walking around on their stumps unaware. Is anyone out there?
  Does anyone care?
Straining and swaying alone, (no support), stripped of their weapons
  as the dragons cavort,
plotting and preening (along for the ride), What terrible queen then
  allows them to hide?
Dear God, do you have one who'll take on the task? To go down and
  remove the chameleon's mask?
It's hard and so strong and invisible, too, if there's someone who's
  brave enough, tell me then who?

For if we stop feeding the dragons at night, they won't have the
strength to put up a fight.
The reason they snarl is to make us afraid and demand is their
  cyclical terrorists blade.
If the babies are burning, so then are we, for we're one and the same,
  oh why can't we see?
So the next time they ask for a succulent toe, remember the beat of
  your heart and say no.
For the innocent cries of the babes are your tears, and the dragons
  you feed are only your fears.

Suzanne Bradley

Requiem

The time has come to step ashore;
This fragile bark of flesh I need no more.

I do not go away; still remain
Though now my life seems changed, it is the same.

Some may recall my gentle jest of "long repose,"
When life on earth for me would gently close.

But how could I enjoy a heavenly mirth
When those I dearly love still strive on earth.

Beside my lonely grave look up above,
Pour out your deepest thoughts, for in my love,

My heart will open wide in quick concern
And plead with God to send you some return.

Until we all can sing that Grand Amen,
I wish no rest, no requiem.

Therese Pike

Tainted Clouds

Far off over the new horizon they hover somberly,
twisting with unrest as they are blown from place to place.
As they draw closer I could see they were as sad as I,
for these tainted clouds wept for all the sorrow they've seen.
They preach to us by reflecting our own images down upon the Earth,
revealing both the beauty and despair we share with each other.
While some are seen easily others lie in obscure shapes and shadows,
but the impact they have can only be seen within ourselves.

Philip W. Cromer

"Hungry Time"

The Children are crying out
This is not the time to do without
It's feeding time, but the plates are empty
The firesides are cold and dark
The pots remain unused.

Their mothers sit and wait for their fathers to return.
Hoping against hope that there would be some food
But alas! their hopes are dashed
The food never come
It's "Hungry Time" again.

The Children tired of crying and waiting
Fall asleep-hungry
It's only in their dreams can they find peace
They dream of the food their bodies so desperately need.

Alas! the morning sun comes streaming through.
The dream has passed
And reality is at hand
What is there to look forward to
Nothing but "Hungry times" again.

Karietha Marks

Secretaries Clerks

Whether a secretary or a clerk,
This is one person that is no jerk.
They are assigned so much work that it's not funny,
Yet they eventually get the job whether rainy or sunny.

It takes a unique person to do what they do,
Yet each one gets their job done — Do you?
What would a boss be without these dedicated people?
They would topple right off their steeple.

Now, not one of them is perfect you know,
Some are fast and some are slow;
But the same could be said about us,
So don't you be the one to fuss.

I'm proud of them each and everyone,
They are always working under the gun.
Thanks for all the paper work that's done,
And the many errands that you've run.

I've come in with many of you over the years,
I've seen you in laughter and in tears;
Yet you're there and doing a job that's needed,
Often unappreciated and unheeded. God bless!

J. H. Blackman Jr.

"The River" Runs To It

This river water run at the back of our land
This land was mostly sand, my dad was a farmer
I have seen—my—dad, broke as he could be
With 3 kids and wife to feed
fall to his knees
As things lay heavy on his chest.
Hard—times, what dad called it
River water's got high, water's got low
We wondered was those cotton field's going to grow
This fall, could it be white as snow
Would it be fit to take to the gin!
Or was we going have to pull
That — cotton — again.

Wanda Wood

57

Gone Forever

You only lived for a short while, and in
this little time you made lots of people smile.
Now it's a cry because you chose to die. We all
know life isn't a cherry pie and may your soul
rest up in the sky. We will meet again someday
but as for today all I can do is pray. For you
this was a way out but in reality you punk
out. We know we must move on but it's so
hard with you gone. We hope you're happy where
you are because now you are so far, and now
all I have to show for it are the emotional
scars. A star shines for you at night and God
knows it's the prettiest little sight. We all
believe God took you in his arms because
you and I both know he will do no harm.
We want to know why but the answer lies
between you and the man above the sky.
You are loved by so many people and may
you rest in peace because at peace is where you are at.

Teresa Jones

Live Today!

Be gay, be gay,
This night, this day,
Take happiness on the way,
For tomorrow, tomorrow,
Tomorrow what?
Who knows what cheer may come to clear the drear?
What gloom will come to chase the bloom of youth
To some unknown hiding-place?
Tomorrow?

Who knows what with the dawn
May come to challenge brain and brawn?
Who knows?

Ah, better that we never know
What joy, what woe,
Lies down the road that we must take,
On which fate has placed her stake,
The birds yet sing and flowers bloom,
Perhaps....
Yes, 'tis better so.

Pauline Bingenheimer Harris

Untitled

Today is father's day,
this poem just for you,
for the best dad in the whole wide world,
and the sweetest man too.
You're always there to cheer me on,
and pick me up when I've fallen down,
always there to hold my hand,
loving me ever when I'm a down.
So I wrote this poem just for you,
to tell you how much I care,
how happy I am just to know,
how many more years we'll share,
I love you Dad

Teresa Taylor

To Grandmother

You are eighty-four years old today they say,
Tho your hair is silver you don't act that way,
For you are always around, here and about,
To see if that gas in the stove is turned out.

Then there's the dogs you feed each day,
They love you so, as to give up their play,
To follow you around as a guide I'd say,
For they - know you are old - in their own way.

There are many more things I could mention,
Enough to bring around a big convention.
But I am just like so many and the rest,
I know that you have and can pass the test.

Now the few short lines that you read above,
Are just a small symbol to you, of my love.
But my comparison for you I implore,
Will be so highly blessed on the Golden Shore.

So happy birthday grandmother dear,
I say with a true heart filled with cheer.
May years to come - bring more your way,
So again to you - I can say "happy birthday."

Omegia Williamson

Mother Can't Be Replaced

Mother can't be replaced.
Those things she has done for you can't be erased.
She tells you, you should live as a certain pace.
Mother is like a lawyer, she pleads your case.
When we get too high in life.
She tells us to make haste,
And of me down.
Mother tells us to live day by day,
Always pray.
For God will show us the way,
The food mother cooks has a good taste.
If mother loves her children she chastises them,
The Bible says train a child while he is young,
And the way he will not depart from it,
Show mother love everyday.
For she won't be with you always.
Show mother love while she is living,
All her life she has been giving.

Robert D. Johnson

"Dedicated to the King of Prussia Vol. Fire Co."

Volunteers are the greatest,
Though sometimes they'd like to rest.
To give of your time and ask nothing
Puts you right up there with the best.

Thanks from the "Ladies Artillery"
For all the things you've done.
You've helped us in so many ways,
It's hard to pinpoint one.

Some bought or sold Entertainment Books,
Help came from many places.
We made some money but still had fun
At all of our Night at the Races.

Some painted sills and planted shrubs
Some set up tables and chairs,
You've helped us cook, and even clean
At our Breakfast and other affairs.

Firemen and Members (Active and Social)
Have come to answer our call.
Your support means everything to us;
We thank you-One and All!

Lenore Irene Runkle

Untitled

Crying kindness never before has been
though wishes in masses that haven't come true yet
What matters when the sun will only convulse hang dance
in waters riddled by moonbeams and people
will live as they wouldn't like to
and for a moment (how vague beautiful) every breath from trees and
    solid earth is
infinitesimally dying while someone else is becoming ignorant.
    Shyness squeezes
so and but sitting with this damp place
this your poem is wrenched from my heart (acute wondering life). Some
soon or later day perhaps an in particular someone shall talk to me.
There is so much in the world that most can be blind to when they're
    pretending
to live and nearly everyone will kill for happiness (think of the
    insects) yet somehow
people have wished
for everything (many in thoughtless pretenses) and listening is
    unbearable
in this world where chattered twilight
hovers

Rachel Bennett

Friendship And Sorrow

Only a heart having broken into, can shed a tear and feel it cut through.
Grieved and laden, my heart at my feet, my friend has been taken
no more to compete.
Will the laughter of spring once more arise? Will ever I smile or see
with my eyes, the joy abounding the clear blue skies? Life is a sweet
fulfillment to bear, I'll go on alone I know not where.
Spring and summer will meet one day, I feel my lost friend would
heartily say
"Life is a joy, give it your most, for I have gone to a greater Host."
As I travel on my heart amiss, my friend you know not the emptiness.
Life goes on, each day a bit brighter, the hurt is dulling, growing lighter.
Memories of you, recalled in my head, a friend such as you will never be dead.
You've left me dear friend tho' I'll think every day, the happiness
you brought in passing my way.
Though tragedy and sorrow came my way, you stood there beside me each
step of the day. I'll strive on, as I flounder each sunrise I see,
to be the person you wanted for me. Thank you again where ever you
rest I'll try very hard to be my best.
Rest in peace my wonderful friend, life moving on it is time to begin.

Peggy Lake

Untitled

I am a woman who walks alone
    through contradictions.
I am beautiful, gracefully at ease,
I am an ugly child, with scarred up knees.
A walking portrayal of copied actresses
    I've seen,
But more myself than I could say
    with a scream.
    I am day.
    I am night.
    I welcome the sun in,
    Then I shut out its light.
Waiting to meet myself somewhere inside
    a dream,
To discover who I am, and everything that
    could mean.

Tammy Heintz

You And I

We have traveled together as man and wife
    through its hills and valleys, the road of life.
The warmth and love we have learned to share
    has held us together with loving care
Along the way, OUR LORD, gave his blessings to our need
    and three beautiful children grew from our seed.
To fill our lives with happiness and joy
    Two beautiful girls, and a handsome boy.

The memories of those bygone years
    Have burned deep within my heart, to still my fears.
The path that lay before us, we know not where it leads.
    OUR LORD will be our guide, His love will fill our needs.
Let us continue our journey down the road in life.
    Together you and I, as man and wife.
For how swiftly the years have gone by.
    Sense that day we wed, my beloved,
        You and I.

Raymond L. Bryce

Eulogy (The Death Of A City)

This small town has been hanging on
    through struggle and strife.
Down through the ages it has had to
    fight to maintain city life.
People come and people go.
People are what makes up the flow.
Sometimes she reaps prosperity
    and sometimes despair.
People go to larger cities for bargains galore!
The consumer has to maintain his store!
Small towns may become like some people I know.
Complacent, uncaring and unkind.
No friendly handshake or a happy hello.
Your business is appreciated, I want you to know!
Unknowingly we may be putting this city to rest.
What to do? What to do? Invest! Invest!

Mary E. Brannan

Mistress

She walks, clothed in sadness,
Through the twilight of an
Aether of Strife and Madness,
Which retreats unto itself
In Her presence as if
A gentle, parting Sea;
She absorbs all that is Pure in the Dark
And all that is Dismal in the Light
In an enchanting
Dance of
Intrigue and Deceit;
Beauty so openly wraps itself
Around Her, like so many
Strands of delicate thread,
Embracing the whole in a
Tightly woven fabric which veils something
Unknown;
Nothing in her wake remains unchanged as She walks,
Clothed in innocence, through the
Twilight.

Mike W. Browning

Through Years And Through Time

Just as always
Through years and through time
That flame in the sky has burned
As I burn with desire
For as long as this world has been
Through years and through time
The ocean has caressed the shore with loving patience
As my eyes enfold and hold you
Even as the incessant wind
Through years and through time
Has stirred a hundred billion branches, leaves and trees
So your love has stirred my soul and moves me endlessly
While this ground we call the earth
Through years and through time
Has yielded up her fruits
So I would give you all that is mine and that I am
Just as always
Two circles in balance - complete - yet touching the other
Just as always
I have been here for you
        Mark L. Saurs

Flower Of Life

Loving flower that glistens in the sun,
Thy reflection is radiant in wonder.
As the seedling of the self
Is planted in the soil of the soul
The vibration of birth is present.
As the waters the seedling
With pace and joy from thy heart
A loving flower doth peck its head
Through the soil in amazement
And feels the warmth of being.
Thy wondrous beauty excites all of nature,
For there is not another like you.
All are blessed by your being,
You give to the oneness of all
And a great healing takes place
As thy eyes open to behold
The universe at play!!!
        William J. Fenchak

'Tis My Eyes To See

'Tis my eyes to see not the America I once knew.
'Tis my eyes to see "Gulf War" Veterans and their families suffering mysterious diseases that could possibly be cured if not for the love of money.
'Tis my eyes to see "Gulf War" Veterans divorced due to symptoms that mimic sexually transmitted diseases.
'Tis my eyes to see denial of proper medical attention for "Gulf War" Veterans.

'Tis my eyes to see my deceased Brother-in-Law telling me that he loved me before going forward into Kuwait and Iraq - I wondered, what is it that he did not tell me?
'Tis my eyes to see medical professionals telling me, "why did you wait to come back home to the U.S. before getting sick?"

'Tis my eyes to see African-American soldiers discriminated against and denied opportunities while wearing the same uniform as their colleagues.
'Tis my eyes to see, what has happened to the America I once knew?
'Tis my eyes to see, will God spare America?
        William J. Simmons Sr.

Words Of Kindness

Say something kind to your neighbor,
To a friend a greeting of cheer.
To your loved ones a word of endearment,
Something tender to dry up a tear.

Give praise to the hosts of deserving,
Say a prayer for someone in need.
A simple "please" said, or "thank you"
Can make a day better indeed.

Say something wise to the children,
Be firm and strong if you must!
But always be sure what you utter,
Are words you know they can trust.

Don't say words cruel and thoughtless,
They can cut through a heart like a knife,
Keep them in check whatever you do,
Or you'll sadden and burden a life.

Use only the words of comfort and strength,
And those that can sting - never say,
For the words you use to stranger or friend,
Can brighten or ruin a day!
        Marianne L. Reed

Songs Of Dawn

One voice alone sings his endless tune,
To alert those seeking a new sunrise due;
A wake up call this lovely is so serene,
The different nationalities are only heard not seen.

More voices join in to reach that perfect blend,
First a few, then hundreds more descend;
The lyrics are unique and yet the same,
Over and over again their territory they claim.

They are bold, yet delicate to the touch,
The colors of their birth right are bright and such;
Was it the dove, robin, bob white or raven today?
Our Lord, made them all and to him we are thankful with praise.
        Wynter Bryte

To A Dedicated Missionary

   You are truly a great inspiration
to all people.
   Your heart is made of gold, and
with a soul only for the Lord.
   May you be blest with all the
goodness of the earth.
   There are very few people that
can compare to your love and devotion anywhere.
   God has chosen you to travel the
world a far, because as His helper your are a shining star.
   May you always be blest with
everything that makes you happiest.
   I will close this poem but
not my heart, with God by your side from Him
   you will never depart.
        Marilyn J. Stephens

Nature's Tonic

I have a secret spot that's surrounded by trees where I go when I want
to be alone. And I lie in the grass on the breast of the earth among
leaves by the wind tossed and blown. Once more I feel freedom and
that special peace that I seek when I come to this spot. And as I
hear the breeze gently rustle the leaves, I feel contentment I almost forgot.

Then I unload my pockets of life's unfulfilled dreams and
reminiscently toss them aside. But when I look around at the sturdy
old Oaks, I gently reload them with pride. For show me the man; may
he be rich or poor, red, yellow, black or white. That's never known
the pain of one broken dream. Should that take the zeal from my fight?

When I hear the ripple of that tiny stream that so faithfully trickles
along. I again feel the courage to walk life's stony path facing foes
with a will firm and strong. As I bask in the warmth of the sun's
golden glow that has dipped toward the hills in the west. Once more
I'm remade, feeling eager to go and reface life with a new zest.

That's why I will come to this favorite old spot when I begin to feel
life's tedious weight. 'Cause a sip from the breast of this old
Mother Earth is a tonic no man can formulate. After my day with
nature, at night as I gaze at the moon and many stars so small. I
feel grateful giving thanks to the source of that tonic. Yes, God is
the maker of it all.

Louise Kolb

Nurse's Prayer

Dear Lord, I am thankful to be a nurse,
To care for patients and be on first,
I want to grow in knowledge and skills
To fill the needs in my chosen field.

Dear Lord, please give me courage and strength
To deal with issues to the fullest length,
My dream includes the strength of mind
To do my best for human kind.

Dear Lord, I ask that wisdom be
A part of me that patients see,
That I am able to readily perceive
All the things that my patients need.

Dear Lord, please help me gain assurance
As I care for patients with all endurance,
Again, I am thankful to be a nurse,
To do my best and stay on first.

Mary Frances Crown

Legacy

I'll leave a candle in the window,
 to cast the banner of a light;
and hover vigil near this pilgrim,
 that flickers softly in the night.

And if its shadows should grow stronger
 than the brightness that remains,
my hand will hold it steady so the light
 can bear the flame.

Some may pass unseeing, never knowing it was there;
 yet even as the glow is dimmed, its whisper fills the air.

Deep in the quick
 untended sparks give rise to other flames;
so candles spared may pass to those whose lights
 have other names.

Kara Lianne Pierce

"Textures of Interpretation"

The castles of my imagination explode with colors.
To experience the pain and wonderment of it all
treads and imposes itself on me.
A garden of fears, deep-rooted and plentiful.
I am different, special you see.
I am the talented one.
I can swim as far as my imagination takes me.
I cannot represent these people,
fore I am one of a kind.
Sort of like a shadow from a lost unknown time.
I quiver with emotion. I've got enough to go around.
Strange, like a stranger in fact.
Never following close behind but leading the way.
Festive and spirited, my body dances with
feelings that were once dormant and few.

Rebecca Chambliss

Oh How I Wish

Oh how I wish to be a bird
To fly with freedom and soar the skies
Until that day I am shot down.

Oh how I wish to be a tree
To have children climb and build in my branches
Until that day I am chopped down.

Oh how I wish to be a house
To have people live inside and take care of me
Until that day I am torn down.

Oh how I wish to be a swing
To have children play and have fun on me
Until that day I get rusty and abandoned

Oh how I wish to live a life
To have peace and happiness
Until that day I die.

Karen Fritz

A Memory

I stalled as long as I could.
To get there, I wore a coat with a hood.

The trip I knew was rugged and cold.
It took courage, but I had to be bold.

To start down the road,
To a place that was not my abode.

And hope that there were pages, left to be used.
Pages that were not often perused.

The prices were not up to date,
For anything one might want to buy, it was just too late.

Upon arrival I would sit on the seat,
That due to Mother nature had lost all its heat.

When the job to be done was complete.
I headed back up the path in full retreat.

The return trip was long and frigid.
When I returned to the house, I was nearly rigid.

After that I was careful what I consumed,
As I didn't want the trip outback resumed.

Time has changed many things I abhor.
Now, I don't have to make, that trip outback anymore.

Robert H. Ver Steeg Sr.

A Prayer For Meg

Tonight I make a special wish
to God above, "Please grant me this -
There is a girl, like my own child
who's been away for quite a while.
She's with her mom; away from home
with some strange man she's never known.
His name, to her is father, now
the third one that she's had somehow.
Please, oh please, dear God above
in all your mercy and your love
hear my cry, my plea tonight
and please make all these wrong things right
Give us the strength to carry on
and believe that someday she'll not be gone.
Until that day I continue to ask
(I know for you this is not a task)
Please keep her safe and well intact
and make her conscious of this fact:
That we are here, her family
and that someday she too will be." Amen

Laura Lizyness

Time

When time unfolds a hoary web
To grasp, to hold, to keep
When time this web does further thread
Then do mortals weep.

The years role in one by one
Treasured memories there, their ways do wend
For whatever life from womb hath sprung
There its narrowed path doth end.

Morris Mitzner

A Contented Mind

Oh what a great joy it surely must be
To have a contented mind
To know that you've done all you wanted to do
And found all you wanted to find.
You've been to all places you want to go to
And seen everything sometimes twice
So now you are happy to settle back home
And enjoy all the things that are nice.

Ah! Don't let them tell you need to buck up
And start on your travels again
Sure if you are happy to be where you are
Surrounded by family and friends
They probably envy you more than you know
To be free from all modern day trends.

So do as you like and enjoy yourself now
You're doing what you want to do
It took many years to come to this stage
Of sheer contentment and joy
Look after yourself, be happy to find
The wonderful contented mind.

Peggy Jammaer

Untitled

Where we were carefree and young
  we walked in the cornfield in the summer heat
  we walked in the fields with prickly hay stubble and scratchy dry
    wildflowers
  we walked in the dry wagon tracks with green grassy middles and
    pretended a long-ago time
while the grasshoppers jumped a welcome in front of our feet

Oh, those were happy times
  filled with the quiet of summer days in the fields

Ruth J. Waske

Lost Heroes

I have been lucky enough
To have known two men that I call heroes
The first was my husband
He served four years in the Navy
During the Viet Nam War
Living experiences most of us only see in the movies
On June 13 of 1993, exactly one month after turning 43
A few days before Father's Day
He saved our son from drowning
And lost his own life doing so
The second man was a very dear friend
He was a very special man who only wanted to do good
He was a police officer who people looked up to
And everyone who met him liked and respected him
He was just that kind of guy
He was brave and tried keeping his pain to himself
He said why trouble others with something they can't change
He was only 27 when brain cancer took him away
On September 8 of 1995
Yes, they were both heroes to me!

Shirley Bundridge

Parents

Parents were created by God the most high
  to help us little creatures they call kids
They are the greatest people we little
  ones know
They are the ones who nourish our growing
  bodies and cuddle us when we cry
We tell them our problems as they come
  and go
They tell us right from wrong, so we won't
  get hurt away or at home
Sometimes they can get their messages
  across by just singing a gentle love song
Parents teach us how to brush, sit,
  eat properly, to share, and how to
  get the hair looking nice with a comb
We sometimes get the extra change
  that clutters their ever - jangling pockets
Parents were created by God the most
  high to help us little creatures they
  call kids

Phoebe Biggerstaff

Be Cool! Stay In School!

It is important to do your homework.
To learn responsibility for your work.
It is most important to be yourself.
Not to try to be someone else.
Everyone is special in their own way.
You can learn something new every day.
It is always better to talk, than to fight.
You will grow and prosper, and do what's right.
It is important to love and to share.
For the best things in life will always be there.
It is important to do your best.
There will be time for play and rest.
When it comes time for you to graduate.
You know you did it, and you will feel great!
When everything is said and done.
Now you have something special to look back on.
You stayed in school and gave your best.
Now you can accomplish all the rest.
You can help someone else how to be cool.
To show them how to stay in school.

Melodie L. Southard-Resa

My Grandson

He's a handsome young boy of seven;
To me, he's a gift from heaven.

He's lean and strong with dark hair and blue eyes;
He has a heart that is twice his size.
He's warm and friendly, loving and kind.
Which makes him ever present on my mind.
He's a bundle of feelings - happy, sad, sometimes quiet and shy;
His minds always working creative, keen and sly.
He's interesting, curious, fun, and quick;
I hate to tell him goodbye or ever miss a trick.
His laugh is full and loud;
It gives you a lift and puts you on a cloud,
When I say to him, "Richard, I love you!"
And he says, "Grandma, I love you too!"
That changes my whole world to sunny from blue!

Yes, he's a handsome young boy of seven;
To me he's a gift from heaven.

Sandra L. Gookin

Street Waltz

We dance on darkened streets
to music of nature and our own chatter.
Birds wake up to our footsteps
before the stars disappear and dawn breaks open.

I look for your shining light as a welcome beacon.
From opposite sides our feet unite on the dark ribbon
and join to sound out a familiar cadence
while our mouths hum along with their rhythm.

A new day begins to tell our story.
It's the story of a desire to improve...
with vows to move more gracefully
and heartfelt hope to glide through the hard steps.

At times we turn our heads
to look at the miles traveled over the years.
Were our choices always wise?
We ask each other and ourselves... sometimes.

When the dance is finished we often linger
but then we part, and move our separate ways,
living the music composed that morning
and remembering the steps to our street waltz.

P. J. Brix

Constellations

My Grandpa sets me upon his shoulders, as we walk into the night,
To see the moon and stars, which are shining, oh, so bright.
As we walk to the top of the hill, to get as close as we can be,
He turns me around and around, and points them out to me.
There's the Milky Way, as white as snow,
And over there is Orion, putting on his show.
The Big and Little Dippers are shining just for me,
I know, because Grandpa whispered it was so, you see.
The moon is full and shining bright, so very clear to see.
I can see its eyes and nose and mouth, it looks so sad to me.
I say to Grandpa. "The moon is crying, why is he so sad?"
He said, "No he is not crying, in fact he's very glad,
That we are out here watching him and all his friends, the stars".
I look again and see that he is right, the moon is winking
  merrily at Mars.
I wave good-by as we turn to go back down the hill,
"We'll be back again someday, yes, we surely will".

Marie E. Martinez

The Killing Grounds

On the killing grounds is where it all began. We trusted them enough
to show them around our land. From tens to twenties they swept, yet
we did not know that soon they'd set up towns where we have slept.
Taking all of our customs and secret ways of life, they ended so many
with guns and the sharp blade of a knife. The lucky ones have died in
honor while the rest rot in a three inch jail cell, I'd call it hell.
Raping our women, killing the men, we'll never know all of our
children. Split as a strong tribe into three's, pushed off our homes
we cry on our knees.

They say we are savages because how we believe, but we do have a God.
He's always given us water for our thirst, who has put us on this land
not forever but first.

The killing grounds on which we have given our lives. Shaping their
government on what we believe, our hopes and dreams will they ever
succeed. Has all that we've done to preserve this land, be just a
memory or once again shall we go back to the way that it use to be
with us killing with a spear in our hand.

The killing grounds on which it ended. The question still lies;
the white man should we have befriended?

Kasie D. Jones

Lead Me On...

Lead me on from the hilltop
  to the valley below
Lead me on through the dreams
  of whispers from your echo
Lead me on past the heartache
  stings of my eyes, swells of tears
Lead me on away from questions
  of clues to lead for answers
  I beg and ponder for years
Lead me on with the memories
  to rejoice with smiles and laughter
Lead me on to the future
  where someday we'll meet hereafter
Lead me on full of love
  for I'm changed from your midas touch
Lead me on never forgetting
  of how I truly and deeply
  love you so much
I know you'll be there in heart and mind
  to push me on, to lead me on.

Marcelle Franklin

Coupling

Return
To the warmth of my body
The comfort of my soul

Take from me all that you need
My love has few boundaries
It is made rich through what you give to me
Unknowingly

Look into my eyes and see the face of love
It is your own
You don't know

A sweet, distant ache begins to grow and
You ride within the wave of its release
Unaware of body knowing soul

Take from me all that you need
Look into my eyes and see the face of love
It is your own
You don't know

Virginia McCabe

Worry No Longer, My Child

Will my eyes ever close
To the worries of the world?
Will my heart ever beat contentedly?
Will my ears be deaf
To these unwanted words spoken?
Will my hands ever lie still
Besides the few hours I do sleep?
Will my nose never have to smell
The bitter corruption?
Will my soul ever be at ease
Instead of riddled with problems?

But, if my eyes close, I have nightmares,
And when I'm content, I bore easily.
When there is silence, my mind edges on sanity,
And if my hands lie still, I couldn't write.
If I couldn't smell corruption, something would feel wrong,
And when my soul does ease, I will die,
But have life in Heaven, with God, and
I will have to worry no longer
Of any questions, ever again.

Starla Fox

The Reason He Came

The King of Kings came down to earth
To visit lowly man.
He did not come to relieve poverty or want
Nor, to clean up the land.

He came in the form of a little babe
Who in a manger lay.
He made his home with the cattle
And slept on a bed of hay.

He came to us as a Saviour
To each and every man.
He lived and died to save us all
From each and every land.

He lived a perfect life
In his short 33 year life span.
And left a perfect pattern to follow
For every woman, child and man!

He paid the highest price ever paid
For a debt he did not owe.
He gave himself upon the cross
Because he loved us so.

Martha Housewright

Kindred Spirits

In my dreams we rode crystal stallions through an enchanted forest
together to a magical place of gardens and waterfalls, and as we
floated through them, the mysteries of youth everlasting and true
friendship were revealed.
It was a land of intoxication. Like bewildered foals we frolicked
through a fantasia,. though tied to invisible threads of
emotion...for how can we rest until the secret has been dispelled?

Suddenly in the twilight, a bit of sinking sun spread a dusty,
pink-orange across the horizon like an illuminated blanket of hope.
In silence a winged creature formed a mirage in the dusk. With a
sense of urgency we ride like the wind into a sprinkling, beckoning
veil of rose petals that fade across the sky.
But we are like oak trees gaping at our own shadows which we can never
grasp. Then a sudden profound thought sends an earthquake through the
center of our beings, and like a chain reaction, the glowing meadows
crumble into fragments of love...passion...hate...confusion.
A thrashing yet soothing whirlwind of wisdom picks them up scattering
them all around the horizon of our souls. Then finally in the shady,
purple depth of a flower scented aftermath, there emerges an ocean of
memories that shrink from words...and the realization that the real
treasure of life lies in the beauty of a moment. We were there.

Katrina Kirkpatrick

Perseverance

The pinnacled mountain, the sandy salt shells,
Tolls clap in the belfry which everyday tells.

How far have we travelled toward far-reaching goals?
Need we be the chosen for whom the bell tolls?

Setting sight on a meaning, demeaning the truth,
Rewardless, unchallenged, defending uncouth.

Maintaining dream-lofty and screaming decries,
To surrender frustration, like pariah dies.

Response to the challenge pries effortless voice,
Lean ease ward in solace, relinquish the choice.

Herculean our effort if only to fail.
Unmoor begs the harbinger, then to set sail.

The slashing waves torment, life's sinew falls short,
Swirling current abysmal drowns call to abort.

Retreat destination as mocking gulls sweep,
Of hopeless spent reason, while briny tears weep.

Then ferocious storm passes enduring light breeze,
Nobility's future, once more to high seas.

Marshall D. McDorman Jr.

Peace

Peace be with you my friend
Tomorrow I will tell you again
In time, of need, in time of pain
God will not let you go insane.

Deep down He knows just how you feel
Get on your knees and you kneel
For I have been where you are
I've walked a lonely path, without a star.

Peace be with you my friend
Tomorrow I will tell you again
Sometimes the path seems lonely and dry
Look to God, for He can hear you cry.

God will never give up on you
He's a loving God and never cruel
So... whenever you feel down and out
Just know you have a friend with plenty of clout.

God is here for you and for me
Open your eyes... Can't you see?
Peace be with you my friend
Tomorrow I will tell you again.

Karen Birdsong

Women's Rights

Born Isabella Baumfree, a black woman slave
Took the name, Sojourner Truth, preaching the
Truth to all she met
Born thirteen children, most sold for slaves and
Taught to be brave
Crusader against slavery and woman's rights yet to be set
Never been helped into carriages, as of yet
Never been helped over puddles, or given the best place
She plowed and planted in places where she was kept
Gathered in her barns to rest, was not her taste
Sent from heaven for woman's rights was her grace
She preached "Woman are just as capable as men."
This was her argument, even with her race
A man should be a husband and a friend
Ain't I a woman?" Please set me free
I am a woman, give me the right to be ME!

Monica Chase

Cranes

Cranes.
Trumpeting over the bosque flyway,
Their cries catch my heartbeat
And tune it to eons-old rhythms.

Cranes.
They herald the coming of frost,
The hope of safety and food on the resting grounds,
And the promise of future love and mating.

Cranes.
I see you against the Fall sky,
Wingtips feeling the nuances of each breeze.
And I feel dread, knowing the hunter lies in wait.

I want to lose myself in the wild abandon of your dance.
I want to see the valley from your lofty view.
I want to shield your soft downy breast from the murderous pellets.

My heart aches in the azure-skied October sunshine.
I shall have none of my desires.
Only my heartbeat, tuned to yours, and a prayer,
Shall go South with you.

Pam McKenzie

As The Moon Sparks The Snow

Howling at the moon
Tumbling in the snow
Gifts of life brought us here
We bow down to that magic God
Blessing this moment
Grateful that circumstance had been no other way
For if it had been
If we had not grown to be howlers and tumblers
Would we be on our knees, humbled
As the moon sparks the snow.

Vicki M. Moore

Lines

Addressed to the congregation of St. James' Lutheran Church, of Union Bridge, on its proposal to solve its financial problems by dismissing its pastor

When Jonah, call'd to preach at Nineveh,
   Turn'd tail and fled for Tarshish in a ship,
God, to chastise, play'd havoc with the sea
   And toss'd the boat ('twas not a pleasant trip).
The crew (no saints on stormy Galilee),
   'Twixt praying, cursing, retching, and a nip
Of grog (we may suppose), with one accord
Cried out, "Let's throw the preacher overboard."

We at St. James', while bounc'd on seas financial,
   Can understand whose Joppan tars' anxiety,
But since Communion wine is less substantial
   To numb than grog, we act with more sobriety
Than any nigh-to-drowning seagoing man. Shall
   We toss the pastor out? No, let's not try it; he
Would soon be miss'd; moreoever, truth to tell, he
Is much too tall to fit a fish's belly.

Richard Eichman

Angel Songs

Angel songs, they sound so sweet.
Unto the Lord, each mourning they meet.
As they receive there wings, harps play in the sky.
They wore golden Hay-lo's, as they grace the Lords eye.
Each given a mission, by the Lord himself.
Go unto the world, create happiness and health.
As angels descend, to take care of there chore.
Angel songs echo, for the Lord they adore.

Sylvia E. Sproule

Twenty And One

My beautiful child you are
   twenty and one.
I know not your fullest potential.
You were plucked as a rose bud, not yet unfolded.
The bud of your being is the beauty I know.
That beauty dwells within me nourishing and sustaining,
Each petal fragile and fulfilling.
Your struggle to reach the fullness of bloom
Binds me forever to the reverence of life.
I weep now that you are twenty and one.
Not for the shortness of your stay,
But for the longing of the shortness again.
And a longing for the bud to unfold bringing forth the fullness
   of life and the
Beauty of your Being at
   Twenty and One.

Phyllis Rollins

Sonnet #1

To be apart from thee, my sweetest king
'Twill grieve my soul and pierce my wounded heart
No more with love a chastened soul to sing
A poisoned arrow rents my self apart.
No more to taste the passion of your kiss
Or hear the sweetness of your tender sigh
Or see your face and share your loving bliss
But left adrift to ponder love gone by.
Another maid your wand'ring eye has turned
With burning glance, a pledge of heated flesh
So cheaply spent to buy a soul that burned
Ensnared and cursed because the two did mesh.
Grief filled, my soul knows darkness and sorrow
Eternal rest bring peace upon morrow.

Laura A. Rager

Ancestral Soul

Deep within his eyes they lie,
Twinkling lights that see
from hundreds and thousands of years ago,
Watching, unnerving me.

He wasn't disturbed by their presence,
But allowed them to see about,
While sharing a common awareness,
Impressions of the world without.

Shadows of those of long ago
Alive within his soul
Peering upon the modern world,
An audience, at a show.

And when those eyes turned to me,
I wondered if they saw
In the light of their reflection,
Recognition, filled with awe.

Lucy Walters

Love Is ......

Love is when you're away
Wanting you back every day.

Love is the tears that swell in my eyes
Whenever we have to say goodbye.

Love is knowing when I'm out of sight
You will think of me both day and night.

Love is when everything is said and done
Knowing that you're the only one!

My love is all these things and more
Because I never meant "I love You" like this before!

Victoria Duncan

65

Wings Of A Magic Carpet

Aloft in the heavens is a magic carpet, bright, faithfully ascends
two kids-at-heart in flight, to embrace glee of soaring height
and frolic its reveling waves of light.
Enchanting journeys on mystic craft, as a seabreeze-cradled raft!

"World of Garp!" Kinfolks cried. "Senseless reason," pity sighed!
Dimensional realm, wonders of two, zealous dreams known by few.
Love abounds jubilant rapture, kids-at-heart share and capture.
Old sonnets, nary an end, as youth discovers MEANING OF FRIEND!
Thoughts differed, oft altered, soulmate bonds ne'er faltered.

Yet, TRESPASSING FEARS, as time traveled fast, brought shadows
and tears when yesterdays passed. Through shatter of Earth's twisting
rain, the magic carpet began to wane! With woeful regress,
did it realize, "When trusting hearts of kids grow wise
to a wailful world of bold, tender hearts-of-kids grow old?"

Enveloping wings, halo surround, can vessel, sound, not be found?
Where's that twinkle of light, majestic form, sailing on rainbows
after the storm, and sprinkling golddust along the way,
sheerly to celebrate the "birth of a day?"

Beyond the blue horizon, a band of angels wait.
Look! The magic carpet...servant of The Gate!
    R. Sarah Farrar

Gilded Cage

Two little birdies sitting in a cage
unbeknownst to them, Daddy's in a rage.
The cage door opened, coaxing them to come out
luring them to the doorway, where they could fly away without a doubt.
Daddy fixed Mom this time for sure
Getting rid of her pets should be easy to endure.
He says she spends more time with the birds, or anything other than with him,
it's a wonder he doesn't just relax or go for a swim.
And leave her alone to enjoy life at its best
and chat with her little friends, or entertain a guest.
But we know this would never happen in our happy little home
because friends are not welcome, it's best to be alone
Alone with the family and his sometimes twisted ways
of which I have seen many, which have lasted for days.
Nothing goes right and it's usually someone else's fault
Someone should just tell him to go pound salt!
    M. A. Koman

Spirit

With the stealth of a panther, a stranger slipped into my soul,
Uncovering treasure, abandoned long ago.
A gift
Wrapped in reality, trimmed with truth,
Surrendered to the passing of my youth.
Nestled beneath roses, amidst thick of thorn,
Once exposed, a spark is reborn.
Soaring skyward in a flash
A sight to astound
void of sound
Whirling 'round....To face me,
then plummeting down
Towards the ground
My fear surrounds..To embrace me.
As I watch this spirit se free, I become ever bolder,
Granting a kiss, she grazes my cheek and rests upon my shoulder.
I've not again met this stranger to whom
I pledge eternal grace.
If paths should happen to cross once more
My kiss will caress his face.
    Linda Ramsden

The Questioning Of My Sanity

From the cloak of darkness,
under the warmth of linen and flannel,
the space between actuality and imagination,
I came, because you called to me.

I roamed through the desolation, pale subways of cement;
unaccustomed to the stalking of buildings,
endless dead ends and vacant cars...
I caught your shadow flung against the wall —
pressed forward, hungry palm of my hand extended,
the whisper of a name not far behind...
You dissolved into blackness,
merging into one as the street lamps burned dim.

Round and round, I turned in endless circles,
threatened by the blank stares of homeless men,
keeping warm with yesterday's news,
the faces of gypsies who have lost their carnivals.
I become lost among the labyrinth,
Your voice tormenting me, mocking me
questioning my sanity.

I imagined you called.
    N. Tace

You

When I look into your eyes, I see a very sad song,
Unlike the person I've known for so long,
Those beautiful eyes, with a distant gleam,
Screaming to cry out-so it seems.
A man of little words, but much to be said,
A strong mind to win whatever is in his head,
The mind is a powerful thing, but the heart is more so,
I hope someday true peace and love you may know.
I never meant to be a threat,
I just wanted to know what your soul beget,
You see I'm a firm believer in the saying:
"Seek and ye shall find."
And when I sought you I found me.
The story hasn't ended and it may never,
Because the love I have for you can not be severed.
I know our time together was not that long,
But you became a part of me that holds a very special song.
    Krissi Collins

Birth Of An Angel

Nothing special this child seemed to be
Until the day she came to me
Her parents aren't extraordinary
But then again they're not ordinary
For this child was conceived
Out of love that they believed
Would fill their void, would cease their yearning
To share with another a life worth learning
Learning of love, not of malice
Learning to be kind, not to be callous
But instead she's the teacher
Though such a small and innocent creature
For she has taught them life is treasured
Given them knowledge that can't be measured
Who is this Angel that has touched me so
She is my unborn child I have yet to know.
    Ross Taylor

"Only You"

When I was young I used to dream of how love could be
Until this time I used to think it was out of reach
But then I met you and I knew with out a doubt you were the only one for me
For the smiles you give and the love you share shows me how much you
    really care
And when I look into your eyes and see the beauty that lies deep
    inside of you
Oh, how my heart sighs to feel your warm, smooth skin next to mine
    for a love so true
If you could know just how I feel, you would know how much I truly
    love you
For never has there been another to truly earn my heart
I have loved you with all my heart since the very beginning
I know you always ask why, because you wonder what you have
That makes a man like me want to spend the rest of my life with you
And for as long as I've known you... you've never given me any reason
    to want any other thing
Your honesty fills my heart and when you say "I love you" my heart aches
For no matter where I am or what I am doing, I just want to be with you
No one could ever change the way I feel about you
I think of you each and every day
I never want to lose you for my love for you is anchored deep
Let me be the one to care for you, to stand by you, to love you
Promise me you'll give me a chance... to prove to you where I stand
That the love I thought I'd never know...I've found in you
                    I LOVE YOU!

Kevin J. Toczko

I Was A Carpenter

Expert builder - running from hurt.
Up went walls -
A maze - a shell -
No hope of ever getting well.
Depressed alone in a dark hole,
Then — a friend, Healer of my soul!
He held me, loved me, called me by name,
Said "Precious lamb, life won't be the same."
He taught me forgiveness, to let go of the past'
sins forgiven - free at last.
Now when I'm hurt I don't keep it inside,
I take it to Jesus - in him abide.
He listens and tucks me under his wing
Now - rejoicing - a new song to sing.
Down tumbled walls - a new foundation
Jesus! Lord!
My God!
Salvation!

Mardee Haase

The Lone Rider

He rides on a dark steed throughout the world.
Upon the fastest wind he travels,
This lone rider who can never smile.

His job is not like the hunters.
No trap does he set no gun does he carry.
All he has is his bag for collecting.
This lone rider who is ever condemned.

He hates his job for all fear his coming,
Some fear the pain, some fear the unknown.
Most fear the judgment of their deeds.
This lone rider doesn't bring this,
He only takes.

This work he does you might have guessed.
He collects the souls who must take the quest of death.
This lone rider is condemned forever to be the reaper.
He only committed one crime.
He was the first suicide.

Robin Nine

Drugs

Stay away from drugs wherever you go,
Use your brains and just say no,
Keep your bodies clean and strong,
When you do this, you won't go wrong.
You don't need drugs to make you high,
Your natural forces will tell you why,
Drugs will never set you free,
You are sentenced for all eternity.
Do you think it's smart and macho
to make yourself a fool
While "Wise Guys pushers" take your assets
and you become their tool.
Drugs are dope, which make you high and low,
you get so inexplicably involved,
You don't know where to go,
To hospital, to bed, to street or shed,
Sometimes you'll wish you were dead.
So listen to safe advice wherever you go
Just be ready to deliver the
The little word NO

Gavalas

Untitled

From down across the river bright
Very close to the king of light
And from deep inside the deepest woods
Listen He the King of good
He listens for vows being made
And promises of love which will never fade
He looks deep inside to see if hearts are right
For nothing can be hidden from the good King sight
And if He is pleased with all He sees
He'll seal that love which should forever be
And then indeed the two are one
And so they shall forever be joined, in the name
Of God's glorious Son.

Randy Furco

"Early Sweetness"

I lie awake in the stillness of the Dawn,
Waiting for the sound of the alarm,
As the blanket of night fades
Into light shades of the morning haze
Before the world is fully awake
To break into its hurried quake
I hear the sounds of Gods happy Creatures
Going to and fro in their own way
Chattering to each other, as if to say
"Come on," "Get up", it's another beautiful day.

Martha E. Dean

Neatness Counts Only Some Of The Time

A pile of dirty dishes in the sink,
Waiting to be washed and put away.
A pop spill on the kitchen floor un-noticed,
'Til your sock sticks as you walk by.
The laundry hanging over the side of the basket,
Unfolded and in total disarray.
Lint on the carpet crying out,
To be sucked up into the vacuum cleaner.
The throw rugs lying in a heap,
Just waiting to be shook.
Toys scattered all over the living room.
AND WHERE IS MOM?
Sitting on the floor, with her child.
Looking around the room she utters,
"My work will still be here tomorrow...
But what of my child."

Marlene "Molly" Fink

67

Lost Innocence

Innocence lost
waking from the myth of forever young
The price is a high cost
for believing in heroes unsung

Endless cries for rejuvenation
yields unanswerable sighs from a disgruntled few
Reminiscing about that newfound sensation
which now only has space for a breath or two

Enlightening new path to follow
to the other side of the hill
Welcome to the other side of tomorrow
where your parents' shoes are no longer hard to fill.

Maria Yvette Carter

That Gloomy Night

On that gloomy night I went
walking through the cemetery.
The fog enveloped me as IT came into my sight.
Its radiance and beauty
as sculpted as a statue, turned cold.
Its focus turned to peer at me,
right through my soul. I knew, it knew — me.
As quickly as I saw it, it rushed upon me.
I felt it take my life as it gave it back
mixed with its immortality.
I know I will live forever
with that gift it so freely gave,
as long as I hide by day from the burning sun
once my friend, now my enemy.
Now I will live to serve it, hunting life as it does,
for that precious life blood — of humans and the like.
The beauty I saw in it
is now ten times as strong,
as I glance at it through my new eyes.
On that gloomy night I chanced to walk...

Michael Caldwell

Friends

Friendship is like a breath of air, sometimes
    warm and sometimes cold.
A soft breeze blowing here and there, we were
    young and then we suddenly are old.

We search for meaning to our existence in many
    different ways.
Sometimes we are productive and then again we
    waste our days.

Each soul has beauty if we look deep within,
    all reaching for approval, if we but comprehend.

Our hearts are drawn to those we love, whether
    they are good or bad.
We treasure each moment, even when it's sad.

But life, like a breath of air, lasts just a
    little while.
So live, just for the moment, and share a
    loving smile.

Like a precious jewel, cherish your friends!
    Because they can be gone in a twinkle
    like a leaf on the wind.

C. Higginbotham

Restless Goodbye

The autumn sun was bright and strong
Warm breeze blew with fury
Trees and winds rustled sounding like a chant
Tears fall to the ground
Collectively creating the pond of life
Neatly tailored finery in place and still
Displaying a dark yet saddened exterior
Inside the soul screams
Heart aches
The surreal picture of life play its part
Eye to eye, looks don't lie
All the chapters have the same ending
Memories become the last drop of water
Letting go is hard to do
Saying goodbye is harder
Slowly the scene fades

J. R. Blum

Autumn

Ah! Autumn, the season of change and color
    Warm breezes mixing with blustery winds everywhere.
Fading of the flora and fauna
    Mother nature stripping bare.
A season for planting anew
    While biding farewell to summer.
Shorter days and longer nights,
    ...Ever changing weather.
A season for many school activities,
    Pumpkins, gourds, and mums abundant
Football, soccer...the end of baseball.
    Growing piles of firewood neatly stacked.
Crisp air greeting you each morn,
    As autumn does year after year,
A time to reflect and prepare...
    The coming of winter's rapture.

Wanda Gentilini

Our Mother

Merry Christmas, Mother dear
Was a wondrous God that sent you here,
Just like Christ a gift on earth,
But only we acclaim your birth.

Mother, you're bright and ever so jolly,
The house all draped with wreaths of holly,
The Christmas tree so pretty with lights,
Oh Mother, you make home so bright.

We love you Mother, all your seven,
And you're a blessing, straight from Heaven,
For Mother, home, skies and sod,
And even more, we thank thee God.

Opal M. Hellin

The Indian Spirit

This land was once theirs,
we took it away,
and stuck them some place out of the way.

The Indians tell their story
how the soldiers ran them off,
and told them to stay, to stay away.

They smoked their pipes,
made arrows and bows.
This land was theirs for hundreds of years.

This land was theirs,
we ran them off
there eyes full of tears.

Matt Robinson

A Patriot's Prayer

Who am I? A child of a war, a Vietnam hero, or an American whore?
Was I a foolish, suckered soul, or an American patriot, proud and bold
What makes me different from you, or you? Am I not like you, of you,
you? Sure I killed for a cause I thought was just. But Victor or
victim, all turn to dust. Who died by my hand? NVA, Vietcong, all
hard core. But no innocence beings, and no spoils of war. Remember
the blast, the artillery roar? Grenades, and rifles, and those
deadly claymores? Remember the children born unto war? Once their
innocence lost, just trophies of war. Oft' baptized in gore, when
madness reigned, still we cried for more, while bearing the pain.
They pinned some medals on our chests, with a careless nod, no more,
no less. Alone we stood, apart from the rest, were we the worst,
or were the best? Wait! Still hear the jungle, the rockets, the
rain, remember deaths evil mask, etched with pain? Speak to me
softly, and do not stare, and save your judgement, your pity, your
prayer. For every time man tries to rise, above evil's strong and
binding ties another patriot will go, and lead the fight, to spread
the holy glow, of freedoms light. He'll send freedoms eagle, soaring
high, 'cross the hallowed breadth, of heaven's skies. And here at
home, we'll sit and wait, as American patriots meet their fate.
Some will live, and some will die, as freedom's eagle, mourns and
cries. But those who shed their blood and tears, have earned their
place on heaven's tiers. From oppression's cries, these men won't
hide, but face each challenge, filled with pride. Who are these
patriots? Their names I mean. The eagle's guardians, are called
"Marines".

Ray R. Fairman

Childhood Games

in those long-ago days, that long-ago time that is only a memory,
was it the games we played and the friends we made, that fashioned
   lives so happy and free?

Jump Double Dutch or single rope, 'twas only an old clothes line, but
on nimble feet, we kept the beat, miss your turn and it will be mine.

A ten cent ball for throwing jacks, pick them up carefully one by one.
Then it's Twoesy, Threesy can you get them all, before your turn is done?

It's one, two, three O'Leary, your leg must go over the ball,
And then we can play Leany Clappy against the garden wall.

Make the Hopscotch squares so even and straight, and polish a stone to
throw, don't touch the line or you give up your turn, and don't step
in my square as you go.

Mounted on stilts that my Dad made, we felt that we could touch the
sky, clip clop down the street, if they wobble, you must jump down
from on high.

At the end of the day, by the old lamp post, choose up sides for Run
Sheep Run, while folks on the porch for the evening cool, watch over
our childhood fun.

Red rover Red Rover let Mary come over, Oh please just call my name!
How the hours flew by in those long-ago days, and to-morrow will be a
new game.

Could I once again skip to Double Dutch or jump into the Hopscotch
square, would my heart feel the joy of long - ago days, and my life be
without a care?

Children, play the games of my long - ago and may your hearts be light
and free, I'll just sit by my window and watch you and drift back in
my memory.

Mary Elizabeth Williams

The Desert

The desert is a hot place
Where the sun boils the earth's face,
Where flowers bloom in crayon colors,
Where a coyote's voice hollers,
Where rocks stand as statues unconscious,
And where mountains background us.

Mary Anne Simon

The Last Thing I Remember

The last thing I remember that rainy eve
Was the sound of a wreck too close to believe
As I ran to the porch someone shouted to me
That the boy in the street was my son Jeromie

I ran around the corner, it didn't take long
And I prayed to God that my fears were wrong
When I reached the scene my blood ran cold
There he lay unconscious only eighteen years old

I felt I was living a horrible dream
The driver who hit him left the scene
Minutes seemed like hours before help arrived
Desperately I prayed God would keep him alive

I remember how active my son used to be
Now he's locked in a coma fighting desperately
If he could only wake up and return back home
I would grieve no more nor feel so alone

My son has a strong will and courage to survive
It soothes my heart and helps my soul to thrive
I pray he'll be home for the 25th of December
I drift off to sleep, it's the last thing I remember

Marilyn Sue Shane

Emptiness

We looked like sisters,
   we acted like sisters
But we were best friends
Until one day
Another girl comes along
Funnier, smarter, prettier
Her new best friend
But what about me?
My feelings torn,
   I'm left to suffer
In the middle of a road
   that takes me to a sad world
I hope she understands what she put me through
A place in my heart
   will always be empty.

Lynn Wozniak

"Collective Seclusion"

Sometimes it feels as if
We are standing alone together.
Perhaps covered;
Protected within a shaded, reclusive setting.
Boundaries exist; a canopy of tree tops
Prevent sunshine; massive trunks prevent passage.
Yet, the air is free-flowing, open and honest.
Together we stand
Yet distance separates.
I can hear your breath,
Sense your presence
But I am unable to pinpoint
Your exact location.
I know that you are there
I thought I could find you;
Had hoped we could connect...
But I can only hear the crunch
Of breaking twigs
As you turn to walk
Away.

Regina Sawicki

69

Dreams Of Past And Present

Dreams are part of, what life is made of
We began as children, as dreams of love

We learned our own dreams as we grew
Striving each day to make them come true

Dreams made me wonder, "Who am I?"
Never ever ceasing, to wonder why

Dreams let me know what I wanted to be
Knowing something better was inside of me

Dreams for my own life have come true
Making each day so special and new

Now the dreams of others I want to share
With deep understanding, because I really care

Dreams of the present to you now turn
Wondering about you and what I will learn

I dream of the softness of your voice when we talk
And being beside you when we go for a walk

My dreams are now of peace and tranquility
To share them with you and you with me.

Steven Reiser

What I Would Say To Clifford If I Could

Your death was so sudden
   We didn't have a chance to say goodbye
   Or tell you how much you meant to us.
Why did it have to happen?
   We rage against the cruelty
   And indifference of fate.
Why did it have to be you?
   You were so young, so happy,
   So full of promise.
You missed so many of the good things
   That we were sure were in your future.
You left a large hole in our lives
   Which will never be filled.
You left a hole in my heart
   Which still bleeds.
The tears keep falling
   For my pretty baby, my sweet boy,
   And for my capable, loving adult son.
I miss you terribly and always will.
   Clifford, my son, my sun.

Olive Lehman

A Friend Of Mine

I just saw a friend of mine I haven't seen in years.
We met by chance on the street, and both of us saw tears.
As I walked I saw her face, and recognized her smile.
She saw me as I saw her, so we just walked a while.

As we walked I felt her arm as it held to mine.
As she spoke I felt content seeing her this time.
Even though those times were old we talked of them awhile.
And deep inside of her, I could see a smile.

In and out of life they come, the friends that we all love.
Once their here and then their gone and hardly spoken of.
Then by chance we pass them by and say hello once more.
Hello friend, old friend of mine, friend that I adore.

Then came the time we had to part, and go our separate ways.
The ties were made again we said, but knew they wouldn't stay.
And though I'll think of her awhile since we met that day.
It's plain to see she'll only be a friend that came my way.

Mark A. Moore

Our World

Although yesterday is gone forever,
We must continue to endeavor,
To strive for a better world each day,
As we go along life's arduous way.
We must live in harmony with our neighbors,
To find true happiness from our labors.
We have computers, fast travel and internet,
And many other achievements so don't forget,
It takes only a genuine ambition,
To change the world to a better condition.
Allow each culture to live lives apart,
From coercion and dictation of any sort.
Take pride in yourself and your homeland,
And every country can ultimately be grand.
Hold your head high and live for tomorrow,
In a world without turmoil and sorrow.
Let us strive together to that end,
And you will find contentment my friend.
Yes, yesterday is gone forever,
But look forward and never say never.

Virginia H. Ligon

Don't Be Blinded To The Beauty

With trees standing proud in stately array,
We saw a doe on the hillside today.
She stood in grace, looking around,
While eating foliage from the ground.
She showed no fear as cars passed by,
She just stood there with head held high.

We watched a hawk, glide on the breeze,
Circling higher, up over the trees.
It's hard for man to so conceive,
But the hawk has beauty, I believe.
We can not glide so free as he,
It was a scene that all should see.

In valleys and hills and in all of God's creatures,
There's marvels in everything on Earth that He features.
Traveling cross country, the sights we saw;
Such reverent beauty, to hold in awe.
Don't be blinded to the beauty God gave,
Tour our great land of the free and the brave.

Marlene Campbell

Mother

Sweet are the moments,
   we spent together.
When all of these,
   will remain forever.
Memories in the past,
   should have to linger.
Without someone to love, cherish and care.

Those embraces you gave me, Mother
In your warm tender breast,
   I felt them.
Around my neck
   your soft arm slips.
To reach those eyes,
   all I see is love.

Sweet are the moments
   we spent together my mother.
When all of these will remain forever.
Memories in the past,
   should have to linger.
Without a mother love, cherish and care.

Priscila P. Reginaldo

Ave Christi

In darkness, despair and lonely hours
We think not of angels above
And He reaches down with graceful power
To hold us with his love.
When tears would course down wasted cheeks
And life on Earth would cease,
Our unhappy thoughts are wiped away
When we feel the touch of Heaven's peace.
Ave, Christi, in His we lay faith
To guide us throughout our lives
And when He calls us to come to him
We freely sigh our last sighs.
As frightening dreams may rock our souls,
We wake with minds full of alarm;
But reach out to His Heavenly Presence,
And fall back to sleep in angels' arms.
Ave, Christi, our loving Maker
Who watches us from day to day-
Give us the strength to mirror ourselves
To thine own Heavenly Way.

Katherine Elaine Green

Jigsaw Puzzle

Like the pieces we try to fit,
We turn right and left.
No matter which way,
The picture remains incomplete.

We clear away those old pieces,
Yet their outlines stay,
Frustrating and haunting.
If only we'd turned them upside down.

Like worn toys, the pieces are put away.
We're too fixed for changing shapes,
Too formed to fit another's mold.
Puzzles are for children, anyway.

We then begin pulling ourselves together.
Yet, one piece is missing.
When it appears, there's no turning.
For this eternal child, the puzzle is complete.

Susan D. Kerley

What We Were Then

We were kings and queens and pirates, indestructible and immortal
We were children, but couldn't wait not to be
When the age of ten was considered old, and nothing could hurt us
We would pick up anything and rocks were treasures
There wasn't a tree we couldn't climb and pennies made us rich
We were fearless except for maybe the dark
When monsters were real and we thought we could fly
Band-aids were signs of bravery and we were the most courageous we'd
ever be, when life was forever and adulthood would never come,
But then it did come.
No one knew the hour or day, but suddenly trees weren't so fascinating
Parents didn't seem so tall
We found ourselves eating vegetables, when we'd vowed never to let
them pass our lips
Baths weren't dreaded and our clothes started to match
We stopped swimming when the weather was cold, and naps became
desirable
Catching frogs was replaced by worrying, and playing seemed like
too much work
We lost our courage and everything had germs, and we always washed our
hands and didn't need band-aids as much, and ice cream became less
exciting. But the biggest thing of all was that being an adult didn't
seem as great or as far away, and our biggest dream wasn't to fly, but
instead to be again what we were then.

Leslie L. Donaldson

A Love Of Life...A Life Of Love

Life.. what a wonderful commodity.
We who live it to the fullest are sometimes considered an oddity.
Life is a gift given to be enjoyed!
To turn away from it or fight against its every obstacle is frivolous at best.
The hand you're dealt is the hand you'll play, sometimes more,
sometimes less.
There are cards that can be changed; others cannot.
Life is a whirlpool—moving slowly at first, then moving fast, all the
while drawing you inward.
At best—we live, we love, we share, we surrender.
Live and experience the good and bad, the ups and downs, the big and small.
How are they all?
Who questions the reason why—not I!
Nay, we will not question, we will not ponder; we will bask in His
Sunshine-of-Life.
Lest we dwell on this power of no control—we shan't.
Life leaves in its wake a Cleansing Beauty.
This beauty is shared from generation-to-generation.
A Love of Life... A life of love, such a physical and mental energy!

Marie "Rie" Andrews

These Twelve Hands

Morning till night, no light left insight,
    we worked God's land,
    all of us...twelve hands.

The fence needs mendin', the crops need pickin',
    work for us all twelve hands.
The laundry needs soakin', the supper needs fixin',
    work for us all twelve hands.

Ma did the washin', the cookin' of chicken dumplings,
    the girls scrubbin' dishes, the sewin' of Pa's britches.

Pa tending to the land, the cattle, the barnyard nags,
    the boys did the pickin', the diggin' of the seven-mile strand.

We shared many things, all twelve hands,
    through the bad times we weathered,
    through the good times we shedded.

The work was hard, the days were long,
    nights in bed, seemed more like seconds in our heads....
But every supper we came and joined hands together...
    'round the table we built from the ol'shed,
    we prayed to the Lord for all that we had, but most of all....
    we prayed for these twelve hands.

Wendy Walker

'Love Unspoken'

I was thinking back on times of fondness, of how I felt when you
were near. Perhaps just a girlish infatuation, then again maybe more.
I still get weak when you look at me that way, this memory I reply
in my mind. my childish fantasy recalled, my first kiss
accompanied by a giggle. And how I blushed when you kissed me again.
That memory I still kept in my heart along with your every embrace.
I love how you always seem to take care of everything.
I'd sit back and watch in amazement of how in love we were.
I feel so safe, so protected in your arms.

The most you've ever said to me is when you said nothing at all.
As you moved closer to seal the moment with a kiss,
but you waited till you'd explored every inch of my face.
As if a game I chased your eyes.
And at last you leaned and whispered "I love you" in my ear.
So delicately I could only touch your face and wander about your lips
with my fingers. As you put your hands around my waist and gently
lie me down, you begin to stroke my hair and there I fell asleep,
with that love song you were singing to me still in my head and when
I awoke I found not you, but a rose. Knowing that I could relive the
moment when you return to me, and knowing you'd be mine forever.
Mellowed in my emotions, I recall your 'love unspoken.'

Leah D. Comer

To My Husband, On Our Wedding Day

Since the day our two paths crossed
We've shared many hopes and dreams in life,
And I consider it an honor
You've asked me to be your wife.

The highlight of my every day
Is sharing it with you.
A lifetime doesn't seem long enough
To show the love I feel for you.

To me, you are my life's greatest gift
Sent straight from heaven above.
I couldn't hope for a better man
To share my life and my love.

When I look up at the stars at night
It's very clear to me
That we were meant to be together.
You'll always be a part of me.

So on this day as we say our vows
And our two paths join into one,
May you know how very much I love you, today,
And all the days yet to come.

Tecia R. Bobay

County Fair

People, music, everywhere.
What a treat to go to the County Fair.
Such sounds, such smells, such sheer delight;
All promise pleasure for us tonight.

In the ferris wheel seat I swing 'neath the stars,
My hands firmly grip the iron side bars.
Over the top to dizzying heights,
Below me a sea of shimmering lights.

Out on the midway, more to explore,
Galloping steeds circle their floor.
Wild painted eyes, nostrils aflare,
Rising and falling, shackled in air.

For fifty cents my image changes.
Height and width rearranges.
Face contorts, teeth of brass
All is changed in the house of glass.

Souvenirs in hand, approach the gates,
Just beyond your tram awaits.
Take one look back, a sight so rare,
Glistening, gleaming, glitter of the county fair.

Viola A. Knauf-Kotas

What One Seeks

What one seeks, is it not the warmth of the sun?
What one seeks, is it not the waves of an ocean?
What one seeks, is it not the smell of a flower?
What one seeks, is it not the sound of laughter?
What one seeks, is truly not temporary but eternal,
For the sun darkens, the ocean dries up, the flower
Withers, and the laughter dies.
The sun nor cascades off marble and stone.
The wave still flows but cannot be seen.
The flowers surround me, but I can no longer smell them.
The sound of laughter is gone, instead the air is filled with sorrow.
But they who surround me should be filled with joy...
For nothing escapes me no more.
For all of the beauty that was compares not to
The immense wondrous paradise which is before me forever.
Truly, what one seeks one finds, but it wasn't I who sought,
But I indeed was sought and for
That I am forever grateful.

Kevin Mark Szczepaniak

To The Bridge Over The River Cam

Old bridge that spawned fair city's name,
What ghosts upon thy arch have trod?
Centurions bold, and learned dons,
And dedicated men of God?

Perhaps Augustus passed this way,
Or Byron by this rail has stood.
Did Grey here wax poetically,
Or Erasmus contemplate the rood?

Who raised thee first o'er this calm stream?
Some Celts or Picts or Saxon Lords?
To bear the load of man and steed
Off to meet the warring hordes.

Could be thy birth was humbler though.
Might be 'twas peaceful from the start.
A bridge for travelers passing by,
For farmers, tradesmen, ox and cart.

It matters not, you're here and now,
Above the Cam for all to see.
Alas! I soon bid sad farewell,
And leave behind a part of me.

William M. Champion

A Dream Deferred

(Funeral)
  What is a dream deferred?

Does it fall down from a tree like a leaf
in the depressed season of fall?
Or go up in burning flames as you cry
for 'help' and no one hears your
fatal call?

Does it throw itself at you like someone
poisoned by feelings of love?
Or does it scorn for its life like an
aborted child headed for heaven's
steps above?

Maybe it just separates like a married
nightmare on the verge of divorce.
Or maybe it just fades without pain.

Keri Mixon

"Which Direction"

Gazing out a window, watching tree leaves sway
What is there to tell us, winds true way
Looking at a river, at a height in perspective
Sights of a being, and the mind thus is collective
In which direction does it go, may be what is concealed
Only with a closer look, may a deception be revealed

Look at a picture, what do we surmise
Is it a sunset, or is it of a sunrise
A reflection, a truth, is what we receive
But it may be an opposite, and so thus deceive
Knowledge and curiosity, is what holds the key
As realities illusions, may be what we see

Ronald R. Meseck

Fights '1995'

  A friendship supposed to last forever,
when is it supposed to end? Not never.
  We get into fights every once in a while
but you have a certain something that makes
me smile.
  I hope we never go our separate ways
I wanna be friends till the end of our days.
  But if we should ever be torn apart,
you'll always be deep down in my heart.

Tiffani Good

Satisfaction

It doesn't really matter
what other people think.
Because to me only you matter
and you will week after week.
We have something me, and you,
and I know that when I'm blue,
I'll turn to you, and you'll always be true.
You keep your hopes up high about me,
and you'll see, you'll be happy with me.
Even though sometimes you make me sad.
I just think about all the times
that you didn't make me sad, but glad.

Karen Lee Jimenez

A Child's Eyes

We can hear ourselves talk and believe
   What we say.
Do as you want... it's only today.
Tomorrow brings change... it's gonna
   get better.
Kid ourselves as adults; to a child never.

The truth can be known without
   any words.
You can try to disguise it; they still
   see the hurt.
They don't understand, they just
   wonder why;
Blaming themselves as the days go by.
They hurt worse than you, with all
   they can see;
"What did I do, I'm only three".
Their hurt, their pain is very real.
Worst of all they don't know how
   to deal.
Speak the truth and never lie;
it will come back... in a child's eyes.

Teri L. Gladd

"With Your Eyes"

Can you tell me how you feel,
What you think and see...
-With your eyes?
Can you feel what I feel
And tell me what I think and see
-with your eyes?
Tell me....What's going on in my head?
In my heart?
Will you run away when you know?
Will you hate me when you find out?
Feelings like a waterfall, crashing in my heart.
Scared of what's to come—
I'm holding back- not telling, not saying
In fear of what you might say, might think...might feel...
Will you be scared too?
Do you feel the same?
Can you tell me what I'm feeling—
What I want to tell you?...
Can you see all these things...
-With your eyes?

MonChere Dickson

Life's A Rose

Amid the fragrant petal grows, stalks of green and thorns in rows.
Yet every petal, every leaf, with dew is dipped and sunlight kissed.
But all's important to existence lest it be spoiled, wither, and fade.
So, we too, need roses and thorns, sunshine, rain and storm.
To help us live and give, as a fragrant blooming, rose.

Katherine J. Ison

"Time" In Retirement

A clock for your gift?
Whatever for you ask.
It's regulated you daily
For every appointment and task.

But wait! Take a second look!
There's no alarm or numbers to tell time.
Surely this IS the best gift
To go with this rhyme.

Arise and go when and where you wish.
Now doesn't that seem fair?
No need in retirement to watch the clock
'Cause — WHO CARES?

Sharon Markee

A Fight Against The Bug (Prepare!!!)

Hey, there my friend!
What's wrong with you?
You look so limp, worse than old, wrinkled up blimp.

You can't chew? Whooooo! Well, you never could,
So, that's nothing new.
Ha! Ha! Ha! Ha!

Your throat is sore?
You don't need anymore!
Your bones are aching? Chills? Fever, too? Mercy!!

My friend, please tell me what is wrong with you!
Why so many questions?
I caught the wrong bug, can't you see?

But, but, but, please..... don't come near me!
Please don't tell that bug about my family.
I think you caught the Beijing Bee.
Hee! Hee! Hee! Hee!

Next time, don't look for a bug.
Be slow and avoid that kind of buggy luv.
Look for someone who will give you a healthy hug.
All right!!! Achoooooooo!!

A. V. Little

Wary

Smell the smoke
   When
All books become paperback.

Heed the heat
   When
The last Hero dies.

Feel the Flames
   When
The Music of the Lute becomes synthesized.

Inevitably, the Inferno
   When
The Voice of the Poet is silenced

Ronnie Pearce

Remember Me

Together, my love, we'll sail through the sunset
   with millions of stars ready to guide our way
Flowing down to the mist of our future
   we'll let all of the emptiness go astray

To see us walk down to our life together
   makes my twinkling eyes get misty
If ever the fruit of our love grows sour
   I pray, my love, — Remember me

Mylene T. Abing

"Mom's Gone"

How do you do what you're supposed to do
　　When all you do is cry?

How do you live like you used to live
　　When your mom, your friend, just died?

How do you go from high to low
　　without it affecting you?

How do you live without your mom
　　when you're not used too?

How do you get through the nights and days?
　　When all you do is cry?

How do the tears keep coming out
　　when you know your eyes are dry?

When will it stop, the hurt, the pain.
　　When will it stop, the shame, the blame?

Does it stop or can it stop?
　　What do you do to help?
　　　　Rose McCurdy

For What Reason

So when did love really matter?
When did the one I cared for...care for me?
When was my life anymore than mindless chatter
And chasing childhood dreams
Tell me, when ever did love matter?
And what rhythm drives this soul so incomplete
To a destiny so distant and obscure
Where the mannequins and mirages all compete
For what reason am I living, I'm not sure

I push my feet through crowded streets with names unknown
And the shackles of strange fortunes greet me there
Halting indecision chills me to the bone
But tell me, if you can, does love care?

Anxiety streams down frames of frosted windows
While cluttered gutters tide with graven fears
Pleasure hints like blinking eyes in distant innuendos
Has love yet cared? Will love care in million years?
Will love exact a worthy measure, should I live a million years?
　　　D. Sank Smith

Here's How

How do you wear a friendly smile
When everything goes so wrong?
You keep your chin up
Through the last mile;
And say to yourself,
Life's a song.
You say a kind word
To a stranger you meet.
Go out of your way to be nice.
All though the day
Those things you repeat.
Don't do them just once or twice.
Soon others greet you in a similar way.
They smile when they greet a friend too
And your heart will dance and skip and sway
For you've made things worthwhile being you.
　　　Virginia Null Miles

Remember Me

Do not grieve for me
When I have gone away,
I will be with you day by day,
When the dew is on the grass
You'll think of me in days that are past
When we shared the first meal of the day
You will remember, I haven't gone away.
You are the child in the corner of the yard
You are digging oh so very hard
Looking for the future in bulb and weed
The things that grow and replenish life in need
Life in need of love
Life in need of care
You are looking for the mother
You no longer think is there
Truly I did not leave you, I am every where
In the tulip garden, in the air
I am always with you
Every where.
　　　Margaret Fox Bawer

The Cycle Of Life

When I was born, I entered the world crying
When I shall leave this world, the tears will come again in dying.

When I was born, I had but one strand of hair
Now in my old age, my hair is no longer there.

As I entered this world, my teeth were not there
As I age, there are less and less to spare.

When I was born, my eyes could barely see and I could hardly hear
Now I am the same, in my golden years.

As I came into this world, I could not speak
As the years pass, my words became less and meek.

When I was born, I was unable to eat, unless I was fed
Now my arms are too weak, so please feed me again.

As I entered this world, my body was weak and I could not talk
Now my child, I need your help to walk.

So listen all my children, as we took care of you
Now we are your children, now that our days are almost through.

So birth and old age are one in the same
We need to help one another, that's the name of life's game.

Life is a Cycle from birth to old age
It is the same as we entered and same as we became.
　　　Kathleen Goga

"Life - Complex/Simplicity"

How can a person have no soul
When the fire within humans so cold
To lose one's mind is a common thing
If you lose your heart it often stings
Yet what does it take to loose your soul
How many have one when they get old
Do we die inside with our bodies to follow
While living in a world that's often too shallow
When in love life is grand and always fun
Is that all that matters once life's said and done
Without love life really never seems to matter
To be alone is to watch all your dreams shatter
I guess to make it simple I'll end with this
There's nothing better in life than having someone to kiss
　　　Miguel Andres del Amo

By The Stream

The fall moon was full as she walked by the stream,
When out of the night came a screech, then a scream.

The water gushed red.
Someone was - dead?

She continued to walk, though shaking with fear,
till a rustling of leaves crackled in her ear.

Someone was there. Her mind raced, "Oh God, where?"
As she approached the still body, she was shown the cruel facts,
On the bank of the stream lay a rusty old axe.

In the distance she saw him. He stared straight at her.
She raced down the path where the sycamores were.

She cried out in desperation, but no one could hear,
And all she could see was the man coming near.

Her heart pounded fast. She fell to the ground.
Her legs wouldn't move. She knew she was bound.

The sullen-faced stranger found out where she lay,
picked up the axe and started her way.

Her eyes become blurry and all she could see,
was the rusty old axe that he used viciously.

Vivian O. Heard

The Black And White Of Years To Come

I long for the feeling down deep in my heart
When races come together, instead of being apart
People talk out of their mouths, not always hearing what they say.
How they'll feel, when faced, may not be the same way.
Being brought up in the deep south, where races didn't mix.
My own attitude and inner soul searched, my thinking I had to fix.

I remember my God said He created and loved all men
None was better, whatever the color, we all would sin.
But he'd still love us all, whether we were black or white.
He's deeply saddened when we turn on each other and fight.
He and I agree we need to find a common ground
Where every race may find compassion so love can bound.

My prayer for the future, a world of peace and harmony.
May each person say "Let it start within me."
To forgive one another, understand and love each race.
May my compassion for others, come smiling on my face.
And the future be filled with bright colors. Alright!
Not the harshness of white nor darkness of night.

Linda Gibson

Life And Love In All Seasons

The snows are soon forgot of winters past
When spring brings warmth and floral blooms to light,
And love begins to urge the heart beat fast—
Its passion surges forth both day and night.
Then follows summer with its longer days:
It's time to enjoy the greenness of the trees,
The mellowness of love in tender ways,
The scent of flowers on a gentle breeze.
Soon autumn starts to lessen daylight hours,
But compensates with brightly-colored leaves,
Then they turn brown, come down in showers,
As if to show that nature also grieves.
Now winter's back-so cold! What will it bring?
Love shivers, waiting for another spring.

William F. Band

What Will You Dare?

Will you dare to go bare
When the fox and the hare
Play tag-a-long out on the moors?
Will you paint yourself blue
Like the Picts used to do
And send Romans off running for swords?
Will you dance 'round the fire
When the flames shoot up higher
Than even the stars and the moon?
Will you hold your girl tight
On a Saturday night?
Will you kiss her and cause her to swoon?
Will you live your life free
As whom you wish to be
And not at another's command?
Will you plant your two feet
In the middle of the street
And against the cruel world make your stand?

Richard L. Parker

Last Goodbye

You said before you left
When the sun comes up each day
    it will be me, smiling at you
You will miss me but please don't cry.
When the moon comes up I'll be
    saying good night my darling.
God is taking me first but don't be sad
'Cause every cloud that drifts by
    I'll be saying hello
And when the wind blows, and the
    Thunder rolls, the lightening flashes,
It will be me saying how much
    I love you.
'Til then, sweetheart, I'll wait for you,
    just beyond the moon.

Ruth Wagner

In Flight

In flight we were
When the sun slid down the day,
Like a funnel,   pulling its orange veil of lit cinders.

In flight, the wild geese shooting north from the barrel of a gun.
Land rolls out like the tide.
A wake of warm dust curls behind us.
And you with your head in the wind, take my life between your fingers.
Your agile wrists twist the road before it's ridden.

And suddenly night —
My body,   body of stars,
Constellation of moths below a garden lamp.
The bumps of my skin assault you, small army of lust.
The universe hangs low tonight — clouds move fast,
Pelting night at my sides —
My bare belly like nuts.

You speak in a voice
Below the rumble of the engine, between the wind in each ear.
The back of your head does not compare
To the wireless bulbs flashing.
In the trees,   flash, flashing like a coal mine hot with diamonds.

L. Lee Abelard

Trees

A seed starts so small,
yet grows so tall.
It will provide shade for the kids to rest,
and also a place for a bird to make a nest.
It is a great home for many,
although it started out as small as a penny.

Mickey Schutzenhofer

The Little Bush Lady

There is a little bush lady that lives under the tree,
When the wind blows she waves at me.
The little bush lady under the tree.
Her dress is green, she a sight to be seen.
The little bush lady under the tree.
When the cold wind begin to blow her dress
   of green turns to gold.
The little bush lady under the tree.
When the cold snow begins to fly she can kiss
   her gold dress goodbye.
The little bush lady under the tree.
She stands there cold and bare not even a
   nest of robins in her hair.
The little bush lady under the tree
Then the warm winds begins to blow.
Her dress of green begins to grow.
The little bush lady under the tree.
And when the warm winds blow she waves at me
The little bush lady under the tree

   Rosalie Taylor

Why!

It seems that every thing comes to why?
When things start going right you ask why?
When something jumps in your path to mess things up... you ask why?
Or when you finally get on the
   right path and life is starting to
   go the way you want it... here it comes again.... WHY!
The why can't be answered, because
   it's the test given to you so
   that your faith will be strengthened
   and also to let you know that
   you only have to answer the door...
For answering the door the lesson
   that is there will answer the why?
So let everything come to why
   then open your heart and listen.....

   Nancy K. Ahrens

Dear Little Brother....

Dear Little Brother,,
   When we were small, we'd yell and fight
but we'd forget why, so it became alright

   If I needed a playmate, he'd always be there,
we'd definitely fight, but we would also share back then.

   If someone else would pick a fight with him,
I'd be the one to stick up for him.

   If I needed a friend, I'd just go up stairs
and he'd be there.

He may not say he does, but I know he cares

When he was hurt I felt so bad,
   when he was alright,
      I was glad.

We've caused each other a lot of tears
   throughout the years.
I hope someday the Lord Jesus will turn it all, around.
There can never be another,
then a big sisters love for a little brother.

   Sharon Appell

Reaching The Goal

When your brain is on break, and you make a mistake.
When your pride has taken all it can take.
When you feel down, and it's taking a toll,
Just concentrate on reaching the goal.

If you try your best, but it's just not enough.
If your school work seems to be getting too tough,
Yet you know you can do it deep down in your soul,
Then you've almost succeeded in reaching the goal.

Then, when in yourself you believe,
All that you've worked for, you'll finally retrieve,
Because you start to improve, and you're on a roll,
It will sure feel good to have reached the goal.

After your goal has been reached, life goes on.
We very seldom think about that which is gone,
Until down memory lane, we take a lengthy stroll,
And then, just all of a sudden, remember
Reaching the goal.

   Robin L. Stombaugh

A Soldier's Face

No one would ever know how close you get with God
When you're a soldier.
His face reflects it all with moments of happiness and sadness.
Thus he is like this;
He cries with sorrow but smiles with tomorrow;
The grimace of pain with sometimes nothing to gain;
The love they have for each other,
So much closer than that for a brother;
No one will ever know, or go where they go.
Today is like every other day, they belong in harm's way.
He shows some wear and tear, the burden for others not to bear.
For there is no other place like that of a soldier's face.

   Velda E. Max Welch

Comfort's Embrace

As moonlight spills onto the heart of an angry city
Where bullets lace the streets, where sirens go unnoticed
And screams of anguish go unheard
Two lovers lay entwined in a safe haven all their own
Where the only sound is the beating of hearts - as two bodies become one
Where screams turn into sighs of pleasure
As love's sweet breath mingles in the air
And in a world filled with millions - tonight there's only them
No prying eyes can breach their glorious Heaven's gate
No rules of polite society can deny them what they seek
There's only a gentle communication where no words are ever spoken
Two hearts that understand a passion where no explanation is ever needed
The only need they share is one of consolation
Their long limbs wrapped around each other in a comforting embrace
For the sun will surely rise too soon and the spell will have been broken
A new day will have begun where reality will seep in
So the two lovers make the most of the hours they have left together
To reach the sky and touch the stars, holding moonbeams in their hands
For tonight there is no tomorrow and yesterday has never been
There is only right here, this moment, to taste the fruit of Paradise

   Regina Auger

Broken Spirit

You broke my body, so how do I mend
You bent my mind, will I ever be right again,
You ran my life as if it was yours
Opening and closing all of my emotional doors,
I'm ok now, I want you too know
It took the step of leaving you and
Someone else's love to show
that I'm not as bad as you made me to be
thank you again for setting me free.

   Sharon Snyder Gambler

Beauty To Behold

I walked today in a forest covered with snow
Where no man had walked before me for there were no
human tracks to show

Just the bear the turkey and wild deer
And I'm sure there were many others, although I could not
See them I could feel their presence there near.

The forest was ghostly quiet except for an occasional sound
Of a branch breaking from the weight of the snow and falling to the ground

The snow sparkled like diamonds glittering and twinkling in the sun
And it caused me to stop and stand in awe and feel the omnipotent
Power of a much greater and higher one.

God made our world so beautiful yet we seldom take the time
To really see and enjoy the simple snowflake as it glistens
And brightly shines

I hope that I can always take the time to listen and slow down
And see all the beauty around me and hear all the wonderful sounds

If we would all find time from our hurried life to listen and behold
We would find the earth is full of beauty and wonders yet untold.

Virginia F. Hansford

Empty Winter

Standing in a dark, lifeless place at dusk,
where only silhouetted trees are seen,
looking as if they are overused brooms standing on end.
One gigantic tree standing above many tiny ones,
looking as if it is a giant towering over smaller village people.
The trees oddly shaped, from being without leaves for so long;
the ground covered in snow, rough from animal tracks.
There is hardly any movement but a slow breeze,
barely ruffling the bare branches,
like a small child trying to move an adult.
This is a gloomy place, where I wish not to return.

Lindsey K. Benton

The Holy Shore

We stand here at the shore
Where the land and sea meet
And the seagulls soar
So close to our feet.

What is it that we seek?
Why is our understanding so poor?
To God everything is so neat
And perfect within its form.

We question, what is it all for?
But God said that life's tribulations will keep.
Then God gave us a door,
And said all we have to do is open and seek.

God has an answer for the troubles we meet.
Like the shells on the shore
Beneath our feet,
They are there before us within our reach.

So open your eyes and seek.
Stretch your hand out to that holy shore.
Take that faithful leap.
And you will see what it is all for.

Stephen McEndree

Generic Girl

Nylons strut their stuff down runways
where the legs used to wear silk.
Baby blue eyes stare out of formerly pretty brown ones.
Is the plastic chorus you rap on flat surfaces
any better than that produced by the girl whose
Keratine didn't come form Sally's Beauty Supply?
Sometimes the new Sunlit Bronze Number
Thirty-two doesn't match your naturally caramel skin.
Or is ultraviolet tan from Ban de soleil the
"tone of the month"?
Who says that Hedi's brilliant rouge locks swing
higher than your technicolor tropical punch weave?
Were your bouncing new silicone t*ts worth
going under the knife?
You tend to pop E-Z Sleep instead of Nytol while
Daddy complains about the wrinkle-free cottons
you sport over your padded behind.
"Why don't they just leave things alone?" Daddy says.
Daddy knows that attempts just shouldn't be made
to make cotton nor humans perfect.

Taryn Stewart

My Galleries

There is a road sign on the way to my makeshift gallery
Where the midnight holds the moonlight like white fire in the sky.
Where whirlwinds in a summer breeze come out and you can plainly see
A falling cloud above my head and my past swelling in my eyes.

There is a smile on the way to a faithfulness I know.
And when I run to take it my thoughts slip fast away
To a place I will not hear them — to a place I may not go
Till I find her smile upon my lips and ask her what to say.

But, my God, way back in my makeshift gallery
Where my room is dark and the moon is dark and flowers and the sun
Where you're used to things and you forget to see too easily
And the clouds just go too slow (to-fro) to jump the gun and run.

Like children, we held hands and ran away from what was real.
And sometimes kids like dancing when they know they've won their game.
I don't want to be grown up if it ain't being what you feel.
I'd just grow old right here and say it's all the same.
(And road signs dancing in my head and spelling out your name.)

Travis L. Seay

God Promised Us

God promised us a life filled with peace, joy and love
where the saints in heaven would surround us from above
He said the road we must travel will be long and hard
but he promised never to leave us, never to be apart.

God promised me a man that would love me always
He said you'd comfort and protect me at night as well as days
He did not say you'd be a knight on a big shining horse
but a meek and humble man, serving God of course

God promised us a family and a small potter home
God said he'd never leave us, God said we're not alone
So I waited for you and waited until one day you came
God made me a promise and his words we're just that plain.

Lynn Lillard

Holidays

Out on the beach
where the seagulls cry
their squawk-squawk claims as the girls walk by
in the rapidly taming sun
in the bloody caravan of souls
in the torrential sands they run.

I wandered alone
where the fruitful ones lie
in their latter days waiting to die
on the filthy tidal dunes they won
in the splendid picnic-parade of noon
in the teeming surf-bubble's fun

And the seagulls sigh
while the old men gawk
at what is the matter and the teenagers' talk
in the strangled skylight's early haze
in a game of volleyball endlessly played
on the indentured people's holidays.

Mark Hamilton

Imagine

Imagine being in a log cabin in a very quiet place,
Where there is no one around for miles, not even a trace.

Imagine lying near a fireplace on a bear skin rug,
Wrapped in each other's arms, that give a great big hug.

Sipping on some wine, and looking into each other's eyes,
Enjoying each other's body warmth where you lie.

Kissing so very gently from your head down to your toes,
Where this feeling will end, nobody knows.

Listening to some soft music and the crackling of the fire,
With all of this around you, makes your passion grow even higher.

With all the gentle touches and soft whispers in your ear,
You feel so content and loved holding each other so near.

Making love to each other, you feel so complete,
You love that person so very much, no one could compete.

Imagine how heavenly peaceful and thrilled you feel inside,
Your feeling will show in your eyes that you couldn't hide.

Savor the moments you have, just like you plan,
Tell each other how much you love them while you still can.

Mary E. Tackett

A Child's Life

They run like fragile colts,
Where us older fear to tread.
Head first and with eyes open, with no malice, fear, or dead.
They can see an open bottle,
and wonder how far is far.
Their worlds of boundless magic, that can't be reached by car.
They fill our lives with laughter,
with smile, tears, hugs and noise.
They make us ever thankful for all our happiness and joys.
We fix their broken toys,
and kiss away their tears.
We listen to their dreams, and chase away their fears.
And when we watch them sleeping,
so innocent and young,
they make us see through them
all life's battles can be won.
We teach them to be honest.
And keep them free from strife.
Try to show them what they'll need to know,
to be the best they can at life.

Kelly Valle

Still Water

Still water is calm as the deep blue sea...
Where you can watch from far under that great big palm tree.
The ocean waves roar in a dramatic sound
as the tides slowly move in touching ground.
The seagulls fly in the neutral blue sky,
in such a silence it makes you wonder why...
Everything around me suddenly becomes still
the breeze from the ocean gives me such a soft chill,
Sitting in the sand watching the sun go down...
has me wondering why I'm sitting with such a frown.
Could it be that still water has my thoughts
in such a freeze...
So deep that I'm crying on bended knees
All around me everything looks so bold...
I reach out with tears and find there is nobody there to hold.
As the night slowly comes to an end...
I walk the sandy trails with my imaginary friend.

Stacy Kimbel

We Must Go On

We have no right to question the hand which we were dealt,
Whether it be for happiness or the pain that we have felt.
The life that we are given, is from the Chosen One,
And the challenges that we face will not always be much fun.

There has to be a purpose for the life that we are given,
To try to find that answer we have to go on livin'.
We live everyday dealing with our highs and our lows,
Believing that someday, God will surely let us know.

We should take life everyday and try to do our best,
To conquer all our needs and to fulfill our requests.
We shall cherish our days for they are precious and few,
Knowing it is only a matter of time, before it can be taken from you.

It makes no difference being young or old, or black or white,
We can all look to Heaven and see His stars shining bright.
For us to keep complaining, is truly not our right,
For the world God has given us is really a beautiful site.

We must never underestimate the power of His hand,
Only keeping in mind, it is by our side that He will stand.
We should always take the time, and not be afraid to pray,
To thank the Lord above, for giving us each day.

Karen Kyer

Reflections

In distant lands there stands a door,
Which holds the key to time.
Windswept with pleas to release its memories,
But not revealing its find.
Remembrance took my hand one day,
And asked me for a dance.
And leapt away in frosted bounds;
Giving only one chance.

To blink an eye was all the time
That door needed to show,
Why my chance could come but once
To look upon then go.
More than that would wrench my soul
From my body's hold.
And steal my mind away from me,
Giving it to all who showed
That hate has teeth, and sorrow claws,
But truth has the worst bite of all.

K. Hoffmann

The Mirror Of Truth

Today is a mirror
which reflects the past
a love-wrought legacy
of memories that last

Take me where thy dreams are twined
thy sleeps abode in a corner of the night
where seraphs laugh with delight
their golden eyes shining bright

Your hand, wandering across time
will find me in need
the path which you lead
can end in paradise

The flame shudders under darkness
a candle dances, alive
I watch and fantasize
this light and never dies is like my love for you

There above me, singing in the garden
dulcet like a grace
she fashions hearts
into shapes she desires

Wayne Bielaga

Quiet Desperation

A calm, quiet breeze shadowed by desperate winds
Which torment the valley of forgotten sins

That which was faltered and left far behind
Is brought to the forefront of a life lived divine

The treasures of the past hold their curses below
When all's been erased, the slate always shall know

The past holds on tight though you try to let go
Because that which you've done is your greatest foe

And though you're forgiven and God shall forget
Your heart beats so surely with thoughts of regret

Now that you have been tested but failed to prepare
The retake is waiting just as long as you care

Tears flow through the valley of mortal temptation
Shedding the past in quiet desperation

William J. Salyers Jr.

A Poet's Song

I've written many pieces
While chewin' ma bacca an' that
Drinking beer, eating chips
Smokin' cigs and getting fat.

I sent some poems to publishers
(I was hoping for an honest trade)
They give me money, I get more brew...
Oh I was hopin' to have it made.

But nothing came of it
My submissions received the same
Disinterest. Discarded leaves that held my thoughts
And carried my worthless name.

I wonder what is it that I'm missing
In my repertoire
I plead my cases, share my causes,
Debate, allude, and spar.

Well, finally I wrote a poem
I thought was a sure bet
It fell through (whoop-dee-do)
So, I ain't been published yet.

Velma S. Pack

Deep In An Ending

I lie alone, next to him
while past love greets new suffering.
There is no peace that comes with sleep,
The heart will choose what it believes.

My nights, they echo emptiness
not one of my invited guests...
It stays too long; sleeps in my bed
taking all of me that's left.

Once again, I face the price
I will pay to feel this life.
With all its pain and joy disguised;
at times the price is not so high...

But then some night creeps slow to dawn
colored with the lost and gone.
Pictures framed but never done...
Some art requires meaning.

I watch him and he watches me.
Neither is the first to leave.
We both make time the enemy...
but it's love, not time now ending.

Sheila Stone

Old Romance

The lights are turned off
Who flipped the switch?
Who stole the wood to the fire?
Only dark is clear
Only ash remains.

The lights are turned off
And black has no feeling
Black has no soul, black has nothing to give
Nothing to live
But black don't burn like red-yellow fire
And black don't make your eyes dance
Black don't lie
'Cause there is nothing to see.

Who burned the wood?
Let it smelter to ash
Nothing left to feel
Nothing left to smell
There's no fire to light the black
And no desire to look back
The lights are turned off.

Neina Chambers

The Little Girl Within

There's a little girl inside of me
Whose life is one of pain
She never feels the sunshine
She only feels the rain
When people try to love her
She runs away to hide
She's built a wall around her
She lets no one come inside
She grew up in a house without any hugs
Without hearing the words I love you so
She grew up in a house that was bitter
She wasn't allowed to grow
Now she lives in a woman's body
And only she can tell them apart
Although there really isn't much difference
Because we share the same aching heart

Kim Zaker

On Loneliness

When feeling alone, like no one cares, I try to remember those
Who have come with me. All those within-if I can remember them,
And what they've done. I know they'll help me now, when the road
Ahead is hard to see, blinded by the hoarded tears, cried now.

Blurred images I find, coming at me, no realities-my mind filled with
Confusion. Thoughts and scenes so changed from how it was! And I
Search, failing to see anything familiar looking to me. Oh, now I
See! I'm looking at one of their histories! Their life! But it's me!
We are one!

Sometimes that remembering can bring the comfort I need, sometimes
It only accents the losses I've had along the way-loved ones, family,
Fantasies, hopes, dreams, plans. And memories that should be mine!
Only now, slowly, being returning to me, as my parts within share.

Sometimes, the injustice of all of this-those mistakes, hurts, scars-
From years ago, hurt deeply. How I paid then, paid since, and am
Still paying! In trying to reclaim my inner selves for myself, and
Recover my life, I still pay! For their abuse of me-that first tore
My mind asunder!

Sometimes nothing changes my feelings, my outlook, or helps me to get
Through the hours, except that there is always tomorrow. And with it,
The chance that some longed for peace of mind be found, and that the
Day might spark the tiniest ray of hope, in the dying embers of my Soul.

Kathleen C. Rinker

Winter

Winter is a stingy, graying old man
who rains down his horrid poison endlessly
and will not relent,
spoiling everyone's fun
who has bushy, snowy eyebrows
and blizzards for eyes
who has wrinkly mahogany flesh
like a hoary, drooping elephant.
Winter is an old man
who spitefully paints dark, ashen clouds
and an angry sky
who throws hailstones from that angry sky
who enters our world so swiftly and suddenly,
unwelcome,
refusing to leave till spring.

Melissa Parrish

Reminiscences '45

Here's to the Dad I happened to get
Who worked in the cold damp mines
To feed and clothe and shelter me
And pretend they were happy times.

He built a house with his own two hands
My mother was there by his side
He fell from a bucket in the open pit
He mended and took another ride.

He walked five miles in the blinding snow
To buy me a pretty red dress
So that I could look good when I sang
My solo at my very best.

He wrote a poem in my autograph book
In his 4th grade simplicity
There was more love in the simple rhyme
Than a dad with a PH.D.

The demons got him away from me
After his work was done
Feeding, clothing and loving me
I love him still. Now he's gone

M. Julia Duval

Thoughts Of A Mother

What do you do with a child, independent,
  who's always done her own thing?

What do you do with a child, so naive,
  except keep her under your wing?

What do you do when that child is a woman,
  so lovely, so trusting, so shy?

You must let her go and pray for the best,
  but whenever she's hurt, you cry.

You pray the day never comes she won't need you
  to be there, to comfort, to love.

You see, being a mother is special; forever;
  a lifetime; a gift from above.

Shirley A. Benson

Lady Magenta

This is a ballad to my confidant, Lady Magenta
whose gentle voice and bold words sing
a mystical lullaby in my heart.
Bright and sensitive eyes cradle me in a tight embrace;
nurturing with the nectar of pure love,
comforting with the warmth of a mother's breasts.
I am deeply touched by the intimacy in our encounter,
because when I need to be heard
Lady Magenta opens her heart
enveloping me in the couch of her inner being.
My heart has given birth to a tender love
conceived by the caress of her words
resonating inside me.
Why protect feelings aroused by our exchange?
We all need to be told that we are held in deep regard,
especially when tending to another's heart.
So I write this for life, for love, for you
My gentle confidant, Lady Magenta.

Karen Gutheit

All I Ever Wanted

All I ever wanted was one man to love. And to love me.
Whose words of endearment were ones of comfort and truth.
Whose thoughts of me would be etched, down to the smallest detail,
in his mind and bring a smile to his face as it warmed his heart.
A man whose joy meant surprising me in the middle of the day with
something silly or loving or something as simple as a call, just because...
A man whose attention to my words would give him new insight to a part
of me he hadn't known or when he closed his eyes he could still see my smile.
I don't need much nor do I ask for much.
Maybe a hand to hold or two arms to enfold me, a kiss or two and,
perhaps, a shoulder to lean on; and every so often a look that would
say "You're mine and I'm glad I found you."
So many years have past.
Many tears have fallen. Many lonely nights, birthdays, and holidays
have come and gone.
False hopes and false words I've had many. I've dreamt the dreams of
fools always hoping and waiting. Each time losing more of my soul.
My heart is no longer whole. I've given away too many pieces.
Is this my destiny to suffer the pains of a broken heart or the
loneliness of a leper, when all I ever wanted was one man to love.

Sandra L. Thomas

The Test

I set my goals to be a champion.
  Why did I fail my quest?

I reached for the stars and didn't make it
  Did I do my best?

I practiced hard and I practiced long
  Why was I weak
when I should have been strong?

I lay here, head in hands, befallen, conquered
  The champion standing over me
declaring his victory.

I had the potential, the tools, the heart of a lion,
  Why is my heart broken?
Losing's worse than dying.

They said "Good Job", "Get 'em next time!"
  "You did your best."
But as I lay here with tears in my eyes;
  I'm no champion,
  I failed the test
            Shawn Walters

Despite The Answer In My Hand

But why,
Why I often ask myself.

Things appear cloudy on a clear day.
Clouds, derived from my own perspiration at the time unknown,
are raining on my private parade.
Did not mean to create them, just did.
Had to get where I wanted to go, and to see what I wanted to see.

Yet now, I am here, and I fear that when I chose my road I knew
that it was inevitable to mislead myself, for I am not seeing what I
wanted to see, and no longer remember what it was.

As light, time passes irreversibly through a window and burns the
skin of the one who does not move, but kills the same the one whom
spends theirs in total darkness.
Yet, part of me lies here burned and the other blackened, despite
knowledge of my cure.

But why, why I often ask myself.
            Trevor W. Voeltz

Then A Hand

Silent tears brim with questions.
"Why me Lord?
'Tis too much to bear."
Yet, his grace cradles my soul
As my God whispers,
"Trust me and know that I care."

Then, a hand penetrates my grief.
Then, a hand reaches through my isolation.
Then, a hand extends kindness, compassion.
A gentle touch soothes my aching heart
As my God whispers,
"Trust me and know that I care."

The "whys" dissolve in understanding
The moment I risk to share my burden;
Hoping one day I too will become a hand
Reaching out to another
Whose "Whys" are too much to bear
As our God whispers,
"Trust me and know that I care."
            Maggie Josiah

Love And Hate

Why must we have hate, when we can love
Why must we look down, when there's someone above
Why do we fight to get what we want
Why do we always have to be number one
Do we have to judge other people and make them feel weak
Isn't there peace in the world that we must all seek
Do we have to be one color to have to belong
Can we be different, can we all be strong
Can we like one another and accept each other
Why don't we give it a chance just to be together
We can all be friends, if we only try
We don't have to see tears, no one has to die
Just be your own self, but believe in others too
They need to be accepted like they need to accept you
Don't be a stranger to those that you need
We were born just the same, we were like a seed
That grew up to learn and to hope and to dream
We are part of this world, we can work as a team
Just look in the mirror and give it a start
You'll see a special person right in your heart.
            Marjorie Albano

"Life's Dream"

Come upon the midnight morn to never be the same, our life before
will never be as tomorrows' finally came.
To be the same would be for naught as the past can never be,
our judgements may be different but together we may see.
By knowing who and why we are there seems to come the day, when
all our thoughts and queries may somehow show the way.
As all shall come to pass and memories do recall, the good and
bad of life and relationships most of all.
Shall we become the players or witnesses from afar, no matter
which you play remember who you are.
The toll of time is plenty and results will vary too, just keep
an intrinsic heart and rewards will come to you.
As all will stand as shadows on judgement day to come, there
is that special place reserved for only some.
Then all will come to light and there is where we'll be, I hope
your path is straight and someday I may see.
A hand outstretched to guide me from here to him above, a hand
to which I promise my everlasting love.
Then all shall come to pass and my dreams will all come true,
I'll be in heavenly bliss spending eternity with you.
            Sandra Roskoski

Fresh Tears

These fresh tears that fill my eyes
will soon fall to the earth,

Sent forth from where emotions lie
installed in me at birth.

Another friend has passed, I question why
and ponder life's true worth.

My tears are for these friends I've known
and also for you and me,

For in this life the seeds we've sown
don't always come to be.
            Stephen Yoham

Winter Lullaby

Hush child, and go to sleep, 'tis only whirling winds you hear.
Winter is upon us, and the northern winds must blow.
Hush child, and go to sleep, 'tis only angel's wings you hear.
Look! Softly, silently, floating gently down.
Falling secretly upon a hushed and sleeping world,
Is a white winter robe to blanket sleeping gardens,
And cover barren trees.
Hush child, and go to sleep, 'tis only stardust that you see.
It's gentle as a tiny kitten, and playful as a wooly lamb.
Soft as velvet, fine as silk, is the magic mist of moon beams.
Hush child, and go to sleep, 'tis only God's own snow you see.
It's cold out there with the white mist a'falling
and the warmth of the fire has now lost its glow.
So snuggle in bed and close your bright eyes,
Sleep sweetly my child, sleep sweet.
Tomorrow my child, you'll wake to see,
A frosty white world of fantasy!

Mary Margaret Bown

Braces

Braces, braces! What a pest.
Wires, bands, and all the rest!

Metal jammed into my head.
I wish my dentist soon was dead!

He caused all this. It's plain to see.
How dreadful could these train tracks be?

A tighten here. Adjustments there.
This irritates beyond compare!

I'm trapped inside this stupid place
with toothpaste fusing to my face.

And all you do is look and grin
and wipe the water from my chin.

You think it's funny? I know you do
since it's me here instead of you.

Sitting here is such a bore.
I think my face is getting sore.

Take this bloody gauze away!
Can't we do this some other day?

Look at me! My mouth's a mess!
Braces, braces! What a pest!

Stacey Elza

One More Day In Life

Dawn has come,
With pinks and blues,
The world is cast over with soft grey hues;

Morning has come,
The sky is clear,
The birds are singing with unusual cheer;

Noon has come,
The day is fair,
The sun is shining like long golden hair;

Dusk has come,
The world is fading,
Time stops as if it were waiting;

Night has come,
Not a sound to be heard,
Except the good-night call of a far away bird.

Margot Laporte

Life's Fulfillment

You've made it through these twelve school years,
With a lot of hard work, laughter and tears;

We've watched you grow from a toddler to a young man,
Now it's up to you to make your stand,
The road to success is in your hands;

It's a tough world out there...
There's heartache and laughter, there's work and there's fun,
But, your goal you can achieve if you walk and don't run;

Whatever it be, hold your head high,
With determination and faith, the limit's the sky;

Greet each new day with a prayer and a smile,
Keep a positive attitude, you'll find it worthwhile;

Often times your put to the test,
All that is asked is that you give it your best;

Patience, persistence, and endurance is the key,
Never give up, someday you'll see;

Success is not measured by worldly things gained,
But rather by knowledge and wisdom obtained;

Remember, you have one life to live,
Trust in God, and the answers He'll give.

Sharon L. Coleman

The Virgin And The Unicorn

There was a magic land somewhere, in the far forgotten past,
With animals that are no more nor spells that they could cast.
But at night in the dark when Noah's ark, slipped off into the mist,
The unicorn held the virgin and, oh, so gently kissed.

To our remorse, that horn-ed horse missed out on the animal boat.
And now the unicorn is gone, lives not in that land remote.
But the horn-end horse still lives, of course, beneath the Arctic sea.
The narwhal plays in its watery ways, swims there in the islands lee.

When virgins play on a sunny day, or a brand new summer morn,
Under stars so bright on a moonless night, you'll know your soul's reborn.
In the pale twilight, when you've said, "Good night." Remember the
    one honored beast.
And wonder now that the horse is gone, just where do the virgins feast?

Richard A. Hein

Morning

Day unfurls like a rug
with banners of dew everywhere
The sun follows on a path of glory
lighting up the world
Birds serenade God with songs of praise
The morning star goes back into its place
And the moon hangs in another sky
continuing its eternal journey
Leaving us the morning like the awake of a ship
Night creatures return to their lairs and dens
bands of light beam through velvet skies
Darkness turns to glorious light
All the dewdrops of the earth
Become prisms shimmering in brilliance
Into all this magnificence, mankind steps forth
hopefully into the morning
Another new day adding to the ancient pages of time.

Mitty Helene Burchick

A Bright Day

It was a bright fall day
With brown and gold leaves falling to the ground
They made a lovely sound
When they crushed under my feet as I walked to town.

I passed fields of golden corn
And vine covered land with dots of orange
I saw a scarecrow dressed in colors bright
With a crow on his arm looking left and right.

The streets were bright with shop windows dressed in a festive air
And laughing children running everywhere
Dressed in bright costumes with bags in hand
Yelling "trick or treat" to all the land.

And as I walked home at a happy pace
With memories of a child's smiling face
And brown and gold leaves crushing under my feet
I thought "this bright fall day has been a real treat!"

Pat Palm

Unknown Freedom

As it flies it seems so free
With color oh so bright
Flying high among the trees
Bringing the dull day to light

I wonder do it realize the freedom it has
In this world full of crime
Freedom of the past
Instead now a world against time

Fly, fly, high in the sky
Never touch down
Or then you too may cry
When you see our town

Oh how I wish your wings were heavier
Or that I was lighter
So you may carry me to heaven
Or just a little bit higher

I long to be like you
Flying wild morning, noon, and evening
And to have your beauty too
But most of all your freedom

Willene Spice Washington

Among The Autumn's Glowing

I glance out my frosty window,
With its intricate designs;
Fancy prisms of crystal white show,
With various etchings from Jack Frosts' fines.

Rushing out my misty doorway,
I enter not into a world of gloom;
But instead a wonderful palace of finest pleasures,
'Tis an artist's gallery room.

Crispy northern breezes are now blowing,
Among the foggy pathways birth;
Where the newness of the morning,
Greets my day with each vapored breath.

Then cadential geese above me share their migrating tunes,
Cascading down upon the over hanging leaves of royal hues;
As they brush by my shoulders here and there a squirrel is scurrying,
Storing up his choicest harvests among the steaming ground he's quilting.

It is at dawning with her rosy gracing,
That I meet each day a fresh;
When with my Creator spreads its special holy rays,
All nature seems at its best among the Autumn's glowing.

Thomas F. Hall

Fallen Leaf

I look into her brown eyes of beauty
with long curly hair
    Underneath the skin of body
I see a heart of love and care
    She rides the winds with gentleness
And I see her in dreams of love
    She keeps me happy with greatness
With her swift graciousness of a dove
    Alas I came around
But I am too late for my dream
    in my shadow I hear a cry sound
As I look into the life of a fallen leaf

Timm Abel

Casualties Of War

To my dearest friend; Ignorance, hate and fear feed the beast.
With love my dearest daughter; a life so unwillingly given.
Our only son, our only child; A once strong body beaten and withered.
Dedicated father; graduations that will never be seen.
Beloved Mother; Lonely children must rock themselves to sleep tonight.
My love, My life; A brilliant soul finally freed from the pain.
Research, Spokesman, Politics, Celebrities.
Despite education and warnings, the Beast still Hungers.
Still epitaphs being written, still the Quilt grows.
The war wages on; and as in every war Casualties have fallen.
For all the forgotten, the ones who have no square to tell their tale of tragedy,
Rest now weary soldiers, you time has ended.
It is time for new soldiers to follow, new voices to lead the Fight.
Your valiant struggle against prejudice and hate have given those
who will follow a chance for dignity and compassion.
There is a brutal killer among us, Its name is AIDS, Its victims,
    Human Beings
For them I offer this small prayer, so that no one's fight ever go
    unnoticed again.
May God have Mercy on all our souls.

C. L. Osborn

Untitled

Green, ashy meadows envelop my white soft toes.
With swift lightness, I mirror her steps.
Soft, in the grass, I touch her hair as she smiles, and I cry.
She is of the wind as I will never be.
I dance in her light trying to ignore my cascading shadows
ever surrounding me.
She holds my hand, and her warmth penetrates me.
She is a petal, and I a thorn.
Her eyes sway and close,
brown as the trunk of the tree we lie under
when we are too tired to dance any longer.
As we rest, she sings.
Her voice mingles with the sound of water tumbling over rocks.
I imagine that is what Heaven would sound like.
She skips, as I wobble across the slippery brook,
until we reach the leaves on the other side.
She puts a golden one in my hair,
and I smile, while she cries.

Katrina Juujarvi

My Plea

I've often wondered what eternal life
would be, I sang in church choir "How
great thou art" and "Nearer my God to thee."
Now at my passing may loved ones hear my plea.
    Please don't cry or mourn for me
what lies before you is a shell, an empty
body. Instead of weeping, you should silently
applaud. For another soul has left the earth
and returned to heaven, and to God.

Leslie A. Maus

New World At Night Fall

The shades of night do fall, when it comes in first of all.
With the night come the nocturnal creatures, great and small.
They hunt and are hunted with bait, great and small.
Out comes humans and animals, who fight, one an all.
To exist, after all night vanquishes, is most gratifying of all.
We made it through night fall.
Even night can bring its beauty in repose.
To show all littlest creatures great and small.
Even in snow fall, tracks show where they all are.
These who do not hunt, find the beauty in repose.
Soft, cuddly, big gruffy, in colors of evening, will show its peaceful pose.

Sharon Ferguson

The Cloud Parade

Here from my early curbside seat,
    With vast and unimpeded view,
As dark of night takes its retreat
    And dawn casts up its now faint hue,

The marchers in their coats of gray
    Have lined up on the avenue,
And start their movement north today
    As though by some celestial cue.

While overhead the cirrus strands
    Take on the daybreak pink of dawn,
As growing light spreads out its bands
    Of tints the rising sun turns on.

Cumulonimbus clouds stand tall,
    Their heads all fringed in brilliant gold,
And now their dingy gray coats fall,
    As myriad shades of pearl unfold.

The avenue of sea now gleams,
    As marchers move in ponderous line.
The morning sun is up and beams
    At plodding hulks above the brine.

Stoughton Atwood

Guardian Angel

A black knight riding into the night
With words of wisdom sounding so right.

Words that speak volumes penetrating the soul,
Cutting confusion that keeps me unwhole.

Everything you say is on money.
So much insight, it's almost funny.

Someone to rescue me, it's hard to believe.
A Guardian Angel just like I perceived.

Someone to listen and really understand,
To believe in me and respect who I am.

You came with a mission to arrest my duress.
Somehow you seem to know what's best.

How deep the meaning, you'll never know.
But with your lead, I feel good to go.

You're heavy on my mind and on my heart.
Seems we've been soul mates from the start.

The truth is the truth will set us free.
Words can't express how much you mean to me.

Sibyl Myers

My Feeble Lord

From his short tired neck, his bald head drooping down,
withered cheeks, broad lips, nose flattening with frown,
his hands dangling, he walks with feet staggering,
and in all these I trace the treasure of old tunes lingering.
Those tunes tell of the bygone times' telling test
and how we danced together without rest to do our best.

O, I behold him, now, lying quiet on his bed,
bearing the burden of life that he led,
calm and cold towards the worldly things,
yet I feel his silent songs for me he often sings.
I care not whether heaven or hell is here
while my beloved lord is near to give me a good cheer.
My lord though feeble, is the fountain of all my courage
and all my might to move a mountain during all my voyage.

Leela T. Gharpure

Souls In Debt

Sit beneath a dying tree
Withered winds enrapture me
Listen to its subtle voice
Crying, Dying, Screaming...Pain
Dance beneath a star-kissed sky
Twirling, swirling...don't know why

Here I am, arms spread wide
Come and take me by your side
Catch me if you can, slow one
The chase is on, but will ya win
Is it my voice that ya hear in your head
Do ya hear bells ringing, sweet chimes, you're dead

Dare ya walk out of this place alone
Do you fear what hides in the shadows of your home
Will ya awaken once you sleep
Or is it death's sweet hunger sleepin' at your feet
Questions asked, answers never heard
Your death is near, ya better listen to my words

Kasey Lee Gerlach

Untitled

Tepid wanders the creating abundance, there
Within a caption of momentary flourish,
To gain that circle of strength, wherein
Time slides its following change.
When may growth in eternal display,
Release of fortune right, then weigh,
Those who abide their humble home, a cornice
Of which the bearing wind deflects.
Cannot the wishing convey its cause, select
A path in nature's realm, confer
Its wealth with wondrous visage,
For this one may ascend tilling fields, again
From a proving wildflower still,
Together of a wholeness forever of will.

Michael Price

Death

I wake up not knowing where I am
Wondering around this dark distant land
Try to fathom, but I don't know what I feel
Searching for life I ask myself, "is this for real?"
Walking around this dark empty place
I see coming toward me a familiar face
It was death coming forth to embrace me
It was life yearning to release me
I accepted death with open arms
I felt the reaper comforting with all his bizarre charms
death picked me up and carried me away
I died on that unusual day.

Kristin Crawford

Letting God

One candle burning bright on a very special night. It glistens soft within your eyes. I see a tear fall from your face, catch a glimpse of something new. You're crying now, please tell me why but I will never know.

It's time you see for us to part, there is no room within my heart. Sorry now to see you go but someday soon we will both know.

You take my hand and hold me tight. For this is our last final night.

Oh my baby please don't cry, you will know the reason why. It's showing in your eyes right now, and always makes me want to cry.

Only for a moment now kiss and say goodbye. Our love will be there unseen unheard. Absurd as it sounds, but I love you so, that's why I must let you go.

Renee Faith Nelson

"Without"

Without "light," the beauty of a sunrise cannot be envisioned.
Without "darkness," the brilliance of the stars cannot be seen.
Without love, the heart begins to wither.
Without discontent, we may never strive to become all we can be.
Without having to seek the approval of others, we can begin to accept who we really are.
Without "limitations," we may never challenge our "responsible" limits.
Without empathy, we close the door of understanding toward another person's pain.
Without an open mind, we create attitudes that can alienate a potential friend.
Without temptation, we may never experience the serenity of faith.
Without forgiveness, we lack the ability to accept our own mistakes.
Without trust, we may never take the risk to believe that there is good in all things.
Without deprivation, we may never experience the joy of having our needs met.
Without sensitivity, we lose the ability to be a caring and genuine person.
Without suffering, we may never come to know God or a Higher Power that is waiting to comfort us with spiritual goodness and awareness.
In retrospect, to be "WITHOUT" is often necessary to motivate and nurture the person "WITHIN".

Nancy D. Fudge

Play Actor

Moving ourselves to center stage,
Without ever knowing our lines,
Only our designs,
Many of us spend our entire lives,
Feinting and posturing about;

Not until life's end confessing,
We lived out all our days professing,
Ourselves as persons we know us not to be;
We got caught up in the moment,
Along with all the other actors,

Caught up in life's stage lights,
And we like they could not,
Jump the trace nor break the trance,
Until the melody of life's last dance,
Faded from our self centered memory;

Many at life's end lament,
For an encore, another chance,
Never realizing and so sad,
The only illumination of life we ever had,
Or ever sought...was that of our own.

William L. Ryle Jr.

Small Pleasures

Have you ever awakened just before dawn,
wondering what makes life worthwhile and feel right...
Is it the birds or the trees that we live alongside,
or a soft wind that blows so gently at night!

Have you ever journeyed down an old country road,
late in the morn as the day is unfolding...
Only to discover a field of sunflowers,
all bent toward the sun, their faces turned and holding!

Have you every enjoyed a warm summer breeze,
or felt the glow of the sun on your face....
Have you seen the leaves dancing,
atop the trees like glittering lace!

Have you ever watched a child,
gather lightning bugs in a mason jar...
Or have someone smile and gently hold your hand,
because they love you - just the way you are!

Have you ever thought,
that's just the way it's meant to be...
These small pleasures in life,
are simply there for you and me!

Karen S. Watson

Tori

Like a butterfly with no direction you dance in the gardens of the world, seeking a beautiful place with beautiful people.

Reality escapes you - you connect in a perpendicular world, a time and space unknown to other creatures.

You fly on the wind with no effort, contemplating time.

Your energy is consumed not in getting to a destination, but deciding which direction to go.

No one can capture you, cage you, or steal your timeless beauty.

You are too sharp and too vigilant to let anyone ruffle your wings of freedom.

You yawn at fate and the craziness around you.

Your clear-sight reassures you the future is promising for those who find joy in the ordinary world.

So you leave your worries behind and dance your dance of life.

Stephanie Barfield

Retirement

If I were retired, what would I do?
Would I rise early as the morning dew?
Or would I sleep for a week or two?

There would be time for lots of play,
and maybe some fishing every day.
Can you imagine spending time that way?

Maybe a few trips would be in store —
off to the mountains and then the sea shore.
If those trips go well, there will be more.

There would also be time to write a book.
It would make friends stop and take a look
To see if I really did write that book.

Retirement has finally come my way.
Oh what, oh what will I do today?
Who ever thought I would feel dismay?

Rowena Barnes

Constancy

You have been grave and gracious with my song
wounded worn wondering at my uneven rage
in times of failing when all paths are long

'Mid madness thund'ring of born-sightless throng
turning your fakir's eyes to my bespattered page
you have been grave and gracious with my song

'Mid sadness hearing death's unyielding gong
sharing finale on our crumbling stage
in times of failing when all paths are long

'Mid gladness draped in passion's torn sarong
mute to what night's stumbling steps presaged
you have been grave and gracious with my song

'Mid drouth and flowering shorn heart felled or strong
daring youth's rivers scarred by fear's tumbling sage
in times of failing when all paths are long

You have come guiltless back where you belong
Bonded in constancy shriven by prudent age
In times of failing when all paths are long
you have been grave and gracious with my song

Ruth Shireman

Have You Seen God?

Some people have asked; Have you seen God? And I responds:
Yes each time I wake up and see the fiery red sun,
how each tree branches out differently, and the birds
that are like angles and I say, "Yes, I have seen God!"

I go further on to say, when I'm able to hear the sound
of waves rushing up to the shore, and walk through
fields of wildflowers, when I'm able to realize how each human
being is different, I say again, "Yes I have seen God!"

Some people have wondered if there is a God. I respond:
Look at the different seasons. Who makes them change?
Not man. Each individual should search deep into
one's own heart and ask: Have I seen God? I have.

MaryAnn Ablack

Face Value

I don't understand why I ran so far away
yes, you're confused as to why now I stay.
I search for the girl I used to be
she's there no more, now this is me.
I searched for answers I could not find
when you stood right there, knowing them all the time.
We fit together like the sun and the sky,
and yet to one another we deny
The trueness of our beginning to which we vowed
of who we are here and now.
To go forth, to overcome what challenges lie ahead
there's no "I" in team, is what is said.
To truly go on forgive and forget
although deep inside I know, it's not over yet.
It never will be if we dwell on the past,
neither will we, it just won't last.
For I cannot control how or what you think
if I could misconception would be gone in a blink.
There'd be no more worry, it would all go away
if you'd let yourself believe I'm here to stay.

Mary Jane La Tulippe-Herberger

My Mother-In-Law, My Friend

The days have turned into weeks, the weeks have turned into years.
Yesterday seems long ago, my eyes still burn with tears.

Memories of happy times still live within my heart.
The crippling pain of losing you no longer tears me apart.

That doesn't mean that losing you is easier to bear.
Only that as time has passed the pain is lighter here.

There's so much I feel you're missing, many things we'll never share.
Don't ever think I've forgotten you or that I've ceased to care.

Your opinion I valued so highly, your advice always so sincere.
The future is mine to face alone since you're no longer near.

The guidance you freely extended, your sympathetic ear,
Will never be replaced with me for to you no one can compare.

There's a part of you that's with me in the things here I can't tell,
For not only were you my mother-in-law, you were my dear friend as well.

Sally J. Dunbar

The Lovers

She lay before him, barren
Yet deep within her breast
Burned the fires of anticipation
For the transformation

She raged with desire
As he gently lifted her to his breast
Ever so slowly sifting her supple richness
Between his fingers

Her ecstasy soared amongst the stars
And knocked at the very gates of heaven
As he gently stroked the furrow of life
From the depths of her being she cried,
"I will bear you fruit! I will bear you fruit!"

Although he heard not her declarations of love
He smiled knowingly
And then the farmer planted the tiny seed
In mother earth
And awaited the transformation.

R. Alexander FitzGerald

N.F.L. Football 95-96

So you are surprised you've made Super Bowl Fame.
Yet it wasn't easy winning that Championship Game.
Even before you won that division
You weren't satisfied looking at the team's revision.

Well, it's the start of a brand new season.
Fans keep cheering for only one reason.
Jacksonville and Carolina are new kids on the block.
Everyone wants to cream them in shock.

It is hard to say who is the best.
'Cause no one stands out above the rest.
Great players and fans in the N.F.L. kept this game going.
All old fans kept cheering and never stopped roaring.

Joe Montana, Joe Namath, Jim Plunkett, Bart Starr
  and Len Dawson were great quarterbacks.
While Calvin Hill, Larry Csonka, Jim Kiick, Marcus Allen
  and Eric Dickerson were great running backs.

Football is known to be rough,
but no one in the N.F.L. says players aren't tough.
Everyone must agree football is a very exciting sport.
It has a lot more excitement than on a basketball court.

Swarup Misra

"The Heart Has Soul"

I only wanted your heart
Yet, you gave me your soul.
You tell me you love me...
I believe you so.

You inspire me... to be the best I can be
Two hearts together, beating separately.
I tell you, I love you —
That you'll always be mine.

Loving you is emotional...
Experiences divine —
Take me with you to the heavens
We'll have a great time.

The splendor of making love to you
Till the end of time.
Sharing moments of this life together
Just a matter of mind.

Two souls on a journey
Walking hand in hand
Is life's purest pleasure
It's yours and it's mine.

Karen Vanni

My Wife

Through good times and bad times,
You are always there;
All those wonderful memories,
Have been a joy to share;
Your everlasting love for me,
A treasure I'll always keep;
To reach that love on top of a mountain,
No climb would be too steep;
Many riches and wealth can be obtained,
During the course of life;
And if these possessions I did have,
I'd trade them all for my wife.

Mark W. Bennett

Whispers In The Dark

We are never truly apart you know.
You are always with me.
That has been true since the very first day we spoke...

I don't know how or why, but there was an instant connection,
Something irrevocable that happened that day.

And now, no matter where I go or what I do,
Some part of you is always with me.

Some diminutive yet crucial part of you is there,
Just next to my ear, just by my shoulder, keeping me whole.

That irrefutable little hint of you that is with me always,
Like the reassuring voice of a mother for her child,
When the night gathers near and imagined fears blossom from
nowhere.

Like whispers in the dark, the reassuring warmth of your presence,
Keeps me safe from the loneliness that reaches out for me in the night

Robert L. Mikels

Metaphor Poem To God

You are as soft as a fallen snowflake in a winter's storm
You are as soft as a rose petal blooming
You are as joyful as a singing bird
You are as strong as an oak tree with branches providing protection
You are as soft as a baby's bottom
You are as beautiful as a rainbow
You are loved by me.

Kelly Williams

Dear Mom

Mom, I love you very much
You are tender, sweet and loving
Your the best Mom on earth
We are two birds glistening in the sun
You are warm hearted and pretty
Now we can cuddle and even if the time goes fast
I'll remember the moments
You try too hard to please people
You should get a medal and a trophy
I'm so glad God made mothers to love and depend on
You really deserve a reward
All of these feelings come from my spirit and my soul
And especially from the thoughts about my one and only mother
You
All the wonderful things I have to say about you
Can't even be told in a year
In my eyes you are a flower shining in the sun
And I will always love you

Shannon Stash

Infinite Beauty

In loving memory of Wayne A. Bradley: July 24, 1962 - April 26, 1991
When I think of life's most infinite beauty
You are the words and I am the melody
Perfection and heaven right here on the ground
The only harmony for my heart and mind
My only soul mate...forever—once for all time
Inferior attempts many have tried
Few truly realized the man you were inside
The words trusted me with the meekness and timidity
I, the melody, understood the gentleness and sensitivity
Love—a rare treasure...its warmth and sensuality
No other will ever touch my soul or integrally inspire me
Whenever I think of life's most infinite beauty
Past or present you're the only perfect words to unify this melody
You're no longer with me, so alone I face each dawn
Now the song has ended, but regretfully, the melody, I...linger on

Sherry E. Travis

"No Where Bound"

It seems like waiting at the train stop with no ticket in your hand
You can feel the great adventure you won't take across this land
Without a destination and no where you have to be
Ride to non-existing places, when you get there you'll find me.

The hills and curves and tunnels that aren't there will feel so real
And please smile at the waitress when she doesn't bring your noontime meal
When the whistle isn't blowing, but you hear it just the same...
And no conductor in the engine car calls off his list of names.

Remember that you have "no power" to make these things "not happen"
And make sure you "thought" you knew real well that man who isn't captain.

Buy a ticket, take a ride, on "no where bound express"
The cost is cheap and leads to heartache, pain, and undo stress.
The passing sign said "welcome, you are no where" and "you're lost"
It's time to stop this "no where" train... it's time that I got off.

Michaeline Ann Crooks

Young Again

To be young again; oh, those were the days.
You didn't get into trouble, it was "Just a phase".
Writing on the walls and shoving candy up your nose;
Playing "This little piggy" on those tiny little toes.

No problems with money, school or love back then,
Neither was shaving your legs or the hair on your chin.
Playing in the rain with siblings and peers,
Taking a bath, washing behind your neck and ears.

Living in a world with any sin.
Oh, what I would give to be five years old again.

Roni Lyn Peterson

Empty Words Broken Hearts

You didn't have to say what you said
You didn't have to do all that you did
In the middle of all said and done you left
Making me feel bereft

Empty words
So many broken hearts

Empty words
That tear us apart

Empty words
That are revealed

Empty Words
Can't hear - we become concealed

Sheryl Dutcher

"Charleston - The Roxbury Echo"

Suffer all ye little children.
You - have been afflicted
with the plague of yesterday.
You - are the victims -
of the inability of mankind -
to cope with the changing times of today
or to progress from the boundaries -
Of his own ignorance and maladjustments.

For you - there will be no peace.
For you - there will be no green fields and daffodils.
For you - there will be no blue skies and lullabies.
For you - there will be no gentle rains -
only storms and hurricanes.
For you - there is no hope for tomorrow -
only pain, grief and sorrow.

So sing your freedom songs -
and make your pledges of tomorrow -
as you listen to your echoes -
running rampant through the halls.
Remember - the bell of freedom rings.

Robert Lee Wood

"Goodbye My Love Goodbye"

I was mentally, physically, and emotionally attached to you. When
you left me, you left me blue. I loved you with all my heart and
soul-and you gave me nothing, nothing at all. You told me you
loved me and I loved you too. But when it really came down to it,
it was all untrue. When you left you took a part of my heart. I
gave everything I had to you, everything from the start.
But when you left you tore it all apart.
Now that you're gone, I feel so alone.
But it is getting easier, the loneliness is slowly gone.
I look back at all the time gone by
how the time did fly-
I hope you're happy with someone new
I am no longer lonely or feeling blue.
My loneliness has passed all is said and done
If I had to do over I'd do it all again
for you were my first love and that will never die
all I have to say is
good-bye my love good-bye!

Kristina Shuda

Chains Of Imprisonment

I was so in love with you in years long past,
you stood and promised you would love me too.
It was too much to hope our love would last
your need of instant power and money was a clue.

Money controls and imprisons those you want to rule.
You forgot love grows in the presence of openness.
Now, it is hopeless, as I have been played for a fool.
Oh, that there was trust to end this empty loneliness.

Where is the freedom to pursue the gift of my life?
I am bound with shackles of lies, used to confine.
Inner self will now brake the fetters off your wife.
Liberty! My bondage is gone, my life free to define...

Ramona Welch

Babies - Children - Adults

At first you water them, and then they start to sprout,

You nurture them with love, and understanding,
You teach them guidelines, rules and boundaries.

You watch them grow, and feel proud of the steps they've taken.

If you don't keep watering them, and teaching them,
they wander aimlessly,
They soon rebel against everything they were taught.

The parents blame the School system, and Society.
The true place to put the blame, is on themselves.

As the Child becomes an Adult, and struggles to get by,
they wonder why life is so hard on them.

Again the Parents blame Society, and damn the Judicial system.
The true place to lay the blame is on themselves.

So, a kind word to those growing and to those that are watching them grow.

Stop! Speak Up! Ask Questions!

Stop all that which is wrong, and take the blame,
both Young and Old, and then and only then,
will things become easier on the Child, the Adult, and Society,
and who knows, even the world.

Nannette Ary

A Picnic Rendezvous

Our meeting was nice, the conversation was great.
You thanked me for the lunch, which, I remember, you ate;
But you made a remark that wasn't quite true!
That "All I gave you was a sandwich!" That made me feel blue.
'Cause the truth of the matter, I hasten to say,
Is that I gave you much more, that very same day.

How much we overlook; how quick we forget
The sweetest things in life and without which we'd fret.
For had you thought before you spoke, you would not have said those words,
'Cause it was not true! A great big lie! And strictly for the birds!

When you examine the facts, I'm sure you'll agree
That an apology is owed by you - to me!
For a sandwich is not all that I gave you, my dear;
Deep down in that bag, a fudge brownie was there!

Vivian Ayoub

Mother

Mother, you had brought me into this world,
You were there when I took my first steps
  and spoke my first words.
Mother, you were there to make the hurt go away.
You stayed up with me when I was sick.
Mother, we didn't live in any place fancy.
We did have a roof over our heads
  and we did have each other.
Mother, you taught me many things growing up.
You showed me what is right from wrong.
Mother, you had many different talents.
You showed me cooking, sewing and crocheting.
Mother, you showed me how to be a mother.
You enjoyed being a Grandmother
  also doing things for your Grandchildren.
Mother, you ended up getting real sick.
Now I was there for you when you needed me.
Mother, your system couldn't take it anymore.
You have just passed on, but you are now at rest.
Mother, you were and always will be my inspiration!

    Susan Moore

Down By The Water

Down by the water,
You won't suffer.
If you just let the water,
Cleanse you of your sins.

Oh, the water, it is going to purify you
And make you innocent, again.

Let the water,
Come into your skin.
And the water,
Will make your blood rich, again.

Let the water flow through your veins,
For, I know you were in pain.

Down by the water,
You won't suffer
If you just let the water,
Cleanse you of your sins.

I promise,
You won't suffer,
Down by the water.

    Ninna Milliken

The Walk

"You're slow, Grandpa Ike, and you creak at the knee
You'll have to speed up to go walking with me.
I can run, Grandpa Ike, as fast as can be
No one I know is faster than me.
You're bent, Grandpa Ike, you need glasses to see
I'm strong and I'm young, as straight as a tree.
Your face is all blotched, wrinkled, and grainy;
Your hands are too big they're knobby and veiny.
You're old, Grandpa Ike, and your head is so shiny;
There's hair in your ears and your nose is not tiny.
There's a dog coming, Gramps, and he's barking and growling.
Dogs scare me sometimes with their sniffing and howling.
You're brave, Grandpa Ike, you made him look sick
You chased him away with your voice and a stick.
There's a hill coming up and I'm tired as can be.
For all that I said, would you still carry me?
You're strong, Grandpa Ike, you carry me with ease
I guess you can still do whatever you please."

    Michael Gormly

Our Eternal Love...A Valentine Message

I remember the beginning when our love was so very new,
Young hearts drawn together with a pledge sincere and true.
An eternal love, a flame ever so bright,
One that continues and glows like a shining light.

For now and always this unity firmly bound
With many blessings through the years, we've found.
Cherished memories that make us merry and sad,
Together we always make the best of what we have.

Each day a new journey with you,
In the distance a melody drifts through.
Success, challenge, acquisitions and reams,
I've always shared your dearest dreams.

Seasons change and blossoms carefully fed
As our love is tenderly nourished by sweet things said.
Peacefully I gaze at our tree-laden lot,
Knowing whatever the years bring, you will forget me not.

    Rosemary G. Krieger

To Tex

Beloved pet, your searching eyes are closed;
Your drooping ear is stiff - to droop no more
While silent furry corpse is now transposed
Beneath the soil in which you kept your store
Of biscuits, bones, and other valued things.
I cherish memories of the childhood games
We used to play, especially when the Spring's
Warm sun enlivened our two youthful frames.

I still can feel your cold nose nuzzled snug
Within my hand; dear pet, you proved your love
And keen desire to please by every tug
Of upheld paw, which was your offer of
Your friendship to the end. Now all is stilled—
And left is emptiness which can't be filled.

    Maxine L. Parker

US - An Ode To My Love

My love, you make my life worthwhile
Your sweet caress, your lovely smile
If you should leave and go away
I would forever have last night and today
Tomorrow may never get here
But for this moment I thank you dear
I was a lost soul, no urge to live
You brought me back with the love you give
I ask no promise and none I give
But hope you are here as long as I live
Our secret moments we must steal
Our love we must conceal
Oh God look down on us we pray
And make our love right one day

    Vivian Millard

"My Darling Angie"

You are my Darling Angie
you're as sweet as cotton candy
sometimes you are a little bit crazy
but when were out your always a lady
I know you can be naughty but nice
that's what makes you the love of my life
There's nothing between us that we have to hide
and I pray someday you will be my bride
you are so perfect in every way
that's why I think of you night and day
like I said before you are my Darling Angie
Just so sweet as cotton candy

    Robert T. Skinner

The Goddess

Your hair is like rays of golden sunshine,
Your touch, as tender as butterfly's wings,
Your eyes like that of two oceans beyond the horizon,
Your skin as soft as the petals of a rose,
Your lips as sweet as honey,
Your body, so sensuous, and caressable,
Just the mere thought of you drives me wild with desire,
How could God endow you with such beauty?
I feel so lucky, just to be in your presence,
The sun and the moon are jealous of your radiance,
You are the epitome of Love and Beauty,
The venus of all my dreams and fantasies,
I just want to fall on my knees and worship you.
You are my Goddess and I, your slave,
Your beauty holds me captive,
You heat me up and I explode like a firecracker,
The things that you do and say, I just lose all control,
Cupid's arrows have pierced my tender heart, and filled it with love,
Are you of this Earth?
No, thou are a Goddess, sent to bring joy into my little heart.

Lowell O. Hillocks

You

My heart beats to the sound of your name.
Your voice echoes inside.
Not a lover, not a friend,
What are you?
A part of me that will never die yet cannot live.
My foreboding idol,
I envy your simplicity.
My mind is haunted by thoughts of you.
You are me and I am you.
This I cherish.

Liz Quinn

The Man In The Moon

If no one seems to listen,
Your words just fly away with the wind,
Just wait until the night falls,
Then look to the sky to find a friend.

The man in the moon is waiting
For you to call his name,
Then the kindness and listening roll in
And take over your unbearable pain.

He may seem to be a little busy,
Or he may be covered up by a cloud.
That doesn't mean you still can't be heard,
But you may need to speak a little loud.

I've looked for help all over,
But the man in the moon is always there.
He always seems to listen
And he seems to never cease to care.

All good things come to an end,
Our friend goes away too soon,
How we long to spend another night
Depending on the man in the moon.

Robin Shupe

Does Equal Rights Mean Look Alikes

In today's world when I look around I see,
That young men and women look alike to me.
Earrings, boxer shorts, neck ties, long hair,
Everyone makes a statement by what they wear.
Can you keep the distinction in daughter and son,
And still have room for equal rights for everyone.

Diana Ingram

Pride

He wrapped his dark hand around the boy's; like this it said.
The same hand that was calloused with work,
The one that had worked so hard for so long,
Now was careful and gentle.

The boy looked up with a smile so sweet and innocent,
And the old man's lined face smoothed into a grin.
Then the boy plucked the strings and giggled out loud,
And the man looked at the banjo that made the sound.

It was torn and dirty with a hard life of work,
It was a token of his race, passed down generations.
And now this young boy was learning to play
The beaten-up, worn-out, tired old banjo.

"Pride," said the man with a tear in his eye,
"Is the name of that tune."
And the boy in response whispered, "Pride!"
And plucked the strings again.

Although battered under the work of harsh hands,
The old man knew its beauty was found
With a simple smile and flick of the hand;
Playing a tune called "Pride."

Jacob Thomas

Purity Of A Dove

The fresh open hole
The rising of the sole

The crow perched above the stone
Sings the song of ones left alone

The opening of the heavens gives a welcome from above
Enter in with the purity of a dove

Left behind those evil ways
Six feet under where the body lays

Streets of gold, angels wings
Thunder clashes, heaven sings

Desolate place where the devil plays
Fear and evil is portrayed

Safe from harm up above
Surrounded with the purity of a dove

Erica Marie Webb

The Field

Flowers budding through the ground
  The rich musty smell of fertile soil
    The warmth of a sun soaked shed
      Outlets waves of heat
        Grass and ground are littered alike with debris from
        Foreplaced events
This makes up the field's spirit

Sawdust scattered in a small piles
  The wind with an icy grip
    Whips round my figure
      Dandelions adorn the field like freckles
      Grass and pine perfumes the air
This makes the field's face

Beneath the surface are hiding many reclusive
  Creatures
    Tires in strewn,
      Moist, and waterlogged piles
        Weeds design elaborately across the track
This makes up the field's physical being

Jessica E. Johnson

Black

Black is what you see when
you're sleeping.
And what you'll see when
you die.
Black is the black board
I see every day in class.
The colour of my phone.
And the colour of some binders
we carry every day.
Black is the darkness we
see every night.
A dark alley without a light.
Black could be your eye
after a fight.
A song sung by queen.
Black is a wicked cat on
Halloween
Black is what I feel sometimes
far away out of touch
on my own, all alone.

Tanya DeCaire

I Forgot You

I forgot you -
Your birthday is March 28
Your favorite color was red
You were my best friend -
I forgot you.

You played the accordion
You painted and took photographs
You were an athlete
You baked, sewed, crocheted
You were an honor student
You drove and worked in an office
You cold do anything
I forgot you.

I still feel the pain
From time to time
In a place reserved
For you.
You forgot me.

Janet Young

Danielle

When you were born
you touched our hearts,
a sweet little baby so
cute and so smart.

Although you were only
with us for such a short time,
our memories of you will
last a lifetime.

Now the time has come
that we must say good-bye,
don't worry little angel,
the Lord will be with you
in that great big sky.

You'll always be in our
prayers and hearts,
we love you and miss
you although we're apart.

Kelly Doyle, August 14, 1995

Right To Death

At foetus stage,
You threatened me with abortion,
Cursed me for nine moons,
Relieved you ushered me,
Skip my world,
Yes death is my fundamental right,
As life is to you.

I turn a street brat,
Bastard my name,
Eyes in deep sunken sockets,
Parched lips,
Ribs reflecting sunlight,
And coiled hollow intestines,
Rumbling dissonant tunes,
All left for dead.

Then an air burial,
With no coffin or grave,
Flies singing hymnals,
Twenty something vulture squawks,
And maggots on palatable meal.

Francis Peter Odhiambo

Why Can't A Dog Be More Like A Cat?

Why is a cat not more like a dog,
You say, I say
A cat is more than a dog.
A dog can retrieve.
So can a cat
Retrieve shiny things crumpled in balls.
A dog will love you...messy thing.
A cat loves too
But waits for permission,
Politely and tidily.
Dogs must be bathed.
Cats bathe themselves.
Dogs must be walked.
Cats get their exercise
By finding mock friends.
Dogs must be aired to do their business;
Then leave it for you to clean up.
While cats, bless them, do it in boxes
And, to boot, will cover it up!

Militza Haig

Siesta

To Andrée
The morning loneliness today, again,
You mixed it into your black coffee
Cold
It passes
Through your dry trachea

The midday loneliness
You pricked it with the fork
Uncounted times
Slashed it into uncounted pieces
And swallowed it with uncounted
Knots

The evening loneliness
You diluted it into tea
Into exorcism
Into a mute, unwanted song

The waxy loneliness
You lit it lively in the summer chapel
And you burn everything
In rotten waters
With your eye turned away.

Dragos Chima

Louisa

Louisa when we met
You looked so good
Louisa when we danced
My quiet shook
Asked you out
Wasn't sure you'd come
Louisa wasn't it fun
Not remembering not caring
Not even knowing your name
Walked to the place
Afraid you'd not show
Counted the clock
Worried, I rose to go
Louisa you showed up
I have to tell you
It was quite a shock
Never would I have
Believed it
Louisa the Roar
You made me smile

Bill Durward

Inspired By Laurie

I talked; and
you listened.

I spoke of loneliness;
and you shared.

I grieved of loss;
and your eyes moistened.

I cried;
and your comforting arms replied.

I felt; and
you knelt.

I smiled; and
you talked assurance.

I laughed; and
you spoke of hope.

I walked away;
you've had a long day.

You filled my brush
with the colors of the rainbow.

Allen Knopp

Untitled

At first I disliked you,
you caused a lot of pain.
You made me feel blue
There was a lot of strain.

I just wasn't ready
it was all so new.
I still had my teddy,
and my mommy too.

I was filled with fear
and unsure of myself.
Nothing was clear
not even my health.

But slowly as I held you near
a feeling grew in me,
my mind became so clear
and I began to think of we.

And now I fill with fear again
as you start out to school,
and now returns the hurt and pain
as I release you to the cruel.

Sandra Delmore

My Friend

In the darkness
   you are my light,
In my despair
   your are my hope,
In my fear
   your are my security,
In my sorrow
   your are my joy,
In my wandering
   your are my guiding hand,
In my life
   you hold my heart,
In my heart
   you hold my love,
Although my body quakes with uncertainty
   you remain solid,
For in my soul
   you are my friend.

Ray Pierce

Appearances

Tall and gangly
yet so full,
thin
yet rounded,
brown and plain
yet beautiful.
With each new growth
white and pink
then green
it's a wonder
something we see
most everyday can seem so
magnificent
but yet others look at it
so plainly
just remember
that the way you look at things
or people may be the way
others look at you.

Angela MacInnis

Shoes

Oh, you beautiful old shoes
Ye tired old loafers
Lined with the fleece of time
Kissed and cursed by the dew
But so aged and blue
And so beaten
At the mercy of the spider mite
You still are sweet relics of my youth
I recall that era...sublime.

So now, you shabby old mules
Ye shrunken old warriors
Beggars in the slush and ooze
Who dropped you in this gutter to die?
Oh, still married you lie
But humiliated
On the threshold of eternal doom
Well, adieu to you, from us who knew
And loved, blue suede shoes

Helen C. Gattinger

Caring People

Counting the flowers on the wall
   writing poems to pass the time
     till someone takes notice of me

Watching hearts being broken and
   people falling in love but the
     lonely poetry writer

For no one cares about the lonely
   and disabled people just themselves
     instead of other people
     as well as themselves

Disabled and lonely are people to
   just asking for a little bit of
   help and friendship

For it's not what's on the outside
   of people that counts, it's what
     is in the heart and on the in
     side of a person that counts

Dale Stewart

Beauty Of The Sky

Your beauty is hard to comprehend,
with your shades so brilliant
and mellow, spectacular shades
pulled across your infinite
canvas, creating stylish clouds
of colored puff and imaginative
creatures, you'll always be an
enigma in my mind.

Abby Rae Fisher

P.E.I. Days

Warm bright days
With the sun's golden rays,
Shining upon fields of corn.
The meadows so green,
Everywhere can be seen,
The earth in its splendor adorned.

Butterflies flutter from leaf to leaf,
A gentle spray upon the reef,
The smell of salt from the sea,
And the swaying leaves of a tree.

This is the picture in my mind,
of days of yore, days gone by,
Along the shores of P.E.I.

The breeze would catch the scent of sea
And quickly bring it o'er to me.
The sunlight danced upon the waves,
Seagulls swooped and laughed and played.
A gentle sighing in my breast,
Tells me I am happy, I'm at rest.

Susan Furness

Autumn

Autumn is a lady,
With Auburn hair unbound,
She trips across the fairest land
In a colored gown!
She touches softly all the green,
She spreads her skirts just like
  A Queen-then
Sinks so softly into sleep,
Is covered with the snow and sleet,
And so begins to dream!

Betty M. Avery

Game Of Chance

Why does my soul pain
With the absence of your touch
I thought I could be alone
But I was wrong, you mean too much
Where can I turn
To find a true love again
As long as you are gone
All is under rain
I wish I could prove
My love so strong
But I cannot say, although I wish
How I do feel
Being bound by a promise
Makes my ache more real
As days go by
Our lives but a dance
I will stand by the wall
Waiting for another chance.

Stacy Heffernan

Choices

Our world is full of rainbows
With promised pots of gold
A myriad of garden paths
And numerous leaders bold
With too many drums athrobbing
The rhythm is obscure
Too many truths are glided
What do we know for sure?
With all of the windmills turning
Who knows which one to fight?
And all of the candles burning
Is there one left to light?
Our space and minds are so burdened
With a confusion of things
Too many pipes a-calling
And too many naked kings

Ann Cosh

Fairy Tales Can Come True

If I were locked in a tower
With no way to be set free
Would you ride up on your white horse
Just to find me?

If I were dancing with you
And at midnight disappeared in the air
Would you tell all your guards
And search for me everywhere?

If I ate a poisoned apple
That a wicked queen did make
Would you search for me in the forest
Then embrace me so I'd like?

If I pricked my finger
And my rest became so deep,
Would you kiss me so I'd wake
From that dreadful asleep?

But if your love is really true
Then all I need to hear,
Is that I am your princess
And you will always be near.

Anna Rozbicka

Baby

Together we shared our love
With hopes from above
We want to be good Moms and Dads
So we can bring up our lass or Lads
We have our love to Share
All we want is what's Fair
Lord please don't say Maybe
Please let us have a Baby.

John P. Martens

Hope

Soaring high above the clouds
with his wings unfurled;
Thinking thoughts to cure the ills
of all upon the world.
Alas! Unless they shall want change
no matter what the price.
The world and all the souls within
shall be a sacrifice!
But lo, what's this I see below
that shines bright as a star?
A soul cries out for help to come
in time and from afar.
The tears he sheds are not in vain
for soon they all will see.
For He shall come to save us all
and set the whole world free!
The ills and evils of the world
shall be chained and smitten.
Just read and heed the word of God
and believe as it is written!

Lanna Sherrie Saunders

Velvet Falling Snow (Extended Care's)

Old worn souls
with frames more fragile
than a butterfly wing
wake to grace these halls
for yet another day

Lines mapped across their brows
highlight the years
that brought them to this place

They'll sit again
eyes moistened with hope
waiting for an image
from their other time
They'll plead
to be taken home again
They'll cry and beg to die

Hey you... in that wheelchair
sitting all alone
I see no tears
but I hear you cry
whatever could be wrong?

Ariel Harmatuik

The Pain Of Not Knowing

The pain of not knowing
Who you are,
The pain of not knowing
What you are doing,
The pain of not knowing
Why you are here,
Should be taken as an experience-pill
Necessary to effect a knowledge-cure
In an endless seeker's life.

Pradipan Michael F. Berens

To Be Alone

A man came up to me today,
With fire in his eyes.
I asked him how was life,
And he replied full of lies.

The terror on his face,
Pushed me back a step.
As I searched for words,
I could see he wasn't here yet.

The trembling in his hands,
Shook violently at his side.
As I reached out to him,
He turned and ran to hide.

I followed for some time
Hoping he would turn back to me.
He looked back many times,
But upped his step considerably.

I lost him in the night,
Some distance from my home,
And at this point I realized,
He was terrified to be alone.

Walter A. Barbosa

The Eagle

O mighty eagle your wings top the sky
with aerial surge, and gliding high
show mountains and the plains
a graceful skill. Your hunters pains
betray a noble predator
who views with scorns the imitator man.
Who's hideous wreck of smell
and noise, ugly sheen, and fell
pollution feigns the aerial master.
This intrusion breeds disaster.
Long after man gives us the sky
which is your home, you will fly
as sovereign should, a regal show
for God above and man below.

Bruce Harding

"Finiter"

How many more hollow nests
Will my ear nudge out
On my feather tick pillow
To fit my face just right?

I fear the span from
The warmth when I leave it
To the next nestling
Closes in too quickly.

How many toothpick trees
From the porcelain pig
To dislodge the mini orts
From repast to repast?
Not too many more I think.
Big one's any way.

There is a number
As each milli-second
Turns finite to finiter.

James Taylor

Too Late

Blank pages of the nineties
Will inherit history books,
As authors search frustrated
For achievement of man's work.

More wars are on the increase
Causing death and heartfelt pain,
There's homelessness, and poverty
Recession strikes again.

The wildlife search for sanctuary.
Pollution freely flows,
Our natures cloaked in acid rain.
Destruction starts to grow.

Man is a fool unto himself
Destroying all God made.
He will not get a second chance,
It's now too late to pray.

Valerie Taber

Mommy's Love

Little child, small child
why do you
shed such small bitter tears?

Mommy has gone
And I don't know where
Daddy says that
She went to heaven
But where is heaven?
Is it in Canada?
Can I visit her?
Why did she leave me?

Hush my child
And be still
Soon you will grow
In mind then
You will know the answers
But I have one more
Very important question
Does Mommy still love me?

Jennifer Paul

Returnity

I met a man in Kingston
Who said his name was Mike
And he was Cree

He asked for money
E'en tho' his pockets jingled
And I gave him all I had
From you via me

We talked of death
And how we wished to be remembered
Then he said something
That startled me

When I die, I want these words
Inscribed upon my tombstone
Coming back, to Returnity

Carolyn Allen

Poor Me

I can never be fully
Who I'm supposed to be
I don't have the right body
The right mommy
I was born at the wrong time
The wrong God-forsaken place
If only I'd been
All that I'm not
I'd be rich and famous
The model woman
With a face worth millions
Living in Beverly Hills
I'd have all the clothes all the food
  -that wouldn't ruin my figure
And married with children
Who'd obey my every direction
Each the apple of my eye
To perfection.. too bad
  -I'd only be living
In fiction

Mary Angela Nangini

The Oppressed's Prayer

Our leaders
Who are in state mansions
Hacked be your bodies
Your destruction come
Your fall be planned on earth
As well as blessed by heaven.
Give us this day our daily dues.
Bear our furious ravage
As we bear your ravages against us.
And plead not to us into compassion
To deliver you from evil
For yours from us is the venom
The choler and the fury
Now and forever.
Amen.

Gerald M. M. Matovu

The Ghost Named Harry

There was a ghost named Harry,
Who always tried to marry,
He once tried Heather,
But she wore leather,
So Harry isn't married.

That same ghost named Harry,
Still wanted to marry,
The next day he tried Jean,
But she wore jeans,
Still Harry isn't married.

A friend of Harry's,
Said he should marry,
So he tried Bombar,
But she went to the bar,
Right now Harry isn't married.

Harry was tried of trying to marry
So he asked his friend Kari,
She said "way out",
Harry laid about,
Now Harry is married to Kari.

Kim Hildebrand

Thoughts

Feeling the touch of the morning dew
While being carried away into the heart
Of remembrance
Longing for feelings that belong
to the past
with the realization that you have
touched eternity
tracing back the sands of time
while standing at the very crest of
the earth
gazing through mists
which in reality is another
beginning
a need to be
a total commitment of self
not to be stilled by
simple interactions
but to continue with sensitivity and
understanding.

Emily B. Phillips

To Gwyneth and Bob

I sit and try to write the words
  Which always came so free.
But now I just can't get them right.
  It's ne'er been hard for me.

I try, and try, to push my pen
  But the words escape my eye.
And then I realize the truth.
  I don't want to say "goodbye!"

To share some time along life's path
  Has been a gift for me.
To see a couple so in love
  The way it's meant to be.

Your teachings surely hit the mark
  Upon this path I trod.
And helped me understand and feel
  The presence of our God.

So I shall close, without goodbye,
  And tears I shall not weep,
For in my heart there'll always be
  A part of you I'll keep.

Cheryl Barker

A Tribute To Mothers

We've seen the halls in Nashville
  where they honour all great stars,
Like Hank and Jim and Roy and Bill,
  all there with their guitars.

  In Hollywood a special street
   has names of Movie Stars
  There is a special place of honour
   for famous horses, dogs and cars.

We haven't seen a special place
  for honouring our Mother
When God created her you know
  He made her like no other.

  That's why out in this busy world
   there is no special place
  Where memory of her precious love
   in any hall could grace.

And so within the soul of man
  where God has His own space
He saved a spot eternally
  and called it "Mother's Place".

Marcery A. Vannatter

Untitled

Uncertainty
Where am I going
What am I doing
These I can answer
It is my heart
Body and soul
Which I do not understand
My mind cries out
Then it shouts for joy
It follows the lead of my heart
Perhaps I have gone mad
Or have merely realized
Just how truly sane
I really am.

Troy Hopkins

Remembering Him

You think your world has ended
When your love and you must part.
He may not be there with you,
But he lives within your heart.
The years you spent together,
Will never go away.
He'll be there beside you,
To help you on your way.
Days may be sad and lonely,
And you are filled with grief,
Just remember that his passing,
Was to him a great relief.
How much pain he suffered,
Not even you could know.
He put on his smiling face,
And didn't let it show
Now, for you the time has come,
To lock him in your heart,
And go on with your living,
Till you'll meet and never part.

Genevieve McMitchell

Sleep

In the quiet of the night
When you let your thoughts go free,
As the velvet darkness laps you
It's like drifting on a sea
Of soothing, tranquil beauty.
Becalmed and full of peace,
Sounds murmur, whisper, fade away
Until at last they cease.
Languor steals across you,
Relaxed and unaware
You slip into the arms of sleep
And they close with loving care.

Mary Brown

The Real Me

If you look at me
  What do you see?
Do you see me on the
  Outside or in?
It's usually on the
  Outside and not the in.
It does not take
  A lot of intelligence
To look deep down in
  A person.
Next time will you look
  Deep down too?

Amarjit Sanghera

Ageless Love

Love knows not age
When it's blessed from up above,
for we all want to care
for someone that we love.

Age shouldn't be a barrier
for what is in the heart,
Because with all the blessings
you shouldn't be apart.

The circle is eternal
the gold is something pure,
An expression of true love
and a love that's ever sure.

So when you take the step
remember the above,
Age does not matter
when your heart is filled with love.

Marion Thibault

"Mother"

Mother cries,
when I say goodbye.
She closes her eyes,
and hopes to see,
her children alive.
No sorrow is greater,
than for a mother,
who cries,
lovingly for the arrival,
of her child.
Life can be gone,
when you don't know why,
she can't stop to smile.
She cries,
and pleas
for her child to be set free,
but no one listens,
no one cares,
for that mother,
can only cry, in despair.

A. De Vellis

Life

Gone are the days
when fight was fair—
defence with word or fist.

Now mercy's it;
how will it be?
In life — no guarantee.

Quick, swift,
to the heart—
dead before he had a start;

his killer—
crazy, stressed, alone—
had no reason of his own.

Modern man boasts of his glory.
He invented this whole story.
What is life to him?

Evelyn Grace Chang

"In Memory"

Now he's gone
What more can I say?
Just last Saturday
He passed away.

His time had come
Without any warning
When he hit the wharf
On that cold winter morning.

It's such a loss
He had to die
We sit and mourn
And ask, "Why?"

An empty void
Replaces the space he filled
He took part of us all
The day he was killed.

Now it's over
Why does life have to end?
Goodbye, Robin
Our dear, dear friend.

Bunny Allen

"Sole" Quest

Who am I? What's my purpose?
What is "quality of life"?
It's hard to find reason for being
In my heart I only find strife...
   I've never felt valued or cherished,
   or felt any measure of worth.
   My days are spent feeling lonely.
   How did I even survive my birth?!
I need someone who will love me
hold me like I've never been held;
to make me feel that I'm special
and my heart and my spirit have jelled.
   Only then can I bare to take a look
   to risk - to see inside;
   to try to determine "for what I came,"
   and why I never died.

Kathy Montgomery

The Enemy

The orders are clear,
What all men fear;
Locate and terminate all life.

Human life form scanned,
No chance for this man;
It has now ceased to exist.

Only one life form remains,
It must play the game;
Kill or be killed.

Scanning possible locations,
No signs of habitation;
It's just a matter of time.

Lines of communication vandalized,
Modes of transport immobilized;
Countdown to extinction draws nearer.

All this energy wasted over a man,
I now realize what I am;
I am the only enemy that exists.

George Loverdos

Untitled

Wha but Fred should fete this day?
Wha else could mak us a' sae gay?
Up and toast Reid, now ye may,
A sonsie lass has he.

From Auld Scotia's shores he came,
Eager to toil in his new hame;
Sweet Dorothy soon will bear his name,
A bonnie lad has she.

So tak your Dorothy, Fred sincere,
And live for many a fruitful year,
Fail in daily kisses ne'er,
Faithful lovers be.

Such loving troths all lands unite
To help end wars, a cursed blight,
So Fred and Dorothy's bairns may sight
Rab Burns's *liberty*.

Come brothers a', rejoice this night,
Your pleasures do our Fred delight;
Auld Lang Syne shall reign in might,
Workers—friends must be!

Art Meyer

"Mindy Tran"

We'll plant a tree in her memory
We'll nurture it with care
And when our souls are troubled
We'll seek our solace there

This tree shall be a symbol
Of peace and joy and love
Sent docon on the wings of angels
From our heavenly Lord Above

Margaret Shiskin

The Purging

We live only to serve
We were born only for your pleasure
We exist only to entertain

Pain, sweet pain
Come pain and cleanse
Cleanse the heart, the soul, the mind

Come heart to bleed
Forever
The endless love of life

Heart to heart, soul to soul
Mind to mind, strength to strength

Love commits the unexplainable crime
Cold fire, lead feather, bright smoke,
Suspended time,
Beautiful pain

Jill Robar

Wild Steed

Have you seen a wild steed,
To the wind he pays no heed,
He jumps, he runs, he rears in play
Until the first light of the day
Then he is silent, still and grave.
His beauty is more than the sunlight
   and waves
Yet they go by him, ignoring his cries
Although they triumph the depths of
   the skies.

Andrea Hill

Cosmic Connection

Even though
we have known each other
for only a very short time,
together
we have struck a chord
that resonates
through the non-existence
of time.
You and I
have gifts beyond measure
to explore
together and apart.
Our meeting started reverberations
that will resonate
for all existence.
Distance may separate our bodies
but never our souls.
We are
reconnecting soul-mates
for a purpose.
Linda Boutet

Waiting

She stands there at the station
Watching the trains come in,
Waiting to see if he will come
Back to her arms again.

But in and out the trains do come,
And his face she cannot find,
And in the darkness she waits alone
Sure that he'll come with time.

Then after pacing up and down,
Almost through the night
The late, late train, finally arrives.
It was such a wonderful sight.

She searches the crowd to find him,
And running towards her he comes
With love and joy and passion
Into her arms he runs.

She knows her waiting is over,
Their life together has begun,
And neither a word is spoken
The two shall now become one!
Mary Koroscil

Where Am I

I am sitting on a wooden bench.
Watching and listening
as the water falls into the river.
I can feel a cool mist on my face.

I can see the flowers blossom
as the sun shines on them.
Their fragrance
reminds me of their peaceful freedom.

The grass is so green
the weather so warm,
and in the distance
I can hear children's laughter.

As hours pass,
it seems like minutes.
The sun is setting
and it is time for me to go.

But still a smile is on my face,
for I know tomorrow
I'll be back here with you
in Heaven.

Diana Del Monte-Rigby

Was I Only Dreaming

Where has the love gone
Was I only dreaming
Childhood dreams of warmth
Grown-up dreams of passion

Where has the glow gone
The glow I need so badly
Has it gone behind a cloud
Drifted out to sea

Where has the laughter gone
of happiness long past
The smiles have all faded
The joy all disappeared

Where has the love gone
Was I only dreaming
Joan Lynch

Untitled

"Come with me",
   was all he said.
"Come with me",
   he begged.
"Come with me"
   "Where?" I asked.
"To a special place,
   filled with love and caring.
There is nothing to do,
   except be happy.
Few are invited".
   "Why me," I asked.
"To come with me,
   you must be special".
"I
   will go
   with you."
Was what I said.
   And then I died.
Tamara Baxter

Untitled

The clouds are peaceful,
upon this dreary night,
The earth is still
and the water has froze.
The bears are hibernating
and the squirrels are hiding
The camp grounds are closed,
and bowling is in.
The dead are being moved
to that arch in the sky,
and the land that was warm
has now turned cold.
Corina Benoit

"Places"

Fly me away to tomorrow
To see the dreams I've dreamt
Shake off the chains of past
Like a lonely ghost's last laugh
Tomorrow's a place
I haven't been to yet
Yesterday's a place
I can't go back
Today's a place
   To live
      And love
         And laugh.
Derrick Swain

Up The Hill Side

A long carpet darkish green
Up the hill side this could be seen

Little ants moving from side to side
In the green they could hide

People picking green tea leaves
Bundling them up in big heaves

Gigantic rocks between the greenery
Oh what a lovely bit of scenery

The cool soft breeze blowing our hair
In the wind flying everywhere

Buds open and the flowers bloom
Fragrance of flowers in the air soon

Water splashing down on rocks
Like the white silk we sew our frocks

Up the hill side you could see
This lovely bit of scenic beauty.
Madhu Hewakapuge

The Ocean In You

The ocean in you
unrelenting, mystical energy
giving you
strength
endurance
integrity
drown yourself
in its depths
rhythms
visions
transformations
beyond the boundaries
of your imagination
embrace
celebrate
the ocean in you
Jennifer F. Austin

Inner Strength

Thus comes the night
Under the starlit skies
She prays for strength
As her spirit dies

The woman she's become
Must face the man
That helped give her life
Then hurt her and ran

She sits and discusses
All the pain through the years
As the little girl within her
Sheds all her tears

The little girl's been imprisoned
The time's come for her reward
The woman gains the strength
To cut the paternal cord

The little girl's free
She flies by the woman's side
The woman looks her father in the eye
Then she walks away with pride
Deborah LeDrew

The Dance

We moved along a mystic path
Twirling as we went
Our laughter was like music
So sweet and innocent

Our step was light and carefree
Like dancing on the wind
Time somehow seemed to vanish, as
Love rushed us round the bend

We moved with wild abandon
Our spirit in our feet
Oblivious to the distant drum
We danced to our own beat

THEN DARKNESS FELL UPON US
OUR FEET STOPPED IN MIDAIR
OUR DANCE WAS INTERRUPTED
OUR MUSIC WAS IMPAIRED

Though fate has stepped between us
And split our paths apart
Our souls remain united
Dancing on within our hearts

Maryanne Hawkins

On Wings Of Wrath

On wings of wrath, what fury flings
Tumultuous darts? What horror brings
That darkest hour of midnight's fate?
All man has sinned. Is it too late?

In piercing wind, what infant cry
Re-echoes over mountain high?
So innocent, this hungry child!
Are God and man not reconciled?

A hellish cry in terror's pain!
A mother seeks her child in vain,
And others lost in fear repeat
The moaning of a land's defeat.

That gentle, inner calm destroyed,
As arms and armaments deployed,
Slay one and then a thousand more.
Another here, another score.

The fire and fumes of war rise high,
Blackening nature's perfect sky,
As men and boys sentenced to die,
With all the world still wond'ring why.

W. Diane Van Zwol

Listen

Listen to the water
  trickling by,
Creeping slowly pass my eyes.

Listen to the wind
  through the trees,
What song does it sing to me?

It whispers softly in my ear,
  listen to your heart,
  so you may hear.

Let there be honesty
  and trust
To live together, it's a must.

  Love and peace
  and harmony
That's all it takes to truly be.

Open up your mind
  so you may see
What mother Earth needs you to be.

Kim Guiltner

I Long For The Marlboro

She comes through open windows
touching everyone
who lies in her path
When you wake, you wonder
if anything is real
until she slides
her shadow
against every limb and appointment
towering beneath the beauty
Until the curtains
brush against the arms
of thin, beautiful men
she waits
for a moment when she won't be heard
pressing scars upon darkness
to open the door
to bring you walking
to ancient ritual.

Sarah Hajes

A Senior's Dream

Wouldn't it be nice
  to turn back time
Be young again
  when all was fine

The excitement back then
  so much to do
The plans you made
  and wished come true.

With each new dawn
  we're a little older
It's then we realize
  fate gets bolder

The sunset of life
  too soon appears
And memories begin
  of those wonderful years.

Jimmy Embro

Take Time

Take time to smell the roses
To touch the morning dew
To enjoy the midday sunshine
To study the sky so blue

Take time to say "I love you"
To give away a smile
To touch a child lovingly
To sit and read awhile

Take time to ease a heartache
To help a friend in need
To spread a little joy around
Take time, you will succeed

If everyone would take the time
What a wonderful world it could be
Time for laughter, time for fun
A better place for you and me

The hands of time are passing
Don't sit alone and pine
Life really could be wonderful
If only you would take time

Shirley J. Srigley

The Marionettes

Like the marionettes, we are tied
to the walls of our destiny.
We are the witnesses of crimes,
but we have to keep silent.
We can not let the walls fall apart
because that would be the end.
Still, there is no beginning.

We are marionettes and we are tied.
We can not do anything.
We are just created to be.
Yet, our being is limited
With borders we have made.

Like the marionettes, we are tied
and nothing can save us
from the darkness within us
The walls are not responsible for stopping the light.
We are.

For we are just marionettes. Machines.
Or hellish dolls asking for forgiveness
from the light we have never seen.

Dunja Metikos

Untitled

I am writing to you
To the power that be
To see how to get
A publisher for me.
I don't know who else
I could turn to and ask
It seems to be
A difficult task!
I have a few books
Of this way cool prose
And I know they will tickle
The most pedigreed nose!
So if you could find it
Within your grasp
To help me at all
I will soon make you gasp!!

Shelly Schwan

Spiders Web

Of fine spun silk you weave your work,
to sparkle in the sun.

You hang it on a fence post,
and then your job is done.

Its beauty is enticing
to all who dare to tread,

But touch your satin pillow
and they're caught up in your bed.

The air is warm, the sun is high,
the moon will soon be near,

To offer brilliant vigilance
upon your tender sphere.

Then comes the dew to ravage you,
and your labour so intense,

Your will is strong, so you'll carry on,
to the other side of the fence.

Melanie Tetlock

"January Crystals"

Rising a'morn before the sun
To see it climb the rim,
Brilliant rays pass clouds of storm
Snow so deep, ice covered forms
Take shape before my eyes,
Orange and red flame up the sky;
Shapes, iridescent, crystal bright,
Frozen; I stood in shivering delight
Spectacular trees of feathered glass
Creaking and crackling, but "alas",
By heat of sun, rare beauty flits
Returning to the winters grips.

Elizabeth Pearl

A Leaf In The Wind

There was no time
To say hello,
Nor say goodbye.

The moment fled.
I'll never know
If you and I

Could fly aloft
And hand in hand
Melt into space.

The dream recedes,
Your steps, your voice,
All but your face.

Since that vision
Nothing, ever
Will be the same.

But now you're gone
And I forgot
to ask your name...

Paul Ember

Fiery Skies

How hard it is,
  to say goodbye,
Without a tear,
  without a cry.

Instead of tears,
  falling down like rain,
Look far beyond,
  far from the pain.

Draw tears from your eyes,
  and smile instead,
You've got the memories,
  deep inside your head.

You know you'll need him,
  till your love burns away,
But no matter what,
  the memory will always stay.

Corisa Chamberlain

Sweet Aura

O to bathe in your sweet aura
  To be drenched by your tears of joy.
  To be inside your masculine arms.
  To be a warm blanket wrapped around
Your swift beating heart.
  To have your hands caress my soul
  To have smothered by your love.
  To have you for eternity.
And to die in your loving arms.

Catherine A. Turjanica

Untitled

What a wonderful life
To live as a flower
One without soil, water;
But power.

To bask in the sunshine
In a delicate urn
Admired for beauty, fragrance;
Adjourn.

To wilt in the sunshine
Because no one could bear
The burden of soil, water;
Of care.

To die in the sunshine
On a ledge in a pose
Shrivelled by hunger; remembered
A rose.

Joanne Tofflemire

Cup Of Cheer

Crawled into my bottle now
To get out I don't know how
Take my mind, my pain, I weep
All the demons put to sleep

Said, "I'm lonely" some old fool
Tried to teach me life's new rules
But I'm stubborn, 'cause I'm young
That's the special song I've sung

So pity me, I have no time
But sit here and drink my wine
Waste my nights, wreck my life
Drown my sorrow and my strife

Ask me favors? I think not
Inside this bottle's all I've got
So come join me, my sweet dear
In my pitiful cup of cheer

Mark Rehman

Country Inn

This is a place where people go
To flee from city life,
The quiet here is filled with peace
Not fear that stalks the night.

Trees cascade the hills around,
The pond that tranquil rests.
'Tis constant fed by babbling stream
Gathers memories, now and past.

The keepers of this wondrous place,
Believed right from the start.
That butterflies and birds and clouds
Might fuel a tired heart.

This Inn defies the sudden changes
Of modern techno themes.
Allows the spirit to fly free,
Escape to future dreams.

Ann Kehoe

Time

Time: Master of our destiny,
Reaching a divine galaxy.
Happiness and splendor.
Silent: unknowingly.
Vanished forever.

Rose Carinci

Children Of God

Shells on a beach...
tiny, fragile, unique
all colours
different patterns
different shapes
infinite in their variety
yet part of the wholeness
called creation.
How could I begin to choose
the most beautiful?

People in a world....
tiny, fragile, unique
all colours
different patterns
different shapes
infinite in their variety
yet part of the wholeness
called creation.
How could God begin to choose
the most beautiful?

Arlene Kropp

Where?

Water from a spring gushes out
tinsel like fantasy
only to fade, like cowboy days
a firecracker's glory.

Why was I my father's decaying seed,
my mother's never child
a fleeting subtle shadow
and nothing more?

Richard G. Garwood

Insomnia

Tic toc, tic toc
Time keeps going
Hour after hour
It's the same time showing

12:00 o'clock tomorrow is
12:00 o'clock today
But today is tomorrow
And the time still slips away

The days are so long
They never seem to end.
Long straight and narrow
Without a bend

Night turns to day
And day turns to night
But when night turns to day
It doesn't mean it's light.

Try to sleep; Try to rest
It doesn't matter when
Because you can't close your eyes
And the day never ends.

Hope Gladue

My Girls

One has hair of honey brown,
The other eyes of deepest blue.
One has a kind and loving heart,
The other a laugh that touches you.

And sometimes when I'm feeling sad,
With sorrows more than I can bear,
Those eyes of blue, that honey hair,
They comfort me, my treasures rare.

Sylvia Poletto

Walking Home

I walk wearily
Through the drunken dusk
That has set the sky aflame
With my burning desires.

My way is long
And I must reach Home.

I must reach Home
Before it is dark.
I must reach Home
Before the flames are out.

Raghava S. Mani

Surrender Your Kingdoms

Golden beads of sweat form lace
Thoughts of surrender, put into place
Can you keep within my realm
Or would you watch from far off film
My mind is open
I'm wide for you
Lick my lips
I'd die for you

Feel my thoughts within my brain
Feel the blood course through my veins
Within your power you set me free
My head goes back, you hear me scream

Surrender to me
Thoughts brand-new
Open me up to all that you do
Broaden horizons of yellow and blue
Grant me the kingdoms of your world and you

Renee Patenaude

Gravity

She holds me down
This mystical energy
Embracing me in her strength

A wild spirit soars
To the sky
Circling the moon
Racing with the stars
Yet still she holds
Me down

Trapped under her skin
I lay under
The blackness
Of the midnight sky
My mind swims with
Her mystical energy

My goddess walks by
My side
Holding me down
Trapped by her skin

Thea Alix Pichurski

War

They live in hunger,
They live in fear.
Their troubles grow worse,
Their people disappear.
Their children cry,
For their heroes die.
In war,
In peace,
In your sweet sorrow.
Hoping to see light,
Hoping for a tomorrow.

Hagit Levy

Flower Flower

Flower flower how do you grow
This is one thing I do not know.

Straight and tall is how you will stand
Wide and vast you cover our land.

A seed in the ground is how you start
All grown up you capture my heart.

Your colours dance your petals sway,
Smelling your fragrance makes my day.

Your matchless beauty, endless grace
Always put a smile upon my face.

But flower flower how do you grow
This is still one thing I do not know.

Kurt J. Weggler

A Part Of My Soul

This is more than a hobby,
This is more than fun and games
Laughter, tears, part of my soul
Sometimes wild and sometimes tame.

It's not like stamp collection,
This is a part of my life.
Remove writing and words
And in my heart plunge a knife.

Don't plan on the great novel.
Don't plan on becoming rich.
Don't plan on quick and easy,
Due less to hits, and more miss.

I don't mean to be somber
For I'm glad of my power,
To express rage, and hatred,
And love, and hearts, and flowers.

This is more than a hobby,
This is more than fun and games,
On paper I leave my soul
Not needed is my name.

Jane Searles

The Story In My Eyes

If my eyes could tell you a story,
They wouldn't tell you,
What I've seen, or where I've been,
They would tell you a story,
Of what I've yet to do.

The shores I long to walk on,
Mountains I dream to climb,
The Ocean's I wish to explore,
And the Sun Sets,
I yearn to see,

So when you look in my eyes,
See in them, what I've yet to do,
Instead of what I've never done.

Tara-Lynn Bryar

Heaven's Door

They drink all day long,
They think nothing shall go wrong.
I tell them each day,
I hate watching them live this way.
Yet they go on with their drinking,
It confuses my thinking.
I wish they would quit,
Or even cut down a bit.
Their always in a fight.
I need to get away, so I just might.
I will miss them so.
I can't live this way anymore.
I feel like knocking on heaven's door.
I just want to get out.
I hate hearing them shout.
I couldn't live this way anymore.
I went knocking on heaven's door.

Laura-Lee McCarthy

Sarah's Garden

The trees are dark, majestic-tall
They rim the edges of the hill
The water in the pool lies still
And like a mirror reflects all.
The grass, still green, awaits the snow
Its winter blanket, cool and white
Will help it sleep both night and day.
To wake refreshed in spring I tro'
Upon the fence the vines hang on
Torn with the autumn's chilly blast
Some brown and withered leaves hang on
They too will go-their will near gone
Around the garden there's no cheer
No happy laughter fills the air
No longer plays young Sarah there
But she'll be back when spring is here.

Harry James Carlisle

Autumn Memories

When I see the trees in the forest.
They gather together so close.
Bringing back colorful memories,
Of days gone by.
I find myself wishing once again,
You were at my side.

A chestnut tree stands alone.
Our names still carved in the bark.
Never cut down or drawn upon,
Not even rain washed it away.

We laughed and rolled in autumn leaves,
Picked up nuts from the ground.
Dirt roads led us to believe
We were in love.
They look us so far.

The smell of wet autumn leaves,
The fires that burnt near by.
Each time this season comes,
My heart cries for you,
And for the memories.

Maureen Cushing Butler

"Memories"

Along darkened paths,
They clear my way.
And lead me back,
To yesterday.

They've made me happy,
They've made me sad.
They remind me of,
Times I once had.

I see my youth,
And days long past,
It is amazing how long,
These memories can last.

It's not up in my head,
Where these thoughts stay.
It is the depths of my heart,
Where forever they shall lay.

Angela Lynn Abraham

A Birthday Poem 22-01-92

Where have all the years gone to?
They brought changes in me and you!
Your hair is gone - your sight is nil
But don't despair, I love you still!

You drive me crazy, every chance
You lead me in a merry dance
I am living in the eye of a hurricane
But you will always be my man!

How did all those pounds appear?
We never saw them coming near!
You have some extra hills and dells
But you will always ring my bells!

Our life goes up, our life goes down
We often smile, we sometimes frown!
Who knows the future what's yet to come
But you'll always be my #1 !!

Erika Solivo

White Rolling Foam

White rolling foam with a vengeance
These waves crash onto the shore
And behind each wave is an eddy
To twist and turn those caught there

High pointed waves with white caps
Cause an undertow, down below
So don't get caught in the curl
Or down to the bottom you'll go

The waves just keep piling higher
As the wind increases their speed
Where they rise to laugh at the sky
As a challenge to all passers by

It's great to watch the white caps
But treat these waves with care
Because they want to pull you down
If your playing and not aware

It's white rolling foam with a vengeance
And it changes the shape of the shore
Because once the storm has ended
Nothing will be the same as before

Don Simpson

You

There is only you
There was always only you
There will always be only you.

Your presence filled my mind
Your beauty blinded me to all else
Your passion flooded my senses
And left me breathless.
You are my heart, my soul,
My very life.
So much a part of me
That I cannot exist without you.

There is only you
There was always only you
There will always be only you.

Linden Jordan

Little Deeds

There are the little drops of water;
There are the little grains of sand;
There are the little birds and flowers,
Helping make our beauteous land.

Let's not forget the little deeds -
Those little acts so kind and true,
That help each other on life's path
And bring the sunshine through.

A kindly word and a laugh to be shared;
The clasp of a friendly hand —
Are little things along the way
To be cherished ever in our land.

Little deeds are hidden blessings
With no great burst of show,
But edging in to bring their cheer
Like little seeds to sow and grow.

Evelyne Day

If I Never Knew You

If I never knew you,
Then what would have been?
Would I still be me?
Would you still be you?

If I never knew you,
We would never have to part,
I would never be hurt,
You would never break my heart.

If I never knew you,
How could I have seen,
Just how strange but special,
One night could have ever been?

If I never knew you,
I would never see,
That something I was missing,
That you gave to me.

I will always miss you,
When we have to part,
But you always will,
Be in my heart.

Lindsay McGillivray

The Whiskin Wind

I'm sitting on a solid rock
The wind goes whiskin by
And the clouds are like a jet plane
A'roarin cross the sky.

The ocean spray is picked up high
When a gust of wind blows at it
Against the rocky undercliff
And down to the beach below it.

All day the wind is blowin
And into the murky night
With natures mighty energy
The trees they shake with fright.

But peace is in the offing
And soon the birds will sing
Today it's old man winter
Tomorrow it is spring.

Alan G. Saunders

L'enfant

"Be ye not weary of well-doing"
   The wayside pulpit said,
And the words resounded deeply
   In the labyrinth of my head.
Then I heard a little whisper,
   "I'm not so sure about that,"
And as she slipped her hand in mine,
   Her words pierced at my heart.
This child had more wisdom than
   All the grown-ups knew,
And the tear that would have fallen,
   Hung like morning dew.

Jessica Dingwall-Boak

My First Love

Deep and blue
The water churns
Smashing with ferocity
Against the rocks
Whirlpools of nothing
Empty and swirling

You and I are like the ocean
Never ceasing
Never silent
Storms brew within us
Washing away debris
Cleansing our souls
Rejuvenating our minds

Lashing out in anger and pain
The fight of the waves
Becomes us

Soon the fight is over
The water smiles
And falls quiet

Keri Sauer

Spring Once More

The snow melts.
The earth uncovered shivers gently.
The air is still - waiting the
   birth of spring.
Hush! The earth softly sings for
   those who hear...
Faithful birds sing -
   joyfully accepting that
   spring is near.

Annie Lyon

Morning's Gentle Touch

The morning sun shone on me
The warmth surrounded my chest,
It longed to soothe the pain I felt
From death's ensnarement.

The chilly vipers of its grasp
Had held me far too long,
But now the gentle warmth of love
Brought wonders to my eyes.

God's nearness surrounded me
As I fought to lose the pain,
The leaves, the plants, the sunshine
Reminded me that all was in His plan.

Darlene Erho

Failed Attempt At Rapture

The smell of stretching grass,
The taste of settled dust,
The entrancing season of life.

Children run by me laughing,
The sticky fingers of summer.
Popsicle sticks blow on the street.

The sound of the fingered sax,
The intent of a lost musician.
Coins tossed in disarray.

Dogs sweat with broken smiles,
Branches spit their youth with
The patience of the tide.

A slight breeze tickles my lash
As the sky opens and yawns.
The peacefulness is unbearable.

I wish they could see me.
I do believe they could love me.
Empty words. The blindness is forever.

Sarah J. Fodey

Loneliness

The silence kills,
The stillness chills,
Enduring, quiet pain.
I cry for noise!
This thing destroys!
I call out loud in vain.

An empty room,
The silence wounds,
It hammers in my ears.
I look around,
Hope for a sound,
Confirming all my fears.

I am alone,
My longing known
To me, myself and I.
No use to scream,
I'm in a dream,
Where loneliness abides.

Christine Dueck

My Cat

Calico cat came
Purring, to sit on my lap.
Cadging cat cuddles.

Jeannene Hadikin

Sky Blue

Have you ever noticed the color of
the sky my friend?
It is blue
But not just any blue
A blue that can make you happy or sad
It could make your day or
ruin your night
And, it could even make a difference
in a bet you had with a friend
Depending on whether the Leafs
won that night
The blue of the Leafs my friend
The blue of the Leafs

Yuri Hatanaka

Inside

The moon is high
The sky dull
No one lives here
No one at all.

Everything is empty
So very sad
Nothing cheery
Nothing glad.

Endlessly seeking an unsung hero
To set free
The multitude of love
Inside......me

Lori Multon

Untitled

The darkness hides the tears
The silence drowns the cries
Too much pain and lonely years
Remains hidden in darkened eyes.
Looking down without a sign
Of a broken heart so full of pain
Endless tears that turn her blind
Are only heard by gentle rain.
Now a stranger to this life
She tries to lock the past away
It's cutting deeper than a knife
The ugly scar that always stays.
Things are lost and left behind
Never will we see
The emptiness in soul and mind
It's how it had to be.
Quiet, cold, and lonely nights
No-one knows the hurt she feels
Kept away from any rights
And love that cold and darkness steals.

Shawna Miller

Dear Grandma

As time withers on.
The body ages,
But as time withers on,
The soul is enriched,
So on your birthday,
Don't measure the age
of your body,
Celebrate the eternal
youth of your soul.

Greg Paulsen

The Ocean

The sparkle of the ocean
the seaweed and the tide
the waves - pounding crescendos
the spray, the salt, alive -

With crabs, shells and starfish
treasures waiting to be found
and children eagerly searching
so pails and shovels abound.

The tide is out! - we quickly run
barefoot across the sand
through puddles, mush and gushy stuff
far out as we possibly can.

The evening calm comes in with the tide
the ocean vast and still
lovers walk hand in hand
captivated by its spell.

The sun ablaze with reddened haze
sinks slowly from our view
a beautiful end to a glorious day
with love, from God, to you!

Judie Suda

Slowly Fade Away

Slowly fade away
the price to pay you cannot stay
a moment this day

You thought you has beauty
you thought you could last
in the end came the duty
and it came too fast

In the form of the sun and the form
of the rain they used to be fun
but now they cause pain

Remember your past
you must not forget
you had gone in a blast
you lived all wet

It's over now so leave in grace
slowly bow cause you've lost face

You should've known you should've prepared
even though you were shown you proudly dared

You didn't believe and so you fell
you'll never receive the glory in hell.

Linda Prescott

Reminisce

The other day I walked by,
The place where we first danced,
And suddenly I found myself,
In a long abiding trance.
Then I went to the spot,
Where you and I first kissed,
It's then I realized,
I was beginning to reminisce.
I remember all the things you said,
And the touch of your hand,
I remember how cute you looked,
When you thought you were in command.
I think of you all the time,
And all the things I miss,
Once in awhile I come back to this spot,
Just to sit and reminisce.

Dianne Smith

Galaxies Beyond

Beyond the Solar System
the one that we know,
The gravity changes
from high to low.

Stars, moons, and planets,
far, far away,
Some burning, some freezing
or like a mid summer's day.

Dark, black holes,
which no one has seen,
or maybe some creatures
ferocious and mean.

Asteroids and comets
flying through space,
Whizzing right past
at a very fast pace.

So when you think
of the planet you're on,
Think of those galaxies
the galaxies beyond.

Christine Eagleson

Forever

To you, whom I give the key.
The one that unlocks my heart
Releasing my soul.
I bring it forth for you.

Forever more we shall be one
Our love to rise above all else.
Like a bird in the sky
Our hearts will soar.

So now I am giving it to you,
The key that unlocks forever.

Katherine Amundson

In Memory

I will paint my face pretty
the morning of early June,
as flowers do when they wake
from mid-winter gloom.

I will dawn at noon
the morning of early June,
as sparrows tend to do
and sing a song for two.

I will dress in beads of rice
the morning of early June,
as maidens do when they grant
the red rose its dew.

I will cry till late
the morning of early June,
the afternoon or evening perhaps
as some trees tend to do...

And I will reach at night the moon,
and in the morning of early June
I will have the angels sleep
my aching heart in tune.

Elisa Ibarrola

Untitled

I hear the wind
The leaves talk of it
They tell their stories
Of times long ago
And those to come
They speak of the truth
To those who listen
Alas, no one listens
Few venture into the garden
They have forgotten
How to get there
They have long ago forgotten
How to listen
Perhaps the song of the chimes
Will help them to remember
How to listen
To hear the stories
And know their truth

Victoria Hartleib

Sacrifices Or Reality?!

The thoughts of a madman,
The laughter of a child,
The breaking point of sanity,
The danger of problems piled.

The shatter of all happiness,
The remnants of a knowing grin,
To be the one who always loses,
To forgive you is a sin.

The pain I feel inside,
Like my soul was ripped apart,
Drowning in confusion,
Feeling the coldness of your heart.

I am alone inside myself,
Not able to stop the mistakes,
I watch my life like a film,
With no rewind and no next takes.

The tears that racked my body,
Have left me feeling drained,
The reality of contempt,
The bitterness of rage.

Jamie-Lynn Bennett

The Empty Seat

The deep color of the red wine.
The fragrant aroma of the gallant meal.
The flicker of the lighted candle.
The empty coldness of your seat.

The shining of the silver goblet.
The last ring of the dinner bell.
The meal is served,
To the empty coldness of your seat.

The silk napkin laid across my lap.
The china plates shine brightly.
I look down the long dinner table,
To the empty coldness of your seat.

The wine and aroma are gone.
The silver and china no longer shine.
Though one thing still lingers on,
The empty coldness of your seat.

Tanya Pomaranski

The Get Away

In this lonely place
The distant post of
Sorrow one's feels.

Without a single light
Among the clouds
Confused and toiled.

It is now morning,
But cannot get away
Words are useless this day.

'Til the moon and stars
Come and led the way
- - to the dance floor..

Minh Ha

A Peddlar's Heart

Oh, twilight eve dispel,
The darkest depth of night,
Cast shadows on his mask,
Mock, his foolish plight.

No fear upon thy palette,
Cascading jewels of light,
Their brilliant hues shall vanquish,
Pierce thy ebon night.

His icy chasm yearns,
To suffocate, this wretched vagabond,
To claim his empty soul,
The peddlar's dream is gone.

He travels down, the misty path,
Obscure his quest, now dim,
He awaits, the gnarled hand to snare,
His heart be lost on talon wing.

Succumb to death, his heart descends,
Down, that murky sea below,
Yet, if he bore the sword of hope,
The rays of truth he'd know.

Cynthia Padecky Dingwell

The Child And The Man

A child is inside a man's body...
The child is trying to escape himself.
And the man is trying to set him free,
The child wants to educate himself.
So he will be a child no more,
And the man wants to help this child.
So he can be rid of the child.
To be just a man and that's all.

But the child never stops learning.
'Cause the man has so much to give.
So the man will never be just a man,
'Cause the child will always be there.

The child may become frustrated.
For he knows he can never leave,
And the man may become the same,
For his goal is never achieved.

But if the man and the child could accept one
     another,
And learn to live and let be.
Then both of their tasks can be finished.
For accepting is how you're set free.

Norine Hong

My Pursuit

I remember the night of the accident,
the cars, the crash, the sirens.
The blood on the pavement,
bodies all around.

I remember the smell of the hospital,
the needles, the doctors, the nurses.
The blood on the floor,
bodies all around.

I remember your funeral,
the people, the tears, the flowers.
The blood is all gone,
bodies all around.

I remember the night that I died,
the sadness, the cliff, the drop.
The blood in the car
my body all around.

I remember the day we met again,
the tunnel, the light, the clouds.
The blood is on the earth,
angels all around.

Paula Train

The Rose Garden

A luxurious house stands
the backyard precisely landscaped
in the middle, a rose garden
beautiful, elegant, and tender
petals carefully molded
leaves shaped in perfection
admired and loved by all
caressed with gentle hands.
In the center grows a weed
lonely, isolated, and desperate
struggling for survival
leaves sparse and ragged
despised and rejected by all
its efforts destroyed in a moment
by the cruel hand of one gardener.

Alanna Manchak

Untitled

Mom loved God's beautiful flowers
That's where she spent hours and hours
We remember a hill so sandy and bare
We remember Mom saying
We'll plant flowers there
She spaded and planted
The work was so hard
The results were there
In her beautiful yard
The evenings were scented
With flowers so rare
She smiled on the hours
That she had spent there
Her mind was at peace
In her garden of love
May God grant her peace
In his garden above.

Linda Watt

Untitled

People
Often feel
Weak and alone
Except when they
Rise together

Tanya Alicia Schwartz

"My Mom"

There's a very special woman
  that's oh, so dear to me,
And I am very proud to say
  I'm part of her family.

When I was young, she'd comfort me
  and wipe my tearful eyes,
Through heartache, pain and sorrow
  she'd clear my cloudy skies.

She gave me, many happy times
  throughout my growing years,
And even though I'm older now
  her love, do I hold dear.

Her tender touch, her smiling face
  there'll never be another,
For who could ever take the place
  of such a special mother

Mom, I know the words aren't said
  as often as they may,
But mom, I really love you
  in my heart, you'll always stay.

Bonnie Bellemore

Someone Said

Someone said that someone said
That your love was untrue
That they saw you with another
Holding hands out in plain view.

Someone said that someone said
That she was tall and lean
That she was oh so beautiful
Like you said I should have been.

Someone said that someone said
That you would find a way
To break it to me gently
That your love had gone astray.

What someone said that someone said
Has broken my heart in two
How will I continue to go on
If what someone said is true.

Wanda G. Maitland

Loneliness

Among the many appetites
That subject the nature of man.
There's one that gnaws at us the most
That we fail to understand.

It's ever present in disguise
Of silence, work and pleasure,
With no respect for age or post
And often the subject of leisure.

This constant craving appetite
Is so often entertained
We never seek its company,
But to avoid it is in vain.

It plays the main on those alone
And those whom grief has stricken
It cowardly attacks the young
And those whom ill has smitten.

There is no cure in medicine
To prevent such helplessness,
But Someone made a human drug
Called "Friends-to-Loneliness."

Rosemary Hayes

Today

I'm through with the strife
That comes with this life.
I'm "looking ahead" no more.
  I live for today
  Nor wish it away
Neither linger in days of yore.

I take today's joys
Not pine for the toys
That eased my heart yesterday.
  I haven't in mind
  What tomorrow I'll find
I live for today, just today.

And as I endeavor
To live in true measure
This life friends would have me live.
  I find in my soul
  As the days onward roll,
The joy life can really give.

E. Lyla Bradley

For The Sake Of Dignity

Forbidden pleasures
sweltering
in the back of my mind.
Intriguingly intense
images
of a strong arousal.
Creating tingles
of excitement,
increasingly present.
Pushing vibrantly
towards consummation
of an affair.
Stolen affections
without satisfaction.
Pure lust
with a bitter aftertaste.

Roswita J. Briffa

Life Lessons

Life lessons:
Sweet dreams,
Hard work,
Soft kisses,
Warm hugs,
Meaningful deeds,
Gut hunches/feelings,
Heartfelt embraces,
Children's laughter,
Parents hopes,
Family values, integrity,
Challenges, acceptance,
Bittersweet moments,
Despair, hope,
Disappointment, joy,
Anger, comfort,
Release, peace,
Torment, bliss,
Birth, death,
Strength... life lessons!

Hilda C. S. Smith

My Love For You

I remember the day we first met.
Such joy I felt when I saw you there.
The loneliness I felt, disappeared,
And for you alone, I began to care.

I remember our very first date.
A long walk under the stars above.
Holding hands, talking 'til late,
And this was the day, I fell in love.

The day we wed, so special to me.
The vows we made, so serious,
So deeply ingrained in my memory,
And the future, looked so mysterious.

Remember the day we first saw her.
Those rosy cheeks and deep blue eyes,
Our baby's little fingers and tiny toes,
Together we began the rest of our lives.

Tell me your plans, your joys, your sorrows
And all of the dreams you have for tomorrow
For I love you more each passing day
More than a poem could ever say.

Sonia Knippshild

Lonely Spirit

Lonely spirit, bereft of pain,
Striving back to body gain.
Bewildered, hopeless, wondering scared,
How the rest of body fared.

Aimless drifting, far and wide,
Searching for a place to hide.
The shock of leaving body, still,
Remembered with an endless chill.

Now, other spirits gather near,
They too, have that look of fear.
Is this the gathering of the few,
Seeking life to embrace anew.

Or is life form now, a thing of past,
And we, destined to life of fast.

Kenneth Russell

For Sale-By Owner

Rusted out mower
stands still; defeated
in an untamed jungle

Paint peeling flaking
tired, old shingles
hail-battered siding

Exhausted foundation
lists to the lee
straining its moorings

Lying in wait
for the end of the world
relief from cohesion

Paul Trottier

Ballerinas

Ballerina gracefully dancing,
like leaves going down a river.
Ballerinas jumping,
like Kangaroos prancing.
Ballerinas moving and swaying,
like trees in the wind.
Ballerinas doing the splits,
like two branches breaking.

Jackie Baran

Love

Love is like a diamond
Sparkling, shining, glowing,
It shines on the outside
And glows from within.
Without love there is no pride,
With hate there is sin.
If you have known love
Keep it in your heart, for when
Love dies, it crumbles like
A leaf in the Autumn Wind.

Joan McCormick

Untitled

My star lights up the velvet night
spangled eye, glittered white.
In your depths I've wallowed deep
your serene sublime soothes me in sleep.
How I search amidst the ashy dusk
caressed by its balmy, softened musk.
Your arms enfold me in my fear
in solitude, your presence near.
And, through this life I'll amble on
finding love in the hope you shone.

Yvonne Ballard

Sometimes

I feel the need to die;
Sometimes.
The pain I feel the tears I cry;
Are they worth it?
Most times.

Joy flashes like lightning;
At times.
Love is life and children laughing
Beyond question;
Sometimes.

Silky strings, life's fragile web,
Other times,
Tangles or breaks and hope ebbs.
I do doubt it.
At times.

I feel the weight of life
Most times.
But the lightness after the grief,
Is a blessing;
Sometimes.

Suzanne Swan

Escape

Everybody creates their own escape.
Some by working, some by sleeping,
some by loving and some by exploring.

Others may use humour by laughing away
the pain and tears of life.

Others may dream of what
the future may bring,
and all the memorable events
the past has given.

But some will never find their escape
for they are trapped
within the realms of reality
with not other place to go.

These few will eventually escape
by walking out the doors of the living,
just to enter the world of the dead.

Janine Groot

Untitled

Despair, hurt, deceit
so much pain and anger
forever present and unrelenting
Emotions are churning and burning
twirling around and around
like a hurricane bent on destruction

Will it ever stop
Will it ever leave me be
Or shall it always be here
To torture me.

Cassandra Mellersh

The Flower

A flower growing in a garden,
So full of life, and a part of life.
The sun shines, and the rain falls,
The flower blossoms.
A girl, living and learning,
So full of curiosity,
Experiencing life's pleasures.
She meets a boy,
He need her, teaches her, and
Soon he loves her.
She blossoms, then
The sky becomes cloudy, and
The rain becomes snow,
The flower wilts, and
A heart is broken.

Evelyn McCaffrey

Blue On Blue

The water spreads out blue on blue
so deep, so still, it beckons you,
to slow your thoughts,
and drop your cares,
and lay your self down
someplace where
soldier trees stands guard o'er you
where peace and God are blue on blue

Shirley Atkins

Summer Snows

What might melt - warm these summer
snows what blight darkens the
immortal soul, how long the eclipse
it is difficult to know through
these relentless snows.

O' what might these winds to this
spirit have known, a tapestry
rich and in full detail worm,
void of color of presence there,
unrevealing before all spirits cares.

Wretched is the spirit which mourns the
rivers flow, fading impressions in
the drifting snows eternity
stripped of her frills and blows,
and these relentless snows

What might melt - warm these summer
snows what fitful scheme on a
the Gods do know, with colder
winds than heat hell knows,
and these relentless snows.

James Boag

Evening By The Shore

The sun slips
smoothly behind
mystic melon light
that glows - hovers
on the tree line -
then reaches
for the night's
blue velvet cover.

Paddles
gently dipped
drip on the silence.

A crescent moon
free falls
between day
and night.

A loon's haunting wail
strokes the weary lake
and in its wake
a dragon fly flits by

And wings a poem on its way.

Frances Thompson

For Eyes That Might See

Beautiful and bright hued man apes
slowly and deliberately dismantled
the planet of their birth
in homage to the God of sands.

How may the weaving of inks
on wood skins
ever challenge the course
of electronic Babylon?

The ironic fortune
of corrupted dominance
is ultimately a failure
to regenerate as a species
once this perfect Eden
has been destroyed.

Only guardians of life
may pass to the stars.

Gary Supp

The Little Bird

Up upon a window sill,
Sits a little bird,
Singing softly in the wind,
With not a feather stirred.

Sing, sweet little bird, sing,
For your song is so sweet,
Can you see the other birds,
Singing in the street?

"Come join us," they sing,
"In our merry tune."
"You don't have to be alone,
Come join us, make it soon!"

Look up on the window sill,
The little bird is gone,
It has left to join the others,
To join them in their song!

Lana Marie Roberts

Ships In The Sea

The ships in the sea
Sit still for the night
Letting the fog be their blanket.

Singing a song of friends
Come and gone
And moaning out their sorrows.

I listen to their monotone chorus
And long for a chance to sit and sing
With the ships in the sea
While the fog makes me a blanket.

Jessica Anderson

Geraldean

The flower of love is but a
   single rose.
Unequal to none as everyone knows
Its satin petals, its fragrance
   supreme.
Brings to the heart, a heavenly dream.

But, if this flower was allowed
   to bloom, and brought to you in
   this very room.

It would whither of shame.
As it couldn't compete with
   the beauty of you;
Or the sound of your name.

James E. Cossette

The Shiniest Star

Grandma, Grandma where could you be,
since you left I'm very lonely
Up above. So far away
I lay awake and start to pray
Grandma, Grandma what can I do
I lay here for hours thinking of you.

When I try to sleep at night
Through my window the Brightest light.
Grandma, Grandma when you were young
me and you had so much fun.
Laying beneath the quilt you made
feeling safe and unafraid.
Grandma, Grandma you will always
be the biggest and shiniest star I see.
With you up there so far above
you shine on me with all your love
Grandma, Grandma I miss you so
When I was young I did not know
That you would ever go so far
And turn into the shiniest star.

Cindy Lewis

Wallpaper-Induced

I entered
shut the door
undressed and sat.
In seconds
my eyes examined the wall
the design, so smooth
the imagery, so real
my mind connected.
Nine minutes later
three knocks on the door
stopped my slumber.
I left
flushing nothing.

Lekan Sola Odutayo

My Friend

You my very special friend
Should know
That you bring me joy
And laughter
You add rainbows
To my day
You give me calm
When storms threaten to
Carry me away
And if you play me
A sad slow melody
I will cry
You have taught me that it is O.K.
To cry after all
Tears shed the sadness
Surrounding our soul
Thank you for being
My special friend

Connie Marie Madge

Jesus

He's just another poor boy,
shifting with the burden of youth.
Burning in the fires of hell;
grappling for the warmth of truth.

His clothes are stained and torn,
carrying wood in both hands.
He's to be our salvation;
our guide to the promised land.

We crucified His mind and body,
forbade Him to live.
He gazed down from the cross
and asked the Father to forgive.

At the right hand of His father,
Jesus sits and scans the earth
for people full of love and forgiveness;
people who have self-worth.

May the Lord be kind to His people
and the people love their Lord.
For each depends on the other,
as we approach the end of the world.

Catherine E. Obacz

Reaching The Stars

A little girl beginning school
She knows not what to say or do,
So many friends this young child makes
She learns to give as well as take.

Do the best that you can
Her mother would say,
Leave the rest to the Lord
He'll show you the way.

The days, the years, they slipped away
Oh how she studied
And how she prayed.

She goes off to college
She follows her dream,
A new door has opened
A new life begins.

Her prayers are all answered
Friends come to her aid,
They have heard of her longings
They share in her love,
Of becoming a teacher... a servant of God.

Rita Flinkert

Did Not Wake

I held her cold hand,
She did not wake.
I whispered sweet endearments,
But she did not wake.
I stared at her pale face,
Sweet as an angel,
But still she did not wake.
My tears fell upon her cheek,
But she did not wake.
I knew she was gone,
But I did not believe,
Such a sweet soul,
Could be taken.

Christine Matheson

Late Bloomer

As a glorious daisy
shades of gold to crimson
spiral within my soul.
Cool caressing breath
soothes my scorched
and blistered heart.
As others concede and wither
radiantly I burst
into the autumn of my days.

Rhonda Gayle

The Challenger

Listen! Hark! I hear a sound
Seven voices leaving ground
The "Challenger" is on its way
The experiment is on today!

They left the earth on record time
Friends and loved ones left behind
The laughing cheering crowd below
Waving as they heaven ward go.

They were chosen for the crew
Everyone their part to do
Everyone was shocked - dismayed
To see the twisting it displayed.

It twisted, turned, and burst in flames
The pieces dropped to earth again
People cried, no one could help
Only sadness could be felt.

The emptiness, space shuttle gone
Wonder what did go wrong
Goodbye earth, goodbye friends
Hello God - We meet again!

Mary I. Field Goodman

Change

Less than this I smile
On your face moves shadow
Onto eyes silhouetting grey waves.

Memory decides to forget
Haunting weather instead...
Bass sounds lying on fog.

Turn around, twirl, choose
Not night, but luminous blues
Offering.

Sylvia Parent

If I Could

No
say it isn't so
I cannot bear the pain
I cannot stand
I cannot take
I wish I could
I cannot stand the thought
of any harm to you
I cannot take the hurt
the bad, the dreams, the shame
I cannot bear the burden
placed upon your back
I wish I could
I'd take the load
if I could know for whom it was
I weep
I weep not in shame
I weep in sorrow
for your pain

Diane Brazeau

In The Still Quiet Of The Morning

In the still quiet of the morning
   say a silent prayer
For God is listening
   He is everywhere
Pray for strength to
   meet the day
For guidance from above
Pray for the sick and
   the suffering
For God is Love
And in His own
   mysterious way
He works His miracles
   every day.

Gladys E. Weaver

Blackness

Did you ever watch a teardrop
roll down a face?
So fast, so furious
having fought so hard to be free.

Have you ever seen a young girl
stand all alone?
So small, so silent
She fights so hard to be free.

Did you ever feel pain so great
you become numb with it?
The Girl, the Tear, the Pain
She wants that numbness
Anything to make the pain go away.
Anything.
She plots in that silence.
And she prays.
Desperately.
Hopelessly.
Do not ask what she prays for.

Marlo Dianne Foss

"To All Who Write"

Write until the light welcomes,
Right through the writer's syndromes.
Pen or pencil in your hand
Chart a course across the land.
Long and weary you must be,
Cramped, and brain in agony.
Perhaps, your body writhed with pains
As each stroke inscribed remains.
Endure the toil till the night
When your soul bespeaks the light;
And, once again, the shadows
Dare, and dauntless be the throes
Which threatens. For fight you must.
Mighty men of valour thrust,
Either with pen or sword in hand,
Frontiers of the mind or land.
So it is from age to age.
So it is on history's page.

Lloyd R. Maloney III

Three Chimneys

Today I went to Grandma's place,
remembered all these years
Where she and Grandpa toiled so hard,
as earnest pioneers.

Their little home, abandoned,
was razed by summer fires.
The blackened chimneys, all that stood
as witness to their lives.

I walked among the chimneys,
searching for a trace,
Of all the things I knew and loved,
about this special place.

Then suddenly, I saw a drift
of Belladonna lilies,
in pink profusion growing there,
nodding in the breeze.

This was Grandma's legacy,
her gift that would not die,
I picked a bunch of lilies,
and said a soft, 'Good-bye.'

Dorothy Vize-Smith

Friends Meet On The Train

Dear Friend,
Remember the poem you wrote for me
While riding on the train,
Well, dear young man
Your words were not in vain.
The words you left me with
I have kept for many a day
It crossed my mind to reply,
Because before too long time will fly.
Your friendly face and company
Were just what I needed,
They filled the time and miles
As the train chugged along awhile.
May your future be filled with friends
And your journey through life easy.
For you have a knack of giving of yourself
When you meet someone you never knew before.
Riding on the train.

Shirley V. E. Butner

Summer Evening

The first stars are out.

Deep blue from above
pushes the
sunset off the earth.

Mother appear
in doorways
anxiously
looking for their
children.

A boy on a
bicycle
noiselessly
changing gears
whizzing by
hoping no one
is watching
his race against
curfew.

Sandra May Doerksen

Untitled

Hope:
    Precious moons
        that light the sky.
    Till morning suns
        do kiss our eye.

Hope:
    Gentle rains
        that drizzle slow
    till clearing skies
        caress our quo.

Hope:
    Babies cry
        that whimpers free
    till mother makes.
        upon their plea.

Hope:
    Envy all
        that trying wills
    Till flanders field.
        impairs our skills.

Dave L. Wright

The Humming Bird

I am hummingbird.
Playing in the flowers
Wings humming happily
Wait, what's that?
I spot an eagle
He is soaring over me
I dash into the flowers
The eagle fly's away
I am safe now
I started to play again
I am happy
When the sun set
I said good bye
Good bye to flowers
I went to bed
In the dark,
All alone,
Till the light of another day.

Kaitlyn O'Neill

The Disco Girls

Stroboscopes slice the time;
parameters go quiet berserk
- the feline, half-naked girls
staccato hang or staccato jerk,
leaning on the deathly white,
hacking blades of light.

We have the weaning
of the first-year first-born
in tight pants and bare navels
swinging around to the music
their knees swaying from side to side
to give their protruding buttocks
a sexy waggle.

Oh ye demons which lie
locked in every wench;
do pray for their souls
- these girl-women; not to be
without the communication,
social contact and etiquette
their parents lost before them.

Paul C. Sandison

Worthy Of Salt

Single pinches sting and offend
Palmfuls preserve the oppressed
Friends are bonded together by this
But if it loses its potency
It has become useless.

Salt runs through the veins
Of all we creatures
Gulp the sea
Taste the saltiness of the scattered
The bitter, confused, found.

Salt from the earth
Make up the finest beings
God culled from cherished soil.
Penetrate, cure and clean
They spill over all lands to redeem.

Brackish and determined
Unwavering grains flavor all the earth
They are witness to the effects of its wonders
And worthless salt
They are not.

Debra V. Rodgers

Her Once Delicate Soul

I see her delicate features
Painted on with the utmost care,
I'm almost appalled by her beauty
Which beckons from behind
The glass doors,
Her dress is of soft velvet
Trimmed with beautiful lace,
Her bonnet doesn't quite cover
The blonde ringlets which
Frame her face.
She is the most enchanting one
I have ever seen.
I can't resist so I open the doors
But alas,
Disaster struck,
And I look all around me in dismay.
For her once beautiful soul
Lay shattered all around me.

Nancy Joyce Garbish

Goodbye

When you're sad
Or when you're mad
Come talk to me
And then you'll see

I'll calm you down
Remove that frown
Use my heart
For not to part

Keep this with you
While I am away
Reminding you I'm thinking
of you every single day.

Although I miss you so much
With your soft loving touch
I know when I return.
For you my heart will yearn.

I long to be with you
Every single day
Every time I see you
Don't go, don't go I pray.

Candice Darlington

Kicking Stones

Standing here, kicking stones.
One of the lost with
no way up, no way down.
Heaven and hell denied.
Waiting for tomorrow
to come and pass me by.
Both love and hate denied.
No one ever loved me
as much as I loved them.
It could have made me cry.
I wish that no one had
left me alone,
surrounded by broken crosses
and broken bones.
Shorn of wing and heart
and thrust from home.
A loss of everything.
Which leaves me
standing here, kicking stones.

Mark Killam

Walk With Me

Walk with me...
    On this path called life
    For together we can find our way
    And hand in hand
    We shall overcome any obstacle...

Walk with me...
    To the rivers edge
    Through the towering trees
    To where the birds sing
    And the sun never fades...

Walk with me...
    Up the rolling hills
    To where the grass is green
    And everything is quiet
    Where time stands still...

Walk with me...
    Until you can no longer
    And there where you stop
    To rest your weary self
    So shall I, and there we'll remain
    Together...

Nancy Kruk

The Picture Frame

Hanging there
On the wall in a
Picture frame so small.
He in uniform so blue-
Standing tall, erect, and true.
Also beside him his lovely queen.
She in yellow lace with green.
Ne'er in all the world had she
Seen as brave a man as he.
And yes, they married were
To be, and live near
Glensdale by the
Rolling sea.

Yvonne Steffler

Impressions

The soft light shines
On the green grass.
A small bird dines
On a large bass.

Light shines down and wakes
Flowers on the bush.
Clouds pass over, takes
Light back in a rush.

Down the rain comes, falling
Patters over treetops.
Gentle music calling
Rumbles over hilltops.

Now the clouds are moving on,
Bringing rain to other shores.
But the day has come and gone,
The sunlight has shut its doors.

Gentle light of rose at sunset
Sends the bird back to his bed.
And although he knows it not yet,
The whole sky is blazing red.

Elwing

Creation

Yesterday I lay my hand
On some snow stuck to a rock,
And through the heat of my hand
I created water.

Today the water is gone
And it is I who lie
On the great white rock
Waiting for the sun's warmth
To penetrate me
And let my mind float
With the clouds above.

Len Phillips

Moisture

A Drop
  of water,

  Fell
    upon a leaf.

    Tingled
      down its spine,

      And sank
        into the soil.

Sandra M. Sherren

A Fireflies Plight

I sat in the back
on a hot summers night,
when my eyes discovered
an old familiar sight,
the dance of a firefly
enjoying the night.

My memories of youth
when I was so young,
at night I would see
by the thousands
the fire fly's flight.

Indifferent then was I
on a hot summers night,
now I take notice
for the past seven nights,
one lonely
fire fly's flight.

Dennis L. Hallé

Unicorn Song

I am a figment
of your imagination
I am an Image of your soul

I steal through your thoughts
and beat
against your heart.

I am your wellspring
I am the wind
Whispering in your ear.

You'll never hold
my immaterial spirit.

For I'll slip through
your fingers,
like a siren's song

And echo
in your
Deepest Desire

For I am a figment of your imagination
I am an image of your soul.

Rhoda Yakichuk

Broken Dreams

Countless V's
of snowhite beauty
stretch across the autumn sky -
plaintive cries
of farewell to the North
pierce early morning silence -
wings grown strong in summer sun
eat up the miles -
eager to escape the coming winter -
steady southbound - never wavering -
stopping just for food and rest.

In the grain field
death is waiting,
well disguised in harmless stature -
and a sudden burst of fire
shatters dreams of warmth and sun.

Joyce Slobogian

The Sound Of Silence

The silent calls
of lonely souls
The price of war
that takes its toll.

Eternal cries
of hungry ones
Now laid to rest
by silent guns.

Sounding echoes
of children's cries
Through walls of tears
that blind their eyes.

Tranquil passing
hands of time
Knows no limits
for one to climb.

A peaceful sleep
where angels soar
Abiding love
and death no more.

Brandon Maharaj

A Silent Toast

At Christmas time I start to think,
Of friends that once I knew.
A silent toast I always drink,
To friends who are so few.
Though years may come;
And time rolls by.
The memories live forever.
If. In your heart,
You ne'er regret,
The laughs you had together,
So...Drink a silent toast with me.
'Twas fate brought us together,
And though we journey far apart.
The memories, the Memories live forever.

Jack Western

"Baby Daughter"

Today I became a father
of a lovely baby daughter
she has the bluest blue eyes
her hair is just like gold
her cheeks are soft and chubby
her hands are white as snow
she is my little darling
and how I love her so
today I became a father
of this lovely baby daughter.

Robert E. Allarie

Mom

She is my friend
My best friend
When I am sad
She comforts me.
When I am happy.
She laughs with me
And when I need her
She is always there for me.
My friend
My best friend
My mom.

Sandra McCullough

Truth

See the torrents of rain,
Oceans, lakes and rivers overflow,
Floods that will rise and destroy
All over the world,
This is mother Earth's strongest ploy.
Disease will dare to claim
The lives of children
Before they can grow.
Black skies, black rain
Oh there is so much pain
As a war is raged in the heavens.
Listen, God is speaking
All angels, prophets, saints and guides
No longer can we hide
We have found the truth we are seeking
With God we will side
The heavens will shine with a new light
All darkness will be gone
We have all waited so long to hear God's song
Hallelujah - a brand new dawn.

Allen Wright

Life

Of infant days we have no mind
Obscure are they, and far behind,
At first we walked, then soon we spoke,
In much the way of all wee folk.

Interests new soon came along
Replacing child-hood's fun and song,
Knowledge to gain, was the intent
So to local school we were sent.

Treasured memories to us convey
A teenaged world so blithe and gay,
Those happy voices raised in song
To only youth could they belong.

Longing for the day to come
When young adults we would become,
Then making home for ones we love,
And asking guide from God above.

It mattered not what size the task
We'd bring to Him, and humbly ask,
Then, true to ancient promise made
In His own way, came to our aid.

Elva B. Mellish

Immortality

Remember me, Oh Lord,
Not in my time of greatest sorrow
But in my times of greatest joy.
It is then, I am most able to believe
In you.

Your hope
Your glory
Your power

In my dreams I see your love.
Do not judge me for what I believe
Only for who I am,
Inside.
Remember me, oh Lord
For I will be forgotten
After I am gone from this earth.
But in you I will live on
Forever.

D. J. Bourne

"Confused"

Not wanted.
Nor needed.
Nobody cares.

Left out.
And forgotten.
No one's aware.

Just a presence.
Of no real consequence.
How will I fare?

When I'm not wanted,
Nor needed,
And nobody cares.

C. Elizabeth Heffern

Beauty At Its Best

A child is born a miracle
No-one can say it's less
Like a flower, nurtured with love
That God will surely bless.

We patiently wait for it to bloom
Watching stages day by day.
Hard to tell how tall it stands
Until it flowers, one can't say.

A rose of pinks and reds
With cheeks of blush the same
Like a lily to be sure
Pure, without any shame.

Morning glory, forget-me-nots
A child does compare.
Each new day, brings more joy.
Cherished memories of one so fair.

To hold a flower in your hand
Is to hold a child to your heart
And wonder at its perfection
I thank God He did take part.

Olive Martin

Untitled

In the middle of nowhere,
no one around,
the revving of motors,
the only sound.

The gears all get changed,
from high into low,
so nothing is wrecked,
we go really slow.

The rush that you get,
from hitting every tree,
you just keep on driving,
unable to see.

The mud on the window,
the rain's coming down,
the sun it has left us,
we head back to town.

Driving that beast,
just one more bend,
you think to yourself,
"I don't want this to end."

Heidi Zilkie

Refreshing

A hot, humid summer day
No movement is too much
No coolness found in shade
People lying on the grass
Across the street is a beach
Cool water in the lake
Run there, jump in
So cold and relaxing
Don't want to go to the surface
You stay down, sinking further
The bottom appears
Your lungs start to burn
You propel upwards
But it is too late
You lose consciousness

Michelle Gabowicz

No More Tears

The rain is falling
No it is my teardrops
Crying for the love I miss
But never the love I lost
Your love will always be with me
But I can't hold you
Like I use to
That is what I miss
The touch
The feeling
Of your arms around me
Someday the sun will shine
The teardrops will fall no more
From my eyes
Only from the heavens above.

Betty Campbell

EMOTIVE MISERY/LONELINESS

Don't ask me to exist
my soul's...
        fantasies
I cannot resist
        for long.

Constance Demyris Helton

On The Shores Of Time

I see in the cool blue water...
my reflection
cold and pale.
My face cracks
with every ripple.
Wisps of light
separate my features
in painless dissection.

I see in the cool blue water...
Tiny stones
washed smooth
from time.
Eternity abounds me.
For I as you,
am only a stone
On the shores of time.

Wayne Beaton

Hands

My eyes touch
my mother's hands:
Surrounded in satin.
A shell now empty
lies alone.
A dazed soul
swallowed in painful
moments that linger,
on dusk filled time.
Grief on-going never
to end.
A life in mid-sentence,
Stopped.
But not finished?
Questions are asked
in an empty room.
Answers are blowing
through a haze of infinity.

Diane Howard

Mother Most Dear

You have gone from me now
My Mother most dear
I look for you always
But you are never near

My heart it will break
I loved you so much
My Mother most dear
I long for your touch

When will I see you
How long must I wait
My Mother most dear
do not leave it too late

My dreams are so empty
and night I do fear
So come to me soon
My Mother most dear

Roni Cooper

Immortality

It seems so easy
mixing sun and seas
earth
air
water
fire

Guides us to the Labyrinths
Theatres of artistic creativity
Wandering.
Draped in confusion
Partake of this luxury
in this land of great
awakening

Carmen Mohn

Mrrrrow

Sleek shadow
Mighty hunter
Gallant mouser
Yowling challenge
Adversaries fly

Happy furball
Softly purring
Paws akneading
Twitching slightly
Dreaming as you lie.

Hilary Blythe

Mama And Papa

When I was a baby you sheltered
me from all bad.

Now that I'm older and understand
how much you did for me mother and dad.

You both treated me like I was
a priceless bar of gold.

Listen to your parents I was always told.

I appreciate you more and more
each day, for all the love you
showed me in each and every way.

When the day finally arrives where
we must part,
You both know that there will always
be so many happy memories of you
in my heart.

Ana Leanaro

Nature's Hand

I sit with quiet splendor to
marvel at the sunset and
paint this art from word before
its memory fades.

Far from the every day
high a top this golden hill
I watch as sunlight gives
autumn its fiery glow.

With quill to ready and
palates of words from my ink
I try to hold the glory of
this day and feeling it's left behind.

As I wonder back and stop
to look soon I understand that
nature's hand truly capture it
best in the beauty of a flowers
bloom for which autumn's frost
has come too soon.

Zoltan Alex Papp

Infinity

Microcosms,
macrocosms...
always
raging against
timelessness of agonies
and
the human condition
so small...small...small
caught in the vortex
of the crucible of suffering.

Even so
essential quality
of living
abides
with mercy
ongoing and godly
bringing hope
and substantively
faith raises
with splendour.

Mona Fair

Untitled

We
look
to
tomorrow.

Seeing
ourself
as
today.
Little
remembering,
tomorrow
is a dream,
yesterday
is
a memory,
and
all
the
changes
between.

Louise M. Goudie

Untitled

Randomly ripping apart
  lives that should
  be for always together,
separating hearts
tearing away love
  Time—
without care, without justice
creates the wounds
  they say it heals.
The salt—
  Time has a way of
  changing things.
I wish time would have stopped
  when I knew you loved me.

Dayna Manweiler

Circle Of Wisdom

When my Father told me what he thought
Little could I see
I thought he was out of touch
With my world and me

I thought that wisdom shone on me
And all then that I did
And that I knew best for all my ways
My ways were at my bid

it seems to me when I look back
How foolish then was I
And how I have learned so many things
As the years have gone by

It is wisdom that we gain I guess
As years and time goes by
I now can see who then was wise
And it certainly was not I

For now I better understand
But little can I see
Why the young cannot understand
When they talk with me

David L. Lank

110

Sundown

When the last glow of the sun
Lightens up the burning sky
When the birds sing their night song
A golden dream comes from up high

When the flowers close their eyes
All the trees look old and wise
They take on a silvery glow
And their shadows seem to grow

Then the night falls from above
And the stars show all their love
When the moon is rising high
Dreams are falling from the sky

Peace on Earth, peace in the sky
I'm close to God, don't ask me why
Peace in my soul.

Elli Matthiesen

Reality Check

Days go on
life may still be going on
but for the unfortunate
society doesn't see the loss
of another human race
whose soul
can't be met
to the rest of its life.

Just its own
and the lives around
praying the worst won't come around
and hit them from behind.

Too blind to see
a loss of another
opens up to see
its own.

Gerard Giardino

Natasha's Birthday

It is noon in Vancouver.
Let's start anew.
Scruff away the top layer
Spritz all over with pink wine
Now blend with the fingertips.
Sprinkle bittersweet shavings
Of Hershey's best delight
Pluck pansies, tulips, daffodils
(In kid-gloved hands)
Spin a homemade ribbon
Blanket everything in white.
She has arrived at thirty-five
Join her at her house
Where the rooms are bright and cool.
Celebrate, celebrate
There will be hugging,
And gifts, and sugary treats.
The sun is high above
So come inside.

Yoshino Kerravala

Reconciliation

Where every peace-unlike this tare
Is bound to fury-hopeful there.
For in your fold of movement tear.
The carnal lure toward sanctity.

All fear subsides as wills embrace.
No pain, no hurt-only to see your face.

Herman W. Scholz

Silent Anger

Shadows of the past haunt our minds
leaving patches of guilt scattered
here and there like leaves after
an Autumn storm.

Our hearts hum a mournful tune
remembering words that should
not have been spoken.

Our angry souls distort their meaning
and keep us both frozen with fear
and a sense of having failed.

Come sweet Love! Melt our hardened
hearts so that the warm wind of
love and understanding can blow
the leaves away.

Irene Gillard Schurter

Water Falls

Thunder rolls,
Laughs and chuckles
Crashing
Thrashing
Pulse after continuous pulse

Monstrously flows,
  and tumbles
Downward

A jump,
A leap,...
A promise.

Leslie MacPherson

Living Death

Strange, I'm in this place
.....just yesterday.....
naturally tamed and nothing to blame
Strange to be in this state
overwhelmed and tranced in deep thought
  To stoically gape
  at this crimson color tree
  the wind's ingenue breeze
  trickling through the leaves
  to suddenly seize
  and flow to the east
  A reflection of my own energy
Until I connect to my sixth sense
living is more painful than death
I can manifest to suicide
discern to one's right
Strange I'm in this place
to feel the unknown, yet
create it to be known
Strange to be in this state

Kore Siddoo

True Friendship

A seed of friendship slowly it grows,
It very slowly unfolds.
Trustingly, lovingly it grows,
Deeper in strength and warmth.
It doesn't have claws of greed,
Doesn't rob you of your needs,
True friendship is like a pillar.
Beside you it stands firm and strong,
Letting you draw strength from it,
When you are weak and down.

Helen Lagergren

Halle-lu-ja Halle-lu-ja

Holy Lord I love you.
Jesus I adore you.
Mighty king I praise your name,
Precious lamb of God, I sing.
Halle-lu-ja, Halle-lu-ja.

Jesus you're my Saviour.
Jesus you're my Healer.
You're the Father's only Son.
Who died for all my sins.
Halle-lu-ja, Halle-lu-ja.

All the days I'll praise you,
Love you and uphold you.
I will glorify you Lord.
In all the earth below.
Halle-lu-ja, Halle-lu-ja.

Zion's trumpets sounding.
Holy Saints ascending.
Heaven's gates are open wide.
With angels leading them inside.
Halle-lu-ja, Halle-lu-ja.

Clara H. Henning Eckert

Untitled

I've asked a thousand questions.
I've told a million lies.
I've looked to the heavens.
I've seen stars in your eyes.

I've heard it all before.
I'll do it all again.
Some things will be different.
Nothing will change though.

Everyone around me is laughing.
I can see their tears.
They all wear brave faces.
I can smell their fears.

They embrace me, so they can stab me.
I let them, because my spirit won't die.
It will live forever.
Will their lies?

If you ask me "Why?"
My answer will be "Why Not?"
If you don't understand, I won't mind.
After all, ignorance is not a crime.

Marc Moon

Untitled

Hi 'ya pop
It's me, your Ause,
My days are full, but
I thought I'd pause.
I miss you lots
Oh, every day
I hope you're happy
In every way.
Henry says to say hi,
But to come here,
He's still shy.
Our lives go on
With work and play
I just thought I'd
Stop and say,
That even though
We're far apart
Never for a minute
Do you leave my heart.

Audrey Smith

The Night Calls

The night calls to me,
Its cloak of darkness wraps around me,
Protecting me from the dagger - like
rays of light upon my skin.

Tonight I must feed
Like a cobra, I wait for my prey,
And strike when they least expect
Their life force absorbed into mine.

My name written in red
In the book of eternal damnation.
I am and forever will be a vampire.

Jo-Anne Nina Sewlal

Of Friendships And Flowers

Friendship's like a flower;
It starts off as a seed.
You give it love and sunshine
And everything it needs.

It soon begins to blossom
And grow for weeks on end.
And soon you may find out
You've more than just a friend.

You've more than a pal,
An acquaintance off the street.
You have yourself a soul mate
And that you just can't beat.

This friendship will survive
Through tough times and much more
Just like a flower through the storm.
You can't wish for much more.

Angela Chapman

Poor Me

When it rains,
it pours
Good luck or bad,
The roller coaster of life
One minute you're happy,
The next, you're sad.

Trying to be optimistic,
Looking for a calm,
How much can life take from you
How much can always go wrong?

Is it the money,
or could it be love.
That makes us feel complete?

Having all the above
shouldn't make a difference,
It's the way we feel inside
that counts,
Expectations,
that we can only meet.

Cindy Willard

The Storm Within

As I sit all alone,
Isolated and forlorn,
Tears begin to form,
I'm afraid I'll create a storm,
Someone please come and comfort me,
Make me laugh with glee,
The summer is all but gone,
Soon winter will be upon,
If only I could see,
What the future holds for me...

Coleen Craigie

Nothing

It was like a hole in space
It had no meaning or place
froze by the unbearable pain
life purposely insane

To most it was unsolved
but to me, it always revolved,
a part of my life
like a delicate child or wife

Majestic beauty
an unseen nudity
feared by most,
but to me, a loving host

Has it all been but a dream
as I scream my final scream
It was my get away
my place to go and lay

Submitted to its deliverance
I have never left since
created just for me
How I feel so open and free...

James Wood

As You Sit

As you sit,
 it bounces into my kitchen
 rolls down the corridor
 and disappears into the den.
Oh, that the sun should hide!
Cracked marble tops welcome me inside
 and I enter.
Your luminescent cigarette
 mocks me as you
 wave it back and forth.
And it is as if I
 weren't aware anymore.
I rock, stop, then rock again.
And as the red seeps from my lips
 I request another chance
 But you have bounced past my grip.

Martina Blaskovic

Kaleidoscope

A kaleidoscope of color
Is what friends bring to me
My newest friend is a real great gal
By the name of Stephanie.

We shared a room for six long days,
With many a lovely chat,
Of tunes and trips, of folks and kids
And different things like that.

We got to know each other,
A mutual bond was struck.
Our Kaleidoscope of color
Has brought us lots of luck.

I had to leave my brand new friend
So she'll get a whole lot better.
Then, we can have a few more chats,
And it won't be about the weather.

So, Stephanie dear, here's hoping
That you will get good news.
And our kaleidoscope of color
Will give off bright, new hues.

Irene Grech

Relationships

To find love unintentionally
Is to do one's heart good
The sharing of secrets
And it's privacy understood

This won't hide fault
With unconditional love
The keeping of feelings
Are known only by above

Suppressed anger causes disputes
Communication is the only key
Figuring out any problems
True love will be stress free

Knowing someone's there to encourage
And promise their life to you forever
Having love without any boundaries
Will bring the happiness of a couple together

Love makes seriousness
Adventure adds laughter
Imperfection may have sadness
And they'll live happily ever after

Trina Bokor

Viva Mandela

To be jailed for one man's belief.
Is this just cause for a man's grief.
Of only wanting his homeland back.
Freed is this man to fight the plight.
Between blacks and whites.
To unify a world racism and hate.
Stand tall for what is right.
Open their eyes to mankind's plight.
We are both the same you and I.
So let prejudices lie.
One love, one nation.
He has a dream.

Loree Nicholson

My Mask

Sometimes what I say
Is not what I feel.
Sometimes the smile on my face
Is not real.

Sometimes I laugh
When I want to cry,
And sometimes there is
A lot more to my sigh.

Sometimes I tell you I'm strong
When I'm weak.
Sometimes it's just your arms
That I seek.

So you've got to look deeper
If you want to know me,
Because sometimes I go further
Than just what you see.

Stephanie Karen Ratcliff

One Puzzle Piece

One missing puzzle piece
Is no big deal.
It doesn't really affect
The "Big Picture"...
Or does it?
What if it is the piece to explain
Why a child has nightmares?
What if it is the piece to explain
Why a seventeen-year-old
Would shoot himself
In his parents' basement?
What if it is the piece to explain
A divorce to a five-year-old?
What if it is the piece to tell
The world that AIDS
Can't murder us anymore?
What if it is the piece
That gives us the answers?

Brandy Maisine

Refrigerator Love

Your kiss
Is like a fine gravy
That makes potatoes
Appear to be the garnish

Undressing
You makes me feel
Like the vanilla ice cream
Underneath the cherry.

I always like the cherry best.

A fresh plate of lasagna
Is how I feel
When I hold you
Under the covers.

And a glass of milk
To wash it all down.

Jon-Paul Decosse

Sweet Dreams Yesterday

The love of your life
Is a stranger today,
Loneliness, emptiness,
Puzzled dismay.

The bills quickly mount,
Overwhelm, override
Any time for romance
Between groom and his bride.

Sweet dreams of yesterday
Sadly defiled, through
Ephemeral sand-castles
Built by a child.

Sweet dreams of yesterday
Fairy-tale wife, his lover,
Their mother, illusory life
That eluded the dreamer...
Was there a Prince Charming
On a Charger so wild..
Or was true life locked up
In the heart of a child.

M. Mickey Turnbull

Passages

Our marriage
Is a dark pool
A whirling vortex
Of hurt and fear

It is windowpanes
Dusty and dim
A reflection of years
In neglect

Spiritually bereft
With haunting images
Flitting ghostlike
Through empty halls

Hope and love
Flicker dimly in its hearth
Dampered in its ignorance
And blindness

A winters breath
Ladders over the saddened heart
And splinters
Into two separate paths.

Gail Stefanie Reeves

Late Love

Fall is flouting
Its colors o'er the land.
As a Master Artist
In bold relief
Its brazen colors stand.
Demanding, with one wild exotic cry,
"Behold my beauty, ere I die.
Winter comes too soon,
And stark I'll stand
Silhouetting the sky,
Unnoticed by passers by."
So, you come to me with love
Because you see me, in the
Embers of my fall.
Time will fade the colors
From my brow.
Will you love me then,
As you love me now?
Nature teaches all
Winter follows fall.

Gertrude Machan

Civilization

There is a crucible
Into which we place ourselves early
Continually grinding away
With pestle after pestle
Of disregard for ourselves

The grit of society
Acceptance, appreciation, belonging
Combines together
To pulverize our being
Into shapelessness

Conformity reduces us
To fine powder for easier handling
Packaged and contained
We are once again together
But never again whole.

Susanne C. Worth

Summer Solstice

The sun melts a liquid gold
Into the blue of ocean cold
The stars appear and shoot the night
Diamond streaked ebony
Shimmering bright
The wind whips up
The night creatures dance
Into the glow of a moonbeam's trance
The curtain of dark
Rises slowly to light
Here becomes the day
The day before night

Grant McLachlan

The Wind

On a warm summer day,
    in the heat of the sun,
    the wind is
    a welcome companion.

The hands of the wind
    caress my skin and
    rustle through my hair
    in a gentle, cooling embrace.

I am not alone.

Whispering through the trees
    and tickling through the grass
    the wind has
    kissed the world.

Maureen Smith

Good Morning

I open my eyes and gaze
In the early morning light
The sky is all ablaze,
As the morning greets the night.

Night creatures hurry off,
Feathered friends take flight.
Along with furry friend in the ruff.
As twinkling stars say goodnight.

The morning sun soon arises
White clouds drift quietly overhead
Bringing the day's many surprises.
People tumble quickly from a bed.

Children's voices greet the day
Bright faces and starry eyed
Parents hurry them and their way
To try the things never tried.

Sarah E. Marks

I Love You

I love you when I'm sleeping,
I love you when I'm weeping.

I love you when I'm dreaming,
I love you when I'm screaming.

I love you when I'm crying,
I'd even love you if I were dying.

I love you when I'm working.
I love you because I do.
I love you.

Nathalie Bureau

The Music Of Nature

The lapping wavelets sing a song
In steady rhythm with the tide.
The rustling wind descants along
While swaying tress conduct with pride.

No sharp baton, no heavy beat,
Yet harmony and cadence thrive,
While flowers and grass all take a seat
To hear this music, so alive.

The choir of birds all sing their tune
And fill the air with music calm.
The bees just hum in "clair de lune"
And flood the scene with soothing balm.

These sounds provide serenity
To quiet the spirit of the earth,
And lead us all in harmony
To live and love with peace and mirth.

Henrietta Daniel

Invader

Bedroom window
in plain sight
wide open
to the midnight sky

With augmented vision
he watches
crazed
craving

Hidden
obscured
by brush

Engulfed
in an
unhallowed
fantasia

The exotic predator
motionless
unrevealed
watching
as you reveal

Mohammad Sharizan Murni

Nature's Balance

The speckled spider
in its spun wheel
fat and malignant,
waiting and still.

Winds from the river
raise their strum
straining the strands
in the turbulent sun.

Urgent repairs
send spider scurrying
to spin a long cord
that will swing to the rim.

Wind raises its tempo:
spider sling misses—
snaps with a jerk
to drop its small load...

Switching of hazards
from prey to the spider
leaves lopsided a web,
squares well in the sun.

M. A. Flower

Blue Jay

Blue Jay, Blue Jay
In a tree

Blue Jay, Blue Jay
Come to me

Blue Jay, Blue Jay,
Fly so high

Blue Jay, Blue Jay
In the sky

Blue Jay, Blue Jay
Say goodbye

Ewa Buzny

Words Of Denial

How are you?
  I'm doing fine.
(I'm going crazy,)
  (I'm losing my mind)

Is it me, or was it you?
  were they memories,
are they true?
  God I wish I knew.

I'd like to say,
  I'm okay!
life wasn't bad,
  it just seemed that way.

The nightmares over,
  "none was true"
now I can be,
  just like you.

Jackie Melia

Autumn

Every September
I yearn to start walking
And wander towards the South,
Away from mankind and civilization,
Under an azure blue sky
And white clouds with silver lining
Under flocks of birds
Travelling in my direction.
I yearn to be alone
Among green-orange trees
And yellow, ripening fields
And to look into deep blue-green waters.
I want to find my soul again
That has been lost and forgotten
In the haste of modern life.
And when all is calm inside
And I have found myself
I'll think of you.

Frederika Kammerer

Life

Did you ever wonder,
How we got here,
And why we were put here?

What created us,
And what created it,
How did it all begin?

The world began,
And one day will end,
But in between is still uncertain.

Nancy L. Ross

Always

Like a flower that blooms every spring,
I will always think of you.
Like the tides forever rolling in,
I will always think of you.

And though the nighttime turns to day,
From you I will never turn away.
And as the seasons come to pass,
I know my love for you will last.

The rain may fall but it's soon to go,
And in my heart I will always know,
That like the endless stars above,
I will always think of you my love.

Kelly Boyle

Truth By Reflection

Deceitful senses
I trust you no longer
blind to idle promises
deaf to the enticing song
of young angels born already vile

I pare myself down
pure intuition
so as to catch
in brief reflection
in words disjointed
in fleeting scent
or in shadow of gesture
the truth by reflection
that has so long eluded me.

And my blood flows
along the invisible drill
traced by grief's nail
before the fear of being myself
should make me already die a little
in the discord between two deaf silences.

Diego Bastianutti

Of My Past

As I walk down the paths of life
I see the tears on those I pass
They cry for me
And the child of my past.

They hear the words I say
And feel the pain in me
But what was, was
That was the child in my past.

There in the past I lay dying
No hope, no future for me.
The tears and pain
Of the child in my past.

Inside I feel the life returning
The hope for life
A new beginning
For the child of my past.

As I walk down the paths of life
I see the smiles of those I pass
They laugh for me
And the child of my past...Me.

Kirstine D. Jensen

Through Lovers Eyes

When I look into your eyes
I see the smiles of love we share
And when you hold me in your arms
I could spend forever there

We share such a special love
It's forever, faithful, true
Your love for me is unconditional
As is my love for you

The feelings we have for each other
Are best spoken from the heart
They seem to form a special bond
Which can never be torn apart

As our eyes tell us a story
That only we will understand
We embrace the future
Together hand in hand

Jennifer Giroux

Solace In Beauty

Love is bright
I see it in your eyes
Stay with me tonight
I'll show you what love is
Solace in beauty

It shines in your eyes
I feel it in your sweet caress
You're there when I call
Be there when I fall
Solace in beauty

You're such a focus for my life
I need you to stay
To hear you're gentle voice
Is the perfect ending to my day
Solace in beauty

You were there for me then
You're here for me now
You'll be with me forever
I close my eyes in peace as I find
Solace in beauty

Karen Millett

Fall

As I walk out from my cottage,
I see fall everywhere.
The leaves are quickly turning
And wild geese are in the air.

Partridge seasons open
But not one can be found.
The coloured leaves and needles
Are lying all around.

My footsteps make a crunching sound.
As through the woods I go.
I sometimes see a deer or two.
A buck, a fawn or doe.

Their tracks are almost everywhere,
From their little cloven hoofs.
And sometimes I see tracks of bear
As I go walking through.

This is my favorite time of year
And I like to leave the town
And enjoy the beauty of nature
In the country all around.

Laura Kargus

"A Sister's Prayer"

To you God in heaven,
I pray for your guidance.
Please put my brother's turmoil,
Into a past of silence.

He is too good of a person,
To be experiencing this kind of pain.
Please show him the warmth of the sun,
And call off this chilling rain.

He has a long road of healing,
Spread out in front of his eyes.
There is so much hope for him,
And this he must realize.

I pray to you to show him,
The path to recovery.
To help him laugh instead of cry,
To rid him of this misery.

I hope this prayer I write,
Will soon be answered by you.
It is of the most importance,
You help to pull him through.

Stephanie Leckey

The Oblong Box

The box was oblong.

Wrapped around, with crimson silk.
I picked it up,

And gently, shock it all about.
It was not heavy,
There was no scent,
There was no card.

It was a secret box.
And inside — maybe,
A diamond ring,
A beautiful pearl,
A dusting of gold,
A ray of sunshine,
A captured rain-bow,
Or a moon-beam.

Or, was it a phantom thing?
A thought maybe — or a wish.
That lay inside, this "OBLONG BOX".
Wrapped around in crimson silk.

Mary Sproule

"I'm Still Young At Heart"

Oh how the years have gone by fast.
I may have grown old but
"I'm still young at heart!!!"

I still love to see the sunshine,
The flowers bloom.
"Oh where have my glasses gone?"

I still love to listen to music,
The radio playing my favorite song,
"But we've missed placed
my hearing aide."

Though at times my memory may fade
"I'm still young at heart."

Teresa Lillehei

The Eagle

As dusk is descending.
  I look up high
A bird is flying
  up yonder, in the sky.

So graceful it moves
  swirling, twirling, in the wind
Suddenly it begins to glide
  as if on a gigantic slide.

With a final swoop
  it grabs its prey
On that Hillside
  so far away.

Whirling around, the eagle does fly
  and heads for the trees
It's almost "Goodbye".

Still clutching his prey
  and soon, out of sight
That flight of the eagle
  with all his might
as if he was saying "Goodnight"

Harold Waring

Mother, What's On The Page

I see you in that deathbed
I know you do not see me
Your eyes are hollow and innocent
  as a newborn
  You have come full circle
  ashes to ashes
For now I know you as you were
  no better than you know me as I am

Delusions of life
  Numb the sting of mortality
Do you enjoy this Nostalgic Delirium
Will you ever know again reality
  if but for a moment
  Long enough
    to help me say goodbye
    my love
    For I cannot bear to see you this way
    And you will never remember me again

Bruce Tulloch

Once Again Lord

Once again Lord
I kneel
On my knees with tears
On my fists
Daring me not to cry.
Once again Lord
I pray
For a swollen belly
Filled with the breath
Of a life within mine.
Once again Lord
I plead,
Questioning you Lord
Even though
I know you hear.
Once again Lord
I pray for your life to fill mine,
I pray for your patience to help mine,
...And I pray for your will
  ...Not mine.

Hilda Van Gyssel

My Grandfather

I hold you in my heart,
I hold you in my soul;
Even though you're gone,
I don't want to let you go.

I miss you very dearly,
I wish that you were here;
If only I could see you,
If only you were near.

Laura Bedard

Nothing Lasts For Ever

Since the years have passed;
I have been able to understand,
that nothing lasts for ever.
You meet someone,
and then it's gone.
Just like water evaporates.
Just like people die and don't come back.
The time runs and you still there,
missing someone with no pain.
No pain to be able to understand;
That nothing lasts for ever.

Maria Luisa Ponce

The Measure Of A Friend

The colour of his skin?
I hadn't noticed that it was different!
I just smiled as I saw him smile-
the dark moustache, so dark
against the ivory of his teeth.
His eyes were dark;
they, too, danced in the laughter.
His touch was gentle,
his voice sincere...
I just sat and listened,
then whispered the response.
He set the pace
with his uniqueness;
he generated peace
with his tranquility.
Sure, he's darker than I,
and speaks of far-off places
but, the colour of his skin....
I hadn't noticed
that it made a difference!

Kathryn Wiley

Anyway And Always

Every night when it is late
I go out unto the terrace.
Outstretched to the sea, to the sky,
I speak a soft good-night to thee.

I know you speak,
Though I cannot hear.
I cannot see, but
I know you are there.

I wrap around the
sky we share,
and say a soft good-night
to thee.

And even though, you cannot hear
I say it anyway,
A soft good-night to you, My Captain,
I am there with you always.

Deanne M. Elms

Anorexic Rest

Although I am at rest now,
I feel turmoil inside,
I can see my mother's face,
And there's nowhere I can hide,

Her tears are acid through my heart,
Which aches although it does not beat,
I long to feel her hand in mine,
And hear her words, gentle and sweet.

It's too late now to change the past,
And still my mother knows not why,
I lay in this eternal bed,
Dear God! Why did I have to die?

I never meant to go this far,
I never meant to die,
I wish that she could hear these words,
As I watch her cry.

I wanted to please, and achieve my goals,
But now it will never be,
I sometimes think it was my fault,
And only death would set me free.

Sheri Monk

For You

I do not miss you,
I feel no remorse.
I will not mourn you,
I'll keep on my course.

And yes, I remember
the times that we had.
And yes, you stuck with me
when the times were bad.

But I do not care
'cause those days are gone;
and don't try to contact me
from the great beyond.

I do not miss you,
yet, I wish you well.
And the next time I see you,
I'll see you in hell.

Allison Crowe

I'm Sorry

So sorry
I didn't call you
on your birthday but
neither did you on mine

So sorry I told you
we're no longer family
that in my mind
you've died

But in my heart
you'll always be there
and much to my dismay
for I would sooner love
to see you gone
gone every far away

You question why?
My words so harsh
I'm appalled you can't understand

But what can I expect
(too much I guess)
from a lonely, dying man

Danielle Harris

Summers Past

When all is still and darkness falls,
I close my eyes and dream.
Of summer days and love gone by,
of walking by the stream.

I dream of cabins by the beach,
And nights spent on the sand.
Of making love 'neath starry skies,
And walking hand in hand.

Of puppy dogs and ice cream cones,
That melt too fast to eat.
And dancing barefoot in the rain,
To soothe the summer's heat.

When all is still and darkness falls,
And it's still too hot to sleep.
I dream of summers spent in youth,
And hang my head and weep.

Susan Wickert

Angel

As I look into my heart
I can see your eyes
I can see the smile on your face
And I can hear your words
Words of advice
That echo in my mind
Words that make me laugh
And words that make me cry

You taught me to believe
In myself
And in others
You taught me not to be so shy
And always made sure I had a smile
I know now where you are
You are the angel
In my heart

Jeff Hart

Solitude

Look out to the
horizon and tell
us what you see.

SOLITUDE.

Look into the
depths of your
soul and tell
us what you see.

SOLITUDE.

Take comfort in
the loneliness, that
is all there is
left to do.

SOLITUDE.

Look into the
darkest part of your
solitude and tell
us what you see.

ME IN THE DARK
LOOKING AT THE HORIZON.

Stephen Vettese

116

Days Gone By

Children, lovers, seasons gone by
hard working responsibilities
left her frail, weak and bent
gnarled, swollen arthritic hands
She remembers a young taunt body
supple with pleasures and warmth
children, lovers, seasons gone by
freedom is present now, peaceful
She gathers the memories and smiles
in a withered, aching body
like a shade, she pulls them down
before the sunset of death
to join her children, lovers
is seasons of life now past.

Annie McNutt

The Truth

Fiction
Happy, friendly
Laughing, talking, singing
Friends, companions, enemies, wars
Crying, screaming, shouting
Black, white
Reality

Jade Swark

"Thoughts"

As I look around at the wondrous things
God has put upon our earth,
The cool green grass of summertime
The early morn's rosy birth,
The rocks of grey, the sky so blue,
The trees so slender tall
Stretching out their leafy arms
To the one God of us all.

It makes one wonder doesn't it,
Just wherein the real truth lies,
When I see the strife today
It makes me want to cry,
This world was so freely given
To us who are mankind
But despair hate, greed and gold
Always want to rule our minds!

Carole Lench

Untitled

I have a little dog,
Giorgio is his name,
He loves to greet the people,
He treats them all the same.

To him it doesn't matter,
If you're thin, or overweight,
A smiles all it takes,
And he thinks you're really great.

To him you could be black, or white,
He doesn't seem to mind,
Because when all is said and done,
All dogs are color blind.

K. Mel Sprackman

Starting On The Work Force

Just turned 18 thinking about
getting a job. Think about
your friend. Bob is also thinking
about getting a job.
Remember to save some money
when you get married you
have some money to support your honey
it pays to start saving
at a younger age
because when you get older
you will have something to
show for your age
being poor at an older age
makes your face at times age
having to worry at times
will depress you a lot of times
save and later buy a new car
you will be happy to have a new car
when you retire you will
feel content to retire

David Kehler

Canada?

See with no redemption
gather in congregation
witness disintegration
without hope of salvation
is this a united nation
on the brink of separation
pray for unification
or freeze in our stagnation
no more admiration
a country in mutilation
is there a solution
Or are we beyond redemption?

Paul Terence Rees-Jones

Jessie's Journey

Jessie's journey, I admire
Full of hope fond desire
All the effort not in vain
Disease to conquer, research to gain
Through the day and through the night
Sometimes clouded over
Sometimes shining bright
The path to cure the dreadful ill
Jessie's journey can fulfill.

J. Kennedy

My Life

My life, like a battle ground,
Full of fear and anger.
It's as death is always around.
Our lives are forever in danger.

Hoping our love is strong;
Like a fearful boar.
As he reaches his heights
of its glorious fulfilling moments.

Always holding onto life,
as if it were hanging.
Hanging from a ledge.
But not yet falling to the end.

I'm always scared;
Scared of what the end will bring.
And what will happen,
After the end of time.

Lisa Wevers

"Life"

From where do you come from
From where do you go.
When all there is, is here.

Life is an adventure,
Time races on by.
You push on ahead
You want to try.
Learning new things
You've just begun.
To live and explore,
You want even the sun.

Travel the world.
Fly high in the sky.
Climb up a mountain,
Dive deep in the sea,
Filled with experiences,
Peaceful and free;
You'll come home.

Ruth P. Shores

Sleepless Nights

My heart won't stop thumping
From the happiness I feel,
When I think of you, darling,
It all seems so unreal.

But, I'm glad it's not
Cause I love you so much,
I'm so happy I've got you
To hold and to touch.

But, it's just past midnight
And I'm feelin' so blue,
Cause you're on this shift
And I just don't know what to do.

I toss and I turn,
Then I turn on the light,
I watch my smoke burn
Until the wee hours of the night.

I butt my smoke out,
I switch off the light,
Now you know, with no doubt
Why I can't sleep at night!

Carol R. Moore

Hollow Eyes

Looking in/out
from hollow
eyes
I sort through
the debris
Discarding the disguise
and then
I find myself,
The real true
me

Shannon Hussey

"Soul Searching"

Nature is life in a closing jail
From fearing creatures
To the ones that fight
From struggling beings
To surviving fire
Nature is life in a closing jail;
Searching for the soul of men.

Carla Viscarra B.

117

U - Wait

A plea for justice
From a black prophet
In a nearby pulpit
Commands death without notice.

A plea for power and might
From an arrogant Fuhrer
In far away lands to conquer
Crushes God's lambs on sight.

A plea for surrender
From a ruthless militant
In country rich and vibrant
Sends oil in smoke, homes on fire.

A plea for national unity
From a tearful prime minister
In a political country matter
Divides brothers and sisters bitterly.

A message of love and peace
From a crucified savior
In a holy land of yester
Grants humanity a new lease.

Maurice A. Gauthier

Tempra Ocean

Open water, Gately sea
   for wake I dare
   you to compare
Skies above, ruffle so high
come the wide tide
Morning walk, in the shore side
find the free breeze, to clear the mind
Ruffling about, to see the skies a mist
   and know the distance is a test

Sharp rocks you prevail
to feel your soul sliding briskly
fresh breeze brush against your cheeks
knowing tomorrow,
   will shadow the peeks,
   you seek!

Yvette Mary Deleff

Untitled

Heart felt tears
for the loved one
that died

Cry a memory
to say goodbye

A belief in the angels
that shed the light

Know in your heart
that everything
is all right

Bill Bainbridge

Nature

Planting new trees,
Flowers to grow by the lake,
So soft and so slow,
Enjoying nature's beauty
Out and about.
Flowers blooming in and out
Don't pluck a flower
It has a life
Just show it off to a friend in sight.

Reema Mahbubani

Forever For Now

He sat and wept upon his arm
For she had gone away.
He cursed himself for taking love
For it brought pain today.

For every second she was gone
He shed another tear.
The affection she had shone on him
Had now begun to sear.

The world around him would disappear
With a smile loving glance.
He was blinded by her poisoned kiss
And her murderous romance.

She gave her love to him
But to others just as well.
And now because she loves so much,
He sits in loving hell.

Always to her, meant only a while.
And so she'd never stay.
Eternally was a year or so.
And forever, just a day.

Jeffrey Kelly

Daddy Love

Hold my hand little one
For I will lead the way,
Soon your eyes will be open
And walking on your way.

Hold my hand little one
For daddy will keep you safe,
Smell the flowers and take a run
I'll help you find your place.

Hold my hand little one
For the years are flying by,
Your dressing up and leaving home
It's hard to say goodbye.

Hold my hand little one
You can walk me to the door,
Life's been full of love for us
And for you there's so much more.

Kendra Grant

The Ring of Eternity

Tonight I watch a bright blue flame,
Flicker in the light,
This fire is everlasting,
Its ember always alight.
The fire I watch is from our souls,
Reflecting in the stone,
The one you placed upon my finger,
Encircling the heart that you own.
Some say true love is a gift,
Euphoric beyond compare,
I prove to thee my love thine true,
Expressed by your ring I wear.
Our meeting was a destiny,
A pledge to eternal love,
The kind that rocks the earth we're on,
And warms the Heaven above.
Please never doubt my passion,
For its color will never fade,
May our love shine on forever,
As long as Heaven can wait!

Leanne Anderson

Isolation

Crags on 'stormy mountain'
fathoms deep with snow
icy finger beckon
its secrets I would know.

(On yonder ledge)
gale winds, ice cracking
snow sifting, churning,
packing.

Element's fury spent.
awesome silence,
chalk white, aloneness
intense.

Hole me 'stormy mountain'
above the tinselled earth
where isolation bares the mind
to healing and rebirth!

Mary-Esther Bean Warke

My God's Creation

The green, luscious grass
falls between my toes.
Feeling cool to the touch,
sweet to my breath.

As I breathe in nature's
own beautiful perfume,
I feel a calmness
wash away my fears.

Alone with our nature.
God's pride and God's joy.
I feel as though a blanket
has embraced my living soul.

The leaves and the flowers
caress the winds song.
Adding their music
with one already sung.

This is my God's creation,
his blanket of love.
If we don't take care of it,
our safety will be all gone.

Melissa Leu

Untitled

He comes to me at night sometimes
Eyes red and full of lies
Speaking a foreign language
Cryptic little rhymes.
He knows just what to tell me
But every time I lose
Because I tell myself it will never be
And yet he is so smooth;
He knows just how to touch me,
Pours over me like a wave,
He knows I need to touch him back
And I think I know his game.
He knows my body well
And my mind even better,
He makes my life a heaven and hell
And my eyes even wetter
Than my body with his entwined
Savoring like wine
The pleasure that was his
And the emotions that were mine.

Arla Carlson

Untitled

Regally he sat
eyes cruel
and condemning.

Beneath the
high vaulted ceiling
he stared from
the cold concrete bench,
his throne of poverty
erected in the
great train place
in his honour.

Across the marbled floor
hatred spewed out aimed at
arrogance flaunted by
the commoners
who paraded through his court.

They cowered with guilt
unable to escape his eye,
they stood convicted
by the judge who begged.

Bruce Coulter

Winter

When winter comes snow falls
everywhere. Children laugh, make
snowmen too. I love the winter.
I think you do too. The winter comes
and the winter goes, so get ready for
winter. You will have fun too. When
winter goes I get ready for Spring.
I miss the cold winter days when
the children laugh and play. I
will see you next year. Goodbye my
lovely cold winter days. Goodbye my friend.

Nancy Medeiros

My Kingdom

If Earth was my kingdom
Everyone would have freedom
There would be no prejudice
There would be no lies
There would be no commitment
There would be no cries
There would be no bitterness
There would be no sadness
There would be no best or worst
There would be no hurt
Everyone would be equal
Everything would be fair
Everybody would be happy
Because they would know I care

Natalie Grenon

Images

When people look at me,
Do they see my scars?
Do they see my cuts and bruises?
Or do they see only a dark shadow?
I wish I knew what others could see
As they are looking at me.
When I wear an empty smile,
Is it seen as dishonest.
Sometimes I think others see right through me.
I can look into a mirror and only see a mirror.
If I can't find myself,
how are others to believe I'm not
just a reflection?

Caitlin Allerton

Seeing Blind

Passing through and seeing nothing.
Enshrouded by mists of blindness.

Unable to notice those around me.
My perception is a coldness.

Living a fantasy of dreams and ideas.
So far from the truth.

Being hurt in mind and soul.
My emotion floods forth.

To no appreciation.
To affection unreturned.

Once again I start at nothing.
But faith, hope and the cold.

Lauran Hill

Anciently New

Perched on a small hill-
Drawn into a drama;
Perhaps the opening act has ended
For the trees applaud!

A drama of great age
Continuous yet curiously new;
Whispering pines herald the dance,
With the tune borne on the wind.

Stag horns swaying in time
Laugh; adding words
As a chorus, encouraging
Butterflies and bees in counterpoint.

Radical change-
As all transforms -
Gnashing and trashing
Bolts and torrents!

Soon enough the theme resumes,
The wind to caress
From the forest into the soul;
A pattern anciently new.

Peter McIntyre

The Sky's Your Limit

Each day brings new beginnings,
Don't let your life drift by,
Visit friends, who share your thoughts,
And hold your head up high.

Wear a smile upon your lips,
Carry love within your heart,
You'll make it in the outside world,
All you have to do is start.

Make some plans, set your goals,
don't waste another minute,
Just use that hidden inner strength,
You'll see - the sky's your limit.

Move on ahead and don't look back,
Your strength will grow each day,
You'll find that peace within your mind,
You thought you lost one dismal day.

Karen Kinslow

The World Today

The world cries out, in sad despair,
Does not your brother care,
Colour creed, it matters not,
So be it your brothers lot.

Can he not stretch his hand in peace,
Defeating want, that wars may cease,
The hands of time, are wearing thin,
What price the victors win.

Man in his restless state of mind,
Cannot seem to find,
The common bond, that all must share,
To love his brothers, everywhere.

Yet there is this never ending seed
Of man's in humanity, and greed
Which seems to show, its ugly face
A weakness, of the human race.

Man must realize, this world we share.
Has been left to him in care,
He must in time, learn to live in peace,
So that war and want, forever cease

Sener David Bowman

What Is Life?

What is life to you, my friend?
    Do you have joy or pain?
And as you journey on through life
    Do you have peace or strain?

Is there guilt or hopelessness
    Confusion all around?
Is there restlessness of mind?
    By fear do you seem bound?

One there is who understands
    Your every thought and tear;
Jesus is God's Son who came
    To rid you of all fear.

He gave His life upon a cross;
    He took away your sin;
He rose again and He's alive;
    He longs to reign within.

Accept Him as you Saviour, friend;
    He'll give new life today;
He'll guide you in His plan for you,
    And be with you always.

Muriel J. Stephenson

A Better Day

When you feel lonely and grey
Do not be afraid or worry
Cause no one will know,
And no one will be sorry

"We understand" is what they say
But, it doesn't change anything
Cause the feelings stay.

No matter how deeply sad you feel
Right now, remember there will be,
There must be, a better day!
Then you will wonder
What was there to be so sad about
Anyway?

Remember those sad feelings?
They were never meant to stay

Remember there will always
Be
A better day!

Antonia Arcilesi

119

Deepest Desire

With the passion of my soul
  Do I request thee
With a yearning so deep
  Do I long for thee
And when I can no longer hold
  the pain within my bowels
You come to me so quietly
  so peacefully
  so calm
As droplets of mist upon my face
  does your presence kiss me
I am no longer of myself
  but I belong to you
My will
  my conscience my all
These have I surrendered,
  with so great a desire
That in turn
I may manifest a mirrored Image.
of so lovely a one as you.

Silvana Sellick

The 11 Cent Speech

Penny for your thoughts,
Dime for your soul.

This price is the toll
11 cent is all the world.

Pay the dime,
But save your mind.

In a torn down world
Is a torn down mind.

Pay the cent,
Let the soul repent.

Wish on the dime,
Save your penny another time.

God made man
Gave him 11 cent, 2 coins.

The devil asked for the 10,
The world took the 1.

Kevin Crook

The Fear

Rising up from within
Deceiving the mind
Strangling the heart
Fighting survival
Indifference to suffering
Prejudice, ignorance
Intolerance of differences
Allowance of injustice
Tolerance of violence
Forever searching
Never satisfied
Unfulfilled
Lost faith
Lost hope
Crushed soul

Joy Kelly-Bratt

Somos De Los Pocos

Hovering over the Alberta prairie
days pass like insects
illuminated by the four o'clock sun.
It is
at these otherwise well-defined
moments
that I've noticed light-
weight curtains will stir even
with the slightest breeze.
...almost as if one's own breathing
could move them to sway,
changing the shadows
on the old brown
tile floor.

Christopher Collom

Dark Stranger

A face among the shadows,
Dark, mysterious.

Hiding from the light,
Hunting the damned.

Taunting the evil ones,
Playing with the minds of the Innocents.

Stalking the world,
By the light of the moon.

The faint howl of the wolves,
In the distance.
Staking their claim.

Anticipating the exhilaration,
Of the kill.

As does the sly, graceful demon,
In the shadows.

Tiffany Puhl

Dry October

Africa, a cold country
Cracked clay sun's cooking-plate
Tree bone fingers poke into dead air
For whom the rains came too late
On land laid bare

Rain, the oldest god alive
Create tunnels of green
In water wash colour give
Merciless survive to live

Rain pumps green blood
Into veins of breasts and leaves
Laid dormant in the womb all along
To feed the birth of young

Swollen drunk rivers bend and punch
The naked fist unleashed for living
As sleep awakens with death
Gasping for their breath
To drown on rain thanksgiving

Karl de Haan

The Pond

A character in our play,
muddy bottomed mirror of the summer's day,
ran on until the end of our imagining.

Its part was dashing,
full of high adventure,
and a little dangerous.

But all the same,
it was a friendly body
of bass, pickerel, frogs and eel.

And in its sparkling embrace,
we swam, and rowed, fished the days,
till we grew up and went away.

James J. Hillmann

Time To

Things have changed
They say
Times have changed
It's time to go
To leave it all behind
The darkness that surrounded me
The chains that bound me
Broken
It's over
I'm free

Jennifer Landaiche

I Saw

I saw a face the other day;
they looked at me, and turned away.
"I'm trying to be like Christ", I said,
but that was all inside my head.

They remember when I'd crossed the line
it hurt my heart, it closed my mind
to all the mean things done to me,
the scar's still there - a gun to me.

I couldn't change in front of them,
It hurt too much - no joy, no friend.
And so they laughed and talked out loud,
I won't give in - or be unproud.

I saw a face the other day;
they looked at me and turned away.
I've changed my life, I now can smile
No bitter there, the sweet is wild!

Cheryl J. Thompson

Say Goodbye

We are their pride and joy
  they laughed and cried with us
  helping us through
  the best and worst of times
Now we are to say goodbye
  to start off on a journey
  they have already taken
  They wish us good luck,
  but still bear the pain of loss
  on their faces
They watch us go
  a tear in their eye
  a smile on their lips
  See you soon and good luck
  they'll say
  - Thank you so much -
We love you so much
  it is hard to
  say goodbye...

JoAnna Modrow

But... Excelled Any Other Rejoicing!

The dawn before sunrise, the post-sunset twilight.
The rainbow-colors seven fill my heart with light;
The running rivulets and swimming swans a bit coy
Overbream my mind with a lot of spright and joy!

My senses all are being cajoled by cooing cuckoos
And nightingales that sing even in the trees of goos;
My liver know no bounds of delight when it rains
Dripping in the month of shravan that on lovers reigns!

Roaming over the hills and hillocks of himalayas
Covered with snow reflecting sun-moon ray's sagas
Lifts my soul sublime with bliss to the feet of God!
Then all other organs of my body with merry-making nod!

But the joy, the delight, the merriment that I had on seeing
The first flower born to my wife excels away other rejoicing!!

Ashwinbhai D. Patel

Black

As the light comes dimmer
The pupil of my eye grows larger
Surrounded by darkness
My pupil grows bigger and bigger
Until it explodes into a pool of tears not yet separated
I close my eyes
The tears trickle down my cheek
As the room is dark
So is my mind
Which encloses my soul
There's a scratching in my ears
Like fingernails across a blackboard
It sends chills rolling down my spine
I grit my teeth to tolerate the scratching
As I do to tolerate the cruelty of life
Life itself is printed in black
Soon to be smudged by the hands of fate

Jennifer Kiler

A Loved One's Life

The song of a hummingbird only lasts so long;
The power of a hurricane is only so strong.
The peacefulness of darkness only lasts one night;
The images of paradise are only in your sight.
Memories once so strong slowly fade away;
Echoes of pain diminish, one accepts what's not to stay.
Relationships thought to last forever is only one dream;
Frustrations held and released is only one loud scream.
The heat that erupts through summer comes only once a year;
And the care one has for you won't always be there.
Staring at love's life slowly draining away;
To change the truth there is nothing one can do nor say
Limits to all aspects, why is there no limit to pain?
Acting to feel joy yet the pain one cannot feign.
The loved one lies right before one's own very eyes.
None can imagine how hard it is to tell pitiful lies,
Saying he will fully recover when we both know he won't,
Saying they know the truth when it's clear they don't,
What can one say to someone who's been more than a Father and a Friend?
Just how much is one allowed to feel when a loved one's life might end?

Andrea Chang

My Prayer

Oh! Lord, show me thy will and thy way
That I might live in our world of today
Give me of thy graces from above
That I may bestow them upon those I love
Grant one only...thy way of life
Deaden my heart to this world of strife.

Florence Fava-McCliman

olive juice

im missing you
the pictures in my room help in some ways
and make it harder in other ways
i knew this would be tough
and ive prepared myself mentally
since the summer and it helps a bit

i never told you that i was preparing
cos i didnt want you to have to think about it

anyway i trust
that the Lord will keep us together
even if there is distance between us
and right now
im leaning on him to get me through
its going to be tough but im in it for the long haul

and i trust that God has plans for us
that we cant even begin to imagine or dream of

David Andrew Chapman

"Where And When"

Where is that quietude we search for
The peace, serenity that we seek,
And hope someday to find.
A place that we could call our own
A haven not too far from home
Where the sun sets and casts a golden glow
That illuminates the skies above,
As nighttime slowly descends upon us.
The ducks and geese they slowly glide across the pond
And the stillness fills the air so that all you can hear
Is the good-night chatter from the ducks
As they cross the water to the other side.
We found such a place not too far from home
If you look hard enough, you could find it too.

Al Schwartz

Satan's Power

When men no longer cheat and lie, Satan will give up and die.
The only power he can ever know, is what we by misdeeds bestow.
We give to him his power to hold, when we trespass and breath the fold.
If all men lived the laws they know, Satan's strength would cease to grow.

In truth, he'd lose his power en masse, over men and women of every class;
Strife and conflict would all cease; Neighbors then could live in peace.
Our world would then from wars be free; all men enjoy true liberty.
Man could then in sheer faith pursue, what he was sent on earth to do.

If we could each serve one another; each man to everyone a brother;
Think of all that could be done, to make this life a pleasant one.
Our "swords of war" could all be bent, to plowshares and our means be spent
For worthy cause and doing good, in perfecting mankind as it should.

The world would then be purged of sin, and each noble child of God
    could win
The glorious promise He has given, "to save each worthy soul in Heaven."
If we'd achieve this blessed state, and arrive at Heaven's gate,
It'll be when we seize the Devil's might, and through obedience
    win the fight.

Because the only power he can ever know, is what we by misdeeds bestow.
So, when men no longer cheat and lie, Satan will just give up and die.

Hugh W. Homer

The Dog I Wished I Had

The dog I wished I had, would be the dog I dreamed of.
The dog I wished I had, would be so faithful to me.
The dog I wished I had, would have the sweetest bark.
The dog I wished I had, is the dog that's in my heart.

Jenifer Slobogian

"Friends To The End"

The first day....our eyes locked
The next day.....our hearts locked
From the very first moment we knew we'd be friends to the end.
We wish for each other only what we wish for ourselves,
  Love, understanding, contentment, and growth
For without love, we can't be open or understand. Without the
glow of contentment we really can't grow and without growth the
can not live.
The electricity between us, could light the world for years,
Our unspoken bond, could seal the cracks of a thousand dams,
The love we have for each other could stop the war of the worlds
You and I have something together no one else seems to have, a
river that runs deep inside, that not many can understand. This
river connects us like a never ending sea, because between the first
day, and the next, we knew we'd be friends to the end.

    Georgene Messina

Futility

In the wine press of my mind
The naked feet of my thoughts go around and around,
Pressing out the purple wine of my desire,
But all of the flasks are broken.

In the cauldron of my soul
Music seethes like white hot gold,
But the moulds of expression are lost.

In the garden of my heart
The soil is moist and warm,
The roses of love should grow well there,
But the seeds have been eaten by worms and bloom not.

    Donald S. Burgis

A Final Good-Bye

At the airport -
The mother, gathering up her belongings:
Her coat, her purse, her bag and the child,
and pressing towards the boarding gate.
The child beating on the mother;
beating, beating with unconvincing anger.
The father who could have made it right
would never be there again,
and the mother - caught in that
choiceless moment of resignation -
stood there and took the blow and
took it and took it and took it.

    Helga Ruth-Mueller

Untitled

Of all the things I have ever lost, I miss my mind
the most. Of all the things I have never had, I
miss the thing I had the most. It is a queen
time in this old world and I will never go.
It is strait and narrow the way I go.
No one most ever know but I knew her well.
She lived with a pack of wolves. She was
a worrier and a flower. I will not miss her.
Since I have not my heart anymore. Beloved gone
and gone is my heart and thought of hope.
Which my love is made of end a heartless fool I will die.

    Ed Albietz

"Treasures"

Please tell me, you whom my heart desires.
The most beautiful among all women,
Whose big brown eyes are full of orneriness
  yet so beautiful with innocence and charm.
My friendship, is it enough to quench your thirsts?
My love, will you allow it to feed the hunger
  in your heart?
I have not fine silver, precious jewels nor gold
  to offer you.
Commitment, devotion, my heart and my life
  are the only treasures I am blessed with,
    to give you, in our friendship and love.

    Bliss Eugene Weeks Jr.

Buried Treasure

Buried under an old mesquite tree you will fine a great deal of money
The money will be in the form of gold.
Too heavy for one man to hold.

This buried treasure is not for any human because it belongs to the
devil or other evil creatures that you can't see.
You must take all of the treasure if you seek the tree.
If you cannot then the devil will take thee.

A woman whose great great grand father found the tree tells the story
you will see.
This man was strong and didn't believe in old stories.

He was cleaning his property and came across the mesquite tree.
He found entangled in its roots a gold coin and there it stood.
He cut the coin loose the from the tree and went along happily.

But when he arrived at his house problems had been aroused.

His family became sick as sick can be with cancer and death.
Bad luck had been taken from the tree.

The coin was taken to a church to try and bless it, and its curse.

To Mexico it must go!

Everyone was afraid but the decision was made.
On this trail we must go.
Problems followed us every where we go.

We reached this church with faith so strong where the coin can do no wrong.
After the coin was given to the church our life and luck returned.

The coin was placed on display outside of the church where it stays
till this day.

    Blanca E. Gonzalez

Words

How does one write words that flow through
the mind like a river, each one meaning
something important and passing on by, and
only God can put them together.
Words of yesterday bringing on the future of tomorrow,
and yet words flow then the mind like streams going into a river.
Some are lost and gone forever catching on things
and holding fast, and yet I know it won't last.
Words of wisdom, words of cheer, words of sadness and words of tears.
Sometimes we wish we could take a word back
again and find it's too late we lost a friend,
and then this that word, oh we wish we'd
of said, but its too late, cause their dead.
So take each word, and pause a minute,
and make each one count, for your in it.
For God will hold us accountable for each
word no matter how small, and only then
him we can say the right words for all.

    Edna M. Kerns

The Meaning Of Truth

I wonder if anyone really knows
The "Meaning of Truth", as the saying goes.
Is it only what we choose to believe,
Or simply beyond our power to conceive?

Is it shown in our living day by day,
Or do far too many fall by the way?
Is it shown by faith in our fellow man?
Is it just the same as when time began?

The "Meaning of Truth" — what a solid ring!
In our hearts it should be a precious thing.
"Do not bear false witness," sayeth the Lord.
"Love thy neighbor as thyself," is His word.

If we all live just as our God commands.
Peace and love shall prevail throughout all lands.
Then the tree will grow as the twig was bent
The "Meaning of Truth" will be evident.

Charlotte I. Kreiser

My Husband

The man who has given me his heart.
The man I've loved from the very start.
The man who has shown me how much he cares.
The man I know will always be there.
The man who's my strength each day that goes by.
The man whose shoulder I use to cry.
The man who has given me a reason to live.
The man who makes my love for him so easy to give.
The man whose smile lights up my life.
The man who makes me feel important as a wife.
The man who is motivated by affection and love.
The man who loves me as much as our God above.

Catherine Davis

Our Worst Disease

A disease is a sickness of the body or the mind
The list is quite extensive a disease of every kind
A disease can make us feel bad or it can take our life
And I find that all people can catch a disease
Though he be red, yellow, black, or white

Diseases are acquired in many ways, all are subject to some
They can be by inheritance, or it can be where you call home
They can be caused by viruses, or where you choose to roam
They can be caused by lifestyle, or the pets that you own
But of all the diseases I can have, I can think of only one

I can think of only one that rates top of the bad
Only one if I had to catch would really make me mad
This disease I write of hurts all. We feel pain every day
But those hurt by it would be spared if we would only pray
It is such a senseless disease, one which we can take away

The disease that I write of, has to be the disease of hate
In which thousands of people die from it, we see it every day
God would still love me, if my life a cancer should take
But I don't want to stand before God, being filled with the
Disease of hate

Billy M. Hancock

Yellow-Fire

The winter snows ooze meltingly away
Somewhere in the dank woods a lonely bird sings
The pale yellow sun summons all living things
Tender green timidly greets the vernal day
Man's heart thrills anew to Earth's awakening
Something glorious is born in the crucible of spring
 FORSYTHIA!

Irma Marcia Roth

Summersoft And Dreaming

Sitting by the window
   the life of the world drifts in and
   envelops me, cradling me in a
   web of sounds, a tapestry of
   textures, a collage of
     colors, the lilting, laughing life
     of a summer's day

My sightless eyes envision
   quiet dreams,
   my ears hear the gentle sound of
     growing things,
   and when I take her hand, her laughter
     trickles over me like the
   soft evening rain, patterning a lullaby
     on my upturned face
     ...making me smile

Dean Lim

The Work Of The Hand Of God

Today I took a quiet walk in the woods near my home town.
The leaves were yellow, red, and gold, and many had fallen down.
As I walked along in the cool fresh air through the yellow goldenrod.
I knew this beauty had to be the work of the hand of God.

As I walked along the pathway there were wild flowers everywhere.
I knew these things were put here for everyone to share.
Down a gently sloping hillside on a carpet of soft green sod.
To the swiftly flowing river the work of the hand of God.

If some day you are down in spirit and the days seem without end.
Take a quiet walk in the woods nearby, I'm sure you will find a friend.
He is there in the trees and flowers, everywhere on the Earth you trod.
It is there for everyone to see, the work of the hand of God.

Edward V. Seese

Misfortune Of A Damaged Man

Headlong against the raging midnight storm I wearily plod
The howling wind inflicts my painful ears with scarlet punishment
And stinging sleet invades, bombards defenseless cheeks,
Involuntary tears meander toward their frigid deaths.

The liquor at the noisy bar was little consolation,
The unexpected goodbye note she left had drained my soul
A forlorn streetlamp, distant, faint, uncaring
Is just a feeble glow behind the swirling, blinding snow.

My brandied breath paints varnished frostings on my hapless lips
With frozen feet I contemplate how leather soles cannot compete
Against the boastful challenge of the icy walk
Step after frenzied step I falter, then on will alone, trudge on.

Onward, insanely onward, to a house that once was a home
Just one more block to go, freezing, wheezing, reeling from the cold
The merciless gale assaults the too-thin coat
I shiver, shudder, fall and curse the mindless knives in my knees.

Desperate now, and numb with anguish and with biting chill
I stagger up the slippery step and fumble for elusive keys
Anticipating comfort from the roaring hearth and fire inside
Now panic, too. Remember, though, the door might be unlocked...

Gordon Dean Schlundt

To Many Leaders

Be a doll, fetch this for me
Stay until your tasks (and mine) are done
Eat lunch at your desk, customers hate voice mail
You haven't finished your degree yet!
Stop!
Is this why I was born?

Jennifer Leola Mummey-Brewer

Untitled

Racism is in the air.
The hate prevails everywhere.
We can't escape from this sad situation,
Or even have hope for a peaceful nation,
No one race is superior to all,
But the one who believes that, most likely will fall.
We all have to learn to love one another,
So just open your heart to your sister or brother.
Love sees no color as far as I'm concerned,
But it always seems if your different, you most frequently get burned.
The idea of love is so hard to create,
Because we can't free the world from all this racist hate.
Orange, yellow, black, or white,
We're all seen the same in God's light.
So free yourself from the ignorance of man,
And make our nation a happy land.

Jessica Stevens

Please Don't Smoke

The Surgeon General says "PLEASE DON'T SMOKE"
The harm it does your body is no joke.
It will ruin your lungs, and make you sick,
that's why it's called a cancer stick.

Now cancer sticks are small and round
and are very easy to be found.
So do yourself a real good deed
and don't puff on the dirty old weed.

When you light one up it starts you coughing
and adds another nail to your coffin.
So if you want to live to a ripe old age
then read and heed what's on this page.

Let's pay attention to the medical group
They know the facts — they have the scoop.
Put out those cigarettes — start life anew
LIFE OUR DEATH — IT'S UP TO YOU.

Fred G. McFarland Sr.

Seasons In Pennsylvania

In the Spring when the Dogwood trees are in full bloom,
The green forests are spotted with white.
And when the green rolling hills are covered with pink wildflowers,
It is a beautiful sight!

Lightening bugs are in abundance,
In the air on a warm Summer night,
Flitting around here and there,
Like little blinking Christmas lights.

The prettiest time of year in the east,
Is probably in the Fall.
The temperature starts dropping,
And you watch in awe....

As the leaves start changing colors,
From green to hues of brown,
Yellow, red and orange,
Before they all fall down...

And cover the forest floor.
As they blow to and fro...
Before Winter descends again,
With a white blanket of snow.

Barbara K. Floyd

Just The Other Day

Just the other day, I went to visit Mother
The gathering in her honor.
We were all to be there: my aunts, my uncles,
Her nieces, her nephews, my sister, my brother.

Just the other day, she wore the blue gown
Worn once before to her third child's wedding.
The scarf 'round her head covered that spot.
'Twas perfect in color and matching.
The shawl 'round her shoulders to protect her from chill
Was nothing but netting, but angelic looking.

Just the other day, it was time to say goodbye
And kneeling at her side, I felt the coolness rise.
I don't ever remember her arm so smooth, so tender.
Her lips did not move when I smudged the color.
Under the rouge, I could tell the pallor.

Just the other day, I heard, "It's time, it's time."
Time to put the lid on her box
And cover her beautiful face.
I don't call that time, I call that the end.

Anna M. Kearney

Fuzzy Tail And The Winged Ballet

In my yard and trees they play,
The fuzzy tail and the winged ballet.

Sometimes with my window they collide
But when I check, off they glide.

My granddaughter laughs with glee
When their bathing she does see.

The fuzzy tail from the bird bath laps,
He drinks his water just like a cat.

The pretty black capped chick-a-dee
Has lots of songs he sing to me.

The gold finches, I do feed,
With the cold and wind it's food they need.

The little sapsucker thought he might
With me enjoy a little bite.

A big blue jay visited me today,
So all the little ones flew away.

The funny birds and silly squirrel
All can give quite a twirl,
As they in my front yard play;
The fuzzy tail and the winged ballet.

JoEllen Reynolds

Sonnet I

To feel the gentle flowing wind like lace,
The fragrance of the lofty pines on high.
O, for the gift to wake a long silent race,
To stand aloft and reach to touch the sky.

The seasons come and swiftly go their way,
With mysteries that cannot be explained,
And hide the simple life of yesterday;
Will there be beauty with what remains?

Is man too blind and bitter not to care,
Or hear the music of the rippling stream,
Will he propose to dam it, how dare-
Whence comes the future generation's dreams?

Dean Ransom

The Eye Of The Lord

Distractions abound at every corner,
the eye is amused by every picture.

The eye is in focus. Its view is voracious.
It sees and it sees and it sees and it sees.

Cataracts moves in, the focus grows dim.
The view is now tainted, shapes start to swim.

The eye must now wait, it listens within.
Clear focus comes, from the guiding of others.

The mind closes in, a new view develops.
Seeing is different, fresh and renewed.

The Eye of the Lord, brightens the light,
shapes what is seen, worry - released.

Distractions depart, focus is clearer.
Seeing now new, seeing now true.

Jeffrey G. Bohan

Twin Zodiac

Twins in spirit traveling through time and space
The depth of your feelings projected through unseen forces
As I see the pain etched on your face.

 Twin zodiac

To know, to feel what is in your soul coming to settle within my own.
Without knowing you and without speaking
Weathering the stillness of being alone.

 Twin zodiac

Time blows through eternity
Embraced in kindred, chaste and pure
So close that my mind holds your key:

 Twin zodiac

Ablaze with wonderment, orchestrated by infinity
To feel this oneness - to be able to know another
Through unseen forces that be
Yes, you are my sister and my brother,
 Twin zodiac

Joan O'Latta

Colored Emotion

Colored emotion filling me up inside.
The deep black is depression, harder to hide.
Color me purple for the anger, things not right.
Blue is the sorrow, the loss, deep as the sky at midnight.
Red colors my passion for the love I yearn, but still haven't found.
Vivid yellow is the happiness I feel when I make music, a beautiful sound.
Green is my envy I have for those with the existence of true love.
White is the purity of the love I'd give, so elegant like a dove.
The passionate longing to make love, the brightest neon pink.
The dreary gray, it fills my days, washing out happiness in a blink.
Gold is the glamour and fame I hope to someday find.
All these colors I see; and black is the only emotion that keeps
coming to mind.

Jeannie Anne Mathis

A Shooting Star

Once I saw a shooting
star fly across the sky.
I wonder how it got here
let me think and find out why.
Even though it went so fast.
I want this sight to always last.
I slipt under the covers and went to sleep.
But the wish I made I'll always keep.

Crystal Copp

Rain

I love the storm, the rain it brings
 the cool refreshing new of spring
The clouds, the sky, unleash their power
 to bring to me, a summer shower

The air, so thick, so close, so wet
 refreshes memories, I can't forget
The thunders rolls,—I clench my hand
 as lightning walks across the land

The skies unfold, from up above
 I spend the hours in making love
I borrow strength from rain and wind
 to be as one,—to be its twin

The skies will clear, the rain has passed
 and I'll be left, refreshed, at last
The sun will set,—in reds and golds
 in a sky washed clean, with colors bold

The rain is love
 from Heaven,—hurled
God's blessings,—rain
 upon the world.

Frank E. Konieska

Don't Want To Let Go

 It is so very difficult for me to grasp and accept
The concept itself that you are gone away from this Earth
 The cold, chilling aura of Death swept in and fought you
Until your frail and aged body could take no more and surrendered
 But, don't you ever worry, I never see you as a quitter
I still see that special twinkle in your blue eyes and I can
 Still hear that soft-spoken voice and jovial laugh of yours
I am being selfish when I long to have you back, I know that
 People tell me that you're not suffering anymore
But, tell me this, were you suffering before?
 Because I will see you again in the Afterlife, I will not
Tell you "Good-bye," but rather, I will say to you...
 "Until Then"

Andrea Marie Bledsoe

Why Me?

Figures hovering over me as if to be operated on.
The cold night entraps my emotions and pain.
What terrible thing had I done to deserve this?
Time moves fast.
Slow is time.
I am smothered in a blanket of horror.
Is this fiction or reality?
Am I in a movie?
My pain does not exist.
Why me?
Pain envelops my battered torso and heart.
Memories of last night play in my head like a movie.
The projector must be broken for I only see last night.
It doesn't cease.
I can distinctively remember last night.
I have forgotten the morning.
Paranoia.
I have died.
I am born.
Why me?

Hector Montano

Happy Birthday Jesus

After their bedtime story, and kneeling beside their beds,
The children with hearts o'er flowing quietly bowed their heads.

They prayed:
Dear Jesus, Mommy told us that your birthday's almost here,
We've learned so much about you throughout this passing year.

She said you came from heaven as a real-life baby boy,
Down to a lowly stable, and the angels sang for joy.

I wish I could have given you my quilt for your manger bed,
And you could have had my pillow underneath your little head.

We know about the things you did, your love-filled ministry.
You caused the lame to walk again, and made the blind to see.

You were so very kind and good, but it made us want to cry
When Daddy said they nailed you on a cross so you would die.

We're glad that you're in heaven now and watch over us each day.
You guide our footsteps and our lives so please hear us when we say

We love you, dear Lord Jesus, and at Christmas once again,
We wish you "Happy Birthday" - In your name we pray.

Evelyn Masek

What Happened?

Silence is broken. The people who suffered have spoken.
The bells of the churches will ring,
no more beatings, rejoice, now sing.
Purple is the color, yet it is black that we see.
She's dead now, he sent her flowers.
Little did he know, he set her free.

The beatings and the pain, all done with a slash.
When does it all stop? How long does it have to last?
Children screaming; crying in their beds.
Listening to their mothers, finding out later,
their mother is dead.

When will this violence come to an end?
When will all the emotional and physical scars mend?
Will they have to die in order for it all to stop?
Will it be life they have to drop?

So, stand tall, with us, let's not fight at all.
We have to band together, together for all.
We have created a unity, one and all.
Stand together, stand together, one and all....

Deborah L. Bobeck

"Hillbilly Angel"

It was a warm misty afternoon as the young cowboy was riding through
the beautiful green country side. The white tip mountains rose up
all around him. Then all of a sudden there she was........

She was standing in a field of wild flowers, all dressed in white.
Her hair hung down her back and was as black and shiny as the wings
of a raven. There she stood, barefoot, with her hands raised towards
heaven, the rain falling softly upon her face.

She turned slowly towards him, and the smile that came upon her face
made the sun come out and white fluffy clouds dance at her feet. She
had eyes that would out-shine the stars on a clear dark night. He
knew, at that moment, he was looking at a "Hillbilly Angel".

She came towards him with the movement of a white swan. He dismounted
his pony, took her small hand in his and asked her name. That was the
beginning...he would ride the hills by night to court her...she would
gather the wild flowers by day to win his love.

They swam in the cool mountain streams and rode his pony through the
beautiful hillside in the moon light. He would kiss her warm lips,
as she reached out to touch his soul.

They were married there on her mountain top....she to her cowboy, him
to his beautiful, "Hillbilly Angel"...

Diane Paulson

Remember

Remember, remember well I shall always
The beautiful apparition which approached
Real I could not believe this angel to be
And real you became with your first spoken words.
Babble yes, I'm sure I made little sense
Knowledge has never been lost so fast
I went from speaking the language of a grown up
To that of a fool within seconds.
Yet you wished to remain and speak with me
I must say the second time around
Became somewhat easier.

David W. Shoptaw

Song Of The Century

Nearing the final anchorage, but months away
The battered good ship CENTURY, sailing surely
And stridently through the murky water, ready for rest
Yet avoiding a persistence of rocks and shoals.

This ship began in pleasant twilight of horse and buggy,
Then came EDISON, light and sound,
The ship's wake intersecting ripples of various impact,
VOLTA, OHM'S LAW, AMPERE, FARADAY, EINSTEIN,
RELATIVITY,
HIROSHIMA.

Following along came a voice from the clouds,
"ONE SMALL STEP FOR MAN..."

Then came the TRANSISTOR AND ITS ILK.

Now the weary ship in view of its final port
Finds its way blocked by construction
Of a flashy new vessel making ready for the next century.

Bright with Ersatz paint, atomic power,
Computer guided, zealous with confidence to avoid
Ancient ripples in the old stream.

Joseph Earl Taylor

An Evening Full Of Stars

An evening full of stars
The bankrupt spirit hog-ties the eager heart
Myopic vision obscures the vastness of possibilities
The distant star of possibility shines
    lightly on the disturbed soul
The heartbeat of ethereal dreams
The stanchion of hope carries the restive heart
Ethereal dreams gilding mundane aspirations
The tempered spirit pilots focused revelation
    from a throng of disordered desires
The veneration of hope, the reverence of vision

Christopher Nessa

Interpretation Of Autumn

The days grow shorter
the air becomes colder
birds begin their annual journey to a
more pleasant climate
flowers begin to fade
leaves begin to change and for awhile
the scenery is beautiful in a burst of color
then the leaves begin to drop
the color begins to fade
now the world is a cold, drab place
void of color and warmth
but life continues though dormant
in anticipation of the upcoming Spring.

Angela Spranger

"Love In The Autumn Season Of Life"

Young love laughs and boasts of its claim, makes folly of love among
the aging and lame.
Days once lived, careless and wild, fills the mind of a once innocent child.
The young and foolish, emotions so fragile, feels that love's reserved
for the young and agile.
But they too, will sometime see, that love is meant also, for the elderly.
The aging soul who's learned from the past, a far better way to a love that lasts.
Strands of gray replace the gold, yet I'd never trade young love for
the quality of old.
The heart stays young for those who know, just how to live and think
and grow.
A love that understands another, forgives slights done to each other.
The autumn of life contains much wealth, combined with wisdom and the
blessing of health.
Then add to these, a special someone who'll share, life's final
seasons with tender care.
The love of youth, so sensitive, naive, still centers 'round its' own
and "what's in it for me".
The love shared by two in the autumn season, can fulfill as no young
love can. Living by faith without human reason, combined with God's
love and infinite plan.

Jane Roscoe

The Rose

Did you ever wonder what happens to that beautiful rose?
   That seems to wither and die when the cold wind blows
It bows its head and is blanketed by snow
   Waiting for that moment to rise again and grow

Now when spring arrives and the weather warms
   And the snow melts and the sun alarms
All the world to awake and open up its eyes
   To bring back the rose that never dies.

That rose lives on like the love in my heart
   And the winter wind is the hurt when we're apart
But your smile is the sun that warms me so
   And my love for you continues to grow

Like that rose so beautiful in the summer breeze
   Is your beauty that only my eye sees
That rose and my love are two of a kind
   They'll both live forever and I'm sure you'll find.

When that cold wind blows and it starts to snow
   My love like that rose won't die, it'll grow
Stronger with each passing season of the year
   And last forever this I promise you, dear

Barry W. Wurst

Untitled

Are the big things in life so important
that we can't accept the small
there are doubts about our future
should we heed their call
we all climb life's ladder
and sometimes we succeed
but are we really happy
with the glory that we see
our world is full of wonders
of every size and form
we can all embrace them
when we escape from the norm
but what if we cared about our world
and the daily riches that she brings
then we could take the chance
on enjoying the little things

Charli Prowell

Existence Is Festive

The absence of your sweet aroma stirs a paining whine
That seems to grow with in me with every memory of mine.
The love I long, I've known, will thicken over time
Our wisdom will allow us a long romantic dine.

Young love we have, it tingles in our blood
I taste it in our kisses
...and feel in every hug.

Once thought of in my younger days
that true love was really built,
but what do young ones know
but the warmth of grandma's quilt.

The absence of true love
may plant with in us want
but to receive it in our hearts
we'll chant the happy songs that haunt.

Alyssa Gipe

His Hands

His hands were soft and gentle
That was a long time ago.
He used to play and goof around
that too was a long time ago.
He had once rode a bike and went to school
how long ago that was.
Threw the years his hands toughened
everything he did made its own harsh mark.
That like so much else, was a long time ago.
As time passed he grew older and had children,
each one leaving a mark, for every child he worked harder
so long ago
Here comes the grandchildren, then the great
From piggybacks and tractor rides, they kept him busy.
All of the years have had their role for every mark there is a story.
Now if you hold his hands, you feel all the hard work that went into them.
His hands were soft and gentle.

Elizabeth M. Plummer

Conformity

Of late it did occur to me,
that prejudice has to be
the worst of all iniquities.
Disclosing improprieties, with sometimes
much resiliency, remaining without
decency, a part of all humanity
one fragment of the recipe by which
we live our lives.

This makes me with perplexity,
then wonder with adversity,
That even if society, reversed itself
entirely, would there be enough
integrity, sincerity, and honesty,
With which we in all certainty
would wipe out all the hate?
I fear it's much too late!

Cynthia Critchfield

Rekindling The Basics

Roots are to flowers like verses are to poetry
that personifies the cornerstone of our relationship -
expression of feelings, listening, and empathy.

The roots of a flower are the essence of its existence
The strength of the base will determine its persistence

Nourishment is required to sustain the life of the bloom,
Sufficient sunlight for warmth and water to consume.

As we grow accustomed to the blossom, its needs may be neglected.
underexposure to fertile soil leaves the roots unprotected.

The flower we once adored has withered away.
Were we preoccupied with ourselves and allowed the other to stray?

So grows a relationship complacent over time.
We tend to lose sight of the sentimental things,
like listening attentively to our partner's feelings and differences to
    compromise

Rekindling the basics of effective communication
will fortify our love and prolong its duration.

The passion which thrives between us can be discerned light years away,
as we renew our wedding vows while our grandchildren look on and say,
"How did both of you remain together so long?"
We would reply to their query, that our groundwork was strong.

Roots are to flowers like verses are to poetry
that embodies the foundation of our relationship -
expression of feelings, listening, and empathy.

Barry Zabielinski

Nature, My Mistress

Let love of mistress ne'er bond me of it,
That our lips may ne'er touch to kiss;
Simply a union of souls to which
By words unspoken we must submit
To a reality we must forget,
For all we own is but a package of a kit.
To have a whim or wish, it might be this:
That graced by heather's dew still forming
While daylight frustrates morning's mist
We work our thoughts to fit
What others miss. To them the loss
That cost them all the bliss of Nature
Yet Nature is itself adorning
When lips that touch don't kiss.

Donald A. Driskell

I've Got God On Hold

Operator, operator, please dial
that number one more time.
I, think I must of pressed the wrong button.
I, heard a dial tone,
I, saw another light starting to blight.
This switch board keeps ringing
and I know I put God on hold.
Which number was it I can't
remember, which one was it.
Oh! God! please hold on.
Buzzzzzz....Charlotte Voldarski
Please, check that number and
please try again...click...
Operator. Operator.

Charlotte Voldarski

Dialogue

Tell me the pillowing of my soul
    that lies in the darkness of
    unforeseen events
Taken from its seam of dissatisfaction
The journey of a thousand years

You have made it to be of
    unshadowed significance,
    foretold it
Left it to be given to the princes
    of high innuendo
Befallen in time, bestowed

Left to travel the inroads of bourne
    to let out the many cries of solitude
    to torment the given allies
    to fortify the grains of love annoyed

For when it came to pass
Having been given a shape
    yet seen as dungeon
Allied with the shadow
    of love as yet fulfilled.

Asha Ariel Aleia

In Memory Of My Brother

When people die, when does the pain go away?
That is something nobody can say
Three years have passed is it still o.k. to cry?
Three years have gone by can I still ask questions why?
When people die what do you do?
If you still think of them do they still think of you?
Questions like this linger in my mind
Someone to answer them is hard to find
Stuff like this is hard for me to say
Through this poem is the only way
As I sit alone my tears start to flow
I start to think why did he have to go?
Everyone thinks of this that's true
But I still didn't find the right answers did you?
Sometimes I think of the fun we had
Both the good times and the bad
Sometimes it helps cure the pain
But the pain comes back and I feel the same
I know we'll see each other in the end
But will you be my brother or my friend?

Amber Chutko

Untitled

You might think I don't know anything
That I'm just a little girl
To you, my feelings don't mean a thing
You don't even want to hear my words
Well you're wrong about me this time
I know people pretty well
From outside you can't see the mind
You have to look deeper to tell
I might've been naive, 'cause I trusted you at first
I didn't expect what you did
Partly, it might've been my fault
Only I because I felt for it
Right now, please don't explain yourself
And don't apologize to me
You can't bring back the time, it's too late
You'll have to live with it.

Anna Pikina

128

The Repair Job

I needed to fix the thingamabob,
That hooked on the end of the bobble.
I needed a clacker with a half inch knob
And a drill that fit half on a cobble.

I went to the store in search of my tools,
Without them I couldn't begin,
But, while they had shimmers and pluckers and gools,
They had nothing with a flange made of tin.

'Use a musker', they said, 'with a lopsided eye,
And a solid round base should suffice."
"But," I protested, "I'd then have to buy
A left-handed croak packed in ice."

So I guess for now I'll delay my task,
And maybe some day I'll do it,
I'll still have to use a right-handed trask.
But, then I must get a round tuit.

Howard L. Peterson

The Sound Of Twilight

What is the sound of the bark of a tree,
that grows on the bank of a river?

Or what is the sound of a twinkling star,
that sparkles in the night time sky?

What is the sound of an autumn breeze,
that rustle the leaves of a tree at twilight?

The sound of a tree is hard to hear,
but the voice of the star
and the sight of the breeze,
both bring words of love to me.

I heard the news that she was gone,
gone to her eternal rest,
I saw the smile upon her face,
and knew that she had passed the test.

I wandered out and gazed into the evening sky,
and saw a star that twinkled more than all the rest.

Then from out of the night,
the voice came strong and clear.
Carried on the evening breeze
It spoke to me of love and eternal rest.

John F. Tucker

Evensong

At evensong I walk among the flowers,
That drift along the garden path I know.
Their fragrance triggers many memories
Of places known to me from long ago.

I hear the song birds' haunting melody;
A rhapsody unmatched by works of man.
Their cheery notes fall on my aching soul
And lift my mood, as only music can.

My thoughts return to scenes of yesterday;
Of childhood's happy languid summer days.
I trace my route back down the trails of time
And wrap contentment round me like a haze.

Fireflies gather with their tiny lights;
Darkness comes and settles round my head.
I thank my Father for His wondrous gifts,
Turn off my light and snuggle into bed.

Anna K. Shoemaker

Lonely Streets

I walk the lonely streets at night, I am very much aware,
That danger is all around me, but I do not even care.
For I am very much alone, and life is hard to live,
What makes it even worse, I have a lot to give.
But no one needs a lonely soul, and so they look away.
I have not one to talk to, no one to smile and say,
Hello to you, I hope you're well, and it's a lovely day.
I have no home to go to, no fire to sit beside,
No bed for me to sleep in, no car to take a ride.
I yearn to have a someone, that I could call my own.
I wish I had some supper, but I don't even have a bone.
I survive, at least for now,
Why am I alive?
But heaven waits for me someday, for that alone I strive.

Clifford Palmer King

Mystery Of Darkness

Come with me and you will see, the darkness and the mystery,
that combine to cause calamity,
in the middle of the night.
Fear starts out with a staring gaze, then walks you through an
imagined maze, to either a splendid or scary place,
spirit is set adrift.
You try to shriek but nothing is released, you can't outrun the
horrible beast, you believe in existence, for nothing has ceased,
you think your life is over.
But when eyes awake you realize, that terror's not reality nor is it
lies, and all the strange creatures recognized,
are an opaque memory.
Memory strains to remember but soon will forget,
what mind tries to conceive the soul will omit, all dismays will
then beset, the body can't escape.
The enigma is over but ears will hear, voices in the night that
are drawing near, the dread returns that had since disappeared,
nightmare begins once more.

Diane Smith

Blades Of Grass

I never knew
That blades of grass could glisten so.
The day was late, the sun hung low
And the fresh young grass
Waving in the gentle breeze
Glistened as if coated by the rain,
Yet it was dry.
A million diamonds sparkled there
As the young blades
Caught long, low rays of sunshine
And made them dance.
The day grew late and calm replaced the breeze
The diamonds lost their sparkle
As they grew still.
And then as twilight fell the glow went, too.
But beauty did remain
The deep rich beauty of a soft green velvet carpet.
The shades of green
Grew darker-darker-darker
Then blended with the night.

Iva P. Owings

Dinner Music

Sea Sends her message up onto the Land
Speaks softly of her tales with grains of Sand,
But she can reign a harsh and bitter fight
And turn white sand into a thing of might
To sting and cut the very heart of one
To send clouds veiling off the setting sun.
Be not amazed at Beauty's Tender Flask
This lady holds a many headed mask.

Dorothy Alice Wall

129

Poetry Writing

I've concluded that my thoughts are moreless expressions,
that are developed with so much care,
The developed thoughts are devised carefully,
to create something pleasing to the ear,
You must select the exact words, to hear the rhythm flow,
A format so unique, that's arranged row by row.
As each phrase's is relinquished, it must be forceful with each sound,
For your orchestrating verses of wisdom, let the
people hear it all around town,
Writing is an art, that takes a lot of logic within,
It's amazing how you must put so much interest
in your work, you must do this again and again,
Tell your narrative story, perhaps someone will see the light,
Arrange it verse by verse, write all through the night,
The pen is mightier than the sword, you'll challenge any opponent.
There's an art in Poetry Writing, never a dull moment.

James Theodore Ross

The Risen

In the old world, the Roman world,
that ancient life of law, power,
and force ever mind and will.

Rose a man not interested in the things
of the ceasers. A man a world into himself.

So separate, so different from
things material. A man who saw
no death, believed in no death.

Possessed of the future of man
risen from the base and unto
the higher more real world.

Leaving behind a small sign.
A cloth showing the very cheating of his death.
A sigh of the power within us all.

We are the rising.
Our destiny his to be the risen.

James Eichor

Grandma

Well look here, it is 1995,
Thank the Lord you're still alive.

You'll go most any place whenever you can,
As long as you can sit and not have to stand.

No matter what my problem may be,
You always have time to talk to me.

When I am sitting in church saying my prayers,
I can hear you and your cane coming from anywhere.

You are remarkable woman as we all can see,
With a few false teeth and artificial knee.

Don't let her fool you with that sweet smile,
She can get her dandruff up when she gets riled.

You're seventy-nine and you look just fine,
Even if some days you don't feel like you're in your prime.

We all laugh and share this day,
As I tell you I love you in my special way.

Alice K. Gallenstein

"Autumn"

Can you smell the Autumn in the air,
Taste the cotton candy at the County Fair,
Touch the ice of the first frost glare,
and see the summer no where.

Summer is spent but Fall is nigh,
Walk on the leaves that fall from high,
Look through the fog to a darker sky,
and see a snowflake so alone and shy.

Yet from that darker sky must come,
The Indian Summer's summer sun,
Hear the stirring Collage songs and hum,
Their melody with the beat of the drum.

The new found summer temperature tease,
The old summer clothes of stately trees,
But the old clothes go with the nippy breeze,
and nature settles down to its first big freeze.

John C. Tuttle

Someone Who Listens

He is very strong in the mind
talking with him he seems very kind.

When you speak, you know he is there
he always listens when you say a prayer.

As mighty and strong as he may be
sometimes he will let a painful soul free.

He does this for a reason, not to be bad
just remember he is there if you're feeling sad.

He knows when you're sick and feeling down
someone you know who will always be around.

A man of patience, a man of love
He is a gracious man from above.

A man who knows pain and takes away tears
People know him as "God" and will for years.

Jimmy Bengtson

But Where Is That Song, Waiting To Be?

The guitar on its stand beckons me.
Taking care of life delays the art.
But where is that song, waiting to be?

Childhood ends, survival becomes key
getting ahead, grand work appears smart.
The guitar on its stand beckons me.

Jobs, marriage, kids bouncing on my knee
responsibility, I play the part.
But where is that song, waiting to be?

Fleeting ascent through years, now forty
reflecting on my unfulfilled heart.
The guitar on its stand beckons me.

There is no trade for God's generosity
love and experiences fill the cart.
But where is that song, waiting to be?

The time, conflict, possibility,
yet drowning efforts never depart.
The guitar on its stand beckons me.
But where is that song, waiting to be?

Bruce J. Irvine

It Is

A madman holding onto memories and dreams,
surrounded by simplicity and somewhere...
Somewhere the screams of entities can be heard,
like a tree in a grassy field on the hot plains of Texas.

The shade covers me in memory,...and the winter wind?
The winter wind cuts through my heart.
Where have the dragonflies gone, have they died in the mist?
Do the stars still dance upon the water, does romance?...

A fraction of a moment sacrificed in silence without movement.
  ...and nobody heard it, and nobody felt it.
The dark azure night wind whips through the weeping willow,
the fireflies dance madly, insanely filling the night with laughter.

  ...and your eyes, where have they gone? the darkness hides them,
the light will never let them be known, only in the shadows can I see your soul,
only in autumn does your spirit sing to me...let the teardrops fall
my dear, like red leaves of fire spiralling...spiralling madly to their end.

The harvester has come, my spirit has died, captured...captured in the night
devoured by shadows,...laughter rings in the halls.
your teardrops fall my dear, did you really think love would last forever?
Did you really think the dragonflies would be there?

Joseph Bonaventure Gonzales

Life Together, Beginning

You are entering a sacred space
Surrounded by light.
You will be together inside.
From the depth of your union
Your vision can reach far and wide.

Should the light become murky
And the flame become weak,
Remember who you were
When each other you did seek.

When your union faces
Its greatest stress,
You will discover yet another part
Of the strength you each possess.

If you both live well past one hundred years,
You will not uncover all the treasures
That lie within you.

Remember, you are whole.
You each contain
More than enough
To feed both of your souls.

Barry C. Saiff

Lost Chalice

There was a boat, that was put in a moat, which
surrounded a palace, wherein dwelt the golden chalice. The drawbridge
did draw at the king's call, the night of the chalice ball. They began
to dance all night long, to the golden chalice songs. Then this night
there came a fog, so they sent out a servant to get more logs.
When he came back in from the night, out broke a fight with twelve
knights. It began over a maiden as always seems to be, where I
heard a knight say something very rudely. So I and the servants hid
under the king's table, that was overturned by the knights of the
chalice table. Then at that time the king began to scream, "Stop this
nonsense all you fiends." At that moment they all stopped in their
tracks, and the king with all his knights began to laugh.
He then said, "Bring me my chalice with some wine." But the golden
chalice they could never find, so who took me and where am I?

Frank J. Florio

Chillin'

Glistening gold, shimmering bright,
Sunshine flickering, blinding my sight.
Boat rockin' gently, life carefree and light.

Early morning breezes, dancin' in my hair,
Clouds rolling slowly, seaweed in the air.
Another new beginning, another day of care.

Chillin' to music, smooth rhythm and rhyme,
Sounds beatin' softly, body pulsing to time.
Memories flowing—mellow thoughts, paradigms.

Sounds of nature, pitches high and low,
Animated creatures, running to and fro.
Life in its simplicity, no worries, no woe.

Eyelids heavy, blackness closing in,
Sweet smell of summer, let it never end.
Savor precious moments, yield to nature's whim.

Life waits for no one, moments gone again,
Future's my destination, past is where I've been.
Lazy days, exciting nights, chillin' with friends.

Bessie H. Sharpe

Loyalty And Trust

Around them flowers bloom
Sunflowers, violets, from dawn until noon
Two souls in deep embrace
A gentle touch upon her face

Eyes sparkle, like diamonds in a ring
In the tree tops, little birds sing
Hearts are pounding, as he draws her near
Upon her face, falls a single tear

He draws her ever closer, touching her lips
Barely stroking them, with his fingertips
Gently running his fingers through her hair
She knows in her heart, love is there

Trust and loyalty, he knows well
His love for her is deep, she can tell
Another tear rolls down her cheek
Streaming downward, like a tiny glittering creek

Happiness is hers this sunny day
For she knows in her heart, he will stay
Her prayers were answered, by God above
She has finally found the perfect love

Joseph D. Osborne

"U"

A poem,
        Strong, detailing every crevice of your soul
a verse,
        so sweet, Angel's voices could not make it whole

Even a sketch surrounded by a bright frame of Gold,

        will try...and try hard yes
but never can maintain or capture the Great
Beauty U possess.

As if touched by Perfection, by the very hands of our Lord
  U surpass everything imaginable
    with pure love which gleams deep from your core.
U, J o y, B e a u t y, H a p p i n e s s, L o v e,
        and U.

  all that is good begins and ends with U, for it was U
        good was invented.
U are a symbol of my life & dreams, of everything I know as
        right.
        Come...bring your presence to me
          so I may love U with all my
            m i g h t.

Calvin Richardson Jr.

Night Vision

Traveling through the dark, searching for the route,
straining to make visual sense of all that surrounds me:
I note each turn, each hill or bridge,
convinced I recognize them from the time before.

Oh, deceptive night that robs us of our certainty and comfort!
Like nocturnal creatures rendered sightless in the day
for want of nighttime cues,
we disdainful humans are humbled by mutations of the night.

To travel in the blackness of the mind with only archetypes
of ancient memory (synaptic guides of inward journey),
would offer sagacity of sight.
(It is not to search for enemies, but to find again the soul).
Might then we comprehend the need for vision in the dark.

Ann R. Langdon

Death Without Life After

Black very black, it is immensely black and deep. The water stand
still so motionless, not emitting a singe into the blackness of the
night. Listen for the sounds of the night, can you not hear? All are
in a hypnotic state, a trace; calm, noiseless and asleep. The night
thick and hollow, are you listening with the your ear perched against
its side? Can you hear the voice of the pit, luring you to join him
in this sacred nothingness.

Nothing can penetrate this blackness, nothing can permeate this
atmosphere; no fragrance, no light on grief or pain. Why then is it
be avoid? It is not sweet, and enticing and eternally bliss? It is
not the Utopia that man, through the ages, has searched so
desperately for, or the fountain of the youth, for all is ageless
there. It is a treasure but unconventionally so, for this treasure
finds you. He wraps you into the folds of his garments secure and
unyielding. Your eyes adjust to darkness, clearly you see now that
you are not alone...Many are there who have gone before you and many
shall follow after. Can you hear the voice of the pit luring you to
join him in this sacred nothingness?

Rev. (SGM) Harvey J. Lester

Perfect Love

Night has fallen; day is done.
Still, I wait for that special One.
That stranger, known yet unknown,
since time immemorial.

Spanning the vastness of a star-splendored
universe,
traveling onward with no time for sleep,
the breath of His voice touches my soul.
The gentleness of His love wraps itself
around my shoulders.

I lay contentedly, nestled in a cloud
of happiness never found in the world
or mortals.
I am, at this moment, surrounded by
Perfect Love.

Jeanette Lovelady

The American Melting-Pot

Do strangers passing on the street
Speak as tho' you are a friend?
I always reply, but it is a puzzle.
Is it because I am the result
Of a really mixed genealogy?
With maternal Scot and Irish
And paternal German and French ancestors,
It is possible I resemble many others
In physical form, coloring and facial expression.
It pleases me to think that I am the result
Of the so-called American Melting Pot.

Dorothy Bieber Bliss

Step By Step With You Lord

Step by step, O Lord, we move with you each day;
Step by step, O Lord, you lead us on our way.
Each and every breath we do take
We know it came from you who did create.

Step by step we seek your favor,
Believing miracles to us will come.
Singing praises to you, our father.
For you are our God, the only one.

So God Jehovah we praise your name,
Singing songs to you again.
Your word of promise to us is kept,
When we honor you, step by step.

Allen W. O'Dowd

I Am...

On the brisk days of fall I ruffle the leaves and tug at their
stems trying to free the orange and yellow foliage.

On a chilly September morning I slowly move through the mist
that crawls upon the banks of the shore.

At noon I soar with the great eagle as his wings glide upon me
on his majestic flight in search of food.

Once evening arrives I dive down from the heavens to play through
the fallen leaves as a child would.

Then before I rest I move softly through your window at night and
whisper, "good night".

On early winter mornings I am the fog that creeps upwards from
mountain sides.

On a frozen afternoon I slowly bring a snowflake down to kiss your cheek.

I am the twinkling blue between the stars and you on the darkest of nights.

I glide over the waters late at night when you can't sleep, in the
still of the night you hear me and turn, but there is nothing.

I am the wind.

Joy Renee Sigmon

The Koi Pond

Glinting
Steely silver and flashing flame
Carp
Mouths puckered and enormous
Saucer eyes
Arrested in perpetual wonder
Dart among water lilies and
Nibble at the deep emerald sky and onyx palms
Reflected in a topsy-turvy
Aqueous world that
Echoes
Silent serendipity sounds of
Serenity.

Elizabeth Pelaez Norris

Blocks Of Joy

She was four
Stacking her ABC blocks one upon the other.
Eyes shining with each new block on the tower.
A squeal of delight as the tower comes tumbling down.
She begins again to build with blocks of joy.

She is four and forty
Someone else is building the tower - block upon block.
She is at the bottom - they are not blocks of joy.
Will one more block bring the tower crashing down?

Or will some mother-hand gently remove the blocks one-by-one?
And give her back her blocks of joy?

Betty Dickman

I Don't Want To Go Home

I don't want to go home
Starting as a child you dream of a big home
As you get older, you realize
You have parents with no ambition
You live in a house that is filthy
The clothes you wear are a daily EMBARRASSMENT

I don't want to go home
Deep down you do love your parents
Remember your dream, make it come true, believe in yourself
Don't forget where you come from

I don't want to go home
You can stop the cycle, you have that taste of WANT
As soon as it is legal, move out on your own
Be responsible for yourself
Work hard, don't loose your ambition
It's hard work, you have the taste of want, you are not alone
There are many more ROSES among the thorns

James S. Bakula

Skid Row Man

Sitting in a corner dark and awful cold,
Staring at the bread crumbs, all covered with mold,
He asks himself a question, to which he must reply,
Looking for the answer he begins to tell a lie.

It's early in the morning, just after break of dawn,
The fog is all around him, the man lets out a yawn,
His hands they start to shake, and he begins to think,
Where will he go now he needs that morning drink.

He walks on down the alley, and digs amongst the trash,
In there he finds a bottle someone forgot to smash,
He smiles rather shyly and wipes away the dirt,
And puts the bottle to his mouth and forgets about the hurt.

He's been doing this forever, at least it seems that way to him,
He must have started sometime, he can't remember when,
Drunken and alone now he ends another day,
Sitting in his corner there is nothing more to say.

David A. Herbeck

The Golden Boy

The Golden Boy so big and strong
Stands tall and firm to the golden song
With hair of gold and teeth of ivory
So records it in her diary

The Golden Boy is truly handsome
His eyes are sparkling sapphire and diamond
His heart is true, his mind is quick
He feeds the poor and heals the sick

He tries his mightiest for war to cease
He prays to God for joy and peace
He wakes up to the cries of Heaven
He finds out he is not forgiven

He went to hell and then came back
Truth and wisdom he does not lack
He gives hope to the many lost
A lowly price for a lofty cost

There is an end to this old story
For he is fact gives all the glory
To the Golden Man who sent him here
To save every man far and near

Arthur H. Presley

The Old Log House

The old log house where so many were born,
Stands faded and tattered, and so forlorn.
It's filled with passions, and dreams, and things.
It's known love, and laughter, and hate it seems.

The children that grew up there,
Have known love, and hate, and despair.
They've all moved on to other places,
But the old log house remembers their faces.

The logs were fashioned with love and care,
By the father who brought the mother there.
But some how their love was lost along the way,
And the old log house is the one left to pay.

It sits there and slowly weathers down.
Its family has moved closer to town.
It remembers the laughter of the children and their fun.
It knows how their life had begun.

The old log house will slowly fade away,
But its memories will hang on till the dying day.
Someone will find a log here and there.
But the memories will be everywhere.

Joyce Procell

My Soul

A wall, high and strong,
Stands against the elements of earth
Defies all and consumes itself with cursèd pride.
Though parts may crumble, disintegrate,
And fall silently, painfully to the ground
The whole, outwardly, appears solid and intact.

Many visitors come to climb the weathered sides,
To feast on the glory of a higher view.
Onward they tramp, oblivious to the crumbling stone.
Each steps opens wounds and scars of rock,
That tumble to the ground—broken and lost,
And only the tear-filled rain consoles.

Winds may whip and shriek,
Or tear into small, exposed and vulnerable rock,
The sun may even beat down in anguishing torture
And people may rip at its very core,
But the wall will remain mostly whole, yet still alone
And only the tear-filled rain from above—weeps.

Jessica Little

Please Jesus, Bring Home My Dad

The saddest words, did I ever hear, was the night my little boy spent in prayer. "Jesus he said, tell Dad I love him and I care. "Please Jesus bring home my dad." I won't be a bad boy anymore, I'm growing up, I will be a good boy. I'm old now, I'm four. Jesus, my dad is my best friend, can I see my daddy again? Please Jesus, bring home my dad. Can you have him to come back to stay? I'll pick up my blocks and put my toys away. I promise to listen to my dad each and everyday. Please Jesus, bring home my dad. When my big sister goes to bed and does cry and I know too she is sad, and the reason why, is she loves and misses her dad. Please Jesus don't let her feel bad. Please Jesus, bring home my dad. We want our dad back for evermore, I had so much fun with him, washing the car and wrestling on the floor. My daddy used to call me his little buddy or his big little man, but I'm only four and don't understand. Please Jesus, bring home my dad. My daddy taught us how to pray, that was a long time ago before some man took my daddy away. Jesus, if you are up in the sky somewhere, please hear my tiny prayer. Please Jesus, bring home my dad. Jesus, I don't want to anymore be blue, I want to hear my daddy, again say, "I love you!" Oh yeah, before I end, I thank you and remember, my sister, my brother and I, need you to "Please Jesus, bring home my dad!"

Arthur D. Gelinas Jr.

Speak to Me

Speak to me, speak to me, speak to me.
Speak to me with your heart, your eyes, a touch of your lips,
Your smile, a gesture of your hands - anything to understand.
Speak to me with a shrug of your shoulders, a wink - tears
Running down your cheek. Yes speak to me with your warm caress,
Everything saying yes. Speak to me anyway you know how,
But not just in words - blow me a kiss, don't look away,
Reach out your fingertips, for when ours touch - they speak to me,
    speak to me of love.
Come embrace me, let me hear your heart - oh to smell you
    near says and says and says.
If all that could be said was written or spoken, then the artist
Would never paint nor music heard to convey the depths and breaths
That mere words cannot or will not or should not ever say.
We are body, mind, and spirit beings - let our spirits loose.
So smile with your eyes, your hands and feet which are now running
    towards me.
Not a word - yet we know our open arms mean acceptance, and need,
    and want.
So speak to me, yes speak to me - just to me.

John H. Rives

your light

you enter the room in song to delight
space moves so still, inviting it's right
you enter my mind, thoughts tangle enthralled
from heaven you turn, how safely you call
you enter my dreams, an angel your guise
sweet fortune to prayers doubt dare not deny
you enter my world, excitement so calming
hope beckons my heart, trust softly following
you enter my past without knowing how
forgiving my pain, peace guarding it now
you enter the place kissed gently by tears
changing my life, cheating my fears
you enter my faith, belief in your hand
this chance ours to take, God's love is the plan
you enter my soul, not a sound no sight
time circles embraced, I'm home in your light

Cindy Giannini

Where Have All Those Hands Been

A little girl who for a picture could pose,
Soon began to pick her nose.

A man who looked like an unmade bed,
Soon began to scratch his head.

And the man who had a heavy cold,
Was blowing his nose out loud and bold!

Add hands that rub grimy banisters on their way,
And those taking out trash to save time that day.

Just who are these people you well may ask.
I hesitate and cringe to mention their task.

They're the ones in the church, in each and every pew,
Who turn around and extend to you

Their hands, and you're expected to shake them,
But sometimes you don't really want to take them.

Because seasons come with their influx of flu
And other transmittable diseases too.

So let's give a nod, a word of peace or two
Thus sparing each other the germs we accrue.

Let's leave the hand shaking to politicians
Receive the Lord in our hands in A-1 condition.

Frances Chepiga

Many Loves

Sometimes love brings heartache and pain
Sometimes love's an experience to gain
Sometimes love can be beautiful for two
Sometimes love is given only by you
Sometimes love's felt for reasons that are wrong
Sometimes love goes on too long
Sometimes love is used when you're lonely
Sometimes love is for your gain only
Sometimes love will go your way
Sometimes love brings happiness to stay
Whichever love you choose to pursue
Make sure it's the one that's right for you
Love is sure to come around
But you mustn't let it get you down
We all must experience what love brings our life
But as long as we survive each struggles and strife
We'll gain the knowledge that keeps us above
Those things that make us give upon love

Julie A. Calvert

A Child's Life

A child's life is but a game
Sometimes good wins, sometimes evil remains
A child's life is but a voice
Sometimes it's high, sometimes it's low
A child's life is but a season
One month it's winter, the next summer
A child's life is but a race
You may get gold or silver
A child's life is but a face
Sometimes it's smiling, sometimes it's frowning
A child's life is all but dull.

Cameron J. Searcy

Faith

My answering machine blinks and plays a message quite blurred;
Something about a wreck that's occurred.
It's my best friend, I hope she's all right;
I'll grab extra clothes so I can stay through the night.
The doctor informs me, she is in a comatose state;
As I hold her hand, I tell her, by your side I will wait.
Two days have passed she still lays perfectly still;
I wonder when she awakes how much pain she will feel.
Day three has arrived and everything is the same;
There is still no response when I call out her name.
The fifth day is here, I don't know how much more I can take;
Dear Lord, if you hear me, please let her wake.
On the day of the sixth her eyes opened wide;
Here I am as I promised, I'm right by your side
She spoke not a word, although I could understand;
I started to cry when I felt her gripping may hand.
It's been a year now and she's doing fair;
Thank you, Dear Lord, for answering my prayer.

Brandi Anne Merlau

Daughter

I love you with a love so strong, it bursts within my heart.
Some times I feel so close to you, some times we're worlds apart.
I only want the best for you, but don't know how to say it.
So then I take it to the Lord, for it's easier to pray it.
A mother does not always say the things she wants to say.
Instead she says "clean up your room, and put your clothes away."
The days are short and time so fast, the things we wish to do,
are oft left to tomorrow, but tomorrows are too few.
You've always been a precious girl, a joy to me and Dad.
Your beauty blooms within, without; to know you makes me glad.
We may not always understand the ways of one another,
but the bond of love's unbreakable, between a daughter and a mother.

Cecelia Assunto

A Rose

It's been a while since I have allowed
someone to climb the wall and touch my heart.
Imagine, I have downed the wall and allowed my soul to be seen.
I feel exposed, yet relieved, as if for the first time, about to burst

I have told innermost thoughts of stars and fire. Of lightning and
visions, of destinies and past. Never expressing my thoughts
except to myself. Never allowing my soul to be exposed.

I remember pain or smiles, hurt or happy. But to feel my pain smile
and experience a happy hurt, is not soon overshadowed.
To see you with that rose, my heart squeezed with pain and smiled.
My body hurt without your touch, but was happy to be near.

To go out of your way for me, my soul now cries.
How do I cover myself? How do I keep what has been hidden
from being exposed? My heart has always seen light,
and dances out in the sun, breaks and mends.

My soul now peeks from the shadow, but I always keep it back.
Should I allow it the same chance that my heart carelessly takes?

My soul is like China, if broken, it won't mend.
Like fine wine, saved, to be savored.
Like a snowflake, it melts on touch. Like your rose, delicate.

Jessie A. Honeywood

Tears

What are tears? What are they for?
Some say they're nothing, but I think they're more.

Tears fall during laughter, sorrow or pain.
Did you know that God cries? For that is the rain.

But why does he cry? What does it mean?
Tears are so confusing, I just want to scream.

He cries for the lonely, the hurt and the sick.
He cries for the poor teenagers, whose hearts have been tricked.

My heart has been tricked quite a few times,
"Let's just be friends", that's a terrible line.

I hear that a lot, too often I think,
And each time I heart it, my heart still sinks.

But back to my question, what is a tear?
Why do we shed them, if they're so often feared?

My question has an answer, that might never be found.
By the time I've found the answer, I may be heaven bound.

Belle Harris Penrose

"Love Is A Blessing"

Life without love is nothing at all
Some people climb and others they fall
Some people search for something to do
I found my treasure when I met you

Me without you I'm lost in the gloom
Everything glows when your in the room
When your away thoughts of you will prevail
I can always touch you by telephone or mail

Love Is a blessing that many can't buy
Some people find it and others will try
Seek and have faith but never despair
Look in lonely places and you will find love there
Look for lonely faces and you will find love there.

Albert J. Wasko

What Color Is Spring?

What color is spring?
Some people ask.
I'd like to know, too
If you don't mind a task.
When you look around you, you can always see,
The colors around you seem ultimately free.
The color green is all around,
In the trees and on the ground.
The color is blue is in the sky,
If you look up, you can see blue birds passing by.
The yellow dandelions sway in the breeze.
While children laugh, with brown dirt on their knees.
There are so many colors in spring.
Sometimes I just want to sing.
So go and watch the white clouds go by.
You will lay on the ground and sigh.
While you're there, you'll feel like a king.
And I will ask,
What color is spring?

Hilary Snyder

Science Fiction

Into the past, throughout the years.
Some laughter, some tears.
I think of the times good and bad that me
and my family had.
into the future I cannot see what
will happen to my family and me.
into space beyond the clouds.
Toward the sun were heading now.
Above the clouds in a spaceship.
I see a floating paper clip.
Use your imagination and you can go
anywhere you want to go.

Amanda Jones

Honor Of The Dead

Battles we have won, battles we have lost,
Some got away, but many paid the cost,
Standing alone among the best,
Some lived on, many laid to rest,
Some were just soldiers,
Many with medals on their chest,
Cease the fire, it's getting higher,
One man fighting for his life,
But most of all he's fighting for his country,
Not for heroism, but for pride and freedom,
Why do I speak of these words of memories of the past,
Hoping that many will hear and they will last,
Some say the worst battles are just ahead,
This is in honor of the dead,
It's time to lay your weary head.

Daryl Marker

"Us Girls"

Some of us laugh, some of us cry;
Some are wimps, some want to fly,
Some like to tackle, some like to sit;
Some sip tea, some like to spit.
Some are dirty, some are clean;
Some are sweet, some are mean.
Some are aggressive, and some are laid back,
Some like to hug, some like to whack.
Some are just both types shown above here,
One or the other; courage or fear.
We all have a unique combination you see;
And this makes up our personality.

Julie DeLouis

Evolution Of Man?

Garden full of primordial people.
Some are angelic and follow the primrose path.
Some are misoneistic and demand quid pro quo.
Misoneists sound like puff adders when meeting the pure and meek.

Beautiful, fragrant flowers growing everywhere, but go unnoticed,
    unappreciated.
Stones gathered and loads grows heavier and heavier.
Stones are piled on the flowers, choking growth.
Flowers die, only dead stems left.

Bodies bend lower as roving eyes search ground, seeking stones of venom.
Stones thrown at angelic people-a hit! Infection!
Now all gather sticks and stones, all want to control.
Sticks and stones fly over fuming ground.

Stale, rank odor of hatred overwhelming in the air.
No compromise, no understanding prevails as time passes.
They slither along bare, rocky ground, seeking battle.
Just chance or evolution of man?

Gladys M. Honeycutt

Solid...Like A Rock

You say you're like a rock,
  solid, hard and sure.
A rock is but a cluster of sand,
  hard and molded throughout the land.
A rock can be broken from the mountain top,
  then tumble to the land below.
Get heated by the scorching sun,
  and weathered by the pouring rain.
Then kicked about to and fro,
  finally reaching the ocean's depths below.
Broken to pebbles, to grains of sand once more,
  We stand; so solid; like a rock; no more.

Deborah Pamela Ida

Untitled

As I sit listening to the sounds of summers twilight,
soft, restful, WAITING,
for the curtain of fall, easing DOWN
WAITING, for winter
asleep, yet not, renewing, restful
WAITING, for the blanket to be drawn off,
WAITING, for spring
Awakening, renewing

Colleen Stone

Is A Rose Is A Rose Is A Rose?

Rose of beginnings
Soft pink of new-born petals
Innocently reaching for solutions
Ever budding to the scarlet rush of full bloom

Rose of life
Darkening red petals of blood
Blooms falling from grace
Wilting in the intensity of loneliness

Rose of endings
Luminescent ivory petals
Smooth; beautiful in glory
Blooming to meanings older than beginnings

Chandra Weghorst

Secret Of Life

There's so much in life we'll never understand
So we plan for our future we believe that we can
• We all fall in love
That's the way it should be
Then our whole life depends
On our hope, hearts and dreams
I believe everyone lives
Their life their own way
The good or the bad
They except day to day
The unbelievers think
The glass is half full
Maybe that is one reason
Their dreams don't come true
So fill up your glass
Always follow your dreams
Your heart will guide you
As tough as it seems
The reality is dreams keep us alive
So keep on believing that's the secret of life

Dorane Dee Bejarano

Untitled

Sickly, peeling bark masks the thriving roots,
so unlike the leaves that hang limply on skeletons.
My mother stands proudly,
flaunting the mottled mask
that cloaks her inner beauty.
Her bark flakes away, floating lazily to the green carpet,
exposing vulnerable flesh that shies away from Nature's fondling fingertips.
Brilliant colored bees swarm around, dropping from their hives of branches
to rush to her protection.
They plaster their veined wings around her trunk,
melting against the bare flesh,
blinding Nature's eyes so that she can't strike.
But she rips the leafy coat away,
drawing syrupy blood that oozes to the ground,
my mother's tears mixed in.
Alone, she is an island in the midst of the cold green sea of grass.
Her arms reach out for support,
painting the sky's slate gray canvas
with dark shadows.

Ellen Rubinstein

Peaches

She came into our lives so long ago
So scared, so small, and so unloved by all
We took her in and watched her grow
Our hearts full of love when she gave life to little ones
She loved us and we loved her
So we gave her the name PEACHES
I sit here and write this for soon she will be gone
Death will come and take her life
But she will always live on in our hearts and in her son
For she was here through all the moves, the ups and downs
She sat with me when I was ill
And made me well with her love and loud purr
Now it is my turn to be there for her
I know that I can't make her well
Like she has done so many times for me
But I will make her proud
For she is my favorite pet in the world
And there will never be another Peaches

Julie M. Cork

When You Surf The Internet

There is no place for cats or dogs,
so please don't bring a pet.
Just bring your mate or friend along,
when you surf the Internet.

Be sure to check out the URLs
and Gophers, don't forget.
This will help you go more places,
when you surf the Internet.

There are many things to see and learn
that will interest you, I bet.
And you'll have no food to buy or gas to burn,
when you surf the Internet.

There is no need to ride or hike,
get hot, cold, or wet,
drive a car or ride a bike,
when you surf the Internet.

So get aboard and don't delay,
being of the Super Set.
You'll never regret the day,
when you surf the Internet.

Joseph D. Rudloff

Wind Walker

The great spirit has sent the eagle and the hawk,
So I may believe on the wind I might walk.

The buffalo is my brother, and all animals that be,
I am part of the land and part of the sea.

My spirit dances like the camp fires at night,
And my heart is one with the wind tonight.

The coyote howls at the big, bright moon,
And the stars are like diamonds that shine,
And my soul is filled by the beauty I see.
For this land that I call mine.

And when the great spirit calls my name,
To join him in the sky,
I shall leave all this beauty behind,
And my spirit will fly.

Then I will join the eagle and the hawk
And the great spirit in the sky,
And be as the wind passing in time,
I shall look back and remember,
This once was mine...

Dominick Cadile

Untitled

I want to write a poem, but I don't know what to say.
So I just sit and scribble, for most of the day.
I have all these thoughts, buried deep within my heart.
But how to write them down, I don't know where to start.

Everything gets jumbled up, and doesn't come out right.
Words get all twisted, my grammar is a sight.
If I thought that they cared, what was on my mind.
The thoughts would surely come, I know the words I'd find.

But they think I'm just a dreamer, in a silly sort of way.
That I waste my time trying, to think of things to say.
How can I make them understand, that I only want to share.
What's on my mind, and in my heart, and just how much I care.

I want to write a poem, but I don't know what to do.
Should I write it down, then share it with a few.
Or keep it to myself, locked up so they won't see.
How much a simple poem shows so much of me.

Gloria Brown

Someone Is Out There

No one loves you, so why should you care?
So go ahead and do it, go for the dare.
With a gun in one hand, and a mask on your face.
You looked in the mirror and your heart started to race.
You jumped through the window and got cut on the glass.
You thought no one was home and started to bash.
You saw a shadow, and then the man.
You didn't think twice about the gun in his hand.
You got so confused, and started to run.
Then, without warning, he shot his gun.
You felt the bullet as it burst through your shirt.
And didn't realize then just how much it hurt.
You can change yourself, it ain't too late.
And I know you can do it, you can change your fate.
No one loves you so why should you care?
If you look a little harder you'll see that I'm here.
I want you stop before you die.
Because I have no tears left to cry.
So when you think no ones there, before you go and take the dare.
Read this poem and you will know there is someone out there who
    really cares.

April Engdahl

The Pope In America

Compassion creased the eyes of his face,
So gentle were his hands,
And from within his spirit spoke
To every girl and man.
His love poured forth to those who came
To see him in our land.
His life he gave to serve the Lord
Just as it had been planned.

If I had nothing more from life
Than to love as this one has,
Without condition, price, or gain,
What greater gift for man.
For love is life, and life is love
This promise from above.
You take the gift, you give you life,
And so, pass on, the love.

Jamie Brown

The Auction

One day I was awfully bored and had nothing I could do
So for a country walk I went my anxious spirit for to sooth.
And as I passed a huge ole house, I heard an auctioneer
Playing people for their bids on an antique straight back chair.
So I ventured forth to sit and listen to his cadence
And very soon I got caught up in buying things I shouldn't.
But there among the treasures dear were so many memories
Of times of old when I was young and my spirit seemed so free.
So I bought a students desk with ink well and quill pin
And very soon I was taken back to my early school days again.
And a lantern like I use to use to light my way to bed
To the attic room dark and warm, and my goosedown feather bed.
There were tools just like my dad used and taught me to respect.
And a rolling pin like my mother used to make her plump delicious biscuits.
And the furnishings galore, just like my grandmom had.
There were books and bikes and pots and pans, and I was very glad,
That for awhile one summer day I had nothing I could do.
And ventured out in the countryside to explore my life anew.

Brenda Johnson

Mother

Mother is a lifelong inspiration
So devoted, energetic and pure.
Gave forgiveness without hesitation.
For many a heartache authored a cure.

She was blessed with immeasurable love,
Supplying a soft shoulder to cry on,
And when I needed one, gave me a shove.
Life just isn't the same since she's gone.

Oh but I still have all those memories,
To elate me as I know she would do.
Has provided me with so many stories,
So heartwarming, satisfying and true.

All part of the legacy she left me,
Protecting me from ever being sad,
Surely 'twas part of God's plan don't you see,
That my mother so dear still makes me glad.

Fred Coley

"The Willow"

Down by the brook with its water
So clear stands an old willow
Tree to see and sometimes hear

Its branches are so huge and its
Height so tall, like a swaying giant
You hope never to fall

In winter she sleeps by the frozen
Brook till spring breaks its ice
And opens her book, her leaves
Are then so beautiful and small
Which will clothe the giant until next fall

Time takes its toll of most
Everything but until the willow
Falls we pray to see her again in the spring

Henry Ward Stradley

"Someone Cares"

When there's times in our life that we feel
So alone, when our heart's in despair and all
Hope seems to be gone, those times when we
Think how unfair it all seems and we just
Want to give up and let go of our dreams.
It may be that we know only suffering and pain
And the dawn of a new day just brings more
Of the same. When we feel there's no reason to
Exist here on earth or that life has no meaning
And we've lost our self-worth. When darkness
surrounds us and we're at the end of our rope
Lift your eyes toward Jesus and renew all lost hope.
Let our hearts not be troubled have faith and
Believe our burdens he will lift and such peace
we will receive. He will walk by our side down
the road of life only he can help ease all our
sorrow and strife. He died for our sins so that
we might live so don't ever doubt him or the love that
he gives, it's love unconditional and there's no cost
and he's there to guide us anytime we feel lost...

Anne Pope

Primitive

Objects in nature expanding her earth.
She is lost in distractions contracting her.
Beginning, she breathes and weeps the colors of the earth.
Now, her heart drums slow in the wind.
She sees once again the moody shadow.
She knows her rhythm.

Debbie Penuel

Flames Of Death

Thick dark clouds of dangerous
smoke!

Two fire fighters helplessly
choke.

Trapped inside an inferno of flames—
Yet no one remembers their names!

The flames grew fierce as it headed
their way.

"Bring in more water!" I heard the Captain
say.

The collapsing of cement, the bonfire of
wood!

All hopes were lost as it's been understood.

Like a beacon in the night appear a tremendous
glow!

From the "Flames of Death" that took our
unknown heroes.

Hector J. Williams

A Child's Summer Dance

It was a beautiful summer day. So warm and fresh. The air smelled of sweet flowers and just passed rain. The grass was a brilliant green, speckled with white. The sky was a tender blue, with soft, cool clouds.

A butterfly, small and delicate, catches the eye of a gentle child. She dances after the butterfly; a dance only a child knows. Her bare feet press the grass gently to the ground. Her hands, like that of a baby doll, reach for the soft, delicate creature. Her hair of spun gold catches the breeze, and as she turns her musical giggle whispers in my ear. Her blue eyes shine of sweet child happiness and her smile was so innocent.

Heather Blair

Angel Face

The radiantly soft sunrise reminds me of your beauty; an absolutely slow walk among the flowers reminds me of your beauty; the changing of autumn leaves from green to gold reminds me of your beauty
The inviting smiles you always have remind me of your beauty
As long as I live, you'll always be my Little Angel Face.

Your playful energy, the gentle way you've treated your friends
Your humane sense of sharing, your many questions and curiosities
Yes, I am happy to be a part of what you've become
You're young; you're innocent and oh, you're so free spirited
It's a joy to watch you grow; it's a joy to watch you expand
As long as life lasts, you'll forever be my Little Angel Face.

You're becoming a woman; it's in your thoughtful eyes
You're becoming a woman; warm and wise, You're becoming a woman;
with a sense of self; you'll be a woman with a heart of gold
Please be a woman who will always be my Little Angel Face. It's a

joyful feeling to anticipate one's daughter becoming self-sufficient
It's a joyful feeling to watch one's daughter becoming independent
And oh, it's so joyful to watch one's daughter grow and explore
Please, know what beauty it is on becoming a woman, and always remember
No matter where life leads you, you'll always be my Little Angel Face.

Irvin E. Prince

Come To Your House, My Brother

Empty closets
Skeleton hangers clack the echoing walls
Jackets folded flat in stacks for packing
Easy chairs, shrouded in white linen
Trophies, wound in sheets and napkins
Preciously carried out

Dust-heaved oaken chest
Its cargo resting in velvet—
How can the chill box be moved
Without spilling the vinegar and gall?

Don't pack the diamonds
Wear them loudly in the narrow room
And take down the picture
Of the lilies of the field
Which today is the same as yesterday
Lift it
Gently

Arlene Pourroy

Ice Crystals

Watching for the iceman on a hot summer's day,
Sitting on the front porch, thirsty from our play,
Looking out for "Toto," a nice Italian man,
Big strong arms, with a deep summer tan.

He rode a horse and wagon, up and down the block,
Calling out "ice" and then would stop,
Mother sent you out for a "ten cents piece,"
Toto cut it quick, in one fast crease.

As he cut, the chips would fly,
Clean, cool icicles in the sky,
Crystal treasures you wanted so much,
Melting quickly to your warm hand touch.

When his work was over and he was set to leave,
Taking out his ice pick, wiped it on his sleeve,
"Who would like some ice," he would laugh and say,
And sucking on that ice, surely made our day.

So running after Toto, and saying "thanks, goodbye,"
On many a hot summer's day, I can still see icy crystals fly.

Frank G. Vurture

Me

God soul am I who pities me.
Sitting in a room with nothing to see.
Looking around at the battered walls.
Seeing the men and all the dirt balls.
Wishing I was a butter fly, flying around.
I lay and listen and there is not a sound.
I wish I was a china doll.
All dressed up and going to a ball.
No that's not me, as your can see.
I am not as tall as I would like to be.
There is an old saying you are growing like a need.
No that's not me for they chopped off all the seeds
The seeds all blew away one windy day
When she went out to play.
Now this need has grown up, but not very tall.
She hopes she is loved by all
When the trees shed their leaves in the face.

Dorothy A. Miller

"Love Lost"

Where is love when love is gone,
Sings the singer of the song;
Has it flown to a distant shore
When love isn't any more?

Where is the sun when it is gone,
Leaving us in the dark—all alone;
Taking its warmth from the golden sand
And leaving a cold and frightened man?

Where are the stars on a starless night,
Leaving only a blue-black velvet in sight;
Taking away our inspiration,
Leaving us only trepidation.

Just where is love when it has vaporized?
Where's the sun and stars when not in empty skies?
Where do they go when they disappear,
Leaving us empty and full of fear?
Leaving us alone, to sit and muse—
Our emptiness and loneliness ourselves to diffuse.

Just where do all of these things go?
Does anyone ever really know?

Alice L. McIlvaine

Visitation

It's a long time
    Since I could go out on my own.
I went here and there.
Saw Tom Graham—
    there's one growing old.
Stopped in at the church.
    The steps are steeper than I remember.
The inside was dark, real quiet—and empty, too.
When my eyes adjusted to the gloom
    I felt better,
    Wandered down the aisle and looked about.
The red glow of a candle
    beckoned me aside
    to sit and rest.
So, I stayed to visit Jesus.
He seemed lonely.

Carl Henry

To Brighten The Night

She sits in a corner, and cries to the night.
    She's so out of touch, she's far out of sight.
Lonely is her heart and helpless is her quest,
    She needs a sign of hope, so that she may feel her best.
But where will love come from if not from you?
    Where will peace shine and show itself true?
The answer, my friend, is deep in the night,
    It's shining itself with a silent special light.
Her tears will not dry the sorrow is real.
    But how can she stop when it's pain she does feel?
Will no one reach out and put to an end,
    What's stealing her love and playing pretend.
Yet when will new moments reach out their young hands,
    And wipe her tears dry, like sharp desert sands.
The answer, my friend, is deep in the night,
    It's shining itself with a silent special light,
This Light is more Holy, more holier than I,
    It bursts into eternity and brightens the sky.

Heidi M. Eilenberger

Women

When viewed through a man's eyes,
She's not just the opposite sex,
Or the object of his desire.

She is beautiful, fun, and exciting
Although still elusive to us.

She's a companion to share life with,
and to encourage us in life and its endeavors

Women, now they have knowledge,
especially in matters of the heart.

Through a man's eyes she's successful.
Not just in life, or her thoughts,
But, he knows where she is and what she wants.

But, the true one greatest thing about a woman is,
that no matter how smart you are, or how long you live.
To our dying day as a man you will never ever,
be able to understand or to figure them out.

So, men heed these words of advice,
"Just don't ever try too."

Frank Martellaro

My Mom...

She's not a famous scholar, or a poet with a pen.
She's not a ballerina, full of grace, small and thin.
She doesn't own a mansion high upon a hill.
But she has one thing, you can always feel.

A heart full of love for everyone you see.
'Cause Jesus lives within her heart for all eternity.
Her name is Jewel, the greatest gem,
She shines brighter than gold.

I'm thankful God has blessed me,
To have her to hug and hold.
I'm proud to say that she's my mom,
The dearest thing to me.
If happiness is what you seek, a loving mom's the key.

Angie Wells

Death's Different Faces

I will know you best when you walk the Earth.
She will know you best when you gracefully fall
toward the Earth with the rest of the snowflakes
on a snowy winter day.

He will know you best when you walk through the
shining gates of heaven, or when you make your
descent through the fiery pits of hell.

They will know you best when you wear your golden
halo, or when you look at your sins through the
fire of life.

We will know you best when we follow your voyage
through the endless corridors of death.

Alan Crawford

Personification Poem

I saw happiness clearly;
She was like a flower and a star.
She turned and smiled with her hair in the wind;
I saw her bluest eyes and darkest skin.
And heard her soft angelic voice;
And I felt peace within me.

Fara Saliceti

The Whore

A hard core whore is hard to beat
She tricks in the pad, she tricks on the street.
She will take your last dollar
She will give her last dime
She'll take the rap - she'll pull the time.
She's cold, she's hard, she's soft, she's sweet
She'll trick in the pad, she'll trick on the street.
She works in the sunshine, she works in the rain
She wears a smile to cover her pain.
She hides from the law, she runs from the pimp,
She's often maltreated for her hustling attempt.
But there's one thing to know about this hard core gal,
She makes a good wife, she makes a good pal.
She has deep feelings of guilt and regret,
often stays high just to for-get.
On bended knees she often prays,
for faith and for-giveness of her yesterdays.
She's one of God's Children, she's one of a kind,
This hard core whore with the dollar in mind.

Dorothy M. Hughes

Finish

My friend of means left today.
She penned her last words very clear.
A stranger message I've yet to see,
Written in haste, and directed to me.

A veil of gloom filled my heart.
Tears slid down my face, as I read the
Words written there, that I could not erase.

So sad the message before me now,
Grief clouds my recall.
"Goodbye my friend, I'm ending it all."
Written by a diamond on the mirror in my hall.

Jean D. Clements

Discrimination

In spring, the daffodil, bring hope and fun.
She lifts her cups, to catch the rain and sun.
The crocus, gallantly pushes through the snow,
And her beautiful colors, leads us where to go.
The pansies, roam, in so very many places,
To show off their colors, on we smiling faces.
Hush! You, who call dandelions weeds.
They brighten up the world, with their flying seeds.
They are all lovely — but I must confess,
I know, I have chosen the very best!
"It's wrong!", 'tis said, to discriminate
But to me the Daisy, is first rate.

Dorothy Friedman

Untitled

She looked into his eyes from across the room
She knew in the depths of her soul that he would get in
She could not let him touch her being, he would take away the
safety she had always known
He would challenge her strength, make her realize it was only
her she was hiding from
If she looked too deeply into his eyes, she would have to
search her soul
He broke away the first piece
She was never to be the same again
There is no turning back now
He has touched her...
Touched her in a place she did not know was there

Julee Spencer-Nickles

Who Is This Woman?

A woman who is a child, a woman who is a mother,
  She is love, and beauty, who is this woman?
A member of the violent revolution, she is angry.
  She is a school drop-out, she has been abused, and used.
A wife, and lover, a child of the ghetto, a child of poverty,
  Who is this woman? Who is this woman? Who is this woman?
This strong, verbal woman. A woman who is angry as hell.
  A woman who can hate like anyone else, and more.
Who is this woman? Who is this woman? Who is this?
  The man who loves her, is aware of her true self.
Who is this woman? A woman who will play at a game of wits,
  And cleverness, a woman who is neither saint, or sinner,
Who is this woman, this woman is all those things and more.
  Who is this woman? Who is this woman? Who is this woman?
  A strong black woman.

Ann Thomas

Why Me

I saw a client looking in the mirror one day
She could not talk
But her eyes were saying a lot.
Her eyes were saying
Why me?
I came and stood beside her.
She looked at me, and there was a tear
Coming from only one eye
I reached out to hold her
She took one step back and
Looked at me again.
She pushed me up to the mirror,
And put her hand on my face
I looked at her and her eyes said,
I see your tears, I asked
My self, Why me?

Bernadette Everett

Old Lady And Her Cat

Together on the couch they nap.
She all stretched out, he on her lap.
For many months, since just a kitten,
With one another, they've been smitten.
The love they have, is plain to see.
He on her lap, head on her knee.
She strokes his back, and he will purr.
And with a paw, he will stroke her.
It matters not, that she's grown old,
For cats have, nine lives, I'm told.
The greatest thing, in life, they've found.
That love makes, the world go round.
She loves him, and he loves her.
She will smile, and he will purr.
Between the two, there is no gap.
She all the stretched out, he on her lap.

Ethel Crownover

Heartfelt

Tears roll slowly down her face
Shame and feelings of disgrace
Her sadness grows deep down inside
Feelings she no longer wants to hide
The desire she has, to show
The feelings she has but does not know
How to show her feelings outside
They are stubbornly stuck inside
She longs for tenderness shown on her face
Beauty, gentleness and grace
The softness in those eyes so blue
Tell of a heart that is so true
Pure and gentle
So sentimental

Deborah Beachler

Violet

The sky was drunk with a neverending haze
Shades of violet deposited from days
Nightfall suffocates many who ask
The reason we die cold in this mask

Now he's wearing a whirlpool to fill the vicious void
Silent shadows wailing, now evil's overjoyed
He was found dead by the poem
The thick, blood red verses from his heart
Marooned feeling maroon
On the darkest side of the moon
Alone in his room
The hope fades - the hope cascades

She was warm and simple in a violet blast
Color left in his eyes from past
The wind howls at the blind who ask
The reason she remains behind the glass

He was found dead by the poem
The thick, blood red verses of his heart

Clint Gray

Life Of Love

Life is a journey on an earthly plane -
  Senses and sounds, visions and pain
Joys and laughter, bitter sweet
  A soul journey, a spiritual retreat.

Smiles and hugs, given and shared
  With friends, lovers and others who cared.
There is no compass - paths undefined
  Yet the white light guides — eases the mind.

Believe it and live it
  Love is all.
Given it comes back
  A golden ball.

Constance M. Ferris

it or Not?

They seldom understand me.
  Seldom understand who i am or what i am.
  Not to say that i am different. Just unique.
  They tell me i am strange.

Strange because
  i know things they don't know
  i can do things they can't do
  i am something they are not.

They even claim to hate me.
  Because even though i am what i am, i'm still beautiful.
  Good. And they say i shouldn't be
  Which makes no sense to me.

Well i still love them.
  Love them so much that i have begun to hate them.
  Just how they hate.
  Hate the things they don't understand.

i think they want me or maybe they don't.
  To tell you the truth i really don't care.
  It's funny how i always understand them yet
  They seldom understand me.

Alana Benoit

Desert Blue Car

Move the tires
Scrape the wheels
Lick the oil
Wash the mad stains on the wheel in hand
The car's kind of dusty in desert land
Blue, which beams to the sky
Blue, we don't ask why
Don't want to know
Dizzy, dizzy car, the engine runs in idle
Kick the sands, desert kind of beauty
Blue has turned to desert, salt, and rust
of this car we no longer lust
Blue chips of paint, it's a memory
Sad, sick, and song
Horror, it's gone
The horror is still there....

Christopher Furner

Then Suddenly

Feather-streaked pink and mauve clouds
scamper across the sky, beckoning us
to Brandt Trace Farm,
long green stretch surrounded by trees.
We lean against the white board fence,
no horses in sight this evening,
watch cloud color deepen minute by minute
from inner shell blush to rose,
brightening now to apricot gold scalloped
and long neon streaks of cerise,
proscenium across the distance.
A guttural sound pebbles the air.
"Can you hear them?" You ask.
Seven Canada geese in V formation
are flying away. You call, "Wahonk! Wahonk!"
"Do you think they heard you?"
"Wait," you whisper close to my ear.
Minutes pass in silence. Then suddenly
geese circle over our heads calling in unison,
like an embrace—from nowhere and everywhere.

Evalyn Pierpoint Gill

Eyes That Speak

Eyes designed to receive
   say so much.
They are beautiful and gentle;
Yet their power can break hearts
   and destroy.
Such power contained in such subtleness.
What do your eyes say? And mine?
Can you hear?
What colors do you see?
Eyes can warm a cold winter day,
   make the loneliest secure,
   and move mountains.
Yes, eyes are the gateway to the heart!
Listen to the eyes of people,
   respect their power,
   and be warmed by their touch.
They're crying to be heard;
   sometimes demand.
Yes, eyes designed to receive, say so much!
P.S. Can you hear?

Brian Forsythe

Storms

The little bird up in the tree
Sat on her nest so pa-tient-ly.
The ill wind blew, the rain poured down
That made me sad, it made me frown.
The storm continued day after day
She just sat there so cold and hungry and grey.

The baby bird peeped from under her wing
That made me so happy I could sing.
My life has taken a new meaning, you see
Since I saw that little bird up in the tree.
When the wind and rain and life's storms blow
I'll look up to GOD, quit feeling so low.

Bernice Farnsley

The Eagle's Cry

She is walking on the beach, letting the
sand crumble between her toes.
   For once in her busy life,
   her mind seems to be at peace.
She isn't worrying about her test on Monday,
or her recent disagreement with her parents.
   For once her thoughts are drifting away
   with the wind.
She is acutely aware of the unfamiliar noises
that surrounds her,
   and she can sense the eagle's stare
   the one that is perched up in a tree somewhere.
It is almost as if their spirits seem to connect.
Maybe it's because they are both just trying to survive.
   Then suddenly her calming peace is disturbed
   by the sound of chains cutting through a tree,
and from somewhere in the distance
she can hear the eagle's cry
pleading, begging, not to die!

Jennifer Landes

Smile At Simplicity

Civilization is a hallucination to
Sages in a world of ignorance
Imaginary life dwells in
The light of technology
An ancient intrusion
Manipulating the aura for
An unleashed environment
Intent is evident
It all makes sense

Jeffrey A. Chicklowski

Drops Of Rain

When I see the drops of rain
Rivuleting down the window pane
I wonder if those self-same drops
Could ever come back again
Would they have a long journey to the sea
Or maybe a rest in a shrub or tree
Tiny though the drops of rain may be
They have power beyond you and me
They can wear away an earthen dam
Give life to a thirsting man
Feed the fields of golden grain
Turn the earth all green again
Tagging a little drop of rain
Is beyond the scope of any man
Only God has the master plan.

Alice M. Hutt

The Ballad Of Sadie And B.C.

Sadie's a dog, B.C.'s a cat
  Sadie wants to get along but
B.C. will have none of that

  Sadie comes over to play and
B.C. says to go away

  They are neighbors, this is so,
but B.C. wishes Sadie would go

  Sadie wags and B.C. arches
Sadie smiles-B.C. frowns

  B.C. hisses and looks like a raccoon
Sadie slinks and is ready to swoon

  B.C. attacks, she howls, she hisses
She claws and scratches and says "I'll get ya"

  We opened the glass door
and to her surprise,
  The dog could now get inside

B.C. in reverse, four feet in retreat

  It's so embarrassing when you get cold feet!
Gina Bunker

In Silence

I see leaves swirling before a chasing wind
rustling down silently to the ground.
I swirl through those leaves
in silence.
I touch the snow as it melts on my face,
Feel each snowflake dance silently on my lashes.
I dance through the fallen snow
in silence.

I inhale perfume of the daffodils
That nod and sigh silently for refreshing rain.
I breathe in the sweet fragrance
in silence.

I taste the salty spray of the ocean
As it rolls frothy caresses silently onto the shore.
I splash in the foamy whiteness
in silence.

I can hear the song in those senses
that help me enjoy each silent season.
And my life is a spiritual praise
in silence.
Diana Y. Berberian

He Called Me Son

Angered four years running...
Running from fear and frustration...
After a mere murdering of the masses.
Those faces carved of order called it
  Protecting our nation.
Oh is that what I did?
The man with the silver chip on
  his shoulder thinks so.
"Job well done, son. Have a few beers upon
  return to port and shake it all off."
He called me son.
Hope he's proud of his hundredth born.
Don't worry, dad,
I'll wipe my mouth clean and flush
  my guilt into the sea.
Isn't that how you do it?
Your knees frosting with numbness?
Your back aching and stomach knotting?
But don't worry, dad,
I'll wipe my mouth clean.
Jon C. Kremp

"Rolling Thunder"

Rolling Thunder, it looks best in black.
Rolling Thunder, leader of the pack.
Rolling Thunder, the chrome it gleams.
Rolling Thunder, its power beams.
Rolling Thunder, riding cross-country is a must.
Rolling Thunder, the words said, "Eat my dust."
Rolling Thunder, an American dream.
Rolling Thunder, the real wild thing.
Rolling Thunder, its power reigns.
Rolling Thunder, Harley and Davidson were their last names.
Bryon G. Beck

The Dream

I was born to dream and have them come true, they appear
right out of the blue. I wished for a car and then a house
and that's what I got. Then I dreamed of getting a wife and
some kids and to come rich. I got my wife then the kids, I
haven't yet to become right. But, I'm not stuck in a cold
ditch. Next I dreamed of being an inventor. What a wish as
I'm getting bigger. This wish has come true and I'm getting
bolder. Any one can do it. Give it a thought and some time, let
it ferment like a good wine. At first it will smolder and
then you'll make it. So start off small, then go as big as you
want!!! Don't feel blue, it's all up to you. Good luck.
The dreamer, bill sawyers
Bill Sawyers

Mom's Theory

It's okay to have a feeling — it doesn't mean it's good or bad,
right or wrong. Just a feeling.

After you have a feeling, it goes to the brain and becomes a thought.

Thought is good or bad, right or wrong.
Then thought travels through the brain to the next place of decision.

Decision is to think good or bad, right or wrong,
as decision travels through the brain to the next stop of consequence.

Consequence is an action of good or bad, right or wrong.
Then consequence travels to the last stop of all — the heart, happy or sad.

Just a feeling and it's your choice.
Dee Fox-Manning

"Kisses For The Stranger"

If I were to kiss you
Right now
At this very moment of thought,
My pent up passions
Would fuse my skin
Right to your essence.

I would never let you go.

Forever, as for as long as the moment lasted,
I would be an aura about you
And you, mine.

In the moist, throbbing touch
Of lips to lips,
I would own you,
And hold your spirit in abeyance
Suspended in a free-fall.

So inside your consciousness would I be
That you would never be able
To release my future
Without letting go of yours, as well.
Judith Bernstein

A Buggy Ride To The Gristmill

Never shall I forget that trip to Monte Ne Gristmill,
Riding behind "Old Nick", pulling the one - horse shay.
It shall always remain an impressionable thrill,
Leaving a vivid, indelible imprint upon my life today.

Mother rigidly sat on the high seat, holding the lines in hand;
While Grandmother steadied brother, sitting at her feet,
And I was twisting and turning to enjoy my Ozark Fairyland;
Yet constantly struggling to hold on to the old buggy seat.

I'm still fascinated by those iron buggy tires, hitting the rocks,
Making sparks fly upward, downward, and in every direction,
But when that wolf chased a deer across the road, I was in shock,
Suddenly from all of us there was a screaming reaction.

Fascinated by all the sights along the roadside,
Brother and I found plenty to entertain.
Suddenly "Old Nick" reared, jerked the buggy and shied,
When a shrill whistle announced the coming Frisco Train.

Again I would like to view that Panorama scene,
Beneath those Ozark skies of azure blue,
And take a trip to that unique, beautiful Monte Ne, serene;
While taking grain to the gristmill down Esculapia Avenue.

Aileen Fielding

The Spring

Spring has sprung in a wondrous rush...
Rich green grass emerges thick and plush.

Nature's fragrance, "ode -de breeze"...
Perfumes the air from blossom heavy trees.

A kaleidoscope of color at every glance...
As fluttering birds do the spring-time dance.

The softening soil is nurtured in a bath of showers...
While the warming sun gives birth to abundant flowers.

Bountiful sweet scents and glorious sights are nature's gift...
To winter weary hearts it brings a welcome lift.

Inhale its intoxicating presence for too soon it's gone...
The beauty fades quickly, as the dusk follows dawn.

Be awed that mother nature created such a thing...
This wondrous event, this miraculous spring.

Cathy Holzer

"Salvation's Tree"

A silhouette atop a hill,
Revealed a cross by death made still.
  A blameless Lamb salvation bought,
  And broke the chains man's sins had wrought.

A crown of thorns... pierced hands and feet,
Fulfilled what scriptures had decreed.
  To free mankind a price be paid,
  ... On Calvary's tree all blame was laid.

Cries from the cross resound no more,
God's precious Son cruel pain endured.
  A pittance price of silver paid,
  Greed held the heart of trust betrayed.

Atoning blood cleansed white my soul,
God's gift of grace helps keep me whole.
  No longer lingers guilt today,
  The price was paid... the Lamb obeyed.
    ALLELUIA!

Frances Kovacs

Burn

Through the memories I do comb
Remembering, dreaming, yet sitting all alone
I can't imagine where it all went wrong
we were both so happy for so long
In my big dark corner I sit wasting time
My life has become a riddle, not a rhyme
I thought it would never end
My heart shall never mend
without your laughter in my mind
I feel so empty and trapped inside
without you it all has no meaning
every day is only a pain-filled routine
I dream of the day you might return
but the memories only seem to burn.

Hilary Disney

Succubus

Nightly squall awakens spirit, but the body still
remains.

Self poised in episodic entropy, contained within the
fragments of control.

Exorcise the dipsomaniac, disinter the devil with a
spiritual bouquet.

Abscission... Circumcision...
Abscond from sight... Enters at night...
Quiescence lost.

Donald Tasney

My World

I strive to be genuine in a plastic world
Regardless of the price
I need to know that what I do is my choice
Not just a roll of the dice.

I strive to be genuine in a plastic world
Using all I possess
To meet the terms of life in every respect
Be it failure or success.

I strive to be genuine in a plastic world
With what my God has given
Only then will I know I have done my best
Building a bridge to heaven.

Faithe C. Snedden

Old Man Winter

Autumn leaves are falling, brilliant colors...
Reds, rusts, yellows and oranges,
They tell us Old Man Winter will soon be here.

Crops are harvested, houses are cleaned, schools are opened,
Football starts and baseball ends,
Old Man Winter will soon be here.

Birds migrate, rabbits burrow, bears hibernate,
The day short and the nights long,
Soon Old Man Winter will be here.

Jack-O-Lanterns stare, there are goblins everywhere!
Their screams are in the air!
Old Man Winter is coming, Beware!

Pumpkin pies, cranberry sauce, sweet potatoes, vegetables,
Turkey, pudding and cakes, Parades of many kinds,
Symbolize Thanksgiving,
Old Man Winter's just around the corner.

The wind is blowing fiercely, the air is bitterly cold,
Dark clouds are hanging low,
Suddenly, oh so suddenly, it begins to snow!
Old Man Winter is finally here!

Brenda L. Messner

An Autumn Canticle

Golden leaves descend like teardrops,
Red leaves fall like drops of blood.

The clear, bell-like blue of the overarching sky,
Forms a tranquil backdrop for the colorful leaves.

White, fleecy clouds floating lazily by,
Soothe and uplift our drooping spirits.

The golden warmth of the sun reaches our inner being,
We relax with the message given by the colors of autumn.

Be wise, be wise, counsels Yellow; be strong, be strong, bids Red;
Overcome, overcome, charges Orange; all's well, all's well, Azure beams.

Nature drifts toward the restful white of winter,
Retreating in a blaze of glory and soft breezes.

As the long days shorten to equal the dark nights,
We are called to quiet contemplation of Being.

The vibration of our spirit slows to harmonize with nature,
With the muting of the tones of life in winter.

Peace, peace, murmurs White; love, love, whispers Pink;
Seek me, seek me, breathes Blue; all will be revealed, promises Black.

We rest secure knowing that the panorama of autumn color reflects
The wholeness of the Divinity's care for each of us, His children.

Jean Whipple Thomas

Red

Red is spicy, spicy is red.
Red is fall, leaves fall.
Leaves are red.
Balloons are red.
Candy is red.
Lava is red.
Red, red, it's everywhere.
Red is blood.
Red is wine.
Red is a P.E. star.
Red is a dictionary.
Like I said, red is everywhere.
Red is rubies.
Red is the stripes on the American Flag, and red are hearts.

Jerry Miguel

Muse Of Seasons

The blast of Winter's hoary breath
Recedes in apt fatigue
As wispy veils to nought but tout
The breasts of Spring's intrigue

The virtuoso cocks his ear
And hearkens to the strains
Of symphonies he strums on strings
Of Summer evening rains

The loom is splashed with transient scraps
Enhancing as it weaves
Flamboyant quilts embroidered
In the hues of Autumn leaves

But time does gauge the depth of rimes
Opaqueness on the panes
And calculates the marvel
Of mystique that never wanes

And lyrics merged with tempo
Render concerts of rapport
With vagabond resplendence
Strewn across the comos floor

Alysia Hayward

Spirits Aflame Through Senior Games

Again and again, look about for a Senior Olympic Game,
Really full of gaiety, adventure and fame.
Participants are special seniors; their ageing ignored,
While capacity and talents are eagerly explored.
Friendly events have thrills and laughter in store;
Yearly, cities and states fervently acclaim,
Convivial comradeship and fun galore,
Ardently continuing all enhanced lives through.
Games are for athletes and community volunteers, too.
Now many spirited events are awaiting neighbors and you.
Ah, proudly, too, you will be greeting family names,
Signing and sharing with kinfolk at Senior Games.

George A. Meffan

Our World

Living the street life is not what you think it is, but an image of reality.
People, hungry and cold, fighting for their lives.
Every night, it's a nightmare of the worst kind.
Most of the people involved consider themselves normal, but does a person really know what normal is?
Can you tell me difference between fantasy and reality?
Maybe one day people might do as they please in this street life, a crazy merry go round of people and places.
So keep yourself entertained as the earth revolves and time and people change.
Hopefully one day, everyone will have a destination.

Jacqueline Danford

"Soldiers Of What Army?"

We are soldiers of what army?
Ready to fist fight, taking hits to extreme ends!
Using bad languages, knives, and guns,
not to be caught, living dangerously, ready to run,

Faster than lightning, the diseases are spread,
young people taken early, obituaries to be read,
educated, in which way? All so tough!
Are we made of a special kind of stuff?

Bullets, and knives, kill you, no education! No concern!
Reality aimed to strike, too late! Haven't we learned?
A blessing to live, the battle to fight, Jesus has won,
he didn't want the message, sent by the enemies gun!

The sun so beautiful, the radiance so strong,
The moon shines bright, all night long,
The battle is fought, to make things right,

We are soldiers of what army?
We are soldiers of what army?

Had to ask this twice!

Cynthia D. Robinson

Summits

Clarity of an uncommon hue,
radiance cleaves a cool zephyr.
Facing the life source gives renewal-
well worth the task, half completed.
Air thinning makes one draw deep,
pausing to capture vast images
before making a descent into loamy intoxication.

James L. Root

Untitled

Listen.
Quiet now.
Can you hear it?
Can you?
Blissful plane of harmony.
The earth in all its glory.
Proclaiming to all, its health, its vitality.
The trees....the water....the air.
All is as it should be.....now.
All is as it was.....before.
Listen.
Quiet now.
Can you hear it?
can you....?

Julie Amanollahi

Shall It Be Right? Shall It Be Wrong?

To kill the beast is to, kill the source. Thou must be
prosecuted then if done wrong. Right? Thus being the
day when man and beast become one beast is
then off the hook am I right? Wrong. Of the day they
'fess up to the bad deeds done in nature, they from
on have the bounds of shackles on the shackle less
mind that engulfs them to do what they do not want.
All mighty one puts a curse of frivolous behavior to
follow them, is it to the ends of the earth? No.
It is to become very dolt and diverse. Not like regular
insanity but just enough to make them realize that
thou became powerless in the arms of an embittered,
incognitoed to make a merciless man. When realized the
beast began to make excruciating pleas to the all
mighty one who commands.
Shall it be right? Shall it be wrong?

Rebecca Anne Codd

Queen

Her name is Woman. Carrier of the royal seed. Born a nubian
princess, strongly empowered to be queen.

Her skin, earthy brown. Hips, wide and round. A spirit blessed by
God. Born to be strong, upholding, not hard.

Her body, the tool that increases her race. She's the life-line of
her people. She knows her royal place.

It's beside her nubian king. Not beneath his royal feet. Their
Creator made them equal. Beside him is her seat.

Apart they each are one. Not half, nothing less than a whole. Each a
complete person, together fulfilling their own role.

She's more than a small portion. A whole person, you see.

God created this nubian queen with mind, with body, and with a
spirit to set free.

Alvette Chase

Brand New Angels

Brand new angels tease the clouds,
Sketching mystic pictures in the sky,
Infants shining out of blue,
Old men seem to hear their coo,

Symphony winglets fly in view,
Melting notes to play on cue,
Lightening strikes the drum as thunder,
Falling notes! Earth drinks in wonder!!

Dorothy W. Risavy

Children Have No Colors Just Dreams

Imagination conquers the world, without any fears,
Precious little jewels, with innocent ideas;
The life we live should be of total honesty,
The portrait we paint can influence their destiny.

Children are God's esteemed gift into our hands,
Let's exhibit love, and take a firm stand;
It's up to us to continuously plant the seed,
Observe the growth, and replenish the need.

They behold thoughts we cease to touch,
Their probing minds perceive and ponder a bit much;
Nothing is impossible to them, it seems,
Of a truth, children have no colors, just dreams.

If their innocence we abuse and stain,
Negativity will dominate the fragments that remain;
It's time to modify our motives, and sharpen our tools,
And become more diligent in teaching the golden rules.

Let's unite and make their fantasies realities,
By keeping their minds focused with the possibilities;
Help them accomplish their scenarios through constructive means,
Yes, children have no colors, just dreams.

Evelyn B. Gourdine

Eagle Shadow

Time left me on a rock of craggy, granite stone
Pondering the things of life and all I've ever known
A shadow crossed the desert floor and painted across my face
A lesson in living, a lesson in love, in this blessed place.

The shadow flew above me then, aloft on broad spread wings
Passing over and into me the spirit of living things
I wondered how it could survive in this land of barren souls
I cast aside my worries then and watched answers unfold.

We can choose to fly above the worry and the strife
And reach across the barrier and help another's life
This message from the ancients, set forth to learn that day
Take what we need, give what we can, each in our own small way.

Perched upon cathedral rock, the desert helped me find
Simple, gentle reason to the musings in my mind
I rid my life of confusion on this desert soliloquy
But nothing quite as sure and free, as this shadow passing over me.

Bobbie J. Herring

The City

Why is the city so violent and frightening,
Polluted, messy, and informal?
Why does it seems so hazy and enclosed,
But to its people normal?

The traffic light flashing red,
Behind it a noisy car horn,
Wouldn't you like to live in the
  suburbs instead,
Or be awakened by the wailing of a new born?

Geoffrey Bockelmann

Perhaps

Perhaps you look at me and don't know what you're seeing...
Perhaps you don't see anything at all...
Perhaps our time is shorter here then we have acknowledged...
  and then again,
Perhaps our time will go on for many years to come...
Perhaps the sun will shine,
Perhaps the rain will fall,
Perhaps the wind will blow us away from it all...
I guess it doesn't matter which of the "perhaps" come true....
As long as you can see me and I can see you.

Elisabeth Brooks

146

T.V. Commercials

Dancing ants, are chugging beer.
  Polar bears, keep this soda near.
Hemorrhoidal pads, keep swelling nil.
  Use these condoms, or get none still.
Football heroes, argue with a toon.
  Drum beating bunnies, won't die soon.
Squeeze a roll, it's incredibly soft.
  Stick to our glue, it'll hold you aloft.
Be self conscious, give a hoot.
  Wear these briefs, with dancing fruit.
Call us fresh, we sell roses.
  Odorous feet, may offend noses.
Dancing raisins, strumming guitar.
  Diarrheic medicines, let you ride far.
On the phones, romance for you.
  Chocolate bits, sabotaging to be blue.
Candies spewing, from the ground.
  Chew two tabs, bring bloating down.
Holsteins climbing, up the graphs.
  Commercial ads, brought lots of laughs.

Allison L. Cochran

Sunny Days

Honey, just a large towel, some cool drinks,
Please honey, don't forget some baby oil.
Let me gentle sooth over my baby, as she
Lays there on the sand, on sunny days.
Beautiful, sunny days, my baby and I, just us
Two, sharing our love together, just you,
And I, honey, just you, and I.
On the beach, on sunny days,
As the world pass us by, we see,
Only the nice things we do.
Honey, let me put some oil all over you.
Beautiful sunny days,
Honey, just a large towel,
Baby oil, just you
And I, on Sunny days.

Evon R. Clake

To Fight The Good Battle

Oh Kindly Being, to whom we all pray,
Please help me, to safely, get through this day.

Each life is a battle, as we learn wrong from right.
My weapons, to win, are your strength and your might.

Help me, always, to make the right choice.
Help me control the sound of my voice.

Help me speak gently, and kindly to others;
For aren't we all, merely sisters and brothers?

Help me be responsible for that which I do;
To be giving, compassionate, and loving too.

Help me deal honestly with each woman and man;
No matter his color, religion or land.

Help me, when there's injustice, to bravely step in;
And always to recognize the right, from the sin.

Help me say I'm sorry, when someone's been hurt;
By something I've said, or a tone that was curt.

Help me when others are unkind to me
To turn the other cheek, and draw strength from thee.

And, when at last, this life's battle is done
Please help me to make it a battle well won.

Eileen Oakes Bender

Hunting

The four dogs played by the tracks,
playing the game they knew so well;
although they felt no fear of the catcher,
the heavy fog that clouded their path
was flowing thick into their throats.

The four dogs played by the tracks,
hoping to grow up and live in a house,
but still eager to wake up to the smell
of the hot garbage on a summer's day.

The four dogs played by the tracks,
hoping for a collision course, one
that would set them apart, but
they just sat on the hot steel strips
waiting for the coming of the train.

Denos Myrmingos

The Pit Of Dreams

To the sleep I took my lazy, to the demons, angels, lace
Pillow wilted with my crazy, seeing past my pretty face
Went to wander with the witches, came to teach the demon's dance
Here to dig the goblin's ditches and to weave the vampire's trance.
Not the real world here to frighten, to twist and turn and scream
Ravens weep as feathers whiten, tearing at my dress' seam.
Mountains glow with dripping thunder, ocean waves their tides do crack
Ants to rocks they live there under, trains and deer befriend no track
May souls and bodies longer linger, fireflies wave their tricky spots
Walls of nothing pierce the finger, time to sing while culture trots.
Grassy stones to guide my wander, whirling pools of crystal rain
Lions play to join my fonder, bloody wounds produce no pain
Wilder thoughts my feeling glory, purple clouds they glisten fire.
Tears of salt while deeper story, gliding splash of wet desire
Rivers warm with vibrant color, lonely fear caressed by love
Sharpest swords to lose by duller, moon is governed by the dove.
Smiles are made without a money, hearts beat fonder while they age
Streams flow backwards bitter honey, passion swarms with broken rage.

Buck Christensen

From My Window

Held together with just a wooden edge, some windows draw a beautiful picture. Only to be redrawn with the slightest movement. The ever-changing picture from my window.

A border of white brick surrounds the picture. Small bugs bounce against the screen. You follow them with your eyes but they lead you only to the magnificent yet almost invisible net that was spun by a spider just days ago.

Uncut grass and blowing weeds. They give you an unknowing feeling about what lies within them. To the left one squirrel chases another up a tree only to unexpectedly round a dying branch,
then back down to the ground. Back into the mysterious weeds that surround everything.
Into the background a lake mirrors the blinding image of a setting, summer's day sun. Covered up by the towering mountains, bringing darkness and night to the surrounding land. Allowing all to sleep quietly.

When you walk away from the window you think- another day, another picture, but you do not realize that the picture you just walked away from will never be seen again.

Andrew Kuntemeier

Above And Below

Above and below, I look both ways, but still I see nothing.
Perhaps there is something passing me by, but for
now it manages to evade me.

All that I seek is all that I ask, a life without pain.
Maybe that too will pass me by,
above or below me.

Edward Lessard

Elias

Friendships can be unexplainable, so it seems at times.
Perhaps to completely understand every friendship is impossible.

The mingling of two spirits, one seeking the other, is the
hidden plan of One who knows that present needs are to be
shared with one who is being himself, chosen for this special
task of helping a lonely spirit so adrift that our spirits unite
only for a time.

Oh, why do you fear this happening so? Are you so afraid to
have him know you and what you stand for? He is what he is,
but his eyes gave him away as a different individual, one
different from any other we have ever encountered.

Our parting was for the best! Did we discover in so brief a
moment the purpose for such a short relationship? Who is to say?

Within our hearts, memories will endure until we shall see
our souls united unto the Eternal Kingdom.

Jim Logan

Friend Or Foe

Street wise I may be.
People wise I'm quite naive.
For if a friend you claim to be.
Then as a friend, it shall be.
As my heart opens wide to thee,
With no pain felt by me.
Then truly you are a friend acclaimed by me.

But if my heart opens wide to thee.
As with pain and torment felt by me.
Then truly thine is mine enemy.

Jeanne Clouseau

Shadows Of Freedom

I remember the place, I remember the time, but it seems so long ago
People were proud and happy to be, friends were forever more
The sun would rise and with each new day there was more hope than the
    day before
You could smile, laugh and even dream, of all that was to be
The past was good, the future bright, destiny lie just ahead
With each step, we paved our way, on a road through the unknown
But it did not matter where we were headed, progression was always good.

Civilization has evolved through slavery, war, freedom and riots
    and now we've come full circle again
Freedom and equality are one in the same, slavery has a new face
it includes black, white, yellow and red, people of all races
The struggle has been hard, more for some then for others, but we all
    loose in the end
Promises have been broken, the rich get richer and politicians just
    don't care.

The system has failed, police are corrupt, doing drugs, murder and maim
We lock our doors in disbelief and try to survive from within
But sooner or later they will come for you, there really is no way out
The fight is not for one, but for us all, there is plenty of work to do
If you spend all of your time hiding inside, when can you try on
    the other man's shoes
It's always someone else, never us, We're waiting for the right sign
But as you can see it's up to you and me, I just hope there is still
    enough time.

Juanita Young

"As Life Turns A Page"

As life turns a page
people come and go
Memories start to fade
New ones start to grow.

As life turns a page
And the world hits a crisis
Technology's expensive, but works they say
Why not use love, it's priceless.

As life turns a page
And people leave us here
Nothing much to say
But prove the things we fear.

As life turns a page
patience will overcome
you'll wait forever and a day
To see the turtle run.

Crystal Pingleton

Winter's Window

Snow falling
Past half-drawn curtains.
    Beyond fog frosted glass, shingles of ice hang dripping
    Pointed reflections dance as delicate flakes
    Gently float toward the frozen furrow below.

No footsteps
Crunching through the crisp surface of freshly-fallen snow.
    Not a print trekking its way over the expanse
    Marring the scarless face of this serene view.

Near and far
A blanket of powdery white is majestically coated over the
    early morning ground.
    Gracefully bowing tree limbs are adorned with new-found beauty,
    Fences copiously capped with tufts of sparkle,
    And a gentle wind wisps over untouched hills, buffing its
    surface to a wintery shine.

Not a sound
But the gentle caress of my breath upon your shoulder.
    Snuggled under warm covers, your cheek against mine -
    A kiss brushed across your lips tantalizes all senses to awareness.

You awake
To a snowy New Year's morning!

David A. Sharp

Star Bright

"Over here Billy, I'm open.
Pass me the ball!"
Mike stood watching behind the fence.
Mike could have told you it was bad call.

Mike's eyes gleamed
As the watched the game.
Mike longed to play,
But not for fame.

"Please, oh, Please,"
Thought Mike, "let me
Play in the game."
(His wish wouldn't be.)

To rid himself of
His morbid condition,
Mike's plan was to cause
His own extinction.

People learned of his death.
All they could say of him was kind.
Had Mike only known that
The fence was in his mind.

Damian Huertas Jr.

148

Window Of Dreams

I can see clearly through the pain,
Pain or pane - the words interchange.
The barrier that shields me from my dreams is invisible.
The window in the wall allows a glimpse into the Eden of unchallenged
potential.... but no passage.

The wall is long and seems unending.
Many are ahead of you - many push to get ahead.
I can see the carnage of those who ran for the window in a dash of
  daring desperation.
They line the path like the refuse of an auto junk yard.
Crippled of their dreams, they beg for help until their voices fail
and their dreams transform into a mindless scavenger hunt.

The struggle between hope and despair keeps me in line.
Occasionally, a brilliant light like the beam of a magnifying glass
  focuses on the line.
A silent prayer of unison hope paralyses the line
as the light surrounds its selected incumbent.
For this one the wall is removed and inexplicably their dreams become
  reality.
All others wonder, "Why can't it be me?".

I will stay in line and look through the pane...
I'll feel the pain.
As long as I can see the window, I can dream the dream.

Alice B. Moody

Our Nation's Outlook

Destroying our nation comes from within,
Overpowered by alcohol, drugs and sin.
The cowardly assailants swiftly begin
Plots that will bring our lives to an end.

Someone is gassing our subways, crashing our trains,
And planting terrorism within our brains.
Citizens' bodies are dragged through the dirt;
While their crosses and flags are burnt.

Doorstep bombs are blasting, and living has reasonable doubt.
Yet, terminating freedom won't turn evil about.
Our blinded minds must learn to see
With awakening intelligence, we'll discover the enemy.

Carolyn F. Peck

Allen's Desire

Miles lay between; leagues keep us apart.
Over fields of gold and green,
Over forests, rivers, and streams.
Through many towns, over countless hills,
Across ravines, and over the stones.
Bounding, bounding; I'm constantly running, I'm constantly wanting.

Together again; embracing once more.
At peace we relax, her hand in mine,
Worries forgotten for a short time.
Happy, content, we sit side by side,
Later, we know, we must say good-bye.
Pounding, pounding; my heart keeps on racing, I'm constantly yearning.

Leagues and miles; they separate once more.
Memories of joy and peace contain,
The agony, the hurt, and the pain.
The fires are raging within,
I await to see her again.
My heart trembles; my heart quivers, and yet my heart still desires.

Jeff Crawford

'Comes The Light'

Back from where they once roamed
over bluest waters and frothing foam
they've come together and some alone
they've come to see the light come home.
  Once where there was only dark
cold and barren and ghostly stark
they answer to bells with an earthly tone
they've come to see the light come home.
  Though forests full of crying wolves
on carriages led by pounding hooves
over grassy meadows and streets of stone
they've come to see the light come home.
  It's come from behind a shadow of sorrow
from hate and death and lost tomorrows
to shine again like polished chrome
they've come to see the light come home.
  At last a taming of the wild
a smile will show on every child
and all can reap what they have sown
as once again the light comes home.

James Robinson

Benjamin

  I see your big blue eyes looking,
out at our huge world,
I wonder what you see,
What you are thinking about.
  I wonder what you'll do today?
will you look at a book,
Swing on the swing set,
make something with your play-doh,
or chase the dog around?
  Well, tomorrow is another busy day for
Benjamin

Carol Schaffer

Sisters

When we were all little girls
Our mother put our hair in curls.
I would bounce with sheer delight
And my curls would stay so tight.
It wasn't so for all my sisters
Whose curls fell out with slight wind's whispers.
As we grew older we drifted apart,
Only one sister remains close in my heart.

Harriet S. Pandolfo

I'm The Dreamer

In this world you have to be smart, athletic, or pretty,
Or people say, "It is, oh, such a pity."
But I am of a different race than this.
I'm the dreamer; I'm the dreamer.

I dream of castles and of love.
In my fantasies I dream of heaven above,
And people will look at me and sigh,
"She's the dreamer; she's the dreamer."

Some day all my dreams will come true,
And no one on that day will rue,
For only peace and no fighting are here.
I'm the dreamer; I'm the dreamer.

In my dreams we live in harmony,
And you're all a little like me,
For we all have secret hopes and dreams.
We're all the dreamers; we're all the dreamers.

Elspeth DeLeurere

Ode To Middle Age

Even though we're in our forties, we're still going strong.
Our memories are sharp as ever, they're just not quite as long.

We used to have such tight, firm butts, that we could really wiggle,
Now they're soft and ripple-y and when we walk they jiggle.

Our sparkling eyes that when we laughed, danced with mischievous
twinkles, are bloodshot now from straining all day and surrounded by
bags and wrinkles.

Our slender waists were trim and flat, our legs firm and defined, But
now our tummies hang out in front, and our fannies hang out behind.

Our muscles and joints have became the home of all sorts of aches and pains,
Our bodies are falling apart so fast—but not as fast as our brains.

We walk in a room, we look around, don't know why we came here at all.
We pick up the phone to dial a friend, it's ringing, now who did I call?

We go to the store for bread and milk, not much, we'll keep the list
in our head. We spend eighty-four dollars and fifty cents, and
come home without the bread!

We lose our keys, our purses, our shoes, can't find our car in the lot,
And anywhere we decide to go, we get lost more often than not.

But we don't care if we're getting old, it's our right to complain and
to fuss, Though we're falling apart and our minds aren't sharp,
there's always somebody older than us.

Barbara W. Brown

9 Months, 3 Weeks, And 6 Days

9 stands for the time we fed the flame,
  our love burning uncontrollably that no one could tame.
   Like a forest on fire engulfed in passion,
    our love was not a thing to ration.

3 is for the times you made me sad,
  when things were just getting out of hand.
   When lightning struck and rain poured down,
    like a disease or a plaque through an old town.

6 is for the days we spent all alone,
  when we wished from this cruel world we'd flown.
   To float and fly,
    away from our problems in the breeze.
     Like the wind through the valleys and trees.

9 times 3, times 6 are the years,
  I'd wait for you, through all of my tears.
   When you'd come back to me and say,
    "From this day forward, together we'll stay."

Aryck Matthew Arthur

Why Take The Time?

I save the old newspapers so David will have more trees to climb;
Our children deserve a future without all the trash we unnecessarily
  leave behind.
I save plastic grocery bags so Josh won't have a dump as his backyard;
Reduce, Reuse, Recycle, this takes so little effort and it's not so very hard.
Just saving the Dr. Pepper cans or the Sunday paper will count;
As we show our kids what saving God's green Earth is all about.
So set aside your plastic jugs and save out the tin vegetable cans,
Let's all work together so our children will succeed in their future plans.
Set the example, because children learn from what they see,
We can show them how easy, preservation and conservation can be.
I take the time to recycle so my boys will be able to see,
How very important two of God's gift, like children and the Earth, are to me.

Debra Wilcox

May 3, 1995 Nicole Brown Ronald Goldman

Someone who just deserved to live, like me and you and all the
others. No one had the right to ever touch her, when she was born
she didn't know anyone would hurt her in this way. Now she's gone so
far far away, and her babies have been robbed of a great mother they
loved and adored, and admired. Why oh why did you do this to someone
who only lived for her children, she was here just like me and you,
and all the beautiful things her and her children would do. She
didn't deserve to die in such an ugly way, someone left these ugly
memories for her family everyday. This person will definitely have to
pay. Nicole's friend Ronald also had a name, no one seems to remember
his name, He died in vain. He was a person just like me and you, He
needs to be remembered too. So speak his name, Don't act as if he
didn't exist He didn't deserve to go this way. He should still be
here today. No one deserves to die this way. People are so heartless
when it comes to these two, They don't realize the damage they do.
These are two people who shouldn't have died at all, but someone took
there life from under them as they stood. I know today they should
be here, they really should. Their families are so empty without them
here today. Please just remember they should be here today. Remember
their names RONALD GOLDMAN AND NICOLE BROWN and please
stop being heartless today, and stop hurting the family that way. Because
someday you'll be judged in a very real way, and all you've said and
done will not go unpunished at all someday. Everything you've said
and done about Ronald and Nicole will come to haunt you and punish
you someday.

Dolly Aceves

Sometimes I Wonder...

Sometimes I wonder my God made us like we are,
Or who we are,
Why we feel certain ways,
Why we like certain things,

Sometimes I sit back and wonder,
Why are there stars in the skies,
Other planets in the galaxy,
Or why grass is green,
Or just why is there an earth at all,

Sometimes I wonder what I would do,
If I had no one to talk to,
No one to love,
No one to be there when times get rough,
If I had no family,
Nothing to call my own,

Sometimes I wonder about the future,
What will it bring,
How will my life change?
  "Sometimes I Wonder!"

Erica Gwaltney

The Path Not Taken

The path not taken, can be so long.
Or can be the magical short cut home.
So often we stand at the crossroad of life
And see how our path is filled with strife.

We wonder about the path not taken,
Where there's peace for the heart, and spirit awakens.
But we stood at the crossroads and dallied along,
Taking the path that led us wrong.

We wander through the briar and bramble,
And bear the marks of this paths ramble —
When the path not taken looks so serene,
No briars to scratch — this path is clean.

And in our hearts as we plod along,
We know the path we took was wrong.
The path not taken is free from care,
And peace and contentment reigneth there.

Ida Marie Lee

Bikin' Cross Time

I lived here once—was long ago,
or was that someone else?
Two different lives—two different roads,
my heart within me melts.
We drive down streets, now strangers claim—
down lanes while memory clears.
Nostalgia plays its ghost-like games.
Reality fights tears.
It hurts to come back to the start,
'cause home's not here today.
You took my hand—I won your heart—
life's trail led us away.
Rev up your bike—kick up the stand,
the past must keep its own.
In silence let me grieve this land—
the place I once called home.
The wind, our friend, feels free as we
make tracks across past times.
I'll not look back—ahead's the sea—
thanks, hon, you made it mine.

Carrol A. Buntin

The Eyes of a Child

To watch a falling leaf flitter in the air;
Or the tiny puffs of dandelion scatter everywhere.
To see large colorful dragons, and unicorns with flowing manes;
While clouds, like fluffy lambs, frolic here and there.
Kites, balloons, the propellers on planes,
Butterflies, kittens, and tracks, full of trains;
All things beautiful - free, and wild
Oh, to see the world through the eyes of a child!

Janice J. Jones

Corners

Is life for the strong
Or the strong minded?

The hunter or the hunted?
Do they realize what is life?

The sport is here
But are they willing to play?

The circle of life has many sharp corners...
Are you ready to turn or turn around?

Chelsea Hoffman

Moving Through Me

Whether I'm in the valley, the plains
    or on a mountain high,
If I'm walking, running, bicycling
    or even decided to fly,
God is moving through me.

God is moving through me
    with every breath I take,
God is moving through me
    with every move I make.

Even when I'm angry, happy, sick or well
    or feel almost at my end,
I can rest assure that
    God is yet my friend.

When I listen to jazz, sang the blues, gospel
    or move to rock and roll,
You must know the truth
    that might be yet untold.

It is God moving through me.
God is Life!

Helen Ruth Johnson

Stay Focused On The Divine Light

No matter how dark the day,
    Or how pitch black the night,
I must continue to stay focused,
    Being guided by God's divine light.

It takes some periods of darkness,
    Before some can see the light of hope.
So God provides our every need,
    By giving us the strength to cope.

Sometimes the light is very dim,
    Sometimes it shines so very bright.
It is up to you and me to always know,
    That we must keep it in our sight.

It is truly wonderful,
    Always to have one or more plans divine.
God intends for all of us to see the light;
    For it shines eternally for all of mankind.

So, keep in mind how important it is,
    To constantly do our part.
We have a divine duty to stay focused,
    To radiate peace and love from the heart.

Joyce G. Moore

Collision

Should the fury and comfort of the sea be ceased
Or can we achieve a global peace?
When we choose to indulge in fields unknown,
We dismiss the beauty of an eternal stone.
Create the miseries and virtually ignore
The sensual attraction of a virgin shore.
This is the choice of the undecided,
These are the feelings of souls divided.
The world was ours for reasons unknown
Will reap the effects of what we've sown.
Destroy in the name of profits and then
Decide what minuscule problems to mend.
We cannot survive without earth's soul
And cannot ignore the ultimate toll
This is the choice of the undecided
These are the feelings of souls divided
This is the decision for you to confide
This is what happens when souls collide.

Bradford Anderson Barnes

Saving The World

I am not trying to save the world
    or bring about peace in all the nations under the sun.

I know the sorrows of many
    often seem to out weigh the sorrows of one.

In this hypocritical utopian existence
    our soldiers stand ready in arms
        to be sent away to other countries
            when their back yard is crawling with tolerated harms.

When the real wars are fought with money
    instead of cannons blaring through the night,
        we flex our might battalions of muscle
            only to die by the economic light.

We say it isn't fair,
    but the trade deficits mount,
        foreign ownership climbs
            and we're getting bought out.

NO. I am not trying to save the world.

Let the lines be drawn;
    tend to your own sheep
        before they're gone.

Benjamin Wilkins

Untitled

A flower blossoms only by
  opening its petals to the Sun
A turtle moves only by
  pulling his head and legs out of his shell
A caterpillar only becomes a butterfly by
  overpowering his way out of his cocoon
A human only becomes a being by
  opening himself and his heart
  to the wonders of the world.

Bonnie Risinger

Moonlight Dancing

There's moonlight on the window shining with its special glow
onto the couple dancing inside the room.
You can hear the music the faint sound of laughter
down the long narrow hall of no return.
It is so much ease then the pain of the past
Living in the dreams of yesterday and magic nights of so long ago.
I can't count the times that I've been asked?
Do you have a picture?
I have to say yes I do I have many pictures but I can never show them
to you for the very heart that holds them all belongs to you.
When I am feeling sad there is one thing I can do.
I can find my escape into that very room.
The doorway is open and I am waiting there for you
follow the dancers footsteps into my dream.
No one can take these things from me.
The pictures and the dancing for only you and I have the key
No one else can enter only you.
For you are the other half of the couple
Dancing inside our very special room.

Alma Jean Epps

Life

Be still my heart for there is no pain in death;
Only without Love my heart is there pain;

Does this mean that in love there is life;
and without there is none;

Does this mean that life without love brings despair;
and life with love brings a heart's repair;

My heart, what is that I feel;
Is that a faint beat that I feel;

Does this mean love still exists and my heart is in repair,
Does this mean that even in pain there is love;

Keep beating my heart for I guess there is still love
Keep beating my heart for I guess there is life after all.

Greg Ferguson

Untitled

Time can only hold one thing
One thing can only hold you
When time runs out
Can you still hold on to a dream
Days forgotten and time lost
Do not look back
And do not return to the dirty hotel
Where your mind was destroyed
When do you say it is enough
Why do you want to give up
How can you give in and never hold the only one you want

Bryce L. Williamson

Love Eternal

In your eyes, my heart did matriculate.
Only with you does it communicate.
Simpleness becomes the tower.
Petals falling from the tiniest flower.
Eclipsing a view, my sight now infinite.
The world smalling every single minute.
Ever holding my hand I shall carry the world in the other.
  In people's vanity, thinking of others and what they see.
Your reflection in my eyes, I'm the best I can possibly be.
That pain may find me someday.
The love I have now, will always stay.
Love does not falter.
Like Christ at an altar.
  The time has come, I'm wandering alone.
A simple waive a talk on the phone.
Your simplest thoughts bring the sun.
On dreary land where night's never done.
Joy for those who find them and stay.
My chance has passed remember till forever,
The day.

David M. Lopez

How Can It Be?

Waking in the morning with you is only a dream and here in reality I
only see my pillow. Your hair lying there, your face so fair, and all
I see is my pillow. Your breath in my ear, I feel you so near, then
all I feel is my pillow. I wake up and frown, there's rain coming
down, I reach out and hug my pillow. How can it be that you aren't
with me and all that I've got is this pillow?

John L. Bollinger

Only Connection

Longing for your touch while I sit here alone,
Only connection, the telephone.
Hearing your voice brings me real great pleasure
But touching your body is my real life treasure.
Climb aboard, let's take a ride, we'll see
What's waiting on the other side.
Friendship or love, for us it's the same, the fire
That's burning is in able to tame.
Feeling your lips brings my thought's to a hold,
Hoping this passion will never grow old.
The path which we lead, to the place is unknown,
For the only connection, the telephone.

Heidi Schmidt

Dr. Martin Luther King Jr.

Dr. King was a man of courage,
one who rendered all of his service.
Dr. King was honest and true,
one who fought to take his brothers through.
Dr. King was a man of fame,
by no means was he ashamed.
Dr. King fought a good fight, and advised
his people to hold on tight.
Dr. King was a God sent angel, one who realized
his life was in danger.
Dr. King was not a sitter, but one who was known
to be no quitter.
Dr. King was a freedom fighter,
one who knew that the future would be brighter.
Dr. King was the best that we had,
but we know his soul is free at last!

Brenda Nettles Robinson

Gasping For Meaning

One person's truth is another's fantasy.
One person's choice is another's destiny.

Keep on dreaming of days ahead,
And follow your path like a thread.

Never mind your restless heart;
Just keep focused when you start.

No need to ask, or say, or do;
Just remember that He's there, too.

Confusion will dominate once in a while;
But your faith will eventually produce a smile.

Your head will feel swelled up and tight;
And that's when you must stay and fight.

You're gasping for meaning and losing control;
Quiet your mind and hear what is told.

The curious will know;
The humble will show.

Gasping for meaning...Gasping for meaning;
Quiet your mind...Quiet your mind;
Listen....Listen;
Know...Know.

Janie Corona Alaniz

One + One = One

If our Father created
One male with unusual attributes
And one female with similar attributes
And equally favored them spiritually
To nourish one unit, a family,
Then, the rights of
All men and all women are proportioned equally.

Doris Snyder

Reaction

Through a green, flowered jungle I chanced to stray,
On, what to me, was a lovely day.
When through the brush came a Lions roar, and down the path,
At a limping gait, came a mangy beast in the hands of fate.
It stopped and lay on the jungle floor,
And licked its aching paw once more;
Where an ugly thorn stuck from its flesh.
To my mind's eye a legend flashed,
Of a timid man in a foreign land,
Who stood in the stead where I chanced to stand.
A man by the name of Androcles,
   Who removed the thorn, which did offend,
And made, of the beast, a life long friend.
Cloud this beast, perchance, one day help me?
Who ever knows what one's needs might be.
By these thoughts bolstered, I pulled the thorn.
   With one mighty, powerful, vicious blow,
It sent me sprawling in bewildered woe.
There was no warmth in my soul that day,
Though the beast didn't limp as it walked away.

Jay A. Meservy

Prediction

If, when you go to Hell, a crowd
Of demons asks you why
You swagger and you walk so proud
And hold your head so high.

Just tell them that you broke the heart
Of one who loved you well
And laughed to think you were so smart.
You'll get along in Hell.

John M. Bunn

White Roses

White roses bloom in early May
On a plant given on Valentine's Day
By a lover now so far away.

The rosebush in its dormant state,
By its appearance did not foretell its fate
To grow luxuriant by the garden gate

With dancing blossoms of purest white,
Which in carefree clusters reflecting bright,
Rival by day the crystalline stars at night.

But when day is over or just begun,
In the soft glows of setting or rising sun—
In the solitude through which old memories run—

The blossoms blush in the quiet hush,
And remembering she's no longer here,
Dewdrops swell and fall like tears.

Grady Thrasher

One Memory Of San Francisco

Plops of rain
   on a greenhouse window
Falling like tears
   down a widow's face
The lit night black and clear
   as if steam from an Erie railroad engine had blown it clean.

Outside....
   Vines intertwined with brick
   fat chunks of green leaves
   others slim as tendrils hanging
   and quivering like trellises in the wind.

Inside....
   Candlelight and wine
   bits of veal chewed and swallowed but not tasted
   fingers intertwined and smiles exchanged
   with rain silently plopping on a greenhouse window.

Chloe Pollock Molnar

The Crystal Ball

While gazing into life's crystal ball
on a clear, warm summer night
I silently watched the darkness fall,
with the moon not yet in sight.

Ah, and the sky, softly lit with stars
filled the air with moods of love
and transparent clouds of planet Mars
created silhouettes high above.

And sweet Venus, looking her best that eve,
crept sensuously into my view;
garbed in thin clouds, so not to deceive
her rare beauty, known only to few.

Yes, stars and planets were all in place
as nature had intended them to be;
not one mistake was there to erase,
yet I searched, 'til sleep crept over me...

Anthony Skoien

153

To Inca

Inca, Oh Inca, in your death throes wait,
 Old dog ravaged by a cancerous fate,
Faithful companion for nearly two year,
 But this eve is our last now I do fear.
Your sunken eyes and shallow breath foretell,
 All hope will end in a rather short spell.
The dawn shall break but nevermore with you,
 So farewell was said with sunset's sad adieu.
But iron willed Inca held on through the night,
 Her status unchanged as the stars took flight.
Crept passed her form on way to the field,
 Where our stranger's distrust first time did yield.
Must I now go check the cattle alone,
 When I see the trailing figure of fur and bone.
Staggering now to join me in one last romp,
 Tearfully, I rushed to where she did slump.
Buried her that day beside two of my best,
 With Missey and Heidi under oak tree now rest.
Lay forever gently on her Oh Earth,
 She that offered me all she was worth.

 James M. Pitt

"St. Petersburg, Goodnight"

 The ocean just swallowed the sun
Oh, what a beautiful sight
The sun splashed rays, over ocean and sprays
and kissed St. Petersburg goodnight.

 Jack Smithson

Rose Glass

Water cleanses the body but not the mind.
Oh the things you do when drunk with wine.
Never knowing where you will awake; opening up
Your soul and allowing your heart to break.
With shattered hope you now exist.
Remembering the temptation that you could not resist.
Now an empty shell is all you have for a heart.
Forced to share a dream of which you have no part.

Water cleanses the boy but not the mind.
Some scars last forever; this you will find.
The only hope you have is to forget;
A near impossible task, you can almost bet.
Left no choice but to live or die,
You hide the pain and on the inside you cry.
You spend your remaining hours in pain.
Is it worth it? Are your sorrows in vain?

 Chad Lee

Just A Tear Away

Lachrymose oh lachrymose
oft I've felt thy saline boast
rushing from your hiding place
to gleam and glitter on my face

Lachrymose my lachrymose
of all thy skills I love the most
that which comes as if heaven sent
to ease my soul ere my heart is rent

Lachrymose sweet lachrymose
so glad I am to be your host
keeping the day from being oh so long
taking from the night its miserable song

 Emel MacKenzie

"Quiet Legacy"

In effort to pass on, or beget a small whisper
of timeless truths, the ones that really matter.
The fragmented moments of time experienced,
through the hours and seconds, thoughts have gathered.

Through kin, friendship and acquaintances,
from each; collected pearls of wisdom, precious or not.
Lessons were learned from each treasured one,
Some were valued, yet many were painful ones.

Each encounter, a memory to be stored,
With a bit of ground gained toward peace of mind
In every lifetime our paths stumble and waver,
Uncertain steps toward age and wisdom.

Pray-listen to the wind, the surf or silence,
they offer forgiveness, smiles and peace.
And to one who would ponder these feeble ramblings
A simple yet priceless message to thee I bequeath

 Cynthia C. Craig

Talk to Me

The feelings run through my mind
Of the world so fast
As I think of the times
we've walked together side by side,
I think I have fallen in love
Yes, with you,
your smile and your personality,
The way you talk softly and secretly to me
Or the way you hold my hand
with comfort and security
I look in your eyes and I see that
I do want to be with you
I know you're shy,
but tell me how you fell about things in your life,
about friends or events you've been through
don't lie or keep secrets from me,
because I love and care about you,
Please talk to me, I'll always be willing to talk to you

 Amber R. Smith

Dilemma

To what do we credit the emotional cost
Of riding the waves of ecstasy.
To battle the fear of losing control
Of how we perceive our destiny?

We create scenarios of loves gain or loss
And burden our souls unnecessarily.
Why not leave it alone; savor what we have
And enjoy the journey indefinitely?

If I loved you would I lose some of myself?
Am I willing to chance that I might fail?
If unwilling to give, I may never receive,
Thus imprisoned in a self-made jail.

 Annette M. Autry

"Playing In The Dirt"

I watch them through my window,
not to close to be seen.
For it is not a moment I was meant to be part of
but thankful to have seen.

For it warms a mother's heart to watch them together.
A father and son bonding, playing in the dirt.

As they plant the flowers and sit back to watch them grow.
I'll step back too and cry for the love that grows.

 Jeanne Wolfinger-Brown

Untitled

Take this hand and feel my fear
  of my life fading away with each passing year.
Never taking just one-instead taking all
  along the trail of life and its bumps and falls.
A touch of the hand a blink of the eye
  you've lived your life but still wonder why.

A fountain of youth I thought I could buy
  but Revlon and L'Oreal only covered the lie.
With the pass of days like a long rolling river
  you see a strange face staring back in the mirror.
Not much can be done and nothing can be said
  to the life you lead or what is to be led.

Jason Shull

Deluded Ego

How dare we speak with certain haughty pride
Of man's divine supremacy on Earth!

So blinded we who stupidity elide
The irrefutable and wondrous worth
Of every bird and plant and beastly birth,
We thrust the varied life on Nature's tree
Beyond the pale of grace and virtue's girth
And think with gross impunity that we
Alone bear Heaven's stamp of pedigree.

Deluded man extols his power of thought
And reasoned sense, but obviates the curse:
With great dexterity of mind he's caught
Within his web of reasoning diverse,
He drowns himself in eddied thought inverse
And, even thus submerged, he raises claim
To rule the earth, the very universe.

How sad that man presumes to boast his name
Though evidence reduces him to shame.

Angela M. Lovett

On Parting At Commencement

Despair of parting conquers all else born
Of human hope and childish longing trust,
A gruesome lamia, ambushed in the hearts
Of those who dare to crave for what is just.
The sun once high, now faltering low, is hid
In hungry clouds that strive to blot the last
Of struggling rays. They too once dared to hope
That future days might still be blessed by past.
To ease the gaping wound we dream in light
Of optimistic Romeo's "sweet sorrow"
That Fate might flaunt his scepter, take his quill,
And scribe, "They two shall meet tomorrow."
Perchance when two are met and sworn to love
That hands are joined and grasped with iron glove.

Donald M. Kladstrup

Sunken Ships

Sunken ships that feel no pain
Of all the sailors who once were slain
Lay dormant in their place of rest
While victorious foes enjoy quest

Be not these lonely ships forgotten
Long aft the masts that are now rotten
But remember these ships that sailed so bold
In years gone past, in days of old

Jeffrey W. Godsey

Love In The Air

So often I think of your eyes and face
Of how you make me happy and how you take me to a calm place.

Calm place where everything is just so beautiful.
For you are my lady—my heaven so beautiful.

So beautiful that makes my heart pound with happiness.
Because you never let me be sad or dwell in sadness.

You pick me up and give me the inspiration of life.
Because we are together — like water is with a tide.

A tide that flows so calm and beautiful on the shore.
Our love is like the seagulls above as they sweep down but
always seem to soar.

Soar into the air and feel so free.
If it's one thing I know is that I love you and that you love me.

Brian Cline

Travelling With The Kudzu

1-65, Mobile to Birmingham. A steamy August
of hot cloudy skies leaden with outbursts
of lightning and rain, and heat
rippling from the asphalt.

From the car window, at the right
suddenly appears an enchanting forest
with giant structures reminiscent
of a Goblin valley but sculpted
in foliage, not stone.

Trees and bushes shrouded in green
leafy vines that silently creep
enveloping even the wind,
in their mysterious enclosure.

They reach out as if to engulf
the highway and its occupants
in their depths. Tempting me
to flee into the cool quietness
of this sanctuary.

Janice R. Lindgren

Fond Remembrances

He tells her of his day,
  of his trials and his rewards.
He speaks to her of days gone bye,
  the days of their courtship and their innocent fun.
He talks of their children; the difficult boy and
  the predictable daughter.
He smiles as he remembers how she cried at daughter's wedding,
  heartbroken at the loss of her child.
He laughs as he recalls how she sighed when junior wed,
  for she never believed that boy would settle down.
He reminds her of their joy at the birth
  of their first grandchild.
He thanks her for enriching his life, for standing by and
  encouraging him.
As he prepares to leave, he kneels, and brushing aside the
  twigs, he sets on her grave the roses; one for each year
  together, fifty in all.
And bidding her goodbye, he retires to their home.

Hugh Carino

World Of Dreams

A gentle breeze rolls across my face. It reminds me
of his gentle ways. The sweetness of a child and yet the
strength of a wild tiger. I close my eyes in the pale
mists of the moonlight. I hear his voice echoing through
the dark corners of my thoughts. I can't even
think as I close my eyes his shadow... his soul over
takes my mind. Putting his picture upon my wall
I feel so weak; his mesmerizing blue eyes penetrate through
my body, I can't even think. I wonder, has he ever loved?
Will he ever love me? Then I feel the burning warmth of his
hands upon my face... A rush of fear stirs within me I don't want
to open my eyes, if I do, my world of dreams will fall, he will
no longer be there... And my heart will shatter to the burning
warmth of the earth. I try and close my eyes just one more time. I try
and see his blue eyes and his sweetness of a child. And suddenly
there he is he reaches out and I grab his hands we are one.

Delpha Kennison

Grandma's House

Memories of a long time past,
Of grandma's house will forever last;
Where the love of family come together,
Creating a bond that will last forever.

The old milk barn where we used to play,
Still stands in the field like yesterday;
Papa sitting under the China berry tree,
With his walking stick he'd draw pictures for me;

We would sit on the porch making Christmas wishes,
While the women in the kitchen were washing dishes;
The old clock ticking was a soothing sound,
Pictures of long ago being passed around:

The old out house standing alone to the side,
The weather beaten door swinging open wide;
Cows roaming the fields eating crisp golden grains,
Cooling off with an early autumns rain:

All of these are memories of childhood days,
Life has changed so much in so many ways;
But the memories keep my childhood alive,
And I'll tell them to Grandma in heaven when I arrive:

Angela Payton

Untitled

I sat alone on an Island
  Of despair
  Of pain
  Of numbness
I thought that death was my only option
  I tried
  I failed
  I learned
That I was not alone in my depression
  My urge to die
  My pain
I grew
Now life is my option
  Love too
My Island is now a continent
So vast I shall spend my life
  Exploring it

Andrea M. Rice

Autumn's Falling Leaves

Falling leaves tell a tale
Of birds and bees, winds and hail.

Fiery red sunsets and others lemon pale,
Soothing summer rains and an Autumn gale.

They've seen cloudless skies and rippling streams
And dark gray heavens with lightning beams.

They blossomed in spring so bright and green,
Fluttering gracefully for all to be seen.

They beautified the atmosphere with dignity and grace,
God's gift to mankind, nothing can take its place.

They've weathered the storms and sheltered the birds,
Now their glorious Autumn colors are flying in herds.

Pinks, tangerines and reds - yellows, oranges and brown,
All brilliant spectacular hues, they keep tumbling down.

They're brushed and swept and packed so tight,
But only temporarily, they'll be out of sight.

'Twill be many a year ere they see the light of day,
But mother nature will nurse them, while with her they stay.

Back to earth they return to manufacture new leaves,
To await their rebirth - and their swaying in the breeze.

Harriet Marks

When Your Life Is Over

When your life is over what shall become
Of all you were and all you had done
All your friends will care no more
Of what you went through before.

To all our friends we say goodbye
As it approaches the day we die.
The curse is life brought upon us all
In years we rise, in seconds we fall.

Can anyone, or thing ease the pain
Of a tormented soul that lives in vain.
Without purpose or reason to be
There is after all no hope for me.

This fiery grave for you and me
Someday we shall be set free.
We will never know the reasons why
Not until the day we die.

Clint Rennick

"Jonquils and Snowdrops"

Jonquils and snowdrops are all that remain
Of a garden once lovingly tended.
They first flourished, these harbingers of spring,
In a gracious era that has ended.

Did the jonquils come from the childhood home
Of a languishing, homesick bride?
Did their pale golden beauty give her strength
To become stalwart at her husband's side?

Were the snowdrops planted near a window
Of a house that was here long ago?
Where they placed there to appease a child
Who was too ill to play in the snow?

I could imagine a thousand stories
About compassion, joy, and pain.
But only of this, can I be sure -
Jonquils and snowdrops are all that remain.

Ann McCutchen Beattie

For: Curt

In our relationship we have no trust
now we are only what memories have made us

Seeking something we'll never find
for it's hidden deep inside this broken heart of mine.

Aimlessly searching it will never be found.
Tears fill silently not making a sound.

Looking and trying so desperately
Looking for love I know was meant to be.

I've never known a love so true
I never wanted to be without you.

Searching for something that was long ago lost.
Searching looking, willing to pay any cost.

Amanda Elam

Pain

Pain forgotten, so therefore unseen,
Now, visibly here, what does this mean?

It never seemed to hurt this much,
I had strength I thought could never be touched.

This pain, it drowns me, help me up.
It now seems half empty, my life, my cup.

Many feelings are hurt, but can't be made better,
My wrists, as I write, every second look redder...

Alisha Merrick Mateer

Memories

Today is Monday morning
Now each day seems the same
My children they have left me to seek fortune
and fame
As I gaze upon their pictures hanging on the wall
I wonder if they ever think of me at all
Sitting at vigil those nights
Didn't leave them out of sight
To ease their little bodies in fever and in pain
But to them no longer I have any claim
Now... what's a mother to do
How does she start her life ANEW
Part of this great big world, I know they must be
But... they also still belong to ME.

Diane Slobodin

Oklahoma

You wake same as before,
Nothing different, all the same,
Bright faces greet you as you eat,
Conversation stirs just as any other day,
A glance tells you it's that time,
In go the kids and off to day care,
You say goodbye just as before,
And smiles tell you everything is all right,
You drive away.
BOOM!
Your tires screech as you come to a stop,
Looking back with fear you see,
Black smoke raising far in the air,
Turning back your heart fills with fear,
You get out thinking,
"Are they ok." "Are they dead."
You search frantically through the crowds,
Your heart sinks and you start to cry,
No longer a daddy,
You say Goodbye.

Jeffry A. Hocker

You Are God's Gift To Me

I stand naked before you,
not unclothed but open - no secrets held in.
I knew soon after we began you would be the one I would uncover my
deepest secrets to.

And you - you didn't disappear
You listened, drank it in and asked...."Is there anything else?"

You heard the places I'd been
Felt my hurt
I began to know it didn't matter.

Little things of the past that had to be shared
The barbs and arrows that were coated with the poison of cruelty

You helped me know I've come so far
I'll never have to be in that hurting place again.

I started to see myself as I really am
Finally able to say, "I Can - I Am - I Will Be!"

The darkness I've been through
The light I've come to see
Your gift of acceptance is
God's gift to me.

Deirdre L. Hayes

"From Dark To Light"

I was in the dark for so long,
Not knowing who I was, where I belonged.
Aimlessly, I rushed around,
Never hearing a word or a sound.
My heart always ached, was full of woe.
Until there wasn't anything left, no where to go.
Life wasn't worth living anymore,
Then something happened as I was about to close the door,
A spirit filled me with amazing grace,
I finally felt I was in the right place.
I needed so much to follow this lead,
My prayers, at last, were answered indeed!
Life became full; blessed with love,
Divine intervention sent me a Dove.
To bring me peace, serenity and joy,
Now, I can pass this on to my own little boy.
I have gotten a second chance to live happy on this land,
The child I could never have now holds me by the hand.

Cynthia Buehler

Lives

You should believe in fate,
   Not in hate.
As I sit here looking up at God,
   My mind, suddenly went into a fog.
I begin to think of the homeless,
   Who have nothing in life, but loneliness.
There faces are filled with sadness,
   While our's are filled with gladness.
In the Winter they sit there frozen and cold,
   Just waiting to grow old.
Crying and Dying............
Why must this be happening.
I do not know what to say.

Alexandra Stangl

What Is "It"

Some people live or at best they exist
Not even aware of the joy they have missed
For it isn't a thing that you buy at a store
Or hastily borrow from the house next door
It's not something you plant in the early spring
And wait for the rain and warm weather to bring
And yet it can grow and become very strong
Or if the fates will it, not last very long
It's not found in a pot on a window sill
Or something you leave, or bequeath in a will
You can't hold it to see in the palm of your hand
Nor will it appear upon your command
And yet you can take it wherever you go
It can be right there with you and not even show
If you have it you've guessed by now what it is
It's a bond we call friendship
And it's all ours to give

Dianna Mount

A Bed Of Roses

Life is a bed of roses, petals and stems
Not a wooly blanket with rosy silk hem
Rosy pink flowers arranged as sheets
Thorns in the shadows prick the feet

Life is a bed of roses, how dare they mean sweet
Life has its bitters and rocky hard streets
Be patient with non-sense, friend the power
Sleep with your head on a pillow of flowers

Life is a bed of roses, a partner you need
Enjoy the fragrance, look out for the greed
Stem the corners, watch over your shoulder
A sweet heart partner keeps out the colder

Life is a bed of roses, pink yellow and red
Beware the dangerous golden thread
Shimmering temptation objects in life
The rose is a flower, the stem is a knife

Dean Glorso

Rainbow

I saw a rainbow after a storm.
Not a little piece of one
Not only half the arch
But a brilliant
Six color
Full
Shining arch
Stretching from one horizon
To the other.
And through the shimmering colors of light
I saw the trees behind it
Glistening
Caressing the beautiful stripes.

Debra E. Norris

My Birthday

I have something to say, so come here.
  My birthday has rolled around again this year.
It has done that many times before;
  but the number doesn't matter to me anymore.
It's the event I like to celebrate.
  So, when asked out, I don't hesitate.
It's family and friends that make it worthwhile.
  I always celebrate my birthday in style.
"We're all getting old", I'm sure you're heard.
  But to me, "Old" is just a three letter word.

Billie Stafford

A Love Hate World

Love is everlasting, but very scary.
Nobody knows real love, but you hear
the words "I love you" all the time!
Hate is so strong, but keeps growing
in a place we call HOME. It grows so
large that it takes over every thing
it sees or touches! It wants to
control.
The world is so large, seems like there is no
ending. Why, do we struggle to survive?
It is made up of so many interesting
miracles that we don't begin to understand.
We try to make a world of our own,
to make up for the bad times.
But you will have to wake up and face
reality sometimes...

Joseph D. Manz

A World Without Trees

Imagine a world without beautiful trees,
No woods for a peaceful walk.
No luscious green above our heads,
as quietly we talk.

No shade on a hot summer's day,
No fruit in summertime.
A treehouse never could be build,
in trees for kids to climb.

And where would lovers carve a heart,
and squirrels climb up and down.
No trees for birds to make a nest,
or bees to fly around.

From small to tall, they stately stand,
leaves swaying in the breeze.
How beautiful the world becomes,
because God gave us trees.

Catharina M. Rinta

My Life

My life, not always so peaceful and sane once wild and untamed, with
no restraint.

Now it all makes sense, I understand, you can never find a needle in
the sand. Especially when you are running so fast, that you don't
know where you saw it last.

That needle is like my heart, I never slowed down to let my feeling start.

Then I opened my eyes and I quit believing all the lies.

I know now that all I needed, was not what I had begged and pleaded!

I needed love and someone to trust, not a one night stand and a
feeling of lust.

Now finally someone has come along and showed me the life I was
living was wrong.

I never thought I could be treated this way. Now all I wish for is
that he will stay.

But is this feeling real, or am I just wasting my time. If only I
could tell if this heaven or hell.

It feels like heaven, but you never know, it could turn to hell in a
week or so.

Angie R. Etterle

Heaven

In that city that is four square
No need for sun or moan there
God himself will be abundant light
There will even be no more night

All the gates of pearl are made
Even the streets with gold are laid
All the beauty, beyond are imagination
Is only the greatest of his creation

Heaven God made for the humble and true
Faithful people like me and you
Serving, trusting, and obeying day by day
So someday Heaven will be our eternal stay

Esther Hillmer

Fear And Hope

One last cry, one last tear means you have
no more to fear. For your fear has become
a greater thing. It is a thing called HOPE.
For your hope can help you cope with the
struggles that life will most often bring.
Emotions may cry but they often lie. Lie to
bring someone or something closer than life
ever could. Fear may bring things near, but
as long as you have your hope there is
nothing more to fear than life and the battles
of true love for one person to another...

Andrea Walker

To Brothers And Baseball

I played the game, no one remembers the name,
No Hall of Fame; Just a young man on pasture
   of green, many times unseen.
The crack of the bat, the ball; The home green over the wall.
The long shot, the streak hot; and all
   the time the eagle eye fixed to race for the longest fly.

The curve, the slider, the in shoot the out,
Step up to the plate, give it a clout.
The line drive; The Texas League fly,
I've had my share, I've given it a ride.

The golden sun, count every run;
Don't look back, steal the sack.
Run like the wind, then do it again.
Move to the right, then the other way,
Tog the bases twice — a double play.

All the time the senses real,
At calls good and bad, that make me feel.
That tomorrow will be a better day,
And my Brother and I, will come to play,
Again; on the pastures of green.

Jack De Young

"Tempus Fugit"

Passing years their imprint leave;
   No decade quite the same—
   Some good some bad
   Some better some worse
   A special one claims fame!

Still living costs soar skyward,
   How ever can we ends meet?
   Then providence comes to our rescue
   And gets us on our feet!

We always want more,
   Prosperity we crave—
   And perhaps the next decade
   Will with gold the streets pave!

Araminta S. Blowe

Black Is Beautiful

No glaring flashing neons,
No car's arrogant honk,
No cycle's angry zaroom,
No billowing clouds of smoke.

Only the man in the moon's gentle smile,
Only the kitten's musical meow
   as she pads silently after June bugs,
Only my lover's slumberful sighs.

Black is beautiful,
Between 3 and 4 in the morning.
   Beckie Bixby

Untitled

I walk along the cold, hard sidewalks wondering where my
next dinner would come on.
The wind whips through my tattered coat as I bend my
head to protect myself from the cold stares and harsh words
The alley next to a huge department store is my "bedroom" for the
night.
Rabid rats and human shadows are my companions for the evening.
In the morning I panhandle for a few hours before
settling back down.
"Sir, do you have a coin to spare?"
"Get a job ya' bum," a passer-by says.
"Ma'am do you have a coin to spare?"
"Yes dear," an old lady says. "Now go with God".
Some people don't say anything at all. They lift up their collars
and walk on.
I made two dollars and forty six cents today. Not bad, huh?
Maybe I'll eat at the shelter and save my money for another day.
I think a person of fourteen is a survivor after a year.
I get scared and lonely and wonder if I'd be dead one morning.
I sometimes wish I was a child untitled.
   Catherine A. Knight

Warning

You, there, sent out to chart
New subdivisions in old universes,
To search, dig, test the surfaces of space,
And learn of life on planets yet unknown
   (If life there is or was
      Or yet may be or cannot be),
What if — what if, one day
Your rocket might return
To find no welcome,
And no one to care what you have found,
Earth having died, meanwhile,
Of long neglect?
   Helen M. Crocker

The White Tiger

Runs so fast, runs so free.
Never last, as you can see.
So very pretty, yet so mean.
Find a kitty, in the scene.
One so smart, and so brave.
From your heart, you would save.
He is strong and dangerous too.
Stay where you belong, and he won't bother you.
He'll hide in trees, and lay on your lawn.
He'll chase the bees, when he knows you're gone.
The whites tiger knows he must leave.
Like the pedals of a rose.
He'll fly through the air, with a breeze.
   Christine Schultz

You, I And The World

There is so much on the mind,
Never knowing which road to find.

So scared to lose the home,
So afraid to be left alone.

Life is so tough for you and me
Never knowing how things will turn out to be.

Always trying to make ends meet.
Our love is our only treat.

No matter what, we have each other.
Never to lose one another!

Jody Anne Witt

One Day At A Time

We live our lives day by day
Never knowing what we're going to say
Learning to live, and learning to die
Taking each moment as life passes by
Saying I'm sorry for things we've done wrong
Or saying thank-you if someone helped you along
Never forgetting that special friend-
Who come along and helped you 'til the end
Being there when times got tough
And remembering how things used to be
But dwelling on the future
And to live your life all it's worth
Trusting your heart to guide you along
Through the many trials and temptations
The devil places before us
Always putting God first in our lives
And always remembering-
We live our lives one day at a time

Bethany Laird

Forever Gold

To measure the wealth of a poet
   never count the coins in his purse,
For the true value of his possessions
   look to his heart for the number of verse.

For the rich man, his wealth has a limit
   on his gold, he must forever depend.
But the poet has a fortune forever
   as the rhyme in his heart has no end.

Constance Vail Hughes

In A Race For Survival

The roles of predator and prey are not good or evil, one could say.
Neither kindly or cruel, but it is Nature's way.
The lives of plants and animals are all intertwined.
But there's a mankind who acts without a mind.
What makes us think we can say.
What is the best for Nature's way?
I truly feel...
The needs and concern are real.
As these forests are lost.
What will be the cost?
A plant may hold the key to a cure,
Only to perish under boot or blade in the next year.
What man ignores year after year.
The problem should be more than clear.
What must be done?
Will you join or run?
What will be our fate?
Will it be too late?

Jessica L. Goodroad

The Flight Of The Bobtail Plane

Suddenly, and up from behind a grove of tall pine trees,
Navigating upon the face of the air with the mightiest of ease,
It comes with the greatest bombardment of the sound of a jet.
The path upon which it travels is almost always round;
"It's the bobtail plane!"
I always quickly get myself outside having no time to lose,
To see the mighty airplane whenever I hear that sound of it
coming on; because in a moment it appears, and in a split
second it's gone.
"It's the bobtail plane!"
It flies low over my house as if for my sole observation;
A triangle of a unmarked craft a-hailing from no known nation.
It comes in the color of old gold, and once a like craft came
In the color of silver, of the days of old.
"It's the bobtail plane!"
It comes in the spring at the time of the hummingbirds and bees,
Flying as if in a hurry, down, through, and among the trees;
It seems to burn the wind instead of any kind of oil or gasoline.
It's the most wonderful airplane I have ever seen.
"It's the bobtail plane!" My neighbor's children cry out.

Jessica E. Walters

Untitled

Somewhere down that long and winding lonely trail
My thoughts of you kept me moving every step
So on I went and hoping them the wind you sail
And now those thoughts and verse I hope you would accept

And to me the rhymes were songs and songs of many bars
Some warm and touching, others smooth and sublime
Far to many to record, 'twould be easier to count the stars
For now I'll give you these, the rest some other time

That cold and lofty mountain loomed ahead, and on I did go,
Step by step and verse by verse dreaming to the end
The way became steeper and the trail covered with snow
But hugs and snugs were my thoughts for you to send

I did gaze about, east and west and everywhere,
When at the top so high and steep a precipice
And thought to send a kiss for someone I did care
So, commanded I the gusty wind to carry that kiss

And as hikes are finished, no more mountains to traverse
These lines, strings of my heart are for you to be the keeper of
One step closer, intertwined, our lives become the verse
According to Him who made us, Who owns the mountain and the stars
   above

Barry Schutt

"Beth"

To Beth with curls and teeth like pearls
My son may look like Clark Gable
But you have legs like Betty Grable
You brought joy into my son's life
The day you became his loving wife.
You learned to cook his favorite dishes
You have fulfilled all his wishes
Your house is clean-not a germ
And you give me a terrific "Perm"
I'm sure your kids will agree
No better mother can there be
Hats off to you
May your skies be blue
If I could have another
I would like to be your mother!

Annabelle Urso

160

Osmosis — Me And The Sea

Look ahead—Friend, see upon the Clear—
My ship it sails, e'er so gently, the wind to bring it Near

Can you feel the strength within its bows—'Tis minute
    a speck of Light

Look ahead—slowly she nears, the sea is her home,
    her best is in Flight

The light is white against the sails, the clouds in contrast—
dark blue
    if only to be lost between the two of them—
    my dream of life come True

Look—A far—A head—Can you See?

The ship and I we share, the most common bond for us,
my friend,
    our love—the ocean and its warm salt Air

But, alas, the sailing ship is gone, outlining shadows
remain

Into the sunset—that speck of Light—will gently return
Again

Jeannine Simonian

Sunday Best

I rode out into the bright sunlight,
My old horse began to put up a fight.
I had no time for his games,
For I was no a list of wanted names.
I galloped off toward the west,
Wearing my Sunday best.
I rode into the dark night,
And slept till morning bright.
Off I go again on my own,
It was hard for my horse to walk on the stone.
I stopped in a far away place
I thought my tracks they could not trace
Evidently I was wrong,
They traced my tracks all night long.
I was to be hung at morn,
But it's okay because my Sunday dress is torn.

Amanda Kendall

Passing of Life

He was an interesting man,
My neighbor across the street.
He was the happiest man,
I probably will ever meet.

He appeared to those with lesser tastes,
As aloof and lacking in charm.
He cared for his roses day after day,
With a passion hard to disarm.

Fortunate for me one afternoon,
I walked up and stood by his side.
His body bent over a beautiful rose,
His nose was stuck deep inside.

I cleared my voice with a polite ahem!
He turned and looked at me.
"If you have an interest in roses, he said,
I have one you really must see."

We slowly walked to the garden in back,
Where the best of his roses grew.
He stopped by the one that blooms once in life.
I knew he knew that I knew.

Jerry Holland

My Heart's Desire

The beach is near, the bay is in sight
My memory's clear on foggy nights;
Short-term or long my standards don't change
What I need and want seems to remain...
    the same.
To love and be loved with a solid respect,
Treated humanely with no show of neglect;
Just common kindness with absence of malice,
Is all I require and my heart's desire.

When the sun goes down and the moon is high
I want to lie in contentment under the sky
And have all my faculties calmed and unnerved:
Camaraderie and understanding is what I yearn.

Debby Mohler

Finale

I'm skin and bones and my blood's running cold.
My Hound dog's mourning. We're both getting old.
Old Hound twitches and turns in his sleep.
I lay awake counting sheep.
We used to run through woods and fields.
We soaked up the sun and now we take pills.
We don't attend our favorite haunts.
We move slow. We're stiff in our joints.
He has his water and I have my tea.
We breathe harder and we can't hardly see.
We've lost our stout and we're ready to go.
Time's running out. We both know it's so.
Yep, Old Hound, we've always known
We're off to town and the Old Age Home.

Bertie Currington Patano

Untitled

Anger fills me
My heart thumps hard with pain
My mind is trapped and frustrated
...Someone is yelling

I try to explain
Without harsh words
A cruel tone of voice answers me
...Words strike back at me like knives (choked)

My soul longs for her understand
And even sometimes...my thoughts pictures
My fist across her face (yelling)
...In reality...I would never

"It's been a hard day,
It's the end of the week" (happily)
Seems to be the excuse every time (angrily)

But I can't stop it.
It's like a train, she's bigger than I am
I want to stop it, but I can't.
I'm only 14, what do I know.
Mom's probably right anyway.

Julie Carreira

When I Go To Sleep

When I go to sleep at night,
My dreams are never filled with fright,
For God's angels come and say to me,
That when I'm asleep my soul will be free,
I will explore the dreams waiting for me.

And for the first ray of sunlight, I can't wait,
For the good Lord to open a new days gate,
And a chance to see the sun once more,
And live in freedom as always before.

Bobby Gambrel

Birth Of A Grandchild

Tears of joy well within my eyes.
My heart swells with love.
Another grandchild is born,
an angel from above.
God, I thank thee for this wee one's health.
I thank you for the chance to see my children's children
and feel great spiritual wealth.
So much in life I don't understand
the awesome beauty of a sunrise;
the marvel of a grain of sand.
The sea, the forests, all treasures given,
and now this - a tiny bit of heaven.
My dreams transpired, my goals achieved.
This new baby is one reason why I believe.

Dorothy Weyrauch

Restless Soul

I sit here listening to the soft rhythm.
My heart beating silently.
I wonder where the people are tonight.

Sweeping sand, flags flying,
Oh, sweet sanity, where are you leading me?

Whispering moon, what are you saying?
Tell me about your love, life, thoughts.

I follow blindly, unknowing, uncaring.
Singing without a voice, thinking without a thought.

Forgotten dreams, memories erased,
I'm longing for something.
Crying with hollow tears, crying.
In darkness, I disappear.

Oh, sweet sanity, what am I doing?
Questions with answers hidden.
Standing in the middle of the world,
So unaware, so simply complex.

My heart swells with emptiness.
I appear only in pulses.
Come and go, gone.

Carma R. Cooper

Untitled

I wander through the dark alley way.
My hands groping for a sense of direction
As I gaze in petrified night
And a river of coldness clasps me in a fierce embrace

I see flickering images of the sacred bible,
the laughter that last danced upon my
friend's lips, the numerous fleeting
glimpses of the sunshine tossing
its bands of golden hair in my face

And I hear the voice of my father
and a part of my chest rafts
up in attention and I stand as straight as
a military soldier
Expecting him to shower me with a hailstorm,
And then the incessant noise of laughter,
and words I remembered in
my childhood that reduced
me into the tufts of a dandelion's
head-carried away by the wind
nothing more than just an ant soaring through the wind.

Amy Huang

Communication

We walked across the summer-fallow field
My cousin Nellie, and my Dad and me
The stubbled fields lay dreaming in the sun
She reached to every glowing poplar tree.

Each berry bush glowing leaf with crimson leaf aflame
With autumn colors, russet, gold and wine
Bordered the bluffs, now painted yellow gold
Shouted in color from each tangled vine.

In autumn hush, bereft of bee and bird
Save for the wild geese, in the summer sky
Honking some warning of a winter's chill
Dipping an arc, a summer's sad "good-bye"

We walked across the old potato patch
In autumn magic, void of summer sound
Thoughts rose in us too deep for common words
And spilled in silence on the frozen ground.

Carmen Elsie Ross

"Hold On"

Closing my eyes just one more time
   My body closing in, the darkness surrounds,
Floating away, as the tide crashes in
   Reaching for air or maybe familiar sounds.
Drowning in my thoughts, a picture of you
   Beauty resting in the silk - feel the peace.
Mountains of trees that whisper my name,
   Fields of sand, never beginning, never ending
Stars on the sidewalk, chanting those of fame
   Clouds roaring across the grey bliss sky
Thunder shouting - bolts of light crashing close by.
   Help, help me, for I am lost and cannot regain sight,
Forgetting that I laid down to rest, on this cold, dreary night.
   Hold my hand, come with me - as I take you to a far away place.
Rainbows of color - gold at either end,
   Birds singing on a rooftop, ready to share their song
Canals full of water, soon a message they will send.
   Gongs of the church steeple in full force - another day has
      brought forth light,
Only keeping me from HOLDING ON, to the dreams of last night.

James R. Fleming

On Bombing Serbs In Bosnia, 1995

How the old hates fester, suppurate, and roil!
Muslim, Serb, Croatian blood still soaks the soil.
U.N. planes, our surgeon scalpels, lance a boil.
Late as harbingers of peace, they slash the moil.
Shades of Sophie, Francis Ferdinand, Gavrilo toil!
(The second try successful, Princip is the foil)
Like a giant serpent, horrid years uncoil,
and Sarajevo stinks, reeks of Hapsburg oil!

Our bombs blast bacilli of their sullen hate;
do not though disinfect these addled lives of fate.
To wait so long to act is just about too late,
may not bring peace, but only aggravate.
Mohammed is their prophet, they die at Heaven's gate.

Why, then, if Serbs be such fools to make no room
for one another on this lonely Earth, the loom
which weaves our common fate or doom,
though hope spring eternal from a shrivelled womb,
there's no future if shrouded in a tomb.

Gerald A. Somers

Dragonflies

Whales in the ocean...swim in the
murky water.
Want to be consumed, surrounded, enclosed.
Long for the sky.
Long for the clouds.
Light with the color white.
Porous sky; full of holes. Gift of
flight worth more than life itself.

Finally.

The day comes. All are given wings. Head
for the sky. The sun destroys them. Obliterates them.
They are transformed. Now dragons rule the
air. Breathe fire
and live a
Dream.

Allan Klinge

Thoughts

Mother is such a complicated word
Much deeper than the songs and poems tell us.
And when mother, Mom, or Mama is
Getting ready to go home to God forever
The word—and the world change.

Memories flood the mind
Without discrimination or cessation
The good, the bad,the sweet, the sour
All blend in a bitter sweet potion
Impossible to walk away from.

You gave me strength and weakness,
Joy and pain, loving and distance,
Character and need, independence and fear,
Insight and problems. You did the best you could.
That's what mothers do. I know—I'm a Mom too.

So as I prepare to let you go
And think of all that we have shared
I want to tell you thanks for
Helping shape the "Who I am"
The one who's free to follow the wind—because of you.

Joan Halligan

A Child's Gaze

Innocence, perceived in the eye of the child
Moves the hostile to be mild.
Then loving, and love reflected in the child's gaze
Provokes an inner-glow in the adult,
One that stays, at least as long as does the child.
For all men know that innocence is a fleeting substance.
When mixed with the passions it produces something less than itself,
But an event as great as a child's gaze
Provokes the adult to remember far back to his youthful days.
Then more occurs.
A transformation?
No.
Just a renewed meaning of happiness.
A yearning to hold the age of four?
No, just the desire to be pure one more.

Allen Glenn

Old

He sits in his favorite chair
Confused and all alone
Waiting for a call from someone
His hand rests on the phone
A home filled with the past
But with no one to share
Wonder's why he's forgotten
And why nobody seems to care
He opens his photograph album
And sends himself back in time
Familiar but lost faces stare back at him
Memories of yesterday slowly fade from his mind

David Doumani

Nature's Wrath

Sent back along the path
Condemned... That's natures wrath
once more the search through vacant eyes
another life of compromise.
Guide my hand oh force of fate
Draw me to my true soul mate.
Born again my life's anew
How many lifetimes searching for you?
Know not your name nor face
Know not the time nor place
Our eyes will meet we then will know
A promise given long ago.
Etched inside my beating heart
Taken with me from the start.
So many life times I've walked this path
Condemned... That's natures wrath.

Kerrie McHugh

The Race

Knots tumble and turn acids begin to churn.
Cold sweats and clammy hands
Everyone makes demands.
There's only one way out.

Little voices inside your head every minute you begin to dread.
Each day is harder and longer
Learning you're getting stronger and stronger.
There's only one way out.

Your life's turned into a staircase.
Each day a slow paced race
Down, down, up, down in the pit. I'm never going to finish it.
There's only one way out.

You can't eat, you can't sleep you're digging your grave ever so deep.
Your body and soul growing ever so weak.
Professional help you need to seek
There's only one way out.

You can climb the staircase high, so high.
To everyone it's all been just a lie.
Don't give up, don't give in, this is one race you have to win.
There's only one way out.

Crystal Goldade

Old Woman (With Alzheimers)

Sitting in a gray mist of confusion and fear,
Clothing askew, body weak and awkward,
Not able to discern, only wear
The banner of old age, on a face
Already too crowded with life's ravages.

A memory of a hand on hers,
A fleeting, floating glimpse of an eternity ago,
Clinging babes and joy filled years
Are in the gray mist, away from here.
She fills the time with useless gestures
Of someone graciously unaware.

Margaret Ann Milliken

Entice

Colors blending into one another and sun fading into night,
churches struggling against combat ...... entice.

I am daunt as I strive to untangle thoughts ......
dastardly lifting my eyes toward softly greying skies to see
an image in my mind and wait for clear reflection.

Misanthrope and pugnacious, but knowing I am of acrimonious feelings.

Hoping this mountain I gaze at will share her strength ...,
her pebbles beneath my feet, each representing a weakness, as life itself.

Ashamed and unchristian feelings await as I desperately try to
elucidate my uncertain burdens.

A desperate scene performed by conscience and realism......
yesterday ————incubus,
today ————faith in mankind————

L O V E
Lil Williams

Christmas Is...

Christmas is a time of happy living,
Christmas is a time of joyful giving.
Christmas is a time of love and share,
Christmas is time with those who care.

Christmas is a time when bells all ring,
To celebrate the birth of a tiny king.
Christmas is a time when the world stands still,
To take time for peace and sharing goodwill.

Christmas is having a family around,
Christmas is hearing many happy sounds.
Christmas is memories of when you were young,
Christmas is carols, and stockings hung.

Christmas is tradition from days of old,
To warm the heart from winter cold.
Christmas is a time for thankful praise,
To God...for the blessings of Christmas days.

Glenna MacNeil

My Dreams

I have thoughts in the back of my mind which are buried very deep,
But these thoughts are free to wander as I'm fast asleep.
I have pictures of these thoughts which sometimes seem quite real,
They have a power over me which can change the way I feel.
I might awake in a cold sweat if my dream was intense or chilling,
Or I might toss and turn all night if my dream was suspenseful or thrilling.
If my dream was sad I may awake with tear stains on my cheeks,
If my dream was scary I may not want to fall asleep for weeks.
I don't always remember the dreams I have although I wish I could,
And sometimes the ones I do remember are not always understood.

Sandra Barlow

Children Of The World

We should love all children
Children that make this world so special
They have new dreams to live by
Hopes in life as wonderful can be.

Children of the World
They expect the good things to teach them
Learn from what they hear and see
They are the future.

Children of the World
Their beautiful smile will bring peace to mankind
Vanish troubles and sorrow
Show them this world is the best place can be
Help to have a solid chain
Lead to the on-going generation
They are the children of the World!

Maria Luisa Delaney

Good Neighbors, Talk

Cat and Dog sat down to talk,
Cat said, "Meow", Dog said, "Stop!";
Cat huffed up and began to stare,
Dog jumped up and said, "Hair!, Hair!";
He slapped the Pussy Cat on the nose,
Cat pounced forward and bit his toes,
Dog grabbed Cat and gave her a fling,
Cat charged back into the ring,
"It's my turn now, let me show you how!";
She scratched his eyes and bit his ears,
Dog couldn't see his way for tears;
Cat was sorry, and licked his jaw,
Dog was still angry and bit her paw,
"I'll not fight back," said Cat aglow,
"It's really only place or show,
"Death always wins at war";
"You have your ways and I have mine,
From how we look to the way we dine,"
Dog said, "You're right, I'm sorry too,
Fighting isn't the thing to do." "Lets talk".

Elsie Joye Smith

Attraction

A walk so effortless,
carrying himself with such utter self-confidence,
her eyes hungrily took in the sight of him,
his dark hair,
glistening with highlights
in the bright sun,
his towering height and magnificent physique,
reluctantly forced to admit
that she found him very attractive
and the thrill ran through her,
she wondered if his appeal
was sheerly physical,
just looking at him
was making tingles run through her,
bringing a peculiar warmth
to her insides.

Valerie Lynn Marie Zimmel

The Wetlands ...

A chilly breeze that outsets from dawn to dusk,
Blessedness of the peaceful, comfort of a meadow.
Standing before it is a silent, motionless forest,
Nevertheless there circling it is nature of all kinds
with emotion towards the moist of the ground
along with the air.

What a spectacular, sacred place ...
Tim Giesbrecht

The American Dream

The American dream - now a cruel twisted nightmare.
Cardboard mansions on empty foundation dreams.
International power!
Unrivalled defense from foreign invasion.
Missiles poised.

Its shell is impenetrable.
Billions of dollars have achieved peace of mind.
Perhaps the yolk of the egg has since died
And the shell protects man's decline.

Children with guns
Internal invasion.
And the faces I see on the news look familiar.
They cry the same language.
Social programs fading to grey
Education misspelled
And war over oil.

If the egg continues to rot still tomorrow.
This priceless shell will be deemed just a fake
And no one will buy the American dream.

Peter Cassidy

War

Take away your death and war,
Can't you see, I can take no more.
Life I do so cherish, it is so very dear.
Oh, please help me Lord, I cannot live in fear.

I sit awaiting another sun,
Clutching my heart within my gun,
Not knowing if I will live or die,
Please dear God, I know not why,

I have now felt, the agony and pain,
Knowing I'm a victim, of those insane,
Please help me release this horrified dream,
For peace, for peace, for peace I scream.

I have searched for better ways,
To help me through these ungodly days,
Now there's no more time for me to decide,
For I am burning away inside.

So this is now my end,
On this land that I defend,
It is now my turn to die,
Oh God, I wish I knew why.

Billy M. Yacusiw

"Expression Of Love"

Sometimes words
  cannot express the gratitude
   and appreciation meant for you today
    for being wonderful parents to the daughter we share

Sometimes words
  cannot express the joy
   for the love and warmth you have shown me
    by allowing me to be part of your extended family

Sometimes words
  can build a bridge
   may we cross cautiously
    with love and understanding
     in sharing and caring
      for each other and each other's feelings
Thank you for being there when I could not and
Thank you for to be open to a relationship!

Joyce Ramer

Let The City Sleep Tonight

Another city night is upon us,
Can you hear the shouts and cries?
Tonight will be a restless night,
One full of anger and lies.

There's a couple in their apartment,
They are shouting loudly, yet in vain.
Both not understanding each other,
Only causing more and more pain.

A little girl lies in the alley,
Cold and full of hurt.
Her eyes are closed and stained from tears
And her face is smudged with dirt.

An old man lies by the coffee shop,
His eyes so full of tears.
His head is low, as he cries.
All he want is, happy years.

God, you know how to help them!
Please, just make things right.
No one deserves to live like this,
'Let the city sleep tonight.'

Camie Chanasyk

Requiem For A Yellow Dog

Just an old yellow dog who died alone,
By the side of the interstate,
Bruised and bloodied then cast aside,
As by the hand of fate.

Now old yellow dogs don't count for much,
In the realm of higher worth,
Yet who can deny there's none so true,
As a faithful old dog of uncertain birth.

Just for a moment let me eulogize,
To the multitudinous mutts of various size,
For there's none so sincere as a friendly mutt's gaze,
With its tail wagging 'welcome', while licking your face.

Jumping and barking and chasing the leaves,
Sniffing the grass and visiting trees.
Always a welcome when arriving at home,
And sad at the parting when left all alone.

But now it's time to drive away,
I'll think of you another day.
So to your memory, this small tribute,
I raise my hand in fond salute.

Frank T. Paterson

Dear Friend

I see the pain in your eyes that haunts me;
But your heart rejoices.

I feel the suffering in the sound of your voice;
But your heart is mellow.

I hear the anger in your silent footsteps;
But your heart holds compassion.

I sense the fear of unknown tomorrows:
But in your heart is resilience.

I taste the beauty of a brighter today:
For your heart is love.

With all my being I cherish your strength,
your courage, and your wisdom:
For you mold each day with blessedness.

Marlene Buffie-Brown

Untitled

The wheel of life has turned;
By the hand whose thinking was blurred.
That hand is lifeless from now on.
The thinking has ceased to go on.

The hollow glamour of alcohol
Filled you with all its empty calls.
Following blindly on weekends,
Fooling yourself and your friends.

Why didn't people help you
'Cause for so long they knew.
They just laughed and carried on,
Not realizing that one day you'd be gone.

That day when I saw you;
I did not think too
Much, that it would be the last.
That in the end you'd drive too fast.

Therefore when driving home,
Do it sober or just phone.
Life is too short for that risk.
Oh young one you will be missed.

Kelly A. Weste

Screaming Red And Black

No sooner than a field is littered,
By some, the very least worth littering,
Will hindsight show -
we cannot render dirty waters pure and glistening,
when our minds are violated impure and imprisoned.

This garden is our wasteland,
our children's playground.
if we break it-it is broken...our Eden, our porcelain.

And can we really abideth forever?

We are the descendants of the earth,
With holes burrowed in her heart up to her skin.
Ozone levels do not sink in,
When politicians swear they've fixed the thing.

Still, tiny saplings grow in concrete cracked rows,
Nature struggles.. though mens' minds refuse to know.

Matteo Castelli

The Meaning Of Life

He searched through the desert, mountains and sky,
but still could not find the meaning of life,
He searched villages, cities and towns,
but still it was nowhere to be found,

He went to churches, temples and shrines,
but still, he was not yet satisfied,
He went to the holy rabbis and priests,
but not even they, could fulfill all his needs,

He questioned all the philosophers and scholars,
and even tried to buy happiness with dollars,
He bought a big house and a fantasy wife,
but still could not find the meaning of life,

Exhausted of search, he stood on the edge,
and questioned himself, if he wanted to live,
He had searched through both, the depths and the heights,
but still could not find the meaning of life,

But when he began to search his heart and his soul,
the mystery of life began to unfold,
When he opened his eyes, he was blinded with light,
in his heart he had found the meaning of life.

Jeffrey Copenace

Remember

Do as you wish to whom you want
But remember my dear friend
It's the ones you were the kindest to
That count most in the end.

When the day arrives for final peace
And a guilt free trip you want
It's the love you give that counts the most
To those who must go on.

No matter what your goal in life
What you're striving to obtain
The ones you love before you leave
Are the memories that remain.

Be nice to all and you can't lose
No matter where you go,
Whatever good is left of you
The whole wide world will know.

Margaret Moquin

"Angel Of Grace"

The sun may die, the world crumble,
but nothing matters, only your eyes.
Oh angel of grace, poetry you state.

Your beauty, the greatest sight,
precious gold colors your hair
and your smile, to me, brings light,
your sweet complexion so fair.

You've capture my mind and it can't break free,
you've taken my soul, and it cannot flee.

Only for you my heart does ache.
Only for you my heart does wait.

My life feels so empty, my heart is in pain.
Without your company, everyday there is rain.

I do not wish neither life or health, nor the air I breathe.
I do not wish all that is wealth, only you do I need.

Please come to me, don't let me cry, alone in the shadow.
Please stay by me, don't let me die, I want to see the morrow.

But should my love you deny, one lonely place for me to go.
To my grave, there I must lie, to life without you, I answer no...

Phong-Phanh Hanphiboune

Think About It

A solitary tear rolls down her face,
But none can tell with all the raindrops on her face.
She thinks of the man who left her,
The body she gave up.
She thinks it's too late for her,
Too late for love.
Quietly she sobs for a love that was lost,
Why should she live?
Carefully she lifts the gun she holds in her hand,
Checks to make sure there is nothing to stop her.
To the heavens she screams,
"Why?"
As she carefully maneuvers to where she lost her beloved.
She hesitates.
Is it worth it?
STOP!
In the rain a broken woman cries for lost love,
But instead of learning about real love,
She decides to leave the world she blames for all her problems.

Elisabeth Jutzeler

Just Because I'm Deaf

I tried screaming out in the night
But no one heard me.

When I try to talk to someone
they don't understand me.

The only sound that I can make,
you hear in disgust,
not giving me another chance.

I went out to walk
and saw people running, playing, laughing
They come up to me and try talk to me
But I back away.

When I reply
When I try to explain,
How I feel
You wouldn't willing to listen

Do you dislike me,
just because I can't hear
I can't agree with what you want me to be.
Because I'm Deaf.

Miranda Ireland

True Beauty

True Beauty lies in your perfect face,
but it is much more than just skin deep.
Your soul through your sparkling eyes
with a brilliant light that you can't see.

The mirrors cannot reveal
the brilliance of your soul
and you need not live forever
in the darkness within your mind.

As long as I have known you
I've always seen that light,
I feel in love with it just as I fell in love with you.
My love will never fade
even with my death
it will shine on even after
all the lights are out.

Christine Knutson

Angels Here On Earth

I didn't know there were angels here on earth
But I realized on the night I'd given birth
She was sent from up above
Down to mom and dad to love
Now I know there are angels here on earth

He took the starlight from the sky
To add that twinkle in her eye
And on her face he painted a perfect smile
And every time I hold her near
I thank God he sent her here
Now I know there are angels here on earth

She has blessed us with her laughter
She brought sunshine where there was rain
She is all we've ever dreamed of
She was worth the wait and pain

And now before I close my eyes
I pray to the Lord above
For sending us our special angel
Whom we cherish with all our love.

Catherine MacMullin

A Song For Enzo

Enzo is fragile like fading lily petals
but he sit up valse-like, crystal-eyed
gripping your hand like there's no tomorrow
and sings to you a song that settles
even my cynicism; a shaky tremolo, a tide
that rushes in to erase all sorrow.

Whom shall we honour the lily or the rose?
The past is like a face in the mirror after a shower's end
the future like crushed glass on black asphalt
but this beautiful shell of Enzo knows
the cancer holding his hand will not bend
the backbone of his race, the crystal of his face, nor halt
the embrace, the faith of those gathered here
amidst the counters and the tubes, the collective fear.

Jim Head

For One

To love for one is overpowering.
But for two is torture.
Love is never ending; as far as you can count.
One.
Torn apart is mine heart.
Toil and tumult serge.
For one a kiss.
For two an embrace.
For three without me.
For four I throw myself upon death's door.
An answer...
of love for none.
Lacking embrace of a dismal sense.
Long for a kiss...
better off,
just without.

Amanda Moreau

"You Should Not Complain"

One door is open to everybody, door to the grave,
But door to life is open to somebody only.
God is not a democrat, does not like fairness.
He likes somebody better than someone
But you should not blame him for it,

He is the being of the ability of giving somebody life,
And taking it back at his will.
God is not love, but the being of whim,
But you should not blame him.

The happiest man in the fleeting world is the man
Who does not think about anything but living his life
To the moment of his death.
God loves anyone, that is his only fairness.

You, who chance to be given life, should not worried
About your life,
Not think about the meaning of life,
Not think about death,
That may always be near you.

Kiyoshi Takashima

She Sits At Peace

She sat in her chair as the cool sea winds danced
around her head. I watched her from close by yet far away.
I wonder what she was thinking when she, with eyes that had
seen a war, watched the gulls swoop down and sail above the
green ocean wave. Many times she had seen the same sights
but still never grew tired of them. It was there that she
was at peace. It was there that I was at peace just
watching my Nan who was watching the sea.

Lorne Oliver

The Man At His Window

The Man is sitting by his window
But does not see out
For he is contemplating on life and love
Or is he thinking of nothing at all.

The man sits by his window
With a gentle smile upon his lips
For he is a handsome gent
Adored by women and men alike.

The man sits at his window
Thinking God knows what
He is control of himself
Never straying from his thoughts.

The man sits at the window
Believing he is alone
However, dark clouds are slipping by
Waiting, waiting, waiting.

Why does the man sit at his window?
Does he await for friends or a lover?
Or does he plot to assassinate his King?
No one knows for sure, but the man looks perturbed.

Ruth McMillan

Torn Between Two Lands

There is a land of what I do and the way I do it
But before I seek that land, I have to feel the heart and
soul of someone I love
And the way I know this, is because I feel lonely without
that hand
I feel why was I born, what was the meaning for it
I want both but I can only have one,
I think in my head it is not fair, because I want more than
just a heart and a soul, I want peace and harmony
So the one I choose is the best one,
I think I want true love with the bare necessities not just
half, I want it all.

Ronald William Squires

David

Eight and twenty years is not a long time
But a lifetime
In which I revealed to you, the ragged ribbons
of my soul.
The very essence of me was in the sunshine glow
of the roses I lavished upon you.
You laughed and caressed me with kisses,
soft as butterfly wings.
In our mind's eye we dwelt in a faerie world
Where there are no secret meetings, coded glances
or whispered endearments.
Your warm embrace blanketed me from reality -
You sheltered me from condemnation and scorn.
But hostility mizzled in and you could not,
or would not, protect me forever.
Alone, I must go - yet again into the twilight
of the unknown.
My ashes scattered to the four winds and
over the bay
My only epitaph - He was gay!

Evelyn J. Hall

"A Clouded Dream"

It was mid fall of 1988,
busy getting ready for the life I was ready to take.
To see your smile and eyes that lit up,
as I walked down the aisle - just me and my Pop.
I said my vows, and you said yours,
the way I felt I knew that I had scored.
I knew that then nothing could ever part us,
the way I felt was absolutely fabulous.
I had beautiful dreams of nothing but happiness,
little did I know I was filled with loneliness.
If only you would hear and feel me when I trembled,
to love and hold me when I crumbled,
to tell me what you were feeling,
to see the hurt in my eyes,
but all I heard were the lies
the lies that clouded my dream but I saw the light,
the light that was only meant for me.

Doris F. Pretzer-Weir

My Mother's Love

Deep within her tear-filled eyes
Burns a love that ever shines
For day and night she nurtures me
Not caring of the time
My disabilities cause her hardships
Yet she never shows a sign
For the love within her caring heart
Does ease the pain in mine
I try to show her how much I care
I'll endear her to my heart
For I love my Mom in every way
I wish we could never part
Those countless hours she spent with me
On all those many hospital stays
And through them all her love would shine
To brighten my darkest days
I know someday that God will come
To take me to His "home with no cares"
And there I'll wait, standing tall
To say "Thank you and I love you Mom" for always being there.

David O. Bayford

God's Gift - Spring

Flowers of yesterday bloom once again,
  Brighten up with the showers of rain,
Cheer up the sick, make richer the poor,
  Oh how I long to see you once more.

Grass that is hidden 'neath white snowy bed
  Waiting for Spring time, to lift up its head,
And cover the hillside, so it will be seen
  A beautiful blanket of Emerald green.

Trees with their branches so ragged and bare,
  Looking like death as they wave in the air,
Soon little buds on the branch will appear,
  Bursting to leaves as the summer draws near.

Tulips and Daffodils in all of their color,
  Seeming, in beauty, to out do each other,
Bright yellow petals, with touches of red,
  Standing like soldiers, by Generals led.

Soon summer sun will be warming the earth,
  Giving the feeling of having new birth,
Each season that comes, its beauty will bring
  But greatest of all, God's gift of the Spring.

Grace Muriel Kilcup

Mysterious Winters Night

One cold winters night the moon shining
bright, the stars giving glow in the skies,
I was alone thinking out loud, when a
voice in the distance I heard.
It came closer and closer then a tap
on my window it seemed.
As I looked out my window a shadow
past by, it was then I opened the door
so slow, but to my surprise, there were
no one around, not even a track in the snow.
I went back inside, and sat for awhile,
wondering what it could be, soon the
telephone rang, with news, my dad passed away,
and he had been asking for me.

Ethel McGregor

Two Pennies

Two pennies on the table laid
Both with their heads straight up
One tarnished brown, one shining bright
Both share the same sunlight
Their years of mint time not far apart
Their journeys by different hands
Both suffered abuse and over use
The bright penny immune from outside perils
The blemished one scratched from sticks and stones
Both coins mature now and old in years
Each draws from the other's strengths
As their different faces now lie side by side
Like old lovers from years gone by
Apart from their days of youth, together again
Lying side by side
Strength by strength

Myrna Mackey

Soul Of A Nation

Now we unveil the Soul of our Nation
Born through McKenzie King Declaration
Here we hold high the dreams of the People
That aim to mould children fit for the many empty steeples
Patriots and goodwishers, we seen then rise
That create "the school of life"; and the Devise.

Like the pioneers shall be cut in forest the Spaces
But is in the mind; where fears and doubts have traces
Again this work shall receive the Crown
As are made new conquest to profit cities, towns

Again all is born in hard work and sweat
That nature provides and God protects
These bear the fruits that Canada Profits
To these we toast and say "Prosit".

We return Canada to be "The Land of Promise"
We remove the pantywaists that make only Pumice
We open to the common people the eyes
To again think soberly; and make the new Device
To adopt again "sweat and sacrifices" and make progress
Remove the greed that only their side stress.

D. Milani

If One's Soul

If one's soul can hope and live to breathe,
and learn to have faith in one's belief,
then one can stand free and true,
without the chill of feeling blue,
let life not pass one by,
one is too young to die.

Rowena Edwards

Life

The ever moving, ever changing complexity of color, of form,
blown to distant civilizations.
The water sweeps the sands bitter intakes
to be washed again and again a million times over.
Processes, clarity, to determine, to strive
to fail, to defeat, to be defeated.

The spirited walk, walked by generations before...
the inclination of youth, who drives recklessly into
forgotten paths,
the stability of middle age
the agility of the child
the fragility of aging,
to that of what's beyond.

Nicole Andersen

Blossom

Open roses send sweet, sweet fragrances
Blossoming beautifully, grabbing life
Vision improves as rose petals expand
Scents so lovely with roses in full bloom
Some flowers can fade, losing their value
Roses keep forever, scent they may lose
A place inside her heart hopefully stays
Love lasts a lifetime keeping strength and beauty
As a rose will remain in full blossom

Dustin Rutsatz

Before You Go!

Sitting there in a yellow chair
Blending in like nothing but air;
Trying so hard to breath out "Hello"
Saying you love me before you go.
I look into your light blue eyes
Taken over by sobbing cries
I see your sick, yellow, thin body
Your collar bone revealed, gross and gaudy;
Closed your eyes and gone to sleep
Into amazing dreams you will creep.
Lying there suffering, stiff as wood
Living and fighting if you could
So now I will say my final word
And always remember that you have heard
Although it is strong and tremendously bright
You have my permission to walk into the Light.

Lisa Cunningham

A Game Of Paintball

Here comes the adventurous players trotting through the fields,
Beware up in front and back because they have no shields.

It is a game of exercise, with watchful eyes and graceful skill.
But most of all, a fun-action type of sport and not a game to kill.

They're well equipped with gear and wearing camouflaged clothes.
There's even some wearing steel-toe boots with rubber-bottom soles.

Shots can be heard beyond surround sound,
When zeroing in your target, you've got one-man down.

Dusk soon approaches and ends their day of play.
Some tired, sore, and dirty; yet, they cheer to a
crazed-wargame day.

Christine Boulerice

169

On Blessings

The Bible Warns to those who think they stand
BEWARE, lest thinking you stand, you're found to fall
At I. S. P. ninety five, some with their band
Left disillusioned; none had heard their call
And so I have a question; please hear me;
Can you read me? Did you return home glad?
Or did you pout, and tell the world you're mad?
Midst all the hype, did you a Senator see?
Senator McCarthy taught me; signed my book
I was impressed; felt like I was gathering fruit
It's good to have some notes through which to look
Ira Westreich lectured; then followed suit
MY final joy, resulting from this quest?
Mabel; adding her blessings to the rest.

Margaret I. Coates

My Sister

We were friends right from the start
Being the same right from the heart
To share a room was meant to be
You were you and I was me
Through the night we'd talk and sing
We'd go to sleep wondering what tomorrow would bring
Growing together and walking in stride
You are my sister, I say it with pride
Some times were bad, some times were good
Through it all, there you stood
Through our teens we went a stray
Now true friends forever we'll stay
as bright as the morning sun may shine,
I'm glad you are a sister of mine.

Maryann Henderson

A Silent Heart

Behold the young girl sitting there, still with silent stare.
Behold her image and keep it in your mind.
In her eyes you see the memories of all that has gone before,
and from her heart sings a future she is longing for.

Watch her as she slowly rises to meet the ocean breeze,
and reach with open arms to welcome the mighty seas.

She seems frail as she walks along the shore.
Dwarfed by the vastness of sky meeting earth.
Beneath her feet the grains of endless time carry her away.

Tania Ryan

A Painter Stands Upon A Cliff And Turns Doubt Into Certainty

Carol Ann Duffy, "Poem In Oils"

No field of rye
behind his back, no catch
today,
the kids have gone
astray;
mourning sea-gulls try
in vain to chat the fog
away;
gray color on gray canvas;
not a still life, though.

Timothy McNeal

"The Beginning Of Eternity"

The beginning of eternity
Begins here,
As the dusk merges into the Night
And the night into the dawn,
And the dawn into the day...

How does the beginning of Eternity feel?
No one can say for sure,
But to me it feels sad
And sometimes quite frightening.
I know I can't look back
And nor do I dare enquire into the Future
Shrouded in Mystery...

With only a Book in my trembling hands
I pass through the doors of Eternity...

Afsana L. Pasha

You Are That

Throughout the ether I have been.
Before time;
Since the Beginning; Before the Beginning
I am the Void.

I am sunbeams glancing off the raindrops,
And melodiously intertwined notes in music.
Twin stars; a dividing cell;
Molecules dancing in gaseous material,
The lonely call of the loon in a thunder storm.

Clay, the potter, the pot,
The emptiness and the fullness of the pot,
I am.

Provider of food
And the food,
I am the cook and the act of eating.

You will find me as the largest Galaxy of space,
Or as the smallest molecule of Space between the Galaxies.

I am the reflection in your mirror.
See Me.
See your Self.

Valerie Beattie-Dolan

Who Will Inherit The Whoozit?

They tell me I should make a will,
Before, as they say, I'm over the hill!
But now some problems come to light,
How to divide so 'they' won't fight.
Possessions I have very few,
Money, even less, 'tis true;
A jar of 'loonies' stashed away
May be for a rainy day?
But who gets what? How can I decide?
Certain stuff just won't divide;
Someone wants this; I've promised that;
And I really must provide for the cat!
Would someone want this oddball heirloom?
Or simply say - I haven't room.
I must give some serious thought to this
Because I have a secret wish;
That some of my favorites may survive
And keep a memory alive.

Peggy Garnot

170

The Lord Is Near

When your world of sunshine
Becomes a world of rain
Full of sorrow
Full of pain
Remember, the Lord is near.

When you need someone to share
Your thoughts and sorrows
Your triumphs and defeats
Your hope for many morrows
Remember, the Lord is near.

When you need sympathetic ears
To listen to your troubles
When you need someone to calm your fears
When you need someone to understand
Remember, the Lord is near.

Never hesitate to talk to Him
He always finds the time to listen
However busy He may be
So next time you need someone who cares
Remember, the Lord is near.

Lynn Ellis

Charlie Chaplin

The poet who left no words
because he spoke to the soul.
Who but he could describe love without
staining it?

He spoke of bitterness,
with a smile covered
with truth; he described poverty.
He showed us life, death, and politics.
He paid with his name,
his daring ideals. But this did not
quench the aura of his gaze,
nor the warm silhouette that moved
as he walked, that marvelous way of
walking and not going. He left roads;
some still unwalked, some still unfinished.

This roads remind
whomever wants to walk
the long and narrow way of art.
The figure of an invisible man
will be always one step ahead.

Arturo Lazo

Untitled

There is a little girl who cries.
Because everything she's heard are lies.
She's all alone with no hope.
And is too young to know how to cope.
Her beautiful eyes are stained with tears.
And her lonely nights are filled with fears.
So young and innocent. It isn't fair.
To have a life where no one cares.
Who will tuck her in, and sing to her at night?
Who will hold her when she's filled with fright?
Each time her dreams are broke, she dies.
There is a little girl who cries.

Andrea deBoer

Nurse's Desire

My life is going to be sublime. I'm going to
    be a nurse sometime.
I had a dream when I was nine I'm going
    to be a nurse sometime.
To study and do what God would do.
Would be pleasant and rewarding too.
Now I'm eleven and feel the same
My goal is onward, I'll head for fame
I love people - God's chosen clan
He's calling me, I'll follow His plan
To care for souls and bring them cheer
To let them know that thou art near
I'm off to college and happy indeed
Head of the class. I must succeed
I'm nineteen now and my cap is white
I do not fear the darkest night.
Thank you to my Mom and Dad
They led me on the path of right.

Mary Barnard

The Plague Of Life

A: is for acid that gets in your blood.
B: is for Bile that sludges like mud:
C: is for Cholesterol from too much fat
D: please don't touch the salt
E: It's time to sit down and eat the calories will reach right down
    to your feet.
F: forget it all just for today someone said splurge it's Muriel's
    birthday.
G: is for gout, gastric ulcer and gall: why? did we come to this
    festive ball:
H: is when your hair starts dropping out, maybe just maybe we'd
rather
    have gout.
I: bi said the Newfie in his speech, eats lots of fish: drink
    Newfoundland screech;
J: is Jack strap itch if you set in the sand it could be a bitch.
The rest of the Alphabet is not worth, repeating the way things are
going we'll soon be done eating, it seems like a waste, and it seems
you can't win, for the apple in the Garden has caused all this sin.

Muriel Jack

Prairie Retreat

I stood on the prairie and breathed in the quietness-
Away from the human race.
And bathed in the beauty of blessed peace -
So free from the harried pace.
I drank in the words of the songbirds with such
Sweet melodies,
And knew that the city could never be home to me.
For such a short time the world was mine -
The sun drenched earth lay at my feet.
So with sweet regret as I left -
I vowed to return to my prairie retreat.

Doris Bolig

Meeting Place

Locking the twelve floor prison door.
An escape down the stairs instead of with stone face stares.
A breathless travel to a clearing in the wood.
Then to creep, and faintly the heart flutters.
A crisp, golden carpet beneath two warming feet.
One, two, one, two
The silent rhythm of this place toots a musical, magical flute.
Caught within its grip, pulled along and now the heart flutters wildly.
For to unravel this adventure of such simplicity is knowing
who waits just ahead.

Linda Cutler

The Quiet Drummer

With soft-footed tread he moves through life, although
Aware of every moment of every day.
Attuned to life he feels its vibrant flow
Deep in his soul, in his own quiet way.

Sensitive to sound, he hears so clear and sweet
The pulsating tempo of the earth, the air,
In every fibre of his being, with every beat
Of his gentle heart, he's conscious of it there.

And he must answer with a rhythm of his own,
Let free the harmony that forever hums
And reverberates through sinew, blood and bone.
He finds release in cacophony of drums.

This instrument, its language ever heard
Through centuries of time, its ancient sound
Sending its messages in rhythmic word,
Throbbing its tribal beat for miles around.

The quiet drummer finds this way to vent
The music's rising swell within, and when
The pounding, rolling energy is spent,
Puts down his sticks until it builds again.

Eileen Clayton Vincent

Summers Passing

Watching autumn leaves blow by
August winds split the sky
Warm summer days we'll miss
Shortened days, sun's lingering kiss

Mother nature's tender care
Comforts us with constant stare
We sit by fireside light
Hypnotized under heaven's night

Just per chance we might see
A falling star for you and me
You cuddle me I hold you tight
Thoughts of spring are our delight

Warm winds of March blow our way
Soon we'll enjoy a longer day
April's showers bathe earth's frozen face
The buds of life show a trace

With life renewed we think back
Where late last fall summer passed
Amidst autumn leaves where they lay
We'll inhale a brand new spring day

Jack A. Bradbury

The World Awaits

So still near the water, the animals stare
At the trees and the flowers around.
I wonder in silence who here really cares
But I'm quiet, I'll make not a sound.

I may be right, for I pray I am not wrong
But the world is ours to share.
The trees are ours as is the birds' song,
Likewise, the land and the air.

We can't be content here living in fear
Of the destruction of life and the end.
We'll sit as animals all disappear,
A rip in our fibre too deep to mend.

Am I asking too much from all those around
To build up our world instead of tearing it down?

Kristy Fisher

Who Are You

As beautiful, as an orchid in the moonlight.
At night, all my dreams, you fulfill.
With eyes, blue as heaven at twilight.
You give me your love, and its thrills.

And then, once again, here comes morning
Last night, was not real, just a hopeful dream.
You awake, cold and strange and so frigid.
Like a thistle with prickly leaves.

Like a weeping willow, you leave me.
Alone languid and blue
Wishing you would reveal to me,
This secret you hold within you.

By day, you're like a tumbleweed
So scorched, confused, windblown
I pray for the night, when as a daffodil,
You will meet this willow tree.

Muriel Rosevear, Timmins, Ontario

Together

Together two people stood alone in the world as one;
As well it might have been for any deeply loving pair,
But the strength and fortitude of one over shadowed all,
And soon they were no longer two as one, but one of two.
The passage of time indicated not that one was gone,
But that a loss of individuality had occurred,
And been replaced with a mimicking tribute to the other;
So one did not realize that there was not two.
A pair of hands came to guide and reassure, to offer salvation,
To address the departed and call it back to life,
To give back to the two that which had been dormant,
To bring into awareness that only by blending,
And not by absorbing, can two people survive as one.
So with renewed courage and not disregarding the struggle,
The pair made a revitalized effort to stand together again.
This time the consumption of one would not prevail,
For they both knew that in order to make a fulfilling one,
...........They must be two.

Ruth Lawrence

Innerspace

Now take a dive and journey with me,
As we swim far down, into the sea.
Sparkling crystals dance over its top.
We're following a sea path that never will stop.

Brightly coloured fish swim right by
And flap their fins as if to say, "Hi!"
But suddenly we're frozen right into our tracks,
Because the feeling of danger behind our backs.

Almost afraid to turn our heads:
And when we do, relief's clearly read.
For it was only a harmless school of fish,
Looking for their favorite afternoon dish.

The colours so beautiful in this underground world;
We now watch a water plant curl and uncurl.
Every move made is so graceful all the time.
For that's what makes the sea a poetry line.

Amanda Lamers

Mysteries Of Life

The mysteries of life surround us
As we are challenged everyday
A new life begins in an instant and one is taken away.
Sometimes we may question and wonder why events take place as they do
But there is a reason and place for everything
And there is nothing that we can do.
We must trust our internal instinct and know that we are loved.
And hope and pray for immunity with our leader up above.

Michelle Fletcher

The Sanity Station

They'd gather round to get their fill,
as to prevent themselves from becoming ill.
The sanity station would commence, imparting each with a dose of sense
and as desire was forbidden, they'd take a grey tablet to be ridden
of silly whims and petty dreams, replacing each with concrete themes,
For it was written Lad and Lass must everyday attend this mass, and
how grey parents did insist that grey children not resist, for they
might grow old and never know that what they'd reap was
what they sowed.
As in the fringes across the way they might not save for a rainy day.
Life in the fringes thus was spent as grey folk knew it was not meant.
It was rumored that the colored folk would listen as their
children spoke, and furthermore, it would seem, they'd encourage
them to dream!
However they knew the foolishness of this way,
for long ago before the grey, there had been more colored kids
and horrid scraps that they would find revealed a world of constant
change, where everyday would hold a range of emotions one could
not control and thus would rend a tortured soul.
No they preferred this modern way-where all was even, square and grey.

Jenny Frank

Legacy

Feel my loving kisses against your cheek,
As the wind whispers across your face

Hear my care - free joyous laughter,
As the birds serenades the dawn

Feel my proud smile beam down upon you,
With the glory of the sun's rays

See my love for you,
In the tears of your unborn children

Feel my astonishing new found freedom,
As an eagle takes flight

Do not weep along side the rain,
For only then can a rainbow ever appear

Lisa Piatek

Life

Life is a bird upon the wind.
As the bird proceeds with its flight,
the wind is its helper,
guiding it along.
The breeze can get vicious,
not caring about the fate of the bird.
Yet the bird is strong,
it will continue its flight.
As a bird upon the wind,
our journeys are not done.
Our winds do not overpower us,
they simply make our journeys a challenge.

Tara Andrews

The Lost Ones

The inky night trickles toward the horizon,
As starry nibs empty their fears.
Scrolling wildly from margin to margin,
The heavens peppered with their passionate pleas.
Smudged here and there with a tear of starlight,
Sprinkled with the gold dust of celestial pens.

As captives consumed by cells of choking gas,
As prisoners chained in fetters of isolation,
Ensnared within a prison of infinity,
Stars signal to mother Earth for delivery.
Would they wail and wretch but were their
Speeches not seized by the dark mouth of an abyss.

Certain that life's secrets abide in hearts of stars,
Man waits below, camouflaged by shimmering clouds.
Stalking with hunger the bodies above,
Craving for the wisdom which flows through their veins.
Though he has eyes of glass and steel, he cannot see
The stars of the sky are as much lost as he.

Mary Elizabeth Cool

Day's Duty

I am concerned today as always,
As seemingly wasted moments I do pass,
What's my purpose? What's my work?
I should really begin the task.

Should I look at my plights daily?
Or save them up for once a week?
With out over analysing, I'd take the tally,
All the things making me loose my sleep.

When I take a hard look around me,
Everything seems relatively safe and sound,
And all the while I was steadily progressing
Then my feelings of pride become very profound.

Dianne Camire-Griffiths

The Four Seasons

O how I love the joys of spring,
As nature unfolds her new work to begin
The plants push their way, up through the hard ground,
Working vigorously with never a sound.

Then summer arrives in a blaze of great colour
The flowers showing off their beauty to one another
Nodding their heads in a mark of ascent
Showing approval of each new event.

As Autumn creeps in the trees shed their leaves
Wafting gently to the ground, caught by the morning breeze
There they lay exposed to the elements from on high
In an expression of loneliness to each passerby.

Winter appears feeling cold and damp
With frost in the mornings that nobody wants
There is snow in the mountains and rain from the hills
One looks forward to spring as they fight of the chills.

These are the four seasons, God so ordained
For the use of man, and so they have remained
Now each season comes whatever the weather
Just think and marvel, how God put them all together.

Eleanor Cochrane

Living

The kettle was black
as midnight,
A symbol of our life,
black with unhappiness,
misery,......Finally our own place,

I teetered carrying the weight of living
the handle squeaked as I walked,
The steps too high, I peered through
feeling tiny, helpless

My mother's face mirrored my own,
I felt her hope, saw her happiness,
she lifted me up, holding onto life
lifting my body and spirit towards the sun.
Moving in..

The darkness lifted, the kettle scrubbed
a symbol of hope, a new life
away from the darkness, the blackness
it shone with life and hope
our place, our shelter, we lived...

In hope of living....

Sandra Foehr

Remembrance Day

Does everyone remember,
as I remember you
The way that you had died,
and that they put you through.
When I think of all the lives you've saved,
but to have to lose your own.
Was it really worth it?
    We will never know.

I remember how you said to me, that you'd return someday;
But that dream did not come true,
The way we know each other, and how you said good bye.
Even though I trusted you
I thought that you may die.
Would we still have our freedom,
if you would have stayed?
    We will never know.

The freedom that you gave us will continue to grow and grow.
As does the pain I feel, because you had to go.
I will always miss you.
    But you will never know.

Geoff Foster

The Tunnel Of Darkness And Light

Where am I,
as I lay neither here nor there?
Darkness all around with not a sound.
My mind cries silently,
"Help, someone, anyone",
but there's only silence.
Fast, I go through this tunnel of darkness
Now, there's light at its end.
Oh, with such brightness.
The feeling of leaving one's self
is now so very strong.
But it's wrong,
this feeling of leaving.
It must be kept at bay
because I know, today is not my day.
I must, with all my inner strength
fight its entire length.
For now, my need here,
is greater than there.

Margarete Berglund

Tears

Tears of joy, sadness and grief
Are something that I will always have to keep
For, every occasion has a different kind of tear
Whether it's joy, happiness or fear.
    But, there's one thing you should hear,
Never try to stop a tear.
For, a tear is a big part of your life
Whether it's a tear of shame or a tear of pride.
    All these tears represent only you
These tears do what nobody else can do
They never leave your side
So, there's no place for you to hide
    Always open up to a tear
Whether it's a tear of happiness or a tear of fear.

Kiran Dulku

"Spring Of Depression"

If your mind is in darkness,
And your spirit is in the night,
The strongest sun will start to shine,
To block out the darkest light.

Evil and fear, can be combined,
Problems can cause a troubled mind,
But the source of power deep within,
Can make a better, world to live in.

Heart and soul, can mean a lot,
Remember, worry, isn't bought,
The giver of life, is much more stronger,
Keep your chin up, and you'll last much longer.

Doug A. Wonch

To Make You My Friend

Standing alone, I spotted you from across the room,
And your eyes captured my heart and soul.
I cannot explain it, but I feel an unusual attraction to you,
And I would give anything to make you my friend.
It's been a while, and we've gotten close,
Blind faith I've given freely to you.
I cannot stop my desire, though with it comes a type of fear,
But I would give anything to make you my friend.
I've gone farther with you than I should have,
But my longing overrides my guilt.
You want more from me, and scary thing is,
I'd still give anything to make you my friend.
Alone I lie here, covered in blood,
Bruised from head to toe, you stole my innocence
A few more painful moments, I am now dead,
And I gave everything to make you my friend.

Chelsea Strom

Mother

Remember all those boys I would phone
and you would tell me to just leave them alone.
    Remember all that make up I wore
and you would say "I liked you better before."
    Remember when I went on my first date
and you grounded me for being late.
    But now as time has gone by, all your rules
I've come to see why...
    I am who I am today because of you,
and all the caring that you do.
    I just want to let you know
that I know you were right,
    And now I thank God for a mother like
you every night.

Kristin Raemisch

174

Passing Years...

I glance into the mirror
And what do I see?
Someone merely a shadow
Who was formerly me!

For time has passed by.....
Fires, banked low, once so high -
Striving, ambition, achievements too,
No longer inflame, as they used to do.

My health declines - old age, I guess;
My eyes grow dim, and I walk much less.
The joints grow stiff and surely creak,
Glad I am that the mind's not weak!

Why do I wail, and why do I moan?
When children, now grown, leave me quite alone;
Yet I've many friends, oh yes, quite a few!
Retirements planned, so I've lots to do!

Back to the mirror for just one more glance,
It's enough to make all my spirits just dance!
Times ever change, still hope glows anew,
Life has a Design meant for me...meant for you!

Gertrude G. Rodd

My Little Miracle

You came into my life
And turned it all around
You made my nights sleepless
And there are days that I still
    haven't found

Your demands are of my every moment
And you've tested my inner strengths
Your dependence is entirely upon me
And you've challenged my patience to the
    greatest of lengths

Your smiles light up my world
And your frowns tear it apart
Your giggles brighten my every day
And your teardrops break my heart

Your are truly my little miracle
And my love you've unconditionally won
You are my angel sent straight from Heaven
And I shall cherish you always,
    my precious son.

Toby J. Owles

Friend

Time has slowly passed my friend since I've called your name.
And things have really changed, you have not been the same.

It seems like only yesterday since you called me friend.
But today I stand here wondering if this is the end.

Your friendship meant the world to me, it was all that I had.
But I don't know what I did to make things so bad.

The few memories that we shared are now nothing but a sigh.
And as much as it hurts inside you'll never see me cry.

I hear you whisper harsh words things so unkind.
To think you were my friend, how could I be so blind.

You say you don't need friendship, so I'll go my separate way.
And some how I will try to forget those harsh words that you say.

I thought that you cared my friend, I guess that I was wrong.
But I know time will heal me because I am strong.

I gave you my trust, respect and honesty, and wonder how it could be.
That someone as special as you in my life could take that away from me.

Maybe one day we'll meet again my friend and make a true amends.
But until then I hope that I can find another worthy friend.

Christina M. Frenza

Best Fishing Story

The sky was grey and the ocean dark,
And the whitecaps did a dance
And leaning against a sun bleached log
Was an old "Tar" who seemed in a trance.

For it's here he comes every day
To watch the ships sail by
To smell the salt air and feel the cool breeze
And on his memories he does rely.

Year after year he fished the "Grand Banks"
Working hard till late at night
Braving the storms, landing his catch,
His holds were loaded, oh what a sight.

But nature has a way of slowing us down
And his time had come to stay home
"Exiled" to the land, were his hidden thoughts,
Never more shall the seas I roam.

But each day goes by and he sits on his log
And the children of the town come down
They sit and listen to the tales he spins,
Best fishing story going round.

Evelyn Randall

Untitled

When the twilight surrenders the sun to the night
And the moon once again is bright regent
A strange yet a welcome feeling sweeps o'er me
The aura I sense is your presence
I think of the many times we two
Stood hand-in-hand in this unreal landscape
And pledged our love eternally true
But love took wings and escaped
For now when I stand in this very same place
I wonder if it ever was real
The excitement, the vista, the moon on your face
Are all lost on times turning mill wheel.

Donald P. Foston

Our Time

Millions of little windows fill the sky.
And the moon big and bright.

The only thing that we can truly call our own,
is this place, is this time in the night.

Here we can sit, and think, and
leave reality behind.

Where we can laugh, and dream, and
find total peace of mind.

Here we embrace each other, and
reassure our love.
All beneath the endless sky, and
the moon that hangs above.

This time it is forever, yet all a memory.
But no one will share that time,
that place.
No one like you and me.

Amber Evans

175

Rainbow

The storm had just ended,
And the caressing wind was stroking my hair.
With the repetitive sound of crashing waves on the shore,
I sat there without care.

The tears of despair pitter-pattered softly,
Into the endless sea.
The rainbow was nowhere to be found,
Where was He?

Tranquility and serenity found a place in my heart,
While the clouds shed a soft yellow light.
The Angels were singing and whispering my name,
Peace and Love were holding me tight.

After gazing back one last time, I advanced,
For in the distance I could see,
The glittering rainbow,
For it was no other then He.

Monique Louise LeBlanc

Daddy's Little Angels

My life has changed in many ways
And somewhere along the path
God granted me two wishes
And he said they both would last

They came with little fingers
And tiny little toes
They came one after the other
And stood there in a row

With both their smiling faces
They can light up any house
And turn it upside down
And still be quiet as a mouse

But they're growing into beauties
And I'm proud that I'm their dad
For too soon they'll go their separate ways
And this will make me sad

For of all the things I've done till now
These two both take the prize
They are everything I've wanted
They sparkle in my eyes

Bryan Forbes

Back From The Road

Let me go back a ways from the road
    And sit on that far hill,
Where the grass is so much greener
    The air so sweet and still.

Let me go back from the road
    Away from the rushing crowds,
Where one could sit on the soft green grass
    And watch the billowing clouds.

I'll sit there on that far hill
    And try to understand,
Whatever could have happened
    To all my girlhood plans.

Was I so young and so naive
    To think that all my plans,
Would all fall into place
    With just the flick of a hand.

Let me go back again from the road
    And sit on that far hill,
To see if all my hopes and dreams
    Are waiting for me still.

Irene M. Clow

Songs Of Sweet Delight

He comes each morn with dawns first light
And sings a song for me.
He has the stage as I sit back
And listen, gratefully.

Although his tune is much the same
As the day before,
I never seem to get enough
And always want for more.

He's yet to miss a morning
And is not ever late,
I'm always sure to find him there
Perched on my back gate.

When he's done his melody,
'Songs of Sweet Delight',
He leaves his modest podium
And enters into flight.

I often wonder why he comes
And sings his songs for free,
For there's never been a single thing
That he's once asked of me.

Sherry L. Waltham

A Lonely Child

She watches the world from the secluded room,
And silent tears begin to fall
She strives to seek her place
Yet she is paralyzed from the call.

Without you enduring within her heart,
The child shall never see
What you have planned for her in life,
And what she is to be.

Soothe her soul, oh Lord
Although you may be a stranger
Hold her close to your heart
And steer her far from danger.

Why she refuses to invite you in
Remains an answer unknown
That only you know dear God
Yet she chooses to remain alone.

A lonely girl with tears on her face
In a room forsaken and bare
I pray that Lord you shall watch over her
And show her that you care.

Shawna Lessard

Reflections

What makes us do the things we do?
And say the things we say?
And act decisively, or not, as we live out each day!
We understand so little, yet we understand so much?
Our fleshly notice thrives, or what we see, and feel and touch!
A new born baby's cry, can being a smile
expose the face of those dear parents that time cannot erase!
Yet that same cry of hunger and of pain,
case be the cry, the cry, never to be heard again!
Man is a man of perplexity,
of happiness, and anxiety.
It's not an easy road we tread,
never knowing what's ahead!
It's only when we stop awhile,
and discovered who we really are,
made in the image of own creator God,
to fellowship along with him..!
"Own only obstacle in SIN!"

Barbara McDonald

176

I Think Of You

One night I looked upon the setting sun so bright and so true
And right away I thought of you and everything you do

One night I looked upon all the stars in the skies
and right away I thought of you and your beautiful eyes

One morning I dared to watch an eagle gliding across the sky, so blue
and right away I thought of you so graceful and so true

One night I looked upon a full moon in all its splendour
and right away I thought of you so sweet and so tender

One morning I woke wondering what I was to do
and than I realized how much I truly love you.

Brian DeVisser

My Secret Place

I had a secret place where I used to love to sit
and read.
  Tip-toeing into mother's room, a huge trunk closet
awaited me.
  All around hung our racks of clothes like a bower
of friendly trees.
  I would imagine them rustling back and forth
in my hidden glen.
  So cozy and quiet with a light to see, the book I
was reading that fancied me.
  Sitting cross-legged on a cushion, nibbling an apple
and sipping a cup of tea,
  My favorite book today is, "King Arthur and His Knights."
  In their colorful garb and armour jousting on
horseback as they fight.
  Someone has called disturbing my empire of freedom
through books.
  I must go set the table for supper and probably cook.
  There are simple meals to get ready, is my family's refrain.
  Everyone should have a hide-away place far from the world's
domain.

Correen L. Robinson

My Mother

You gave me life and cared for me,
And never slept till comfort me.
You caught me when I fell,
And felt the pain I couldn't tell.
You swept it very patiently,
The tear that fell impatiently
You wept when I did wrong.
And taught me to be strong.
You prized me for my best,
Enduring me to quest.
You held me through blues and chill,
Sharing, cheering when I was ill.
You smiled at silly things I did,
And taught me etiquette to live
Me, a part of you and shall remain for ever,
My mom, my best friend will forget you never.

Nazima Z. Shaikh

Abandoned Flight

Last night as I lay in my bed, I heard a rumble over head
A storm is in the air, I fear, the gentle rumble not far from here
A rush of lightning through the sky, flashing, dazzling, way on high.
Now the rain begins to patter down, to quench the earth for flowers grown
And lull my sleep in a rhythmic way, from a curtained sky, to end the day
I ride the clouds and chase the storm, and dodge the rain until the dawn
I dance above the clouds on high, beneath the stars in an electric sky
Now I wake - it is dawn - did I really hear a storm?

Joyce P. Brecknock

Unheard Whispers

I feel empty inside....my soul seems hollow,
And my cries echo inside of my being looking for escape.
I'm trying, maybe too hard, to be what is expected and what is
also expected.
I lie awake with confusion, looking ahead for answers, searching
behind for comfort,
Yet, being faced with the present.
I hide, I smile, and I fall apart inside.
I cling to things I love,
A cotton blanket,
A pen and paper,
A book and a cool autumn breeze.
Here I look for security and escape.
Wishing to be different, knowing I am no different.
Longing,
Always longing,
For my childhood laughter,
A lullaby that sings me into tranquillity.
Filled with dreams, always dreams,
And perhaps, nothing more.

Sandra Merk

Don't Leave Me

When in the spring the lilacs bloom, when hearts are gay
And love is young and all the world is bright and new
My thoughts begin and end with you;
Don't leave me then, don't leave me then
You cannot leave me then.

When summer winds blow soft and warm and roses climb the
Garden wall, when white clouds sail the endless sky
And life is sweet and full of joy;
Don't leave me then, don't leave me then
You cannot leave me then.

When in the misty autumn haze red leaves dance in the
Restless breeze and high above the evergreens
The golden harvest moon;
Don't leave me then, don't leave me then
You cannot leave me then.

When winter sweeps across the land your touch is like
An icy hand and silently the snowflakes fall
Into my frozen heart;
You left me then you left me then
Why did you leave me then?

Karin Kuskis

Abortion

A baby bird fell out of its nest
And landed on a tree,
No LIFE, No breath, no covering, no cries
No shouts of glee.

The baby's skin was wrinkles and balding
With no hair.
The baby's mouth was open and breathing
In no air.

The mother lie there snoozing
Like sawing through a tree,
Waiting for the bough to break,
Waiting to be free.

Dianne F. Baiton

Precious Daughter

If I could turn the clock back
And know then what I know today
How different things might be
I hope and pray, they still could change today.

Perhaps you would still have chosen
To live your life this way
I guess I'll never know now
If you would always be away.

I hope a day will come soon
Before it might be too late
That we can sit and have a talk
And discuss what steps to take.

There is nothing more I want to do
But help you.
There is nothing I can do
Until you want help too.

You are growing into a stranger
This really breaks my heart
The girl for whom I would give my life
Is tearing us apart.

Elizabeth O'Brien

My Love For You

I love you with all my heart,
And it tears me up inside when we are apart.
Every minute of the day you're on my mind,
Love like ours is a hard thing to find.

I love you more than you could know,
And I would die if you were to go .
My feelings for you I just can't hide,
You make me feel so happy deep down inside.

I care for you so very much,
And it is like magic every time we touch.
You are as beautiful as a rose,
I guess my love for you really shows.

You mean everything to me,
My love for you is so easy to see.
So before I go I would like to say,
I love you in each and every way.

Tracey Sullivan

First Born

I shake and tremble as I hold your mother's hand,
And in the middle of life's miracle
I ride, she sees,
Her brave knight has a love story
Pouring from his eyes ——
I'm humbled.

My heart beats time on time,
And in your presence,
It cries out to be your hero,
The protector of your way ——
I'm small.

I awkwardly caress you in my arms,
And through my tears
I whisper,
Your home is not a palace,
You need a cradle,
Son ——

I love you,
I'm your father.

Darryl Patterson

"My Dear"

You were nineteen, when first we met,
And I was then eighteen
You smiled at me, and in my heart
I felt a glow unseen.

We went on dates, and then we wed.
On a September day.
Our life together had begun
Our love with us did stay.

We had our share of joy and pain.
And many friends so true.
And through years, our love remained
And my whole life was you.

So suddenly, one day in May, you left me all alone
With memories so wonderful
That I am proud to own.

I would not wish for you, my dear
This ache within my heart,
I thank thee God, when we shall meet
And never have to part.

Kathleen I. Olmsted

Autumn

Colors, colors, vivid colors are appearing all around.
And I see some of the leaves gently twirling to the ground.
Is it Autumn time already, did the season change that soon?
Will the birds fly south again, ducks and geese and yes the loon!
I am thankful for the summer, pretty flowers, green, green grass,
But now comes the yellow harvest, children all go back to class.
Oh so many vegetables are now ripening on the field
and the apple trees are laden, giving us a big, big yield.
Lord we know that you are waiting, watching us on Earth below
Are your children giving fruit? Yes we know, You love us so!

Help us, as we went through Springtime, Summer days and into Fall
so to spend our days on Earth loving You Lord most of all!

E. Bos

Cleopatra

My maids have done their magic work at last,
and I in all my glory as a queen
look through the shadowed gloom to mirrored night,
where Anthony, my lord, has reached his throne.
I long to be the regent of his eye,
and stretch my wrist toward the gentle fig.
I feel a subtle sting,
and chill flows up;
then great birds' wings take forth my golden soul,
like noon's high sun in heaven's priestly hands.
And I for Anthony cry out,
wanting his lordship like a yearning child
to see my beauty coming from afar,
arrayed by light in my soul's shining dress.

Ian MacLennan

A Boy And A Castle Of Sand

Everyday I wake and begin my active day
Always pursuing a dream, I'm very busy you see.
Gathering things I need and my confidence with me
Out to a familiar spot, the place I like to play.

Designing plans magnificent and built from level sand
The opportunities and securities, things I like to share.
Usually drawing some interest and occasionally one to care
An experience so enriching, something out of hand.

A prince courting a princess and nothing more to say
Except the tides will change, washing all away.

Meia

My Little One

His hair is sandy and his eyes are blue,
And he does anything you want him to do,
My husband got custody of my little son,
Oh! How I love him, I love the little one.

His father and I are separated you see,
He said I tied him down so I set him free,
Well enough of that and back to my son,
He walks and he talks, he's two years plus one.

As he walked in the room with a smile on his face,
And he ran over to me with such poise and such grace,
He kissed me and hugged me with all of his might,
And he said, to me, "hey mommy you got me tonight!"

As I sat there with tears filling my eyes,
He said to me, "mommy please don't cry",
At that point I pulled my son closed to my heart,
And I prayed silently that we would never part.

Well the next day came so quick and so fast,
And I finally realize this time could not last,
As he stood in the car and he waved goodbye,
I said, "see you next week honey" with tears in my eyes.

Cindy Kelly

Jet Black To Shining Pink

On losing a spouse, after many years of constant happiness
and great enthusiasm for life together, everything crashes
on one with a final abruptness.

Shock to one's system numbs the brain - undoing all control
of concentration and sense of balance - resulting in extreme
weakness, prolonged fatigue and lack of interest! There is a
sensation of a huge blanket floating overhead and not sufficient
energy to throw it off or get out from under.

In brief, those are the first symptoms of being alone!
Yes! Alone! Oh so alone!

Much praying to God our Father - begging for strength to
encounter the activities of each day - one day at a time.
Time, usually measured in years, gives one hope for a new life
in the future.

And finally, looking skyward, one observes the clouds with
silver linings and shining hot pink casts.
It can and does happen! There are better days ahead!

When reflecting on the happy days once shared, one realizes
one must live for today and seek out the shining pink for tomorrow.

Floris M. Wilkie

For The Moment

Your gentle hand caresses my face
and for the moment we embrace
For the moment we are filled with love
and the moon shines down from above
For the moment we share an intimate kiss
this I know I shall always miss
For the moment you and I slowly dance
caught in each others caring glance
For the moment our souls are one
and the song is far from done
For the moment we start to believe
that the other shall never leave
For the moment I caught your eye
and I knew it was time to say good-bye

Jennifer Comack

Ode To Winter

The days are shorter now that summer's gone
And birds are heading south toward the sun.
The garden bared of colour, sound or cheer
Is resting for the advent of another year.

The rain and clouds appear as sunshine fades.
And overhead a thunder storm pervades
The heavens, and e'en the dog is scared, and waits
Beneath the table till the storm abates.

Then frosty days and chilling air are here
Bringing blue skies and brightness everywhere.
The earth is hard and crunchy underfoot.
And ice appears upon the nearby brook.

'Tis then we hope the roots of summer's heath
Are safe beneath the harsh and frosty breath.
While we await their entrance from the earth
We sleep and dream about the dawn of birth.

Rita J. Thompson

When You Are Depressed

When you are depressed and down,
And all roads seem...to close...
When you feel; you are among thorns
No one to behave like a fragrant rose?

When the sky looks so cloudy and dark,
And you feel helpless, and can't cope
Don't you please, then be discouraged
There is sunshine, there is hope!

Lift your soul, and heart, and spirit...
Look to heaven...go on your knees...
And believe in a helping; Higher power
In God, who is able...and oversees

Tell Him freely all your troubles...
Sincerely, for you're on friendly ground
And trust me...I know Him so well
His loving help will be around.

Don't ignore this help from heaven...
Nor even waver,...'cause help is real...
Soon you will see rays of sunshine
And I am sure, that thrilled you will feel!

John Ivan Jakovac Sr.

The Body

A twisted limb, a pallored face,
An acrid smell, an evil taste,
A mattress soaked with sinful grime,
A tight wound watch keeps pointless time,
One soul companion, Man's Best Friend,
Bears witness to his master's end,
And still beyond he will not leave,
In unknown ways begins to grieve.

No memories of errors made,
No hopes and dreams of better days,
No daughter with a goodbye kiss,
No mother with a final wish,
But just we guests, in unity,
We prise you from your dignity,
And through the cleansing Reaper's smoke,
Forgive us if we share a joke.

Gary Ritchie

Clown

What do you see when you look at me?
Am I all that you expected I'd be?
When things go wrong and you're feeling down,
do I cheer you up by playing the clown?
Yes, I go through life with a smile on my face
for I know there are times when a grin can erase
your cares, when I enter stage left, the fool;
Laughter, it's said, is to the jester's tool.

Now, how many times can you recall,
was that smile on my face not real at all.
Did you truly not know it was all a gaffe;
That a wounded soul hides behind a laugh?
When you cry, when you tell me of your heartache,
do I tell you how often I've felt mine break;
That sometimes the clown really feels dying?
Look closer then friend, you clown is crying.

Beverley A. Josephson

water

As a river pours its soul into the fresh ocean
All the waves of joy and drops of cheer
They come together to relax and abate
I want to pour myself into you
All my good times and memories of you
I want them to join together and calm
But all I do is thrash into you
Waves towering over me and I cannot swim
I have forgotten how to move with the water
How to breathe through the waves
And I lay lifeless at the bottom of the deep blue
Reaching towards a light as the water ripples overhead
I will never be.

Sara Infanti

"Nancy"

As little girls we shared our toys, our dreams and
All the treasures we could find
But all too soon our carefree childhood would
soon be left behind

Though life took us down separate paths
The bond remained so true
Never forgetting one another
My dearest friend was you

Then God called you home to be with Him
Where there'd be pain no more
Now another Angel's by His throne because
you opened Heavens door.

My cherished thoughts and memories keep you
ever near
And with the passing of time
God willing we'll be to-gether once more

Love - - - - - -
The friend you left behind

Judy Serson

Change Of Seasons

Autumn - the season when
    all the countryside takes on
        a glow of colour - gay, but sad
            with promise of inevitable change.

Much like the way
    we mortals live;
        an ever changing spectrum
            through the years.

With every minute's passing
    we grasp
        with funnel hands
            for memories to cherish,

Then fleetingly they
    sweep away - and leave
        within their wake
            an emptiness of life unlived.

Laura W. Fisher

The Circle Of The Seasons

As the leaves begin to fall, the wind whirls by,
All the colours of the earth, disappear and begin to die,
We see the flowers that were once beautiful and bright,
We feel the days become colder, the flowers fade into the night,
The days become so short, the nights come so fast,
The snow begins to fall, the fall becomes the past,
Through the chilling winter the darkness takes hold of the land,
In the stillness of the night, you feel the cold upon your hand,
The suns warmth caresses your face,
Suddenly you notice that Spring has taken its place,
The trees come alive with radiant colour green,
The scent of flowers evokes a reminiscent scene,
The flowers appear with a hue of colour that sets a summers glow,
With starry nights and lazy days, in our hearts we all know,
Another season arrives, but suddenly is gone,
The circle of the Seasons continues on and on.

Anne Marie Renaud

Dangerous Minds

As I look in the mirror and I see my reflection.
All that I see is a dangerous complexion
The rain has a shadow that falls on my face.
The shadow's of a tear, and each one in its place
to hold you and love you is easy to do.
Hoping and praying that we can get through.
Don't ever want to be left behind.
Scared and frightened of your dangerous mind.

I see you in my thoughts, each minute of day.
Stay in my arms forever, don't ever go away
I wish I could make you my bullet proof man.
I want to protect you but...I don't think I can.
I wish that I could but I don't have the power.
Yet! the power of love can pass through each hour.
If I had a reason to life, I would find...
that everyone has a dangerous mind.

Carmen Brown

The True Face of Justice

In a silent moment I pause to consider
All of my youthful idealism and wanton vigor.
There were so many visions of justice that I carried with me
Walking and toiling in faith, clinging to truth to set the captive free.

There was many a day I stood tall and strong
Fully anticipating that the journey would belong.
Awaiting that great moment when the day of reckoning would finally come
And end my weary journey on that narrow road home.

I fought the bureaucratic and influential
And I didn't back down to the strong-hold tactics of the
    upper-affluential
Never doubting that virtue would reign
And conquer the plaguing, deadly pain.

Now I sit in silence, a broken man,
Not understanding their insolence and partisan.
I spoke meekly, but they chose not to hear
I cried out in distress, but they only stopped to jeer.

My words were like the lilting music from a lute.
They listened and pondered and knew the truth
Yet they resolved to deny that such a thing could ever be
Once they realized that the words were emanating from me.

Judy Dunsworth

The One I Love

Even though the meeting was not from some book
all it took was just one look
I had to meet her, this I knew
the feeling in me was simply new
with eyes of hazel and a slight touch of green
an unforeseen beauty is what I mean.
Raised and nurtured from the olden ways
she knows what she wants, for this I'll stay
one small touch from her delicate soft hands
brings out the boy from inside this man
and the slightest kiss from her tender sweet lips
makes me wonder what I truly have missed.
She speaks to me like a true dear friend
and this I'll keep till the end
trust, honesty, respect we seem to share
no question about it, I really do care
she's natural, sweet, warm, and sincere
at times I miss her and wish she were near
our times together are precious and few
it's easy to see why I'm falling for you.

Rob Fiorido

Grandmother

I look out my window, I glance at the clouds
all I see is my dreamland ... my home to me,
I see the family seated at the dinner table...
eating your delicious roast and apple pie...

We all walk in your garden of yellow roses
springing into bloom,
when the sunlight hits their petals...
the rays bring joy and happiness to our family

You gave each and everyone of us your tender loving care
...........just like the petals on your roses...........

You taught us to be strong and stand up for what we believe in
You were always there to hold us through the bad times

You would put your baby soft hands on top of ours and say
... "I love you darlin'" ......

Michelle King

Ode; To The Howling Of Wolf

Eyes...
    agleam like ripened autumn corn
    or hot sun blasting splendor on late morn
Burn...
    from his wary face
    at odds now with all former passive trace
And howling out his restive-sounding tale
In eerie, wild, high-scaled cascading wail
    with throat thrust high, sharp-angled to the moon
    in strident voice as haunting as the loon
He stands...
    Defiant
    cloaked in thick, wind-ruffled furs
Fostering within me profound thrill
    whenever this moon ritual occurs.

Barbara Jean Hawkins

Destiny

Should I forget that we ever met
Adrift in a boat on life's waters afloat
Propelled by the force of destiny.

Should I forget that when we met
To you my lark I gave my heart
At the point of the sword of destiny.

Should I forget that we only met
Forever to part and to the break my heart
Torn apart by the hands of destiny.

Can I forget my ambition, my aim
O' Love of my youth, to you attain
Was condemned by the voice of destiny.

I cannot forget nor will I attempt
To forget that I lost my heart at the cost
Of my happiness, submitted to destiny.

Ray Simons

Tribute To A Witch

Dark and jagged rocks
add overalls and fluffy frocks
newt eyes and frog legs
chicken bones and billboard pegs
simmer and sizzle
Pterodactyl from an archaeologist's chisel
Neanderthal blood and marrow
mixed with the breath of Tutankhamen the pharaoh
stir in a clay vase and bury in the ground
twenty-one days thereafter swallow it down
nine months later
the return of the Magical Creator.

Tania John Caleekal

Looking At Sydney Harbour Bridge

Etched against a sapphire sky,
A lacy arc stands proud and high:
Crystal waves bejewelled with sun;
Soaring birds frolicking in fun.

Convicts, chained, sunk in bleak despair,
Gained hope and strength in this land fair.
And free men coming in their wake.
March bravely on for Freedom's sake.

May hearts and hope like bells do ring,
And every voice in faith does sing:
"Let Freedom reign upon this Shore.
And Peace and Plenty evermore!"

Margaret-Anne Tseng

The Potentate Of Applegate

The administrate and magistrate of tiny little Applegate
Activate a candidate to find a better potentate
The potentate's a reprobate sole purpose to intoxicate
Said reprobate does postulate his better side accentuate
With hopes that he'll regenerate he plans his name to vindicate
Instead those men who propagate do instigate a delegate
To associate with potentate his actions to investigate
Said delegate does interrogate and to his peers enunciate
On words that serve to irritate and views that seem to fluctuate
To abbreviate the potentate on a plan begins to meditate
To mitigate this conflagrat' his opponents he'll eradicate
To annihilate the administrate he turns him on the magistrate
In town hall they do congregate and wages they do confiscate
The candidate they motivate to congratulate the potentate
Who was able to invigorate a campaign though but a reprobate
This story serves to demonstrate indeed it serves to obligate
Each one of us to concentrate on a leader we can imitate
For new administrate and magistrate now endure this fickle advocate
The reprobate who's potentate of tiny little Applegate

Brenda Bottas

The Coloured Leaves

I saw them leave the mother tree
accompanied by a host of others
They danced and fluttered in the breeze
They played like sisters do with brothers.

Their dresses oh! How beautiful
Their gaiety new found
They twirled and flipped and floated
Until they reached the ground.

To lie and die beneath the snow
While winds blow fierce and cold
They all turn brown and fade away
The yellow red and gold.

Sometimes I think I'm like a leaf
Born to a special tree
Distinct in character and looks
There's no one just like me.

Please God, I pray, make me to be
A leaf that fits your plan,
Teach me to love to work to play
And be a friend to man.

Verna Callan

The Ships Above

The murm'ring whales play in the waves
Above the ships within their graves.
They frolic in the windblown spume
In God's aquatic living room.
They live off fish; we harvest them.
Are they not fish? Are we not men?
If they are beasts and we sublime
Why use harpoons? Why not use line?
And Captain Ahab wants to laugh
Within his watery cenotaph, while Moby Dick's whole family
Is ground up by our industry.
Who knows what crazed group of men
Might kill God's last Leviathan.
To never see a whale again, to see but ships, to see but men.

But what if God pulls in His line
Before that last whale's found,
And burns up all the ships at sea
And all men on their ground...

And leaves the whales within the waves
Above the ships within their graves?

H. Allan Armstrong

Wondering

I walk through this world and wonder,
About the wind, the rain, the thunder
And of the times that now are past,
And how long the earth will last.
I feel the pain of cut down trees,
The starving, the lonely, I hear their pleas.
The cries of the unborn, the old, the poor
And those who are dying, no hope for a cure.
I watch as the rich gain complete control,
And I tremble in fear for their very soul.
We've fallen from the knowledge that we once knew
And accepted the illusions around us as true.
It won't be long before it comes to pass
That there will be no food, no air, no grass.
All those on earth will wither and die.
The sad part is they won't know why.

Shirley Nelson

My Friend

I love to write poetry, especially the rhyming kind,
about a lot things that came to my mind.
There are many people who merit special praise
and I like to do it, in different Poetical ways.

One deserving praise, is God the great Creator,
who sent His only Son, to be the world's Saviour.
His love is beyond comprehension, in a world of sin
but if we invite Him, our hearts He'll enter in.

When we give Him first place, things work out somehow
so it's really important, to think about this now
We need not be afraid of what lies ahead,
just trust, let go and let Him instead.

We couldn't find a better Friend, to me He is true
and I hope, that you know Him too.
When feeling hurt and down, I tell Him all about it
then in His great love, He lifts me up in spirit.

The moral of this poem is very plain to see,
that if you are sad and lonely, you needn't be.
Let my dearest Friend, be your Friend too
then you'll have joy, peace, contentment and life anew.

Dorothy J. Parr

The Eyes Of A Woman

I looked into the eyes of a woman who was given a line.
A woman who had been hurt too many times.
This time the pain was more than she could bear.
To love a married man, filled her with fear.
I looked into the eyes of a woman,
   who fail for words so sweet.
It didn't take much time, to sweep
   her off her feet.
He bought her gifts, and he brought her flowers,
They went for walks, and talked for hours.
She fell for a man, who filled her with lies,
Than walked away, refusing to hear her cries.
He denied his loving her, and turned the other cheek.
While she lay alone too hurt to sleep.
I looked into the eyes of a woman who was all alone
Only to realize the eyes I was looking into were my own.

Marlene Nichol

A Wild Place

A wild place at evening-
A wash of western gold
Precedes a red magnificence,
A sunset cavern, staining half the sky,
That sinks and fades, dissolved in vesper grey.

The lucent world is gone;
There is a moon, new-sprung,
Which hides in velvet boughs
As dusk more sweet than any city knows
Comes deep, and deeper still, in wilderness
Where thrusting rocks bestride the loneliness land.

The silver crescent soars, and there are stars,
While short impatient hours repel the night:
The living spectrum turns, to cast in pearl
The hour when spinning earth uncloaks
A wild place at dawn.

Kathleen M. Haley

What Is The Significance Of The Poppy?

It's been some time since the world was at war
A time hated by both the rich and the poor
Where men of all ages unselfishly fought
For peace and love that could not be bought.

Men of all nations fought and died
And people with sadness watched and cried
The world at war was no pretty sight
With gunshots that rang throughout the night.

Soldiers strong and soldiers brave
Now most lie in unmarked graves.
They fought for freedom in a world of hate
As families watched and saw their fate.

Buried in fields where poppies thrive
Year after year they still survive
Proving to the world as the seasons shift
The quality of their precious gift.

So the next time you see a poppy bloom
Remember those who discovered doom
For the freedom they gave up with no expectations
A new world for us with new generations.

Richard Krim

Of Silhouettes And Shadows

The eagle
A tapestry of flight
sewing an arc into the sky
through it, touching it
A delicate masterpiece
hewn by a master carpenter
At night myriads twinkle their applause
Moon escorts the silhouette across the pebbled sky
stretching pinions heed to chimes in the smouldering wind
In time the shadows tattered wisps are cut out of the night
and pasted onto the scrolling hues of morning
waking the world from the sandman's lullabies
The breadth soars across the floor of heaven
brushing the sea of trees and mountain peaks
A crisp, dark shadow of lightning
gleaning life out of freedom
Then the eagle weaves into twilight
bidding the sun, return again
a giant glowing furnace
deep in the western sky

Kirk Bartha

No Colour

A flag of no colour is a coward's flag.
  A symbol of surrender and loss.
A bloodless face on a corpse so still.
  A nation's loss of will.

The paint is there, the canvas is bare.
  The palette is in the hand of the creator.
So simple it seems to create those dreams.
  No painting, no colour, no painter.

The fabric is cut, the needle is thread.
  The colours are all provided.
To blend and mingle seem so simple.
  No design, no colour, no weaver.

There is no time, the metal is molten.
  It must be shaped before it sets.
So easy to bend at the right time.
  No shape, no colour, no metal worker.

A generation has gone another has come.
  With all the colours therein.
To paint, to weave, to wrought.
  No painter, no weaver, no metal worker.

Robert Madhosingh

The Star

There, before my window I saw
a star, no normal star. 'Twas a special
star, 'twas a green star, it was as big
as a carriage pulled by horses.
I thought, thought hard dreaming about space.
When all of the sudden, the land
below the castle was full of green,
glowing green the special star came
through the latched window, approached
me, turned into an angel, "art thou going
to murder me." A soft sweet
reply whispered, no you are special.
The beautiful white angel started
fading, before she was gone
she said, "Remember you will
boldly go where no one has gone
before." The green lifted off the
damp grass, then a star fell
from the dark night sky.

Jarett Hughes

A Baby Is Born

In the still and quiet of the night,
A sound rings out to awaken the culling peace.
It's like a voice calling out to all around,
Praise God, a baby has been born.
This miracle that has always been,
Brings forth the fruit to be seen.
Another creation molded by God.
This human, this wonder, to be awed.
A bit of heaven, a bit of earth,
Worked divinely together to create this birth.
Know in truth, this wonderful "Child of Light,"
Has come to earth, to make things right.
So cherish forever this precious soul,
Let love, peace and harmony be your ultimate goal.

Shirley M. Fisher

The Smile

I am lucky for I have been given a smile which glows in my heart.
A smile which is full of mischief, laughter, and a world of love.
A smile that is true, trustworthy, and never deceiving.
A contagious smile, that can even lighten the heaviest of hearts.

If I could be granted but one wish;
It would be that the world could close their eyes and see this smile.
A smile which radiates a glow and warmth that replaces hate and fear,
with love and laughter.

I am lucky for I have been given this smile;
a gift of love.
All I have to do is close my eyes,
and I see this smile, which will live in my heart forever!

Leslie-Ann Reber

Alone

In the still of the night
A small and fragile creature passes through the streets.
There is only the sound of falling rain penetrating
The deathly eerie silence as she stands alone beneath the sky.

As she stands and ponders, the world becomes
a large envelope sealing and trapping her in.
She is alone, but treasures the thoughts
of her loved one who is far away.

As the rains begin to pound against her face,
the world around her becomes a rapidly spinning top.
She becomes frightened and desperate, reaching
out yet finds no one there.

The storm passes and again it is serene and calm.
Yet, she stands alone.

Karen Harty

Dreamer

Lonely times seeking a spiritual calm
A sensitive companion with whom to share
An intimate moment in which we remain
Understanding and loving each other's space.
Whispering memories, our link in life
Through all these trials we have cared
And our strength grows in blind faith

My days have been filled with the wonders of you.
For I have been touched by your gentle warm ways
Closer still, in the nights to come
Knowing the conflicts guiding our paths
Building a bridge of eternity
That will always be there,
No matter what roads we travel apart
Deep contentment lies here in my heart
Among priceless treasure of yesterday's past

Paula Sinclair

Deaths Gift

The incredible journey to unknown places;
a feeling of constant elation and freedom;
the ability to never want or need again;
a totally blind journey into the spectacular after-life.

For death brings nothing but dreams,
the ability to grasp what never could be reached in life.

Life is precious for those living
but is hell for those who have journeyed beyond the black
curtain, crossed the line that separates life and death.

For in death, all senses are lost
but are replaced with one sense far superior than any other,
that is the sense of life.

David MacEachern

The Dancer

This I love:

    To watch you your body
    a scissor cut of pulse
    your boots neat
    light and strong the flow
    of you like a
    mercury drum beating

This I desire:

    To savour this mating of heartbeat
    and stream
    to let it melt on my tongue like snowflakes

This I own:
    My longing like a polished hall waiting
    for dancers

Edgar H. Schmidt

Reflection

If time should cease to render me,
A place to stand, a place to be.
Would I not plead the quest for life,
And prove myself by toil, by strife.
The man who dares to question time,
And settles for less than is sublime,
Does he not scrape the edge of guilt
When faced with evils he has built?

Or, is he found blameless in the eyes of fate,
Because forces compelled him-innovate.
Moribund from whence I came,
I chose beauty and cherished the same.
He chose grandeur ensconced in foil,
And gained his wealth from humus soil.
Condom him! And let me be,
Or does that prove me guilty as he.

Mary Lou A. LeClair

Far Away

Far away, waiting for me
A place I know is my destiny
A place where peace and love rules all
A place where all mankind stands tall

Far beyond the morning sun
Far beyond the rays of light shun
The warmth and life which is given here
Is given by one who is always near

Far away one's dreams come true
For in this place fantasies drew
Which once was dreamt, is dreamt no more
Miracles made and memories stored

Far beyond the tumbling hills
The luscious greens of grass stand still
Instead of this, a bed of love
One made with only the fabrics from above

Far away, waiting for me
A place I know is my destiny
A place so glorious, cherished by everyone
A place, far away, called Heaven

Karen Munn

A Pioneer Mother

She was a little old lady, with shoulders bent
A pioneer who came west, and lived in a tent
Her family were grow, and moved far away,
Left her alone, an the old homestead to stay

She grew more feeble, and her mind wandered a bit
Spent hours in her rocker, with yarn to knit
One night when the weather was bitterly cold,
Our Father, called her into His fold.

In the darkness and cold she lay
There was no one to kneel and pray.
No minister to give a comforting word.
Just the howl of the wind could be heard.

As the shadow of death, came closing in
The rooms was lit with a halo sheen
A angel in shimmering white stood there
Gently touched the brow once so fair

Gently closed the tired eyes, once so bright
Folded the hands that had worked, from morning to night
Whispered so softly, you are no longer alone
The Father, has sent me, to take you Home.

Margaret North

Vanity Fair

What is it in a woman that creates a need to be
A person other than herself, for all the world to see?
A major part of every day spent looking in the mirror,
And spending more for pantyhose just because they're sheerer.
False fingernails and lashes, wigs and padded bras;
And even phony beauty marks...all for a good cause.
Now they make contact lenses to change her shade of eyes,
If you ask her hairdresser all you'll get is lies.
A girdle holds in everything a woman shouldn't have there;
Bathing suits allow a tan in places you can't see where.
Putting on her face can be a serious operation, for
Nothing else takes so much time as make-up application,
She'll buy her shoes a size too small, so her feet won't look as big.
In public, she'll eat daintily... never like a pig.
Her aim in life? To look her best, no matter where or when;
No matter how much time it takes, or how much she must spend.
She'll have all that is needed to change her total look,
And what she doesn't know she can find out from beauty books.
So when you see a woman, give your eyes a feast
But keep in mind the beauty might really be a beast!

Myrna L. Blumberg

Spirit Caller

Darkness falls over the lake
A murky fog blankets the crystal waters
The luminescent moon and stars
Awakens the black sky
giving as eerie light to every rippling wave.
In the thick of the fog
A figure appears.
A loon whose beauty is as intoxicating
As its voice
Out of the stillness of the night
Comes a ghostly, echoing sound
a vibration that can awaken spirits
The loon is the spirit caller.
Every call is said
To bring all spirits of nature alive.
To set them free
Through the night and day
The loon will sing her song,
Until all of Mother Earth's children
Are at peace.

Lisa Anne Mostowy

Fireside

Sitting in front of a fire burning bright
A lovely way to spend the night
Time to relax, time to reflect
Time to think.

So many things can be seen
It's somewhat like a dream
Watching the leaping amber flames
Cuddled in a favorite chair.

Crackling, crackling in a darkened room
Imaginations can run wild
Flames making odd shapes on the walls
Thinking of things long forgotten

One should take more time
To enjoy the ordinary things
Like a shimmering, warm glowing fire
And all the pleasures it can bring.

It's so very important
To take time with family and friends
Because before we know it
It all comes to an end.

Elizabeth Hale

Broken Promise

Crying within, the man is humbled by what has transpired:
A love which healed him so, to his bewilderment, has expired.
Once again a significant other has departed
leaving the man to dwell in sorrow, broken-hearted.

He ponders the three words he passionately spoke of
when asked by her what he was thinking of.
Sadly the man realizes that the words he uttered that day
are what caused the one he so dearly cherished to run away.

"I love you...But every time I speak these words,
   they all tend to run away ."
Approaching and embracing him she whispers, "I will not go astray."
Comforted at long last, he took her reply to heart...
Finally assured by a love that she would never depart.

But what anguishes the man is what she promised him
and the way she responded in the most caring mannerism
after being told of his fears..
Holding him and soothing him, kissing him...wiping away his tears.

Weeping in the dark, the man repeats that promise she had once made
and reminds her of the things she had said.
But she is unable to hear him, she has already departed
leaving the man to dwell in sorrow, broken-hearted.

Garry D. Ladobruk

Come Walk With Me

Come walk with me to a place that others cannot see,
A living and vibrant place, a place that will always be.
This place that we are going to is not so far away,
This place is always available, you can even go today.

Come walk with me through a place that others cannot see.
A place though very old is young if you want it to be.
This place is filled with treasures that all belong to you.
This place is beautiful and spacious as the sky is blue.

Come walk with me to this place for a while we can abide,
Among all the wonderful things that are forever by our side,
This place will release us from this thing we call time,
Though we cannot stay it will always be yours and it's mine.

Come walk with me through a place that others cannot see.
For it is the very heart and soul of you and of me.
If this place seems strange and it is hard for you to see,
Come walk with me...hold my hand...as we go to a place called memories.

Kathy Zekveld

Through The Ages

So long ago, stood side by side
A handsome groom and blushing bride,
Whose hands together they will hold
And hoping prayer for the future untold.

For they travel, this road of life
With a sacred vow of husband and wife,
Together they have watched their children grown
And then had children of their own.

Good friends to some they may be
But loving grandparents they are to me,
They gave me something that I now share
The gift of love, generosity and care.

And as I grow up I begin to see
The love they offer unconditionally,
And grateful always I shall remain
And someday may return the same.

And now still stood their side by side
The handsome groom and blushing bride,
A living example they portray
That true love never fades away.

Melissa Seifert

Untitled

A sparkle of light that opens your mind
A gentle touch that is warm and kind

A soft spoken voice tells right from wrong
Lulled to sleep with tenderness and song

Exploring the world, learning to crawl
Brought to your feet, standing tall

Discovering life, the one you live
That to take is selfish and to love is to give

Out in the world first seems strange
But experience provides a means to arrange

There is fear that wells up from inside
But strength and confidence must abide

A twist of fate turns faith into query
Let hope guide us when this makes us weary

Life is like a sunny day
And with day, there is night

And with night, there is morning
And in our mourning, there is light.

Ivan Clough

Friends

He walked along the road of life,
A friendless man was he.
Until he met a worthless tramp
Who bade him home to tea.

They sat and drank, and laughed and talked
About the way life bends.
Before the sun set late that eve,
The two became good friends.

He walked along the road of life,
A friendless man was he.
A worthless tramp became his friend,
A better man he'll be.

Linda Rowe Belak

Magic Love

Love is a feeling, a feeling so real,
A feeling that no one could ever steal.
You're above the world, high on a cloud,
You want to tell your sweetheart, scream it out loud.
There are no secrets, nothing's a surprise,
When he comes around there's a sparkle in your eyes.
His smile so perfect, and oh so bright,
It shines like the moon and lights up the night.
Love is magic, there are no strings,
And when you're in love it's the most wonderful thing.

Tahnya Parachuk

View From High Rise Window

The trees reach up tall and straight
A deep and verdant green.
The river winds all shade and light
Slightly serpentine.
The hills shrouded deep in mist
Reach trembling to the sky.
The crows lift strident voices
Wake up world here am I.
The traffic whishes up and down the street
Swift flashes of color bright.
Like toys pushed by impatient hands
Trying to beat the light.
Houses like tiny boxes
Peek out among the trees
Lawns spread with doll house furniture
And flowers can be seen.
Gardens in perfect squares
With neat and tiny rows
Tended by miniature beings
Laboring - impatient to see it grow

Shirley Hyderman

A Friend

Amidst the waves of melting snow
A breathless seed begins to grow
From blankets of clouds so vast and dim
A gleam of light protrudes within
Then engulfed by the elders so clearly forlorn
A calf, to the dying herd, is born
And so as nature carves its path
Our fellow man cries out with wrath
For his barren life, so frigid, alone
To the millions of stars he has never known
When suddenly the moon enhances the sun
And the rivers half wildly begin to run
As the glories of nature, to earth's needs do bend
Man reaps the ultimate pleasure, a friend
For one who can see nature's beauties unbound
Through the eyes of another, they then
hear the sound
Of an unspoken bondage that lingers within
A space that can only be filled by a friend

Brenda Deley Baillargeon

186

The Gentleman's Hello

When I woke up to face the morning light, everything looked so gray;
The clouds looked dark and haunting, and there wasn't a sunshine's ray.
The branches on trees were all bent down, and the birds seemed unable
   to sing,
Why, even the beautiful sound of the churchbells were missing the life
   in their ring!

I was determined everything would go wrong today, and even a little more,
So it wasn't surprising when my toast burned, and my orange juice fell
   on the floor.
I was off to work in a huff and a puff, wishing today would fly.
When an elderly gent with a smile on his face, gave me a cheery "Hi!"

And then, as I listened, I was sure that I heard a little bird sing,
And the church bells sounded so beautiful, with their strong and
   vibrant ring.
As I lifted my eyes toward the heavens, there wasn't a cloud in the way,
But a lovely shining light, in the form of a sunshine's ray.

Then, in spite of myself, I had to smile or at least give an overly large grin,
For I realized in my selfish way, what a terrible day this could have been.
"It seems to me the world might be a better place," I said to myself
   with a sigh,
If there were more old gents on a cloudy day, to give you that
   special, cheery "Hi!"

Karen Jewell

The Promise Of Love

Mama always said,
"Don't make promises you can't keep."
So without your love
These words I cannot speak.

But if I could, such love you would feel
Bound more tightly, more tightly than steel.
Fired more accurately than Cupid could point.
Blessed more sweetly than the Gods could anoint.
Fought for more gallantly than a knight's chivalrous deed.
Brought to life more miraculously than a child from a seed.
Tended more carefully than a farmer sows his field.
Needed more preciously than the air we must breathe.
Felt more frequently than the pounding of my heart.
Enjoyed everlastingly like the love from which we start.

Mama always said,
"Don't make promise you can't keep."
So without your love
These words I cannot speak.

But if I could...

John William Fister

A Day In My Life

Of childhood past, remembered in glee,
Oh! Wouldn't it be nice to relive thee?
Watching my children roll in some hay
Set my memory on instant replay
Back to that magical old yard I went
to relive a memorable childhood event.
Sitting under a guava tree,
all too happy and quite carefree
I observed an eclipse
at the tender age of six
The sky was flame red
horrible thoughts came to my head
Thinking the world was coming to an end
Almost caused me to go around the bend
Up the tree I climbed to better the view
Perched on a limb and stared at that scarlet hue
On the way down, my neck got caught
I struggled to get free, like a fluttering moth
That day I gave everyone such a fright
Uncle chopped the tree down with all his might.

Aneela Hamid Taylor

The End Of It

It seemed so dreary, so pointless,
One more day, no dollar, all in distress.
To be what I am is of little matter.
I long to just be with, just no chatter,
Because I am is why, life is so solitaire,
Alone, never learning life's social flair.
This is where I sit never to be around,
Woman, child, maybe a dog for simple sound.
My crime is one of despair and depression,
The pair happen daily in rapid succession.
Of this I know, it is not a purposeful act.
Yet one where one cuts no slack.
So here we go again, down paths of pain.
Will I feel the light ever touch me again?

Seth Wertz

Father Tom Peyton Has Found The Bell

*Dedicated to Father Thomas Joseph Peyton for his 20th Anniversary;
April 27, 1994; Sacred Heart Parish, Savannah, Georgia*
Ding! Dong! Dell!
Father Tom Peyton has found the bell.

Climbing up to the steeple on the ladder,
He was determined, so it did not matter.

If that bell could talk at all,
Imagine it saying, "Watch your step, Father Tom, Please don't fall".

Birds made a haven in the steeple,
Now, it is clean out for the maintenance people.

With all his humor, sincerity and vim,
We honor and pray from Him.

We hope Father Tom's kidney stones have gone to rest,
So when he pulls the rope of the bell, he will not have stress.

Although Father Tom is tall and slim,
He is like a tree with reaching out limbs.

As the bell tolls around the community, it has a message to tell,
"Father Tom Peyton has found the bell."

Lois Russell

Eternity

U
took
my hand
in your hand
We walked together
for many miles we saw
the beginning of no man's
land We searched for eternity
on the nile You taught me about
the ultimate universe Together we
would go off to another world Perhaps
take a turn in reverse Or just remain here
on the planet earth You listened to me in pain
Helped me struggle through the walks of life Kept
me from being vain Told me that life's not sugar or
spice For you to find yourself, you said you must ride
high and steer low Life's greatest treasures will soon be
ahead For you and I only know that we have been together somewhere, sometime before But for now You are my gift and I am yours
Until we meet again and travel further in another place, another time.

Leslie Duttenhofer

"Thoughts Of You"

Of all things good or bad
You're the best of what I've had.
Of all the things happy or sad
You're the happiest of all lads.

You're the icing on my cake
My dessert of desserts.
You're the ice cream in my shake
You're the best of what I make.

You're the blood running in my veins
You are the life that keeps me living
The oxygen that feeds my brain
You are what keeps me sane.

Our life is finely sealed
Because you are you.
I love you still
My life you will always fill.

Ann M. Clancy

The Birds

Powerful,
Your wings beat the air,
The force creates a gentle breeze
Where there is none.
Quietly,
You soar through the skies.
The image of you inspires awe
And the dream of flight.
Swiftly,
You dive at your prey.
Your strength frightens people
And captivates them.
Fiercely,
You rip the flesh of your meal.
It repulses some
Yet mesmerizes me.
Slowly,
You return to the air.
The world stares in admiration
And I am among them.

Julia Wantland

A Friend

I need not understand
You will always be there
To be a sister to me
As I need you to be
To understand me
With no contradiction or
ridiculing, to be
I need not understand
You will always be at
hand
To be there to listen
Whatever may be my reason

Crissy Mae Kibbons

"Oh The Honeymoon Is Over"

Oh the honeymoon is over
you are no rover

Mother nature is like that
you get no pat on the back

You do not have to rave
you will be put in a grave.

Oh the honeymoon is over.

Francis DeGruy

My Peppi

When I first saw you I knew
you were the one for me.
Eight years to be the
sunshine in my day,
my star by night,
if you had your way.

When sorrow touched and I
would cry,
I knew you understood,
For I could see the comfort
in your eye,
if only you could.

You were once lost,
I vowed to find you
long before the frost.

My heart is now sad,
my eyes they weep,
beneath earth's crust
my Peppi sleeps.

Betty Lee

Midst

You were my father
You were supposed to be there
You weren't

How was I to know
How was I supposed to learn
Without you

Am I missing something
What you forgot to give me
I earned on my own

I tried to remember you
I tried to care
But I got lost in the midst

That's behind me
I made it through somehow
Some days I doubt myself
Some days I don't

Jean Louise Codianni

Bird On A Wing

Bird on a wing
You touch the heavens
Then like an Angel you descend
Such beauty and innocence
No other so graceful
Yet none are so subject to the wind

The freedom you possess
Your carefree style
Beware, the thunder calls
Heavy rains will come
Darkness will fill the skies
No one can catch you when you fall

Bird on a wing
So hard to get close to
But never too far away
Travelled far and wide
With no companion
I hope to join you there some day

Dan Kalena

Christmas Prayer

Oh, Lord, we adore your Holy name;
You taught us how to give,
    Lights of love -
    Carols of praise -
Life you gave that we might live.

Lord, bless our Christmas Season
And fill our hearts with love,
    As we share -
    Your ceaseless care -
Abundant blessings from above.

Darlene B. Cox

"A Piece Of Heaven"

Heaven above is no match
You see for the wonder
that stands in front of me.
Gaggles of backyard memories
abound, I can see my kin all around.
Grandma, grandpa, mom and dad,
everyone is happy no one is sad.
Dogs chasing cats, cats chasing
dogs around the old maple
through the orchard by the "Mog"
Some are still here,
Some now gone
Memories forever is my heart's song.
Heaven above is no match
you see. For I have a piece
of heaven right here with me.

Donna L. Lobdell-Monroe

As One

How can you love someone
You hardly know?
When you can see their heart
When you can read their soul

Your silence speaks volumes
Of the weaknesses you hide
Your life flashes before me
When I look into your eyes

Give me your heart
Put your trust in me
Allow me to love you
To set you free

Take my hand
Take shelter in my love
'Cause two wounded hearts
Beat best as one...

Christina R. Montgomery

A Friend's Farewell

How can one say, "Good-bye"?
With lump in throat, tear in eye?

With sadden words tripping off the lip?
Or wise cracks from off the hip?

I know not how to do these well.
Sorrow within myself does swell

But knowing friends will always be
The only phrase to you from me.

"See you later and take care.
We'll meet again, sometime, somewhere."

James W. Arnold

188

Shame On You

Shame on you!
  You did not to
    What love required.
    Fired, fired

Will you be
  from heaven's shore. You'll see.
    In this land
      your hand, your hand

Turned the killer loose.
  Now your goose
    has been cooked.
    Overlooked

The evidence.
  You will not advance
    to a higher plain.
      "Life is not a game",

Say the Lord.
  Hear His word
    from on High!
      "You will fry.!

Gerda A. Saul

Silent Invader

  Something's coming!
You can't hide!
It's to be feared
like a flooding tide!

  Run if you can,
or be chained down!
For if you're trapped
you will be bound!

  Struggle hard!
Resist fast!
If you don't breathe hard
you will breathe your last!

  It's coming faster!
It's not kind!
You see, it will
invade your mind!

  If you're strong
you might abide!
You're fighting against
your darker side!!

Corina M. Cook

Christmas

I always like Christmas best
You can see your relatives
eat turkey dinner
enjoy presents
and trees
and cookies
lots of fun
also stockings
and Santa Claus
at the mall
and hear the
Christmas songs
everywhere
at the church
we celebrate Jesus Christ
being born on
Christmas Day by
the Virgin Mary in a manger
in Bethlehem.

Alyson Weaver

Love At Last

My love at last I've found you
You are my sweetest dream
You are the one I've searched for
You've made my life supreme.

I prayed that I would find you
And hold you close my dear
I can't believe you love me
Please keep me ever near.

Whisper to me sweet things
Of love and happiness
And make me one true promise
That you'll never love me less.

At last we're here together
At last we've found true love
You're mine to hold forever
I know there is a heaven
  and God is up above....

Alice D. Stermer

Again

Tomorrow it shines
yesterday it wept.
The green land,
the charred life
separates from the stained
glues to the pure.
Soft and young it brings
wealth and joy.
Temporary songs
to sing today
gone tomorrow, forgotten.
Another day passed,
another life born,
brought forth, taken forever.
Wondering, contemplating.
Is it next? The answer is not said
but whispered, faintly
unheard by the wind, uncared for
lost in the glory of hope,
left only to your memory.

Alexandra Grivsky

Good Bye Mother (A Brief Pantoum)

Good bye Mother I must go.
Yes, your love - this I know,
But to begin my life...I must
So from your heart please trust!

Yes, your love, this I know,
I'm in my summer and still grow,
So from your heart please trust;
For seeking life is what I lust!

I'm in my summer and still grow,
Where the winds take me, I will go.
For seeking life is what I lust!
Carpe diem, "In God We Trust!!"

Where the winds take me, I will go,
So from your heart please trust.
Yes, your love - this I know,
But like a flower in summer, I must grow!

Geri Cribbs

"Captured Sunshine"

Captured sunshine, obscured by clouds,
yearns to break free.
Feel the power, and the warmth,
but you cannot see.
The way I feel, I cannot wait,
but you are afraid.
The cloud is strong, and hard to break,
the light just starts to fade.
Listen to me, remember this,
because there is no doubt.
Inside of you, there is a spark,
that no one can put out.
The love for me, I know is there,
I hope that it is true.
Nothing more, to do or say,
except for "I LOVE YOU!"

John Kroeber

Bless This Home

Alley near 4th and Main
Ya know jus' down the street
Behin' that fancy new church
Found a new box.

It's a big son of a gun
Trash man missed it
Grabbed it and ran
To 4th near the streetlight.

Packed my stuff in it
Room to spare
It's warm - heavy duty kind
Streetlight can't get in.

God bless the church
For leavin' that box
Mansion on 4th Street
God bless this home.

Ginny Spencer

Man

The human man - a wonderfully
  wrought being
Rarely thinks of whence he came.
I marvel at the concept of it all -
Each intricate part in perfection tuned.
To function in perfect harmony
Starting of comparatively nothingness
And at each stage within its
  mother's womb,
Nestled in warmth and security
Growing into God's plan -
For no other could fathom
  or duplicate
The delicate perfection
That is the human man.

Bernice R. Kuhn

The Sea

I see a ship across the sea from
Where I dare to stand.
I often feel the need to flee,
And yet, I never can.
The time has come for me to leave.

I feel the sand beneath my feet.
Oh, what a welcome sight it is
To stand among a sea of weeds,
And feel this lovely breeze
Within me.

Inez Farmer

Forever

If every word I said
Would make you laugh
I'd speak forever

If every tear I shed
Would be for you
I'd cry forever

If every step I took
Would bring me closer to you
We'd be together

If we were together
'Till the day we die
We'd live forever

All is said is true
I'd do it all for you
If you'd be at my side

Forever.

Jesus Delatorre

Freedom

My heart
would cross
a darkened sea
on paths of moon gold
stretching far
beyond the shadow
of a caged bird
whose earthbound dirge
beats on—
her weary song
confined to notes
no longer free
to rise toward Heaven
on wings,
but held to earth
by slender threads
perceived as rules,
not written
by the hand of God.

Barbara Frank

Race

   What is race? Just another
word for separation. Who expects
to cope with anyone, being
separated from others?
   What is race? another
worldly division. Are we not all
human beings trying to
accomplish life? It keeps us
away causing prejudice.
   What is prejudice? Another
word for hatred. Keeping as away
from each other, hating each
other for the decades to come.
   Why do the whites hate
the hispanics? why do the blacks
hate the whites? why do the
Hispanics hate the Asians?,
Because the prejudice of
today's society. That is the
separation we call race.

Jennifer Shaver

Beautiful Love

A beautiful love fills my heart,
   Wonderful love,
And a wonderful smile, touched my heart,
   Smile at me always,
Touch my heart always.

Franklin J. Warren

"Gazing Back"

Nineteen hundred sixty three,
wondered why some weren't free.
In the school bus we would ride,
in one part of town tried to hide.
Passing stops where others waited,
throwing rocks, like us they hated.
Gazing back, eyes would cry,
even then, I knew why.
Rode back home on a city bus,
line on the floor, them from us.
One old woman sitting near,
smiled friendly, ate a pear.
She got off, out the back door,
in her hood folk were poor.
Gazing back, eyes would cry,
even now, I know why.

Jack Overfield

To Die Alone

No one should die alone
Without their love ones
By their side.

Everyone needs to feel loved,
Even if it's just to hold their hand.
Especially when death is
Knocking on their door.

You see it in their face,
You see it in their body,
Death creeps slowly
Like a dark, black shadow.

You tell them that it's okay,
That it will be alright,
But is it really?

You ask are you in pain?
Do you feel cold?
The blank stare is your only response.

So if I'm dying,
Please hold my hand,
For I don't want to die alone.

Brenda Lee Wark

My One Night Stand

The way that you left me,
Without any goodbyes,
A touch, or soft kind words,
Has made me feel hopeless.
In your eyes, I see now,
I was just like the dirt
With no value at all.

I guess you proved to me:
How unwise I can be;
That a man will use you;
Leave you when you are blue,
As he makes others glad.
The next time he comes back
He will be seeing red.

April Ferry

Sandy Beaches

I love the sandy beach,
with water just within
my reach.

I love the beach calm.
Blue water, the way
the salt just floats around.

Jeniece Bridgforth

"A Childhood Reflection"

   Scattered planks underneath
with varied hues of lime
colored moss growing plankton;
Barnacles firmly gripping on
the half shell ostentatiously
   defying the grime;

   Feeling the sizzling sensation
of the noon swelter —
like a fowl dancing frenetically
on a hot plate;

   Grazing the gauntlet-flanked
strings weighted with bait, immersed
to coax the Blue Bays—and
enjoying the mystery of the
tug; - Yanked-in;

   Polluted habitat contamination adjoining
sluffing mates peering into the milieu of murk
infighting tolerance with a tempered jerk
   — If you believe in reincarnation
   don't come back as a crab!!

David Pritchett Sr.

Stars On Earth

So many stars fill the sky,
With their beauty and love.
We wonder at their light
How it never fades away.
Of all the stars in the sky,
They all are bright.

Yet there are billions on earth,
Only a few succeed to be stars.
Just a few show their love.
Many fall into traps,
Without light or hope.
But only a few have the courage
To shine like the stars above.

Asma Syed

The Novice

Snow falling ever so slight,
   with the smallest of breeze.
What a great sight,
   gliding over these trees.

Up high in the air,
   seeing everywhere.
Soon we will be there,
   as we ride this chair.

Skies on my feet,
   poles in my hand.
Life can be sweet,
   and certainly grand.

As we near the top,
   I prepare to hop.
Instead I drop,
   Kerplop.

Christopher J. Coco

If You Were Mine

Your glance being anticipated
With smile assiduously hunted;
You drift through desolate mind;
YOU ARE ALL I'VE EVER WANTED.

Your eyes needing love,
And heart craving a beat,
A day without you
Is a lifetime of defeat.

With promises luridly existing
Through integral essence;
Your life cannot be complete
Without my presence.

I lust your every thought,
Your every word, your every breath,
When I seize them all,
My soul will have conquered DEATH.

The malediction of endless dream
Arrests the seconds of time;
Gives me an extra minute
To think: If You Were Mine.

Emily Mae Erstine

Reaching

When darkness falls
with orange and blues,

When quiet sounds float
through your soul,

I raise my hand
to reach.

I reach with all
my heart.
My emptiness grips
and screams.

Fill my soul,
Fill my life,
Fill me.

Darkness now is
black but calm.

I have reached
until I can reach no more.

Cindy Carter

What If Man Could Live Forever?

What if man could live forever
With no fear of death atone.
What if man could live forever
And could call his life his own.

What if man could live forever
And he never would grow old.
What if man could live forever
With no claim upon his soul.

What if man could live forever
With no regard for time or tide
In a life with no tomorrow
With no need for God, as guide.

What if man could live forever
Would you make the choice to live,
Or would you leave this magic potion
And your share to others give?

Jewel Ambrose

It's Not Easy

I walk down the halls
   with my head down.
I'm not popular and
   not so smart.
But I study really hard
   to get good grades.
My friends and I
   like to study a lot.
They all seem so smart.
I'm probably just average.
People think I'm perfect.
I'm not.
Maybe it's because I hang out
   with smart, perfect people.
Maybe.
Now I have to live up to those standards.
They expect too much of me.
No one understands.
It's just not that easy.

Christina Chung

Seeing The Fall

As I walk through the fields
with my eyes aiming at the sky
like a telescope,
I fall to the ground
with my shoe regrettably untied.
I get up,
brush off,
and head for home
for a band aid
and some sweet, pumpkin pie.

Ben Annunziato

The Sounds Of Music

The soaring notes of a violin
With its highs and lows
And lyrical beat.

The rhythm
That makes the body
Sway and throb
To the pulsing beat of a drum.

A heart that pounds
To the memory of loves.
And tears that come to the eyes.

A song that makes feet tap,
Of special times
And friendships shared.
Of memories that never die.

The soaring sounds of music,
The universal language
Of love and dreams and hope
How sweet and poignant they are.

Eleanor Kerness

Hope

In a world such as this filled
with drugs, crime, racism and
hate,
I hear a cry pierce the night,
It is a cry for peace
It is a plea for a better world
it is hope.

Dawn Marie Cudak

Two Fish In The Desert

Two fish in the desert
with hopes to survive
swimming the waters
searching for life

Their births days apart
but, of opposite sex
placed in this desert
to face the ultimate test

In site of each other
yet, unable to touch
their voices cry out
their desires, and wants

The male swears an oath
of blood, with a knife
to be the other's protector
and guardian, for life

Two fish in the desert
each, fighting for life
one needs the other
one needs to survive

Bradley S. Hartliep

Nothing Compares To You

The morning sun shining bright
   with golden rays from up above
Pales in all its radiant glory
   To the beauty of you my love

The stars in all their magnificence
   can grant a wish they say
But the magic you give to me
   Fills my every night and day

A rainbow with its many colors
   holds gold at the end 'tis true
But all the gold in their world
   can't compare to a smile from you

The earth in all its majesty
   with flowers and trees all around
cannot compare to your greatness
   or this love for you I've found

So for you my love I am thankful
   and for all to me you give
You have filled my life with love
and by your side I'll forever live

Gary K. Farlow

Memory Bliss

You make me feel so special
   when we're together
But...
Have I been walking
   in sadness,
Staring into the dark
   and lonely unknown?
When I say that
   I love you...
I want you to believe me
   without a doubt in
your heart.
When I feel lonely and
   upset, I want to know
that you will be there,
   so we can walk that
crooked road together,
   hand in hand.

Jennifer Groszewski

191

The Family Tree

Our family tree stands tall and proud,
With branches reaching wide,
To gather in the warmth of God's sun
And shelter those who reside.

With roots firmly embedded
In foundation of faith and love,
The strength of generations
Supports each branch above.

As each new branch is added,
And each new twig is born,
The rustle of leaves whispers from all
"We'll keep you safe and warm"

When life's storms may stir our leaves,
Our branches shake and bend,
We'll weather it all together,
And be stronger in the end.

So, wherever life's journey takes you,
No matter where you may be,
There's always a place of honor for you
Here on our "family tree."

Janice Sweeney LaPorte

Spring And Summer

Nature has smiled upon us again
With blossoms of red, white and pink,
With the mystery and beauty of it all
It should make us stop and think.

The grass and many of the trees
Are taking on their coat of green,
With this and many early flowers
Just adds more beauty to the scene.

As spring gradually goes into summer
And the children are out of school,
There'll be vacations and times of fun
At picnic grounds and swimming pools.

The season of spring and summer
Is a joyous time to live,
We can enjoy the things of nature
And give thanks to one who gives.

Audrey B. Gilliam

Here And There

When heat of summer blends
With autumn's gentle breeze,
My car is wont to take me
Wherever I would please.

Time was when kith and kin
Provided me with fare,
But memories remind me
I'm better here than there.

My cousin is a genial host,
Her meals beyond compare,
But other than her sumptuous board
I'm better here than there.

My classmates are in nursing homes
Receiving loving care,
But then again, it all boils down,
I'm better here than there.

And when I've reached those Pearly Gates,
In answer to my prayer,
You know I will look down and say,
"I'm better here than there".

Bernice Nash Crawford

Say No Drugs

A joint in your mouth
Will ruin the brain.
Wine in your system
Will do the same.
Snortin' that coke
Can kill you, too.
You better listen to
What I am telling you.

Drugs ain't cool
At all my friend.
Saying no to drugs
Is when you win.
Don't be like other kids
And be a fool.
Cause drugs, my friend
Just ain't cool.

Greg L. Cooper

Wilderness Requiem

With the thought of what was
will never be
the intrusion kept growing,
but nothing gained.
Days pass
and the land yet forgotten.
A scarred forest
is all that's left.
The life and beauty it holds
is thrown away.
An enchanted land
dispensed at man's will.
The thought wasn't much,
but of silence and death.
Engulfing the wild parts
which lay
cold and still.

Dorcus Cudney

Beautiful Day

It's such a beautiful day
Why inside you want to stay?
The Sun has come, and chased the rain.
Why in there you still remain?
Inside is not the place to be.
Come out,
You can let your spirit free.
All the gray clouds have passed away.
So come
Let's enjoy this beautiful day.
The Sun is shining.
The skies are blue.
Even the birds are singing too.
That's why to you,
I want to shout.
Don't stay inside,
Come on out.

Delores Webb

Ode To A Butterfly

Oh butterfly, butterfly,
Why do you flutter by?
Across the sky,
Across the field,
And across my windshield?

Beverly Ryder

Friends

If we are just good Friends
why do I feel this way
about you.

If we are just good Friends
why can't I live without
you.

If we are just good Friends
and I wonder where you are
when you are not home at night,
I get so upset.

If we are just good Friends
I should not feel like this,
wondering whom the woman is
that you kiss.

If we are just good Friends
and that's all we'll ever be,
I hope this feeling
that I have for you will
Painlessly leave me.

Erika Olson

Like A Mother

There's a woman in my life,
Whose always there for me.
You would think she was my mother,
But she isn't, now you see.

I enjoy going to see her,
To share with her my life.
The good, the bad, the joys, the sad
And all the world's strife.

When things go bad within my life,
There is trouble or some strife,
She lends a hand, an ear, a heart
And brings sunshine to my life.

But when I'm very happy
And news for me is good,
She's always happy for me,
Like a real mother should.

She may not of been my mother
When my life on earth did start.
But she really is a mother
In the bottom of my heart.

Charlotte Legate

The Little Shepherd Boy

When first I saw that shining star
Whom shepherds saw from near and far
I knew so deep within my heart
That I would play a special part.

So to the stable I made my way
To see the Christ Child where he lay
His mother was so dear and sweet
And precious gifts lay at His feet.

I saw and looked upon the Child
So tiny sweet, so meek and mild
The wonder of it all was new
A gift from God for me and you.

I bid good wishes to them all
And went my way as I recall
To spread the word both near and far
About the Babe and shining star.

Carolyn Vanderhoef

Someone Else

I hear a giggle behind closed doors.
Who is it I wonder?
A voice I do not recognize.
Suddenly, I hear your voice, my love.
I wonder what is going on.
I do not want to believe
You'd ever hurt me.

I put my ear against the door.
I hear the door creak open;
I look inside, only to see you holding

Someone else in your arms.
I see you caressing her,
The way you caress me.
I close my eyes praying,
This is only a dream.
I open my eyes in hope,
But...how awful to see you
Kissing her the way you kiss me.
I wonder to myself what have I
done to make you seek someone else?

Jenny L. Gall

Untitled

There was a President named Bill
who had a wife named Hillary
They had a family tree
with only three
His wife said dear
and whispered in his ear
So they did have twin
and the election he did win
His rival named Dole
ever so much did boil

Boyd Van Horne

I Stood Alone

I stood alone that moon-lit night
White shadows danced along the shore
And teardrops fell, reflecting like
The silver stars at heavens door...

The gentle waves caressed my feet
And washed upon the waiting sands
The silent screams that echoed deep
Could not be smothered with my hands...

I stared beyond the endless sea
While numbness filled my broken heart
And sank into each memory
That stretched itself across the dark...

The winds were cool against my face
As ghostly whispers high above
Dissolved me in a dreams embrace
That hungered for a distant love...

I stood there 'til the break of day
And waited for my tears to dry
Then, slowly, as I turned away
I hung my head and said goodbye.

Helen Dodge

Our Charles

Charles went on ahead tonight
We buried him under the trees
His coal black body will nourish
These snow white birch
Our diminished world goes on.

Judson W. Holmes Sr.

Reflections On The Black

Black is not always black
White is not always white
There are sometimes only shades of grey
If you look closely it's not quite
Purely black or purely white

This is not how it should be
Between you and me

What is the difference what is without
When we're the same within
We hurt, we cry, we feel pain
How we are inside has nothing to do
With the color of our skin

And I repeat again and again
Black is not always black
White is not always white
You feel hurt, I feel pain
Together we can blend the grey
Our dreams are the same
And we'll make it.....

Together.

Judy Kay Hart

Desert Whispers

The desert calls...
whispers of ancient voices
riding the wind

The mystery of life full
in its power to compel you
to imbibe of its deep intoxication.

Called to the ritual of planting,
you, spirits two,
seek the harvest of peace
that transcends all understanding.

Through the ascendancy of growing,
you stretch to the stars in the sky,
hung from the canopy
of your own realization

The fruit of Heaven bearing
the seed of freedom
planted in your hearts.

Carl V. Hitchens Jr.

Bright Night

There's a place that we can go
Where the winters green
And the summers snow

When the raindrops rise
We awake into REM
Where the dogs cockle-doo
At the growls of a hen

As the horses eat slop
And the pigs run a thon
All the sheep are a jealous
Of the wolves wooling on

Then the moons rays arise
In the first light of day
And the sun takes disguise
As the night fades away

Yes maybe we'll go
   Maybe one sunny eve
   To the place in my dreams
      Where no hearts deceived.

Gina Esposito

Always

We're living in the here and now
   where life seems hard to bear,
Because of sin that entered in but
   good news is near;
For we're living in the "in between"
   and God's presence is here,
In all we see and taste and touch
   and also what we hear.

E. Joyce Matheny

Parents

She ties your shoe
When your too small
She combs your hair
When your not too tall

He reads a book
While you look
Tucks you sung
Gives a hug

They loan the car
Provide the gas
Wait without sleep
Till they know
Where you are

They prepare you for life
To be free from strife

They're gone too soon
Before you knew
You didn't say goodbye
And Thank You.

Jacqueline M. Lindberg

Gray Is Just A Color

What does it mean
when your hair turns to gray?
Does it mean that you're old,
that youth's slipped away?

To say that one's old
is just so absurd,
for gray is just a color,
and old's just a word.

Some people are vain
and they try to dye it.
Each gray hair, means wisdom.
so don't try to hide it.

Your mistakes you have made,
and from them you've learned.
You've shared much with many,
as your dark hair has turned.

You have beautiful memories.
and thoughts you can share,
you take pride in knowing,
you have gray in your hair.

Dolly Brown

God's Hands

God is always with you,
when you need His care.
He'll always have nourishment,
and a helping hand to share.

He'll always be there for you,
even when you've sinned.
God will always love you,
as a father and a friend.

Jennifer Lynn Weathers

Blizzard

Warning! Waiting, waiting
When will it start?
Winds and howls and blowing
Penetrate the fibers of your heart.

Flakes begin their downward course
Natures mighty lashes carry on
Swirling, twirling, blinding force
Tossing the earth with scorn.

Life grinds to a standstill,
Prisoners in a world of white
Blizzard must have its fill
Before the passing night.
Barbara A. Butt

In Heaven We Sleep

There are times in our life
When we become restless
Our jobs are tough
Our nights are sleepless
We struggle all day
As well as all night
Praying someday
God will hear our plight
When things go bad
As they sometimes do
Trust in God
He will help you through
Whether it's a gentle breeze
Caressing your hair
Or a warm tender smile
From someone who cares
His love for you
Runs far and deep
So worry no more...
In Heaven We sleep.
Dawn M. Williams

Suzanne

My heart aches at the years gone by
When others lives mixed with ours
Kept us afar and occupied
Life strayed beyond our powers.

But now in our middle years
our paths have crossed once more
Let's make the most of minutes shared
This time love will endure.

Can this be real?
The Great Spirit smiles on me?
Have I found the love I've sought
To last through eternity?

Suzanne I'm under your spell
So do as you wish with me
As much love as you're able to give
For as long as it's to be.

I can offer trust and honesty
and true caring, through and through
I only want to add to your life
By giving my love to you.
Dick Conradi

Take It To Him

I'm looking forward to the day
When no more tears are shed
When we are through trudging
On the path that Jesus led.

Though He had it so much worse
This is the hardest we've ever known.
And when He is beside us
It seems like we're alone.

But only because we've drifted away
From His warm and caring touch
And as we cry, He cries too
Because He cares for us so much

So when you have a problem
That tears into your heart.
Take it to the Lord above
And realize, from you, he will never part.
Jamie M. Clegg

Is It A Strange Thing?

Is it a strange thing,
When my heart cannot sing,
When my soul is filled with fear,
When my eyes shed many a tear?

Is it a strange thing,
When my worries to God I bring,
When joy is turned to sorrow,
When it's difficult to face tomorrow?

Is it a strange thing,
When trouble hurts as a sting,
When my heart is broken in dearth,
When my spirit is cast down to earth?

No, it's not a strange thing at all,
As long as on Him my soul shall call,
Who shall wipe away each tear,
Who shall calm every fear.

It is a strange thing not to rest,
In Him, of Whom our spirits are blest,
The Healer of the broken heart,
Who, in all our sorrows has a part.
Gene Griffin

A Mother's Prayer

You are my only child
When I'm alone with you
Though you have brother's and sister's
That are my children too
Each ones joys and sorrows
Are as though they were my own
While we commune together
In the quiet time alone
If wishes could bring you riches
And love and happiness to
My prayers would surely be answered
Because of my love for you
But God gives us each a blessing
And with it happiness to
So my child seek God's wisdom
And all He can give to you.
Alice Morris Bolser

Heat That Taco!

The crowd booed
when I declared Taco my favorite food.
It didn't make sense
why everyone was so tense.
Tacos are easy to digest,
and you never need to go
to the medicine chest.

The fillings vary
from dietary
to calamari,
since restaurants want
to please every dignitary.

My favorite hangout
is Taco Bell
and I don't care
who you tell.
Walk up to the counter
with ease,
and say - Heat that
Taco please!
Derek Laurila

To Sow A Seed

The days were long ago indeed
When He went out to plant a seed
To make this world so wide and bright
For every one to see thy light
For all of us were meant to be
Like stars above so we can see
The ocean and the sky of blue
The sound of birth in every tune
The bloom of every precious tree
What lies behind this gift of free
The breathe of air is within us all
He is always present to make a call
To take what is his very own
And call us back into His home
Irena L. Turiansky Johnson

Do You Hear My Prayer?

Sometimes it's hard to say a prayer
  when Christmas time is near.
You wonder if there is a God when
  heartache turns to fear.
That's when I think of Christmas past
  bringing a happy tear,
Waiting for my dad to come so we
  could all be near.
He always had faith in the Lord
  above, with thirteen mouths to feed,
And on his truck a special gift to put
  under our Christmas tree.
Now we wait for Mom to come from
  selling Christmas trees,
Hoping she'll be safe and sound and
  see her Christmas Eve.
Thinking of their fears untold
  makes me realize
My prayers are answered every day.
With faith, our God's alive.
Joslyn Perron

"Autumn"

There comes a certain time,
when all the leaves shall fall
The trees will stand there watching,
remaining strong and tall
They know the leaves must go,
but still, wish they could stay.
Remembering all the times,
when life was happy and gay.
New leaves will come,
and seasons pass.
Flowers will grow,
so will the grass.
Not for long,
they know it won't last.
Then one day,
all of a sudden!
The branches are bare,
the leaves are all gone.
Winter is coming,
goodbye, sweet dawn.

Alexandra Masem

Faded Love

Time slips away so fast,
what was my future is now my past.
My life that was young-now is old,
with no more stories to be told.

Just a faded memory,
and some pictures I can't see,
Just an old heart feeling young,
now that my songs have all been sung.

Life's been always good to me,
with many friends and family.
My time is short I must agree,
but only God - He holds the key.

Irene E. DeOnofrio

Sunny Sunflower

Please tell me Sunny sunflower
What made you grow so high?
Far above my head you tower
Like a golden crown up in the sky.

What made you king of my flower bed
Standing ever so bright and gay
While the bees buss on your yellow head
And the butterflies around you play?

How can you stare at the sun so bright
Nodding and turning your head all day
Following the sun from morn until night
And waving in the breeze that way?

Please tell me golden sunflower
With the greatest blossom of all—
Where do you get such power
To stand up there so tall?

Alma A. Lindsey

White Wall Wooden Rail

White wall wooden rail
Tiny lady - so frail
Your mind is where
Not cheer - despair
To you I reach
I wish to help
Recognizing you
Within my self...

Heather Priestley

Try Again

I try so hard at
what I'm good
at in life.

I never know what
I may have at my
finger tips.

Even though I win
or lose I know I'll
never give up on
life.

Jermey McLain

A Reputation

People make of their own life
What ever their gratification
I am sure there is strife
But one makes his own reputation.

Certainly we all make mistakes
We would not be human if we didn't
No one is ever so strong
As to let some acts be omitted.

We have a lot of trials
Sometimes great is temptation
We seek to hide our smiles
At the mention of a reputation.

A reputation is what others think
No one ever knows for sure
People see too much at one blink
And say too much sometimes to endure.

As long as we have a conscience clear
And our love and hearts are true
Let others talk, repeat and hear
But I will never stop loving you.

June L. Arnold

The Beauty Of Life

The beginning of summer —
    What a wonderful time.
Birds, flowers, butterflies
    And weather sublime.

We sit in the grass
    And watch the clouds in the sky.
We enjoy balmy days
    As the time passes by.

Then comes autumn
    With leaves all aglow.
We'll soon have winter
    With the beautiful snow.

The promise of spring then
    Is not far behind.
In each year and each day,
    There's joy we can find.

Doris C. Cumbo

Waiting For Sleep

The warmth of your voice
Sounds deep within my brain
As I wait for sleep.
To dream...
That I might listen to its evenness
Forever.

Elizabeth Peter

Anniversary

How can I love you more than I do?
We've only had fifty years together!
Fifty short years out of all the years -
past, present, and future.
Just a drop out of all the rain
that's fallen,
Or one snowflake out of all the
winter storms,
Or one ray of the sun.
One song of a bird,
One blade of grass,
One seashell on the shore...

Fifty years ago,
My love was like an embryo,
But now it's just beginning
to be born,
Ready to live
on, into eternity.

Elna Vickers

Mary's Conceiving

Two wills with love's heart
Were drawn from the start
To their wooing, by God's great decree;
A gift of great pleasure,
A love without measure
Mary's joy and response had to be.

An angelic addressing,
All grace sweetly pressing,
Enraptured and captured was she;
Love's gentle alluring,
The maid's patient enduring
Elevation of soul, pure and free.

The Lord's secret scheming
Won her in the dreaming,
A child of her own she received;
Humanity won
Divinity's son
When Mary her dear child conceived.

Irene Broussard, O.P.

Untitled

Perhaps he sometimes slipped a bit
well, so have you.
Perhaps, something he ought to quit
well, so should you.
Perhaps, he may have faltered—why?
Why all men do, and so have I.
You must admit, unless you lie,
that so have you.
Perhaps, if we would stop and think,
both I and you,
When painting someone black as ink,
as one folks do;
Perhaps, if we would recollect,
Perfection we would not expect,
But just a man halfway correct,
Like me and you!

Ellen Billingsley

Untitled

Hello, my child,
Welcome to our world.
We've been waiting your arrival;
Wondering what you would be like.
A boy or girl;
Blue eyed or brown,
Blonde or brunette.

Please accept, little one,
My faults.
Because, you see, I'm new at this
And I am not perfect.

But I will try,
Please bear with me.
As we learn together,
To accept one another.

Hello, my child
Welcome to our world.

Althea Hurst

Where Have All The Heroes Gone?

Where are all the heroes?
We need some inspiration,
Politicians promise help
We watch in desperation.

Health Care, Welfare, Our Defense
For Votes these they embrace,
But Someone has to foot the bill,
Leave that to a future race.

Crime in the streets, senseless death
Shoot-outs, Robbery, Rape,
Where's a cop to help us now?
Indicted — on video tape!

The Victims dead, the Criminals free
Where did Justice flee?
The "O.J. Cruise" just left the dock,
It's headed out to sea.

The New Generation needs someone to trust
Faith and Hope are at issue,
Where have all the Heroes gone?
Oh, John Wayne, we miss you!

Bonnie Best

Teach Me

Sometimes in our life,
We all make mistakes,
Taking things in strife,
And wanting all the breaks,

But...
Within each of our lives,
And deep within our souls,
There lies a surprise,
That cuts into our goals,

It is a thing called learning,
That teaches each of us,
Who have that yearning,
Not to raise a fuss,
But to always find the truth,

So, I must agree,
"Teach me and I will be quiet,
Show me where I've been wrong!"

Bertie Langdon

Without You

Without you I cannot fly,
way up into the big blue sky,
above the clouds where heavens lie,
I can only watch my life pass me by.

Without you I cannot feel so high,
above the hell where I fry,
and the sorrow that makes me cry,
I can only close my eyes.

Without you I can only ask why,
must I be a lonely guy,
no matter how hard I try,
I can only let out a sigh.

Without you my heart runs dry,
and is in a tie,
about that I cannot lie,
I can only watch myself die.

Doug Fenske

Freedom

The day we met, my life
was changed forever. You offered
me something I thought no
longer existed. A safe, neutral
place to allow my soul to
run free. Be who I am and
never worrying about having
to hide. You gently reached down
into my very being and softly
coaxed out parts of me I'd long
since forgotten. Time can erase
many things, but it can
never destroy who we really
are. A long time ago I fell in
love and at the same time I made
a bargain with the devil on a
contract for my soul.

Jennifer Pearl Winland

Seems Only Yesterday

Seems only yesterday I saw you
walking, patched pants and all
down red-clayed rutted roads
to school and friends and home again,
I loved you then — and now.

Seems only yesterday I heard you
laughing, red cheeked and all
down hollows full of wonder trails
to school and friends and home again,
I loved you then — and now.

Seems only yesterday I touched you
warming, self near stove and all
down stairs well-worn with footprints
to school and friends and home again,
I loved you then — and now.

Seems only yesterday,
to school and friends and home again,
I loved you then — and now.

James W. Kelz

In My Own Backyard

When I got up this morning
Walked across the floor
I stretched and yawned,
As I went to my door.

There to my amazement
The beauty that I saw
Sun-beams glistening through the trees,
I just stood in awe!

Oh, the dazzle and the sparkle
As the sun-beams danced with glee
From the ice that hung there
At the top of all the trees.

Suddenly, I found myself
In a world all of my own
Of such rare beauty, peace, and calm
As I stood there all alone.

In my world of crystal
I hadn't traveled far
For the beauty I was caught up in
Was IN MY OWN BACKYARD!

Betty Stigall

Color My World

Roses are red
Violets are blue
I'm going to bed
'Cause I have the flu.

Amra Geschwentner

"The Waters Of Life"

A woman kneels on the ground two
vases are at her side.
Behind her a star shaped sun with
seven stars beside.
A bird sits on a shrub symbolizing
the soul.
The water is life the wind gently
blows.
She reaches for a vase then reaches
for the other.
She slowly fills one while spilling
the other.
The waters of life, the gifts of the
spirit.
The song the bird sings only few
will hear it.

Cynthia D. Kanz

Butterfly

The butterflies dancing
Upon their rock
No band playing
Their wings moving
To the all nature band
As they fly about
Like angels they dance
For god upon His rock
They come from out
Among his trees
To dance the butterfly waltz
Circling their rock
As His nature sings
From God's water fall Springs
His melody rings
Their dance will bring
Love upon his rock

Douglas C. Reed

Morning Kiss

Sweet moisture
Upon my lips,
Your touch is soft
As morning mist,
Tangled hair all askew
Clinging bunching
Form intimate new.
Daylight dances on the walls,
muffled moans,
And much, much more.
Small bugs scurry across the floor.

Joe R. Donaldson

Ode To Nicole

Her life is like a teeter totter
up and down up and down
She had a son and a daughter
Where's the justice in this town?
She was bruised and she was battered
and she knew one day he'd do her in
with all her hopes and dreams shattered
by an unbelievable heinous sin.
Where's the justice in this town?
Now she's six feet under
and he's roaming free-
All her life's plans put asunder
because of his raging killing spree.
He had lots of money for the
lawyers' fee - What would
happen if it were you or me?
Where's the justice in this town?

Audrey Ames

Alone In The World

Alone in the world was I
Until the day you happened by.
There was instant harmony
The beginning of a profound melody
We shared bountiful pleasures
That suffocated all past pains.
But then the cold black day came
That love or fate would not change
And you prepared to die.
Today a blue rose grows where
You lie, it brings beauty to the
World as you once did.
And for I, because of you thrive.

Dana Holt

The Service

You lie in bronze,
U.S. World War II
American flag draped.

I do not hear
words spoken
or songs sung,
I think only of
our happy childhood,
packing lunches to wander
unexplored lonely trails
that only cows made,
always to find flowers
or an empty bird's nest
at the end.

Peace be with you,
little brother,
for it is found
nowhere else.

Clover B. Gibson

Speed

It began innocently!

The night engulfed with stars
Twinkling through frost-laden
Trees that seemed to zip past.

Headlights bounced on black elastic
Stretched tightly in front of boys
Who loved speed.

Swiftly the road rolled beneath
Much like a kitten
Darting under a couch.

Suddenly a curve - lights became a
Ferris wheel tumbling over - metal
Crunching, glass breaking, debris
Flying - gasp!

Silence - death!

Galena Fulkerson

A Letter to Pop

I'm sitting here tonight
   trying to figure how to write
A letter to Pop, who was my Dad
   with several points to get across
   just to explain my profound loss.

Little girls are supposed to be
   their father's little princess
   his pride and joy.
I'm supposed to say
   How could you? How dare you?
I'll never understand why.
All of which make you unable to deny.
No more pretending from you
   or minimizing
I will not allow.

Then I get to call you names
   to get you to finally see my pain.
But the letter, like me, you'll just toss out
   and then say "What's this all about?"

Danene Whitney

Untitled

Gray walls squared,
   Trapped souls that dared.
Hidden from sight,
   Like some form of blight.

Hate, ridicule, shame the rule,
   Ever present, the looming duel.
Strike out, strike in
   Oh our damnable sins.
Keeping us bound,
   To a silence within.

Charles Moore

To Mama

Clouds covered and darkened the sky
   today.
I turned me round 179 degrees
Before I spied a single break;
And thought,
As faith had turned me round and round
To see this break,
Must needs a steadfast faith
To see a break
When one is not apparent.

Charlene Thompson

Practice What You Preach

Why can't we all just get along,
together we can make this
country strong.
I'm teaching my daughter my
next of kin, that it doesn't
matter the color of skin.
If more parents could
preach this lesson, maybe this
world would have less aggression.
Bitterness hatred what does
it teach, that peace and
contentment can't be reached.
So let's have families sit
together and try to make this
country better.
Doesn't matter single parent
or married, this message
must be quickly carried.

Denise Mary Pittman

Tale Of The Twins

Beware the twins.

They are each other's beloved.
Together they share eternity.
Spirits conjoined.

They are each other's likeness.
Differences are illusive.
Split center.

Love one, hurt the other.
Hurt one, face the other.
Severed brains.

Beware your pride.

They are mystics ever chanting.
Mind the archaic song.
Femme fatale.

Mistresses of the hunt.
Run for your life.
Discarded amour.

Passionate embrace.
Devotion unscathed.
Look upon them with homage.

Elizabeth Electra Hurd

Memories

In memory where we are free
to travel far and near,
Meeting friends we haven't seen
and places we hold dear.
It seems so long since I have
gone adventuring alone.
The childhood scenes are very clear.
but yesterday has flown.
In those yesteryears I find a
comfort to embrace, loving family,
friends, God's guidance and His
Grace.
All this within my memory has
value I must keep,
Until with His great wisdom
He beckons me to sleep.

June Marie Hilton Grant

My Spiritual Angel

To stay away from drinking
To save my life and my wife
Please - somebody help me!

Close your mouth and
Lock it tight
Open it only to eat
And talk

When you want liquor
Remember to lock your mouth
My spiritual Angel says
It will become a habit

Dear Angel, you are right
For 2 months I have been good
Instead of a drink, I think
Lock your mouth!
Thank You, spiritual Angel
I love you.

Anne Warner

Field Of Clover

Lay me down in a field of clover
To rest my weary head.
I will lay here in all my sorrow
For I know I will soon be dead.

The rifle's bullet showed no mercy
As it knocked me to the ground.
Blood and death are all around me
To heaven or hell I will soon be bound.

All my comrades are fighting fiercely;
Some have fallen by my side.
The enemy they overpower us,
Soon we will all go out like the tide.

Pain shutters throughout my body
For my time is growing near.
For many days in this field of clover
The smell of death will linger here.

My vision keeps growing dimmer
As the lights go slowly out.
I close my eyes, the pain is easing
As merciful death comes quickly about.

Frank W. Stutsman

The Stolen Kiss

I think that I would be remiss
To remember not the stolen kiss
I never added to the score
But would have liked six dozen more
Six dozen twice is one four-four
I think that I should steal some more
But why not simply steal the miss
And keep her ever near to kiss

Hubert I. Shifler

Untitled

Your smile is a beacon of light
to a tiny, little ship
on a starless night
guiding its sail
so it can prevail
and return to its safe haven
and once again, oath it the raven

Craig Meyer

Give Up

Dear life, pull the knife
to open up, too say I give up
is it always going to be like this
waiting and wondering if it's
ever going to change
for the better, maybe

Dear mom open my palm
I'm relentless and I'm depressed
I want to know what life could offer
devastated and always a bother
to people around me
why can't I see

Dear Lord, here's my sword
I'll give it in, to release this sin
I have so much more in return to give
laughing and crying to live
my life my way
should I stay?

Brian C. Elliott

Hidden Fear

The times felt dark, cold and scary
　To one so young, so wet and weary
Into the water he came
　like a demon from Hell
"GO AWAY, LEAVE ME ALONE"
　I wanted to yell
Why does he do it
　Can't he leave me alone
Caressing and touching
　my body so wet and cold
"HELP ME, HELP ME"
　I wanted to yell
This person seemed nice
　I saw it everyday
The fun I had in the water
　I swam and played
But then he came into the water
　and all the fun faded away
This stranger came and touched me
　in an awful way of rage.

Jennifer Gouthier

Midnight Gladiolus

I am listening in
to my Borgia soul:
my cruel instincts,
my corrupted unconscious.
My kind and educated self
highly disapproves.

In the end I read my own verdict.
The midnight blue flower
lies collapsed
into a pale blue hole,
a taste of failure
in my mouth
like a desiccated petal.

Itala Langmar

"Nature"

We have a great creator,
to give us such beautiful nature.
All kinds of trees,
blow in the breeze.
Some of the limbs,
Are so very slim.
The brightness of the sun,
lets children have their fun.
At times the rain,
may not be tame.
We pull all the weeds,
then plant the seeds.
To plant a flower,
and watch it grow.
Gives me the power,
not to move slow.
The moon comes out at night,
and it's a terrific sight.
When I looked at it last night,
I saw a bat in flight.

Carol C. Lombard

My Prayer

Thank you Lord, that I am able
To get up and walk to the table
That I can see the morning light
Even though it's not as bright
That I can see the falling rain
Dripping down my window pane
That I can see a cheery smile
That brightens my day, for a while
These things are not so much
When you are young and still in touch.
So thanks again, for blessings dear
With your dear Lord, I have no fear
I'll bless each day I have at home
I know dear Lord, I'm not alone.

Francel Rietz

"The Name"

My everlasting life this means
to find out who You are,
and a title or descriptive word
can tell me much, I've heard.

But something's missing
it's not the same,
what I need is a name.

Robbed from many and myself,
by the "thinking" man's philosophy
the ignorant man's pride,
a beautiful name they've tried to hide.

Fight, as hard as they do
it will prove to be of no avail,
because His word cannot fail.

Even backed by fallen angels
they cannot hide the true God's name,
now when I shout "Hallelu-Jah"
you will know to praise Jehovah!

Eric Pranausk

Gifts

Across the waters misty haze
To far horizons I often gaze,
And marvel as I look
On things not made by man
Nor found in book
The setting sun's brilliant hue
As it sinks beyond my view,
And, as day fades into night,
Myriads of stars dusky light,
Silver moonbeams gleaming o'er
Rippling waves and sandy shore.
All of these
God's gifts of beauty
Bestowed by him
Though love, not duty,
Have been ours since time began,
And should strengthen
The soul of every man.

Irene McKinnon

Our Scenic World

Planning spacious sight seeing trips
To enjoy world scenes so far and wide
Also perchance renew old friendships
Scenery that even God couldn't hide

The planet earth has sights galore
Availing to us all a godsend stage
Giving those views pleasures and more
At this time of our modern viewing age

Traveling by car, plane or by train
It's needed suitable transportation
To see mountains, valleys and plains
Massive green fields of vegetation

Plans complete-off on that merry way
With excitement we wonder and ponder
About worldly sights with great array
So off we go to the wild blue yonder.

Joachim C. Mosbrucker

The Window

Her world is confined
To a room dark and drab
Her hours spent lying in bed

Her health has been taken
Her faith has been shaken
Her mind has a need to be fed.

So gracious this lady
Her age is past eighty
The traces of beauty remain

The frail and so thin
Such strength from within
A spirit that can't be restrained

They opened her window
The world once again
To her life, new meaning would give

The world would embrace her
She welcomed it back
Through the light of
The window, she lives.

June Dedmon

Four Seasons

Embrace me 'neath vernal bowers
Till spring and summer wed.
Kiss me o'er the summer
Till the rose its petals shed.
Love me, when the snow is new,
And the down is soft and warm.
Then I shall love thee forever,
When our flower of love is born.

Edward C. Lauber

Whispered Silence

Whispered silence
Throughout the room
Fresh cut flowers
Continue to bloom

White leather couch
By an open window I lay
Breeze tickles my skin
A ray of sun creeps through the shade

Smell the sweetness
Breathing deeply
Draining my thoughts
Relaxed completely

Take the glass
From the table beside me
White tablets, white poison
Set me free

Flower's scent
Carried by the breeze
I close my eyes
And fall permanently asleep.

Jacey Jay

A Tribute To Rose McGrath

You have passed into eternal peace;
Through heaven's golden portal.
I wish that it were here on earth,
That you could be immortal.

I am saddened by your passing;
My heart is filled with pain.
But there is comfort knowing,
My loss is heaven's gain.

You share your home in glory land.
With the best friend I ever had.
So if some day, your paths should cross,
Please say hello to Dad.

When we gather for a family feast;
Every woman, child and fellow.
You are truly missed, to say the least,
'Cause no one brings the jello.

Byron L. Doepker

Untitled

I wish only to know her
thoughts. If only my eyes were
more than eyes, that I might
see past, the spoken and the
physical. That I might live
inside her, as does the heart
that confesses, its undying
love for me. I fear there is
something amiss, that my
heart has not the courage to know...

Fred King

My Lord And King

You have given me LIFE to me
    Though your death on Calvary
And forever I will sing
    My Lord and King.

I was wandering aimlessly
    With no purpose I could see
When in love you rescued me
    You took my hand.

For a century I've been told
    Of the glories I'll behold,
What a grand jubilee
    With my Savior and King!

You are coming back for me
    Through the clouds so rapidly
In an instant I'll be changed,
    Given a wondrous body!

Oh how happy I will be
    When your face at last I'll see
There to live eternally
    With my Lord and King

DaleWilloughby,

Captain, U.S. Marine Corps (Retired)

A Valley On Fire

Every leaf shined,
those that remained,
in the fire and wine.

Strong and undaunted
while merciless winds
through valleys haunted.

This time of year
bears such a new world
to smell, see and hear.

Many, sudden changes,
yet exhilarating crispness
across the mountain ranges.

A sky of blue
offers background
to bare-branched hues.

Beauty beyond a brush
with so many men is lost
for they can't feel the hush.

Joan M. Hoffman

Sixteen

I've just begun to live in
this world.
To hurt and understand
why.
To hate be hated and yet
to love.
A world of laughter, tears
and fears.
A time to live.
A time to die.
Some are happy.
Some are sad.
The snow is cold.
The sun gets hot.
Don't give up.
Give it all you've got and
Live in this world as
You change so often.

Cynthia S. Tilton

November Morn

The air is crisp and cool,
This November morn
And the nearly bear trees,
Continues shedding their leaves,
One by one
They fall to the ground,
Ever so quiet
Never, much of a sound.
With all the sun's warmth,
Yet, not as warm as before
Has caused,
That which was once green
To change to rustic yellow, burnt reds,
And colors that magnifies the seen.
How funny it is,
That I should put on a coat,
While leaves continue to fall
From the mighty shedding oaks.

Debra Mossman

"You And They"

While, I am sitting here
Thinking, how people are
They're all wrapped up
in their mighty armor
Ready to attack anyone
that comes near
so protect yourself and
make them fear
For YOU are mightier than THEY
Let them know that
games aren't to be played
If you win or lose
Raise your head up high
Because YOU not THEY have reached
all limits to the sky.

Darlene Jones

The Angel's Book

I saw a picture of two angels.
    They were looking at a book.
I could not read the pages.
    But I could read the angel's looks.

They seemed to be concerned about
    something they had read.
Could it be a list of prayers
    prayed beside the children's beds?
Should they go and help that one?
    Should they intervene?
I hope they do. I hope it's soon.
    I hope it's Molly Green.

A precious girl of seven
    brings so many loving smiles.
A little piece of heaven
    that we need between our miles.
If she's allowed to stay here,
    think of the love she could spare!
I just know that they will come and help.
    Yes, I know the Angels care.

JoAnn Guest

School Boy

He looked so sick
So pale and wan
He's better now
The bus has gone.

Florence Kammin

The Rescuers

Hearts wrenched and full of tears
they are the RESCUERS

People laughing, people crying,
people living, people dying
but they are the RESCUERS

Push three buttons and you shall find
these men and women aren't far behind
because they are the RESCUERS

Big ones, small ones,
Short and tall ones
they are the rescuers

A real-life super hero
every child's dream
still they are the RESCUERS

Sometimes they don't succeed
things just go wrong
but they pick themselves up and
move right along
because they are still the RESCUERS

Brian Lewis

Life's Song

Life is fleeting, death is certain
There's no holding hands with time,
Tears of laughter, tears of sorrow
Young or old we know the rhyme.

Pain and parting one more lesson
On this journey we must learn,
Dance in life's eternal circle
Though we leave, we must return.

Dust we are to dust returning
Dust will always grow the rose,
The rose is life, in all perfection
Round and round the circle goes.

Weep no tears for those departed
Shed the body learn to fly,
Death like birth, completes circle
There's no ending when we die.

Gloria Norwood

The Fork In The Road

We started out together.
    There was so much to see
We stumbled over every stone,
    But you walked close to me.

Why did the way divide? For two
    It was just wide enough.
But one road led to logic
    And one road led to love.

And I chose love, you, logic.
    Dear kind companion, how
Could you have done it? But you did,
    And I can't see you now.

Emily FitzHugh

Believe My Love

"High across the mountain tops
Splashed across the sea
My love for you will never die
As long as you believe"

Elaina Moyer

A Birth Control

Once upon a rift of time
There was a good Lady,
Who thought in due time,
I'm having too many babies.
To her doctor she soon went
And her thoughts did relent.
To the Lady, Doc gave some good news;
Drink lots of fresh orange juice.
Asked the lady — "Before or After?"
With a soft smile, face of red,
A chuckle, a bit of laughter,
Doc calmly replied "Instead."

Ellis C. Lynn

Untitled

Don't shed a tear
    there is no need
People die today
    from simple greed.
Don't ever cry
    over such a small thing
But feel the pain
    of a birds broken wing.
Cry not for
    your little pain
But cry for others
    starving in vain.
And when you feel
    you have to cry
Cry for those
    who shouldn't die.

Donna Jean Fitzgerald

Keep Me In Mind

The ocean's not forever
There has to be an end
This man's not so clever
With his round opinions
It's my life on this vessel
It's not that I don't care
One man's quest for answers
Is a non-believers dare
Keep me in mind, keep me in mind
First it wasn't easy
To look and not see home
Sailing down through rushing waves
Our ship was all alone
Waking up to seagulls
I shed my disbelief
Knowing now the earth is round
Are sure for those who seek
Keep me in mind
Keep me in mind

Norbert D. Chanley II

Sometimes

    Sometime I just lay
there and try to sleep.
Sometimes I just lay
there and weep, but then
I realize why I
shouldn't weep.
It's because I have
you to dream about
in my sleep.

Cassandra Messingham

Untitled

If time is a river,
Then I'm on the shore,
On a sandbar,
Soft but solid.

I feel the sun on my shoulders,
The sand between my toes;
I stand still
While time flows past me.

I let it, turning my face
Back to somewhere safer:
Childhood, maybe,
Or earlier still.

Jennifer L. Painter

Appreciate The View

The flowers in the field
Their fragrance do yield
Their beauty is unsurpassed
As they sway upon a sea of grass.

There are so many colors
As one looks at the flowers
Their beauty we can appreciate
Only if time we take.

There are many reds and blues
As well as other colors of many hues
And how they sparkle in the dew
That keeps those colors fresh and new.

It would do us good to sit and ponder
To see what is in front of us
Instead of gazing over yonder
Wishing for what we think is grander.

We need to take the time me and you
To look at those colors a new
But often there are so few
Who really look at such a view.

Beverly J. D. Samuelson

Children Of The Earth

Their smiles warm you
Their cries sadden you
You can feel sympathy
But the children show it
They don't care
What people think of them
For they are all innocent
In the Lord's eyes
They roam free
Like creatures of the Earth
Combined in one as the Earth
The Earth's sadness they can feel
The Earth's happiness they can share
All the feelings of the Earth
Are in these children
Children of the Earth

April Green

A Summer Night

The moon nestles comfortably in
the velvet sky
A king, surrounded by his
courtiers, the laughing stars.

The grass echoes the wind.
Like lovers in a moonlit night
They whisper softly to each other
Reflecting the other's mood.

Betty J. Williams

A Rain Drop

I stood beneath a tree,
    The world was fresh and sweet;
A shower had passed by,
    Leaving mud beneath my feet.

Now the sun was shining.
    As I gazed on high -
A flash - as of a diamond,
    Caught my wandering eye.

A branch had bathed in rain.
    And at its very tip -
Hung a lovely rain drop,
    Just about to slip!

As I beheld its beauty,
    For just that shining moment -
My memory had that picture,
    That Mr. Rain had sent.

Now when I walk a muddy trail,
    Striving for the top -
I look on high and remember,
    The beauty of one rain drop!

Jean Hicks

Reflections

Like a mirror, crystal clear
    the words I write reflect
        Inmost thoughts of heart and mind
            that can't be held in check

Speak softly, o my heart
    search deeply words to find
        Meditate to draw them up
            my heart does stir my mind

Words like whispers dwell within
    they beckon for release
        True feelings long to be expressed
            reflections bring me peace

Donna E. Green

Springtime

Have you ever wondered through
The woods in early springtime
And marveled at this amazing
World of yours and mine.

Have you ever seen a robin
Take a bath in morning dew
Then fly to the top of a tree
To enjoy the magnificent view.

Have you ever watched a daisy
Push through the ground, its head
After a long winter's nap
In its warm earthly bed.

Have you ever seen a mockingbird
Perched high upon a limb
Singing its song so sweetly
It seems almost like a hymn.

To see Mother Nature bring forth
All her beauty so bold
Is such a wonderful sight
For one's eyes to behold.

Betty M. Harris

The Wheel Of Time

Through the sands of glass
    The wheel of time churns.
Oceans shift their mass
    The fire of Heaven burns.

Mountains rise and fall
    Like nations among men.
Who will hear its call
    And remember what has been?

When time stands still
    And the stars are all as one
Life will be there to fill
    The hole of the fallen sun.

Like the seed into grass
    Man fails and he learns
Ages come and pass
    The wheel of time turns.

Duke Willis

Never To Forget

There is so much I need in my life;
The warmth feeling in a home,
were love is being felt.

But these things I must do without,
I must save the tears that flow -
like an endless river.
For I shall be in need of them
for a long, long, time.

By night there is no silence on my part.
For I am afflicted and poor.
I wish to God to pray attention to the
voice of my entreaties.

To give ear to my prayer without lips
of deception.

Cindy Joseth Agreda

The Blue And The Grey

The fighting is over.
The war is lost.
The battles are finished
And what was the cost?

The dead and the wounded;
The maimed and the mourned;
Their bodies lie broken,
Twisted and torn.

The gray mist of morning
Lies heavy and still.
The sun peeks from behind
The green wooded hill.

The guns and the cannons
Sit silent and cold.
Oh, the lives they have taken!
The brave and the bold!

And where is the victor?
What is his reward?

Peace for all eternity
In the house of the Lord.

Jeanette Carmean

Dreams

Everybody dreams,
the very young, the very old;
Everybody has a secret,
dreams they never told;
Everybody, at sometime,
has wished upon a star,
blown out the candles on a cake,
had hopes that drifted afar;
Everybody dreams,
but dreams don't often come true;
Yet mine have because
I have you!

Duane M. Heimann

Love's Candle

In the flame of a candle
The truth you cannot handle
The love that was stranded
In the flame of a candle
The kiss not remembered
The body that surrendered
In the flame of a candle
The heart that beat
For loves special treat
In the flame of a candle
The love that's around
The future that surrounds
In the flame of candle
The love that began
with the touch of a hand
In the flame of a candle
The demise that was shout
As the flame burned out.

Jenelle Hanlon

Life's Tree

On a budding branch
The spring sunlight dances.....
Life begins.

On a leafy branch
The tempest fell....
Dark summer's tears.

On a colorful branch
The harvest moon shone...
A waning tribute.

On a withered branch
The snow listened....
Winter's silence.

Donald K. Oster

The Future?

It's too bad no ear has heard
the silence that now goes on
Life died that day to gain this peace
ev'ry life form is gone

Only spirits tell the story
of life once on this land
And the day that it was ended
by man's uncaring hand

The rivers, winds, and rains
the only sounds that now exist
Ask us,
Does this need to happen
or must this peace be missed

Gregg Bremers

Ka' Nowa Ma: And I Give

Naked with anger, I am naked.
The sea is angry, pure with anger.
As the souls fly from battle
They fly afraid.

But I fear none
I will be mad with painted anger.
I will chase fear,
And fortify my heart with fire.

I give my body to chase
the souls and all the stars
I give my world
A feast.

I am dying in battle
So come all to remember mercy.
Remember love, the sea of red earth.
Remember this and keep watch above.

Remember anger out of nothing,
Naked and painted,
Painted alone,
Kills the one that loves alone.

Chanz Skeffington

Loveliness

A lovely woman,
The petal of a rose,
The song of the trees,
When it snows;
The fragrance of spring air.

The song of nature,
At evening's repose,
The peace of sunset,
With its golden glows,
The beauty of a maiden fair.

The soul of man sees;
Beauty from inside grows;
Nature bestows.
The unseen hand sows.
It's always there.

Charles McKinley

Life Is Like...

Life is like a gravel road,
The more bumps, the harder it is.

But the farther you go,
the easier it will get.

And soon that road
will smooth out.

The more you learn,
the easier it will be.

And sooner or later your life,
will smooth out too!

Your life has curves that,
are the hopes and dreams for oneself.

The dead ends represent,
the hopes and dreams that fail.

But as you learn,
you choose a different path.

That path could lead to a,
paved road.

Or a new beginning,
to a better end.

Jennifer Holbrook

A Mother's Eyes

You can't describe in words
the love you feel from your
mother's eyes.
Too often we forget to look,
for fear of shame and pain.
We turn our back and walk
away to scared to look
ahead. She sees our
pain and runs ahead to
tell us it's alright.
"Share your pain with me
my son, I love you oh so much ."
Don't be afraid to look at
these eyes the ones that love you so.
For all the gifts we ask
of life, none are so great as this.
The eyes of a mother are a
gift from God to show
us all just how much
she really cares.

Steven Wilcox

Masks

The masks we wear
The looks we see
Are all just props
Of a fantasy
Behind these props
Are ones who hold
Are ones who pull
The fantasy
The dream
Until we see
Until we hear
We will never know
How life feels.

Alice Peng

My Father's Love

I wander through the paths of pain,
The hearts of men I sought in vain.
Journeys traveled far and wide,
To find the love I lack inside.

But no one loved and no one cared,
I finally fell alone and scared.
On my knees my spirit torn,
I lift my eyes, a light is born.

A gentle whisper calls my name
He says "in Me there is no shame."
I ask the Lord "how can this be"?
He says "I died to set you free".

"But can your blood erase my sin?"
He says "just ask and I'll come in."
He showed me that I had been blind
The love I sought I'd left behind.

I didn't need to search and roam,
A father's love awaits at home.

The answer now I knew I had.
The purest love was in my dad.

Jennifer M. Raymond

Canyon

Canyon,
The Grand Canyon,
Deep, curvy, long and wide,
Ancient, stone colored layers,
Gorgeous.

Adam Frady

Earth

The air was moist
The fog was low
And grass growing
From the light dew.

The deer walked over
To a nearby stream
Being ever so quiet
With their young ones.

The fog then rose
Up into the sky
They now are clouds
Blanketing the trees.

The sun beams shone
There was a breeze in the air
All was peaceful
On the little touch of earth.

Jesse Rieg

Alone

I stand there in the dark alone
   The darkness of the night
overpowers me.
   Rain beats to the ground
      like a whipping stick
I neither see life or death,
   light or dark.
   I am forever here,
   Until the day you
      come and free me.

Anil Nambiar

Going Home

We drank it smooth
the dark, warm liquid

We drank it slowly
while we watched her go
drowning in the strange arms of the sea
can't you hear it calling me
can't you feel its sharp misty breath
whisper my painful name
it calls to me
so I must go home now
where the darkness drowns all emotion
you cannot hurt me anymore
none of you
I would rather be threatened
by the scarred depths of the sea
Goodbye, it is calling to me

Jennifer Creach

Déja Vu

On Granny's wide veranda
The creaking swing-song
Lulls my little one to sleep.
Fireflies explore the twilight,
Darting, twinkling.
A honeysuckle breeze
Sets wind chimes tinkling.
My mother sits beside me,
Savors with me
Sounds of children's laughter
As they play at Hide and Seek.
We share a smile,
Remembering
When carefree voices
Calling in the early summer dark
Were ours.

Betty Henry Young

Until You Return

Last night I gazed into
the dark sky above and
in it I could see no light.
No moon, no stars, to fill
it with beauty.
Only an endless black void
which reflected in my heart.
My spirit felt the lonely
darkness, and a tear of despair
ran down my cheek.
And I said to myself...
Brave heart be true, for like the
moon in the sky returns with
light anew, so too will your
light come back to you.
It's just the beginning of a
new circle within the life of you.

Billie Butler

Dance

Look at my dance
The dance of life
The mystery and power
Emerged from sun
To bring you light
To waken your soul
And feed your spirit
Follow me then
With open heart
We'll climb the sun
And read the stone

Eva Idrian

Untitled

The white of the snow,
The cold of the air
A figure bent down,
On top of a stair.

The dark of the night,
The sweetness of wind.
She's only hoping,
That she hasn't sinned.

The sudden rush,
Of her blood to her face.
Just because of a thought,
That she couldn't erase.

The ever lasting winter,
The never ending thoughts.
If she could sing them away,
Like the thin, black notes.

Anna Agadjanyan

Dad

He was a good Husband and Dad
The best that we could of had
He touched a lot of folks
With his humor and his jokes
Now that he is in Heaven at last
We can reflect on the past
Dad was one of a kind
Whose memories will never leave my mind
Please rest in peace, Jack
I only wish you could come back
But when I am feeling blue
I will always think of you
So please watch over us from up there
Because we know you still care.

John W. Roberson

My Garden

I walked into my garden
That's where I learned to pray.
I gazed with joy at beauty
God sends us every day.
The sunshine is His happy smile
The dew drops are His tears
Colors sprinkle from His palette,
In my garden there are no fears.
When life becomes a burden,
And sadness fills my day
I steal into my garden
'Tis heaven, and there I pray!

Anna Ribbeck

I'm Free

I can fly like a bird
that's never heard
and without a word
   I'm free

I play with my friends
the fun never ends
so playful and glee
   I'm free

After a hard day
there's nothing to say
no one to see but a cup of tea
   I'm free

On a cold night
the moon shines bright
but I'm safe and snug and
   I'm free

No where to go
No one to see
Just me...
   I'm free

Asha Atkinson

"Sweet Freedom"

Don't lose that freedom
That you have with you today
For tomorrow it may be
Far-far away.
Freedom is a gift
That we fought for and won!
It's a beautiful thing to have;
It can also be lots of fun —
I've lost my freedom for now,
but I'm fighting to get it back,
This time when I get it
I'll definitely give no slack;
I'll never lose that freedom
Nor will I give it back!
For our freedom is the greatest gift
That cannot be taken back.
Sweet, sweet freedom,
Here you are today;
I've learned to do what's right,
So here you are to stay.

John Matthew Cannell

I Remember A Rose

I remember a rose
that once grew
and such colors
splashed my eyes
but that was
so very long ago,
time passes,
memories fade,
soon I shall remember
it not, as I did then
those once bright colors
will bear a touch more gray.
A loss that only my soul
will remember and describe to God
in ways,
words can never know

James E. Morris

Untitled

Who is he
that judges me
whom can't be judged himself.

And who am I
not to sigh
as time upon a shelf.

For does it please thy soul
to watch me grow
my body wrapped in chains.

To live my life
through pain and strife
till nothing else remains.

I've seen your heart's
and I've played the parts
of all your wicked ways.

But now it's you
who say are true
A sinner always pays...

LEO

Yearning

What is it that I'm doing,
That isn't part of me.
What is it that I yearn for,
Where do I long to be?
Somewhere there's an answer
To all these questions now.
I am searching for them strongly,
Yet I'm unsure how.
Why aren't things more clear for me,
More easily understood.
There must be something missing here,
I'm sure it's only good!
I search by day and pray by night
My quest should happen swiftly,
To piece this puzzle that I'm in,
For something doesn't fit me.
I'm not doing much of anything,
That makes my day exciting,
It's mostly just my routine life,
Except today, I'm writing...

Cecile Marie Bell

"Looking At Life"

Life is one big window;
    That each of us looks through.
Each person sees it differently;
    Each eye a different view.

Some see a life that's full of love;
    And some a life of fame.
Still others peer with discontent;
    And some with pure disdain.

If where you're at is not quite right,
    Then nurture what you've got.
Just do your best at what you do;
    Things will improve a lot!

If what you do is much too hard;
    Then take another view.
Expand yourself!, climb up that hill!;
    Perspectives will be new!

So follow where your heart will lead;
    Get rid of all your strife.
Contentment is the remedy;
    It is the fruit of life!

Eva J. Correia

Friendship

Friendship is a priceless gift
That can't be bought or sold
Its value is far greater than
Mountains made of gold.
If you should ask God
for a gift,
Be thankful if he sends
not diamonds, pearls,
or riches,
But the love and trust
of friends

Francisco Jauregui

I Wish

I wish to be more
than a drop of water
that flows within
your stream of thought
wetting your conscious briefly
then drying up
for lack of nourishment

I wish to be a spring
from which you can drink deeply
a well
forever full

Barbara R. Culpepper

Highways Of Life

Like the yellow center line—my life is
steady with happiness until
a disruption occurs and
the line becomes dotted.
Letting my happiness
pass me on,
leaving loneliness, sadness, or anger
to fill its spot.
Soon, the line becomes steady again,
and I go on following it until
God decides it is time for my
yellow line to come to its end.

Jo Haney

The Holy Part

The way we always hold each other
Tells me I've not been loved before
There've been other arms around me
They always left me wanting more

You don't have to say you love me
I need no proof, I've seen your soul
We don't brag about our feelings
They're much too sacred to be told

You taught me I should never let
My fear of love keep me from heaven
So when you asked to take me there
A voice told me, you better let him

Unlike some who came before you
I found someone who really cares
Our love has built a special shrine
A place that only we can share

That's our holy part, the holy part
The passion that we share is like a work of art
But what we feel, the part that is so real
Is the holy part, the holy part

Anne Stokes

Sunflowers

Vibrant yellows, smiling faces
Sun-streaked petals, dew kissed leaves
Like golden fields of wheat
A treasure of happiness
just waiting to be opened
The flowing of the wind through
the tender yet strong petals
makes a heavenly sound
a sound so beautiful
only the angels can hear it
the sunflower is not only
a thing of beauty but
it is also a sign of strength
not only does it possess
beauty outside but
inside as well

Amber Wilson

Elegy Of A Soldier

Young to old, old to young
Such is war, to all or some
Life and love, death and sorrow
This is the truth, and the horror

The scars on bodies tell not all
Our eyes will show what hurt the soul
Pain and terror, joy and relief
These are what we have hidden deep

In the jungles, in the paddies
From the Delta, to the DMZ
We screamed out our frustrations
As our lives were taken from us

We fight the battles when we are asked
And some condemn us for our task
A warrior lives, a warrior dies
And yet we ask for none to cry

Dave Roark

If Not For The Poet's Pen...

Ideas for eternity
Subtle abstract imagery
Told by those worthy
In the art of poetry

Tone, rhythm, and rhyme
Encompassing all of time
Scanning, meter, symmetry
Techniques of poetry

Eloquent style and form
A poet at his art
But all a poem is
Cries from a poet's heart

Soar to heights perilous
Like Icarus
To resurrect a mind dead
Like Lazarus

So what of reality
But a mass of obscurity
For if not for the poet's pen
Who will tell the world of men

Enrique J. Ruiz

"Gray"

Somewhere in the shades of gray
Still lie black and white
Indifferences can turn to hope
Hate won over by the light.

Look into the depths of gray
Confusion - nothing's real
Shadows closely guard the heart
Only love can break the seal.

Hear the Siren songs of gray
Feel the tangible grip of night
Lies shine brightly, visible beauty
While the truth stays out of sight.

Mists of gray - swift to descend
Opposition disappears
No one moves forward, and no one back,
Nobody seems to care.

Amy Engebretsen

"O Silver Moon"

Shining through the darkened
starlit sky,
creatures come out
while others lie.

Filling her time,
March emerges strong.
Aires, the fire sign,
marches to his throne.

The howling werewolf of myth
dances at your fullest light.
Green earthly plants are bitten
by bats along their flight.

The left eye of God watches
as the sun is gone.
Because the earth is dark,
doesn't mean we're alone.

Earl Barnes

My Reflection

My reflection in the water
staring back at me
My reflection of the past and
the remembrance of being
By using my reflection as a mirror
I search for my own person
By finding my reflection
I know who I am
Without my reflection
I am lost

C. Huston Wamsley

To My Mother

With silver hair and folded hands
Stained by the toil and strife,
On mothers day the world depicts,
The setting sun of life.

Dear God we thank you for the gifts
That come from thee alone.
And chiefly for that mothers love
Which is so much like your own.

We pray that you will greatly bless
Our mother on this day,
With treasures from thy mighty store
That will never pass away.

Her love is like an Island
In the ocean of life,... vast and wide.
A peaceful, quite shelter,
From the wind and rain and tide.

Mother's heart was made for loving,
The kind no other knows.
God in heaven ever keep it
Pure as the whitest snow.

Charles R. Nowlin

Seedlings

English ivy grows under my tree
Spreading in all directions.
Its simple beauty is a source
Of pleasure to me and quiets my mind.
A portion grows beyond
The shaded protection
Of the limbs above.
The summer sun scorches
Some of the leaves while
Others remain unscathed
Reminding me of another
Garden I tended.
Two baby girls grew under my heart
From one seed.
One was ready to greet the sun
But one was not.
Nature's beauty
And Tree of Knowledge
Yields both.

Diane Harvey

Untitled

Now is the time for brightest lights
On the shortest darkest winter nights
Now is the time for "Silent Night"
Now is the time to sing again
Peace on earth, good will to men.

Jeffrey Alan Lovvorn

Imagine

Imagine being on a
Spaceship or on a
far off world.

Imagine being a
deep sea diver
on the ocean floor.

Imagine being a
dinosaur or having
a planet all your own.

Imagine being on
the inside of your
body fighting a bad green.

Imagine being a
dolphin swimming and
playing in the sun.

Imagine what you
could be or where
you could put yourself.

Jamey Woodruff

"With Death Comes Life"

Heart that yearns, for its dying love
soul that speaks of what thou loves
spirit that feels,
the pain and the hurt.

The sadness you feel
when loved ones die
the ones you knew and loved dearly
but now they are all gone.

Betrayed by one you love
once she was so dear to you
but now you feel lost,
your just lost in your own misery.

But time will soon heal
all the broken hearts
along with the pain,
and the doubts in our hearts

Alicia Villasenor

Foreclosure

Oozing from my pores,
sorghum of self-hatred.

Sown by the farmer
of inappropriate seeds.

Gummy, black sludge
coats my tongue,
leaves vile tastes in my mouth.
Tars my guts
with sticky pitch.

A mire, determined to nurture
the evil planted in my roots
for eternity.

Howls shoot silently
from my throat, begging
release of the fetid fruit
growing inside.

Through this mourning,
his shadow blocks
watery sun.

Foreclosing my future.

EmJay League

Looks

Sometimes people glance,
Sometimes people stare,
Other times you look around
And no one is there.
Someday you will see me,
Someday I'll be there,
That day you won't glance
At me
That day you will stare.
I will send a smile
Out your way,
You will open up your heart,
Catch my smile and put it
Where it will stay.
When you look outside
During the day,
Open your heart
And let my smile out to play.
For all you have is my smile,
Keep it happy so it will shine.

Elizabeth Walker

Time

Time has ways of giving chances
Sometimes as raunchy as exotic dances
Causing tremors in the heart
Or shooting arrows in the dark
Making choices that goes unheeded
Creating sorrows that comes unneeded
Imposing fitful sleepless nights
A handful of sunshine orange and bright
How much time is anyone given -
No one knows, but is hauntingly driven
To a destiny that's not foretold
Until fate appears big and bold
Straining needlessly, to hold on to life
Straining hard to down play strife
Each day life is an agency
Living in a sense of urgency
Running out of time — time is a loan
Run, run, while you can
   Time marches on

Juanita Fisher

Without You

   Living in the past, is not
something I can do,
   but, living in the present, means
I would have to live without you.
   I keep wondering why you left,
and never said goodbye,
   but, there is nothing I can do,
except keep wondering why?
   I think back on what happened,
and still cannot understand,
   but, even with you here, an
explanation, I could not demand.
   You see, you were never mine,
we were never together,
   we could have never been in
love, especially not forever.

Donna Waite

My Sister

My sister you bug me,
My sister you're a pest,
Although you can't see,
I think you're the best
My sister I think I love you!

Danielle Sheffler

Eagles

I love Eagles as they
soar to the sky

Always watching how high
they fly

It's funny how they just
zoom by

They fly around turning
every tide.

They spread their wings
soft and wide

Swooping down like a big
long slide

Always enjoying a free
feeling ride.

They are such beautiful
birds.

In flight, soaring
without words.

Cliff Larson

The Earth And Me

The sap of a tree,
So sweet as the blood of my heart.
The bud of a flower,
So pretty as the soul of my body.
The hotness of day,
The coldness of night,
The blue water of the sea,
The darkness of night.
The brightness of day,
The stars of night.
As the sun fades away,
I fall asleep.
The moon shines above me,
As I fall into deep sleep.

Billy Dillon

A Message To Our Grandchild,
With Love!

Sweet little baby
So soft and warm,
Nestled in your blanket,
Safe from harm.

You came from love,
And precious, too.
You are all the things
We hold so true.

Hope for the future
We pray will be ...peace,
And prosperity for all to see.
We wish you well, and
We hopefully trust,

Your generation will bring
The best for all of us.
So sleep well, little grandchild,
In this blanket of love,

May the Lord bless
And keep you, and guide you
From the heavens above.

Helen Cline

Pollution

The world started out
   so neat so clean
It was like nothing you could imagine
   as pure as a dream
But then came along the cars
   and the fires
They said it wouldn't harm us
   but they were such liars
They polluted our waters
   and tore down our trees
They didn't ask they didn't care
   they just took our vital needs.
But things are going to get worse
   if nothings done
Necessities will be scare
   and soon there will be none
So if nobody does anything
   cause no one dares
Then everybody's going to suffer and die
   simply because not everyone cares.

Anne Masters

Adolescent Arrest

So many with fond memories
So much lack of growth
So great are the obstacles
So wide idealistic selves

So few with future sensories
So little there can't be both
So small are the debacles
So narrow the shelves

Summit never reached
Slide is on same side of hill
No tools of climb
Holding onto a crevice

Of age has peaked
Conflicts can kill
Values of another time
How to solve the premise

Carl Casteel

Listen To The Angels

Angels from the heavens
So lightly fly about
Caring, healing angels
That make us have no doubt

Some are walking, some are talking,
some are listening, too
kindness, fairness, gentleness
Are the only words they choose

Revealing our life's purpose
As they laugh and sing with glee
"Be all that you are."
"Be all that you can be!"

Courage, strength and wisdom
Are the messages they send
Making our own destiny
A treasure to extend

Messages are brought to all
Who awaken to the call
As we journey - You and Me
And learn to love unconditionally

Carolyn A. Henderson

"Time"

Say - time is passing,
  So fast! So fast!
Yesterday's vanished,
  And - today's here at last!

Day turns to night,
  It's always been so.
But - let's stop the hours,
  And not let them go!

My, oh, my
  Tomorrow is here
Today is yesterday
It's like that, all year.

So, we're back to today!
That's what tomorrow became.
  Yes, time is flying by,
It's always the same.

  How will we handle it?
What to do? What to do?
  One day at a time, dear
For me - and, for you!

Florine Holley

Butterflies And Elephants

Butterflies and elephants
So different in every way
One is small and elegant
The other big and strong
Who would say God made one wrong

Just as butterflies and elephants
He made people different too
As you see you are not like me
And he did not make me like you
Who would say He made one wrong

Butterflies and elephants
And everything that lives
He gave each uniqueness
A beauty of its own
Who would say God did things wrong

Butterflies and elephants
A reason for each birth
A purpose here on earth
Who would say God did things wrong

Joyce Degrand

Untitled

  Look at your glass mirror reflected
smiles with you plastic finger pointed
me... mocked and laughed at in this box
I sit in the corner and decay forgotten
and lost my world evaporates before your eyes.

Christian Dolias

Untitled

Photos in an album
smiles
Best friends
Our images overlapping
Like good times
Where have you been
We are young and innocent
awaiting the real world
I live through this moment
I long for this moment

Jill K. Edwards

Coming Of Age

As a little bundle in mothers arms
Sleeping soundly, safe from harm
Growing, changing every passing day
Crawling, walking, content at play
Learning more as time goes by
Of mother earth and the deep blue sky
Life experiences thus challenge me
To break the chains that set me free
I wish to reach beyond the clouds
Return to thy maker, happy, proud

Jonna Beam

Who Will Warm The Children?

Who will warm the children
sleeping in Death's cold arm?
Who will look in on them
protecting them from harm?

Their bodies may not remain
for Death is a physical thorn.
It's sharp and ready to tear
children from where they were born.

Their memories are still intact,
though loved ones unable to hear.
God clearly remembers each one,
individually, holding them dear.

He will warm the children
lying in Death's cold grave.
He will resurrect them,
each one, their given day.

Dawn A. Scholze

Evening

I walk slowly down to the brook,
Sit beneath the willow and look
At the sun sinking in the west.
  It's evening.

The sky all red with a fiery glow,
In yonder distance cattle low,
Chipmunks peek from a nearby tree,
They're used to seeing the sight of me.
  It's evening.

I hear the babble of the brook,
Watch dragon flies flit about this nook.
While frogs chant their merry tune,
Away far off a lonely loon.
  It's evening.

When the sun sinks beneath the hill,
Comes then the call of the whippoorwill.
Contentment like this is my quest,
It's the time of day I like the best.
  It's evening.

Hazel Barnes

The Ant

The ant, he crawls and crawls,
seemingly going no where.
But, as I watch him,
I find,
that he goes everywhere,
everywhere I cannot.
Because, you see,
the ant is my hopes, my dreams,
my fears, and me.

Cassie Walker

My Sister

She's a very special person,
She's always there for me.
I feel so warm and safe,
With her I love to be.

I sometimes get to thinking,
She's getting on in years.
She's not healthy as she used to be,
It fills me full of fears.

I know she won't always be around,
And it scares me half to death.
I don't know how I'd cope,
It from my life she left.

I think, I hope she knows,
Just how much I love her.
She's my very best friend,
I'm so glad she's my sister.

Beverly K. Schultz

Changes In Seasons

Mother nature has her gowns,
She dresses earth in them.
And she changes all the seasons,
for lot and lots of different reasons.

White for the cold and soft snow
Springtime has a summer glow
Golden for the fall's stiff leaves
Summer's dressed in bright pink sleeves

This cycle goes around and round,
changing colors on the ground.

And the sky turns grey to white,
Winter darkness to summer light.

From the golden and brown blanket
to the green and yellow trinkets,

Nature changes all year 'round
with her different, gorgeous gowns.

Jennifer Montsinger

Our Family

This family of ours
Shall never part
For there's a special love
Deep in our hearts.
Days shall come
When we shed the tears.
From joy and from sorrow
Throughout the new year.
Things have been said
And things have been done
But the love in our hearts
Shall still go on
I care for my family
And I know they care too
So let's share our feelings
The way we're supposed to.

Christine Helwig

Haiku From A Work In Progress

The seasons come back
like an address you keep from
letter to letter

Christopher Brunski

"Love At First Sight"

From the second I
   saw you,

It was love at first
   sight.

I knew that I'd feel
   this way.

It pains me to love
   you,

Not knowing if you
   love me back.

And every time I look
at you, I feel happy
and overjoyed.

But there's always pain
in my heart because I
know that you're not
   mine.

Amanda Baukol

I Wondered

I looked back to yesterday,
Saw my reflection in its face.

What happened to fair play
And belief in better days.

I wondered...

Was it youthful energy fantasy,
Maybe fear of middle age.

I looked forward to tomorrow
And felt decades of sorrow.

I wondered...

I spent my twilight years in anger
Seeing the present full of danger.

A half of century filled with unfounded
Dreams and conquered wishes.

I looked in the mirror and saw my face.
Drained of life and full of fate.

What happened to yesterday.

I wondered...

Diane Williams

"The Last Buffalo"

I am the last of the buffalo
roaming through the field
I am the last of the buffalo
can you see how I feel?
I am the last of the buffalo
searching for a mate,
Will it be God, man or I, who
decides my fate?
I am the last of the buffalo
let me go my way,
to graze, to run, to sleep and play.

Aaron Davis

Sister's Palace

I woke up to a cow bell,
reminding me of the chimes
sounding in the alley

over the thyme and basil,
potted herbs
in the seclusion

of the courted yard,
coffee with black
and grounded strength

wafting through the wires
and within

the high-wooden boards
keeping to themselves,

Carbon sprouting in
a fruiting barrel, and
the cow bell nailed nearby.

Heather Fortinberry

Tears

A tear falls,
Reflecting the sadness,
Of broken hearts,
Lost dreams,
And aching souls.

A tear falls,
Revealing not a soldier,
But a man,
Who feels and understands fears.

A tear falls,
And forgotten promises are remembered,
And wishes are made,
For a second chance at life and love.

A tear falls,
In joy as black polished boots,
Touch the blessed soil of home,
A tear falls in silence.

A tear falls in thanks.

Bentley N. Williams Jr.

Quiet Intensity

A bat flutters overhead,
   Reeling
   Teetering
   Diving
   Traversing its dizzying path
      against a backdrop of haze.
Gritty, suntanned fingers on the beach
   grip a string.
Animated eyes
   watch the bat
   struggle
      to stay aloft.

Jane E. Squires

Portrait of Sara Chang

Celestial flower dancing,
Moving when music's emotion
Compels her, beautiful,
Sensitive beyond belief,
Still a child, trailing
Glory from her muse.

Clyde Beakley

Anticipation

One
   red
      strawberry
Eaten while waiting for you
Savoring the luscious fruit
So sweet
So juicy
I wonder if the taste
Will seem as delicious
After
   you
      arrive

Julie A. Kittinger Hunkar

What Is Life?

Memories I have,
Recollections I don't,
People I'll remember,
Names I won't,
Like this it will continue,
To go on for years,
Until the day I die,
My family in tears,
Though I am young,
My thoughts they are clear,
And when I sleep,
My thoughts reappear,
Reminding me of what is right,
Now and then all through the night,
So there you see,
What life means to me.

Gina Karst

Unforgettable

You left just as you came to me
Quietly without a word
Your first hello was just a smile
Your last goodbye I never heard

But life goes on and time will tell
Just how much you mean to me
When in a sweet and better place
Your precious face I'll see

Should the stars all burn away
And the sun deserts the sky
No, not even then my sweet
Shall my love for you die

John R. Geary

Papa

   A man
Quick to love, quick to laugh.

   A man
Ready to help, ready to trust.

   A man
With a hand out to support others,
   not a hand out for his own wants.

   A man
Full of caricature, full of wisdom.

   A man
Full of compassion, full of love.
   A man
I treasure, I adore.

   A man
Loved by all, especially me.
   A grandson.

Don McLeod Jr.

Desolation

My heart is a grey stone weight
pulling me; concave empty body,
shivers and cracks,
shredded memory
burns my soul
tears of hatred fall to nothing
and I am dead and lonely;
no one will ever be able to find me.
I hide myself in disguised gaieties
fighting the jealousy
completely remembering,
but nothing left to go back to.
So I burn my ashes, and you
are gone forever.

Jessimy Blasberg

Lakota

She was a Lakota woman
proud and strong
and she knew she would
always have a place to belong

Her heritage was her own
and her blood was pure
for the Lakota woman
had much to endure.

Her path was not always easy,
and her road was not
always smooth, but
courage and strength always
took hold.
Even during the whiteman's
endless pursuit of yellow gold.

She bore children and made
warriors out of boys
where bow and arrows
and knives were their only toys.

The Lakota woman, proud and true. Honor
pride and war is all she knew.

Deborah L. Reddell

To Jerry

You are the infinite onward
projectionist
with a gist about your torso
casually woven
   in
spring fall dementia glisten!
And listen
to the chords fall unto yearning
like stagnant dream-sickles
   punch
   through rough core
   and a whimsical heart
   slick from the passion
   of angelic communes
   passing through time
   slipping through hands
     stopping/receiving
     the virtual day
     encumbered
     never forgotten

James Patrick Sinisi

Your Memory

Sadness
Pouring from within.
I try to conquer;
I try to fight.
I always fail.
Your memory overwhelms me,
I can not resist.
You are never in sight,
Yet always in mind.
How can I leave your memory behind?
I can't get over what you did,
And I can't get over you.
It isn't fair.
I can't seem to move on.
I'm stuck in the past,
Without a future.

Amy Leeper

Prayer Of Love

Heavenly Father up above
Please protect the one I love
Keep him always safe and sound
No matter where he may be found
Teach him to know
As I teach him to see
That I love him
And he loves me
Please dear Father help me to be
The kind of girl he wants of me
Grant me this, oh Lord
And I'll be content
For the boy I love with all my might
I'll say this prayer every night

Beverly Trygar

Being Strong

Oh dear Lord
Please hear what I say
Answer my prayers
each and every day.

Guide me through
this difficult test
help me to see
your way is the best.

Give me strength
to endure what I must
Give me guidance
to never lose trust.

Show me the path
that I must take,
knowing I'm forgiven
if I make a mistake.

Soften my heart, Lord
so I can see
always loving you
is where I want to be.

Jayelee M. Stone

Exorcism

Do demons really walk around?
Play havoc with the populace?
Cause wars, famine, and disaster?
They may; but we do it faster.

Helen Stuart

Invictus

Do not drop the satin
pillow gently
on my face,
point to calendars,
scurry about with clocks
reproving fingers to your lips.

Bring me a silver
casket, line it with
raven's wings,
invite me in,
and I will leap astride
waving my arms like Teddy
at San Juan.

I am presumptuous.
I will not
courteously stand aside,
for these same bones
walk. The calendar
cannot be argued with
but I do not believe.

Eva Holmquist

Winter Frolic

The ice twinkling on the trees,
Piles of snow hug your knees.
Snowball fights are so much fun,
With such high snow you can not run.
School is canceled every day,
And everybody says hurray!
You reach down to get some snow,
You lose your footing and away you go.
Down the road you can not halt,
What happened to the plows and salt?
Suddenly you tripped and fell,
And now you have a long story to tell.
You said you better get on your way,
Before night turns instead of day.
You walked and walked forever it seemed,
Then you awoke, it was only a dream.

Jennifer Sanders

Sarajevo (Bosnia-Herzegovina)

The screams of children
Pierce the smoke filled air.
Silent adults choke down fear.
Body parts fall like rain,
No peace is found.
The oracles of religion
Are set aside,
To satisfy the demons of death.
The confusion of men's minds
Speak meaningless words.
Death stalks the streets
Like a lion seeking its prey.
No prayers are heard.
No bloodshed averted.
No love endured.
No peace held.
The God of love weeps!

David C. Eddy

"Dawn To Dusk"

As I sit upon this Cliff,
Overlooking the sea,
Asking God about my end,
And how close can it be?

From birth, on the farm.
Through childhood and adolescence,
I never did anyone any harm,
But, I had my share of pestilence.

As I grew into adulthood
Through thick and thin,
I look back now and wonder,
Why did I fault and sin?

I'm sure God will forgive me,
For living such a fast pace,
As I look up to Heaven,
Tears roll down my face.

Glorious God in Heaven,
What sinner been I,
I'm ready to repent
For a Life well spent.

Harold L. Sargent

Death Waited

The air was warm with Spring
Outside the hospital room.
But inside the quiet halls...
Were filled with dark gloom.

Death waited...for the moment,
For which God had ordained.
A bird sang...a quickened breath-
And then...death acclaimed!

God called the mortal man
From the bed on which he lay
To the Heavens above.
And then death went away!

No more anguish or pain,
No more worry or fears.
But a loved one remains
Just a sob and her tears.

Cries that fell on deaf ears,
A touch he could not feel-
One last..long look...A
Broken heart only God could heal.

Bobbye Tubbs

Untitled

I once loved
Or maybe twice in life
But pain remains
The ardent hound snapping
At my heels I am
Running
Running gaining strength
And distance running
Out of time I die
A little running
Running love
Into screaming
Amber flames of hell
I douse the burning
blackened heart with
Sour wine
And die a little
Running
Running
Running

JoAnn W. Bernard

Memories

Everything will one day be
Only a dim distant memory
And whether good or bad
I can't relive what I had.

An ailment may eventually come
That makes my life wearisome
And stops the busy activity
Of my brain and my body.

If I cannot hold in memory
Loved ones most dear to me
Then I dread not to perish
If I can't recall what I cherish.

Then let me return, as all must
From where we come back to dust.
Was my life a pleasant memory?
Is there anyone to cherish me?

Cherry E. Jones

A Questioning Heart

You gave me a friend
One to cherish and admire,
But I got confused
And may have lost the entire.
For the sake of a question
I should have brought to you;
Could I take it all back
And start up anew?
I just didn't want to get hurt
For the pain I could not stand;
My family was already broken
And I needed a helping hand.
Could this relationship be fixed
And work once again,
Or should I just give it all up
To avoid heartbreak or pain?
I'm praying with sincerity
Hoping you'll hear my humble cry.
Help me decide to say hello again
Or just say good-bye.

Anna-Marie Cecrle

Snowfall

Oh, the loveliest sight in winter,
  One I'm sure you'd like to know,
Is a meadow full of pine trees
  All with bonnets made of snow.

Snowflakes dancing on the breezes
  Are the lightest things there are,
Once I caught one in my hand
  And there I held - a star;

But it melted, oh so quickly,
  And a tear welled in my eye
Till I looked toward the Heavens
  And more stars were in the sky,

Floating lightly, resting softly,
  Heaping mounds of airy white
In the meadow, glen and forest,
  'twas an awe-inspiring sight.

And I thought as downy lightness
  Sifted tall on rail and post,
Of the many glorious wonders
  Mortals know with God as host.

Fannie Peterson

"Nightmare"

The blue water
once calm
now angry
crashing, thrashing
I look down
fleetingly, frightened
At the rocks
with their evil, crooked grins
I am helpless looking in
too late
too late
cruel world
cruel fate
one passing moment
the ground releasing my feet
I awaken
too shaken
to even speak

Alissa Martin

Where Are You? Where Am I?

Do we still exist
on the same celestial ball?

Do we still possess
the same dichotomous form?

Or has your spirit shed its skin
and gone to Glory?

We want you "home"...
but perhaps you are.

Cynthia Thomas

Sequoia Song

Redwood tree, Sequoia grows
On hallowed ground.
Ancient ones, in timeless place,
Enchantment found,
The quiet holy sound,
Of a millenium.

Forest shrine, a mystic grove,
Deathless life abound.
Day by day, time after time
The seasons come,
And the years succumb
To a millenium.

Evergreen, O Conifer
From tiny seeds may grow.
Long ago, fell to the ground,
And the pinecone knows,
Of life unbound,
For a millenium.

Debra Miles Newkirk

The Gates

The gates have softly sealed now
On all the things we knew.
The tears have gently whispered
The last I love you too.

In parting, pain and sorrow
Comes into life so strong
It rips upon my inner soul
And make it seems so wrong.

And yet, someday I'll find him.
I'll hold him close to me.
We'll walk and talk together
In God's Eternity.

Arlene E. Rambough

Seasons

Love is

the whisper of a fresh breeze
on a summer noon
the tap of a fallen leaf
on an autumn eve
the sight of a tender flake
on a winter night
the taste of a sweet raindrop
on a spring morn.

Love is

the lashing rage of the wind
the barren emptiness of the trees
the frozen stillness of the grounds
the flooded frenzy of the rivers.

Love is

coming home
to the warmth of your embrace
all year around.

Harshi Syal

Eagle In Heaven

As the eagle flew by
On a summer day
He went very high
To be on his way
To meet the clouds
So nearer to God
The closer he got
A good feeling came to him
To see that he flew
A little too high
For he was there
On this summer day
In a wonderful place
Called heaven.

Dänya Vanzura-Rogers

Wind Of Freedom

I felt cold and alone,
On a dark, dreary night,
But a warm, subtle wind,
Brought my spirit to light.

My emotions were stirred,
To a slight discontent,
With hopes to soar freely,
And no wish for descent.

Follow your desires,
And travel your sky,
I can't hold you, Wind of Freedom,
Nor will I try.

You've given me a gift,
I was too blind to see,
The true course to freedom,
Is hidden in me.

This vision did capture,
What no words can say,
Perhaps I too,
Will be Wind someday...

Janice A. Johnston

Poetry Writing

Poetry is a free form
Of word after word;
Written about anything
You've ever seen or heard.

Take a little time
Focus on one subject.
Write everything about it,
No word or thought reject.

Give yourself a challenge
Like a word describing a trait.
Ponder and write all you can,
It could change your fate.

Turn that chosen word
Over and over in your mind.
Think of people you know
In whom this trait you find.

Write down each variance
Found in those you know,
And from the ideas collected
A wonderful poem will flow.

John W. Henderson

Fireflies In A Rainstorm

Small mirrors
of the World Above
Parodies
of the Greater Brilliance

Sparks of Light
Defending against the Darkness
Links
to the realm
of Faerie

The Magic
of Fire
and Rain

for where Light and Darkness
intertwine
Anything is possible.

Ilona M. Cookman

Relief

I was weary and tired
Of the toils of this life;
Living through worry,
Sorrow and strife.

I felt the need and
Lack of some love
It was the blessing
Of God up above.

Then, when I found it
The peace that I feel;
Make all of my worries
Seem so unreal.

I've forgotten the weariness
The sorrows and care;
The toils of this world,
Are not even there.

I feel light headed
Care free and gay
For Jesus has taken
My care all away.

Alma Elizabeth Elder

Raindrop Song

Listen to the pitter-patter
of the raindrop song,
Hear the sound of what the matter
singing sweet and long,
Gently falling for an hour
into eager earth,
Soon the blossom of the flower
blooms into its birth,
See a flutter butterfly
light upon a pink,
Where raindrop from the big blue sky
is sip of water drink,
Raindrop sings its liquid note
natures gift to nourish,
Golden sun in sky a-float
we see above and cherish.

Amelia Nyers

Drifting

Listen to the quiet
of the morning
after the night
and before the dawn.

A time of its own...
yet in limbo
A separate zone
between the realms

Of dark's sleep
bright's waking.
Thoughts creep...
weaving in and out

Of altered states
of time and place.
We weight their traits
on drifter's scales.

Soon shades of the night
slowly give way.
Dreams take flight,
but memories stay.

Barbara Wicke Scialdone

Still Moon

Upward I take council
of the moon's overflow
a dream-state cup
this gift to know

Virtuous recompense,
quiet, tranquil wonder.
Outward stretched arms,
dreamy summer.

In flux it continues
never ending away
defiant flit
ever at bay.

Give me resurrection
forever, scorn be gone.
Where is my dawn
of the new morn?

In quiet I ponder
in search of my fullness
Stay mine old moon!
Be still, be nigh.

Donald R. Gray I

An Old Soul

I've stood at the edge
of the deepest river,
and looked into
its eternal soul.
Its waves ripple
to hide the secrets
and the passions never told.

I've been at the foot
of the highest mountain,
able to image
its unending peak;
And envisioned immortal footsteps
discovering the answers
we all seek.

I've been in the eye
of the freest wind,
its unburdened spirit carried me away
through every obstruction,
reaching here and now,
for tomorrow from yesterday.

Jamila Kibibi

My Masterpiece

I used to dream
Of being a writer,
Or a poet, reciting prose.
What I found
When I looked around,
Was my masterpiece sucking his toes.

I used to dream
Of being a designer,
A cherry red dress and a cape.
What I found
When I looked down,
My masterpiece wanted grape.

I used to dream
Of having it all,
It's plain to all I have won.
Because every night
I rock him gently to sleep
For my masterpiece is my son.

Jane A. Klemm

Ode To Democracy In Nigeria

My penchant is dead
Obituary page reading.
For the news.
The passing of autocracy.
Soldiers saccharin.
The dagger on democracy.
Autocracy alive.
My penchant is dead.
Intimidation ahoy.
Sour government agog.
Soldiers in vogue.
Autocracy alive.
My penchant is dead.
The columns are filled.
The people are killed.
My penchant is dead.
When is the news?
Where is democracy?
Autocracy alive.
My penchant is dead.

Alex Edema

Thomas Crow

My wife you ask?
O yes I loved her, and cherished
 her too.
But 'twas I who trapped her, for
 she was always home, I but
 twice a week
I liked it that way
"A woman has no place out of doors,"
 I told her
But oh how I loved her, cared for
 her
Though - she did not feel loved, nor
 give unto me as I unto her.
For 'twas her hand which placed
 arsenic in the champagne at
 dinner that night
And 'twas I who looked her straight
 in the eye and died...

Jill Berrier

Crone Revealed

False images lie within mirrors
nursed by illusive mind imagery,
transporting a sixties face into
a twenties memory...while

A photo in newsprint evidences
reality, exposing each linear
indentation in a face, eulogizing
an earthly voyage of existence. . .

A jolt giving substance to time
spent living, loving, and
regretting hours spent or
not spent in caring —
Revealing roadways to rapture,
pathways to sorrow and grief,
lines of fun and laughter —
each encased in crevices of
painful decisions.

Yet the image maker, still passive,
 refuses to confront
the uncontrollable process of maturity.

Beth Scott

Life

  Life is like a road,
Nowhere to run, hide or
go; some go fast and
some go slow, but there's
no where to go. There are
bumps and there are curves
and there are accidents,
but we survive, yes, we
survive, but one day that
road ends, after all the
bumps and curves and accidents
we finally find our way home.

Alison Day

Who I Am

I am like the water of a lake
my soul searching for the sea
Some of my strength that shall be;
a comfort for a few loved ones.
If I become negative
I stand alone on sandy ground
but all in all I come around
the Lord God I have found.

Becca Dunn

Wish

Life all alone
Nothing is clear
Death is my wish
Without you here

Once I was kind
Now I can hate
Look in the mirror
Death cannot wait

What has become
Of this life that I live
You took my love
Now there's nothing to give

Ending my life
My friend is this blade
The pain is so good
My smile soon fades

My wish has been granted
But no one can tell
I'm still all alone
But burning in hell

Christopher DeWildt

Always Have You

Walking through life
Not thinking of reality,
Being in a dream,
living a fantasy.

Not realizing that someday
the man I adore,
will no longer be
the loving man from before.

Friends are all I have
to comfort my heart
to listen to my problems
and help me find a new start.

Are you sent from Heaven above
to take away my pain?
To stay with me always,
so I never go insane?

Then no matter what I say,
no matter what I do,
can I be honestly sure,
that I'll always have you?

Jodi Fechtelkotter

Part Of The World

Let me be part of the world,
not bury my head in the ground
and let things slide by me
like pictures on a screen;
not to get involved.
Let me help where help is needed
use my talents for the good of man,
Be the world flat or round.
I want to be part of the world,
not that my name be known far and wide
but to know I've given something
to the growth and changes,
on this earth in which
I can take pride.
I want to feel it in my bones
and in my soul,
To feel that depth of satisfaction
that this world is mine
and I am part of it.
Only then will I feel whole.

Dorothy J. MacKenzie

"Bottomless Sea"

My heart lie not in the timber of time
Nor in the grass departed
Beneath the sand under the sea
My heart reaches clearest

Storms turned into mountains despair
Of time everlasting into a dawn
With springtime blooming in prime
Young in serenity old in confusion

My heart rested on a rock solum
In the sea with beauty in slumber
Never lost or rediscovered
My heart hears nothing

Judith Hostetter

Onward Till Dawn

Walking along the dusty dirt path,
No real destination in mind;
Having no idea where I'm at,
Not knowing what I'll find.

Dwelling not upon the past,
Letting bygones be bygones;
Memories of old slipping away fast,
While I march onward till dawn.

Obstacles come and block my way;
I somehow find a path through.
Night soon blends into day,
And eventually, eve is born anew.

Someday, I'll remember this place,
And the day my journey started on;
But as of now, life's only a race,
And I'm just marching onward till dawn.

Emily Siska

The Light Will Come

Why am I left with hurt
No one else on earth can help?
Why does God not see the pain,
And agony, I've felt?

Are dreams worth struggling for?
They come and go with ease,
No power of mine can stop them,
Nor can I ask God, "Please".

I can't cope with my heart,
It's bound with memories
I only wait - for the light
To help me cross the seas.

Inez McLain

"A Token Of Love"

Lord as I ponder,
my thoughts of way yonder,
it's easy to offer you praise.
And as I surrender
my all and remember,
I'm even more amazed.

I can never repay you,
but help me obey you,
as a token of my gratitude.

Your love ever lifts me,
my soul longs to bless thee.
As a token I offer you praise.

Brenda Maynor

Southern Lady

Such grace! Such charm!
No one could quite compare,
To the Southern genteel lady,
With the silver stylish hair.

Her smile is oh so warm,
If just a little tight.
A genuine steel magnolia,
Her step so quick, so light.

A lady first and foremost,
A stalwart to behold
A stronghold for her children.
Tactful, sweet, and bold.

Her posture's almost perfect,
Her grammar is superb.
Her manners most impeccable;
Goodness in deeds and words.

She knows just how to comfort,
She knows just when to calm.
She's genuine Southern Lady,
Who can make a house a home.

Gail Walls

You And I

You and I will always be,
no matter what hardships we see.
Through good or bad, happy or sad,
you and I will always be.
Through sunshine or rain we will
always remain the same. Tho' years
may pass our dreams will last.
When we grow old and gray
We will remain young in our
hearts, because you and I will always be.

Ellen Covington

Air

Out of the water, out of the sky
never seen
nor heard
nor smelt
creeping
bubbling
floating
it comes; it is
never wanted
always needed
never thought of, but always
on the mind
prayed for, screamed for
by the hopeless, helpless
slurping
gasping
sighing
AIR

Carrie Nelson

I Can Still Feel It

I can still feel it,
    my heart crushing inside of me.
I can still feel it,
    my tears rolling down my cheeks.
I can still feel it,
    and I'll feel it forever.
But somehow, even after all this,
    I am glad that
I can still feel it.

Judith A. Mixner

The Walk Of Life

As you walk along, your trail of life
never pause to stair
upon the ground, beneath your feet
for now is all that's there

Hold your head, up high and strong
look as far as you can see
if you continue step by step
soon that's where you'll be

Now and then, turn around
and look at what you've past
but not for long, or you will find
your not walking very fast

There may be times, it seems as though
it's an endless upward stride
but never fear, for at the top
of every hill there is a slide

Jessica Kaempfer

Daddy

The man you love is
near and dear
with a loving smile and
charm, so great
you thought he was
a hero.
You thought he could
do no wrong
so who is this man
who loves you so,
I think you know

Jennifer Frink

"Missed"

I once had a daughter
    named Michele.
She was my best pal.
She drew close to God
She was all that I had
She was never bad
Then it was very sad
I was all alone
Because he called her home
But she is in a
    better place then me.

Carol Evans

My Room

Don't let me guess
My room is a mess
My blankets are down
With no happy frown
My door is shut
With big cuts
But I don't give
It's the place
Where I live...

Chelsea Linsley

My Beloved Mary

It has been oh! so long
My ordeals so hard to bear
I can only find real comfort
In thinking of you who care.

I have sailed on the high seas
I have marched on foreign terrain
But the greatest torture I know
Is to have you too far such pain.

This war has torn us apart
And at times it makes me ponder
There must be truth in the adage.
Absents makes the heart grow fonder.

I eagerly await for that day
When this conflagration will end
To Triumphantly with joy return
To my love my life I will spend.

I never for a moment forget you
Rather it's on the contrary
I think of you always and always
For I love you my beloved Mary.

Benjamin W. Siravo

mid-night shadows

within the horizon
my mind's highway goes
beyond the archway
into adventurous dreams,
where visual conquest
purses primitive self
only to find heritage
on yesterday's corner...
so, inner self is exposed
to ceremonial rituals,
as life endeavors bond
to emulate the ancient's,
allowing those "chosen"
to sculpture the creed
for life's peace keepers
to step the alley ways...
wisps of past fragrances
come to pledge images
that silhouette my spirit
honing life by star glow....

Edward Robert Lang

Ode To South Africa

How I weep for you,
my long lost land...
Where hate has brought despair.
I ask this question of you,
one and all,
no matter what your colour...
Why have you sacrificed our land,
(of milk and honey)
for all that anger that you harbour?
Set it free! Cry no more!
For you hold the key to life...
The wounds must heal.
So yes, take time for this,
but do not let it hinder...
The joining of a Nation,
(at Peace)
The goal for which we strive!
Always faithful...

Ingrid Smith

"I Had No Means To Shout!"

My dream of life has come to be;
My hope has come to me.
I can call to someone through my hands,
and all the world can see.
If I can keep this dream alive,
I might be known throughout
to sail the oceans and sail the skies
with all my inspiring shout.
My heart is full.
My hope is great.
My story I will tell;
My thoughts come rapidly to mind,
and my feelings tumble out.
My eyes are words,
My hands are thoughts;
My heart is full of fear,
As I begin my journey through my words
to teach the world the things my heart will tell
   about.
If I can impart to you what I know to be the truth,
My mind is better than I dreamed to wish,
and soon you will know about
the things my heart has wished to say,
but had no means to shout.

Charles Martel Hale, Jr.

Prayer

Oh! Lord, ambition sears my breast.
   My heart's a-stir with wild unrest.
I yearn for all the greater things...
   Sage's wisdom, sport of kings.

Contentment ne'er has been my lot;
   I want to be what I am not.
Oh! Lord, make me content to be
   In humble cottage by the sea

With breakers splashing on the shore....
   Lord, let me not desire more.
Oh! Lord, let me be satisfied
   To live my life beside the tide.

Let me know my heart's desire
   Before the embers of a fire.
Let me find contentment where
   The seagulls swoop from salty air.

May I breathe the salty air,
   Feel the seabreeze in my hair,
And let me be content to end
   My life with just one faithful friend.

Doris Rafferty

Where Is The Dawn?

The sky is darkening
like my mood.
I feel isolated
from the earth.

I turn a full circle.
There is no joy or light.
If the dawn doesn't come soon
I will be in the darkness forever.

Where did it go -
the light in my heart?
Was it plucked from me
for a reason-

Like an off key guitar string
with a twang?
Will I ever know the answer?
Where is the dawn?

Jill S. Collier

Summer Breeze

As the summer breeze hits
my face, I think of the winds
touch. So smooth so quiet, so
calm. It is not always this way,
wind can be cruel and Murderous.
I do not believe the wind can be
deadly. But it is. Cruel the wind
but at the same, time Calm.
Quiet, the wind but so loud.
The wind can fly forever and ever.
Never stopping for a rest. You
can not see it nor touch it. But it
is there welcoming you,
sometimes with a sweet kiss of
air or a poisonous breath. It plays
with you by sweeping through you hair,
and entertains you by singing in the
trees. Laughing and giggling. Going
around and around while it dances on
the ground. Singing in Delight.

Christina R. Rogers

Sister Of Mine

I have a sister, I love o' so
much, who's helped me with
problems no one else would
touch.
   She's been by my side through
sorrow and pain and helped
ease the heart full of so much
strain. Now the love I feel for
this sister of mine is so very
strong words cannot define.
   We've partied we've laughed
we've crawled and we've cried
"but through the years she stayed
by my side. Now the moral to
this poem is so very clear"
   That God should give everyone
a sister so dear
   "As mine"

Joyce A. Murphy

A True Friend

One in a million;
more precious than gold.
Far beyond caring,
generous and kind.

Must be content;
share laughter and joy.
Also will feel
your sickness and pain.

Your happiness
comes before theirs.
Innermost secrets
will never be told.

Will sacrifice all;
be at your defense.
Rejoice in your fortune
when they go deprived.

Have a true friend
give praises to God!
Real gift from Heaven;
an angel of love.

Jan Loudin

Summer

Smelling pollen rising in the
Mid day air
A soft warm refreshing
Breeze
Bees buzzing happily from
Flower to flower
Birds singing in sweet
Melodies
As they sore high in the pale
Blue sky
Tracing shadows on the
Ground
By the suns bright
Glow
Children splashing in the
Ocean waters
The rapidly roaring waves
Colliding into rocks
Soon the sun sets over the horizon
And a new day begins

Julie Rossi

Full Moon Circle

Full moon circle while I sleep
meet the dawn souls deep
all my secrets daylight keep
full moon circle while I sleep

Smell of pinetree, see the sun
remembering on that silent run
I found my Maker in a book
the truth I found, the oak tree shook

Taste of almond, hear the harp
feeling air grace my heart
the horizon soars to sheep
full moon circle while I sleep

Brothers, sisters, mothers, fathers
circle crystals glow to grow far
when the red starts to snatch
the truth I found, the Maker match

Full moon circle while I sleep
meet the dawn souls deep
all my secrets daylight keep
full moon circle while I sleep

Jeffrey Robert McCusker

Being There

Coming close to the one you love
   means going through their heartache.
Carrying the burden when they cannot
   and leading the way when they do.
Holding their hand in a time of grief,
   lending an ear when needed.
Walking down each hard road
   and going barefoot part of the way.
Kissing all the bruises, left by
   others brutality and carelessness.

Go through the pain, grief, and anger
   of your loved ones life
Take your loved one though yours
   and you will both come out
With a greater understanding
   and a love that is unbeatable.

Becky Vinson

"Take My Hand"

   Take my hand O Lord walk with
me, to the promised land.
Where the streets are made of gold,
and the beauty, to great to behold.
The light is always shining bright
there is no need for darkness or night.
There is no sadness or sorrow.
No worries of the to-morrow
Where my soul is set free, and for
ever more with you shall be.
Take my hand O Lord, that I
may now walk with thee, through
all of eternity.

Georgia D. Hunter

Dad

In memory of a man,
many loved and do miss.
He was thoughtful of others,
and did what he could.
He was kind and tender
hearted.
Many say he was one in
a million
He will always be
remembered for he was
my Dad.

Charlene Barnhart

Softer Petals

Flowers, nature's natural blooms.
Makes me smile, the colors so blessed!
Petals so silky, Oh! so soft!!!
Leaves of moisten - filled with dew!
They have freedom, to grow.
No matter where they go!
Flowers show freedom to me,
And wisdom beyond enlightening!

Carla S. Pampain

Reality Against Love

Reality is for what we live
Love is for what we know is real
Reality can be hard to face
Love can be hard to feel
Reality is all around
Love is body and soul
Reality must consist of all smarts
Love must consist of all emotions
In the end reality is against love
As love is against reality

Jessica Halaska

Untitled

My emotions
Like waves of the sea
Thrashing about
Causing confusion
Blowing out
Leaving misunderstanding
Be careful
Follow each wave
Know its beginning
Discover its end
Learn to calm these waves
My emotions

Beth Gnatiuk

Birds Of All Kind

Birds of all kind
Like to sit in their nest and dine.

There are Parrots
They like to bite on carrots.

There is an owl
The owl to howl.

Birds of all kind
Do the birds live in a tree that's pine?

Jennifer Schifano

Birds With Wings

Birds with wings
Like to sing...
And fly up into the sky
To see all kinds of things.
To see the sun arise
In the cool morning spring
It's fun to be a bird
With pretty long wings
And to sing a nice pretty song
And to sing it all day long
That has a pretty ring
And it's not a silly thing...

Gale Simpson

First Summer In Dixie

I wore the oppressive August air
Like a wet winter coat
And breathed laboriously, consciously,
As though no longer an involuntary act.

The impatiens hung like dead men
And the grass, dry and brittle
Like an old woman's hair,
Lay flat and in want of chlorophyll.

The sun beat down
With the tenacity of a burrowing tick,
And not a cloud dared
Cross its indomitable path.

Somewhere in the distance
I thought I smelled lemons,
And it was almost enough to keep me
Outside a few moments more.

But alas, I retired
To my air conditioner, iced tea,
And memories of Canada.

Gordon Heins

The Allspice Of Life

When you're young and full of ginger,
Life is mostly pretty nice.
Full of little childish capers.
Full of mystery and spice.

Later still we learn to curry
Favor with the gods of thyme.
Seek the sesame of riches —
Stretch the hours of our prime.

Now it's time for us to ponder
What we have besides our age.
Hopefully we'll face what's cumin
Like the wise and honored sage!

Audrey M. Botz

Sanity

Insanity

Darkening figures dancing on the wall Sun going west to follow the call The call to sleep, the call to dream The night is calling drowning the screams Light fading fast soon to be gone Leaving my past following the sun Falling deep into a trance Hypnotic figures begin to dance Lost amongst a floating myst Caressing my body, paining amethyst Forever falling down a bottomless hole The pain so intense to pierce a soul Ecstasy in pain, so pure a fire As to burn into my deepest desire Afire but not burnt, the pain hasn't ceased Inside a roar brought forth by the Beast The beast within begins to growl Exodus it wants to commence its prowl Ripping through My spirit cleaved Raping, killing, its appetite appeased It feeds upon the pain inside Burning! Burning! Fire Abide! Within my soul find your home Draw the beast from its roam Bring the beast to where it belongs To the burning fire it forever longs Emerges a tiger cloaked in white To guard the fire and challenge the fight I am tired and want to sleep In the endless, peaceful keep Instead I live alone in pain the wondrous joy that keeps me sane I leapt ahead but did not move What of this world is yet to prove Avoiding Love to remove all doubt I step behind and lose my route Afraid to be happy for the pain it will cause To be content the uneasiness gnaws memories of former pain fester inside: I insane.

I insane

Cat-Astrophy

Margie MacFee was a spinster; she lived all alone with her cat.
He was a magnificent creature, sleek coat, tabby stripes, and all that.
As a girl, Miss MacFee was a beauty, but that beauty had faded away.
She'd lost her true love in the trenches. To new suitors she'd sadly
  said "Nay".

Margie was sorting the contents of a chest she'd received from afar.
A bottle of strange shape she noticed, fluorescent with age, sealed with tar.
She cracked off the odd looking stopper. In a flash and a cloud there appeared
a genie of splendid proportions! "Three wishes, Mistress, are assured."

Margie, of course, was quite startled. Thinking quickly, she said,
  "I would wish
To be rich; not have to count pennies!" "It's done. Full of diamonds
  this dish!"
"Next I would like to be nineteen." Said the genie, "Voila!" and 'twas so.
The wrinkles were gone. She was ravishing; a virgin aroused to love's glow.

"And last?" She thought for a moment. "Transform my dear puss to a king."
Pouf! Stood beside her a dream man, so handsome it make her heart sing!
Into his strong arms she yielded; her passion could not be delayed.
As he kissed her ear lobe, he whispered, "Aren't you sorry now you had
  me spayed?"

Malise J. Graham

To Young Seafarers

You have a gift for seeing Nature's way:
A bat against the starlit sky, the whale's breath on the bay.

As a young explorer, lured far from home,
You're like a fearless sandpiper that tempts the ocean's foam.

Share your views of Earth, serving as a guide,
And send the currents of your thoughts to push the larger tide.

If your valued friends turn and walk away,
Forgive their ignorance, and bridge their gulf another day.

Those hard times, when a person puts you down,
are temporary scribbles on your beach of higher ground.

Guard your self esteem, and trust God's gift of love,
When sailing on the sea of life where waves loom high above.

And when you have self doubts, repeat this lifelong rule:
"My mind and personality will always bring me through."

Katharine D. Barrett

Underwater

Beneath this sea of turmoil, there must lie
A bed of understanding.
How do the sands of time lay there motionless,
Against the great tide of influence?
What makes something so soft, so hard to move?
For millions of years with nothing more than
True conviction each granule supports the other.
Without regret, and without purpose.
Except to bear against the tide.

Russell Foisey

One Step

A lonely heart and single tear are wrenched against his brain,
A bloody sword of battles fought against a world that's quite insane,
A childhood fear, the reaper's sneer, inched just beyond the grasp,
The decided pace upon the race is one step beyond the last.

With armor pierced, he swayed and winced, and drank of bitter ale,
He knew that he survived the war because he'd been to hell,
And to his dismay, there it lay, it was written in the sand,
The decided fate, we all must wait, is guided by our hand.

Upon the mountains and in the trees he forged on patiently,
Marvelled by majestic scenes and sequoia pageantry,
And there in sight, of perfect light, in which he had been blind,
The decided skew of that to view, is perspect of our own minds.

A screaming souls romantic verse chimes soft about the breeze,
A graceful timbrel melody that dances among the leaves,
In rhapsodies of pure devout, in cries of ecstasy,
The decided tones of lover's moans are sung in harmony.

The touch of earth and kiss of sky had brought him to his knees,
An angel hovered over him and caressed him selflessly,
With waves of love and tides of joy so intensely never felt,
She said "the decided cheer that reappears is that of which
  you've dealt."

Steve Roark

Snaggletooth And Stone

The Rock of Gibraltar, a face turned to stone,
A business man look, he can stand on his own.

Life's tough decisions, to manage affairs,
Risk losing or winning, each challenge he bears.

This stoic figure sets down to eat,
Looks 'cross the room and sees Snaggletooth seat.

A grotesque looking man, poor, wretched and dirty
Should be 'long further in life, the man must be thirty.

Stone looks away searching deep in his heart.
Life's fate is quite strange but what is his part?

He rises up slowly, perhaps this is his lot.
Walks to the stranger with a meal that's hot.

Sets it before him, they exchange but a glance.
A weak "Bless you" is muttered; Fulfilling a chance.

Karen Y. LaBarbera

Trapped In A Light

I was trapped in a light
A light that stayed, and wouldn't go away.
Even though you try and try to close your
eyes the light is still there.

Trapped in a light that is so powerful.
It could blind you if you looked up with sorrow.
It is so powerful that it can blind you with sweetness.
Trapped, in a light, what does that really mean?

Sara Ann Bartels

A Child's Mind

A child's mind is full of thought, is full of fun.
A child's mind is full of toys, lots of fun for girls and boys.
A child's mind is like a blank slate, unruined.
It's not too late to fill that slate full of things, only good.
But if we fill them with bad things,
However great or small, we may find no child at all.

A child's mind is like a snowflake, white, pure, clean.
But if we are not careful, a clean child's mind
May soon become a dream.
The mind of a child is precious more than money, rubies, or sapphires.
It sparkles like a diamond.
It is purer than gold.

A child's mind is a beautiful thing, like a blooming flower.
If we don't save it, it may become a thing of the past.
Now I ask you is this fair?
Filled with gangs, drugs, violence, and war,
We look into a child's mind no more.

Kurtis D. Miller

"18 Years And On My Own"

A pause it was, a wanderer saw
A cross road he came to, which way?
 Maybe he knew

Not a long road these feet have walked
But a smooth one not by far
Clouds and rain with sunshine some
Hills and rocky cliffs, a beach but one.

But a wrong path chosen, a short cut then
Hazardous, but right
New people, new worlds, new ways.

Experiencing greed, death, fear
Accepted were teachings
Which nourished, built and grew
Denied are friends, love, contentment

Ever to be moving, losing, gaining
A looking, a searching, so few close to his heart
That much more to endure.

A pause it was, The wanderer saw
 A cross road he came to.
 Which way?

Richard J. P. Kowalski

For The Love Of You

Looking forward to seeing it everyday,
That delectable smile that comes across your face.
I would walk a thousand miles,
Fly around the world,
Drive from state to state,
And swim the ocean blue,
All for the love of you.

Like birds of a feather,
We will flock together.
I would be by your side,
Holding your hand,
Because I am your woman,
And you are my man,
It's all for the love of you.

Tasteful memories of you and I,
Bonded by all eternity,
Dreaming every night,
Crying when you are away,
Anxious once again to hold you tight,
All for the love of you.

Shannon L. Myricks

Just In Time

To witness a petal drop from a rose
A desert storm or dew form
on grass early in the morn

To arrive in time for an unannounced celebration
To catch the eye of the one in the room for you

To know a heart with no words
To walk in fields with the birds
Not to lose the voices under the music
Not to lose sight to the sun
Not to fall when free enough to run

To scathe the sky with a mammoth love
To touch the moon drunk with passion
To see a star fall
To hear a mother's call as the sun once more escapes the day

Is enough for me
To endure the rest
Whatever it may be

Sanford O. Bruce III

My Mountain

A magnetic force was beckoning,
A desire needing a reckoning.
Mountains, trees, and pine cones, of course,
Nature's way of radiating a healing source.

Mt. Spokane, off to the North East
Was calling for a spiritual feast.
Saturday, a day meant to be outside,
The decision was made to take a ride.

An overpowering calmness was given me
By the message of the whispering tree.
Mountain sitting gives such a peace,
My soul consumed the release.

Heaven came down and touched my soul
As the peace filled the empty hole.
The presence of God was evident
As the fear and despair just went.

Descent from the mountain was slowly made
As plans for the return were mindfully laid.
Daily, return is made to my mountain peak,
Where the presence of God I again seek.

Melba Rae Vick

Darby

We had us a promise, Dawna, Darby and me; come hell or high water,
a family we'd be.
I shouldn't feel sadness, I'll wipe away tears; Momma's known true
love, a lifetime of years.
So listen up Babe, good buddy, best friend; what we've had together,
no-way will it end!
Your memory I'll carry, we won't be apart; our love will always beat
deep in my heart.

Thanks for showing true dignity and strength; so loyal, such honor,
you've gone the full length.
Don't worry about us, Princess, don't be concerned; you've been the
best teacher, the lesson's are learned.
It's okay to sleep now, rest your little heady; close your sweet
eyes, anytime you're ready.
Just "one minute", till you're having a blast; doing all "fun" things,
we've enjoyed in the past.

Many happy returns, Baby, you deserve a good rest; be proud Darby
Caldwell, you've given your best!

Momma Loves You...

Susan C. Caldwell

Moments of Tranquility

Morning...In the midst of Fall
  a flurry of unrelenting winds
  brings leaves all aflutter,
  heaping them in an array
  of color beneath our feet...as

High noon...hastens shadows of yet another
  season, the harvest is completed
  and the seeds scattered to lie
  in wait of another Spring bloom.

Early evening...the sun glances eastward,
  coloring all that lies in its wake,
  a subtle nuance of rust, as the deep
  brown ridge along the hillside
  clearly defines the evening sky.

All the while...evoking a sense of grace and tranquility
for all who pause within her presence...NOVEMBER

  Sandra L. Shields-Herzstein

A Friend

A friend is someone you can count on in good times and in bad
A friend is someone you can lean on when you're feeling down and sad
A friend will show all their courage when yours is somewhere lost
A friend will give you anything no matter what the cost
A friend is someone who will protect you when you somehow seem too weak
And will be there for you no matter what day of the week
The one who will always lead you when you just want to follow
The one whose heart is always full and never will seem hollow
The one who will always step down when you are in the spot light
Or when you seem to stumble they'll make it all seem right
They are the ones that make it warm when it starts becoming cold
The one who always makes you feel young when you start feeling old
A friend is the one who will guide you along a path you choose
And will always be beside you whether you win or lose
They are the ones who comfort you and wipe away the tears
And will hold your hand securely even when the hour is near
A friend is someone you can always count on to give you a great big hug
But most of all a friend is someone that you can truly love.

  A. Wemhoff

A Perfect Blend

FRIENDSHIP is the sum total of its partners;
  A Friend laughs when you think you are funny.
  A Friend can often finish your sentence from unspoken thought.
  A Friend accepts your faults as mere imperfections.
  A Friend always find time to share herself.

FRIENDSHIP is built with mutual trust, faith and love;
  A Friend never leaves you alone in your loneliness.
  A Friend always leaves her door open along dark passages.
  A Friend makes unbearable pain tolerable.
  A Friend is God's gift of faith and love.

FRIENDSHIP is security because of acceptance;
  A Friend knows what lies beneath a surface mask worn for
  protection of her heart.
  A Friend bolsters your fragile ego; never condemning,
  always accepting.
  A Friend silence is acceptance, never disinterest.
  A Friend offers truth wrapped in sincerity and love.

FRIENDSHIP has feelings as the roots of its relationship;
  Love is the key to open communication and friendship.
  A Friend never holds a grudge; she forgives.
  A Friend offers a strong hand to steady your trembling.
  A Friend always listens with both her heart and her ears.

  Phyllis Schoepflin

A Frown, A Smile

A frown, not a smile, lay unconsciously on your lips.
A frown, not a smile, thinking of your disasters, your conflicts.
From your thoughts you try to get away.
You wander, you roam and you stray.
On the dark streets you contest,
always trying to be the best.

A frown, not a smile, lay unconsciously on your lips.
A frown, not a smile, thinking of your disasters, your conflicts.
You search for a place in which you call home;
a base, a shelter, a dome.
But instead, you let God lead your life
and unlike the devil you will not strife.

Then, you will have...
A smile, not a frown, laying peacefully on your lips.
A smile, not a frown, thinking of joy and happiness.

  Melissa Scott

The Gift

One long and dark December night,
A gift from God came into sight;
God's gift to us was a baby boy,
To bring the world a lot of joy.

He grew up to be a man,
And taught the Word throughout the land;
He healed the sick, the lame, the blind,
The man named "JESUS" was very kind.

Then one day, great sadness came,
The man named "JESUS" was put to shame;
Soldiers nailed Him to the cross, left Him there to die,
It was a price He paid for all, so sad it makes you cry.

Jesus lives in Heaven now, a city made of gold,
One day we'll live there with Him the Bible stories told.
God's gift was the greatest gift that anyone could give,
I'm glad for this gift from God, so all mankind can live.

  Wanda L. Kiser

Love Changes

Alone...
A glance began a love so fresh, so new
Anticipation is exalted as they want to know each other better
Weakness comes over her as he speaks
Confidence is gained due to his acknowledgment
Courting began because of feelings so strong, so real
Together...
Apologies are repeated-they are growing apart
Time cannot heal their wounds
Reality sets in-they know the relationship can not work
Weariness begins to take its toll-they are fighting a losing battle
Acceptance occurs - it is over and they must face it
Alone...

  Mechelle Lewin

Creation

As a dove takes flight
A glimmering sun shines over the vast horizon
The marriage between earth and sky
A flowering bud opens to show its beauty
its fragrance captivating
The rumble of God-like thunder
permeates throughout the heavens
Alas, the wondrous ocean crashes upon shore
as if to awaken it
A breath of life
as a child cries out
Thus a beginning
A miracle
Creation

  Patricia A. Horoszewski

218

Beauty Is...

Beauty is...
A leafless tree at night
with black sky all around, and newly fallen snow
that covers the barren ground.

Beauty is...
Waves of rippling water

washing over the sands,like the Holiest of waters
that cleanses the Lord's hands.

Beauty is ...
The burnt orange sun at dusk,
that falls behind the mountainside.
An object so exquisite, there's nothing bad to hide.

Beauty is...
The gracefulness and ease
of a Stallion running wild.
The miracle of birth that a mother gives a child.

Beauty is...
what you feel inside,
and know in your heart is true.
Beauty truly comes from deep inside of you.

Stephanie Gille

A Harvest Wind

A little cool this morning
a little death in the air.
Mean ,this morning,
like the wind through your hair.
Too bitter to gather
the fruits of our labor,
better to weather the cold in together!

Wait for the sun
to warm our cold hearts.
Linger at your leisure
'til the harvest may start.
Let the gold of the grain remain on the stalk,
let the reaper go waiting,
while we sit and talk.

Come to me, come to me,
come to me now.
Winter's sure comin'
no leaf on the bough.

Robert Harold Overton

Untitled

Across the misty hazy moor
A little (lonely) fawn
is laying upon the cold, tall grass so green
all alone by itself
its thoughts wandering

Inside myself I am that fawn
so (lonely) and so scared
afraid of the troubles
that face me
and my future that awaits me

Rise Scott

January Moonlight

January moonlight a-shinin'; through the pine;
A million stars a-twinklin' as if keepin' time
To some heavenly music which seems to stir my heart
As I stir a-singin' in the early dark.

Don't know why I'm happy; don't know why I'm gay;
Don't know why my youngish hear keeps thumpin' this a way
I guess it's just a livin' among such friends as mine
That keeps me calm and happy, and laughin' all the time!

Pearl E. Lucas

Daybreak

Flickering lights dance across the water
A lone loon calls a greeting to the sun
Stillness, quiet, waiting, waiting

Birds give voice in joyous abandon
Insects humming, fish jumping
Life begins

Throbbing noise rips through air and water
Raucous voices call out greetings
Death of all sound, waiting, waiting

Invaders gone, stillness of air
No ripple of water
World pausing to breathe

Birds give voice in joyous abandon
Insects humming, fish jumping
Life begins, again.

Phyllis Jeanette M. Priest-Gastent

My Christmas Wish

This Christmas wish is all from me - to have hearts like they could be
A loving family all filled up with cheer - not a hateful family filled up
    with tears

We have grown together a long time you see and that's the way that it
    should be
We can't bring back the past and change mistakes
But only live on and cure all of our hates

It is told to me that we are stuck with each other
That is because of our Father and Mother

Being together in this very special way
Is the only thing that I ask for on my Christmas day

To let my family know that presents don't matter
The only thing I want is to hear their chatter
To set our feelings aside and not be torn
Is a tradition that must go on

Instead of exchanging a gift, if only our hearts we would lift
To know that we matter each day of our lives
That we are a family that has survived

So, my wish - to always be together
No matter what storms we may all weather.
To make this Christmas the most special of them all
By being together and having a ball.

Wendy René Henry

The Deadly Jewel

There in the window atop a tall building leans
a man. His shadowy figure watches and waits.
His hands sweat and the molded metal beckons.
In the parade travels a man with increasing power.
This man's guided waves are surrounded with shields
of flesh. In front of him, there is a grassy hill with
a fence. Cheering crowds conceal the hidden quest.
A triangulating horror is complete through a clap
of thunder. The window is empty and the object
hidden, but the man's existence is reconciled when
the blue and gold legs pronounce his deed. Threats
of exposure are in the air. There are others, but
they will not be known. For his efforts, he will
receive payment in the form of a gem. Unknowing,
unsuspecting when it will be delivered, it's too late
for him to refuse as the dark, dark jewel is a Ruby.

Val Nadin Jr.

Evening Shades

Black against crimson
A multitude of wings
Rankled in no formation
Reflections and shadows cast on ripples below
Engines raised to overtake
Trucks laden beyond capacity
Crumbling roads laboring under the onslaught
Of monsoon rains and spinning wheels
Pipes laid with no function along earth dug trenches
Forever trenches...
A lone tamarind tree in the midst of fumes
A cow stares moodily into nowhere
Past a child pumping water
Into an earthen pot
Headlights flash - a horn bellows
Western cuts and polished shoes within
Passing a laden truck
Birds settle, rises again
Black against grey, shadows eat away
The realities of a city

Shonali Chandy

Life Is Like A River

It has a beginning
A natural birth of nature that grows
and thrives on a destined course.

It's weakened by obstacles along the way,
then strengthened by tributaries day to day.
It bends with uncertainty as it continues to flow,
confusing at times, just where to go.

It's straight with direction as it moves along,
with bubbles and ripples, blending in song.
It has springs of freshness, vibrant with life,
marred with stagnation, motionless strife.

It has depths of turmoil, uncertain but true,
followed by shallows of clearness, crystal blue.
It's rapid with excitement, then calm and serene,
destined with character, sometimes demean.

It's shared for pleasures, tragedy as well,
amid falls and turns, it's sometimes hell.
It subsides to infinity, as it ebbs away,
but from another source, is born again on another day.

Walter A. Reinhardt

The Most Beautiful Beast

High upon the mountain peaks, where the sun shines,
A nest lies.
Within it, eggs lie; born of a non-existent being.
A noise is heard . . . an eagle's cry.
The creature is seen upon the above peak.
Feathers to fur; bird to the king of beast.
Magnificent from tail to beak.
Talons grip the rock and feathered wings lie flat; flawless.
Behind it, the moss is crushed,
Beneath great lion's paws.
What is this great beast?
You wonder as you gaze upon this majestic creature.
As huge and powerful as it seems; you fear it not in the least.
This, the most beautiful beast.

Shaun Rieth

A Dieter's Lament

Today I start the Diet
A never ending Quest
A hundred pounds to lose
It will take six months at best

Now we've got to go on vacation
For which you wait all year
In lay in the sand and relax
and drink cases of beer

So now comes the great decision
Good health or good fun
For when your with a friend you never stop with one

The Devil paves the way
With tough decisions through life
The easy way always down hill
The right way full of strife

So what the hell's a guy to do?
With a hundred pounds to lose
I think I'll cut down on the food
But stick with a little booze!

A Pour Soul

Richard L. Balliet

Changing Seasons

The closing of the hot summer night etches a memory of
A passion that was from long ago when we allowed ourselves to be one
Lovemaking was a symphony, perfect timing, and harmonious notes
A moment when lovers were inseparable
The earth trembled and volcanoes erupted
Fall approaches and your voice whispers in the call of the wind

Your caress and warm breath rejuvenates my skin
Your arms embrace me and your tongue caresses my knees
Touching your finger tips with my mouth as I feel you enter me
We are one...again...the way it was before

Your love inspired me to dream,
Looking at the world through your eyes
I found strengths to believe
We walked the same road together our lives parallel

Too soon the howling winter breeze will arrive
Seeing the glistening frost I long to hike the hilltops and
Hear the mountains echo your name

Spending nights alone by the fires glow
Reading books of poetry and travels
Where dreams rest at the beginning, waiting to be believed

Karyn Briggs

A Warning To Heed

Working on a ship we sometimes see
  a sad situation we wish wouldn't be.
One day I saw a small bird die all alone.
  To me a stranger, but to God it was known.
A sense of sadness and loss came over me
  to witness such a lonely death at sea.
I sat and wondered, as I gave a long sigh.
  Why do these birds come out here to die?
To pass us by would be for their best,
  but they see us and decided to stop for a rest.
Then they have them a drink or maybe a meal,
  and by mistake consume something that kills.
If we could write what a bird could read,
  each ship would have a banner, a warning to heed.
"This place is toxic!! So please stay away!!!"
  Then they could enjoy living for another day!!!

Mark K. Stewart

Childhoods End

The world child is hard and cruel
A place without reason to the duel
A place were the small, the helpless, the pure
Are soiled and ruined even murdered without cures

But things you are coming to understand
Only hours have you gazed at the wonder land
The awe inspiring vastness of a world
That was never yours and doomed your pearls

So run child run while you can
Run from the darkness of the promiseland
Run child run even faster
The evils upon you to destroy your pastures

Can a child created from rancid dead flush
Become a man of love and lust
But child poor child have you even a soul
You will die in your future as your past unfolds

If only you could fly away from here
Free of hate free of fear
You would drift in the breeze to the edge of the world
And live in the wind as it swirls
Lorin Dean Hamilton

See Off

Whiter than verdant the maidenhair shows,
A precursor for beyond a curved mountain road
The little church and cemetery enfold.
Tender steeple reaches ridgetop monuments.
The way continues past granite and wood
Downward winding to another clapboard church
And cemetery this time downslope from worship.
Two-toned green hemlock branches edge
The field of vision gradually gravitating from
Dunn's Creek Baptist Church because you can hear it to
Dunn's Rock Baptist Church because you can see it.
*Back up above and down once again: Hogsed off one side ending,
Becky down the back, See Off past marble and sanctuary,
Two-Seventy-Six bending to the French Broad,
And long before you cross riverwide sheen,
Connastee twisting off numbered highway —
Pavement scene from resting place to place.*
Keith T. Holtsclaw

Love

Love
A simple word to speak
A complex emotion to feel
Sometimes the search for it is bleak
For some base it on sexual appeal

Love
Some see it as a plague
Some as a disease
The signs are vague
With the ability to bring one to their knees

Love
Others see it as a blessing
And more see it as a gift
The benefits are baffling
The changes are swift

Love
The one thing that brings the world together
When all else is tearing us apart
For this there can be no impostor
It can only be found in our heart
Keren Wilde

Untitled

I sit alone in the middle of a crowd
a single in a world of pairs
searching for a right in a universe of wrong
abandoned from birth in my mother's arms.

I have spent my life screaming at the deaf
and waiting a response from the mute
and still I stand lost and confused
waiting to be enlighten by the darkness.

I walk a straight line down a crooked path
follow a schedule of an unplanned trip
remain flexible in a society of rigidness
and yet I still stand here wondering why:

I stand alone.
A. Riley

Why?

Some things happen you don't understand
A small child taken by an unseen hand.
A girl struggling jumps from a bridge,
I can't help but ask, why didn't she want to live?
Everyday people hate and destroy
Treating our world like a child's play toy
Black or white, what's the difference?
Skin's a color not a hindrance.
Guns and wars we've been fighting forever
Can't we just be happy living together?
Rachel Draper

Always A Daughter

A little girl, that is so cute and sweet
A smile on her face, that is just hard to beat
The hug that she gives you, right from the start
The love that is there, comes straight from her heart
The first words she'll speak, you'll wait to hear
The first time she cries, and you see a tear
The laughter she makes, when having some fun
The nap that she takes, that's in the warm sun
Sometimes she'll pout, to get her own way
Or look to be held, at least once in the day
She'll start to grow up, and you will grow too
For your heart knows, what lies ahead for you
Her teenage years, will seem to fly by
You'll look back in time, and ask yourself why
She is no longer a child, she's grown up too fast
You wished for a childhood, that would always last
Now that she's grown, and a woman you'll see
But in your heart a daughter, she will always be.
Vincent Cea

"Moon Poem"

Silver sphere up in the starry skies
A source of wonder for all our eyes
Beneath your light there will always be
A world of romance and mystery
Wise old owl sits speaking to the night
Silver moth spreads its wings and takes flight
Modest ladies wear their skirts up high
The shy man sings, but doesn't know why
Out in the courtyard young lovers dance
In a place where fate rules over chance
Shane A. Beck

Peace

A mountain range painted delicately with snow.
A spring breeze whispering to the trees.
A stream giggling ever so softly.
The fragrance of a rose just born.
A star-filled sky on a warm summer night.
A rain shower cooling the sun-warmed ground.
A forest calm, yet alive.
A mystical fog hiding some unknown beauty.
The sun sparkling on a morning's dew.
Peace is in nature's beauty.

Tonya Danz

Peace For Life

The definition of peace includes quiet,
A state or period of calm within,
Agreement to end the hostilities of war,
So a state of tranquillity can begin.

Peace may be felt in a gentle breeze,
Or in the calm before a storm.
Personal peace is mercurial like life,
With no special formula or form.

Today, the world is one neighborhood,
With conflict in numerous backyards.
Efforts for peace should be equal for all,
Or the watch may be enemy guards.

We fight, write, negotiate and often pray,
For common ground to plow and sow,
Some fertile seeds of freedom and peace,
That will sprout amid doubt and grow.

We must increase all peace negotiations!
Revise efforts that move too slow!
If heads are bowed by mushroom clouds,
Peace will come, but who will know?

Louise Wright

Us

Our love is like a roller coaster
a thrilling and exciting ride
once your strapped into the seat
you cannot run and hide

It's the ups and downs that we go through
that make our love so fine
and so I pray most every day
it will last till the end of time

With this poem to show my love
that I will give to you
so you can see with your own eyes
my love will always be true

Thomas M. Walker

"The Champion"

A champion is someone who gives their
all even when they can't.
A champion is someone who will fight
until the very last second.
A champion is someone who has no
fears and feels no pain.
A champion is someone with good
sportsmanship and doesn't gloat at victory.
A champion is someone who will
work as a team or work as one.
A champion is anyone who wants to be.

Stacy Jane Hubbard

What I Ask Of You

A smile of the simplest kind.
A word of the purest honest truth.
A love like the innocence of youth.
A dream for all eternity.
A laughter filled with happiness.
A heart that beats in tune to mine.
A tear that flows and always grows.
A magic filled with destiny.
A simple dream, of the purest kind.
A heart like yours, and a heart like mine.
Believing in love and in truth for all time.
Letting go of your heart and mine...
Leaving all of the crime behind...
Never again will it make us blind.
A love of such the simple kind.
Beats in time with this love of mine.
Soon you will free me...
And always believe me...
For my darling what I say is true,
And this is what I ask of you.

Tina Rigney

Feuding In The Mountains

Listen, teen-agers, and you shall hear
About the shotgun wedding of Johnny O'Lear
And a pink-cheeked lassie named Patsy Lee
Deep in the mountains of East Tennessee.

Young Johnny was the son of Soul-Saver O'Lear,
Hell-fire preacher and Devil-Killer mountaineer;
Patsy's Pa was big, gun-totin' Lukey Lee,
Head of the largest moonshining family in East Tennessee.

Lukey Lee caught the young pair one summer day
Making love in the barn on a bed of hay;
He grabbed his gun and horse, after tying Johnny to a tree,
And galloped to O'Lear's church to say when the wedding would be.

The startled preacher, at the wrong end of Lukey's gun,
Agreed that, next Sunday week, the deed would be done;
Lukey hurried back across the mountain side
And alerted his family as soon as Johnny was untied.

On wedding-day morning eight carts full of Lees
Joined dozens of O'Lears under the churchyard trees;
After songs, prayers and vows, without a gun drawn,
They ate O'Lear food and drank Lee booze—the feud was plumb gone!

Marjorie Robbins

The Town On The Hill

How quiet on this mountain top
Above our bustling town.
One by one we gather here
While those who bring us shed a tear
And lay our casket down.

Beneath the somber granite sky
Side by side we rest.
Near friends with whom we laughed and played,
With whom we danced, and worked and prayed.
Our closeness now is blessed.

We taught your children, healed your ill.
Speak our names out loud.
We built your town, shared in your dreams,
Governed, worked, and fished your streams.
One day you'll join our crowd.

Stroll slowly by our resting place.
There's history here, dear friend.
Heritage in names and dates,
In stories that each stone relates,
Where past and present blend.

Lyn Edwards Asselin

222

Colors

Why does the pigment beneath the skin
Affect how we treat people?

Is a tan man any better than a non-tan?
Or a white man, more wise than a black man?
I THINK NOT!

Veronica L. Amey

A Hero's Tale

Dark are dreams, of doom and woe
After reading tales of old.
Of Elves and Men, and mighty Valar,
War against a great Foe, with much valor.
Beren One-Handed, and beautiful Luthien
Took by stealth of Evil's crown,
One bright shining Silmaril.
Passed vile Carcharoth on the way down.
Thus was their sad fate carried out.

Strong, bold, cunning: Beren son of Barahir,
Wise and warm-hearted, loving was Luthien
Luthien, Luthien, fair Tinuviel,
Daughter of Thingol and Melian.
Immortal was she, before Beren was slain,
Wherewith she went: Straight to Death's domain.
There they met again, and left together
Flesh that will die, but love that lasts forever,
Luthien, Luthien, fair Tinuviel,
Live in peace where the shadows dwell,
And I will write thy tale to tell.

Matthew J. Powers

Springtime

Today was so warm and fresh, the air
after spring thundershowers smelled
so clean and sweet,
my heart wandered out the window
and hurried off to meet
a thousand memories—
long, sun-filled days, wild rain
and windy skies,
the rich and fragrant earth
when over all the landscape lies
a gypsy mood, a charming, carefree warmth—
such memories that brought a
bright, exquisite pain,
a poignant sadness;
but still withal my heart went
tripping down the rain-swept lane
to meet the spring with gladness.

Ruth V. Cox

"Ornamental Roses"

Miniature roses again shall appear,
Again they will blossom, for spring is near.

Oh, roses be dapple, have blossom and cheer,
Let roses have season, and grace on us here.

Having burnish on hilltops, and also on vail,
Again miniature roses will emboss this trail.

Blossoming in inches, having petals begem,
They again shall be flawless, having buds upon them.

Those miniature roses that we all treasure,
Say that spring is here, and in good measure.

Lani D. Dunham

Discarded Love

I can't even repeat the beat of my heart
against my pillow as I cried.
It was so full of sorrow and so void of hope
and too like despair
which
is at all times empty.
I had opened up my heart to you
but all you did was watch it bleed.
I bled to death waiting for you
to see this love inside of me.
Eventually the love grew cold
and left an empty hollow hurt
which to this day
reminds me still
of that love
I held for thee.

Shanna Eakins

Dazzle, Dazzle

The sky dazzled me when I looked up at it.
All blues, reds, pinks and purples.

Then I saw an airplane
that looked like a shooting star.

Then it got dark
and all the stars twinkled
and dazzled me again.

Then I went to bed
and dreamt that I went to Canada.
There was a full moon
and it was so pretty on the water.

Matthew D. Drost

"Open Your Eyes And See"

Open your eyes and see,
all of the pollution in the air
and on the earth.

Open your eyes and see,
all of the violence and crime
that goes on behind your back.

Open your eyes and see,
all of the young kids who think
that doing drugs and smoking
pot is cool.

Open your eyes and see,
the suffering kids that live in poor places.
They have no home, no money and some of them no family.

Open your eyes and see,
the enormous hole in our
quickly fading ozone.

Open your eyes and see,
people are cutting off our
supplies of oxygen, by cutting
down our rain forests and jungles.

Katie Elmore

The Field

I'm here in the field where all I see
And hear is the grass waving like the sea
The wind wishing through the trees
The little bunny's chasing butterflies
The Field, Oh The Field
The perfume smell of the butter cups
The sun flowers
The Field, Oh The Field

Kendra Rae Howard

Choices

I don't know what you are going to do!
All that I know is that I don't want to lose you
I look into your eyes,
And I see you've been telling me lies.
Is drugs worth losing me?
If so I guess we were not meant to be.
I lay awake in bed,
Thinking about all you have said.
About how you're only out to have fun
But you're fun is killing me hon.
You might not think it is a crime.
But don't you see I'm paying the time
Cuz I sit around here feeling sad,
When I think about all we could of had.
If you love me as much as you say
Then you'll stop this game you sorted to play.

Melissa Peters

The Past

I look at your picture and remember the past,
All that was said and what didn't last
The memories that save all the times that we shared,
And the time that you told me that you always cared,
The things that you said and the things that you gave,
Will always be things that now I can save,
The roses you gave me that withered and died,
The cards that you gave me all the times that I cried,
The pictures they took of love as it grew
But the ones that I cherish are the memories of you.

Stephanie Schendel

I Remember

I remember well when I was just a lad
All the crazy sayings that my parents had
With children of my own, I'm at the point of crazy
Mama always said "You'll pay for your raising."

Plenty of times we tried to leave home
Thinking it fun to be on our own
Daddy was right, he knew weren't able
"You'll do as I say if you put your feet under my table."

The things we saw our parents do
We always thought we could do them to
We always planned to get our own way
"Don't do as I do, do as I say."

The things we would ask, the things we could try
No matter the answer, we always asked "Why"
To get the right answer, great lengths we would go
But always the same "Because I said so."

Now if you're still young, and think you're so cool
And have no reasons to follow their rules
You argue with then, say things you'll regret
"Believe me, you don't know everything yet."

Mary T. Fulcher

I'll Always Remember You!

If life lasts a lingering minute
And love but a moment or two.
I'm content that you once were in it
For I'll always remember you.
I will save all the treasures you gave me
To last my lifetime through.
Time will unfold what is destined
But, I'll always remember you!

Paula Franz

"Behind The Mask"

Behind the mask, no one can see,
All the pain inside of me.
It hides my secrets from long ago.
So many secrets, I too don't know.
The mask protects me from all my fears.
It lets out screams but hides my tears.

Behind the mask, all that you see,
Is someone else who is not me.
I've changed my ways from long ago,
But don't ask why, I too don't know.
The mask has helped me to conquer my fears.
When I become weak, the mask reappears.

'Cause behind the mask, I am much stronger
And then I don't need to worry much longer.

Marina Rios

The Golden Ager

Here's face that smiles with merry eyes alight,
    All twinkling gay and merriment and fun,
That those who view will never know the height
    And breath of battle fiercely fought and won!
Smiles must be born that blanket hemlock tears,
    And merry laugh erect a blanking screen:
Erase all view of muddled brackish fears, to shield
    The young from glimpsing ordeal's scene.
For once the bleak drear face of death stood there,
    Bold met the mortal's eye, turned then and left
A wound untenable: great bleeding cleft.
    Yet soul survived, to walk the one kind road
Of love, and build for other's safe abode.

B. J. Jeffrey

Ever-Glowing Horizon

Sliding steadily down shifting mountainside.
    Alone.
    Afraid.
My cries of distress answered
    by outstretched hand
    by desperate beckonings.

Moment of hope invokes courage to risk.
Now I dangle,
    naked and exposed beneath tenacious hold.

Tireless, unfailing, pulling the whole of my weight.
Your memory fixed on days afore.
"You shall, you must, you will stand beside me once again".

Suddenly, a foothold.
I step...you pull...strong arms embrace my frazzled soul.

Resolute arm upon my shoulder
Turns me away from engulfing darkness.

Together we depart,
Faces set toward ever-glowing horizon.

Renee J. Irish

Crystal Lilacs

Frost came late to my garden last Spring,
And overnight a magic spell was wrought.
For in the early morning's light,
Crystal Lilacs filled the air
With frozen perfume fit to scent the beauty
Of a Snow Queen's raven hair.
I know this, for my love was there.

Virginia A. Tomlin

Alone In Silence

In the darkness my Brother waits,
alone and afraid of things to come,
unable to reach out to anyone.

In the time it takes to blink an eye,
the darkness now silent, the hurt now gone.

If only he'd known the pain would pass on,
like a runner who passes the baton.

I now wait alone and afraid,
the Brother who's hearts filled with sorrow,
who's minds filled with pain.

Time will continue, the sun will shine on,
children continue to play as through nothing
is wrong.

Like a story with no ending, a road that goes on.

I wait for the day the pain will be gone.

Ralph L. Ruiz

Sirens

Out they come piercing the night
Alone I lie in shivering fright
Shoved beneath my pillow is a weary head
Crying and wishing to be dead.

Run to lock the door and latch the shudder
On they come, getting louder and louder.
They won't find me, oh not tonight
I'll run, I'll hide, I'll take flight.

Flee far and fast from this beast
For tonight, this night she will not feast
To devour my dreams and hopes is her ploy
Leave me alone, for I'm just a boy.

Hauntingly, the sirens continue to scream
Hunting me down while awake and in dream
Fatigued am I, yet, still no sleep
For in my dreams the sirens still creep.

Patrick D. Sandoval

Mansion Up High

We have been through pain and grief,
along the way there stands disbelief.
We lose our self in this world today,
All we have to do is get down and pray.

We have to climb our hills and mountains,
But what we have waiting is golden fountains.
There is a mansion setting way up high,
and all around it the angel's fly.

We keep ourselves bottled up inside,
But with Gods love we will abide.
We vow our hearts for eternity,
and the garden of eden awaits for me.

So lay your troubles by you side,
and in the golden chariot you will ride.
With God's angels there to steer,
Don't hesitate another year.

Take God's wisdom and his love,
It will come to you on a wing of a dove.
And to his arms we will fly,
To his mansion in the sky.

William T. McMullen

My Garden Speaks To Me

My garden speaks to me in many subtle ways;
Although no words are spoken in the messages it conveys.
My garden whispers daily that it's grateful for my care;
For there's a special bond between us that only we two share.

In the early, misty mornings when I walk among my trees;
My garden sends its fragrant perfume to mingle with the breeze.
And when I'm sad and lonely and filled with deep despair,
My garden stirs the leaves around me to let me know it's there.

My garden is my mentor, it has taught me all I know.
It taught me how to create it and how to make it grow.
My garden is my treasure chest that opens every day;
To dazzle me with colors that take my breath away.

My garden serenades me with song birds in its trees,
And sends rainbow-colored butterflies to flutter in the breeze.
It beckons little furry creatures to gather round my feet,
I'm so glad I planted it, for it has made my life complete.

Nelly Anita Robinson

The Child Of The Universe

Do not compare yourself to others for
Always there will be a greater and a smaller
Person than yourself.

Take kindly to the council of years gracefully
Surrendering the things of youth.
And do not distress yourself with imaginations
For many years are born of fatigue
And loneliness.

Neither be cynical about love for in the
Face of all aridity and disenchantment
It is perennial as the grass.
But do not let this blind you as to
What Victor there is many people strive
For high ideas and everywhere,
Life is full of heroism.

You are a child of the universe and no less than
The trees and the stars, you have every
Right to be here and whether or not it is
Clear to you, no doubt the universe is unfolding
As it should be.

Patrick Amponsah

Fourth Of July, An American Celebration

Many happy returns of the year
America, Uncle Sam, you and I.
For two centuries we have grown
we have reaped what we've sewn
a country filled with love, faith and pride.

When we came-what we brought
we see each day
So give your heart, give your all
you'll find a way

Happy Birthday USA
we salute you on this day
for helping make our special
dreams come true

From our islands - across the oceans
from our countries - far and near
Happy Birthday America
and many happy returns of the year.

Sheldon J. Dubow

Untitled

You are looking for yourself
among thousands of people.
You won't find it. You are burying your hopes
and wake to live again.
Again you snatch the avowals,
grasp the empty words
and you're driven to desperation again.
And you want to vanish. One more time.
Wait! Don't let be destroyed!
Look at yourself from the side,
will to glance at your soul.
Don't make your last step,
before there's no way out,
anymore.

Katie Krakowiak

Questions And Answers

Where have all the great poets gone?
Among what poets do I belong?
Where are Wordsworth, Shelley, and Keats?
Are my poems worthy; are my poems strong?
Do my poems have an original beat?
Do they suggest some magical feat?
Can I compare my poems to those gods?
Do gods exist or do we merely cheat?
Am I an original or a carbon sheet?

The romanticized poets have all gone away.
Like no other poets am I; I pray.
Poets of poetry lost their beat.
My poems will linger throughout the day.
Poetry is life; my thoughts it displays.
They evoke my dreams and all my hopes.
To please myself is my heart's way.
The word is God; my words are popes.
In this image my words will cope.

Michael R. Catanzaro

The Safety Pin

You love your ribbons and cherish them
And also your buttons and bows
But when these are gone, without safety pins
How would you hold your clothes

Have you ever been to a midnight party
With only the clothes you were wearing
When your face grew red with sickly dread
Cause you felt your britches tearing

Along the wall, and down the hall
You creep with caution untold
You feel the wind dance
Through the tear in your pants my, but it's awfully cold

You must make haste, there's no time to waste
For someone may come in
You reach back there, and fasten the tear
With the aid of a safety pin

You say a prayer for half an hour
You pray right there and then
Down on your knees, with folded hands
You give thanks to a safety pin

Leon Totten

The Country Drunk

He drinks whiskey the home
and anywhere he may roam,
behind the tobacco barn,
or in the field of yellow corn.
He drinks it where I've seen a mouse
scurrying about in the smokehouse,
He's told me a fib
about drinking it in the corn crib.
He hid it for a rainy day
in the cow barn which stores the hay.
The woodshed holds empty bottles
of that which he enjoyed when he was idle.
The henhouse was spared
because when he entered, their wings flared.
All the mules in the stables
know the stories are not fables.

Margaret Glidewell Poole

Moonlit Walk

We walk along together by the moonlight
And are bathed in the darkness of night
Ever so often we stop and gaze up at the sky
And watch the stars-n-moon glisten up so high
You enfold me in your arms
And tell me you'll always keep me from harm
I guess we've known it all along
That in your arms is where I belong
You are my friend yet so much more
And our love will soar and soar
I can't imagine my life without you
Because your love always shines through
As we continue our moonlit walk
It's almost as if the heavens talk
And tell us we were meant to be
As the stars shine down on you and me

Rebekah Anne Breakwell

Men Of Pure Heart

If people would begin today
And ask God's grace to find a way
To raise the world from dark despair
Help could come forth from everywhere.
They should make a very strict vow,
Of exemplary conduct! Now!
"To think first! and, not do or say
Anything to harm or dismay!"
For that would only add fuel
To hate's blazing flames, so cruel!
That nations rise against nations
And "teens" make streets battle-stations.
God told us to love each other
Obey! Reach out to another,
Our troubled world yearns for peace! Life!
Free and clear of all global strife.
Oh men, of pure heart! Humane!
Start to heal humanity's pain
Make the "WORLD" a safe place to be
Through prayer, justice, hope, endlessly!

Laura E. Miller

Untitled

Yesterday is but a figment of our imaginations,
    (at least what we can remember);
Tomorrow will never come,
    (at least not today);
Today is a dream,
Spend it with me.

C. A. Klentzman

The Garden

How lovely a seedling kind hands had planted
And climbing it reached to full size
But as years tarried on, day and night passed us by
A disease had begun to arise

Saddened and grieved for its beauty was lost
The decision was clear to my mind
With axe in hand and purpose of heart
No help for the tree I could find

Cut it down, dig it up were the words I could hear
So patiently set out to my plan
And in doing so planted a garden of love
With my spirit and help of no man

Then one night with round moon high up in the sky
At my garden in worship to You
I saw how my life had been diseased like the tree
And changing, You made me all new

Today in my garden my heart is for You
Today there is no more decay
My tomorrows are calling with pain far behind
Your kind hands took the past far away

N. Jeanne Murray

Shades Of Blue Light

Blues, I love you, wild Northwest Pacific blues,

Slate blue of a calmly rippled bay, which doubles
    and dances shoreline and edging trees,

Deep sea aqua, intersected by a path of mirrored sun-gold,

Choppy, open-ocean, marine blue, dotted white to the world's
    edge with wind caps,

Even shiny man-made royals: Kayak hulls, rain tarp plastic
    and gear-bag opaques,

Horizon gray blue, touching and supporting the paler, wan
    edge of sky's majestic canopy,

Distant layered mountains, range upon range of dark purple
    blues, thrusts of mass and of mystery,

A heaven of midnight blue and its gradations, embedding the
    tracking stars in their appointed orbits,

Blue-black shadows, edging and defining the pounded sea tracks,
    the rocky coastlines and the covering forests,

And not least, the steel blue of a beloved's eyes,
    that can marvel too at the rich palette of this vast ocean world.

Virginia Hoyte

Waves

When you sit on the beach
And feel the sand at your feet
And hear the seagulls circling in the air
And smell the salty water
And see and hear the gentle lapping of the waves against the shore
The waves are the things that stand out
You could listen to them for hours
As haunting as a ghost's scream
As gentle as mother's touch
Just another rhythm
And then look at the shapes of the waves
The curling tops
The sacred touch
Lapping against the shore
Giving you that haunting feeling
Waves

Melissa Tuckman

Surrender Gracefully

When body parts begin to sag
And days are long- and hours drag-
Think back to youth and days of yore,
When you could hear and things weren't sore.

All joints would move and you could sing,
And did remember everything.
Were never lost and rarely teary,
And fell asleep where you were weary.

When you could savor things of taste
And sprinted when in need of haste.
You could detect by sense or smell
If food was fresh or old and stale.

Who can say what's right or wrong
'Bout being old and living long.
Who decides what one should think?
Or how to dress or what to drink?

This once a man and twice a child,
Is not for sissies, meek and mild.
So one must do, what once he did-
Indulge yourself! Act like a kid!

Selwyn Murray

Fill Us In

Sometimes at night I throw my sleep away,
And decorate my mind with things I wish you'd say.
Then I'll shake - shake my head and turn,
and realize what I have to learn.

I've got to be sure if your love is love that is serious,
The way that we carry on just make it not clear to us.

So fill us in
Let's stop talking in the wind.
I think we've got something here
more than just good friends.

I can't set my self up for a big let down,
I need a mutual feeling to bring my confidence around.

So fill us in
Let's stop talking in the wind.
I think we've got something here
more than just good friends.

J. P. Martin

Last Kiss

To touch a lover's lips one last time
And feel the tingling sensation through your body
Feeling your heart pounding out of control
Just to remember the touch of the skin
The warmth of the body heat between two
My body still trembles at just the thought
To hold that moment in time forever
And never forget the deep love and passion
To seal the memory in your mind
The electrifying feeling from head to toe
To feel alive throughout your entire soul
Knowing forever in your heart you will hold
Wishing for it not to go away
At once the feeling was supposed to last an eternity
Feeling so lucky to have felt this at least once
Some have never felt it so true and won't

Sherri Warstler

227

Important Things

I built a castle with my hands
  And filled each room with treasures rare.
Then thieves broke in when I was gone,
  If only I had stayed right there.

A garden I had planted once
  Of every fragrance far and wide,
An early frost came through one night,
  And all my fragile flowers died.

My fortune I had hidden well
  And no man knew wherein it laid.
I came one day to take it back
  But found that it had all decayed.

I've found that things in life don't last
  As long as we would like them to.
I've seen things more important now
  Like people such as me and you.

Wesley K. Curtis

"The Dream"

I feel asleep last night.
And had a strange, but wonderful dream.
One of God's angels came down to take me
on a long long flight.
As I went up into the dark night.
I began to see more and more bright light.
What a beautiful sight to see.
I saw so many pretty things.
Angels with gold trimmed wings.
Birds that could really sing.
Then I saw heavens gates open wide
And there standing inside was God and
my first born baby boy.
What a blessed joy to see other members
of my family all with my first born baby boy.

Margaret Lewis

Dichotomy

We are the ones who speak in poems
And have leapt from reality's edge,
Yet survive the fatal fall.
We follow the God with His prophecies as our guide,
And hold our swords to the sky.
We stand tall
With a hand over our hearts
And view a glowing moon that fills the sky.
The raven flies above us
And speaks to us of lies.
You say you know us,
But you don't know both halves.
This Void inside our hearts
Consumes us as we fly.
Out of our Void a light shines.
The sub-human and heartless it blinds.
All that's left here are our words;
They live on after we die.
We are the ones who speak in poems.

Seth R. Sams

For Grammy

Grammy is very old now, her dark hair has turned gray
And her blue eye's have faded, somewhere along the way.

Still Grammy sings to me with a smile on her face
And a heart full of love, she sings Amazing Grace.

Her eyes are full of wisdom, there's a softness in her voice
And she has taught my heart how to love and to rejoice.

She says: Go in peace and grow in love
And do all those things you've been dreaming of
Listen to your heart, walk tall and proud
Hear that song in your soul and sing it out loud.

Grammy sings a hymn, for me just one more time
As I drift off to sleep I hear the hour chime.

I dream of climbing mountains, of flying in clear skies
I dream I am a hero as the sun begins to rise.

I will always love her, I have her eyes of blue
And Grammy, when I'm grown up I hope I'm just like you.

So I'll: Go in peace and grow in love
And do all those things that I'm dreaming of.
I'll listen to my heart, walk tall and proud
Hear that song in my soul and sing it out loud.

Pam Spencer

Kiss The Wind

It was on a beautiful Autumn day,
and I had journeyed to my favorite place,
to a lake, where always it seems,
the waters are at peace,
touched only and slightly, by a peaceful breeze;
And while standing there gazing out over the waters,
I thought to myself,
Heaven must be like this!
and then leaning out over the railing,
I calmly swore to return again,
and gave the wind a kiss!

Russell D. Nolen

Storms

The wind blows
And I see misty Korean mountaintops
Smell the salty ocean of the Korean Sea
Hear the clackity-clack of the train as I travel from station to station
Feel the pinch of warm fingers on my cheek as the wrinkly
  grandmothers tell me I'm pretty and then scold my mother
  because I seem cold.

The rain falls
And I'm reminded of typhoons with warm rain, not cold
The world so wet there's not an inch of dry
Rusty brown floodwaters swirling and rising past my hips as I
  trudge up the hill to school
A musty, renewing smell lingering over the earth
With a small break in the grey sky as the Filipino sun shines for
  a moment and then disappears.

A clap of thunder jostles me back to the present
The majestic mountains and rainy seasons scamper back to their
  hiding places in the crevices of my mind
I sigh, and wish they would remain.

Ruth Strong

228

Love Lost

She glides along with incredible grace
And I watch, loving her beautiful face,
I yearn to feel her hands' warm, soft touch
But "No" from her would pain me too much.

For years I would watch her with all my care.
In hopes hers, with timid me, she should share,
But never could I fulfill my desire
For courage is something I do not sire.

Lonely years go by with me never bold
Places, faces have changed; I have grown old.
My aching heart wearies, my aged mind slows
And yet, her delicate face still glows.

When love is not returned, a heart is pained,
But when love's not offered, nothing is gained.

Rey Ranido-Remolacio

The Blind Date

Tonight's the night
    And is she a beauty
As I don my top hat and tails
    I jostle my memory
How long has it been?
    I've been waiting
And I'm psyched
My expedition begins
    I expertly spurt to arrive before my competition
Traffic is harrowing
    as I enter the vestibule
It is dark and sweltering
    The air is moist
Intoxicating desire fills my senses
Without warning, I spot her
    But she's not alone
My head is spinning, my tail left behind
    We fuse
Victorious and Fulfilled
    A zygote now

Toni McGuire

What Is A Friend?

A friend is one you can lean on
And is there through the hurt and fear.
A friend is one you can talk to
And one who is very dear.
A friend knows how to comfort
In a time of need,
One who always listens
And is trustworthy, indeed.
You can tell a friend a secret
And never have a doubt
They won't tell a living soul —
Wild horses couldn't drag it out.
A friend is a shoulder to cry on
When someone breaks your heart
And when you're too tired to go on living
It's a friend who helps you start.
Now you see what a friend means to me.
You can figure out the rest:
You're the only one who fits the bill.
You are the absolute best!

Laurie Pratt

Autumn Reverie

The wind is blowing so cold
And leaves are whipping around.
The colors are gone and trees are bare,
As the rest fall to the ground
While I sit here thinking of seasons past
As time moves swiftly along.

Why am I growing so old?
Make time stand still — but for a moment.
Time that will last an eternity.
As I wish for things grand
That can happen to me
I dream of things that used to be.
Yes, let time stand still for eternity.

Leslie Whalen

Beyond

Man was not made to sit ashore
and let his boat to rot at pier;
He early sprang to take the oar,
to face the winds and waves that roar,
to seek afar a new frontier...

Man's craving for the hidden core
of life, made humans shift their gear
for higher stakes-through mounting fear-,
and outer space we now explore
in capsules blasting from the rear....

Today, as never felt before,
what lies beyond, to man is dear....
No longer we the odds ignore;
yet we still hope, in search of more,
however much we've granted here.
...FOR MAN WAS BORN A PIONEER.

Ruben Ortiz-Lamadrid

Untitled

And now I must bury my face into your soft comfort
And let your welcoming shadows hide me from revealing light.
Will you accept me as your own?
Will you comfort my sorrows and lessen my pain?
Will you let me show you my saddened soul?
Will you not run away as others have done?
I'm ready for your knowledge, the knowledge of the night.
That hides and protects and cures.
Perhaps tomorrow I can once again show my face.
Perhaps that night run to you once more.

Krista Barber

My World Of Friends

In this world I live in my own little space,
And my thoughts are not biased by creed or by race.
I accept any friendship that is offered to me,
And if you're in need, a friend I will be.

I feel sorry for those who live in a clique.
They only have time for friends that they pick.
And those who aren't picked and are left in the dust;
Acceptance in cliques is all that they lust.

All of those people with greed as their friend,
Who want everything but don't want to spend;
Power and money is all they live for.
I wish they'd realize that a friend would give more.

Everyone is different in this world of mine,
But my friends are as numerous as stars that shine.
So next time you're feeling lost and alone,
Just come to me and you'll feel right at home.

Melissa Olson

My Tree

My tree, it stands so great and grand,
And pleads to heaven for a helping hand.
For soon the kiss of death will come,
As jack frost paints his pandemonium.
Upon each leaf he misses none.
My tree is now bare, cold and scared.
With all her leaves around her feet.
She'll have six months of quiet sleep.
Then one morn, still a chill in the air,
A robin comes to nest in her hair.
He sings a song of love and content,
And woke her from her sleep of
Dormant.
She reached to heaven, and thanked God
Again, for another chance of life's return.
She budded and blossomed, and
Fussed all spring.
To prove to me she was gracious thing,

Virginia E. Tomsa

In This Corner

You, who boxed your way so elegantly, carried by brassless angel wings
and Purple Heart brass. Street warring and nameless whoring at every
banged out corner. You, who dined on pizza fondue and lived a
fast-food life, who marveled at penny pitches and stick-balled wins.
You rose above the monkey grime sensitive to murder and the likes.
Boxing your way through tribal orientations and railroad suicide.
Imbibe of ethereal top dog wine stomped on only by heroes for heroes.

Count with me how much you've overcome. Come, sit next to me and
count. On fingers, on toes and back to fingers, short on digits we
are for survival recognitions. You, you who boxed your way so
eloquently winning unseeable medals of honor so shiny with bright,
your mind needs shade from the glare.

Stepped out your front door only to land in Viet Nam lunge and
slug dodging. You who were born chosen, gangly with wisdom
and brained with handsome gallantry...who would have suspected.
My veteran of life at such a modest age, I bow at your presence
and kiss your feet callused with golden eggshells fragrance
with baby powder. The mask about your face, one of unnamed humility
not of snivel. I am yours.

Nancy G. Oxman

Something That Lasted

They came, a race of iron, of fiery dreams,
And raised their oaken walls on solid sills,
And roofed with riven shingles sturdy beams,
And dropped in rows some bulbs of daffodils.

Today they moulder—all that's mortal must.
The walls have rotted that they built to last;
Their very sills of stone have sunk to dust.
The daffodils waved blithely as I passed.

Patrick Brophy

An Easier Time

I still see the green in the trees and the grass
    and the blue in the sky above.
I hear the sound of the robin's call
    blend with the coo of the dove

I picture the stream in the meadow below
    and the pond where we use to swim.
Remember the water as cold as ice?
    the way we got warm again?

There were no problems to life back then
    at least not for you and me.
Loving each other our only chore
    and love our only fee.

Robert Reed

"The Mirror"

If you could see through the window of heart,
And see the fortress I have built.
If you could see through the window of my mind.
You would see the weaving web of time.
If you could unravel the thread that sets
The weave in motion,
And find the mysteries of life,
That leads us to our wanting heights,
If you could find the stairs that lead to all beginnings,
And be the first to see the face of Christ,
And if you could see through the window of my soul,
You would see the things that are so dear to me,
You would see my world as just beginning,
God's world in perfect harmony.

Shirley Schroeter Brunner

Time To Pay

It's time to pay the price for our bigotry,
and self-righteous pomposity.
To pay for the price of bondage.
To pay for the enforcement of suffering.
To pay a price that we can only compensate with blood.
To pay for a bomb in an Alabama church.
To pay for laws named Jim Crow.

It's time for us to pay.

To pay for a bullet,
that brought down a reverend.
To pay for the blows and bruises,
on a man named King.
It's time to reap the bitter harvest,
and the sorrows for our sins.
It's time to open our racist eye,
to understand the price to pay.
Orenthal James Simpson;
Not guilty.

C. W. Gordon

Tears Of Love

She was with me in the beginning
    and she taught me how to live.
She was always there for every encounter
    that life would so vehemently give.
She enriched my life with her wisdom,
    by showing me the importance of love.
She always gave what she could of herself,
    which originated from heaven above.
She walked me through each phase of my life,
    knowing when to hold me and when to let go.
She was the light in my darkest hours,
    guiding me, with a warm soft glow.

Then, in the final moments of her life,
    as I wiped the tears from her eyes.
I knew that the greatest gift of all,
    was her love, which will never die.

Karen L. Curry

A New Season

A lone batter, the crowd is tuned out
as the pitcher stands with poise and little doubt
the center fielder finds position in his stance
an uproarious crowd, yet there is still silence.

A warm sun and little overcast, as was predicted
no wind to be felt, another perfect day has been resurrected
the weather to be envied by all
as the home plate umpire stands and yells "Let's play ball!"

Kevin Scott Atkins

When Can I Cry?

Her only son was being buried that day,
  And she was my lifelong friend.
She married very young, and moved faraway
  But our friendship did not end.

The very next week in a traffic accident,
  A mother, a father and two children died.
We visited and comforted each time we went,
  And soon all their tears were dried.

A beautiful wedding was on the next week,
  Both bride and groom known to all.
The ceremony, the environment, I could hardly speak
  With friends on hand to the wall.

Tragedies, triumphs, tears pain: part of every life.
The preacher, a friend, a confidant stands by
  through the strife.
We rejoice at birth, other times we sigh,
The pastor must survive it all, and wonder
  when can I cry!

Mary Miller Walker

Beneath A Tree

If we could take time out each day
And sit down beneath a tree,
And view the scenery near and far
What a picture that would be.

In our minds we could travel many a mile
Without much effort on our part.
We could meet new friends and share their joy
With a smile and a willing heart.

Maybe help someone along the way
Whose burden is heavy with care,
Or smooth the path down a stony road
For the stranger. We're willing to share.

Now come with me down that shady lane
Let us laugh and sing, I implore
Don't linger behind on wasted time.
God gave us this land to explore.

So come along and share my dream
As we travel over land and sea.
Oh, the many things we can see and do
When we're sitting beneath a tree.

Mabel Sebens

Grandma's Garden

She often walks to her garden in the mist of dawn alone,
And sits beneath the maple tree in her rocking chair, her throne.
She alone is its only human refugee,
And she gazes upon the beauty as she sips her cup of tea.

Dawn's tears of dewdrops are tiny sparkling stars upon green,
As sunbeams gently caress them and the air is so fresh and clean.
There's a scent of nature's bouquet of flowers, spruce and pine.
To eternally stay in this paradise would surely be divine.

The birds whistle sweet melodies as they flitter from tree to tree,
And there are bees buzzing and butterflies fluttering so free.
The flowers and blades of grass waltz in the gentle breeze,
But the brilliance of autumn leaves is a sight that does please.

Oh but to be in her garden is where she truly wishes to be,
But only in her mind is her garden of beauty and tranquility.
For she can no longer see clearly as she's old and almost blind,
But to have once seen this beauty she thanks God for being so kind.

It is now my turn to sit in grandma's rocking chair,
And each day's dawn in her garden to her I say a prayer.
For I am grateful to see what she must have once seen,
In her garden so beautiful and serene.

Willetta Goodrich

Still Here

At times not my will but my fathers, give one hundred percent
and sometimes more. Give withholding nothing, give with no regard
for what's given back. Still here in the Lord he knows the heart
and that's a fact.

Still here over and over and over again journey deeper
within. What's being accomplished may endure even until the end,
but it's just a comfort to know, that Jesus cares for he is
an ever and ever friend.

Still here and there: To and fro may love conquer all,
don't waste Gods unconditional love, do encourage the heart
with his word. Worry not of your thoughts, just continue to
give, the devil can't be conquered unless we try. Edify one
to another, just follow the word and not your own thoughts, you'll
find he's still giving blessings when we do as we ought.

Still here: Me and my master, reaching out trying to touch,
make a connection to a once torn and shattered heart, desiring
only to wipe away the tears, mend the broken pieces, just staying
with Jesus growing stronger together rather than apart. Still
here I've given to you a valued possession my heart.

Robert C. Wallace Jr.

Upon Sleeping, Upon Awakening, Upon Being

In a world where darkness runs free with light
and spirits roam with childlike vigor
as demons of sadness covet the earth and flesh
sleeping princess awaken from a dream to find
  all the nightmares of a blessing lurk behind an unclosed door
I see and can not move

This land I cross alone
this land it lies in truth
  lies reveal such truth
this land it speaks through stone
  I see then why should I move?
All this I bear witness with a beaten horse named blue

My sleeping king he says to me
"take your powers from the ground"
"kill my prince he sleeps too much"
"all that I am is here to be found, and all that I see is such"
"my lands you shall cross alone bearing witness with a beaten horse
  named blue"

Scott Ertel

Mountains

As mountains reach to touch the heav'ns in vain,
And stretch their tow'ring crests above this earth,
Above this earth and all there in, sublime,
To man each gives a picture of true mirth,
Yet each may work with might and main to gain,
Supremacy, but no one gains the throne,
For each may work with might and main to gain,
But they were placed steadfast to stay, not 'tain.

So selfish man, his eye on heights so high,
Doth stretch his arms their length; he may come nigh,
Or even reach those heights so long desired,
But what can he attain of things desired,
For each may struggle all his life to gain,
But all is left behind, attained in vain.

Lawrence A. Bonker

231

Autumn Leaves

When September wraps itself around August
And summer's fruit fade into autumn's frost
The leaves dance in each day's gust
And shiver in each chilling night

They struggle against each northern attack
Each storm and perilous gale
A mad fluster of oranges, yellows, and reds
Resounds the sleeping forest

When yellow soon dominates the forest
And they are drained of all strength
They succumb to the wrath of autumn
And the forest sheds yellow tears

Carried away to their resting place
Beneath the dissolving canopy
They wither away, crumble, and perish
At the foot of each bare oak and birch

When autumn comes around again
And exhales its bitter cold breath
Can I hold on until April comes
Or will I perish like the rest

Nicholas Roy

My Favorite Time Of The Year

As the summer loses its grip
And the air has a slight chill
I know that fall is drawing near
This is my favorite time of the year.

The leaves start to change to a brilliant color
As mother nature unleashes her magic
It is such a beauty for the eye to behold
That at any price this sight would be sold.

The nights seem so pleasant
As you drift off to sleep
The cool air surrounding you
Makes your dreams run so deep.

If I could freeze one moment in time
I would hold this one dear
And cherish forever
As this is my favorite time of the year.

Wayne G. Daniel

Coda

When I have fears that I may cease to be
and the Fast Forward has been set for me,
I'm really not afraid for I've lived madly;
when it is time to go I shall leave gladly.
Few, if any, past regrets - no future fear
will hamper my departure from this sphere.
Somehow I know that I will not be late
for all the wondrous glories that await.
Tempted at times to take an early leave,
I could not if there is but one to grieve.

And since Time never stops but moves along,
there are few moments for my simple song;
I must be certain that I daily say
"I love you," to my loved ones in some way.

Mary Jane Richeimer

The Roses

I dearly miss the roses
And the meaning that they had;
Instead of enjoying their beauty
I look at them now and I'm sad.

The long stems and the beautiful colors
That brightened up the room;
The smell of their sweet fragrance
Now emphasizes my gloom.

The buds, they were so perfect
And in time, their petals would spread;
But they still needed nurturing
Or soon they would be dead.

Although you give them all the love and care
Even the petals start to turn black;
The leaves go colorless and start to fall
And they turn brittle and crack.

Your love for me was like the rose
Because neither could last a lifetime;
You can take away the roses and your love
But the memories of you will stay mine.

Syl Valverde

Pearl The Pretty Pumpkin

Most pumpkin are boys,
  and their name is Jack.

But in farmer Johnson's garden,
  in the first row, at the very back,

There's a teeny weeny pumpkin,
  which is perfectly round.

It is a beautiful golden color,
  and its green leaves spread upon the ground.

There is something different about this pumpkin.
  She is little girl.

This dainty lady is definitely no jack-o-lantern,
  as you can tell by her lovely name, Pearl!

Loretta Tollis

Something To Remember

The best things in life are always free
And these are the things that mean most to me
The smile of a friend, a pat on the back
And someone who cares if you're on the right track
A walk in the woods by a quiet stream
A place in the shade to sit and dream
The beauties of nature are ours to embrace
And take care of all things with pride and grace
We pass but once along life's way
Let's stop look and listen, ere we call it a day

Russell Fenimore

Hara-Kiri

You choke me with your gentle glances
and touch that threatens to make me overflow.
I don't know the words to ask you to stay, even for a moment,
while razor blades dance in my head one more,
singing salty music of lust, begging me to release
their lightning edges into my life-giving bloodstream.
Let me hold you close, please, just for a second.
I promise I will let you go, return to the typical teenage relationship
now in progress, with little sisters and unheralded anniversaries.
But now, this instant, not Monday morning, I need a magic spell
to cross the time span between now and when we met,
to the moment in which it was perfect, before my personality
began to get in the way.

Sarah Walters

Danny

"Grandma, why are you crying?", the young boy asked;
  and thoughts of her son came rushing from the past.
She grasped his hand just a little tighter
  hoping this visit would make her burden lighter.
She took her grandson and walked to the Wall;
  there in the third row was her Danny among them all.
"That's my dad's name," his voice spoke with a crack.
  "I'm not the only one whose Dad's not coming back."
"Yes, we lost your dad as did others too,"
  as over Danny's name their fingers traced through.
"He and many others fought and died in Viet Nam;
  and we must keep on living the very best we can."
"Your dad was tall, so handsome and proud.
  He wanted you to be a man-not just one of a crowd.
You have the color of his hair, the smile and sparkle of his eyes.
  We must try to accept and understand why so many dads had to die."

Maureen L. Hornung

Untitled

We want to say thank you for all that you do-
And to say that you are appreciated for just being you.

The depth of your caring and understanding is so deep
we've looked for it in others but no one can compete.

The value of your presence, constant by our sides-
I don't believe you know the strength that you provide.

Through your honesty and openness we're more than
  child and mother-
We've become close friends, I think able to depend
  on one another.

No other person in this world views us in such a light-
As to appreciate her children so even when they've not done right.

Looking at ourselves through your eyes it's no wonder
  how we've grown-
To be such positive individuals successful on our own.

You've truly done a wonderful thing raising us as we are-
And no mother could do better I'm sure, if we
  looked both near and far.

So on this Mother's Day, we wish you many blessings-
Happiness for your todays, fulfillment in all your tomorrows.

Shari Adams

For A Friend

I would like to reach out
And touch your day with a smile
To imprint upon your heart
The memory of happiness
I wish for you the joy of autumn
As well as the hope of spring
May you know the warmth of friends
On the coldest winter days
And the cool touch of kindness
When no medicine can ease the pain
I wish for you my friend
Sunshine to light your soul
Where dark shadows used to grow
And the prayers of loved ones
To lift you up when the burden of caring
Weighs heavy on your shoulders
These things I wish for you, because
In a very special way...I love you.

Leslie Hillhouse

My Prayer

I pray every night that God will guide you
  And touch your soul with faith
So you may be happy and over your sickness
  And always feel comfortably safe

I don't know why you feel so bad
  About the person you see
When you look in the mirror and walk away
  Shaking your head disgustedly

You should learn to talk it out
  Whenever you feel unsure
About what you ate or what you did
  Or that you're insecure

For once I wish you could see yourself
  Through someone else's eyes
For you would see a stunning beauty
  Buried deep beneath the lies

But for now I know that all I can do
  Is tell you how much I care
And hope that every single night
  God is answering my prayer.

Kimberly W. Van Deest

Living In His Light

I wander restless through the night,
and try to fight the loser's fight.
I often feel so all alone,
I open the door, but there's no one at home.
Something, someone keeps pushing me down,
but, no I've got to win that crown.
And when at last I learn to stand,
then I will mightily reach for his hand.
At last I will make known my plight,
For I will be living in His light.

I must remain, I must contain living in His light.
I must believe, I must receive living in His light.

Tammy L. Chaney

Homerun Ball

With a warm gentle breeze we all settle in
and waited, for the game to begin

with the greasy smell of hot-dogs
and the sour smell of beer
a young man yelled,
"get'em right here"

a big man,
lumbered to the plate
people all around us
said he was really great

the pitcher eyed the man
and nervously he paced
this was an important game,
this was the pennant race

he pitched the ball,
very very fast
and then all we heard
was in incredibly, defining crack

the ball flew up over the outfield wall,
and guess what, I caught that homerun ball.

Robert LeNeve

"Goose Bumps"

When I listen to the Star-Spangled Banner play,
  and watch our nation's flag unfurl each day.
Nostalgia begins within an inward grin,
  How thankful I am to have you within.
I got "Goose Bumps".

Lord, I feel there is something for me to say.
  Just as we talked the other day.
We talked of things in life that thrill.
  As we talked, I felt glorious chill.
I got "Goose Bumps".

Gracious Lord, When I pray,
  You speak so clearly as to say,
How you love us, even today.
  I got "Goose Bumps".

Kenneth W. Hammer

Sandcastle And Dreams

Come be with me...
And we can watch the sunset
While the sand sifts through our toes,
And a quiet gentle breeze blows through our hair.

Come be with me...
And as we walk along the shore
The only sound for miles around is the whisper
Of an echo as our kisses float along the night time air.

Come be with me...
And we can build a castle made of sand
And dreams, and all the things that lovers seem to
Cherish when the wonder of discovery is still new.

Come be with me...
And we can play the night away
Till the waves wash down the castle
And all that's left are dreams and sand and you.

Maryann Ziga

Sensations

The rain bears the scent of a crisp, white, linen sheet,
And we can wrap ourselves in its soothing simplicity.
It keeps us cool and safe,
In the heat of the tormenting summer night.

It pours down on our foreheads; a tall cold glass of water,
To wash away all the strain of time.

Beneath our feet, it scurries into the crevices,
Of the Earth's wrinkled face.

And though man looks into the sky and curses
The omnipotent black clouds he finds floating there,
We, you and I, will always be
Wrapped and hidden from the world,
In its sullen, gray shadows.

Snow Taylor

Fragile Life

As lightning and thunder crashes to the ground,
Another day goes by not feeling too sound,
Living a life trying to make the right decision,
Hoping God might give me that one great vision,
Of what to do with my life so bleak,
So many places to go and seek,
Not going back to that same old way of life,
Learning to do things that will build my new life,
Please, God, help me to find my true place,
Don't let me drift any more as in space.

Philip L. Potts II

Brandon

A baby cries
  and when he no longer cries,
The world cries.
Babies are meant to experience
  the wonderment of their tiny world,
The love in their mother's eyes.

  Babies are not supposed to die.

Your short time upon this earth
  touched loved ones near and afar.
We who never saw you, long to know you.
Those who never would have met you
  grieve your loss.
Just as they celebrate an unknown baby's birth.

  Babies are the hope for a better world.

A baby's death is not God's will.
  God is loving and welcomes
His children with open arms.
Perhaps that is why He gives us memories
  and the ability to smile again, after the pain.

  Babies live forever in our mind's eye.

Patricia J. Whitney

I Never Told You Goodbye

I made you smile, giggle, laugh, but also cry
And when I left I never told you goodbye
We went here and there and all about
I didn't say goodbye the day I walked out
There's been no other from that day on
I've lived my life lonely and withdrawn
I've thought of you every day of the year
Picturing your face I shed many a tear
The years went by slowly and I grew old
The memories of you were worth more than gold
If one more time I could have touched your hand
Walked you down the beach on the golden sand
One more smile would have crossed my lips
One more time I would have been in loves grips
But now I'm old and my days are through
A life of happiness is what I wanted for you.

Rodney Stamper

Sorrow Of My Heart

The sorrow of my heart is great, it burdens my every step
And when I stop to think sorrow becomes regret

To regret every step one's made is very sad indeed
When the sorrow becomes too heavy, then there is a need

The need is for different times, of happiness and joy
But the happiness seems so shallow, the other just a ploy

For soon come along the changes, that disturbs and upsets
And everything is gone, the safety lines and nets

The sorrow returns anew to strike at a every corner
Nothing is left untouched, you become like a mourner

The tears come to your eyes and your heart seems to burst
And nothing seems to ease the pain, you go from bad to worse

They say the eyes are the mirror of a persons soul
Then mine would show the lonely, empty, unfilled hole

I think of my past, the people that I have known
I think of my future, and hope that I have grown

I think of every thing in life beginning with the Womb
Of what my life will mean when I'm in the Tomb

Where is the gladness of which I once was part
The only thing that is left, is the Sorrow of My Heart

Thomas D. Whittaker

Never Far Behind

I wish I could wrap my arms around you
And wipe away your tears.
I would do anything to ease your pain
And release you from your fears.

I cannot help you for this is your battle
But I will always support you.
Though at times you may feel alone
I am always with you.

To be your support
When you feel weak.
To be your guide on the darkest street.

I am always a few steps behind
To catch you if you fall.
To lift you up again
And make you stand tall.

For you will conquer this battle
Just like the rest,
And the lessons you have learned
   will make you stronger
Because you withstood the test.

Kelly Lee Lynch

'Treasured Love'

Musicians sing sweet melodies of love
And with their songs give pleasure to the ear
By wise and witful lyrics so they prove
With each concordant breath to all that hear
The universal heralds of delight
Likewise the gourmet chef does serenade
The tongue appealing to the appetite
Presents to taste his palatal parade
And so it is with eyes and hands and nose
To see a rainbow born of sky and storm
To touch fine cloth or smell a scented rose
All these the pleasures of the senses form
   Yet none enrich my heart comparedly
   To that with which your love has given me.

R. F. Stancill

"From The Heart"

Dear Teri, this is exactly as my heart dictated it. God sent us an angel from heaven in 1973 cause he wanted to share her with us for all eternity. You'll know her when you see her, causes she has no peer. She's even a stand out among angels, her beauty will evoke a tear. She caught eye in an instant in oh so many ways. She's a charm that's most radiant right there in heaven's rays. To say that she is precious will only do for a start for she's many time above that and will quickly steal your heart.

Her eyes move clear than diamonds are a beauty to behold. They seem to look right through you to tease you inner soul. I bring you to heaven each day dear in the prayers that I say just for you. But an angel doesn't need prayers, dear cause that angel is you. You certainly

have beautiful parents to have raised such a sweet girl as you. What a shame dear parents like yours are oh so very few. Since we are so much alike we're meant to have much fun. Since we are so much alike I'm glad I met you, hon. You have the manner of an angel, you're serene as a saint. Oh, if I had the talent what a picture I could paint!

I hope I'm not too bold, dear, in what I'm penning here. Cause God is right behind me whispering all this in my ear. This is my whole confession, dear, of what you mean to me. I've poured my heart out, darling, for you and the world to see. I cannot end this poem as you shall plainly see. Cause Teri and I will be here through all eternity.

William H. Nichols

Painted Shadow

Mirrored, close to the kneeling child
Another kneels to watch her there
But darkened gaze no answer yields
To eager glance the first would share.

No echoing sound from Gemini child
Though moving lips like movement brings,
And ear hears only one soft voice
The plaintive song the first child sings.

The azure pool shares azure sky
And flowered frocks the two have worn
Are one bouquet reflected there
A drift of petals waterborne.

Lost deep in wonder both do share,
The radiant sheen of sunstruck hair
An aureole rings round the other child
Strange garb for a shadow to wear.

Then fingers touch, a gentle touch,
Rippling the lovely azure sky
To scatter the petals and quiet the song
And a cloud stole the mirrored child.

Selene Smith

My Grandmother's Love

It's unconditional - a grandmother so loving, so kind
   Another would be so hard to find.
The childhood memories there are so many: The egg hunts,
catching lightning bugs, and slumber parties with cousins,
   These are memories to have and to hold, by the dozens.
It's OK, grandmother would say as flour and sugar I would spill,
   Learning to make cookies was always a big thrill.
Angels and Santas we would cut out for Christmas,
   These are such simple times with Grandmother I miss.
Fond memories of Papaw, whom I miss everyday,
   Mamaw took care of, so much, as he lay.
He was so sick and died so young on that day,
   The love of Grandmother was there as she pray, for she knew God's
   plan was greater than they.
Now I hear tell grandmother was a real cowgirl, horses she'd ride,
   She could tame a wild horse and people would ah! as she rode
   with such pride.
I love you so much for the many times we've shared.
   The patience you've shown can't be compared.
Your Vicks rub downs followed by our taking turns reading Bible
   verses in bed,
Soon we both nodded off to slumber land with peaceful thoughts in our heads.

Ruth Walker

Playfully Admonished

Blue skies
are an artist's canvas.
Painted puffy white clouds
with mystical motions.
A land far below contains
   the creatures of the Creator.
Children. Cute little boys and pretty little girls,
Colorblindly playing.
Fulfilling Life's potential enjoyments.
See-saws, swings, sandboxes, grass and light breezes.
Peaceful,
Harmonious,
A temporary dream.

Neil West

Comfort

All the struggles and pains of mine
are just a learning block in time.
Lessons not to be used by me alone;
looking back will be a stepping stone...
To prepare me for a much bigger task
bow will this help me God, I ask?
Not to help you my child, the reply
a comfort for another as the years go by.
The comfort that you offer is for me to take and share.
With so many blessings I have an illness with no cure,
whatever lies ahead of me, please help me to endure.
As the trials come my way your will for me be done
and may my work for you on earth have only just begun.
Help me to know each day I face a purpose and a plan
as each one passes, we both smile, and continue hand and hand.

Kimberli D. Hargnett

My Little Box Of Times And Dreams

Many of the times I share and dream.
Are so happy times I see. For when they come
it seems so slow, but all to fast they seem
to go. One happy time you think will last, but
all to soon it seems to pass.
The dreams you seem to have at times
come and go like little rhymes. I want to
keep my times and dreams in a box tied with
string. So when I wake to find them gone
There they are tied tight and strong. Then
I know they will never be gone.

Lori Smith

Where Are We Going

Where does this life lead us... down the road and back
Are we really willing, what is it that we lack?
Are we so afraid of walking? To take that step of faith...
So we're content to stay behind
And wait... and wait... and wait...
What is it that we're hoping for; what is it that we need?
What will we do to get it?
Will we sow a little seed?

So, where does this life lead us?
And would you like to go?
Let's set some goals, let's plant some seeds
And sow... and sow... and sow...
And when this life is over, and we have to give account;
We can boldly say that we lost track
And didn't measure the amount.
We worked and worked... and gave and gave...
Until our life was through.
The legacy was left behind
That God could work through me and you!

Susan R. Keck

Because

"Because" is not an answer.
"Because" is not a reason.
"Because" is not a good excuse.
"Because" is not a rational statement.
"Because" is a continuum of status-quo.
"Because" is not a result.
"Because" is not an action.
"Because" will not result in action.
"Because" is not an indication of agreement.
"Because" is not definite.
"Because" is unacceptable.
WHY?
"BECAUSE!"

William J. Mader

Billy And The Bear

Billy went hunting with his bow and
arrow, hoping to kill a deer but never
thought about a bear. He strolled along
down through the woods, not having any
fear all he had upon his mind was just to see a deer.

The weather was beautiful, everything
was calm and still. You could hear the
sound of your footsteps as you walked along the hills.

He had walked a lot that day and was
getting tired and hungry and he knew it
was getting late; so he sat down to rest
a spell and eat a piece of cake.

He leaned back, stretched out his arms
enjoying the mountain air, heard a noise
behind him, turned and looked, there stood
a bear. It scared them both half to death,
but the bear stood still and so did Bill.

Neither one knew what to do. Then
the bear began to prance, Bill he wet
his pants and they both turned around and flew.

Oscar Neal

A Haunting Image In My Mind

Silver blue shades of day light fades,
As dark shadowy fingers of night descend.
Changing the light of day,
Into deep shades of night's ebony.

Lonely winds of night lightly stir,
Softly tantalizing feathers of thought.
Bringing forth an image haloed softly of light,
An image of love's dream shadow.

Yet I can't but wonder in night's dim thought,
Thoughts that seem as reel as reel.
'Tis this image only a hopeful misty dream,
Or be she real and not a dream.

Dark shadowy images of night spinning,
Spinning their ever present haunting melodies.
Tempting a weary mind to dream,
Dreams of that dream or of reality.

Thoughts drifting aimlessly through a billowing night,
Ever seeking more than those occasional glimpses.
Yea more a solid image of that spirit's face,
That haunts the recesses of this weary mind.

Stan L. Guyer

Summer Nights

The setting sun is sinking low,
As gentle breezes softly blow.
Our work is done, we sit down to rest,
A bull frog croaks, birds go to their nest.
Locust are singing, fire-flies fly,
They turn on their lights and light up the sky.
The moon comes up and the stars start to appear,
Night is upon us, bedtime is near.
As we lay in our bed we hear the hoot of an owl,
And in a far distance a coyotes' howl.
Soon dawn will appear and we'll be on our way,
Off to work to start a new day.
We rush through the day till it comes to an end,
Then hurry home and we know once again,
That the setting sun is sinking low,
As gentle breezes softly blow.

Tula R. Gillespie

"The Blue Bird"

Remember the little blue bird
As he fluttered along
So very small a bird was he
But his color bold and strong

As we sat alone together
Our hearts heavy with fear
We spied the little fellow
We knew that God was near

While we watched this little bird
With his beautiful blue so rare
He lifted our heavy hearts a moment
From a world that's often cruel and unfair

He seemed to us to be a sign
From our Heavenly Father above
That no matter how rough our road
We'll always have the beauty of His love

Mary Beth Dunn

The Final Kiss

I saw an old man on a park bench today
As I was on my way home
I wanted to stop; see what he had to say
But thought it was best left alone

Because I don't want to know what it is
With those tired old eyes he's seen
And I don't want to know where it is
With those tired old legs he's been

I just want to know what he thinks
It is in life he has missed
And I want to know what he will feel
When at last death's face he's kissed.

Sherrell Van Leusden

Through Closed Eyes

I looked around the corner and saw a man fighting with the air
as if it were his only true foe.

His spirit was that of a fighter and it rose with each passing moment
for he knew he was a winner.

With each movement that he made his eyes became wider
and the smile upon his face became more pronounced.
Life was his to live as he wanted, on his own terms.
His hands were like lightening and in a flash...in a flash...
In a flash a man lay before me that was only a shell of what was.
His cheeks hollowed, his eyes sunken.

Almost nothing of what I knew before and yet,
oh that beautiful spirit,
that fighter within him, that love for life.

The months did pass and aided by family he fought.
But he could only fight for so long, and so hard.
And while his spirit continued his body could not.
Because of his body, his spirit shall fight on in the memory of those
   he left behind.

Mitchell Blank

Cause And Effect

Thunder raises its mighty voice
As if roaring on its own.
You are here only because
Lightening has come and gone.

Roar, rumble and make your noise
You're head in much repetition.
Surely your mystery is not hid
Lightening is your motivation.

Windows and doors shake and rattle
In response to your boisterous sound
Proudly you march until no more
Your cause dashes silently to the ground.

Is it possible you're more than you seem?
You rumbled, you grumbled, you said,
No, you're simply a fleeting thing
Born when lightening raises its head.

Loreta Durham

"While You're Away"

Slowly my tears fall down my face,
As I'm praying for God's amazing grace;

I miss you so much, while you're away,
Please God help me through another day;

Time goes by, like we don't belong,
But God always helps me with a song;

Our love is stronger, while we're apart,
For God fills the emptiness in my heart;

I can't wait to hold you in my arms,
So we can thank God for keeping us from harm;

One more night I'm all alone,
Watching and waiting by the telephone;

Sweet dreams I'll have to be with you,
And patiently waiting I'll be true:

Patti Webster

Falling Leaves

The clouds gather and the sky turns gray,
As she walks in the grass that is turning this day.
And the rain starts falling so gentle to the ground,
As she walks through the grass, with leaves falling round.

She looks at the fruit hanging low to the ground,
And smiles at the sweet taste and remembers his touch.
He planted that tree and she loved him so much
As she walks through the grass, with leaves falling round.

That noisy old barn with the roof coming down,
He never had fixed, as she hears its loud sound.
And wishes he was here so tall and so strong,
As she walks through the grass, with leaves falling round.

A sad tear runs down the still pretty face,
As she sees his work with each steady pace,
And the rain still falling so gentle to the ground,
As she walks through the grass, with leaves falling round.

G. Wm. (Bill) Lewis

237

Sorrow Is A Song

Just as you turn up the volume
As the first notes of the song rise to your ears
So do the tears well up in your eyes
And a lump rises to your throat.

The music courses rapidly through your body
And you can feel the beat pulsing inside you
From your head to your toes.

The overwhelming grief surges powerfully through you
And the unshed tears mix with your blood.

The music surrounds you, penetrates you, engulfs you
As does your unceasing anguish.

You are drowning in the sea of the melody.
You are drowning in the sound of your sobs.

The music softly caresses your cheek.
The tears tickle your skin as they slowly trickle down your face.

The last notes of the song die away.
Yet the music still lingers in your ears
As the sorrow still lingers in your heart.

Renee Hill

May Heaven's God Have Mercy On Our Souls

May Heaven's God have mercy on our souls
As the world suffers man's most dreaded blight
The bible's last chapter, it has foretold

We could do no wrong, so mighty and bold
Fifty's child saw a future so bright
May Heaven's God have mercy on our souls

Dark does humanity's future unfold
Seventy's child saw but bleak black night
The bible's last chapter, it has foretold

See now! How cheaply life was bought and sold
Too late we question great deeds in hindsight
May Heaven's God have mercy on our souls

Seething nations clenched tight in Anger's hold
Ninety's child sees and trembles in fright
The bible's last chapter, it has foretold

Beware! Nuclear darkness, deadly, cold
Bright flash - searing wind - doomed is Earth of old
May Heaven's God have mercy on our souls
The bible's last chapter, it has foretold

Patricia Howard

Quality Time?

In order to enjoy the leisurely life
As we now envision it,
We must pattern it, play-act it
To forgive our time-loss.
We buy machines designed to promote efficiency:
Cuisinarts, bread makers, pasta makers,
Mixers for decadent desserts,
Espresso-makers for decadent coffees.
We spend our time in the kitchen
Making 'home-made' everything for company:
Push-button engineering—but is it cooking?
We could be playing with our children,
Discovering the mysteries of life with them,
But no! The nanny has that privilege.

We'll do that on another day
The day-that-never-comes:
Play a family game of Cootie
And eat packaged, instant pizza.

Miri Hargus

You And Me

People wonder about you and me
as we walk down the halls together.
People can laugh and stare all they want
But I will still love you forever.

Skin to skin just you and me
I'd love you forever can't you see.
I'm knee deep in love that came from your heart
I want you to know that we'll never part.

I need the love that makes me feel right.
I need that love from you tonight.

Scott Klassen

The Music Still Sings Blue

The rocking chairs go back and forth — each on or off a beat
As weathered as two gentlemen, perched on each time-worn seat
Straw hat and felt fedora top skin shades of brown and black
And dual cigars unlighted; Slim Jim sits with soft-shoe Jack

Between them time is mostly spent on talk of yesterday
And after queried weather, there is not much more to say
Unless a passing traveler stops there — restful on the road
In endless search of novelties and living legends-told

Then locals knowing history will often join right in
The plea for a blue melody — of other times past when:
"Hey Jim, give us a good song, "ole school" — but not too long
A cool and haunting melody about a man done wrong"

A play at "some" reluctance then the stage soon sets again
Slim Jim smiles them an answer as the serenade begins
Much smoother than black velvet, raw soul croons just like a threat
Involvement in the music reaffirmed by mounting sweat

Harmonica to sweetly scent a verse well-sung's refrain
While tapping feet to music soothes and clapping hands sustain
As one song begs another applause prompts — then bids — adieu
Each sits and smiles approval that the music still sings blue.

Pamela Kelly Phillips

The Flower He Gave Me

Zuzu's petals never looked so grand
As when they sat on my table
The table, in the kitchen, of the house we rent
Surrounded by books
In a vase much too big for its slender frame
Even at night Zuzu's petals still smile
Though their innocence be opened up and laid
    bare for all to see
And when the petals grow, in grace, to shriveled
    memories right before my eyes...
I am not ashamed
I will keep those petals in a delicate crystal tray
I will keep them on the table, in the kitchen, of the
    house we rent...
And smile

Kimberly L. Ashby

Untitled

May the good Lord bless and guide you
as you travel down life's road.
Today is the beginning of a story yet untold.
Hand in hand you go forth
your hearts within you sing
a new life now beginning with
the exchanging of a ring
God's love will sustain you
through the trials of your life
stronger now together
forever man and wife.

Rose Rokoski

238

The Passing Of Time

He held the dagger that took her life. No one knew. No one saw.
At least that's what we're told. I was a child and believed what
I was told, but now I'm grown and I've begun to wonder. I've seen
things that made me know that everything is not what it seems.

Mama's waiting for us, I know it's true. She's a part of heaven.
That's that woman we all knew. HATE, JEALOUSY, RAGE, AND
    VIOLENCE...
LET THE MOON SHINE, LET THE DOG HOWL, THERE'S
GOING TO BE BLOOD SPILLED. And I can still hear her cry.
And all her cries were snuffed out. I've been told that blood cries out
to God for vindication during a wrongful death. I'm just wondering what
God will do to make everything work out right.

People say I'm like my Mom...But the night I let the pain
win out, I did for dad what he did for her. And now I feel better,
'cause we're all part of the same big picture.

M. G. Rutland

The Ocean

The moon in the water
at night is so gentle,
and that is you.

The mid day sun on the water
is rough and strong,
and that is also you.

I am not afraid of what you are
for you are so many things
and can be yet still more.

Nor am I afraid of what you have been...
for you have all those waves behind you now.

Only do I desire to plunge into
all those things at once in you.

I see them-
am exhilarated by them...

And so love the feel of you
as you wrap yourself around me.

I walk into you willing, wantingly...
hoping to drown in the ocean
of your sweet embrace.

Vincent Cantwell

The River

Sometimes we'd walk down to the river
at night, just before daylight. We'd lie
there and look up at the stars, and try
to guess which ones were Venus, Saturn,
and Mars. We use to sit there and he'd hold
me tight, and we wouldn't let go till the
morning light. Then we'd go back to lives
we lead before, but each night we'd meet back
at that cold river shore. But things are different
than they were before, we no longer meet at that
cold river shore. And we no longer look up at the
stars trying to guess which ones are Venus, Saturn and Mars.
And he no longer holds me tight, till the morning light.
Why did God have to take him so soon, now my heart is
just an empty room. Even though he's looking down at me
from above, I will never have another love.

Tasha R. Lewis

Forever and 'Till'

Forever and 'till' the end you'll be
    at the heart and in the soul of me

Our memories will always be there
    a reminder that you still care

The love in your heart will never die
    no matter how long or hard I cry

Your caring tone will never change
    no matter how far the distance or range

You'll be there when the hurt is through
    to point me toward the path that's true

With you to be there and make me laugh
    I'll never stray the lighted path

I'll never venture into the dark
    I'll never bear the troubled mark

No one can ever break my bond with you
    your bond with me is just as true

I'll be there for you 'till' the end
    I'll stand beside you as your friend

Time is all it takes to show
    just how far our friendship will go.

Sara Fuller

A Woman Is

A woman is like a delicate flower, whose petals blow
Away with the wind, but can stand as strong as a rock,
Just to be there for her man.

A woman can work twelve hours a day, and still run a
Household, she can know your deepest thoughts without even being told.

A woman can give you a smile on a dark and dreary day,
And fill your world with sunshine, as you go along your way.

A woman can be the most beautiful thing, you ever lay eyes
Upon, but treat her bad and she'll walk away, leaving you all alone.

A woman is a loving soul, for she is your true Queen. She'll
Make you feel like no other can, show you love like you've never seen.

A woman can be as gentle as a lamb, bring pleasure through
All your days, but cross her and she'll take you down,
Break your spirit in many ways.

So put her on a pedestal, show your love for her and then,
Respect your Queen through all her days, and she will
Forever be your friend.

Renea A. Simmons

Relinquish

Gotta turn this so called life around
Before I run myself into the ground
A second chance to me was dealt
A repeat of this should never be felt

I had them all fooled myself as well
So I thought, and quickly I fell
Strong and resistant like no other
I am alive and fine, but then I wonder

The realization of my contrasts with life
To take it or leave it, my biggest strife
Contemplations I never thought would enter my mind
Searching for excuses or misinterpreting what I find

Impressionable, but human, I tend to forget
Constantly doing what I later on regret
Careful what I wish, getting what I want
Aware of what is right, as the wrong is there to haunt

Katie Sundstedt

Memories

I wandered alone again today,
Back to our little cabin where we used to play.
Birds sang in the trees not far away.
The sun shone brightly,
it was such a good day.

All the world looked so beautiful,
as I stood by the old door.
Everything looked the same
as my memories returned once more.

Happy voices of my children
swimming in the lake near by.
It all seemed so real,
I wanted to cry.
But things are different now
My children are both grown.
Many loved ones now live
in their Heavenly home.

Oh, how can this be? Those days are now past.
Life must go on
But my memories last.

Voncile T. Ledbetter

Bea's Song

Quietly she comes on the evening breeze
bathed with the moon's gentle light,
a vision, no a dream come to seduce.
Silent torment, purveyor of the night.

In the quiet hours, when my mind drifts,
unfettered by convention,
not confined by need.
Myself only left,
no direction
fading.

What is this specter of which I speak,
without form, yet with substance?
Real yet a fantasy, its meaning I seek,
souls bereft, the placid torment LOVE.
For what is can be no more,
and what was is itself ever found.

Steve Nelson

Tennessee Morning

Your beauty in the morning can not
be compared.
The bird's song is so soothing,
the soft due is in the air.

Gentle is the moisture upon the blades of grass.
The sweetness of the flowers,
if we could only make it last.

The stillness of the sunrise
without a whisper of a breeze.
You inter with each breath I take,
you touch the soul of every tree.

It is this time of everyday
that starts us on our way.
Through many directions we must take
Through many decisions we must make

I will always cherish this gift from God above.
The special time of morning,
given to us with his love.

Mary Fecteau

The Silent Audience

There is a large, open room warmed only by the sun
Beaming windows of light onto the wooden floor.

Mirrors own one of the four walls, reflecting shadows of pigeons
As they flutter by the open windows.

A young woman dressed in a leotard and tights steps into the room,
Enticed by the original bare beauty of the space before her.

She runs silently to the windows and peeks out
Breathing in the peacefulness of the morning.

She steps back from the window and turns just enough so that
The sunlight will warm her back as she stretches.

She places a graceful hand lightly on the bar, her face glowing
As her dainty feet move perfectly with her long flowing arms.

Every move is perfectly controlled...a flawless performance,
But why, and for whom?

No one is in the room to give her a standing ovation.
No one is there to throw roses at her feet.
No, her audience is greater than any to be found in this world.

She turns away from the bar smiling, takes two might leaps,
And whispers, "for Him, I dance for Him!"

Sunnye Collins

The Essence Of Me

Describing the essence of me is a difficult task
Because don't you think we all wear a mask?
Who am I? What am I? I wish that I knew
The answers are known to just a privileged few.
We must peel off the layers, one by one.
It's a lot of work and not much fun.
We begin with our genes, our genetic code,
Which help form our thoughts in our childhood abode.
Our experiences count as well as our schooling.
But if we are what we eat, who are we fooling?
I am what I am, just a romantic soul.
An incurable optimist with an impossible goal.
Perhaps in my next life, if there is reincarnation.
I'll know the right answer with a complete explanation.

Roxie Wintz

My Maw Maw

My Maw-Maw holds a special place in my heart.
Because in my days of growing up she played a big part.
My Maw-Maw had loving and thoughtful ways,
And I will always remember and cherish those days.

My Maw-Maw taught me wrong from right.
She put love and kindness in front of sight.
She taught me how to sew and cook.
My Maw-Maw always gave and never took.

My Maw-Maw knew just what to do,
When I was sad, lonesome, or blue.
I could listen to her sing all day long,
Because you could hear warmth and peacefulness in her song.

My Maw-Maw had enduring patience and time for me.
Whenever I needed her there she would be.
I hope that when I'm a grandmother my grandkids can say,
That I'm just like My Maw Maw Era Mae.

Regina Frazier Newman

This Time

It's gonna be different this time
because I've made up my mind

No more procrastination
no more of my life just a wasting
I've grown tired of Idle preoccupation

It's gonna be different; I know
because I can feel it in my soul
Don't need anyone to tell me so

THIS TIME I'VE GOT CONTROL!!!

Not gonna be affected or scared by life's rejections
Will not allow anyone to smear my perfections
My mind and spirit is ready to challenge all objections

It's time to pursue life and make connections
This life is leading towards a new direction
THIS TIME.

Stephanie Fluker

Tears

I shed a lot of tears today,
Because my beloved husband has passed away.

His days were numbered long ago,
The disease that invaded his body continued to grow.

I ask myself why did he die first,
The sorrow and pain in my heart overwhelmingly hurts.

My mind and body feels numb,
I dread to see our friends and relatives come.

They say things to comfort me,
But they have no idea how empty my world will be.

I shed a lot of tears today,
My beloved husband was buried in a place far away.

I shed some tears today,
I gave my husband's clothes away.

No longer will I find socks and shoes around the house,
Our dream house is now empty without my spouse.

I wish I could go back in time to relive the pleasurable times,
Now they are treasured memories in my mind.

I shed a few tears today,
I discovered I have to make decisions about my future in a new way.

Patricia L. Rusinko

"One Man In A Million"

Don't judge me by the color you see,
  because you are looking at a human being.
Don't judge me by the features of my face,
  because I am a member of the human race.
There is just one race - the human race.

Don't ask me if I'm black or white,
  I might be either one tonight.
Don't lay any "guilt trips" on me, I am not responsible for history.
I am a human being, I have a right to be free.

Don't try to erase who I am because I do not fit into your plans.
I have a right to be here too, just as much, maybe more than you.

Don't try to take my life - get one of your own.
Don't rob me of my land and then call it home.
Don't criticize the way I pray - God understand what I say.
Don't put me down for who I am.

  I am a human.
  I am a man.

Tony Bethel

Deliverance

The chains that have kept me in bondage have
been broken.

The shackles that have caused me poverty of
spirit have been torn loose.

My mind has been set free and like an eagle
soaring about in the open sky I look down
upon the heads of the people wishing with my
whole heart that they could know my joy.

The spiritual emptiness I once knew is gone
forever and for the first time feel the
Loving Hand Of God.

The dark and dismal world of yesterday is
lost in obscurity and the paradise that has
eluded me has finally been found.

A new Day has dawned which has brought
enlightenment and I see the sun shinning with
a brilliance in the distant horizon beckoning
me to come forward.

Yes, I have been delivered since I started
calling God...MOTHER.

Virginia A. Bucher

Winds Of Time

Long before my time and yours, before primates walked on all fours;
Before snow-capped mountains and clear running streams, before
Mozart and Aristotle could even dream dreams. There was such a
deepening darkness that nothing could be seen, a blackness which
consumed all that was; it went unchecked and roamed free. Soon light
was created, thus separating the blackness from all that was; the
bright light shone upon a barren sphere; the warm winds enveloped all
that we hold so very dear. Together the sun and winds nurtured
the barren fields, it seemed the Heavens poured forth and breathed life
into the very first streams. Warm winds again did blow, they carried
moisture to the mountains, which capped their peaks with snow. Yet,
alone was this place we now hold so very dear, that man was formed as a
likeness of the Creator to watch over that which we now hold so very
dear. When the warm winds again did blow, man was given, a companion,
and they roamed freely, as two. Eras and epochs and periods did pass,
until no part of the world was alone from their mass. And they took
openly from that which we now hold so very dear. And the winds
proclaimed hunger and pain, for now no one could take anything as free:
They ravished the hillside and seas and fought over that which we hold
so very dear. They soon levelled the mountains, burned off the
fields, and poisoned the streams. And smoke rose heavily over them
until the air was unclean. They blackened out the sun, which made the
warm winds turn cool; they diverted the streams and the barrenness
grew. Famines created diseases, which altered their gene pool, until
plight took the last two. There was such a deepening darkness that
nothing could be seen, a blackness which consumed all that was; it
went unchecked and roamed free. And soon light was created...

William T. Boyd

A Poem On Freedom

To be is a gift!
Being is freedom!
Freedom is a gift!
I must give it to myself,
For, if it is given to me
I will not respect it.
If I do not respect the gift of freedom,
I cannot respect my Self,
then,
I am burdened with the past.
Freedom will not survive
the awesome load of the past.
Freedom is a gift I must seek
and find for myself....
through being.... who I AM.

Patricia M. Guest

241

Natural Selection

I stand alone roaring
Being tormented by spirits
Spun around on a tumultuous wind
Tossed to and fro this way and that

Searching begging for the eye of the storm
Praying for the calm peaceful center
An island of tranquility sprawled
In the midst of torments

I am the four winds spinning around
Controlling the tides and surf
Changing the course of rivers
Eroding the mountains and rocks

Calling on the elements to serve my purpose
I have been here since the beginning of time
Choosing the course of events
Picking the kings, electing presidents

Beware of my roaring
For I am an animal preying in the night
Devouring the souls of men
Practicing natural selection

Samuel Del Gore

Reflection

Reflection, refraction, the way light moves, the way light augments; bent and broken in many fragments can we see the world in several places, varied faces In the mirror on the wall, do you recall, the places that we hold, the places light won't go What is there, is it really known; a world of its own...Reality, reflection, the unknown depending on the light or lack there of; day or night, what makes it right Can we separate, recall...Does it matter much at all Do you know now...Can you feel, the poignant memories, the world of our dreams our social upbringings, our unifying theme...the American way Empty people, empty places, living days and night go by, without or real reason why Altruism, all to kind...Who knows what they left behind In their post, or their future days...no one knows, no one says So in these reflections on the wall; is it social grace, lives' them, lives' place or is it chaos and decay; survival in the oddest way, that reflects upon these walls windows to our souls, our cause... To our life, to our way Reflection, refraction; the reality, the sublime, can be a gift or so unkind...What's in our mind Do we understand these places, different races, different faces to life's mystery, to not knowing why...to the picture behind the wall; beyond he grasp of those who know it all To the spiritual, the abyss, the places we resist...To the forces so unknown, they drive as all, they take us home to the spaces that we hold, the places light won't go...To the infinity of our souls

Maria Helen Brown

Abandoned Lamb

Your eyes burn angrily as spinning daggers embed in her back; beseeching answers, I oblige to be your beacon. As I ponder at the window, clouds wash the sky; their fury unleashing on a dip in the road, just as they did when I was five. My body betrays my past like the tributaries of my palms. The serpent struck for reasons unbeknownst to me, even after twenty-three years. A ferocious sting, though secondary to the constant pain in my belly, subsided by a teaspoon of peanut butter or grapes salvaged from the crows. Congestion of cots provided warmth on winter nights as the absence of our parents during holidays lured the men in the red trucks. Age and experience transformed my green eyes to blue. They linger on you, imploring consideration of all sacrifices. Though as I see it, you were the lucky one; the one she gave away.

Mary Withenack

He Just A Little Man

He's eighteen he thinks he's a man, he works real hard he does the best that he can he's just a little man. He shaves once a week he try's to keep his hair cut but then he looks in the mirror and and wished that he look tough he's just a little man.

When your eighteen it's really hard to know who your friends really are, some just want to ride in your car some want to know how much money you got so you can help pay for their beer and their pot then he ask himself is this all I got he's just a little man. He don't make enough to live on his own and he hates like hell living at home he's just a little man.

He's eighteen he thinks he's a man he works real hard he does the best that he can he just a little man, he shaves once a week he try's to keep his hair cut but then he looks in the mirror and wish he look tough he's just a little man.

His Mom and his dad they don't understand they treat him like a kid but they call him a man he don't understand. But one day he'll grow up he'll look in the mirror and know that he looks tough he'll be a man, he'll have a place to call his home and a little boy to call his own, and then one day he'll hear himself say he's just a little man.

Yvonne Schwartzbeck

Night Of Conception

I stood in the doorway
between warm you and
the glowing moonlight;
Somewhere I knew

I looked back at
those soft browns,
my direction toward the stark moon.
It was full, you know.
Over my shoulder there was this passion
and it kept me alive
accepting this moment
when I must leave unafraid
My lips about to
express love for all you
stayed stationary, the words choked in my throat
And I know you knew, too.

It happened that night.
It captured me
and for what it was,
'I love you' wasn't enough.

Maya Payne

Old Railroaders

Old railroad men, wore a striped cap
Bib overalls and underwear, with a flap
Rough and ready, and always on time
With a railroad watch, on the railroad line.

Those days we will always miss
The toot on the whistle, or watch them switch
They left home, any hour to go
Take care of the train, in rain or snow,

Three meals a day, they didn't pop pills
They used their wits, to have a thrill.
With no computer, they used their brain
To get from city to city, on their big train.

The locomotive had a cowcatcher in front
It cleared the tracks without any stunts
Passengers were happy though tired and worn
Riding the milk run home in the early morn.

Lloyd Rexford

Pure Love

Blue skies, full moons, white fluffy clouds, a summer sunset,
Birds singing early in the morning, Colored leaves in the fall,
These Things remind me of you all and all...
  Mountain streams, Wild flowers growing in the fields, A Rainbow
after a spring shower, A Winter snow storm when everything
is all white, crisp and pure, These Things are you for sure...
  A doe and her fawn, A robin in her nest waiting for hers to be
born, all the spring flowers in full bloom, in my heart, for
you, there is plenty of room...
  When I'm in your arms everything is beautiful, there is no
pain. You make everything all right...
  When I'm with you, it seems I have only to gain, you make
everything beautiful in sight!!

Robin J. Irvin

Clouds Black

Black clouds come; - Black clouds blow.
Black clouds are in the valley below.
Maka Unci's rains came;
that's really Mother Earth's name.
Black Clouds come....Black clouds go.
When they come and where they go,...nobody knows.
But, the green grass grows.

Corn to plant; ... corn to hoe.
Buffalo come; ... buffalo go.
Now buffalo graze in the valley below.
Now, hides to scrap, hides to sew.
for daily work there is no lack,
With little papoose upon her back.
All this is needed for a man and his wife;
this you see is the hoop of life.

Black clouds come, — black clouds go,...when they come
and where they go, nobody knows.
Now-Black clouds again in the valley below.
Yet....the green grass grows.

Roger Kies

Untitled

In a world infected with violence
blood runs through the cities
like pollution in a river
where we look over and embrace
in peace mimicking the rolling waves
that stretch beyond our sight
collecting the filth of all place
through crimes of hate and crimes of love
producing tears of sorrow from the pain
as broken hearts so often do.
Staring at the water and calm we are divided
between the passion we seek
and expression through writing
find ourselves gazing into the setting sun
in awe of the beauty of the quiet light
that leaves no reason for thought of
the approaching darkness which eventually covers it all.

Krista Port

The End Of Belief

Infinite inane repetition of a sickening child's song
Broken promises falling by the wayside
Like scales from my eyes
World I knew to be real, illusion before my clawing hands
Lies told in hopeful deception
Reality built of sand
Blowing now before me
Promises circling my feet as my dreams disappear into the maelstrom
Joining the motes which sting my eyes
Without tears to shed for the freezing of my heart

Lisa Combest

"Left Out" In Elementary School

Foot long smiles complimented with laughter.
Blooming ideas giving birth to dreams;
Winking back at those eyes in the corner,
For sure, we'll get married, at least it seems.
It's time to sing, but instead we snicker,
Fabulously joined, like enduring streams.

Razor edged mocking easily rapes you,
Dirty looks screaming at your nothingness;
Rumors produced by the popular crew.
Extended arm dying for tenderness.
Companionship assumed: words to live by.
Savagery is king to those who win
Great memories that will never untie.

Kristi Potts

Your Soul

If your soul was a color I think it'd be blue.
Blue like the ocean.
Rough when angry yet calmly beautiful at peace.
Or blue like the sky.
A vast never-ending world that's out of reach.
Maybe Cookie Monster blue.
A furry wild and hungry monster.
Or perhaps a bluebird.
Free to fly and sing beautiful songs that open every heart.
Dark blue like the pride in our American flag.
A symbol that waves freely in the breezes.
Or maybe just beautiful baby blue like your eyes
which are the windows to your soul.

Karen Williams

Starship

You're flying, flying, flying, sailing through the stars, past
bluish Earth, the Moon and scarlet Mars. Accelerating,
speeding up, stars streaming by, a silvery shower
of asteroids powdering the sky, past Jupiter and
Saturn, huge and bright, Uranus, with its icy
rings, an orb of emerald light. Pale
blue Neptune, flashing quickly by.
Now you've passed Pluto,
a pale blot in the sky.
The ship leaps ahead,
starlight streaking,
engines roaring,
a swift bird
in flight as
you jump
forward
faster
than
light!

Laura Durkay

Harvest Moon

Brilliant, luminous, large orange moon
Brightly shining in blackest silk nights
Clouds shroud eerie shadows around her waist
She nods her head slightly and suggests
A voice that is not formed upon her lips
Whispers so delicate that they cannot be heard
They can only be felt by the beat of the heart
Seducing, enticing she pulls you to her chest
And in her haunting embrace you regress
The ebb and tide of the September moon
The earthly beauty reminiscing harvest days

Sharon Madison

A Solution For Some An Answer To All

We are generations who have cried for years,
Both sides have shed the shameless tears.
We have silently prayed and we have yelled our plea.
Let us forgive and for once, be free.
The damage we're doing now will forever last.
Yet, we still blame our actions on the past.
Blacks killing whites, whites killing blacks,
How long will this senseless violence last?,
We cannot begin anew by blaming history,
It all starts here with just you and me.
It's bad enough to kill due to the color of skin,
Now we are dying due to the color of clothes we're in.
The solution for some has become tragic "drive-bys".
Caught in the cross fire an innocent child dies.
We need to pull our values from off the back shelves.
Instead of looking down the barrel of a gun,
We need take a lasting look inside our selves.

Sandra Komendo

Autumn Tragedy

Siblings at play one crispy fall evening. Our
breath-streams illumined by yardlight beaming
upon cool, rosy faces. Feet circling below
outstretching arms. We surrender to vertigo,
self-induced. As dominoes we fall to the leaf-trampled
ground. Then, dizziness done, we continue our play.
A furry farm kitten slips swiftly beneath my thistled
bare feet; unexpectedly twists in drunken-like
spinning. We hear a soft thud, and Fluffy is still.
I cradle her carefully to my pounding heart.
Tears pool onto warm, shiny fur as I stare into
Fluffy's green eyes, slowly dimming. While frozen in
incomprehension and grief, my kitten is torn from my arms.
My father 's face looms, contorted with rage, as he
assails me for causing the death of my cat.
Stinging, open-palmed punishment brings pain,
searing hot, and blisters my tender behind.
The anger I feel surpasses my grief.

I comprehend, now, his weakness and pain. Yet,
fifty years later, remnants of anger remain!

Oleta Oveson

"Perfecting Espresso"

I am the promise of a new day...
Bringing hopes and dreams to be filled of generations passed.
Unique in my identity-culturally and powerfully inspired in tradition,
I possess personality, potential, charisma, and class.

I am the other sister...
The one that you rarely hear about but often see.
I too, am a gutsy depiction of a soul in America...
A piece of the melting pot is in me!

I am what they call Espresso.
Not a deep mocha nor a honey glaze,
But just as rich in style today
As I was yesterday.

Our world is filled with those who often see, but do not observe,
Those who hear, but do not listen-or take heed,
Those who wish to know answers, but do not ask questions,
And those who seek, but are afraid to find...that's not me.

I wish to create a path out of a vague trail that
Takes me to a place that I've never been before.
Leading the way with a strong vision...
For the rest to follow-today and ever more.

Sunshearay N. Gonzalez

Sunday Fun In The Park

The warmth of the spring sunny day with a cloudless sky overhead
brought forth laughter of children rollicking to and fro,
barking dogs, playing tag, rolling hoops, throwing balls, bicycling
and other activities enjoyed by all.

A Drake and his mate with their quacking ducklings in tow
swam by on the rippling lake.
A scene bestowed to the crowd's delight
by their oha's, aha's and sigh's they did make.

There were sailboats of various sizes and shapes
made from paper, cardboard and wood by young hearts of all ages,
competing with the wind as they raced on the lake.

Colored balloons flying high above in the breeze,
as carefree children below ran gleefully free.

Soothing music flowed forth from the bandstand,
people gathered to sing and to dance,
while others just listened, bringing peace to the soul,
you could tell at a glance.

Sunday's anticipated, excitement in hearts, worries forgotten,
fun from the start, even acting like children once again,
for this one day a week in the park.

Marolyn E. Baker

Seashore

The children are fervently working to
build their sand castles, strollers
walking back and forth along the sandy
  seashore.

Its beauty really engulf me, as I gaze
from shore to sea, then sea to shore
  repeatedly.
No other scene could possibly match the
  beauty found here.
Nor the way it arouses your senses.

So I perch upon a log to gaze a little
more, as the waves roll in and wash into
  shore.
My nostrils are filled with the smell of
salt, my ears with the pounding waves.
A strange tingling mellow sensation passes
over me, as if everything is all right, and
not at odds as we know it to be.

Madaline Cornish-Coleman

My Cat

Eyes so fiery in the night
burning like a candle bright,
giving the night an eerie glow,
then to turn around and go outing
her light.

Her touch in all my splendor receive,
at day or night I want her to leave
me in quiet time..., but it seems
like her quiet time is mine.

A friend to me she'll always be
glaring, peering, inquisitive.
Yet like a child, not knowing
whether to take the chance or leave it be,
That friend my dears is my cat HEIDI.

Sherryann Woodroffe

244

The Corporate Dream

What is a dream
   but a strange configuration of little bits and pieces of life

From the time the world first began
   the same scenes are played over and over again in our minds

Innate fears, irreversible moments, uncontrollable situations,
   childhood insecurities

A mountain road that narrows
   the car slides our of control
    the bridge swings side to side
     the edge so near
Morning comes, the dreams change, the insecurities fade, control is hard
The same scenes play over and over.

Terri Miller

"When Times Get Hard"

We've made it through most of our sorrows,
But at this time
I've got to ask you
What about our tomorrows?
Will your heart be there for me
Like my heart is for you
Because if it isn't, I don't know what I will do.
I've tried so hard to keep you here
But lately my heart is living in fear.
And sometimes I wonder,
Will you be here?
When times get hard.
Just know that I'm there for you
Through good times and bad
I've been here all along
Through the ones we've had.

Renika McQueen

The Four Seasons

Summer was hot
But autumn has fallen apart
I'll be glad when winter is gone
And the colorful spring has begun.

Like the four seasons life keeps changing.
At first one is happy, and content, and
Nobody or anything can make it wrong, but
Suddenly everything is gone.
Or so it seems, you feel empty, and cheated
Like you can't go on.
It's a struggle but, one must be strong.
Learn to live, and live to learn.
Because there must be hope on the horizon.
And when you accept what nature has done.
Then you will know you're new life has just begun.

Maria L. Putt

Untitled

I would not bother you
but bothering you is so natural to me.
I would never take up your time
but I can't get enough of it.

You are all the things called possibilities
and you tantalize my sensibilities
and I am incomplete without you
and even with you.
So I swallow hard
and seem to know
I must go and look else where.
Oh, I am not there - else where!
But I stand a chance.
I love you. Goodbye.

Robert L. Lasnier

Friends And Lovers

Friends can be lovers is what the songs say,
But can lovers be friends or does it get in the way?
If given the choice, which would it be?
Friends or lovers, or you or me?
The light in your eyes shows me you care,
But if I needed you would you be there?
I loved you once, I love you twice,
I love you against my own advice,
We've both been hurt, this I know,
But the past is the past, we have to let go,
My love for you came strong and fast,
A love I know deep down will last,
Maybe someday you will feel that way too,
But until that time I'll have to hide it from you,
Without you in it my life would be nothing,
So I'll settle for friends—at least it's something.

Patricia A. DeMarco

As Long As The Song Bird Sang

She lasted as long as the song bird sang
but guns spewed bullets that flew faster than their fluttering wings
and the songs stopped short and so then did her life.

This is a story of a child that died
    too early
the alarm clock rang
and it was a very long night
and instead of pressing the snooze switch
    was now on off
and the respirator stopped her breathing
and she died for you wanting to sleep
    a little longer
she wanted her life to be.

Tick tock, tick, tock, and the father that she made believe would give
her life and held so much compassion only had enough to cross his line
and invade her child-mind as she sits
as an adult now still not understanding the
lives of the children,
because where is the child that stood naked in the shower just knowing
that she had heard the last of the song bird sing.

Tatiana Mudrak

When Will I Awake?

A smile used to live on my face
But has moved to a different place

My heart was warm but has now turned cold
And the feelings of sadness have begun to unfold

The skies around me have changed to gray
While the happiness within me has gone away

The only thing on my mind was you
And my hoping that love between us would come true

A bond was there that seemed so real
Yet a great deal of doubt was all I could feel

Every chance I got I'd look into your eyes
And somehow or another they'd take me by surprise

But I guess the feelings weren't what they seemed
Yes, they were only things that I dreamed

All I can do now is fight the heartache
And maybe one day from this deep loneliness awake...

Steve Jefferson

245

Sensing Eradication

The rays of dawn elicited of sweat from his brow,
But he could not see the morning sun.
The snare banged slowly with intimidating tension,
But he could not see by whom it was done.

A crow cawed as it flew over head,
But he could not see nary a feather.
The gentle breeze filled his nostrils with floral fragrance,
But he could not see any of the heather.

The cotton absorbed the wetness from his mouth,
But he could not see the design of the stifling fabric,
His back ached against the hardness of the adobe,
But he could not see the stalwart wall of brick.

The stone under foot caused his feet to sweat,
But the could not see the composition of flooring coal.
Latin oration weaved a path of deliverance to his ears,
But he could not see the one who spoke to save his soul.

He heard the words of readiness, and the subsequent cocking,
But he could not see the terminators' weapons smoke.
His senses strained for any indication of impending death,
But he could not see his demise because he suddenly awoke.

Raymond R. LeClair

Why Me?

Did it really happen? Was it just a dream? I tried to run away
but he ran faster. I tried to fight it, but he held me tighter.
I ask myself...why me?
Did I ask for it? Was it something that just happened? I tried to
get it out of my head, but every time I saw him, I'd get flashbacks.
I ask myself...why me?
Am I suppose to share my pain with someone? Do I just keep it all
bundled up inside? Will other people think I'm not any good? Does
God still love me for what happened? Was it God's fault? Was it in
God's plan for me, so I'd be a stronger person?
I ask myself...why me?
I'm running, but why do I keep running back into his abusive arms?
Is it my fault because I think that's the way love is supposed to be?
I'm hurting, trying to find a way out, but I keep running in circles.
Will I ever reach that point where I'm happy again?
I ask myself...why me?

Rebekah Ramirez

Winning Isn't Everything

I've practiced hard, I want to win,
But I know,
Winning isn't everything.

My parents are proud, I think I've done well,
But if I don't win, I'll know,
It isn't everything.

I have a new costume and contest shoes,
And I still know,
Winning isn't everything.

I've encouraged my friends; it's time to go on,
But I know,
Winning isn't everything.

I didn't win, but that's okay,
Because I know,
Winning isn't everything.

I'll work to improve; I'll still do my best,
Because,
Doing my best is everything!

Sarah Hanson

"Oh Boy!"

I wanted a girl, I was sure you were one,
but instead I wound up with a new baby son.
No pink frilly dresses or little pink shoes
I guess for now blue suits and blue booties will do,
You are kind of cute in a boyish way,
And I do love to hold you and rock all day.
You're warm and cuddly and you smell so sweet
I hug you so close I can feel your heartbeat.
My love for you grows more and more everyday,
Who wanted a baby girl anyway!

Wendy Sunderman

A Thing Called Dope!

It didn't have to happen
But it did.
They say I don't know, because I was a kid.
I took one puff
And I began my skid.

All my folks and all my friends
Can't believe the things I did.
I lied and stole,
I didn't know
I lost my soul.

In one more day I'll be twelve
But I'll never know,
Because I am in hell.

Listen to me
I am in jail
And have no hope
All because I tried
Thing called dope!

Thurman Wright

For My Sons (A Single Mother's Cry)

A child is born from two — I know
But left to grow with one alone

This task is hard and lonely too,
For there's no one else but me and you.

My little one — if not for you
what of me, that is so true

You have given me so much joy, courage and strength
As no one else has
I owe you my life as it is today.

I'll do my best to care for and love you
As a mother should

And one day I shall let you go,

Be Strong, be gentle, be good my sons
And know that your mother will never be far

Marisela Perera Prado

"Paul"

I feel like I'm viewing Auschwitz,
But that's my brother laying there
Head shaved, gaped mouth toothless,
Eyes opened in death's grim stare.

Naked, draped partly in a linen sheet,
The huge tumors are now in plain sight.
They called from the home to announce his death,
And that's why I'm here tonight.

Alone I walked into his room, oh my God!!
I thought he would look like asleep,
But I feel like I'm viewing Auschwitz
And in nightmares this image, I'll keep.

Sue Benigni

Aged Mother

Your eyes can still evince some spark of youth,
But mostly they appear too rheumy, tired
As if the happy past with tears expired
And you are left with only scraps of truth...

I see your fingers, gnarled and trembling there,
A numbing coldness in them always, now:
Once-supple limbs, each one become a brittle bough;
You pluck and touch and fondle things with care.

The words that I am speaking pass you by,
Not locked in silence, still you miss their sound.
Where love and death in such few words surround
The sadness of my loss foreseen; I cry:

Oh how can I express this frightful fear?
If suffering will make you slip down notch by notch,
I cannot bear to have you dying as I watch!
My own death whispers faintly in my ear.

Marlene Carey

The Dream

You remind me of a dream,
But no ordinary dream,
A dream no man would ever forget,
The dream of all dreams.

A dream about you,
A woman with enchanting beauty,
And eyes that I could become lost in for days,
The dream of all dreams.

The feeling I experienced,
While I stared deep into your eyes,
Is one I may never feel again as I lie and die,
The dream of all dreams.

Nervous and cautious,
I leaned forward for a kiss,
A rush of adrenaline and ecstatic pleasure consumed me,
The dream of all dreams.

How could I ever explain,
The meeting of an absolute angel,
I must have been at the top of Jacob's ladder,
The dream of all dreams.

Kevin D. St. Clergy

Untitled

To know me is to love me,
but not necessarily to love everything about me.
To love me is to criticize me,
but not in a cruel way or expecting results overnight.
To criticize me is to help me,
this means telling me when I'm wrong as well as when I'm right.
To help me is to encourage me,
give compliments periodically or just a mere kiss on the lips.
To encourage me is to enable me to grow,
help me to learn, teach me to learn, but be patient also.
With growth there comes mistakes,
mine will be made so let me make them.
But along with this growth comes a love,
so powerful and intense that it will overwhelm you in time!

Sheree Denise Collins

Making It Together

I do not ask that our life together be one of constant ease,
But only that it be a life where we try to please.

You've never asked for jewels so rare,
What ever you wanted I tried to see it was there.

I do not wish for fickle fame or fortunes garish touch.
All I ask is that we never have too little or too much.

Our marriage is perhaps an extraordinary find,
As a wife you are one of a kind.

Our marriage was not based on a house and lands,
Nor was it based on other material demands.

The years together have given us memories from day to day,
May we hold fast to them that none may slip away.

J. Howard Campbell

Grandma's Last Request

I wished I could have had, a chance to say good-bye.
But the Lord knew ahead of time, that it would only make you cry.

Please try to wash away from your eyes, those tears you shed for me,
For I am now in the Promised Land, where I really want to be.

He knew my body was tired and weak, and that I had tried to do my best.
That is why the Lord that night, put my soul to rest.

I have no pain or heartaches, and I will never have no more.
For I have reached my destination upon the Golden Shore.

May each day find your spirit, to be stronger in Faith my child.
For God has promised Grandma to see you again in a little while.

Patricia Davis

Discovering A Friend

Friends come and go
But the truly friends stay in touch
It may be because deep inside themselves
They have discovered someone who can teach them much
And it is from these friends of ours
That we watch, listen, and learn
Studying the greater aspects of their ways
And letting their judgments cause our opinions to turn
Our ideas change, and become more focused
Because we see more clearly through a friends eyes
It sheds a new perspective on the event
And the breadth of our viewpoint has become more wise
The friends that will have this effect will be so ever hard to find
For now our sights are narrow
But with each true friends discovery
Comes an opening of the mind

Michael Harmon

Alone or By Myself?

The human soul
Can be seen in the imagination-
I see
Light
Patterns of pastels
Like press-board
In the shape of the body.
And we float around this empty void of a universe
Alone, by ourselves
But I have found you
And if you hold me close enough, tight enough,
Maybe we'll fuse
And become one
So even if I'm by myself,
I won't be alone.

Lisa Borowski

Constant Companion

They say time heals all wounds.
But there's no guarantee a scar won't be left behind.
They say you can get rid of skeletons in the closet.
But there's no guarantee a bone or two won't remain.

Live for tomorrow, not days gone by.
Forget the past, live for the present.
These things are easier said than done.

Footprints wash away with rain and time.
Even photographs fade as the years pass by.
Our past we carry with us always.

It is indeed a very powerful thing.
It cannot be erased, nor can it be altered.
There is no turning back.

Our past serves as a constant reminder of where we've been.
Often it reminds us of things we wish could be forgotten.
The reality is we can't change it no matter how hard we try.

It becomes an enemy we battle over time.
Therefore we must look at our past and learn to accept it.
It is a constant companion that will not go away.
Whether it becomes our friend or our enemy is in our hands.

Sherry Severson

My Castle In The Clouds

There are many castles in this world today,
But they all have been man-made.
But there is one that man hasn't seen,
And it's the one that my Jesus has built for me.
In this castle there's a royal banquet hall,
And it is set with a wedding feast for us all,
And at the end sits my King on the throne
Waiting patiently for me to come home.
To my castle in the clouds
That's waiting for me,
And it is nestled in my God's glory
And it is made of pure gold,
My castle in the clouds is my eternal home.

Vickie R. King

Untitled

I watch the children running by,
But they don't notice my gazing, gawking eye,
I long to get up and join their crowd,
Hoping to make my parents proud.
Why is it so hard to enter that group?
Why must I stay here and feel so cooped?
Feeling alone is how it must be.
I'm a loner, a shy girl, a girl no one sees.
I'm the girl you never talk to,
The one in the corner with an eye of tearful blue.
I'm the girl whose smile you never returned,
The girl with half of her body burned.
Don't pity me when you stare.
I pity your biased glare!

Lisa Hartkemeyer

Warm Memories

Warm memories torn by shadows
Call upon you like a whisper in the night
Taking you back to yesteryear of staying forever young.
A teardrop softly falls upon your cheek as you look
into your lovers eye's.
Whispering's of warm memories cloud his mind as he
gently takes your hand.
Drifting in this pool of memories he softly whisper's
"Will you marry me?"
Looking into his misty blue eye's, warm memories call
upon us in the shadows of our minds to say "stay forever young."

Nellie E. Shields

Your Love

There was a time I said good-bye,
But when I see you and I realize I still love you,
I begin to cry.

I can't believe I gave you away.
Now I want your love back,
That feeling grows stronger everyday.

Your heart was so big and your love was so good.
I wish that somehow I could get everything we had back,
You don't know how much I wish I could.

Now, I realize when I said good-bye, you did to.
So I want you to know that I am really sorry,
And I am still in love with you.

Kimberly Joy Baumruck

How To Describe Me

My Skin is white
But you will often see me in black.
Some people tell me it's all out of whack.
People asked me if I'm depressed
Or if someone died.
If you ask these questions
They'll all be denied.

If you see me on a good day
You will see me in Blue.
These colors represent
All that I've been through
I've been through some bad times
And I've been through some good.
These colors may not represent
The things that you think they should.
But these colors
That best describe me
Black and Blue
This is the way that I feel.

Kari Wheeler

Daddy You're Gone, But You're Not Far Away

Daddy you're gone
but you're not far away,
your body might be dead
but your spirit is with me today.
The things that we shared soon passed away,
but the memories we hold get stronger each passing day!
One day I will die and see you again,
only to realize you were not just a father,
but a beautiful friend.
Take care where you're at, because I know you're safe and well,
it's just sometimes here alone and without you that's hell.
But soon I must realize, and often I do
my life is just a passing moment and then I will be with you.
Daddy take care, I will see you soon.

Rodney J. Niehaus

"To You, My Love"

I thank you for giving me your life—
by giving me your whole self as my wife.
We may shout and fight as we go through life,
but no one could take your place as my wife.

We are not as young as we used to be—
but God has given us a lot more to see.
May our lives together in the next years to come,
be full of joy and love that comes to some.

Then in the end, whoever goes first—
may the one that is left, keep happy and for love, not thrusts.
And then in heaven with our Lord we will be
to love and be happy for all eternity.

Lester J. Ames

You're The Reason

Brittany, my love for you can't be measured
By a gift, or a bouquet of flowers;
Nor, should I be able to express it with words,
Does the day contain enough hours.

From our very first evening together,
There was something exciting and new;
For suddenly my life had new meaning,
Then I realized that something was you.

You've given me joy beyond measure,
For exceeding my fondest dream;
And you've made our home a castle,
So baby, that makes you a queen.

You're the reason my life is worth living for,
You seem to always put my needs first;
You must be my own special angel,
You've made the past ten years heaven on earth.

Luke Joubert

A Wife Of Noble Character

A wife of noble character is much desired
By a husband seeking to place on his head,
A crown which says nobility required
Each and every one my wife has met.

For she is a crown to me and all must see
That the Lord is good beyond all measure.
In choosing a wife that would be good for me,
A crown, and all its noble pleasure.

I walk, my head up high as a crown should be,
As I display all its gems and precious stones.
Its brilliance and glory for all to see,
My wife as nourishment to my bones.

For the Lord blessed me with my wife,
And anointed her with nobility for me.
Separated especially to enhance my life,
As my children, friends, and all will see.

Robert Perez

Susan

Susan sits in her rocking chair,
Calico dress and long brown hair,
She stares at her field, the chores still undone.
She sighs and she rocks. She waits for her son.

Susan looks at his baby book,
Passages to the past, came take a look,
He's gone now, but he'll be back.
And she rocks from forth to back.

Susan sits in her rocking chair,
Ragged dress and long grey hair,
She stares at the field, closes her eyes,
Thinks of her son, wails and cries.

Susan looks up, and whom should see?
"My son! My son has come back to me!"
In tottered clothes and sweat on his face,
He runs to sit next to her place.

He holds her in a warm embrace,
But no expressions takes her face,
Her arms are limp, she seems sedate,
And he knows he is too late.

Noelle Knutsen

A silent cry that echoes all night long
Can only harken those who have sung and know
It is the lost children's story and song

Who are these children, why don't they belong
What causes them to make this cry in woe
This silent cry that echoes all night long

So why can no one hear, has sympathy gone
If only they know what they say so low
What is the lost children's story and song

Does one, to understand, need to be young
Or just be able to hear a sad wind blow
A silent cry that echoes all night long

Can you not hear if you are much too strong
Or just if you have too much weight to tow
To this the lost children's story and song

Do these lost children seem to be lost in a throng
Is this the reason why they cry to a foe
A silent cry that echoes all night long
Who hears the lost children's story and song

Rebecca J. Bernemann

God's Flower Garden

Close your eyes for just a moment.
Can you see heaven when you do?
Can you see God in His garden of flowers?
Making each one as beautiful as you.
He starts with just the tiniest seed.
And plants it with loving care.
Before he can even realize it,
The seed is a blossom, with beauty so rare.
We, too, compare to God's flowers,
Each Mother is blessed from above.
God sends forth the tiniest seed, and then;
We, too, have a blossom to love.

Yvonne Unroe

"Near Time To Catch The Train"

Can't you hear her coming down the line
Can't you hear her coming with her mournful whine
The soul train is calling for those whose time has come
Just pray she passes by on this nightly run

She's calling to some with her lonesome cry
"your time is coming...it's time to say goodbye"
Not all can hear on the nightly run
But all will board her when your time has come

One day - she will stop with her sorrowful cry
For the souls she's called to make the trip
When I hear her call for the very last time, I know
she will be loaded with those long lost friends of mine.

Can't you hear her calling..
Can't you hear her cry...
For those long lost friends of mine.

Paul W. Newman

Carry Me Home

The wind dust blows beneath my wings.
Carry me, carry me home.
I've traveled far and oh so hard.
Carry me, carry me home.
Through flakes of snow and drops of rain,
Through desert sand and all terrain,
Through dark of night and bright of day.
Carry me, carry me home.
My mission, is not to fail.
To see you is my goal.
For you are the light that guides my wings.
Carry me, carry me home.

Monique E. Alexander

"One Earth"

Taking care of earth because it takes
care of us.
Ending the pollution and finding a
better solution.
With everything it has and all it has
to offer, we must keep in mind, there
is only one earth and so many that
suffer.
Great mountains, high seas, deserts and
all make earth what it's meant to be.
Blue skies, green land and forests
that never seem to end.
This is a gift God has given. A gift that's
home for all of us to live in.

Sonya Contractor

Enough

O when will madness cease its sway,
Careering ravenously, drunkenly
Through the streets,
A silent and shadowy spectre with frozen risus
Leering lewdly from stonecold features
Absent all reason,
All compassion,
All humanity,
All thought?
We sacrifice our brightest,
Our most promising,
At the altar of arsenals,
And when any unreasoned subhuman
Can wield ignorance in the shape of a .38
We face danger far greater than did
Earlier citizens, centuries ago, fortunate enough to exist
Before the Age of the Quick Kill: now it's as easy to
End a life as it is to snap off a light switch.
Daily the compact and deadly force of the .22s, .38s, and .45s
Blows bloody holes through the peaceful innocence of our lives.

Timothy H. Hite

Thoughts By The Sea

Sitting here on the beach, feeling the gentle caress of the sun and wind,
We know when we are heartbroken or burdened, God's love will mend.
To hear the roar of the sea, so deep and wide
Gives us a greater feeling of God inside.
Watching the waves pound and break against the shore
Makes us ever aware of His love forevermore.

Seeing the seagulls gracefully flying by,
Reminds us of how much He cares for you and I.
So we ask how much does God really care and Love
How deep is the ocean, how high the sky above?
And as our boat rocks on life's stormy sea,
May we remember God is always there to calm you and me.
He will ride with us through all the storms,
For her is our life Preserver as we lean on His everlasting arms.

Lou Hill

My Future

Ghosts of my past piercing your present
clouding your future
The healing has begun
not too late
To see the beauty of the friend that is she
not too late
To reacquaint me with myself
not too late
To take my brain off the shelf
take a look and see the friend that is she

Ross R. Gallegos

Silhouette

In early mornings pink and golden hues
Caress with their rays, her hair and warm thy
Face and touch thy heart and with shades of blues,
Thine eyes twinkle at my face and flutter my
Heart and love's wrath surrounds me in a trance
That snares my soul into eternity
And with a sweep of demure eyes and glance
Turns and walks into the fathomless sea.
Thunder sounding and lightning striking earth
I turn away; at the call of my name
I scan the horizon and see rebirth
A vision before me appears the same
Only the time of years past have changed and
Thine silhouette has become of thine land.

Melissa Gruber

Carolina Hills

There's no time like April in these
    Carolina Hills,
When nature wakes her flowers,
    and beauty in them instills.
When the golden eagle on Grandfather
    spreads her wings and flies
Up, up over the treetops and on into the skies.

Where over Table Rock the stately birds do fly,
And sing their tuneful songs soaring
    high in the sky,
And looking down into the valley where
    the graceful deer do graze,
Among the grassy meadows and the early morning haze.

In these Carolina mountains where
    the air is pure and clean
Where flowers grow in profusion,
    And the grass is always green.
There let me live in happiness
    until the day I die,
And then among their beauty, forever let me lie.

Mada Franklin Carswell

Catpaws

Leaves dropping from trees,
catpaws chasing them on the ground below,
chasing, catching falling leaves.
Autumn zephyrs yellow, gold and red,
scampering with the falling leaves.

Leaves dropping from trees,
catpaws playing scatter 'neath the boughs,
scattering the tears of weeping trees.
There's music in the falling leaves,
autumn wind blends in to harmonize.

Leaves dropping from trees,
music on the wind until each branch is bare,
catpaws clutching, scuffing, scattering;
leaves falling, branches cold and bare
and catpaws creep away to other toys.

Mahlon H. LaVasseur

Life Is A Challenge, Be Prepared To Fight

Everyday I thank God for taking care of me.
'Cause ain't no telling what tomorrow will bring.
That's why I trust God with all my needs.
The world don't care or owe me anything.
Everyday some broken heart wipes away a tear.
A child has been slain in their prime of life.
Many are controlled by wants and fear.
Many are slaves to drugs, corruption, grief and strife.
Many are slaves to a system that don't treat them right.
Life is a challenge, be prepared to fight.
Education is one of life's greatest tools.
Potential for mind development is unlimited.
If wisdom and understanding is allowed to rule,
Fear of limitation is ended.
When a stand is taken against negative intrusion,
A mind is free to seek solution when creativity abounds.
Success is the result of ideals, not illusions.
Through realization of what builds or brings down,
Learn to recognize wrong from right.
Life is a challenge, be prepared to fight.

William M. Callands Jr.

"Restless Night"

I get deep without sleep
Cause the way my mind is weird
My thoughts rise above me, like smoke from a fire
My pen strokes this page, because I'm just so tired.

Over my head, the moon a burning ember,
Crosses the sky, it's chasing September.
Those who come by with tales of woe,
On a journey through life it seems to slow,
But in my heart a visitor unseen I harbor,
Now he's hear in my head holding a egg by farber,
Follow a pathway were I haven't been.
On a watery moon beam that I haven't seen,

Sounds and darkness that others fear,
I sit in quiet splendor, feeling quite queer,
Rise my soul, above my being.
Without eyes, look what I'm seeing.

Steady hand, my mind is bending
peace and caring, you I'm sending
Dream will come and fill my sleep.
So please be quiet, not a peep!

Walter Bauer

Help Me!

Help me oh God to survive this pain
Certainly, surely, I've gone insane,
So many feelings of hurt and disgust
Brought on by a daughter I thought I could trust!

What happened to my years of glory?
For sixteen years I've told her story,
The most wonderful daughter a mother could have
A happiness that's turned so sad.

I loved this child with all my heart.
Is this love falling apart?
Can I forgive and put aside
All this pain I cannot hide?

Sweet memories, they flood my mind
Taking me back to another time,
Of inner peace and a heart content
All these feelings have gone and went.

I'm waiting for God to intervene
He has to help me change this scene
For this hell I can endure no longer
Please help me God to get much stronger.

Sonya Poston

Time

Our lives are made of circles,
Circles without end,

Sometimes we merge as lovers,
Sometimes we meet as friends.

We've known each other before,
You know, in this grand old cosmic dance,

Two souls joyfully dancing intertwined,
Two souls sadly dancing apart.

And each time, after,
Only the energy remains,

The energy of love and emotion,
Healing and washing away the pain.

Its strength pulling us together,
Its power sometimes pushing us apart.

Every time we have a chance renewed,
To choose each other once more,

To soar again
On eagle's wings,

To be again,
As One.

William H. Murphy

Halleu Yah!

I've watched the moon ride high in the sky, watched the dark clouds saying 'Goodbye' to a year that's soon to end. Feeling the chill in the Autumnal night - a night that seems steeped with fright through eerie shapes that lay hard by - Black trees, dark rocks and dried leaves that fly - like bats that swirl in the muted glow.
In the dark, we are not seen so there is no one to know - of the spirits lost in the 'I don't know' of life and its darker side. But, even though we do not know, we know life still abides, for there's no despair in the darkened air while the Moon reflects from Heaven's Chair the Almighty Light that resideth there!

Patricia A. Henderson

Christmas Memories

From the Christmas of our past
Come the memories that will last

Whether we were rich or poor
Our memories of Christmas endure

When once we were young, and then when we are old
Our memories will be of Christmas, and the stories we told

So come join and celebrate, be a child once more
For our memories of Christmas, are forever more

So let the angels sound their horns
To tell the world, that a child is born
That this child was born, on Christmas morn

For Christmas comes but once a year, and may friendships never cease
For while we're on this planet Earth, let's wish each other peace

So may peace be with you, throughout all time
For the child was born, for all mankind

R. David Fordham

City Of Angels

Are there magic powers in these early morning hours
Confused by the "box of entertainment"
Time passing, the news of days gone wrong
Watching slapstick animals sing their jovial songs

1995 we just couldn't keep justice alive
The victims had no chance
One the victim of love, one the victim of circumstance

No chance to survive.
A racial separation they carelessly revived

How did I end up here;
In this city of Fear.
Drugs the Devils persuader
The great mental invader
Gangs, Ghettos, AIDS, the homeless and their plight
Cast aside by a system you just can't fight

Compton, L.A., the streets where you lay
I'm sorry when you're cold at night.

The cartoon Characters keep on singing
A small relief they are somehow bringing.
The room fades to black, there is no turning back.

Laura S. Brady

Metamorphosis

Ebb and flow of unstable emotion,
Confused, overwhelmed, frustration.
Soothe the spirit, enhance the mind,
Yesterday lingers behind.
Fiery horizon discloses your path.
Smiles return, begin to laugh.
Community embraces unconditional love.
Turbulent waters subside, flying white dove.
Cries of anguish fulfilled with hope.
Set free strangling rope.
Ever present glowing Light.
Opulent robes, omniscient white.
Sensitive, calming azure eyes,
Rip away the senseless lies.
Born again to serve humbling life,
Erase insurmountable moments of strife.
Come my friend, join me now,
Stumbling knees, awkward bow.
Connect with future, universe one.
The battle, you have won.

Linda Harple Bowman

Will There Be A Tomorrow

As I walk through this desolate land I wonder
Could it have once been the lush green forests my ancestors spoke of
Naked trees withering under the blazing sun cry out for help
Animals gasp their last breath
And darkness fills the sky
Wait
There is a single ray of light far in the distance
I run increasing my speed with each step
Finally
I am there
Tall bushy trees provide shade while animals scamper around happily
A clear blue lake is the core of my surroundings
As I breathe in the fresh air
I notice a young boy and girl planting a sapling
Perhaps there is hope after all

Kristin Krumm

It Happens, I'm Sure

Wandering through the forest I came upon a sight
confusing my feelings with curiosity and fright.

Ahead a little ways was a giant teddy bear
looking pretty, but still giving me a scare.

I approached it carefully, watching close,
being brave I think, but I'm not one to boast.

Then noticing movement in those big eyes it had
seemed to watch me, but wasn't acting bad;

Suddenly it moved — holding out its paw;
my first thought was, "watch out for a claw."

But my feet wouldn't move, they seemed to be froze;
the closer it came, the more tensions rose.

Only inches away, its expression was the same,
I still didn't know if this bear was tame.

In a soft tone, I complimented its style
and its beautiful coat; cringing all the while.

Its paw then touched my shoulder, with a gentle nudge;
now I was worried — too scared to budge.

Then I heard its voice, erasing every fear,
"IT'S TIME TO GET UP," mom said so clear.

Richard Berry

Triangles Of Life

The mind is the center of all,
Controlling your feelings, thoughts, and actions.
Dreams make their own figures,
Contrasting the conscious with the unconscious mind.
Differences between the colors, black and white;
Show us how different reality is to dreams.
Yet, there are times when there is no variation;
the grey shadows of life.
No one can say what actually makes up the shadows.
They seem to be just another triangle;
In the Triangles of Life.

Maria Kotsialiotis

The Dream Maker

(For Joseph Cornell)
He gathers dreams in tiny boxes
corners filled with flotsam
Castaways of his heart.

Alchemists blending, a leitmotif of fluted shells;
pitted thimbles and tattered, tinted prints.
Boxes, plastered with familiar jetsam
porcelain dolls in whopping surprise
nailed to walls
with other derelict treasures.

Boxes, set in touching order
hits of whiplash, snapping stiff-necked minds
I follow his eloquence
It traps me
shocks,
like his limbless dolls, paper heavens, wooden parrots
stages without curtain-calls
or moody actors
Boxes, talking back
with real crystal balls.

Phyllis Grover

252

Killer

Is it in the poisoned air or the polluted waters?
Could it be in spoiled food or simply in our genes?
Where ever it may be it's killing our sons and our daughters.
Either it's in our lungs, our breasts or our colons, heck even
   in our blood cells.
No matter where it hits it always hurts our hearts the most.
It's everywhere these days, where was it years and years ago?
It was here recently, thriving on its friendly host.
It's unstoppable, unfair, he was so innocent, so strong.
It must be stopped, it will be stopped.
We're helpless at this point and can just ask, "when and how long?"

Kim Casto

Homeland

Who but God but God alone
Could provide that special throne
Cradled in our Mothers womb, no sins to atone
A haven, a Homeland of our own

We are released the cord is broken
Received by gentle hands, a loving token
Born into that cozy family place
So full, so very full of God's special grace.

My Homeland, a country steeped in memories so great
The heather, the bracken, the moors, the open gate
The sight of wild primroses, bluebells, daffodils still dampen the eyes
A loving family sharing those special joys
A Homeland can last for some, for all life's span
For others there will be so many moves to meet Gods special plan.
Whichever the case, memories will be so paramount
Fellowship, love, patience, sadness, but only receiving Christ will count
Our final home, beyond the very needs of life
A Homeland where there will be no strife
God for us in Jesus Christ alone
God with us, the Holy Spirit, all our Sins to atone.

Lawrence Hutchinson

Amulet Of Gold

Is it fire reflected in your eyes or lightning
Creating those flashing flecks of Gold, exciting?
Is it warmth from your body or goodness in your Soul?
Have I struck a vein of oil or an overflowing pot of Gold?

Is the glow from the strength of your being?
Or has warmth melted the Gold within your heart?
Is it an outpouring of your virtue and honesty,
Spilling forth to brighten my days on Mother Earth?

It's akin to starlight sparkling o'er lonely fields at night,
Seaside waves, crashing, filling me with sensual delight,
Riverlets of life's most valued treasures abounding,
Solid as mountains and cliffs without measure, astounding.

Peering into your eyes, shimmering gold and green,
Borne silently, radiating, although unseen,
I confront the amulet of sincerity you draw upon,
Receiving your gift of love and day's new dawn.

Lynn C. Davis

Royal Smile For D-Day

While viewing Normandy's tearful scenes,
D-Day's old heroes, tales of valor,
Countless crosses gleamed.
A frame paused upon Euro's eminence and sheen,
Presidents, prime ministers, princes and queens.

On chance I caught a fleeting smile
Amid hosts of placid reflecting faces.
A smile of knowing rapture.
An instant only shutters capture,
In crowded places.

A gracious beam induced by genteel clasp,
A kiss of hand, by Czech Republic's President,
A tall gallant uniformed man.
The lovely recipient beautiful to be seen?
'Twas Sovereign Beatrix The Netherlands' Queen.

A. R. Jack Banks

Daughter

As many mistakes as a Daughter makes,
Dad always made sure I made my own,
He let me decide either right or wrong,
He just stood by my side,
To catch me either left or right,
Where I fell, he was there,
To pick me up and set me on my way, to take life day by day.

Daughter, Dad would say,
Either cry or laugh, walk or run,
Dad is here by your side,
In your heart always I'll stay,
Loving thought and memories too, dad will never go away.

Dad is looking down from up above,
Still standing by your side,
To hold you up when you cry,
To find that strength you have from way down inside,
Dad will never go away.

Just look way up above, see the brightest star,
It's me daughter, watching from above,
Dad will never go away.

Peggy McAlpine

"Of Faith's Rules"

At the archdiocese a tree came forth
damned to die standing
to put up with an ancestral calamity
cockades and slashed barks
the shower of holy water onto chandelier's foliage
left it with anxiety on edge
a shelter from its darkness grows
to imbibe the mutant entrance's facade
bit by bit, branches crowd over the piazza
foreigners are frequent on Good Friday
by the time every hostess hangs up his dresses
while a perpetual tree
is trampling on God's land devoted to man
it's about a quiet and tranquil expectancy
the autumnal spoliation
which converts the paving stones
in a ravage court yard.

Tony Ravelo

A Dark, Dark Day

It was a dark
  Dark
    Day.
  It was a cloudy and cold and gloomy day.
    The trees didn't sway
    The birds didn't sing
      I felt something wasn't right.

All of a sudden I heard something,
the two words that would change my life for ever
  and
    ever
      and
        ever.
        DAD
          DIED.
  I felt all hope was lost; the only thing I could think of
was two simple words,
  DAD
    DIED.

  T. J. Graf

Untitled

A return to nothingness,
dark, bleak, and foreboding
will the light ever penetrate it?
or will the darkness envelop time
Distant clap of thunder heard
rolling is wistfully, like an enchantress
warning of eminent storms
approaching nearer as time passes.
Electricity filling the air
tingling sensations spur my every nerve
excitement occupying my mind
converging with my listless soul.
The future marched like a timely drummer
bringing music to my ears
is the music magic or meaning?
will it halt the darkness around me?

  Paula M. Borkowski

Cat's Ears Doth See

It's beginning again,
Daylight's in
Sarasota. Beside during which animals sing
Monti from couch did wing
Swiftly from veranda door
For
Pleasant songs of birds,
This day's starting was heard
Through the ears of Giuseppi Monti.

That's happy state
In Florida state.

Cat's ears doth see
The Supreme Being's birds.

  Rosa Leonora Galfano

The Harvest

After the harvest comes death.
Death of a farmer's heart, soul, and land.
His offerings come from his calloused hands,
Raised above to thank Him.

After the shadows appear past
  the hill of plowed earth,
The sun proceeds to fade.
Man sheds upon the earth a tear,
  A tear of blood, a stain of blood.
Growing is over and sorrow has come.

The background holds a dark and menacing future
  like the clouds before a storm.
Before him there holds an army of life
  foreboding to him.
The seeds once planted are no longer thought about.
The golden fields of wheat are lost as man cowers
  to his fields.

As hands raise above once again to thank Him,
The realization of the end is near.
The end of his life and the end of his life in his harvest.

  Susan L. W. Sommer

From Clattered Reality Sparks A Flare

Existence.
Deceived by confusion and incapability
disorientation
discomfort from chains of conformity and insufficiency
disorientation
mirror of society, rain

Hope.
Drawn by the gift of inspiration
Ignites an intimate reality
capabilities
Consciousness connected with discipline
capabilities
sparks a flare
sunlight
life.

  Michael A. Jost

The Trail

I pause, my eyes glimpse an inviting trail there,
Deep into the forest, shaded from sun's glare,
A tempting pathway, to its mysteries I'm drawn.
Will it fill my dreams as some places I've gone?

Past crystal clear lakes, a spectacular sight,
Surrounded by great peaks with their patches of white,
Like ancient sentinels guarding all about,
Blue waters disturbed only by breeze or trout.

Where one can watch tranquilly the dawning day,
From first bits of light, which are but shades of gray,
To constantly changing pinks and coral hue,
Then salmon, yellows, and finally pale blue.

To the highest peaks, past where stunted trees live,
Where deep winter's ice causes great rocks to give,
High up where one may spy the great eagle soar,
But a speck, circling above the valley floor.

Where quiet softly settles as daylight wanes,
Warmed by a campfire, mortal cares one disdains.
Smoke hangs in treetops, coals surrender last glow,
And stars in heaven become inspiring show.

  Lee W. Peterson

"Wild Friends"

Shades in summer. Cool reflection
Defection from heat. Pleasant reception.
Chill in autumn. Seeking cold subjection
Ice in winter. Scurrying squirrels.
Birth of spring. All joyfully sing.
Time for the bear; sleepily uncurls
To face our seasons for all the right reasons.
To reject man I choose to turn
To assemble with those who churn
In the wild to discover my friends.
The wild ones whom I will defend.
Hope will I inspire to those therein.
Thoughts I will never forget
To those many creatures that I've met.

Tommy Rhodes

At First

A look, a glance, the brush of a hand
Discriminate, indecision
Comfort and peace, conversation
Stretching the spirit
Expanding the soul

A smile, a laugh, the tickling match
Familiarity, closeness, contact
Horizons of friendship, exercising the mind
New dimensions of consciousness
Defining the soul

A touch, a caress, the first kiss
Decision, indiscriminate
Conquering comfort zones of initial peace
Deepening and broadening the souls
Searching for something more

Clasped hands, new demands
A glance, a gaze, the step
Decision
Beginning

Sarah Marie Erickson

Waif

Lost child on a street in Reciefe,
Distant image, go out of my dreams.
I do not want to walk amid the refuse,
Stench and boiling flies again.

Who will know you?
Who will know the little urchins
Of the Rua Marquis Olinda?
Will it be a kind heart, a good Samaritan,
Or say it be only God?

And what of this God,
Champion of the masses,
Leader of the spectral paraders
That follow the invisible chain that links
Them to Rome and beyond.
A faith moment, an augenblick in time.

Gentle waif, disperse now
To an eternity of hunger and desolation
Cleansed by the God darkness.

Weep not for Adonis!

J. E. Zedalis

Leave Something Good Behind

Do nice things for the ones you love,
Do something kind;
Should you leave this world tomorrow,
Leave something good behind.

Give your heart to a special friend,
Ask for nothing in return;
Because their love is a special gift,
Something you must earn.

For the special people in your life,
Share in their good times and in the bad;
Always close by when they need you,
Be the best friend, they ever had,

Share what's in your heart,
Show them that you care;
It will see them through,
All those times you won't be there.

You gave to me, your love and friendship,
In return, I gave you mine;
Should I leave this world tomorrow,
I will leave something good behind.

Kim Parker

Homeless

You, who have no home and no soft place to lay your head,
Do you have memories to keep you warm on cold dark nights?
Do you dream of other days when you sheltered in a home
With family and friends to share your fire?
Did you think then of others who lived out on the streets
Bereft of all they once held dear?
Did you ever think that someday you would end up there?
Now you wonder, "How did I come to this?
Will the world be poorer at my passing? Who will care?"

Now tormenting cold seeps through your ragged clothes
As nightfall brings its penetrating chill.
In the long night hunger adds its pangs to unforgiving stone
And again you wonder, "How did I come to this?"
Sometimes a shelter offers food, a bed and a friendly word,
But others are uncaring and do not see your pain.
As time goes by you die another death each day
And wonder through the depths of your despair,
"Will the world be poorer at my passing? Who will care?"

Nellie L. Truxal

Innocence

Innocent child of youth
Do you really know the truth
Of what is happening today
Of what the young are trying to say

Does it really matter anymore
What lies beyond life's last door
To open it may not be a sin
But who is really trying to get in

The old may be wanting to leave
And the young are wanting to believe
So are you then a product of the old
Or a mistake of the young so bold.

For who can say of what will be
Perhaps the blind who really do see
Who will take us from this pain and sorrow
And who will promise us a better tomorrow

Perhaps the day will come when you will see
And you can tell us all of what will be
But then one day you too will lose your youth
And need to ask of those who really know the truth

Michael Rains

Does She Love Me?

I love my Gabrielle with all my heart,
  Does she the same I truly ponder.
Through the deadly deserts I would struggle,
  But does she love me, I truly ponder.
I would sail the seas dark and dreary,
  But does she love me still I ponder.
Over the mountains capped with snow,
  But does she love me I still don't know.

I bought my Gabrielle a rose one day,
  But does she love me, I yet don't know.
I wrote her a poem of my passion,
  But does she love me, I yet don't know.
I bought her a ring of gold one day,
  But does she love me, I yet don't know.
I expressed my benevolence to my Gabrielle,
  And does she love me? I'll never know.

   Rusty West

A Fond Illusion

When a friendship is lost, does it ever return
Does trust and faith once it's gone, ever come back
Does the bitter disappointment ever go away
Do you follow your heart, or do you hold back
Fearing the pain will return.
Do you doubt and wonder or do you simply say,
I turned this over to God knowing that if it is his will,
We would be together again.
So, if it starts to happen, how do you react
Can you put aside the fear, the doubt, the mistrust
How strong is your faith, is it deep enough
Can you accept what is happening
Or must you stop it with your doubts.
Must you hold to the struggle within yourself
Or can you allow this to unfold as it will
Let it play to its end, whatever it might be
If it doesn't work, what will be lost
For the friend has been gone for such a long, long time
Let things unfold - Don't stand in the way
Be open, be honest, hold onto the faith.

   Sharon K. Stackpole

Sweet Child

Sweet child of mine
Don't give me that line
I knew when I saw the sign
You were lagging far behind

If only you could know
How life can make us low
And things are harder as we grow
And life is not one big show

Through the day you run your pace
Not knowing the many things you face
In days to come you must find your place
Among the humane race

Of trouble I hope you steer clear
It often slips up from the rear
To me you are so very dear
I wish you could always stay near

Of all the advice I could relay
I would tell you to pray each day
Try always to do what you say
And never ever forget how to play

   Theresa Floyd

Untitled

Whistling through the breath of life
Dramatizing the world with precision
Nurturing the seeds of our time
Glorifying the growth of succession

Like the wind that blows through the fire
He's maximizing each flame to its vastness
Like the snow that melts under pressure
He's magnifying each drop to its fullness

Expressing the mind without heart
Terrifying the all with induction
Exciting the young without hope
Influencing the old with addiction

Like the hive that enriches the bee
He's implementing each sting with exactness
Like the rose that develops the prick
He's executing each wound with preciseness

Death
You take the life that lives among us
Giving the dead a life below us

   Timmy D. Saeed

Sticky Valentine

I once received a valentine, its heart
  drawn all askew,
Fashioned by two sticky hands with
  paper, crayon and glue.
Bereft of frills and lace, 'twas true,
Yet no treasure found on earth
Could buy my sticky valentine;
There's no measure for love's worth.
Yes, the world can keep its sweet
  bouquets and cards bought from a store,
The cellophane - wrapped candy hearts,
  or gold and jewels galore...
If I was granted one last wish,
I'm sure what it would be:
Just one small, sticky valentine
Whose heart belongs to me.

   Sandra M. Van Kouwenberg

Sisters

They grow from the earth, beautiful, giving birth.
Drinking the sun.
Strong, swaying.
Spreading their seeds.
The essence of power, the enriching fragrance of a flower.
Gathered in the garden of life, among the thistle and thorns.
You see their beauty, touch their soul... admire from afar.
Wondering if they know the simple pleasures they give,
to some lonely stranger passing by.
Different flowers in the same garden, how lovely when in bloom...
Then they hide to protect themselves from some impending gloom.
Sunshine comes, eyes open!
They tell each other it's safe... to grow tall and strong.
Some entwine... one grows alone.
Step back and look at the garden.
An artist he has mastered.
There will never be a place as lovely,
as the garden I call sisters.

   Kim Craig-Woodworth

Mother's Dreams

Something still exists after the twilight has subsided
Drop by drop of sorrow as fleeting and as unnamed
A journey of a thousand miles is only a departure
Forgotten days are left behind.

A little star reigning over the multicolored sky
Eastern language dominating the West
You still remember your origin and your motherhood
You offer your private feelings to the wind and the clouds.

The string of the past is covered with mist
The direction of march flooded with lights
Mother's nursing her expectations and loves
For her son hopeful and bright future

Mother imagines the space which separates
The round earth has switched the direction of danger
How could she describe her happiness
When seeing her son as in a dream.

The beautiful dream which prolongs the vitality of life
Mother's counting the years of old age
And says to herself: Man's power is limited
Still hoping for her son's return for the time of communion.

Quang Thanh

Blue Green Bay Silent Prayer

Take my thoughts far, far away to the Blue Green Bay
Drown any sadness in the Sea of Sorrow
So it will not twist my mind tomorrow!
Take my Soul and cleanse it and help me
So I cannot ever lose quickness of mind and Spirit!
Slow me down to a much softer pace
As I do not want to fall flat on my face!
Each time one falls to the ground, it gets
Much harder to lift one's self up, so!
Take my body and mind and make it strong and quick
So there is nothing I cannot lick!
Hold me up by a nice strong string, dear Lord,
And I promise to always do my best at everything!
Take my heart and make it pure and clean
And you'll always see my face has a beam!
Scrub me and cleanse me so I will never step
So far out of line throughout this eternity!
If you'll do all these things in your own sure way
Lord, I'll say goodbye until tomorrow day!
It's really wonderful one can always pray!

Valerie Hall Stetson

The Children

The sun and stars both shine bright
During the day and by night

The children are precious that are on this planet
Some of the time people think they are made of granite

They need some discipline and to be loved
They don't deserve to be hit or shoved

Children should be taught right from wrong
And their love for God should be strong

They grow up so very fast
So enjoy them while they last

For one day they will be gone
And you will sing a sad song

But the light in your heart will burn bright
During the day, and the night

So, for the short time they are with you
Love and care for them the way you ought to.

Vickie S. Captain

Rt. 14

Cars are whizzing past,
each afraid of being last.
Billboards are flashing by,
too fast to read with naked eye.
A red light looms up ahead;
I must stop or I could be dead.
A man's love affair with his car,
surpasses everything by far.
Where is everybody going?
'Twould be nice to be knowing.
I'm tired and hungry, want to get away.
OOPS! I just passed "Ye Olde Cafe".
Oh well, there's other eateries down the line,
the selection of which will be all mine.
Wow! there's a new one I do believe,
I'll pull in there my hunger to relieve.
I must turn around soon, and reverse my path,
or else I'll incur my boss's wrath.
Next weekend if I'm alive,
I'll go for a drive on 45.

Mildred E. Kragh

Mindscape

Beloveds and enemies ripple through my memories-
Each coloring a different dimension of my personality palette-
A jumbling pasture of co-mingling flowers-
Such sweet- some bitter- herbs of my ego garden-
Random reapings flavor my disposition-
I cannot plough asunder the bitter-
Nor mulch the sweet-
They are rooted in my mindscape and know no gardener-
They are the blood of my conscience, and the salt in
my wounds-
Grow gently, my garden of revelations-

You are me.

Vickie E. Munden

Winter Night Miracles

The milk-white frost crept over the land,
Each corner, each edge, was fringed in pearl,
The frosty powder covered the ground,
And swept over it in a gentle swirl.

A house, outlined by sparkling snow,
Inside, snuggled warm, was filled with dreams,
The roof had soft, airy collar of white,
That sparkled like fire by the moonshine beams.

Smoke curled upward from the tall chimney,
Each snowflake gleamed like a spark
As the thin moonshine fell on the snow,
They shone in the surrounding dark.

Surani Joshua

Watching Over You

When I'm gone
Don't worry
I'll always be there for you
Watching from far above
Wishing I was till there with all of you
But glad I've moved on to a better place
Where I have no worries or fears
But don't worry
I'll always be there for you
Watching over you
Watching from far above
Forever

Tina Baran

"The Four Seasons"

"Winter, Spring, Summer or Fall,
Each season we wait for every year
The Winter months bring the cold and snow,
Also skiing, sledding, and much good cheer."

"Coming inside from the cold outdoors,
Enjoying that warmth of the fireplace
Everyone is comfy and friendly,
Hot toddies to satisfy each ruddy face."

Some folks enjoy the Spring the most,
The weather seems the best
Flowers bloom, the fish are nibbling,
A great time to vacation, with lots of rest."

"The Summer can be delightful,
Its warmth can help a lot
For swimming, jogging, and camping too,
And a Cola that hits the spot."

"Fall cannot be too far behind,
It's time to think about school, we're told
How fast the Seasons pass us by,
I've enjoyed them all, whether hot or cold."

Marty Rollin

In the next port, in the next town

You walked out in the cold night
Each step moving the present into the past
The last good-bye was still echoing
The last touch of hands slipping away, fading
Time dripped in silence, twisted in pain
Slow melt from glaciers of thousands of years
I stood up and left the suffocating emptiness of the cafe

Tell me again the story of salmon fishing
Dall sheep and brown bear hunting
Dog mushing and Aleutian volcanoes erupting
Take me back to Resurrection Bay
Where porpoises dance at the bow of the boat
To lead us to the blue waters where sea lions sleep in the sun
While cormorants cut their black silhouettes
Against the white snow of Mount Alice
Return with me to the pier where fishermen unload
The last catch of halibut in sunset's golden light
Before they gather in the bar with floors covered of sawdust
Where coffee blends its aroma
To the smell of scotch, sea salt and musk
Then tell me again that our journey isn't over
And in the next port, in the next town we will meet
For adventure knows no respite and to its call we must heed.

Alyssa James

Reunion Light

Silence sung above the silhouettes shivering simultaneously.
Eager to embrace each ebb of events, embedded with eloquency
And absent-minded to an aggressive anarchy arising amidst,
The twain teamed in tandem to take on the titanic twist
Fate had flung ferociously in the field of their future.
Naive nor narcotic, neither nonchalantly noted nature.
Blessed and bearing burdens of a beginning bitterness,
Reunion restored them with reassurance and relevance.

Spring sunlight sparkled on shades of silvery green
Dawn danced upon dew-made diamonds of the emerald scene.
Bringing the burning, brilliance of a fresh desire,
Light lanced a lifetime of languished love and set afire
What Winter's wicked winds whipped and whiled away.
Flames filled the firmament fending off foes of yesterday
Teaching them thankfulness is tethered to tomorrow,
Given in grace, guided by God, and granted without sorrow.

Virginia Sullivan

Mansion In The Sky

We may not live in a mansion, while on this
    earth we tread,
It may be a humble dwelling with little or no
    frills instead.
But there is one thing on which we can rely
Someday, when we meet our Maker, we'll have a
    mansion in the sky.
Many many years ago, He came to prepare a place
    for you
For it was what His Father had instructed him to do
And all He asked for in return was that the ten
    commandments we keep
That we love one another, live by the golden rule
    from the time we wake till we sleep.
Over the years from these rules we've often gone astray
And we keep right on down the wrong path with each
    new passing day
So let us search our very soul and those commandments buy
So our spirit will one day enter the Kingdom of Heaven
    in that Mansion in the Sky.

Marion A. Richards

My Friend

Was it anger? Pity? Shame?
Emotions swirled as I marked the changes in you:
    Gaunt frame
    Clothes sagging, bagging, flapping,
    Hair shoulder length, greasy, separated into
        dirty-blonde clumps,
    Gait slow, careful, hesitant,
Yet you spoke and from your eyes there was a bright spark of
    life
    recognition
    interest
    concern
    affability

In that feeble body the soul of you was captive,
    Still knowing
        reaching
        loving
        caring
And I wept!

Lillie B. Brewer

Love Enough

Ageless dreams of one another,
    endless vows spoken true,
Sweetest words of sweet surrender,
    flow like time between the two.

Hold them close, you must remember,
    Keep them somewhere in your mind,
For changes come as stormy weather,
    And soon enough the two shall find.

That love in words can't stand the weather,
    Words fall apart when times are rough,
To stay the storm and stay together,
    There must be LOVE ENOUGH.

Richard Pinkston

City By Night

It is a lady dressed in midnight blue
Enhanced by jewels in clever symmetry,
A gracious maid unswayed by public view,
For truth, not fickle praise, shall keep her free.

It is a lighted Christmas tree unique
Within whose branches countless blessings lie,
Both small and great - that men of stout physique
Would count as naught should freedom die.

By night a city is a crystal glass
Reflecting God's own starry sky above,
Reflecting freedom it cannot surpass,
Serene in peace held fast by silent love.

Cautiously, still the dawn creeps in on night,
And lamps humbly submit to day's great light.

Marian Fortkamp

Untitled

Neither the brightest day, nor the darkest night, can
erase your memory from my heart and mind.
It's not time or distance that keeps us apart, it's the
words that we left unsaid, from your heart and mine.

We've always had each other to lean on, no matter
the challenge that we had to face.
Somehow we've avoided talking about the warmth,
happiness and need, that we find in the other's embrace.

The closeness that I feel and share with you, is one
no other will ever know.
It's this special friendship that we share, that makes
it impossible for me to let the depth of my feelings show

We still hold one another and try to minimize,
the love, that is there in our eyes.

We talk for hours at times, hoping the other will
say the words that need to be said. Before we become
more than friends, the rest of our lives.

Larry T. Murrell

Lost Love

We were a couple everyone noticed and saw.
Everyone thought our relationship could never fall.

At one time I loved you, and I still do.
You always loved me and thought I'd always be true.

I lost your faith and I lost your trust.
Now I lost you, and to go on, I must.

You betrayed me with words alone.
I betrayed you with ways that I've outgrown.

I couldn't love at all this much
If it wasn't for your ways and such.

When I decided you were the one I'd adore.
I promised myself I'd betrayed you no more.

You already left me because that was your choice.
Everyday now I'll hear your voice.

I know now, that our love has come to an end.
Hopefully forever you'll be my friend.

Rachel Martinez

"Who Am I...?"

Everything I believe, has been sown
Everything I am, has been reaped

A moment hasn't gone by, where I am either
A planter of tomorrows, or yesterday's reaper

I am alive, but I am death
Everything I eat, once had breath

My thoughts create, but I am not God
I'm trapped in time, in this flesh and blood

Memories of the past, visions of tomorrow
Caught between two thieves, it's emotions I swallow

I am always alone, searching for my truths
And living the lies, because that's all I knew

Brothers and sisters, we are lost in time
Preaching each other's perception, which is yours or mine?

"Who am I...?"

Into the darkness, I'm roaming around
Searching for what...?, but it must be found!

Then through the blackness it comes, shining the path so bright
"I am finally found," I said...as I entered the light!!

Thomas "TJ" Dombrowski

Tania, My Beloved

Your hair, my daughter, soft and wavy,
    Eyes so large and deeply brown,
Shaded by your lovely lashes; long and black and curling round
    Cheeks so plump and pink and rosy;
Nose so small, a wee bit tilted; lips so soft and always tender
    On your face your smiles weren't stilted,
But big and wide and generously given, with just a wee bit of a dimple
    Your dear face registered your love for God,
And faith He'd care for your wants so simple.

We do miss you so, our only daughter,
    But God also wanted you, my dear;
Your eager face full of loving laughter is gone from here and up to there.
    It's so dreary here, and lonely;
Hope you are happy there, my Sweet;
    From your home here so low and earthly, you've gone to heavenly
    mansions great.
You built your mansion up in heaven by your good deeds here below.
    Eight short years to us were given— Years of pleasure as you know;
And these short years we'll always treasure as the years may pass us by.
    Yes, we loved you without measure and we'll see you, by and by.

Zena G. Nicol

Too Busy

I've had something on my mind,
Ever since I was nine.
I keep remembering when my dad was in the hospital
It was a building that was very tall.
Fifth floor
I thought it was a bore.
That's when he made everyone but me leave the room.
Little did I know he'd soon he in a tomb.
He wanted to talk privately to me,
But I was too busy.
I ignored
In my mind for all this time was where it was stored.
He had to die,
And I was too busy to say, "goodbye."

Karyn Steinert

Voices Of TV's Family

Father:
  Faring better than most, I suppose, I would that there were more.
  For living, the life I live is a drag...
  What more is there in store?

  The more I have, the more I want...
  Avarice is my name. No other pursuit to call my own...
  Grabbing is my game.

Daughter:
  Used and abused, but just as I choose...
  My morals are right there in place.
  Every third time I'm asked I supply
  Fornication so he can save face.

Mother:
  Well, well, what have we here? What rank of monster are you?
  How did you turn out the way that you are?
  I really haven't a clue.

  All I did was my very own thing...
  Everyone has a right to do it.
  They said every woman should see to herself...
  Don't tell me now that I blew it.

  Mary K. Williams

Grandfather's Delight

A daughter is born with all giving thanks
Fatherhood, motherhood time passes by.
A daughter is married, with all giving thanks,
Fatherhood, motherhood, time passes by.

Unaware is the mind of pending forthcoming
While rising, working, housekeeping chores.
But genes are working the miracle forthcoming
While rising, working, housekeeping chores.

A son is born 'tis grandfather's delight,
The miracle granting a gift of each moment
A reflection of self, grandfather's delight,
The miracle granting a gift of each moment

  Richard A. Ruth IV

My Liquid Amber Trees

From my studio window, the scene there
  Fills my soul with the wonders of nature.
With my arms folded on the sill I stare,
  And my mind adrift, I dream the future.

Summer has fled, Autumn brings a muted sun
  Reflecting glow from liquid amber trees.
The walls in my room with new colors done
  Fills it with beauty that brings joy to me.

I love the trees that shield from Summer's heat,
  Provides background beauty in shining green,
Tall and stately, guards our garden retreat,
  While we bask in peace that endows the scene.

One tree, colored amber of burnished hue,
  Which Autumn polishes with brush of gold,
Another is red/brown, not amber true,
  A color her own, defiantly bold!

Then comes the Winter with snow, sleet and rain,
  Giving rest from their labors, while they dream
That Spring ends their slumber so they may reign
  In splendor of their new mantle of green.

  Thelma Jo Parker

Longing

I'm longing for a time in my mind to find...
Find what my soul is searching for.
Knowledge, religion, love, hate.
What is my fate?
The path which I am taking is unknown.
There is no guidance to show me,
There is no light to lead my way.
Riding the moment in a land of darkness
With a mind undecided and time racing the unknown.
Mind and soul reaching and searching.
For what?
The answers to it all or the answers to nothing?
The mind is lost in thought to find the soul
Which has lost itself in darkness.
Determined, but tiring, to find what is mine -
Peace for my soul.
Then there will be
Peace for my mind.

  Paul J. Caparratto

What If

What if we controlled time...went back to when our lives were
fine...when we were free...to be whoever we wanted to be...
I'd do it for you...would you do it for me?

What if you were ready...to go steady...and I was leaning...towards
agreeing...would we ever try...or...simply pass it by?

What if I were a bait...to a special twist of fate...would time
really matter...or... would things only scatter? Would you really
want to see what kind of life it could be if you were involved with me?

What if I didn't say no...how far would you go? Who would be your
concern? Is this just time you're looking to burn?

How would you feel if my feelings for you weren't
real...but...simply a backed-up desire...of needing to spread a bit
of fire? What if I fell in love with you? What would you advise me to do?
Would you truly care? Would you be there?

What else can I say?

I'm in disarray...

and just sitting here...wondering...
WHAT...IF.........

  LaWander D. Patrick

Tribute To My Wife, Sylvia

We think of angels up on high
Floating around there in the sky.
They have no faults, a pristine life
They lead, without a care or strife.

We try to match their high ideals
To get a taste of how it feels
To have such qualities so rare
But often we yield to despair.

Sometimes we're good, sometimes we're bad
At times we're glad, other times sad.
But angels here are hard to find
You're apt to meet the other kind.

Don't look up high, give up the search
Right here on earth is where she's perched.
An angel by another name
'cept Sylvia is not the same.

So stay down here and spread your cheers
And warm friendship for many years.

  Sidney Goldscheider

"Around And Around We Go"

SUMMER, oh SUMMER, where have you gone -?
  You've made such a fleeting call;
You warmed our hearts with your shining rays,
  Those rays which ushered in FALL.

The greens transferred into colors,
  Of orange, of red and of maize,
A foretaste of nature reshedding,
  To prepare for long WINTER days.

The frost - so white and so vivid,
  The snow on the brow of the hill,
The parks - so quiet and peaceful,
  The beaches so icy and still.

Then sudden new life sprouts before us,
  As the birds in the morning do sing,
The first and sure indication
  That WINTER is turning to SPRING.

The circle is now completed,
  We start all over again,
The SPRING will turn into SUMMER,
  We're back to where we have been.

Marjorie M. Lynch

Dear David

At eighteen years of mature age,
You've build a solid growing base,
To enter the journey of adulthood,
And search and find your lively good.

Forget the play, it does not matter,
The world is waiting to be always better,
For you, on this earth, there is no time,
Your wisdom will uncover and you'll be fine.

My advice to you: be always fair,
And honest, patient and for others to care,
Than the law of Karma is not a concern,
For the Love you give shall always return.

Only son of mine, I love you dear,
Whether you're far, or whether you're near,
Life is a wonder, just let it flow,
Give God a chance for blessings to show.

Dick Martin Haas

My Sister

From the time I was little to present day,
You've always been there to show me the way.
You're my sister, my mother and my best friend,
The person on whom I can always depend.

You know dear sis, you mean the world to me,
A better sister there could never be.

So have a wonderful birthday
  And many, many more,
From the heart of the sister I
  Know you adore!!

Cindy Goruik

Mysterious

Then he pulled the trigger...
you started to run.
He pulled out a gun,
but while you were going you thought he was insane.
He said to come to the lane,
but would not tell his name.
A mysterious figure came,
when the black birds flew away.
On a dark and misty day,

Sean Magee

"Time"

Time is as precious as giving birth.
You're not here that long to have a dark world
When you're on this earth.
Time goes slow and time goes fast,
You never know how it's going to turn out or
If it's going to last.
Time has a way of taking away the pain,
But never will time stand still and stay the same.
Time with you I will chase
Because it's such a timeless place
Time takes us to where we want to be.
Time will tell you will see.
Time with you is a mystical thing
For you've taken me places I've never been.
Time with you makes my love and happiness so free.
Time with you I want to go on till eternity.
Time, I want to spend the rest of my time with you
I hope you want that time too!

Pamela Bohun McClure

Winning Ways

Plaudits come and plaudits go,
  You're hero for a day.
The ringing cheers will fade too soon
  You made the winning play.

Yet true strength comes in daily shots
  Without overt display.
By those who stay the rugged course
  Who forge on day by day

To battle life's adversities
  With honest toil and pride,
Mindful of his brother's needs,
  And sometimes steps aside.

I see it in the kindly eye,
  The understanding smile,
And shun the spot light, though they may,
  They're winners - by a mile!

Majorie E. Davidson

Macbeth's Decline

Macbeth, Macbeth, you started out well,
Your wife and weird witches, that's how you fell.
Thane of Cawdor just wasn't enough,
For Lady Macbeth demanded you tough.
King Duncan sure paid for being naive,
That you would kill him, he'd never believe.
With dagger in hand you bludgeoned him deep,
Your soul is gone, Macbeth gets no sleep.
Banquo was next, an axe in the back,
Your conscience now gone, a coward's attack.
From hero to villain in such a short time,
Macduff's wife and children, now that was a crime.
Her mind now absent, that Lady Macbeth,
She stood at the stairwell, then leapt to her death.
The English were coming, that much you knew.
Your men fled the castle, why die for you?
The gates were rammed open, in the troops ran,
You showed no fear except for one man.
Macduff was hell-bent, you couldn't defend,
He chopped off your head, a quite fitting end.

Wayde Darren Henry

Little One

Suspended in your mother's womb
Your picture is of all the things to come
  —the future held in such a small being
  —your potential is boundless
  —we cannot fear the unknown
Little One, your name is Hope

Floating rhythmically in your chamber
Your every movement shows you will succeed
  —little heart beating rapidly
  —you are like a small beacon
  —lighting the way for the world
Little One, your name is Faith

Growing in harmony with your mother's body
You are caressed with loving fingertips
  —promised a loving home
  —welcomed to a caring family
  —heralded like a King's arrival
Little One, your name is Baby

    Joyce Ray

Why You?

Why you? I don't have a clue
Your physical appearance isn't the best
But your brown eyes draw me to you
And resisting you is the ultimate test.

Your smile is goofy but sincere
Every time I hear you coming near
I wait to see your sweet face
Only to realize that for me you have no place.

We are very different you and I
So I don't think it will work out
But when you happen to catch my eye
I forget that I'm always in doubt.

Your faults fade away when I look at you
Because I find you're so real and true
Your superficial beauty isn't the best
But your inner beauty is like none of the rest.

    Sylvie Viau

Nature's Heartbeat

When you sing springs new songs again,
your new children growing, their heartbeats begin,
old ones greet new ones, since they have always been there,
telling soil stories, new surface to air.

When you hum summers days away,
your sunned grown up children will lazily lay,
the gusts will send warnings through the trees,
but happy are greens who dance in the breeze.

In your autumns you whisper life's names
your nudeness grows fast, you are ashamed,
you cry silently, your body grows thin,
for you loose your coloured children again to the wind

It worries me so to see you again,
to look at you closely and see your frozen pain,
For your winters are cold, your frozen rough skin,
but I listen closely...
your silent heart beats within.

    Michelle Kretz

Neighbourly "Mews"

If you have children, you can bet
Your neighbours never will forget
  To give complaints and tips aplenty
  About them till they're one and twenty.
They'll say your child is just a brat,
Spoiled, uncontrolled and things like that.
    They'll put your ego on the skids
    With snide remarks about your kids!
And strange to say, the paragon,
The one who can talk on and on,
  Who knows the fancy from the fact,
  And spurns that little thing called tact,
The one whose knowledge drives you wild,
Possesses neither chick nor child.

    Edith Virtine Carey

Eerie Silence

I'm walking through a dark, silent forest
Your face is everywhere and in everything
I can feel your presence tingle down my spine
Oh, I can hear the leaves rustling
Your face suddenly disappears
Oh, the sound of the leaves rustling becomes louder

    Catherine S. Ho

Your Bedroom Eyes

Cool, classic, calm, and bold
Your eyes hold me, softly as they move across the room.

You touch me softly,
You hold me tight and slowly, as we embrace
I look deep into your eyes and see love and kindness.

Before we go to sleep,
Your mine to keep,
As we hold each other into the night,
you move slowly so I do not wake.
When the morning is almost near you whisper, "I
love you." into my ear.

When I see you awake in the morning,
you smile and in a deep whisper your eyes say hello.

As we get up and go our separate ways during the day.
Your eyes say good-bye.
After you leave I think of them all day.

    Eric Barrett

As You Are Now

As you are now, so once was I.
Young, lithe, and lean and stepping spry.
My eyes were bright - no strain to see,
My youthful spirit soaring free.

The aches and pains were absent then.
I could burn the candle at both ends.
And start another day anew;
Without a thought that I'd get through.

Old age creeps up insidiously.
So strong to frail - how can this be?
Have patience with love, so at the end of the day,
I'll feel honoured and valued and not in the way.

You will one day be here too.
It's hard to imagine, but oh so true.
So take time out, and think of me.
Inside my head, I am twenty-three.

    Mary Smith

Undying Love

If you watch the sky turn night into dawn
You'll see the beautiful shades of morning hue
Kissing all of the land with a radiant warmth

If you watch the mountains close enough
You'll see them wrapping their beauty around the sun
Releasing all the beautiful colors of their love

Watching the two of you
You see what is seen when you watch the mountains
    hug the sun or the night turn to the light of dawn
You see something so pure and beautiful
Something that is meant to be and will last forever

An Undying Love for one another
Susan L. Luff

Revelation

Losing your way is not a crime;
you'll find the path if given time.
Time to explore worlds high and low,
time not to know which way to go.
With an ounce of smarts, and a heart of gold,
you'll find the key to the lock you behold.
When you fall on the love thought was lost,
or step past a boarder you've never crossed,
you'll know what you knew,
to yourself you'll be true,
and you'll see the path is made for you.

Though strain and strive the strong survive.

Deanne Cameron

When You Look Back Upon A Thing

When you look back upon a thing that was old when you were young
You wonder after it, where it's been and where it's going
When you find that thing when you are much older and much more
    complicated
You feel your relationship between time and yourself desiring rate
When you find out that you never had a strong bonding like you first thought
You realize that time has always been in control and your just another
    person living in it.

Jasen Molnar

I Will Always Carry You, My Child

I will always carry you, my child;
you will never be a heavy burden to me,
but you will always be a sweet bundle of joy.

From the time of your conception,
I have carried you in my womb,
with a mother's expectant joy and wonders -
    Will you be a boy or girl?
    How will you look like?
    How heavy and how long will you be born?

At last! I have the rapture of carrying you, for the first time,
God's most wonderful creation, in the hollow of my hands,
to gaze with your father at your beautiful, innocent, peaceful face,
to hold you close, so very small, so very light, so very warm,
and to thank God for His most wonderful gift of love, my treasure.

And as you grow up and become heavier,
with love and care, I still continue to carry you,
including all your fears, your worries, your struggles and disappointments;
with God's help, I will always carry you all the time, everywhere
and even in my life beyond, I will always carry you in my memory, prayers,
and always there is God, supporting my hands to carry you.

Concepcion Romana Saavedra

Mother

Oh, mother dear I cannot forget the first time I saw you
You were as gentle and kind so perfect I thought.
I was so proud, even boasted to myself and others.
As I looked out in wonder across the meadow, I thought am I real?
Why am so lucky to have such a wonderful mother.
Besides being mother, you were my companion, teacher, friend, and advisor.
In turn, I was your wood gatherer, inventor, and occasional advisor.
Mother, you remember the invention, a time piece, a mere sundial.
And of course the humane mousetrap long before there was such a thing.
Ssh mother I know what you're thinking, don't say a word.
Yes you remember, I know 'cause mothers almost never forget.
Bonita Starr

Do You Hear What I Hear?

It's funny, don't you think, about things that go bump in the night?
You suddenly wake up and then you listen... you would swear that
    you'd heard a sound.

You're just on the verge of dozing off, you know, at that time
"just before?" When quickly your heart beats, your pulse rate
increases. That noise again; my God, what is it?

Your eyes are wide open, your ears are attuned, to every slight
    sound around you.
Your head it starts roaring, now you can't hear a thing.
You're sure that someone is near.

The walls play witness to the macabre dance of the shadows about,
moving ever closer. The dark will play tricks and make you look
harder at all the shapes that surround you.

You're sure everything's locked, but there's always a chance,
You've missed that one window in the porch at the back.

You're waging a war within yourself by asking the question,
"Should I go look?" You berate yourself, you have no mercy. You're
just being silly again.
You close your eyes and try not to hear those eerie sounds all around.
"There's nothing there" you keep telling yourself, as you wait for
    sleep to come.

It will happen again on another black night and no one else will hear.
Those bumps around you, those scrapes on the floor,
You hope it's only your imagination.

Catherine Ann Fitzpatrick

Birthday Cake Poem

Make a wish. C'mon. This is the best time.
You know what to do.
When you're a baby, they blow out the candles and you don't understand.
Or care. The cake's too good.

Then when you're bit older, you wish for the impossible.
I wish I was a ballerina, a princess, a fireman.
I wish I had that pony.

When you're a pre-teen, it's I wish Scott like me,
I wish I had a Nintendo, I wish my boobs would grow.

When you're much older, wishing is childish.
I'll blow out the candles, but I'm NOT going to wish!
(I wish my husband were here)

And when you miss the princess, the ballerina, and fireman,
You blow out the candles, saying, What could I wish for?
You're all here. (I wish I had a Porsche and not a V.W. bug)

Then you watch grandchildren blow them out.
And you don't understand. Or care. The cake's too good.
So. Make a wish.
A good one. C'mon.
Heather Hnatiw

The Terror Inside You

I am like an evil shadow.
You can't run from me, you can't hide from me.
I am inside you pulsing through your veins.
My fatal poison eats away at your tissue,
Slowly killing you.

I am your worst nightmare,
You keep running but you can't break free.
It is a nightmare that tells a story,
A story of pain and of fear.
It is a story that forces you to stare death in the face.

While you look into my eyes
You can look away and let me consume you,
Or you can stare deep into my cold, dark heartless eyes.
You can stare me down and make me look away first,
You can yell at me and tell me you don't want to die.
That you will not die, that you will kill me first
Only then can you win, only then can you defeat me.
You have to kill or be killed, but do you have the strength?

Jennifer Esbjerg

Domestica

Gone are those rosy coloured days when you promised me the moon
You can pay the piper but I'd like to call the tune.

You swore to me in bed - you said I'd be queen of all that comes
But wealth and riches passed me by leaving babes with dirty bums.

And kiddies crying in that night "Where's my mum?; I want a light,
My tummy hurts; I need a wee; Please mummy come and sleep with me!"

Oh what I'd give for eight straight hours uninterrupted sleep
And not a single bedmate instead of my boys in a heap.

And someone to make me breakfast, lunch and dinner, and run my bath;
And someone to take out the garbage and someone to shovel the path.
But you sit here in front of the T.V. set saying "Honey you're 5 minutes late
I said I wanted my supper. The ball game starts at eight."

What if I said "Well get it yourself I'm never cooking again
And as for the housework, hire a maid, it goes against my grain."?

But I stand here counting the minutes till the casserole is done
Trying to ignore the dismal roar of my fair haired second son.

And after the minutes I count the days till the kids are all in school
And live in my head where I'm truly queen, and ruler of all I rule.

Cassandra Vinckers

Unexpectedly

I came into your office, we talked about the weather
you came into my dreams and changed my life forever
and it happened...unexpectedly.

The attraction wasn't instant, it didn't happen overnight
it grew over months and months until the time was right
And then it happened...unexpectedly.

I drove around with nervous fear not knowing what you'd say
when I professed the truth to you in my bold and forceful way
And then it happened...unexpectedly.

You didn't run, you didn't hide and you didn't laugh at me
you sat and smiled and took my hand and my spirit was set free...
and it happened...unexpectedly.

And now the time we spend together is peaceful, safe and warm
we laugh and talk and share our thoughts in each other's arms
and it happened...unexpectedly.

Now we know the situation isn't perfect, it isn't even right
in the eyes of those who sit and stare when we go out at night
but it happened...unexpectedly.

Everyday is a new day...where will our future go?
We pray and look to the one above for only He shall know
and it goes on...unexpectedly.

Jo Ann E. Comeau

For Our Country

You fought for our country.
You brought peace to our country.
You risked your lives for our country.
You knew you might not come back.
But you fought for our country.
You knew you might lose friends
And your family might lose you,
But you fought for our country.

I have so much to be thankful for...

If it weren't for you, I might not have been born a Canadian.
If it weren't for you, I might not have had an education.
If it weren't for you, my parents might not have been able to vote freely.
If it weren't for you, my classmates might not have included many cultures.

As I grow up and learn to appreciate all of our great qualities,
I hope that I will always remember never to judge others by their
  colour or the country from which they have come.
I hope that I will always remember to keep this great country of ours
  a land where everyone is welcomed.

You fought for our country.
You brought peace to our country.
You risked your lives for our country.

Thank you, for all you have done, for all of us

Allison Rae Bartok

His Garden

When someone you love goes away
You ask yourself why and if it's really fair
God has a secret and that secret is time
We don't know when
We don't know who
He takes them in His garden
and there He keeps them warm
Don't cry today
Don't cry tomorrow
For He has them safe
For He has them now.

Daniela Bruno

Tender Captive

You are the sun, that coaxes me to bloom.
You are the soft spray from a wave, that makes me content.
You are the gentle breeze, that blows my hair and makes me happy.
You are the wind, that makes me feel wild, alive.
You are the oil, that makes me feel warm.
You are the beach in early eve, that makes me feel at peace.
You are the smell of an autumn day, that makes me feel adventurous.
You make me laugh, you make me sigh.
You make adrenaline race through me.
You make me passionate.
You give me reality.
I love you and always will.
You make me feel vulnerable, you make me feel strong.
You make me feel feminine.
You make me cry for wanting you.
You are steadfast and true
  You are my love.
  You are my soul.

Wendy MacCabe-Chapman

264

Eternity

Days have passed ever so quickly
yet my love for you still runs slowly.

Through good times and bad
our feelings never change
our emotions are true and our love remains.

Holding you close and feeling you near
surrounded by warmth hoping it will never disappear.

One year has gone by
and our love is stronger than ever,
you are the one for me I'll leave you never.

Your brown eyes, dark like chocolate
Your smooth caressing hands, soft like snow
make me feel comfortable, secure and
I never want to let go.

What we have is something special
I hope we last forever, cause having you near me
Makes my love for you stronger.

I hope we last for eternity,
I love you forever more.

Natalie Kalms

Unus

I may not climb a mountain
yet in my mind I'm halfway there.
If you could see through my eyes, feel through my heart
you'd know it's something we all share.

I may not fly with the wings of an Eagle
though I sail through the air with his spirit.
I hear the same sounds, sing the same melody.
In completion, we are all connected.

I may not run with a Gazelle
still I am moved by her beauty and grace.
I rise to the possibility, alike in curiosity.
Equal in chemistry, it's just a different face.

I may not be the "heroines of the day"
simply their courage gives me inspiration.
I stand for what I believe, admit when wrong
and any other difference is an illusion.

Kirstin Wandschneider

Only A Rose

He stood silently beside her resting place,
Yes, he stood there all alone,
He did not want to leave her side,
There was no one waiting at home.

Lovingly, he clutched it to his breast,
What his thoughts were, he alone knows,
But a smile lit up his wrinkled face,
As he tenderly caressed the rose.

The rose was his wife's favorite flower,
And each caress was a wind-blown kiss,
Bringing back those beautiful memories,
Of happiness and of bliss.

His heart was filled with sadness,
A tear flowed from his eye,
He gently kissed the rose he held,
And blew it to the sky.

His lips moved as he whispered,
A message of undying love,
And a longing to be together again,
As promised, in the land above.

William C. Ott

My Eyes Are Bleeding

Fragile, are the thorns embedded within my soul.
Wretched, are the sensations bestowed within my heart.
Silence rejoice!
Darkness foreshadows!
  AH HAIL, the dreamers dream,
      the white knight,
      the white picket fence.
  AH HAIL, the innocent dreamer,
      who's life looms in
      the shadows of the light.
Sweet, is the sorrow embellished within my twisted soul.
Love, is the demented devourer within my forgiving heart.
Broken arrows!
Dead flowers!
  AH HAIL, the dreamers dream,
      the delicate touch, the sweet kiss.
  AH HAIL, the imaginary soul who's
      flower wisdom is amongst the torn and faded.
Forever the wicket white, an intruder of death
Forever the shroud of a dream, a hypnotic medieval spell.

Carolyn McKinnon

The Deep Blue Sea

Guilty, guilty
World of hatred.
Last night,
I dreamt I
Wasn't in bed.

Under, under,
The deep blue sea.
Where I could - breath as though...I'm free.
Salt and Seaweed
In mine eyes,
Remembered me of
Days gone by.

"Cry, cry, little fish,
and come unto thee."
"For there I set your

Dreams to me!!!"
And if God therefore,
Put you on the shore,
To rescue you, from sin.
At least you could say!
"Well, I've been there -
To a place where-
I know me!!!

Ruth L. Stone

The Rock Dam

Trapped in the artist's hands are the expressions of an open mind.
Words take not the place of creations so warming and kind.

Mysterious is life's palette with its primaries and naturals.
Maturity is blessed with color to have black and white as pupils.

All is placed and taken by the one who is the giver.
The chosen blind, born with sight must face the force of the river.

To see not the hues of beauty is live in the pitchiness of black.
A stone blocking the current as time produces the fatal crack.

Life must be lived in the way of the flow, and follow natures demands.
Erosion will touch those that stand with the rocks that are damned.

Anthony Gatto

On My Own

Living on the edge, always in danger
Wondering where the next thrill will come from
Looking for fun and excitement on the streets
Getting in trouble and laughing it off
Nothing can hurt me now, I'm on my own

Now that I'm on my own
Nothing and nobody can hurt me
On my own

Roaming the streets and towns
Looking for something or someone
To help me find myself
Before I destroy myself
Now that I'm on my own

Nicole Rosemary Nystrom

Without You

Without you I am miserable
Without you I go insane
Without you I cry all night
From all the hurt and pain.
Without you I am nothing
Just a face in the crowd
Without you I try to find my way
But that I've not yet found.
Without you my life is incomplete
I know there's something wrong
Without you I wish you would come back soon
You've been away to long.
Without you I can't see your face
I wish we hadn't part
Without you though you're far away
You're always in my heart.
Without you I miss you
I miss you so much
I remember you, I cry for you
Without you.

Robin McGauley

Rainbow Of Nations

A rainbow is not a rainbow
Without its many colours
A world is not a world
Without its many nations,

For a world is like a rainbow
Each colour represents a nation
Each nation represents a colour

For if the world was one nation
It would not be a beautiful world
For if a rainbow was one colour
It would not be a beautiful rainbow

But when different colours come together
It forms a pot of gold
But when different nations come together
It brings joy untold
for the world we live in is
A
Beautiful rainbow of nations

Alexander Jannetta

The Eagle

Of all the birds I ever see, the eagle is the most pretty.
With eyes of blue and wings of gold, he is always brave and bold.
And as he glides so gracefully flying overhead of me,
I think that it is plain to see the eagle's always loved by me.

Erin Malette

Speculations On A Martian Desert

There is deathless humor about these winds
    without air which only pink crystal sand
        can inhale. The thought of life makes us wince
            at sixty histories of threats unmanned,
doomed before the fire that they cannot spark.
    Perhaps our pale long shadows descended
        once here, commanding some grandiose ark
            whose memory in Egyptian ash ended
in Napoleon's maze of rubied conquest.
    We think rubber scalps and nickel bellies
        brought their hand and zeal to their very best,
            yet ninety years and thirty Schaparellis
found no seed of trace, canals nor fortress.
    But the turtle sands still slip their ancient
        undertow, burying the frozen mistress
            Mars in bed, her infertile womb translucent.

John Kelso

Toast To A Bride

As you travel down the highway of life,
with your husband at your side,
may you always be as loving a wife,
as the day he took you as his bride
May grey skies never follow you,
no dark clouds up above,
May sunshine always land on you,
and shower you with love
If ever a dark cloud comes your way,
to mar your wedded bliss,
just remember this happy day,
and seal it with a kiss
When your hair has turned to silver-grey,
and you have climbed the highest hill,
may you never forget this happy day,
the day you said those words, "I will".

Helen Dupuis

Smiles

Smiles just seem to be fading away
With the toil and strife going on today.
There used to be smiles, and joking around
But now you find there's few to be found.

The people these days just all seem to frown
With no smiles left for they are all seem down.
A smile could be given because it is free.
Making people happy, especially me.

People need something to give them a lift
So smile and they'll think they've been given a gift.
Then maybe, they in turn will find
Returning it gives them some peace of mind.

Their hearts just might lighten up a bit
Making them now seem happy and fit.
For now they can handle what comes their way
And be happy to say, "What a wonderful day".

Vena Humphrey

My Love

My love, you've changed my life in more ways than one
Where there once was darkness, you gave me sun
You took away the sadness, and put a smile on my face
You have changed my life in so many ways

You're amazing my love, a real gift in deed.
Here, take my hand, I trust you, you lead.
Take me into tomorrow with you I've no fear
I'll follow where ever you go, I'll always be near

Like the moon with the sun-they're never far apart
Like you with me - together forever in my heart.

Barb Francis

Breath Together

Gone are the days with whom I shared my life secretly for some months
With the same breath, ate and felt together.
When I was a cluster of living cells with little tiny brains
Holding my happiness and pains of my close partner.

Accompanied me like little puppy kangaroo in her swollen water-melon
With Himalayan confluence of Gangotary and Jumnotary's passion.
Pain and love's seesaw played very well till I become clever
And the silent eavesdropper of her future dreams.

I was so naive to kick and hit brutally in her sacred cottage
To ponder my thirst and hunger like civilization of stone age.
But she kept me like Hebrew (Moses) till I perceived magic rays of
Divine strength so that I can see her face.

Now I am the statue of love and pain standing unaltered among
Numerous tides of forgotten emotions
Which I earned during my formation.

Dalbir Sangione

Untitled

Have you ridden o'er the upland in the searing burning heat
With the sage-tang in your nostrils from the west?
Have you faced Dakota prairie in November wind and sleet
With a thousand miles from nowhere for a test?

Have you done a deal of searching for the lovely and the true
For the dream-girl who awaits you by the shore?
When you find her she'll be smiling and her smile is all for you
And you'll hide her in your heart for evermore.

Far-beyond a northern river where the beavers slap their tails
I was sure I'd found an answer that I sought
'til I found my little flower had been broken by the gales,
In their fury what a havoc they had wrought.

So I'm riding sad and lonely down a pathway of the past
That is carpeted with needles of the pine,
And this winding pathway leads me to the fields of green at last
And the river where we wandered for a time.

J. Colin Keppel

A Bride's Tears

She stood alone that October morn
  with tears of sorrow on her face
Her grandma's dress is what she'd worn
  and danced with death with flawless grace
Her hair a golden woven mass
  with stars among it gaily placed
And through her heart she'd gently pass
  her last dream dreamt, and in her haste
She let the silver demon drop
  and one last breath perhaps she'd take
Once more her heart would beat then stop
  before she fell never to wake
She took the freedom so longed for
  and fled from this hellish place
And from this earth she flew at last
  with tears of joy on her face
  She stood alone that October past

Amy Reid

Treasures

A small boy, pail in hand, blue hat
Wanders down the path toward me smiling.
What marvels does that pail contain?
Wriggling creatures of delight make his eyes sparkle.
And I wonder who has the greater treasure - he or I?

Dale Herman

As Time Rolls On

From the beginning of time life flows along,
With our dreams and our hopes we start out strong,
As life races on we do all that we can
To ensure a legacy for the next generation of man.
Life is good, life is sweet, we are still on the run,
Trying to meet life's demands before the next setting sun.
Aging rolls along, half my life is gone
Will I meet the next half with a cheerful song?
Age creeps along slowing me down, I now want to sleep
My body grows weak, my mind's at rest, why do I weep.
I remember now the things I have done when time was mine,
Aging is on the climb with the passing of time.
I now have the time but aging brings me down,
Aging flows on, aging is all around.
I remember now that aging is time
Aging is long, aging will no longer be mine.
Now it's time to remember what went wrong,
With the aging of time I have sung my song.
Longevity has been mine, aging with time
Giving me sweet memories that will always be mine.

Weonia Hutton

Vampire Love

I love him with my heart and soul
with my body I worship him
he seems unaware, cold, empty
I am losing myself

He drains my passion with a sudden whim
he is still empty, dissatisfied,
alone
I am losing myself

I can think, dream only of him
Being without his touch is a physical pain
My life is forfeit to my desires
I am lost

Love awakens a hunger never to be satisfied.

Andrea Colby

The Birth Of A Drum

With one chop the tree is felled.
With another a section is separated,
The other parts discarded for the worms and termites to devour.

Strong sculptor's hands grasp this vulgar piece of tree.

They start chipping away at the rings of pride which once inhabited
  this old stump.
His character enters the drum as it is carved into the maker's desired shape.
His hands are old and the age shows dexterity.
The age reveals a dignity which he polishes into the stump.
Gouging out the life of another tree in millions,
Using crude meagre instruments to execute his trade,
A passage is formed;
A transformation takes place: from an old tree to a tunnel to another
time and tradition.

Looking for a skin to complete the passage,
A strong one, with a history,
A history spanning decades, perhaps centuries.
He stretches the skin across the frame.
With every pull its thinness becomes more pronounced.
He fastens the skin to the frame.

As hand hits drum, the voices of centuries passed are sounded;
The voices of martyrs, heroes, and nature resound in that one beat.

Andrew Miller

Such A Fool

I sit staring off into space
Wishing I did not feel so out of place.
I am trying so hard not to fall apart
But I should never have given away my heart.

I feel like such a fool with each tear I fight
As I lay hugging my pillow each night.
Listening with hope for the telephone to ring
Feeling the hurt the silence does bring.

You have not called, nor have I seen you
And I am at a loss as to what to do.
I miss you so much that I cannot believe it is so
That you would walk away and not let me know.

Joanne Fabrizius

The Vampire

Everyday there's longing and pain,
wishing for change as swift as the rain!
Never wishing it upon another,
to be a Vampire is to suffer!

Only those who have lived the curse,
know that dying is not the worst!
To prey on the living of the sun,
is not a thing that can be undone!

To live in darkness without Light,
is a battle and a flight!
The blood of innocents so sweet and pure,
is the only thing we hold dear!

Nothing is worth the price that you pay,
never to see another day!
Loved ones are lost to you forever,
while you live on as another!

Angela Biefer

Free Flight

Sun shining
wind blowing
trees swaying in the breeze
two hawks gliding overhead
hunting, searching
seeking their prey in midday
sailing high and low
wind currents lifting them, drifting them
taking them where they want to go
effortlessly, gracefully
they move with the breeze
scanning, meeting, crossing paths
weaving patterns with their flight
like a sensuous pas de deux
moving together
travelling up and away into the beyond

Velma Schwabe

His Touch

Autumnal tints and cooler evening
Will give us hints of Summer's leaving,
And, so imprints its red leaves grieving.

Bemoan a song of Summer's dying,
Before long, tree leaves are flying,
The cool breeze, strong, from trees starts prying.

Yellow and orange are some leaves who
Begin to change their natural hue,
They do rearrange the green tree's view.

The Master Painter will add His touch,
And, like last year, still does it such,
His paint is time, love is His brush.

Douglas Peters

Friendship

Oh, my friend!
Why won't you accept my friendship the way it is?
Whenever you're feeling blue,
Why won't you let me lend you my shoulder to cry on and comfort you?
Whenever you're troubled
Why won't you pour your troubles on me and let me help you?
Whenever we share a good laugh and merry times together
my heart overflows with happiness.
But whenever there's tension or you won't talk to me and not tell me why,
I search my heart to try to find out if I have offended you,
I find nothing
and that throws me into the deepest black hole there ever was.
I'm here for you, through thick and thin,
and I'll always be there whenever you need me.
We trust each other.
We always have.
Friendship is the deepest love anyone can ever have.
A friend is for life.
If you break your friendship with me,
oh, I know my heart shall break and never heal again.

Karina Laari

Heart

A man waits as he thinks to himself "I shouldn't have."
Why he thinks is only his own speaking in innocence.
The man dressed in white, what does this man hold but victory or fate.
Man and wife sit in a room and listen to the fate of this man.
Not one, two, but three times decided that this man return to the place
   of the sick.
The man's heart races with fear of leaving this world when he knows
   it is not his time.
Why this man returns is only his own doing of 4000 chemicals into a
   love filled body.
Love for who, but family and friends.
As he lies down his worried head his mind lingers to 93% chance of living.
But also to what he knows could happen to his love filled heart if
   something were to go wrong.
Without an incision he knows his life is shortened.
A new man now walks from an old room of worries to one of hope
He realizes that he will live a happier, healthier, fuller life.
He walks, now knowing it is ok to walk a bit further.
My grandfather had to have a triple bypass and he ended up having
quadruple and he is alive and well as ever. So for anyone who is now
scared like My grandfather was just remember, While in the shadow of
death a sunshine of life and happiness is waiting.

Justin Reid

He Is A Friend

He is a friend,
Who will listen to your problems,
About life and its little whims.

He is a friend,
Who will lend a helping hand,
When your chores are in a demand.

He is a friend,
Who will laugh at your funniest jokes,
And return them with all kinds of pokes.

He is a friend,
Who will take you to a hockey game,
And sometimes call the referee a bad name.

He is a friend,
That you'll want to have forever,
Until life will reach to never,

He is a pal, a buddy, a side kick,
But most of all,
He is a friend

John Merits

"Never End"

In Memory of Janie Anderson
They say that when you lose somebody
who meant a lot to you
The pain and sorrow you're feeling
will get the best of you
Well I tried not to cry
but the pain I'm feeling inside
is getting harder, day by day
it feels as though, this grieving will never mend.

They say to live, is to love someday
Then they're taken away from you
I really miss you, I don't know what to do
I can cry each and every night
but that won't bring you back
there's so many things I wish I had said
but the love you gave me, will never, ever, end
Anita Paul

Happy 80th Birthday

What can I say 'bout a lady now 80
Who looks like she's still 65?
She's pretty, she's witty, incredibly gritty
Since many a fall she's survived.

Her kindness is legion throughout every season
When friends arrive at her door;
So it's not surprising the numbers keep rising,
There always is room for one more!

She's a wonderful Mother, Grandmother, and Aunt,
Seems her mission in life's to give pleasure;
So on HER Special Day I'm delighted to say
My sister-in-law is a TREASURE!

So CHEERS TO THIS LADY
This "girl" who's now 80
Who looks like she's still 65!
MAY YOUR ANCHOR STILL HOLD
AS LIFE'S SEASONS UNFOLD,
AND GOD'S LOVE ALWAYS BE BY YOUR SIDE!
Marjorie Archer

Resurrection Morn

God knew there was no other one
who could atone except His Son.
The only sacrifice: His blood
with water mingled, stains the mud.
Sudden insight! "This must truly be
the Son of God upon this tree!"
The heavens weep, the veil is split;
the keys of Death are retrieved from the Pit.
No more curse — the ransom's paid;
God's majesty and power displayed —
Satan's head bruised by Woman's Seed
Just as God through Moses decreed.

Great stone rolled back, seal broke asunder —
Pure Life from Death proclaimed in thunder!
E'en before dawn lights up the sky,
The One they'd heard cry, "Tetelesti!"
Breaks Death's dark grip and walks out free
From Empty tomb to Victory!

Hallelujah!
Muriel C. Morgan

Rebirth

Lightly and softly, the autumn breeze,
Whispers through the colored leaves;

Silently, slowly, they gently fall,
Baring the trees so slim and tall;

Forming a protective coat, it seems,
over the seeds of flowers and weeds;

Then, when winter comes with its cold
Frosts and snows and winds so bold

They lay in comfort, and wait for spring,
and listen to hear the robins sing.

When mother nature sounds her horn
They rise, fresh and new in the April's Morn.
Muriel White

Cherished More Than A Rose . . .

I silently prayed
  while walking home one stormy night
Asking the Lord: "Where did I go wrong?
  My heart is full of pain."

Then...instantaneously fell some nourishing rain
  in the form of a R O S E
that I couldn't see in the dead of night
  for.....it came in a spiritual light.

A strong, fatherly voice queried my soul
  "Do you want to be a crushed weed?
  or a cherished R O S E ?"

"Why...a Rose" I answered through my tears.
  "Then protect your stem with the firmness of thorns -
  and strength of my love
    so your heart's petals will remain soft and tender -
    not bitter and torn.
You're my child
  worth more than a Rose....
    born with a gift of Free Will - to choose
    on whether to Win or to lose."
G. Inga Sigurdson

Death Is Arriving

She lies in her bed,
  while God lets her suffer.

My family says,
  "It's time for her to go."

I tell them, "No! She's too young."
  But God does not listen.

She died the next night, 10:30 p.m.

I didn't get to say
  I love you or, to even say Goodbye.

I don't blame God,
  but I wonder why she had to die.

Everyone, but me, have said their Goodbyes
  and their I love You's.

But now she's gone
  and I can't do anything about it.

So, the next day came and
  I went to her grave.
    I said "Goodbye"
    I said "I love you"

And now it's O.K. for her to go.
Jaqueline E. Smith

Untitled

A vampire is an immortal soul,
Which feeds on blood that is warm not cold
If so he then shall mourn in the beauty of the night
And suffer slowly and painfully to a bright

They shall never see the sunrise again
They will perish into windblown dust
Blood of youth of society coursed sweetly through their veins
But one thing hurts the good in a vampire
The killing for feeding is unbearable
But God kills indiscriminately,
And so shall we!

Elaina Pang

Twenty Lines Or Less?

I just could not find a poem with Twenty Lines or Less
Which completes the whole story the way I know best
So, I have decided to take a little while
To give you a taste of my rhyming style!

I understand your dilemma, needing Twenty Lines or Less
But I'd only leave you hanging, you would never know the rest
If, for instance I attempted, my poem of "Toe Joe"
All the facts of my story, you would just have to know.

"Shades of Blackness" and "Decisions" are poems of our time
With "Bag Lady, Nightmare Alley, Lotto Six Forty-Nine"
Need those extra few lines, beyond your limitations
Of Twenty Lines or Less, as states your stipulations.

Some folks delight in details, don't leave them in the air
Still others need not very much to make their thoughts all clear
But, mostly it depends upon, just what you wish to say
And if you need just Twenty Lines your message to convey.

Although my inspirations entertain a lengthier style
And to satisfy a craving heart, can go that extra mile
I must admit your contest here, did put me to the test
Seems I can write much shorter tales with Twenty Lines or Less.

Evelyn Musgrave

A Hug From A Friend

A hug from a friend is something we all need
Whether we laugh and smile, or cry and weep
At any time, for reason of whatever sort
It encourages, it comforts, it offers support.
In its strength there's no need to stand alone
Because a hug is like returning home.
It expresses what words cannot say
It heals, it will take the pain away
It's priceless, it cannot be replaced or bought
Not with money or gold in any amount.
Unequalled is the hug from a friend
It's every time it's given
And conveys all the feelings of a friendship true,
With love and care, I give this hug to you.

Cristina Auriti

Two

On two little legs he came running to me
Two sparkling eyes beaming above them.
With two little lips he implanted a kiss.
The children — How dearly we love them!

With two little hands he extended a gift,
A paper heart colored in crayon.
I gathered him up and I cuddled him close
And gave him my shoulder to lay on.

The two little arms that encircled my neck
Instilled in me feelings of pride,
For the heart that he gave wasn't paper at all;
'Twas the living one beating inside.

Dorothy M. Hough

Children

Let's not take for granted, the life of a child,
Whether naughty or nice, complacent or wild,
Just continue to nurture, to love and to mould,
For there's nothing more precious to have and to hold.

When life is beginning to seem too unruly,
They'll look up at you and say "I love you truly"
Then all of your troubles, somehow melt away,
With those few little words, which brighten your day.

When you finally think, you've got it all sewn up,
You turn around and there stands a grown up,
No more skinned up knees, no more sloppy kisses,
No more messy rooms, or sinks full of dishes.

All you have left are your fond memories,
Of the way they climbed mountains and swam cross the seas,
Though you know in your heart, 'twas the sandpile and lake,
What you wouldn't give for one more double take,
Of the children who grew up too soon and too fast,
So let's not take for granted, and thank God memories last.

Terri Robinson

Hole In My Heart

There's a hole in my heart
Where your love used to be
The pain was tremendous
When you went away from me
Silently crying when no one could see
There's a hole in my heart
Where your love used to be.

They say memories fade and pain dissipates
The hole will get smaller
I'll mend and will wait
There's a hole in my heart
Where your love used to be
There's a hole in my heart that no one can see.

You're cherished very dearly
There's nothing more to say
I made that clear on your dying day
There's a hole in my heart
Where your love used to be
There's a hole in my heart but you will stay with me
Forever, forever, forever.

Joyce Stewart

Peradeniya Campus

Where the mighty Mahaweli meanders along,
    Where the verdant canopied rain trees throng,
Where the road to Galaha winds through the valley,
    There, where my heart reposes, to leave - a folly?

The Senate building stands on stilts concrete,
    Like a gaunt reminder of a past city of East,
Flanked by hills where fine teas grew
    Now replaced by Halls, great and new.

Marrs and Marcus, the hills dominate,
    And Sanghamitta, a 'Walled-off Astoria' made
To secure 'gals' in their pristine youth
    From nasty barbs, and males uncouth.

The bridge too narrow, for traffic vehicular,
    Spans the river, now so popular
An avenue for boys of Akbar-Nell Hall,
    To meet the girls under willows tall.

On the grounds where once the golfers strode,
    Stands a faculty, today the abode
Of lads and lasses, Lanka's pick
    Learning the art of healing the sick.

Peter Seneviratna

Untitled

I once dreamt of a fire at night at night
Where painted in the flames to me came a name
Of someone I knew in the sight of light

Where written was his name, right in the flame
Deceiving the light of the fiery pyre
Like a liar shadowing his soul in shame

To me he claimed to try to rise higher
Or to wane and die and indeed to bleed
All of his sins from within through the fire

From the silky flames a figure is freed
And high it floated like smoke and took flight
And then I could see that the fire did read:

I once dreamt of a fire at night at night
I once dreamt of a beacon of white light

Mike Bethune

The Walkways

There is a boardwalk in my garden,
Where I spend many hours alone —
Down through my flower garden,
Back of my country home.

I enjoy a nice flower garden —
I think flowers are so sweet,
Like Pansies and Primroses with Petunias—
All in bloom around my feet.

When alone in my flower garden,
I think it is no sin —
If my heart floats like the pollen,
Searching new blooms in the wind.

Along the house is a slab walk —
Beside it Tulips grow and bloom,
And many friends stand and talk —
While! over head the Swallows swoom.

William J. Lambert

"The Game Remains"

Not in ostentatious stadiums
where egos run rampant
where agents, lawyers, and owners roam
where money makes the calls
But in the streets, the backyards, the playgrounds
in the hearts of the children
with those who will pay
just for the privilege to play
the sun
the dirt
the grass
the pocket of a glove
the sweetspot of a bat
the beauty
the purity
the essence
The GAME REMAINS

Paul Armstrong

Exploitation

I was a cannibal,
until I heard the painful cries of man;
and I ate the animals and the fish,
until I heard their screams for mercy;
and I ate the plants,
until I heard their whispers of distress.
Now as I sit alone judging my life,
I am left with nothing but feelings of remorse.

Iyad Matuk

Tintagel

There is a place that I well know,
Where Arthur's knights once trod,
And ocean waves reflect the glow,
Of sunsets made by God.

The fading sun each summer night,
Burns purple, red, and gold,
A heaven-sent, ethereal light,
As day starts to enfold.

Where fire-fringed clouds drift on the air,
A romantic fantasy,
Where man can dream with little care,
In musing reverie.

A glowing cloud, I see appear
King Arthur clothed in gold,
Then Lancelot and Guinevere,
Just as the legend's told.

'Tis but a dream; to me it's real,
An eternal touch of joy,
A preter place where I just feel,
At home - I am a boy!

Ernest Smale

An Early Beginning

We were just dozing off on that September morn,
When your Dad called to say that you soon would be born.

Aunt Squish and Grandma got up with great haste,
And rushed to the car with no time to waste.

We hoped to see you arrive on the scene,
But Mommy was tired and not very keen.

So out in the hall we waited, excited with joy,
To find out if you were a girl or a boy.

We heard happy voices and then a wee cry,
And we let our tears flow and released a big sigh.

It was 6:25 when Mommy had her first glance,
And five minutes later, Dad gave us our chance.

To hold you and kiss you and be thrilled with you so,
And we really had difficulty in letting you go.

It was only the start of your new little life,
But something we will never from our memory wipe.

Sharon Badgley

In The Light Of The Storm

Blue eyes shine brightly in the light of the storm.
When your brother was taken away, at first I could not see, only clouds.
I will not stop my tears for him.
He will always be a part of me.
But, you are here, and your blue eyes shine.
You are also a part of him.
When you smile, you laugh, and tease, I see him there in you.
My love for him will never die.
He was here for only fifteen years.
I shared those fifteen years with him.
I will cherish my memories of him forever.
You are here still.
You have a world of love to give.
I have world of love for you.
When you smile, laugh, and tease, you help to ease my pain.
I will cherish every moment I have with you.
You are a gift of love.
I will do all I can to keep you safe and warm.
Your blue eyes shine brightly in the light of the storm.

Ruth Sabatula

271

The Seasons Of Romance

How restless are the days of spring
When yearning desires blossom
Shy, naive eyes meet and rapidly part
Cautious gazes return with astounding precision

Smiles emerge with childlike simplicity
While the hands of life's clock hold still
Cupid defeats the unsuspecting duo
A blush of crimson envelops their facades

Dreams are shared, aspirations revealed
Tender lips press together in a first union
Gentle caresses bring shivers and tingles
Loving embraces breed welcomed security

The mercury rose with passion
But an end to the dog days nears
Verdure changes to hues of scarlet, pumpkin, and gold
Emotions commence to stir

Cupid cold-heartedly retrieves his arrow
A single curling leaf flutters to the ground
Tears flow freely as interlocking fingers slip apart
But a minute piece of love's pie remains

Katherine A. Stein

When Does It Stop?

The pain, the suffering and all the despair.
When will it stop? Doesn't anyone care?

The people are screaming, the children they cry.
For whatever the reason, won't you please tell me why?

Make the noise stop! Please make it cease!
The worry, the fear, form a permanent crease.

The enemy periled, through torrents of rain,
Not thinking the plan was to cause us much pain.

The children are sleeping, when the enemy comes.
All they've had for dinner, is water and crumbs.

The suffering, the pain, the killing, the tears,
All this and more, for so many years.

Make it all stop! Oh make it all cease!
Won't someone listen, to this little voice, please?

When I look in your eyes, I see hatred and fear.
Please stop the violence, just stop it right here!

I'm tired of crying, over someone's else's loss.
The result is not worth it, it's just not worth the cost.

When the war's over, when the guns stop their noise,
Then, only then, sir, my heart will rejoice.

Jaime-Lynne Gallant

Journey Through The Autumn

Close your eyes while we listen and hope for a dream
We're surrounded by country, such a mystical theme
There we'll capture the sky for its radiant blue
Savor sunset and sunrise in shimmering dew
We embrace with our thoughts, in the clouds up above
With our blanket of clover wrapped in beauty and love
And drink from its splendor so pleasantly pure
Nature's gift for her children to partake and endure
For the heat has now left us shed not but one tear
Only summer now gone while the autumn draws near
With its colors all changing in mosaic portray
Our great lake's high white caps, a fearsome display
Autumns breathtaking air, how inspiring and sharp
Hear the wind singing to us though an eerie tuned harp
Behold the aurora, her dance to delight
They claim it's when lovers should shine just as bright
That is just how we are, so unique yet so tender
Engulfed by a season where our souls will surrender

Robin L. Cross

Neighbors

What would we all do without neighbors
    When troubles come, clouding our sky?
One might as well live on an island
    Alone, where no one will shout, "Hi!"

When wishing to go on vacation
    To visit a son or a daughter
We simply toss keys to our neighbors
    Saying, "please give our house plants some water."

"Will you see that our cat gets some breakfast
    And fresh air at least once a day?
Will you make sure the paper's not scattered
    By winds that could blow it away?"

"Please watch that the children don't litter
    Or throw things. Please keep the gate shut:
And when the grass gets a bit lengthy
    Will you try and see that it gets cut?"

God bless all good neighbors and love them:
    They're always on hand to assist you.
They'll tell you to have a good journey
    And when you come back how they've missed you.

Lilian McCullagh

Mysterious Night

At early evening time when all is calming down,
when the slowly sinking sun makes twilight gone.
The insects come alive and slowly fly around,
some of them are creeping, and many others chirping.

Their soft music is preluding, as the night is approaching,
now the dark is settling, and upcoming stars are twinkling.
The frogs are awakening, their concert is in the making,
it's their high time for courting, nature is well going.

Then the crescendo in sound as more frogs come around,
Their high light in the night, to keep up with new life.
Now the moon is upcoming and shooting stars are falling,
in the mystery of night, strange sounds are causing fright.

And now an unseen owl is wooing, a lonely dog is howling,
Frightened in the night, in the mystery of silvery moonlight.
And the concert is on going as a gentle wind is blowing,
from the fields of hay, perfume scent floating in the air.

Then far in the universe, stars are closing their sleepy eyes,
as the upcoming sun's golden rays bathing the fields in haze.
And up in the height a ditty of the lark flutters in the air,
praising the Lord almighty for his wondrous nature and care.

John Kerekes

The Making Of Gold

The rim, thy shank, the vessel
wet,
with Spring's water.
Beset the lead.
Wandering of towns, of Earth and sky
what a violence, the clouds would cry.
Lorn of bode, almost like crust.
Sheaves of laughter pile rye.

Forward young buds of Neptune's delight
cross the Asian desert, bright.
Could this be a marksman ye, who lamented
the sacred fountains shore.
Under the fiery ore.

The giant red orb, Axle Rose, cosmic and great
burning flour from mills of late,
Mata Hari magenta and green, loving the ore
of gold unseen.
Arian fairies, sylphs set in gold
The calendar burning, from time so old.

Marko Kiansten

Blue White Haze

How I cling to those days with the blue White Haze,
When the earth is wrapped in scented warmth.
I remember them well, for all they can give.
When the summer sun reaches into the depths of a soul,
To heal the wounds left behind from the unforgiving cold.

How I cling to those days with the Blue White Haze,
Our Creator's masterpiece, indeed.
Do we see, smell, feel, and touch all that which He has made?
Each day, so new, yet never to age,
For by dawn, the Master turns yet another page.

How I cling to those days with the Blue White Haze,
Softly washed hues, its outline not seen.
Ingest with pleasure this feast before thee,
Become straight and strong and know you are blessed.
Pale gold, purple, rose and blues are readied for your rest.

Should you choose the beauty of these days,
And the skies begin to gray.
You won't despair, but feel joy and peace,
For memories of days gone by, will keep thee.
For now you have become the apple in our maker's eye.

Diane Farr

My Favorite Things

When I'm feeling sad and weary
When the day is dull and dreary

It's time to turn to thoughts of things
That makes me smile, that happiness brings

Special memories, old friends and places
Looking at my grandsons' faces

A little blonde head at my side with a book
Turning the pages so we both can look.

Listening to my grandsons' laughter,
The sound remains a long time after.

A long quiet walk on a sandy beach
That stretches as far as the eye can reach.

Watching a sunset, smelling a rose,
The scent of a woodfire in my nose.

Bob Seger's music, getting lost in book
Leaving my troubles and cares on a hook.

I'm suddenly warm with a feeling of love
I look up, and the sun is shining above.

Jean Timm

Confused

One moment I'm up, the next I'm down,
when should I smile, when should I frown?
It's not that I need to try, it's natural with you
if your looking upset, of course I'll be blue.
There's been times I've been overwhelmed with happiness,
It appeared the sun would never rest.
Then I sense the fullness of your absence,
Although I see you their "really" your not.
Should I try and win or maybe I should pass,
Maybe all my hearts emotions will shatter like glass.
I'm really confused - that - I hope you can see,
I feel I'm with you "yet" your not with me.
Are you really in love or just surrounded by mist,
Heaven knows, I really can't taste our last kiss
I'm so confused, do you love me - truly care,
Maybe it's emotions you really can't share!

Kathryn Morrison

Untitled

There was a moment in time
when I ceased to be
the day you stole childhood away from me
I was your hostage, shackled-up in your lies
you fed me nothing but pain and sour lullabies
You jailed me up far too long
and took away my youthful song.

Where am I now I cannot say
'cept distant from my yesterday
abundant strength unlocked your dreary cell
'till God came down and rang my freedom bell
Yet not quite there on future paths
I often question what tomorrow has.

It seems my hope will let time fly on
'till I reach tomorrow when today is gone.
Fearless and free I will look back to see,
that sad child that once was...me.

Ann Politis

Untitled

Dream merchant, dream merchant sell me a dream
When gypsy moon maiden sails on sky sea
Bring chimera rapture to awaken my scream
Drunken gardenia blossom reverie

Deliver a knight on steed bold and blue
To champion my maidenhood prize
Or matador courageous and true
With deep honey cacao eyes

Make me a celtic queen of intrepid bouquet
Conquering emerald isle with brandished sword
Or flamenco dancer in brilliant array
Passionate posturing in each spanish chord

Fill my cup with cimmerian blood red wine
Parchment tome of great Alexandrian Hall
Food of Atlantis on which I may dine
Golden sun dried Mayan Temple Wall

Dream merchant, dream merchant I beseech thee
Guide me to know what I want, what I need
Harmonize the journey of my soul odyssey
For the child has awoken as woman I bleed.

Donna Lee Piper

Pioneer Living

Moon, moon shining bright,
What a glorious, glorious sight,
In the little log house,
Lives a little black mouse;
I have my place with pollution and smog,
Big Maple is lonesome, expecting a hug,
Nice to take a walk by the creek and see,
All the creatures in the waters, stare at me...
Take a drive to those little country towns,
And laugh from all those drunken clowns,
Moon, moon shining bright,
What a beautiful, beautiful sight,
Everything looks scary in the dark,
Here and there the dogs they bark,
Winding river, with dark waters,
I used to be a Farmer's daughter;
Fresh, country air;
But who cares?
Everything is gone...
Visiting is no more fun.

Minnie Dowhaniuk

Friends

We've shared a lot of special times, and confessed to all our fears
We've laughed at each others silly jokes, and shed a lot of tears

It seems we were inseparable, but things are different now
It doesn't mean we're not best friends, but things have changed somehow

Our priorities are different than the way they were before
Our dreams have so much colour, and our future holds much more

We now have much more friends that we hold dear in our heart
But the one thing that hasn't changed is that we haven't grown apart

Maybe one day we will, maybe when we're old
But I know the memory of you, I will always hold

Maybe when we're famous we'll sometimes meet for brunch
And when we're not so busy, we'll meet at twelve for lunch

I know I sound real sappy, but right now I do not care
We have a special friendship, so many secrets shared

No guy can come between us, no argument, no fight
Because we can't get mad, and because we're really tight

I thought I'd tell you now, before it gets too late
Like when you're married with children, and move to another state

So now I'll end this poem, by saying your a true friend
And that we have a friendship that will probably never end!

Oriel Ramcharran

"The Flower"

The new flower begins life soft and white;
Welcoming the sunlight and reaching for the sky.

Then the rains come pouring down,
Covering the land.
The virgin white is replaced by blue
As the flower gets it first taste of real life.

As the young flower views a more graceful one,
A shade of green takes over the woeful blue.

And all the while that it dwells
In its envious state,
A dark hue of purple oppresses the green.

As the aging flower sees
The error of its passions,
A light shade of red tints its aging petals.

Its sinless heart now stained,
The flower shrinks in a hue of yellow
Away from the world; away from the light.

Time passes by and the flower is now old.
Robbed of all youth and innocence,
The flower is, at last, enveloped in black...

Lisa Schussler

For An Instant

For an instant, a moment in time,
we were together, you and I.
Now that moment is gone, never to return.

For that instant, that moment in time,
everything felt right, felt as it should be,
as I realized you love me.

But we had tempted fate,
had gone against the odds.
We were torn apart,
through no fault of our own.

Now I'm left with the memories
of that instant, that moment in time.
Of what was never meant to be.
My only consolation is that you're
suffering too, because you still love me.

Candice McDonald

The Tree, The Wind, And I

I was looking at a tree one day
We were one the tree and I
The breeze helped the tree whisper a sigh
And I knew that sigh; it relates to you and I
The deep emotions pent up inside so easy to release
Have a deep sigh!
The feeling of relief so sublime,
A simple thing, the trees and wind
They help each other, such love a kindling
Shouldn't you and I?
Be like the trees and wind
A simple thing, friends in nature; such deep reply
Helping keep life simple with a whisper and a sigh!

Josef Paul

Bermuda Triangle

Separated by the sea of a bed,
We were held immobile by our expectations.
We failed to notice
Hamilton playing host to the wind,
Blowing the streets clean of life.

Gathering clouds cast unseen foreshadows.
Across the open louvre windows of our room.
Palms rattled and shook.
Light escaped.
We remained captives,
In a cage smaller than the bed we shared.

The exterior
Wind whipped world
Never touched
The you. The I.
Never breathed life into the we.

Prisca Mary Campbell

Nursing Home Volunteers

As we think about you, we liken you to flowers
We take this time to thank you for brightening up our hours.
We really do appreciate the many things you do,
You fill our hearts with sunshine, our thanks go out to you.

Sometimes when our days are long and needing times of cheer,
It makes us glad when we look up and see a volunteer.
Volunteer means many things - kind, helpful, friend
Someone we can know and trust, in whom we can depend.

Flowers shed a fragrance that's sweet beyond compare,
Just like a volunteer who takes time out to care.
And as each flower is different with a beauty all its own,
So it is with each of you as kindnesses are shown.

As you walk around our home, cheering up our way
You're like spring flowers strewn about to lighten up our day.
Our home becomes a garden path, a pleasure to behold
And just in case you didn't know - you're worth your weight in gold!

Betty Boddy

Dreaming

Thinking of you as we plow the deep ocean
Watching the bow wave with deeper emotion
Living again those moments divine
When I asked and you answered that you would be mine
The stars in the heavens and a new moon on high
These jewels of God all shine in the sky
All these I would give for a glimpse of my Jean
Enthroned in my heart like a beautiful queen

Gord Littler

Porcelain Marionettes

We are born such precious dolls
We see the sun's loving waves bathe
our hearts, clear our minds and bring us peace
And as the Earth and sky come together the dolls dance...
now but not forever.

As time slowly swims by we are merging toward darkness.
We shut our minds, our hearts, away from the sun
away from our peace.
Our faces harden, our limbs stiffen and ropes bind us
to the patterns of the lost.
And we become porcelain marionettes destined to dance
at our masters command.

But now we are old, our porcelain painted faces have faded,
our limbs are cracked, our ropes are torn.
We are placed upon a shelf to be forgotten.
All too soon we realize
that we have always been simple rag dolls
fated to dance in the very same fashion
into the very same gardens of stone.

Kinga Nowak

The Day To Remember

Looking back in the minute of silence,
We realize how much we have left behind us,
People were killing and fighting and dying,
Others were mourning and red-eyed and crying,
Friends and relatives fighting and dying at war;
Peace is what we should strive for.

Some were at camps or fighting and slaving,
Races and cultures repeatedly saying,
"Will today be the final day of the war?"
Peace is what we should strive for.

Remember the people who fought to be free,
The ones who died for you and for me,
Some wear the poppies which are coloured dark red,
To signify bloodshed and all those who are dead,
Those people are dead because of the war;
Peace is what we should strive for.

So realize now that war's not fun and games,
It is death, violence, and blood all the same,
The mighty lion is tame compared to a war;
Peace is what you should strive for.

Robbie Hillstead

Today

This is a time of great violence
We piss on this earth and sit on the fence,
All getting to see with little pretense
The crap on T.V. that never relents.

Fighting each other, both you and I see
Killing our brothers, not a pretty thing be

Let's strengthen our hearts and our minds,
Search for our stars, now's the time
For a better tomorrow
When all young minds may shine.

Waking up from this slumber
To truly be all we can be
Let's bet words make great weapons
And books be the key!

Chris Garside

The Joy Inside

The beauty in the world is hard to find these days,
We must search within to find other special ways.

Outside our doors men and armies will fight,
Inside my home I tuck my baby in tight.
The world is stained, rusted. My baby took his first step,
In me he trusted. The vast waters are no longer fresh,
My hungry child will suckle at my breast.

The rainforest perishes each day limb by limb,
I read his favorite bedtime story, the lights are dim.

A light shower means acid rain falls from our skies,
My son searches my soul through his beaming bright eyes.

Each day puts the earth through more strain. Baby is teething,
My arms help ease his pain. The world around us is falling apart,
My sweet son is able to warm my heart.

The sun warms the earth more with each passing day,
A floppy blue sunhat shades him as he sits in the sand to play.

Your loving eyes speak to me before you fall asleep,
I promise to you, a clean world I will try to keep.

Sleep with tender dreams of tomorrow,
We will figure a way to repay the things we borrow.

Audrey Tamar Anderson

Bend A Bit

Sometimes life can be so hard - we have to bend a bit,
We have to learn to give - before we ever get.
So you remember this my friend, and share a little blame,
For when God created us, he made us all the same.
You take the beggar on the street - he was a man of pride
One careless step, one thoughtless deed, and now his face he hides.
But maybe we could help to restore this man's broken pride
I think God would love us more, if He knew we tried.
But this is not the theme to-day, as life goes rushing by -
"It's take what you can get - never mind the other guy."
But when we are called to Heaven - up around God's Great Throne -
We are all treated equal - no one is left alone.
So why not help your fellow man and learn to bend a bit,
And remember - before you get - you have to learn to give.

E. F. Steinhoff

Death Came Calling

We had just made love.
We both lay spent and dreamy.

Death came calling my name.
It sat on my chest like an elephant.

She reached for the phone to save me.
They came like avenging angels.
Faces in the dark surround me.
I hear their voices as they fight to save me.

I see her face in the crowd.
She sends me her strength across the room.

Rushing now for the hospital.
I see the Emergency doors open.
I relax and the lights go out.

Two days later I find her face again,
waiting for me by the bed,
as I climb out of the dark.

Death has gone home.
Life begins again.

Glen M. McKay

275

Wandering In The Dark

Past, present and future we walk.
We ask amiss; unprotected we fight
and lose, and wonder how and why.
In darkness being is senseless and silent.
In our fear we are comfortable,
Unknowing the destruction of our own will.
Once innocent; then choose and turn
Away, we wander in that darkness.
From Innocence; turn and grow in
Grace, we walk and live in light.
In darkness will and power battle man.
Know the truth, seek the light and
Submit our will.
Darkness dies; the battle is won,
We have found our way.

Alexandra Swinimer

A Leaf For All Seasons

Spring has sprung, oh glorious day, as little buds the trees we spray,
We are so young, we are so free, to paint the boughs in velvet green.

She comes and visits to check and see,
As covering the trees we must be,
Being so happy in the summer sun,
Shining and whispering of new life begun.

Days are warm and wonderfully gay,
Below us, happy children play,
Blankets of green lay at our feet,
Love and laughter can be heard so sweet.

Soon time passes and we must prepare,
For different colours we must wear,
Varied greatly in shade and hue,
Upon the hilltop a spectacular view!

Suddenly, the season is for us to leave,
Letting go of our home, letting go of our dream,
Floating to the ground together we lie
Our time is gone, we must die!

Don't fret and please don't weep, you see we aren't dead we're fast asleep!

Adelene Gushue

Calamitous

Gazing at the stars above,
We are both, young and in love.
I hold your hand, and you mine,
Your touch as pure, as a dove.

In your eyes, the stars they shine.
You say with me, you'll forever be fine.
I bring you close, and hold you tight.
As we softly kiss, and sip white wine.

Across the sky, a shooting light.
Falls, from the moon so bright.
I envision it is us, going on a ride.
Oh how I wish, there is no end to this night.

As we leave for home, side by side.
All over the world, they could hear how I cried.
For that car that hit into your side,
Did not hear you scream, for you instantly died.

John Baumhartner

Family

When we are all together
We always have such fun.
We laugh and joke and even cry;
My daughters and my sons.

Through times when they were growing up
I may not have always agreed
On things they've said, or things they've done
But tried to give them the lead.

To learn from mistakes that they have made,
From school to friends they've had,
They all grew up so beautifully
I'm proud and very glad.

To say that they're my children
Who used to fight each day
God as my judge, I Love Those Kids
Until my dying day.

Michele Stableford

The Stars

Beautiful stars, silvery dots in the sky that light the
Way down the mountain side.
How mysterious you are, so far away and yet so near.
Falling stars, wishing stars. Is it true that wishes
Come true when one of you lights up the sky with a spark
So bright that children love to see and lovers dream about?

Standing on top of the mountain, or walking by the sea shore,
I have seen the beauty of a starry night, so bright a night
That shadows escorted people enjoying the night air as
They happily walked laughing, singing accompanied by the
Melody of sound coming from the crickets, frogs and many
Other creatures of the night.

Wonderful stars, the merriment which you bring to people
As they gaze at you, remains within to be expressed in
Stories for children on a cloudy night.

Jorge Luis Serrano-Estrada

Fall

Red green, orange green, brown tips, and yellow.
Water rippling, lapping the crumbling concrete gray,
Where fresh black bars mirror in the weedy murk.
Treasures there for Mallard all alone
dipping, bobbing, rejected by the other ducks, chased,
his moulting plumage pecked and pulled.
Fat lazy carp sliding under,
ignored by duck - equal size, so no contest.
Both lonesome, alone, or in such different states
uncomprehending the other.
Putta putta, a late cruiser,
rocking the Mallard up and down,
hooting to the sculls, whose backs to the sound,
sweating at the oars, swish plup, swish plup
cannot see or hear the danger.
The harsh crying of blue Jays
gathering for warmer climes, as the hard sun
blinding directly into dazzled eyes
frenzies tiny insects, dancing summer's
dying rites.

Janet M. Last

Another New Day

As I gazed from my window one morning,
Watching two Blue Jays at play,
The sun breaking through the clouds in the sky,
I thanked "God" for another new day.

With my dog up the mountain I wandered,
And sat on a rock for a spell,
My eyes looked up to the heavens.
And I felt in my heart all was well.

The country around me so splendid,
Clothed, by nature's own hand,
In colors to show of "God's" glory,
Of this wonderful world that "He" planned.

What a great pity man spoils it,
By violence, hatred, and greed,
Why can't man all live together,
Race, colour, or creed.

'Tis a beautiful world that "He" made us,
So let's all live together and say
Thank you "God" for this life that you gave me,
Thank "You" for another new day.

Jessie Davidson

Childhood

I sit here beside a babbling brook
Watching children run hither and yon
And I daydream of my childhood days
When life was so carefree and fun
Never a care to mar my days
For a child does not worry 'bout life
They accept what is theirs to have
And worry not of what they don't
For the sun and the sky beckons
They enjoy what is God's gift to them
The flowers, green grass, and tall trees
Oh a child is so innocent and free
And I sit here daydreaming and yearn
For things that have long passed for me
For the days that I cannot recapture
And for things that were never to be

Heather Sampson-Butz

Maybe

You can forgive me all my lies,
Watch my every move with carrying eyes,
Be always there for me
Always help me to see the reality,
You can give me your hand when I'm scared of a friendly ghost,
Touch me when I need it most,
Or just simply give me something
That I cannot get on my own.
  And then I'll whisper - "You can come in..."
  And maybe I'll let you to win,
  Maybe I'll show you regard,
  And maybe, just for you, I'll open my anxious heart.
Maybe I'll let you to turn off the light
And ignite the candles on a cold winter night.

Katherine Majewska

Proposal

The day you asked me to be your wife
was the happiest day of my life.
You are the prince only I could dream of when I was five.
Now, you're here beside me
you make me feel so alive
I now wear the diamond you gave me
you love me and that I can see.
Money and articles are petty
compared to the feelings we have for each other
they are so small, they just don't matter
you've made me see life through the stars - your sparkling eyes
I feel so comfortable with you
I don't have to put on a disguise
you are the only one in life that I need my friend.
And I long to love you and live with you until the end.
I hope and dream as the time grows nearer to our wedding day
I love you; there's so much more to say
one day soon we'll be husband and wife
all I want to do is make you happy
for all the days of my life

Louise Blahovici

The Price Of Alcohol

A Couple a' beers at me favorite bah
Was all the stranger said.
My reason for breathing was taken away,
Her name has been etched in stone.

My name too will soon be added,
To that stone which marks my love.
Some lead through the heart will reunite us...
If God forgives me.

I swear I didn't see 'er he said to the court,
As if this was a valid defence!
I haven't seen her either...
Or talked to her, kissed her...
Held her.

The stranger began to quiver,
As his sentence became airborne.
I don't want to spend me life in prison!
Yeah? And I just want my wife back.

Jeremy Travis

Going Home

Carved on a birch in a yard well treed
Was a heart with initials we could still clearly read

Peeled back with age was the red brick siding
Stories within for years had been hiding

A hole in the chimney the size of a football
Condemned sings decorated every wall

The porch to the house was no longer attached
Birds in the eaves waiting to be hatched

Ah what a sight we saw that day
Where once as youngsters we were happily at play

Years were not kind and my heart felt pity
For our childhood home up in Dawson City

Charlotte Hughes

First Jump

I want to fly, as in my dreams
Want to take the leap of faith required
To make those dreams come true

Cold rushing wind screams its hunger for me.
I am pulled out and away into the frightening unknown

Fabric flaps and suddenly —Peace, Tranquillity, Euphoria
As I check my life lines and listen to the wind whisper
Seductions.

I am spellbound by my desire all at once
to look, to feel, to sing, to laugh, to cry out in sheer bliss and

Flirt with the wind

I now see how easily Icarus was hypnotized by the illusion of freedom
and the temptation of the air.

The voice of my Daedalus crackles,
Ripping through this reverie,
Reminding that the jealous planet reclaims me.

Reluctantly I heed my lessons and meet with the fury of gravity

but not even the jarring reality of solid earth can steal away
this ecstasy of dream-flying

Still coursing through my blood.

Laurel Tokuda

Of Tomorrow...

Have you ever seen a sky of such crystal mirrored in blue -
wandering and free.
    Yes, once I...now, only white scars across its hue.
Have you ever seen mountains rise as swirling clouds give chase -
whispering to the heavens.
    Yes, once I...now, only naked a treeless and barren face.
Have you ever seen rivers sparkle a golden glitter as they dance -
quenching a thirsty land.
    Yes, once I...now, the black desecration of life's diminishing chance.
Have you ever seen trees of emerald towering and free -
piercing sky holding earth.
    Yes, once I...now, only you need always destroy to be.
Have you ever seen life so regal living hunter with prey -
respect for necessity.
    Yes, once I...now, you arrogantly assume the right of judgement day.
Have you ever seen a world born not knowing conflict or death -
no anguish or despair.
    Yes, once I...now, not since you took your first breath.
Have you ever seen a tomorrow where not a shadow cast on the earth -
paradise never lost.
    Yes, once I...now, only chaos since the dawn of your birth.
Have you ever seen a world bequeathed in trust to no longer keep -
living and time all spent.
    Yes, once I...now for all your kind will soon lonely sleep.
And do you remember a living blue-green world so lush and just -
all life emerging as one.
    Perhaps, once I....now, even my memories have turned to dust.

Mario Pennetta

Gold And Silver

    Gold is like Summer
The Summer sun spreads its beautiful golden rays across the land.

    Silver is like Winter
The Winter clouds drop a silvery mist of ice crystals to the ground.

    Gold is like a Lion
A lion who's goldish, muscular body sways proudly in the bright sun
    radiance.

    Silver is like a Wolf
A wolf who howls his sad distant song to the moon.

Kristina Coupland

To Be Led Or To Lead

The gentle lamb so soft and cuddly
Waiting to be led to greener pastures
By his master the Shepherd
Safe with the flock

The ferocious wolf so hard and deadly
Waiting to eat
By his own will he survives through hardship
and perseveres

And through it all they both live
They both take a mate
The gentle lamb may have many
For his life he is given

But the wolf will take but one
And through his life remain
For wolves mate for life
And the strongest wolves lead the pack

John Thomas McCormack

Windows From The Outside

I often stood by storefront windows
Viewing each with critic's eye
The merchant's best-display, dispose
To enter in that I may buy.
Jumbled potpourri take shape, reside
In continuity after impressions coalesce
To patterns of choice the mind's eye can address
From my standing viewpoint-windows from the outside.

I often sat where the trains chugged by
In lowly grass near bands of steel
I jumped and waved-then a warm goodbye
To the caboose's window and the click of wheels.
Now all is past when time hitched a ride
To mega markets and transit trains
And the computer age rather than simple lanes
Create chaotic choices-windows from the outside.

Richard Roberts

Universal Love

A cool winter night, with snow so soft, it's like down,
Unmarked, unprinted by prowlers of the night.
The moon full, lighting the sky with diamonds, it see's a couple
    lying below,
Embedded in the snow, while in soft embrace.
Naked for the heaven's above that listen to the soft murmurs of love.
Two of God's children folding to one, coming together, falling apart.
Little flakes of snow flutter ever so softly.
Taking refuge on the soft white flesh.
Feeling the body heat, they form into tiny droplets of moisture.
Then the moon with all its glory, listen for breathing but there is none.
The stars see eyelids close.
The sky see's the entwined lovers in deep sleep.
The flakes while landing feel the warmth turn stone cold.
And God, seeing, hearing, feeling everything,
Reaches down and takes them into his loving arms.
Brings them, his children, home, to Heaven where they belong.

Diana Strader

Natural Equation

Whether bug, bird, animal, person
The male being the exactness of the female;
Their being identical—flesh, blood, mind,
Their reason inverted—genital, voice, purpose;
Inverted reason, male and female,
Identical beings, female and male,
Natural reflections forming a natural whole.

Debbie Hamilton

Marriage

This marriage is blessed from heaven above,
United together a life full of love,
The groom at the altar waiting to first see,
The beautiful bride his wife to be.

The vows that you say, you'll honor each day,
Your love for one another will show in many ways,
With the things you do and the ways you touch,
In the years to come will mean so much.

Life's path is never straight and true,
But with each other you'll always get through,
Growing closer together with the passing of time,
I will always be yours, you will always be mine.

A long time you have waited to find one another,
Always a true friend but also a lover,
Love, honor and cherish for the rest of your lives,
Together forever you will be husband and wife.

Donald R. Sprunt

Letting Go

I watch you through eyes from afar
Trying vainly to spread the mist
To catch a glimpse of you.
I pray that I night be able
To stretch out a steadying hand
To guide your faltering footsteps
Away from the edge of the abyss.
No one has told us of the intensity of faith
In which we would need to rely upon,
In you, in God and in ourselves, as mothers.
Tread surely, my child,
And know that our love
Awaits quietly in the shadows,
Ready - should you ever need to draw upon it.

Beryl Cheater

Cloud Of Desire

Sculpting a cloud to the image of my essence,
Under the light of apprehension; I study patience.
I gather memories slowly, quietly.
Who will oppose their tranquillity?
I lay aware as I wait.
Longing for my fate,
Eager for a consciousness.
Knowing that this timelessness,
Was not meant for me.
The cloud will remain, silent witness,
Spectator of my foolishness;
For I have yearned to exist.
I have dared crave, beg, even insist
In a warm, cozy womb to be woven
Expecting, desiring, hoping, wishing even,
That no one would, willingly or not, slay me
Until I had a chance to be.
Is the purpose of being, worth my desire?
I wished I could answer.

Sylvie Pratte

Born Again

And let's move on, you say,
Trying different places, seeing other faces,
Dropping some of your traditions,
Life is taking a new definition.
And on your own heading to the unknown!
You pick yourself a new homeland.
With all the warmth it welcomes you.
Like a mother protects you,
Hugs you, helps you reach your dream.
Hey! I'm born again!... you scream.

You dig your roots deep in its grounds
You search, you find; you fall, you rise
And to your own surprise...
You are only searching for the old,
Longing only for your past
Renewing all your former habits
Not giving your chosen home its credits.
Afraid to mingle with the new,
You hide yourself behind a mask
And ask:...Am I truly born again?!

Alice Hanna

Good And Not So Good

Experienced from a far, innocent up close
Two opposites, yet one person
Two faces, two souls, yet the same person.

Is this possible to be experienced yet innocent?
Can a person cross from either and then return?
Is it realistic for innocence in a foreign world?

Maybe for some who have yet to understand
the workings of the foreign land.
Yet innocence in a foreign society can disappear

Into experience in a matter of seconds
If one is not careful.
One must protect their innocence until ready for

Experience.
But when is that?
One can be

Experience from afar, innocent up close
Two opposites, yet one person
Two faces, two souls, yet the same person

Lisa Foster

The Vision

One night, as I tossed and turned in my bed,
    Trying desperately to rest my weary head.
I spotted a shape in the vanity mirror,
    That made my whole body shiver.
Closing my eyes in a fright,
    With the hope of avoiding the dark light.
I knew there was more to my tension,
    And that I had uncovered a whole new dimension.
My heart raced as I opened my eyes,
    Hoping and praying there would be no surprise.
To my utter dismay while turning my head,
    She stood patiently waiting on top of my bed.
I traced her black silhouette against my powder blue curtain,
    Only to discover that she was indeed the Virgin.
Quickly, I plunged underneath the blanket,
    To prevent myself from becoming frantic.
Could it be possible that I had seen an apparition,
    Or maybe..., just maybe I simply had a vision.

Karen Maria Santos

The Swamp

A most disdainful sight, to see the rotting
trees and grass.
The roots that have no function, but to topple
monsters of the past.
The stagnant water pools of rain, and melted snow
on this terrain.
And yet to other eyes are seen a picture, blue,
browns, yellows, green
The greens of life anew, reaching for the sky
of blue to form the monsters once again.
The insects, reptiles that romp, and start the
cycle of the swamp.

Cyril D. Butt

"The Hidden Treasure"

Many shall seek but few shall find the hidden
treasure which is only Mine, share I shall with
those that seek My Name to always keep.
   My pearl is worth more than silver or gold
and can never, no never be bought or sold,
neither fame nor fortune can purchase My treasure
only the soul that is Mine forever, when the day
has come for you to see My pearl in all its
splendor, stay you will never to leave The One
Who is The Sender.
   The net that is cast into the sea shall gather
up all off thee, the chosen and defiled it shall
reap, the chosen will have a place to keep, the
defiled will know what it's like to weep.
   On high the chosen will know Him well, the
defiled will know what it's like in hell.

Rosalind Whalen

Modern Living

Troubled waters, death in time.
Toxic waste, islands of grime.
Holes in the ozone, fish on the shore.
Modern day life till life is no more.
Blood in the waters, acid, the skies,
ruining creation, burning our eyes.
Children with sickness like never before.
Is our future filled waiting at death's door?
Poisoned bodies. Poisoned minds
realizing sure death through new research, new finds.
Killing our offspring by force and by feed.
Killing creation through poisoned seed.
Who will clean up this nation of ours
before permanent damage and permanent scars?

Mary S. Watt

The Days Ahead

Yesterday has past
Today is yet to last
And tomorrow will gain another friend.
But someday this world will end
And leave yesterday the very last.

We all know we need this earth
Let us give our loves worth
So their will be a yesterday a today and tomorrow
And we can live our lives without sorrow.

Let their be many days ahead
So we never have to bury the dead
Now that you have read
I hope this poem will be said,
In the days ahead

Debbie Abeling

"On Perceptions"

Who am I, except what I am perceived to be?
To the one who pre-judges me,
I am not who I am
But who I am expected to be.
Am I simple-minded and uncomplicated?
Possibly...
Am I wise and complex?
I could be that too, but...
What you see is what you want to see
And you have already pre-judged me
So what you see may very well be what is in you
And not necessarily a reflection of the real me.
I would really like you to see me
Yes, the same me that I see
But, is there still such a possibility
After this well-intentioned society
Has dictated that a particular label
Must be appropriate and just,
For one who looks like me?

Horace Benjamin

Forever Young

Take my hand and walk with me
To the land of time gone by,
It's down the road of yesterday
To a place of golden sky,
Where time stands still, and peace abides
Where memories song is sung,
There within the heart of hearts
You remain, forever young.
Time may change the landscape
But the earth is still the same,
All that grows upon it
Recalls from whence it came,
Yet even with the changes
Though all the bells are rung,
There within the heart of hearts
You remain, forever young.

Beatrice Brayshaw

Spring Is Come

Spring is come, hark you heralds all
To the first faint flutterings of robin song,
And the bittersweet scent of earth
New warm from a sun too long cold.

It is time; the world is re-awakened
In the pearl-pink buds of quince
And the shy and tender green of shoots
New-sprung from the forest loam.

Skies are blue; winter cloud has fled
Before the unspoken promise now fulfilled.
Many a heart beats fast as life is born anew,
To breathe the silken zephyrs of another spring.

Shine on sun; sing to me of warmer days to come,
And velvet nights when crickets sing.
Oh, for the homely drone of bees
And hummingbirds buzzing in the wisteria vine.

Sandra Matskiw

Solitude

It is time for the blazing sun
To sink into the ebony depths of the tranquil ocean;
The scarlet hue reflects off its glass-like surface.
A lone form
Glides through the rippling sea
Murmuring its woeful song.
Its solitary call
Reaches the eagles who soar high
In the vast, golden sky
And extend into the deepest abyss
Of Neptune's creation.
The sun vanishes into the shadowy sea
Ignoring the pleas
Of the moaning creature.
And as the milky sphere
Ascends into the blackening sky,
The woeful song of the whale dissolves
Until only the echoes of its cry
Can be heard in our minds.

Cynthia Renee Burke

My Heart Cried

Oh! To be there again, my heart cried.
To see the clouds, slowly drifting by.
The tall pine's, the snow-cap peaks,
reaching high into the sky.
The tiny cabin in the valley below,
beckon's me back, yet again,
to play in the deep, soft snow.
I watch the dark, grey smoke rise high
from the chimney stack, only to blend with
the snow-cap peaks, and disappear again.
My heart cries for the solitude and piece
I once found there; will I ever! See it again?
My heart cried.

Corinne Gostick

Heritage Day

I am glad to be here on this day
to see the children so happy and gay

To see the streets alive with people
and to hear the bell in the ol' church steeple

To see the horses trot along once more
to deliver the produce to the merchant's door

I am glad our town has been restored
to see this day has made my spirit soar

The town fell to ruin when the gold rush died
after the fire, few buildings survived

Then came the vandal's and looter's too
they came in swarms like the locust do

The damage they were doing hurt me so
for, you see, I am buried six feet below

To see the destruction and carelessness
is more than a soul can bear

So, it gives me great joy and pride today
to see our town restored this way

Perhaps, if more people care the way you do
on the next Heritage Day, they'll be honouring you, too!

Sylvia Hurd

When You Look At Each Other

Remember when you look at each other,
To see each other your friend.
Yes to see each other as friends,
Who love each other with Unconditional Love.

When you look into each other's eyes,
Let there be Trust that never dies.
Forgive each other when there's wrong,
And love will stay strong.

My dear friends, there will be difficult times.
But remember back when, you first grew to love each other,
And love will conquer all! Yes love will conquer all.

Please Build each other Up, and not tear each other down.
Because this is God's Kind of Love that never falls down.
I know that this is all true,
When you are soulmates from the heart.
And what God has joined together,
Let no one take them apart.

Tracy Marontate

Gold Reminds Me Of You

My brother said to me, listen for it is the time
To say goodbye and when we meet again,
We may be just another nutrient
In this vast universe

For 'tho we've travelled high in the sky
Over land and sea, and often-times met
And enjoyed each other's company,
I fear you'll not be back this way again
But please keep faith with me.

And when my ashes are scattered
Over the Frazer River, say a prayer
And remember me - my love of God, family,
Gold-panning, books taken from the shelf
And sincere company.

When you, with my brothers and my sisters,
Gather to pay homage and reminisce,
Know that 'tho my ashes are scattered,
Yet shall I live abundantly,
Within the fullness
Of your memories.

Suzie Cooper

A Picture For Mom And Dad

If I could only find the words
To paint the picture in my heart,
I'd tell the world to stop and view
My greatest single work of art.

I'd paint a glowing summer scene
With golden sun and cloudless sky,
And stately mountains looking on
Where miles of velvet meadow lie.

I'd make the meadow green and free,
As wide-eyed as my childish ways.
The warm and lustrous sun would keep
Your kindness, strength and gentle praise.

The ancient mighty mountain range
Would guard the years you've helped me through.
The sapphire dome of endless sky
Would hold the love I have for you.

Alas! I have at my command
But scribblings from a poet's hand...
Just words to frame a work of art
They are for you, drawn from my heart.

Larissa Ramsky Covato

281

Where Angels Fear To Fly

I woke today to find my sorrow still with me.
To live each day, is to live an eternity.
A shell of a man, a shadow of my former self.
I ask myself why I continue this meaningless existence that is
    now my life.
Each day offering a new nightmare of her memory.
I find myself in a daze, wondering about my sanity.
Happiness is just a memory, a dream, one which I'll never reach.
Sleep is my only rescue from my living hell, even then you invade
    my thoughts to haunt me.
In a crowded room, or all alone, I'm consumed by this empty
    loneliness from which I can barely survive.
The hurt and pain I endure is only overcome by the fear,
    the fear of continuing on, the fear of what's left of my life.
Our time together was just a beginning, I wanted a lifetime.
I guess young love's naivete, has gotten the best of me.
Love, a complex word, a word that can make one man happy,
    but can kill another.
Trust in love again? Never! I now realize I only have one friend...
    myself.
Angels fear to fly in love, now so do I.
That's where angels fear to fly.

Jay Cooke

I Have Come Home

To the chill of wintry weather,
To life's tempestuous fires,
I have come home.
And I salute you my country, haunting shadow of my destiny
that stalks the horizons of my birthright...
I greet you, adoptive mother of my waking
that quells the cries that knew no quelling
in the gentle cradle that saw me bred...
I embrace you, cold comfort of my tested soul,
my taint and my purge,
that rifles the treasures of my being
in wanton search of gifts discriminate...
I applaud you, sounding-board of my resilience,
reluctant echo of my strength,
that would not mute a soul unmuted
by the mediocrity that saw it bred.

Marlene Jones

Untitled

I'm always in a hurry
To go to those nowhere places;
The side streets and waterfronts
Of other people's histories.
Meeting in unmarked midnights
The revellers of romance or debauchery;
And we dance the dance of strangers
Some we know as fellow journeyman.

Madrigals and marigolds
Violins weeping down the alleys of dawn
Cobblestones and asphalt pathways
Familiar only to the very lonely
Or those brave enough to seek love out.
Summer sand in city buses
The only reminder of the traveller's passing
From those foreign shores beyond our street.

I'm always in a hurry
To be calmed by the leaving.

Nancy Kelly

Untitled

In facing reality, I do not face truth, for I am not able
to find truth in reality. The life I lead is not my own.
It is merely one created in order to appease those whose
only goal in life is to live: a daily grind of waking up,
going to that place of employment which seems to give some people
a sense of warped pride, returning home where sleep overtakes me.
As I sleep however, I dream of a colorful existence: of peace, of
serenity, of solitude, where only the impossible is possible. It is
here where I long to remain, not only in my dreams, but forever. I am
however, forced to live that day to monotony, in a black and white world.

I have not yet been able to break the restraints. I have not
yet broken those rules which bind, not only me, but also the
faceless masses of which I am simply another faceless figure, lost,
still searching. I do not have the strength yet. But I do not worry.
For in time, that power will become mine, or rather ours; all of those
ghostly shadows who will soon come to life. It will be forever and
always. And it is this thought which keeps me alive in this endless
struggle which can only be seen as reality when I am asleep.
It will not be this way forever. Therefore, we must dream!!

Valerija Nerad

Tick Tock

The pendulum of time goes on and on.
To balance consciousness oh the vibrations,
The inclination is to swing in time
Is to swing from and for each other by using this moment in time
By going into the darkest places of time to share your light
You are so like a burning candle and shining ever so bright
For all to see. Joyously go forward freedom wisdom
Flowing freely through the river of life
Your pendulum is important for all, courage to accept
The beauty of being as the pendulum of life goes on and on.
Tick tock, tick tock and so it goes

Gloria Froystadvag

The Fate Of Nature

A calm day - a free way
'Tis opposite, the weather is, from decades ago
A freighter of might became a ship of fright
A raging storm so hungry for life - such strife
    Did they batter down the hatches?
Did they have to navigate - so close to Paradise
    Gitchee Gumee sealed their fate.
Twenty nine perished aboard that ribbon of steel
    Sliced in half by Nature
    Devoured by the Creature
Many prayers were whispered that night
frozen in the darkness - so peaceful down below
The Edmund Fitzgerald - its destination failed
All hopes of survival let go.
God bless them
Ne'er forget them
Superior shall ne'er be tamed
Death is the name of its ebbing game
Ominous silence - the tune of its ruin
A Nightmare that never awakes.

Robert Brown

A Soldiers Eyes

He arose to awaken,
Tired and shaken,
Wrapped in a bandage,
To cover the damage.

He had suffered in the wee hours of dawn,
He was now relaxed and calm.
The only disturbance left on the mind of the soldier now,
Was the question, how?

He desperately tried to hold onto the pain,
But it came down like thunder and rain.
You have to understand the pain was so deep,
So the soldier battled not to weep.
He could not sustain the hurt and pain in his eyes.

This experience of war had made him so wise.
In a flash he saw the light,
the decision wasn't right.
The white sheets were covered in red.
In the few seconds the soldier was dead.

Amber Van Steenbergen

Time

With what do you fill your hours my friend?
Time is a fleeting with none to lend.
Days are consumed with many a task,
What is accomplished - you may ask?
Propelled by work and burdened with care
No time for quality friendship to share.
Do you wander about from day to day,
Weeks run to months, into years of disarray
With no particular direction to follow,
And results in turn are fruitless and hollow?
Time is a limited resource, my dear
Use it wisely or it may disappear.
Identify early your eternal goal
What's the purpose with regard to your soul?
Do activities clutter or seek that end,
Distractions may dictate a selfish trend.
Focus and prioritize with goals in view,
Tailor the future with relevance for you.
You investments mirror the sweat of your brow,
Remember, time is of the essence, we only have "NOW!"

Carolyn Sinclair

Life's Maze

As time strides onward, we must follow our days
Through the months, into years, life's relentless maze
Where we seek and discover, find pleasure and sorrow,
Learn to dream and to love and share hope for tomorrow;
Where we tease as we play, and we laugh and we cry,
See the wonders of Spring, watch the clouds in the sky;
Know the warmth and affection of friends by a fire,
Feel the well-kindled flame of a passion's desire;
Hear the birds sing at sunrise, fear the silence of night,
Be amused by dark shadows that dance in the light;
Enjoy expressions of music, or a chorus of voices,
Climb a hill, take a trip, or be forced to make choices.
Come, walk with me now as we wonder and care.
Could we join in our search for an interlude there
In our maze, where we try to see round each new bend?
Oh please hold my hand tightly, beautiful teacher, my friend.

Edward Gilbert Reid

Purpose, Life Still Clears At One Hundred Years

You've lived one hundred years,
Through family's careers,
Teaching God will share tears,
You enjoy your new dears.

Rockets, atoms one hears,
In car ride home nears,
Wars, peace, depression fears,
From good history veers.

Your teaching, board careers,
Gave a circle that cheers,
Heaven's hopes, earth's, death's fears
Let God guide by His cheers.

Doug Currie

Black Coal

Seven days and seven nights and all the times they make,
Through fallen gold; through whitened cold
And a thirst they could not slake.
For every dawn had spawned new hope
Whose roots were in the earth,
While every sun that walked the dust
Was like a new found birth.

Hosts of hearts has gone towards the etching in the sky,
A steel web with gossamer thread
Where the wheel of fortune rides.
It spins around
As dreams go down held by a string of steel,
The hope of kids,
In the coal he digs,
Seems the only thing that is real.

Ron MacIntyre

Through A Child's Eyes

Through a child's eyes she sees much sorrow,
Through a child's eyes she wonders if she wants
  to see tomorrow,
A child's innocence was taken in the dark,
The next day her family takes her to the park,
She cries in silence every night,
She wishes she was a bird so she could
  take a flight,
The child still has many growing years,
She wonders how she will overcome her fears,
The child felt she had lost her soul,
All she wished for was to become whole,
The child's higher power carried her through
  her sorrow,
So she could one day see a brighter
  tomorrow.

Jacqueline Meierhofer

"Like A Tree"

Children are like a tree;
They must be given the right to grow;
Their roots must be fed with all that nature has to offer;
Their bark not abuse by human hands;
Their leaves kept away from pollution;
With all care given, there should be no reason
not to grow strong and tall,
and "Like a Tree" free from scars
they too will reproduce again and again;
So when you see a child treat it well
as they too will become our new and
unspoiled generation.

Marie L. Beaulieu

Guardian Angel

A nicer girl he'd never known, a prettier girl quite rare
Thoughts of her invaded his sleep, her eyes, smile, voice and hair.
Knowing that he would never deserve someone of such quality
He resigned himself to the hope he'd seen her in "Eternity".

Soulmates can be bound by borders of various kinds and types
And sometimes never united till meeting in the next life.
Where earthly boundaries are erased, politics, religion and race
And all that really matters is that each find happiness.

And if other ties don't bind them, all other factors are right
Both hearts will get another chance to set all the records straight.
"Death", alone will ensure reunion, sad though is the fact
One soul must precede the another, into death, but may come back.

He prayed he'd be the first to go, then visit with her once again
He'd be her Guardian Angel, and shield her from all pain.
To guide, guard and protect her, from all injury and harm
The rest of her sweet earthly life be within reach of her arms.

Then one day they will meet again, eyes sparkling with delight
Smiles, hugs and passionate kisses will fill that day and night.
To that day he will look forward, for that place he'll anticipate
Their lives will be much better than would be their earthly fate.

George Patrick Coleman

Two Souls Parting

The parting of two souls, such a weary feeling.
Though it is only for a while, these two souls find it hard to smile.
Forever in my heart, never will I part.
From a love so true, like my love for you.
The parting of two souls, stirs up loneliness and despair.
Still these souls search and find hope,
And with their loneliness they will surely cope.
The parting of two souls, such a weary feeling.
Forever in my mind, never will I find.
A friendship so strong, to each other we belong.
The parting of two souls, stirs up loneliness and despair.
But really these souls do care.
They are separate, but not for long.
Certainly their love will grow strong.
And their hope are set on meeting again.
The hearts of these souls, together will burn.
And to be together, they do yearn.
The parting of two souls, such a weary feeling.
"Two souls parting"
The parting of two souls...

Clinton W. J. Collins

Death

Death; it seems so final Lord, to my human finite mind;
Though I know it's just a stepping stone to life of another kind.

I cannot see beyond my grief as he lays limp and cold;
Then put into the dark, dark ground, never again to hold.

I know that soul is all that counts, and body is naught but dust;
That's why, though grieved, I can look up, 'cause in You he did trust.

It's beyond my comprehension, Lord, that is why I fear;
My only consolation, is that he held You near.

You alone know all things, Lord, You alone can see;
Why it's best he be with You, and not left here with me.

You know how much I loved him, Lord, but You must've loved him more;
So now I'll trust him to Your care, 'til we meet on Heaven's Shore.

When my time has finally come, then I'll better understand;
For Jesus, Himself, will guide me, He'll take me by the hand.

That's when I will truly say, "O, Death, where is thy sting";
For God will open up my eyes, and I'll know everything.

Death...it seems so final, Lord, to my human finite mind;
Though I know it's just a stepping stone, to life of another kind.

Gloria Reid

The Miracle

There was a time, so long ago-when always I would pray,
This need with-in, so strong it was-just would not go away,
Please God, one tiny little soul-is that too much to ask?
My God, I felt, did not respond-was this to great a task?

The time passed by, my faith still strong-I must believe, I must,
God will decide if it's to be-In God I placed my trust,
The years went by, "give up, they said-it's just not meant to be,"
Be still, my heart, they do not know-what God has planned for me,

God housed this soul for many years-unique, so kind, so bright,
In heaven it was God's right hand-never out of sight,
God knew that soon the time would come-when they would have to part,
The soul was getting restless-though its leave would break God's Heart,

'It must be some-one special-or I'll never let it go,'
So God dispensed the angels-they alone were sure to know,
Who on earth was worthy-who will love it as I do?
And so became 'The Miracle'-'The Miracle' that was 'You'!

Denise van Kessel

Precious Gifts

The day will come when I take my last breath,
They'll lay me to rest, shortly after my death.
But I'll continue to live in a very special way,
My presence will be felt, every single day.

I'll leave you my eyes, that will constantly see,
Leading you to light and setting darkness free.
The sky is bright blue and the grass a deep green,
I give you these gifts, that I've always seen.

The skin that I leave you, will cover the scars,
I'll see your pain mend from beyond the stars.
My kidney or liver you'll need to survive,
This gift from me, now keeps you alive.

The heart that keeps beating, was special to me,
When you feel my love pounding, I'm sure you'll agree.
It's felt pain and sorrow, followed by grief,
But moments like that, for you will be brief.

With each passing day, your sadness will fade,
Someone did listen as you silently prayed.
So I trust in you, to take care of my heart,
For my soul will be broken, if it's ever torn apart.

Karen Halls

My Father's Shoes

Tonight I know I am my father's son, as I stand here in his shoes.
They were a gift beyond all others he gave, when he gave them up for new.

They were a part of him I seldom saw, the times when he was glad.
He wore them like a badge of honour, when he walked a gentler path.

Tonight I wear these shoes of his, though my path be not so smooth.
I walk the rain to find the tears, that haunted me in my youth.

I taste the moistness that clings to lip, but mere raindrops cannot deceive.
My eyes do burn and my throat is strained, but a tear I cannot free.

So I ponder on sadness I have met, to trick my heart's resolve.
But stands firm the thick and hardened dam, or cracks to foretell the fall.

I turn inside myself with rage, for that which I've become.
Until at last I finally see, I am my father's son.

But then at last a tear does form, and another falls and dies.
I know the love that tears my soul, because I've seen it in your eyes.

So tonight I stand and face my path, and thank you for these shoes.
They were a gift beyond all others you gave, when you gave them up for new.

Paul W. B. Carey

My Eyes

My eyes see many beautiful things,
they see a view of a light blue sky
and in it, a gorgeous unicorn with golden wings,
that can fly ever so high.

Other times my eyes will see
many mountains with peaks of soft snow,
and down below a deep blue sea
that never stops and will always flow.

My eyes, they see something called nature,
something natural, something called beauty,
Everything so sweet and pure,
Everything so wild and free.

Renee Christine Rush

Winter's Coming

As the leaves change colour while still on the trees
They fall and they flutter and dance in the breeze,

The frost veils the land like a white satin sheet
And the trees look like people with white fuzzy feet,

The bears get ready for a long winter's nap
And the children stay snuggled on Mom's cosy lap,

The birds all fly south where the weather is warm
As we prepare for our first winter storm,

The snow starts to fall and covers the ground
And if we all listen we won't hear a sound,

A blanket of snow on this wintry day
And the laughter of children outside while they play,

The children make angels as they lay in the snow
Then we all stop to listen and hear the wind blow,

Now our winter is over we get ready for spring
And if we all listen we will hear the birds sing!

David A. Christie

Hope's Hiding Place

Two walking in the snow remarked,
There's beauty in her crystalline
Enchantments, hope hides there for,
Only summer, reveals her advancements,

This spring no heady victory holds
For me, better to hide in winter's shield
Where hope is hidden yet as seasons
Pass us, oh! Those airy lofty heights;

Of summer's sublime embrace, forever
Chasing winter's subtle hidings, as
Spring times light will someday
Bring; hope's effervescence with a

Bouquet; held for summer's warmer
Clime, when bitterness of hopes duress
Will be eliminated; by fond and
Loving clasp of summers bold caress.

John Small

To My Daughter

I see you walking towards school across
the playground, alone, walking with long,
floral - legged strides, the pinkness of your
jacket, like a confident assertion of self,
contrasting sharply with the somberness
of the day.
I feel a small twinge of regret at
your growth. I remember my own feelings
at six and wonder what your own are ...
When you're alone... and I'm watching you.

Lesley Taylor

Untitled

The road winds down through the hill to the sea
There on the beach, walks a girl so lonely
Head bowed, she thinks of a time gone by
Tears fall from her eyes as the remembers
His hands, long and tanned.

Slowly she turns to the sky and smiles
A presence she feels
Reaching out her hand,
She touches the fingertips of that wonderful man

His hand holds her and she turns with a smile
To look into the face of the man that
She loves

"All is well he said" Then he vanished in air
She reached out once more
But he wasn't there
As she turned to leave
She smiled as the place, where his hand
held hers in a brief embrace.

Shirley Robinson

Heart Wanted

Eyes have looked at me, yet
there is so much they don't see.
Arms have held me and hands have
touched,
But pain and fear don't make love
worth much.
Someone who can see the real me
inside,
Someone who knows I have nothing to
hide.
I want love, honestly, and loyal trust,
I don't want second hand lust.
I want to be cared for and loved,
Something true sent from the stars above.
My heart is cold, it feels haunted,
From someone special, there is a heart
wanted.

M. L. Allaway

From Within

There is no right
There is no wrong
Only the weak
Only the strong
Be patient, there could not be one without the other
we need right and wrong or we just wouldn't bother
If you truly believe in something
"Live it out"
But tread softly, there are those that may get hurt
Learn to know yourself
Grow to love yourself
As seasons change, so do we
This is part of our history
What was old back then, may now be new
So keep an open mind and think things through
Leave the doors open
Let the fresh air in
Listen to the words nature has spoken
And start from within

Philip B. Amo

285

Of Mothers

Conscious and Unconscious Minds meet
there is no separation I knew you
The essence of my being; before I was even
a heartbeat.
Flesh within flesh.

My own fetus speaks to me
in Energies
and Vibrations
It's gentle kindness and sweet innocence
Swish, swirl, bump, flex
A telepathic song of movement.
Words have no meaning we speak only in hearts.

The void begins with a tiny ache,
then the gaping wound.
Fear, and unforgivable regrets.
Bonds break and are lost but never die.

We will always be tied- you and I
In flesh, In spirit.
The song is unsung.
Drip, Drop, Tic Toc.

    Nadien Carroll

As I Sit By My Window

As I sit by my window and the light starts to fade
There are memories of the past I hold dear
I think of a father who has long been at rest
And a mother who lies very near.

And many a friend has left me alone
And gone to that home in the sky
Perhaps I will join them, when my work here is done
And I reach the sweet bye and bye.

You've been good to me Lord as I've traveled through life
'though many's the time I have failed
Still I've know all along that your hand was in mine
What a comfort to know that you cared.

I see the dear children, so happy and gay
And I wonder what their future will be
And I earnestly pray as I sit here alone
That these children will come to know thee.

I'm so thankful that Jesus came into my heart
And my sins are forgiven it's true
'though many are lost in this troubled old world
I know my dear Savior, do you?

    Albert D. Ellis

Taking Chances

If there's one thing in life I've learned
There are many events that can be turned
We cannot always sit around and wait
If you don't try, you may begin to hate
If something in life means a lot to you
Fight for it and time will tell you it's true
It may seem it's impossible to win
But open your eyes wide, and don't give in
If you walk away and don't even try
Many things in life will pass you by
Life is about learning and making mistakes
Take chances and you may open many gates
So open your eyes and take a quick glance
Nothings ever lost, by taking a chance
Although for reasons we may never see
Event's in life are always meant to be
So never give up in time to find
All of the answers that will ease your mind.

    Lisa Horvath

Age Of Mind

They say that age is just a state of mind.
Then why, as I look into the mirror of time,
the image I see isn't kind.
The eyes so clear and full of vitality,
while the body deteriorates towards the walk to life's gate.
Shrinking away till life is just a fray of memories,
pouring out all that remains for reminiscing.
So let us pray that we may stay,
with the hope that there will be a strong hand to guide the way.
For growing old can break the soul,
without a hold on tomorrow's glow,
of living for today.

    Kim Lewis

"The Weather Of Our Love"

The sun was out, when you were here today,
Then the rain came, when you went away.
The thunder roared, the lightning struck,
The winds blew strong, my mind amuck.
I loved you dearly, for so very long,
Only to find, your love for me was gone.
You said you'd be there, forever and a day,
Then why was it easy, for you to go away?
My mind was rolling, from love to revenge,
I wanted to hurt you, my heart to avenge.
I couldn't think straight, I wanted to die,
How could you do this, how could you lie?
My world, my life, I thought so complete,
With you, with me, not a drop of conceit.
Sharing and caring, dreams and our hope,
Sunny days, soft breezes, no storms to cope.
All gone, my heart swings in silent space,
Heartache and pain now shows on my face...

    Betty (Goldaline) Dalton

Angel

They say earth is crammed with heaven.
Then it must be true, that angels are in our midst.
I met one this morning.
I wonder if she realizes that her thoughtful gesture
at lifting another's soul,
has allowed her to replace the wings
that have been damaged
and weakened by the occasional fall.

Numerous attempts at diverting those who
come off the path is just an indication
that perhaps the route was to be avoided.
Her wings torn and weathered, she has managed
to dust them off and continue on course.

With an encouraging word she redirects those
who fall off the path and eases them back
on route to their destination.

Wherever we are on course,
she reminds us,
our destination is the same.

    Samm

Darest I Think

The man who loves nature!
The man who loves the sun and the moon!
The man who loves the universe!
The man who loves all human emotions and feelings!
The man who loves the man!
The man who loves himself!
But love the man, who searches and tolerate himself,
For the love of man.
  Darest I think!

    Thomas C. Gilbertson

My Angel

I turned over this morning feeling cold and alone,
Then I saw him lying next to me, Breathing softly,
arms stretched high over his head,
I thought as I gazed in wonder at him, how beautiful,
He looks so peaceful and content lying there,
He looks like an angel with his long raven coloured
hair fanned out like a halo,
His rugged masculine personality gone now
while in deep deep sleep, he in sleep is beauty,
an angelic aura surrounding him,
I watch him sleep, afraid to awaken him,
Lest my angel be gone,
The love I feel for him overpowers me,
I lean down to kiss my angel, he pulls me near to him,
I'm no longer feeling cold, no longer alone,
Look next to you when searching for beauty,
Look to your heart when searching for an angel,
It's there, you'll find it.

Wanda Lorie

Choices

Waves angrily smash against the rock.
Their cries of torment fill the air...
    no control.
Yet, just on the other shore,
Like waves lap gently against their boundary
Knowing they are at rest...
    cared for.
Touching the shore.
Then pulled to the depths again.
The process repeats, both pulled to depth...
    unknown.
Some continue to smash,
    inflicting pain with peace so near.
Others continue to lap,
    resting securely in the care of the Creator.

Lilianne Davidson

Delayed Until Christmas

Yesterday - gazing out my window
the world was frozen and solid
but awkwardly dull and khaki.
a stale, static state
had winter suspended caught in mid-air.
Her first day hung indefinitely
in tight elastic tension.
The whole atmosphere was on edge
so anxious to topple.
Stunting the natural rhythm of life and breath,
mother nature held us on the verge of...

Today - gazing out my window
finally, release
barriers were broken and tension snapped.
Then the rubble had been rewound
with lengths of gauze and cotton batting.
The snowy world felt fresh - brand new
appropriately gift-wrapped just in time.
Now her rhythm (and mine)
could return to relaxed respiration... once again.

Valerie Angus

Why?

The day is finally dawning,
The world is now alive,
The parents are all crying,
Tears run from their eyes,
The others try to hush them,
And put them back to sleep,
But they will never understand,
It's not fair they weep,
The children in the war fields will never see the light,
Because of selfishness,
They have been murdered in the night,
If we had seen the warnings,
Coming clear and fast,
We would never have seen the hate,
Or seen the killing blast,
Why?

Cynthia Cotton

Desire

As she struggles with each and every flap,
The wind is there to give her a firm, quick slap.
Yet she continues to push towards her distant destination.
Nothing on this earth can break her concentration.
The wind, often merciless, is finally on her side,
Giving her a chance for a well deserved glide.
But nothing lasts forever, as she soon discovers,
As her peaceful glide becomes a standstill hover.
Once again, she must struggle with the all too powerful wind.
Never reaching what lies ahead; Only seeing where she's been.
Something inside her refuses to let her stop.
At last, she takes a rest on a bare tree top.
With her new strength and courage, she takes to flight;
And before long her destination is in sight.
She's determined to look ahead and never look back,
But the wind comes up for one final attack.
To no avail, the wind has little effect.
For there is one thing it seems to neglect.
Not everyone has the desire, but the desire is in everyone.

Ruth Ellen Wilson

Love Of Mother

   Mother dear, your so far away, you're flying in
the wind. I don't know what to say.
   The love, the pain, the hurt, the tears, mother Dear
it's been a lifetime of years.
   The fun we've had I can't explain, but mother
dear the memories won't go away. I love you
so more than words can say, I just can't
understand how we float away.
   The heavens above I hear are so green, I hope
for you mother, it's not just a dream.
Mother dear you're darn-tooten, if you come
to earth, I'll come scootin.
Because I remember what you said to me
you are going up to mommy,
I wish you were staying here with me.

Kim M. Smolski

Mother Planet

The earth is me, I am the earth.
Tears of the earth, One drop Two drops
dropped to outer space and converted to stars.
Whispering to my soul,
"In spite of all the things you've done to me
and whatever you do or not,
I love you, I do love you, I just love you, I only love you.
Everyone of you is each one of the stars living within me,
brilliantly shining my adorable alter egos."

Rieko Momoi

"Lost"

Dedicated to: Grandma
A "lost" person is one who struggles with
the truth inside. People who are
"lost" fight with emotional pain,
confusion and hurting. For a
person who's "lost," their
heartache and frustrations are
hidden, this person is unable to
see that there is a
HERO
within themselves. A "lost" soul is one
who might struggle with the unknown.
These people that are "lost" are like
stars with NO shine left in them.

Nicole Hopke

Darktime

It's weird that when the sun goes out everything is changed,
The trees, the clouds, and shadows, all seem to be re-arranged!
There are monsters creeping up the ceiling, and monsters under the bed,
Although you're just "imagining" them, at least that's what mother said.
Yet you can hear their ten inch claws clicking on the floor,
And there's always those frightening ghosts moaning at the door.
You'd go and run to mother's room yet your feet are made of lead,
But they're only there when you think they're there, at least that's
    what father said,
There's a pack of angry wolves outside howling at the wind,
You're lucky you locked the curtains down, of course they're only pinned.
You think they might not be so scary if they didn't eat you and make
    you dead
But they're only dangerous when they're hungry, at least that's what
    I always said.

Allison Myrah

"Epitaph"

Bravely carved from disaster
The thing flourished and grew
Amid confusion
Carefully, it allowed
Conflicts pitted fight to conquer
To gain stability
Until the test of time erupted.

Slowly the thing was crushed
By lock of frankness and restrictions
Insensitivity and silence
And soon the last fragments
Of reality were sucked dry.

Alas! A sharp blade cut the thing's flesh
And out gushed rivers of trust.
It was torn shred, by tiny shred,
Until its bones reeked of
Deception, and it lay dead
In a pool of twisted half truths
Only to be identified
As the manipulated corpse of friendship.

Noreen B. Keats

Untitled

Why a world of many faces
Status, pride and greed is its game
Love and kindness smooths the surface
And men be equal in his reign
Face to face in a mirror, man will see
The shadow close behind him is really what is he

Marie H. Danielson

Inner Sky

Searching for something beautiful,
the streets are ravished and torn.

Hoping for a concordant peace,
the shots rip through hearts and homes.

Believing in truth and innocence,
a child huddles in terror.

Wanting an abode of happiness,
the desolate homeless shiver through the night.

The mind spins on its swivel eye,
crying for a piece of bright blue sky.

Corinne Kessel

Life: The Production

The words I did not hear, the faces were not seen.
The smirks were assumed because of jealousy, not
of hate and disgust.
The laughter and smiles warmed my cold, frozen
heart.
But those smiles had no meaning because they were
of pity.
The acts of friendship were false but well acted.
We were all actors, playing characters on a stage,
performing a play with false joys and pleasures.
But when we were alone to ponder, we realized that
the play is over and we must find a new part to play.
Whether it is one we like, we cannot tell until it
is too late to change roles.
I see the crowds dwindle, the applause grows softer.
My fame is coming to an end.
There will be other plays.
We may not have the same roles but we will always be
in the same production.
The production that is my sad and lonely existence.

Andrew T. Randall

Ten Seconds To Light

Standing tall with hands held...
The smell of lace binds my eyes...
Seconds of anticipation sends
    a nervous energy through my body.
I feel my pulse in my fingertips
    as I squeeze my fists tighter.
This is taking forever...
What am I saying?
My life passes, faster than a lightening flash.
I can't help but to see colours...
Reds, blues, purples, yellows, then black.
The five who held my life in their hands...
    never knew me.

Brad Henderson

There's More To Me

Please don't look through me
The sadness and fear is not what I want you to see
There's more to me
I can feel the strength with in me
Strength that can soar beyond the sadness and
Reach out

Please don't look through me
The sadness and fear is not what I want you to see
There's more to me
There is no fear in the eyes that I look in to
Beyond the fear, there's great victory
There's more to me

Lisa Di Pietrantonio

288

An Amputation

Two months have gone since I have been alone.
The shock and grief have been too much to bear.
But time has dulled the first bleak unbelief,
My mind has now accepted emptiness,
    But not my body.

When first we began our married life
We slept spoon fashion, bodies melded in
A quiet closeness, after making love,
Then comfort and affection kept the habit.

But now I feel, when suddenly I wake,
For one brief instant sense of being held;
A body at my back, an arm across;
An instant only, then I'm wide awake.

Now I can remember reading how
An amputated limb can still be felt,
How empty space can still be filled with pain
So now I know about a missing limb;
I now have my own amputation.

Opal Otto

We Don't Have Time To Dream

Environment and Ozone layer seem to be theme;
The scientists are saying we don't have time to dream.
We have the answer in our hands; the time to act is now,
when we contribute to that goal; we all can take a bow.
A fit and healthy planet is the wish for all mankind,
But it won't happen on its own, we have to take the time,
Recycle this, recycle that, be careful with your sprays,
So we can pass on to our children many fruitful days.
It doesn't matter if you're rich or poor or sick or well,
The same applies to everyone, for we can never sell
This planet that God gave us, when we don't like the scene,
The scientists are saying we don't have time to dream.
The haunting sunset from the shore,
We've seen so many time before,
The snowcapped mountains in their might,
And we believe we have the right,
To take for granted all these things,
Bestowed on peasants, bestowed on kings,
Protect the worldly forests, and all their woody beams,
Perhaps we should be saying we don't have time to dream.

Lilian Evans

The Final Storm

The winds of change call forth
    the restless child of eternity.
Prepare yourself-time is running short.
    A great change is coming!

Listen! Can you not hear? Look! Can you not see?
    The secret voice of the whispering wind?
Building, becoming a rage now; the guardian trees weep.
    A great storm is coming!

Stars, standing vaguely vigilant in their endless plight
    look on, as promises long foretold, are fulfilled,
here, at the end of humanity's long, endless, night.
    Can you feel it? Don't you know? Change is near!

Put your houses in order, oh, great nations of this world.
    Lest you be caught asleep, unprepared
as Gaia aligns herself with the Heavens.
    Their storm banner unfurled shouting, change is coming!

Make your stand, all people of this earth.
    Stand tall, stand true; the time, now, is very near.
There is no turning back, prophecy calls forth
    the great storm, the great change! Do you hear?

Lee Walker-de Souza

Questions

I never quite realized nor understood
the purpose of oneself;

Was I to love oneself or another or
does it really matter?
Who knows? Who cares? No one.
Nobody has the answers.....
Questions that I will always have;

Was I to understand the person who
is of great difference from me.
Searching within each soul but there
was nothing to be found;
I wondered everywhere - got lost
in deep darkness.
And the questions were still there;

Was I to hate people within I don't belong...
Or must I ignore them?
But the will of revenge I can't let go.
So you see I have mixed feeling of
three - what is good? and what is
bad? are just questions I have to ask thee.

Aimee Beboso

Orchards And Pastures...

Apple orchards and pastures, lavish buds that flourish,
the placid edges of nature, in my senses they nourish.
Honeyed bouquets, provide such comforting thoughts,
greet me tenderly with gifts, that can never be bought.

Bound together in fertile carpets, so broad and so green,
mingling throughout the grass, wild flowers are seen.
The bees start their day, with endless motion of flight,
tireless wings go on gathering, all the nectar in sight.

No shadow of pretense, for each day is so grand,
these treasures taken for granted, are seen on the land.
So much is accomplished, as they fly to and fro,
all blossoms are kissed by the bees, row after row.

Humming birds hovering, acquiring their share,
gladdened together in harmony, so lovely and fair.
Secluded and peaceful, it provides comfort to me,
these are just some of the gifts, in the orchard I see.

An intimate peace is inviting, if I take time to look,
some foliage and petals, I have pressed in a book.
Apple orchards and pastures, soft buzzing of wings,
much more than treasures, that thoughts often bring.

Harold A. Sutton

We Should Always Remember

Do you remember, the day's gone by.
The ones who were hurt, and the one's who have died?
The guns that were shot, the bombs that explode.
The ones who felt, to there country they owed.
Or are all of your feelings, just back in your mind.
Do you just forget about them, you leave them all behind.
They died for you, so you can be free.
To live your life, the way it should be.
Do you see those rows, of people who are gone?
Do you realize that when they died,
    this war was not wrong?
These people who sacrificed there lives
They are the ones who heard the screams
Now it's up to both you and I,
To continue their dreams.
But the dreams are all lost if we don't
    Remember...

Penny M. Schrader

289

In The Shadows Of The Night

In the pitch, solemn, black of night,
The new young birch quivered in fright.
The full dusk moon hovered above,
Two young hearts fell in love.
In the shadows of the night.

Moon beams sent quivering rays,
A frosting of silver upon everything laid.
He held her hand on the mossy boulder,
Wishing forever he could hold her.
In the shadows of the night.

Voices of spirits echoes in the trees,
Leaving trickles of laughter not yet seen.
Feeble stars twinkled in the sky,
Like the sparkling jewels deep in her eyes.
In the shadows of the night.

Around a face of creamy pearl,
Luminescent locks of chocolate curled.
Their lips softly brushed together,
That moment will live forever.
In the shadows of the night.

Jennifer Jean Houden

The Snowy Night

A blanket of white covers the ground.
The new fallen snow is all abound.
The children wrapped tight in their parkas will play,
Make snow forts and snowmen throughout the whole day.

But now 'tis the night, there's peace on the earth.
By my feet, a warm fire burns in the hearth.
The stars all punch holes in the dark of the night,
And the moon on the snow is a breath-taking sight.

The wind whistles by in the cool snowy night,
Catching snowflakes that are dancing in the fading moonlight.
The trees are all capped; the world is serene,
It's something that only appears in a dream.

I look up in the sky, and I thank God for life.
I thank God for friends, for family, my wife.
But mostly I thank Him for the beauty on earth,
As the fire dies down in the back of the hearth.

It's late, and I'm tired, so I head back to bed,
With all of these thoughts going round in my head.
I slip in the sheets, and turn off the light,
And I wish for you all a wonderful night.

Robert Taylor Redden

"Friendship"

If I can be your friend and be to you
The kind of friend you are entitled to.
If I can share the hardship that you bear
And in the sharing know that I've been fair.
If I can see good fortune come to you
And not regret I've missed good fortune too.
If I can see you lovin' and be glad
To share that Love that I always had.
If I can learn to fight when you must fight
But first to know that within that it is right.
If I can stay by you when you are wrong
And in temptations prove myself as strong.
If I can take a hurt and yet can smile
And know that feeling hurts is worth while.
If I can spend a year alone with you
And love you all the more when it was through.
I think that then you'd know I was your friend
And I would stay that way - till the end.

Theo Ohlhausen

After The Separation

A wooden leg seeks to replace
The muscles, bones, sinews, blood and nerves
Of yesterday's fondest hopes and memories.

But after it has been shattered ...
Mangled and crushed beyond recognition,
The once vital limb, bereft of its pristine charm,
Will shudder at the joyless prospect of its own decay.

Its dreams of co-existence will spurn reality's laughter
While dreams of wishful thoughts and deep conviction
Will spawn idyllic futures that beggar forgiveness
And make mockery of the once impressive Whole.

A needless amputation will induce much more than trauma
For there is no reason, compromise, fair play or euphemism,
No solace or recompense that can justify to a healthy body
The unconscionable dismemberment of its cherished being.

After the Separation
The amputee will be too angry, her loss too devastating,
Her regrets too many, her disappointment too great.
But her greatest torment will be this cryptic gibe and epitaph:
"Before you spat in God's face, you should have counted your blessings."

Karl Gordon

Fantasy Hill

Where are the thoughts of lovers tonight?
The moon and the stars, an eagle in flight.
Trees swaying gently, the waters are still.
Contentment's been found on Fantasy Hill.

Their dreams are as endless as the stars of the night.
Laying quiet, so gently, their thoughts take on flight.
Slowly they drift through their Fantasy Land.
Creating, exploring, they go hand in hand.

Trees of all colours, mountains so high.
Beauty so vast, they both want to cry.
But back they must go, realities calling.
Their minds stop drifting, they both start falling.

Time has slipped by as fast as the sands.
Both minds are back from their Fantasy Land.
The grass is so wet, this all feels so wrong.
Nothing to remember but their Fantasy Song.

Where are the thoughts of lovers tonight?
The moon and the stars, an eagle in flight.
Trees swaying gently, the waters aren't still.
Contentment's been lost on Fantasy Hill.

Gail D. Smith

The Parent's Promise

I gave each of you life, my best accomplishment yet,
The memory of which I won't soon forget;
Each beautiful and special in your own way,
You fill us with happiness each waking day.
We want to love and teach you all that we know,
And give you the space that you each need to grow.
We promise to treat you with dignity and respect,
We'll try not to say things we know we'll regret.
Patience and understanding, we may struggle to keep,
But the most peaceful of angels you are when you sleep.
We'll protect you and keep you out of harm's way,
We'll treasure and be proud of you for all of our days;
And all that we ask of each one of you.
Is that to yourselves and each other you will always be true;
Be there for each other, long after we're gone,
And in your hearts and minds we will live on.
We promise we love you with all of our heart,
A promise we'll keep 'til death do us part.

Vicky Caruana

Reflections Of Youth

I hear the sounds of summer-time, relaxing, soft and sweet,
The memories of childhood dreams,
Warm sand, soft winds, bare feet.
And somewhere down in memory's lane, a melody comes through,
Out dancing under starry skies and happy times I knew.

The summer birds with songs so sweet,
And the lonesome call of the loon,
The insects flit and fly about,
They will be gone too soon.
The hazy skies that make one dream,
The red ball of sunset's glow,
The majestic outline of the trees,
Familiar scenes I know.

And now that twilight years are mine,
And movements are so slow,
The ebb and flow of youth is past
But my heart is all aglow!
I sit and think about my life,
And the joys of my childhood home,
I am not sad because I know, the best is yet to come.

Rita M. Havey

Emerald Lake

A precious jewel, a setting so divine
The Master Jeweller's hand did thus create
A Masterpiece, a thing of beauty rare
A setting for the senses thus to sate.

A million carats of delight you give
Set in a cusp of mountain peaks so proud.
Adorned by sides of verdant green escrolled
And wreathed by the soft down of fleecy clouds.

In pristine splendour thus you lie becalmed
Your emerald beauty glistens in the sun
He must have smiled at this His handiwork
And felt a glow of pride in what He'd done.

Norman L. Ibsen

Before The Hammers And The Saws!

The sky is as blue as the light blue sea
The living things are as alive as a tree
The air is pure but shall not be seen,
This is the way it use to be
Before the hammers and the saws
there was once a tree that appeared near a rock
As solid as my heart the tree was
broken into little bits and pieces
that shall be returned as a token
Although there is still trees, flowers
and a light blue sea but that
shall never be as living as they
used to be.

Natalie Verney

Simple Things

My heart has treasured simple things,
The dewy freshness that morning brings.
A wish upon an evening star,
A mockingbird's sweet repertoire.
A hammock under swaying trees,
A midnight stroll amidst cool breeze.
A fireplace on wintery nights,
A hill top view of distant city lights.
Now, life holds serious times, it's true,
But thoughts such as these have pulled me through.
For my fears and my worries they take up wings,
When I remember these simple things.

Ronald H. Goldkind

Dad

What are you there, old man?
The light that shone and showed your pain is dimmed.
They say it's out and gone, but no
What light is quenched that burns so fiercely in my heart?

Rest now, in the arms of God, yet stay with me
Your laughter - sparkling eyes and gentle spirit never fading.

Hands, hair, voice and bearing; each shrug and shift and shuffle
Sweet anguish in remembering
How graciously you spent yourself
To make them rich who came within your scope.

And such a doubt that rages deep within
Will I be worthy?

Gavin Lister

The Little Man

Out of the cradle of water, I took my first breath in space.
The light that opened my eyes smiled at me with boundless compassion.
"Fear not the unknown my child, you are not alone." I heard a soft whisper.
"Not just hear, but listen to the little man, he will be the
guide." The light slowly faded.
When the bumps on the long winding path were rough, I tried
to twist and twirl.
But bowed down to the kind voice only to walk upright and clear.
Nimble and arrogant, I pushed my way through ignoring
the frail and the helpless.
Till he earnestly asked me to be humble and generous.
When end was all that mattered most, whatever the means,
He pleaded with me to feel the pain of others.
Frustrated I argued, till my voice became faint and remote.
Still, he never left me alone for a single minute.
As I approach the finish line, I feel the Bliss.
Because I knew, I listened to the little man not just heard.

Kamala Roy

I Feel It Too

The hurt is deep
The hurt is strong
The pain continues on and on
The pain is hurting you I feel it too

I hear you crying in the night
I hear the same, the frightening pain
I see the shadow coming near
I see the fear that you prepare
The pain is tearing you apart
I feel it too

The memories so deep so fresh, the painful scares they still rest
The terrible spell of unhappy doubts
Is now living inside your heart
The pain will descend upon you
And I, will feel it too

Maybe love will come back someday
And like inside your heart
The happiness will comfort you, the pain will depart
You have always deserved to be happy and when you are
I will feel it too

Laura Peddell

291

The Hands That Knit

Whose hands? My hands?
The hands dance their solitary dance,
Caressing the yarn, singing around the fluffy pile.
My hands used to be dancers, knitters, my hands used to knit:
Bread, poetry, songs.
My hands used to knit songs for the little children.
Do you know? My hands have grown silent, immobile
They don't knit anymore, they don't sing anymore.
They rest by the river, counting stones, counting dead leaves, alone.
Your hands. Do your hands knit?
Do you knit dreams or do you knit desolation dresses,
Or bitter gowns for solitary women?
Don't answer me. I'd rather have them cut off.
Maybe in my hands sleep the hands of my mother,
Or of the mother of my mother.
The primal mother knitting for the first time ever,
Sometimes awakens in me
And a little sunshine sprouts from my hands, little by little
One finger following the other slowly.
Maybe I will knit a colorful scarf to murmur and illuminate your face.

Violeta San Juan

The Real World

The smog the smoke we'll all soon choke.
The gray air that smothers, the pollution that covers.

We dream of there being none of that stuff
but, we still don't know it may be a bluff.

We see in our minds the green grass that grows,
the clean air that blows, on our windows.

The leaves that are shuffling up in the trees,
the poor little children yelling, "help me please."

There coughing and wheezing,
some choking or sneezing.

With nothing to save them,
we'll kneel down and pray for them.

The real world can be sad,
and also be bad.

With people dying,
and their families crying.

Buried in soil fresh from its birth,
or maybe in toxic, against Mother Earth.

We dream of there being no wars or fights,
but what can we say. Reality bites!

Alexis L. Quistberg

Realization

The face before me I know I have seen,
The girl seems familiar in my mind,
Her eyes tell me tales of where she has been,
Her face is soft, her expression is kind.
But her tears tell me a different tale:
She is sad and lonely and needs to feel
Secure and safe, but tears slowly trail
That whisper to me that her pain is real.
"Who am I?" She asks, as she shakes her head,
Desperately pleading with me, taking
My hand.
"Can you help me to know?" she says.
"Can you stop my tears and stop my shaking?"
Then suddenly who she is is clearer:
A reflection of me in the mirror.

Adrienne Dunn

Halloween Night

The black cat arches his back in fright,
The ghosts and goblins are out tonight.
The halloween witch will ride her broom,
Casting her shadow across the moon.

The graveyard tombstones begin to shake,
What slept below is now awake.
From dusk 'til dawn you hear them moan,
One night each year, the earth they roam.

Each time this chilling stories told,
Your blood by now is running cold.
So lock your doors and windows tight,
For this my friend is, "Halloween Night!!

Elaine Page

Complexity

The stranger I always fail to see.
The friend I sometimes regret to praise.
Feelings I was withheld to sense.
His nature I inexorably despise.

What lacks my intellect he knows,
What perspective I didn't see he shows,
Through the road of uncertainty he leads,
Perseverance to righteousness he seeks.

Derailed from the truth he tolerates,
Situations for himself he creates.
Slightly to work up to righteousness,
Intellect is arrested in presumptuousness.

The intricate beauty he appreciates,
Only to dwell in reality,
Of the water that ebbs away,
Consanguinity of the past has come to stay.

In the mind it is conceived,
Complexity of life and has believed,
Fate of the heart he will await,
Softness of the beat a fervent state.

Angelo M. Aguila

My Birthday Poem

The day has come within my life, as I walk on down my path.
The first part of my journey ends and now begins the last.
So I sit down by the water's edge, on the river bank.
Where it was I first saw you and give to you my thanks.

"Thank you for my birth and life when I was young.
Thank you for all I am today and all I may become.
You have given to me everything, that was and is and will be.
And now I give myself to you, with a life of serving thee.

Know that I am with you, as I have always been.
And as I will be forever, within the soul of me.
Nothing you could ever do, could sway my love for you.
My heart will be forever more, remaining eternally true.

I have shared your sadness and heard your silent cries.
And I have witnessed your glory, with my naked eyes.
My love is as a gentle breeze, my love is as the sea.
My love is as the universe, all wrapped inside of me.

So if one part should falter and some day blow away.
All would fill the empty void, to ensure my love would stay.
Now I wish to create a miracle, a gift to you from me.
An ending of all living strife and a genesis of life that's free."

William Albert Simmons

Autumn Days

The first change is in the air,
The first fall of the leaves,
The first change in colour
Are the first signs of Autumn.

Fall brings an explosion of colour,
Red, green, yellow, orange and brown.
The colour of the leaves are beautiful,
It's nature changing right before our eyes.

Autumn is a time to celebrate
The Thanksgiving holiday.
It brings much happiness,
To family and friends.

The cool breeze in the air,
it's kind of relaxing and easy to enjoy,
People's interest gets sparked when they see,
nature's leaves changing.
These are the Autumn days.

Cheryl Lyn Constantineau

The Morning Paper

Oh, the lies you've shared with the masses
    The filth and truth you've exposed
    Black deeds coloured with metaphors
    Heaven's hell etched on fragile white pages
World events ooze from the four corners and
    Culminate daily on your blank passionless face.

Shaking my head slowly, nothing to do with me
    Coffee on my lips, facts hard to believe
    Opinions and judgments some of which I agree
    Merely, interesting parables of my own reality
    Graphic details in snapshots, spiting images I'm told
    How you sensationalize man's living stories
    Spewing shock filled revelations... as they unfold.

Depiction after depiction where, distress, death,
    Destruction and despair makeup the news
    A dismal chronicle of how you entertain, inform
    And cheat us out of an optimistic start to the day
Yet, tomorrow, humanity's curse, comfort and
    Conscience will lie innocently on the doorstep
Yes, of course, my precious morning paper...

Bronton Wraye

Transition

Wandering. Lost. Alone.
The familiar left behind.
Warnings, fears ignored.
From within a voice - listen:
Go on, go forward!!
The forest is dark
Strange voices and strange noises
Increasing my anxiety, my fear.
Light?
Is that the voice calling?
This road? This destiny?
Exhausted. Walking, walking. Darkness.

Nightfall dawning.
A ray of knowing touching the earth, heart and soul.
Clear road
Not lost after all!
Celebration!
New beginnings in my heart.
Dancing and song.

Elke Hamel

Getting Ready At The North Pole

Santa Claus is busy getting big and fat
The elves are stuffing Santa's sack
Mrs. Claus is sewing Santa's ripped suit
While shelves are packed with dolls and trains
that go toot toot!

Santa's ready he's rearing to go
No stop right there he can't Oh No!
His sleigh isn't ready his reindeer aren't hooked
There still in the barn they have to be took

Now Santa's ready he is all packed up
He has dolls and trains and even a pup
Look he is going, going gone
And he won't be back till tomorrow at dawn.

Amber Martinat

Imagine If...

Imagine a world where mankind ceased to exist.
The Earth would probably sigh in relief
Its precious ecosystems safe from destruction.
The giants of the sea would reclaim their home
Their voices raised in celebration.
The great span of the condor would once again grace the sky
No longer under the threat of extinction.
It would be a world at peace with itself.

It is mankind who takes advantage.
Pushing nature aside for his own purposes.
Turning a blind eye to the abuse of the world.

Imagine a world where nature ceased to exist.
Could mankind survive?

Tracy Bennett

The Tree Of Love

Who really is our family?
The earth, the sea, the sun above
That warms our soul and gives us strength
Or those near our hearts who express their love?

That love comes without demands.
It's a part of eternity but our life it spans.
It never dies through winter's deep freeze.
It can't be cut down like a forest of trees.

Those trees that have no love to give
Build shelters from the piercing cold.
When we allow someone inside
The walls that guard our hearts and hold
Our deepest fears; our needs.
We then have made our family.
We've found the love that's like a tree.
Deep-rooted, strong, protective, complete.

Bonita Welton MacPherson

Untitled

When you're alone and cold, no one to hold your hand
The earth seems flat, no adventure at all

The days go by, the pain subsides to memories
The nights are cold, and so it shows I'm crying

The world has grown to love the hurt and forget the pain
Let's hurt someone and do it all over again

The winter nights and aging trees, wilt just as though leaves
and our fear of God and Love of evil has but one moment to trace the
past and burn the future.

Michele J. Nouvion

Autumn's Splendor

A hushed, cool dampness fills the air,
The dewy dampness stirs
Like sleepy, heavy, lazy wings
Of a large and tired bird.
The stirring breeze picks up the sound
Of a crow beyond the rill
An answering Jay screams greetings
From its wood upon the hill
The reaping is done, the fields are plowed
There's a brown and austere note
Then the sun beams forth
On autumn blessed trees
That light up
To boast and gloat

Afton Gillespie

Agent Orange

I will never forget that cold December day
The day it quietly fell upon us
Slowly descending along the way
My eyes started to water, my head started to buzz
I was dying, a slow and painful death
My men were screaming
A silent scream
They were grasping at their throats,
Trying to breathe
I watched them
As they drew their last breath
The breath that brought them nothing,
But a poisoning death
One by one, they fell to the ground
It was literally killing,
Everyone!
I will never forget that cold December day
The day it silently fell upon us.
Killing everyone along the way.

Pamela McPhee

The Merging Of...

Silence - in the night,
the dark brings upon us such secrets
and mysteries.

Noise - in the day,
the light brings with it, the splendor of
surprises.

Two mountains, side-by-side, silent and
still, never knowing day or night.

The glimpse of yellow grass beneath the
thin layer of snow - glistening in
the day and the night.

Day and night merges and becomes dawn
what each day of our lives, are part of.

Grace Vega

The Candle

The light flickers threatening to blow out
The candle down to its dying point
Any sudden movement, any sudden doubt
   Could blow the candle out
You'll be alone with nobody, nobody at all
   Don't blow the candle out
A whisper, small and quiet, unknown but yet known
Cutting the silence like a sharp knife
Glistening in the pale moonlight
The light may be the last light you see
So... Be careful
   Don't blow the candle out

Amy Collins

Ode To The Human Spirit

The silence of the hollowed halls shattered with the wail of new life
The cry was long and demanding, needing something far beyond the reach
   of man
The trilling voice begged for refuge from the hostile world, as well
   as sweet solace and unstipulated love
The being behind the sound recognized the reality of his position
Life granted him the chance to be distinct individual, to ensue one
   self-fulfilling project in the course
And, despite the anxieties erupting, he clung to the strange human
   urge to survive, the barriers facing this tiny life were immense
But from the first echo of his voice
the once 'trivial' soul confirmed the erroneous thinking of society
He decided that he would govern his life and command its destiny and
he did. He left his imprint on the world; refused to be forgotten.
He wanted to be remembered in the hearts of all. The small person
behind the wail accomplished what could never be done He rose above
the trials life presented him. And when he had completed his earthly
tasks, he was not ashamed; he was proud. And his voice ebbed at the
edge of the universe never to be heard again. But no one forgot the
wait of new life, which broke the silence of the hollowed halls.

Andrea Lee Dennis

In Remembrance

When European war broke out
The countries honor was at stake
The sons of service volunteered
And the great sacrifice did make

Two minutes silence two minutes thought
Two minutes silence for those who fought
For those who fought suffered and died
For those who young lives were sacrificed
Two minutes silence with lowered head
Two minutes spent on thoughts of our dead

Thoughts of our dead of whom we are proud
Thoughts of them now in heaven above
Who gave up their lives that we may live
Two minutes silence with lowered head
Two minutes thoughts to think of our dead

Elizabeth Hart

Heavenly Paradise

Why so many people are scared of death I will never know.
The chance for a new beginning to leave all past woes.

It's true there's no proof of heaven but it's nice to think,
After we leave all this behind there's another link,

A link into another world better than our own.
Where peace and happiness prosper, a paradise home.

I'm not talking about white clouds, gold halos or God.
Just a place of rest for angels in their own small pod.

Each pod consists of dreams not lived but always have been yearned.
Them wanting this experience to see what wasn't learned.

To me life after life exists if you just believe.
So when your time down here is done have no fear to leave.

Christine Wolfram

Life And Death

Some people say that life is like a
   stormy, dark night;
Always full of unpredictable adventures.
Yet these same people would say that death is
   dark and cold.
Same as the storm of life.

Totally opposite ends of the world,
yet so closely related.

Melanie Woode

"To Be Ruler Of Such A Magical World"

The moon reflected, the air was still, a lone deer silhouetted on hill.
The breeze was fresh and whispered through the trees,
The chirp of the insects replaced the hum of the bees.
The water lapped gently around the lake's edge,
The birds and the hares slept in wood and in hedge.
The frost settled crisply on the grass and the stones,
A wonderful feeling crept into my bones.
The stars twinkled down upon the water black and deep,
Every human, except I, was comfortably asleep.
This world was my own from now until morn,
My own special refuge until the dawn would be born.
The crystal sparkle of a dewdrop upon a single flower,
A rainbow traced against the sky after an unexpected shower.
The first faint rays of sunshine fall gently upon the ground,
The air is warm and moving with different smells and sound.
The grass will crunch beneath my feet,
The dark disperses the shapes will meet.
The clouds will form, converge and float,
There is no more cold, I shed my coat.
I wander home abdicating my world,
Waiting for another night, to its magic be hurled.

   Pauline May

Just A Thought

Why can't people be like trees? Trees are strong but flexible,
the branches bend gently with a light breeze,
or they bend deeper, and turn when the storm is raging,
Always straightening to their original height.
When the storm is wild, when lightening strikes
a branch may break or a trunk will snap.
When the branches break off the tree heals itself,
the branches remains strong as is lays on the ground,
even when the trunk has broken the roots remain strong and deep,
the trunk lays its head down but still retains its strength.
Once a year the tree looses its cloak, it's laid bare for all to see.
We are sad when the leaves fall, we rejoice when they return
We get shelter, warmth and comfort from a tree.
Why can't people bend and turn, why do we feel shame
when we snap the odd branch, why are we afraid
to lay our heads down, why are we condemned when we lay our hearts bare.
Why can't we help each other with the dignity of a tree.

   Dorothy Aspinall

Untitled

Like a crimson corpse in the sky
the blood-soaked sun lays down to die

   Trading morning for mourning
   fading, scorning a warming

Sinking, swirling, a thousand black holes
to oneness and God send back the souls

   Here they will forever pray
   here they will forever stay

From a fierce double hurricane
comes a sheer sorrow, fury, pain

   Tears of blood fast from its eyes
   fears do flood past as it cries:

   High again, take my place, rise!
Lies of men make me face my demise

   Mike Bethune

The Beach

The sun rose to greet the ocean as I walked along the beach
The birds flew all around me and called out a welcome screech

The surfers in the water left their troubles on the sand
They sat astride their surfboards searching for a wave
on which to take a stand

The wet sand was cool and soothing to the bottoms of my feet
A cool wind blew upon me and the sun reached down
to offer me its heat

The ocean offered me its treasures that it washed up on the sand
There were shells of every color and I reached into
the water and placed them in my hand

At dusk the sun set upon the ocean in a fiery orange blaze
As it spread across the water at its beauty I would gaze

The pounding of the waves was like sweet music to my ears
They seemed to say come back some day! We'll be here for years

With this place I fell in love right from the very start
The memories of my time there remain forever in my heart

   Marietta Okell

Eternity

Eternity! How to mark and single out?
The Beginning of all beginnings, the Wide Twilight
Covering Void - till my sneezing 'Ego-Rise'
Lending a mark, cuts twilight in Time
Adorning sight with Day and Night.
Eternity - a throbbing mirror awaiting a face
To reflect; or twitching touch in fingers hidden
Before their clutching the cup of wine.
What is the end of all endings beyond?
The closing of the book of mortal deeds
My mad pursuits - good and bad and barren, all;
Call it else a tray of action-fruits, full to the rim.
Eternity - without Beginning and the End, is fixed
With reference to me and me alone.
It belongs to me; if I were not to be
Lost and gone is Eternity.

   Sikander Toufiq

Alone

You walk the city streets alone with nobody by your side.
The alleys are your home.
Some people nod or say "hello" as they pass
Sometimes offering change
But many turn their heads and look the other way
Not wanting to accept the real truth.
The sadness is that it is everywhere
Nobody knowing what to do to help, many not even caring.
Denial is the word of the day.

I see you in the distance, coming nearer,
But I will not change the course of my path.
Although I cannot change the world or open people's eyes,
If I can bring a smile to your lips or some joy to your day
It also brings happiness to my world.

So when I see you on the street, I won't simply pass you by.
From me you will get a big, warm smile, and a friendly "hi".
So when I see you coming my way, I will not turn around the bend.
Although I can't change the world, I can surely be your friend.

   Karyn Dawn

Dear Friend, I Heard You Cry

When the sunshine will turn his back on you,
The air and water will ignore you,
The Lord our Father will pick you up.
Like the lights of Heaven you will shine.

Back and forth, good memories will come
To join us together forever.
Don't be afraid to meet the great King.
Both He and I will always love you.

In my heart the soul is sensitive,
It will sing to you as a prayer.
Into saddest, my eyes will look.
Bubbles of water will clean my cheeks.

Forever my heart's a friend of yours.
Forever my soul is trusting yours.
For you and for me the world will praise.
With someone else you will trade bodies.

When the big mountains will dance with me
And my only soul will run away,
The bright lights of God will enter me.
I'll be able to see you again.

Fabienne Aubuchon

Only In Dreams

It only happens in my dreams
that you can carry me away,
It could never happen in real life
cause of what the people say.

They all would talk about us,
or just stop and stare,
wondering why are they together?
And that kind of pain, I just can't bare.

So we sit apart and alone,
thinking of how our life could be
if people would only realize,
just stop and realize, what we see.

How we see age as only a number,
to us it doesn't mean a thing,
there shouldn't be a barrier on love
cause of all the happiness it brings.

But as of now all this love
can only take place in our dreams,
cause the world doesn't see love for what it is;
only for what it seems.

Jenny VanDer Meersch

Love

I've understood every word, I've understood very well, thank you.
That things have changed, that flowers have bloomed.
Why can't you understand that if you zap and leave, love will also pass?
I just want you to know...
I'd search for your heart, even if you import it elsewhere,
I will give you all options as long as you will still love me.
I will find the languages needed to sing your laments.
I just want you to know...
The magic formulas of the Marabout's of Africa?
Yes, I'll recite them without remorse, as long as you will still love me.
I will make myself new, just to add a spark to the smoke
I will become the others if that's your desire,
Their games will become our own, if that's your wish.
I will change myself into gold...
As long as you will love me.

Elizabeth D'Angelo

True Love

As the sun slowly rises, I look to see
That the man I love is still here with me.
Holding me close in a tight, warm embrace
His hands move to gently caress my face.
He whispers sweet words of romance in my ear,
Knowing we'll be together year after year.
I feel safe and secure with him by my side,
All my wishes and dreams, to him I'll confide.
He's the man I want to be with till the day I die,
Conquering all - together - this we will try.
As the sun slowly sets behind the horizon I see
That I've found true love and that's
    the way it'll always be.

Angela Gallant

The Soul Translucent

Feet press small footprints in grass
that springs dishevelled, waving upwards
Toward the light which glows through
muslin sheets, tugging against clothes' pegs
lining the wire which spans the heavens

Above the boy who searches in the dandelion
hoping to find an answer to the yellow circle
opened above the green blades between his toes—

An entirety glimpsed, caught, frozen in a moment
of emptiness reflected in the stillness of the
boy's wide blue eyes

Only to be vaguely forgotten, as the dandelion is trampled
under the staggering feet of the boy who in an
ecstasy of excitement follows the distraction
of an itinerant bee flying free in his daily rounds

From flower to flower, ignorant of the struggle
amid the damp sheets as the boy pushes, stumbles,
and rises again in a busy endless search for a moment lost,
forever, in the little garden, under the laundry glowing
yellow in the morning light.

John Thomas Donald

Memories

Our memories seem but like a dream,
that somehow makes one wonder.
Could that really happen or did it seem
only in a daydreamer's hunger.
To search for fantasies of make believe,
just like child-like behavior in jest.
When in reality we, as adults still perceive
to be like little children, when oppressed.
It seems like yesterday that we were young,
but decades march along the path of time,
bringing days of rain and sunshine to our minds.
How precious are these moments one by one.
Time races onward, oh how very fast,
and time after time we wish to hold this past.
Just for awhile, but it is not so,
for we just grow older and on we go.
To try to reap our glorious past,
memories of dear ones gone at last,
to Heaven's Gates that glitter and shine,
as we hold them fast in our hearts and minds.

Dina Venturini

Sonnet

(for M. W.)
Looking 'round myself I see
that everything I know is thee.
Without, I live, each day a chore,
I see our hours in times before.
We seem to lie there in my bed,
The willow is thy bowing head.
My own brow bears a tortured crease,
I close my eyes, the pain to cease.
I am undone, you are more clear
in darkness, methinks thou art here!
Heaven and earth must I remember.
A flame's forced down; a smoldering ember
now is two, but from one heart.
So we are one; now torn apart.

Lindsay Milner

Sharings

My Bill, we've shared love and laughter
tears and pain
at times we did things
that may have been insane.

We've shared the birth of our three sons
their growing and accomplishments
the ups and downs of a relationship
and we emerged with a stronger sense.

We've shared the love of nature
canoeing and bush walks
camping in the cold and wet snow
and witnessing majestic flocks.

I'm grateful for the things we've shared
when we were side by side
today I share my sorrow with God
and accept my day in stride.

Gloria Claypole

My Guide

You've guided me through life's paths,
Teaching me right from wrong.
You've held my hand through rough times,
Teaching me to be strong.

Your trust in me as my leader,
Your confidence my guide.
Your kindness is my comfort,
Your honesty I stand beside.

I want to thank you for your wisdom,
And letting me be true.
I want to thank you for your love,
And just for being you.

Even though the time may come,
When we're made to part.
The miles may be distant,
But you'll always be in my heart.

The good times and the bad times,
You've always pulled me through.
What else can I say to you Mommy?
Except that "I love you".

Farah C. Thombs

Harley Man

Dressed in black leathers; handsome and lean
Tanned like a gypsy; spontaneous and free
He mounts a precision-built, black, Harley machine
A full-throated roar escapes as he turns the key
And off he glides down the road to parts unknown
Noble as a knight riding his fiery stead.
Across borders and highways, he ventures alone
Never knowing where fickle fate's path may lead
He conquers life's obstacles with a confident smile
His only enemies are boredom and sorrow
At a roadside cafe, he'll seek refuge for awhile
He lights up a smoke, orders coffee and ponders tomorrow
People take notice when he walks through the door
But they need not fear the tall, dark stranger sitting there
For he is a sensitive and passionate man whom women adore
An articulate vagabond who captivates audiences everywhere.
As dusk begins to fall, he bids a hasty farewell
He jumps on his Harley and turns the key in the ignition
With another passing day and a new story to tell
He embarks on his next adventurous mission.

Patricia Capote

To Bee Or Not To Be

"O fierce warrior in thy suit of black and yellow, thrust not thy
 sword at me.
If thou heed'st not my warning, then lifeless wilt thou be."

"Ha, I fear thee not, O stalwart one, for set thine eyes on me.
I bear with me a mighty sword and what hast thou with thee?"

"I have nought but mine own two hands, yet a staunch young knight I be;
A fight to the finish thou shalt have, for I shall not flee from thee."

Brandishing his sword in hand, like lightning the rogue did fly.
The bold young knight stood fast his ground and uttered not a cry.

The battle raged; 'twas short but fierce, for the knight much strength had he.
Grasped he the knave with his own two hands and flung him to his knee.

The warrior lay upon the ground, so close to death though he.
But the knight with pity in his heart, declared, "Bee, off with thee."

Darlene Van Laar

In A Manger Lain

Over the stable where Jesus lay
Swaddled and lying in a manger of hay;
Came a star shining bright with a glorious light
To guide the shepherds to him this night.

Three wise men from the east also came;
Bearing gifts for the babe, in a manger lain;
Gifts of Frankincense, myrrh and gold
They gave to the babe in the manger, as foretold.

The King of Kings was born that day;
In such humility where he lay;
From the House of David, as foretold
By many, many prophets of old.

A babe in a manger they came to see.
Our Messiah, our Saviour He was born to be:
In a lowly manger, He was born to die,
That we who believe may reign with Him on high.

Our salvation He came to give;
That those who believe might forever live:
Sing praise to His name, all ye people sing praise,
To the Babe born in a stable, and in a manger lain.

Muriel Bostock

Bitter-Sweet

We played and enjoyed the warmth of the
  sunshine
The grass a soft green carpet gave way to the
night
as we lay silently beneath the
  sky
Wrapped up in the wishes of the
  stars

Content with the feeling of warmth
drifting off on a cushion of the midnight
  air

Dreams and fantasies come true
lit up like a stage by the light of the
  moon

Only to awaken to the realities of another
  day
Searching for the answers of
  tomorrow

    Judy Bougie

Sunset Dialogue

I watched the sun go down
suffusing the sky with colours
from another world
The vivacious brutality of orange hues
Tempered with the discreet timidity of blues
What a wondrous Hand that creates poetry
With music and paints with sculptured shapes

The might of an endless inspiration
The crescendo of a high-powered reunion
As the colours mingle, separate
Lost in a harmonious dance high above Man's reach

Colours of dreams, reds of insane passions
That I could reach into your colorful souls
Lost in the vortex of your flamboyant pride

Say no more for the sun is no more
I and my thousand throats will shout an encore
To a vain sky, lost in the knowledge
That part of my soul has disappeared
With the blues that my heart has seared.

    June Vel

The Climber

The weather changes
suddenly
The climber is trapped
huddled over shivering
Shielded by an overhanging boulder
trying to keep warm
not succeeding.
"Think warm" he grunts
as he loses the feeling from his feet.
The climber starts to think absently of his family:
"I can't wait to see your next game Johnny"
"Wait till Maria sees the ring that I bought her"
"I shouldn't have gone ahead of the group"
"as soon as this storm stops
I've got to get down."
The climber realizes
that he can't feel his legs,
nor move his arms,
and suddenly finds himself hoping
that they'll find his body.

    Jeffrey Lingwood

I Bear A Charmed Life

Conversations on the phone. Trivialities.
Such a bother to a busy, busy boy.
I know the fury of your smile,
the fueled rage within your mirthless snicker.
I feel no sorrow for the plumber
who's feeding fires in this hate connection.
Right now you're merely taking practice shots.
I know the target of your competition slugs,
the rod of your brain lightning.
Tonight the chicken won't be cooked enough,
I'll incorrectly squeeze the lemon wedge,
the salad dressing won't stick right, perhaps
we're out of ice cream, juice or milk.
Cinderella, castle disappears.
I always know the moments.
I'll raise my hands to God for intervention.
Like every night before, He'll be asleep.

    Ev McTaggart

Ocean Waves

Ocean waves, ebbing and flowing,
Struggling to merge with one.

Reaching the shore to meet one's love
Only to shatter in disappointment; scattered.

Exhausted, not despaired,
Tormented, not discouraged,
Flowing again, renewed with inner strength.
Lashing back again with ecstatic refrain.
I shall endeavor to meet once more,
Humming new songs; bringing new rhythms,
Stylishly adorned.

Leaping, fluttering, whirling, swirling,
Gathering momentum with new vitality;
With new harmony.

Giggling, chuckling; we will laugh.
Singing, dancing; I shall return.
We will meet again.

Rolling, yearning, rapturous and ecstatic,
Triumphantly marching,
Until I merge with my love.

    Madhu Varshney

Inside Our Self

Crushed as severely as a rose petal
Strangled of moisture
Our soul withers, as life giving tears
Freeze on barren creativity.
The intricate web of beliefs not our own
Binds tight, yet live within the
Narrow strands of generations past
We continue, existing
On batteries of motive and drive not ours
Never questing for altered consciousness
Only answers to fulfill an emptiness which torments;
Clamoring to be heard past cement walls
unknowingly placed by ourselves.

    Brenda Kennedy

Shadow Of Night

There is no darkness for me only shadows
Shadows are places without light that can be seen
There would be darkness if not for the moon
The moon gives light and the light gives the shadows
The night is one giant shadow

    Jeffrey Neeser

Rent-To-Own

Cracked Naugahyde, plaid in neutrals.
Starkly, parts and pieces stood,
stacked upon the dusty cement patio.
Filtered strands of sunlight touched upon the crushed cushions,
intertwining briefly with the breezes breathing hesitantly
upon the backs of the old, worn covers.
Olefin nap, gently lifted,
returned to diminished form when movement paused.

Plush cushions of soft black, brushed nylon, velveteen;
large plump forms surrounding square black tables,
as yet unlined with memories,
the inevitable circles and burns.
"Rent-to-own!" "Twenty-four monthly payments..."
Wistful spirals of cigarette smoke swirled about the room,
deceptively beautiful,
caressing the covers with silver.

Andrea Lynn Moen

Dinner

The spaghetti scattered indiscriminately
Staining the fragile, white fabric of intimacy
Bright red tears mingled with anger
The broken stoneware carelessly fell
Chipping the delicate, unfinished pattern of trust.

Hands trembling, she bends to clean up the pain
Sifting through the tangled mess of broken promises
She finds forgotten pieces of self respect
That were caught in the tasteless layers of denial
Her tears turn to bitter sweet hunger.

How does one take the brutal reality of war
Set against the backdrop of the kitchen table
Fought with the hurt and anger of yesterday's pain?
How does one dine in peace with strangers of love?
Perhaps...

One could change the menu...

Lenora Richardson

Hollow Passage Of Time

The ancients lie with battle cries
Spanning cross the main,
Where pure by chance, an awkward stance
Fails to distance pain.

Friends trained and lost, with farthest cost
To mark the bloody day,
Where debts unpaid and prayers proclaimed
Fell beside the way.

When pressing on, the group responds
Retracing half his steps,
The past was dim, a youthful limb
The fearsome battle kept.

He ponders now, explaining how
As nightmares often show,
If time withstands the spoils of man
When countries choose to grow.

For now he'll last, to tell of past
Memories that remain.
Another year towards distant cheers
To join them once again.

Rob Currie

Albatross

She felt she was the albatross.
Somewhere, welded, in her
was the knowing that she could not be
in rhythm with the step the others danced.
Shamed, she locked her doors.
Would not, could not lose
the aura of burden.
Not hers to carry but hers to be.
And locked within her walls
the shadows of perception toyed
but would not let her see.
That each dancer strove to step in time
and ached to sing in key.

Katherine Groven

Sometimes

Does that mean I'm insane
Sometimes my feet don't touch the ground
    for reasons I'm not sure of

Sometimes
    if only I would jump
I'm sure that I would fly
Soaring far above the world
Clear thoughts yet
    wondering why

So much has changed or
    is everything the same
Does that mean I'm insane
    frightened

With a push of a button THEY
Can manipulate my brain
Too many buttons, too much pain
    frightened
        Sometimes

Dafney D. Roberge

Tears Are In My Eyes

When I see her holding hands with a new guy
Sometimes it makes me wonder why
Oh, the tears are in my eyes again
Lord, it's giving me so much pain

Why does she have to go away
I was hoping that she'll stay
Oh, the tears are in my eyes again
Pouring hard like a falling rain

L....ady, you've got the love I need
I....know for sure someday we'll meet
S....uch a warm hearted woman indeed
A....ll I know you're very gentle and sweet.

Where do you think I'd go from here
You're the only one I ever wanted dear
Oh, the tears are in my eyes again
This long distance love affair's driving me insane

You broke all the rules of the game
Now they're saying that I should be blamed
Oh, the tears are in my eyes again
If only they knew she's got looks and brain

Yandhi T. Cranddent

My Dearest

Your touch is like a new born babe
Soft as you hold me
Your love is like a wandering brook
It flows through me
As I watch you from a distance
My heart say's
I'm yours with no resistance
Though we haven't been together for that long
I know our love will always be strong
I hope and I pray that we never part
For my dearest
I could never go on with a broken heart

Jeannette Kowk

My Presence

As the petals of a rosebud unfold,
So will My Presence in you,
Open the bud of purity in your soul.
The petals unfurl, drinking in
My light and love,
Gently falling as the dew,
Unfolding in My wisdom and truth.

Until, in glorious perfection,
Blending with Me in bliss divine,
A holy love, forever new and unfolding,
Infinitely more beautiful, moment by moment,
Eternally expanding, and

Exploding! into
Vast oceans of shimmering light,
Filled with radiant love,
Calm, yet seething with activity,
The timeless hum of creation,
The source of all life,
The Presence within.

Violet Shaw

Again, Again

You came back into my life
so very carefully,
A friend I was hoping.

Releasing my anger,
slowly grown,
I allowed my love, once again to be shown

Good times we had
the barriers down
We talked, we laughed
My mind hid the haunting memories of the past.

The hope was there once again
Would we make it this time, my friend?

But time did tell
as again and again
I found, I must say goodbye
to my husband...my lover
and my friend.

Judy Laking

Sisters

Sisters are there to help you out,
Sisters are there when you're in doubt.

Sisters are there to stand by you,
Sisters are there to love when it's due.

Sisters are there to show that they care,
Sisters are there to be as a pair.

Sisters are there when you need a friend,
Because with sisters the love never ends.

Suzanne Cormier

Goodbye My Friend

For fourteen years, Max was always by my side
So today, my grief - I cannot hide

Max was my best friend
And we were always together until the end

Together every day we walked
It never mattered that no-one talked

He always made me smile
For him, I would gladly go that extra mile

I gave him the best of everything
Including his daily chewy ring

He loved to drive with me in the car
Even if our destination was not far

With him, all my joys and sorrows I shared
And he needed no words to show he cared

Today, when I saw him lying there so still
I felt a void, I knew nothing else would ever fill

Please tell me what I'm supposed to do
Oh Lord, if I only knew

Please tell me why my best friend had to die
Before I even got to say goodbye

Karen Suchinski

The Wayside Cross

There's an old wooden cross, near a village I see,
so serene, how it looks over fields of grain
turning to the cross, the flowers sway and bow
God bless all they seem to say.

In a vale stands a large wooden cross so sublime
amid flowers wild and vines intertwined,
people stop and gaze, in awe and wondering eyes,
God is here, God has love for all.

At the turn of a field, there's a large holy cross
sheltered by cedar trees, daisies stirring nearby —
a rosary there, waiting for you to pray,
faith and love, the pioneer way.

Helen Moyer

God's Creation

God was lonely for creation
So he used imagination
On the first day he decided
Day and night should be divided.

On day two, at his will
Came heaven and earth, oh! what a thrill
To our delight on day three
The Lord created land and sea.

The fourth day then, for everyone
Our Lord gave us the moon and sun
On the fifth as was his wish
He gladly gave us fowl and fish.

The sixth day then was oh! so grand
Because that day came beast and man
Set aside from all the rest
The seventh day our Lord did rest.

John F. Carpenter

A Pond

Our pond is really a thing of delight
So clear and sparkling, the ripples so bright.
The fish enjoy the water clear,
I Think they know they have no fear
They glide around too fast to measure
To see them jump gives us great pleasure.
The birds fly down and take a drink,
Then fly away as quick as a wink.
A duck wanders in and swims around
Then off he goes to further ground.
Dragon flies of various hues,
The reeds that sparkle with the dews.
The breeze that shakes the trees to laughter,
Then bends them down to reflect in the water.
The air is full of buzzing bees,
Croaking frogs and dancing trees.
So good to sit and look around
To see and hear the sights and sounds
And know that nature smiles upon our pond.

Kaye Sheldon

The Works Of God

Just look around you can't deny the wondrous works of God.
So beautiful it speaks of peace, his nature filled with awe.
Look at the sky the shades of blue, how they change within a day.
The clouds so fluffy like cotton balls and in a moment fade away.
The sun so bright you can not look with the naked eye.
The birds they soar upon the wind so very, very high.
See the birds how beautiful, each unique in color,
As God painted each bird he made, no one is like the other.
The flowers also a pretty sight they cast you in a spell.
And as you watch God sends a breeze and they cast off their smell.
Oh the pleasure of all God made, there's beauty you can't deny.
For even the trees lift up their limbs, to God they glorify.
The birds sing such a pleasant song, so pleasant to the ear.
For they know the Lord their maker is very, very near.
When the rain falls from the sky it dances on the ground,
The bouncing of the raindrops it is a peaceful sound.
The raging of a thunderstorm it catches our attention,
There's something about its beauty only watching it can mention.
And yet when it's over, a picture freshly painted,
And a peaceful stillness, only God has created.

Theresa G. Harrison

The Power Within The Bottle

The bottle perches on the counter
snickering at me,
enticing you.
The power within is too terrorizing to comprehend.
Once you start, it's impossible to stop;
for it is compromised of control;
directing, dominating your every move.
The potential potency frightens me
like an evil demon possesses a soul.
Your thoughts are distorted,
your actions are abusive,
your attitude is apprehensive.
Your bitter, brutal comments lash out
agonizing me.
I live my life in pain, suffering and in fear
of the bottle;
of the power within the bottle.

Donna Waines

Midnight Highways

I love the lonely roads,
Smooth with rain,
On cool October nights.
Twinkling farm lights play hide and seek,
Through the green soldiers
Bowing to my transport.
The road slinkys up and down, up and down,
Up and down,
Under the glowing blanketed sky.
Two columns of light,
Followed by its car,
Pass into an abyss.
Swish!
Tonight, I slide home.

Kimberley Enns

Our View

Sometimes a whale, amongst ducks afloat.
Smooth and majestic, sails the boat.

United and proud, are my geese.
Perched and alone, the heron's at peace.

Across from the mountain, reflect the trees.
Fish jump tempting, the men on the seas.

Quiet and sneaky, goes the seal,
As he constantly looks, for another meal.

Playful and happy, are the otters at play.
The sun sets with brilliance, at the end of the day.

Glimmering, shimmering shines the moon.
Romance without cost, echo's the loon.

Lynn Babcock

Maggie At 90

The memories flow together now as streams flow into rivers

Great rivers course side by side, the emerald Thompson briefly skirting the muddy Fraser, before the currents cloud its shimmering green

Both are lost at the ocean's door, a trillion drops of sparkling memory bound together

Boundless ocean, sum of the old woman's life and love and feeling

For the listener still bound by chains of measured time, her flowing memories seem confused

Be patient; to hear does not matter if we know the lost son of 60 years ago or the great grandchild found

First, second and third husbands, not counted nor compared, but in one love

The widow's memories are her reflection on life and death

Through her we always knew the brilliance of life, now fading gently

In inevitable death, her sparkling memory will shine through the ocean's deep.

Audrey Spence-Thomas

Christmas Wish List

What do I want for Christmas?
Six little words with a wealth of meaning.....

Of material goods I have no need,
For spiritual blessings I would plead.
An end to hunger and fear worldwide;
All races and colours stand side by side;
Free to worship, each in their own way,
Welcoming peace here on earth every day.

Families together, healthy, happy faces;
Everyone visiting old familiar places.
Through windows, softly glowing in the dark,
Glimpses of friendship and love are the spark,
Lighting the spirit of this holiday season.
Keep it year 'round, defying all reason.

White Christmas! What a dazzling sight!
Sparkling crystals, prisms of pure light.
Candles gently glowing, drawing us nigh;
Fragrant trees gleaming, reaching on high;
Wreaths hanging on doors - "Welcome, friend."
Joy to the world...peace without end.

Marilyn Johnson

"George And Harley's Mitzvahs"

Cats die; owners live—
"Sir George"; "Pretty Kitty, Harley".
Why do cats have 9 lives?
Do cats take on their owner's stress; what do cats give?

Cats always land on their feet.
Cats always rub against your legs.
Cats always listen to you.
Cats always cuddle you when your heart's broken;
Cats are always so sweet.

Owners in the 90's get Aids, Cancer.
Owners in the 90's want companionship
at any age, stage, phase of life.

Cats in the 90's get: shots/needles
for viruses/diseases, de-clawed for living inside,
neutered for pesty pet control.
Cats in the 90's get crystals with no lancer
so, Cats die; owners live.

Judy Kirchmeier

Untitled

My city has a wolfish determination
Silent running, close, perhaps unseen
To ground level, a child of earth-formed instincts.

It is lying still, alert;
Beneath a cool moonless night, shadowless,
That I sensed its arrival, blood to blood.
Wanting to greet this elegance of pure power
Yet, my life demanded stillness - - steady heart strokes.

Perhaps I dreamed, as its scent washed my skin
But I think not, perhaps only a wishing time.
It's the surviving, you know,
One more season of city created death breaths
This, and revelling in a new season's coming.
Wary with half remembered sharing of other lives
My steps are stronger with its arrival.

Take my hand, I know so well this beauty.

La Loba Cuento

Untitled

You will climb one day
Shyly from the moist earth
Peer at the enchanting sunlight
The supple green of your tendrils, pure and fragile
Curving coyly upwards, trembling with anxiety
You culminate into a bud, one day
In the dark recesses of your mind, you dream
An aberrant gossamer of colours, a tingling web of fragrance
While nature awaits to kiss your future lips
To drink the nectar from your heart
Oh! You shy little bride of nature
With the softest of whispers you unfurl
In all your daintiness, one day
Holding out your petals, breathe in the blue sky
Listen to the soft murmurs of the wind
Emboldened, you look around, bathe in the warm light
And then, fall asleep under the stars
Drooping with exhaustion, dreaming another dawn
Cringing from the reality
Which will see you... wilt

George Jacob

Reflections

When I was a young child I used to cry late at night, as the wind
shrieked and the rain clawed at my window. Terror would clutch my
heart as the monsters of my imagination came to play in the shadows
of my bedroom. As my sobs became audible, my mother would come and
comfort me. She would hold me in her arms and rock me back to sleep.

When I was a teenager I used to lie late at night, as the rain pelted
down and the wind rattled my window, thinking of the meaning of life,
death, eternity and other such intellectual things. I thought of my
dreams, goals, desires and the people with whom I would share them.
The world was mine to conquer and as I yelled a gruff goodnight to
my mother I would enter a dream world of women, friends, adventures
and dreams.

When I was a young man I used to plan late at night, as the rain
monotonously poured down and the wind groaned at my window. Visions
of wealth, power and challenge danced around me in all their splendor.
I barely thought of the one with the large brown eyes that I had
passed over because there would be plenty-even more beautiful to come.
As I finished a letter to my mother I fell asleep and entered the
world where I was king.

Kathryn June Gillies

Carrying The Torch

The crimson of the poppies petals,
Shows dull against the rusting medals.
The crosses, still standing tall, towering
Amid the graves below.

We are the carriers. Alive to-day-
We live, we stand, and thank the way,
Brave men fought, although they lay,
In flanders fields so far away.

We with courage hold, and stand against the foe:
Living, guarding peace, row by row-
The torch is ours, we've held it high;
In memory of you, who fought and died.
So sleep in peace where the poppies grow-
Sleep in peace-
Row by row!

Linda Ann McGeorge-Scheelar

The Unknown "The Circle Of Life"

As I stand at the door of the unknown, I take a look around,
should I knock and enter? Or be still and not make a sound.
I have no luggage with me, once I enter I'll stay awhile,
all I need is a heart full of love, and have a friendly smile.
I see the door is now open, this place is beautiful and bright,
these flowers I've never seen before, what a wonderful sight.
Down the long-long pathway I see some friends of mine,
I knew they'd be here to greet me, although it's been some time.
There was no need to worry, the unknown is quite clear,
I think I'll stay forever, now that I have no fear.

Norma M. Stroobandt

Days Of Grace

So many stolen days from winter, when the sun has
   shone so bright.
The skies have been dramatic, fluffy clouds of white.
We know it is not April, for snow and ice abound.
As we watch the river force its wave, to a crackling,
   lively sound.

A winter on the Prairies, but in the Foothills nestled tight.
Calgary has its own sweet song on hilltops that delight.
With vistas of the mountains, or valleys deep below.
We revel in the moment, for one thing we all know.

This month, or moment, each day we face.
We cannot deem to be, the same within each season,
   for nature here is free.
She is capricious, kind and loving, or tormenting,
   cold and cruel.
As we live within her boundaries, and bend to let her rule.

Jean Mears

A Prayer For Faith

Dear Lord, show me the golden path
Shine your glorifying light upon my heart.
Give me complete faith in your divine presence.
Your abiding love warms my soul
Like sun on a beach,
With the warm sand under my feet.
Your voice to my heart,
Is as gentle ocean waves,
Lapping against the shore.
Build me soul of steel,
Soften my heart with your glory.
Grant me eternal life.
To be by your side in heaven
Is my only desire.

Chris Bateman

United Again

I am sitting beside her, holding her hand,
she's breathing her last.
But she continues to smile and tell me about him,
her man, her love.
As she speaks of the way he looked at her,
her eyes sparkle.
She speaks of the day they met, the times they shared,
the whispered secrets.
Her face brightens as she speaks of the birth
of all her children.
Tears enter her eyes as she recalls the day she lost
the only man she loved.
A flash of pain eases across her face,
she continues to smile.
At last her breathing slows; she slips away,
she's now gone.
Into the promised land where they will be,
united again.

Vernanda Deleeuw

Beauty Is Forever

Returning to the pew
   she watches the candle.
Tall, slender, white.
   Beautiful in form.
Its young flame
   flickers in the breeze
   of passing communicants.

In her youth
   she too was lovely,
slim, upright, alive.
   Now white hair
crowns her wrinkled face her aged eyes are dimmed
   Her foot steps falter.

The service ends
   the old lady hobbles to the door
her radiant face aglow.

The candle too will waste,
   lines from the melting taper
will run and form
   a new beauty on an old waxen body.

Phyilis Moore

One Man's Dream

There she stood, within the moon light
She was lovely as the sky's brightness
caressing was her smile, softly did she sing
Sweet where her words
real was her presence
the passion of her was intense

A lone star shoots across the sky
in flame never to remain and like the star was once
There she stood no more

Sadness touches his heart
bowing his head he whispers
may my eyes fall upon your grace once more
There in a forest, within the moonlight
He walks alone in memory of a girl

One man's dream, and in an instant glimpse
There was a small taste of that dream
He holds his dream close and patience
For the day when His thirst.
Shall be quenched and the dream
   shall remain.

Gentleness
Opens
Doors

Paul D. Thompson

Dad

June 15th 94 at 8 a.m., here no more
Sadly missed as you can see,
I know you're in heaven waiting for me.
When your time came, you had no say
We know you fought this,
Day by day.
You were one of a kind, I can hope to be
To raise my children,
The way you raised me.
Getting on with my life I'm trying to do,
But that will never stop me
Of thinking of you...

Bill Armstrong

Part-Time Father

I look at her with a heart felt longing.
She looks at me, knowing, yet unknowing.
She seeks a reason for the familiarity,
unable to realize that it is heredity.

She smiles and laughs. My heart melts.
My inner turmoil is temporarily quelled.
She is absolutely perfect in every way,
gaining knowledge and growth with each passing day.

She cries, and I rush to her side.
Concern and worry mingling with my pride.
With a comforting hand, and a gentle caress,
I do my best to ease her stress.

She falls asleep in my loving arms
knowing that I could never do her any harm.
A bond of trust begins to take shape.
A feeling that I shall never let abate.

She awakes, and looks me in the eye.
I smile broadly, while inside I cry,
for our visit together is coming to an end.
The pain in my soul will never mend.

Robert C. King

Last Good-Bye

The house lies quiet tonight
She left me without saying good-bye
She lied her head upon my lap
And slowly slipped away.

She was everything to me
I poured all I had into her
When she got sick I tried to be strong
But to watch her weaken reduced me.

She never stopped loving
From the day it began to the last hour she loved
Though the pain was intense she'd smile
I felt her pain in the core of my heart.

when I could, I'd hold her
She felt safe in the grips of my arms
I prayed each night for healing
To remove this cursed sickness from her.

Take not from me my love
I love her with all that I am
Goodnight my sweet, rest well
You'll always remain in my heart.

D. Scott Chatterson

Love

Her golden looks caress a moon-swathed pillow.
She lays, her heaving breasts, replete now.
We have loved the night away in sweetest passion,
In requited love we pass the brief sensation.
She breathes a sigh of happy satisfaction
And dreams a dream of primal adoration.
And yet throughout she held herself apart
Not anxious to reveal her hidden heart.
But yet, at last, in complete and final dissolution
She gives herself in splendid resolution.
Now spent, she lays, limbs a kimber,
Peaceful now and free and limber,
Soft curves in moonlight, passion rendered
In love sublime complete surrender.
Then she stirs amid the wakeful stars
And strives to gather what is hers.
And now she sleeps in gratification
A deep content and satiation.
She sleeps!

David Levingbird

A Little Girl's Faith

The little girl walked slowly up to her father's grave
She laid down some pretty red roses,
Then stood looking oh so brave.

She got down on her tiny knees and looked towards the sky
With tears running down her cheeks she said,
"Why did my Daddy die?"

God, I never even knew him; you took him when I was so small
All I know of him is the stories that others tell me, that's all.

Oh God, please be nice to my Daddy and give him a kiss for me
Tell him I'll see him someday and then I will sit on his knee.

Dear God, I know I am lucky cause I have a Mommy, you see
There are many kids who have neither,
So thanks for your kindness to me.

The little girl rose slowly and began to walk away
Then looking back she whispered,
"Dear Daddy, I'll see you someday."

Linda Skelhorn

Blue Solitude

The winds are gusting outside
sharp pellets of snow burn the skin.
I crawl into my snow fort
kneel on the ground
and light my candle.
The calm blue air
comforts me,
numbness overtakes me
joy buried deep within me
begins to warm my body.
Nobody to share my peace with
except my cats
that jump on my lap
jarring me out of my silent world.
Even though my knees are burning with cold
I decide to sit a while longer
so they can warm their little feet.

Linda Elmi

Twilight: Michael At Three O'Clock

I linger between two worlds -
Shadows or either side;
Sadness on one - joy on the other.
I'm scared - I feel so alone - I don't belong.
Where is she?

They cry for me - I know she's there,
It is dark - I see a light.
I am deaf, yet music fills my head -
I hurt, but I can't feel it anymore.
I am waiting for her to come and take me.

Don't cry for me, I love you
I'll be one step away
And I won't be alone.
Help me! I feel so alone,
And yet ... she comes.

I feel her hand caressing me -
I knew she'd come!
Goodbye. I love you.

Linda Follis

304

Ode To Men

Dignity
Self denied
Islands oceans apart
From wimps to warriors
Fear of the inner spirit
Beer and pretzels are not enough anymore
Alone with feelings hidden behind the facade of manhood
Power brokers devising tactics used to control the very
   essence of life
What was once masked now exploding through a
   self-addressed enveloped
Little boys we forget don't want to grow up just play
Struggling to guard the sanctuary of the soul
Help sought not found
Childhood pain unrealized
Silent crying
Seeking.

Hans Stupan

Quest

Been travelling the road of life
searching to find out what's wrong and what's right
wondering when this journey will end
so I may find peace in my life's once again.

Been searching my life for a dream
not even knowing where I'm going or where I've been
to find a place where people really love
to see if there's a hell below or heaven above.

Been hunting for so long
that all my fears and worries have gone
this path leading me down the road of self knowledge
gaining wisdom not found in any school or college.

Been on this road for too long
and now the years have come and gone
only to find I didn't have to run
for the answer was there my journey had begun...

Everything I was looking for was inside of me.

Carmen Maja Nagoda

The River's End

In life the river winds,
Searching for the end,
As it empties into the sea,
It becomes one with all other rivers.

The bird flies free
yet it is part of the wind
which answers to the land,
They all join at the river's end.

People fight the way
pushing and pulling to change eternity
it is all for naught
For all will be known at the river's end.

Better to flow like the river from the beginning of life,
to live as you will die, to be one now as you will be later.

The river will not change its course
it will not stop or run uphill,
fighting the river will do no good
it will flow on, no matter what is done.

So be one and flow and all will fall from you
till all that remains is the river flowing to its end.

Kurt Nordli

In And Out

A monster of earth, taking a bite
Scratching his way out from inside
Bits and pieces under his nails
Pale and dirty he is out again

Keeping his distance, observing the sight
He chooses you to help him decide
Shall he stay calm or will he fight
For your respect to get back his pride

He is so vigorous, looking into your eyes
And you are helpless against all his might
Frozen and scared like a figure of stone
You keep silent on the edge of the skydome

Another step closer, you wish to disappear
You'll sooner jump then let him near
Now for the hero it was all very clear
Pity for self is the center of fear

Now he wants to enter the way where he come from
His mother heard, Gaea swallowed him whole
Nothing is ever the way it appears
You'll eventually die, but he will always be here

Julia Novikova

Black Cap

The mother of my soul is screaming for its seeds today,
Scratching, clawing at my innards,
   sneering in entirety.
Jeering at attempts to clutch a happy state,
   mocking me for all I am.
I crackle
   with bristling unsated rage,
Glaring at my spark of fire
Wishing it away, yet cajoling
   it to stay.
Alerted to my self destruction
   is my meditative mind,
Singing songs in an effort to remain
   detached and ignorant
   of my urgent state of mind.
My famished core is feeding on my doubt,
Its madcap craven hypocrisy
   poisons and infiltrates me
   without clearance of consent.

Rivka Claman

Destiny

We closed our eyes as mother nature died,
Save the air, save the trees, save the world, she cried.
To care for the earth to mankind she must show,
So, a delicate web from a silken thread she wove.
Take heed to my words, cherish earth, she said,
Respect it, she warned or many tears you will shed.
But her warning ignored we continued the destruction,
The web collapsed with no hope for reconstruction.
To mankind she presented dark, rich, fertile soil,
But the chemicals injected caused quite a turmoil.
The mighty wind which once frolicked with my hair,
Now cease to blow, relief cease to share.
Once brimming with life and a deep sky blue,
the ocean turns murky, what a pitiful hue.
This could be our future if we choose,
But not if we recycle, reduce, and reuse.

Sivanny Selvakumar

The Storm

The skies were full of darkness, distinctive winds
Rushed hastily throughout the leaves
Some scattering about on the ground

I watched from high above the landscape as the streaks of
power danced with gaiety free of all opposition.
Taking command of the heavens,
the further demonstration of the Ruler's force,
was the chamber's echo that deafened all sound around.

Damp smell permeated the surrounding land.
Within brief moments life's dew poured from the dark,
creating with it a new sound
as if a new instrument had been added to the majestic
sound of a symphony.

My awe was peaked again
by the grandeur of the Creator's play
as the orchestra of the heavens prepared for its close.
I looked upward and felt connected to it all;
part of and yet not.
My participation was as a member
in the audience of existence.

Laurent Christiaens

Silence

Silence sits and watches our reactions to each other as we enter a room...
The excitement, the desire, the pain, the anger, the resentment...
Silence feeds the questions that loom in our minds
of each other, the future - the present.

Silence has become a member of our family - accompanying us every
moment we are together - feeling very comfortable in our home....
often more comfortable than we do.

I look at you and feel myself wondering how you're doing, what you're
feeling and wanting to ask you to hold me tightly in your arms.
Your presence makes me miss you, your eyes break my heart.
My questions multiply, the pain wells - it's then that I can feel the
comfort of a familiar hand on my shoulder... SILENCE.

I watch you again as you leave the room, wanting so desperately to
reach out to let you know I'm still here and through all the confusion
I still care.
That there must be some way our worlds can re-connect.
In the distance our eyes meet and once again I am painfully
reminded of what has so thoroughly engaged us...
SILENCE.

Diana Vaton

Giving

Unveiling the secrets of your heart, be speak of giving.
Roaring embryo fragments, seeking out your soul in grief.
Still the child in you, weaning thoughts, yearning to relive.
Reminiscing on brooks caress,
    mountain's dew heights and valley's tears.
For to withhold is to perish, not knowing what it means.
When you give of yourself, what you truly give is every real.
To liberate the giant within you, between sorrow and glee.
To be wary in your solitude, and joyful in your gleams.
To awaken too much tenderness, mindful of what it keeps.
Two hearts reflected, guiding life to its stream.
In entrenching on thought-belief of non deserving,
    would be life-law wrong doing.
Turn about weals hurting, and prey on another sun of loving.

Nicolas Akkaoui

Free As A Dove!

All the pain,
rinsed down the drain,
all the hurt,
washed away like dirt,
I wash myself free of him,
and soon the memories will dim,
the bruises will go away.
As the fear lives within me everyday,
A life with him would lead to brutal length,
to love my child will give me strength,

Now in my bed as I lie,
I dream of happiness for my daughter and I,
the memories of him left to die,
I'm free to laugh and I'm free to cry,
I'm free to feel and I'm free to love,
finally I'm free, as free as a dove.

A. Haines

Victoria - We Love Thee!

Hail Victoria, the city that we love, where people come to live and
    revel in her setting sun.
Her Majestic name emblems a great queen; where warmer breezes blow
    and there's little snow.
O' Victoria our land of glory - City of Gardens - flowers we count
    one by one.
Where grass is forever green; - parks galore - exciting activities,
    and there's more.
O' Victoria, our beautiful home - we love thee! We welcome visitors
    from lands afar and host a seasonal show of flags unfurled in an
    annual yacht Swiftsure!
O' Victoria, our glorious land - our home.
O' Victoria doesn't matter where we roam, we always want to come back
    home.
O' Victoria our home - we love thee!
Liquid sunshine sometimes prevail but seldom do we get hail.
Magnificent birds in flight - even quail.
Blue skies to view, - the mountain streams rush to the surf,
    sand and sea - the deep blue waters where the salmon run.
Victoria, beautiful garden city of the world. Victoria where culinary
    feasts delight everyone!
So proud O' Victoria, the capital of beautiful B.C. - where mountain
    peaks o'er land and sea.
O' Victoria our beautiful home, we love thee.
O' Victoria, we love thee!

Frances Gill Fraser

Charity Unto Thee

Beloved cease thy weeping and embrace thy tormenter no
longer. Thou doth arise with harrowing impressions and thy
frame is delicate from midnight dreams. Thy visage art smeared
with tear drops. Doth thy mind and thy heart linger in anguish?
Thy art comforted by an abundance of faithful charity. Anguish
shall not command thy spirit. Thy faith to believe abides within
thee. Receive thy blessing of Godly love. Mercy comes to rescind
thy tormenter. Silence thy weeping and hail thy victory. Sweet
joys shield thy heart form pain. Peace delivers thy mind from
captivity and appeases thy spirit with gentleness and goodness.
Charities manifest themselves and renew thy spirit within thee.
Godly love abides within thee forever. Thy Beloved.

Cynthia Daniels

Till We Meet Again

There wasn't time to say
"Good Bye"
When I think of it, I
want to cry
I know you knew I loved
you, Joe
Because I always told
you so
But still, I wanted to
embrace,
To hold you close, to
stroke your face
There was so much I
wanted to say
Before I could, you
went away
I'll see you soon,
we've got a date
I'll meet you at the
"Golden Gate"

Virginia Hannon

March Wind

Over land and seas I travel
Over houses and barns, and
Fields, creeks and meadows
Over every golden shore.

I travel here, I travel there,
I have selfish, bless.
I go my way, without delay
Help no one in distress

You hear me in the timber
You hear me everywhere
You hear me especially in March.
For I sent you shivering then.

I'm the wind
You're sure to know
So goodbye
For here I go.

Mildred P. Rieselman

Tapestries Woven

Subtle beginnings, a beguiling smile,
vibrant eyes that implore an approach.
Casually we greet at once at ease,
your lilting voice spellbinding,
caressing me like a gentle breeze.

Two paths have now become one
your hand held in mine,
as fingers clasp
so our souls entwine.

This gesture alone so eloquent,
a simple gift taken to heart.
Encompassing all we've shared
kindred souls, never apart.

Richard S. Misener

Untitled

An angel's wings
a butterfly's
Wispy, whispering, soft
Light in the air
Sparked by God
delicate as gossamer
A web of intricacy
Love can be like this
And snap with one word.

Linda F. Miller

Untitled

Perched on my arm I can see,
A bird, blue as the sea, I wonder,
If he has the power to fly.
Why does he sit with me.

In the rays of the fiery sun,
Waiting for this heat to be done,
I give shelter to the Jay,
Who watches the young children run.

Instantly the cold sets in
I can feel Jack Frost's frigid grin.
My little friend, soon flies away.
The food is gone and he looks thin.

When she decides to wake me.
My green coat with amaze thee
I love to sit and think, damn,
It's good to be a tree.

Michael Braga

"White Lights And Black Roses"

And so I pass into oblivion within
a blinking of your eye
And the echoes of a gunshot continue
ringing in your mind
Time will ever be eternal, trapped
within your soul
And lost upon the endless darkening
sky within this cold
Behind me I leave nothing, immortality
not my case
To follow numberless shooting stars
in the heavens I do chase
And forever in your memory my
face goes through its poses
And all I have to give to you is
white lights and black roses

Liticia M. Smith

The Book Of Life

One more page in the story of life.
A chapter unfolded.
A book resting on the shelf
once to turn back the pages
to see how far we have gone.

Then turning forward
to journey on.
Making our mark,
a hope,
not to be forgotten.

A statement made
and left to be told.
A chapter is done and
the next to be written.

Self as the author.
The soul as the pen.
Our creator the inspiration.
Death the next chapter to be written.

Melissa Tuma

Diamonds

Life can be
a diamond in disguise
so shiny and bright
when loves in your path
so deadly dull
when your all alone

So many facets
to our little gem
love hope and to understand
and truth
that is as wide as the sky
is the crown of this gem

So my dear friend
I hope and pray
when you come, that you'll say
you'll be my diamond
the light of my life
my meaning to fight

Rebecca Mone Dove

Sunshine In The Rain

A thought keeps coming to my mind,
A dream I've kept down deep inside.
I want to know what love's about,
I want to know, without a doubt.
I want to be held in your arms,
And know that I am safe from harm.
I want to know that what I feel
Is something warm, and kind, and real.
I have weathered some stormy skies,
And you can see it in my eyes.
I have felt a lot of pain
And wished for sunshine in the rain.
But now I see the clouds are breakin',
And I wonder if maybe I'm mistaken,
But maybe I see something in you
That can change those grey skies to blue.
So take my hand, and hold it tight.
Protect me from the angry night.
Now I feel I can be strong,
Because I've found where I belong.

Shannon Wrisner

True Life

Love on blowing breeze
A heaven dream
Life, a birthing death
Angel, wing dipped in blood
God, planning or destined
Dying, dying, dead
Where I do not know
Knowing I wish not
Loving in all hoping
Hoping in all truth
Crying a tear of nothing
Nothing born, but not of bliss
Kissing not of sense, but of mind
Knowing it all
And yet, knowing nothing

Ryan Keith

Untitled

MARRIAGE
A life-long plan
Designed by God
For you and me
To join together and become one.

It involves a love
That only comes from God
A love that is unconditional
Understanding and forgiving.

MARRIAGE

Is a plan for us
To experience what only
God can create when we
allow him to take control.

A gift and a privilege
When God blesses us
as we grow together
in love and in Christ.

Martha K. Boucher

Definition Of Love

There is a love that stirs the heart
    A love that gives it rest.
There is an all enduring love
    A love that stands each test.
There is a love that grows with years
    Through turmoil, doubt and strife.
A love that feeds a hungry heart
    Fulfills another life.
There is a love that needs no words
    To tell its depth and height.
A love that ever seeks to give.
    That love is always right.

Wilma R. Ray

Time Flies

January is here
a new year begins
soon February appears
when did the new year end?
March comes along
spring is almost here
April rains sprinkle
and thoughts are too dear
May gives us flowers
June, July, the sun
August is the season
the start of school for some
September the winds are coming
October it has begun
November the snow is falling
in more ways than one
December is for children
so innocent and care free
and then before we know it
again it's January!

Monica Mohart

Mountains

Oh, the beauty that is seen
all around us, shades of green.
Living, breathing plants and trees
spread further than the eyes can see.
Up and down the hilly land
held steady by clay, dirt, and sand.
Black top asphalt intrudes within.
Water flows around the bend.

Kimberly Burley

The Sea Of Time

Alone I walked by the sea
A sea bird's call upon the breeze
The waves' thunder filled the air
A peaceful scene without a care

A pearly shell by the dune
A foot print of I know not whom
The dark blue water looms to call
To wipe the traces left by one and all

And so it will come to pass
The sea will consume everything at last
And wipe the slate of history's past
And with it every trace of me

Miklos Sipos

Shimmering Light

Penetrating through the sea
A shimmering light that comes
Beneath the sea
There is a glorious beauty of light
Down below
Countless fish that come and go
The light guides the fish
Through the sea
And no one can help them
Not even me

Maria T. Chaydez

Dead Wood

Of length and breadth this world over
A sight most commonly seen
Was the prevail of growth around us all
Replete with animate sheen

Trees once abundant and all a 'clutter
when genesis come to be
Were habitat to life, rife with wing
nursing on loamy mead

Our planets growth of flora
once said to be unended
is threatened by the very life
to whom it gives provender

To log the forests around us
presents litigious need
others deplete their wooded growth
glutting the markets greed

Indecision plagues the future
we must debate our right
do we farm Gods given manna
or risk environmental sight

Thomas M. Esser

The Yellow Bow

It's only a small yellow bow
A simple reminder to pray
For the courageous men and women
Who are in the Middle East today.

Maybe it's a loved one
Or someone you don't know.
Either way they need our prayers,
Probably more than it shows.

Won't you take a moment,
A special moment today,
To pray for their protection
And their safe return to the USA

Sue Gibson

I Have...

A memory that I remember
A song that I sing
A thought that I have thought through
A feeling that I feel
And a you I won't forget.

Lora Tasset

Love

Love is like a bridge,
A string or a rope.
Connecting two people together,
and the world has to cope.

You never know,
who or when.
If today or tomorrow,
a stranger or a friend.

The moment it happens
you will know.
For only then,
shall your love grow!

Shanna M. Butler

To My Brother

The sun shines on my face
A tear falls from my eye
Where are you my brother?
Did you hear my cry?

I reach out to hold you
But nothing reaches back
I try to touch your picture
But the frame just seems to crack

No words from your mouth
Not even your charming smile
Just your face appears
To bring back my inner child

I know where you are now
Yet, I still don't know why
But at least your loving memories
Will take way all the sad goodbyes.

Melissa Florio

Salvation

As a rose kisses the morning dew
A tear falls from the sky
A choir of angels are singing
A song for thy
The wind doth howl and carry
The sins of all mankind
But our souls shall overcome it
If not all life would die
But fear not for our purity
And fear not for our friends
Fear for our souls and blessings
God's powers have no ends

And emerge shall we in Eden
A kingdom of balance and grace
It is filled with crystallized moonlight
Twill save the human race

Laura A. Kirkpatrick

Evening Time

With ev'ning comes,
A time of rest,
Through the day, long,
I've done my best.

I like to work,
The long day through,
When ev'ning comes,
I sit with you.

To sit and dream,
Of what could be,
Just you and I,
Is what I see.

What's life about?
I've often thought,
Without your love,
It's all for naught.

William H. Ball

Rhianna

Six hours is not enough
A week is too long
Look in her eyes you'll see
Her innocence
Her will to learn
Watch her at play
Hear her laughter
The sound of her voice
Her temperament
And individuality
I want to show her
The world
I wish to learn again
What it's like to be
A child
All in six hours
My time is up
I love you baby
I'll pick you up
Next week

Steven Cruz

A Little Smile Can Last A While

A little smile can last
A while it will fill your heart
forever. A smile is something to show
any way even on your Darkest Day
then, and now, and forever.
A smile is something for every
one to see because it doesn't cost
one Brown Penny always now and forever
So when you start to smile
your friends will too but, you'll know
who put that special smile in you.

Niki Dula

Clouds

Look above see the wonder from
above, see the pictures we
can make. Tell a story to a
mate. Clouds that move slow
are safe. Clouds moving fast
fell us there is a change coming
our way. The clouds do so much
more up there in outer space.

Susan Balsley

An End To Darkness

The blade slashes
Across the fleshy throat
Of a demon.
The angels rejoice.
Even their goodness
Does not allow them
To feel remorse.
His death is a victory
In the eyes of God.
No sad song shall be sung.
The heavens unite
And bathe in his blood.
They give light to the darkness
That once pulsed through his veins.
Evil has been eliminated.
The demon is dead.

Tami Osborne

LA Sunset

The sky
afire with light.
Clouds, seldom seen
incensed at coming night

The embers
fanned by solar winds
burst with light and fade

The breeze dies.
The embers darken.
The leaves, silhouetted still
pause

Linda Robeck

I Thought Of You Tonight

I thought of you while on watch
against the foe.

I saw your beautiful smile when
the silver moonbeams glistened
off the golden rice straw
in the fields terraced below.

The starts twinkled like your eyes
when I look into them.

But more than a twinkle - a spark.
A spark, no a flame
Blazing out of control,
engulfing the entire forest
Like my love for you.

Yes, I thought of you tonight
Just like I think of you
every moment of the day.

E. Glenn Sanford

Identity

Lost in the search for identity
Amid a world with no serenity
Dreading fates tempting lure
While life's experience is obscured
Through the haste enacted by time...
However far the searchers climb
Never attaining the egos peak
Till the last while all is defeat
Fate grants a boost upon the flower
So immortality may brush the power.

Peggy L. Nuckols

A Friend Of Mine

A friend of mine died today
Aids taking his life away
A father, a husband, a friend
Never more to see again
His visions of time to spend
With a wife, a daughter, a friend
Time no more his will be
The heavens are now his to see
A friend of mine died today
Aids taking his life away
A breath no more he shall need
The angels of heaven are his to see
Memories of my friend and me
Are all I have left here with me
Tears will flow as time passes
Never more my friend to see
A friend of mine died today
Aids taking his life away
In pain no more will he be
Never far from my memories

Shawn D. Vaughn

Homing

Master sun glazes
All things
Green to yesterday
The night sky dance
Enters the song
In South America
Hearts and arrows
Measure
Grapes to wine
And culture wheeling
Cultures yes me
O so far
I maybe you
Felt as
Songs of all
Firmly pleasing
This is my temple
Or template
As I grope
Where stars whirl

Kevin K. Ferrin

Honesty To Keep

I am but an orphan lost at sea
Alone in wilderness, compromised
Interpreted in a vacuum
Collide not with facts to see

I am but an urchin fatefully in neglect
Charisma in fantasy absorbed
Consistently in life's wreck

Am I but a layman
Jurisprudent constantly in a dive
Strained through the verbiage
In salient effort to survive

Am I but another victim, off stage
To colored strobe lights
That my name is justice
Not all men seek my fight

You may seek me in the back room
Jury room, or street; although
In an effort to survive alone
I need all honesty to keep

William E. Dickinson

Indigence

We squander such a wealth of dreams
Along with all our youth,
Are prodigal of pity, love,
Of valor and of truth.
So costly is this price of life
That, in the end, we find
We are so drained of our reserves
Of will, of heart, of mind,
That even the brave cannot support
The burden of their fears,
And only the happy can afford
The luxury of tears.

Waverly L. Hemenway

Secrets

Sometimes malicious
Always delicious,
Sometimes saddening
Always maddening.
Drives you crazy,
Shrouded and hazy,
Dark and deep
Hard to keep
Secrets.

Mary McGovern

Untitled

My mother told me
"always smile at everyone
even if they don't."
So I smiled at him
and he finally saw me,
but did not smile back,
so I felt once more
the hurt of looking too hard,
and began again.
I'll just show myself
as I am at that moment,
it's much easier.
And besides sometimes
I suppose I smile too much.
My cheeks really hurt!
Now what should I do
quit smiling altogether
or smile when I want?

Olivia Briggs

Home

Bubbles of chatter
amidst a heated crowd
a thundering sound of music
sneaking through the mass of confusion
of a rowdy, untidy room
a strike 3 for the yanks
as a teenage boy howls
and opens the volume a bit more loud
a shrilling call, a boisterous shout
as laughingly they live
my home
where warmth and love and feelings show
my heart aches to be there once more.

Maria Persaud

Fall

As I walked
  among the trees
I saw the pretty
  golden leaves
And as they twirled
  around and around
They fell asleep
  upon the ground

Nikobie Bellamy

Little Guest

A wonderful thing has happened
An act of God you could say
An amazing gift that we'll receive
About nine months away.

We have created a new life
A mom and dad we'll be
A child to love and care for
A child you and I conceived.

It may not be perfect timing
But I feel the Lord knows best
He obviously thinks we're ready
For our blessed little guest.

Robin Lynn Strole

A World Of War

It's not just a bomb dropping plane.
An invasion of troops upon a shore.
Welcome to the real world.
A world raging of war.

Drugs sold to the young and curious,
By dealers dancing to a dollar,
Poisoned minds of future leaders.
too innocent to stand and holler.

Mother nature does the twist,
Hurricanes bombard our shores,
Volcanoes spew a river of fire,
Quakes rattle our doors.

The rape of a pretty woman,
Mugging seniors for an easy kill,
Stealing and selling of newborn babies,
This is not God's will

Fighting an enemy we cannot see.
Marching into battle blind,
Did God have the right idea,
Leaving this world of war behind?

Randy Overton

Thanks?

For the money,
  and a bed,
A place to hang my hat,
  a place to lay my head.
A cozy fire to warm my bones,
  fine music to feed my soul.
What is the missing link?
  Love, I think!

Lois L. Gitchell

Farewell To Summer

Leaves move gently now like hands
  and as they wave good-bye,

The sky joins in
  by darkening...

The wind, can only sigh.

Tears from heaven pit-a-pat
  upon my window pane,

Oh, how we'll miss
  her loveliness...

Until she comes again.

Roberta R. Simulis

The Goblins Are Coming

Lock your doors,
And bar the windows.

The night is clear,
The wind - O how it blows.

Put out the Jack - O - Lantern,
And turn out the lights.

They have waited all year,
Just for this night.

Pick up your feet,
And put out the treats.

They will soon be here,
But please don't fear.

For you see,
They are not after you and me,
All they want is the treats.

The Goblins they are coming.

Sandra Nabors

In Carelessness

You took the petals of a rose
And carelessly tossed them away
Never to lend its scent on summer.

You stood and laughed
As the wind blew them about,
Yet you failed to see in them my heart.

In careless pride and selfishness
You tossed my dreams, one by one,
To drift away, like a broken melody.

Valija P. Tubbs

A Paratrooper's Leap Of Faith

I leap! I leap, into the sky
And float upon the quiet air.
I ride the eddies of the wind
And let them waft me where they dare.

I see Earth beckoning from below,
Its grassy arms outstretched to me,
To grasp me when I land - too soon!
For I have touched Eternity.

Today I flew with the angels;
I saw where the Guardians trod.
I heard the whisper of their wings
While cradled in the hands of God.

My mind is tired. I long to sleep;
And in my dreams once more I'll leap.

Maureen Mills Ladds

The Measure Of A Man

To raise up high the mighty bow
and down a nameless, faceless foe.
To don the fleeting crown of glory
and be the hero of the story.
Is this the measure of a man?

To reach the pinnacle of fame
and always win the senseless game.
To march victorious through the field,
a place in history forever sealed.
Is this the measure of a man?

Or is it more a gallant mission
to dream one lonely, far-off vision.
To risk a mighty, fearful fall
and gain a height unknown to all.

To learn the lessons of the past
and seek the truth in all at last.
To darkness be a shining star
The measure of a man by far.

Tim R. Bridges

A Love Letter

The Lord has set my soul on fire
And filled me with His mighty touch
May I never grow lukewarm or cold
His love for me just means so much

I hunger and thirst for righteousness
Talking about the Lord is my delight
I read His word for understanding
He's on my mind both day and night

His love for me is beyond measure
It knows no limits or bounds
He waited for me patiently to repent
And then He turned my life around

I want to get to know Him better
He draws me closer the more I pray
Sometimes my feelings will overwhelm me
The Holy Spirit gives utterance for words I
cannot say

My love for Him keeps growing
I pray that it will always be that way
May the honeymoon never be over
And by His side I'll always stay

Robyn Davis

"Where Dreams Have Been"

I see blue lakes
and flowering vines.
Rainbow colors
and nature signs.
One midnight hour
from a distant hill,
I saw more blue lakes
asleep and still.
While across the sky
they glowed and glowed
the moon and the stars
and the clouds they rode,
I caught a glance
of scenes unfold,
that none would believe
even if I told.
I would love to see
Those things again,
just for an instant
where dreams have been.

Wanda Jones

Missing You

I miss you so very much,

My heart burns for your soft lips
and gentle touch,

Why you had to leave I don't know;
I really cared although it did not show,

I always thought our relationship would
stay strong,
Now that you're gone I find I was wrong.

Melissa M. Ziemer

The Reunion

Aunt May sat in her rocking chair
And glared at people everywhere
John passed out beer or cokes
And told his usual old stale jokes
Ezra quoted from the books (Bible)
And gave the beer boys dirty looks
Will then read his latest verse
'Bout Grandma falling from the hearse
It look them hours and hours to find
The body they had left behind

Daisy modeled Grandma's clothes
Tim tripped her up and broke her nose
Jimmy bobbed off Nellie's curls
And chased the other little girls
Joe shot Peter from a tree
We picked the buckshot from his knee
Alice drowned but who should care
She'd been told not to go there

Consider these things all in all
We really truly had a ball.

Ralph Zeigler

Tenderly I Surrendered

Gently you took my vulnerability
and held it tenderly in the arms
of your profound understanding.

Like a flower that blossoms when
winter is spent and spring is
on the horizon ... I surrendered.

Mazell Parker

Moons

The autumn moon is waxing
And hits me right between the eyes
Catching my conscious relaxing
So much to my surprise
That scarcely I felt my heart stop
And shivers wrapped my spine
I thought I saw a shooting star drop
The night the world was mine

Too much for me to remember
Like stars never really go away
A night to live forever
The night that was my day

The summer moon is waning
And the sky has become my heart
Catching my clouds fading
Wishing upon a star
Scarcely I see, feel forever
With a quick God sent eye
I'll forget this moon come never
And always believe in the sky

Rip

will you sit with me
and hold my hand as i reach
the end of time?

will you ponder me
later when i'm gone
beyond your fingers reach?

can you hold me fondly
first in the closet
of your heart's loving thoughts?

will you rescue times
of love possessed
in whirlpools deepened by tears,
withered...
yet in sight.

Mary Kay Stalley

Dawn

As the sun begins to rise,
And hopelessness melts away,
I realize with comfort,
It's the start of another day.

The past shall drift behind us,
And tomorrow shall come at will,
We have begun another day,
And there'll be another day still.

Life may treat us humbly,
Or impose an unjustly fate,
But we choose our own tomorrow,
We choose our own mind's state.

Though death eventually finds us,
And forthwith we fade and are gone,
We can rest with reassurance,
That our children will have a dawn

Owen Li

Spirit With You

Tears flow from your eyes because of me
And I feel the deepness of your sorrow
But I want to relieve your pain
So I'll tell you of tomorrow

I flowed down a narrow darkness
Until I saw the light
Then a hand stretched out to me
To assure me it's alright

As the light surrounded me
And cleansed me from within
Then I felt total peace
For I was released from sin

Now I am truly free
I never knew how it was
With so much love around me
I wonder...what's the fuss?

I needed to tell you this
To let you know it's true
Even if it doesn't seem like it
My spirit is always with you

Sonja La Rue Tracey

Daughter

You give me that smile
And I know why I'm here
To care for you, to count on
I'll always be near

No one could replace you
Or ever will
Your hugs and your laughter
I'll never have my fill

Your feelings, your secrets
They'll be safe with me
I'll hold you tight
Then set you free

You can travel the world
From here to the end
I will still be here
Your mother, Your friend

Marie Snyder

"My Son"

My son, I so love you
And I really do miss you
My son, you're in my heart
And I hate for us to be apart

My son, I miss your warm smile
And our walks mile upon mile
My son, you've brought me joy
For you are my loving little boy

My son, I wish you were near
And your voice I could hear
My son, we may be miles apart
But you'll always be in my heart

My son, you take care of yourself
And I'm always here if you need my help
My son, I'm sorry I can't be with you
And to share life with you

My son, don't ever forget me
And out of your life don't put me
My son, I sure do miss you
And my heart aches to be with you

Steven Bounds

Unconditional Love

Talk softly to my soul - old friend,
and I will listen well.
Of your triumphs and your sorrows,
I know you've much to tell.

Cry gently in my arms - old friend,
and I will wipe your tears.
Let out all of your emotions,
your joys and too,... your fears.

Look deep inside my heart - old friend,
and there, I know you'll find,
a love so unconditional...
the ties forever bind.

Paula Lynn Slovick

Autumn Leaves

Vivacious and vibrant leaves astray
bountiful fire colored bouquet
reflect upon a shining gold sky
and float amidst wispy winds high
while sailing aground to fastly fray.

Michele Marie Hall

Lasting Love

May happiness be yours
And life be good to you,
May you find lasting joy
In everything you do.

May all your steps be guided
By the brightest star above,
May each and every day you live
Be filled with honest love.

May your journey through these waters
Be a kind and gentle sea,
And if you find the waters rough
May you remember me.

For I will still be waiting
As I vowed the day you left,
Yes! I'll still be waiting
As I promised, till my death.

I will calm the troubled waters
Honest love I'll give to you,
I'll do my best to bring you joy
In everything you do.

Rosemarie Booth

Love Is Where

Love is where you see it
And love is where you feel it
Love is where you touch it
And love is where you show it
Love is where in your heart
And love is in your soul
Love is where in your mind
Love is in a feel
Love is in a touch
Love is in giving
And love is in caring
Love is in all your being
Love is in knowing it in your mind
Love is all in your emotions
Love is where -
   where you have it!

Pat Boyd

Midnight Crawlers

I like to hear the crickets chirp
and make that beautiful sound at night.
I like to hear the wind blow to the
ground as it sweetly whispers
"sleep tight."
As I slowly pull down my bedroom shade,
I look at the moon above.
I see it's the color of a pale white
with bright twinkling stars above.

I tuck myself into my bed holding
my bunny real tight,
As I go to sleep the wind scares
away all of my bad dreams with
a terrible, terrible fright.

Then I kiss my rabbit on the nose,
as I sleepily say "good night"
My covers are above me and my bed
is all warm, as a kiss of the
wind says "sleep tight."

Lauren W. Carter

Peace

Is there a place where peace prevails
And people are not divided?
Where color, faith or shape of eyes,
Aren't constantly derided?
Must greed and envy lead the way
And honor be forsaken?
Must torture rule and children die
So more land can be taken?
Will there always be contention?
Can't we learn from one another?
And try to live in harmony,
True sister and true brother.
If there's a God for each on high
Who made this earth we live on,
His tears must fall perpetually
To see our self-destruction!

A. Myra D'Gabriel

Memory Past

As I sit and gaze out my window
And see the trees and grass so green
I'm reminded of my childhood days
When all you had to do was play
All things seemed beautiful then
How come they don't today?
Is it because we work so hard
That we forget to play?

Sarah J. Joy

Blind Trust

Hurt is pain that plagues the heart,
And shreds it vein by vein.
Crying is torture building up inside,
Till it falls out the eyes like rain.
No matter the spasms it might endure,
The heart opens its arms out wide.
And let grief and hopelessness,
Take company deep inside.
The heart trusts completely,
That what it craves will be given.
While the possessor has other plans,
Then the life that they are living.
The possessor gives the love it wants,
Then gradually takes it away.
And leaves the heart hungry, waiting,
For the next criminal to come its way.

Kim Anderson

Peace

I gaze across the azure sky,
And watch the sunset glow,
I see the night birds winging by,
As homeward-bound they go.

The days are often filled with noise,
The city sounds and such,
As far as peace may be concerned,
Some days don't offer much.

But as each day come to a close,
And the WORLD is put to rest,
The deep serenity of night,
Is welcomed and is blest.

The cool breeze slowly filters in,
Shadows replace the light,
And with this transformation comes,
The gentle PEACE of night.

Sister Stephen Marie Driscoll

"Thoughts Of You"

I would like to share my thoughts,
    And spend my life with you.
That would be very special,
    Knowing that my dream had come true.

At times, I have nice thoughts,
    About how my life might be.
Having you there around,
    To share your love with me.

It makes me very happy,
    Just knowing that you're there.
I sometimes have thoughts about,
    How much you really care.

I have had many thoughts of you,
    Throughout each and every day.
There are feelings from within me,
    That I feel a need to say.

I would like to have the time,
    To express just how I feel.
To tell you that I love you,
    And my thoughts of you are real.

Steven R. Williams

Flow Of Life

In man, life flows to every cell
And that it flows, man knows it well.
But what life is, no human knows,
or why through living things it flows.

Man only knows that life has cause;
And life responds to Nature's Laws.

Robert C. Quinn

As Jesus Did

With the exception of Christ
and the salvation by Him,
what more could we ask
than a true friend?

With their hearts set on Christ
are the friends I am drawn to,
to strengthen my faith,
ever lean onto.

To sustain and support,
He commanded us in John
to love each other,
"Do as I've done."

I want you to know that,
through the Grace He did send,
I love you very much...
You are that friend

Karen Vencel

When The Leaves Of Autumn Fall

When the leaves of autumn fall,
And the snows of winter near,
That's the time I cherish most,
Reminding me of when you were here.

When the tides of oceans rise,
And the crowded birds of summer fly,
Then will the festive moods begin,
In which you and I will at last abide.

Orlando Joseph Machado

The Setting Of Life

As the days grow longer,
And the sun begins to set,
I start to think about my life,
And the struggles fought within.
No one knows how hard it's been,
With all this worry and strife.
But soon the sun will set,
And I will be stronger.

As the day turns to night,
And I lay down to rest,
My life flashes in front of me,
And I see I've lost my way.
What reason is there to stay?
I can't seem to see, but
I will give it best,
To try and find the light.

Tracy Krause

Our Father's Hand

Sometimes storm clouds may gather
And the sun refuse to shine,
But it does not really matter
As tomorrow may be fine.

Our world seems in a turmoil
With unrest in every land.
Many things we sometimes question
And we do not understand.

So with faith and hope and courage
And a great amount of love.
We can safely, leave the future
In our Father's hand above.

Orville J. Loucks

Prelude To Death

   On the prettiest day
and the warmest of all nights

   It creeps and it stings
the clueless and the bright

   It searches and it preys
on the strong and the stray

   No prejudice against color
or sex's it may

   Innocent nor guilty
if one be of choice

   While the clock ticks
the hunter shows no remorse

   Searching for the one
whose time has run out

   He'll leave with his prey
A definite conquest no doubt

Stacie Knighton

How To Search?

The divine recognition of falsehood.
As the radiant energy of childhood,
Takes over the mind and thought,
I know something there is to be sought.
What there could be,
Is defiantly for me.
I simply do not know how to search.

Sean Milner

I Have Seen Jesus

I have seen Jesus
And this is how I feel
It's people like you
Who make Him "So Real".

He's the sun in my mornings
My stars in the night
He's Winter, Summer and Spring
He is my everything.

I'm glad that I meet Him
As oft as I do
I meet Him each time
I meet people like you.

Theresa M. Ebert

Day By Day

If yesterday was tomorrow,
and tomorrow was today
we'd know more about our future,
and how to chart our way.

Since yesterday has come and gone,
tomorrow yet to come,
we'll have to deal with just today,
and ponder the unknown.

So living day to day is still,
the best way to proceed,
to meet each challenge when it comes,
and deal with every need.

I know what happened yesterday,
tomorrow is a dream.
Today is now reality
and going well it seems.

With faith and hope an ally,
a challenge is ahead,
to deal with just tomorrow
for yesterdays are dead!

Truman R. Purtle

The Attic Where We Keep Our Souls

You have no idea who lives here
And yet you climb the stairs...
Believing that you'll find the key
Unlocking your despairs.

A moldy odor lingers
Through these hallways, dark and cold.
On every side are doorways
To the secrets left untold.

Within us all are closets
Where we keep what brings us pain
Our minds become our attics
Where our lonely souls remain.

We keep searching for the answers,
But they're locked so deep inside.
They too are in our attics
Where our lonely souls must hide.

Tracy A. Mignone

Fade Away

I walked away from you
And you watched me go
Now all I have are memories
Of the days with you long ago
I thought I had all the answers
I thought I was so right
Because you never called
Or put up any kind of fight
Communication was the key
And I didn't try
I thought you had changed
I thought I would die
I can't make a move towards you
You're the unreachable one
I guess nothing will change
What's done is done
But, I miss you still
And think of you from day to day
For in my thoughts
You will never fade away

Sarah Moore

A Wedding Toast

Since this moment is so special
    And your feelings are so true.
Here are my best wishes for you both
    And my advice to you.

Should troubles come your way now
    As you start on this new life,
Remember how you feel today
    About your special wife.

If things go wrong ignore the thoughts
    And logic in your head.
And make your judgements based upon
    What's in your heart instead.

Just look into her dancing eyes
    And think of what you'd miss.
Then tell her that you're sorry -
    And seal it with a kiss.

So let this moment be the one
    Remembered as the start -
When you and she first joined your hands
    And God first joined your hearts.

R. Michael Roman

Untitled

Though your troubles may be many
And your Joys be very few
never give up the battle
Victory is in store for you
Though you try your very best
and never seem to win or gain
Remember you have a purpose
A single goal to claim
even when the chips are down
and no one's on your side
You always have something
You always have your pride
So when your dreams crumble
and the winds blow them away
Remember there's tomorrow
for tomorrow's another day
So never say life's worthless
or think of yourself as poor
For what lies in the future
Only God knows for sure!

Paula Babcock

An Ode To A Miniature Schnauzer

I love you my bearded dame
and your scroungy big behind
which wiggles without shame
with every smelly find.

I love your sexy bites
uninhibited anywhere
who's to squelch your rights
to kiss or bite or tear.

Your love for a juicy steak
like any expensive doll
just a naughty little fake
No wonder I went for a fall.

Pedro C. Cabral

Two's

Toys lay
    another day done.

Two tired children,
    can't take any more fun!

Sleep in their eyes
    thumbs in their mouth.

Bobbing heads
    in a few minutes they are out!

Mary Saarinen

My Mom And Dad

    My Mom and Dad
are so nice and kind,
When I talk to my Mom
her eyes shine.
    When I'm sad, I go
to my Dad, he makes me
feel safe and glad,
    That I have a Mom and Dad.

Kristin Komrosky

Moments

The sky holds the stars
as a mother holds her child
as the frame holds a picture
as I hold my memories.

A moment passes by
like a stranger on the street
and the breath of a whisper
melts away from my ear.

Leaves fall to the ground
as children fall to sleep
as words fall to silence
as the soldier falls to pain.

Sound echoes back
like the ebb of a river
and the destiny of the past
carries me back and forth.

The sun fades to blue
as colors fade from wash
as the chorus fades away
as I fade into my shadow.

Nicole Speulda

Snowflake Power

Behold! The lovely snowflakes
As delicate as can be.
They are elegant as the finest lace
And are beautiful to see.

They are so light and feathery
As they drift gently to the ground.
They are dainty as they fall
All are silent not a sound.

Now where are the lovely snowflakes?
Where did they all go?
They all joined forces
And now we call them snow.

They have worked together
Stopping all man made things.
Now we know the power
That the lovely snowflakes bring.

Why can't we be like snowflakes
And work together too?
If we would all join forces
Just think what we could do!

Luella Knauss Potts

Death Is My Name

I come to take you home
As I lay sleeping on
This blanket of peace.

My pain is gone and
I am at rest now.
I feel good about
The peace I found

My soul wave with the wind
God has come to
Take me home

I pain no more!
Cause the tears are gone

God has come
To take me home
To the enter peace
That I have found

Vivian L. McCoy

My Love

My love is like a mountain stream
as pure and clear as it can be.
Winding through canyons
beautiful and green
Stretching as far as my eyes can see.
There have been rapids,
which I've navigated with ease.
Boulders and dams
and large fallen trees
Have blocked my path,
but my love finds its way
through the smallest of cracks.
Ahead I hear the thundering sound
of a waterfall, no way to turn around.
As I go over the edge I reach out,
Looking for something to stifle my doubt.
Finally I find what I've been looking for
And I hold on with all my might.
Of course, it's your hand I hold
And together I know we will win this fight.

Kim Grimes

Ashlee And I

Oft times I hear these whispered sounds,
as soft as snow flakes sifting down.

When all alone, they come to me,
And fill my heart with instant glee.

Because I know she's here; she cares.
She pats my cheek and tweaks my hair.

Most people say this can't be so;
she left this world two years ago.

A love so strong can pave the way,
for these visits that make my day.

While all doubts continue to grow.
Ashlee and I really do know.

Lela L. Carter

A Place Called Mother Lane

We may not agree on everything
As we would like it's true
But there's a place in Mother Lane
Where I meet in thought with you.
And always as we hug and kiss
As closely as can be
Quite magically, the hours take on
New happiness for me
And it's grand to know that always
Through cloudy days or fair
Whenever I walk down Mother Lane
I'll find you waiting there.

Marissa Epstein

At Last

At last I don't need you.
At last I don't love you.
I found someone else,
Who rose completely above you.

At last I'm not begging
At last I'm not pleading
I found someone else
Who gives me love I've been needing

At last I don't cry
At last I don't care
I found someone else
Who's willing to share

At last!

Lisa Olive

To Bob

You came into my life
and we walked the same
pathway for a while.

We shared friendship,
companionship, and real
camaraderie without guile.

What could have been was not.
What might have been was not to be.
What was—was
And I am grateful.

Marie Sturdivant

WISHING ON A SATELLITE

WISHING ON A SATELLITE
AT THE TIME I THOUGHT IT WAS
THE RIGHT THING TO DO. I MISTOOK
IT FOR A STAR BECAUSE OF ITS SHINE.
HOW WAS I TO KNOW YOU WEREN'T TRUE?

THE MOON'S FOOL GOLD GLITTERED FALSELY
LIKE JEWELS CLOSE BY. I SHOULD HAVE
KNOWN. REAL STARS ARE CLOSER
EVEN AT A DISTANCE. THEIR BRIGHTNESS
ALWAYS REMAINS.

REAL STARS LIVE
REAL STARS DIE
LEAVING A BLACK HOLE IN OUR UNIVERSE.

SATELLITES SEEM TO SHINE FOREVER
AND ARE REPLACED BY MORE.

IT'S HARD TO TELL WHO TO DEPEND ON
IT'S HARD TO TELL WHICH ONES ARE REAL
THERE ARE MORE SATELLITES THAN STARS
ILLUMINATING THE UNIVERSE AND BURNING THE MUSIC.

Michelle Pecora Elsbree

Like A Garden

Like a watered garden
awakening from a winter rest...
Lush, verdant garden
alive with promise
and breathless in its promise.

Like a fruitful garden
where perennial promises are kept...
Sweet, fragrant garden with
new hopes planted in waiting soil,
stroked, kissed by sun's caress.

Like a hidden garden
serene within my heart of hearts...
Silent, tranquil garden
where I walk with God
and listen to His words.

Like an Eden Garden
my heart, my soul unfolds...
Cherished, enchanted garden
tended by the Divine Gardener
who holds his garden dear!

M. Ann Stamm

Victory With Jesus

I have victory in Jesus as I turn
Away from sin, to keep serving my
Dear Lord, because through him
I know I'll win...

Victory with Jesus as I live my life
Day by day, the sins I have
Committed, are all washed away.

I'm thinking of my Lord in
Heaven above, my blessed Salvation,
And his spiritual love...

I have my victory in Jesus, from
All my trouble and pain, because
With my Lord and saviour
I have everything to gain.

I love my Lord, my God, and
My father, for He's forever in my
Heart, my treasure forever,
And we will never ever part.

Timothy Lee Linam

Ginosko

I see a star with its five points,
Away up in the sky;
Because it glows with dazzling fire,
I know that I am I.

It points above with shiny spire,
To distant cloud and haze;
I hear the distant thunder roar,
And know I live my days.

I feel the rain come pouring down,
To quench the thirst of earth;
Reminiscent of the liquid that
Was present at my birth.

I taste the drops that have come down,
'Tis pleasant to my soul,
The star above flicks its delight
To contemplate the whole.

I smell the fragrance of the mist
That rises from the mead;
The star above with its five points,
Agrees that I'm indeed.

Richard LeRoy Anderson

Empty Nest

Waving goodbye
Be careful!
Take care of yourself
the same way I have taken care of you
all of your life - until now

Good luck
I'm so proud!
I am bereft - desolate!
Be careful!
Tearing hunks of my heart from me
wounding my soul
taking my reason for existing
Be careful!
Love yourself as I have loved you
I'm left behind
Love myself as I have loved you?
How will I do that?
Can I? Goodbye
Don't go! Please
Be careful!

Rosemarie Edwards

Friend

One morning at the chime of six
    Before the daylight came
I saw the winter's icy tracks
    On every window pane.

Glancing through the glazing
    And with surprise to find
All bundled up a tiny friend
    Near by the closing line.

I must invite her in thought I
    'Twould be polite to do
Her title gives her grace for such
    She's far from home, I knew

Pushing window pane ajar
    Extending welcome tie
Madame Lady Bug stepped in
    Pleasured just as I.

Virginia Pillsbury Cantrell

Curiosity

Sometimes people
believe in things
that others only fantasize;

You seat yourself
to a journey of the unknown
more like a dream
but, maybe reality;

Questioning intelligence
of a higher source
can put you down
so you feel worse;

Stumbling across
the wonders of the world
can inspire
creative minds which
we all desire.

Tamara Malhas

"Send Him Home"

Lord, you know what I'm asking tonight;
Beneath the stars so big and bright.
I want you to send him home,
And for his heart to never roam.

The fear that was between us
On that cold starry night.
The care that lies between us
That fills us both with fright.

I just pray at this moment
That when his time is done
You'll be merciful to us both
And send him safely home.

I pray that someday
He'll realize that I care
And he'll stand by my side
And know I want him there.

Kelly Jo Middleton

Visit With Mom

I came to visit the other day
Beside your grave I knelt to pray
Just one more time I'd love to see
That Dear sweet face, smile at me
Touch your hand, stroke your hair
Let you know I really care.
As I rise tenderly
I'm glad I had this talk with thee.

Phyllis Francis

Prayer

Help me reach the balance
between rising moon and setting sun

help me reach the balance
between the water and the shore

help me reach this balance
of night and day

and, in balance,
help others to balance

Siri D. Galliano

Death

Swaying in the sand of death
  Birds surround death arrives
Not knowing where to turn
  Just seeking deliverance.

Listen. People are being silent
  Ready to kill
  Please don't take me
  We all are going to die.

Three more are demolished
  checking for the answers
  Living a life of madness
  Die, die, die

I hate you
  Get out of my face
  I don't need you, Die.

Death don't play
Have to go someday
Maybe now, maybe later
Death knocking every hour
You could be next...

LaToya Larry

"To My Wife"

When I awake each morning,
Blessed with all I see
The one that makes my life worth while,
Lies sleeping next to me.

And when I fall asleep at night,
It's peaceful and serene
To have her nestle in my arms,
My love, My Wife, Darlene.

I hope the day will never come,
When I awake to find
A loneliness I can't describe,
To know I'm left behind.

Or have her find that I've gone first,
And she would need me still
It really doesn't seem quite fair,
And yet may be God's will.

But rather would I hope and pray,
Our end will all be planned
So both of us could meet our Lord,
Together, hand in hand...

Peter Kern

Nature's Reminder

Sing birds and make me feel lonely,
Blow breeze and make me feel sad,
Shine sun and make me long for
My blue-eyed, handsome lad.

Mother Nature, it's not your fault
That you remind me of last year.
But this year he's with another,
And I dare not shed a tear.

So sing birds, and I won't feel lonely,
Blow breeze, and I won't feel sad,
Shine sun and watch me be happy,
For my blue-eyed, handsome lad.

Sherry L. Rifley

Untitled

I love it when at night the rain
Blows against my windowpane
And thunder rumbles overhead
When I'm all tucked up
Warm in bed

I love it when the snow and sleet
Dances down the icy street
I watch my breath form overhead
When I'm all tucked up
Warm in bed.

I love it when the witches fly
On their brooms up in the sky
Cause they can't see my sleepy head
When I'm all tucked up
Warm in bed

I know somewhere way up high
God looks down across his sky
And reaches out to touch my head
And tucks me up
All warm in bed.

Rita Johnson

Seraphims To Greet You

Goldfish dance and swirl,
Blue birthday balloons soar high
Whispers to your son
While whooping cranes wisp by

Solar flares, inward dares
Cuttlefish in Indonesia
Rabbits on wing, roses in Spring
Sirens Seraphims to greet you

Bring wines from southern vineyards
Porcelain plates of fine cheese
Slice some warm fresh French bread
Absorb the balmy breeze

Butterflies carried your far
Orcas called your name
Lilacs laced your neck
Could you ever be the same?

Dolphins white and grey are friends to thee
Travel other worlds to set you free.

Ross Watkins

Blue

Blue.
Blue is a cool color.
Blue is a blueberry.
Blue will be our friend.
Blue is the color of the sky.
Blue is the color of my house.
Blue is the color of a blue pen,
Blue is the color of my science book.
Blue is my favorite color.
  The blue end.

Matthew Hawley

"Whispering Wind"

Softly, very softly, the gentle
Breeze did sigh,
  "Our summer sun is waning,
  How swiftly she passed by.
  The golden hue of autumn
  is reflected on her face.
  And winter soon will follow
  With snow to take her place."

Margaret Kohler

316

Unforgettable

To John Cejka

I got a glimpse of him.
Body, the triangle shape.
He disappears...
The music tickles my ears, and
here he is, asking for a dance.
Too late!
I am completely speechless.
His hand is touching my back,
Something blooms from that,
It comes to my heart,
    goes to my lips,
        to my eyes, and
        to my mind.
It radiates!
I am enveloped by the love.
Let's the music not to stop,
seize this and
step into eternity.

Krystyna Alina Dabrowska

"Come To Me"

Come to me
Bring me all your cares and heartaches
Come to me
I know just what to do
Come to me
Let me share your pain and sorrow
Come to me
And I will see you through

I know just what you need
I know how to solve your problems
If you just give them to me
I will help you
I'm always by your side
Always there to lead and guide you
Why not give me a try
I'm waiting here for you

I'll never let you down
    I'll never let you fall
I'm always right on time
    I'll never fail you

Linda R. Kent

The Sun

The fearless sun
Brings with him
The song of day

For he embraces the sky
Dominating the blue
Humming in tune with his stride

The notes so clear
As if crying for the earth
His voice so pure
As to cleanse its wounds

The healing so divine
The night rides in
Taking with it his song

Ryan Mitchell Moser

Mom's Chores

Said the mother, "I've nothing to do
But breakfast and dinner and lunch,
And the various needs of the crew,
And the problems of all of the bunch."

Mack Hobson

Broken Promises

Stitch me together with
Broken promises
Yet to be.
Let me count them
Silently, in my head
As I begin to dream.
Count them on my fingers
And on my toes
Then I will begin again.
I will let them squeeze out,
Burning onto my face
Down my cheeks,
I will taste them on my lips.
Until, finally, I forget and
Wash them away with Love.

Marya DeRaad

Then And Now

Broom Sedge blowing in the wind
Broom Sedge broom is sweeping still
When I close my eyes.
I recall a childhood day
Broom Sedge broom to sweep the clay
When root to root between the trees
I cleared a place to play.
Open now my eyes.
Broom Sedge blowing in the wind
Broom Sedge broom is sweeping still
Sweeping short each summer day
Dust of time along the way.

Susan Carlton Smith Cavanagh

Having Few Memories

The child daydreams
Builds sandcastles
Of expectations
For the keeper
Of the dreams.

Lucie Glenn

Untitled

Whose eyes watched the killing
But did not heed its warning
Whose eyes
So full of tears
Streaming down his innocent cheeks
As he watched
All in a flash she was gone
But, still he ran outside
Asking if she was all right
She could not answer
As her lifeless eyes stared up at his
His life had revolved around her
She had brought the life into his eyes
And then it was back
It struck the boy as it did his mother
Because the boy
Whose eyes watched the killing
Did not heed its warning
Lightning, flash
And then, he too, was gone

Rebecca A. Holzman

Alone

A teardrop falls
But has no voice.
It comes from nowhere,
Its burden heavy.
Travelling easily
Through valleys of wrinkles
And falling from face
To breast, its existence
Meaningful nothingness.
Shimmering, beautiful,
Leaving a glimmering path
And diminishing, gone.
Another, not so beautiful,
Not unique, for the path
Is made and it must follow.

Kimberly Dietert

Prairie Wind

"Breezy today", the weatherman said.
But how do you suppose
that weatherman knew
Our friend would
come to call today?

That fashion fanatic
who tosses the hair
to give one and all
the windswept look.

He rattles the windows
and knocks at the door.
He does everything but ring the bell.

And when at last he coaxes me,
to see who it is at my door.
That naughty friend,
Like a wayward child,
Holds his breath and slips away.

LaVerne Schroeder

Hope

Darkness surrounds me
But just up ahead
A tiny light flickers
I leap from my bed.

As I run at full steam
Toward that tiny flame,
My hopes start to rise;
There's less and less pain.

What's that break in the blackness
That makes my heart sing?
What's that minuscule wattage
Absorbing the sting?

And then I remember
From Mama's prized Book
That Someone so special
The darkness forsook;

Replaced it with light,
Hope, goodness, mercy and love.
I'm loved and I'm cared for
Praise God from above.

Lynn Rankin

Along Life's Way

We can count all of the years
But never the joys
That we have had along life's way
Family and friends who love us
Sharing and caring - our every day.
Our homes where we live
Our Church where we pray
Our work - and our leisure
Yes - blessing each day

I think of that old familiar song.
That many of us have sung.

"Count your many blessings
Name them one by one...
And it will surprise you
What the Lord has done."

Norma Davis

I Want To Be Free

As I sit here alone
But not wanting to be alone
I know I want to be free
My eyes are burning and there
Are signs of ageing under my eyes
Why because I want to be free
My mind is constantly racing and
My stress level is high
Why because I want to be free
But I am mother and a wife and
My priories will not allow me
To be free
I'm trapped in a place
I don't want to be
I want to go home
But I'm not at home
Will that set me free
I'll never know unless I go
So off I go on that journey
To be free.

Michelle Taylor

Blankets

Slowly
but surely
the blanket
encircled her small shoulders
keeping her warm and
protected
from cold and hate

Once the blanket was removed,
this junior Columbus
with a sunshine smile
slowly dawning
realized that it was not the
wool and cotton that had been providing
that warmth that protection

Katie DiSalvo

A Breath Of Mind

Swallowed alive
by the sound of thought
drifting through my quiet shell,
My lungs breathe
raw smoke of dreams,
where phantoms dance
in dervish glee to songs
plucked by the darkling harp.

William Draganza

"You"

I stood on the threshold of despair
but then I looked and you were there
like you always are (forever),
I tumbled through space without
a parachute, landed on
the caress of your love (unscarred),
I rode the white water falls
tumbling, tumbling over rocks and
waves, only to end up in the
life jacket of love (unharmed).
You stand at the end of my
rainbow, colorful, hopeful and
with promise (always).

Sara Allen

I Love Walter

He is short in height
but when we're together he gives me hype.

I know he is passionate because
he proves it to me when we're on a date.

No matter what time of day or
night he calls, I will be climbing the walls.

When I'm in his arms, that is allthat is wrote.
He whispers in my ear baby do you need a coat.

LaWanda J. Hicks

Untitled

I long to love you
but you long to leave me.
In bitterness I stand so true.
Kindness of the foolish heart
made me flee to you.
From one little glance I knew that we'd
be friends forever more,
but I didn't know that I'd fall so hard
for you like I had before.

Katie Foster

A Convicts Account

Take a boy at any age trapped
by the system, locked in a cage.
Unable to cry from fear of being
weak, unable to cry for fear of being beat.
Like dungeons of old and days within
filled with hatred, violence, and sin.
Now he's grown older and down
for his race a hardened convict he'll
spit in your face!
Paroled to the street's without a
trade a living for him just can't be
made in his bitter rage for his lack
to provide he grabs for the gun and
quickens his stride.
He's not mad at you, so don't be
afraid, he's mad at the system against
what they've made, so the next boy
you see give him a chance, cause the boy
in this poem was me long since past!

William D. Zappa

Sounds of Life

Outside the wondrous sounds of life
call from every corner,

to remind us of the many things
which we are not aware.

The beauty of the miracles
of which we are truly graced,

comes from a mystical being
far too great to dare.

Lisa P. Smialek

"The Little Things In Life"

The little things in life
can bring me so much joy
like a smile on the face
of a little girl or boy,
like the very first snowflake
of the winter season,
like a cinnamon oat meal cookie
without a single raisin,
like a beautiful rainbow
after a heavy storm,
like a blanket out of the drier
cozy and warm.
If people took the time
to notice the simple, little
things, imagine how much
happiness each new day
would bring.

Maura Green

A Song To A Rosebud

Oh, tiny, little rosebud.
Can't you hear or see?
Don't you know that summer's here
Won't you talk to me?

My pretty, little rosebud.
Can't you hear my song?
You only sit and drink up sunbeams;
All the whole day long.

Wondrous, little rosebud;
Mother natures child.
Can it be that the country rose;
Is your cousin, fair and wild?

Shirley Gabrielson

Reflections

Mirrored images
captured in space,
Fleeting memories
of time and place.
Shadows, Silhouettes,
a spectrum of hue,
Blending and shaping
emerging in view.
Radiating emotions
encompassed in frame,
Frayed edges
without refrain.
Vanishing visions,
fractions of light,
Inspiring moments,
taking flight

Reflections.....

Marsha Pilger

Aura

Autumn
Catalogues
Promises unfulfilled,
Peels
Opaque desire of summer,
Disarms
With color, symmetry
Senses sought.
Gold
Orange
Vermilion
Brown
Sere!
Wither verdant
Immortality?

Mary McKeel

"Sadness"

The pull on my heart
causes a tremble in my body.
My life seems different
now.
Sadness is setting in
faster than I can prepare for.
My heart is crumbling
to pieces like an old building in
an earthquake.
Soon there won't be anything
to save, it'll be gone and so will I.
So someone out there, please
grab my hand and show my heart the
way to recovery.

Nicole J. Froelich

The Dance

Stomach to stomach,
chest to breast -
wrapped in a blanket of sensual sound,
the warm breath that preludes
a gentle caress
is held by the soft throat
where pulse beat is found.
Two bodies together,
cheek next to cheek -
moving together
as mind and flesh meet;
the birth of a romance
in music's embrace -
christened by rhythm,
and wedded by beat.

Marybeth Francis

Dandelions

Flowing jewels in the night,
Dandelions we are.
Sure and without doubt,
Plentiful yellow and green.

Secrets are hidden in our stems,
Spilling out in bright buds.
Picking up to travel afar,
To again share our wealth.

Sweet, warm air of summer,
We have again begun our journey
On the backs of wind lifts.
The memories remain - golden!

Thomas Robert Huetz

Trembling Hands

Trembling hands hold the phone,
clasping every word

A shaking voice cries to God,
"Help me, dear oh Lord."

Crying eyes look to heaven,
praying to hold his hand;

Cold and dead lies my father
deep within the land

Wishful thoughts ignore the truth;
I must be fast asleep

But facts of death slap me hard,
and lies my heart won't keep

I wander blankly 'round in circles
with a stale stare

Tomorrow as the sun awakens,
father won't be there

Trembling hands drops the phone,
their words I cannot hear

A shaking voice asks my mother,
"Does God see my tears?"

Katherine Galluzzo

Ode To New York

Antiseptic buildings, antiseptic lives
Clean
Straight
No frills.
Red, brown, or grey
Cold, damp, not gay.
A feeling of warmth, joy
They express these not.
No seats, no real nooks,
Or even crannies for crooks
No place to seek or even
To hide, or places to group
Or places to gather together
Like grandma's back stoop.
But do they tell a story,
Do they spin their own clean yarn?
Their own germ-free listerine line
Do they emulate our city folk's
lives? As day by day we go to
our antiseptic hives!

Robert T. Bate

A Desert Sunrise

Out of the blackest gloom of Chaos
Comes the first pale hope of dawn,
Like a wisp of inconsistent vapor
Gathering substance from its spawn.

Growing, each suspended moment,
'Til at length a beam break free,
And at once the night is melted
And creeps away to secrecy.

Shadows scurry into hiding,
Hell's furnace door ajar.
A blazing crescent breaks the surface,
Dispelling from the sky each star.

Then at last the door swings open
Pouring liquid flame into the morn.
And with soul-inflaming beauty,
A desert sun is born.

Keith C. Chastain

Judge Me Not

Judge me not by the
color of skin but deep
down inside where the
beauty begins, cause we
all have to live in this
world together through
earthquakes and storms
through all kinds of weather.

Be kind to one another
love your neighbors and
treat them like brothers.

No matter if black or
if white just try and
love them anyway
which is only right.

The madness must stop
and come to the end.
let's try to get along
let's try and be friends.

Laura S. White

Moon Child

The moon child I am
Comes out in early morn
Before the babe's awake,
Before the night is shorn.

The moon child I am
Knows these hours are most holy.
And I walk and run in wonder,
As the sun peeks in slowly.

The moon child I am
Is so happy that she's free.
I love the wonder of this world,
Drink its nectar like a bee.

The moon child I am
Loves the stillness and the dark,
And rolls over gladly
To days of sand and sun so stark.

I'm the lucky, smiling moon child
Who has all that she can need.
I'm the blessed child of life,
Who on life's love, need only feed.

Sherry L. Cass

Life In The Middle

Pieces of the puzzle
Coordinator of life
I ask who am I
Professional, mother or wife.

Words of unwritten songs
Slave to success
What do I really care
Of my own happiness.

Fragments of broken bones
Caretaker of the frail
Mom and Dad how can I
Be the nightingale.

Colors of the palette
Provider of love
What do I believe
That exists from above.

Divided are the nations
Future seems a riddle
Where am I
Life in the middle.

Rose Helinski

Menu

Sizzling bacon
Crisp and brown
Eggs over-easy
Best in town.
Fried potatoes
Skins and all
Toast and jam
Tops it all.
Golden waffles
Not too crisp
Sausage links
In the dish.
Cereal with
ice cold milk
Slides right down
Smooth as silk.
Orange juice
Freshly squeezed
Come and get it
If you please.

Linda Bacic

Nighttime

Nighttime
Dark and light,
Quiet,
Stars shine bright.

Looking far,
Searching,
Beyond a star.
Dreaming,

What will I be?
Wondering,
Who will I be?
Thinking,

What the future will bring?
Hoping,
I can bring my family everything.
Thanking,

God for everything.
Wishing,
I could hear the birds sing.
Dreaming.

Nicholas Angstadt

Of Joy And Pain

A humming bird, gathering nectar,
darts from flower to flower, then
caught by a breeze, soars higher,
and is gone in the wind.

Joy, on wings of a bird, flies
through the soul, intoxicates
rapturously, sails to the sky,
and is lost in the clouds.

Pain, descends like a vulture,
devouring joy as the wind,
the hummer, leaving despair,
and the soul cries for hope.

A bird comes back to flowers,
as joy will return to the soul
drink deep its honeyed rapture
and pain dissolves in its cup.

Mary Kendall Hersey

Dat

Daniel Arthur Taylor Boy,
Dave's and Stacey's pride and joy.
Tiny, handsome, little man,
Bringing all the love he can.

Kicking, crawling, throwing toys,
Crying, screaming, making noise.
Bottles, binkies, other joys,
Now come forth and quell the noise.

Driving parents to despair,
Happy you are not a pair.
Sleepless nights and tired days,
Cause new parents to be amazed.

Changing diapers, baby chores,
Midnight feedings, walking floors.
Little boys, who are so small,
Sometimes make no sense at all.

We thank you Lord in Heaven above,
For this little boy, so full of love.

A. H. Whaley

Beyond Night

Continuation of love
Dawning at the dusk
An endless trust
Bound by sincerity.

Stacy Philp

Hashbane

Quietly slipping,
day toward night.
Full moon rising,
silver light.
Elves laughing,
in happy delight.
Pixies dancing,
fairies in flight.
Leprechauns holding,
their gold tight.
Witch's brooms,
swooping as kites.
Wizards casting,
enchantments of fright.
Spirits out moving,
to great heights.
Ah, but dawn,
makes all things right.
Then again comes,
The - NIGHT!

William B. Stanwix

In Memoriam...

Damned with birth and doomed to living,
Death has found him unforgiving.
A bastard fruit of "not-known" seed
The sin of a "no-name" womb.

Who remembered mocking laughter
And the tears that followed after,
Till his spirit, dimmed forever,
Retreated to the tomb.

There he chose a fatal pleasure
A macabre fount of treasure
Where the solitary measure
Is the need...

Owen L. Burkhart

Fleeting Images

Days; drab, difficult
    deteriorating
last week a flicker
    of recognition perhaps
Euphoria emanated from bedside
    a glimpse from the past
Viewing the future
    eyes closed, yet seeing
Angels?
    Loved ones?
Those gone before?
    Reaching out
Touching the face of God.

Maxine Aldinger

Death Be Still

Death be still!! I'm coming!
Do not be in such a rush.
You frighten me a little,
Get behind me - give a push.

You've waited quite a while for this
But I never looked your way.
Yet now I'm old - all loved ones gone
And I need a place to stay.

Michelle Stewart

Can Anybody Hear Me?

Can anybody hear me?
Does anybody care?
I'm lost and can not find my way.
Is anybody there?

Is somebody out there
To wipe away my fears?
Is somebody out there
That can chase away my fears?

Please! If you can hear me,
Give a little shout.
I'm trapped in a world of darkness
And I'm trying to get out.

Is anybody out there?
Does anybody hear?
Will somebody please help me?
I'm blinded by fear.

If you can hear me
Please make me aware.
I know you can hear me.
Please answer my prayer.

Melissa Miller

Forever Engraved

The sickness, it spreads
dying eyes each day.
To pain, I yield
left now only to pray.
Trusting, trust not
for thy words, they are lies.
Sympathy, embrace not
thy memory quickly dies.
Your hurt, it has spread
to the depths of my heart.
Renew, Revive
I search of new start.
No speech, no knowledge
thy memory has no place.
Thy kindness, thy hurt
forever engraved in my face.

Meghan Cuccia

Our Love

Love me forever
Don't ever let me go.
Let's stay in each others arms
So we won't feel alone.

Love me tonight,
Until we see the morning light.
Let us always be lovers,
Let us always be friends.

Our love we have between us,
Will never end.
Cause we was meant to be together.
Till love becomes a sin.

When love becomes a sin,
Then we shall both be guilty.
Cause there's nothing that will stop us,
Not even angels sent from God.

Cause I'm a heaven sent angel myself, when
God holds our love.
So we shall never be punished, if love
becomes a sin.
Cause God knows he can trust me,
Since I do belong to him.

Karen Hogue

No Fear

As we see our lives passing,
down avenues of hope.
We get caught up in traffic,
Makes living tough to cope.

We must have faith in knowing,
Our problems will solved.
With every action taken,
There's one more to evolve.

If we use the fear inside us
As opportunities to grow.
Be courageous as we walk the line,
Have faith in what we know.

It's not the fear of falling,
That seems to make life hard,
For falling brings us down to earth,
This fear we disregard.

If we learn life's lessons wisely,
Down the road to inner truth.
Our lives will be much richer,
Souls of everlasting youth.

Steven James Qualls

Rose Quartz

A slick heart shaped stone
from Egyptian times...
Affection, love, and trust
thrived from PHARAOH's hand.
A beguiled Gypsy listening to
a new companions woes...
Rocks float leisurely near the
grassy shore.
Fragments of luminous roses
lay scattered upon her withering hands.
Now, a child mystified
beyond the Elysian Fields
Looking for her favorite pebble....
QUARTZ.
Is she a Princess clad gauzy
or the lady in BLACK? Only a
Celtic bard knows...
The enigma...ROSE QUARTZ

Dreams

Dreams....
Dreams can be beautiful,
as beautiful as can be.
They make you joyful,
and so, so happy.
Your dreams can be of a friend,
and might not be wanted to end.
But when dreams are scary,
and upsetting, and frightening.
You wake up screaming,
or crying or grasping your head.
Sacred, silent shadows,
that seem they'd rather swallow,
you than comfort you instead.
But dreams have always been,
And dreams will always be.
They come and go as they please,
so unexpectedly.
Dreams......

Tamara Mohammed

Complexatively

Man dreams
dreams of future gains
of peace, money or
better yet, "Women!"

That special female
his companion, mate
wife is a better term.

Man dreams
sometimes nightmarish thoughts
of possible failures
money woes, but always
shakes these negative thoughts away.
Positive thoughts take over,
dream wife, house and family
man dreams
complex thoughts.

Robert J. DiGennaro

Smitten

Submerge me in thy beauty.
  Drown me with thine eyes.
Whisper soft the summer winds bestow.
  Thy words upon my ears.
Lifting up from me.
  The passing of the years.
Through the times we shared.
  No passion may compare!
I live for the moments.
  My senses feel you near!
Basking in your aura.
  No time for fear.
Love has fully enlightened.
  I need not be frightened.
Love like the sunlight.
  Enhances all, must enthrall.
None may know true happiness.
  Till they are smitten.
Somewhere in the book of life.
  Surely it is written!

Ronald Bunce

The First Shadow Of Sunset

At the first shadow of sunset.
Dusk starts closing in.
Covering daylight with its shroud.
Waiting for night to begin.

People light their candles.
Fighting back the dark.
Wolves howl in the distance.
And the dogs begin to bark.

Mist drifts amongst the trees.
And it covers up the ground.
The darkness moves on stealthy feet.
Not making any sound.

The children listen to the tales.
Filled with unknown fright,
Of all the things that creep around.
In the mist of the darkest night.

At the first shadow of sunset.
Nyx soars across the sky.
Bringing stars and darkness.
But no reason why.

Michelle Lima

Agony

The agony of not knowing
Empty stairs across the hall
A love kept from showing
To the one he loved most of all.

The agony of not knowing
The emptiness inside
The love that is kept from growing
Can be seen as they pass by.

The agony of not knowing
The tears in her eyes
As she keeps hoping
She breaks down and cries

The agony of not knowing
What they feel inside
They keep hearing whispers
Why is love so blind?

The agony of not knowing
The pain that is swept away
The new love that is found
It will never be the same.

Lynsie Newman

School

I hate it,
Every time I go, I have a fit,
It's a catastrophe,
I know everyone will laugh at me,
Every problem I answer,
It turns out to be a disaster,
If only the day went faster,
School is the worst foe,
I've ever known,
So why do I have to go?

Youseph Haiderzad

Jesus

Mary had a little Lamb,
He was Jesus Christ, Her Son.
He came to sacrifice His life,
For each and everyone.

Mary Rita Bock

Untitled

A perfect match, that's what we are.
Everyone asked, "how do you know when
  you're in love?"
All I can say is, "you just know."
It's a feeling down deep inside,
that you can't quite explain.
A feeling that you would gladly
  give and spend your life
  with this person. This one person.
A perfect match that's what we are.

To me he is, as Adam was to Eve.
Yet, no damn apple is going to tempt me.
A perfect match that's what we are.

Libby Shultz

Laugh

Build for yourself a strong box
fasten each part with care
fit it with hasp and padlock
and out all your troubles there.

Hide therein all your failures
and each bitter cup you quaff
then lock all your heartache within it
and sit on the lid and laugh.

Tell no one of it
never its secrets share
drop in your cares and worries
keep them forever there.

Hide them from sight so completely
that the world will never dream half
then fasten the top down surely
and sit on the lid and laugh

Marie Redonn

Lost Love

Unspoken words
Feelings divine
My love was lost
But I knew it was mine

Moments of breathlessness
Was it really meant to be
Life dealt a cruel hand
Thus, you were taken from me

Will you be with me forever
Yes, I was told
It is you who I will cherish
With you I want to grow old

Then that fateful night came
And you were no longer here
You are now far away
But in my heart you are near

I will never forget you
For I will see you in time
My love is now gone
But I knew it was mine.

Tanya D. Schulte

Heaven

  Floating around the sky so bright,
Going to Heaven in one flight.

  Pillows all around me,
Looking down at the sea.

  Laying down feeling tight,
Knowing I am safe tonight.

Lexie Barton

Good-Bye With A Smile

Memories of the past,
Feelings that live on inside.
Forever and ever, on and on,
Never to forget...
The time we shared together,
Weekends at the beach.
Skiing through the night,
Holidays of closeness and warmth.
Then the time came,
And we said "Good-bye"
We still have memories,
Which always leave us with a smile.

Tara Stokes

A Smile

A smile is a frown in reverse
filtered through the brain
regenerated from the heart
and then expressed
with the lips
and through the eyes

Norman F. Potter

Proud Poetpourri

Play with words is fun;
Finding fitting adjective
To make clear scenes blurred.
Quite complete word robe
Is a writer's top must, though
Keep competition.
Magic of a name
May burgeon austerity
Or simplicity.
Analogy proves
Worth continuity:
Bind sparks and sparkle.
Penning poetry
Language rhythmical, shares
Beauty exalted.

J. Wayne Lindquist

Lavender

  First blue sky in a long time;
First blue sky in the Morn.
No more saying goodbye, blue sky,
I bid farewell to my Love instead
refusing to keep Her from Her desires.
Obstacles constrict me,
the Greyness Saddens me
my Heart is Lonely!
Without Her...
I wait for the blue sky a long time
to save me from me ache,
and now that it's here,
I won't let go!

Sandra Falicki

Dust

Millions of tiny specks
float around my room.
Each one is a little world.
When I dust, I kill them.

That is why I don't dust.

Rachel Chadderdon

Loneliness

The snow way up on the mountain top
flowed down with the wind and rain
the cries echoing in the canyon
came out like the screams of pain

The loneliness of a place so high
where the winds will always blow
the deserted little hut that stands
is a vision of my soul

Lorraine Janshen

"Seasonal Change"

  There are not too many
flowers left,
  God is performing an act of theft,
He is taking the beautiful flowers away,
So many people wish they could stay,
We save a single red rose,
Though one of the last,
We press it, and save it,
In remembrance of the past.

Lauren B. Kunach

Freedom's Symbol

The red white and blue of you
Flying high in the sun before noon.

Arcing the entrance to Freedom's Place.
Blood spilled defending your grace-
Seas that protect your lands -
Stars mark states taking stands.

You have done so much
To guide our souls
Yet efforts of vanity
They mark your goals.

Those that disgrace your deed
Do not understand the need.
Your place in sight
As a guide every day,
Every night.

Reminding those that believe
They can achieve
Anything
Inside the gates
Of Freedom's Place.

Mary J. Swiderski

Time After Time

He hits you once
He hits you twice
How many times will
You sacrifice for him
Leaving behind a family
That loves you so
Why won't you take our advice
Time after time
Our hearts are breaking
Watching your life pass you by
Please stop the lies and
Come back to us.

Theresa L. Gilley

"The Gift of Life"

Bless the folk who pray
For a small infant in their town
Who desperately needs a "transplant"
So his small life will abound.

This child's name is Tommy
A fighting little guy
Whose life lays in the balance
Amidst his tender cries.

It's hard to grasp that one must die
In order that one may live
Oh God be with the loved ones
Who must sacrificially give.

Please give strength to Tommy's family
Friends and relatives
Who are praying for his healing
Each and every day he lives.

You too gave Your Son
That others too may live
Thank you now for patience
And the healing that You give.

We ask in Your Precious Name.

Amen.

Ruth S. Sippel

We'll Never Be Apart

We've known each other
for about three years,
we've shared lots of happiness
we've shed lots of tears.
Both of us love
to be in each other's heart,
it was fate that brought us together
but destiny tore us apart.
Even though our minds are one
our bodies are as two,
we bring each other joy
in almost all the things we do.
We know it in our minds
we feel it in our hearts,
we love each other dearly
we'll never be apart.

Shandrea Carroll

Youth

A fig
for freud
and his sprouting plants!

Violence and sex
marked my generation
because it was not able
to be earlier than itself.

My youth
leaped upon ancestors
to create an ego-independence!

We do not wish
to live long on earth:
one tarzan-scream worth
more than any civilization!

Patrick R. Penland

Remember Me

Remember me always,
For I'll remember you.
Our souls are connected,
No matter how far apart we are.

Remember my smiling face,
Always cheering you on.
I am always on your side,
In good and in bad.

Remember my love for you,
My love that never ends.
Remember me always,
For I'll remember you.

Nicole Harman

The Awaking

She reflected back in time
For the answer she would find
Does the cross she's made from lead
Exist only in her head?
And as the spirit sings so pure
She could never ask for more
For even through the daily dung
She knows life has just begun!

Kathy Dorney

Self-Esteem

Words with a debonair ring
from a heart that is stunned
the path has been cut
you feel the sting,
    An attitude suffering
a plunging tail spin
where has the pilot gone?
Automation has failed,
    Weight in the mind
on the body
in the soul
self-esteem on the counter balance
the fulcrum is off
acknowledge and move on.

Philip Warren

"Day Break"

As when the sun lifts
From behind the clouds,
And spreads on the horizon,
A golden hue, like a shroud,
And things begin to stir,
That during the night stood still,
And there's no longer,
Sound (song) of the whippoorwill,
Day is come.

Olivia McDougald-Jones

Why I Love Him

He gets hyper
From drinking fruit punch
And eating
Halloween candy.
He helps little kids
Cheat playing poker.
His eyes light a
Candle in my heart
And he would hold
My hand if
My fish died.

Kelly Sullivan

Who Is This Jesus?

Jesus shed His blood for us
From sin He set us free.
He loves us very, very, much
To hang upon that tree!
To be placed in a grave
For sins He didn't do
Showed how much He cared
Yes, he cares for me and you.
On the third day, He arose again
His work was not quite done
He come to Earth to help us
Yes, to help everyone!
Jesus is in Heaven now
Preparing us a place
The people who accepted Him
Whose sins He did erase!
Soon there will come the Greatest Day
The world has ever known
When Jesus takes His Born Again Christians
To their Heavenly Home!

Natalie McWilliams

"Florida Dawn"

Sunshine creeps slowly over the roof
Gently wrapping the orange tree
In a soft caress

Dark green tree
Covered with a sparkling necklace
Of diamond dew drops

Oranges like little suns
Radiates gold
In a nest of green

The still damp grass
Shimmers
In the early morning light

Hope springs eternal
In the new
Florida dawn

B. Dewitt Alexander

Ghosts

Ghosts floating in the air
Ghosts are floating everywhere
Ghosts at day and night
Ghosts are within my sight
As they go floating by
I wonder, I wonder why
Flow those ghosts got so high
As they gather into crowds
They appear to just be clouds

Steven Toy

A Moment

A moment,
Give me a moment of your time,
Touch my life with your laughter,
Warm my spirit with your fire.
I would ask for more
But know it can not be,
So will be grateful for each
Second that we pass together,
And treasure it and shelter
The flame of memory until
The day when it can be
Rekindled and kept alive
And growing for eternity.

Sandra Matteson Dusch

323

At The Bunny Hutch

At the Bunny Hutch
Glistening snow covers everything.
The bunnies have thick warm fur,
It is winter.
At the bunny Hutch,
Baby animals are born,
The bunnies tenderly eat the new grass,
It is spring.
At the Bunny Hutch,
The hot sun shines down,
It is summer.
At the Bunny Hutch,
Leaves blow about in the breeze,
The bunnies snuggle into their soft beds,
It is fall.
A year goes by,
Yet, it stays a timeless treasure in my heart.
At the Bunny Hutch.

Miranda Lee Gohde

Happy Birthday Mom

If I could give a rose for every
    great thing you've done
And if I could change all that's sad,
    I would change it to fun
It wouldn't be enough, for you deserve
    much more
So what my wish is for you, is to
    have happiness galore
What you are to me is "one of a kind at
    it's best,"
Which to me in my book is being
    above the rest
I thank you mom for holding my hand
    along the way
Please take the time for yourself,
    and have a happy birthday

Tina Marie Conner

Our Mother, Dora's Roses

There must be so many flowers
Growing in Heaven above
Many Roses growing
For Roses were our Mother's Love.

She tended, oh, so many
While she was here, below
She had a "Special" formula
Which always made them grow.

Most certain - she had patience
And, an unending care
She pruned and watered carefully
As she worked in silent prayer.

No doubt, that God watched her
Gardening every day - and said;
"I have a Job for Dora
When she 'Comes Home' to stay".

For now, that you are gone, Dear One
And I see a Rose of Special hue,
I cannot, but think, "Oh, Mother",
God gave their care to you.

Phyllis Chavez-Bradley

Summer's End

The day before fall
    had come to an end;
As crickets sang out
    the last love song when;

The air grew cool, fresh, and clean;
    As the forest began its colorful
    scene;

Winter is near and the wind will
    blow;
And we'll soon shelter from the
    cold winter snow;

Yet dreaming of spring with
    flowers in bloom;
Can lift my spirit from the cold,
    gray, gloom.

William J. Prater

Fathering

The color of our love
has changed again
having run a spectrum

    Now she has a beau
    a bairn
    that I am supposed to share

Betrayed by my own bedding
and guilty in any court
of law or heart

    For wanting what was
    the sentence is to accept
    what will be

Or to spin
in
perpetual adolescence

W. Turner

Biographica E=MC2

Einstein studied the stars.
He knew there was Mars.
He accepted no flaws,
In mathematical laws.

He challenged no God,
And studied very hard
Sciences of man
When he saw the plan.

He grew quite weary
Seeking a theory
To explain that zone
To our world, unknown.

He at last laid bare
E=MC2
And, it came to be
The Einstein theory.

The world wanted proof,
So he kept aloof.
We thought him a dreamer
Until Hiroshima.

Michael Max Liebman

"Hi Mommy, It's Me"

Once a young boy knew her
He loved her with all his heart
Until that final lonely day
It tore his soul apart.

He never showed his feelings
No hurt, no pain, no tears
He thought he could forget them
Through all his thirty-four years.

He found out that he couldn't
So he decided to end his life
Behind he left his loved ones
His two kids and his wife.

He didn't realize how he hurt them
He forgot what he went through
He's now where no one can hurt him
Where he can't feel sad or blue.

Now he's up in heaven
Where he's always wanted to be
His first words to her
Were "Hi Mommy, It's me".

Lindsay Rice

The Hope Of Life

He was a son, he was a brother.
He was a father, he was a lover.
Then in a flicker of an eye,
Darkness came and filled his sky.
Would he see his children grow?
Would he see the yearly snow?

His daily life now upside down
His silent screams, a steady sound.
Quiet was his normal way
Could he please stay today?
Is it time to say goodbye?
No, by damn, he did cry.

As he shivered head to toe.
He knew fear and pity to be foe.
He vowed to fight for all he's worth
To stay here on this sweet, sweet earth.
He's known hope, he's known love
Now he sends his prayers above.
In praise of those who helped him through
And turned the sky back gold and blue.

Linda A. Fruehwald

Purple In Teal Abandonment

Desert drenched in moonlight....
Her eyes flash stars at me tonight.
She gives her love, till break of day;
When others come, take her away.

Amid the morning skies of teal
And indigo, they land to steal
From me the one and only friend,
Upon whom all my needs depend.

Far out to the heavens flew
The spaceship - and my loved one too.
Abducted by aliens - she left me
Waiting here on Earth, so lonely.

Beyond forever's end I fear...
She never will again appear!
I gaze intently at the sky;
While stellar dust gets in my eye.

Kristiana

"The Woman I Admire"

"Is someone to be desired"
"Her smile is like the breeze"
"One glance at her"
"You would be at eased"
"She is my mother"
"No one could fill her space"
"So don't even bother"
"She taught me all I know"
"And gave me a chance to grow"
"I love her dearly"
"Thank God for her I now see clearly"
"Every day in Every way"
"Her love keeps me going"
"Without her my life would be boring"
"Every night I go to bed"
"I thank the Lord for her instead"
"I love you mom"
"You are my inspiration"
The woman I admire
That everyone desire

Kay R. Japsi

To Make A Witches Brew

To make a witches brew,
Here's what you do.
Throw in a rat,
Toss in a bat.
In goes an old shoe,
A cat with the flu.
The cauldron burns and bubbles,
Everything that went in, doubles.
Dump in all kinds of slimy bugs,
Especially ugly slugs.
Tongues of dogs,
Toes of frogs.
To cool it off,
Add a horse's cough.
To make a witches brew,
Here's what you do.

Mandie R. Crist

That Special Clown

This special clown means so much to me.
He's one of my favorites, he's
the one I love to see...
All the fun times we had,
I can't forget. He's the
greatest clown I've ever met.
He was happy all the time,
and funny. He always
made me laugh. When he did
magic tricks he would make me
smile. Then after, I could not
see him for a while. He came
back with a smile. He sat down.
I said to him you're a special clown.

Rachael Jaime

The Day Always Ends

Bright mirrors flashing.
Horses prancing. Round and round
they go. Carousel.

Horses up and down.
Mirrors round and round. Why does
It all seem so sad?

Frozen leaps. Midway
shut down. Sadness takes over
The merry-go-round.

William C. Tremmel

Rainbow Of Life

Life is dark black corners,
Holding hopeful dreams,
Hiding sorrowful tragedies.

Life is hot red flames,
Glowing within each spirit,
Fading away with each death.

Life is rough blue rapids,
Splashing hearts with love,
Crashing souls into hate.

Life is cool purple mist,
Covering over obstacles,
Blinding vision from goals.

Life is soft white pillows,
Comforting frightening falls,
Suffocating with mounting stress.

Life is
  a rainbow.

Shone Buswell

The Search

The darkness it engulfs me,
holds me down 'til I can not see.
The light, the light
where could it be,
it shines for others, I can see.
I've searched so high,
I've searched so low
for the joy that came so long ago.
I've searched for Love,
I've searched for Light,
anything to fill the hole.
My days they come, my days they go,
but seldom do they stir my soul.
What is it that I want and need
that seems so far away?
Is it the joys within my grasp,
the feelings yet to be?
If only the courage to try
would just come over me.

Linda Sklenar

The Procrastinator

Dawn arises
Hope awakens
  It rests
  Be cautious
Night falls
Despair decides
  You descend
  Are dead
  But alive
Fire's hot
  Too late
  To forgive
Too early
  To forget

Travers M. Wall

Gone Away

Gone away, far into a different land,
into a different world gone,
So far, see the different
people. See the different
things, the world of weirdness,
the world of earth.

Kelsi Newby

Knowing

Tears
Hurting cavity where my heart resides.
Who are you, my love?
I knew you yesterday.
Now...
How is it that I know you so well,
And you know me so little?
Perhaps I do not know you.
Yet, I love you.
Such mingled joy and pain
Is a mystery too great.
I must simply hand it to God...
For Him to unravel
Or not
As He sees fit.

Susie Miller

Artemis

As I step into the sultry evening air
I am embraced.
Its sensuous touch surrounds me,
bathes me, encompasses me.
I am a silhouette,
a shadow of myself
against the velvet backdrop.
The gentle whisper of the wind
with its faintly-lipped words
encircles me and I am caressed
by its pouty-mouthed kisses.
My skin is translucent, alive,
paled by an even paler light.
I am one with the sister moon-goddess,
my countenance
a reflection of her aesthetic beauty
as she envelops me
in her Cimmerian mantle of darkness.

Karen Kennedy

A Life Once On "E"

A genie gave me three wishes.
I asked for strength deep inside.
I asked for wisdom.
Last, I asked for pride.

She just snapped her fingers,
and quick as an eye blink,
my skin darkened,
and my hair began to kink.

To my surprise she said that
I now have two wishes left.

Terrance Tyree Whitehead

A Crying Shame

Don't leave me in this crib tonight
I do not want to stay
I'll Scream my head off, if you leave
- Until I get my way -
But.. if you do not leave me now
Then I may never know...
The value of my sleeping
All on my very own!
Thought I may SCREAM with all my might
It really is a must
That you prevail and win this fight
To teach me how to trust

Melanie Horrigan

The Question

Do you see?
I cannot comprehend
the catastrophe
of loving one such as thee.

Should I try
or will you make me cry?

What's been done to you before
tears out pieces of your soul.
It hinders you from seeing,
you can't help but wreck my soul.

Could this be?
Not allowing your heart to die.
Can you stop;
have you forgotten how to cry?

Do you concede the truth?
To a truth you want to see.

Do you see the bitter end?
Do you make it so?
Just to know, the end.

K. C. Watkins

A No. 1 Grandma

Today I feel all alone,
I can't believe you're gone.
I want to walk with you,
I want to talk with you.
I want to be together.
Always and forever.

Now all that's left is a shell,
Of my Grandma I knew well.
I can't see your colorful eyes,
And sit with you close beside.
I know you had to go away,
But I've always wished you'd stay.

In spirit we walk together,
Your spirit will carry on forever.
One day I know we'll meet again,
In heaven where we'll begin.
To talk of old and new alike,
And to me this will be alright!
I love you Grandma.

Kim Kennedy

Untitled

From out of you came me
I can't think but I can breath
follow you blindly into the light
I maybe wrong
I maybe right
from behind the scratchy voice
cigarette choke hold
cigarettes of choice

From out of me came you
black hair and finger nails
I'll paint you too
might as well bbarbie perfume
you give me an expression
you almost died
I called you twice

Standing together hundred and withered
we use our powers to complain about weather
I've got some and you do too
you called me or I called you

Tom Hunt

A Grain Of Sand

Lord, there are people
I come in contact with
each and every day
that have a tendency to
irritate and rub me wrong
in many a different way.

It begins early every morn
and goes on til the end of day.
I wish I'd not been born
to toil like that each day.

Let me be like an oyster
when a grain of sand
enters between its shell
and slowly begins
the process of irritation
to produce a precious pearl.

Pedro G. Colon Jr.

Today

Today
I come to you
in peace
healed and happy,
rejoicing in beauty
about me
above me
within me.
I recall times
too many
when I could come
only in tears.
But today
I come to you
in love.
Glad for all things,
glad to be me
knowing you.

Tris Stephanic

My Wish

If I had one wish to make,
I don't know what it would be;
I'd try to make a difference
For all mankind to see.
Stop the wars in all the world,
If only for a day;
Take the time to show them
That war is not the way!
Why not feed the hungry,
Or give good health to all?
Make the ones that cannot walk
Stand so straight and tall.
Stop the hate and all the fear
That some have in their heart;
Show them love and kindness,
It would surely be a start!
Wouldn't it be wonderful
To make these all come true?
It really is quite possible,
It only takes ME and YOU!

Odessa A. Szumita

Quatrain

Low above a woodland ridge
In virgin beauty bright
Is hung the pendant evening star
About the throat of night.

Shirley Butler Donnelly

Dreamlight (For Delta)

I close my eyes and dream.
I dream of a light.
A dreamlight which opens up my soul,
and wipes it clean.
I speak to this dreamlight.
"Dreamlight, talk to me.
I'll listen to your words."
"Dreamlight, let me talk to you.
Listen to my words."
"Dreamlight, let me touch you
and you can touch me."
"Dreamlight, I want you to know this.
You have inspired me deeply."
"Dreamlight, please don't burn out.
I want you to exist forever.
Without a light in my dreams,
I cry alone in the dark."

Michael J. Nepper

Our Search Is Over

Our eyes meet
I feel I know you.
We speak as if long time friends
The silent moments are comfortable.
With your arms around me
Our lips meet, so warm, so right.
Our paths have crossed
Many times over the years.
Now our search is over
We know we belong together.
All those years we felt we had lost
Helped us grow and mature
So when we finally met
We were ready to love
With all our heart, body and soul.

Suzie Eppler

Immortal Kiss

For love cannot escape me now.
I feel you'll take it with somehow
Through long expanse of time and then...
    return to me yet once again
Like pages opening a book
    my memory peeks inside and look...
You're there with me,
    and oh what bliss
    enraptured
    in immortal kiss.

Sonya Allison Thorne

I Forgive

I forgive you for what you said,
I forgive because Jesus did;
The filthy words that passed your lips
Have caused me in Christ to be hid.

At first those words cut me to shreds
And sent me to a world of sin,
But there was Someone standing by,
And through His love he took me in.

Because of you I've come to know
Him and He's become my dear friend;
Now He's my constant companion
And will be till the end.

Mary L. Shelton

A Hometown

You have a home town.
I have a home town.
My hometown is called Stop Light City.
My hometown is in the midwest.
I hope people who take illegal drugs.
Will stop in my hometown.
And I hope people will stop
abusing drugs to overseas.
And God bless my hometown.

Yes, really yours too,
God bless your town too.

V. Tyler

The Artless Major

For one brief moment in my life
I joined the world of art
Had one short fling of headiness,
But could not find the spark.
Then once again I raised my hand
To pen immortal words
That men would sing for endless time
And weep, such beauty yet unheard.
This candle too, a feeble flame, soon
Dimmed, a flickering light
A pinpoint in a sky of stars,
Unseen in darkest night.
No Grandma Mose within my soul
Do I purport to be
Nor Dylan Thomas' golden words
Attributed to me.
But time to time I'll fashion thoughts
Upon some sheet of rag
And hope to reach a spark in you
Wherein your spirits flag.

Ralph L. Rowbotham

The Gift Of My Life

I heard a little bird sing today
  I knew the Lord was there.
And then I heard a happy cricket
  sing in the cool night air.
My mama said God is everywhere
  and I believe it's true.
Because even when the storm is gone
  He sends a rainbow through.
But more than this, I know He is there
because God gave to me
the gift of my life, with all His love
He set my spirit free.

Renee Robinson

Longing

Your soft lips
I long to kiss
Your strong hands
I long to hold
Your tender words
I long to hear
Your sensuous body
I long to be pressed against mine
But these things I cannot have
Because you belong to someone else
And so do I
I long for the day
When we can be together
But for today I dream
And in my dreams
You love me

Melissa Langley

Because We're Friends

Because we're friends
I know on you I can depend
To keep love within our hearts
Even when we're far apart
For some days we may not get to talk
Or even go out for a walk

To brighten my darkest day
You know those special words to say
You tell me how much you care
In what I do, and the life we share
For God knew my heart was for you
And I know his word is true

God gave you to me for all eternity
For through our love, I gained maturity
He gave me the type of friend I need
Not one who is irresponsible or conceited
But one as loving as caring as you
This, my friend, is why I love you

Kimberly Templeton

Weeping

Under the weeping willow tree
I lay making love to thee
The wind was blowing through
my hair and my body so cool and bare
Under the weeping willow tree
The night was falling I could hear
your voice calling softly to me
Our bodies were running free under
the weeping willow tree when I
made love to thee

Patricia Struckman

"Trapped"

Trapped inside myself
I long to be free
Yet, I know I'm the one
who created this captivity

Once I had a window
where I had a view
but being the introvert
that I am
I closed the window, too.

No amount of pain
outside the wall
could be as painful
as feeling nothing at all.

Many times I've tried to put
this scenario on the shelf
yet, I still remain
trapped inside myself.

Micky Thompson

The Loss I Held Within

Thoughts of forgiveness
I shall always carry.
A fear that I hide
I shall always keep.
A memory of joy
I shall always remember.
The trust within
I shall always treasure.
A secret so deep
I shall never deny.

Vanessa Washington

Where Have All The Flowers Gone?

Where have all the flowers gone?
I look around and all I see,
is darkness, dirt and buildings
where the flowers used to be.

No longer do the flowers grow,
but buildings, one by one,
slowly, leaving nothing for
Mother Nature to show what she has done.

Man has taken over
all the beauty of the land,
leaving nothing made with love,
but something made with hand.

The ponds no longer live,
the sun no longer shines,
the birds no longer sing,
but yet, man, still, he dines.

Plant a seed here and you will see,
You will get nothing, not even a tiny tree.
Soon we will get nothing,
not even a You or Me.

Tasha Bortzfield

Love, Wisdom, Truth

I love self.
I love mother.
I love father.
I love the UNIVERSE!

Wisdom doth age acquire.
Wisdom doth we call upon
Wisdom doth cometh with
  lessons learned.
Wisdom doth calm a weary
  soul found.

Truth elude me not!
Truth eludes us when love
  is not a part.
Truth eludes when thought
  is not from the start.
Truth eludes when prayers are
  not from the heart.

Seek ye love!
Seek ye wisdom!
Seek ye truth-forevermore!

Vivian Hester Bennerson

Breaking Up

I love you so much
I love you so true
Can't believe I broke up
With someone like you

I regret what I did
But I was so mad
Now that I did that
I'm always so sad

Come back to me
We'll go out again
This time it'll work
Forever Amen

Kristi Derenne

Consequence

I put it away.
I meant to return,
  and retrieve it someday.
I did not want
  to leave it behind.
But, I had so much
  on my mind.
I pictured it always,
  waiting there.
I did not realize
  it needed love and care.
So, I neglected it,
  and it did not survive.
I have lost tomorrow.
  My dream has died.

Penny Caldwell

Slave

The stench is very strong
I must hold out however long.
Many miles from home
I am weary to the bone.

We row by day and night
still no land in sight.
Painful blisters on my hand,
Pig slop is not for man.

Aboard this cruel ship
I feel the devil's whip.
I smell death in this galley
And want so to be free.

Hatred burns in my brain,
While captors inflict pain.
Will I die before I go insane?
I pray for strength to break chain.

Willie A. Buchanan

Life's Journey

As I walk along life's journey,
I often wonder....about the crossroads,
The many detours along the way,
How many paths there were.

I wonder if....
I had a guiding angel,
To direct which way to turn.
And if she chose the paths I took?

As I walk along life's journey
I wonder about the crossroads,
About the detours along the way.
Were they paths I was meant to take?

I wonder about those directions
About my guiding angel,
And the paths I took.
Were they mine or hers?

S. Irene Bender

Mirror

I look in the mirror
I see sadness
My eyes start to water
But why bother,
Looking in this mirror
Shows something I don't
Like to see.
Why they say?
Because
I see me.

Miguel Chavarria

Sunday Evening, Late August 1992

Walking my dogs,
I saw God's hand
Holding the world,
Gigantic fingers,
Grabbing the earth.

A car passed, windows up,
Driver, staring at the road,
Ignoring the heavens.

Indoors, people looked at shadows
Flickering on tubes,
Toyed with remotes, shouted at kids,
Ate, drank, flushed
During commercials.

Then God let go,
My dogs got anxious,
And darkness repossessed the world.

Richard Tuerk

You Are So Wonderful

All of my life
I searched around and now I have found
Everything that I hoped for and more
You're all I ever needed
Key to my destiny
You are so wonderful
Wonderful
Oh, yes you are
In my life you brought love, happiness,
Joy and understanding
You are the key to my every dream
My guiding light,
through the day and the night
You are so wonderful

All the heaven I need to make me feel
the joy you give that makes me smile
more and more each day

You are so wonderful
Wonderful...wonderful...

Willie McKinney Jr.

Doggie

Doggie, doggie what do you see?
I see a lamb looking at me.
Lamb, lamb what do you see?
I see a brown bear looking
at me, with a happy face.

Mei West

Shadow Boxing

Morning sun through the window;
I see my shadow on your body,
  my form against yours.

I move my arm,
  to be sure I see me.
With my hands,
  I form a barking dog,
  I form a quacking duck.

You stir, as a bird in flight
  crosses your back.
Sorry—
I didn't know my shadow
  could move you.

Patricia DiSandro

Thoughts On A Star

Oh star up in the lonely sky
I see your light as night draws nigh
It fills my heart with strange delight
As I enjoy your beauty bright.

I gaze and gaze at your distant light
So far away in the lonely night
And wonder if by some strange chance
You are returning my searching glance.
Do people such as you and me
Live far away by a distant sea
Do they know life and all its joy?
Do they wage wars that all destroy?

Alas for me I'll never know
If mountains rise and rivers flow
If people live and work and play
On that strange star so far away
Oh star so far off in the sky
You do not heed my lonely sigh
But sail along with beauty bright
Into the dark mysterious night

Marie D. Walklet

By Bad Co'd (My Bad Cold)

Plug Nose Tightly And Read
I ca't breathe, OH WOE IS BE!
  I think I have a co'd!
By head is full, by eyes are red,
  I ache and feel so o'd!

I ca't taste or sbell by food—
  Whatever shall I do?
I guess I'll sit and blow by dose
  Ad give by co'd to you!

Oh, dow I see you pulli'g back—
  You have doe sy'pathy!
So go ahead ad leave be here
  To die id bisery!

Before you go, I'll ask wud thi'g—
  Thed you'll be "fadsy free",
Cub closer dow, please wipe by brow,
  AH-CHOOO!...Oh, pardod be!!

Yvonne Dieffenbacher

Voice Of The Raisin

The time is here. I hum my tune.
I think I sound a little nasal.
I watch for cues and know that soon
We all will face the great appraisal.

Our Father Walnut quotes our missal,
Of duty and tradition long,
His bushy eyebrows all abristle,
Demanding our most perfect song.

My Sister Celery twists and turns,
She fears her fibers are askew.
I try to soothe her as she learns
We're soon to be in public view.

Dear Mother Apple holds us all
Together with her quite voice.
I nestle close and feel so tall,
I'm ready now for this day's choice.

But as I wait to serve this world,
I will admit my secret wish,
To reach the heights with flag unfurled,
And run glissando round the dish.

Vivienne Federico

Moms

Just yesterday, it was
I tried to understand,
it made no sense,
none at all.

How could it be,
that you've left me?
I miss your troubled
eyes, your smiling face,
tears fall from my face.

I miss you so.
I don't know where to go,
or where to turn.
You're gone forever,
good-bye

Mary Ann Lockwood

What Have You Done?

What have you done to me?
I used to be in control
No memories of stories of old
Or of love long gone cold

Then you came with sweet, soft words
and before I realized
I was totally mesmerized

Mesmerized by words of love
and passion so sweet
I alone could not retreat.

What will you do with me?
Now that you have control

Katrina Oliver

Return Daze

The silence is deafening!
I wait for a noise
The quiet seems louder
Than both of the boy!
No beat of a radio,
No creak of a floor,
No flush of a toilet,
No slam of a door!
(I've prayed like a fool!)
For both of the boys
Have gone back to school!
Thoughts fill my head,
Daydreams of fun,
But all these aren't possible
'Til my work is done.
I pick up and straighten,
I wash and I dust.
It all looks so clean now!
My Lord, here's their bus!!!

Lana F. Teeters

From The Shadows

In the shadows
I wait for my chance
My chance to attack
Always present
Never expected
I creep up
Set in
Break you down
Until there is nothing you can do
To escape my wrath
I am
Depression

Ryan M. Lockner

Cheap Thrills In Antelope Park

No one told me
I was going to hell
Last night in Antelope Park.
No one asked me to
Compare and contrast
The ultimate question
On poverty and death.

My eyes were free
To play the burning puzzle
Adrift in the Nebraska sky,
Watch water slip over soft stone
At a child's playful gait,
Take in all that's offered
By this gift of rattled contractions.

There are other events
To witness in the dark,
I know autumn begins
At my home, just like yours.
Paint any picture you desire,
It's all done for cheap thrills.

Michael D. Dunekacke

The War Of Right And Wrong

Out across the dusty lane
I watch as smiles turn to disdain
As both apposing sides now grunt
From problems I must now confront.
Which road is best for me to take,
And will that answer heal this ache,
Or is that answer just a fake?
The night is neither light nor dark.
It's hiding face gives me a start.
Which answer do I claim as mine?
Which one to me will be most kind?
The fast and easy road looks bright
And I could hide my sin from sight.
The other way would take more work
To prove to others I have worth.
I question all the long night through
Before I know what I must do.
Though others may defame my name,
In moral truths I'll stake my claim.

Lanita Sue Creech

In A Moment Of Despair

Softly
I whisper my lover's plea.
hoping
you will return to me,
knowing
it will never be,
losing all my sanity.

William T. Mitchell Jr.

Sense Of You

In every breath you breathed
I would smell the fragrance of the air,
And the softness of your flesh
I would touch with tenderness and care;
In the quiet beating of your heart
I would hear the lovers' faint sighs,
And the sadness of the earth
I would wipe from your tearful eyes;

But in your mouth
I would taste the truth.

Mick Fitzpatrick

Untitled

I am always last in line,
I'd give anything to be first.
Is this all a sign?
That I will always be the worst.

I am never quick enough,
Always too slow.
Should life be this tough?
I don't know where to go.

I am always last in line,
Why can't I be first?
Even second would be fine,
Maybe I'm just cursed.

Loretta Jeffcoat

The Gift Of Life....

The gift of life is so special
if given a chance to life
Some do not get that chance
an others just can't take it
So when you are given the chance
God has given to you, don't blow it
Cause the life sometimes want make it
So be strong
Cause the gift of life has to make it
Don't be afraid to shed a tear
Cause everybody has their on fear
So if you don't get a chance
to give the gift of life, remember
Their is all ways a life that, you
Can be a gift so special to....

Naomil Burch

"Grant Me This Eight"

Will you give me your heart
If mine shall be its last
Will you give me your love
No matter what's in the past

Can I touch your soul
It will be treated lust I see fit
Can I be in your life
I yearn to be a part of it

Will you give me your trust
I will guard it with my life
Will you give me your faith
To be trothed as your wife

Can you leave me a sign
To show me you care
Can you swear on a promise
You'll always be there

If you can and are willing
To grant me this eight
Then a family of course
Is what we'll create

Kathrine Martinez

"What Is"

What is pain
If not for reward
In the end

What is need
If not for help
The Lord sends

And what is finality
If in the end
There isn't a new beginning

Robin T. McIe

The Awakening

Fear has been my keeper,
Ignorance has been my shield;
Passion has been my desire,
Illusion is my veneer.

The grey clouds have begun to part,
I am in awe of what I have missed;
Each passing moment is now revered,
While I weigh the burden of my choices.

The heart struggles with itself,
Challenged by the finite mind;
Nature is also a fragile friend,
Whom, I too have abandoned.

No one can feel my inner pain,
The shield has done its job well;
Like a child emerging from the womb,
I sense a rebirth. The fool awakens!

Roy Milton Waldt Jr.

Scared To Death

I'm frightened.
I'm scared.
I'm always watching my back.
It's a pain I can't bear.
If I keep feeling this way,
I just may go crazy.
I'm scared to death,
that you might try to kill my baby.
Now, I do
As I am told.
You frighten me,
because you are big and bold.
I want help.
But I know I won't get it.
You promised me if I tell anybody,
I will regret it.
So now I listen.
I do as you say.
And I know there's no hope
for this way of life to go away.

Maria Jefferson

Untitled

I feel so cold and alone,
in a hole of my own.
I map and I groan,
Can't you see me?
I feel great pains
as my tears pour like rain,
I believe I'm not sane.
Do you hear me?
I star holes through the walls
I try to rise... but still fall
my world makes no sense at all
can you help me?
Thoughts run through my mind
as I pass away time,
my fears lie here in this thyme,
Do you care?

Melissa Davis

"Christmas"

Christ was born upon this day
   in a land across the sea,

He gave His son upon a tree
   to die for you and me.

Risen again, how sweet the thought,
   as we sing aloud His praise.

In Him I find my strength and peace
   upon my worst of days.

Soon again I'll see His face,
   my heart shall fill with joy,

To sing His praise beside His throne
   my voice He shall employ.

My thoughts will turn to friends below,
   I'll watch their every step,

Assist them in their hardest trials
   they're bound to intercept.

Some day you too can see His face...
   "Eternal Life" to have...
   'tis only this the price you pay...
   "Believe"...and ye shall have...

Patrick A. Hughes

Evanescence

Beauty is a thing that comes and goes
In baby's smile, or in a rose
In leafy shadows from a tree
In words
Between you and me.

From life's beginning to its close,
Beauty is a thing that comes and goes.
Beauty flies on silent wings.
You can't hold on
To some beautiful things.

Rilla Black

Rainbow Song

Glistening drops
In colorful flight,
Tiny spheres
Refracting light.
Myriad hues
From reds to blues.
A waterfall prism
Cascading from heaven,
Bending its knee
In supplication.
Shooting arrows
Of beauty
Behold
With great pleasure,
This taut bow
Of nature.
Welcome
Rain's treasure.

Mary E. Quandt

Stars

What is a star?
Is it yellow?
Look up at the sky do you see them?
Are they in heaven or the sky?
They are neat to look at.

Linnae Marceau

You Are The Word

I want to be like Jesus,
   In everything I do.
I want to be like Jesus,
   Always faithful, kind and true.

I want to help the sinner,
   In his time of need.
Into his fertile soul,
   I will plant your seed.

I will feed the hungry,
   Your heavn'ly bread I'll give.
And restore the dying,
   Then in you they will live.

I will heal the cripple,
   That they may walk to you.
I will give you all the glory,
   You are the WORD, tried and true.

Peter A. Gregorio

Life

In love there's life
In life there's death
Where to turn...
My heart holds dear

A lady so sweet
Knowing when to speak
A heart so full
With room to grow

Now where to go

Richard E. Wilcox Jr.

Untitled

I scream out for him
   in my dreams
But he did not hear
I reached out for him
   in my thoughts
But he could not feel
I have searched for
   him all my life
But he did not see
For his spirit is wild
   and never can be tamed

Melissa Farnam

Images

Swirling, swimming images
in my mind's eye have formed.
Memories of yesterday meld
with tomorrow's dreams.
Shifting, swaying,
they focus, vanish,
flitting in and out.
Melting, molding, taking shape
in the fertile, futile
imagination, fascination
of uncertainty.
Tomorrow, today.
Past, present.
Together they beguile us,
will us with possibilities.
Beginnings, endings,
slowly take shape
in the reflection
of who we were, are,
and could yet be.

Mark D. Maddy

Moon Madness In The Night

The full moon rushes, fervent
In striking souls below.
They cringe and hide in horror,
Crying before each blow.

The little people wander,
Each one a differed task.
You cannot see the terror
Behind each 'madness' mask.

Their minds entombed in darkness;
Emotions wrought in hell,
But none can warn of evil.
No, none dare ever tell.

So, on and on, they ponder
The way it best be done.
Malicious deeds are plenty;
No sanctions to be won.

When dawn comes creeping onward
It peeps on thwarted bud
To watch the bodies rotting,
And trickling of the blood.

V. L. Chamness

Untitled

Misery completes my anguish
in sudden overload of confusion

Mirrors mock the pain and suffering
I shall never make known.

Eating inside of me
my feelings numb to understanding

Gothic times prevail in my
desire called life.

Rhea Colwill

The Christmas Star

The star that shone on Christmas day,
In that small town so far away,
Was sent by God, from up above
To tell the people of His love.

He placed it in a sky of blue,
A beacon, for all those who knew.
Shepherds on the hill that night,
Marvelled at the wondrous sight.

Wise men trav'ling from afar,
Were guided by the glorious star.
To the manger they were led,
To our savior's lowly bed.

Proudly there it shone on high,
Never wavering in the sky.
Telling all who saw the light,
Christ is born on earth this night.

Richard L. Hardesty

True Joy

True joy,
is children smiling.

True joy,
is a child's laugh.

So much about children
can show true joy.

Children,
are true joy.

Pierangeli

An Emotion

You can find it all around,
In the air, and on the ground.

It is always seen,
And is considered green.

Love, and hate all mixed in one,
An emotion that can't ever be fun.

It's a crime,
Showing up all the time.

Growing bigger, and bigger,
Something you just can't trigger.

Always can be felt,
Will it ever melt?

It's a bubble that just won't burst,
Jealousy is a major curse.

Melissa Lukose

Still Moon On The Way To The Train

Still moon hovers
In the dark blue presence
Of the sky.

The air heavy,
Quiet in the heat;
Little sound
Save Katy-dids
And crickets.

On the platform
A light breeze blows
Breaking the stillness.

> I fly through
> Hot dark quiet
> On my way
> To the train.

Sarah Park

My Friend

You came to me
In the darkest Despair of my life
You rose from the blackness
Like a brilliant star
And you showered me
With your wonderful light
And filled me with love
You've given me peace
Renewed my hope
Your strength stills my fears
And makes me stronger
You're a wise and powerful teacher
Thank You
For being my friend.

William Corwin

The Tree

The tree is so tall,
it stands so proud.
It's shade for all,
the few and the crowd.
It's home to many,
like birds and squirrels.
The animals think it's cozy,
when the snow comes in swirls.

Shirley Cox

Think Right

Think right
In the light bright
To unite
People of earth-site

Think right
Not to fight
Just to show might
On earth-satellite

Think right
For future bright
And use best foresight
To see the people's plight

Think right
Day and night
For human right
To share peace, progress, prosperity alright

Think right
Don't hesitate slight
And unite to unite
That's a thought real and right.

Patel Motibhai C.

In The Potter's Hands

Though I shall return to dust,
In the Potters' Hands I trust.
'Ere this lump of clay were rolled
I was cast without a mold;
Shaped uniquely from above,
With His everlasting love.
Though by sin I am diseased,
Never has his loving ceased,
For my soul is highly priced;
Paid by blood of Brother Christ.
On the tree he washed my soul,
Raised me up and made me whole.
Thank thee mighty God for all.
I await Thy judgment call.
By His grace I do atone;
Never more to walk alone.
As I rise and shed this crust,
In the Potters Hands I trust.

Wayne R. McLaughlin Sr.

The Journey

First it starts with footsteps,
in the right direction,
Next is steps of faith,
in the right book's section,
then we go to hope,
that shines through the night,
Next is the gift of love,
that in our heart shines bright.

The next step is of sacrifice,
the one and only son,
Afterwards, the step is mourning,
this poem's almost done,
The next step is of peace,
these people came to meet,
The final step is resurrection,
The journey is complete.

Karri Johnson

Twinkle Twinkle Far Away Star!

Twinkle twinkle little star
in the sky so bright and far.
With other stars and bigger moons
You're like a baby watching cartoons.
Will I get the wish I'm asking for
Or be shot down to the ocean floor?
Answer me you Little Star
Can't you hear me, are you too far
Maybe I'll still get my wish
If I fly away and send a kiss.
I'll go so far no one will find me
Hey, it could happen! Probably.

Robert Mealer

Numbers

I have seen a hundred dreams
In the sparkle of his eyes
I have sensed a thousand schemes
In the shivers of his sighs

I have touched a million stars
Since he came and made me whole
I have felt a billion scars
That he burned into my soul

I have cried a zillion tears
Since the day he said goodbye
He had whispered in my ears
An infinity of lies

Suzannah Kuhn

Crossfire

A deadly plague rages
in the street,
A drug crisis crack is cheap
A mother son dies and she weep
His bullet ridden body lay
at her feet
As the car drove by
He was sprayed with Gunfire
there were fears and tears
He was always in the street
He was into dusk, candy, and horse
but he had a choice
the neighborhood was a combat zone
now he gone
His mother wonder about this generation
If they are going to get an education
Her son was caught in a crossfire
Now she must say good bye
family and friends are hurt
and cry

Maxcine Fuller

Untitled

I looked for me
In your eyes

Your heart beat
And mine responded

You cried
And I tasted tears

I lost myself
In your shadow

I need to see
Sunshine again.

Lamont Curtis

Evening Theater

Take a long country walk,
in the summer, if you can.
In the stillness of twilight,
tune in to live, accented
broadcasts of insect tales,
rendered from their green
earthly beds,
listen to feathered friends as
they chirp drowsily in
bowed branches above,
daydream at dusk, in the
smoky view,
feel the tease of evening's
soft breeze, when the air
is oh, so cool.
And don't you hurry,
when night unfolds to
offer a dark and cozy
comforter to every
present guest.

Serene T. Marshall

Two Lovers

Two lovers are born
   in the twilights last
   showing
Two lovers about to become one
They share the feeling
They share the need
They fulfill the wanting desire
   as they follow their trail
      on passions high wire
Not sure of what their doing
Not sure of where they are
Just sure of wanting to be
Two lovers
   living for the moment
   savouring the ecstasy
Getting lost in the whirlwind
   of emotions
As they lay
   two lovers in love

Maria Martin

God's Garden

Well, I'm just a tiny seed
In this garden God decided to plant
Everyday he gives me sunshine
And the things I need ne surely grants
Earth is like a giant greenhouse
Where everyone could live in peace
If everyone knew the planter
All our problems then would cease
He fertilizes us with love
Gives each of us the right amount
God knows how many seeds he's sowed
He never has to count
Sometimes his flowers wilter
And they fall gently to the ground
They then slowly loose their color
And the roots by which they were bound
God can pick up that wiltered flower
And by the touch of his gentle hand
Place it gently in the garden
Of Heaven's holy land

Onda M. Hill

"The Place"

As I gaze at your image,
in this picture of mine,
my heart races quickly,
it must be a sign.

Your beauty captures me,
and my mind drifts away,
to a place in my soul,
that I wish I could stay.

For at this place,
my heart is as warm as the sun,
and I dream of that day,
when two become one.

I know in my heart,
my dream will come true,
for I recognize this place,
each time I'm with you!

Stephen J. Szypula

An Educator's Will

I long for days,
in which life stays,
a peaceful place.

I long for time,
which could be personally mine,
in a peaceful place.

I wish for all to learn,
to be good and kind,
in a peaceful place.

I wish for all to see,
my students glee,
in a peaceful place.

I live today,
I live for always,
hoping for a peaceful place.

Ronald Malabed

Life

You come into the world
Innocent and wanting love
You look for an adult to teach you.

You reach your teens
Struggling through the doubtful years
Finally making it to adulthood.

You are an adult
It is not as easy as you thought,
But you had good leadership.

Now you are a parent,
You hope, you try, you pray,
That you set a good example,

Only time will tell!

Shirley Gregg

Dream...

To dream, to dream, of love on wing
Is a lovely, many-splendored thing;
To hold you near when I am sad
Is something else that makes me glad.

In all the days I've loved and lost
I hope that you might someday cross;
The wide blue waters of the land
And give to me your lovely hand.

I cannot say to you how much
The feelings of my soul you touch;
It makes the world revolve around
When I have searched, and you I found.

There's no one else like you above
There's no one else I'd rather love;
But if you tire of me some day,
I'll hide my tears and go my way.

Steve Mitchell

A Desert Walk

The quietness of the desert,
  is a place to go for a walk.
With Saguaro cactus standing so tall,
  you can almost hear them talk.

They say, "Look at the sunset,
  the colors paint the sky".
They talk of roadrunners, dove or quail,
  and jackrabbits scampering by.

And if you're really quiet,
  you might hear the hoot of an owl.
A snake or a lizard through the brush,
  or a coyote yelping his howl.

What they used to call the wild west,
  has through the years got tame.
So many of us have moved from the north,
  to seek out fortune and fame.

But don't destroy our desert,
  please let the wildlife stay.
Cause walking through this wonderland,
  is a joy along life's way.

Mary Jane Greleski

The Beauty Of The Autumn

The beauty of the Autumn
Is a scene beyond compare,
With the grandeur of all seasons
In this lovely land so fair.

I view the trees in splendor
As their colors richly glow,
Knowing well it was not man's painting
But it was God that made them so.

Then I ask myself this question,
"How can man deny the fact
That there is a God eternal,
One that holds the world intact?"

When you see the leaves in color,
Yellow, brown, rich gold, and red;
Don't forget the greatest Artist
And in reverence bow your head.

Give Him thanks for Autumn beauty,
Praise His name for beauty grand;
For the beauty of the Autumn
Is the painting of His hand.

Viola E. Rowe

"An Angel For You"

An Angel on your shoulder
is all you'll ever need,
An eternal reminder
of God's amazing deeds.
Angels guide, protect and counsel us
and keep the Devil far away.
They are charged to follow us
to keep us in light's way.
Always good, sincere and true;
Angels are heaven-sent just for you.

LaVinia Rothrock Goudie

The Chairlift

A chairlift for a stairway
Is important, let's agree;
It's doubly so for two-way rides,
Both up and down, you see.
When going up you see no stairs,
Just glide on slanting plane;
And going down, forget your caress
For coasting is your gain.

Whichever way you ride the chair,
For going up or down,
You're quite as free to come and go
As anywhere in town.
At first one might be tempted
To take this simple view,
'A chairlift ain't important
Till the passenger is you!'

Royal F. Peterson

My Grandfather

Look, my child, that cloud in heaven
Is like a horse-just see!
And the rider is a child.
His eyes, two stars, shine brilliantly.

Keep this picture in your mind,
Before it vanishes, do!
When you grow up, when you're a man,
I'll buy a real horse for you.

But from my old back now get off!
By what I have said, set store.
You will be riding a real horse.
And I'll be your horse no more.

Then as life goes, following
Its usual course,
Your grandchild will the rider be,
And you will be his horse.

Walter W. Artzt

Sibling Love

A sibling's Love
Is neverending,
No matter what,
Always come forward
And let them know
How much you care!

Tell them daily
or show them often,
How much you Love them.
Because, one day
They might not be
there to share!

Tammy D. Howard

Thanks For Thorns

To give thanks in every situation
  is sometimes hard to do,
When the body is racked with pain
  it's hard to say "Thank you!"

Or if there's a physical problem
  for which there is no cure,
or if we've lost a loved one
  It is difficult to endure.

We thank Him for the roses
  but never once for the thorn.
We're always glad for the good times
  but for the bad times we mourn.

When a cherished bond has been broken
  It's hard to feel peaceful and meek.
We must learn to thank Him always
  He gives us strength when we're weak.

So let us be thankful for all things
  Let's thank Him as all Christians should,
He will show Mercy in trouble,
  We must always believe GOD IS GOOD.

Lillian T. Johnson

Inheritance

What is this my Father hands me?
Is this to be my fate?
He hands me fear, prejudice,
a world of pain and hate.
I cannot see the way to follow.
Is this to be my life?
His left him one of hope and prosperity,
mine left only strife.
I wonder if he didn't care,
or tried only to fail?
Does he understand and know
he left his children hell!
You ask why so many in my generation
try to escape through death.
Can't you see my loving Father,
there's simply nothing left?

Sam L. Douthitt

Maybe I Should've Waited

15 seconds
is what it could take
15 seconds
could make or break

Feelings so true
feelings so deep
but it is you I want
for me to keep

15 seconds
so long so little
15 seconds
so very brittle

Time must've went slower
or faster that night
but I know it didn't
not to mortal sight

15 seconds
a clock is a deadly knife
15 seconds
could have saved a life.

Mike Jones

Bye-Bye Fly

My eyes become heavy
It is getting late
Dreams of sleeping
I just can't wait
Lay me down to sleep
Keep it quiet, not a peep
Into bed I quickly fell
Now at peace, I rest well
My eyes now barely open
Do I dream?... I'm hopin'
In silence I hear a fly
It lands on my arm
I mean it no harm
I shoo it away
It comes back to stay
"Fly, leave me be"
I won't swat thee
The fly is still there
Now I don't care
SPLAT!!! Bye-bye fly
S. Van Tassell

Time Is The Essence Of Life

It waits for no one
It passes so quickly
and yet so slow
It controls the hours
of wake and sleep
It is the factor when we laugh
and when we weep
Time gives us moments of joy
And it allows for healing
Time keeps hours and days apart
and yet together
Time is the essence of life.
Sandy Wagner

I Found an Arrowhead

I found an arrowhead today,
  It set my mind awhirl;
I thought of him who sent it forth,
  A man in ancient world.

I wondered if he missed his mark,
  And hungry went to bed;
I wondered was he young or old,
  That one with skin so red.

I marveled at perfected skill,
  To make a stone so right;
I marveled at its sawtooth edge,
  Cut in the flint so white.

I wondered if his heart did beat,
  With fears of any kind;
Or did he have a faith and hope,
  A love for all mankind.

I wondered if he knew our God,
  Whate'er the name might be;
I thanked the Lord for arrowheads,
  And all in them I see.
Thomas L. Neely

By Quietened Night

In quiet by night and darkness still,
A night light burns to aid my quill.
With thoughts in flow of sleep no need,
A minds a-stir in making plans.
No talk from near to notions halt,
By chiming bell the night slips on,
My plan now made to puzzles solve.
Alison Latham

The Petals Of Life

Life is like a rosebush
It starts out as a seed,
Then it grows and flourishes
As you too grow and flourish.

The young plant is like an infant;
Soft and very vulnerable,
the slightest wind can hurt so much.

The bush grows and strengthens,
as the baby grows and strengthens.
Then one day the bush stands alone,
as the toddler will too stand alone.

Young roses appear slowly
each petal opening bright and sure.
The full flower will one day close,
petals falling one by one
like tears shed over someone gone.

As the aging rosebush withers and dies
So do we, one by one —
now the cycle of life must begin again
like the rosebush does each season.
Kelly Steepleton

Missing Richard

Will the sadness ever go away?
It will with time is what they say.
That may be true in the light of day,
but in the still of night
sorrow finds its way.
Into your heart
it silently steals,
grabbing on tight
such sadness you feel.
Life beckons on,
but you never lose sight
of the one you will miss
in the still of night.
Michele Fletcher

Halloween

  There'll be goblins and
ghosts and witches on brooms
and big jack-o-lanterns that
sing scary tunes
  It's Halloween that time
of year. When everyone has
that kind of fun fear.
  There'll be bobbing for
apples and parties galore and
trick or treaters at everyone's door
  Come one come all it's Halloween
night a beautiful scary frightful delight
Carolyn A. Jensen

"Alive"

Puppies are love,
Children and treasured,
Flowers are bloomed,
We're all part of life.
Like birds of a feather.
And if by chance
Or even a reason.
Remember your pleasing
Be happy or glad.
  Don't be mad.
E. Scullion

Pipsqueak

My kitten, at noonday
Contented and free,
In sunshine naps dreaming
Of things yet to be.

Fish for his supper,
A romp with the dog.
His mistress to cuddle him.
A prowl through the fog.

Then cruelly my flashbulb
Interrupts his reflections.
He stares at me with amber eyes
While weighing my intentions.

As he mutters his displeasure
His eyelids gently close.
Chin on paw, whiskers atwitch,
My kitten's in repose.

I sometimes feel that I might be
Content through all eternity
If I could at the same time feel
Relaxed and yet alert as he.
Genevra Richards

Roar

Blood red skies dare glisten,
Coloured by iron trails of
Defiant red crayon and fairy dust
My tiny hand print against the heavens.
My body dark and cool with
August wet,
I feel wind stories and
The cosmic travels of raindrops.
I swallow these tales whole and
Drown in luscious vitality.
Barefoot and wet-swept,
I cling to cast-iron railings and
Howl in untamed pleasure
At my tempest splendour.

The earth moves to meet me.
Jennifer Jeynes

Symphony Of Passion

We were so patient about our being,
collecting numbers, hours, seconds,
all the moments of loving,
nothing passed without a note,
everything impressed, created memories.
We simply did not leave it
to the earth, wind, fire and water.
We kept our own time,
from not being to being,
to overflowing with love,
until everything came together
raising up our trembling bodies
into a symphony of passion.
How can we forget when we were born?
Out of all the things we dreamed
in the spaces of our souls,
close to the edge of the eternal fire,
with our senses as guiding stars
all the secret doors opened for us:
The here and know - the you and me.
Peter W. Jedlicka

Household Hardship

Father yells,
Mother tells,
the children to go to bed.
Mother says, "It is past that time,
there is school tomorrow."
Father screams, "Black and blue
is what I'll do, if your not in bed."
The children scramble to get on their P.J.'s.
Mother tells Father not to be so harsh,
but it is hard when he is a military man.
"Calm down," she says, soothing her crying babies.
They fall fast asleep with their mother at their side.
Father and Mother keep right on yelling at one another,
but it is not a fight but a mere argument.

Jonathan Bridges

Where Has Character Gone?

There is a culprit out there,
    mother of all friends!
We Americans are its victims,
    least-wise so it seems.

Is terrorism her name?
Is stress her game?
Is valium the answer to this pain?

Oklahoma City? NRA?
Hey, I'm proud to be an American
But what's with it in the good ole USA?

Where is my old Grandpa,
his hobo weed and sassafras tea,
the blackened coffee pot,
the old pump sixteen
leaning, gleaming against the Lum Benson Tree?

Where has character gone?

George C. Irvine

There Will Be Another Spring

Almost the end - not quite,
More of darkness than of light
Time of slowing down, ending and dying
Season of asking, seeking, and why-ing.

I'm in the November of my life
Looking for peace and quiet, not strife.
I'm finished seeking answers for questions asked
As I attempt to complete my God-given task.

When His plans for me are complete
My life will truly be replete
With all His love and caring
Which He's given me for sharing.

I may never know the reasons
For the changes through my seasons,
But I know what the changes will bring
And there will be another spring.

My new spring may not be here
But the thought of that holds no fear.
My new life, which I'm heading toward
Will be one of joy at the feet of the Lord.

Diane Scaife

"Big Brother"

The lad grew stronger as days passed by,
More in the mind than being tall.

They now called him "Man of the house",
A title he did not desire at all.

To be so young and yet so wise,
Was not his final goal in life.

But there are times when things occur,
Bringing with them tears and strife.

Though most would bend he dare not,
Too many rely on him you see.

So like it or not he must prevail,
And keep his strength for sis and me.

David E. Woll

Miss Jourdan

May I remark upon your most delightful face..
    Miss Jourdan.
the way the sunlight dances in your hair..
Azure eyes beneath a parasol of lace..
the paleness of the room when you're not there.
and may I pray you'll notice me one day,
    Miss Jourdan..
I'll hear you gaily laugh and call my name.
You'll run to me and hold me, and whisper you adore me,
intoxicate me with your rare perfume...
But if I fail (and clearly this is not my plan)
then I will simply, softly, fade from view..
and someday if they ask me to recall
the sweetest love of all
then I'll say, Miss Jourdan, I remember you.

Carolyn Wynn

Dusk To Dawn

The road is so rocky
Miles and miles of it I see
The burden gets so heavy
Oh please...just let me be

Will the darkness brighten sometime real soon?
Or, do I have a life-sentence of doom
(sometime later)...

I heard a voice say
"If you want a brighter day
Get down on your knees and begin to pray"

So I prayed a while
I prayed into the night

The voice said again, "Now you will see the light!
Just stay sincere, my child, when you pray...
And soon those burdens will go away!"

Angela Anderson

Halloween

Ghosts, witches and goblins come and see.
Little creatures hiding behind every tree.
Come find your candy and hear the screams.
Work together in trick-or-treat teams.

After it's over, you'll go home to your bed.
While visions of hauntings dance in your heads.
You're safe for now but better beware.
For Halloween's coming again next year.

Ashlee Erin Clendening

For I Believe Him

In the early years I walked with a love, He told me of his power and might; that I would soon delight and I believed him.

We walked endless days of playing haze, I learned of strength and saving grace; soon I would have to take my place and I believed him.

The endless days, they fade away; a new love now soon to vow.
For I believed him.

The storms they raged, the tempest played.
I learned of pain while stumbling down, soon I would have to stand
  my ground.
For I believed him.

A call from yesterday pointing the way, an uneasy twist of fate that day.
I learned to loose in order to gain.
For I believed him.

I follow forward for my Lord, he says he needs me in this war
  and I believe him.
O' Satan, you've had me down for a while, but I'm up now.
My Father promises a better day when Jacob shall return this way
  and I believe him.

The day springs forward, I know it now.
My heart is free from your evil vow.
A wife of youth awaits her love, a precious seed from God above.
For I believed him.

Beverly R. Nett

"Rise Up And Live"

Take up thy bed and walk with your guiding
merciful and Angelic 'Light' that
overcome the cruel and blackened
darkness of the guilty past that man will
never let you forget. Ah, so sad!

But thanks be to God, Jesus, and the
Holy Spirit. These three powerful
teams do mightily forgive
and forget also. "Hallelujah"

I looked upon the pink rose bush today
and was deeply touched and comforted,
bye the almost one dozen pink roses,
just for me and for you.

Could it be thy answer - as the hushed
still quietness of the now calmed
morning dove. "Selah"

Just as I am, oh! Lamb of God,
I come, 'I come.' Thank you
and abiding love.

Bert Rivett

The Mother, The Killer

The new child wandered around the house,
  looking for its sorrowful mother.
The mother, the killer.
  The killer of child life.
    The aborter of humanity.
The child walked to his mother,
  and vomited on her head.
She didn't know what had happened.
She felt the child's soul present.
The mother reached forward,
  to try and touch her baby's soft flesh.
But she felt nothing.....
    GUILT was all she felt.
She wished that she had never killed her child.
But it was too late.
The baby then looked up toward the sky
  and was carried to heaven.
But the mother had to rot,
Living on this cruel earth.

John Duffey

Sweet Memories Of Mom

As I sit here and enjoy the view
Memories of mother come shining through

I was only ten when she passed away
But oh how I remember all those caring days

A mother of eight, the youngest only a year
She left us all with our greatest fear

What will happen to all of us, how can we survive
"Easily" she answered, by strength and power instilled in pride

A loving mother who fought cancer for many, many years
Living with the fear and pain through all her hidden tears

She did not want to be remembered for her pain and illness
Rather for her years of love and caring she made her business

From the beginning she chose the man of her life
One that was strong and caring—she called him "Mr. Right"

Yes, her husband, our Dad, the man who would carry on
Whether good or bad decisions, he was never truly wrong

He cared for his children and raised us till we were all grown
And for that we love him deeply, as now we're on our own

Memories of mother and the time that has passed by
Will stay with us forever, until the day we die

Irene B. Melancon

A Funny Thing Happened

A funny thing happened on my way to the park, a salesman tried to sell me a smile; a small crowd had gathered around him, so I stopped and listened a while;

He had a warm, caring face, chubby pinchable cheeks, and a big fedora on his head;
"Step right up, they're sellin' fast," then he turned to me and he said-

"For you little lady, I'd like to sell you a smile, it'll only cost ten bucks; a week long grin with a giggle is 30, but that's the happy package deluxe."

"I haven't much money," I sadly said, "could you let me just sample a few?" "I normally don't give away samples," he said, "but I'll do it just for you."

He was truly, without any doubt, the master of his trade; but little did he know that bright sunny day, of the numerous friends he had made.

He finally sold me, "How much?" I asked, "I'll take a smile, size large"; he wrapped up my smile, in a pretty pink bow, and said, "This one's on me, no charge."

Charron M. Hunter

Motherhood

She holds the newborn to her bosom
  Marveling at the child she has blossomed
After nine months of discomfort and stress
  Her life is enriched by the child she is blessed

She will guide the child down the road of life
  Being there through life's perils and strife
Watching the child nurture and grow
  Sometimes going too fast -
Sometimes, going too slow

Wondering what the future holds
  In store for her child
Will the child blossom like a flower
  Or, like a weed, grow wild
"I will do everything in my power"
  She thinks, with a smile,
"To give the love and guidance
  That only a mother can
To her child."

Robert L. Gamboa

Untitled

Seeking the mysterious wonders of God,
Many interpretations are fabricated, nothing but frauds.

Astrology illuminates the stars and the skies,
Though does not highlight, where the soul goes when a man dies.

Mythology is a man's' theory, proclaiming his own interpretations,
None of which can prepare you for what's in REVELATIONS.

In the soon forth coming days ahead,
Don't believe these fabrications and end up being misled.

For you don't want to miss the first coming of Christ,
Caught up in foolish folly, which only the enemy enticed.

Debra K. Pearson

Blackberry Delight

When it was berry pickin' time and the weather just right,
mamma and us children would put on our long sleeve shirts,
old blue jeans and start out really early, just before daylight,
in search of a blackberry patch.

We would pick and pick until our buckets were full,
some might say we were berry pickin' fools.
We would spend all afternoon cookin' the berries down into preserves
and jam.
The jars of berries setting on the shelves looked so grand,
it was a lot of work, but we'd do it again.
Just about bedtime we would begin to scratch
from the chiggers we all got in the blackberry patch,
but time would soon take care of that.

When Thanksgiving Day rolled around and dinner was served,
Mamma would bring out the steaming hot blackberry cobbler and preserves.
It was pure delight!
We could hardly wait to get a bite.
You could see the pride in Mamma's eyes, her home cookin' was hard
  to match.
I shall always remember Mamma, her cobblers and the times we all spent
in the blackberry patch.

Juanita Jones Lunsford

Journey To Before

Two suitcases wait beside the door, Mother is weeping, but wishing him
luck. I sit on the rust-colored carpet in the corner of a darkened
hall streams of mumbling tears pour down flushed faces. I bolt to my
room, yet quiet enough to hear the sounds of snails conversing of eternity.

Not enough memories of clubhouses, camping trips, and secret
handshakes to fill my head. Not enough monsters turned silent when
the lights are turned on. Not enough picnics, and puzzles, and
neighborhood softball games to play.

Those few are gone now. As though scissors are cutting, cutting them
from my mind. Those few are gone now, too.

Not enough nights to drift to sleep and know I would still have a
family in the morning. Not enough days of laughing, and smiling, and
horsing around. For those days are gone now.

My tears are all gone now, since there are not enough memories to hold
them so tight. My tears are all now, because there is too much "Not Enough."

As I step off my train, a man stands. Waiting by the door, his arms
one wide to greet me. Too wide, too innocent, too forgotten. Too
much of before, and not enough of now. And yet, like a child's trust
in Band-Aids, I cling to the man from my past.

Jamie Barthell

The Royal Within Thyself

Be thee loyal to the 'royal' within thyself
  Loyally stow thy royalty on thy sovereign's shelf.
As royal blood has been planted deep in the soil,
  So in each soul is planted deeply the 'royal'.

Is the 'royal' dedicated to the queen, the king?
  Or could it be that royalty is a common thing?
If royalty is not a common thing as commonly found,
  Could it be an uncommon common thing, not dirt, not ground

A special bit of royalty exists within each soul,
  A special bit of royalty without soul is not whole.
A little bit of royalty, regal like a precious stone,
  A little bit of royalty leaving each soul not alone.

Something dignity needs to make it regal royal,
  Something royalty needs as water requires fire to boil.
Splendid and king like are true royal families.
  Splendid and sovereign are tall strong trees.

Be loyal to the oaths, the codes that guide our destiny,
  Be loyal to precedents that serve us unerringly,
Be loyal to tales of the giant, the prince and the elf,
  Be loyal to your life's role, the 'royal' within thyself.

Gerald G. Larsen

Love

Love is like a treasure, lasting through all time.
Love you cannot measure, especially yours and mine.

Love is like a mountain, it's an uphill climb.
Love you have to work at, almost all the time.

Love is like a soft breeze, blowing through the day.
Love is being comfortable, in that special way.

Love is like a summer rain, that makes the flowers grow.
Love is caring and sharing, the good times and the low.

Love is like a violent storm, that blows across the sea.
Everyone has their ups and downs, just talk it over with me.

Love is like a moonlight night, light shimmering all around.
Love needs to be spoken aloud, to stay on solid ground.

Love is like a Saturday, kind of easy and slow.
Love is what you make it, ours will last I know.

Barbara Knight Smith

A Voice Now Silent....

A voice now silent still echoes in my mind.
Love from beyond crosses distance and time.
Six feet and twenty years keeps us apart,
Undying love inside this broken heart.
Tears still fall after all these years,
The little boy inside this man still cares.
Can't run from memories or from the past,
Lord knows I've tried and it didn't last.
I feel I'm in my own world, stuck back in the past,
Never really growing old, but dying really fast.
Am I going crazy, have I gone insane?
Not going with the flow, need to stay the same.
Had some things to stay, never got the time
A voice now silent still echoes in my mind.
I know one thing for sure, dear angle up above.
Until the day I die, I'll forever be in love.
They say that a man, should never bare his soul
But a man who never does, is never really whole.
To all of those concerned, now you really see
I'm not the man of stone, I appear to be.

Donald J. Keith Jr.

"My Son"

When a baby, sweet and gentle,
Lovable, and full of glee,
How I loved this little baby,
No one ever knows but me.

Then he grew a little older,
Didn't want to play, you see
Took to fishing, and to hunting,
Didn't have no need for me.

I decided this was normal,
For this son of mine, alas
So I said, you can't go fishing
Till you swim as well as Cast.

Then one day he met his gal,
He said Mom, she is a wow
She's got blond hair and wears white shorts
And right then blended two more hearts.

Della Starkey

Yesterdays - Past Tomorrows

Yesterdays are past "tomorrows,"
Lost hopes, lost plans, lost schemes!
They hold no vision of things to come
And are filled with empty dreams.
By living each day to its fullest,
All motives - clean and pure;
Memories sweet then can be gleaned
When our tomorrows are no more.
Tomorrows are gifts that are given
By the hand of a loving God;
They are dreams we may never conquer,
All our hopes—gone and scattered abroad.
Yet today we can live and take pleasure
In the goodness that God sends our way,
For tomorrow may be an unfulfilled dream;
We must live for the moment—TODAY.

Becky Ostrzycki

My Dreams Near The Sea

How peaceful the sound of the ocean's roar.
Looking at the bright reflecting water
As I am standing near the ocean's floor,
The sand on my bare feet becomes hotter.
A place in the world I'm hoping to find,
It seems far away in a place that's rare.
I stand near the water for peace of mind.
Beyond the horizon, you wonder what's there
When the sun starts to set over the hill,
The day becomes night when we start to dream.
Whatever the future holds is God's will,
He'll stand by us, nothing is too extreme.
This place I've been to hope and aspire
Has helped me find my every desire.

Dana Blusius

Together Forever

From the moment I met you and
looked in your eyes.
I knew we would be together forever.
From the moment we touched and held each
other close.
I knew we would be together forever.
The moment our lips touched I knew that
you and you alone would be forever mine.

Crystal Hughes

Vacation

Flying into a new landscape,
look around to the ground below.
The microscopic specks on our earth seem smaller still.
The flat green areas, like a patchwork quilt.
The spaces of red and green and yellow up above,
are rows and rows of tulips down below.
You land and arrive to see your family with tears in their eyes;
for they have only seen you but few times in your life.
They are so surprised to see you and your growth.
Happiness fills your heart.
Love comes quickly there.
Getting to know your family which otherwise would be lost.
Being in a new land,
that others don't see.

Alexandra Bottemanne

With God All Things Are Possible

With God all things are possible, the proof is very clear.
Look around at all the beauty He has placed for us here.
Ohio is the Buckeye State, we cherish oh so dear.

"With God all things are possible," our motto we uphold.
The hills, the plains, the rivers and trees,
Are part of the story told.

Our scarlet carnation is representation
Of the blood christ shed so bold,
He died on the cross so we might not have loss
Of our soul while growing old.

Something big is what Ohio stands for.
Seven men from our state and only God
Knows how many more will become leaders
Of our country, the highest of rank.
The President of the United States to be most bold and frank.

Our pennant shaped flag, Ohio flies the only one of its kind.
Search the world over and try to find
Something as nice to see,
But could there ever be a state
As dear as Ohio is to me?

Ellis Denlinger

Land Before Time

Long time ago the sky was not beautiful,
long time ago the sun was not bright,
The earth was lonely and over all by ashes,
Long time ago the earth was not alive.

All it surface was fiery and hot, the sky was red, the moon was gone.

There were no stars, the trees did not exist
The river never had a place where to be

Until one day an angel came to Earth
And pretty things he only brought with him

He brought the sun, the animals, the light;
He brought the trees and the beautiful stars

He made man, important creature of all
He brought the sun, the animals, the light;
He brought the trees and the beautiful stars

He made man, important creature of all
He brought the winter, spring, summer and fall

But then a devil came to earth and only sadness he brought with him

Then came the tear, then came the sob
These substituted happiness and love.

This is the story of how the earth really became what it is today.

Jezabel Ayo

Falling Back To 1975

The tremor of your music quivers through me
long before I reach the driveway. Angry
through the front door, I am seized by the tender
voice of Neil Young singing about why.
I trip over a chord and plunge into a memory, chilled
by the echo of my mother screaming
turn it down turn it off be quiet don't talk don't breathe don't . . .
Standing frigid and mute, I just listen.

I know you are in your room chasing answers to those plucking questions
swearing at the someone who gave you false hope,
lied about these being your best years.
I can tell you I have felt the pain of walking
without direction in the crowded halls with thousands of others -
I can't tell you why
so I won't tell you to turn the music down.

Anita D. Shumake

Time

In a little white house across the street
Lives a dear old man, and it seems
That all day long on his porch in the sun,
He watches the world and dreams.

The light is gone from his deep set eyes
And his once brawny hands are still.
Though his hair is thin and silvery grey,
His memories time cannot kill.
He recalls the days of his long lost youth;
What happy days he knew—
Christmas at Grandma's, a home run hit, and
A date, in his buggy, with Sue.

And now and then, across his face
Will come a tender smile,
And down his weathered wrinkled cheeks
Rolls a tear of self denial.

It seems to us who look from without
That time is cruel and unwise,
But to the old man, who looks from within
Time's a blessing in disguise!

Deane Query

Delicate Things

Wee!
Little!
Diminutive!
Petite!
Tiny delicate things reflect God's kindness and gentleness.

Teeny humming birds with gossamer wings.
Wee new born soft and pink.
Petite butterflies with glittering colors on their flittering wings.
Small bees busily gathering pollen from golden flowers are soon gone
   with a blink.
Tiny delicate things reflect God's kindness and gentleness.

Little tadpoles and polliwogs swimming in a pond.
Small green grasshoppers jumping from place to place with all their might.
Wee lady bugs resting on a leaf eating aphids of which they are fond.
Diminutive webs made by little spiders sparkle with dew drops in the
   morning sunlight.
Tiny delicate things reflect God's kindness and gentleness.

Joanne Marie Lake

Paddle Softly

Paddle softly
Listen to Mother Earth breathe deeply
See Her calmness smooth the water's surface
Feel Her move the lake beneath us
As we move through time
My little girl and I
Paddle softly.

We pause on the water and lean over the side together
Carefully, we touch the water lightly,
With one finger each.
Into the magic mirror we gaze at one another.
She giggles, enjoying the cool wetness
On this warm North Shore afternoon.
We savor this peaceful moment alone
Enriching our souls.
Time passes.
Will she remember?
My little girl and I.
On our journey
Paddling softly.

Debra A. Savageau

Cleaning The Walk

I hate to do a lot of jobs
Like scrubbing pans or making corn cobs
But what I despise and would rather eat chalk
Is sweeping and cleaning my father's front walk
I'm twelve years old; I don't have such a great back
It's so excruciating to clean some tiny, tiny crack
Why even bother I said to my father

Now readers and fans I had a plan
I went outside to sweep the front walk
And (ha ha ha) I played that old game where you're not aloud to talk
Was it some kind of disease that came from odd bees?
Or did I get it in school from a sickly child's sneeze?

It was too late I lipped to my worried dad
The sidewalk disease had gotten too bad
I would die unless (oh here comes the best)
I don't clean the walk and leave it a mess
My father caught on and gave me a broom
He scolded me proper then sent me to my room

So hear little children, clean your front walk
Or you really will lose your tongue and not able to talk

Jaime Fritsch

Changing Scenery Again

Once again we've found a place
Like home
But as soon as we feel settled
Orders in hand, it's time again to roam

The boxes will come
Many good-byes will be said
A part of us will awaken
That which we thought was dead

All the treasures we bought with such care
Will soon be tossed and crushed
Loaded into a moving truck
Our apartment then empty and hushed

Soon too will come a parade of new faces
The dance of new friendships will begin
The longing to stay in our comfort
We'll face with our usual chagrin

The scenery keeps on changing
Faces and places blending with the years
Someday we'll be home
And when we do, be listening for the cheers!!

Jacqueline Cammarato

Untitled

My friend is...
  like a mirror through which I can see,
  all the things I ought to be.
My friend never speaks out
  just quietly reflects
  and so, therefore, has nothing to expect.
But for these gifts, what must one
  give in return...
Loyalty, honestly, love...firm.
My friend is...
  God, a best one, my husband or child,
  family, with whom I can sit a while.
My friend is...
  anyone, really, with whom I'm willing to see
All the things I ought to be.

Gloria Jacobs

Unwrapping

The fog covers the face of the river
Like a grey cashmere muffler,
Wrapping itself around the hills,
Stilling sound,
Pulling time,
Lapsing rescinding memory.
A silhouetted bear moves with
Noiseless footsteps
Scavenging for reserpine root
On his way to the slumber cave.
The silver rod with its hairy sinuous leaves
Clustered with sylvan flowers
Glistens wetly at the
Spiralling snail.
Disturbed by the reverberation of the phone,
With echoes chasing the silence,
The fog moves, the muffler unwraps
A shining gift of beauty,
The river stippled with sun
Like the freckles on a trout.

Irma Garbarino

'Capturing My Attention, Captured My Heart'

Your glittering smile shines as bright as the sun.
  Lights up my world.
Your sweet voice sounds as charming as a soft melody.
  Holds peace and compassion.
Your delicate touch feels as comforting as your love.
  It makes me sedate.
Your vibrant eyes sparkle as brilliant as diamonds.
  Brings me new life.
Through your eyes, I experience a warmth and passion
that one only dreams of becoming a part of.

Larger that life is your Heart!
Its radiant energy is as potent as the love it offers.
With every beat I fall more deeply in love with you.

To a lifetime of laughter, love, companionship, and
Good health. I want to devote my love to you.
May we join hands to preserve, grow, and prosper
Together. I love you and would honor and cherish
A lifetime of happiness.

Gregory P. Franzke

The Gambler

The machine was a beauty with its flashing
lights and its cards. The announcements of games
and with them their rewards.
  At first it took quarters and one dollar bills.
Only the gambler knows, how exciting it feels.
  It seemed to be taking away from the game. To
have to stop playing to go and make change.
  The clerks became annoyed with it, just the
same. To take care of this problem, things must be rearranged.
  The machines are improving, now they take fives
and tens. The gambler keeps feeding the machine, but
never does he win.
  Time is passing, as he sinks deeper into the hole.
Suddenly he realizes, it's taking hold of his soul.
  If by chance he gets lucky, he's touched by God
above. Reaching down, He brings him from evil and
fills him with love.

Catha D. Newman

Life After Life

Lifted up to who-knows-where
  Lights and darkness filling the air
  Sun in your face, wind in your hair
Alive and free and without a care

Take away to something new
  Not knowing where. . .or by who?
  Somewhere the skies are always blue
And everyone loves you for you

Leaving the earth you know so well
  Hoping you won't end up in hell
  If heaven awaits at the angel's bell
  Whatever you find. . .you cannot tell

Allison Leeuw

Within The Leaves Of An Aspen

Within the boundaries of a tranquil, dynamic forest,
lies an Aspen with brilliant leaves,
standing out in a parade of green,
it quietly whispers a song to us.

The icy wind streams down from the mountainside,
acting as a messenger of time,
and soon the frail Aspen reveals its splendid golden colors,
leaving the carpet of red, yellow and orange to bare its legend.

It returns to the womb of the earth to hibernate,
and is sheltered by winter's frosty snow,
but in this sea of whiteness the chorus continues to grow,
being sung by the dreams of others and carried by the comfort of nature,

and from this cradle the sun rises and paints the sky with warmth,
as the Aspen awakens from a fog of confusion, blinking with the joy
  of rebirth,
and just as the quiet Aspen...we hum the song within our hearts,
as we leave our footprints embedded in the enchanted earth to carry
on the legend.

Brian Keithline

Porcelain Heart

Broken into pieces, waiting for help,
just to be picked up and placed on a shelf.

How lonely it seems with the boys all gone,
All by myself with a heart that is torn.

Where is the laughter that we all once knew,
It slowly disappeared, as the kids all grew.

So what will become of me, a toy that's been forgotten,
Sitting on a shelf with a heart that is broken.

Alisa Lynne Owen

A Hamden Landmark

Just beyond the fairways green,
Lies a unique mountain - a magnificent scene.

Unlike many counterparts that reach for the sky,
This wonder of nature stretches for miles - lengthwise.

Formed like a huge Goliath, laid down for an endless sleep,
One must follow a long, marked trail - to find its oversize feet.

From the greening of its leafy cover in early spring,
To the golden, brown blanket it puts on in the fall,
This creation of nature renews life - in us all.

For centuries now, this rocky wonder had reclined in quiet repose,
Waiting for a name that would fit - I suppose.

So in spite of man's mindless effort to destroy,
This great mountain has remained defiant,
And is proudly known as, "The Sleeping Giant".

Harry F. Hoffman

Let Me Not Rest In Joyful Turmoil

Let me not rest in joyful turmoil,
Let me not die in sweet pain,
Let not my heart beat in heavy toil,
For it may forever be slain...
Love me enough and let me survive,
This torment of insecurities,
Your passion is what makes me alive,
Share it with me, set this mind in peace...
Say you love me or say you will,
Let this soul be glad forever,
Let my heart live to tell,
The joy with you in this life of wonder...
Let me carry you to our paradise,
As we embrace the birth of our sunrise...

Eusebio C. Noblefranca Jr.

"The Merry-Go-Round"

Ride the twirling, whirling merry-go-round.
Let it dizzy your senses with its magic.
Horses, lions, rabbits, gondolas...
(Let's see, have I missed any?...)
Well, perhaps so...
But those painted abstractions,
Stationary on their moving plat form
Delight, relax, captivate the senses,
Give charm and grace to the lacquered livestock.
And the music...
The sound of the calliope, the cymbal's clash,
The tin-pan sounds of the drums
Whirling through the air excite the senses.

Take but a moment to be a child again.
Round and round...never too fast...but exhilarating!
To the last circuit...to reign in your horse, or lion.
Or whatever magic beast you were riding.
Then you step off that enchantment...
But promise to come back to ride another day.

Chet E. Blair

Untitled

It's not the fact that when you're born
It is for you to die -
Nor, when you softly say Hello
You turn and say Goodbye -
But, what you've thought and said and done
In time, that's measured HOW -
Your acts today will be what counts -
The In-Between is NOW!

Jayne Dickson

Untitled

The sands of the hour glass are running still
Lesser and lesser to more and more
You can't stop the changes from happening
Or know the future before it comes
We have sand for each of our friends
That flow constantly through our life
Only God controls the flow of sand
How fast or slow they will go
But sometimes when the bottom is full
And the time with your friend has run out
God will reach down with his hand
and rotate the glass once again.

Chad Hewett

Leaving

As the evening sun goes down
leaving the skies a red and blue
You left me with just my dreams
and all I ever shared with you

Parting was so sudden
giving neither a chance to ask why
Full realization came to me
when I heard you say good-bye

So I'll just put my feeling high upon the shelf
And keep hoping for a fresh new start
even though there are no tears in my eyes
they are carried in my heart

Floyd Keeton

Untitled

The winds of fall are in the air
Leaves are rustling everywhere
Children are hurrying back to school
Leaving behind the fun of the summer pool.
Parents are thinking of Christmas, not far!
Possibly wondering about that new car.
New shoes here, new coats there
The needs many, extra money is rare.
Big sister Anne's Beau come to court,
The carefree days are oh so short.
Mom and Dad get a hug,
And then with a glance,
She's rushing out, not to be late for the dance.
Soon it's spring and summer is here, and,
Again comes the winds of fall in the air.

Doris Newsum Hull

Risk

Should we call you a fool for the chances you take
Knowing within the jeopardy, there lies certain fate

An enticement that beckons your inner soul
And guides you toward an inscrutable role

You cling like a leech to a mountain's highest peak
Knowing one wrong deportment means certain surcease

Yet at the end of it all, what eminence do you gain
But the risk of eternal demise from life's chain

So go on and take liberty with your destiny
But I shall stay determined to reach mine risk-free

Big Joe Leming

Inconsolable Grief With Mourning

This husband of mine we're to bury today,
Leaves a hole in my fabric of life,
There breathes not man who can mend it, I know,
The loss cuts through my soul like a knife.

Attentive, considerate, conscientious, and true,
Was My Love since the first day we met,
Never spoke he an unkind word to me,
Not a moment with him I regret.

My Darling is borne in that hearse up ahead,
Oh, Daughter, I'll miss your dad so!
Our lives entwined like the weave of his shroud,
But soon we'll be parted, I know.

My own life without him can never go on,
Friends and family my sorrow can't share,
Oh, where will I go, Oh, what will I do?
I could write a new book on despair.

Pull into that driveway, just yonder ahead!
The preacher and diggers will wait.
Let's check out that sale in the yard by the road,
For Depression Glass saucers and plates!

David Lockard Brooks

Love

"Love me you will forever, come what may;
Leave me you won't, not ever," so you say.
Although I love you more and more each day,
Who are we to know what will come our way?

Let's love each other while we're still together;
Waste it not on thoughts of stormy weather.
Love me wild, love me strong, and love me tender,
As I love you, 'cause that's all that matters.

Are we to love on another as always?
Or shall we say our goodbye, comes one day?
Will our love go away or will it stay?
Whichever way, baby, it'll be OK.

Should one day we'll be on our separate ways,
Never think that one of us has betrayed.
Soon enough someone new's gonna come your way,
And you'll be singing love again one day.

Huyvan T. Vu

"A Ghost's Last Request"

Catch the whispers in the wind and hear the demon's cry.
Leave me now to sleep, within the earth I'll lie.
Death will come in silent flight.
With raven's wings he soars.
Come my child and rest, sorrow feel no more.
From death I'll wake in heaven, its gates will open wide.
And all the sadness that I feel will be left on the other side.
Tomorrow comes to quickly at least that's what they say,
but for me dawn's not last enough it's still a day away.
Though I suppose I now have time to sing to you my song;
to tell you not to cry, through it all I was wrong.
Goodbye, now! I love you well.
My heart to you I truly gave.
So if you feel alone just call.....
   by bringing flower to my grave.

Andrea C. Mitchell

Longing

Gazing into the depth of the glass
Leaning over, hoping to see more
than herself staring back.
Questioning the mirror
and hoping to see something different,
something better once more.
To see something beautiful and youthful
again would be divine.
Gazing into the eyes and soul of Cinderella
instead of the ugly stepmother.
Where the lines of experience are washed away
and replaced by a radiant glow.
The longing for that day when she'll
be proud again is too far to comprehend.
Proud
and not ashamed to smile back.

Jennifer Guillot

Who Filled My Empty Dreams

When I think about the times we've spent together, the memories and laughter that we share, these times we have are built on special moments, and as all of those that really know we care.

When I look into your eyes I see the future, for you knowing what I'm thinking brings me home, and I know above it all you understand me, in my life with you I'm always free to roam.

Roam in that special stroll of happiness, the place we go to find the love we've missed, it's now our time to share our lives together, in contempt I hold a Love as this.

How could being this close be anything but wonderful, if apart we move together as the sun, goes beyond the cloud to form a rainbow, to the end of earth from where it had begun.

A promise that was made of no destroying, we can have this promise in our lives, to embrace reality as it's given to us, for what binds us to the Love will be the ties.

I could have searched my life to find the answers, the faceless being found only in my sleep, but as thoughts of you just sauntered in my conscience, it was you I found
"Who Filled My Empty Dreams."

Cheryl Lynn Rainey

Eye Of The Storm

Buddha sighs, "Change...change..."
Lao Tsu Shouts, "Let BE, do naught."
God whispers, "Let go,
   turmoiled self,
   untangle the knots,
   embrace change.
Fearful self,
yield, let BE,
embrace non-action.
   Cluttered self,
   relinquish ten-thousand things,
   embrace the jewel. Let go,
Turmoiled, fearful, cluttered self,
Breathe deeply, center the heart, be still.
Plunge into God's 'eye' in the calm of the storms."

Estelle Marie Meyer

"Sew, Sow"

Dating back from early times, and to the present day,
Ladies, on occasion, gather and spend time in a special way.
They form a "sewing circle," and with cloth and thread in hand,
They "create" a unique piece of work, as only they together can.

This makes me think of life, and how we "sow" with different means.
Not with cloth and thread but with qualities of human beings.
Some use Love and Kindness to help their fellow man,
While others grab for themselves, everything they can.

It would be wise to remember, as we travel life's roads unknown,
That HE is watching from above; we're never entirely on our own.
Then, once life's journey's over, and HE finally "Calls us Home,"
Each of us will have our turn to reap EXACTLY what we have "sown!"

Jody A. Jakesch

The Woods In Spring

Tender green, the woods in spring,
Laced with dogwoods, virgin white,
Wild flowers, sprinkled at thy feet,
Earth reborn from Winters blight.

A carpet pink, spring beauties spread,
With quaker ladies, small and prim,
Along the path in shady nooks,
Jack in the pulpit stands tall and trim,

Umbrellas green, mandrakes unfurl,
While violets shy, nod their heads.
Indian pipes, so ghostly white,
Spring up from pine needle beds.

From hidden boughs, the birds sweet song,
Bursts forth, with clarion call,
A magic place, the woods in Spring,
Earths renewal, proclaimed to all.

Hazel F. Shaffer

Ivy Lane

I watch the bar ditches fill with rain,
Knowing soon I will be wading along Ivy Lane.

The rain will stop for a little while,
Long enough to make Mama smile.

I will run and climb and play chase,
Even have a bicycle race.

My friends and I will go to the old brick wall,
Walking, and balancing, so we don't fall.

We will walk to Five Mile Creek,
And after that play hide and seek.

My brothers, my sister, my friends, and me,
I know we are as happy as we can be.

The day will end and the clouds will hover,
And Mama will call us home to supper.

This bed, this home, this Ivy Lane,
Form the links in my life's chain.

Ava Linda Gibbons

Untitled

A dreamer is an individual who plants a tree
   knowing it won't be big enough to climb
until he is too old to climb it...

D. Slas

Child

Tiny lass on a pallet, lying alone,
Kicking and squealing and rolling around;
Listening so quietly as someone approaches,
Waiting but wary as someone bends down.

Beautiful blue eyes and curly brown hair,
Slender and pale, like her daddy in form;
Ever pleasant, not crying, little hand in her mouth,
Did no one see trouble the day she was born?

To LeBonheur in Memphis, the best in the South,
Doctors testing, researching, not finding a clue;
Continuing seizures, epilepsy they say,
What is the answer? We're still asking you.

Frustrations, tired muscles, with cries of despair,
Our prayers still fly heavenward day after day;
What can we do next? Where can we go?
"We'll try again soon," says neurologist Maye.

Come love her, caress her, little angel of two,
She'll smile, turn her head, until she can find
Your voice, your touch—they are her guides,
Dear God, help us all; our Meghan is blind!

Juanita Jean Riddle

Alex

A chasing glance, an abrupt, turn of the head
Juvenile response to Daddy's loving call
Awake as the Crescent Man blows out the lights
Alex, your desires, Daddy knows them all

Sentences without words, you clearly speak
for your wants exceed your years
The thoughts and the emotions that you feel
are an initiation to a family's most guarded fears

Soft hands will carry you
though you will thrust them away
Life is to be lived by me, I hear
every moment in time of every day

You cannot really on that which has borne you
nor can the owl, the turtle, the bear
Each new experiences transports a lesson
it isn't people but events we share

Finally, you could do well without me
but intelligence and creativity aren't yours alone
So Alex, take it and caress it
and never reject the giving hand yet unknown

David C. Mahood

"The Future"

If I could see beyond the grave
Just where I'm begin loud
And know my heart is right with God
Laying there sleeping side by side
If I knew my children were saved
Waiting for Jesus to come
I'd sleep on until judgment day
When he calls me and my love ones
We know we can't see beyond the grave
Where every spray of flowers they laid
When Jesus says "where is they beautiful flock
Here they are Lord, I haven't forgot."
What a wonderful day it will be then
To leave this old world of
suffering and sin.

Hilda Marie Layton

The Seven Towers

Seven towers rise by the desert's shore;
  Just seven towers, and not one more.
The first stands for greed with no light from within;
  Those deep inside its walls can't laugh or even grin.
The second is the tallest — Religion is its game—
  A dark priest walks its turrets...he doesn't have a name.
The third is off a muddy path; its column quite erect.
  Lust is what it stands for — its love is not direct.
The fourth is for the losers; its message clear is fear.
  (Some go inside for just a day but last throughout the year.)
The fifth stands way away; all lost in guilt and need
  It has its many farmers with their deeds and bags of seed.
A sixth form stands upright there; beneath the noonday Sun.
  A blind man sits in front of it while brandishing a gun.
Anger drives his violence; he duels without a care
  He rises from necessity; he fights on any dare.
The seventh has a chimney, and smoke comes up from it.
  The cooks are little people, who never throw a fit.
Their seven doors stand open, for business day and night;
No matter if it's raining, or of the sky is bright.

    Jeff Teitelbaum

I Stumble Not In Vain

One day as I was walking down a lovely winding road,
Just seeing half the beauties there, just bearing half my load,
I struck my sandal on a rock so sharp it cut my toe,
And knew that treading there was more than easy come and go.

I paused to see what was the thing that caused my little pain,
And, behold, I was repaid and yet again:
For as I paused, a bright-winged bird alighted in a tree;
I listened to the red bird's song and felt it meant for me;
But as I paused my throbbing toe beckoned to my glance,
And, ere my eyes fell down to it, I saw the rock, by chance:
The more I looked, the less I saw the rock that stumped my toe;
Instead I slowly saw the rock on which I stumbled so;
And in the sun, its colors shown more bright than bloody sock,
Until I knew there'd always be a rainbow in that rock.

There's just one bigger, better thought which now I entertain;
It is a truth that I must learn — I stumble not in vain;
Though hard this fact to keep in mind — still harder to explain;
I know because I realize now that beauty outlasts pain.

    Helen Svadlenak

The Shawl

Out of Heaven came a gift
  Just for those who need a lift.
By hand woven, woolen and warm,
  Help for those amidst man's storm.

As you give so shall you receive,
  Shawl was passed to ones in need,
  Only given to plant God's seed.

Given three times, it always came back
  Just when I felt the greatest lack.
Six years passed, the shawl was worn
  By those others born to mourn.

Now the shawl has returned to me,
  And as I wear it, you will see
The pain that was born to give to thee:
  The knowledge of Christ's love for eternity.

    Bettie P. Mitchell

A New World

I ran
Jumped
It covered me
I felt it go from my head to my toes
So fast I couldn't stop it

The water took away my worries
A new life had begun for me
I looked up at my old world
Foggy
Boring
I could fly carelessly through the new sky

I shot from side to side
Up and down
As if I were a minnow
Shooting
Fast as lightning
Then drifting lazily

Here in my new world

    Chad Caswell

Trusting Jesus

In my deepest, darkest moment,
Jesus has held my hand,
Bringing me to victory,
For Him I take a stand.

If He can't take me out of a situation,
He always walks me through,
I'm totally in awe,
At the things, together, we can do.

A difficult circumstance,
That I don't understand,
Or an illness or tragedy,
Is taken care of with His command.

The love and support He surrounds me with,
Through family or a friend,
Lets me have peace inside,
Helping me to mend.

In Jesus I can completely trust,
And on Him always depend,
Knowing He will be here,
From the beginning to the end.

    Barbara Freeborn

Jealousy

If I have something, you want it too
Jealousy can ruin everything between me and you.

You have your things and I have mine.
You say not being friends will be just fine.

The silent treatment and ugly looks that you give,
Makes me say "you need Jesus" so I'll forgive.

The way I live my life is my own personal business.
Living life to the fullest makes me the realist.

Me, myself, and I is all that I can be.
I'll always remember the person inside is totally unique.

    Chyla Q. Rucker

344

"Father Time"

I've heard the wintery winds blow
I've watched the rivers as to the sea they flow
I've wept for the old that winter and die
Yet I still get cold chills when I hear
a newborn cry.

Even after a million sun sets
I still feel the loneliness that one sometime gets
When brother fights brother
And the human race fear's and distrust each other

I've seen love, laughter and tears
And I've watched bravery, hate and fear
I've stood with the rich, the famous and the strong of mind
I've wept for the weak, the poor and the blind.

I've been alone on many a bleak night
Not knowing which way to turn left or right
Yet with the help of a power much stronger than mine
I set the pace, and am called father time

Frank H. Dust

"A Dying Paradise"

The world is dead!
I've these knots in my gut, nightmares plague my sleep.
oh, why the hell won't they stop!
the world is spinning, were moving backwards.
Here we're crying,
we're fighting.
we're all dying!
do you care anymore? not enough
What is love? show me. The emotion is dead!
take a gun to your head! Does anyone care?! of course not!
your pretty life means too much!
don't turn around, I won't go away!
I won't go away! I'm already pounding at your door!
can you deal with reality?!
crazed monsters and dying angels we are,
caught somewhere between heaven and hell.
where is the rain, where's the snow, innocence?... gone!
the world is spinning too fast only to explode!

Bernie Soto

When Falls Come

I've walked the woods this Fall,
I've seen the birch, the willow and the oak
Turn to the beaten gold of mines.
The maples stood in rich straw-gold,
As elms were clothed in saffron.

I lingered where the willow slants the stream,
Its olive leaves all slashed in veins of crimson.
The beeches held great flares of living flame,
Vying with their golden clouds
The moss upon an ancient oak.

But when those myriad leaves have passed,
Blown by the winds across the world,
And a few brave tatters still remain;
Those stark bare branches must stand forth,
Sentinels 'gainst the cold to come.

Andy Marshall

A Honey Of A Bee

Oh, little bee, I watch you making honey
In the bright days that are so sunny
Kissing each flower when the sun arises,
You make them feel like special prizes
You open their bodies with each visit
Trip after trip, your charm is exquisite!!

Charlotte M. Williams

Trick-Or-Sleep

I can't get to sleep tonight. There's snoring going on.
I've listened to these snores before, sometimes right 'till dawn.

I put my fingers in my ears, but the racket travels through,
I wonder if there are other homes with snorers in them too.

I wonder how those other kinds in their rumbling houses sleep.
Do they put their minds on other things, like counting woolly sheep?

Or is it I'm the only one with walls that shake and rattle?
Where drifting off to peaceful rest becomes a nightly battle?

I'm running out of patience, I've counted 'till I'm blue.
Not a thing is working. I must try something new.

So I try some snoring of my own. The loudest snoring yet.
It's a little trick I'm proud of and really don't regret.

For very soon the snorer stops! Me too, and all is still.
The snorer asks, "Are you alright? From here you sound quite ill."

And in a flash I'm sound asleep, quite glad my trick succeeded.
It's one I'm sure I won't forget, the next time that it's needed!

Carol Katterjohn

On Stage Everyone

I've been on this stage of life quite a while,
I've been made to cry, laugh and smile.
I've been found wanting and abundantly filled,
The conductor of this play has me gloriously thrilled.

He did not promise I would know every line,
He said just do your best, all will be fine,
Study your part from the script I have gave,
It will guide all from cradle unto the grave.

When you are unsure, the future you can't see,
Don't hesitate to call upon me.
I will dim the bright lights, the curtains I'll raise,
I am waiting to hear, your applause and praise.

Oh God may I perform your approval to gain,
that my life may not have been played out in vain.
Not for a gold cup or statuette to have striven,
but that I may be blessed by you with a home in heaven.

James A. Jackson

Breaking The Rules

Today I am no longer considered a young man
I've become a mature individual overnight, without warning
How could this happen, no one asked me
Older, Thirty years older
No!
There must be some misunderstanding
As they say, you're only as old as you feel
I'm staying the vibrant, crafty soul that I am
Original - Untamed
This is who I am
Breaking all the rules
For the best is yet to come.

Cheri A. Lucas

Who Will Play?

The wind is playing wild and happy games today,
It chuckles in a soft but most mischievous way.
The tiny pines wave branches as she hurries by,
The oaks bow slowly down with a reluctant sigh.
The birches rustle to acknowledge that she came,
While daisies dip down gently and join to play the game.
Out on the placid lake where the jolly wind blows
Little fairies leave small footprints from their tiny toes.
How joyously she sounds as hurriedly she passes
Then dances far away into the tall, rustling grasses.

Jean A. Cook

Love Come Rescue Me

Love, love come rescue me.
It's the only way to make me feel safe,
It's my only oblivion, my only escape.
The pain I feel, the pain I know,
it hurts so much; that I just want to go...
No not home, No not ever,
I want to fly like a bird-of-a-feather,
fly far away to the Golden Gates,
anywhere as long as I am safe.
Love, love come see me through.
Through the hard times, I have to go through.
No way will I be happy, No way will I see fit.
Unless I'm in it, it is the only way to get rid of it.
Cupid and Venus the Gods of love,
point me in the direction, show me a dove,
give me a clue. Considering the facts I need to, I need to,
   Be rescued by love....

Jairmene L. Robinson

He, Who Shares My Heart

I look at his dear face, which I know so well,
It's relaxed in sleep, and still for a spell.
That gentle face, that gives laughter, anger and tears,
Has been beside me for the past forty-plus years.

I love that face, crowned by tousled white hair,
It holds crinkly blue eyes, that show love and care.
The mouth is always smiling, and very rare to offend,
His friendship is worthy, as one can always depend.

His family adores him, as it should be,
He brings light into our lives, especially me.
We've been so fortunate, never having been apart,
He's my beloved Husband, whom God sent to share my heart.

Beverly J. Johnson

Untitled

Hey You,
It's me.
It's someone you might never see.
I'm curled up underneath a black cloud.
Afraid of the dark and afraid to crawl out.
I don't want to hide from you, my starving need.
No need to lie - me to you or you to me.
Will you leave or save me from my storm.
To help me mend what has been torn?
My pain needs innocent shelter to heal.
Guided toward a path that is real.
Your circle of dark secrets need to be mine.
For within my soul a bright light has a need to shine.
To be someone and to be whole.
Never to be captured away from my soul.
Grab a hold of my hand, I'm fading away.
Yours with love,
Forever and a day.

Deborah Brooks

Empty Page

I turn away from the dark, cold stares.
It's beginning to seem as if no one cares.
No one wants to take time to discover what's inside.
It seems as if they've already made up their mind.
They think I'm different and just plain weird.
Why is it everyone runs when I come near?
No one seems to understand.
There's nothing I can do about the way I am.
I sometimes wish I had someone I could call a friend.
But I don't think this heart would be easy to mend.
I don't think things will ever change.
I guess my life will never be anything but an empty page.

Chandra Bales

Quickening

Voiceless, blind, the spastic fish retracts.
Its lease expired, the statistic tenant peels free,
stealing back into itself - clear, red, exact,
slamming into oxygen, a bioptic slice of glee.
Draining onto metal, it claims its Ziploc home.
The absent ex-lover, the murderous anesthetized host -
both will keep captive grief and wake to their bodies alone,
twisting feline out of the bedclothes, lost.
For these pathetic three, no divine funereal march;
the parasite bastard will die as the dove,
the ex-lover will forget the strong and sexual arch
of her back, and she will deny that they ever made love.
But when the two lament the "should have been,"
he will remember their possible king, and she the fallen queen.

Bonnie L. Miranda

"A Letter To Heaven"

Please give this letter to my dad.
It's his Birthday and I'm very sad.

Please put this letter in his hand.
Because it's impossible from this land.

Can't pick up the phone to call you.
Nor have a coffee joke and scare you.

I wake up each day to say Good Morning.
Only to realize I'm still mourning.

We were so close and yet so poor.
But you always said to strive for more.

We had our fights and would grit our teeth.
But in the end we would always meet.

I miss you more each and every day.
And would really truly love to say:
Happy Birthday

Bonnie Lish

Son

When I look at you, so handsome, willowy and tall,
it's hard to believe you are a product of my womb so small.
Into a young man you have grown,
so many things I should have said and done; if only I had known.
weeks, months and years, so quickly they passed,
I had hoped forever your childhood would last.
The tears in my eyes well up and fall, for now I realize,
it wasn't enough . . . giving my all.
Please remember, I tried my best,
I hope I have prepared you for life's long, hard test.
A mother's love is undaunted, tireless and true,
I hope your life will be filled with others,
who love you as I do.

Ann M. Lisota

"My Special Chest"

   A great big chest I'm getting today.
It's coming to me from such a long way.
I've wanted one since I was small,
with varnish and wood, with cedared walls.
   When it arrives we will sand it smooth.
Then put the varnish in every groove.
I'll fill it with my own special things;
Like keepsakes, trinkets, and jeweled rings.
Maybe some clothes and blankets for fall.
Please don't forget those scented moth balls.
   When I open it up in the following years.
The scents and the fragrances, nostalgia and tears;
Will come back to me, like my child's request;
When I grow up mommy, can I have your cedar chest?

Amy Seiders

Power Play

Alive and well the way life shapes
It's called stepping out of the shadows
Magic on slick shredded pebbles
Like walking through flower-strewn meadows.

Stubborn "I can'ts"
Replaced with pliable "I cans"
Stepping stones to victory
The keys that fit the plans.

Success like health and well-being
Even the smallest starry symbol
Fluffy feeling of its sweet taste
On light tiptoes ever so nimble.

Beth Sudduth Wills

I Saw The Face Of Jesus

I saw the face of Jesus in a flower of many hues.
Its brightness made my eyes grow dim and
I pledged my faith anew.

I saw the face of Jesus in a beggar by the road.
His burdens seemed so heavy, but I did
nothing to lighten his load.

I saw the face of Jesus in a happy child at play.
His face was filled with love and trust,
It lifted my spirit that day.

I saw the face of Jesus in a woman filled with pain.
Her starving child lay in her arms,
And I bowed my head in shame.

Do I show Jesus in my face,
to those I meet each day?
or do they see my self-content
as I go my busy way.

Lord slow me down that I may see the needs of the
suffering each day. Let them see Jesus in me
as I travel along life's way.

Edna L. DeWitt

Mother Earth

The earth's strategy is very unknown,
it's as mysterious as the ozone.
For layers of time are buried beneath,
which we identify with modern techniques.
Were guided by knowledge collected with time,
persuaded with evidence on artifacts we find.
We pursue the past of treasures below,
hoping mother earth will give up her load.
She pleads, shed tears and gives off steam,
to warn intruders to leave her be.
They continue to excavate and abrade,
only to discover what's beyond the grave.
Her empty hole is filled with darkness,
perhaps the hurt man has brought her.
She wants to be loved and nourished,
her vegetation to grow and not perish.
The earth will engineer and maintain,
if man kind will hearken and apprehend.
The earth is silent and does not speak,
she gives augury to those who seek.

Catherine C. Mondragon

The Perfect Gift

If I could give the world a gift what would it be?
It would be people who care enough to help others in need.
People who know when a friend is troubled.
People who you can tell stories to and they will not grumble.
People who know how to get what they want without hurting others.
People who treat everybody like their own family; like
    their sisters and brothers.
People who can give away all their money and still be
    happy with themselves.
People who do not change their identity for anyone else.
If I could give the world a gift it would be caring, sensitive people.

Heather Ivey

Crystal Hours

Our time alone was a crystal hour
It was soft light and love
As we held the power
In a world wrapped around by a crystal hour

Years ago for the genocide done to our nations
Our ancestors dragged from palatial homes
On Carolina plantations
The spirit gave us the tie that binds
Evolved living waves crossing miles and times
To heal the pain of the crying minds

Though the faces change as the rivers wind
The way of the spirit cannot be denied
And the intricate lace of the lifeline plan
Makes us survivors in a war torn land

A war torn world turns its back in its quest for gold
As the Blue Crystal Gem Stone Stories unfold
With healing songs and flowers and ribbons of rain
Drowning the madness of the sons of Cain
Blue Crystal Gem Stone ways in Crystal Hours
Are lifetimes of love in Ivory Towers

Janet Hyatt

On A Rock

I built my castle by the sea,
It was made of sand, you see.
It was a place to do my dreaming,
And watch the water gleaming.
Dreams and sand alone, do not make for a strong abode.
And I saw my castle erode.
I tried again to build a more modest home with wood,
It would surely resist what it could.
It was still on the sandy beach,
And I found troubled waters it too could still reach.
Perhaps a home of brick, would do the trick.
But the sand, on that too made its demand.
Further back from shifting sand, I again made my stand.
Now on solid rock I've built my fort within,
The most comforting place I've ever been.
From this most beautiful place,
I am ready to deal with whatever I'm asked to face.
Here at last, I will complete my task.
And know it is here I can find, that elusive peace of mind.

Betty Beecher Blough

A Lover And A Friend

Once there was a time I thought I'd never love again.
I thought never would I believe the term "A lover and a friend".
But that now seems oh so long ago,
how I got along without you I will never know;
but if you go I surely know I'll never love again.
For now I know the meaning of a lover and a friend.

Glenn K. Donaldson

My Love I Thought I Would Never Have

You came into my life one cold January day.
It was love at first sight in each and every way.
It was just so great the way
everything clicked together.
I didn't think things could get any better.
I never thought that I would feel like this.
I kept thinking something was greatly amiss.
My life never ever goes this way.
And I waited for your call each and every day.
The sound of your voice still
excites me when you call.
I'm not afraid of being
in love anymore at all.
I'm so very happy to be a part of your life.
I hope one day to be your wife.
It took me forty years to find someone like you.
And I will always always be true to you.

Diane Kay Schultz

My House Is Empty Now

This my house is empty now, a shadow of what used to be.
It used to run and jump and play, but now its eyes don't see.
It used to love and laugh and touch all that were near to me,
But my house is empty now... No feeling of pain or glee.
It used to hunt and fish, and through the woods walk on a sunny day.
Play guitar, sing a song... sometimes off key.
It loved the fragrance of Spring, a dew droplet, a bee,
And it loved the Autumn of the year—spent most of it alone with me,
enjoying the sights and sounds while bowhunting from a tree.
But my house is empty now, just a shadow of what used to be.
Its ears don't hear falling rain on a tin roof, or the sizzle of frying bacon.
It can't feel the small child's hand, or the touch of a young wife taken.
It can't smell new mown hay or can't walk barefoot in the grass.
For my house is empty now, just a shadow of the past.
Yes, my house is empty now and soon will planted be,
'neath the boughs of a great white oak overlooking life's troubled sea.
But, if planted, will again spring forth and the former a shadow be
of my new home there taken somewhere in eternity.

Jim Dabney

Away

Only I hold the key.
It unlocks a place I go to be free.

Here, good memories are all that remain, spun into stories, often
retold. Tied in ribbons, kept in tins of silver and gold.

Small humble houses dot these lands.
Laced in ivy, made from cobble stones, earth and sand.

Rock walls hang heavy with honey suckle vine, neither created to confine.
Sometimes I bring along the spirit of a few close friends, they are
strong enough to let the other guy win.

We walk for hours with hardly a word.
They know they're important, don't have to be heard.

Sunlit valleys dance with pink daisies, poppies, and daffodil, those
in shadow have treasures to behold.
Water falls, spring lizards, crickets and toad, each evening their
ageless songs unfold.

Everyone's secrets are all safe and still, I keep mine in the tall
grasses, just at the foot of those hills.

Though I would like, some of theses territories are best left
undisturbed, laid to rest and forever unknown.
This sun never completely sets on any given day, it leaves just a
glimmer, for me to find my way, home.

Gladys A. Hall

Reaching For The Light

The dying tree reaches for the beckoning sunlight.
It stretches up to the merciless, high window that is challenging it.
The window towers over the domestic plant,
And the tree begs for the sun's nourishment,
But the tree is condemned to death and must reach the distant light source.
Its outstretched branches reach higher and higher in darkness.
Its destination comes closer, mocking the sickly plant.
The thin, discolored tree reaches upward until it knows
   it can no longer endure the arid and barren soil.
And then, just as the tree is about to give up, it happens...
The ever-forgiving light restores the forsaken tree,
And shoots of new green foliage appear on the twisted branches,
Growth that symbolizes its victory over its grim fate,
And the strength to conquer all that defies the resurrected tree.

Jill Schwartz

Strength Of Color

Yellow is lightness... beauty and laughter
It signifies joy and the love we're all after
It's caring and tenderness in the embrace of a friend
An innocent smile of a child in your heart to the end.

Yellow is lightening! Fierce, powerful, mighty
When the wills of the world clash with the Almighty;
Its brilliance and splendor show both the future and past
From the threat of the fire to the vivid rainbow's cast.

Yellow is majestic in each golden petal of a flower
And the light in gentle raindrops of a warm summer shower,
While its magnitude fills every size and dimension
It creeps in and quietly commands your attention.

Yellow is hope from the breaking rays of dawn
To the last glow of sunset as the ivory moonlight turns on,
It touches your heart when you're feeling insecure
And steadies your footsteps until they are sure.

Yellow is strength... darkness must always obey
Even one fragile glimmer of a gossamer ray.

Heidi L. Pedersen

Dying Young

It's the virus that never heals.
It makes you crave for no more meals.
You lie in bed and look so pale,
Your tiny bones so weak and frail.

I ask God why it happened to you,
And to make your body strong like brand new.
To see you look like a lump of clay,
And pray that you make it through the day.

I look back on the days when you were sick,
And ask myself, is this some mean trick?

But the day when you were put to rest,
I thought to myself, it was for the best

Because God took you to a better place,
Where no more pain you'd have to face.
I don't think about the day you died,
Only the memories when we laughed and cried.

Elishia Ann Moore

My Poem

My poem is about a certain book
It is one into which we all should look.
It teaches us to watch and pray,
And to live faithfully every day.

This book has very significant features,
And has brought forth many teachers.
The greatest of them, you all know —
He had love for friend and foe.

He gave his life, for Adam's sin,
That those who wish, may live again.
Yes, you guessed him from the start!
He is God's Son, after His own heart!

The book is unique, and we do adore
The short stories, poems, and adventures galore.
Romances, novels, and mysteries
Lead us to laws and biographies.

The conclusion gives us hope and light
For a long, long future — happy and bright.
It is a source very reliable — Yes,
It is God's Word, the HOLY BIBLE!!!

Arloween E. Cody

My Attic Is Haunted!

My attic is haunted, I tell you!
It is full of ghosts, witches, goblins, and more!
They lurk and hide all day
and they wail 'til night, just to play!

Play with what, you ask!
With my mind, I say!!!
I'll call it frightening, and they'll call it play.

These goals make magic spells,
(and some have fainting smells....)

MY ATTIC IS HAUNTED!
So what do you say about these things?
Huh? What do you think? Oh, no! My pen's
running out of ink!

Heather Good

A Single Rose

A single rose I give to you,
It is for your heart that is so true.
Your love is a special kind,
One that is so hard to find.

When I am down, you are there,
Always showing that you care.
You give a meaning to my days,
You do things in special ways.

Our time together seems to go so fast,
Sometimes I wonder if we will last.
You seem to always be there,
You make life seem so fair.

No requirements do you put on our love,
Sometimes I think you were sent from above.
Your presence is all that I need,
From your love I want to feed.

You make my day so bright,
Your lovely face is a precious sight.
You make me want to live,
To you, a single Rose I do give.

George Chenette

"Wave"

He walks in the room and I am tempted
It hits me and I become delusioned
I feel as if my soul has been dented
Cold fingers caress my tongue-illusioned
His naked body sears my burning eyes
Surroundings are swirling mass of color
Far up above me I see red, black skies
In collision of worlds mine is duller
You course through my veins as a part of me
My every thought revolves around you
When I am with you I would never flee
Your affection helps me to make it through
Your love for me burns like acid inside
When tripping with you I am satisfied

Jennifer Beale

Demons

"What of it?!" I screeched as I raced for the door.
It followed - then stopped - and sat on the floor.
I couldn't help but be puzzled by this turn of events,
which were happening so quickly - not making much sense.
For I knew it was filled with questions and answers I loathed to hear,
But I knew it would always be a few steps behind
So very near!
It follows - it stops - it's everywhere I go
Questioning - reasoning - carrying on so!
But I notice when around people it slips quietly away
Only to return at the end of the day.
To argue, to fuss, over things done and said
Until I grow weary and collapse on my bed.
Only to wake in the morning with which I will find
It sitting in a corner - just biding its time.
To resume its attack with gusto and relish,
Quite frankly at times I find it quite hellish.
So why do I put up with this aggravating nonsense?
Because my dear friend - it is only my conscience!

David Scherer

Untitled

I have a dream...
    it flies on the wings of the wind,
    whispers in the tops of trees,
    blows across the lake making ripples in the reflections,
    falls to earth with the rain
        and rises again to the clouds,
    follows moonbeams through my open window
        and into my unconscious mind.
But I know it is there
    because I am alive and happy
And somehow...
    I can feel it growing inside
        being nurtured and strengthened
            until one day
    it will at last come true.

Jo E. Moore

A Mother's Love

Her precious son, amid life's hurts and harms,
Is safe from ill, clasped in his Mother's arms.

His countless needs, proclaiming stern demands,
Are met by deeds performed by Mother's hands.

His childish words blurt out his childish fears;
Peace comes because they're heard by Mother's ears.

He has his faults. He sometimes acts unwise.
But He's a gem viewed through his Mother's eyes.

This gift from God, sent to her from above,
Shall e'er rejoice in his dear Mother's love.

Joseph A. Crane

349

Untitled

It's fantastic, it's beautiful, it's sublime.
It finds pathways through the entire force, it's mine.

Who and what decided on this way through heaven and hell?
There is always a limit to environment, this we know well

Enough to call a halt to the foolishness of borrowing time.
There's only one way to go, and it's mine.

Will I rub my eyes and see clearly through this mist,
Knowing it's all been laid out there so I'd never be missed?

Where I've opened doors they now swing back and forth,
When I've decided this is right, it now points East, West, South, North.

There can be limits for the maiden, but there's choice.
For in breaking the silence, there now is a voice

That speaks, that answers, that clearly states
There's everything now selected, because of the FATES...

Anita Halbert

My Son

The stubborn golden lock of hair will never stay in place;
It dangles on the forehead of his tiny-featured face.
Those deep, dark pools of wonder that can pierce my very heart
Come alive with sparkling mischief and the love that they impart.
His freckled little button nose wrinkles up in stubborn haste
When correcting his behavior's not in keeping with his taste.
Those firm and gently-contoured lips that purse when he's "so mad"
Are much like those belonging to the man I love - his dad.
The ways and means he uses make refusals very hard -
Like the special straggly daisies gathered for me from our yard.
He is impish, yet angelic, when attention he has won.
And I'm proud to call that precious little man of mine "My Son."

Janet D. McKinstry

During Fall

The first day of all is in September,
  It continues till mid December.
During fall leaves start changing colors,
  to red, orange, yellow, and many others.
They start falling from the trees,
  swaying back and forth in the breeze.
Squirrels scatter everywhere,
  searching for nuts here and there.
Geese are flying south each day,
  we'll see them again in the month of May.

Andrea Robertson

Every Two Hours And Nine Minutes

While lying in my bed one night, I looked outside and saw a light.
It blinked across the sky real slow, I thought it was a UFO.

I checked the clock at 9:01 and then looked back - the light was gone!
Was I dreaming? I wasn't certain. I decided not to close the curtain.

I stayed there watching from my bed, while scary pictures filled my head.
Like aliens of monstrous size; I grabbed the sheets and closed my eyes.

I woke up at 11:10. The blinking light was back again.
I thought, "Stay calm and have no fear." As I watched the light, it disappeared.

I could not sleep, I just kept guard. What if it landed in my yard?
"Ok, that's it!" I said, "I'm crazy. I'm getting up, I won't be lazy."

I searched my mind for ways to cope, and then I thought -
  DAD'S TELESCOPE!
I aimed it at the moon and stars. I thought I caught a glimpse of Mars.

I gazed the sky for sights unseen. My clock was reading 1:19.
Right on schedule the light arose. I was so scared, my fingers froze.

I finally focused on the sky. And then I laughed, and this is why.
What caused my fears? What did I see? Just U.S. Air, Flight 103!

Bonnie Lee Prendiville

This Bond

Sometimes it's so sad to be alone,
isolated away from your loved ones at home!
But your mind can out you there with them, if you let it go,
the thoughts, the dreams, the memories are so sacred, I know!

I want to tell you that being stuck in here,
has given my reflections a chance to clear!
I've had the fortune to travel deep inside my soul,
and duel with my emotions that continue to roll!

I've felt the winds blow around in my cavernous head,
stirring up the dust that I thought was long lost and dead!
My appetite for a loving family and questions I can't remove,
reminds me of the treasure I have in you that's filled up this groove!

The pool of memories have opened my eyes from within,
and target this wondrous feeling of joy, again and again!
My family in you, and love, makes me exhibit just how fond,
Point blank it's you, Heather, Damian, and Teresa, that's powering this bond!

James Goss

Look Where God Has Brought Us

A chosen peculiar people
Is what we are today;
Through bondage, toils and struggles,
Our God supplied The Way.
We now are His Anointed—
Vessels blessed, preserved through strife;
The Debt owed is a challenge:
SUBMIT OUR WILL TO GOD FOR LIFE!

The Soil within our Vessels
Should be fertile in God's Truth,
His Seed of Love be EXERCISED
And SHARED, starting from youth!
The Oil from His Anointing
Should freely flow from us
To others, who have yet to know
Reality through trust.

And as our peculiar number
Continues to increase,
Let's pray for Uniformity
That seals each mind in PEACE.

Janet M. Gant

Shady Place

Can I do as I think? Can my mind comprehend?
Is it yes or is it no? Is it him I depend?

Should I love him or will he leave me? What's it going to be?
Scattered thoughts of love in my mind, Answers set me free.

  I close my eyes and wonder what life has put me through,
  The constant tears of not knowing what I'm suppose to do.

  I rest my soul so softly in a very special place,
  Escaping from reality, it's called my Shady Place.

  Here is where I hide my feelings, somewhere I'd feel secure
  No feel of fear or confusion, just love that I'll endure.

  My heart no longer trembles with no fret of what's to face
  That's why I often drift to my special Shady place.

  Whenever I need to go there, I cry myself to sleep
  My Shady Place I run to and my sanity is what is keeps.

Arlene M. Montoya

The Dove

The dove in flight so strong and free
is how I wish my soul to be
to soar above the days and nights
in solitude upon midflight
he plays among the silver clouds
and watches people on the ground
in emptiness their hearts cry out
for their own anger and their own doubt
they store their love upon a shelf
continue to within themselves
the dove he rests in thoughts and dreams
and bathes himself in golden streams
he shakes his head in sympathy
the way he looks at you and me
then on he goes to sing his songs
for happiness
to him belongs

Christy L. Sheehan

Growing Older

To grow older, but not grow old,
Is a gift you give yourself.
This truth through the years has been told.
You cannot rust on shelf.

Rocking chairs are wasted motion.
You move but you go nowhere.
You live with a selfish notion,
And you lose the will to care.

Don't gaze in your mirror and moan.
View the world through your window.
Do Good -, it's a way to atone,
As your road becomes narrow.

This fills growing older with zest,
And give later years great worth.
It brings to Life new interest,
And makes a Heaven on Earth.

Just heed the Lord, in Joyful Trust.
Help each Sister and Brother.
Ere Death makes us ashes and dust,
He warned, "Love one another."

Joseph J. Blanchfield

Just One More Day

When day is done and shadows fade
Into the night I kneel and pray
To ask the Lord for one more day.
When morning comes and the dew has fallen
The grass is green and the creeks are swollen
Comes another new day for the Lord has spoken
He tries to make us understand to love
One another the best we can.
He's understanding and he's just
To know Him is to love him and that is a must
No one knows what tomorrow brings,
Maybe the sunshine or maybe rain.
But if it is sunshine on a bright sunny
Day, maybe the little children can go out and play
He loves the rivers, the mountains, the birds and trees
God loves us all as you can see.
He has a plan for us to do, he is wise
And very thoughtful too.
The time for the Lord and me to say
Another new day is on the way.

Dorothy Currier

My Precious Sam

If only I had tossed the bone away
   Instead of sharing it impulsively with you,
My precious Sam, you'd still be here today,
   And I'd be watching for your every cue.

I loved you more than words can ever say.
   God knows I'd ne'er have hurt you by intent.
May He forgive my harming you, I pray.
   The grief I'm bearing now will not relent.

I long for you each time I look around.
   I miss your gentle tapping at the door,
Your curling up and resting on the ground,
   Your pawing at my knee for treats galore.

You blessed our home with happiness and joy.
   When you were here I never felt forlorn.
You entertained me as you squeaked a toy.
   Your soft black form our landscape did adorn.

No other dog can ever take your place.
   My love for you will surely never die.
Time can't memories of you erase.
   My Sammie, may you rest with God on high.

Cynthia J. Arnold

Season Of Dreams

A ray of sunshine streaks in warmth across your face.
Inevitably the floor creaks as you begin life's pace.

Through quilts of colored leaves many folks call a bother;
Simply served by natures breeze an enigmatic mother.

Skipping some stones lightly into the calm bay;
Following their touch quietly and observe the play.

Heart stopping honkings of geese over the bay;
Mindless of my longings they point the way.

Inhale the crisp night above the marvel of sparkling sights;
You are free as a dove your mind has held your flights.

Soon overcome by visions of sleep the day suddenly dies;
Trivial problems undoubtedly will keep heading off through the skies.

Jerry Weggum

It's Christmas Time In Buckeye Land

The evergreens are a beautiful sight
   In the fields of snow so still and white.
The streams have lost their rushing roar,
   Stilled until springtime comes once more.
Majestic hills silently stand.
   It's Christmas time in Buckeye Land.

The far off sound of the hunter's gun
   Starts a white tailed deer on a frightened run.
The squirrel is asleep in a big den tree,
   His dreams are peaceful and worry free.
Through the sky above flies a wild goose band.
   It's Christmas time in Buckeye Land.

A noise outside makes the children pause.
   They think each sound is Santa Claus
So we give them a bath and put them to bed,
   But they won't sleep until prayers are said.
Then we pray together the way God had it planned.
   It's Christmas Time in Buckeye Land.

Donald B. Evans

351

The Lost Tree

I remember you standing,
In the center of my life.
You were the fire that burned bright,
Within the memoirs of my heart.

And in my dreams you spoke to me,
Of great new things that I could see.
You made me sure that I'd become,
A solemn person, in touch with one.

Throughout ours days you held your ground.
You held us all together bound.
Until that one but fateful day,
I found you lost, and I had stayed.

The world did changed, since that one day.
I found you gone, and I had stayed.
Without your memoirs, I'd carried on.
Without my script, I'm lost, you're gone.

You are the lost tree of my life.
Deep in my heart, you still burn bright.
Since you been gone you're my lost tree.
And, I'll not forget your hopes for me.

Carlos C. Torres

"The Hero"

We stood there at the airport
In tears and dressed in black
Oh what a sad occasion
Our son was coming back

I saw the flag draped coffin
As they rolled it off the plane
My heart stood still, I couldn't breathe
I've never felt such pain

I fought to gain composure
And hold my head up high
But in my mind, all I could think
Is why did he have to die

My son is gone forever
I whisper as I cry
Someone please explain to me
Why he had to die —

Joan R. Smith

Mom

When the doctor came, shaking his head side to side
In shock and dismay, I remember "No" I cried
It was so unbelievable, it just couldn't be true
Our mother's work here on earth was through

We went home in shock and sat starry eyed
Over and over in our mind, we said, "She died"
Somehow, though it just couldn't be true
We needed our mother more than anyone knew

We went through the motions, the very next day
Picking out her clothes in which she would lay
Who would be singing and who would pray
And who would carry her on that dreadful day

Sunday came with the sun shining bright
We buried our Mother, it took all our might
We're so full of pain, anger, hate and despite
We've carried these feelings through many a night

Understanding has dawned on us in bits and pieces
But the pain in our heart just never ceases
We remember her every day with a crying bout
We miss her, we love her, each day is harder a mother without

Connie Sluss

Single Heartache

My 5 year old came home tonight, from the weekend with her Dad,
In one of those moods again, half angry, half sad.

I'm the one on whom she chooses to lay the blame,
I moved her out, I changed her life, and nothing is the same.

I must admit for 5 years old she has adapted fairly well,
But, then again, on Sunday nights, she shoots my weekend all to hell.

There are only so many reasons that a 5 year old can relate to,
I just hope she understands I did what I had to do.

When she gets older I'll try to make her see
That a life for her Dad and me was an impossibility.

Then, when she knows the story and the reasons that are true,
I hope she will turn and say "How proud I am of you!"

Julie M. Behan

Unseen Nude

Cloth: the sign of extending disbelief
In natural beauty; A cloaking ledge
For unheeded guilt harbored in Mind's reef,
Born with Adam's tasted fruit of knowledge.
Sacred scriptures preach strict conformity,
Bequeath shields over the human portrait:
Art unjustly hid by vulgarity
Fallaciously feared; Fear ordered by writ.
Search beyond words breed by the falsely sage.
Unhusk shame, bare thy untainted sculpture.
Reveal one's bald self, doff civilization's cage:
Find Expression in Man's raw signature.
Scare not. Carry yourself nude and open;
Possess, know, feel you're under no burden.

Jacob Callcut

Fragile Beauty

Who can resist new fallen snow when winter winds no longer blow?
In my yard so fresh and clean, I sculptured there a great snow queen.
A silver wreath adorned her head,
   and a rose bud mouth from ribbons red.
Two chunks of coal cut right for size,
   my snow queen had dark lovely eyes.
An empty spool tucked in between, a dainty nose for my snow queen.
Christmas garlands on her dress, draped around with great finesse.
A work of art, I felt such pride, but all too soon that beauty died.
At night there came a spring time rain, my snow queen is not the same.
That sweet young face that held no guile, now wears a Mona Lisa smile,
A haughty look and twisted nose and not a hint of queenly pose.
Chunks of coal and garlands bright, lay at her feet, a messy sight.
Cleaning up there in the rain, to those around I must explain,
While they stand by and laugh at me, how such a mess has come to be.

Erminne Stamper

In My Eyes

In my eyes, you are the rose that smells so sweet
In my eyes, you are the feeling of defeat
In my eyes, you are the liquid to my thirst
In my eyes, you are not a second, but a first
In my eyes, you are the happiness to my soul
In my eyes, you are the feeling when I reach that special goal
In my eyes, you are the sun that dries my tears
In my eyes, you are the one that eases all my fears
In my eyes, you are my tomorrow
In my eyes, you are my joy, not my sorrow
In my eyes, you are the blood in my heart
In my eyes, you are a big part
I want you to know, I'm here till the end
I want you to know I love you, my girlfriend

Eric Vargas

"A Mother's Hall Of Fame"

If there ever is a hall of fame for Mothers, ours will be honored in gold!
We will miss her presence, but cherish all the memories and good
times that in our hearts we all hold.
If we listen close we can hear her say: Don't be sad and don't weep for me.
There's no more pain, and I prefer to stay: I'll wait here in heaven
for my family.
Even though there's an empty feeling in our lives, and in our
hearts for our Mother Dear.
We need only to look around at all the love and memories she left
behind, she's still here!
We thank you God that in this wonderful ladies life we all had a part.
For as long as we live, our Mother will be in the Mother's Hall of
Fame deep inside our hearts!

Dora F. Lewis

To Be A Leader........

Being a leader is harder than you'd think
In fact, sometimes, it can even stink!
People yell and get mad at you,
But still you know what you have to do...
Make the smart decision- whether popular or not,
And if you do they'll realize that they've got...
A leader that wants the very best for them,
Even if it means a little giving in.
Good leaders know how to criticize
Without cutting you down a size.
So next time a leader tells you to do
Something that just doesn't appeal to you
Think about this poem, and maybe then you'll see...
They're just being the leaders they were cut out to be!

Carrie DeLaquil

The Open Mouth Of F. D. R.

Nothing was ever so dear
In any Depression year,
as the Open Mouth of F. D. R.
Banishing fear, the confidence of a nation restoring,
Uttering cheer, rendering population spirit's soaring;
Proclaiming dire destitution at an end;
Shouting measures for the idle to work begin.
Cry for freedom throughout the world,
Vision for a peace keeping structure unfurled.
The Nazi terror will be repelled;
The degradation of humanity utterly quelled.
Though his Closed Mouth utters no sound,
His spirit shall be eternally bound.

John R. Green

Requiem II

Trees flee towards blue sky
in an attempt to escape this death.
I stand silently beneath,
lost in a field of irregular grey squares
set against solid green,
and I know that nothing leaves this place.

Within these delicately kept green grass plots of white marble,
threatening caucasian statues of Jesus and Mary do not impress me.
They are insignificant next to this cracked slab of ancient stone,
thriving but forgotten in its dense private garden.

She, and I, and the vines have not given up
they struggled with thick cruel stone until after years
of battle it yielded, bursting with a thunderous crack,
and the vines stormed through
the small flower placed at her head long ago
has grown into a vigorous shrub adorned with glimmering red buds
which feed bright passionate bees as golden butterflies dance
across this exhausted grey marker
a shining black and blue lizard hurries to join his friends.

Joshua Edwards

A World Of Silence

I watched a little girl at play
in a world of silence today.
To see her smile, laugh and play.
She was so happy, it really made my day!
You see this little girl couldn't hear or speak.
But, she accepted everything in
stride because she lived this way all her life.
To imagine how it would be, never
to be able to hear your mother yell
"Dinner is ready now."
To never hear the birds sing or the
telephone ring, to never be able to say
what you want or where you want to go.
To live in a world of silence, to try
to understand, why your living in a different land.
What a life that must be, and yet to be so happy.
It makes you wonder, why we can't be happy
with all we have.

Brenda G. Smith

Woodland Wonder

I took a walk today
In a secluded woodland way
My heart was treated to many treasures
Far beyond any human measure
A graceful deer who looked at me
As if to say "come follow me"
She did not leap in alarm
I am sure she knew I meant no harm
The creek was flowing quiet and serene
It did its share to complete the scene
Trees of red, orange and brilliant yellow
Could not help but make me feel mellow
The sky so blue with clouds fluffy and white
Made a truly awesome sight
I left the woodland with a heart filled with love
For all I had seen was from God up above

Elizabeth R. Miller

I Saw My Mommy's Spirit Bloom Today

for Mark Browning
I lingered for a while today
In a field of golden daffodils.
Quickened by a gentle breeze,
They danced and nodded under a gleaming sun
As it ascended to the top of the bright blue sky.
I saw my Mommy's spirit bloom today.

One faultless blossom turned its face to me,
A drop of morning dew still clinging to its yellow cup.
When I touched its radiant face,
The luminescent drop fell softly to my hand.
It lay shimmering there like a tiny tear.
I saw my Mommy's spirit bloom today.

Dozens of golden daffodils were blooming
In that freshening field where I stood today.
But only one so rightly formed, so newly made
That it held a glistening tear to shed,
Then it turned away to show the light to me.
I saw my Mommy's spirit bloom today.

Once more, I touched its shining head,
And took it in my hand.
I carried home my Mommy Flower
And Pop-Pop took it up to where she lay
So it could guide her to the light.
I saw my Mommy's spirit bloom today.

Joyce Browning

353

God's Gentle Hands

By the early mist I awake in my tent,
  in a cool campground near a lake.
The birds are singing, the lake is rippling
  as I start to light a fire.
I wake the other campers and we eat breakfast.
Then, in the foggy mist, we cast and fish all day.
We catch bass, catfish and some nice trout for dinner.
What a fine catch that day indeed!
So now we eat a delicious fish dinner.
We went to bed that night in a land of gleaming stars.
We went to sleep in the rest of God's gentle hands.

  Jonathan Kralick

Memories

As I see you everyday my mind often wonders and sight of you places me
  in a complete daze.
My feelings race and my heart begins to beat at such a fast pace, that
  I am placed in a haze.
Life for me has definitely changed since meeting you and a stronger
  person I have become.
The memories of you often cloud my mind throughout my days and
  sometimes it becomes too much to take.
I often miss the times we spent together, if not speaking just being near.
I often study the movement of your lips when you would speak even
  though often I didn't hear and sometimes didn't care.
I have come to realize as times forward things will never be the same
  but forgiveness is the key which you could give me
  and I could give you.
Many obstacles will always be thrown at us as life moves on but no
  matter how big or small they may always be overcome.
So the hurt that has plague us needs to end and the goodness we can
  offer each other needs to begin.
Memories may be bad and some memories may be good but as life moves
  forward no memory is worth losing a friend.

  Guy Shannon Jones

Loneliness Causes

Minds to reel with thoughts of loss;
Imaginations to run wild;
Self-confidence to dwindle;
Nerves to be frayed;
Hearts to feel empty;
Souls to seek contact;
Eyes to shed tears of self-pity;
Ears to listen for footsteps;
Mouths to speak words of regret;
Feet to walk with no destination;
Hands to write poems of loneliness;
And time to pass slowly - into wasted moments.

  Elizabeth A. Green

sea of love

i'm standing in the sea — the froth swirls 'round and 'round
i'm standing in the sea — the blazing sun pounds on my back
i'm standing in the sea — my feet are cold yet hot
for i'm standing in the sea the mystic sea of love

the waves are high — they grow alarmingly with each move
the waves are high — they fold and collapse to form undertows
the waves are high — their motion drags me under
for the waves are high in the sea the mystic sea of love

i cannot resist — the fury of the water mounts higher
i cannot resist — the tempests rage inside me
i cannot resist — i have lost the strife
for i'm drowning in the sea the mystic sea of love

  Duane S. Farnell

Christmas Eve

My thoughts, tonight, are of us, dear
  I'm writing them down for you.
Are your thoughts of the friends you are with
  Or do you think of me, too?

A Christmas Eve twilight is falling
  Long shadows have carried the sun.
Small lights, twinkling through the darkness
  Seem to tell me that day is done.

I'm all alone in the room, dear,
  And yet, I'm not lonely nor blue.
For dearest, I'm thinking that next year,
  I may be alone, just with you.
Alone in our own room, together
  Looking out, on a twilight like this,
Held close in your arms, in your heart, deer,
  And telling our love by a kiss.

I hope that my thoughts come true,
  I pray every night that they will,
We'll both just keep hoping, and praying,
  That God, our great wish, may fulfill.

  Edward T. Kitchen

Guardian Angel

As I sit here gazing into the wide open skies,
I'm wondering what are your fears,
what are your dreams.

I see you walk through life with heavy burdens,
will it be I to help you through them.

I see you now with so much pain in your heart,
let me be there to help you make a fresh start.

Though sometimes we choose to walk through life alone,
there are those who will be by your side 'til the fears are gone.

Only a few are chosen to go through life
with a guardian angel by their side,
to see that dreams are dreamt.

  Geraldine Stettina

Something Good Will Come My Way

I'm the root of a flower that blows in the wind.
I'm the soul of many men.
Opposition comes everyday. But, I am still able to say,
"Something good will come my way."

I'm the little sail boat on a dark river's bend.
Not real sure if I'll get a good wind.
But, when it comes my way, surely I'll sail that day.
Into an ocean so bright, then I'll know, I'll be all right.

But, my enemy is Father Time.
Don't want to hear his clocks chime.
Because I'll know I'm running out of time,
To get my peace of mind.

"Hold on!" I'll say. "Just give me another day!"
Because I'm still able to say.
"SOMETHING GOOD WILL COME MY WAY!"

  Angela Walker Kea

Paint

I'll paint my mood, in shades of blue.
I'll sketch your lips, so they know what to do.
I'll trace a hand to wipe your tears.
And a look to calm all of your fears.
A silhouette of dark and light
While we hold each other tight
I'll paint a sun to warm your heart
Swearing that we'll never part
I'll paint the truth to show how I feel
Try to make you completely real.
I'll use a brush so light and fine
I'll draw you close and make you mine.
I'll draw the years, passing by.
So much to learn, so much to try.
And with this ring, our lives will start
Promising that, you're in my heart.
I offer what you can not buy.
Devoted love, until we die.

Amber Force, Age 14

My Wild Flowers

Walking down another path,
I'll find you...
Slowly closing another gap,
Getting closer...
Closer to you...
I've seen you through the tall green grass,
Like a symbol of...
Fire...
Fire within you....
  Like my wild flowers

Angela M. Perri

The Hurt Will Still Go On

I know inside your heart is breaking.
I'll do everything I can to prevent the aching.
It's been four years the hurt has went on.
Even though she may be gone.
The hurt will still go on.

This experience should have taught you not to take life for granite.
And though you thought that I didn't mean it.
Believe me it's true that the pain will end.
But the hurt will still go on.

She still lives in your heart.
You see her at night and even when it's light.
No one knows why she had to part.
And the hurt will still go on.

Now that you're gone.
I see no reason to live on.
So for me the hurt will be twice as painful.
But the hurt will still go on.

April McDavid

Lies

Don't tell me you love me if it's only a lie
If you're going to lie to me then please say, "Goodbye"
When we are alone and when we're together
You make me feel as if it could last forever
Then tomorrow comes and your feelings for me have changed
But my feelings for you will always remain
I try to please you but I don't know how
How do I know what you want from me now
You always ask for more than I can give
All that I want is to love you and live
When I see the hateful look in your eye
I know the love you professed was only a lie
There seems to be no more reason to live
I've given to you all I can give

Heather Koski

The Transcendence Of Aging

Clocks would run backwards
If they were built that way,
But time would still advance.
The cosmic stopwatch was set,
And time advances, advances.

Moss settles into the crevices
Of the old faces,
Having rolled and rocked
A billion split seconds,
Old faces,
Caring too much to stop running,
Sweeping hands about them:
Slower, faster.

Their dance is to a time noted for each one differently,
And time advances differently,
Measure by different measure,
Until each life lasts
The same length of cosmic time.

Dan Kerley Jr.

Passionate Forces

If the forces of compassion were not driven by love.
If the clouds floating by were not creations of God.

If this world were to crumble beneath our very feet,
Who would resurrect your being would you experience total defeat?

Now is the time to welcome him in,
Meditate on his glory acquire his consent.

Sometimes starting over seems like a mountain of a task,
But he'll guide you, opening doors, if only you will ask.

But he will expect something in return,
That you study his laws and desire to live what you've learned.

No, he doesn't expect us to be perfect
  That task is beyond our control,
But only to pray for direction
  Allowing him our personalities to re-mold.

Elaine D. West

Food For Thoughts Garden

I believe on all this earth the most beautiful gardens would grow
  If sown with seeds of true friendship with love not for show.
Planting love, life and kindness, thoughtfulness, souls and deeds,
  We would all be happy gardeners if we'd only plant those seeds.
While travelling along life's pathway disappointments are very few
  When time was taken to plant those seeds, you harvest the same when due.
If ever you feel a failure your garden didn't grow like it should,
  Always try replanting as any good gardener would.
Good Gardens need cultivation, weeds may cause you some gloom,
  Remember, some of the ugliest weeds has the most beautiful bloom.
Patience the tool of production, at times the sweat from the brow,
  Or maybe it's teardrops moisture that sprouts the seeds somehow.
Of course it needs lots of sunshine, your smile could mean so much,
  To grow your friendship garden "Be yourself with GOD'S TOUCH".

Dorothy W. Young

Under Our Willow Tree

Sitting under our sad willow tree
I think of the days of you and me
We told each other secrets and stories,
we shared our hopes, dreams, and glories
Under the branches of this tree,
you held me passionately
You were never cruel in any way,
but now you've gone away
To a higher place no one sees,
I hope they have willow trees.

Jennifer Baker

If I Could...

If I could take an hour from eternity divine
I'd pick a peaceful, happy one - no obstacles to climb.

If I could take a day to settle calm and clear
that's the place I'd want to be - year after wrenching year.

If I could take a week and turn it into gold
In a melancholy search - the treasure to behold.

If I could take a month to briskly wash away
A very careful choice - the consequences weigh

If I could take a year out of the hands of time
I would not take a yesteryear - they are not friends of mine.

I'd look into the future and find a pleasant rose
A 'morrow your upon the thorn - passing no more foes.

Joye Leach-Henrie

If I Was An Angel

If I was an angel, I'd live up in heaven,
I'd make my bed on cloud number seven.
My wings would be big, all shiny and bright,
I would wash and scrub them, spotlessly white.
When it was dark, I could fly near and far,
And I would look like a shooting star
Living in heaven, it's sunny and warm,
The days are filled with heavenly charm.
Over my loved ones, I would watch and protect,
To do all the things, that angels expect.
The biggest surprise for someone would be,
Is to walk into heaven and bump into me.

Gary L. Skinner

My Dream

I have a dream,
I would like to share.
It's about me, so don't even try to say,
how stuck up I'm being.

I wish for a guy,
to come my way.
Caring,
and fulfilling all my needs.

He would love me,
and I would love him back.
For it would be so easy,
Since he is the one.

I will love him so much,
I know I will.
For my pain would be gone,
because of my sweet dream.

Elizabeth Mason

A Walk In The Rain

On my way home, I took a detour
I went down a street that had no name
I saw a building and entered through the door
After a few minutes, I left, and it started to rain
I walked and walked, looking for some way home
The way I had gone, I was lost
The street, it was empty, and I was on my own
All to my stupid curiosity, Oh, what a cost!
My head hung low with no pride, just shame
And yet I continued, shuffling through the rain
I saw a bird, singing a melodic song
Open its wings and fly away
Oh, how I would trade my life back
For to change that one cursed day!

Alan Heckner

I Am

I am outgoing and love sports
I wonder why people die tragically
I can hear voices that tell me right from wrong
I see obstacles that are before me
I want to do something for someone they will never forget
I am outgoing and love sports

I pretend that I,m the best athlete in the world
I feel that life is going to be difficult in the future
I touch stars that represent people that are special to me
I worry that I might die young
I cry for the thought or parting with my best friend
I am outgoing and love sports

I understand the meaning of friendship
I say you never fail until you quit
I dream of playing college basketball
I try to understand things that make no sense to me
I hope this world will become a better place
I am outgoing and love sports

Amber Ames

Disunity

When I take a look at this cruel world,
  I wonder why it has to be

A world filled with so much hatred
  Such disunity.

Again, we've begun to divide,
  Using our outer selves as our guide.

It's so hard for some to understand
  that respect is all that we demand.

Equality is what we strive for.
  Yet, our inner potential some choose to ignore.

When will the ignorance no longer be?
  When will we overcome this disunity?

Start to ask yourself these things,
  And maybe you will realize

What a nicer place this world would be
  If everyone opened their minds and their eyes?

Fredericka Lanier

"Who Am I"

I hide behind a mask for so long it seems.
I wonder who I am!
Lost in thinking what people
thought.
I wonder who I am!
Right I always tried to do
but wrong it always was.
I always try to do my best
but best was not good enough.
The mask is to hide the
many tears, I shed from hurtful
words that many people said!
I wonder who I am!
I try so hard to please that
all I ever wanted was for
someone to love me.
But with that love comes a condition
The mask must come off
and you must love me for
who I am and not for who I'm not

Carla J. Strella

356

Melancholia

Should I fall into the depths of melancholia,
I will wallow in its arms,
and weep upon its shoulders.
Should the poisoned passion press upon my heavy heart,
I will push the limits of its tolerant pain,
and place no boundaries for its stay.

Racked in sobs from shivering sloth,
it melts the iron that made the shield,
and prepares the way for what was killed.
For in its blackened heart of hearts,
it mourns the death of an ancient me,
and welcome life to peer on new possibilities.

Then once I've writhed in pity's sake,
and the sludge of misery has blessed me free;
I will rise and smile to greet the morning sun,
and view the world once hid from me.
And then I'll sing a song so joyously,
to praise the strength of the soul in me.

Cynthia H. Delgado

Autumn Age

Shades of cinnamon surround me as I stand in the autumn wood.
I will go no further than the end of the path
for fear of losing my footing.
I want no one else to trouble over me,
I've seen the harm that can do.
Only the good spirit protects the bird with a broken wing
and with time it mends.
I am never alone here in the woods,
the beasts all scurry around me.
I see the birds fly aloft,
Oh that I could be that free again...
maybe ... someday.

Debbra M. Ream

You Will Never

To keep the world from finding out about the wrong that I had done
I went ahead and sacrificed what might have been a son.

It might have been a daughter but the result would have been the same.
Murder is what I said do no matter what you call its name.

If abortion is the thing you have decided to do
Let me tell you a few things you will never go through.

You will never hear their laughter or kiss away their tears.
You will never share their dreams or explain away their fears.

You will never hear them sing or talk
You will never see them run or walk

You will never get a chance to hear
All their words that become so dear.

You will never have a chance to see
What your child would have grown up to be

Grace E. Smith

Lost Love

Sweet innocent love and pain
I try to let you go but you still remain

In my heart you remained so long
To try to forget you, could it be so wrong

I let you go so long before
Cause you didn't understand that I wanted more

Now I dream that I'll find you again
To take the place of all those other men

At night I pray to the heavens above
That I might find you again my dear lost love

Christina Farrell Rogers

Seven Up At Sun Up

Seven up at Sun Up
I watch with awe
Seventy-three seconds, Boom! Boom!
Disaster!

I watch with awe
The craft explodes, white smoke engulfs it
Disaster!
I want to help— it's hopeless

The craft explodes, white smoke engulfs it
My heart goes out for you
I want to help— it's hopeless
Seven courageous people, dead

My heart goes out for you
What thoughts go through your mind
Seven courageous people, dead
Your destiny fixed, too late to turn back

What thoughts go through your mind
Seventy-three seconds, Boom! Boom!
Your destiny, fixed, too late to turn back
Seven Up at Sun Up

Anna M. Reyes

When I Am Lonely

One day not very long ago,
    I was walking down a lonely path
And I was given a thought or two of which are so true.
    For when I think that I am all alone
I truly am not all alone at all.
    For from today, tomorrow, and from hence forth.
God is always with me as I walk to and fro.
    And in all that I do, whether I be walking, working,
Playing,
Or even sleeping, he is there,
    Right by my side giving to me the strength and the
Encouragement that I lack so that I can make it through the day.
Therefore encouraging me from day to day.
    For from pulse to pulse as my heart beats, likewise
Through which God restores my soul daily through his love.
    For from day to day, when I am lonely
I truly am not alone,
    But God is my very shadow as I walk to and fro.

James Juergensen

Daddy's Little Girl

I remember how it used to be
I was so young and so carefree
But now Daddy's feelings of love are gone
With only our memories to carry on

Daddy and I would always play
"That's Daddy's little girl," they'd say
I'm not sure where it all went
Because it seemed heaven-sent

Now I wonder if he still cares for me
And at night, does he think of me?
If only I could turn back the hands of time
I'd be Daddy's one and only valentine

And though our feelings are hard to show
I want Daddy to always know
Whatever he's doing and wherever he is
In my heart, his spirit always lives

Daddy, please know I will always care
And I pray one day our love we'll share
Even though our love's in a whirl
I'll always be Daddy's Little Girl

Jessica Slonaker

357

"Weep When They're Born"

On a cold winter's day
I was getting prepared for you
to come into my life.
There was no doubt in my mind
that I wanted you, because I had
fought everyone to keep you.
People talked, and looked down on me
I had made my choice
not to listen to anyone's voice.
The years have come and gone
Now you are almost grown.
Through the years
we have shed many tears!
When I see you standing so tall and strong.
I thank God I chose to weep
when you were born.

Doris Thompson

Learning To Live Again

I hold my head high
I walk tall and proud
I'm learning to live again

I used to wake up lonely
And go home sad
I hold my high

Life wasn't worth living
Every day was as blue as could be
I'm learning to live again

I decided to end my life. What was the point
Of life if it isn't lived?
I hold my head high

I looked deep within myself
Was there something worth salvaging? I thought not.
I'm learning live to again

But when I looked deeper I found
Riches of goodness inside me
I hold my head high
I'm learning to live again

Delfina Homen

Rising Water

Waters rise though I'm out of harms way,
I view scenes of the flood TV channels portray.
See others in pain, left homeless and lost,
Hardship and suffering, how heavy the cost
To learn letting go.
The somber grey sky blends in with the ground,
In a mud soggy gutter a child's toy is found.
Victims stand helpless, look beaten and strained,
knowing that nature cannot be contained.
Some struggle to help, to save what they can,
filling hundreds and hundreds of bags of sand.
As rivers spill over and streams swiftly rise,
Tears of compassion fill humanity's eyes.
Community bonds with each drop of rain,
Why must we learn through so much pain?

Beverly A. Chinello

Darkness

I fear it, for It controls me.
I try to hide from It, but It seeks me out.
It visits so often, I almost enjoy It.
It gives me a sense of completeness
—the dreadness of the Darkness.

The silence of the Darkness rings in my ears.
My vision belongs to the Darkness.
I feel It
I smell It
I can almost taste It.

The taunting voice commands me to move but I cannot,
For the Darkness resides in
my lungs
my stomach
the bottom of my soul.

It envelopes me — invades me.
It suffocates me — paralyzes me.
Its secret method gnaws at me.
It continues on and on forever until It becomes me
— and I am free.

Corey W. Whaley

The Serpent

He clenches his fangs into my heart.
I try and I try to break them apart.
The pain that I feel is only my own,
while his venom seeps out of my heart,
through my bones.
I feel his warmth to the tips of my fingers.
As I lay on the bed, through the air his scent lingers.
He won't let me be, though I beg and I plead.
He slithers inside me, and there plants his seed.
As I open my eyes I lie there in fear,
for I know that he loathes me and thirsts for my tears.
How can I break free from his wretched deceit!
When I feel him inside me it becomes bitter-sweet.

Bernardine Irish

"I Believe"

I believe that we should be treated equally.
I think that we should make a difference.
I see that there is destruction of a rainforest every day.
I feel like I can make a commitment to the world.
I can believe in myself if I tried my best.
I hear someone calling me in a distance.
I love being someone else if I just pretend.
I believe that we should be treated equally.
I read to my brother or sister if they are lonely.
I could climb the rope in gymnastics if I believed in myself.
I am just plain me!
No one can change the way I...
    look...
        dress...
            or... the way I...
                feel.
I picture that I am helping
    someone in the future.
I believe that we should be treated equally
I believe in myself and no one can stop me!

Jessica MacIntosh

"Our Homes"

As I go back through my memories, now that I'm growing old,
I think of all our houses, we either bought or sold.
As I walk through everyone of them, through the windows of my mind.
A special memory fills my heart, and each was one of a kind.
The one that comes to mind now, hold memories oh! so sweet,
A big old house in Iowa, when we lived on Huron St.
Our two little girls grew up there, went to school and on their way,
Left memories, dolls and cars and me, I miss them so today,
A lonely tear keeps dancing and falling down my face,
As I think of all the things we did in each and every place.
Everyone has a little corner or nook within my heart,
Doesn't matter whether old or new, each played a special part.
It fit our needs and protected us from the rain and snow and cold,
And held us in its arms so close, from our youth till now we're old.
They've heard our children's laughter and watched our family grow,
But a house needs love to make it a home and God to make it so.

Deloris Grandgenett

The Rose

A rose is a rose
I suppose
It grows and grows
just like Pinocchio's nose
It is red like a tomato
My friend told me it was a potato
so I showed it to my Uncle Kato
He told me it wasn't a tomato or a potato
He said it was a rose
So I stuck it up my nose
and I tried to get it out with my toes.
I guess it would help if I took off my panty hose.

Christine Riggs

Midnight Walk On A Star-Filled Night

In the silvery light of a full midnight moon
    I strolled through a beautiful, fragrant park
Dreaming of many years gone by too soon
    Gazing upon brilliant stars that made the night not dark

As that heaven of diamonds shone down on me
    Like a thousand glittering eyes
A sudden wave of peace and serenity
    Touched me with the deep, blue shade of the quiet skies

On this lonesome night I'd wonderingly hear
    The silence of the crisp, unmoving air
And when I peered into the lake, so crystal clear
    I saw the nearby willows with lovely drooping hair

With tears in my eyes like dewdrops they posed
    I recalled the most precious moments during my life
Tender and delicate as the flowers they closed
    While music rang in my ears like wavering notes from a fife

In that one earnest dream my mind eagerly met
    As I strode back home in heavenly delight
A pure tranquility I'd never forget
    On my midnight walk on a star-filled night

Julie Lieu

Beliefs

I still believe,
I still believe,
'Cause after all is said and done,
I am still alive.
And the boots have come and trampled on me,
Yet I am still alive
Because the sun has kissed me and loved me always before.
And because that I am strong there's a chance that I will grow,
This I know.
'Cause I am still alive.

Danielle Rene Owens

Of Festering Crimes

Of festering crimes in my heart
I still hope that will never part
The seeds of time have gone away
Please stay with me for one more day
Let my wounds heal through the night
For you'll be gone when mornings light
The razors ripped out my jagged soul
Now I'm half no longer whole
Of festering crimes I did commit
Now I lay at the bottomless pit
No matter which way I twist or turn
For all eternity I will continue to burn
Pain pierces my heart like cold blooded ice
So unfaithful the deed I must pay the price
I wither and scream but mostly I cry
For all of my sins I'll surely die
My eternal soul now blackened out of sight
Now I sit here alone in the darkness of night
This eternal torture please end it I pray
For you've only been gone for just one day

Andrew Balasa

Losing You

Even though it's over,
I still feel the same...
I'm trying to move on,
But there's still a steady flame.

I know you were looking out for me,
And thought it was for the best,
You never intended to hurt me,
But why did our relationship have to be put to rest...

The fact that you've given up on me is very hard to see,
You've locked up all your love,
And taken away the key...

What did I do to deserve this?
Your going to want me back.
Do you really care about me?
The ability to understand all of this,
Is something that I lack.

When I thin of all the memories,
I know the love we had was true...
Will there be a second chance?
Because I can't risk losing you...

Jacqueline Dee Cambron

The Ocean

Land and water meet,
I stand on its playground.
The water washes over my feet pulling the sand and my footprints away.
I think of a mother cleaning her yard,
sweeping the pollution of mankind away.
Its strength—power—a final frontier?
Buried secrets—waiting to be found.

The water sparkles like diamonds in the sunlight.
Breathe deep, smell the ocean.
Lick lips, taste the salt air.
Waves splash, a seagull squawks.
It caters to no one—accepts everyone.
Daily tides—serenity—stability—generation after generation.

Ann Cosimini

Untitled

Tonight during fighting fierce and intense
I stabbed someone in self-defense.
Then face-to-face in a hole we lay
With the horror of death on display.
At first his face only showed surprise,
Then pain and fear filled his eyes.
His bloody chest rattled with every breath,
Until at last came the quiet of death.
The light of the flares showed he was just a youth
And made me realize the awful truth:
That war bears a terrible cost
In the senseless waste of young lives lost,
And the future of the world as a whole
Suffers the loss of every soul.

Brad Baber

Perfect

I idolize you. Your life I envy.
I see you in the halls, smiling with your beautiful smile,
And I can see how your life is perfect.

You're the best at everything you do—EVERYthing you do.
You're the top of your class, captain of this and captain of that.
I wish my life was as perfect as yours.

You're friends with everyone.
Even the most out-of-place people, including me.
I saw you in the hall today and you smiled at me
And I see how your life is so perfect.

I saw you laugh in the hall today with all of your friends
And I wished I had them too.
And I hate you for having friends, but not really hate.
I just wish I could have your perfect life.

When I heard the news, my heart fell to the floor.
How could you put that gun to your head and not want to live?
I was angry that you ended the life I wanted.

I idolized you. Your life, I envied.
I saw you in the halls, smiling with your beautiful smile
And I couldn't see how your life was not perfect.

Jessica Tucker

As You Sit From Afar?

As I sit from afar
I see you.
I want to talk but I can't.
Were so different in ways that are of my imagination
As I sit from afar
I think to myself.
If things were only different
If maybe I were someone else
If only you could see me as I see you.
As I sit from afar
I lean back wishing.
Wishing that you would look up and see me.
Give me a sign.
You are so strong
so powerful.
As I sit from afar
I dream that one day you will see
me and rescue me.
What do you do
as you sit from afar?

Jaclyn E. Peterson

I Paint What I See

I see a rainbow shoot across the sky
I see the rain and leaves blow by
I see the shadows of night
Fall before my eyes.

Oh, but ya wonder will it be alright
Love, is the thunder
That's splitting the night
Crash away rainfall
Splash away light
Thunder take me far from here tonight.

Imagine a way of creating your dreams.
Imagination is a way of life it seems
The sunshine's so simple, the rain is so hard
And ya wonder where it's goin', is it gonna be far?

So ya paint pretty pictures
I paint what I see
Give colors to life
Give the sky to the sea.

Or is it just me—or is it just me?

Brian Alan Knowles

A Walk Along The Creek

As I wander, using a trained eye,
I see the history of change.
The rocks speak, but not to the untrained,
to one of knowledge, the language is common.

As I look at a small creek, I see the pieces
of creation. Some are battered and broken,
some are round, telling a story of great travel,
others are sharp, just starting journey, these
are the sedimentary builders.

Farther up stream, I see the carvings of erosion,
and others the weathering has warn down.
I scoop up rocks here and there, my hope is to find
a diamond, but all I come home with is quartz.

It will be added to my collection of travels,
for a man is not judged on his money and power,
but on his ability to look past the scenery and listen
to what the rocks are saying.

Daniel D. Duncan

Autumn's Inspiration

Through my small closed window
I see the hints of change randomly strike
at the predictability of summer's green,
and notice myself in the tree.
Reaching out like the limb she stands on,
inching precariously and persistently,
looking down, frightened;
then focusing ahead, determined.
I notice from this place in here
that out there her every second is a risk.
Every muscle, breath, thought, move, look,
absorbed in moving outward,
changing at pace with the leaves.
She wants only to connect with life,
to not let the passage pass her by,
or miss the beauty of passion
embodied in autumn's fire in the trees.
She seeks to dare,
to step out into love
from this safe but lonely place in here.

Jen M. Putney

Life Anew

I lie in somber, I move no more
I see the heavens golden door
I stop, I fear I can't go on
I hear my family edge me on
My loved ones come from near and far
They bring me gifts I share from a star
I hear the talking, the I love you's,
Goodbye
I see the tears but I can not cry
I lay beside you still breath in my blood
My body is with you, my soul has moved
on
I try to reach out, a touch, maybe smile
I'd scream just to tell you the holly joy
I feel, this new life I found
This new life is real

Doug Odegaard

"Grandparents"

Grandparents are kind and very loving
  I say;
So I want you to know
Grandparents, I really do love
  you;
Grandparents, will be there
  so you can tell them
  a secret or two;
Please don't worry, they won't tell a soul;
  like some sisters or brothers
  I know!
Grandparents, are wise and generous
  and some hilarious too
Grandparent, I just want to say
  I really do love you!

Rashé Athena Bronner

Buried Treasure

In search of something to make me remember him
I rummaged through what jumbled belongings I still possessed.
Rather than priceless mementos and rare antiques,
I found tattered shirts once gently touched by his scent.
Instead of precious heirlooms to display my lineage,
I located only a few frayed sweaters and pile of faded photos.

I explored all the closets and all the drawers.
I dug through all the boxes and had to give up with nothing in hand.
In a huff of disappointment I walked to the unlit window.
With eyes searching the somber darkness of the night,
I suddenly found what I had been seeking.

I discovered my answer right there in the reflection.
Staring into the glass was the face of the young girl he had loved.
Looking back at me was the daughter he would've fought to protect.
Right there were the cheeks he used to tenderly kiss goodnight.
The exact same brown eyes that had adored him with all her heart.
There I saw who I had been and what I had become.
There in the shadows I found that the most perfect gift
I'll ever need to remember him is inside of me.

Jayne A. Love

Seeing And Hearing

When things seem, too hard to stand
I look for a quiet place, just to sit
Maybe by a rock, with a quiet running spring
Are in the sun, in the middle of a field
Sometimes under the shade, of a big old oak
But no matter how I may feel, are where I go
I can still hear, the still quiet voice of God
In everything he has made, for you and me.

David L. Thomas

Love The Now

Lazy, lovely fall days.
I resemble them,
For I have such caring
For the new person in my life.
I could draws away just every sunlit hour,
Dreaming of him
With his manly form and human compassion.
He is not mine to hold,
But I treasure each minute spent in his presence.
Our sharing and caring is so wonderful in its sameness.
I am so blessed to have found this new friend.
Once again I am born anew
For having found this fine human being.
Every life increases our own.
Mine is filled with such dividends, ten fold,
Because, in just this present moment,
He is here.

Jo Piper

Memories

As I kissed Sis good-bye today and she smiled through the pain,
I remembered how much life we've shared with sunshine and rain.

Life has been full of ups and downs,
  but she was always there for us all.
She taught me how to play hop-scotch and how to catch a ball.
She helped me build my first play house and rock my doll baby.
I was quite a tom-boy but she was such a lady.

On my first day of school, I took her hand as I waved good-bye to
  Dad and Mother.
I knew everything would be alright because I was with Sis and my
  big brother.

And then she grew up and became a beautiful bride,
I nervously lit each candle with joy and so much pride.
As the years went by, she was blessed with two little girls.
We could rock our real babies now and toss their golden curls.

As she cooked and sewed and cared for her family,
I always knew she was just a phone call away and she always had
  time for me.
And when her day is done and the sun is setting low,
  she'll walk into her garden and watch the flowers grow.

Joyce Lawhorn Schultz

Afraid

I remember
I remember like a heart striking nightmare
My body will not let me forget
I see it
I see her face
Wet with tears
It is my mother
"I love you," I whisper
She turns her wet face from my tenuous body
Where is she?
Where is my sister?
Having fun with her friends?
Lying dead in the gutter?
My mother does not listen
She is afraid
She is afraid to see my sister
The phone rings
My mother does not listen
She is afraid
I am afraid

Cathlene Pineda

Untitled

Afraid is the only word to use
I realize I have so much to lose
For the first time that I can recall
I finally have it all
And if I were to lose her, it would surely kill me
I just wish there was a way I could make her see
Before I met her I was an empty shell
Content to continue the act I knew so well
But she showed me life offers so much
And this she showed me with just her touch
Now each day I look forward to what it might bring
When I'm close to her, I know how it must feel to be a king
I pray I can make her as happy as me
Then she will finally see
Just how much I really love her

Jeffery Shatwell

The Saranac River Flows

As I sit in my cabin where the Saranac flows,
I often wonder if anyone knows,
Just where it comes and where it goes.
The love of nature on its banks
Of greatest beauty it surely ranks.
I kneel and pray to give God thanks,
As she flows along here and there.
A view of white face is in the air
Along it flows to Franklin Falls dam,
It twists and turns like a little old clam.
On into the narrows and Woodrif bay
If you have been there, I am sure you would want to stay.
Of such beauty and peace is more than I can say
Please dear God keep this forever wild,
I want to remember it just as a child,
When her waters finally reaches the sea
I hope today and always it will be free.

Gertrude Chamberlin

Never Said

I never said I'd be what you want me to be
I never said I'd be all things to all people
I never said I'd be patient and kind and easy to know

I said I'd live in Lebanon and eat tabbouleh and baba ghanoush
I said I'd read "Crazy Jane. . ." by the fire and drink Irish coffee
I said the owls on my farm would cry, "Ke-e-e-sh! Ke-e-e-sh!"
   not "Who - Who - Who - Who!"
I said I'd be whatever it takes

I never said I'd take Buddhist temples in Bangkok
   or shoot mirrored office buildings in Hong Kong
I never said I'd snap wrinkled widows in Sidon
I never imagined a living room gallery

I never said I'd write poetry about the Great Kirghiz Khan
I never said I'd jet to Jordan and Jedda and try on cultures like skin
I never knew I'd have to travel so far from Taylor Valley
I never knew I'd have to scale the Alps before I saw the mountain
   in my own backyard

Jane Cass

Untitled

Death is coming or so it seems
I have lost the memories of all my dreams
All good things are in the past
My next dream could be my last
When I'm gone I want to leave behind a memory
Will you promise to always remember me?
I am sorry that I made you so angry and mad
But your harsh words left me so terribly sad
The fire within me will never again burn
And now I have nowhere left to turn.

Amber Piel

A Christmas Thank You

"Dear Mom and Dad,
I never knew....but you were always there.

In weakness and stubbornness of youth,
I erected walls and shut you out.

Did I change? When?
How did I grow strong enough to let you in?

Does youth always resist familial vulnerability?
Does adult compassion give birth from childish rebellion?

I will not speculate or dwell upon missed opportunities and
years lost for really knowing you—they are gone.

Please forgive our sad past. Rejoice with me now
in the awareness of our unconditional acceptance and love.

I FINALLY lowered my walls and found you...
waiting for me. Thanks!"

Donna Walker

Jealousy

Is it that I want you to see or rather
I need you to want me
A maze of sexual obsessions
Lure me into the shallowness of this phrase - Jealousy -
A primal ritual of instinct
to desire whatever you possess
A yearning to become one flesh
when your touch is for another
A lust to become one mind
when your thoughts begin to wander
So easily provoke, so hard to
explain, for it is better to know
who you are than what I seek
Pause for a moment to ponder
what could be the cause,
what could be the why,
Our vanity falls to insecurity,
Our innocence falls prey to
the selfishness of a phrase
Jealousy...

John V. O'Flaherty

Untitled

While daydreaming, a flash sparked. I must write!
I need to be poet. Oh, that I might.
Panic and anxiety to me came.
Woe! The thoughts and theme were one and the same.
How do I voice them with verve, love and care?
Good grief! Was my intellect not aware?
I searched the caverns of my mind over
For the muse of rhyme; to grasp, to hold her.
Alas! I guessed it was not meant to be.
Where were the fruits of my bountiful tree?
To my surprise, the key was bright as day.
Scribe these very words, seeking else to say.
So I did. Behold, the poetry done!
Now I can rejoice. Indeed, that was fun.

Joseph J. Bloyder

To Protect And Serve

As I approach you look at me
I can see the fear in your eyes
But why do you fear me?
As I get closer you clinch your purse,
If you only knew, I took the oath to protect and serve.
Yes, the one you fear will give his life for you.

Allan B. Samson

362

My Two Fathers

Memories of my earthly father reveal how much
  I love him.
I wanted to be with him, help him, walk with him
  and hold his hand.
I wanted to obey him, please him and would be hurt
  if he was angry with me.
And when it was time for him to come home from
  work, I would anxiously wait for him to open
  the door of our home.

May I love you Heavenly Father as my earthly father.
May I want to be in your presence, walking with
  you and allowing your hand to lead me so that
  you may not be angry or hurt by my sinfulness.
May your word saturate my thoughts so that others
  may see a difference within me.
And may I anxiously wait for your coming and the
  day when you will open the door to your home.

    Grace Hulstedt

The First Snow of the Season

The first snow of the season, fell last night.
I looked out in wonder, at this beautiful sight.
There was no wind, all things were serene,
and everything out there, was spotless and clean.

There was a stillness, in the air,
not a sound could be heard anywhere.
The blanket of snow had covered all things,
This wonderful sight, made one want to sing.

Children loved it, when snow they would see.
They would jump up and down, and shout with glee.
Out came their sleds, down the hill they would go,
there was nothing better, than all this snow.

As I looked out, at this new fallen snow,
I knew that soon, it would quickly go.
It would be trampled by so many feet,
]and cars driving by, their schedules to keep.

Clean white snow, is like the beginning of life,
when all seems so rosy, and things are all right.
Then trouble sets in, it's like snow turned to slush,
your loved one is gone, your heart is crushed.

    Jennie Wiora

I'm Getting Bigger Now!

I'm getting bigger now, my mommy told me.
I looked in the mirror just to check and see.
Here I am standing up tall.
I remember when I could only crawl.
Well, there's my face, it's smiling back at me.
I now have teeth where space used to be.
I have two arms and I can catch a ball.
I make my mommy mad when I put my fingers on the wall.
My legs seem long and kind of out of place.
But I know how to tie my own shoelace.
I now have feelings both good and bad.
I like the happy feelings more than the sad.
Sometimes new things are a little scary to me.
A hug and a kiss can make it all history.
Today is my first day, I am starting school.
I can reach the drinking fountain without standing on a stool.
WOW! My mommy was right, I am a bigger me!
I'm still standing here looking, and I like what I see.

    Carol Morton

Midnight Mystery

After dark,
I look up at the night sky and wonder,
I see the haze around the moon and ponder about other planets.
I hear the melodic murmur of night owls and question nature,
Why do some animals stay awake at night?
Why do wolves howl at the moon?
The light glimmer through the tall pines set shadows over the
mountains land,
As I see all of this I think about all creation.
Why is the moon round?
Why are people smart and animals aren't?
All of these questions flow through my mind like a rushing river,
as I think about life.

    Daniel Dickey

The Midnight Ride Of The Lorelton Fire Drill

Hurrah for 12 A.M.!
I like the LOUD klaxon sound!
Whenever the P.M. ends,
To the TOWERS we are sent.

Later, home again we go
Once more to bed or to TV,
Safe again and happy to see,
Always we are glad to shout
The olde LORE school, inside and out.

Judy Stout, bless your kind, kind, heart
We need you there and here thou art
Even now planning another wee hours event
Which Jeff will welcome, along with Kent.

And so we will all pile out
Short, tall, small and stout
To the TOWERS again
This time better at 3 A.M.!

    Gordon D. Patterson Jr.,
    former 4th grade student at Lore School now resident at Lorelton

Remembering

Lord I pray, forgive wrongs of my past
I know you hold my future now,
Keep me from going back some how,
As long as my life shall last.

Give me love and understanding,
To share with my friends you have given.
Keep watch over me and guide me tenderly,
Reach for my hand and walk with me.

With all my heart, I say I'm sorry
If I speak my mind more than I should.
Sometimes when my friends let me down
And a smiling face can not be found.

As I start my day each morning,
Show me how to walk in your light.
Share your peace with me night or day,
That I may give thanks when I kneel to pray.

    Gloria Ray

Wind Swept

As each morning dawn to evening dusk betrays,
Hereupon continuing hourglass wind swept days,
Thereupon realizing materially wind swept dreams,
Whereupon using awakening wind swept minds,
Oh, keep us in neverending wind swept times,
And, hold fast to the treasure-trove of memories.

    Ann D'Alessandro

The 3 W's

WAYS
I know what happened to you is so bad,
And if you had your way you would want to be dead.
I dread each day to see you this way
And if I had my say,
You would have your way.
WHERE
Where do we go from here?
Is it close, far, or near?
I don't know, I guess of fear,
Cause I know death may be near.
Yet I go on knowing in fear
That I may be gone with the year.
WHY
Why did this have to happen to you and me?
I thought I went through enough with your Father, Mother, and me.
Now it comes down to you and me.
Can I have the strength to hold to what I'm supposed to be.
Lord knows I'll try, but sometimes I want to die.

Genie Staggs

Where Did You Go

I saw you there, staring at me.
I know I saw you, where can you be.
'Twas it just a vision, a dream or a prayer,
That I wanted so badly for you to be there.
To see the smile upon your face,
To live in the memory of your infinite grace.
Oh where did you go, I know it was you.
If you care at all, come back into view.
Let me feast my eyes, upon your body strong,
Take in your warmth, before you are gone.
Oh please reappear, don't leave me like this,
Come give me a hug, a warm tender kiss.
Then you may go.

Izella L. Satterfield

Ode To A Tall Pear Tree

He wore his Air Force uniform,
I knew he would soon be leaving.
We searched for a place to be alone.
Down in the meadow close to my home
We found it beneath a tall pear tree
On that spring night in nineteen forty-three.

If there was a better place to be, we didn't care about it
As we spread his Air Force blanket, beneath the tall pear tree.
At first, I thought about prying eyes,
But soon it really didn't matter,
All I cared about was he and I
Making love there on that blanket, beneath the tall pear tree.

This was the beginning of a love that lasted fifty years.
Now I often walk down into that meadow
And stand beneath the splendid tall pear tree.
Now he is gone and I'm alone.
But the memories linger on
As I wipe away the tears.

I see two red birds perched on a limb.
I think how lucky for them making love in the tall tree.

Anna Lee Kyrkpatrick

Memories Run Through

So many things running through my mind.
I just don't know what I'm trying to find.

My thoughts, I hide.
I just can't let you see my other side.

For if I did my heart might melt.
Over flowing with pain I've felt.

I only wanted that one wish,
But instead it ended just like this.

We both said good-bye,
But yet I still had to cry.

A part of me was dying
And inside crying.

You'll never understand how hard it is to hide
I've still got to try to keep it inside.

So laying down, memories running through
I'll cry knowing you never even had a clue.

Christina Parker

God's Music

In the wee small hours of the night
    I heard the lilting song of a mockingbird.
His repertoire included notes borrowed from Kinfolk,
    Lifting my spirit to heights unspeakable.
And I knew that it was yet another way
    God used to let me know of His love for me!

As I lay there enjoying every sweet note of that song;
    In the stillness of the night
I became aware of other musical sounds in God's symphony.
    The rustle of the breeze in the trees,
    The call of a frog that seemed to appear from nowhere,
Because God was sending gentle rain to water His greenery.

Right then, I sent forth my prayer of thanks and praise
    To the Father of all the Universe,
That, because of His great love for me
    I can enjoy His handiwork every moment of my life.

Claire Ross

You

I feel your warm breath on my skin
I hear the rustle of linen as you move carefully beside me
Trying so hard not to wake me
I keep my eyes closed to savor this feeling
I reach across the pillow to touch you, but you're not there

I see you walk across the room
You stand beside the window, gazing at the street below
Shadows play upon your face in the moonlight
I cannot quite see your eyes from here
You face is turned away from me
You don't know I am watching you
You stand so still so close to me
But you seem so far away
I wonder what you're thinking

You move away from the window
My eyes are closed, I don't want you to know
My sleep has been broken by thoughts of you
You sit on the edge of the bed, I think you are watching me
I keep my eyes closed to savor this feeling

Hillary Gould

Innocence

Led Zeppelin screaming a big legged woman ain't got no soul,
I have a soul, not apparent at the time
To any of the boys having their way with me
Appearing happy, at fifteen
Yet so sad, screaming within
Unknowing of the harm they did
I just laid there as the next would enter my body
My soul a virgin never touched — a lock in which
The key they did not own,
This I would not give them
Too scared to say yes or no, never giving permission or refusal!
Appearing to like me, oh they loved me, just not in public
I was always recognized in the halls
They wanted me
My innocence
My gift to them — everyday it was not me but my shell
My soul will be a gift to myself
And the finder of the key

Heidi Rumph

My Son

I have a son who won't do right
I have a son who was a star so bright.

I have a son who has no fears
I have a son who throws me dares.

I have a son who is now eighteen
I have a son who turned me mean.

I have a son who was raised by a single parent
I have a son who is never congruent.

I have a son who thinks he knows it all
I have a son who (with that attitude) will one day fall.

I have a son who treats me like dirt
I have a son who doesn't care who he hurts.

I have a son who uses me
I have a son who I rarely see.

I have a son who wonders why I've changed
I have a son who now thinks I'm quite strange.

I have a son who I know no more
I have a son who (I know) one day the police will come for.

I have a son who is a sloven
I have a son who, no matter what, I'll keep on loving.

Gail Veronica Brooks

Illusion

In the park I was walking on a night so warm and clear, wishing
I had the power to bring you here.
Knowing I'm human and things don't happen that way, still thinking
in my mind I would like to see you this day.
Sitting by the water I saw a picture of you, wiping my eyes saying
this couldn't be true.
As I looked a little closer the water seem to begin to move, then I
started asking myself what does this prove.
An illusion was about to happen but I didn't care, to have you in my
arms I would give anything to have you there.
You began to look real to me your skin was very wet, maybe my mind
put you there in an imaginary net.
You came out the water as a mermaid, a goddess, or a queen, strutting
your nude body creating a sinuous scene.
This is the moment I always thought of... the right time at last, I
want to make love to you now, now before this time pass.
As water rolled down your body from your lips to your knees, I
enjoyed catching the drops until I felt you were pleased.
When the passion was over I felt the illusion fading away, maybe I'll
come back tomorrow to see you another day.

Ivory Shelton Jr.

"Too Old To Cry"

I guess I never realized how lonely I could be,
I guess I never thought you'd get rid of me.
Your love was never sweeter than the day you said goodbye.
You'll never know how much it hurts, 'cause I'm too old to cry.

If I knew then what I know now, you'd still be kissing me,
instead there's someone else's lips where my lips long to be.
I say hello and wish you the best each time you pass by.
But you'll never know how much it hurts 'cause I'm too old to cry.

Your love was never sweeter than the day you walked away.
When I can't sleep, I don't count sheep, I count the mistakes I've made.
I can't believe you left me,
no matter how much I try.
You'll never know how much it hurts 'cause I'm too old to cry.

It seems so strange to be alone.
I thought we'd never part.
The tears that fall you won't see, 'cause they're falling from my heart.
I guess I'll go through life without love.
I'd guess I'd rather die,
Than let you know how much it hurts, 'cause I'm too old to cry.

Amberley Wright

The Days Between

It's the hardest thing when we part,
I get this aching inside my heart,
That reminds me it may be a while,
'Till I hold you close, 'till I see you smile.

It hurts too much just to think,
That we'll be apart and I'm on the brink,
Of losing composure and breaking down,
And going somewhere I can't be found,
'Till I can finally be back with you,
There's nothing I'd rather do.

Not a day goes by that I don't wish
To hear your voice, to feel your kiss,
The only way I endure these days between,
Is knowing there'll be a day I'll see
you again.

Anna K. Howell

I Still Love You

I sat down today, the first time in a while that
I gave myself a break.
I realized something today,
something that I have been denying
for what seems like an eternity.
You are gone.
You are no longer mine yet you are all that I want.
But you are still gone.
All is silent.
Although the silence between us will never be broken,
I can still hear your sweet voice.
But all is still silent.
I am alone.
There are others all around me
and I feel your presence.
But I am still alone.
I love you.
I dream of you all the time
and you tell me I must go on.
But I still love you.

Dawn Lavender

365

Reflections

I passed a mirror on a wall,
I gasped at the reflection that I saw.

Someone who looked hollow and cold,
No longer young not exactly old.

The tears that have spilled down that face,
Stopped by laughter in just a trace.

I see the heartbreak along with the hurt,
I see the pain that lies inside.

I shut my eyes to the figure before me,
I shield my heart from that pain.

I open my eyes to a matching tear,
Use all the strength from the vision in the mirror.

Jane Clayton-Cornell

Emotionally Unstable

Nervously I let my eyes wander
I felt your presence
A touch upon my finger

The musty smell of cigarettes
A scent I learned to forget

I long to hear my name roll of your tongue
Those three pretty syllables
A masquerade of what is yet to come

Through your eyes I steal secrets from your heart
You haven't found what's behind my facade

Your ignorance hurts me
The intellectual side of me screams
I feel stupid in your shadow

Angélique L. Emile

"Precious Moments"

As we kissed each other for the first time,
I... felt the soft, white sands of
  Siesta Key beneath my feet;

  Saw you wading in the waters of
  Waikiki as the sun set within;

  Heard the soothing sounds of sea gulls and
  Surf from all the beaches I'd been before;

  Smelled a fantastic forest of flowers
  In late spring, early summer;

  Tasted your precious lips of
  Parignon, aged to perfection.

May I kiss you again?

James Patrick Wilbanks

Leaving

Saying goodbye to my very close friends,
I felt tears forming in my eyes, one by one.
I got in the car
I closed my eyes,
It was as if I was leaving forever.
I just wanted to shout, "I don't wanna leave!
Let me stay!"
Tears were now streaming down my face.
The car started drifting away.
My hands were pressed against the window,
looking back; watching my house,
friends, and my old life fainting slowly away.

Abby Hertz

"Call Upon Me"

On the day you found out about it
I felt the pain you felt, I cried with you
I longed to reach out from heaven, gently
wrap my arms around you
and comfort you
I wanted to wipe the tears away, tell
you everything was going to be okay
But I couldn't because you didn't call
upon my name
oh, but you can now and I will take
the hurt and pain away
For I am God, I can do anything
I died on the cross for you
I took all the stripes on my back for you
So just say my name and pour out
all your feelings to me
For I will listen to everything
you have to say
and then if you believe in me
I will take all your hurt away

Joetta Valdez

Resurrecting A Secret

Living up on this mountain - up so high
I feel like I could touch the sky!

The moon becomes so intoxicating - almost exhilarating
Crescendoing
Like a shooting star.

This hot August morning
Lulls me rather than disturbs me.

The noonday sun is suddenly on the run
Pouring richly through me.

Melting into silence as I
Listen to the steeple bells ring.
Hindsight - newborn sunrise -
Promising me a brighter spring.

And although I'm far away -
I'll resurrect this one little secret...
  As I live up on this mountain,
  Up so high - I exile into the night -
  To the top, top - toppest point of the mountain
  And quietly - with bright, bright eyes -
  I whisper your name into the lit - up night sky.

Dianna L. Starkweather

Am I?

Bumped and moving in a crowded sea,
I feel life all around, but no one touches me.
Faces zoom in, then out.
Barely anyone notices, though I shout, I shout!

Down from the heights, I marvel at the city lights.
Alas! No response, acknowledgement is returned nor received.
I must return to the deafening quiet once again.
Is there not one I can truly call friend?

Though exhausted from my efforts, my fears, my loneliness;
I desperately search for the portal, try to bridge the gap.
I must enter, be accepted. I want to belong!
What can I do? Who in this universe have I wronged?

I will reflect again, stare deep within.
Complete my penance for whatever the sin.
Time continues to slip away for getting it right.
Is my destiny to become but a shadow of the night?

Edward J. Dixon Jr.

Death Angel

The death angel is knocking on my door
I feel it deep within my core.

My mother is waiting to let the death angel in
She has long past paid for all her sins.

She fought a hard battle all her life
She longs for peace, an end to her strife.

All her treasures have gone by the way
She feels a burden wherever she stays.

She's living in her memories of days gone by
She's waiting and watching though she knows not why.

All she wants is a warm smile and
a loving touch
From those she loves so much.

Lord I leave her in your care as I tuck her
in for the night
I pray you will let me see her smile
in the early morning light.

Judith Phillips

Reality

I am now alone
I feel as if you've left me here to die
So every day I think of you and then begin to cry

All my fears and all my dreams
in you I did confide
And all these things you took with you
my hopes, my love...my pride

We had our time together
Now that world's a memory
We joked, laughed, and talked but now
You won't acknowledge me

Where are you now?
Together for eternity is what I thought we'd be
I was so blind, but now I realize
you're not in love with me

Reality is the bullet
in my wounded heart
Only a word-but I can see
That's what's keeping us apart

Blanca I. Cintron

Great Soul

With prayers on and fear gripping me,
I enter the room with a crest fallen face.

There she lies with her eyes closed,
looks like she's sleeping,
but the sights set me weeping.

A touch of mine and a call of "Grandma"
Makes her eyes blink, and fix her gaze at me.

Tears stroll out marking her happiness,
her trembling hands hold my petite face.

She is sick and weak, only whispers come out,
her eyelids flutter fast
and come to a sudden rest.

Gripping her hands I bend my head,
and thrust my mind
in praise of this noble soul.

Chandran Manickavasagam

My College Lad

From babyhood till home was left behind
I crept each night into his room, wondering
If drafts, perhaps, or covers strewn I'd find.
'Twas sweet to stand and see Nature sublime
Change boy to man; lightly I'd touch his brow
And turn away, knowing that naught stays time.

In college now the lad is far away;
And I must creep into his room just in thoughts,
Through which, I feel, to him I can convey
My prayer he grow in wisdom and in grace.
He seems as near as when I tucked the quilt
Around his form and kissed his precious face.

I know at last it's mind that keeps us near
To our loved ones, far nearer than body can.
For this did Christ leave earth to reappear
A spirit soul, that closer He might stand
To those He loved, yea even yet more close
Than when he touched them with a healing hand?

Halkaline Kirk Bergsten

Dissevered

(for Olga)
As I wander through this weary land,
I come across a bird, a tree, a flower,
And I'm reminded of your gentle hand,
The stars o'erhead that sparkled grand:
Oh, to go back to such sweet hour!

But how shall I remember Love:
By the currents of the roaring river
Or the smooth silent soar of the dove
That circles high as I search Above?
My soul turns small and shivers.

And what shall happen when memories fade
To new delights that replace the old?
I know too well that Yesterday is made,
But for it, Tomorrow I soon would trade
Just hoping for some stronger hold.

Sometimes I wonder if I'm not wrong
That Time's pace has been a little fast:
So quickly all whiles we shared are gone.
Of the opera we are but a simple song,
But to you I shall remain steadfast!

Ben Bentrup

The Vision

Descending in all her majestic beauty,
I catch a glimpse of her glorious profile.
Gold and tender - stretching on for eternity.
Her colors run from bright and brilliant, to faded and opaque.
So few times have I seen her power,
I am overwhelmed and mesmerized by the sight -
There stretching from one side of the horizon clear to the other -
It is now that she makes herself visible to me,
I fall on my knees in honor of her presence, and
Feel honored to witness this.
Once again, amidst a brutal storm,
The bright star we call the sun sets and
A full rainbow appears -
It is Mother Nature in all her power, grace and beauty.

Jenny Shelton

About Partings

Only muteness from the strangled chords,
I cannot speak, I can't afford
  Good-bye.
Severance like unwelcome abscision,
  Good-bye.
A hand wave parts the cloud of rue
While glassy tears diffuse the view,
A hollow heart and wordless lips, an
obscure fission,
  Good-bye.
A bottomless place but brimming with images
like a mirror.
  Good-bye
Reflects the breaking of connections.
There is no twilight, only darkness and light.
  Good-bye
But I take you with me.
   Elizabeth Segedin

I Am The Ghost

I am oblivion...
I am obscure...
I am everything... yet,
I am nothing...

Divine, eternal, abysmal...
Devoid, ephemeral, shallow...

Void of solidity, I seep through every corner of consciousness.
  Unnoticed... Underestimated...

The Ghost I am...

I shall leave my mark upon the sun for all to acknowledge and remember
  me by...
For my solitude has provided me with what I need to create my own
  reality...
For without it I would not have survived to this day...
Don't need your religion... Don't need your paradise...
I am the incarnation of fire...
and I need nothing more than what I can fathom within the depths of my
  own mind...

Oblivion I am...
Obscure I am...
Everything I am... yet.
Nothing I am...
I am the ghost... and your reality, values and one-sided opinions are
  mine to toy with...
   Chris Carlucci

Union

Apollo you sliced me in two.
I am empty.
All that I am is half of what I could be,
Half of what is.

Apollo, I pray, unite me.
My lover and I will embrace;
Matching emptiness to emptiness,
Becoming whole, complete,
One.
   Jorge Mayo

To The Children Of The Night

To the children of the night.
I am calling out to you.
Have sympathy for just one lone wolf.
He is blindly staggering in the painful light of day.
Trapped, until the key of eternity is upheld.
His fledgling peers are unfortunate to be so deaf
to the music of the night.
But, oh! how they unknowingly suffocate him.
Unknowingly they torment him.
Unknowingly they kill him.
His misery is his knowledge.
In the depth of his being an unbeknownst seed has sprouted.
It endlessly perils from the lack of nourishment.
The dominion of the dark side.
Don't ignore my pleas.
Just one of your immortal kisses.
Just one cold touch.
And you will process my soul.
My absolute.
   David Trausch

Man Of Two Worlds "The Inter-Racial Inter-Ethnic Child"

I am a man of two worlds
I am a child of two cultures
I am the brightness of day
I am the darkness of night
Love is what created me
Hate is what is killing me

  Understand me for I am a mere child facing the world—alone
  Longing for acceptance and in search of a true—home
  Unable to speak the tongue of one of my worlds
  I am ridiculed, shunned—labeled of fake
  The other of my worlds gazes upon my golden brown skin in fear
  Exclaiming in a thunderous manner that I do not belong
  At times I feel as if I cannot go on, but I must

   I was created by the love and the unity of a man and a woman
   I am the child of two colliding races, cultures, and worlds
   I am a bridge that spans together these two worlds.

    I beg thee do not let another tear drop fall, instead accept me
    for who I am
    I am a man of two worlds
    I am a man of two cultures. Hate is what is killing me
   Federico Valadez Jr.

What Should Have Been...

My hopes and dreams I so willingly sacrificed for you;
I always knew the joy you took in seeing me so blue.
Still, I want you to want me; I want the love I am due.
I would sacrifice it all, if you'd tell me we'll never be through.

All that I've done to retain your love, so many plights;
A love that was never mine, too many lost days and nights.
I chose to believe your credo, your wants over my rights.
So what do I do now? Now that I know we'll never reach the heights.

You've taught me well, I'm wiser now. I see it's on my soul you dine;
All that I've done to retain what should have never been mine.
I give it all back to you, these years of misery are thine.
Now that I've weathered the storm, it's time for me to shine.

What we have is over. I wish you well, but I cannot stay.
It will be tough, I know, but I'll be stronger come what may.
Because I will finally be leading life my own way.
I won't be your victim anymore, yours is a price I don't have to pay.
For I've found the hope of a better love today.
My own.
   Alex Colby

Now I Too Must Die

My job is done, the war is won, and all may know the truth,
I aimed, I shot, I fired. Now there's nothing left to shoot.
I've seen men cry. I've seen men die.
I've seen man's share of pain,
But I'd never thought, I'd be the one,
whom all would put to blame.
Some say I shot him purposely, that's why I tried to run.
But I swear I did not mean to, when I shot him with my gun.
A taken life from my country,
is all because of I,
My lack of responsibility,
has caused one man to die.
May this soldier rest in peace, and might he please forgive,
for it's not fair that he is dead, and I the one to live.
But I'll see him at the crossroads, for so guilty I have felt.
So I guess there's one solution,
I will have to kill myself.
And now I pull the trigger, with just one thing on my mind,
I killed my country's soldier,
and now I too must die.

Dante Lee

From The Book Of The Black Crow

see that Scarecrow in the sun's shadow-
hung there as though a trophy from a battle,
i heard Him breathe with the strength of a "coward,"
until He bowed His head after three painful hours.

the black birds had lashed out His side.
one crowed three times that He was stuffed and just a lie.
"He's not really the Farmer of this land," they said,
as they dug holes in both His feet and His hands.

for three days the crows stayed gathered at a distance-
to find the Scarecrow's demise was only a pretense.
there! there! the Farmer rose from behind a wall of stone-
to take back the land; to take back His own.

Julie Bowring

Room With A View

The walls, bathed in an opal luminescence,
hum with quivering expectation and meet the floor
with a hard, disappointed thud.
Once again they rise, reaching for the Ceiling of Destiny.
Dreams floating above all reality;
Hope makes another sinewy journey to Truth.

Heather Clardy

Think On These Things

Sometimes I think
How very much like
A bunch of pearl onions
My daughters are.
All have lovely, delicate, thin skins
With layer upon layer of complex emotions,
Variations of sentiments.
Each is firm in her resolve,
Adamant in her opinions,
Impenetrable in her innermost feelings,
Unyielding in determination
And absolutely sure of the love of her father.
Just as the onion is all onion,
Each daughter is strictly all female.
To uncover just one layer of their intricate makeup,
Makes me cry.

Flora Adams

"Daddy's Love"

Dad you mean so much to us, and we just want to say
How much we wish you happiness on this your special day

We have so many memories of cherished childhood days
When you and mom made our house a home and loved us come what may

It's the little things you did for us, that stay forever in our minds
Like five pairs of perfectly polished shoes on Sunday mornings we'd find

Also on the T.V. top, five one dollar bills in a row
One-tenth of your hard earned income and off to church we'd go

Although you worked in a cotton mill and took your lunch in a jar
You always taught us to just do our best and be proud of who we are

They say that if you spare the rod, you'll surely spoil the kid
But all it took was that look from you and we were sorry for what we did

So, today as we pause and honor you on this your special day
As we bow our heads and close our eyes and we begin to pray....

For fathers here and everywhere we thank the good Lord above
But most of all we thank Him for you and for our "Daddy's Love!"

Judy Rogers West

Something In Me

Something in me can't ignore—
how much I miss you.

Something in me can't forget—
how it once felt to kiss you.

Something in the way we talked,
the hopes and times we've shared—

Reminds me that in our own way—
we loved and even cared.

Something in me keeps repeating—
there are good times still ahead.

Something in my heart feels,
there are fond words to be said.

Something in me senses—
we've passed through our darkest weather.

And something in me keeps saying—
why can't we get back together?

Corinna Robinson

Untitled

How many deaths to make "History"?
How many slaves for a failing "Civilization"
consumed by drugs, bribery and their retinue of defects?
How many cases of "Sida Mental" for our
factitious powers...?
How many heretics for a Church, C.A.R. which
earthly advantages and a hierarchy of
small filthy corrupt the faith
in our God...?
How many humiliated men for a little hope
in Life?...
How much compassion and understanding for
a human being debased, diminished by Society?...
How many yearnings, gestures, stewed over words
"To Be Loved"?...

Questions without answer
Questions eternal
For all life formed with a back bone,
For all mankind for whom the goal is man

Jean-Elie Gilles

Teacher To Child

Oh, my child you are so meek,
How I long your heart to seek,
There is beauty in the mind of every child
I can see that beauty when you smile.

When you come to take your seat,
Then your eyes and mine will meet.
To hold your hand in mine, is a joy to me untold.
When you speak to me, your thoughts, to me unfold.

To the child that wants to know, how the buds on fruit trees grow.
Then my answer to him would be,
Heavenly Father helps you see.
With all his love and all his care,
We can all be angels fair.
Like the fruit trees in the spring, good fruits we all must bring.

Don't you know my child, my love, that you came from up above.
With all God's wondrous help,
I've been called to guide your step.

Some might say their class is best, but, I know from all the rest,
That you, are more than sweet to me, you are beautiful too, you see.
First to reach you, then to teach you, is my goal.

Helen F. Price

Little Green Bottle

Little green bottle on the strand
How did you wash to this watered sand?
Who blew your curves and filled you up?
What lips drank the fill-ed cup?

Did your life emerge way upstream?
Had you any questing dream?
How long have you lain in this sullied sand
Before my eyes asked "Why" and "And"?
Does it mirth your heart and soul
To see the Eddys take their toll?

I lift you up and launch you in the stream
Once again you have a dream.
Little green bottle, with just a glance,
I gifted you a second chance,
And when you hear that siren's call
You may still win it all!

Think not, alas, of only cost
But loving less the more is lost.
Better yet the love that fails
Than hearts imprisoned, bound in jails.

Hal Johnson

Concept Of Singularity

Too many times I ask the wrong questions.
"How can you love a fool?"
She said back at me
"You ask the wrong question."
The she molded by mind.
From that day on I asked no questions
Unless it was with me in mind.

The next time I saw her
I asked her a question
"How can I not love a fool?"
She turned at me
And gave me a smile
And said, "Now you're starting to learn."

I went my own way
And asked many questions
The way I had been taught to do.
Surprising the others; I was no longer the fool.
I dropped to my knees,
And gave praises of thanks
For the love I found within.

David Kagie

How?

How can I tell you that I'm in love with you
How can I tell you I'm falling for you
How can I tell you that I think that you are
the one and only one for me
How can I say that I want you for me and no one else
How can I say that I want us to be together forever
and never be separated so I'm going to just come out
and say it....
I want you to love me not as a friend but as two
lovers deeply in love I want you to stay with me and
put up with me and never leave me
I want what ever would make you happy when we're
together and promise me that we'll always be in
deeply in love together.

Iannette Velez

Butterfly

Butterfly
  Hovering with wings poised to fly;
    Free from the cumbersome life of a worm;
    Free, at last, from the dark cocoon.

Jesus Christ
  Lifted up through the clouds in the sky;
    Free from the cumbersome life of a man;
    Free, at last, from the darkened tomb.

You and I
  Lifted, by Christ, from the miry clay;
    Free, at last, from sin and strife;
    Free to live the victorious life,
    Like the butterfly.

Doris Faust McGuinn

What The Statue Of Liberty Means To Us Today

Tribute to
Hope
Eternal

Standing in the harbor of an awesome metropolis
This lady, a symbol of hopes, dreams, and liberty,
Awaits all who come to our land, United States of America.
The lighted torch is held high to show the way—
Undaunted by the storms and tribulations in life that
Everyone encounters, whether young or old, rich or poor.

On the tablet which our lady holds is our declaration,
Fundamental in establishing and upholding the freedoms we hold dear.

Love, liberty, and law must combine efforts
In maintaining what our forefathers initiated for us.
Before us lie the many challenges, as well as the obstacles.
Encouragement from our lady is omnipotent,
Rendering strength and diligence needed in our endeavors.
The Statute of Liberty, a gift of friendship from France, remains
Youthful, giving courage to all who gaze upon her, hoping
  that God will bless America forever.

Bernice H. Palazzo

Untitled

Warriors are beaten
heroes are hung by society
using death as examples for paths for the future
the future is set because
it's already been lived
get rid of the past and
take a chance
individuality leads to dead ends
togetherness, teams, and unity
is the way to overcome the fear of man
and the past

Damon J. Billingsley

I Dream of Him

I dream of Him
Holding me, loving me
I dream of him
Speaking passionately, caressing me with his sweet voice
I dream of him
Touching me in no way any other has
I dream of him
Kissing my time worn and tired body
I dream of him
Laying in my arms listening to my heart beat only for him
I dream of him
Kissing me in no way any other has
I dream of him
Loving me, loving him
I dream of him
Love

Heather Lunsford

"God"

God, more constant than day turning to night.
Holding far more steady than the beat within
the heart.

His devotion stretches across an never ending
reach; with understanding that exceeds the
incredible.

God, the perpetual omnipotent eminence of the
universe, reigning with all rank and authority
over heaven and earth.

All Hail! give reverence and praise unto God;
to whom alone is worthy of:

Ann J. Marshall

Which Lane?

The snail's so timid and content, below his shiny shell.
His world is peaceful and quite slow, but pleasant just as well.

Should we ride upon his coach, observe the beauty about...
Or travel upon the spider's back, and take the faster route?

Work all day to spin our web, soon filled with innocent prey.
Suck out their blood, their liveliness, getting wealthier all the way.

What a life that spider lives, he feeds our hungriest frenzy.
Feared by all the other insects, but admired for independence.

The snail he is more subtle, he lives out every day,
Wondering what enjoyments next, not concerned with status or pay.

Noticed not is the quiet slug, and care not a bit does he,
For who are all the other bugs, they're no delicacy.

He will continue the slower route, as sand runs through the glass.
Enthralled with every moment, as his calmness comes to last.

The spider or the snail, the journey a tough choice,
whichever road, we each must choose,
and in that life we should rejoice.

Catherine Baker

Untitled

Gentleman on my mail route
Had a big pine tree he wanted out
Missing the shade I thought a pity
Made a marker with this ditty
"Big old tree was doing fine
Fir its shade I truly pine"
Gentleman thought the marker appropriate
Called me the mail man poet Laureate

Gerald C. Wackerfuss

The Touch

The touch of The Master's Hand will turn your life around...
His Spirit will come upon you like the wind without a sound!

The touch of the Master's Hand will create you anew...
His Spirit knows all you have done and all you will do!

The touch of the Master's Hand will bring perfect peace...
His Spirit fills your heart with joy that will never cease!

The touch of The Master's Hand will calm your deepest fear...
His Spirit is The Comforter, The Helper, who is always near!

The touch of The Master's Hand will save you eternally...
His Spirit is the only truth whose knowledge sets you free!

The touch of The Master's Hand will allow your eyes to see...
His Spirit lifts the veil of all who are blinded spiritually!

The touch of The Master's Hand is the gift of God's grace...
His Spirit will dwell within your being so life you may face!

The touch of The Master's Hand comes only from God above...
His Spirit will abide in your heart, evidence of His love!

Judith M. Perkins

Restless Nocturne

Warm is the night.
  High the moon guards with its light.
This is the time for lovers
  To capture the stars, fling back the bars,
Seize love's swift flight.

True love is spring.
  'Dawn of affection wakening.
My love will go unheeded.
  Dark night seems to pall; fog covers all.
Envy is king.

Light up the sky,
  So I can sing and not cry,
While I lie scheming, longing,
  And taste bitter wine for love not mine.
Wry lullaby.

Mem'ries still creep.
  Just let me dream and not weep.
Cradle me with your night songs.
  Blow gently, O breeze, rustle the leaves.
Sing me to sleep...deep sleep.

Bonnie Allen Schmidt

Echos Of Summer

The winter beach is sad and still.
High above the gulls call shrill.
The sand is smooth - no footprints left
The beach is silent, cold, bereft
Of all the shouts and noisy clamor
Of a lovely sun kissed summer.
A restless tide leaves shells upon the sands,
Uncollected by children's sunbronzed hands.

I still hear the laughter of many old friends;
And the whisper of lovers as day nears end.
It is sad to leave the lonely beach behind.
The enchanting summer still lives in my mind.
The waves repeat their pounding murmur
But all I can hear are echoes of summer

Joan Millard

371

Your Little Boy

You laugh! In credulous! You yawn,
He's chasing butterflies on the lawn.
And following every step you take
While others dream, they're not awake!

How swift the time, this little lad
You held him in your arms, the first you had.
A miracle; almost, so you thought
A gift so wondrous, God had wrought!

The years go by so very fast
And childhood days that ought to last;
But dads and moms they never will
Quite understand the love, the thrill

Of seeing him grow to manhood strong,
How could it be, it wasn't long
That he was just a little lad,
This precious gift; this son you had.

And so life moves for every one
He isn't just for us; we shun
The thought, too soon, he's on his way,
This little boy, you had, just yesterday.

Helen Bazet Ostheimer

Thanksgiving Wishes

They really talk of giving thanks,
Here where the air always stinks;
And where the lights are always on,
Never enough space or lawn.

Kind of makes you wonder why,
Saying thanks is sometimes a lie;
Give me the strength to change my mind,
In between the screaming and lying.

Vowing to do things when all this is done,
Inviting a chosen few to help;
Never to know right now if we've won,
Getting our wonderful ideas felt.

Will we all really give thanks,
In our pods, our cells, or even the "tanks";
Saying we will and crossing our hearts,
Hearing the 'you ain't got no smarts'.

Eating still with that locked up rush,
hearing the quick momentary hush;
Say thanks for me because I just can't,
it smothers and grasps and sticks and I won't!

JoAnne M. McKinney

Summer Night

Come dance with me tonight, my love,
Here beneath the trees.
Together we'll slip away
And our bodies gently sway
Like two reeds caressed by the summer breeze.
Lost in the moonlight reflected in our eyes
We kiss, and the evening sighs.

Come lie with me tonight, my love,
Here beneath the sky.
Together we'll embrace,
Making love while our hearts race
To the urgent rhythm of our passion's cry;
Until at last our bodies relent
And together we lie spent beneath the morning sky,
As the echoes of the night's passions slowly die.

Frank A. Fetta

My Beloved Jami Jo

Her love filled my emptiness, Her touch eased my pain.
Her smile brought the sunshine, when all around was rain.

Her eyes are more beautiful, than the starry sky.
Her lips are as soft, as a lullaby.

Her laughter reached the heavens, Her heart could melt the snow.
Her love I still hold close to me, my beloved Jami Jo.

She showed me falling in love, was something I could do.
I loved her with all my heart, my love for her was true.

What she saw in me, I guess I'll never know.
She made me the man I am today, my beloved Jami Jo.

All the happiness that she brought, was followed by the pain.
She took with her the sunshine, and left with me the rain.

The rain poured down confusion, as I watched her go.
Why my life is without her, to this day I do not know.

Each and every day, my love for her still grows.
She'll always mean the world to me, my beloved Jami Jo.

Someday we'll be together, someday soon I only hope.
I long to hold her next to me, my beloved Jami Jo.

Cory Jensen

Sheila Kaye Paglusch

She smiles with all of her heart and soul
Her eyes sparkle and glisten like gold
Even though I know so little about her
I feel a warming bond begin to take hold
Letting time and feelings create something special
And each day reveals new wonders as the future unfolds

Keys to the doors of the heart and mind
Are always changing and the locks are ever so hard to find
Yesterday follows close behind, leaving today with less to trust
Emotions are blind, finding the truth becomes a must

Passion burns deep as two now become one
A new beginning filled with hope and desire
Giving love a chance to be born again
Life has many wonderful gifts to bear
United with faith, together to share
She came to me with open arms and will
Closer to the heart our affections instill
Holding on forever to this conscious reality

Brian H. McCormack

The Mirror Image

She danced along the corridor
Her eyes bright and shining.
"Cattie is in love," they said.
But she knew more than they.

She walked along the river banks
Her shaw blowing in the breeze.
"Cattie is at peace," they said.
But she felt more they.

She ran through the tangled brush
Her dress catching on the thorns.
"Cattie is forever happy," they said.
But she felt more than they.

She dashed around the big oak trees
Her face exposed to the moonlight.
"Cattie has found her one true love," they said.
But she heard more than they.

She found her way to the cliff
The rocks crashing down after her.
"Cattie is at fault," they said.
But her soul knew more than they.

Andrea Lawruk

My Prayer

Give me strength, O Lord I pray,
Help me make it through each day.

Give me air and open sky,
Where white clouds go drifting by.

Help the children to be good,
Help us be as people should.

Bless my family, one and all,
Bless good people great and small.

Oh, dear Lord, please love me too,
for this is my prayer and request to you.

John Butler

Almost Goodbye

Love knots wound tightly through the years,
  Held us both together.
Bumps in the cord of life,
  were something to hold onto.
As I lost my grip,
  your circle around me tightened.
And in your misery, my heart grew weak.
Love I thought was lost, heightened.
  Our future no longer bleak.
What was that something, we try to define?
Fate or forgiveness that brought such joy sublime.

Carol Rose Petrunich

Heart, Heart, Heart....

I want to shout, I love you.
  Heaven, Heaven, Heaven...
I want to scream, I need you.
I want you to know , that I care for you.
  Never, never, ever...
I will desert you...
  Always, always, always...
I will love you...
I am on my knees...
I am exposing my weakness to you...
  Please, please, please...
Consider my poor heart.
Take me and do whatever you want..
I will be submissive to you.
I will soothe your pain.
I will satiate your desire.
I want to win your love.
I want to capture your heart.
  Now and forever!!!

Dorleus Chrysler

"Knowledge Well Kept"

Times well written, but time, not yet heard.
Hard for him to speak, so you read his word.

Possessing a power, to help them all.
Neglecting his own self, so soon shall he fall.

Now the choices he has, and will always know.
Realizing his own strength, the determination to glow.

An image so breath taking, an image in stone.
He must see, that he is not alone.

To break a mold, that's keeping him in.
Nothing shall stop him, not even his sin.

With all behind him, he will start to send.
His own journey from the start, and all through the end.

Jon Hughes

"Bluebirds"

Hush, listen to the quiet of the morning
Hear the singing, happy singing of the Bluebirds
Each one celebrating life and all its wonders
Each one heralding the brightness of the sunshine
Each one calling to the other through the shadows
Each one flitting through the breezes and the fragrance
Each one playing with my thoughts of days gone by.

In my life I've seen the happiness of Bluebirds
With their fragile wings, their sweet melodic sounds
I have touched their world, so near the wondrous heavens
I have sensed their thoughts, and they have known mine too.

As each day, I fly the heavens with the Bluebirds
As I touch their world and sense the meaning there
I release a few protected, cherished memories
Saved from magic moments found along life's way.

Hush, listen to the quiet of the morning
To the Bluebirds moving swiftly through the air
They will share with you a few exciting stories
Gleaned from memories and thoughts in days gone by.

Frank Thomson

"The Darker Hours"

Although I have wings now this beautiful summer day; they are yet healed from my battle wounds. Wounds? Physical or mental? Doesn't both feel the pain? Mine do! Sometimes more than others. Off all alone, on my own, I yet search for one to follow. Show me the phenomenal art of flight: The feel of the winds whisper upon my skin; gazing upon lands and seas below; I only want to know! Why has the Lord blessed me with these wings; except to fly where He commands? Yet; if man was to capture me, my spirit could not soar: I could live no more! Most people have no desire to learn the simplest facts of life; let alone to comprehend flight! My mind is so full that if I could sleep, I'd be afraid too: What in God's name do I do? Follow my heart, my minds most innermost thoughts? Or follow my heart because the law say's I must. Yet if I'm not completely free, I will die you see. Unstable? Cocyss? Cuckoo? Or perhaps totally sane. Wanting to give love, joy, and peace; no pain! Perhaps I will learn; when you tell some people your all, they then seem to watch for your stumble, and even perhaps your fall. But, I did not stumble and fall: I simply took my first flight in front of you all!! There I shall remain: Wrong? Or Right? Is it you who has the power to decide? No matter anyway now; we've come upon the darker hours.

Donna Faye Eager-Stoneking

Hand In Hand

"Take my hand," he said, "We'll go to a quiet place."
He whispered softly in my ear with his hands upon my face.

And right behind I followed leaving no trace in the snow,
He stopped and turned around, "Far away is where we'll go."

It was very cold and I shivered with every shake,
I thought someone was watching every move we would make.

It felt so good to run away, it felt so good to be free,
But I knew back home that they were really missing me.

But I didn't care, because I had him there.

"Lay right here and don't make a sound,
and put your head faced towards the ground."

He did the same as I could see,
"I love you my princess, and remember me!"

"Here is this gun and on the count of three,
I'll shoot you and you shoot me."

So we counted and three did come,
I would have used my sense if I had some.

"Wake up!" they cried in their demand,
but we just lay still "Hand in Hand."

Amber K. Martinez

Muted Shades Of Gray

She was a victim nearly all her life.
He was just there on the wrong night.

They are the forgotten - Ron and Nicole.
Each day that passed
We lost a piece of our soul.

Bringing in the money, fueling the fight,
The media feeds the frenzy
While they preach what's right.

At any cost, they play the game.
In search of the truth,
But they know only how to blame.

Just how do we make it right?
How do we get past
The Black and The White?

I want to find that place -
That precious place of muted gray.
Maybe there, the pain will fade away.

Heather Alayne

"Father And Son"

He watches as you struggle to become the very best you can.
He tries not to over extend his helping hand
Father knows and understands, he to was
once in your shoes, trying to become a man.

When your son makes a mistake
to him it seems so tall.
Until father takes his hand
and says, don't worry son it was small.

As you grow it may seem he is hard on you at times
when you get out of line, you will hear him say,
my wish for you son is that you grow to understand,
my purpose is to teach you to become a man.

Knowing that once you grasp the meaning of life
You to have become a man and stand very tall.
May you remember your Fathers teachings
how once he to, must have been small.

You may even look at your own son someday and shake your head,
hear yourself repeating the same words your father once said.
My wish for you son, is for you to grow to understand
My purpose is to teach you to become a man.

Evelyn Creasey

The Path

I took the path where a man did wait.
He took my hand and said, "I'm here to walk with
you to Heaven's gate.

You have come a long way and are weary.
God is with you tho, and your burdens he
will carry.

God has called you to leave your loving wife.
The one who has helped you through such
terrible strife.

Now God will help her carry on, for her
loving husband has been called home.

You have called many to the alter, and implored
them not to falter.

For God's kingdom is our reward, where angels
sing in sweet accord.

So please kiss your loved ones good-bye, for
you are going to your home on high.

Your Lord is waiting with arms wide open
with loving words softly spoken."

Donna Dotzert

Hero

I saw him standing there through the darkness of the storm
He stood there in a long, black trench coat and hat, holding an
    umbrella to shield himself from the falling rain
His eyes were pools of black, so mysterious and unknown
He had no smile and he had no frown
The expression of his face was just plain, no happiness yet no anger
He looked so scary yet so kind
He looked at me in mystery and fear
This man was my hero, this man was my friend
He helped me up and made me strong
He gave me courage and took away my fear
He smiled when he held me and cried when I fell
He was kind and loving, taking off his jacket to wrap around me to
    keep me warm and dry
He turned my life around, he gave me a reason to live
He made all my fears turn to joy
He made all my tears turn to smiles
He turned me from weak to strong
He made my cold and lonely heart turn to warm and compassionate
He made me able to love for this man was my hero

Christine Houston

Messed Up But Good

A poor little bear was loosing his hair.
He said, "Oh dear! What's happened?
I wish I knew, for I sure would do
whatever it took to stop it."
"Come here dear, have no fear.
You're just as sweet without it,"
said mother bear, as she swept up the hair
where the little fellow had lost it.
I'll make you a robe that reaches your toes,
and we'll say you have the flu.
It's just a little white lie,
and we'll tell them better by and by.
That's just about the best we can do.
I'll do what you say if there's no other way,
but it sure is hard to accept it.
I'll tell you what I think, the whole deal stinks.
Mother nature took the ball and dropped it.

Betty B. Holmes

Generations

Moses with a black face, tanned leather hands
He is the one whose spirit, moved
Drops to the water, and on bent knees
Sculpts the land, brings back fertile soil
Sells the bounty for his family, stores up all the grain.

Rain falls on his bare back
Summer rain of Missouri comes
Fallen water from Godlike hands
Holding land his father never owned
He is Moses with a blackened face.

Rhythms fall through heavy feet
Trodden down through decades told
Stories in their slow beating, working, living,
The worn out shoes, handed down, broken souls
He remembers lullaby night songs, chanting of his brothers' rhyme
While suckling at his mother's breast.

Carey Buczwinski

Dr. Butz - A Valentine All Year

Keeping folks healthy has long been his line,
He is known by some as Doc Valentine.

Two thousand babies, he started their lives;
Now they're all grown up with husbands and wives.

When called in the night, no matter how cold,
He was always right there to care for his fold.

From measles and mumps or just the plain flu,
He knew how to fix it and just what to do.

For fifty-one years he gave it his best,
Now he deserves a long happy rest.

He loves to go dancing with Lou as his mate,
They go quite early, and often stay late.

During his life he did have some sorrow,
But he came right back to live for tomorrow.

We wish him happiness and years of good joys,
And thank you also from all of our boys.

Barney Jonen

I Can Love

God chose to love, it didn't just come to be,
he demonstrated his love for you and me.
When he sacrificed his only son upon the tree,
making a way to heaven for us to be,
alongside him for eternity.
And now he has taught me to choose,
someone to love I cannot refuse.
Your the one I will forever love,
I'm thankful for the gift from above.
My strength will not wane in loving you.
As long as I let my God shine through.
His power will not fade as years roll by
and I will love you till the day I die.
So I thank my God for sending you
and made a way for me to love true.
And so it is I've made the choice,
until the day I hear his voice,
express approval like he did with the dove
and say "This is my son, through whom I love."

Fred Highhouse

"Letting Go"

Have you ever felt a touch that you just can't forget?
Have you ever had a memory that you really did regret?

Have you ever loved someone with your whole heart and soul?
Have you ever had a feeling that you just can't control?

Have you ever looked into his eyes and felt the love that was there?
Have you ever wanted to tell him how much you really care?

Have you ever needed someone and you didn't understand why?
Has he ever held you in his arms and made you want to cry?

Have you ever tried to win his love until there was nothing left to do?
Have you ever longed to hear him say the words I love you?

Have you ever thought of him when your all alone at night?
Have you ever wanted to tell him that his love could make things right?

Have you ever had so many feelings that you just couldn't show?
Have you ever loved someone enough to let him go?

Carla Thrasher

The Rockies Made History

The Colorado Rockies baseball team
    Has indeed proven itself to the fans
"A miracle in Blake Street" states the theme
    Of early hopes only few gave a chance
From the offense came the "Blake Street Bombers"
    ...Dante, Walker, Castilla, and "The Cat"
Since these fearsome foursome led in homers,
    Our prospects looked good whenever they'd bat
And oh what pitching...wicked with a flare
    In starters like Ritz and Holmes for the saves
Though, an occasional ring from the "bear",
    The Rockies made history with the Braves
In only three years of their existence,
    Against all the odds, they made the playoffs!
The current of Don Baylor's influence
    Sparked the league's quickest post-season send-offs
Along with great cheers they've won from their fans,
    They've earned the praises of former critics
Who, in 'ninety-five saw them build a stance
    That will merit respect in 'ninety-six.

Bob G. Martinez

All The World Loves A Clown

All through life, I've wanted to be.
Happy and fearless, and feeling so free.

I've said my lines, but I cannot feel.
What do I say, when nothing's real?

Behind this smile, who but I can see?
The outfit of a clown, how it has become me.

I make them laugh to displace their frown.
Part perfected, the way of a clown.

I blow my horn, a performance to please.
Patience and pampering, no effort of ease.

And sing and dance, with feeling so free.
Bringing smiles of wonder at what life can be.

My outside world is one great stage.
I've played my part as I'm trapped in a maze.

I want to wash this make-up away.
But then for the show, how many will stay?

One day I'll shower and end this charade.
I deserve an award for this part that I've played.

My final act, to remove this frown,
For all the world loves a clown.

Grace M. Brown

Lover's Apprehension

The minute movements give it away.
Hands jerk in small erratic motions
or clench, remain rigid, whiten.
Would that a verbal sedative could relax this nervousness,
but one can only sit and experience
the gut wrenching twist that accompanies
a view of the skeletal,
the exposed skull beneath the flesh,
and the motive behind the word.
Glances become signs.
The eyes speak ancient tongues,
betraying the real within the facade,
either refusing or confirming the anxiety.

Remove that mask!
William S. expressed the truth.
but we can deny him.

Jean-Paul Corriveau

Peace: A Plea For Children

I watch you standing there alone,
Hair gently frolicking to the music of
a summer's night breeze.
Your pitiful frail silhouette once sculptured
by the hand of a mighty artist,
now stands forever seared by war.
The sadness in your eyes tells a story
of irreducible pain and suffering.
Can you ever trust again?
Can your sadness turn to joy?
Is there room for forgiveness in your heart?
Will the sound of bare hands digging in the
rubble of war ever stop?
Take my hand child; lead me, help me
to see your suffering.
Then we can take that first step together.
Take my hand child; we will seek peace.
Take my hand child; we will forgive.
Take my hand child; we will stand
together against war.

Arlene Sherma

Interlude

Resting on a hilltop where strong
gusts of wind swirl, I willingly yield
to forces lifting - twisting me
till I am freed from earth. Green fields
below forgotten as I rise
to greater heights than eagles soar...
higher still piercing sun - shot clouds
into quiet where winds rush to more.
At last I view the vast unknown -
surely, this concealed life must be
more real than all imagining...
not mine to touch but mine to see
are beckoning worlds beyond my reach
and huge clusters of stars in sleep -
only mortal - I waken - look
heavenward unfulfilled and weep.

Jorian

Restless Tendencies

He speaks to me in the quiet of the night - while the stars watch
guard and the sun lay sleeping. I listen for his words but can
only hear a whisper - translucent as the wind and as soothing as
a lullaby. He then tucks me in with a petal soft kiss - so many
miles but my heart breathes it in - bathing me in love,
protecting me like a soft blanket.
And then he cries, warm salt that wets his cheeks, for his youth
makes him weep - that sweet bird that flew away.
Maybe I'm that bird whose wings he wants to fly with - soaring
through the sky, kissing the moon goodnight.

Angela N. Babb

Conquest Of Life

Don't let the numerous little things, so much a part of life
Grow into massive troubles, filled with toil and strife.
Don't turn away in anger if a loved one makes you sad
You can smooth away most troubles if your path is paved with "Glad".
It don't take much to change the scene of doubt and fear to love
If you pause to read between the lines and trust in God above,
To keep happy through your years of life, you need
Patience unrestrained,
Then for every heartache conquered, a sweetness of life is Gained,
So when thoughtless words are spoken and feelings of hurt remain.
Remember, no two people think just alike. No two think just the same,
So work together, share together, let a difference be your guide
You will find your years rewarded if you are walking side by side.

Ellen W. Carpenter

Oh Lonely House

Oh lonely house against the sky you sit and watch the world go by,
grey weathered boards no windows panes so vulnerable to clouds of rain
With sagging doors front steps all gone and someone ought to mow the lawn,
Who came and lived within your walls who laughed and played along
  your halls,
What happened when the sun went down mothers gathered children
  all around,
with lullabies and words of love along with prayers to God above,
to keep them safe all through the night to wrap them in loves warm respite,
until the gentle nod of dawn awakens all from sleep's sweet song,
to start the day a fresh a new with glistening drops of morning dew,
to sparkle on the sun kissed rays with heartfelt love to fill the days
With cotton clouds high in the sky where rushing little breezes sigh,
Oh lonely house against the night wrapped in the arms of cool moonlight,
with gaping holes and weeds so high I stop and think when I pass by,
what made the people come and go I wonder, but, I'll never know!

Joan Overton Hogue

My Happy Little Clown

You are my happy little clown that stands on his hands, rolls in the
grass as the people are laughing. Your happy face well light up the
world with laughter and make every one forget his troubles for a
little while. As you grow your heart well reach out to the lost and sad.
You my little clown well give them hope and laughter back in there
lives once again. Your spirit is full of love, and kindness.
As clowns give to all they see you to well be out there giving to the
world. Remember God gave this beautiful spirit to you as you are to
give it away, where ever you go. As I give this blessing as clowns
give to all God gave each one of us a light to follow. Yours is my
happy little clown.

Connie Varner

Life Is Like A Travelling Circus

Life is like a travelling circus,
  going from town to town like a deadly plague,
  towns folk watch intensely,
  clowns on a high wire,
  balancing two unequals, high stepping to a beat.
A crowd roars with anticipation,
  as monkey-men perform unrealistic tricks,
  so many strangers at the carny's village,
  or is it a strange village.
The sunsets on the horizon,
  And the big wheel comes to a halt,
  the young are reborn,
  and the elderly fade away.

Donald W. Droelle

An Ode To A Struggling Lady

I was married to a lover very happily
God saw fit to take him from me
I struggled and struggled all alone
Finally met a man I thought was his clone
But he wanted to make a puppet of me
So here I am again alone and free

I struggle and struggled all alone
Trying to keep up my house and make a home
Then low and behold! I met another guy
When I consented to marriage, my kids said "WHY"?
But marry him I did, because I was free
Alas, we are parted because of his fee
He wanted my money and possessions too
Now what is a lonely lady to do?

I struggle and struggle to keep up my place
I try to act carefree to save my face
From here on out I will wing it alone!
Unless a nice fellow comes by then I'll be gone!

Helen Davis

Majesty Of The Sky

Eagle of power! Fly in the sky!
God gave you the "magic eye",
To see, and understand all from above!

Majestic beauty in brown color of earth mother.
Magnetic energy from the sun...magnificent!
Wings of strength..."Tailored laces",
Of feathers fit for fright...Powerful!

Face as white as a cloud...wise! Noble
Talons and beak of sharpness,
Plunge into the water...pierce
Your fish! Forebearing, loyal!!

Spread your wings in contentment
As you fly!! Majesty of the sky!!
Dedicated, and, delicate in your way,
Greet God for us in salutation of honor!!

Noble, and, proud eagle, symbol of our
nation...the United State of America...grand!
Thank you Lord for the noble eagle symbol
Of our nation...majesty of the sky!

Anita M. Diaz

X

Thirty-seven hour manic raging in my head,
"God damn you for abusing me," innards boil and yell,
To war paint, whispers, I wish only to be dead.

Agent orange flash back of captive child's dread,
Lurks in holy water shadows rippling acid kiss toll bell;
Thirty-seven hour manic raging in my head.

Futility and hate shrapnel every plank I tread;
Ancestral mind game stupors, "Fine, Thank you, I am well,"
To war paint, whispers, I wish only to be dead.

Battery acid shelling, cerebral bloodshed,
Echoes wrath of holy gargoyle, divine gangrening hell;
Thirty-seven hour manic raging in my head.

Your sickness you gave me, merciless heart of lead,
I need your deprivation, maternal driblets to quell,
War paint, whispers, wishes only to be dead.

Psychotic ambush sends me groping for the flower petal meds,
Therapeutic folly, all treatment's faltered, fell;
Thirty-seven hour manic raging in my head,
War paint, whispers, I wish only to be dead.

Jane Huntzicker

In Its Season

Flying through the crisp, clean, cool air
Gliding down at its own leisure
Watching everything down below grow larger and larger
Soaring high as a gust of wind blows through
Tasting the last golden rays of the sun as the night takes over
Reaching its destination, the land, with a plop only a cat could hear
Is a red, yellow, brown, fragile leaf
In the middle of the fair season of autumn.

Elizabeth Mani

Untitled

A diamond glass holds a ruby sea
Gentle waves wash upon sunlit shores
Truth
A bottle of starry sky and gentle breeze

The maker drinks eternally
From the inner fires
Of distant suns
And fuels the spirit of humans
With the raw material of creation

Joshua Biernbaum

Untitled

Now I lay me down to sleep...

Please add me to your list of
    God bless Mother, Daddy...etc, etc.

I am about to be a new life.
My birth mother is troubled -
    she looked and found a loving, caring
    family.

I understand.

I hear the joy
the overwhelming love of my chosen family.
I hear you, my mother
I hear you, my father
...and my loving sister.
It will all be OK

I understand.

My world is waiting
I am happy
I have a future
    my security...my family.

I pray the Lord my soul to keep...

Brenda Hayden

Recollections

Through times of joy and times of tears
Go back in time some forty two years
I wed my bride till death do us part
She had most surely stolen my heart

We had a girl and then another
My bride was truly a good mother
After one more girl we had a boy
Then another brother increased our joy

Our children were a great source of pride
Then came the time they were gone far and wide
My bride and I were again alone
Looking forward to the times the kids come home

The number of grandchildren came to nine
They used to be ours but are now only mine
My bride has gone these past two years
How long does it take to stop the tears?

I put together the lines above
In recollection of all that love.

Clinton A. Leef Sr.

Recovery

Straining at the seams
    From the tautness
Plaguing this spirit with pain
How can the struggle be strengthening
    When pain keeps coming again?

Vying to conquer the anger,
    The hurt, the rejection, the strain
What becomes of this loving soul
    When the apparition keeps coming again?

Stinging from each caring mention
    Of the strength of character I possess
Though meant to relieve and be assuring
    Sometimes it adds to the stress

Knowing one day it'll be better
    I keep the faith to go on
Challenged by what I can handle
    Growing since I was born!

Dorothy A. Coleman

A Porcelain Face

A porcelain face emerges in the Pacific blue
   glassy-eyed papio erupting out of nuclear explosions
   roughly-scarred Hanauma, once pristine and inviting
   disfigured Koolaus—for precedence and progress

A discordant voice cries out in despair
   too long forsaken
   too little possessed
   too much to withstand

A cold facade has wrinkled the old charm
   pseudo-smiles
   candied alohas
   calculated mahalos

And the soul freezes
   at white ginger bruising
   at sweet melodies ebbing
   at resounding rhythms fading

And the pain is crystallizing into a silence
   uncharacteristic
   unbearable
   unbelievable

     Jeannette Okamura

Untitled

Your Dad said: "We must write to our son
   Get busy and hurry now let's get this done!"
We've been thinking a lot, while sitting 'round here,
   Your Graduation Day, is getting so near.
The first steps are over, of struggle and strife,
   You've earned your diploma, AND won a Sweet WIFE
Your goal now is Law, aim well, and aim true,
   We think you are lucky, and hope you do too!
To say we are proud, is putting it mild,
   Now what to send you, is driving us wild.
We haven't a hint, or even a clue,
   We are stymied, now what should we do?
We thought of a typewriter, or a book of Law
   We couldn't agree-wound up in a draw;
An idea came, we thought it was bright
   We hope our idea, suits you just right
Enclosed is a check we wish it was more
   We'll see you soon, please open the door
Good luck, best wishes, our love, come your way
   From your Dad, your Mom, and your sister M.J.

     Faye A. Laughlin

To The Finish Line

It's all been about you and I and about our ancestors' glory and pain,
It's been written down for all of us to read in this story book of fame,
To obtain the direction and to answer the questions
To what is good and to what is evil in it the balance hangs,
And to what is left yet to come and to what is left yet to be gained,
And to yet how many more there are that need to still be named,
For we already know that were all caught between to
What is right and to what is left to be in this great game,
So onward we go with life's quest its journey to fulfill its aim,
For on this books pages the question of tomorrow and eternity still remains,

     David M. Johnson

I See A New Day Dawning

Now glancing out my window I awoke to an early morning heavy fog. I gazed out into the distance and I see the autumn leaves there under the trees covered with frost. I used to gaze into your eyes and see no lies, but now I gaze up to the evening stars, and like the blue morning sky I look upon you again with my bright blue eyes

I gaze out into the distance thinking of only you of how we used to kiss and hold each other close. I believe that's what I loved about you the most. Oh, the way your brown eyes would light up when the noon day sun came shining through the trees. I'm thinking what will I do today since you're gone away. As I wipe another tear away you saw there, in the distance I felt and heard from my heart a melancholy tune for the two of us. Now the bright shining moon up above sends me a message of a melancholy mood of you my love.

The day is warm, the sky a bright blue. Since you went away I've cried almost everyday over you. You left my aching heart behind in another place and time. What can I do or say, but only brush the tears away. The night was very dark, the evening sky like black velvet decorated with bright stars above, and a shining silver moon which made me feel a melancholy mood and totally lost and not in love with you. When the bright rays of a moonlight would appear, I would wish to hold only you near - if only I could end the loneliness I feel now everyday, if only you would come back and take me away. I know a person can come back after so many years gone away....

     Audrey Meilhammer

Go, Baby, Go

When you feel too tired and slow;
Fuel up and go, baby, go;
For sitting back only spins your wheels;
Get up, run, and go, baby, go.

When you feel too weak and despaired;
Do not tell the world of your weaknesses;
For it is your secret and your secret alone;
Put your doubts aside;
Then understand that weaknesses are a test of strengths,
And go, baby, go.

When you feel a subject of harsh criticism;
Turn your cheek and compliment another;
For it is kind words that make a person;
Hold no grudges on those against you;
Find courage in your actions,
And go, baby, go.

Make peace with yourself;
For it is within one's self that joy can be found;
Give praise to your wisdom,
And show others the way to go, baby, go.

     Bonnie L. Warner

Sunshine

Your beauty to me is beyond compare
From your smile to your loving stare.
My love for you has no end
Till the end of time, in my soul you'll be within.

The way you hold me in your arms
Calms me like the evening stars.
Your smooth soft sweet kiss
Is like honey on my lips.
When you talk so smooth and soft
You stir my blood to a crescendoing loft.
Your beautiful eyes look right threw
Letting me know how much you love me too.

In your hands you hold my heart
With their comforting grace, we will not part.
The Lord has granted me a chance
With his grace I'll take my stance,
To keep my vows to you and him
Until the time he takes us within.

     Chris P. Larsen

Hopper's Early Sunday

Rusty Red Rows Roll Right and Reverse,
floating as they do
on an asphalt river,
awash in the burlap-thick glow
of A.M. anticipation.

No jungle this....
Instead just a curtain,
         a drape,
               a baffle.

It hides the lives of those entombed,
hidden, isolated by its gate.

They can look out;
Only I can look in.

    Thomas V. Saluzzi

Falling Leaves

A leaf, yellow, green, and orange,
Flutters softly to the ground,
To be pushed on by another gust of wind
Soon dying wilting in the hot sun.

Then another is to be brought
To this tortuous death, making
Green grass a graveyard for leaves,
And the trees bare as stalks.

But the leaves decorate where they die
Making it more beautiful than ever,
And soon they're blown away
Just to be replaced by more again and again...

    A. Randall Guenthner

Flutterby

Velvety orange and black, caught by surprise
flying up from underneath a dandelion she'd stooped to pick

Squealing with delight
eyes uplifted, arms reaching, legs twisting, turning
no thought to where her feet might land
All senses alive and following its airborne dance

Finally to rest it came on a dandelion nearby
Dropping all collected flowers she fluidly knelt beside it
straight down, bended knees at chest, bottom inches off the ground
That easy child kneel no adult can do with grace

Eyes wide she explored, caressed, communed
inviting it ever closer - Reserved still
yet with desire and glee she beckoned - Not directly
not to her finger, nor to her hand but to the flower she held to it
That would be enough

As she watched the flutterby she watched me too
Her glances quick and full
sharing pure and simple
take my breath away

    Sandy H. S. McClintock

No Help

    Confusion spreads over me like a thick blanket of fog. Never have I felt like this before. The devils and good doers talk at me. They are no good. No help. No one. They have all abandoned me when I needed them and not helped when I did.
    Somebody screams in darkness but no one will touch them. I reach for the light, but will not be saved. Everything is far from grasp. The air is harsh and I cannot breathe. Someday the pain will end, and darkness will be forever more.

    Laura Johnson

Standing Stones

I stood at the edge of the entrance and I found that I could not focus on any particular one. They all at once held my study; bleached white stones standing in the sun. A continuous and unbroken terrain of pallid reliability.

The work on this garden was done with fervid consideration and Harmonious symmetry. The black paths that curl through this garden are generous in heir submission of receiving observers.

The atmosphere is swollen with light and mood, emotion and fluctuation. One could not help but feel a sense of confusion and ponderance for these stones of assignment.

On one generous path it's where suddenly I recalled a view of the neighboring garden in the distance, a reserve relation. The path unexpectedly stretched before me into an assembly of grand, dark, dignified and sheltering trees.

I recalled the passing, the gathering, the submergence. This is his part of the garden, this companionship of standing stones. I distinguished each from that uniform viewpoint, this landscape of whiteness.

Surrounded by unbroken terrain and tireless symmetry of bleached white stones I turned and there before me was what I had come for, to see his garden, his name, his standing stone...

    H. Arrington Lewis

Carolyn Sue

Tears flow freely from the heart
For a sister's love dearest from the start
Blonde hair, blue eyes and skin so fair
Her life was lived as hard as she dared

Far too young to give up life
Only God knew what was in sight
He took her home to live with him
To be an angel to sing, "Amen"

Her death was such a tragedy
I could never see the strategy
Why her life ended so soon
Life for her was totally doomed

Even tho' she had to go
Her love she left me with a glow
She'll always live inside my heart
For the loss of her pierces like a dart.

    Linda Brannan Sadler

The Doctor

The Doc arrives, with his plans so many...
For at least there's twenty, he has to see!
Memos to check, papers piled under arm high -
Are seen by patients, who utter a sigh.

Patients go in and patients come out...
Seems "I'm" called last, without a doubt!
I've READ every book I've brought with me
And they're good, but it's DOC "I" want to see!

"Mrs. Newman, it's your turn to see Doc now",
The nurse calls out, as I utter a silent shout!
I wonder NOW how long before I get to see him -
My Doctor I've waited for...since 9 A.M.!

He's a mighty good Doctor, that he is...
DOCTORING all those patients, that are HIS!
So whatever your health or the case may be...
Be mighty GRATEFUL, the DOCTOR, you got to see!

    Ruth Emily Newman

My Mother's Love

My Mother's love is uniquely different to him and her and me.
For his Mother and her Mother are V.E.R.Y. different from mine.
His Mother was young and beautiful; hers, a bit reserved.
My Mother was wise and thoughtful with a silent bold nerve.
Our Mother was kind and strong, giving to the end.
She taught us all to give to life the best that we have in us; to do
our best in every endeavor, whether it succeed or fail. To look upon
life with both eyes open and to "always be yourself."

While this lady of which I speak was known in different ways, one
thing went unquestioned, unchallenged to this day.

We, each one, knew the other was my Mother's only child.

Linda M. Young

"Do Not Weep For Me"

Do not weep for me,
For if you understand where I've been
and where I am, there will be no tears.
Though my life has ended here on earth;
I'm just starting a new one with my heavenly father.

I realize that you all feel a void and that
my chair at the table is empty,
But if you look back and remember all the happy
times we've had;
I will always be there... in spirit!

So do not weep for me.
For when you look to the sky and see a bright star shining;
It will be me, looking down on those I have left behind.

Mae M. Zimmerman

Jesus

Friend, there is someone I'd like you to meet,
For in him you will find He knows no defeat.

It is He who has conquered death, Hell, and the grave,
And without Him your soul can never be saved.

If you'll open your heart and let him come in,
He will give you new life and free you from sin.

He will become your closest friend,
He will go with you until the end.

This man that I speak of is Jesus you see,
The one who has died just for you and me.

Patrick Vandivier

Untitled

My companion shall be the Earth
For in the Earth
My hands do hold
all of Life.

Truly
all that ever was
or will be
is the Earth.

She knows.

My companion shall be wise
and keenly attune to mystery;
of this universe by more than mere conception.
Possessing knowledge
and radiating
Love.

Surely
My choice
is a good one.

Maerushka Danko Ognibene

Holden Beach Bridge (The Bridge Was Torn Down To Make Way For A Road)

I am the bridge at Holden Beach
For many years I've stood
Above the deep and beneath the sky
As proud as a soldier would

I've been the path for many souls
To cross from land to sea
I've opened up my silver gates
To set the sailboats free

I've lasted through the gallant storms
The winds and watered gales
And then the peace is again restored
As the fishermen tell their tales

It's time to change, I've gotten old
It's time for me to sleep
And tho' the new road takes my place
My memories I will keep

Tammy Brinker

Wouldn't Stop There

If I could bare my soul for you to see; in the age that best is suited for me.
I'd bring us back to a time in mind; in the sixty's where all search
  and some find...
    But I wouldn't stop there.
I'd tell you of the love I've known; the friends I've watched die and
  my many homes.
I'd speak of hard times we all go through and what I feel when I just
  walk with you.
    NO, I wouldn't stop there. I'd touch your soul with reality...
    Who are you and what are we?
If I could let you within my walls; I'd share my utmost all.
I'd walk with you in the night; Talk if need be:
    But it would, in silence, also be right.
I could tell you my feelings of the friendship that's grown:
    And how I hope you're never left alone.
I would stop our walking to space at the stars, then thank the Lord
  you are what you are.
Then I imagine after all thoughts are clear:
    Try as I might... I wouldn't STOP there.

Tracy L. Howes

War And Peace

For battles the entire surface of this earth is very narrow
For peace a single conference table is big enough.

  World's entire ammunitions are very little for a war
  A single dialogue for bringing peace is big enough.

Every bullet, every bomb, and every mine is the enemy of mankind
Even a small explosive leaves damaged environment behind.

  A few nice words bring happiness, progress, and prosperity
  Hostile words, guns, and explosives bring destruction and adversity.

Save! Save! Save! The world's present population
Save! Save! Save! The future of the coming generation.

Syed M. Wakil Ahmed

Winter Assault

Jack Frost tapped me on the shoulder.
Frigid from his icy fingers, I shiver.
Their continuous massage penetrates.
Lances sharp through thick woolen garments.
Mind - numbing tentacles start to pervade.
My last coherent thought has crystallized.
    S.O.S.

Patricia Bunkoske

Grandmother

Your love for us will stay on earth
For that is where you gave us birth.

Grandfather, a good father, you were his wife
Two sons, two daughters, to fill up your life.

The four children, they grew up so fast
But, the grandchildren, we will share the past.

The children laughed, at times they cried, and
Harder yet at times they lied

But they told us grandma was always there, her
Wisdom and guidance she was willing to share.

Everything you had you shared,
You were our grandma we knew you cared.

You welcomed us with open arms, a warm smile, a hug and a kiss,
That more than anything is what we will miss.

Well grandma, we have to say good-bye for now
But the hard part is we really don't know how.

We all love you so very much
Through our prayers we will keep in touch.

So as we lay you down to sleep,
We know the Lord your soul will keep.

Shelley J. Winders

Ghost Dance

And the music played, then came the dawn
For the dance had lasted all night long
And we had danced you and me
On a floor of glass.
We were Ginger and Fred
You wrote a tux, my dress was red.
All around the floor we danced
Our feet so quick and sure
Light as a feather we were.
At last the music ended,
The floor turned to sand
Dawn's early light, we awoke as we must
To view the empty room, except
For the footprints in the dust.

Rhoda Gleason Brosious

Till Memories Are Gone

Great is the thanks I owe for the good things,
For the good fortune of a long healthy life,
For the burning passions of a loving wife;
Warm scented evenings that jasmine brings.

The kindness of mothers from whom life comes
Their guiding hand, their selfless gift of love,
And their warmth that rivals the sun above
Precious jewels to which my heart succumbs.

Luminous nights and low starry eyed skies,
The magic of moonbeams gently through trees
And the rustle of leaves on a night breeze;
For the luminous love making of fireflies

Praises be raised to him above all men,
For simple things, for the dreams that he weaves
The peace and quiet that falls amidst the din;
For this last breath to which all my hope cleaves.

Upon the door of death I stand alone,
Till memories of lovers and wives are gone.

Rudolph Hammitt

"For My Children"

For my children, for my life
For the ones, that are worth a fight
Time has passed...
Time has gone by...
Time I lost not having you all by my side.
Many nights I've cried alone,
Many days I spent by the phone
Longing to hear your sweet little voices
longing to hear just some noises.
But for you my children,
my darlings, my dears,
I'll be there to take away all your fears...
To dry your tears and kiss you goodnight
To hug and tell you everything will be alright
Someday soon just you wait and see
the Lord's gonna bring you all back home to me.

Kathy Hudson

To Be Loved

The noise of the crickets sing tonight
For their is love and joy in the air.
Happiness brings smiles to many people's faces,
Whom they don't know.
The moon sparkles an endless shine
Into the water by the shore,
Where they rest.
A single lily grows between them,
As they hold each other in their arms;
And as their soft tender lips touch each others
Many tears will follow;
People will look at each other
And have a desire to be loved,
Like they loved each other.
And when it's three a night,
A silence would be heard
Followed by a baby cry.
For this is the spot where it happened,
When a girl who couldn't swim
Tried to save her only love.

Sara Webb

The Thief

My heart is heavy with grief,
For there is a black dressed thief,
His job is to take the living's lives away,
Young and old both have to pay.

Sarah Minges

The Blanket

Old Mother Earth was cold last night
For winter had stripped her bare.
The leaves were gone from all of the trees
And the fields had nothing to wear.
I know she was cold, for as I lay in my bed
I felt her shiver and shake, then she grew calm.
When I awoke I found no need for alarm,
For God had provided a Blanket,
Yes! a blanket of snow;
To keep old mother earth warm.

Kathryn Phelps Fowler

Cold Ashes

Flow free oh tears,
For your lost love,
For he shall not return.
If he would,
You'd only find cold ashes,
Where fire once burned.
You might recall his embrace.
His kiss may even leave a trace,
Of warmth as embers do... when they are turned.

Yet, remember how very, very long ago,
That fire sparked and burned.
If you chance to lay with him again
In search of once known bliss,
You'll awaken to find the chill returned,
Cold ashes strewn amiss,
So place your feet upon the floor,
Your clothing rearrange.
Cross the room, close the door.
Dismiss your gloom, unleash your fears,
Just let your tears, flow free.

Karen Allen McKitric

To The Pitifully Desperate

The desperate person shall prosper, as all the loving do,
Forever searching pitifully for the love they thought they knew.
Perhaps a stab of jealousy broke their heart in two,
Or maybe searching pitifully is just what the loving do.
Either way, the pitiful, being the desperate and true,
Will never love another as long as the desperate do.
Though the hands of time will turn their hands a
     thousand times past two,
The time to give their hearts away is never quite past due.
That is how the pitiful, in their desperateness, do choose,
To deny the love they truly deserve and receive the hearts they drew.
Will the desperate ever learn to love as the pitiful tend to do,
Or must they live in pity and sorrow living their love untrue?
As many thoughts pass in our minds and many left to brew,
One flows true for everyone as light hits morning dew:
The loving shall prosper, desperate, in their perilous life anew,
To pity those aside their love amongst the desperately true.

Stacy Roberts

Kleo, Patches And Whiskers Baby

Kleo, Patches and Whiskers Baby
Form a trio of cats in our home
They like to eat, sleep and play
And are curious as they roam.

Kleo, our calico cat, has a black patch on her head
She's bold, talkative and feisty, too.
She likes to drink cold water from the tap
It's something she has to do.

Patches, also a calico, is the shy one
With a red patch on her head
Her meows sometimes sound like a billy goat
When she's half asleep in bed.

And Whiskers Baby is a large, orange cat.
He's a lover, not a fighter,
We love him for that and for being one of our trio
Along with Patches and Sister Kleo.

Sharlee L. Lewis

Alphabet Soup

I can say my A, B, C's,
     Forward or backward, with equal ease.
You can, too, if you will listen,
     Then try to use my easy system.

To say them backward, learn by threes,
     Except for two letters, W and V.
Learn by threes, except for that one "two,"
     And you'll find, they're easy for you.

When you practice, go from Z toward A.
     As you add new groups, you learn more that way.
Combine new groups, to form a string of six,
     And it gets easier yet, with that sort of mix.

Now that I've told you, I'll show you the way,
     That it looks in print, what you will say:
"ZYX and WV, UTS and RQP, ONM and LKJ, IHG and FED."
     Now all you have left is a "CBA."

Purnel L. Collicott

The Zone

The Zone, (thu zone) n., adj., adv., pron.,
     [Fr. zone; L. zona, Gr. zone]
     1. Lift of an elevator.
     2. Focus of a telescope.
     3. Light of a laser.
     4. Strength of steel.
     5. Charge of electricity.
     6. Power of a symbol.
     7. Peace of a sunset.
     8. Freedom of wings.
     9. Urgency of birth.
     10. Joy of ecstasy.

The Zone, v.
     Surrender.

The Zone, pres. perf.
     meaning nothing and meaning everything.

Minnietta Millard

Planting Shade Trees That You Don't Sit Under

God has many shade trees in His garden of love,
     Free for the asking from above.
The species are noted for their beauty and shade.
     They grow very well in the everglades.
There is no time to sit in the shade,
     Because of the problems man has made.

Children are yearning for love in all lands,
     To make them happy and to feel grand.
Some are suffering from criminal acts.
     Some are abused, but fear to state facts.
Some are hungry and malnourished, you know,
     Many discern it, and their bodies do show.

What about the elderly who are thrown in rest homes
     Wondering where their children are, who roam?
These problems exist among all races of men,
     Black, white, yellow, and red skin.
Let's all band together who are physically fit,
     In the shade, we have no time to sit.

Ruth Golson

Universe Dreamers

Break the surface with your glistening body
Frolic with others in the liquid that is your life
Protect and marvel your young
For you are a dolphin
Let us stare into your eyes
Let us learn the secrets of the Universe
You have many answers
We have many questions
Teach us, try to be patient
Guide us through your world
Help us to preserves both our worlds
For you are a dolphin and a teacher of many.

Neil Jon Klein

My Godchild

My Godchild is something I hold very dear,
From birthday to birthday, year after year.

Godparent, the title, can mean quite a load,
To continue the love down a parents' wish road.

I don't always shine like some Godparents do,
But perfection's not what is expected from you.

Special feelings abound in my Godchild with love,
Like the title was given, from God up above.

Good times and laughter we've shared without doubt,
Living and loving, that's what it's about.

Should distance between us seem never to end,
My Godchild will always have love and a friend.

Lois A. Ouellette

Humidity

It draws thoughts of you
from deep within.
It brings them out to dance
upon my skin.
They play. They tease. They bring me joy;
a smile.
Evaporating; here for just awhile.
It's hot, so return they do
those thoughts of you,
to dance, to sparkle
like drops of dew.
Again and again
the dance goes on.
The thoughts change to dreams
and the comes dawn.
With dawn comes the sun; the heat.
Dreams fade to thoughts
returning of you.
Again for the dance,
a silent dance with truth.

Michael P. Manning

Untitled

Life is an enigma
Full of apprehension and confusion
Who's right?—Who's wrong?
How are we to know.

Are people in their own world really sane?
We corrupt what is good,
We waste what is rare.
So, do we see the world through the eyes of "an idiot,
full of sound and fury,
signifying nothing?"*
Who is to know...

Luci M. Locsin

* - *Quote from Shakespeare's* Macbeth

God Loves Me

I was only six
full of funny tricks
and thoughts and things,
So I did something silly
while in church one day
I didn't think anyone was
looking my way-

Everything looked so dark and dim,
Maybe I was doing it just for Him;
So I turned on all the lights I could find
I didn't think that He'd mind.

It all looked so pretty and bright,
Like I had brought in the sunlight,
But then the bell ringer went and told
My sister that I was bold,
It seemed everyone looked at me angrily,
And my silent answer was "God Loves Me."

Kate Noone

"Defeat"

Pools of fire spit forth their bitter truths
Fumes engulfed the nostril spirits
As we viewed the lifeless limbs left lying
Had we proved our point
Of course we had
We had taught them all a lesson they won't soon forget
Or had they already forgotten
As they faded to their new threshold
Victory did not seem so sweet
Nor did the sweat and blood that had mixed upon our lips
We gazed into each others eyes
Longing for assurance
Puzzled stares abundant
As we mounted our steeds
And rode off in defeat

Larry N. Smith

Ryan's Gift

Early morning hour
Gentle beat of sweet April showers,
Solemn Palm Sunday.
Goodbye my friend,
Your guardian angel shone for the last time.

Wisdom beyond your tender years.
You eased prejudice; calmed fears.
Your soaring forgiveness unchained us from hate
Allowing us to act with compassion.

In silence, you endured endless pain.
No tears, no complaints.
Now there is no pain for you are free.
We promise to keep alive your memory.
Your gift to us was your courage and dignity.

Kimberly Marchbanks

Thy

Between the ivy lies a man of copper field and velvet hand.
The breathes no more for life loved be but spent alone.
This seed bath perished, the ancestors woe to see the man that
lives no more.

Lisa M. Herrick

Autumn Script

Geese fly overhead through passing mists.
  Ghosts with soul stirring voices
  that echo skyward, and beyond.

The Dawn, bright with false promise.
  The warmth that never quite comes.
  The air, thick and damp and chill!
  Yet, somehow Autumn refreshed!

Fragrant leaves and dying things
  scent the air. A crisp fragrance!
  A flavor of the seasons turning on.
  Hints of life are packed away
  in seeds and nuts and tubery-things.

Autumn is a time for remembering...
  The "Good year", the past days,
  all captured
  in the Autumn haze.

As Autumn writes a new-script
  of the "rest" to come....
  Deep in the blankets
  of wintry sleep!
    Mark Matthews

Octopus

Suction cupped tentacles, fluidly unreeling
Giant slinky probes, constantly feeling
Four arms leading, sensing a route
Four arms holding, then releasing in suit
A shifting giant amoeba, coated with goo
An amorphic mass, clinging like glue
A spongy soft head, a digestive bladder
A thousand muscles controlled by little gray matter
The body curls up like a small beach ball
Then stretches out from wall to wall
It maneuvers deliberately, a movie in slow motion
Two eyes are watching, showing no emotion
A masterpiece of art, or an evolutionary quirk
A functional form of an abstract work.
    Tom Rundquist

The Watch

Discipline, Courageous, Proud,
Giving their lives for humanity,
Who are they who keep the Watch?
The Soldier that guards the portals of freedom.

Together they stand, an immovable rock of power,
Keeps our nation strong every hour,
Who are they who keep the Watch?
The Soldier that guards the portals of freedom.

Unselfish, unrelenting, strong and does not hesitate to go when duty calls,
To sow their seeds of freedom anywhere in this world needed,
Who are they who keep the Watch?
The Soldier that guards the portals of freedom.

Every race and color,
United in friendship above all others,
Who are they who keep the Watch?
The Soldier that guards the portals of freedom.

Keep our shores free by night and day,
So that we can live peaceably along the way,
Who are they who keep the Watch?
The Soldier that guards the portals of freedom - Our Country.
    Judy W. Nash

The Color Of God

What color is God, you ask of me.
God is the color you want Him to be.
He's the color of truth, the color of love,
The blue of the ocean, pearly grey of the dove.

He's the bright golden yellow of sunrise at dawn,
He's the sparkle of dew as it lies on the lawn.
He's as brown as the earth, and as white as the snow,
He's a soft velvet black like the wings of a crow,

The purple of sage, the color of thyme,
Red like a rose, or a glass of fine wine.
What color is God, you ask of me.
He's the God of creation, ALL color is He.
    Omega Smith

An Ode To The Children Who Died

Goodbye our little children,
God loaned you to us for just a little while,
We know the Angels came to lead you to that
  heavenly shore,
Where you can rest in peace forevermore.
May you laugh and play with all the little cherubs,
and sing in God's Angelic Choir of girls and boys.
When we hear the Angels singing,
We'll know that you are happy.
So, goodbye our little Angels, and we'll see you
  in just a little while.
Rest in peace sweet baby child!
    Ruby LaNell Bowen

Untitled

Jesus was given for loved ones,
God's commitment to show,
His life was the ultimate symbol,
Of how he loves us so.
So when you get roses,
Watch them bloom and watch them die,
And then think about Jesus,
The thorns, the blood, the tomb, the sky!
    Kevin Ontman

The Executive's Loss

Glorious sunrise,
golden rays radiate through cirrus clouds,
wasted on the Executive whose
eyes scan the freeway traffic looking
for accelerating breaks first here, now there.
Even on second chance
when Sol bounds over
skyscrapers to bounce
playfully among hued plated glass,
the mind diverts to last minute
changes in the corporate report,
cellular in hand, legs
racing to the nearest lift to the day's agenda.
The journey home,
sunset but a memory in the purple sky,
replays of the harried day flash through an ever-desensitizing mind.
Finally, tired and alone, suit jacket slung across the shoulder, key in door,
"I'm home," she wearily sighs
into the sleeping house.
    Norma L. Morris

Cherokee Spirit

My world has almost disappeared. The Trail of Tears is so long gone. But the tears still fall. For we are forced to live in the white man's world. They promised that we would never be discriminated against; they lied. For this and many other things that they lied about, I know that their word is no good. We shall all die at the hands of them. My heritage and many others' heritage is dying with us. We must teach our children our ways. Before it disappears all together. I am ready to die for my heritage! I shall teach my children to be proud of who they are. I have a white man's blood in me. I may look like a white man. But I am Cherokee Indian and I shall always be.

When I perish, I hope the Great Spirit takes my soul. So I may still watch over my loved ones for eternity.

Marie West

Autonomy Without Discipline

God, Himself, had second thoughts when the world
grew much too harsh to handle.
"What have I done but created a killer,
a thief and a vandal. Can I live with that?

The answer was "no", so He summoned the rain
to wash away his mistakes.
Forty days and forty nights is what He used
for everyone's sakes to right the wrongs He'd done.

Said He to Noah, "Gather up only in pairs
all that live and breathes for Me
so that you create anew
a wiser few from the ones who've gone astray.

Here we are in a world of empowerment,
racing to climb its ladder
to make unreproachable decisions.
It doesn't matter how poorly we behave.

The few who experience power surges
and lust for all they can take
-an inch, a mile, the universe-only want to
make or break. Is it time to begin again?

Kay Lohner

For Your Special Day

May the special love you share today
Grow even deeper—along life's way.
Let nothing ever tear you apart;
Always stay close...in your mind and your heart.

Forever have your friendship strong
Building memories together as you go along.
For there is nothing stronger that two people can share,
Than the bond of trust and having each other near.

So, as we celebrate your special day,
To you these words we'd like to say:
May God bless you from up above;
With lots of laughter, much happiness and
Everlasting love!

Linda D. Super

A New Friend Of Mine

I found a new friend,
He is gentle, kind, honest and sincere.
He makes me laugh.

I have only known him for a short time.
I am at ease with him.
I look forward to our time together.

I may be a hopeless romantic.
I must believe in fairy tales.
For I have found my Prince Charming.

Thank your for the opportunity of being your friend.

Terri Lyn Schaefer

"The Tulip"

Beneath the bush that's filled with roses,
Grows a tulip, pink and gold—
It tells me that where she reposes-
Lies her body, not her soul.

Up in heaven she is waiting
Looking down with loving eyes
Knowing, and anticipating -
The day when I shall soon arrive

Love in life we shared together
Love in death will be the same-
God will bless our love forever-
Give back the girl that shared my name

Life is short none know the hour
My times running out I know
Thank you God, for this pretty flower
Blooming where her roses grow—

Nathaniel W. Powers

The Sunset

I love to watch the sunset just you and I
Hand in hand looking in each other's eyes.
Just to know that we're together
And to know that it's forever.
As we look at each other with a great big smile
We knew that it was all worthwhile.
We were there for each other
Through the good times and the bad
No matter what kind of problems we had.
Nothing could ever pull us apart
'Cause we knew we belonged together right from the start.
You whisper in my ear everything I want to hear
I tell you I love you and want you near
For when I'm with you, I have no fear.
Our love grows better and stronger everyday
Even when you're far away.
You're my husband and my best friend
You're the one I can always depend.
I love to watch the sunset with you
You make all my dreams come true. I love you.

Sharon Smith

Graveyard Of Dreams

Life is a mystery, and so it seems, we may plan
hard, and work hard to fulfill our life's dreams.

As we grow older, and wiser we learn, all those
plans and the dreams, have taken new turns.

Soon we're aware dreams don't always come true,
for while we're making plans, life has made them for you.

So we take each dream, one at a time, and lay it
to rest, thinking life is unkind.

If you have faith, and love in your heart, not all
of your dreams will you see fall apart.

You might mourn for a while, for all healing takes
time, and then with our healing, a new dream comes to mind.

Patricia Hoglund

At-One-Ment

I and my father are one not two,
He does my bidding and I follow through;
Together we are a powerful force,
And pave a wonderful winning course;
He knows my needs before I do,
And makes sure my choices are fair and true;
For when I am one with my Higher Source,
I live life fully with no remorse.

Lana Schreiber

385

The Awakening

You lure me to lie beside you,
Have I lulled you to sleep?
Laughter seems swollen in your lungs.
Is this for keeps?
I remember the song of Poseidon.
The water poured forth his whispers,
And your nearness numbed my sorrow.
Can you hear the rain fall upon your face?
Perhaps that is why you are cold.
Your eyes are like lichen on stone.
Why are your eyes white, now?
Skin rigid and gray—won't you grasp my hand?
I want to see your face as soft as it once was.
But now your shadow flows from your heart.
You leave to the sea alone.
Off to other beds, other hands.

Katherine D. Parr

Every Day Lonely; Lonely Every Day

I know, I know, I spend money I don't
Have, on things I don't need, or for people who
Never remember Christmas or my birthday.
In short those who don't really give a damn about me.

I know why I do it too. For an instant, when
The clerk takes my card, my cash; when I hear
The sound of the register, for a split instant
I feel a small connection with that person
And loneliness takes a half step backward
for just an instant.

Paul N. Knowles

Ageless Universes

Ageless universes
  have stood in awe
To watch the child as he deciphers
    Life's benevolent questions.
    Wondering as they did so
      What the young lad must be experiencing
        At that exact moment in time.
The child looks up, to see the universe at its best,
  And then looks down
    As though he wished the universe in its entirety would dissolve
    At that very instant.

Colliding with one another, fusing as one
  The child is devoured by the universe
    Question, yet unanswered.

Susan Kay Crouse

The Sacrificial Lamb

One winter night as cold as ice a child was born to man,
he came in peace and love from God but died with nails in his hands.
For his mission in life was to fight a good fight to save
those who did not know,
that God is the way, the truth, and the light and through his
word they could spiritually grow.
Even as a child he taught men who desired to know the way
to the book of life,
so they could change the way they live and trust in God to
remove their strife.
When he completed his mission, hung on the cross and looked
back on the people he'd blessed,
with his last little breaths he asked his father to render the
sinners blameless.

Lynn Ames

The Simple Life

In younger years he swam the seas.
He climbed the mountains high.
As years passed on and dreams grew dim, he was asking why?
he thought about the country and how it all has changed.
He thought about the time he spent and how it passed him by.
Years ago when he was young and very much alive,
Life was easy going and simple, yet fulfilling,
But years kept passing quicker and time began to fly.
The Old man in the rocker was part of simple life.
The old man laid to rest now.
He's back to simple life among the stars so bright and clear,
Up in heaven's light.
No one came to say goodbye, no one knew his name,
But there beneath that head stone, lies the man of simple life.

Richard L. Horton

Night Strolls

  Through my window I watched a cat,
he crossed the road and stopped to scratch,
  A dog out for his evening stroll,
thought this is one cat he could roll.
  I heard a thump
and then I saw, Upon the fence
the cat did jump.
  The dog howled and howled,
but the cat cared less he was on the prowl.
  Wake up the neighborhood? Yes indeed!
  People yelling!
  Dog howling!
  Cat meowing!
  So ends a peaceful night for me.

Mary L. Smith

What We Wish We Could Say Now

He wasn't always the greatest man in the world.
He had his faults just as each of us do.
We sometimes think of only the bad in people.
Wouldn't it be better to think of the best?
Once one is gone that is when we think of the
better in a person.

Now it is too late to tell them anything good.
Nobody is perfect, we all know that.
So try and realize the best of a person before it is
  TOO LATE
What we wish we could say,
  SAY NOW!!!

Tammy Heying

April Twelfth Nineteen Ninety Four

In memory of Shane Huskey (August 27, 1975 - April 12, 1994)
  He was so happy for most of his life,
He has a beautiful baby and a loving wife.
  They were only married for a couple of weeks,
But they knew in their hearts it was love they seeked.
  She found out she was pregnant once more,
Without knowing he wasn't going to walk through the door.
  At eight o'clock that night the telephone rings,
How could we know what it would bring.
  I saw my mom's face and knew something was wrong,
I cried for weeks my brother was gone.
  It was raining so hard he couldn't see where he was going,
He took the chance without knowing.
  I couldn't believe what happened to my brother,
Oh God why couldn't you have taken another?

Nicholas J. Caron

Out Of Sight

He knows your face but not those eyes
He knows of darkness but not of lights

The colours of flowers - birds in the sky
Not able to see that certain smile

When summer turns into autumn leaves
And falling snow in the winter's breeze

A running horse - A boxing fight
And also miss a guiding light

Not to notice the grasses grow
To miss a sunset an evening's glow

That autumn forest - A river's stream
He heard of these but has not seen

Sebastian

Christ Is Risen

Christ is Risen - He is risen indeed!
He made a sacrifice so that we may see;
That through his light and by the power of his ways -
All can be conquered - day by day.

Out of 3,000 promises he has made to us
All that he asks is for us to trust.
With nothing to lose, yet Eternal Life to gain -
How could we not give our lives to this man?

He is the Holy one - with Heaven's Angels all about -
One for each of us, so let's sing and shout;
"Jesus is Lord, the only son of our Father",
Let's praise His name and get people to follow!

For He is the way, the truth and the life.
Through Him things happen — he's our way to survive.
His creations are beautiful, from the grass to the skies;
But can you imagine how gorgeous if we looked through his eyes?

He loves us so dearly, each one of us the same;
For we are His children, and that will never change.
Christ is Risen! He is Risen indeed!
So let's all join hands, and follow His lead!!!

Sandra Horton

"Down Home Memories"

My Pa Havard got up at four, to build a fire in the ol' cook stove.
He made water biscuit in the long wooden tray, that would always
brighten my day. The brown flour gravy, he made with water, would make
anyone stand up and holler. Many times there would be a knock at the
door, pa always said "you'll come on in, soldiers would be standing
there galore, with a grin, you see, it was back in the forties,
during World War Two, and soldiers were abound. They were on
maneuvers, sleeping on the ground. Sometimes water had to be added,
and made the gravy a "little thin," but Pa always said, "you'll come on
in." The long wooden table was all aglow, with the coal-oil lamps
flickering low. We all took our places on the benches made of planks.
And bowed our heads, while Pa gave thanks I always felt Pa did his
part, taking these brave home sick soldiers into his home and heart.
Pa is gone to heaven, that I know, but the memories of his love and
cookin', will always remain with me wherever I go.

Kathleen H. Gill

Friends

I have special Gemini, he's very dear to me.
He's always warm and gentle whene'er he speaks to me.
He tells me I don't know him, and I guess it's really true.
He just has a certain charm that makes me feel I'm free from harm.
And when he calls me on the phone, I'm thrilled to hear his voice
Because he's brief but pleasant, and my phone number was his choice.
So you can see he's very special and charming as can be.
I just wish his next birthday, he wasn't eighty-three.

Mary Lazarus

Grandpa

Looking up at Grandpa always made me smile,
    He spun twisty tales every little while,
Since a young Huck, to an old Grandpa Finn,
    Everyone loved irrepressible him.

He was the one we followed about,
    Knowing that sooner or later he'd flout
The mischievous things he'd done as a lad,
    Some of them cute, and some pretty bad!

Then observing the looks on our young faces
    He'd throw back his head - abandon all graces;
He'd roar with laughter until his eyes run,
    Then back to his work - still chuckling from fun.

I took the challenge to grow a twig tree;
    He'd said I could grow even marbles, you see.
Today that tree stands thirty years high,
    Its foliage is thick against the blue sky.

At twilight time with his sight growing dim,
    When health was failing, life seemed a bit grim,
He still had his charm when he'd smile and say,
    "Ma, she's brought sunshine in with her today."

Laural J. Wolford

Untitled

Momma, he said I have pretty eyes.
He stroked my hair and kissed me gently.
I thought he was opening his heart to me.
I didn't know he was saying good-bye. Softly.

And when they leave, I remember your leaving.
I remember stroking your hair (what was left of it)
and kissing you gently.
You opened up your heart to me and said good-bye. Gracefully.

And those that knew me then say I've changed.
They wish I'd get over it - (but they still have their mothers).
They watch, as I become indifferent.
I walk defiantly on this psuedo-God driven path,
just wanting to reach the next destination - intact.

And when they leave,
I die inside.
I wait for sleep, and you,
to stroke my hair and kiss me gently.
I want you to tell me how to let go
with the kind of dignity you'd be proud of.
It's quiet.

Patricia Steffes

Requiem For A Paradox

He was an enemy; he was a friend,
He was a hellraiser; he was a godsend.
He made me laugh; he made me cry,
I will surely miss him; I'm glad to see him die.
He was a loving husband; he had a mistress,
He was very shy; his voice was hard to miss.
He has left us; he is with us all,
He is in our hearts forever; he will be forgotten by fall.
He was a complicated man; he was easy to define,
He stood up for what he believed; he'd run at trouble's first sign.
His life made no sense; his life was a contradiction,
He easily made friends; he easily caused friction.
Perhaps he was in the middle; neither one nor the other,
He was common among people; yet like no other,
My eulogy for him is done; for some it will begin soon,
The requiem for a paradox; is sung with an uncertain tune.

Kyle B. Lee

Frog Fatality

Another frog went crazy last night.
He was leaping through streets of "paradise."
Frogs nowhere.
Warts bare, shoddy pad,
  looks like it used to be his homestead.
There he was,
  leaping around.
Water dried up in his pond.
Head down, eyes to the ground,
  looking for pads of which he was fond.

That's why he went hopping crazy.
His jungle and pond were his life.
He went crazy from fear of homelessness,
  from loneliness for other frogs,
His only support system through all his strife.

So he's leaping through streets of "paradise".
Frogs nowhere.
Mother Nature not there.
Another frog gone crazy.
Man to blame everywhere.

Kathleen Ann Schoenberger

"Death of a Soldier"

Oh death! Thy touch is dark and chilled,
He was only nineteen when he was killed.
My world is dark and has slowed its pace
As I look upon my brother's face.
A blood-stained uniform he wears
The reason why? Because he cared.
He cared for you and enough for me
To die for his country; that we might be free.
How brave they are! Look how bold they fight
For the flag with colors of red, blue and white.
Why God took him, I don't understand
But God, I trust you! He's now in your hands.
My heart is breaking, as you well know,
It's just because I love him so.
Dear Robert, you're gone, we'll see you no more
Until we reach that heavenly shore;
Then oh what a glorious day that will be
No more separations, together we will be!

Sharon Dianne Wood

Someone Special

He came with rough, calloused hands to do what he could.
He went away with friends of all faiths, color, and background.
He worked the land and benefited from nature's bounty
  proudly boasting of the reddest, ripest tomatoes
  by the 4th of July.
He delivered mail in the bitter cold as well as in the
  heat of summer for the satisfaction of knowing
  the peace such communication would bring to a Mother
  whose son was away at war or the joy that brought news
  of a new baby's birth, a graduation, a wedding, any event
  that would change not only an individual, but also the world.
He was privileged to live and grow old enough to see eighty-two.
  In that span of time, he laughed and loved,
  and lost his wife of forty years.
He was respect and commitment.
He was...my Dad!

Louise Elpers

Jesus Waits For You

There is no friend in the world for me
He went to Calvary
For He cared so much for me
That he died on Calvary
You can have this friend too
For he also loves you
His blessings will be the same
Bless his Holy name
For He is the blessed light
He knows what is right
Jesus's name is so sweet
We'll be glad to lay our crown at his feet
Jesus shed his precious blood
For it is the cleansing flood
If you take your sins to the cross
You can count them as loss
Please take Jesus too
For he's waiting on you

Richard Grimes Jr.

"My Boy"

Written for Kris Patrick Burnau, my son. June 25, 1993
First he was my baby, then he was my sweet little boy.
He would run through my yard with his dog, and a tiny toy.

He grew and grew as his childhood slipped away so fast.
Such pride in my heart, watching the years fly quickly past.

He came to the end of his school years, for me that was very hard.
Now, only memories, of how he once used to play out in my yard.
Tonight he passed me in the hallway, as he headed out for a date.
Lowering my eyes to hide my tears, I said, "try not to be too late."

He stopped, turned around and grabbed me up in a whirl,
As he softly said, "Mom, you'll always be my favorite girl."

His hair smelled so clean, and his Polo cologne smelled so grand.
Told me one thing for sure, my baby, my little boy, was now a grown man.

Nancy S. Burnau

Fall

Listen!
Hear the rushing brook,
and the deer walking.
Watch the birds flutter from tree to tree,
and see glorious fall leaves float silently down.
This is the cloak of fall,
nature's lustrous cape of
brilliant colors and sounds,
woven from threads of magnificent,
fiery red leaves,
sparkling water,
and royal blue skies.
Sit quiet and still,
and you will see
all of this and more.
Maybe, if you're quiet and still enough,
for long enough,
you will see and hear
the leaves change color.

Megan M. McKnight

The Dying Dragon

I watched the dragon everyday
He'd come up close then fly away
One day I never heard his chime
Nor did he tell his little rhyme
Later that night when I should've been in bed
I followed the moon filled with teary dread
I fell with a wave on a grassy floor
The entrance to a cave through a big brown door
The dragon sprawled upon the ground
Barrels of blood spilled all around
I sat at his side and started to weep
Hoping he was just asleep
I looked at his head
And knew he was dead
So I left him to the dark gloomy cave
Which was now a dead dragon's grave

Melissa Bingham

In The Coffee Shop

Her hands show years of hard work and pain
Her body knows there is no more to gain
She leans back and sighs
Her face she lifts up
She opens her eyes
She lifts up her cup
The liquid runs down
Her parched, dry throat
She makes not a sound
Just gets up, and gets her coat.

Stacey Dianne Salmon

Loving Care

The young disabled girl was so surprising.
Her heart and strength keep rising.
She is unable to talk.
Also she will never walk.
But the girl gets help riding a pony,
She sits up there while being held on by Tony.
The pony helps her to build up her muscle tone,
The pony is her best friend that she will not leave alone.
They show love for one another,
This takes stress off her mother.

Stephanie C. Husky

Silent Pictures

I once had a friend I thought I knew
Her intimate feelings, promises to
But as I watch her secrets unfold
Her memories deep down, that have never been told
To know the way she thinks or how her mind works
To know why she smiles
When behind evil lurks
Why do I give her everything
And always receive nothing in return
Why do I help her out
When I'm the one to get burned
But I give her a kiss anyway
And silently say goodbye
As I watch her walk down the street
Still hiding her innocent lies
She never looked back
But that was the way it was meant to be
Still struggling alone with her pain and agony
For eternity

Michelle Saldivar

"Nancy"

A woman of the world, yes—so they say,
Her tears like ours, fall on a rainy day.
Surviving alone and making her way, her smile covers all emotion.
Her temper is short; love is her potion.
Her stride is doubled, her talk somewhat jumbled,
She dances the wind; her tower not crumbled.
Her life is a novel, the end yet a question.
Her dreams are high, to us some mere mention.
Her friends are many, the song comes on strong;
Her eyes are the notes; the world sings along.
She argues and listens, both at the same time.
Ruffle her feathers, her face becomes mime.
Her riches but few, her happiness encumbered;
The feelings she shares seem to come on like thunder.
Her awkward grace is appreciated by all.
IS IT ACTING OR REAL—THAT LAST CLUMSY FALL?
So let's hear it for "NANCY", the queen of the floor;
She's one heck of a sister, I can't ask for more!

Margaret Metot

Unknown Love

She comes upon the wings of the white dove,
Her touch is true, her love unfair.
I gaze in wonder, is she my true love?
This confusion encompasses me, is it my heart I should share?

Thee I truly love, yet I'm alone in the dark.
My fire rages, what am I to do?
It is thee I truly love, but what is this spark,
Do I stay with the old or go with the new?

Her warmth blankets me from the world outside,
But is that where I long to be?
Is it from the world that I should hide?
Who is it I love, her or me or she?

It is thee I love, but for her I would die.
I don't know how it happened, or when or why.

Shane Garner

Eraser

Here in time a glass brakes
Here in time a lover cries
Here in time a gun goes off
Here in time someone moves on
Here in time someone is following their dreams
Here in time someone is finding their inner child
Here in time I wish to turn back
Here in time someone is dying of aids
Here in time a rich man laughs
Here in time someone is born
Here in time someone is having sex for the 1st time
Here in time someone is alone
Here in time we are all erased

Katie De Mattia

Untitled

You have to speak to Marcus when you see him.
He's child-like now and repeats his hello until you answer.
But if you take the time to stop and talk,
you can catch glimpses of a once-learned man.
I've been told he spoke several languages.
During the good times his vocabulary is still extensive
and you sense he's well-read.
But most days now, he's satisfied with a friendly greeting.

Pat Avery

Darkness

Darkness, hidden from sight,
hidden in corners,
hidden from light.

It's the sheet that covers,
the sleeping at night,
crushing the hope
on its raging flight.

Spilling slowly into the sky,
Darkness will convey,
turning black to white of eye,
banishing the sun's ray.

And yet, darkness is hidden in the light,
haunting our lonely hearts.
Darkness, a nightmare, turn and fight!
soon enigma starts.

Darkness is what you can not see,
but feel in every way.
Darkness knows no black or white,
Darkness, name of grey.

Leah Albin

A Prison

An unforgivable act he had done, a crime so
Hideous that he could tell no one, so, with
Walls of blame and bars of shame, a prison he
Did build. He bound himself with the chains
Of desolation and placed himself in a cell of
Isolation.

For years, he longed to be free from the torment
That made him flee. Then, he remembered his
Father's grace, as from the world he hid his face.
Before the throne of God he made his plea, and
Waited anxiously for his decree.

A pardon for him, God did proclaim; thus, setting
Him free from his guilt and shame.

C. A. Howard

The Clam's Dance

Eyes of green, smile so bright
hides rivers of pain the color of night
confusion sets in, will she ever know
what it is she wants, will he tell her so?

Opposite energy always brings them there
to the one place they both can share
the wishes, desires of every being
the dance brings the heat they both are feeling

She tries to deny the tingle she feels
when he unmasks his feelings, sometimes so real
He battles his own ghosts of confusion
not knowing if he should love, she could be an intrusion

His mask may change from dawn to day
what's in his heart he's afraid to say
Her heart aches, can she withstand
all the emotion he buries in sand?

Yet her eyes remain bright and her smile still shines
Her walls get stronger with passing of time
when he unveils his mask, he just may see
She's gone on, cannot wait, for him to be...hers

Natalie Nickell

Untitled

Ambrosia is the Blood of Christ
His body is the Bread
satan spoke with a dimpled smile recalling how He bled
his eloquence was unsurpassed...
so we gave him the floor
he said,
"Blood's for barbarians, flesh offers so much more"

He Jew's an outcast satan said, standing outside your door
tell Him the welcome mat is only there as a decor
He Jew comes knocking everyday but do not let Him pass
though He recites I am Alpha, Omega, First and Last
He Jew's a beggar...
tattered, at the threshold, indiscreet
"the welcome mat's immaculate, far too clean for bare feet"
ambrosia is the Blood of Christ,
utopia's the Bread
remember you reap what you sow, remember how He bled
for Jesus is the welcome mat before the heaven's door
it seems this world knows nothing of what welcome mats are for

Robert Hellom

The Rookie Angler

From the pier of the Great Lake the Rookie Angler cast his line.
His excitement was obvious in this his first fishing experience.
His goal to enjoy the day and to catch his first fish.

In the distance a sailboat passed before his eyes to unknown destinations.
He watched it navigate the choppy waves until it was out of sight.

A tug on his line brings him instantly alert.
He rapidly begins to reel in his line.
To his dismay the hook is full of seaweed and nothing else.
He baits his hook and once again casts his line.

An hour passes then another without a bite.
Finally he feels a tug on his line that he's sure is his elusive catch.
He slowly reels in his line, then erupts with joy at the sight of his fish.

What type of fish he did not know.
How much it weighed he did not care.
It mattered not that this would be his sole catch of the day.

It was the challenge of the catch.
The excitement of the day.
That made the Rookie Angler a Fisherman.

Thomas M. Roszman

Fairy Lake

A little boy went walking along a summer's shore,
His eyes were filled with wonder, his ears with quiet's roar.
The pathway grew more dense around the fairy lake
As green touched green above him while below in forest brake
The sunlight fell in droplets making radiant pools of light.

Cicadas played their violins and bird voice called to bird.
The leaves above him rustled, the lake was softly whirled
As a gentle wind moved eagerly to tag its friends at play.
The little boy held out his arms to carry the wind away
But slipping through his fingers it touched his hair in flight.

Now the day was all aglow, fairies glimmered from the lake
And the green of forest shimmered while below in tangled brake
The elfin creatures scurried. The little boy came, in his play
To the green along the shore but as he neared the edge it broke
   and swam away
And a billion greenish tadpoles sparkled in his sight.

Margaret D. De Jong

Peace

I dream about Lyonesse's lady as I lie beneath a chestnut tree.
Hopelessly lost in what was and what could be.
The king's crown of lost memory weighs heavy upon my brow.
It was a brief shining time.
It was a time of the legend's quest.
The storyteller's told their stories in metered rhyme.
Do I seek Auther's grail at Castle Perilous or rebuild Camelot?
Where the Pendragon's decide what is and is not.
Will we sit again at a table round?
Can knights again find common ground?
When it's our time once more,
The king will return through a temporal door.
Camelot will be as it was before,
This time I'll make it last forevermore.

R. Dale Smith

I Will Just Stand Here

Dreams that once knew reality;
Hopes that once knew life;
Emotions contained in a shallow vase
My past, I wish was forgotten;
My future is uncertain.
Changes are hard to make;
Time, I wish could stop.
I am lost in a forgotten land.

Silence, I wish I had.
I stand at the crossroads of my life.
I have two paths to choose from
Which path, which direction, should I take?
I will just stand here,
And wait for someone to show me the way.

Travis Mitchell Pokorney

Remembering Us

I remember the first time I saw your face.
How fast my heart started to race.
And when I looked in your eyes so deep.
I knew it was your love I wanted to keep.

Yes, it's true we didn't know each other long.
But, I knew that you were the one.
And who cares what other people may say.
I want you in my life from day to day.

I think of all the times we had.
The good and the bad.
And no matter what happens now.
I know we can work it out somehow.

Rather you believe this or not.
I feel it deep in my heart.
It's you and it's me.
Together for eternity.

Mariann Burson

Dandelion

Dandelion,
How I envy you,
So sure of who you are.
With your roots firmly and intricately
    woven into the earth,
And your head held high.
The soil around you is so solid
    and familiar and constant
That you smile with the knowledge
    that no mere wind can ever unsettle you,
And you flourish...

Nancy Cope

Reflections

I look at pictures, past and present, and what do I see?
    How I grew to who I am, and what I have yet to be...

I listen to loved ones, the stories they tell, and the things they
    say, and I get an idea of how I am perceived today...

I glance at my reflection and what do I see?
    The physical traits of a body that defines "Me"...

Can anyone really see "Me"
When what matters lies inside??...
Yes...
    Through the people I touch,
    the difference I make,
    and what I leave behind.

Kathryn J. Barcomb

"To My Dear Sister"

My only sister lives so very far away -
How I wish I could see her one day!
We both have large families -
but her people are near her -
Whereas most of mine live far away -
I have hopes of seeing them -
but sister - I miss you every day!
It almost makes me cry - for
I do hope I'll see you before I die!

We both seem to be too poor
to transport ourselves to the others' door -

Your friendly disposition is a delight -
Everyone loves you and this is your due
I want you to know - that I love you too!

Why does it have to be like this -
Letters are our bridge - there is no kiss -
Please know that I love you nevertheless -

I send my love - though there can be no caress.

Sweet and vivacious is what you are -
My only sister - beloved from afar! .

Lorena Barrett

Snow

Winter with the white snow,
How it is constantly falling from the sky high
    above to the ground below.
    Snow,
How it blows and throws,
    Falling, blowing, swirling,
Constantly descending and twirling
    Each crystal of ice
Gracefully descending.
    Forming, becoming, accumulating,
A blanket of newly formed snow.

Lee Pond

My Love For You

My love, for you, is so, so deep.
I dream, about you, when I sleep.
I dream, about you, when I woke.
I pray, my love, for you, you'll take.
If you refuse, I know, my heart will break.
I'll go to bed, and weep, and weep,
Until at last, I fall asleep.
My love, for you, is so, so deep.
I always, thought, you felt, the same,
Not just, playing, some sort of game.

Marjorie H. Lockwood

Memories of Erin

No matter how many spring times, or
How many years may pass

I have all these pictures of you
My favorite is the one I carry in my heart

The memories of you are like sparkles and
shimmers on the stream of time
Each reflecting its own moment of beauty and time

You make the world brighter just by being in it.

You have a talent for chasing away
clouds and painting rainbows
Launching dreams like kites in an endless sky
For building sand castles that don't wash away

The memories in my heart are here to stay
You are a gift of life whose worth
Cannot be measured except by the heart

Kirk Clark

Learn Well

I want to teach all children to know,
How to live and get along in this world below.
Good character traits we must possess,
Develop them carefully, there will be a test.

We all must learn right from wrong
Obey and trust as we journey along.
Thinking clearly from day to day,
Fold your hands and learn to pray.

Show respect and responsibility too,
Both will greatly benefit you.
Enter carefully the self-control gate
Begin now, don't hesitate.
Learn the facts of life values,
Be kind and obedient too,
There's a lot of learning we must do.

Remember always to walk up-right
Happiness will lead you into the night.
So start this day to become a better you,
Our world will be a friendlier place, because of you.

Rose Branch Gibson

It Really Doesn't Matter

It really doesn't matter are the words you speak most frequently
However, it really doesn't matter since the words mean not a thing to me

You became part of my life when things were looking gray
And I found myself wanting you with each passing day

The words it really doesn't matter are used most carelessly
You see I don't understand as you mean the world to me

Don't say it really doesn't matter
As I can see it in your eyes and feel it in your touch
Inside you are a sensitive caring man whom I love very much

Wherever the road of life may take us
Whether we are together or apart
It really doesn't matter you will always be in my heart

Sharon Spachner

"A Friend Indeed"

I've searched my mind, and a dictionary or two.
Hunting a word, to prove worthy of you.
A word that would fit you like a sexy tight dress-
I'm sorry! Let me rephrase that, like a—
Think, think, think! "Stink fits a mess."
No- I'm only kidding! I just like to see you smile.
But to fit you with a word has stumped me for a while.
For you're not my mother, my wife nor lover.
But when I was cold, you gave me cover.
When I was hungry, you fed me.
When I was weary, you gave me rest.
When I was lost and confused, to help me, you tried your best.
So it's in Love and Admiration, that I do hold you dear.
And it's your Love in return, that I do persevere.
So what can I call you, what word could it be?
The best I can think of- is that you're
"A Friend Indeed!"

Rocky Allen Marshall

"Why Are Some Men So Violent"

Guys beat their girlfriends,
Husbands beat their wives,
Don't they realize there messing up your lives?

They make you scared,
They make you worry,
They make you want to leave in a hurry.

They beat you once,
Say it will never happen again,
They beat you twice,
Say the same thing over again.

They used being drunk or high
for an excuse, so it's your fault
and you have to take the abuse.

It's not your fault, it never it.
He shouldn't hit you, no matter what you did!
Just because you wouldn't sleep with him,
and made him really mad, doesn't
mean he has the right to hurt you, and make you really sad.

Just cause he's a man doesn't mean he has the
right, so try your hardest and PUT UP A FIGHT!

Kelley-Ann Wheeler

Autumn Hymn

Waste not these days of loveliness
Hushed gold drenched hours
Forgotten in eternities long past
Skyline of tourmaline silk draped low
Against as Joseph's coat on valley, hill and tree
Ballerina wisps of grey blue chiffon wreathing o'er
Pyramidal altars of sacrificial leaves
Blazing offerings to stay the cold, dark Gods.
Murmurings arrows of starling speed across the crisping sky
Calling out in the loneliness of time
Wild geese wheeling down
Cry out in their paean of farewell
The swirling, wild, defiant blaze
Before in somber dullness she beds to sleep
Nature - flamenco dancer in opalescent flame
Vibrant to the crescendo
God's own choreography
Heed
Oh my heart — heed
Waste not these lovely days

Maria Day Simonson

Second Place

I should have known when I saw your face.
I always knew
  I would come in second place.
Why did I even bother?
  Always something better to do,
Always something neater and new.
  Can't you see, I need you now?
Not tomorrow, just today.
I may not have exactly needed you then,
  But now I need you more than ever.
Always when I'm feeling blue,
  You come along with someone new.
Always something better to do,
  Always something neater and new.
Well, now I'm gone,
  And how do you feel?
To some it might seem like a great ordeal,
  But to you, what do you care?
Always something better to do,
  Always something neater and new.

    Leyna Reeves

Body And Soul

What does it matter what clothes I wear?
I am in pain and you don't seem to care.

My life can't be found in the pages you read.
You say you have answers, I continue to bleed.

You don't want to hear what I have to say.
You discount who I am if I don't see things your way.

I can't be content with things of this earth.
They bring no satisfaction. They deny self worth.

Once in a while we see eye to eye.
But those times are few and I continue to die.

You are so strong, while I am weak.
Self gratification you want, self denial I seek.

Will we spend the rest of this life
in constant turmoil, in constant strife?

I know the answer and so do you.
I will be victor when this battle is through.

For you are but dust and you will pass away.
But I'll be with my Lord in eternity.

    Patricia Baxter

Untitled

Oh, I want to love! But it is not allowed.
I am pushed away, then forced to come close.
And I am still recovering from being rejected.
But I want to be close; oh, I hunger for a warm touch, a loving glance
The glance would say: "I adore you," and the eyes would melt the
flesh and embrace the soul.
Yet, tears stream down the face of one continuously weakened by heartache.
Pain the consequence of love forgotten - is paramount inside and
colors the countenance with grays and blues.
And I await a revelation, hoping and praying...
Soon, though, I will not linger, hoping that the hurt is realized.
I will escaped the darkness over me, and my path will be renewed.
Tenderness gliding toward me will be welcomed and I will not die.
Amid the twists of love forgotten, I will smile again.
Oh, I want to love!

    Mary Paula Hatam

Time

As I travel down the paths of expected roads
I am so tempted to hike through the woods.
The roads would be much faster so I am told,
but one would then miss the flowers growing along the sunlit trails.

For time is not saved on a computer disc for corrections made later.
Time is not a stack of old books laying on the shelves,
for those are only memories.

Time is the layer of dust resting on those books,
living throughout each page.

Whether time is a memory of laughter,
or a memory of regret.

One should always go back and dust the books.
At least to remember time.

    Kyla Karr

Loving...

The first day I saw you
  I became we
  one became two
  There was no more rain
  The sky was blue
The first day we met
  Shorter days
  Longer nights
No, I'm not in loving yet...
The first day we touched
Oh, how it meant so much
I'm almost there...
The first day we kissed
  I knew you I would miss
The first night you held me in your arms
  I knew there was a heaven up above
And now right now
  "I am in love"

    Mar-cia Fur-tick

Untitled

  Someday when I am old I hope
I can look back on my life and smile.
  To think of all the good and special
times I would of had.
  To look at the pictures of my
children and grandchildren and be proud.
  To look into my husband's eyes and
be happy of the love we have shared.
  It's funny but when you are young
you wish your life away. You jump
ahead because you want to know the
future so it will be easier, you think.
  Yet when you are old you want to
take it slow. One day at a time.
  Maybe we should listen to the
old people.

    Kimberly Hartig

Could This Be Love

The feeling I get when you're by my side. Could this be love
I feel inside. Could it be. That you and me. Are meant to be
together. Forever and ever. Since the beginning of time we've
been friends. Must our friendship grow or end. We've been
through so much you and I. We usually see eye to eye. You
buy me flowers when I'm down. You always come around. I can
cry on your shoulder. You seem so much bolder. You're there
for me when I'm in a bind. It seems as though we read each
others' minds. The feeling I get when you're by my side. Could
this be love I feel inside.

    Lindsey Marie Korte

"Be There"

I can see the hurt behind the laughter.
I can see the tears coming right after.

You're crying out for the pain to end.
Those are the signals I see you send.

You are reaching out for a helping hand,
but not many people seem to understand.

I asked what was wrong, but you did not reply.
I don't know what, and I don't know why.

It is none of my business, I just wanted to help.
I saw you hurting, and that's what my heart felt.

If you need a shoulder, my shoulder is near.
If you need someone to talk to, I will listen and hear.

I'll stay by your side as long as you need me.
That friend who will listen is who I want to be.

I won't ignore you, or push you away.
I will listen closely, and I will stay.

You don't have to be best friends to be there,
You can be, just a friend who really does care.

We may not be close, but I really care.
I will listen to you, and I will always be there.

Sandy Smith

"I Love You"

As ecstasy fills the room we're in
I can't but help it, I need to pretend
That you and I are together again
and will be forever, until the end.
I know this will never happen my dear
But there is always a chance I do not fear
You want this too, I see it in your eyes
Just knowing this makes me want to cry.
Why can't we forget about the past
It will help us embark a new beginning fast
I need you this you might not know
So if we speak our minds it will help us grow.
There is still just one thing I need to tell
You'll probably wish me straight to hell
So anyway honey, this is my cue
I can't stress it more but, I love you!

Theresa Macy

Cheers

To thou that is divine, whose taste is like wine.
I cherish you in thought, through the times that we fought.
I loved you tenderly, I loved you splendidly.
With love always and forever, forever, always and together.
My passion like a fever, my thoughts to never leave her.
To you I would look, with my life an open book.
The hands ticked round, in your love I did drown.
Through stories you did write, with your wants I delight.
To long, lonely nights, to the what ifs and mights.
To the countless words spoken, our years of love unbroken.
To the good and the bad, to the happy and the sad.
I give thanks to you, for the things you do.
So to you I give with cheers, many, more lovely years.

Peter McArthur

Fading Memory

When I saw you, I was mesmerized
  I closed my eyes and tried to visualize,
The picture of your face
  Your sweet smile in my mind,
The caressing sound of your voice,
  The kisses that stopped time.
Our last embrace, when we said good-bye
  Warmed my heart and my eyes began to cry,
I called out your name
  Though my lips did not speak,
I summoned you with my soul
  My voice was too weak.
I ran after you
  My feet still to their place,
Screaming out my love
  Into the empty space.
Gone are my tomorrows
  Lost in yesterday,
Clinging to a precious memory
  That is slowly fading away.

Naomi D. Durr

Dawn of the End

  It was almost dawn.
I could see the bright orange of
the sun coming over the mountain.
  The ground all moisten with dew,
leaves fluttering carefree to the ground,
  Animals roamed freely about.
And the sky was so blue.

  As I looked into
the clear clean stream, nearby,
I saw something glittering, and
wondered what it was.
  As I bent down to
pick it up, a chill shot down
my spine.
  For how I knew that one day,
that all this beautiful wildlife
would soon be destroyed.
  It was a nineteen-sixty
nine—dime

Mark Edward Ennis

"Why"

In my pain and misery.
I cried and said, "Oh Lord Why me?"

He seemed to say with a smile,
Tho I was blue,
"My child, my child
Why not you?"

"Don't you know though the way grows long
In your weakness I am made strong?"

"Yes, I asked God to spare me,
If it was His will,
But yet they led me up to Calvary's Hill."

"I died for you that you might live,
And only one thing I asked you to give."

"Just give yourself and lean on me,
Bring your burdens and be made free."

I cried, "oh Lord, I'm so ashamed.
Forgive me when I cry and complain."

And then in my tears and misery
I cried and said, "Oh Lord, Why not me?"

Margie J. Rose

I Forgot To Pray

I didn't THANK GOD this morning as I rose to face another day
I didn't bother to ask him to 'show me the way,'
I forgot to tell Him how I needed Him so until suddenly I
realized, I didn't know which way to go.

I didn't THANK GOD this evening for his Son, Jesus Christ and
I failed to tell Him what a difference He has made in my life.
I just simply did not say to GOD Oh Thank You so much, for
all you have given me, your grace, your love and such.

Now, I always STOP - just after opening my eyes, to first
look upward toward the beautiful blue skies and then, in humility
I bow my head and say, Thank You Lord for I could have been
dead. I Thank him for all that he has brought me through
and I tell him how much I love Him, Oh I do, don't you?

So whenever you get so bogged down and forget to pray, be
reminded the Lord keeps you, each and every day. And the
way we can Praise Him is to do the very best that we can,
Stop! Pray! And ask for guidance and he will keep blessing
you, over, over and over again.

Tisha Horn

That Night

Right before dawn, we got up
I didn't know when and why
Coincidentally, that was what I thought
But with her body moving around
And the sexy atmosphere I found
She easily got caught
I knew it wasn't true
It was a trick
A sweet nice one
I happily bought
I played dumb, resistant
But deep inside I knew
It was a losing battle I should've never fought

Kamal M. Elkhalil

My Mother's Tears

In the tunnels of my soul
I do hold

Images of my Mother's Tears
her desires, wants and fears.

Locked in the back of my mind
are my Mother's eyes.
And they are WET and shining all the time.

Hidden in my heart,
are all my Mother's hopes and schemes.
Did I steal my Mother's Dreams?

Did I silence the song my mother hears?
Am I the reason for my mother's tears?

Sharonda Pugh

Destiny

Dedicated to the "Wolf" from the "Flame"
You are the moon and I am the sun.
I feel deep in my heart that you are the one.
   Do you believe in soul-mates?
I never believed it was true,
until the moment, that I meet you!
   How could something so wrong,
feel so right? I can't
   help myself I tried to
put up a fight.
   We have a cosmic like "Relationship"
that I hope will never end
   Just always remember "you've
got a friend"!

Lisa Marino

"Motherless Soul"

A deep darkness will forever be embedded into my soul
I don't understand God's purpose; I don't understand His goal.
My mother's love was unconditional and true
A love that no other can every try to do
She would carry me gently in her loving arms
Sing me a lullaby, protecting me from all harms
Her touch was so gentle; her voice so sweet
I was her life- together we were complete
All this is true, or so I was told
For my mother was never given a chance to grow old
A year and six months I was, before this fall
Too innocent to know; too young to recall
This is the mother that God gave to me
I only know her through other people's memory
I grew up an orphaned little boy
Now I am a man, who just doesn't understand
God's purpose or God's plan.
What could have been his goal?
To leave me- a motherless soul...

Lynn Pangelinan

Respite

In the quiet corners of my sometimes raging mind
I escape the clutches of mortality
And journey the night sublime.

Though customary not at all, my sense come unchained
To a lightness—an unheaviness-
Climbing life's last refrain?

No, my soul journeys the day with mind and flesh-
Still of nature's breath I remain,
And surrender as miracle's guest.

For only the unseen hands of heaven evoke such a will
To transport my spirit beyond myself
Yet leave my person still.

And I am here, but not, and unforgiving fears are gone-
I beseech you, my quiet respite,
Carry me home, carry me home.

Rebecca Dixon

On Becoming Invisible

On becoming invisible
   I fade
      I wither
         I die

All of me that was
   Is no more
All that could be
   Cannot

Do not be bothered by my disappearance
   For it is of no concern to you
You will not be aware that I am gone
   For you were not aware that I was here

On being invisible
   I
      am
         no
            more

Kim Neubauer

395

Reality

I am now alone
I feel as if you've left me here to die
So every day I think of you and then begin to cry

All my fears and all my dreams
in you I did confide
And all these things you took with you
my hopes, my love...my pride

We had our time together
Now that world's a memory
We joked, laughed, and talked but now
You won't acknowledge me

Where are you now?
Together for eternity is what I thought we'd be
I was so blind, but now I realize
you're not in love with me

Reality is the bullet
in my wounded heart
Only a word-but I can see
That's what's keeping us apart

Blanca I. Cintron

The Intriguing Presence Of The Wind

The wind is like love, love cannot be seen, only felt.
I feel the wind against my bare skin, when it glides across
    my body it reminds me of your hands.
The wind carries me away, where everything is pure and natural.
There are no sins and no impurities.
I am surrounded by exotic flowers, with their vibrant colors
    flaunting at me.
The sun peeks at me through the trees, yet I do not notice it
    watching me, but I feel its presence.
Suddenly, the warmth leaves me and the sky darkens and begins to rain.
The lightening is audacious and strikes in divergent directions and
    I feel belittled by the encroaching of the storm.
The myriad of raindrops trickle down my body though the wind
    returns and licks them off of my skin.
When the wind is touching me I feel a sense of protection and
    exposing myself I feel its lips kiss me all over.
The wind sometimes whispers in my ear and tells me secrets that
    I promise never to share. I speak of my most inner thoughts,
    and the wind never judges me, nor does the wind disapprove.
I trust the wind, therefore, I love the wind. The wind is you.

Melissa Penn

Eclipse Of The Heart

As I stand beneath the stars in the sky,
I gaze in amazement and wonder why.
A love so true and strong as ours,
a love that should have never died.

As the sun shines bright all the day through,
upon occasion the moon obscures the view.
As the world around us becomes brightly dim,
it's like our love that's come to an end.

The love that we had is like the sun above,
its light filters our souls with rays so loved.
As time goes by the rays grow dim,
a shadow is cast on us so grim.

When we were together our love shown bright,
now that we're apart it's always night.
I've search my soul and all of its parts,
there I found a total eclipse of the heart.

L. David Henson

My Mountain

It stands in majestic beauty. I am but a grain of sand as
    I gaze upwards and feel its strength.
It is the spring of time, of new life and new beginnings.
It is the summer of plenty as we feed our souls with
    greenery that sustains our lives.
The glorious color of fall refreshes my memory of
    patchwork quilts, and the feel of completion.
The winter is quiet. The softly fallen snow buffers sounds
    of birds and animals searching for survival.
The pines sway in a gentle breeze and protect the existence
    of things to come.

My mountain has come full circle from beginning of time. It
    has weathered the scars of man, has refused to succumb.

I too, have come full circle. I have seen the spring of
    new beginnings, young love; the summer of gratitude;
    the fall of fading and weakening.

The winter of my life has brought a quietness and serenity.
Man, woman have come, they have gone,
    but my mountain will always be.

Sallie T. Fariss

"To Mother-In-Law With Love"

Although my real mom lives far away
I get to talk to my other mom nearly everyday.
You're warm of heart and kind of soul
And when God created you he threw away the mold.
You're the mom of the son I love
And for both of you I thank the good Lord above.
We're lucky to have you share in our life
Through joy, sorrow, good times and strife.
You add so much to all our days
In all your little special mother ways.
As Moms go, you are first rate
And your granddaughter thinks you're pretty great.
I hear your name from her everyday
And know she loves you in a special way.
And so do I as you must know
Just like your love for us you're quick to show.
So on this special day, hope we find you with a smile
Love you much from son, daughter-in-law, and bay girl child.

Kathy Edrington

Alone

I've got no one to share love with.
I go through life alone...
    And always have. I'd give anything to
be on Cupid's throne.
    So here I sit in the dark,
expressing my feeling from poem to poem.
    A secret admirer I would have,
and in my head we'd roam.
    We'd sit upon the cloud in the sky with the stars
brightly shining above.
    And as rainbows and fireworks light the sunset sky,
we'd embrace through the songs of love.
    Then I'd wake up once again, out of my fantasy.
Feeling like a vulnerable child with a broken heart,
I punch holes in the walls of reality.

Robert C. Ervin Jr.

Sgt. Richard Cruse

I was just a Rookie, new upon the road.
I had a Training Sgt., who I thought had grown old.
He drove me round the county, on every old back road.
As we stopped the speeder, he would only scold.
We stopped at the coffee shop, had a cup or two.
I listened to his stories, remembering quite a few.
He constantly reminded me, I would pay my dues.
I was just a rookie, relatively new.

I wrote reports, took complaints, papers I did serve.
This old training Sgt., really had the nerve.
He taught me that my duty, was to protect,
Defend and serve, the ordinary man.
As time went on I realized, in him I had a friend.
No matter what the problem, on him I could depend.
He taught me every story, had another side.
He helped me make decisions, before anybody died.

I can even tell you, the thing he stressed the most,
Remember, God.. the Father, his Son... Christ, the Holy Ghost.

Shari Cummings

Untitled

Enchanted world
I have fallen into confusion
This mission is unattainable
At times we wonder has it been reached?

Wondering....
We dissolve into time.
This cycle, brings hurt, and tranquility?
We burn... but we wonder?
Chain linked heart never once apart
Fleeting the vicious deceit
Escape a triangle of conceit
...slip into precious moments...
Retreat.
The stillness, neither alone
Nor, concrete.

Behind the blinded mind undefined...
Slicing at thou passionate crime.
Least remorse
Least confine!
Live the total escape.

Mike Sardina

The Sounds Of The Night

It is the night
I hear the misty mountains
It lets out a sound of not happiness but of fright.

The river cries out a wistful moan
Cry made of not body but soul.

The trees sing a song
Of not sweet but horror
But as the night ends the sounds get poor poorer.

But I know somewhere there is a sun
And with that light there is a dawn.

And as the sun awakens these sounds go away
And all that is coming is a bright new day.

Linde Murugan

Alone

In the still of the night, my heart all alone
I heard the wind just beginning to blow,
The moon turning blue, what a horrid sight
Who shall be the one to get up
Not I for I am the one who is alone in the dark
But with all the things in my way
What shall I do
It is hard to see my way through
But wait I heard the owl hooting away
Maybe I will be able to follow the way
Now I know it's got to be, only me
So away I go with all my might
To find the window just in sight
With all the noises I hear
I only want to hear the shutting of all my fears
I knew I could do it for I am the one
Alone in the dark.

Susan Annette Zika

In My Father's Closet

Time passes by all too soon
I hold on to precious things, what's dear to me
Memories contemplated
You're only what I see

In my Father's closet
Oh! How this flower blooms
A portrait come to life
Lighting up this darkened room

When you think that life has let you down
And you feel as though you've been misunderstood
when you always wear a frown
And life, you say, seems no good

When you think that life is so unfair
Full of hate, and not of love
There's always someone there
There's always God above

May the Lord comfort you
Rest assured, He will
In times of tribulation and relief
You can believe He'll be your Father still...

Suzi Bumbera

A Message

Son I have a message for you.
I hope you'll find it to be true.

Love your mother and your wife,
bless them with respect not strife.

Love your brother and your sister too
in the end they'll be there for you.

Friendship will help you in many ways
and sustain you in the darkest days.

Conflict and failure can bring you down
but God will be there to help you off the ground.

Be strong in heart, mind, and soul.
This and friendship with the Lord shall make you whole.

Love your girlfriend as you would your sister.
After all would you want someone to mistreat her?

If you do what is noble, right, and true,
I know that you'll always pull through.

Try your best in all you do but if you
fail I'll still love you.

And son no matter what you do, I just want you
to know that I'll always be proud of you.

Zak Wilson

Gone Fishing

A circle from a fish which jumped out from the shores:
I hurriedly dress, grab my pole and my oars.
My dog, my boat, my tackle and me,
Away from the bank and now floating free.

I'm anxious to see what prize I will take
When my lure hits the surface of my Juniper lake.
I can now settle back with a sigh and a smile
And listen to bird calls, each in their own style.

No nibbles, no bites, no tugs on the line,
But care less could I - I'm feeling just fine;
Although I'll admit if my dog had his wish,
I'd reel in my line and throw him a fish.

Alas, it's not to be, but my God's peace is real.
All the beauty around me, the calmness I feel;
I can say without the use of any obscenity,
"Please fish - don't bite and disturb my serenity!"

Marx S. Nathan

Good Bye My Son

You've been gone so short a time, the pain, so fresh, so new,
I keep remembering you as a child, watched you as you grew.
We tried to guide your footsteps, to smooth your path but knew
That each of us must try our wings and so away you flew.

The years, they pass so quickly and as time rushed on past,
We are left with memories like movies, run too fast.
I knew there were things I'd like to do and things I'd like to say,
And then, Oh God! You took him, you took our son away.

Our dreams like vapors melt away and the fog that shroud my brain
Slows even more these feet of clay, sharpens this awful pain.
Lord help him know how much we cared, Help us! Hear our cry,
Draw us closer to those you spared as we bid our son good-bye.

Shirley Colton

Hang Your Head In Shame

I know we have the same blood
I know I am to forgive you,
Love you, and always be there
  But I hang my head in shame
God says to love your enemies,
It's harder not to do so when your a member of the family
  But I hang my head in shame
You hurt me as a child in more ways than one
Your love for me was not instinctive
You crossed too many boundaries
  But I hang my head in shame
I can not give my heart and love to you anymore
My pain is to deep
I ask the Lord to please forgive me
  But I hang my head in shame
I can not carry this burden anymore
It wasn't mine from the beginning...
You hang your head in shame

Melissa K. Boeddeker

Nightfall

When I go to bed, I think of my Mama
I look by the window, I look at the sky
adorned with millions star
and I wander which if them is my dear Ma'
I think if she have the duty of cleaning the sky,
dusting and cooking 'n pray.
I imagine the angels so happy 'n gay
because Mama is baking
pies of peaches, strawberries 'n cherries
sweetened with love as she always does.

Susana Matos Martinez

Knowing

You know me (I know). You pave the way (I journey). You tell a story (I listen). You are music (I dance).

You have known me for centuries, through millennia of oceans and fire, of terra cotta and green, swirling change and time that stands still with your touch. Some might see a river, you capture the essence of water flowing over stones as the sounds describe the texture below. Few have never seen a clear sky speckled with stars, but you emanate the light of each.

You touch me (I feel). You speak (I smile). You sense me (I sigh).

In thousands of years, in only moment I react to you and we are both transformed, attracted, magnetic. Your eyes find beyond the common blue and gold a spirit colorless as crystal and air, a spirit that shines like a prism in sunlight, reflections of your love.

You guide (I follow). You are light (I see). You are home (I settle).

With you my heart is home. Home, where the characters required in the scenes of living can momentarily fade to black. Home where the actors unmask and there is no script. The persona of the soul you have uncovered can be alive, joyful, impromptu and fresh, spirited or calm knowing and learning, here at home. Home, where we are not required to define or prove. A haven where hearts embrace and know...

You glance (I brighten). You sooth (I heal). You know me (I Love You).

Kim Morrison

My Little Peanut

I watched you while you were sleeping
I looked at your face so sweet and innocent
You looked so peaceful and content
I wish I could have joined you
To wherever your dreams had taken you
You know I would follow you anywhere
Doing anything for you
For you hold a piece of my heart
Just hearing you say my name
Just looking at me with your big blue eyes
Makes me smile
To you I give the sun
So all your days will be bright
To you I give my hand
So you will never be alone
For you are my sister's first child
And My Little Peanut

Stacey Elliott

The First Snow of the Season

The first snow of the season, fell last night.
I looked out in wonder, at this beautiful sight.
There was no wind, all things were serene,
and everything out there, was spotless and clean.

There was a stillness, in the air,
not a sound could be heard anywhere.
The blanket of snow had covered all things,
This wonderful sight, made one want to sing.

Children loved it, when snow they would see.
They would jump up and down, and shout with glee.
Out came their sleds, down the hill they would go,
there was nothing better, than all this snow.

As I looked out, at this new fallen snow,
I knew that soon, it would quickly go.
It would be trampled by so many feet,
]and cars driving by, their schedules to keep.

Clean white snow, is like the beginning of life,
when all seems so rosy, and things are all right.
Then trouble sets in, it's like snow turned to slush,
your loved one is gone, your heart is crushed.

Jennie Wiora

398

Friends

Friends of mine mean a lot to me.
I love them for what they are and
not for what I'd like them to be.

I have friends small, medium, and tall;
Anyone of them would help me if I should fall.

It has never mattered to me their age,
I find something I like in every stage.

The innocence of the young and the wisdom of the old
Are what make life worthwhile, and I don't have to be told!

If we could just accept people the way that they are,
We would have so many friends and be richer by far.

Material things have never meant much to me,
But, you know, I'm rich, as rich can be.

Friends made me that way,
And, Lord, I just want to say,
Thank you, Lord, for sending
each of them my way.

Shirley Jean Walker

Untitled

I love you for who you are, not what you are or what you have
I love you for the way I feel when I'm with you,
   only to cherish that feeling when I'm away
I love you for all the sharing and caring you give me
I love you for the time that you make for me in your life and heart
I love you because after all you say and do sometimes
   you think it's a waste of time.
I love you because you cry at nights unaware where
   i'm coming from at times
I love you for loving me the only way you know how, totally.

Raymond Louis Bickers

Trains Are Forever

When I was a very little girl,
I loved to play "Choo Choo" and swirl.

My brother let me play with his train.
While he tried carefully to refrain.

"Choo Choo" I'd scream in my high pitched voice!
So he would ask me for my choice.

The engine blew smoke out of its stack,
And the caboose lights shown on the track.

The milk car pitched cans here and there.
While the cattle car, one handled with care.

The switches changed the lights from red and green,
And one can shift the animals in the farm scene.

However, there was only one thing I wanted to do.
That was blow the whistle and yell, "Choo Choo"!

I still love to laugh and play with trains today.
My brother gave me two trains on my 50th birthday.

Lynda Jean Bryant

The Kingdom Of The Lord

YOU are gone from us forever, but you still live
in our hearts and memories. You are in a place, where there
is no pain, no disease, no arthritic stricken hands; you will
be able to run with your brothers and sisters, as if you were
children again. You will now know the kingdom of the Lord, for
now you will dwell with him for all eternity. I hope and pray
that you are at peace and can rest now...

Yvonne C. Orem

Irene

I dreamed I saw you tonight.
I mean, I really dreamed I saw you.
I'm not just writing it down because it sounds good. .
And the dream was so real I swear I touched your hand again.

And it was you girl.
Your head attached to your body.
But not exactly the way it was.
Maybe a little bit heavier.
Living not far from where you used to live.
   (Where I used to live)

And it's no use, I can't get you or what you said out of my head.
By any of my normal convictions of
Smoke, drink, running two miles, or riding my bike to the waterfront
threatening to jump in-only to realize; Myself.
And ride back home again.

"Yes you are too late. No we can't start it all over again!"
Like a tape loop plays over and over in my head.
And in other faces, I see your face,
And in other eyes, I see your eyes,
And every headlight that passes me from the opposite way
I see the question 'WHY'.

Robert Mark Browm

To An Old Friend

I miss.
I miss the days of secrets shared,
a friend I knew who really cared.
Who didn't boast or look down on me.
One who let me be me.

I laugh.
I laugh at the fun times we had,
not worrying about if our hair looked bad.
Giggling, talking, sharing dreams,
that's what friendship really means.

I remember.
I remember you were there when my grandpa died.
In my hardest time you stood by my side.
All the bad times that we went through,
we lived them together, me and you.

I wish.
I wish I could find another one,
a kindred spirit filled with fun.
A friend to cheer me up when I'm feeling blue,
someone special, just like you.

Sara Marino

Mirror Image

Looking in a mirror, I do not like what
I see.
   In my eyes, I see a soul longing to
soar, yet trapped by fear.
   The smile upon my face, hides my
pain, lies to the world.
   My eyes look through everyone, searching
for understanding, yet my search never ends.
   My lips speak of forgiveness, which
never comes.
   My heart desires love, it is written
upon my face.
   In my eyes there are stories of love
lost, of a heart broken, over and over.
   Looking in a mirror I see the
real me, I do not like what I see.

Melissa Nelson

Riding The Cusp Of Happiness

Riding the cusp of happiness, I feel alone yet together.
I miss those I love, yet many I care for are present.
When all are happy, I am happy.
When those around me smile, I am inclined to duplicate.
The value of friendship shines so bright it blinds me.

It's been said you don't know what you've got 'till it's gone
  I say you don't know what you've got 'till you see it, feel it,
  until you truly witness your surroundings.

I want to write, to tell those around me of the partnership I feel.
  To share my experience, my Utopia confined.
Confined by the thoughts and feelings of the rest. True expression
  eludes them, true emotion dealt with, toyed with, then quietly
  tossed aside.

Sometimes I sit alone and question my thoughts. Am I an impartial
  judge of my experience, or simply a witness condemned by bias?
I'm not sure which, but have faith in one certain.

How does one express that which must be seen? That which must be
  seen to be heard, felt to be understood, absorbed to be retrieved.

How does one express that which overwhelms him?
Anticipation robs thoughts objective.
  Thomas Murphy

The Wonderful Face

His face blesses my dreams,
I never want to awake.
His sweet face was like a beautiful flower,
That kept on growing in my mind.
When I saw his face I felt joy,
I could never feel anything else.
But the person behind the face has drifted,
Drifted away from us forever,
But his face will soon be filled,
With such lovely memories,
That we will never forget,
His sweet young face.
  Katie Umbehauer

Untitled

I think about the down-pour of my life.
I ponder what was, what is, and what never should have been.
I look towards the future.
Who knows what will occur by then?
I attempt to search within myself to find the person that was.
That person is gone.
She grew up.
All I can think about is how my life has gone wrong.
I can't be who I want to be.
I am restricted to what society expects.
I am not sure what that is.
I am just reaching for whatever I can get.
  Michele Alison Strong

Baseball

Back in the streets of my New York home town.
I remember the dreams I used to dream.
I had my brother's glove, old hand-me-down.
I used it always in my daily games.
I remember the way it used to be
Walking out on the field on a warm day.
The way my teammates were always with me.
We were synchronized, clockwork, every play.
Now I am here living out my dream scheme.
My ears ringing with the sound of the ding.
Playing on a field with a different team.
I am glad I know how to play this thing,
The game that I play with a ball
The joy and magic of the game baseball!
  Matthew Teutsch

The Face In the "Pain"

On gazing through my window evening last,
I saw clouds of gauzy gray glide past
To reveal a wistful moon hanging oh so high,
And tree limbs like white lace against the sky.
I peered through the glass to see the night so black
And to see a thousand stars peering back.
Many lonely thoughts drifted through my mind
Leaving tear-strewn trails of sadness behind.
Looking back on years filled with anguish and strife,
Subsisting on sorrows in a regrettable life.
Then I noticed a face staring back at me
Another lonely figure overcome with misery.
I studied her face and then started in surprise
To see so many tears streaming from her cheerless eyes.
Misery overtook her in ways I could not know
Her despair and her hopelessness in her face did show.
In silence I did sympathize; I shared her agonies;
I moved a little closer in an effort to appease
But, wait — the face in the pane, weary worn and creased with care
I looked closer in shocked dismay to see my own face mirrored there.
  Patricia A. Curtis

What I See

As I looked into the darkness,
I saw my fears come to life.
I saw the edge of morality,
The line between wrong and right.
I thought about the choices
I'd made along the way,
When suddenly I realized
The world was no longer gray.
Reflections of the past
Are ways to improve upon the future.
But when you dwell too much in the past
It threatens to impress itself upon the present.
As the dawn of the day brings hope to all
So does the presence of love bring joy.
As the sun reaches its peak in the sky,
Our hopes continue to soar
In an unending endeavor to reach
That mystical place on high.
  Melanye L. Francisco

Garden Of Eden

As I soar among the stars and gaze on earth below
I see all God's creations and marvelous things that grow
The lovely blue forget-me not, the high sunflower stalk
The daffodils, the crocus buds beside a garden walk
A clump of pinks, a tulip bed, a green and trailing vine
Azaleas blooming white and red beside a stately pine
A bush of purple lilac along a high stone wall
Marigolds with orange heads and iris, straight and tall
Bush after bush of royal roses swaying in the breeze
And pansies shyly bending low, beneath the tall oak trees
So as I soar among the stars and gaze on earth below
With clarity a thought occurs and suddenly I know
the Eden God prepared for us is really close at hand
It stretches lush and blooming across our verdant land
To properly care for paradise, so the task is not too hard
God dropped down bits and pieces in every man's back yard
  Olive M. Lani

"Mom And Dad"

When I look into their face,
I see gladness and happiness inside of them,
but when one goes away,
you only have the memories,
and a picture of his face,
but you know that in your
heart he will never go away,
and with his love he left behind,
the pain and tears He blew away.

Remembering my dad who
past away...

Mary Carmen Ruiz

Mt. Olive

Perched above the hill, across the fields
I see it waiting
with doors open wide
for all to come and receive
the Spirit
the wood, chipped like tree bark
holds windows, dusty with cracks
surrounded by a once bread-white sparkle
turned yellow with age
Still, it never loses the burgundy
grace
always kneeling
the same humble way,
before the sky
a loyal steeple as two hands
in constant prayer.

Kimberly White

Ophelia's Poem

As I stare into the water below,
I see not the person I knew long ago.
A silent tear rolls down her cheek
and yet I know not why she weeps.
My father dead, he lives no more
speared by the man I love's cursed sword.
Hamlet's life spent on a foreign shore
I wish my living to be no more.
The tie that binds me to this life,
I wish to break and end my strife.
The water flecked with green and gold,
how welcoming its arms to hold.

Kelsey Swensen

I See You There

I see you there, huddled close, your tiny hands trembling
I see you there but I can't hold you and stop you from shaking
I see you there, although my vision is distorted by my tears
For I can't go back in time and protect you
I see you there, noticing that your pain is not coming from the outside world
It's coming from the space you call love and life
I see you there as you grow and mature
I want to show you who it is that is hurting you
I want you to see so that you will come to my arms for protection
I see you there, only now you are sobbing and clutching your bleeding heart
"What happened", I scream
And now I realize what happened, so I step back ashamed
For I saw you there and wanted you to see what was hurting you
So finally you saw, and the pain was unbearable
And still I can not help, for now the pain is worse, its source being exposed
I see you there, your body calm now your face hidden, embarrassed
    that I know
And I shed a tear because you're numb and no longer able to feel the bruises
As I turn to go, I look once more
I see you there, alone

Tiffany Rae Hardy

My Friend, My Self

I can see you, my friend, my self!!!
I sense in you moments of soaring passion.
I see you in experiences of sheer ecstasy,
In breathless screams of deep loneliness and despair.
In the sensations of individual perspective.
    In the unity of oneness...
The celebration of life/life's.
May your soul ring a eternal amen.
Radiating from the essence of your being
My friend... I can see you,
In the multi dimensions of life.

Orvis A. Hollobaugh

Things

Whenever I have a depressing day,
I sit and write what I need to say.

To me this is therapy, to you it is absurd,
I need to express myself with my own simple words.

The need is overwhelming, something inside me screams,
I let the words flow though no one else may know what they mean.

I know, I can feel each word,
Like a mighty eagle or a baby hummingbird.

Words are our life, well at least mine,
They don't come to my lips, but only when I write a line.

Inspiration is never a problem because of the sorrow I feel,
There are wounds deep down, they're inside, they won't heal.

I feel too strongly about too many things,
I'm scared of the night and what dreams it may bring.

Someday it will stop and I'll be at peace,
This is the day I live for, or dream of, at least.

Mattie A. Snell

This Prayer, I Pray

Rays glisten dew, ov'r hills far away.
I sit ... stare, words I know not, say.

Vacant hours from now, farther down the road.
Your face no longer seen, good-bye, not so told.

Our God, He knows we are, I know He can see.
No interruption of friendship bond, between you and me.

I pray for you, strength, in time to come.
Harmonies with others, comrades of some.

May wisdom He give unto you, guide every step you take.
For faith, hope you hold, shall remain, not break.

When days become hectic, I pray He provide peace.
So when storms, rains come, he can make them cease.

This, my only wish, a prayer that will be, so prayed.
Every minute passes, every night, every day.

For you my dearest of friends, this prayer I do pray;
God, hold our hands, to touch; each we go, our separate way.

Laurie D. Greer

Untitled

You called...
I wept for you, dear friend,
In your silent world
    Without a human voice;
No birds in song,
No listening to the raindrops on the roof;
Only the thundering
    Of your own internal clock...
I wept for you, dear friend,
    When you called.

Margaret Plenk

The Knowledge

Outwardly still, inwardly swirling
  I stare at the moon
    Alone with my pain.

The clouds endlessly move across the face
  of the sky,
Even as my feelings move through my soul.

Upon reflection, as of a wind clearing the clouds,
  I found an inner peace;
with the clear, bright knowledge - a full moon
  in a deep black sky;
that love is all we need to disavow the dark.

this love need not be of a man,
  But of humanity
Family, friends, spirituality...
The greatest love we must sustain
  Is love of self and identity.

  Kathy Mashburn

Still

With all the answers I have
  I still walk on unfamiliar ground;
I still seek to learn,
  I still look around.

And though I feel I've learned so much,
  I still must learn much more:
I still must struggle
I still must stretch
  To open that unopened door.

Yes, with all the answers I have
  Many questions still abound
And I still must strive to submit myself
  (by my own choice)
To trust in that guiding hand
  And follow that still small voice.

  Ronald Wendel

Brief (??) Case

A briefcase, to my side is bound
I think it weights about ten thousand pounds
Did you ever wonder why they call it brief
The reports and papers just give me grief
Is it because it's little smaller
Than a steamer trunk, which is a bit taller
It's packed with more than one can think
The only thing missing is the kitchen sink
The trouble is; to get it shut
I have to run over it with a truck
I wish someday they would invent
One with a lock that didn't bend
And spread its contents at my feet
When I'm jaywalking across a busy street
But in the end, I'm willing to bet
It's a helluva lot lighter than my filing cabinet.

  Karen L. Catozzi

Divided Love

In crowded streets I'll look for you.
In lonely sleep I'll long for you.
In the falling rain I'll weep for you.
In fatal pain I'll cry for you.
In summers breeze I'll think of you.
When I'm on my knees I'll beg for you.
When you want me near I'll run for you.
And as long as you want I'll wait for you.

  Steven Johnson

Still Loved

I want him back, my mind's a mist.
I thought I could change what was on God's list.
I know it happened, it makes me cry.
Why did Rod have to die?
For every happy thought I shed a tear.
For I know that Rod cannot be here.
What did he do? Why could it be,
That God took him from the world and me.
He was a good man, he did nothing wrong.
He took his dying brave and strong.
I loved him dearly and now he's to rest.
But I have to realize it was for the best.
I still get sad, but then I think of how
He is out of pain and happier now.
Rod, I will see you in heaven. When I have no clue.
But until that day remember, I still love you.

  Ryan Clover

Why Can't You Love Me

Why can't you love me?
I truly don't understand
You said you were a Christian
Who is suppose to give love unconditionally
Without looking for something in return.

When I am down you are suppose to lift me up.
When I cry you are suppose to wipe away my tears.
When I am hungry you are suppose to feed me.
When I am pain you are suppose to comfort me.
When I am lonely you are suppose to be my friend.

You say that I am too independent
But independents look for love too.
Someone to befriend them, to hold them,
To share tears of sadness and joy.
Remember life is not forever
And each second should be cherished
For we know not when our days may end
So, why can't you love me and let me know;
I have a good friend.

  Samella Burse

A Four Letter Word

As I turn out the lights and softly close the door,
  I turn and I whisper,
"Take care of him please, he means so much to me."
  Home is a four letter word.

I open the door to my office a usual,
  the phone rings and the day has started.
Children absent, irate parents, tired teachers,
  Work is just a four letter word.

As I slowly walk and open the door,
  A whisper comes to me,
"I took care of him, a little more tired,
  but he is fine."
Home is a wonderful four letter word.

  Marylou Crothers

Parsing The Fourth Dimension Of O.J.'S Unconscious

I was Orenthaling through Brentwood the other night, when
in a sudden flash to my senses I was transported to
Chappaquiddick Island at nearly twice the speed of light.

Now, to my surprise, I'm home again in Brentwood all safe
and sound, but something is vaguely missing.

Perhaps I will travel again soon.

  Larry R. Vandervert

402

"Only You"

I took in the air as if it were my last breath,
I wandered my mind as I fought with myself,
I could see in my heart, a picture clear and so true,
I paced through the darkness seeing only you,

I loathed the stars and lashed out at the earth,
I screamed out in passion and fell in my hurt,
I was blinded by ignorance and deafened by pain,
I was lost in the silence as I smothered in blame,

Your voice is in the wind and your eyes in the sky,
Your lips are the rain and your smile my only light,
My mind now numb, but my heart cradling the truth,
I cry in vain for my love, I search for only you,

The darkness now my companion, no moonlight to be seen,
I grope through my madness, with but one dream,
To touch your face and to hold your heart near,
To stop this endless searching, finding you here.

Robin Garrison

I Was Lost

The whole world started to close in on me.
I was lost.
My eyes began to shake
my legs felt like rubber.
I was lost.
I walked around in circles
each step I took crushed more and more
of my hope of being rescued.
I was lost.
I sat down on a log to think.
I thought being lost is like an ant trying to find
its way through a 5,000 foot maze.
Or maybe being lost is like a seven year old youth
struggling to find his way home.
I got up
off the old log I was sitting on and started crying out...
Mom! Mom!
My voice fell to a whisper...
Mom, mom.
I was lost.

Peter Stenson

Gift

Once upon a time
I was moved to write rhyme
That talent was given to me:
By the Almighty - knowingly
For with it, I have the unique tool
To share heart-felt thoughts of this fool
To joke and story tell, ...all in good fun
With inspirational thoughts, now and again a pun
There is true pleasure and great enjoyment
In helping others see their own self deployment....
Of their great worth, value and relationship, as I can
In the eyes of both God and man
Inspiration comes about 'special' people or their acts
Because I have been granted the ability to write those facts
Some call it perception - but credit not me
'For all things are possible through Him', you see
I am just now beginning to discover
Introspectively, things I should have sought earlier to uncover
I know not why, other than to fully trust
Some day, for Him, This Gift will count for something AUGUST.

Robert E. Kersey

The First Fifty Years

For fifty years
I was only permitted to lightly touch your surface
As a child I was obedient
As a woman, I am still that child
We play with polite conversation, my babies beauty, my husbands status
Unspoken are the loneliness and the sadness that reside in my soul
If I let you see my pain,
You will have to face your own imperfection
so I silence myself
trying to sustain your approval and semi-love

I have many secrets
Innocently, one blossoms and bares fruit,
huge and ripe, refusing to be suppressed
Your unvoiced judgement cries in my head
I watch the universe between us expand and grow
As you silently push me away, I deflate, I crumble,
Yet still, I reach out for compassion, for love,
but the only contact I make is with the air
In the end I have to accept into every cell of my self.
Your heart is dead and always was.
Mother as you turn from me, the rest of my years can be finally free

Sheila McGuinn

"Staring into the Golden Dome"

Staring up into the golden dome,
I watched a bee floating from square to square,
thinking it must have found its long lost
golden honeycomb hive and touching on nothing
but cold, hard stone - touching on each bit
of gold and caramel, coming up dry and
bitter sweet - round and round the circular
formation of the tiles on the dome, each time
going back to stop on a missed bit of potential
triumph the yellow and black almost
blending into the tiles and hiding the bee from my
view for who knows how long, is it gone or just
disappeared into the mosaic to find the other
lost travellers who have been sucked into the
sweet honey feeling of finding the dream—
it reappears at the center of the dome, golden,
beautiful, lost, finally accepting its mistaken home
and shattered dreams, the bee floats softly off
into the sunlight - up, up, up, it flies, on its way to
the sun it seems, and off to another disappointment

Tiffany Krell

Neighbors

I watched my neighbors spade and hoe,
I watched him rake, and watched him sow
And set new plants, out in a row,
I watched him trim, and watched him weed.

And, here and there, set out a seed,
And do the things all garden's need
I watched him everyday to see,
How glad a gardener's, work can be.

But I knew not that he watched me,
I looked across the fence last night
And oh, it was a lovely sight,
With blossoms gold and red and bright.

I saw my neighbor pluck each fair,
New bloom with love and tender care
I cried when every, stalk was bare,
But when I rose at dawn today.

Upon my topmost doorstep lay,
A dewy red and gold bouquet.

Mary Townsend Cook

"The Journey"

Please allow me a moment of time,
I will take you away, to a place without crime.

This journey of ours will consist not of travel,
The ground not of earth, the roads not of gravel.

And oh, do not bother to pack up your wares,
Where you are going, not one soul will care.

By now you must wonder, where could this place be?
Is it in space, or maybe the sea?

No genders exist, no people of color,
No hatred, no friends, not even your mother.

And to throw you again, you've been there before,
It's your mind that I speak of, way down in the core.

It's one little feeling, just one and not more,
The emotion of happiness that makes your heart soar.

When you feel this motion, you have not a care,
The world is at bay, your troubles not there.

So next time you visit, take time to enjoy,
It's your lifetime present, it's life's little toy.

Richard Edwards

"Silent Screams"

I wish I could take, those tears all away,
I wish I could wash, those fears at bay,
I can't, I'm powerless, I'm unable you see,
It's really not up, to you or me.
We're put on this earth, from that day of birth
Our bodies are built, with memories of pain
The heartaches and laughter, they're one in the same,
They both serve a purpose, we're to blind to see
Broken teddy bears, broken dreams
Never ending, the pain just grows, when will it stop, no one knows,
Shattered Barbie dolls, heads detached, clothes so tattered,
Nothings attached, - busted fire truck, toys all gone,
Where does the child go, when everything's wrong?
They enter adulthood, thinking, yeah...that's what they should
Broken teddy bears, silent screams,
Shattered Barbie dolls, how cruel it seems,
Their sojourn of heartache, those memories of pain
God'll take away, those broken dreams,
Of busted Barb dolls, and silent screams!

Leah Karen Wiley

Waiting For Baby

As I wait for the arrival of our first baby
(I wonder are we ready)
Then I think of course...not really...well maybe.

There are so many questions that run through my head
That keep me thinking despite the books I've read.

I know nature will help guide us through,
but I can't help but wonder what we'll do.

I wonder will we be good parents to this precious one
then I think of the great job our parents have done.

I can only think of happy thoughts towards this bundle of joy
No matter if it's a girl or a boy.

I know it's hard work and life will change a lot,
and this can't help run through every thought.

So, I take a deep breath and let out a sigh,
and for the moment my worries pass by.

Vicki L. Wells

Limited Warranty

Unfortunately **IT** has returned; maybe secretly I knew **IT** would.
I wonder if **IT** ever truly left, or just hid **ITSELF** away for awhile.
I believed, or actually desperately hoped
That **IT** would become lost in the total confusion:
Left in my hospital room, pushed away and forgotten, unable to find
   ITS way home.
I know now that didn't happen.
Slowly things began changing, nothing for the better.
Mind unraveling, I feel the firm, tightening grasp,
And soon the intolerable pain.
The pathway has been re-opened: Newly paved.
I wake up frightened, knowing I'm not alone.
Shutting my eyes tightly, I sneak a quick, paralyzed peek,
However, **IT** would not retreat, a confrontation was mandatory.
Looking into **ITS** eyes, I hesitate, swallow hard, then panic.
Struggling to hold on, trying not to slip away
I fight with all my soul, but finally I lose.
So now I must face **IT** - against my will I'm forced to submit.
Trembling, I take **ITS** hand, and **IT** leads me back.
The journey is unpleasant, yet all too familiar.
Shortly we arrive: **IT'S** taken me back to the beginning...

Lisa DeGuglielmo

I Am

I am one who can see other worlds and touch someone's soul
I wonder why the young and the brilliant's lives are taken
I hear the clash of good and evil in a battle for the soul of a
   human being
I see a faint light of hope in a dismal future
I want all to be free of hunger and want
I am one who can see other worlds and touch someone's soul.

I pretend to help the world
I feel the beat of a heart no one cares for
I touch the soul of a forgotten person
I worry of the future of the world
I cry over what may be, but has not yet happened
I am one who can see other worlds and touch someone's soul.

I understand the responsibility of being a human
I say all are good at heart, but too many do not show it
I dream of the coming of the end of the world
I try to change negative to positive
I hope I can make a difference
I am one who can see other worlds and touch someone's soul.

Richard E. Laux

Reality

I looked inside my soul and wondered what I'd see.
I wondered what memories were still trapped inside of me.

I thought I saw a small child afraid to go to sleep.
I thought I saw my mother when she had just been beat.

I thought I heard loud voices raging in the night.
I thought I heard an angel say "it will be all right".

I thought I felt great pain, my heart was broke in two.
I thought I was all alone and didn't know what to do.

I looked again inside my soul and could not believe my eyes.
For what I thought was exactly right this reality is mine.

Tammy Taylor-Vaughn

When I Was A Child

When I was a child
I would dreamily stare at the snow
Plotting the tunnels to places only I could go

When I was a child,
I would look into the sun
Pretending I was invisible to everyone

When I was a child
I would ride along gazing at the moon
Wishing this rocket would take me there soon

When I was a child
I would pretend I was Katrina
A world famous ballerina

When I was a child
I hated when my mom rang the dinner bell
Because my circus horse tripped and fell

When I was a child
I was the last to be picked for the team
Probably because I liked to daydream

Now that I am all grownup, I am even a few feet taller
and waiting for my business caller

Sometimes I still fantasize that I own this enterprise.

Kathleen Cook

What I Know Now

If given another chance
I would fall more wisely
knowing what I now know

Perhaps choosing a soulmate
When our hair streaks gray
And we need glasses for almost everything

Possibly escaping the pain
And even holding on to the passion
The ultimate gift of grace

Kind and gentle in
The small everyday minutes

Wanting to see me,
Touch me, hold me, tell me...

The eyes and the laughter
Both windows
Reflecting the soul and
Speaking the love

Love to be cherished
Not squandered
Maybe, perhaps there is still time...

Marilyn Peyton Corbin

Count Your Blessings

My problems weighed heavy, as I knelt to pray;
I'd forgotten to count my Blessings
Here's the lesson I learned one day.

As I took up the Good Book,
'Twas then that I realized;
I had over estimated my problems' size.

As my thoughts turned to God above,
Disappointments disappeared;
Happiness was there, I knew I must never despair.

So why not count your blessings?
This lesson with you I must share;
God will always listen,
And eternally answer each pray'r.

Pauline Jackson Jessup

Untitled

God felt man would be lonely
If he did not have a pet
Some kind of furry animal
That gets smelly when it's wet.

A dog or a cat to worry about
When vacations came around
That "What are we going to do with Fritz?"
When Kennel space cannot be found.

I've had many pets throughout my life
Dogs, cats, canaries too
But when Shieba used up all nine lives
I said no more pets for you.

But now my wife is looking around.
A new dog to be friend
And offer it a home with newspapered floors
When it's ready to move in.

I'll clean up and feed it, go for a walk
Veterinarians will leave me poor
It will get more attention than I've ever had
Why can't I be her dog-du-jour.

Ted Marshall

Along The Way

How can I miss the one I don't know?
If I wait and wait will he ever show?
Give me a sign, some way to know
Will he ever come? Yes or no?

I know what he's like, can't picture his face.
And no one on earth could take his place.
And if I should find him, did he wait for me
Or as they say and so shall it be?

Is he still out there or just in my mind?
Will it take forever or just a short time?
To find him and love him as I know it should be
Do you think that he's out there looking for me?

And if we should meet on the street someday
Will we then know, or just walk away?

I guess it's a chance, a chance I must take
Because he's out there and I must wait.
So give me the strength to wait a long time
Give me the strength so hard to find
And please let me wake every day
With the hope that I'll find him - along the way...

Robin Bray

Soft

I sat hugging my knees with my toes in the sand.

Sifting the soft crystals through my fingers, I felt every grain as
If it were the nape of my child's neck.

The golden fingers of the sun reached down to caress my shoulders
Relieving the aches and pains of my life; calming my breath.

I watched as the waves gently stroked and pulled at the shoreline
As if to say: Come with me. I'll take you to the sunset where the
Colors lovingly hide the blemishes of the world, where things can
Be more than they seem, a place where yearning stops.

Come with me where living begins with an unquenchable fire,
Thirsting to give what is to be taken, then returning it to the
Sand where I have thrust my feet deep into its heart, begging for
The truth I can't find.

I feel the softening sun letting me go, tenderly persuading me to
Find the way.

Maria Carpenter

Unspeakable Love

If I could only find something to show
If only there was some way for you to know
Those wonderful feelings I feel inside
Those sincere feelings of love that I have no need to hide
Words are no where near enough to say
The way I feel about you everyday
Please listen to these words I say
And try to remember them every minute of each day
When we fight it gives me such tremendous pain
Sometimes it damn near drives me insane
Do not ever doubt my love for you
Cause it will always be there if you want it too.
I really wish someday
There will be words that say
Every thing you mean to me
And everything I see life with you to be.

Mike Gardner

Nana's Girl

I wonder where my life would be
If this child had not been born
She came at such a lonely time
On a sunny, bright spring morn

Her name will be Keeley
My heart and love she's won
I'll hear her cry, and watch her grow
This daughter of my son.

I would that I could keep her small
And keep her from all pain
Give her a life full of sunshine and joy
With never a day of rain.

She is growing up, as well she should
The years go by in a whirl
And when she's grown, and I am gone
She will still be Nana's girl.

Margaret McGrory

Someone's Daydream

Everything starts by being someone's daydream
If you reach for the stars you will see
There's a light shining down illuminating your path
Now it's your choice which road it will be

And while you are searching and dreaming your dreams
Keep eyes open, head up and be strong
For sometimes things happen beyond our control
Life's not perfect ... at least not for long

Tho' on one hand I wish I could spare you the pain
That life's journeys are certain to bring
To protect you from harm and the pain in your path
And to make only happiness sing

But if I could do this and as much as I'd like
I would have to choose this to not do
For in order to help you prepare for your life
Is to show that it's inside of you

You already have them, the keys to success
The ability, knowledge and more ...
The potential to be just whatever you want
Don't be frightened to open the door.

Kris Schumacher

A Communion Meditation

If you have a burden that's too heavy to bear,
    If your heart is weighed down with sorrow and care,
If the light on your pathway is dimmed by your tears.
    I've good news for you, you've a Father who cares!

He cares when you're happy, he cares when you're sad,
    He loves you when good, and when you are bad.
For His love has been given so full and so free
    To bring peace to the hearts of both you and me.

His love was made known to all men on earth,
    And God became man through Bethlehem's birth.
But His great heart was broken for you and for me,
    When God gave His son on Calvary's tree.

So today as we bow at the altar and pray,
    And partake of Communion on this Holy Day,
May we offer ourselves to the Father above
    To be channels of grace and mercy and love.

Raymond W. O. Knowles

Right For You

What can I do to make it right for you?
I'll die for you, I'll cry for you,
But what does it take to make it right for you?
The names you name mean something to me
The scars you wear tear slashes through me
I'll think for you, I'll breath for you,
But what does it take to get through to you?
I know that you know that a good time's hard,
Easier to feel or to disregard
A message written in hidden places,
A lifetime of trusting familiar faces
But a promise made within your reach
Is slipping through your fingers
The labor of fulfillment
Even stronger, ever lingers
I'll bleed for you the need for you to penetrate the prison
That holds your soul's undying goal in suspended animation
To see with you and be with you, the only things that I can do
But how can I make it right for you?
The endless start is the fight for you

K. A. Wandlass

No Failure, Just Faith

If I look and see failure lurking
I'll look him in the eye and say
I refuse to be your successful partner.

To failure, I'll say I walk by faith
In Jesus. I'm made fearfully and
Wonderful in the image of my Lord,
Jesus Christ who never fails.

Walking in God is no failure
There is always success on the inside of me
I release the success of God within me
Now I let it flow out and on out in winning.

"For greater is he that's within me
Than he that is in the world."
I am totally victorious by being
"A person spelling failure as faith abiding
In Lord of Lords unto riches eternally."

I have the "I can do" attitude; and the "I
Can be" attitude of all I want to be
Because of the Jesus power in me telling me
I'm a winner and a conqueror to overcome all!

Margaret S. Green-Zoladek

I'm Saved!

Ask me why I'm special and
   I'll tell you that I'm saved.
By the grace of God's forgiving heart,
   My sin wrought debt He waived.

God's mercy and His love for me
   Stretch beyond my deepest understanding,
Yet God loves me just the way I am,
   My faith and trust's all He's demanding.

He pours His power into me,
   He lifts my spirit up.
When I humbly bow before His throne,
   He offers me His cup.

Speaking through His Holy word,
   his Spirit ministers to me.
His great wisdom, power, strength and truth
   Set my spirit singing, soaring free.

Even though I stumble badly
   And I fall from time to time,
Staring straight into the Devil's eyes
   God declares, "This one is mine!"
      Robert Jackson

"To Mother"

When I look to the clouds on a summer day
   I'll think of you.
When I see the colored leaves fall swiftly to the ground
   I'll think of you.
When the snowflakes sparkle on a cold winter day
   I'll think of you.
When the spring flowers bloom with color all around
   I'll think of you.
When the night breezes blow gently on a quiet evening
   I'll think of you.
When the birds sing sweetly a melody of song
   I'll think of you.
When the rain falls softly on the window pane
   I'll think of you.
When a rainbow shines in the southern sky
   I'll think of you.
When the sun sets in the west to a golden glow
   I'll think of you.
Till we meet again in heaven Mother
   I'll think of you.
      Rosemary Dilley

Scrapbook Memories

As I take my scrapbook, from its place on the shelf;
   "I'll visit old memories," I say to myself.
Petals of a prom rose lace the first page;
   Pressed in loving memory, they are withered with age.
The yellowed pages show a couple hand-in-hand,
   A sunset behind them, as they stroll in the sand.
Through the pages of time, I view my husband and I,
   And relive our wedding, with a peaceful sigh.
Souvenirs of my children grace the book,
   And I laugh aloud at all the pictures I took.
Our family vacations and celebrated trips,
   Are revealed through postcards and airline slips.
Anniversary cards mark the passage of years;
   I smile with the memory and brush away tears.
I touch pictures of grandchildren sitting on my knee,
   And smile at the grandmother I am happy to be.
Seeing family together is a lovely to behold;
   The joyful peace given cannot be bought or sold.
As my scrapbook of life is closed with a sigh,
   I thank God for memories of times gone by...
      Patrice Thomas

I Need You

Sitting here, all alone at night
I'm just thinking of you
So I had to take the time and write

I just can't fright it, I need to have near
My heart just breaks in two
As my eyes begin to tear

I need you, more than words can say
The illusion is in my head
But the reality is so far away

I know there's no way, that my hopes can be
Because the feelings that I have for you
Are not same that you have for me

But I can dream, now and forever more
You'll always be on my mind
'Cause that's what dreams are for.
      Tom Mattocks

Standing At The Crossroads Again

I'm standing at the crossroads once again my life.
I'm pretty sure I've been here, maybe once, maybe twice.
Although it doesn't look the same, my heart tells me it is.

The paths that lie before me, which one do I take?
I'll stop and look behind me, "just for old times sake."
Now which can do I take?
What decision do I make?

To continue on as I am, well that just doesn't seem right.
It's time to decide which one is right.

So I'll pray and ask the Lord to lead me unto the right path,
And to give me strength to continue on.

To stay on the path and not to stray,
To pray the path will lead me closer to the Lord,
A deeper understanding of an ever lasting love.
And life as he had meant for me to live a life's work.
      Sandy Dunn

Skin

No matter how hard I try, they won't let me in.

They tell me I'm equal, but when the unthinkable happens,
I'm quickly accused regardless of where or who I am.

They tell me color, race, and sex is against their standards,
but I appear and I'm denied.

No matter how hard I try, they won't let me in.

They say I'm ugly, dirty, and represent evil, but they use the
sun to gain my shade.

They say it's the land of the free and opportunist, but I'm denied,
although my forefathers and mothers, brothers, and sisters helped
to build this country.

No matter how hard I try, they won't let me in. It's sad they can't
realize by now, I'm only skin.
      Phyllis Floyd-Greenidge

The Mind's Eye

Pictures, ever appearing in the mind's eye.
Innumerable, fleeting, flashing;
A blink brings another into focus.
Only a glance to spare; so much more awaits.
A brief pause here, there, then drawn on.
Wanting a closer look, but reaching for what lies beyond.
Another, and then another, ever appearing in the mind's eye.
      Mary Carol Weeks

Goodbye

I will never forget this painful, farewell
I'm saying goodbye, still loving you.
If you ever loved me. I could never tell
Perhaps you loved me too.

This sad and crazy passion
that rooted so deep in me
may not be love, may not be affection
may just be desire for thee

The memory of a kiss forever will stay
My heart tells me that I can't forget
And when alone, knowing that you are away
My love like a plant will grow every day

Goodbye my darling and happiness too
With this goodbye, my most beautiful dream dies inside me
I'm saying goodbye for the rest of my life,
life that I will spend crying for you

And, when the last tear drop from my eyes has fallen
And my life of agony gets to an end
With your name in my lips and facing the sky
there will be no more pain in the final goodbye

Rafael Leon

The Autumn's Grasp

Outside the leaves sprinkle down
In a sea of leaves you begin to drown

The sky is the clearest blue
The bright yellow sun looks down on you

As you lay in the leaves and gaze
The sky gives way to a crisp autumn breeze

And just as the breeze passes by
A dark midnight blue covers the sky

And up comes the large rounded moon
And you know this feeling will be over soon

Because now comes the Autumn's night chill
But yet the trees remain still

And then you go into your warm house leaving the cold behind
As you lookout the window at the multi-colored trees one last time

J. T. Edwards

You Are Always There

When I think of all I have done,
In a world full of despair.
Trusting in so many people,
Who really did not even care.
But then, I remember how Jesus loved
And died for me,
Way back on Calvary.
The heavy burden of the cross and
My sins he did not have to bare.
Oh, how many times, can I say thank you, Lord
For you are always there.

Thank you, Lord for you love.
Thank you, Lord for looking down from above.
Thank you Lord for hearing me when I call.
Thank you Lord for picking me up when I fall.
Thank you Lord for bringing comfort to my soul.
Thank you, Lord for making me whole.
Thank you, Lord for showing me you care.
Thank you, Lord for you are always there.

Robin L. Oliver

A Touch Of Friendship

It happened this year, at the convention held at Washington, D.C.
In August, on the sixth, this tiny act of friendship
Between two aspiring poets, a mother and a husband.
Joined by daughter and wife they had breakfast, had said goodbye and
had parted to go
Home, the couple to Hawaii, the mother and daughter to Chicago.
Little did they know that later that day, there would be
An unusual meeting between the two, and once again, each other they
would see.
Who told the mother to ride on the side near the descending escalator?
And the husband to ride on the side close to the ascending escalator?
For, as the escalators kept moving, just at midpoint between the floors
The poets suddenly saw each other going in opposite directions
It was the mother who had first seen her friend and voiced a happy greeting
With beaming smiles, leaning over with arms extended
They were able to touch each other's fingers for a very fleeting
moment, because
The escalators would not pause and kept on moving, of course.
That mere touch of fingers, strangely, has left an impression very dear to me
And carefully, I have tucked the touch in a recess of my heart.
Today, as I reminisce
That fleeting touch I find, is more precious to me, than a look, a
hug, or a tiny kiss
The tender touch of fingers, my heart will forever embrace
This touch was a touch of friendship, which time can never erase.

Yoshiyuki Otoshi

Eye Of The Storm

A long time ago, I never thought it would be me, a fragile bird
In flight from the storm, heading South,
Flapping my wings so furiously only to be chased by the rain, soon to be hail
Flying away to stay clear of the turbulence but to no avail.

As soon as the sun's rays would peak from behind a cloud
I'd try to slow down to listen to the whispers of the wind and wait
For the sun to shine bright so I could fly with the warmth of the sun's arms.
Yearning to be caressed by such radiance, such beauty
For even just a fleeting moment. Following the music of hope not despair,
Of love and trust not fear.

My wings slowing pace could not last for long, the storm has not ended
Feathers continue to be tattered and torn
Soft and frail, tough and strong, which will be which and when?

Will the storm die or will we become one?
Can any part of the innocence be mended?
Lost in the eye but blinded by the light
I see the lucky ones flying so well, no turbulence,
Only a few boundaries. Nothing following them, nothing lurking
From behind a cloud, nothing waiting ahead of them.
Beautiful shadows. The sun shining.
Envious of birds so free, a long time ago that was once me.

Marla Katz

"My One True Love"

My one true love awaits for me,
In the darkness of the sea.
Go my sheep away from me
And rest upon the river's knee.
My love is so true
Said the sea of the deep blue
and I will always wait for you.
Carry on toward the sun
And you shall always love young.
For this is the moment our love has just begun.
See the waves crash ashore
My one true love I do adore.
Come with me
Ride the sea
My one true love, one are we.

Maigen Green

408

Winds Of Change

Death leaves a found cause for lost love;
in grief we seek inspiration from above.
Our love heightens the depth of our sorrow;
we dry our tears with time borrowed.
Shouldering the pain left behind,
the haunting void stays to remind.
We are suddenly asked to grow
and to accept life is no more.
Not knowing if and whom to forgive,
we search questions to die and live.
We do not understand why it happens;
what is taken must be given.
In seasons passing, we grow together and apart;
the spirit of our friend kindles in our heart.
Blessed by the one who touched us,
we envision what once was.
The gifts of God are deeply appreciated;
how we wish we were not separated.
With gratitude we thank the Almighty;
to love and to return love in infinity.

Rama R. Nerella

"Ginger 6-14-64"

In her veins, flows my blood.
In her heart, holds all my love...

In her eyes, I see my face.
In her carriage, I see only grace...

In her deeds, she succeeds, where I never could.
In her manner, what I never understood...

In her smile, elusive glee.
In her laughter, all the love she has brought me...

In her speech, clear and kind.
In her spirit, brings another to mind...

In her hands, all I hold dear.
In her life, I will always be near...

In her praises, I will speak.
In her devotion, I will ever seek...

Love, Mom.

Pali

Life's Monsters

As a child my fears were of the night,
In the eerie dark there was no light.
Monsters, Goblins, filled my dreams,
A muffled cry, please hear my screams.
The light comes on, I'm now okay.
My parents chased the monsters away.

Monsters or bullies you were always there,
To wipe my tears and show you care.
I've since moved away and I'm older now.
The monster's still there, but different somehow.
They've left my dreams and the eerie night.
And haunt my life during broad daylight.

The stresses of life have the monster's head
Just like the terrors that were under my bed.
When my fears become to much to bear,
It's you I can count on to always be there.
A phone call home, the comforting sound
of an emotional hug, your arms all around.

The light comes on, I'm now okay.
My parents still chase the monsters away.

Robert M. Cox

Broken Hearts

The loneliness of time echoes
in the empty halls of life. Each time the
clock ticks another heart is broken as another
heart mends. But it's only temporary for the mind
can play some cruel tricks. The hollow sounds
that cry for a mutual love ring in the ears
of an invisible soul, stalking and walking
down an alley, somewhere we will never know.
As the story goes on, you will find that you
you were only a pawn in a game, where
kings and queens really do exist or so it
seems. But as you move the time fades,
as the knight raids, you come to a point
where there is no return. When the game
is over and so is the love you made.

C. Yvonne Burton

Garden

I put you in the light of day,
in the wind your flowers sway.
I pick your dirty weeds away,
so you can blossom one more day.
I give you water when you're dry,
to hold your beauty beneath the sky.
The love I give is unconditionally yours,
I'll try to heal your weeping sores.
Under skies of lightning storms,
you know you're safe, and that you're warm.
So blossom garden, blossom for me
make your beauty shine for eternity.

J. Justin Woods

Behold!

Behold! the mountains of life...
In them you will find
The valley of despair and the land of hope
The hills of trust and the gully of failure
The trail of faith, the peak of success
The boulders of grief, the stepping stones of joy
The uncommon fruit of love
The rainbows of friendship
The avalanches of problems...
Through it all runs the river of truth

So, choose your path carefully
To avoid valleys and gullies
To watch out for boulders
Only receive small portions of avalanches
See many rainbows, climb many hills
Take the stepping stones when available
Eat often of the fruit
Achieve a few peaks
And follow the course of the river

Rebekah Jones

Seasons

Spring is like the new born, so wide eyed
innocent and small.
Summer is like the teen aged, blooming,
impertinent tall.
Autumn is like the middle aged
vibrant, colorful, effervescent too!
winter is like the elderly staunch,
mellowed, weathered, reminiscing true.

Katherine M. Marana

Golden Gown

Speak to me, earth creature,
in your native tongue.
Build your castle on the highest peak
and leave a sacred torch burning for me.
For I come within with warmth of heart,
seeking my sleeping maiden
whose love enchants me evermore.
She is the beauty I adore.
Fair maiden with her silken skin
and golden gown like heaven's radiance.
My angel sleeps on satin sheets.
I'd die to be those satin sheets.
As I search the castle catacombs
For the scent of sweet perfume,
I'll find my maiden sleeping sound-
on a cloud of satin in a golden gown.

Mark Blackard

Independence

I imagined it. Intimidated. Incrementally, ideas identified.
Invigorating. Intense. Individual!
No one. Nameless. Not needing. Numb. Nervous?
Don't despair. Dream. Direction determined. Dance!
Exceptional energy. Enjoyable encounter. Endless expectations
examined. Enough!
Pity/pride: Painful process. Passion/principle: Personal plan.
Patience/progress: Persistence pays.
Eyes explore. Eagerly engage. Express empathy. Easily evaluate.
Explain.
Never! Nonetheless, nice. Neither negative nor naive.
Definitely distracted. Discouraged? Decide. Do. Demand daring.
Essential. Each event: educational. Every elation: empowering!
New name, naturally. Now, nurturing.
Childhood circumstance, consequences coming:
(Cruelty causes complication. Concern calms confusion. Caring
creates compassion.)
Everlasting!

Wendy Madison

The Black Oasis

for my Tim and Melissa
Extreme yet graceful, salvation of the scarlet angels.
Irresistible ivory devotion tears away at my restless mind as
phydelic poison is interlocking my soul and fears
impurity pulsates within me slowly distorting the mundane silence
Forever engraving myself on two nameless hearts as they two
   as one arise from darkness into each other forever.
I am an infamous mind breathless and frightened by the neverending
echo blind folded I'll pursue the purity of the glistening black
oasis overshadowed by hypnotizing lightning and mystified by the
   musical outsider in the sky.
Grasping at the legacy of faded heartache and an intimate
   genocide of those I love.
Fears of falling inward, reclusion to a point of no return as
hysterical rage radiates from my every direction.
A forceful draft arrives interrupting my sleep I rise, reaction
   to my unjustifiable denial of this morbid massacre.
Solemnly I wait anticipating my final outcry
a one sided sacrifice dissolving from myself.
As this dream mutates I am alone on my ledge
I am myself the only enemy.

Star Christine Havird

The Cemetery

Down the road and across the street -
Is a place of silence where many sleep.
It's usually empty, few people around -
Always quiet with manicured grounds.
There are stones of white, black and red -
And near some are flag holders made of lead.
The flags represent the wars they fought -
To make us free and the lessons they taught.
There are colorful flowers, wreaths made of vines -
There are trees of oak, maple and pine.
Blessed with God's love and all His grace -
Someday I'll be there taking my place.

Marion Kerr-Snyder

By Myself

Why do I feel so alone?
Is anybody out there?
I'm enclosed in a secret place,
A place where no one shall find me.
I'll sit and wait to be found,
But I'm forgotten.
Nobody will know I was gone,
Nobody knew I was here,
I'm forgotten.
Nobody wants me.
Like the shoe on the shelf with a scuff mark.
With no companion.
I'm where people stare at me and laugh.
Will I be alone forever?
Will I ever be found?
Will I ever be able to look at someone
and say "I love you"?
I don't know.

Lori Menard

Old Man Time

When Old Man Time makes up his mind there
is nothing that anyone can do to change it.
When he decides it is time for things to change no matter
what anyone does to try and stop him he always
prevails in the end.
Old Man Time is never in a hurry
he just takes as much time as he needs to bring
about change that he feels the world needs.
It may take Old Man Time days, weeks, months,
years, or even centuries to bring about changes
but when his changes come they are so immense
that they can be compared to an upheaval in the universe.

Trasha N. Hickman

The Unsuspected Fall

A quick little slip on ice and snow,
Is quite an experience, ask me I know.
With a broken bone, and severe pain,
You think you are dying or going insane.

A trip to the doctor for that hard white cast,
Then walking on crutches is quite a task.
The things you could easily do before,
Are out of the question, even opening a door.

You sit with a pillow, and a bag of ice,
And hope that this ordeal soon will pass.
Your family are great, with their sympathetic looks,
As you sit in your chair with a pile of books.

You lie in bed and ponder your fate,
About things undone, or that canceled date.
As time goes by, I know I will mend,
With the help of my family, loved ones, and friends.

Martha Clark Burford

"Hope"

Why are you cast down, oh my soul? Review you hope in God!
Is this a testing of your faith, or God's chastening rod?
You need not be disquieted, for God's still on his throne.
He never has nor never will, forsake his very own.

The storm clouds gather, the billows roll, but God is still the same.
He makes a way through each storm, for those who trust his name.
He is the Saviour of the soul, and the body too.
And what is established by his Word, is forever true.

You can fully trust him each day, as you walk the road of life.
Though obstacles are encountered along the way, that will engender strife.
But God has promised those who overcome, full victory at the end.
So, no matter what, at the end of life, we shall go to be with him.

   H. Fitzgerald Durbin

If

To erase a tale that has never been told,
is to tell a tale that will never be erased.

To live a life that has never been lived,
is to never live a life at all.

To read a story in a magazine, would not be a story
if never wrote.

So to be a prisoner, you would not be a prisoner,
if there were no jail.

To be a guard in a jail, if there were no jail,
There'd be no guard.

When man lived in a cave, when there was no cave,
He lived.

But with Christ we find that we stand,
But without Christ, we'll never see Beulah Land.

   Rufus F. Crump

Eternal Reflections

When we recall the wars of old,
It always makes our blood run cold,
If we would only look within
And realize where we have been
You'd think we'd learn from past mistakes.

Our world now reels in its earthquakes
Only God alone can make
And cause the stubborn will to break
If we would only let God in to rule and reign from within,
How peaceful this world would be....
As all men live eternally.

   Patricia Casto

Love

Love is like a rose.
It blooms and it grows.
If you love someone a great deal
Happiness is what you feel.
Love should be true
And always be new.
If you love someone enough
It doesn't matter if they are tough.
Love is a very special thing.
You should treat that person like a king.
When love comes, you'll know it
And the person will show it.
So if you see love coming
A beautiful song, you will be humming.

   Kristyn Mount

And Yet

And yet...I still dream of my youth.
It came so fast, the silver crown,
and then, so smooth
the multi symptom aging gown
embracing me,
silently.

And yet...I still dream of my youth.
For when I look towards the sky,
in each of myriads of stars that lit the night,
I find the truth,
I'm part of it,
infinity.

I'll never die.
I'll multiply: Specks of dust on this star.
As for my soul, my soul will fly
where there is no matter and no pain,
and there will reign,
eternally.

   Maria del Carmen Smit

Untitled

My heart may beat to the beat of a different drum.
It can thunder and rage as the whirling winds.
And as I climb that mountain which is at the
   highest summit.
I may fall a thousand times.
To reach for what I cannot see.
To hope that one day no longer shall I succumb to the vanity.
Of a useless cause.
Inside that heart is a different song.
A barely audible hum.
That longs, and yearns to find.
Just simple unconditional love.
When I reach that fountain.
I will plunge, to drink.
Of it richest rhymes.
And when I get there.
I know I will find.
Not only myself, but each and everyone of you.
Who helped me get there.
One step at a time.

   Ofelia S. Martinez

Pop

Pop is just a little word, it isn't very impressive
It carries no Academic message.
There is no College, where such a title can be bestowed.
Of the millions of men in this great World
Only one man I called Pop.
Quiet and gentle he spoke not of love
But showed it in everything he did.
Seven days a week he labored in his shop
From the crack of dawn until it got dark.
Never asked for a thing, only that his family be happy and well
He lived a poor man and died a poor man, but he left me great wealth
A proud name and priceless memories.
I sorely miss him and wish he was here so that I could say,
Thank you Pop for your strength and love.
I now have a family of my own, when I hear the word Pop
Of all the people in this world, I know my children are near.
It's just a little word, but it has a big meaning
To me it has a wonderful sound
I'll wear it like a badge of Honor
As long as I'm around.

   Sidney Taiz

411

Money

Money is green with a successful face of value.
It could bring happiness or sadness.
Money can bring joy or success for those.
A piece of paper with a former dead president.
But you need money to live and survive in your residence.
A bill payment or a new car.
How much money did you save? Will it get you far?
Money can bring changes or disasters.
More education and knowledge is the key to success.
Money can't bring life, but money can cause death.
It could help the unfortunate, disabled or the less.
They say the more you give the more you receive.
How many people you think sit back and believe?
Money is like a piece of power, it could make you or brake you.
The history of our money goes on and on, whether it's greater or not.
Technology and more technology the world keeps changing.
Gods money keeps circulating as time keeps ticking.
Do you follow economical trends on where your money goes
and where it ends?

Marquel D. Waites

In Life You Pay

In life you pay for everything you do
It definitely did not bypass me and you

But we wonder why is it happening like this
It merely feels that we've been dissed

I suppose I realize why this is occurring to me
I am paying the price for what I did, you see

I was never a wonderful daughter, nor an honest friend
I had even deceived my boyfriend

But are those reasons enough to pay the price?
For conducting in a manner that was not right?

You just wish it all came to an end
So that you won't keep going through this pain

I can't help but wonder when it will end
Would it occur when the Bible is at hand

It's really hard to climb that ladder
When everything just keeps getting harder

Just when I feel I'm going ahead
I fall flat on my face
Not looking forward to another day.

Marilyn Ayala

"Tita"

Growing up I used to take you everywhere,
It didn't matter where, you didn't care

You got on my bike and rode facing the back,
You were so cute, you looked like a nap sack

We would ride to my friends or to the park,
And hang out there until it got dark

You were there so often, they made you mascot,
We were the only school with a mascot/tot

But when I tried to sneak out without you,
You'd run to the door and beg me, "Me too"

Through your tears, "Tita, Tita" was all you would say,
Knowing I would never leave you crying that way

I'd open the door, dry your eyes and say "Okay, Okay,"
Took your hand, put you on the bike and be gone most of the day

Now you're all grown up, married and will soon be moving away,
I just wanna run to the door and beg you to "Please, Please Stay"

"TITA, TITA DON'T LEAVE ME, OKAY?"

Lori K. Lau Castaneda

Life

What is life? Life is a precious thing, for
it is one of Gods best creations, but not all
people can see although it is staring them in
the face. Look to this day for it is life the
very life of life... For yesterday is already
a dream and tomorrow is only a vision. But
every day makes every yesterday a dream of
happiness and every tomorrow a vision of
Hope!!

Natosha R. Rue

Hugs

A hug is like a band aid,
it makes you feel all better.
It makes you feel all warm inside
when there is nasty weather.

I get hugs from dad and mom,
those hugs always make me calm.
I also get hugs from cousins,
from all of them I get a dozen.

But the hugs I get from Gramps and Grams,
are the hugs that make me who I am.
They're the hugs that make me
happy, nice, and sweet,
just like taffy.

Their hugs say
"Hey, your the best."
"You're `A' number one, on the grandkid test!"

Their hugs are perfect to the brim,
'cuz they've had practice giving them.

Kari Nichole Tanner

Give Someone A Smile

Give someone a smile, today,
It may help them in some special way.
They may feel discouraged, sad and blue,
And may need a smile from a person such as you.
So, give that special gift, someone's spirit you may lift,
Give someone a smile, today.

Virginia C. Blaich

Lost Love

I don't know just where to start,
It must be somewhere in my heart,
I don't know who or what to blame
For all my sins that I'm ashamed.

As a child, I went to sunday school
and learned about the golden rule.
Respect, loyal and trust my parents taught,
But love is something they forgot.

In my own backward and sinful way
I kept on living from day to day
Doing things wrong and later thought
Of how to cover up the plot.

My friends, family and children too,
Paid for my sins the same as you.
Oh! How I paid for what it cost
For the love that I must have lost,
Dear God some day before I part
Please put it somewhere in my heart.

Mamie L. Medrano

The Prairie

It is the crack of dawn and there is much to see.
It seems you can hear the mountain roar,
and see the great eagle soar.
The scenery someone would find simple,
does not see beyond the human eye.
As I walk through the prairie it is like an ocean;
it seems as if the grassland will never end.
This prairie so desolate, quiet, is really full of life.
Things you would never see,
is like a door an key.
It is waiting for a person to unlock it.
It is waiting for a person to release the magic.
I do not understand when they
Just say prairie, for it is extraordinary.

Meghan Betz

Love

Love can be like the beauty of Art
It should be strong enough to bring everyone
together, not push everyone Apart.

Love can be given in more ways than just one
By writing someone a letter or poem
or simply just someone over the pane.

Love can be nicely dressed up just like our Pope
He is one who puts more love in hearts
and also gives our world more hope.

Love has been around for many centuries
That is how most people out of love
made their families.

Love should not just be given to some but to all
Whether you're white, black, red, yellow
or simply because you're short or tall

If we all learn to love and try less to fight
This world would be as beautiful as the stars at night

This poem was about love as you all can see
If everyone takes my advice, we can all live very happily.

Michael A. Wallen

Reality

It shows sadness.
It shows gladness.
It is called happiness by some.
Others, call it worrisome.
It consumes many.
But, some deny it.
Some, believe it is confusing and unwilling.
Some, believe it is as clear as a star.
It is.

Kenneth Speicher

It'll Be Me

When the wind blows gently through your hair
It'll be me flying free
When the stars above twinkle softly
It'll be me winking at you
When the tree branches gently brush your window
It'll be me saying "I'm here"
When you cry and feel a sense of comfort
It'll be me holding you
When your grief is over and happy thoughts remain
It'll be me, with you, forever

Lynda L. Spotz

Synesthia's Autumn Rain

The rain feels gray.
It tastes of sorrow and remembrance.
It smells of lifeless leaves falling to earth.
It sounds like cedar sighing.

The rain smells silver.
It looks wistful and woebegone.
It taste of bitter and biting threnody.
It feels like invisible color.

The rain sounds blue.
It smells of loneliness and misfortune.
It tastes of foxglove and nightshade.
It looks wretched and barren.

Rain whispers a rainbow, and
Autumn is a broken bubble.

Mary-Frazier Paul

"Feelings"

Another day, I hope and pray - to make
it through another day. I go to school,
I hurt no one. Another day, too soon not
done. They talk about me, I don't care,
they talk about me and they stare. I
don't know why they make fun of me,
I don't know why, they just don't see.
I'm just like them, I'm just the same.
Another day, another game. Don't they
see, I don't want to play, another game,
another day. Get to know me, no more games,
I have a face, I have a name. If you
knew me, you might find, I'm really
nice, I'm really kind. Get to know me, know
my name, I'm just like you, we're all the
same. Another day, I hope and pray, to
make it through another day.

Mandi Meyrick

A Matter Of Trust

I was there, so were others.
It was a long way off, in distance and time.

We came from every corner, every walk of life.
We were troubled, we were proud.
We believed in what we were doing.

Ours was a club, a fraternity, a lodge;
Never have men had a more common purpose.
We were misguided, perhaps so were others.
Still we gave all that we had.

It was more than a war - it was a matter of trust.
When men are sent onto the field, no
matter the pursuit, it comes down to this.
Those who send must be as devoted as those sent;
There can be no compromise!

Death is a high price; its investment must be worthy.
Perhaps those who ran sensed this -
perhaps they were smart. We were expendable.

I will never forget those who died, and those wounded.
They believed and trusted in me. And I in them!

Mike Falcon

413

"The Psaltery"

The music was coming from a psaltery
It was something so unique and wonderful
I thought I stood in the midst of heaven
Enraptured by the sweetest tones I've ever heard.

Never have I been so moved before
The music touched the very depths of my soul
The sensation was so hard to describe
A marvelous experience to be retained forever.

The musician used a plectrum of bone
And the songs he sang were in Spanish
He stroked the strings in a caress
His agile fingers gliding in tenderness.

This ancient triangle of strings
In my memory, a happy adventure
Bordered on the sublime and I was thrilled
Until a fly fell in and died in my cup of coffee.

Lela Melanie Peterson

When You Wear A Smile

When you wear a smile, it will go a long while;
It will change your skies from gray to blue.
It will lift and lighten your face.
It will give you peace and grace.
And you will know that GOD is there with you.

When the Devil comes around, He wants us to wear a frown
He will try to give us the "D's" and be cast down.
Now what are the "D's" you ask of me?
I will tell you and then you will see.

D is for DOUBT, with these "D's", we all have our bouts.
D is for DEVIL, he is D- EVIL.
D is for DISCOURAGE. Those folks we must encourage.
D is for DISSOLUTION. Some need a new birth transfusion.
D is for DOWN, so look up, and SMILE, like a happy
   clown; and then the Devil can't stay around.

   WHEN YOU WEAR A SMILE!

Shirley Ann Sanders

The Antique Shop

I found an antique shop in old Sutter Creek
It's a place in the foothills with real narrow streets
A gold rush town where mining has ceased
So enticed was I by its western mystique
I had to come back in a couple of weeks

In the month of October with fall colored leaves
I returned once again with the girl of my dreams
Together we browsed for an hour it seems
before entering a shop near a bridge and a stream
It was there that we found after looking around
A most narrative treasure of classical themes

So the rest of the day we walked and we talked
about things that were old and things that were not
We hugged once or twice and we smiled a lot
Then we drove the car home with the book we had bought

With visions of October still fresh in my mind
I cherish the treasure from that moment in time
For it wasn't the book a favorite Dickens of mine
but our love that I value with the passing of time

Theodore Lampron

The Follower

The follower chooses someone.
It's always there when it chooses.
The follower has chosen someone.
It's always there when it chooses.
The follower won't quit following me.
It's always there when it chooses.
I asked it to leave me alone, but it won't.
It's always there when it chooses.
Nobody knows it's there, but the follower and me.

It's always there when it chooses.
Finally, it has chosen someone else.
It's always there when it chooses.

Shilo Johnsen

A Portrayal Of Peace: A Tribute to Claude Monet

Peace is a simple word yet complexed by its meaning;
It's an intangible condition that exists in a painting.
Tranquil, sedative, imperturbable, and true,
Peace conveys hints of love and amity, too.
Soothing while encompassing us, this lone word,
Peace is its name, so lulling it's unheard.
Numerous in forms, the source, a simple modesty,
Seemingly hidden from many, a missed opportunity.
This source may well be an excursion for some
To a meadow that's vacant with nature in blossom.
Others find peace with an enjoyable hobby
Or a stroll down a beach with companions in harmony.
And yet, perhaps the most alluring of sources around
Is the sight of a bridge with petals abound.
It's a joyous impression full of colors much spirited,
But of reticent charm with all turmoil abated.
Life's at its height in this view that's quite quiescent,
A solacing scene aroused not by a resident;
So, to enjoy a beautiful peace, one must fondly
Gaze upon Monet's Japanese Bridge at Giverny.

Susan Dianne Tompkins

"Daddy Dearest"

Daddy dearest, where did you go?
It's been so long and I have missed you so.
And Daddy dearest please don't lie,
I thought you were gone for good, I
thought you had said goodbye.
Oh God Daddy dearest, don't hurt me now,
I've forgotten how to take it. I just don't remember how.
It's been so lonely not to have you here,
when all those memories linger so intolerably near!
And Daddy Dearest will you hug me once more?
To ease the pain, my body is so tired and sore.
Oh, and daddy, will you read me to sleep?
And help me pray the Lord for my soul to keep?
Daddy Dearest, please stay until tomorrow.
So I can talk to you a little more to ease the sorrow.
And Daddy Dearest, before you go, I just want to say I love you so.
Yes Daddy, I understand that you have to
Leave, I'll be alright, can't you see?
Oh my God Daddy! Don't fly away!
I'll miss you so much, please Daddy, please stay.

Melissa Nicole Mullinax

Sisyphus Revisited

Lantern in hand, I navigate the corridors of hope.
   Just ahead, a will-o'-the-wisp beckons:
Love, slyly cloaked in comfort's guise, teasing
   With seductive mien.
A yearning kiss shapes my lips
   As I rush, headlong, into temptation's web,
Helpless to resist what I ought,
   And the kiss becomes a primal scream.

Veronica Sattler

My Soul's Storming

There's a storm in my soul and it's developing its voice.
It's beginning to rumble and growl and thunder and moan and it's
   coming soon...
I'm going to let that voice out and it's going to ROAR at the world to
tell everyone the truth.
The earth knows the true value of a real storm-can feel it, can hear
   it...never forgets it.
My storm is full of anger and rage and questions that begin with WHY?
It will find its victims and let them know the effect they have had
   on my clouds.
My storm will tell those who did the damage exactly what lightning shower
and thunder pounding is theirs...what they need to know and feel.
And when my storm makes its way through—fully and completely letting
   it all out, there will be a rainbow.
The rainbow is my heart which can see a clear soul coming out.
And that is when new life springs. When my soul's storm erupts, has
its fury and then subsides, there will be a beauty and peace that
the earth has seen only in a few glimpses from heaven.
It will be seen by all in my smile and my eyes; which are the windows
   to my heart and soul.
Because for the first time, my smile is true and my heart is pure...
Yes, there's a storm in my soul and its voice is rising.

   Tamara McIntyre

Tree In The Rain

My heart is rainsoaked - like this tree
Its branches stripped of leaves,
Are deathly still
Are hung with raindrops chill.
And heavy as the raindrops, quivering caught,
Is this my thought
That parts to break
Its truth into the hollow of my ache,
My heart, that hears its lonely part foretold,
And knows that on itself, alone,
It must depend,
Even to the very end.

   Raymond R. Osenga

Perfect

Today I sought the perfect shell;
Its definition, I knew well.

Perfect color, shape defined,
precise ridges, colors refined.

But today, as I walked the sands by the sea,
The shells that seemed to call to me

Were the broken pieces, ravaged and small,
The shells that looked not like shells at all.

Tossed by the waves over the years,
Of endless ocean and salty tears,

They reminded me of people I know
Whose broken lives leave them nowhere to go.

Misfits in society
washed by the tide, until nowhere you see

The perfect color, shape or size.
Sure makes you stop to realize

That all of us are useful in different ways
on various jobs, on various days.

Is this lesson for others to learn as well?
Only time and tide will tell!

   Patty Barrett

"Tell Me How"

Tell me how can you stop the rain from falling down.
It's like trying to stop the world from turning around.
People here and there, what's going on we're all
human so get use to it and try to get along.
   This world may seem large to each and everyone,
but it's small to many and few.
So tell me how? This world needs to heal,
life is not easy for us all. Just look around you.
   There are children who needs love and understanding,
people with no homes and no food to eat. We all need
to think? Walk a mile in each other's shoes.
Try to lend a helping hand. Than maybe we can all call
this world a promise land.
   Tell me how can we learn to love one another,
embrace one another's soul and heart. We shouldn't have to wait
until one departs to express our love and understanding.
   Tell me how can we be God's children and not
try to take a stand. Man can't live by bread alone.
Let's mend our hate and selfishness, try to learn to love each other.

   Tell me how?

   Monica Carson

October

October is upon us, it came hauntingly quick...
it's my favorite season, if I had to pick,
because the leaves are all changing, their colors so bold...
no longer just green, they are bright crimson and gold.

They give up their home of a branch long and sturdy...
and fall to the ground, as they twirl whirlie birdie,
they lay scattered and crisp as we rake up a pile,
but then a thought comes to mind, which makes us all smile...
for what is more fun on a cool autumn day,
than to pick a huge mound to fall on and play.

This month brings us wonders to both see and feel,
so the end of our summer is no great big deal...
go outside to smell the crisp autumn air,
let the breezes of fall ruffle your hair...
watch a flock of birds fly south for the season,
just enjoy October, whatever your reason.

   Kathy Nelson

Divorced And Fifty

This is where I am now - but where is it?
It's not the "Isn't this heaven" type place I expected to be.
Nor the paradise waiting with open arms to calm me.

I've waited for years, cried those tears,
Had those fears and for what?
Expecting with time, that life would be mine,
But the treasures of life I have not.
I've got "none of the above", nor real joy, no true love.
Oh how sad, just too bad for me!

Now, I know where I've been - the fun I had then -
And the future just had to get better
But I think "futures" been here or is terribly near
And I've come to my senses at last.
So what I profess is what you would guess
That better is all in the past!

So here is where I am now - still spinning my wheels,
Still waiting for thrills.
Now shooting for life everlasting.

I still have great hopes, pray I can cope
And find out where I am before passing.

   Sue Eyler Stitely

415

Baseball

There is a game that's called baseball.
It's played by many, and loved by all.
I watch and listen to the game
Each play, each hit, they have a name

A thief, when caught a judge he faces
But in this game, they steal the bases
The umpire shouts with hands up high;
He calls a foul, he calls a fly.

He calls a strike,but all keep playing
What is this funny game talk he's saying?
How can these things be understood?
If he'd talk English — then I would.

Out of the bull-pen players run;
But I've yet to see a bull in one.
The Cardinals, White Sox - any name.
I'll still cheer on this famous game.

Wilma Buller

The Beauty Of Nature

The Beauty of Nature is shown everywhere,
It's shown when the moonlight twinkles with care.
It's shown when the dove moves across the sky.
And how it shows love even though it's way up high.
The Beauty of Nature is shown when a
Dolphin swims through the water.
It's just like you looking at your new born daughter.
It's like a flower when it goes into bloom.
Or when a new sight comes into loom.
The Beauty of Nature is when a rainbow appears.
Or when a child is happy and sheds a few tears.
So next time you see something that has to
Do with the beauty of nature.
Enjoy it, share it, and thank God for.
Creating this treasure.

Lindsay Scully

Read Life

I've always been told,
"It's the books you carry that lead you through life."
I carry books of
Laughter at Christmas time,
Big birthday surprises,
And constant love from family members.
All of my books end in "...happily ever after."
Not all my African brothers and sisters carry my same books.
I've read some of their books.
I've read about terror screams in the night hours,
Games with guns just for fun,
Beatings leaving brothers and sisters soulless.
I've read about infants being traded to feed crack addictions,
Children raising themselves in the cold rainy streets,
Babies not even fortunate enough to taste life being ripped apart in
    dark alley ways.
If we are all from the same blood,
Then how did our books become so different?

Natasha Likkel

Secrets

In our hearts lie the deepest secrets
known only to God and Universe.
Our hopes, fears, joys and insecurities
all instilled in that one, small package.

Pride swells the heart, pain breaks it,
hope keeps it beating until we are once
again able to dream.

Lorraine J. Steinmetz

Canadian Geese

I saw some long neckers fly overhead today;
It's the time of year they leave without delay.

Good weather men are this long necker crew;
They bring us the seasons with little ado.

Autumn days, golden and gray;
The long neckers honk as they depart to the sparrow and jay.

In spring the bright skies are darkened with patches of Vees;
As long neckers return with the gentle spring breeze.

Perhaps if the weather men took the long neckers' route;
Our forecast would be more accurate without a doubt.

Meanwhile, for those of us that are a year or more;
We scan the skies from season to season, believing in long necker lore.

Lois Osborn

"A Heart Isn't Clay"

A heart isn't clay that you sit down to mold
it's there from the start, it's there when you're old

With uncertain feelings nourished by love
given to us from the good Lord above

Sometimes I feel that it's made of thin glass
that's easily shattered by pains of the past

But keeps beating strong although torn and tattered
listen to your heart for it knows all that matters

LeAnn Pisar

The Homestead

The old house stands in a desolate state of late.
Its weathered old walls once chinked with slate
have cracked and sagged and withered.

With painful pulse and half-drawn breath I wait
while long gone dreams of long gone days
flitter and gambol in childish ways.

I walk down the lane to the watering trough while aloft
swallows swoop in the sun's first rays,
and dandelions wave in sunburst leis.

There in the field by a rusting harrow, a sparrow
flits from a spike to a bending seat
where once a boy had leaped.

The old elms wave in the lonely breeze, and leaves
tumble and spiral with restless ease
to build the mantle of autumn.

C. Jay Blank

Sun Upon My Face

I've heard the song of birds, it's true, so many times before
I've felt the sunlight warm my face and fill my every pore
Yet now with your love, finally, safe within my heart
These simple gifts today now cause tears of joy to start

For a great man once said that he could only dare to dream
Of the warmth of love's true passion upon his face to beam
Like the great orb of sunlight shining from the sky
And then, and only then, could he feel free to die
Die in peace knowing that he at last possessed
The sunlight of true love and bathed in its caress

I've shared some great adventures with lifelong friends and laughed,
Laughed in the face of trials, knowing "this too shall pass"
I've weathered many storms in my young and tender years
I've felt the rain envelop me and mix with bitter tears

Look into my eyes, love, of those tears there's not a trace
Hand in hand beside you, the world's a brighter place
For the sun, dear, at last, now shines upon my face

Monica Lynn

Inheritance

All that I know of their early years
I've learned from family stories
Which focus on my parents' love,
Its birth, its life, its glories.

Then came those years which shaped my life,
A life their love conceived,
As I bore witness to those things
In which they both believed...

Like honor, truth and loyalty
And the faith that made them one.
Plus playful laughter, dance and song
And the freedom to have fun.

I do believe they taught me well,
Not just by their instructions,
But by the way they lived their lives...
Both brief yet grand productions.

Kathleen Martin

The Ordinary World

I've seen the world (or maybe half!) and fought a war or two;
I've tried my hand at industry and had my share of brew.
I've lived and loved and sung and played, and prayed when things got tough,
But always got the breaks and life got squared-up soon enough.

Although there seemed to be no way that life could offer more,
There was at times a yearning for a yet-unopened door.
The scenes were vague, as in a dream, but seemed to say to me
That out there somewhere, somehow, there was something more to see.

I was doing nothing special, on an early, dreary morn,
Just walking off a too-late night; but then a quest was born!
My path wound up around a knoll, and there before my eye,
The sun, behind me, opened up and glorified the sky.

The valley there in front of me was yet to catch the light,
But just a touch of mistiness was lifting off the night.
The shadows crept down off the distant hills in perfect line,
And when the moment passed the only shadow left was mine.

I stood in awe of what I'd seen a hundred times before.
A simple act of Nature's law had thrilled me to the core!
And, standing there, alone, a gentle zephyr 'round me swirled;
I'd caught the fleeting beauty of the ordinary world.

Morton Wood Jr.

Oh, Hibiscus!

Oh, Hibiscus
Jewel colors that delight the eye;
Glorious trumpet sublime,
Lift your dewy face toward the sun
Receive its kiss, then steal away when day is done.
Oh, Hibiscus!

Oh, Hibiscus!
Your color spectrum reaches heavens door
To touch our hearts, and yet, we asked for more.
You give the sweetness of your flower breath,
And sound your trumpet splendor
Without rest.
Oh, Hibiscus!

Oh, Hibiscus!
More precious are your blossoms
Than the Midas touch, we strive for more perfection as we must.
You greet each day with rainbow colors bright,
Then gently fold your petals
And steal away at night.
Oh, Hibiscus!

Sibyl Jarvis Pischke

Today, Tomorrow Forever

The trees on either side of the street
Join hands above my head.
They make a lighted tunnel for me to enter, then pass through.
I taste a bit of heaven as their shining glory
Illuminates me.

Reds and golds are all aglow,
A haven of beauty surrounds me.
Oh, grasp it while you can, for soon the glory fades away,
The trees are bare, darkness fills the air.
I go to sleep and dream.

When I awake, again there's beauty everywhere!
The branches once so black and bare are glistening
With pure white snow.
The trees, the fields, the fence posts are a sight to behold,
But, oh, so cold!

One day all will perfect be again; I'll never mourn or feel a pain.
The autumn glory, the wonder of winter will all be wrapped in one.
My soul will never die and I will never cry again!
I'll live and love and laugh and play
Oh, glorious day!

Ruth M. Sanders

Please Teach Me

Unlike you I have no name, no title, to show others where I stand.
Just a mass of this and that, cluttered in my life, just an ordinary
me, so I ask in you to teach me! How do I make others feel what I
feel? With smiles or tears, or memories that will last for years.
PLEASE TEACH ME!

How do I fill someone's soul with the past or future, or touch their
heart where no one else could? Do my words draw out any excitement
or fear, do I make them tremble or glow, for if I can't should I
let go? PLEASE TEACH ME!

Do I offer feelings that will stay with them for the rest of their life, or
give them a warming on a cold winter night? I ASK YOU TO TEACH ME!

How do I take ordinary paint and canvas and turn it into the softness
of one's smile, movement of their tears, wet to the touch, children
looking at God and make them real? PLEASE TEACH ME!

How can I take from me what is inside my inner soul, my life my
dreams and my heartbeat, my tears and my happiness and lay them
all out in front of you, and help you feel and touch all that I can
see, for if I can't I don't want to be? PLEASE TEACH ME!

How do I take love and show feeling? The softness, the warmth, two
bodies in the center of time, two hearts now beating as one, all senses
intertwined, all movement exploding into one pair's mind.
PLEASE TEACH ME!

How can they take it with them to store it in their mind, or hold it
close enough to bring it back another time. How do I talk about or
show a rainbow when all skies are gray, or show a mother's love when
her children have now gone away? PLEASE TEACH ME!

Help me to lay a part of one's soul out in the air, and let it melt
one's heart that cares. A tremble of myself, a promise of ones
tomorrow, my thoughts to be passed down from our children unto theirs
and theirs unto forever's tomorrow. For my need is still and will
always be your ultimate goal, IF YOU TAKE THE TIME TO TEACH ME!

Stephen John Redman

Colorful Leaves

When I go outside and I see orange and red and yellow
leaves whipping in the wind.
And the leaves were so pretty I was amazed to see
so many
It just took my breath away.
Then when I saw them land on the ground
I just ran out into them and
started throwing them up into the air.

Karen Keith

"Me"

I am me and no one else,
just my quiet and personal self.

I do things different from others,
never copied from another.

The way I act, talk and speak —
these are the things which make me unique.

I see things from a different view,
never ever the same as you.

I know one day when I die,
the world will continue and pass me by.

It's just hard for me to conceive;
that never will there be another quite like me.

Lorraine Marie Welsch

The Things You Didn't Say

You didn't say a word
Just walked out the door,
I thought you'd never love me, that was for sure.

I never made you happy,
Nothing I ever did,
You always said you loved me,
But inside you never did.

You gave me everything
All that you could,
But you never loved me, not even in my
childhood.

All the things you said hurt
But what really hurts is what you never said.

The silence is here, everyday, haunting me
from day to day,
All those things you didn't say.

Stacy Lyster

"An Aubade To Marguerite"

Oh, the anguish of a lost sister
Kept me awake most the night
Her zealous gift of laughter
Made our youthful pranks so right
Her hair was shiny, very dark
Her body slim, oh, so lithesome
Ofttimes we dashed into the park
Where she'd create some lyrical phenomenon
I miss her most when I enjoy
The very things she loved to do
I cherish the memorable joy
Of a sibling's exotic view
Of life, which is no more
Her charming antics I well knew
And treasure those gifts
From days of yore.

Mary John Hunter

Untitled

Once you and I
know as the best term,
yet, we become strangers for years...
You and I both known as the occurred.
How strange - we are not in the best of term,
yet, become the well and like in the flow years
among the thousands and from the so call place...

Till today, I still wonder
as I eye back through the yesterdays,
we met and smile, yet,
not known how we become the ghost for thee and you for I

Won S. Ng

Friendship

It's getting up in the morning
Knowing that somebody cares,
It's that feeling of quiet contentment
That sneaks up on you unawares.

It's what gives you the mem'ries to cherish
When things somehow go bad,
It's the phone call, or letter that comes in the mail
When you're feeling low, or sad.

It's the person who tells you to "Hang in there!"
To never give up the fight,
Who encourages, flatters, and stands by you
Till things become all right.

It's the difference it's made in your way of life
When you've had a friend or two
With whom you can chat, and frankly discuss
The problems that life hands to you.

Friendship is one of life's greatest gifts,
More precious than silver or gold,
But to have a friend, you must be a friend,
At least, that's what I am told.

Mildred J. Katemopoulos

My Angels In Heaven

Two little boys so rowdy and rough
Laughing and playing and all that stuff
But their room is quiet now, no noise at all
As I look through their things and I recall

The things that they did
The things that they said
The kisses I gave them
When I put them to bed

What will I do now
How can I go on
When the light of my life
Is suddenly gone

Am I still a mother
With my babies gone
When Mother's Day comes
Can I still carry on

My sweet little angels, Mama's little men
Please don't forget me and all that we've been
Just keep laughing and playing and my love I'll send
'Til I see you in heaven and hold you again.

Peggy Davis

Daydream

Standing in a dense forest listening to the rustling of
leaves in the breeze, feeling the biting chill
of the winter air against my bare cheek
I hear a voice calling out to me, "where are you?"
the wind blows harder and the snow begins to fall;
a blanket of death covers the hard earth,
a voice echoes in my head - but it isn't real, is it?
a cackling voice echoes through the trees
I can't find it - can't make out the words then sharp loud booming
"RUN" - an order.
I run: fast, hard, strong
and get nowhere.
Lost and trapped in the dense forest.
voices in my head admonishing my deeds;
I run - but can't escape - I fall to the ground and close my eyes
the blanket covers me and freezes my mind,
I dream of breaking away from yesterday
being stuck in today and running towards
a tomorrow I will never live to see.

Sara Kirsten Evans

418

Dying Without You

I'm dying without you, I thought you should know. When you left I saw a light, my breath got short. I can't see you anymore. The only thing I can see are the memories of us in my mind. They linger around like dreams that will never be again. I'm starting to float to the light. My dreams and memories of us are lingering around more and more, twisting and turning the tears out my eyes. This light is getting brighter now, my breath is all so short. I'm almost there, as my soul is squeezed of life, 'cause of you. For I think of all our times together, all the joy and happiness, it is killing me deep down inside. I'm here now. Well it is time to say good-bye, 'cause I'm dying, you see. Dying without you.

Katherine A. Leitch

Blind Faith

May faith firmly uphold and lead you
Let fear float distantly behind
When midnight falls upon your day.
Just throw out your hands and feel your way.

Faith is not what the eye doth see
Pressing through the dark and gloom
Faith is what the heart believes can be,
Busy bringing its goal into reality.

Faith takes a convinced stand
And gathers the soil with two main hands,
Faith has power, faith has might
It keeps toiling through sorrow, and the night

For it's true, what my mother
Used to sometimes say
When darkness encircles your river,
Trust yourself, trust God, and feel your way.

Clontine Waygallo

Sun

Oh Sun, oh mighty Sun; shine upon us.
Let us revel in your magnificent glory.
You giver of light, let us bask in your warmth and splendor.
Come, inspire us and fill us with joy.
Let the merry birds sing their praises to you.

Oh Sun, oh mighty Sun; greet the morning
with your blessed golden beams.
Let the animals dash beneath you, contented with living.
Show your fair face to the world.
Let one and all gaze upon you proving their faithfulness toward you.

Oh Sun, oh mighty Sun; bestow hope upon us.
Let the many diverse cultures come together as one.
Share and encourage your vast wisdom of the ages.
Let us become enlightened by you,
For we appreciate and love you oh Sun; oh mighty Sun.

Leann Woodmansee

The Leaf In Fall

It explodes with colors
Jubilant reds and sunset oranges.
Yellow and green separate
And mixed - rainbow.

It has never been more beautiful
It has never been more alive.
It is as glorious as any of God's nature now.

It falls to the ground.
It dies, the cycle continues.
We watch and admire and praise.

Mary Donna Kelley

"Daughter To Mother"

Well, mother, I tell you:
Life for me ain't been no beautiful dress.
It's had snags in it,
And rips,
And tears,
And spotted up with stains
But all the time
I have been adding on to my dress
I have been putting on lace
And bright new buttons
And I have been putting little silk flowers over
The spotted stains.
And I added new string to the rips and tears.
I have had people to laugh at me in my dress
But I don't care;
I'm still going to add to my dress.
It's going to be kind of hard,
But don't you worry, Mama,
I'm not going to give up
For life, for me ain't been no beautiful dress.

Melissa Carol Young

Condemned To Live

The worst punishment is not to be punished.
Life in prison would have been pleasant enough
even death's row would have its compensations,
flowers, cards, protestations of love,
would people the cell,
money would accrue
while you waited for a governor to pardon you....
Now life will be your jailer
and life is without mercy.
Remembered eyes will study you
from a younger face,
spring rain on the roof
will be like blood
dripping on pavement,
your golf club will burn in your hand
like the heft of a knife,
and a woman's body
no matter how much you pay her
will be like a glove
you can never quite fit into.

LoVerne W. Brown

Time To Wonder

Stop to wonder, but not ask why?
  Life will not heed to pass you by.
Many have pondered to question of many,
  To pass both by - to stand both and steady.
To question a few is but okay with time,
  To wonder to long it to search but not find.
Walk - not to run you see and but still,
  Questions are answered by you and life's will.
Some not to be answered is a probable fear,
  Answers are vague and not always clear.
Meant not to be found it has happened that way,
  Many will walk and many will stay.
To move is but best - to walk but to rest,
  Ask a question or few - A few or a less.
Make sure to keep moving to make rhythms through,
  Life answers to questions not meant to be knew.

Laura Turcotte

"The Human Search For Meaning"

The endless search for meaning engulfs my aching soul.
Life's delicate transitions bars my revered goal.
What is this life I ponder? Why hide the answer true?
Are mystery and illusion the blinds we can't see through?

How long it takes a tree to grow; How long it takes a flower.
The flash of lightning cross the sky and thunder roars with power.
A gull in flight above the seas, an eagle soars majestically.
Rain falls tranquil on the ground; a rainbow's formed romantically.

The glaring brightness of the sun, its ray of heat and light.
The glow of moonlight from darkened skies, the somber of the night.
The twinkling of starlit wonder with dreams we hold and breathe.
The wonderment of all creation; is this what we believe?

The search for Life and Meaning is surrounding us in love.
The beauty of this world, from earth and skies above.
Can't you see this beauty, the meaning and the sign?
A Creator so specific. I'm speaking of God, Divine.

Worthy Schonfeld

Grandma Was Like A Flower

Like a flower from seed, she started.
Like a flower she did grow, with many sprouts that came along.
Like a flower she blossomed and was best pick of the bunch.
Like a flower she did wilt, a little cranky at times,
rejecting the gardeners help to stand up.
Like a flower she did die-it only saddens me now, that I didn't
come to the garden often enough to see her beauty, but I'm
just a sprout growing so far away.

We are just seeds in God's hands.

Thomas Posey

"My Daughter"

She is the sunrise shining bright,
Like a flower unfolding to the light.
Her cheeks the color of a cardinal's wing,
She's the sweet music that angels sing.
She has the freshness of a morning's dew,
With all the loveliness of a rainbow's hue.
She has the heaven like song of a nightingale,
With all the imagination of a fairy tale.
She has a spirit that is wild and free,
She is a miracle from God sent special to me.
She's like a story that has just begun,
Of love, laughter, delight and lots of fun.

Susan Roth-Weitzel

Mind Game

Spirit coursing through ravaged soul
Like a raging river through well-known borders flow.
Leaving an indelible print,
Ensuring strife, unerringly sent.

Oh wretched soul! Gain no release?
Upon storm tossed shores of subconsciousness
Imprisoned memories sown in pain;
Shackled with fear, recalled never again.

Held hostage by a moment, internalized blame.
Betrayed within a thousand times, multiplied shame.
Sheer terror lurks authored by history.
Unwittingly played out the macabre mystery.

Rosemarie Shafer

Shadows Of Peace

The shadows fell around the sleeping child,
Like a soft blanket of comfort and silence.

The breeze blows soft against the lace curtains,
Making the shadows dance around the room,
Like small watchful angels, to protect the sleeping infant.

The moonlight of the lake, dances with the breeze to create,
Shapes of new fairy tales of the heart and imagination.

The dreams of peace engulf the sweet child's mind,
The fragrance of the mountain air, brings the certainty,
That tomorrow will come, with new rays of hope and love.

Safety and peace are shared by all, who enter within.
The sweet wall of the silent sweet stranger of sleep.

Kayleen Marie Huxhold

Larue

She moves into my mind
Like a swirling snow deep in winter
A rising light glowing in my dark mind
As a flake of snow like unto no other

Where is sanity in the dark abyss
It's there behind her dark bright almond eyes
A will of iron and steel clothed in silk
Her character is true she is steadfast

In my minds eye I look upon her sweet self
To behold her is to have my heart pierced

Was all this suffering, all this humiliation,
All this love demanded to open my eyes
To be lifted up and delivered from myself

My heart is touched with the thought
of how a beautiful and magnificent spirit she is

Without her my strivings will be without yield
My wants no my needs only she can fulfill

I hold within myself a strong consolation
That I can flee to her refuge to lay
Hold upon her hope set before us.

William David Baker

Eagle's In Flight

High over the cliff an eagle flies
   like an angel in the sky,
Watching her eaglets in their nest
   just wondering how they'll stand the test,
She puts sharp thorns for them to set
   not much comfort they will ever get,
Then one day she will give her call
   out of the nest you'll have to fall,
Then swoops down under from below
   her love for them she has to show,
The day will come they'll leave her side
   and from the storms they will have to hide,
So as the raging sea now rolls
   and hunger grips their very soul,
A promise was made for a flood no more
   as God opened up the door,
A rainbow shines across the sky
   for the eagles as they fly.

Nina Eddings

Sea Gulls

Deep, deep sea, with waves towering o'er,
Like dark blue-green pyramids,
lashing, falling in sprays of
Heavenly blue-white foam.
The ripples of the tide reaching out,
Splashing o'er the rocks, whispering
to the inlets, mooring ore the sounds,
Ripples of the waves make patters like little fans,
With white beads of foam and brilliant
prisms glistening in the sun.
White cumulus clouds, propelled by the wind,
So Lofty and white and hanging like
puffs of white down,
Drifting along, as though on wings,
Hanging precariously against a blue sky.
Sea gulls screeching, flying as though
on the wings of a song,
As they dive, dipping their wings and
soaring above,
Free and happy creatures, to my envying.

Mary Geneva H. Herd

Apples And Oranges

You grew your lies
Like fruits on barbed wire vines
Then you chased me
Right into your painful web
I foraged for sustenance
Only to find a token of your affection
A locket keepsake filled with ashes of promise
Clutching my grief in my mind
And my heart in my hands
In an attempt to please
Could you send me away to repair
My nakedness was not allowed
A veil to shield my vulnerability
I wear my scabs like mourning badges of black
Press my heart into my chest
I bleed, I breathe
To steal these waves
About my eyes
And escape

Melissa Ross

Elusive Beauty

I slink unidentified behind a wall of grasses, that is a barrier.
Like dust, I travel freely, whenever to whatever.
I remain hidden to the eye, behind the trees, my ancient guardians.

I lay motionless, waiting, waiting.
Suddenly I am being chased; the whiz of a bullet passes by me!
To them I am no creature of beauty, but merely a fur.

I am out of breath, unlike the wind which breathes harshly against
my face. I leap to limitless time,
forcing my legs, body and mind forward.

I race across the deeply wooded land while branches grab at me,
reaching for me
I stop short and listen;
listen for those who pursue me, but there is no one, no one.

I breathe hard, raggedly, like the last breath of a rising wind.
I stand erect, alert, aware.
The trees and grasses are my kinsmen; swaying in a mesmerizing dance,

while I, the Wolf, stand proud.

Meredith Carlson

"Summer Sky"

Fleecy cloud's floating way up high,
Like snowy drifts across the sky;
Blue here and there, like a tiny face,
Peeking through curtains of creamy lace!!

Slowly the fleecy clouds drift away,
Like melting snow on summers day;
Leaving the sky so clear and blue,
With only the sun a shining through!

The golden sun with rays so bright,
That warms the earth with its magic light.
Then sunset brings fleecy clouds on high,
And draws a lacy curtain across the sky!!

Pauline A. Turner

The Value Of A Seed

Spring rains fall so whisper soft
Like feather floating slowly aloft.
They gently moisten the thirsty earth,
But few take time to know their worth.
Far, far beneath the ground we see,
New life has begun to be set free.
The tiniest speck that knew not life,
Has begun its struggle through endless strife.
Through layer upon layer of cold, hard dirt,
The seedling has climbed since its birth.
On a bright sunny day after much time has passed,
This seedling will finally peek its head at last.
Oh what triumph, oh what success.
But how could this seedling ever possibly guess,
After all the hard work and struggles it's gone through,
So anxious to begin its life a new
To the world there was little value in this tiny seed.
People will view it as only a weed.

Vivi Radford

Tears

My tears fall from my face
  like the raindrops out of darkness;
Descending downward, on and on
  like parachutists from a plane;
Wetness clenching my skin
  like water over rocks on a stream;
Tears continue to fall,
  reflections of my life splash before me;
Lightning and thunder commence
  as my problems render answering;
Rain pours from the sky,
  my head begins to swirl;
Over and over lightning flashes
  always a sign of more tears;
A rainbow forms that promises
  us our problems are not everlasting;
The tears quit falling
  the clouds drift away,
Everything returns to normal
  until another day.

Trina Sue Haasis

421

Transcendence

Love of my heart, life's most integral part.
Lingering in a misty space your grace
Now filled with the essence of your presence.
Image of a face in filigree case
Is your photograph in tissue wrapped.
I relive the moments, recall comments
And review the past like a movie fast
Remembrances in celluloid stacked.
Expecting, hoping to find you again
In some obscure land - listening to the band.
Evasive vacillation - vacuum packed
Where all waiting lovers stand back to back.
Reaching out I lay my hand on your hand
And life will begin all over again.

Mirtha G. Moreno

The Rain

As I lay here in bed
Listening to the constant melodious thrum of the rain
I think of one of the summers past
How as we came to the end of our crick walk
The sky clouded over and thunder boomed in the distance
Then it started to rain at first in large separated drops
Then it started to come down harder
We walked along the road fishing poles in hand
It was like a monsoon
It was warm and coming down in a solid stream
We started to run as the rain got steadier
Laughing with free spirited glee
Looking to the sky
With a feeling of freedom and purity

Megan Fraley

Our Worlds

The tank is very full of life,
Little fishes spotted and some with stripes.
It's a free world to them, you know,
For they are always on the go.
You can sit and watch them swim and play,
They never tire and are never found
Just sitting around.
On the move they flip their tail,
Little do they know they're in their jail;
A happy place it must be
For little fishes of the sea.

There are no sharks or wiggle tails,
No octopi or killer whales,
It must be nice to have a world so safe and sound,
Have glass to look through all around;
Do you suppose man's this way, too —
Walled in his cell, working his way to heaven
    or hell?
Only time will tell, and you can bet
There's no way out that we know yet.

Warren Atchison

"Did I Forget"

Did I forget to thank You Lord
For the prayers you answered me,
When all went wrong and the one I loved
Was far across the sea.
Did I forget to thank You Lord
For the peace you helped us win,
For the faith and hope You gave our boys
When all looked mighty grim.
Did I forget to thank You Lord
For the safe return of John,
If I forgot, forgive me please,
My thanks to you from this day on.

Inez Jack

Ode To Spider

Teeny, tiny, little spider,
Little head and body wider,
Dark black fur like pointy spindles...
You come out as daylight dwindles.

In the dark I see your eyes,
Glinting black (those little spies!).
I hear your feet run up my wall,
Then cross my ceiling hear you crawl.

Your furry legs brush past my nose
(I feel your little spider toes!).
When I'm fast asleep and dreaming,
You stare at me, those black eyes gleaming.

Well, the time has come for you to die,
I'll squish you flat, then stop and sigh.
I see you looking at my shoe...
Now just hold still as I step on you.

Spider, spider, time to crush you,
Spider, spider, time to mush you,
When I step, you'll feel a stitch,
Then all your spider legs will twitch!

Kirsten Dahler

Good-Bye My Love, Good-Bye

Good-bye my love
Long have I dreamed of this moment
Yet I never thought the day would come
But time doesn't stand still, the day is here
And so again I say
Good-bye my love, good-bye.

Good-bye my love
The moments we have shared I will treasure always
Dear and loving they will remain to me
But time won't stand still, the day is here
and so again I say
Good-bye my love, good-bye.

Good-bye my love
Today is here and another love is on the way
But he will never hold the place in my heart that you have
Time never stands still, the day is gone
For one last time I say
Good-bye my love, good-bye.

Theresa M. Pearson

Untitled

Just a few words of things in prayer
for the time with my friend, I was able to share.
Peaceful moments talking of life,
of all the good and all the strife.
A bit of food we both ate,
sharing our Lord, it was great.
Than you God for all you do
please keep my heart forever true.
Protect me from all evil ways
let my faith never be in a haze.
Mostly Lord, thanks for my friend
please help soul fully mend.
Fill him with the Holy Ghost
for him Lord, I make this toast.
This friend to me is such a gift
his inspiration gives me a lift.
So thanks again from the bottom of my heart.
And God don't let us ever part.

Jerry Mulligan

Gentle Hoax

Gray green moments
Cold with life
Telling stories
Masking cries
Machine gun fire
Mental notes
Melting Together
To the source

Tasting Power
Crawling begging
Screaming God
Falling silent
Rising again
like drops in the ocean

Gordon Laird

God Children

Children are not bits of
    clay
To mold and to model
    in a carefree way
Children are people
    small person of love
The sweetest of blessing
    God sent from above
    to cherish and watch over.
To laugh with play
To hold in our arms
at end of each day
each child is a miracle
An answer to prayer
for the heart of
child
has the love of
God there
God bless my boys Jason, Jerry

Marilee Hudyma

Skiing

At breakfast time we stop to eat,
Cinnamon buns and other treats.
Up the mountain we start to drive,
Until we reach the top by five.
In the parking lot we stop,
The car's so cold we put up the top.
We don our skis and mittens too,
In the process I lost a shoe.
Down the hill we start to go,
People pass us 'cause we're so slow.
Somehow my brother crossed his skis,
And flew into a bunch of trees.
As I was going up the lift,
I fell and landed in a drift.
It's time to go, it has been fun,
But I'm sure glad that skiing's done.

Kelsey MacDonald

God in the Sky

Bugs crawling on the ground,
Birds in the trees.
God in the sky,
What a wonderful place to be.

Sweet smell from the flowers,
Honey from the bees.

They thank God for the earth,
With a little help from me.

Whitney Agassiz

Grief

The morning fingers of the light
Chase away the fears of night-
The dreams that rob me of my sleep,
The memories it hurts to keep,
All dissolve and fade away
At the coming of the day.

The sun, it shines and warms the earth
calling each creature to its birth-
Begs us all to laugh and love,
and dance beneath the skies above;
To make the most of this new day
And chase all fears and grief away.

But this is what I cannot do
Because the day, it brings not you.
You have left this earthly life,
Left me full of pain and strife.
The grief is more than I can bear-
It robs me of my every care.
And there is nothing I can do,
For there was only one of you.

Andrea Vandeyck

(the future)?

please
change the future
        it cannot be changed

please
stop the future
        it is already here

no
this is now
i mean
what is about to happen
        like yesterday

no
like tomorrow
            it already passed

Michael Henning

Moms

"Feed me!" Here.
"Change me!" There.
Sleep now!
So amazing, "Wow!"

"Mom!" Here.
"Help!" There.
"Please, can we?"
"Did you hear me?"

Girlfriends here.
Boyfriends there.
"Can I go too?"
"So, where were you?"

Young tears here.
New loves there.
Families to care for.
Babies no more.

Love here.
More love there.
Daughters and sons.
Moms!

Judith Johnsey

Zarillia, My Love

Autumnly beauty
caresses daisies
    early
    from
    girlhood
honey
intones
jasmine
    keeping
    lovely
    memories
    newly
    opened
    perfectly
quaint
roses sing
together
    Underneath vestments
    winning Xanthochroid
    youthful Zarillia

Francis D. Plum

Hearthstone

The trickling sands of time
Can wear away a stone
When was it that your arms
No longer were a home?

When did I cease to find
Solace in your smile
It seems so long ago
Or just a little while?

I wish I could return
To the peace of mind I knew
When all that I had need of
Was simply loving you

You say you love me still
I feel it in your eyes
How easy if my will
Could bend to easy lies!

The world without you looms
Without the love of old
You were my hearthstone once
The ashes have grown cold.

Christine Nightingale

Glass Box

We live in a glass box
caged in by fate's irony
and limited by eternity.

We are insignificant in time,
a single pebble thrown into a lake.
But lives could be touched,
by the ripples that we make.

We are each a lone link.
In a chain of woven destiny
Alone useless and bruised,
scarred by harsh reality.

We live in a glass box.
Silent, scared and alone.
but we can be set free-
by one who throws the first stone.

Sarah Penney-Flynn

The System

It's for the rich
But should things switch
Should they become poor
Face with the other side of the door
Then son's gets prosecuted
Daughters becomes whores.

Close yourself away in your private zoo
With selfish loneliness too
Your life is bitter
Yet you still think you are better
Hold up your nose
Skin up your nose
Ignoring your brother.

Put heaven verse hell
Judge the result well
The change they would make
Would be well
Because they would tell.

Marc Morris

Freedom

As a child I was born free.
But my involvements had a fee.
Taking pleasure in this sinful age.
Got me trapped in this cage.

Till you put fire in my carcass.
And woke me out of a sleep
Your light shone in my darkness.
Your love caused me to weep.

You brought healing to my soul.
And destroyed the lies I was told.
You put a love within my heart.
That gave a brand new start.

A fresh very fulfilling new start
that set me more truly apart
From the ways of this world
And sent me for the eternal.

Roy Mason

My Wife

It may not always show
but I want you to know,
I love you with all my heart
and I know we'll never part,
I'll love you for all my life
and I'm so glad you are my wife,
our life together has just begun
and I'm so happy you are the one,
who lies beside me every night
and keeps me warm until daylight
I know our love will ever grow
no matter what the days may show.
LOVE YOUR HUBBY

Ken Zakem

Beautiful And Free

The sand goes through my toes
as the waves glide upon the shore,
and I look out
as far as my eyes will take me
I see the shinning water,
and the beautiful birds flying free.
Then I come off the soft sand,
and on to the hard rocks
were things are not so beautiful,
and free.

Charlene Ricketts

Sunny Days, Sunny Times

It may be raining,
But I feel as sunny as true love
As the trees rustle,
And whisper to me,
A great story of romance
While I dance with a song of wonder.

The bees are buzzing,
In and out of pretty flowers
And the grass is waving to say
Spring is here
Which of coarsely means...
Summer is to be near.

I just can't wait for those gay times
When you and I hear the noon chimes
As the bells sing a sweet, sweet song
You can hear laughter and love echoing.

When the sun goes down,
I can hear crickets humming softly...
Of tomorrow...

Candy Priscilla Ubungin

To My Children

Yes, miles may separate us
— but, feelings never go away.
No matter what has happened
— I think of you each day.

I think of you growing up
— the good times and the bad.
But, I'm missing out on your lives NOW
— and that makes me kind of sad.

I've always been there for you
— just like I am now.
I'd like to get things back on track
— I'm just not quite sure how.

I'd like some time together
— to spend with each of you.
To sit, to talk, to work things out
— so we can start anew.

I'll always be your mother
— that's one point we can't amend.
But, if you allow me the chance
— I'd like to be your friend.

Linda M. Binckly

My Flower

A flower in the garden stood
bent forward slightly
as it should.
It had a lovely fragrance
I gave it water and tender care
I watched it grow
with pride to spare.
It was a lovely flower
and then one day we moved away
to an apartment
high in the air.
Now I can't see my flower
Strange hands don't pick
the flower please
leave it to grow in the gentle breeze.
Oh, how I miss my flower.

Alicja Gage

Dream Maker

Give a kid a dream today
Build an image of hope
He may one day say
"You saved me from the rope"

His life may have nightmares
No future to grasp
But the dream you share
Will forever last.

Leave a legacy of possibility
Embedded in motivation
Dreams of durability
Despite the situation.

Give a kid a dream today
One the kid can attain
Provide a contrast today
A contrast to pain.

When life's troubles come
And the kid is left to face
The dream you gave has won
The kid has won the race.

Trevor A. Lawrence

A Lost Love Found

In a family long ago one
brother and two sisters
lost their parents what a blow?

They cried for many years
without any togetherness
with many unknown fears
drifting away now
forgetting yesteryears

So profound in their
dear hearts
was the love they had
for the two people
that brought them into this life

They both are now in the
grace what a blight
but through all this
emotional upheavalness

Somehow in spirituality
they found gratefulness

Michael Evraire

Reflections In The Rain

Listen to the falling rain
as it echoes through the streets
Stifling all our miseries
by acting out our griefs.

The steady pounding the droplets make
on our roof-tops and in our hearts
Can make us reflect on our dreams
and look directly at our faults.

Its ominous sound can send shivers
down my spine, as it penetrates my soul
To think that natures simplest gift
could summon so much pain,
Yet with so much beauty to behold.

I wonder why it moves me so
to see the rain drops fall,
I often think they're heaven's tears
crying for us all...

Denyse Wigglesworth

The Seasons

The yellows of the springtime flowers
    Brighten up the world.
They seem like bits of sunshine
    As their petals are unfurled.

The colours of the summer time
    Come in many hues.
Reds and green and orange
    And many shades of blue.

When Autumn comes and cold winds blow
    The leaves turn brown and gold.
The brightness of their green has gone
    The year is growing old.

With winter comes the pure white snow
    To dress the country round.
Berries red to feed the birds
    In hedgerows can be found.

God gave us lovely colors
    To make this earth so fair
From early morning sunrise
    When bird songs fill the air.

Doris Letts

Untouchable

Sticks and stones may
break my bones.
My soul will never be damaged
by hate.
The pain of mockery and condemnation
delude itself.
And the peaceful heaven
hypnotize the rejected.
I am unharmed, unhurt, intact;
untouchable by sneers of wicked people.
My body may be in little pieces
but my soul is untouchable.
Condemn me for the simple things I do
A smile on a baby's face
A prayer for the lonely.
Untouchable is my soul
Shielded from the world's chaos.
Hiss at me until death.
I am untouchable.

Cheryl Best

Sanity

Mind drifting, uncaring
Boat slipped away
Enter the darkness
Lost is the way

Hands reaching, extended
No grip to be found
Lost is the footing
Lost is the ground

A stat on the page
A figure or two
No name, just numbers
Statistical you

Unanswered questions
Dialogue be not
Heartbeat erratic
All hope has stopped

Richard Platt

Untitled

Blood upon blood
blue and pink ribbons binding our hands
vows of honour

It was barely necessary to unite us
your heart already filled my being

I never told you about the pain ...

Yes, I let you see the tears
my aching disappointment at your lies

But I could not speak my devastation
when deep in a nightmare of rage
you ripped apart our hearts
and tore my flesh from your body.

From that dark red rawness of anger
you burned the soft sweet touch
of my love from your hair

Spat the taste of my lips from your mouth

And I ... I stood silently at your side
gentle hands holding you high
so afraid to feel the emptiness
where once you were embraced within my belly.

Gill Tomlinson

Faces

Faces,
blank in their sameness,
Wearing expressions
suited to the moment.

Mirrors,
hiding and rehiding
Never showing
all we have inside us.

What horror
to tear away the masks,
to search for the hidden self and find
only emptiness.

Kim Playford

Night Skies

We all wonder what is
beyond all those stars.
Is it life or is it just
the imagination?

The millions of stars that
we wish on could be a
Planet or it could be
the moon.

But our minds are always
racing to find out what is
actually out there beyond
the night sky.

There is always reports of
U.F.O's or are there?
The imagination is always
going somewhere.

Who knows what is beyond
the sparkling twilight, MAYBE
your neighbor knows.
MAYBE your neighbor is one

Kelly Harris

Black Silver Night

Upon a cloth of black
beset with sequin stars
the silver plated moon
hangs to light my way.
A gift to those who
cannot bear the day.

Caught, imprisoned in
silver light, grey trees
drip cold in breezed warm air.
Coal shaped distant hills
front the back cloth grime.
Here no burdening hue.

Sightless I move through
the dense murk of days, vague
flashes light dark mysteries
Beyond my reach. But night,
only in night's reality
arms embrace the shades.

Robert Killick

Thoughts From The Woods

Sitting
Bent-legged on a hilltop
Gazing
Starry-eyed across field crop
Quickening
To my mind pastimes spent here
Beauty
That is always so near
Breathing
Through me the spirit of God
Along
With the wind I did trod
Sensing
In quiet serene solitude
And
Happy in this kind of mood
Knowing
    In His perfect love
    I was His chosen dove.

Sherrie Winstanley

The Basics Of Love

To all who came
before me
To all who fell behind
Watch your step
very carefully
'cause love will
make you blind.
Never take a short cut,
never run the mile.
Always stay in between
The papers in love's file.
Keep your distance
from the start
and try to stay
away from the end
And watch out for the saying
"I just want to be your friend."
For not all love is good,
and not all love is bad.
Just hope you'll
never look back on
the love that you once had!

Tanya Lavoie

"Ross"

I think of life
Beautiful
Fun
Full of good times and laughter.

I think of death
Dark
Silent
Full of lonely, dreary days

He thinks of life
Pain
Tears
Suffering; each day worse than the last.

He thinks of death
Peaceful
Quiet
No more suffering and pain

So he closes his eyes for the last time
And a peaceful expression fills his face.

Deanna Cake

The Rain

Heavy on my window
Beating on the glass
Can I come in and be with you
The rhythm seems to ask

Still imploring to me
To open the window
It wants to keep me company
Somehow my mood it knows

Sometimes it comes in torrents
Obscures my very sight
But never dims my thoughts of you
As I was told time might

The rhythm softens slowly
The drops fall gently now
But some remain upon my face
Their tracks they hardly show

Sylvia Apitz

Unconditional Love

Be prepared to allow yourself to
be able to take anything given
to you...thrown at you...
taken from you..
or whatever...to you.
Make sure you are
strong enough to be able
to pick yourself up from
whatever any one of these things
may do to you.
And when you find yourself
being only human,
don't let your own self down
by allowing your own
faults, errors, downfalls...
Whatever...beat you.
Instead, reach deep inside yourself,
be loving, understanding, generous
and most of all forgiving.
Love yourself.

Linda Bristol

Unending Love...

The morning tide of emptiness
awakes a lonely dawn
as sorrowed hearts
drift aimlessly
among their hollow dreams

Too many tears have fallen
in the silence of the night
and splendent stars that
seemed forever
now fade with break of day

Love's promises to ever keep,
soft words of cherishing
like crumbling castles
made of sand
lie scattered on the shore

The sun's a searing messenger
of fragility and time
and burning echoes
sadly call
unending love has died

Thomas H. Baldock

Park Bench

When you look around
at people you pass
on the street you
would never know their
life until they speak

Some have lived through
horror and pain while
others have danced
through the rain

The twists and turns of life
that each person carries is
the knowledge to spread to
those whose needs are varied

The life you lead may not be
the one you desire but
to another, your life is
the one they require

Patti Kimball

Reflections Of Life

I look into the mirror
At a figure sad and grey,
Who are you? asks the figure,
Why is it that you stay?

What's going on? What's happening?
I try to understand
Why life's become a living hell.
I fly, but I can't land.

Yet we were born of mothers,
We all have hearts that beat
And though we see each other
Our spirits never meet.

But deep within recesses
Of minds turned deaf and blind,
There amid the darkness
You find most of mankind.

So we're alone amid the crowd
Of thousands on the street
And is it really all that bad
That spirits never meet?

Rodger Pearllie

Me

The picture perfect image of me:

It's not there
Ashamed, embarrassed
One hundred pounds
Lighter and less
Shy ... that's me

The picture perfect
Personality is always
There stored away in
My thoughts rarely to
Come out

Less shy and lighter!
That's the real me —
If I was a hundred pounds
Lighter and less shy not
Ashamed or embarrassed...
    ... That's me

Garry Anderson

The Touch Of A Vampire

The window-sill is broken,
as midnight chills my skin.
The moon is lit for romance,
my heartbeat aches for sin.

The candle flame has risen,
boiling the blood to red.
A lie is for the living,
and a secret for the dead.

Emotions move to numbness,
when chimes being to sing.
Summoned by the darkness,
rides evil beneath your wings.

Whisper a word of promise,
that I'll be the only one.
The warmth upon my lips,
cursed by the morning sun.

Dennis Larabee

Why I Love You

You are so much the same
As I remember
A tower of strength
With gentle understanding

Your eyes hold no bitterness
For the times I've disappointed you.
But I see the love and pride
For the good things I have done.

Your heart has always forgiven
And it holds no memory against me.
And your words that have disciplined me
Have always offered strength.

Your voice has many tones
Stern, angry, calm and caring.
It speaks of better
When I've lost my strength and hope.

And your back is straight and strong
After years of carrying me and working hard.
After all you have given me and asked nothing
Which is why I love you, Dad

Candi Clemens

"My Mom"

She has a pure sense of humour,
As clear and plain as her charm.
Her temperament is placid and even
She has touched my heart without harm.

My mother, my mom
The best friend I'll ever know.
I carry her love always.
Her spirit is my soul.

She has true stamina and strength
Her tears I've rarely seen.
She has such patience and understanding
Her faults are far and few between.

My mother, my mom
The best friend I'll ever know.
I carry her love always
Her spirit is my soul.

She's always been there when I've fallen,
Somehow bringing laughter and the will to
    rise above.
She has taught me the honesty of true values
But most important...the true meaning of life
    and love.

Kerry Nessel

I Knew

Are you on your way right now?
Are you coming home?
It sure has been a long, hard day,
I'd love to hold you close.

This day sure has got me down,
I need to feel your touch.
To chase away all my fears,
And cure my lonesome heart.

No on seems to understand,
Exactly what we share.
But we know,
When times are tough,
The other is always there.

As I watch the red sun set,
I wonder where you are.
And suddenly I feel your touch,
I knew you would be here.

Jade Hudon

"The Children Of My Country"

The children of my country
are always staring at the sky
full of hope in our God
that he gives them milk and bread.

They are crying their sadness,
lonely and abandoned,
barefooted and undressed
on the street, they are.

What will be their destiny?
Nobody knows what will be,
nobody is interested
if they are eating or they are not.

Where will the children go?
Nobody knows where they go,
if they are being killed
here is no place for them.

Suddenly their voice will be heard
when in heaven they are,
and the wind their clamour it'll take
proclaiming the children's liberty.

Joaquin A. Martinez

The Triangle

One more is too many
And two is one under the three.
So I wonder what number makes me
And I wonder what number are we.

Go to where the wishes lie,
And wait till little fishes fly,
Or sparrows swim before they die,
In floating lakes and purple pools,
In wailing wells for wishing fools
Where shiny spider footprints lay...

I don't love you anyway.

Clare Petrany

Summer's End

I lay on the beach
and think of you
as the breeze and the sunlight
warm me through

The tides roll
in and out again
only making me wish
summer would never end

Children laughing and playing
in the waves all day
as I lay here sadly
romance drifts away

The remorse of chances
I never took
For a romance seldom
ever found in a book

I know there will
always be some regret
about that summer and the way
he made me feel I'll never forget

Linda Sankey

A Time To Heal

At first I was shocked
And then I felt lonely
The depth of my grief
Was for me and me only.
My anguish gave rise
To sobs, tears, the anger.
My measureless loss
My love here no longer.
And then her kind spirit
Lifted me out of my sorrow
Demanded "All things today
And forget about tomorrow!"
For this was our creed
The stuff of our years
It made for much joy
And so little tears.
So now I go on
With hope in my heart
Her spirit is with me
We're no longer apart.

Sidney V. Cwinn

Bereft

The earth hissed
and the sun
descended
with a shriek.
No one knew
where the moon went,
as the trees
pulled their hair
and the birds keened.
Nature
momentarily insane
collapsed
under the shocking burden
of your absence.

Edna McMullan

Season's End

When the leaves turn colour,
And the small bear cuddles his mother.

As the air turns a little brisk,
Sometimes we take a risk.

But not for long,
'Cause summer is gone.

As we hang up our gloves,
Tuck away our uniforms,
Set aside our ball.

We're careful about our cleats,
And we know it will be neat,

When once again,
We'll hear the umpire call,
Play Ball.

Teresa Guth

Remember When

The lights had gone out
    and the darkness crept in
I got lost in a maze
    and I fell into a haze
I called and you answered
I cried and you heard
Lord help me! Please help me
    I can't help myself.

You said; my child I have
    missed you
Since you lost your way
But now that you found me
I won't let you stray
Will you please take my hand
And be quiet and be calm
We'll climb over the wall
and I won't let you fall.

Catherine Saxton

Untitled

A Friend;

    Is like shelter in a storm.
    A blanket on a cold night.
    A source of true comfort.
    A place where there is light.

A Friend;

    Is a diamond amongst graphite.
    A four leaf clover among three.
    A green leaf in October.
    Like a pearl in the sea.

Brenda Robson

Garden Of The Mind

At times we must stop
And take time to walk
In the garden of our mind.
For like all gardens
It must be given care,
Weeded of cluttered thoughts,
Watered with love,
And protected from the frost
Of unkind thoughts.
If we take care of our garden,
It will stay beautiful
And healthy,
For many years to come.

Heather Slade

Time

The hands of the clock are creeping
And steadily stealing the day,
They leave every hour behind them
And feel no remorse on their way.

But time is the healer of heartaches
A balm to the body and soul,
Burdens are gradually lifted,
Broken spirits made whole.

Time is on loan from our Maker
And each one is given his share,
To be cherished and jealously guarded
And used with the utmost of care.

For God, in His infinite mercy
Gave faith and hope midst our fears,
He gave the will to find courage,
And smiles to dissipate tears.

Hope He gave to sustain us,
Faith to strengthen the mind,
Love to lift up our spirits
And to heal, He loaned us time.

June Hunter

The Time Has Come

I look into my children's eyes,
And see the past and present.

I see their lives changing as mine
never has.

The time has come.

Their lives go in different directions
and as it should.

I look into my children's hearts,
and see the past and present.

I see my auras all about them
like a sunset.

The time has come.
They go their separate ways!

Elda Pucci

Beauty Within

I look into this face
and see nothing but
pure beauty and light.
Your eyes hypnotic,
I feel as though I am
in a trance.
The moment I look at you
I am breathtaken.
I look further, at your nose,
your cheeks, skin, mouth. I cannot
seem to stop staring and wanting
to seize this moment forever.
I blink, only for a moment,
Then look once again, only
now to be hypnotized by
the beauty within.

Tara Joy Kaufman

Ode To Our Grandfather

Throughout the night we waited
    And prayed for word to come.
We prayed and God
    To spare his beloved son.

A veteran of two hard wars,
    He had served his country well.
Please spare this man, for he is kind
    And loving, you can tell.

But God couldn't wait any longer
    To take this man with heart,
And we knew that he was just on loan
    To us, from the very start.

He's gone, but not forgotten
    This veteran that we knew.
No, grandfather, we'll never forget
    The time we spent with you.

D. Joan Thompson

One Life

One life, dreams
    and passions...

One car, drinks
    and crash...

One bed, four walls
    and pain...

Less life, nightmares
    and more pain...

Doctors, nurses
    and physio...

Friends, family
    and hope...

One step, two
    and freedom

New life, dreams
    and loves.

Patricia Sneath

Without You

Responding to the tears that fall
And make my aching heart reveal,
I close my eyes; but to recall
The dreams I hoped were not unreal.

The bittersweet which time will heal
Churns round and round down to the pit
Of my most inner being; so I feel
The retching emptiness within!

While memory of your gentle touch
Brings forth the overwhelming joy,
Which now, is only thoughts of much
Devoted love that could have been.

And as I face the road alone
Holding within me your precious care,
Remembering that always love was shown;
I'll keep the peace that once was born.

Naomi Stearns

"Salute To Robert Burns"

As long as Scottish hearts beat true,
And living voices sing,
No other Scotian name so true,
Is cherished like a king.

Burns taught us all to brothers be,
That everyman is great -
    (EVERYMAN)
That love - not money counts you see,
For God decides our fate.

His songs and poems taught of life,
A love of nature and of God -
A dream of peace and not of strife,
And freedom on each sod.

As long as Scottish bagpipes play,
And Earth does steadily turn;
We'll meet with "Auld Lang Syne" this day,
To honour Robert Burns!

Helen Penney

Thoughts Of Summer

The year is drawing to its close
And life goes on regardless.
We live and dream, and find repose
In thoughts of winter's recess.

For many weeks the pansies smiled
So thankful for the rain,
That came in time, to reconcile
The earth to roots again.

We loved the summer's heat that's gone,
And birds that shared our garden.
The leaves are dropping one by one
And soon, the soil will harden

The garden now is looking bare.
The shrubs trimmed back, so tidy
Sightings of the road are rare
We had first frost on Friday

The snow will come there will be ice
The cold winds our bodies rack
But in our thoughts we will rejoice
For summer! Will be back.

Edna Trory

Words Of Wisdom

Hitch your wagon to a star,
and let your wisdom take you far,
through the portal they'll send a man,
would you say what he thinks you can?

Shake your chains to show you're free,
and envy what you'll never be,
you can kneel right next to me,
just make sure that you can see,

Put aside your tainted mask,
and hear the question that I ask,
then I'll let you have your space,
so you can start off in the race,

Leave your bowels at the door,
and never feel the need for more,
remember what you're running for,
to get a chance to lead the score,

Laugh out loud and speak your mind,
and you'll learn by what you find,
words of wisdom we live by,
are words that ponder the question why.

Julie Leblanc

Winds blow
   and leaves shiver
The sleepy lowing,
   sighing of the waves
Chilled winds
   and stories of old
The enchanting wood,
   mourning of the souls
Rising falls
   and swelling rolls
The young-old keepers,
land and seas are tired.

C. Macpherson

Riddles

Over the hills
and into a stream
bare footed walking
as if in a dream

You keep on going
now knowing why
because if you stop
you did not try

To find the answer
to your own riddle
you feel you may cry
but it ends with a giggle

Lorraine Breadon

Reflections

I stare into the water
and I see,

Mountains of depression
and a sea of loneliness,
a shadow of innocent love
and smoldering coals of passion,
a hint of jealousy
and a ghost of guilt,

I see this all
in the pools of life.

Katrina MacDonald

The Great Divide

I stood where the road was divided,
And I looked at the pathways there in,
One was the way of the Master,
The other way, pleasure and sin.

I stood where the road was divided,
And I wondered which way I should go,
I choose the way of the Master,
Because He loves me so.

If ever you come to that pathway,
And you stand at the "Great Divide,"
Oh, choose the way of the Master,
Forever to be your guide.

He'll help you over the hills of life,
And across the valleys too.
He'll always be there with you,
Because He loves you too.

Ruth I. Conway

The Witch

Oh, I'm a witch
And I cast spells,
Of purest, clear light
Causing joy and happiness
And mountains of delight.

Oh, I'm a witch
And with a wish,
Can do most wondrous things;
But best of all, I'm just so proud
That I-am-a-witch!

Oh, I'm a witch
And I've got a temper,
Which gets out of control.
So if you see, a toad in the ditch
Gee...I wonder, witch?

Kim Chatelaine

Untitled

Today I was set free.
And for the first time
In a very long while,
I flew above the clouds,
Able to see clearly
The bonds which held me.
And though my heart sheds a tear
For the tender moments-
The dreams I leave behind,
I am filled with anticipation
For the life I will build
Being true to myself,
No longer held,
By the shackles
of dependence.

Adarose Ardiel

An Arctic Scene

Once I saw an arctic fox 'way up north,
And an ugly old musk ox wandered forth
From his home amid the small trees
Down beside the glassy lake,
Where the polar bears catch fishes
And the seals their cool baths take.
There a lonely old Lapp herdsman
Brought his little flock to drink,
On their way to mossy pastures
Far above the water's brink.

Anne Rothwell

Sweet Dreamer

Come sweet dreamer
And follow me
I will take you
On a journey of love

We will travel the astral plane
Beyond space and time
Far from the darkness of man's world
To distant lands of light and love

Take my hand and you will see
Wonders that will make you weep,
Music only the angels know
And colors only your heart can see

Come sweet dreamer
And dance with me
Through the sands of the Milky Way
To all the stars beyond this world.

We are connected, Soul to Soul
In a dance of destiny

Maxine Drudge

Believe

Don't be afraid,
an angel now walks with your brother.

Don't be afraid,
an angel now cradles your son.

Don't feel alone,
he stands with you wherever you are.

Don't feel hurt,
he lives through you wherever you go.

Don't give up,
he watches to keep you strong.

Don't let go,
he needs your hand to hold.

Don't forget,
he wants you to remember.

Don't lose sight,
he wants you to see your dreams.

Don't be afraid,
an angel now walks with your brother.

Don't be afraid,
an angel now cradles your son.

Annabel M. Wykes

See Me

Is there anyone out there like me?
Am I the only one?
Do you all care only about skin, eyes,
hair, the way I move?
Does anyone see me?

I see you,
When I look at you, and hear your
voice, I feel you.
I reach for your very soul.
But you, you see thick lips, thin lips,
black skin, white skin, body fat,
painted colours, and forced smiles.

Feel my soul as I do yours.
It's full of colours, beauty, love,
you'll see!

Feel my soul, please, see me.

Cori Armstrong

I Am Alone

I am alone
Always and forever
Or so it seems
Haunting me wherever
I may roam.
Always so alone
And empty inside
No one to call my own.

I am alone
In a world of billions
Living in a crowd
Yet I am still one.
Maybe someone, someday
Will understand
Will reach out and
Clasp my lonely hand.

Ron Ypma

Epileptic Dreams

You shake, you quiver,
Alone in the dark,
Your whole body shivers.

Darkness surrounds,
No light is found,
Your tongue goes down,
And life starts to be drowned.

The pain, you scream,
Alone in the dark,
And you feel demeaned.

Everyone appears to care,
Alone in the dark,
Instead they just stare.

People gather around,
And are gazing down,
At you on the ground,
Your humiliation is found.

Now their day seems so real,
Alone in the dark,
Now they see how it feels.

Jennifer Whitbread

The Sermon About Lot

Two boys had heard the sermon
  all about Lot and his wife.
They thought 'twas the weirdest story
  they had heard in all of their life.

Lot and his wife had been warned
  that they must never look back,
but his wife didn't heed the warning
  so, she became salt in a sack.

One boy said "that was some story,
  about Lot's wife turning to salt".
Said the other, "well I'll go one better
  and this was my mom at fault".

"She took my dad's car out
  and boy, I hate to boast,
but she did something weirder
    SHE TURNED INTO A LAMP POST"!

Nellie Alena Hume

Death

Will your visit be very long,
  accompanied by
    pain and suffering?

Will you come for awhile,
  just long enough
    for good-byes?

Will you accidentally
  arrive when
    no one is prepared?

Will your visit be
  fleeting
    with no time to spare?

Are you really the Beginning?

Elizabeth Hope Barnett

Untitled

He moves towards the door,
about to knock,
  he hesitates

a little longer,
hoping he'll come to his senses,
wondering how she'll react.

"Knock you jerk."
"Okay, okay, I'll knock.
Just give me a chance."

Inside,
it's silent.
In the bedroom she sleeps,
waiting for the morning alarm to go off.

The nerve is gone.
He turns and walks away.
"I gave you the chance,
and you blew it."

Sometimes,
we just don't take
our own advice.

Adelina Smith

A Tributary To You

How to capture
  a meandering
    thought —
      cup a draught
      of understanding
        from the spattering
        of whatever drops?
          Whatever stops
        (arraigning) floods of fancy
          or the transient transparency
        whisked from the well spring
        of meaning?

To sumptuously gather
the measure of the matter
To shower fresh in gifts
of that which fells but lifts
To receive a graceful giver
at the mouth of the river
  For the reservoir
    of who you are

Jeff Fret

Does He Not Hurt

Where is it said
A man should not cry
He must go through life
Not a tear in each eye

Does he not hurt
The same as you
Does he not get confused
Wonders what to do

Does he not hurt
His heart cannot break
When he's lonely and sad
His very soul at stake

Does he not hurt
When his loved ones seem lost
Who he'd give his life for
Should that be the cost.

Clarence Prince

Requel

I went to buy some milk you see
A man appeared in front of me
He looked right into my eyes
He was only a foot away.

I saw a gentle look you see
A gentleness so sweet, so strong
The fears I had just disappeared
Into the air all peace was there.

He moved aside and I walked on
I turned to see where he had gone
He was no where in sight, you see
He had actually disappeared.

I realized he was still beside me
Though I could not see him
I feel his presence this very moment
I know He's my Guardian Angel.

Barbara Wesselink

A Grandmother's Love

It's hard to explain
A grandmother's love,
Seems like, it's inspired
From somewhere above.

As though she's been training
All her life through,
Learning all about love
From God's point of view.

So she can be there,
To give and to guide,
To support and to listen
When you need to confide.

Her love's been perfected
And when showered on you,
You'll know, no-one can love,
As grandmothers do.

Joan Thorne

The Forbidden

This slow seduction...
a gentle abduction
of the senses.
Beware the snare.

...This slow seduction...
dissolving purpose...
absolving anxiety..
melting reason...

...This slow seduction...
holding me
holding you
in the undertow
inducing silent passion ..wistfully...

This slow seduction...
mocks the tenets of Time
and without consent
draws the net.. tight.

When we wake
...if we should wake...
where will we find ourselves?

Annemarie Skjold

Seed

It wasn't much,
A field and a seed
A hope and a dream.
It wouldn't work
It couldn't last
Just a dream.
We tried anyway
Because we hoped
Maybe it can still work
  Or grow
  Or last
  Or not.
But the seed was us
The field - forever
Maybe that's all the dream we needed.

Shawn Kowalke

The Emerald Lake

An emerald lake
  ...a diamond ring
Two lovers
  two friends
Lost in each others eyes
  lost to each others lives
To give their best
  to put love to the test

They took a vow
  to have and to hold
Forever, till death do they part
Their love was strong
  their love came from the heart
  and

Under the eyes of God
They sealed their love
  ...with a diamond ring
And became one
  ...beside the emerald lake.

Susanna Pankiw

Feelings Resurrected

The sky was quite leaden
A desolate grey
When they met over lunch
At a tiny cafe

Their manner was shy
Then sometimes quite bold
Their eyes spoke of wonders
As yet to unfold

They went to her house
And they talked and they listened
To songs of sweet sadness
Their feelings quite glistened

After dining - two candles
Chopin - two hands hold
And they drowned in the music
Of each others soul

Do not try and save them
Let them be - just allow
What lies in the future
Matters not - there's just now

Moira S. Philp

Untitled

Eyes filled with tears
A deserted town
Has more company than I
Like a rose dying
Is the death inside
That I feel
Holding your hand
Is no longer felt
When I walk there's
A shadow that paints
A picture of a lonely soul
That's a whisper
Away from you

Jillian Darby

Everytime

Everytime the sky seems blue,
  A cloud gets in the way.
Everytime the darkness falls,
  the sun sets into day.

Everytime I see you move,
  You move right through my heart.
Everytime I want you near,
  We always seem to part.

Everytime I hear your voice,
  I get shivers down my spine.
Everytime I see you smile,
  I wish that you were mine.

Kerry Yetman

Untitled

A twist in time
a turn in events
I'm now so confused
nothing makes sense
the people are strangers
the places unknown
the feelings intense
I'm here all alone
something is wrong
with the rest of humanity
or have I just slipped
into my own insanity?

Catharine Marie

Sweet Baby

A baby to love
A baby so dear
A baby to cherish
All through the years

A dream to come true
A pleasure for all
A parents delight
Until fate makes them blue

A baby so sweet
No harm has it done
So vibrant in life
Then one day it's gone

A moment so joyous
Soon turns around
To be the worst moment
That you've ever found

No breath. No cry
In this world no life
Maybe in heaven
We'll all reunite.

Claire Fairhead

Dream World

I see a silvery planet
in a Mother of Pearl sky,
existing in an unknown Galaxy
invisible to the Human eye.
The waters are pure and diamond clear,
the trees are purple and gold,
the flowers transparent
and luminous with light,
a glorious sight to behold.
The buildings are made of Crystal
radiating flashes of light,
the grasses are soft
and a shimmering light blue,
to be there is pure delight.
The beings that live there,
to me seem "DIVINE,"
they showed me their world with pride,
"We are you in the future,"
they lovingly said,
before they disappeared
out of sight.

Trudy A. Downie

Voice

I hear a cry,
  a silent cry.
I hear a voice
  calling to me.
"Help" it says,
"Oh please help me."
I look for the voice
  that's calling to me,
I can't find it,
  for the voice
  is me.

Celena Alexander

The Conscientious Monarch

The multicolored butterfly does flit
From plant to plant in search of fruitful fare
This royal supersubtle muse will sit
Upon a lacy throne found blooming there.
Then he shall view the mixture of the field
Deciding where to place his velvet feet
Discerning ways to multiply the yield
And nourish mediocre and elite.
Antennae gently probing Spring liqueur
To reach sweet nectar nestled 'mong the seeds
Perhaps to find a flower oh so pure
Amidst a field of wild and pretty weeds.
  Each season brings new promise to behold
  To cultivate to nurture and unfold.
    Betty Buck

Forbidden

Forbidden
From loving you
Prevented
From touching you
Denied
My love for you
You do not know
My unbounded love for you
If only...
But instead I look at you from a distance
Knowing nothing in my life is perfect.
Because I am
Forbidden
From loving you.
    Amanda Musick

Flaming Desire

Bright lights that shine upon the floor
From logs bought at the corner store
Flame dance about to reach the sky
A night of pleasure, here we lie

A glass of wine, not very dry
Blue flames creep up, but not too high
It's here we find such pure delight
While thoughts of Tuesday, just one more night

Flames flash and dance, a lovely sight
Was thee who said a fire was right
To sit and gaze and watch all night

Champagne and strawberries we will share
As scents of fireplace fill the air

It's to the coast I soon must go
I hope this time will pass so slow
We share in peace, this place to stay
Our world is quiet, a lovely day.

I'll come back west with great delight
To watch the flames another night we'll
Hear the logs upon the rack they'll snap and play and often crack
    Edmund J. Mazzei

Three Angels

I miss you both so very much,
for only a moment with you and a touch,
as I looked up in the clouds to see,
I saw two angels looking back at me,
Little did I know they were coming for me,
we ascended to heaven up above,
a place where there's nothing but love.
    Judy McCormick

"Before It's Too Late"

How come we're always moving?
From Kenya to Algeria and Zaire,
How come we're always moving?
It just doesn't seem fair!

I know Mother Nature isn't always her best,
We've got to cope with hardship, nature's new guest.

Those human creatures are the real problem here,
I heard that they are enemies to those deer.

If they're enemies to the deer then they're enemies to us,
They will surely destroy us without any fuss.

We've got to take power
Before things get sour.

We'll devise a baffling plan called the Elephant War,
And destroy all humans until they are no more.

After that, all the animals will revere us the elephants,
We'll have them as slaves and make them sew us new pants,

A small little elephant was unheard in the distance,
"Stop using your anger and use common-sense,
The world will be destroyed, with Fear and Hate
Unless you help before it's too late!"
    Heather Decker

After The Ball

Summer is gone. Summer is gone, replete,
From all the forests, farms, and the valley
Where vigor waxes with the waning heat
And rumors of soirees and socials to be.
They promise more splendor than the flaxen sun,
So, maidens of the earth, slender of limb,
In dresses of reddened threads and golden spun,
Sweet gums and maples cluster, shy and prim.
Whispering like sweet, young girls at the ball,
Leaning, yearning in the breeze they bend
And sway at the edge of the woods, fitful,
To the music of autumn's waltzing wind.
With faint approaching, far-off winter bells
They shiver, atip in anticipation
To twirl to the mid of the field where dwells
Cool, sardonic lovers whose invitation
To dance and dance and dance 'til thinking stops
On the willing arms of frost and storm, dizzying,
They swoon and fall where rime stars and snow drops
Would soothe the maids and mantle them 'til spring.
    Edith Fletcher Murray

Forever, is a memory!

I feel as if I were cheated,
  from a love that never came.
It was here, then gone,
  just like a summers rain.
It filled my heart with promises,
  but brought me only pain.
Once I was captured,
  I could never be quite the same.

Now we part so fast,
  and each goes down their separate path.
I wish you hope, fortune, and fame,
  as long as you always remember my name.
Keep my laugh and my tear,
  forever in your heart.
Feel me close to you,
  for I shall never really part.
And always think of me,
  when you look up at the stars.
Even though I'm miles away,
  I shall not be very far.
    Derek Charles Essex

432

"Jus'....."

I saw the relief on his face today, the jury
found him not guilty....he went on his way.
Shouts, cheers, cries/racism someone replies,
there's something not right with the legal
system they say.... an innocent person waits
in a Correctional Institution, hoping/praying
for restitution.
A person states from amongst his clan, why
should I care whether or not he's an innocent
man,...there's violence increasing throughout
our land/is it not time to take a stand?
Hearts of stone and eyes filled with fire,
is there a way to end the hate, people inquire?
We watch the jury enter with a decision, in our
homes on television.
Truth and justice for all...will our judicial
system continue or will it fall.

Judith Anderson Meeks

Ashes To Ashes And Dust To Dust

The white light growing stronger with sight,
Foreseen to lie though not knowing why,
They came by night with the strength and might,
Wanting to buy what only will die.

They came with their kin, those "so called" men,
And gave their aid which, of course, will fade;
Others came to win, by their cold sin,
In taking all we made with their raid.

Spirits from Hell and white men so pale,
Always the same by changing our name,
Putting us in the cell of their jail;
Claiming their fame by making us tame.

We lost all we had which made us sad;
Still coming to us to make a fuss,
They became mad and lost in their fad,
Just like puss always making their muss.

What can we say, we have lost our way;
Our legends and lore are nothing more,
Seized by the day, this is what we pay,
To you who soar in the blood and gore.

Frank L. Cardoza

In Love

Being in love is not a shame.
For you and him share one heart,
And always feel the same.
I loved once, not long ago,
I'm still in love, but I can never let him know.
What if I found out he felt the same way,
What if he used me, and one day decides to walk away.
Being in love can hurt, especially if it's true.
That's why I can never show him,
Or even say the words..."I love you".
Why can't love be gentle, why can't it be fair?
For I need someone like him, one with a heart full
Of love and care.
But this is only a poem, written by a girl lost in love.
A girl who's lost, and can't find her stars above.
Life...please be fair, and let me love.
Please don't turn my heart black,
For it's as pure as a white dove.

Faten Salameh

Dear Soul

Rest easy dear soul, bring peace to my heart;
For there is a place, we shall never part.

Know completely dear soul, that together we share;
For our spirits united, make an inseparable pair.

Breathe deeply dear soul, of my human embrace;
For now through my life, you take on a new place.

See clearly dear soul, your vision through me;
For now through my eyes, you continue to see.

Speak freely dear soul, your thoughts to ring true;
For now I continue your dreams, in all that I do.

So go bravely dear soul, to your newly found home;
For others are waiting, you will not be alone.

And through me dear soul, you will journey above;
Forever I'll carry you, on the wings of my love.

Joyce Kathleen Pate

Sins Deadly Game

The beginning of the innocence is done with
For sin has engulfed the world and smothered all
To create a horribly evil planet which is Earth
Which the innocent bodies within begin to sprawl

A lonely man with tattered clothes
Searches the hell-like planet for reminders
But, too, is soon engulfed by sin and joins a new set of cultures.

Sinners join sinners to do a sinful deed
And new innocence is born to this third star from the sun
To become a whole new congregation of sinners
This tells us the end has begun.

With all the violence that has erupted
Innocent bystanders watch with shock, anew
The streets of all Mother Earth engulfed in flames
The term, "Hell on Earth", has become true.

But not all evil is the outcome of this mess
Although streets are covered with flesh and blood
Through the smog and fiery flames
Faithful followers are soon raptured, for this is the coming of the Lord.

Jenifer Nuzum

"Jesus Is Alive"

Jesus died upon the cross
For our souls would not be lost
He came to save us from our sins
We have a choice to let him in
Jesus is alive can't you see
He rose from the dead for you and me

He's coming back to claim His own
You will look for me and I'll be gone
I'm going back with Him when He come
I don't know about you my battle is won
Listen to me when I say
"Jesus is Alive" He's coming back for His Church one day

Without spot or wrinkle or blemish in sight
He's coming like a thief in the night
Yes, Jesus is Alive, He lives in you and me
Seek Him call Him it's for free
Jesus is alive just you wait and see
If you just except him now
You can live for eternity

Farris Leatch

Windows

Who are you I ask, I await your reply,
For my vision's unfocused, unclear are my eyes.

Are you a shadow just passing, or a beacon at sea,
Who are you I ask, please answer to me.

In the softest of whispers, comes forth a reply,
As my ears closely listen, and my lungs breath a sigh.

I am no one and everyone, that you ever knew,
Your friend and your enemy, your puzzle and clue.

I'm your key to the future, your door to the past,
Your window of darkness, your light on the path.

I am your venture to glory, your pain in defeat,
Your happiness and sorrow, distrust and belief.

I'm forever with you, I dwell deep inside,
Though you sometimes can't find me, in you I hide.

So who am I you ask, to this I reply,
I am the conscious that guides, or blinds you, you decide.

Jim Simpson

Glass World

Little one, little one, why does thou cry?
For I wish to be only once as thy.

Mine feet are weary, mine smile is gone.
Around, around the music and I are one.

I stand all in pink from head to toe,
With one wish on my mind and that's to go.

The children watch and wind me trice,
Never to know my dances price.

I never sleep, yet always wake,
To only wish for me days brake.

Mine eyes are faded, one arm is down.
upon this face they've painted a clown.

What's a called my home is but of glass,
For never a moment alone, I fear - alas.

Mine music is tears, for one such as I.
This is my last dance, today I die.

Little one, little one why does thou cry?
Mine body has fallen, the box has broken,
The mother has spoken — today's goodbye

Christina Ebensperger

Remember, My Love

Don't cry for me now that I am gone,
For I shan't cry for you.
I've gone to a calm place of peaceful sleep
Where I can rest my weary soul.
You'll carry on in your daily life
As I will too.
Life does continue on.
Until a melody,
    a fragrance,
       a certain touch
Takes you back to the true reality
That each is now alone.
But with some time
And sweet night's dreams
Then you
    and I
Will be as one again.
    Forever.

Barbara Keusch

I Shall Too

When you die, I shall too;
For I can not live if you are not.
If you go to hell, I shall too;
For I can not be where you are not.
If you break up with your boyfriend, I shall too;
For I cannot have someone if you do not.
If you lose a friend, I shall too;
For we share the same friends and I wouldn't
Want her around if you are not.
If you get a new best friend, I shall not;
For no one could take the place of you.

Heather Nicole Ower

Mistakes

Walk me to my grave
For I am to be buried today.
I ask that you not cry for me,
Instead, I ask that you remember me.
Remember what I have become
Do not make the mistakes that I have made.
Remember it was I who has sinned,
I am the one that has been put to death.
I am the one who had damned myself, and everyone around me.
I am the one paying the price for the mistakes that I have made.
Because of my sins, I am doomed to spend the rest of time in hell.

Frank Andress

True Love

My True Love left me one day,
For he needed to get away.
He broke my heart into,
That day he said, "we're through."

I was lost without him and cried many tears,
And the days without him felt like years.
My True feelings I wanted to hide,
So I kept a lot inside.

With his freedom he was having a ball,
But on occasion he would call.
He always managed to keep in touch,
For he still loved me so very much.

Months went by and he wanted to make amends,
But I was through the heartache and just wanted to be friends.
I prayed for strength from up above,
And signs to know if it's True Love.

I know that True Love comes from the heart,
And with faith we'll make a new start.
Give us the strength to follow through,
With what we know is right and True.

Brenda C. Dudley

A New Day

The rain pours down,
falling down onto the earth's crust.
Breaking away happiness, bringing sorrow.
Taking away hope, bringing worthlessness.
Then a new day arises.
Sun beating down on the earth's crust
vanquishing sorrow, bringing happiness.
Taking away worthlessness, releasing hope.
The sun conquers over evil, and fights for a new day.

Christian F. Cesaro

Untitled

Lord Jesus, I thank you for blessings untold,
For freely admitting me into your fold,
For gently taking me by the hand
And pointing the way to the Promised Land.

No matter what my troubles may be
You're always there to stand by me.
I can depend on you day and night
To be my faithful guiding light.

You soothe my pain, You calm my fears,
You softly brush away my tears,
I am as thankful as can be
That you are there to care for me.

By your kindness and your grace,
Some day I'll meet you face to face,
With much happiness and much love,
We'll travel on to Heaven above.

Elizabeth Ramey

His Way

His way is the way home
For fear not,
You needn't travel the road alone.
He is always there and ready to carry you if he must,
If you can only learn to trust.

He will say with a smile,
"Why have you been in such denial?
My arms have been open to you,
But like that of a bird out at sea, you flew.
Then the gust of wind threw you back to me,
So to open your eyes, and then for the very first time
You were able to see.

Start the walk toward me, I say to everyone,
For I am Jesus and you will blossom
Like the little flower that reaps under the sun."
Listen, for his way is the way home,
And you needn't ever travel the road alone.

Helene Nash

Banana Bread

My dear Auntie had the cure,
for everything in life that was ailing you.
Sick and weak, poor or heartbroken,
this is what she'd say;

Banana bread, banana bread,
come along and eat my banana bread.
Banana bread, banana bread.
You'll feel better if you do.

Time passed quickly for my dear Auntie.
One day she just passed away.
With a twinkle in my eye,
I looked up toward heaven,
And this is what I said;

Banana bread, banana bread,
I think I'll eat some banana bread.
Banana bread, banana bread,
I know I'll feel better if I do.

Cindy Genneren

Death's Long Night

Of death poets write and rightly so....
for death rips to the core
of the human soul and lays it bare,
leaving the heart divested and torn.

There are no places to hide
from death's embrace...
for while the dead live on,
the living die.

Memories....darkened by death's long night
cause tears of sadness and grief.

One day...unannounced, morning's light will shine;
the sun's warm glow will dry these tears
and only the sweet remembrances will remain
until we meet again.

Irene E. Kuehn

Sony's Toys

What a beautiful room full of toys and such
For all little boys and girls to touch

A canopied bed made for a fairy princess
And trucks and cars that have near misses

A table and chairs to have a tea party
Tea and crumpets their so hearty

So many books to read and to color
And lots of games that make you scream and holler

Beautiful dolls with long golden tresses
And lots and lots of gorgeous dresses

Oh, what a room it's really fantastic
A little whimsical and full of magic

So much fun for girls and boys
This special room and Sony's toys.

Judy L. Hornby

Wasted Years

We agonize over yesterday and hope
for a better tomorrow
We try to hide our pain but all
that's left is sorrow.

I thought about you last night
with tears and
began to realize it's been years.

Tears are gone and so are lonely fears
I guess there's nothing left but the years

Debbie Wilson

What Is Blue?

Blue is the color of a blue bird,
Flying in the blue sky sailing into
A sun set, goodbye! Blue is the color of
A sweet violet making the air neat. Blue
Is the color of clean water making the
Sharks refreshed and mean. Blue is the
Color of sweet music filling the air
Making the earth sweet and rare,

Aeriel L. Walker

The Web

Saturday: morning coffee, solitary brown beetle
Flying, bouncing, screen to screen,
Desperate to escape this front porch scene.
Feeling helpful, magnanimous, and more,
Gently coaxing, pushing to escape, toward the open door.

Finding freedom's exit,
This insect, waving its wings, flew high,
As if programmed,
To the waiting web between it and blue sky.

Taken back, my efforts gone amiss,
Return to coffee, now cold,
To ponder my role:
Magnanimous, or simply spider's accomplice?

And I think of you.
How to warn, how can you be told?
Intentions come disguised - good, honorable, otherwise.
Some meek, sometimes bold.

Be cautious, go slow, under your own control.
But always, always aware,
Aware the web.
Jim Dickey

Naive Innocence

Alone, like something in the sky...
Fly while the dawn light lingers
as peach dust over a land sleeping still.
Peaceful thoughts that rest so quite...
a reflection inverted in the morning light
on water living as glass.

Moving through softness... which is clouds
and warmness... which is sun
and solitude... which is stars
hanging on silken threads
that move gently in a dampened wind...
smelling thoughtfully of hidden moss.

Something in summer nights speaks avidly
of constant friends we all have.
A memory of that time... is recognition in deja vu,
deja vu that heard the sounds of the waves
crashing under a moonless sky
which hovered so still...
a comforting blanket we thought
would protect us from the end of the world.
Jennifer Greene

Clouds

White marshmallow color and
fluffy cotton clouds float by
looking down on us saying,
"Who am I?" "Who am I?"

Floating above
and in the giant circus of the great tent
sometimes saying, "Hello, how are you?"
Or maybe just waving a
sweet bye, bye

Away up yonder,
looking over there a bird, a snake, a crocodile
crawling by a man all bent.
And here we are together, the cotton
candy circus in our heavenly sky.
Carol Oliverius

Singing At Supper

My Gram, as usual, wrote the commandments.
First among them, "Children shall not sing at the table."
Too serious, the work of surviving hard times,
For singing at the table.

My mother, trained in those no-nonsense ways,
Could no more contain her love of fun,
Than hide the smell of her good cooking.

When Bud and I would pester her,
"What's for supper?"
She'd say, "Wind pudding and rabbit tracks!"
Leaving us a word puzzle to gnaw on.

Not your business, child to know
If the money envelope is empty,
If the canning lasts the winter,
If the corner store gives credit.

For she could take nothing
And make of it something so wonderful,
That I should have sung at the table,
I should have sung and sung.
Barbara Armbruster

Schubert

Child in the mountains at night,
fireflies were piercing the fields
sprinkling the scent of the hay,
someone was singing there down by the lake;
music was seizing the dark,
lights other side of the lake,
grasses occasionally lit.
"Schubert" suggested a voice;
no one remembered the song,
always remaining unknown
sweeter than anything else.
Later it came back again
now with its name,
Schubert "The Youth at the Spring."
Friends called their daughter "Louisa"
also because of the song;
then it was shortened to "Lou"
ending the spell held so long.
Audrey Wilson

The Cave

Dragons guarding the barriers of my soul
Firebreathers around me
Occasionally singeing me as they devour.
They are my only protectors.

I created such hideous life
And yet I love them.
I have many skeletons around me.
They have consumed much since I began.

I have to exert great strength
To will them to their nest of stones.
I feel free sometimes when they're asleep
Curled together like elegant ribbons.

Reflected in their bottomless eyes
I lose myself in that place.
Only I know how fragile it is here
No one enters.

I turn myself from the darkness
The dragons breath on my back
Powerful yet comforting and warm
I'll soon return.
Howard E. Franklin Jr.

They Come, They Go

A Humming bird sat on my finger.

Standing in a woods, outstretched arm like the branch of a tree,
finger pointed horizontally to see
if one of the birds would land on me.

Then showing no fear, a slight buzz the only sound,
it sat on my hand, weightless I found.

What wonder, as it looked at me, and I looking back could see
its red throat, all this bird, that thought me a tree.

Soon it was away, that thing of the wild.
A poignant example, much like a child.

Children darting, darting to who knows where?
Darting, away, away, and we who care,
can only hope, as they go,
they will slow,

be like the bird, look for the chance,
Find time to rest on a friendly branch.

John E. Kelly

Mommie And Daddy, I Can't Take It Anymore

Daddy and mommie, all you do is fight and
fight, day and night
you don't care who is right or wrong
all you want to do is harm!
Mommie and daddy, what will happen to me
if you and daddy are taken away from me
Daddy and mommie you are hurting each
other, you see, but you both are really hurting me!
Please don't fight, and hit any more.
Because mommie and daddy, my little heart
Just can't take too much more.
I love you both, can't you see, so please
mommie and daddy, stop hurting each other and me.
Just hold each other tight, instead of starting a fight
So mommie and daddy, when you are going
To start to fight, just remember, what I
told you, it hurts my little heart.
As this little heart
can't take no more.

Barbara Brauer

Cabala

Look upon the savior child—the last drop of liquid
feigned
forsaken to be had——by the demagogues arena,

Man's final chance
woman's final hope
human's first glimpse

So the woman went her way—and got lost in the he-man's jungle
While nine inch nails hold open wounds no one can lick

And the women weep
And the men wail

And the he-man swings about—on cordless connections
through his concrete jungle
while the female corruptor gathers appealing poison for their
feast and nothing really changes—the voices are too subtle

Like cycles of earth and life - no one hears.
    the river's falling rain,
    the whisper of the leaves as they rustle
    the ageless words of the savior child across the summer breezes

    and the woman weeps
    and the man wails

Janis L. Matuga

Love Dreams

I don't know exactly what it was that made me care and caused me to feel,
    What it was that made me care and feel for you so true.
And I'm not sure of the exact moment or the day in time,
    That exact day I fell in Love with you.

I don't know why I did fall so hard and fall so fast,
    Why I fell so fast for you at this point in time.
I don't know why I didn't pay more attention to the warnings,
    Why I simply chose to ignore all the signs.

I don't know if it was your laugh, your soft voice or simply the look
    in your eyes,
    These things I would long for so deeply and so much.
Maybe it was your friendship and your thoughts and your dreams of true love,
    I'll never forget your passion... and feeling the need of your touch.

I don't know why I opened up and let you so deep inside,
    Why I let you inside me so deep and so near.
I don't know why my heart wasn't more careful of the pain,
    Why my heart got confused and over came all the fear.

I don't know why you made me feel you were so different and so special,
    You stood out from the rest or so it did seem.
But now I do know I'll feel a fool as I stop and I realize,
    When I wake up to realize...you were only just a dream.

Brendon James

"Lost Friend"

On Mother's Day, when I awoke,
Fate had played a cruel joke.
When it was time to eat,
You were not purring at my feet.

Some time during the night,
You must have been filled with fright.
After slipping through the door,
Your curiosity was aroused a little more.

Being chased was no thrill.
Just hiding and trying to be still.
Hoping to get home safe and sound,
Not knowing that you wouldn't be found.

I hope and pray each day,
That some day soon, if I may.
On my door step, you will be,
Waiting just for me.

Oh, how my heart will pound,
Just seeing you safe and sound.
After being lost for so long,
My heart will burst with a song.

Helen M. Wettlaufer

Reason

A thought, just one, it sparks it all. I clutch my soul, to stop the fall
The fall to Hell, the fall to death. I try in vain to catch my breath
My heart and mind, they are in strife, one cries for death, one cries life
My heart erupts with hurt and sorrow. My mind calls out, wait for tomorrow
These emotions which I feel so strong. Will float away, when comes the dawn
Then everything will seem all right. But what about tomorrow night
Then this wish, it will return. In the pit of hate, my soul will churn
Why end it now, life will improve. The pain will pass, and love will soothe
It did not before, why should it after. To the optimist, I respond with laughter
Disappointment rules my existence. Now is the time, to end the penance
I believe that I have suffered enough. When the tough get going,
    the going gets tough
My soul erupts in rage and pain
And finally, I slit the vein

Benjamin P. Fagan

Loneliness

Do you know what it is like to be alone?
Facing that which is unknown.
You sit all day and stare at the walls
And look down those long dark halls.
It must be sad to face this life
Where you have nothing but sorrow and strife.
Alone you are, and alone you will be
Until you mind is made up that you want to be free.
Your mind must wonder and probably blank
But I tell you this, and I want to be frank.
If you dare to sit there, and be alone
Then nobody wants to hear you mumble and groan
But if by chance you wanna let go
Get right up and let someone know.
Loneliness is no place to be
For you, for them, or even for me.

Charlotte Jean Taylor

Those Eyes

Eyes that whisper the truth to my soul,
Eyes that sing a song to my heart,
Eyes that cry with pain of the past,
Eyes that speak of love and joy.

Eyes that love with a tender little wink,
Eyes that scold with a squint and a stare,
Eyes that sigh with a roll and raised brow,
Eyes that smile their own crinkly smile.

Eyes that leave the past behind,
Eyes that guide a child's future path,
Eyes that have seen both bad and good,
Eyes that still have much to see.

Eyes that say much more than words,
Eyes that meet mine and embrace my soul,
Eyes that provide me with a feeling so safe,
Eyes that say I'll always be with you.

The eyes of my hero,
The eyes of my future,
The eyes of my LOVE!

Christina R. Ochoa

The Sparrow's Zealot

Sparrow's Zealot has deep faith in something that may not
exist and is creating a cult based on her exclusive beliefs.

Sparrow's Zealot numbs the talons she sinks into your back
and invades the landscape of your mind while you sleep.

I am the sparrow. Perched precariously on a branch that is
splitting beneath me while struggling to fly with wings that
have been clipped.

I wear my vulnerableness like a badge and Sparrow's Zealot
preys on those who share my position. She ensnares you from
behind and drags you into the depths of her practice.

"What you have been forced to believe is wrong because I know I am right."

Beware the Sparrow's Zealot! Don't trust that shining smile
and those winning ways. She only wants to change you and add
one more to here league of mindless, programmed zombies.

She doesn't care where you are coming from she merely wants
you to know her background. Sparrow's Zealot wants to share
what she brands as a wonderful gift but she wants you to
ignore her shallow, pointless existence.
Confidence in my own principles is unshaken by the Zealot's efforts.

Alice Schaefer

Forever

Sometimes the fun you had comes to an end.
Except the love that you had to lend.
For love is never a one time thing,
Because if you love that person it ain't a fling,
At times you know the leaves turn brown,
But the times you've had should not bring you down,
They should be great memories of love,
And your head should not be down but high and above,
The geese fly south to get out of the cold,
But it reminds you of a person you would still like to hold,
And that special relationship might bring you apart,
But that person will be with you forever in your heart.

David J. Borunda

The Last Indian From Bunches Creek

The Indians have gone now from Bunches Creek
Except one, who still lingers on
Now in his late autumn he struggles
But soon he too will be gone.

If I'm here to witness his passing
I'll mourn him more than the rest
To most he's an old drunken indian
But to me he's the best of the best.

He treats me like I was a brother
Shares long-guarded secrets with me
Tells stories of times gone forever
As long ago things used to be.

He talks about bear hunts and fishing
And of "INDIAN" things that he's done
About walking on tall distant mountains
That reach toward the now setting sun.

Tho his sun seems now slowly setting
Over life's last mountain so tall
The very last Indian from Bunches Creek
May be the last Indian of all.

Fred Ray Holbrook

A Christmas Vacation Happening

We awoke early and took a ride on a narrow gauge railway.
    Everywhere we turned, we saw God's work placed on display.
On one side, a deep gorge with a river running through.
    Mountains on the other side, very close! Unable to view!

Icicles from ledges hung and frozen waterfalls of blue;
    Myriad tracks crossing unblemished snow; some we knew.
Some were made by animals, others by snowmobiles were made.
    We are amazed to suddenly come upon these forest glades

The engine blew steam and we saw rainbows, a-glimmering.
    The stream passed under us so very brightly shimmering.
The engine belched coal smoke; away flew the many sparks.
. At Cascade Canyon the train stopped; we all disembarked.

The people, no matter their age, were as children in play.
    Excited with all the snow, this was their special day.
They built snowmen, tossed snowballs, posed on the engine.
    Reboarding the train, our spirits high on a new dimension.

Just as wondrous the return trip, the same sights to view.
    On the return angle, the scenes seemed different and new.
Our mountain train-ride came slowly to an end in the town,
    New memories to take home to reminisce, to renown.

Ada Stein

438

Dream Girl

See the girl in my dreams who will get me by
Every time I even think of her, I begin to sigh
Can I ever be with her ever again?
If you know, can you tell me when?

I cannot stand all of this false gossip
My heart feels as it is on a rocking ship
I do not know why these accusations are here
All I can say is that she is my dear

I care for her and I pray for her
I have never loved anyone as much
If only we were together as we once were
It would only be perfect to feel her touch

She is very special to me
Can she only see the truth inside
All I want is for us to be
I will also learn her rules to abide

I love her so
She is my girl and only mine
I would love to have this conception real
This young woman is called Lea, my sweet wine

Dale A. Woodworth

Billy Chinook

Out of the west, a spy satellite slithers in.
Everything is visible to this invisible spy in the sky.
To the East are the Blue Mountains of Oregon and Idaho.
It traces the Columbia river from its westward destiny
to its northern origins. Behind it, the truly blue Pacific.
To the south, it can distinguish Lake Klamath
from the shimmering mirages of the Sunshine State.

This eye in the sky sees all, yet knows nothing.
It doesn't know what to make of a peculiar regularity
taken on by some eroded gullies and ruts.
All that time has left to mark the great medicine road.
The course sailed by thousands of prairie schooners
riding the wave of manifest destiny a century and a half ago

Nor does it know what to make of the ruins of a chiefs house
on the Indian Reservation below.
The all seeing eye can find no trace
of this chiefs footprints that he made
as a young man walking with Captain Fremont
against the grain to manifest destiny.

Time has erased them.

Harry Paget

When Death Comes

Death waits for no one.
Every life that is lost.
Ten times the amount is born.
With memories and pain we wonder why.
Why do someone so good have to die?
Why must their be an end?
So many obstacles one must cross
life is a giver and a taker
Either blood sweat or tears.
You will meet your maker -

An eternal lost you will have to overcome.
Tears will burst from as aching heart.
Healing together will give life a new start.
No one knows why when or where.
The one that believe will have no fear.
Sooner or later death will knock on your door
The pallbearers will carry you home.
For after this gathering I'll be all alone.
This is my last goodbye for I'm forever gone
With respect may you rest in peace (RIP).

John Boyce

Untitled

To all the poets who've ever dreamed,
Ever loved,
Ever smiled.... or so it seemed,
Ever cried,
Ever mourned,
For a love who has died,
Ever looked upon a bright new day,
Ever kissed,
Ever wished someone in the past had stayed,
Ever wished, ever prayed,
Ever wandered far and strayed,
To all the poets who've ever shared,
Their feelings inside,
Ever cared, for what is right,
Ever dared, to tempt fate,
Ever fared, good or bad,
To all the poets who've ever wished,
"If I only knew."
To all the poets out there,
We salute you!

Alan Lucchetti

When I Am Alone

Sometimes I feel alone...
  Even when others are there...
Sometimes I feel alone...
  And feel there's nobody anywhere...
Who's as lonely as me...
  No man is an island...
That's plain to see...
  But sometimes I feel like an island...
As deserted as can be...
  Then, when I get on my knees to pray...
The loneliness disappears...
  I tell Jesus what I have to say...
And you know what? He always hears...
  He's a friend, like no other
To trust and obey...
  More special than an earthly sister or brother...
Then I suddenly feel o.k!!

Ann Berg McKenney

A Special Visit On Father's Day

I went to see them both today, but didn't have too much to say;
  Even though thoughts filled my head, I felt somewhere those
  thoughts were read;
In loving memory I gave, an arrangement to place on their grave;
  Through sadness, a strange peace I found, as I stood there on that
  lonely ground.

I was Daddy's little girl, sometimes he was my only world;
  Although I missed them both this day, I missed him in a special way:
He'd make me say, "I love you best," and I mostly always did;
  It wasn't that I loved Mom less, but I was just a kid.

He never had to lift a hand, I didn't want to lose his praise;
  In a raised voice, he could command, and put me in my place;
I was Daddy's little girl, he held me on his knee;
  He was the best dad in the world, at least, he was to me.

My daddy had a handsome face, with eyes of deep, deep blue;
  Till he got sick, there was no trace, of the pain that he went through;
He had more strength than many men, holding down two jobs most every day;
But one battle he could not win, though doctors tried with their x-rays.

His dark brown hair began to gray, as he became weaker day-by-day;
  'Twas cancer that ended his short life here, and I miss him more
  each passing year;
I'm trying to be the best I can, someday I'll see him in that land;
  Of happy days and endless sun, if I, a crown of life, have won.

Carolyn Rebecca Cauthen

In My Lifetime

In my life I've seen good and bad in it all,
even though I've always tried to do what was right.
It seems that there's always someone there to put up
some sort of fight when we're trying to do what's right.
In my lifetime, I've witnessed a lot of racism,
Whether it was about the color of skin or that a person
wasn't good enough to be called a friend,
because of their background or income.
Day by day I see the constant struggle of families
trying to stay together as one.
We can all say, it's hard, we've seen it.
When they have things such as adultery, abuse and the
recession of money trying to hold them back.
In my lifetime I've seen a lot of hearts and trust broken.
But, I feel with a little help from everyone,
was as a nation can rise through it all.

Exie M. Williams

A Nurse's Reflection On Alzheimer Residents

For those placed in my care each day-I will be constant-I will stay.
Even though bewildered I try to impart all of the feelings that crowd
my heart. They once led strong productive lives-these sons and
daughters-husbands and wives. Before they wore the frightened masks
their lives were purposeful and filled with tasks. The men will show
a weathered hand from reaping harvests of well worked land. The bloom
of youth has vanished from faces of women whose children live in other
places. Their home is now like a foreign land and they are lost-
they've misplaced life's plan. These frightened souls with questioning
stares must understand that someone cares. They are so grateful for
everything-give a smile, a hug and they're remembering, maybe a time in
earlier years when they comforted someone and wiped away tears. Perhaps
they used a soothing voice-not out of duty but out of choice, to help a
loved one find their way even if only for a minute each day. It is so
hard on the families-knowing the way they used to be. They ask why
does it have to be this way that the one they loved has been taken
away. They think they are left with an empty shell of a former self
they once so well. But each of them has so much to give even if it's
an alternative life they live. They still remember kindness and love
and most do not question our God above. And if I question what God's
purpose may be, the answer, I think, is to humble me.

Cheryl King

War

War is blanket; a darkness, a blindness,
   eternal fight quenches all heavenly flame.
Don't stop, keep on fighting; save only yourself now;
   killing all others leaves no one to blame.

Children are running; all wide eyed and crying,
   everywhere people are fearful, and hate.
Flee away lonely, behind loved ones dying,
   hope that a bullet does not seal your fate.

Around you is chaos; and terror and bloodshed;
   survivors, once stalwart, are crippled and lame.
Some can still win now, but too many lie dead;
   all are pulled into this dangerous game.

Then comes a warming; a dawning, a brightening,
   golden light shining on every face.
War is forgotten, the curse has been lifted,
   leaving light bathing the whole human race.

Deirdre Hess

To Each His Own (Let It Be Written)

Let it be written as it's been said a thousand times over,
Etched in my brain from the bone of an ass,
That those who live with rabid dogs live rabid lives,
With not the hint of remorse nor regret,
Just a tainted soul,
That when the moon sets and the sun sinks to the depths of darkness,
A greater evil arises,
The evil that beckons mind and soul.
One who's watched inhumane acts of cruelty and violence,
One who's watched what they have gotten away with and caught their
foolish flaws.
Lack of mind control,
Lack of patience,
Only to be damned on Earth by mere mortals,
Caged and treated like swine,
And the minister of pain appointed by his peers,
Travels to his jolly home on the hill,
By mocking the Holy Book in which their laws were derived from,
Need we not forget "Judge Not Less Ye Be Judged Thyself."

David Morgan

Silent Wings

Why oh why do butterflies fly,
   especially so high - around in the sky,
Is it magic that you fly so high,
   with vibrant colors and spotted tongues,
Those flighty insects passively succumb
   to be a creature of flight!
Such power, such might,
   a strong sensation to posses in life,
To avoid troubles, sorrow, and strife!!

Betsy Wilson

My Mother My Friend

Sitting alone I can feel her presence, as the combined
energy of life surges through my veins.
She is able to sense when I'm hurt or feeling lonely,
and wills me a map to re-route the pain.
By herself, she has taught me survival in a world
so unjust and unkind.
I've learned to forgive those who judge and degrade
for they were raised to be prejudiced and blind.
Our bond is so strong that communication may be silent,
understanding without having to talk.
She is the light that surrounds me each day of my life,
revealing the footsteps that I will soon walk.
Since being the only hero I revere in my heart, on top
of the pedestal she will always stay.
I ask God to protect and bless her with a much deserved
long happy life for she is my mother, my friend, who has
paved my way.

Biley Riddlesperger

The River

Thoughts of you run like a river through my brain
Each wave each ripple driving me insane.

Through all pores it seeps, quenching every nerve
Try as I might, this flood I can not curb.

At long last I rest
But it won't be long before a new one will crest.

In time I will drown and will know no more
These things of you I knew before.

Drema D. Rubinoff

440

My Special Place

Soft, caring, dark green, redwood trees
embrace a small, crystal, clear lake
that's smooth as
baby soft skin
a small, blue and white sailboat
tiptoeing across the lake
Orange, blazing sun striking the
water at just the right angle
making it glisten like tinsel
on a white Christmas day
looking up at the beautifully, clear, sky
I notice the faint outline of the
tall, brown mountains wanting to be
closer
My small, brown cabin
awaiting my arrival
I lay there thanking God
for the life I live.

Jennifer Frizzell

Mothering

Mothers you are special, ALL on God's created
earth, and only he knows your magnifying worth.

You give of yourselves to nurture your young.
It seems you go on and on and never get done.

You are stand in's for your children so that they
will always share in fun!

You laugh, then you cry; because sometimes it
seems so hard that you hold it all in and it feels
like you are going to die.

You portray your roles in a most elegant way.
You know what you have given, is in your child's
hearts to stay.

You wait for "thank you's", you wait for "smiles"
and in anticipation those thoughts seem like miles.

You don't ask for much; but you would like to be
thought of as giving the "MIDAS TOUCH"

For all of you children everywhere, please understand
us, because we will always be there!

Janice E. Wilson

Wilderness

Walking in the wilderness - it's a lovely sight.
During the morning or during the night.
In the golden sun or romantic moonlight.

Watching the animals - large and small,
As they run through the trees that stand so tall.
Or listen to the birds as they give their call.

Going through the Wilderness is so much fun.
Whether you walk real slow or decide to run.

It's such a great feeling - on a brisk Autumn day,
To lay on the ground or a small pile of hay,
And watch the animals as they play.

To hear the screech of an owl at night.
Or see a Bluejay in its flight.
Yes this is Wilderness in all its delight.

Ivan L. Smith

When I Dream Of You

You are close by, near to the touch. All around us, darkness
drowns all. You are dressed in black, your hair gently blowing in the breeze.
You stand alone, a glowing light surrounds you. No sound can be
heard, just me breathing. Your already pale skin is paler, your
already long hair longer. My eyes drink in every detail, for I have
not seen you in a while.
No sunlight can reach us here, just the eerie glow around you
gives us light. Your movements are few; are you unsure or is it
because you haven't moved in a while?
You have changed, but you are still the same person I fell in love
with. I have never met you, I have only seen you from afar.
I remember when it happened, I would have died too, but I couldn't.
When I dream of you, you are not dead. You are alive and we are
not here, in this place.
You extend your hand to me, and I take your pale hands in mine.
Forever bonded, forever in friendship.
When I dream of you, you love me too...

Amanda Reagan

"Whispers On The Wind"

Hearts break in warm silence...
Dreaming of the dream.

Eyes open and close again...
Things are not as they seem.

Uttered words of now and then...
 Whispers on the wind.

Hands held high over aching heads...
Reaching for invisible salvation.

Feet go stumbling down the beaten path...
One vision, one God, and one nation.

Uttered words of now and then...
 Whispers on the wind.

Lungs inhale time and reality...
Searching for purpose and matter.

Minds spin on as did those before...
Thoughts come in order and then scatter.

Uttered words of now and then...
 Whispers on the wind.

Allison L. Dunn

Mom

The pangs of your death grip my innermost being
 draining the very life right out of me.
How do I survive without your gentle ways,
 and the sound of your voice caressing my ears,
 letting me know everything will be okay, in your own special way?
Your shelter evades me now and I'm a lonely child
 in the wilderness of life.
How do I go on, when the thought of finding you gone,
 consumes me unto a death of my own?
Your pictures remind me of your absence,
 and only stir up the volume of emptiness I live in without you here
You've gone where I have longed to be;
 home to our Father, the lover of we.
I want to see you again and feel the warmth of His touch in your embrace.
These things I would say to you now, if I only had the chance;
 yet opportunity has not afforded me one.
So I shall go on loving and living to the Son,
 and trust one day soon my prayer will come true;
 to stand with God in Heaven, greeted by angels,
 and ultimately,...you.

John I. McLeod

Daniel Varoujan

Did you hear the winds...
Down from Mount Arafat?
Where an earthquake birthed the cradle
Of the human race - in its face.

Mount Arafat looms bight in the clouds
Mystical, aloof and draped in shrouds
And legends of long ago...
In perpetual snow.

High above the frontiers of Turkey
Iran and Armenia...
By ancient Persian legend
The Mother of the World.

Ancient armies bloodstained your valleys
'Midst Armenia's mountains on your stied....
Music from your terror - heard far and wide
When your poet cried....and died.

Jeanne Aya Duncan

Don't Drink The Water

Don't drink the water for its poison runs deep,
Don't drink the water, or your soul it will keep.
Don't drink the water, or your wounds will never heal,
Don't drink the water, or your heart will never feel.
Don't drink the water, do not you understand?
Put down that golden goblet which you hold in your hand!
Cannot you hear me, cannot you read?
That sign right in front you so bright indeed!
I say unto you again, listen to me!
Or in that dark place you will surely be!
As a last resort, in front of him I jumped.
Drank the water, then in his arms my cold body slumped.
He scowled and dropped me,
Walked away and muttered "I was thirstier than he."

Forrest Reinke

Child, There's Hope

Deep inside... are you sad?
Does something make you really mad?
Do you feel that life is so unfair?
What's the use... who really cares?

You're not alone; there are others too.
You can't always tell without some clue.
You're not the first, and won't be last,
Who's living daily behind a mask.

No matter what you're going through,
There are some who truly believe in you.
As hopeless, at times, your days may seem,
Keep looking to the future and always believe.

You may not be able to change what's now.
Some day you'll be on your own, somehow.
So go for a dream, as you are Special.
For nothing, in life, stays the same forever!

Barb Kawa

Untitled

A dancing wreath with burning candles came into my dream
Children's voices laughing
An ocean lit by moonbeams
The spirit knows a kindred heart
In the middle of the night
And wants to share the meaning of a magical, mystical flight
Lives begin in passions lust and
End in distant blowing dust
Angels earn their wings with love
To guide earthly spirits to the world above

Catherine Frinier

The One Up Above

Can you feel the heat from the rays of the sun?
Do you sense the fear, when behind you a stranger runs?
I myself from the sun feel the heat,
I myself fear, when behind me I hear running feet.

Don't take it for granted, you have someone to love.
Don't get too enchanted, thank the one up above.
For he guides you through life, from beginning to end.
Don't stab him in the back with a knife, for he is a true friend.

Not everyone will approve of you,
Not everyone will show that they care.
In our hearts we all carry the truth,
Be careful, it's a cruel world out there.

If you haven't found someone you care to love,
Maybe it's just not the right time or place.
He placed us on this earth to love,
Regardless of color, sex, or race.

Just remember,
The one up above is here for you.
Just remember,
When you feel no one loves you, he died on the cross for you.

Carmen S. Alicea

Life

Do you hear what I hear?
Do you see what I see?
Do you know what I know?
I listen, do you listen!
I see, do you see!
It's life all around us.
Did you feel it?
Did you touch it?
Did it just pass you by?
Life is a mysterious thing.
One day you can be here the next your gone.
But when will it happen?
How will you know?
Can you see death, feel it, see it, touch it?
No! Why do you ask, because death you
Can not feel see or touch!
But life is something precious and something
You can always feel, touch and see.

Amy Rae Starcher

My Friend

How old is old, I ponder within,
Do you pick your friends, by age - fat or thin?
To me, age resides all in the mind,
I love a friend because they are kind;
Arthritis sets in, come teenage - whatever,
My best friends call, there's a change in the weather;
Neither cosmetics, nor hair color to me will make —
A difference when someone cares for my sake;
There are those special folk you always hold dear,
Ready to help, share in a fear;
No one is called - by age, clothing or health,
We can't put it off, even with wealth;
Heaven's our destination - our longing end;
So why not on earth be a real good friend.

Colleen A. Sinnaeve

"Do We Take Time"

In the hurried schedule of daily living,
  Do we take time to think of God?
Of blessings without number, given with love,
  Do we take time?

Do we stop for one brief moment,
  To still our tongues in angry haste,
Words we can't recapture, gone to waste?
  Do we take time?

Do we appreciate loved ones more in absence,
  Than we did when they were here?
Are we too busy to dispel a tear?
  Do we take time?

We must stop and linger for awhile,
  In quiet reflection, so we can know of God's perfection.
It is all around us, if we would but see,
  It is there to enjoy, and it's all free!
    But — do we take time?
      Do we take time?
      Elise L. Siegel

Battlefields

When you hear the cry of battle and the rattle of the spears,
Do not walk among the shadows where there lurks a thousand fears;
Nay! Walk bravely in the forefront with banners shining bright!
Aye! March bravely where others may see your shining light.

When you walk down the pathways ten thousands trod before,
And troubles walk beside you by the tens and by the scores,
The crowds they cry out "FAILURE" as defeats are laid to you;
Ah! But the victories are more precious when they are so very few.

In the time and times unending perhaps we'll learn a better tune,
Compassion and forbearance, understanding is our boon;
When the foe who stands before us is perplexed at every turn
For those they sought to join in combat have refused to even learn.

Now the "victors" have no glory, no wounds of which to boast,
No strategies of battle, no over whelming host;
No hard won battle ground, nor heroes of the fight,
Only murderers and villains shall show their strength and might.
    Emmett E. Miller

The Tornado

You came like a thief in the night
Destroying our home and treasures we loved
You put our little town in peril and fright
As you lowered your funnel of terror from above.

You showed no mercy for our forests of trees
Mowing down everything in your path
You brought us all to prayer and our knees
As you continued mile after mile with your fury and wrath.

You may have won the battle
But you never won the war
You may have caused our nerves to rattle
Because of you we are stronger than before.

God spared us our lives as we were gone when you hit
It was only material things you destroyed
With our love for each other and health that is fit
We'll go on with our lives though you caused in it a void.
    Evelyn C. Bohn

The Sun Will Come Out Tomorrow

The sun will come out tomorrow
despite how it rains today,
But reach out and thank God
for the things he gives you each day.
There are times when we deal with things
that we really don't understand.
But remember, the Lord never draws back his hand.
In his hands are the answers to life.
The hurt, anger, love and strife.
Learning to accept is hardest of all.
But dealing with so, you'll never fall.
Courage and strength are what I admire most of you,
taking charge and doing what is expected of you.
But just as the sun comes after the rain
Happiness and love come after the pain.
So don't give up hope, for soon you will see,
that God really loves you, and the same goes for me!
    Debbyette Ruiz

Grandma Is My Name

Ah, that name, it comes floating gently to my ear,
Delights my senses, makes me feel quite dear.
It pleased me from the very start,
It's always tugging at my heart,
Wrapping me in a cozy warmth I can't explain;
Grandma is my name.
When spoken by a little child,
A toddler less than three,
It makes me feel as tho' God Himself were
Reaching down to me.
His breath a fragrant summer breeze,
That touches my very soul,
And leaves me with protective strength
I never thought I'd know.
Grandma's here my precious one, she's looking at your sweet face.
She loves you with a tenderness that will never be erased.
She'll cradle you, and comfort you, until she's very old,
Then pray for you continually, till heaven you behold.
    Gerri Daniels Harding

Gilead

Calamity struck—
Defeating,
Devastating.
Downed, I struggled to be upright once more,
Determined to survive.
Family, spouse told me, "Be strong",
Said to me, "Persevere",
Spoke the words already born inside my brain, ricocheting through
my consciousness.
Still I reeled.
Until
Silently, my friend came,
Enfolded me in strong embrace
And let me lean awhile.
    Jeanne Dyer Coleman

Hail To The Chief

Hail to the chief played the band
But in a far away distant land
A similar tune rang through the ear
Of similar people waiting to hear
What a similar leader had to say
But I can tell you it's the same old play
That's been around for quite awhile
With many acts that are terribly vile
And even the audience has a part
But why do they ask when does it start
    Bobby Jenkins

Letter

Dear Southern Soldier,
Debra is my name,
and I write to you in extreme pain.
How did you ever stand that fight?,
going through hunger well into the night.
You fought for your way of life,
Solely to protect your children and wife.
The South was doomed from the very start,
But you couldn't give up 'cause it was in your heart.
As a Southern soldier, your name was not great,
But the whole damned war was rooted in hate.
So I ask you kindly, right now, right here,
How did you ever take control of your fear?
In your place, I would have failed,
But you, unjustly, were put in jail.
Thank you sir for teaching me,
What the values in life really should be.
A home, a family, a piece of mind,
Is what we'd like the world to find.

Debra Gentilella

Untitled

Don't open the door death is behind.
Death could come from the person you think most kind.
Don't go outside, it's snickering behind that tree
You are going to step in the trap and never again be free.

Darkness falls, as the heavens crash to the ground.
Satan's slaves running round and round.
You'll never again see that glimpse of hope
You are gasping for air as your neck rejects the rope.

You drop to the ground watching the last flicker of light
little voices inside saying it's too late to fight.
Suddenly your soul begins to rise. Now you are gone
the banjo of the devil, plays the victory song.

Annette Vislisel

Here Comes The Sunrise

Open your eyes, see the sunrise
Dawn on the darkness, as love comes alive
It may seem too cold, it may be real dark
But open your eyes, and unlock your heart
Crawl out of the corner
Get up off the ground
Open your eyes
There is light to be found
The light is in you
It's been there all along
Get out of the dark, and know you are strong
The sunrise is in you
Warming your heart
You have your love, what more do you want?
Open your eyes, the storm, it has passed
It left you alone, but get up at last
Open your eyes, love's coming alive
And the dawn's on the darkness
Here comes the sunrise

Jennifer Wymer

Winter

Winds will be blowing cold and clear;
As the long winter is drawing near,
Joyous Holidays will soon be here;
Windows will be full of Christmas cheer.

Snow will be falling and glittering so bright;
While children will be playing with delight,
Houses will be painted all snowy white;
Stars in the heavens will be our guiding light.

Barbara Quatroche

Dark Night

Oh, why is this that I now forsaken?
  Darkness, darkness, around me there.
What this? Hath brought me here,
  To this dark night of thy soul.

I cry out to thee, but I cannot see
  Abandon me not, for I will walk your walk
Only one word doth it take, speaketh to me!

My soul cries out in one long hymn
  To know you, to hold you, one moment only.

Torn am I, between these worlds, where I go, I know not.
  My mind I cannot clear, for fear alone.

Is it because of her? I so desperately seek
  To be held one moment, and want another
For I have so long waited, to gaze upon this beauty.

This love of mine, quenched only by you
  To give her this forlorn heart,
  Desire buried so deep.
Cannot I awaken, this dark night of thy soul.

Shine here now, oh, light of my life!

John F. Kay

Magic

Your name says it all.

Like silk you'd glide up the court,
Dancing from left to right.
Your skills were unmatched,
Your precision deadly,
Like shooting down Birds in springtime.

You made mediocre players into stars
and super players even better.
Your team mates were well Worthy of your exploits.
You made the game a worldwide spectacle,
Truly a "fantastic" show.

Your mistakes on the court were rare,
and it seems unjust that the one you made off it
  was so devastating.

Alexis Dujan

Into The Wind

When I was the age of three
Daddy fashioned a broomstick horse for me
Horsey became my faithful friend
As we would go racing — into the wind.

I was barely grown when I met a boy
Our love became a fulfilling joy
We knew our life was a special blend
As we would go dancing — into the wind

The precious years were never long
Life was good — filled with our song
With sons our happiness did ascend
As we would go laughing — into the wind.

Cool summer breezes were refreshing
Too soon winter's blasts turned cold
I sit by a lonely fireside warming
As calendar years change me to old.

Springtime season will be approaching
To a new beginning never to end
When I join my departed loved ones
As we go flying together — into the wind.

Cynthia Wiggins

444

Visiting The Mennonite Quilter

She screened her looks with her lashes;
Curiosity swept over her,
But her manners kept her from staring.

They were gaudy, too many colors,
Half naked in their shorts,
Bedecked with dangly earrings.

They crowed at her work
Talking of their own quilt
More thought about than worked on for ten years.

She tried to focus back on the rhythm
Of the needle in and out,
with its comforting regularity.

But she wondered why did they
Just talk about admiring simplicity,
when they had made other choices in life?

Joann Hansen Haggerty

The Walk

As I walk, the light fades and the shadows begin to creep.

Down a black alley, bums coward in the cold, damp dark
of cardboard boxes.

Children play deadly games of lust, desire and greed,
woven from the threads of deceit.

Profanities stain the walls of a colorless and angry world.

Rivers of blood streak the hard, unrelenting and endless land.

Filth and sickness oozes from every porous dwelling,
spreading as a plague.

The smell of death lingers in the air as a dense, enveloping fog.

Overcome by these sights, I walk in misery!!

Donna Leigh Williams

"Small Treasures"

Immune to all ages, race, and creed barriers
countless numbers of tiny orbs
in an assortment of rainbow colours
randomly embody a crystal world.

Shiny as marbles
but so much more enticing.
Their quiet invitation is accepted
for a quarter.

Clink- Twist- Clatter

With care I remove the small treasure
just purchased.
Ahhhhhhhhh- the sweet aroma.

A moment or two of
vigorous exercise -

"s-nnn-aaa-ppp!" -
"P-O-P!"

I savor the excitement
yet.....
with a trace of irritation this sticky sugar
plastered on my face.

Annette H. Baldao

"Awake!"

Awake, Awake;
    couldn't sleep for goodness Sake
Stuffed up Head; can't stay in Bed
Mind in a Swirl;
    things to do, watch them Whirl
Mom is home in her Parlor;
    Close enough if we Howler
Has her space, relax and Rest;
    getting better is a Conquest
Friends she has to luncheon and Fun;
    worries are lightening, that's one
Sister will come to visit Mom;
    she can't travel till she gets strong
Time is precious, make every minute Count;
    having her here, my treasures Mount
Fortunate I've been, parents special by Far;
    jewels they are, twinkle like a Star
Raised to love and Care; I hold that so Dear
Mom it's nice your Home; you no long will Roam

Julia Huett

Christmas

What do you want, was asked the little boy?
Cookies, candy and an electronic toy.

What is the purpose, do you know?
Getting presents and kissed under the mistletoe.

Whose birthday is celebrated at this time?
I am getting lots of presents so it must be mine.

Do you know what Christmas means?
Santa Claus comes and wintry scenes.

Ah, the meaning of Christmas is so plain to me,
The birth of Christ is for eternity.

Rejoice, rejoice the feeling in my heart,
Knowing Christ plays such an important part.

Enjoy the Christmas season as we have grown to know.
Celebration with family and friends that we love so.

Charles Herrera

Hear The Heart

Wondering, moments of reflection,
Controllable despair, illusory grief.
Stability of time though ever so short,
lends sadness to contentment, learning
how life's summer will end.

Anxiety enters the door and is a constant
companion. Hear the spirits, hear the heart,
time is vanishing. Darkness is near, timeless
and shaped. The end is hazy, clouded by
the unknown. Loneliness is a fight to bestow.

Memories abound, O' so grand a memory.
The door was shut but opened again, continue
the climb, persist in the struggle, and dream
the dream. Any dream will do.

Bret K. Webster

I Question

Rash, troubled, turbulent, angry youth of today
Caught in the web of frenzied rhetoric of would be Zealots
Following blindly, mindlessly unsure of purpose
By what divine right do you destroy and desecrate our altars
Before you have earned the knowledge and desire to build a
better temple.

Doris M. Crabtree

Inside The Mirrored Room

Living inside the mirrored room, a cramped
Confined space despite all the bright reflections
Of myself in infinite variations,
I gaze entranced at all the endless
Images in ceaseless poses. This small
World is all I know, these tight and petty
Grimaces and smirks of me, as I adjust
My smile and fix my hair. Sometimes I long
To see what lies outside this room, to
Open up one of the many mirrored
Windows and look out beyond the countless
Portraits of myself reflected on cold
And brittle surfaces. If I could just
Get past the thrall of all these mocking
Illusions of myself on fragile
Coated glass that shatters my very soul
Into a million fine, pale particles
Of dust.

Alexandra Collins Dickerman

Gateway

Gateway to hell dark, lonely, and sad.
Condemned for all eternity.
Like a burning river engulfing your soul until all that
surrounds you is blackness.
Hard and rough, never to return.
Hearts alone in the cold, black night.
Painful as a sword through the center of love.
Deserted, bound up inside by hate, anger, and sadness.
The screams, the horrors of a life one lived, echo through
your hollow soul, turning your nauseous stomach until you do
not want to exist any longer.
Fear and rage boil up from somewhere deep within you
and push forward, never to be condoned or released.
You have lost all consciousness yet you know where you are.
This is the gateway to hell, forward is the pain and
suffering you will feel.
No longer is there choice.

Jennifer Hillyer

"That Night I Heard"

A breeze at my feet, and a light overhead,
Comes the beat of words, I dread.
The time on the clock is nine to ten,
But I hear no tock, only the sound of my pen.
A room a bluster, a heart beating hard.
The courage I muster, and my sanity to guard.
Sound through the walls, a painful thought,
Hearing the noise I will say, "I forgot!"
A rustling I hear as I fight my internal fear.
Ten O'three, is what is read, and finally I hear
Nothing being said.
A voice risen in silence, broke the even of my sleep,
Words mostly of defiance and voice of one who weeps.
But for now all I feel is a breeze at my feet,
And a light overhead, comes the beat
Of words that tonight, I dread.

Jenny Dee

Missing You

You left this world when I was not present
But I returned to see you set free
You and I had a special bond
That belonged only to you and me
Although you were not my mother
I felt as close as a daughter could be
I kneeled to touch your hand and kiss your face
As you lay to rest so peacefully
I whispered "Goodbye Mother"
Will you miss me?

Bettie J. Williams

Nightmare

My nightmare hits me every night. It
comes around to give me a fright. All I
see is him sitting there, then I see it
happen. His heart attack was a massive
one, he had no chance to carry on. But
yet, he was so very young. That night
on the crowded dance floor my uncle left
me, and I saw him no more. With him
he took my happiness, away with him
went my joy. Instead of happiness, the
tears came flooding in. I only saw
him once more, that was at the
funeral. I wish my nightmare would
come no more. I don't want to be
scared anymore!

Cassandra N. Wendel

Accidents Of Birth And Other Natural Disasters

In the deepest recesses of my mind
   cold camouflages warmth
   darkness obscures light
Silence cascades to a deafening height.

In the deepest recesses of my mind
thoughts incubate, but are never born.
Invocations evoke ancient ebony rites,
the truth of which remain unspoken,
until at last the Seventh Seal is broken
and the Revelations pour forth.

Deborah A. Ross

Subset

Come to me shallow princess of dust.
Close my eyes- let clouds come to mind.
Release the grip on the world's worn crust;
Slide away- leaving confusion behind.

Take me to a place where tomorrow lives;
Just beyond the yellow painted lines.
Unleash everything this world has to give;
The silence of screaming- how bright the stars shine!

Unravel my memory, your magic seeps in.
Spinning and twirling, your games are learned.
I see the end, but I can't remember; where did it begin?
Keep me here just one more hour. For this have I yearned

Safe from the pain and the loud pantomime;
The desires that sleeping can bring after time.

Brooke Tuma

Reflections

I wanted to help to be there for you
   But you held back
   Oh girl it would have helped us both
Oh how my heart cried tears for your pain!
I wanted to hold you for a moment
   to soften the blow
   But we couldn't connect, how sad
Oh how my heart cried tears for your pain!
You let me hold you in private moments
   though few
   Others quickly filled my space
   Silent tears from a near distance
Oh how my heart and soul cried tears for your
   pain and sorrow!
Oh how God's heart cried for my loneliness
Maybe one day.

John G. Zimmerer

Vagabond Dream

Look at the boy
Choking the air with dust as he runs
   and runs
Pursuing the hairy helmet
   in and out
Among the briars and branches,
Brown and musty green mixing
In a humdrum pattern,
Suiting this inverted taco with a tail
Perfectly. As the armadillo rests, amazingly hid,
The boy looks, he knows his goal is near,
The mask is removed,
The mad chase continues
As the animal goes here and there
Weaving the untraceable.
Almost, oh so close, comes the boy
To grabbing the tail. But the armadillo,
Antagonizing, moves quicker.

Everyone cheers the boy on,
Knowing he can't win.

    John Vaught

Father's Love Ended

The old man gazed at the empty spot;
Charred, blackened, barren smoking spot.
He asked himself why the blaze so hot,
which took his love that could love not?

It once had been his favorite place,
He called it home by his lost grace.
Its wood, a weathered unfinished face,
Here, on weekends to peace he'd race.

It once was built on four stilts standing,
Porch roof of aluminum siding,
One bulb mid way the whole room lighting,
Woods surrounding, never ending.

Late one night a fire burnt queerly,
Killing the one father loved dearly,
End the affair; no more to be.
Birds fly, snakes slither, deer run swiftly away.

    Gretchen M. Koenig

The Loop

The world encompasses me in prosaic patterns.
Changing hues and colors as the past rolls round
in a never ending circle.
Its beginning cannot be found.
Faster and faster spins the spider's web,
in the past and present,
caught up in the now.

The world encompasses me in prosaic patterns.
Persistence of time, moving backward.
Roots of the unknown are known.
Slower and slower, slipping into subconscious.
Realizing the unfamiliar,
caught up in the past.

The world encompasses me in prosaic patterns.
Pestilence of memory, creation depleted.
The past rolls round in an immortal circle.
Halt to a stop.
A realization of the unperceived
becomes faithlessness,
caught up in the present.

    Christine C. Milborrow

Elegy for Michael

There must be a need for more angels in heaven
   'cause God in His knowledge has taken my son.
When I'm really in pain, I may ask God, "Why?"
   Lord, I don't understand why he needed to die!

My life is so lonely - without purpose now;
   I know I'll survive, but I'm not sure just how.
I'll try to help others and perhaps find someone
   to help mend my heart from the loss of my son.

I see him in the clouds and hear him in the wind.
   Snowflakes are his kisses; his touch is in the rain.
My son seems much closer when God's wonder does perform
   the beauty of a rainbow produced by sun and storm.

Whatever the reason for my grief and despair,
   I know someone needs me and I'm willing to share
the love and compassion my heart still contains,
   to help solve the problems and help heal the pains.

God, I ask forgiveness for questioning your plan;
   there must be a reason (unknown to me, mere man).
Lord, be patient with me if again I ask, "Why?"
   It will be a long time before all my tears dry!

    Dolores E. Sampson

Shadows

The light falls across the room,
casting shadows on the unpainted wall

The odor of smoking wood drifts
through the cracks in the door

Childish laughter can be heard
whispering against the clinking
of spoons and bowl

The woman, with hands worn and calloused
smiles gently
sssssh children
you'll wake the others

Now the house is alive with
laughter, rustling,
at the sound of the slam of the door,

You can hear the cooing of the woman
as the shadows move
slowly to and fro

    Ina L. Ateshkadi

Fall

Promenading mountainous hillsides
cascade beautiful pillows of
fall colors.

Gloriously radiating far reflections,
Simultaneously demonstrating dances
when challenged, completely flowing.

Gracefulness enhances wonderment,
freely allowing point of origin, to
echo the countryside.

Colorfully synchronized in assembly,
brightly resembling a biological
choreography of mystery.

Majestically performing its version of overtures,
similar to a rendition of a conducted symphonic melody.

Delightfully announcing closure,
displaying the, "Grand Finale" of fall splendor.
Brilliantly presenting cast
production of future season's magical arrival.

    Barbara M. Blau

Soul's Compromise

What subtle feeling overwrought thou
Candy cane conscience is the only allow;
To lose sight of life, to put it behind
And sit in the flowers in everyone's mind...
But is there a pit
Beneath where we sit
Where blackness and sorrow
Lie waiting tomorrow?
To be so unaware
The joy?...or the SCARE?
This candy cane conscience, it limits my mind
It makes me feel useless, it makes me feel blind
To see all these people accept it so well
For me, I cannot...it's literally HELL!
My mind slips and stumbles in accepting this joke
Of candy cane conscience, simple life and a coke.

Ann Crowley Justel

In Time

Love - it's such a simple word, four letters, if you will
Can send you soaring through the clouds or tumbling down a hill.

In early days it was with ease I gave my heart away.
I opened up to share my life, so sure that it would stay.

But nothing's promised, it's been said, and that, I found, was true.
Forever ended much too soon and my heart broke in two.

Decades have passed since early days, my heart is not so soft.
Now when love knocks upon my door I hide up in my loft.

It is not true, it's all a dream, I know it is not so.
And yet it comes repeatedly but I just let it go.

I do not want to bear the pain that comes from up above
Each time that I have let my heart be taken in by love.

But now and then I let myself enjoy what love can give
And hope that I can come to terms before I cease to live.

Gloria Owens

God's Eye Is Upon Me

No one can tell you of its essence.
Can impart to you, the anguish and suffering.
Not until it has dwelled with you intimately,
Will you know loneliness.

Nothing can replace the feel of the outline of his face.
The lusciousness of his lips, the comfort of his arms.
In desperation, I reach for him,
When I awake in the twilight hours.
The sheets are cold, there is no warm body next to me.
Death has taken him-I am alone.

But, have I ever really been alone?
I commune with my heavenly father,
I have an avenue to the very throne room of God.
The only one who is willing and completely able,
To satisfy my every need.

I go to him in my prayer, and lay my heartaches at his feet
He is always with me, he will never leave me.
His love and grace know no boundaries.

Joy does come with the rising of the sun.

Deborah Phelps

Clouds

Clouds drifting by in each a lazy way
Can change their shape and size.
They challenge your imagination
Inventing face and figures in the skies.

If I could be a cloud for a day
Oh what fun it would be
To float from one creation to another
Knowing I would finally revert back to me.

Bernadine Carroll

My Past

My past is well known, as the future lies unknown.
Can anyone even guess what the future holds in my hands?
Does anyone have a clue or even a slightest guess?
I think the future can only read its self.
It whispers, the future, quietly and patiently waiting.
You can only hear these words if you can stop and listen,
Not with your ears but with your heart.
You have to believe in your self to get anywhere in life.

Abby Fernandez

Learning To Fly

With the gift of strength and optimism
came a gift to soar high above the mountains.

In an unopened sky of mysteries, you set me free
to travel my own way, but not to fly unguided
   across the course of life.

I follow a guide...
to learn and live in the world of unforeseen dreams
to struggle and overcome the barren grounds I hunger
to hold my heart and protect my dreams from the destiny of despair
to risk traveling the cloudy sky, to find a dream or hidden wonder
to confide and listen to the nature of promise
to send a smile and shed tears with those cherished souls
to love and be loved by beauty and kindness
to simulate the learned truths of a mother and a mentor

With your gift of friendship and unselfish acts
I have learned from the master of flight,
to soar high above the mountains

But never will I fly without you as my guide,
   across the course of life.

Amy Litchfield

Memory House

I'd like to live in a house
By the side of a road,
Where by a small stream
I once played.
My memory goes back to my childhood,
As I sit 'neath the willow tree shade,
There the meadow sweeps back.
To a tall picket fence,
And the grass is as green as can be,
And cows are grazing both black and white
As far as I can see,
And I think if I ever build a home it will be.
At the curve of a brook where a small stream flows
Where a cedar tree stands
And where black-eyed Susans grow!

Edna N. Koch

"The Car-Strangled Spanner"

Oh say can you see
By the dawn's early light

While so crowded we sail
In the headlight's white gleaming;

"Tween road stripes and bright cars
On our perilous flight

Through the jammed cars we strive
To go gallantly streaming;

While the tail-light's red glare
The exhaust-fumes in air

Gave proof through the night
That the crowd was still there!

Oh, say does that Car-strangled Spanner yet pave
The way between our jobs, and the homes of the brave?'

Diana B. Swann

Out Flanked

It's bad enough to be surrounded
by pressure
But now I'm being attacked from the inside
If this keeps up, people will start to think
I'm as crazy as I think I am
Afraid to sleep, closing my eyes
only invites the nightmares in
Beautiful dreams quickly
metamorphosis into a glimpse
of the pit-fiendish apparitions
dancing in the flames
celebrating the death of the soul

Jim Lamoreaux

What Is Riches

Riches can't be a measured
by money or material things,
riches is the grace and mercy sent from God
from up above,
riches is always in health, spirit and most of
all having love.

Riches can be from a smile
from someone who loves you so much,
always to be with you and
give their tender loving touch.

Always think of all of the sunshine that
warms you through and through,
but remember there are the unfortunate that
can't do the things you do.

Count all your riches as blessings
and dare not to despair,
just remember the rich and the
riches comes from God's loving care.

Bernie L. Tompkins

Heartbroken

I lean against the cold wall, and glare out my window
'cause it's been over two months now, yet it feels like eleven more
since we've last spoken a word, and shared a memory
tears rain from my eyes as I am constantly reminded of you
what has happened....that I do not know
you made me a promise of best friends forever-
you and I together as one
and now we are split, but for what reason so unclear,
my heart will forever be healing, but I can not
go on to that day until I know one answer
WHY?

Andrea Z. Dubsky

Walk With Me

My feet disturb the sleeping street
by kicking pebbles, as I walk in solitude.

Homes neatly line the street. I spy neighbors
glances from faces through window laces
a Robin sings my name, I won't be gone long.
Walk with me. At the river's edge I stop to fish awhile.

Look at the calf standing by its mother, small and frail,
he stumbles when she licks him. Walk with me.

A quiet comfort consumes me
while amber heavens warn of nightfall.

It's time to turn around kicking pebbles,
as I walk at sunset in chilly solitude.

Eveline Smith

Silent Heartache

My heart cried out to you tonight,
But you were not there to hold me tight.
I thought you were going to be here by my side
But you never heard me when I cried.
Everyone keeps leaving my life,
no one realizes being alone cuts my heart like a knife.
I want to give you my heart,
But we are so far apart.
You should know how much it hurts
For someone to leave your life forever.
I cry inside every time we are not together.
Can't you realize my heart is not strong,
It breaks each time you are gone.

Faline A. White

Why The Free Bird Won't Sing

I wonder why birds fly in formations and groups,
but why the deer hunt alone.
I question the silence before an afternoon storm
that sends all the animals home.
I ask the lion in the zoo to quit pacing.
because I know he has nowhere to roam.
I wonder why the buzzard circles and drops
and why he circles and rises again.
And I wonder why trees drop leaves in autumn,
to only grow more upon spring's early rain.

But I know why babies cry just after waking up
and adults, before falling asleep.
I know why children think cartoons are funny,
and parents, the children they keep.
I know why the watched pot never boils,
and why people are afraid they're too deep.
I know why mothers hold their children too close
and why fathers keep too far away.
And I know this fear that I'm speaking too much
is the fear I have nothing to say.

Jenni Hass

Clear Waters

Shimmering with silver lace
Beneath the rays of the sun,
Swaying and winking, whispering with
Movements so gentle and
Tinkling with shy laughter,
Clear and cool and sweet and loving,
Soothing and comforting with
Feelings of crystal green and blue,
Angels and spirits dipping playfully in and out of
Gentle ripples - beautiful - and
Shimmering with silver lace
Beneath the rays of the sun.

Adésanya

A Family Of Love

Often things happen, that we don't understand
But we rest assured, it's all in God's Plan
We worry and fret, and we try to pray
The words won't come, we don't know what to say.
God gives us wisdom, to think things through
We don't know where to start, or what we should do.
We won't give up on Life, we won't throw it away
We take it as it comes, just day by day
But right before the Storm, there always comes a Calm
And we turn our Bibles, to the 23rd Psalm.
So Brother dear we Love you, and as we kneel and Pray
We know the Lord will Bless you, as you start a brand new day.
We thank God for the Blessings, and Friends within his sight
With all the Prayers we've Offered, we know you'll be alright
So listen Little Brother, it's all left up to you
Take a hold of your Life, and I know you'll see it through
Let all the World know, that you 're in Command
And anything is possible, if you hold on to God's hand.

Joyce A. Baker

A Rose

A rose has fallen from the earth,
But to Heaven it did float.
Love ones are like flowers,
We may only have them for months, years or hours.
These wonderful flowers are put here to grow and shine,
To make our lives happier, yes yours and mine.
When the flowers fall to the earth,
We're left with a loss and such a hurt.
But as we turn the pages in our mind,
We can recall such wonderful and happy times.
These memories no one can take away,
We can hold on to them and bring them out on lonely sad days.
Memories are something no one but you own,
Your special things, yours alone.
So remember your fallen rose,
With a warm heart and love aglow,
And let these lovely memories flow.

Barbara Dail

Wasted Tears

There are times when tears should fall,
but there are times when they shouldn't come at all.
I despise those wasted tears,
those that pour from unexpected fears.
That fear of not knowing what will come,
because of something someone's done.
Those tears full of worry and concern
for those who never listen, never learn.
I wish those tears didn't have to be,
and the one who causes those fears could see
the anguish and pain from their stupidity.
I do not hate those special tears
those that come when miracles appear,
for they are not useless, but needed.
They are not caused by someone conceited.
Tears of love, happiness, and celebration
are wonderful, they don't fall in desperation.
I hope the thing that results in wasteful tears,
Will someday vanish, just disappear.

Joni E. Starnes

The Phenomenon

I was running with my dog, like I do everyday.
But something upset me in an unusual way.

There was a body by the road, cold to my tough.
And I couldn't tell the gender that much.

Then the body rose to a ninety degree.
And I could see the body was me.

She said, "your running days are over and your dog is at a lost
Because there will be an accident and you will be tossed

I thought I'd try to warn you before it's too late
But you and your maker have a date."

As I dashed back onto the road, to the house I went.
To put it all together, what didn't make sense.

At the same time the next day, my dog wouldn't go.
And I made a smart remark like "so".

I ran my fastest that day, the fog was as thick as tar.
The flashback, the body, my dog and the car!!!

Fatima Smith

Hope Of The Last Wise King

Words may hint at many things,
    But silence sails on silver wings
To tell of what the future brings
    A bold brave eagle decries and sings
Of the last hope of a wise king.

The thought is transformed into sound
    Those who hear it must look around
And remember what the people found
    In the cities beneath the bitter ground
Where the last wise king was crowned.

He filled their lives with poetry
    And furnished each, a chance to see
The reason why they came to be
    With the inner wisdom to be free
From a world of pain and misery.

Then he began to wonder why
    Each of them must one day die
So he climbed a tower to the sky
    And with a tear of gladness in his eye
He taught the children how to fly.

Cherie Rizzo

Moms

Moms are for loving,
But not for shoving.
The way they show they care,
Puts love in the air.
So, I just want to share
We should all shout Hooray!
For a special Mother's Day.

We should hug and kiss
And let them bask in their bliss.
To give them some candy
Is just about dandy.
To give them flowers is good,
If only every day I could.
But that's for beginners.
To give them love is for the real winners!

Amy Rannals

The Door In The Wall

There is a door in the wall,
But no one knows quite where it leads...

To a playground, a castle, a courtyard,
Or where ever you want it to be...

It is up to you, what you want to do,
You can stay out or you can go in...

But there is only one thing to unlock that door,
Which you can have or you can possess...

It's not only the key to happiness,
But also the key to success!

Jonathan Hewson

Together

They say that being apart makes the heart grow fonder.
But it is a cruel joke.
I could not stand being without you for no longer than a few minutes.
Every time you leave my side a pain grows inside my heart.
And the only cure is you.
Then when you return I am strong again and in your arms.
Your warm embrace secures me and I can feel the love flow
  throughout your body.
I could never have survived in this world without you.
Together in our hearts and our minds we can never be apart.
And the love that we have created that has bonded us, will
  never be broken.

Harry E. Williams III

A Mother's Pain

I may still be young and not wise to the world,
But I would do anything to get back my little girl.
The pain and the joy of bringing a child to this earth,
The joy of a newborn brought to my hearth.
Strawberry blonde hair and sky blue eyes,
She became the first true love of my life.
Her first step, her first word remembered,
Until it all ended in '94 in December.
A craving for more beer, a decision gone bad,
In my life, she was the best thing I ever had.
Samantha Lynn is the name given her at birth,
Though she won't be my only child, she was my only first.
To never be able to hold her in my arms again,
To only have the memories of things that have been.
Perfect little hands and small delicate little feet,
Never to know the joy of all the people she'd meet.
Taken prematurely from a world that is cruel,
Only the good die young, for that is the rule.
For all the decisions I have made, my life will never be the same,
The death of my only child, the most excruciating mother's pain.

Colandra Lynn Pentecost

Untitled

He's said goodbye before this, that we could just be friends
But he always seemed to change his mind and come right back again

But this time he wasn't kidding; he really had to go
and now the truth of what should be, I guess I'll never know

The rules have changed- the game is getting harder than before
I thought I knew the book by heart, but now I'm not so sure

The way things had been going made me think that things were fine
But then he told me to give up, it wasn't worth the trying

So now I'm trying to see just what my life is all about
It used to be so good but now I think that I want out

I'm really sad to see we won't be like we were before
Because I always thought that you and me were made for so much more!

Jessica Reynolds

To Hannibal Holmes From All Of Us

Good-bye Hannibal, we know that you have to go;
but don't forget that we will miss you so...!
Fifteen years is a long, long, time, it's a big slice of one's life
time; but see it not as a waste of time.
From you we have learnt the true meaning of brotherhood, and a
character refined.
You are always there in times of need to share solid wisdom that you
truly breathe.
We will miss you I know, but do believe your marks you have left.
Engrafted in our hearts are the sincerity of your smile,
the warmth of your eyes where we see the remarkable
Spirit of your soul.
So go forth now with all our blessings and leave similar prints
with those whom you will find....

Cleopatra Brown

Together At Last

We were young and full of hope
But Daddy's dreams couldn't cope.
So we had a parting of the ways
To ponder things of better days.

We made mistakes throughout the years
With broken hearts and shedding tears.
Our lives seemed empty and up-ended
In marriages deceived and suspended.

We faced the day and tried to be tough
But remembering and dreaming weren't enough.
Maybe soon the time could be right
And maybe, just maybe, we'd be in love's light.

We are older now, the years have passed by
But blessed by a God who cares why.
Finally, together, a love so vast
With no one to say "too young, won't last".

Elizabeth W. Collins

Atomic Astromic

The blast was bungotchka,
Bungotchka was the blast;
Eerie luminosity, luminous iridescence;
Bend back, bend back,
Unearthly flash which must not be seen.

Epochal, cosmical,
An upworld light;
Fabulous, forbidden, energetically expansion;
Sky-splitting boom-boom,
Smashing, ker-mashing poompf.

Down-crushing finale,
Fomentation ghastly;
Fireball, doomsday, orangey burst—
Earth shouting thunder—
Man was there too.

Celestial wisdom, likewise an atom—
Split it, Prometheus,
And side by side
Match atomic astromic
With guidance bungotchka.

Henry S. Patricoff

"Love In Autumn"

Sunlight danced across my brow
As I walked on this autumn day
I thought of you and all of life's treasure
And could not of its depth and splendour measure.

Jason Signor

Robin Ascending

Sky-like, bright among the pebbles blended
brown in garden leaves,
I heard a scratch of what I took to be
grass thunder; felt weightlessness

of what I later learned was flight.
I felt the lift; the liquid rivers'
gentle tremble in your hard hand.
After this, a sense of my descent

to leaves that spun last fall, got tangled
in the wind as colored stars that tried
to fly and landed in the garden. Before
you wandered freely over earth,

did you, as I did, hear a crack? For I
saw black sky broken and attacked bright slivers and again
attacked - attacked until I burst
from one shell to another singing first

a rough song, hard song; the gravel chirp of thirst.
Today, I rose and kept on rising.
I carried on my wings your round blue universe.

Bob Russell

"Long Drive Home"

Often times I drive by, the years gone by have
    brought pictures to my mind
Per chance I'd see a light, the things we could have
    done that were spoken of.
From afar I stare into a place that could give a dream its home
Custom built by two, furnished countless open doors
Reflections off the waters held inside, shone crystalline
    angels on walls of white.
Whispers from the forests told its stories to other lands
Now they're the only friends, and the road that leads
    to nowhere is its only hand.
The sky is now its only roof, and
It wants to feel like it belongs with where the people are.
The mountains are the city's walls
And they hear the cries
And fear they'll be torn down.
    Solitaire where is your piece of mind
gone through days - just to find - what was left behind -
lift the blind - to a time - you may find -
a peaceful stare - in its solitaire

Brian K. Holz

The Warmest Place

Warmer than the desert sun,
Brighter than any valued stone,
Exists a place God smiles upon
Belonging to us alone.

This place has no boundaries,
No government or rules.
Survival of its reign depends
On Love that never cools.

To find it now, where do we start?
Leave compass and map behind.
Our world should learn to follow in kind-
The example of a mother's heart.

Alice Novak

The Stones

The sun with its golden rays
breaks through the fog and the mist.

It begins to cast shadows of the
stones, nothing more peaceful
than this.

Someone stands with a child close
to one of those graves.

The child needs to know the how and
the why, so his family history
can be saved.

The flags that fly beside the stones
are signs that they didn't die in vain.

The stones are etched with names and dates
some new, some of old, but all with memories
that remain.

They fought for our freedom and peace and
to show us the right path no matter the way.

As you stand beside those stones, to honor
and remember, be sure to Thank God and them
this Memorial Day.

Ann Moody

The Singing Forest

Out among God's great Sequoias
Branches reaching ever upward
Tall and straight they tower o'er us
Like the love of Christ empowers us.

How I long in this life about me
To add beauty to my time
That my life, in its surroundings
Will be stately as the Pine.

For what if in God's eye of wisdom
He sees each tree as life's for Him
Then the forest is a choir
Singing refulgent joy from within.

How harmoniously they blend their voices
Reaching arms out to each other
Does it say to us, with voices
How to live in harmony with our brother?

Or does the Redwood live his life, and me mine,
And no co-relation intertwined,
Ah, their unvoiced longings
Show to us, a Life Sublime...

Ida Rena Strouse

Sad Farewell

So freely it comes and goes.
Born into this world, taken from this world.
Sometimes silently, sometimes out with a BANG.

It soars like a bird on the breeze
It flies like a ship on the sea.
Sometimes torrent and tortured
Sometimes calm and serene.

"I feel lost and lonely," it moans to the stars
Silently whispers to the clouds,
I'm gone again, I'm back again
Hello again, farewell again
To see you again, be you again
Farewell again

Angelia Rohde

Miracles

Sunrise, sunset
Blue sky, gray sky or red
The sun, the moon, the stars
Majestic mountains, lush valleys
The rivers and streams and oceans
Lightning, thunder, and a downpour of rain
Gentle spring rain
Crocus, daffodils and roses
Green, yellow, orange and red leaves
all on a tree simultaneously
Kittens and puppies and baby chicks
Monkeys and giraffes, rhinoceroses and whales
The intricacies of the human body
The birth of a baby
The love of a parent
The rainbow in the sky
Who can deny God?

Jeanette Stone

Love You Left

The pain has escalated to the peak;
Blood leisurely seeps done the cheek.
Teardrops are far from watery and clear;
Thick red lines, streaming down from the fear.
A vigorous ogre is taking my life;
Heart lashed into pieces by a razor sharp knife.
Disappointment creeps up my spine and wraps all around;
Legs trembling so fast, I drop to the ground.
Fingers tingling, as numbness sets into the brain;
The love you have left me, will always remain.

Debbie Dean

Night Falls

Blue darkness falls across the sea
Blackness covers the sky in purple hues
Stars bleed their light into the night
Salty cold air glides off the water
I am alone in this sharp beauty

Sharp moist wind envelopes me
My body curls against the warm sand
My soul rises high towards the blue moon
Naked in thought, naked in emotion
There are no words for this night.

Sharp yellow eyes peer out of the woods
Dancing like devils, glowing like a wild fire
Interloping his head thought the pines
The wolf gazes at the lonely soul by the waters edge
Turning slowly to watch the sky for all its glory.

The wind blows once again
Carrying me off into the stars
Carrying me off into the night
The night has fallen again
And with it, I fall...

James A. Hulsmann

Feeling Love Lost

Through an opening sky, feelings flow through
as to warm like the sun on a pale face.
Suddenly closing up as if a frown drops unwanted,
as do rain drops fall like tears.
To travel down the cheeks until they ar so softly tasted on
the tip of the tongue.
And it shall linger on.

Christoph Schmitt

The Million Man March in 1995

They came to the nation's capital in Washington, D.C.
Black men by the hundreds of thousands for all the world to see

The skeptics were surprised that so many came out
Responsibility and atonement was what it was about

It was a moving experience for those who were there
They were proud to be a part of this historic affair

Black men from the east, from the North, West and South
Came to be counted did not wish to be left out

Big men and strong men with tears on their faces
Greeted each other, hugged each other, with warm brotherly embraces

It was a day of atonement though some did not agree
With the man who had planned this day of unity

It was the message not the man, that brought these men out
A statement of unity was what is was about

Black men by the hundreds of thousands came to show that they can
Stand together, bond together, when the situation demands

Alberta A. Gray

To My Husband On Our 25th Wedding Anniversary

Beneath Cherry Blossoms pink
    Beside the Tidal Basin
You in Navy Blue, me from Tennessee
    'Twas the spring of our years

Distant war, separation and uncertainties
    Ships and seas and far-away ports
Our letters joined us across the miles

Civilian clothes replaced the Navy Blue
    A new start in a golden state
We marveled at our off-spring

You joked at my burnt offerings
    Praised my achievements
Encouraged my ambitions

Tho I'm a nagger and a shrew
    My heart still skips a beat
Seeing you at end of day

Now the days grow shorter, the nights grow longer
    But our love grows stronger
The Best is yet to be —
    'TIS THE AUTUMN OF OUR YEARS

Bess Carrier

Trackings

I have seen the deer prints in the woods,
behind the house
On several evenings now.
I love to feel their nearness.
I remain amazed at their courage, returning
to inhabit a place of sadness,
of decimation.

Do they come because they can go nowhere else?
Or does a place of sorrow require continued
explorations, a digging out and sifting through
of pain, before it can become memory?
Perhaps even the saddest answer can be borne
once it is spoken.

I cannot believe they return without a message,
but I do not find it in their hoof prints.
I would like to believe that loss begets wisdom
And so at night, when the woods are black,
I watch for them from my window, waiting
for a sign, a sound
something more than silence.

Gail Johnston

Grown Up

I'm all grown up. — Even Mommy says it true,
　because I can walk out to the bus with
　　just me and not us two.

I go to Nursery School with my grown up cousin
　Lou, who has learned to listen—share his
　　toys and recite a little of
　　　Winnie the Pooh.

Mommy is very proud with all I've learned to
　do—like feed the dog, put away my toys
　　and take my nap when I am through.

So, Grandma don't call me Baby Willie —I know
　it isn't true. But it still makes a big
　　man like me—feel a little blue.

　　Hetty F. Noble

A Known Stranger

Long ago he was just an ordinary stranger.
Because he lived in a strange land very far away,
where cock crow at dawn heralds the birth of a new day,
as the village slowly awakens to embrace the coming day.

One day you came to know the stranger.
Because in response to need, he journeyed to your land.
As time passed, he learned the customs of the new land
and although he yearns for home, your friendship keeps him glad.

Life in this foreign land could sometimes be wonderful.
Because with hard work and luck, the reward may be bountiful.
As the stranger image fades, your friendship becomes joyful.
And you hope and pray the relationship continues to be meaningful.

Looking at him, you no longer see an ordinary stranger.
Because you choose to see a good friend, rather than a known stranger.
As the evening sun sets, you stroll with your stranger
and wonder whether this known stranger will always be dear.

　　Anthony A. Ikaiddi

"Nobody's Fault"

High atop a mountain I sat one chilly night, to watch a most
beautiful and very unusual sight. The moon was a golden sliver of
light and the sparkling stars were quite exceptionally bright.

As the darkness descended into an ebony night, the view was an
incredibly awesome sight. Two brilliant beams of both red and blue
laser lights, shot across the valley to several distant sites.

Difference in the measurements would show movement but not why, that's
for the geologists to decipher using "Q" sheets and the equation of
"PI". Occasionally a gust of wind would trumpet and then die, as I
continued my vigilance with just a sigh.

Throughout the night the desert creatures serenaded a song to the
moon, as the ground gently swayed to the rhythm of the tune.
Perhaps on the night of a big full moon, the San Andreas will
announce herself but hopefully not soon.

When the San Andreas dances with her might, all of California will
have such a terrible fright! So, should you see a bright magenta
light, it's only the USGS possibly checking your site.

On that night the measurements revealed a small slip on the fault, but
the attack on my senses continues and will not HALT! I do realize
it's "NOBODY'S FAULT", it's just a period of a HIGH SEISMIC
　ASSAULT!

　　Allison Rhoden

Beyond The Stars

Beyond the stars in the fathomless skies
　beautiful and Holy city lies—
And in that land, our Saviour lives
　Within his kingdom, where he constantly gives
To those upon earth, his boundless love.
　Always, he watches and prays, there above.
In that sanctified land, there is no night,
　For the Glory of God gives comfort and light.
There can be no pain-or sorrow-nor tears
　Purest love will abide and banish all fears.
Nothing will harm us, for no evil thing mars
　The wonders which wait for us - beyond the stars.

　　Dorothy Black

Life Fist

Tiny fist, dark with birth's blood,
Beating...beating the bright, white air;
Wail, thin, weak with tired emotion,
Eyes clenched tight from life's lucid glare.

Chapped fist, smeared with friend's blood,
Beating...beating his pale, white face;
Wail, angry with child's fury,
Eyes filled with life's hatred stare.

Teenage fist, dark with rival's blood,
Beating...beating the stubble chin;
Scream of rage primeval,
Eyes hot with life's passion bare.

Aged fist, dark with own death-blood,
Clutching...clutching the bright, white air;
Wail, thin, weak with tired emotion,
Eyes closed tight from life's lucid glare.

　　Colleen Freeman Gordin

My Life My Nightmare

Do you know how it feels to
be sick and alone? Do you know
how it feels to have had to like in a
run down dump to call my home? The
only true friend I ever had is now in an
urn he is ashes!!! I turned to people and asked for help
all they did was abandon me. Walking
in blizzards is part of my life
pulling a heavy can't all alone, to the
dump that I had called my
home. Even though I seem
So different to you, I'm
human I have feelings
and I need love too!!!

　　Bonnie Rinert

Soul Mate

God has someone out there that he wants us to
　be joined to.
A soul mate that fits us like no other. One that
　complements one another.
One that will be a friend as well as a lover.
　One that will want to discover the world with
no other. One there to wipe away the tears and
　sorrows. One to look forward to happy tomorrows.
Sharing special times and happiness too.
　One to be there when the world knocks the hell
out of you. Two souls joined by God first and
　sprinkled with his grace.
A love they will know when they meet face to face.
　Yes! A soul mate.....

　　Angelia M. Beavers

Speak To My Soul

For years my Silent Soul lay hidden deep within
Barely noticed, never pushy, expressing only now and then.
This timid entity began to glow, began to blossom, began to grow.
Began imparting its wisdom to me, swept out the cobwebs so I could see
Cleared out old sorrows, old doubts and old fears
And gave me a new way to live out my years.
It sings and it dances and tells me what's real
It's now my best friend and I like how it feels.
Don't talk to my ego, my ego has fled
My old way of thinking has dropped away — dead.
My soul is my contact with Allness and love
My soul is my hope and my reason to live.
It's custom tailored to fit like a glove.
We grew up together, increasing in love.
If you want to impress me or want me to hear
Then speak to my Soul the dearest of dears.

Jean Myers

A Child

A tiny hand,
barely as big as my thumb,
Gently curls around my finger.
A small, wrinkled face,
   is turned ever so slightly toward me.
Her eyes are closed in a restless sleep.
   She sighs.
For a moment, her lips press into a gentle
   smile.
I touch them.
She moves slightly
   and turns closer to me.
Will she ever know
   how she touched me this day?

Jill Edwards

Run Over

After school, Sam and I used to run
barefooted through the brambles and
weeds to get under the Route 97 bridge.
We would climb carefully up the bank,
avoiding the slippery grass that dared
to fling us to the bottom of the
shallow, muddy creek.

After picking our way onto the diagonal
wall that held the bridge in place, we
would lie in an excited flurry, waiting
for the semi-trucks to run over us.
When only a few inches separated their
massive tires and our faces, we would
scream and hurl insults at them, cursing
and yelling until our eyes bulged. But
our peeps and squeals were buried beneath
an avalanche of noise and unrestrained power.

Then silence crashed down just as hard,
shattering around our ears, while the
diesel fumes drifted down, and up into our noses.

Jennifer B. Jones

Rocky Mountain Autumn

Majestic, distant peaks have changed to variegated blue,
And valley floors are carpeted in brown and golden hue.
The sparse, still clinging leaves of Aspen share a private joke,
And yellow Willows spar with raucous shrubs of Oak.

The dwindling lakes and lazy streams all hold the bright blue sky,
Reflecting ordered geese who start their southbound flight on high.
Then, marching up the hills, grey Sagebrush crowds the Goldenrod,
And only fools could venture here and miss the hand of God.

Betty R. Baker

For Susie

Far off in silent distance,
barefoot in a shallow stream she knelt.
Her hair, by the wind, was charmed to dance;
kingdoms of daylight upon it dwelt.

Eyes of evening sky as seen through a gentle rain;
a hue for which all description lie,
shade without a name.

To the gazeless face of water below
her sorrowless hand enciphers—
endless despairs, dreams and desires,
unspeakable things and things left unspoken
float out on gentle rings unbroken.

Whilst slipping further down the stream,
my thoughts as much alone,
my mind recalled what mine eyes had seen,
my heart—what it was shown.

Far off in the silent distance,
barefoot in the shallow stream she knelt.
Her hair, by the wind, was charmed to dance,
and kingdoms of daylight upon it dwelt.

John Lambert

Untitled

A MOTHER'S LOVE IS ALWAYS THERE -
   at times you think she doesn't care -

She's there with you in silent prayers,
   Her hands that mend the clothes you wear,
      Your meals she prepared for you each day,
      Her soft spoken voice that helped your
         blues away.

With the hustle-n-bustle off to school,
   the homework that she helped me do -
      Achievements, there were many of,
      Happy faces - Gold Stars

A Mother's Love Is Always There -
   Her helping hands to show she cares,
      Her voice of wisdom that she shares,
      is that of Mother's Love.

Janet L. Lincks

From The Heart

October one, nineteen ninety five
At one p.m. he took a bride
With all the happiness and the joy
Today I lost my little boy
With vivid memories, both good and sad
I remembered his childhood, as I said a prayer
God let them be happy, live a long life as one
The little boy I lost, today was my son!
He became a man, to cleave to his wife
His childlike ways, he has put aside
A good husband, I'm sure he will be -
Hopefully a father, of one, two or three!
God bless and keep them all, in the palm of His hand
The little boy God gave me, today's a grown man!

Esther M. Langford

Aileen

I watched the stars tonight so glorious in their brilliance
And the color of the sky was a satin pink
And then I marveled at the splendor
And the beauty of the heavens
I wondered too if you can see me watching
The night is clear enough
Are you there?

Jeanne F. Pratt

A New Beginning

If you look at the stars in the sky tonight
At first it is a beautiful sight
The twinkling light of each little one
Lighting the sky like a very big sun

Now count the stars and you will see
The numbers last eternity
Now imagine each one is a person you love
Smiling down from way up above

Part of life is learning the truth
That a very precious thing is youth
It only last for so long
Before you know, it is gone

Death is a stage we must all go through
Though hard to handle, we can pull through
Because every death means a brand new life
The incredible joy to a husband and wife

So every time you are sad and low
Because of someone's time to go
Just think of all the joy it's bringing
A brand new life, a new beginning.

Amy Peterson

Emily

And the strong sun beat straight down
As your friends gathered around

And the familiar college green
gleamed as bright as ever I had seen

Oh, my, time does pass
since I lay out there with you, skipping class

More memories began to flow back
So many I could not keep track

And the flowers your favorite vibrant blue
So strangely exactly like you

And as my heart grew a little tighter
the sun shined down a little brighter

And I knew it was you
this brightness I knew

As it shined from above
I could feel all your love

I am so aware
that life is unfair

Tragedy one can never sever
but Em, your love is forever

Danielle Silverman

The Chess Game

You maneuver into position
as you play the game.
With skill, finesse and cunning
you swiftly stake your claim.

I know exactly what you are doing,
but I am fascinated by the art,
with the precision, the planning and the timing,
and how they become an interwoven part
of the excitement and the appeal.

I was caught up in the intrigue
while you, with your usual charm and care,
manipulated the rook and caught me unaware.
Check Mate!
I had to smile.
Only you, would understand why.

Juanita L. Merritt

Guardian Angels

Life's plan is often uncertain and dim
as we walk so frail and bowed with care
let your spirit rise, have faith within
for the Lord ever watches and is there

He will sustain you in times of sorrow
and shed light onto your darkest way
you will know surely there is tomorrow
and it will be a brighter, happier day

So look up, know and understand with me
how God's plan includes Guardian Angels
to watch, care, and love us for eternity
leading our footsteps to where he dwells

In heaven, a home of purest radiant light
of mysterious beauty and glorious hosts
who whisper to us saying, that the night
is but a veil of eternal love so close

Joanna Gilbert-Hilton

Conversations

Your tiny fingers curl around mine
as we converse with our eyes over your dinner-time bottle.
Our discussion fulfills and gratifies without a word ever being spoken.
Words are trivial, unnecessary, when our eyes are able to say it all.

You are an amazement to me.
I want to see the world as you do—
your life is fresh, innocent, so beloved.
I am in awe that you indicate your pleasures by the way you squeal
and wiggle with laughter as the tree blows in the breeze,
or as the car drives down the road,
or at the pot of colorful flowers that sits on the stoop.
Whatever the motivation, your delight is pure and it invokes in me
a feeling so radiant and deep I believe I may explode
if I don't immediately reach down and smother your face with kisses.

Your fingers tighten around mine
for you crave my attention in no uncertain terms.
Your eyes dance, invite me to play.
The bottle is ignored, your smile infectious.
Nourishment given up for another.
Let's talk a while instead.

Julie Elizabeth Faulconer

The Kings On High

The silver kings were silhouetted by a spectrum of color
As they traversed o'er the earth with the evening wind.

I sat beneath those majestic kings on high and probed
My mind for inner peace and eternal joy.

As these kings hung aloft o'er my head, I was filled with an
unsurpassable and indescribable feeling of joy.

These tremendously vast domes of silver and red
blown along with the setting sun were kind, warm and peaceful.

These things of glory offered protection and comfort
from the troubles of the surrounding world.

I climbed aboard a majestic king of beauty and strength
and gave my spirit to be blown past time itself.

My soul, my spirit, were cast aloft to dance with
the silver kings and the evening wind.

I was carried from earth below to a wonderful land,
where I was but one in a sea of happiness.

We flowed along, into the keystones of our mind;
we found ourselves in the present time once more.

Oh so great, this journey of tranquility and joy,
that I await the king of kings once more, beneath those very skies.

John Paoli

Sunset

I see the dazzle of gold upon ruby
As the sun sets in the ring of the sky
This treasure is so overwhelming
That my breath come out in a sigh.

And surrounding the orb of the heavens
As though cushioning its descent
Are zephyr clouds in pastel hues
In wondrous beauty blent.

Could the jewels mined from earth's deepness
Compare to this glory I see?
I'm transfixed by the radiance of color
That spills from the sky to the sea.

What words could poets engender
To even say it in part
The fullness with which this splendor
Possesses and fills up my heart.

The lavender of dusk now
Settles like sheerest chiffon
As I watch God's stage from my window
While the drama of sunset plays on.

Ann Susan Crow

The Shadows Light

So soft my mind wanders against the gentle angst;
As the strippers shed their skin, and true colors flare in
unbridled sin.
Birds float and perch, and my thoughts concede, to a pursuit
called home...
For I can be but only me!?, a soul entrapped in a crevasse
of pain, lurking ever so gently towards you.
Passing breezes flourish throughout, blood stained trails
upon mother earth, and her children walk in chains,
Pushed forward with every shifting change of the current.
Slips the sun from view vanquished by the night, as her
young ones consume the sky, unable to fully capture the
darkness.
But try and attempt is all the shadow can conceive, with the
lack of light;
So sleeps he does upon this hours, and sleeps he will.
    As my mind will gently wander,
      What anger swells within the boundary of the night?
        For it is upon these hours in which I seek,
          The Shadows Light....

Jeff Prouty

Winter Days Gone By

The wind blows cold, across a frozen lake,
as the Creator sends, the first snowflake.
A young boy stands, on unsure skates,
while older brother glides by, no hesitate.
On wobbly legs, like a yearling fawn,
spirit free and new, like breaking dawn.
Youth brings unbridled passion, no tree too high,
yet skin their knee, just a moment cry.
I reminisce of joys, heart's pounding sigh,
with happy thoughts, of winter days gone by.

Greg Breach

Halloween Moon

Darkness entranced the night,
As the bats took to their flight.
An eerie chill enshrouds the air;
as the Halloween moon doth appear.

Shadows were long, the night time
was still, night birds were calling
over the hill.

The moon was full, what an evil sight,
but that's how it is on a Halloween night.

The night time was still, though
'twas not like June, I could not
escape, from the Halloween moon.

Carolyn Bouchez

Through The Eyes Of Glory

The bombs flew.
As tensions grew.
Soon a Mad-man would see,
What had come to be.

At first he tried to deny our powers,
but after the first couple of hours,
the air belonged to us,
and a capital city was all but dust.

Then the ground attack began.
Which should have brought glory to Saddam.
But his forces were weak, and spirits were low,
and the worry He did, started to show.

The end came quick as our Nation cheered,
It wasn't as bad as we had feared.
But even through the eyes of glory,
we knew this wasn't the end, of this sad story.

Guy T. Lousberg

Sonnet To My Dear Friend

Our friendship's like some rare and precious jewels
As rich in depth of color as the blood
Red ruby that encompasses the smouldering fuels
Of banked yet glowing fires of friendly love.

Yet it creates a diamond sparkle when we're merry;
Glittering like the flash of fiery crystal light
In a twinkling diadem of spotlights fairy
Reflecting delight; enhancing every sight.

And in a time of loneliness or bitter woe
Our friendship's like a sapphire, rich and blue,
Where lights are deep within the stone and glow
With tender succor or with comfort ever true.

Friendship's jewels thus lie within the jewel box of my heart
Treasured e'en more when we find ourselves apart.

Dorothea M. Eiler

Daydream

Looking out into the bright blue sky, I
begin to daydream. Dreaming of childhood
memories, and the things yet to come. Not of
flying through the air on wings, as some may
do. Dreaming of riding a horse in an open
pasture with bright green grass will suit me
just fine. Or perhaps sailing on a brand new
sailboat on a clear, sunny day. As I stare
deep into my own little world, I hear whispers
of people - people past and present call to me,
"Come, look and see what your future holds for you."
As I begin to awaken, I notice I am just
a normal kid daydreaming out of a window.

Christine Heathman

Dark City Wildlife

Dust begins darkness of lights untamed,
as late night covers the city.
Crawlers of insomnia claim its domain,
homeless is its committee.
Criminally, the nights made for those,
who wander around unseen.
Grave-yard shifts dangerously exposed,
to violence through its extreme.
Are unconscious ears aware, for instance,
of villains who prowl about.
Larger cities all night entertainments,
can bring, Dr. Hydes, demons out.
Pitch blackness consoles the eyes, and this,
the rave of culprits entirely.
You must, and cannot be remiss,
they'll rob quick and very quietly.
Alert yourself if you live there,
the attractions can swallow you whole.
Statistics as they are prepared,
becomes you as stories unfold.

Jacqulin Deloris Williams

Hopes And Dreams

I soar high on a wind that protects me,
As it puts me in the greatest danger I have ever faced.
I can see the whole world from here,
With a hundred-thousand hopes and dreams
For everyone who lives there,
But only a few, a handful stand out.
Because they can say they did it.
Their hopes were made reachable,
Their dreams turned into reality,
As they soar high upon a wind they created.

Debbi Steimel

Early Morning Prayer At Glinodo

God's voice can be heard in the morning air
As it breathes across my face.
In the trees as the sound becomes swishing
across the darkened sky.
In the swell of the waters at the edge of the lake,
I envision Him speaking in my mind's eye.

His voice imitates the crickets' chirping.
A cat's paws pouncing
From my lap onto the unyielding, wooden deck,
And in the purr rr r-ful sounds at my breast
before its leave-taking.
In a silent man's nearby footsteps
Measured in synchrony of the bowel's awakening.

Geese adrift emitting a cacophony of honking
And crows matching the foul in "caws" drowning.
  "Caw"...."Caw"...."Caw"

  "Aah"...."Aah"...."Aah"
Of the gentle breath that enters and leaves me,
Spirit within ... to and fro.
All this is my early morning prayer at Glinodo.

Julia Calvin-Coll

Longer Than Forever

As long as the grass shall grow,
And the sun shall shine.
From the depths of the darkest ocean,
To the sparkle of the farthest star.
Much more than all of this are my feelings for you.
Secrets of my soul to you I've told
And the keys to my heart you hold.

Christine Byrd

Most Especially Autumn

Today was most especially Autumn.
As I walked a country road,
The afternoon sun rested over fields and trees
Spreading iridescent amber glow
Which seemed to gentle all the world on any side of me
And outlined multi-colored trees in their last magnificence
Before the silent winter came.
Half-way home,
The peace of it entered all the chaos of my day
And muted all my memory to softer sound
That somewhere, deep within,
My mind would reach and touch
The quiet strength of life within.
Solitude filled the lonely corners
Once again, to drive away my fears.

Today was most especially Autumn on this road
And all the fruitful dying thrust my vision far beyond the fields.
And as I walked the last hill which starts its climb beyond the bridge,
I knew that, for some briefest time,
The pilgrim had come home.

Jeannette Goglia

In The Silence Of Our Room

In the silence of our room,
As I am lying close to you,
Listening to the rhythm of your breathing,
As I lie awake and dreaming.
In the silence of our room.

Thinking now of yesterdays,
And our beckoning tomorrows.
Of happy times we shared,
And even times of sorrow.
In the silence of our room.

What a privilege it is to share,
In such a happy life.
Knowing you're my husband, dear,
And I'm your loving wife.
In the silence of our room.

Betty Burke Myers

"Offer God A Little Help"

One summer while on vacation I went to the beach to play. Water water as far as the eye could see. Can you imagine our God pouring every drop there? And He did it without any help!

While I was there like most kids will do, I dug in the sand to build a sand castle too. I must have dug for hours and never ran out of sand. Then I heard that still small voice inside me say, "there's plenty" God put it there himself, and he did it without any help.

I still remember one winter, when we went to the mountains to ski, I can recall hills and more hills and some I couldn't see. God placed them there according to their size, just for man to enjoy. Boy! What power to do what without any help.

But you all must know all about the power our God has, you give up one of your days off just to come to His house to worship Him. But what about that family just down the street, or that person you work next to. Are they saved or are they on their way to Hell.

Now God's in the saving business and He hasn't yet retired. I just as much as he loves you, HE still loves them too. Although He has the Power and could do it by Himself. If you really love and trust Him, YOU'D OFFER GOD A LITTLE HELP.

James D. Keoun

Utopia

All is quiet on the high hilltop.
As colorful flowers dot the land with beauty, and
golden green grass shuffles in the breeze
while lovers lie in happiness

All is quiet on the ocean and shore.
As sparkles float eternally on the water, and
a smooth, warm wind fills the air
where the stressed find peace

All is quiet on the sun-setting horizon.
As majestic colors enrich the sky, and
powerful clouds stand in their glory
while the whole world holds its breath

All is quiet in the night sky.
As a silver moon watches over the world, and
millions of stars smile like angels
where the hurt can finally hide

All is quiet inside two hearts.
As you put your hand to my cheek, and
gaze into my frightened eyes
while everything ends, in silence

Julia M. Perla

Classmates Forever

Only ten short years ago, we met
   As classmates warm and true,
We've met again to see old friends,
   And memories renew.

Some precious ones have gone to rest,
   We miss them oh so much,
And others suffer untold pain,
   They need a special touch.

Some fifty years have come and gone,
   The time goes swiftly by,
But friendships that we made back then
   Will never, never die.

Hail Woodlawn High School still rings true,
   It was a special place,
And even yet our fondest thoughts
   No one will e'er erase.

My dear, dear classmates we all know
   That each of us must die,
So let's stay true that one day we
   Will join hands in the sky.

George H. Harwell

The Greatest Gift

The wind blew the night was cold
as an icicle stick. The silence broke
off with a cry of an innocent child

who is this child? there is no answer,
but the wind and the cry on the stairs
of an innocent child.

who are this people that dare to forget,
the life so precious that comes from above.

And only He who knows our hearts,
will once again give us this gift, with
more than love.
For He cares, and sees us where we stand,
and dare not disturb our silence, that
dwells within.
For He respects our inner thoughts
and fears, and only we can change and
see what God can do if you let Him in.

Connie Sarinana

Masterpiece Of Life

Babies are but a blank canvas, or wood, waiting for the carver's knife.
As adults we must use this surface to create, a "Masterpiece of Life."
"Suffer the little children," said our saviour good and true; but I
don't think He meant they should suffer, at the hands of me and you.

"Spare the rod and spoil the child," should mean discipline fair and
firm; mixed with love and affection, for that is how they learn.
They should never be beaten or starved, neglected or abused. They
should be taught discipline, love, and guidance; but never be misused.

This blank surface is waiting, for the artist's knife or brush.
The picture or sculpture it becomes, depends entirely on us.
We adults must be the ones, with strokes firm and sure,
who create the picture of life, on this surface blank and pure.

A child is like a hothouse orchid, grown in a climate of love.
Nurtured and tended, trained as it grows, it will climb to the heavens
above. If neglected it will die, overtending, it cannot bear.
It needs the freedom to grow on its own, but to know that we are there.

So give your child its freedom, but keep a firm hold on the reins;
to guide it around life's pitfalls, but never put it in chains.
Give it love and guidance, but give it room to grow, and nine times
out of ten, it will grow up to be, someone you are proud to know!

Barbara J. Benson

For A World

The day is gone, the darkness falls into the wings of night,
As a feather drifts down, from an eagle in its flight,

I see lights of a village, gleam through the rain and mist,
And feelings of sadness covers me, my soul cannot resist,

Feelings of sadness and longing, that is burdened only with pain,
And resembles sorrow only, as the mist resembles rain.

Come hold me gently, come listen as I lay,
Sooth this restless feeling, banish thoughts of the past day,

Not of the grand life, not of man's sublime,
Whose distant footsteps echo, through the corridors of time,

If each man wrote a poem, it would be the way to his heart,
All races would surrender, and falling of tears would start,

All weapons would be banished, for war we would have no need,
We would only see each others color, by our personalities.

The music of the poets, would be heard aloud by all,
And the love for human nature, would be our only call,

Our long days of labor, would turn to a labor of love,
And everyone would agree, that enough is enough.

Jessica Merritt

My Love Is Lost

But now life seems different
around me since my love is gone.
And I can't see further than the dawn.
Other people see my loneliness.
Even in the light, I see the darkness of the night.
And still try not to think of our fight.
When I left you in the pale moon light,
you saw the coldness in my eyes.
But it was not to your surprise.
Through the pain and the tears,
there were the happy years.
I should not be the one to blame,
even though you caused me so much pain.
My heart is broken and nothing is left unspoken.

Jessica Stokes

Mother, Did You Call?

Oh, Blessed, Blessed Lady, how may we serve you?
Are you calling, beckoning, leading us to renew?
Through God's light and grace, we'll act as one
And follow your path until our days are done.

Virginal Mother, Mediatrix for humanity,
Would you help us shed our daily vanity?
So, like you, we'll be prepared for the call.
Unworthy servants, may we give you our all?

Your roses are a sign from the heavens above;
A holy presence is with us, a fullness of love.
Proper prayers fill our hearts, atoning, adoring;
God's holy gifts into our lives have been pouring.

We want to be with you forever, Mother so blessed.
Let us do your will and aid those distressed.
Although bound to this world by both time and space,
Through loving service, we'll earn your Son's grace.

Mary, our Mother, answer our plea
And tell us how best to serve thee.

Claire S. Satta

What Color

What color are my tears
Are they many colored like the days
Or do they stay a simple shade of grey
Do I grieve for the world and its crimes
Or only for what is mine
What color are my tears
Are they scarlet like the blood that stains my hands
Or only silver strands
Do I grieve for the life I wish I had lead
Or for the life I must live instead
Will I ever be able to name my fears
Will I ever be able to find the cures.
What must I see
What must I be
To solve the problems of my tormented soul
Or my fragment goal.
What color?

Jennifer-Méchelle Dean

Dodee And Andy

Dodee and Andy, I do declare,
Are the funniest pets, anywhere.

Stonewall Dodee is an English bulldog.
Some say she's as ugly as a bullfrog.
Some say she's as rough as can be,
But I know she's as gentle as a little baby.

She loves and protects Scott and Colette.
And is the best watch dog I've ever met.
She doesn't have to bark or bite.
Just one look at her, gives them the fright!

Now Andy Allspice is a Myna bird.
Right now he only says one little word.
When he's in the right mood he says, "hello".
I hope he'll say more, but I don't know!
He squawks and whistles most of the time,
And often plays with his bells and chimes.

Dodee and Andy are very happily
Two nice additions to our family!

Charlotte Crane

Untitled

Have you ever noticed that the waves in the ocean
  are never still
always changing their mood...
at first they come in crashing, ready for anything-
  they want to stay
but then,
something scares them
  so they retreat back slowly
  to being safe...
only to return once again
  ready to start new.

Our relationship reminds me of the waves,
  staying for only short periods at a time
but always returning to where
  we feel safe.....
    alone.

Dawn F. Scheeler

Thanksgiving Time

Within the pattern of times and seasons
Are all the happenings of today;
Sometimes it seems they come without reasons;
Soon they all will become yesterday.

Experience teaches; lessons are learned
From the gladness, struggle, or sorrow;
And testings that come should never be spurned
There will be thanksgiving tomorrow.

Times and the seasons keep passing along,
Planting "deeds" in a long yesterday;
Then will come harvest, made joyful with song
Through an eternal Thanksgiving Day.

Fern M. Cooper

Soul Storm

To see things now at this remove, I have the chance to wonder
  are all my dreams and private muse to fade as distant thunder?
By others wise they were pronounced a bit too ill conceived
  and this consensus of opinion-should it be believed?

When truth is false and lies are truth, I put my stock in these.
  Ignore the set, pursue the dreams-it is my soul I please! Yet...
In my private moments when it's but me, alone,
  I have as my companion the seeds of doubt they've sown.

I gather up my courage thrown round me like a coat
  to warm me from the chilling winds and break the ice of rote.
Is it enough to keep me safe, fearing what's ahead?
  Is it me or is it they-the source of all my dread?

Beyond-the seminal force! Feel its powerful embrace!
  Confront the wrathful currents that toss you from this place.
This struggle leads to stunning heights, a stony precipice
  Beware, below on rocky shoals the swirling, roiling mist...

I see reflections of myself, tossed upon the tide,
  but oddly by the tempest cleansed and hope along, astride
To take me to a greater height where I shall fear no more
  to face the path ahead of me and knock upon your door.

David M. Russo

Like A Rose

Our love was like a red rose. We promised to cherish
and obey till death do us part. But the day he parted,
my life grew dim. And my red rose thus turn black as
the midnight sky. So I lay at night and weep and stare
at a picture of him. And remember our love as a red
rose. A rose nearly complete. A rose almost perfectly
bloomed. But all I can do is lay at night and dream
of my sweet till the earliest morning light.

Amanda Gross

Heaven

The foaming crystal waters roll in caressing the sands.
Approaching, they strike the rocks and glide over them
in a smooth and gentle manner.
When they reach the sand, they are quickly drawn back.
The steaming bits of sand burn the soft and
delicate fingers of the rising waters.
The trees begin to laugh and whisper.
The mountains can't help but join in with
all the gay and jovial voices.
The laughter vibrates the earth.
The fragments of rock are jolted from their homes
and embark on a thrilling journey down the steep crags.
The plush cotton clouds float over the peaks of the mountain
forming intricate designs in the azure sky.
The seagulls soar overhead, shrilling their cries of excitement.
The tourists swarm in numbers and stroll up the long pathway
in search of a glimpse of heaven.

Amanda Mainer

Lonely Is The Heart

Lonely is the heart who longs for another.
Another heart who mirrors the emotions of the first.
Another heart who knows that great love shared by two.
Another heart who desires the safe haven of an embrace.
Lonely is the heart who longs for you.

Lonely is the heart who yearns for love and tenderness.
Another heart who gives gentleness with a caress.
Another heart who's arms offer strength and security.
Another heart who's shoulders lend understanding and compassion.
Lonely is the heart who yearns for your love and tenderness.

Lonely is the heart who suffers separation.
Another heart who feels the pain of distance.
Another heart who cries at the passing of time.
Another heart who cherishes the memories of yesterday.
Lonely is the heart who suffers being separated from you.

Lonely is the heart who dreams of tomorrow.
Another heart who echoes hope and aspiration.
Another heart who softly reassures that love abounds.
Another heart who patiently awaits the arrival of the dawn.
Lonely is the heart who dreams of a tomorrow with you.

Gina B. Graves

Autumn

As the green chlorophyll drains from the leaf
Announcing its own epitaph from life,
Its greatest glory begins.
The radiance of all the remaining colors
Exceeds that of all but the distant sun
And nearest rainbow. It is only for the
Human eye to see the aura of Autumn.

The forest becomes a cathedral for worship
In the brevity of the leaves terminal days.
And suddenly, a severance of the stem from the branch
Of life is complete, and the anthem of Fall ceases.

The leaf quietly and distinctly lands
Upon the earth to serve its Maker as a cradle
For its mother. It will rise again
And canopy all living things with its
Green umbrella, and later the prisms of Autumn.

Arlen Curtis Matson

"Nothing Is Forever"

When you think happiness has found you
and your heart seems to feel all aglow,
It don't seem very long, before those sadden blue
skies come along
and the thrill that you once felt somehow
has magically gone.

When you think love has made your life worthwhile
You watch smiles turn into tears
You grow old, and start to wonder
how you made it through all those years.

Money has come so easily, success with it
right along
to find it was only temporary
cause nothing really lasts very long.

Enjoy today what makes your happy
store memories of all those good old days
Because "nothing lasts forever"
and tomorrow is a brand new day!

Carol Ann Eigenhauser

Dreams

Pursue your dreams from day to night,
and you will find what is truly right.
Never stop to take a break,
or you shall lose what's at stake.
you must follow your heart at all times,
if your heart beats true you will hear no rhymes.
But if one day night never falls,
don't you cry or don't you bawl.
If one day you start to snore,
or just give up or try no more.
and if one day you lose your way,
you have just let your dreams fly away.

Amber Lynn Williams

A Fight Between Friends

The sun is down I should be sleeping
And yet I lie awake still weeping,
The thought of our best friendship ending
The tears the rage still never ending
I wish this friendship would always stay
But I am hurt by what you say
Our thoughts were once all meaningful
We talked about the lives we hold,
Our lives were one but now are two.
I wonder how I will get through
Through this trouble, through this pain,
This is one lesson that I must gain.
This gift of friendship will all ways stay
And it can not be thrown away
Are you blind or can you see
All this pain you inflict on me
Our friendships done and I'm alone
Lying in my room at home
I care so much and wonder why all
All I want to do is cry.

Angela Loconto

Untitled

It's amazing how often I think of you
and wonder if you're thinking of me.
Maybe accidentally, at the same time each day,
we both remember and smile
if only for a second.
Maybe you notice the moon at the same time
I'm so far away admiring its beauty;
or maybe a song will remind you of me
just as I am humming its soothing melody.
Perhaps you are thinking of me now,
as I'm thinking of you and maybe,
just maybe
you miss me.

DeAnza Pattison-Church

Look Up My Child

When life is more than you can bear,
  and when it seems that no one cares;
When everyone is insincere,
  look up my child for I am here.
In times of trouble and you feel lost,
  where can you go that has no cost?
Search your heart and have no fear,
  look up my child for I am here.
With a weakened heart on the darkest night;
  look up my child and see the light.
When all else fails, be sincere;
  look up my child for I am here.
The Lord thy God is all you need,
  and prayer will plant the very seed.
Fear not my child I'm ever near;
  look up my child for I am here.

Dennis W. Baxter

Have You Lived?

Have you ever looked in a big oak tree
And watched the squirrels play,
Or seen a family lose a child
And watched a mother pray?

Have you seen the wildflowers in the spring
When they first begin to bloom?
Have you watched a handicapped person
Try to make it across the room?

Have you smelled the wild rose beside the road
As you wandered on your way,
Or stopped to talk to little kids
And listened to what they say?

Have you smelled the dust of a summer rain
When it first begins to fall?
Have you ever helped a stranger
Or anyone else at all?

If you can't stop and help someone
Or find some time to give,
Perhaps you're just existing friend
And you need to begin to live.

Billy G. Jennings

Forty— Time Marches On — MAHS Class Of '55

Time marches on and we're still going strong.
  A little slower, but better, like vintage wine.
We must admit it's been quite a climb.
  Forty years to be exact, but what a joy at looking back,
Only to relive those years in one's own mind.
  Lots of joys, lots of sorrows, but let's all look to tomorrows.
Try to savor our times together, for some may not weather, much more time.
  I'm glad to see you all, now let's try to have a ball,
and enjoy this special time.

Cela Beckey Spearman

Fear To Believe

To believe a person, but fear their words,
And to hurt the mass, but to be unwise.
So now everyone must deeply despise.
The little she knows, she flies like the birds.
The air isn't clear for her, like the herds.
Can she feel the grief she causes with lies?
The burden of tries is shown by the eyes,
And the way she cries. No one even turns.
I can sense it coming around again.
Anxiously I wait to come through the door,
But not to my alarm she wants to mend.
Now her reasonings will go to the floor.
She will understand that this is the end,
The one I used to trust, I trust no more.

Anne Marie Jones

'Tis Christmas Again

'Tis Christmas again, our "unique" son,
And through the snow, you will come,
Not a reindeer sleigh, but a sleigh that has wings,
To come to Florida, to get some "things",
From ole' Mom and Dad
But we are so glad you are comin'
We spend all the days singin' and hummin'
You'll make our Christmas great,
Even though we can't "skate",
We'll all be together,
And whatever the weather,

WE CAN SWIM!
ENJOY!

Beverly J. Williams

Like The Wind

With a grizzle beard
And the winds of winter
Whispering through Fall leaves
A peaceful thought lights up in me
Like the calmness of waves
Lumbering to shore,
I feel strong,
Ready to endure the repetitious
Cycles of seasons
That I've grown to know,
Like friends in swing sets when I was ten,
Even though I've never seen them again,
I still know they're out there somewhere
Like the wind.

David Michael White

"Surrounded With Desert Sands, Winds"

I stand surrounded by desert sands, winds
And swirling dust of ages pass by me.
I am reminded of the earthly sins
That come from loving one's self, not the three.

If to accomplish good through charity
We must learn to not fear the punishment.
Love God and neighbors. We should let it be
That every action displays temperament.

Our souls are desolate, barren, wastelands.
The feelings are reserved and sparsely shown.
We wonder what Future brings, in whose hands
Our lives are held, we see, and they are ours.

I look down dunes. Across the horizon
Wind is covering prints of past attacks.
I see tents, hints of civilizations,
But do I see the future or the past?

Josie Tibbitts

Gravelines

Epitaphs
and such matters
as please the eye
and calm the soul,
are better left unwritten,
left unsaid.
There is nothing in memorial
but memory,
and such memory of no sure sweetness as
memory uncalled.

Close the well-meant, foolish mouth -
buried deep in comfort is the heart of sorrow.

I know....

And if you must,
when I am dead,
write silly, gentle things of me,
be kind, write only this.

James Laughlin

Arise

For all the days I hoped, and all the nights I cried,
And sometimes when I wished or wondered what if I had tried?

Through all the days I grasped for peace, yet was denied my dreams,
A seed of strength grew in me, a substitute it seems.

For every time I was thrown down, I raised up twice as strong.
I learned to laugh and spit in the face of the fears I've held so long.

From the remains of scorn and pain, has arisen a better man,
One with self respect and pride who triumphs for he can.

The pain, it now just glances off, my smile, no longer fake.
They can take my heart and soul and life but my will shall never break.

Alone and strong, I've found my peace of mind.
They could never understand, I've stopped wondering why they're so blind.

Branden Wiley

Reflections

There were times I've loved you to much
And sometimes I thought not at all

But I know I could never meet another like you...
And I hope you feel that way to...For I am
writing this dear, to say in words...that I love you.

There was times we were at the top of a mountain.
And sometimes we were down in the pits.

But we both learned together, with Christ we can make it
No matter what comes in our midst.

"Caring" and "Thoughtful" and "Wonderful" are words
I seldom say, though I think of you quite often...In
my own special way.

Elizabeth Richburg

Untitled

The ocean seems to be kin my soul,
as I lay my eyes upon its beauty, it
entrances me, its beauty beyond word's sings
to my ears, whispering "watch me and I'll carry your
woes away" "cry and hurt no more for I will dance
and show you the beauty of the light", as the light
caresses upon the waves showing the depths of its intensity.
All the while seducing me ever more. Never
will I forget its gift of serenity. For in my mind's eye
I ever so caught a glimpse of the truth, the promises
of heaven.

Diana L. Scoville

A Resolve

I shall spread my wings in the worldly wind
And soar to the Heavens so my soul be undimmed.
I shall rise in each morning with a trusting heart
That from my Father's will I shall never part.
I shall seek the Earth's music, never heeding the din,
So the beauty of God can live within.
I shall trust that the road I've taken so far
Is one God directed, and I'll follow His star.
I shall live in expectancy that the Lord will provide
And ever be near me, my Friend by my side.
I will dodge Satan's arrows of mistrust and doubt,
And will help to show others what God is about.
I will let go the past the could hinder my heart
From loving, forgiving, from doing God's part.
I will study, will seek Him in living and prayer,
And will try to search only the good and the fair.
Let the word, therefore, flower within me, I pray,
That I may reflect Thee in every way.
In worldly distraction, when glitter I see,
Let me know that Thy grace is sufficient for me.

Carolyn Row Barber

"Life's Journey"

I walked along life's road today
and saw the sky so blue and gray
I heard a voice from heaven say
"Child, follow me, kneel and pray."

I stood beside a friend today
and touched the heart of God
the moments rare and very dear
His scarred hands showed, how much he cared.

O sinner come your burden share
and place it at His feet
then trust the savior and entreat
His mercy to repeat.

How long will you, your life destroy
for earthly pleasures and employ
He gave His life for you to see
how much he loved, He died for thee.

Jerry G. Ryan

The Snail's Secret

He looked at the snail
And saw its secret

Gently
He picked it up

Patiently
He held it and waited

Slowly it crawled out
It was whole
But its shell was cracked and wet

Suddenly
Wet droplets multiplied along each crack

Forcefully
The surfacing droplets shattered the shell

Skillfully
He felt it and watched

Gently he placed it in the grass
Threw away the shell
And, its secret became part of him

Carol Dolan

The Coat

My Dad's coat was a treasure, he wore it with pride
and pleasure, it matched his eyes of blue you could
see the love in his eyes shining through, it was
tattered and torn, from the work that he did to
feed his hungry kids, but that didn't stop him from
braving the wind, because in his heart he knew we
were God send, and even on Sunday, when he went to
pray he wore that old coat with a smile on his
face, for others look on the outside of man, but God
looks on the goodness that comes from within, so now
you see why I'm proud of my Dad, he's the best friend
a girl ever had.

Jerri Beeler

The Starflower And The Tumbleweed

She was blown across the plains
And over the mountains from the Northland;
the harsh Wyoming wind at her back —
weary and ragged, her roots bare and broken.
The trail ended on the Taos plateau —
(The Mountain soothes my wounded spirit —
The distant drums stir my soul.
Now I can rest in peace amid the fragrant sage and chamisa
— finally home again...
Innumerable moons... a half-century's harvests —)

The Full Moon paused in his walk across the heavens
and watched as the old tumbleweed bounced along the prairie;
it mattered not where —-
The tumbleweed came to rest, entangling the Star Flower.
The touch!... A spark of life!
She sensed a familiar longing as the Tumbleweed
caught up the dying Star Flower...
"It's you!" She clung inconsciously to the Tumbleweed.
"Yes," he replied, "my journey is at last ended...
I knew you'd come home again."

Helena Brewer Cox

Look Upward, Traveler

He passed a beggar on the street,
And never slacked his pace.
He didn't care if his need was great,
He never paused to see his face.
Then a blind man stopped to cross a street,
The white cane so clear to see,
Yet this traveler only saw his feet,
And hurried by oblivious, as any one could be.
As time wore on, this traveler
Grew weary of the passing scene.
He pondered o'er these foolish things,
How a man could be so mean.
He said to himself that such a one
Could never, ever be!
But as he looked in the mirror, he gasped,
"My God, that one is me!
Since then, on seeing some unfortunate one,
He'll never pass him by.
He remembers the phrase,
"But for the grace of God, surely there am I".

Benjamin Millman

Face

Lines not connecting, but crossing with age.
A deep cracked sliver created by rage.
Scornful black onyx hidden from shame.
A reservoir of silence, remember my name?
Everyone has a rembrandt they don't really see.
Born down from history, their own branch of tree.
Created by sex, religion and race.
The spirit is alive, we're only a face.

Jeff Geraci

What's Wrong With The World Today?

I am an old woman of seventy-nine,
and looking around me, just trying to find —
What's wrong with the world today????

I'm trying and trying to think can it be
The world that I live in, or could it be me?
I'm finding it hard to perceive that the things going on are only
getting worse.
Can't we come to some agreement, to put things in reverse?
I think we can.

If we all get together,
put our arms around each other,
to sing and act as one,

We could turn this thing around,
Pray and fall upon the ground,
to the Lord far up above, for help —

If we do it as one, peace and love will be won,
so-please, join in with me and PRAY —

We can over come it all -
and stand up straight and tall -
Before God our King.

Genevieve Hopf Pagel

My Son

I knew you ere I saw your face
And longed to clasp you in safe embrace
You were 'neath my heart, inside of me
Not yet ready to be outside and free.

I knew you ere I saw your face
Puckered and pink in disgruntled grimace
Clinging to life with tenacity
Not yet ready to be outside of me.

I knew you ere I saw your face
Full of laughter that lilted with grace
Blue eyes sparkling with impish glee
Growing and learning about being free.

I knew you ere I saw your face
Though the lilting voice turned to bass
You were racing far too speedily
Not yet ready to be outside and free.

I knew you ere I saw your face
And sorely miss your loving embrace
You are in my heart forever, my son
Now outside, have you freedom won?

Elaine E. Kelso

"I Can Help"

When things go wrong, as the occasionally do
and life's tangled web starts to turn your blue skies gray
You're not asking to stay — but you pray for one more day
Just lay your head on my shoulders and everything will be alright

When the road you travel has been paved with broken promises
and the funds are low and the debts are high
you can't seem to smile, all you do is sigh
rest in my arms if you must, but never quit and the future will
always look bright

Remember a person needs to fail before they can be a success
and without doubt every cloud has a silver lining
even though at the time, it doesn't seem possible
just take my hand, I'll take you to the promiseland and you'll
see the light
We need to keep rolling on, win or lose
Stick to the fight when we think we're out
Because it's these times when everything seems lost
That we must join together and not lose sight.

John Giovanini

"Let Your Heart Heal"

Time will take the hurt away
  and life will still go on.
Your dad wouldn't want it any other way
  Be happy he'd say "my son."
Your father was a special man
  There's a closeness you'll hold near
I'm sure he was your favorite fan
  Yet memories at times just won't seem clear.
You are his son; I know he was proud
  And I'm sure you feel the same
Though he wasn't the type to say it out loud
  He loved you, he gave you his name.
Remember the good times always
  Do your best to forget the bad
When you have those sad days,
  Just think about your dad.
There never is a right time
  For someone you love to leave
Cherish your memories, it's not a crime
  And don't be afraid to grieve!

Denise Arlene Sveinson

The Wind

The wind howls like a wolf to the moon
And its strength is like a blow from a rod.
It roars like a mighty lion
And its strength is from the hand of God.

It whistles through the trees at night
And stirs the lifeless branches.
The wind blows across the land
and past the old cattle ranches.

It helps the ocean to roll
So smoothly to the shore.
It helps the bold Eagle to soar
And the Eagle's burden it bore.

Caleb Fenter

Tears Sizzle In The Rain

A tear, smooth, glides across your smiling face,
And it seeps onto my skin and sizzles into the rain.

The rain splatters upon my pores and burns.
It stings existing sores, but your tears,

Again they're on my face and again,
There they sizzle into the rain.

I don't let them in my old, weak, sores.
They'll never heal if they're always torn.

You think your tears are the remedy,
But I'm not sure, so they can't come in.

I cover my sores, and the rain comes through,
But tears of love, I can't let near.

I'm afraid to try such unknown cure.
It might heal old sores, but then again...

...It may only cause NEW sores.

That's why when you cry on me,
Your tears only sizzle in the rain.

John Eric Eddy

A Face

A face is nothing, but a covering on a clock.
A face is covering for a coffee pot.
A face is something that I can't describe.
A face is something to never hide.

Aleiha Marie Godfrey

Untitled

The mystical magic of the evening stars
and illumination of the radiant rays from
the moon bring out lovers. For there is no
secret to share and no blame to bare,
for the soul is so clear. The mystical
evening air holds essence of love so dear.
All is at peace when love succumbs to
the breeze of the air. The entanglement
of hearts and souls mingle with the stars
and the rays of the moon to join two
souls together that only the brilliant stars
at night know their destiny.

Ella L. Wilborn

How I Feel

I feel the ground beneath my feet as I walk,
And I think darkness within my soul
because within my mind I feel society has been unjust.
But on a more positive tip, I feel that I need to think
above what people have thought.
As I walk alone, as a man, through the phases of life there
is no need to turn back on ignorance.
Because how I feel, is that society is too blind to see that
they are the ones portraying the definition of the word
ignorance.
But above all this sadness, on how I feel, is now on how I felt.

Abram Rodriguez

Faith

Who do I talk to, I talk to the wind
  and I talk to summer rain

And it's nice to talk to the starry sky
  when the night is on the wane

When the air is filled with the joyful sound,
  of songs by the robin and thrush

I have found that beauty surrounds me,
  unveiled by the morning's first blush

When I speak of these friends all around me
  it really isn't that odd

For the sound that I hear and I cherish
  is truly the voice of my God.

John D. Smith

Living In The Black History Of The Bible

O God, from my youth thou hast taught me
and I still proclaim thy wondrous deeds
so even to old age and gray hairs for those of us
that are Young and Restless in which we only have
One Life to Live for Jesus said I am the bread of
life As the World Turns for men who have turned
the world upside down have come here also to see
The Guiding Light to guide me with thy counsel
and afterward thou wilt receive me to glory for
All My Children in the spirit himself bearing
witness with our spirit that we are All My Children
of God has the Days of Our Lives, for this day
is a day of good news celebrating Black History
in Another World, Loving one another has
Bold and Beautiful, living in the Black History
of the Bible of Greater Garth Chapel African
Methodist Episcopal Church in the sweet hour of
prayer we'll all end up in General Hospital in
Heaven.

Dorothy Smith Houston

465

"When I Look At You"

It sure took more than time to be where we are
And I can't say it's just a memory
As I look into your eyes, staring back at me now
There's a love that's forever to see.

All those moments spent with you
Those times aren't lost to memory
Like a timeless paperback story
Those years with you
I plainly see
When I look at you looking at me.

All the children have gone off into starting new lives
Raising some kids of their own
Guess we did them some good after all these years
Without you this house wouldn't be home.

All those moments spent with you
Those times aren't lost to memory
Like a timeless paperback story
Those years with you
I plainly see
When I look at you looking at me.

Christopher B. Ransom

Creation Stood Still

I was sure I had lived about all I could live
  And had seen all there was to be seen.
I enjoyed all the days which had something to give;
  And endured all the times that were lean.

Looking back on hello's and goodbye's that I've shared
  When we played little games just for fun
Although some with their tears, let me know that they cared
  I don't know that I loved even one.

Until now, when it's late in this life's rapid pace
  Am I fortuned to learn what I've missed.
For I've now seen the love on your face
  And I've learned what it is to be kissed.

Who could say where it leads, or what fate has in store
  While we gamble with laughter and tears
But you know in your heart that I'll love you much more
  As the days lengthen out into years.

And then ages from now, I would know such a thrill
  Should you choose to recall with a smile
That for one precious moment - "Creation Stood Still"
  And my darling, we lived for a while.

Doris Coffman

Shadows

I am living in the company of shadows that flutter
And grow; dancing, prancing, winding and writhing,
Increasing and grinning a gargoyle's grin,
Touching; and jumping out of reach
As day shows through, changing then to flickering bits of dust,
Floating in the air, changed to nothing, harmless,
And no longer breathing phantoms of my fear,
Forgotten memories of pain and panic.
The day becomes an ordinary thing of walking, talking,
But shadowless, with light and sound,
And hope and faith. Until nighttime comes, somber and chill
That brings overcasting shadows hiding light,
And specters begin to move around me here;
And all my dread returns, leaving me
In trembling terror as the shadows
Start their midnight promenading, twisting
Teasing, laughing at my loneliness and despair,
'Til the daylight comes, chasing, circling,
Frolicking, shining bright, probing, prying,
Searching, bearing with it confidence and trust.

Dreda Hill

Remember

Just like the cosmic sands that tick away all times past, present
  and future, even times that never were and never will be,
I think of you constantly.

It has been a long time since I last felt your warmness,
touched you and heard your vocal utterings,
I think of you constantly.

But now, oh now, I am glad.
Glad I could glimpse you for just a little while-for such a short while.

I could feel your soul reaching out to mine,
your mind reaching out to my mind,
you reaching out to me in a way unique to all but us.

Just as the sun reaches out to the sky in the morn'
and brings it from darkness into light
exposing its all for each other to see,

That's the way it was.
That's the way I want it to be.

John W. Gunn Jr.

"Do Angels Have Wings?"

Did you think all angels have wings?
And fly around heaven all day,
Strumming golden harp strings
While heavenly music they play?
Well, no doubt some of them do.

But the ones that eyes can see
Ministering to our many needs,
Walk among us and seem to be
Mortals, doing vital, mortal deeds.
How could we live without them?!

Some of them wear uniforms of white,
With stethoscopes and all such things,
Or a smile that is heavenly bright
With garb of blue, with badges and rings.
They don't even know they are angels!

Some carry burdens great, and frowns
Sometimes appear—they need wings!
Struggling here, earning their crowns
Trudging through the storm, she sings—
One angel I know, who has red hair!

Hallie H. Walter

Weeds

Could I have the strength
  and endurance of a weed?
Seeded itself with help of the wind
Lives and thrives in a crack
  in the cement
Strong determined to grow
  not lament
Hot sun, drought, trespassers on their home
  cars, trucks, cats, dogs, Reeboks
If weeds can live out a life
I can face all obstacles and thrive
  I will survive!

Hazel Risk

466

A November Morning

There is frosting on the grass
  And diamonds on the trees;
But high upon the mountains
  There are stranger things than these.
Snow while peaks still with golden aspen
  Shivering in the icy breeze;
Mingled with bright red maples about to freeze.

Against the far horizon
  Etched clear and bold
  Are tall pine trees;
  That have turned blue
  And white in the cold.

The snow geese have flown
  In "V" shaped wedges to the south.
All the leaves have been blown down
  And drifted into the hedges all around.
The fat bears are hibernating,
  After feasting on everything to be found.
Out of an ashen sky snow is falling to the ground.

    Billie Perry Prpich

The Pattern Of Life

Sometimes in our life there seems endless toil
And days without rest and ease,
And sometimes come days of boundless joy
Like wonderful melodies;
There are also the days of peaceful times,
The days without pain or care,
And these are the days when our soaring souls
Seem floating away on the air.

But God has meant our days to blend
With times of joy and pain,
And often with these His boundless love
Comes welling back again;
And although in our lives the pattern is dim
It will become clear when we dwell with Him.

    Jessie H. White

Sounds Of The Echoing Past

Feelings reverberate throughout the depth
And core of the human soul that cries out.
But throughout this depth of darkness,
It reaches out in hopes
Of touching a tangible form;
Instead, only to be wrapped in an arc
Within its own embrace.

There's no glimmer of light
To penetrate the depth, and like
A tumbling block, it collapses upon itself.

It rest awhile, inside its own embrace,
Trying to deny the calamity of—
The reverberating sounds of the past,
Knowing, that the sounds can only be
An echo that's rapidly diminishing.

It cradles itself in this form of denial,
Expecting the sounds of the echoing past
To strengthen its will;
But the sounds—Can No Longer Be!

    Joan E. Gettry

Partners

As young lovers, we confronted marriage
And commenced our journey as partners.

Our promises, our intentions
Desire, idealism, commitment.

As "Mama and Daddy," we kissed tiny fingers
And caressed tender skin. We became a family.

Our joy, our pride
Innocence, energy, challenge.

As professionals, we experienced independence,
Yet support and respect seemed to thrive.

Our responsibilities, our careers
Fatigue, communication, accomplishment.

As parents of young adults, we reflect on life
And wonder at how quickly the years have passed.

Our children, our sons
Attainment, maturity, pride.

As a seasoned couple, we treasure one another
And gain strength and satisfaction from our bond.

Best friends, husband and wife
Love, devotion, fulfillment.

    Diane Bailey

Who Could Be Like A Poet!

Who could be like a poet,
and be able to express his feelings in a poem!
To ease his pain,
To throw away the oppression,
The brutal weight of my affliction,
That so cruelly torments my life.

How many times I have wanted
to open my heart to someone,
To talk heartily,
But as soon as I see
a gesture of doubt, or suspicion,
I have locked my lips, with the key of silence...

And I have thought,
Who could be like a poet,
and express his feelings in a poem!

    Hilda P. Perez

Silent Voices: A Requiem To The Civilians Of Bosnia

They lie there; at the confluence of man's brutish instincts for war and avarice.
  They lie there; caught in a nobelian crossfire, dying without the
    benefit of a farewell kiss or even a hug.
      They lie there; many in mass graves, buried unceremoniously as
        a testament to the inevitable savagery of war.

They lie there; dismembered parts of a previous whole, yearning for
  corporal unity. Hapless victims of the ferocious fury of
  kalashnikovs, ubiquitous mines and mortar shells.
    They are trapped there, innocent losers in the bloody banal
    battles to balkanize the balkans. The silent voices
      beckon to us increasingly loudly to stop the madness...
        But, is anyone listening? Let us listen to the
        loud wails of their tears and the pulsations of
          their aching hearts. Let us discard our cloak
          of indifference to this orgy of
            orgy of annihilation-in-slow-motion.

    Chike Nzerue

A Forever Friend

We met when we were very young,
And always knew right then,
If we worked hard and stood our ground,
We would be forever friends.

Then life did everything it could,
To draw a wedge between us.
We worked very hard, and stood our ground.
We realized we still needed "US."

Then we spent some years apart,
Developing and growing.
Fate saw our path together again,
Fate... it is all knowing,

Our lives were always meant to touch,
And now I truly understand;
Everybody needs to have,
The love of a "Forever Friend!"

Cindy Fraser

Poetry Is...

Poetry is...
An expression of feeling,
A link between reality and make-believe.
A way to show emotions,
A time to feel vulnerable.
Strength, love, weakness,
Anger, infatuation, lust
Bitterness, uncertainty, hate,
Rage, hurt, and frustration.
An escape from the world,
An escape from one's self.
Poetry is life.
Or, is it...
  Life is poetry?

Carrie Anne Schmidt

It's Christmas Time

A church steeple, a cross, blessed quietness,
an evening prayer meeting.
An open bible, good tidings of great joy,
a congregation on bended knee.
Silent night — holy night
a church choir softly singing.
It's Christmas — holy, sacred,
the Christ and beautiful.
— "Christmas" —
For God so loved the world.
A sign given by an angel of the Lord
Grace and Truth — Lamb of light.
Heaven descending to earth
A BABY, a KING, a SAVIOUR
and wonderful!
— It's Christmas time —
EMMANUEL - "God with us"
HEAVEN BORN, PRINCE of PEACE...

Harold R. Carlson

Toast

Here's to you, my love, he uttered next
And gladly took the glass she offerèd.
She gazed at him serenely, quite unvexed,
And saw in him that same look mirrorèd.
Oh surely he had seen the deadly dust
Administered by dainty fingertips.
Yet loved he her 'til diamonds turn to rust,
So raised he then the glass unto his lips.
Looked deeply he into her fiery eye
and thought *oh, what a lovely way to die.*

Erica Michelle James

The Old Piano

Etudes and scales are such a bore,
An eight-year-old trying to learn a score.
A teacher beside me I really dislike,
Oh, how I wish she would just take a hike.
A slap on the wrist 'cause I play a wrong note,
Such a waste of money, it will all come to naught.
Now my teacher has gone, gone away with the years,
I remember her guidance, I paid with some tears.
Innocent youth, not knowing the values of teaching,
Until we are grown, we appreciate its meaning.
We cannot go back except in Nostalgia,
Old precious times we try to recapture,
With a retentive mind and a desire to play,
How I wish I could thank my teacher today,
'Cause I've a lovely new piano, Beethoven I play.
My strict tutor in her wisdom said, "Lessons never end."
I realize now my old piano teacher was a friend.

Goldie Carlova

Angelene

Nestled close to heaven, a house of wood and stone
An Appalachian woman, her name was Angelene
Tending to her garden, a seedling yet ungrown
A love so everlasting, like some unanswered dream

A precious, little darling, denied her time to play
She never was considered her parents' pride and joy
For they disguised their caring with selfishness and shame
Acceptance was the only only child's choice

One day a young adult knelt down beside two graves
She wished if only love could be just like a bird
Gliding in the wind and flying unafraid
To nestle in the clouds of love so well-deserved

A house of ash and pebble, and high above with wings
An Appalachian angel, her name is Angelene

Joseph M. Forgacs

Thank You Lord For Randall

Thank you Lord for sending me joy,
An angel disguised as a red haired boy.
You made him perfect in every way,
For this I thank you Lord every day.
In my darkest hour he was my light,
For this I thank you Lord every night.
For sixteen years he filled life with joy,
This angel disguised as a red haired boy.
Thank you Lord for those wonderful years,
Just knowing him was worth all the tears.
Lord I miss him so very much,
His beautiful smile and tender touch.
I love him Lord but you love him more,
Thank you for welcoming him at your door.
Thank you Lord for sending me joy,
An angel disguised as a red haired boy.
Amen.

Dorothy F. Peterson

Alone With Me

I'm in New Jersey, and I've made new friends, but I am
alone with me.
It's a big city, and crowded here, but I am
alone with me.
I have friends at the gym, and work, and school, still
I am alone with me.
Coming from the south, I am not the same, I can't fit in, that's
why I am alone with me.
Florida is my home, that's were I belong, and until I go
back, I will be alone with me.

Dawn Lynn Cline

Your Flittering Blues Eyes

Amigo Mio, don't be afraid to have your look of glittering's for me.
Amigo Mio, because glittering's in your eyes are beautifuls.
Amigo Mio, because looking at you, I see things with you in joy!
Amigo Mio, may your glittering's blues eyes, shine through me.
Amigo Mio, your glittering's blues eyes, turn my thoughts always in you.
Amigo Mio, in your glittering's blues eyes, I see a grateful heart!
Amigo Mio, in your glittering's blues eyes, you have: Courage and wisdom,
Amigo Mio, in your glittering's blues eyes, I see a wonderfulness of you,
Amigo Mio, in your glittering's blues eyes, I see love and patience.
Amigo Mio, in your glittering's blues eyes, be yourself as you are,
Amigo Mio, in your glittering's blues eyes, I can see your sensitive's,
Amigo Mio, may our hearts, have glittering's, always to Each others!

Dolores Maria Bolivar-Brauet

My Father

A carpenter skilled in his labor
Always helpful to his neighbor
Loving, caring, courteous father
His children are never a bother
He always has time for them,
And they can share their problems with him.
He'll give you his last dollar
And sometimes he can really scream and holler
A man of strength.
With an imagination of great length
He drives a big truck
And he likes to make an honest buck.
He likes to tell a good joke
And listen to stories from old folk.
He likes to have a good time.
And rarely has an extra dime.
Whether it be using a power saw,
Or swinging a big maul
There's nothing he can't do,
And you'd like him too.

James Beatty

Things

There are things that words cannot express,
  although you are unduly impressed.

There are things you know should be done,
  but where does the inspiration come from?

There are thing that are not meant to be.

Who is to be the judge of such things as these?

There are things that can disappoint,
  as well as serve as inspiration to the higher point.

There are things that cannot be explained,
  such as, why don't things happen as ordained.

There are things that bring only peace and quiet.

Of these, I am quite sure, as I have found them abiding
  in the Church of God, where only peace and quiet reigns.

Barbara McFall

For This Is The Cup Of My Blood....

It was offered to me as a cup of salvation, a representation of acceptance.
But I could not accept nor could I deny for I had no words.
As I knelt boiling in my shame, trying to make peace with the decision
I had just made. The air quickly dried the path from where my tear came.
And it was presented to me, the answer, an alternative for which I can accept.
With speech not, I took from it and from it received freedom and from
freedom I received peace and from peace I gained acceptance.
With my brain as my sword and my heart as my shield I need not shudder
behind my tongue. For the way may not seem clear, but if I continue
along the path I shall not be lost.

Jason Whittier

Ice-Cream

You're my ice-cream, I was fourteen
Although I couldn't afford it you gave me a cornet

I was licking it up right in front of you
I would have swallowed it whole if you had asked me to

You're my ice-cream, I was new on the scene
I blushed at your prices but I tasted all your ices

I jumped in your van with my school bag and tie
Some strawberry sauce and a flake in your eye

Climbing the hill waiting for the sound of the bell
Climbing the hill waiting for the sound of the bell
Climbing the hill waiting for the sound of the bell
Climbing the hill waiting for the sound of the bell

You're my ice-cream, my double-scoop dream
Oranges and lemons that send me to heaven

And I never paid for a single whip
Including the screwball-mint-choc-chip

You're my ice-cream, I was fourteen
Remember the polythene, you're my ice-cream

Joseph Rye

Thus Saith The Lord

I've sat on the mountain top
alone with the birds.
I've sat in on court hearings
and heard others prayers; every word.
On my throne I sit all alone,
at the same time I visit everyone's home.
  I AM OMNIPRESENT!

I know about crime, I know about war,
I know about the obstacles behind every door.
I know the truth, I even know the lies.
Everything that exist, I made, and I know why.
  I AM OMNISCIENT!

I am the beginning as well as the end.
I am your savior, your salvation,
As well as your friend.
I am everywhere at one time
and all knowledge is mine.
  I AM OMNIPOTENT!

  ....Thus Saith The Lord
Gregory L. Clark Sr.

Waiting

Alone at night I wait for you.
Alone at night with the air so true.
All is silent and all is calm.
When from the forest I hear a song.
A song that is silent but rich in tone.
A song that is chilling right to the bone.
As I try to figure out the bird that sings,
While listening to the melody it brings,
It reminds me of the better times.
It reminds me of a churches chimes.
Now the bird that sung now sings no more.
Which makes me feel so sad and poor.
So now I must wait and wait I will do.
I'm sitting here waiting, waiting for you.

Catherine DeJohn

Growing Older

The years so swiftly have passed by
Almost in the blink of an eye.

Joys were many, sorrows too
With family and friends-
TOGETHER
We'll make it through.

Our steps are slower, our knees don't bend
We just can't do it, no need to pretend.

Our eyesight is dimming, can't see as well,
Are we complaining? If we are, please don't tell.

Life is still sweet as the years roll by
How often we think of our home in the sky.

We dream of a place with silver and gold
We just can't admit that we're growing old.

To all of our loved ones as we bid them adieu
Life has been good, hope it's good to you.

And as we slowly hobble on our way
We silently wish for just one more day!

Cleopha Homan Link

Our Cat

You are our family pet
All you do is lay or set
Your comfortable in our home, and eating
our table scraps
When there are no table scraps
You'll eat dry cat food perhaps
Your a good friend to have around
You seldom make a sound
Now and then you get the run of the house
If you had to, could you catch a mouse?
How lucky you are to have such a life of ease
When you get comfy cozy
Your thoughts to everyone are stay away please.

Janice Weber

Memories Of Yesteryear

Out on the hilltop
  All weathered and bleak
Stands an old sheep wagon
  The symbol of sheep.

The old canvas roof flaps in the wind
  The bows look up at the stars
There's holes in the floor the tongue is a wreck
And the wheels will turn nevermore.

From where I now sit all wrinkled and gray
Fond memories return of yesterday
  I can still hear the bleating
On the evening bed ground
  There's no duplicating that musical sound.

Melancholy by sunshine lugubrious by rain
She withstood the droughts,
  The blizzards, misuse and strains
You could see her white cover for many a mile
And the comforts she offered brought many a smile.

Now that we're both battered we're old and we're gray
I want to rebuild her as she was yesterday.

Bill Norton

For Your Love

Cathi, since the first moment you were our baby girl
All we wanted, was to show our love, and care for you
To give you happiness, and you share your life with us
Having you to love us wholly, with a devotion and true
In a way, that we can always bond a wholehearted trust

Causes for your unwarranted outlook on life today
Has hurt us deeply as surely as you hurt, but we know
Everything will be done we can, to get it back again
Leaving no doubt for you, and because we want to show
Causes for you, a new life in your heart and your hand

Only you have the power to talk to and make your mind
Make these decisions, for the good of your livelihood
Ever to ease your mind and heart, so you have not to dare
Hoping these words have helped you to know, that we would
Ever be aware we love you, we want us united, and we care

Places like where you are, are not for the likes of you
Look around you, and think about the wonderment of the why
Even realize at the same time, this doesn't have to be
Assure yourself of our love for you, and for yours we cry
Ever again, we love you, miss you, and want you by our side

Jimmy Lee

A Mother's Love

So much love, so much joy,
All this and more for my little boy.
  Love began from the start,
Upon site it filled my heart.
  Everyday he'll do something new,
Oh how fast those days flew.
  There will be laughter, there will be tears,
So many memories to fill all the years.
  Take pictures, take notes so not to forget,
For life is so short, no room for regret.
  One day just a boy, then he's a man,
Hopes and dreams from mom, he'll be all he can.
  So much love, so much joy,
All this and more from my little boy.

Debra J. De Jesus

Insanity

My mind screams in the darkest night, a scream so cold and dark;
All the fears begin to creep in; hell leaves its evil mark.

Reality begins to fade my mind tries to hold on;
My mind screams in agony but all sanity is gone.

The world begins to twist and turn, the light is turning dim;
I can feel the darkness coming I cry out unto them.

Sounds are bleeding into my head, won't this noise ever end?
The darkness is coming closer, the darkness is my friend

I am a stranger to myself the thoughts have all faded
This world begins to appear, this world I created.

The pain seem to be seeping in, why won't it go away?
I want to unleash the pain; I will make this world pay.

My life starts to fade away, reality moves on;
The ending is becoming closer, all existence is gone.

Jeremy A. Pack

Friendship

A friend sees you through good times and bad.
A friend will hug, kiss, share, laugh and cry with you,
  usually picking the right time to say and do the right thing.
You can be yourself when you're with a friend.
Friends can love each other freely and with confidence.
A good friendship should never be taken lightly or for granted
  because it is truly a gift from God.

Frankie Kober

Heaven's Claim

Red roses, gifts I have given
Alive they are, for those unliving
These long few stems, I tend with care
Gates have opened, in heaven is where

As the rain falls, I sense his tears
To die alone, so young in years
His life so full, of jest and toil
Three roses I lay, upon his soil

Two steps I take, familiar name of stone
To lose another, a child I have known
A disease so strange, pilfered a face
Few prayers I read, more roses I place

Four steps I take, an empty grave
One rose left, I dared to save
I hope they are placed, my roses with care
The gates reopened, in heaven, I'm there!

Jennie Santiago

Farewell Brother

Across arid deserts or the Great Plains
Across the oceans or e'en - sugar canes
He'd journeyed on ward forever more
Until he'd reached that Heavenly shore.
Amid GOD's forests and peaks unknown
And through vast wasteland, overgrown
To the spots he'd never been before
In his journey to that Heavenly shore.
Across the expanse of the Sierra Nevada
To hear shrill music of the Cicada
To the Odd Fellow Temple with its open door
Where he lingered e'er reaching Heaven's Shore.
For life itself - is a journey complete
Before he could reach his Heavenly Seat
And his travels rambled from shore to shore
E'er he'd made it unto that Heavenly door.
FAREWELL - DEAR BROTHER - adios to you
Until we all meet again - up there too
We shall miss you greatly, and will evermore
AS YOU REST IN PEACE UPON HIS HEAVENLY SHORE...

Elma M. Rasor

Peace In The Valley

It was twilight when five browsing deer slowly made their way
across the field to the kidney shape pond. A gray wolf was
drinking from the pond. He quenched his thirst and then moved
on. A chipmunk and a squirrel scampered along the ground,
each animal intent on the mission it was on.

Alyce M. Nielson

The Lonely Soul

The wind was blowing a bitter breeze
Across the barren plain.
All life was still, as time stood still,
Except for one lonely soul.

No one knew who the stranger was,
Or did they dare to ask.
For there was a darkness around him
That no one would approach.
Only one man knew who he was,
And his reasons for being there.
He knew he was death,
And his time had come,
To become part of that barren plain.
He was not scarred to go with him
For now there would be peace within.

Deborah Pike

A Mother's Test

I peeked into my daughter's room,
across my face swept clouds of gloom.
What has happened? What took place?
A look of anguish crossed my face.

Clothes strewn all over, the bed unmade,
the pillow with a dent in it where her head had laid.

"Don't get excited", says she, "it'll be tidied up in a jiffy!"

Several hours later I again mount the stairs.
Opening her door, I'm caught unawares.

There is it before me, the same old mess.
These are the trials of bringing up daughter, I guess.

What can we do, we mothers all?
Shall we close our eyes or maybe bawl?
Or berate our daughters and punish them too?
Would that be better than to sit and stew?

I guess we should recall when we were that age,
when our mothers had to go through our "growing up" stage.

So cheer up you mothers, please don't fret.
Our little gal will grow up yet!

Janet Erickson

Retrospect

The gentle dusk of twilight is a stole
About the lovely shoulders of the coming night
A mood in which the facets of the day
Reviewed will make the record seem more bright

Perhaps the parting with a loved and cherished one
Still lingers with a touch of sadness still
Much better than the page be marred and dark
With anger strife or hurt that will not heal

Like bright and gleaning wings of butterflies
the treasures tones will linger that is past
the darker shadows slip so fast away
Like clouds on sunny days that do not last.

And when the whole is blended we will see.
a tracing of the pattern and our part
the hours that only once is ours to fill.
With which to be content or sad of heart.

Gladys M. Little

"The Drum - Major"

M artin sits on the throne of martyrdom
A rticulate spokesman for the masses
R eflective beacon of twenty-two million
T ried, tested among all classes
I nspiration to evoke the shining truth
N ever will that spirit be extinguished
   (How long will it take?)
L ove, peace, justice cried the drum-major
U nite black and white or perish
T he moment of truth is fast approaching
H eed to the fact that the fate of one man
E ventually becomes the fate of all men
R eaching all race, color and ideology
   (How long will it take?)
K ing, Kennedy, Evers and the Forgotten Four
I nside our collective conscience we implore
N o more deeds of infamy can this nation endure
G one to the promised land, free at last!
   FREE AT LAST!!
   (How long will it take?)

James Bynoe

Reflections Of A Child

A mother is a flower hidden among the trees
A wonder to behold like the wind upon the sea.

The softness of her touch upon a child's head
The strength of her love when the child's feeling sad.

The beauty shining from her eyes as she looks upon her own
The wonder of her love as the child matures and grows.

A Mother is the harbour in the stormy sea of life
A place to put our heads and hearts when overcome by strife.

Always there to shelter us, to lift us up with love
Always there to counsel us, the hand within the glove.

We look to our Mother as the flower to the sun
With worship and love to warm us in life just begun.

We look to our Mother as a friend in mid-life
To walk beside, laugh and share, as a daughter, a mother, a wife.

The Mother (once a flower) feeling low; now in need
The Child (once a seedling) now is strong as the tree.

Now it is our turn to comfort and to hold
The parent held so dear to us, our strength must be bold.

The strength and love sowed within us so very long ago
Now matured and ready to share — with a Mother feeling low.

Clara J. Wilson McVay

The Wanderers

It could be called insanity—the way I am drawn to you.
A Wandering moon attracted to your orbit,
Your magnetic force pulling me closer, against my resistance.

As your insistence grows stronger, the more I hold back;
A rubber band stretching to its elastic limit,
The potential to snap at any slight provocation.

I should feel violated by your assumptions, but instead
I am compelled by you; your intoxicating stare,
It burns through my facade, burns through my game.
Your hollow laugh taunts me; empty of emotions,
Pregnant with desires that are not your own.

I roam the narrow path between obsession and repulsion.
You keep me at odds with your erotic voice and flippant words.
Daring me with your movements, revolting me with your actions.
My fixation increases with every breath; whether to abhor or adore.

I know not which to follow, so I choose the trail of the Wanderer.
I will walk the delicate line between adornment and aversion for Eternity.

I know that you will follow my path. You are a Wanderer, too.

Angel Filip

Traveler

  Life, has been
a very wide road for me. I've been to places
that, I'll never see.

  Gone down streets
that meet me. Shaking hands with enemies. Smelled
flowers that will never bloom, taste water that I
didn't drink.

  Dream while I
was awake. Slept, as I stood in lines. Dance
with-out music.

  (Just traveling)
  Held adults...that...
once were babies. Flew; and it wasn't on Delta.
Prayed, and I wasn't saved. Laugh with-out the
wine. Looked in eyes that are now closed.
Had you traveled any of these roads before? Then...welcome back.

John D. Freeman

His Dream

Swirling wind of satin black,
  a velvet touch across the back.
Two who bathe in silver dust,
  will join this eve in love and lust.
Eternal starlight acts a shield,
  by lover's kiss the scar is healed
From long remembered parallel,
  when wary heart had tasted Hell.
Tortured soul, besieged through time,
  one moment free from guilt sublime.
Heart for heart, soul for soul,
  the pain is fading far below.
Flesh will yield to pleasures craved
  through yearning fire the spirit saved.
A perfect orb will rule this night,
  fiercely burning pale blue light,
upon the two who stand alone
  beneath its jeweled nocturnal throne.
Night will hold here evermore,
  and they will soar the moonswept shore.

Jessica Johnston

"A Simple Thing Called Love"

A touch that is tender, tender and light.
A touch that is tender, indestructible with might.
Eyes that have the sparkle,
of a fresh morning stream.
Lips of softness and loving delight.
A smile exasperating as a summer's night dream.
A thought to share, never asking to care.
Feelings of happiness and that of togetherness.
The bearing of children and loving them always.
Those hard and good times,
and memories that amaze.
So share with someone, with God's kindness, the things above.
Then you will soon learn how great and magnificent,
is that simple thing called love.

Henry Glass

Depression

A state of anxiety, with twisted and distorted feelings of fear.
A time of distance and despair, that seems to stand still.
It is as if a dark hole has opened and swallowed the hope of life.
Thoughts and memories seem to puncture the heart like a spear.
Allowing life to pour out of the body quickly and painfully.
A time when loneliness, takes over life like a disease and
swallows the soul into darkness.

Depression sneaks up on you slowly, but attacks the central nerve
and takes the body captive and leaves little time for a contemplated plan.

Depression is a disease that eats up the life that we have or
(once knew). Because we have lost the key to unlock the freedom
that exist to shut out the deadly disease that seeks to take over
the soul and kill the body.

Gina A. Whitacre

Goin' Nowhere

I' gonna dilly-dally all day long,
A-rockin' in my chair, singin' a song,
The dog's a-barkin' but I do not care,
Sittin', a-rockin' I'm goin' nowhere!
Looked out my window and what did I see?
An old bird-feeder and a cedar tree.
The phone's a-ringin' but I won't get up;
My rhythm rockin' I won't interrupt,
Someone's a-knockin'; just let 'em stand there,
I'll sit here a-rockin' — goin' nowhere!

Dana Elizabeth Orchard

Inside Me

Inside me there is a place of quiet calm,
a sweet retreat where there is balm.

Amidst the memories of time
a place refreshing and sublime.

It is my place of quick escape
with no long lines or cause to wait.

Quite suddenly I take me there
and breathe the freedom in the air.

Behold, such bounty from which to draw!
my senses are enthralled, in awe.

I touch the beauty all around
and tune me in to each small sound.

There are soothing whispers of content
and joyous laughter being sent.

I drift among the smiling faces
and there reclaim the warm embraces.

There wafts a fragrance in the air;
it seems to come from everywhere.

I seldom find I am alone
when to my secret place I roam.

Carolyn Gilbert

Rock And World Collecting

From out of me, suddenly, up welled
a splattered belch of boulders fell
irregular rocks, word patterns dropped
from out my heavy mind, I unwind.
Taming my irregular. I find
the jagged shapes of my shattered images.

Irregular white gray boulders crashed
into a rich green field to rocky grass.
Black letters on a white page? Are these
red, cracked pink, gray rough rocks; colorless?
Dirt brown does camouflage the gaudiness
of alpha quartz and quirky feldspar.

My thoughts are also filled with color.
My bones are well, my mind a stutter.
My ragged lines reflect my utter
need to express my feelings thus.
As an old man of poetry, I must reject
I don't understand the current feel good mess.

Joseph M. Donatelli

Depression

It has come to obscure all joy,
A smile is the most difficult task.
It surrounds me like a cloak.
A pegasus come to take me away,
Where we fly nobody knows.
No - I am not angry,
No - I am not sad.
Joy has simply been blocked out,
As clouds catch the sunlight.
Alone - with thoughts that mar the soul.
Happiness is not wanted,
To be punished and harmed is what I deserve.
We are flying through the night sky.
No moon, no stars, no light reaches us,
We fly into darkness.
I am wrapped in the dark cloak.
Smiles live in a far away land.
Everything is black.
It has come to take me away.

Beth Ann Frechette

"Fleeting Moments"

I dream of beauty I have seen!
A single flower in a sea of green,
A wispy cloud against a sky of blue,
A blade of grass weighed down by drops of morning dew.
A baby robin perched upon a tree,
A massive wave upon an angry sea,
A whole town blanketed by snow
Beneath a dreary sky that hides the sun's warm glow.
Ice covered trees that sparkle in the light
Like countless diamonds - what a sight!
The lightning flash with thunder's roar,
The drenching rain on sea and shore,
The crescent moon, the stars so bright,
A soaring eagle on its upward flight.
The snow capped peaks, the waterfall,
A lonesome pine, so straight and tall.
The shimmering rainbow though it quickly fades,
Brings hope anew to a world that waits
For daily wonders that bring such pleasure
To those who care to truly treasure.

Johanna Haug

Why Me?

Awakened eyes surface on a face drowned in sleep,
A shrill alarm whines into deaf ears,
A hand gropes into the darkness to slap the lighted "snooze",
A time card has been punched on another endless day...

Students jump into their beetles and race to get stuck in traffic,
Scarcely a parking spot is available in an empty parking structure,
Speeding to the bookstore; prices gouge gold from penniless students,
School is a fun place...

The 5 o'clock whistle blows on a clock with no hands,
The students retire once more from a formal place with no names,
The assignment of would be classes become regurgitated with ink,
To home before the rising sun sets on lamp lit paths...

Back in beetles students blast through gridlock bi-ways; but
Before long drowsiness overcomes whiles I bed and the stop watch is
    reset on a never ending rut.

Dave Shun

'Skippy Was First'

A hearing dog can happily give
A profoundly deaf child a good life to live.

Our "Skippy", the prototype hearing dog,
Helped bring our Linda from a silent fog.

The telephone, and the doorbell, too,
Were no longer ignored, as soon as she knew

Her world was filled with many new things—
Love and beauty and songs to sing,

Words and sounds and barks of joy,
Even a pretty musical toy!

The love, protection and self-confidence
Were gifts gladly given by this dog immense,

For sense, scents, cents, and play,
Are part of a hearing dog's every day.

No wonder when God planned
To name this friend,

His own name, spelled backwards,
He chose to send.

Helen J. Prichard

473

A Piece Of Paper...

A piece of paper is strong in that it can speak your feelings,
A piece of paper is weak in that is cab easily be crumpled or torn,
But if like a piece of paper our marriage is crumpled in careless hands;
Together we shall iron it out...
And if like a piece of paper our marriage is torn in two;
Together we shall it back together.
A piece of paper is strong in that in can declare many different thoughts,
A piece of paper is weak in that its words can be faded and it
can discolor and become brittle over time,
But if like the words on a piece of paper our love becomes discolored
by lies and deceit;
Together we shall whiten it with bleach...
And if like a piece of paper our love becomes brittle from illness
and hard times;
Together we will have learned to handle it with the care required
to make it last for always...
Our love and our marriage is in this way like a piece of paper.

Dawn M. Jaqua

A Little While

He ran to me around age three, his blonde hair was a flying.
A memory had returned to him, to tell me he was trying,

As I listened to the words he said, so wise for one so small.
He said one day as the angles played, he heard his Jesus call.

His Jesus ask if he would come and fill my life with joy
His tiny wings, he gave up then to be my little boy.

He said ok, that he would try, for just a little while.
I wondered at his story, and now remember with a smile.

At nine he came to know the Lord, he gave his heart forever
As quickly days turned into years, as he made our lives much better.

He was all boy, as we all knew, and a friend to all who needed.
He silently waited for the call, his time almost depleted.

Then in the twinkling of a eye, Jesus called him home.
His angel wings are now replaced, as he sits near God's great throne.

He stayed his time, and brightened our lives
His little while completed.

Ada Lynn Kirk

The Old House

That old house stood amid the yard.
A massive farm, watching; on guard.

Its beams were rotting under the ground.
Upstairs, in rooms, treasures were found.

Under the flooring and out of sight,
paper dolls found, with much delight!

They belonged to an age out of the past.
Still mom's and Kit's-but found at last.

In the cellar made dry and warm long ago,
a shoe-form found; whose we don't know.

There are smells familiar only to there
  (and old places).
To remember them now puts smiles
  or our faces!

We'll always remember the times we spent there-
when we pass by that spot that is now so bare.

Brenda Campbell

Nostalgia

There is a longing inside me,
A longing I cannot repress,
A feeling of melancholy has lodged itself in my breast.
The shrill sharp cry of a seagull beckons my thoughts to review
a panorama of pictures from a childhood I once knew.
In my mind's eye I see meadows, strewn with flowers of white, lilac
and gold, nodding as if to greet me, a chorus of a thousand fold.
I see the blooming heather, a royal purple hue,
covering sand dunes in patches
where the white sand glimmers through.
Now the cries of the seagull are fading.
A soft shadow covers my view
and within my heart there is gladness,
for the childhood made anew.

Johanna R. Warren

The Past

As I look in the mirror I'm starting to see.
A lonely sad face looking at me.

The past all before me, I see in my face.
All the hurting memories that time won't erase.

The past steals the present, pain fills my heart.
While all of these memories refuse to depart.

A prisoner of yesterday, locked in the past.
How long before my heart will free itself at last?

For only by seeking new love will I find.
The power to erase these thoughts from my mind.

As I look in the mirror I'm starting to see.
It's time to let go, It's time to be free.

Daniel Gerkin

A Look Into Myself

I look into myself and find,
a little girl with peace of mind,
hopes and dreams, ideas galore,
leaving fulfilled, wanting nothing more.

I look into myself and find,
family and friends so good and kind,
a group of friends who like me for me,
and a loving bunch of family.

I look into myself and find,
my childhood years going far behind,
from the age of a toddler I'm now growing old,
growing more independent, outspoken, and bold.

I look into my heart and find,
a love so deep, a love so blind,
love for music and learning, and many more things,
love my God, my friends, and my family brings.

I look into my life and find,
a little girl with peace of mind.

Janelle Cotter

A Star

I think I know how a star must feel...
A cauldron of light and heat,
Flames shooting exultant streaks
Against the blackness of space.

And yet, some being on a distant planet,
Stopping to contemplate the night,
Will say, "What a bright and lovely star.
How cold and lonely is its light."

And....he may be right.

Jo Ann Duchesneau

474

A Golden Circle

The ring bends around the finger,
A golden, shimmering circle of trust.
There, forever, it will linger
To mark the commitment and thrust
Of the meaning of "two as one."
And with strong, spirit-filled wings,
Fly around the sun
To share our lives and all beautiful things.
   The ring forever.
   The promise is clear.
   The love, how clever!
   Means God is near.
     James H. Harper

Gnarled Pine

Standing on the mountain side I see
a gnarled and lonely old pine tree,
looking down on the valley below
watching the people come and go.

How long have you been standing
there on the rocky ground so lonely
and bare. As you stand alone on your
perch so high, has time and worry passed
you by.
I often come by light of day to
watch the birds and squirrels play, and
smell the fragrance of the pine, in
a lonely solitude that is mine.
     Herbert W. Funk

Lord Ned

Along the shores of KyJaVee, beside the Sacred Indigo Sea,
a frigid williwaw blows down from the Mountains of Jabah,
and dark vapors swirl in restless flight.

Beneath the haloed Virgin Three Moon Sisters of the Night,
a jagged bolt of pyrolight ignites the darkness,
and the rumbling of thunder-trills rolls through the distant hills.

There, upon the star-raked bluffs, overlooking the sacred sea,
beneath the phosphorous sister moons at their points of perigee,
the great Lord Ned did vow to wed and bed the sisters three.

"Oh, great Lord, 'tis voodoo," Ned's wise men all implored. "The
virgins do bewitch thee. Oh, Lord 'tis plain to see. Thou cannot
love. Thou cannot wed. Thou cannot bed the sisters three. We state
it most emphatically: 'tis an impossibility."
But, Lord Ned did not agree. Such talk just made him angry.

So, for ninety years Ned struggled
—by the second, by the minute, by the hour—
to construct a crystal tower that would reach the sisters three.
But, the task was far beyond the great Lord's frail ability.

And, eventually, he failed, as his wise men did foresee.
And the crystal tower collapsed and was covered by the sea.
And the great Lord Ned died alone in his bed moonstruck by lunacy.
     John Weldon Wood Jr.

A Natural Born Leader Reece

More than merely ambition, or
A desire to get ahead... there was
The ever-unsettling recognition of
An unclaimed furtherance within
His soul; there were lights
To shine, but only with reasons - and
only eventually would there be claim!
He thought to know, without fully
Knowing, of all that possibly there could be
Only a little farther on...
Up there, just ahead.
     Canadia Collins

Beat The Drums Slowly

Beat the drums slowly, and lowly with love.
A dear soul has gone to his home far above.
Bravely he fought, still more gallant he died.
Defending his country with honor and pride.

The flag-covered coffin, a loved one enshrouds,
So beat the drums slowly, and keep your heads bowed
A riderless horse plods despondently slow,
Empty boots in the saddle, as onward the goes.

A Master, no longer to guide the loose rein;
No one in the saddle to pat the short mane.
Beat the drums slowly and lowly with tears,
For the weary young soldier who died without fear.

Beyond line of duty and love for another,
He gave his own life, to save a black brother.
Now God in His heaven has welcomed him home...
So beat the drums slowly, while lonely hearts moan.
     Dorothy A. McLachlan

Valentine's Day

A special day, a loving day
A day when roses bloom
A peaceful day
A day when hate and sorrow is forgotten
Love and joy remembered
The heart a symbol resembling a shield
To protect us from evil
But what Valentine's Day really means
Is to learn to follow in Jesus's path
To know love and to be a servant to one another
As peace reigns in the heart.
     Gregory C. Garritani

Morro Bay

The gulls woke us in the morning and sang all day.
A cup of coffee warmed our chill away.
The mist was more magical than words could say.
The fog lifting from the water took our breath away,
as we watched from a dock on Morro Bay.

A man and his dog strolled the pier until they faded to gray.
The birds inspected each vessel for the catch of the day.
Surfers were up early to catch the big wave.
The rocks extended so high that we were amazed,
as we walked on the peninsula at Morro Bay.

Boat captains sail out to sea and catch fish for their pay.
They harmonize with the sights and sounds of nature at play.
The sun and the stars and the moon provide the perfect array.
But we have so far to go that we can no longer delay.
I kick a stone and walk away,
as we look back and fall to our knees and pray.

Thank You Lord for this place called Morro Bay.
     James V. McGowan

Things That Are Nothing Without The Other

A flower without rain
A caboose without a train
A well without water
A teeter without a totter
A bell without a ring
A bird that doesn't sing
A desert without sand
A women without a good man
A clam without a shell
And you the woman I love to keep me well.
     Alex Chesragi

A Salute To Mayou

I rise to great thee, a curtsey or a hug, if I may
A chosen one propounded by, the vibrant words you say

A gift from God, to tell of your, prose of life
Some spirited established of slavery past and the livelihood of strife
But it, is God who gives and the balancer, of all our life

Though, somewhat like Jeremiah, who open not his mouth
But, oh! What joy that God can give in the temple, of his house
It was levy high, one morning, on the pulse, of the president prose
He gave you a gift, to lift the spirit of all the people souls

You have the lights of God that can draw
One from, one step, to another and for the better
He has shown what a black woman can do
Indeed the blessings was in the united states president letter

He guided moses when he protested and God knew his speech was lame
He knows all our problems, he loves all his children, no color, the same
Extras, extra, extra read all about, her pronounced fame
Hear, hear, hear what God and the U.S.A. president proclaimed

On the pulse, of God blessings and in your very soul
You are his star and the adornments of your poems unfold
He open your mouth and blessed your heart; your prose and poems are told.

Cleator Rose Clay

Zachary

Zachary Thomas Delph
A child less long than his name
Kitten soft- wee and pink
A perfect, but miniature man.

Zachary
Arms flying- feet kicking
Bird mouth, frantic and searching
mercurial moods- wondering eyes
Intense, knit brow- Mysterious words- Lightning smile.

Zachary
Brand new-Wondrous creation
Parents' treasure-Grandparents' delight
Bundle of mystery- of love, hope and promise

Zachary
Sculpted by God.

Alice DeRossi

Stalemate

The days bend up and down
a calloused see saw ride,
tip-tip
pictures,
reflections of things too obscure to be deemed important.
Ornery and undetected,
our effort passes just out of sight under us,
making only its feeling known.
Calm and brutish, give all to me.
I want the strain on my back,
weakness in my knees,
ache in my head.
I'll accept you and promise to be faithful;
After all
I let you give me no choice.

Joseph Lamperez

Trix And RC

He angled across the street in front of me:
A box of Trix cradled in his left arm
A can of RC dangling from the hand of his right.
His clothes, a bright red sweater and dark slacks, were worn.
The cuff of his left sock hung like a mud flap over his left heel.
He walked with determination - gaze straight ahead.
For some reason he caught my attention.
Days later I recall the moment.
Where is God for him?
Where is God for me?
The two of us - nameless to each other - crossed paths on a September Day.
I remember the moment.
God is such as experience.

Donna M. Williams

The Sword

Its edge is strong, long, and sharp
a blade for a warrior, it quickens the heart
a weapon of power, a symbol of faith
steel finger of fire, cold talisman of strength
there's a soul held inside, forged deep in its heart
a blood hungry demon, thirsts, to tear things apart
It has no real master, knows no true friend
it has but one passion, to murder and rend

But a man's passion stirs, behold the naked blade
a hand grasps the hilt, richly engraved
the thrill of cold steel, held tight in ones grasp
brings visions of battles, and yanks forth a gasp

Though men of true courage, whose hearts hold no hate
have picked up the sword, and made themselves great
the sword cares not whose blood it may drink
and will fight for a good man, or strike down a saint

The evils men do to further their wage
cause the sword to behave in one of two ways
to further the cause of evil rewards
or to stop the world evils in the name of the Lord

Eugene G. McDaniel

God's Garden

The rose that smells so sweet and mild
A babbling brook that just runs wild.
Birds that sing as they fly in the air
Little animals that don't seem to care.
Living in God's garden.

Trees that stand so straight and tall
Bearing the seasons spring, summer, winter and fall.
The sun that shines to warm the day
Autumn winds blowing falling leaves away.
Living in God's garden.

Stars that come out to brighten the sky
Meteorites that just go zipping by.
The moon that shines so big and bright
Clouds that roll completely out of sight.
Living in God's garden.

I close my eyes and I can see
This beautiful garden where I'd like to be.
When my time here on earth is done
Maybe I will be a lucky one.
Living in God's garden.

Florence B. Green

One Great Weekend

One great weekend in the Month of May
5 of our Grandchildren came to stay
a couple of nights and a couple of days
it was so much fun in so many ways

They sing and they dance and on Roller Blades skate
All through the park and out through the gate,
Down to the creek and toss in some rocks,
Check out the new little covey of ducks.

Cory, Kyle, Lindsay and Meghan and Sven
They made Grandma feel "almost" young again.
Thank goodness for McDonald's, they make things so right
We all had time for fun so we slept good at night.

Curl up on the floor or in a big cozy chair
As long as Grandpa and Grandma are there you can sleep anywhere.
We all watched the Lion King 2 or 3 times.
What a glorious movie, fits our grandchildren fine.

When the weekend was over and I took the kids home
I wrote a note to my sons and to the kids moms.
I told them how good their children had been,
and that anytime they'd let me I'd keep them again.

June Crafton

So I Dance

Ready to give up my love. So I dance. Let me show you what love does.
You pass up the chance. The night begins to fall. So I dance. Still,
your expression says to hell with it all. You dared to even take a
glance. I can feel you calling out to me. So I dance. I can sense
the love you truly need. Again, you pass up the chance. To me, lust
and the need exist. So I dance. The self-mission is to be the giver
of bliss. Selfishly, you close your eyes. So I dance. It created
distance in disguise. Watching you pretending not to watch me look.
So I dance. A link to reality like an open book. Willing and able
debuts at last. So I dance. I take you back to innocence. Your body
shivers at the thought of our first dance. I just want to feel your
rhythm. So I dance. You realize you have nothing to lose. Unity of
minds leap for the chance. All was needed was one touch of my hand.
So I dance. The touch had come and gone before you could get a clear
glance. You become a victim of change again. So I dance. Accept the
challenge with texture, soul, and more importantly, substance. It
had already happened in another life. So I dance. Like before, about
lust and needs, I lied. Besides, love doesn't know how to turn around.
So I dance. This dream woman that I found never would've given me
the chance. What's left for me is to either dance or die. No need to
question why. Dance or say good-bye. So I dance.

Eric L. Crisp

Hand In Hand

Isn't it funny how worried we were, when you first started school.
You marched through those doors, sat yourself down, you were ready to rule.
As the years passed by, we watched you grow and your mind consumed
    much knowledge.
Isn't it funny how worried we are, now that you are off to college.

We know in our hearts, you will do just fine in whatever you choose to do.
But, if times get tough and you need a friend, we will always be here for you.
We love you son, you've made us proud, as you've grown into a fine
    young man.
Always remember, if times get tough, reach out we will grasp your hand

Off you go with our blessings, we will miss you very much.
Let us know how things are going and always keep in touch.
Until you, yourself becomes a parent, will you then understand.
How difficult it is a parent, to release your child's hand.

Hand in hand we guided you, we taught you right from wrong.
Please take all that we've taught you son and it will keep you strong.
For in a world of weakness, ones life can waste away.
Remember where you came from son and you will be okay.

Beverly D. Johns

July 4, 1776

Today is cause for great celebration
Let freedom ring throughout our nation
The flag is born, a Ross creation
No man lives without dedication

Life goes on and some will die
That others live and you and I
Have no fear our fathers lied
With "Give Me Liberty", don't deny.

Today our fellow man may be
Of Irish or German descendancy
Of Latin, French, or even Swede
Without regard to color or creed

To these men who gave their lives
We owe so much, both you and I.
This flag, a symbol that freedom thrives,
Should be honored, protected and eulogized.

Fenner W. Steward

The Pilgrimage

Scorching winds shrieked powerfully
through the dense crowd
Shoulder to shoulder
Proud, angry, diligent
to the Pilgrimage

The restless words plunged deep
into the murky abyss of hatred...
Firing the spirits of resolution
Children's voices crying out with conviction
come home...

Confused, the hurricane of humanity
wrestles with these words of change
A message strong repeating
dignity, heritage, love
While others only blamed, condemned and threatened...

A million faces, a million men,
a million times demand to be heard...
Our sisters, our brothers, our children,
heal these wounds of difference
As pilgrims, as crusaders of peace and equality...

Dorothy Forrest

FIBS Warning

This is copyright protected.
Violators will be inspected by virtual reality.
Charges merit pennysworth per word or minimum wage per page.
Spouse honors checks without question.
USA dollar donations do inspire.
For permitivity in copy privileges, as is, retain credits and
send SASE (self-addressed stamped envelope) by return receipt.
Resemblance to reality is solely for fictionalized refreshment.
Make no changes. Smile for huckleberry stickers for trademarks.
Author is not responsible (nor liable for opinions).
Accentuate the positive. Proceed with care for generations.
***This is triple star rated
by Raft Rock Songsters Anonymous in Authorships.
Superinformation Freeway
endorses fictitious names of corporate sponsors.
NOTE: No Hurtleberries.
These are not allowed. Focus is on issuances not personables.
Upon notice, any questionables are transferred to Commentary Notes.
Space is pending for News P.R. (by Promotional Rates)
- for "Free World" News only!

Jacklyn L. Shaw (AKA Samuella Clemency)

Vacation Flashback

Wings glared on the reflecting pool,
Seconds before the jet touched down.
All kinds of planes were sucking up fuel.
His ears popped as his brain skipped 'round.

"Look!" he said, "Daddy once flew in choppers."

First Arlington and soon after
They were at the Mall, paused in line.
Smiles mingled with children's laughter.
What a splendid day, warm and fine!

"...miss the skies," He mused, "I loved those choppers."

It arose in dust at their feet,
A domino, one black game piece
That grew and shimmered in the heat,
Then towered, causing sound to cease.

A noise echoed, "God, the blood, the choppers."

His wife's voice spoke, amid the pall,
"This is now, it's another life."
Yet he knew pain in that black wall,
Etched with waste of life after life.

She pointed, "Honey, they're corporate 'copters."
Eve Lewis-Chase

Stormy Night

A stormy night is the black panther,
Ready to pounce upon me and devour my innocuousness.
The moon is the eye of the watching panther,
Who anticipated its own rage,
It stares at me.
Sharp teeth of lightning slice through the dark evening void,
Like a silvery-white dagger,
It cuts me.
Roaring thunder pierces the calmness which awaited so
patiently for me.
Claws of rain eager to slash through the thick black hollow,
As it smells my fear.
But the panther fades away,
The rain subsides,
And all that I see is still a sky.
Abigail Ramirez

Somewhere Tonight

Somewhere tonight, a fire is burning
raging through the pits of hell we call earth.
Somewhere tonight, a baby cries
screaming in pain from the starvation for love.
Somewhere tonight, a man kills in cold blood
hoping that the helplessness will go away.
Somewhere, evil is born
in the church of our Lord.
Somewhere, money falls
because the country cannot keep it.
Somewhere tonight, a reporter jumps from delusion
saying there are no good stories to be told.
Somewhere, chaos thrives
in a place where order is multiplied.
Somewhere tonight, a voice is taken believing words aren't important.
Somewhere the adolescent failed life's hard and grueling test.
Somewhere tonight, she died.
Angela Cavicchi

The Friend

Gather the days and hold them close,
Remembering the joys that mattered most.
For tears and sadness a trifling thing,
Take wing when in your heart you hear
Me bring.
Messages that are forever abounding, with
Hope, good tidings, and ethereal surroundings.
Hold fast to your faith as you run the straight
race. Imbued by my power, my love and my grace.
For I am your friend, unseen though I be.
Yet I know I have found the same in thee.

Lift up your heart now the race has been run.
Your journey to paradise has just begun.
Trusting and faithful without fear of the foe,
Lift up your face now to the heavenly glow.
You have trod the rough road to your journey's
End. So come unto me now for I am your friend.
Tilly Roders

Monsoon

One belch of thunder and the rains came down
Relentlessly, incessantly
Destruction laced with wrath

Parched throats lifted
Arms in welcome stretched
Crusted, cracked, the ground a sponge became

Thirsty rivers drank to roaring tumult
Rocky crags were masquerades of green
And crops in death throes grasped God's gift of being

Madras, Bombay to Delhi
Pelting torrents, black umbrellas
Empty bellies

Sleepers, sardine-packed
Once paved Calcutta's streets
Till driving downpour drove them to retreats and stayed to reign

Puppeteer, Mistress Monsoon, makes India dance
And lures her to new life
In a love-hate romance
Muryl Anderson

The Rose

You remind me of a beautiful red rose.
Red, which stands for love.
Crushed velvet petals... so soft... so tender.
Leaves of green, envy.
But be careful of the thorn,
Which drains life with a touch.
Life is the blood within one's being.
Blood provides romance, patience and whispers of virtue!

You are the rose whose petals are falling off,
One by one.
The envious green runs from your leaves.
Your thorns show more now than ever,
Looking for life to drain and destroy.
But that thorn shall grow weak and brittle,
For the last drop of blood that gives me life...
Always will give me life...thus kills the rose!
Tammy N. Cunningham

Depression Hovers O'er My Heart

Depression hovers o'er my heart,
It's filled with sorrow and grief,
Desolate and apart,
My aching soul weeps for peace.

Friends and family gather round,
Yet I feel lost at sea,
Caught in a terrible thunderstorm,
Of life and its tragedies.

Why can't the world just stop,
Just for a little while?
To give me time to take a breath,
And hopefully make a smile.

But oh no, the world keeps turning,
Each day just passes me by,
While yet my heart is ever yearning,
For someone to relieve my sighs.

Depression hovers o'er my heart,
It's filled with sorrow and grief,
Desolate and apart,
My aching soul weeps for peace.

Melissa M. Schultz

Tribute To A Mother

Watching a child grow up,
It's hard to let them know;
The way of the world is hard.
But still you let them go.

You worry and you pray
That they can weather the storm;
You'll pass along the tools,
With which they will perform.

A child's life changes constantly,
The road is long and rough;
Many times you pick them up,
It never seems to be enough.

A world grown cold and hard
Will challenge the rules you made.
What can we give in return,
For the dues that you have paid?

We honor you on this day,
For the love you always give.
God bless you and God keep you;
Thanks for the life we live.

Olive Morris

Dreams Of Love

It's not about money,
It's not about fame.
The person who has the most,
Doesn't always win the game.

In the game of life,
The rules are so few.
Yet everyone is so confused.
The ones who want the most,
Are the ones who usually lose.

Yet life is so simple,
And the few want so much.
When all I really want in life,
Is to feel her gentle touch.

Some may call me a dreamer,
But dreamers are so few.
Could they deny my simply dream:
To have a love that's true?

Matthew T. Kimball

Reflect The Mountain

Life is like a mountain,
It's rough,
Yet beautiful.
It reflects something special.

A mountain has only a peak to reach.
Its roughness never leaves
And its beauty is only seen.

Life has a never ending goal.
Its roughness never holds
But its beauty is internal,
Throughout the human soul.

Priscilla Leedom

September Fair Song

That time of year has come again!
It's the Washington State Fair!
It's time for hot dogs and cold pop
And displays are everywhere.

But sad to say, I'm staying home.
I'll mope around... just bored!
My car is broken down, you see,
And the bus I can't afford!

They've raised the fare to travel there
From ten cents to one dollar.
I think that they are cheating me...
And it makes me want to "holler"!

If fares increase on other routes,
I don't think I'd really care.
But for this route I don't consider
The increased fair fare, fair!

Wes Kunkel

Just Like Me

When I look around
It's then I see
People are hurting
Just like me.

Faces that smile
Yet their hearts are cut deep
Voices that laugh
Yet sob in their sleep.

People so different,
But so much the same;
Regardless of culture
Or nation or name,

One thing in common
All around I can see,
People need Jesus
Just like me.

Michelle Stephens

Beyond A Dream

It doesn't hang all steady together,
like a puppet tightly woven;
It unravels freely to create forever,
A masterpiece of wonders to be proven.

It looks beyond like a picture-book,
to search freely up and over;
Exploring new, unfamiliar ways,
Like a wandering vagabond or rover.

Sarah Wyatt

Evening

As the mosquito murmurs maneuvering
its way to fat feasts.

As the moon moves high casting
mystery in the sky.

As the magic moonlight makes known
all manner of form, all life below.

As the miracle of the milky-way
Mars and Mercury, meteors stray.

As immortal stars meander
Across measureless morbid dark;

As all this cosmic drama moves
A mere mortal stands mesmerized

In the middle of all magnificence
Mind in the maelstrom — Me.

Maria Burden

Family

There is a certain family
I've grown to love a lot.
They have so much going
things I haven't got.
Like, sitting all together
at breakfast, lunch, and dinner
And going down to grandma's,
just to share their love.
It seems they are so happy
every single day.
Oh, I wish I had a family
I'd even be willing to pay.

Vivian I. Woodley

Untitled

Sunny days and painted skies
June gloom haze, winds lullabies
Spring, summer, winter, fall,
My minds blindness missed them all
Children laughing, a bubbly brook
Up to heaven I will look
And thank God for another day
That He has chose to pass my way.

Russanna Gilmore

A Mother's Passing

When I was small
Just a young baby
I loved you mom

Growing with you
Each and everyday
I loved you mom

Even when things
Didn't go my way
I loved you mom.

Through the walks
And talks of life
I loved you mom

When I was grown
Living on my own
I loved you mom

Independence my lesson learned
Kept my mind strong and stern
You loved me mom

Marie Crawford

Untitled

If you need someone to listen
Just call out.
I'll be there in no time
Without a doubt.

If you're sad and crying
In a moment of desperation.
Don't hesitate to call on me
You need no invitation.

If you're in trouble
And everyone has turned away.
You can count on me
Any time of the day.

When your troubles are over
And you're feeling very carefree.
Do me a favor...
Don't forget about me.

Rebecca Budzinski

Changing

I believe we change
  Just like the seasons.
Spring is a time of
  Awakening and growing.

Summer we play and go
  Dancing with all the new
Things we found in the
  Springtime.

Fall a time when we
  Start slowing down and
Spend time reflecting
  On everything new we
Have learned.

Winter a time for
  Resting and quiet and
For me, a time for
  Waiting! Waiting! Waiting!
For another new spring!

Marilyn A. McNeill

Undying Love

Love is a wonderful feeling;
  just occurring unknowingly.
It is liked a fire burning;
  in the heart incessantly.

Love is forever so true;
  for those who are true.
Not letting obstacle hinders;
  nor hatred interferes.

Love is unchanging;
  though year's passing.
It is rooted deeply;
  in a heart so lovely.

Love is unending;
  though life's terminating.
It's a gift from above;
  to the world created with love.

Maria Georgina Camero

The Bluejay's Demise

Scolding, eating all the day
Keeping other birds away
From the food that is in the pan
All your feathered friends you ban

Eat, eat, eat scold and eat.

Now the squirrel would like a bite
Oh! No, you propose a fight
Go away you four footed scamp
How dare you invade my camp

Scold, scold, scold, and eat, eat, eat.

Now this morning you're not there
Putting on your lofty air!
Showing off your suit of blue
My goodness, just where are you

Scolding, scolding and eating, eating.

Aha! Mangled feathers on the ground
A beak, a pair of feet I've found
Alas! You've come to your demise
It must have been quite a surprise

When the cat did eat, eat, eat.

Mabel M. Miller

Graduation

It came to pass
last Saturday noon,
clear as glass,
but all too soon.

My daughter's graduation
and I was so proud,
feeling joy and adulation
I'm on top of the clouds.

Now from here
she's on her own,
but she need not fear
she'll never be alone.

As time passes on
I'll wait to see,
how her being gone
has an affect on me.

Alas, now I'm feeling
a little sorrow,
because I'm now dealing
with a new tomorrow.

Thomas M. McCurdy

The Eternal Quest

The pond without a ripple
Lay still and placid
And the dragonfly has landed
On the stiletto edge of a fragile reed.

Unmindful of Chernobyl
And the Vesuvian ash
And the games of dominoes
The nations play.

I, too, must seek my peace
My silence, the equilibrium
Of my soul
Amidst the din and rattle
Of my world.

Romulo Habla Estareja

No Answers-Time

What is life if it hurts?
Learn from your mistakes, but as time
passes what is it worth?

Time runs fast, take the future
and leave the past.

Too many line on your face,
This time cannot erase.

How old are you to age before
The time heals the pain?

Sorrow you must feel, but soon
Comes the rain.

Cleanse you it will, but time
does not come alone.

Scars it will bring - just accept
It and leave you it will.

Alone at last with the future and the past.
Because time may erase the
pain, but soon you must

Remember, and answer me,
really with time exactly what is it you have gained?

Karen J. Colangelo

Wife's Risks

Love me
Leave me
Always be true
Believe in you
Believe in me too... I do

Maturity
Security
Always alone
Heart's gone
Growing strong... what's wrong?

Live to be one hundred
Give until no more
Love for a life time

Come on! Come on! Come on!

Nothing's forever
Some things end never
Understandings are clues
Emotions run high
Oh my eyes... cry... bye!

Dream dreams depending on you.

Patricia F. Johnson

Surrender

Thoughts fall through me
Like a frantic rain
Held over by pregnant clouds
Of poison.
As in childhood,
Nothing is contained easily.
I find myself
Spilling over you
While rivers of dreams
And waterfalls of fear
Escape my embrace,
Weakening my resistance
And softening my heart.

Tamerin Corn

O Love, How Hard Enough

How hard enough
Life would be
With only its hardship
And adversity;
How sad then we should add
Such discord to life's strain
And anger or heartache to obtain
Petty kingdoms for selfish gain—
Or to look at loneliness
And call it freedom,
To look away from suffering
And say it is a fair lot.

Peace waits for Patience
To have her perfect work in us;
And Love—that still, small guide
Doth never hide,
But alike with Wisdom cries
Listen! Listen! Listen what your heart beats
From the Ancient of Days until Omega:
Love, O Love, . . . how hard enough.

Wesley Allen Riddle

Spinning

Life is spinning round us
   Like a circus ride
But you and I have gotten off
   To share love for a little while
Life can get so crowded
   I need time alone with you
To show my love responsibly
   In all I say and do
Just a touch from your hand
   The warmth of your eyes

If I always have you near me
   I know I have nothing to fear
Because you looked so deep in me
   And found I was so dear
I had a life of only spinning
   Until you stopped the ride
I took myself on weeks ago
   Because love skipped me by
Just a touch from your hand
   A word from your heart

Tamala A. Gumble

Free Spirit

Judge not by miles, but steps taken
Like a new day, the spirit will awaken
To face a road least taken
Because love has been forsaken.

Long and winding this path I travel
Past and future to unravel
Never knowing at which turn
What fence to mend or bridge to burn

Carrying only faith and trust
I walk this road I know I must
To sow a flower or a weed
I can not tell which one I seed.

Even when the days are dreary
And the load I shoulder makes me weary
I will carry on to tempt my fate
Embracing love and spurning hate.

Weaving slowly my tapestry
For at journey's end I'll stand and see
What person I turned out to be
The truth shall set my spirit free.

Marie Frisco

Lion Eyes

Makes me angry aggressive hard
like a protective lion
when I hear all the lies
the sad, the mad
eyes
see the truth, see the death
the agony, the fear
intensifying hate
spawning hidden voices
penetrative, clouded
visions slash beliefs
crucifying thoughts
neglected, unprotected
life dies
in all the
lies

Steve Caruso

Stars

Ghostly golden fingers
   like arrows from the sun
rend the clouds
they split the dark
   another day's begun.

The never ending struggle
   between the dark and light
has come again
and turned again
   as day defeats the night.

Now darkness slowly spreads
   like a blanket in the sky
it stretches out
across the land
   and day gives way tonight.

But night time has a failing
   the blanket, it has holes
it can't hold back
the shining light
   a million stars still glow.

L. D. Lewis

"Requiescat"

As I lay here alone
   Living in eternity,
I vaguely recall
   How I longed to be here
Relieved of the longings
   Never to see fulfilled.

Don't let there be a rebirth!
Don't play my life again
   Unchanging...
In a different time and place.

I'll remember..
   The aches...
The same empty sadness...
   Afraid...
But not recalling why.

   Oh, Death, my Comforter
My friend and constant companion
Stay by my side; don't leave me.
   Embrace my forever
In the power of your love.

Maritza Blandino Farnan

Realusion-The Paradox

I ask you now to come with me
Look at the sound of a falling tree
Or are you deaf - and cannot see
The illusion of reality?

Scientists will rant and rave
Of atoms and ions and electrode rays
But the concrete is abstract to me
And fiction is fact eventually.

So come with me and you will see
The clearness of complexity.

Shawn Coupe

No Way Out

Standing at the gates of heaven,
Looking back on my life.
I see the things I miss the most,
My children and my wife.
How could it be, I died so soon,
And left them in this plight.
I vowed to never leave them,
Yet I had no chance to fight.
He snuck up from behind me,
And killed me straight away.
What is it with the gangs,
That make them act this way.
To get in is real easy,
To leave their is no hope,
My killer got me out,
My killer was a rope.
It hurt to leave my family,
But now they are safe to stay.
I gave my life for theirs,
But they'll never know my way.

Trevor H. Ross

"The Unveiling"

The easiest thing on earth to see is
         LOVE
It is merely without structure
WITHIN these outward feelings,
yet, never void before my inner vision.
I hear its music through your heartbeat,
knowing its spirit evinces
from THE SOUL of its own art.
Just as your mind portrays its
beauty, my eye looks upon
its warmth, and captures the
essence of its TRUE colors.

The easiest thing on earth to see, is
         LOVE
When looking at it through you.

Sara Bradford Ware

Love

   Love is important,
   Love is to share, if you don't
love, you're lost somewhere.
   Love is like magic, don't waste
any more, follow your heart, and
go through that door.
   Love is like flowers,
   Love is like snow,
   Love is the best thing ever known
Sometimes love's easy,
Sometimes love's hard,
   and sometimes people just
break your heart.

Kyla Bryanna Duncan

Friendship

Quivering, silver drop of dew
Luscious, vibrant deepness of green
Contrast of rose
Soft against thorns,
Red against brown,
Vibrance against desolation,
Sharing of beauty-unashamed
No thorny protection,
Open.

Richard Pine

Dear Life

Her need in his velvet nostrils
makes a slave of the forest king.
A duet, older than memory, begins.
Spirits of earth and air
dance with acrobatic abandon
through strangely silent meadows.
Echoes of leaden thunder
shatter his antlered existence.
As she flees on wings of fear,
hooves barely gracing the earth,
life quickens within.

Paul M. Schummer

Feast of Seasons

A feast of seasons
   marching one by one
they come at us like clockwork
   while we spin around the sun
they are free for the taking
   and to be enjoyed by everyone
so long as we take the time and notice
   that nature can be a lot of fun
If we find that we missed one or two
   the world will forgive us
and bring forth seasons anew

Luigi Baldini

I See, I Feel

Eyes closed,
Meditation...
Yesterday's Arise.
I see, I feel, I shout, I cry
Until... Eyes opened, seeing...
Still Yesterday.

Eyes closed,
Meditation...
Tomorrows float by.
I see, I feel, I laugh, I sigh
Until... Eyes opened, hoping...
Still tomorrow.

Eyes Closed,
Meditation,
Today!
I shout, I laugh, I cry, I sigh
Until... Eyes opened, knowing...
Yes! Tomorrow.

Laura Jerney

The Birth Of Man

Sun and Sky come together in a blaze
merging for an instant.
Falling to earth,
The product of their creativity.
Fire and Ice,
lie entwined on the sand,
so a consciousness is born.
It is a being of opposites
each other needing the other
to make a whole.
It is logic and emotion,
truth and lies,
good and bad,
life and death.
The creature rises from sleep,
and takes form from shapelessness.
Leaves ignorance for knowledge
and is no longer nameless,
for it takes the name...
MAN

Robert Sigety

Love Unspoke

(For Jody)
What lighted soul doth yonder shine
'mid dimmer sparks below?
'Tis one who claims my tender heart
but nought my love he knows.

O secret guarded in my breast
be silent lest you yield
to tempter's guileful trickery
my affection to reveal.

For love unspoke grows stronger still,
its object more beloved,
and passion cannot be refused
if never spoken of.

Karen Butter Jenkins

Untitled

Chaotic dreams fill the
   minds of the bizarre.
Stability is the name of
   the game.
Insanity is the only way
   to win.
Freaks dance in the heads
of the lonely and insecure.
They grasp for reality, but
only grab something unreal.
Screams envelope the room,
while tears bounce at the
   ground.
The colors are a bliss,
while nothing in their lives
   are ever fulfilled.

Tymra P. Harris

Friendship

Friendship is an esprit
of silent equanimity,
holding the soul with
contentment
giving the heart reason,
helping the mind to see.

Karen Crider

Untitled

Less than a feeling
more than a thought
wants to continue
wants to be stopped
Heaven and hell
and all in between
these are the places
that I have been
Holding on tight
and then letting go
Lost in the fiery, icy snow
Quaking and shaking
and lying quite still
looking from mountain to valley to hill
Bridges are tossed
yet chasms are crossed
in the spectrum, the moment
between feeling and thought

Kristine Ramirez

Undressing A Mountain

In the distance stands a
mountain hidden from view
Behind a foggy curtain
The sun peeks through and
makes a hole in the mist
Finally the mountain
Raises her arms and lifts
Her filmy clothing slowly
Over her head and flings
Them to the skies
They float around her
Ever so gently in feathery
Wisps until she stands
Undressed, unashamed
Her contour again in
Full view, her feet
Firmly on the ground.

Marjorie DeHaut Abner

Lord You Gave Me Another Mountain

Lord you gave me another mountain to climb,
They get steeper and steeper all the time,
How will I make it to the top?
The pain and agony won't stop,
I hear the echo in the valley below,
How much higher will I have to go?
I hope the plateau is near,
But it is just a memory I fear,
The snow covered peak,
This is what I seek,
At my journey's end,
I will have no more mountains
to climb my friend.

Margie Chisom

No One's Good, No One's Bad

Some of us are different in
one certain way we all
have feelings. Some of
us laugh some of us
cry some of us live and
some die.

But we all have
heart's love and joy
no one's better than
any other.

Michelle Blalock

482

Forward Planning

Forward planning.
Multi - facet action.
The knowledge of others.
Small changes.
Mobility.

I am very much aware
thoughts stray, unwind.
Afterwards, frustrated,
Confidence.

Of this formula for success,
I slide away from problems.
I write a poem.

Decision!
Primed by my own knowledge,
patch up solutions,
forward planning.

Walter Liggett

Music Of The Four Seasons

Music where the water falls,
Music where the linnet calls,
Welcome music of the spring,
Bringing life to bud and wing!

Music where the crickets lie,
Music where wild waves beat high,
Summer calls with laughing breeze,
Croaking frogs and buzzing bees!

Music where the wild winds blow,
Music where dry leaves fall low,
On the plains the coyote's cry
Ushers lonely autumn by.

Music where tall pines are split,
Where the crackling fires are lit.
Music of the winter tells
With cold crisp snow and tinkling bells!

Rochelle Vickey

Unrequited Mother Love

In my longing I reach for you
My dream child.
I comb your long, blonde hair
with my kisses,
and my teardrops bathe your face.

Oh, to touch you, to be with you,
if just for a little while.
Never is such a long time,
and I've carried you in
my heart forever.

I can't say goodbye!
I can't give you up!
But reality intrudes.
Maybe the hurt will someday heal.

In the meantime though,
I comb your hair with my kisses,
and my teardrops bathe your face.

I love you.

Sandra L. Renauer

Love

I am consciousness
my name is oneness
I exist when I surrender
to love
time and space collide
I hold the hand of God
infinite understanding is experienced
I am alive with joy
my fears subside
I am filled with light
all is given to me
and nothing is kept from me
the kingdom of Christ within me
is granted unto me and unto you
for ours is the world
if all that remains is love

Scott Devon

The Search

The wheels of life will turn
My shattered soul will burn
From darkness to light
My essence takes flight
Searching for my sacred love
Torn apart from up above
The spell of matter cast on me
Shall be released when I find thee
The curse of loneliness will lift
When I get thy love as a gift.

Mario R. Denis II

"One Is Not Enough"

If I had but one wish,
My wish would be,
Peace throughout the world,
So souls could be set free.

No more hate,
From one man to another.
To live and love,
As sister and brother.

For every disease,
There would be a cure.
For an immoral thought,
A new mind so pure.

No more fighting
Over sex, creed or race.
For people to walk together,
And rise at their own pace.

One wish is not enough,
To work for my plan.
So please wish with me,
Every child, woman and man.

Winnie C. Hart

No One Else

No matter who
or
what the distractions
in life
that I have encountered,
my thoughts
have always
come back to you.

Richard L. Walton

Friends

Friends will be there if you
need them

Because that's a friend.

Friends will not let you down,
or let you frown
Them talking to you is so nice
just the sound.

I tell you that a friend
is someone will always be there
for you

A friend is nice that's what
they do.

Lani Kauffman

Stillborn

Look into the face of death
Never feel your baby's breath

Never worry, never sigh
Never hear your baby cry

Never feel your baby's soft skin
Never in a diaper will you put a pin

Never see your baby walk
Never hear your baby talk

Never watch your child grow
Never will he see the snow

Never see your baby's smile
As you think, was it all worthwhile?

For he has gone far away
And you'll see him sooner, day by day

Kyle Colleen Pratt

Night Moves

A door slams
Night must be almost over.
Tiny Steps - Pad, Pad, Pad
Coming closer to my bed.
Small body searches for mine,
Self's smaller echo conforming
to the small of my back.

Another door - opens, closes.
More gently this time.
Steps heavy enough to leave
traces in the carpet.
A second body comes to nest.

Then constant motion.
Heads knock, knees collide,
Limbs probe and unite with others
Like creeping vines round an old brick wall.

I watch shadows play with sleeping faces
As a river may caress a far shore,
Until two voices break the silence
And night moves on.

Karen F. Russ

Untitled

Love is not a thing to buy or sell
Or the silly patter of voices to tell...
It is of heaven born
To be cherished from the dawn...

C. B. Lax

"Someday Soon"

Someday there will be no pain
No dark clouds or pouring rain
No shining sun no glowing moon
I'm going home someday soon

No bolt of lightning across the sky
or rolling thunder from mountains high
Changing seasons I'll not see
For in God's paradise I'll be

As time passes we know not when
Our final journey we'll begin
And the only voice that I will hear
Is my guardian angel as he draws near

Sent just for me from God above
To show is everlasting love
So I'll never have to be alone
Someday soon I'll be going home.

Kenneth Dean Young

The Eight Wonder

Like the mystery of space
No man truly knows
Like the softness and the beauty
Of the first spring rose
Like the untamed desert
And the wonders it holds
You're a well of inspiration
With a never ending flow
You should never be conquered
You should never be tamed
You're like the light of the sun
You have an undying flame,
They say there are seven
Seven wonders of the world
But there's no greater wonder
Than, too become a woman from a girl
So now there are eight
Eight wonders too behold
A mystery to be explored
Not a prize to control

Keith Robinson

To Face The World Alone

Stacy stood alone in the corner
No one would ever join her
Could she ever sing or laugh
    or talk on the phone
Or would she just stand here
    all alone
When the other girls planned
    a party or sleepover
Stacy would wish they would
    include her
Maybe someone, someday would
    see across the outside
And over to the corner
    they would stride

Trang Hoang

Grey Rain

Some eyes settle gold-flecked soil,
others absorb azure sky,
but the man of my ceiling
in the long fall night
opens his eyes, grey,
full of clouds, laden
with passion for
soaking my ground.

Robin M. Phillips

the smell of rain...

I walk quietly through the darkness,
no star in sight.
    the silence broken by a pin point,
    a splash on my skin.
at first just one,
    then another.
        the wetness tingles my sensations.
        nothing seen, all is felt.
a rush of freshness floods my senses.
    wetness increases, smell intensifies
    the smell of rain...
        so charming, only a hint.
        so hidden, so bold.
        so mysterious, so known.
a smell longed for;
    dripping with life.
        so powerful, overwhelming... unseen.
i thirst for the smell of the rain,
    quenching my worries, my troubles.
        refreshing to my soul.

Kip Kuhn

Reflections

Insignificant I
None care
Inside I cry
People unaware;

Time has not corrected
Pain I feel
Love for me neglected
Death my pain will steal.

A lonely hurting part of me
I carefully force a smile,
Afraid to believe; can it be
At last I matter for a while.

Marion D. Arnold

Untitled

Wretched be thy name, for I am pain
Nor for anger nor for transgression
For she knows I am maim
Yearn for anger, no for aggression
Blessed be thy name for she is gain
Yearn for love, yearn for kindness
For I know she is maim
Yearn for love no for fineness
She finds beauty without I
I find beauty within she
For she so close yet so far
For I so far yet so near
    I reach out to pull her near
    I realize she's an image in a mirror

Leah Dummich

Meant To Be

Where we really meant to be,
Or am I livin' in a fantasy
Can my love be this strong
To have lasted so long
The pain my heart has bared
And all the cries I teared
The memory of how we used to be
And our future not even I can see
Is this my life long love
Or will he soon travel like a dove.
Maybe one day we will see
If we were the one's meant to be

Kelly A. Shirey

The Poet's Heart

The poet's heart is full of ink
Not of blood as one may think
You cut me then watch me bleed
In black and white for all to read
Sketchy lines, the canvas stained
Drip by drop 'til naught remained
The poet's heart, clean once more
Emptied, vacant, as before
Sure to fill 'neath another's smile
Bit by bit through sunny miles
To overflow again in time
For love, or cruelty, in rhyme
And so it goes, this special breed
Creates his best art as he bleeds.

Kristy Ann Blankenship

Untitled

Take it easy.
Not so much,
All at once.
Just relax,
And easily glide in.
Let your thoughts wander.
The freedom of your mind
    letting go,
        falling,
            looking down,
You're walking on ice.
Easy now,
Don't slip up.
You'll lose your mind.

Linde Coffey

The Pharisee, The Publican

Our Lord often warns us
    not to compare ourselves with others,
Accusing them to be
    not as holy as thee.

The Pharisee seeking God's help
    based on the fact,
He was better and not like
    the Publican in the back.

We know whose prayer was heard
    before God's Holy Throne,
The Publican in the back
    sorrow for the goodness he lacked.

Accept God's gift
    not looking to others,
To see what we lack.

Rejoice in your gifts
    of family and friends,
Thank God for your talents
    and use them for Him.

M. Rosemond

A Play

Bohemian: Hey, policeman.
Policeman: Hello.
(pause)
Policeman: Where you going, boy?
Bohemian: To the show.
Policeman: Seen it.
Bohemian: Don't tell me the ending.
Policeman: They all end the same.
Bohemian: So what's the answer?
Policeman: Crowd control.
Bohemian: Seen it.

J. Damien Simpson

Charades

Standing in front
of a tilted mirror
in the attic,

too-big shoes
on the first grade
feet unbalanced.

Feathers and lace
with stale perfume,
and a sheet—

a makeshift gown—
trips the feet...
and the gloved,

too-small hands
catch their balance
in the dust.

Lindsay Bertram

Sign Of Love

A rose is a sign
Of love,
Rain is a tear
From above,
Spring is a sign
Of life,
A ring is a sign
Of a wife,
Laughter is a sign
Of happiness, and brings
Sound to the wilderness,
Children are a sign
Of joy,
Kind of like buying
A new toy,
Warm is something in
The heart,
That's where love starts.

Kim Sterling Knapp

"In Search Of Self"

Traveling the path
of my heart and your words
"To thine own self be true..."

But whose truth?
Which self?

Nightlogues with meghosts
Echoes of past encounters
Suddenly clear.

My truth or theirs?
Windmill or giant?
Princess or whore?

To rebuild the cliff
from these shattered remains
And piece together the colors
of a Never-Neverland rainbow.

My scattered vision
refracted
in their broken mirror.

Margaret M. Abel-Quintero

The Hummingbird

I saw you through the window,
of our kitchen door today.
A flash of red, a glint of green.
And then you flew away.

But soon you come back.
With a buzz and a tweet.
To quench your thirst
for the nectar so sweet.

You stayed quite busy.
All summer long.
Till I said good-bye in August
to your sweet little song.

Maybe next spring
I'll see you again.
But good-bye till then.
You sweet little friend.

Lavonda G. Overholt

A Soul United

A hunger, a need
  Of safety received
To sleep all night
  Without the fright
Of demons chasing
  Nightmares facing
Childhood past
  Horrors that last
Wailing inside
  Fears that reside
To be at peace
  A final release
Two halves - one whole
  Child and adult - one soul

Theta J. Zornes

The Forest Of The Rest Of My Life

I walk into the forest
of the rest of my life!
I feel the sun
filtering through
mingling with
the energy of the trees
The flashes of light
wrap me in knowledge
helping me through the night
welcoming me
into a new adventure
that will undoubtedly ensue
as I go forth with the
wisdom and knowledge gained
from all the hard knocks of life
unhealthily attained.
The forest has become
as a labyrinth for me
with new discoveries
behind every tree.

Patricia Horwell

Untitled

  As seasons do change
only our eyes can really see
the beauty of colors
that nature can bring,
we see all the views
as we can always admire
oh what beauty can we desire

Mario Gonzalez

Victory

Who's a candidate for the president
Of the U.S.
I don't see where it is all leading
Lots of people do
That is politics.

I already tried it
He come by to see me
I'll see him sometime this week
We couldn't very well get going until
We had our guy.

What do you do
I guess I just wanted to see if
What's he look like
I will still be here
I am going to holiday morning.

Mike Barkoot

The Queen And The Joker

I had always been so sure
of what I wanted and felt,
But I didn't look closely
at the cards I was dealt.

Within that playing hand
was a card I could not see.
He was hiding behind the Queen,
winking and laughing at me.

Don't bet on your Heart,
you may not realize all at stake.
The Queen of Hearts is not strong
and will easily break.

The Queen of Hearts is deceiving,
so look long at your hand.
Watch closely, for strong she is not
and alone will never stand.

Her strength comes from the Joker
who uses her as a tool,
to hide behind her beauty
and play you for a fool.

Marie Johnson

He Died Plowin'

The doctors told him,
"Old Man, you're gonna die."
So he hitched up old Buck
to the plow
And died where he had lived —
In the fields.
Plantin' and plowin',
Feedin' a family of five children,
The old woman and himself.
He died shoutin',
"Haw mule, you flopeared sonofabitch!
I'll cuss you 'til a fly won't light
on you!"

He died in the brown earth
with dirt under his fingernails
and a smile on his face.

Venita Morgan-Caldwell

Untitled

Beautiful rainbow
On a humid summer day
Soon it will be gone

Reagan Lunn

Home Free

Conferring beastly honors
On fallen foe alike
We measure not the gentle lost
But turn in lone respite.

We gather sickness to us
And feign an awkward calm
We fester in some costly guilt
And shun the beggar's palm.

So return me to my sullen spaces
Ferry forth my dawn
I feel less burdened by the breeze,
Less like the anchored pawn.

I pander free in time alone
Consequences will remind
That fauna of the current clime
Regress to liken kind.

I bequeath this stoddard fortress
To those who would remand
That questions bear confinement
My salve soon turns to sand.

J. Toby Kolp

To Rob

Where did you go, Rob,
On the day you died?

Did you become a teardrop
As my daughter cried?

Did you become an angel
Providing comfort at her side?

Did you become a moonbeam
To lighten her dark tide?

Did you become a loving Word
To comfort and to guide?

Did you become a rainbow
To color her gray sky?

Did you become the Truth
As she prayed it was a lie?

Did you become the Answer
To her question, "Why, oh why?"

Loretta Allen Cash

The Illusion

I hear the wind blow,
on this misty, silent
night with an illusion.

Alone, yet words echo
upon the shores of my
imagination, the right
words, you'll say.

I'm focused on a vision,
of you and I, looking out
to sea, throwing stones
skipping the shadow waters.

I ask, where am I?, Walking
this sandy path, listening to
the waves hit the mellow
   shores.

I'm with an illusion,
my friend when I'm alone....

Wesley Alexander

"Ink Blob"

Ink blob, ink blob
on this page
what a holy mess I've made
This piece of paper
Now a stage
A folded over table aid
Two colors now
I dare to gage
dues of which my fingers paid
Blue yellow blob
that dries with age
As colors change and somewhat fade
This blob of ink
Upon this page
in which blue yellow fingers wade

Steve Rice

Summer Rain

Sometimes it falls in sprinkles fine
On this thirsty lawn of mine
Making sure each blade of grass
Sparkles like a mirrored glass

Then there are times when droplets fall
So big and bouncy like a ball
And rivulets form to run around
On down to lowest parts of ground

A puddle here, a puddle there
Where little birds their bathing share
And children wading back and forth
Create a picture of much worth

All at once the sun shines through
Between the clouds of gray and blue
We're thankful God has once again
Washed our air with gentle rain!

M. B. Reniker

The Bat's Wish

A fog flew off
on wings of white
fast forward
in the realm of night.

Hung upside-down
a bat asleep
was dreaming wishes
wild and deep.

Oh sky-night queen,
next Halloween,
I ask of thee,
oh let me be,
thanks to your power,
a purple passion flower.

A fog flew off
on wings of white
fast forward
in the realm of night.

Margot Nicolaus

On Jean And Randy's Wedding Day

Dearest Jean and Randy,
on your Wedding Day,
Saturday, December 2, 1995,
May all your seconds, minutes,
Hours, and years together,
From this day forward be,
Dreams to come true,
Wishes be granted,
Filled with Love, Joy,
Friendship, Respect, and Warmth,
Needs and desires fulfilled
Problems so small, as angels
Float away on clouds,
All this and more,
Your sister wishes,
For eternal peace,
Happiness, God's love,
And most of all,
This poem will last, as long,
As your love lasts, for each other.

Love, Vicky Halliday

Knowledge

I was taught
one and one
makes two—
and Santa Claus
brings toys.

No one taught
I'd be
the scattered dust
of stars—
nor who would laugh
when the universe explodes.

Milton L. Marks

Untitled

"I have no name,
only a face"
a face I've seen
a thousand times,
a thousand places.

A rugged face,
beautiful eyes,
her cheek bones high,
her hair is dark,
I've seen her twice.

A grandma pushes a
cart full of junk,
her face is lined,
her distant gaze
seems set past time.

A young girl stares
out from a page,
a magazine
from far away,
when will we speak?

Susan Jane Kohut

Fishers

I cannot see city-silvered windows
Only icy blue faces on the shore.
Who am I?
One of the fisher people
Who fish away their dreams;
And, when the night stars
Lanterns are,
We turn back down the valley path
With hymns of sorrow
In our visions lost
To sleep—
God-haunted.

Margaret Johanson

Anchor

Waves slip past me
Opportunities lost.
Memories swell, surge
Threaten to suck me down
To timeless depths.
Sand shifts under my feet,
Ungrounded.
Each wave a choice, a loss
Possibilities gone.

I yearn to let myself
Be swept away,
Riding the crest
Of each new wave.
Yet here I stand,
Secured
To your assurgent shore
By your need of me.

Lisa Michael-Good

Some things Change

Is there pain in everything I see
Or is it
Some crazy world inside of me
Or is it
The colors of life, so let it be

Some things change
Some say I am strange
They don't know
What's in my brain
Some things change

There are others like me
Up in the stars
Someday I will find
Others who, have the same mind

Money can buy a lot
But it can't buy sanity
Wine helps me escape
Forget all the red tape
Something else I must hate

Robert Lenzen

Untitled

We should never walk in the
shadows of the past, for they
are cast by the sun of the
future, shining through the
world of the past.

J. Patrick Egan

Rain

As I fall upon the gentle grass
or slide down an umbrella of red,
I could fall upon the yellow plain
or upon somebody's head.

As I fall down the sky of gray
so many things I see,
a vulture looking for his next prey
or a queen honeybee.

I think how much I help the earth
the flowers begin to rise,
I help grow the cherries
for those delicious cherry pies.

As I soak up to the ground
and evaporate again,
don't worry I'll be back
'cause I'm a gift from God, one he likes to send.

Nikki Wrenfro

"Selena"

Selena was our hope
our sorrow,
and she would never
ever be forgotten after
death, her soul would
be safe with someone
very special, and that
person is everyone's
best friend, God.
Selena would never
ever be apart, she
would always be in
our hearts, and if we
listen to our hearts
and ourselves, you
would maybe get to
listen what her voice
says in peace.

Megan Lyman

Everlasting Hope

As I look through my window,
Out over a rolling sea,
I see a beautiful vision,
It's your face, it seems to me.

With it comes haunting memories,
Of when I was young and gay,
Of when I used to court you
And we traveled, the highest highways.

To-day I am old
My hair has turned gray,
But I still have that hope
Of finding you, my love; some day.

You left me on a shaded lawn
Where the orange blossoms grow,
You were to meet me to-morrow,
But where did you go?

I still look for you on that shaded lawn,
Hoping someday you'll appear,
So I can hold you close to my heart
Call you my own, my dear.

Martin Edwin Peterson

Oklahoma

Oklahoma is my home,
Over its fields I like to roam.
Oklahoma is the land of
the red man.
It's also in the shape of
a frying pan.
The white man came and
took the red man's home,
And shot the buffalo
that liked to roam.
The red man walked
a trail of tears.
While the white man
was causing many fears.

Tanner Jones

Peace

Peace is silence
    Peace is Christmas
on a sunny day in June
Peace is like a morning
    glory that sparkles with
    the dew
Peace is healing, peace is
    Trust, truth and time
Without action that
    doesn't lead to despair

Sharlene Gagnon

A Yellow Rose Of Friendship

A beauty of nature
    picked from the garden of a friend
So simple a picture
    but, so rare a blend
A personification for those who
    share genuine friendship
    throughout life with you
Like unto this rose
    a perfection of yellow hue
in time will wither, and be gone
but, the beauty of it lingers on

With cherished thoughts of
    such a friend in you.

B. J. Rust

Minus Signs

Curved roads, minus signs
Poly-directional, hightech
Dreams, multi-orgasmic
Patterns within, without
The minds eyes
Of Kafka, Goethe, Kerouac
Sweet desire, minus signs
Fantasy wheel, archaic
Reality, single-minded
Truth, abound
The soul's parched reality
Of Dante, Crowley, Poe
Sweet existence, minus signs
Abstract, pearl white
Roadways, poly-morphous
Paradoxical, cluttered
The truth's bigot
Of Roger, of Rediron, of Wowo
Of madness, minus signs

Roger A. Lipe

Untitled

Reaching and grabbing tight
pulling forward with all its might
there it goes
I watch it float away
I never knew it could be taken that way

Gasping for air. It's not really clear
what I'm doing here
it's not for fun no time to sin
looking around, caving in,
backing up falling down

I cover this hole with my feeble hands
this pain in my chest I can not stand
I look up at you, you're smiling
I'm dying

Licking the blood that drips down your arm
Your evil is half your charm

So this is how it is to be done
You get it all
I get none.

Marjorie Jacko

There

I wake up in the dark of night
Reaching for your hand
But you are not there.
I search a sun-filled day
For a trace of your welcoming smile
But you are not there.
I have looked so long and lonely
For a glimpse of love
Reflecting the love I have to give.
And long for the day I find
That you were always there.

Shari Burdick Hemphill

Time Wasted

Moments spent
REFLECTING
On things past.
REMEMBERING,
Recalling memories
Left far behind
And yet so near.
MOODS,
Unexplainable,
Unshakable.
They must be
MEMORIES long buried,
Forgotten;
REFLECTIONS of emotions
Which haunt me against my will.
MEMORIES best forgotten;
Moments spent
REFLECTING:
Time wasted.

Kathy J. Cook

Untitled

Traveling with family is fun
Riding from dawn to setting sun
Looking for beauty on the way
And places we would like to stay
But we must move on and on
Looking forward to another dawn.

Louise Pinion Wilson

Musings Of A Septuagenarian

Do the ashes
Resting in the grate
Remember the all consuming flame
That danced and leaped
And made all things bright again

These ashes may be content
Not to flare brightly
Throwing flickering shadows
At the dark
Then wane

Do seeds of warmth
Still remain
At the center of those coals
To once again bring fire to life
With joy and hurt and love and pain

These things may best
Be past and done
And to let the dead ashes
Be at rest
And final peace at last attain

William Hollopeter Sr.

Jungle Night

Darkness diving
Rhythmic thriving
Speaks the night with voices driving.
Restless walking
Nightsounds taking
Shadows peaceful creatures stalking.
Silence rising
Springs surprising
Padded footsteps dark disguising.
Slowly beating
Night now heating
Dawn's soft fingers lightly fleeting.
Shadows fleeing
Daylight seeing
Darkness' safety ceases being.
Quiet.
Watchful.
Waiting.

Melissa A. Alliston

'Ode To The Cancerian'

Oh, ride the tides
Ride the waves with me
The ocean currents swift
The fluid of life — the sea

As the waters respond
To the glow of the moon
So the inner me
Responds to the sea

As waves peak and valley
So my life unfolds
As the sky reflects the blue
My soul is renewed

Immerse me in thy power
Oh waves of the sea
As my spirit becomes one
With thee for eternity

Linda L. Crews

"My Little Jewels"

God sent a precious jewel
Right out of heaven's joy,
And now it shines within our home
It is our baby boy.

God sent another jewel
A precious little pearl,
He sent it straight into our home
To be our baby girl.

God only loaned these jewels,
He wants them back you see.
But oh the sunshine they have brought
Since He loaned them to me.

I pray for guidance every day
To train these jewels right,
And then when they return to Him
They'll still be shining bright.

Phoebe Ferguson Law

Car Crash

The telephone rings
rings, rings.

Finally Mom answers it.
It's Dad. He has been in a car crash.

It feels like my life is over.
Like I've just run off of a cliff.

As we drive down to pick up Dad,
my stomach rolls
rolls and rolls
over and over again and again.

Not a bump but just one cut.
My dad's all right.
"I love you, Dad, with all of my heart.
I'm so happy you're all right."

Victoria Walters

"Dawn"

When I see the sun,
rising with all its beautiful hues;
I have only one thought, my love,
it is for you.

The dew on the grass;
the birds flying to their nest.

The flowers leaning toward the sun;
nature's stirring has just begun.

Dawn to start anew;
how many more or how many few?

Mary Green Kelly

Morning Magic

Coffee pot percolating
Rosy sun escalating
Crowings of a rooster burly
The magic of a morning early.

Dewdrops clinging tenaciously
Cool wind blowing graciously
Robin bursting with joyous strumming
A magic mornings soothing humming.

Stars rolling up in a carpet blue
Sparkling sun playing peek-a-boo
Purple and pink spreading like a shroud
Morning magic painted on the clouds.

Teresa J. Taylor

Untitled

Miles build easy
roads follow roads
days turn years
    time to stop.
Can't outrun myself
fooled them all
    they don't know me.
Temples throb, sweaty palms,
my nervous stammer.
Unmask myself?
Reveal it all.
    See me here
        as I wish to be
your disapproval means nothing
    anymore.
Prove myself? Belittle myself for you?
    I think not. Not anymore.
You understand nothing
    'cause I fooled even you.

Robert William Powers Jr.

the first time I saw...

there she was
rocking in emptiness

a little one
curled in sorrow
waiting...

as I moved
to her,
her shoulders
choking for comfort
she whispered,
"i'm so glad you're here"

and the moment
of meeting her arms
flooded with tears
for I had made
her wait
22 years

and there I sat
beside my child
beside myself.

Susan H. Roden

Say You Still Love Me

Say you still love me
Say our love is the same
I know you were untrue
But, I was the one to blame.

I'm sorry for what I did
I know I was wrong
Let's forgive and forget
And I know we'll get along.

We were once happy
But we had a silly fight
Please come back
Don't just say I might.

You know I love you
And I promise to be true
Please come back
And let's say I do.

Pamela Hill

Walking Pacific Coast Trail

I appear poised like a pelican,
Scattering my spirit into voices
of sand. The Pacific chooses
to go on, bringing messages

that taste of salt. At the edge
of this slender sweep, I translate
the syllables of mermaids nervously
lamenting in a tantrum of seaweed.

From the Pacific I hear my own
departure trumpet into a separate moment,
a bridge I can cross over,
a beginning for my life to drink from.

From the Pacific the middle of life
holds a candle in a wind of echoes.
Into my life whales pass after years
of captivity, knowing the way homeward.

In the distance the celestial Bear
lights an avenue to the moon,
and I can never go back
from where I came.

Baloian

Earth's Sorrow

    Rushing waterfalls and splashing
seas,
    What can be as beautiful as
this can be,
    Is it the birds that chirp
or the mice that squeak,
    Is it the wave of a whale or
a fish that leaps,
    Is it a silk bow or
a feathered crow,
    Will my great, great
grandchildren be able to see,
    The things that are so
normal to me?

Robyn R. Hasty

Through Grandpa's Eyes

Through grandpa's eyes they
    see so much love
Those lucky Hoefer kids
    brought down from Heaven above...

Since the day they were born
    grandpa found a new joy,
They were as gracious to him
    as a child's first toy.

As he watches them grow
    with tears in his eyes
He remembers moments that
are special, as simple good-byes.

All five love their grandpa
    as much as he does them
Cause they realize, who they
    are, stems from him.

He takes them to Colorado,
    the place that he loves,
To show them the creation
from their God above.

Ruth Hoefer

Restless Night No More

Doors ajar, window open,
Shade half mast,
Roaring thunder,
Thoughts of past.

Crickets chirping,
Croaking frog,
Piercing lightning,
Barking dog.

Curtain swaying,
Blinding light,
Mind is wandering
Through the night.

Youth long gone
Left far behind,
Endless wonder.....
Was all done right?

Raindrops falling,
Soothing sound.
Heard God's voice -
Now, peace I've found.

Waltraud A. Meyer

"To Cupid"

Oh! Great symbol of love,
sharpen, your arrow above
and aim it down;
turn the ones who scorn around.

His "Ego" embittered
tour up by sorrow.
The miracle is coming up;
the queen of music
begins to play in his last...

The notes are floating
as little dolls colored;
happiness is coming
you will know why!

Santina Arizoni Tatar

Shepherdess

Shepherdess, with staff in hand
She cares for the little lambs
With quiet step and simple dress
Her song floats over the wilderness.

The mountain's height
What a pleasant sight
The path she takes is no mistake
Her master has a destined plan
She welcomes the touch of His hand.

Miriam McIntire

My Singing Soul

Flowering Melody
Sings in my soul
laughing, smiling
spinning dizzily
voices mix
like a river rushing
joining the rocks
tumbling in a lovely dance
hearts beating
a tempo in unison

Melissa Keys

Visiting With Grandma

I'm visiting with Grandma.
She don't have much to say.
She just listens to me talk
About the dreams I have today.

I tell her all my hopes,
My troubles and my fears,
And the warmth within her heart
Dries away my tears.

I close my eyes and I can see
Her gentle loving smile,
Feel her hands upon my shoulders
Because I've hurt for quite a while.

And yet, she's oh so distant.
The clock ticks on and on.
I wish we'd had more time,
But those days forever now are gone.

And although I can no longer hold her,
All her memories I will save
When I'm visiting with grandma
Visiting with grandma at her grave.

Robert Silva

Our Sunshine

Aunt Mae was a wonderful lady
    She touched so many lives...
Brothers, sisters and little tots
    Yes, even her nephews' wives.

Her mother taught her early in life
    To always walk close to the Lord
And His caring ways were reflected
    Through his love that she had stored.

A companion, a helper, a friend,
    A counselor and even a mother
She was all these things to all of us
    In one way or another.

But today our hearts are heavy
    As the time of parting has come
How will we go on without her?
    We feel just so helpless and numb.

Then soon comes a warm strange feeling
    A light glows so brightly, it shines!
We know in an instant she's not gone
    'Cause she's here, through His mystical
signs.

A niece, Sandy A. Wiest

Siren

Alone on the island
She waits.
The next suitor comes
Time for bait?

Tempting melodies
Charm from within
Reach out and touch me
She calls to him.

Weep, weep poor Innocence
Secretly.
You are so lonely
For company.

The curse falls upon you
In a flash
Irresistible desire equals
The crash!

Lisa Southerland

Change

In dark and silence,
shy,
my soul changed its clothes.

Katerina Stoykova

Eyes Of The Wolf

Surroundings of white
Silence
The cold intense
    yet not penetrating
Tranquility
The land a living thing
All is known
    to my eyes
Nothing is not heard
Taste of life
    a salty warmth
Voices on the wind
Reuniting comfort
    a lifelong friend
I live and breath
There is no tomorrow
    no yesterday
Only the wind and earth
    and life
I am one with it

Kevin Kirkpatrick

The Statesman

Superficial smile
Sincere lies
Artificial lights
Shine in his eyes
His truth is just
A false disguise
To bait the trap he sets

He crafts his words
Adjusts his face
Epitome
Of charm and grace
He weaves his noose
Of silk and lace
To sweetly embrace his prey

E. Michelle Justice

The Early Morning Wild

The doe graciously
sipped water
from the sparkling
lake, and the buck
watched over her
in admiration as
the dew droplets
evaporated in the
morning sunshine.

The doe and buck
evaporate into
the woods as dusk
lays a dark blanket
over the fields
leaving the crickets
to sing soprano
in the motionless
night.

Tracy Senour

Own Little World

Civilized society Saturday night
Sirens wail to a shadowy flight
Still the dealer's close at hand
Back by popular demand

Under a lamppost she barters her fate
A four-wheel motel room awaits
Her dreams are a blank biography
As the car door opens anxiously

Like poison vines creeping wall to wall
Self-esteemed graffiti scrawl
The signatures of conscienceless pride
Drowning authors of a rising tide

One is company, two's a crowd
Lower the volume, this life's too loud
Who wins when all is said and done
The beating heart or the loaded gun

Protected in my hotel womb
From a city as cold and dark as a tomb
I'll stay here in my own little world
O.K. here in my own little world

Keith Steinbaum

"To My Love"

    When I am near you my
skin screams out for your touch
    When you finally touch me
I cry out for more
    Each touch so sweet and
Innocent makes every minute
in your arms grander than before
    Your lips are so sweet and
soft, they invite me for more.
    Each taste of you makes it
harder to resist.
    Each touch makes me go
wild for more
    When I wake in the morning
your name is on my lips
    The look in your eyes makes
my body ache for you morning
and night
    My heart burns for the
love I feel for you always and forever!!

Krietha L. Slone

Afloat

Four white oars
Slicing in unison
Three golden orbs
Make up the center
A choice
Of two golden chains
dangling down to the bed
of my watery resting place

Swimming in dreams

Sandra Murphy

Morning Light

Oh what a peaceful place I see
    so early in the morning
Before the sun is fully free
    of the eastern boundary
Tiny footprints in the sand
    busy was the night
Now a new day is at hand
    swept in by golden light

Mary St. Cyr

The Sweet Violet And The Honey Bee

A little flower in the park
Smiled as a bee passed by.
The little bee just tipped his hat,
And the flower blinked an eye.

The little bee circled about
And returned for the flower's name.
The flower's violet perfume
Made the bee quite tame.

He asked, "Do you have any sweets?
I want some for my comb;
I'm trying to make some honey
Back at my old sweet home."

The flower said, "Just help yourself
To my sweet scented nectar."
The little bee just hurried off,
And came back with the rector.

William F. Hoffman

Death

Standing before the stone,
Snow falling to numb feet,
   Another play with a new cast,
   To dwell in the forever past,
No escape, Death's hands await.

T. Joseph Egan

Life

As life travels,
So builds the past.
The future becomes
Memories transcend.

Time irrelevant,
Space unhindered.
The mind ponders,
Mere reality.

Life inconsistent,
Real complexity.
Problems persist,
Only answers evade.

Hindsight is perfect,
Vision unbound.
Seeking tomorrow,
Life is experience.

Stephen V. Miller

The Impoverished

  Impoverished by a world,
So harsh and cold.
  That cares for none,
Not even its old;
  So they cast them aside,
And into the street.
  A paper bag for breakfast,
No shoes for their feet.
  Yes these are the people,
You'll never hear sing,
  As they run from the night.
And the Treachery it brings.

Lawrence Capparelli

Dumb Country Dog

I'm a dumb country dog,
So I've been told.
I'm a dumb country dog,
Like to lay in the road.

I'm a dumb country dog,
Not too big or too little.
Like to lay in the road,
Not the side, but the middle.

I'm a dumb country dog,
Just somebody's old hound.
And I'm not getting up,
That's right, go around.

Suzanne E. Higgins

The Victory

The story of God's matchless love,
  So real, so pure, so true,
Is often told, yet never old:
  A story ever new.

He gave His Son—His only one
  To die on Calvary.
That Son He gave all men to save,
  And all means even me.

'Twas God's great plan that every man
  Might through that Son be free.
The cross He bore became a door
  To greatest victory.

Those rugged nails, those cruel nails,
  The crown of thorns He wore,
The suffering there no one could share
  The agony He bore.

He gladly died—thus crucified
  For sinners great and small.
He loved so well, no tongue can tell
  The beauty of it all.

Veda Ridpath

"Knowledge"

Until it's lost, it isn't found,
so some thing's can't be claimed.

Discoveries,
Uncoveries,
These are much the same.

It's ignorance,
and lack of learn,
That causes us most grief;

We think, we find,
and loose our mind;
Seeking what is brief.

Intangible,
unscanable,
True Treasures are unseen.

The here-and-now,
and yesterday,
tomorrow's disbelief.

Paul Scott Winkler

Our First Kiss

Our first kiss was so soft, so warm
So tender and sweet, so much so
As to cause my mind
To faint from surprise,
And my heart to leap for joy
At the mere touch of you!
Press ever nearer to me!
Let my love hold you,
As my arms enfold you,
Licking lips and sucking tongues,
That have for so long yearned
For love's sweet feast!
Cling to me tighter, don't ever release,
Suck in my soul, come on baby, come on
Kiss me harder and deeper,
Kiss me rough, kiss me long
Kiss me ever so passionately, then
Kiss me over and over again!

Maurice Weldon Young

Sorry, Fact or Fiction 1996

Those timeless words
So vain and so shallow
Taken by others
and used without morals
What do they mean?
Why are they said?
Why don't they mind?
Or do they even know?
They are the representatives
of hoax and dread
I often ponder
these questions in my mind
Does the hand that hits
grieve with such ease?
And why does the tongue
use it so lightly?
Those timeless words
What do they truly mean?

Sheharazade Sheerahamad

American Heart

America had to make a stand
So we were sent to a foreign land
Many hearts reach out to you
Many hearts stand fast and true
We hope that you won't be there long
Until then stand proud, stand strong.

I. Kay Casey

Bondage!

"They" say you took him, Lord.
Somehow, I can't believe that!
He meant so much to me
Do you need him more than I?
Him with the tousled head,
And battered knee?

His stagecoach and bat are
Awaiting him still
Just like "Little Boy Blue's!"
His dream of a horse of his very own
Was just about to come true.

My need for his laughter
His shining blue eyes
I'm sure 'twill never cease.
'Til we meet "over there"
And I hear his, "Hi Mom",
I'll never know release.

Katharine P. Rowland

Tragedy At The Lake

In this complicated world
sometimes wrong seems right
As Susan Smith's sorrow
took over mind and sight.
The tragedy of Alex and Michael
is so hard to understand
When two precious lives were taken
by their own mother's hands.
A life of sorrow and disappointment
led to Susan Smith's big mistake
By strapping her children in the car
letting it roll into the lake.
Now the children lie in their graves
their father and family heartbroken
Susan says she is sorry
true words I'm sure when spoken.
At last the trial is over
the verdict is prison for life
May God in her life intervene
helping to conquer fear and strife.

Naomi Haigler

Spite Man

I encountered a man the other day
spite beamed from his very soul
pity I thought
such a sour pity
such a small heart
such a small life
no room for the sentimental
no room for love
no room for emotion
no room for meaning
he packed only one thing in his soul
the ignorance of hate
the center of his being
like a bad motel
cracked and dry
filth and spiders in every free nook
ready to break down
and fall apart
until it's gone
when nobody goes there anymore

Vince Mewhirter

Untitled

Beautiful
standing
wind in my hair
sand warm
under my feet
you closer
than the beat of my heart
a breath of the air
I breathe
washing around me
in the lapping sea
rocking my soul with
comfort
wholeness
peace

Lorelee J. Rude

"Rainbow"

A shower forms in the skies;
The rain stops and the wind dies.
The clouds sparkle and the sun shows;
Several beautiful colored rainbows.

Loretta Felts

"The Wind"

There are two windmills
standing in different yards
reminiscent of time gone past.

Their blades mostly broken
and their skeletons rusted fast.

What was the power that once
moved their massive arms?

The wind caught and harnessed
to provide comfort within their farms.

C. Beckermeyer

Old Bow Hunter's Lament

The fawns were oh so pretty
Standing with their ma
I couldn't kill their mother
I was looking for their pa.

I paid my license money
A very goodly fee
I couldn't kill their mother
'Cause I would be killing three.

Now I am getting hungry
And feeling kind of blue
I really need some venison
To cook into a stew.

I am getting pretty edgy
And feeling kind of glum
As I sit and wait so patiently
For the buck that does not come.

Lyle D. Jensen

Sunrise

Early morning skies
Still dark from night,
Capture your attention
As they become light.

Slowly, life stirs
On this beautiful morn,
Time to recollect
On the years since you were born.

There are things to do,
Time always runs out,
While we are so busy,
Going about.

But if you can capture a sunrise
And witness its awe,
Such different colors,
All without flaw.

Sunrises are such a promise,
Another day to try
To do the things you've always wanted,
But never found the time.

Susan Webb Warren

Sunrise

Slowly, in the morning distance,
    Sunrise arose from bed;
She looked so very beautiful
    With the blush of morning red.

As she shook her tresses
    With the bits of golden hue,
She gave to the morning's dimness,
    The lightness that was due.

Opal Williams Shank

"Shady Lady"

"By the roadside, hot and dusty,
Stood an oak tree, old and musty,
From its branches, tired and heavy,
Came a stirring, slow but steady,
Some leaves older, high and lofty,
Began to flutter, very softly,
Then a wind came, heavy laden,
From their moorings, some were shaken,
Down they circled, twisting lower,
Mixed with droplets, in a shower,
Instant lightning, bright and flashing,
Rolling thunder, loud and crashing,
Soon the raindrops, wet and teary,
Filled the branches, now not weary,
Then the old tree, washed up brightly,
Raised its posture, ever slightly,
Like a monarch, like a lady,
By the roadside, cool and shady."

Leo D. Ames

The Hitchhiking Sailor

By the roadside, dressed in white
Stood he, graceful and polite.
An outstretched arm, and upturned thumb
Still so long, heavy and numb.

His grief was too much to bear,
But he must despite despair.
Behind he was leaving his love
In the trusting care of God above.

Tomorrow he must sail the sea.
There wasn't a sailor sadder than he,
The hitchhiking sailor by the roadside
Trying so desperately to hitch a ride.

Wanda Swint

Voice

I hear it.

Into my ear,
Straight through my mind,
Down to my soul.

The whisper of a demon,
Big heart as black as coal.

Draft coming through the window,
Brings a voice on the wind,
Icy tongue; not that of a friend.

Every night haunting,
For the rest of my life.

Blank eyes staring into the night.

Leah Henninger

Chill Verse

When the sun goes down
stretch out
lay back
put your feet up.
THEN
as the sun sets
AND
the heat leaves
your side of the planet
wipe away
your last drop of sweat
and just
CHILL

Marlene Montgomery

A Home-Less Man's Plea

Streets of broken promises
Streets of pain, that is where
I live on streets of shame.

A humble man with tattered clothes,
and weary blood-shot eyes.
I stand watching, as face-less people
pass me by.
"Hey mister can you spare a dime"

Why can't you see me - I am alive!
To my existence you are blind.
Stop! Look into my eyes,
for you will see that you are,
merely a reflection of me.

So please have some compassion
for me, a fellow human being.

For one day you may awaken to
see that, I am you and you are me.

Linda Yantin

An American Tale

  Quickness of a coyote
  Strength of a bear
  Smoke from a tepee
Red skin and long black hair
  Eyes of an eagle
  Grace of a doe
  Lies of the white's
The power of a bow
  Hunters by name
  Warriors untamed
"Heathens, mostly" some claimed
  Then the white man came
  Stole their hides
  Settled their lands
  Spent their pride
Gathered and drove like buffalo
  A child's cry
  Blood on fresh fallen snow

Nathan Hyde

Hole For One

As a young boy of seven
Strolled slowly on his way
Through a back field all grown
to meet his bus that one day

Handicapped was that boy
Scorned when he would run
Legs that worked poorly
He felt hated by everyone

If only to be home
From that awful hateful school
To miss the bus at morning
Mother would let him home as a rule

Down through the field thinking
He remembered this little hole
Large enough to fall in
Surely away the bus would roll

It worked like a sweet charm
He was home to plan some fun
A way to erase the mean people
He had his hole for one.

Larry J. Hileman

4 P.M. In México

The dawn broke beautifully,
Sun peeking, breaking the clouds.

The air flowed breezy, promising heat.
Gradually,
And comfortably,
The heat came.

Perhaps too much.

She smiled, feeling the warmth,
The warmth coming naturally.

RAIN.
Without warning.
Unable to find shelter.
Getting soaked.
Heat still lingering,
Yet the rain making her shiver.

Then the rain stopped.

She stood there still shivering,
Knowing the heat of the next day would dry her.

Sylvia J. Martínez

Untitled

Sun down
Sunset
Clouds
Storm
Thunder
Showers
Rain
Skies
Clear
Blue sky
Birds flying
Waters
Fresh ocean
Breezes
Mountains

Suzanne Lilly

Sea Of Emotions

The storm erupts
Swirling, churning through my head
Which may do I turn?
Pulling me one way
I feel safe and protected
Pulling me the other way
I find no direction.
The battle pages on
As I try to get a foothold.
It's like climbing a mountain,
Neverending.
The storm erupts, then it calms
Leaving me wondering what has happened.

Paula Deitch

Untitled

Stare
the essential dream
would produce
a picture,
I think,
of a worship,
sad and smooth
never away from power
beneath behind above.

Lori Strongin

A Silo Beckons

Erect, strong,
symbol of fertility,
your voice echoes
abundance, life.

Only I see the
beautiful composite
of life in the mosaic
of your stony walls,

melding, blending
with the greenery
that softens and
surrounds you.

Nestling in the rolling
hills you reach out
and I linger
in your embrace

Mary D. Hayes

My Child

A child so near but yet so far,
takes the place that once was ajar.
She brings happiness and contentment
to this place, but for some reason
I keep making a big mistake.
The child is mine as so you've learned.
I want to be near her at all times,
but I have some fears that will take
some time.
Until those fears are afar,
my child is safe in another one's arms.
Here someday
I'll break the chain, then my
child and I will be one again.

Yvette Seabolt

Standing Still

Standing at nature's door
Taking my breath away, I enter
Enriched with beauty
I stand still
Listening to sounds of wisdom
The animals, lead the way
Approaching, the rushing stream
Seeing my reflection
I stand still
Reaching high into the sky
I hug, the old tree
Feeling its vibrations of speech
I stand still
Standing on earths blanket of silk
Feeling the sway of the grass
Smelling the fragrance, of the flowers
I stand still
Gathering, my thoughts
Reaching paths end
I stand still

Peggy Pike

Twinkle, Twinkle, Little Ear

Twinkle, twinkle, little ear.
Tell me, tell me, what you hear.
Hope it's good, not bad.
Hope it's happy, not sad.
Twinkle, twinkle, little ear.
Tell me, tell me, what you hear.

Sabrina Kempfer

493

Love Of Years

Love is like a candle light
that burns and never dies.
It is within the two of you
as it lights up your lives.

As each day comes and goes,
they all add up to years.
The good is all that lingers
within those dried up tears.

Your children they are grown and gone
from within your home,
and yet they lives reflect the love
that you your-selves have known.

As you now stand together
as you have always done,
the candle light is burning bright,
for you shall always be as one.

Susan Lewis

Wide-Mouth Frog

There once was a wide-mouth frog,
That couldn't see good in the fog.
He jumped in a lake,
In it was a snake,
And now he can't see at all.

Melinda Reynolds

Someone Left Me

Someone left me
That dark and stormy night
Someone I loved
Left me, for another
For someone else
Someone left me
That dark and cold night
Someone I cared for
Left me
There to bake my sheds of
Tears away
Someone left me
That dark and stormy night
For another
For someone else
That I cared for
They left me alone
There to back my
Tears.....
....away...

Tovah France

A Beauty Within

There is a certain beauty
that each one of us do possess.
Not shown by one's appearance
or the mask of fancy dress.

For this beauty goes much deeper
and blossoms in many ways.
A writer,poet, and musician -
on paper their true emotion displays.

Such a beauty has no limit...
Its limbs spread both far and wide.
A painter, sculptor, and designer -
among their talents it can divide.

As the flower begins to open
and reveals the beauty you possess,
use it to reach other's hearts
with only yourself to impress.

Ron Titus

Felinity

Stretched out like a rubber band
that has lost its elasticity

The Cat yawns and wraps
her self around
the chipped clay pot

Black-tipped fur glowing
rising and falling
with each breath
one paw crossed over the other
her tail swishing even in sleep

The day drops behind
cream colored curtains
but the Cat does not awake

Krista Alvarez

My Prayer

Oh, God,
  That I might use
  My tongue for Thee.
  That through the years
  My voice might be
  A lilt of love
  To souls in agony.
  This is MY PRAYER!

Mary Anne Miller

A Little Confused

Just a line to say I'm living,
That I'm not among the dead,
Though I'm getting more forgetful
and I'm more confused in the head.

For sometimes I can't remember
When I gaze at the foot of the bed
If I must get up for something,
Or I've just come from there.

And there are times when it is dark out,
With my bandanna on my head,
I don't know if I'm retiring, or
Just getting out of bed.

And I'm before the "fridge" so often
My mind is filled with doubt,
Have I just put food away, or
Have I come to take some out.

This may sound absurd,
But I'm sorry for the past,
Please don't let this be the last,
So remember, I do love you.

Michael Jones

April Or June

The cool breeze
that lifts my hair
and refreshes me
tempts me
to succumb to
the seduction of
my senses to
Spring's refreshing-ness
of new life
and fragrances that
stimulate memories...
freedoms..
of childhood days
and adolescent loves.

Rebekah C. Frantz

The Last Sunflower

Oh, little flower of the sun
that stood through wind and shower,
hang low your lovely golden head,
for it is your final hour!

Your fair sisters all have fallen,
their slender bodies 'round you lie,
their golden crowns upon Earth's bosom
they lie asleeping, 'neath the sky.

Oh, once your shining faces
did greet the morning sun,
while little honey bees did kiss——
your petals, one by one!

Lay down your golden head
upon your Mother, Earth,
for winds and time their havoc reaped
so sleep, my pretty one, sleep!

William McRae

Coming Home

I knew as I knelt to pray
  that the angels
would come that day.
For they had been just out of sight
  watching
throughout the night.
She had struggled so hard to stay
  but a golden heart
  stopped beating today.
Loving arms would circle her tight
  as they brought her
  into heaven's shining light.
The pain that had held her dear face
  was replaced
  with God's loving Grace.
She knew she had come home
  as God beckoned
  from his glorious throne.

Shirley Hartline

Death's Black Angel

Fetter the days, Hoary the nights
  The black angel of death
Awaiting! To take final flight.

Bitter cold, icy, That final day
  I mourned! I wept!
The vale of breath fading away.

Couched, She lay so still
  Mortally wounded!
Smote! I felt the chill.

The days of yore, "Forever Gone!"
  Swift as the wind
Thou ruddy cloak, Now art wan.

Oh! Bitter grave, Thou cannot take
  Give back my love!
Souls thou have will awake.

Can't thou not shew remorse?
  Vagabond! Black angel of death,
Yet! Thou taketh life by force.

Oh! Smitten grave, Thou will cease
The angel of life will re-lease.

Ruth Crawford

Child Man

Rigid jaw and hard fixed eyes
The boy prepared for life's surprise.
Don't touch! Don't speak!
Don't disturb the shell,
that gives me peace!

Paging through the textbooks' fluff
A frozen clock it's time so tough.
Don't touch! Don't speak!
Don't disturb the shell,
that gives me peace!

Throbbing veins with savage beats
His daily life demands raw meat.
Don't touch! Don't speak!
Don't disturb the shell,
that gives me peace!

Clear to see the hurt and pain
Too bad nobody knows his name.
Don't touch! Don't speak!
Don't disturb the shell,
that denies him peace!

Kathy Leonard

The Great Outdoors

The window is open
The cool crisp January air
Is drifting in
Refreshing an tingling
Tantalizing and inviting
Beckoning me to the great outdoors

I must go
I can't refrain from thoughts
Of wandering over hill and dale
It is calling me, beckoning me
To the great outdoors

I must go
Walk through the cool crisp air
I must go
Run run run
Through the once tall green grass

This I must do
Before the cold icy winds of winter
Once again comes to
The great outdoors

Robert Andrew Thompson

Promise

When it's hard to get going,
  the day is soon done,
and we haven't moved a thing,
  let alone have some fun.

The hours we have wasted,
  and too numerous to mention,
although they were spent,
  with the best of intention.

We make ourselves the promise
  tomorrow will be different;
time will be better spent,
  and we look back on accomplishment.

Just look at those promises,
  we intended to keep!
they reach such a height,
  we never can leap.

Luke N. Baxter

Memories

I was by your side
The day you said "Good-bye"
I didn't want to believe it
But I know it was for good
All the pain you went through
It was in me to
It was hard to take the facts
That you were going to be gone for good
Now what was I going to do without you
I was scared to move closer to another
Since you meant the world to me
For so many days, I cried for you
Wanting you to come back
But I know you wouldn't
You were millions of miles away
And you place was just right for you
Soon I started to understand
That you were looking down on me
And when I needed you
All I had to do was pray.

Tammy Anhalt

Our River Road Farm

The buildings are white
The fields are green
It's the prettiest farm
I've ever seen.

The Blue Earth River
Deep and wide
Runs silent past
The eastern side.

I vow our farm
Will never see
A button weed
As tall as me.

This farm of ours
Has raised our nine
All healthy as
The tallest pine.

Our Blue black earth
Which named our town
Produces crops
Of world renown.

Richard Ralph Quaday

Moonbeams And Surprise Lilies

On a sultry summer night,
the full moon
sheds its cool light,
in a silvery glow,

Mingling with
the potent perfume
of pink-petalled lilies
that bloom
on
leafless
stalks,
as they rise
from their warm beds.

Like languishing lovers
and pent up poets,
who has not longed for
the unfettered freedom of
naked ladies
bathing
in moonbeams?

Susan E. Even

The Sound

The whistle of a flute
The gentle violin bowing
With a toot, toot, toot, toot, toot.
And a violin F (Sharp) flowing.
The piano keys the music
While a clarinet softly flows.
The orchestra director cues it.
While the trumpet player blows.
All instruments in harmony
All together all at once.
This could turn out to be
the most beautiful sound, and it was.

Natalie Cruz

Ode To A Geode

Beauty endures
The heart of rock
Truth is pure
The soul a lock

Known from without
The heart a rind
Understood from without
The soul will blind

Known from within
The beauty of youth
Understood from within
A gem of truth

Flesh will fade
Time will tire
But what's inside
Will not expire

Robert L. Miller

Recovering

As I sit here in
The light of my soul,
  There's a brightness that
Shines like a star
  A sparkle of life,
That dwells within
  Sometimes I feel the darkness
of humanity that surrounds this
  old heart of mine
To fear is to live as I
  Come to find a new freedom
within in my own soul,
  a freedom that moves me
To love.

Trish McFayden

Untitled

The moon shines once a night
The sun lights once a day
Nature is true to its sight
Its innocence will never give way
Only man's ignorance will destroy it
When religion is in turmoil
The belief are among the prophets
In common and different soil
To tear down God's domain
As things don't seem fair
And then to feel the shame
When God shows no despair
To feel God's presence
Is to respect his creation

Seireyrith Thonn

495

You

You are the sunshine
  The light when all is dark.
The flower
  Not the weed.
The inspiration
  Not the uninspired.
The vast beautiful ocean
  Not the pollution.
All that is joyful
  Not what is painful.
What is beautiful
  Not the ugliness.
The fullness
  Not the emptiness.
The beauty of the changing seasons
  Not the darkness and cold of winter
My friend, not my enemy.
I have opened my heart and now
  You illuminate it...

Michelle L. Jennings

Since You Don't Love Me...

Since you don't love me...
The moon never more
it's coming out without you,
and my stars night will be only that,
a sad night
dark, empty...

Since you don't love me,
already I don't care about it
if the life, it's my own dead,
when you're near to me
it's same when you're so far,
I prefer to be dead
to finish with this double martyrdom.
Martyrdom because I can't
take you out of my heart;
and martyrdom....
Because I don't want.

Since you don't love me..
I don't want to recognize that the loneliness
.....hurt.

Luis A. Pozo

Dimensional Triangle

A dank and never ending midnight
  the moons full light.
Brooding, menacing upon the waters
  tars did sit by candlelight.
Floating atop the fathoms,
  weep and groan.
Battalions manning the oars
  at ramming speed,
Then silence ..... alone.
The indigo deep begins to speak:
"'Twas their sentence reliving the
Judgement decree forever,
  not eternally...
But into nothingness
  annihilation is the cease."
To face deaths existence without hope,
Never to have day, sun and cloud.
    But eerie lapping, sea water tapping
    the hulls face, silently
    ... old tars by candlelights flicker.

Emily Fleming

The Gift

I saw a flower on
the mountain so high

It was nodding its head
up, toward the sky

The pedals so soft and
laden with dew

Its color was vibrant, but
with a beautiful hue

The stem with leaves, but
not a thorn in sight

And the fragrance it shared
was a special delight

Beauty like this could only
come from God's hand

He made it for all
all over this land

So when you see a flower
with its head titled high

Thank God for his gift,
it's for both you and I.

Randy Wynn

Mother

Mother, send me a picture,
the portrait in my head, just
isn't enough.
I long for your touch, the
smell of your skin, your grin.

Teach me more mother,
now I think I understand.
Every loving word you've said,
your amazing power of insight,
I want to know this too.
I want to be like you.

Mother your my epitome of beauty,
you've taught me everything I know.
My soul glows in your footsteps.
I wish to walk beside you
to the kingdom of wisdom.

All my creations I emanate for you,
make you proud of your little boy.
I love you so much, I cry laughing.
Thank you.

Park A. Adams

Embark

Close the light and dare to keep
The sight of mountains, high and steep
  Of legends bold
  And dreams of gold;
Drift off into boundless sleep.

Rush on, rush on, like whispers creep,
The endless lands and treasures deep.
  God's grace unfold
  To loves untold;
Dream on in boundless sleep.

Arise again to labors reap,
Till there, anon, the mystery keep
  Those tales untold
  And legends bold;
Then sail into boundless sleep.

Matthew Snow

"Jesus"

When I look up, in
  the sky:
It's than I remember, why
  "Jesus" died:
He died to save us, all
  from sin:
If we'll open our hearts, and
  just let him in:
We have to depart, from our
  old way of living:
Just think of what, he has
  already given:
If we want to see, "Heavens
  Gracious Shore":
We have to first, open
  the door:
If we'll do this, we
  will see:
"Heavens" everything, we've
  heard it to be:

Mary Lou Parsons

Because Of You

The grass is so much greener now
  The sky is a deeper blue.
I can't help but think somehow
  That it's all because of you.

When we first met, I thought,
  It was only in friendship's due.
But now my heart is full of love
  And it's all because of you.

Our love is so much different
  From the love of any two
Our love is bigger than life itself
  And it's all because of you.

It's easier to meet the roughest day
  And smiles come easier, too.
My life now has a purpose
  And I'll spend it loving you.

Robert Lee Holloway

Snow

I sit and wonder at
The snow as it falls,
Sometimes in silent beauty,
Or in bitter frozen squalls.
    SNOW
Covering all with its whiteness,
And its crystallized beauty.
Then to shovel and plow
It is our civic duty.
    SNOW
How nature could make
Such a wondrous dust,
And to make each flake unique,
Wow, how God must have fussed!
    SNOW
It's a shame that most people
Can't see the beauty or enjoy,
The best thing of winter
Nature's winterland toy.
    SNOW
It's clean, white, and refreshing.
And it's quite able to be,
Whatever your imagination is,
It's that simple you see!
    SNOW

Terry Ward

My Love For Thee

My eyes tell the story
The story of you and me
My heart holds the picture
Of our every fantasy
The physical attraction
The way that we made love
The way that you kiss me
Like an angel from above
With lips so soft
And skin so brown
I feel the love between us
Going round and round
Like a ring of diamonds and gold
That's how precious you are to me
I'll cherish all our time together
For all eternity.

Mary Bannister

Christmas

A child was born quite long ago
the story surely you all know.
He came to save us from our sin,
A place in heaven we would win.
This then is what we now share
A change in life, if we should dare.
So think not on what you might miss,
but rather friend just think of this:
An anniversary of life's great dedication
the result quite simply, our salvation!

C. Alan Lynch

Unfair

The wailing
the suffering
the bleeding
a madman
deranged killer
crazed coward
plants it
runs
doesn't look back
doesn't care
BOOM
the wailing
the suffering
the bleeding
where are the children?
Hundreds killed
lives lost
tears shed
the world
is breaking

Sarah Long

Today

TODAY
  The sun is shining,
  the wind is blowing,
  the world is turning.
TODAY
  Your eyes are glowing,
  your hair is shining,
  your love is showing.
TODAY of all days...
  I can show you my love is true,
  my heart is taken
TODAY is Valentine's Day

Katy Coker

The Last Sunrise

That August morning
The sun shined bright,
She laid in pain
Thankful she made it
Through the night.
With all her strength
She raised her head
Into the rising sun she stared
With every heavy breath
She knew it's time -
She turned away
And slowly dying
She knew that she could
Rest in peace.
She saw the sun rise
One last time.
And although the sun
Shined bright.
It felt very gloomy
Inside my heart.

Lana Mazover

The Dawn Of A New Day

Get up in the morning
the sun's not yet up
I make up some coffee
and pour out a cup.
Get showered and dressed
it's off to work I go.
It's Monday again
how can it be so?
My mood is so somber
I'm having a fit
I'm tired and I'm cranky
why put myself through it?
I think of my little ones
and know of their needs
their lives are a mystery
who knows where it leads.
I just know that I want
to do all that I can
the sunrise is beautiful
it's all part of a plan.

Kathleen Urban

Paradise

I love this tree
The tall strength as well in me
The large majesty over time
The gentle wind that comes in
Catching the sun in play
It runs through me
The gentleness of being
Its golden leaves on air
I rest my soul in your arms
And let my mind go on
On away through the wandering
Endless windows into the distance
I view the sense of something
Touched by a belonging need
A pattern a cycle a weave
In this pleasure of Innocence
Tied to the Natural dance
There is the freedom
In paradise
Sometimes lost

Livingston R. Webb

"Floating Down the Forest"

Floating down the forest
The trees so far away,
My heart has been captive
My loneliness is stealing its stay.

My thoughts are only torture
to my withering soul,
My being aches to feel your skin
your arms such love they show.

Can't you sense my aching?
Feel my heart break for you?
Can't you feel my sorrow?
My restless soul wants to run to you.

The forest is gone now,
replaced with buildings.
I float so far from the forest.
The trees are gone now,
just like you are gone now.

Laura Marie Cookson

"The Last Memory"

Sitting alone once again,
the waves caressing her ivory skin.
She walks along the distant shore,
I wonder what her love was for?
I wish to see her one last time,
to hold her hand close in mine.
I know the time will never be but
just a part of my memory.
I swallow my tears and try to be brave,
as I look down at her lonely grave.
And I place the roses by her side,
as the rain slowly does subside.
I turn to leave and hope you are,
as happy as that big bright star.
Your soul, at last is finally free,
you will live forever in my memory.

Rusty Hill

Status Petals Drop

I've smelled the roses
their exquisite fragrance
lifted my spirit to enriching beauty
(rapture enticing, ecstasy rare).

But, as gold bars have melted
Red petals have fallen
Ah, my freed soul remembers
While I stoop to whiff the violets.
Purity

Pat Troisi

I Wish It Were All Over Now Wife

Twenty seventh of July
Theo my dear brother
today on the road to Auvers
I painted my last picture
evening the end of the day
wheat fields clouded dark sky
lovely sunflowers here and there
the road
red spots
the men
shape nearly sketch
between uninterruptedly flowing
colors of the river
church somewhere on the hills
still you can hear bells
and reflective echo of shots.

Krzysztof Dabrowiecki

Three Friends

Three friends, still visit my mind,
Their faces I clearly see.
They loved me. I loved them.
No others were ever so kind.

Their names I no longer recall,
But buddies forever we'll be.
They backed me. I backed them.
I cried on hearing their fall.

In body bags they zipped them black,
No explanation e'er given at all.
I mourned me. I mourned them.
But never, would they ever be back!

Well twenty-five years have passed,
Since those men went on to God.
But, O so much, must still be done,
For the past to be put in the past.

What? You ask, must I do still?
I'm not sure it can never be done.
But I'd like to say good-bye, and over their
    coffins cry,
And dear God, get their blood off of Bill!
William E. Oldham

Someone Forgot To Give

Some people dwell in "shanty towns"
their problems...very real

There are no lights surrounding them
sometimes just constant fear

No newsmen come around to see...
no congressman to call

No place to hang a coat or hat;
no pictures on a wall

Just silent tears and empty stares;
just wonder what will be

Some "shanty town" where people live
not far from all to see

Another day on thing is sure
the sun will always shine

Another day to wander there
from "shanty town" to "town"

For "shanty towns" will always be
wherever homeless live

Somewhere, sometime where homeless are...
someone forgot to give.
Ruth Hill

Fear

If you think that you can't,
Then you won't,
If you fear that you won't,
The fear will frighten you.
The if fear frightens your soul,
They you'll never gain the strength,
And thus the courage to become you.
And you'll simply be existing,
Existing got within yourself,
But the fear within your true self.
Onelia Molina

God's Hand

God touched His hand to the ground.
There flowers grew in leaps and bounds.
The scent of fragrance filled the air.
So many colors He made with care.
When outside, the beauty I see,
I feel He made them just for me.
Vicky Moore

An Alzheimer's Cry

Within the dark recesses of my mind
    there is no calendar of time
Naught but transient words and faces
Aliens my world embraces
They come and go freely yet unbidden
    memory and reason now is hidden
I speak yet with no definition
I walk yet have no destination
I eat and sleep yet know not why
I do not smile nor laugh or cry
I am not deaf, yet I hear naught
I am not blind, yet I see not
I have no emotion, yet I feel anger
I have no fear, for what is danger
I pace, I pace, I seek freedom
Free me Father - to thy Kingdom.
Louise Patterson

Time

Another day is dawning;
There is no time for yawning.

Do your work today;
Tonight give thanks and pray.

Then all day tomorrow;
There will be no sorrow.

As you think of yesterday;
"No time was wasted," you may say.

This could be your life's guide,
As you lift your head in pride.
Pearl E. Smith

Celestial

With 'all' and 'nothing' both.
There was a deep hole
A vast vacuum ahead
Just 'nothing' was spread.
I found myself alone
just owning my own.
And stepped ahead ...
I screamed
"Is there any......?
There answer were many,
Came on the wings of air
Telling me 'some' is there.
I guessed there was an end.
I begin to walk towards that trend.
I found at last that end
that answered me...assured me....
In the deep celestial quiet
"I am" it said "with you".
I saw, I felt
That was 'YOU'.
Navneet Sandhu

My Life

I was born, raised alone, I see
There was no one else, just me
To share or squabble with each other
I wish I'd had a sister or brother.

I married too young, I do now know
Never a child with that happy glow
But much too old for my years
Grew up too fast, I really fear.

Worked real hard all my life
To get ahead through all the strife
Things did work out so very well
I never became a ne'er-do-well,

I am the last of the five generations
I'm the oldest now of those relations
God gave me much to be thankful for
So life to me was never a bore.

Don't grieve for me when I am gone
I've lived a full life so very long
I am ready if God calls for me
To live with my family in eternity
Kay Heinke

On My Mind

When I close my eyes
There you are
In the darkness
There you stand
Alone
Spotlighted by my love.
Even though you can't always
Be everywhere I go
You will always be with me
Whenever I close my eyes
Because you are always
On my mind.
Raymond E. Niemann

"Death"

If I died tomorrow
There'd be no sorrow
No there'd be no pain
For I know there'd be rain
I hope that you'll forget me
And let my remains be
No I really don't care
About the way they fix my hair
For I shall be dead
Laying in my resting bed

For if I died tomorrow
There'd be no sorrow
Life would resume
And I shall assume
That I wouldn't be missed
By those who never knew my kiss
Nor knew my hatred and pain
For I have drowned in the rain
Of those I've hurt and maimed
For I am the soul of the unnamed.
Mary Juliet Lohnes

"Ghost"

Ghost, ghost
You are my host
You make me toast
You ghost!
Sharon Gieder

Men

Men are so confusing.
They are easy to upset.
They are easy to hurt.
They are sometimes easy to please.

Men are so moody.
You never know what to say to them.
You never know how to act around them.
You never know what will upset them.

Men are so different.
Some are gentlemen.
Some are jerks.
Some are handsome.
Misty Truitt

Tiger's Eyes

A tiger's eyes,
They glisten, they gleam.
But the tiger's eyes,
Are not what they seem.

A tiger's eyes,
Seem to glow in the night.
A yellowish color
That is soft and is bright.

A tiger's eyes,
A mystery within.
A mystery held
For all who can win.

To win you must first
Learn to succeed,
To understand
All that you need.

That the key
To the tiger's eyes.
The key to the mystery,
Held deep inside.
Kara E. Dodge

Dreams

Dreams go fast and far
they go by trains,
they go by cars.

Dreams are good
dreams are bad.
If you dream you
might be mad.

If you dream in your sleep,
it might make you weep.

Dreams are especially fun,
if you are the one.

So dream very carefully
because dreams can be fun.
Sylvia Lewis

Printed Product

Between the walls of leather bound,
thin paper pages will be found.

Upon each page words are penned,
fruitful thoughts to comprehend.

What would I do without this pleasure?
This is how I spend my leisure.
Susan Wright

The Spoon

They're all jealous of me.
They have to be.

Snuggling with my silver sister
so perfectly. I'm cozy.

Puddles of pastel milk fill me.
Pink hearts, blue diamonds—
It's morning.

Where am I going?
Into the sugar bowl
where white sweetness surrounds me.
I'll nap here all day, maybe.

A sneaky someone lifts me
into light for a midnight bite.
I'm sinking sticky into saliva—
being bathed by a wet baby kiss.
Stephanie Lee

A Child's Fairy

I love little fairies
    They're so sweet to behold
They're loving and caring
    or so I've been told.

Guarding young children
    Throughout the earth
A sweet little fairy
    For each child's birth.

The woodlands do twinkle
    From each fairy's light
They're watching their children
    Throughout the night.

No harm will befall you
    Sleep ever so sound
You'll awake in the morning
    To love all around.
Linda J. Borden

Ending The Hate

The blending of all the hands,
This could be our sign,
For the hour glass of sand,
Is running out of time.
Come closer together,
To unite as one,
Because we don't have forever,
For this battle to be won.
Let us go to this place,
Where everyone is equal,
Not divided by face,
But togetherness is legal.
It's just around the block,
This door of conclusion,
Which a few of us unlocked,
In this world of confusion.
If a couple more opened their minds,
And gave a suggestion,
Then maybe we would find,
The answer to this question.
Lisa White

The Ebb And Flow Of Humanity

To what depth this heart endures
this mind cannot conceive.
Passage go swiftly, on
winds of time—may
you mercifully haunt the
abysmal caverns of this
old abandoned heart.
Oh God, what conflict
beleaguers me is
cruel human frailty
when torn between the
cold logistics of
this enamelled mind,
and of heart strings incessantly
longing for that
what forever can
never be.
Of this my hell
my curse shall be...
the ebb and flow of humanity.
Sylvia Sepulveda Sandoval

I'm Not Alone

I'm not alone -
Tho' trouble may assail me -
My steps may falter -
And my dim eyes fail me.
I'm not the first to have
Such pain to bear -
It's all around me.
But in my faith, I share
The hope of peace,
And quiet release, from pain
Both for myself, and those
For whom I care.

I'm not alone -
For kind hands offer to me
The help to make it
Through each lonely day.
And now I understand
So much more clearly,
His words -
"I am the life, the truth, the way."
Mildred Judd Smyth

Seasons Cycle

As sun so sadly turns to rain
Those drops then turn to snow-
Year after year, time and again
That's the way the seasons go-

Leaves so green, then brown, then fall
Trees left dismal, dead, and bare-
Hearing the echo, mother nature's call
Before she chills once warm air-

Snow flakes fill gray empty skies
Now so wintery for sure-
We wished for snow we can't deny
Now wish for sun much more-

Then daylight's seen much longer
The frozen land begins to melt-
Warmth replaces chilling air
We recently had felt-

Abundant colors start to bloom
Children play as birds are singing-
We all know this is the time
The seasons cycle is beginning-
Tazz Anderson

Untitled

You raped my heart
Though you never knew

And left me
virgin
For none but
you.

Sarah Priscilla Thomas

Spiritual Reunion

The taste of rain upon my tongue;
Thy sweet celestial angels hum.
   I struggle through the endless night;
Without thee love, no strength to fight.
   So here I stand at heavens gate,
No more my weary soul to wait.
   And earthly hearts no more to know;
Of sacred dreams shared long ago.
   Oh golden gates you open wide;
And I abide and come inside.
   With awesome wonder do I see;
My sweet love awaits for me!

Sherry Schrammel

Time

While doing things I love to do,
Time passes quickly, this is true.
But lab'ring on a job undone,
Or working 'neath a burning sun
The minutes into hours turn.
The sun my back proceeds to burn.
And if I want the hours to be gone
As I think two, old time says one.

Time passes not when one needs so.
The man can barely even go
Forward and progress at all.
He's as slow as fleas are small.
Upon its delay when one relies,
Time O time, so quickly flies.

Roy Carr

Untitled

The goal is set before us,
   To be together at last.
How long for a life of trust,
   And not of hate, like the past?

Man and wife, thus we will be,
   On some beautiful day.
Love and trust will be the key,
   For both of us to stay.

Together we will grow,
   Not apart like the rest.
We were the greatest seed,
   ever sown,
   A relationship in which the
   Lord has blessed.

Sara L. Richter

Untitled

To behold a miracle is a treasured joy
To behold a son is my only boy

To concede to being truly blessed
To admit a matter of a simple jest

To acknowledge my most cherished lives
To bestow on men as future wives

Patricia Montaño

End Of An Era

Order drapes like a garment
   To clothe and hide
Till roustabouts disassemble
   And cast the tent aside.

The show was given extra time
   To sell her colorful wares
But in the end she folded
   As all such brief affairs.

We thought the entertainment
   Would hold their eyes and ears,
But interest waned, and eyes were drawn
   To distant other years.

Trice D. Yemm

I Have No Mouth...Yet I Must Scream

To release the inner anguish
To control my thoughts and yours
With one loud scream
Paralyzing your emotions
Leaving your heart in turmoil
Confusion sweeping through your brain
HEARING, SEEING, TOUCHING, SMELLING
TASTING, the bitterness of my despair
Altering your senses
Wishing you weren't YOU
Do you wish to be me?

You Can Not.
I Can Not.
I Shall Not.

I have no mouth,
   yet I must.....
   SCREAM.

Liz Beth Ann Collyge

I Don't Want Friends That Bad

I don't want friends that bad,
To do what is a new fad.
To smoke in the bathrooms,
and chew in the classrooms.

I don't want friends that bad,
To do things I never had.
To even doing drugs,
When I could have some hugs.

Jesus is my best friend.
He'll give me a helping hand,
When I am very sad.
I do want friends that bad.

Tim Meadows

Untitled

The winds carry your cries
to me, I'm coming, with the
night's moon I search to hear,
   "You Love Me"
from the core of your soul!

We are one, but did we miss
our "flight", so we failed, next
departure not known! we fight
to be know for all that there is.

Only then do we realize "our
knowing" was now our time
"Chosen"! a race from within
we fight from the past!

Kim Lumsden

An Old Pro

Handle the problems that begin
   to flow.
Don't panic if it should start
   to snow.
Put it together, learn how to
   to sew.
Keep your head up, go straight
   as an arrow.
Don't be afraid, just
   say no.
It will come natural, as
   you grow.
How simple it sounded, from
   an old pro.
As he preached, to the
   young doe.
His eyes were filled with a
   special glow.
A leader he was of an
   old show.

Patricia Goskowski Kubus

My Eagle, My Love

To soar with my Eagle,
to know life is nearby.
To sway form the mountains,
knowing any time, I could die.

Going through the tunnel of change,
knowing every day and night.
Flying. Blinded and out of rage.
Knowing I might.

With my wings out-stretched wide,
knowing the mountains are near.
If I hit, I may live, and yet die.
Is it humans, I want to fear?

All I ever wanted was freedom,
just like a friend from no where.
Is there a million or just one,
Is it death I fear?

When I flew with my Eagle, My Love,
We used to fly so high.
Knowing my Eagle, was my Love,
Together we died.

D. Bobeck

"Am I Too Busy?"

Am I too busy
To lend a helping hand
Or reach out to one who's hurting
And try to understand

Am I too busy
To even send a card
To encourage one who's going through
A trial that's very hard

Do I make excuses
For the things I don't get to
Convince myself there's not enough time
To do all I have to do

If others were as busy
As I always seem to be
Would anyone have the time
To ever be there for me

Oh-may I make the time
To lift others up in prayer
And never be too busy
To show them that I care

Lona S. Galyon

Care Bears

Take the time to lend a hand
  to listen
    to understand
      TAKE CARE...

Take the time to play
  to reflect
    to relate
      TAKE CARE....

Take the time to smile
  to laugh
    to cry
      TAKE CARE...

Take the time to share
  to hug
    to love
      TAKE CARE....

Monica L. Monsrud

Farewell

I tried starting over
To make the world as one
Don't ask Him the question why
Your answer never comes

So won't you please, please me
Hey let's just let it be
Everyone just come together
Now don't you weep for me

All you need is love, love
So don't let me down
Let's all give peace a chance
And show them what we've found

Do you want to know a secret
Life's road isn't very long
The dreams I spoke of in my life
Shouldn't end because I'm gone

I bid you all farewell
I'm with lucy in the sky
Christ you know it isn't easy
For them all to say goodbye

Michael DeMicco

That's Life

I couldn't wait when I was young
To reach the age of twenty one
The things I'd do, the things I'd see
And thought of no one, only me.
I made a list and kept it where
I could cross it off, if time to spare.
I worked and played so very hard
I soon forgot the old scorecard.
Now life goes on at a faster pace
With graying hair and wrinkled face
At 82 I've left behind that
Silly list that I had signed.
I've seen the happiness and pain
That living life will surely bring
I've loved and lost so many others
My son, husband and both the mothers
Yet through it all God gives me grace
To show the world a smiling face.

Opal L. Ray

Teacher

The time has come
To say good-bye
To books and friends
And Teachers too
I will have lots of friends
And books a thousand more
But oh! beloved Teacher
None other just like you
You taught me from the start
To read and write so well
You taught me how to color
My life a thousand ways
You always were my Friend
My loyal confidant
You saved me from the problems
That were straight ahead
I don't know how to pay
For all your dedication
All I can say is thank you
From the bottom of my heart

Mina Quintero

Final Rest

Rest is something we must do
To see life through and through
We all rest failing to believe
That you can not be reprieved

Some say they are afraid to do it
Just look around we all go through it
only failing to see the truth
That our final rest is our proof

We all know what the final rest is
You're lying upon your death bed
You lay down hoping to awake
Everyone knows there's no escape

Richard A. Thomas Jr.

Gang Awareness

When the gangs run
To see their friends
Each of them stealing a
Benz
They can't stop fighting,
To see the light.
Instead they run to see a
Fight.
But because
Their eyes are closed.
They get hit and they get dosed.
To stop this fighting
We need to seek the problem.
Run, run, to the nearest digits,
Jump on the phone
And stop those midgets.

Kyle Jensen

Love

Love that is hoarded, moulds at last
until we know someday, the only thing
we ever have is what we give away.

And kindness that is never used, but
hidden all alone, will slowly harden
until it is as hard as any stone.

It is the thing we always hold that we
will lose some day, the only thing
we ever have is what we give away.

Mattie Elaine Cooper

Travel Story

There's no ticket like a book
To take us miles away,
Nor any view to look
Than colored page display.

A grand knight you can be
Of graceful stature long ago,
Riding out for chivalry
With golden sword and bow.

A pilot now, you cruise the sky
Tread the heaven's light and space,
Wish forever you could fly
Make a circle, dive, zoom, rise!

Captain, captain! You are called
There's a light amidst the shore,
Let our glorious flag unfold
Home at last, the frigate's roar.

Oh! Your dreams, the book fulfill
Be it summer, be it winter,
Miles of travel, life's thrill,
All at once throughout the year.

Miguel Mojado Jr.

My Father

I awoke that night
To the smell of my father.
It filled the room
And there, in the silver gray light
Sat the real man my father.

Freed from his fears and
Grain quickened anger.
I hear thoughts of his love.
Take refuge in his strength.
Breathe his essence through my skin.

Touch the gray shirt smell of him.
I'm awake,
I leave the room and return.
He still fills my nose,
The factory man who was my father.

Slowly he fades.
I feel the promise of guidance.
We'll share a journey yet to come.
I know the truth of your love.
Quiet giant from my youth.

Susan Featheringill

A Make Of Me

Sick I lie, just gazing over
To where truth died, and bled all over
Like a plant torn by its root
With crying ground lying mute
I had hope, but you spit
In the fire that I lit
You control me no more
My revolting little sore
Has grown up and spread its wings
And inside of me it sings.
Who are you, and who am I?
Just a flicker in the sky
Just a drop of tainted blood
Piece of earth in piles of mud
You're the friend I never had
You're the clown that made me sad
You're the love I never found
You're the mouth that made no sound.
In your hell, you'll finally see
You are not a make of me

Seva Gunitskiy

Critical Thinker

Is it not a learning experience,
To wonder why things are?
To think of how it could be,
And not to find it so bizarre.

Oh, how does fate do it,
When it places you where it does?
Your life as you know it,
And the role you play, because;
It's not all so very easy
Sometimes it can be a pain.
The problems that exceed you
Non stop in the middle of the rain.
The circumstances that surround us,
As we play the teeter totter of life.
You have your ups, downs;
Possibly a middle ground.

Stop! Take a breathe,
Because you'll be alright!

Michael Dean Robinett

My Friend

If each step you take through life
  today brings nothing but despair,
Then reach out my friend and take my
  hand and I will walk with you.
So many times when I was blue and
  knew not where to turn,
You took my hand and walked with
  me and I never felt alone.
We shared so much together, embraced
  each other's fears,
You found the strength when I had
  none and together we were strong.
Though we know not what the future
  holds, tomorrow come what may.
Nothing will lift my spirits as high
  as you my friend, by my side.

Shirley Ryan George

For The Love Of A Child

It is a tragedy when a child dies
too soon, like a flower unable to
bloom. I feel sad and I care, but
the experience of having a child I
am unable to share. Unable to
see the child be. Here is what
Sarah would look like to me.
Like the sun her hair is the color
of a flame in which her mother's
is the same. The sparkle of the
blue skies shows in Sarah's eyes.
Her smile is so contagious that
anyone sad would feel glad.
For the love of a child lost in the
past, trust in God and
the grief will not last.

Suzanne Robinson

Why

Why do birds fly?
Why does math multiply?
Why do people stop and stare?
Why does cruelty have to glare?
Why do creatures hide?
Why do children like to ride?
With all the questions at our hands,
Why do we answer in our heads?

Rachael Graves

True Love Waits

True love never withers,
True love never fades,
True love only grows
In beautiful waves.

True love never angers,
True love finds no fault,
True love only praises
And uplifts the soul.

True love never gripes,
True love complains not,
True love only thanks,
And gives back to you.

True love does not hate,
True love won't despise,
True love only gives,
Through your fault and pride.

True love does not lust,
True love does not pine,
True love only waits,
Patient and kind.

Tiffany Davey

Handlebars

Handlebars strong and gentle
  turns corners up - until
deep brown headlights hooded by
evening dusk are a twinkle
  Hang on - listen to the sound
of life lived in abundance,
  Still more corners to take
Beneath the roughen exterior - gentle
Streams of fuel flow as churning
rapids - ebbing through content
meadows, caressing every sloping
rock, pebble and cove.
  Riding high in the King Queen
seat of life.

Mary Edwards

The Lamb's Eye Heals

Two o'clock
Under a plum sky
Crickets chirp

The House sleeps
Quickly I come to
The clouds knit

Shadows fall
I pull up my sheets
Sleep pines on

Nicholas Hayes

One In Bloom

One in bloom
unfolds true self
opening wide from
inside to out
reaching towards the sky
while firmly planted on earth
scattering the seeds of harmony
the process natural
when left to nature itself

Mary McDevitt

Giving

Give and give, and...
Unlock the gates of Heaven
If thus favoured
That's the mark of nobility
It's blessedness

It negates His giving grace
To give this morn
With an eye skewed to receive
The next eve
Keep giving, for He who gives
Gives it back

But...don't give
When you ought not
For such giving and taking
Cast dreary shadows
Giving no relief to recipient
And the giver too, no buffer

They are curses in essence
They unleash the blights of hell
And stalls growth at best.

Paul Owusu-Aduening

The Bosk

Lording over Mother's breast,
Verdant-laced fingers, silent,
Reach out to touch the sun

While thickened shadow prevails
Beneath lichen arms,
Yielding haven to His creatures.

Fed from loins as old as Time,
Breath deeply
That which pristine has made,

And ever valiant against darkness,
Shields us from the callous night
To blanket us unto the dawn...

Kate Breslin

Sun Of A Night

In the quiet of the night there are
very strange sounds and mysterious
fights often you imagine you see,
things that just aren't there.
You find yourself lost in visions
and just a slight jerk of your head
will bring you out of a blind stare.

The quiet of night often leaves you
waiting for the morning light to come.
You embrace the night with caution,
for you know not what it holds.
There is something in the night
that everyone is afraid of
it could be death sickness...

LeeVester L. Clay

The Dove

There is a bird that's called a dove,
Who is full of peace and love.
If only humans were like the dove,
Always full of peace and love.
Then we wouldn't have to see,
All the violence in our streets.
The dove holds out a helping hand,
But so few of us understand,
How a small bird called the dove,
Can give out so much peace and love.

Kerry Weichey

Fishing Vessel

Upon all oceans, deep and blue
Vessels made, for the master's use

Casting our nets side to side
by his blessing fish do arrive

From port to starboard, forward and aft
his floating power always will last

A royal mast riggings of strength
rudders and keels by ships length

Our helm is him from the heart
a guiding lighthouse all in part

When stormwaves crash upon our bow
In his perfection, we conquer somehow

A life ships mystery he did send
Teaching us, be fishers of men

Thomas A. Mayer

A Candle

It stands alone in its mold,
waiting for a striking blaze.

The glowing spark warms the heart,
as the flame begins to dance.

While staring into the brilliant glow,
time seems to slip away.

As the light grows dim,
the shadows move in.

Soon the wick will flicker,
no longer will this fire burn.

Tonia Ann Philipp

The Spring In New York

When in New York come Spring
Wake up around Everything
The butterflies at once
Spin in a happy dance.

But I unobserved the Spring
I wait and ask to everything
Why am I quite alone
and my Heart sleeps very long.

I do not see butterflies at once,
Which play with the wind a happy dance
I listen to the radio song
Who open my door to be long.

You enter my door and kiss me,
and in my heart come in spring,
I love around everything
The butterflies at once
Spin a very happy dance.

When in New York come Spring
Wake up around Everything.

Leonid Tsygan

His She And Me

I sometimes wonder,
    what their eyes do see,
    when he laughs with me,
    but kisses she.
because, it's funny how His her, and
    she can be
    two totally different people,
    to He and Me.
    And yet to others,
    her, is just one she.

Liz Slane

The Birth Of Christ

On Christmas morn a babe
    was born,
So tender, loving, and kind.
The stars in the heavens came
    close to the earth.
    Oh, how they did shine!
The angels sang their sweet
    little hymns,
Peace on earth good will toward men.
The shepherds left their flocks so small,
To witness the greatest birth of all.

Stephen R. Gray

Still Alone

You've been alone
way too long.
You feel and do
What you want to do.
When she's in your life
You treat her like a queen,
But since you've been alone
You forget that she's your thing.
You wanna please
and take care.
You wanna hear,
But you can't tell.
When you've been alone
You forget all your feelings.
And when she comes along
You're still alone.

Kasey M. Hiatt

Becoming Our Dad

You came into our lives.
    We did not need you.
You brought your ways.
    We did not know you.
But you married our Mom,
    We went along with you.

You brought your discipline.
    We did not always have that.
You made demands of us.
    We begin to understand
You made us feel secure.
    We felt comfortable with you.
You married our Mom.
    We began to like you.

You showed us you cared.
    We began to care, too.
You helped make us a family.
    We accepted you.
You married our Mom.
    We love you!

Linda K. Sadler

Invisible

I try with all my heart not to cry,
when I'm not seen or rather ignored.
How can my dark skin not be noticed
in the bright of day?

I wonder can I really fit in to a world
that has left me out.
Where is my place in a place
that does not welcome me?

How can my heart be loved by people
who can't see me?

Shilynda Scott

Untitled

I gave you my heart,
    what else did you want?
Now that you gone,
    your ghost comes to haunt.

I gave you my love,
    I gave all that I could.
Now I know,
    I gave more than I should.

I dedicated my life,
    To serving only you.
Now that you're gone,
    I have nothing left to do.

I do not know,
    where we went wrong.
I tried to show,
    My love was strong.

I guess this is good-bye,
    though it doesn't have to be,
But I will be strong,
    and try to find me.

Kelly Greathouse

What Makes A Poem?

What makes a poem?
What ever you feel:
The secrets of rain
On a window pane,
The smell of a rose
Or of cowboy clothes,
The sound of a flute
Or a foghorn hoot,
The taste of cake
Or a fresh water lake,
The touch of grass
Or an ice glass,
The shout of noon
Or the silent moon,
A stand still leaf
Or a rolling wheel,
Laughter and grief:
Whatever you feel.

Teresalee Hope Roundy

Wonder

I wonder each day
    what God would do
if he came to - day
    looking for you

Would he like what he sees
    or turn his head in shame
Do you know where your at?
    would you know that he came.

If you think of this rhyme
    as your day starts to begin
would it be any different
    would it be closer to him?

If this is the case
    put this on your mirror
we all need reminders
    Our life he can steer

Ken Beeler

Abortion

What is ever happening,
What is going on?
"Mom", I try to scream,
But my little voice is gone.

"Why me?" I say,
As the doctor proceeds.
"I could have met,
All of your needs."

I would have loved you,
Oh, so very much.
I've never even felt,
Your motherly touch.

Why do you do this
"Mommy, no please!!"
They've taken me out,
Like a sickly disease.

I will still love you,
I'll try to forgive,
But I'll never understand,
"Mommy, why couldn't I live?"

Kristin Dawn Carr

Time

Those endless days of summer,
When all of us were small,
The trees that whispered softly,
The breeze that seemed to call,

The plans we made, when we grew up,
That never were fulfilled,
Still in my mind as time goes by,
Were all enchanted filled,

As I think back, to years gone by,
I wish that time stood still,
Because I can't recapture,
Those memories, my heart has filled...

Kathee M. Felty

The White Dove

It was the noon of yesterday
when I returned back home
and I was greeted on my street
by a white dove.
Its tail was opened so wide
and looked like a peacock,
and looked me straight in the
eyes and sat on my head.
"I bring the news from the
Middle East, a land of bloody mess,
and I whisper in your ears
they are going to be friends.
The enemies of yesterdays
will come to terms this week
and shake hands in our land
for better days ahead.
There will be witness of our best
and the world will watch
when the heads of Israel
shake hands with Arafat.

Sophia Demas

A Stranger Over Time

You told me once,
when I was small,
to never talk to strangers.
Don't you remember
That's what you taught me?

Does that mean, Mom,
I can't talk to you,
even though I'm bigger?
Don't you get it?
Can't you see?
Mom, you're a stranger
A stranger now to me.

Noemey Wilford

Unborn Memories

I long for the days
When the earth was green,
The air was pure,
And the waters were clean.

I have missed these things
Very much already,
But I think it is even worse
For the unborn children.

They will all grow up
Not to have memories like this,
Never to know the earth,
Was a beautiful place to live.

I will not be here to share
All the wonders I have seen,
To all children not yet here,
They will have unborn memories.

Ralf Sutton

West Virginia

A walk by the water's edge
when the eventide has fallen,

Where the pools form little ripplets
Where the rushing water's falling,

And the mountains seem so close
you can hold them in your hand,

Where the woods form little hollows
airy quiet lies on the land,

For there is no sense of time
deep-woods deer make not the sound,

No, the trees are never stirred,
such a gentle peace is found,

Come walk the wood and mountain,
Come roam the forest glade,
Come share a bit of God that's free,
in a place that HE's handmade.

Melissa Dean Burdette

In Your Heart

Laying
with my thoughts of you,

Seeing
my dreams come true.

Wanting
to be a part,

Forever
in your heart.

Kimberly R. Pallante Berriman

Did You Stand?

Did you stand?
When the flag went by
your hat off
Your right hand over your heart?

Did you stand?
When you saw the Red,
White and Blue
Old Glory waving for freedom?

Did you stand?
Thinking of our boys who
did not return
And we are here
because of them?

Did you stand?
As the Stars and Stripes went by
your hat off,
your right hand over your heart?

Did you stand?

Shirley Holvick Leisman

Reach

Defenses are surrendered
when the need
exceeds the risk,
exposure chosen
over singularity.
In the mirror of their eyes
we face the fear
rejection holds,
a reflection
too true to bear
alone.
Dawn's vision
or retreat of dusk,
pain's threshold,
if it must be crossed,
presents the choice.
So cry.
Time, not words,
makes ragged edges smooth.
Love is never wrong.

Liz Hile

Living Rose

I met her one day
when the sky was blue
her eyes shone like diamonds
she was sweet as the morning dew

With her smile so sweet
and her laughter so pure
I knew she was the answer
and her love was the cure

And just like a white rose
that's planted in the spring
her love it will be nourished
and joy it will bring

Her love it will blossom
her love it will grow
and her seeds will be spread
where ever she may go

William O. Whiting

"All My Feelings About You"

You make me smile
when there is no happiness left.
All I have to do is watch
the enormous happy smile come across
your handsome happy face.
You make the sun shine
when there is no shine left
on my dark gloomy days.
All I have to do is look
into your brightly lit eyes.
All I have to do when I am sad
is close my eyes.
All I see is a huggable,
lovable, attractive young man
that lights up all my days with
bright glorious sunshine
and lots of joy and laughter.

Lauren L. Lucas

Why Worry

Why worry
When you can pray
Turn from sadness
To joy each day

You have a father
In heaven who cares
Gives you daily blessings
And doesn't forget to share.

Each new day
Is a free gift
Look up and say thanks
For giving me a lift

When would I be?
Without God's love
His hand is on me
Reaching from above

My creator is strong
This thrills my heart
Some day I'll be with him
And we will never part.

Sara L. Fox

Time

Where does it come from and
Where does it go.
This invisible source that we value so.
We measure it off in minutes
and days, and watch it go by
in so many ways.

We call it precious, yet we waste
it with ease.
And act like we have all the
time that we please.
But someday we'll find that we
wasted so much.
That our hourglass of time will
be gone from our touch.

Shirley Warner

"In My Garden Of Memories"

In my garden of memories,
where I will always be,
dreaming of my happy past,
I wish again to see.

In my garden of memories,
there are no lonely, dreary days,
the sun is always shining
and friends are here to stay.

The flowers in my garden,
are friends I knew and loved,
the fragrance of their memory,
still lingers from above.

Oh, how I wish my garden clock
would reverse it self in time,
and I once more could see my friends,
when they were in their prime.

But I know too well that this can't be,
when time has gone it ends,
so, with longing I will always be,
in my garden of memories.

Manuel Schwartz

Some Like It Hot

We seem to be often at odds
    Where room temperature concerned.
The thermostat's up, and she nods
    When I ask her why it's thus turned.

Where room temperature is concerned,
    The thermostat must be on HOT.
When I ask her why it's thus turned,
    I say that I wish it were not.

The thermostat must be on HOT —
    She says that's the way it must be.
I say that I wish it were not
    Because all this heat's killing me.

She says that's the way it must be,
    When out to her trailer I roam.
Because all this heat's killing me,
    I'm packing up and going home!

When out to her trailer I roam,
    The thermostat up, and she nods
While I'm packing up and going home.
    We seem to be often at odds.

Loraine O. Funk

"You'll Always Be Near"

God love you darling
Wherever you are
Thoughts are with you
Near and afar.
I loved you darling
I always will
I'll miss you honey
Time just stands still.
Now you're with Jesus
The one you held dear;
No longer sadness
Not even a tear.
I'll think of you darling
Fond memories held dear,
There will be no sorrow
You'll always be near.

Ruth M. Fuqua

Littlest One

My precious little boy.
Who brings me pain and joy.
Who shares with me a place,
A different sort of space.
With childish wonder he takes life in.
And in his impish little grin
I see the insect on the ground.
I watch the T.V. with no sound.
I talk to him with my hands
He looks up and he understands.
He is my son you see.
His name is Jeremy.
He's not like you and me.
For him the wind blows quietly.
Waves crash in silence on the shore.
There is no slamming of the door.
The popcorn pops soundlessly.
You see, he's not like you and me.
He is my son, my Jeremy.
And he is deaf.

Paulina Stowers

A Best Friend

A Best Friend is someone
Who means so very much.
A friend who will always care
And always keep in touch.

A Best Friend will guide you
Through your dark and gloomy days
And make the good times better
With their loving, thoughtful ways.

A Best Friend is someone
Who is there to share your tears.
To reassure your hopes and dreams
And cast away your fears.

A Best Friend is someone
Who has been there from the start.
Who will never let you down
And will never leave your heart.

A Best Friend is someone
Who will be there through and through.
That's why I am so happy;
Cause my Best Friend is You!

E. E. Nichole Billings

A Friend

I speak of a friend
Who's always there;
For when I'm troubled
She seems to care.

Her advice and counsel
She freely gives away.
When I come to her with problems,
She gives me the time of day.

Her humorous nature
Is always present.
Her big, wide smile
Is like the moon as a crescent.

She can be serious
Or even be mean.
And when she calls my full name
I don't want to be seen!

But she's very special;
She's like no other;
I speak, of course,
Of my dear mother.

Mark Young

A Mother's Ode

My dearest son
  who's brought such joy
Ever since a little boy
Who always smiles
  when life looks glum
And to his Mother
  a loving son

So proud and strong
  tender and warm
Dearest Steven
  you truly belong
For life's rewards
  make dreams come true
For one so dear
  and, son, that's you
    Valerie J. Gaspardo

A Night Of Dreaming

Dreaming is like fantasizing,
Will my dreams ever come true?
It's sad that I have to start realizing
That the morning's come anew.
In my dreams I enter,
A whole world of my own,
Where I can be the center.
Of a place I've always known,
A place of everlasting,
Gleaming twilights pink and blue,
My dream world is so wonderful,
Would you like to join me too?
But sometimes they are violent,
And those dreams can be strange.
But at least I wake up in the sun,
To notice nothing's changed.
Yet across the horizon the sun dips low,
And the whole world now is seeming,
A dark, mysterious, wonderful place,
As I enter a night of dreaming.
    Rachel Chung

Untitled

A little stranger
  Will soon visit you
And you will dress it in
  Pink or maybe blue
Someone to be loved-
  Yes cuddled too
With hair like sunshine
  And eyes sky blue
You will teach him and guide
  Him and tell things true
And hope he will always
  Be a credit to you
But remember this is
  A free soul who
Is not of you
  But only passing through.
    Vera Frederick

Whispers Of Love

Whispers on the wind
your gentle voice I hear
falling softly, like a mist
so lovely, when at first we kissed
whispers; sweet, enticing sounds
ecstasy in love abounds
and lo, at times, no words we need
when, in our hearts, our senses lead.
    Kenneth W. Raker

Evolution

In finding me, do I lose you?
Will you have other things to do?
Are you near and here to stay?
Or will you need to go away
To find a fluffy, vapid thing
Who'll worship you and to you cling?
That was me not long ago;
There was so much I did not know.
Where there was a gaping HOLE,
Now there's me escaping WHOLE.
I want you here to be with me
Because you like just what you see:
Someone who is finally free!

So, then, can we both be free?
Free to be...just you and me?

I want you here, but I won't lean.
Can you know just what I mean?
    Teddi Buttry

Nature

Water trickling through thickets;
winding downward sings.
Can you hear it?

Meadow lark balancing on a
reed, cocks its head, side
to side,
Eyes so shiny, sings!
Trickling water, meadow lark,
  Harmony.
    Mary S. Sneed

Joseph T. Johnson III

What you be doin' comin' 'round here
wit' yo sad face, checkin' on me?
I ain't dead yet.
Me, I got moves inside
of me that you young folk only dream of.
I hears you talkin' 'bout me
like I ain't even here.
Sometimes, I jes sets here
and acts like I don't hear nothin'.
Don't be thinkin' I can't figure out
what's what.
I've already done what you haven't even
thought 'bout doin'.
For now, I'll jes be settin' here,
watchin' my stories,
checkin' out them pretty nurses
and the old ladies who try to catch my eye.
Don't be worrin' 'bout me, now.
Go on wit yoself, child!
I gots things to do.
    Lisa A. Peterson

Witches

Witches are wondrous
Witches are free
Witches are not like you and me

Spells and potions are what they like
You better beware for Halloween Night

Ghosts and goblins are scary too
But when witches come
They put a spell on you
    Tonya Pierce

Shadows

From the shadows I watch you
  with adoring eyes.
  If only you'd look back at me
  and see how my heart flies.
I want to profess my love for you
  I want to tell you how I feel.
  I want to make my dreams for us
  became alive and real.
When I look at your beautiful face,
  my heart cries out "I love you!"
  I want you to feel the same about me,
  I want you to love me, too.
But if I told you all these things,
  I know you'd laugh at me.
  You'd think I was just a silly girl,
  you'd think our love could never be.
So in the shadows I once watched you from,
  now I silently cry.
  But if you'd simply smile at me,
  maybe next time I won't be so shy.
    Lena Abella

Cuddly Evening

A young teenage girl
with an ironic sense of humor
plays viola at
the dining room table.
She's got rhythm.

A third-grade boy
skips through
the apartment and
bubbles over with questions.
He rushes through homework
to play Nintendo.

A middle-aged mom
washes dishes and
listens to the viola.
She stops the third
grader and checks that
he's done all his homework.

After hugs, we go
to bed feeling satisfied
    Susan D. Archer

Roads Of Destiny

As one finds destiny
  with each passing day,
They learn of the lessons
  that one must pay.

The roads twist and turn
  in so many ways,
You must choose one wisely
  for there's where it lays.

So with this thought in mind
  choose as you may,
For the choices you make
  in your destiny stay.
    Mandy Lovin

Missing You

It's autumn time again,
    With every falling leaf I cry
When I remember you,
    And when we said goodbye.

Each new day brings thoughts of you
In such a loving, gentle way
I know you're gone from me
But within my life upon this earth,
    You will forever be.

Some days are filled with memories,
of all the days that used to be.
Some days are filled with tears,
and others filled with fears.
But you love remains within my heart
    since all the days we've been apart.

Lucille Tompkins

Remember Me

As I sit alone
with nothing to do
memories come back
and I think of you
    I smile to myself
    as a thought comes to mind
    a tear slides down my cheek
    thinking of another time

When you remember me
If you remember me

Sometimes I dream
they seem so real
when I open my eyes
there's so much I feel
    You've stolen a part of me
    never to be replaced
    I still feel your touch
    I still see your face

When you remember me
If you remember me

TeResa Samples

Walk With The Lord

When you're down and out
With nowhere to go
Just talk to the Lord
For he loves you so

He'll walk along beside you
All of the way
You'll never be lost
Night or day

Tell him your troubles
And hold to your faith
He'll lead you and guide you
Along the right path

His love never fades
Though the way be dim
Just hold to his hand
And walk along with him

A peace will be felt
And a glow in your life
As you walk with the Lord
Both day and night

Margaret Spillman

"Treat Me Gently"

When I am old, please treat me
With respect that I am due.
I have lived for many years,
Helped changed the world for you.

My memory may be failing,
My eyesight going bad,
My halting walk and trembling talk
Make those around me sad.

I may speak harsh, or not at all,
My muscles may not move.
My skin and bones break easily,
My health may not improve.

But I'm still that same person
That I have always been,
So treat me gently, young one,
'Til I'm at rest in Him.

Martha A. McCartney

Makoye-Kin

The lone one of legend
With the eyes like a man
Remains as he has been
For all of his life

In the winter twilight
Gray one standing in the snow
Viewed but somehow recondite
Substance and shadow

Unlike his four-legged brethren
He made precious little meat
Forced to stalk two-legged men
His soul made deplete

In the Godforsaken jungle
First, unarmed, not to the hilt
Dispatching absent ritual
To serve to ease the guilt

He has lain down his robe
His spirit no longer rife
Dying well is less than tragic
He has led a sacred life.

Terita Maria Savoy

Treasured Friends

Friendships are treasures that mature
with time,
Enhancing the quality, as the aging
of wine.

In life you will travel through
journeys that pass,
With friends of the moment that
vow it will last.

But, when the moment of truth
finds you in bed,
Searching your mind for all that
was said.

You may be surprised, as you sift
through the sand,
Your friends can be counted on
fingers of one hand.

R. S. Ashton

If Love Was...

If love was but a mountain
With you upon its top
I'd climb so I could hold you
Not until then would I stop

If love was a vast ocean
With you on distant shore
I'd sail my boat through storm and rain
And swim when its sails tore

If love was the blue heavens
With you on lofty whites
I'd fly the quest to find you
I'd soar to endless heights

And if your love were all these things
I'd solemnly pray to the Lord
That I might conquer everything
And have you as reward

But love is not a mountain
Or an ocean nor the sky
It's this feeling deep within us
Mine for you I won't deny

Thomas J. O'Leary

Why Am I Alone?

Do I choose to exist
without one
to which my soul can commune?
Or is it simply because
I choose a road that
others wish not to travel upon?

Why am I alone?

Am I like the prophet of old,
who thought
he was in love existence?
Or am I rather blinded
by my own emotions that I
cannot see those who travel with me?

Marie Goins

Desperate And All Alone

Desperate and all alone
without sun and water,
the flower shriveled up and died.

Desperate and all alone
without clothes and shelter,
the boy grew weak and was weary.

Desperate and all alone
without its mother's care
the puppy was sad and afraid.

Desperate and all alone
wandering about in unhappiness,
is the man without Jesus Christ.

Vibrant and full of life
walking in happiness and love,
is the man with Jesus Christ.

Desperate and all alone?
    or
Vibrant and full of life?

Tammy Lynn Hazzard

The Sands Of Time

Here I sit, on the sands of time,
Wondering what tomorrow brings.
Here I sit
Watching the world and its busy ways.
Putting my feelings on paper.
Watching the sun's playful rays
Dancing on water.
So bright, so light.

Here I sit
Watching the waves
In, out,
In, out,
Like a dance practiced so many times.

Children racing back and forth
Leaving footprints on the sand,
Only to be washed away.
They are in the past,
Never to be walked on again.
On the sands of time.

Meghan Rowland

Listen Here!

You never heard a thing I said,
Words cannot penetrate your head,
I talk until my face is blue,
The words just skip right over you!

I tell you where I put your tools,
The ones you piled upon the stools,
You look everywhere except the place,
Where I just told you to your face!

You search and search complaining still,
Want me to help you if I will,
Oh, do be quite, and open your eyes,
One cannot see with mouth so wide.

So when I tire of all the scam,
I open up the drawer you slammed,
The tools are there as I surmised,
Right before your very eyes!

Zelma Lorine Alford

If Not For You

If not for you, where would I be now?
Would I be somewhere alone?

If not for you, would I know how?
Would I have made it on my own?

If not for you, where would be my soul?
Would I know the joy I've had?

If not for you, as I grow old,
Sweet memories,
Mom and dad

C. Douglas Cozart

Untitled

Poems are words
written in quiet
after the tumult
when the somber
the joyous
the halting hours
are lived through.

Norma Ring

Longing

You are what I want.
You are what I need.
To give your heart,
Would set me free.

You are the one that holds the key.

Share your heart.
Share your needs.
Maybe that will also set you free.

You are my love,
And you'll always be.
Please, give some to me.

You are the one that makes me cry,
But still you are the gem in my eye.

You can be tender.
You can be strong.
For you it is I long.

Sharon Kae Bagby

The Darkness Of Love

In a room well lit
you can only see the
darkness of your mind

Even as your heart grows
stronger the light creeps
slowly behind

But can you pull the
switch that you left in time

Still only the darkness
of love you will find

Time can save what's
on your mind if you
find light and a peace of mind

Paul A. Felix

The Lonely Dove

At last my love,
You flew away.
Spread your wings
Just like the dove
That cast me peace
But never sings.

I feel you near,
Feathers upon my face
Warm with grace.

In your flight
I am the wind,
And if you were scaled
I am the sea.
I am the sun
In your garden of death.
The soil in which you rest,
And the life you can't endure.
Live in my heart,
Take ease in my mind,
And walk in the path of my fate.

Michelle L. Shields

Special Friend

A special friend is someone
You hold close to your heart
And never want to leave for long
And never be apart
They always seem to know
Just how you feel and why
And they always seem to be there
When you feel the need to cry
They love you just because you're you
And don't ask any more
Because you have that special bond
That only friends are for
They test you-they try you
But only cause they care
And then you know the reason
Why friends are always there
They make you happy-make you sad
They are there to help you grow
And always hold that special bond
That only Good friends know.

Patricia A. Dotter

What You Tell Me

You tell me,
You love my hair.
You love the things I do.
This is what you tell me.

You tell me,
You'll always be there.
You'll always care.
You'll always be my unbiased opinion.
This is what you tell me.

You tell me,
This is meant to be.
This is our fate.
This is what love is.
This is what you tell me.

What you tell me
May be true.
But sometimes,
I love you,
Is what you need to tell me.

Lisa Wimer

To Catch A Star

To catch a star
You must reach out into the darkness
And trust the light
To drive you forth
And carry you safely
To the place where stars are made
And when you touch your very own star
Then you will see
That it is possible
For you to catch a star
But as you grasp it in your hands
The light lets go
And if believe you do not
Then you will fall into the darkness
And you will drop your star
But if believe you do
Hold on tight to your star
For you know the light is still there
Walking with you
Ready to catch you when you fall

Kathleen Clevenger

From My Heart

You are a special lady
you really touched my soul
and every time I look at you
I go out of control
you amaze me with your beauty
you take my breath away
and when I want to talk to you
I don't know what to say
I want to say you're beautiful
I want to say you're sweet
I want to say I love you
but baby I'm so weak.
Mario E. Zugasti

Passion In Reverse

Stay away from me
You shadow of my past
Stay away from me
The love that couldn't last
All the hurt and pain
Memories in vain
Forget the dreams, that lore
My love is there no more
I cannot longer take
Not even for you sake
That my heart will break
I will forget, be free
Stay away, away from me.
Karin Dovring

Your Tears

For the tears
you shed,
for the loss
you live,
for the promises
you didn't keep,
for the emptiness
you not yet conceive.

For the dreams
that vanished in the air,
for all the times
I despaired,
for all the memories
I've cried alone,
for the great pain
you will suffer,
I pray to God he looks your way.
Rosa M. Diaz

For Us You Do Weep

A day long ago
You stood tall and proud;
Watching and smiling
At all the things around.
But now, weeping willow,
For us you do weep.
Standing sadly and only
Looking down,
Trying not to see
All of the evils that surround.
Oh, beautiful willow,
You've bowed your head
To pray for our sins,
So that one day we might
See you stand tall again.
Samantha Peterson

Dee

On the day you were born
you were dimpled and sweet
from the tip of your nose
to your cute little feet.

As the years quickly passed
you were such a dear child
your personality remained sweet
and your manner was mild.

As you got to your teens
you were a joy to my heart
and our closeness and love
grew right from the start.

I've been with you through your problems
and you've been with me through mine
and no matter what else happened
we always turned out fine

Now that many years have passed
my love for you is true
and my prayers each night will always be
that I'm still loved by you.
Phyllis Maudsley

Untitled

When I first saw you.
You were so tiny and new.
So precious and a marvel to see.
Just to think you came from me.
You are a wonder of my love.
That came from the heavens above.
It's no wonder who you are,
Or who you've become.
You're where all my love comes from.
Your beauty always shines through.
With a love that is so true.
You are a blessing to me.
One that I know will always be.
S. Nault

Untitled

The day slowly approaches
You will finally be gone
My heart slowly begins to break
Dreading that day for so long.

My closest and dearest friend
Who has become to mean so much
Leaves behind wonderful memories
Of that warm forgotten touch.

Tread lightly upon my heart
When you come to say goodbye
Take your time in leaving
Hold me when I begin to cry.

There is no doubt in my mind
You will be deeply missed
Your laughter, your gentle smile
The memory of when we first kissed.

How will I say goodbye
To a man I care so much for?
I don't know what else to do
But walk you out and sadly close the door.
Lori A. Culver

"Happy Birthday"

A year has come and a year has gone,
You're still a part of me;
You may be getting older,
But much better too, you see.

My Love for you is more today,
Than yesterday by far;
But tomorrow's Love will be the best,
Like old wine aged in a jar.

So hold my hand, look into my eyes,
Touch me with a smile;
As Love touches both our hearts,
We linger embraced awhile.

When we release and go away,
My Love for you is strong;
Our minds will be united in Love,
And this cannot be wrong.

With this thought of Love in mind,
And in my awkward way;
I would like to take a moment of time,
And wish you a HAPPY BIRTHDAY.
William R. Cotten

History Lesson

The day that history stopped,
Was not a day to seize.
Darkness came with thunder,
And Hell began to freeze.
The day that History stopped,
Death came on the breeze.
There was no time to wonder,
Not even heaven heard the pleas.
The day that History stopped,
No one could save the trees.
Mankind made the blunder,
And Hell began to freeze.
Rob Henley

Side By Side

As we walk through life,
Let's do it side by side.
There'll be no mountain too high.
There'll be no ocean too wide.

No problem will be too large.
There's nothing we can't beat.
We'll walk together in the cold.
We'll walk together in the heat.

We'll face every obstacle.
Yes, we'll overcome them all.
We'll always boost the other.
We'll scale every wall.

Sure we'll have some tough times.
Sometimes life will be mean.
But as long as we're together,
We'll fulfill all our dreams.

We'll always come out ahead.
We'll never fall behind.
I'll always be yours
And you'll always be mine.
Cosby S. Haddock Jr.

Untitled

G race more precious than diamonds or gold
R edemption the merciful gift to all of his fold
A gift not of works, but grace by faith alone we are told
C harity of grace by Christ who shed his blood so bold
E ternal salvation from a saviour, creator from days of old

G race has justified, just-if-I'd-never did wrong
R epentance assured it for such peace I did long
A ccepted into Christs grace were we all belong
C omfort in grace, in peace, thankful in song
E nimity destroyed by grace victory echoed as a gong

G race never to late as the thief on the cross
R ighteous by faith forgiven of all his dross
A live in Christ because of his grace, all is not loss
C hrist more tender in grace than silk fibre in floss
E scaped in his blood, brighter than the luster of gloss

G race is sufficient for more I shall not ask
R est a gift of grace that we so firmly clasp
A h! Grace given free we could not receive it by task
C learly we see all it has done, yet so hard to grasp
E ndless grace one must secure as with a hasp

Willard Nernberg

"The Mask"

Mind games
pretending
you pretend like it was a game
a play, presenting a fabulous actor
the mask
that covers your face every time I see you
disguise the truth
but what in fact is the truth
no effort put forth
unless you have your mask on
and then you have your own reasons for it
do you enjoy playing with my mind
with my heart?
after all the years of silence
who was I fooling but myself
you have taken my trust and my blood
and you have taken my respect for you
put the mask back on
but I don't want to watch
you play

Jen Leno

Every Baby's Plea (Abortion)

Oh, Mother, sweetly within your womb I lie,
Praying that you will not let me die.
Every limb on my body is growing,
And even my little ears are showing.

Pumpity, pump goes my little heart.
Hey, my little body is getting ready to start!
Can you feel my foot kick your side?
I feel like I'm sliding down a big slide.

Please, Mommy, take me all the way through:
Don't do to me what other Mothers do.
Some day to you I might be a joy,
Maybe some gifted little girl or boy.

I love you Mommy and now in you I rest;
Awaiting the day to be held to your breast.
Seeing the joy that your eyes will possess,
As you sing and rock me to sleep none-the-less.

Patricia Foreman

"Of Ladies And Light"

Oh, Ladies of lustful, and of virtuous kind,
Please open your hearts to a few thoughts of mine.
You see, in my travels, of near and of far,
I've occasioned, to unlock the secret of stars.
For as much as they are, on a midsummer's night,
Like your eyes, brilliant diamonds of astral delight.
They are, but a candle, when held in compare,
To the fires raging wild, in the souls of the fair.
Now, I sense your resistance, your reasonable doubt,
To submit to the fact that I've figured this out.
Yet, the truth lies in waiting; a wish, I decree!...
In the stars, in yourself, you must first believe.

Kevin W. Ferguson

This Is My Heart

This is my heart, I give it to you.
Please don't walk on it, for it's very true.
For it loves you. And that comes straight
from the heart.
Once it was broken, and badly bent.
Bruised and raptured by time.
Searching for true love.
So this is my heart, I give it to you.
Will you love it? The way I love you.

Keith Reading

Death Of A Bird

There I sat upon the floor
playing a game and laughing galore
and then the news was brought to me
that she lay dying not much worse could it be
the game stopped, and all was hushed
the thump of the stairs was clear and rushed
the thump I recall more than the word
she had passed on, the death of a bird
a bird more beautiful than art can portray
more graceful and elegant than the words I can say
I walked out of the room that was suddenly still
and made no sound which took all of my will
I locked myself away with my despair
with all of my strife and no other care
I was told my bird had felt no pain
but in my heart it did rain
I know that day that I cried
and tried to convince myself my grandmother had not died
I loved her much, and will always remember that awful day
that my bird flew away

Anastacia Deinstadt

Blossoming Friendship

We've never seen a poem yet, comparing friends to flowers,
Perhaps no poet has been blessed by friends as grand as ours.

Flowers, like friends, are all distinct in size and shape and name,
No matter if they appear alike, you will find no two the same.

The strength of the stem and curve of the petals set them each a part,
What makes them all so similar is the way they cheer our heart.

The colour they bring into our lives - more vibrant than the sun -
Will not be dulled by cloud or night, it cannot be outdone.

It's when they bloom we look to them, to brighten up our days,
They surround us in their glory, and we gather their bouquets.

They give us gifts that can't be bought - a treasure chest of wealth,
Trust, respect, serenity, and a stronger sense of self.

God's gift to us is friendship, He provides us with the seeds,
So we plant and tend these gardens with our hearts and our good deeds.

Corrie Dunlop

The Dawning

Ah sleep
Perchance to dream
Of flowers blowing in the wind
And fields of grass so lush and green
Hiding delights waiting to be seen.
And birds so graceful in their flight
Winging us peacefully through the night
To dawns beginning, watching as nights curtain withdrew
To awaken the sun with a shower of dew.

Carol Fielding

Dogs I Knew

Shep, and Ranger, Lucky, and Blackie,
Penny, and Butch, Bibs, Candy, and Tuffy;
A furry, cold nosed, tail-wagging, squirming,
A cuddling, protective procession of boyhood dogs
Keeps wandering through my memories.

Tailing rabbits, pointing pheasants,
Fighting skunks, chasing cats,
Announcing cars, and playing games.
Whining, with pain of Porcupine quills,
Trap-crushed paws, and needless cruelty
Of vicious children; I see them all again...

Shaking hands, licking wounds,
Standing fierce beside me, warning the stranger.
Rushing to greet me home from school or work.
Nuzzling, in sympathy with childhood woes, and grownup worries,
Bringing happy pictures to my weary mind.

Fred R. Woeppel

Peace

When buzzard and dove fly the sky together
    Peace will be here
But who will feed the buzzard?
When foxes pass the suckling lambs and let them be
    Peace will be here
But how will the fox survive?
When lioness rests with the doe
    Peace will be here
But who will feed her hungry cubs?

Beasts their own kind will not kill
But man, who has reason and free will
Will kill a brother for his own ambition
Without a thought or inhibition.

Only when man curbs his greed
And sees another's urgent need
    Will peace be here.

Joan E. Clark

The Purple Turtle

The purple turtle crawled
Over the rocks
To where an old lady was
Washing some sox
He craw led u behind her
And she gave a scream
He was the first purple turtle
That she's ever seen
Into the stream he went with a splash
Off to her home she went with a dash
When she got there she was all out of breath
That purple turtle near scared her to death
In bed she had nightmares all through the night
It took her a week
To get over her fright.

James Kennedy

"Child Upon His Mother's Bosom"

Child upon his Mother's Bosom.
Patient, waiting, fussing, 'till he's fed.
Thinking, mother's 'tention awesome.
After, he's fed, she puts him to bed.

Silently, by his bed she stood.
Watching, every little detail.
Lately, he did not look so good.
Lately, he seemed, a little pale.

She had been watching him for hours.
The wall-clock, it ticked silently.
The air filled with scent of flowers.
She paced, up, and down, restlessly.

She was getting very anxious.
Tight, were the muscles in her neck.
It would be very merciless.
If the Lord, also took him back.

Only, a short two years ago,
She had lost another baby.
She cried to God, it wouldn't be so,
not this one, not even, may-be.

Hendricus P. Zwinkels

Heartfelt

Hours pass, days fade, love blossoms
Passion in the heart beats with natural breaths
New found love grows deeper within the soul
Tenderness and warmth flood life
Heart thinking begins
Sacrifices, frustrations and longing
seem worthwhile
To long is to please
Being as one unites two
Fondness is distance not kept
Heaven is love....
and love is what I'm in with you

Janice Pelletier

For Brandy

In which ever way the wind blows
Our souls are separated but will re-unite
As we climb upon wild horses
And are traveling across the sanded sea
We will once again meet
And a dove will guide our ways
So that one day the darkness ends
The dusk will be removed from my vision
There I will see you standing before me
It will have been an unforgettable turning
Each dawning and setting of the sun
The remembrance of the past
Seeming so unimaginable
The chances are even
I will see you again
Not mattering how long it takes my soul
To wonder in the path of yours
Goodbye

Kimberly Davies

Ding A Ding, Ding

Hurray no more winter! Mother Nature accommodates us by opening her gates. My heart rejoices and springs up to the odors so sweet. From roots unseen every blooming tree has birds busy building their nests singing ding a ding, ding. The vallies peek over to watch millions of buds unmask their tenderness and sweetness. Everything is right with the world. What a magnificent time of the year! Ding a ding, ding.

Marlene Clements

One More Time Daddy

I'm looking for you, yet you cannot be found.
Our paths have never crossed, yet we are still bound.

A part of me will always be with you.
Even though each other we never knew.

We've never met but you must part
You'll always be deep within my heart.

You've made a choice I cannot bear.
If only I was there then maybe I'd dare.

A choice without love, no hope can be found
Yet deep in our souls we are still bound.

One more time Daddy, a chance for us to meet.
Please one more time Daddy, I shall not claim defeat

A chance to prove I am your child
Your choice to ignore me when you were young and wild

Give me the hope I've never had before.
Open your arms if I ever walk through your door.

Let me be your little girl, and then,
Give me the love you could not way back when.

Susan Robinson

My Special Someone

Gone is the day that we're together
Our great memories I'll always remember.
The thing you gave will always be treasured,
For the love we shared can't be measured.

Always go to our tree,
Where we always stay when we're free,
And read the engravings,
That were always inspiring.

Time is running,
And that's why I've been worrying.
Time can't wait,
And with that, I learned to hate.

Now that you're back,
Both of us will find our luck.
We are really meant for each other,
So let's face the future together.

April Marie Cruz

Choosing Friends

Throughout life, we all make choices.
Our dreams, our goals, controlled by voices.
Voices heard by only me,
my love, my friends, who will they be?

We look to others, to show the way,
Mothers and fathers, both say nay.
Words of wisdom, they do provide,
"All the answers, in your heart do hide."

Search within and then you'll know,
Down which path that you should go.
Walk your path and walk it true,
And all you seek, will walk with you.

Through hard work, your dreams come true,
Achieving goals, depends on you.
Our love, we meet sometimes by chance,
But never do we take a second glance.

Our friends we limit, sometimes too few.
Those we trust, we call them true.
We talk, we listen, we laugh, we cry,
True friendship, is one that will never die.

John Henri Commanda

Dear Mommy Mommy Mommy (Alias SNAPDRAGON)

I do not think it funny
Or even kind of punny,
That you should spend such money,
On seeds and weeds and hoses
For centipedes with noses.
Your family, it growses,
And always it proposes
That you stop smelling roses.
To spend such time with greenery,
And miss us lovely scenery,
Seems to me OBSCENERY!

Carol-Ann Chretien

Why?

Why don't people hear me, or see me
or even believe in me?

When I needed someone, who was there,
Nobody!

Everybody expects me to be kind, happy, nice,
Why?

I don't want to be always be,
but now that's what is expected.

But I give up, why resist,
Am I just supposed to go on.

Roseann Shuflita

Conundrum Or Pun

Conundrum: As per the dictionary; a puzzle, a joke, a pun,
Or a play on words, twisted all around for fun.
Now Quasimodo needed help to ring his church bell,
Up went the signs, and all around town he did tell.
Next day a man with no arms showed up and did apply,
Don't tell me you can ring the bell, what can you pull the rope by?
Running towards the bell, he leaped and struck it with his face,
Upon my word, Quasimodo cried, you'll get blood all over the place,
Master, please give me a chance to show you, just one more try,
Off he ran, leaped, missed and through the window did fly.
Running rapidly down four flights Quasimodo tripped and almost fell,
Peasants asked, do you know this man; no, he replied, but his face
   rings a bell.
Up till now, I bet you thought this was funny,
Now take a second look, all it is; is punny.

Anne Sawchuk

"Mop-Up"

The office flood was a sight to see
operations manager was here at 0230

Supervisor got the call
to get here quick
'cause water was pouring in creating quite a slick

Off she went to the tanker base and believe you me
it was not a wild goose chase

It was a sight to behold
water pouring in
from two ceiling holes

The office was in chaos
with paperwork all a-wash
monitors and dispatch
were looking quite sloshed

A mop-up crew at the air tanker base??
Talk about a turn-about face!!

Lorraine Marshall

Blanket Of Silk

I looked inside of myself
Only to find a small frighten child.
Holding tightly to a blanket of silk.

Security and comfort is found beneath this blanket
Hiding behind its warmth,
how cozy it makes me feel.
I sit in my corner, sucking my thumb.

I'm sheltered from all my fears,
almost a sense of being isolated
from the people around me.

Freedom, fairy tales and happiness.
My blanket of silk.
Bethany Kenneally

I'll Drink To That

Does the hue of drink forget the real world?
Only the person supping of the nectar feels.
Is everyday life so hard to take?
Creating a false life does not uphold reality.
Then why does each new day bring unawareness
I ask, drinking in more relief to facing the
Problems of living another false day.
Oh the goodness of the night and the dread of the morning.
One's body is unable to sustain the falseness
Of the liquid to the real world.
One day I'll wake and make it as a real person.
Until that time I imbibe on pleasures
Of my own making, and find it easier to survive.
Sandy Findlay

To American Indians

Kain dried his knife and went to say his prayers
Only one drop of blood is still remaining
And land, stripped naked, for the wake is waiting
Kain dried his knife and went to say his prayers.

Blue ceiling of sky cathedral vaults up
In funeral rhythm hooves are trembling
Army of sparkling knives cuts soil like fresh baked bread
Its own children disowned and without it.

Kain dried his knife and went to say his prayers,
Only one drop of blood is still remaining,
And land, stripped naked, for the wake is waiting,
Concrete and iron would not drink it up.
Nadia Ondricek

Poets

Poets are pace-setters
Only found in high IQs
Every time they are in thought
To interpret and reveal the world,
So that peace may reign.

Perpetual visionaries
Of the earth and nature
Ever recording
The endless cycle of idea and action,
Shrouded in the planet we live in.

Painstaking poets of the universe
Oddly treated in days of yore
Ever remember to be steadfast
To perfect your heroic job,
So you may have your fill.
E. J. Nwoko

One Year To The Day!

Here it is September 13th, 1981
One year to the day, that Terry was on his run,
This brave young man, he went quite away...
And Terry you will always be remembered, every single day.

The task he performed, was really quite the thing
As he started running across Canada, in that very early spring,
Along those highways, up and down...
Terry always smiled, and never frowned.

Now a lot of people, are raising money, for the cancer fund
But there isn't a single soul, who will complete Terry's run,
No not a sister, or brother or even a friend....
For where Terry had to stop, his run did end.

Your cancer finally took its toll, Terry before you reached your goal
I know in my heart Terry, that you gave it your all, heart and soul,
And Terry I know, that you did your very best...
With your terrific run from east to west.

Terry I don't really know, what else there is that I can say
But that you are still, my only thought of hero, to this very day,
For you were a young, ambitious man, who did your own thing...
With you magnificent run, in that very early spring.
Darwin A. Huffman

Ego

Id and Super Ego are an interesting pair
One concerned with self
The other consumed with fair

Id clothed in the Devil's dress
Superego in adorned in
Gowns of those who will bless

Evil Id shelters our hidden desires
Tickles the fancy
Sizzles, and lights the fires

Holding back, toeing that line
Goodness is Superego
Holds us all to be proud and fine

Always a struggle between the two
Leaving the EGO in the middle
For me and for you!
Nansi Busch

Just For Awhile

Well wife my dear we are growing old
Own life's work will soon be through
Our steps that were once so light and gay
Now are flattering, and slow.

But this life down here
Is not forever, It's only
just for awhile
It's only the beginning of the life here after.
But here it is just for awhile.

Down here we plan in the early morning
To do something really grand
Only to find when day is over
Were only done half what we'd planed

But this life down here is not forever
It's only just for awhile
It's only the beginning of the life
here after
But here it is just for awhile.
Hazel D. Leahy

The Colors Of Swe Dagon Pagoda

It isn't yet noon and the warmth is still quite bearable.

Near the White Elephants a young girl in longyi threads
ondulating like a bright and slight reed on a wavelet.

An old woman on her knees cries by the shrine of a nat,
she lits up a few candles while monks in safran attire
walk by one behind the other,
mute under the cool shade of their large dark-red umbrellas.

Black birds are stealing the rice of yesterdays offerings;
sucking a cheroot businessmen haggle with their fingers
and oh...

...a stray dog has just urinated against a nat's dress
pastel blue, pink and green with touches of gold and silver.

A tall lady who has to ask for an urgent favour
beats the gong to call the Buddha's attention and further
some carvings have half-smoked cheroots planted into their mouths.

It was those days by gone of nineteen-sixty-two,
the days before the coup.

Who will now restore after the monsoon rains the colors
of the temple guardians, its nats mischievous or kind? Who?

No land should let its legends die.
Madeleine Micheloud

Once Upon A Time

You used to look so happy,
   once upon a time.
You would smile at the sun,
   now you shade your eyes from the glare.
You sit alone in the blackness of
   your room.
Not looking really, just blank stares at the walls.
Eyes that used to shine, now are
   just glazed over.
You liked adventure, now just surviving
   another day is adventure to you.
You are always flying in the sky,
   never coming down.
You are now afraid of the world.
Fearing everyone about you, now
   it's you and your pills, injections,
   snorts and hoots.
Oh dear God, let him help you.
It's much too late for me to start.
Once upon a time, you were alive,
   now you just sit and stare...
Sue E. Brosseau

Loneliness

A bleak mountain looking out to the grey sea,
On the summit, a lonely man.

Loneliness,
Like the harsh cry of the jackdaw,
The mournful wail of the loon.

The looming shadow of the pine tree,
Perched on an icy peak.
There, you hear the lonely howls of the wolves.

The cold distant moon
To which they lift their heads,
Casts a pale light on the woeful creatures.

Drifting around, everywhere,
Those same empty eyes,
That same blank look,
And that same wild grief.
Angela Koh Ying Si

Untitled

I, myself, was an actor
On the stage of life.
In the limelight, in the darkness
Coming and going as I pleased.
A clown whose face masked the tears,
The sorrow beneath mine eyes.
Giving bodily love to those who
Crave, to taste my tempting flesh.
A succulent beauty, lo and behold
Warm to touch but still I'm cold.
The laughter, the lights, the performance
I give - an act, all a play.
Just to satisfy what others want
To get through yet another day.
Sacha Gollop

The Lonely One

The wind blows into his white hair, as he sits alone
   on an old bench stuck in the sand.
Always gazing into space as the cold waves and foam beat into the land.

He gets up and walks away with shoulders slumped and head bowed down,
A far away look in cold blue eyes that constantly frown.

Who did he suddenly leave in great haste?
Never caring for those sad tears of waste.
He loved once and never again took up with the so-to-voce of love.
L. Evans

A Soldier Lost In Time

   The clouds go rolling softly by,
On a soft warm summers night,
The gentle breeze and rustling trees, it's such a peaceful sight,

   A silvery moon, on silent watch
Like a soldier lost in time,
A gentle old familiar face, soothing fears of every kind,

   Then suddenly the spell is broke,
By a far off distant cry,
The howling of a lonely wolf, followed by a whimpering sigh,

   An owl with eyes as sharp as glass,
Circling with talons open wide,
Watching for a startled mouse, with no place left to hide,

   A mother deer breathing soft,
A young one nestled near,
Keen ears twitching to and fro, for every noise to hear,

   And while we sleep our minds at peace,
For your sake and for mine,
The moon will watch for ever-more,
Like a soldier lost in time.
Keith Timbers

The Gift

Lord, thank you for sending Your son,
No others would willingly come,
He left the safety of Your side,
Knowing Your plan would not be done until He died,

For a brief time, He joined the human race,
A burden of love He carried with abundant grace,
He taught and reasoned so that we might learn,
To accept our Father's love was all He yearned,

As they lead Him up that hill,
Obediently still, He followed Your will,
The world only saw the end as He hung on the tree,
Not realizing that His death was to set us free.
Greg Kerr

Macaw And Me

It is there,
On a branch, watching me.
Its flaming eyes
Ignite brittle
Memories.
It waits.
Patiently.
Lighting my empty stare.
Deep charcoal eyes purify my soul.
I, Transfixed, feel the warmth of
Macaw's glowing, blinking embers.
I look at Macaw; Macaw looks at me.
We wait for each other
to make the first move. Nothing happens.
Raging flames of silence engulf us. Memories
dance around me, burn me, wound me, hypnotize me,
Consume me. Macaw defies me to douse it,
but I can't extinguish its flickering, comforting illumination.
Macaw has beguiled me, enchanted me, taken me under its wing.
My memories are Macaw's dreams.

David Gambrill

Lady Atlantic

Gentle moisture on my face, caused by accumulation.
Oh so close to body of woman Atlantic.
Beauty of her movement.
Gently, gracefully, meeting her lover shore.
The smell of her.
The sound of her giving of all she has.
Are you as frightened for you as I?
A woman!
My beautiful Atlantic.
To no respect have you,
Except from me.
A reputation, misleading.
A wife.
Oh so willing and fulfilling.
The gifts you gave to numerous to count.
Tears they fall.
They took from you, but never gave.
Savagely raping my dear one,
Bruised and broken they leave you now.
Oh great lady Atlantic.

Brenda Curry

Lamentation

I hear a voice
Oh! How it cries,
It wails!
It electrifies the skies.

I hear a voice
Oh! How it cries,
It wails! To the four winds it flies.

I hear a voice
Oh! How it cries,
Me! Me! Me! It wails!
I'm the one it lies.

I hear a voice
Insistently it cries
Not you! Not you! It wails! I'm the one it lies.

I hear a voice
Desperately it cries
Not you! Not you! Me! Me! It cries.

Still is the voice
Silently it cries,
Forever lost is the voice... Something in me dies.

George E. Moore

Resume

I am about to draft, a copy TODAY
of the essential evil, called RESUME.
Some call it Bio-Data, some CURRICULUM-VITAE
and that reminds me, of my new SILKY TIE
which definitely soon, I am going to WEAR
when hopefully, for an Interview I APPEAR.
I will always look ahead, and never in the REAR.
You also take heart, oh my friend, oh my PEER.

I AM GOING TO GET A JOB THIS YEAR. (AMEN)

I remember when my goals, were not that CLEAR
the job was so far, but seemed so NEAR
of rejection and failure, so great was the FEAR
Certificates and Diplomas, I was about to TEAR
and listen to me, if my voice you can HEAR.
Just for a moment, please lend me your EAR.
This state of joblessness, I just can't BEAR.
It brings along with, frustration so SHEER
so painful at times, OH DEAR, OH DEAR
but never again, I will shed a single TEAR.

I AM GOING TO GET A JOB THIS YEAR. (AMEN)

Zubair H. Malik

The Person Inside

So many times I've been told not to care,
Of the cruelty others express.
I knew long ago that the world was not fair,
Yet there's something that I must confess.

There is something about me that others despise,
Something I can't comprehend.
Perhaps my appearance, my looks or my size,
Have kept me from getting a friend.

I've always tried so desperately,
To be like everyone else.
Yet still in my mind I've known privately,
I am destined to just be myself.

I can only stand alone,
And hear them whisper my name.
None of my actions they seem to condone,
Just because I'm not the same.

I guess nothing can be done,
I can't sit there and lie.
I can't go with them and share in their fun,
Just like always, I'll stay here and cry.

Tina Garbas

Invaluable Lessons

Invaluable lessons
Of puddles that riddled through the lines
Drawn by a stick
As I Envisioned Rivers
Flowing
Transporting leaves and logs
No heavier than a twig
Lessons of ants
Running tiny little armies
Carrying the injured by back
I would be upon my elbows
With the wistful, wondering eyes of a child
Simply amazed
Amazed to have ten fingers and ten toes
Two eyes, a mouth and nose
Amazed to think that life
Is something greater than myself
And that I
Was much too young to be perplexed.

Maureen Bomberry

515

Untitled

The tenderness
of it sweeps o'er me like the gentle hand of spring.
I watch as the buds bloom,
in amazement,
as if it were the first time.
I sip slowly the memories I will endure
and even treasure,
someday.
As the beauty surrounds me,
I will embrace it with open arms,
wanting never to let it go
I do.
It will always be there,
for I will never lose sight.
    Helen Anne Leach

What Happened To Our Love

You used to hang on every word I'd say
Now you can hardly wait, to get away.
I ask you to help; or give me a hand;
I have to ask often, or force, or demand.

The only time you want me; is when we're in bed
if I want to talk; you watch T.V. instead.
You used to look at me with love in your eyes.
I don't know, maybe it's time we said our good-byes.

I still love you though; and my heart would break,
but this isn't good; how much more can I take?
I wish I knew; what happened to our lives.
Maybe this is what happens to all husbands and wives.

I promised myself, I'm not wearing my ring
the symbol unbroken circle doesn't mean anything
I miss, and I long for my very best friend.
I wish you could fall in love with me; all over again.
    Lynne Pederson

Ontario Budget

  The new Ontario budget is here.
Now many people have a new fear.
What is going to happen in the coming year.
Anything of value must be held dear.
Which can be sold later, for food and occasional beer.

  We live in a country of great hope.
Which they tell us, they can keep afloat.
As long as the people have a warm coat.
They may not end up like people of the boat.
    Bradley Caskanette

Deserted

What happened to years of love and affection
Now gone,
Replaced by what?
A loneliness so deep
A pain that defies detection.
So cover up
and place a wall between
Another who may desire to show intention.
No
It cannot be!!
For never again could I stand desertion.
    Olive Boyd-Bukowiecki

Mom

Not a day goes by and I think of you,
Not a week goes by and I quote something
You used to say,
I still cry when I wish I could talk with you,
But I know it's with God that you stay.
    Denise Mota

I Left My Heart In Williamsville

I left my heart in Williamsville in the city of Amherst of the greater Buffalo
north of New York on the Canadian border.

I left my heart in Williamsville in the fall when the winds of the north
blow through Ontario letting the last leaves fall on the ground
as a remembrance of my lost youth.

I left my heart in Williamsville in the winter when the winds of the plains
breeze through Erie leaving thousands of stars flying in the sky
in the whitish glow of the moon,

I left my heart in Williamsville in the spring when the multi-color
Shades of grass and the strength of the flowers
Had overcome the past winter.

I keep and leave my heart in Williamsville in the summer
When the blooming of the flowers is scenting the air
And Tommy's baskets are flying in the air
Rob's baseballs are sliding and gliding
Rick's footballs are bouncing and rebounding
And the clear voice of Lori is humming in the air
And a multitude of Tans is giving the summer its peaceful pace
In the glow of the clover and the sounds of the Rovers.

This is my Williamsville the Williamsville I love.
    Franco Crivelli

I Don't Remember The War

I don't remember the war; though I still feel mournful;
Nor does my father remember the war;
Sometimes he too feels sorrowful.

I don't remember the war;
I was told there's been more than one;
I've been told of the one with the Germans;
The one that we won.

I don't remember the war; In a way I'm glad;
The horrible things that happened;
Would surely make me sad.

I don't remember the war; my grandfather does;
I don't want to ask him if he was in the war;
But I'm sure he was.

I don't remember the war;
There's supposed to be more to come;
I hope I'm not around then;
If I'm not, I'll be luckier than some.

I don't remember the war; except for once a year;
When we remember those who died for our country;
And those who died in fear.
    Tammy Lynne McKinnon

Seasons Of Life

My body awakes as the trees burst forth
New life is all around,
Summer heat and scents lull the senses
Time marches on,
Red and yellow streak through the trees
My body once again grows weary,
Cold, stark, white covers the land
I am still, lifeless and grey,
    Marie Schoenmakers

Remembrance Day

Our fields are empty now.
No screaming, fighting, dying.
Just the whistling of the wind through the weeds.
The soldiers are gone now.
Only the memories of those who left and those who had to stay, remain.
We wear poppies now.
For those who died.
Not just for us, or their country or for future generations
But to end all wars.
The wars do not stop though.
The fighting goes on.
We should remember not only those who have died
But also those who are still dying.
Still fighting to end all wars.
The fields are empty now.
No screaming, fighting, everyone is dead.
That is how all the wars shall end, when no one is here to fight them.
If humanity will not live in peace, humanity will not live.
Remember on the eleventh day of the eleventh month,
Why our fields are empty now.

Brian Ward

Superior And Inferior, Not: Who Is The Mule Who Defined Equality?

Equality does not exist in society?
No one recognizes variety.
Be it one's job, family, friends, schools,
We are all in separate pools.
Each on individual stools
Of thought,
We have sought
Out.
One can not shout,
One can not boast,
Without someone having a roast.

Why does one not see but
Instead judge?
We will not budge.
Parce qu' equality is 5/5=1.
It exists mathematically
Not society systematically.

Il y a no such thing as 100% truths, because human beings are nothing
More than telephone booths.

Mia Hill

This Country Of Mine

What will happen in years to come
No one can say not even the young
To live in this country
To be one of a kind
Is to live in Canada
This country of mine

They would like to see you fall to the ground
To take away your sights and sounds
Your customs your heritage are ours to be proud
To pass onto our children
To be one of a crowd.

Your trees shall stand tall
Your rivers will flow from ocean to ocean
From spring to the snow
So let them surround you
With their threats and their time
For in years to come you'll still stand
This country of mine.

Marilyn Galloway

The Cross And His Blood

The cross holds safety for my weary soul
No matter the valley, my Lord's in control.
He sees all my sorrows, He knows all my fears
When I whisper His name, I know He will hear,
He patiently waits for my faintest cry
In mercy He answers with softest reply,
"I chose the cross gladly to set your soul free
My blood I shed freely on Calvary's tree,
To free you from bondage of sin and despair
In agony I suffered and bore your sins there,
Each blood drop brought cleansing to your dying soul
My death has redeemed you and made your life whole,
My blood purchased victory, when for you I was slain
I heard your heart's cry when so humbly you came,
To the foot of that cross stained with blood so divine
The angels rejoiced when I claimed you as mine,
For my blood purchased ransom to those who are lost
They find redemption and pardon at the foot of the cross."

Mary Young

Don't Blame Me

My sigh changed into a sick hysterical laugh.
No, I'm not crazy, you are.
You made it, not me, I just put it off.
Now you will all thank me.

I hit the button over and over again.
As I did it, my laughter got louder and louder.
Maybe so loud that it covered the sound made by the button.
But now everyone is going to know me.

And then they will ask me why did I do it?
I'll say, for everyone to know me.
And then they will ask me, how do I feel?
I'll answer by saying, popular.

I stepped outside now, to smell the air.
But all I could smell was smoke.
I needed a drink from the ocean.
But it was milky ash.

Now they won't ask me.
Because there's no life around, not a person, animal or tree.
How do I feel, I don't quite know.
I guess I'm a little scared.

Rhonda Basaraba

Stolen

My people, so at peace.
No fears, no anger or pains to release.
We live upon this rich bountiful land,
Sought or intruded by no other man.
My people have lived here so long and so free,
Our land is the lock and we cherish the key.
The others arrived and our peace is now gone,
A dead spirit lays, where the bright sun once shone.
We did not foresee, this awful dark day,
When the Indians land would be taken away.

Melanie Weber

Summer's Gone

The beaches now are quiet and lonely
No children playing in the sand,
Quietly leaves have changed their colour
Autumn reigns throughout the land
Cooler now October breezes
Leaves fall gently to the ground.
To make a blanket for the winter
Each leaf in place without a sound.

Joy LaPierre

'Tears Of Love'

Days seem difficult to go by.
Nights still harder to pass by.
 Thoughts so muddled bringing tears to eyes.
 Heart so heavy of painful cries.
Was it yesterday when I left?
It's hard to tell since I have never slept.
 Oh the pain cuts through my heart.
 My dreams seem shattered since we are apart.
It seems so easy to go in eternal sleep.
Where life is lifeless and promises not harder to keep.
 Memories are so fresh as far as I know.
 They hurt and just won't go.
Such was my love that you couldn't hold.
For you were scared and couldn't be bold.
 No matter whatever you do.
 Every breath I take is just for you.
Hate me, shut me if that's what you want to do
But give me few moments of life to survive just for you.

Harman Ahluwalia

Untitled

Still running, the young child was desperate for a
new sacrament. From the temple, there was another
mind-change. A new level of ritual. Landing without
words in a rock covered haven. Hiding from evolution.
Have you seen the interior? The child stood there,
towards unknown symbols. The quiet ones are secretly
starving. So now we need to burn their homes and their
saviors. Smile and exit the labyrinth. Are you done?
Enter the age of judgement. An
under-world of history.
Time and greed.
Sit in the corner and read.
Of the beyond, there are illusions
that are necessary for the story
to be complete.
Now, I know the silence,
and the serpents.
The gardeners and the citizens.
Your spiritual teacher (-guru-)
and the end.

Duncan D. Harry

A Waste Of Air

My first breath, morning of March 28, 1966.

Time passes and I waste more air.
 Needed air for everyone else.

I look outside and see no real happiness.
 On television, I hear and see all about torment and pain.
 Real life horror, it scares me.
 Everyone I talk to, has no good reason to be happy.

Tonight I sit here alone as usual, in more ways then one.
 In my heart I am empty.

My mother called today, really has nothing to say.
 She has no clue what I am about.

"Friends", what are they, can anyone really say that they know what
the word means.
 Why can't "God" come and save us from this eternal "hell" we live in?

Money is the root of life, yet it destroys life.
 Peace should be among us.

If I could, I would become an Eagle and fly away forever.
 I want the courage to be free to do the things I want without restrictions.

My head hurts...
 My last breath...

Steve Prete

Time

Today I walked amidst the rain
My toughs were of you
Of the times when we were young and free
Where has the time gone

The words left unspoken
That are held so dear to me now
You have gone so quickly
Why have I waited so long to think of you

Is time the master, the one who holds the key?
To our lives and then we hope
When time is slowly ebbing away
Can we lock the clock of time

To take the dreams once we knew
Amidst the rain I thought of you
For thoughts are only rainbows
They fade, like dreams, like the rain

If now was like tomorrow,
And yesterday was a chance again
I'd hold you in my arms so tenderly
Amidst the rain, to wish you back again.

Ruth Beter

The Rose

Beneath the withered rose, petals lay strewn about
My saddened heart in sympathy wants to cry and shout
Stay for just another day, maybe two or more
Let your beauty linger, let it be as it was before
Your petals crushed beneath the feet of countless passersby
Who never thought to look below but trampled right on by
They never stopped on summer days to smell your sweet bouquet
Which you so freely gave to us on each and every day
Winter is approaching, and moving in quite fast
Fear not my gentle rose, for her bitter cold can't last
Soon spring will follow with her warm and gentle rain
And you too shall rise and cease your slumber once again
Fear not you gentle flower with your ever-sweet perfume
The Spring will come and summer too and once again you'll bloom
Once again my gentle rose you'll heave a happy sigh
And force your shoots through now thawed ground and reach toward the sky

Eleanor D. Morrison-Gardner

My Mother

When I was just a toddler,
My mother used to say,
That people needed our loving hearts,
And then she taught me to pray.

We prayed for the homeless,
The hungry, the needy, the ill,
Asking God to reach down and bless them,
So their lives might be changed by His will.

We also prayed for the crippled,
And people who could not hear,
The blind, babies, and elders,
And then I saw a tear.

The tears came down, one by one,
Throughout the rest of the prayer.
Mom's heart so sweet, and mind so kind,
She had something special to share.

She quietly wiped her tears away,
And then, ended our prayer.
I'll never forget the way she was,
So loving and full of care.

Wendy Marie Barnes

518

The Unforgiven

When the love of my life walked out that door,
My heart was crushed and fell to the floor.

My chest stopped moving, my voice was weak,
My eyes swelled, and I was a freak.

A mistake I made, I can't undo. The love I have, I give to you.

Your heart is warm, your soul is caring,
The love we have, I want to keep sharing.

You are dear to me, I want you to know,
Together, our love can grow.

I was foolish, immature and dumb.
Now, my mistakes have made me numb.

Life was so precious, with you by my side,
Now I feel like I have died.

If I could turn back the hours of time,
I would erase my foolish crime.

My worst nightmare might come true. I could lose you.

A person I love is slipping away,
I want us to be happy. There must be a way.

Anything you ask, I will do, only because I LOVE YOU.

Cindy Litwinski

Inside Out

I lie here thinking, time unknown,
My heart aching for those at home.
A tear emerges my heart is shattered,
My mind confused, becoming battered.
I long for her and her graceful presence,
To me she is my life's full essence.
For me she bore a life - my token
My love for him could not be spoken,
The pair, my joy and sometimes sorrow,
I strive for them a great tomorrow.
Resent me not my mind untold,
Stand beside me, be strong and bold.
My self relieved, my greed my pains,
The pair my duo, my greatest gains.

Nicholas Gouvis

The Guardian

Like a fireman's boots standing ready for duty,
My father's leg stands guard at his bedside,
An extension of a vital man once whole and complete.
A fearing man who was a soldier,
His days of Glory misted in history.
A crested sock reaches high to warm its ever cool surface,
Its shoe a mirror of spit polish shine.
In readiness it stands, to await first alarm,
Set not for action to save the world
But await dawn's light
When slumber's rest has soothed the weary stump
Naked but for cotton sheets stretched over imaginary toes.
This leg has travelled many miles
A visitor on worldwide shores.
Sailing over azure seas, flying cobalt skies,
Trudging over desert sands and valleys of sweet green,
Step by step in unison, man and appliance.
As each grows weary with reality
Evening brings earned rest with freedom of appendage.

Norma Jean Thompson

Fate

Dedicated to Alice Watson
Like an angel she descends upon me from the heavens, and from
my dreams, a soft warm glow surrounds her.
She embraces me, wraps me in her loving warmth.
In her arms I'm taken to heaven.
Her kiss
Lips, soft, smooth, press against mine, my heart begins to race.
We make love.
It's no longer her and I, we are one, united.
She's gone
Without her there is only emptiness, although it's only temporary
It feels like eternity
Us. Together we are whole, full of love laughter, happiness and joy.
It's a bond stronger than any other, only to be broken by death.
But even then it will never be completely destroyed.
For she will always be there, deep in my heart.

Tim Komasara

The Healing Of Time

My best friend, my lover, gone, is no more
My comfort, my strength and all those things
Life was loving each other and the sons we shared
Gone forever is the wind beneath my wings.

Gone is the passion that once was
As is the touching, the holding and the kissing
The intimacy, closeness and shared moments
All that and much more is now missing.

The desires and dreams of the future
Shattered by death, replaced by despair
A constant companion, the loneliness and pain
I wonder, why me, this is so unfair.

Life isn't worth living, its meaning is lost
An ache deep inside this broken heart of mine
The tears keep flowing, how can I go on
People say, have patience to heal, one day at a time.

What's left, yes, I have my memories
To fill my sleepless nights, my mind of the past
The year has been hard, the heartache fading
I've had to let go, peace comes at long last.

Shirley Penner

The Salmon

The sun shone bright in the clear blue sky - the salmon knew that he must die
He remembered when he'd been - a small white smoult with a silv'ry sheen
Then he was living in the sea - swimming wild and swimming free
He grew there for several years - joyful, carefree, free from fears
One day he knew to go - back to his hatchling river home
He joined a group swimming river bound - they all travelled in a pinkish mound
Through the streams and lakes and pools - past those gaping human fools
Leaping falls and dodging bears - fighting rapids, gaining tears
In fins and tails several died - our hero salmon always tried
To swim the distance to his river dear - joy free, careful, full of fear
He made it there and swam and found - a comely female, also bound
Their eggs were laid and fertilized too - there was nothing more that they could do
As the sun rises high in the clear blue skies - the salmon gasps his last - and dies.

Tracey McGowan

My Wonderful Trip

Over the Andes we flew, such glorious sights to unfold
Mountain peaks covered with snow, their tips sticking out above clouds
The Captain and crew were most gracious, what wonderful care and control
What a lovely experience watching all the things I had heard of unfurl
The climb to the top of Machu Picchu was beyond belief, Moon Valley a
  glimpse of another world.
The ride through the fjords was wonderful, little Switzerland a sight to behold.
Bariloche was like heaven, what fun to hike and see
The glaciers in the distance, and have folks wave to me.
The dinner and dance at Buenos Aires was great, the dude ranch a
  huge success,
Iguaccu Falls was unbelievable, the heat and humidity nearly did
  everyone in.
At Rio the scenery was gorgeous, the mountain ride was great fun
Being tossed back and forth together, we laughed and hollered like kids.
The party at night was stupendous, the lights and reflections like dreams
How we laughed and enjoyed the beautiful sights as we acted like
  kings and queens.
The little boats moving slowly at Manaus and Leticia what fun,
The Amazon days are unforgettable, oh, to live them again!
Bagota ended the journey, the mountain tram very exciting
The farewell supper was the thrill of my life as I was chosen
  as hostess that night.
After fifty-three days this trip ended all too soon, leaving
  me wishing I was doing it all over again!

Gwen McLean

Natures Will

Rain falling lightly on leaves turning gold,
Mother nature spreading her blanket of white sparkling snow.
Jack frost early in season does his dance on window panes,
Hearing migrating calls of vast ascending cranes.
Fall is upon the hand, winter on the way;
Trees looking empty, waiting silently for warm summer days.
Nature has its disguise, reposed yet mystic.
Man does his evils, industry, pollution, so selfishly,
Will it turn back the tide to engulf his pride,
Possessions and dignity.
The days grew shorter for the wide wild North
Aggression, depression always striving forth.

Dale Edwin Wagner

The Flame

Everyday I walk past him.
Most times, I pretend he is invisible.
He is dressed with a pair of ragged old jeans and a t-shirt
  with the markings of several wears.

I quickly walk past him and hope he doesn't talk to me.
I try to isolate myself from him by concentrating on my day
  and what lies ahead.
But his eyes see me and the flame dwindles.

He holds a newspaper that pleads for spare change.
Nobody has the time to dig in their pockets. Not even me.

Everyday it's is the same routine. He never speaks.
He just stands there silently and waits.
He waits for the moment that someone walks up to him and offers
  a consoling word or an understanding look.
But no one ever does, and the flame becomes a spark.

There may be the occasional time where a person may give him a
  few loose coins in exchange for the newspaper.
But, they always scurry away before a word is exchanged.
Maybe they are afraid of seeing something familiar in his eyes.
Or perhaps, they are blinded by their own realities.
I just hope that one day I too, see light again and the flame will re-ignite.

Isabel I. Marangoni

Untitled

You are ...
More beautiful than the stone mullions in a gothic window,
a soft sculpture forever immortalized in my mind and heart,
the montage I've been trying to put together my whole life,
a gazebo where my soul finds shelter and rest,
the definition of eclectic, which triggers my passion,
you are all colors at their brightest intensity,
many tones of the same hue,
my future and my nostalgia,
where I look to achieve my greatest potential,
You are ... my renaissance.

Roger Desforges

Time

Days going,
Months passing,
Decades falling away,
Life becomes more complicated,
The world more fast paced,
The world gains age,
And the days seem shorter,
Things that are here today, may be gone tomorrow,
Today a flower thrives,
Days later it has life no more,
Centuries quickly go by, for time waits for no one,
What is here today may be a memory one day from now.
With a twist and a turn, it is two years later,
Then two more,
So don't say I'm too young,
Nor say it's too early,
For the next decade is just a heart beat away,
Time waits for....no one.

Nikki Rampersad

Moments

Standing alone facing oncoming moments
Moments which go by quicker as I age
Age that takes away my dreams of youth
Youth wasted by careless deeds and thoughts
Thought created in a state of confusion
Confusion brought on in my haste to be older
Older too long in a lifetime too short
Short moments melded together as I
Stand alone, waiting, facing old age
and the end of my oncoming moments.

Patricia Livingston

Forever An Image

A form shimmers upon the water's edge where I stand,
Misted eyes watching as it glistens with a shine.
You are a ripple upon the water's surface,
An image that I wish was mine.

You are a wrinkle upon the water's wave,
Shivering on a pool of blue.
Tears come, instead of courage,
Leaving no whisper from my lips saying I love you.

So I guess you'll just always be a form shattering the still
  of the calm
A reflection of imagination silhouetted upon the water line.
Just a beautiful image,
An image that will never be mine.

Heather Mathewson

"Our Two Different World"

Your beauty hail from Middle East,
  Mine talent and skill start at Far East;
Leave my homeland, love ones to serve your kingdom,
  Traditions, cultures and life styles amazed my boredom.

At the market with gorgeous friends and you do shop,
  Select and buy what's new for you to take part;
In the counter you paid and our eyes meet-glued cause a stop,
  Two people met from diff'rent world had just start.

True, eyes the window of our soul;
  My stay in your oil-rich land shouldn't be in contract,
Since that day; your smiles, voices and
  looked stare a fool;
Seeing you again with a chat could lead an attract.
Different world and religion could be our gap,
  being friend or lover is just like a nap;
After a dream from slept it's all past,
  thinking you in my life is always a cast.

   Aurelio Haber

Untitled

I can still remember the day you left,
Me standing there,
The tears falling down my face,
As you walked away.
You walked away with your bag in hand,
And tears streaming down your face.
Now all I do is sit and remember,
The joyful times we spent together.
I loved you with all my heart,
And now my heart is broken,
You broke my heart and now I sit in sorrow.

   Candice Leanne Korsch

Through Xavier's Eyes

Perhaps a thought,
Maybe a feeling, or just...
A mirrored image of how I feel...

In throes of passion found we
Beloved, burning...Timing lost
But without care
For it was found...
A face of ashen as you walked by,
Deepened eyes taken aback
But soured in a haze of pain.
How weakening it is...
Leaving the very walls of the soul unprotected
Beauty...you kept walking
But in the distance a feeble heart is heard...
For all that is everything
And everything that is nothing...
A battle.
No complacency. Only desperation in suave tones.
For it is you, and only you...
Through Xavier's eyes.

   Kimberly-Ann Dore

Clouds

Fragile covering where angels rest their wings
Moisture laden softness resting on Earth's shoulders
Cosmic imagery where solar rays recharge
Visualize my vertigo, let the stillness touch you
Shadows imprint on traces of tomorrow
Seek the sunrise hidden by today
Disappear in solitude, let the whispers cry
Softly.

   Emmett Patrick Finnegan

Marriage Cage Wife

She peers through the bars
Marriage cage wife barely sees cracks now
Her mink like features have molted with time
Bones are brittle nails become soft easy to peel
Empty shell of what once she was

Brief seconds cage is unguarded
She fumbles with the lock
Tries to pick it with her shrivelled nails
Then the children call cement hardens over the lock

Beautiful eyes, beautiful bodies
My children they are the cracks of sunlight in the cage
When bars squeeze tight she holds their gentle bodies
In her arms air is fresh with them

At night legs spread open, not for him
Not for his pintop mind
Not for his pinching barb wire body
Or his flimsy cutting knife
It is for the sunlight through the bars
The gentle bodies. The fresh air. The children.
That she is resigned to her cage and lives in an empty Shell

   Barbara Frewin

Soothing Waves

Walking on the beach again -
making footprints on the sands of time
collecting seashells, or is it memories
of a broken past, long forgotten
that brings me back here - once more.

An unconscious longing to hear:
the lashing, soothing sounds of waves
calling soul back to the cradle of life,
where once it was rocked and caressed,
safe as a child in its mother's arm.

Fluid and free like the ocean -
a cry of the heart drowned out long ago
by heavy winds amidst sands of time;
a potential pearl in the ocean deep
waiting to be polished and restored.

Slowly the sacred tools are gathered,
as life shapes and sculpts its vessels,
connecting the past with the present;
soul restores her shattered dreams -
to the sound of ocean waves, healing within.

   Ida A. Rasmussen

Why?

This world of ours is such a beautiful place
making a home for the human race
why can't we live in peace?

This creation we have works so well
its birth and growth and intricate cell
why do we mar it by wars?

This privilege we enjoy to live in this land
to love our neighbour and take a stand
why do we find it so hard?

Our great responsibility, day in and day out
is to give back to the world more than we take out
why do we procrastinate?

Let's hope we can wake up before it's too late
and stop the world's violence, war and hate.
We can if we try!

I ask these questions of the world at large
and to every human being I throw a charge
please do something.

   Edna M. Richardson

Moods And Textures

Sun-drenched snow trickles down meandering mountain streams.
Majestic evergreens take on s sharp green and let off a thirsty scent.

Desert hills come alive with green. Bunches of bright yellow
flowers nestled amongst creamy shrubs dot velvety slopes.

Delicate blossoms paint the valley with peaceful colours.
Sadly, the blossoms slowly drift down to cover the ground
with their random blanket.

Sweet succulent fruit ripens as the valley soars with heat.
Cooling breezes are found as restful eyes watch the sun
bounce its sparkling rays across the waters.

Days quicken into night, fresh air fills the soul as the
heaven display its tapestry of stars.

Splashes of yellow and gold adorn the trees. Gentle breezes
whirl through the trees causing natures song and dance.

Falls harvest is abundant, the pumpkin has seen its night.
Silently snow drifts down upon the landscape and its beauty
renews the valley with life. To begin again...

Sandra Kennedy

Babies

New born babies in the hospital,
loving mother's holding them with care.
Sleeping so peacefully,
watching them in the nursery.
Nurses taking care of them as their own,
though parents and family are the ones proud.
Learning something new everyday,
babies crawling, walking and talking.
Soon will grow up and won't be babies anymore.
First day of school then graduating soon.
Before you know it they will be having
babies of their own.

Dana Nielsen

"The Girl I Love"

Eulogist may say you're really
Lovely looking and daughter of beauty
Infrangible is what you mean to me
Fondled with such love of a visionary

Archetype you are this poem is ever made
Beauty of yours a pattern of this
Exposition of what your personality is
Though you're shy and a little bit timid

Hospitality of yours is deeply appreciated
In entertaining friends with liberality and kindness
Natty gesture of yours also proved to be
Obviously speaking you're really good to me

Chirography is also one of my hobbies
Exploring my knowledge to share with you someday
Nonchalance I'm not in so many ways
Care for everything is what I'm trying to be

Eventually this is only just a poem
Dedicated to you by my very own
In so many poem that I've ever made
Creating like this poem is a matter of high respect.

Joel T. Espedido

And Two Become One

As gently as the evening breeze sweep over the moonlight waters.
Love enters two hearts, and two become one.

As silently as the dawn washes away the last remnants of night,
Light enters two hearts, and two become one.

Love-kept a mystery to all; held forever captive within.
Till that one special moment in time when,
Hearts open upon one another, and two become one.
As with all new born life, if given no light of tenderness,
Love will wither and cease to exist.
But when nurtured with loving hands;
Hearts intertwine, souls unite, and two become one.

Love-ignited becomes a flame
Which unites two people in a bond so strong time itself cannot break it.

For, when love enters two heart,...two become one.

Roberta K. White

Late Winter

I wandered in our bush, today
Looking for signs of spring —
A little shoot beside a stump
A robin on the wing

But the ground is still hard, underfoot
The branches, bare and brittle
The dogs still have their fur coats on
And...I mind that wind, a little

I didn't always long for spring
The way I do, of late
It seemed, then, we had just begun
To ski and slide or skate

When spring came, then, it brought with it
Long days upon the land
With sunburnt faces, tired backs
And blisters on the hands

And so it is the same today
For those still into farming
But as for me and maybe you
Retirement is quite charming

Thelma Fiebig

"Faith"

A little angel sat upon my windowsill;
Looking confused and alone.
Her eyes wide and a look of sadness.
I asked, what was wrong? She gazed up and replied,
I am sad because the one I am to watch over
has turned away from God and the power of love.
I have tried to understand that at times people do this,
and I'm trying to find something for her to believe in,
so God may fill her heart with love and passion for life again.
If only she would believe for a moment,
I could give her, her heart back whole and pure.
A moment they say lasts a life time,
I wish people would understand how true this really is.
As the Angel looked away, a tear slid from my eyes,
then warmness overtook me.
I looked back at the Angel, she winked and then I knew.

Michelle R. Hutchison

Portraiture

Close the door softly, don't make a sound
Look and see what I've just found.
Three little kittens the size of mice
Cocoa, black a shade of spice.

Rubbery legs and tiny scared mew
This world is different, entirely new.
Innocent tongues and sleepy slit eyes
Did you know, out of three, two will be guys?

The box in the corner is beginning to age
What once was their world - now is their cage.
Lions and tigers these wee kittens have made
After they've fed they hate to be bathed.

Just like children, they grow then scatter
Mothers and fathers get left with the platter!

Arlene Dubinsky

'Home Town Nostalgia'

EIGHTEEN YEARS...

Longing of getting married, new things, new country, new life.

Longing for children, dear beautiful affectionate children.

Longing to see them growing up, anxious to go to
school to learn it all.
Happy times, sad times, all go by quickly.

Longing to finally go home to the little town up the
hills. Sorrows, sadness a loved one is no longer, we
never see each other again!

Longing for this life apart from all, was nothing but an
illusion. We only live once, the days are getting shorter.
The little town on the hill top is far far away, the vision
darkens... Things bigger than us keep us tied,
the children fly away from the nest, to make other nests.

Longing to see them happy. But what is this life?

A forever longing that will be with us for an eternity!

Deanna Del Monte

The Day Shift

Darkness lingers on through the dawn,
Long fingers soothing the sorrowing brow of a harsh new day.

Light - weary of these times, cries softly to herself. The grief of
men has brought her beside the Stream of Fears, where rests a soldier,
sleeping at the turn of tide, hands resting, as if in slumber, lie by
his bloodied side.
Head turned towards the lightening skies - pleading, helpless and deprived.

The Light turns to enfold him, like a mother to an ailing child.

Darkness - impatient, turns to go,
to desert the Light, who surveys the land with frightened eyes.

As he leaves, the Darkness turns - she is weeping into the Stream of Fears.

Young men, strewn, inert - more than she can bear, and in the dawn,
shades of crimson - reflections from hopeless battle cries,
mirrored in the colours of the blood red skies.

The Light of day shivers, and races, calling to the darkness - afraid to see.
He replies softly, impatience abated; 'I am the Darkness, yet
in the blackness of the night, I tremble, you are not along Light - I too
weep into the Stream of Fears.'
And the Darkness lingers on through the dawn
long fingers soothing the sorrowing brow of a harsh new day.

Anna NicLeòid NicLaomainn

"Magic Mist"

Pure as ivory, and white as snow,
Lived a magical horse, from long ago.
A pearl white horn, adorned his head,
In the garden of twilight all green and red,
He roamed the land with witches and wizards,
Lived among wild creatures, fire dragons and lizards,
Goblins and goonies, and star dust fairies,
Eating grass and roots, and nibbled wild berries.
In the enchanted kingdom, lived many trolls,
And every rainbow, had a real pot of gold.
In a far away castle, a good King and Queen,
On the edge of the moat, lived a witch that was mean.
The red witch, haunted, in the Mountain of Bells,
With her potions and lotions, and caldron spells.
A two - headed serpent inhabited the lake,
And lunched on all travellers, in his wake.
It was known, that the horned horse did exist,
And lived free and wild, in the magic forest mist.
A dream, a myth, about a pure white horse,
If we believe in dreams, we must believe of course.

Pat Korell

The Silence Of The Children

From April 19th., 1995, Canadians watched T.V. day and night,
Live coverage of the Oklahoma City's bombing plight,
Ten days, maybe more, we looked and prayed,
For the victims of this needless carnage.
My thoughts forever will remain on 'The Silence of the Children.'
The baby girl so still, in the arms of a fireman,
The dear little boy being carried by his mother,
Safe, as blood slowly trickles down his forehead.
Another quiet scene, the small hand of a boy
Gently patting the back of an adult in mourning.
At the memorial service, there were the 'The Teddy Bears,'
Silent symbols of those who'll never be here,
Each mourner hugged a teddy bear for their loved ones,
Edye Smith hugged two, for Chase and Colton, her lost sons .
Sometime later that week, a saddened husband
Spoke of his wife, a victim - a would-have-been mother,
His only consolation, they are together,
This unborn child, forever silent, with its mother.
The clean-up ended, the healing has begun in Oklahoma City,
However, 'The Silence of the Children' is imprinted for all eternity.

Eleanor E. MacDonald

Listen

Listen with me to the cries,
Listen to the call of living as it dies.
Listen to the cry of the young,
Listen to the call of the tongue.
Listen to the damage caused by a word,
Listen to the continuous want of a sword.
Listen to the suffocation of nature,
Listen to the scream of every creature.
Listen to the lockup of conscience,
Listen to the breakdown of cultures.
Listen to the squeak of hunger,
And understand the pain of the younger.

Najwa Raslan

Unidentified

This poem has no meaning, no words of advice or terms of endearment
it is about nothing that means anything
something that could mean what isn't possible and everything that
could explain the unexplainable
it is the possibility if the impossible and the passage to the
impassable the meaningfulness is the emptiness of this poem

Teresa Binkle

A Summer Symphony

Soft white clouds sail placidly by
Like puffs of cotton in the sky,
While the earth below waits parched and dry
For the wetness to begin.

The dust is carried up in the air
Then settles slowly here and there,
To powder a leaf, a branch, a pear
And linger for a time.

A sudden hush comes to the land
Then darkness follows as if planned,
A symphony by an unknown hand
'Tis summers' thunderstorm.

Thunder claps and lightening shines
Electricity crackles in jagged lines,
The rain is a torrent against the vines
'Til the dust is gone once more.

Then when the storm is finally through
And skies return to their former blue,
The sun glows bright and the earth seems new
Serenity rules again.

Walter Taras Chownyk

The Magic Of God

The morning dew, and the still of the night
Like murmur of the trees, a beautiful starlight
A child holding his mother's hand.
Everything, around you, animal or man.
Just let go your imagination
Is there anything wrong with God's creation
If your man would respect His laws.
The world would be a better place to live
Make peace with God and yourself
And take a share of his blessing
For the magic of God is all around you
His perfection is there for you to see
God is the greatest magician
No human can be that good.
Who can make earth, skies and oceans.
Without even a piece of wood.
Isn't it wonderful to know
That such a God is our Father
Just let your love, grow and grow
For that wonderful creator

Denise Bidner

An Audience Of Great Magnitude

Watching, always watching us.
Like larvae under a microscope.
He sees us with his millions of eyes.
Never missing a step anyone takes.
Through a picture screen of great detail, he watches, and sets the stars.
One tragic error and we're pulled off the stage by a mighty hand.
He is a great admirer of our short skits and soap opera lives.
He also knows that such things are harmful and demanding.
After eons of watching he never gets tired but merely changes
channels at periods in our lives.

Jeff Rupert

An Ode To Canada

From the four corners of this vast land,
Its many different people mingle and stand,
Blending together within Canada's core,
With their bits of tradition and lore,
Sounds of varied tongues and music we hear
Reaching out to each other; showing we care,
That's what makes this country so rich and so free
Canada's potpourri of you and me.

Catherine Weller

Love Flow

Warm water rolls on
Like blood from an open wound.
It travels over pebbles that frown
Like eyes of a saddening clown.

I can not cage you, surround, or dam you
For your destination is unknown.
I try to understand you
Before you take away what you have shown.
Tell me who you really are
Before our day is through.
Help me make sense of this
So I do not feel used.
Where will you be tomorrow
Who will you come to know.
Are you so afraid to stay
Where love is known to flow.

Ronald Gordon Waller

Lost And Found

Lost in the shadows of anger and pain
Life is very isolated, am I going insane?
Why is our chosen path so unfair?
You try so hard but get nowhere

You can only see ruin and sorrow
Praying for the sun, to shine tomorrow
Friends try to help but what can they do
you know in your own mind, it's all up to you

Take a look inside, what do you find?
Pieces of a puzzle, that needs to be put together
On each piece, you see clouds of confusion, torment and tears
How do you solve this puzzle?
It takes time, to fit each piece back into place.

Dallas Watts

Secret Confession

And to all my greatest desires,
Lies the truth that remains unknown.
I am your biggest secret admirer,
But I am too scared to let it be shown.

This confession is too risky,
You may be better off without a clue.
The thought of rejection frightens me,
But one day you'll see what's true.

Until that day arrives, how must I react?
With our all too complex lives,
Knowing that feelings were the one thing you lacked.

I think back to all the laughter we've shared,
All the fun we have together.
Hoping that you would be the first who cared,
But knowing that your smiles changed like the weather.

My one and only dream, is that you could be mine.
I watch whose direction you lean, each and every time.

So maybe with this poem, I will finally get through.
Side by side or on the phone,
All I want is you...

Erin Colleen Moran

Shane

Every time I see a rain drop, I think of you.
It reminds me of your talent, heart, and soul too.
You were a hero to everyone in my eyes,
You were so special it hurts to say goodbye.
But now you're free, there's no more pain.
I'll never forget you,
I love you Shane.

Shannon Hookey

A New World?

1789 ... and people shout
Liberty, Fraternity, Equality
and the astounded privileged ask: what's it all about?
But the peasants revolt against their misery.

New constitutions, bills of right
are drafted by rulers with all their might
Democracy!! Let the people rule
Let no-one feel he is a mule.

1989 and we still hear cries
For Liberty, Equality, Fraternity
But too many are engulfed by their bias
Too few have learnt from our History

Sylvia J. Thomas

Peace Times

The rain has passed over
leaving the air clean,
the flowers bloom and the fields are green.
These are peaceful times.

The wind has stirred
the leaves of the trees,
whispered through the hair of my love and me.
These are peaceful times.

But, the rain once fell on the world like stones
you and I were alone,
but then I found you and together we learned
hard weather leaves and the sun returns
to peaceful times.

Now the sun shines
on our children as they play
and we can finally say
these are peaceful times.

At last we have our
peaceful times.

Tammy Dasti

The Oklahoma Disaster

The heartless mistakes evil can bring
Leaves devastation, sorrow, and guilt
A life taken leaves no glory
For now, all mourn.

Rejoice in heaven's name
Pay your respect to those whom are lost
In grave all your griefs with endearment
For now, all mourn.

A tearless surrender is immense
A once close soul is taken
The heaven's bow down their heads
For now all mourn.

Hate is felt alive today
Life accepts all faults
God now lives in disbelief
For none shall mourn again.

Nancy Huntley

You

You are the first thing that comes into my mind when
I wake up and the last thing that enters my mind when I
go to sleep.
When I'm having a bad day, and everything has gone
wrong I only need one glimpse of your face to make it
better.

Kristen Bellissimo

Flight Of The Falcon

Across the savage sea and shore,
Lead through the centuries in flight,
Comes the falcon and its lore
Great hunter, leader, survivor, warrior,
Keen observer, symbolic in spirit,
Hawklike, fierce, bold, and swift!

Compact body, so strong and symmetric,
Such lovely powerful wings so intense,
Soar and hurtle the skies and the winds
Shift short sturdy legs to reel and lift,
Vice grip talons like cold cunning steel,
Striking their screeching prey to keel!

Lives the falcon, symbolic in spirit,
A mighty master raising its large head,
Riveting eyes scream in absolute triumph!
Across the savage sea and shore,
Where still comes the piercing night,
Dark, dark as a raven's wings once more!

Kimberly J. Jones

South End Optimism

Perched as we are, here on the fringes of respectability
Just two blocks from King's Square, we look southward.
We stroll the streets in anticipation
Knowing that our inquisitive eyes will find
Not the pleasures of the flesh, but the delights of the voyeur.

In one window along St. James a too-bright red rose is newly placed
Amid the broken ornaments and snagged sheers,
Plastic petals perfectly arranged to off-set the sagging frame.

On Broad the door of the Sally Ann store swings outward
And a girl of nearly eleven moves daintily over the puddles
In her two dollar black-patent flats.
She is merrily unaware that their dubious shine
Is rivalled by the oily hair spread across her shoulders.

Along an alley on Wentworth a new clothesline pole gleams.
The hapless housewife, leaning out the second story window,
Hopes that the grey underwear and bedraggled sheets renew themselves
As she wearily pushes them toward the shiny pole.
Is proximity worth anything? If not, she has
So little of value.

L. M. Young

Musing

I gaze on a lovely sunset
Just over the hill by the sea,
Thinking could I but dwell in that glory
'Twould unfold life's mystery.

I'd know how stars in their glory
Hold sway o'er each life below,
How the moon in its soft, subtle beauty
Directs the tides in their flow.

How the world keeps turning always
Like a puppet on a string,
With no visible hand there to guide it,
Yet ordered in everything.

Why robins come with the springtime,
Each singing a love-song gay,
As a valentine sent to a sweetheart
That brightens the live-long day.

How two hearts meet, as a magnet
To itself will draw its own,
And though sundered the pathway they travel
Nevermore are they quiet alone.

Esther Frances Jenner

Roots

Roots are like tentacles reaching out far and wide
Just like our grandparents who toiled side by side.
As they struggled and toiled to develop this land,
more and more did they realize they needed a hand.
One day in their leisure and to their surprise,
A new seed was planted to nourish with pride.
A new son or daughter God gave them with glee
As a new generation was begun, can you see.
As the years came and went and the roots they did grow,
More were added in number with much zeal to bestow.
It is only natural as everyone knows,
That roots get tangled as everything grows.
As time was a passing, weary bodies we see,
Some roots were cut off from the trunk of the tree.
But the tree is still standing, many roots still remain;
bound together in love with fond memories sustained.
May all generations continue in love;
With peace "n" contentment from the Father above.

Joyce Kuruliak

Button

It was in the Spring when he came to us,
Just five weeks old - he made no fuss.
I could hold him right in my one hand,
He would snuggle there, our "Little Man".

He gave us joy beyond all measure,
Whatever he did, he gave us pleasure,
He loved to run and play 'football',
He'd run so fast, though his legs were small.

At home when, Dad, was away at work,
He would protect us, he wouldn't shirk,
When someone knocked upon the door,
He'd bark and we knew we were safe, for sure.

This year, the summer has come and gone,
The days are short and the nights are long,
We could not guess that he'd soon be gone,
Never to be with us in our home.

He was killed by 'Charlie' in his own backyard,
And we all have found it very hard.
Yes, he has gone - but he's not forgotten,
He will always be our Best Friend, Button.

June C. Phippen

The Friendly Demons

She looks at the familiar faces; laughing, talking
  (jeering, mocking)

She allows them to hug her
  (maul her)

They kiss her cheeks
  (suck her spirit)

Their malignant happiness forces a cloud of hate to
  encircle her benign spirit.

They are her enemy, her demon.
But they are her friends.

They paralyze her thoughts and censor her emotions.
But they are her security.

They are dissecting her soul bit by bit.
She knows it. She feels it.

But everyone is oblivious to her silent screams.
There is no escape
There will soon be nothing left of her.

It will soon be over.

At last.

Kerry Beckstead

Immortality

I delivered myself into the temptations of evil and justly,
I've been resurrected into eternal damnation.
I've explored the world over through countless centuries,
Each bringing new births of madness.

A composition of music plays in the back of my mind.
I watch and listen in majestic trees, ready to pounce like a wild cat.
I hear murmurs from across the globe and,
Find myself awakening to the sweet essence of maidens far far away.

I am the monster that men fear and that women find irresistible.
I hunger for life, for I am nothing inside.
I devour every light and every movement presented before me.
I play amongst society, then strip them of their worth.

The consumption of passion has withered away,
As I stare gazing into the new horror of pavement and stone.
I have witnessed poetic courtships and nature at its greatest,
And now, only to find mechanical instruments of man's very own
  imagination.

Jolie M. Vermette-Hooper

Forbidden Fruit

Temptation cries out to me behind the golden gates.
Its voice belongs to my heart, or rather the Devil who masks as fate.
The Demon's voice is cunning and strong
Even though his intentions I know are of the wrong.
Lucifer is safe there in my soul, resting on its pyre,
Knowing that I have succumbed to her touch,
And to Cupid's fire.
She began the crimson blaze within my soul
With the wink of her eye, and made me whole.
In those pools the stars and heaven reside,
In short, the passage to Eden
Which for Adam was denied.
I alone carry the burden of sin each time I see her smile
Or smell her fragrant skin.
I gave my heart to someone who does not belong to me,
Yet the eternal inner voice promised that she would set me free.
She is the object of both my desire and pain.
For this I am condemned to live the life of Cain.
To trample the earth forever alone,
Without her warmth and without a home.

Danial Lam

I Love You, Grandma!

Grandma tonight your last wish came true
It's time to say "Good-bye" to you.
I've never been afraid to show you my love.
I'm happy for you - you're with Grandpa above.
You're together again, after so many years
It's this that somehow calms my fears.
I love you! I love you! I love you so much!
I can feel it now - your gentle touch.
You've given me so much over the years
Memories that fill me with laughter and tears!
I'll cherish our Sunday telephone calls,
Your overnight stays and our walks through the malls.
You've always been such a BIG part of my life!
I remember your smile as I became Cecil's wife.
"Thank you, Grandma" for all you've done!
I'll remember you with each setting sun.
You'll always be with me - in my heart each day!
"I love you" is easier than "Good-Bye" to say.
And so that's how I'll end this poem for you
"I love you, Grandma! - I love you, true!!"

Gwen G. Morrow

Untitled

There is nothing to be afraid of they said,
it's only the rain and the wind.
But it was the rain and the wind that took you away from me.
There is nothing to be afraid of they said, it's only darkness.
But you went to darkness and never came back.
There is nothing to be afraid of they said,
it's just a reflection in a piece of glass.
But in the glass I can see the rain,
wind and darkness and I am afraid.

Above, the trees and across the
sparkling water my spirit flies escaping
the darkness. As free as an eagle
racing against time I can fly without leaving. I can die and be.

There is a place for me in this world, somewhere I have been before.
It's a place I go, in my head, when I want to be alone.
The sun is always shining, and it never rains or snows.
There is no need for tears in this place, there is no pain.
I can be alone but never lonely.
One day I will find this place, but for now
it is just a place in my head.

Wendy Hall

Grandma

What is a grandma? Funny you should ask.
It's one step greater than a mother task.

It's a Chance to sit back when you see things go wrong.
And not say a word, cause you'd never cause harm.

You wait for the grandchildren to come for a visit.
The house chores can wait and everything in it.
The time for the children flies by so fast.
You want to make each moment last.

We color the pictures, bake muffins too.
And talk about every animal there is in a zoo.
A walk in the forest, a swing in the park.
The explaining we do, not to be afraid of the dark.

Yes all grandma's are special.
Ask any grandchild
It's also our privilege to sit and spoil them awhile.

Lorraine Rochon

Dangers Of Love

They met on a hot sunny summer day.
It was love at first sight.
He sang a song of love.
This made her fly high as a kite.

They went for walks along the sandy beach;
They watched the stars and moon.
He taught her a lesson of love;
They knew they'd be together soon.

There was one problem.
He lived far away.
They called and wrote each other.
They started to grow apart, some people did say.

The calls stopped; she had no clue why.
Then she got a call which answered the reason why.
She heard a woman's voice calling to him.
This is when she started to cry.

Someone has taken over his heart.
I have no more tears left to cry.
I just have memories in my heart.
Now my heart is healing from the left over scars.

Alice Beaudoin

Starting Over

I married a man, he treated me so bad,
It was like a nightmare, the worst I'd ever had.
In sickness and health, for richer or poor;
I promised I'd love him forever more.

I tried and I tried for so many years,
Through sleepless nights and endless tears.
My love turned to hate, I just gave up trying
I was tired of fighting, exhausted from crying.

I left my home town on a warm summer day,
I tried starting over, thousands of miles away.
At first I was scared, was I making a mistake
Should I try one more time just for old times sake.

Then one summer night you held me in your arms
You stole my heart, with all of your charms.
Now life has new meaning, for good reason it seems,
I'm starting over with the man of my dreams.

Marie Butler

Too Late For Time, Pray

A lonely gaze and a desperate clasp to hold on to what is slipping past.
It waits for no one, time, as it slips by; wishing he could have,
	knowing he should have, sadness, dampened eyes.
She knowingly smiles with calmness and grace, to him a familiar
	comfort, oh, the beauty of her face.
His lips quiver, a struggle to speak; Not much heard from a shallow
	breath and a body weak,
He prays, I'm sorry Lord Please show me a sign, that you forgive
	me Jesus this one last time.
For all the hurt and all the pain, and for the things I've said I'd
	never do again.
Watch over my wife, our children too; If I am to leave, I leave them to you.
She knows his fear and tries to comfort him by smiling again, but,
	both want peace, to just end all the pain.
I'll hold you darling, you won't be alone; Know how much I love
	you when the Lord takes you home.
If I could have one last wish, a chance to go back; I'd build on our
	strengths and not what we lacked.
To look for the good in those that we care for, and know true love,
	we don't value anymore.
Are you there darling? I can't hold on too long;
	I can't see your face but, I hear angels and song.
A squeeze of the hands, one last kiss on his face,
	and life left his body to that heavenly place.

Michael C. Hunter

Defeated

I hear a voice inside my head
It talks me through the things I dread
It says stand tall, you can do it
Just listen close I'll help you through it.
Just hold on tight you can do it
Oh but wait, you just blew it.
You opened the door and let them through it
Oh why do you let them do it?
They knock you down with just a look, one cruel word that's all it took.

You feel the pain deep down inside, soon the tears they fall from your eyes.

You try to hide the pain you feel, but they all see it, they know it's real.

Catherine D. Bonnici

Ode To The Organ

The most majestic sound in all the spheres
It surely was not made for human ears,
But for those of more exalted beings
For it contains the wonder of the eons.
Octaves, flatted fifths, diminished sevenths,
Celebrate the music of the heavens
Here on earth.

When I am tense or struck by grief or illness,
Its music brings me sudden, inner stillness
Blown by sonorous airs, I float away,
But let the notes I leave behind still play.
Harmony can reach no greater height
Swelling through churches bathed in candlelight.
Pedals with their numerous vibrations,
More meaningful than all of math's equations
Transport me to another time and place
Where I can cease to run this mortal race.

Celestial chords of Messiaen provide
A royal bouquet, a feast of delight.
There is no earthly food that could ensure
Repleteness so satisfying and pure.

Jean E. Wilder

My Lancelot

The treadmill turns no more for me
It stopped and set my senses free,
This love so pure, so well deserved
Just for this day, has been preserved.

No dreaming feeds this love's desires
Reality fuels our heart's own fires,
Though well you think of me today
Keep well that thought, I hope and pray.

White knight has battered down the wall
That black knight built before its fall,
The chains of ills are now unbound
My life will soar through this love found,

And, should it end, my soul will be
Forever shackled, never free.

Paula Suckling

Moonlight

The waves had a glitter of moonlight,
It shone upon the mast with a glow.
The ship was ready for battle,
The sailors were ready to go.

Their sabres made not a rattle,
The captain called from below
The sailors rushed to attention,
Time seemed to go slow.

They saw a ship on the horizon,
A cry went up in the night "Man the Guns"
"Bang" "bang" shattered the night
The water lit up like the sun.

The mast was set a blaze.
Across the sea went the cannons roar.
The enemies abandoned ship
And swam to the near shore.

They watched the galleon sink.
Deep beneath the oily waves,
And those unlucky sailors
Were taken to their graves.

And now when the waves pound against the shore,
They call the name of sailors that they had swallowed up before.

Teale Nevada Phelps Bondaroff

Gone Forever

Look at my friend in the shadows
It seems like she's withering away
I run to try and catch her
I know she'll be gone any day

Her brown hair and eyes aren't as shiny
The disease she has just can't be cured
I tell her that it could be deadly.
She knows but won't let me be heard

She never goes out into public
She says she can't bear to be seen
I don't see her getting excited
Her last wish was to be crowned a queen

My good friend has now vanished from sight
Her vibrant smile I shall never again see
I still talk to her knowing she won't answer
But in my heart she always shall be.

Tish Taggart

Would That I Should Never Be Silent Again

You were always unapproachable, or perhaps
it seemed so
I repressed any notions to share my thoughts
with you
This loss of expression weighed heavy
I know...
For now you yearn for shared strength to help
you pull through.
Melting my defences; emotions exposed, desperate for
the chance to share.
Sensing panic, abandoning all, I pray you allow
my concern, my care.
Though we fear the unknown, a glory has been
discovered...
For the meaning of life is expressed LOVE and through
diversity; this we have uncovered.

Paula Goldade

Metalmorphosis

in Gastown is a little world.
It is a shop, a place of chrysalids.
Here old bricks turn into gold.

Metalphysically, it is God welding,
cutting the shards with fire-scissors.
See, there, the one with the dark glasses
in the back, torch forging, bellows bending.

And the Voice saying, let there be
copper-clusters of birds, dogwood-sprays,
metal boats, sunflowers other metal-alchemy.

For the dead, it is a resurrection
from old scrap, a sort of re-creation.

For the quick, a hammering,
let a new face peer out of the old plate,
a re-coloring by the salt of mettle,
a healing, metalbolically.

E. C. Barton

Untitled

The Moon drops His sparkling tears
Into the dark, quiet night.
"Why must I always be alone," cries Moon?
I stretch my arms, open wide,
But I can never reach far enough
To comfort my lonely friend.
And still the tears sparkle in the sky
As moon and I cry.

Ruth-Anne Yeo

528

Way-Lyn Ranch

Fletchers have an awesome spread
It goes by the name "WayLyn"
A - One hundred and sixty acre ranch
Where folks can "come on in".
The ranchhouse is on a hilltop
With the valley spread below
And I can't imaging a prettier place
In the sunlight or covered in snow.
The Birch trees and the corrals
And the haying fields all around
With a pretty lawn and white stained fence
Lets you know God's hands have touched this ground.
Cattle are grazing and horses roam
And soon a golf course we'll see
Spread across this rolling range
For the pleasure of Wayne's company.
Hospitality abounds in this friendly place
Where old friends are welcome always
May God's grace continue to bless you all
And you'll find peace for the rest of your days.

Helen Lott

The Joy Of Light

Oh how great the sun in the sky.
It gives me strength and
warmth from deep inside.
It gives life and meaning
on dark rainy days.
Even as we sleep it
never looses its rays.
As I reflect in my later years.
Those clouds would come
those clouds of tears.
I looked deep inside that night.
Then I moved slowly toward a glowing light.
What a joy to behold,
the light I could see.
Was mankind's soul brighter
than any sun could be.

Bruce Olivier

In Awe Of You

A single raindrop fell, landing on a leaf, inclined in a half circle.
It gently swayed. I knew not if from the weight,
Or the warm summer breeze, and gently slid downward,
Leaving a shiny trail, and reaching the edge, paused.
It became elongated, begging to fall, yet clinging to the edge,
Hanging like a trapeze artist, defying gravity and testing its strength.
I snatched a chance to see it. Sunlight glimmered off its edge,
Its cleanliness and purity so plain, so unblemished by cruel fate,
The ravages of sin, or distress of loss,
The mystery of cold, or choking of bad luck.
It possessed a child's charm, simple and exquisite, impossible to recreate,
Helpless, I surrendered and stared in wonderment.

Last night, you were like that raindrop. I wanted to hug and kiss you.
But did not, for fear of smashing the magic. Merlin was at work.
I felt like a vessel, being hauled by a tug, connected yet powerless.
You possessed a wizardry, spinning charm by the sack full.
I was enchanted, as if in a trance. I lost the gift of choice, my mind quiet.
Thoughts, usually rushing at speed, almost stopped, as I gazed at you.
Every one of my senses worked feverishly to capture the you before me.

Chris Rygier

Inspiration

Look through a window if you want to be inspired
It frames such masterpieces in galleries you'll not find.
Take a common poplar that throughout the seasons grows;
Each day a different canvass of glorious colours it unfolds.

Seasons surge with exhilaration your soul cannot contain,
After the brush has painted winter, rebirth will come again.
In the springtime hang red catkins, so brilliant in the cold;
Sunlight transforms summer leaves to silver and autumn's to pure gold.

Yesterday you saw buds opening and the little bits of green,
Today the foliage darkened and you welcomed summer in,
And tomorrow's rain might bring rainbows in the droplets left behind.
Ah! The warmth of summer lingers as beauteous thoughts are intertwined!

Doris D. Fediuk

Children Of Light And Dark

I take a breath and look around
Is the world embedded in chaos and
corruption?
Or are my fears a claim totally unfound
"Humans are generally born good but can
become what society dictates to them!"
Innocent as a blind child within thy
mother's womb
Should soon open its eyes to

A world forged in complexities
"Children of Light, Thou art so when
born; dirtied under the influence of
our morals that seem to be breaking down"
Is society to blame for a child's inner
most struggles form the time he or she
grows?....
Until the time he or is no longer a-
round!!!

Samir Goel

Shadows

The Shadow of the night,
Is the opposite of the morning light,

The morning comes and then disappears,
Just like a poor kid in fear,

But too young, he can't seem to swallow,
The difficulties in life stuck in his shadow,

He has that uncoloured thing following him,
For every step he does, just like a kid in love,

But that child has lost his breath,
His shadow's gone, in life of death.

Linda G. Thibault

Infatuation

Tide ebbs and flows,
  Infatuation comes and goes.
Each lapping wave scratches a tortuous mark,
  Along the shoreline in my heart of hearts.
See the myriad ripples on the sand?
  Count out how many if you can!
Higher and higher breaks the wave,
  More and more bubbles prick and fade away.
Though build I in vain many break-waters round and round,
  Still the rolling breakers into the harbour of my heart rout.
And the receded rushing tide's laid here and there, everywhere,
  The little sacred cockles of my heart very bare.
If the moon is the shadow behind the tide,
  Infatuation? Tell-tale sign of true love hard to find!

Ezekiel Lloyd

Migraines - The Devil's Fire

The fire that's burning in my brain
Is the devil's roaring flame.
Once it's reached the centre core,
I'm sure to go insane.

The coals that are formed by the devil's fire,
Are my eyeballs, burning red;
And my only friends and companion,
Are my pillows and my bed.

I'd never wish them on anyone,
Worst enemy or friend.
It's bad enough they're driving me
Somewhere around the bend.

Good-bye to pain and torment
And the fiery flames of hell.
Someday I'll see the end of pain,
Yes, someday I'll be well.

So to all who feel the flames of hell,
Fight back with all you've got.
Take on a positive frame of mind,
And get you...he will not.

Idella N. E. Born

The Moon Is My Friend

I sit in the sand staring me straight in my face,
is a moon with beauty and grace.

As it shines its power on the sea
it makes me feel alive and I know I am free.

Escaping from the darkness, I don't need to hide,
the moon is there to protect me from my fears I feel inside.

Up and down it rises soon my problems disappear,
the moon is my friend who is always near.

Wanting to touch it, moving it to a place,
seeing its brightness with happiness on my face.

Then moon is my friend who will never leave me,
he has all the power in the world as you can see.

The moon may not be able to hug me or give me a nudge,
but he is always there to talk to with my kindness and love.

Angela Slifka

Pastoral

A light has anointed my fever this morn,
　Inspiring a reverent calm.
A breeze has refreshened my soul this morn,
　Bestowing a comforting balm.
I feel at peace with the gods this day,
　The tempest has been becalmed.
And thus, for now, I may rest this day
　And embrace this renascent dawn.

The faeries must be rejoicing this eve,
　For the woods are alive with song.
The nymphs and the sprites must be dancing this eve
　In their delicate magic gowns,
For the stars are out bright and clear this night,
　And there thunder no piercing alarms.
I believe I will pause, I will lie this night,
　In the arms of a sanctified calm.

Robert H. W. Hook

Militia Extremists

Boom, boom went the bomb.
Innocent people went down.
Babies, children, young and old.
All met their doom I've been told.

The concrete building is now a tomb.
People from around the world,
Came to help those people of doom.
Why this city of Oklahoma?

These terrorists thought from the Middle East,
None but our own right wing extremists.
We'll not be defeated in our town,
Certainly these terrorists will go down.

Fellow Americans people alike,
It could happen again in our strife,
Lets get these terrorists alive,
Before anymore bombs threaten our lives.

Whatever extremists your going to jail.
Your judgement day is here.
Your lives will be lost in the electric chair.
The F.B.I. have them there.

Mary Lou McKnight

Alone

Alone, kneeling,
In the mist of a bare desert,
Far from the people...
Alone.
Far from humanity
Far from everything,
But yet so near;
Surrounded by people
In a crowded room
But not really...
Alone.
A thorn amongst a rose bush,
Belying the image,
Drawing the attention of penetrating eyes.
Welcomed by voices
But not really, - false...
Alone.

Kala Kathir

Incense

Incense burning in the night
In the midnight darkness there's a flare...a light
It slips away, but embers stay
To burn until it's gone...burned out...decayed.

Ashes fall, but the smell is strong
Beautiful smoke fills the room like a song
Embers fade, but ashes stay
The smell lingers on like memories of summer days.

Stephanie Waddell

Grandmotherly Advice

As you grow older you will see
Important are friends and family.

Money and things are nice in life
But no guarantee against trouble and strife.

Some advice for you, do what is right
And have a goal to keep in sight.

Forget past wrongs, be happy and gay,
Prepare for the future, but live for today.

Toni Corner

Someone

The sky is dark, rain is falling,
In the distance a voice is calling
Over meadows, across the sea
And yet, someone still misses me.

Clouds move about from here to there
As if they didn't have a care,
Across the heavens wide and free,
And yet, her thoughts are still with me.

We were young, our love so strong
Three weeks wed before I'd gone
Across the waters deep and fierce,
The night's long storm, one life did pierce.

The years have passed, the young grow old,
But love is cherished as of gold,
My Captain brave, his ship at sea,
And, still someone is missing me.

Today is Monday, the sky is blue
There is but one last task to do,
The service short, at rest to sea,
Someone - no longer misses me.

Lilly R. Fougere

Power

The crowd stares at the elephant
in the center of the ring

One crack from the sequined circus trainer
forces the elephant to sit with his trunk held high

Faint carousel music whispers
through the tent from the merry-go-round

Children wiggle in their seats
"Is it time to ride on his back?"

The smell of popcorn
forms line-ups at the concession stand

   The spotlight glares on the elephant's back
   Shrieks of laughter pierce his ears
   People surround him

He breaks
   pacing around the ring
   swinging his trunk
   roaring a helpless cry

   until the armed vet shoots

He staggers stumbles
and slumps to the ground

Kate Cooper

For My Dad - My Day Of Atonement

Suddenly I saw a knight
in metal armour coming o'er the glen
He was dressed in gold and silver colours
And he was my friend
He threw off his ancient helmet
And much to my surprise
I beheld my late father sent to me from heavenly skies
And good were his intentions: to stop the worldly wise. -
He talked of ancient trees and gems
And goods galore found in heaven's store
Then, suddenly he disappeared from view
And I was left alone -
   an old dying self
Learning from the worldly wise
Emerging into the world anew.

Ann E. Cowan

The Cottage

On a tranquil lake, north of Parry Sound,
In a quiet setting, we have found,
With natures beauty all abound,
A cottage built high, upon the ground.

With jutting rock and sifting sand,
We've come to love this northern land
With panorama e'er so grand,
Mother nature needs no helping hand.

The silver birch sway gently in the breeze,
With sighing sound and graceful ease
We know now here forever lies,
A secluded, peaceful paradise.

As dawn replaces moonlight glow,
We will peace, now and forever know.
In the magic of the shimmering lake,
A second look at life we take.

An enlightening holiday, we found
For those of us, who are city bound.
We will forever miss Nature's sound
As leave we take, from this high ground.

Moira McAllister

Flames Of Love

A lovers tale left unread,
In a letter full of God's pure dread,
Unspoken words of royal lace,
Hidden without a single trace.

In the trunk below the floor,
A lovers tale dead to adore,
On a paper fringed by eternal fire,
Showing each persons lofty desire.

Without a hope of a lovers crime,
Is a lovers poem written without rhyme,
A lovers tale of sadness and mourn,
With the watchful eyes of her lovers scorn.

Lost forever in the flame,
Burns a lad without a dame,
Of death or murder or suicide,
A lovers tale in which I confide.

A lovers tale with a saddening phrase,
A lovers tale in a lovers phase,
A lovers tale to show I care,
A lovers tale of a lovers dare.

Leanne Danelisky

Self Discovery-Self Destruction

In my constant quest for perfection, I have created the most
imperfect woman.
To be accepted and loved I slander myself.
And when loved and accepted I secretly do my best to destroy it.
Wanting it so.
Yet destroying it before it destroys me.
Those who failed to exploit the good in me created the bad with
their words and gestures.
Hearing the slanderous words about myself to myself constantly,
believing them always.
They are the evil that destroys what good I may have.
And now when left with no one but myself I complete the task
daily by what I do and say to myself.
I pray that one day I will meet the soul either within myself or
in another with strength enough to make me feel equal to all others.
Or even to put me one inch above them so I might see where
I belong.

Deborah Ruhloff

Demystification

Disorganization leads to the dislocation of
important information, and if I had the inclination
I'd come to the realization that the frustration
of last minute preparation could use some consideration.

Were I not prone to procrastination
I could change this situation ...

But it is my observation that total organization
like temptation can lead to the devastation of our
self creation for there evolves a limitation to any
new sensation as avoidance of relaxation becomes
one's primary occupation.

Without hesitation I declare my situation
my recreation for after aggravation comes
revitalization and gratification.

And so I extend this invitation for transformation:
Drop now your reservations -
it will be a splendid vacation!
Nix your habit of seriation and live life as a
celebration of complications, expectations and
communication!

Teri Strain

If I Could Live Forever

Watching the night through my dark window, not able to see day,
I'm living forever not able to die, watching the people
in my life go on with their lives not having to stay.
My feelings I can't explain,
I never ever want to feel an ounce of pain.
I keep watching my offspring die one by one, I don't
know if I can take it anymore seeing them all go,
I keep saying to myself should I have taken the
chance or should I have just said no?
What would of happened if I did say no?
Would I have been dead or living a life alone?
When I'm alone I think,
How my life is passing with just a blink.
I have no one who loves and cares,
Whose things they would offer to share.
But my choice is settled I am what I am,
Living forever in a vampire clan.

Tania Bongelli

Poverty

Lightning shot across the sky
Illuminating the smirk of evil.
The grin of satanism ran through
The streets laden with blood soaked rubble.

The laugh echoed through the streets
Which were as silent as a grave.
Filled with terror, the homeless scattered
Into the unknown darkness.

Little did the innocent know that soon
The raucous underworld being would
Lift its veil; to reveal its diaphanous face
Filled with contempt for the living.

Many feeble people lay askew
Like plucked daisies.
Throbbing with the anxiety that
The land-born hydra brings.

Tormented, alone, horrified,
Shocked and patronized;
They slowly awake
To the land of the living.

Mary Blais

Stained Glass

I do not know who I see in the mirror. Sometimes I see beauty illuminated by love and other times I see ugliness possessed by hate. I see laughter in a smile full of dreams and sadness moistened by loneliness. I see passion that is fueled by madness and kissed by desire. I see a maze of contradictions tangled in not knowing who I am. I see a lot, but do I see me?

I see the unwavering stare of the mirror piercing my mask and beckoning my soul. I see fear permeating my pores and scaring my potential. I see the residue of abuse colouring my perception and distorting my view. I see mysteries in a shadow protected by a grin and the reality in a tear dripping with pain. I see a world of complexity revealing an unsettling picture of who I am. I see a lot, but is it me?

I see a story written all over my face with lines eager to be understood. I see a complexion of expressions moving me with their insight and vision. I see eyes focussing on the truth, drawing me closer to the light of my strength and away from the darkness of my weaknesses. I see a glow spirited by acceptance and a warmth nursed by grace. I see a worth revitalized by seeing and an attitude changed by belief. I see an abundance of gifts offering me encouragement as I begin to know who I am. I see a lot, I see me.

Ladona Constantina Dawes

Please Come To Me My Children

Please come to me my children, let me but keep you near
If you would only listen, I'd help you through the years.
But children seldom hear you, though not to be unkind
They have so many things to do and so much on their minds.
They couldn't live without you, they would exist it's true
But children need a mother's love and their father's too.
From the miracle of childbirth, till their grown-up years,
Love nourished and protected them, extinguished all their fears.
Molded by environment and all their trust in you
Absorbing every moment before their plight is through.
If only we could help them, forestall the pain today
But they never ever heed you, regardless how you pray.
Once their childhood's over and they've babies of their own,
Partaking parent's torment, they'll wish they'd only known.
We all learn things the hard way, so often do we say
"If only I could start again, I would do that, this way!"
Thus, come to me my children, in errs of wrong no blame
Let one but help the other, in learning there's no shame.
Too soon our paths will widen, you'll branch out on your own
But the tools I lay beside you can make your house, a home!

Ann Dudley Duncan

All Things Natural

Frozen trees stretch tortured limbs up to the empty skies.
If you listen closely you can hear their mournful cries.
For each heart that is broken a twisted tree is grown.
From our salty, saddened tears a great forest can be sown.
Rocks lie on the ground like cruelly broken bones.
They come from the souls of those people without homes.
You see the flowers joyfully bobbing in the breeze.
They are hopes of the people whose hearts will not be squeezed.
Then winter comes and destroys all we know.
It covers the ground with cold-hearted snow.
But our hopes are not dead, merely asleep for a while.
They'll come back again in the spring with a nod and a smile.
For all that is natural a feeling has been felt.
So accept the life that Fate, to you, has dealt.

Krista McLaren

The Cup Of Cold Water

Saviour Lord I ask again,
If Thou wilt consecrate my pen;
Guided by this feeble hand,
Instructed by a dullard brain:
Though weak I be, yet through Thy Grace,
My weakness You can erase,
All efforts by Thy spirit led,
Then may some hungry soul be fed,
Some broken life touched by Thee, Lord,
And strengthened by Thy gracious word?
That through my hand You did allow
A cooling touch on a fevered brow!
If some small way I this attain,
My life, my hopes were not in vain.

Mary Dubois

Gone Is Life So Quickly

Past goodly bye.
I'd the pain.
And read book on Cain.
Looked through the pain.
Not free, life.
Be in the garden!
Place in the Son.
Life is too real.
Hear, see, meet, and read - but raised to buy and buy.
Gone is life so quickly.

Passed goodly by.
Eyed the pane and red book on cane.
Looked through the pane.
Knot-free life.
Bee in the garden.
Place in the sun.
Life is to reel.
Here, sea meet and reed.
But razed, two.
By and by, gone is life so quickly.

Aneela Nayani

I Wonder

I wonder what the colour is of her hair.
I wonder what she'd do if I was there.

I wonder what she's really like.
And if her parents really care;

I wonder what her smile is like;
And if she has dark or light hair.

I wonder if she has brothers and sisters,
Who really love her and care;

But, still I wonder she'd do if I were there;

I wonder what colour are her eyes,
I wonder how she waves her good-byes.

I wonder how many friends she's made;
I wonder if she's ever been afraid;

I wonder what the colour is of her hair;
I wonder what she's do if I were there.

I wonder if she knows what she wants to be;
And if she'll know about me.

Kaye Magee

An Ode To A Winnipeg School

As I walked down the halls of a Winnipeg school.
I wonder to myself just who is the fool!
There are teachers in slacks, students in jeans,
No where can proper attire be seen.
There is writing on the wall, paper on the floor.
Oh how our parents would abhor,
Never in their day would this be allowed
They and their peers were much to proud.
As I turned to go from where I had came.
I heard from a far a most beautiful refrain.
Their on the stage dressed in blue and gold,
was the most beautiful sight you could ever behold.
with faces a glow and head held up high.
Their voices seemed to reached to the sky.
I stood in awe, with tears in my eyes.
Were these the students I had just be rated?
Never let it be said, to days youth don't care!
You know without doubt they would gladly share,
Any of the work, all of the pain
Just to hear their own refrain.

Elsie Babiak

Adieu

Tonight is a night of peace
I wish to share it with you
For every day spent
Caught up in the wind-swept drama of life
Each minute of this evening
Will represent a moment of triumph
For every tear shed in recent past
Each second of this evening
Will represent a moment of happiness
And as I gaze at the stars
That all our fondest wishes grant
With the warmth of your hand in mine
I can simply say adieu
For I have nothing left to wish for.

Shari L. Morehouse

I Wish

I wish the hands of time could turn and not take life away
I wish our loved ones held so dear could forever with us stay
If only we could know when young the experience of life
To be more tolerant and calm avoiding any strife
But that's the lesson taught to us as we pass through life's sea
We all have different ways and thoughts - how boring it would be
If everyone was made the same, just think how one can learn
From other people's good points until it is our turn
To say goodbye to this life and leave all stress behind
Forever then to rest in peace with content untroubled mind.

Barbara A. Pellikka

Golden Love

I wear your ring upon my finger, through every day I live,
I wear it proud, because it stands for the love you always give
I take it off to protect from hate, I take it off to see,
If anything has stained or broken, the love between you and me.
Someday's the ring, it won't come off. Others it fits just right,
Sometimes I throw your golden ring, after a terrible fight.
This ring has its special glow, and when I don't know what to do,
I rub my fingers over it, it sends me a part of you.
Your priceless ring can not be seen, by the human eye,
It is only seen with our hearts, therefore it will never die.
If you betray me, down the drain your precious ring shall roll,
For on my finger sits not only your ring, but your everlasting soul.
Stay with me always and forever, and so our love will linger.
I'll always cherish and look at you, through your ring upon my finger.

Melissa Wooldridge

The Search

With silver in my pocket bulging to burst
I went looking for desires of the heart
Without preference of premeditated design
Wanting fancy to decide what I sought
The marketplace was filled with a throng
Of seekers' and sellers' and choicest wares
Each time the heart skipped a beat and it found
Its fancy, my coin was short or it had been sold.

I remonstrated with self to look for something else
But conviction makes no compromise
The second best could not even come close
In an iota to my first dearer choice
I saw beauty being sold and every virtue
The power of money trading the soul
And what with loads of silver one could not buy
Was going cheap for a piece of gold!

Despondent my footsteps I homewards turned
Desires shelved in the recesses of the heart
Knowing on the concourse when reality meets hope
It's mostly hope which empty handed returns...

Vinay Benjamin

Dad's Garden

Fond memories of my childhood days:
I went into a lush green garden to play.
Tulips and crocuses of early spring,
I enjoyed my old wooden swing.
Trellis of roses with their heads held high,
Delicate blossoms stretching to the sky,
Beauteous colors of pink, white and gold,
It was a wonderful sight to behold.
People came from near and far,
My father gave them a tour of the yard.
Many a bouquet of roses, larkspur and fern,
Father was thanked with a smile in return.

Mary T. Theobald

Last Night

Last night I stirred. With sleep-fogged gaze,
I watched you as you slept.
So angel-like in many ways I very nearly wept.

Your faced peeked out from ruffled quilt
and pillow 'neath your chin.
I gazed at you and keenly felt a stirring deep within.

In this the girl who years ago I took to be my bride?
Is this the one who loves me so
and lies here by my side?

So quiet then in bed you lay...
with radiance glowing through.
How perfect seems the coming day to start it next to you.

So many thoughts went through my mind
of times we laughed and played.
So filled with love of every kind...
I hope they never fade.

I looked again to strengthen those sweet memories I'll keep.
I kissed your brow and cuddled close and then fell back to sleep.

Why did I wake? I cannot tell the wherefor or the when.
I only know last night I fell in love with you again.

S. Oltman Stoker

Our Dance

On a warm summer day in the land north of the Wandering River,
I watched an eagle soar in lazy spirals on an up draught high above the pines.

When I thought of you, my heart joined him and I knew by the power
of his wings, by the strong beating of his heart, that this eagle
was the love between us.

I was carried far into the summer sky and, as I watched, a gentle
breeze carved you from a cloud. I took you in my arms,

And as we danced

I became afraid of the power of the eagle and yet drawn by it.
My mind said no but my heart would not, could not, will not,
compromise. Your vision has set me free.

The eagle is with us, the wind whispers our love through the pines,
encouraging us to soar, to dance, to throw caution to the wind.

Oh how I love to dance with you.

Our love will last till the rivers run dry, the wind ceases to
blow, and the eagle can no longer fly. Our hearts beat with the
same rhythm. Our souls are one in different bodies; the dance can
never be as beautiful as when we do it together.

Dennis R. Cooper

I Want To Be

I want to be real, I want to be happy,
I want to be an artist, but my drawing is crappy.

I want to create, but I'm low on creativity.
I want to be strong, but I have too much self-pity.

I want to laugh, I want to cry,
But most of all, I'm afraid to try.

I want to be successful in the eyes of my parents,
But the world's running out of big circus tents.

I want to have children, to love and to scold,
Yet I'm a child still, so young and too bold.

I want to be psychic, yet I'm afraid of the future,
So little is left even now, nothing is for sure.

I want this and that, and that over there,
Yet I never seem to have any money to spare.

I want an end to world hate, famine and war,
But for one alone the road is too dangerous, too far.

I want to see people who care like I do,
Who feel these same fears like me and you.

I want all to have freedom, oh, don't you see
A person without freedom can never want to be.

Teresa Lou Riley

Serenity

Before I lay down to sleep
I try to sort my thoughts so deep;
To realize my faults and dreams
Thinking of past lies and schemes;
The times wasted and people hurt
My life of drinking was simply dirt;
The idea of believing in a higher power
Is beginning to make better thoughts flower;
Life is such a beautiful thing
Now once again good thoughts can sing;
Depression fading every day
Life of sobriety is such a better way;
Love in my heart I now can show
Where past thoughts were full of woe;
The future now looks very bright
Serenity now comes, as I rest at night.

Corey Tennison

But Tonight

As I look up to the heavens
I try to see your smiling face
But no matter how I look at the clouds
There is no trace
I see horsies and rabbits and little puppies too!
But there's no sign of you.

But I feel you in my heart every minute of the day
Still I wonder, is this feeling real or am I imagining, this way
I'm always praying to the Lord for a sign from up-above
Just to let me know that all is right, and you are loved

All I need is a whisper or a little hug, to know you're there
Right beside me all the time
I need to be aware

I know the Lord will take care of you
I know you're safe and sound
But tonight, I'm awfully lonely
So I'll still pray for you to be around

Wanda Ouellette

Letting Go

I thought he knew how much I really cared,
I thought he'd remember the times we shared.
He probably thought our relationship wasn't meant to be,
But he's wrong again, because he is the one for me.

I still love him but he doesn't love me,
I feel like I've drowned in a deep blue sea.
He remains nameless as he always will,
I remember the past, I sit very still.

My heart has been broken and I should move on,
I should try to forget that he is now gone.
I hope he remembers the great times we had,
I miss him so much, I feel lonely and sad.

I don't want to say good-bye to my sweetheart,
I wish that we could've just decided to restart.
I hope one day he'll realize that I loved him so much,
He was the one for me, I remember his gentle touch.

He's moved on with his life which does not include me,
But letting him go is something that's not meant to be.
Always remember that my love for him was true,
He was my first love, I hope I was his too.

Antonietta Balsamo

Suicide

I've seen the leaves that changed with seasons,
I think and feel for what reasons
My life is not worth very much
How can I help to keep in touch,
Please don't let me breathe this day,
Why in this life must I pay.
I feel no hope, I see no light,
My heart it breaks, it's just not right,
I've reached so low
I can't come back
I can't move on
All I see is black.
I leave this life in which I came,
I leave with nothing but my name.

Leah Stapleton

Sibling Rivalry

Here's to you Oh Radiant One;
I take off my hat
And bow lowly because I'm no one,
I'm certain of that.

You shed light upon the world and warm
The coldest of days;
Lush fields you make grow with such charms,
I admire your ways.

But let not your pride swell to new heights,
My dear brother Sun;
You give way, to sister Moon, at night:
Who's the stronger One?

Sean Dupel

Faces

I sit here in the dim lighted room and see many other faces around me.
I start to wonder if I'm the only one who hurts inside.
With all their smiling faces and their laughter and joy,
They all seem so happy to be alive.
They don't have any big problems or worries,
except those they can't help, but have.
I have real problems.
The kind that dig and carve a hole right out of my heart.
On the outside, a mere shadow of mine projects
the happy-go- lucky person who pretends to get around.
But, the shadow deep within-
he lurks beneath a shattered soul.
One that cannot be replaced by little compliments
given by those other faces.
'Tis a shadow seen by not even the closest of friends
but by the person herself-
ME.

Lucia Marzano

It's Fall

As I look up in the sky,
I see the birds are flying by,
I hear the birds sing,
When I wear my diamond ring,
I hear the leaves blowing,
When I hear the wind blow,
And that's when I know that falls going to go,
And when fall goes the wind goes,
The leaves go and everything goes,
So go, go, go, for here comes the cold snow,
  Ho, Ho, Ho.

Cindy P. Vigario

Unconfirmed Reality

Hidden in my past is unconfirmed reality
I need to know who I look like,
Who I act like,
WHO I AM!

I have no quarrel with my past
nor with the role my adoptive parents cast.
They taught me an appreciation of music and dance
They gave me support and every chance.

But as I grew up and had my own family
I looked at them and began to see THEIR reality:
Who they look like, who they act like,
Who they are — but I still don't know ME!

And so I travel on a journey
to find out about my own genetic history,
to find that missing part of me
and perhaps discover my "unconfirmed reality"

Jackie Briggs

"I See"

I see an old man in rags, fast asleep
I see on old house, abandoned because of a fire,
Where no one lives, all boarded up,
I see a teardrop fall from a woman's cheek,
  no place to go, no home to call her own,
Where will she stay? Where can she stay?
I see a child crying in the street, hungry, lost, no food to eat,
I see a dog roaming the hills, alone, looking for shelter, a bone to seek,
I see a cat with kittens, born in the wild, too soon to die.

In life, in my dreams, these myriad things I see.
I ask, where is the answer?
Are these unchangeable dreams?
I see what I have, what they do not have,
I see God needs me to help,
To help those others have forgotten.

What can I do? How can I help?
By giving, by caring, by sharing what I have,
I see a way to help my neighbour less fortunate that I.
I pray for an answers, for courage to help.

I see a teardrop change to a smile,
I see a dream come true.

Cheryl M. Parker

A Night Alone

Something comes over me,
I see colors that never before were ever present in the stars.
I hear the heart beat of an honest man,
Living in the soul of a guitar.
My senses have a new desire,
One of a passion before unclear.
Suddenly it is brightened by a glow of unconditional joy.
The colors engulf my mind.
As they pour into a soul reborn.
Direction is a new path,
As clear as a foggy morn.
A haze covers like a wet dew.
What can be seen through the cloud
But the true tale of a vision,
And a fuzzy outline.
It's clearer now than ever.
Then suddenly the urge subsides,
And it turns into a new day.

Anyone got the time?

Rachelle Richards

A Child Untold

Looking back yesterday, when you said goodbye,
I searched myself, for the reason I cried.
Was it because, you'd left me alone?
Or was it because of our child untold?

I know the child, is the reason I cried,
And thinking about it, I understand why.
For what do you have, to offer this child?
When you've always treated me, so very wild.

Will it be like you, or take after me?
This is the question I'll wait and see.
Will it succeed, or do as we've done,
Just run around looking for fun?

I guess you do, have the right to know.
But if I tell you, will you still go?
Maybe you'd change, but that would be new,
For your deepest cares, have always been you.

Now that you've left me, for someone new.
Not knowing or caring, that I'm really 'two'.
I really don't know what will become of this mess.
I hope for this child's sake, it'll turn out the best.

Karen Fletcher

Mystica

When we met
I saw a rainbow painted across your face
I never realized how seven colors
Could be so beautiful.
When we touched your warm, loving hands
Warmed mine from the chill of the evening.
Your gleaming eyes of sunshine
Brightened my rainy and cloudy afternoons.
The streak of blue in your pupils
Reminded me of a freshwater lake.
The peachy-orange color of your skin
Matched the scales of the leaping salmon.
When you tousled your gorgeous brown hair
I smelled the sweet aroma of chocolate cake.
Your broad shoulders
Were firmer than any stone boulder.
And your pale pink lips
Spoke every word that existed.
But what exists now?
You are gone and my world is black.

Kristin Ann Fung

"This Summer"

Such a wonderful summer, the sun was so hot,
I really was proud of the tan that I got,
I haven't been out much for many a year,
But this year was different, my folks, would be here,
They all arrived, from near and from far,
Most came by aeroplane, some came by car.

I worried a lot about where would they sleep,
What kind of food to buy, what should I keep,
In the fridge, or the freezer, and what will they do?
See the lakes, the museum, the parks or the zoo?
I had no need to worry and no need to fuss,
The reason they came here was just to see us.

We did things together, we laughed and we shared,
We were happy, and mostly we loved and we cared,
The days are still sunny, the sun not so hot,
And now it is fading, that tan that I got,
But not so my memories, they are forever,
This summer I won't forget, will I? No never.

June E. McGhee

Roses Die When Love Does

I rushed out of the room as soon as those words of hurt had been said.
I ran down a lonely hallway, tears flowing down my face.
I could not believe what I had just heard.

I pushed open a door that led to the outside world,
and felt pain.
A pain so deep, it pierced right through my heart.
I glanced down at the roses he had given me,
before he broke my heart.

I watched my blood mixing with the roses I clutched.
A red so deep, so pure, it seemed as though the thorns had drawn
blood from within my heart.

Still I kept running, his words of hurt ringing in my ears
over and over again.
Why did he have to break my heart?

I had to face the truth. It was all over.
The love that he had once felt for me had died,
Died too soon.
That's when I noticed that the roses had died too.
Died too soon.

Shenoor Jenna Hajee

536

Flowers Of Fate

Standing in a distant meadow
I looked about and saw
One thousand buds of color
Protruding through the thaw

Row upon row, heads held high
Their petals fluttered free
A pungent garden of fragrance
Dancing gently in the breeze

And breathing in the crisp of air
I knelt onto the earth
Then picked one stem, for to tell
And prove to me its worth

Slow, one by one, I pulled apart
With fingers clothed in glove
And passed my dream to the fate of the flowers
To determine my springtime love.

Kathleen Brown

The Rose

I'm beautiful, but I could hurt you.
I look strong, but I am fragile and need to be treated with care.
I can be ruined, either petal by petal or all at once, I'm left
with the same result. Nothing.
If you bring me home with you, I will give you everything, my life.
After the short time you'll spend with me, I'll die.
You will either watch me droop and shrivel up, or you'll throw me
away like any other piece of trash.
Either way you will forget about me; forever and someday soon you
will bring home another.

Carrie Jones

I Wonder?

Another school year ends and as
I look around my class.
One question comes to mind just
one I have to ask.
Which child did I touch which
child did I reach.
Did I do my job or is there one I
couldn't teach.
I taught them all the basics to read
and write and add.
But in my heart today I'm feeling both
a little glad and sad.
For they are going on for many years to come.
And I will always wonder did I reach that certain one
Will they remember me and all I've tried to do
Please tell me that I reached them tell me I got through
As they leave today I have nothing more to do but wish
them all the best
On their journey through grade two.

Sandra Lee Ward

Untitled

Sometimes I can't understand
How you came into my life.
But I'm so glad that you did,
Because you are what makes me life complete.

You have made such a big
Difference in my life,
I never thought anyone could.
Not in the way that you have.

And that's why I thank God
For you every night.
Because I would be nothing
Without you in my life.

Helen Klassen

My Grampie

My grampie, Bill Murphy was a very special man,
I hope he knew that I was one of his biggest fans.
I wish that I could give him just one more hug and kiss,
It is true that it's my grampie that I really, dearly miss.
At the early age of sixty-six, my grampie passed away,
I miss him even more and more, each and every day.
He had the biggest, kindest heart, and he was very nice,
But now his soul soars in heaven, soaring high with Christ.
I think of grampie all the time, I have wonderful memories,
Like when he wore his nice beige shorts, with socks pulled up to his knees.
He always liked to sleep a lot, at all our piano shows,
After, he'd get us all ice cream, and give us each a rose.
Grampie liked to eat peanuts, sardines, and chocolate bars,
He also liked the taste of jam my grammie made in jars.
Whenever he came to visit us, he always brought a treat,
My grampie was a thoughtful man, a grampie you could not beat.
My grampie liked fiddled music, and loved an Irish beat,
He used to take us to the Dairy Queen to buy us a sundae to eat.
I miss a lot of little things my grampie used to do,
Grampie, it's hard to say good-bye to someone I loved as
    much as you.

Meg Murphy

I Remember The Time

I remember the time, when I was the one...

I can't stop thinking of your touch in my skin,
I heard you knocking. My heart let you in.

You picked up my old life, put it back on the tracks,
Yet now since you've been gone, my life wants you back.

You were the one I always dreamed of,
I knew right away, that this could be love.

I remember the time, when I was the one...
I remember the time, now I look what I've done...

When a dream comes along, I grab it and hold,
I protect it, cherish it, and treat it like gold.

I've learned with some pain, not to grab and hold,
A dream is not something to be brought or sold.

I remember the time, now look what I've done.

Michael Lewis

Forever?

My life is dark, I am alone in my sadness,
I have no one to hold, no one to caress.
For he has left my life forever,
He was my friend not only my lover.
I would confide my darkest secrets,
I loved him I have no regrets.
I would dial the number to listen to his breath,
I would stand inside my hell and hold the hand of death.
For he was there through night and day,
He would listen to my thoughts and what I had to say.
He was in my life for so very long,
Now it's time to just move on.
He played it as though it was a game,
And now I will never be the same.
Why does love hurt, the pain is so strong,
It feels so right yet it is so wrong.
Everyone says he's not coming back ever,
All I need to know is...
    Does the pain last forever?

Tamara Archambeault

Caught In The Middle

As I lie here with tears in my eyes
I gather my thoughts and realize,
At times I feel as if no one cares for me
and that is one thing in life that scares me.

I cry myself to sleep at night
But always in darkness, with no light
I cry out loud hoping someone will hear me
Maybe it would comfort me to have someone near me.

I love my family and they love me
but why can't they see what it's like to be —
    the middle child.
Tammi Lean

What Is Fame?

I dreamt someday I'd be a success
I felt from the beginning I would be the best
Perhaps politics would be my game
Maybe as a surgeon I'd have my fame
A lawyer or author could bring me great wealth
I could be famous in spite of myself
As time went by and I didn't achieve
The status of success which belonged to me
I resound myself I'd never be on top
I was sure to this day I was merely a flop
But the lights came on and the crowds did cheer
And at this moment I knew why I was here
I could make babies with a wink of an eye
And mothers would gleam as I would pass by
Children always greet me as I arrive into town
You see dear people I'm the circus clown
Muriel Elaine Buick

Read My Eyes

So many things I want to tell you
I feel I have to say
But my tongue is tied in a double knot
With each passing day.

Every day goes by, one by one.
And one by one I see them slip away.
Another day wasted, where we can't be together
Another day unshared.

I see and hear your name
And it brings me pain, when it should bring joy.
All because my mouth can't utter
Three simple little words

So I must hope, that you will see all my love
For you in my eyes, and dream
That someday in the future it will be
Only you and I.
Denise McIntyre

Life's Linger

As the weariness of death draws near,
I drown in sorrow but I have no fear.
For when I leave this world I'll have no pain,
Just the contentedness like the falling rain.
As the air grows colder and my own sun sets,
I drift deeper in the light but I haven't
gone my farthest yet.
And when I slipped away I heard the cries
of the world,
And I found the pain in this - the pain I
Unfurled.
Ashley Rochefort

Blackened To Light

With the pain and isolation of what I have created
I create more of what I do not want to live
Choosing to be happy, free, and living to not be berated
With desolate truths of what I have created, I just want to give

The battle of life rages on in my head, reality is not all that bad
It is seeing the dark turn to light, ever so slowly, as life passes me by
Covering the pain with a smile, may work for awhile, to me that is sad
Going deep to the core where black is the shade, I see the faith...
    then...I sigh

To see is the first step, learn is the next: Living at life's pace, that is what's hard
A reality created solely from fear...has blackened...many a year
Turning this boat around, in the midst of a storm, I must put up my guard
Throwing away what I lived so far, starting over, where do I steer

Blackened by my beliefs, they blackened how I perceived the world.
All that is good can be made out to be bad, and all that is bad opens
for pain. Blackened by my beliefs, they blackened how I received the
world. All that is good helped me realize, in all my pain, there is a
lesson to gain.

Discourteous battles are fought from within, it's easier to run than to
fight. Blackened by doubt, regret, fear, helplessness, desolation
and screams. Challenging each day as a battle to be won, leads to the
altruistic sight. Gaining courage to win the fight from within, seems
like fairy tale dreams...
Ralph Steven Herceg

Earth's Paradise

While standing here in sunshine's silver sheen,
I contemplate God's rich creative power:
From lowly plants to stately trees that tower,
And point the way whence all these glories stream.

Canoes glide o'er the silver lake serene;
Glad bird's song sweetens each enchanted hour;
And round the shores, from every hedge and bower
Contentment, beauty, grandeur reign supreme.

Ah, can it be, that here in Paradise,
Amid such symphony of sound and sight,
My languid heart is slow to realize
The full extent - the breadth, the depth, the height -
Of nature's bounteous beauty? Touch these eyes,
This heart, that I might savour each delight.
Clifford W. Ketchum

Tales

Tales of old, and tales of yore,
I come to lay before your door,
Loves lost, loves found, proud ships run aground,
And the plunder is rich on the rocks by the shore.

And the plunder is rich on the rocks by the shore.

A young soldier alone in a far foreign land,
Saw a vision of his love reaching out for his hand,
As he reach out for hers she just faded away.
And he sighed as he wondered to whom he should pray.

And he sighed as he wondered to whom he should pray.

A bold prince on his steed is seen riding one day,
On a quest he must go, from his lady, away,
But he called as he crested the top of the mound,
His words lost on the wind in a soft sighing sound.

His words lost on the wind is a soft sighing sound.

On a sea tossed with stars, is a ship made of light,
Its crew the lost souls who must wander the night.
They saves those they can, but the rest they must leave,
To be mourned by their loved ones who now are bereaved.

To be mourned by their loved ones who now are bereaved.
J. M. Tamarynn

538

I Love You

I cannot promise you that I will not change
I cannot promise you that I will not have many different moods
I cannot promise you that I will not hurt your feelings sometimes
I cannot promise you that I will not be erratic
I cannot promise you that I will always be strong
I cannot promise you that my faults will not show
  But
I can promise you that I will always be supportive of you
I do promise you that
I will share my thoughts and feelings with you
I do promise you that
I will give you freedom to be yourself
I do promise you that
I will understand everything that you do
I do promise you that
I will be completely honest with you I do promise you that
I will laugh and cry with you I do promise you that
I will help you achieve all your goals
  But
Most of all I do promise you that I'll love you

Pierre Lambert

Same

I can feel the tension of the racial slurs
I can feel the aggression of the black peoples anger
I am white but am I pure
I might be the exception for any rule
What I mean, what I'm saying
Is I'm not racist in any way
But a racist man that is white
Looks at me and thinks he can confide
So I hear more racial ignorance, than I can believe
They think that I agree with them
cause the colour that they see
These same people won't say it to their faces
Just looks at them with untrusting faces
It's more mental than physical but still causes the same pain
And this is what creates all this negativity today
When I hear someone saying racial slurs I think what a shame
What if, it was the same person you put down
Was the one that saved you from a burning house
Would you still hate him just the same
Or realize, as people we're all the same.

Manolis Zontanos

Blind

Help me!
I am lost in a world of heartlessness.
In the solid, grey mass of blinded
ignorance, is there a break to let in
the golden rays of truth, understanding,
love... and peace?
Everywhere I look there is evil; there
is judgement; there is pain.
Save me from the pollution of human
kind; hating for the pleasure of hating;
killing for the pleasure of killing; lying
for the pleasure of lying.
Like leeches that cling to the minds
of the young, naive and vulnerable,
they infect and corrupt.
This disease has no reason, or
rhyme, yet it spreads through the
population like wildfire.
Filling the heads of the ignorant
with shadows of fear and half truths.

Nicole Butler

Riddle

I,
I am light from the darkness.
I am order in the chaos.
I am as steady as a rock
yet in a state of constant flux.

I,
I am as ancient as the Cosmos,
Yet as young as a newborn child.
I am the single most primordial being,
Yet am so abstract that I remain a Mystery.

I,
I am the source of all life,
And I am to where all must return to upon Death.
Everyone knows me,
Yet to most I am a stranger.

You know me
What am I?

Sarah Bowdidge

Dream Child

I am a child of the heavens, the stars
I am but a dream, dreaming its web of truth and joy
Come dream with me.

Mine is a dream of laughter of play
My reality is but a wisp away

On the back of the great golden dragon
We'll soar for many seconds, for many days.

We'll rest upon fluffy pink cherry clouds
We'll join in the chorus of chorus' above

To fly through the night mists with fairies
To dance to evergreen dance with elves
To ride the deer and stroke the bear

Mine is a reality that only the dreamer shares
That only the free may know that only a few come to realize
Come dream with me
I am a child of the heavens, the stars!

Lisa Hostrawser

Bulgur Is Vulgar

When guest at a gourmet banquet Middle East
I all alone beweep my outcast state:
There's falafel in olive oil begreased;
I look on eggplant and bewail my fate.
A minted buttermilk and radish soup,
Then shish kabobs with fava bean kookoo
Are guaranteed to make my taste buds droop;
Grape leaves, savory stuffed, are hard to chew.
I say, leave pureed chickpeas to the Turks;
The Greeks may have moussaka, feta cheese;
Moroccans prize couscous (They have their quirks!)
Yogurt becomes the Berbers: I allow all these.
I say to each his own, for pity's sake,
And as for me, I think I'll stick with steak!

Lois MacDonald

December 6

Dedicated to the fourteen young women who were killed at Montreal University in Canada

One time we knew you,
however now we only remember
you. Even if we can not see
your beauty, your presence will
still belong in our hearts.

We will always remember
those simple mornings, when you
looked through the window while
the birds sang your personal
freedom.

We can not believe from
our hands, so quickly you
slipped away, so young you left
our breaking hearts. We now
know you can not be by our side
any more.

Sleep away young maidens,
dream freely my daughters.
Shall you never be disturbed by
anything or anyone again.

Jose Miguel Gutierrez Sanchez

"My Golden Angel"

Your glow is soft and whispers gentle I long to
Hold you in my arms. Behind you left your
Little twin forever grateful I will be.

The piercing silence of your birth will
Always echo in my mind. For you my baby
I'll always love and hold you dearly in my heart.

Now in heaven you will be my golden angel
From afar, each time I see a flash of light
I know it's you near that shining star.
Our worlds are two my little son but you'll
Always be my special one.

Love, Mommy
Celeste O'Reilly-Baker

Nephew

Today my sister came to call and brought her only son.
His visit home long overdue, now he was twenty-one.
It flashed across my mind the thought, maybe every auntie's fear,
The world's too big to keep in touch with those that we hold dear.

I remembered how chubby and cute he had been and how Auntie he'd try
to beguile.
He'd cock his head to a side with a smirk, then the smirk would break
into a smile.
I would read him a story and then he would say, "Now Auntie, I tell you.
I had a great big *birfday* cake and Auntie, now *I'n* two!"

Now here was this long lean stranger, his hair even starting to thin,
But as he reached to give me a kinfolk hug, a smirk broke into a grin.
I covered my thoughts with the words he said but then perhaps he knew,
For I could have swore the words I heard were "Auntie, now *I'n* two!"

Donna Dempsey

Clouds

Fleecy cream clouds like frolicking lambs
cover the landscape as far as eye scans
chased by the wind over meadow and dell
casting a happy quite magical spell.
So much we perceive brings joy to the heart,
clouds, birds and trees all play their part.
Wondrous and yet majestic the plan
The "fly in the ointment" most often is "MAN."

Ralph E. "Buddy" Sullivan

"Dad"

My Dad was great, the very best,
His smile always topped the rest.
But you got sick and had to leave,
And still it is so hard to believe.
But they picked you and took you away,
And you'd be here if I had my say.
Oh Dad we always loved you so,
But answer a question, did you have to go?
You were the man we could always trust,
To make us happy, you never had to fuss.
But now you're gone for your final rest,
And, as I say, you were the best.
But you died so fast it isn't fair,
But the Love for you will always be there.
So, Dad, you know, cause you had to go,
The Love for you will always show.
No one else can take your place,
Or have your smile upon their face.
Dad you know I'll always Love,
So take care from Heaven above.

Lisa Kirk

God Never

God never once intended, that true love should ever be.
Hidden somewhere in the darkness, where no one could ever see.
God never once intended, that true love should ever hide.
Otherwise before the whole world,
Jesus never would have died.

God never once intended, anyone should be so blind.
They would be lost in the darkness, with his path too hard to find.
God never once intended, we should live in fear and grief.
He says we've done that to ourselves.
Through sin and disbelief.

God never once intended, anyone should ever be.
Losing out on him and heaven, lost in hell eternally.
But surely God intended, when his son was on the cross.
That his dying there would save us.
Letting us gain from his loss.

Paul Ranger

Winter's Promise

Behold the shining mantle of the world!
Hidden is the brown and wearied earth;
Soft-sleeping, their tiny tendrils yet unfurled
Rest the leafed heralds of Spring's birth.

Into the diamond light of sparkling field
I gaze - a vision of all time I see,
The promise of what stirring Spring will yield,
The radiance of glories still to be.

The glittering panorama disappears,
An iridescent beauty hovers there.
The rainbow-tinted mist, dispersing, clears,
And lo! 'Tis Spring is subtle raiment fair.

The trees all gowned in dainty elfin green,
Murmur in the gentle whispering wind
Of joys, which in Spring's dawning are unseen
But with Summer's sweet fulfillment life will find.

So does the world, which now in darkness gropes,
Seek in Spring's miracle, promises of Peace.
Just as quiescent Winter knows the power of hope
So shall we find Life's Spring when strife shall cease.

Evelyn A. Power

The Drifting Wind

All alone as I stand here
Here, at the edge of the pond looking into the glistening water
I visualize an image - an image that once existed.
Two people together as one
Their faces hold smiles - smiles that bring forth the contentment
between them.
There is a drifting wind:
A wind calmly blowing thorough my hair giving me a chill of emptiness.
Apparent is the look in their eyes - eyes that posses a twinkle
Brighter than the sun's sparkle on the water.
All is tranquil with utmost silence - silence sustaining a laughter from afar
That is fading in the drifting wind.
Now, slowly beginning to swell are my eyes - eyes only seeing a
blurred image
That was reflected clearly as if on a mirror.
Into the water a tear drops - drops and shatters the image that once was
It too is slipping away with the wind
As I stand here alone without motion
In the Drifting wind.

Josie Novielli-Moro

Freedom

At a dizzying height, she soars
Her sleek body slicing the wind.
Glancing below, a field
Of those beneath
In their final resting place.

Tilting her wings, she glides
Gracefully down, and rests
Upon one of many white crosses
Of victory - freedom for those to come -
Yet defeat - the stillness of many hearts,
Once beating, full of life.

As she flies away,
The dove, spreading peace
Beneath her wings, spies
A blanket of poppies
Opening, welcoming the new day
Changed forever by those
In Flanders field.

Jan Augert

A Companion Of Summer

Each night her head falls gracefully to sleep,
Her long arms fold beneath the dark ocean,
The bustling town is but a quiet heap
That waits for her to make her first motion.

Her friend, the moon shines over the Blue Coast,
Revealing each night the wonder to be
Young lovers, sharing thoughts they think of most,
All while she lay in her calm reverie.

When she awakens she gives life to all,
The trees, the birds, seem to dance in her rays,
The warmth of her smile - a welcoming call
To the worshippers who bathe in her gaze.

The town comes alive when she is aglow,
Only to wane when she is out of sight,
Her strength is an energy which does flow
Into the horizon that masks her light.

Laura Andreozzi

My Wife, My Friend

She may be small, but she is taller than life.
Her heart is soft and flowing with love.
Her mind is open and full of knowledge.
Her warmth will fill you, if you are cold.
An adventurer in her own way.
Takes life by the horns and takes it for a ride.
She belongs to no-one, but one.
She may not see but not to be fooled.
Her hands open ideas to her mind.
Her friends are many and cherished.
She will pick you up and lend a hand.
Her tears are real and shed sadness.
Her laughter is true and full joy as we.
She is as one and as true as life.
She is a woman, she is my being.
She is my best friend, my one and only.
She is my wife.

Curtis Yakichuk

Shine On

Heaven opened up its gate and let a nymph slip in,
Her eyes were full of laughter and her heart was full of fun,
Her spirit free of all restraints fell into loving arms,
And Heaven was a brighter place, she was a shining star.
But before she journeyed onward she looked from whence she came.
She saw the pain and suffering of those she left behind
And her heart filled up with sorrow,
She had to pause, to hesitate,
Would they be all right tomorrow?
She lingered at the gate and a tear rolled down her face
For she couldn't leave this place.
Then gentle fingers took her hand and led her through the night,
And Heaven was a brighter place in the dawning day.

So when you want to see her face
Look to the bright sky
She's tending baby angels,
And looking out for You and I.

She was, She is, A Shining Star.

Tammy Lee Teneycke

Sweet Dreams And Lollipops

A little girl looks around a room,
Her eyes, huge and vacant and seem to loom
Her face is distraught and her hair is tangled and knotted
If only someone cared enough to notice.

Her dress is black and torn,
She smells of time and soot and her shoes are worn.
Her parents are somewhere amongst other people
In heaps of decay and bloody bodies amongst the remains
of a broken church steeple.

The decay and smell is making her nauseous
So she slowly gets up being cautious
She remembers the bomb bursting in the air,
The wind wildly blowing through her hair,
The turn of her lifetime searching to find,
The parents that she left behind.

She remembers their smiles and happy faces
Now turned to screams and chaotic places
She remembers her religion, that she is a Jew
But the only people who really ever knew
Were the people that killed in World War 2.

Sarah Zebruck

Redecorator

She paws the ground with her mighty hoof,
her body a lashing hot flame, ready to leap.
She spurs the earth as if she can fly.
Her bold dark mysterious eyes hold the secrets
of her unknown fierce wild heart.
Her body sleek without a flaw.
She comes running toward me,
my arms outstretched in a warm embrace.
She belongs to me, she is mine.
We are one together.
She runs with more infuriating speed,
her body the picture of superb power.
Her eyes are like darting fire.
But still I am not afraid.
Only I can ride and tame the unimaginable
fury that torments her soul.
Only she can find the hidden love
within me that is meant just for her.

Kellye Woods

The Sun And The Moon

The sun springs upon the Moon,
Her army of Light quickly defeating the Darkness.
The Moon calls for retreat,
His Stars back away, all eyes on the enemy.
For some time, the Moon regroups,
Planning his next attack.
While the Sun makes camp,
and waits for the time.

The Moon marches over the horizon,
the Stars reclaim their place in the sky.
The Sun runs in terror,
Rainbows and Clouds flee to the west.
And Darkness claims the sky again,
waiting, patiently, for the time
when Light springs up again,
to begin the Day, and end the Night.

Chris Hodgson

An Eye In A Keyhole

Shadow of hell be not over me, but cast a darkness as I write.
Help me feel anesthesia, but great awareness of this night.
Creature, grant me but one interview to define your coldness
   and your curse
An anecdote; a single passage from good to the worse.
I ask not you lay down your hone'd tine, or direct your eyes to the wall,
To drop your cloak outside the door - to beg, to cry, to lust or to crawl.
Just to be near to thoughts. To entice silence as I pen your life,
And be still as I watch your form, as you would to my plight.

Forgive me, I cannot trust night; so I won't shake your hand to bid farewell.
Nor a smile forget my pleasant face - return now to your hell fire cell.
Yet do leave with understanding, leave not with my pure bright soul.
Take with you your darkness - your presence you dole.

Shadow of hell be beneath me, let me rest for I shiver fast.
Never to meet again in this life, this hot black thought we've passed.
I find it hard to thank-you, I shook no pleasure, nor did find...
A feeling, yes, but so unpleasant. A invitation for death to dine.

'Neath the curtain of dusk I now sit,
The horned pilgarlic now long gone.
I gave to it nothing - and still,
The moment scared me...to death.

Raelene Holtner

Remembering You

I whisper it to you my sweet child, echoes of what I've longed to hear. Traces of memories and bittersweet voices have now become hollow within my soul. I sweep the dust off a treasure long since buried. In a twirl, it vanishes and leaves me. Surrounded in wisps of clouds, I catch a glimpse of times past.

The door beckons me to open it, but what shall I find? A cradle which is bare, empty, and void of your existence. Back and forth, back and forth, I rock you, knowing it is not for the sake of slumber.

As I bend over and pick you up, my arms are filled only with the air around me. A lullaby rings through my ears, but only I can hear the melody. Bedtime stories I read to you, no questions do I hear.

I must leave this room now, for you have given me the key to open a new door. Although I can never capture this moment again, I will cherish it with all my heart. For you, my child, have set me free.

Lori Smith

The Pain He Drags Along

He shuffles, he staggers; He swaggers, he floats
He straggles, he slides; He waddles, he shifts
He ambles, he plods; He shimmers, he roams
As he deftly walks the city streets
And daily navigates the faceless crowd
Obsessed with his self-imposed unpleasantness
No one seems to care or wants to know
No one seeks to meet this weirdo in his turf or terms
Not even in the common ground of one humanity
Where all that unites abound
All they see is ugliness, the noisy ungovernable self
Obstinate and uninfluencable they assume
Offensive, provocative, unlikable and nonconformist
What is more, inattentive to life's approved details
They claim it's all in the gene, or worse
How come they're so sure, and they never see
The burden he drags along, the shafts he's trying to dodge
The pain that frames his smile, the sorrow that swells his heart
How come they do not know his wounds, his shame, his needs
How come they do not know and do not see and do not care

Sam Ifejika

The Father, The Son

I came across a chap one day, who told me how to be.
He spoke of morals, values, words, he said he'd make me see,
How wrong I was in all I thought, he said He'd show me light.
Being then still very young, I declared, "you must be right!"
He took my mind and stretched it out, I soared amidst his thoughts,
He molded, sculpted shaped and changed, I soaked in all he taught.
His words were gold I stored and kept, not knowing that one day,
I'd take all this and question it, and throw a lot away.

Now it lies away somewhere, a heap of tarnished steel,
I have found my own gold mine which shows me how to feel.
I now have my own small chap, to whom I give my gold.
He soaks it in and always does, exactly as he's told.

Sometimes it seems like it's a waste for I know he will not keep,
The gold I give, he'll throw away, and bury very deep.
But maybe once, throughout his life he'll stop to think and say,
my father told me this was right, and that shall make my day.

Matt Swoboda

542

A Fisherman's Flight

On a fisherman's flight
he sees nothing in sight.
Looks around and
hears not a sound.
Sticks out his pole,
looks for his soul.
I could sail forever and the end
I would get there never.
Ocean so vast
everywhere present is past
What I'm fishing for
I've never caught before.
When I catch the fish I will find myself
and sail no more.

Darryl Horrocks

Dad

He was my knight in shining armor
He is graying at the temples
My dad has broad shoulders, a big smile.

But then he left me. All alone, by myself
Well not by my self, there was my mother and brother
But when he left a light went out of my life

He calls, but not often
He doesn't know the sound of my voice
I don't think he ever did.

I don't know him the way I should
I know him as a friend, distant relative.
Not as my father, my dad

He has broad shoulders, a big smile
He is graying at the temples
My dad was my knight in shining armor

But then he left and a light went out of my life...
               Dad.

Alesha Schmidt

God's Perfect Creation

One day God decided to create something perfect
He had only created miracles that were necessities as yet
Something to love and fill us with devotion
Something that would be God's perfect creation

This gift would always be around us to love
A most wondrous gift from our Lord God above
And if your loss is that special loved one may die
Keep your faith no matter how hard it may be to try

Because just like in the Bible it tells us to believe
That this gift is something that will never really leave
You may not be able to see the power surrounding you
But it's there by your side no matter what you do

This feeling will be around you, until your dying days
And this power will guide and protect you in wondrous ways
I hope you realize why this creation is like no other
Because there's only one person it could have been

And that was my mother

Lorna Martins

The Birdhouse

The birdhouse was built when Chris was young
He had Dave to guide him as he begun
To saw and to hammer it all together
So it would be strong in all kinds of weather.

We have it outside where it looks best
A starling inside it, is building a nest
We watch with interest, each day that we look
With grasses and sticks inside that she took.

The robin is squatting atop on the roof
He's guarding the nest and now doesn't move
For this is their place - they've made up their mind
And a better house they couldn't find.

Now Chris is so proud of this one little house
With the door at the front as small as a mouse
No curtains or beds that one can see
This plain little house is even rent free!

Now we're looking forward to that special day
When we find those eggs there that she did lay
More songs to be sung with these little birds
Much joy they will bring as nature stirs.

Blanche Gerard

The Chickadee

Against the backdrop of the freshly-fallen snow
he comes to life—
A tiny, swift, distinct dynamo on wings.

With rapid whimsical movements, he flits
in and out of the tree-cover
his round delicate body fluffed fully in the crisp cold.

Suddenly he alights in my upheld hand
and I am filled with awe.

I so want to caress him — but I must not,
for against my hand-size, he is infinitesimal
and he honors me with his trust.

Lucille Robinson

Treasures

My time has passed of youth and gold, and in its wondrous place
Has taken hold an awful scar that time cannot erase.
Behind the eyes of knowledge there lies eternal truth
That youth is wasted on the young who do not know its use.

So unto each and every child, I pray you hear my words.
Let not your heart be soiled now, for you are like the birds.
Completely free of cares and ties, from tree to tree you leap
Do not forget to look around, these memories you'll keep.

To each new morn, do greet the day with open wings and fly
To every leaf bestow your touch and know what you've gone by.
The skies are yours to travel now, your head above the clouds
And on your skin feel satin drops of rain soaked through your shrouds.

Let not your fellow travellers lead, but let them share your space
And through your skies, your friends, your world, your youth will
   quickly race.
The innocence in everyone is captured through the years
And very soon you're sure to find it's drowned in aged tears.

This loss I fear is permanent, though no-one knows but why
So try to hold young treasures close, Remember how to fly.

Cheryl Lee Vallee

Life

A childhood that never was
  hard work from dawn to dusk
  daydreams, fantasies, was there time
  for a child growing up on the farm
  a childhood forever lost
A young woman full of hope falls in love
  in the city to start anew
  this is different, the struggle
  to fulfill their dreams
  of home and family
A mother who loved so tenderly
  caring for her children, sacrifices
  that were made to give a warm and
  happy home
A mother grand and great
  a time for sharing memories, to reflect of times gone by
  but life is cruel and dealt a blow
  there she sits, no touch, no hello
  are there daydreams, fantasies, no one knows
  her golden age forever lost

  Eleanor Parr

Untitled

The so low feeling is back
Happiness and feeling are something I lack

My friends help but I runs to deep.
My soul is fighting but It's down to a peep

I feel so alone and no one can help me.
Maybe I'm invisible and no one can see.

Why is it here is something I'd like to know
The answer to that is waiting to show.

Happiness is lost with nothing left to feel
I feel like I'm fake but what I'm feel is real.

No one seems to notice or no one seems to care
people think I'm nothing but I have so much to share.

People like to shun me, push or fight
Like am I lost and I have no rights.

The fear no longer tearing at my heart
the tears no longer play their part.

I have lost touch with joy and gladness
nothing left but pain and sadness.

  Margaret Hunter

A Strong Tower

"Follow me, follow me," it was the voice of God;
Guiding me to a place, His feet already trod.
Not sure where I was heading; the place was not in sight;
He guided me by His Spirit, He led me by His light.
Then in the distance I saw a tower reach up into the clouds;
He appeared upon the tower when I heard His voice aloud.
"Come climb unto this tower"! There were no stairs in sight;
"Just take a step, I'll do the rest, you'll make it up alright."
Then at the top, He disappeared through a narrow door;
"Where are you Lord? I cried aloud, I couldn't see Him anymore.
He brought me to a place where the sick and helpless were all around,
Handicapped and in special chairs and most were sitting down.
Looking around I peered before me to a long dark corridor;
And all across its path there was a closed door after door.
I had a hopeless, eery feeling for those bound and shut in tight;
They needed the touch of a loving hand to help everything seem alright.
Then gazing out a window that surrounded the tall tower
I looked upon the busy people not knowing the need or hour.
A peaceful place of refuge, a healing place of rest and love;
A Strong Tower, we are all called to be a part off.

  Sylvia Levack (McLellan)

Thunderstorm

Pound your anvil.
Growl and shake the trembling heavens.
Flash and dash your sheets of rain
Against the darkened houses down below.
Drench and quench the parched land.
Mutter in your distant passage
With shafts of blue light in the curtains
Of your ragged gray clouds.
Run the rain beaded on the window pane.
Strew the drabbled blossoms on the grass
Green wakened 'neath its yellow thatch,
And let the sparrow in the furrow
Of the eaves trough
Sing praises to your awesome bounty.

  Freda K. Thomas

Too Old, Yet Too Young!

  Twelve years old in your mother's eyes,
growing up so fast! Just a baby in your
Father's eyes taking your first steps.

  Pressure going round and round, your world
just keeps spinning. Life and what it means
to you never stops changing.
  Decisions too hard to make. Test and jobs you
can't take. You are too old, then too young.
Why is life so off and on?

  You hope for some slack. You run fast
to an older age. Then you wish to go back.

  First you are told to listen then to speak your mind.
Where is the balance you are supposed to find?

  Ideal looks, ideal grades, ideal friends, you may
have to say, we aren't all models. We all can't
get A's. We don't all hang with the "in" crowd.

  But, Hey, to get through the week, you need some
heart. Let's all try to get a head start!

  Jaclyn Christie

Sea Of Dreams

Pain stricken hearts, tear filled eyes
Grieving for a love lost, wondering why.
A bursting of energy, so alive, so free
Came into her life, swept her off her feet.
Their love was young, their love was strong
Stronger than the sun that shines above.
The hopes and the dreams they shared with each other
Were dreams that would never come true, not ever.
His ego had been broken, the boys she bared for him
Had been a token.
Of their love lost, in a sea of Dreams.

She gave up, he let go
Something went wrong, felt he didn't belong.
Desperate and frightened, he gave in to fear
Took his own life, and now he's not here.
No Father for her kids, no loving good-night kiss.
She's missing him, her love was true
Their dreams have all been swept away
In a sea so blue.

  Jeannette Gimza

Pigeon Dance

Leaves are green on trees;
Grass covers all the lawns.

Dance, dance, dance, female pigeon, small and tiny,
Stalks with her head high, gone is the usual timidness;

Dance, dance, dance, the male, big and bright,
Goes after with his beak lower hide, none is the daily arrogance.

She strides up and down, ignoring anything around;
Back and forth he is waltzing, to her love signal is twittering.

She strolls high and low, devotee is accepted to follow
Her away from the flock into the bush having their sweet romance.

Eggs laid, babies hatched, the busy mother performs her duty;
While adherent mate is gone, ardent lover not around.

Leaves are red falling;
Grass is withered thinning.

Dance, dance, dance, order of the day resumes;
Brutal as ever the male pigeon beaks the female into submission.

Andy Xu

My Mother

How very lucky I have been
God gave her to me.
A mother who taught me so much
And gave so willingly

Each day she taught me many things
How to grow and understand
She taught me compassion
And how to lend a helping hand

Though her life was filled with hardship
She suffered heartaches, illness and pain
She taught me how to deal with them
Never give up and how to begin again.

She taught me how to clean and cook
How to bake, sew and mend
She taught me unconditional love
The meaning of friend

She taught me we aren't perfect
And it's ok not to be
Just do your best she always said
That's good enough for me.

Mary Gaudet

Loneliness

We have been together, oh, so long, Sweetheart.
God called you, now you're gone.

Here am I at home alone - it's not the best.
There's something binding me called loneliness.
I get up and try to push it away,
But loneliness comes back again.

Then all of a sudden I saw the bright glow.
I saw you, my Angel, resting on the end of a rainbow.
I stood there and stared seeing you, Angel, lying there.
I saw you smile and then I knew I was going back to you.

My Angel came flying down to me to rest.
I put my arms around you and then came happiness.
I'm as happy as can be,
For now I have no more loneliness.

Leonard R. Levaillant

Frozen Memories

Slowly set the sun in horizon, spreading a spell of gloom on earth
Gently arose the memories, that lay frozen in my tormented heart
Suddenly flashed, the pleasant unforgettable days of my childhood
Fondly caressed and petted by my loving father in a luxury home.

He cherished me like a flower, fed me with love untold
He carried me in his arms, I slumbered on his bosom
He fed me with love and love was all that the gave
He called me "Sweety" I was his world.

The sense of serenity, that surrounded his charming countenance was
remarkable, the spontaneous and gleaming smiles of his, bewitched everyone
who set eyes on him
The dark black eyes of his, keep haunting me day and night
The tall slender figure of his, traverses along singing merry hai.

I had a friend, a philosopher, a guide, it was he, my loving father
I waited in sun and rain, for the return of my loving father
I hear his voice echo "Sweety", but no more my loving father
I stand! I gaze! I look! where? where? where is my loving father?

There were tears in his eyes, when he descried tears in my eyes
I am in tears today, he is no more, he is gone to the land of the dead
There remains his memories frozen and hardened in my lonely heart
Never to be defrosted, never to be forgotten, but to be told and retold.

Pushpam Wignarajah

Night Is

Night is...a clear night looking up at a full moon
   gazing at the pinpricks of light
   in a black velvet sky
   and sometimes
   the silver streak of a shooting star.
   Watching the fork lightning spear the darkness
   and the crash and boom of thunder
Night is...the crackle and sizzle of a bonfire
   flames licking upward
   feeling hot on my skin.
   The legions of crickets chirping
   and in the distance
   the mournful wail of a siren
Night is...the lemony smell
   of a citronella candle burning.
   The persistent buzz of mosquitoes
   darting in front of my face.
   Riding my motorcycle on the solitary ribbon of blacktop
   no destination in mind-riding for riding's sake.
Night is...when I feel truly alive.

Matthew Emmett

The Crystal Spring

I went to the spring I was tired and worn
Full of tears and sorrow and most forlorn.

I knelt down by the spring and looked into its depth
Nothing was there, I wept and I wept.

Then a voice within said, "Look down again,
There is water there to soothe your pain."

The water bubbled so cool and bright
And filled my soul with its sparkling Light.

I drank and I drank from this Crystal Spring
Bringing hope and joy into everything.

The Water of Life can be dark as night
But also can shine with a sparkling Light.

When the world is dark and life seems in vain
Look for the Crystal Spring again.

Ruth Fletcher

Mirrors Never Lie

In the mirror you see a face
Full of beauty, life and grace
Throughout the path, the journey of life
You embrace the love but the hurt cuts like a knife

Where's the source of your fear?
People, places and most of all friends, seem to disappear
The vows we seem to take
And the promises we break

We must walk, bound to the crosses we must bear
They say in love and war all is fair
We stumble through our best and hope not to fall
If we do will anyone be there at all?

And at the end of this rocky, winding path
You find you are the comfort, your own rod and staff
You will look back in that mirror and reflected you see
You are the sole comfort, all you'll ever be

Michelle Dipardo

Love Is A Funny Thing

You know, love is a funny thing, you don't know
from time to time.
What really is going to happen, with someone
that you call "mine"
People wonder day and night, if they'll ever fall in love
Some even kneel and pray, to our God high above.
Love is a funny thing, it's really hard to say
What's going to happen in the future or what's
going to happen today
Everyone dreams of finding someone that will be true
But it's hard to find someone, who is a little new.
I never thought in my life, I would ever fall in love.
Now I know that I am wrong, as God picked
her out from high above.
Now I'll tell you a simple thing, love...
is a funny thing.

Allan Gourd

Life's Journey

We embark on a journey
From the first moment we take breath,
That takes we know not where,
Until the moment of our death.

Our sojourn is by sight, by sound,
By smell, and yes, by feel.
Our path is always winding
Both true and yet unreal.

To live is to scale the burgeoning heights
And to suffer the unfathomable lows.
To partake of the nectar
Whose taste only God knows.

We awaken each day
To adventure, great or small
But how each of us will experience it,
Is the greatest mystery of all.

Let us know passion! Let us know joy!
Let us know fear and excitement!
For what else is life,
But the ultimate enticement?

Michelle Alarie

Their Speech

Your words come like young birds
From nests of woven water
To flutter in small streams.
Your speech knits the earth and sky together.
  The bride answers her groom

When you talk, the seasons speak.
I pray forever after:
May you nest in woven wool;
May your speech bathe in young water.

Joan Gordon

Autumn's Splendor

A glow of orange and bronze, red and gold
From nature's beauty autumn unfolds.
A harvest of plenty can be seem everywhere
Enticing and bewitching a glorious fall fair.
A cornucopia of earth's many treasures
Surrounds and brightens the earth beyond measure.
Colorful and warming as a soft fire's glow
We are drawn even closer to this wondrous show.
Each new season is a marvel to behold
We have seen them miraculously unfold.
Nothing surpasses the beauty and grandeur
Of a Thanksgiving from autumn's splendor.

Elizabeth Zurba

Our Valley

When God created this valley
From Kamloops past Vavenby
He made it look like Heaven
Just for you and me

He added the North Thompson
For green and scenery
He made it look like Heaven
Just for you and me

There is a fellow from Vancouver
That wants to turn the river south
He wants to dig a channel and add a water spout

We want our valley as it is
We want our greenery
Just leave God's creation
That he left for you and me

Milton R. Caul

"All Things Great"

All things great,
from a tiny seed nurtured
with sun and rain and love;
of which the greatest is love,
for without it there is no sun no rain.
The greatest gift, a shower of love,
shortest becomes tallest, smallest turns to grand.
Time passes by and yet
still stand tall;
all things great,
from a tiny nurtured seed!

William J. Whyte

A Cold Shoulder

Icy gusts of wind blowing,
Freezing the hearts of all,
People wond'ring what they're showing,
Wond'ring if they should answer its call.

When the air's beginning its blows,
It whistles a loud, fierce tune,
And every single person knows,
That winter will be here soon.

Then the snow begins to fly,
Storms are traveling our way,
All across the wide, gray sky,
And the weather starts to play.

Now Jack Frost is laughing,
Painting scratchy pictures on the window,
For he knows what is still coming,
The trees join in swaying to and fro.

"Little children hide from me,
You'll soon see I'm not nice,
For I will let the storms blow free,
I am Jack Frost, King of Ice!"
Erin McInrue

October's Wind

Each October on a moonless night
Freedom of soul is my passport to flight
Sweet elusive wind you come
Before the snow flies, when summer's gone

October's wind you call to me
"Spread your wings, rise up and see"

Breaking through the cloudy shore
Mortal woes exist no more
High above their swirling masses
We race through times uncharted passes

Visions in time your gift to me
For this one night - serenity

This night the wind becomes my lover
Playing, soaring together we hover
But all too soon the glimmer of sun
Our sign this magic night is done

We've lived a hundred lives before
With each October's flight - one more
A last caress - earthbound again
'Til next comes calling - October's Wind
Theresa Divell

"Three Seasons"

Three seasons on which I grow, A soul born free;
Free from wars hate!
A child's innocence hides in me, A virgins eyes unknown
in today's world.
In three seasons, when was I alone, to roam free;
Free without the worries and fears:
Unscarred from the hardships of life's dealings;
When was it that one was able to think and return
To a forgotten past without seeing what you want to see;
But to see what is actually there to be seen:
In three seasons, I have been sheltered from within,
Naked to be looked upon
by all who wish to look:
In three seasons I have grown.....
Andrew Pond

A Poet

He writes words on paper,
    forming thoughts - creating inception.
Then like a gushing tide the words begin to flow,
    stronger with each passage the passion rises.
A beginning gradually intensifying
    with every line, every stanza.
Ideas flowing through the quatrains
    magniloquent as he writes.

He is an artist,
    painting pictures with words - 'tapestries'.
With every trust and confidence in his words,
    the masterpiece unfolds.
He rejuvenates the spirit
    refreshing every movement, every twinge of life.
No fallacies, no qualms,
    his idea clearly justified.

He is an artist
    painting tapestries with words.
Patricia J. Andrew

Love Forever

I shall love the Lord forever...
    Forever and a day,
I shall love the Lord forever,
    Who stole my heart away.

I never would have known, had I been blind to see
How he just showed me his kindness, which often showed in me.

I will cherish fondest moments, from the day that we first met
They will stay with me forever, until we meet again.

He often eased my sorrow, and helped me ease the pain
He really was a blessing, who walked into my life that day.

I won't forget his guidance, he showed me in his way,
Who guided me to sunshine, and brought back life to me.

He had a heart of gold, which helped me day by day,
He had a way about him, and helped me on my way.

He charged the world about me, and taught me tenderness,
I thank the Lord above me, for his warm and thoughtfulness.

My deep appreciation for, giving me a break
It really had a meaning, I never would have dreamed.
Shirl MacLeod

Precious Moments

My Darling; thou has so much to be desired.
For thou art the blossom of my youth, that
causes my heart to quiver.
Thou art a rose that blooms in the evening;
and awaits the morning dew.
Thine lips, are lips of softness; such as thine heart.
Thine eyes, are such as pebbles;
reflecting its gems.
Oh, my darling;
Let not our hearts depart, but,
Let our hearts unite as one.
Let our hearts embrace together;
Such as the sunrise embraces the day.
And in the evening;
Let our hearts embrace each other,
Such as the sunset embraces the night.
For what good is there a tear; without feeling
Or a love; without knowing
Let tomorrow speak of itself,
And let this moment be ours; forever.
George V. Lonsdale

Untitled

O death, what a sad thought
For the man who lives for all his possessions
Who rejoice in everything he's got
And can still taste the joy of living

But death, you are welcome
By those who are miserable and weak
Or to the old man tired and worn
For whom life has no more meaning

Do not fear when death is coming
Remember those who came before and after
It's the will of God for all human beings
Just accept the decision of the Master

Remember there's a time for everything
Like a time to be sad and a time to sing
A time to laugh, a time to cry
And there's a time to be born, and a time to die

Claudette Lambert

"Mudpies"

Face off at the sandpile,
For the boys and me,
There were six of us,
So each team had three.
I got the mud.
He got no mud.
He only said he got mud,
To draw no blood.
We got painful berries,
To throw at ourselves.
We should have started a governmental force,
For we loved to hand out our hell.
The towering trees indicated natural auditoriums,
And birds were our inattentive audience.
C.O.P.S., super heroes, G.I. Joe,
Toys had so much flowering radiance.
Those fairy tale days were when pain felt different,
Before the temptations came.
There is still one thing to keep me optimistic,
It is all still a game.

Jan Hrubin

Distant Light

Rest in peace and do not fear,
  For out the darkness will appear,
    A host of angels drawing near.

And as your reach that distant light
  Friends and family will come in sight,
    To ease you to a new domain,
      Free of suffering and all pain,

Let them guide you to a place,
  Until we join you in eternal grace.

Wendy C. Maximilian

Soulmates

I could live without you, but it wouldn't be the same.
For who would share my happiness, who would share my pain....
I'd still hear the songbirds trill, but miss the meaning of their song
I could weather any storm but, who would give me calm....
I'd still wake with morning's light but, lose the purpose to my day
I'd still wander from my path and who would help me find my way....
You are deepest part of me, the anchor for my soul
You are the sun behind my cloud, that makes me blossom, makes me whole.
We walk together, hand in hand but grow in knowing, one on one
If I am torn from this sharing, my soul would slowly come undone...

Patricia Jones

A Father I Would Be

Am I a father, doing what he should?
For my family, do I seek what is good?
Do I all my love with them share?
Do my actions show how much I care?

Loving Father, you my example should be,
Guided by the Holy Spirit living in me,
To my wife and children be a good dad,
Let me be the best dad they ever had.

Show me how to teach them God's Word,
The greatest story anyone has heard.
How it can make our lives much better,
By obeying God's commands to the letter.

Let me, my family, to You daily bring,
Father let's us drink of the Living Spring.
From the well of living Water renewed,
From within, the love of God exude.

Giving my family into Thy tender care,
With one another, Jesus love to share.
Living for the family that I now love,
Proven worthy of blessings from above.

W. G. McClain

Oh For A Life

Oh for a life with no struggles and strife
For me it was not meant to be
The ache and the pain
The death and the bane
How stressful it has been for me
The lost loves and lost friends
For me never ends
Tears and sadness in this long life are mine
The loneliness and tears
All down through the years
So in death when it comes shall I shine
God in your mercy when my life is o'er
Let Your light shine bright on my face
Your mercy I beg
Your forgiveness I seek
And pray Death finds me solace and peace

Margaret R. Sell

"The Little Light House"

The little light house stood on guard
  for many, many years.
It's saved many many a life
  spared many many tears.
It's braved the storms and shed its light
  o'er many an ocean wave.
On many a dark and stormy night
  many a ship it's saved
from crashing on the unseen rocks
  scattered along the shore.
I hope it stands and guards the seas
  for many many more.
The foghorn moans its mournful cries.
"Beware", it seems to say.
"Down there many a brave ship lies
  'cause it couldn't find its way.
I hope my light lights up the waves
  to show where tempest's tossed
and ne'er again while I'm on guard
  will any lives be lost."

Irene Stead

Thoughts At The Death Of Day

The sun goes wearily down in the west
for its nightly rest
And with that comes to an awful end
A perfectly sad and ailing day
A day which began with a sensuous hope
Brought along with it the sadness I couldn't cope

Perhaps the night will bring some relief
As in dreams I do strongly believe
But I do not dream to become a king
I only dream of a simple thing
That the sun will rise again
Bringing a little happiness and take away
all this pain
For tomorrow I shall become
What I could not be today
I only dream
of a fine - Day.

Gagan Badyal

The Power Of Prayer

There is guidance and grade
for each challenge we face;
There is peace and comfort to space,
you will find quiet rest
In God who knows best
If you go to the Lord with your prayer.

When black clouds fill the sky
and your dreams go awry,
And your hopes fade into the air,
courage and strength can be found,
And new peace can abound
If you go to the Lord with your prayer.

When life sends you some new disappointment
that you find you're unable to bear;
There is help for each task
if you will just ask
if you go to the Lord with your prayer.

Bea Nacey

Autumn Lost

Shadows from a low sun
Follow the slow stream.
Into the smooth curves
Life's ribbon flows.
Reds and browns furnish
A fallen crown of leaves.
The forest stands high
Above its masterpiece.
Miles lose their way
As the river sighs.
Home lies in everything seen.

Cloud crests in a determined sky,
And sweeps indifference from
An autumn lost. Birds aroused
Beat their path to where danger's passed.
We now await the mystery of winter,
Under snow clouds massing.
The Overlord's cloak reappears,
Silent and absolute.

Richard Morton

"Our Heritage"

I walked along a worn woodland trail,
Flowers growing thick along the way.
I heard the sudden rushing of a quail,
It took flight and quickly sped away.

A lake sparkled far down in the valley,
And forest stretched miles from its shore.
Mother Nature shines in all her glory,
While in the breeze a mighty eagle soars.

I stopped and looked at all this beauty,
Much more than the mind could gauge.
I took a moment to reflect on this great country,
And thanked God for our heritage.

Randy Hann

Flowers

Flowers are bright
Flowers are gay,
Flowers are always there to say:
"Thank you, best wishes, congratulations, get well,
things will get better in every way.
Remember we grow better on a rainy day."
From the spring of our life, until our call
Flowers will be there big and tall.
Flowers so delicate
Flowers so bold
Each having something special to hold.
Like the flower, you and me,
are special and sweet as we can be,
for in your hearts we too can see,
No matter how different each is to grow,
we all have our glory and our glow.

Cecile Cloutier Cartmill

The Lion And The Eagle

The pretty lion lying in his pretty little nest
Flies like the eagle in his head while he rest
The clouds and the wonder
The poacher and his thunder
Awake the pretty lion from the sky and his rest
Never beat the lion even at the poachers best

The silent soaring eagle in the still surrounding sky
Looks upon the lion smiling in his resting mind
Hear the eagle scream
Break the lion from his dream
Peering from his perch as the poacher starts his search
Lion dashing rapidly into the jungle's lurch

Ryan Lotecki

Bleak

His life ended earlier than anyone planned
Fate was forced into his own hands
the shattered soul could take it no more
"I'll end it abruptly" he thought as he swore
went to the wrecker, got rid of his car
down the street with a gun, into the bar
had a few drinks to dull the pain
Didn't help much, his tears fell like rain
Walked out around midnight, onto the street
The lonely young man, not a soul did he greet
Got to his home, put his hands to his head
Pondered a moment, knelt by his bed
Saying "Lord I can't take it my life is a mess
I'm pulling the trigger, you handle the rest."

Michael S. Grenier

An American Deity

Young he was and sound 'in wind and limb',
Fit and tanned, bareheaded, toothy, slim;
Rich, he was, of vocabulary and purse,
Bore away he be, in a wagon, not a hearse.
Draped in a flag, his form, of garish stripes and stars,
Followed slowly by lesser men in motor cars.
It all began, they say, in a killing frost,
A cold replicated later when he was lost.
Abbreviated poesy marked the spot,
On which commenced the reign of Camelot,
Where a bogus royalty came into view
As desideratum, thus embraced as true.
We revel in our freedoms, howe'er expressed
And yet seem not offended, nor depressed
By those to whom the title 'Born to Rule'
Applies; from journalist to scholar, foe to fool,
The dust of glamour thrown into the skies,
Blurs such lines and tidily binds our eyes.
What quality should leaders most possess
Strength, grace, honesty, success?

Peter M. Jakobsen

Night Panes

Glittering light - diffuse - moonlit
filtered through cruciform, veiled
shy clouds - floating - drifting in
and out of view, darkness all
encompassing, enclosing my
thin shaft of iridescent light
seeking - narrowing - expanding
vision lost, vision seen, vision provoked.
Thought of darkened wonder, painful
surrender, reconciliation the fern
reaches for the softly shed light.

Karen W. Mooney

A Sign

As I sit and listen to the thunder
Feel the rain
And see the lightening
I wonder what my future holds

Tomorrow, and I safe on the street
Or will I be wished away
And see my picture on a telephone pole

In years to come, steady income or poverty line
Happy marriage or just a statistic
Thriving country or war torn nation

And after that, the joy of childbirth
Or death and disease
Before that day arrives

Oh with so much ponder
Even now I feel the pain
Should the future be frightening
And yet... suddenly I don't feel cold

I look up and see a ray of sunshine
A ray of hope... a sign

Colleen Clarkson

Winter Solstice

You wake up one morning, unusually late.
Everything's dark for it's that time of year;
But something feels different about this certain date.
You look around carefully, with uncanny speed;
You find nothing missing, but there's a feeling in the air,
Which leads you to the window to see this special deed.
Your hand, though shaky, slowly lifts the blind as you squint at the sight
Of a brilliant sea of silvery light.
Suddenly you realize what deed was done; for where there was
A brown earth all bare, there is now a shining blanket which before your eyes
Is transforming into a lake of radiant sunrise.
This snow softly sculptured the ground
Without a single solitary sound.
As you step into the light outside,
You smell the scents of your childhood days,
Hear the melody that nature plays,
And remember those same, beautiful sunbeams
That used to make the life in you gleam.
It is comforting to know that God does care
And gives us gifts we thought were not there.

Joel Alexander McKenzie

Remembrance Day

Remember the war in the past years
Everybody had lots of fears

Loved ones died while they where fighting
And what we are remembering

People cried, people were sad
The whole world felt bad

It's like you have an empty feeling
And it will never be heeling

Thousands of soldiers died
In the whole world wide

We demand no more war
Because our hearts have been torn before

Let the children of tomorrow
Be safe to grow
Let's at least
Wish for world peace

Christine Vincent

Life Or Death

Is this life or is this death,
Every breath I take of this death,
Seems like an eternity,
A lifetime,
A future.

For what shall become of us in the future,
What shall become of us,
The world,
Everyone.
Shall everyone of this world die or,
Shall everyone live.

For death might even be better than life.
Death might be the light and,
Life might be the darkness,
Of this hellish death.

Derek Gauthier

On The Brink

We Canadians are so unhappy, so critical
Ever torn by dual language
Always resentful of the other
Never live and let live always pushing and shoving
Why can't we compromise and enjoy one another?

Our country is peopled by immigrants
We are paranoid that they will overshadow
Oust others from the workplace
Bring down the neighborhood
They want only to be accepted, their work judged fairly
Their customs honoured, not embraced

We are obsessed by our governments
Fine until in office, our judges and police corrupt and unfair
Ask only that our leaders be strong, fair, accountable
Heap praise on our law enforcers
They are trying to do their job

We must stand up, be strong, stop grumbling
And be proud, proud of all we have
The beauty, the cleanliness, the security, the opportunities
We are on the brink of greatness.

Claire McIntosh

Life's Tapestry

Life, like a tapestry, rich with feeling,
Ever revealing, its riches to me,
Each season casts, its colorful past,
Weaving soft hues, in my memory.

Hearts delight, my silvery knight,
Stitches of strength, in my tapestry.
Beautiful threads, shimmering gold,
Memories of all of my babies I hold.

Happy times, magenta; sad, subdued,
Melancholy moments, yellow hued.
Love, like soft fabric, comfortably worn,
Mosaic design, makes up, my life's form.

Reflections, alive, with intensity,
Constantly awed, by all that I see,
The texture of life, that is longing to be,
Entwined in the textile, of life's tapestry.

Maureen Palmer

Solitude

Sometimes I just like to be alone.
Even though I know I'm never alone.
I revel in the peace of a quiet Sunday.
Freedom to do as I please, as long as I'm hurting no-one.

In the spring and summer I revel in the beauty of it.
I go to the Gillies Lake Park.
There are friendly people walking and talking together.
I see the birds and feel the solitude.

Sometimes I like to be around other people.
But when I like solitude it is there.
Walking with a friend and discussing life.
It is good to be compatible with another person.

But I am always talking to God.
I feel the Holy Spirit giving me peace, filling the void.
This is something I wish every person would have.
Then the world would be a better place.

The universe is a big place to contemplate.
But with meaning in life comes peace.
Understanding brings strength to fight the hard times.
But most of all I like the gift of solitude.

Gerald Keyes

I'm Canadian

30,000 Feet up in the sky
Escaping the highlands can't understand why
No knowledge of this formatic land
A brighter future was the initial plan

Canada, offers citizens glory and freedom
Open arms to foreign struggle giving hope and happiness
Shipping resource worldwide each day surviving the poor feeding the hungry

Maritime troubles 27 million share the grief
Quebec wants out let's stay together let's have belief
Ontario industry drives breath taking scenery it provides
Saskatchewan, a Canadian farmers paradise, N.H.L, dreams kids skate on
   its ice
Manitobans are the coolest folks climate is rough making them tough
Alberta, BC, share rocky mountain high oil, logging in demand in supply
Territory wildlife cannot be beat take off poachers just retreat

Free trade deals with our neighbors below
They'd be lost without us in the north American flow
A native home welcome makes you glad you came
The past has passed look ahead racism is still a losing game

Harry Keyworth

The Destroyer

Only sad to say that not everyone is wise
enough to see the destroyer and those who do may
not admit or know how to change its evil ways.

Until we sacrifice and do justice for ourselves,
that is when some of the suffering will stop.

We have to win the battle by changing or starting
to realize that we must fight until we feel safe within ourselves.

The destroyer can weaken us but we have to
grow stronger. We have to win the battle to diminish
this destroyer.

Then we shall feel as one, feel whole and for
once feel secure within ourselves.

It's all the matter of knowing your own strengths
So remember, if you're feeling vulnerable the
enemy will attack; so stay on guard and know
that the Destroyer is always lurking for its next victim.

Nicole M. Greenwood

Waiting Child

The child sits quietly bemused,
engrossed in a treasure - his find.
His mother beside him is sleeping;
he is patient, contented, resigned.

His three year old mind probes it deeper,
this red toy in the palms of entreat.
He ponders when Mother will awaken;
why so many tonight sleep in the street.

With honest gaze, eyes wide, lips pursed;
boundless love and trust reach where ever he treads.
To fathom this thing life with the elders;
Oh, to learn and explore what's ahead!

At the curb of this dusty old dirt road,
in this poor country in Europe-even now,
this tear stained young boy continues his waiting;
belly tight, leg bleeding, sweating brow.

Mother's body beside has been pummeled;
bloody shroud, sniper fire, soul's undone.
The child awaits innocent 'midst the slaughter;
in his hand rolls the shell of a gun.

Simon J. Varricchio

Time For Change

Now a days the news might as well be rated "R".
Eight year olds with guns, it's gone too far.
Kids are killin' kids, children killin' mothers,
shot the father, why not do the brothers?

Thinkin' you're the main man 'cause you got a big gun.
Always on the run, sounds like lots of fun.
You say you do what you do
'Cause your parents beat you.
Well, that's in the past.
How long must the anger last?

It's time for a change in society.
Love or war, what's it gonna be?
Hear the children screamin'.
Man they're only dreamin',
Of a love that isn't there.
Tell me truly, do you care?
If you do then you can see
That it's time for a change in society

Wessley Dyck

Summer Memories

We have a cottage on a river, that is part of the Trent Canal,
Each morning around 6 a.m. a Blue heron comes to call
He stealthily walks along the dock watching for fish or frog,
Sometimes it's hard to see him in the early morning fog.

A Woodpecker often wakes us, tapping on the drainpipe on the wall
And many times a day, the Hummingbirds pay a call.
As we boat along the river other boaters smile and wave,
It's a polite habit, I hope the waterway will save.

I like to use our paddle boat, in the cool of eventide,
The Swallows swirl around us, adding enchantment to the ride.
A family of Chipmunks have a nest in our storage shed
And Coons sneak around at night, hoping to be fed.

At the end of summer, I see and often recall
Canada Geese in formation and their rousing good-bye call.
So when Summer is over and the Winter days grow long.
These memories of Summer keep my heart warm and strong.

Pauline Ireland

Unread

The lonely soul in the cold pouring rain,
Each drop whispers sadness and pain,
Blended into salty tears,
Nothing is as it appears,

Can't plant seeds without the land,
Alone barefoot in the cool, wet sand,
Poetic heart, open and free,
A kind spirit no one will see,

Open wide the disfigured cover,
Turn the pages, a yearned for lover,
Romantic words, long to be spoken,
From a human heart shattered and broken,

Sharon L. Cliff

Evening Tea With Two Cousins

Their coffee table
Deep and glossy like a pool
Would hold the white mugs
Like baby ducks

And as the evening hugged the town house window
We, the guests
Drowsy and smiling and far from home
Would lean through the gentle lamplight
To hold our tiny birds close
And kiss their warm, smooth feathers

Erin O'Hara

Sourdough Miners

A hill of Gold overlooking a shaft of claims
Drowning in a whiskey river of shame
As the sourdough miners trek and hike
Old timers dreaming of one last strike

Down in the depth of a coal dust shaft
Breathing air of pollution in an underground blast
A quarry of black rock is waiting for the drill
Deep in the earth not one rail cart is still

This town's sin was placed on the backs of gold greedy men
For gold stealing was a claim jumpers bullet riddled road to the state pen
A baby doe ghost mine lost to a fables dream of John Taber
And chinese coolies were the back bone of gold fever labor

A sawdust saloon of whiskey and wicked gun play miners
One more shanty town of broken down old timers
As these grubby miners were seeking a fortune as "gold fever" was their thrill
Silver and gold was the dream of a future on "snob hill"

Now gold dust was the inspiration for this tin cup town
As gamblers, miners of boom town glory was their sad frown
Frenchies was a gambler's paradise of pretty whiskey saloon girls
Only a ghost of a town left to the spirit of lost silver mining pearls

Donald Jardine

Just Because

Just because I never say it
Doesn't mean my love's not there
Just because I never hold you
Doesn't mean that I don't care

Just because I hide my feelings
Doesn't mean I'm heartless
Just because I don't keep track of things
Doesn't mean I'm careless

Just because I love you
I wrote down this simple phrase
Just because I care for you
My heart, for you, is full of praise

Andrew Mitchell

Silence

Silence...
  Do you hear it,
  Do you feel it,
    Why does it come again and again?
    Just when I think the light will shine,
      Silence comes
    And takes it away.
Silence....
  Nobody comes, nobody calls,
    Where are they who said they care?
    Alone again behind these walls,
      Silence grows
    As they stay away.
Silence.....
  I can't take it,
  I won't take it,
    Why should I live like this anymore?
    Suitcase packed with all that I have,
      Silence stays
    As I walk away.

Evelyn Krawchuk

552

The Best Years Of Your Life

Society silicone, implanted in your mind
Do what is right, or you will find
Labels plastered to your brain,
Crying tears of acid rain.

Childhood is just a phase
Preparation for the maze.
Life is just an empty page,
'Till you scream in teenage rage.

Futuristic, funny faces,
We have come to take your places.
Mixed-up, screwed-up, dumb as dirt
Cut us down and we still hurt.

We lie and kill, we cheat and steal
'Cause we don't understand the deal.
Confusion diffuses through our souls
Forced to accept the hardest roles.

Scapegoats, we all take the blame,
Start out early, to keep us tame.
Put up with all the pain and strife,
These are the best years of your life.

Alicia Cox

Cynthia

She had the wisdom of a thousand lives
Disguised by the face of umblemished innocence.
Her skin was softer than the petals of a rose
Nurtured by the sweet dew of spring.
The mystery and beauty of the universe
Was captured in her eyes
And she could convey the secrets of the ages
With a single glance.
With a tender smile and gentle touch
She erased the pain of a lifetime.
And as I lay there in the warmth of her shadow
She whispered me her name with a voice so gentle
It could hush the night..."Cynthia".

Mark O'Krafka

.... Belly Quest ...

Weldfridge,....but contrare
    discovery inst midriff
Phantoms art cotton fluff
Nort spinetap any calorie count
Who's beeline trip is a bogwaste trap
    Sugarlane....how doth we padlock
Temptation sweet where variety rules
Saucer eyes fuel gainst yoyo digits lies
    truth shakes a wardrobe finger.
Cheat not too often; aroma's blemish is to linger.
    Wink denial and proof evident
flavour rival!
Cholestral cupboard
Heaven's above! Handles of love.
Shadowland...have you starburst mirror?
Models wee bikini; dreamy crown and roses.
    Mind's over matter
Contempt versus fate in strong debate
    Outbreak this fad weight
And end thy waist mistake in the name of food's sake!

Sonia L. Bodnar

Diamonds And Daggers

Eyes
Diamonds determined to dream,
Brilliantly flashing the blue, gold and silver
Of untarnished life.
Together embracing the warm flood of future,
The ocean of family, quick to their eyes.
Eyes
Daggers of mutual distrust;
His outwardly rejecting
The lethargic slump of her shoulders.
Hers - vacant pools of nothingness,
Reflecting only, the inner darkness of her life
Passive perhaps,
Until the full tide of love
Brings wisdom to pain,
And patinas the present with the silver in life.

Susan Stewart

Why?

A brand new life pulsing within,
Devastation, confusion, elation abound
Too premature for life's greatest joy-
Decisions so complex,
Painful times to endure.

Never before so large, life's journey ahead,
Valleys of despair - the hurt so profound
Unselfish maturity, you grow very strong,
Still questioning why — and wondering
Will there be peace - can you survive and go on?

Too quickly you must learn,
Right and wrong — not black and white
Your head remains the ruler, even though your heart breaks,
A love not thought possible, is experienced through him,
How is this so beautiful, and painful all in one?

Never to forget a distant miracle to love
Your heart knows for sure - someday you'll meet again
Life's greatest gift is a child - you've given that today
You loved him enough, you were able to say good-bye.

Beverley Templar

Untitled

Ishtar, in search of her beloved
Descended from the highest Heaven
And knocked upon the gates of Earth.
"Who is it that knocks?"
Cried the Angel of the Presence.
"It is I, Ishtar, the Mother of Heaven."
"Remove your celestial wings,
your radiant crown, and luminous robe,
If you must enter," replied the angel.
Without wings and the power to reascend;
Without the crown of divine memory;
Naked and without her astral light;
She entered through the eastern gate
In perfect splendor and radiant glory.

She came in your perfect form my beloved;
Perfect in every way.

Serosh Haroutunian

Memories Of Henry Drummond

In early days; dis Silver Town was famous tru de world
De story dat old timers tell would make your straight hair curl;
Des spend a few days every year to celebrate dis place
All de people dat you meet will have a happy face.
  Henry Drummond came to stay, he was a doctor man
  De population was so big, der was so room to stand;
  He's do his best to help de sick and make dem all back well
  Small hospital, not many beds, must have been real hell!
He's live in cabin on de hill dats overlooks de town.
After he's pass in a few years, de cabin she's fall down,
De fire place still stand, de same is now a monument
In his spare, she's write some poems about some big event.
  She's always use de french accent when she's write up a poem
  Dat make you laugh out loud and always tink of home;
  Dat one of Old Batiste, who fall in de Stovepine hole
  De girl's boyfriend won't pull him out till he gets de girl.
De years slip by, old timers pass, dats history in the making
Get Grummonds book and read it all - start at the beginning
When you get tru, you will agree has was a clever man
Go to the cairn, stop and think, you'll really feel quite grand.

Haretey Houston

Mournful

She mourns in the Pasture,
crying softly with her head hung low.
Her lover has left her,
but forever will she love him so.

He was her life soul mate,
and she never will forget this day.
The memories will haunt her,
of friends and family surrounding his grave.

Without him she's all alone.
She has no family just a home.
Now, the house will be empty,
just like her heart, fragmentary.

She does not know how,
but her life will have to go on.
She knows that it will be hard,
but he'd want this now that he's gone.

Heather Marceniuk

Dessert Ice

Out nestled in the trees
countless dreams float about the streams
Where footprints once were
are now vanished from time but not from mind.
Stones fly with emotion from innocent palms
landmarking arrival.
Close but yet so far many strive to touch the stars.
Wind apparel, blue, yellow, sapphire
cries out with love and desire,
Hearts flutter with trueness and splendor
counting days but years of thunder.
Green barrets of clean spoken wonder
dance about like a ballet of untamed pleasure.
Many worries, doubts a wander
through moonlight saffron cobblestone streets plunder.
Emerald green to magenta pink,
eyes of mahogany look about and think,
this shady crystal ball know as earth
is it really a world at all
or does its majestic starbright seem to...

Lisa Giroday

Count The Cost

When temptation and evil knocks.
Count the cost before you open the door.
Stop!
Take a long hard look at all who will be affected
You owe it to all concerned.

When a thought of infidelity arises in your heart
Snuff it out immediately without hesitation.
For its flame will consume your very soul.
It won't be quenched till its ravenous appetite is fulfilled
Stop, and count the cost.

Times are hard.
Wants and needs are great
Entertain not the idea of unjust gain or evil scheming.
Their end is nothing short of destruction.
Stop, and count the cost.

Let wisdom be your companion
And righteousness your guiding light
Turn a deaf ear to deception's call
And a blind eye to unjustifiable's way.
Stop, and count the cost.

Paulyne Cascanette

The Edge

To the edge of green cliffs
Look over
See your reflection in the water,
Rocks falling
Your face rippling away into the distant shores
You see your life
As a kid swimming in the water
The waves hitting his back
Then curling over,
Curl after curl
Day after day
To the edge where we push our parents
To the edge where we live!

Kelly Williams

An Everlasting Love

How much do we love thee?
Look up at the stars in the sky.
How many do you see?
That's how much we love you, we wouldn't lie!

How much do we miss you, when you're not here?
Look around you, see the people with sadness in their eyes.
Multiply that sadness times ten and you're getting near.
That's how much we miss you, don't you hear the heavy sighs?

As we sit here waiting for your return, we wonder,
do you all miss us too?
We tell ourselves, it's best for them to wander,
for here, there's just not much for them to do!

Oh how we long to see your faces.
Sometimes, I think I see a tear in papa's eye.
Secretly, I pretend to feel your sweet embraces.
But, wait, we mustn't, they tell us not to cry!

Mary Elaine Feltner

Colorful Walk In Autumn

As summer turns to fall, and the
leaves turn all brown
I wonder where the golden leaves are
bound and the evening shadows host
the fallen leaves, as they fall forever
to the ground

I listen for the autumn sounds,
the falling acorns thump to the ground
Squirrels scoot around storing up all
their treasures for the winters bound

As the cool nights turn to winter I
will always remember the colorful
walk through the autumn leaves
Betty W. Smith

Reaching For The Stars

Reach for the stars.
Lay hold of life's opportunities.
Let your eyes see visions of greatness.
Never lose sight of what you can be.

Set out for the goal,
feet planted firmly on the ground.
With a steadfast hope
and an impassioned zeal,
seek our your dreams,
keeping faith in the unseen reality.
Anthony Bontempo

Every Drop Of Your Love

Being in love with you is so much fun.
La la means I love you.

Zip-a-dee-doo-dah you're the best thing
since candy, yum yum eatum-up.
Your sweetness is my weakness, that's
why I love you so.

O la de da you're number one in my
book. I can make you feel good and
please your mind. I qualify and
satisfy.

I love every little thing about you.
Ain't nothing you can do to make me
Stop loving you. We belong together.

Say you love me honey.
Juanita Shine

Violence

Drugs,
Knives stabbing,
Gunfire ringing out,
Poverty, abuse, rape, murder.
Evil!
Barbara Ann Miller

The Conservatives' Creed

Widows, orphans and spineless men:
judgement of righteousness
by unbound sin
and choir mouths hot with vowels.
    O come,
let us worship and fall down
to gain salvation for a house
dried to tinder to burn alone.
David Thomson

Kindred Spirit

So blue was the sky,
    just moments ago.
Children playing, bustling streets,
    the scenario,
    life.
Then, silence instantaneous,
    followed by a chorus of voices,
    oh! Terrible roar...
Young and old,
    in one mere breath
of fire, and fury.
    Without warning,
I rise with 3 million,
    to survey the charred
and wounded landscape,
    wondering what might have been,
if peace and harmony
    had reigned supreme.
David T. Potash

Untitled

Yes I am a doctor—
Just a plain and mortal man—
And I do for all my patients—
The very best I can—
But at times deep in my heart—
I get an awful throb—
When people expect of me—
What you can only get from God—
Oh' yes, I may save a life—
When God wills it done—
But I cannot keep a life down here—
When God has called it home—
So remember friends to say a prayer—
For that is good and proper—
And remember, I am not your God—
I am just, your family doctor.
Thomas B. McGowan

Through And Through

Inside my heart there's a feeling,
I've never experienced before.
A feeling that comes once in life,
it opens many a door.

Only one that I've ever known
could make this feeling stay.
He brought it to me long ago,
but I realize it in just one day.

Since then I found my happiness,
he made the bad times end.
He came into my life, I feel,
to start it over again.

If you've never had this,
you'll know it when you do,
because it seems so strong inside,
It burns you through and through.
Amy Laine

When I Lay Me Down To Die

When I lay me down to die,
Let no tear drop stain thy eye.
For I have tasted earthly love;
And caught a glimpse of that above.
Now, I can never really die.
Harold G. Oswald

My Dad

I lost my dad today.
I've feeling now. I've never known.
I'm empty, sad and lonely
His presence with me on this
earth, gone forever.
He was a good dad, loving,
caring and giving
He shared with me his
strength and wisdom
Grateful, I will always be
His job here was completed,
he had to go away
He walks with God, of that
I'm sure, and until we
meet again someday, his
memory will live in my
heart and mind all the
days of my life.
Carmella Lacertoso

The Power Of Love

The crickets are singing
It's time to write
Another poem
Blessed in the night

They come from where
I do not know
Pearls of wisdom
With the power to show...

The importance of love
It's the heart of all
Without it, we falter
With it, we're tall

It brings us together
It has the power to heal
It opens our hearts
To that which is real

The power of love
Will open the door
It will heal the pain
And oneness restore
Debra J. Lenter

Last Wishes

It's just my body
it's not really me
mine you can't destroy
not even in your dreams
burn up the body
I don't need it any more
it was good while it lasted
but the body is just a whore
to be used for a while
used and thrown away
for its memory a smile
no money to pay
let it float on the wind
or top the manure pile
give it back to the Earth
let it rest in style
maybe in a growing thing
could be dust on a rock
but ask a dead man to care
and he will not
Jeffrey N. Glaze

Shopping

Our pretty money comes from well fair.
It's not dirty and green like yours.
We buy powdered milk and yellow boxes.
All kinds of yellow boxes.

We are special with our
cream colored money.
I know
cause when Mama pulls it out
people look.

Jennifer Lee Bame

The Winter Sky

The winter sky called out to me
Its colors grey and pink to see;
And as I watched there came in view
Through shifting clouds a summer blue.

I seemed to see a castle there
Standing so tall just in the air,
While in the distance I could see
A horseman coming hastily.

But then the clouds did cover all,
The horseman and my castle tall;
No longer was the pink in view,
Nor was the lovely summer blue.

Helen Minetree Bowles

The Old Oak Tree

On top of a hill stands an old oak tree,
Its branches bent with age,
This place is full of memories
from a child's life.

Under this tree I would sit,
I'd come here to read or just
to think, sometimes to cry
sometimes to laugh.
I'd hang from its branches on a
hot summer's day.

Oh how many memories
I have of that place!
But that was long ago.
I have grown and moved away.
Someday, I promise myself, I'll
go back there and sit under
the branches of that old oak tree.

Dana Eaton

Down To The Pond

The pond is always calling us;
It beckons through the year.
The summons is so very strong;
We hear it loud and clear.

Down to the pond in spring we stroll,
To sit and dream with fishing pole.

Down to the pond in heat we dash,
To swim and float and dive and splash.

Down to the pond in fall we tramp,
To build a fire, cookout and camp.

Down to the pond is snow we slide,
To skate and race and fall and glide.

The pond is always calling us;
Its message to make known.
"Come spend your carefree days with me,
For you will soon be grown."

Connie Morrow Vincent

To My Husband

As I awoke the other morning,
  It was your birthday, by chance.
I was disoriented,
  In somewhat of a trance.

It seemed I saw a baby,
  Nestled in his mother's arms
And every one around them,
  Was quite taken by his charms.

Then the scene had shifted,
  And I saw a little lad;
As he scampered in the garden,
  Playing baseball with his dad.

Again I saw another scene,
  A young man filled with pride;
Standing at the altar,
  With his new wife by his side.

Of this one thing I'm certain,
  After 50 years arm in arm;
You may be getting older,
  But you haven't lost your charm.

Ella Leonard

"Bold And Beautiful"

The color spectrum of the sky,
it shines like never before.
The clouds roam free and
the sun follows a path that
will never break. The rain
falls and covers the ground.
The reflection is bold and beautiful.

Holly Allana Hobson

If You Keep Searching For Love

If you keep searching for love
It may never appear,
All that you find
Is a sigh and a tear.

But if for a moment
You simply don't try,
Then love could be there
In the blink of an eye.

And you may soon feel
A lover's embrace,
Touched by a smile
Upon his sweet face.

Christa Morgenthaler

Life Strife

My life has its ups and its downs
It also wanes and waxes.
While I sit here in tears
Controlling my fears
Wondering how will I pay for my taxes.

Gerry Spangler

Lincoln

Lincoln's name will live forever
Immortal never growing dim
Numbered with the great of history
Causing all to honor him
One who made the Union sacred
Leaving peace among the states
Not condemning, just forgiving,
  those who showed weak human traits

Irene Hayes

"Love, To Me"

Love, to me,
Is your smiling face
And love, to me,
Is your constant grace.
Love, to me,
Is sharing your tears
And love, to me,
Is knowing your fears.
Love, to me,
Is the magic we share
And love, to me,
Is knowing you care.
Love, to me,
Is when I'm with you
And love, to me
Is you.

Craig J. Weatherford

The Man I Love

The man I love
Is tall and handsome.
He takes me
Where I wish.

The man I love
Lets me cry on his shoulder,
And never ever lets anyone hurt me.

The man I love
Has a love of his own,
But loves me still the same.
For the man that I love
Can bear no shame.
Since I am his little girl!

Audra Angelique Renaud

Greater Than Ours

The love of the Lord above
Is stronger than thy own!
For Jesus is the Son of God
And his blood did He shed.

The light of the Lord above
Is mightier than our own!
Light as a Saviour did He come
And brought me to His thrown.

The peace of the Lord above
Is greater than our own!
God's peace is what I longed for,
Peace for ever more.

Christina Wang

"When Our Souls Will Rise?"

The water of the salty ocean
is rising and rising up
high in the sky
in the form of vapor,
and for the good of the world
it rains back on the earth
in the form of water
pure and sweet.

O God! When! Our souls
will rise up and up
and shower on this earth
in the form of love and mercy,
to heal the pain and suffering
of the peoples on this world.

Dhiraj Shah

Thoughts Of Dismay

What used to be once united
Is now falling apart
Your angered words you threw
Now you've broken my heart

Things we've done together
Happiness we shared
Memories we made
Now I wonder if you really cared

The beginning of each tomorrow
I wanted to be with you
My hopes my dreams my future plans
Were all prepared for two.

Now it's dark
The clouds have moved in.
And oh! I feel
I'm alone...once again.

CeCelia LaBarr

Silence

Some people think that silence
Is golden, and though that's true,
Silence in a house of boys
Would be something very new.

At night time when they're sleeping
And silence does prevail,
It's sad to think it won't be long
'Til childhood soon sets sail.

So, though silence can be golden
I look forward to each day,
To watch my young boys grow to men
With laughter and rowdy play.

For soon enough the house will have
A silence all its own,
When children no longer come to play
And all my boys are grown.

Brenda W. Hodges

Sometimes I Wonder

Is a Black man really Black?
Is a White man really White?
Is a Butterfly made from butter,
then just take off into flight?

Who wins the race of racism?
Is the prize a Winner's Cup?
Why do we chop a tree down,
and then go and cut it up?

Will Hopscotch make you drunk?
Will Scatter make you run?
When old folk finally lose their teeth,
do they really chew their gum?

Sometimes I just don't understand
the things that people say.
But I'll keep listening carefully
every night and every day.

And one day when I'm old enough
to talk like people talk,
the next thing I will learn to do
is walk like people walk.

Don Walker

My Favorite Brunette

My favorite brunette
Is a darling I love
So tiny and sweet
Sent from heaven above

I've waited so long
I've hunted so high
I finally found
the apple of my eye.

Only four foot seven
weighs eighty five pounds
God gave her to me
On American grounds

She's tiny and sweet
And something to cherish
God keep us together
Till the day that we perish

John H. Zehren

That Old White Woman Speaks

I remember his look
into my soul
touching me in places
long ago sealed away
in deep chambers
of my heart.

No stranger in these places
it knew the yearning
and longing there
crying to be heard.

At that moment
we were one
as we had been
since time began.

Just his look
into my soul
giving me strength
hope and new life
having no other color save Love.

Alma Garrison

New Life

I am so glad you came
into my life,
I am so glad you gave
your life for me,
I am so glad you set
my spirit free,
I am redeemed, reborn
anew,
reconciled unto you
O, God.

I was a sinner,
but you saved me.
I was slow, but
you held me fast.
My faith was broken,
but you healed me.
You, My awesome God.

Joi Vormelker

Motoring With Friends
(Or Independence)

When you don't know where you're headed
Into freedom or a trap,
Anxiety leaves you puzzled
And all choices are befuzzled,
Get a map!

When destination seems confusing,
And you have no loving lap,
All problems seem unsolvable
And pitfalls all are probable,
Get a map!

When a car you are not driving
And the driver is a snap,
He might say all so enthusing
While forward we are cruising,
Take a nap!

Now if I have not informed you,
Traveling troubles will entrap.
I will give you of my aid though
Cannot find you a safe shade so,
Get a map!

Donna G. Davis

Words

Words come tumbling down my arm,
Infusing eager fingers.
Rushing, whispering,
Swirling, shouting,
Pushing, shoving,
Clamoring voices.

They strip away
Concealing fabric.
Reveal the me I am.
Expose my mind
To naked freedom.
Word - love rules,
Insatiable.

Dalton G. Crum

Two Kinds Of Peace

Bright lights,
Infant squints and sounds alarm.
Warm arms,
Reassure with soft embrace.
Fear not,
No harm will come if Mama's here.

Red sun,
A child feels its ardent glow.
Green fields,
Gentle dampness brings delight.
Repose,
Nature's warmth abounds, it's safe.

Dark night,
Old man squints and softly moans.
Lover, won't assure with gentle voice.
Distrust, always haunts his dreaded place.

Needle, nearly gives a numbing grace.
Pillow, it is not a soft embrace.
Nature, soon again the peace he'll face.

Joe Collina

557

Blue

Blue sky,
Indigo blue.
It matches the color
In my heart. Sky, will you lend me
Some stars?

Blue eyes,
Cornflower blue!
Innocence shines through you.
Reluctance, too, perhaps, and fear
Of love.

Blue sea,
Mirror smooth and flat.
Yesterday all aroar
With tearing winds and crashing waves.
Now stilled.

Blue sky,
Frame for an arch
Of gentle pastel shades.
This iris tells me there is sun
And Hope!

Elizabeth McNally

Sister With Red Hair

I am the one who writes the words.

Why?

I look at her and know that

She

Is the only true poetry there is.

She would never think to capture herself
In verse, though;

She doesn't like cages.

Jacklyn E. Stroud

My Friend

I see your face before me
In the twilight of the day
As memories of you steal in
The chase my blues away.

You came to me in friendship
And as love between us grew,
I opened up my life to you,
As friends so often do.

You brought to me the sunshine
When my days had all been blue,
You put a new song in my heart
And brought me life anew.

I shared the secrets of my heart,
You opened yours to me.
We gave each other parts of us
That no one else could see.

For all the things you've given me,
For all the joy you send,
No wonder when my day is through
I think of you, my Friend.

Darlene Trevino

Passage

Last night as summer lay dying
  In the stillness of moving time
I sat in vigil for the passage
  Remembering the gift she freely gave

Quietly, with only a zephyr to murmur
  She went her mournful way
Promising to me in her passage
  Another year, another summer

Deril K. Mays

Remember The Rainbow

Look, there's a rainbow
In the sky above
Remember God's promise,
Remember His love.

After the darkest night
The sun will rise and shine
After coldest winter
The flowers will bloom again

When grief and sorrow
Turn the heart to yearning
Remember God's promise
Of the rainbow's returning.

Joy after sorrow,
Peace after pain.
Blue skies and sunshine
After the rain.

Frances West

Touch Me

Silver hair shimmers
in the moonlit breeze.
All the curls beckon, saying,
"come touch me."
They flutter and flirt
with my fingertips
and curl up in welcome
with a soft silken grip.

Donna Niquette

Each Poem

Each poem is like a chapter
In the book of life, it seems
Comprised of facts or fiction
Or, of memories or dreams

Broken down to topic sentences
In an outline sort of form
And briefly drawing pictures
As a message is passed on

In short form variations
Whether rhyming, whether not
Each line will pass to readers
The paragraphs of thought

A poem can tell a story
With so very little words
And uses very little paper
When compared to narratives

Dennis Wheeler

A Mood

As fog rolls in from the ocean
In silence slowly enfolding
Meadow and cliff and tree,
Veiling the face of the sun,
So over my soul there creeps
A sadness heavy and vague
Hiding the gate of dreams
Leaving no way of escape.

Even those that I love
Seem suddenly strange and cold
Beyond the sound of my voice,
Subtly changed and remote,
Unable to feel or respond.

I long for some way to express
Formless intangible things,
I long for the voice of the wind
Wailing mankind's despair.
I long for gray wet woods
Branches dripping with rain
So Nature might share with me the unreason-
ing grief of the soul.

Margaret Herman Peters

"Imperfections"

The flower grows inside me now.
In my heart is where I'm free.
Remembering childhood thoughts,
And playing childhood games.
Reminisce, all the same.

My heart asks for you know.
My soul beckons for you.
Do you think you're in love too?
I remember thinking...
Never would anyone love me.
I'd just say let me be,
With my imperfections.
Can you cure that infection?

Abby Laib

A Motivated Dream

I dreamed that I was drifting
In a skiff, upon a pond,
Waves were rocking me asleep
As I drifted there, on and on.

The moon was shining brightly
As leaves came falling down.
Also, drifting on the water,
Some landing on the ground.

As if, blessed from heaven
The sky lighted up so bright,
Lightning floated through it,
As I was drifting in the night.

The sky was clear as crystal,
Except splashes of honey brown,
Here and there clouds drifted,
Then drops came falling down.

To God, my thoughts were open
Accepting knowledge I was to know,
Directing me, in deep wisdom
And inspiring me where to go.

Eileen Corey Norwood

Remember Me

The blur of fleeting time
   Impedes my ability to separate
   Reality from illusion
It can make one stop or forge ahead
   An impulsive intrusion
Time can stir or strip the mind
   To leave you in confusion
It can cleanse your heart and
   Free the soul with total absolution.

Only time can tell of
   Where it has been and
   Where it soon will be
It can visit sorrow then
   Move to where there's glee
Time is always in a hurry
   Seems always on a spree
As it slips through my grasp
   To leave an eerie mystery
I wonder if time has passed me by
   And won't remember me.

Joseph Binder

Angel

I'm no angel;
I'm not who they needed me to be.

   Dealt the King of Diamonds
   Awakened with a start
   Boundless

I'm no angel;
I didn't do what they wanted me to do.

   Controversy surrounds the uncertain
   Pulled by action
   Explored

I'm no angel;
I'm not what they expected.

   Strengthened with desire
   Consciousness of spirit
   Uplifted

I'm no angel;
I'm not what they had.

   Growing with knowledge
   Learning semantics of life
   Discovered.

Jihan Murad

She's Great To Me

She's great to me,
I'm not sure why.
Been so nice to me has she.
She had just past my eyes by.
I was so mean to her.

Everyday I say,
I love her that's for sure.
I know that today.
I love her genuine and pure.

On everyday she is loved by me,
For I love her.
Me loved by she?
To prove it I'd buy her a house, a car,
   a diamond, a fur.
I'd do anything

I'm in love with you.
Cos' that she is you!

Jason Mayeu

A Mother's Plea

I am Mother Earth... Hear my plea.
I'm here to nurture you. Help me!
Hear me, so I may give you life.
Nurture me and avoid strife.
We can start now. Let's begin.
If we all care we can all win.
I feel Great Love, yet... I'm in pain.
Such destruction... Even our rain...
My rivers no longer run pure.
Before we die let's find a cure.
My top soil must be revived.
If we are all to say "we survived".
And my mysterious Ocean...
Filled with my deepest emotion.
Is crying out. Listen to her!!!
No longer are things as they were.
You have multiplied and filled me.
Now I beg you to "Hear my Plea".
I need you to honestly care.
This pain I can no longer bare.

Jane McWilliams

First Kiss

I remember it so well,
I'll never forget the night
You held my hand so gently,
you pulled me close and tight.

You looked so sweetly in my eyes,
and pulled my face so near.
I knew the time was coming,
that moment it was clear.

You brought your face much closer,
and placed your lips on mine.
my mind was in a whirlwind,
but the world stood still in time.

I'll never forget that experience,
and that night, I sure will miss.
But with you I fell in love.
and with you was my first kiss.

Carmen D. Welch

Oh, It Feels Good To Be A Friend

It MUST be a sinking feeling
If you do not have a friend
Someone with a kind voice-so appealing
To tell you, it is NOT the end.

A Puppy might be so friendly indeed
It certainly may help one along
But to BE THERE and talk when in need
Fills your heart with a song.

When you yourself - hit a low
What a better way to ascend
Not a Doctor needed to spend your dough
But just go out and be a friend.

Many people are in a crowd all day
But if one person an ear can lend
What more is there to say
Oh, it feels good to be a friend.

Arline R. Gaugler

A New Beginning

Oh, woe, render me friendless
if you are my only friend.
Cast me out and offer
no reprimand.

Pity me not, and keep quiet
your merciless command;
for I dare not be controlled
by your stringent hand.

Woe, go away from this day,
depart, darkness, from my door;
forever sweetly refrain
from knocking here again.

Weary I am, pained
your imprisoning strain
dragging mysterious miseries chain
through the brandied decor of my life.

Oh, woe - eternal woe,
fret not for my demise
at your parting, for I
shall go on.

Gwindale Person

Scent In The Air

When I see him there so tall and quiet,
I wonder what is he thinking?
Is it about me?
Does he know I am here?
He looks up like he sees someone.
Could it be me?
He smiles.
Is it at me?
He is waving.
Is he waving at me?
Should I wave?
He is walking this way.
Should I walk?
He walked on by.
It was like I was not even there.
I am alone.
The only thing left to remind me of him
Is the scent in the air.

Ginger Laurin Nooft

"I Wonder"

As I lay here
I wonder
If you love me
As much as I love you
I wonder if you'll care
When I cry
Or if you'll care when I'm gone
I care for you too much
That's why I hurt inside
Because you'll be gone someday
And I'll be here left to cry.

Joavan Fischer

Butterfly And The Nurse

I'm so old
I want to die.
I'm so old
I want to cry.
Why can't I be a butterfly?

Why? Why? Do you want to die?
Fight for life!
Please don't cry,
God's not ready for a butterfly.

Dora D. Pemberton

"Come And See New Life In Me"

Come to Me, my little dove;
I wish to set you free:
   I am here to give my love;
There's new life in Me.
   Come to Me, my faithful child;
Continue to follow Me:
   Be not as the desert wild;
There's new life in Me.
   Come to Me, my precious one;
I Love you eternally:
   Follow Me, the battles won;
There's new life in Me...
   Come my Love, Come and See;
The new life, give I to thee.

Candy Fitzroy Weiss

Love Faithfully

Someday soon
I will take you to the moon.
On it we will have a ball
for I shall never let you fall.
You are so very dear.
I think of you more fondly each
day of the year.
I will hold you in my arms
and keep you from any harm.
For I would forever cry
If you should die.
For I couldn't bear
anybody else's care
May our life together be so bright
For I wouldn't want to lose my sight.
Because you bring so much light to my life.
and I would make a wonderful wife.
May we never part
For it will break my heart.

April Wood

"To My Unborn Child"

My love is unconditional
I will raise you, best I can
You will always feel my love
For that has been God's plan

You will never be alone
I will follow each step you take
I will always stand beside you
Whatever choices you should make

My love will be your guidance
And my strength will see you through
And whatever life may deal
I will be right here for you

Carol A. Chandler

Untitled

Often - it seems
I lead a life
of quiet (or not so quiet) desperation

But then I share
with someone else
who also has this feeling

And still find that
two desperates
make one too desperate

Alone - I cope
I cannot bear
to share - and yet not share

Ervin J. Larsen

The Morning After

In the morning when you leave me,
I will have known last night was wrong.
But for now the only thing that matters
is tonight I'm in your arms.

I know you do not love me but
I can make myself believe, that
I am your one and only, and
forever we will be.

From time to time I will
feel guilt, and maybe even shame,
but with the light and the lovers,
in time they always fade.

And in the morning when you leave me,
I'll have no one else to blame,
so I'll forget it ever happened,
and go on as nothing's changed.

Dawn Kenney

Helpless

I watched you waste away
I watched
Do you understand?
I watched and shuddered
I shivered, I shook
With sobs of pity, of pity
I'm sorry, but pity it was, and wonder
I wondered why? Why?
Are you listening?
Why? For who?
For him? For us? For you?
For what? What?
What do you see in the mirror?
The mirror lies, it lies
I didn't stop the lies
I let them live
I couldn't speak to save your life
I watched
Do you know what I'm saying?
I watched you die.

Camisha A. Russell

My Decision

Today I met a girl today
I was quite surprised to hear her say
I have been saved by Jesus you see and
He has set my soul free.
I looked at her and soon I knew
What she had I wanted too.
She said she once was in a gang
She had no pride nor no shame
And that was when the darkness came.
She said that in her prison cell
She fell down on her knees
It was obvious God heard her pleas.
So she said I could have it too
Jesus is waiting to deliver you
So listen people to what I say
Because of Jesus I'm here today!

Joan Mlcak

Word Porridge

Kitchen violence
Goes with slow knives
That cut all thought of competence
Until all you know you know
Is how to keep things
From boiling over

Gail Barton

Schindler's List

The lost are lost.
I was not there.
I could not save
Nor can I now.
What's past is past,
But tomorrow lies
Across my path.
Who's there in need
That I should see?
What would you, Lord,
Require of me?
Whose name is on
My list...today?

Ann Dillon

No Chance For Retrieval

A loss of my innocence -
I was a fool to an illusion.
I've often looked back and hence;
The mistake has already been done.

There is no turning back -
No retrieval of respect.
In love I have no knack.
On my life this will reflect.

Andi Bailey

Autumn Is Coming

In the fall,
I walk slowly.
I see green leaves
That become golden.

A strange mystery involves
Flowers, plants and trees,
A yellowish magic that prepares
All of them for sleep.

The air is lethargic
And the sun wants peace.
Golden autumn is coming
And is transforming
Valleys, mountains and hills.

Concepcion McNeal

"On The Wharfs Of Boothbay Village"

On the wharfs of Boothbay Village,
I traverse the creaky, fishy boards,
Smell the algae - laden lobster traps,
Hear the cries of hungry gulls as they
   search for scraps,
See healthy men at their sea work,
Breathe in the salty winds with
   pennants flying,
Gaze towards sailboats, Southport and
   the southern rocky coast,
See the coming of fall in the changing
   colors of deciduous leaves further
   inland,
And the hourly chime of a little white
   New England church behind me reminds
   one of a more tranquil time in America.

John S. Gale

Growing Up

Lying in my crib,
I thought what a wonderful world
I was in
Being protected from all the violence
And problems in the world.

But growing up
I realized Mommy and Daddy weren't
Always going to come when
I cried for them.

Growing up I realized things
Were much tougher than I thought.

Growing up
I realized not everyone
Has learned the rule "Share"
And not everyone followed the rule,
"Be nice to other people."

Growing up
I realized I've got a lot more
Growing up to do!!

Erin Amanda Connelly

To Avis

I love you more now than then.
I think of it now and again.
In High School we met,
Later married and yet,
I love you more now than then.

Married for better or worse,
You got second, I got first.
Four children were born
Yes, before we were worn.
I love you more now than then.

You and I have come a long way.
Forty-four years and a day.
Rough roads in the past,
But they did not last.
I love you more now than then.

Sure we belong together;
Have come through all kinds of weather.
And I want to say
I pray we will stay.
I love you more now than then.

Ernest C. Anthony

My Angel Up Above

Every now and then,
I think of how it used to be.
When you were here with me.

I loved you and you loved me.
How I can tell isn't very important.
You are in my life forever,
And you will always be in my heart.

No matter where you are,
Whether it's near or far
Eventually I will see you again.
Don't know when.
Don't know where.

But I promise you one thing.
You will forever be mine,
And I will always love you.

Desiree T. Figueroa

Just Clouds

I see a goat leaping up a hill.
I see someone home in bed looking quite ill.

I see a lonely lady without a date.
I see a man rushing because he's late.

I see a sea serpent breathing fire.
I even see three birds singing in a choir.

If you think what I say is a lie...
Then just look at the clouds in the sky.

Jennifer L. Van Beber

Deciduous Death

In a deciduous moment of death,
I see.
For when there's nothing left to do,
but flee.
Like birds in a flock,
it's natures clock,
What a colorful death it will be.
To perform such a task,
is all we could ask,
for without them we'd die,
no air in the sky.
What a glorious death it will be.

George Hacklin Jr.

To Whom I Love

I think of you everyday
I remember your embrace,
I love to hear your words
And see your handsome face

Even though we are apart
I think of loving you,
And the wait is rough
But I know we'll see it through

Because you I have found
To be with great passion,
One who is truly devoted
We believe in like fashion

Oh I am deeply in love
With you eternally mine,
And my soul is fortunate
To have one who is so fine...
And two hearts that entwine

Jacqueline Beth Wright

For Daddy

Sit in my chair, old man,
I placed it there for you.

Sit in my chair, old man,
And let me sweat for you.

Sit in my chair, old man,
Rest your weary bone.

Sit in my chair, old man,
Divulge your days by gone.

Sit in my chair, old man,
Review the things you've done.

Sit in my chair, old man,
And be glad, the race you've won.

Sit in that chair, old man,
Adjust your attitude.

Sit in your chair, old man,
Prepare, for GOD'S interlude.

Doug Barnes

"Peaceful Man"

I respect you as a person.
I love you as a friend.
I am overcome by feelings now
    that I just can't comprehend.

I've met so many men like you
    along this path I walk,
But no persons ever moved me
    like you did the night we talked.

Your voice was wrapped in gentleness,
    Your eyes conveyed a trust,
Your mood was calm and peaceful
    like the earth is after dusk.

And yet if we had somehow met in
    another place and time,
I may be more in love with you than
    I tell you in this rhyme.

Joanie Reilly

While Waiting

I feel you moving,
    I know you are there.
I wonder what you look like,
    And what color is your hair.

I wonder if you are a boy,
    I wonder if you are a girl.
I just know whichever you are,
    My love for you will be fulfilled.

I'm starting to get scared,
    As your arrival gets near.
I want everything perfect,
    When it's your time to appear.

I try to do all right,
    though sometimes I do wrong.
I'm working as hard as I can,
    To make you very strong.

So I hope you feel my love,
    As my heart keeps beating for you.
Because I love you more than anything,
    And I'll love you all your years through.

Julie Pollard

Tears Fall In My Heart

I know you have emotions
I know that you may cry
But you could never know
Not as well as I

You could not know
How much it means
To have a silent cry
You could not hurt as much as I

So you say you cry
But you do it with your eye
True tears fall in your heart
Never in your eye

Never in your life
Have you hurt as much as I
Until you've stopped yourself
To have a silent cry

Next time that you cry
Stop to question why
Remember, tears fall in your heart
Never in your eyes

Emily Mayes

Something Wonderful

I knew my body was old and worn out.
I knew I was very sick.
But as you see,
Something wonderful happened.
Now I am much better.
See what I can do.
I can move my arms without pain.
I can walk without falling.
I can move and twist my body with ease.
I am not cold any more.
My mind is clear.
My voice is strong.
Why don't you look at me?
Have you gone blind?
Why don't you listen to me?
Have you gone deaf?
You should be joyous at my recovery.
Not moping around and crying.
By the way, why are you crying?
Did somebody die?

Don DePriest

Long After The Hunt

With hand on head
    I gaze into my dog's eyes.
I see the faraway fields
    And the flushing birds.

In these moments
    The birds and the fields
        And the dog and I are one.

George W. Welsh

My Love

In the ways of the world
I found a girl.
My life to change,
Or just rearrange.
A special friend
to never end.
Depression will not conquer
Nor fear will not stop her.
The way I feel will never yield,
Toward the lady of the world.

Joshua Springthorpe

"Mom"

When I look back through all the years
I find it easy to see.
Just how many-many tears
You prevented from falling on me.

You made our clothes and all our meals
And worked to help out Dad
To you it was never any "Big Deal"
And you gave it all you had.

Today you're in your "Golden Years"
Your hair is a beautiful white
And now my eyes fill up with tears
As I wish with all my might

That we could travel back in time
So's I could once again
Have that chance that once was mine
To say "I LOVE YOU" as I should have said
    back then.

Alice Jacques Belanger

Heavenly Voyage

In that peaceful meditation,
I climbed upon my favorite cloud
Soaring upwards to the other side
Where many angels travel
And I saw the smiling faces
of my departed family and friend
who were as happy to see me
as I was to see them.
And in that brief time
the heavenly and
earthly beings felt
the assurance that
our spirit has no end.

Judy Dandridge

Summer Day

As I stared at the morning dew,
I began to whistle a familiar tune,
Other tunes came to mind,
Tunes of a forgotten time,
Yes, a past, left behind.

Dinner's over, time to work,
Now I pick up the old pitch fork,
Hay in the barn, hay on the ground,
I can find hay all around,
Hay, like a soul, needing to be found.

While sunlight falls on fields of grain,
And family works to bring in the hay,
As birds fly over in the sky,
I look up at the clouds and sigh,
"Alas," I think, another day gone by.

Jo Ann Brandon

No Second Chances

We're down by a run
I advance to the plate;
My teammates are cheering
I now own their fate.

He hurls the ball
I swing and I miss;
I hear from the crowd
Some boos and a hiss.

I fall to the ground
A tear in my eye;
If this happens again
I feel I may cry.

I regain my strength
And take one last attempt;
He goes into the wind-up
I swing and I hit.

So if there's a lesson
To be learned by this;
Never give up
No matter how many times you miss.

Jason Williams

At The Party

He liked her bubble-gum sensuality and
hopscotch fingers that touched his
when she spoke of why
Kafka didn't have a metamorphosis and
how Karen Silkwood really got killed
and wanted to feel her legs around his
on any lonely Sunday in Detroit

Donna R. Brenneis

Catalysts of Time

The changing wheels of fortune,
How fickle and unsure.
And yet they say what must be said,
Those catalysts of time
That make us grow
Or fade;
It's we who change.

For life continues at its fearsome pace
With these obstacles to love and bliss.
These trolls draw near
With lambs of warmth and beauty;
It's we who make the choice to view,
When crashing on our lives will come,
Unwanted and unwelcome,
Guests of time to wreck our faith.

Or, if within our strength and courage,
We shall boldly see
Sweet memories of the past,
Expectant hope for things to come.

Clifford Van Sickle

Shadows Of Yesterday

Shadows of yesterday
Hovering — always near
As a reminder of better days
And of feelings held dear

As reminders of laughter
And good things shared
Of bright lights and glitter
And lived as we dared

Hot rods and burgers
Were the staple of the day
Never once caring
What others might say

We look at our grand kids
And wonder what to say
To them about their
Shadows of today

Jim Brogan

A Christmas Gathering

A family gathering in the late
hours of Christmas dawn
reminds me of the same day
of years long gone.

Gaming and feasting with
too much to say
has turned to a table
of hate and dismay.

The den would be filled
with happiness and smiles,
but all that is left now
are evil eyes beyond miles.

Year to year
out unity abandons us
leaving only a
lonely Christmas.

Heather Nicole Haste

They Will Never Know

I am here;
Hope is there.
They are there;
I am here.
They will never know.

Yes, They care;
But, still-alone.
The pain I know;
It leaves me here.
They will never know.

They reach to know,
But, no one knows;
The pain I know.
The pain I will always know.
They will never know.

It is too painful for others to know;
To know the pain I know.
So, I keep my pain, for I know;
They will never know.
They will never know.

Heather Eidbo

Let Me Lead You To The Lord

Let me lead you to the Lord
Hold my hand, oh Brother dear
Let Him take away the sorrow
Let Him wipe away the tear

I know your loss is painful
I know you hurt inside
But trust our Lord and Savior
And He will give you light

Once you turn your life to Jesus
He will take you in His hand
And turn your sorrow and sadness
Into happiness again

All you need to do is trust in Him
And believe in Jesus Christ
For the gift is freely given
Through His loving sacrifice

Nothing is impossible
For our Lord and God above
For in Him....is the way
For He is love.

Diana Swift

His Little Girl

He works alone,
his troubles never to be seen
except through the occasional tears
which trickle gently down his
somber face.
I try to reach out
but there is no door
and I am left alone to be a child
forever...
frozen in space and time
No matter what age I become,
how many children I bear,
or where I travel with my dreams,
I will always be
His little girl;
And never grown-up enough
to help brush away
those tears.

Heidi Elizabeth Philipsen

Swift Wind

There once was an Indian boy,
His name was Swift Wind.
He was very nice and thoughtful,
Always had a hand to lend.

Then one day,
As I was playing with him.
He was playing on a tree,
When he fell off of a limb.

"Help," I cried,
I was so very scared.
But Swift Wind lay calm,
He didn't get up; he did not dare.

I bent down by him,
Down in the sun.
As he laughed weakly he said,
"Do not fret little one."

He now lay in heaven,
Up on cloud nine.
He's in everyone's heart,
Especially mine.

Ashley Rice

November Challenge

Autumn haze is everywhere-
   Hills are purple through the trees,
Leaves fall softly on the air
   As webs float on the breeze.
Hunters in their coats of red
   Stalk the fields and trail.
Guns with a load of lead
   Aim to kill without fail.
The elk and white tailed deer
   Feeding on the frosty grass
Sense the danger ever near,
   Hide until the hunters pass
Some game is bound to fall,
   victim of a well aimed shell.
Later, friends and family all
   hear the tales their hunters tell.

Gladys E. Kendall

Comparison

Have you ever chanced to stop
High upon a mountain top?
How big you feel, so stately tall
'Cause things below appear so small.

Then go you on your way - descend
The dusty road 'round the bend,
Observe the mountain towering high,
Reaching upward toward the sky.

You're not so big, now, after all;
You're really very, very small.

Elizabeth A. TePoarten

A Promise To Myself

If I am going to give my
glorious, good self to a man
and be the best friend and
lover he ever had, then
he had better be as good
or better than I am.

Carolyn Vero Maddelena

Just A Boy

Got to understand the lad,
He's not eager to be bad,
If the right, he always knew,
He would be as big as you;
Were he now exceedingly wise,
He'd be just about your size;
When he does things that annoy,
Don't forget... he's just a boy.

Just a boy, who needs a friend,
Patient and kindly, to the end,
Needs a counselor, who will show
Him the things he wants to know;
Take him with you when you walk,
Listen, when he wants to talk,
His companionship, enjoy,
Don't forget... he's just a boy.

Ed Antin

Ear To Ear

Ear to Ear...
Hear a voice,
Someone's crying.
Feel a feeling,
Now your sighing.
Want to hold them,
You don't know them.
What to do,
Someone crying.
Now it's you.
Hear a voice
   Ear to ear.

Jeanmarie Todd

One Spirit, One God

O Mighty Spirit in the sky,
He who makes the eagles fly,
Help my spirit cope with the pain,
Fill my heart with hope,
Help me to love again.
O Mighty Spirit in the sky,
He who has an eagle's eye,
Watch over us, keep us for another day,
Teach us to walk in your loving way.
O Mighty Spirit in the sky,
He who makes the eagles cry,
Reach out your loving hands from where
   the mighty waters flow;
To dry desert sands and yonder still to
   where the winter's wind doth blow,
O Mighty Spirit, keep us, teach us, so
   your loving way all will know.

Corrine Pendleton

"Goodbye"

I know we've been together
For so many years,
And now you're leaving,
So it's hard to fight the tears.

I know we've been friends
Right down to the core,
But how I've wished
We could have been more.

I wish we'd stay together,
But we have to be apart,
So I'm letting you know
That you're always in my heart.

Andrew D. Wicks

563

March Music

March is a mad musician.
He whines and whistles and roars.
I wonder where his music goes
When it lifts and rushes and soars?

Sometimes it's loud and boisterous
With its notes and raucous bong.
Sometimes it's gentle and soft
And whispers a lullaby song.

He chants wild fierce melodies,
Or hums a soft soothing strain.
Oft in the night he sings the blues,
With a mild and haunting refrain.

He leads a giant orchestra
As he wields a fiery baton
First brilliant and harsh, then tuneful
As a pastoral scene he has drawn.

I like March with his caprices
And whimsical ditties so gay.
Include with all this comes in
His song to me, "Happy Birthday!"

Evelyn Slade

My Cat Smokey

My cat Smokey is gray and white
he sleeps in bed with me at night.
He stretches out and
starts to purr and waits for me
to rub his fur. If I stop he'll raise
his head and pretty soon jumps off
the bed. He wanders all around
the house I guess he's looking for
a mouse. The only mouse that he
will find will be his toy, the wind
up kind. I think he finds the house
too quiet, since everyone sleeps at
night. He comes back, jumps on my
bed and curls himself around
the top of my head.
Settle in Smokey, it's too late to play,
time for that tomorrow, a brand new day!!

Allison Nichole Waldschmidt

I Don't Know What To Believe And Think

He shows signs of love
He shows signs of hate
Which does he feel for me,
If only I knew
Oh what shall I do
This matter cannot wait
I like him so
Never want him to go
Yet he still makes me cry
I cannot lie
I will surely die
If he ever walks out of my life
I don't know what to believe
What should I perceive of his actions
I don't know what to think
If I just blink
Will he disappear?
Please stay close to me
My sweet dear

Deana McDonald

Seattle Misses The Sun

Seattle misses the sun,
  he dries up all the rain.
And when the clouds appear,
  she doesn't know when
she'll see him again.

He brings her light,
  and makes her feel blessed.
But when he leaves her,
  Seattle's depressed.

His return brings joy,
  and satisfies her life.
He takes away her anguish and strife.

The day goes by,
  and evening is near.
She dreads the moment
  when he passes from here.

And when the night comes creeping,
  and Seattle's sun adjourns,
She lays there faintly sleeping,
  dreaming of his return.

Amber Wnek

Clothesline

You
have plucked out my last nerve,
Strung it up taut
Between tree branches.
Pins bite down on it
To hang heavy wet sheets,
And crows sit on it,
Preening their feathers.

Danielle Catherine Dodder

Family Reunion

The loved ones we have lost from life
  Have gone to greater heights
They are now up there with angels
  And all the saints alike.
The stress, the pain and earthly things
  Are now a part of the past
For they walk the streets of heaven
  So for them we should be most glad.
Perhaps some time in the future
  When our Father calls us home
We can all gather together again
  And our "Family Reunion" can resume.

Carole French

Hope

From one small light in Israel
Have come ten million more
To glow more brightly year by year,
Till night-time shuts its door.

So strongly shines the Father's love
In hearts, one here, one there,
That soon the radiance from above
Will light men everywhere,

And push the darkness back again
Where death and demons flee,
Until the glow from Heaven's Star
Is spread from sea to sea.

Then earth will vibrate with the sound
Of praise to Him who came
To warm our cold and empty lives,
So we can hope again.

Audrey L. Robertson

Freedom

Hate
Hate with its snow and sleet,
Burning red like Hell's fire.
Hate with its foolish ways,
Devouring everything good.

Gone are the sunny spring and
summer days.
Flowers, beaches, birds;
everything happy
gone.

Left in their place is
war
Hatred's child.

If only we could find love.
Love is poison to hate and war.
With love we could find
FREEDOM

Anna Prior

Untitled

Hesitate and attack
Grooves and fills
Up and down the off beat expressions.

Manipulating fibers of wood
Nimble wrists and fingers fluttering
Legs and feet accentuating
The ends and beginnings of feelings.

Timing of a metronome
Doubling and cutting the edge of lyrics
Transcribed by him - "The Professor"

African jungle beats - driving
In the thumping of a bass drum
Crack of the snare
Ping of the ride

A multiplicity of sounds and range
Splashing and swishing
Crashing and ringing
Amplified by electronics
Pounding through my body

An expression of concentration, driven by
determination.

Andrew J. Jasie

Nine Meeting Nine

Sing the way you love,
Go blind and hate tomorrow.

Yes, in magic and prophecy.
Heart penetrates the show.

Seal the pain, fair false unity. . .
But the flood exalts the plain.

If not from joy, then for experience
And if not now, then yesterday.

Day won't find it, isolate the night;
Uniform the flame, confess the light.

City-light wanting sunshine,
So guiltily runs the street — away.

Born in the dark, growing darker;
Born in the morning, may day mourning.

Would that a vow at that spot
Were not stealing.

Who can puzzle, who can clear
The moment, the desire, the fear?

Andrew T. Moo

My Backyard

There are crows in my back yard
Giving doom and death.
My fears reappear
When the darkness becomes my light.

The dark memories and twisted love
Shroud my eyes like a woolen glove.
Making my heart a pump
Having no love.

Crows in my back yard
Giving doom and death.
When sunlight turns to night
That's when all fears come to sight.

Always there to turn me
Against me.
Never showing a glimpse of light
To end the fight.

Crows in my back yard
Giving doom and death.
All my fears are here
For the crows fly tonight.

Jana Hightower

An Alaskan Greeting

A warm hello
From the land of snow
Where the temperature dips
To sixty below
And the trapdoor of
Your long underwear
Is weather stripped
So your derriere
Is protected from
The flying snow
When those icy northern
Tail winds blow.

Dick Mealey

Why Do Angels Cry

Outside the rain is falling
From a silent sky.
Absently, I wonder
Why do the Angels cry?
I look up to the Heavens,
Searching for a star.
Once again I wonder,
Who are they crying for?

Do they cry for an old love,
Or a broken heart like mine?
Do they weep for the millions,
Who are lost in time?

The raindrops fall unending,
And flow on to the sea.
Like a sea of teardrops,
Shed for empty souls like me.
Who can't forget the sweetness
Of some old memory.
Tonight as the rain falls,
The Angels cry for me.

Barbara Hall

"Ruins, Roads And Rulers"

Family - rape and restrictions
Freedom - ravenous and restless
Faith - radiant and regal
Mobile Nirvana
Our heart's desire
As she and I drive
From family to faith
Freedom! Aye! There's the rub
Freedom to make a wrong turn
Freedom to get a flat tire
Freedom to crash!
Better to crash than to stay home
Being the family
Ravaged by rape and restrictions
Radiant and regal
Not she nor I, but he
Ravenous and restless
Are we
To enter the gates of the kingdom

Bryant Brewer

Back In 1513

Upon this date long years ago
Four Hundred Twenty Nine
A rover happened on a spot
He couldn't half define.

This daring Spanish traveler
(Named - something de Balboa)
Disclosed the greatest water-show,
Since one that featured Noah.

It seems that he was barging 'round,
And spied the huge Pacific;
And ever since all history
Has called the deed "terrific".

But though it is the largest hunk
Of wet, with dry around it,
I read the news and goodness me
I wish he'd never found it!

Betty Thompson-Stafford

Untitled

No regrets.
For laughter shone like ribbons
    wrapped and wound around
    the days like flowers
    in a vase that was our life.

No regrets.
We learned too much together
    reaching ever forward
    and beyond our daily world;
    we gained too much.

No regrets.
time will melt the sharpened edge,
    but never dim the gleam
    of what was good and right
    and such a part of me.

No regrets.
The special place inside my heart
    will always be the same.
    No one else will ever reach me here,
    this place that holds dear only you.

Debra S. Berg

My Loss

Let me not cry with your passing away.
For in my heart, you'll always
Be here to stay.
It's for my loss and
Loneliness, that I weep.
For I know that you have
Peaceful sleep.
While I, who remain behind,
Am hurt and lonely at the love and
Friendship, that I have lost.
Yet in my heart, you
Will always be
A comforting memory.

Evelyn Bush

Four Seasons For A Flower

SPRING is the time, the right time
For all the great sunshine
And for all the rainy days
To bring us new sprouting flowers

SUMMER is the growing time,
It's the time for showing
What all you have to offer
And to be proud of who you are

FALL is soon arriving,
With the cool breezes
The time has come for every flower,
To lose their leaves

WINTER is the time of year,
When every flower knows
Their hours are best spent sleeping,
For the new beginning that happens every spring

James T. Lamb

Abused

You've been abused;
feeling quite used.
The anger and the rage,
just won't go away.
Please take my advise;
don't even think twice.
Stand up and stand tall,
don't let it make you fall.

I know it hurts now;
inside it brings you down.
The frustration that you feel,
don't let it guide your will.
For the anger and the rage;
takes some time to fade.
Your life will go on
like beginning a new song.

Deb Gloyd

In God's Hands

Memories of you are with us here,
Even though you are not.
Close to our hearts we hold them dear
Of you we think allot.

In God's hands, he holds you well,
No more pain for you.
For this I know cause God did tell,
And words he speaks are true.

There's not a day that does go by,
That we can't see your face.
We try to smile instead of cry,
For we know your in a happy place.

Janet Spicer

Road Of Life

The road stretches long and wide
Far in front of me.
There's no telling where I'm headed,
Or where I'm going to be.

I'm not going to give up.
I'll ride it to the very end.
Will not stop and pull off
When it begins to turn and bend.

I've traveled so far now,
With so much more to go.
It will be easy at times
And tough at others, I know.

Some shortcuts will tempt you
Pass them up, I recommend.
Ride it complete and to its fullest,
And ride it to the very end.

Amanda Leigh Davis

The Phoenix

Now I lie and live each moment,
Every hour, and every word.
And the time, which once so fast went,
Drags — and snares me like a bird
In a net of deepest yearning,
And your smile comes shining through;
Only hastening the burning
Of my soul for want of you.

Waking all the sleeping passion
That we both had thought was dead;
Till it flames in such a fashion —
Like a wild fire that has spread.
Scorching sacred, secret meetings,
Razing rendezvous we knew;
So my heart must still its beating
To escape from thoughts of you.

Frederick Hanna

Peace On Earth

The suns forever rising,
every day that passes by.
Like the beauty of a sunset,
across the western sky....
Like the warmth that fills my heart,
while I watch our children play.
Like the little bits of beauty,
that are over looked each day...
There's so much anger in a lifetime,
that doesn't need to be.
So much grief and sadness,
We pretend that we don't see...
We all must work together,
To rid our world of hate.
We may not have tomorrow.
Because of unknown fate....
Our children are our future,
So please for what it's worth.
Let them have the chance,
To live in peace on earth...

Heather West

Respect

Don't take advantage of me
And I will serve you.

Don't command me
And I will obey you.

Dianna L. Antos

Living

Every month
  Every day
    Every hour
      Every minute
        Every second

    THINK
Feel
  enjoy
    suffer
Go on day by day
sometimes up, sometimes down

Dreams come true, dreams are destroyed
Dreams change, dreams are modified

Live every day with whatever it brings
do your best at all times
  SO

You can look back.....
be happy and proud

and in the same way at the same time
look forward to the future

Gloria Morales

In The Still Of The Night

As the darkness of night
Erases the lightness of day
A new dawning appears
Just moments away...

In the still of the night
All contemplates a surrender
To what must and not be
A new horizon awaits...

All which contains
The whispers of the darkened sky
Recesses the slumber
Gracing the still of the nigh...

Peaceful waters settled
Within their silent flow
Awaiting morning's near due light
Of dawn's preeminent glow.

Janet S. McMillin

Life's Departure

Did you ever watch the thread of life
ebb slowly from a man;
Gently stroke the fevered brow,
and grasp the flailing hand?

In some small way, attempt to ease,
departure from this life;
Struggle with each gasping breath,
and pray an end to strife?

To see a body, proud and strong,
grow weaker day by day
Oft makes me wonder, how it is,
that God could plan this way!

Yet steps upon this path of death
are due for every man;
My prayer shall be, with dignity,
Death quickly takes my hand.

Joyce Rash Nevinger

"No Time To Grow"

Today's pace is so frantic
each second on the go.
With mundane tasks innumerable.
we have no time to grow.

The pressures of our life styles
tend to stifle our thoughts so.
We're omitting things important,
we have no time to grow.

Big business flows as usual,
enjoyment's turned on low.
"I'll take the time tomorrow"
we have no time to grow.

If my curtain call comes early
there's one sure thing I know.
I will have missed out on a lot,
I've not had time to grow...

Bethany C. Marini

Untitled

With Eternity in mind
each moment is lived,
With trials and love
So precious to give.

Our life doth soar
for the race is on,
Aware of the Orchestra
of sound and song.

The beauty of laughter
and the cry of man,
Should always be heard
in our hearts, first hand.

Life's journey is grooming
refining mind and heart,
Empowered along the way
with Hope, we start.

Alice L. Gerecke

Never Part

We live the lives of many
each day that passes by.
We laughed and cried at simple things
and sometimes wondered why.

The times we remember most
and stick deep in our hearts,
from fishing in the deepest dark
to soccer in the park.

You were always there for us
to make sunshine out of rain.
To heal the cuts and scratches
and all the little pains.

Our lives will never be the same
without you by our side.
You are very special and you
will never part our minds.

Denny Buck

The Milk Man Is Gone

The frothing of dawn
Brought the white man there
Almost at my feet.
I miss the clink
The bouncing frosty bottles
Bobbing down the street.

John L. Mazzuca

Pride

In tune with tradition,
dress in dashiki
glorious like Japanese
in Kimono.
Squat outdoors barefoot
arrogant as Californian
on beach.
With fingers-
oblivious to jeers
from civilized friends
for shelving
acquired western manner
of cutlery-
Pick and knead
fufu from mortar
dip in bitterleaf soup,
Swallow large clumps.
Proud like Chinese
using chopsticks.

Ifejika Okonkwo

"Dreams"

Dedicated to James Totten
Dreams forgotten,
Dreams remembered,
Dreams of you and me.
Seeing you, touching you.
Dreams forgotten,
Dreams remembered,
Dreams become a reality.

Elizabeth Huie-Norris

There and Back

I watched as a rose petal fell
down, down, and farther yet
into the abyss of deadly hell
then it touched the ground
its cries of rage made no sound
but somewhere they were found
for the wind did come and set it free
up, up, and farther yet
as far as the eye can see

Arlo J. Smith

A Trip To The Doctor

Oh no ill ill
Doc doc doc

Hurt hurt whine whine
Hot hot hot

Look look listen listen
Wiggle wiggle wiggle

Poke poke feel feel
Tickle tickle tickle

Sick sick x-rays
Pill pill pill

Scream scream shot shot
Still still still

Pain pain cry cry
Moan moan moan

Sucker sucker sticker sticker
Home home home

Billie C. Hayes

In Answer To Your Question

How many ways
Do I love you?
Dear one
Need you ask?
When I diaper the baby.
Take out the garbage,
And share in your every task.

How many ways
Do I love you?
Sweetheart,
Please, just count
And when you reach a thousand,
You'll be close
To the right amount.

Grace S. Kane

"Gutter Language"

Be done with gutter language!
Disgusting, loud or lewd.
No unclean word should surface:
Reveal me "in the Nude"!
Swearing - taking my Lord's Name
In vain, or tossed around
Like garbage, in the gutter
Gives life a morbid sound!

Should not our lips yield good fruit
If all the heart be sweet?
Our many words "reveal" us
With some I can't repeat!
The tongue is like a rudder
That leads the heart along
To deeds that are disgraceful
And rob the heart of song!

Lord, make my heart a fountain
Of cool, clear water - fresh!
That flows with sweetness ever,
Revealing righteousness!

Alma M. Keen

The Wind

The wind is a friend,
diffusing Indian summer's smog,
turning windmills and turbines,
bringing winter's cold, snow, and rain,
and ultimately creating new life
throughout the universe.

Gladys Schantz

Is It Over?

Trying to find out what I
   did wrong,
I am left with a sad
   love song.
All the things we did
   together, hoping
we can last forever.
   Here I am
crying over you, I
   don't know what
to do.
   Now that your
gone, I feel so lost.
   I don't know
what to do
   I still love you

Jasmine Medina

Dear Imagination

Dear imagination with all my
daydreams, hopes, and fears;
you have been with me through
my childhood years.
You have taken me to my
dreamland, so very far away,
and there you showed me a
quaint and unusual way.

Dear imagination deep in the
back of my mind;
you have taken me to places
some awkward, some kind.
You've shown me what
might've and could've been done
but always took me back
to reality where I had begun.

Jacqueline S. Hall

The Chill

Somewhere, lost in the
   cycles of my life
I feel a destructive chill.

It breathes a breath
   as cold as ice
And at night,
   It freezes my dreams.

Connie Altman

The Rolling Stone

Knocked out of its rock bed,
cultured by sand and water,
sculpted by time and tide,
indeed this rolling stone
gathers no moss.

Forever it retains its gloss
and rolls down the stream
sleeping on its dream.

Its leaping brain waves
subside within the walls
engraving patterns
on the memory shores.

When it reaches the sea,
it'll form an island
on which it can raise
its evergreen dreams.

Francis Madassery

Loving

People who do their best
do not compare with the rest.
The love we have will last
until the day we pass.
To be in love with such a lady
brightens the days that are shady.
To see your smile so warm and bright
is such a sensuous delight.
To touch and feel and caress
are gifts of love truly blessed.
All of this I say to you
to let you know I'm anew.
My heart is warmed by your touch
I'm just saying: I LOVE YOU VERY MUCH!

Harlon Farr

Blindness

Shadows of darkness come
creeping through the blind,
upsetting the righteousness
of the human mind.

Man's morals are now
quickly degrading
and his respect and pride
are continually fading.

His concept of love and sanctity
are frightening.
Yet, he says his irresponsible
world is brightening.

How can he stand there
with God all around
and claim that life is a joke,
with a frown?

When once he shall
acquire his sight,
never will he be blind
to the night.

Carol Kleiber Zwahr

My Precious Treasure

No Monetary value
    could ever be paced
On the beautiful features
    of your face
No sapphires could ever shine
    as beautifully as your eyes
No string of pearls
    could be compared
    to your grin or smile
No lottery fortune would
    mean as much
    as a hug from you
    or your touch
And no one else could
    ever have a precious
    treasure like mine.

Beth Hamilton

Precious Gems

Grandma has a treasure chest
    come child, take a peek inside
I gathered all the smiles I could
    as I watched you with great pride
Then I collected the many joys
    you brought me through the years
And yes there is a special place
    for all your pearly tears
But most precious of all the gems for me
    are the diamonds in my heart
For they are the sparkles in your eyes
    that only Grandma can see.

Carmella DeGidio

While Looking Out To Sea

From far
Beyond the line
Where Heaven's blue kisses
The sea's darker green
The pulling might
Of submerged dreams
Reaches out
Again
And again.

Byron Kohn

This Year

Here it is, this year
Cold coming in
Cold going out.

Somewhere in
Between there will
Be flowers to bloom,
Rains and snows to
Fall — suns to shine
Moons to rise
This year there will
Be births and there
Will be Deaths
I know this year
Is no different
From others, except
For one thing
    This is this Year!

Becky Hunter

Dream

I lie down
Close my eyes
A wave of darkness
Serenity
The mist clears
A dream begins.
I can see you
But your face is hidden
I know I love you
But I do not know you
Stretch out your arms
Hold me close
I am happy
So peaceful.
You start to fade
I cry out
You wave good bye
Blow a kiss
I awake
And dream of you.

Jenny Campbell

Untitled

Raindrops crashing into the panes,
    Clinging for a moment and then
Stretching into long streams.
Wrapped in the soundless crashing
    I feel your love.
Unsteady repetitions of rain
    Numbly awakes me to a profound ache.
Parched I scan the sky
    For signs of fullness
Then it falls,
    Boosting me into believing
We will always love each other.

Ann P. Shields

Sad Blind Girl

A blind girl sits in a chair
as lonely as can be, has no
friends nor enemies, but she
can hear as good as mouse
though, she starts to cry
probably not knowing why
but I guess it's because
she's sad inside.

Jessica M. Lanning

"Health And Freedom"

Please dear Rock of Ages
cleft for me, let me cling
upon 'Thee' for awhile,
for a touch of real class,

and - anointing oil graspings
of long awaited desire and
golden dreams.

Bluebirds of happiness singing
in the heavenly trees and
finding their truly beloved
and Godly mates for evermore
Selah!

The ornate and artistry workmanship
from their creator woven
as a threading pattern of
"Standing Ovation"

Anne Rivett

A Child's Eye

Blue as the ocean,
clear as the sky.
The innocence is there
in a child's eye.

Pain and sorrow in the world,
a child asks 'why'?
Tomorrow always looks brighter
in a child's eye.

Life has trust and smiles,
it's full of sickness and tears.
Through a child's eye
there's no such thing as fears.

The child lives the dream,
shares the vision, then dies.
There is no more pain, no hurting
in a child's eye.

Dark as the ocean,
grey as the sky;
Life is too short
in the child's eye.

Andrea M. Solari

She Called Today

She called today.
Centered in her eighteenth year.
Hearing new versions of the truth,
Stroking still bruised images,
Feeling a slipping grip,
Knowing the pain of disillusionment.
Building and altering as she goes,
Returning to the familiar as she must.
Just for a moment,
Not to stay.
Just to drink from her spring of origin,
Only for a moment.
Testing her grounding,
Stability sought,
Pain fought,
A beautiful creation in progress
She called today!

Carolyn Cramer

Special

Where in all this land
Can you see
Something special
Special as me

A symbol of my country
School children say a
Pledge to
While service men and
Women are so proud
To salute me

Yet the saddest thing
I see, are the tears
Of a mother and father
When they see me,
As I lay covering someone
Who served their
Country same as me

Yes I am special
Special as can be
As I fly over the hard of the free
Cloamar Suiters

Twisted Fate

What it is, is it
Can it change, it can
What leads can follow
What follows can lead
All, falls down, get up
No layin' or strayin'
Maintain, lead and follow
Walk light, belt tight
Hold trust all might
Done, now up or down
Look around another trail
Others - fear they fail
Calm sea do sail
Storm break or build
Know well — gate
No twisted fate

Jimmy Oral Brown Jr.

Going Home

When I hear my Father's voice,
Calling me to join Him,
The lights around me dim.
But my spirit says rejoice.

Going home, going home,
Rejoice, I'm going home.

See the story of my life,
His love will replace
All the hurt and the strife,
Yes, I'm healed by His grace.

Those who went home before me,
Show the way through the dark.
Then, we see a tiny spark,
A light that reaches to me.

That light of joy surrounds me,
And I know the greatest love,
Indescribable love.
All is clear — with harmony.

Going home, going home.
Rejoice, I'm going home.

Gloria Bassett

Rain

Rain falling
calling me to come
speak in
the tongue of the old ones
Who forgotten
sleep until my soul
Awakens them
from the darkness
Of disbelief
I sing to you hear
The voice
of pain and joy and love
You until
the end of time remembered
That forever
could be so short seems
Impossible dreams
shared with the rain
Rain falling
Jenny Minniti-Shippey

O Canada!

The Stanley Cup was won
By Toronto Maple Leafs.
The final game had ended, and
Detroit floundered on the reef.

The score was four to nothing,
It could have been much more.
The people in the gardens yelled
DETROIT! - but no score.

Toronto really backchecked.
Their passing was superb!
And when the game was ended
Detroit got the bird.

Once more Toronto has the Cup!
It sure won't be the last.
Detroit really bit the dust
But they won't give up - they're fast!

Frances White Woodward

Success

Success is not measured,
by others but by the individual.

Success is not something you buy,
but something you earn.

It's the feeling you get inside,
when you know you have done,
your very best.

Success feels so good,
it makes you feel,
powerful enough to take,
on a new challenge.

Success is not measured,
in giant leaps,
but in small steps.

Success may be the first time,
someone writes their name,
or becoming the first woman president.

Success feels so good.

Jessica Anne Rhodes

Just Me!!!

Don't you see we love you
but you can't be true.
Just one girl at a time
to you is a crime.
You are the biggest bluff
because one isn't enough.
You go with two or three
why can't it be just me?
I gave you all I had
but you still left me sad.
You are all I want now
and, I know, that somehow
I will make you see
that all you need... is me!!

April Phillips

Untitled

Yesterday I didn't know him
  But today I do
Now I'm a different person
With a peace that fills me
  through and through.
And now I know that as
  the tomorrows come their way
I'll just wake up saying
  "Thank you Lord"
for another beautiful day.

Judy Edwards

Untitled

To live is not just to survive,
but to take chances and risks.
To go not for glory,
but for self-awareness.
To go not with caution,
but to answer the call of the wild.
To not worry about the consequences,
but to live for the moment;
RIGHT HERE, RIGHT NOW.

Danielle N. Dionisio

"The Debt"

She was a mother of four
But she was so much more.
She gave us her heart
For which we all tore.
The time has now come
To repay this debt.
For she has not once
Shown signs of regret.
She is loving and caring
To her girl and three boys.
She gave up her life
To us four joy.
Now I repay
With all of my might.
To honor and cherish
And not again fight.
I give you my love
Forever more
From here-on-out
It's peace and not war.

David S. Arnold

569

School

During the summer I was lazy,
But school is now driving me crazy!
I wish I was at home in my bed,
But I'm at school instead.
At home I could sleep all day,
But here it's all work and no play.
I have no more to say,
So bye 'til another day!

Becky Lofton

Divorce Leaves A Child Forgotten

Oh, It was grand
but now the hour glass is out of sand
They just don't get along
Yet I'm supposed to be strong
Quivering in bed all night
pretending not to hear them fight
wishing ThEY would sit in a corner
lying in bed like a mourner
Each rude comment
Would take away time well spent
To then feel guilt
and lead a life unfulfilled
In court, they make a choice
without ever hearing my voice
I used to love their touch
to one now alcohol is a crutch
There's no family meal on a holiday
and no vacation for the family to get away
Yet somehow I think I'd be sane
If it all were the same

Brian T. Moore

Remembering

My heart is still for a moment.
But my mind races...and races.
On thoughts of yesteryears.
Remembering the pain and sorrow.
Yet today we talk like old friends.
But I still remember.
And because I do remember
Trust and you will never
Come together!

Alma E. Jordan

Hear My Prayer

I'm wondering why
But may never know
our Lord doesn't explain
or tell us so

He does things as he pleases
and thinks they should be
we don't have to understand.
We don't have to agree...

It's true I've done wrong
made so many mistakes
please don't take my daughter
and let me take her place

I know it's not the same
since now I am old
but my baby will grow
and is someone you can mold

So father, hear the prayer
that I say every night
Please grant Danielle
a second chance at life

Annie Pena

A Child's Treasure

My room is not a pirate's den,
But it has a special treasure.
Not one of golden coins and jewels,
Next to mine those hold no measure.

It's not a very fancy chest,
It has no lock or key;
But the things in it are far more rare
Than ever sailed the sea.

My treasure chest is—just a box,
As plain as plain can be;
But every toy that's tucked inside
Is a special one to me.

My Jack-in-the-Box pops up to say,
"Good day, my little friend!
Please play with us, and have your fun
'Til day has reached its end."

Who'd ever want a pirate's chest
With coins and jewels of gold;
When they could have a chest of toys
To play with, love, and hold?

Carol Bleakley

Land To Believe

This land is my land they will say,
but how can this be a strong black
man from the inner city. This land
is my land as I here the song ringing
through my ears, but how could
this be there's no justice here, but
prejudice everywhere. This land is
my land they will preach, but it
can't be, because they cut and beat
us down like we're trees. This
land is my land I continue to here
there's no truth to this, because
this land wasn't made for my
black brothers nor my black sisters
to live and be free. This land is not
my land I will say until we eliminate
hate and prejudice in the world
today. Is this land really my land?
I continue to ask.

Christopher Barber

Tolling Of The Bell

I am swift... I am slow
But do try to let you know
Through happy sounds of
      laughter... I may appear
Sometimes reaching... for
      those most dear
So vigorously, I am fought
But time from me...
      cannot be bought
Hints of me... can be detected
Tho unannounced, I am expected.
There is no barrier to age...
Fate steps in... to write her page.
Impartially chosen... all dear souls
Pre-destined... is when the bell tolls.
For all men... someone weeps
You will meet me... when your
      heart sleeps
I am DEATH... the robber of BREATH!

Dorothy M. Carani

Transmigration

If there was pain, she showed no sign
But daily took her place in line.
As evening came, I poured the wine.

We'd shared a former life so fine
It blurred the present, hers and mine.
If there was pain, she showed no sign.

On dogwood days the blazing shine
Of eastern fire called us to dine.
As evening came, I poured the wine.

On poached islands we would twine
Both flesh and muse - a lusty shrine.
If there was pain, she showed no sign.

But here and now will not resign.
Instead they fix their own design.
As evening came, I poured the wine.

The invite came. Who could decline
That final trip in rough hewn pine?
If there was pain, she showed no sign.
As evening came, I poured the wine.

John R. Hamburg

Death

What a harsh word for some
But a sweet word to me
When will this day ever come
When will he sweep me off my feet
Why must I cry, Why must I sigh
I just want to be in the sky up high
I want to touch the moon and stars
I want to sit on a cloud under a tree
Where I see angels around me
Where everyone is free
To some death is a sin
To me death is like a pin
You poke yourself you bleed
I poke myself I've been freed
There is not much to say
I will just wait
Wait until that one day
Once I catch his bait
He will take me away
Just take me away.

Janet Esho

Contrary Winds

Alone in a storm without hope,
Brings a fear no one can explain
To whom can we turn who will care
About our agony and pain.

The One who offers peace of mind
Can rebuke the wind and the sea
We recognize awesome power,
Christ arose after dark Calv'ry!

Those who believe will not perish,
For God sent His begotten Son,
To bring redemption to mankind
Available to everyone!

The question is, do you have faith
To withstand the storms in your path?
God's promise of eternal life
Will remove all fear of God's wrath.

Let us be anxious for nothing
The Lord is always very near,
With thanksgiving make requests known,
HIS own child's voice He's sure to hear!

Carolyn Marquis

Contentment

The music came to me,
Borne on the summer air.
It lifted me and took me
To a place beyond compare.

There were no words to the song
That filled my heart with gladness.
My mind was quiet and at peace,
There was no room for sadness.

I want to stay, I cannot go.
Contentment cast its spell on me,
The music is much louder now,
I close my eyes yet still I see.

Allow me to stay, I beg of you,
I cannot go away.
It seems so near to paradise,
A year seems like a day.

I drift through time and space,
I fall into a dream less sleep,
The music slows, it's quiet now,
I sense the loss and then I weep.

Carol D. Eboch

People

People are different in many ways
Born throughout the year
On many different days

Some are black some are white
Many are heavy many are light

Some have families
Some have none

When you put us together
We are all as one!!

Heather Fournier

Black Is Me!

Black is beautiful.
Black is me.
Black is the color you see on me.
Black is my nature.
Black is my pride.
Black is all I can be so I stride.
Higher with my blackness and pride.
I am proud of what I am.
And I can't change the fact.
Black will always be a part of me.

SO THAT MEANS I'M BLACK!

Andrana LeGendre

The Beauty Of Nature

The beauty of nature is all around;
Birds cawing and singing is the only sound.

As the breeze makes a gentle
appearance each day;
Honeysuckle and golden rod in rhythm
do sway.

Scents of heather and cedar caress
the air;
So clean and so fresh, so soothing,
so fair.

The cool emerald grass, and crystal
blue skies above;
It's the beauty of nature sharing
her love...

JoAnn Anderson

The Edge Of America

At the edge of America
beside the oceans on the beach
and the cities that crowd its shores
you'll find the mobs of the unwanted,
forgotten and exiled
the lost
the beaten
the losers and lunatics
the ambitious wanderers
hungry souls from third world countries
Lost drunks from southern ghettoes
and last and least
a starving artist
peeling his eyes
in the middle of the mad mob
at the edge of the world.

Frank Cruz

Companion

Come
Beside me
And stay

Why
Is it easy to feel,
But hard to say?

Come
Stay close.
I need you.

Why
Is there such emptiness
Without you?

Bruce R. Schulman

"The Price"

I see One struggle up the hill,
Beneath a crushing weight;
His body gasps for life,
Yet, no loss of faith, no hate.

They raise Him between two sinners,
And lots for His garb they cast;
Has God forsaken this Man?
Can not His cup be passed?

They gave Him soured drink,
And beat Him with bramble and thorn;
Yet He asked they be forgiven;
He bore them love, not scorn.

Then I saw His life slowly leave
Through the nail holes in His hand;
His body striped by rod and whip
Shadowed darkness across the land.

I looked into His eyes; He, into my soul;
Then it was that I could see;
With His life He'd paid the price,
And bought me eternity.

Buck Elder

Separate Ways

If one day we should part
and go our separate ways,
may the memory of our love
and good times that we shared,
exist within us throughout our lives
and may we forget our faults,
and think of each other
in the fondest way.

Encarnacion O. Bravo

Untitled

Light is life
beginning as a seed
at the center of our being
waiting to be a flame

As it touches the heart
warmth seeps into it
slowly melting the obscurities
letting it flow through arteries

Breaking down the walls of unfeeling
bursting through veins
singing loudly inside the soul
shining forth from the eyes

Making a person whole and glowing
with the aftermath
of the tremendous fire
becoming what we call - LOVE.

Carmen L. Harris

"Sing Yourself A Love Song"

Sing yourself a love song
Before you go to sleep

Sing yourself a love song
And know it comes from me

Hug yourself real tightly
Whenever the day seems long
I'll be there thinking of you
And listening to your song

If I can't always hold you
With love the way I feel

Hold yourself so tightly
And know our love is real

Sing yourself a love song
My love's in every key

Sing yourself a love song
And know it comes from me

Betty Wheeler

Blessings

The beauty of the Lily
  be upon your mountains high
The Rose of Sharon touch
  your peaks making sorrows sigh
The Morning Star guide
  you each day into his rest
The faithful of Adonai
  make your union blessed.

The winds of grace blow
  upon the covenant made today
Rivers of wisdom flow
  from the Ancient of all days
Spirit of life draw near,
  spirit of union come
With reverberating chorus
  "Thy will, O Lord, be done"

Della M. Prater

Kindred Souls

As we walk through our time
Aware of each exchange
We flow through life
to grow you must retain
to each your time will come
and the two will become the one

Beth A. Miller

571

Untitled

This is how I'm looking
at you is why me cause I,
thought you told me no matter
what you do I still will like
you and will do those things
with you like we planned to do.
    I think that you are a
special friend to me cause you
know how I feel inside all the
time now it is oh Brita will
find herself somehow somewhere
but I've been telling you.
I'm trying too alright what do
you want from me. My world is
very dark right now.

Brita Segerhammar

Sweets SunSet

The sunsets
At the end of another day
The moon rises
High above our heads
Shining over the ocean
The waves crashing
Against the shore
The beat of your heart
In rhythm with life
Your hands so warm
Your lips so soft
I look deep into your eyes
A love that I lost

Anthony Rodriguez

Mirage

To many you are glass
at first sight
Cloudy

But to One
But as the light reflects
They discover truly

That you are a precious and special
    Gem of beauty, such beauty

You control whether others
see you as glass or Gem

All but one were fooled
But he later paid the ultimate price

Broken from within....

Joseph H. Gaines, Jr.

Torment

For who am I,
As vast as God is?
How dare I be
To blame for this.

Nor, who may I be,
The one to blame God?
'Cause my pain is great;
But, worthy I'm not.

Their purpose fulfilled;
God's perfect plan.
And because I loved much,
With grief I must stand!

Ima Jo Crews

The Shades Of Autumn

I watch the leaves of autumn
As they drift down to the ground.
I get lost among their colors
Of yellow, orange, and brown.

I hear the leaves of autumn
As they crinkle, swish, and crack.
The jog the memories of my mind
And sweetly call me back.

I visit scenes of childhood
That were special through the years.
I remember loved ones now passed on.
I shed some gentle tears.

My mind drifts back in autumn
To choices I have made.
How different would my life be now
If different cards I'd played?

I love the shades of autumn
In yellow, orange, and brown.
For it's among the shades of autumn
The best memories can be found.

Deborah Kirk Pettus

Night Rain

Sheets of silver tassels
    as they dance with blackened garm
are lonely silent couples
    who are joined with arm and arm
I'm sitting at my window
    am the only one who stayed
to watch these sad performers
    after all have closed the day
Entranced unto their presence
    with intoxicating spice
I listen as they whisper
    to the ground in sacrifice
To understand this poem
    doesn't come without a tear
'tis all I have to offer
    as they embrace

Charles Todd Beuk

"So Long Dad"

The Angels smiled upon him,
As they called him from this earth.
They had made a reservation
For this man of wit and worth.

And though our hearts were saddened,
As we sent him on his way,
He had earned this long vacation
Which he'd longed for more each day.

May his mem'ry live forever,
As he joins that "Golden Throng",
And 'tis not good-bye we're saying,
Just we'll miss you, and so long...

Geraldine Fields

The Dust Bath

Daybreak finds
A velvet devil
Housed in feline form
Encroaching like cancer
To extinguish the life
Of an aerial brother
Too careless in dust
To guard against death.

David B. Clair

Gentle Wind

I have kissed before the gentle wind
as the soft rays of the sun caress
when every breath is of another
and light is all you see

I have walked beside the lonely night
in silence forgotten by the world
when every whisper is of love
and darkness is your friend

I have spoken to the restless sea
and heard her weep when times are gloom
the memories of my love remain
but a mystery to me

Jacob Broussard

Miracles

Today - I saw a miracle
As rain fell from the sky.
Today - I saw a miracle
As several birds flew by.

Again - a miracle I saw
A young child's smiling face!
That miracle once more appeared
Hands folded - saying Grace..

Each breath I breathe - a miracle,
Each step I take or run.
Each sight I'm privileged to see
Beneath God's shining sun.

Todays - to me - a miracle,
Tomorrow - hopefully!
I pray you know the blessedness
Of miracles to be.

Eileen M. Taylor

"Spruce Tree"

I think that I shall never be,
as lively as this lovely tree.
I've lived my years and now I'm bent,
in such a way my life is spent.

Its scent is fresh upon the air,
in rain and snow and wind to bear.
Reaching up to skies so high,
living proof of years gone by.

Comes the time for me to bend,
like burdened boughs upon this tree.
I love its human stature great,
knowing all who feel their fate —

It's GOD who loves this tree!

Bertha West

Night Music

Music tickles your ear
As it plays through the night
Flutes softly sing
Your eyes begin to fall

Slowly you drift off to sleep
Saxophones share their thoughts
Drums keep a steady beat
With the beating of your heart
You fight to stay awake

Clarinets calmly chant
French horns warmly whisper
Finally you can't fight it
You fall into a deep sleep

Alayne Crick

He Writes

A writer breathes his every word
As it flows from pen to page
Like blood pumping through his veins
He gives it life without age

He captures each moment
He suspends it in time
The mark of a true artist
Regardless of his kind

He lives briefly then dies
But his words linger on
They often become immortal
Long after he is gone

Yet he continues to write
With verse and with rhyme
Leaving what will survive
To be determined by time.

Barbara A. Turpin

Ode To Michael And Alex

We saw Mommy looking at us
As into our seats we were strapped
Mommy was driving the car
The door opened and we were alone.

Alone we sank in the water
Mommy was standing outside
Looking at us with sad eyes
But we could no longer escape.

Mommy, don't cry for us
We've gone beyond the darkness
Always together...forever waiting
Waiting for you to come home.

Evelyn S. Krug

Memory

While gazing through the recent past
As if though through the looking glass
I see a vase upon a shelf
A solitary rose once stood.

A name once scribed
Was vague, not clear
But holding near the glass so dear
Could be made out to say
For Dearest Serita Ann.

Anthony DeWayne Greene

Angels My Friends

Angels hold a special place in my heart,
As I walk my path in life we
    shall never part.
Over hill and dale we glide
With my angel at my side.
While evening stars shine so bright,
I sleep so peacefully through the night
Angels are guardians of hope and love,
Sent to us from heaven above.
To share our life with us until it ends.
And forever we shall be with our
    Angel friends,
Angels forever by my side.

Elizabeth A. Leick

"The Shining Light"

As I wake up in the morning,
    As I view the shining light,
I see the evidence of God's creation
    When the sun is shining bright.

I look toward the heavens,
    Ask the Lord to lead my way,
That my feet will not falter,
    Or lead me the wrong way.

When I travel down life's pathway,
    At the dawning of the day,
With God's road map there before me
    As I read and humbly pray.

O yes, there are trials and temptation
    Along life's rugged way,
But God has promised never to forsake
    If I follow the road map there before me,
I will never lose my way.

Gladys Webb

To My Classmates Of 1938

The hands of time spin backward
as I see you standing there.
What's happened to all those books
you carried everywhere?
Say, can that be chalk dust
you've gotten in your hair?
And who are all those youngsters
I can not help but stare.
They remind me so of someone
that I have seen somewhere.
Of course! The time is sixty-three,
not nineteen thirty-eight!
I don't know what came over me,
It must be getting late.
It's just because I'm getting old
There can be no doubt of it.
And when I look at you
I see you haven't aged a bit!

John O'Donnell

My Violin

My violin is one magical thing,
As I run my bow across the strings.
Playing the Mozart "Serenade in G."
Flowing from my violin so freely.
As the audience listens quietly,
It gives my heart and violin joy
When we end and get a standing ovation.

Andrew Shoemaker

Untitled

Sail off into the sea.
As far as your eyes can see.
Out into the deep blue.
Aqua, lavender, and sea foam, too.
Out to your hearts content.
Without anyone's consent.
To a place where dreams come true.
For both me and you.
So sail off into the sea.
As far as your eyes can see.

Carrie A. Haehnel

Temptation

It shimmers in its brilliance,
    As facets catch the light;
While rainbow colors dance about,
    The temptress of my sight.

It holds me with its beauty,
    And beckons me to take;
But wanting what must never be,
    Would be a grave mistake.

Don't let its luster fool you,
    For once you've taken hold,
You then become the captive,
    As it robs you of your soul.

For things aren't always as they seem,
    And 'All that glitters, isn't gold,'
As you find the prize of greatest value,
    Was the very thing you sold.

Take heed these words I've spoken,
    Don't let this moment pass;
Don't find you've traded diamonds,
    For a broken piece of glass.

Denise Zofcin

Brandy

Duane has a dog, calls her Brandy,
As a watch dog, she's a Dandy.
She obeys when hearing his call.
Loves their game of fetching a ball.
When Brandy runs, she seems to sail
On a cloud of air, whipping her tail.
Shares his pleasure, when he is glad.
Offers comfort, when he is sad.
Gives him kisses that are wetter,
Though not human, she is better!

Bernice DiBernardinis

Piecework

Yesterday lies at my feet,
    as a crumpled garment.

A raiment pieced together,
    threads woven long ago.

A shroud I've worn,
    Albeit ill-fitting.

Now I address the future—
    Naked.

Cloaked invisibly,
    in my childhood dreams.

Weaving fantasies forgotten,
    treasures lost on the path.

Today, I stitch my place
    in time.

Searching to reclaim
    the child—
    in ME.

Connie K. Ciufo

a spot of blood on the paper
an opened vein, a gushing flow
of the rush of fact and fantasy
i am startlingly exposed
to the probing eyes of all who read
and think and judge
this birth my inner self exposed
my soul of lines and verse

Carei Cutler

My Best Gift

My favorite birthday gift
Arrived today for me.
It was from my grandmother.
I like to sit on her knee.

She knows I will like this,
She knows it's the key
To make my day happy,
It's special for me.

It's not just the colors
As bright as the sea.
I know how to say it,
It's just perfect for me!

A short time has passed
And it's still fun to see.
But now it's not as great
As I thought it would be.

But there is a happy ending
Yes, the best gift for me
Is the box that it came in
With so many possibilities!

Ashley Regan

Shadows Of Memories

Shadows of memories
are residents here.
They fear to love
and love in fear.

Shadows of memories
are what lurk here
ever present,
but never near

Shadows of memories
I grasp to hold
Escape through windows
open to the cold.

Shadows of memories
too firm to move
too shadowy to hold
too painful to lose.

They are memories
lost to time.
Only their shadows
are left behind.

Danielle Wiltse

"Lucy"

The things I can do
  are phenomenal and glorious
The pain that I cause
  is historic and infamous
The time that I have
  is provided from below
The place from which I come
  no one dares to go
The purpose to serve
  I'm a tool of destruction
The things I'm against
  is human construction
The powers I have
  are handed down to me
The feats I accomplish
  are graded by Lucy
The one that I'm for
  will rise once again
Against God's evil will
  and the angels within

Eriq Tews

Life

Feelings
Are mixed like drinks
You add a little courage
Then some pride
Give in dignity
And shake it like tide
Put a dash of sensation
A teaspoon of passion
Stir in some romance
And shake up the action
Now sprinkle some spice
And look what you've created
A life full of hope
A life for a nation

Jackie Lowe

My Love

Big round lights
  antiseptic smell
"It's over now
  You have a girl"
But where were you,
  My love

Easter dresses
  Play skinned knees
Friendship rings
  On Christmas trees
But where were you,
  My love

High school proms
  Friends off to war
Our college coed
  A child no more
But where were you,
  My love.

Gladys O. Pitt

Interrogation

Question after question
Answering to the beat;
When will it ever end
I must not let it bother me.

I've done something wrong
They can't find it out;
Asking all the wrong questions
But I will never tell.

If insanity is what they're after
I just could be at fault;
For question after question
Neither will give up

Janelle Lynn Maydak

Your Special

I miss our daily contact
By person or by phone
I miss seeing any movement
'Cause you're not at home
You became a big part of me
As the days grew into years
We leaned on each other
Through our joys and our fears
And so your missed so very much
That I would like you to know
You're a very special friend
I'm glad I got to know.

Iva L. Foor

"The Skeptics"

They say that you can't hear
And you can't see
There in the hereafter -
But, what do they know!

I can't believe that all my words
And all my tears
Have been in vain
Here in the left behind.

All the things I feel
And sense within me -
They have to be part of something
Binding our two worlds.

How could they know
And feel and see -
They've never been inside my soul.
They've never loved you!

Eleanor Hausa-Josephs

Convictions

With my eyes, I see the skies
And wonder what is to come.
People talk, and others mock
And question where I am from.

With my nose, I smell a rose
And think of who made it be.
I say Lord, many ignore
But they want eternity.

With my ear, I am told to hear
All of what the world may say.
The command, destroy the man
Who has put you here today.

With my mouth, I scream and shout
And they stop to give a glare.
In their eyes, I see demise,
They do not accept what I share.

With my mind, I will stay kind
For I know the end will be good.
He paid the cost, died on the cross
So I must do what I should.

Brock Chesbro

Through The Day

I wake up each morning
And wonder,
How will I get through the day
Without you.
So many tears remind me of you.

As I go about my daily tasks,
I hear news I want to share.
I rush to tell you,
But my heart reminds me
And my steps grow slow.

But I do not dwell in darkness,
So many happy memories
Light my way, and I remember
All the good times, and that
Is how I make it through the day.

I know that when my time comes
To join you,
You'll reach out and take my hand,
Your welcoming arms will guide me
As I make it through that final day.

Fannie M. Kelley

"Curves Versus Lines"

The year when I was twenty-two,
And weighed just ninety-nine;
I wished I had a few more curves
And not so many lines.
But now when I am sixty-two
With still no curves nor lines;
I don't mind being sixty-two,
But oh, — how I wish I weighed
Ninety-nine!

Frances Emmons

"When I Die"

When I die, don't weep for me.
and to my funeral wear, blue
and pink and red and green.
don't grieve and don't despair.
I lived I loved and saw my
children born. After that my
God decided to take to my home
When to my grave you come, put
daisies at my head, then kneel
and make a wish, when you
go just leave a smile and seal
it with a kiss. And time to
time when you return see the
daises grow and know that
someday soon you'll join me,
as hand in hand will prance
through the streets of heaven, and
watch the daisies dance.

Dorothy E. Dalton

My Life, My Love

On our Anniversary,
    And through the many years,
Please always know, my Darling,
    That my love for you endears.

You are my Life, my Love —
    My Groom of twenty-one;
The answer to my prayers,
    My Blessing from Above.

Sweet memories we've treasured
    For fifty, plus one, years —
Two children, reared so lovingly,
    Have brought us four more Dears.

I cannot put to words,
    How much you mean to me -
You've made my dreams come true;
    My Life, My Love, it's You!

Happy Anniversary, My Darling,
    I love you more than ever;
The World belongs to Us -
    Please, God, let it be forever!

Dolores M. Moeller

A Beautiful Rose

A rose made out of stone,
A rose that's all alone.
As beautiful as can be,
that which no one can see.
A rose that's no where to be found,
Where no one walks, or no one
talks, or even makes a sound.
    A rose that wants to
    be loved,
    to be loved from up above...

Breana Walters

The Artist

She worked throughout the night
And through the early morn.
Her art was a wondrous sight,
When I awoke at dawn.

As the sun climbed in the sky,
The vista made me stand in awe;
Its beauty caused me to sigh
And wish that I could paint or draw.

The bare trees seemed spun with glass
A Venetian artisan would revere,
And as the sun danced on the grass,
A million diamonds did appear.

I didn't mind the slippery path
That Held me captive in my home,
For Mother Nature plied her craft,
And I really had no need to roam.

Eleanora Feucht

Portrait Of An Empty Heart

Just for a moment
And the moment soon fades
To the quiet dark mysteries of time

This moment of peace
That's forsaken me so
slips away with the blink of an eye

So cold are the nights
When the chill that you feel
Is all coming out from the inside

So long lasts the sounds
Repeating the nightmares
Echoes from out of the emptiness

Under the surface
Animosity hides
The vulnerable loneliness there

A tear in the dark
That not one man can see
Is the only prize for survival

Amy Lynne Goeringer

I Wonder Why

I sat by my window
and stared at the sky,
then began to wonder why...

I wonder why the sky is blue,
I wonder why I can speak to you.
I wonder why the grass is green,
or anything else I've ever seen.

I wonder why the dogs can bark,
I wonder why it gets so dark.
I wonder why the sun gives light,
then wonder why it gets so bright.

I just don't know why...
Why can't I fly?
All I do... is wonder why.

Geneva Roman

To My Love,

I have looked into your eyes
And seen Heaven.
I have heard Angels weep
upon seeing such Beauty.

My heart soars
full of thoughts
of Hope,
And mixed blessings.
Wondering if you could ever
Feel the same for me.

For years now
I have dreamed
of such a vision,
of holding you in my arms,
wishing for Dreams to come true.

I've been kissed
under the shower
of a pale moon glow,
By your lips...
the sweetest I've ever known.

Jim Kelley

Life's Path

You must travel your path
and seek out your destiny
study your realm
so you may find
your own quest
for your questions of life.
And to know what's to come
but study what is past
so shall your mind reach
for voids far and vast.

Craig C. Kelsey

For One Lost Little One

Once, Jesus said go leave the flock
    And rescue one lost sheep.
This youth a chicken's life would save
    Within a dark well deep.

Yes, down he climbed full sixty feet,
    And there he drowned, brave boy,
This lad of Egypt swept away,
    The undercurrent's toy.

His sister and two brothers went
    The youth below to save.
Two neighbors went to rescue them,
    For all, a watery grave.

All six they drew to daylight out,
    All dead, from Egypt's well,
With them the chicken still alive,
    The clucking-truth to tell.

Everett Francis Briggs

Life

He took a dream
And fashioned it with mighty hand
Into a spark of radiance,
Into a whisper of His voice,
Into a shadow of His thought,
Into beauty infinite;
Then adding the ingredient
Of love, breathed His breath into it,
Placed it in its mother's womb,
And smiled on it and called it "life".

Ann S. Word

"God's World"

To converse with those we love
And receive a wonderful blessing
Makes the sky much bluer above
And life a lot less distressing.

Today the sun is shining bright
And God's world is all aglow
The beautiful stars I see at night
Makes my spirit rise and grow.

At night when God pulls the shade
And it's time for prayer and rest
I softly kneel for my prayer
And know I have passed the test.

When the morning breaks calm and fair
And God's service I start to do
I often care about things out there
And serve Him as he would want me to.

Bernadine Ayers Evans

Strive To Be Neat

Young men, pull your pants up
And put your shirt tails in.
Wear your belt around your waist
And keep suspenders in proper place.

Please try to be neat!
Pull your breeches up in the seat
Don't let them Lag while on the street.

Turn your caps around
Stop wearing them backwards
Like a clown
Wear the bill over your face,
Then you won't look
So much out of place.

To make your educational life complete,
You must always strive to be neat

Whether at work or at play,
Remember neatness counts every day.

Henry B. Heath

Let's Pretend

I'm flying high on gilded wings,
And on the way a raindrop sings
That up ahead near Rainbow's End
Is the Land of Nod and Let's Pretend.

What is real and what is not
Means little to us who have got
Imagination in the extreme
So that we can wander in a dream.

Thoughts of love and riches go
Round and round in the ebb and flow.
What matters most, as dreamers know,
Are lovely thoughts in the afterglow.

Speak not to me of what might be
Unless it's of beauty for eternity.
Life can always be a grand surprise
For those who possess enchanted eyes.

It's delightful to drift upon a cloud,
Looking down at the human crowd.
It's fun to follow my star and soar,
Knowing I'll always have dreams galore.

Calvin W. Haywood

Qualities

To weep,
And not decry the pain;
To hope,
And not despair at unfulfillment;
To sing—
Deep into myriad caverns—
And not lose heart
At the resounding silence:
These are the qualities
For which I pray.

Harry Bartron

Shades Of Gray

How can I say goodbye
And not begin to cry

What are the words to say
There are so many shades of gray

So near and yet so far
You say that's just the way you are

Yes, I know how much you care
I feel it in the way you stare

Many words are never spoken
But the bond will not be broken

Even though I'm far away
A part of me will always stay

Nearer than you'll ever know
Closer than I'll ever show

How can I say goodbye
And not begin to cry

What are the words to say
There are so many shades of gray

Chari Lynn Gates

The Poetry Contest

One day I picked up a newspaper
And, Lo, what did I see
A notice on a poetry contest
I thought, "This is for me!"

I real all the instructions
Of when, and where, and why;
But down close to the bottom
A sentence caught my eye.

It said that anyone could enter
Any subject, or any style.
With the address in bold letters
Boy! I began to smile.

I search for pen and paper
And words danced in my head
I mused on what to write about
Something interesting to be read.

But the sentence that tripped me up
Said, "lines no more than twenty."
For me, of course, that's not enough.
But, for them, I'm sure it's plenty!

Earlene R. Nicholson

Clanging Steel

Life is but a mockery,
And death a thing unreal,
And there is nothing tangible,
Save loudly clanging steel.

Edwin A. Weinberg

Forever Very Near

And so the house is quiet now
and laughter comes no more,
I often sit and wonder why
I've never felt this way before.
And every room seems empty
like my saddened heart each day,
the silence that's around me
I wish would go away.
And even when my loved ones
are near me for awhile,
it's hard to stop a tear
for just one little smile.
But then I stop and think
of all the precious times we've had,
and that fills my heart with loving joy
and makes me feel so glad.
So now I'll cling to every thought
of when you once were here,
and know I'll always have you
forever very near.

Deborah A. Sosa

Remember Me

Remember me in candlelight,
And laughing in the sun.
Hear the river sing my song,
As the living waters run.

I'd rather be the sunlight,
Than the falling rain.
Let my memory bring you laughter,
And take away the pain.

See me in the moonlight,
Feel me on the wind.
In the rhythm of the endless sea,
You'll find me once again.

Christina C. Sorrell

I Lay Her Down

Now that her tiny clothes
and infant toys
have been tenderly packed away,
I must let her go
so I can live.

I must lay her down
so the sharp edge
of the sleepless nights
are no more.
I must.

Carved within my heart
her precious, tiny face
will forever remain.

I'll always remember
the feel of her soul
because it's now
a bas-relief of mine.

Jackie Peters

Reflection

For a man who is a clown is
a way of thought.
In front of the mirror covering
his reflection.
What does he really cover?
His face?
or
A way of life?

Crystal Kramer

Nocturne

The night breathes softly,
And in the dying light
One faint star is winking,
Pinned on the breast of night.
Soft velvet mountains watching
The curtain of the sky
As it draws across the heavens,
Another day will die.
The trees stand cool and silent,
Wait for the opening strain
Of night's unfailing symphony
Played by the wind again.
The crickets tune their violins
And hum a bar or two,
The wind takes up the melody
In tones of gray and blue.
While far off, from the distant hill
Insistent as the dawn
The wistful call of whip-poor-will,
Pianissimo - then gone.

Gertrude M. Taylor

Thunder In The Distance

Thunder in the distance
And in an instant;
Lightning flashes, and dashes,
From cloud to cloud;
Followed by its thunder clapping loud.
I heard the thundering sound,
I spun my head around;
I saw one lightning bolt,
Shoot from one cloud,
Through three others,
And into the ground.
If the storm is weak and slow,
Then along the ridge the storm will go;
"But," if the storm is strong,
It will jump the ridge,
And flood the bridge;
And make you think:
How much food is in the fridge?

Charles E. Rogers Jr.

Let Me Be Your Friend

Let me be your friend today,
And I will chase your blues away.

Let me be your friend tonight,
And I will be your guiding light.

Let me be your friend tomorrow,
So that I can share your sorrow.

Let me be your friend next week,
So for a friend you need not seek.

Let me be your friend next year,
So that you need never fear.

But until then will you allow,
Me to be your friend right now.

Edward S. Deli

New Challenge

As I approach
a great new height
I fight the competition.

Bonnie Bosman

"Shadows On The Wall"

I feel their presence,
and I see their shapes.
I sit there stunned,
with mouth agape!

I've seen these faces
somewhere before!
Rushing in, running out,
of my front or back door!

I still hear their voices,
and the games they played.
The quarrels they had,
and the friends they made.

The times they were sick,
I would feel it, too.
Their pain became mine,
all moms know it's true!

So, these shadows I see,
when the lights are low.
Remind me of the angels,
that we made in the snow.

Bernita Lolley

Little Miracles

From the moment he was born,
and I looked upon his face.
I knew it from that moment
that he had made a place.

Deep inside my heart he laid,
and forever he will be.
A part of me I'll keep inside
for no one else to see.

The love that I have for him,
there's nothing to compare.
I thought he took it all from me,
and there was none to spare.

But then another miracle,
and I knew that it was true.
From the moment I held her in my arms,
and looked in eyes of blue.

The love that I have for them
is deeper than the sea.
For my son and daughter,
and forever it will be.

Jennifer T. Boltinhouse

New Baby

There is a time and place
And I have lost the time.

The hands were clear to me a space ago;
Each segment held its own.

But now the spinning lines have taken
up a speed beyond belief.

And I find
there is no time.

Dolores Rogers

A Lantern

Dog
Tall, black
Runs around
Slobbers, messy
Big

Erin Deters

Untitled

I'd hand you my freedom
and give you my soul.
I'd hand you my life
and give myself, whole.
I'd draw myself closer
but you're never near.
To me you're a stranger
to you I am queer.
You act as you hate me
yet I show you love
you can not sedate me
when push turns to shove
The truth is I want you
bottom line, you do not
so this leaves me astray
though I've hissed and I've fought
Now, I'll try to forget you
though I still haven't met you
I'll always regret you
so now I must say it is sorrow, goodbye

Iztac Lucero

Your Love

When I look up to the heavens,
and gaze upon the stars,
I see in them your eyes of love
and know that you are there.

Or when the sun has risen high
and warmed us with its glow,
I'm reminded of your love, and
the warmth that it bestows.

And, when I see a rainbow spread
Its colors across the sky
I'm reminded of the way your
love spreads across our lives.

So dear father, in all the
beauty given us, by God's own
Loving hand, I know that
your in heaven above, and
Embracing us in your love.

Audrey Clarke Nettik

To Loudly Try

I want to swim in the sky
and fly in the river
I want to loudly try
than to quietly quiver

I want to get lost some day
and be found a better man
Than to be the same everyday
not knowing if I can

I want to think clearly
in order to decide
Than to rage emotionally
for the sake of pride

I want to look tyranny in the eye
and make it give in
Than to whimper and cry
and let it win

I want to be more
than just to be
I want to live life
than to have life live me

Hammad Khan

Shadow Of Love

I have a shadow that follows me
And each day it grows and grows
If only it would talk
To tell me what it knows

When night comes, I'm not alone
My friend, the shadow, is still with me
I think he feels I love him so
But he wonders what will be

The days go by one by one
My little shadow is still a bother
But you see, I don't really mind
Because he's just my loving brother.

I hope he's with me always
Until the end of time
So I can watch his shadow
Out grow mine.

Bonnie Link

Unsung Heroes

They bring in the light,
And conquer the hate.
They set all things right,
And make the world great.

Against them is that vile foe
It feasts on young one's souls.
The vital heart, it cannot grow
In this darkness, alone it rules.

Reason is what makes it run
And wounds that mighty beast.
It flees away from that brilliant sun,
Till it finds a current feast.

They take up that mighty task
With no chance of gaining treasure.
Their purpose needs not a mask,
Only love can be their pleasure.

Send the beast down to its hell,
Give it no chance to gain glory.
Don't fall for that evil spell
But, oh yes, do tell its story.

Joshua Ray

Fire

Fire is a living growing being,
And burns in the hearts of every one.
It's consuming and heavy breathing
Laughing at us just for fun.

It burns strong when we're together,
And cinders down when were apart.
May our souls stay a flame forever
In the furnace deep in our heart.

May the heated furnace stay a lit,
Fueled by the love that we claim.
Staked to the heat be it,
By the passions that we aim.

We burn and burn each other,
Till none can stand the pain.
The hot flames above us hover,
And the furnace withstands the strain.

Until the flames have stopped,
and weakens to an amber glow.
Then the fire can not be topped,
And the passions cease to flow.

Carl Patterson

Cowboy Is His Name

There's a hundred years of history
and a hundred before that

All gather in the thinking
going on beneath this hat.

The cold flame burns within him
until his skins as cold as ice.

And the dues he paid to get here
are worth every sacrifice.

All the miles spent sleepy driving.
All the money down the drain.

All the ifs, I's and nearly's
and all bandages and pain

And all the girls tears left dry
and all the fearers and fight.

Are all a small down payment
on the ride he makes tonight

It's love, guts and glory
and one mortal chance at fame.

His legacy is Rodeo
And cowboy is his name.

Bill Ryder

A Morning Dream

One morning as I lay sleeping;
An angel appeared in a dream.
I wondered as it approached me;
What this hovering being might mean.

As I pondered and wondered;
Christ crucified appeared in the sky.
He hung on the cross there before me;
The angel, Christ crucified and I.

My heart, mind, and soul,
Were so moved by this scene.
It all came upon me so clear;
A moment so serene.

There beyond the angel and Jesus;
A sunrise so beautiful to see.
As this picture before me unfolded;
I knew that God's hand had touched me.

I felt love and hope sprout inside my heart;
As I felt all my sins and failures depart.
I know my Lord who died on that tree;
Has never and will never forsake even me.

Charles A. Gordner

No More Frown

The moods of life, they
always change. Day to day,
hour by hour. The way that
I feel, the way that I look.
The mood of the minute
happens to be good. Happy
at times, not sad anymore,
pleasant thoughts, and dreams
race through my mind. I
notice now that, the
thoughts that I think, they
just happen all to be sweet.
With a smile on my face
the day will go on, happy
now, no more frown.

Ginger Rakovec

Untitled

Where am I
Am I in heaven
How did I lose my way
When I was just with Steven

I remembered brightness
But it was normal
I remembered darkness
Which was unusual

Three, big, strong devils
Out numbered us
All dressed in vinyls
Ready to do their task

All shook up in fear
We obeyed every command
Are we supposed to be here
To please their every demands

What is to become of tomorrow
When there's crime everywhere
Every person full of sorrows
Making the world turn to scare.

Eileen Magallanes

Reflection

Moments of meaning
always give birth
to memories of Mother's face.

In perils of life
the blue in her eyes
seemed to heal with power and grace.

Yet tragedy fell
and expressions of sorrow
froze in the pit of her soul.

Now reflections of passage
pierce mysteries of being
in the image so like our own.

Oh dear God, we see you
and what we are to be
in this woman so tender of heart.

May we never lose sight
of the gift of our life
and the beauty of Mother's face.

Jeanette Angela Drzymkowski

Fall Arrives

Many days have come, have gone
Along with summer nights, were long
With lake side walks to be alone
Days heat, nights heat must be borne

Days work to earn the bread
Be done to keep them fed
Long days before the bed
Days heat, nights heat must be said

Strength I need just to endure
Complete this day I must insure
Life's toil to finish will continue
Day heat, nights heat, then surrender

Relief my soul perceives 'fore morning
Sleep is easy, restful dawning
No more days of heat and morning
Days cool, nights cool repeats my longing

Joseph Chautin

Ants

Hurry-scurry in a flurry
All the little ants they go
Here and there, everywhere
Marching onward in a row

Helter-skelter dash for shelter
Every time I come and go
Hither-thither all a dither
In all directions high and low

Round n' round homeward bound
Aimless wander to and fro
Willy-nilly sort of silly
Where is home? How do they know?

Tugging, lugging barely budging
Fussing over food in tow
Hurry-scurry in a flurry
All the little ants they go

Elizabeth J. Grigson

Missouri

I've lived in Missouri
All my life.
It isn't such
A bad life.

We have spring,
Summer, winter, and fall.
Man, all the seasons,
I love them all!

There are friendly people.
I've met quite a few
That are never too busy
To bid you A-DO.

We have places to shop
Until one drops.
Schools to attend
And fences to mend.

Whenever I travel
Or wherever I roam,
I cannot wait to get back
To God's country, Missouri, my home.

Bonnie Mann

Sunday Morning

A quiet Sunday morning
All except you asleep.
The cat sits on the window sill warning
The birds their distance to keep.

The sun rises slowly overheard
To start its way across the sky,
While you lay in your bed,
Needing to rise—and wondering why!

Church bells ring far and wide;
A busy day's just ahead.
The newspaper rests on the lawn outside
While deeper under the covers you slide.

Take pleasure in this quiet Sunday,
At least, for a while,
For tomorrow's a work day
And bound to be a trial!

Dorothy G. Wilson

My One True Love

I know I've made lots of mistakes,
All along the way.
But I just wanted you to know,
What I need to say.

I loved you once, I love you now,
And I want you to know.
That you will always be in my life,
No matter where I go.

For God had given me your love,
He let us be together.
And I will keep you in my heart,
For now and forever.

But you have gone off by yourself,
To be with someone new.
And I just wish that I could say,
"My darling, I love you."

Now close your eyes and think of me,
Remember what I say.
"You'll always be my one true love,
Forever and a day."

Jay Knight

Untitled

The sun labored to rise
Against the heavy dew of morning.
Autumn resisted summer's warmth
And welcomed winter's cool.
Brightly splendored were the sunsets
As long necked birds pointed south
With their instinctive mates in flight,
Always looking toward tomorrow,
Never back to an unchangeable past.
Sure as day and night they flew
With strong assurance of their needs.
If only we could be so sure
Of all that life and love will leave.

Harlan L. Vague

Seasons

I struggle now, as out I gaze
  across the lonely hill,
To penetrate the ghostly haze,
  their memory to instill.
I'm thankful as I look around
  and see the beauty in this land,
The barren trees, the frosty ground,
  where God has laid his hand.
The months fly by
  and spring draws near,
A time of growth
  we all hold dear.
As winter's grip begins to fade,
  it's time to think of plans we made.
Our spirits rise up with the sun,
  another season has begun.
But time goes by, as we all know,
  and soon the North wind it will blow.
The long dark nights will soon return,
  for summer skies again we'll yearn.

Emmett Burleson

Desire

So I am wandering
Across the crystal fields of desire.
Upon my shoulder
The timid spider
Does not frighten me.
In my hands
The blue flower of sensual tenderness
I am giving to you,
Who follows the path of the wolf,
Within you
Gentleness and strength.
For you,
Guardian of the greatest magic
I am singing my song
Thus shall vanish
All shadows of fear

Christiane Langer-Rowlee

Wasted

Powers from
a time
when time
was
forgotten
nothing
existed
outside
of
immortality.
Wasting
the
non-existing
time
from which
our minds
are
grown.

Elizabeth Bruhnke

A Mother's Poem To Her Children

I give you this on Mothers Day
  A tender loving heart
To carry with you all the time
  When we are near or far apart.

A glowing smile, a sweet embrace
  Meant just for you alone
With words and deeds to signify
  You are my very own.

Encouragement when needed most
  A sincere helping hand
With aid of any kind or sort
  To show I understand.

And I will try my remaining years
  To help your dreams come true
By saying each and every day
  A little prayer for you.

For the wonders that are around me
  Make me realize so well
That the worthwhile things of living
  Are around me where I dwell.

Bonnie B. Kirkham

The Rose

Memories sweet with fragrance of,
A single rose from you,
Plucked hurriedly from the fence row,
Midst thorns and weeds it grew.

Crimson in its glory,
Damp with morning dew,
Reflections of my younger years,
When dreams and passions grew.

Now, tucked between old pages,
Crumpled, lifeless, true!
Forgotten, through the years,
The rose, and me and you.

Catherine Cross

Untitled

The month October oft' implies
A season born while another dies...
Scenes of orange, red and gold
Change the shade of nature's soul.
The bite of morn has yet returned
And crystal frost has, too, confirmed
That Summer's heat has faded past
And bowed to Fall's relief at last.
A subtle shift from sultry days
To Autumn's cool and kinder ways;
A crisp wind sweeps across your face
And blows away without a trace...
Amid the swirl of falling leaves,
The final breath of Summer breathes.

Debi Cleland

These Are The Things Of The Ocean

Old pieces of China dish
A sea anemone, a starfish
These are the things of the ocean
A jellyfish and a killer whale
A manta ray with a very long tail
These are the things of the ocean
Tall sea grass
A large sea bass
These are the things of the ocean
You can hear the sea gulls call
As you play with a big beach ball
These are the things of the ocean
And now you've had fun
But the day is done
There is no more
Time to explore
So say goodbye to the things you've seen
The sea, the sand and the sea weed that's green
All the things of the ocean

Jaynie Schonbrod

The Dream

I watched him lying there asleep,
a man with a little boy's face;
with puckered mouth and face serene,
I wondered who was in his dream?
Does he see a boy with tousled hair
laughing and playing without a care?
Or does he see a man full grown
facing his future still unknown?
or does he see his sordid past
where demons rule and love and beauty
are outcasts?
I wonder which of these are true;
I'll never know, will you?

Elaine Mokhiber

As I Awake From My Sleep

As I awake from my sleep
A new day did I see,
I think of all the ways
That "God" has been good to me,
He has always been beside me
Everywhere I go,
No matter what I'm doing
And love, he always show,
As I travel through this world
Not knowing where I'm bound,
No matter what my sorrow
He'll never let me down,
As my days grow shorter
And my nights grow dull and gray,
He's always there beside me
He'll never turn me away,
As I arose from my sleep
To face a brand new day,
He picked me up and holds me
And starts me on my way.

Harold Jackson

"A Tribute To The Inanimate" (The Clock)

From ancient times to modern days,
 a mandate for us all
Was issued by the little clock
 the tyrant on the wall.

With undisputed power, he is in
 full command,
We find our hearts are racing
 to keep up with "little hands".

"He" sets our pace relentlessly
We are unaware of time,
We are unaware the pulse of life
Is competing with the chime.

Antoinette Putrino

Dream Boy

My dream boy would be
A great guy to me
A man so great and strong
He could love me all day long

He would kiss me every night
Outside by the moonlight
He would love me every time
I kiss him cause he's mine

I'll love him to the end
Of the earth when God will send
Jesus who hopefully part us never
So we can stay together forever

In heaven we shall love
Even though we are above
We are not below
And we will not bestow

Caitlin Norem

My Sullen Reign

Your beauty is captivity
A destiny that's unfolding
Your shadows like a demon
A love my heart's been holding
Your structures like a mirror
Sincere but not to boast
Attachments seem dissected
Floating by the coast

Your beauty is reality
A blessing with God's seal
Your shadows like an angel
My recent wounds you've healed
Your visions seem familiar
Hovering far above
Consciousness reflected
A spectrum of my love

Jason Pickens

What A Sound

Snap! It's perfect a man is dead.
A cold white hand
points to the floor.
EYE'S STARE
Feel the pain that was there.
Click! It's perfect
What a sound.
A crumbled note lay's on the floor.
EYE'S STARE
Feel the pain that was there.
Crunch! It's perfect
a bottle on hand.
Smashed to the floor
EYE'S STARE.
Feel the pain that was there.

A hand that could of been held,
A note that lead's to no where,
A scar that can't be removed,
GO AHEAD- LOOK AND STARE...
cause the pain is still there.

David Shaw

Untitled

Inside my heart I feel a warmth,
A certainty, fulfillment;
A knowing.

I look into your eyes and I
Begin to smile;
This smile is a contagious thing
For you return it.

You touch me and I melt
Beneath your fingertips.
We come together in a tender embrace
A union of rapidly pulsating hearts.

Inside my heart I feel a warmth,
A certainty, fulfillment,
A knowing, I feel you.

Jennifer Arnold-Champagne

Tiger Swallow Tail

Paint the scent of tawny morning,
A breath of dew on this window,
To catch one seed of feeling,
A root to know you - again.
To greet golden stars
And walk with you.

Tear the vines
From these branches,
To breathe the stormy bank of our river
Again, these feet taste cool stone,
These fingers drink of water!
This skin drenched in you.

Sing this song silent,
Rise and fall - my breeze,
And have this dreadful machine!
Stolen by the tide in a dream,
Where truth unwinds - a single string.

Exhaust the spool, in banded green,
To flutter full, before our dying streak;
Beyond sight?   Cast off, despondent cocoon.

August Bering

"Lord, Fashion Us In Thy Mold"

Lord, fashion us in they mold,
As you our shepherd
Lead us to Thy fold,
Made pure our heart and soul,
That we'll follow thee thy way to know,
How marvelous - how wondrous is
Thy gracious love,
That only comes from thee in heaven
above.

Thy Blessings to fall on us in rays
of shining light,
Ever shining bright,
To bring us joyful peace
Held in they gracious love that'll
Never cease,
May we in thy word of truth
grow and increase
That we'll truly be with thee at peace.

Inez Smeeks

Hare Up To Nowhere

The pig with very little hair
went to the market square
and bought a brown hare.

It hopped around everywhere
and seemed to be in despair
because it didn't have a pair.

So the pig sold the hare
to an old lady with long hair.
She tied up the tail
of the now very frail
brown little hare
to her own long hair.

The bunny lost hope
and stopped to hop around
anywhere and everywhere.

The hare sang a sad song:
Sunny days are over
for this little bunny....

Gloria Francis

Break Of Dawn

As I arose one morning
A bird flew on my sill

He sang his song so sweetly
And I listened very still

I marveled at his high notes
The melodious sounds he made

Of all my quiet moments
This was one I wouldn't trade

I asked him why he sang like that
He answered high and shrill

I sing to my Creator, because
this is what He wills.

Brenda J. Brown

Untitled

I will never be
A beautiful rose
A glorious orchid
Or a majestic tree,

But God leaves me free
To strive to become
The very best friend
The world will ever see,

It's up to you and me
In each of our lifetimes
To become as perfect as
We can possibly be.

Donald Shiles

In The Country

How I love the peaceful country
Where all you hear are crickets calling
Where cleanness fills the sky of blue
And sometimes a star is falling

How nice if all the world could be
So cozy, smooth and quiet
Instead of cities full of fear
And thieves and death and riot

I wish each person in the world
Could know a life like this
To each and everyone, I'm sure
It'd seem like God's sweet kiss.

Margo L. Clonts

My Father's Hands

Each day my father's hands I see
Hard, but warm and tenderly,
Hands each day I clearly see
Gift o' his a-give t' me.
Each day those hands I clearly see
Tough, and warm and tenderly
Touch to life — a clutch of steel,
Grip a tool or work a wheel.
Besting, testing — childish fun,
Playful cuff that weighs a ton,
Hold your hand or push a plane
—Tasseled veins swing in the rain,
Swing along me by my side
Wise and wondrous things inside,
Scent of wood and silent pride
Swing along me by my side.

Each day my brothers' hands I see,
Gift a father give t' me.

David Glaser

"Happiness Is Up To Me"

My happiness is up to me,
A gift I give myself.
All my negativity
Belongs upon the shelf.

God has given me so much.
Sometimes I fail to see.
I need the ever loving touch
That he can offer me.

Life is short, but meant to live,
Why waste a single day?
So I must think more positive,
And try to live his way.

Cheryl Rodriguez

The Power Of My Word

I stand not upon a stage,
with audience to entertain.
Nor have I sung a song,
no recognition to my gain.
Crowds gather not around me,
as do the rehearsed mime.
Tho unknown I have strength,
through my poetic rhyme.
My passion and inner growth,
it's only a mere reflection.
My beauty and my effect,
lie in my written expression.
Ink, paper and emotion,
in vain, if left unheard.
Unread it's strongly diluted,
the power of my word.
Feeling's and event's lived,
on shelve's and together bound.
The power of my word:
If read, a voice with sound.

Alisa Garner

Don't Look At Me And See Black!

Don't look at me like that
Look at my heart which is not black
Look at my sole which hold the key to my life

Don't look at me and see black
Look at my eyes that show the care for you that I feel
Look at my face that show the love that I feel

Don't look at me because I'm black
Look at my hands that are willing to lift you to a
place you need to be, laced and entwined in yours

Don't look at me and see black
Look at me and see a human being that walks,
feel and need like you
Look at you, look at me, SEE!

Shirrell W. McDuffie

"Angela"

She caught my attention by saying "please excuse me; I'm sorry." I looked around but could see no one as I stood and waited for the light to turn green. But this lady's voice was so warm and sincere; it gave me no reason to worry. Was she my angel who guards me here though she whom I have never seen.

I continued to say my prayers as I had always done. For I was hoping she would appear and speak to me one more time. She made me more aware that she was near but I did not hear or see an angel, not one. I praised her in my prayers and asked God to reward her; For speaking to me was not a crime.

I knew not what to call her but thought that "Angela" would be an appropriate name. I then talked to "Angela" in my prayers in hope that she would appear to me. She called my name as I slept; This is how she came. I opened my eyes to an angelic shadow on my wall; it was she.

Nine days later she came again flying and flipping with her acrobatic dance. She landed directly in front of me so I could see the divine beauty in her face. "Angela" is so elegant wearing her gold lace that she kept me in a heavenly trance. Tiny lights were all about her so I could see her beauty and grace.

I am impatient for late nights arrival to see my guardian angel in her majestic glory. As I look up from my pillow I see thousands of wings going in every direction. When "Angela's" work is done she leaves as a portrait photo and that ends my story. My story is truthful as to how it is happening so I'm sure it need no correction.

Raymond G. Brancho

San Padre

When first I came to these sun kissed shores, I spent my time
looking at the sand, for gifts deposited there.

But now that I am about to leave, I crave the view of the open sea,
for the memory may have to last me for eternity.

How can I say goodbye to the sea, because of its importance to me?
This symbol of infinity, renews my very being.

Mary Helen Borland

America

Millions found refuge on thy shore
Modest dreams come true and spirits soar.
Goodness gave thee a saintly name
Belief in mankind eternal fame.

H. Peter Zell

Across The River

One day I was on the top of the icy road.
Looking down, deep black river was flowing.
Scary eyes, I looked around the bridge.
Nothing there, I cried.

Small voice called me across the river
"Look toward the east side"
I began to turn around my sight.
There was small bridge.

My two feet with soldier boots was
Coming down the icy road.
Strange iron bridge was there
Scary eyes, I crossed the river.

"Welcome to this land, follow me"
The little girl pointed the white stairs
I was climbing up the white stairs
Up-ward the top of the white hill.

Looking back across the river I saw
My parents sad faces, I cried.
"Come on this way" small voice called me
I began to march toward the green road.

Sun Myung Lee

Love

Love can hurt
Love can sting
Love is capable of many things.

Love is joy
Love is pain
You may be in love again and again.

Love your father
Love your mother
And even love your older brother.

Love can be given
Love can be gotten
Love can also be long forgotten.

The more you give
The more you get
You can even love someone you've just met.

Love is about kindness
And about caring
And love is all about sharing

Selvi Sriranganathan

Flies With Butterflies

Forever more in flowered and through.
Love flows around and through.
In yellow daffodils she may yield,
Evermore to her children be true.

Sun her smile to light each day,
With her smile to remind us of her love.
In the rain and clouds of grey,
To water flowers from tears above.

Hear her soft voice in the soft breeze,
Believe in her love as the wind covers you.
Under her loving arms feel at ease,
Tomorrow still there she's true.

Tommy Dorsey plays for her now,
Even Glenn Miller and his big band.
Remember those bubbles floating and wow,
Forever she will have that music at hand.

Listen Sandra and Stephen for she feels peace,
In all Gods creatures there lies that good which is.
Everything God created is only a short lease,
She is Gods heaven just as angels are his.

Stephen R. Dwyer

When Do Love Hurts?

When do love hurts?
Love hurts when you feeling blue and purple.
Love hurts when the other partner is just not
there anymore to comfort you or massage you.
Love hurts when there's no more friendship
out of the relationship.
Love hurts when your "ex" partner is tuning
you out of the mind.
Love hurts when you're crying and the partner
is not there to pamper you and say
"I Love You".

Lakeisha Bowman

Love Is...

Love is a word, when said as kind.
Love is a feeling, which some only hide.
Love is a memory, when thought in the mind.
Love is an emotion, when it's left behind.
Love is my life, which I hold for you inside.

Stacy L. Green

True Love

Love is talking and laughing, it's spending time together,
Love is honesty, sharing and caring about each other.

Respecting one another and encouragement too,
Standing behind each other, no matter what we have to do.

Love is working out differences and being each other's strengths,
It's being there for each other and going to great lengths.

Love is a friendship, you can't get anywhere else,
To talk to them about it, always seems to help.

Love is romance, the heart feels fulfilled,
Though at times it can be difficult, it takes a lot of will.

It may not come easy, and sometimes it hurts,
But in the end it will be worth it, it may take some work.

Love is a commitment to one another,
Because if it's true love, there shouldn't be desires for others.

Paula J. Candelaria

The China Closet

I could barely see the treasures there,
Lovely crystal everywhere.

Tiny cups and the silver urn
that always made my young heart yearn.

The scent of chocolates,
that homey smell.

When the doors were open
I could always tell.

Comforting, security,
It meant the very world to me.

The doors of glass kept me apart
from all those things that filled my heart.

That closet held a stately place.
It represented charm and grace.

The mystery, the gleam, the joy.
It all was there for a little boy.

And though the years have quickly flown,
that little boy now is fully grown,

It's clear to see why it meant so much.
It was mother's love, it was mother's touch.

Marie Alosa

Love's Special Light

Loves' special light of a woman and man,
Loves' special light are all of God's plan.
Love for a child, born out of love,
Loves' special light from God up above.
Love's special light helps makes our day,
Love isn't love, if you don't give it away.
Love is sincere if you're really in love,
Love is so simple, it fits like a glove.
Love is so simple, fulfilling and blind,
Love is a feeling, it's never unkind.
Love is for sharing, and I have a hunch,
Love can be fruitful, it feels of so much.
Love is for young and love is for old,
Love's special light never grows cold.
It surrounds and it warms, whether near or by far,
Its special light shines wherever you are,
Loves's special light always makes a good day,
Love is so beautiful, please give it away.
God's love is shining when you're finally done,
Love brings you home, when your life's battles' won.

Shirley Allen

Pennies

Pennies copper-lighting my days
make rainy-day finds and sunshine surprise...
one, two, three!

Arizona mountain-path pennies,
driveway, sidewalk, and parking lot coins,
join Grandpa's pocket-pennies washed and shiny,
while Grandma's purse pennies accumulate speedily
from hoarded change.

Penny searches challenge my ways,
Urging me onward to creative spots not yet revealed.
Finding-penny hopes disappear
When bottle-caps and chewing-gum abound.
Then hidden shadow rounds pop up to delight evening walks;
daylight glisteners lie scattered on restaurant floors...
Where will the next ones be?

My gifts to you
clink merrily from your deft three-year-old fingers
to nestle securely in your penny-saving bank...
Pennies copper-lighting your days.

Margaret A. Lort

Untitled

A teacher who gives her all
Makes a difference-no matter how small
You help a child's mind to grow
And teach them what they need to know
The love you extend is evidence
Which makes it hard to lose your patience
With each child you give your time
And help their success to climb
You help them with their special need
Because of you, they will succeed
With you kind and loving hand
You help the children understand
To face the future unafraid
And prepare them for the 3rd grade
The teaching you do is beautiful
Kayla thinks you're wonderful
For "Teacher of the Year" you'd be nominee
And I must say, I do agree
You'd be a winner every year
Because your teaching is sincere

Theresa Canfield

The Wyoming Wind

In the West you'll find a wind that no
Man can tame,
The Wyoming wind is its name,
It so gently kisses the golden wheat
Fields, in whispering rows of waves,
Laying it over softly, yet every little
Grain it saves.
Yet in the mountains you feel its
Chilling sting, and see its strength in
The drifting snow,
Endless, whipping, twirling, when it
Begins to blow.
In the West you'll find a wind that no
Man can tame,
The Wyoming wind is its name.

Sharon Hood

Memories

MEMORIES-down on the farm in the Tarheel State,
Many are faded, but many more are great.
I can see the fields, golden with grain,
I can hear the old rain crow cawing for rain,
I remember the forests surrounding the land,
Surely, no doubt, made by GOD'S HANDS.
The redbuds and violets popped out in the spring,
You could almost hear the yellow bells ring.
The summers were busy, filling jars with jelly and jam.
Then, down to the old swim hole, just below the dam.
The fall, the busiest time of the year,
To shirk our duties, we did not dare.
I loved the winters-off to school I would go,
Trudging in the mud, playing in the snow.
MEMORIES-No worries, no secrets to hide,
And in all that HERITAGE there lies my pride.
Deep in my mind are memories of yore,
Kept in my heart are many, many more.

Katherine H. Matthews

Through Angela's Eyes

As we walk around the lawn
Many things we come upon.
Very ordinary things to me,
To a child of two, they're a delight to see
A small toad hoping on the ground
A squeal of joy when it was found.
A red bird chirping in a tree,
was another thrill to see.
A flower bush, a big red rose
"That smells good" to her little nose.
Big white ducks on the pond.
They say "quack" "Quack, Quack" she responds.
Her little dog is there, wagging his tail
"Grandma, look"! It's just a snail
If we'd view the world as a two-year old
Think of all the beauty we'd behold.

Louise Aaron

Wake Up Call

I wake up to the brightness of the morning sun
My eyes opening to the day that just begun
I looked out the window to the old oak tree
to the song that the sparrow sung just for me
I walked to the bathroom at a staggering pace
And looked in the mirror at my early morning face
My hair was all tangled into a terrible mess
Twisting and twirling like a rat's straw nest
My cheeks were all puffy and a bright brilliant red
And then I realized it was time to go back to bed

Thomas Grogan

I Am Your Child — Oh God

May I always walk with you by my side
May I keep my heart full of love and not pride
May I grow with your knowledge and wisdom and truth
And live my life so that there will be proof
    That I am your child - Oh God

May my countenance shine with your light
And my eyes remain clear and bright.
May I always be willing to help those in need
And remain humble enough to follow your lead
So the whole world will know as I come and go
    That I am your child - Oh God

May I keep my mind stayed on you,
Though my friends may become very few.
May I honestly study and follow your word
And be gentle and trusting as each little bird
Knowing you will take care of my physical needs
And train my spirit and soul through my deeds,
That only your words from my mouth will come out
And as I develop, there will be no doubt
    That I am your child - Oh God

Kandi Moore

"Guardian Angel"

You are here in spirit but not in the flesh.
Memories of fond, happy, good times
always make me smile in the worst of times.
I always have comfort, feeling you
here, although you are far you feel so near.
I really miss seeing you face to face.
So all I need to is look up
to the sky, and feel that I
see you eye to eye.
So now I will smile instead of frown.
Please keep watching over me, for
your wings will eventually set me free.

Sarah Gentile

Awakening

Christmas past, childhood gone
Memories of happy moments
Pressured, responsibilities, adulthood.
Grow up quickly we show our youth.
It begins with the loss of a child's first tooth.
Hurry, hurry! Walk and talk
Be a girl or boy...grow up!
Childhood should be a joy!
Slow down...savor each phase
There's days of leisure and pleasures untold
Beauty, brotherhood, nature, reflection
"Oh, to be young again!" A common refrain
    Stop Enjoy Live Again
      Memories...

Noel Marie Sanders

Success

Heartbeats high pulses race,
Memories pass at star speed pace.
The game begins and then deletes,
Will we win or reach defeat.
Will we smile or shall we cry?
Don't you realize it's our last try.
The road to success has many directions,
Only you can create the colorful dimensions.
So now is time, the moments at hand,
Both doubt and fear have both been banned.

Tony Stevens

Reason Not - My Love

I have come to the conclusion that love goes beyond reason. The mind may have the capacity to reason; however the heart knows reason not; only passion! Likened to savage my passion absorbs me. Though my thoughts envision sacrifice; the desire of my heart breeds hope. In the torment of my yearning lies a state of anxiety where all reality is abandoned in compulsive imprisoned emotions. The unsatisfying actuality thus far brings only the strongest disapproval from the mind. As necessary self-preservation contradicts the doubtless power of my passionate desire. The consequences therefore lie in realistic devastation. Warning, risk, danger, possible regret; threat of a broken heart; severed nerves of pain! The disillusion of my discontent is destroying my endurance with an exhausting effect. Moreso, the realm of my consciousness lives in mental duress. Distressed, fragile, and weak, my incurable optimism awaits the audience in you. For the essential part of this devouring passionate desire is useless without the object of its affection; which in turn promotes this hopeless obsession.

Pamela Ann Wood

Retrospective In Green

Cool shadows in shade of palm
Mock the heat of fury
Lurking just out of sight.

Strained silence blankets the fields
Where they fell like toddler's toys
Wondering why it had to be forever.

Each brother's tale a moment lingers
In the air between embittered foes
Dancing with the paradox of war.

Like Theseus each returns
Without friend Pirithous
Gasping from his trip to the Underworld.

Poison tears through broken dreams
As faces bob past their boats
Floating nightly away from greener pastures.

Ted E. Karatinos

The Once Mighty Land

The sun still shines, still warm and good, but it is all in vain.
Moderate winds blow a song of mourning across the barren land.
The cities, once full of life, silent now; no sounds anywhere.
The sky, once full of jets and planes, empty now — just a few clouds.
Clocks that once told time have stopped — time itself no more.
Once there were days and weeks and months; no one now to care.
Just a wasteland; the once proud people never to return again.
Greed was the reason. Big people got bigger, small people smaller.
Fighting soon began as hunger and fear swept all across the land.
Starvation and panic soon had all in their mighty hands.

The end came swiftly, as time was now against them, slowly ticking
   away the hope.
Then there was no one to tell someone of this once mighty land.

Timothy E. Steineger

The End Of Life

I once walked the beaches of Tampa.
My hair once brown and my eyes once full of sparkle.
Then I was young and full of life.
Looking back, it makes me sad, to think I am now so frail.
How quickly the years pass and the summers fly.
Today, the only thing I look forward to is dying.
"Supper is ready," the nurses always say as they wheel me to bed.
I only look forward to dying.

Quincy Thomas Marr

The Brain Of Death

Class beginning
Mom came in
She said, weeping, that we had to go to the hospital
My heart pounding
As the hospital sign got closer closer
Till we were in
But why? No one was sick then I glanced around
Dad? Where was Dad?
He was only having headaches
Nothing serious
Then I was thinking of all the people it could have been
My Grandmother or Grandfathers
It could be anybody
When they called us to go see this some one that I did not know
My Mom, Brother and I all went into this room of mystery
Dad was lying there on the bed
He had just finished having brain surgery
He had a brain tumor
Relief came into my body Dad was all right now I was too

Mandy King

Wondrous Moments

Lightly walk upon the dewy, green, grass
Moon shining upon the little stream
the stream slowly flows, and frogs croak
Wondrous sounds of crickets playing a violin
Oh the beauty of sounds and sights
Maybe occurring only in ones dream

You swirl in a dance, with the rhythm of sounding nature
As the dew caresses your feet and toes
On and on you dance as the music of nature flows
Lighting bugs flash on and off in tune

Off in the distance an owl adds his voice
to celebrate the moment
The fresh clean fragrance of pine fills your being
You want to memorize the rhythm, of a special time
For soon it will pass, as it's turning fall
These lovely sights and sounds will be again
Maybe to someone else's treasured heart
And the beauty of it all will forever chime

Rita McNulty

Night Owl

Sitting on the windowsill
moonlight fills the midnight.
The owl, Consistence, watches me
through beady eyes in snow white hair.
In faith I can but do none else
than meet in turn her soul deep gaze,
and follow through into her eyes
to search her mind for lore as well.
Though white snow falls
and rain pours down,
still Consistence waits outside the glass
to duel in silent battles fought
through thoughts and images sought from me.

Mary Rachael Peacock

Hope In The Mystical Dance...

Life is a trance to the mystical dance.
My soul is a flower in the universe,
I am here with so much fear.
Hope is a shooting star, forever is where we are.

Mark Cohen

585

"Thoughts"

I think about you night and day,
More than I could ever say.
Your gleam, your smile, your gentle touch,
I dream about you ever so much.

The night is very quiet and calm,
You have my love in your palm.
If words was just a precious passing,
My thoughts of you are for the asking.

If color is the block between us,
I'm white, you're black, there's no big fuss.
Time is fast and we can't wait,
There's no time for everyone's hate.

Let them make their own friends,
Our thoughts for love is our sins,
So here we are between two lives,
I'm old, you're young, we have no wives.

Time, pressure and unneeded fate,
We'll stop their awful, stupid hate.
So remember all the goods times we sought,
Let it go, we're in each other's thoughts.

Steven L. Austin

It's Time To Say Goodbye To "Mother"

As much as I hate saying goodbye, it's been two months since the morning you died,
Oh how we all cried, it was hard to except what I knew to be true, my sisters tried to tell me, she who lie in the box was you.
As I looked in disbelief, I tried hard to see,
Looking for the mother I once knew,
I looked and looked,
I still couldn't see you,
Deep in my heart I knew where you were,
Rocking in the arms of Jesus looking down on earth so far,
The celebration everyone had for you was grand.
Standing room only, hand to hand,
As we all sat side by side, I couldn't help hearing my brother cry,
"Why Mommy? It's not fair, she shouldn't be lying there, oh God, it's just not fair, it's not fair,"
As I turned to Daddy he had tears in his eyes,
How brave he was telling us not to cry, he said "You had gone to a better place,"
No more pain, no more suffering from this earthly race,
You are dammed in hell, but in heaven you rise,
Some day he would again be at your side, "don't cry children, she's out of danger now, be happy, be glad for her not sad,
If you live right, you will reunite",
So I say goodbye for now, I'll see you in the future. I'll love you always Mommy.

Muriel McCoy

Teen-Age Tides Of Sanctum

Anguish is ubiquitous among the masses. From one mourning to the next it devours the falling and the fallen in one malevolent snap of its well toothed grin. The agony of despair grinds their spines of esteem beyond recognition. Digested by insecurity, their vigor is burnt, and excreted in the forms of low self-esteem and drug induced states. Their reality yields no truth. LSD spiders fly and paisley chickens go cluck, cluck; sorry pal your time is up!
The neurons hiss and the dendrites fry. While the twilights sleep wraps them in a false blanket of hope.
All falls to foulness and their future dies...

Sean H. Cardones

Light

Outside the glass door the shrubbery stood,
Moving slightly in the light breeze,
Sharing its beauty with all that it could.
The rain had left on it but one small drop,
And on that drop shined a ray of the sun.
It sparkled and flashed a white light
So bright until its course had run.
If one small drop so much light could make
How much light from a shower could God take?

My life I've lived to a full eighty two.
The rain fell freely as I tried my duty to do.
God smoothed and led his way for me
With the light from his spirit I could clearly see.
He changed my heart to one who cared,
With many so needy my life I shared.
As now those many long years are spent
There is still a small drop not yet lent.
Got knows when from me it will be rent.

Mary Ellen Roberts

My Sons

When they were small, I felt the glory of Eve
must shine about me as I watched them
play and grow.

The days seemed full and endless and unheeded
by me they flowed.

And suddenly the time has gone —
great changes wrought —
without my planning —
without my thought.

The big house, now it empty stands.
I gaze at my unused hands
And thankful though my heart may be
For all the past joys heaped on me,
A part of me is gone forever.

Margaret Ficzere Mc Lean

Why?

When days are going great and I enjoy the beautiful skies
My body tells me something is wrong
And I ask WHY?

Why can't I spend more time with my beautiful wife
See my grandchildren smiling, laughing, giggling
Enjoy talking with my dear friends
Might I ask WHY?

I have worked so hard for so many years
Given of my time to help those who need
Heeded the call when it arose
It seems so unfair
Might I ask WHY?

Anger, I suppose is what I'm feeling
Remorse for undone dreams
Regret for many things never spoken
I don't want to leave
Might I ask WHY?

WHY?

Nancy Rounds

A Twelfth Of A Year

Thirty days, a month, a twelfth of a year
My darling, my love, my precious dear,

I've searched, I've waited, I've longed to be near
A woman whose love was warm and sincere,

Through empty days that harbored lonely nights
My spirit slumbered in hopes of a light,

A glow, a glimmer, a beam, the dove
You've beckoned the dawn and with it my love,

I cherish, I covet, I embrace this day
In hopes, in dreams, in every way I pray,

That I'm the one that God has sent
To love, to comfort your soul content,

In thirty days, a month, a twelfth of a year
My darling, my love, I am here.

Rod Knowlton

To My Child

When first you were entrusted into my keeping,
My desire was to give you the benefit of my knowledge,
My wisdom but not my fears,
To shield you from darkening skies,
That you may be graced with golden sunshine.

I would counsel you so you would not know,
The heartaches of this life.
You would know laughter rather than tears,
And joy instead of sorrow.

But you eluded me and went your own way,
The path you traveled was not smooth.
It was turbulent and rocky.
Sometimes black clouds were all around you.
You persevered and found the light.

I know now that this is the way it had to be,
For you are your own person.
I could not spare you.
I could only love you,
For you are wiser than I.
You know you are the master of your own destiny.

Marion P. Ackerman

Lost Love

As I awaken I see a light
my eyes are closed but the light shines ever so brightly
there is a window that shows a budding flower
it has opened slightly so that only a little color shows
it feels so warm and enticing
it makes my heart smile like it hasn't in a long time
I watch the flower and it begins to blossom a little more
and the warmth spreads slowly throughout my body

Suddenly I feel a change and
the bud begins to close

As my eyes begin to open I see it fading away
I close my eyes and want it to open want the warmth to return
but it doesn't
will it, can it?

Michael K. Tyson

My Work Companion, Chip

A new time era is being ushered in
My genderless partner is ready to begin;
Sitting upon my desk, as smart as a whip
Programmed for many jobs, my friend Chip.

It's strictly business, no small talk at all
But the company says ole' Chip is really on the ball;
Chip's memory is great when all goes well
Just following the program, doin' it swell.

Work, work, work, twenty four hours per day
Chip's making me look bad by requiring no pay;
No medical insurance and Chip's never late for work,
Sometimes ole' Chip makes me look like a jerk.

My partner is perfect, I've heard some people say
And will most likely replace you one day.
With death or retirement, they say Chip is easy to replace
There are no benefits and they don't even consider race;

But let me tell you a secret, Chip is not perfect yet
I can tell by all the home phone calls that I get;
It's HELP! HELP! ALARM! Please come to work for something's not right!
Someday I'll say, "Sorry my friend, I'm retired". It's all yours tonight.

Ronald E. Blacklock

Dreaming

As I gaze into your eyes under a full moon
My hands begin to sweat wondering if the words will come soon
It is so hard to say what I feel in my heart
When it was words of love right from the very start.
The feelings I feel must hide and inside keep
it seems the only time I have you is in my sleep
You could break the chain from my heart and set it free
if only you'd rush to my arms and kiss me
Thoughts of my fingers running through your golden hair
laughing, talking, exchanging ideas we both share
I wish our stars would cross very soon
the honor I'd feel just being in the same room
It's hard to put on paper what I feel in my heart
when it seems you're the one I've searched for from the very start
for it seems every breath I take no matter what I do
it's for no one else, just only for you
I know we haven't even met, yet
just thinking of you and never to forget
maybe my dreams may come true when I wish upon a star
but until they do I'll just worship you from afar

Robert C. Schmidt

I'm Here

I know who I am and know what I want—
My heart is in your hands-The feelings
won't stop.
I see your smile and miss your touch.
To stand by your side—Am I asking too much?
I know you're confused—Not sure where to turn.
Just let down your shield—You will never get burned.
All that I am is all that you see. You are in my
heart, why can't you believe—That life is real
and so is love.
We can make it together with a prayer from above.

Karen Marie Eiring

Nature

Nature rolls; giving us strength
Nature breathes; giving us wind
Nature brings birth; spring to summer
My heart rises to my throat when I see animals die
I may not be perfect, but with me nature is.

Tom Isabell

587

Like Father Like Son

My little eyes would watch you, every night and day.
My little ears would listen, to every word you'd say.
My little feet were eager, to fit into your shoes.
And this little boy would try, to walk and talk like you.
Now sitting in the window, watching for your pick-up truck.
Is something I remember, causes you rarely did show up
You always were my idol, and the wisest of the wise.
And in my mind about you, no suspicions ever rise.
Now how could my young ears and eyes come to be so blind?
I guess cause when you'd take those drinks,
You'd seem to feel so fine.
You always set examples, in everything you'd do.
But what about your boy, who wants to be like you.
Now when there's pain and sorrow I will always stop and think.
The time I sat right next to you, and watched you take that drink.

Walter James Wilson

"Love Is Many Things"

My love is many things.
My love is like the time of spring.
When a birds heart seeks to sing.
My love is like a breath of life to live.
For all that's in my heart to give.
My love is like a dark moon lit night.
Where the mysteriousness of heated passion, clash at fight.
My love is like soldiers of war.
Making a lonely women's heart soar.
My love is like a seeking wanderer in times of heated sands.
Where hearts of undying love meet unfinished plans.
My love is like what dreams are made of.
Given, it is the gift of "God's" eternal love.
My love is many things, 2x
My love is me, this I know for sure.
For a gift of giving, to you I give my love forevermore.

Robert Young

My Only Regret

Today as I sit here, beneath the great oak
My mind travels back to nights long ago.
We sat by the fire with our backs to this tree
I'd look to your eyes, and wait patiently.
You sat by my side, my hand you would hold
The silence you filled with the stories you told.
The love in your voice, the dreams we shared
Your words were like music filling the air.
Our time together went by so fast
I took for granted it would always last.
Now you've gone on to another place
Never again shall I see your face.
The memories I treasure and can never forget
Never saying goodbye is my only regret.

Marjorie Cunningham

Family Tree

My family is like a tree.
My mother is the trunk, our support.
My grandmother are the limbs holding our love.
My brother are the leaves that dangle with joy.
I am the bark that protects all of us.
And the flower is my father which was blown away from the storm of
    divorce.

Louis A. Flenner III

Come Back

Hi, my name is Shana;
My nickname is banana.
I once had a dog;
Who sat on a frog.
The frog jumped up high;
The dog flew in the sky.

He never came back! You know what I think?
He sat on a tack
That was on a cloud.
I bet he bow-wowed!

As I think I'll take a drink,
And go back to the sink to do the dishes.
I bet he wishes, he was back with me
So he could put his paw on my knee.

But before I go
I would like to say
On this very wonderful day
That I miss him,
I wish I could kiss him!
He's my pet dog, shame on that frog!

Shana Williams

Suffer No Longer

Suffer no longer
    My people help is on the way
    Our heavenly father is sending
    Someone to take the pain away

    Some of you think that we don't care,
    Since, we're in another land, but don't
    Forget my brothers and sisters, we're
    All willing to lend a hand

    I know we have struggled all our lives,
    But won't I'll be wonderful when we
    Reach the heavenly skies

    Forgive us, because it took so long
    I know a lot of us need to find our
    Way home, but we need to know
    Will you except us with open arms to
Suffer no l-o-n-g-e-r

Shonda R. Brown

A Wonderfully Busy Day

"Mommy, mommy I wet the bed",
My preschooler woke me up and said.
Groggily the sheets to the laundry I take.
I need a shower; the baby awakes.

Rush, rush the kids get dressed and eat.
Quickly to preschool; Do we have treats?
Brushing through snarls and tangles of hair,
My second grader scrambles; her backpack is where?

The baby opens the sliding door with pride!
Out shoots the dog...no longer inside.
Time for lunch; both kids come home today.
After school it's homework; a soccer game to play!

Dinner is quick, "Yuck...Mom what is it?"
Bathtime for three; I hope they all fit!
PJ's are on, everyone is nestled in bed.
Books are quietly chosen; three stories to be read.

Finally all is quiet; at an end to today's races.
Yet I saw love and wonderment and smiles on their faces.
As the day went zooming by us too quickly once again,
There's no place on earth I'd rather have been!!!

Laura McEllen

A Trip To Outer Space

I would like to go to outer space.
My rocket ship would go so high without a trace.
I would look out the window and see the man in the moon's face.
I'd stop at Saturn and Mars, refuel at Jupiter and see some stars.
My ship would go light years fast, that I can't even grasp
What a year At Last!

Stan Blank

Osmosis — Me And The Sea

Look ahead—Friend, see upon the Clear—
My ship it sails, e'er so gently, the wind to bring it Near

Can you feel the strength within its bows—'Tis minute
   a speck of Light

Look ahead—slowly she nears, the sea is her home,
   her best is in Flight

The light is white against the sails, the clouds in contrast—
dark blue
   if only to be lost between the two of them—
   my dream of life come True

Look—A far—A head—Can you See?

The ship and I we share, the most common bond for us,
my friend,
   our love—the ocean and its warm salt Air

But, alas, the sailing ship is gone, outlining shadows
remain

Into the sunset—that speck of Light—will gently return
Again

Jeannine Simonian

Song Of Myself

My hair is brown; my eyes are green like jade.
My skin is like milk chocolate.
I am happy like a bright summer day,
But when I'm sad, I am a cloud ready to rain.
When infuriated, I boil over like a pot.
But now and again, I retire like a badger to her homely set,
Or go to my room like a mouse in her safe hole.
Sometimes I feel like I could burst with excitement,
Like a balloon with too much helium.
I can be ferocious like a lion catching its prey
But then, I will be gentle as a purring cat.
That is the song of myself.

Yfa Kretzschmar

Our Love

Seeing lovers holding hands...I think of you.
My thoughts of you breath the sweetness of honeysuckle
blowing in the wind.

Will I grow to resent you? By chance will fate
take you away from me...Will tomorrow bring
health and prosperity?

Will lonely nights always find my heart empty and
void of the closeness of you, that you and I
could share as one...

Am I to be denied your love...
Time is unpredictable and tomorrow waits
for no one, but do we simply wave and flow
like that waters running deep...forever

Shirley A. Turnbo

Mourning Never Falls

You are the sweetest of memories, the richest of
my thoughts today. Tomorrow's pain will be washed away
by the blaze of emotion your existence emits
through my body.

The absent of my life in yours creates an endless
void of guilt, maturing my vanity as I know it.
Only you can moderate my direction,
sweep my life away from infection,
and close the door on my mutinous thrust.

No words need spoken nor your face be shown.
For your being alone renders freedom
from the chains of evil that had bound my soul.
I nurse the expressionless gift
your birth has bestowed upon my heart,
which no one can take away or blemish,
which will be carried with me throughout
my pilgrimage.

If destiny shall release our separation, or not.
I will hold you dear until I leave,
via demise.

Mikel K. Myers

Mine Is Not The Only Voice

All my life my mouth had been gagged;
My voice had never been heard.
My mouth was bound with secrets that stifled my voice
Just as effectively as a piece of torn material wrapped tightly
around my mouth.
Just when I thought I would never hear the sound of my own voice.
God removed the gag that had always extinguished my voice.
Finally, I was free to speak and I sang the most beautiful song.
I was astounded by the beauty and strength of my own voice.
The melody was distinctly my own and the lyrics told the story of my life.
It was truly exquisite.
There are others who have truly beautiful songs to sing;
Unfortunately, their voices remain silent.
Although one day, their voices will be heard
And what a wonderful chorus it will be.
For, mine is not the only voice.

Kimberly Cosby

Night Life

Moon shadows pass in gliding paths as
Needled boughs in concert scratch at
Silent sighs the dark slips past.

Mountains black, hulk in packs—
Waiting for the resurrection.

Echoes crack the granite peaks
From wanton beat of bony racks.
Bellowed screams scorch the trees
And melt to moans—as ritual gore runs to grass.

Stalkers pace, with dripping lips-senses quick-
Prey relents.
Serene at Mother's feet -
Lay the feed of bloody meat.

Before the burning brow clears the east -
To die the dampness in its heat -
Silence holds a shroud of peace - and
Night is pleased.

Madeline H. Lucas

"Life In The 90's"

Poverty guns black or white,
Neither one is wrong or right,
Endless battles constant killing,
Why must youth be young and willing,
No one wins we all lose,
Do you think it's your right or must you choose,
War or peace it's your decision,
It's youth to youth a head on collision,
Open your eyes to see past your fears,
Good or bad we all shed tears,
So you go on and live you lives,
But think of this with your guns and knives,
Some day you'll need a helping hand,
But who can help if no one stands?

Tanya Johnson

Broken Spirit

You say you'll love me until the day I die
never did I know being your woman would
be the reason why.

You broke my spirit and then you broke
my bones, you tried to choke me and said
you would never leave me alone.

And the truth be known when I decided to leave,
you would not stand in my way no matter how
I bleed.

So if you're still with that person who hurts
you so, remember that you're the only one
that can make the decision to go.
    SO BE STRONG

Lee Piland

I'll Always Remember, But I'll Never Understand Why

Lord, you gave me a very precious gift though I
never fully understood your plans for giving me what you
had. What I will always remember is you gave me this
precious little child that grew to learn, love and share.
That made us laugh and sometimes cry. This precious
gift lives no more for he has gone to heaven above.
Such a brave little soldier who fought his battle, when
he heard his masters call, he departed from this earth,
no farewells not even a goodbye. He didn't go alone
for part of me went with him. No, I asked no questions,
but I did not understand why such a precious little
gift left early from this land. No one will ever know,
but the Lord Almighty. For I thank Him for that
little time he let him be with us. Though life without
him will be hard to bear, we know he rests better
in the life filled up above.

Sarah West

Untitled

Young George the Vet was free as an eagle,
No cares, no worries, except cows and beagles.
Until one night after a couple of drinks,
He said to himself, this life sorta stinks.
What I need is a wife, both gentle and sweet,
Who will wash my clothes, and kneel at my feet.
It didn't take him long to find sweet thing,
And he rushed right out and bought her a ring.
This poem could be over about George my friend,
But he wanted you to know the bitter end.
My God, he said, I must have lost my mind,
I laid down with a lamb and got up with a lion.

William A. Alexander Sr.

The Flower

Our friendship was like a seed,
new, fresh and exciting
and with nourishment and time it grew more mature.
Until one day, unexpectedly, the flower bloomed into love.

Now more than ever we tried our best to keep the flower in bloom.
And for a while we looked at the magnificent flower, as we looked at
    our love,
both beautiful, new, refreshing and enjoyable.

Together we stared at the sweet sight in a daze,
as we felt for each other.

Until one day I stopped looking at our flower from a distance.
I saw time was all we had.
As I grew closer I saw our flower,
beautiful as it was, wilting at the edges.

I turned to you for support, only to find you weren't there.
And I knew right then, as I turned back to the flower,
petals, petals of our relationship fell to the ground one by one.

I felt a small bit of hope, so I turned to you once more for support,
only to find you have planted another seed.

Racheal Anne Mercer

As The City Awakes

As the city awakes
    Night turns into breaking dawn
Another day is coming on
Quiet stillness, is filled with sound
The piercing noise, of the alarm
As the city awakes
    Darkness, is once again gone
People hurrying, and rushing along
To their jobs, they've had so very long
Kids to school, their told be strong
As the city awakes
    You say there goes another day, as you yawn
But ready to do it again, when six o'clock
    comes around
Yes, as night turns into breaking dawn
Another day, is coming on
As the city awakes

Mary Foucault

T-God

Why must the pain continue to repress me
    No longer can I live without memories of you
    Constantly with me, like the night which will always follow the day
Just like the darkness your presence, or lack,
    Creeps upon the light of my happiness, until, it is drowned out
    Constantly am I trying to fill my mind with joyful thoughts
    Only to fail and watch them drift away, like white clouds on the
    like white clouds on the wind, replaced by thoughts of you...
    Rain clouds that hide my inner sun
The tears fall like rain
    I can not breathe for the tight noose around my heart
    Every time the darkness comes it tightens another notch
    One day I will hang, and fall
Only you can save me
    Give me your love, loosen the noose that suffocates my heart,
    Release me from the cold night, enfold me in your arms, protect me,
    Guide me to the light
Or if you will not, I will relinquish my one last point of light,
    To create an extra star in your nights

Kerri Sheehan

590

Remember

I know we'll meet again,
No matter the distance between,
Remembering the "Good Ole Days,"
The memories we've shared,

Others will come and go,
Leaving laughter and tears,
Thinking of the past times,
Now called "Wonder Years,"

I often set and think of you,
And wonder what went wrong,
But we can't dwell on our past experiences,
Just think of our new life here and now together, forever,

But I know you cannot hide,
The feelings of "Remember When,"
Just keep my love in your heart,
For advice now and then,

Don't ever lose your goals, my friend,
Don't ever turn your heart away,
For when you open your eyes,
I'll be there for you each and every day.

Karen L. Coleman

Mind And Body

You and I we are the same,
No matter what I say or how I feel.
I always stay the same inside
And you can never truly change.
We will always belong to the same soul.
I am your thoughts and you are my action.
Together we control.
So you see, together we must stay.
I am your courage, you are my strength.
And the world goes on around us.
So why not go on together?
I am feeling, you are touch
If only we could agree.
I am thought, you are sight.
Together we will see.
Once I wished we could part,
but, now I'm glad to be.
To explain we must tell you that
I am mind, You are body
And the unity of us becomes me.

Trisha Poole

I'm There (The Philosophy Of Unwanted Complacency)

No matter what I do
No matter what I want to be
The future holds no change
I'm there

I will do what I must
I will be what I am
No change
No future
I'm there

There is where I'm at
There is where I'll stay
There is here
My future is here
My future is upon me
You would think that I would have little pressure or pain knowing
I'm there

I'm not happy here
But, I'm there

Steven William Bleser

You Would Never Lie

You said you would never lie, that you'd always be true
No matter what we went through
I thought it was a dream, then it became a reality
A little bit to short of an eternity
We went through a lot and you were still there
In a some what distant form, but at least you pretended that you cared
You tried to let me down easy through my constant pleading
You knew that one more scratch could cause bleeding
The next heart to be broken is bound to be mine
You're too far from the truth to go back but you said
    you would never lie

Kellie Saloga

No!!! God Is Not Your Toy

I sit and wonder about some folks who think life is just a game
No real clue of where they're going, no clue from where they came
Everything seems to be one **BIG JOKE**, they think time belongs to them
I'm not talking about some little child, can you believe the are
   GROWN MEN
What a waste, God what a shame, so many gifts inside
They're covered up with so much junk, consumed by so much pride
They laugh and smile like what's the deal, there is nothing wrong with me
They don't even know who woke them up, gave them sight so they can see
No God Is Not Your Play Toy, you owe Him **ALL** your **PRAISE**
If it wasn't for the strength He gives, your arms you couldn't raise
He woke you up and gave you life, a chance to make it right
Instead of saying **YES** to Him, all you do is buck and fight
No God Is Not Your Play Toy, someone to push aside
Slip and slide all you want, there's still **NO PLACE** to hide
Every knee **ONE DAY WILL BOW** and declare that **HE IS LORD**
They'll shout it all in unison, they'll be on one accord
No God Is Not Your Play Toy, rise up and take a stand
You say you're not a little boy, then **WAKE UP** and be **A MAN!**

Marganette Epps

To The Hardworking

You work, work, work,
No time to play
Since a "wee bairn", you work
You try to relax and are told
To work
No one cares
Yet, you work harder; and it makes you stronger.
They say hard work and determination pays off,
When? And will it ever? Even with the questions and the cold hearts
And not getting to do what you deserve. You still are working hard!
Maybe, one day you and I will get our just rewards, one day, one day!

Osomwonken J. Igbinosun

The Way...

   The way you were there for me when
nobody else was. It was sweet and kind.
   The way you offered me a place to
stay or someone to talk to. It gave me
piece of mind.
   The way you smiled and talked to me.
It gave me something to think about.
   The way you gave me advice. I felt
there was nothing at all to doubt.
   The way you held me in your arms.
It gave me a reason not to cry.
   The way you understood. It made me
never want to die.

Renee Dutton

Alone

I didn't have a sparkling diamond
nor a band of gold to caress my finger...
Nor a satin and white laced gown... to hide the shame.
I didn't have a veil dropping over my shoulders
Nor a sweetheart to say, "I do". And change my name.

But I had a life within me... and I knew that I loved it dear...
Alone I would carry my child with gladness.
Even though the world looked down upon me...
I knew my child would soon be here.

How I prayed each night to Jesus...
Who above all could understand...
And if ever a friend I needed...
He would always hold my hand.

Then when the time came for delivery...
I looked to God who created man...
And I thanked Him for my baby...
For it could have all been in His plan...

How I remembered God in all His glory...
Left His beautiful heavenly throne...
Became a child in the Virgin Mary...
Had now given me a child to call my own.

Vesta L. Pollard

Friends

Walking side by side feeling peacefulness,
Not knowing about the real word racism.
Best friends from the heart, feeling happiness,
Never showing any kind of pessimism.
Black and white friends can be like day and night,
Sharing each special moment together.
Arm in arm like soldiers ready to fight,
Two friends stand ready to defend each other.
Marching in step not caring what others think,
More concerned about where the two might drink.
Conversation between a companion
Comes easily to kids in unison.
    The two friends could be considered an outcast,
    But decide their friendship should forever last.

Lorena April Reynolds

My Street

'Twas "Whispering Trail" they called my street,
Not knowing where I'd be,
A pleasant, peaceful place to live
For people just like me.

How little did they realize
They day they named my street
That I would choose this quiet place
Where friends galore I'd meet.

My happy thoughts of other homes
Soon vanished from my mind;
The joy I found on Whispering Trail
Was never hard to find;

For flowering trees and chirping birds
And lawns so trim and neat,
With friendly smiles along the way,
Made Whispering trail a treat.

Vada Lord

Peace

A state of mind free to all who seek
Not only for the strong, but those who are weak
It comes from many sources, driving out evil forces
Standing strong in troubled times
It shapes hearts, and renews minds
Replacing sadness with joy divine
Restoring souls like yours and mine
Hold on to this sustaining force
For it will keep you on the right course
Do not be robbed by a common thief
Stay in the war, the war for peace.

Susia Smallwood

The Christmas Tree Out In My Yard

Out in my yard there's a Christmas tree,
Not rooted and stuck in the ground;
But a tree with no needles or branches,
Quite skinny and hard to be found.

It's a tree that was given one Christmas
Some seasons ago and long past;
From a sweetheart who will always be with me,
Alive in my soul 'til the last.

My sweetheart has moved on and left me,
He says he was never here;
But out in my yard there's a Christmas tree
Standing there, year after year.

In the heat of the sun and the wintery moon,
The tree and I wait night and day
When the roots will regrow,
And the branches will know
That life starts again with Jose.

Susan Cullen

Cassandra

Cassandra should have warned us, should have shrieked and cried.
Not that we could have changed anything,
no would we have believed her had she screamed her dreadful message.
But the way things were our hearts were trembling with anticipation to
    welcome spring.
The winter had been bleak and hard making our longing more intense.
And then April came, and though full grown was hard to catch.
Golden forsythia was forced to climb through snow filled yards.
Kites flew but needed weighted tails to meet the March like winds.
Children decked in snow pants hurried home, clomping in boots where
sneakers should have danced.
Croci made a bold attempt but froze before their color was complete.
Skunk Cabbage grew as always in the swamps, but there were few to notice
or to find the Hepatica sweet and pink hidden under frozen leaves.
Weeks passed and May was gone.
Still the forecast snow was heard.
Instead of Red-Winged Black Birds flying free, Chickadees still sought
the oft-filled tray.
"Yea", and again I say, "Yea, Cassandra should have moaned aloud for
    us to hear."

Marian McIver Prochnik

Father

Caring, loving, trustworthy too.
Not very old, yet not very new.
All the places to go and people to see,
all through my life he has been there for me.
When I'm in trouble he's there at my side,
even for my mother his loving bride.

Melissa Beck

Trust This Voice

There is a voice within me that knows the truth,
not the loud voice in my mind that screams for my attention,
but the quiet voice in my soul that gently whispers

It offers me a life of love and possibility,
a life filled with joy and sharing,
of truly living, not just surviving

It doesn't force itself upon me,
or ask the impossible of me,
but always speaks the truth if I'll only listen

It knows I am the perfect one for what is asked,
When the time is right and which path to take,
only asking me to accept without fear or question

This is the voice I was born with,
the one that guides and protects me
I will not be afraid to follow,
I have only to trust and surrender

Terry J. Novak

'Him'

Never together, but always close
Nothing to me but a memory,
Of the brother I loved the most

When I'm in need, he's always there
Like a shadow, an angel,
A ghost, howling in the cold night air

So few precious years, I looked up to him
My brother, my idol,
Now just a voice in the wind

The only brother that I had, the greatest person I know
I don't know what to do,
It's too hard to let him go

He's there in my sleep, he's there in my mind
Jerking out painful teardrops,
One at a time

Never together, but always close
Nothing to me but a memory,
Of the brother I loved most...

Michael J. Brenner

Night Song

Slowly the day slips to its end,
Now spring the shadows here and yon;
I watch the swans fold to their rest
And see the sun set 'neath the pond.

Light sinks silently into dark,
Birds on boughs are nestled together;
While cricket choruses mount in song
To tell us of tomorrow's weather.

In yonder forest guardian trees
Over all their limbs have spread;
Ever shielding those beneath
Who keep the forest for their bed.

God, grant us peace when daylight fades,
And guard our rest through darkest night;
That with the calm of endless changes
You'll gently lead us to the Light.

Lee Bradley

The First Day Of The Rest Of My Life

A two-year separation; it's taken its toll,
now time that we ended this menacing role.
Lawyers, accountants, and CPA's,
a checkbook gone completely astray.
Will it be possible to regain control?

A quarter century of both joy and tears,
and four lovely children who are so dear.
Our commitment genuinely true,
hard to believe it's finally through.
Bittersweet memories will fade through the years.

The lawyers are set to present their sides,
the judge finally enters, "All please rise."
Testimony is long and grueling,
we wait the judge's final ruling.
Fate for our futures will be a surprise.

The deed is done, I'm no longer a wife,
I hope there won't be more pain or strife.
Loneliness fades with each new day,
as new horizons make their way.
It's the first day of the rest of my life.

Yvonne Puls

Sweet Baby

Baby, Baby you were such a delight,
Now you live where the stars are so bright.

Your time on Earth was short yet sweet,
Someday again we will meet.

Until then I think of you daily,
Loving, caring and always praying.

Your weeks were few,
But every one had much love for you.

Gifts were bought and plans were made,
Our memories will never fade.

You cried and laughed and even loved,
You were a child that was thought a lot of.

I think from day one that maybe you knew,
You were to be one of Gods chosen few.

You left this life with spirit and grace,
You gave me a tear and a smile for my face.

I know the plan God has for you,
With your ability you can do.

Don't worry about us little one,
Our days filled with sadness are over and done.

We think of you now with love and a grin,
For your suffering is over and Heaven you're in.

Vicki Hansen

My Mother

Through these eyes of mind I see, memories of a century.
Of a loving husband, family, and a day that lives in infamy.
Through these eyes of mine I see, one hundred years of history.

Through these ears of mind I hear, kind words spoken oh so dear.
Of children laughing far and near, of cries of anguish and of fear,
Through these ears of mine I hear, one hundred years of hope and cheer.

Now my eyes are failing fast, my ears are about to hear their last.
My thoughts are of my happy past, I'll get to meet my God at last.
I have no sorrow about my past, my life has really been a blast.

I am so lucky to be alive, for one hundred years and five.

Lee Churchill

593

The Twilight Of My Years

A young face gone, and age lines drawn; in the twilight of my years.

Three children have grown and a husband has gone; in the twilight of my years.

Memories serve to bring a tear to eyes that can barely see.

Sweet laughter of grandchildren to ears that can hardly hear.

In dozing dreams, a future seen, of a husband with whom to reunite; in the twilight of my years-when God sends his heavenly light.

MaryAnn Penrod

I Dream Of You

I think of you among my dreams
   of silhouettes on moonlit streams.
I cross the through time to another space,
   amidst the stars I see your face,
      And I ask, ..."do you think of me?"
Then you disappear but I hear your voice,
   so I follow, for I have no choice.
I reach for you through the galaxy
   where I feel your touch so tenderly,
      And you ask, ..."did you think of me?"
.....Then I dreamed that you
   dream of me.

Sally Jean Rappolt

A Season Past

The seasons gone of blossoms sweet.
Of singing birds and driving heat.
The trees have stopped their budding blooms,
Around the bend, the winter looms.

The air grows crisp and night grows long,
And all of nature sings the song,
Of lullaby and quiet rest.
Another year, she's past the test.

For many it's a somber cry.
Not time for birth, but time to die.
But let us look beyond the gray,
Beyond the cold and shortened day.

All things are set upon a course,
We live, we die, with some remorse.
And just like nature, come to bloom,
Again, in God's green living room.

Tammy A. Davis

A Vote For Fall

If I were a poet, I would write
Of the beauty we've seen today
Truly we've seen many a magnificent sight
As we journeyed up Princeton way.

It's been a mild day in mid October,
Only partially sunny at best
We left at ten-thirty from Mount Tabor
Where the trees were not yet fully dressed.

Oh for the words to convey
The beauty we've been able to behold,
Of all the color along the way,
The green, yellow, orange, red, and gold.

If there should be an election of the seasons,
While I see beauty in them all,
I can't just give all the reasons,
But I think I'd vote for the fall.

Marvin A. Lawrence

Amorous

Our love is like the pearliness
Of the first winter snow,
And like the morning's mist
Our love will protect us from woe.

Our love is like a billowing river,
It will always flow,
It will never wither
Like a flower when it's cold.

Our love is like the immensity of space,
It has no limitations.
And like the weave of delicate lace,
We are together, there are no separations.

Our love is like the morning sun,
Sparkling off a frozen lake.
It is amorous not numb,
Our desire's we will always take.

Our love is like the natural light,
Of the stars that glow and glare.
And by the moon that illuminates the night,
This love we will always share.

Paula Holden

Going Barefoot In The Summer

When I was a child, I went barefoot most
of the long hot summers.
   I loved to feel the grass under my feet
It was soft and cool, and felt like velvet too.
   At times I walked on hard pebbles and stones,
that would make my feet hurt even my bones.
   Then I would walk in puddles and streams,
My feet would feel great, and I like a queen.
   Back on the dirt paths, my aches would return,
And my whole body wanted to yell and scream.
   But before I knew it, I was back home,
Soaking my feet, and vowing never again to roam.
   It has been quite a while, since I was that child,
Yet I will never forget, the summers I spent,
   Going barefoot and running free and wild.
How I long for the past and all that I did,
   As I grew up in my barefeet as a small kid.
It was the simple life in mine 40 on third street,
   And what I wouldn't give to have that treat
of going again in my little barefeet!

Rose Ann Hazy Pruchnik

Untitled

As I stare out across the meadow I hear the hiss
of the surrounding trees as if they are telling secrets.
The billowing clouds dance to form pictures
as I lie within a patch of daisies.
He loves me........He loves me not.
For that I shall never know, I think,
as I softly pluck the petals from their centers.
A sparrow is flying overhead and she whispers...summer is here.
The wind turns to a roar over the trees
and my pictures within the clouds begin to change,
forming new pictures, and then spreading out,
to form no pictures at all.
My fantasy is gone.
The glow of the afternoon sun is slowly falling asleep
and I feel a raindrop meet my nose.
Soon the earth is crying like a baby
and my daisies were getting their evening shower
I shut my eyes and lay peacefully, and think of what
God is planning to do next.

Kelly Markferding

Desert Landscape

The Living landscape — carved — elicits quiet memories
Of transient ages... ageless eons past.
A face — crease-lined—
Elicits quieter memories still, of a Life in memorial.
The face... like Creation,
Seems withered, windblown... parched,
Yet — splendidly settled — it is, indeed, singly sculpted...
Duly accepting... graciously given
Both beauty and character
By the same dictatorial winds... of Time!

Robert E. Jones

Forgotten Stars

When my rationality goes twittering over the hills,
(oh chant thee threnodies for my rationality.)
Samphire dies upon its home by the vast-unknown sea.
(oh he will never, never rest, except...)
Far and long, far and long then goes he
(oh he ever unrests; ever, ever until...)
Far amid flaxen, long amid dark—flaxen and dark.
(oh he the sad-seeking, the not-finding.)
Low and mournly dirges he his swift longing.
(oh when the sad-mouthed, scarlet-crimson? Where?)
His shroud is cold, his shroud is dark, light-dropped.
(oh slow-unnourished his unknown undying.)
The black flowers stand whisper-still by the alone sea,
(the black flowers shiver in the ice of his ungone passing.)
When he, all-enfolding in his coming-going, stays.
(is this, ah this then, the no-unrest, the long Where?)
Ah here, on the dust scraped from forgotten stars. Here.
(Samphire lives. He, resting, rests, finds. Flaxen? The dark? No.
His, alas, are only black flowers and ancient stardrif.)

Paul Van Gieson

I Believe In Jesus

I believe in Jesus, I believe in God.
Oh, His wonderful path one must trod.

To reach the Holy prize,
We must be baptized.

God is love,
He sends rain and sunshine from above.

From the dead, He was raised.
Let His name be praised.

Confess His name,
And He will free you from your blame.

Love your enemies, this is what Jesus taught.
Oh, we must never forget, with a price we were bought.

Jesus is Lord,
Why must we walk on the devil's sinful cutting board?

God is the world's light that shines all about.
Satan can never blow this out.

God sent His only Son to die,
On the cross for everyone, 'tis the reason why.

Why must others in Christ choose not to abide,
This could lead to suicide.

Nathan Dudenbostel

Untitled

Oh why does it have to hurt so much
Oh why is the pain so great
When all I had in my heart was love
Oh why did I find out too late

But the sun will surely rise again
And it will shine on as before
But its light will be dimmed its sparkle gone
Because I won't love anymore

But then when I think of the joys that we shared
And the love and the trust we found
It's worth the tears and worth the fears
For that special love to abound

So again I'll place my heart in peril
And again I'll risk the pain
And feel sorry for those that won't
Who will never experience the gain

Peter J. Moeller

Christmas Time

Oh, Christmas time is so wonderful and gay
on a red tablecloth, food, drink and popcorn balls on display
warm feelings with fire crackling from logs on the hearth
as I gaze out my window and see
a blanket of white covering the earth
trees loaded with pine cones, a blue jay and some squirrels
and a pond frozen over, I see ice skaters a twirl
horses pulling a surrey, coming up the country lane
they seem to be snorting,
and snow is glistening on their manes
some carolers are now gathering and starting to sing
and in the distance I see the old church
and faintly hear the bells ring
and I can vision the manger scene with baby Jesus dear
Mary and Joseph with faces aglow, hovering near
Yes, peace and joy seem to fill the air
truly, Christmas is a wonderful time of the year.

Martha Teegarden

Innocence

It walks the paths of dancing leaves, free falling laughter
on butterfly wings,
With abandon, never measured, a smile of light-pure-delight
fresh from God's warm embrace.
A signature of trust it ensues,
Love unfathomable it imbues,
A baby's smile reveals its truth,
Innocence, thy name is beauty.

Lois Marie Thompson

Full Circle

Bleakness, black and gray scattered heaps,
Nothing in sight,
As far as an eye could see.
Mounds of cracked boulders and ash,
Nothing moving except the wind,
Swirling, sifting the ashes.
Not a sound, no one to hear,
No blue skies up above,
Man's tinkering with a force,
Beyond his understanding,
It has come full circle,
From Adam to atom.

Oma B. Reed

"Fishing"

My husband, and I love to go fishing
　on Cedar Creek lake.
When spring time comes we can hardly wait.
We get into the truck with the boat, and
　head for the lake.
Ten minutes of time is all it takes.
We stop at the bait shop, and buy our bait.
Then there we are at the lake.
We get into the boat, and head for our favorite spot.
　We cast our line to see what kind of
　　fish we can find.
It might be a croppie, bass, catfish, or blue guile.
but what ever the fish is, it's a thrill.
When darkness is up on us, and the sun is set.
We head home with our day's catch.
Fishing on Cedar Creek lake is so relaxing,
　and so much fun.
My husband and I have a good night's rest
　after our day's fishing is done.

Virginia C. Bolton

Hard Up

Awakened, Sweaty
on tattered dirty sheets
I lay: Alone
Among these empty walls
I speak your Hallowed name
Pausing, for the echo...
Inhale
Tasting old perfume of Lost dreams
Was it a dream?
I ponder....
As I reach for a drink...
　Maybe?
But the damn scratches on my back still sting.

Robert A. Long

Life's Fabric I Weave

The threads of life we use are fragile and fine,
On the day I was born God gave me mine.
I must be careful not to tangle the thread,
But weave the fabric with care, as God's word has said.

There are days I'm more confident, and as an eagle soars,
I work more to achieve than ever before.
If my threads break by the worry of life,
I call on Jesus, he's my help and guide.

He mends the broken threads and then says, now try again
To keep weaving the fabric and if I fail again.
He don't forget I'm just learning today,
How to be a weaver that will weave more perfect each day.

It takes much prayer and a watchful eye to weave the threads of life.
He came to earth and lived, he knows the grief and strife.
The fabric must be beautiful, not a spot or wrinkle to be found,
For the fabric I am weaving, it will be my wedding gown.

At the marriage supper of the lamb,
　all the saints will be dressed in white,
And the angels will be singing, it will be a glorious sight.
Jesus will be the one to greet us, welcome home we will hear Him say,
When the door of heaven opens for us, what a wonderful day.

Ruth E. Thompson

The Riddle Of Existence

I am a bloody creature;
Once a man had to endure my sin.
An evil being I am, laced with
A dark past. A woman even died from my
Sweet, but bitter touch, only to awaken
With a new life.
A starry sense of self you will see
Within me, if you are so fortunate.
New life is spurred from me,
Like that of a newly sprung tree.
A treat I may be,
If you want me.
Guess my life,
If you dare...

Stephanie A. Stauffer

Time After Time....

Children oh, how quick they learn
once the story told, of fights and
wars of long ago that hurt both
young and old.

Crying out, they die of hunger
for all the world to see, I can't
believe, not then not now this one
day might be me.

Efforts fail, world peace on edge
the blind leading the blind.
Yes at fault, place the blame no longer in
there minds.

See, look here the children
eyes, the stories here ten fold
Of course who cares time after time
the children they are told....

Walter Dean Ramsdell

Snowfall

I saw the snow start falling down
One cold and blustering winter day
Gazing through my window.
Whipped by the wind, it swirled about
in quiet disarray, carpeting the earth below
in pure white sparkling magic

It snowed and snowed, throughout the day
filling every nook and cranny,
So heavy at times, you couldn't see
Beyond the view, of shrubs and tree
Thickening with the passing of time,

Towards, the gathering dusk, it stopped,
Revealing the wonderland it had created.
The setting sun left a sight
of heavenly pink, reflected
On branches, tipped and laden
Down with snow
Like frosting on a cake,

Ruth A. Merolillo

Untitled

Draw me the Wind and where it blows.
Paint me a snow storm and why it snows.
Show me a ghost who remembers why she died.
Bring me the scepter of hemlock and I will decline.

But if death be a great vessel who sails the endless seas
Then give me a Bismarck and I'll trick her into taking me.
Then tomorrow will be the sunshine with rays to touch my cheeks
And forever a simple rainbow to have and hold for keeps.

Sharron Hazlett

Embracing Our Roots

I was born in nineteen hundred and sixty three
One hundred years after the Emancipation Proclamation came to be.
Embracing our roots to the motherland where we were free
Nubian kings and queens as far as the eye could see!!

Up came slavery which brought us to the U.S.
Freedom taken away in this awful mess.
They wouldn't let our ancestor learn to read or write
The goal of freedom always in their sight.

The root of economic wealth was gained on our people's back
Our reward, an EEO, Civil Rights and Affirmative Action attack!!
Goals are okay for everything outside of our community
Affirmative Action sets goals to help achieve equal opportunity.

Embracing our roots allow us to appreciate from where we came
Uplifting the sacrificers and trailblazers who stayed in the game.
In spite of all the obstacles we will succeed
Being a Lockett or married to one is all you'll ever need!!

From Africa to slavery, to sharecroppers, to migrants, to great cooks
to crew leaders, to educators, to pharmacists, to
developers, to coaches, to programmers, to attorneys,
to physical therapists, to doctors, to entrepreneurs, to corrections
and to the military!

Thomas E. Lockett

Untitled

Freshets of spirited laughter spangles from your brow.
One line of hinted malaise attached by your very now.
Should cumulus clouds pass over and you bow a tired eye.
Walk not blindly through abeckoning hidden in sweet disguise.

What makes us laugh what make us cry.
Emotions strung on like beaded pearls become loose,
No knot, no noose.
Gems of truth. What are secrets to youth?

Flights of fallacy rearing up
Thinks us immortal, begging for more.
While times of sadness and great grief
beat down our "so-called" protected door.
Our lives soon filled to overflowing
even when it's had its fill, and the
fairytale is left not knowing, but
the message leaves one clue
the meaning of life and the making
of anew.

Rhonda Fintel

The Emptiness Of The Empty Nest

The leaves fell.
Only the occasional cries of a blackbird
Disturbed my solitude.
All the flowers were gone
Except for
A single chrysanthemum.

As I gazed
At the empty house in silence,
I was overpowered
By a feeling of
Melancholy and loneliness.

Victor Huang

Walk On

I walked alone through the bright circle, pushing
onward to the beginning of life.
Each day new encounters, new faces, new shades of grey.
I walked on through the sparkling embers of broken
hearts and shattered dreams, holding, fantasy at my side.
I walked on through empty promises, broken vases,
shattered blood.
I walked along the trail of faded dreams, loosing
energy. Coming close to the world above, never
knowing the feeling of love.
I walked on through valleys of tears, where pain
flows like gushing streams of crystal crashing
fearlessly upon Jaded Stone.
As I now look back at each step, each twist,
each curve of fatality. I wonder;
have these passages forged out a
subtle underlined map of my voyage to
come?

Melissa Blaisdell

Ashley

To see you is to see the blossom
opening at first dawn, the soft
delicate natural beauty of a flower

To hear your voice is to smell the fragrance
of the violet, while listening to the
birds sing up in the trees

To know you is to see and feel the soft
glow of the summer setting sun into the
shimmering ocean from a hilltop

To be part of you is to be part of the star
filled evening sky where you can see
into the darkness forever.

To love you is to wake up every
morning happy to be alive and watching
you grow another day

Ron Peloquin

If I Could Change

I wonder if there's anyone I would really rather be,
    or if there's someone out there who's wanting to be me?
In moments of decision, we think we would like to change,
    to take our lives of disarray and completely rearrange.
But would I want to give away these precious memories,
    those loving moments from the past that mean so much to me?

I've sat and quandered deeply and thought of who I'd be
    if I could just be anyone instead of being me.
I guess I thought of everyone with lots of wealth and fame,
    from movie stars to princesses with big important names.
But then I thought how much I'd lose if I were to be another.
    I'd have lost what means the most to me—the chance to be your mother.

Linda Henderson

Windows

A gentle breeze travels within our soul
    Passion and hope abound untapped
Free the passage that allows us to grow
    Images will remain while the words fade away
Golden years arrive after the touch of light
    When the window is broken it's not a matter of intent
To be partially graced is something to behold
    The essence of the opening will bring out fears
When the young are privileged nothing is known
    To the aged appreciation never can be lost
Slide it open as easy as this breeze
    You will never be forgotten for unrecognized deeds

Tony Nikolenko

Untitled

Mihara
or in plainer terms my heart

Lies in a mass of crippling confusion
laden by burdens long ingrained
fears endowed
to unforeseen and overpowering strength

How things became so bad
- I know not
I know only that phobia afflicts me - seizes me - now
playing me the bigger fool through its domineering control

...for Mihara
it is not so idiotic a thing to adore you
- no, to the contrary
'tis idiotic to withhold this
precious intelligence from you
particularly in a world so precious as this one
where a second chance to act or speak or both might easily ne'er come.

Kat Jaske

Blessings

Have you seen a rainbow after the rain
Or seen rain drops hanging on a line?
Have you seen a snow top mountain
Reaching high up in the sky?

Or seen foot prints in the snow
Or heard a coyote calling to his mate
Or an owl hoot in a tree? I have

Have you seen the patterns made by drifting desert sand
Or carpets of desert wild flowers in the spring?
Or bees gather nectar from blossoms on a tree
Or heard the cry of a lonely whippoorwill?

Have you seen waves as they crash back onto shore
Or a sea gull dive and catch a fish
Or a tree shaped by ocean winds, I have.

Have you watched a setting sun at closing of the day
And seen the glorious colors left behind
Have you stood and gazed in wonder at
The beauty of it all?

If you have seen and heard these things - my friend
Then you too have been truly blessed - I have

Niola Parrish

Loving An Older Man

If we compared the number of years marked by a calendar.
Or the number of sunsets you have seen,
I would fall behind only because of
time.
If we compared our accomplishments,
or what we've come to know,
I would fall behind only because of
experience.
But if we compared what it felt like to laugh
with each other,
or compared the feel of being touched with a smile,
and making love with true passion,
than we share equal time.

Pamela J. Charter

Crime And Pain

I do not know what makes mankind turn to crime and pain
Or what burdens we must carry to want to spread this stain

Has simple faith gone to the wind, is this the source of pain
That few have faith in God above and to fellow man complain

Is no child taught respect today or pride in a job well done
Or are they simply left to learn the prize is taken, never won

What has happened to society that many of us expect
That home and food will be provided and we need not pay the check

Hard work is not degrading, respect not much to ask
If you ever hope to rise above and accept your rightful task

When this nation turns from God and rejects Him, one and all
The angels will cry in Heaven for the nation about to fall

So instill in the children a faith rooted deep
That as this nation's future, they will be His to keep

Teach them respect and to care for the ill
To honor their parents and walk in His will

Allow guidance from Heaven in lessons taught here
That the children will keep them and never know fear

Lord stop this madness, the crime and the pain
And with your precious blood, cleanse mankind's sinful stain

Marie B. Wurtz

Our Life

When our life began as one
Our future was so uncertain.
As time passed us by,
Our dreams became reality.

We are what love means!
You have brought sunshine to my sky
That was once doomed a lifetime of rain.

Together we've shared more pain and sorrow
Than one deserves in a lifetime.
Now, replaced with laughter and happiness,
Pain and sorrow are just a memory.

The lessons God taught us
Always seemed so unfair,
Somehow we've stayed strong
Still standing on our feet.

Throughout all the sadness,
I never dreamed
One could love,
As much as I love you.

Pamela Jean Howard

Measuring The Cup Within

The cup may look half empty but in reality to others, it is half full
Our measure could be affected by our life's gravitational pull.
Negative attitudes can decrease our measure's, positive thinking
Can yield untold treasures
Treasures more precious than silver or gold
Not necessarily monetary but food for the soul.
When your cup looks half empty, stand back and look again
Look for the sunshine in spite of the rain.

A cup's measure of time depends on your outlook within.
You may feel broken when it is only a bad bend.
Fill your cup to the brim from the power within.
All along life's highways, we encounter potholes and ruts.
We must never be discouraged from refilling our cups.
Life will never be perfect on this we can depend.
Our secret weapon is to harness the power within.
When we find our cups filled to the brim.
Look around at our neighbors and share the cup with them.

J. Harris Jefferson

Lyric Movement

Pleasure dances brought me
out this evening.
Icy tears sear across cheeks,
burning in the sights of now.
Visions will make recollections of
ribbons setting rhythms, building and falling
with crescendos of stone and steel.
You sing a constant harmony
to this racing beat.

I cannot lead you as we are singular
partners.
Gentle urgings make a silky passage
between lines while hour upon hour slip by.
Smooth skin trembles under my hand,
heat rises and flows with cutting edge towards
a core that shouts elation.
Intertwined, breath and pulse, I cling to my
final minutes of the passing darkness.
A tired smile reflects promise in tomorrow.

Seamus Gregg

The Frustration Of Mother-Nature

My fifteen-year-old daughter seems to be stuck in the cocoon of her
own caterpillar-ness. On some days she pops through the end of her
entrapment and views the world with hopeful eyes. At other times she
uses drugs and alcohol to lull her into the sleep she perceives as
peaceful, or to propel her temporarily into the near-death risks she
perceives as excitement.

Occasionally the world is her fantasy come true, and she prepares for
    her escape to it.
But too often she remembers old pain and abandonment and so remains
    shut up inside.

Like the caterpillar she gorges herself toward maturity, except she
    smokes the grass instead of eating it.

All she needs for success rests inside the cylindrical bed where she
sometimes lies motionless. Gathered in with her are all the
values, standards and ethics that will make for contented living.
Wrapped around her like the silk cocoon is enough goodness and good
sense to last her lifetime. But they can only mature when she bravely
bursts forth into the beauty of her butterfly-self.

She doesn't seem to know the prison door opens from inside—out;
Like the caterpillar, she is held captive only by herself.

Katherine L. Carlton

The L. A. Riot

City burning, stomachs churning:
Panic, fright throughout the night.
Verdict shocking, nation rocking,
Anger, tears, hate and fears.

Batons flailing, curses...wailing;
Jury not hung, senses wrung.
Tempers wearing, passions flaring,
Pent up anguish through the years.

Conflagration, torches flung;
Cries of bitterness are sung.
Burning, looting, senseless shooting;
If in the way, one dies that day.

Guns reloading, minds exploding;
Your time has come, you can not run.
Hopes are shattered, burned and battered;
Once a goal now blackened hole.

We cry for peace and quick release
From all this strife and loss of life,
But hate and greed this night is theirs
To burn and kill...not hear our prayers.

Merle W. Kinne

Ignorance Is Deadly

Away from the right way, down the wrong Ave.
Peace and unity is what we need to have
To keep us going, but some are never-knowing
Shortening our futures and lives are just blowing
Away in the winds of trials and tribulations,
Never having knowledge of the times and situations
But that's okay because I'm here to make it happen
With strong words that will spark some reaction
Like the strike of a match to the fuse of a bomb.
Brothers and sisters, do you know where I'm coming from?
Knowledge of self is a very easy task,
But do you want it that's the question I got to ask
Of my people because there are some that I see
that seem to lean to the repeating of history
which is not fair to the youth that are up and coming.
Blind to life that's why they are learning
to be the best the best they can be
Because ignorance is deadly.

Raymond E. Harris

Spirit Of The Seasons

Winter is like the quietness and
Peacefulness of your inner self.

Spring rain is like a purifying
Shower to cleanse your outer-self
And mother earth.

Summer is like the brightest
And warmest glow in you heart and soul.

Thunder and lightening are the incredible
Energy of one's passions for love and life

Fog is like the cloak of your
Spirituality.

Autumn is like the change of a
Beautiful ending to a breathtaking reawakening.

Pamela Phillips

Festival

Lights dance around my mind,
People flow across the floor,
The band strikes up another tune,
Let's hear just one more.

The dresses swirl in pure delight,
Friendly smiles flash from the door,
And all the while, the band plays on,
I want to hear just one more.

Colors filling every empty space.
Is this real? I don't know for sure.
The music takes me places I've never been,
I can't wait to hear just one more.

If I was lost, then now I am home.
If I was sick, then this is my cure.
I know I must go, but I don't want to leave,
Please, let me hear just one more.

This could all be a lazy summer dream,
Or a deadly predator, with a sugar-sweet lure.
But still, don't ever wake me up.
I need to hear just one more.

Tabitha Wilson

599

Life Unusual Life

An unusual thing, life seems to me
people in pain, is all I see.

Many scarred by love, this I have found
most marriages these days, don't stand ground.

Family problems always butting in.
Is this life? Do you ever win?

Should we lead life simple, take it slow?
Shouldn't our life be, the way we want it to go.?
Tina Davis

Fire Underwaterfall

On the cheek of the nocturnal visage
Perceive the light of the Persian Night
Admire this eve's ignescent image
Let's ground the flight O' the future's plight

To play in the silver mirrored pools
Beneath the prancing procession of stars
Not to be repressed and crowded by rules
Freedom — the evening is ours

And the nubilous night is your chorus
Your voice crescendos in melic array
The dragons and wolves are upon us
I am your safety O' cammoufler

Your brilliance shines through me whene'er I call
Like glowing fire, under waterfall
Zacchariah A. Craig

Merchant Mane

Unhindered spirits?
Perhaps ignorance.
Heads held at full mast
shirking only at the whim of the larger hand.
Introduction of the banshee to a soul.
What is duty?
The finally buckle -
the sweeping brush?
Might I should be in the morrow of my dreams.
Yes - dreams. How can you not ask?
Into the battle we carry one another, knowing we will never win.
When death comes nigh for me - 'twas I who merely carried the mouth of bees.
Never more than a gesture?
With a kick in the ribs death awaits, I am impatient.
And he -
he will bare a medal upon his chest.
At night he will hear the echo of my last words - see my last breath on the mist - just over there - dancing in the crystal truth of a tear.
Lisa Sowards

Poem Of Life

or

Who Threw These Marbles Out There

The Earth a beautiful and unique
place full of mystery and intrigue
and different peoples who threw these
marbles out here. The sun, moon, earth
and 7 planets the brain its wiggly terminal
of knowledge what makes people think the
way they do, the water a mystical being in
itself the life force of all things. It moves
with emotion and power with its beauty and grace
the sun the most powerful entity of all how it
shines through us all to brighten our days.
Who threw these marbles out here.
Liz Harriton

"Her Name Is Cho Cho"

I am an old lady with senile ailment.
Please don't pity me!
I have the most precious pet.
My "Hearing Aid Dog" name Cho Cho.
She signals me when phone rings
a knock at door or smoke alarm activates.
How does she signal me?
Cho Cho taps my leg or hops on bed
swats my face to - "Wake up!
After feeding time she drops a
doggie biscuit at my feet
as if to say, "Thanks."
When talking on my special phone
She is quite possessive
Paws the cord, a silent hint, "Enough!"
Nighttime sleeping next to me
Curled on an old torn Jacket
That is her special private property.
My beloved Cho Cho. I am blessed.
Virginia Blair

To Be Free

To be free, oh...how I want to be free
Please let me go - I want to be free

"Freedom"
I've never known what that is
since I can remember I've been bound, stifled,
locked in a lonely cage
unable to grow,
to live

Many seasons have passed
always cold and grey
when is the sun going to break through
so I can see
so I can feel
the light of day

This prison I live in
so dark
so cold
will I ever walk
those streets of gold...
Lisa Gain

"A Matter Of Time"

Time to us is a lesson taught, as a
Poor old soul lays on a harlem's cot.
A cold blank daze contains dried last tears,
This once youthful glance has now succumbed to
years. And the voice within dwells no more,
For death has entered....yet...closed the door.
  Oh, yes it's just a matter of time,
That a flowering soul withers then leaves
Behind, in parting, woe such a sorrow bitter.
But...even youth is spared not, as a poor old
Soul lays on a harlem's cot. A lesson at whose
Expense is a lesson taught...
And in time, sad to say, a life forgot.
Kemberly Jo Duckett

Three Loves

Days and years, come and pass-forever,
  Some see joys in life - some - never.
   Nature, friends and life's endeavor,
    Three loves - we dare not sever.
Lyle McLeod

My Comfort Zone

Like Sealy, strong and supportive
Posture pleasing and positively pampering.
I understand the universal ugliness of urbanity
Which whips weathered wayfarers,
And repair a ripped rear or reduce its redness
By the beleaguered back of basketball's bounce
Tantalizing the toes of tennis tournaments.

Like Jordan jumping with justifiable jewels.
A fanatically frightening fountain of fortitude.
Coolly comforting, calmly controlling, crispy charging.
I indulge intensely into Ur ideal image I Am.
However hard the hill to hoe,
my mouth's member melts with memory of mountain-top moments with U.

Like Christmas itself,
We were born in the August of life relational mangered.
And my quiet quest is to make U as cozy with me as I am with U.

H. L. Patrick Davis

To Take A Bow

It seemed for a lifetime I had waited,
Prayed, fantasized, hoped, and anticipated.

For the day to come when all would hear,
The hail and acclamation from my peers.

I had imagined the scenario, as it would unfold,
And could feel their faces of praises to behold.

Then there I was, wearing a brand new tam, looking years younger than
my age,
And reciting my very, very best works, page by page.

The audience was hushed, I had their total attention,
Hearing only my verses, and the background music I have failed to mention.

Then I waited to hear their deafening applause,
Stone silence was it, and my heart took pause.

Soon came giggles, soft whisperings, and the flipping of a program,
Sweaty, awkward, and old I slumped and lost my tam.

Please tell me what do I do now? Please tell me what do I do now?
When from behind the curtain I heard..."Hey lady, just take a bow!"

Mary Kay Uraga

"A Tribute To Them"

First it was theirs, but it was taken.
Promises were made, but were forsaken.
First they were wild, but peaceful.
Now have been tamed, and they are ashamed.
Where have the gone to?
Out towards the blue?
Why did we harm our friends?
When we could have just made amends.
It would have been so easy.
Life could have been so calm and breezy.
We are the ones who should be blamed.
We are the ones who should be ashamed.

Sandy Willman

Untitled

Upon a rock a light house stood
Sending out light to ships at sea
They sailed from all parts
Of the planet earth
Knowing it would be there for eternity
They could not find their way alone
But had to depend on the light that shone
So they were able to travel far
By the light of the light house
And every star.

Letitia M. Solomon

When I Was Young

I climbed to the tops of trees
proudly wore cherry blossoms wreaths
thought I knew earth's spring—when I was young

I baked mud cakes, chased my summer rainbows
gathered winter's starlight in
held golden spires of sunrise—when I was young

But now that I have walked the stony steps
and marshes, dark and cold
waded ankle deep in soft, sweet clover

Welcomed winds both fierce and friendly
known miracles and moments
that hold onto forever

I've found a holy grace along the hallowed way
and thrill to spring that leaps within my heart
in ways that could not be—when I was young

Doris Patricia Hays Toppen

Fall Returns

...Fall returns.
Pumpkins, indian summer
Coolish nights, leaves rustling along the yards and in the driveways
Scare crows and harvest time
Ma's homemade jelly and turkeys baking in the kitchen
Sister getting excited about the season's different decorations
Bright colors-leaves, scarves, Pa's bright flannels, indian corn
and glowing pumpkins
Fall is again here
Football games with an apple afterwards
Kids running, jumping, always chattering
The last picnic before the snow flies
Politicians
Lovers walking in the park hand in hand
Bright nights with golden moons and tree branches reaching for the sky
Thoughts of Christmas with the tree and presents-
Snuggled in bed on a frosty night with a great book
It's fall-that's for sure!

Richard Scott O'Connor

A Very Special Patient

I heard a soul go to heaven today
Quietly and quickly she went on her way.
How can we measure her 86 years.
We knew not enough of her joys and her fears.
We really knew her for such a very short time,
But I'll say with pride that she was a patient of mine.
Her last five weeks were of pain without end,
She faced it with courage and faith in "Her Friend."
She had battled for years with a fatal disease
But her smile never faltered nor did she forget to say please.
I remember her saying last week with a grin,
"You're a nice girl, but this medicine is a sin."
To meet her was to like her, to care for her was a pleasure.
Because I knew in my heart here is one of God's treasures.
She was struggling for a breath when Jesus came by.
He took her hand in His and I heard her soul go by.
My tears then were selfish of this I am sure
As I knew for her illness there could be no cure.
I'll remember her example - at least I will try
To be ready as she was when Jesus stops by.

Pat Smith

A Tribute To "Onyx" (November 24, 1987-April 1, 1995)

There's a new patter of paw prints
quietly strolling up above,
they belong to my little girl, Onyx,
my special gift of love.

With a coat that's black as the still of night,
a touch of auburn reflecting the sky,
the demeanor of a Princess,
a gem that's treasured and prized.

Eyes that sparkle like moonbeams,
gleaming of a mahogany glaze,
attentive to the scope of her domain,
her wisdom - an intricate maze.

To all she shined in virtue,
willingly confided all her trust
for the delicacy of a gentle hand,
suppressing any action of rebuke.

And those of us now left behind
recalling the memories she brought,
knew from the moment we met her,
that her love would capture our hearts.

Patricia Wells

Perhaps

I sometimes have trouble with the word perhaps
Quite often it leads me into unusual traps.

Perhaps leaves a great deal of doubt with me
It must be a first cousin to the word maybe.

Today I wonder what the weather will be
Perhaps I'd better take a wrap with me.

I hope that these plans will work today
Perhaps I'd better find an alternate way.

I keep wondering if the market might collapse
My broker slyly smiled and said, "It might perhaps."

At Vegas I was talked into a game of craps
Do you think I can win? My friend said, "Perhaps."

Perhaps finds its way into so many schemes,
And quite frequently slips into my nightly dreams.

I keep trying to face life's problems like a man,
And with a little bit of help Lord! Perhaps I can.

Leonard J. Western

Life

Life
Radiating a smile of both innocence and tranquility
Being true to your ideals is the breath of life
Hushing a tear
And hiding your fears
Life
Growing in maturity
Then strengthening your morality
Being true to your ideals is the breath of life
Sharing the sorrow and the grief
The reprimand and the happiness
Life
Wishing for love, hope and peace
Admiring what is to come
Being true to your ideals is the breath of life
Cherishing good moments
Giving yourself time to reminisce
Life
Being true to your ideals is the breath of life

Liza Gonzalez

Untitled

I dream of the golden splendor of the sun as it casts its
rays upon the earth.
The long grass, windswept and restless, whispers across
the vast plains.
It is soft and gentle as it caresses my skin.
Absence of another sound, the silence is music to my ears and
a relief to all of my senses.
Autumn has once again begun.
The suns radiance helps to paint the foliage with such
brilliant colors.
The breeze brings with it the sweet smell of death.
Not saddening however; for after the thaw, comes the dawning
of re-creation: New Life more brilliant each time.

Krista Shaw

May You Always

May you always ride the rainbow,
  Reach every pot of gold,
  Smile brighter than the sunshine,
  Shake your fears - be strong and bold.

May you always blossom friendships,
  Catch every falling star,
  Emphasize togetherness,
  Spread love both near and far.

May you always chase your fantasies,
  Get caught up in your dreams,
  Let the shadows fall behind you;
  Not all is what it seems.

May you always show compassion,
  Laugh and cry and care,
  Share that special magic,
  Know I'm always there.

Millie Lindsay

I Am Love

I've tasted the wind
reached out for a star
crossed the waters both near and far

I've walked the desert
in the heat of the day
and chilled to the night
on the grounds were I lay

I've climbed the mountains
on my way to the sky
and kissed the clouds as they drifted by

I've gathered dust on my
feet from this old earth
and will never cease to wonder
of a human birth

And cry when I see the ruin of war
and to the needy I will open my door

By now you may have wondered
just who I am I'm not an angel nor am I a man
  I am love

William J. Zanoviak

Dr. Andrew Bragdon

Damsel in distress I was, until you gave me hope for a future.
Readiness to face any problems I may be having.
Always there for me when I needed answers.
New life you, and their others, have handed to me.
Dedication to helping other epileptics, such as myself.
Realist in you...not a visionary, such as myself.
Excellent bedside manners...something most doctors lack.
Wisdom of Solomon...you found the cause of my seizures,
   which other doctors couldn't do.
Big smile on your face, which always put me at ease.
Respectful of a patients wishes and opinions.
Always ready to listen to any questions I may have...and
   usually able to give me an answer, right there and then.
Great way of explaining things to me...in layman's terms.
Delightful personality...can always make me smile.
Optimism you have for pessimists...such as myself.
Never a hopeless or doubtful thought...always positive.
Thank you for my freedom!

Lisa-Marie Kinsman

Selfish Love

Visions blurred
real pain now
Oh how I thought no one was around
rough waters in a hold came rushing through the dam
Not knowing where to go but still they ran
What love could do is touch my hands
but everything strived for had all washed away
Now fate had to find its way
A selfish couple ran and looked around
than the water took them down
I said man, I wouldn't care
but I was here first before you were
Than out of the blue I saw your eyes
and we both dove in at the same time
though we tried and cried
We knew it was the Lords way
For selfishness had taken over their lives
And they met their fate
As the sun set sad in our hearts
We both looked and walked away

Kim Wickman

"Mother"

As you look back across the years,
recalling laughter and sometimes tears.
You feel the pain unlike no other...
the loss of your beloved mother.

She gave you life and taught you how,
to love the things that you love now
Her job here done, she's earned a break;
it's time for you, her lead to take.

And if you think, you'll come to see,
she's with you yet...In memory!
No longer bound by earth's constraints;
in heaven now, she ranks with saints.

Those things she loved are still here yet.
She taught you well, so don't forget...
that if there is a God above,
in his hands, now, she rests...In love!

Ken Moodyman

Mystery

The Radiance of your presence surrounds me, in the solitude of my
red rock aerie.
Angel voices carried gently on the breeze, echo the cries of the
human race.
Seated, gazing into infinity, soft purple grey mist languidly fills
the valley below, and
Dusks mystic light floods the ravine now obscured from my view.
Silence, permits me to hear whispered words borne on air,
And all God's creatures on the earth below, cry out the human
suffering, while humanly we stand in despair, not knowing, not see
seeing, not being, just here.
Our grief and confusion wraps endlessly on all we survey, as we
search for the light to guide our way to peaceful tomorrows.
I'm called to attention on each days journey, never knowing how
I've arrived in this space.
Now that you have my attention,
What is it you want me to know?

Stella Grove

January Evening

The light of day in night, a night to warm
   reflected in the moon, the glow, falling on the headlights
Warm for winter, a little too much old love on the radio
   ears remember what they said
Horns are blaring, so I'll move away...
   away to the quiet
Warm for winter, I shouldn't be sweating
   Yesterday plays again "I believe..." It ends.
I've found the place of moon beams, the dots appear on the sky
   start shining, start blinking
Connected they draw a picture
   She smiles in this one, at me, I don't know
At her, He can dream.
A little warm for winter,
   No chill to match the soul
Too many stars are flying,
   None to wish on at all.

Mark Beamen

A Thirty Something Single Women

Remnants of broken relationships stored deep in the hearts corner.
Reminders of different lives where everything had an order.
Routines marked the passing days temporarily filling up the void.
Creating a false sense of security.
Never realizing how much of me was destroyed.

Where will I get sex?
What will I do on Saturday night?
Who will be my Husband? Boyfriend? Date?
Why can't I find Mr. Right?

I think I will cut and dye my hair. Spend money until it hurts.
Eat a lot of chocolate. Read self-help books.
Analyze myself. Experience rebirth.

Ignore the ticking time clock, watching
Other women marry and have children.
Pretending that a single woman has a worthwhile life.
Living alone was always my dream.

I will hold my head up high never letting them see the pain.
Smile pretty and play a young woman's game.
Maybe I will win. Maybe hope I can sustain.

Linda Arvio

Perspective

A virile Hector strode into the room,
Resplendent in his uniform of war;
His Trojan helmet topped with flowing plume,
While in his hands his spear and shield he bore.

He only came to bid a fond farewell
To his young wife and his beloved son.
His gaze seemed fierce as on the two it fell,
So, Astyanax to Andronache did run.

But Hector then laid down the shield and spear,
And, smiling, took the helmet from his head;
And when his son beheld that face so dear,
He ran now to his father's side, instead.

And so it is with what we do not know;
We look upon a friend and see a foe.

Marilyn H. Parry

A Child's Imagination

I see the stars,
Resting upon the night's heavy palm,
To shine brightly, then fade away,
Before the sun's fingers touch the horizon.
I dream of being a star.

I hear the birds
Chirping gaily to the beautiful day's arrival,
Brushing the morning dew
With their soft, feathery wings.
I wish I were a bird.

I smell the roses,
Faint in the summer air.
Raindrops trickling down their pointed leaves
Like tiny spectrums dangling on a thread.
I wish I were a rose.

I dream of being any of these,
But I am not.
I am only a helpless human child,
With imagination as
My only weapon against life.

Kristi Leonard

Realities Of Age

Some years ago, while I still had my mate,
Retirement brought decisions regarding our fate.
"Should we this," or, "should we that" was the theme of our day...
Ideas that would help us as we traveled life's way.

We found that illness was a deciding factor.
To be, or NOT to be, in this world, an "actor".
Our decision was "yes"...there was no need to be
A drone on our friends...on our family.

Bare essentials were told, and not much more;
Days ahead would reveal what was "in store".
No need to burden our loved ones too soon.
Meantime, we'd plan our "trip to the moon."

Selling our home to a neighbor next door...
Remodelling our cottage, right on the shore
Of a lake, where we'd spent much of our time
Would be pleasant for us, and things turned out fine!

We lived there, in peace, for several more years.
Folks came to see us, including our "dears".
The minimal work, now...expenses as well,
Fit in so comfortably, 'til our time of "farewell".

Valerie A. Lange

Autumn Muse

Autumn came drifting in,
 Riding on the back of a summer wind.
Falling gently on the lawn
 With a hint of unsuspecting chill.

A woolly caterpillar crawls across the blacktop.
 Never knowing how close it came
To not reaching its destiny.
 It continues up the curb searching for its cold retreat.

I sit in the old porch swing,
 Wishing the quiet evening could linger on.
How quick is the closing,
 Of a gentle peaceful time.

Robert H. Thomas

The Ride

 Just like a bronco coming out of the shoot
Riding the wind for the thrill, not the loot
 Wild was fun, like a roller coaster ride
Taking life in, and all in stride
 Home was a "Thought", the road was the way
Doing the new, the street everyday
 So hold on to that horse but soon let go
For the world is a play ground
 But also a place to grow

Rheba Wadsworth

Dancing Upon The Mountains

Down the great mountains
roll tumbling stones of power.
Trees grow ever so strong.
Winds roar through rustling leaves,
dancing upon the mountains.

Massive trees scattered one by one,
shed shadows upon the earth's ground;
scarred in all their natural beauty
jagged and standing proud.
Weeping weeds dancing all around.

The morning sun brings a glorious light
from the heavens above.
Children laughing, playing, singing and chanting.
Mothers caring, praising, cleaning and cooking.
Fathers working, thinking, eating and sleeping.

Sooner than we think,
stars, moon and darkness shower down upon us.
Yet, in our minds we can still recall the morning light.
What more do you think?

Lori Guinn

Untitled

 Our garden is full of flowers; fenced with shrubs, lilacs and
roses. It is part of the Garden of Eden; it has bright light. We
were born and brought up in Bloudan; Bloudan, our father and
mother, has enough harvest and fruit for everyone. In Bloudan
we live like brothers and sisters in peace.

 On the top of your mountain we build the castles and the
beautiful buildings. The gentle breeze smells like perfume and
incense. Wherever you go you will never find better and higher
than Bloudan. All the gentle and the sweet talk, the beauty, the
pride, the dignity; The songs we are singing on her beauty.

People love each other and they live in harmony.

God gave all beautiful things and completed our beloved town Bloudan.
 God bless and save Bloudan

Nasif E. Dehabey

604

Fourteen

My daughter wades through piles of
rumpled flannels
discarded plumage

Layered, even armored
in black and grays
silvered chains

Thank God there is no body piercing

Gone...
the fuzzy pinks
my princess in a rhinestone tiara
waving a sparkling wand

Gone...
the tiny spirit
perched in her room of bunnies and ponies
hearts and lavender

Now, the CD's are spinning
the bass throbbing
her room a cavern of posters and incense

Waiting.. for the passage
When the bunnies reappear
　　　Robin H. Wintz

Lifetimes

In another time we were together
Running through the secret passages
of castles
Laughing like girls at the tricks we'd play
on others

In another time we were torn apart
Learning the lessons in life that make us different
Experiencing the hurts that make us smart

In another time we were lost
Searching for shelter in clouds of smoke
that blew away
Catering our feelings and love to people,
no matter the cost

In this time we are reunited
A little beat up and confused,
yet still able to feel
Reassuring each other that all is okay,
and in our own ways, will remain
"sighted"

　　　Lisa Brune

World Gone Wrong

People runnin' 'round, as fast as they can go
　Rushing to their destinations, going with the flow.
So bogged down with worthless longings,
　Things to make their lives' complete
Missing the meaning for their being,
　As they march along to their own beat.
"One more dollar", "one more meeting",
　We hear the people say. . .
All the while their days are fleeting. . .Vanishing away.

"What is the point?", we all must ask
　Before our time runs out
Or truly, our lives will be a waste,
　Of this, there is no doubt.
Take this moment, this one now—
　for it could be your last—
And seek the Lover of your soul,
　Before this time is past.
For close by waits the Answer you've searched for
　Your whole lifelong,
And you will find your one true home— beyond this world gone wrong

　　　Rae Punzel

Untitled

What is freedom?
Said a voice to me from way,
way up high in a tree.
"Come down from there this instant!," I said,
then quickly added.
"Who said you could go up there?"
Suddenly out ran a squirrel
then out flew a bird
but out from that tree
came not another word.
Then as I turned and walked away
I still managed to hear the voice say.
This tree you see it does not belong to you
it belongs to the free.
　　　Marius Jan Jaskowski

One Day In The Life Of....

It is very early in the morning just starting to come light and the
sand is cold, and hard-packed under my naked feet. The gossamer veils
of mist drift silently among the still sleeping sand dunes, and it is
quiet, so very, very quiet! Even the waves have quietened the ripples
as they foam gently up on to the beach and as gently are sucked back
into the waiting ocean.

Suddenly, as with the fanfare of a thousand golden trumpets heralding
the new day, the sky turns from pale to deepest gold, from pale pink
to a flaming glorious red.

What a gift I have been given - a whole, new, untouched day - with
nothing at all yet imprinted upon it - Tabula Rasa - to do with as I
will, for good or evil. What a priceless gift. And when it is all
over and these blazing, triumphant, trumpets are sounding the coming
of evening in the western sky, nothing I have done that day, committed
or omitted, can be changed. Forever, that day which has come and is
now going and will never until after eternity come again, cannot
be changed by a single word or deed, after it is gone.

Just one day - but of such is life made: Seconds, minutes, hours and
days, one by one, one at a time, inexorably they grow in their glory
from dawn 'til dusk until they finally fade away forever. Gone!

　　　Q. Eileen Ward

Good-Bye Uncle Johnny

I tread slowly along the water's edge.
Sand sifts silently between my toes,
releasing its tenacious hold on the beach,
a poignant reminder of life's changes,
the beginnings and the endings.

Just as the ocean endlessly massages the beach,
your spirit will remain in my heart
all my days and beyond.
Even now, I see you strolling the sandy beaches,
sun glinting off your back,
as you patiently seek the perfect or unusual shell.

Just as the sea gently plucks grains of sand from the shore,
tears escape my eyes, slowly rolling down my cheeks.
I miss your wink and mischievous grin,
your stories of life in Mexico,
your generous warmth and sense of humor.
I miss your love
and I miss not having the chance to say,
"Good-bye, Uncle Johnny. I love you."

　　　Sherry Settle

Feather!

One day I looked up in the sky, and
saw a single feather, it gently passed
among the trees, and landed on the meadow.
I could not help but wonder why, this feather
blew astray, and then I heard the masters
voice, a whisper and a gentle breath away.
He said when the weather gets too hot, there
must be time for change, a little pruning here,
and a little preening there, causes life to break
forth in the chain.
So blow little feather, blow as you wish, to a
place that's called heaven, that no one should miss.
And here's a small reminisce, so that you could see,
I gave to you that feather, so you would come to me.

Kathryn J. Millard

Beyond Tomorrow

Beyond tomorrow peek into joy
Scan universe atlas thought employ

Day by day shadow in sun stride
across pathway by one's side

Blessings downfall - become shadow neat
off tree bough through meadow streak

Today earthling think high above cloud
Rainbow arc pot of gold proud

Hope is suncast after storm blast
Journey forward - earth burden behind at last

Experience in mind - take morning's hand
Let calm one's pathway on land

Rest in peace of gentle night dark
Night fall dew to await morn spark

Fresh day with new element shadow land
Move beside one with new plan

Beyond tomorrow promised land solar sigh
For one's soul is written plan solar high

J. Rose Vetter

As Is

Know me as I really am is all I ask of you.
See me as I truly exist; this is done by few.

I do not aim to look better than I am in your eyes.
So don't look too highly on me and my faults disguise.

Accept my weaknesses, one and all, but you needn't like them.
Give me your strength when I need it; don't ask 'why?' Ask, 'when?'

Praise my virtues no matter how small they seem to you.
I'll accept your praise humbly and strive to return it too.

Judge me not by words of others, but let me prove to you
that every fiber of my being seeks only what is true.

Don't think you know how I feel, ask and I will tell.
Don't think you thought you knew or you'll never know me well.

Don't change me to a pattern of living that isn't me.
I want to be as I am, as I exist; not what should be.

I am not asking to be loved, but only to be known.
Need you be shown that I am what I am alone?

Here I am, I want to cry. This is me - she lives
Only as one, always the same and in the end "As is".

Lois Wegner

The Boy

He sits in his chair awkwardly watching,
seeing all movements, hearing every word.
His hair, the color of soft see-through blond,
lays neatly combed and parted to the side.
His eyes are a handsome, electric blue,
even a deeper blue than his father's.
His cheeks are still as soft as the first day;
cheeks everyone enjoys loving and kissing.
He has his own laugh and will rarely cry,
except when dad leaves him with the sitter.
Strong enough to stand, but he still can't walk,
going by Andrew Michael; Blake Andrew,
the names of my unborn, unconceived son,
this little boy I see in all my dreams.

Robert D. Edwards

Untitled

Sometimes our earthly burdens
seem more than we can bear.
We must always remember
how much our Heavenly Father cares.

He feels the pain and agony
that we are going through.
He carried that pain to Calvary,
as He died for me and you.

He sees every tear as it
trickles down our face.
He reaches down His mighty hand
our tears to erase.

So I ask You Heavenly Father, for
strength and comfort for each new day.
For a smile or a kind word to share with another,
who may be hurting as they pass my way.

Father, I give You honor and glory
in this trial that's come my way.
May some good come from this,
to someone's life, I pray.

Patricia Anne Copsey

Rainbow's And Such

Pretty, pretty rainbow up in the sky.
Seems I could touch you if I could but fly.
Pretty colors, all in a row,
God seems to have them lined up just so.

Pretty, pretty butterfly go as you will.
It seems you are never still.
Pretty butterfly gliding through the air,
my you certainly have a flair.

Pretty, pretty Mr. Robin way up in the tree,
right there where you're supposed to be.
With a little red vest looking so proud,
five little birdies chirping so loud.

These help to from the beauty of the earth
made by God not man.
All things bright and beautiful were
made by His hand.
All these things come from above,
with the promise of our dear Savior's love.

Maggie Stevens

"Secret Retreat"

Twittering birds near a mountain stream
Serenading tiny forest inhabitants unseen
Sunlight reflected on strewn dappled leaves
Creating a serene and wondrous scene

The muted murmur of an echo
Emanating from a mountain waterfall
Cascading jeweled tinged tears of water
Upon the barrier of a stone wall

A carpet of moss caressing tired feet
In this wonderful idyllic retreat
Nestled close by reaching up the sky
A circle of pines in beauty did vie

This sylvan glade in the forest deep
Knows the secret of why I weep
Daisies nestle in this hidden dell
Rest assured that daisies will not tell

Kathleen R. Jazwienski

"There Really Is Love After Abuse"

There are three kinds of abuse in relationships today, mental,
  sexual, and physical,
They are all real, they all can kill, and none are phony or mythical.
When you've gone through all three for a number of years,
The day comes when you have to escape, using all your courage and
  hiding all the fears.
It's been seven years since escaping from hell, for which there are regrets,
You wonder if the scars will ever heal, if you will get back your self
  confidence, and self respect.
After a while you build a wall around yourself, not letting anyone near,
You are safe and alone, always holding in the past fears.
Then one day comes when you least expect it,
You meet a man who is sweet, caring, and treats you with respect.
It's a God send to meet someone who accepts you for you are and
  understands,
A rare quality in today's world to find someone who is a true gentleman.
After all the years of being treated like a nothing and used,
You keep pinching yourself when you realize there really is love after abuse.

Patty Nichols

Phantom Daughter

Only I can enter the room through a doorway
  shaped in your image
    Inside sits the kaleidoscope
      that now contains you

Scraps and sounds that no longer belong to the outside world
  Feelings
    stacked neatly
      and not so neatly
        Some serious and silent, some still laughing

You were a Baking Powder Twin with porcelain skin
  You were beautiful, delightful
    always laughing
  Your feet were perpetually moving
    busy late

I never dreamt that you could evaporate
  leaving a chalk outline
    etched so deeply inside me
  The lines ooze pleasure
    on occasion
  more often the substance is phantom child pain

Patsy Dorrell Dawson

A Mother's Cry

Mother cries: At the pain of birth
She cries: When her child is sick or hurt
She cries: When they go to school
She cries: When they break her Golden Rules
She cries: For joy she is so proud
She cries: At the mistakes they make
Mother cries: When her child is grown up
She cries: When she sees them go away
She cries: Hoping they're not in harm's way
She cries: When they're from her protecting arms
She cries: When they forget to come around
She cries: Wondering if they're alright
She cries: As the years roll on by
Oh! Will the child cry after the Mother is gone?

Sarah Altice Cassell

The Man And The Wren

One night when a wren was upon her nest,
She happened to look down and saw a man at rest
She thought and thought and tried to figure why
For she knew not this man nor could he fly.

Did he walk or run only to fall,
Was he lost or hurt from chasing a call
So she chirped and chirped to awake his sleep
Looked down at his place that seemed very deep.

All of a sudden he sat up and said,
Thank you Mrs. Wren for I have mistaken my bed,
Now I am on my way the night is late
And for you Mrs. Wren I shall open the gate.

Wayne A. Smith

My Mother, My Friend

I miss my Mother, I miss my friend,
She is gone,
I am never to see her again.

So many missed chances, too many days gone,
Some filled with beauty,
Some when I was wrong.

I enjoyed her;
Her warmth; Her comfort;

I'll remember our laughter;
Her confidence in me.

She gave me life, she gave me love,
I miss my Mother,
I miss my friend.

Patricia Fallis Thorn

The Birth Of The Laurah Elizabeth

The S.S. Cyprys was your maiden mother's name
She mated with the Mighty Monarch
  Hence the Laurah Elizabeth came
Although they were but two ships passing in the night
  Nothing more could they be
Yet they produced a Laurah Elizabeth
  Out of their passionate sea
Even though the S.S. Cyprys and the Mighty Monarch
Sail no more
  Long sail the Laurah Elizabeth
They produced in years before.

Theresa Key

My Favorite Pal

Baby is a small hamster all tan and white,
She may be a rodent, but still very bright.
Has a cute little nose with eyes that are black,
Friendliness or shyness she does not lack.
This animal likes to be in the grass outside,
I know it would drown in the ocean tide.
She listens and listens and doesn't make a sound,
Plays in the wheel which goes round and round.
She sleeps in the morning and is up at night,
Boy! Sometimes she is quite a sight.
And stays in a cage most of the day,
By night she is frisky and ready to play.
Constantly trying her hardest to get to the floor,
Watch out! Or she'll be out the door.
In September Baby could enter a hamster race,
Most definitely win with her quick pace.
If you were lucky, you'd have one too,
Then you would never be blue.
I love this Baby more and more every day,
I guess this is all I have to say.

Theresa M. Stallone

Mother's Wisdom

"A buttermilk sky,"
she observes with a sigh
as we watch the late sunlight
watercolor the cloud furrows.

Soft, but weathered hands
testify to her stewardship of the land,
as she expertly peels the skin from 'round an apple
in a single curling ringlet.

The same hands firm the fertile garden soil
over another seed,
and relieve the moist, warm earth
from the clutches of yet another weed.

Simple observations and appreciations
she passes on to her grandchildren and daughters.
By gentle advice, examples, and simple guidance
she teaches them to calm rough waters.

Without being asked or told,
she continues to care for young and old.
And as her children grow,
in many ways they need her so.

Karen Sigl

My Pet Is The Best Because

She meeteth me at the doorway.
She waggeth her little tail.
She sitteth beside me as I read my daily mail.
If I want to talk, she listens well.
If it's a secret, she won't tell.
She's a ray of sunshine for my golden years.
She's there to cheer me if I feel like tears.
The friendship that we share, is plain for all to see.
My dog shows the world that she belongs to me.

Lillian Nordman

Late

There I sat alone and scared
So afraid he didn't care
As time went by I started to cry
Then he came walking by
He gave me a rose and asked for a toast
I guess I was wrong it just seemed so long
I hold him so dearly to my heart
And when he's not there I fall apart.

Kimberly Putzer

Dried Roses

Scarlet turned to maroon
  she was arranging a bunch
    of dried roses in a vase.
"Throw them away," he kissed her hand
  "they are dead. I'll give you another
    bouquet."
"No, they are not dead,
  they are only dried."
"When they wither, they are dying
  and when they are dried
    they are dead."
"No — when they wither, they are transforming
  and when they are dried
    they are transformed.
A rose is dried,
  but it's still a rose
    still a rose, still a rose.
It's transcended to eternity
  above life and beyond death."

Wang Wei

"Mothers-In-Laws"

Now a mother knows that after her daughters marriage
She will soon return pushing a rubber-tired baby carriage.
Now a mother knows that after her son leaves the warm nest
She has already seen, and has known his inadvertent best.

A bride can call her mother for any number of minor things.
But if a groom calls his mother he's tied to her apron strings.
A brides' mother offers advice: that's considered very nice.
A groom's mother is butting in: she has committed a mortal sin.

There is a policy every young couple simply must obey.
From his folks you must stay far, very far away.
If this letter painfully stabs your heart!
Remember this....it's not too late for a brand new start!

Katie Manna

To Stasia Ousley

My grandmother is very special to me,
She's all you'd want a grandmother to be,
Kind and gentle, and full of love,
For her I thank God above.

Twelve kids she and Grandpa birthed and raised,
For that alone she should be praised.
They never had a lot, and at times things were rough,
But they made it through, their love was enough.

Although years ago, Grandpa passed away,
I know when he looks down, he's proud of her today.
She's very special lady, one of a kind.
And I'm proud to say she is a grandmother of mine.

Whenever you need someone, she's always there,
To lend a hand or just let you know she cares.
Whether the role be a mother or grandma,
In all of our hearts, she is the best of all!

Susan Ousley

The Tree

Aged with wisdom
Scarred with the past

Future rushes upon it
Never more will the tree see its home

Technology is its death
Industrial growth is its grave digger

One last stand
Never more will the world see its beauty.

Kristi G. Evans

608

My Mom

She's intelligent, knowledgeable and wise
She's expert, clever and skillful ... MY MOM.

She's exhilarating, inspiring and heartening
She's dedicated, focused and devoted ... MY MOM.

She's energy, strength and vigor
She's deliberate, considerate and thoughtful ... MY MOM.

She's candid, open and sincere
She's upfront, honest and truthful ... MY MOM.

She's shy, modest and humble
She's kind, merciful and gracious .. MY MOM.

She's comic, happy and witty
She's delightful, joyful and charming ... MY MOM.

She's beautiful, graceful and elegant
She's radiant, bright and shinning ... MY MOM.

She's joyful, glad and happy
She's appeasing, calming and peaceful ... MY MOM.

She's caring, kind and loving
There's no other person in the world like ... MY MOM.

Richard Ur

Looking Ahead

When I never again see the sunrise
 shining on shimmering seas
Nor the birds on the wings, or hear them sing
 as they nest in the nearby trees
When I never again see the moon or stars
 as they brighten up the night
Or feel the glow of the warming sun
 as it gives us life and light
When I never again see the flowers bloom
 or the garden's great delight
Or never again hear the patter of rain
 or hear the wind in the night
When I never again see the sunset
 or feel the evening breeze
When the Lord says "come" and it, is time to go
 I'll relinquish it all as a dream
He has prepared a far lovelier place
 in the realm of eternity
And I know He is waiting to welcome me there
 what a wonderful time that will be

Ruby Bryant

Ways To Peace

Jesus worked with the poor countries
 showing us the way.
We should put forth efforts to assist
 the homeless in our land.
It was Jesus who loved the unlovable with
 understanding and peace.
We, too should follow in HIS WAY so that
 hatred and war will cease.
Frequently, we can use our talents in the
 works of art,
To show that we love other nations with all of
 our hearts.
With all the many sounds from our music and songs,
We can express our thoughts of love what will last
 for long.
And some day Jesus will come and Joyfully Say,
 "Well Done My Faithful Ones."

Mary Rose Shoemaker

Shroud

Struggling free from this sticky mesh
Shredded strands cling in my hair
I wet my lips and taste the sting
Of acetate and something clear
My arms hang long from such wild trial
My chest is heavy to suck this air
Beads of sweat dry on my brow
And in my heart, that's silent there

What is this darkened, loving place
With whom I share such restfulness
Of stars and wondrous, blackness wide
This mother's womb; this faceless shrine
Many before me have traveled here
And many yet will travel still
They stood and stand on this bare hill
Plateau of longing and dreams fulfilled
Trinity:
Love, Cover and Benevolent Smile
Shroud their new guest
In most peaceful quiet

for awhile.

Susan J. Rowland

Those Golden Years

As we grow older, year after year
Signs of good health do disappear.
Aches and pains find their way
To ruin an otherwise perfect day.

Which goes first, teeth or hair?
At least these we can repair.
Wear false teeth and perhaps a wig.
Now then, don't we feel big!

Of course, we cannot see as well
Cataracts are starting to grow and dwell.
The voices we hear are not as loud.
We'd wear a hearing aide if we weren't so proud.

One more thing, we'll have to admit.
We're not exactly physically fit.
Additional pounds have been added too.
Somehow, right out of the blue.

If you think we're complaining, you're very wrong
'Cause even though we're not as strong
We live life to the fullest, and so it appears
We do what we can in those "Golden Years".

Maxine McNeil

Kirsti's Smile

As I stand here and watch my precious, little one sleep.
So many thoughts rush into my mind and I begin to weep.
I'd like to keep her here resting all comfortable and warm.
In the safety of her bed, nothing can cause her harm.
The nightmares of her illness are never far away.
For a healthier tomorrow each night we always pray.
Each day we wake to find the sunlight shining in.
Just as the sun rises, we are sure to see her smiling face again.
To see her smile, you'd never know the horrors she has faced.
But with a smile, she just goes on as if they've been erased.
I watch her laughing and singing as she runs to play.
I've tried to bring her comfort while the doctors have their way.
Don't ask me how I bear the pain, or what gets me through.
Just look into those smiling eyes and forget your problems too.

Sondra Baiel

Reservations Before And After The Climax Of The Sunset Limited

Amtrak trains: Days no more at Union Stations?
Silver sails along silver rails?

Come along and ride these trains.
Listen to the black pullman porters whistling "Shuffle off to Buffalo."

Sing with them "Wabash Cannonball," "Chattanooga Choo-Choo,"
"Midnight Special," "Orange Blossom Special," "Sixteen Tons," as
red sunsets close another day for silver sails along silver rails.

Night draws its ruffled curtain.
It starts to rain.
A man in the diner
beats his guitar
to
pitter
patter.

All engine wheels must be extinct! Tons have broken arrows!
At a thunderous, stoic tongue, Burton Crowtree asked Clayton, his
Cherokee son! "Why can't the government fix the tracks?" "Aren't they
steal American hells with loved ones steel locked in their Lucifered jails?"

Thomas R. Shoemake

Poem Of Proposal

It's been quite awhile dear, quite too long
Since a poem from me came your way.
So I know you won't mind if, here and now,
I recite this one to you today.

Filled with soft thoughts of you...love for you
And plans for us as a couple to be.
Neither too plain nor fancy these words of mine,
I guess you could say they're just like me.

Nearly five years have passed so quickly by
And I'll remember always our first slow dance.
Half of those years you've patiently waited
For me to be willing to take another chance.

But when two people love and care as much
As you and I do for each other,
There's no sense at all in living apart...
And no reasons to look for another.

So, with this poem of proposal just read to you
That nerves would not permit me to memorize...
I ask you now, love of my life,
Will you marry me and forever share our lives?

Reed Kays

The Lost Smile

It was kindergarten picture time,
So proudly, did I dress my son!
In a little white shirt and sweater vest
of grey and wine,
Navy pants and neat bow tie.
No one could top this little guy!
Off he went as sparkling as the sun,
What a very special day,
We would never forget this one!
Finally it was the day for the pictures
to arrive,
We could hardly wait to see his little
face come alive.
What a perfect picture of my son, Paul,
Just one little thing,
There was no smile at all!
When I asked why he didn't smile,
His reply was really worthwhile!
I did smile, Mom, he said most sincere,
But, the man just didn't put it there!

Patricia Kiser

Eternal Seconds

The mosaic with all its hues
Sits before me, inviting.
My fingers slide along the smooth surface,
The spirits enter...

Blue. For the water.
The cool splashing upon my skin,
The love envelopes me once again.
my hand is held.

Blue. For the sky.
The breeze catches my voice,
Carrying it to a mountain.
And my hand is warm.

The flowers intoxicate us,
The waters rhythm pulls at our eyes.
The breeze pulls, it's pulling me away...no..no..
My hand is frozen and white once again.

I glance about the room.
The stained glass matches the flowers.
I wipe the tears from my eyes,
And I go to say good-bye to the past.

Naomi Wender

Met My Match

Young boy ice skating, strong as an ox,
Skating down center ice, through block after block.
Stick held tightly close to his chest,
Puck to the net, he was at his best.
Team circling round him, patting his back,
Nice goal, go take a break, let us have a crack.
Smiling broadly, gliding back to the bench,
Hopping over the boards, teeth somewhat clenched.
We're in the third period, twenty seconds to go,
Putting ox on the ice, it was time for a show.
Hitting him hard to do him some harm,
The buzzer rang, I shook his hand, he had just one arm.

Lois Gregg

A Moment Ago

A moment ago, looked in on my son,
sleeping, the sins of the day
washed away with the evening bath
his face bathed in angelic glow

Marvelled at the rising of innocence
to the surface of the face
released by the honesty of truthful sleep

Beauty in a virgin mind
his mind awash in the realm of dreams
mirrored above on the calm waters of his countenance

Fragile little butterfly,
the transition you must make
is not a pretty one
but make it you must
so that someday

A moment in the future
you may stand here
looking down on your own son's purity
and grieve for
the loss of your own

H. Bruce Logsdon

The Miracle Of Nature

When autumn's leaves
Slide down their banisters of air
And land upon the carpet
Of their living room,
They then invite the sun
Through the canopy of their home
To caress the fertile soil they made below;
To give incentive to the seeds
That lie dormant in the mold
That they may thrust their way
Out of the damp and leafy womb
For all the world
To wonder and behold
As they embrace
Their day of glory in full bloom.

Rupert James Herrick

Time

Time,
Slowly ticking by,
It seems so long ago when the sun shined;

Rain,
Like tears,
Fall from the sky,
And clouds drift slowly by;

One day,
The sun will shine,
The rain will dry,
And the clouds will disappear;

Everything happens in time.

Stacy Snukis

These Arms

These arms once held you close,
So close to my heart.

These arms encircled you with comfort,
When you were frightened, or lonely, or hurt.

And these arms picked you up
When you slipped in your dance.

These arms learned to stretch,
As your circle ever widened.

You ran into these arms less often.

But once in a while these arms,
Would catch you as you danced by.

Then one day these arms stretched so far,
They snapped.

These arms watched in disbelief,
As you danced away.

These broken arms tried to stretch ever further,
In a vain attempt to catch you.

Now these arms are empty,
But this heart is still full.

And these arms are learning to wait.

Susie Hamilton

My Sweet Puppy Weezer

My little angel,
so full of life.
Playing and jumping,
without thinking twice.
The mistake he made,
took on too much,
died shortly there after.
Our hearts he's stolen,
his love taken away.
The memories will stay,
together we'll be another day.
There will always be a place in my heart.
For my cute little puppy,
with no time to start.

Melissa Himschoot

The Shade Of Night

I breathe in time to the drops of rain.
So gently they touch, yet I feel pain.
Nowhere to hide. There's no place for shelter.
I'm trapped outside, in summer, in swelter.

There is no sun where I am standing.
I run through darkness, my lungs expanding.
Quicker and quicker the rain drops fall.
No time for rest. No time to crawl.

Grim Reaper laughing. He whispers my name.
He's dominated wild animals too fierce to tame.
Sweat pours out my body. There's no more salt to yield.
Realizing He's been defeated, before me Grim Reaper kneeled.

A gift of admiration, He bestowed upon me a key.
It unlocked a door. I'm still outside, but now I'm able to see.
I stand in its threshold not knowing what to do.
Ominous clouds scream above me. The sun is breaking through.

I breath in time to the drops of rain.
So gently they touch, yet I feel pain...

Stephen McCarney

Lady In Waiting

Eyes bloodshot; nose dripping; what do we care?
So what if the sheen has gone out of her hair!

Zipper at "half-mast"; nothing that fits;
Seems that go popping whenever she sits!

Digestion queasy; Dill pickles at night:
And a tendency sometimes to look for a fight!

Provocative; precious; So tender, appealing!
Dear little girl to whom love is revealing

Creation; fulfillment; self-immolation;
The blessing - The heartaches - the whole of creation!

Eyes bloodshot! nose dripping; what do we care;
The Madonna-like aura she sheds everywhere

Is a beauty of Soul that envelops her being.
This is the whole of her—this what we're seeing.

Radiance; Loveliness; sweet ecstasy;
Our dear little daughter! A MOTHER TO BE!

Peg Schomer

611

This Disease

I have so much to live for.
So, why can't I just live?
I'm really only existing.
There's so much more I want to give.

I'm not the deceitful person,
hat this disease has make me become.
I'm trapped inside my own mind.
And this disease has become my friend.

Sometimes I pretend that I am fine.
And life is really, just grand!
Then reality stares me in the face.
And this disease gets what it demands.

Anorexia Nervosa is the disease I'm referring
It has successfully taken over my life.
My relief comes, when I sleep at night.
And this disease, each day, I'll fight.

Lori Rodgers

Barbara Elaine

Lips that taste of candy cane.
So young to spun the bottle game.
Summer hay rides with my flame.

On through school our love stayed the same.
Playing in the hay, moon lite window pane,
A kiss in the dark was are aim.

Us sixteen and far from being tame.
You're parents now leaving, your boarding the train.
We hold each other; I kiss you again.
I care not who looks; I am not ashamed.

In the years that past the letters still came.
Our love was still strong; your images etch in my brain.

School now over, to love and fame.
A ring for your finger; the telephone rang.
Your mother crying. My heart went still to hear your name.

She lies there so still; Pneumonia was to blame.
Her eyes last closed; Her heart is cold, Mine aflame.
My eternal life you claim,
Her lips still tasted of candy cane,
Barbara Elaine...

Ronald Brissette

Illusions of Grandeur

Illusions of Grandeur?
Soft and gentle,
  were the kisses.
When our eyes would meet from across a distance,
  were the smiles.
The strength of your manhood,
  were the embraces.
The quiet, peaceful times we spent together,
  were spoken words essential?
Illusions of grandeur?

Ruth A. Glanzman

Apart

  You've abandoned my soul and so I must prevail against the sorrow that is in me.
  But this task will not be easy, because my desire and love is so strong for you. I need to sort out my confusion and start realizing that we are drifting apart.
  We made or mistakes and then paid for them. Now we're not together.
  I die inside thinking that maybe we don't have a chance again. I sit and listen for the phone to ring to hear your voice tell me you want us to be together again. But will that ever be possible?

Michelle Harper

Quiet Season

Through glowing wreaths of frosted pane,
soft moonlight sleeps upon the floor;
While shadows lie on winter's plane,
as night wind sings outside my door;
The silent woods in darkness hide,
with rising smoke against the sky;
To untouched snow the wedded bride,
an owl sounds out loud its cry;
Soon into sleep I'm falling fast,
I softly lie upon the bed;
These stories told of winters past,
now dancing round inside my head.

Neil Bergstrom

Echoes

The willow branch low over the pond spoke to the rising mist,
  softly.
"Where are you going now so early as the sun and the moon pass
  in their flight?"
Answering as it rose:
"We are the cries, the pleas, the secrets, the whispers, the joys, the tears,
Of innocent young hearts.
We come always now when night and day mingle -
To give the young maidens once more their voices,
Who stood on the cliff, looked down to the pond and exposed
  their souls - to it - their trusted friend."
So the willow branch strained, to hear the souls utterance.
A myriad of voices, spanning hundreds of years.
Some asking questions, some giving answers, some shouting,
  some merely a tear.
All confiding.
All regardless of time -
Trying to discover the Truth of Living.

Leah Moore

Winds Of Age

She was a shining light, unlike any other,
Some called her friend, I called her Mother.

She taught me love, by loving me.
She taught me faith, she believed in me.

She gave me wings, she set me free,
All the while, she prayed for me.

She taught me bravery, to fight for what's right,
To know that darkness is followed by light.
Our Heavenly Father recently called her home,
I was told I have cancer - I feel so alone.

The night is endless, I'm filled with despair,
Can anyone hear me? Does anyone care?

Like the sun, she was my warmth and light,
My strength and comfort, both day and night.

Darkness has come, the sun has gone down,
The winds of age have left no sound.

Peace comes to me - at last I can say,
At the end of life's journey, I'll see her someday.

Mary Ann McCormick

Without A Clue

The world we live in is hard and cruel,
The blade of life is dual,
There is a constant fight for power and fuel,
but why me who feels like the mule?
Each day I wake, I wake in a daze,
Each day I wonder, I wonder what happened to past days,
Each day is clouded with haze,
but each day I fight through the walls of my maze!

Paul M. Cicero

Elusive Crappie

Some call them paper mouth,
Some just say crappie.
All fisherman know this sly critter.
They're well known among the waters,
The elusive crappie.

They come quickly in the later afternoon,
As the sun is setting;
While the water is warmed before evening.

Swiftly they come to nab the little minnows,
Swimming free and easy near the shore.
And in a matter of minutes, they leave as
Quickly as they came. They are no more.
Where they hide in the day, no one knows.
Very few will be caught by chance,
In the bright of day.
And not as often as we pray.

The elusive crappie will remain a mystery,
While fisherman scratch their heads,
Wondering where have they gone,
The elusive crappie.
        Nancy M. Piekarski

Nature

There is much more to nature than what it seems,
some people see
animals, hills and trees.
But like I said, there is much more.
If you're in the country, it's out of your own front door.
It's peaceful, no pollution and no worries, you see,
you can think about life under the shade of a tree.
Let your bad times wash away as you dip into a lake.
When you are in nature there is no mistake.
Just like I said there is much more than it seems,
Now I bet you think there is more than
animals, hills and trees.
        Tina Maria Cofer

I Am A Flower

I am a flower in a meadow though no one
speaks my name, I watch the days come and
go but my life remains the same. On days
of sun, I stand erect, my beauty all do see,
on days of rain, I'm slightly bent, no one
will notice me. I watch my pedals fall
before me as the seasons they do change.
I am no longer a beautiful flower and no
one knows my name, my soul is filled with
sorrow, my thoughts become so dim, then
someone picks me up, because they know
what's within, As I stood erect, never did
they see, they knew I needed love and was
full of beauty. I've returned to myself,
as he who helped me knows, I am a
flower, a beautiful flower, I am a
bright red rose.
        Stephanie Wisecup

Peace

Let there be peace within our country.
Take away the hatred that fills our land of freedom.
Let us dare to cross our bridges and travel through our tunnels.
Still the noise of bombs bursting within our buildings.
Clear the smoke of the arson's match.
Stop the flow of blood in our streets.
Silence the wailing child.
Comfort the grieving parents.
Let us turn hatred into love and work together to bring peace
To all.
        Lois A. Pratte

Our Misty Lee

Those August days around the pool,
    Splashing and giggling all the while;
You peeking out to watch the fun,
    Not able to join—But we could.

Bicycle rides around the block,
    Roller skates up and down the drive;
A chair on wheels to take your ride,
    Not able to play—But we could.

Jumping the back fence everyday,
    Running in and out the screen door;
Air through a tube to help you breathe,
    Couldn't go outside—But we could.

That fall afternoon a friend came to call,
    But we were all scattered in the wind;
His coming was quiet and unannounced,
    Couldn't hear him knocking—But you could.
        Patricia A. Conley

Falling Forty-Five Stories Without A Parachute

Have you ever seen the inside of a cloud, or felt the morning dew
squish between your toes, or are you to busy in your tower of glass
and power to acknowledge the little things in life; the beat of a new
baby's heart, thump, thump, thump, thump, the rhythm of life, the
music of history. Can't you bring yourself down from your high chair
without falling to the floor in a pool of flesh, bones and bad karma?
The humming bird she swoops by without as much as a good-bye kiss, or
see you again sometime. Do you feel like this? Like the honey suckle
that is raped of its glory, of its essence, taken from it by a swifter
kite. The wheels of the wagon go 'round and 'round, but no one is at
the reins. The horses, they pull dead weight, and yet nobody thanks
them for bringing it home: Much like the candle that burns and gives
good light, emitting that beautiful yellowish glow, while putting your
hand up to the warm light only to snuff it out, just so you can smell
the smoke. And are you then, just five stories from the ground when
you phone 911 with your great feat of technology just to say, "I'm
going to be late for supper!"
        Robert-Andrew McFarlane

My Country 'Tis Of Thee

We meet and converse
    standing around coffee machines
Idle conversation
Masters of the mundane
    is what we have become
Programmed clock-watchers begun at an early age
Big wallets with little souls
Regurgitating spoonfed information
Minds empty of original thought
Bodies full of original sin
Those who do not conform are outcast
There is no room for philosophers
    Teachers
    Thinkers
Fortune 500 is the superior race in the last quarter
    (these days) of the twentieth century
Money makes the world go 'round
Poets and lovers push the wheel
        J. Terrence Roche

Untitled

I think of her.
 Starting life is easy:
 energy is absorbed.
 Creating life is never ending:
 it is not to be ignored.
I walk slowly under her eyes.
 The action of creation is
 a passage to non-perception,
 where the tunnel leads you
 in infinite directions.
We look at each other -
There is ignition.
 Spiraling funnels of direction, searching,
 only to find conception.
I touch her thigh and death smiles.
 Fires quenched
 Desires fulfilled
 Emptiness awaits
 Coherence - once again - overtakes.

Playing with life can lead to death, and death not ends it.

 Shawn Lutz

Priceless Heart

The mist from his harmful acts
still lingers in the air,
embracing my being, my heart, my soul
leaving more than I can bear.

The twisted hands of fate comes like a thief,
robbing me of what I've tried to hide.
This thief has no honor, no concern,
he takes what is rightly mine.

I have no protection against this horrid man,
he's powerful, persistent, and does what he feels.
He comes in the day-he comes in the night
and for his pleasure he steals.

Maybe he's unaware of what he has just done
he has taken a piece of art.
This man stole nothing of cheap value,
but ran off with my Priceless Heart.

 Susan K. Kappus

A Past Runs Quickly Over Now

Howl enough louder near the moons past light.
Still, steal time glides softer than before.
Bless the sweet smell of anchors pulled from lake bottoms.
Then, count your fingers once by one;
Drum them fingers on tree wood, there's fun!

Seems Mom's in the box that fortune turns. Our hearts
held gently by her breath; "Give a little take a lot".
Alone with a bag of coins the jazz of jingle leads that road.

A past runs quickly over now. First the eyes, then the teeth,
the liver next and fire is frightened from the belly.
Sly dances start low in the line, groan follows leg,
leg pushes heart and witless brain drives. Drives!
The ancient butt over the edge of the cushioned bed.

Iron whispers, kissed warm cheeks,
bodies turn slowly hiding from the light.
Silent queen of doors, poised for the touch,
a squalid touch, then out for another day.

 Lou Garcia

A Little Girl Left All Alone

A little girl with golden curls,
Stood along the road,
With tear filled eyes,
As though she had such a heavy load,
I asked her if I could help in anyway,
She said I don't know why my Mommie left me today,
Without Mommie there is no home,
I'm just a little girl left all alone.

Will you write to my Mommie?
And tell her I need her to bathe me,
And to brush and comb my hair,
Without her here, everything seems so bare,
If she loved me why did she go?
When she knew I needed her so,
Without a Mommie there is no home.
I'm just a little girl left all alone.

I can't go to sleep without Mommie to tuck me in,
I need her so, my little heart to mend.
Tell her I love her, to please come home.
I'm just a little girl left all alone.

 Naomi B. Runkles

Planet Earth

What man has done to planet earth has caused extreme harm,
Stripped it of most of its beauty and charm
For his own personal gain.
If the earth could talk, it would cry out in severe pain.
Man has polluted the water and air,
Which is so very unfair.
The time has come to call a truce
And get more into cleaning up the earth from decades of abuse.
So lets all wise up while we can
Before the planet is completely destroyed by man.

 Keith D. Peeler

The Storm

Early afternoon
Sun beats down on the thirsty land
The dry wind is slowly gracing its presence
It was a sweaty sunbaked day

Weather is cooling
As the sky starts drooling
Rain comes tumbling down
Lightning lights up the sky
Thunder keeps churning

Raindrops drench everything in its way
The waterless land is now an ocean
Trees, flowers, and bushes were relieved
The scorching weather was now over

The storm has ceased
Dark clouds part for the sun
Rainbows glisten through the sun
What a beautiful day.

 Patricia Strom

Untitled

 As I sit here with my thoughts, silently
talking to a God of my understanding,
the memories of all the hours, the days,
and the years that have since past in my life.
They come to me as waves of a
never ending ocean upon which I ponder,
and ask this God of my understanding,
why? He simply replies in a whisper, why not.
As I sit here with my thoughts, I
sincerely know I am not alone.

 Lorri J. Crable

Aerial Artistry

Steel wings glisten with the
  sun's shimmering reflections
as the jet journeys across
  Heaven's expansive canvas;
leaving lavish strokes of
  soft, pearl, swirling furls,
  filmy, feathery, transparent trails.
Eventually, these spirals are converted —
  stretching, straying
  sheer opalescent tapers;
  ... now distantly fading
  into lucid vapors...

   Patricia J. Erickson

Midnight Gazing

Lying on my back,
Surrounded by September air and hay
My breath sprints
To catch up with my heart.

Gazing into the deep blue basin
As the fiery oven fades away,
Milk spills across the bowl
Cutting silvery rivers through the sparkling sugar.

Greek deities climb up past the trees, rising higher
Never ever blinking.

Through the dark looking glass
Darts the twenty-first century.
Speeding right behind are the people who have to catch it.

But what do we, us two and three,
Care of spilled milk and technology?
For our giddy laughs dip out happiness
Pin back the nightly bogey man
With the Bowman's arrow and string.

These, the stars and wonders of the sky,
They are all comrades making the dark and night friends of ours.

   Katie Karnehm

An Autumn End

The most brittle and reluctant floated from retiring trees,
sweeping along the tattered path we often strolled upon.
The gray pond mirrored its jagged edge of rock,
matching the sky in its effort to exaggerate fall's color.
Even her sweater was a bulky gray, but for a red rose arrowed
between her arm and chest.
Her fine, honey hair danced with the leaves, teasing
hunched shoulders.
Two beggars searching for elusive change, our hands dug deep
inside worn Levis.
The cotton collar pressed her ears, a futile attempt against
the brisk chill.
Stepping in place to the season's symphony of autumn,
we met to say goodbye.
A warm embrace, I cupped her face and she was gone.
A red rose floated in the pond.

   Robert W. Wilson

On Psychoanalysis

Humpty Dumpty sat on a wall
That masochist was doomed to fall
He tempted fate and fate said yes
That sick, sick egg wound up a mess

Some say that egg wasn't loved by his mother
And some say that egg had a rival brother
But whether or not the cause be found
That cracked up egg can't leave the ground.

   Teresa Tealey

"Storming Nights, Lovers Light"

The darkness is like death, no light to be found.
Swirling winds and swaying trees are the only sounds.

Separated by miles but connected at the heart.
I pray for your safety and begin to cry in the dark.

Having only one wish, that you were here.
To wrap your arms around me and take away the fear.

Night and day my thoughts consist of you my lover.
But my craving for you tonight is like no other.

I dream that you are here, stroking my hair.
We speak of our love and show each other how much we care.

In the dancing candle light we embrace in a kiss.
I awake from my dream and it's you I still miss.

With every effort I try to escape the fear of the night.
And I began to dream of your smile, your whole face it lights.

The sparkle in your eyes appear to be so real.
Your strong but tender hands I can almost feel.

Again I awake and suddenly discover,
that the night was made short by the thoughts of my lover.

It was you, that had carried me through the storm.
And I realized, that our love will never be torn!

   Leslie Paige Taylor

God's Wedding Day Bouquet

Here, take this soaring soul that is me.
Take my hand, for in your hand...mine becomes beautiful.
Bless you for walking so near me..your step is like soft
whispers of doves and angels.
You are the sun, streaking down through majestic branches of
the Lodge Pole Pine.

Now I am awake. I am no longer a shapeless dream in the mist.
I have NOW become you..part and counterpart.
If love is food for the soul, then today our eyes hold before
us two souls becoming one, nourished and replenished into perfect harmony.

Like dusty keys of a Baldwin, untouched, talent undiscovered,
until slender, loving fingers stroke the ivory nerves into a
Sonata of two lives, brought together by our loving Creator.

Like a withered blue bell, a parched bud waiting for the gift
of life...a rainfall from heave refreshing the petals...morning
sunlight peeking over a mountain, the wild fragrant sprays turn
to face the sun...love blooms.

And so begins a new life for James and Ellie, precious flowers
gathered unto His bouquet of sweet song.

   Rubye Jean Stroup

A Cure All

Feeling depressed?
Take some of this medicine of mine,
Go out doors, leave your chores behind,
Feel the warm sun not strong but kind,
Smell the fragrance of the warm earth sublime,
Its sweet perfume will soon remind,
That spring is here and winter behind,
The crocus has bloomed and gone on its way.
To return on yet another day,
The lilac too its bloom has passed.
Now roses are budding and ready to blast,
All this leaves no room for pain,
So here I'll stay and meditate,
No better medicine to date.

   Patricia Gavin

His Winds

Strong winds blowing as if mysterious melodies
Tapping on the windows, the winds beckon to me

I am in here, seemingly snug and secure
While outside, all these unfamiliar noises I can hear

What was that rustling sound I now heard
Could it be someone, or am I being absurd

Why won't I look out of my window to see
Is my imagination now taking control of me

Motions of winds continue to whistle through the tree tops
I wish these blustery currents of air would now stop

Sometimes I wonder if wind could be God's way to free
All the things of this earth from clutter and debris

But, does He have to blow so hard tonight
His powerful breath is filling me with a fright

    Marilyn Bublitz Berning

Train Station

Deep sighs - unspoken messages conveyed;
tattered coat, mud-covered, once discarded;
frayed, dirty shirt; cold fingers through ripped gloves;
thin pants of polyester, unfashionably torn;
mismatched socks; worn-through shoes;
newspaper blanket; fetal positioning;
smell of urine; stench of defeat;
cold, dead eyes;
broken dreams.

Footsteps - sharp, purposeful echoes;
Sleek overcoats; warm, impeccable;
Single needle tailoring; cheerful paisley;
Dry-cleaned pants, fashionably pressed;
Brand-name socks; patent leather shoes;
Gleaming, black briefcases; straight, proud posturing;
Smell of cologne; scent of power;
Cold, determined eyes - focused, firm;
Leaving behind
broken dreams.

    Walfrido Yanuario

Pictures of Grandpa

The pictures keep on falling on to my
    tear-stained face,
They scatter round me like rockets
    returning from outer space.
Each holding a special memory
    a time, a place, a face,
I try to push them away, but this just
    brings them closer.
I begin to look at each picture, and realize
    how special are, I then discover that,
I shouldn't cry over your being gone;
I should be happy that you suffer no more,
for now you are where you wanted to be,
with Grandma is all could see.
you wanted to talk to her,
    but she wouldn't answer back,
what you didn't know, is that her
    presence you did not lack.
But now that you are with her way up above,
You are reunited with your love.

    Tolene Borkhuis

My Darling

God never sent a sweeter thing upon this earth to dwell
Than my darling little baby, and I love her so well,
    With eyes deep blue as noon day sky
    And hair of golden brown,
A little mouth all smiling too, and dimples deep and round.

I was once so lonely, and sighed the whole day long.
Now the days are brighter and always filled with song.
    The days were dark and dreary,
    And were so awfully glum;
Now the days go swiftly, because my baby has come.

Her basket sitting here, her walker over there,
She keeps the place all covered with playthings, every where.
    She fills the day with sunshine,
    With her little babbling tongue;
For she calls "Mama" and "Dada" and it sounds as if 'twas sung.

    Ruth Mills Grant

Ode To My Grandfather

A grandfather with a special key
    that a grandchild only can see

A key of love and understanding
    a key of hope and banding

A grandfather who fought in the war
    a grandfather who would give so much more

For this grandchild soon to be
    but not for him to be able to see

A grandfather true in both spirit and heart
    but smoking tore him apart

For smoking is as deadly as can be
    I'm afraid my grandfather paid the fee

For the fee was the gift of life
    and taking the fee he left his wife

Chris my brother did not see him
    but part of him will always be within him

His name was Ralph Longobardo a goodhearted man
    and I was his biggest fan

Smoking is bad and it comes down to this
    that my grandfather died and him I surely do miss

    Nicholas Longobardo

Stars For Barb

I had a dream, one summer night,
that all the stars which shine so bright,
fell like gold dust from the sky,
as we stood and watched, and wondered why.

When I awoke, it seemed to me,
my dream was real...but it couldn't be!
But that same night, as I stood outside,
I suddenly knew how my dream applied.

For like tiny stars, they twinkle bright,
playing in my yard each night.
Children scrambling to and fro...
jumping to catch them when they glow.

Twinkle bright, each fallen star,
captured in a Mason Jar.
Reluctant we are to let you go,
but we can't hold on to a star, and so...

You're free again to fly away.
come back little star, another day.

    Susan E. Snyder

Life

Life is on earth
That begins with birth it can be worthwhile
Starting off as a child then you cry
Let me tell you why you're at that stage
Before you become a teenage
When you're able to hold cup
That's when you're growing up
Now you're a teen with a high self-esteem
You want to hang out and do
You still need to be cared for and loved, too
It's called affection and care
It starts at home not here and there
Without this, it's not your fault
Now you've become an adult it's all about being right or wrong
Life can be valuable and long
Don't be fast (living) in the wrong kind of class
The wrong neighborhood
Can stop your life from being good
We all know (that) killing is a sin
Enjoy life, before it comes to an end.
Sonja Lynn Williams

Hurricane

You may hear the dreadful stories of hurricanes
that brought great destruction
and along with that
came great disfunction.

But, you'll never know the dreadful feeling
until you've been all alone in a house,
no one there, not even a mouse.

There's someone knocking at your door,
who it is, is all a blur;
it's a hurricane, it wants to come in,
it wants to take you for a spin.

You board all your windows, you lock all your doors,
you wish you were eating chocolate s'mores
by a bonfire nice and warm,
away from this very dreadful storm.

The storm has passed now, it's all gone by.
You look up in the sky
and smile at the bright, new shiny day
and the storm so far, far away.
Verina Robiller

Rest of My Life

Darkness is a sky
that constantly covers me
I just need some light
So I can breathe
Troubles are an every day occurrence
I just need you
To give me some reassurance
Will I be able to make it through the rest of my life

Hatred is a disease
That lives inside us all some are so addicted
the pain is hard to recall
no one knows the reason for living
But we must adapt to the bodies we have been given
Will I be able to make it through the rest of my life
I just wish I had a hint of the future
Then I would know if it's worth all the torture
Maybe one day I'll seethe light and smile forever
But until that day the battle in my head will last forever
will I be able to make it through the rest of my life
Warren Quinn

If I Went Back In Spring

The angels sang there in the spring on
that farm where I was born and raised.

I would sit in an old tire hung from
an ancient maple tree and look upon the
pure white display all over the old apple
tree. It was spring and I heard the angels sing.

From side to side and as far as I could
see, the peach trees were showing
their glorious, fluttering pink blossoms
welcoming the spring and waiting to hear
the song of the angels again.

I wonder, if I returned, would it all
be different and gone?
Could I again hear the angels sing
if I went back in spring?
Marie Nolte

This Thing Called My Soul

This thing called my soul is a bottomless hole
That feeds off my tears and my pain.
The more and more I think of it, it leads
Me to think I'm insane.
I know there are answers I know there are ways.
If there is a God he knows that
I pray.
So tell me why there are highs, but mainly
Lows, because I know this is not what I chose.
Ryan McMurtry

Angel Child

It is my song
That I am different.
Hey, World! May I join in?
Is there room for me?
I speak my own language,
I move on my own way,
I hear my own tune
And I see far beyond.
Who has the handicap?
Is it really me?
I have been challenged to strive harder.
And success is sweet.
This world is better for I have touched it.
For others, I need to be here.
From me many learn a little bit more.
Would I choose to be the same?
Not a chance.
I'm perfect just the way I am.
And I sing a Heavenly song.
M. Cynda Bongiovani

Forgiveness

How beautiful to me the words
That Jesus spoke, one awful day,
When hung beside him on the Cross
A thief, who cried, "Remember me!"
These words of cheer Christ spoke to him,
"I truly say to thee, today
In heaven thou shalt dwell with me;"
Oh, Christ, who spoke those thrilling words
While dying, mortal man to save,
Teach me forgiveness by Thy grace,
And fit me for Thy home above!
Priscilla J. Tolson

Wardrobe For The Future

Someday we'll have devises, to put in our ears;
That let us hear the truth, spoken by our peers.

We'll have very special glasses, to put on our face;
That let us see clearly, the person, not the race.

There will be hats and caps, to wear atop our head;
That permits total retention, after each book that's read.

Now our "Wardrobe For The Future", is almost complete;
We'll also need smart shoes, to put on our feet.

They'll always be pointed, exactly in the right direction;
And our dresses and pants, material of total protection.

The accessories are worn, each color a mood control;
Pulsing shades of light, for our nerves to console.

We will heal our bodies, just by thinking it's cured;
A life of at least two hundred, would be well assured.

We'll only have to eat, just one meal a day;
That will leave more time, for work and for play.

The "Wardrobe For The Future", is a concept, an aspiration;
The "mother of invention", is need and imagination.

S. Brownlee-Cobb

Satan's Lair

Was a foolish thing to think
That Satan's lair was fire
When all about me evil ice and snowy storms devour.
And merciless winds with full force
That carry forks that sting.
And what about the pelting hail
That hits one's face to no avail?
Only he could bring.

Tell me, no! It's not of God!
The cruel cold that freezes the hearts
Of mortal man.
This is not God's plan!
And spits up gusts of fury
In fearful children.
It is not!

Only eyes of cool-cobalt blue
Could delight in the chill damp
That creeps into the souls of sin.
Only he could stir, watch and grin...
Only Satan.

Kara L. Davis

Friendship

You played a hymn
That strengthened me one day.
Gave me the laughter of your lips and eyes,
The touch of your hand on mine,
Then turned away —
Yet, left these memories.
Ah, yes, you brought strange sunlight to my gloom.
So carelessly you gave this gift so fair.
As we passed through that closed, cross-lighted room,
My heart was lifted to God - with you there.
Yes, with the aid of your whispered prayer.

Marion Crusselle

Classic Of A Lifetime

Every life has meaning, every life has purpose,
    The ability to make a difference.
At the end of your life's story,
    When looking back through the pages,
If one could only see, how a word, how an action effected another's.
    How a simple, kind gesture changed a day,
A page in a stranger's life.
    What an important verse contained in your life's novel.
One that makes a great contribution to the library of the world.

Oh, if we could only glimpse at another's page.
    See reasons for words, understanding for actions.
I believe we would see more smiles given,
    Less negative words spoken.
In the end, each smile and helping hand,
    Not only makes a significant difference in another's life,
But after reading, as you place your book upon the shelf,
    You would be left with the feeling of great accomplishment.
For you will be an author of a classic,
    Among the stories of your fellow man.

Lisa Thomas O'Brien

Under Night

The black tide draws high, to regress and subside, under Night.
The awake and wide-eyed look inside and confide, under Night.
The dawn fellow sleeps while the Night creature peeps, under Night.
The still of the air, with its secrets to bear,
and when listened to fair, can arouse quite a scare-
or a curious stare,
under Night.
The Moon overhead paints the ground in Sun's stead,
on the doors of the dead, and the dormant life's head,
under Night.
The Day casts its light - in exchange, it is right
But behind waits the Night, poised and geared to take flight.
When she finally draws near, those of soul never fear,
for salvation lie here, in a nocturnal cheer,
under Night.

Mike Nelson

Thanks To You

I think of the past and you come into my mind
The bad times we had, so many sleepless nights
The worry I forced on you when anger filled my heart
The times because of me we had to be apart
Now the bad times are over, you pulled me through every one
And it's thanks to you all that anger is now gone
You stayed by my side no matter what I did
Your faith in me was strong, you encouraged me to live
At times I didn't show how strong my faith was in you
Now I hope these words will make up for things I didn't do
I never could have made it without your love and support
Your kinds words and hugs always filled me with warmth
On your special day I want to give that warmth to you
To tell you how I love you and thanks for all you do
I have came a long way in my life full of pain
But I never could have done it without you leading the way
Mother you have been the best,
My heart you hold in your hands
Thank you for giving me life and including me in your plans.

Tammi L. Yates

Season

Spring is here and animals are playing.
The bears have finished hibernating.

Summer came but there was no rain.
It was as hot as a boiling pot.

Autumn sprang into yellows, oranges, reds
And browns all over the town.
Leaves started falling to the ground.

Winter was here and it started to snow.
Pine trees were scattered high and low.

Rohit Davé

A Full Moon

The world-a battleground between lightness and darkness
The body-a soldier
The mind-a vast, open universe containing numerous stars
Stars-like memories-not always visible,
Nonetheless, always present

Memories-set in patterns-
Accept the constellations of your life
The moon-forever present-
Illuminating our minds, giving light-
Watch your step, lest you stumble-blindly-and fall

A half-moon-a crescent-ignorance-defeat
A full moon-knowledge-passion-desire

An eclipse of the mind
Danger-
Walking in darkness-stars growing dim
Overwhelming despair-

Examine the universe of your life
Avoid an eclipse
Polish your cherished stars

Always walk with a full moon

Katie Fletcher

Marshmallow Skies

Marshmallow skies, autumn colors everywhere,
The clouds, grey tinged like they were
Roasted over a prairie campfire;
Clouds floating aimlessly in a sea of azure blue!

The mountains-capped with snow,
In amongst the green of the evergreens;
Farther down the bushes-with red and yellow aglow,
The artistry of nature's paint brush.

The howling winds threaten to blow us away,
Sending tumbleweeds tumbling aimlessly
Across the desert-dry prairie;
And sending our kittens scurrying for cover!

It seems that the mountains are special,
The ever changing rock and shadow formations,
Snow in July, hot dry winds in fall,
Elk coming into town in the winter; can you top that?
So now I will enjoy the clouds,
God's marshmallows, ever-changing,
The greens and whites, yellows and reds,
Of autumn in Montana!

Lorraine Wentz

Annual Birth Of Summer

The misted colors of lavender, gray and blue hues
The crashing of white foamy fluff against rocky resistance

The flapping and distant cries of airborne creatures.
How soon we forget at Winter's birth

The soft sweet song of voices in the breeze
The gentle caress of the calm surf enveloping our very being.

In peaceful content the annual event of summer brings
Nature's magnificent aura to be devoured once again.

Mary S. Caliri

Welcome To The Night

As the sun hides its face from the world
The darkness begins to dance around me
My eyes become one with the night
Welcome to my world
The night is my home
As the moon bathes me in its light
The power begins to flow through my veins
I run to the place where my sadness washes away
I'll take you there
To a place where the moon shines with the darkness
Here is the place where we can be alone
Let our hearts be as one
Take my hand and look into my eyes
Here there is no fear of our love
Please don't be afraid
I only wish to spend this night with you
Welcome to the night

Nathan Fenn

Rape Of The Roses

Most didn't notice
    the day roses were raped.
They only occasionally
    glanced over at the garden.

They just stood there...
    ...I just stood there,
        listening to their screams,
            watching their bones being
                crushed and their faces being smashed
                    into ground mulch.

Why don't you stop his
    rude thrusting knife?
Why don't I stop him from
    this meaningless rape?

They are screaming!!
    Screaming at the indignation showed to them.
        They weren't expecting this...
            ...I didn't expect this.
    Perhaps that's why we are
        both screaming——silently screaming.

C. R. Peer

I Have Often Wondered

I have often wondered how I could repay
The love and the care I received each day
From a mother and father who would give all they had
To keep their children from turning out bad
Remember how every day they would drive you to school
How they tried to teach you the golden rule
Remember how you ranted and raved and gave out a loud shout
When with your friends they would not let you go out
Let me tell you friend, they gave you a little bit of themselves
Each day
And that is something you can never repay

Richard Loos

Inbetween Age

This inbetween age, this age thirteen,
The days are long to me they seem.
Too old for dolls, too young to date.
Too young for a boy's heart to captivate.

My young teen life seen page by page
Shows me, in this, the inbetween age.
This inbetween age will come and go
In each teen's life, they tell me so.

This inbetween age, will it ever end?
Will this, my inbetween age, ever mend?
TV, sodas, history books,
Language Arts and pretty looks.

This, my friends, is a summary,
Of this inbetween age, this age of me.
This inbetween age can sometimes be blue,
But one of these days I'll be grown up, too.

Nancy T. Smaragdis

A Poet I Must Be

Some days when I awaken and nothing seems to rhyme
the days grow long and weary in the space of creeping time
then I read a favorite poem and my mind begins to clear
as the beauty and the rhythm gives my a mind cause to cheer
and the thoughts expressed so simply in the poets written line
opens worlds of grace and wonder as the sun begins to shine.

The joy I get from others must somehow be repaid
it costs no gold or silver for the effort that he made
the poet asked for nothing for the pleasure I received
a gift so freely given must somehow be perceived
as a letter that's unanswered except in poetry
to honest repay the gift I must a poet be.

E. Lawrence Brevik

We Try

We try to teach our young ones,
The difference between right and wrong.
But we're never quite sure,
How well we've done...

Maybe we may be able to teach with songs.
For words spoken in this form,
Seems to get through to them...
And they may be glad that they were born.

Besides this may be our only chance,
To get our point across.
For we tend to forget and even dance...
That we once were like them.

We only need to let them know,
That we were once in their shoes.
Then just maybe, maybe they'll understand,
Why we don't want to hear or read about them in the news.

Robin F. Fazel

Waiting For The Day

As dawn stretches her fingers over the land,
The earth begins to awaken.
Dreams of the night before vanish,
And life is renewed for the coming day.
The sun spreads its warmth,
As the spirits of the world begin to move.
New adventures wait to be discovered,
Mischievous souls search for trouble.
Unique experiences a part of daily living,
The process of learning never ending.
The day ebbs away, making way for night.
We'll wait for the day to come again.

Melissa Dawn Warden

The Dream's Not Gone

The dream's not lost.
The dream still lives,
Though he is gone and now the dream will not be his.

The dream survives
And it can grow
If hearts are strong and we will share all that we know

About hope and faith and spirit;
About healing and forgiveness;
About love.

The dream's alive.
It's burning bright
As memories flood our hearts and fire our inner light.

And we join hands to share the dream,
To build a future held together by the seam
Of hope and faith and spirit;
Of healing and forgiveness;
Of love ... of love.

The dream's not gone,
The dream survives.
The dream will grow.
I can see it in your eyes.

Rita M. Ramsay

September 24, 1975

A terror shriek engulfs the night
The dreamy bliss now utter fright
Storm struck with a violent power
And ravaged the harvest at the blackest hour

A trembling voice muttered prayers in the dark
The trees are uprooted, fields are stark
Wind burned her face and rain stung her lips
Red curtains streamed and white sheets ripped

God winced in pain from the gruesome sight
But a saint had been born that night
And Satan's wrath had cracked the soil
His tempers raged and fury boiled

Angels watched in shrouds of black
With their wings pinned to their backs
The plump little cherubs watched the rising sun
And mourned their brother, the battle done

The peace came swift with hardly a fight
For the eyes of the babe never saw the light
The wasted dreams and futures planned
So hard to let go or understand

B. J. Critchley

Mother Earth, Mother And Child

The scent of the ocean air,
the feeling of closeness to the earth
    when you roll around in the sand,
the scene of the full moon in between clouds at dusk,
the plain flavor of fresh fallen snow-
nature gives these combinations of beauty in many ways.
Spirituality lies within this connection
    that surrounds us with pure elements.
The intense emotion of the bonding between mother and child,
the sound and feel of a little heartbeat,
the smiling face,
to really smell your baby,
the animalistic sense of knowing: this belongs to you;
the peacefulness, the harmony,
the being in touch with mother earth,
    in step with the perpetual universe -
this everlasting love seems beyond the exhilaration
    of existence.

Tania L. Schuttelhofer

No More Forgiveness

As the footsteps drew closer
The drums sounded out the soldier's heartbeats
Thump-thump, thump-thump, thump-thump
Over the green grassy hills
Through the crystal river
Around the giant oak tree—KABOOM
The sound of murder echoed threw the valley
As the masked slayer's
Shot and killed each other
At the end only a few stood
As they looked across each rolling hill
There lay the innocent people of which were killed
As they all walked slowly back
The presents of guilt took hold of their
Souls and would not let go
Before they had a chance to say we're sorry
Death took hold; now no one stands free
No one stands alive, no one stands to tell
The other's we're so sorry; please forgive us
For we were wrong.

Tesona Lynn Stepp

Thoughts: 34814 Day 128

The passing of time has given us insight.
The events that have been requested have come to pass.
The new existence is on the horizon.
Alone but not alone but possibly alone forever.

Will the time hold the emotion?
Will the emotion bring the love?
Will the love endure the entire breadth of what is required?

You are the beauty which I have come to know.
You are the understanding which has come to accept.
You are the warmth which has endured the pressure.

Guilt holds no positive value.
You are not the cause or the effect.
Let they who choose to judge not be judged,
   but come to understand and
   accept their true meaning in this
   reality.

You hold a special in my heart.
You are a special part of my life.
Where will you be in the history of tomorrow's past?

Raymond E. Janssen

A Symphony Of Love

On the days the sun doesn't shine, in the clouds I see
   the face of thine.
The ocean breeze whispers to the trees, and tells
   them all to sing to me.
The birds are quick with a melody, and dance and
   play like a show for me.
I watch their acrobatics in the air, and wish that
   I could, for a moment be there.
On the days the sun doesn't shine, the ocean
   breathes life into all that it finds
Ferns wildly swaying, leaves tumble and dive, a
   soft misty rain adds glitter and light
The loud spicy smell of wet rocks and pine.
I taste the sweet breath of the ocean in the sky.
On the days the sun doesn't shine, I'll be
   outside with the wild things I find.
Jumping from logs and dancing in mist, I'll be
   found with my love........
      the ocean's sweet kiss.

Stephanie Torres

Moment Of Life

In Indian Summer
Today I watched the sun set in the October evening sky
The fiery orange and red-a stark contrast against the infinite blue.

I felt the crisp north wind blowing cool against my skin
And...I thought of you.

I heard a sparrow singing in an autumn-yellow tree
And I stood still and absorbed the sights and sounds around me.

I felt a peace within - that's been missing far too long
I closed my eyes and heard an ancient native song.

A voice deep within my soul said, "See and feel the harmony.
You can harvest your dreams...if you'll only set them free."

This is Indian Summer with all its splendor!
God sends this vibrant season before the coming winter.

Awaken and see and feel the beauty that prompted me to write this.
Look, and listen, listen closely...and be sure not to miss...

The meaning in this moment of life.

Marsha Patterson

Birds

I like birds.
The flying,
The hopping,
and walking of a bird.

The tweeting,
the chirping,
and singing I have heard.

The pecking,
the pulling,
and tugging of the worm.

The slurping,
the munching,
and never gets a germ.

Room 1Y Winners, Winchester Elementary School, Winchester IL

Wisdom Of The Sea

I walked along the rocky shore and words of wisdom spoke to me
The fog was thick with salty air, I felt Gods grace amidst the sea
Within each wave a stories told of life's uncanny sorrow
The crashing waves, the whispering voice, He told me of tomorrow
A squall appeared with darkened skies and lightening struck the land
Life's existence thus appeared to me like writing in the sand
Washed away in little time no chance for praise or penance
No words are spoke, just swept away to serve a lifelong sentence
From crashing waves against the stones, I heard the cries of pain
The wailing words of wisdom from the lives that lived in vain
They pondered times of lust, without faith, without fears
Their souls like eyes of evil weeping only words of tears
The devils voice, it spoke to me, I raised to see his face
When I looked up it disappeared, my image in its place
I knew right then my life had changed, A story I've to tell
I'd heard the voice of heaven and I'd seen the souls of hell
When I awoke the squall was gone a hope surrounded me
I'd learned life's questioned meaning from the stories of the sea.

Mike Poynter

Broken Hearts In The Heartland

I tried to write a poem, describing that awful day.
The gates of hell burst open and blew my heart away.
Springtime In Oklahoma, The Smell Of Breakfast In The Air.
Children at the bus stop, innocence, without a care.

The rumble of distant thunder, fire and brimstone filled the sky.
The people moved like statues as they watched the children die.
I heard the rush of angel wings as through the smoke they came.
They wrapped their arms around us, nothing will ever be the same.

I saw the snow white robes of angels as far as the eye could see.
They were singing, "Oh what you do to the least of these, you also do to me".
Yes, angels come from heaven on that awful day, they cuddled you in
their arms, my love, and softly flew away.

My heart cries out in anger, bitterness and pain.
How can I forgive them, again, again?
For God so loved the world, as cruel as it may be,
But God loves that warped and twisted soul as much as He loves me.

E. Frank Sisson

Rooftop

The intrinsic light twinkles in the distance.
The glowing moon of brilliance,
gleaming full of passion,
playing above the rippling body of blue; you ration.
With sounds of echoing laughter and pleasure,
surrounded by the infinite twilight; I treasure.

An orange glow embodies the heavens.
As the hypnotic laser web spindles throughout
and dictates the sermon.
Drops of life parachute down
and land of the unsuspecting ground.
It digests this Godly juice
and in return evolves their fruitful roots.
Exploding up through the underground night,
they burst into the sunlight.

Playing in the friendly breeze who cares.
The kind that tickles behind the ears.
This radiant earth gives them this light
and in return they do take flight.

Steven Jaffray

An Autumn Day

What glorious days, the Autumn brings,
The golden sun with its color schemes
Brings a joy of gladness to one's heart,
When mother nature plays her part.
The leaves stand out, with splendor and beauty;
The sun sets on their auburn colors
What joy to see; How this can be
What glorious days to nature's duty
When the sun sets low, and the leaves are falling,
The wind then shares the work of art
The trees are bare, for the winter's rest
For mother nature did her part

Mary Fanucci

"My Life"

When I was young I gave no thought of getting old someday
The Golden Years as they were called were many years away.
Being young and having fun to me was really nifty
Until a friend gave me a charm, it was Gold, and it said "50"

Think not about the Golden Years, your life has not been lost
Some how, some way, you've done it all and cared not what the cost.
When I was young I'd fall in love, a new beau every day
And heartbreaks too....they come with love
My eyes would always stray.
I've seen the sad times come and go, loved ones born and moved away
I was gaining on the Golden Years, the Gold had turned to gray.

Life's road has many curves and turns, it's mighty rough at times....
The hills are steep, the valley's deep, you have to watch the signs.
I've had happiness and turmoil, but love was always there,
I always gave more than I got, for I was taught to care.

I'd like to think I didn't waste my life a single minute,
I've lived it to the fullest, like a race I had to win it.

Someday my loved ones will join me...and when their days are ore'
I'll be listening through Heaven's Keyhole waiting at Heaven's door.

Margie A. Spencer

The Bible

If I could write down everything
the good Lord's ever shown me
the books they'd make would cover the earth,
and fill the deepest sea.

He's shown me oh, so many things
my feeble mind can't recall
from answers to things that seem so big,
to things that are micro-small

Yes, everything I've ever asked
to see and be made clear
He's opened up these earthly eyes
so at spiritual things I may peer

This ain't no Gift made just for me
He'd do the same for you
If you would take the time to hear
What He would have you do

And friend you're never gonna hear it
from a little bird
It only comes when we spend time
In God's most Holy Word. The Bible

Michael Angelo Polley

The heart cry of the people

The violence on the streets
the heart cry of the people
the downfall of our government
the heart cry of the people
the abortion, "oh" how many
the heart cry of the people
prayer taken out the schools
the heart cry of the people
the hungry, the empty people
the heart cry of the people
the agony of nothingness
the heart cry of the people
the breakdown of the homes
the heart cry of the people, concern more for safety of
the animals than our children
the heart cry of the people
the remembering what happened in Hitler's
time when the people became apathetic
the heart cry of the people
the healing, the knowing there is value to life
the heart cry of the people

Shirley I. Mertz

The House For All

The house had magic,
The house had charm.
The little house within the woods was a home for all.
For all those sick and all those dead.
All those with hate, and all with despair.
They were trapped in the house,
The house of evil.
The Angels they came to set them free.
Set them free from the house
In the door, through the window,
Down the chimney.
The Angels, they came.
With the grace of God they made
It in, only to gasp and fly away.
They left the house, the house for all.
The house that still remains.

Linda Skalski

Winter Night

Dark, cold and forbidding
The lake's a gaping hole.
Its movement frozen solid
By winter's blowing soul.

The night is filled with silence.
There are no sounds at all,
Except the hooting of an owl
Who sings his lonely call.

The darkness of the evening sky
Is lit by lunar light.
The full moon shines upon the lake
With moon beams of the night.

The sleeping trees surround the lake.
They dance their winter dance,
As gale winds blow right through their boughs
Without a passing glance.

And then the clouds begin to form,
And with them comes the snow.
Dropping crystal, frosty flakes
On every naked bough.

Sheila B. Roark

"Ode To Boots"

Why are you here? As I look into her eyes
The last thing I wanted an attachment or ties

When it comes to pets I've had the best
She got her call from heaven, had to leave our nest

A black little fur ball who took away my heart
She had the starring role, not just a minor part

Some time goes by, the hurt starts to heal
In walks this kitten she's staying for real

Out to the pet store; here I find I'm lost
What do cats need, and look at the cost!

The caring creeps in, next trip's to the vet
Can't deny it any longer I've now got a pet

I'm learning it slowly a cat's not a dog
She won't even run with me when I go for a jog

I listen for the collar bell if I'm to find her at all
Heaven only knows, she won't come when I call

A white footed tiger, we need a name that suits
Welcome to our home, I think we'll call you "Boots"

Kathleen K. Inglesby

One Step Forward, Two Steps

African-American, Black, Colored, Darky, Girl, N****r...
The list goes on and on
Each word seems to be a new part
Of a cruel and hateful song.

You judge me by what you see,
And allow that to become a boundary between you and me.
But what happened to not judging the cover of a book,
Is society really made on the basis of looks?

Get to know me for who I am,
Don't always be so ready to slam.
Don't listen to what you hear,
And let that be your guiding ear.

Read the pages, hear its story.
The words inside might be your morning glory.
If your want to hate, first hear me speak.
Are my words so strong that they make you weak?

You don't even know me, how I feel, what makes me tick,
But you are the first one willing to make a judgement, oh so quick.
No, it's not that I'm hard.
I'm simply a lonely spade in a deck of cards.

Michelle Rose

Truth

Bury me not where I might see
the many changes coming to be
though change is good to a large degree
but change for change sake is fallacy.

Bury me not where I might see
another war to "set me free"
for my freedom lies in the love of man
in a universe together where all began.

Bury me not where the wind blows cold
where icy promises are given so bold
a windy day has so much to say
if you listen and hear - then obey.

Bury me not in the eyes of deceit
this travesty of man we must defeat
our harmony lies in honesty and truth,
holding our nature, our destiny and our youth.

Just bury me in the quiet of a day
where my light and energy are on display
only then will the truth be forever known
in the stillness and solitude of the moment shown.

Sherry Stevens Johnson

Geezer

I looked today and found much -
the many songs, smiles long ago,
the foolish love of life, the drinks,
slow crawling tears of joy :

   I'm not sure why I can see you
old geezer or what the old term means ?
Some say a geezer can be any man over forty
possibly passed his prime but extremely happy.

Slip behind the thoughts, open your heart
to long ago hurts, feel its warm building
of old memory shot into my artery ....
How you loved a few songs ago.

   Someday the old geezer I watched drink-
up life and sing "Danny Boy" will be me
And this world he left with me, well, it's like
Joe Cocker's "YOU ARE SO BEAUTIFUL".

Ted Rose

Love's Ember

Two people sparked an embers glow
The month of June a year ago

With passions kindle loves fire did grow
It blazed up bright, forever to go

Then storms came, with a cold winds blow
And loves ember dimmed under December's snow

No fuel to feed, loves fire burned slow
A spark, a flicker, not much to show

With no tender tinder, or passions flow
The ember lies smothered, and does not glow

Has it died, is it gone, stacked in a row?
Or waiting, glowing, just below

R. L. Steen

Peace Arrives In A Storm

If only she could awaken
The nightmare would be gone
Only there's no way to move a muscle
There's something like a space suit on

Realizing now she is not asleep
She calls, "Dear God hear my cry
These arms and legs won't move
Please God don't let me die

From this hospital, I want to go home
A little girl needs me, so does her daddy, too
Please forgive me of all my sins
So I can work for them and you"

Instantly a calmness surrounds her
Peace and love upon her mangled body fell
There He stood, all clothed in white
With these words, "have no fear, all is well"

Victoria Milligan

The Choice

Do not resuscitate the chilling words charged through my churning mind
The nurse's voice was kind. The form explained how I could designate
some how could ensure my wishes be obeyed if some mishap
of surgeon's hand entrap my life behind a dark unyielding door.
Or should I fail to wake from sleep induced when anesthetic fails
and that flat final line on screen produced the doctors last betrayals

Such morbid thoughts, unfettered in my brain,
obscured the voice of reasoning's domain.
Now weary from the pre-op tests endured
and from the endless questioning, inured,
I hear the words, "You do not have to sign."
But if I don't will living death be mine?"
With stroke of pen, my fate decreed by law,
I go beyond to some uncharted shore.
Responsibility to choose I fear
to face, and mutely hand to him to bear
that load. He whom I trust, let him decide
what future lies for me on turning tide.

Pat McQuiston

Dreams

Slipping into a dreamlike state as our subconscious becomes awake for the occasional welcomed dream, while other cause us to shake. The extent of emotion varies as we escape into a world of restful silence where our lives become the movie plot as in comedy, or scene of violence.

Recapturing images that may appear to have come from a previous life entering the hidden rooms of our minds, the dreams encompassing joy and strife. The clutter during our waking hours becomes transferred into life's mystery as we lose the image of who we think we are, placed into virtual reality.

It's during these times we can fully escape into another distant land lost is the world of apprehension and turmoil that sometimes gets out of hand. When travelling back to childhood memories or in a situation of fear becoming like a frightened child, mutely crying out for someone to hear.

Unable to be heard as we toss and turn with murmurs during the darkened night, lacking control of the demons invading our sleep causing incomprehensible fright. Later waking up with disbelief that it didn't really happen that way; that we're safe and sound in our own protective space and really are okay.

Perhaps we discover during sleep the honesty of self and who we're destined to be frequently clinging to the invisible yearning to recapture youthful facsimile. Gaining insight through experiences we had while our conscious body was in sleep rousing from a restful slumber revitalized, with recollections to zealously keep.

L. J. Burmeister

A Trial

Here I lay upon the beach,
The ocean so easily within my reach.
Gazing up into the sky
One lone teardrop I do cry.
"Why?" I cry out in the night.
And then my Jesus shows the light;
"Have patience child, I am here,
For I am always very near.
I will bring you through this trial,
And hold your hand every step-every mile."
In that second my burden released,
And in my heart was joy and peace.

Michelle G. Tison

Mistakes

I look at the man, the one who just a minute ago I hated.
The one who had laughed at me, the one who had made a mistake.
I look at him and wonder, What is he thinking?
Is he thinking, perhaps, of all the times people had laughed at him?
Is he thinking of the time when he went to school with his shoes on the wrong feet? The time everyone had pointed and laughed?
Or he is thinking about his son, the one away at college?
Maybe he is thinking about his mother, the one who left him this past month.
There is so much to a person, if you only see between the lines.
When I find myself mad, I have to think: That person hasn't had a wonderful life.
I have to think, that is the same person who ate dinner alone last night.
I have to think, that person was the one who once, with the gentleness of a mother, taught his daughter to dance.
I have to think, that is the man who can make cold hearts warm.
I have to think, that person deserves another chance, not revenge.
I have to think, we all have erasers on our pencils.
Because we all make mistakes.

Kristin Wainright

624

"No More Fairy Tales"

I don't believe in silly fairy tales any more.
The only "Prince" I ever knew was someone's dog.
No knights in shining armor to approach me by the score;
(Perhaps the dragons ate them all, the fiendish hogs!)

I've never lost a shoe, then found it with a charming man attached;
(I guess huaraches don't attract like heels of glass).
No poisoned fruit has ever warranted my rescue from attack
By evil witches...though I've known some in my past!

I heard a tale once, as a child, of some cruel witch's curse.
She changed her prince into a frog, (when spurned, of course).
The only thing which could release him was a kiss from a fair maid,
So for a while I tried, but all I got was warts!

Who thought that it was good to brainwash children with such tales?
All that "happily ever after" stuff is cruel!
I know it devastated me to learn in truth love often fails.
But now that I know better, I'm no naive fool.

So please don't try and read to me before I go to bed,
Of castles, damsels in distress, and other lore.
I think I'll just resign myself to life in this cruel world instead.
At least I know each day what real life holds in store.

Marsha Strawser

Autumn

When it's autumn I feel free,
The orange leaves are rustling,
The black, night sky is soft,
The trees are becoming bare,
The season for turkey or maybe some candy.

I feel free as a bird,
Love is in the air,
It's windy now but a different wind,
A cool breeze instead of a warm breeze
Winter is coming,
And soon white confetti will
Cover the ground,
The famous fall colors, copper,
Brown, orange, yellow, red, and white,
I feel light and golden

Maggy Desmond

Our Love

I love you for all times
the PAST-PRESENT and the FUTURE
I love you and you're all mine
I'm yours, solely yours and I'm glad
Content I am even though it's sad
That day - That blesseth day will soon appear
No more worries, Fears nor Tears
Knowing that each day won't always be the same
Striving, devoting, committing in His name
Believing, Trusting, Dedicating seem so right
Loving each other more with each passing night
Understanding that God has a plan for us all
He put us together, never to let us fall
Obstacles, setbacks are all part of knowing
We will be together all for the showing
My love for you is pure as can be
It's real, everlasting, honest - You'll see
The two of us together from the start
Will never - Shall never be separated a part

Marlene Miller

Potters Field

On the prowl and prairies of the cities they roam,
The poor and forgotten that can't call it home,
They never had the time to take a good clean s**t,
Now they dead and gone, to some worthless pit.

Lovers now been, now lovers be gone, and I am tellin'
    ya now it didn't take long.
So listen in on this rhyme and verse as you cruise
    along, aside of this unmarked hearse.

There's nobody there to say so-long, good-bye, cause
Nary a tear be shed for you on this, your last long
Drive, on a lonely road, a lonely sign, as the band
Plays out another mournful cry! Cause duty calls on
Some other wasted being, with wasted hopes and wasted
    dreams of the poor and forgotten that can't call
    it home, on a grassy knoll, it's the same old song.
There be an eerie sound of a Whippoorwill on a windy
    morn and a wind-soaked chill.

No matter no cost, no wise man's sayins, too late for
    song, too late for prayin', darker yet and darker
    still, as ya make your way to Potters Field.

Mickey Genner James

The Lord's Replay

When I was little, I couldn't understand;
The powerful works of this mighty man.
I was told He moved mountains,
And separated the sea;
And I know He died on a cross for me.
This mighty man is the King of Kings.
And oh what joy His name does bring
As I grew older, I still couldn't see;
Why in this world He'd choose someone like me,
For I am a sinner, and this I'll admit.
I thought I'd wind up in the devil's pit,
But by His grace, my way has been made,
And at his feet, my sins have been laid,
So I knelt down on bended knee,
And ask the Lord all about me,
"Why did you choose me? I asked with a sigh.
"Because I love you," was the Lord's reply.

Mary Ellen Gilbert

The Music Of Laughter

Some gifts from the Lord can be seen by our eyes
    The purple in rainbows, and deep sapphire skies
Those soft tender looks between mother and child
    Show God has looked down—and probably smiled.

The talents He gives often come in disguise
    Knowing how to make friends, or to grow extra wise
To write, and to sing, heal the sick and the lame
    Bring the Spirit of God, and to some He gives fame.

To laugh at our foibles God surely has meant
    And few greater gifts down from Heaven are sent
For laughter, each day, plays an important part
    So live all that's life with a warm "merry heart."

Wilma F. Barry

Were Your Kisses Or Mine?

Your kisses,
and my kisses,
a desperate mix of two dark oral lakes,
where aimlessly navigated
powerful marine velvet tongues
of everchanging licks,
surrounded by your lips and mine,
wrestling in a neverending elliptic fight,
lost in the night,
robbing our moans
as they set fire to the shadows.

The dawn, in vain invaded our desire;
and, in this tangle of sighs,
and, in this yearning to love each other,
it did not matter to know
which kisses were yours
or mine.

Humberto Claveria

Before The Wedding

Nubile
parsimonious hop
  scotch   wry
cunning lingo

Linger
Consummate later
Let simmer   longer
Allow an exploration before immersion
Stand with your naked shadow licking the outside curtain
a brief, *ACCIDENTAL* view down your shirt
an aborted sidelonging gaze

Anticipating.

Arran Fisher

The Last Voyage

The wind, the sea, the revelry
the gulls make o'er their flights,
no sounds so sweet shall ever meet
these ears attuned by right.
No smells as fine as the pungent brine,
The tang of the salty sea,
The sight I'll save of the foamy wave
Though blinded now I be.
So, I'll tender my bark for a one last lark
To only God knows where,
With my hand on the stern
I'll surely learn
What beckons me out there.

Marian Feigelson

Sun Rise

Whispering fireflies lead the blind man to the edge of
the lake, where he baptizes his soul, and soothes his visions
of dreams. Standing as still, as the blackness in his head,
while tiny fish nibble at his ruff, thick soled feet.
Swooping bats wake him from his interpeace, as the night
melts to day, while the love of mother nature turns his
blackness to red. So he pulls his sight stick from the
honey rich mud, and proceeds to travel his birth map.
Ancient tales once spoke of a man of great wisdom, and
beauty who lacked one gift, the gift of sight. Could this be
the man who stands in front of me, on this lake side, of hot
summer night, as the sun rises, and reflects the beauty of
crystey fairies off the calm, untamed tears of GOD.

Rudolph John Tighe

Damn

Damn the ones who hurt us,
Damn rejection and unrequited love,
Damn the gremlins that live in my car and computer,
Damn the mall rats, damn the all!
Damn the old ladies, who all look the same,
Damn the old men who can't play the game,
Damn all the jocks and the sports that created them,
Damn Californians, for they are superficial,
Damn the stupid who don't seek to be taught.
Damn what I can't change.

Scott M. Palmer

Oedipus Complex

Henry was obfuscated, the feelings were strange.
At twenty five he was a psychological wreck.
The shame, the turmoil, with whom could he confide?
That the object of his sexual desires, was his own mother.

Thomas' shock was quite apparent
his best friend, Oedipus complex, it was sick.
"Maybe if you married someone of your age",
you could overcome this in time", he advised.

It had been a year of blissful married life
he loved and cherished his beautiful wife.
Now the guilt and shame was overpowered
by the fear that his friend knew of his dreaded past.

The decision was final, the friend had to be eliminated.
A picnic was arranged, a plot was hatched.
He took his friend aside, confronted him,
a fight broke out and a chilling scream was heard.

The wife looked down from the edge of the cliff.
She found some help and made her way down.
The body was turned over and she was asked, "What was his name?".
Weeping uncontrollably she replied, "Henry... Henry Thomas".

Mythyly Putcha

Blaze

To hell with women.
To hell with life.
To hell with work.
To hell with strife.
Down with evil,
Likewise good.
Damned be things
That are as they should.
All is tasted.
All is won.
There's nothing new
Save death alone.

Nicholas A. Sica

The "Many" Were There

Well, the reunion is over and the hall is all clear.
The "many" showed up both from far and from near.

Everyone was happy to see one another,
Each Uncle and Aunt, and Sister and Brother.

It was a gala affair no one can deny,
To meet once yearly, they suggested to try.

They danced and gave thanks and wrote stories for the show
I was there too, so I ought to know.

The love and the caring came shining through,
Any sad memories from the past have now washed away too.

Patricia Wilkerson

626

Secret Voice

Kiss me, at a time and place so hidden,
Touch me, at a room, in a house, on a hill,
Lick me, I'm so dirty under your nail,
And hear me, on a night so quiet and still,

I want you in me, you masculine wave,
A feeling within me,
Breaking at my loins,
And hidden in my swollen embassy,

I love to touch your sweeping brow,
And hunt with the cats in the graveyard,
You kiss my lips and draw blood,
From a heart so deep garnet,

You are so new at this, my sweet kitty,
I love you, dearest emotion,
Play with me tonight as the sun sleeps,

Pray upon the stolen shadows with
   A voice so numb,
I call to you in my secret voice.

Kimberly Patryk

Dallas/Phallic

Arches arcing stratospheric
Firmament fixation
Frenetic flow of traffic
Frenzied, fiendish pace
Aortic/Thoracic, heartfelt isolation
Real time. Real space.
Wistful embraces.
   "Hey! Wha' sup, man?"
   You be in Dallas, boy.

Some officious yuppie jogger
Grunting, panting
Sweating bullets for approval
Mount the corporate ladder
   Piss me off, man!
   Take your pristine Porsche
   And drive yourself to Yuppie HELL!
Archer/Torture, William Tell Effect
You miss the mark...
   Big D you're killing me -
   You be in Dallas, boy.

James B. McGuire

A Dentist Lament

A woman came to the dentist with pain you wouldn't believe
Crying in despair, "please give me relief,"
"Which one is the culprit?" The dentist inquired
"Oh you find it, you're the expert, I am so tired."

He pulled a molar with some disdain
"That's not it", she screamed with pain,
Another was extracted and again she cried out
"You didn't get it" bursting with a shout.

Finally due to her stubbornness all were gone except one
The pain prevailed, it was a son-of-a-gun,
Then the forceps on the last tooth did surround
Released with a jerk, it was nowhere to be found.

He rushed her to the hospital laden with fear
The x-rays revealed the lungs and stomach to be clear,
Then the gastroenterologist came on the scene
Nothing visible in the bowel to be gleaned.

As a last resort to the proctologist she went
He placed her on the table, head down and knees well bent,
The proctoscope inserted and low and behold
"Wow!! There's a tooth there, to the dentist you must go"

Dr. Henry H. Seifer

Susan

To love a woman —
To love your self
feelings which cannot be.

But Are
But Are —

Breasts on Breasts
Slide beyond safety.
Silent dry tears
tear my body —
your touch cradles.

My soul is alive.
Life stops.
Frozen in the moment

I exist
I exist
I exist

I am at home.

Doris Jeanette

Is It Hot

Is it hot enough for you
Is it hot enough for me

As the sky gets darker
I'm sure we will see

Is it as hot as a burning river or the sun set afire

Is your man just a man or A sexual loving liar

Does he burn holes in your heart
And tear you apart

Or do you do it to him

Should I listen to you,
Oh, what should I do

I don't know how far to go
I don't know if you're gonna blow, but I think it'll be pretty soon

Is yours and mine as hot as his
If you don't go soon I'm gonna fiz

Oh, it's so hot it's gonna pop

And he's so good you just can't top

I don't know if she can stop I'll ask again my rockin friend

Is your and mine as hot as his. I don't know the answer
and hope you agree But yes I think it is

Amanda Pack

Goodness

Goodness flows from the heart
Always do good deeds and never stop...

Goodness will keep you strong in God's word
Goodness is a word spoken sometimes not heard...

Always do good unto others
As you would have them do good by you...

Remember Goodness mean Good
Like Love means Love to....

So never ever stop the Goodness.....

Verleen R. Green

Falling In Love To Stay

Like glowing rays shining through
A cloudy day.
A tender touch like cooling waters,
Yet with a
Spark of electricity that warms the
Innermost part of one's being.
A twisting knot that to some would
Be pain, but to one in love it
Is the swelling
Of joy, yearning to burst within.
A diamond-like
Sparkle in the eyes-glowing from
The deepest depth
Of a lover's soul, allowing all to know the secret
Place in the back of the mind that causes the smile
That plays upon their lips.
The carefree bliss they know is theirs
And the special gift they know they are to each other.
This shows all that lovers really can fall in love to stay.

Melissa A. Frey

Heart Felt

A heart waits in hesitation to portray emotion inside;
A heart breaks at every thought of ne'er being contrived.
Looking into the eyes, a deep sense of strength is felt;
What power this is and that in the mind is not dealt.
Surely this feeling does not belong in the premises so dwelled;
For it should be a shattering sight to band this on a shelf.
But how indolent and effortless it would occur to set it all alone;
Or otherwise set it free to capture the one it's always known.
To the privy one to whom this feeling in the heart does belong;
Don't allow this gallantry to linger of be put aside too long.
For an undeviating love this willing heart not much longer can await;
Come take this hand and allow for eternity this heart to elate.

Jennie Blackmon

Brown Eyes

Brown eyes glistening.
A lost star in the darkness.
So deep, so strong, so blessed.

Only I see your pain, and feel your bereft sorrow.
Why me? You look to ask.
Only my heart knows your deepest desire.

Brown eyes, you're glossy. Crystals of melted ice form.
Slowly our down your cheek, to the very tip of your breast.

Still you smile.

Brown eyes, through you I see.
Together we share our pain and anguish.

Like the close of day, Brown eyes, why stay?
The weariness of your body,
and the sighing in your voice will finally lay still.
Your heart will be at rest.

Brown eyes we are one. Look close, it's me.
You see, I am lonely, but not alone.
No more Brown eyes.

Close, Close. Rest in peace.

Jessica Blanding

The Dream

Sitting on a pedestal
Alone all around is darkness
Look deep, deep into the heart of a person
You once loved.
Understand love is a mysterious thing
Not to know which way it will go
Scared to know the truth
Look into my eyes
What do you see
Darkness where the truth is found
Feel my heart, hold me tight
Tears on my pillow, where you once lay
So many far from your heart
When we'll we ever learn
A vague memory of a smile I once remember
But it was only a dream
Back on the pedestal sitting alone
In my world of darkness

Michele Barela

A Poet's Master

Cautious, careful and ever so slowly,
Always alert, almost focused,
The angry, but well meaning metaphor,
Spun the web tighter and tighter.

Mellow, mighty and now so swiftly,
Every movement, every thought,
Offered a subtle and serene view
While others only wondered.

Fast, fervent but never so quietly.
Each moment, each glance,
Inside the small curved crevice,
Lay the soft and silent
Never ending, unwinding, unwilling
Explanation of it all.

Max Phelyne

Life's Journey

When we began our life together,
And joined two lives into one,
We said we'd keep our vows forever;
Then our journey we'd begun.

Our journey began at the bottom
Of a curvy mountain road,
And we often thought we'd welcome
Some help to carry our load.

Just when our curvy road seemed roughest,
New lives were given us then,
And to our journey they added zest,
Giving strength to hike again.

Now our journey's end is drawing near;
And we've reached the mountain's peak;
There's no place I'd rather be than here;
We've found what we came to seek.

Lenora J. Smith

In The Master's Hands

Here I stand in a baron land in heat of an August day;
and look aghast at stormy past and clouds that make it gray.

I'll say aloud that I'm not proud of a past with wrongs each day;
if life behind could speak its mind for ere' ashamed I'd stay.

The futures blown by winds unknown and reeks of winds gone by;
it harbors fear and threatens tear with methods mean and sly.

I'd like to hope yet bleakly grope to a future kept at bay;
and growing old become less bold turned tired weak and gray.

Distraught I'd be with what I see as through this life I trod;
'cept here I stand held by the hand stretched from the arm of God.

Life's thunderous noise stilled by his voice he speaks and all is calm;
His voice brings hope so I can cope His words are life's true balm.

The past is burned and lessons learned though lived or just displayed;
with wisdom gained we march ahead or watch and be dismayed.

The past is set the future met within the masters plan;
today is mine and life will change by giving all I can.

The futures great, adventures date one day or many years;
I challenge thrills accept the spills or shrink from it with fears.

Now God He is and man I am and worlds He commands;
let foul winds blow and storms rage so I'm safe within his hands.

James F. Bard

I Love You Dear With All My Heart

I love you dear with all my heart
And only God can make us part.

Four score and seven years ago today
My Daddy said those words to Mom that way
And as he held her hands he whispered low
I want you and all the world to know.

I love you dear with all my heart
And only God can make us part.

Well here I am with you again today
Saying those old words the same old way
And as I hold your hands and whisper low
I love you more than silver and gold.

I love you dear with all my heart
And only God can make us part.

Ten years have passed and here alone I stand
Laying roses on this saddened land
And as I kneel beside your grave
I only hope that you can hear me say

I love you dear with all my heart
And only God has now made us part.

Edward F. Benvin

Morning

The ebony shroud is gently pierced
by the light of a new dawn.
Dream shadows yield to the starkness of a white
bedroom wall.
The fleeting life of morning runs its course on
a tightrope tethered between the promises of
the past and the hopes of the future.
The moment of waking, like the faces of Janus,
presents an eclipse of temporary realities — the
candor of day prevailing over the obscurities
of furtive darkness.
Morpheus pivots to meet Helios,
and succumbs to his brilliance.

Marty Toren

All But The Dancer

The tiny pink toe shoes are on the wall
And other things from when she was small
Posters and pictures of beautiful things
In her deserted room, the telephone rings
With grace and beauty is how she danced
Her life for ballet is what she had chanced
She could have gone far the people say
She could have but won't because of that day
A party with friends, she'd be home by one
She didn't know you could die from fun
Going home in the car she didn't think
That maybe her friends had too much to drink
They swerved and sped up, the road wet with rain
It was fun, they laughed, death was merely a game
But everyone screamed as they head for a tree
The driver had turned, she didn't see
All lost consciousness as the car did a flip
They all lived but the dancer, who hadn't had a sip

Elizabeth Hargrove

To Mother And Father On The Death Of Their Child

There's a corner up in Heaven, where the little babies play,
And our Blessed Mother watches all throughout the live long day.

They're a happy lot these babies, sure the reason's very plain,
For they've missed the world's contagion,
    came unscathed without its pain.

'Tis an angel band they call them, and you both should happy be,
You're the parents of an Angel, 'cause your baby's there you see.

Yes and smiling down upon you, with innocence sublime,
Waiting, watching, for the parents it will meet again in time.

You should never be rebellious, rather thank a loving God,
For your little guardian Angel, as along life's way you plod.

With a faith that never falters, clasping - catch the other's hand,
Pledge yourself to meet your baby, in the better, happy land.

Glorianne Blythe

An Ode From A Secret Admirer

My dreams are saturated with your presence.
And when the full moon rises in the east.
My admiration for you grows ever stronger,
As my passions become overwhelming beast.

So long now I have secretly admired you.
Is it love or a never ending infatuation?
In dreams, I adore and caress you,
But reality present another situation.

From afar, I watch all of your movements.
I love your walk, your stance and your demeanor.
My eyes consume your physical being,
And my desire makes my other senses so much keener.

In my heart, I'm your secret admirer.
And in my mind, I have only one wish.
That one day I will have a special place in your heart,
And be able to seal it there forever with a kiss.

Emma L. Sanford

Sonnet To Freedom

After all undeserving, who bragged their boast in vain,
Are forgotten, though they would be fain,
To be remembered, there will be a name,
Whose white honor is a symbol of true greatness.
He begged the world for nothing less
Than justice for all.
And although he died, he did not fall,
Down into the abyss of the ages.
His name is spoken on the stages,
On which is played
His story spoken yesterday,
But still revered.
No matter if he is not here,
From there, he hears
His great name spoken well.
From that pedestal it never fell,
Or will fall until the last of times.
What is that name that all men in speak in reverence?
From now until their departure hence?
    That name is Freedom.

Angelique Anne Warner

Our Children

Drugs are red and drugs are blue, our children
are too blue, it's true, we teach them simply to
just say no, be strong and not rough, but is it enough
to just say no? I ask you, my so called friend,
how can I win? My father, where have you been?
Hey mister, stay away from my sister; or ask my undercover
lover; my unemployed brother; and say hello to my
Alcoholic mother who taught her children single handed
Don't be late, sit up straight; be neat, and look both ways
before crossing the street; crime is sometimes Blind - so be
aware that drug don't care and remember children it's
always cool to stay in school. I ask you will we ever
rediscover the natural high of life? Wake up and smell the
Roses stop living the hell and stay out of the cell.
Can't you see the disaster, lets fire the master of
the pushers, the abusers, what a sad excuse for the
users, yet we are the accusers - wake up! Face the
reality in our society, I'm too red, and feeling bad,
we don't have to be sad lets stand up and say
No more children dead....our children!

Francine D. Donley

Victory

Life passes through the transformation
as Death materializes,
The spirit slips into heaven space
and the body becomes a shell.

The energy once contained
will become a vapor.

At what point did death knock?
Was it when the actual breathing stopped?
Or, could it be, is it possible
it came unaware
before that final gasp of air?

Perhaps life and death collide
and like the thunderous rolling tide,
explosions ripping within the soul
and then one day you finally know.

It is good to be prepared
for do not let Death rip you unaware.
So, slowly as the light glows dim,
be assured that in death you win.

Nancy E. Molitor

Canine Love

Silhouettes of NIGHT HAWKS flying yonder,
As howling WOLVES...in the forest wander.
An OWL screeching, hungrily for its food,
Eyeing a RODENT below, with a serious mood.
A wisp of smoke went floating lazily by,
As the Moon was lighting the evening sky.
A HUNTER by the fire, a pipe at his lips,
Pours hot coffee, and takes a few sips.
His COMPANION sat silently listening in fear,
The rustling of leaves.... Something was near!
He turns as a bundle of fur began its attack,
Pouncing and snapping it nips at his back.
Twisting and turning, he hollers out loud,
Glancing behind him, at what made him proud.
He turns quickly, grabbing hold of the paws,
To protect himself, from a slash of those claws.
No harm was done, and when at last it was over,
HE reaches to hug an old friend, his dog ROVER.

Larry J. Valenzio

Untitled

He came into my life.
Asked me to be his wife.
Said he wanted me for life.
Stabbed me with a knife.
Broke my heart.
Said we should be apart.
I wanted to die.
He made me cry.
He was unhappy too.
He didn't know what to do.
Eventually he came back with tears in his eyes.
He wanted no more goodbyes.
He said he still loved me and wanted to live with me.
I said we'd have to see.
I had to decide what was best for me.
Well now we're back together.
Hopefully forever and ever.
If it doesn't last.
He'll be in my past.
He won't have a second chance.

Janet K. Strupp

"While The Heavenly Hosts' Are At Play"

As little De Aurdrez sleep, he grins, chuckle and snatch
at the air, but at one glimpse at the little fellow, usually
there's nothing there. When the sitter comes about, he beings
to shiver and cry; apparently the heavenly host's has spoken
goodbye...
    "While the Heavenly Hosts' are at play, light emerges
off the heavenly plains, every hosts' at their station, bringing
on the Northern rains.

    The little old lady, with her afflictions she bares'
not alone, by faith she is made whole; that appointed
angel carry's' her cry, then the chief corner stone heals
her soul. Yes, behind flesh and blood principalities of old
strive hard, but what can stand against the word of truth,
in which strongholds are torn apart...

    "While the Heavenly Hosts' are at play, light emerges
off the heavenly plains, every hosts' at their station,
bringing on the Northern rains.

    As the wretched Man, walks daily alone, lusting world of
despair, not even knowing the hosts' of heaven can count
every grain o his hair...

Michael James Craig

Apples Of Gold In Pictures Of Silver

Tell you loved ones you love them as often as you can,
Be a friend indeed, when they have a need;
Warm their hearts with your smile;
Help them find their purpose in life,
Always, giving encouraging advice.

Tell them how beautiful they are like flowers;
in a field all colors and sizes;
Each one beautiful in its own way;
God created all of us this way!

Tell them you care and that you will be there;
In good times, and bad times, in happy times and sad;
Always, be kind and gentle in the words you speak
For we all must go through life's 'Seasons'

Tell them how special they are today, tomorrow, and forever;
Try to see good in all they do!
So, love each other everyday!
Because, we know not when we or they maybe called away.

Remember, to smile and say "Thank You", for the gifts God has given you!
As the Proverbs say "A world fitly spoken is like Apples of Gold
In Pictures of Silver"

Janis A. Haggerty

"I Bore It All"

You bore me out of love, expectation, planning and hope. Years
belonged to weeping cries not knowing if reality would and loom into
the day. You created my life plan to include fashion, career,
etiquette, character unspotted like ivory soap floating. I emerged
tall, intelligent with thirsts of curiosity intᴈ every motion
inquiring, reading every message inspiring, even coping with despair
eluding. My love for you dismissed the obvious, hurting evidences of
your emotional jealousy webbing around the weave spider, loveless
relationships void of respect, caring and responsibility.

The years coming are not kind, another generation springs to find
horror in mother's love, directions muddled where the breast milk
soothes the sibling, secures the sibling, and yet you cry sunken in
your own mire of rejection and anguish, and obvious loneliness amid
those earlier ones who cared. End this, end this now! Let not
another crawl through times alone where only you can secure the ends
of fate. A fate that already topped my destiny to not reaching the
journals of understanding, you didn't mild me into society's fold, you
sit and rock lashed with misunderstandings of hope. My heart and my
being love you, give me an injection of toughness, nurture my
sensitivity with strength, lay your wisdom on my mind so that I avoid
foolish trappings. I will stand, I will fall, I will call upon he
sapping in seasons tall. In spite of...I will prevail.

Elaine Cruz

Conversation Piece

Thought to be well endowed with reason
but given much to their own phantasies,
two talking males found it the perfect season
to enlarge upon fond memories.
The first one was attracted by the eyes,
portraying the sum total of the whole.
The second was more cautious to apprise,
and opted for the body and soul.
There were no takers for the orphaned mind.
Incognizant of such perceptive matter
the intellect of wits was left behind
to later be disposed of with the latter.

And so, the two in solemn unity
divided up the doubtful subject - me.

Patricia Adzima-LaFave

Jason

This poem is dedicated to my retarded brother.
His eyes have seen pastures of green, and skies of the deepest blue.
But in his mind, unlike our own, he doesn't remember the hue.
Though, window panes, and Nintendo games in his everyday life exist,
His memories, and abilities could all fit on a short list.
His life will be an eternity, but really he doesn't know
That the hands of time although they strike, in his mind the age won't show.
But, pity not, nor be ashamed, for the "gifted" one is he,
Because through his life he'll only know,
A life of childish glee.

C. Scott Schuler

Where To Go

'Tis said that one should go with the flow
But it's taking me where I don't wish to go
I've drifted onto some foreign shore
One which I didn't plan to explore
So I'm not gonna go with this flow anymore.

Yes, from here on I'll be bucking the tide
And striving to get to the others side
And tho it may be a more difficult ride
No longer will my soul feed denied.

Margaret Ray

"Fell The Ashes Upon The Ground"

Fell the ashes upon the ground,
But not was heard a single sound.
For to speak would promise a similar fate,
Because of his greed, because of his hate.
Beaten, tortured, starved, and killed,
Their fate he'd horribly sealed.
Thousands and thousands tragically defaced,
Because of their Forefathers heritage and race.
Thousands witnessed the deaths of others,
Friends, comrades, acquaintances, brothers.
Those who've survived; bitter, scorned,
Have to themselves solemnly sworn.
Never a word, never a sound,
For remembered are,
The ashes upon the ground.

Jennifer D. Holmes

Love And Hate

I loved you ever since the first grade.
But now I look at you and all I can do is degrade.
I used to look at you and fall apart.
But not now, ever since you broke my heart.
I used to listen to everyone call you names,
    and never said anything about it.
But now I am included in the shame,
    and I am not guilty one bit.
Everyone used to call you a slack.
But now I hate you because you talk about me
    behind my back.
You were my first crush.
Trying to forget about you, hopefully a rush
How could you do this to me, don't you know what love means?
I guess you don't have that in your genes.
I used to love you, but that was then.
And now I hate you.
Love and hate.
Now and then.

Danielle Dragone

631

Peaceful Solutions

Peace is in the air
But to all it is not so fair,
To some it shall never be theirs
Systems fail, and reason cease, to exist
But water and blood flow in all the seasons...

The accords, and treaties are proclaimed
And signed in the end
All will be undermined; the mentally created or the heavenly ordained divine
Share the same soil for the eternal human toil.
This alone should give reason enough for our love to maintain.

Peace starts from the soul, the blood and the mind,
It is forever held in all our hearts
It must be made from the heart's mind
To lay down all of death tools, or prepare for tears for all mankind..
Chris Duncan

Know Me....

You said that you don't know me,
but you have heard me crying in my room.
You claimed you have not seen me!
Yet only yesterday.......

You saw me wandering;
half-clad in the corridor
my body weary from drunkenness
my face covered with sweat mixed with tears.

You might have asked: what is the matter with that lady?

What is wrong, and why she acts that way?
But at this very moment today

Half wakened from a sad, and turbulent dream

I sway between nightmare's tormenteous grips
Reaching....
Calling....
Trying to clasp the edge of reality.
The sun is here in the sky
Bringing its bright daylight into my very being!

And I wait for its touch!

For my redemption!!!!
Silvia Ruth Guardi

Together Forever

You may leave one day
But your soul will be here to stay
You may go away but your love and
happiness you shared will never despair
You find your own life
But your life will stay with ours forever
You may go to your new home
But ours will always be yours
You will always be a part of us
in our souls near or far
You will come and you will go
But wherever you are
You will still be with us in our prayers
We will miss you
You will miss us
We will always be a family
near or far
Amber Joy Hill

Ties Of Love

When left with lovers, ebbs away its flavor,
By joss to capricious Luna forever subjected,
With her waxing to madness love is bursting,
And yet, in her waning, only taste of sorrows.

When left with lovers, ebbs away its splendor,
Save to Venus temple forever left consecrated,
Under her auspices the flame of love burning,
In life and into death bound by unbreakable laws.

So it was sworn, that day of blissful ardor,
Under Gods' eyes our hymen we celebrated,
No death shall part us, oath ever binding,
Where love's folly goes, there our path follows.

So it must be if we lose our mutual fervor,
Come, guardian of vows to such task appointed,
To us, while our hearts are still touching,
Slain us together with your mighty blows.

So be it in this world of unending clamor,
That in full triumph love eternally resuscitated
By truth and purity returns peace and soothing,
And the promise of ever beautiful tomorrows.
Toru Kawahara

Fragile, Handle With Care

The enchanting rain forest
calls out to the still night
the strong wind whispers
with all of its might
alluring are the trees
standing so tall
the huge tree canopy like a wall
covers and hides
the animals away
forest animals frolic and play
miraculously waterfalls dance off the rocks
while exotic birds chirp and talk
it rains
life within the forest air
remember the rain forest
fragile, handle with care
Alexandria N. Neely

Can You Still Run?

She asks with concern in her voice and worry in her eyes.
Can you still run? I look at her with a smile on my face but sadness
   in my heart.
Knowing what she might have to face in the future.
"Everyone is different. There are many courses this problem can take"
"But as for me, no, I cannot run."
   Only in my spirit can I still run up a green grassy hill.
   Only in my spirit can I still skip along a shady park path.
   Only in my spirit can I still run up the stairs.
   Only in my memory can I still run in out of the cold windy weather
   or walk along the beach.
   Only in my heart can I still dance to the music.
   But as real as it may seem, it is only in my dreams I still soar
   and glide with ease.
   There is no effort or pain, no heavy dragging feet.
   In my spirit and in my dreams my heart is so light,
   My steps are so sure and my arms are still strong and
   Yes I can still run!
Linda R. Marshall

Love No More

Sea of salt
Crusted tears dripped
The roaring of his soul as it fled
Vacant eyes that stare
A skeleton moldering on the shore
His love thrust a dagger into his breast
The day she spoke the words
I love no more
It whirled around, around in his head
A silent scream, madness descended
And the wind toyed with disheveled hair
A mist appeared and gathered him in
As vacant bloodshot eyes stared,
Spitting sea foam splayed the air
While the sea, gently rocking, carried him to bed.

Diana Dolhancyk

A Colorado Memory

A magpie flitting in the Colorado sky
Curiously catches the black dog's eye.
Curving in an arc, resting on a limb,
On with the chase, the black dog's whim.

Fly away, magpie, out in space.
Hurry up, black dog, win your race.
Wings outspread, black and white,
The magpie's flight, what a beautiful sight.

Black dog racing, barking with the wind,
"Where you going, my fine feathered friend?"
Circling around as if to tease
The magpie dips, then hurriedly flees.

Over the ridge with its beckoning call,
Daring the black dog, jumping the wall,
With a flutter of wings, then up to the sky,
"Oh, black dog, black dog, why can't you fly?"

J. Boswell Sims

A Homeless Poem!

Hopelessness and despair and freedom - "yes"?
Dirt and crud and bugs
encompass my being!
Thinking is so muddled!
From stress and strife and abuse
Only I and right kind of help will
bring me through:
And God help me; only if I want too!

Shirley D. Parsons

The Eyes Of Saturday

With the blueness of Summer Sun Sky
For eyes of Saturday angels sigh
With the blueness of summer sun sky
For eyes of Saturday angels cry.

When the coldness of Wednesday has found me'
In the eyes of Saturday will I glory
When the coldness of Wednesday has found me
In the eyes of Saturday lies the story.

With the glitter of diamonds before me
To eyes of Saturday my heart will sing
With the glitter of diamonds before me
In eyes of Saturday my soul takes wing.

To the eyes of Saturday the music plays
With the eyes of Saturday my heart stays
With the blueness of Summer Sun sky
When no eyes of Saturday I ——

David Murphy

The One Up Above

Can you feel the heat from the rays of the sun?
Do you sense the fear, when behind you a stranger runs?
I myself from the sun feel the heat,
I myself fear, when behind me I hear running feet.

Don't take it for granted, you have someone to love.
Don't get too enchanted, thank the one up above.
For he guides you through life, from beginning to end.
Don't stab him in the back with a knife, for he is a true friend.

Not everyone will approve of you,
Not everyone will show that they care.
In our hearts we all carry the truth,
Be careful, it's a cruel world out there.

If you haven't found someone you care to love,
Maybe it's just not the right time or place.
He placed us on this earth to love,
Regardless of color, sex, or race.

Just remember,
The one up above is here for you.
Just remember,
When you feel no one loves you, he died on the cross for you.

Carmen S. Alicea

Eminence Of Doubt

It arrived in pace like an opportunity in time
Doubted by the experience once never tried.
Confidence was not for the moments to and from
My body cushioned in comfort, but numb to the bone
People all about, whispers and words of none I heard.

I closed my eyes and counted to three
My darkness was light that journeyed through the wind.
The minutes came much too fast, the seconds too slow
Risky indeed, but there was no turning back
I was captivated and gripped by an unrelenting fear.

Suddenly a thought and calm walked in,
Reassured and reminded that it didn't have to be
While the world travelled under me and into the past
The clouds descended quickly from the rising roar I knew
Would carry out its purpose and bring me through again.

Edward Leake

The Wall

Smiles pervades thee not this place, and silent whispers from lips escapes, from somber souls who have no face.

To see loved ones again brings a beating of the heart, but to hasten escape brings death across that winding rampart, and the guards and the towers and the wire razor edged, for years have separated and detoured those wishing to cross that concrete ledge, but to across and to live is a hope for most, though not many have journeyed and on the other side boast.

It is difficult to understand the reasonings of a sadistic mind, how they hate, murder and maim their fellow human kind.

Listen to the sounds from the other side, listen to the joy, to the laughter, and wings labors for freedom as it hitches a ride. It soars ever skyward above that abhorred wall, and freedom beckons from the rooftops with its desirable call, and it enters the breasts of every man woman and child, and hope strengthens hearts that the wall hath beguiled.

So down the wall came, with a sudden demise, and freedom landed safely with tears in its eyes. Tears for the mother who longed to see her son, tears for those seeking loved ones, and found they had none, tears for a nation divided and now not at all, but no tears were falling for the death of the wall

Ronal Patterson

633

Love

There is a light that shines, that you cannot see,
Even in darkness, it seems not to be.
The light of which I'm speaking of
Is the light in your heart that is known as Love.
It cannot be seen with the naked eye
But it shines as brightly as the sky.
You would not know what I'm speaking of
If you haven't experienced a thing called Love.
It's a light that warms you from inside out
It's a powerful light without a doubt
It's a light that can travel around the world
Like a shooting star from where it was hurled
It's a light you'll never forget
And something you'll never regret
Though you can't see it with your eyes
If you ever find it, you'll recognize
The thing that I have spoken of
Is a thing I know called Love.

Hal Proctor

The Dream

The world is a calm and peaceful place.
Everyone greets with a warm embrace.

No one gets sick and no one can die.
There are no tears or reasons to cry.

Every family has food on their table.
There are no worries for jobs are stable.

There are no storms or face earthquakes.
Smiles are real and no one is fake.

No child is left without his care.
Each couple is a perfect pair.

There is no smog or pollution.
Love has become the solution.

Each house is sturdy and never will fall.
The flowers smell fresh and the trees stand tall.

People chat and laugh along.
The birds above sing a song.

Everyone is working as a team.
Then I awake, it was just a dream.

Stephanie Jones

African Diamond

Captivating and Mysterious
exists a strand of hair created unlike all others
a tangible oracle whispering wondrous tales of ancient times
Like soft clouds of wrinkled cotton, these intricately woven fibers
mirror romantic rhythms and velvet vibrations,
a medley of personalities, passions and poetry
Intriguing all with its unique design this timeless and talented chameleon
ripples, unravels, curves, locks, folds, loops, twists...!
Its lustrous growth always winding upward into the heavens
Yet our African Diamond has been misunderstood, an enigma to many,
even to those from whose heads it grows!
Hated Despised Abused Cursed Loathed Resented—by souls who feel
    betrayed
For them their African hair, like brittle coal crying out into a desperate night,
crumbles wearily into thirsty dust, secrets of sweet beauty unsung, unseen
but African hair that is
Cherished Protected Respected Nurtured Embraced
like the celestial sun tenderly pouring its amber rays over rich ebony coals,
gives birth to
a divine and perfect sculpture of rare and exotic symmetry,
our African Hair, the African Diamond!

Raina L. Marie

By The Wayside/Sea Song

I have cradled anemones,
Feathered dandelions,
Petaled roses,
Captured the minute life of wildflowers,
Toed leaves aside and
Stubbed the stones of summer lanes
That carpet through the colour
    of perfume and memory....
And in the night the sea
Cradles me
In white-foamed glory in the moon,
Lifts me on the green scent on the tide,
Tumbling, and rising, casting on the beach
    a residue of stars

Sally Diamond

Never Alone

You'll never have to be alone if you'll only walk with me.
For I will show you where to go; alone you'll never be.
There may be times you'll feel so lost, that no one seems to care.
But there is One who understands and all your troubles share.
You do not keep your thoughts within, nor troubles in your heart.
For in this world of love, true friends will never part
and so we never walk alone unless it's where we choose.
But in our hearts we know we'll have too much to lose.
For what on earth of what we gain are good deeds that we sow.
We are not put on earth alone it's what we do and know.
And so you do not walk alone there's things you must abide.
You'll always get the help you need with God there by your side
if only you will just believe or think that no one cares
for in this world of beauty God is everywhere.
There may be times you'll wander or be far away from home
If you will only trust in God you'll never feel alone.
And so in life no matter what you'll never have no fear.
If you will only trust in Him you'll always feel him near.
And so this day into the years, whatever they will be,
I know I'll never feel alone for God will walk with me.

A. O. Leatherberry

Life's Journey

Love me today, tonight and tomorrow
    For I won't leave in times of sorrow.
Love me with honesty, commitment and belief
    Always make arguments short and brief.
For one day you'll wake, to find you're alone
    So never cast shadows, nor rock, nor stone.
For love is the way this world should turn.
    Never be harsh, cold nor stern.
Love yourself first, and others will see.
    What a wonderful journey, our lives can be.

Lisa M. Copeland

Children Grow Up

As you lay quiet, asleep in your beds,
I go over the day and the words that we said.
It was a good day, we laughed and we talked,
We sang and we danced, then went for a walk.
Your hands in mine were warm and soft,
If only this could last forever I thought.
But soon you'll grow up and be on your way,
We will no longer laugh and dance through the day.
I will cherish the memories that we've made together,
And deep in my heart they will stay forever.

Cindy M. Setka

Sweet Heaven

Mommie, tonight I'm asking Jesus to come into my heart,
  For in my life He's a great big part.
I know He loves me more than anyone,
  More than you Mom, and Mimi too.
Tonight I'm going to dream of Heaven
  and I know it's full of candy through and through.
I know it's full of sucker trees, we can pick them as we please.
I just know the grass is made of green chewing gum,
  I just know I'm going to want some.
The roads are made of gumdrops- I do believe
Chocolate pudding mud for trees to grow out of,
  Which I know I'll be sure to love.
Chocolate bar roofs on the houses up there,
  Which make up a place none can compare.
I dream about Heaven a lot and I know it's a wonderful place
  full of cotton candy snow where kool-aid rivers flow,
I'm sure Heaven's the most wonderful
  and sweetest place I'll ever know.

Rosalee R. Dyer

The Gift Of Love

The Gift of Love is two eyes,
full of hope and wonder, delight and innocence.
The Gift of Love is two tiny hands,
open and grasping,
searching and accepting,
gentle and playful, innocent.
The Gift of Love is a smile,
it caresses your being,
warms your heart,
brings life to your spirit.
The Gift of Love is a touch,
a hug anytime, a kiss anytime,
holding hands, playing pat-a-cake.
The Gift of Love is a cry,
a call of hunger, a need for consolement,
a longing for touch,
a need for companionship, contentment.
The Gift of Love is a laughter,
enchanting and contagious, innocent.
The Gift of Love is a Child, irreplaceable.

Pam Walton

Wings Of An Eagle

When you can't take anymore, break the chains off the door
Go fly on the wings of an eagle

When the pain never ends, it acts like a friend
Go fly on the wings of an eagle

When tears run down your face, their salt you can taste
Go fly on the wings of an eagle

The eagle will fly, high in the sky
Over all the enemies you know

The eagle will soar, to the cliff tops and more
Fly high in the sky

When abuse comes, run child, run
Fly high on the wings of an eagle

When words cut you into, don't know what to do
Go fly on the wings of an eagle

You will find peace and rest as you lay in the nest
Go fly on the wings of an eagle

Two eyelids to see straight into the sun
His power comes from on high

When you have given it all, there's still time to stand tall
When we fly on the wings of an eagle

Katherine Clore

Torn Between Two

The snow that melted, by the roadside dirty, gave a
grim impression, for to worry.
The night that fell gave darkness and hue, an impending
blackness, as I looked at you.
My bags lay packed, and exit I must, for your profanity
spewed, no more can I trust. My infant's face photographed
and framed, shall comfort my departure, I have not lived
in vain. Your hands grasp all that I own, beseeching me,
to forge out, and leave this home.
Before I depart, my child shall come with me, for he
is my savior comfort I find in he. I cling to his
softness, and hold on tight, but the furor of the moment
gives a terrible fright. Neither one shall set him free,
And in God we trust, how could this be?
The cries from the babe ring out in the night, then
silence falls upon my ears, I view a horrible sight.
All that I love lies lifeless and still, I clench my
hand at the sky, God is this thy will?

Heidi Grucci

A Victory...

Just a tough, small town girl
Growing up in a cruel world,
Independence was her claim,
All the world she was to gain...

And with this she went forth,
High expectations for what they're worth,
She wanted some identity,
And searched the ends of earth...

She possessed a thirst for knowledge
But her confusion only grew,
With the lies that she was told,
Deceit was all she knew...

So many things she needs to learn
So blinded by her quest,
Almost captured by deception, and all it can suggest...

Yet some days she felt untouchable, no one could stop her now...
But in the midst of Glory, still lies an untold story...

Renata Marie Izzi

Rebirth

I've been given the chance to live again.
  Hallelujah, Hallelujah
  The land has come.

He saved me from all my sins.
He's opened up the gates of heaven and let me in.
As I closed my eyes I felt him within.
And he replied walk to the light my child.
For the true and only love lies within.
So take my hand and follow me.
For I am the only one who can set you free.
Just look in my eyes and you will see.
I remember thinking to myself is
this a dream or is it reality.

When he touched my hand I knew
it could only be the Lord, my God,
my saviour for no one else has the
touch to heal all wounds.

So I opened my heart and set my love free.
For he has given me the chance to live again.

Christina Marie Englehart

The Skeleton Complex

Baby born from a junkie's womb
Having no choice of her destiny of doom
Days are just days and nights are simply nights
Soon a walking skeleton composed of frights
Bones that are fragile and easily broken
Mishaps and mistreatment are her black token
Here to mocked, a constant menace to mankind
No happiness or foundation shall she find
Bones dry and brittle as an autumn leaf
To have no meat is not beyond belief
She shall travel back to her place of doom
To a dark abyss which is her eternal tomb
Never to feel again Never to be heard
Never to hear another chiding word

Rhonda Fontenot

I Feel No Fear

My daddy was a bad man.
  He used to beat me wild.
Now I have a lover
  Who takes away the pain

There still are many doubts and fears
  From the first time around.
Abuse is hard to put aside
  New trust is hard to find.

The traumas, pains and memories
  Have claimed their hateful toll.
I search for peace; at times it comes.
  I feel the one I love

I think there's help from the Lord above.
  My life is filled with love
It feels so real that I feel alive
  When we share our love.

Florinda Oles

I Know A Little Boy

I know a little boy who loves to run and play.
He wakes up with a smile to start each and every day.

And as I watch him grow I thank the Lord above,
for giving me a child who is so full of love.

And as the years go by and he becomes a man,
He will make his own choices and develop his own plan.

And I will be there if he needs advice or just to talk to someone, because
I know a little boy who will always be my son.

Donna Barton

Raindrops

I hear them, raindrops in the treetops.
Here at my home, I hear them,
slowly caressing each leaf as they fall.
Raindrops I see sitting here at my windowsill,
raindrops falling to the ground.

Like tears of someone who cries of such sadness.
The raindrops are the tears of me,
and the sky is the center of my emotions.
My sadness comes from deep down inside,
from the one who only cries
me and only me.

I cry deep down inside,
but on the surface happiness pretends to lurk.
I do not want to feel pain inside.
I can't keep it a secret,
but still I hide,
from the world I do not know.

Kimberly Diane Hurst

Life On Planet Earth

Things are sadly different here, ...Your TV's, telephone and beer!
  Hustle bustle everywhere, with barely time to say a prayer!
Rainbow flowers growing wild,...sniffled perhaps when once a child!
  Surf and sand, NO TIME TO PLAY....tomorrow is another day.
Education, years and years,.... ROCKET-POWERED ENGINEERS...
  10 K Megabytes of speed, ... Always re-defining "need".
Compu-graphics, Neon Lights....Fiber optics, Concord Flights,
  Seminars and Training camps,...What became of oil lamps???
80 some odd waster years, ... WORKING, STRIVING, FIGHTING
  FEARS,...
  Trying hard to get ahead, until one day, you WAKE UP dead!!
Overnight your babes are grown, ... aged and crippled, ALL ALONE!
  Here today and gone tomorrow,....Life goes on, NO TIME FOR
  SORROW!
Sun comes up and sun goes down,.... ceiling fans go round and round,..
  Two steps forward, one behind,... all in sync., ALL ARE BLIND!
POLITICIANS, WAR and BATTLE,. "Puppets", slaughtered just like cattle!
  Rushing to your own disaster, ... GETTING NOWHERE, that much
  faster
POISONED STREAMS, POLLUTED AIR, ..too convenient NOT TO
  CARE!
  COMPLETE EXTINCTION GROWING NEAR,...
  Things are SADLY different here!!!

Toni Melton-Treworgy

Wandern

I wonder if he knows
I am here.

Each time he passes my temperature rises,
and my blood runs cold.

I wonder if he knows
I am under his mystical spell.

So enchanted, that even a deep rumble
of the earth I rest my feet upon,
could not break its barrier.

I wonder if he knows
that time is modified

Never ceasing to stay for fear of dying;
only to be born again to die.

My love grows impatient
I wonder if he knows...

Carol Hoover

The Days Are Long And Lonely

The days are long and lonely and the nights go by so slow
I can only wish when you return, our love will continue to grow
It seems so empty without you, here by my side
I miss the precious moments, with you I could confide
I try to think of cheerful thoughts, with a smile on my face
But at night it becomes difficult, to forget your gentle embrace
I know the time is nearing, when you will come back home
Counting the minutes, the hours, the days I feel so all alone
The days are long and lonely and the nights go by so slow
I can only wish when you return, our love will continue to grow

Debra Kay Hershberger

I WHISPERED IN GOD'S EAR

I whispered in God's ear one night that AIDS was killing me
I cried that this was not my end but knew this was to be
I whispered in God's ear one night that a cure would not come late
But I soon got sick and weaker I knew this was my fate

I whispered in God's ear one night I'll try to be very strong
But felt I was betrayed by life I was a good person I did nothing wrong
I whispered in God's ear one night my family, and friends have sorrow
How can I help even myself when I may be gone by tomorrow

I whispered in God's ear one night please help me to live on
To help those who need my help to guide them when I am gone
Then all of a sudden God whispered to me my son you can rejoice
You will help those who need it most you are my TOOL my LOVE
   my VOICE

So off with you and start your work I promise it will not be painful
You are needed by so many prayers my son you are a guardian ANGEL
Take care of the flock I assign to you and love them as if they were your own
Then one day you will guide each one to my Kingdom your very home

Pamela J. Locke

"Riches"

Each time I think of us,
I feel I've found my fortune.
Success and prosperity are ill-conceived notions.
Misrepresented materialism; modern man's malpractice.

I look at those around me:
Scenes of souls still searching.
Always wanting more, displeased with what they have.
Possessive of possessions; passion's passing pleasures.

I search within myself for truth,
A flame feeds new-found freedom.
My dark side submerges; rebirth begins.
Self-knowledge needs no negative notions.

Happiness lies not in money, power, or property.
Fulfillment's fruits found not within but between.
Being with you, I am enlightened.
Our relationship reaps rich rewards.

We've grown so close together,
Two intertwined in immeasurable interests, intellect, and intimacy.
Our wealth concealed inside our hearts.
Success's secrets sealed in two shared souls.

David W. Mitchell

A Gift Of Christmas

When going through my Christmas things
   I found to my delight,
   the many things I'd put away
      completely out of sight.

So I would like to share these things
   with friends and family too,
   in baskets filled with cones and bows;
      I'm sending on to you.

Where in this blessed Holiday
   we share with ones do dear,
   and pray that health and happiness be
      their throughout the year.
Now when the Christmas Season's done,
   and gift are put away,
   you'll always know the love I sent
      is never fay away!

Marion Garrett

"After Our First Date"

When I awoke this morning
I had you on my mind
I thought I'd let you know it
By dropping you a line.

Here's hoping you are feeling fine
And happy as can be
And maybe, just maybe you may have had
One little thought of me.

I asked our God to bless you,
Give you strength for each new day
And show you love and courage
And help you on your way.

As your day progresses
May all things turn out right
And may you find you'll have peace of mind
As day turns into night.

Curtis W. Gordon

Following The Light

I feel your arms wrapped around me Jesus
I hear you whispering softly in my ear
I know that soon, I will be with you in heaven
And now, I have nothing to fear
My guardian angels are beside me
To take me to the promised land
The path that I've followed, here on earth
Will lead me to your waiting hands
Following the light,
Seeing God so near
This is what I have been waiting for
To see you open the door
Following the light,
To peace and comfort evermore
Praising and worshipping day and night
I'm glad to be following the light

Peggy A. Tipton

Lady

One time in the darkness of loneliness felt
I spoke to the Father I asked for His help
I prayed for a someone a soft gentle touch
A female a Christian a woman of such
His answer came to me as often seems to
A message of guidance that led me to you
A woman has beauty she's pleasant to sight
But lady is star shine the heavenly light
If one such existed in likely it seemed
A person, a someone, a quest for a dream
To fine her to hold her the angel of love
To seek among mortals a gift from above
Soon after I meet her I know how I feel
My prayers were now answered, my dreams were now real
Do prayers receive answers I'd have to say yes
One word does describe you and lady is best

Silas Webb

637

In Black And Brown Town

The Barrio; Logan Heights...In San Diego that's BLACK AND
  BROWN TOWN.
I was born, raised and schooled in BLACK AND BROWN TOWN.
I went to college and work far from life on the streets of
BLACK AND BROWN TOWN.
Later, I returned to teach at a high school in BLACK AND BROWN TOWN.
I taught ethnic pride and "fired" students up; then lost my job
teaching in BLACK AND BROWN TOWN.
But all 'twas not lost; I then taught, traveled and learned all over
the world; but never forgetting I came from BLACK AND BROWN TOWN.
And now, I'm happier than ever to once again be teaching in
BLACK AND BROWN TOWN.
I am amazed by the apathy and lack of ambition in the lives of my
wonderful students in BLACK AND BROWN TOWN.
Now I ask myself: "Why do Blacks act so loud and foolish? And why
are browns so timid and shy in the classrooms of BLACK AND
  BROWN TOWN?"
But, with patience and enthusiasm galore, I'll make heroes of each
and every student I teach in BLACK AND BROWN TOWN.
And, surely the truest measure of human success will be in the number
of Y.O.U. students soon to be able to learn, work and travel all over
the world; but never forgetting they came from BLACK AND
  BROWN TOWN!

  Bob Moss

Come And You Will Find Me

Leave all your possessions far behind,
I will give you treasures of another kind.
Search, for you alone can find me,
where the pearly white sands meet the sea.
Come and you will find me, waiting here,
take me into your arms to hold so dear.

Let us clasp our hands together for evermore,
as we stroll this private golden shore.
Smell my hair as the winds take a dip,
and taste salty waters from my lips.
Come, and you will find me, come my love,
release your heart, soaring far, far above.

Your eyes look through me, as sky's clear blue,
mine to watch shades of pebbles hue.
Waves will wash us and drift out to sea,
come searching My Love,
and you alone will find me.

  Peg Riedel

I Will Dream

Last night I dreamed a dream I wish I had not dreamt.
In all the confusion of the dream, few things I understood what they meant.
Now here I am dreaming this dream again.
This terrible dream full of sin.
I dreamed of you, I dreamed of me,
I dreamed of you and me, I dreamed of a we.
I dreamt of that perfect time when I could make love to you.
This terrible awful dream that can not come true,
And I wish I would dream no dreams of you.
But this night as I sleep, the dark under my eyes
Will fill with thoughts of you, truths I wished were lies.
So this night these dreams I pray will go away,
So that I can look at you in the light of day
Without having to think of my silent thoughts at night,
My terrible awful horrid dreams that from my mind will not take flight.
This evening I will dream dreams I wish I would not dream,
And even though I say I don't, I will understand what they mean.

  Melanie Wienecke

In Memory Of

In memory of the times we had.
In memory of the songs we sang.
In memory of the dreams we shared.
In memory of the places we went.

I sing this song in memory of you!

In memory of the holidays.
In memory of the decorations so bright.
In memory of the streets at night.
In memory of such great delight!

I sing this song in memory of you!

In memory of the love we shared.
In memory of the hugs we've given.
In memory of the nights that passed.
In memory of the days that didn't last.

My dears, I sing this song in memory of you!

  Beth Anne Wilson

"Upon This Hill"

Upon this hill; I gently stand a while,
In my eyes; there shows a tear, on my face a smile.

I reminisce of days gone by, when I was younger too,
Now time; has made its mark, but I remember you.

Upon this hill; we played as kids, imaginations running wild
We made promises, we wouldn't keep; but it seem like fun,
all the while.

Upon this hill; above the school, I kissed 'Mary Jean',
Lustful youth; with no cares, my world so serene.

Upon this hill; I've seen seasons pass, as I became a man
And upon this hill, I just thank god, for who I am.

Upon this hill; I've seen our friends,
Laid gently beneath the sod
Upon this hill, I've watched the clouds
Roll by, and I've talked to God

Upon this hill; I've shared my life,
With memories they'll never take away
And upon this hill; I hope to rest,
When god calls me home someday.

  Mitchell A. Stanley

Blow Out

My heart is a spare tire stuck
in snow   deep tread marks show
the skid on glassy
cinders and blue frayed
cloth   frozen earth is tossed
from the spinning   leaving scars
on underbrush   and patches
of ashes fill my mouth   rocking
to and fro in a strange
rhythm   rocking to and fro as a child's
cradle would   but the wrong
tune   alone   abandoned
on black ice   my eyes search
for you in a sweeter
time   the village tow
truck won't be needed

  Mimi Eagan

638

A Season Foretold

In the sweet summer, I heard my heart above the soft, warm breeze.
In the binnacle of my soul, I saw you standing there without a sorrow.
It became lucid in your explanation. You asked me "Please..."
And with your words, you were the elucidator of tomorrow.
I was fearful of our dreams of forever and actuality.
We saw two roads to take, the two roads to choose.
And we each chose our own vitality.
We acknowledged in that choice what we would both loose.
So when we whispered our farewells in the morning dew,
I stole a fragment of our past together,
To reminisce about the dreams that were once true...
About the season foretold as forever.

Sara Vanderhei

The Span Of Life

Gamblers will say that all life is a game,
In which you can also bluff and can raise;
While others will say that life stays the same,
For it is pre-ordained in all ways.

But the true soul knows that on-coming death
Is a part of any greater life span;
It must come and go as a daily breath,
A part of a non-fathomable plan.

The way to live is enjoy what you can,
For life is to be loved and be felt;
This soul so laughs and so loves in his span,
And gladly plays the cards that he is dealt.

William Lex Coplen

The Stalker

Nowhere is where the driveway empties into the pot-holed-paved
intersection.
I once read cement was this nonsense made of limestone;
scraps of dead little clams
The parking lot is vacant; under the moon white lines accentuated.
Right sixty feet northward drifts a flirtatious neon sign.
Glazed glass bulbs have gone out,
now reading: BROOKVIL E DIN R
Peering through the window, again, elders are cozy;
so many maladies between them.
The waitress is wiry and bond, tossing charcoal roots to the side.
She piles up crepes and slabs of cheesecake.
It was rancid 36 hours ago, hours crusted on the sides.
That's what I saw, right sixty feet southward.

Andrea Pantor

"Old"

He looked at her and thought, is that my young wife?
Is she the one that was so gay and full of life?
Is she that girl that thrilled at a kite in the sky.
She who watched it dip and dive and flutter
    with hop in her eye?
Is she the one that arose before dawn to
    pour coffee in a cup, and watch the sun come up?
Is she the one that could skip, sing and run,
    and spend the whole day in the sun?
Who is that old woman with the wrinkled
    skin an graying hair?
What happened to my love that was so fair?
    she slowly raised her head and thought,
    who is that old man?
The one who is stooped and has gray hair.
    It that really my love over there in
    that rocking chair?

Martha Waid Walker

I Found The Way

As I was driving down this road, I saw a holy sign.
It said, come one come all, so I stopped and got in line.
Someone had opened a godly store, where everything was free.
As I, traveled down the aisle, this man walked up to me.
A ray of sunshine accompanied him, and a smile was on his face.
He said, welcome my son, come shop with me, so we strolled
Around this place.
First on a list was repentance, I had heard of this holy act.
Within a heavenly bundle is how this item was packed.
High on a shelf and far to the back wa this thing called love.
With a open heart and out stretched arms, he gave a bit of a shove.
Then came faith, along with hope, I knew I'd need a lot
While growing up my mother loved me but that's all the love I got.
Last on my list was salvation, I said I don't need this.
He said you've earned all you received, so take some my child,
I insist.
As I got to the counter to pay, I said, I don't have a cent.
This son of man looked in my eye and said, pain in full, repent.

Clifford O. Procter

Do You Know?

Indifference in men is the meaning of hate.
    It's apathy saying that love holds no weight.

Then hate is the chosen tool of a man
    Relentlessly battling his own Divine Plan.

Yet hate, when seen through the sage's eyes,
    Is the veiling of Truth; Love's total disguise.

Then, what is wrong as compared to right,
    But another step as we journey toward light.

And what's a mistake, whether big or small,
    But a road in the map of Divinity's all.

What is fear, but a call to the wise,
    To bring to awareness, Love in its guise.

Love is the answer, as me and you.
    So choose, at this moment, false image or true!

Veronica Grogan

Lost Love

Her name as sweet as a song inspired
Its flowing sounds leave aught to be desired
Its rhythm as soft as moonbeams striking a chord
Its pulse beating out a tantalizing rhapsody.

Her eyes so deep, so stirred, so quickly defiant,
In sheer hypnotic to their depth of soul
In spirit so strong, of confusion and conflict
Of fight, of drive and a dream to unfold.

Your eyes look to meet hers
Subdued and lost for words,
Her haunting spirit within you a storm creates
of desire, of despair, of help yet of hurt.

Her dream she clutches hard to bosom
And leaves not room for more,
She has me tangled in her hair
She has me fettered in despair.

I pray thee, release me in thy mercy
So I can breathe again
Or take me to your breast
to be at peace again.

Philip Rosenberg

Dream On My Pillow

There's a dream on my pillow
Just waiting there for me
If sleep comes tonight
Your sweet face I'll see

So I follow my heart and turn down the light
I place my head on my pillow so tight
I toss and turn and curse the night
No sleep to come, no dream in sight

It's four in the morning with a few hours left
Before I get up and have to get dressed
Then in a second you were here
In your eyes, not even one tear
But a smile on your face
All dressed up wearing white lace

There's a dream on my pillow
I dreamed it last night
We got married
By dawn's early light

Avonell Blackburn

Untitled

Life is a book filled with joys and sorrows
Life is a book of money yesterday and tomorrows
God wrote your book and he also wrote mine
He wrote them both so they could intertwine.
He filled them with love of family and friends
He filled them with love from beginning to end.
But when your book came I am end
My book had lost a very great friend.
I turn my pages only to find
You are out of sight but in my mind.
For God has left me a treasure so wonderful
    and great
He left me memories of you - as you
    enter his gate.

Mary De Cesare

Desperation

Life is cruel and cold,
like one's heart...to be sought after but not to hold.
As I listen to the soft pitter patter of rain
eroding away soil our Lord made for man to claim.
I wonder what lies beneath it all...
could it be water, more soil, or lifeless bodies
unclaimed by this cold and cruel life?
They say a picture's worth a thousand words,
if I painted mine it would be black and cold.
For the sun never shines where life doesn't lie,
as the birds will never sing until they've learnt to fly.
Mother Nature is something truly to behold,
she has life that blooms,
NOT BLACK, CRUEL, and COLD!

Michelle Foster

Friendly Tendrils

I opened my cupboard and to my surprise
My potatoes had roots, growing out of their eyes.
And they made me think of my very dear friend
Whom I had not seen for months upon end.
So I called her and said, "Tear your schedule in two.
Come visit me bringing some spuds that are new."
She laughed and she said, "I was thinking of you.
My carrots have sprouted. Can you spare a few?"
I knew what she meant when she made the remark.
Friendship, like roots can grow in the dark.

Mary Meeker

Love

Loving God first is always right,
Loving thy self is next in life,
Loving everybody is not hard to do,
If your heart is right you'll find it to be true,
hate come's from a very, very sick mind,
And will destroy the person in little or no time,
With love in your heart you will always do good,
you will help mother nature to do things it should,
every child you can talk to you will teach them well,
words of wisdom will ring a bell,
love all animals they are here for a reason,
love the birds they are here for a season,
love your family because they are dear to your heart,
    love your friends is also smart,
we were created to love each other,
everybody should think of one another as a sister or brother,
life would be great if there was no hate,
there would be no wars and peace would be our golden gate,
everyday our heart would shine,
a loving light to the end of time.

Joe Light

Our Love

Time creeps along slowly,
minutes seem like hours here without you.
Loneliness like a vast ocean,
miles and miles of nothing but blue.
Thoughts of you fading in and out,
though you're so far your presence is so near.
Memories of happiness and bliss,
run through my mind like clouds on a windy day.
Our love, bright like the sun,
always shining, giving me warmth and comfort.
Nature surrounds me,
constantly reminding me of our brief time together.

Lorrie Ann Mendonca

Sonnet For My Father

Faded the pictures, all but one, of you:
Morning, your time of day, you sitting there,
Half up the steps, bent down to tie your shoe,
Sun on your thin gray face and wisps of hair.

"I'll be all right," you say with quiet smile,
"I'll hoe a bit, I guess—or cut the grass."
We drive away, shouting, "Take care the while."
You wave goodbye. How quickly life's loves pass,

Gone the green days and voices dear, so dear.
Oh, my unseeing eyes, how blind to Now!
Moving lips mute—and deaf my youthful ear.
Father, might you have made me know, somehow,
To press the moments ere they sped away,
To note each Now of Never—yesterday.

Phyllis Lahti

"If Only"

If only I could be loved
    The ways that I've loved
If only someone could give a little
    The ways I've gave a lot
If only someone could cry one tear
    The ways I've cried one million
If only someone could just touch
    The ways I've touched with my heart
    But one day I'll have the love,
    the giveness, the tears and the touch that I deserve
If only I could get the chance to have my love I "Need"

Ruah Guy

640

The Path Of Goodness

Who walks the path without a heart
Must see themselves beheld in beauty
Neither for pleasure's soothe nor ego's part
Rather for undivided destiny's duty

For neither brick nor stone may halt
The growth of the rising earth's colorful life
Where man's foot has fallen in grateful fault
So that he too grows from every strife

While direction shows itself from the core
Women and men begin to explore uniqueness gift
Eternal within; earth kisses sky while ocean's roar
Touching the person along the path 'til spirits uplift

With a smile so magically big
So colorfully together and all
A quantum heart that sings
Loves to rise and not to fall

Damon Vallese

Untitled

You captivate me...
My mind...
My body,
My soul
(Completely).
I am spellbound...
With the way,
Your eyes look into me
and not through me.
How they people into the recesses
of my mind.
Through corridors of realities that cease,
to exist.
I am breathless..
with the way,
your lips embrace mine
like a lost love found.
How they seem to touch upon every fiber,
of my being.
As you carefully caress my willing flesh.

Mia C. Proctor

She And Her Son

She's depressed and alone.
No one here to call her own.
Her only child died at the age of two.
She was so depressed that she didn't know what to do.
She stopped eating drinking and even sleeping.
She just sits there weeping.
If you try to talk to her,
She will just want to know, "what for?".
One night she finally went to sleep,
At least that's what I thought when I took a peep.
This sleep wasn't temporarily,
It was permanently.
I didn't want her to leave,
But in my mind, I believed,
She was in Heaven with her son,
Praising Lord God, number one.
Now they're back together,
Side-by-side for the better.

Nicole Mason

Gypsy Wagon

Once festive abode of the Pharaoh's folk,
   Now fading colors, peeling paint,
Hanging traces and mossy weathered oak,
   Your deep song lost, tongue lying silent,
   No longer accused of devilment.
Spoked wheels, iron-rimmed, stilled,
   By a dark-eyed familia's abandonment,
Your "Dukes of Little Egypt" long banished.

   A relic beside an elm as ancient,
A rootless vagabond left in a British field,
   Marked by a leaf-filled Norman moat.
What life have your priests of Isis found?

LaVedi Lafferty

Dreams

What are they? Mostly fantasies and hopes.
Of different places and mountains slopes.
Of things I wish, but have not obtained.
Of a love so perfect, that I have not gained.
My dreams are of sunrises fresh and clear.
And a day that's not wasted that I can hold dear.
Of sunsets and rainbows and beauty untold.
Of someone to touch, to love and to hold.
A dream of a lover, in which I can believe.
All of my dreams, around him I'll weave.
The dream of God's beauty put here on earth.
Of laughter and music, happiness and birth.
Someday I'll find him and I'll be complete.
For dreams must be shared for life to be sweet.

Myrl Moody

"On To"

On to live another life
On to love another man

She dies and brings sorrow to us,
but is born again and brings joy to another
On to live another life

She loved one man,
He cries out for her
but tonight she is with another
On to love another man

He kneels at her grave, wishing it is
only a nightmare in which he will awaken
He knows it is true, but does not want
to say good-bye, does not want to let go.
On to love another, but he is now
On to love another

Melissa Mitchell

One Dark Hole

In the meaning of life there is one dark hole,
This is where I sit all alone,
No one there but me, all my friends are in the light
Fight as I might, I never get to the light
The dark has taken me as his friend,
He'll never let me see the light again
As my friends see me they run
Side by side, they see darkness and I

The dark hole I sit in is a large one in fact
Many people come in, all of them go out
Darkness lets everyone go but me,
Oh, will you come in and talk to me!

Cynthia Allen

"The Watchers"

Someday out here within the sky,
  Our tiny point of light will die,
Then sparkle in the watchers' eye,
  Of distant worlds left floating by.

We'll scatter far, past scenes once near.
  Our small demise, someone may hear.
We'll echo through an endless year,
  Awake somewhere the watchers' ear.

We'll crumble and through darkness fall,
  A tiny speck, a floating ball.
Then time is up, and gone are all.
  None answer to the watchers' call

They heard our birth, the sun had dawned.
  They looked for us from worlds beyond.
But left have we, and all are gone.
  And still the watchers wonder on.

So may it be, the watchers find,
  Our world before they're left behind.
    Rachel M. Bailey

Spirit Of The Seasons

Winter is like the quietness and
Peacefulness of your inner self.

Spring rain is like a purifying
Shower to cleanse your outer-self
And mother earth.

Summer is like the brightest
And warmest glow in you heart and soul.

Thunder and lightening are the incredible
Energy of one's passions for love and life

Fog is like the cloak of your
Spirituality.

Autumn is like the change of a
Beautiful ending to a breathtaking reawakening.
    Pamela Phillips

It's My Turn

All of a sudden there she was staring back at me, that
person I saw my mother become to be. Like her, my
eyes are also still clear but they now tote those inevitable
bags, and should I worry that my flesh has begun to sag?

Oh I don't fear this process called aging...I just hope
that, like my mother, my mind remains engaging!
    L. L. Braxton

Rainbows

As Rainbows are beautiful in there splendor,
Rainbows are the completion of one thing, and
a promise of a new beginning. As I stand at
the end of my Rainbow, I can see no pot of
Gold. Oh' but I do see the beauty of God in
all of His creations, even the Rainbows of Life
are very beautiful. Rainbows are very pretty
gift from God with a promise of a new beginning.
May you always find a new beginning in the Lord
at the end of each Rainbow of Life.
    Charles E. Chancellor

The Time Of Nourishment

The winds gather and meet
  Reluctantly, the saplings are chilled to the core
From the two clouds the rain pours
  O you and I better watch out for it looks like a war

From the two clouds the rain pours
  Out from the sky there is a lightning flash
Though the old man snores
  The black sides of the two clouds clash

Long the clouds pour forth their tears
  The time passes as though it were lent
But it is not rare, it happens throughout the years
  Since it is a time of nourishment

The ferns and irises receive their soak
  The roses are ready for the stage of pink
From the rain there becomes a moat
  Of which a creek forms and animals drink

From these things there is life
  And from these things people have hope to live
So, my friends, do not weep and put forth strife
  For it is not us but the heavens that give
    David E. Grim

Fatherless

I looked in the mirror. And what did I not see.
Reminiscences of a father, that I have yet to meet.

The braveness of your conception has left a scar of pain.
A child's heart longing for a father, who left to be unclaimed.

You father, have not been available to fulfill my needs.
But that's okay, my heart's not filled with hatred with hatred of greed.

I don't hate you for human nature error.
I just don't know what to see, when I look in the mirror.

The mirror holds a divine emptiness for me,
when I gaze into it, a reality of you I cannot see.

I can't imagine the real me because I don't know you.
I have my mothers eyes, but what do I have resembles you?

We have yet to meet face to face, because, you
left me without an ounce to trace.

I am fatherless!
    Nona B. Hubbard

Just One Sip

All I want is just one sip, one drop of water upon my lips.
Send momma to the well, try to find out the secret she won't tell.
Send momma to get a little more. Haven't got a dime; we must be poor.
Momma, poor momma, oh how she cries.
She doesn't know it, but me and the Lord, we know she tries.
We haven't gone to school in years.
The only thing we study are each other's tears.
I try to care for the younger ones as best I can.
Everyone in town says momma, she needs a man.
My momma don't like to be dependent on some else, you see.
That's how we live, she says that's just the way it has to be.
Poor little Jimmie, oh how that boy lies.
Momma says, "Leave 'em alone," but it's hard sometimes.
I never asked my momma for a bicycle, or a puppy, and such.
In fact, I never asked for very much.
But, for now, all I want is just one sip,
One drop of water upon my lips.
Send momma to the well, try to find out the secret she won't tell.
Send momma to get a little more.
Haven't got a dime, but we'll never be poor.
    Melody A. Carswell

"Afflicted Waters"

With the illusion of promise so invitingly serene
She is the dreaded waters, MELANCHOLY
Misery is the fate for swimming her seas.
Blackest sin or unimaginable desire?
Tempted by the answers, he dives
Into an emotional whirlpool of lies
Struggling against the depths of murky iciness
Arms outstretched in a macabre embrace
Unbearable silent screams
Awaiting a joyous rescue that never comes
Currents too powerful to resist - he succumbs ...
A desolate surrender since there is no merciful death
Deafening sounds of her waves crashing relentlessly against
the shore
HOVERING IN ALL HER GLORY, MELANCHOLY ROARS
"WELCOME TO MY
LAGOON OF LOVE!"
The tide comes.

Amber R. Shakir

The Status Of A Dandelion

Dandelion seed floating by, a pale white wisp in a cold blue
sky, softly whispers for me to hear, singing songs for the
imaginative ear, singing the blues. I made a wish on a
shooting star, sailing by away off far, I saw the star wink
at me, something only the imaginative see, what's to lose?
Our world is a dying race, with no more place, for my
imagination to roar, or watch starfish on the shore, all in
my brain. No more fun only technology, and everything turns
out, technically, no more roses no more wine, no more time
to watch the moon shine, our world is insane. When I look
inside I see the snow, flurrying down and landing on my
nose, cold and white it settles with a chill, and piling
higher and higher still, I feel the silent peace a field of
flowers blowing gently in the wind, and to think only around
the cobblestone bend, it really is there to say good
morning, gracefully adorning, and never to cease, if only we
could learn to see, the world is so peaceful imaginatively,
not to far away and always there for me and
all you have to do, is learn to see,
dandelion seed floating by...

Natasha Boyer

Flames Of Death

Thick dark clouds of dangerous
smoke!

Two fire fighters helplessly
choke.

Trapped inside an inferno of flames—
Yet no one remembers their names!

The flames grew fierce as it headed
their way.

"Bring in more water!" I heard the Captain
say.

The collapsing of cement, the bonfire of
wood!

All hopes were lost as it's been understood.

Like a beacon in the night appear a tremendous
glow!

From the "Flames of Death" that took our
unknown heroes.

Hector J. Williams

To A Wonderful Lady

Here's to the lady, over whom that I dote
    So much I think of her, yet no poem have I wrote
I am not alone in my praise, of this gem
    Friends, family and neighbors feel the same of this femme
Her daughter knows, she's a woman of grace
    And her kindness shows, just look at her face
There's stories and odes, and tales of her praise
    And many would help, her halo to raise
To Kenny and Mark, she's Ma, or it's Mum
    She is still their mother, but also their chum
The grandchildren love her, they are at ease by her side
    They share my feelings, of my wonderful bride
All our love, upon you we bestow
    You're always in our hearts dear, I am sure that you know
Your character, no words or expressions could taint
    Your beauty, on canvas, only Michelangelo could paint
And so life goes on, one year after another
    So God Bless this Lady, my wife and your mother.

Peter McEwen

My Friends, My Friends

They think to help me,
So they think;
They talk behind my back
In whispers as a pack;
Ah, my friends, my friends.

They think to help me,
So they think;
They arrange my affairs hidden from sight
With plans and schemes hatched in the night;
Ah, my friends, my friends.

They think to help me,
So they think;
They tell me naught of what they do,
Yet expect my goodwill to so accrue;
Ah, my friends, my friends.

They think to help me,
So they think;
They visit upon me pain, not pleasure,
Their help hurts beyond all measure;
Ah, my friends, my friends.

Joseph S. Fulda

Victor's Broken Heart

A pure, clean love, unconditional and
sole, flows in the heart.
Envy and jealousy, walking hand in hand,
knocking at the door.
The wind whispers forever, our souls
become endless, one person exists between
the two.
A touch from my hand, the sweet has gone
sour, a stench follows the death of our
song.
Each breath intoxicates your air, leaving
you gasping, searching for the truth.
A dream turned into a nightmare, boiling
at the blood, tearing at the heart.
The sound of one hand clap echoes,
loneliness numbs my body, there is no
feeling in your heart.
I close my eyes trying to deny my
touch of filth, cutting my hand,
breaking your heart.

Michele Higgins

Tear Stained Letters

So many tear stained letters
Stacked in many separate piles,
A girl rips them one by one to tatters
It's been like this for a while.

No one to talk to when needed her family seemed turned away,
And oh, now she cried and pleased but no one helped to her dismay.

Then it happened on a clear night
She turned toward the starry sky,
raised her sharp shining knife
and then quickly said good-bye

She looked beautiful in her casket
her cheeks even looked a little rosy
Surrounded by flowers in baskets she looked peaceful and cozy

Why was all anyone could say if they only knew how she felt
To her everyone seemed turned away
If they could only feel what she felt

But ifs and maybes can't fix anything and no one will
know to whom where all those tears stained letters
But there is one more thing if she had
turned to God would things have been better?

Summer Bowman

Untitled

Walking in the late evening with my girl on gas light
street with the sounds of Moonlit Serenade coming from a tavern nearby.
Two children helplessly in love. Her head on my shoulder,
my arm around her waist, We strolled for what seemed to be
mere short minutes - turning out to be hours. Solving every
problem the world could dish out. Our love for each other could
resist through the ages for all times! Saying goodnight at the end
of the evening. Standing on the front porch a dim light shines
from a lamp near the window, casting shades of yellow gold on
her skin. I seek the kiss which bears goodnight.
With eyes closed my body leans, fumbling, searching for
her lips. With short minute "peck", the task was over.
A shy goodnight was whispered as she opened the door,
Her eyes were gleaming, I love you!
The door shut behind her, as I turned towards the front
steps heading towards the gate.
Walking alone down the gas light street. With the sound
of Moonlit Serenade coming from a nearby tavern, I knew that I was in Love!

Paul M. Young

To Know The Season That We Call Fall

A crisp, vivacious breeze toying with my hair, along with
Swirling eddies of cascading leaves playing in the wind,

Quickly arouse my keen senses to the reality that, once
Again, that season known as fall is in the air.

The sky is a vivid, clear blue, devoid of any intrusive
Clouds; sunlight shines from that oh, so melancholy angle,

From which long shadows emanate to fall across the earth
Like echoing latticed shrouds.

Trees aflame with leaves in fiery paint-box colors of
Oranges, golds, yellows and reds, undulating rhythmically in
The wake of the tormenting wind,

So that their shaken leaves will ever so gracefully glide
Downward to meet their earthly beds.

Hark, the scratchy sounds of rakes I hear, the piquant aroma
Of burning leaves titillates my nostrils,

But soon the thick smoke will begin to clear.
To know the season that we call fall, we must indulge our 5
senses
So that we may experience the wonder of it all.

Sandra L. Smith

Poetry

There are little bits of poetry
that filter through my mind,
but it's hard to find a pencil at the time.

As I'm driving, while I'm working,
even dreaming, I will find
there's a certain flow of words that seem to rhyme.

But, of course, there is no paper
or a place on which to write
and I think I can remember just a few.

But it's not at all that easy,
it's a struggle and a fight,
to recall that certain phrase, or maybe two.

So it seems the key to poetry
is hearing from above,
it's not necessary that it be in print.

There are angels up there talking
and their words are filled with love,
if you'll listen, you'll be richer than the mint.

Yes, I hear a lot of poetry, too beautiful to write,
it's not written - it's projected - and it's blessed - with all HIS might!

Donald L. Bratten

The Daydreams Of A Boy...

Running through the backyard to chase a butterfly...

Climbing up a big tall tree and gazing at the sky...

Dreaming that I have big wings and could soar up in the air...

I would fly around the world I'd fly everywhere...

Or, no maybe I would be a jet pilot
that would fly his plane so fast...

I would pass by all the other planes
and people would clap as I flew past...

Or maybe I'll be a firefighter, saving people each day...

Riding on a big red truck Beeping cars out of my way...

Or maybe I'll be a little boy just for a while longer...

Until I grow up like my Dad, then I will be much stronger...

And for now I'll still climb trees and chase all kinds of bugs...

And when I am tired from all my hard work
I will go see my mom for some hugs...

Michele Mariejka

"Desert Storm"

Desert storm, desert storm.
The eagles in the night is flying overhead,
Because the Mother of war will not do
What is right,
Come out of Kuwait or lose your life.

The tanks are moving through the sand.
In hope that the foot soldiers will get
there in time, for the President's demand.
Come out of Kuwait by high noon, or
else the snuffer will find you soon.

One by sea and two by land.
The gulf of Persian was polluted, by
Saddam Hussain's hands.
Come out of Kuwait or lose your life.
United States are winning this fight.

The black smoke of oil is blazing fire.
Smell of death and flesh in the sky.
Clouds are hanging heavy over the desert's sand.
This all started by Saddam Hussain's Hands.

Geneva Franklin Ruffin

644

The Wind And The Desert Sands

As the wind blow through the desert sands
The howling tell its presence
The sands swirls and shuffle,
It settles, creates bowls
And scatter along coast lines
'Tis the journey the wind makes occur
If you were there and the wind meets the sands
It swirls, whispers and graze your eyes
Its strength is told
The desert stays still and beckons the wind
You can hear the bawling when the wind arrive
Why shuffle me says the sands
To cool you says the wind
Each day, and night your are scorched by sun.
'Tis duty for I to restore.
For why, 'tis my duty I do
The swirl, the graze and the shuffle for me to see
Your whispers tells my presence
T'is the nature of desert sands
When the wind blows. (Across).

Charles Ihejeto

Dinner At The Ancestral Home, Ripley Tennessee

There is a way the air gets outside, just before a big family meal.
The lull of evening as it falls across your eyes like hair.
Everyone's skin the color of Indian corn in the lowering sun.
I could smell the colors of the food. We were as big as our eyes.

I, with more hunger for us than for the cornbread of potatoes,
watched the eyes and the mouths, could feel the voices pouring
over me, running over me like my mother's fingertips on my back
when I was burning with fever as a child.

We were many children and we were as big as our eyes.
The food spread across the table like an old oil painting,
the many female hands passing in front of my face,
masculine voices as rick as custard warming my body into my chair.

My big family has a thing for big food in big bowls.
When we gather or knocking knees make a rhythm we lean into.
When we have dinner there is a great explosion of talking.
I can almost see the bursting of fire around our mouths.

Everything comes from us. Our hands and arms thrust forward
into the table. We make any excuse to touch one another.
And act like we don't notice.

Laura Tucker

The Mask

Remove the mask, sweet child and reveal your heart
The mask is only worn by fools. I again beseech you
cast it off!

With full smiling lips, the mask revels
In certain convivial actions.

But tell me child.
Do your lips really frown with pain?

The mask shows eyes of royal blue
frolicking in gaiety and joy.

Now tell me child. do your eyes dance in their spheres,
or do they weep and cry?

In honest innocence answer me child.
Are you and the mask the same?

Reluctantly the mask removes and all that is there to see,
is the innocent child weeping in fear and pain.

For that is what all wish to see,
No pain, no suffering, only love, only happiness,
only the Mask, not me.

Missy Nason

Angie's Pain

Angie was a tall, stout and lonely girl,
The neighborhood kids were always mean to her,
Her parents would beat her unmercifully,
Echoes of her screams permeated the air,
They were sounds of excruciating pain,
As an animal caught in a trap.

Wished I could've rescued her,
But I was only a child.

Teasing her was a daily event,
Often she'd screamed uncontrollably
In order to escape the pain,
The pain of being ridiculed.

As a lone flower in a desert place,
Angie thirsted for love,
Should anyone endure such pain,
I often asked myself, why?

Without warning she pops into my mind,
I can hear her screams,
They have lingered for thirty years,
Angie, I hope you're in an OCEAN of LOVE.

David Jones

Yes I Can!!

Black like me is hard to see,
the stereo types and wanna bee's.
I live in the shadows in a world of despair,
because of my color, which is quite rare.
No one can see the world like me,
through rose colored lenses, struggling to be free.
I asked Him why, this curse on me,
the color of my skin so dark and ugly.
He lifted my eyes to the sky to see,
He made me special, the best to be.....
I'm glad He made me the way I am,
a woman of color who knows she can.
Can change the world who's in demand,
of colorful people, OH YES I CAN!!!!

Donna Lugardo

Oy Vey, My Knee

Why is this knee be so painful to me?
The surgeon said how great it would be;
that I could jump-up and run right off the gurney,
just a few hours after replacement surgery.

But he failed to mention
the pain, the swelling and pure agony,
of having a virgin joint placed into me.

My neighbor, a gent, twenty years older than me,
danced the lambada after receiving two replacementee's.
Even the nurse who pre-oped me,
Strutted around on her newly conjoined knee.

So why am I tortured with pain and misery,
peeing in a bag with great humility?

I should have known,
something would go wrong for me,
when I woke up and found
Kathy Bates doing my physical therapy!

Linda Syputa

645

Autumn

They wait not meekly for their death to knell,
The trees and bushes in the autumn scene.
No sombre-hued and furtive last farewell,
No mourning for the vanished summer green.

Magnificently garbed, in vibrant tones,
Mocking the sun, the rainbow and the flowers;
From purest ivory, pale as old bleached bones,
To lavish gold, with all its dazzling powers.

Copper, bronze, they shine like jewels bright,
Glowing like a fiercely flaming fire,
Every leaf becomes a shining light,
Every tree becomes a brilliant pyre.

Red as a sunset in the evening sky,
Their beauty sings a promise to the earth;
Glorious and undefeated as they die,
That death is just a prelude to rebirth.

Jean Buzan

"The Life Of The Elderly"

The life of the elderly is important to everyone,
They are special to our new generations,
To all of us, Mother, Father, Daughter, and Son,
No matter where you go, you will hear their conversations.

The life of the elderly both women and men,
Some of them are sick, while other are well,
We want to hear their stories of way back when,
In their loving hearts they want to tell,

All about the time when they were young,
I remember mother told me one day,
It was great hearing the song they sung,
I wouldn't want to take of children today,

It doesn't matter if the elderly are black or white,
They know Jesus will love them with all of his heart,
Wherever they go they will be alright,
Life of the elderly is special from the start.

Margaret L. Rodkey

A Belief

I believe in more than a rising sun,
This granted; but for all and one.
Not what I see or feel alone...
That which is, unproven, through eternity blown.

I believe in mankind past and present
As one in a struggle, on a dream bent
To fulfill a destiny, to create
Each hour with purpose, never to wait.

I believe more than fundamental morality
Will preserve a future lashed together to be
United; of love neither for self or state
But to encompass incipience to end, to exhilarate.

Arta Beverly

The Love Of My Life

You're an Oaktree that protects me from the rain,
You are the rainbow that puts a smile on my face,
Just like a flower, always there to cheer me up.
A sunset on a beautiful day,
Always by my side,
You're like the wind that sweeps me off my feet,
You're an eagle always looking over me.
Warm, summer rain that just melts my insides.

Christina Gayle Long

Eileen

Poor Eileen
those who knew you back then say
who could have known
this wrinkled bald mess
was her high school's beauty queen.
Certainly not the neighborhood kids
or the man at the corner store
who sells her denial in a bottle
that she drinks from a brown paper bag.
Tourists toss her a coin
when they see her pushing her pathetic little cart
with her dirty cans
and toothless grin.
She wouldn't have it any other way.
Poor Eileen they say,
but poor Eileen knows better.

Cera Lane

The Fruit Of Love

For forty years,
  through the birthing of four children and the arrival of ten
    grandchildren,
Walter and Eunice remained faithful and loyal
  like the deep blue sky to the dark brown earth, a face shining on a face.
He, a refined truck driver, did not know how to foul his mouth with
  imprecations; and she, a petite secretary, delicate and gracious,
    like a meadow flower waiting for her wandering bee.

When death dared to tear apart their cosmos,
  they held tight to each other in spite of their reformational split.
He a Lutheran; she a Roman Catholic-grace and law, perhaps;
  but in between their deep blue love, the Big "C" had grown in
    Walter's skull-too deep to operate, too far along for chemotherapy.
Then Eunice bonded with Walter like a mother to her child,
  reading to him those grace-filled devotions-
    morning, noon, and evening: she a metaphysical nurse.
And he held her bedside hand tightly, not letting her go into the
  night, while easing him into his.

Gordon Beck

Thank You Father

Thank you father for;
  Thy gentle voice,
  To guide me to make the right choice.
  And for the abundant gifts You've given me,
  Even in my times of trial, You spoil me.

Thank Your Father for;
  Thy empathetic ear,
  Whatever I say, I know Thou will hear.
  However foolish or silly it may seem,
  You listen, and help me achieve every dream.

Thank You Father for;
  Thy loving embrace,
  Where I can find no better place.
  You drive away my fears,
  And wipe away my tears.

Thank You Father for;
  My brother's strong, broad shoulders,
  To carry my burden, He carries my boulders.
  Who could have greater love for me?
  Than one who gave His life for me.

JoLene Joy Elmer

Masters Hand

I do not know what's happened
to our life planned from the start
I only know my love for you
goes deep within my heart.
We used to talk of days gone by,
of things we did the same
We'd hold each other lovingly
and speak each others name.
We'd often talk of days to be,
of walking hand-in-hand
While strolling on some lovely beach
barefoot in the sand
And there the words, "I love you,"
would be written, as if I'd planned.
Though the tide will wash up on the shore
and smoothen out the sand
Those three words will be there still
images on the land
For the words you see, though thought by me,
were placed by the masters hand.

George C. Tetrault

Live Each Day As Your Last Day

Don't worry about what people say about you. Live your life like today was your last day. Life is too short to ponder on what I should have done. God has given you an opportunity to live another day. Enjoy yourself don't worry about petty circumstances. Focus on things that will make a difference in your life or someone else's. There is no promise to you or anyone else that you will see another day. Enjoy this day, with a positive attitude, knowing that today may be your last day.

Linda L. Miller

An Alliterative Autumnal Glance At Rural Colorado Country

September showers touch and trickle from leaves,
trickily transforming them into Van Gogh visions.

Night winds blanch panes of pavilions and
shuttered-down shops, leaving their silvery
symbol of solitude.

A russet-brown road wends its way through
patches of pompous pumpkins, presumptive
in a shrouded sun as scuttling, stingy
squirrels stash and stockpile.

Then it winds in the distance toward impending
hills where winter and its icy intrusion lurks
and laughs.

Bob Roades

Watchful Eye

Beyond the hills that slope to form the concrete
Valleys like the sun sloping its beams: Beyond
the water that purls its shining blue flow,
Ferries are drifting
As artful as dolphins weaving waves of foam
Beneath a revolving moon.
Unsettling winds among the columns: Ashore is
the city that twists its glass towers,
Flaunts a dazzling wealth
As electric as lightning scorching skies of gray
above a fevered locus.
I keep this watch and sketch the scene,
Hiding myself in an astral shroud: Mournful
in my task, of the bitter end I bring.

I cry to you from a forlorn throne.

Joan B. Hayes

Untitled

With all good intentions
What is it that makes me wonder
And daydream about holding someone
In my arms to love - putting it simply
I cannot deny my physical need
But what's making it so painful
Is the emotional absence of a body with a heart and mind to care for
Just when I've come to accept my fate of loneliness
An emotion stronger than I can imagine come from somewhere
Deep in my psyche and slaps my heart.
Pounding with a desire over whelming my senses
I rub the inside of my thighs and moan.
I moan once for the erotic impulse to taste myself and
Twice for the ache in my soul to cease and cry no more.

Tracey L. Dawkins

Red Coals Turn Gray

It all began in the dusk of the year
when the wind was cold and gray,
Inside our hearts warmed coals of love
that we swore to fan each day.

As we basked in the warmth of the days and nights
Months faded into years
Two babes were born in the joyful years,
then the red coals began to turn gray.

We worked, we cleaned, we went our ways
Our hearts grew colder each day.
The babes grew fairer and brought much joy
brought a flicker of warmth so needed.

But, again in the dusk of the year
after a bakers dozen
The wind blew cold, the wind blew gray
Only our babes felt the warmth of the day.

Our oath was ripped, our ties were torn
its death left us in shambles.
We live today for the hope of the day
that our hearts will glow once more.

Jolene R. Constance

Beautiful Day Gone

Breathe deeply, gaze toward the shore
where our love was anchored once before
The sea-gull sails above me alone
the sand-castle dream has turned to stone
and the long beautiful day is gone

Freedom's roar to me is a sickening crash
of hopes on rocks and the outgoing tide
But still I must endure the blast
or drown in sorrow from sea to sky

Charles A. Lemley

Daddy

I sigh, then cry, and then ask
"Why?" "Why did my Daddy have to die?"
He was so young and I was too
"Why Daddy why did God have to take you?"
It's like a race that we just couldn't win...
A life together our family had just began.
We lost the race and each other too...
But Daddy...
"I still love you!"

Betty N. Fuller

Soul Mate

Tears running down side of my face —
Wishing my best friend... sitting in this place
Our lives so different and far apart —
When together our souls... touch at the heart
If one should slip and take a fall —
The other jumps to their feet... as strong as a wall
True, honest friends will always exist —
Treating the other... like that special gift
Sometimes there is an unpredictable course —
But love will succeed with all force
Words that are spoke... will open the gate —
My best friend... my Soul Mate.

Lambert Keglovich

Grandma's House

Grandma's house is a very big house
With lots of room to run
With lots of room to have fun
Grandma never gets mad
And she never seems sad
Sometimes Grandpa's there
Even though he doesn't have much hair
Now Grandma is kind a short and plump
And she sure can't jump
I love it when we go out to play
Because if I get dirty she says it's okay
The dirt will wash away with a bath
Then she'll tell a funny story
An we will laugh and laugh
Grandma's house is a very big house
With lots of room to run
With lots of room to have fun

C. E. Foster

In Memory of Dee Dee 1944-1948

FATHER,
Would that I could say the things that lie so deep within.
I fear this earthly voice is much too weak and thin,
To penetrate the realm where all things have begun,
The Heavenly Rest your arms where nestles now my absent son.

I love Thee, Father, but I miss him so.
If Thou art saddened by my grief, I wanted You to know.
It's not because my babe is there with Thee,
But just because he is so far from me.

I know the beauty of Your love for me,
As to my lips Thou dost Thine ear incline.
And so I learn that all my love for him is
But a fleeting glimpse of Thine.

Away with tears and heartaches in the night.
He hasn't left me for some unknown land.
It's joy to find that every time I talk with Thee,
He's at Thy side and I can hold his other hand.

Gladys Allende

Reflection

Lord, I thank you for the gift of life you have bestowed on me.
You have kept me safe throughout the years, without you,
how empty my heart would be.

You are always with me, never forsaking, giving needed wisdom
each day. You teach me patience and how to forgive others as
I travel along life's highway.

So many fiery trials come to test and pull me down. But I must
not give up, only trust in you and continue toward my crown.

Some sweet day you will call me home and I will see you face to
face. Unspeakable joy, oh what glory, to be in your embrace.

My life on earth will then be over, I will cut that final cord.
My Lord will say, "Well done, faithful servant, welcome to the
joy of the Lord."

Jacqueline Pasini

"Old Grandma"

Two uglies do not a pretty make
You kids behave, for goodness sake!
On the parch sat old grandma in bonnet and shawl
Watching we children far, fight and brawl.

This tit far tat has got to cease
Come now give this old body some grace,
When disaster struck she took us in
From a babe in arms to one almost ten.

Say many say sir, thank you and please
Before going to bed, get one your knees.
Love many, truck few, away paddle your own canoe
This she taught we, he honest and true.

Now grandma's gone, her life is history
How wise old words still ring in my ears
Solving my problems soothing my fears.

Would that world leader heeded today
Which serve old grandma had to say.
Simple words of advice but hard to take
"Two uglies do not a greatly make!"

Mary A. Drennon

Your Gentle Touch

I miss your gentle touch,
Your loving words and glances.

I miss your gentle touch,
You were my life's romances.

Sometime, somehow, the words will start to flow,
So I can erase the hurt that your passing made grow.

My heart aches for your gentle touch,
Your kiss, how I dream of such.

My heart screams and cries,
But there are no tears in my eyes.

The tears are private and must not show, they are mine,
Only you and I should know.

I miss your gentle touch, your loving words and glances,
I miss your gentle touch, each memory your love enhances.

I have entered their world, I'm lost.
As if winter had returned, I'm over taken with a chilling frost.

Alice Elek

Lauralee

Bright brown eyes stare into green
Mirroring each other's soul
The love flowing through could not be seen

But it was centuries old

The wonder of tiny hands and feet
I explored to my delight
This little darling, but hours old
Was the angel of my life

I sought to find the perfect name
For this tiny part of me
I remember a song from years gone by
Yes, she will be my Lauralee

Many years have passed since that afternoon
How quickly they have flown
My tiny baby is all grown up
And has a daughter of her own

Such times we had in her growing years
And she's weathered some stormy seas
But though years pass, I will never forget
When I first held my Lauralee

Marlene Waldron

Monsoon

One belch of thunder and the rains came down
Relentlessly, incessantly
Destruction laced with wrath

Parched throats lifted
Arms in welcome stretched
Crusted, cracked, the ground a sponge became

Thirsty rivers drank to roaring tumult
Rocky crags were masquerades of green
And crops in death throes grasped God's gift of being

Madras, Bombay to Delhi
Pelting torrents, black umbrellas
Empty bellies

Sleepers, sardine-packed
Once paved Calcutta's streets
'Til driving downpour drove them to retreats and stayed to reign

Puppeteer, Mistress Monsoon, makes India dance
And lures her to new life
In a love-hate romance

Muryl Anderson

Losing Someone

The hardest times,
Are when you lose someone you love,
Someone you loved so dearly,
Someone who could make you laugh,
Now that they're gone.
The laughter has vanished and turned into tears.
Tears of grief, the only thing left are memories,
Memories, good and bad,
But there's nothing you can do to bring them back.
As much as you would like too.
You know you can't.
And that makes you feel helpless,
The only thing you can do is move on,
Move on and take life for what it is,
Accept what you got today.
And what you will have tomorrow.
Just let those around share your pain.
And live through this with you,
Someone who loved you is gone,
But don't forget the others who also love you.

Tara Smith

In Memory Of Life

*Written in memory of my father Willard L. Ashcraft,
who died August 10, 1971*
Weep if you must, for the living,
but not for the one who is gone.
His passing has made him a free man.
Now is the time to be strong.
Remember him not with sadness
but with love and happiness too,
tho' you may not be able to see him
he'll always be part of you.
Remember his smile and the way be looked
when he sat in his favorite chair.
Think of the fun you've had with him,
and his love that was constantly there.
Thank God that this wonderful person
shared your life for so many years,
and remembering all of the good things,
you'll find that there's no roam for tears.
Don't bury his memory in sorrow,
keep it alive and bright,
then he'll never be very far from you
he'll only be out of your sight.

Norma Ashcraft Banman

My Last Speeches

Just a moment the cosmos begins,
Just a moment, bang went the cosmos,
The dew trickles, the mist dispels,
Like a beep in a deep,
All a while a while.

My tongue is cleaved to my upper groove,
My slimy water has dried up in bits,
And drought has kinged the orchard of my throat.
Where heaviness are the adversaries of my heart,
And my branched fingers clasp my sunset jaw.

My gimlet sight accomplish immortality,
Bridging the sojourn of my inner parts,
In a hot stream where tissues are wrinkled,
And bitter are the foams she formed,
Just to climax an in-apt inheritance

The whirling sound fell on my deaf lobes
where my heritage has lost all quarrels,
street songs have not my legs' jive
Oh! Speeches I deeply uttered, yet inaudible.

Francis Anat Okolo

Futile Solidarity

Alone again, Why is this so hard for me? Does my every moment have to be filled? Some say, "If I only had more time"; I've got nothing but time. Having time strips me of my motivation. Not being busy is laxing for me, thus I accomplish less. Or do I really do the same? Only seemingly less due to the absence of business. Alone again, my time alone is not well spent. It is wasted. Interaction is the spark for motivation. Solidarity diminishes my spark, but comradity ignites my senses. Yes, interaction, this stirs my emotions. For some, time alone can be used to reflect. To some this is useful, to me it is futile. Discussion solves more than reflection. Soleness is not necessary when companionship is savored. I sometimes feign the need to be alone, soon after I am bitter. Only returning following good talks with friends, acquaintances, strangers. Reveries are difficult for it entails oneness. Reality, however, encompasses interactions amongst beings which shape souls. Privacy is an overrated enigma. Although at times exhausting company builds a person. It's a matter of knowledge and exchange not present in solidarity. Thus, if needs for isolation occur don't retract, but expand, share, discuss, learn, find, discover and solve.

Daniel Timmerman

649

Eggs Can't Fly

My darling son,
Tiny perfect hands and feet,
Toes like grains of rice, eyes sealed shut.

How you fought to live.
At birth you cried a tiny mewing cry.
My heart, so long submerged in dread, floated up at the sound.

And live you did, daily changing, growing.
The miracle of life inside glass walls for all the world to see.
Long before I touched you, you touched us all
With your strength and determination.
Our little wonder, you seemed too good to be true.

Aysa, your name means "the healer."
You did the best you could and then relied on us.
I shall always ask myself why I wasn't quite enough a mother for you.
I failed you somehow.

Perhaps you were again pushed too soon from your nest
As yet no feathers, no wings, and eggs can't fly.
My tiny son, once more we held you close then tucked you in to sleep, forever.
Perhaps where you're going eggs can fly... please try.

Lynn Varughese

Believe

Life is simple, good to me,
I believe in all I see!

Simple pleasures in abundance,
Someone to share the same.
Windswept whispers to a cloud,
Children to bear my name.

Forever lasting happiness,
Of which I've not deserved.
His giving so unselfish,
In my heart a "Whole" reserved.

Hardships in abundance,
Windswept cries sent to a cloud.
Pain riddled in my silence,
Suffering to him aloud.

I am not to wonder why,
My faith put to a test.
But to know my destiny,
As I lay down to rest.

Life is short, good to me,
I believe in where I'll be!

Wendy Teodoro

Death

You're walking down a street, someone puts a gun to your head.
They pull the trigger, all of a sudden you're dead.
What did you do to deserve to die?
Why is it no one heard your cry?
Why are people dying for no exact reason?
Why do some killers say I was just teasing?
If you were just teasing, then why is he dead?
Why did you put, that gun to his head?
People kill people, so don't blame the gun.
It is your choice to kill someone just for fun.
What happened to families? What happened to friends?
When you pick up that gun, you choose when his life ends.
Look hard into your self, because it's your time to choose.
How would you feel if you were in that boy's shoes?

Monique Simoneau

Break Up

"I'm going," she said.
I said, "Where to?"
She said, "Somewhere."
"Where's that?" I said.
"No where," she said.
"With someone," I said.
She said, "Maybe."
"Okay," I said.
She said, "You know him".
I said, "Good friend?"
"Sort of," she said.
"The neighbor," I said.
"Not quite," she said.
I said, "Then who?"
"You know," she said.

Miriam Stang

Everlasting Angel

When life has dealt you problems
   And push has come to shove
Try not to stare on downward
   Lift your head and look above.

If you need someone to talk with
   And say what's on your mind
I'm always here to listen
   You just have to take the time

No one can be as true to you
   As I when you're in need
Please take my hand in yours
   And forever I will lead.

At a time you can't find answers
   On your own, don't make a fuss
I'm standing right beside you
   Your lifetime friend JESUS.

Anita Catherine Baker

The Change

Shadows fall at sunset
They cast a morning glow,
Upon the heart of every man
Unsuspected loss and woe

However, when the morning comes,
The hues and blues enrich the earth
These miracles of love,
A promise sent of hope and life
From the master of this love

A guided path throughout our lives
And changing scenes of seasons,
The simple gentle change of man
Like seasons and their reasons

Joanne Denise Samson

650

Memorial Day, Remembering the Soldier

Remembering the Brave

I remember the brave
I remember the soldiers that died
I think about how they must have felt
Shall I fight or shall I hide?

But they fought the battle
They died for you and me
They fought and gave their life
For us, to keep us free

Our precious loved ones went to war
Tears falling from our eyes
Never to return again
My heart, it often cries

As I walk upon the graveyard soil
I ask, why must they fight and die?
I pray there is no World War III
Or there will be no one left to cry

—*Deborah West-Owen*

Untitled

An angel's wings
 a butterfly's
Wispy, whispering, soft
Light in the air
Sparked by God
delicate as gossamer
A web of intricacy
Love can be like this
And snap with one word.

Linda F. Miller

Kindness

Kindness doesn't really need
A purpose to do a kindly deed.
Love is behind it - it is agreed
To plant this ever loving seed.

One shouldn't need to kneel and pray
To have a kindly word to say.
Or help someone along the way.
Or wish a "friend" a blessed day.

Kindness comes from within the heart
It's love, through God, we try to impart.
A ripple effect we strive to start
Love and kindness - A la Carte!

So if you want kindness to come to you;
You must a kindness in turn to do.
But don't just stop to do a few.
The more kindness done - the more blessings too.

Make kindness in your life a reality
So all the world can surely see
That "Christ-like" is what you want to be.
And to live in Heaven through eternity!

Vivian Jean Leslie

Untitled

If you think being a poet is tough,
And periodically, rhyming is rough,
It's really much quicker
To be a limericker ——
And for many, that is enough!

A. Kenneth Yost

A Rose Petal

A rose petal,
a rose for love
A sweet wren
and a gorgeous dove

A rose in a desert,
a cactus on a hillside
The rose died,
the cactus died
For I seek thou secret
of the rose for love

Jenna Phillips

"His Heart Is Always With You"

God blessed you with a son,
A son who made you proud
To be his mom and daddy,
To say, "I love you" loud.

To see his smiling face each day,
You knew this child would be ok.
He cried each time he scraped his knee,
But knew you'd fix it instantly.

He made you smile when you were sad,
And loved you through the good and bad.
To say "I love you Mom and Dad",
You knew what kind of child you had.

God took your child to heaven,
Though we'll never understand,
He'll be well taken care of,
Until you meet again.

Please think of all the good times
With every passing day;
His heart is with you always,
In time you'll be ok.

Susan Watkins

"A Dying Nation"

A Nation of fighting
and a Nation of hate.

A Nation of suffering,
and a Nation of fate.

A Nation of destruction,
and a Nation of war.

A Nation of pain,
and a Nation of poor.

A Nation of hurt,
and a Nation of crying.

A Nation of hard times,
and a Nation of dying.

What is this Nation coming to?

Tracy L. C. Williams Jr.

Untitled

The rain
 As it falls,
Fills my heart
 with a certain contentment
That without the rain,
 or the sadness
There would not be
 flowers of Joy nor buds of
 happiness.

Antoinette S. Oley

"Friends"

Friends like you are hard to find,
 and even harder to hold.
That is why you are the one,
 with a heart of gold.
Even though I'm stuck,
 in this damn place.
You always seem to put,
 a smile on my face.
One thing is for certain
 and I know it's true.
Whenever I am around you,
 I will never be blue.
We become friends,
 right from the start.
And now you hold,
 a special place in my heart.
You are special, that's something no one can deny.
If someone tells you different, you can believe
 it is a lie.
The one thing I must tell you, as this poem ends.
I love no one more, then you my dearest friend.

Marcel Forte

"A Thought"

Weeks and days apart
And even miles to boot,
A yearning so great
 for one to endure,
 in order to survive
 and feel alive,
 some solace in dreams so dear,
 can bring one so near,
 'and then separation
 never appears!

George J. Shapiro

Cycle Of Fear

When one is young,
And has no fear,
He does not care,
If danger is near.

Then one gets older,
And he learns fear,
If not for himself,
But for others near.

And then older still,
Age takes away fear,
There is wisdom gained,
Knowing death is near.

Alton Matheny

Sanctuary

That which I seek
I also seek to be:
A sanctuary.

For I am very strong
And he will also be;
Yet each with a certain
Vulnerability:

The need to find
And the need to be,
even if only occasionally,
A sanctuary.

Sharon F. Wilton

Bombing Of Munich

Within me, I thought buried deep
And hidden in many ways
Quietly I put the past to sleep
And all the yesterdays.

But in my dreams forgotten sounds
Keep ringing in my ears
And horrors dreadful, without bounds
Rekindle all my fears.

Again the night bursts into flame
With a dreading roar.
And all the world is put to shame
While fires skyward soar

Yet through all this I hold my son,
Close, closer, still to me,
While death is taking his very own
Here and there, ruthlessly.

Gusti E. Bechtold

Without You

I am lost
and never to be found.
Since you've left
I have felt nothing.
My life is incomplete
without you.
But soon we will be together.
To talked about times missed.
And I hope when you look upon me,
You see no disgrace
for I try my hardest
to be the best and
I'll never stop thinking
about the times we had
or the time we could've had
For there will always be
a way for us to be together.

April Edwards

Within - Without

When the house is topsy-turvy
  And the kids are all about
And the clouds on the horizon
  Reflect moods, without a doubt;

Should the kids eat on the sofa?
  Should the dogs be in or out?
Should mother keep her mouth shut,
  Hide behind a book and pout?

Never mind that dad relaxes
  In his chair amid the din -
Mother longs for peace and quiet,
  With her paper hides a grin -

Tomorrow to the airport
  Dad takes luggage, kith and kin;
While Mom relaxes happily
  At home with dogs and gin.

Her daily log holds secrets
  Only her eyes know the route;
She quickly learned, turmoil within,
  Ahhhh, peace and calm, without.

Betty McMullen

When You Shall Turn Away

I've felt the rains, lash upon my face
And the wind, pounding on my back
I've heard the far off thunder roll
And watched the lightning crack
Heard the deafening roar of oceans
Churning, shore to shore
I've felt the pulse of all mankind
Throbbing in my breast
Shed tears of blood
Until rivers over ran their beds
I've screamed aloud till I had no voice
And begged to feel no more
I've cursed my fate, and felt the hate
That only love can know
I've died, yet lived, to only die again
I've held you close, than ran away
When you've bid me to stay
And I wake each day
To dread the night
When you shall turn away

Belinda B. Osborne

Free

In morning, the sheets are tangled
around my limbs.
I'm dancing...
the white walls are whispering
and I remember
when last I let you come inside
and I remember when you last
said goodbye.
I'm moving...
slow but surely to the music.
Swaying... arms and legs are trembling.
To be me...
to be me without you
is breathing.

Vanessa Leigh DeRenzis

Our Federation

You ask me what we really do
At meetings where all too few,
Now we are organized you know
To help make our community grow.

Sometimes we take a box of joy
To some small girl or little boy.
Or maybe cookies to the old
To keep them close within our fold.

A song to lift some lonely heart
And for the church are to our part.
A pair of bootee's some may make
Just for our elder member's sake.

Some members keep alert with books
While others plant in lonely nooks.
Still others make a beautiful gown
And each keep litter from our town.

With shelter, clothing and food galore
Who could ask for anything more?
Good job, religion and education
Let's keep it safe with federation.

Merle Schott

Tender Harbors

The dawn's stillness is broken
By an unwelcome shatter
It's knowing you're there
That's all that matters.

The flickering of proud dreams
Now seeming so distant
Can't lessen your love
Deep and persistent.

A single day's journey
Like so many others
This child that greets me
So loved by his mother.

Weariness falls upon me
My day is at an end
I turn my thoughts to you
My love and my friend

For it's in this love of ours
That pain is surrendered
My spirit is nourished
By a heart so tender.

Brian J. Helmlinger

Untitled

I understand
finally
that when we
divorced
my children divorced me

So
somebody buy me a rose
let's open up some wine
we'll hum a tragic tune
and dance in candlelight
for pain is in the air
  and loneliness
    close by
please turn out the lights
please don't watch me cry

...yes...
someone bring me roses
let me weep in clouded moonlight
for pain is in the air
  and loneliness nearby

Annette Lane

Untitled

Our love is like an endless sunset,
forever painted in strong emotions
and bright ever present words of
truth;
Always changing, always becoming
more than it was a moment before.

Our love is painted across our hearts
and minds,
Making us reach for the others heart,
mind, and body.

Our sunset is not perfect, yet it is
beautifully and colorfully painted
in every shade of our love.

Moria J. Doverspike

A Post Card Home

Dear folks,
Helen and I like to walk on the beach,
Guess we'll have to give that up.
We can't move an inch without,
Some kid tagging along.
Take this little girl today,
She pulled at our clothes, nudged,
And beseeched and whew!
Did she smell.
God, can't a person take a vacation,
Without being bothered by these,
Poverty-stricken ignorant people?
Leaves me with a God-damned,
Bad taste in my mouth.
How are the kitty cats?
Helen bought them blue leather collars,
With the sweetest sterling silver bells.
Cutest little trinkets you ever did see.
Thanks for keeping our babies.

Josie Rogers

"My Very Special Friend"

I have a special friend whom I
hold close to my heart, in my life
she's come to play a very important part.
    I wouldn't trade her for anything
because she's simply the best oh,
did I say she's my mom and for
that I feel blessed.
    I love her more than anything
I want her to know, she's part of
what keeps me going, she's still
helping me to grow.
    She'll always be a part of me
Because I need her there for I have
A mother who is completely beyond
compare.

Kimberly Madden

A Dream Gone

I will walk quietly, as if
   I came in a dream.

I will disappear,
   with the coming of the dawn.

I will always think of you,
   as if you were the dream.

A figment of my life,
   that I thought was there.

The love that could have been,
   but was not.

You will fade away
   like the shadow,
      as the cloud covers the sun.

I will be solemn,
   only for a time.
For you were only a dream.

Lina Middleton

Untitled

When I'm down!
I sure need you around!
You're my lift!
That's why you're
My special gift!

Tina Marie Palmer

My First Love

My first love was you,
I didn't mean to fall out
of love and make you feel
Forgive me, I didn't mean to
make you sad.
When I met you, I was so glad.
I'd try my best to be true,
I didn't want to be a fake.
It was times that I would
sit up after dawn, after dawn
wondering, "What went wrong?"
I would pray that we
would see each other again.
Hoping you'd be by yourself
and asking, "Can we
still be friends."
I understand we can't be lover,
but I just want you to know,
"There was no other."

Charlotte McKinney

After All

   What can I do?
   I draw, that's all
   After all.
I am humbled by your disappearing face.
I have hurt others.
It couldn't have been the stars
   That lied to me.
I must have lied to myself;
   My life more fragile
   Than you can imagine.
I get lost in a small space.

Diana Vance

You Are True

I love the lakes
I love the cakes
I love the sea
So I can see
The water blue
So I can know
That you are true.

Laura Hauck

"Black Angel"

She calls me Black Angel;
I often wonder why
Could it be that she thinks of me
as an angel from the sky.

She calls me Black Angel;
This is very true
The name picks me up
when I sometimes feel blue.

It must be a blessing to be
given such a name
I feel that I belong in the
Hall of fame.

She calls me Black Angel;
It's easy to see that she
took care of me
before I was three.

She calls me Black Angel;
What else can I say
I love her dearly
forever and a day.

Michelle B. Arnold

One With The Night

The silence surrounds him,
   in the darkness he cries.
The loneliness won't escape him.
   They become one.

In the moonlight his shadow fades,
   disappearing in the dark.
He surrenders to the night.
   They become one.

The dawn is approaching, there
   is emptiness all around.
In the sunlight he has vanished.
   He is one with the night.

Tonia M. Baker

Frozen Delight

Rainbow colored lips quivering
in the sultry heat of the August sun;
a fleshy tapestry woven of popsicles
and snow cones
Each flick of the tongue,
each chomp of the teeth,
leads to another and yet another
'till all that remain are
splintered sticks crumpled cups
and chilling bliss.

Walter A. Hayes

"Just You"

Inspired by Maria
Is your hair just as silky
   before I run my hand through it?
Are your eyes just as deep
   before I lose myself in them?
Is your smile just as lovely
   before I steal a glance?
Are your hands just as warm and secure
   before I trace them upon your face?
Is your body just as sexy and soft
   before I hold you against me?

And is your voice just as soothing
   before you whisper to me?
Are you always naturally this beautiful
   and breath-taking,
Or do you do it just for me?

Fred C. Torien Nguyen

"So Strong"

It's so deep,
It makes me weep,
This pain I'll never hide.

It rips,
It tears,
I worry; it scares,
This love I have inside.

Never before,
A step through this door.
A tear brings so much pain.

Each breath I take,
I feel a stake,
A love so strong it's insane!!

Larry Lee Schleinger

September Fair Song

That time of year has come again!
It's the Washington State Fair!
It's time for hot dogs and cold pop
And displays are everywhere.

But sad to say, I'm staying home.
I'll mope around... just bored!
My car is broken down, you see,
And the bus I can't afford!

They've raised the fare to travel there
From ten cents to one dollar.
I think that they are cheating me...
And it makes me want to "holler"!

If fares increase on other routes,
I don't think I'd really care.
But for this route I don't consider
The increased fair fare, fair!

Wes Kunkel

Untitled

Ever since we've met,
I've felt so close to you,
you've made me open up,
to things I never knew.
You've given me a chance,
to make my dreams come true,
my dreams of being loved,
and loving someone too.
I'll open up my heart,
so, take me on a ride,
I'll never be afraid,
if you are by my side.
You are what I need,
and I think you need me too,
together there can be,
no other love more true,
than me and you!!

Michelle Arellano

Love Me Now

If your ever going to love me
love me now so I can know
all the sweet and tender words
from which real affection flow
Love me now while I am living
do not wait till I'm gone
and then chisel it in marble
warm love words on ice cold stone
If you've dear sweet words about me
why not whisper them for me.
Don't you know that it would make
me just as happy as happy could be
If you wait till I am sleeping
never to waken here again
There would be a wall between us
and I could not here you then

So dear, if it's just love me any at all
even if it's just a little bit
love me know while I am living
so that I can own and treasure it.

Arlena Smiggart

The Platypus

Evolution morphologically
Mutated all the species
Creating physiologically
Hairy apes from scaly pieces

But locked in form immutable
The duckbill did somehow
By facts now indisputable
Remain both beast and fowl

So regard the odd platypus
For whom the process stuck
Who waddles 'round among us
As a furry, fuzzy duck.

Mark Friedlander Jr.

The Preface

As I write this poem today,
My motives are in view
my hair is quickly turning grey,
And all the bills are due.

Twenty lines or less you say,
Puts the pressure on it's true.
But I've A message to convey,
And this, my first debut.

I wonder what you're looking for,
As my last dime is spent.
I will write A whole lot more,
Just to pay the rent.

All my poems are from my heart,
With A message to portray.
Maybe I could advertise,
And be your protege.

Penny Dunne

To Chris

You are the flame that lights my fire;
My only one desire.
You are the clouds up in the sky,
On which I'd fly so high.

To touch you would be paradise
I'd look into your longing eyes.

When ever you're around,
I want to kiss the ground,
and hear the sound
of your voice.

I look around to see
that you don't notice me.
But soon I will change it all
then it will be my call.

When finally we'll be together,
and all is well and gone.
You'll realize that you were wrong
about me.

Tricia Wozniak

A Croft of Crocuses

Diminutive Crocuses,
Stationary, you tower
Above the long-dormant earth.
Bowed by the blustery breeze,
Your crowns appear to curtsy
To the verdant grass below.
Alone, you herald better
Days ahead—spring's arrival!

Kathryn A. Hager

A Dream Come True

Over the summer
my step father
proved how much
he loved my brother and I
He adopted us
on August 10th 1994.
I was just so happy!
At some points
I thought I could cry.
This is a dream come true
I love you dad forever!

Amanda Saunders

My Baby

I was only a teen
Nowhere to be seen
I was all alone
Shipping from home to home
I didn't even know how far should go
Afraid of what I didn't know

I debate should I keep him
With not much sleepin'
And tears from eyes
I was weepin'
But the morning rise
With a gleam in my eyes
I said "this is a great surprise."

Nine months I shall go
My future unknown
But my brand new baby
Will soon be grown
A life he would lead
Wanting to succeed
A chance he got from me.

Hershelly Nelson

Red

Red is the blood
Of the loved ones, now dead,
Red comes the sunset
As I sleep in my bed.

Red is the rose
On its prickly vine,
Red is the color
Of grapes and of wine.

Red is the fire
Ablaze in my home,
Red is the fox
Wherever she roams.

Red shows the anger
That burns inside me,
Red are my lips
As I scream to be free.

Red is my love
And red is my fear,
And wherever I go
Red shall be near.

Jessica Ross

654

Only You....

Courage comes from deep within
one's soul. Your's shines through,
even the roughest of life's storms.

Your strength is a beacon: that
lights the way, through to the shores of
tomorrow's dreams.

Encouraging, and inspiring ships
to set sail, for unchartered waters:
without fear of failure.

Keep shining for all the tomorrows
to come for today is your beginning;
of living your dream.

Tracy Bertotti

Licenses

At the Registry last week
People lined about, quick
Some leaned on the table
Others in a scramble
Patience was tasked
In the rush to pay tax
Then new faces appeared
First I saw Soyinka
Followed by Angelou
Next was Wa N'Thongo
With Morrison close by
What might bring together
These diverse sages?
Then it hit me
My Driver's Licence was due
Their Poetic Licences were due

Oladimeji Adeoye

Untitled

Barren hills with caps of snow,
Pines, heavy-laden, drooping low,
A pale blue sky without a cloud,
A small log house in winter's shroud,
A red snow fence - marshmallow drifts
Of gleaming white, while o'er them sift
Diamondy snowflakes, fairy toys,
These are but few of Winter's joys!
The southland's color, vivid bowers,
Her topic rich exotic flowers,
Can never in my heart replace
The northland's magic mystic grace.
Her beauty in my heart I store.
Here may I dwell for evermore.

Evelyn P. Hunt

To My Mother

I never thought I'd miss you
Quite this way.

The emptiness I feel
Just won't go away.

You aren't there to listen
When I complain.

Nor advise me to view things
In a different kind of way.

I know you asked
Who will I pick on
When you are gone.

But, damn it maw
You didn't tell me
The hurt would last so long

Lillian Zosh

Our Flag

Our flag is pretty
Red, white and blue
See it in the city
And the country too

If flies up high
On a staff or a pole
A silhouette in the sky
That stirs the soul.

Its stripes of red
For courage stand
And it has led
Many a stirring band

Its stars on darkest blue
One for each state
Count them will you?
Forty eight and then two

It's fifty and you will see
It flying in glory and victory
As we united will have to be
Our dust will be our destiny

Eleanora Julig

The Zephyr

A gentle wind of remembrance
Runs her fingers through my hair.
I smell the sweet aroma,
A fragrance of moments shared.
Unhurriedly she flies,
Over the sea of sweeter times.
Whispering on a wiser breeze-
"Don't forget"-as she passes by.
Arms outstretched she rushes
Through the trees of remaining years-
Sending reminisces cascading-
The leaves of laughter and tears.

Wanda Lynn Proctor

Mindy

My cat's name is Mindy
She is rather long and skinny
She sleeps all day and plays all night
Sometimes giving me quite a fright

Katie Knowles

I Love...

My Mother is the best
She's better than the rest
She may be fat, she isn't tall
But that doesn't matter at all
Her hair is light brown
The color of a mouse
She rarely ever wears a blouse
She dresses like a bum
But she is number one
And that is all that counts
She is a substitute teacher
And she can be quite a mean creature
Mostly, she is kind
And let me remind
I love her
She loves me
So we're a happy
FAMILY.

Tricia Beth Gonwa

Fire

Love is a fire,
stand the right distance away,
give it air and let it breathe,
and you can feel its warmth and beauty;
Stand too far away,
and you feel no warmth at all,
therefore defeating the purpose of
the fire
In the first place;
Get too close
and you could smother the flames or,
worse yet,
you could get burned.

Amy Novak

The Web

Like the spider webs,
Strong hold in the wind
Spun by heads you turn,
Left with hearts you bend.
I drifted into you...captured.

And trapped within your web,
Of intricate design.
The love of mine left helpless,
By the silken hold of time.
I drifted into you...captured.

I have struggled in your web,
Of intimate confine.
A delicate geometry,
As infinite as time.
I drifted into...The Web.

Kevin W. Flinn

"My House Not Made With Hands"

I've found the house I seek dear Lord,
The house not made with hands;
Though I may err and go astray,
It ever near me stands.

The doors are always open,
And his arms are waiting there;
To receive this lonely soul,
And all my troubles share.

He'll take you in and care for you,
He cakes every pain.
He lifts you up into his love,
And cleanses every stain.

Oh come to him, he's waiting
If you're troubled and alone;
He's waiting there with open arms
To make this house your home.

Jannie Griffith

Love And Marriage

Love is like a rose.
    The petals encircle and recline.
They protect with essence..
    And the fragrance is divine!

As the years pass one by one
    Its elegance is ever near..
Pressed between each time capsule..
    Each year is so very dear.

Children come and children go..
    And love is ever a bliss!
Grand children running everywhere
    Is a blessing not to miss

Audie Crockett

Untitled

The black
The white
The good
The bad
The object
The price
The thing
The cost
The truth
The lie
The victim
The scam
The lock
The key
  What does that leave me

You
    Sarah Mitchell

Why Him

Our soldiers are dying.
Their mothers are crying.
People say it's a shame.
As they point the finger to
someone else for the blame.
Their name is chiseled into the wall.
As their mothers get the call.
Your son is dead
He took an enemy bullet.
Their mothers tremble
Fathers mumble "Why him".
The casket is closed.
The flag is folded.
The tomb is molded.
He's placed in a garden of stone.
To be left alone.
As the fathers look around
It wasn't just him it was all of them.
As the trumpets sound a new body is found.
    Brandy Lazarus

In Remembrance

If I could tell you how I feel
Then I'd truly feel I'm real
for I'm not sure within myself
I have given you what I felt.
Up lift my voice, let my feelings soar
so you'll remember me forever more
  for you have gone
  and left me here
  and only God knows
  how I miss you dear.
I have a surprise to show you one day...
And one day you'll see her
Is what I hope for when I pray.

On Mother's Day...this is a greeting
from us to you.
To show you our love is still very true.
We still harbor feelings that wish
You hadn't gone away
From the four of us we'd love to wish you
The Happiest Mothers Day.
    Cheryl L. Smith

If nothing had happened
There would be no question
of my sanity
or my constant fear of losing it
there would be fear of people
places
or things that go bump in the dark
I would be able to stand in the mirror
look and not question
who I am or what I see
without blame or shame
what you said, what I heard,
would be the same thing
there would be no parts
separated, disconnected
or loss of time
I wouldn't be afraid to love or be loved
and I wouldn't fear you
    Kim Wright

A Look In My Eyes

Have a look in my eyes.
They are full of reflection.
They are so penetrating,
They have no satisfaction.
They are spiderful, lionless,
They are lacking some happiness,
They are shark-like and mighty,
They are strangely united,
They are hollow and vain,
They are suffering pain,
Now green, now grayish
They are crying in anguish,
They are deaf for your shrieks,
They are mountain-peaks,
They are hungry for love,
They are down and above,
They are hell, they are heavens,
They are robins and ravens,
They are not at all kind...
But my eyes are not blind.
    Sarah Miller

The River

I tried my beat,
to keep things going.
But I was just a leaf,
in a fast river flowing.

Too small to be seen,
and too light to sink.
I was swept away,
with little time to think.

One minute in the phone,
I end up with a broken heart.
I know my choice was right,
by breaking us apart.

Now I'm on the shore,
watching the waters flow by.
I want to swim again,
as I let out a deep sigh.
    Rachel Swanson

Friendship

Friendship means so very much
To you, to me, to all.
It means our joys and sorrows
And lifts us when we fall.
It rules our lives in may ways
Which we don't understand,
It turns the winter into spring
And lends a helping hand.
I'm thankful for all blessing
Given me each day;
But most of all I'm thankful
For the friends who come my way.
    Margaret Good

"Solitude"

There is no room for our
Togetherness
In your life.
  Although
  I wish I can make it.
See, I have a glass of warm champagne...

You will not carry me
In your arms.
  Although
  You have enough power
  And I want to trust you.
See, I have a glass of warm champagne...

You will not enkindle your body
When you are looking at me.
  Although
  As time goes on
  Everything is possible...
See, I have a glass of warm champagne....

I feel your fingers in my hair.
They are - the best.
    Ewa Sikora

Games

Why did you lie?
Was the tears
real when you cry?.

No more games
or
faces with no names.
A candle that burns
at both ends,
racing against the wind.

Where does it start?
When does it end?

Temporary insanity,
step into the light
of fantasy,
say goodnight.

The show's over,
go on home.
Slip beneath the covers
you're all alone.
    Steve Cochran

Natures Voice

Sunshines made yellow
With pure rays of light,
Eagles glide high
On wings endless flight,
Meadows are brilliant
With colors abound,
And natures made full
Of beauty and sound,
So next time your senses
Take hold of these wonders,
With slow tears of rain
And clouds mighty thunder,
Remember man's greed
Will soon put us under,
For greed brings hate
And hate brings destruction,
For soon will all stroll
Through meadows of nothing.

Elizabeth W. Manke

Lord

Lord, you are life, you are love,
you are the light, you're the very
breath of me, you're the very soul of me.

You're the sound, you're the beauty
of all things, you're the reason
why I write, the reason why I live,
the reason why I hope.

You're the air I breathe, you're
the quietness at the end of a day,
the setting of the sun, the shining
of the stars, the movement of the
waters in the sea, and the Spirit
that lives in me.

Alfreda Johnson Byars

Silent Witness

Why must you drown me with your words
you know I do not desire to hear them

And at the same time you rape my mind
with every question you ask

I do not speak because
you do not know how to listen

A selfish rage boils within you
while I am a silent witness

Andrea P. Dinaro

A Ballad Of Heaven

What does heaven look like?
You tell me.
Is it miles and miles of clouds
Or a shining sea?

Is it birds and flowers;
Possibly trees?
Maybe there's beautiful butterflies
And non-stinging bees.

Is it wide prairies or deserts,
Snow topped mountains?
Could it be a big court yard
With beautiful fountains?

Can you just walk in,
Or need you a key?
So what does heaven look like?
You tell me.

Holly Strickland

Biographies
of
Poets

ABELARD, L. LEE
[b.] July 7, 1973, New York City, NY; [oth. writ.] Omicron Delta Kappa, published: Newsletter Inago (AZ), Old Crow (MA), Small Pond Magazine of Literature (CT), The Paper Salad Poetry Journal (UT)...all as of January 1996.; [pers.] Power, sexuality, discipline, knowledge, power, authorship, democracy, identity, public, power, private, individuality, governmentality, historicity, heresy, propriety, ideology, genealogy, power, riot, surveillance, hegemony, authority, power, revolution, self, property, criticism, penopticism, tyranny, singularity, production, power... "The soul is the prison of the body".; [a.] New York, NY

ABELING, DEBBIE ROSE MAURIE
[b.] February 17, 1957, Toronto, Ontario; [p.] Ludger and Rose Perras; [m.] Uwe Abeling, August 19, 1978; [ch.] Amanda and Daryl; [occ.] Housewife; [pers.] With love and honor to all the good people on this earth. My mom and dad, my husband and children, and to every living creature. May all the power be with us.; [a.] Toronto Ontario, Canada

ABRAHAM, ANGELA LYNN
[b.] July 18, 1975, Niagara Falls, ON; [p.] Elizabeth Abraham; [ed.] Saint Paul High School, Mohawk College of Applied Arts and Technology; [occ.] Student, Radio Broadcasting; [hon.] First Class Honors, Second Class Honors, 1st Place Canada's Wonderland for Ballet, 3rd Place United Nations Peace Contest, and many other Ballet Awards; [oth. writ.] Poems in local newspapers, short story, prose, poems for personal gratification, journals etc.; [pers.] To my mother, without her encouragement and support I would not be where I am today. Blessed be!; [a.] Hamilton Ontario, Canada

ADAMS, DEBORAH SUE
[pen.] Deborah Sue Adams; [b.] February 8, 1952, Little Rock, AR; [p.] Charles Melton Jones and Annie Rachel Ryan (Both Deceased); [m.] Eddie P. Adams, March 24, 1978 (Divorced 1989); [ch.] Pulaski County Special School, District - Mill High School given in the State of Arkansas, the Twenty-First Day of May 1998; [ed.] Just at home trying to relax into the flow of life and let life flow through me with ease; [pers.] I recognize my body as a wondrous and magnificent machine. As soon as I come in contact with other people, I detect the weak points of myself and of the others, with the instruction, the Lord give grace, strength, faith, and courage to carry out everything that we need to carry out, the impossible becomes possible. I love lot of energy. I am like the moon, not like the sun. The sun has light from itself, the moon only reflects the light. For people who have marcolepsy a sleep disorder!; [a.] Little Rock, AR

ADAMS, FLORA BOLLING
[b.] February 26, 1922, VA; [p.] Laura Boggs and Henderson Bolling; [m.] Kelsey Adams, October 22, 1945; [ch.] Karen, Kirk, Rebecca, Mark; [ed.] Flat Gap High School, Radford Teacher's College, University of Maryland - (Master of Education) 1970; [occ.] Retired Educator, Writer of Stories and Poems, Plays, for Upper Elementary Students; [memb.] 1) Alpha Delta Kappa Honorary, 2) Teacher's Sorority International, 2) First Church of Christ, Scientist, 3) Educational Organizations - County, State and National (While Teaching); [hon.]

A few Little Honors while Teaching; [oth. writ.] The U.S. constitution (a play) - Norton Press, a few unpublished stories, plays, songs and poems.; [pers.] I write about ideas which come to me in daily living. To expect anyone to read my writing, I believe it must have some quality of satisfaction whether it be satire, humor, rhyme, adventure or just a ditty.; [a.] Williamsburg, VA

ADAMS, NANCY
[pen.] Nancy Adams; [b.] April 6, 1953, Sacramento, CA; [p.] John Welch, Hazel Welch; [m.] Donald Adams, February 5, 1972; [ch.] Donnie and Marcelina; [ed.] Grant High School (Diploma); [occ.] Teacher's Assistant, Orchard Elementary, Rio Linda, CA; [pers.] I write to inspire people to think, feel, and react. One of my goals is to encourage children to write.; [a.] Sacramento, CA

ADAMS, PARK ALEXANDER
[b.] April 4, 1973, Bellflower, CA; [p.] John and Ingrid Adams; [ed.] Redmond High; [pers.] Life's an infinite song, recording harmonic, our truths and our wrongs. Preparing ourselves since in utero, for divine intervention. To sing along in understanding, without questions of morality. Your voice is your song, life, and living. Sing!; [a.] Vancouver, WA

ADEOYE, OLADIMEJI
[pen.] Penjudge; [b.] September 25, 1964, Lagos, Nigeria; [p.] Thomas Adeoye, Julianah Adeoye; [ed.] Columbia College, Chicago, Nigerian Institute of Journalism, Lagos, Nigeria; [occ.] Editor, African's Digest Magazine.; [memb.] Commonwealth Journalists Association.; [oth. writ.] Author, "The Morning Of A Cup - The Dictatorship Of Ibrahim B. Babangida". Two screenplays, One currently in development.; [pers.] If I can positively influence one person through my writing, then I have done my Job.; [a.] Chicago, IL

AHLUWALIA, HARMAN
[b.] June 23, 1971, Punjab, India; [p.] W. B. Singh Ahluwalia, Baljit Ahluwalia; [ed.] B.Sc. (Med.), B.Ed., Diploma in Marketing Mgt.; [occ.] Live in Care Giver; [hon.] Medals and Certificates given for being Outstanding Student in School and College both in Academics and Extra-Curricular Activities; [oth. writ.] Wrote for school and college magazines from time to time.; [pers.] I believe it's my deepest emotions that flow into words to take the shape of a poem. In my writings I have been influenced by different colors of life but foremost love, which I am still searching for.; [a.] Toronto Ontario, Canada

AKER, DONALD C.
[pen.] D.C.A; [b.] September 14, 1975, Escanaba, MI; [p.] Don Aker, Chris Aker; [ed.] Flat Rock Elementary, Gladstone High, Grand Valley State University; [occ.] College Student; [hon.] Boy Scout Merit, Honor Roll Student, Several Sporting Awards; [oth. writ.] Occasional writings such as: The faith, the day that has gone by, if, (and a song, "She Realizes Now)."; [pers.] My writings come from a feeling within. They come from personal experiences and reflections upon each. My style is quite basic, but my meaning is very heart felt. So my advice to people who love to write is: Keep writing from the heart, it's valuable to life! Enjoy.; [a.] Gladstone, MI

AKKAOUI, NICOLAS
[b.] October 27, 1954, Beirut, Lebanon; [p.] Josephine and Salim; [ed.] College Du Sacre-Coeur Grade 10, Lebanese, French, English, and other Vocational Studies (Book-Keeping, Auto Mechanic, Cooking 6 yrs.); [occ.] Intend to become a Long Term Care Aid; [memb.] Volunteered for the Disabled 1 year; [oth. writ.] Definition of God (My) desolated soul and few other poems, 1st at age 16 in a French essay. Pragmatism and the mantic arts.; [pers.] Giving, love instigated, begins with oneself, to oneself and far beyond, the universal element that knows no greed, color of religion and has no bounds. I am deeply marked by the philosophy of Gibran on life and his wisdom.; [a.] Vancouver, BC

ALEXANDER, MONIQUE E.
[b.] March 9, 1956, Baltimore; [p.] Harriet Vail Wade; [m.] J. Stephen Rutherford, May 26, 1994; [ed.] Winston - Salem State Univ., New Bern Senior High; [occ.] Flight Attendant US Air; [memb] Delta Sigma Theta Sor., Big Brother, Big Sisters; [hon.] Dean's List '77 USSU; [pers.] My relationships, friendships and family and love are the inspirations of my work.; [a.] Charlotte, NC

ALICEA, CARMEN S.
[pen.] Meechy; [b.] November 2, 1968, New Wark, NJ; [ch.] Donald W. Skenandore Jr.; [ed.] South Division High School, Patricia Stevens Career College; [oth. writ.] I have lots of poems of my own, I would be happy to share them with the world.; [pers.] In my heart I believe we are all poets. You just need to find the right person to bring the poet out in you. In my case I have found peace within myself. Search deep inside of yourself and you will find peace.; [a.] Milwaukee, WI

ALLAWAY, MARIAN LYNN
[pen.] Lady Bug; [b.] October 30, 1962, Ottawa, Ontario; [p.] James and Sandra Allaway; [m.] Divorced; [ch.] Amie, Katie, Chelsey; [ed.] Grade 12 Graduate, Business Admin. - NWCC Kitimat BC, Accounting - Kingston Ontario; [occ.] Waitress - Vancouver, BC; [hon.] Singing Award 1990, Female Vocals; [oth. writ.] Several poems not yet published. Some day I hope to publish my own book of poetry.; [pers.] My poems come from my thoughts and my heart. I have been greatly influenced by my daughters and my parents.; [a.] Surrey British Columbia, Canada

ALLEN, CAROLYN
[b.] December 25, 1943, Sydney, Australia; [p.] Hilda Mitchell, John MacDonald; [m.] George Allen, April 29, 1967; [ch.] David Garth; [ed.] Abbotsleigh School for Girls, Sydney University, Ryerson Polytechnical Institute; [occ.] Freelance Writer; [memb.] Concerned Citizens of West Lake, Regent Theatre Foundation; [hon.] Southern Award for Highest Standing First Year, Journalism Program; [oth. writ.] Graduate, Institute of Children Literature, Connecticut; [pers.] I write for pleasure and comfort and to provide a record of personal experiences. That have moved me.; [a.] Picton Ontario, Canada

ALLERTON, CAITLIN
[b.] August 8, 1975, Owen Sound, Ontario, Canada; [ed.] Went to Grey Highlands SS in Flesherton, ON, and then to Georgian College in Barrie - for Business Administration; [oth. writ.] I started writing when I

was very young. I won an award in grade 5 and in grade 6. I had a story I had written on TV Ontario. The show was aired by Heather Conkey, it was narrated and pictures were put to it.; [pers.] I would like to dedicate this poem to my Popa Allenton (the one who always encouraged me to write). I owe him a great thanks.; [a.] Barrie Ontario, Canada

AMES, AMBER
[b.] February 8, 1981, Abilene, TX; [p.] Melanie Ames and Richard; [ed.] High School Freshman at present; [occ.] Student; [hon.] Most Outstanding - Jr. High Art, No. 1 Camper - Camp Champions Many Sports Awards, Softball All Stars - 3 Years.

AMES, LESTER J.
[b.] April 22, 1919, Redfield, SD; [p.] Clara and Joy Ames; [m.] Helen Marie, October 13, 1940; [ch.] Three Children, 10 Grandchildren and 7 Great Grand Children; [ed.] College; [occ.] Retired U.S. Gov.; [memb.] Son of Morway, Central Lutheran Church, Sandie Club; [hon.] Military; [oth. writ.] Ten other poems that were all given to me by God.; [pers.] I love people.

ANDERSEN, NICOLE
[b.] December 2, 1969, London, Ontario; [p.] Erik and Gertrud Andersen; [ed.] High Mowing School - Wilton, NH, Freies Jugend Seminar - Stuttgart - Dalhousie University - Halifax, NS, University of Western Ontario - London, Ontario, In Lingua Teacher Training Center - England; [occ.] ESL Teacher; [a.] Burnaby British Columbia, Canada

ANDERSON, ANGELA
[pen.] Angela Sharron; [b.] April 25, 1968, Chicago, IL; [p.] James and Sharon Wysinger, Edward J. Anderson; [ch.] D. J. and Marcus; [ed.] Kalamazoo Central High, Davenport Bus'ns. College; [occ.] Entrepreneur - "Cuddle Bear Day Care"; [memb.] Christian Life Center: Soprano Choir and Volley-ball; [oth. writ.] High School - Upward Bound Newsletter (Minority Affairs - WMU); [pers.] My endeavor is to be a positive vessel releasing in all mankind, through my gift of writing, the "I can" instead of the "cannot!" Hats off to the great poets who have opened the doors of opportunity for more generations.; [a.] Kalamazoo, MI

ANDERSON, BEAUFORD
[b.] March 22, 1984, Houston, TX; [p.] Katha Anderson, Solomon Mitchell; [ed.] 6th Grade; [occ.] Musician, Student; [memb.] Black Arts Alliance; [oth. writ.] Many other now published writings.; [pers.] My mother always tells me just do the best that you can, follow God's teachings and every thing will be ok.; [a.] Austin, TX

ANDERSON, DIANA L.
[pen.] Sam Anderson; [b.] May 4, 1949, Cherokee, IA; [p.] Donald F. and Lois K. Bengtson; [ch.] Staci and Corinne Anderson; [ed.] B.S. Elementary Education Associate on Mathematics, Southern Oregon State College Ashland, Oregon (1990); [occ.] Substitute Teacher, Painter and Writer; [hon.] President's List and Dean's List (Honors List) 1988-1990; [oth. writ.] "A Rock Rembers Sitting Bull," a poem included in "Mirrors of the Soul," (anthology) published by Modern Poetry Society; [pers.] I believe poetry is obliged to tug at a heart and muse the mind, as we are all obliged to cherish our inherited values.; [a.] Shady Cove, OR

ANDERSON, GARRY
[pen.] Muce; [b.] August 11, 1979, New Market; [p.] Diana and Paul Anderson; [ed.] Attending Grade 11 at Max Cameron Secondary School; [memb.] Powell River Trail Riders Max Cameron Interact Club, Chamber Choir, Jazz Choir, Academy Choir; [hon.] Community Service, Large Block; [oth. writ.] Local newspapers, magazines.; [pers.] I wish to thank Sarah Hamilton for giving me the courage to start writing.; [a.] Powell River British Columbia, Canada

ANDERSON, JOANN
[pen.] JoAnn Anderson; [b.] January 12, 1948, Pittsburgh, PA; [p.] Orlando Visconti and Jennie Carnevale; [ch.] Tracy Dawn and Tammy Linn Anderson; [ed.] Baldwin High School and Alleg. Community College; [occ.] Event Planner for Crown Point Enterprises; [memb.] Fairhaven Social Club; [hon.] Vidal Sasoon/Customer Serv., Uncle Ben's Rice/Customer Service, Curtice Burns/Customer Service, these awards were presented due to going above and beyond in assisting each customer; [oth. writ.] "In The Still Of The Night," "Golden Kitten," "Sweet Little Thing," "Happy Birthday, Angie," "My Dad," "My Mom, The Star," "My Hero," "Smile," "Missing You," "Flowers," "Sleepless Night," "Such A Mess, Not Such A Mess," "My Younger Brother," "Uncertainty," "My Daughters, My Love," "Little Candle," "How Lucky I Am," "A Sigh Of Relief," "Oh! Wondrous Island," "A Mother's Love"; [pers.] I have always loved to write, but I was the only one that ever read any of my poetry. I guess I was rather backward or shy although the above two are not two of my traits. I suppose, I started writing poetry to express my bottled up feelings. I raised two beautiful daughters alone. Of whom I feel very very proud. They are my true inspiration. And of course, my truly beautiful Mom (now deceased) "Jennie."; [a.] Bethel Park, PA

ANDERSON, MURYL
[pen.] Miraslava Andrejciw; [b.] July 5, 1934, Saint Boniface, Manitoba, Canada; [p.] Theophile Andrejciw, Pawlena (Nee Sawchuk); [ed.] King George High, B.C. Teachers College, Copenhagen University, The Sorbonne, Alliance Francaise; [occ.] Director Ukrainian Village Registry, Researcher, Tour Guide; [memb.] National Genealogical Society (NGS), BCGS, MGS-East European Grp., SGS, FEEFS; [hon.] King George Honor Award, Venture Photography Magazine Award; [oth. writ.] Newspaper and magazine articles: Australian Women's Weekly (Sydney), Our Dumb Animals (Boston), Kabul Times, Baghdad News, Amrita patrika Bazar (Calcutta), The Statesman (New Delhi), The West Ender (Vancouver), BCGS Quarterly (Vancouver); [pers.] Author Richard Halliburton inspired me to trek for 10 years around the world. During which I never consciously sought "Spiritually" but was surprised the times it found me, searching for my own Walden's pond.; [a.] Vancouver British Columbia, Canada

ANDREWS, MARIE
[pen.] "Rie"; [b.] October 31, 1948, Saint Louis, MO; [p.] Arthur Rowden and Willemena Riley; [m.] Divorced; [ch.] Felicia Ann, Barry Jr.; [ed.] Vashon High, Lincoln University (MO); [occ.] Secretary/Stenography (U.S. Government); [hon.] Typing Awards, Sustain Superior Awards for 14 Years

Running; [oth. writ.] A collection of poems yet to be published.; [pers.] I create poems of the heart, poems that reflect the current evolutions of people's lives. People's moods or personal conflicts move me to pen some of what I consider my best works!; [a.] San Antonio, TX

ANTOS, DIANNA L.
[b.] July 14, 1947, Herington, KS; [p.] James H. and Dolores M. Debus; [m.] Terry L. Antos, September 1967; [ch.] Anthony L. Antos; [pers.] I wrote this poem in the early years of my marriage when I felt my husband had no respect for me.; [a.] Kansas City, MO

ARCHAMBEAULT, TAMARA
[b.] November 5, 1980, Vancouver, BC; [p.] Corrine, Grandparents: Wally and Gerri; [ed.] Mount Baker Senior Secondary School, Laurie Junior Secondary, Steeples Elementary School Cranbrook; [pers.] I write to express my thoughts and my feelings. I was influenced by the great black poets I have read of.; [a.] Cranbrook, BC

ARCHER, SUSAN
[b.] March 14, 1949, Burlington, WI; [p.] Earl E. Delahoyde Audrey and Smith Delahoyde; [m.] Michael John Archer, October 10, 1992; [ch.] Katie Hable, John Hable, Jill Archer, Aaron Archer; [ed.] Burlington High School, B.S. History Education, University of Wisconsin, Madison, MA Mass Communication, Marguette University; [occ.] Technical Writer for Computer Software; [memb.] Society for Technical Communication (STC), Whitetish Bay Methodist Church; [hon.] Award of Excellence, STC Region 6 Technical Publications Competition; [oth. writ.] Several papers presented at technical/professional conferences, poems and articles published in non-profit publications.; [pers.] For me, writing poetry is away to express deeply felt thoughts and emotions.; [a.] Whitefish Bay, WI

ARELLANO, MICHELLE I.
[b.] May 2, 1966, Honolulu, HI; [p.] Mark and Carol Furukawa; [m.] Artemio Arellano, October 2, 1993; [ch.] Kylie, David, Aniza; [ed.] Pearl City High; [occ.] Domestic Engineer; [pers.] This poem is dedicated to my husband Artemio, who has inspired me into writing poems.; [a.] San Diego, CA

ARMSTEAD, GIRARD DOYLE
[b.] July 27, 1971, Bessemer, AL; [p.] William, Joyce Armstead; [occ.] (Mechanic) U.S. Marines; [pers.] Capitalism survives only with the application of two tools, those tools being superhuman love and superhuman self-discipline.; [a.] Hueytown, AL

ARRIOLA, GAIL EMILY
[b.] June 19, 1958, Austin, TX; [p.] Manuel and Delia Arriola; [m.] James A. Nickell, March 23, 1996; [ed.] BA Art History, California State University, Los Angeles; [occ.] Co-Editor of the Etcetera Newsletter, School of Engineering and Technology - CSULA; [memb.] So. California Women's Caucas for Art, Art Council, Clay Club; [hon.] Dean's List - CSULA '88, '89, National Dean's List '88, '89, Kappa Pi Honor Art Fraternity; [oth. writ.] Articles for the University times - California State University, Los Angeles.

ASHTON, R. S.
[b.] November 3, 1928, Melbourne, FL; [p.] Clarence and Eva Ashton; [m.] Jean Ashton, April 4, 1957; [ch.] Three: Gail, Jeff, Chris; [ed.] High School, College (Three Years) Florida State University; [occ.] Retired, First Union National Bank; [oth. writ.] First fiction novel will be completed by February 96.; [pers.] Decided to write after retirement.; [a.] Jacksonville, FL

ASSELIN, LYN EDWARDS
[b.] April 2, 1921, Oberlion, OH; [p.] Davis Edwards and Jill Edwards Gardner; [m.] Vi Asselin, September 5, 1942; [ch.] Rex Lee, Larry Dean, Sandra Kay, nine grandchildren, 2 greats; [ed.] Graduate 1942 Northwestern University School of Speech; [occ.] Retired after 50 years of active participation in Branson area Tourism, and living on a mountain top 10 miles from bustle of our renowned Country Music Tourist Meca; [memb.] Zeta Phi Eta, Professional Speech Sorority, Past Vice President Dogwood Trails Girl Scout Council, Former Board Member Library Club, Chamber of Commerce, many Community Activities; [hon.] Won my first poetry contest at age 11 in Chautauqua NY, Dean Dennis Award for Interpretation NU 1940, Best Actress NU 1941, Who's Who in MO '74, Prestigious Branson Lakes Area Chamber of Commerce "Pioneer Award" in '95 along with Husband Vi for 50 years of Service and Contributions to the Community; [oth. writ.] Many published articles covering the History of the Ozarks and the growth of Branson. Promotional stories, booklets, and news stories for newspapers and magazines on Ozark tourism.; [pers.] Poetry has always challenged me... the strength, magic and power of conveying emotion and ideas in concise form with precisely chosen words and rhythms. Vachel Lindsay was a family friend and I vividly recall him dancing around a campfire chanting "The Congo" when I was 5.; [a.] Branson, MO

ATKINS, KEVIN S.
[b.] March 28, 1975, Fresno, CA; [ed.] Washington Union High, Kings River Community College; [occ.] Manager, Piccolos Pizza, Fresno, CA; [pers.] My personal and professional accomplishments, including my poetry writing, can be attributed to a very special woman. Thank you Lindsey R. Irion.; [a.] Fresno, CA

ATKINS, SHIRLEY
[pen.] Sam Copper; [b.] Ceylon, Saskatchewan, Canada; [p.] Elizabeth and Albert Vermeulen; [m.] No longer married, November 20, 1954; [ch.] Three Boys and 2 Girls, 10 Grand Children; [ed.] Only High School and then Career College; [occ.] Nurse (L.P.N.), Working in Personal Care Home; [memb.] I was born Shirley Anne Marie (Sam); [oth. writ.] Have written many poems and songs but have never attempted publishing them.; [a.] Selkirk Manitoba, Canada

ATKINSON, ASHA-TALIBAH TESSITA
[pen.] Asha Atkinson; [b.] July 17, 1983, New York, NY; [p.] Kathy Atkinson, Philip Atkinson; [ed.] Herman Schrieber P.S. 279, John Wlson Is. 211; [memb.] Peer Mediation Group, Youth Opportunities United - World Wide Church of God; [hon.] Music Achievement Award; [oth. writ.] "My Sister and Me," "Butterfly," "The Swing"; [pers.] I believe that

writing lifts the spirit and opens the mind. When I write I feel free to express my feelings and stretch my imagination. If more people were writers the world would be a happier place.; [a.] Brooklyn, NY

AUBUCHON, FABIENNE
[b.] October 30, 1979, Saint Isidore, Quebec, Canada; [p.] Helene Dore and Dale Nugent; [occ.] Grade 10 Student at A.S.J.M. High School, Thetford Mines, Quebec, Canada; [oth. writ.] Short stories, songs.; [pers.] Thank you, God, who gives us strength everyday. He loves us. For all the people of my age. I know that life isn't that easy, so never give up. Be positive. God is here.; [a.] Kinnears Mills Quebec, Canada

AURITI, CHRISTINA
[b.] November 29, 1970, Brandon MB, Canada; [p.] Nicola and Dina Auriti; [ed.] Bachelor of Arts from Brandon University, Student of CGA Association of Manitoba; [occ.] Accounting Clerk with Medichair Ltd.; [memb.] Alpha-Beas Calligraphy Guild, Catholic Women's League of Canada, K. A. G. (Klingon Assault Group) of Canada; [hon.] Sister Bernardine Memorial Award for Christian Ethics; [oth. writ.] Some poems published in local fanzine.; [a.] Brandon Manitoba, Canada

AUSTIN, ANN M.
[pen.] The Rapping Teacher; [b.] July 1, 1940, AL; [p.] Willie B. and Lemerle Motley; [m.] Thurman Austin, June 27, 1965; [ch.] Ingrid Ann, Thurman Peron; [ed.] Chambers County Training School - Lafayette, Alabama, Alabama A and M University - Huntsville, Alabama, San Francisco State University, S.F., CA; [occ.] Teacher, Project Director for the San Francisco Unified School District; [memb.] The National Sorority of Phi Delta Kappa, Inc., Beta NU Chapter - Basileus, San Francisco Alliance of Balck School Educators - Executive Board, Alabama A and M Alumni Association, Secretary, Saint Paul Tabernacle Baptist Church - Christian Women of the 21st Century - President; [hon.] Outstanding Service Award - Ella Hill Hutch Community Center - 1995, Phi Delta Kappa - Distinguish Educator Award - 1994, Outstanding Service Award - Ethnic Leadership and Awareness Committee 1993, Distinguished Service Award - District Merchants Association - 1992, Alumni of the Year Award - 1994 Bay Area Alumni Association; [oth. writ.] Working on a "Positive", Rapping Tape. Have been writing poems, for special occasion, since third grade.; [pers.] There is some "good" in all people. "Education is the key that will open the door to all the amenities of a joyous life." All people can learn.; [a.] San Francisco, CA

AUTRY, ANNETTE M.
[pen.] Ashleigh Coe; [b.] January 7, 1938, Elizabeth Town, NC; [p.] R. G. and Annie McDuffie; [ed.] White Oak High School, NC State University; [occ.] President/Owner, All Sport Camping and Housing Inc., Fayetteville, NC; [memb.] Professional Women of Fayetteville, Writers Alliance, Bod. Springlake Little Theatre; [hon.] National Quality RV Dealer of the Year 1980; [oth. writ.] Several poems published in local newspapers and publications articles in RV trade magazines.; [pers.] Worry less about the destination, and enjoy the journey.; [a.] Fayetteville, NC

BABIAK, ELSIE
[b.] November 30, 1920, North Battleford; [p.] Charles and Nellie Dopson; [m.] Joseph Babiak (Deceased), January 1, 1941; [ch.] Seven, 4 boys, 3 girls; [ed.] Grade 10; [occ.] Retired Custodian; [memb.] Ladies Club, Canadian Memorial Club, Rockwood Club 360, Shalome Gardens Writers Club; [oth. writ.] My Biography; [a.] Winnipeg Manitoba, Canada

BACON, STEVE
[b.] July 1, 1953, Sacramento, CA; [p.] Robert C. Bacon and Rose Marie Bacon; [m.] Kelly Bacon, June 23, 1972; [ch.] Benjamin Christian, Elizabeth Kristin; [ed.] San Juan High School; [occ.] Bricklayer, John Jackson Masonry, Sacramento, CA; [a.] North Highlands, CA

BADGLEY, SHARON
[b.] October 3, 1940, Port Arthur, Ontario, Canada; [p.] William and Violet Sutton; [m.] Monte Badgley, June 10, 1966; [ch.] Dawn Leigh Fittpatrick, Sandra Richelle Badgley; [ed.] Grade 12 Commercial Diploma, Port Arthur Commercial and Technical High School; [occ.] Manager, Sales Administration for George Kilk Corporation; [a.] North York Ontario, Canada

BADYAL, GAGAN
[b.] February 11, 1977, India; [occ.] Student; [oth. writ.] Ode to the unknown (A collection of poems); [pers.] One sweetly solemn thought comes to me 'o'er and o'er I am nearer home today than I ever have been before phoebe cary; [a.] Mississauga Ontario, Canada

BAIEL, SONDRA
[b.] January 4, 1971, Flint, MI; [p.] Marc and Sue Swartwood; [m.] Dave Baiel, June 18, 1988; [ch.] Kirsti, Kyle and Kelzi; [ed.] Flushing High School; [occ.] Full-time Wife and Mother; [oth. writ.] Kirsti - The Smiler and Kyle's Birthday; [pers.] I dedicate this poem to my little Kirsti. Cystic Fibrosis has taught you to be a fighter. While you have taught us, to smile through the tears. Thank-you!; [a.] Antioch, TN

BAILEY, DIANE
[b.] November 1, 1951, Meadville, PA; [p.] Willard Flaugh, Shirley Flaugh; [m.] Chip Bailey, November 25, 1972; [ch.] Scott Christopher and Jason Matthew; [ed.] B.S. (Elementary Education), M.Ed. (Reading), East Tennessee State University; [occ.] Reading Teacher; [memb.] National Education Association, Tennessee Education Association, Lamar School Parent Teacher Association.; [hon.] Kappa Delta Pi, Alpha Lambda Delta, Phi Kappa Phi, Dean's List; [oth. writ.] Poems and children's books (unpublished); [pers.] By sharing my personal thoughts and experiences, I hope to influence others to cherish life and its many treasures. I have been personally affected by the works of Emily Dickinson and Carl Sandburg, and have great respect for authors of children's; [a.] Jonesborough, TN

BAILEY, RACHEL MARIE
[b.] May 19, 1978, Greenville, SC; [p.] Mr. and Mrs. Chris and Cindy Bailey; [ed.] 12th Grade High School Student - Central Christian School; [occ.] Student/Sales Clerk; [memb.] Maranatha Baptist Music Committee; [hon.] Honor Roll Student, other

School Award, etc., Principal's Award; [oth. writ.] many other poems, "Harmony of Nature," "Thoughts of Time," etc., (poems won school awards and were printed).; [pers.] I try to present aspects of life in unique perspectives. I want to write from a view point not written from before. I like Tennyson and Poe's poetry.; [a.] Kinards, SC

BAILLARGEON, BRENDA
[pen.] Gabrielle Jean; [b.] January 3, 1950, Montreal, Quebec, Canada; [p.] Jane Parr, Russell Deley; [m.] Jean Baillargeon, December 5, 1992; [ch.] Jason Philip, Belinda Erin; [ed.] Verdun High School, Life; [occ.] Singer, Entertainer; [memb.] Country Music Club of Canada; [oth. writ.] To read what one has written is to know them deeply, and so I offer myself to the world.; [pers.] The path my writing takes is greatly influenced by life.; [a.] Montreal Quebec, Canada

BAITON, DIANNE F.
[pen.] Brea Baiton; [b.] January 16, 1950, Kelvington Saskatchewan, Canada; [p.] Wesley (Deceased) and Marion Baiton; [m.] Wayne Lynch (Fiancee); [ch.] Rhonda Lynn, Harvey Shaun and Lori Anne; [ed.] BA - PSCH, BSW (Bachelor of Social Work); [occ.] Residential Therapeutic Service provides, Regina, Saskatchewan; [memb.] Saskatchewan Social Worker's Assoc and North Central Advisory Board Regina, Saskatchewan; [oth. writ.] Many unpublished; [pers.] Through my poetry, I attempt to draw attention to the social, moral and justice concerns that are current in our communities, I hold an everlasting hope for workable solutions.";
[a.] Regina Saskatchewan, Canada

BAKER, ANITA CATHERINE
[b.] May 27, 1964, Musquodoboit Harbour, Halifax County, NS; [p.] Pauline Russell, Freeman Russell (deceased); [m.] Stephen Baker, August 20, 1988; [ch.] Brandon Mitchell, Aaron Ashley; [ed.] Eastern Shore District High School, Academy of Cosmetology; [memb.] Member of The National Library of Poetry; [hon.] Editor's Choice Award for "Aging Heart" from N.L.O.P.; [oth.writ.] "Aging Heart" was published in the anthology Walk Through Paradise; [pers.] Life is meant to be enjoyed and to experience all that you possibly can, not to be feared and experience nothing.; [a.] Halifax Co. Nova Scotia, Canada

BAKER, CELESTE O'REILLY
[b.] June 1, 1961, London, ON; [m.] Ron Baker, September 7, 1991; [occ.] Homemaker; [pers.] On September 7, 1991, I remarried, I had one son through my first, marriage. My present husband Ron wanted another child so we began our journey with a deep love. Well on February 14, 1994, I have birth to a set of beautiful baby boy one we felt joy, the other sorrow.; [a.] Edmonton Alberta, Canada

BALDIN, LOU
[pen.] Luigi Baldin; [b.] October 7, 1952, Verona, Italy; [p.] Lino and Clelia Baldin; [m.] Nancy J. Baldin, April 7, 1979; [ch.] Angelina, Jennifer; [ed.] 14 years; [occ.] Home Builder; [memb.] Certified Master Builder, HBA; [hon.] Vietnam Era Veteran; [oth. writ.] Two books currently unpublished one a biography the other fiction.; [pers.] Jesus does not need us - he saw us stranded at the side of the road - he stopped and offered us a ride whether we accept

the ride of continue on our own is simply our choice.; [a.] Smithville, MI

BALES, CHANDRA
[b.] August 27, 1980, Hollywood, FL; [p.] Elizabeth Bales (Divorced) and Michael Bales; [occ.] Student; [a.] Grapevine, TX

BANDAROFF, TEALE NEVADA PHELPS
[b.] February 7, 1986, Calgary, Alberta, Canada; [p.] Stan Phelps and Carole Bandaroff; [ed.] Ecole King George School grade 4 French Immersion; [occ.] Student (Artist, Lockey player, writer); [oth. writ.] Boza et Zanba, La grela de 1987, zoo bo's, GorDie Howe, les Flutes, teale and Jared, les Isles on Vivent les Gremlins, Au Bord de la mer, the Adventure of Elmer chicken 1: The Haunted Mansion, 8 realms in chaos, sea others.; [a.] Calgary Alberta, Canada

BARBER, KRISTA
[pen.] Kit Brenna; [b.] April 10, 1979, Santa Clara, CA; [occ.] Student at Monta Vista High School; [memb.] Monta Vista Madrigals; [hon.] Honorable Mention in the Olympiad of the Arts, First place in the Heritage Festivals (Show choir), Scholarship winner from the Michael Mutter Scholarship Fund; [oth. writ.] I am currently working on a reviston of beauty and the beast; [pers.] True beauty is what I love most, and it is what I try to reflect in my work; [a.] Santa Clara, CA

BARD, JAMES F.
[pen.] Jim Bard; [b.] January 18, 1942, Dearborn MI; [p.] Forrest and Elberta Bard; [ch.] Colette, Annette, James Jr.; [ed.] Bethany Bible College - Pastoral Theology; [occ.] Paramedic; [memb.] American Heart Assn., National Assoc. of Emergency Medical Technicians, National Society of Paramedic Instructors; [pers.] To God be The Glory, others be thanked and for the good of all; [a.] Grants Pass, OR

BARELA, MICHELE
[b.] April 6, 1981; [p.] Sarah Barela; [ed.] Attending Walnut High School I am a Freshman; [pers.] Anybody can write poetry. As long as you have a heart.; [a.] Walnut, CA

BARFIELD, STEPHANIE
[b.] July 11, 1977, Naples, Italy; [ed.] Walkefield H.S., Arlington, VA, George Washington University, D.C. School of Business and Public Management; [occ.] Computer Assistant (OA) - GSA/FEDSIM, Falls Church, VA; [hon.] Outstanding Vocational Student for Arlington County (1994-1995), Outstanding Business Student (1994-1995), Crew, Field Hockey, Co-op program, President Future Business Leaders of America (FBLA) (1994-1995); [pers.] It's hard in such a scary world to find your way in life. Writing Allows me to escape the crazines to find myself, my hopes, and my dreams. It allows me to expression I feel. Inside when syaing it does it work.; [a.] Arlington, VA

BARNARD, MARY ANN
[b.] August 10, 1919, Wiarton, Ontario; [p.] Mr. and Mrs. David Collins; [m.] Arch Barnard, September 1, 1945; [occ.] Retired formerly with bell Canada for almost 45 years; [memb.] Baptist Church Bell Canada Pioneers. Hospital Auxiliary Community Living Agricultural Society; [hon.] Special Prizes for baking at Wiarton Owen Sound and Toronto -

Ontario; [oth. writ.] Enjoyed writing poetry as a child - some published in Local papers.; [a.] Wiarton Ontario, Canada

BARRY, WILMA F.
[b.] March 19, 1920, Oakley, KS; [p.] Ralph and Martha Medlin; [m.] H. Lee Barry, M.D., May 16, 1942; [ed.] Elem. and H.S., Oakley, KS, Bachelor Music Education (BME) Univ. of Kansas, Grad School Hours.; [occ.] Home Maker, have taught music and English. Office work woman's Auxiliary to:; [memb.] Sedgwick CO Medical Society, (Past Pres) Kansas State Medical Society, (Past State Pres) and American Medical Society MU Phi Epsilon when and Alumni (Past Pres), Methodist Church order of Eastern Star. Other Music and Education Organizations; [hon.] Vale Dictorian (8th grade), County and State Pres. of Auxiliaries to Kansas Medical Societies Dean's Honor Roll Sr. yr. College. Editor's Choice Awards and Cassette Tapes, 1 Honorable Mention, for poems published Choir Soloist for many years, Wichita KS, International Society of poets.; [oth. writ.] Book: Unpublished "Poems: Memories, and just fun", 2 elem, school plays, and published poem: "Christmas Eng", "I'll wait for you". "To Kristy Ann" "The Rainbows of Faith" (Best poems of 1996). Many unpublished poems.; [pers.] Poetic goal: To write clearly but with enough substance that people will relate to and enjoy my poems. To "Live all thats life with a warm merry heart" is my outlook toward life.; [a.] Las Cruces, NM

BARTON, DONNA D.
[b.] December 23, 1955, Woodward, OK; [p.] Don William and Lou Dailing; [m.] Charles Barton, August 2, 1986; [ch.] Jennifer and Bryan; [ed.] Bachelor Degree in Nursing from Central State University in Edmond Okla.; [occ.] Operating Room Nurse (part-time); [memb.] Association of Operating Room Nurses; [pers.] I wish to thank Charles for letting me take time off from nursing to explore other talents hidden inside of me.; [a.] Irving, TX

BARTON, EDGAR CHARLES
[b.] October 12, 1917, Vancouver, British Columbia; [p.] Ernest Albert Barton and Flossie Kate; [m.] Mary Irene (Nee Fairburn), February 7, 1942; [ch.] Richard and Donald; [ed.] B.A., M.A., University of B.C; [occ.] Retired High School Teacher-English Language and Literature; [oth. writ.] Have some 150 poems, but have never tried to published. My son found the add in a magazine and urged me to enter. I reluctantly complied.; [pers.] My poems are a statement about my beliefs and attitudes concerning past, present and future.; [a.] Vancouver Alberta, Canada

BARTON, ELAINE C.
[b.] February 24, 1931, New York City; [m.] Murray G. Barton, December 26, 1948; [ch.] Francine, Douglas and Gary; [ed.] Evander Childs High Boston University MA from Northwestern University; [occ.] Retired Elementary School Teacher Little Rock, AR, Part time Faculty. The College of St. Rose, Albany, New York; [memb.] League of Women Voters Unitarian Universalist Church Alpha Delta Kappa; [hon.] Graduated Boston University Summa Cum Laude; [oth. writ.] Poem published in Alpha Dleta Kappa yearbook.; [pers.] I write about things which affect me deeply and may stir other kindred spirits.; [a.] North Little Rock, AR

BARTON JR., GLENN LESLIE
[b.] November 27, 1953; [p.] Glenn and Jerri Barton; [m.] Rowena Barton, January 4, 1992; [ed.] De Vry AEET; [occ.] Dream catcher, Route 1 Box 1714, Jeffersonville Ga 31044; [pers.] The mirrored steel of truly whispers free of it's silk sheath, to cave the shape of the soul held tightly beneath.; [a.] Jeffersonville, GA

BARTON, LEXIE P.
[b.] December 31, 1982, Hobbs, NM; [p.] George and Sherry Barton; [ed.] 7th Grade; [oth. writ.] "The Moon," "Angels I," and "Angels II"; [a.] Hobbs, NM

BARTRON, HARRY
[b.] December 26, 1917, Van Etten, NY; [p.] Margaret Cranmer, Fernando Bartron; [m.] Inez Lee Fortner, June 1942; [ch.] Stephen Bartron, Liz Pittenger and Carol Furtick; [ed.] B.A. in English, M.A. in Speech, B.A. (Equivalancy) in Theology; [occ.] Actor, Singer, and writer; [memb.] Screen Actors Guild, Secular Franciscan Order (Catholic), Equity, American Federation of Radio and Television Artists, Dignity, the I am.. Foundation; [hon.] Who's who among students in American Universities and Colleges, Dignity Arch Angel Award, Library of Poetry, California Legistrature Assembly Certificate of Recognition; [oth. writ.] Poem book of poems entitled "Poems of Protest". A novel entitled "Drummer Boy." Book of poems entitled "Quite Another Place."; [a.] Los Angeles, CA

BASTIANUTTI, DIEGO L.
[pen.] Diego Bastianutti; [b.] April 26, 1939, Fiume, Italy; [p.] Luigi Bastianutti and Bianca Tumburns; [m.] Giusy Cecilia Oddo, December 4, 1992; [ch.] Bettina and Lana; [ed.] M.A. Marquette Univ., Ph.D. University of Toronto; [occ.] Professor Spanish/ Italian Liter. Queen's University, Kingston, Canada; [hon.] Vice Consul of Italy for Kingston and Eastern Ontario (1978-1994) First Prize 1994 North American Lyric Poetry Contest (two juries one in Italy one in Canada) For Italian poetry only; [oth. writ.] Critical publications (books and articles) on Spanish literature of the XVI and XVII centuries. Publications on Italian language and literature. Two Volumes of Italian poetry:; [pers.] Poetry has been a love of mine since my school in Italy. Later, in this continent, it has matured as the cathartic expression of my own existential experiences. My poetry has two main influences: The French symbolists and the Italian hermetics. My writing strives to give voice to all those who, in this century of mass migrations in the growing anonymity of homogeneous societies, often mourn unconsciously the loss of their homeland, their language, their sense of belonging, their sense of identity. My writing is an act of faith in the fact that others might recognize their own individuality and their own solitude in mine. Like an Arab wrapped in the silence of his white mantle, I listen to God ripen the grain around my tent.; [a.] Kingston Ontario, Canada

BAUER, WALTER K.
[b.] November 28, 1962, Philadelphia, PA; [p.] Charles and Elsie Bauer; [ch.] Emily Marie Bauer; [ed.] Just enough; [occ.] Student of Life; [pers.] With all my love to my daughter Emily.; [a.] Palmyra, NJ

BAXTER, DENNIS W.
[b.] July 31, 1953, Wichita Falls, TX; [p.] William A. and Gemeva M. Baxter; [m.] Divorced, July 29, 1977; [ch.] Emili Joan Baxter; [ed.] North Mesquite High School, Eastfield College; [occ.] Disabled; [memb.] Mesquite Cumberland, Presbyterian Church - Elder; [hon.] Award of Merit from "World of Poetry"; [pers.] My writing comes from my heart as it is inspired by my Lord and Savior, Jesus Christ.; [a.] Mesquite, TX

BEAULIEU, MARIE
[pen.] Tiante; [b.] May 1933, New Brunswick, Canada; [p.] Rosalie and Joseph Morin; [m.] Lawrence Beaulieu, November 22, 1958; [ed.] 10 Years, Clair New Brunswick, Canada; [occ.] Housewife; [memb.] W.O.T.M., "Woman of the Moose," 1986 Library, 1987 Treasurer, 1989 Chaplain, Friendship Heart and Ring; [pers.] I read poems every day it's my way of relaxing, I also enjoy music, played guitar and a little piano. Always happy! Grand mother of two.; [pers.] Croton Ontario, Canada

BECHTOLD, GUSTI E.
[pen.] William R. Burns; [b.] November 10, 1942, Munich, Germany; [p.] Deceased; [m.] Divorced; [ch.] Four Stepchildren; [ed.] 1/2 Twelve Grade; [occ.] Laundry Machine Operator at Bay Pines; [hon.] From Bay Pines; [oth. writ.] Unpublished other poetry - over the years.

BECK, GORDON A.
[b.] March 21, 1940, Saint Cloud, MN; [p.] Arthur and Bernice Beck; [m.] Sally Ann, June 4, 1966; [ch.] Andrew (28), Gretchen (25), Sarah (18); [ed.] 512 Woodleaf Ct., Kirkwood, Missouri 63122; [occ.] Teacher/Clergyman; [hon.] Masters of Arts from the New School of Social Research in New York and a Masters of Divinity, from Concordia Seminary, St. Louis; [oth. writ.] Devotions for "Portals of Prayer" Published by Concordia Publishing House, St. Louis, MO, Biographies of the Apostles Published by Contemporary Drama Service, Colorado Spring, CO., Screen Play Entitled, the Atwater Saga, a Play about Youthful identity in an all-boys Midwestern Academy, two unpublished set of poems entitled, "Ottersville" and "The Fruits Of The Spirit."; [pers.] In my poetry I strive to celebrate the universal in the common place.; [a.] Kirkwood, MI

BECK, SHANE
[b.] November 21, 1970, Wichita, KS; [ed.] Metro-Meridian High School; [hon.] 1st place Citizenship Award, 5th grade, black school, 1st place in scary story contest, 8th grade in Denver, Colorado; [oth. writ.] Two editorials published in local newspaper, the poem "Message to the children"; [pers.] I believe that if you work hard, good things will happen to you.; [a.] Wichita, KA

BENGTSON, JIMMY D.
[b.] April 23, 1977, Riverside, CA; [p.] Mr. James and Renee Bengtson; [occ.] Student - Riverside Community College; [memb.] Member of a oncology - Hemotology - Teen Group - Loma Linda Childrens Hospital, Lumalinda, CA. Eden Luthern Church, Riverside, CA; [hon.] Honoree in Washington D.C. for my poetry at the 25th Anniversary of the "Candle lighters Foundation". A group in which helps children, as a non-rofit Organization, with deseases like cancer in many loving ways.; [oth. writ.] I was able to publish my 1st poem in my high school newsletter, the year always a junior - I also enjoy writing poetry for or about people whom are close to me very much. A relative or even a friend in need.; [pers.] I am very glad to my say that poetry is a very caring uprise in my life and for others. I feel God has given me a tool, so that I may use this tool, and happily pass it on to others as a gift.; [a.] Riverside, CA

BENJAMIN, HORACE BRUCE HILTON
[b.] Guyana, South America; [p.] James and Doreen Benjamin; [m.] Karen Benjamin, June 25, 1983; [ch.] Ryan Daniel and Jasmine Esther; [ed.] BA Queen's University, Kingston, Ontario Canada; [occ.] Computer Programmer Analyst; [pers.] This effort is my first at documenting any of my thoughts in the form of poetry. I am now encouraged to devote more time in the chronicling of my reflections.; [a.] Toronto Ontario, Canada

BENNERSON, VIVIAN HESTER
[pen.] Shee Shee, Knee Waa/Mother B.; [b.] February 24, 1933, Washington, DC; [p.] Ethel L. Whitaker Hester, Johnnie Hester; [m.] James Alphonso Bennerson (Deceased), August 30, 1955; [ch.] Gregory A., James A. II; [ed.] Vermont College (graduate), New York University, College of the Virgin Islands, Commerce, H.S., NYC, writer Long Ridge Graduate; [occ.] Artist, Counselor, Writer, Lecturer; [memb.] IWWG, (Internat'l Women's Writers Guild), AARP, Crone Network, Elder of Spiritual Femininity; [hon.] Service Award, Virgin Islands Legislature '89, many Plaques Awards, Certificates Boy Scouts of America for Scout, Explorer Groups in Steel Orchestra and Police Pre-Cadets, Director/Co-ordinator PAL (Police Athletic League); [oth. writ.] Anthology on death, several poems published, local magazines, newspapers, dreams and myths mag. My own book entitled "Epheta," universal prayers and thoughts.; [pers.] Wear well your learned "Motherearth," knowledge is life, life is knowledge - accept and utilize what you already have. Know your needs - love self first then others.; [a.] Frederiksted, VI

BENOIT, ALANA
[b.] May 13, 1987, Brooklyn, NY; [p.] Cheryl Benoit; [ed.] Currently a Junior on as a Philip Randolph High School, Class of 1997; [memb.] Girls Choir of New York City, Poet Society, Debate Team as well as other Activities; [hon.] Certificates of Achievement for Programs in and of School; [oth. writ.] I have written several short stories and poems. Currently I am working on my first novel.; [pers.] We live in a very narrow minded society. It is through writing that I am able to express myself freely.; [a.] New York City, NY

BENOIT, CORINA
[b.] January 5, 1974, Calgary, AB; [ed.] Forest Lawn High, Mount Royal College; [occ.] Care giver, Riverbend Day care, Calgary, AB; [memb.] Canadian Child Care Federation

BENSON, SHIRLEY
[b.] February 17, 1941, New Bedford, MA; [p.] Eleanor and Manuel Brown; [m.] Larry Benson, August 14; [ch.] Laurie Ann, and Steve; [ed.] New Bedford Hiott School; [occ.] Admin. Asst.

McAllister General; [memb.] Contractors, Sarasota NAFE (Nat'l Assoc of Female Executives); [oth. writ.] None submitted; [a.] Sarasota, FL

BENVIN, EDWARD F.
[b.] February 11, 1926, McKeesport, PA; [p.] John and Mary Benvin; [m.] Doris Benvin (Deceased), June 1951; [ch.] Stanley, Pamela, Christine, Deborah; [ed.] High School, Army, Air Force; [occ.] Retired; [memb.] UAW Retires American Legion #701 Western Penna Square Dancers Federation, Gateway Campers; [oth. writ.] "I Love You Dear" "Girl Behind The Bar" "Night Beat" "Thanks For These Tears" "Honky Tonk Wife" "Don't Tell Momma"; [pers.] Loves to paint in oils, bird carvings, crafts of all kinds given as gifts; [a.] McKeesport, PA

BERNING, MARILYN
[pen.] Marilyn (Bublitz) Berning; [b.] July 27, 1938, Winoma, MN; [p.] Donald and Helen Bublitz; [m.] William E. Berning, September 13, 1958; [ch.] Jeffrey Wm. Berning, Jason Daniel Berning; [ed.] Spring Valley, Mn. High School, (Life's Experiences); [occ.] Business Owner Homemaker; [memb.] International Society of Poets; [oth. writ.] Several poems working on a book; [pers.] Sometimes it's easier to put into a poem what the heart feels, than to express in other ways. My faith has a part in most of my poems.; [a.] Stewartville, MN

BERRIMAN, KIMBERLY R. PALLANTE
[b.] March 4, 1969, Los Angeles, CA; [p.] Jim and Judi Grieme (Galen Pallante); [ch.] Kori S. Berriman and Alexandra N. McMorris; [ed.] New Berling High School; [occ.] Leasing Consultant; [oth. writ.] Plenty of unpublished, basically "Unseen" poems.; [pers.] I believe there is good in all there is, but that people just have to chose to want it, to find it.; [a.] Tampa, FL

BERTOTTI, TRACY
[pen.] Tracy Bertotti; [b.] April 5, 1964, Perth Amboy; [p.] Bob and Carole Bertotti; [m.] Divorced; [ch.] Crystal, Santino; [ed.] High School and Culinary Arts... With Certification two minor degrees.; [occ.] Executive Chef; Restaurant Owner.; [memb.] American Culinary Fed., National Restaurant Association, American Cancer Society, American Heart Association; [hon.] Numerous awards in the Culinary Arts.; [oth. writ.] Dreams, Through a Mother's Eyes, Starlight.; [pers.] If it weren't for meeting my divine soul mate... my writing would have continued to be unread. I thank him for his encouragement, but more so for his inspiration, and the love he's given.; [a.] Voorhees, NJ

BETHEL, TONY
[b.] Renton, WA; [pers.] "But I said to you, love your enemies, bless those who curse you, do good to those who hate you, and pray for those who spitefully use you and persecute you, that you may be sons of your father in heaven, for the makes his sun rise on the evil and the good." Matthew 5:44-45

BICKERS, RAYMOND LOUIS
[pen.] Sleeper; [b.] May 29, 1957, Norfolk, VA; [p.] Mr. and Mrs. George Bickers; [m.] CTB, September 28, 1980 to June 26, 1995 - Separated; [ch.] Jennifer - Courtney; [ed.] Bayside High School Graduate

1976; [occ.] Petroleum Transfer Specialist (Truck Driver); [memb.] Automotive Club 1976 - Saint Gregory's - The Great Catholic Glee Club, Altar Boy, since 1967; [hon.] Honorable Mention Science Exhibit - Safe Driving Award - 11 Years Running; [oth. writ.] None published - started 1992 - "Heat of Madness," "Sand and Surf," "Pen and Pencil," "Unknown," "Full Moon," Mister moon, "The Line," "The Mirror," "Sweet Dreams," "Alone and Cold," "Unit"; [pers.] Inspiration - my darling. She introduced me to myself that I never existed. Emotionally I was a mishap - now I am complete. Even though we travel on a roller coaster of life - there is always time - for each other.; [a.] Virgin Beach, VA

BIELAGA, WAYNE ALEXANDER
[b.] March 6, 1978, Chicago; [ed.] East Leyden High School; [occ.] Student; [memb.] French Honor Society; [hon.] Won High School Fern Award. Won Young Author's Contest. Won Outdoor Conference championship for 300 Intermediate Hurdles in Track. Received 1st place in prizewrite for fiction genre.; [oth. writ.] Two novels, an anthology, and two collections of poems; [pers.] I am a visionary who uses poetry and other forms of Art to expend limitless energy, and to unravel the mystery of truth. I advice Jim Mocisson as a poet, but value all creative writers.; [a.] River Grove, IL

BIGLER, HELENE L.
[b.] April 13, 1940, Managua, Nicaragua; [ch.] Four-Mark (35), Vickie (34), Chris (33), Teresa (26); [ed.] Compton High School, Coastline Comm. College Institute of Children's Literature; [occ.] Quality, Safety, Environment Compliance Clerk; [memb.] Orange County Public Employees Council for Cities and Districts - President; [hon.] Ethan Fulmer Achievement Award; [pers.] Children-the future. To shape, to mold, to open up the imagination- no greater gift can one give our tomorrows.; [a.] Hemet, CA

BILLINGS, NICHOLE
[b.] September 16, 1981, Mesa, AZ; [p.] Karen M. Billings; [ed.] Valley Christian High School; [occ.] Telemarketer for Bank of America; [memb.] Cheerleading Squad, Mesa First Church of the Nazarene Youth Group; [hon.] Cheerleading, Poetry, Short Story, Signing, Bible Quizzing; [oth. writ.] Many other pieces of poetry which I am hoping to get published soon.; [pers.] I love to write past time. My writings usually deal with love, friends, family and personal experiences.; [a.] Tempe, AZ

BILLINGSLEY, ELLEN
[b.] July 24, 1946, Douglas, AZ; [p.] Herbert and Mildred Estes; [m.] March 1964; [ch.] 1 sons, 1 daughter; [ed.] High School Diploma; [occ.] Ellen passed away May 8, 1993; [hon.] She was Rodeo Queen her Senior year in Dunan, AZ; [oth. writ.] Ellen was a born again Christian and belonged to Baptist Church in Dunean AZ. She did a lot through the church to help other people.

BIXBY, BECKIE
[ed.] Some College lots of life (school of hard knocks?); [occ.] Recently retired after 30 years as paralegal for Grand Island City Attorney's Office; [memb.] Trinity United Methodist Church, GI Municipal Ladies Golf Assoc, National Assoc of

Legal Secretaries, local Crime stoppers Board, local Zoning Board, other humerus things, etc; [hon.] Am certified as a Professional Legal Secretary; [oth. writ.] Placed fourth in national competition sponsored by West Publishing Company and National Assoc of Legal Secretaries in 1995 on subject "How Has New Media Affected the Image of Lawyers."; [pers.] "Never pass up an opportunity, you may not get another chance. Never give up!"; [a.] Grand Island, NE

BLACKBURN, AVONELL
[b.] November 4, 1959, S. Williamson, KY; [p.] James and Dollie Chapman; [m.] John Blackburn, June 26, 1987; [ch.] John Thomas and Desiree; [ed.] Sheldon Clark High School Southern W, VA Community College; [occ.] Housewife; [a.] Fort Gay, WV

BLACKLOCK, RONALD E.
[b.] February 1, 1941, Murphysboro, IL; [p.] Evert D. Blacklock, Etta Lorene Blacklock; [m.] Conne J. Blacklock, May 23, 1987; [ch.] Deanna Marie (7), Ronald Jr. (34), Dennis (33), Kelly (31); [ed.] East Peoria Community High School '59, California State University, Sacramento School of Engineering '73, Metals Engineering Inst., Elem. of Metallurgy '68, The Institute of Biblical Studies '95; [occ.] Development Technician for Caterpillar Inc., Joliet, IL; [memb.] Joliet Loyal Order of Moose, Good Shephard Lutheran Church in Kankaker; [hon.] Life Scout B.S.A., Leadership SW for Scouts, Committees Church and Work; [oth. writ.] America Astray/ Someone will Pay, Young Cowboy Published by National Library of Poetry, others never submitted for publication various topics and songs.; [pers.] My poetry is a poetic expression of feelings on the topic chosen. Sometimes in a serious manner other times with comedy. I enjoy the challenge of creativity with words.; [a.] Wilmington, IL

BLACKMAN JR., J. H.
[b.] May 17, 1932, Jacksonville, FL; [p.] Julius H. and Jennie Blackman Sr.; [m.] Louise W. Blackman, June 8, 1956; [ch.] James Daniel, Benjamin Lee; [ed.] Andrew Jackson High, David Lipscomb University; [occ.] Minister Church of Christ, Faculty Florida School of Preaching, both in Lakeland, Florida; [memb.] North Lakeland Church of Christ, Board of Directors Florida School of Preaching; [oth. writ.] Mostly religious articles and many religious poems.; [a.] Lakeland, FL

BLANKENSHIP, KRISTY ANN
[pen.] Kristy Ann; [b.] July 9, 1960, Bellefonte, KY; [p.] Rose Ann Callahan Blankenship and Ernest Richard Blankenship; [ed.] PhD in Biomedical Sciences at Marshall University, WV 1996, B.A. in Biology and Chemistry at Univ. of Louisville, KY 1983; [memb.] Sierra Club, Greenpeace, and several other environmental groups, Sigma Xi, Women in Science; [oth. writ.] Several Volumes of unsubmitted poetry and essays scientific abstracts; [pers.] I have many passions. I love my land, my family, friends, my God and move. From this love comes all my art. I thank them.; [a.] Cattettsburg, KY

BLEAKLEY, CAROL
[b.] May 13, 1937, Colon, Republic of Panama; [p.] Fred Newhard and Loretta Newhard; [m.] Andrew Bleakley Jr., December 22, 1963; [ch.] Andrew

James, David Thomas; [ed.]Cristobal High, Colorado State College of Education, Montessori early Childhood and Elementary Training, N.C.M.E/San Diego, CA; [occ.] Montessori Teacher, Ramona Community School, Ramona, CA; [oth. writ.] Composed original songs and lyrics and produced an audio cassette of educational songs for learning Ed-u-CA-tunes.; [pers.] Poetry... a special way to share.; [a.] San Diego, CA

BLEDSOE, ANDREA MARIE
[b.] August 11, 1975, Memphis, TN; [p.] Ralph W. Bledsoe Jr. and Martha Ann Bledsoe; [ed.] Memphis Harding Academy - HS, State Technical Institute - College; [occ.] Teacher's Aide at Cheerfield Child Care; [memb.] Member of Germantown, Church of Christ, Participant of Volunteering Committee of Alzheimer's Day Services; [oth. writ.] I am the writer of Germantown Church of Christ's teen newsletter, F.Y.I. I have written six books of poetry for a hobby.; [pers.] Reach for the stars, hold fast to your dreams. But keep your feet on the ground.; [a.] Memphis, IN

BLOYDER, JOSEPH J.
[b.] December 3, 1939; [m.] Linda; [ch.] Jessica and Joseph; [ed.] St. Peter's Prep Parks College of St. Louis Univ; [occ.] Pilot Delta Airlines; [pers.] Poetry is the natural flow of one's intrinsic rhythm.

BLUMBERG, MYRNA LOUISE
[b.] July 9, 1957, Port Alberni, BC; [p.] Norman and Elaine Newberry; [m.] Ross Blumberg, September 26, 1980; [ch.] Three Daughters and Four Grandchildren; [occ.] Matron for the R.C.M.P, in City of Port Alberni; [pers.] I have always enjoyed writing poetry as a hobby and as a form of 'Release.' I believe in laughter as a tool for living. I also enjoy doing genealogical research.; [a.] Port Alberni British Columbia, Canada

BLYTHE, GLORIANNE
[b.] January 23, 1925 (d. March 23, 1958), Cleveland, OH; [ch.] (4) Sandy Jo, Mellanie, Randy, and Patti; [occ.] Deceased; [oth. writ.] "A Fool Was I," "One Summer Night," "A Boy or Girl For Daddy;" [pers.] My lovely and talented mother went to be with the Lord leaving children 10 yr - 5 yr - 3 yr - 3 months. Four years later her son joined her there. We missed her and this publication is a cherished honor to her talent. With all my love Mother, Your Daughter.

BOBAY, TECIA R.
[b.] March 15 1974; [p.] Gerald Bobay and Shirley Bobay; [m.] Robert J. Wiersma, April 20, 1996; [ed.] Leo Jr./Sr. High School; [pers.] I dedicate this poem to my husband, by whom I was inspired.; [a.] Angola, IN

BOBER, FRANCIS J.
[pen.] Frank J. Bober; [b.] September 6, 1942, Adams, MA; [p.] Frank and Josephine Bober; [ed.] High School Degree: Saint Joseph's High - North Adams, MA, Bachelor's Degree and Doctoral Candidacy: Catholic University of America - Washington DC Master's Degree: Saint Vincent College/Seminary - Latrobe, PA; [occ.] Roman Catholic Priest and Chalpain to various Organizations and Institutes; [memb.] MENSA, Knights of Columbus, Washington Astronomy Club, Metropoli-

tan Cosmology Forum, The Planetary Club, and Member of several Teacher and Ethics Organizations; [hon.] Dean Lists, Several Academic Honors, Summa Cum Laude Honor, several Teaching and Organization Skill Awards; [oth. writ.] Several theology and philosophy articles published in local and national newspapers, papers, magazines and book.; [pers.] To seek the truth, to live it and share it with other while experiencing life as fully as possible. I have been greatly influenced by several philosophers, theologians and scientist, especially, A. Einstein, M. Heidegger and several process theologians and philosophers.; [a.] Washington, DC

BOCKUS, HEIDI
[b.] May 17, 1976, Lexington, NE; [pers.] I wrote this poem (To a Dreamer) as a call to action on my part. I often loose sight of "what's worth it" in life that is, serving my maker. The short time in which I've been able to do this (through believing in his son's death in place of my sins), save been the happiest moments of my life.

BODDY, BETTY
[b.] September 30, 1934, Yorkshire, England; [p.] Amy and Stan Welford; [m.] James Roger Boddy, July 31, 1954; [ch.] Christopher, Clarke and Carolyn-Amy; [ed.] Educated in England, Emigrated to Canada 1956; [occ.] Chaplain (non-denominational), to Senior Citizens; [oth. writ.] Community newspaper column. Numerous poems about God's goodness and interpersonal relationships.; [pers.] In a word which rewards by remuneration, I honor volunteers who express the joy of giving which is 'more blessed.'; [a.] Kingston Ontario, Canada

BOLIG, DORIS
[pen.] Dolly Bolig; [b.] May 18, 1941, Medicine Hat, AB; [p.] George and Leona Thompson; [m.] Bernard Bolig, October 22, 1960; [ch.] Shannon, Felicia, Delsie, Jordan; [ed.] Senator Gershaw School, Bow Island, AB; [occ.] Child Care in my Own Home (11 years); [memb.] Parents of the Handicapped Association; [oth. writ.] Poems published in several news papers, self-published three poet books - working on a fourth. A few song - lyrics set to music.; [pers.] Strive to reflect on the basic human emotions that touch us all, therefore writing mostly inspirational poetry.

BOLTON, VIRGINIA C.
[pen.] Chris; [b.] June 22 1931, Russellville, AL; [p.] John William and Lillie M. Henry; [m.] Clovis J. Bolton, January 13, 1950; [ch.] Glenda, Donna, Judy, Deborah; [ed.] Cherokee Voc. High; [occ.] Retired, Love to Cook, Garden, Fish and Write Poetry; [memb.] Church of Christ; [hon.] Plaque with name and gold key for best cook from Jewel Food, two editor's award from The National Library of Poetry.

BONGIOVANI, MARGARET CYNDA
[pen.] M. Cynda Bongiovani; [b.] March 25, 1957, Baltimore, MD; [p.] Anna McGuire, Jack Stafford Sr.; [m.] Steven W. Bongiovani, January 16, 1977; [ch.] Shane Steven, Gianna Cynda; [ed.] University of Maryland, Baltimore Country, Mount Bebron High School; [memb.] Catonsville United Methodist Church, Mount Saint Joseph High School, Mother's Club Executive Board, 1995-1996; [pers.] Children with special needs challenge others to be the very

best they can be. As the mother of a special education student, I write this poem for Gianna, my "Angel Child."; [a.] Ellicott City, MD

BOOTH, ROSEMARIE
[b.] Quincy, MA; [occ.] Office Manager; [oth. writ.] Poetry for my own personal satisfaction.; [pers.] Poetry is a way of expressing feelings that cannot truly be expressed in any other way.!; [a.] Quincy, MA

BORDEN, LINDA J.
[b.] April 8, 1948, Woodbury, NJ; [p.] Ernest R. Borden and Ester Jean Borden; [m.] Ronald E. Steighman, November 15, 1984; [ch.] Jeffrey, Aaron, and B. Justin Myers; [ed.] College (2 years) AL., Christian (Deans list), Graduate Porcelain Doll Making, 17DM Member of 5 Years Study. Studied Sculpting with Lewis Goldstein; [occ.] Sculpting and Original Porcelain Doll Artist (owner of Doll shop) and Artist/Illustrator; [memb.] Trazier Memorial Church, 1 year Secretary of the Cottage Hill Association, Red Cross Donor, member of SAC's Gallery, Chamber of Commerce; [hon.] Junior Olympics, 1 gold medal and 2 silver medals, relay running and 100 yard dash. "Blue Ribbon and best in Show" porcelain Doll, "Ashley." Medalist for walk, A-Thon. for M.S Patients; [oth. writ.] Currently writing a series of children books. "Passing of the Whitetail Deer" for magazine called Buckmasters. Also writing a true life story for reader Digest.; [pers.] We pass this way but once so before I am finished my journey something of my self behind that will be enjoyed for generations. Hopefully I will bring a little sunshine, or a smile into some ones life through my writings.; [a.] Montgomery, AL

BORLAND, MARY HELEN
[b.] April 19, 1941, Santa Fe, NM; [p.] Gerald Leo and Helen B. Davies; [m.] Stephen M. Borland, July 6, 1979, (2nd); [ch.] David, Ron and Frank; [ed.] Santa Fe High graduate; [occ.] Office Manager for Dermatologist Kenneth H. Brooks, M.D. 25 years; [oth. writ.] Just beginning; [pers.] Although I have always expressed myself well in writing, I never thought of writing poetry until I made a 3 day visit to San Padre Island October 1995. I was so struck by the beauty of the ocean by moonlight, I felt compelled to record what I was feeling and seeing. During that period of time I composed several poems about the ocean. The poem I submitted expressed my sadness at having to leave that creative environment so soon. I hope to develop this newly discovered talent further.; [a.] Santa Fe, NM

BORN, IDELLA
[b.] December 3, 1945, Pembroke, Ontario; [p.] Deceased; [m.] Clifford Born, March 20, 1971; [occ.] Housewife (due to a Physical Handicap); [oth. writ.] I have written many poems, a few children's stories and an autobiography which have not been published. This poem will be my first publication.; [pers.] Due to a car/train accident in 1952, which left me physical handicapped, I've had to endure many challenges in my life. I have expressed my feelings and emotions through my writings and I believe it is an inspiration to my family and friends. The works of Robert Browning have been the most influential to me.; [a.] Pembroke Ontario, Canada

BORTZFIELD, TASHA
[b.] March 1, 1979, Chambersburg, PA; [p.] C. Edwards and Judy D. Bortzfield; [ed.] High School Junior; [a.] Waynesboro, PA

BORUNDA, DAVID J.
[pen.] David J. Borunda; [b.] April 4, 1966, El Paso, TX; [p.] Ralph Borunda and Terry Rodriquez; [ed.] Coronado High, ElPaso, TX; [occ.] Freelance Exercise Rider Thoroughbred Race Horses Everywhere U.S.A.; [hon.] Outstanding student DECA (Distributive Education Clubs of America) Senior year High School; [pers.] I write about my own traveling experiences I travel alot and always drive the back roads. You see more and meet more people. There for it gives you more to write about. Bottom line: Dream it, do it and write about it get off the couch!; [a.] El Paso, TX

BOSTOCK, MURIEL CHRISTINE
[b.] July 28, 1944, Welland, Ontario; [p.] William and Christine Shantry; [m.] John Charles Bostock, May 25, 1963; [ch.] David, Janet, Andrew and Cassandra; [ed.] Pelham District High School Fenwick College of New Caledonia. Diploma Nursing Program; [occ.] Registered Nurse; [memb.] Ontario Nurse's Association, College of Nurse's of Ontario Cornerstone Pentecostal Church; [hon.] During my nurse's training, I was awarded 5 scholarships on basis of my high grades; [oth. writ.] This is the first of my works that I have submitted to contests or for publication, although I have written a book full. Some of my works have been published in our Church weekly bulletin. I am currently working on a novel.; [pers.] I am a Born Again in Christian and strive to glorify God in my writings. I believe we all have a God given talent in us. Unfortunately only a few ever discover what their is.; [a.] Keswic Ontario, Canada

BOTTAS, BRENDA
[b.] May 10, 1964, Regina, SK; [p.] Terry and Shirley Smith; [m.] Jim Bottas, June 26, 1982; [ch.] Jamie, Cody, Jesse, Randy; [ed.] Scott Collegiate; [occ.] Home Based Educator and Sears TSA; [pers.] The heart's light shines bright in a poem.; [a.] Regina Saskatchewan, Canada

BOUGIE, JUDITH E.
[b.] June 9, 1949, Toronto, Canada; [p.] Mike and Genevieve Kerr; [m.] Robert Bougie, 1988; [ch.] Jason Robert; [occ.] Victorian Gift Store and Christmas Store; [oth. writ.] I write for personal satisfaction from personal experiences.; [pers.] I enjoy reading poetry of the the romantic period one of my favorite books of poetry is "Wings of Song".

BOWDIDGE, SARAH LYNN
[b.] August 25, 1979; [p.] Carol Bowdidge and Richard Bowdidge; [ed.] I currently attend, Lockerby Composite School, (grade 7). I am in Science and Technology Program; [memb.] Girls Guides, School reach for the Top Team, School, Improve Team Sednet Auditor, (Sednet is like internet except is for Sudbury and Area only); [oth. writ.] I have no other published work. However I am currently writing a series of short stories and other poems.; [pers.] In my poetry I try to show the enigma of our world. I truly enjoy Arthunic Legend and Celtic, Greek and E Egyptian mythology. My work often reflect this interest. "The essential is always invisible."; [a.] Val Caron Ontario, Canada

BOWEN, RUBY LANELL
[b.] October 23, 1931, Albany, OK; [p.] Benjamin Franklin Shipman and Myrtie Mae Purkey Shipman; [m.] Dr. Collin W. Bowen, August 8, 1950; [ch.] Deborah, Susan, Brent and David; [ed.] Honor Grad. of Blue High School, B.S. and Ed. Southeastern Ok State Univ. and Graduate Study at OK Univ. and Ok State Univ and Univ of N. Colo.; [occ.] Housewife and Artist (Oil Painting); [memb.] President of Durant Creative Arts Guild, Delta Kappa Gamma, Pi Omega Pi, retired Teachers, First Baptist Church, AARP; [hon.] Dean's and Pres. List Honor Graduate in all degrees Blue Ribbon on painting "Irises"; [oth. writ.] None pub.; [pers.] Ever since my high school teacher, Mrs. I.W. Brown, made us memorize poetry from American Literature, I have loved it. At times, words just come to me and I got them down, but have never tried to publish them.; [a.] Durant, OK

BOWMAN, LAKEISHA
[pen.] Lakeisha Bowman or Chocolate; [b.] November 30, 1979, Queens; [p.] Jeffann Bowman; [ed.] General Education; [occ.] Attending Bayshore High School; [hon.] School Honor Rolls and School Awards for Poetry; [oth. writ.] Friendship lane, charm, love and sitting here alone and plus many more.; [pers.] I will like to dedicate this poem to all my love ones and bright waters group home. My teachers of Bayshore High School that helped me out at let me not leave out lawrence High.; [a.] Brightwaters, NY

BOWMAN, LINDA HARPLE
[b.] May 7, 1957, Philadelphia, PA; [p.] Ken Harple and Nancy Harple; [m.] Ron R. Bowman, June 21, 1985; [ch.] Ashley (10), Anna (2); [ed.] BS, Accounting, Auburn Univ., MBA, Real Estate, Georgia State Univ.; [occ.] Commercial Mortgage Broker; [memb.] Advent Episcopal Vestry, EFM, Teacher, MCES Tutor, Girl Scouts FOGS Chairperson; [hon.] Phi Kappa Phi, Delta Gamme Sigma; [oth. writ.] Local newspaper, children's literature.; [pers.] Love can touch a heart, change a lite, involve imaginations. Glorious rewards of simplicity.; [a.] Madison, GA

BOYD, JAY E.
[b.] May 6, 1950, Baltimore, MD; [p.] Jay M. Boyd Jr. and Margaret Culler Boyd; [ed.] Friends School, Baltimore (1968), West Virginia Wesleyan College, (B.A. 1972), The Catholic University of America, D.C. (M.A. 1974); [occ.] Editor of Computer Newsletter at the Social Security Administration; [memb.] The International Society of Poets, Kappa Pi Art Honorary, American Delta Kappa Leadership, Honorary, Alpha PSI Omega Drama Honorary; [hon.] Hatfield Fine Arts Award (W.VA. Wesleyan). Dean's list (W.VA. Wesleyan Omicron Delta Kappa, Leadership honorary, (W.VA Wesleyan),. Who's Who in the new poets (1995); [oth. writ.] Poem "Friend... Almost" was published in Echoes from the Silence (1995), poems "All Good Things..." was features on the Sound of Poetry Audio Tape (1995) and published in Beyond The Stars 1995.; [pers.] Diversity is the spice of life. That which makes us different from one another. We should spend more time and effort trying to understand one another and less time hating.; [a.] Reisterstown, MD

BRADBURY, JACK A.
[b.] December 2, 1942, Peterborough, Ontario; [p.] Mr. and Mrs. P. A. Bradbury; [m.] Mary-Jane; [ch.] Roxanne, Martin, Chandelle, Daralynn, Grandchildren, Rhalynn, Corbin; [ed.] Junior High; [occ.] Letter Carrier, Canada Post; [memb.] International Society of Poets - 1995; [hon.] Publication, "Shabby Little House" - Sparkles in the Sand Editor's Choice Award 1995 - "Shabby Little House"; [oth. writ.] Published in several papers, both Alberta and British Columbia; [pers.] "And still it seems, that our dreams, haven't left us at all, they simply wait for us to recall" - from my poem "thoughts" 1990.; [a.] Prince George British Columbia, Canada

BRADLEY, PHYLLIS CHAVEZ
[pen.] Phyllis Chavez-Bradley; [b.] April 6, 1939, New Mexico; [m.] John G. Bradley Jr., February 22, 1963; [ch.] Paize and Tyler Bradley; [ed.] High School - 2 Years of College; [occ.] Housewife - Caregiver; [hon.] Editors Choice Award "Echoes of Yesterday"; [pers.] Keep good thoughts and thinks nothing else.; [a.] West Minster, MD

BRAXTON, LILLIAN L.
[pen.] Lillian L. Braxton; [b.] February 23, 1937, Bronx, NY; [p.] Walter and Lillian Mortenson; [m.] Divorced; [ch.] Brenda Louise Braxton; [ed.] High School, Business School; [occ.] Dental Secretary (and retired Civil Service Employee); [memb.] East Harley Tutorial Services as a Volunteer Tutor; [hon.] A plaque issued by the Montfrod Point Marine Assoc., in recognition of my voluntary services. MPMA is a not for profit organization founded by the first black men inducted into the U.S.A MArine Corp. during WW II; [oth. writ.] Several poems unpublished.; [pers.] If you have a friend keep him (her) so let him (her) not your secrets know for if this friend becomes your foe then all then world your secrets will know.!; [a.] New York, NY

BRAYSHAW, BEATRICE
[b.] December 26, 1938, Edmonton, Alberta; [p.] Gordon and Johanna Campbell; [m.] Glenn H. Brayshaw, June 13, 1957; [ch.] Wanda, Candace, Deanna, Curtis, Marnie; [ed.] High School; [occ.] Housewife; [oth. writ.] I've been writing poetry much all my life. I started keeping some around 1969, so I have a few boxes of my thoughts and feelings. Some lost and forgotten, others under my bed. I refer to them as my therapy.; [pers.] My writings has been inspired by the people and places in my life. Forever young was for my mothers 91st birthday. I was always shy about showing anyone things I wrote the first time they were read in public was at moms funeral. People said really nice things. It gave me the incentive to enter your contest.; [a.] Calgary Alberta, Canada

BRAZEAU, DIANE M.
[b.] February 23, 1961, New Liskeard, Ontario, Canada; [p.] Marcel and Mildred; [m.] Brent G. McAdam, September 11, 1993; [ed.] Post-Secondary; [occ.] Secretary, University of Calgary; [oth. writ.] (Novice Level) - poetry, greeting card copy, articles for submission.; [a.] Calgary Alberta, Canada

BREADON, LORRAINE D.
[b.] November 7, 1958, England; [p.] John and Dorothy Breadon; [m.] I am divorced (parents from N. Ireland); [ch.] Tara and Eric Milner; [ed.] Grade 12 diploma majored in English: I write often since I was a child. I skipped grade due to an English gift;

[occ.] Education; [hon.] Award from Correspondence booklet; [oth. writ.] In local newspaper, hospital and correspondence book he would aid me in publication. He has since passed away; [pers.] Everyone has a gift. With insight you shall cherish it and share it and use it.; [a.] Ajax Ontario, Canada

BREWER, BRYANT L.
[b.] November 7, 1953, Detroit, MI; [p.] Harry and Marjorie Richards; [m.] Tracy J. Schoemaker Brewer, December 13, 1986; [ch.] Angelique Brewer, Rachel Brewer, Zachary Brewer and Brett Shoemaker; [ed.] Southgate High School, University of Michigan, Eastern Michigan University, BS in Music (organ) Concordia College, Central Michigan University; [occ.] Aide for Bay Arenac Intermediate School District and Musician; [memb.] American Guild of Organists, Saginaw Chapter; [hon.] Young Composer of the Year ASCAP; [oth. writ.] Numerous poems songs and compositions.; [pers.] All poems I write are set to music and performed with the band, "Lectric Bebop."; [a.] Pinconning, MI

BRICE, BARBARA A.
[b.] December 8, 1942, Charleston, SC; [p.] Christine Bryan and Hammond D. Bryan; [m.] Billy W. Brice, May 2, 1964; [ch.] Valerie Christina, Lisa Marie and Anthony Howard; [ed.] Frederick Douglas Senior High School, Morgan State University, Coppin State College; [occ.] Retired Elementary School Teacher; [memb.] Iota Phi Lambda Sorority, Inc., The National Sorority of Phi Delta Kappa, Inc., St. Monica's guild of St. James, Episcopal Church; [hon.] Outstanding Teacher (Arlington Elementary School), Outstanding Tutor (Iota Phi Lambda Sorority), Excellence in St. Luke's Oystreach Ministry Certificates for Iota Phi, Invaluable service (Lambda sorority), Outstanding Performance for The Housing Authority of Baltimore City; [oth. writ.] Several poems for area schools, poems for special occasions, personal poems.; [pers.] I find beauty in daily living. I love to give flowers through poetry.; [a.] Baltimore, MD

BRIDGES, TIM R.
[pen.] Tim R. Bridges; [b.] January 15, 1953, Chicago, IL; [p.] Raymond and Mary Bridges; [ed.] St. George H.S. Northeastern Illinois University, University of Illinois Chicago; [occ.] Police Officer, Laboratory Technician, Chicago, IL; [memb.] American Society of Clinical Pathologists, Fraternal Order of Police Emerald Society; [oth. writ.] Several unpublished poems; [pers.] I dedicate my writings to those unsung heroes and their untold deeds that adorn all with such amazing grace.; [a.] Chicago, IL

BRIDGFORTH, JENIECE
[b.] October 26, 1982, Yukon, OK; [p.] Dan Bridgforth and Deana Bridgforth; [ed.] Parkland Elementary, Independence Middle School; [occ.] Student; [memb.] United Methodist Church, Excaliber, Scholastic Club, Yukon Angels Basketball, Yukon Turbos Softball; [hon.] Presidential Scholastic Achievement Award '95

BRIFFA, ROSWITHA
[pen.] Rosvita J. Briffa, Rosvita Testaferrata; [b.] November 25, 1948, Germany; [p.] French Father, German Mother; [m.] John; [ch.] Andrea, Justin and Valerie; [ed.] German High School Diploma; [occ.] Flight Operations Agent for a European Airline; [oth.

writ.] A selection of poetry short stories and travel - documentation. A children's book in progress, - no publication yet.; [pers.] To me, poetry is a reflection of scared emotions, a healing medicine, potion to soothe lover's grief, a song to liberate the spirits of love, an illumination of the soul. I have been greatly inspired by the Minne-Singers of the Middle ages.; [a.] Mississauga Ontario, Canada

BRIGGS, EVERETT FRANCIS
[b.] January 27, 1908, Fitchburg, MA; [p.] Thomas Everett and Mary Lillian Hughes Briggs; [ed.] Postgraduate: S.T.B., Catholic Univ. of america (1933), M.A. in Ed. (Cum Laude), Fordham Univ. (1953), L.H.D. Holy Cross College (1950); [occ.] Ordained priest (1933), Instructor, Maryknoll Seminary, PA (1944-46), Academic Dean, Maryknoll College, NJ (1946-50), Assoc. Pastor, Japanese Catholic parish, L.A. CA (1950-56), Pastor, Catholic Churches of Monongah, WV (1956-72), Adm. St. Barbara's Nursing Home, Monongah, WV (since 1961), Adviser to NGO Dnh-Diem, later Pres. of South Vietnam (1948-50), Chairman, WV State Nursing Home Administrators Advisory Council (1970-74), Prof. of Japanese, U.S.N. V-12 Training Program (1943-44); [memb.] Wheeling Diocese Priests Senate (1971-72), Sons of American Revolution, Founders and Patriots of America, Descendants of Colonial Clergy, Descendants of Mayflower Society, order of Three Crusades, and other Organizations; [hon.] Won National Conference of Christians and Jews: Citation (1954), also American Freedom Foundation Awards, 2. Missionary in Japan (1933-42), repatriated from wartime camps in Japan during WW II; [oth. writ] Has published books and pamphlets in both English and Japanese, as well as poetry in both languages, and musical compositions.; [pers.] "To grow old in love of God and fellowman."; [a.] Monongah, WV

BRIGGS, OLIVIA
[pen.] Olivia Briggs; [b.] June 29, 1919, Marysville, KS; [p.] Leonard Cole, Grace Sale Cole; [m.] Clarence A. Briggs, July 3, 1942; [ch.] Cole Arthur, Paul Darcy and Brian Lee; [ed.] BA, Stephens College, Art Education, University of Kansas; [occ.] Art Teacher, Secretary, Housewife; [memb.] Art Association, Univ. of Colorado, Faculty Wives, Monday Bridge ACBL; [pers.] My interest is composing my thoughts, confined by the classical modern Haiku form.; [a.] Boulder, CO

BRIX, PAMELA
[pen.] P. J. Brix; [b.] October 18, 1955; [p.] Gerald and Marilyn Olson; [m.] Thomas; [ch.] Phillip Marshall, Morgan Arthurs; [ed.] Forestlake High School, Oliver Their Bty College, E., Texas St. U., Central FL Com. College; [occ.] Owner: Bty Salon and Artist; [pers.] Life is wonderful journey controlled by God, where we touch one another. Walking with my friend each morning has been one growth experience of my journey.; [a.] Winter Springs, FL

BRONNER, RASHE ATHENA
[pen.] Rashe; [b.] February 8, 1991, Mount Holly, NJ; [p.] Aileen C. Smith; [ed.] Greenbelt Middle School, Greenbelt MD, 9th Grade; [occ.] Student; [memb.] Leaders of Tomorrow; [hon.] Tutoring Certificate, News Reporter Award 6th Grade; [pers.] I enjoy writing I learned that the the very best way to

deal my feelings is to write. I especially enjoy the writings of Maya Angelou.; [a.] Greenbelt, MD

BROWN, CLEOPATRA AGATHA
[b.] Portland, Jamaica, West Indies; [p.] Clifford Brown and Una Dyee; [ed.] Norman Manley Secondary and Pace University; [occ.] Presently a - Student at Pace University, Pleasantville, NY; [oth. writ.] Several poems, short stories and songs including, "You chased Me," which was published by the National Library of Poetry in the fall of '94! My the writings have not been.; [pers.] Jesus Christ is the essence of my life, he is my reality, he is my purpose for living. Living for him makes me feel totally complete and satisfy. Taking to h in is like taking a ship from a cool running spring that refreshes my whole being. My greatest desire is to live so that everyone can see him through me.; [a.] North White Plains, NY

BROWN, GRACE MARIA
[b.] February 17, 1969, Omaha, NE; [p.] Estelle Brown, Gerald Brown; [ch.] Ronald J. Bozant, III; [ed.] Me Dnogh #35, New Orleans, LA Strayer College, Wash, DC; [occ.] Margaret Analept, U.S. Department of Education, Wash, D.C; [memb.] Alpha Chi - National College Honor Scholarship Society; [hon.] Graduated Cum Laude 4 year Honor Roll Student; [oth. writ.] Personal connection of many poems, unpublished; [pers.] Don't curse the dark, light a candle.; [a.] Capitol Heights, MD

BROWN, MARLENE
[pen.] Marlene Buffie Brown; [b.] January 17, 1938, Winnipeg; [p.] John and Mary Buffie; [m.] Separated; [ch.] Two Boys, One Girl and One Grandchild; [ed.] Graduated High School grade XII 1956. RN from Winnipeg, General Hospital School of Nursing 1960; [occ.] Registered Nurse - General Duty - Day Surgery; [memb.] Member of Toastmaster, International, CTM (Competent Toastmaster 1993) ATM, 1994 (Able Toastmaster) Currently Compiling a Book, an Short Stories and Poems, "The shelhirk,"; [hon.] Mumerous Speaking Awards for Best Speaker, "C.T.M.'s (Toast Masters); [oth. writ.] Short stories and poems in the Delhirk collection.; [pers.] "Memories and emotions are the magical combination and basis of great writings."; [a.] Winnipeg, MN

BROWN, ROBERT MARK
[b.] April 26, 1956, Brooklyn, NY; [p.] Pete and Edith Brown; [ed.] Brooklyn Prep., Brooklyn College; [occ.] School Bus Driver, Bus Trainer, (Teaching other to Drive a School Bus); [memb.]; [hon.] My own book "Twilight Double Header"; [oth. writ.] Twilight double header, a biography that tells a story in form of poems that can be taken out and stand on their own.; [pers.] DYLAM and the beatles open the doors for me. A transplanted new Yomler living in "The valley of the Sun," "People be good to each other, we're all we've got."; [a.] Mesa, AZ

BROWN, SHONDA RENEE
[pen.] Shon; [b.] November 15, 1970, Shreveport, LA; [p.] Lucinda and Timothy Brown; [ch.] La Donovan, Jamal Brown; [ed.] Captain Shreve High School, Shreveport - Bossler Regional Technical Institute (Culinary Arts), Ritter and Associates Cashier, Teller School; [occ.] Homemaker, U.S.

Naval Reservist - Boatswain, Mate Third Class; [pers.] First I want to give thanks to my Heavenly Father, who inspires me. I also want to thank my family and friends for their support. Last and especially not least my be loving son, La'Donovan - you bring me more joy than I've ever known.; [a.] Shreveport, LA

BRUCE III, SANFORD O.
[pen.] Trey Bruce; [b.] March 2, 1971, Brunswick, ME; [p.] Lanny and Donna Bruce; [m.] I am single; [ed.] I am currently a junior at the University of Memphis. I major in Political Science/Int'l Rel; [occ.] I am a bartender at a T.G.I. Fridays; [memb.] The nature Conservancy; [hon.] I have none, but I would like to use this space to welcome my nephew Bradley Kessler to the world. (due in February 96); [oth. writ.] I have about 200 poems, (though this is the first I have ever submitted for publication; [pers.] I dream one human raise will forsake the ignorance of our modern ways embrace the wisdom of the ages. I embrace "Gaia" the Earth Mother.; [a.] Memphis, TN

BRUNNER, SHIRLEY SCHROETER
[b.] February 28,1935, Lawrenceville, IL; [p.] Helen and Arthur Scott; [m.] Pete Schroeter (1st husband deceased), September 29, 1952; [ch.] Debra Diana, David and Dena Schroeter; [ed.] Ervine High School Hesville, Indiana; [occ.] Housewife; [hon.] Correspondence Course with the Ambassador Bible College 2 Awards, 1st November 22, 1989, 2nd September 20, 1993; [pers.] My inspirational for writing has been due to my love of God and family and my church, my faith has always been the lite that has guided me always in everything. I have done, and I read a great deal on many others poetry written very moving.; [a.] Lake Station, IN

BRUUSKI, CHRISTOPHER
[b.] March 30, 1977, Shrewsbury, NJ; [p.] David Peter Bruski and Jill Foster Brunski; [memb.] Glenn could foundation, Alliance Franklaise; [hon.] None in particular; [oth. writ.] Numerous works in progress looking for editors!; [pers.] The greatest teacher of writing, for me, is Johann Sebastian Bach.; [a.] Shrewsbury, NJ

BRYANT, LYNDA JEAN
[pen.] Lynda Jean; [b.] October 13, 1941, Washington, DC; [p.] Virginia Mae Lamm Darden Zierdt and Jesse Robert Darden Sr.; [ed.] Suitland Sr. High School, MD, Eckerd College, FL (BA 1984), and Capitol College, VA (MS 1996); [occ.] Program Manager - Computers, Communications, Controls, and Audio/Visual; [memb.] Washington Farm United Methodist Church, Information Systems Audit and Control (International) Association, and small writing groups; [hon.] Federal Systems Integration and Management Center performance awards, Scholarships, Speaker at the Federal Data Center Directors Interagency Conference ('90) and others business, educational, and church groups; [oth. writ.] Several technical articles published in Federal Computer Week and various personal poems for friends, families, and fellow travelers.; [pers.] I strive to reflect faith, hope, and understanding in all my writings both for fun and business. Communication with each other (worldwide) and GOD is critical. Thanks to my friends and family for the encouragement to learn, write, and persevere towards my dream.; [a.] Alexandria, VA

BRYANT, RUBY
[pen.] Ruby Bryant; [b.] September 16, 1902, Lynden, WA; [p.] Jed and Ethel Parrish; [m.] Robert Heaton (1st husband, deceased), Wendel Byrant (2nd deceased); [ch.] Bethany Heaton, Robert Heaton; [ed.] General, (no College), several Years of Nigh School (1930-1940), Photography Horticulture English Greek; [occ.] Retired, Bible teacher many years ago correspondence for several years; [memb.] Church of Christ (63 yrs), correspondence. Bible study was with people influence about a years, some because preachers, I that I remember special; [hon.] I don't know how much this to remember you decide; [pers.] I have had strange things running around in my head for many years never that they were worth mentioning mostly poetry.; [a.] Redding, CA

BUCHANAN, WILLIE AUTHUR
[pen.] Wylie Buckman; [b.] January 23, 1942, Gary, IN; [p.] Eugene and Josephine; [m.] Mary Lou Buchanan, March 12, 1982; [ch.] Veronica, Nicole, Antwoin; [ed.] Roosevelt High; [occ.] Retired Steel Mill-Worker, Land Lord; [memb.] Shiloh Temple Church; [hon.] World of Poetry; [oth. writ.] Several poems published in local Newspapers, community world.; [pers.] if my writing evokes emotions then I've done what I set, out to do, God bless Mom, dad, 3 brothers, 3 sisters, wife and children.; [a.] Minneapolis, MN

BUCHER, VIRGINIA A.
[p.] Coletta Roethlein Bucher and Arthur Bucher (Father deceased); [occ.] Secretary; [memb.] YWCA, World Wildlife Fund, The Nature Conservancy; [pers.] We must not limit ourselves to only one concept of the Almighty, for in doing so we deprive ourselves and our children of the wealth of the spirit.; [a.] Pittsburgh, PA

BUDZINSKI, REBECCA C.
[b.] December 27, 1971, New Jersey; [p.] Debra and Anthony Yuhasz; [m.] Michael Budzinski, January 30, 1991; [ch.] Ashley Rebecca and Jessie Michael; [ed.] High School Dip; [occ.] Home maker; [memb.] Christian Children's Fund; [pers.] Hope other people enjoy my poems as much as I do.; [a.] Miami, FL

BUICK, MURIEL LOUGH
[b.] August 26, 1948, Belleville, Ontario, Canada; [p.] Howard and Peggy Lough; [m.] William Buick, March 17, 1973; [ch.] Jason William, Kelly Ann; [ed.] Sir George William University - Montreal, Quebec, Cornwall Regional School of Nursing - Registered Nurse; [occ.] Own a Video Store which I Manage with a Small Staff; [memb.] Registered Nurses Association of Ontario; [oth. writ.] I have been writing short stories and poems since 5th or 6th grade and have done several poems for my family including a poem I wrote that is on my mother's head store.; [pers.] My mom was my biggest fan and passed away in July 1991. For years she had carried a poem in her wallet that I wrote when I was 15.; [a.] Perth Ontario, Canada

BUKOWIECKI, OLIVE BOYD
[b.] August 28, 1920, Edinburgh, Scotland; [ed.] Gretna Scotland; [occ.] Retired; [oth. writ.] Diversified; [pers.] I have never found a companion, as companiable as a book.; [a.] Bobcaygeon Ontario, Canada

BULKLEY, JORY COLT
[b.] February 7, 1980, Jillette, WY; [p.] Randy and Jail Bulkey; [ed.] Sophomore - Campbell County High School, Jillette, Wyoming; [occ.] On Family ranch and part time at Campbell County Lockers, Jillette Wyoming; [memb.] 2 year member - Jillette FFA Chapter, 8 year member Campbell County 4-H, Chairman of 4-H and FFA Youth Livestock Sale Committee, 5 year member 4-H Exchange Program; [hon.] 1995 Over all grand champion construction and stylist at Wyoming State Fair. Winning trip to Denver Raind-up and National Stock Show 1995 - High Point Sr. on Livestock Judging Team - Winning trip to State Fair 1995 - 2nd place in young Authors - Contest with Collection of poems; [oth. writ.] Have entered several years in our young Author's Contest with Beth poems and short stories; [pers.] I have always enjoyed writing, being encouraged to write about what I like. That being my way of life - my family, ranching, horse back riding, working with livestock, hunting and nature and her wildlife. I also love to read; [a.] Jillette, WY

BUMBERA, SUZI
[b.] June 17, 1967, Philadelphia; [p.] Dorothy Buckery and Leonard Bukaitis; [m.] Steve, December 31, 1988; [ch.] Amanda Rachel Jesse; [ed.] Commercial Art (certificate) Allied Medical Careers/Certificate); [occ.] Photographer Certified Nursing Assistant; [memb.] Hazleton Area Camera Club; [hon.] 2nd place photography in Expo Competition in 1993 and 1995; [oth. writ.] Am currently working on a book about the humorous joys of motherhood; [pers.] I would like to reach the lost for Christ, through writing and art. The soul is touched through the power of words and prayer.; [a.] Beaver Brook, PA

BUNKOSKE, PATRICIA
[b.] October 23, 1956, Milwaukee, WI; [m.] Ronald Bunkoske, May 8, 1982; [ch.] Janette Fay; [ed.] Greendale High School; [occ.] Inspector, Delco Electronics, Oak Creek, WI; [pers.] Arctic Wiscensin Winters have never thawed from my memory, but the "spring" of my loving family has given me warmth during the bitter cold days.; [a.] Oak Creek, WI

BURGHART, MRS. ALICE G.
[pen.] Alice Gordon Statler; [b.] February 5, 1898, St. Louis, MO; [p.] Maude Both, Statler; [m.] William Joseph Burghart, October 8, 1918; [ch.] 3 daughter, Mary, Lucille and Dorothy; [ed.] 8th Grade in ML Ida, Wish a lifetime reader of history, poetry, graphs - analysis, the classics, everything of interest; [occ.] Died of Parkinson's Decease in April 1971; [oth. writ.] She wrote a letter of indorsement for "Shippy Peanut Butter and won a case of product? She wrote poetry for all three of her daughters as we went through school. See addendum - use whatever.; [pers.] I could write a book about my mother's life and our life with her. She loved reading writing poetry and making up stories, we never needed fairy tales - she made up better ones. She was multi-talented, wonderful sense of humor, but also very melancholy. A light under a bushel!; [a.] Saint Louis, MO

BURGIS, DONALD STAFFORD
[b.] February 17, 1913, Ladylake, FL; [p.] Stafford and June; [ch.] Stafford D. Burgis; [ed.] Grade

School, High School, College - MS Ag. "43", BSA - "41"; [occ.] Retired Research Professor Univ. of Fla. IFAS; [memb.] In Professional Societies they won several - now none; [oth. writ.] 120 scientific publications.; [a.] Bradenton, FL

BURKE, CYNTHIA RENEE
[pen.] Renee Barbin; [b.] December 10, 1976, Portage La Prairie, Manitoba, Canada; [p.] Jocelyne Burke; [ed.] Blessed Sacrament School, University of Alberta; [occ.] Student; [memb.] PETA (Protection for the Ethical Treatment of Animals), WWF (World Wildlife Fund); [hon.] Governor General's Award for Academic Excellence; [pers.] I strive to reflect the pain and beauty of nature by creating a backdrop of emotional experiences that all of humankind can relate to.; [a.] Wainwright Alberta, Canada

BURLEY, KIMBERLY
[b.] May 13, 1967, San Antonio, TX; [p.] Virgil and Ruby Nalley; [m.] Edwin D. Burley, January 24, 1988; [ed.] A.A.S. in Paralegal Technology 1989 Fayetteville Technical Community College B.A. in Psychology - May 1996 - UNC at Charlotte; [memb.] International Society of poets.; [hon.] The National Library of Poetry Editor's Choice Award 1995; [oth. writ.] I have a personal Collection of poems I started in 1993. Two poems published in Anthologies. Poem published in Best Poems of '96; [pers.] I like to write poetry and stories for children. When my emotions are highly charges is when I write the best. And since I'm an emotional person, that happens quite often.; [a.] Concord, NC

BURNAU, NANCY S.
[pen.] "Bick"; [b.] July 25, 1936, Hunting, IN; [p.] Garnet and Fritz Bicken; [ch.] Kimerly Sue, Kurt Thomas, Karla Jane, Karri Renee, Kris and Patrick, Also I have 12 grand children; [ed.] I've been a ceramicist owning my own shop. I've lived and own my own farm for over 30 years; [occ.] I also paint in oils. I belong to Saint Mary Catholic Church, here in Huntington. I've held Offices on Parish Counsen, our Ladies Roasary Sodiality etc, Philosophical Statement; [memb.] My poems to me, are word's that shine like rays' out thorough the window's of my heart. Like a mirror reflect's only good that I find in other's, and for the world to read and enjoy. (Hopefully when I have all of my poems pretend up in one look my family will all buy to enjoy.); [hon.]; [oth. writ.] At present I am finishing a book about "The beauty of having a stroke." And I have written poems as far back as my grade school years. I have writen many things in our Local news paper.; [pers.] I come from a family of 18 children (11 boys and 7 girls) and some of my brothers also write poetry, so does some of the over 100 nieces and nephews, and 60 some great great nieces and naphews with more on the way. We are a really close nit family.; [a.] Huntington, IN

BUSH, EVELYN
[b.] October 7, 1941, Bradford, PA; [p.] Joe and Marie Bishop; [m.] Jesse E. Bush, December 21, 1964; [ch.] Jinny Wozniack, Kandy Zazheis, Cindy Sockbeson and James Tidd; [occ.] Housewife; [memb.] International Society of Poets; [hon.] Editor's Choice Award from the National Library of Poetry; [oth. writ.] Two published in Sparrowgrass anthologies. Many others unpublished.; [pers.] I write from nature and everyday life.; [a.] Franklin, PA

BUTNER, SHIRLEY V. E.
[b.] June 13, 1936, Kinkaid, Saskatchewan, Alberta; [p.] Alvin and Emma Anderson; [ch.] Anita Clarke, Sandra Butner, Wayne Butner; [ed.] Bachelor of Education, U of Alberta, 1980, Royal Conservatory of Toronto, Piano and Voice; [occ.] Teaching, Strathcona County, Alberta, Pianist-Fort Saskatchewan Pioneer Singers Vocalist-back to Pop Chorale, Fort Saskatchewan, Alberta; [memb.] 1976-1978, Executive Member Salisbury High School Band Parents, 1974-1978, Alberta 4H Club, Looma, Alberta, 1971-1972, Alberta Teacher's Association, Executive, Strathcona Country, Alberta; [hon.] 1994, Guest Soloist, Trathcona Retired Teachers, 1994 Guest Soloist, Fort Saskatchewan Community Chorus, Royal conservatory of music examination: Voice grade seven, Honors, Teachers, Leafa McNeil; [oth. Writ.] Who Is The Tooth Fairy? A Day At Your House, A Tribute To A Mother; [pers.] Most of my poems are written for friends and family members, with the hope that they will provide humor, and quiet, as well as a picture of themselves.; [a.] Fort Saskatchewan Alberta, Canada

BUZAN, JEAN MARY
[b.] May 20, 1916, London, England; [p.] Ernest and May Burn (Deceased); [m.] Gordon Frank Buzan (Deceased), September 2, 1939; [ch.] Anthony Peter and Barry Gordon; [ed.] Dip Ad - Ed., University of B.C., M.A.; [occ.] Retired Gerontologist - still freelance lecturer, consultant, writer.; [memb.] Canadian Association of Gerontology, B.C. Association of Gerontology Heartaud Stroke Foundation, Knowledge Network, Use your Head Club, Public Broadcasting Society, Oxfam, Memorial Society of B.C. etc.; [oth. writ.] This is on Teaching English to older Immigrants many articles in various publications. Currently writing books on "successful Aging" "How to spell" and "Memories of a Pet Cat"; [pers.] I've always tried to ensure that the world is a little better for my existence by not knowingly hurting anybody and activity helping where I can. I believe that age peruse is not a relevant measure of worth and that one should "live" until one dies.; [a.] Surrey British Columbia, Canada

BYARS, ALFREDA JOHNSON
[pen.] Freda; [b.] June 16, 1954, Beaumont, TX; [p.] Emanuel W. and Victorian T. Johnson; [m.] Lee Allen Byars, April 20, 1974; [ch.] Lee, Robyn, Lendsay, Hannah and Tabitha; [ed.] Jesse H. Jones Sr. High School, Houston Community College; [occ.] Wife and Mother (Former Occupation - Secretary); [memb.] Trinity Broadcasting Network, Anointed Tabernacle; [oth. writ.] To my Husband, a book of Psalms), that is still in the making.; [pers.] It is the Lord Jesus that is my inspiration and inspires me to write, and my prayer and desire is that he will continue to inspire me to write even more to touch the hearts of men.; [a.] Beaumont, TX

CABRAL, PEDRO C.
[b.] January 28, 1923, Aveiro, Portugal; [p.] Edith Hamilton Chapman and Jose Cabral; [m.] Susan, March 28, 1973; [ch.] Anna; [ed.] MIT (1 year) BU (3 years); [occ.] Retired; [oth. writ.] Write bridge articles for "Australia Bridge World"; [pers.] Most of the poetry I have written is very different and I have lost a lot of it. I like Edgar, Alan Poe and Wordsworth. Avid bridge player. Bridge is my first love.; [a.] Briarcliff Manor, NY

CADIGAN, DARCY
[b.] July 13, 1965, Eugene, OR; [p.] John and Claudine Cadigan; [ch.] Devin, Dillon and Kaithlyn; [occ.] Dry Cleaning Management; [memb.] All Saints Church and Oregon Athletic Club

CALDWELL, SUSAN C.
[pen.] Thoughts by Susan; [b.] February 26, 1946, Bath, England; [p.] Morena Corbin, Lee Morgan (deceased); [ch.] Dawna Lynn Caldwell; [ed.] '63 Los Altos High Calif. San Francisco State Univ., School of Business American Management Assoc., New York NY; [occ.] Consultant; [memb.] Toast Masters International, the National Assoc for Female Executives State of California. Notary Public, ASPCA Volunteer; [hon.] Valued Kalaveras County Women's Crisis Center Volunteer Rotarian Work and Shriner's Volunteer; [oth. writ.] Several poems however this is the first poem submitted for publication.; [pers.] This poem was my way of expressing the depth of the love left for our rottweiler, darby. Darby valiantly fought cancer until 3-2-94 currently she works hermagic from the other side.; [a.] Sunnyvalle, CA

CALEEKAL, TANIA
[b.] December 13, 1984, Guelph, Ontario, Canada; [p.] Ms. Anuppa Caleekal; [ed.] Grade Six; [occ.] Student; [hon.] Young Writer's Literary Competition Award, University of Guelph 1995. University Village Public School Recognition Certificate, Honored for Poetry and Illustrations - 1995; [oth. writ.] A dozen leaves a collection of poems and Illustrations, presented to Wellington County's 9th young writer's conference, "Author, Author" 1995.; [pers.] Always be happy; [a.] Guelph, Ontario, Canada

CALLAN, VERNA
[b.] June 17, 1916, Parry Sound, Ontario, Canada; [p.] Rufus and Mildred Harris; [m.] Arnold (Joe) Callan; [ch.] Wayne, Trudy and Harley; [ed.] Entrance to University Credits Typing, Creative Writing 1 and 2 at Sheridan Community College; [occ.] Retired Senior; [memb.] Attending Private Writing Classes at Present - have Written numerous Poems Stories hope to Publish some; [hon.] Not too many acknowledgement from our Mayor for efficient service at our manor (volunteer); [oth. writ.] Assistant, editor on "Neighborhood new's a small B. monthly 8 pg - paper in Halton county - Milton Ont. Can.; [pers.] "Jesus and others and you a wonderful way to spell joy" I love service others and be involved to share and care is living.; [a.] Milton Ontario, Canada

CALLANDS JR., WILLIAM MCKINLEY
[pen.] Curly Q.; [b.] April 14, 1954, Pittsylvania Co, VA; [p.] McKinley William Callands and Roxie Callands; [m.] Kathleen Kim Moore (intended spouse); [ch.] Antwon N. Tate and Stephon R. Tate; [ed.] Gretma Senior High School; [occ.] Service Agent for a Major Rental Car Company; [memb.] Riceville Baptist Church; [oth. writ.] A book (copyright pending); [pers.] I strive to bring a wareness, to build hope, to feed hungry minds, to bring hope and insight to hurting hearts. My influence is life and the infinite wisdom continually given by God.; [a.] Washington, DC

CAMPBELL, BRENDA
[b.] May 26, 1959, Newberry, MI; [p.] William D. and Maxine J. Campbell; [m.] Raymond W.

Campbell, May 8, 1978; [ch.] Rachael D. and Raymond W. II; [ed.] G.A. High, Purdue University, Home Study Course; [occ.] Cashier for a Large Store Chain, Kalamazoo, MI; [memb.] Greenpeace; [hon.] CNA Certification in MI CST Certification, U.S. wide. Various Plaques and Certificates for Childhood Sports (Tennis, Softball, Snow-mobile safety, Gun safety, Track; [oth. writ.] When I was in 5th grade the Jr. High students chose one of my poems to put in the 7th/8th grade "newspaper" that came out monthly.; [pers.] I have always felt that reading and writing has helped me to grow, both mentally and physically. It is my hope that we may be a country (if not world) of totally literate people who enjoy both reading and writing, and the "wellness" that those actions bring.; [a.] Augusta, MI

CAPARRATTO, PAUL
[b.] December 22, 1976, Springfield, MO; [p.] Cheryl Marsh, Gary Caparratto; [occ.] Student; [oth. writ.] Love You, Miss Trina; [pers.] Poetry should be applicable to a wide range of ages and cultures. It's meaning is what ever you believe it to be.; [a.] Crofton, MD

CAREY, EDITH V.
[b.] August 17, 1915, Kensington, PE Island, Canada; [p.] George Morris, F. Virtine Morris; [m.] Leslie C. Carey, September 16, 1939; [ch.] Philip, Noel and Carolyn; [ed.] HS Stanstead Wesleyan College (Que.), Mt. Allison University, Sackville, New Brunswick, Post Graduate in Dietetics from Hospital for Sick Children, Toronto; [occ.] Getting used to being 80 years "Young"; [memb.] United Church of Canada, Toronto Peal Post Polio Club, Past Polio Penguins Club, Canadian Mental Health Ass.; [hon.] Winner of Dubarry Success Course (Mrs. Toronto '44) - Life Member U.C.W. (Un. Church Women), 50th Wedding Anniversary Party ('89), 80th Birthday Party ('95); [oth. writ.] Many poems over many years, for friends, family members, and just for my own enjoyment. It's a special hobby. This is the first poem I've ever sent anywhere. It's exciting to know it's appreciated by others besides those near and dear!; [pers.] A keen sense of humor and a positive attitude, plus a ready smile, will help you deal with life's adversities.; [a.] Toronto, Ontario, Canada

CARLOVA, GOLDIE
[b.] England; [p.] Isaac Shapero and M. Rachel Shapero; [m.] John Carlova; [ed.] Educated in England, Fashion Designer, Sculptor, Painter. Avid Poetry Reader and Writer my Poems have been Broadcast on Radio Station, W. LBH-1170-KH2, in Mattoon Illinois; [occ.] Assisting my Husband John, who is also a writer, film rights to one of his books. Mistress of the seas" were recently bought by Columbia pictures; [oth. writ.] We are all merely visitors on this earth, leave a good name.; [a.] Lake Forest, CA

CARLSON, ARLA
[b.] May 28, 1977, Nakusp, British Columbia, Canada; [p.] Gordon Carlson, Pauline Carlson; [ed.] J.V. Humphries High School, Kaslo, B.C.; [hon.] English Literature Award, Honor Student; [oth. writ.] Several unpublished poems, plays, and short stories. Articles for on the edge newspaper.; [pers.] My writing reflects my own feelings and experiences.

CARLSON, MEREDITH
[b.] April 13, 1981, Columbia, MO; [p.] John and Linda Carlson; [ed.] Currently in Ninth Grade; [occ.] Student; [hon.] Academic Achievement Award; [pers.] I only try to live by this ancient proverb: "Treat the Earth well. It was not given to you by your parents. It was loaned to you by your children."; [a.] Mexico, MO

CARON, NICHOLAS
[pen.] Nickel; [b.] December 13, 1979, New Smyrna Beach, FL; [p.] Linda Helsel, Walter Helsel; [ed.] Student at Garden Cit High School, 10th grade; [occ.] Student; [memb.] Former Kick Boxing Jr. Feather Weight Champion of Michigan; [oth. writ.] No other writings; [pers.] I thank God for my two beautiful nieces kala Ashley, and Mariah Austin. I also thank my mom Linda, my dad Walter, my brother Brett, my close friends Lorea Kaske, Erin Megd, Melissa Chate.; [a.] Westland, MI

CARR, KRISTIN DAWN
[pen.] Stargazer; [b.] January 18, 1980, Decatur, IL; [p.] Susan and Randal Bird (step dad); [ed.] Bishop Du Bourg H.S St. Louis, MO; [memb.] Pro-life Club S.A.D.D.; [hon.] Many Acedemic Awards; [oth. writ.] I write very often and I have had one other poem published called, "Friendship."; [pers.] Everyone is someone who is important. Keep your head high and do't lose sight of your dreams, and always expect them unexpected.; [a.] Saint Lous, MO

CARREIRA, JULIE
[b.] February 7, 1979, Los Angeles, CA; [p.] Manuel and Linda Carriera; [ed.] Have not finished High School yet, currently am a Junior; [occ.] Student; [memb.] Hamesteaders 4-H of Santa Clara Canty and Homestead High School Colorguard; [hon.] Advanced Photography Individual at the Santa Clara Canty Fair in 1994 and 1995; [oth. writ.] I have written about 20 other poems based on events in my life and about 10 others short stories relating to things I have student in school.; [pers.] The fear of the Lord is the beginning of wisdom. "It is better to have lived one day as a tiger than a thousand years as a sheep - Alison Hargreaves. I Corinthians 13 and Psalms 105:1-3.; [a.] Sunnyvale, CA

CARRIER, BESS
[b.] May 25, 1920, Knoxville, TN; [p.] James Karnes, Clora Karnes; [m.] William Russell Carrier, December 9, 1945; [ch.] David Alan Carrier; [ed.] Knoxville High School Draughon's Bus. College Knoxville, TN; [occ.] Retired Secretary; [memb.] Newspaper Inst. of America, NY 1956; [hon.] Award of Merit Certificate World of Poetry Golden Poet 1991, Word of Poetry; [oth. writ.] Short stories, essays, "Gift of Life" sold guide post mag. never published. Poem "Mijit" published Vaney Valley Pub. School, Ramona, Okla.; [pers.] Influenced by writings of Loren Eisley, Anthropologist Emily Dickinson.; [a.] Sacramento, CA

CARRIGAN III, JOHN R.
[pen.] Jay Carrigan; [b.] March 13, 1962, Rutland, VT; [p.] William and Jacqueline Carrigan; [ed.] GED - Howard County, MD Self Educated and the School of Hard Knocks; [occ.] Jack of all trades; [hon.] 1991 winner of The Silver Loki Award; [oth. writ.] Poems published in several, Native American psychology

newsletters.; [pers.] By facing man's darker nature, we can strive to rise above our own brutality. I have been influenced by the works of E. E. Cummings, H.P. Lovecraft and Gwendolyn Brooks.; [a.] Arlington, VA

CARRISON, ROBIN BAILEY
[pen.] Robin Bailey Carrison; [b.] August 10, 1969, Mississippi; [p.] Joe and Beverly Bailey; [m.] Thomas Carrison

CARSWELL, MELODY A.
[b.] January 7, 1977, Atlanta, GA; [pers.] We are all characters in our own book of memories, and, although we may write our own rough draft, it is not up to us, however, to write the final copy.; [a.] Marietta, GA

CARTER JR., JOHN W.
[pen.] Seth Curtis; [b.] February 7, 1970, Waynesboro, VA; [p.] Wayne and Skip Carter; [ed.] Waynesboro High School Mary Washington College; [occ.] Sales Counselor GEICO, Fredericksburg VA; [memb.] The Salvation Army; [pers.] It has always amazed me how one life can touch the lives of so many others. Poetry to me is a way of expressing my inner self outwardly.; [a.] Fredericksburg, VA

CARUANA, VICKY
[b.] December 21, 1964, Toronto, Ontario; [p.] Victor and Georgina (late) Caruana; [m.] Stephen Weston; [ch.] Stevie, Curtis, Collin; [ed.] Early Childhood Education Diploma and 2 Certificates in Voluntary Sector Management; [occ.] Teaching children with special needs; [memb.] Healthy Communities of Clarington; [pers.] Children are our greatest gift and must be respected, protected and treasured always!; [a.] Courtice, ON

CASS, SHERRY L.
[b.] July 20, 1951, Houston, TX; [p.] Jack Edwards and Joyce Shotwell; [ch.] Cody and Dustin; [ed.] Pearland H.S., University of Houston; [occ.] Administrative Assistant; [oth. writ.] This poem is taken from a collection entitled, Losing the Bonds... finding the Light. I have also written a children's book, Teeny Tiny King, which I hope to publish.; [pers.] Most of my writing is a personal reflection, some serious, some very light. I believe in hope through all of the struggles that life brings, and my desire is to help renew that hope for others.; [a.] Cardiff-by-the-Sea, CA

CASSELL, SARAH ALTICE
[pen.] Sarah Altice Cassell; [b.] May 21, 1949, Franklin County, VA; [p.] Bernard and Ruby Altice; [m.] Jimmy Cassell, October 20, 1990; [ch.] Harnold Jacque and Austin Gillispie; [ed.] Franklin County High School Continuing Ed; [occ.] House-wife; [hon.] 1st Poet Contest; [oth. writ.] I helped my husband write, "McGruff the crime dog," that was accepted by the National Crime Prevention Council in Washington, DC; [pers.] Through the eyes of our children, we can see and believe in tomorrow!; [a.] Bassett, VA

CASSIDY, PETER
[b.] October 4, 1966, Oakville, ON; [p.] Terence and Judith Cassidy; [ed.] B.A. (English), attended Carleton University in Ottawa; [occ.] Teacher's Aid,

at Timmins High and Vocational School; [memb.] OSSTF; [oth. writ.] Several poems that have not ever been submitted for publication. Poetry is a hobby that can be time consuming but rewarding.; [pers.] Winters are long and harsh so I find a lot of my writing occurs during this time.; [a.] Timmins, Ontario, Canada

CASTANEDA, LORI K. LAU
[pen.] April 6, 1960, Honolulu, HI; [m.] Carlos A. Castaneda, September 24, 1994; [ed.] High School; [occ.] Administrative Assistant at Hewlett - Packard Company; [pers.] The poem was written for my sister, Liesl, who growing up used to call me "Tita" (Hawaiian meaning sister). That Christmas she was moving away to Germany to be with her husband.; [a.] Mountain View, CA

CASTELLI, MATTEO
[pen.] Matthew, Matt; [b.] January 18, 1967, Toronto; [p.] Carlo and Nina Castelli; [ed.] University of Toronto - B.Sc., Psychology Special, Minor Philosophy, Graduate Student, Ontario Institute for Studies in Education (Voft.); [occ.] Student, Homemaker, Support Care Worker; [memb.] Families and Friends; [hon.] The Russell Thompson Award (Arts and Literary School Contribution - High School, Grade 13), St. Michael's Christian Fellowship Award, OSSGHD; [oth. writ.] A closeted of voluminous texts, essays, philosophy.. unborn and organic. I.e., None published!... but I hope.; [pers.] Carved, chopped, classified, but innocent in all opened eyes. Beauty is a pollen bravely bound on vulva. Beauty beware - pollen is rendered war, when toxins hit the air.; [a.] Richmond Hill Ontario, Canada

CASTO, PATRICIA
[b.] December 23, 1943, Jacksonville, FL; [p.] Frank and Vivian Makomaski; [m.] Eugene Casto, December 30, 1969; [ch.] Richard and Steven; [ed.] High School Graduate; [memb.] First Assembly of God - Christian Coalition, American Family Assoc. Republican National Committee; [hon.] 1) Jenkins Middle School Plaque - Band, 2) Fifth Place - Duvall County Spelling Bee, 3) Miss Blaze - St. John's Bluff Fire Department; [oth. writ.] 1) Used at Tallahassee State Intercessors, 2) Used at North Fla. Aglow Women's Retreat; [pers.] Have always loved - music, poetry, writing and reading - instilled at an early age from grandmother - Leona Roebuck.; [a.] Ralatka, FL

CATANZARO, MICHAEL R.
[b.] December 7, 1959, Ambler, PA; [p.] Edmond Catanzaro, Betty J. Catanzaro; [ed.] Upper Dublin High School, Temple University (BA), Northeast Louisiana University (MA), University of Toledo (Enrolled in Ph.D. Program); [occ.] English Instructor, University of Toledo, Toledo, OH; [hon.] Sigma Delta Pi, Sigma Tau Delta; [pers.] I do not expect my words to be received as the work of a great writer. I do, however, expect my words to be received as an expression of my individuality and as an attempt to express my thoughts.; [a.] Toledo, OH

CAUL, MILTON
[b.] January 3, 1928, Devlin, Ontario; [p.] Lorne and Mary Caul; [m.] Jean Caul; [ch.] Dane Glen, Barry, Rick, Debra and Shelley; [ed.] Grade 6; [occ.] Retired; [oth. writ.] Life's long road in book after the

storm.; [pers.] Gives me pleasure to write poems. There would be more peace in the world if each and everyone. Would write instead of fight.

CAUTHEN, CAROLYN REBECCA
[pen.] The Poetry Lady; [b.] February 27, 1945, Cheathan Co, Kingston Spring, TN; [p.] Cheathan Edward McElroy and Ruth Judd McElroy; [m.] David Franklin Cauthen, October 18; [ch.] Anita Carol (Black) Steen/Bradley Cheathan Cauthen; [ed.] Grade 1-8 Kimpston Springs Elementary School, 10-12 Belleve High School Graduate, 1 Year Middle Tennessee State College; [occ.] Castodian - Bretwood High School/Cook-Bethany Hills Campgrounds; [memb.] Kingston Springs Church of Christy/International Poetry Society; [hon.] This is my third poem to be published. "Memories of Robert of Christmas won Editor's Choice award in East of the Sunrise; [oth. writ.] "A tribute to God's day" will appear in Best Poems of 1996 antholoy. "What friendship means to me" will appear in the poet's corner of the international poetry society.; [pers.] I am compiling a book of poems called "life before and after mother." It contains thoughts about my childhood and beyond her death in 1992. So far, it has been read by almost every teacher at bratwood High.; [a.] Kingston Springs, TN

CHADHA, AJIT KAUR
[pen.] Jeet/Jeeti; [b.] March 10, 1940; [p.] Mr. Kindan Singh Behl and Mrs. Swarran Kaur Behl; [m.] Mr. Rajendra Naith Chadha, April 8, 19866; [ch.] Two boys and 1 girls; [ed.] MBBS (MD) India and Obsterics worked as a physician for 25 yrs; [occ.] Housewife since 1988; [memb.] AMA, A.C.O.G., I.M.A.N.E., AMDAANA, American Reproductive Society R.I. Medical Society, Providence Medical Association AAPI Association of American Physicians of Indian Origin. Scholar-ship for 2 yrs in High School and 5 yrs of Medical College; [oth. writ.] In punsabi, 2 books, 1) "Mere Hanjhu Meri Muskan", 2) "Nameh." ("Greeting"), 3) Just make a Videotape "Project one advice," a collection of general advise from friends family and acquaintances.; [pers.] To worship one ever existing God to gather his blissful bounties and to be free of all beguile. From Sri Guru Granth Sahib. Sikh religion scripture. 50 Brisas circle.; [a.] East Greenwich, RI

CHAMBERLAIN, CORISA LYNNE
[pen.] Cori, Chris, Shorty; [b.] February 2, 1981, Scarborough; [p.] Lynne and Clyde; [ed.] I attended Poplar Road Junior P.S., Jack Miner Sr. P.S. and am now attending Laurier Collegiate Institute in grade nine. I am above average student and favorite subjects are English, Drama and Arts; [occ.] I am a student; [memb.] Field Hockey and Baseball Teams, Dance (Ballet, Jazz and Tap), Drama Clubs, Children's Television Studios (Modelling School); [hon.] I won silver in an all Scarborough Science Fair, awards and medals in Dance Awards won in the arts (English, Drama, Music and Visual Arts); [oth. writ.] Passing By, Open Your Eyes, No One But You, Homeless Despair, I Confess..., Tearless; [pers.] My poems come from what I'm feeling and thinking in my mind, heart and soul. I try to portray a message in my poems, that people that are feeling that way can relate to. I feel I have a talent and would like to share it with others.; [a.] Scarborough Ontario, Canada

CHAMBERS, NEINA
[b.] March 29, 1975, Pensacola, FL; [p.] Timothy and Teresa Chambers; [ed.] Undergraduate at University of California Los Angeles (UCLA). Major Latin American Studies; [occ.] Student; [oth. writ.] This will be my first publication.; [pers.] My poetry is a journal of the experiences that shape me. I am thankful to the people (family, friends...) who have influenced me - they are all present in my writing.; [a.] Los Angeles, CA

CHAMPION, WILLIAM M.
[b.] January 31, 1932, Edward, MS; [p.] Sid S. Champion, Ruth and C. Champion; [m.] Annette J. Champion, December 27, 1958; [ch.] John W. Laura R.; [ed.] Edwards High, Hinds Jr. Coll, Miss. State Univ., B.S., Univ. of Miss, LL.B., George Washing-ton Univ., LL.M., Harvard Law School; [occ.] Professor of Law, Univ. of Miss.; [memb.] American Bar Assn., Miss. Bar, Phi Delta Phi, Omicron Delta Kappa, United Methodist Church; [hon.] Outstand-ing Teacher, Univ of MS. 1982, Outstanding Teacher, Univ of MS School of Law, 1981, 1987, 1990, 1993; [oth. writ.] Several Articles and a Chapter in a book, all law related.; [pers.] I'm addicted to rhyme and meter.; [a.] Oxford, MS

CHAMPION, WILLIAM M.
[b.] January 31, 1932, Edwards, MS; [p.] Sid S. Champion, Ruth C. Champion; [m.] Annette J. Champion, December 28, 1958; [ch.] John W., Laura R.; [ed.] Edwards High, Hinds Jr. College, Miss. State Univ., Univ. of MS, George Washington Univ., Harvard University; [occ.] Professor of Law; [memb.] Pi Kappa Alpha, Omicron Delta Kappa, Mississippi Bar, American Bar Association, Association for Practical and Prof. Ethics, United Methodist Church; [hon.] Outstanding Teacher - Univ. of Miss. 1982, Outstanding Professor - Univ. of Miss. School of Law 1981, 1987, 1990, 1993.; [oth. writ.] Several articles and one chapter in a book. All law related.; [pers.] I am addicted to rhyme and meter.; [a.] Oxford, MS

CHANCELLOR, CHARLES E.
[pen.] The Old Cowboy - Dream Painter; [b.] November 15, 1946, Wichita, KS; [m.] Katherine (Deceased), July 25, 1965; [ch.] Tony, Terry, Shenelle; [occ.] Retired; [oth. writ.] The Cowboys Midnight Dream, The Cowboy, Angel Flight, A Day With The Lord, Breezes Of Beauty, The Precious One, many more.; [pers.] I try to find beauty in all the earth, men, women, cowboy, horses, beauty of the heart in purity.; [a.] Umatilla, FL

CHANG, ANDREA
[pen.] Andrea Wang; [b.] January 11, 1979, Van Nuys, CA; [p.] Beatrice Wang; [ed.] High School, Mark Keppell Junior; [hon.] Honor Student AP Classes; [pers.] I dedicate this poem to my Grandfather, who passed away in March of 1995. He was a father to me. No matter where he is, he will always have a special place in my heart.; [a.] Monterey Park, CA

CHANLEY II, NORBERT D.
[b.] February 9, 1961, Alexandria, VA; [p.] Norbert Chanley and Lois Chanley; [m.] Diane M. Chanley, April 26, 1991; [ch.] Kara Alyse and Jenna Marie Chanley; [ed.] Graduated 1982 Arizona Medical College, Tucson AZ; [occ.] Respiratory Therapist;

[memb.] American Heart Ass., National Board for Respiratory Care; [oth. writ.] Several other poems for personal use.; [pers.] This is dedicated to my wife and two daughters Kara and Jenna, who I love dearly.; [a.] Colorado Springs, CO

CHASTAIN, KEITH CAMERON
[pen.] Keith C. Chastain; [b.] July 20, 1917, Ibapah, UT; [p.] William Chastain, Armina Brown; [m.] Bernice Zilinsky, March 29, 1958; [ch.] K. Clifford (stp), Sally Susan, David; [ed.] Ibapah Grade, Ibapah, UT, Wasatch Academy High, Mt. Pleasant, UT, BS - CSUN, Northridge CA, MBA, USC, Los Angeles, CA; [occ.] Retired; [pers.] Played Cornet at country dances in 30's. Many dances ended at dawn. Have observed the sun rising out of the Utah Desert many times. In High School I wrote poems in lieu of themes for English Classes.; [a.] Banning, CA

CHAUTIN, JOSEPH
[pen.] J. Chau; [b.] May 7, 1935, Opelousas, LA; [occ.] Cajun Chef; [memb.] Catholic Cursilo, Prairie Ronde, LA; [hon.] Graduate: Dale Carnigie Human Relations Course; [pers.] Hobby: Primitive Art (Cajun Style); [a.] Krotz Springs, LA

CHESBRO, BROCK D.
[pen.] Broderick; [b.] January 24, 1979, Wellsville, KS; [p.] Marvin Chesbro, Sharon Perkins; [ed.] Student at Wellsville High current Grade Junior; [occ.] Student; [hon.] Honor Roll, many Athletic Awards, but no previous Writing Awards; [oth. writ.] Several other unpublished poems that I hope to have published some day.; [pers.] I believe if you write what you truly believe in, all words are beautiful and should be listened to.; [a.] Wellsville, KS

CHOWNYK, WALTER TARAS
[b.] August 10, 1947, Windsor, ON; [p.] Walter Paul and Anne Victoria Chownyk; [occ.] Receptionist, Canadian Mental Health Association; [oth. writ.] "The Tide," published in the book "Dance on the Horizon"; [pers.] Thank you to the following people: My Dad and Mom, My sisters, Julie Cummins and Mary Lou Deans, My brothers-in-law, Paul Cummins and Daniel Deans, My niece, Trice black, My Grandniece, Ashley Blak, my very good friends, Kyoko Yoshida and Murray Patterson, My Aunt Sophie stack; [a.] Vancouver British Columbia, Canada

CHUNG, RACHEL MARIA
[b.] November 13, 1982, Bethesda, MD; [p.] Wing Suen Chung, Anna Mana Chung; [ed.] I am currently in 7th Grade; [occ.] Hard working student of the American School of Asuncion, Paraguay; [memb.] Middle School Newspaper, Drama Club; [hon.] 5th Grade Honor Roll, Literature Certificate for one of the Best Writers in the Class, 7th Grade Drama Medal; [oth. writ.] Many, but none published. This is the first time my work has been noticed.; [pers.] My poem express the importance of dreaming, I believe people should hold on to their dreams. They bring out the best in all of us.; [a.] Asuncion, Paraguay

CHURCHILL, LEE A.
[b.] April 23, 1933, Sand Point, ID; [p.] H.C. Churchill, Olive F. Churchill; [m.] Lanora Wakefield Churchill, November 12, 1977; [ch.] Jeannie Marie, Julie Anne, Charles Lee; [ed.] Grade 12 GED; [occ.] Retired Trucker; [memb.] Unity Church Everett, WA Teamster (retired); [pers.] My ageless mother is my

inspiration in writing poetry. The first poem (not published) was for her 90th birthday. Through these eyes I see was for her 105th. I am working on others in my remarkable family.; [a.] Camno Island, WA

CINTRON, BLANCA
[b.] December 19, 1976, Grand Rapids, MI; [p.] Joseph and Maria Cintron; [ed.] K-4 Grade Attended Schools in Milwaukee, Wis. 5&6 Grade, attended Schools in Newark, NJ 7-12 Grades, attended School in Lawrence, NE; [occ.] Student; [memb.] School Organizations: Choir, Cheerleading, Drama, Journalism, Lower Elementary Teacher's Aide, Volleyball; [hon.] Choral Director's Award, National Honor Choir, Kearny High's Barbershop Quarter, Honor Roll; [pers.] What you learn from pleasure, you'll remember forever.; [a.] Lawrence, NE

CIUFO, CONNIE K.
[pen.] Shyama Mata; [b.] June 12, 1942, Iowa; [p.] Leonard Leola Luttrell and Richard Knoble; [m.] Paul P. Ciufo, December 8, 1990; [ed.] Highlands High School North Highlands, CA. and have Studied Metaphysics for over thirty years - I am a Certified Hypha Yoga Instructor and Certified Massage Technician; [occ.] "Majestic Moments" Photography/Writings; [memb.] Amadors County Arts Council, Amador Artists Association; [hon.] Published in Amador Arts Council Newsletters, Several Photography Awards at Amador County Fairs. I also Produce Photogprahic Post Cards; [pers.] A express the inherent excellence in each moment thru my art medias of writing and photography. I refer to myself as a mystical artist.; [a.] Volcano, CA

CLARDY, HEATHER
[pen.] Heather Clardy; [b.] August 28, 1975, Rapid City, SD; [p.] James P. Clardy Jr., Dora B. Clardy; [ed.] Midland High, Midland College, Midland, Texas, Texas A&M University, College Station, TX 77840; [occ.] Student; [memb.] Prevent Blindness Volunteer March of Dimes Volunteer, Young Republicans; [hon.] Honor Grad - Midland High - June 1993, Academic Decathlon High Medal Winner 1993, National Honor Society, 1992, 1993, Phi Theta Kappa, Fall 1993, Spring 1994, President's List 1994; [oth. writ.] Several poems and stories published in school publications, local newspapers, memorials, also stories for campus publications, "Study Breaks," (Sample enclosed - Stone Walls).; [pers.] Inscribed in my writings are the thoughts from my heart and the pulse of my soul.; [a.] College Station, TX

CLARK, GREGORY L.
[b.] July 20, 1971, Saint Louise, MO; [p.] Sharon Clark and Gregory White; [m.] Wendy W. Clark, August 21, 1993; [ch.] Joseph Jerod, Gregory Lamont and Minni Josephine; [ed.] Visual Performing Arts High Talladega College; [occ.] US Army; [memb.] Omega PSI, PHI fraternity Inc.; [pers.] I try to reflect myself in my writing. One must first be true to himself and everything else will follow. To become something or someone you are not in the pursuit of success inevitably leads to failure.; [a.] Yuma, AZ

CLEGG, JAMIE MICHELLE
[pen.] Jamie M. Clegg; [b.] March 12, 1916, Parkersburg, WV; [p.] Lowell and Cheryl Bungard;

[ed.] Parkersburg High School, International Correspondence Course; [occ.] Child Caretaker; [memb.] Children International, North Shore Animal League, National Wildlife Foundation, The National Children's Cancer Society; [oth. writ.] Many unpublished poems, short stories and one book.; [pers.] I like to try to write about all different topics. I try my best to keep an open mind.; [a.] Davisville, WV

CLONTS, MARGO LYNN
[b.] March 25, 1951, Saint Louis, MO; [p.] Lindell and Christine Clonts; [ed.] Normandy High School, St. Louis MO Columbia College, Columbia, MO; [occ.] Cartographic Technician, USGS, DOI; [hon.] Alpha Sigma Lambda, Dean's List; [oth. writ.] Several poems and articles published in local newspapers.; [pers.] I try to do my best at whatever I attempt. Sometimes it works, sometimes it doesn't but we MUST keep trying.; [a.] Saint James, MO

CLORE, KATHERINE
[b.] January 7, 1945, Laramie, WY; [m.] James Clore, November 19, 1966; [ch.] Two Children; [occ.] House wife - active in jail ministry and Volunteer Works; [memb.]; [hon.] Two Golden Poets (1990 - 1991) Awards, several awards of Merit, poem published 96 "New Voices in American Poetry' 1981, many contests under author - Eddie Lou Cole; [pers.] My writings come from my heart and life experiences. I work with a variety of people and they help influence me. I am a Christian and I give my thanks to God for He inspires me.; [a.] Casper, WY

CLOUGH, IVAN D.
[b.] October 26, 1969, Quebec; [p.] David and Pauline Clough; [ed.] High School Graduate, currently Enrolled in Computer Science at the Limoilou College in Quebec City; [occ.] Plastic Coatings Innovater; [oth. writ.] Several untitled and unpublished poems.; [pers.] Hope is a poem I had written the day after my father passed away from a little longer than a year battle with a terminal brain cancer. Survived by Pauline (wife), Peter, Jason, Ivan (3 sons), susan (mother), Jim brother).; [a.] Quebec, Canada

COCHRAN, ALLISON L.
[pen.] Allison L. Cochran; [b.] May 10, 1957, Coshocton, OH; [p.] Lee G. Cochran and Rosalie T. Goss; [m.] Vernon R. (Salters) Cochran, April 8, 1994; [ch.] Minda K. Deupree; [ed.] Entering Columbus State Community College 1-2, 1996, Majoring in Graphic Communication Technology; [occ.] Student of Life; [hon.] The National Library of Poetry Publication. Thank You!; [oth. writ.] I have amassed over 45 poems since 1973. All but one, so far, have been for personal fulfillment only, never before published. Lyrics for songs written.; [pers.] Always remember, the most unnerving, devastating, instable times of our lives, also often brings forth in us, the most creative, opportunistic, times for change in our lives.. and beyond.; [a.] Coshocton, OH

COCO, CHRISTOPHER J.
[b.] March 29, 1964, Edwards AFB, CA; [p.] Stanley and Mary Coco; [m.] Suzanne Coco, April 10, 1991; [ch.] Zackary Dalton Coco; [ed.] Shermon High, Community College of the Air Force, and Wayland Baptist University; [occ.] Entrepreneur/Dental

Laboratory Technician; [hon.] Summa Cum Laude, the President's Honor Roll, and the Dean's List; [pers.] I hope the Dallas Cowboys win another Super Bowl.; [a.] North Pole, AK

CODIANNI, JEAN LOUISE
[b.] November 16, 1970, Brooklyn, NY; [p.] Lois Pennington and Anthony Codianni; [ed.] Utica College of Syracuse University, BA 1992; [hon.] 16th College Award - Producer, Best Documentary Series; [a.] Hollywood, CA

CODY, ARLOWEEN E.
[b.] February 26, 1935, Cameron Mills, NY; [p.] Harold and Clara Rude; [m.] William R. Cody, June 7, 1958; [ch.] Charles Richard and Jonathan Joel; [ed.] Woodhull High School Graduate 1952; [occ.] Teacher, King's Way Christian Academy, Corning, NY; [memb.] Central Baptist Church Choir; [hon.] Valedictorian - 1952; [oth. writ.] Never tried to write only one other poem. Also as a senior in high school I may try more now.; [pers.] I wrote this as a senior in high school (1952) and kept it all these years. Never had opportunity before to "enter" in any contest to judge its value to anyone else.; [a.] Corning, NY

COFER, TINA MARIA
[b.] January 17, 1985, Fayetteville, NC; [p.] Mark and Jacquie Cofer, Rick and Sheila Schad; [ed.] Still in Elementary School, Honor Roll every year, currently attending Jupiter Elem.; [occ.] Student; [hon.] At age 7, in the 2nd grade one first place for her class in the Cumberland County Young Authors Contest; [pers.] I like to write because it lets me express my feeling in my writings, and especially because it's really fun.; [a.] Jupiter, FL

COLEMAN, GEORGE PATRICK
[b.] November 2, 1958, Sudbury, ON; [p.] William Michael Coleman and Louise Coleman; [m.] Margaret McGuire (Deceased), February 16, 1981; [ed.] Bachelor of Science, University of Toronto 1981, St. Michael's College School with Honors; [occ.] Marketing Account Manager, CP Rail System; [oth. writ.] Many more not submitted for publication... yet.; [pers.] The past will always influence the present and the future and I try to reflect this in my writing.; [a.] Toronto Ontario, Canada

COLEMAN, MADALINE CORNISH
[b.] March 25, 1924, Baltimore, MD; [p.] Joseph and Ethel Cornish; [m.] B. H. Coleman (Deceased June 30, 1985), December 31, 1954; [ch.] Marlene, Bradley and Carla; [ed.] Attended and Graduated Baltimore, Public Schools and Business School, CA Adult Secretarial Classes, and Merritt College/Evening and Saturday; [occ.] Retired; [memb.] None currently; [hon.] Sports Letters in Basketball, Softball and Baseball, Dean's List, Certificate in Administration of Justice; [oth. writ.] Several poems (unpublished), Articles in local newspapers, the post and California Voice, short story (incomplete and unpublished).; [pers.] I believe in doing everything in moderation, and you're never too old to learn.; [a.] Oakland, CA

COLEMAN, SHARON L.
[b.] August 5, 1936, Princeton, IN; [p.] Charles Mauck, Lena Mauck; [m.] Harold L. Coleman, February 16, 1957; [ch.] Tonja Beuligmann and

Tamara Cox; [ed.] Owensville High School, Lockyears Business College, Evansville, IN, attended Classes at Univ. of Evansville, Evansville, IN; [occ.] Bookkeeper and Treasurer of South Gibson School Corp., Ft. Branch, IN; [memb.] Christian Church, Diciples of Christ; [oth. writ.] I have written only three other poems, none have made available for publication at this time.; [pers.] I believe I have been inspired to write in my later years. Hopefully, my writings might be an inspiration especially to young people, my family has been my influence in writing.; [a.] Haubstadt, IN

COLEMAN, SHARON L.
[b.] August 5, 1936, Princeton, IN; [p.] Charles Mauck, Lena Mauck; [m.] Harold L. Coleman; [ch.] Tonja and Tamara; [ed.] Owensville High Sch., Lockyears Business College and University of Evansville; [occ.] Bookkeeper and Treasurer of South Gibson School Corp.; [memb.] First Christian Church, Disciples of Christ, Various Club Organizations; [oth. writ.] Various poems, but never made available for publication.; [a.] Haubstadt, IN

COLEY, FRED WILLIAM
[b.] September 14, 1926, Bedford, IA; [p.] Fred and Emma B. Coley; [m.] Arlene Eleanor, March 28, 1953; [ch.] Bob, Dick, Bill, Mara-Jo; [ed.] 1 yr. University of Omaha; [occ.] Security Guard; [memb.] Church; [oth. writ.] Random poems unpublished; [pers.] This poem was written Mother's Day 1995. Mother had passed away 26 years earlier. The poem reflects my memories of her.; [a.] Griswold, IA

COLLINA, JOSEPH V.
[pen.] Joe Collina; [b.] April 13, 1938, Chicago Heights, IL; [p.] Virgil and Mary Collina; [m.] Mary Robbins Collina, September 14, 1975; [ch.] Daughter (Sherry) Plus Three Grandchildren; [ed.] Purdue University - B.S. 1961, Northwestern University - M.B.A. 1967, John Marshall Law School - J.D. 1975; [occ.] Chief Public Defender, Lake County, Illinois; [memb.] American, Illinois, and Lake County Bar Associations; [oth. writ.] "Out Of Control" a novel scheduled for publication in March of 1996, Northwester Pub. Co.

COLLINS, CLINTON W. J.
[pen.] C. C. Rock; [b.] June 14, 1970, Edmonton, Alberta, Canada; [p.] Bonita, William (Deceased); [m.] Five; [ed.] Grade 12 Diploma; [hon.] Troubadour Award; [oth. writ.] One Summer Night, Love in Life, Prayer, Positive and Negative, Wisdom Street Life, Life and many more; [pers.] "Pay heed to an elders, council or advice, instead of being ignorant, and walking on thin ice."; [a.] North Vancouver British Columbia, Canada

COLLINS, SUNNYE MICHELLE
[pen.] Sunnye Collins; [b.] November 8, 1976, Houston, TX; [p.] Mike and Susan Collins; [ed.] Freshman at Texas, Christian University Major: Deaf Education; [memb.] FCA - Fellowship of Christian Athletes; [hon.] Houston - Vanderbilt Club Book Award for excellence in Creative Writing - 1994; [pers.] Poetry is a quiet room in my heart where I can go to sit with my father Jesus. In that room, we laugh and talk and I just write down whatever he tells me.; [a.] Houston, TX

COLLOM, CHRISTOPHER
[b.] November 18, 1964, Boulder, CO; [p.] Jack Collom and Edeltravo Hopps; [ed.] B.A. - University of Colorado, M.S. - Brigham Young University, Ph.D. - University of Calgary; [occ.] Invertebrate Paleontologist (Molluscs); [memb.] The Human Race; [hon.] The Sun Each Morning, The Stars at Night, etc.; [oth. writ.] Currently compiling my poems into an anthology titled "Instructing the Sun," 25 years of need publisher, blue-eyed poems 1971-1996.; [pers.] Don't leave this earth until you've risked your life (semi-irresponsibly), just to drive home how exceedingly fleeting are our days and fragile our existence.; [a.] Calgary Alberta, Canada

CONNELLY, ERIN AMANDA
[b.] October 25, 1982, Morganton, NC; [p.] Larry Connelly, Clara Connelly; [ed.] Liberty Middle School; [occ.] Student; [memb.] First United Methodist Church Morganton, 4-H Girl Scouts of America, WCC Volunteers, Student Government Assoc.; [hon.] 1995 Morganton Young Citizen of the Year, 94 and '95 Academic Excellent, '94 4-H State Champion in Dance, '94 4-H State Champion in Entomology, 1995 NBA Skills Game Champion; [pers.] Through my teachers inspiration I have improved my gift of writing and for that I am grateful.; [a.] Morganton, NC

CONSTANCE, JOLENE ROYER
[b.] August 25, 1958, Sulphur, LA; [p.] George and Camy Royer; [m.] Divorced; [ch.] Amy Jo Constance, Sara Constance; [ed.] A.A. General Studies (McNeese State Univ. - Lake Charles, LA); [occ.] Library Paraprofessional II, (McNeese University - Frazar Memorial Library); [memb.] Louisiana Library Assoc., Louisiana Library Assoc., Support Staff, Interest Group, Libraries Southwest; [a.] DeQuincy, LA

CONTRACTOR, SONYA
[pen.] Claudia Dawn; [b.] January 25, 1930, Chicago; [p.] Chandrika Contractor; [a.] Chicago, IL

CONWAY, RUTH I.
[b.] April 22, 1926, Mayton, Alberta, Canada; [p.] Clark and Julia, Bennett; [m.] William Conway (now deceased), December 4, 1946; [ch.] Two Girls, One Boy; [occ.] Homemaker; [memb.] United Church, U.C.W.; [hon.] Poem in New American Poetry Anthology, Poem in Great American, Poetry Anthology; [oth. writ.] My own book, "The Concert in the Hall and other Memories," several poems published in local newspapers.; [pers.] My poems are all my own feelings or experiences.; [a.] Olds Alberta, Canada

COOK, KATHLEEN
[b.] August 23, 1969, Royal Oak, MI; [p.] Kay Walling, Bob Hierholzer; [ch.] Amanda Ellen, Rochester High, Wayne State University; [occ.] Self-Employed; [memb.] St. Clair County, Community College, Theater Discipline; [hon.] Dean's List; [pers.] My daughter is my greatest inspiration.; [a.] Avoca, MI

COOKE, JAY
[pen.] Sebastian Amadeus; [b.] 1969, Saskatoon, Saskatchewan; [p.] Robert Cooke, Carole Cooke; [ed.] St. James High School, National Institute of Broadcasting; [occ.] Graphic Technician, Weather

Tech Services Inc. Winnipeg, Manitoba; [memb.] Manitoba Writers Guild Association, Manitoba Sponge Hockey League; [oth. writ.] Poem published in magazine, various poems and songs, currently seeking publication of book, "Shattered Innocence"; [pers.] Having experienced both deep sorrow and great joy, I've found sorrow to be the stronger of the two. Hence the poem. Philosophical statement: No guts, no glory.; [a.] Winnipeg Manitoba, Canada

COOPER, CARMA REBECCA
[pen.] "Becky"; [b.] September 27, 1972, Okinawa, Japan; [p.] Jois J. and Fred M. Cooper; [ed.] Student Studying in London, England, graduated from Roseburg High School; [occ.] College Student, Coaching Basketball, Volleyball and Track; [hon.] Senior Class President, Girls State Representative; [oth. writ.] At 4 yrs. of age, I wrote a song that my Mom published in her Cook Book.; [pers.] My poetry is a sanctuary for my essence of life.; [a.] Roseburg, OR

COPELAND, LISA M.
[pen.] Kaylee Copeland; [b.] December 4, 1966, Fall River, MA; [p.] Donald W. Copeland, Madeline R. Dron; [ed.] B.M.C. Durfee High School, Bristol Community College (Pre-Pro); [occ.] Disabled, hoping to enroll in Medical School soon, Physical Therapy; [memb.] American Museum of Natural History, National Audubon Society, Saint Anthony of Padua (Church); [hon.] Bristol Community College, Dean's List, Starburst Modeling Contest, Second Runner-Up; [oth. writ.] Several poems in which I am waiting to have published. I am currently looking into publishing companies.; [pers.] I have been through many trials and tribulations in my life, and if my poetry (or knowledge) can help at least one person in their life, it would make my life so much more interesting and complete.; [a.] Fall River, MA

COPENANCE, JEFFREY
[b.] August 28, 1978, Kenora, Ontario; [p.] Ed Copenace, Donna Indian; [ed.] Currently attending grade 12 Thomas Aquinas, High School; [hon.] Several Academic Awards throughout High School; [pers.] My poetry is greatly influenced and inspired by my close personal friends and experiences in my young life. Thank you to my best friends and all who support me. To my friend Shauna who encouraged me.; [a.] Kenora Ontario, Canada

COPLEN, WILLIAM LEX
[pen.] William Lex Coplen; [b.] December 11, 1923, Wingo, Kentucky; [p.] Morris Rex and Eva M. Coplen; [m.] Betty J. Coplen, August 23, 1947; [ch.] Mark (son), Scott (son), Robin (daughter); [ed.] Bachelor of Arts Degree in Poli. Sci., Wayne State University; [occ.] Retired from Manager, Staff Services Group, Michigan Consol. Gas Co.; [oth. writ.] Two books published: (1) The Beasties Among Us (And Other Pitfalls of Life), The Beasties Are GAining On Us (Lengthen Your Stride); [pers.] Life is serious, and yet it is made to be laughed at often. The "Laugh Approach" is the only way to defeat "The Beasties" (educated or non-educated people without any common sense).; [a.] Taylor, MI

CORNER, TONI
[b.] October 29, 1928, Italy; [p.] Anna and Rosario Rosati; [ch.] Jeffrey, Greg and Paul; [ed.] H.S.

Diploma, Commercial Course night School University in Languages and Psychology; [occ.] Retired Executive Secretary; [memb.] Humanist Society, Reading Club, Past member - Harmony Inc., Beta Sigma Phi, Hospice Wellington; [hon.] Personal use only; [oth. writ.] Personal use only.; [pers.] Poetry for me is a hobby. Writing is therapy for getting over bad times or also used for celebrating good times.

CORWIN, WILLIAM E.
[b.] April 26, 1957, Norwich, CT; [p.] Laurence Corwin and Mozelle Corwin; [ed.] ASN, Deanza College, Cupertino, CA; [occ.] Registered Nurse, MT Diablo Med. CTR, Concord, CA; [memb.] American Heart Assoc, California Nurses Assoc; [oth. writ.] Several poems published in local community newspaper.; [pers.] I wish to thank my friend Roger Wilkerson for all his help and inspiration.; [a.] Pleasant Hill, CA

COTTEN, WILLIAM R.
[pen.] Bile Cotten; [b.] April 2, 1940, Covington, IN; [p.] Alva and Nellie Cotten; [m.] Single (Widowed); [ch.] Richard W. Cotton; [ed.] 3 1/2 years College: Spokane Falls Comm. College E.W.U., Gonzaga University; [occ.] Electrical Design Engineer; [memb.] Eagles Lodge Aerie #2: Church of Christ; [oth. writ.] Book of personal prose of poetry - unpublished.; [pers.] I write prose and poetry to special people and events in my life. I strive to put to pen and paper those things dar to me in the form of prose and poetry.; [a.] Spokane, WA

COTTER, JANELLE JOY
[b.] December 22, 1981, Peoria, IL; [p.] James and Donna Cotter; [ed.] I am currently an 8th Grader at Holy Cross Lutheran Grade School, and Next Year will go to Concordia Lutheran High School. Both are in Ft. Wayne IN; [occ.] Student; [memb.] Praise Lutheran Church, Chancel Choir, Junior Choir, Jazz Band, Performing Band, Suzuki Orchestra, CLHS Orchestra, School Newspaper Editor, Cheerleading Squad; [hon.] Piano, Violin, and Vocal Awards, Placed 1st in Allen County Poetry Contest, Honor Roll; [oth. writ.] School newspaper articles.; [pers.] I like to write about personal experiences that I have affected my life greatly. It's very difficult for me to make up stories. I am trying to use my God given talents in ways that will praise Him. I hope all you will do the same.; [a.] Fort Wayne, IN

COULTER, BRUCE WALTER BURNS
[b.] September 3, 1932, Cornwall; [p.] Don and Dorothy; [ed.] Bachelor of Social Science, University of Guelph; [occ.] Retail Book Seller; [pers.] Suffism, Existenialism, Experience the moment for all it's worth.; [a.] Owen Sound Ontario, Canada

COUPLAND, KRISTINA
[b.] November 7, 1982, Vancouver, British Columbia, Canada; [p.] George and Lisa Coupland; [ed.] Pacific Academy, Honey - Pitt Meadows Christian School; [occ.] Middle School Student, Grade 8; [pers.] I never thought any of my poems could be printed in a book, but it shows if you but your mind to it anything is possible.; [a.] Maple Ridge British Columbia, Canada

COUSINS, IVAN E.
[b.] November 26, 1929, Baileyville, ME; [p.] Stella (Gower) and Omar Cousins; [m.] Dorothy (Stetson)

Cousins, June 25, 1954; [ch.] Ellen, Julig, Brenda Schenck, Mark Cousins and Karen Miller; [ed.] Woodland Schools (7) yrs. So. Portland Schools - Grad. 1947 Eastern Nazarene College - (3) yrs. U.S. Army 1947 - 1950; [occ.] Retired - Time Study Man; [memb.] Penny Road Church of the Nazarene; [oth. writ.] Nat'l Library of Poetry copy enclosed; [a.] Raleigh, NC

COVATO, LARISSA GLORIA RAMSKY
[pen.] Larissa Ramsky Covato; [b.] April 2, 1959, Toronto, Ontario; [p.] Peter Ramsley, Alexandra Ramsky; [m.] Richard Covato, July 17, 1982; [ch.] Andrew Richard, Jonathan Mark, Michael Adam, Daniel James; [ed.] Trinity College, University of Toronto, (Bachelor of Arts), Ontario Institute for Studies in Education, University of Toronto (Masters of Education, Doctor of Philosophy); [occ.] Computer Consultant, Educator; [memb.] Ontario Science Centre, Metropolitan Toronto Zoological Society, Kortright Centre for Conservation; [hon.] OISE Graduate Scholarship, Faculty Scholar Designation, Dean's List, several undergraduate Scholarship; [oth. writ.] Doctoral thesis in computers in education, technical writings in university, publication poems published in local newspapers university publications.; [pers.] Do not boast about tomorrow, for you do not know what a day may bring forth. Proverbs 27:1; [a.] Toronto Ontario, Canada

COX, DARLENE
[pen.] Darlene (Stadsklev) Cox; [b.] March 26, 1931, Webster, SD; [p.] Edwin Stadsklev and Olga Stadsklev; [m.] Derald K. Cox, April 3, 1953; [ch.] David, Ricky, Loren, Danny, Robin, Kevin; [ed.] Bristol High School, Bristol, SD Northern State Teacher's College, Aberdeen, South Dakota; [occ.] Homemaker, Piano Teacher, Volunteer Piano Teacher at Senior Center; [memb.] Faith Lutheran Church, Faith Lutheran Church Choir, Bear Canyon Senior Center; [hon.] First Place Ribbons on Oil Paintings and other Art Work at State Fairs. Honored by my good husband, six wonderful sons and four beautiful grandchildren; [oth. writ.] Several poems as a child roadside jingle about Burma Shave as teenager - short articles published in Reporter and Farmer, Webster, SD - several poems concerning faith, family, friends, death, life, etc. presently working an collection of poems called "Childhood Memories of the Farm."; [pers.] Since childhood I have been interested in the beauty of poetry. I write as the Lord inspires me with thoughts and words that express my deepest feelings. My desire is that my poetry may be a joy and blessing to others.; [a.] Albuquerque, NM

COX, HELENA BREWER
[pen.] Starflower Brewer, Water Lily; [b.] July 12, 1925, Clarksville, TN; [p.] Harley and Violetta Brewer; [m.] Gerald H. Cox (Deceased), April 21, 1946; [ch.] Kathleen, Karl, John and Karen; [ed.] 1) U.S. Indian School (High) '42, Santa Fe, New Mexico, 2) Southern Baptist Hosp. School of Nursing, 3) Platte College, ("New Orleans, La.) Columbus, NE, Dean's List, 4) Northern N.M. Midwifery Contor, Taos, New Mexico Taos); [occ.] Retired Nurse; [memb.] AG Church, Reach to Recovery, Assn. Surgical Technologists, International Assoc. of Infant Massage Instructors; [hon.] High Honors Graduate, Platte Coll.; [oth. writ.] Several articles published in surgical magazines,

medical several terminology crosswood/word search puzz. Published, two published poems in magazines.; [pers.] Born-again Christian, blessed with a bilcultural heritage, Anglo/ Eastern Cherokee and a deep appreciation for God, family, country, love, nature and life.; [a.] Bridgeport, NE

COX, ROBERT M.
[b.] April 3, 1964, Winslow, AZ; [p.] Gladys and Ted Cox; [m.] Sheila Hiatt Cox, April 17, 1987; [ch.] Kaitlin Brooke and Austin Hiatt; [ed.] BYU - Electronics Engineering Technology - 1995 (graduated with B.S.); [occ.] Novell - Provo, UT; [a.] Orem, UT

CRAIG, MICHAEL JAMES
[pen.] Br. Michael Craig; [b.] April 24, 1975, Detroit, MI; [p.] James Craig Jr., Georgia Craig; [ed.] Paramount High, Huffman High, Jeff. State College; [occ.] Writer, Critical Thinker, Spiritual inspired Poet; [oth. writ.] "A taste of the spiritual realm," the days of vengeance, we are spiritual being, new day I, new day II, the told tales of men, vain customs of man, the journey to the incorrupt, ye shall still stand.; [pers.] All which is good, is by the grace of God, by faith, through Jesus Christ. Each gift that's within man, was given freely, for purpose by the creator on High, therefore I'm inspired by the anointing of the Holy Spirit, for we are only vessels, sewn, in corruption, reaped otherwise into in corruption.; [a.] Birmingham, AL

CRAIGIE, COLEEN
[b.] October 6, 1960, Scotland; [p.] Elizabeth and Colin Craigie; [ch.] Jason, Amanda, Cosmo, Brody; [ed.] Grade 12; [occ.] Hairstylist Student in Cambridge; [memb.] Member of the YMCA; [pers.] The best knowledge is the knowledge of life.; [a.] Cambridge, Canada

CRANDDENT, YANDHI T.
[pen.] Yandhi T. Cranddent; [b.] November 20, 1964, Copenhagen, Denmark; [p.] Former Diplomat, alive and well; [ed.] Vishal Art and Business Management Course (1986), Graduated from Algonquin College, Ottawa, Ontario, Canada; [occ.] Full Time Clerk in Retail; [memb.] (U.F.C.W/ Canada Local 175), United Food Commercial Workers Union of Canada, P.R.O./Canada - So Can; [hon.] High School Honor Diploma in Ottawa, Ontario. "Editor's Choice Award" from the National Library of Poetry in 1995; [oth. writ.] Wrote songs, available through PRO/Canada for copies wrote many poems, one published by "National Library of Poetry" available in - deluxe hard bound - "Sparkles in the Sand"; [pers.] Always believe in your dream, hard work, determination, always be yourself, don't try to be something or someone you're not, but most of all, have alot of love to share!; [a.] Ottawa Ontario, Canada

CRANE, CHARLOTTE
[b.] March 15, 1944, Valparaiso, IN; [p.] Herbert and Celia Brocksmith; [m.] Carl Joseph Crane, February 26, 1962; [ch.] Scott Joseph and Colette Christine; [ed.] Valparaiso High School; [occ.] Q.C. Inspector for T-P Orthodontics, Westville, IN; [memb.] Wannatah Christian Church, Wannatah, IN; [oth. writ.] Non-published poems written about my family.; [pers.] I have two adorable granddaughters, ages 4 and 15 months. I teach 7th and 8th grade sunday school.; [a.] Hanna, IN

CRAWFORD, BERNICE
[b.] February 9, 1905, Detroit, MI; [p.] Charles and Katherine Nash; [m.] Duncan Crawford, September 4, 1931; [ch.] Christine Crawford Doll; [ed.] Grade School at Grindstone City where we lived. Graduated from Bad Ave High School in 1923. Received an A.B. degree from Central University at Mt Pleasant; [occ.] Retired after 30 yrs of teaching in grades (Kdg); [memb.] 2nd Class Girl Scout and later Girl Scout Director. President of two different Study Clubs; [hon.] Received an Award here where I live for Work in Activities; [oth. writ.] "The village song" was composed by me, both words and music.; [pers.] In the poem "Here and there" that I sent is more affective when I read it. The "here" means the place where I am live, a very nice retirement home called "Independence Vilage."; [a.] Frankenmuth, MI

CRAWFORD, DONNA MARIE
[pen.] Marie Crawford; [b.] December 20, 1954, Washington, DC; [p.] Harold and Aileen Hedges; [ch.] 1 - Michael Leonard; [ed.] Largo Senior High School (PE Community, some college), self taught through Reading and Application - life itself; [occ.] Accounting Manager, Supervisor, The Driggs Corp, Capitol Hghts, MD; [oth. writ.] I have written several others poems - all of which have never been published. This is my first experience.; [pers.] never treat anyone any differently than you would expect to be treated. My poems are my feelings. I have been a single parent for 23 yrs. writing is necessary.; [a.] North Beach, MD

CRAWFORD, KRISTIN
[pen.] Kristin; [b.] January 21, 1980, Dallas, TX; [p.] John and Kathy Crawford; [ed.] Grapevine High School; [occ.] Student 10th Grade; [memb.] German Club, Church Youth Group, Sunday School, Plays Guitar; [oth. writ.] Private collection; [pers.] "Nothing ventured, nothing gained."; [a.] Grapevine, TX

CRAWFORD, RUTH
[pen.] Ruthie; [b.] August 2, 1950, Charmco, WV; [p.] Charles R. and Nellie E. Jones; [m.] John E. Crawford, October 25, 1969; [ch.] John R. and Rebecca S.; [ed.] GED completed 10th Grade in Nuttall High School Lookout WV; [occ.] Housewife; [memb.] Hopewell Baptist Church, North American Hunting Club, International Society of Poets; [pers.] Climb to the top of the ladder. Reach out and help others. Always show love and lend a smile to all you meet. Life is a song in the heart and a poem to impart.; [a.] Hico, WV

CREACH, JENNIFER
[pen.] Destiny M. Darrell; [b.] June 24, 1976, Yakima, WA; [p.] Carol Gefre, Darrell Creach (Deceased); [ed.] Zillah High School Yakima Valley College; [oth. writ.] A private collection of poems. None have been read or published.; [pers.] I write about another side. A side brought out by depression and desperation. It is an easy place to hide when everything else haunts or hurts.; [a.] Zillah, WA

CRIBBS, GERI
[b.] March 27, 1970, Long Beach, CA; [p.] Geri and Charlie Cribbs; [m.] Gareth Hooper; [ed.] University Alaska Anchorage; [occ.] Technical Writer, System Intergrators, Inc.; [pers.] Time is a concept which shouldn't be overly watched.; [a.] Sacramento, CA

CRITCHLEY, BRIAN
[pen.] B. J. Fortin; [b.] May 1, 1978, Bayonne, NJ; [p.] James Critchley, (Deceased) and Margaret Critchley; [ed.] Bayonne High School; [memb.] Official Madonna Fan Club; [oth. writ.] Over 60 poems some published in literary Art magazine "Beginnings `96."; [pers.] For me, writing poetry is like giving birth. Each time I write I must did deep and experience unbearable pain to create a work of art which is different from any other and that I feel a heart feel bond to.; [a.] Bayonne, NJ

CROCKETT, AUDIE BAKER
[b.] May 8, 1916, Owens, TX; [p.] Charlie and Ada Baker; [m.] Awbrey C. Crockett, June 28, 1936; [ch.] Jay, Joe, Jean and Jack; [ed.] B.S. degree and Masters degree from howard payne U. Brownwood Tex; [occ.] Retired Teacher; [memb.] Church of Christ Texas retired teachers ass. American Ass. of University of Women; [a.] Coleman, TX

CROMER, PHILIP W.
[b.] September 3, 1971, New York; [p.] Lorraine Cromer; [ed.] Martin County High School, Florida Atlantic University; [occ.] Student Working on B.A.; [oth. writ.] Several poems published in the University newspaper.; [pers.] I strive to see the beauty in all things and reflect them in my writing.; [a.] Stuart, FL

CROOK, KEVIN
[pen.] Kevin "Mull" Crook; [b.] September 12, 1978, Brampton, ON; [ed.] Currently in Heart Lake High School, advanced level, currently studying Art, History, English, Music, Drama; [occ.] Composing Poems and Stories; [hon.] I have received the Chief Scouts Award, My 5 Stars in Cubs, and received the Most Improved Award during my first year of Football; [oth. writ.] I am working on a full-length novel titled the Maye wars, I also have several short stories. In total I have written close to 300 pages of poetry.; [pers.] To remain happy, and find a future for this world we must retain a balance of good and evil, positive and negative. Observe the would outside the human, you will see this.; [a.] Brampton Ontario, Canada

CROOKS, MICHAELINE
[b.] April 8, 1960, Evansville, IN; [p.] Jerry L. Corn and Jane Corn; [ch.] Mackensey Jane Crooks; [ed.] Graduated Boonville High School 1978; [occ.] Mother, Aspring Singer, Writer of poetry; [pers.] If one could find a smile inside maybe then they would find a smile outside?; [a.] Boonville, IN

CROSS, ROBIN LEAH
[b.] July 9, 1972, Thunder Bay, Ontario; [p.] Ronald George, Rosemarie Stanczyk; [m.] Douglas Cross, June 26, 1993; [ch.] Taylor Grace Cross; [ed.] High School; [occ.] Canadian Automobile Association (CAA); [memb.] Northern Air Search and Rescue Association; [oth. writ.] Fictional stories in the local newspaper.; [pers.] My writing is inspired by the breathtaking beauty of my home, on the North Shore of Lake Superior in Ontario, Canada.; [a.] Thunder Bay Ontario, Canada

CROTHERS, MARYLOU
[b.] August 20, 1932, Marquette; [p.] James and Adeline Hudson; [m.] Walter Crothers, December 21, 1970; [ch.] Judy, James, Peter and Holly; [ed.]

High School Graduate; [occ.] Retired; [hon.] Certificate of Achievement from the National Wild Life Federation for "Backyard Wildlife Habitat Program"; [oth. writ.] This is my first; [pers.] Worked 29 years as a Elementary Secretary. I believe that a house is a house, but home is where you hang your memories.; [a.] Marquette, MI

CROW, ANN
[pen.] Ann Susan Crow; [b.] April 18, 1918, Chicago; [p.] Susan and Samuel Drobena; [m.] John Barn Crow, May 1, 1948; [ed.] Northwestern University School of Speech Docontrian Campus, 1945-46 Pr. Drama Study - Fire Machtell; [occ.] Retired Artist but still at Point at Studied with John Down Private Classes, etc sold 200 paintings LA; [memb.] West Valley Artists Assn., CA Machtel Chorale (Oldwhile sponser) Soloist, Lyric Soprano Lansing Michigan paid Church Christ 1st presentative Church Lansing NU; [hon.] Athletic Letter, GAA 3rd year High School Literary Letter Lindflom High School Assistant Editor, the Eagle Sr. Year, Little Theatre (Summers Stock) Michigan State University, Member of Concert Orchestra Lindholm High Chicago FL; [oth. writ.] Rewrote reader shares for television, WBKB, Chicago - State Lake Bldg 12th floor 1942 to 1948 and television associates, inc. wrote radio and TV calms for also acted, WJIM - TV radio 1966 directed shows lansing michigan "Copper kettle" howard finch V.P. Mr. Grass Pres.; [pers.] I believe in the things "that are more excellent," wrote 6 extra stanges to lymm "there is no disappointment in heaven" when I was 13 years old for tabor lutheran church chicago, IL; [a.] Wooland Hills, CA

CRUMP, RUFUS FRANK
[b.] October 7, 1945, Coquille, OR; [p.] Rufus and Mary Crump; [m.] Divorced, 1968-1973; [ch.] Rufus Crump, Greg Crump and Ryan Crump; [ed.] High School, Personnel Management Specialist School and N.C.O. Academy, U.S. Army; [occ.] Laborer; [oth. writ.] Various; [pers.] I have an unpublished book, various other poems and various songs that I have wrote.; [a.] Florence, OR

CRUZ, FAYE ELAINE
[pen.] Elaine; [b.] November 24, 1497, Birmingham, AL; [p.] Holsey and Edmonia Drake; [m.] Divorced; [ch.] Will Patrick Cruz; [ed.] Samuel Ullman High School, Lawson Community College, Shorter College; [occ.] Administrative Assistant (currently employed as a temporary. Permanent position expected soon) Employment terminated after nine years; [memb.] Georgia Poetry Society, Lakewood Church of Christ/Atlanta Inner-City Ministry; [hon.] My life is dedicated to serving mankind through spreading God's Gospel; [oth. writ.] Poems submitted to the Georgia Poetry Society Contests. Awards known in January 1996 and April. Other poems submitted to the National Library of Poetry.; [pers.] My writings are from the heart and life's experiences. My family and friends inspire my dedication to continue writing.; [a.] Marietta, GA

CULPEPPER, BARBARA R.
[b.] June 4, 1948, Lexington, MS; [p.] Sylvester Saffold, Millie Saffold; [m.] Edward Culpepper, July 11, 1964; [ch.] Gwenne Christine, Deborah Denise and David Louis; [ed.] East High School, classes at Hawkeye Community College; [occ.] Administrative

Assistant to the Superintendent of Waterloo Schools; [memb.] Professional Secretaries International, NAACP; [hon.] Achieved CPS (certified professional secretary) rating 6/95; [pers.] "All the beautiful sentiments in the world weigh less than a single lovely action."; [a.] Waterloo, IA

CUMMINGS, SHARI
[b.] April 13, 1955, Iola, WI; [p.] Richi and Barb Ogden; [m.] Roger T. Cummings, August 31, 1974; [ch.] Kaylee, Tabitha, Michael, Joshua and Thomas; [ed.] Iowa Law Enforcement Academy -DSM, IA McConnell Schools - Mpls, MN W. Delaware Community Schools - Manchester, IA; [occ.] Retired Law Enforcement Officer; [memb.] St Joseph's Catholic Church, Del Co. Genealogical Society, Delaware Co. Domestic Violence Services, Del. Co. Foster/Adopture Parents Assoc, International Society of Poets; [hon.] My biggest honor is being a parent. Its my belief the world can be changed one child at a time; [oth. writ.] "Your light" - in famous poems of today - famous poets. Society "Diet" - in Inspirations - I had press, "I am alone" - in beyond the stars National Library of Poetry.; [pers.] I write about everyday thoughts, feelings and experiences hoping someone else may relate to them. In this particular poem "Sgt Cruse" was my training officer and I wrote at to him as a way of saying that you.; [a.] Earlville, IA

CURRIE, DOUG
[b.] March 25, 1960, Hamilton; [p.] Warren and Tean Currie; [ed.] Westmount and Sir Allow Machard Secondary Schools, graduated from southmount SS 1978 Herrity of Waterloo, Faculty at Mathematic 1978 - 1981 Credit Graduate, Molawk College 1986-1987 Graduated Coldities Educations Courses in Micro Computer and Langauge; [occ.] Who Iticial Trunilator, Volunteer Teacher of Senior English as a Volunteer Credit Breachal Evangelist; [memb.] Planetary Society, Reform Party of Canada, West fifth Bible Chapel, H.C.C.F. Humilton Closer Christian Fellowship Adherance involved Truthfully but not Membership; [hon.] Vern Amer. Mathematics Award Grade 8 Kity of Hamilton, Proficiency Award 80% Average Grade 9-12, Community College Graduation Diploma Electronic Data Process 1987; [oth. writ.] Have had on article as the red hill creek expresses published in letter to christian poems, to me scientific hamilton spedalo. Poems some miscellaneous poems, translation into literal English and Romarized Candohero (Yalel) of Clarie character and Pinyin (manduria Rcmarzied of Gospel of John in process) translator of hoter of Clinton horkers new Testament notes into Spanish some prose in Hamilton line Clinton fellow in same.; [pers.] Read hardbook most but not all of my poetry and other writing or from a born of the holy spirit christian perspective explicitly or at least implicity because this is most important to me. I am learning closes and eventually I would like to write poetry in closer or some other language like french.; [a.] Hamilton Ontario, Canada

CURRY, BRENDA
[b.] June 29, 1963, Dartmouth, Nova Scotia, Canada; [p.] Shirley Bezanson; [ed.] Presently pursuing a career change to Youth and Childcare Worker; [occ.] Eletrician; [pers.] Expression of love, to Mom, Pooh, Nadine, Evern and special love to Amanda Lynn. "May Jupiter aspect you, favorably always."; [a.] Edmonton Alberta, Canada

CUTLER, CARCI
[b.] August 15, 1977; [p.] David and Lesa Cutler; [ch.] Dylan Cutler; [occ.] (Wandering) Parent, experiencing the American Irony; [oth. writ.] Local college newspaper; [pers.] Honor, Honesty and love, but the best of these is obedience, in faith love is limitless.

D'ALESSANDRO, ANN
[b.] July 4, 1952, Irvington, NJ; [p.] Anthony and Jean D'Alessandro; [oth. Writ.] Oh Wayward Wind (poem), Wind Swept (poem).

D'ANGELO, ELIZABETH C.
[b.] April 6, 1979, Port Colborne, Ontario; [ed.] Grade 11 at Lakeshore Catholic High School; [occ.] Full Time Student; [hon.] On the Honor Roll for 3 Consecutive Years; [oth. writ.] "My Complicated Kitchen" published in the last issue of "Scaling the Fade of Reason."; [pers.] I believe that if eveyrone lived by this quote, "Today is the beginning of the rest of your life." Everyone's life would be better.; [a.] Port Colborne Ontario, Canada

D'JOHN, MATTHEW
[b.] May 12, 1982, Warren, MI; [p.] Larry D'John, Karen D'John; [ed.] Currently in the 8th Grade at David Jr. High; [memb.] Plays as a starter for 8th grade School Basketball Team; [hon.] American Presidential Academic Award, Straight "A" Student, Honor Roll Awards; [a.] Sterling Heights, MI

DABROWSKA, KRYSTYNA ALINA WANDA
[pen.] Krystyna A. Dabrowska; [b.] January 1, 1952, Poland; [p.] Kazimiera Dabrowska, Jozef Dabrowska; [ed.] Technical High School - Gdansk Polytechnical Institute - Warsaw; [occ.] Mechanical Engineer, Dreis and Krump MFG Co., Chicago, IL; [hon.] Several Awards in Children Art Drawing, Prize for Sport Achievements; [pers.] The mercy of good is above all of his deeds.; [a.] Chicago, IL

DAHLER, KIRSTEN
[pen.] Kirsten Dahler; [b.] December 30, 1975, Winona, MN; [p.] Manely and Jeannie Dahler; [ed.] Winona Senior High School and Winona State University for One Year; [occ.] Just moved to Texas and looking for a Job - I used to be a Cashier; [hon.] I got the "Excellence in Creative Expression" award and the "Herb Hultgren" Art Award in High School; [oth. writ.] None that have been published.; [pers.] I just like to write things that are fun for me, things that make me laugh and visualize what it is I'm writing about. I like to be amused!; [a.] Maxwell, TX

DALTON, BETTY
[pen.] Goldaline; [b.] June 1, 1945, Toronto; [p.] John and Goldaline Crossman (Deceased); [m.] Divorced; [ch.] Tammy and Tom Jr.; [ed.] High School, I.C.S. and Life; [occ.] Trying to Sell my Writings. Disability due to Car Accident; [memb.] Royal Canadian Legion #289; [hon.] Journalism/ Short Story, Writing Diploma 87% Average. Before my Accident I received a Dancing Award and Sport Awards for Bowling, Darts and Softball. Local Papers have published my Poems and "Ask Goldaline" Column; [oth. writ.] Song poems and quotes, poems and short stories, advertising promos, slogans, wedding and birthday personalized poems. At present I am writing a novel called "Skeletons in

his closet" to be finished by the end of 1996.; [pers.] Most of my writings are non-fictional based. In my mothers memory, I trade marked her name for my usage, with my writings.; [a.] Havelock Ontario, Canada

DALTON, DOROTHY ESTELLE
[pen.] Dee Dalton; [b.] March 3, 1932, Madison Heights, VA; [p.] Horsley Burks White and Mary Lillian Hamlet White; [m.] Dead, New Year Eve 1952; [ch.] Koe Blake Dixon (Dead); [ed.] High School Graduate, Night Classes Washington and Lee School from Univ. of Virginia Studied Liturature; [occ.] Geriatric Nurse "Home Care"; [memb.] Rebekahs of Virginia; [hon.] This is the greatest honor that I could have - for my little poem to be published task gon from my heart!; [oth. writ.] Poetry but I write it and tear it up I never felt that it was felt that it was good enough to be published "when I die" is in honor of my son my life has been greatly teached by music and poetry.; [pers.] Classical music and poetry are good for the soul. I started playing piano when I was 4 yrs. old.; [a.] Lynchborg, VA

DANDRIDGE, EULA B.
[pen.] Judy Dandridge; [b.] March 3, 1924, Illinois; [p.] John A. Dandridge and Nannie Hines Dandridge; [ed.] Augusta Tilghman High School and Business College - Paducah, KY, presently attend class in "Psychic Development Dawn of Peace Center-Oxnard, Cal."; [occ.] Retired Office Employee of Studio Transportation Drivers - Teamsters Local 399 in Motion Picture Industry - No Hollywood Calif. BKPR - Computers; [memb.] "Gulls" - Women's Luncheon Club - Oxnard - Channel Island - Benefiting Charities - Friends of the Library - Oxnard - Int. Brotherhood of Teamsters Local Union 399 - Motion Pictures - No. Hollywood Cal.; [hon.] National Honor Society, Augusta Tilgman High School - Paducah, KY, American Legion Scholarship Award - Paducah, KY, Editors Choice Award from the National Library of Poetry - 1994 and 1995; [oth. writ.] Several poems "Friendship" published by Natl. Library of Poetry - in 1994, book "At Days End" (2) "Unforgettable" published in "Edge of Twilight" the poem published in Best poems of 1995, "Hooked on Colorado" - poem published in the Dolores Star Newspaper of Dolores, Colorado, several eulogies.; [pers.] At age 5 moved to Paducah, KY with mother and family, mother - Nannie Dandridge, deceased at aged 96 - loved to make rhymes. Moved to Los Angeles, Cal at age of 20 - then to No. Hollywood and Burbank, Cal. 1983 moved to Shell Beach, Cal. moved to present address in Oxnard, Cal. in March 1990. Special intents - music opera, (ballet, ice skating, spectator) poetry, tennis, ancestors believed to be from family of Martha Dawbridge Curtis Washington, wife of Pres. Greg Washington.; [a.] Oxnard, CA

DANIEL, HENRIETTA
[b.] February 1, 1996, Trinidad; [p.] May and John; [ch.] Nil; [ed.] Ontario Teach Qualification B.Sc. (psychology) - University of Toronto M.Ed - University of Toronto teacher 15 years, principal for 21 years; [occ.] Retired School Principal; [oth. writ.] Several poems some of which were written as a child.; [pers.] Poetry is beautiful. It is the music of words, thoughts, feelings and life writing serves to share these human emotions with others and with posterity.; [a.] Toronto Ontario, Canada

DANIELS, CYNTHIA
[b.] May 15, 1958, Washington, DC; [p.] Robert and Elizabeth Williams; [m.] Scott Daniels; [ch.] Dominica and Darius; [ed.] Chamberlain Vocational High School, University of the District of Columbia; [memb.] Jericho Baptist Church; [pers.] Glory and honor to God for giving me this gift of writing.

DARLINGTON, CANDICE
[b.] June 5, 1978, North Vancouver; [p.] Janis and Dolph Darlington; [ed.] Montroyal Elementary, Handsworth Secondary; [occ.] I coach Baton Twirling; [pers.] Enjoy and love writing poetry.; [a.] North Vancouver British Columbia, Canada

DASTI, TAMMY
[b.] September 14, 1971, Hamilton, Ontario; [p.] Adopted by grandparents, Charles and Rosalind Smith; [ed.] Hons. B.A. from McMaster University. I hope to get my Masters and Ph.D.; [occ.] Student; [memb.] International Society of Poets; [hon.] Editor's Choice Award in both 1994 and 1995 from the N.L.P.; [oth. writ.] "The Solitary Tree," "The Vampire," and "On Poems and Paintings," all appear in N.L.P. anthologies.; [pers.] "Peaceful times" was written as a kind of folk song for a novel that I am working on and hope to publish soon.; [a.] Dundas Ontario, Canada

DAVE, ROHIT K.
[b.] March 21, 1984, Ottawa, IL; [p.] Amar and Lorraine Dave; [ed.] 6th Grade Student at Grundy High; [occ.] Student; [memb.] Fox 43 Kids Club; [hon.] 2 Soccer Trophies, 1 Pine Wood Derby Trophy, 1 Young Author Trophies, 1 D.A.R.E. Essay Medal, 1 Soccer Medal; [oth. writ.] A christmas poem, 2 young author stories.; [pers.] I want to reach the hearts and minds of people through my poetry.; [a.] Ottawa, IL

DAVIDSON, JESSIE
[b.] January 22, 1924, England; [p.] Deceased; [m.] Deceased, December 7, 1952; [ch.] Two; [ed.] English High School; [occ.] Retired; [pers.] This is the first poem, I have published. I was raised by two very loving parents, who taught me to see beauty in all things. If in some small way, my poem can help my fellow man, I shall leave this world a very happy person.; [a.] Langley British Columbia, Canada

DAVIDSON, MARJORIE E.
[b.] January 11, 1924, Portsmouth, England; [p.] Henry C. Dugan and Florence Dugan; [m.] James A. Davidson (Deceased), May 24, 1942; [ch.] Dennis Michael Davidson and Carol Ann; [ed.] Equivalent to grade 10 - Omega St. and Nelson St. School, Portsmouth, Eng.; [occ.] Retired; [memb.] B.C. Heart Assn.; [pers.] Having been motherless since 8 yrs. old, my education has been of secondary concern, with 5 younger siblings, but poetry has come naturally to me since age 11, when a teacher, coming across a recess-time scribbling of one, hauled me - up to over.; [a.] Osoyoos British Columbia, Canada

DAVIES, KIM
[b.] August 20, 1981, Saskatoon, Saskatchewan; [p.] Illa Davies, John Davies; [ed.] Grade 9 at Burt Fox Composite High School, Elementary School; [occ.] School; [oth. writ.] I have only written for myself and my friends.; [pers.] I write about feeling, not always about my personal feelings but about the feelings that other people have.; [a.] Fort Qu'Appelle Saskatchewan, Canada

DAVIS, DONNA G.
[b.] March 23, 1922, Pittsburgh, PA; [ch.] Lynne, Christine and Stephen (three children); [ed.] University of Pittsburgh, Major, Journalism/English; [occ.] Retired, Legal Secretary; [memb.] Abington Players, American, contract Bridges League, Rockville Little Theatre; [oth. writ.] Various poetry through the years.; [pers.] JFK committed, "more poets should be in politics and more politicians should be poets." I've been influenced by poets of New England.; [a.] Gaithersburg, MD

DAVIS, H. L. PATRICK
[b.] September 9, 1965, Mobile, AL; [p.] H. Leroy Davis and Dora M. Davis; [m.] Tracy L. Davis, August 21, 1973; [ed.] Murphy High School, Auburn University; [occ.] Manager, Space Shuttle Astronaut/ Flight Controller Training; [memb.] National Management Association, United Professional Tennis Registry, Kappa Alpha Psi Fraternity Inc., UJIMA Inc.; [oth. writ.]; [pers.] If I can inspire greatness in others through my writing the way that Langston Hughes, Many Angelou, God, Family, and friends have inspired me, then nothing is wasted.; [a.] League City, TX

DAVIS, KARA L.
[b.] April 28, 1956, Grand Rapids, MI; [p.] Howard Jay Myaard and Evelyn Myaard; [m.] Judson P. Davis, October 8, 1979; [ch.] Aaron, Sara, Carla; [ed.] I attended Forest Hills Schools up until 9th Grade - then G.R. Public - Central High - Graduated G.R. Junior, College - 2 Years - and I am planning on going back to college; [occ.] Artist (Draw and Paint Oils and Watercolors), Piano Teacher, Part-Time Sales Woman and Homemaker; [hon.] President's Honor Society in High School - Dean's List in College, 8th Grade - Won 2nd Place out of Class - Science Fair Project; [oth. writ.] Poem published in blodgett hospital newspaper when working as secretary for safety and security dept./ copyright on a collection of poems by Kara Myaard.; [pers.] Possibly, the poem I wrote will be interpreted differently by different people. I wrote it when I was around 20 yrs. of age. Of course, it will remind you of icy-cold weather conditions - but I wanted it to convey a deeper meaning. Being a born again Christian, I feel that it draws a picture of the state of a person's heart - the indifference, anger and rejection towards Christ - and how Satan delights in this!; [a.] Lowell, MI

DAVIS, MELISSA SUE
[pen.] Pandora Dementia; [b.] August 8, 1980, Martin, TN; [p.] Avanda James and Harold Davis; [ed.] Palmersville High School; [memb.] Member of FFA; [hon.] Prettiest Smile, 2nd Maid, Spelling Bee, Athletic Achievement Awards; [oth. writ.] Get away, a dream, an expression of love, feelings, a lost friends, longing.; [pers.] I write simply to express myself, and to emphasize the beauty, fear, and confusion of our world. I've been influenced greatly by poets such as Jim Morrison, Sylvia Plath. Edgar Alan Poe, and Percy Blyshe Shelley.; [a.] Palmersville, TN

DAVIS, NORMA STOEBER
[b.] October 11, 1967, Larimore, MD; [p.] Mr. and Mrs. Fred Alyea; [m.] Stoiber (1st marriage S.C.

Davis died in 1975), August 11, 1931; [ch.] Two Children, Donald Stoiber, Norman Stoiber; [occ.] Retired Librarian, Housewife; [memb.] Church Membership (Zion Methodist) and DAR; [hon.] Just in my own File - or for Friends Occasions; [oth. writ.] Just in my own file - or for friends occasion.; [pers.] Mostly I reflect on the "positive" that the Lord can and does have in our lives. And the other good things in life.; [a.] Marshfield, WI

DAVIS, TAMMY
[b.] December 13, 1963, North Wilkesboro, NC; [p.] Albert Adams, Annie Adams; [m.] Richard Davis; [ch.] Daniel Wayne, Jared Lee, Morgan Annie, Jordan Lorraine; [ed.] West High; [occ.] Mother of Four; [oth. writ.] Have written since childhood. Have always loved the art of poetry. One article published in the Smithfield Herald.; [pers.] Most of my writings reflect personal experience and feelings.; [a.] Smithfield, NC

DAWES, LADONA
[pen.] Constantina; [b.] July 18, 1966, Vancouver; [m.] Winston Dawes, July 23, 1994; [ed.] BA Economics and Communications, MA in Psychology currently Completing; [occ.] Student of Psychology Cashier at Safeway started Writing through a creative Writing Course Jan. 8 - April 10/95; [oth. writ.] Non published material creativity, the teacher, rebellion laughs with defiant wisdom, human kind, a clandescent affair, book currently writing nightscape, to die for.; [pers.] Writing explore allows me to the inner depths of my being transcending beyond that while is good or bad, happy or sad - writing makes me feel at peace and a wide's me.; [a.] Vancouver British Columbia, Canada

DAWKINS, TRACY L.
[pen.] Lady-Bug; [b.] August 13, 1960, Berkeley, CA; [p.] Herbert Dawkins and Lana Blodgett; [ed.] Skyline High, Feather River College; [occ.] Electrician Apprentice, UNCC; [oth. writ.] Novice - Currently writing poems and catering poetry contests at random.; [pers.] In this complex most times, chaotic world, one of the simplest pleasure of life is to wake in the morning with a simple.; [a.] Charlotte, NC

DE BOER, ANDREA
[b.] May 1, 1979, Woodstock, Ontario; [p.] Ralph De Boer, Jean De Boer; [ed.] Student - Grade 11 Huron Park Secondary School; [hon.] Poem Published in 1995 Year Book - Argus. (title - Dedicated to Kurt Cobain) - 3rd Prize; [pers.] I use writing as an outlet for my sadness and anger.; [a.] Innerkip Ontario, Canada

DE PAULA, HENRIQUE
[pen.] Sorcerer; [b.] December 12, 1928, Sao Paulo, Brazil; [p.] Antonio and Amalia De Paula; [m.] Maria Luiza De Paula, May 31, 1958; [ch.] Julio Cesar - Carlos Alberto - Celia - Valerie (in Laws); [ed.] First School and Commercial School; [occ.] Construction and Demolition Laborer. In Brazil I was a Sales Manager for a large Chain of Newspapers; [memb.] American Museum of Natural History. American Association of Retired Persons. The International Society of Poets; [hon.] For the book in the Desert Sun (1993 - The National Library of Poetry) for the Books Dance on the Horizon, Tears of Fire and Edge of Twilight 1994 - The National

Library of Poetry). For the books Best Poems of 1995 and Windows of the Soul (1995 - The National Library of Poetry); [oth. writ.] Many poems, letters and articles printed in local and other cities and states newspapers, in English and Portuguese. In Brazil I wrote many articles about sports for the newspaper Noticias Popular's, in the city of Sao Paulo. Ponto De Encontro, a very serious magazine in Elizabeth, N.J., also print my poems in Portuguese.; [pers.] I hate the liars. The world should be put my side down. The governs, the economy, the educations, the religions, the ects are just slavery, big business. I love to write about everything. In poetry I go from the romantic to the tragic, passing by the humorous. I write what I feel and I was never influenced by any kind of writer or poet.; [a.] Newark, NJ

DEAN, JENNIFER MICHELLE
[pen.] Jenna Dean; [b.] July 8, 1973, Bakersfield, CA; [p.] Cherryl Goff; [m.] Charles Dean; [ch.] Malakii, Raistlin and Majenna; [occ.] Homemaker; [pers.] There is no excuse for stagnations. Thanks and much love to those who made me realize this. Especially you grandmother.; [a.] Parachute, CO

DE CESARE, MARY GELO
[b.] November 21, 1922, New York City; [p.] John and Grace Gelo; [m.] William De Cesare, June 23, 1945; [ch.] Bernadette Morello, Karyn Saar, Jonine Lester; {ed.] New Utrecht High (Brooklyn) and N.Y.U. - Woods Bus. Coll.; [occ.] Retired (Antiques); [memb.] Present President Denville NJ Senior Citizens Chapter I.; [oth. writ.] Unpublished children's stories.

DECOSSE, JON-PAUL
[b.] November 21, 1975, London, Ontario, Canada; [p.] Marilyn and Roger Decosse; [ed.] Sir Wilfrid Laurier Secondary School, London, Ontario, University of Toronto, Faculty of Music, Toronto, Ontario; [occ.] Bass Soloist/Section Lead, Rosedale Presbyterian Church; [hon.] Secondary School Award for "Most Outstanding Contribution to Extra-Curricular Activities," Alexander Kinghorn University Entrance Scholarship; [oth. writ.] Outside of a few publications in High School collections, all my writing is kept to myself and family/friends, in a collection of over 200 pieces of my work.; [pers.] All of my writing is directed towards capturing the spirit of emotion, human or otherwise. Most of my poetic influences have been 20th Century, Canadian poets.; [a.] London Ontario, Canada

DEE, JENNY
[b.] December 12, 1978, Orange, CA; [p.] Donald and Valerie Dee; [ed.] Senior at Garden Valley High School; [occ.] Student and Writer; [memb.] Cheerleader at Garden Valley High; [oth. writ.] A collection of over 169 poems from the last four and a half years.; [pers.] I have been writing since the eight grade, and was inspired by my English teach, Mrs. Landdrum. Every poem I write tells about a certain event in my life.; [a.] Garden Valley, ID

DEFORGE, MICHAEL C.
[b.] December 7, 1949, Montpelier, VT; [p.] Robert and Marjorie DeForge; [m.] Cheryl Ives; [ch.] Angela, Tauni, Sonia, Jasmine, Nova; [ed.] E. Montpelier Elementary, Spaulding High Barre VT, VT College of Norwich University Montpelier, VT;

[occ.] Developmental Disability Specialist; [memb.] Disabled American Veterans; [hon.] Good Conduct Medal USMC, National Defense Medal USMC, Outstanding Service Award, Sterling Area Services D.M.H., Editors Choice Award National Library of Poetry; [oth. writ.] Poems published by National Library of Poetry, studies on file Norwich University Library, many poems, songs, short stories.; [pers.] Portraits in words of the emotion and inner spirit of mankind. Owed by the words of "Samuel Taylor Coleridge."; [a.] Wolcott, VT

DEGIDIO, CARMELLA
[b.] September 4, 1937, Englewood, NJ; [p.] Pellegrino and Palma Giordano; [m.] Michael R. DeGidio, September 7, 1957; [ch.] Michael Charles and Kevin Peter, Grandchildren: Michele and Kimberly Paige; [ed.] Leonia High School, Modern College of Cosmotology; [occ.] Homemaker; [memb.] St. Bernadette's Roman Catholic Church, International Society of Poets; [hon.] Editor's Choice Award; [oth. writ.] Parents heart thoughts published beyond the stars.; [pers.] Feelings cannot be bought, sold or inherited, they are the one possession that can only belong to you.; [a.] Parhin, NJ

DEINSTADT, ANASTACIA LYNN
[b.] September 1, 1981, Nanaimo, BC; [p.] Christine and Brent Deinstadt; [ed.] Continuing; [occ.] ETA Embroidery, Partner in Ownership; [pers.] A creative mind and a strong will take you far in the world.; [a.] Prince Rupert British Columbia, Canada

DEITCH, PAULA
[pen.] Paula Deitch; [b.] July 1, 1976, Metairie, LA; [p.] Ann Deitch, Sam Deitch; [ed.] East Jefferson High; [occ.] American Cancer Society; [pers.] My mother passed on from her fight with cancer in "93." All my poems are my emotional outlits. My personal experiences. No matter how horrible life can get, never let it bring you down.; [a.] Metairie, CA

DELANEY, MARIA LUISA
[pen.] Merlie; [b.] December 6, 1959, Philippines; [p.] Marcelino and Asuncion Celestino; [m.] Joseph Delaney, June 17, 1988; [ch.] Martin Anthony Delaney; [ed.] Roosevelt College, Central College of the Philippines; [occ.] Restaurant Owner/Manager, Delaney's Deli, Dryden, Ontario; [memb.] Multicultural Association, Constituency Association, Member Liberal Party of Canada; [oth. writ.] Several poems published in local newspapers, articles for the local express.; [pers.] The great source of happiness is to love and understanding for one another. I was inspired by great people who created peace.; [a.] Dryden Ontario, Canada

DELEFF, YVETTE MARY
[b.] March 29, 1964, Gander, NF; [p.] Margaret and Wycliff Dyle; [m.] Thomas Edwin Deleff, July 7, 1990; [ch.] Jeromy O'Rein; [ed.] Post Secondary, Registered Nurse, Lethbridge Community College, Fort McMommy - Father Mercedes High School. Dover Junior High NF; [occ.] Rin, gerontology; [memb.] Sancee Social Club - President, NF Calgary Heritage Society - President; [hon.] Achievement in Personal Best; [pers.] Nature, life experiences freedom of natural boundaries and exploration within our environment.; [a.] Calgary Alberta, Canada

DELEURERE, ELSPETH ALEXANDRA
[b.] December 20, 1979, Parsons, WV; [p.] G. Harley DeLeurere, Sharon Hall DeLeurere; [ed.] Tucker County High School; [occ.] Student; [memb.] Hendricks Free Methodist Church, Free Methodist Youth, Youth Christian Club, Future Business Leaders of America, Foreign Language Club, Senior Girl Scouts; [hon.] West Virginia Young Writers Award; [oth. writ.] Articles for "The Parsons Advocate" and "The Voice of the Lion" (Tucker County High School newspaper).; [pers.] It's never too early to start working for your dreams. For God so loved the world, that he gave his only begotten Son, that whosoever beleiveth in him should not perish, but have everlasting life (John 3:16).; [a.] Hendricks, WV

DELGADO, JUAN ANTONIO RAVELO
[pen.] Tony Ravelo; [b.] November 18, 1965, Havana, Cuba; [ed.] B. A. Accounting and Finance, Havana University 1990; [occ.] Bookkeeper; [oth. writ.] Some other poems and essays unpublished.; [pers.] Turn every stone, makes the way.; [a.] Miami, FL

DELI, EDWARD S.
[b.] December 29, 1996, Bradford, PA; [p.] Dorothy and Steven Deli; [ed.] Hillside High School, Hillside NJ currently attending American Bible Academy and RHEMA Bible Correspondence School; [occ.] Full-Time Poet; [memb.] Life-long Cure; [oth. writ.] Let me be your friend previously published "Treasure Poems of America - Winter 1996" Anthology.; [pers.] Anyone or anything can be inspiration but only our heavenly father is true inspiration. There is good in everyone regardless of what you see.; [a.] Draper, UT

DELMORE, SANDRA
[b.] March 27, 1957, Windsor, Ontario; [p.] Donald and June Durham; [m.] Timothy Delmore, March 13, 1976; [ch.] Melissa, Amanda, Daniel; [ed.] Forster Secondary School; [occ.] Administrative Assistant, Richmond Terrace Nursing Home; [oth. writ.] Scrap book full of poetry never before seen by anyone.; [a.] Amherstburg Ontario, Canada

DEMATTIA, KATHRYN E.
[b.] October 21, 1981, Washington, DC; [p.] Tony and Libby De Mattia; [ed.] S. Christa Me Auliffe, New Market Middle School; [occ.] Student; [hon.] Honor Roll Student, Championship Swimmer on the M.A.C. Swim Team; [pers.] All my love goes out to my family. Thanks for always being there and always believing in me. Also thanks for all your support with my swimming and other activities. Dad, I'll never forget to thy own self be true.; [a.] Mount Airy, MD

DEPRIEST, DON
[b.] January 24, 1940, Gobler, MO; [p.] Robert B. and Ester M. DePriest; [m.] Clara A. DePriest, December 26, 1962; [ch.] David Scott and Leigh Anne DePriest; [ed.] M.A. Communication Disorders; [occ.] Speech Pathologist (Traveling); [memb.] American Speech Hearing Assn.; [pers.] I have only been writing poetry for 11 yrs. and only in sports. Most of my work comes from ideas and events in life.; [a.] Marshfield, MO

DEPTUCH, PAMELA ANN
[pen.] Pamela Ann Wood; [b.] March 24, 1959, Los Angeles, CA; [p.] Teddy Griffin; [m.] John W.

Deptuch, November 4, 1994; [ch.] Shane Blue Thompson/Ashley Gray Robertson and Danielle Michell; [oth. writ.] Postcards from heavens, I've noticed, mutual love, savor the wine, speak-up thine heart, my son Shane, forbidden love, just a glance. To name a few.; [pers.] Water a plant, hug a child, steal a kiss, smell fresh muffins, pick some rose's read a book, spread kind words. Today is all we have, yesterday is gone, and we may never have tomorrow, it does not belong to us. Only this moment this breath, that smiles, this tear. And may never have tomorrow, it does not belong to us. Only this moment, this breath, that smile, this tear. And maybe if we embrace the day we will have a life filled with moments and a few success along the way.; [a.] Cottage Grove, OR

DESFORGES, ROGER
[pen.] Roger Desforges; [b.] August 13, 1953, Montreal, Canada; [p.] Roger and Helena; [m.] Debra; [ch.] Jaclyn, Peter; [ed.] Palmdale High, UCLA, McGill University; [occ.] Sales Manager; [oth. writ.] A collection of poems.; [pers.] A part of all that I write, comes from and is dedicated to the memory of my parents.; [a.] Cambridge Ontario, Canada

DESMOND, NITA ANDREA
[pen.] Maggy Desmond; [b.] December 9, 1935, Fairbanks, AK; [p.] Michael C. and Edith A. Desmond; [ed.] 5th Grade; [occ.] Student; [memb.] Band and Chorus; [hon.] Grand Champion Ginger Bread Competition; [oth. writ.] Home Work; [pers.] 10 years old, love to write, like to draw, I have a cat named Ducky and a dog named Angel, and I want to be a vet., tiger trained, and flight attendant, and alive!; [a.] North Pole, AK

DEVON JR., W. SCOTT
[pen.] Scott Devon; [b.] June 20, 1961, Detroit, MI; [p.] Wes and Nancy Devon; [m.] Terri Devon, November 2, 1991; [ed.] BA Michigan State University attended of London M.M. Aquinos College; [occ.] President Cole's Quality Food Inc./ St. Honore Restaurant; [memb.] Board Member/ Trustee Muskegon Museum of Art; [hon.] Who's Who Worldwide; [oth. writ.] Various business articles published.; [pers.] My personal philosophy is involved in the development of my theory of expansionism. An acceptance of our humanity and eternity. Hearts open to feel all eyes open to see all. Minds open to know all and souls open to be all.; [a.] Ada, MI

DEWILDT, CHRISTOPHER
[pen.] Christopher Stevens; [b.] April 23, 1978, Grand Rapids; [p.] Steven and Kathleen DeWildt; [ed.] Class of 1996, Hudsonville High School; [pers.] Music inspires what I write. Without it my papers would be blank.; [a.] Hudsonville, MI

DICKEY, JIM
[b.] June 18, 1940; [ed.] B.S., M.S. Civil Engineering, Auburn University; [occ.] Engineer, Owner, Osprey Galleries, Wildlife Art and Wood Carving Studio; [hon.] U.S. Patent No. 4,206,013; [oth. writ.] Tehnical publications, currently compiling a volume of poetry.: Beasts, Friends, and Others.; [pers.] Life's journies and those encounters a long the way create a set of experiences unique to each individual but having a commonality of those changes,

expectations, decisions and contradictions we all know. Addressing my own private set of Beasts, Friends and Others my hope is to share those, things common and easily recognized by some.; [a.] Panama City Beach, FL

DINGWELL, CYNTHIA PADECKY
[b.] January 10, 1964, Toronto, Ontario, Canada; [p.] Frank and Yolande Padecky; [m.] Stephen Dingwell; [ch.] 4 children, Justin (13), Nicole (10), Brian (8), Luke (2); [oth. writ.] I have written many personal poetic compositions. They usually pertain to my vision, that our world, though in a state of distress and emptiness, still assures the soul of its inner beauty. And as a testimony to its strength, to rise again. I delve in the moments of innocence lost, yet I leave open the door to success and fulfillment. This conflict duels repeatedly, in my work, and how I perceive life.; [pers.] I have felt many dreams, and desires, as I traverse the road which my writing leads me. Sometimes, realizations are unpleasant, and are hard to accept. Maybe, we should discard the wealth od disillusionment and despair, and focus more on our own personal accomplishments, and contributions to society, no matter how minute they may appear at times. Each fulfills a cherished moment in our hearts, to be destroyed by no one. Later, they instill, piece by piece, our own true worth and identity. Displaying our uniqueness. As human beings that we are diverse yet beautiful.; [a.] Newmarket Ontario, Canada

DIXON JR., EDWARD J.
[b.] Pittsburgh, PA; [p.] Edward, Martha (Nee Daly); [m.] Sue; [ch.] Eddie and Katie; [ed.] BA in Economics and MBA Concentrating in Finance from La Salle University; [occ.] Internal Consultant; [pers.] Active in various sports organizations, coach, play basketball and softball, now embarking upon a writing career, one of my hidden dreams.; [a.] Philadelphia, PA

DIXON, REBECCA
[b.] April 20, 1955, Lake Charles, LA; [p.] Newell and Alma Ash; [m.] Michael E. Dixon, June 27, 1992; [ch.] Audrey Swanson, Eric Swanson, Chasity and Michael Dixon; [ed.] West Orange High, Alvin Community College; [occ.] Life Insurance Agent; [memb.] Court Appointed Special Advocates (CASA); [oth. writ.] Not yet published; [pers.] Only my poetry knows me as well as I, for the wealth of my soul has only been revealed to pen and paper.; [a.] Orange, TX

DOBE, KIMBERLEY-ANN
[b.] October 12, 1973, Ottawa, Canada; [p.] Pierrette and George Smith; [ed.] St. Bonaventure Elementary, De La Salle Academy of Arts, Samuel Genest Catholic High School Cite Colligale - Practical Nursing (Graduate Spring of '97); [occ.] Medical Reception at the University of Ottawa Health Services; [memb.] Member of the HIV Primary Care group of Ottawa Carleton; [hon.] Valedictorian (Junior), Bronze Medal in Track, Geography Award; [oth. writ.] Placed first in essay writing competition, have had short stories and poems published in newspapers.; [pers.] When I am writing, I look deep inside myself, feeling emotions that are profound, I imagine, I feel then I write. I am inspired by Elizabeth Literature.; [a.] Ottawa Ontario, Canada

DOHLER, JOANN M.
[b.] September 21, 1941, Chicago, IL; [p.] Leopold (Deceased) and Martha Rottau; [m.] Gunter Dohler (Deceased), August 16, 1975; [ch.] Cary Opiela (son); [ed.] Wilbur Wright College; [occ.] Executive Secretary of the Vice President, Product Operations, Northrop Grumman Corporation, Rolling Meadows, IL; [a.] Palatine, IL

DOLAN, VALERIE BEATTIE
[b.] March 23, 1947, Hamilton, Ontario; [p.] Nina Frampton, Robert Beattie; [m.] James Dolan, December 6, 1985; [ed.] Barton Secondary, McMaster University, George Brown College, Maitreya Buddhist Seminary; [occ.] Executive Director, Bold Park Lodge Incorporated, Hamilton, Ontario; [memb.] 1) Women Who Excel, 2) Hamilton-Wentworth Drug and Alcohol Awareness Committee, 3) Pregnancy, Drugs and Alcohol Committee, 4) Niagara College Advisory Committee, 5) Ontario Federation of Community Mental Health and Addcition Programmes; [oth. writ.] Short stories and poems published in heart paths and women's centre publications.; [pers.] I endeavor to write about my understanding of the universe and my place in it. I have been greatly influenced by Vedantic and Buddhist philosophies.; [a.] Hamilton Ontario, Canada

DOMBROWSKI, THOMAS
[pen.] "TJ"; [b.] January 27, 1965, Chicago, IL; [p.] Marge and Thomas Dombrowski; [occ.] Research and Development, J.C. Enterprises; [oth. writ.] "Endless Love," "Follow the Rainbow," "Listen to the Wind," "I Love the Rain," "Spreading of the Wings"; [pers.] Our perfection, is like looking into the sun...we become blinded to all other perfections. As a wise person once said, "we are blinded by, what eyeglasses we carry from yesterday...and the beliefs of illusions are such a spectacle."; [a.] Elk Grove, IL

DONATELLI, JOSEPH M.
[b.] July 3, 1950; [m.] Marlon, July 30, 1988; [occ.] President Eastern Marble and Granite Inc.; [memb.] Sons of the American Legion, Scotch Plains Business and Professional Association, Building Stone Institute; [oth. writ.] Several poems published articles for trade magazines.

DONLEY, FRANCINE DENISE
[b.] January 26, Chicago, IL; [p.] Daisy M. Donley, Norman Marshall; [ed.] Manierre, Waller High, Loop Community College, Illinois School of Commerce, Dean's List; [occ.] Adm. Assistant/Public Relations; [pers.] It's ok to love to to care for others and it's not selfish to love yourself first... others who care to share will love you for you, if they don't its ok.; [a.] Chicago, IL

DOUMANI, DAVID
[pen.] David Kidd; [b.] July 15, Windsor, Ontario; [m.] Angela Doumani, April 21, 1988; [oth. writ.] I have been writing for a number of years only decided a few months ago to pursue my writing as a potential career. This is the first contest I entered and am pleased to be published on my first attempt.; [pers.] My writing style reflects on human struggle. My inspiration comes from author's Henry Rollins and Jim Carroll.; [a.] Winnipeg Manitoba, Canada

DOVERSPIKE, MARIA
[b.] November 22, 1974, Ontonagon; [p.] Trudy Bartholomew and Gale Doverspike; [ed.] Ontonagon Jr. - Sr. High School Gogibec Community College; [occ.] Secretary/Receptionist Eagle River Health Care Center Inc.; [oth. writ.] Two poems previously published by the National Library of poetry and in a school paper.; [pers.] My poetry is a gather of my lifes experiences. They tell my life story if you look hard enough. I have been writing since I was 13 years old.; [a.] Eagle River, WI

DOVRING, KARIN
[b.] Sweden; [ed.] Born and trained in Sweden, Ph.D. Lund University, invited by Harold Lasswell of Yale Law School to USA as his Associate becuase of her book "Songs of Zion," later American Citizen; [occ.] Communication Analyst, Freelance; [memb.] Honorary Life-Time Member of Societe Jean Jaquer Rousseau in Geneva, Switzerland, Hon. Memeber Advisory Council, International Biographical Centre, Cambridge, England, Foreign Correspondent Rome Italy where husband was on the diplomatic Staff of the United Nations; [hon.] While commuting between Yale and Rome invitred guest lecturer in many American and European universities and in the Vatican as well as for the American Army and Peace Corps; [oth. writ.] Six books in communication analysis among them the classic "Road of Propaganda" (short stories), "No Parking This Side of Heaven" (poems), "Faces in a Mirorr," some of them set to music on cassettes, Hollywood 1995, many articles in communication analysis here and abroad, among them one for a global public of journalists in International Press Institute's Bullettin.; [pers.] My life has given me many aspects but my heart is in poetry.; [a.] Urbana, IL

DRAGONE, DANIELLE
[b.] November 22, 1982, Morristown, NJ; [p.] Leon and Maureen Dragone; [ed.] June '96 graduate St. Peter The Apostle Elementary School, September '96 Oak Knoll School of the Holy Child, Summit, NJ; [occ.] Student; [hon.] Forensics, 1st, 3rd, Finalist; 1st & 2nd Honors in Academics; [oth. writ.] None to Date; [a.] Parsippany, NJ

DRENNON, MARY A.
[b.] February 25, 1921, Lebanon, TN; [p.] Foster and Nelle Andrews; [m.] Malcolm Drennon, December 19, 1945; [ch.] Barbara and Jane; [ed.] Lebanon High, Nashville Business College; [occ.] Retired; [memb.] West End Church of Christ; [pers.] Legally blind 14 years, love to laugh, love people, use talking books, for blinds, invalid husband, house bound.; [a.] Nashville, TN

DRISKELL, DONALD A.
[b.] January 26, 1951, San Diego, CA; [p.] Richard O. Driskell, Lucile G. Driskell; [ed.] Aspen High School, Co. Montana St. University, Mt. Williamsport Area Comm. College, PA; [occ.] Photography; [memb.] Sierra Club, Wilderness Society, Bald Eagle Art League, Wellsboro Art Club; [oth. writ.] Three consecutive "Editors Choice" awards. National Library of Poetry none published.; [pers.] "The god rooted heart blooms in wonderway."; [a.] Wellsboro, PA

DROELLE, DONALD WILLIAM
[b.] August 29, 1974, Detroit, MI; [p.] Joan and Donald Droelle; [ed.] Redford Union High School, Military School "BT" Class "A" School; [occ.] Damage Controlman, U.S. Navy, USS America CV-66; [memb.] Dept. of Defense; [hon.] Gold Key- (Scholastic Art Contest), Navy Achievement Medal, Nato Medal, Various Military Ribbons; [oth. writ.] None published; [pers.] Poetry and art have always been a special thing for me, I encourage all to be creative and out of the ordinary. The navy has been a powerful force throughout the years, I'm proud to have been a part of the organization. Navy power forever.; [a.] Redford, MI

DRUDGE, MAXINE F.
[b.] August 19, 1934, Edmonton, Alberta; [p.] Stewart and Jeanne McLeod; [m.] Divorced; [ch.] Peter, Murray, Alex, John (four son); [ed.] Hons Grade 12, Manitoba, Technical Institute - Secretarial - many years in the Diplomatic Corp Studying Humanity; [occ.] Retired an disability pension - past polio syndrome; [memb.] March of Dimes, Past Polio Committee; [oth. writ.] I am also an artist and have sold many paintings.; [pers.] A near-death experience 20 years age changed my life forever - I believe in the continuation of life and the ultimate good in all people and try. Reflect this in my poetry and paintings.; [a.] Scarborough Ontario, Canada

DUBSKY, ANDREA Z.
[b.] April 14, 1978, Fort Lauderdale, FL; [p.] Paul Dubsky and Zdenka Dubsky; [ed.] Olympic Heights High School; [occ.] Customer Service/Sales Rep. for Service Merchandise Corp. Store, #200 Boca Raton, FL; [memb.] 4-H Club, Humane Society of the U.S. - (HSUS), ASPCA - Prevention of Cruelty to Animals, South Florida Soccer Member, U.S. Olympic Committee; [hon.] Co-Captain High School Girls Soccer, Senior Class "October" Student of the Month, "United we stand America" Essay Winner; [oth. writ.] Editorial in "Soap Opera Digest," "United We Stand America," Essay (winner), various poetry.; [pers.] "You can do anything and everything - if you want it bad enough." And may God bless my family and friends.; [a.] Boca Raton, FL

DUES, BONNIE
[b.] November 9, 1950, Dayton, OH; [p.] Orville and Ruby Helfinstine; [m.] Ron Dues, October 27, 1970; [ch.] Kimberle Ann and Joseph Brian; [ed.] West Carrollton High School, W.C. Ohio. Carousel Beauty School Dayton, Ohio, Palm Beach Beauty School W. Palm Beach Florida; [occ.] Hair Dresser; [oth. writ.] The eyes of a child obituary of my father a child's prayer.; [pers.] I like to write about the emotions a and person I feel deeply about. I like to look for the positive and good things in all people events. Every day is a chance to start all over.; [a.] Port Saint Lucie, FL

DULKU, KIRAN
[b.] August 16, 1979, England; [p.] Kulwant Dulku, Nirvair Dulku; [ed.] Presently in Grade 10; [occ.] Student; [oth. writ.] I have a great interest in poetry. I have many more finished pieces of poetry and I hope to publish my own book someday.; [pers.] Most of my poems are based on my own personal feelings and expressions of every day life.; [a.] Mississauga Ontario, Canada

DUNCAN, CHRISTOPHER E.
[b.] July 22, 1957, Wichita, KS; [p.] Bruce and Sally

Duncan; [m.] Rima A. Haidar/Duncan, September 16, 1990; [ch.] Meera Christopher Duncan; [ed.] AA in General Biology/BA in International Studies/ Business Adm.; [occ.] Work with Family Business Research, Trade and Investment Management; [memb.] President Biological Science Club. while in attendance NEOA and M Jr. College Member of International Business Club WSU collect for looking Foundation, Heart Association and Cancer Society. Have paid various political group, with note that money should begin to government, and now we see the political, budget impass; [oth. writ.] A poem for the mentally starved, my eyes shall never see, till the end.; [pers.] Land, power, money this they all confess with greed. When love is the only need. Belief in something greater than humanity, is the only path to human sanity.; [a.] Wichita, KS

DUNN, ALLISON L.
[b.] April 20, 1975, Birmingham, AL; [p.] Mr. and Mrs. B. Dunn Jr.; [ed.] 2 1/2 Years of College - Majoring in Early Education; [occ.] Student; [hon.] Invited Twice to the Two Week Summer Camp at Brenau University for Exceptionally Talented Student in the Arts, KA (Kappa Alpha Theta) at Auburn University; [oth. writ.] Several poems and one short story published in Firespark's young poet's magazine.; [pers.] I write from my heart. I feel very deeply the emotions that envelope my poetry. Sometimes when life goes to fast, paper is all that will listen. I hope to touch many hearts with the tip of my pen.; [a.] Auburn, AL

DUONG, THANH TUNG
[pen.] Thanh Tri Cao, Quang Thanh; [b.] August 6, 1951, Binh Thuan; [p.] Duong Chuc (Deceased), Nguyen Thi Sang; [ed.] Bo De High School Phan Thiet, Vietnames Academy of Buddhist Van Hanh Saigon, Vietnam; [occ.] Ven. Thich Quang Thanh, President of Bao Quang Temple, Painter and Flowers Arrangement Instructor; [memb.] The Founder of the Vietnamese Buddhist Center for Charitable Services Bao Quang. The General Minister Buddhist in World Order. The General Secretary of Truc Lam Magazine; [hon.] One Gold, Two Silvers and One Bronze Winning Awards on Waterfalls and Flowers Arrangement, Saigon, Vietnam; [oth. writ.] 1995 Collected poems: "The sleeping moon in the cloud." Several Zen's poems and articles about the flowers arrangement and the miniature waterfalls and Bonsai. Philosophies of Buddhism. Zen's flowers. Social affairs...; [pers.] I try to convey in my writing the ideal of struggle for human rights in vietman. I have been very much affected by the sufferings of oppressed people in our present time. I hope that I could create and contribute some works of Art to our culture.; [a.] Garden Grove, CA

DUPUIS, HELEN V.
[pen.] Victoria Agar; [b.] March 21, 1932, Ontario, Canada; [p.] Gordon Eager, Mabel Eager; [m.] Leo Paul Dupuis (Deceased), December 26, 1956; [ed.] Sarawak Elementary, Ont. Canada, Owen Sound Collegiate and Vocational Inst. Ont., Canada; [occ.] Retired Terminal-Operator, Race-Horse Trainer, Restaurant Operator/Owner; [memb.] Grey-Bruse Writers Association, Owen Sound Ont., Canada; [hon.] 25 Year Employee Awards, 25 Year Accident-Free Award, Honorable Mention in Paper in regards to a poem I composed for a retiring Race-Horse, Award for Best Essay, Elementary School; [oth.

writ.] Poems in the form of tributes to retirees. Several un-submitted poems and a children's christmas horse story. Written in 1972.; [pers.] Most of my writings usually relate to things and beauty that surround me each day.; [a.] Wilberforce Ontario, Canada

DURBIN, H. FITZGERALD
[pen.] H. Fitzgerald; [b.] February 18, 1915, Todd, OK; [p.] W. R. Durbin and B. L. Romines; [m.] Nolda Juanita Walker, August 15, 1933; [ch.] Seven; [ed.] Progressive; [occ.] Retired Minister; [memb.] Gen. Council Assembly of God OK., District council of Ass. of God International Society of Poets, Rutherford Inst. C.W.A., C.A.N., A.F..A.; [hon.] Gold Pen Award for Fifty Years of Ministry; [oth. writ.] The man last true love, after the storm working on Autobiography poems in local news paper, Sparrowgrass forum, M.W.M Dexter.; [pers.] Writing poetry is a lot like life. Sometimes it flows rewarding, the more you put in the more you can receive.; [a.] Wyandotte, OK

DURR, NAOMI D.
[pen.] Naomi D.; [b.] June 5, 1963, Magee, MS; [p.] John L. Draughn and Dora Draughn; [m.] Divorced; [ch.] Candis Nicole, Dimitri Christian; [ed.] Graduate 1981 Mt. Olive Attendance Center, Jones Jr. College, future plans to attend William Carey to complete my Education to receive my Master in Education; [occ.] Mt. Olive Attendance Center's Special Ed. Asst. Teacher for the Handicapped; [hon.] Faculty's Committee Parent Teachers Association; [oth. writ.] Two completed unpublished romance novels, Sweet Wing Song, and First Light of Love. An unpublished book of poems and I'm presently writing another novel called from truth to freedom.; [pers.] It is my hope that the publication of Faded Memory will open the door for more of my work to be acknowledged. Thank you National Library of Poetry for my beginning.; [a.] Mount Olive, MS

DUTCHER, SHERYL LYNN
[b.] July 21, 1954, Midland, MI; [p.] Edward Dutcher and Barbara Smith; [ch.] James R. Cruze IV and Janell D. Westbrook; [ed.] Santa Rita High, Phoenix College; [occ.] Certified Nursing Assistant; [oth. writ.] I am working on a book titled the Crimson tree along with my daughter. Another book written on behalf of my friend Tracy Davis and myself titled empty words/broken hearts.; [pers.] Family and friends, especially Joe Foarde have been an influence in my life to write and in writing I reflect on people and circumstances past or present that have affected me in one way or the other. Love to all of you.; [a.] Phoenix, AZ

DYCK, WESSLEY P.
[pen.] Wessley Dyck; [b.] September 8, 1979, Paraguay; [p.] Peter and Adelgunde Dyck; [ed.] Grade Eleven at Garden Valley Collegiate in Winkler; [occ.] Student; [a.] Winkler Manitoba, Canada

DYER, ROSALEE R.
[b.] June 30, 1963, Crossville, TN; [p.] Robert and Ruth Walker; [m.] Larry Dyer, April 30, 1989; [ch.] Kristie Michelle, Corrie Alexandra, Cassie Rea, Chaylin Rosa; [ed.] University of Tennessee, B.S. College of Communications; [occ.] V.P. Tennessee,

Wholesalers, Inc.; [memb.] Crossville First Church of the Nazarene, American Water Ski Assoc.; [hon.] Advertising Scholarship Award at VT, 3 Time Womens Overall State Waterski Title; [oth. writ.] Write various types of poetry and rhymes for my children. Insteads of buying cards - I write my own greeting cards.; [pers.] My life situations, my faith in God, my love for people (especially my family) influences most of my subject matter.; [a.] Crossville, TN

EAGAN, MARY MARTHA
[pen.] Mimi Eagan; [b.] August 28, 1926, Syracuse, NY; [p.] Leo T. Eagan, Eleanor Eagan; [ch.] Margot C. Papworth, Mary Martha C. Wilson, Christopher E. Cheney; [ed.] Franciscan Academy, Syracuse, NY, BA Degree: Georgian Court College, Lakewood, NJ; [memb.] President's Circle, Georgian Court College, A.I.C.R., Local Clubs; [hon.] Several poems published by The National Library of Poetry, Editor's Choice for Poetry; [pers.] I write about everyone and everything I love. They are my teachers. I write about the wasteland of war. I am influenced by everything I read and see, and I store the data, both good and bad, for future use. Robert Frost, Walt Whitman, Anne Sexton, and W. H. Auden have influenced me the most.; [a.] Fayetteville, NY

EAKINS, SHANNA RENEE
[b.] October 8, 1978; [p.] Michael and Cindy Eakins; [ed.] Grinnell Senior High School; [occ.] Intern at the Grinnell Herald Register; [memb.] International Thespian Society; [hon.] Honor Thespian, Best Supporting Actress in One Act Play, Presidential Academic Fitness Award; [oth. writ.] "Because I believe" 1995 Grinellian, Vol.84, articles published in the local paper; [pers.] Yet another in a seemingly endless series of unrequited love, is what prompted me to write this poem. Though each love has broken my heart to some degree, it is with much appreciation that I wish to dedicate this poem to the select few who continued to treat me with respect they can never know the true importance of their actions.; [a.] Grinnell, IA

EBERT, MS. THERESA M.
[b.] March 28, 1933, Pottsville, PA; [p.] Mr. and Mrs. John Sarge; [m.] Deceased, December 9, 1951; [ch.] One Daughter; [ed.] 13 years, grades 1-12 St. Mary's, St. Clair, PA, Mary Queen of Peace and St. Patrick's Pottsville, PA, 1 yr. Penn State, Sch. Campus, PA; [occ.] Semi-retired, Merrow Operator; [memb.] Ladies Guild of Mary Queen of Peace Church and Choir and Certified Religion Teacher for Diocese of Allentown, PA, work all voluntary; [oth. writ.] Various poems about spirituality and nature, mostly I do for self expression and satisfaction.; [pers.] I believe in the goodness of God and in the goodness of God's people and that we should do for others the best we can.; [a.] Pottsville, PA

ECKL, MELISSA JEAN
[b.] May 8, 1980, Milwaukee, WI; [p.] John H. and Barbara Eckl; [ed.] High School student; [occ.] Student; [hon.] Essay contest, 1990 numerous equestrian ribbons, wrote a play in 5th grade, that was performed by my class; [oth. writ.] Poetry, short stories, essays; [a.] Milwaukee, WI

EDDINGS, NINA
[b.] December 14, 1937, Okfuskee, OK; [p.] J. E. and Mary Edmoundson; [m.] Robert Eddings, December 31, 1952; [ch.] Rebecca, Roger and Doyle; [ed.] High School; [occ.] Housewife; [memb.] Pentecostal Holiness Church; [oth. writ.] Several of my poems have been published in the Local Newspaper.; [pers.] My thoughts come from the heart and are mainly from happenings around me and of God's Creation.; [a.] Shawnee, OK

EDER, ELIZABETH
[pen.] Elizabeth Eder; [b.] January 19, 1946, Macomb, IL; [p.] George and Flossie Brown; [m.] Larry W. Eder, May 28, 1994; [ch.] Paula and Merle, (Step-children) Jeremy, Sarah, Caitlin and Zachary; [ed.] High School and Cosmetology; [occ.] Secretary to Athletic Dir, at Lamar CISP; [memb.] First Baptist Church-Needville LCESA, TESA; [hon.] When in High School I received several awards for my music. At present I am the editor of the LCESA newspaper. I am also, church clerk and assistant organist.; [oth. writ.] The China Doll, You Are There, Why Do I Love Thee?, My Mother, Use To!!, It's me you see and many more none of them have been published although my family would like to see a book at my poetry published someday.; [pers.] Most of my writings pertain to personal happenings in my life and in the lives of family and friends. I found that through my writings it was a stress relief and a way to express myself that I couldn't do otherwise.; [a.] Needville, TX

EDWARDS, APRIL RENE
[pen.] A. R. E.; [b.] November 1, 1980, California; [p.] Carolynn Edwards; [ed.] I am a sophomore at Corvallis High School in Corvallis Montana; [memb.] Member in 4-H, member in the Corvallis speech team; [hon.] 4-H awards, fashion reviews for 4-H (second place) Science fair award; [oth. writ.] I've written other poems but only for myself or friends; [pers.] I think that inside of everyone there is a poet, but they just have to reach an inner peace to find that poet; [a.] Corvallis, MT

EDWARDS, JUDY ANN
[b.] November 16, 1946, Toledo, OH; [p.] Virginia and Jewell Farless; [m.] Dennis Edwards; [ch.] Craig Allen; [ed.] Springfield Local High; [occ.] Vice President of Edwards Communications and Alarm Systems, Inc. in Mesa, Arizona; [a.] Mesa, AZ

EDWARDS, ROBERT DUANE
[b.] January 16, 1968, Phoenix, AZ; [p.] Donald A, Kerrie Lynn Edwards; [m.] Amy Lee (Wright), May 22, 1993; [ch.] Donald A. 111, Traci Lynn, (Jon) Watson; [ed.] Oakland High, Eastern Illinois Univ., University of Illinois; [occ.] Substitute Teacher and Graduate Student (Eastern Illinois Univ.); [memb.] Veterans of Foreign Wars, Aircraft Owners and Pilots Association; [oth. writ.] Several non-published poems written for a poetry class at Eastern Univ.; [pers.] The ideas for my poems come from experiences and dreams. (Mostly from things I have observed.) This is one way I can let others enjoy my wonder heart felt experience and dreams.; [a.] Charleston, IL

EDWARDS, ROSEMARIE
[pen.] Rosemarie Edwards; [pers.] My goal is to reach out and touch others through my writings.; [a.] Chicago, IL

EGAN, PATRICK
[b.] July 29, 1929, Lansing MI; [m.] Char, July 23, 1955; [ch.] Five; [ed.] Advanced degrees in Guidance and Counseling; [occ.] Retired Educator, Volunteer - President of the Blue Ridge Center for Lifelong Learning.; [memb.] National Board for Certified Counselors; [oth. writ.] Numerous Educational Article in a a variety of publications; [pers.] It does no good to have the world as your oyster if you can't get it out of the shell.

EICHMAN, RICHARD P.
[p.] Paul and Lenore Eichman; [ed.] Peabody Conservatory of Music, John Hopkins University, Schuler School of Fine Arts; [occ.] Oil portraitist in "old master" tradition, correspondent with the Carrol Country Times; [memb.] Member and organist of St. James' Lutheran Church Union Bridge; [oth. writ.] Wookly column in the Carrol Country Times; [pers.] Chief interest: The English language, its usage and literature influences: In poetry, the British neo-classic poets from pope to Byron, in prose, Sir Walter Scott, Baron Macaulay, and H. W. Fowler; [a.] Union Bridge, MD

EILENBERGER, HEIDI
[pen.] Heidi Marie; [b.] April 19, 1978, Buffalo, NY; [p.] Bruce and Vicki Eilenberger; [ed.] Living Word Academy; [occ.] Sales Associate for Costume Jewelry; [hon.] This is my first; [oth. writ.] Several writings in school newspaper and school literary magazine.; [pers.] My only dream is that people can see the world through my eyes within my poetry.; [a.] Lititz, PA

EILER, DOROTHEA M.
[b.] March 8, 1922, Long Beach, CA; [p.] Charles and Flora Eiler; [m.] January 20, 1944; [ch.] Three children, Two Grandchildren; [ed.] BA UCLA, 1942 MA United States International University, 1966; [occ.] Retired, freelance writer; [oth. writ.] Various National PUBCS. Editorial for various newspapers from the wall street Journal to San Diego Union Tribune, Travel Pieces and Tourist info.; [pers.] There's something about the discipline of sonnet that I like. Usually I feel strongly about the subject, and the form puts my feelings under control.; [a.] Rosarito Beach Baja California, Mexico

EK, DAWN A.
[pen.] Alene Ekler; [b.] December 12, 1920, Momence, IL; [p.] Hilda Bailey Strickland, Frank Strickland; [m.] Thomas Ek, December 12, 1942; [ch.] Paul, David, William; [ed.] Elementary Schools, E. Chicago, Indiana, Novikoff, Chicago, Illinois, Classical Ballet, Sorbonne University, Paris, France, Mme. Preobrajenska, Classical Ballet, Univ. of Musical Arts, Thai Classical Dance, Bangkok, Thailand, Harper College, Writing Courses; [occ.] Retired; [memb.] Chicago Cnic Opera Ballet Co. (1932), Ballet Russe De Monte Carlo (1936), The Michael Morokin Ballet N.Y., Lyric Opera Ballet, Chicago, Lilacia School of Classical Ballet, Owner, Teacher, Lombard, Illinois; [oth. writ.] Short Stories - "The Rap", "Interlude"; [pers.] For happiness and satisfaction, we must act our roles in God's play to the fullest, knowing this life's game is merely one of many, yet to be imagined!; [a.] Leslie, AK

ELLIOTT, BRIAN
[b.] October 20, 1970, Cincinnati, OH; [p.] Judy Mae Handley and Robert Grab Elliott; [ed.] Milford High School; [occ.] District Manager, The Art Works Corp.; [hon.] National Choral Award Thespian; [oth. writ.] One poems published in my High School Paper; [pers.] My poetry is a reflection of me If only everyone could see themselves as only human, our world would be a better place.; [a.] Indianapolis, IN

ELLIOTT, STACEY MARIE
[pen.] Stacey Elliott, Stacey Parks; [b.] April 21, 1972, Baltimore, MD; [p.] John B. Parks, Mary Ann Parks; [m.] James R. Elliott Jr., April 2, 1994; [ed.] Pikesville High School Frostburg State University; [memb.] National Multiple Sclerosis Society, National Audubon Society, National Geographic Society, Whale Adoption Project, Clean Water Action; [oth. writ.] Several other poems published in Frostburg State University's art and literary magazine the "Bittersweet", another poem published by The National Library Of The Poetry in the anthology "Mists of Enchantment".; [pers.] For me, writing puts those intense feelings that are hard to express verbally on paper in words that others can read and experience; [a.] Gaithersburg, MD

ELMER, JOLENE JOY
[b.] July 7, 1972, Phoenix, AZ; [p.] Evan and Nita Elmer; [ed.] Barry Goldwater High, Phoenix College; [occ.] Interpreter for the Deaf For Mesa School District and Personal Respite Care Provider; [memb.] The Church of Jesus Christ of Latter-Day Saints; [hon.] Miss. Lo Mia; [oth. writ.] Working on a Book; [pers.] It's easy for people to say they will die for what they believe in, but how many of us have the strength to live for it.; [a.] Mesa, AZ

ELMI, LINDA
[b.] August 29, 1965, Winnipeg, Manitoba, Canada; [p.] Carlotta and Andrew Krenkewich; [m.] Abdul Jibar Elmi, July 26, 1990; [ed.] University of Manitoba; [occ.] Support worker; [a.] Winnipeg Manitoba, Canada

ELMORE, KATIE
[pen.] Kat; [b.] October 20, 1982, Walnut Creek, CA; [p.] Lynda and Michael Elmore; [occ.] 7th Grade student at Walnut Creek Intermediate "WCI"; [hon.] For soccer I was awarded for the most improved for a straight year; [oth. writ.] Composed many other poems for self expressions and satisfaction; [pers.] I love playing sports and writing poetry. My favorite sports is soccer. I like writing poems about earth and it's environment. Also now it is and how we can help fix it.; [a.] Walnut Creek, CA

ELSBREE, MICHELLE PECORA
[b.] June 16, 1969, Rochester, NY; [m.] Todd M. Elsbree, October 24, 1992; [ed.] Bishop Kearney High School St Bonaventure University B.A. in English; [occ.] Librarian Rochester NY; [hon.] Dean's List in College, Various Scholarship granted at College.; [pers.] I strive to relate my experiences as realistically as possible, whether good or bad, in general and specific ways which may reflect other people's lives.; [a.] Rochester, NY

ELYEA, TRENT
[pen.] Trent Elyea; [b.] July 29, 1956, Collingwood, Ontario, Canada; [p.] Dewey and Jean; [ch.] Emma, Joshua, Justin, Ryan; [ed.] Collingwood Collegiate Institute Ontario Fire College Graduate Seneca

College graduate, Georgian College graduate; [occ.] Fire Captain Clarington Fire Dept.; [memb.] Provincial Federation of Ontario Firefighters, International Association of Fire Investigators, Durham Critical Incident Stress Team.; [hon.] Certified Municipal Manager (CCM); [oth. writ.] Several poems published in Canadian firefighter, poems turned song - firefighters Christmas.; [pers.] The public just does not understand firefighters. Our job is an emotional as it is physical. My poems reflect that both paid and volunteer firefighters deserve a lot of credit.

ELZA, STACEY
[b.] July 24, 1980, Elkins, WV; [p.] Eric and Susan Elza; [occ.] Student; [oth. writ.] First place in the 1995 Christmas Writing Contest held by local paper, the Walter E. Clarke Middle School Literary Anthology 1994, the Socorro Independent School District Literary Anthology 1994, the Morgantown High School Literary Magazine 1995; [a.] Morgantown, WV

EMBRO, JAMES CHRISTOPHER
[pen.] Jimmy; [b.] July 31, Guelph, Ontario, Canada; [p.] Mr. and Mrs. Michael Embro; [m.] Jean Parker (Widowed), August 4, 1947; [ch.] 5 grown-up and away; [ed.] High School Comp., Accomplished Musical Theory (Conservatory) - Musical Director and Composer Arranger; [occ.] Amateur Writer, Lifetime Hobby - "Great" Library; [memb.] Leave of Absence "Musicians" - many years an Orchestra Leader and Dance Band Entertainment; [hon.] Winner "Directors Award", "Musical Directing", 1st Prize "Canadian Music League" Balim Leader and "Conductor", "Composer", and "Arranger" (Music); [oth. writ.] "Hundreds" of Compositions... all put to "Musical Scone"... Complete... Arrangements and "Beautiful" "Very" Interesting!; [pers.] Have been an amateur "Composer" and "Musical Writer" and "Arranger" life-time. Studied theory at Conservatory of Music - had 21 pc. Orchestra "Bio Band" - like "Lawrence Welke" and Sammy Kaye Stylings - Dance Band.; [a.] Guelph Ontario, Canada

ENGLISH, SHERYL J.
[b.] June 23, 1964, Whitehorse Yukon; [p.] Robert English and Lauraine Collier; [ch.] Justin, Darren, Devan; [ed.] Eastern Commerce, Canada College; [occ.] Receptionist/Clerk typist; [hon.] Nominated for the ontario Ministry of Agriculture Terra (Employee) award by peers; [oth. writ.] Published Articles in PDR Notes; [pers.] I been writing poems since I was little, I was my escape a place I could voice my opinion and be heard; [a.] Toronto Ontario, Canada

ENNIS, MARK EDWARD

ENNS, KIMBERLEY
[b.] November 3, 1973, Winnipeg, Manitoba, Canada; [p.] John Enns and Tillie Enns; [ed.] South Delta Senior Secondary BA Degree From Trinity Western University; [memb.] The Planetary Society BC Horse Council Canadian Federation, Trinity Western Alumni Assn South Delta Baptist Church; [hon.] Delta Riding Club Sportsmanship Award; [pers.] I am a firm believer in the statement: What the mind can conceive and the heart believes, the body can achieve!; [a.] Delta British Columbia, Canada

EPPS, ALMA JEAN
[pen.] Alma Jean Epps; [b.] January 20, 1935, Evansville, IN; [p.] Vivian - Newman, Marvin - Townsend; [m.] Melvin Keeton Epps Sr., June 7, 1966; [ch.] Brad Scott, Timothy Allen, Melvin Keeton Jr; [ed.] High Central, Tri State beauty College Elementary School, Emma Roach High hon. in art won draw me contest, designed some of my clothing have a great love for children.; [occ.] Fairlawn School; [memb.] Jehovah Witness I have a great love for God I take care of my mother so I have no member ships at this time; [hon.] Draw me contest excelled in art designed clothe for plays the teaches's at school talked me into sending in my poem.; [oth. writ.] I write many poems, and I have wrote a beautiful song that no one has seen I wrote with my heart not my hand it is my out let away of letting out my feelings"; [pers.] My very deep love of a wonderful man from an Eastern Country that I had give up because of family obligations that I could not turn my back on I have tried to find him since my obligation ended. To no avail.; [a.] Evansville, IN

EPPS, MARGANETTE
[pen.] Margie Epps; [b.] March 22, 1958, Baltimore, MD; [p.] David McFadden, Martha McFadden; [m.] Lonnie Epps Jr., July 24, 1982; [ch.] Tayvon Lajuane Epps, Vernell Chrishawn Epps; [ed.] Paul Laurence Dunbar Senior High School, Community College of the Baltimore, National Education Center; [occ.] Office Secretary II, Dept. of Labor, Licensing and Regulation, Baltimore, Md; [memb.] God's People Union Worship Center on the Ministerial Staff, Praise and Worship Team, Department Head for Intercessory Prayer Group, Department Head of Counselors.; [hon.] Graduated in the top 5% of my graduating class, (Honor Student). Received Phi Beta Kappa Scholarship to attend College, received awards in Shorthand, Typing, and office Practice.; [oth. writ.] I have a compilation of 45 original poems and psalms, on various subjects, in my book entitled - "Moments."; [pers.] My poems and psalms have been divinely inspired by the Holy Spirit. All of my writings contain a prophetic message to the believer, and even more so to the unbeliever.; [a.] Baltimore, MD

ERICKSON, PATRICIA J.
[pen.] Patricia Rindahl Erickson; [b.] February 4, 1939, Valley City, ND; [p.] Melvin (Deceased) and Marie Rindahl; [m.] Gerald Erickson, December 28, 1958; [ch.] Brian Anthony, Steven Shane, Michelle Marie, Wade Matthew, Kristi Ruth; [ed.] Oakes Public High School, St Luke's Nurse's Training (1 yr) Joliet Jr. College; [occ.] Radio announcer for KTIG Christian radio, Pequot Lakes; [memb.] Messiah Lutheran Church, Minnesota Citizens Concerned for life, Inter Varsity Christian Fellowship, Lutherans for life of will country and IL; [hon.] American Legion Constitution Award, Girl's state, student Council, Graduated H.S. and Jr. College with Honors, (President's List); [oth. writ.] Messiah Messenger newsletter articles, Jr. College newspaper ("Blazer") articles and "wordeater" creative with magazine poetry and stories.; [pers.] Inspirational and devotional messages provide means for me to convey encouragement and hope to others by relating the blessings God has given my life.; [a.] Merrifield, MN

ESTAREJA, ROMULO HABLA
[pen.] Ronnie H. Estareja; [b.] October 10, 1939, Philippines; [p.] Domingo and Presentacion Estareja; [m.] Milagros H. Estareja, February 14, 1964; [ch.] Robert and Imelda Estareja; [ed.] Casiguran High School; [occ.] Nurse-Therapist; [oth. writ.] 50 more unpublished original poems.; [pers.] Hoping to touch someone life with love, goodness, truth and beauty-that's why I write.; [a.] San Gabriel, CA

ETESSE, GABRIELLE
[b.] September 7, 1976; [p.] Kathi and George Etesse; [ed.] Sycamore High School, Bowling Green State University; [occ.] College student, Sunday School Teacher; [memb.] Kappa Delta, Sorority Bowling Green State University Honors Program; [hon.] Student of the week Sycamore High School (94-95); [pers.] If you don't try you will never know if you can succeed. Sometimes the best way to heal someone is to say nothing but hear everything.; [a.] Cincinnati, OH

EVANS, BERNADINE AYERS
[b.] July 12, 1923, Grantsville, WV; [p.] Bernard H. Ayers and Sue Ferrell Ayers; [m.] Walter Evans, October 1, 1971; [ch.] Bernard L. Reed; [ed.] Calhoren County High School Institute of Practical Nursing 1962; [occ.] Home keeper; [memb.] American Legion Auxiliary 50 years member, Knotts Memorial Methodist church, 72 year member; [hon.] 50 Years membership in the American Legion Auxiliary Life member of Knotts Memorial Church; [oth. writ.] "Ode to Billie Brown" "Ode to Gene Norris God and Prayer" "Spirit, Hope, Faith and Friends" "God Cares" "Ode to Committee on Aging" "Two Roses Still Grow"; [pers.] I am a Ham Radio I was married to William Reed Operator and Walter Evans I've help cook for the army reserves and Lions club Grantsville also the last mans club; [a.] Grantsville, WV

EVANS, LILIAN
[b.] May 19, 1932, Manchester, England; [p.] James Hassall, Lilian Hassall; [m.] James Evans, January 16, 1954; [ch.] Cheryl, Dianne, Christine, Joanne; [ed.] High School, Loreburn Business College England; [occ.] Home maker; [pers.] I tend to write about emotions and feelings, being a sensitive person myself; [a.] North Vancouver British Columbia, Canada

EVERETT, BERNADETTE
[pen.] Doll; [b.] November 18, 1948, Lynchburg, VA; [p.] Mrs. Beatrice Diuguid; [m.] Daniel, January 30, 1970; [ch.] Daniel Jr., Brandon; [ed.] Campbell County H.S., Central VA. Community College; [occ.] Direct care giver mental retarded (retired); [memb.] Mt. Zion Baptist Church, American Canter; [hon.] Certicates Award in working with the mental retarded; [oth. writ.] Behind the walls my struggle as a black woman I live here; [pers.] I try to let people know that everyone is their own person. No one should pass judgment on anyone for being different.; [a.] Lynchburg, VA

FAIR, MONA E.
[b.] August 12, 1940, Langruth, Manitoba, Canada; [p.] Alma and Steve Thorlakson; [m.] Raymond Fair, December 5, 1959; [ch.] Charles Frederick; [ed.] R.H. King and Winston Churchill Collegiates, Scarborough, ON, post-secondary courses at Ryerson

Polytechnical Institute, Central Baptist Seminary, and University of Waterloo, Grade V111 Piano, Grade 11 Theory, Toronto Conservatory of Music; [memb.] Etobicoke Art Group, Neilson Park Creative Centre, St. Paul's Presbyterian Church, Women Alive, Shaklee Canada, Metropolitan Toronto Chapter-Multiple Sclerosis Society; [oth. writ.] Poem, What I need, Conquest Magazine, 1963, Social column in Etobicoke Advertiser-Guardian, (1971-87), News Report on Joni Eareckson Tada, The Evangelical Baptist (1987); [pers.] I am a committed Christian. I believe that Jesus is the solution for the evil and turmoil in the world. Marana tha.; [a.] Etobicoke Ontario, Canada

FARMER, SILAS
[pen.] Silas Farmer; [b.] December 5, 1946, Bedford, IN; [p.] John and Lucille; [m.] Lois E., September 17, 1976; [ch.] London Taylor; [ed.] B.S., M.S. Indiana Univ., Principal's License; [occ.] Teacher, 4th Grade; [memb.] Woodville Baptist Church, Masonic Lodge No. 228 (Past Master and Secretary) U.S.A.F., Ind. Nat. Guard, Ret.; [hon.] A second place in an anthology.; [oth. writ.] Published in several anthologies.; [pers.] To be able to say what I feel when I see beauty is an awesome feeling. To have someone else say "I could feel that," is a real high for me.; [a.] Mitchell, IN

FARR, DIANE MARIE
[b.] June 11, 1949, Hawkesbury, Ontario, Canada; [p.] Marcel and Laura Sadoquis; [ch.] Lisa Laura Marie, Steven Leonard Marcel, Jason Norman Thomas, Richard Maurice Joseph; [pers.] In my writings, I endeavor to see beauty in a troubled world. Attempting to employ empathy in under- standing the pain and injustice that surrounds us in these ever changing lines.; [a.] Watford Ontario, Canada

FARRAR, R. SARAH
[b.] October 10, 1941, Pittston, PA; [p.] Edward J. Courtney and Susan (Pignatone) Courtney; [m.] Edward B. Farrar, August 20, 1957; [ch.] Michael Edward, Steven Clifford, and Douglas Chance; [ed.] Tucson High, Glendale Community College; [occ.] Real Estate Sales, Services and Investments; [memb.] HBA Sales and Marketing, D.A.V. Aux.; [hon.] Associate of Arts Degree with "High" - Distinction, Phi Theta Kappa, Dean's List; [oth. writ.] Poetry: Crown of Light, The Nightingale, Nature's Connection, The Mask, A Moment Away, (among others); [pers.] I enjoy expressing my deepest perceptions of "truth", in an intense fashion of fantasy, drama, romance and sincerity.; [a.] Glendale, AZ

FARRELL, RONALD
[b.] November 13, 1964, Dallas, Texas; [p.] Cliff and Linda Farrell; [ed.] Oil City Senior High, The Art Institute of Pittsburgh - Associates Degree in Photography; [occ.] Photographer and Part-time Cashier at Toy Store.; [memb.] Played Flute Two Years in School Band, Wresting Team Two years, one Year as Editor and Reporter for School Paper. College - Student Ambassador. 1987 - Church of Scientology.; [hon.] Grade School - Certificate for "Good Reader", College - Certificate for Perfect Attendance, Honor Roll; [pers.] Man is basically good. We're factually spiritual beings. Life is a game that is to be played and won by all, achieving the prize of optimum survival.; [a.] Vero Beach, FL

FARROW, JUNE M.
[pen.] J. Maria; [b.] May 23, 1929, Amesbury, MA; [p.] Wm. and Irene Farrow; [m.] Divorced; [ch.] Baker, Larry, Alex, Dennis, Bryan; [ed.] Public and Private Education in Mass., Calif. and Oregon, California Community College Teaching Credential Securities and Insurance Training; [occ.] Owner/ Mgr. Professional Management Consulting - Business and Language Training; [oth. writ.] Various poems published in National Library of Poetry anthologies.; [pers.] All men have feet of clay. There are no heroes among us. Examine your love for God and neighbour. Therein lies the measure of character.; [a.] Victoria British Columbia, Canada

FAULCONER, JULIE ELIZABETH
[b.] June 15, 1962, Elgin, IL; [p.] Mires C. and Janice E. Stine; [m.] Michael A. Faulconer, April 19, 1986; [ch.] Matthew, Caitlin, Brandon; [ed.] Albert Einstein Sr. High, Frederick Community College; [occ.] Owner, The Perfect Word; [memb.] Hospice of Frederick County; [oth. writ.] Other poems and short, short stories; [pers.] It is my hope that I connect with people by the intimacy of my words.; [a.] Walkersville, MD

FAZEL, ROBIN
[b.] April 6, 1960, Salina, KS; [p.] Phannitta J. Brugger and Danny D. Fazel; [ed.] I received my High School Diploma at Kansas State School for the Visually Handicapped; [pers.] I believe that parents need to came down to the children's way of thinking, instead of forcing the children to go above their minds. And that parents should encourage the children to reach out for their goals. For their influenced should come from their hearts.; [a.] Casper, WY

FECTEAU, MARY
[b.] February 23, 1960, Spokane, WA; [p.] Bruce and Ernestine Siggins; [m.] Pierre, August 15, 1987; [ch.] Peter, Nicole Dorothy; [ed.] Palm Beach Lakes High, North Tech., LPN; [occ.] Homemaker; [pers.] Everyday is a Gift from God. Staring with a Beautiful Sunrise - ending with the Sunset, enjoy it.; [a.] Whitesberg, TN

FEELEY JR., ROBERT WILLIAM
[pen.] Easy; [ed.] Grade 12 Diploma; [occ.] Lic. Auto Body Technician, Lic. Spray Painter, Lic. Welder 2 tickets, taking Architectural course right now hoping to become an architect; [hon.] Won an award for my gingerbread work. Won a beautifica- tion award for landscaping my home. 2 Trophies for my big brother achievements. 3 Trophies for my auto and bike painting. 63 Trophies for my racing cars professionally (5 years).; [oth. writ.] Written short stories (1st. and a 3rd. place), been writing poetry for some years now. I write what I think and feel.; [pers.] I get influenced by my travels and experienced and last but not least my loved ones.

FELIX, PAUL A.
[b.] December 25, 1964, Houston; [p.] Ms. Gladys H. Wright; [m.] Roslyn L. Felix, February 13, 1988; [ch.] Paul A. Felix Jr.; [ed.] Art Institute - Houston G.C. Scarborough High School, Clifton Middle School, K. Smith Ele.; [occ.] Machinist/Free Lance Artist; [hon.] Creative Writing Award; [pers.] Look deep into the wisdom of our Lord, search deep into the heart in which you possess faith. There you will reveal the love that only he can give. If you truly

believe in him. H.S. Church. College Newsletters.; [a.] Houston, TX

FELTNER, MARY ELAINE
[b.] April 5, 1943, Texas; [m.] Gus R.H. Feltner, Jr., June 29, 1963; [ch.] 2 sons, 3 granddaughters, 1 grandson; [ed.] Masters in Education; [occ.] Teacher and Coordinator of Gifted Education; [pers.] I have been inspired by the love of my children and grandchildren and my many students.; [a.] Devine, TX

FELTY, KATHEE M.
[pen.] Kathee M. Felty; [b.] December 10, 1950, Chelsea, MA; [p.] Arthur (J.) and Margaret (M.) Gleason; [m.] Earl R. Felty, August 29, 1986; [ch.] Christopher (E.), Melissa (M.), Amanda (G.); [ed.] Wheeler High School, North Stonington, Conn.; [occ.] Owner of Tanning Salon, Secretary to E.R. Felty Inc., Poet, Part-time - West Berks Crier, Newspaper, Notary; [memb.] National Society of Poetry, International Society of Poetry; [hon.] Editor's Choice Award (1995), The International Poet of Merit Award 1995; [oth. writ.] "Again" published in Carvings in Stone, "Melissa" published " At Waters Edge", "Taylor", "Best Poems of 1996", "Grandmother" published in "Tomorrows Dream", "Time" published in "Beneath The Harvest Moon", several poems published in the Reading Eagle Times - Newspaper, "You Should Be Thankful" published in "Where Dawn Lingers"; [pers.] Love is the beginning and the end, the very essence of mankind, the secret of happiness. Strive to be the best you can be.; [a.] Wernersville, PA

FERGUSON, GREG
[b.] June 27, 1943, Miami, FL; [p.] Donald and Laura; [ch.] Brian Sandy; [occ.] Computer Specialist; [pers.] I wrote this poem to let a friend know that even in total despair, there is always a reason for living, and that there is always love to be given or rec'd.

FERGUSON, KEVIN W.
[b.] June 12, 1961, Barrie, Ontario; [m.] Rosemary Golding; [ch.] Adam, Joshua, Jesse; [ed.] Father Henry Carr S.S., Etobicoke, Ont - Creative Arts, Georgian College, Barrie Campus (Jan. '96), (have not started college as of the date); [occ.] Artisan - Student; [oth. writ.] Earlier poems published in newspapers. Songwriting is of greatest interest, although short stories and a novel are in the works. Life is my inspiration.; [pers.] The plains of my youth are held barren and dry, across great expanse must the memories now fly. Without precious love to guide true, destined flight, I'm afraid all is lost, of the pain I must write.

FERNANDEZ, ABBY C.
[b.] October 2, 1983, Portland, OR; [p.] Adrienne Fernandez Stout, Ron Stout and Kelly Korhonen; [oth. writ.] Listen to the Cries, published in local newspaper.; [pers.] I'm a twelve year old, who enjoys playing softball, and reading The Norton Anthology of Poetry. My poems are often inspired by things I've gone through. My favorite thing about the world today is being here right now.; [a.] Camas, WA

FEROCE, CYNTHIA L.
[b.] Concord, CA; [p.] Kenneth and Nancy Walters; [m.] Anthony Feroce, September '90; [ch.] Kenneth

Feroce; [ed.] Hilton Central High School, Hilton New York; [occ.] Principal Office Assistant, Monroe County Family Court; [oth. writ.] "A Special Gift" published in the Echoes of Yesterday 1995, "With You" published in Best Poems of 1995; [pers.] Life is a gift. A gift we are too consumed to enjoy during the daily grind that we live. Through my poems, I hope to remind myself and others of the purpose to life, and that the simplest of things, can sometimes be the sweetest, so don't consciously overlook it.; [a.] Rochester, NY

FERRAZ, CATHERINE
[pen.] Catherine Weller; [b.] October 28, 1938; [pers.] My motto in this life is ..."For ye have not passed this way here to fore." (Bible O.T.); [a.] Strathmore Alberta, Canada

FIELDING, CAROL
[b.] June, Toronto, Ontario; [p.] Max and Ann Fielding; [ed.] R.T., A.R.T.; [occ.] Retired; [hon.] Editor's Choice Award from National Library of Poetry for 1995; [oth. writ.] Short stories, poems; [pers.] I try to put people's feelings into words. I greatly admire Robert Frost, and Emily Dickinson.; [a.] Sherwood Park Alberta, Canada

FIGUEROA, DESIREE
[b.] September 15, 1980, Woodbridge, VA; [p.] Joanna Woodard, Jose Antonio Figueroa; [ed.] Potomac Senior High School, 10th Grade.; [occ.] High School Student; [memb.] Patriots of Northern Virginia; [oth. writ.] This is my first poem to actually be published. I'm so happy. I didn't think it would ever happen.; [pers.] I just write poems for fun but my friends and family pushed me to enter my poem. And look where it put me. Thanks. Krissy, Tanisha, Mom, and my nephew Angle Shawn. You would never think a 15 year old could do this.; [a.] Woodbridge, VA

FINNEGAN, EMMETT PATRICK
[b.] December 9, 1962, Edmonton, Alberta; [p.] Owen and Jennie Finnegan; [ed.] Grade 12 Diploma, Cowichan Senior Secondary, Duncan, B.C.; [occ.] Supervisor of Cabin Services, Canada 3000 Airlines Ltd.; [hon.] This is the first time I have ever written any poetry and I really enjoy it. I am accomplished dancer and currently studying acting. I have received many dance awards.; [oth. writ.] I have many poems unpublished, that I'd like to write and give to friends/family. This will be my first published poem.; [pers.] I like to be simple yet creative in my writing. I like to express an idea or thought in a different way and make people pause and reflect to see my view.; [a.] Vancouver British Columbia, Canada

FISHER, JUANITA
[b.] January 13, 1934, Winston Salem, NC; [p.] William and Irene Jarrett; [m.] Deceased, June 5, 1959; [ch.] Seven - One; [ed.] High School Graduate 1952, Atkins High School, Winston-Salem, NC; [occ.] Retired; [memb.] Tenant Association; [hon.] Voices of New York, Poetry Readings - Six Community Service Plaques; [oth. writ.] Play "Eny", assortments of poems, Sagus - ODES - on different subjects - People - etc.; [pers.] "I look through your own eyes" and what you can't put out your mouth. Put it on paper."; [a.] Brooklyn, NY

FISHER, SHIRLEY MARIE
[b.] October 16, 1931, Hamilton, Ontario; [p.] Elsie Melvina Fisher and Marquis C. Fisher; [ch.] Linda, Bill, Deborah, Cynthia, Laura; [oth. writ.] I have written 15 other poems.; [pers.] I started to attend "Unity" approximately fifteen years ago, "Unity" teaches metaphysical truths. Approximately eight years ago I became interested in the "Infinite Way" "Teachings" of `Joel Goldsmith'. These poems come through me when I go within myself.; [a.] Hamilton Ontario, Canada

FISTER, JOHN WILLIAM
[b.] October 9, 1959, Windsor, Ontario, Canada; [p.] Mildred, Stanley Joseph; [ch.] Katelyn Autumn, Ryan Johnathan; [ed.] Simon Fraser University, Burnaby, B.C., B. Ed., B.A. Cultural Geography, Minors, Early Childhood and Special Education, Walkerville S.S., Windsor, Ontario.; [occ.] Social Studies, Law Teacher, David Thompson S.S., Vancouver, B.C.; [oth. writ.] A host of unpublished poems, ex. "Lavender and Lilac", "Lines", "Love's Buried Treasure", "Egotesticle", and "One People". Two children's stories, "The Christmas Seals - Nandor and Sheeba", and "Crissy the Christmas Cone".; [pers.] Sometimes satirical, my writings are passionate, philosophical, and personal. My inspiration is drawn from the works of nature and the culturally diverse people of Vancouver.; [a.] Port Coquitlam British Columbia, Canada

FLETCHER, MICHELE L.
[b.] March 14, 1963, Bremerton, WA; [p.] Dorothy and Forrest Gross; [m.] Kenneth W. Fletcher, April 5, 1986; [ch.] Erin Michael, David Wayne and Sarrah Loyce; [ed.] Graduate of Central Kitsap High School, Silverdale, WA; [occ.] Civil Service Employee, Puget Sound Naval Shipy; [pers.] First time published; [a.] Bremerton, WA

FLETCHER, RUTH D.
[b.] December 13, 1931, Toronto, Ontario, Canada; [p.] Harold Sleeth and Mary Wicks Sleeth; [m.] Ronald W. Fletcher, December 24, 1959; [ch.] Andrea Ruth, Ronald Wm. Jr. (Jay); [ed.] Aurora District High School; [occ.] Retired (Former Office Manager); [memb.] Connecting Rainbows Breast Cancer Support Group; [oth. writ.] Nineteen other poems, none published at this time.; [pers.] I started writing poetry in May of 1995 following surgery and treatment for breast cancer. I look upon my poetry as a gift for the poems appear randomly and spontaneously. I call my poetry songs of the spirit and thank God for this gift.; [a.] Newmarket Ontario, Canada

FLORIO, MELISSA
[pen.] Melissa Gabrielle; [b.] June 25, 1977, Los Angeles, CA; [p.] Carmela and Jerry Florio; [ed.] Attended Taravella High School in Florida and now at Florida Atlantic University; [occ.] Dance and Gymnastics instructor for children.; [memb.] I am getting ready to join DEA, Dance Educators of America; [hon.] I won the Presidents Award in 7th grade. I won Choreographer of the Year Award in 10th grade. I won Poem of the Year in 10th grade. Honor Roll through school.; [oth. writ.]I have so many, the list is endless. The poem I won for was called "Cindy" a poem about drug abuse.; [pers.] I write how I feel, I put my words on paper because sometimes they come out better that way. I was

influenced by my mother, my best friend.; [a.] Coral Springs, FL

FLYNN, SARAH PENNEY
[b.] September 16, 1979, Pickering, Ontario; [p.] Herbert and Joan Penney Flynn; [ed.] Presently taking Grade Eleven High School (Honor Student), Pasadena Academy; [occ.] High School Student; [memb.] Church Youth Group Executive (Pentecostal); [hon.] Grades Six through Ten received overall honors awards. Various recognitions received locally for literary pieces.; [oth. writ.] Several pieces written for local publication. Mostly stories and poems for personal use.; [pers.] The blood of my writing tends to come from my own personal struggles, what I consider the injustices and oddities of society, and my experiences of love. Que Sera Sera.; [a.] Pasadena Newfoundland, Canada

FOGLEMAN, HUELANI MEI
[pen.] Mei West; [b.] September 12, 1939, Redwo; [p.] Pualani West, David West; [occ.] Student at Garrison Mill Elementary, Grade K; [pers.] To always dream of wonderful things.

FOISEY, RUSSELL
[pers.] The more you endure, the more you learn and easier life becomes.

FOLLIS, LINDA ANNE
[pen.] Linda Follis; [b.] January 22, 1947, Toronto, Ontario; [p.] John C. Follis, Kay (Lauria) Follis; [ed.] High School; [occ.] Electronic Banking Analyst, Bank of Nova Scotia; [oth. writ.] This is my first submission for publication but I have been writing poetry since 1961.; [pers.] This poem is dedicated to my brother Michael, March 17, 1951 - March 21 '92. Death is a stepping stone.; [a.] East York Ontario, Canada

FORD, ANDREA SHANNON
[b.] August 23, 1972, Plano, TX; [p.] Martha Sue Jackson, Frank Ford; [ch.] Mitchell Lee, Wesley Dillon; [ed.] Pre-Nursing Student University of Texas at Arlington; [occ.] Faculty Lecturer UTA, also student; [memb.] Allied Health Society, Native American Student Association; [hon.] 4.0 GPA at University of Texas at Arlington; [oth. writ.] Several unsubmitted poems not currently published, poetry published in "Messenger" Newsletters in Ft. Worth area.; [pers.] My poetry reflects feelings towards people or situations regarding my experience, strength and hope. I only strive to reach one other who may, through my poetry, no longer feel alone.; [a.] Arlington, TX

FORDHAM, R. DAVID
[pen.] R. David Fordham; [b.] August 9, 1943, Baltimore, MD; [p.] Robert Fordham, Frances Fallon; [m.] Doris Schriefer Fordham, July 5, 1975; [ch.] Robert Benjamin, Margaret Anne; [ed.] University of Maryland, Strayers Business College, University of Baltimore; [occ.] Lawyer - Assistant State's Attorney For Anne Arundel County; [memb.] National District Attorneys Association, Marylands State Attorney's Association, Anne Arundel County Bar Association; [oth. writ.] This is my first published poem.; [pers.] The words of a poem are like music to the human mind.; [a.] Arnold, MD

FORGACS, JOE
[b.] December 9, 1965, Cincinnati, OH; [m.] Christina Worrall, May 20, 1995; [ed.] Bachelor of Science in Geology, University of Cincinnati (1989); [memb.] Big Brothers/Big Sisters of the Bluegrass; [pers.] I have been interested in poetry since I was ten years old. I started writing songs after moving in 1990 to Frankfort, Kentucky. I enjoy challenging myself by writing on a variety of subjects.; [a.] Frankport, KY

FORSYTHE, BRIAN M.
[b.] February 26, 1960, Cape Girardeau, MO; [ed.] North Miami Senior, Diploma 1978, Harding University, BSN, 1991; [occ.] Registered Nurse, BSN, RN, Specializing in Psychiatric Nursing; [pers.] Human Nature, that of our thoughts, feelings, and behaviors, along with nature, that of the world we live in, and share are strong motivated for my waiting. Also much thanks must be given to Donna Walls for inspiration, earl Wescott for encouragement, and to Brenda Forsythe, my sister for loving support always!; [a.] Little Rock, AK

FOSTER, CHRISTY H.
[b.] May 25, 1982, Sacramento, CA; [p.] Shannon Ludwick, Marc Foster, Step Father Dale Ludwick; [occ.] She baby-sits her cousin - Breanna; [memb.] Sunrise Roller Land - she loves to skate and be social with her friends; [oth. writ.] She writes poems for fun.; [pers.] This was a special poem Christy wrote for her Grandfather Jack A. Perry who died 6-29-95. She thought this would be a special way to show how much he meant to her.; [a.] Orangeville, CA

FOSTER, CYNTHIA E.
[pen.] C. E. Foster; [b.] March 13, 1955, La Rochelle, France; [p.] Mr. and Mrs. Charles I. Turner; [m.] Raymond A. Foster, June 4, 1972; [ch.] David 1972, Daniel 1976; [ed.] Father in service went to several schools. Last school attended was Camanche H.S., Camanche, Iowa.; [occ.] K-Mart Merchandiser, K-Mart 7256, about 8 years, Richmond, Va; [hon.] Receive Several K - Chairman's Awards from K-Mart.; [oth. writ.] Aunt Leones, Home, Grandpas Everywhere, not been submitted or published yet.; [pers.] I believe that each of us are God's Miracles. I believe saying a kind word or doing a good deed each day is part of our purpose on this earth.; [a.] Richmond, VA

FOSTER, LISA
[b.] May 18, 1978, Ingersoll, Ontario, Canada; [ed.] Grade 12 student at IDCI in Ingersoll, Ontario, I plan to study anthropology in University.; [hon.] Several poetry publications within my school and county, grade 12 Art Award; [oth. writ.] Very active in the student government, along with many other clubs with my school. Along with a friend, I run a penpal program at school, to help people become aware of places outside of Canada.; [pers.] I believe that the greatest failure in life is not even trying. One of mentors told me that and to this day, that statement makes me finish the things I've started.; [a.] Ingersoll Ontario, Canada

FOSTER, MANDY MICHELLE
[pen.] Michelle Foster; [b.] October 22, 1977, Little Rock, AR; [p.] Andrew Foster and Sandy Jewell; [ch.] Son: Dexter Ray Barton; [ed.] Mena High School Graduate 1996; [occ.] Florist: Stewman's

Florist, Mena, AR; [memb.] FBLA, French Club, FCS, Sports, Science Club, and GCE in High School; [hon.] Honorable Mention in Art Show, October 1995; [oth. writ.] I have many other poems which have not been sent to any publishers or entered in any contests yet.; [pers.] Poetry is best written by the heart, not for assignments, only then can it truly be felt.; [a.] Mena, AR

FOSTON, DON P.
[b.] May 9, 1930, Dartmouth, NS; [p.] Paul and Olive Foston; [m.] Mary Foston, April 18, 1953; [ch.] Douglas Robert, Cheryl Lee; [ed.] Scarboro Coll., Inst., Extensive Training in Graphic Technology; [occ.] Retired; [memb.] Gilbert and Sullivan Society - St. Annes Music and Drama Society, Whitby Jubilee Choir; [hon.] Royal Ontario Museum - For Service in Tutankhamun Treasure Tour; [oth. writ.] Several poems and T.V. play "Amoera" (rejected by Twilight Zone); [pers.] My belief is in the spirit of truth that is in all men.; [a.] Scarboro Ontario, Canada

FOUCAULT, MARY FRANCIS FAITH
[b.] March 23, 1951, Everett, WA; [p.] Ingrid; [m.] Deceased; [ch.] Chastity; [ed.] High School; [hon.] An award from NCA Records, Jeff Roberts Publishing Company, and I'm a Registered Member (lifetime) of Song Writers Club of America; [oth. writ.] I have quite a few songs copy righted (Library of Congress). I have had a lot of poems published by Night Roses, Pickerwood The Acorn, The Advocate, plus many more.; [pers.] I would like to be recognized as being a great poet (while I'm still alive).; [a.] Seattle, WA

FOUGERE, LILLY R.
[pen.] Lilly; [b.] March 15, 1945, Cape Breton, Nova Scotia, Canada; [p.] Madeline and George Fougere; [ed.] High School, School of Nursing, England, Technically Trained by New Brunswick Telephone Company as a Draftswoman.; [occ.] Electronic Draftsperson; [memb.] Elizabeth Fry Society, V.P., numerous Sports Organizations - President, Past-Pres., Player; [hon.] Life-Long Athlete, recipient of many awards; [oth. writ.] Began writing poetry as a young girl and over the years have compiled numerous poems on several subjects. This is my first attempt at sharing my poetry with the public.; [pers.] I am greatly influenced with what I've felt experienced from life's experience as an athlete, volunteer and mother nature.; [a.] Saint John New Brunswick, Canada

FRALEY, MEGAN
[b.] November 28, 1980, Vancouver, WA; [p.] Barbara Ryan and Dan Fraley; [ed.] Grade 9 at Fort Vancouver High and 6-8 at Jason Lee Middle School and K-5 at Fruit Valley Elementary; [occ.] Student; [hon.] Honor Roll; [oth. writ.] Several poems and stories and a few "songs".; [pers.] I write about my experiences and what I feel and I also think that your experiences, whether good or bad can only make you stronger and wiser. As Megan's mother I wish to include her work as a tutor with 3rd. grade students in a behavioral school. Megan also does childcare for her 4 yr.old artistic niece.; [a.] Vancouver, WA

FRANCE, TOVAH
[pen.] Jade; [b.] 1982, Bouldet; [p.] Vida and Richard France; [ed.] Homeschooled; [oth. writ.]

I've written a few stories but I never had them published. I thought about getting my ABC book published but I never got to it.; [a.] Boulder, CO

FRANCIS, GLORIA
[b.] July 22, 1987; [p.] Florency and Francis; [ed.] 3rd Grade, Gifted; [hon.] First Place, Essay Contest on Americanism, First Place, Science Olympiad, Voted Best in Math in the Class, Second Place, Science Fair; [oth. writ.] First Time Stories, Poems.; [pers.] Find a cure for AIDS and other incurable diseases.; [a.] North Miami Beach, FL

FRANCIS, RON K.
[pen.] Bronton Wraye; [b.] June 26, 1954, Edmonton, Alberta; [p.] Alan S. Francis, Betty A. Francis; [ch.] Daughter: Kami A. L. Francis; [ed.] Bach. Broadcast Comm. BCIT, Journalism and Law Studies at Casleton University Ottawa Canada; [occ.] Marketing Coordinator Royal Bank Dominion Securities; [memb.] Federation of B.C. Writers, Nashville Songwriters Association Imt., Pacific Song Writers Association; [oth. writ.] Song Published, "Living with Ghosts", "Investors Night Before Christmas" poem. Short story, "The Santa Inigma". Several articles published in local papers.; [pers.] See with probing eyes beneath the surface of life. Discover what makes it tick! Look for all the good, the bad, the ugly and the beautiful nuances. Paint vivid pictures with words. Be emotionally objective.; [a.] Vancouver British Columbia, Canada

FRANCISCO, MELANYE
[b.] April 17, 1974, Great Lakes, IL; [p.] Victor J. and Joyce S. Francisco (Both Deceased); [ed.] High School Diploma, East Robertson High School 1st-11th grade, McGavock H.S. - 12th Grade; [occ.] U.S. Navy - Aviation Ordnanceman; [memb.] Association of Aviation Ordnanceman; [hon.] Who's Who Among America's Top High School Students - '90-'91 and '91-'92; [oth. writ.] "Standing Strong" to be published in "Echoes of the Silence" by Quill Books.; [pers.] Treat every moment as a precious one because the small things bring the greatest joy.; [a.] Old Hickory, TN

FRANK, BARBARA ANNE
[b.] August 13, 1942, Providence, Rhode Island; [p.] Hubert Slater, Elvira Slater; [m.] Winn B. Frank, May 20, 1967; [ch.] Christopher David, Matthew Slater; [ed.] East Providence High School (R.I.), Ohio Wesleyan University, University of Rhode Island (Graduate School); [memb.] Evangelical Presbyterian, Church of Annapolis; [pers.] Having retired from teaching early to raise my children, I held on to a lifelong dream of writing, which I am now doing. Encouraged by many who have read my work to share it, this is my first submitted poem. I have no idea what you will choose to include. However, I do wish to state that I believe that God has given me a gift that needs to be shared as I strive in my writing to speak truth and encouragement to others. Much of my work reflects the beauty of nature, the gift of life, which includes growth even through physical and emotional pain, and the importance of self-knowledge and acceptance.; [a.] Stevensville, MD

FRANK, CHRISTI
[pen.] Kyrsti; [b.] July 15, 1973, British Columbia, Canada; [p.] Vest Steeves and Robert Frank; [ch.]

Cat - Widz, 13 yrs. old; [ed.] Accounting Diploma, Kwantlen University College; [occ.] Accounting Student; [pers.] My mind was opened to poetry in High School, now I can't close it.; [a.] New Westminster British Columbia, Canada

FRANKLIN, MARCELLE
[b.] June 16, 1973, Los Angeles; [ed.] B.A. in Black Studies, B.A. in Law and Society; [occ.] Songwriter, Student at Univ. of Cal. Santa Barbara; [memb.] Black Student Union, Outreach Program; [hon.] Various Academic Awards including scholarship into Washington Program, Letters of Appreciation for Community Work; [oth. writ.] Seeking to publish 2 compilations of Poetry. Write for various performing artist. Short Stories, "I Need To Know...", "Tender Sweet".; [pers.] We are a creative people. It is up to individual's to foster and express their our creativity. Sometimes words are never heard, however thoughts shall always be expressed. To this I contest with the story of my life.; [a.] Isla Vista, CA

FRASER, FRANCES GILL
[b.] October 4, 1924, Woodside, Nova Scotia, Dartmouth, Canada; [p.] William A. Gill and Mary Dina Gill (Nee Lucas); [m.] William Gordon Fraser, June 24, 1944; [ch.] James Gill Fraser, Lynda Jean Black, Margaret Anne Fraser; [ed.] Grade 12 Woodside School, Dartmouth, N.S., Graduate - St. Peter's Commercial College, Dartmouth, N.S.; [occ.] Retired, Previous employment - Civil Servant Military H.Q. Halifax, N.S., District Manager - World Book Childcraft of Canada Ltd., Winnipeg, Manitoba; [hon.] Pursuit of Excellence - Organization Achievement, Pursuit of Excellence - Personal Achievement, World Book - Childcraft of Canada Ltd.

FREEMAN SR., JOHN D.
[pen.] John D. Freeman Sr.; [b.] April 30, 1960, Shreveport; [m.] Henry Etta Freeman, July 9, 1994; [ed.] Green Oaks High; [occ.] Security Officer (Owners) of a Lawn Service; [oth. writ.] Working on a book, of poetry. Title "Another Opinion".; [pers.] Strive to do your best, and trust God to take care the rest.; [a.] Shreveport, LA

FRENZA, CHRISTINA
[pen.] Christina Frenza; [b.] January 3, 1972, Hamilton, Ontario; [p.] Giuseppe Frenza and Sandra Frenza; [ed.] 1. St. Jean de Brebeuf High School, 2. Sheridan College of Applied Arts and Technology, 3. Mohawk College; [occ.] Sales Clerk for Music Retail Store; [memb.] New Altitude Fitness, Volunteer for Arell Youth Organization for young offenders; [hon.] Honours Diploma from Sheridan College; [oth. writ.] I have a book of unpublished poetry. I have written poetry for weddings/ Anniversaries, I also have unpublished songs which I use in my band.; [pers.] My work is influenced by those in my life who have touched me. My heart and soul is put into everything I write. I am interested in romantic poetry and hope that my poetry touches others.; [a.] Hamilton Ontario, Canada

FRET, JEFF
[b.] December 23, 1962, Canada; [p.] John Fret, Jackie Fret; [ed.] Honours BSe. University of Toronto, Astronomy and Physics; [occ.] Carpenter (Nashwaak Paddles), Part-time; [oth. writ.] Queen's

University Student Paper, '82, 3rd and 4th prize. Accompaniment to photographs (poems) by a friend in a local paper '87. No serious pursuit at publication prior to this contest.; [pers.] Poetry is a rush, a gush, and tidying up the mush, ending up as something causing a hush.; [a.] Toronto Ontario, Canada

FRIDAY, PEARLENE ELIZABETH
[pen.] "God's Precious Pearls"; [b.] October 21, 1949, Jamaica, West Indies; [p.] Mr. Evan Jackson and Late Mrs. Vilyn Jackson; [m.] Thomas Friday, April 16, 1983; [ch.] Christopher, Stephanie, Nicholas and Jonathan; [ed.] High School - Jamaica Chelmsford School of Nursing Essex, England, UK, Registered Nurse and Midwife; [occ.] Registered Nurse (Part-time) and Home-maker; [memb.] Faith Landmarks Ministry; [oth. writ.] Richmond Awakening "What If Jesus Had Been Born In Churchill"; [pers.] My prayer is that my writings which are inspired by the Holy Spirit, will help to provide strength healing and restoration to the reader.; [a.] Midlothian, VA

FRIEDLANDER JR., MARK P.
[b.] July 12, 1930, Washington, DC; [ed.] B.A. Univ. VA 1951, Li.B. Univ. VA 1957; [occ.] Attorney; [memb.] Various Bar Associations; [oth. writ.] Co-Authored: Handbook of Successful, Franchising, Van Nostrand/Reiuhold, 1981, Winning The War Within, Rodale Press, 1986, Higher, Faster and Farther, William Morrow and Co., 1973, Fiug Down and Glory, G.P. Putnam and Sons, N.Y. 1958, The Shakespear Transcripts Ox Bow Press, 1993, Of Love and Laughter, (Poetry), Licensed Posts Publishers, 1995; [pers.] Great Falls, VA

FRITSCH, JAIME GARRETT
[pen.] Jaime Von, The Atomic Germanic; [b.] April 14, 1982, State College, PA; [p.] J. Michael Fritsch, Pat Morrissey; [ed.] Mount Nittany Middle School; [occ.] Student; [memb.] Editor: The Underground Alliance - Journal of Science and Literature, Member: World Footbag Association, Member: National Geographic Society; [hon.] "Pennsylvania Mathematics League" certificate of merit, "Second Place Award of Merit for Outstanding Rocket Design" in 1994 Space Derby, "Third Place Award of Merit for Outstanding Rocket Design" in 1994 Space Derby.; [oth. writ.] Various poems, essays, and short stories for classes.; [pers.] Life on earth is short compared to eternity. Be wise and cautious but live it up.; [a.] State College, PA

FRUEHWALD, LINDA A.
[b.] April 19, 1945, Clarksburg, WV; [p.] Ruth and Vincent Sutphin; [ed.] Fairfax High School Strayer College; [occ.] Research Analyst, Presearch Incorporated, Arlington, VA; [memb.] Alpha Sigma Lambda - Iota Eta Chapter Honor Society; [hon.] Strayer College Dean's List, Associate in Arts Degree - Business Administration, June 1996 Graduate; [a.] Alexandria, VA

FUDGE, NANCY D.
[b.] March 26, 1947, Jacksonville, FL; [p.] William Wilson, Isabel Wilson; [m.] Fiancee - Gordon J. Sweatland; [ch.] Shannon, Carole and Adam Fudge; [ed.] Ribault Sr. High, Concorde Career Institute; [occ.] Human Rights Advocate for people with mental disabilities, State of Florida; [memb.] Human

Rights Advocacy Committee for Mental Health District 4, Fl., Jacksonville Alliance for the Mentally Ill.; [hon.] J.C. Penney Golden Rule, Direct Service Award, Statewide Human Rights Committee, Girl Scouts of America, Jacksonville Alliance for the Mentally Ill; [oth. writ.] Article for the Clay Today Newspaper, several articles in Local and State Newsletters.; [pers.] It is through the written and spoken words of honesty that we are able to tap our inner strength and see over true beauty.; [a.] Orange Park, FL

FULCHER, MARY T.
[pen.] Mary Elsie; [b.] June 27, 1937, Bassett, VA; [p.] Cletus and Dovie Turner; [m.] Richard D. Fulcher, April 14, 1995; [ch.] Donna G. Wells, Lynn Hopkins, Brian W. Byrd; [ed.] Fieldale High School; [occ.] Supervisor with Bassett - Walker Ktg. Co., Inc.; [memb.] Hillcrest Baptist Church, Spencer, VA; [oth. writ.] Several personal poems in my collection, none ever submitted for publication.; [pers.] I strive to re-create happy times as a child in my writings. I have been greatly inspired by my grandchildren.; [a.] Critz, VA

FULLER, BETTY NAOMI
[b.] February 7, 1969, Danbury, CT; [p.] Roberta Barnes, Albert Lawrence (deceased); [ch.] Shea Amber Fuller (age 8); [ed.] Danbury High School, Naugatuck Valley Community College, Norwalk State Technical College; [occ.] Oral Surgery Assistant; [memb.] Tae-Kwon-Do, Bowling, Softball; [hon.] D.E.C.A., High School, JROTC Awards (Rifle Team Commander Award, Flight Commander Award), Tae-Kwon-Do Competition Awards, Varsity Softball Letter in High School; [pers.] "I feel that everyone who reads my poem will be able to relate to it's content in some way."; [a.] Danbury, CT

FULLER, MARK
[b.] December 15, 1964, Gaffney, SC; [p.] Oscar and Joyce Fuller; [ed.] EE - Ga. Tech., Masters of Wood Technology - Univ. of Ga.; [occ.] Wood Technologist; [pers.] My writing reflects personal experiences and explores the wonderous as well as ponderous facets of life. I have been influenced by southern writers and musicians.; [a.] Conyers, GA

FULMER, ELIZABETH
[pen.] Elizabeth Fulmer; [b.] April 17, 1926, Linwood, PA; [m.] Robert L. Fulmer, January 15, 1949; [ch.] Robert Jr., and Barbara, 5 grandchildren; [ed.] P.S. du Pont High School, Thompson's Business School; [occ.] Retired Administrative Secretary; [memb.] Chester Bethel UM Church, Fort Delaware Society, Friends of Gettysburg; [hon.] As church Historian - First Prize in Church History Contest, Delmarva Peninsula Conference; [pers.] I enjoy writing about nature and the beauty of the world.; [a.] Wilmington, DE

FUNK, HERBERT W.
[b.] March 3, 1932, Jefferson, OR; [p.] Myrtle V. Funk; [m.] Berniece M. Funk, December 28, 1961; [ch.] Steven W. Funk, Robyn M. Lentz; [ed.] Milwaukie High School, Milwaukie, Ore.; [occ.] Retired; [memb.] Mt. Carmel Lutheran Church; [oth. writ.] Other poems published in Church Papers and some in Monon News, Monon, Ind.; [pers.] I am active in the church, am currently Vice President of

the church council, I sing in the church choir. My wife and I sing and play at Care Centers and Retirement Homes. I enjoy Hunting and Fishing and all other outdoor activities. I also have four grandchildren.; [a.] Portland, OR

FUNK, LORAINE O.
[b.] July 29, 1924, Cobleskill, NY; [p.] Jesse and Myrtle (Wellman) Oliver; [m.] Divorced; [ch.] Michael, Richard, Ronald, Carleen; [ed.] Chester High School, Chester, NY, Spencer Business School, Computer Courses at College where I worked.; [occ.] Retired - was library Clerk at Suny College of Ag and Tech, Cobleskill, NY; [memb.] ISP - Distinguished Member; [hon.] National Library of Poetry's Editor's Choice Award; [oth. writ.] Many poems, usually for friends or family; [pers.] Talent should be used to bring what joy it may to others, it may lift the spirits of some who need it.; [a.] Laurens, NY

GAFFNEY, IMOGENE
[pen.] Jeanie, Jean Jean Baby; [b.] July 6, 1932, Elmo, TX; [p.] Earl Adkins, Louisa Adkins; [m.] Edward O. Gaffney, July 30, 1955; [ch.] Theresa, Edward O. Jr., Orlando, Cyernard, Regina Darrell; [ed.] Booker T. Washington High School Graduated, Prairie A&M College 1 1/2 yrs; [occ.] Retired nurse; [memb.] Disabled Veterans, Holy Trinity Baptist Church, International Society of Poets, NAACP; [hon.] Newsday Merit Awards, Essay Contest, Christian Service Award, Editor's Choice Award; [oth. writ.] Songs and poems as a hobby unfortunately they were lost due to relocating.; [pers.] I hope to and try to show love through my writing. I would like for love to be so contagious that when one touch anothers hand that he or she, would become infected with same.; [a.] North Babylon, NY

GAIN, LISA
[pen.] Lisa Christian; [b.] December 6, 1965, Mount Kisco, NY; [p.] Robert and Florence Stabe; [m.] George Gain, March 4, 1989; [ch.] Arianna And Caylin; [ed.] Tabernacle Baptist School, Anderson College, Institute of Childrens Literature; [occ.] Homemaker; [pers.] There is still a side of mankind that chooses to turn a blind eye to the sexual, physical and emotional abuse of children and the effects of the abuse in their adult lives. My writing is a reflection of just one suffering child's soul and her dare to hope for her freedom; [a.] Brooksville, FL

GALETKA, JASON
[pen.] Strider; [b.] August 18, 1975, Saint Paul, MN; [p.] Patrick Galetka, Elaine Nicoletti; [ed.] Forest Lake Senior High, Northeast Metro Tech; [occ.] Warehouse Worker; [hon.] Environmental Studies Award; [oth. writ.] Several new stories published in High School newspaper, Environmental Editorial published in Star Tribune; [pers.] It's my goal in life to write a superlative style, so as to craft my work from the Intellectual inks of thought. My ability style is derived from creative thought conjuration along with my treasured thesaurus.; [a.] Forest Lake, MN

GALLANT, JAIME LYNNE
[b.] February 2, 1981, London, Ontario; [p.] Ralph Gallant and Lesley Lamb; [ed.] Currently pursuing grade 9 at St. John's College in Brantford, Ontario, Canada; [occ.] Student; [pers.] At any time, at any age, anyone can do anything; [a.] Brantford Ontario, Canada

GALLENSTEIN, ALICE KAY
[b.] October 20, 1940, Maysville, KY; [p.] Walter and Nancy Austin; [m.] James L. (Buddy) Gallenstein, July 4, 1961; [ch.] Jim II, Elizabeth, Louise, Allison; [ed.] High School - Beautician School; [occ.] Wife - and Grandmother, retired - 1987 as beautician; [memb.] Knights of Columbus Ladies, Auxiliary - Past Pres., St. Patrick Activity Club; [hon.] Lady of the year of K&C Auxiliary 1968-69; [oth. writ.] None published; [pers.] Influenced by my mother who loved to write and tell stories. My poems are of family and friends. I like writing about them. I did not write tell after my mothers death 1965; [a.] Maysville, KY

GALLOWAY, MARILYN
[b.] December 12, 1937, Montreal, Province of Quebec; [p.] John McDowell, Dorothy McDowell; [m.] Ralph Galloway, January 11, 1957; [ch.] Ralph, Karen, Janice Scott, Shane Donald; [ed.] Verdun High, O'Sullivan Business College; [occ.] Homemaker, Mother, Grandmother; [oth. writ.] Short children's stories, other pieces of poetry writer for my children's pleasures; [pers.] My writing's tend to reflect my personal surroundings "ie" my family, and country, animals oceans mountains make me happy and thats what I love to write about; [a.] Richmond British Columbia, Canada

GALLUZZO, KATHERINE L.
[b.] October 18, 1980, Saint Louis, MO; [p.] Stephen and Lois Galluzzo; [ed.] Marquette High School student, Freshman; [occ.] Student; [memb.] High School Volleyball Team, Mixed Choir, Forensics; [hon.] Honor Roll; [pers.] I try to reach people of all kinds with the power of human emotion.; [a.] Chesterfield, MO

GAMBLER, SHARON SNYDER
[pen.] Cheyanne Wolf; [b.] June 13, 1955, Milwaukee, WI; [p.] Mr. John and Mrs. Rosemary Snyder; [ch.] Ezra Patrick; [ed.] St. Augustine Milw Wisc., St. Mary's Academy Milw, Wisc., Milw. Area Tech College (Nursing and Special Development) (Assoc. degree); [occ.] Private duty nurse mother; [memb.] Share program, volunteering for care of the elderly; [hon.] Editor's Choice Award from National Library of Poetry; [oth. writ.] At Water's Edge, National Library of Poetry; [pers.] Dedicated to Bob and Ezra thank you very much for the inspiration and support and love, you gave me to do all this and more. I love you both very much.; [a.] LaMesa, CA

GARNER, ALISA M.
[pen.] Alisa M. Garner; [b.] June 11, 1963, Kissimmee, FL; [p.] Jimmy R. and Rachel N. Garner; [ch.] James Randall; [occ.] Ass. Supervisor of Quality Control; [oth. writ.] Songs, Short stories, Poems; [pers.] You always have control to view tragedies as a teacher and victories as a lesson learned. I love you, To Randy and Mom, for believing when I couldn't.; [a.] Haines City, FL

GASTENT, PHYLLIS M.
[pen.] Phyllis Jeanette M. Priest-Gastent; [b.] June 26, 1944, Danville, IL; [p.] William and Jeanette Priest; [ch.] Lori A. Gastent; [ed.] A.A.S plus Working on B.A., plus some creative writing continuing Education Courses and enrolled right now in Writer's Digest School; [occ.] Assistant to Director, World Learning's International Students of

English Florida and 2nd job AT&T Universal Card Services as a Collections Agent; [memb.] NAFSA, International Teachers/Educators, International Society of Poets, ATT Inter Tribal Council, Watts; [hon.] International Poet of Merit for 1995, Editor's Choice Awards for 2 poems Business Awards, Best Employee, Bookkeeping Awards, Merit Awards; [oth. writ.] National Library Books: Seasons to come, best poets of 1996, Harvest Moon, Tomorrows Dream. In other publications: Southern Anthology of Poetry, Kipling's Foloeys and ATT UCS Associates Press Papers.; [pers.] I have always believed you can do anything or be anything you want as long as you don't hurt anyone else in the process. I also believe that in order to write about life you need to experience it on some level knowing that nothing worthwhile is achieved by by sitting still.; [a.] Jacksonville, FL

GATES, CHARI LYNN
[b.] November 22, 1950, Kalamazoo, MI; [p.] Robert Shultz and Betty Wilson; [m.] Steven C. Gates, May 22, 1982; [ch.] Jeffrey Allen, Kenneth LeVerne, Amy Lynn, Larissa Irene; [ed.] Gobles High School; [occ.] Grandmother; [pers.] Always a student and a teacher be.; [a.] Coloma, MI

GAUTHIER, DEREK
[b.] August 9, 1980, Calgary Alberta, Canada; [p.] Denis, Lynn Gauthier; [ed.] Thomas Haney Secondary School; [occ.] Student; [memb.] Meadow Ridge Knights Football Association; [hon.] Most sports man like, Most Valuable Player; [pers.] Several of my poems are thoughts on life.; [a.] Maple Ridge British Columbia, Canada

GELINAS JR., ARTHUR
[b.] June 16, 1965, Norwich, CT; [p.] Arthur and Lucille Gelinas Sr.; [m.] Cindy Gelinas, April 11, 1994; [ch.] Ashley, Arthur III, Andrew; [ed.] St. Bernard's High School; [occ.] Janitorial Business Owner; [hon.] None, this is the first poem I ever sent in, I have 40 or 50 and a children's story, and songs but I never sent any in.; [oth. writ.] Daddy's Little Girl, Societies Captive, The Day The Easter Bunny Needed Help, A Wish, these are a few of many; [per.] My gift for words comes from my faith in Jesus Christ, and that all our life is about is how we serve and love others.; [a.] Moosup, CT

GENTILELLA, DEBRA
[pen.] Debra; [b.] December 13, 1980, Santa Ana, CA; [p.] Jerri and John Gentilella; [ed.] Attend Chattahoochee High School, Duluth, GA, all Honors Courses, 4.5 CPA, Dean's List; [memb.] Private Service Club, Member on CHS Dance Team; [hon.] 2 Years-helped collect presents for needy families and deliver them at Christmas, made and filled stocking for needy children; [pers.] "My family is my inspiration and with inspiration, one can write or do anything desired.; [a.] Duluth, GA

GERLACH, KASEY LEE
[pen.] KC Gerlach; [b.] August 14, 1978, Sioux Falls, SD; [p.] Elizabeth Dozier, Randy Gerlach; [ed.] Senior at Riggs High School, Pierre, SD; [memb.] Combat Karate Club; [oth. writ.] 1st attempt.

GETTRY, JOAN E.
[b.] Jamaica, West Indies; [p.] Deceased; [m.] Martin D. (Deceased); [ed.] LaGuardia Community College,

Future: Hunter College; [occ.] Homemaker and Student; [memb.] Women's Auxiliary, The N.Y. Medical Center, International Society of Poets; [hon.] Dean's List; [oth. writ.] Enrollment in Institute of Children's Lit. from which I've taken a leave of absence until summer 96. And publication of my new book of poetry, due out early 96.; [pers.] We are surrounded day after day with new growth, both in nature and in the human condition. So recognize those growth as a step forward which should be nurtured like a new-born - with love and caring.; [a.] Beechhurst, NY

GIANNINI, CINDY
[b.] Redwood City, CA; [p.] Don and Bonnie Giannini; [ed.] B.A. Dramatic Arts, UC Berkeley (graduated with honors); [occ.] Project Analyst; [oth. writ.] Short stories, work in progress, script editing; [a.] Tarzana, CA

GIARDINO, GERARD
[pen.] Geronimo; [b.] May 27, 1980, Kasplalex's; [p.] Joe Giardino, Maria Makowski; [ed.] St. Edmons, St. Lucy's, Vital Grandin, Richerd S. Fowler, St. Albert High grade 10; [occ.] High School student with love for doing writing and poetry.; [oth. writ.] Betrail What is These All Around, Hatred Rules The Hungry, Money Just A Cure, Emptiness Inside They, Coldness Around, Death Is Not A Question Just A Fearless Action Dying Of The Infinite Is Nothing More Than Common.; [a.] Saint Albert Alberta, Canada

GIBSON, LINDA
[pen.] Linda Gibson; [b.] April 11, 1945, Waco, TX; [p.] Olin and Doris Skidmore; [m.] Maurice Gibson, June 1979; [ch.] Sean Smith, Staci Smith, Alayna Gibson; [ed.] Abbott High School, Lenials Beauty College; [occ.] Homemaker, Grandmother; [hon.] Trophies/Beauty College; [oth. writ.] Numerous poems for Family and Friends, poem for book at Abbott Centennial; [pers.] My heart communicates it's feelings thru poems. Whether it's sad, happy, comical, or filled with love. The personal lesson I learned from this poem you have, was left out as it was too long.

GIBSON, ROSE B.
[pen.] Rose Branch Gibson; [b.] April 29, 1931, Richmond, VA; [p.] Howard and Annie C. Branch; [m.] Frank E. Gibson, November 20, 1954; [ch.] 3 (2 girls and 1 boy); [ed.] B.A. Degree - VA. Union University, M.A. Degree - Virginia State University. Further graduate study at University Va., Va. Commonwealth University and University of California, L.A.; [occ.] Retired Educator, Writer, Poet., Workshop presentations and demonstrator in Math and Economics; [memb.] Alpha, Kappa Alpha Sorority, Richmond Chapter Dejour's Inc., Eastern Star - Eliz Harris Chapter, Richmond Education Association, National Council Self-Esteem, Virginia Chapter Self-Esteem; [hon.] Economic Council of Va. award for the invention of the Mini Math Thinker's mall for children to enhance Math and Economic skills., Sickle Cell Day Camp award for Children's presentation on Self-Control and Self-Esteem; [oth. writ.] Poetry to enhance self-esteem and self-control in children.; [pers.] I believe, in the power of just being yourself, in the fast that all children are different, in helping children to get going on a new beginning to be self-worthy, all children are special and unique in their own way; [a.] Richmond, VA

GILBERT, CAROLYN P.
[b.] January 8, 1930, Gaskin, FL; [p.] John T. Parish Sr., Stella Parish; [m.] Paul R. Gilbert Sr., February 2, 1952; [ch.] Paul Russell Jr., Stephen Michael; [ed.] BS Florida State University Masters, University of Northern Colorado; [occ.] Retired Teacher, Business Education, Dade County Schools, Miami, FL; [memb.] First Baptist Church, Key Largo, FL (Church Clerk, Sunday School Director, Leader, First Place) Delta Kappa Gamma; [pers.] My life and writing are greatly influenced by the beauty of God's creation and the inner joy of his loving presence.; [a.] Key Largo, FL

GILL, EVALYN PIERPOINT
[p.] Walters L. and Lou O. Pierpoint; [m.] Deceased, John G. Gill; [ch.] Susan Pierpoint Gill, Mary Louise Glenville Gill; [ed.] B.A. Cum Laude Univ. of Colorado, M.A. Central Mich. Univ.; [memb.] Phi Beta Kappa, N.C. Writers Network, N.C. Poetry Society, Poetry Council of N.C.; [hon.] Recipient of Fortner Writer and Community Award from St. Andrews College 1995; [oth. writ.] Poetry publication in such "Little Magazines" as Crucible, Pembroke, Magazine, Award Winning Poetry (N.C. Poetry Society), Southern Poetry Review, International Poetry Review; [pers.] The essence of poetry is to find new connections between unlike things. Poets must be aware of details in nature and the human condition. Through keen perception, poets become more human and broaden the understanding of those who hear and read their work. Poetry can open new worlds and show us wonders we have never imagined.; [a.] Greensboro, NC

GILLES, JEAN-ELIE
[pen.] Item; [b.] November 1, 1963, Jacmel, Haiti; [p.] Orphanie Denis and Elie Gilles; [m.] Single; [ed.] Baccalauriat (1st and 2nd part) (1988) Scholarship of French governmet (1990-1992) Paris and Nice as French Teacher - BA in French (1986); [occ.] Student C.W.U., CBC, Pullman (1993-1996) (WA); [hon.] 2nd Prize of French contest (1983) cultural writing; [oth. writ.] "The Pearls Of Tacmelian Poetry" (1990) 680 pages, anthology of yearnings dialogue (1993), 90 pages In The Footsteps Of Diogens (1995) novel, 250 pages Jacmel, its contribution to Haitian History (1995), History book, 632 pages; [pers.] In my writing, I try not only to reflect the way we can make the difference in this world through our "Weltonschaung" but also investigating who we are and why are we here (on earth).; [a.] Richland, WA

GILLEY, THERESA
[b.] April 2, 1970, Elizabeth City, NC; [p.] Frank Moore and Vickie Michael; [m.] Junior Gilley, January 28, 1995; [ch.] Jeremy Brock; [ed.] Manteo High School and College of the Albemarle; [pers.] Look up in the sky no goal you ever set is to high. Believe in yourself and you will always shine as bright as the stars.

GILLIES, KATHRYN JUNE
[pen.] June Gillies; [b.] July 15, 1975, Trenton Ontario, Canada; [p.] Mr and Mrs Jim Gillies; [ed.] Dunbarton High School, University of Toronto - 2nd year; [occ.] Student in the Basic Medical Sciences; [memb.] Member of Victoria College, University of Toronto; [hon.] Robin Hood Multifoods Scholarship Awards in '94 and '95, (Gr.9) Royal Conservatory of

Music Certificate; [oth. writ.] Several poems published in local newsletters; [pers.] I write for the glory of God and for the enjoyment of my fellow man. Any other reason is useless.; [a.] Pickering Ontario, Canada

GIMZA, JEANNETTE
[pen.] Jeannette Gimza; [b.] April 19, 1960, Toronto; [p.] Don and Jacqueline Rivet; [m.] Richard Gimza, September 22, 1979; [ch.] Steven and Kimberly; [ed.] Runneymede Collegiate, Humber College; [occ.] Wife, mom and writer; [hon.] None, but excelled in the high "Nineties", in both High School and College for both English and Language Arts.; [oth. writ.] Several poems which I am compiling into a book, and have submitted into several publishers.; [pers.] It isn't enough to instill your values on others. You must live by them and believe in them yourself. Only then, will you be respected, your values accepted and others will believe in you.; [a.] Brampton Ontario, Canada

GIRODAY, LISA
[b.] March 23, 1983, Vancouver, British Columbia, Canada; [p.] Mrs. Linda Giroday, Mr. Gordon Giroday; [ed.] Grade 7; [occ.] Student; [memb.] The Canadian Equestrian, Federation and the British Columbia, Hunter/Jumper Association.; [hon.] Several awards in English Equestrian Hunter Horse Events; [oth. writ.] This poem will also be published by the Poetry Institute of Canada in the childrens poetry Book, Friends, Animals, and Rainbows.; [pers.] My experience of writing is not the greatest. I never did dream (beyond my wildest expectations) that I would get this far. When I stated in my poem, "Close but yet so far, many strive to touch the stars!" I meant, fantasies that seem impossible, can be created with one thing persistance! A man once said, "Giving up is like folding your deck. But giving up entirely is like folding up your life!" My motto has always been, imagination creates knowledge, for without imagination the world would be without existance.; [a.] Richmond British Columbia, Canada

GITCHELL, LOIS L.
[b.] April 11, 1927, South Dakota; [m.] Tracy, August 20, 1950; [ch.] Andrea, Vanessa, Denise; [ed.] College; [occ.] Retired; [oth. writ.] I jot down thoughts now and then for my own pleasure.; [pers.] My husband, a retired judge and restaurant myself, and our dog - live by a lake on the rolling plans of South Dakota. The children are grown, the grandchildren (Callie, Cole, Adam and Amy) are growing and we are fine.; [a.] Huron, SD

GLADUE, HOPE
[b.] August 9, 1959, Red Deer, Alberta, Canada; [p.] August B. and Anna M. Provost; [m.] Terry R. Hayduk; [ch.] Christopher, Mandy, Tanner, Amber, Afton and Oksana; [ed.] High School in Red Deer, Ab., Can.; [occ.] Domestic Engineer, full time Mother; [pers.] I have been inspired by the nobleness of my husband and influenced by my experiences throughout my life with my children.; [a.] Sylvan Lake Alberta, Canada

GLASER, DAVID
[b.] September 29, 1919, Brooklyn, NY; [p.] Samuel and Jennie (Oiffer) G.; [m.] Millie Sappol, February 19, 1944; [ch.] Susan, Sherry; [ed.] Student, N.Y. Sch. Indsl. Art, 1937, N.Y. Sch. Contemporary Art,

1947-48, Bklyn. Mus. Art Sch., 1948-50., Illustrator, Cartoonist comic books, Popular mechanics, Electronics Illustrated, Popular Sci., N.Y.C. 1939-42, 46-50, pres.,; [occ.] Painter, Sculptor, Designer, Inventor, Mosamics Co., Bklyn., 1948-50, Art dir., Advt. Mgr. Univ., Loudspeakers, White Plains, N.Y. 1951-60, Owner, Mgr., Graphic Designer, Studio Concepts, Wantagh, N.Y., 1957, Artist Civilian Conservation Corps, Adirondacks, 1936, Tchr. Art Ctr. Island Jewish Sch., Freeport, N.Y., 1959, Newspaper Artist Bering Breeze, Aleutian Islands, 1945-46.; [memb.] Freeport Arts Coun., Allied Artists Am. (pres. 1985-86), Huntington Twp., Art League, DAV, Comic Artist Guild (treas.); [hon.] Art Student's League scholar, 1936, Recipient grand prize for redesign Levitt Home, Printing Industries, N.Y, 1973, Graphic Excellence award Monadnock Mills, 1975, Cert. of Merit Vet. Soc. Am., Artist, Desi Grand award, 1980-82, Award of Excellence, Long Beach Art League, 1989, Numerous Graphics Awards, 1973-84, Poetry Award Nassau County Fine Arts Mus., 1981; [oth. writ.] (Poetry) My Mother Died Dancing, 1960, Three-Man Show Heckscher Mus., Huntington, N.Y., 1964, Exhibited in Group Shows Nat. Art Club, N.Y.C., 1959, Art Directions, 1959, ACA Galleries, 60, Hofstra U., Adelphi U., Nassau Community Coll., 1980, Knickerbocker Artists, Islip Mus., 1983, Wantagh Libr., 1975, Levittown Libr., 1986, Freeport Libr., 1987, Illustrator, Planets (Willie Ley), author, American Indian, Crime and Punishment, Superstition and Parapsychology, 1947-50, inventor process for mass prodn. ceramic and transparent mosaics, silk screen sys. for printing inside compound curves. Designer war posters, visual aids for U.S. Army, 1942-44, Creator comic character for Army newspaper, 1943-46.

GNATIUK, ELIZABETH
[pen.] Beth Gnatiuk; [b.] March 15, 1976, Annapolis, MD; [p.] Alex and Mary F. Gnatiuk; [ed.] Green Run Sr. High; [occ.] Student; [memb.] Thespian Troupe #1625; [hon.] National Honor Society, French National Honor Society, Who's Who of American High School Students; [oth. writ.] I have many other untitled unpublished writings that I am quite proud to possess without acknowledgement; [pers.] My writings reflect my feelings, which are influenced by my life; [a.] Virginia Beach, VA

GODFREY, ALEIHA MARIE
[pen.] Aleiha Godfrey; [b.] January 31, 1981, Bradenton, FL; [p.] Katie Ives and Patrick Godfrey; [ed.] Currently at Bishop Verot High School; [occ.] Student, Freshman; [hon.] Student Class representative for Freshman Council 1995, 1996 J.V. Viking Cheerleader; [oth. writ.] "Weird" published in the 1995 Edition of the Anthology of Poetry by Young Americans.; [pers.] I try to write poems that reflect me. All my writings for either fun or school have part of me in it.; [a.] Fort Myers, FL

GOEL, SAMIR
[b.] March 14, 1976, Revelstoke, British Columbia; [p.] Mr. Hersh Goel, Mrs. Neelima Goel; [ed.] Douglas College, New West, B.C., Studying to Major in Fither, Psychology or Social Work, while hoping to Minor in Political Science; [occ.] Student; [hon.] In High school at Burnaby South Senior Secondary, I attained passport to Education stamps in grades 9, 10, 12, as well as receiving an Outstanding P.E. Student Plaque in Grade 9 (1991);

[pers.] I wish to dedicate this milestone moment to my father, mother, and brother for being the ones I will always love throughout life. I would also like to extend great gratitude to God for blessing me with this beautiful gift that I maybe able to share with others.; [a.] Burnaby British Columbia, Canada

GOGA, KATHLEEN HUSZCZO
[pen.] Katie Huszczo; [b.] December 9, 1946, Hantranck, MI; [p.] Agnes and Henry Huszczo; [m.] Richard Goga, May 21, 1994; [ch.] Anthony, Kevin, Melisa, and Michael; [ed.] Pershing High School, Macomb Comm. College; [occ.] Patient Inq. Rep., Medaphis Corporation; [memb.] Chairperson for United Foundation, Parents Committee CUHS; [hon.] Medical Terminology Certificate, Success Skills for Secretaries, Administrative Assistants, and Support Staff Certificate; [oth. writ.] Presentation for United Foundation; [pers.] I find my family, friends, neighbors, children and people to be the most important things on this earth. I truly value human life and life itself.; [a.] Clinton Township, MI

GOLDBERG, KERRY
[b.] February 28, 1950, Evanston, IL; [p.] Reva and Leonard; [m.] Lisa Vignale, August 19, 1995; [ch.] Jacob and Ryland; [occ.] Personal Fitness Trainer; [pers.] Life is short, so walk slowly.; [a.] Santa Barbara, CA

GOLDFIELD, ROBERT
[pen.] Robert Saul; [b.] June 5, 1935, Philadelphia; [p.] Israel and Mathilda; [m.] Mexicah (Divorce), 12 years; [ch.] Daughter; [ed.] G.E.D. Diploma; [occ.] Retired, was rock band, window cleaner, factory worker, orderly; [hon.] Check ripped on mental Unit - 10,000 Dollars in 1991 American Poetry Anthology.

GONZALEZ, BLANCA ESTELA
[b.] October 14, 1957, McAllen, TX; [p.] Argentina Alvarado Gonzalez and Marcelo Gonzalez Jr.; [ed.] PSJA High School 1976, Pan American University 1980 BA Psychology and Elementary Education Texas A and I University 1985 MA Reading, Texas Teaching Certificates Elementary Education, Psychology, Reading Specialist, Supervision and Mid-Management; [occ.] Reading specialist, Teacher at PSJA North High School, 15 years teaching experience in elementary, secondary, and college; [memb.] Texas Computer Education Association, The International Society of Poets, Poets Society of America, Texas Class room Teachers Association; [hon.] Editor's Choice Award 1994, Poem published in After The Storm, First division for two years in ensemble band, Second Division for one year in ensemble band, Psychology scholarship for tuition, President honor roll; [oth. writ.] Article published in local paper, Poem published in the following in the following books After The Storm, Best of 1996, A Delicate Balance; [pers.] I believe that through education anything will be achieved. A goal is accomplished through hard work and determination. The stars can be reached; [a.] San Juan, TX

GONZALEZ, MARIO
[b.] April 3, 1965, Brooklyn, NY; [p.] Marciano and Ana Gonzalez; [m.] Emily Gonzalez, December 9, 1986; [ch.] Giselle and Anthony; [ed.] Bullard Havens Vocational Technical School, Bridgeport Connecticut; [occ.] Machinist; [a.] Lake Worth, FL

GONZALEZ, SUNSHEARAY N.
[b.] January 25, 1977, Merrillville, IN; [p.] Tanya L. Gonzalez; [ed.] Theodore Roosevelt H.S. (Gary, IN), Hampton University (Hampton, VA); [occ.] Full-time student at Hampton University; [memb.] National Association of Black Journalist, Hampton Script Newspaper Staff; [hon.] Dean's List, N.W.I. Links Scholarship SY 1995-96, Nat'l Sorority of Phi Delta Kappa Inc., Scholarship SY 1995-96; [oth. writ.] Poems and articles published in high school yearbook and school paper (The Roosveltian); [pers.] "Bad things happen.... even to the best of us. When things don't go your way — build a bridge and get over it."; [a.] Gary, IN

GOOD, MARGARET
[b.] February 4, 1933, Torrance County, NM; [p.] Claude and Bertha (Crider) Brown; [m.] Paul W. Good, March 1962; [ch.] Dena Sue Robert's, Edward F. Good, Steven W. Good; [ed.] Ewing School, Torrance County, NM, Estancia High School, Torrance Co., NM, Harding University, Searcy, ARK; [occ.] Retired Secretary; [memb.] Church of Christ, International Society of Poets; [hon.] NM Girls State 1950, High School Salutatorian, Scholarship to Harding College; [oth. writ.] Published in Anthologies, High School (2 yrs) plus Sermons in Poetry College 1 year, Famous Poets Society "Todays Great Poems", and "Famous Poems of Today", National Library of Poetry, Best Poems of 1995, Best Poems of 1996 plus 11 other anthologies by NLP, several poems by Vessel Publishing.; [pers.] I credit my 6,7,8, grade teacher, Eulah Watson, now deceased, for getting me started writing poetry. My writings consist of things with which I am familiar, specific events, people, and religion; [a.] Stephenville, TX

GOODRICH, WILLETTA M.
[b.] July 4, 1952, Newberry, MI; [p.] Ralph K. Smith, Dorothy M. Luoma (mother deceased May 1994); [m.] Gerald L. Goodrich (divorced 6 yrs. but are reuniting), June 30, 1973; [ch.] Jonathan Scott and Jeffery Lee; [ed.] Science Hill High School Johnson City, Tn.; [oth. writ.] I am a novice writer. Although I do have 2 books of poetry near completion. "Tears For Teddy Bears" and "Bits And Pieces". I have many concepts for poetry, short stories, novelettes, and autobiography. I am fulfilling a lifetime dream.; [pers.] "I live within a world of cold and cruel realities. Yet I can escape into a life of dreams and fantasies. For I am a voyageur upon silver moonbeams, in search of Fantasian Dreams".; [a.] Johnson City, TN

GOOKIN, SANDRA L.
[pen.] Sandra L. Gookin; [b.] June 27, 1942, LaJunia, CO; [p.] Esther and Richard Wolfe; [m.] Robert G. Gookin, September 11, 1995 (my 4th marriage); [ch.] Michelle-29 and Christopher-27; [ed.] B.A. English and Psychology (Education and Counseling), M.A. English and Special Ed. (Education and Counseling); [occ.] Co-owner Creative Skills etc. and Amateur Writer; [memb.] Kingsville Women's Club, Colorado Speakers Bureau, Asso. of University Women, Asso. for Curriculum and Educational Development, People to People Internat'l, McRoberts Elem. School PTA, NAS Kingsville Bowling League; [hon.] Who's Who Colorado Speakers Bureau, Who's Who-University Women, Certificate of Achievement - Texas

Teachers Asso., Certificate of Achievement Medical Arts Asso., Buzz Because Awards (3) - Provenant Health Partners St. Anthony North Hospital; [oth. writ.] Unpublished poetry and a few short stories; [pers.] There is no greater feeling than the special bond of grandparents and grandchildren to stimulate a grandchild's knowledge of his/her self worth and their abilities to accomplish their best at whatever they choose in life. Grandparents are a vastly untapped source of educational and social information. They are the link to the past, present and future of our children and grandchildren.; [a.] Kingsville, TX

GORDIN, COLLEEN FREEMAN
[b.] March 16, 1952, Murray, UT; [p.] Herman and Doris Freeman; [m.] Dr. Richard D. Gordin Jr., December 5, 1980; [ch.] Lisa S. Snyder, Michael G. Glabe; [ed.] B.S. University of Utah, M.Ed Utah State University; [occ.] Assistant Principal; [memb.] NASSP, UASSP, NEA, UEA, BEEA, BEAP, Phi Delta Kappa; [oth. writ.] Ancient History Cartoons; [a.] Providence, UT

GORDON, CURTIS W.
[b.] January 23, 1925, Darien, GA; [p.] Mr. and Mrs. T. P. Gordon; [m.] Evelyn Cameron Gordon, September 29, 1948; [ch.] Catherine G. O'Neill, Wanda D. Gordon; [ed.] Ludowici High School; [occ.] Retired, Trainmaster, CSX Railroad (37 years); [memb.] U.T.U. Transportation Union - Honorary Member; Deacon, Calvary Baptist Temple, Savannah, GA; [pers.] Now and then an idea just comes to mind, and I simply sit down and begin to write.; [a.] Savannah, GA

GOSTICK, CORINNE
[b.] July 4, 1932, Saint John, New Brunswick, Canada; [p.] Joseph McLeod, Margaret McLeod; [m.] Donald Edward Gostick, April 11, 1978; [ch.] Philip Paul, Leonard Wayne, Marion Corinne, Sandra Golding; [ed.] High School, Journalism/Short story writing with International Correspondence Schools in Montreal, Quebec/Institute of Children Literature, West Redding, CT; [occ.] Writer; [pers.] All my life I've wanted to write, now that I am retired, I can devote most of my time to it, it is my life! I was surprised and thrilled to learn my poem was selected, and only two days before christmas, what a gift!; [a.] Mactier Ontario, Canada

GOY, DIANE P.
[b.] August 8, 1966, Wilkes-Barre, PA; [p.] Margaret Goy and James Goy Sr.; [m.] Walter A. Gurdock; [ch.] Nicole, Paul Joseph, Desiree Dakota; [ed.] Coughlin High School, McCann's School of Business, W-B Area Vo-Tech; [occ.] Mother and Housewife; [oth. writ.] A poem read during Sunday mass at a local church, Paster Reed, read it.; [pers.] All my poetry is based on experiences and feelings of my past and present life. Based on the bitterness and joy.; [a.] Wilkes-Barre, PA

GRANDGENETT, DELORIS
[b.] June 3, 1933, Mondamin, IA; [p.] Levert and Jessie Layton; [m.] Dwain, October 8, 1950; [ch.] Deborah Crose, Lisa Kenna; [ed.] High School; [occ.] Retired; [hon.] Golden poet award, several poems published in Iowa - Great Lakest - South and California; [oth. writ.] Songs, Raps.

GRAY, CLINT
[b.] April 26, 1974, Ottumwa, IA; [p.] Richard Gray, Tula Gray; [ed.] Eddyville High, Indian Hills Community College; [occ.] Management, Excel Corp, Ottumwa, Iowa; [oth. writ.] Monthly humor article in Ottumwa-based Real Life magazine, currently working on poem compilation called Burgundy Moonlightning, finished book of humor called Superkrud; [pers.] Let your own heart and your own mind do the writing for you. Being naturally unique is a gift for you to unveil.; [a.] Ottumwa, IA

GRAY, MRS. ALBERTA A.
[pen.] Alberta Avery-Gray; [b.] March 23, 1918, Birmingham, AL; [p.] Charles Avery, Larnie Avery; [m.] Marshall Gray, (Deceased), January 20, 1952; [ch.] Marshall C. Gray, Businessman, John C. Gray, Merit Scholar, grandchildren: Phillip McKnight, Michelle Delois, Latoshia Renee, Lolita Marie, Marshall Eric, and Marcus Charles; [ed.] Englewood H.S. Grad., AA Degree, Chicago City College, Wilson Branch, 1 year, DePaul University, 1 year Chicago Teachers College; [occ.] Retired, Administrative Assistant Chicago Public Schools; [memb.] The League of Women Voters, The Chicago Africa Study Travel Group, The Montgomery Place Retirement, Community Poetry Writer's Groups, Montgomery Place "Quality of Life" Committee; [hon.] "Editor's Choice Award, presented by the Nat'l Library of Poetry for "Reflections Of Me" (1995); [oth. writ.] Published in Tomorrow Never Knows, in 1946 - Published a Tabloid Called, "The Wellstown Crier" for the Ida B. Wells Homes. Also wrote two unpublished plays for CUB Scouts. And several poems. At the present am writing a full length novel on African-American Life in A Chicago Community.; [pers.] Motivated and inspired by the talented members of the Southside Art Center-Chicago.; [a.] Chicago, IL

GREEN, JOHN R.
[b.] May 25, 1914; [p.] Rev. John Henry and Mattie Mae Green; [m.] Loretta Irene Sheaffer, October 11, 1952; [ed.] West virginia University 1933-37, Graduated Bexley Hall Theological Seminary (Episcopal) 1947; [occ.] Retired Clergyman; [oth. writ.] Published literature. The Easter of Claudia (Drama), The Easter Moment-Easter Dawn (Poem), and featured contributions in the periodicals, Group Psychotherapy and The Princeton Theological Seminary Journal; [pers.] In my writings I like to reflect the relationship of religious ethics to Society

GREEN, VERLEEN ROSE FLETCHER
[pen.] V. Rose; [b.] October 27, 1963, Pontiac, MI; [p.] Rev. Eddie Fletcher (late) Rosie Lee Fletcher; [ch.] Henry L. Green III; [ed.] Pine Bluff, HS Grad 1981, University Arkansas Pine Bluff, Central Texas College Europe; [occ.] 9 Year U.S. Army Veteran, Inspirational Poet; [memb.] Veteran of Foreign Wars (VFW), (DAV) Disabled Veterans Assoc.; [hon.] (3) Army Good Conduct Medals, Army Achievement Medal (3 Oak Leaf Cluster), Army Commendation Medal (ARCOM) (1Oak Leaf Cluster), (NCOPD-2) NCO Professional Development Ribbons, (NDSM) National Defense Service Medal, (ASR) Army Service Ribbon, (OSR) (2) Overseas Service Ribbon, Vernon L. Bowers Administrative Award of Excellence (88); [oth. writ.] Presently writing two novels "Wrong Side of the Mirror", "Friendly

Deceptions"; [pers.] I strive to up lift peoples spirits with poetry. I am greatly influenced by thought provoking events of everyday life.; [a.] Pine Bluff, AR

GREENIDGE, PHYLLIS FLOYD
[pen.] P. Floyd; [b.] July 23, 1959, Saint Augustine, FL; [p.] Mr. and Mrs. Charles Floyd Jr.; [m.] Bruce Greenidge, August 3, 1991; [ed.] BBA-Tennessee State Univ., MBA (con't) University of Phoenix; [occ.] Fitness and Health Instructor; [memb.] American College of Sports Medicine, IDEA - International Association of Fitness Professional, AFAA - Aerobics And Fitness Association of America, Reebok Professional Instructor's Alliance; [oth. writ.] A book of unpublished poems. Editor and publisher of "Fitness Spotlite" A Fitness Newsletter; [pers.] Through my writing I try to express the injustices of society in hopes that the written words will help to bring about change; [a.] Santa Clara, CA

GREENWOOD, NICOLE MARIE
[b.] April 4, 1972, Kingston, Ontario; [p.] Steve Greenwood and Francine Caron; [ed.] Kingston Vocational Collegiate, Institute, Toronto School of Business, Loyalist College.; [occ.] Student/Server; [memb.] Computer Interact, Member; [hon.] Award for continuing education.; [oth. writ.] I have several personal writings of poetry over the years.; [pers.] I strive to reflect on current emotions or past emotions. I like to also reflect on words of encouragement and the mysteries of wonder.; [a.] Kingston Ontario, Canada

GREER, LAURIE D.
[b.] May 20, 1979, Owensboro, KY; [p.] Sherry Greer, Dargan Settles; [occ.] A Junior at Apollo High School; [memb.] Involved in Christian Student Involvement, FCA, Sonstruck Youth Choir, and part of the writing team for the Academic Team.; [hon.] Young Author's Conference; [oth. writ.] I write for I.S.I. newsletter for my church youth group and I'm on the Literary Staff to publish the Tapestry magazine each year.; [pers.] God blessed me by giving me the words to write this poem for a friend before his leaving for college. Because of this wonderful gift, I strive each day to give all the glory to him through the love and abilities he has placed in my life.; [a.] Owensboro, KY

GRELESKI, MARY JEAN
[pen.] M.J. (The Poetry Lady); [b.] August 14, 1947, Sharon, PA; [p.] Madeline and Henry Vicozi; [m.] Robert J. Greleski, April 9, 1966; [ch.] Pam and Glen Luglan, Dawn and Gary Havunen; [ed.] Farrell High School, Farrell, PA; [occ.] Design Coordinator; [oth. writ.] I write personalized poems for family, friends, etc. Also write about places I've been.; [pers.] I try to reflect life and meaning thru my writings. I like to create a silly or serious biography for people and places. I've only done this for a short time but get much enjoyment with it; [a.] Tucson, AZ

GRIFFITH, JANNIE
[b.] June 23, 1938, Elwood, TX; [p.] Walter Dewitt Ultz, Maggie Jane Matthews Ultz; [m.] Quillen Ed Griffith Sr., February 14, 1958; [ch.] Ronald Lee, Saunda Gail, Quillen Ed Jr., Donna Jean, Charles Allen; [ed.] I had to quit school and go to work when I was in 12th grade (1957). My family was very

poor. I got my GED in December, 1989.; [occ.] Housewife; [memb.] Member of Westside Church of Christ Cleveland, Texas; [oth. writ.] I have copyrights on two (2) songs, but they were never published. "Touch Me" and "Love Hurts" (1976). I have many more poems that nothing has ever been done with. "To My Daddy" is in "The Rainbows End"; [pers.] I have been writing poetry since I was in sixth grade. When I was in high school my poetry helped me through literature. I now write for friends and loved ones. I have always liked to read poetry and religious books.; [a.] Splendora, TX

GRIFFITHS, DIANNE CAMIRE
[b.] April 17, 1957, Kenora Ontario, Canada; [p.] Madeline and Adrien Camire; [m.] Bruce Griffiths, January 13, 1979; [ch.] Nancy, Anthony and Amber; [ed.] Beaver Brae and Lakewood High, Niagara College, Sault College, Confederation College, U of Waterloo, Lakehead University; [occ.] Home maker; [memb.] Canadian Hearing Society; [hon.] Self Gratification; [oth. writ.] "Satisfaction", "Island Sunsets - Pictorial Press", "My Mark", Reflections by Moonlight (National Library of Canada); [pers.] Poetry has always been a part of my life. Without it things wouldn't seem as clear to understand.; [a.] Kenora Ontario, Canada

GRIVSKY, ALEXANDRA
[b.] November 29, 1977, Brussels, Belgium; [p.] Michael and Sophia Grivsky; [ed.] Langley High School, George Mason University; [occ.] Student at George Mason University, Communications Major.; [a.] McLean, VA

GROGAN, THOMAS
[b.] May 3, 1977, Vandenberg AFB, CA; [p.] Donald Grogan and Virginia Grogan; [ed.] Gloucester High School, Institute of Children's Literature; [oth. writ.] Locally written poems and school assignments; [a.] Gloucester, VA

GROOME, VANESSA
[pen.] Vanessa DeRenzis; [b.] May 5, 1972, Philadelphia, PA; [p.] Daniel DeRenzis, Lindsey DeRenzis; [m.] Sean M. Groome, September 29, 1995; [ed.] High School for Creative and Performing Arts., Temple University; [occ.] Customer Service Rep., Chrysler Credit.; [hon.] Magna Cum Laude, Dean's List, Scholarship Recipient, First place winner in Great American Smokeout Essay Contest.; [oth. writ.] Published guest opinion in Philadelphia Daily News.; [pers.] I create for myself - with each word, I express myself and everyone who reads my work shares a piece of my soul. Writing, for me is a form of self-examination.; [a.] Bensalem, PA

GROVE, STELLA
[b.] April 5, 1938, England; [ed.] England, New York New School for Social Research - Art Therapy.; [occ.] Free lance writer and artist.; [oth. writ.] 1994- To the present. In a writing workshop at the Joseph PAPP Theatre NYC - 1995 - 'Mystery' was selected by PBS-CH 13 for 'Voices Of New York' a promotional invitation to poets in NYC.; [per.] Currently writing an illustrating a book, in order to share an experience of hope with others - interests Inc., Meditation - creative writing and painting.; [a.] New York City, NY

GRUBER, MELISSA
[pen.] Vivian Lee; [b.] November 28, 1977, Boise, ID; [p.] The late- Gordon Gruber, Wanda Hosier, and Bob Hosier - Stepdad; [ed.] Emmett High School; [occ.] Student in High School (Senior); [hon.] Publication in School Literary Magazine.; [oth. writ.] A poem and short story published in school literary magazine. Many other poems, short story and short novel.; [pers.] My father always wanted something of his to be published. After he died, I started to write and decided to carry out his dream. This poem is for him and of course my loving mother.; [a.] Emmett, ID

GRUCCI, MRS. HEIDI
[b.] May 22, 1964, Long Island; [p.] Mr. and Mrs. Robert DecArlo; [m.] James J. Grucci, July 15, 1984; [ch.] (One son) Dominick J. Grucci; [ed.] High School Graduate from Bellport High School, 2 years at Suffolk Community College; [occ.] Nurse Aide; [oth. writ.] I have been writing poetry since I was ten years old.; [pers.] All dreams are possible, if the desire is strong enough. And no star is out of our reach.; [a.] North Patchosue, NY

GUARDI, SILVIA
[b.] December 8, 1932, Riga, Latvia; [p.] Janis and Natalija Schultz; [m.] Frank Guardi, April 28, 1959; [ch.] John, Alfredo, Nano, Jennifer; [ed.] Graduate from University of North Dakota, Grand Forks in 1957 with Major in Music and Literature.; [occ.] Foster Grandparent; [memb.] Member of Sigma Alpha Iota, a music Fraternity; [pers.] My ambition is to publish a book of my poems under the title: Crystal Tears, Why Tears? Every person has emotions. These emotions may be sad, or happy. They sometimes surface as tears reflecting an emotion of a particular moment - direct and crystal clear......; [a.] Chicago, IL

GUENTHNER, A. RANDALL
[b.] June 1, 1977, Winter Park, FL; [p.] Ray and Martha Guenthner; [ed.] Embry-Riddle Aeronautical Univ., presently a student of Avionics.; [pers.] Never give up. No matter what the odds, no matter how peppered with failure the past, reach for your dreams, and never, never give up!; [a.] Simpsonville, SC

GUSHUE, ADELENE
[pen.] Addie; [b.] November 2, 1948, Saint Thomas; [p.] Dorothy and Perry Herbert; [m.] Thomas Arthur, April 8, 1978; [ch.] One daughter, Patricia; [ed.] Grade XIII 2 years Lab Technician; [occ.] Medical claims assessor for Ontario Health Insurance; [memb.] Hope Ring, Facilitator for Canadian Labour Congress on Various Committees for Breast Cancer Research; [hon.] Learned rep for United Way of London, just winning over breast cancer.; [oth. writ.] One poem; [pers.] I am a disabled person and could not be active in sports and so I enjoy the nature and try to express and give joy to anyone who reads poetry.; [a.] London Ontario, Canada

GUTIERREZ, JOSE
[pen.] Jose Sanchez; [b.] May 12, 1972, Chile; [p.] Gustavo and Maria Gutierrez; [ed.] DMCI "Gr. 12" Diploma; [occ.] Hotel Hospitality; [memb.] Chilean Association of Winnipeg-MB-Canada; [hon.] In Chile won 1st place in Youth Poetry Award; [oth. writ.] XAISO - Adventures, Keys To My Thoughts,

Tears Never Heard Of; [pers.] Because a woman has the gift of giving life why would anybody take hers and why would she take place in taking a life.; [a.] Winnipeg Manitoba, Canada

GUY, RUAH RENNA
[pen.] Ruah Davis; [b.] January 25, 1955, Baltimore, MD; [p.] Opal and Phil Lee III; [m.] Michael Ray Guy, May 6, 1990; [ch.] Justin Guy and Ruah Gillen Water; [ed.] Mountain Empire College VA, Patterson High (Balto Md); [occ.] Housewife; [memb.] Kingsport Tomorrow; [hon.] Sci. Honors; [pers.] If not for my husband Michael and my children Justin and Ruah and family I would not be loved. I found my real love in (Kpt.) Tennessee my husband Michael for whom has help me all the way; [a.] Kingsport, TN

HAAS, DICK MARTIN
[b.] August 12, 1943, Holland; [m.] Sueko Haas, August 26, 1994; [ed.] B.A. Concordia Univ. Montreal, Que., Canada; [occ.] President, The Compass Group a Training and Learning Organ.; [memb.] Assoc for Study of Dreams, Ontario Speakers Association; [oth. writ.] "Time Reading" (1984), "Dreams, Masks and Angels (1996), Many Articles for Dutch, Japanese and Canadian Magazines; [pers.] To uncover the wisdom and compassion within me and share this healing and creative force with love, patience and humility by nurturing all that's alive on this planet; [a.] Milton Ontario, Canada

HADDOCK JR., CASBY
[b.] August 13, 1930, Jacksonville, FL; [p.] Cosby Haddock Sr., and Reba Clance; [m.] Colleen H. Haddock, May 18, 1986; [ch.] Gary M. Haddock, Diane M. Haddock; [ed.] Bachelor Degree Business Science; [occ.] Retired; [oth. writ.] Only unpublished poems; [a.] Fairplay, CO

HAGER, KATHRYN ANNE
[pen.] Katie Hager; [b.] June 27, 1956, Brooklyn, NY; [p.] William M. Hager, Erna C. Hager; [ed.] St. Thomas Apostle Grammar School, The Mary Louis Academy, Molloy College - BA, C. W. Post University - MS; [occ.] Special Education Elementary Teacher, Henry Viscardi School Albertson, NY; [memb.] Policy Board of Herricks Teacher Consortium Adirondack Council, American Museum of Natural History, Audubon Society, Center for Environmental Educcation, Defenders of Wildlife, The Gorilla Foundation, National Geographic Society, North Shore Animal League, North Wind Under Sea Institute, NYZS The Wildlife Conservation Society, Theodore Roosevelt Sanctuary, The Whaling Museum Society and World Wildlife Fund, The Wilderness Society, Sierra Club; [hon.] Certificate of Appreciation for 15 years of dedicated service at Henry Viscardi School, Dec. 14, 1994, Molloy College Alumni Award, June 7, 1981, Alpha Mu Gamma, Delta Epsilon Sigma, Omicron Alpha Zeta, Psi Chi, Full Scholarship to Molloy College, NYS Regents Scholarship, The Mary Louis Award, Jamaica Rotary Club's Student of the Year Award; [oth. writ.] 145 unpublished poems, one published in the Molloy Forum while I was a senior, "First Flight" published in Songs on the Wind, "Dewdrop at Dawn" published in The Garden of Life, and "Icy Sentinel" published in At Water's Edge (three volumes by The National Library of Poetry).; [pers.]

I strive to convey universal emotions and concerns in my poems. I am greatly influenced by deep faith in God, a love for nature, personal experiences, and an appreciation of the power of language. They are constant themes in my poems.; [a.] Williston Park, NY

HAINES, AUDREY
[b.] February 5, 1975, Edmonton, Alberta; [p.] Ralph and Janet Haines; [ch.] Tessa June Haines; [pers.] This poem was written to remind myself why I left an abusive relationship. With God's help anyone can find strength. God found away through my writing.; [a.] Winnipeg Manitoba, Canada

HAJEE, SHENOOR JENNA
[b.] December 31, 1983, Toronto; [p.] Yasmeen and Nizar Hajee; [occ.] Student at the Hawthorn School for girls; [memb.] Junior Volunteer - Agakhan Ismaili Volunteer Corps, Crescent Town Club, Kalev Institute of Dance, De Santos Martial Arts; [oth. writ.] Poem published by poetry institute of Canada - friends, animals and rainbows; [pers.] "To me, a poem is like a dream, a chain of images, that express the emotions that you feel."; [a.] Toronto Ontario, Canada

HAJES, SARAH
[b.] November 3, 1977, Winnipeg, Manitoba; [p.] Albert and Vera Hajes; [oth. writ.] Waller Avenue, All Canadians (in memory of Stan Rogers), The House and Giant Dawn.; [pers.] Much of my inspiration has come from the writings of Leonard Cohen, Jim Morrison, Tom Waits and also my father, a poet himself. Playing guitar has also led me to transform my poetry into song.; [a.] Brandon Manitoba, Canada

HALE JR., CHARLES MARTEL
[b.] January 2, 1957, New York, NY; [p.] Charles M. and Mary Jane Hale; [ed.] Self-educated, Brain injured, expresses himself verbally through Facilitated Communication only.; [occ.] Attends the Northwest Workshop in Winchester, Virginia; [pers.] "I would like to say that my poem was a cry from the heart to God who allowed me to speak, at long last, through Facilitated Communication, after 35 yrs. of silence."

HALL, EVELYN J.
[b.] March 1936, Ontario, Canada; [m.] Larry Hall (Retired Broadcast Journalist); [occ.] Secretary and Cook (private home); [memb.] Local book club volunteer for local Hospice Association, Charter member of P.H.O.G. local writers' group known as the Port Hope Original Group; [oth. writ.] Book reviews (newspaper) and for Ontario Black History Society Miscellaneous articles for local newspapers and publishers, Articles for the P.H.O.G. magazine; [pers.] Enjoys walking, meditation, gardening and collecting unicorns.; [a.] Port Hope Ontario, Canada

HALL, GLADYS ANN
[b.] June 21, 1947; [m.] Ollie F. Hall; [ch.] Connie Tony RT; [occ.] QA Superintendent; [memb.] ASQC; [pers.] I avoid feeling sorry for myself by staying busy.; [a.] Smyrna, TN

HALL, JOHN KINSER
[pen.] John K. Hall; [b.] December 9, 1940, Tampa, FL; [p.] Malcolm J. Hall, Mary K. Hall; [m.] Janice L. Hall, July 3, 1981; [ch.] Susan E. Fuguet; [ed.]

H.B. Plant High School Tampa, USMC 1959-1963; [occ.] Attorneys Private Research for Law Frims in Florida; [oth. writ.] All published by the National Library of Poetry, evening love, a little happiness, a flag upon an empty box; [pers.] The poems I write are life experiences written from the heart to be shared, so none will feel unique. Just the knowledge that someone else lived these experienced helps us to know we are not alone. Shame your life, share your love; [a.] Winchester, VA

HALL, WENDY
[pers.] This poem is dedicated in memory of my beloved mother, Gladys Nequest, who passed away July 30, 1988.

HALLE, DENNIS LIONEL
[b.] January 4, 1941, Toronto, Ontario; [p.] Leo and Anne (Charuk) Halle; [m.] Ruth Fern Halle, September 27, 1963; [ch.] Grant, Kelly; [ed.] Attended Notre Dame Schools, Welland, Ontario until grade 9, presently completing 12th grade, Sarnia, ON; [occ.] Journey Insulator, Local 95, Ontario, Canada; [memb.] Active in Hunting, Angling and Conservation. Clubs, L.C.A. Sarnia, O.F.A.H., N.F.A.; [pers.] Inspired by my loving grand mother, Mrs. Albertine (Langdon) Halle, deceased, whom loved writing. To her credit was the author of "La Vallee Des Bles D'or." (Roman revised 1983); [a.] Sarnia Ontario, Canada

HALLS, KAREN
[pen.] Lady Blue Bird or bluebird; [b.] February 7, 1960, Woodstock, Ontario; [p.] Wilhelmina and Robert Halls; [ch.] Marci and Matthew Halls; [ed.] High School diploma achieved in 1994 as a mature, working full time, mother of two student. Future goals are education in journalism.; [occ.] Production Associate at Cami Automotive, Ingersol, Ontario; [hon.] This is my first time recognition for any of my poetry.; [oth. writ.] Deligate reports and short articles in Union newsletter. Letters to the editor in local newspaper. Personal poetry for close friends and family.; [pers.] I have a deep inner struggle of not being capable of expressing emotional pain. My soul becomes paper and tears turn to ink and together they create a sense of peace. It gives me the strength to continue my journey of reaching the light at the end of the tunnel.

HAMILTON, LORIN DEAN
[b.] November 10, 1956, Hammond, IN; [p.] Louis and Virginia Hamilton; [m.] Divorced; [ch.] Kristina Dawn and April Nicole; [ed.] Quit in 10th grade and turned part time job to full time. Matinace mechanic and tire man for a local trucking company. Got G.E.D. 1990; [occ.] Owner Operator Truck Driver; [memb.] Teemsters local 714, 17 years; [hon.] 13 Good Driver Award; [oth. writ.] A Wish Upon A Star, A Rose For The Lady, Watching, Rock-N-Roll Music, (and many more); [pers.] If I had only one wish, just one wish to come true, it would be for peace, the whole world through.

HAMILTON, MARK F.
[b.] October 2, 1953, London, England; [p.] Jane and Francis F. Hamilton; [ed.] U. of Calif. Santa Barbara; [occ.] Computer Consultant; [oth. writ.] Poetry Collection, Short Stories, Screen Plays, Non-Fiction Stories, Computer Programs, Math Text Books (18 registered copyrights); [a.] Sedona, AZ

HAMMONS, FRANCES J.
[b.] June 21, 1935, TN; [p.] Veta and Gaiter Lloyd; [m.] James T. Hammons, August 17, 1949; [ch.] Anthony, Louise and Gail; [ed.] 7th grade plus Certified Nurse Aide Training. Worked at Kit Carson Conv. Hospital and Amador Hospital from 1970-1989; [occ.] Housewife, Retired to Breast Cancer in 1989; [oth. writ.] None published but I have written poems for friends anniversaries, and in memory of people as this poem in memory of my son age 2, Anthony killed in a caracci June 3-52; [pers.] I lived on a farm until my parent's were divorced when I was 11 and my mother moved to Calif. bring us 3 kids still at home with her. There were 13 children in my family.; [a.] La Mirada, CA

HANEY, JO
[b.] March 2, 1978, Shattuck, OK; [p.] Red and Joyce Johnson, R. Haney; [ed.] High School Senior at present; [memb.] Has been accepted at the University of Oklahoma and will double major in English and Journalism.; [hon.] 5 County All Star, Western Oklahoma Classic All Star Basketball team.; [pers.] Had knee surgery as a high school athlete (basketball and softball) Idea for this poem came early one morning on the 35 mile drive home from knee re-hab workout. Credit H.S. English Teacher Serena Kauk for the motivation and tools to be a creative writer.

HANN, RANDY
[b.] January 11, 1970, Gander, NF; [p.] Gordon and Monnie Hann; [m.] Paula Hann, July 16, 1994; [ed.] Clarenville Integrated High; [occ.] Bucket Wheel Operator, Syncrude Canada Ltd.; [pers.] I dedicate this poem to the memory of my father, Gordon Hann.; [a.] Fort McMurray Alberta, Canada

HANNON, VIRGINIA
[b.] August 14, 1917, Queens, NY; [p.] Margaret and Fred Miller; [m.] Joseph (Deceased), September 7, 1941; [ch.] Three girls, one boy; [ed.] High School Graduate; [occ.] Retired (from Accounting Dept. NY Tele. Co.); [memb.] Telephone Pioneers of America; [oth. writ.] Composed many poems over the years (for my own pleasure) never entered any contest before; [pers.] My husbands sudden passing inspired me to write this poem. I was able to release my feelings on paper (at 4 AM in the morning) he passed away, June 1993 of non-hodgkins Lymphoma.; [a.] Boynton Beach, FL

HANSFORD, VIRGINIA
[b.] October 6, 1945, WV; [p.] Clarence and Minnie Miller; [m.] David P. Hansford, January 26, 1968; [ch.] Lisa and Rebecca Hansford; [ed.] East Bank High, Carver Career College; [occ.] Hair Stylist; [memb.] U.S. Coast Guard Auxiliary; [oth. writ.] A Limrick published in Jr. High School, several songs and poems not published; [pers.] I try to reflect the beauty of nature in my poems. I have been influenced by the book of psalms in the Bible.; [a.] Chesapeake, WV

HANSON, SARAH
[b.] September 10, 1983, Marion, IL; [p.] Stan and Maribeth Hanson; [ed.] High Honors Student in the 6th grade at Marion Junior High School, Marion, Illinois. Participates in the gifted program.; [memb.] Member of the Illinois State Champion Competition Team of the Heartland Twirling Corps; [hon.] Pre-

teen Miss Southern Illinois, Talent Winner, has won Awards on the Local, State and National Level in Baton Twirling, Business and Professional Women's Club Talent Show Award Winners, Southern Illinois University and John A. Logan Jr. College Guest Performer.; [a.] Marion, IL

HARDY, TIFFANY RAE
[b.] February 28, 1974, Reno, NV; [p.] Robert and Vicki Harshbarger; [m.] Joshua Hardy, October 3, 1992; [ed.] Elko High School, Nevada community College; [occ.] part time secretary, full time ordained minister; [pers.] I miss some, I love some I regret a little, I'm proud of a lot, I hurt sometimes, and I cry but I still laugh, I'm much stronger, and also some weaker, I cherish my past, and welcome my future; [a.] Elko, NV

HARGROVE, ELIZABETH BLAKE
[b.] July 2, 1979, Los Gatos, CA; [p.] Harry and Joan Hargrove; [ed.] Westbriar Elementary, Joyce Kilmer Middle School, Geo C. Marshall High School; [occ.] Student (currently 11th grade); [memb.] National Honor Society, Tri-M Music Honor Society, Geo C. Marshall Symphonic Band, Dakota Team (youth group that travels to S.D. to teach Bible school to the LaKota Indians, church sponsored); [hon.] Several Music (duet and solo) awards. Nominated for Youth for Excellence Awards 1994 and 1995; [oth. writ.] 20 and other poems written for school and/or personal use; [a.] Vienna, VI

HARLESS, JEFF
[b.] April, 22, 1943, Bakersfield, CA; [p.] Lloyd and Violet Harless; [m.] Roberta Harless, August 22, 1993; [ch.] Allan, Elizabeth, Christine, Steve, Traci; [ed.] East Bakersfield H.S., West Valley J.C. Saratoga, CA; [occ.] Floor Covering Contractor; [oth. writ.] Nothing published previously.; [pers.] Influenced by E.A. Poe, Charles Dickens. My poetry is a hobby, instilling pleasure in myself, friends and family.; [a.] San Jose, CA

HARPER, JAMES H.
[pen.] Jim Harder; [b.] September 15, 1949, Jacksonville, TX; [p.] Howard and Ila Cotton Harper; [m.] Christine Johnson Harper, September 4, 1982; [ch.] Timothy and Adam; [ed.] Master's in Education, Stephen F. Austin State University, Nacogdoches, TX; [occ.] Associate Clinical Psychologist, Rusk St. Hosp.; [memb.] North American Association of Masters in Psychology - Trinity Lutheran Church; [hon.] National Honor Society (High School), Psi Chi (national Honor Society in Psychology; [oth. writ.] Previous published in NLP. (Beyond The Stars,) numerous unpublished) poems.; [pers.] The catharsis of poetic expression provides immeasurable joy and allows for feeling life fully.; [a.] Rusk, TX

HARRIS, DANIELLE
[b.] October 19, 1977, London, Ontario; [p.] Ms. Rita Harris; [ed.] John Paul II, Catholic Secondary School; [occ.] High School Student; [memb.] V.W.O. Rowing Club; [oth. writ.] Other poetry, "In her heart" published in school board anthology, "Making Connections", presented to the United Nations - Fall of 1995; [pers.] "When the student is ready, the teacher will appear." For: Michelle Kennedy whose faith, encouragement and support has guided my heart and therefore my pen.; [a.] London Ontario, Canada

HARRIS, PAULINE BINGENHEIMER
[pen.] Polly Harris; [b.] October 14, 1924, Angola, NY; [p.] Philip Bingenheimer, Erna Zempel Bingenheimer; [m.] Price Harris, August 14, 1957; [ed.] Hamburg High, State Teachers College at Buffalo, Albright Art School, Teacher's College, Columbia University, NY; [occ.] 41 years as Art Teacher, retired taught in NY and KY; [memb.] Retired teachers, Paducah - McCracken County, Kentucky Retired Teachers Association; [hon.] Alpha Delta Kappa; [pers.] Reading, writing, painting, listening to music, and gardening are my choices for time investment, discussing, working, and sharing these activities with interested people has created wonderful dividends in my life.; [a.] Paducah, KY

HART, JEFFREY KEY
[b.] January 29, 1976, Vancouver, BC; [p.] Ken and Lynn Hart; [ed.] South Delta Secondary, Presently a student at the University of British Columbia; [occ.] Student; [pers.] I wrote this poem for my friend, Vyanne Neufeld, who passed away on August 25, 1992. She will always be with me and I miss her a great deal.; [a.] Tsawwassen British Columbia, Canada

HART, JUDY KAY
[b.] July 23, 1951, Huntsville, AL; [p.] Douglas N. and Thelma G. Anders; [m.] Charles W. Hart, May 22, 1992; [ch.] Donnie Eiland Jr. and Dawn Marie Eiland; [ed.] High School graduate and am currently enrolled in Children's Institute of Lit. in correspondence course (King High School - Tampa, Florida); [occ.] I am a booking/customer service agent for a cargo ship line; [memb.] I am active in my church as a S.S. Teacher (5th and 6th grade) am Church Librarian, belong to Prison Fellowship Ministries; [oth. writ.] Am currently working on children's stories and have written several poems also want to write romance novels; [pers.] "Black is not always White..." was written after the O.J. verdict. Racial strife hurts my heart and needs to be obliterated. There are enough problems without adding hatred of fellow human beings.; [a.] Tampa, FL

HARTLIEP, BRADLEY
[b.] March 11, 1966, Fargo, ND; [ed.] Catalina H.S., Tucson, AZ, Technical Studies U.S. Air Force and Cochise College Douglas, AZ. Educational Studies, Martin Luther College, New Ulm, MN.; [occ.] Teacher III, Youth Enrichment Services, Centennial Elem., Tucson, AZ.; [oth. writ.] Approx. 450 lines of currently unpublished poetry, including 40 additional lines to "Two Fish in the Desert," several pages of "Early Poetry Attempts" lost a long time ago...; [pers.] Striving to be a positive influence on every child I meet is my life goal. Positively affecting one child's outlook on life is reaching my goal for today.; [a.] Tucson, AZ

HARVEY, DIANE
[b.] September 10, 1942, Dallas, TX; [p.] Aaron and Inez Pederson; [m.] Divorced; [ch.] Kathryn Sue, Susan Kaye (Deceased), Lisa Michelle; [ed.] Adamson High School; [occ.] Customer Service Specialist - McGraw -Hill Publishers, De Soto, TX; [memb.] Earthsave, People for the Ethical Treatment of Animals; [hon.] National Honor Society; [oth. writ.] Enjoy writing poems for friends Birthdays, special occasions, etc.; [pers.] Expressing myself

through poetry enables me to look inside my soul and become real. I was inspired by Bill Moyer's series, "The Language of Life."; [a.] Duncanville, TX

HASTE, HEATHER NICOLE
[b.] October 3, 1975, Raleigh, NC; [p.] Richard and Judy Godwin; [ed.] Broughton High; [a.] Raleigh, NC

HATAM, MARY PAULA
[b.] December 29, 1955, Newport, RI; [p.] Angeline and Michael DeCotis; [m.] Reza Hatam, November 28, 1980; [ch.] Ben 13, Maria 7; [ed.] A.D.N., Tarrant County Jr. College, Ft. Worth, TX and attends University of Pittsburgh, Pittsburgh, PA pursuing B.S.N.; [occ.] Registered Nurse; [pers.] I am just beginning the enjoyment of writing and wish to be an author someday. To me, all actions in life are art and it is up to gifted writers to expound on and appreciate art.; [a.] Irwin, PA

HATANAKA, YURI PER
[b.] September 2, 1968, Tokyo, Japan; [ed.] High School Graduate; [memb.] Action Autonomie, the collective for the defense of rights in mental health in Montreal; [hon.] Concordia University Broomball Championship; [pers.] I strive to find meaning in life through language.; [a.] Dollard-des-Ormeaux Quebec, Canada

HAUCK, LAURA LYNN
[b.] December 23, 1988, Tulsa, OK; [p.] Michael and Donna Hauck; [ed.] In first grade at Arrowhead Elem. in B.A.; [occ.] Student; [memb.] Theatre Arts in B.A. when I take Acting and Musical Theatre.; [oth. writ.] Have written short stories for school; [pers.] Love making people happy whether writing or acting. Want to act and make people laugh when I grow up. It is good to be happy.; [a.] Tulsa, OK

HAUG, JOHANNA
[b.] February 12, 1915; [p.] Herman and Magdalene Leedgens; [m.] Eugene J. Haug (1906-1980), June 27, 1937; [ch.] Eugene H. Gerardine, Norena Bruce, Christine; [ed.] Graduated Washington, Irving H.s. (N.Y.), Brooklyn College Seton Hall, Bucknell U. Lewisburg PA., Ohio U. Ext. Chilicothe O.; [memb.] Several memberships in Philanthropic Org. Beta Chapter alpha Chi Omega Sorority; [hon.] Many but not published; [oth. writ.] It is one's duty to live up to daily responsibilities to best of ability but it is also to appreciate the beauties of nature in all its phases which is what my poem is all about; [pers.] Forth Worth, TX

HAVARIS, MARCIA E.
[b.] June 7, 1957, London, Ontario; [p.] Marjorie and Kenneth Miller; [m.] Christos D. Havaris, July 23, 1989; [ed.] Performer's Associateship of Music-Voice, Teacher's Associateship of Music-Piano, Western Ontario Conservatory of Music, Canada.; [occ.] Teacher of Music and Speech Arts - Miller Academy of Music and Fine Art, London, Ontario, Canada, Vocal Workshops, Lectures and Seminars, Creative Writing and Drawing Workshops. Mask-Making.; [hon.] 1st Prize Winner in Via Rail Photo Contest: "Canada's cities, Towns and Villages" 1987. Photo of, and article about our Gazebo created and built by my husband, Christos. (In Select Homes and Foods, summer 1993.); [oth. writ.] Published in the "Encounter" (part of the London Free Press). Several hundred poems (unpublished).

A collection of writings and photographs: Volume I - "To Parents" (Writings From My Youth, 1972-1983) 1995.; [pers.] Writing is self-expression through words, a creative expansion of the soul in a desire to communicate feelings and to share experiences. I hope that the words I choose will serve to affirm truth and beauty and to inspire faith in God.; [a.] London, Ontario

HAWKINS, MARYANNE
[b.] June 16, 1954, Toronto; [p.] Mary and Michael Lucchetta; [ch.] April and Gregory; [occ.] Quality and Humans Resource Management; [pers.] Creativity is often the offspring of adversity, if one listens to one's inner voice.; [a.] Brampton Ontario, Canada

HAYES, DEIRDRE LUCY
[pen.] Allison Goodwin; [b.] January 17, 1945, New York, NY; [p.] Charles William and Anne L. Hayes; [m.] Thomas E. Williams "Tommy", Spring, 1996; [ch.] Jeff, Jill, Laura and Bryan; [ed.] Dixie Hollins High, St. Pete Fl. Tarrant County Jr. College, Ft. Worth, TX; [occ.] Business Manager, Center St. Counseling Services; [oth. writ.] "Loving Thoughts of You", (Work in Progress - a biographical Fiction not yet completed); [pers.] This poem is one of a collection written in the summer of 1994, and is a reflection of love and acceptance dedicated to "Tommy", the love I've never known before.; [a.] Everman, TX

HAYES, NICHOLAS
[b.] January 25, 1978, Joplin, MO; [p.] Clayton Hayes, Linda Hayes; [ed.] Rock Bridge Sr. High; [occ.] Student; [memb.] Student Environmental Coalition-President, Folio: Literary/Arts Magazine, La Societe Honoraire Franquise; [oth. writ.] Published a Vignette in the '94-'95, issue of Folio.; [pers.] I write to hint at gnosis that language can not portray.; [a.] Columbia, MO

HAYES, ROSEMARY
[b.] July 21, 1945, Saint Patrick's, New Foundland, Canada; [p.] Leo Hayes and the late Mary Hayes; [m.] Robert Barnes; [ch.] Kanti; [ed.] BAH (Bociology), Major Psychology; [memb.] Alumna of Acadia University Wolfville, NS, Canada; [oth. writ.] A collection of unpublished poems; [pers.] I wrote "Loneliness" on November 26, 1967 when I was only 22 years old. I was thousands of miles from home and already feeling very homesick, only a month away from Christmas.; [a.] Hammonds Plains Nova Scotia, Canada

HAYWARD, ALYSIA F.
[b.] February 22, 1925, Rural, OH; [p.] Lina and A. C. Lohbeck; [ch.] 1 Daughter, 2 Sons; [ed.] 9th Grade and G.E.D.; [pers.] Visual impairment is a daily reminder to savor each minute of every hour of every day. Remember words in print, beholds colors, the shape of each flower. Visualize the source of each fragrance and resonance. Be cognizant of the face of a laughing child, the color of the eyes of a loved one reflecting happiness. Record the expression of pain and sadness etched in the countenance of a familiar visage. File in your memory in such order that you can choose one for any occasion that might rise in a future of total darkness.; [a.] Mesa, AZ

HAZZARD, TAMMY LYNN
[pen.] Tammy Lynn Hazzard; [b.] May 2, 1977, Amsterdam, NY; [p.] Havid Hazzard Jr., Sally Hazzard; [ed.] Faith Bible Academy; [pers.] To make myself and others be all that God wants us all to be.; [a.] Fultonville, NY

HEATH, HENRY BLAINEY
[b.] January 20, 1972, Chester, SC; [p.] Sam Thomas and Susie Heath; [m.] Martha Corena Heath, May 30, 1945; [ch.] Susie L., Antoinette; [ed.] B.A. Degree, Major - Elementary Ed., Minor - English, J.C. Smith University; [occ.] Substitute teaching before retiring, served as School Principals and Teacher; [memb.] Phi Beta Sigma, Veterans Club, United Methodist Church, Chancel Choir, Sunday School; [hon.] WW II Combat Star, V.S. Army 4 yrs., Served 3 yrs. in Foreign Service in South West Pacific; [oth. writ.] Mitchell, Mitchell How I love Thee, My Tip Upon the Atlantic Blue, When I Go Home from Tonga; [pers.] Keep smiling and be responsive to the master's dictates.; [a.] Charlotte, NC

HEBERT, REGINA
[b.] January 14, 1951, Durham, NC; [p.] Clarance Wilkerson, Mary Latta; [m.] Maurice Hebert, May 11, 1994; [ch.] Chad Groves, Lisa Gossellin; [ed.] Orange High, Hillsborough, NC, Training Academy Richmond, VA; [occ.] Integon Ins.; [memb.] Cathedral of his Glory the Mother church of church around the world; [oth. writ.] I am writing a book, named "Hearts window."; [pers.] My desire is to reveal the Love of Jesus Christ though my poems.

HECKNER, ALAN
[pen.] Alan Heckner; [b.] August 12, 1977, Weirton, WV; [p.] Gordon and Mileva Heckner; [ed.] Currently attending New York University; [occ.] Student; [pers.] This poem is dedicated to Declan MacManus, Thank You.; [a.] Houston, TX

HEINKE, KATHRYN
[b.] October 5, 1916, Goldbar, WA; [p.] George and Gladys Cross; [m.] Ray R. Heinke, January 24, 1933; [ch.] Ronald Heinke, Arlene Heinke Miller; [ed.] High School - Graduate of Everett, WA High School - class of 1934 1/2; [occ.] Retired - Formerly Licensed Wash. Insurance Agent; [memb.] Rhododendron Chapter of Eastern Star; [hon.] 5 Grandchildren 2 Great Grandchildren; [oth. writ.] Poetry - pertaining family members and friends.; [pers.] Spent most of my time with craft projects, along with knitting and crocheting. Also love to travel when I can.; [a.] Tacoma, WA

HEINTZ, TAMMY
[b.] September 4, 1976; [ed.] Metropolitan State College, Denver, CO; [memb.] Porter Hospice Care Volunteer, President's Circle of Excellence; [hon.] Dean's List, S.P.I., Scholarship Award Winner; [oth. writ.] Several poems published in local underground, magazines and papers; [pers.] You can not seek beauty, you must find it. Every experience can be learned from, and create something of beauty from.; [a.] Denver, CO

HEMENWAY, WAVERLY L.
[b.] July 17, 1937, Alexandria, LA; [p.] Louise Davidson and Paul Hemenway; [m.] Wm. M. Simmons, July 11, 1957, Wm. C. Mueller, March 8, 1979; [ch.] Wm. M. Simmons Jr., Waverly D. Simmons; [ed.] Bolton High School, 2 yrs. Newcomb College, 1 yr. Tulane University; [occ.] Retired; [hon.] National Writers Club Award 1st place, Imagery Division - Poem 'The Seasons' 1954; [oth. writ.] Poetry and humorous, short stories.; [pers.] I love writing within the discipline imposed by classic rhymed and metered verse. These is no thrill to compare with capturing an emotion in the best possible words in the best possible order!; [a.] Newiberia, LA

HEMPHILL, SHARI
[b.] August 29, 1957, Cuba, NY; [p.] Rowland and Eleanor Burdick; [ch.] Stacy and Michael; [ed.] Bolivar High, Nursing School; [occ.] Licensed Practical Nurse; [oth. writ.] Poems for school papers, and local newspaper; [pers.] "I always believe that even in our darkest moments, seeing a sunrise, or hearing birds singing shows us we should still have hope."; [a.] Bolivar, NY

HENNING, JAMES CRAIG
[b.] January 23, 1957, Huntington Park, CA; [p.] Betty Joe Polk (Willis); [ch.] Matthew Henning and Patrick Henning; [ed.] Corona High School 1975; [occ.] Aerospace - Subcontract Administrator, Rockwell International Corporation, Downey, CA; [pers.] Happiness is seen in the eyes of a true romantic and as reflected in our children's smiles.; [a.] Lakewood, CA

HENNING, MICHAEL
[b.] July 19, 1978, Regina, Saskatchewan, Canada; [p.] Barbara Yates Henning, Bruce Henning; [ed.] Graduated 1995 Sheldon Williams Collegiate Regina, SA, ARCT in Violin Performance with Great Distinction from the Toronto Conservatory of Music (1995); [occ.] Student at the University of Calgary; [hon.] Governor General's Gold Medal for Academic Proficiency (1995) and many other scholastic awards, Duke of Edinburgh Gold Medal (1996), numerous local, provincial, and national scholarships and awards for excellence in music performance, including two silver medals from the Toronto Conservatory of Music.; [oth. writ.] Author of approximately 100 poems, or songs, Regina Sun Correspondent, featured Writer for Regina Leader Post; [pers.] The function of art is to make new and complex insights and ideas appealing to ordinary people through inspired innovation. I myself employ striking use of form coupled with contemporary societal, and often startling on surreal, situations and images to communicate the perceived nature of the world and the individual's plate within it.; [a.] Calgary Alberta, Canada

HENRIE, JOYE LEACH
[b.] January 13, 1977, Dallas, TX; [p.] Sheila Hinton and Derrel Leach; [m.] Russell V. Henrie, December 2, 1995; [ed.] High School Diploma - (YCP) Youth Challenge Program N. Little Rock, Arkansas; [occ.] Repair Call Handler with U.S. West Communications; [memb.] Latter Day Saints; [hon.] Various art and painting awards, Civil Air Patrol, Outstanding Cadet; [pers.] My poetry is often not understood, but I write only about my personal experiences, therefore, it's sometimes vague. I never write about things I haven't personally experienced but the "feeling" isn't there.; [a.] Salt Lake City, UT

HENRY, WAYDE DARREN
[pen.] Darren Henry; [b.] May 14, 1963, Calgary, Canada; [p.] Clayton and Joyce Henry (Father Deceased); [ed.] Currently attending Mount Royal College in Calgary with a goal of achieving my degree in Applied Communications (journalism); [occ.] Student at Mount Royal College (Calgary); [hon.] Made the honor roll four times (in a row) prior to attending Mount Royal College.; [oth. writ.] Several commentaries in the Calgary Herald, and several letters to the editor.; [pers.] Never let age stand in the way of your dreams. Age is a hurdle, but a dream can become your future.; [a.] Calgary Alberta, Canada

HENRY, WENDY RENE
[b.] August 9, 1969, Baltimore, MD; [p.] Charles A. Henry and Lynda J. Gutkoska, Alkla Lynda J. Henry; [ed.] Graduated from the Medix School, Feb. 1988 - Glenn Burnie, MD, Graduated from Andover, Senior High School, June 1987 - Linthicum, MD; [occ.] Medical Secretary; [memb.] Saint Benedict Parish; [pers.] I write for everyone and express feelings for thought.

HENSON, DAVID L.
[b.] June 19, 1952, Memphis, TN; [p.] J.C. Henson Jr. and Mary F. Thomas; [m.] Elizabeth A. Henson, July 15, 1988; [ch.] Melody, Leslie, Melinda; [ed.] Graduate - Business College; [occ.] Real Estate Agent; [memb.] Memphis Area Assoc. of Realtors, Tennessee Assoc. of Realtors, National Assoc. of Realtors; [pers.] We are all sons and daughters of God who have lost our way home. God is the same yesterday, today and forever, we have just forgotten who we are and where our home is at.; [a.] Memphis, TN

HERCEG, RALPH STEVEN
[b.] June 5, 1965, Toronto, Ontario; [p.] Jim and Elke Herceg; [ed.] Grade Twelve, College, and Distant learning Psych. plus home study home study in psychology and learning life.; [occ.] A peaceful warrior in daily life training; [memb.] Positive Attitude Training and Volunteer for Human Services many hours, University Psychology; [oth. writ.] Touch from a far truth in lies, a way out, un or non-published works.; [pers.] The one most important relationship is with ourselves and this relationship sadly gets the least effort. I would love to see this change for the good of mankind.; [a.] Guelph Ontario, Canada

HERD, MARY GENEVA H.
[pen.] Holliday; [b.] June 17, 1925, Flat Rock Liberty, SC; [p.] Rev. and Mrs. Simon P., and Georgie Tinsley Holliday; [m.] Grady Loyd Herd, May 12, 1944; [ch.] Daughters: Georgie Lynn, Mary Yvonne, sons: David Michael, Mark Anthony; [ed.] Jr. High/GED; [occ.] Housewife; [oth. writ.] Some of my creative interest include painting, sewing, interior decorating and music, both composition and vocal performance. My poem entitled "Ireland", set to the familiar, "Londondery Aire", is a hauntingly, beautiful tribute to Irish patriots. Other poems and songs such as "Freedom Is", have their roots in my own Judeo-Christian heritage, I always feel compelled to create vivid. Word pictured which like paintings, can inspire the imagination. They reflect my love of nature on reverence for the Creator.; [pers.] "I love my country and I'm proud to be an American." I am of English, Scotch/Irish decent.; [a.] Greenville, SC

HERMAN, MRS. DALE
[m.] Herb; [ch.] 4 children; [ed.] University Degree in English and Philosophy, Laurentian University, Sudbury, Ont. Canada; [pers.] I enjoy life as a grandmother of six. My husband and I live a quiet life and I enjoy writing very much.; [a.] North Bay Ontario, Canada

HERRERA, CAROLINA
[b.] March 8, 1976, McAllen, TX; [p.] Jesus and Martha Herrera; [m.] Jose Felix Escobar, December 23, 1995; [ed.] Graduated, McAllen Memorial High School; [occ.] Working, (receptionist), Avion Travel, Inc.; [memb.] McAllen Folklorico Performers; [hon.] Perfect Attendance, Business Administration, Choir and Dance Awards; [oth. writ.] (Only at school, none published, well, only in school newspapers); [pers.] I believe that each one of us can leave everything behind and start again, but this time learning from our previous mistakes.; [a.] Pharr, TX

HERRICK, LISA M.
[b.] September 16, 1964, San Diego, CA; [p.] Bruce and Sharon Courneya; [m.] John A. Herrick, October 18, 1985; [ch.] Blake Anthony, Brooke Marie; [pers.] The White Knight fades into the distance, dreams perish, living are the memories never forgotten.; [a.] Lino Lakes, MN

HERRICK, RUPERT
[pen.] Rupert Herrick; [b.] March 24, 1929, London, England; [p.] Arthur and Beatrice Whyard; [ch.] Robert and Susan; [ed.] Pasadena City College (Assoc. in Arts Degree); [occ.] Retired; [memb.] Technical Writer for thirty years, was a Member of Society for Tech. Writers and Publishers; [oth. writ.] A few poems and one novel, none published (yet).; [pers.] My sole ambition is to entertain and elate my readers and to enjoy the struggle and renown of its accomplishment.; [a.] Hawkins Bar, CA

HERRING, BOBBIE J.
[b.] July 2, 1948, Lovington, NM; [p.] Bob and Prudy Koonce; [m.] Major Richard C. Chatfield, June, 1990; [ch.] One daughter; [occ.] Hughes Aircraft Electronics Inspector; [memb.] Society of Southwest Authors; [oth. writ.] have been accepted by 'Reminisce' Magazine for a photo and exceptal version of a short story, a poem and personal essay in our journey, a publication in Portland, Or. A poem in Nat'l Library of Poetry, Summer Anthology titled 'Autumnal Gold'; [pers.] My love of the Southwest deserts and concern for the exponentially exploding population has complied me to write after a twenty-five year respite.; [a.] Tulson, AZ

HERSEY, MARY E.
[pen.] Mary Kendall Hersey; [b.] September 10, 1926, Wenatchee, WA; [p.] George Kendall, Ellen Mulloy Kendall; [m.] Walter William (Bill) Hersey, April 27, 1945; [ch.] Carolyn Nelson, Barbara Hersey, Sharon Hersey, Dawn Hersey, Janice Hersey-Beam, Larry Hersey; [ed.] Holy Name Academy, Attended Seattle Univ., and Univ. of Wash.; [occ.] Retired Journalist and Labor Relations Representative,; [memb.] Newspaper Guild, Central Wash. Peace and Environmental Council; [oth. writ.] Staff writer! Wenatchee daily world (1945-46), our times weekly (1964-69), Yakima Herald Republic (copy Ed. 1970-73); [pers.] Poetry is for me a

spiritual expression that seeks a clear focus and a disciplined mind.; [a.] Selah, WA

HERZSTEIN, SANDRA LOUISE SHIELDS
[b.] February 25, 1945, San Francisco, CA; [p.] Frank Shields, Gladys Shields; [m.] David J. Herzstein, March 7, 1980; [ch.] Jeffrey Scott, Matthew Sean; [ed.] Balboa High School, City College of San Francisco; [occ.] Clerical; [memb.] KQED, Nature Conservancy. I'm not sure, the membership. We are members of many org. but only as far as donations are concerned. We are not board or staff members.; [hon.] Chosen 3 times to display photos for photo contest, won 1st prize for one.; [oth. writ.] Have written for 30 years, this is my first submission.; [pers.] Words are fun, and thu them I attempt to convey both beauty and truth, a way to feel connected to all things, an expression of "God's" wonder and wisdom. I have been influenced by many writers, both western and eastern. In particular Haiku. I wish to share what they all have in common, "feeling."; [a.] Fremont, CA

HICKMAN, TRASHA
[b.] February 5, 1977, Loris, SC; [p.] Rupert Hickman, Doris P. Hickman; [occ.] College Student; [hon.] National Honor Society, Senior Beta Club, Who's Who Among American High School Students, 1st Place Global Challenge Winner; [pers.] I believe that there is a writer in everyone waiting to break out.; [a.] Loris, SC

HILEMAN, LARRY J.
[pen.] Finney; [b.] June 13, 1948, York, PA; [p.] Herbert and Alice; [m.] Julie M. Hileman, July 28, 1990; [ch.] Valerie, Christopher, Shawn, Jason; [ed.] Marketing and Business Mgmt. York College at PA; [occ.] (Handicapped) Physically Challenged; [memb.] I have given time to the United Way, Hometown Hospital and Literary Council as a volunteer; [hon.] My honor is to be allowed to contribute, my work to your organizations and to give someone enjoyment.; [oth. writ.] Poems come from my personnel collection; [pers.] My poetry comes from personnel experiences and observations collected over 47 years of life. I strive to reflect the goodness as well as the sadness of existence.; [a.] York, PA

HILL, LOU
[b.] September 4, 1927, Aiken County, SC; [p.] Mr. and Mrs. Jacob Scott; [m.] Robert G. Hill, January 26, 1952; [ch.] Mrs. Ruth Hill O'Briant; [ed.] Aiken High School, Aiken, South Carolina; [occ.] Housewife; [memb.] Darien Baptist Church, Aiken, S.C.; [pers.] I'm writing poetry - I'm inspired by God's Creation and it's beauty that is available to all mankind. Its my desire that all will stop to see the breathtaking scenery and take "Time To Smell That Roses!!"; [a.] Aiken, SC

HILL, PAMELA
[b.] August 6, 1947, Ravenna, OH; [p.] Victor and Hazel Knox (Both Deceased); [ch.] Michelle, Gena, Brenda, Diana; [ed.] Independence High School, Independence, Ohio

HILL, RUSTY
[b.] May 29, 1975, Saint Petersburg, FL; [p.] Richard B. Hill and Melanie D. Winn; [ed.] Southeast High School, Manatte Community College; [occ.]

Assistant Theatre Manager; [pers.] Mainly try to reflect nature, harmony and love in my poetry.; [a.] Fort Walton Beach, FL

HILLOCKS, LOWELL O.
[b.] November 20, 1967, Brooklyn, NY; [p.] Clarence and Rita Hillocks; [m.] Priscilla Yvette Hillocks, June 29, 1988; [ch.] Shanika and Amber Hillocks; [ed.] Uniondale High School, State University of New York College at Old Westburg; [hon.] Enlisted Surface Warfare Specialist, Admiral's Letter of Commendation (US Navy); [oth. writ.] Several other poems written in high school and college.; [pers.] Love is freely given, so freely give love. I have been influenced by early romance poets and the writings of Richard Wright and Maya Angelou.; [a.] Apopka, FL

HINES, DEANNA
[b.] February 25, 1954, Lubbock, TX; [p.] James B. and Dolores Hines; [ed.] A.A. Education - South Plains College, B.G.S. - Indiana - in progress; [occ.] Office manager for the Learning Center, South Plains College, Levelland, TX.; [memb.] WIBC (Women's International Bowling Congress), SPC Staff Club, International Society of Poets, Academy of American Poets Contributing Member; [hon.] Faculty Women's Scholarship 1983, High School Writing Contests (1st place in several poetry contests, 2nd place in short story) writer's guild Silver and Gold poet awards - 1986 and 1987; [oth. writ.] Poems published in over thirty anthologies and poetry reviews, Local Newspapers, College Journals, High School Reunion Booklet...; [pers.] Good poetry is a matter of opinion. The key to popularity is to appeal to those opinions are similar to your own. Currently in awe of Martin Espada's "Genius."; [a.] Levelland, TX

HITCHENS JR., CARL V.
[pen.] Carl Hitchens; [b.] February 19, 1947, Washington, DC; [p.] Carl Hitchens Sr. and Althea Lucas; [m.] Marie Douglas; [ed.] Archbishop Carroll HS, Hampton Inst., Dillard University; [occ.] Poet, short story writer, novelist and essayist, Yoga Teacher; [hon.] Navy Achievement Medal, Yoga Teacher Certificate; [oth. writ.] Short Story, "Sign On The River," published in "Arizona Mandala Newspaper Magazine," several articles in a CWA union newsletter: "The Local Front."; [pers.] I consider my writing and artistry to be an effusion of the spiritual life stream, expressing life's oneness and sanctity through my stories, characters, and imagining's.; [a.] Durham, NC

HITE, TIMOTHY H.
[b.] October 26, 1948, Red Bluff, CA; [p.] William Hite Jr., and Patricia Hite; [m.] Carol E. Hite, June 20, 1970; [ch.] Catherine Elizabeth, Thomas Timothy; [ed.] Pomona High School, Cal. Poly State University, Pomona, B.S., M.A.; [occ.] English Teacher, Montclair High School, Montclair, CA; [memb.] National Education Association, California Teachers Association, California Association of Teachers of English, Coalition to Stop Gun Violence; [oth. writ.] Poem in College Poetry Magazine; [pers.] All my writing energy and ability goes to promote harmonious relationships between people. "An eye for an eye makes the whole world blind." (Ghandi); [a.] La Verne, CA

HOFFMAN, JOAN M.
[b.] March 13, 1966, Okinawa; [p.] Julius E. and Betty C. Hoffman; [ed.] High Point High, West Virginia University, University of Maryland; [occ.] Science and Math Teacher, Glenwood, MS, Glenwood, MD; [memb.] National Wildlife Federation; [hon.] The National Dean's List; [pers.] I am intrigued by words in the way they stir our imagination and memories. In the right combination, they can take us to places, many miles or thoughts away. I mainly try to capture the magnificence I find in nature.; [a.] Greenbelt, MD

HOGLUND, PATRICIA
[b.] October 14, 1948, Queens, NY; [p.] Chester Sadler, Josephine Sadler; [m.] Divorced; [ch.] Dawn-Marie; [ed.] New Utrecht High School, Brooklyn, New York; [occ.] Disable - due to multiple sclerosis; [oth. writ.] Prayer and Inspirational Verse, Greeting Cards, Invitations (general and personalize), Children's Poems and Limericks, Children's Book (pending) humorous poems and songs; [pers.] My daughter was, and still is a large part of my inspiration, everything I taught her as a child was in song and verse. I worked as a hairdresser for many years, a travel agent and last, with a bond firm on Wall St. before my illness forced me to an early retirement. I believe M.S. has taught me to become a more meaningful and spiritual poet. I do more soul searching and writing from my heart than ever before. I hope to someday venture into a new career, "because of M.S. I might find success."; [a.] Brooklyn, NY

HOGUE, JOAN CLAIRE
[pen.] Joan Overton Hogue; [b.] June 27, 1944, Lakewood, NJ; [p.] Carl and Glennie Overton; [m.] Montez Allen Hogue, August 20, 1977; [ch.] Sean, Brent, Ryan Hogue; [ed.] High School Diploma, Southern Regional High School, Manahawkin, New Jersey; [occ.] Assistant to the director of the Addiction Program, for the City and County of Denver.; [oth. writ.] Many poems, nothing published, this is the first time I was have ever entered a contest.; [pers.] I and my twelve siblings grew up under incredible odds, through sheer determination and perseverance we made it. Life is really what you make it, and it is the end results that count. My message to people, especially young people is even though things may seem futile and hopeless, you can always carry your hopes and dreams within your heart.; [a.] Denver, CO

HOGUE, KAREN
[b.] October 5, 1978, Dayton, OH; [p.] Gerald and Ila Hogue; [ed.] 10th and still going (I will be graduating in 1977 or 98); [oth. writ.] I've done a lot of poetry, but none ever published or anything. Here are some and someone different, Something Kind Of Special, To Be Yours, To Remember You When I Go, Missing You, Being Mine, etc...; [pers.] I would like to thank the people who took the time to read my poetry. Thanks so much, this means a lot to me.; [a.] Cookeville, TN

HOLDEN, PAULA L.
[pen.] Paula L. Holden; [b.] March 22, 1964, San Diego, CA; [p.] Hubert and Charlotte Brogdon; [m.] Karl A. Holden Sr., August 7, 1982; [ch.] Karl Edward and Kellen Kenneth; [ed.] Great Falls High School; [occ.] Substitute Education Assistant; [oth.

writ.] Co-author of several children's books; [a.] Cheyenne, WY

HOLDREN, WARREN
[pen.] Warren; [b.] August 7, 1946, Blue Ridge, VA; [p.] Henry Holdren Sr., and Minnie Holdren; [ch.] Alicia Renee Holdren Boles; [ed.] Lord Botetourt HS, ITU Bereau of Education.; [occ.] Office Service Supervisor Sr.; [memb.] National Thespian Society; [hon.] Outstanding Young Men of America, World of Poetry 1986, 1987, 1988, EEOC Chairman and Secretary, Mertierious Service Award, State; [oth. writ.] Local Newspaper articles, Published own book of poetry, published in The Poets Domain, Vols, 1, 2 and 4; [pers.] Don't say it, write it!; [a.] Roanoke, VA

HOLLEY, MRS. FLORINE
[b.] July 26, 1912, Alief, TX; [p.] Minnie and Warner Boyce; [m.] Joe Hill Holley Jr., November 2, 1931; [ch.] Bill Holley and Mary Lou Bass; [ed.] B.S. degree Univ. of Houston and Alief High School; [occ.] Retired teacher and retired music secretary at Braeswood church; [memb.] T.S.T.A, A.C.E., P.T.A., all retired; [pers.] My life has been very blessed by the children I taught, through the years, my loving family and a host a friends, all inspired my writing.; [a.] Houston, TX

HOLMES, BETTY MAHAIR B.
[pen.] Betty B. Holmes; [b.] February 16, 1927, Spaulding, OK; [p.] E.R. and Susie Bryant; [m.] Daniel H. Holmes (Deceased T.M. Mahair), December 21, 1994; [ch.] Thomas (Deceased) Tudy Lane-Mike L.D.; [ed.] Grades through two year High School - G.E.D. at age 50; [occ.] Retired from retail - now very happy newly housewife; [memb.] Distinguished member (by invitation) of International Society of Poets - Southeast Texas writers League Bmt.m TX., Central Church of Christ-Lumberton, TX.; [hon.] Invitation to become a distinguised member International Society of Poets-Nomination as poet of year 1995-Poet of Merit-These honor I am sorry to say did not understand until reread the letter and even more sorry I could not attend and Editor's Choice Award for Poem printed in beyond the stars.; [oth. writ.] Published poem in sparrow grass "Treasured poems of America Fall 1995", poem in "Beyond the Stars." National Library of Poetry poem to be in "Treasured poem of Sparrow Grass of America Summer 1996", poem to be in "Muse to follow" - also one in "Beneath the Harvestmoon". National Library of Poetry; [pers.] I like to paint a picture and tell a story in the words that I write if I am able to accomplish this I am satisfied with the piece I have been trying to create. I love to love with 100% of my heart. Even when you loose someone the tears of the price is worth it.; [a.] Lumberton, TX

HOLMES, JENNIFER D.
[b.] October 24, 1978, Montgomery, AL; [p.] Donnie and Geissla Holmes; [ed.] As of this date, I am in the 11th grade of High School in Highland Home, Alabama; [occ.] Student; [memb.] 4-H Club, Squadron Pride Band (Highland Home Sch.) Annual and Newspaper Staff at Sch. English Club, Mu Alpha Theta; [hon.] Public Speaking - 1st pl. 3 yrs., Science Fair - 1st pl. 5 times, Hoby Ambassador 1995, Band Sec. and Librarian, Currently reporter on Sch. Newspaper Staff; [oth. writ.] Assorted

unpublished poems, 3 speeches for 4-H, Several Term papers for English Literature in Sch., Articles for my newspaper spot; [pers.] Poems, in my opinion, are not for everyone. They are for those who want to read more than a plain word. Hopefully they will inspire us to look at life, not through rose-colored glasses, but through our hearts.; [a.] Highland Home, AL

HOLMES SR., JUDSON W.
[b.] August 25, 1923, Portage, ME; [p.] Prescott and Bessie Holmes; [m.] Hilda Pinette Holmes, June 30, 1946; [ch.] Judson Wilcox, Bonnie Ellen, Steven Scott; [ed.] Maine High School, Equivalency Certificate; [occ.] Retired; [memb.] First Congregational Church, American Legion, 30th Fighter Sqdn. Assoc., Retail Clerks Retirees Club; [pers.] A swinger of birches favorite poet Robert Frost, favorite poem by Longfellow "A Psalm of Life", I collect and take great enjoyment from poetry.; [a.] Santa Barbara, CA

HOLMQUIST, EVA
[pen.] E. N. Holmquist and Eve Holmquist; [b.] January 29, 1921, Forest Lake, MN; [p.] Frederick and Olive Seager Holmquist; [ch.] Heidi Johnson, Gene, Joel, and Robin Smitt; [ed.] BA, V. of Minn., MSW Fresno State Univ.; [occ.] Writer, Retired Social Worker; [oth. writ.] Novel, no certain time, 2 Children's Stories, one a book, one in Highlights for Children, several poems in journals and an anthology; [pers.] My hope is to finish the novel, I am now working on and/or publish one or more of the two novels languishing in my dresser drawer and/or some of the short stories relegated to the same fate.; [a.] Saratoga, CA

HOMEN, DELFINA
[b.] January 23, 1983, San Jose, CA; [p.] Walter and Kathryn Homen; [ed.] In 8th grade now; [occ.] Student; [memb.] Camp Fire, Band; [hon.] Winner of ALA T-shirt Design Contest, Best In Band 1994, 1995, Top Seller for Camp Fire Candy Sale, 1995, Blazer's Essay Winner, Lions Essay Winner, Oregon All-State Band; [pers.] I write my best works when I'm not in the mood to write.; [a.] Amity, OR

HOMER, HUGH W.
[b.] May 5, 1938, Charlo, MT; [p.] Russell Kent and Fay Homer; [m.] Beverly (Hancock) Homer, September 21, 1962; [ch.] Melvin-33, Arlen-28, Mike-25, Debra-29, Serena-27, Nicole-23, LaBretta-21, Sheldon-19, Sandra-17; [ed.] Dixon and Charlo Montana High Schools, High School, College Business and Computer Classes, Tax and Accounting courses; [occ.] Self-Employed R.V. Park Owner/ Operator; [memb.] Operating Engineers Local 701, Good Sam Club; [oth. writ.] A few unpublished poems; [pers.] Believe in high moral principles. Family oriented. Most of worlds problems are cursed by selfishness and greed. I try to portray positive and uplifting ideas in poetry. Have instructed adult business related classes for 15 years.; [a.] Boardman, OR

HONEYCUTT, GLADYS
[ed.] Bachelor of Arts in English, North Carolina State University, Raleigh, NC; [pers.] I use my knowledge by combining it with creativity and hope to create a new understanding. Thanks to the professors who taught me at NCSU.; [a.] Youngsville, NC

HONEYWOOD, JESSIE A.
[b.] November 19, 1951, Chicago, IL; [p.] Enos and Charley Mary Honeywood; [ch.] Hershel Jesse King, Natasha Sheri Dyer; [ed.] Farragut H.S., Wright College, Chicago State College; [oth. writ.] Poetry and versus under work "White Sugar Melts, Brown Sugar Creams", short stories; [pers.] Touch another life in a positive way. A smile, a squeeze of a hand, a kind word, a vote of confidence, a pat on the back, a shoulder to cry on, an encouraging hug. Something to say "I care."; [a.] Chicago, IL

HOOK, ROBERT H. W.
[b.] April 11, 1957, Edmonton, AB; [p.] Mr. and Mrs. H. R. Hook; [m.] P. Jane Hook (Nee Willis), July 28, 1973; [ch.] Christopher Robert, Alexis Jane; [ed.] King's College School, 1969, B.A. (Dalhousie University), 1973, B.Ed. (Acadia University), 1976, LL.B (University of New Brunswick), 1984; [occ.] Lawyer (Previous Teacher, Actor); [memb.] Canadian and Manitoba Bar Association; [hon.] Various; [oth. writ.] Published, History, Softcover, 1984: "An Illustrated History of Rothesay", unpublished and unsubmitted poetry and short stories.; [pers.] Dragons are just bizarre butterflies, though it might be the reverse.; [a.] Winnipeg Manitoba, Canada

HORNBY, JUDY L.
[b.] December 4, 1950, Portland, OR; [m.] Robert S. Hornby, September 27, 1980; [ch.] Robert II; [occ.] Housewife/writer; [pers.] Imagination is the yellow brick road. We should all use it.; [a.] Portland, OR

HORNUNG, MAUREEN L. ANDERSON
[pen.] Maureen L. Hornung; [b.] July 22, 1940, Stephenson, MI; [p.] James La Pointe and Lillian Hanson; [ch.] Jamie, John, Jeff Hornung; [ed.] Galesburg High School, Galesburg, IL, Stephenson Public School (Elem), Stephenson, MI, classes at Carl Sanburg College Galesburg IL, Civil Air Patrol's Great Lakes Region Staff College.; [occ.] Membership Secretary at Knox County Farm Bureau, Galesburg, IL; [memb.] Women Marine Assn., AMVETS, American Legion Aux., AARP, Stearman Restorers Assn.; [hon.] I was one of several winners of a Turkey for saying why I liked winter. (I had it roasted and paid for a complete meal to have it served to 4 men who had nowhere to go for Thanksgiving.) One poem was used by the City of Peoria; [oth. writ.] Several poems published in local newspapers, poem published in 2 books. I had a column in a local newspaper.; [pers.] I usually write from what inspires me most. I write many patriotic/Americana type poems. I have written on request and recited for special occasions.; [a.] Knoxville, IL

HORRIGAN, MELANIE A.
[b.] May 20, 1963, Toledo, OH; [p.] Rich and Patricia Myers; [m.] Patrick K. Horrigan, December 2, 1983; [ch.] Casey Lee 11 yrs. Sarah Michelle 1 yr.; [ed.] High School Graduate, Maumee High School; [occ.] Homemaker; [pers.] Poetry is a wonderful outlet for the outflow of energy children can create in you!; [a.] Maumee, OH

HORTON, RICHARD LEE
[b.] July 25, 1957, Dixon, IL; [p.] Arthur Horton, Bernie Horton; [occ.] Photographer; [pers.] Experiences are memories, memories are forever!; [a.] Dixon, IL

HOWARD, KENDRA
[b.] December 8, 1982, Fort Worth, TX; [p.] Laura and Kenneth; [ed.] I am recently going to Strickland Middle School and I am in 7th grade; [occ.] Going to school; [pers.] I am a 13 year old girl and I live with my parents Laura and Kenneth Howard. In Denton, TX and I go to Strickland Middle School.; [a.] Denton, TX

HOWARD, PAMELA JEAN
[b.] July 11, 1959, Ann Arbor, MI; [p.] Don and Carol Cheever; [m.] Kelly H. Howard, July 9, 1980; [ch.] Chelsea Rae, Cortni Kay; [ed.] Milan High; [occ.] Environmental Management, VAMC Battle Creek, MI; [a.] Delton, MI

HOWDEN, JENNIFER
[pen.] Jen Howden; [b.] February 6, Yorkton, Saskatchewan, Canada; [p.] John and Jean Howden; [ed.] Grade 9; [occ.] Student; [hon.] 1st prize in a remembrance day poem contest, 1992; [oth. writ.] I've wrote many poems for my own enjoyment. As well as poems I've wrote short stories and several novels.; [pers.] I enjoy writing in my spare time for pleasure. I like to capture the beauty of nature and tragic romance.; [a.] Meath Park Saskatchewan, Canada

HOWES, TRACY LYNN
[b.] May 20, 1965, Vernon, CO; [p.] Leroy Howes and Sandra Espling; [ch.] Echo Joy Howes; [ed.] High School Graduate - Dabbled in some College course and Vocational Institutes.; [occ.] Shipper/ Receiving; [memb.] While in school I was very active in sports and clubs, now I'm a member of Motherhood and the working class.; [hon.] I have awards in trophies in most all sports.; [oth. writ.] I've been writing since I was Little so I have books full of unseen words.; [pers.] Being a single parent does for me what my written use to give me margins that I cannot pass or I am unheard and become obsolete. Echo Joy is my written, only heard.; [a.] Dover, NH

HUANG, VICTOR
[pers.] The "Emptiness of the Empty Nest" was a translation of one of his chinese poems.; [a.] Bakersfield, CA

HUBBARD, NONA B.
[b.] September 22, 1965, Chesterfield, SC; [p.] Robert and Sarah B. Bittle; [m.] Mr. Wannamaker Hubbard Jr., September 17, 1988; [ch.] Nickholas Tyee Hubbard and Phillip Antuwan Hubbard; [ed.] Chesterfield High, and Chesterfield - Marl-boro Technical College; [memb.] Mt. Tabor United Methodist Young Adult Choir; [hon.] Pianist for over 15 years; [oth. writ.] School literary magazine and other personal writings; [pers.] Writing is the easiest form of freedom of speech. You are allowed to express yourself freely. It is also remembered by others, because it is written and you can always refer back to it. It is always quoted as it is written.; [a.] Chesterfield, SC

HUBBARD, TRACEY DAWN
[b.] May 9, 1967, Barrys Bay, Ontario; [p.] Doral Almstead and Rick Sawyer; [m.] Michael Lance Hubbard, August 21, 1993; [ch.] Jessica Miranda-Doral, Aug 17, 1994; [ed.] General Vanier Secondary School; [occ.] Mother/Housewife; [memb.] Shaklee; [hon.] Clogging Certificate First

Aid, Bowling, Horeshoes; [oth. writ.] I have had one other poem published in "Poets Corner" of the Toronto Sun. I would like to write a series of children's books someday.; [a.] Kingston Ontario, Canada

HUDYMA, MARILEE
[pen.] Long Legs; [b.] September 23, 1960, Alta, CA; [ch.] Jerry, Jason; [ed.] Grade II; [occ.] Poems and Artwork; [memb.] Church; [hon.] For Art Best Reading and Drawing and some work; [oth.writ.] Kind poems and others; [pers.] I love kids writing and art work.; [a.] Edmonton, KY

HUERTAS JR., DAMIAN
[pen.] Junior Huertas; [b.] March 26, 1978, Fallbrook, CA; [p.] Damian C. Huertas, Mary J. Huertas; [ed.] Fallbrook Union High School; [memb.] California scholastic Federation for 3 years; [hon.] Principal's List all four years at high school; [pers.] I usually try to unmask the flows of today's society. I hope that by reading my poetry, people will strive to change their ways.; [a.] Fallbrook, CA

HUETZ, THOMAS ROBERT
[b.] March, 1, 1967, New Jersey; [p.] John Huetz, Mary Rose Huetz; [ed.] Columbia High School, Trenton State College; [occ.] Promotion Project Manager; [hon.] Dean's List (4 semesters), Eagle Scout - BSA; [oth. writ.] Personal Collection; [pers.] Smile, laugh and be at peace with oneself. I live each day with these 3 ideas, to fill my days completely.; [a.] Denville, NJ

HUFFMAN, DARWIN, A.
[pen.] Darwin A. Huffman; [b.] January 10, 1951, Orillia, Ontario, Canada; [p.] John and Esther Huffman; [ch.] Darwin Frederick Gordon Huffman; [ed.] Grade 10 Park Street Colligate Orillia, Ontario Canada; [occ.] Mid Ontario Disposal Recycling Plant; [memb.] Royal Canadian Legion 21 years.; [oth. writ.] Salute To Terry, Terry Did His Best, Canadian Of The Year, Dad, Recapture My Dream, Our Christmas Remembered, Your Silence Hurts, A Soldier Of The Heart, Have You Ever Wondered, You Ease The Pain.; [a.] Orillia Ontario, Canada

HULL, DORIS NEWSUM
[ed.] Santa Paula High, Santa Paula, CA, Truckee Meadows Community College Reno, NV

HULSTEDT, GRACE
[b.] August 27, 1949, Chicago; [p.] Thomas and Gladys Ellefsen; [m.] Charles Hulstedt, September 4th, 1969; [ch.] Paul and Karin Hulstedt; [ed.] Northern Illinois University Dekalb, Illinois; [occ.] Registered Nurse, B.S.N.; [memb.] Golden Key National Honor Society, Memorial Baptist Church; [hon.] Golden Key National Honor Society, Editor's Choice Award, (National Library of Poetry.; [oth. writ.] The lobby, Dismantled Bailread; [pers.] Majority of my writings reflect the spiritual aspect of life and dependence on God.; [a.] Rockford, IL

HUNKAR, JULIE KITTINGER
[b.] July 25, 1962, Evansville, IN; [p.] Paul and Barbara Kittinger; [m.] Nicholas J. Hunkar, June 21, 1986; [ch.] Alexander John, Kyle Andrew; [ed.] Beauncreek High School, Wright State University; [occ.] Computer Consultant; [hon.] Graduated Magna Cum Laude from WSU, 1st Prize in 1980

Sinclair Community College, Poetry Contest, High School Division; [oth. writ.] Publication in Anthology High School Poetry - 1980; [pers.] The poet that has been most influential to my poetry is e.e. cummings.; [a.] Traverse City, MI

HUNT, EVELYN P.
[b.] March 6, 1925, Fort William, Ontario, Canada; [p.] George and Doris Brownridge; [m.] Cadwell, January 22, 1955; [ch.] Heather, Lesley and Catherine; [ed.] BA - McMaster University, BS - College of St. Scholastic, Cert in Management CSS, Also served in RCAF (Womens Division) in WWII for 2 1/2 yr.; [occ.] Retired, I was a Biochemist and later an Editor and Tech info Mgr at EPA Lab in Duluth; [oth. writ.] A number of poems; [a.] Duluth, MN

HUNTER, MICHAEL C.
[b.] November 17, 1961, Newbrunswick; [p.] Al and Susan Hunter; [ch.] Seven year old girl - Cheyenne Hunter; [ed.] Secondary - Park St. Collegiate Institute/Orillia, Ontario; [occ.] Supervisor for Premier Manufacturing Support Services at Honda Canada, Alliston Ontario; [memb.] Board of Director Member for Orella Home Base Network; [hon.] Daughter of seven years old (Cheyenne Hunter), 1979 Ontario Teenage Olympic, Lifting Champion 2nd in Canada in my class.; [oth. writ.] Inspirational of Educational Material - Blood, Sweat, and Tears? Do it - Anyway! Other poems - single, Together For Christmas, The Secret.; [pers.] I am an aspiring writer, speaker, published dedicated to promoting principle - centered thinking for achieving quality living. My definition of principles: natural laws that govern how the rewards of success are earned.; [a.] Orillia Ontario, Canada

HUNTER, REBECCA GAIL TUCKER
[pen.] Becky Hunter; [b.] June 19, 1943, TN; [p.] Mason and Agnes Tucker; [m.] Richard Allen Hunter, February 24, 1985; [ch.] 1 son; [ed.] Grade thru some college; [occ.] Housewife; [memb.] Woodbury 1st Baptist Church; [oth. writ.] "Kinship"; [pers.] I have to write. My soul finds peace in these words I hear and feel for the are sent to me by God.; [a.] Woodbury, TN

HUNTZICKER, MARTHA JANE
[pen.] Jane Huntzicker, Jane Stipe; [b.] November 7, 1970, Ann Arbor, MI; [p.] Thomas Huntzicker; [ed.] Working on Bachelor at Eastern Michigan University in their Honors Program; [occ.] Student, previously a Technical Translator; [hon.] Member of Golden Key National Honor Society, Member of the Honor Society of Phi Kappa Phi; [pers.] Most of my poetry emanates from journals I keep and reflects events that have affected myself and those around me.; [pers.] Ann Arbor, MI

HURST, KIMBERLY DIANE
[pen.] Kimberly Diane Hurst; [b.] July 16, 1985; [p.] Michael and Diane Hurst; [ed.] 5th grade; [occ.] Student; [memb.] Academically Gifted Program Orchestra; [hon.] Honor Roll, Citizen of the Week, Principal's Honor Roll; [pers.] I strive to be the best writer I can be, and influenced others to write as well.; [a.] Brandon, FL

HUXHOLD, KAYLEEN MARIE
[pen.] Kayleen Marie Huxhold; [b.] December 26, 1960, Saint George, UT; [p.] Orin Dee and Barbara

Barnum; [m.] Steven Glenn Huxhold, March 12, 1980; [ch.] Joshua, Tiffany, Matthew, and Alyscia; [ed.] High School Grad.; [occ.] Mother and Housewife; [pers.] You get out of life what you're willing to put into it.; [a.] Magna, UT

HYATT, JANET
[b.] February 16, 1935, Iowa; [p.] John Hyatt, Mary Hyatt; [ed.] Independent study: Verse of Longfellow Shakespeare, Melody/Rhyme of Burl Ives, Jimmy Dale Gilmore; [hon.] Angel Trimmer Merit Award, Shenandoah Iowa September 1995 for "Flowers for the Living" an inspirational poetic song about little motherless sister Ann and Baby Rose and their father; [oth. writ.] A volume of unsubmitted songs and poems; [pers.] To encourage more consideration of human rights. I find Gerry Spence's soft spoken common sense words to be inspirational.; [a.] Plattsmouth, NE

HYDE, NATHAN S.
[b.] May 29, 1973, Lancaster, OH; [p.] Samuel and Norma Hyde; [pers.] I believe there is a poetic sense of creativeness in everyone either they choose to express it or to admire it, and a dull life bestowed on those who wish to ignore it.; [a.] Lancaster, OH

IBSEN, NORMAN L.
[pen] Norman L. Ibsen; [b.] November 20, 1915, Halifax, NS; [p.] Fred and Minnie Ibsen; [m.] Doreen Mary, December 22, 1945; [ch.] Paul, Donna, Bruce; [ed.] Halifax Academy, Saint Marys College-Dalhousie, University-Halifax-Palmer, College of Chiropractic; [occ.] Chiropractor very active in music, piano and choral; [memb.] Alberta Chiropractic Association, having been in RCAF during war for 5 years-member of Military Service Club.; [hon.] Atlantic Star for action on Atlantic during War Award of Merit for Assisting in Development of Violin Chin rest for the Benit of Violinists; [oth. writ.] Have had poems published in newspapers. Write on local personalities.; [pers.] While still writing feel age gives more to depth and beauty in writing; [a.] Halifax Nova Scotia, Canada

IDRIAN, EVA H.
[pen.] Eva Idrian; [b.] June 17, 1952, Gdansk, Poland; [p.] Zygmunt Szymanski, Janina Idrian; [ed.] M.D. Fine arts - Film, Theater and Television Institute., Lodz-Poland, studied creative writing - YMCA College Chicago; [occ.] Art Gallery-Manager, Show Director and Singer; [hon.] Several poems chosen to be published in Chicago. Never signed author's realize.; [oth. writ.] Working on a novel.; [pers.] I believe in balance in the Universe and in love. God is within us. Everything is here and now. Don't miss it.; [a.] San Francisco, CA

IFEJIKA, SAM
[b.] May 12, 1942, Africa; [p.] Matthias and Christiana Ifejika; [m.] Stella Ifejika, July 1, 1972; [ch.] Barbara Ifejika, John Ifejika; [ed.] LL.B., M.A., Ph.D. (York University, Toronto, Canada); [occ.] Coodinator, Jesuit Refugee Service - Canada; [memb.] Knights of Columbus - Virgil, Toronto (Member of the Board of Directors); [hon.] Ontario Scholar; [oth. writ.] The Insider (Short Stories), Nwamife, 1971 The making of a Nation: Biafra, C. Hurst and Co., London, 1969, Praeger, New York, '70, The New Religion, Rex Collings, London, 1973 (Fiction), plus article and academic writings.; [pers.]

How I wish that all peoples can understand and affirm for themselves our common spiritual destiny. Then they will all see that we are all soul brothers - one people, one race of humanity, one fundamental destiny!; [a.] Toronto Ontario, Canada

IHEJETO, CHARLES
[pen.] Charles Jeto; [b.] June 25 1950, Amaibo Nguru Ngor, Owerri, Nigeria; [p.] Michael, Richeal Ihejeto Kabiri; [ed.] CKS Elem. Sch. Aba Abia St. Saint Patricks College Calaba, Teachers College Eubema Imo St. Texas Southern Univ. Houston TX; [occ.] Teacher; [oth. writ.] Articles published in Africalert. A Houston Based Africa Newspaper Magazine; [pers.] I seek for perfection in my endeavour, the quest to understand the mind and human nature. I have been influence by Chinue Achebe, Syrain Evensi and by ancient writers.; [a.] Houston, TX

IKAIDDI, ANTHONY A.
[b.] October 26 1955, Oron, Nigeria; [p.] (Late) Clement Anthony, Elizabeth Anthony; [ch.] Uwana Ikaiddi, Udeme Ikaiddi; [ed.] Graduate Student (Pharmacology) Florida A&M University, Tallahassee, FL; [occ.] Full time student; [memb.] American Chemical Society; [hon.] 1986 Winner of Time, Magazine College Student Essay, Writing Contest; [oth. writ.] Africa's Future! How Certain? (1986 Winning Essay); [pers.] Poetry, like other literary arts, could be considered to be one of the most beautiful forms of human expression. A Jewish poet once said that every poem is a prayer, but could it also be argued that every prayer is a poem? Maybe.; [a.] Tallahassee, FL

ILACQUA, DAWN
[b.] March 6, 1971, Brentwood, NY; [p.] Rita Ilacqua and Nick Ilacqua Jr.; [ed.] Longwood High School, Suffolk Community College-Early Childhood, Cwpost-Psychology, Stony Brook University BA Social work; [occ.] Social Worker Crest Hall Nursing facility, NY child care little flower children services Wading River, NY; [oth. writ.] Several poems unpublished; [pers.] I am inspired by mother's strength and faith. Philosophical statement- just do it!!!; [a.] Wading River, NY

INEZ, JACK I.
[b.] January 11, 1914, Manhattan, KS; [p.] Calvin, Carrie Insibell; [m.] John (Deceased 1993) April 12, 1936; [ch.] 3 Foster Children; [ed.] High School; [occ.] Widow; [pers.] Poems so are written during W. will spouse was prisoner of Mr. in Germany. Poems express humor family values and my love of nature; [a.] Tacoma, WA

INTERLANDI, ASHLEY
[b.] April 26, 1985, Boynton Beach, FL; [p.] Stacey and Mark Interlandi; [ed.] General Education Manatee Elementary Grade 5; [hon.] (1) 2nd place in school spelling Bee. (2) Application pending school of the Arts; [oth. writ.] Numerous unpublished; [pers.] To other children my age (10 years old) don't become discourage, because you will succeed.; [a.] Lake Worth, FL

IRELAND, MIRANDA
[b.] May 17, 1978, London, Ontario, Canada; [p.] Max and Marsha Ireland; [ed.] Robert School for the Deaf; [hon.] Sport awards, M.V.P Volleyball; [pers.]

My mother and a brother, two sisters are deaf. I have been good influenced for deaf people. I want to be good role model for deaf people include Native people too.; [a.] Onyota'ako Ontario, Canada

ISON, KATHERINE
[pen.] Kat; [b.] January 12, 1953, Isonville, KY; [p.] Mary and Everett Elliott; [m.] Willis J. Ison, August 7, 1970; [ch.] Willis David, William Arlis; [ed.] Park Layne Elementary School, New Carlisle, Ohio, Tecumseh High School, New Carlisle, Ohio.; [occ.] Housewife; [memb.] Sumter Baptist Temple, Weight Watchers Life Member, since May 10, 1989, Walden Book's preferred Reader Club, Block Buster Video.; [oth. writ.] The one and only Christmas Time, Time, Enduring Love, A Solitary Life, Friendship Prayer, Why the Rain, (all of these unpublished at this time.); [pers.] I started writing little ditties to my husband in the early seventies and have been writing ever since. My intent is to encourage through writing. Helen Steiner Rice and Fannie Crosby have inspired me greatly.; [a.] Wedgefield, SC

IVEY, HEATHER
[b.] February 17, 1978, Peoria, IL; [p.] Kathi and Lee Swindell; [ed.] Limestone Walters Elementary, Hewitt Trussville Jr. High, Oltewan High School and Germantown High School; [occ.] Student; [hon.] Presidential Academic Fitness Awards Program, National Jr. Honor Society, Germantown High School PTSA Faculty Choice Award; [pers.] I would like to thank my entire family for their encouragement and support. And a special thanks to Kara who got me started writing.; [a.] Memphis, TN

JACKSON, HAROLD
[b.] October 12, 1934, Saint Louis, MO; [p.] Edward and Florence Jackson; [m.] Divorced, January 18, 1959; [ch.] Sharon D. Caldwell; [ed.] 10th Grade Vashon High School, Divoll Elementary School; [occ.] Machine Operator; [memb.] Rose Hill M.B. Church, Senior Choir Member and Soloist. Little League Baseball Coach of Matthew - Dickey Boys Club.; [hon.] Bowling Base Ball Track; [oth. writ.] About 200 poems

JACOB, GEORGE
[b.] September 5, 1964, Cochin, India; [p.] Academicians (father) Director Grad. Stds. Providence Univ. Taiwan Roc., (mother) Freelance Writer and Botanist; [ed.] M. Sc. (Tech.) and Master of Museum Studies (M.M.St.) University of Toronto, Canada, Double Masters; [occ.] Commonwealth Scholar; [memb.] Executive Council of the Commonwealth Assoc. of Museums for the triennial period 1995-1998 and numerous other Committees of Museums and several Govt. Departments; [hon.] Several awards for Painting and Sketching at National Levels (India), One solo-exhibition of 30 rks, Award the Canadian Commonwealth Fellowship for 1994 in Musicology, At 25 became the youngest Planetasim Director in India (1989); [oth. writ.] 30 Publications on a cross section of topics ranging from Musicology, Aesthetics, Jallfusion, Planetary Sciences, Science Museums, Education and Plusalistic Societies and cross-cultural heritage issues.; [pers.] To touch somebody's heart and uplift somebody, soul by the simplicity and purity of thought expressed them words - spoken or written!; [a.] Etobicoke Ontario, Canada

JAFFRAY, STEVEN
[b.] May 6, 1974, Evanston, IL; [p.] Allan Jaffray, Daisy Jaffray; [ed.] Tremper High, UW-Madison; [occ.] Chef; [hon.] Honors in Biology and Spanish. 2nd Degree black belt in karate.; [oth. writ.] Several yet to be revealed; [pers.] Time is not of the essence, it doesn't even require your presence. Be strong in yourself and in turn there will be wealth.; [a.] Kenosha, WI

JAIME, RACHAEL
[pen.] Ray; [b.] December 26, 1983, Clovis, NM; [p.] Karen L. Jaime; [ed.] Dover Junior, High 6th grade; [memb.] Pioneer Club; [hon.] Honor Roll; [oth. writ.] The One I Love (not published); [pers.] I get my ideas by looking at the beautiful places around me I would like to dedicate this to my Uncle David; [a.] Dover, NH

JAQUA, DAWN MARIE
[pen.] Dawn M. Jaqua; [b.] February 23, 1977, Hunising; [p.] Randy V. and Debbie S. Vining; [m.] Matthew Do Jaqua, September 10, 1994; [ch.] McKayllif Elizabeth Jaqua; [ed.] Superior Central H.S.; [occ.] House wife; [hon.] Name in Who's Who Among American H.S. Students 93/94; [pers.] Out of all of life's regrets I shall never regret the choice of love.; [a.] Chatham, MI

JARDINE, DONALD
[pen.] "The Spoiler"; [b.] March 24, 1940, Renous, New Brunswick, Canada; [p.] Ernest, Helen Jardine; [m.] Beckywylie Jardine, October 15, 1993; [ed.] Moncton New Brunswick Canada; [pers.] I strive to portray an accurate account of history in most of my poems; [a.] Wetaskiwin Alberta, Canada

JASKE, L. KATHLEEN
[pen.] Kat Jaske; [b.] October 17, 1974, Columbus, OH; [p.] Donna Jaske and Carl Jaske; [ed.] Graduate of Upper Arlington High School. Graduate of Wake Forest University with a BA in Psychology and English (double major).; [occ.] I have just graduated from Wake Forest and am doing temporary work until I find a permanent position.; [memb.] I am in the process of joining new organizations since I've just graduated. Will join a track club and probably now.; [hon.] Merit scholar at Wake Forest University. Dean's List every semester. Varsity scholar athlete in the ACC and for Wake Forest University.; [oth. writ.] Was a section editor of our High School year book. Also have been published in "UA News" (articles that is, during high school). A poem "Sit Perhaps Stand" is to be published by Quill books this spring. I've also written several novels I've been trying to publish.; [pers.] "Treat others as you wish to be treated, you never know what you might learn from them." "Life is to be lived not simply a process of being, but of becoming, striving, passion, love, sadness, and melancholy..."; [a.] Winston-Salem, NC

JAZWIENSKI, KATHLEEN R.
[b.] October 23, 1916, Boston, MA; [p.] Andreas T. Kopp-Ellen Gertrude Bell; [m.] Lt. Theodore Jazwienski, September 23, 1946; [ed.] St. Thomas High School U.S.C.G. Institute Courses; [occ.] Housewife; [memb.] Florida A.L. Historians Assc., Nat'l Assc Dept. Historians A.L., American Legion, A.L. Auxiliary, Honor Society Women Legionnaires, Ret. Officer's Wives, National and International Poetry Assc.; [hon.] 4 Yrs. Scholarship (Journalism),

Boston Globe Spelling Champion, A.L. Post 235 National History Winner (1st pl) 1st pl. for Consecutive National Assc. Dept. Historians, American Legion, Numerous Trophies, Cary-Comm. Serv. American Sng P.R.; [oth. writ.] 40 Yrs. History, National Assc. Dept. Historians, 2 Personal Volumes Poetry, in 3 Poetry Assoc., Anthologies 4 Sounds Poetry Cassettes.; [pers.] The lamp of recorded poetry will do wonders in guiding the footsteps of those who follow.; [a.] Fort Walton Beach, FL

JEAN, LISA MARIE
[pen.] Catharine Marie; [b.] December 22, 1975, Hamilton, Ontario, Canada; [ed.] Finished High School, continuing with Post Secondary night classes.; [occ.] Child care, Volunteering; [oth. writ.] Poems, Short Creative Pieces.; [pers.] Seize what you can from the moment, for you may never find it again.; [a.] Hamilton Ontario, Canada

JEFFERSON, STEVE
[pen.] Steve B. Jefferson; [b.] October 27, 1976, Shreveport, LA; [p.] Bill and Pat Jefferson; [ed.] Airline High School; [memb.] Air Force Junior ROTC, also play drums for various local bands; [hon.] Proclamation Award from the Mayor of Bossier City (saved someone's life), award from the fire chief, and the Cadet Humanitarian Award in ROTC (All awards for saving someone's life); [oth. writ.] Had a poem published in "The Seedlings", a city-wide publication, in 3rd grade.; [pers.] I tend to write poems while in certain moods - I wrote this poem when I was depressed about someone I loved but they didn't love me back.; [a.] Bossier City, LA

JENSEN, KYLE
[pen.] Jensen, Kyle; [b.] May 2, 1977, Denton, TX; [p.] Dennis and Donna Jensen; [ed.] Billy Ryan High School; [occ.] Pizza Delivery Boy, Roman's Pizza; [pers.] I'm pushing to see more peace in our America. Which in my mind is falling fast.; [a.] Denton, TX

JOHANSON, MARGARET
[b.] February 5, 1943, Boise, ID; [p.] Harold and Helen Osborne; [m.] Benjamin Johanson, May 15, 1970; [ch.] Ben Jr.; [ed.] Walter Johnson H.S., Muskingum College, Univ. of Montana, American Univ., Univ. of Wash., B.A. English, Seattle Univ.; [occ.] Self-employed Importer; [memb.] Pac. NW Writers; [oth. writ.] Currently working on poems and non-fiction, also a series of essays.; [pers.] My interests are in the areas of Religion, Ecology, Native American spirituality. I enjoy the works of Emerson, Thoreau, Blake, Yeats and Mekton.; [a.] Westport, WA

JOHNSEN, SHILO
[b.] December 7, 1980, Kearney, NE; [p.] Merle Jr., and Crystal Johnsen; [ed.] I am a 9th grader; [hon.] Honor Roll, Social Studies Award; [oth. writ.] The Dreamer, The Honeymoon; [pers.] I would like to succeed knowing that I have something special to look backon.; [a.] Eddyville, NE

JOHNSON, BRENDA
[pen.] B. Daphne Johnson; [b.] October 9, 1946, Mountain Home, AR; [p.] J. C. and Edna L. Watson (Both Deceased); [m.] Harvey E. Johnson, May 2, 1964; [ch.] Jeffrey Wayne and John David II; [ed.]

Graduate of Mtn. Home, Ar., High School, Bachelor of Arts in Bibical Studies from Carolina University of Theology - Working on Masters in Christian Counseling Psychology (from same university); [occ.] Line Haul Driver for Donco Carriers out of Okla. City, OK; [memb.] First Baptist Church, Calico Rock, AR, American Red Brangus Association, Arkansas Cattlemans Association, Past Member of Ozarks Earth Science Club, Half Owner of High Point Red Brangus Farm, where she and husband raise registered cattle.; [oth. writ.] Poem published in the "Clove Collection of Verse" 1969 Vol 2 also "A Collection of Poems by the Arkansas Maryland, Connecticut Society of Poets" and several in newspapers and magazines. Other articles in newspapers.; [pers.] It is my hope to some way reflect a bit of the rural atmosphere in my writings and in the future find ways to introduce others to Christ through my poetry, and other writings.; [a.] Mountain Home, AR

JOHNSON, DAVID MARTIN
[b.] August 8, 1957, Des Moines, IA; [p.] Reverend Martin Johnson, Hazel Marie (Vestal) Johnson; [ch.] Joshua Martin Johnson; [occ.] Des Moines Independent School District; [memb.] Central Assembly of God Church; [oth. writ.] Book called just a simple series of poems volumes I, II, III, IV; [pers.] This poem is dedicated to my son Joshua Martin Johnson, Most influence People I admire and my Dad Bob Dylan; [a.] Des Moines, IA

JOHNSON, HAROLD G.
[pen.] Hal Johnson; [b.] March 12, 1922, North Grafton, MA; [p.] Raymond F. Johnson and Beatrice L. Hargraves; [ch.] Paul, Deedee, Carolyn, Martho, Louisa; [ed.] Grafton H.S., Grafton, Mass. 1934 Boston University, Premed 1934, Harvard Medical School, March 1946, Board Certified in Family Practice; [occ.] Retired sailing, Birding Bridge, Tennis etc.; [memb.] AMA and Florida Med. Soc. American Board of Family Practice; [hon.] Clinical Ass't Professor University of Illinois, Peoria, IL (retired); [oth. writ.] Folk songs; [pers.] Please, God, teach us humans how to wage peace and not war!; [a.] Chillicothe, IL

JOHNSON, HELEN RUTH WILSON
[b.] May 17, 1943, Bartlett, TX; [p.] Juanita Inez Wilson, T. J. Wilson; [m.] Formerly to Herbert R. Johnson, September 24, 1965; [ch.] Alisa Michelle; [ed.] Basic Business Administration, Bachelor of Science in Education; [occ.] Property Investor and Mortgage Analyst; [memb.] National Education Association; [hon.] Toast Masters International Award; [oth. writ.] Several poems for personal collection; [pers.] I believe that mankind should acknowledge the presence of God at all times and know that he is never alone.; [a.] Midland, TX

JOHNSON, IRENA L. TURIANSKY
[b.] Ukraine; [p.] Anthony and Karolina Turiansky; [m.] Major Robert L. Johnson, August 9, 1975; [ch.] Edward S. P. and Paul A. Czekaj; [ed.] Elementary Education - St. Olha Girl's School, Kolomyya, Ukraine, High School, Beauty Culture and Bookkeeping, Newark, New Jersey; [occ.] Retired in Florida; [memb.] Ukrainian American Club of The Palm Beaches, Reserve Officer's Association - Ladies, The Ukrainian National Association, Assumption Catholic Church and Ukrainian Catholic

Church of Miami.; [hon.] Award of Merit - World of Poetry Editor's Choice Award - The National Library of Poetry; [oth. writ.] Autobiography poems in local paper copyright song "Christmas is Forever" on November 22, 1995 "The Turiansky Legacy", a family history, was published.; [pers.] By learning about the famous Ukrainian poet Taras Shevchenko, I knew at an early age that I would enjoy poetry. Growing up with the beauty of nature, I have learned about people, their joys and their sadness. The love of a poem has no ending.; [a.] Pompano Beach, FL

JOHNSON, MICHAEL
[pen.] Mickey Genner James; [b.] August 9, 1948, Martinez; [p.] Elmond and Naomi Johnson; [m.] Dorothy Jean Jefferson, August 31, 1985; [ch.] Andreana Terrdin Johnson; [ed.] Graduation from Ione CA. P.S.I. D. Company L. Company; [occ.] Landscape and gardening service; [memb.] Tamai Brew Masters Committe, North Block Tamal CA.; [hon.] Track and Field 1964 PDSBO Robles - 660 - yd, Run Track and Field Sierra Conservation Corp, 1975; [oth. writ.] Poems, songs some copyright, short stories unpublished; [pers.] Each of us has so much to give something special and uniquely different from any other, unbridled, it be from the be facts of social conditioning; [a.] Oakland, CA

JOHNSON, PATRICIA
[pen.] Faye James; [b.] October 26, 1953, Birming-ham, AL; [p.] Milton James and Mary James; [m.] Milton Johnson, October 20, 1972; [ch.] Timothy Tobias, Janae Chemera, Kachina; [ed.] Morisson School, East side High Al Med Academy, Bite Byte Computer School, Hickey School; [occ.] Dental Assistant Designer, Artist Homemaker; [oth. writ.] Several poems, several songs and several books have been completed.; [pers.] I plan to meet and speak to people through my poems in return they will come to know a small part of me. All creations inspire me.; [a.] Centreville, IL

JOHNSON, SHERRY STEVENS
[b.] March 11, 1952, Jackson Hole, WY; [p.] Danny and Dorothy Stevens; [m.] Divorced 1995; [ch.] Stephanie Hays, Daniel Michael; [ed.] Dubois High, Casper Junior College; [occ.] Massage Therapist; [oth. writ.] Several articles on the history of the area published in Dubois Area History book, several poems pub. in local newspapers and The American Cowboy Poetry Magazine.; [pers.] Pursue what you love to do and success will follow. I am neither educated or well-read in poetry writing. It is my greatest love.; [a.] Dubois, WY

JONES, DAVID
[b.] December 22, 1954, Pinetop, FL; [p.] Clarence Jones, Carrie R. Jones; [m.] Gail I. Jones, December 3, 1976; [ch.] Five; [ed.] Bachelors Business Administration University of North Florida - Jacksonville, FL; [occ.] High School Teacher, Special Education, Baker County High; [memb.] Church of God by Faith; [hon.] Dean's List, Teacher of the Month; [pers.] I write to inspire readers to utilize their full potential. We see life through our binoculars.; [a.] Jacksonville, FL

JONES, PATRICIA MAY
[pen.] Patricia Jones; [b.] August 19, 1946, Ontario, Canada; [p.] Albert (Deceased) and Florence Parrett; [m.] Paul H. Jones, July 6, 1963; [ch.] Donna-Marie,

Kirk, Lorraine; [occ.] Entrepreneur; [memb.] Child Find-Ontario; [oth. writ.] I am accumulating many poems, several children's stories as well as adult short stories but to date, I have not submitted anything; [pers.] Life has not been easy, but still I continue to fixate on the 'positive' of every situation. I am blessed for the ability to share these feelings with a wonderful husband and three terrific children.; [a.] Barrie Ontario, Canada

JONES, STEPHANIE M.
[b.] April 16, 1972, Bedford, PA; [p.] Michael and Sarah Clapper, Paul and Bernice Lohr; [m.] Brian Jones, January 6, 1989; [ch.] Rachel, Rebekah, Stephanie, and Gabriel; [ed.] Bedford Highschool and Hagerstown Junior College; [occ.] Full time mother of four.; [oth. writ.] Poem published in Bedford Gazette. I write mainly for my personal pleasure and fulfillment. Sometimes there is a poem inside of me that must be given life.; [pers.] When it is our time to leave this world we won't care what house we lived in, what kind of car we drove, or even what we looked like. All that will matter are the people we loved, the laughs we shared, and the lives we touched. A special thank you to Tammy and Sarah for their unconditional love and friendship.; [a.] Hagerstown, MD

JONES, TANNER
[pen.] Bryce; [b.] September 5, 1985, Norman, OK; [p.] Michael and Pamela Jones; [ed.] Washington Elem. Piano Student; [occ.] Student; [memb.] Honor Choir - Gifted and Talented; [hon.] Principal Honor Roll; [oth. writ.] Fall is here - I am thankful; [pers.] I have been influenced by the love of my family and my love for reading!; [a.] Norman, OK

JONES, WANDA
[b.] March 8, Harlan, KY; [p.] Andy Pack, Eunice (Lewis) Pack; [m.] Jackson C. Jones; [ch.] Timothy And Jason Jones; [occ.] Housewife and Writer; [oth. writ.] "The Butterfly", "Imagination", these two poems have been published recently; [pers.] I am greatly influenced by Nature Romance and Love. I love animals and include them in my writings.; [a.] Norwood, OH

JOSHUA, SURANI
[b.] July 23, 1982, Pittsburg, PA; [p.] Sarath Joshua and Mangala Joshua; [ed.] Presently in grade eight; [occ.] Presently attending grade eight at Hendrix Jr. High; [hon.] Many children's awards in math, spelling, and writing.; [pers.] I want to make an impression on the world, however small or insignificant, I want to help better the world; [a.] Chandler, AZ

JOST, MICHAEL
[pen.] Mike; [b.] November 29, 1977, Saint Cloud, MN; [p.] Rose Jost and Loren Jost; [ed.] St. Cloud Technical High School; [occ.] Cook, Waiter, Bonanza Restaurant St. Cloud; [memb.] Member of United Christian Children's Fund; [pers.] Nothing maybe considered more noble, than the journey for excellence in everyday living.; [a.] Saint Cloud, MN

JULIG, ELEANORA
[b.] August 28, 1916; [p.] Mr. and Mrs. Robert Froemming; [m.] Carl L. Julig, June 21, 1938; [ch.] Nine; [ed.] Country School Graduate of Alexanddria High School - 2 yr. graduate of St. Cloud Teacher College; [occ.] Retired Living in Nursing Home

KANE, YVONNE B.
[b.] Morgan City, LA; [m.] Patrick Kane; [ch.] Annette Thibodeaux, Susan Mahfouz and Bonnie Guarisco; [ed.] Graduated from High School at Lafayette High, Lafayette, LA; [occ.] Accounting - Union Camp - Lafayette, LA; [oth. writ.] Novel "Child of Love" Short story - "Last of A Kind", poems that have been published. "Memories", "My Song", "Chosen" and "Depression".; [pers.] In my work, I try to express the feelings of others as well as my own. In doing so, I hope others find joy as well as understanding in my writing; [a.] Saint Martinville, LA

KARR, KYLA
[b.] August 13, 1976, Parkersburgh, WV; [p.] A.C. and Sarah Karr; [ed.] Harrison High School, now attending Indiana University; [occ.] Student; [pers.] I write to quietly express myself and my experiences. Also to give back a gift to my grandfather Karr, for he has passed the gift of writing to me.; [a.] Evansville, IN

KARST, GINA
[b.] October 28, 1981, Huntington, IN; [p.] Tammy Arnold and James Karst; [ch.] Julie, Nick, Jarrod, Keith, Kabt; [ed.] 8th Grade; [occ.] A part-time newspaper route; [memb.] A member of 4-H; [pers.] I am not forever, as no one is, but God.; [a.] Bluffton, IN

KAUFMAN, TARA JOY
[pen.] Tara Joy Kaufman; [b.] February 28, 1975, Montreal, Quebec, Canada; [p.] Lynda Pitt-Taylor, Harvey Kaufman; [ed.] Face High School, Dawson College, LaSalle College; [occ.] Student, Camp Co-ordinator; [memb.] C.J.A. (Canadian Jewish Appeal) Camp B'nai B'rith; [hon.] Rod Roy Ski School Honors, Best Staff Award for Camp B'Nai B'rith, Outstanding Leadership Award for C.B.B.; [oth. writ.] Several poems published in High School paper.; [pers.] My writings are the expression of my heart and soul.; [a.] Montreal Quebec, Canada

KAWA, BARB
[b.] June 28, 1947, Mt. Clemens, MI; [m.] Dean Kawa, August 30, 1969; [ch.] Christopher and Chad; [occ.] Paraprofessional at Meridian Public Schools; [pers.] My poems are generally written to family member as my Grandfather did before me. His poem written to me when I was born greatly influenced me. Because of him, I try to touch someone's heart and express my faith.; [a.] Sanford, MI

KAWAHARA, TORU
[pen.] Arako Warthau; [b.] December 14, 1951, Tokyo, Japan; [p.] Fumio and Tcha Kawahara; [m.] Angelique Ryoko Kawahara, October 14, 1978; [ed.] Lycee J. J. Rousseau University of Paris; [occ.] Accountant; [memb.] N.R.C., N.R.A.; [hon.] Literature and Philosophy Honor Student Prizes.; [oth. writ.] A score of poetry (collection) Rebecca's songs (collection); [pers.] My inspiration comes from emotions felt in front of human tragedy and love.; [a.] Los Angeles, CA

KAWURYAN, ANNA MARIA SITI
[b.] Jakarta, Indonesia; [p.] Johannes Soemadiman, Maria Henrika Wadjiah; [m.] Keith Owen Fuglie, December 19, 1990; [ed.] Santa Ursula High School, Jakarta, Indonesia University of Indonesia, Jakarta,

Indonesia University of Minnesota, Minneapolis, Minnesota; [memb.] Ikata Sarjana Ekonomi Indonesia Golden Retriever Rescue, Education and Training, Inc.; [hon.] First in Class, 10th grade, Santa Ursula High School First in Class, 11th grade, Santa Ursula High School Graduated from High School Cum Laude, Santa Ursula High School Award for Classical Guitar, the Music School of Indonesia, Jakarta, Indonesia; [a.] Falls Church, VA

KAY, JOHN
[b.] January 27, 1959, Pontiac, MI; [p.] Donald and Aileen Kay; [m.] Divorced; [ch.] Barbara, Brittany, Lauren; [ed.] High School, 5 yrs. under grad and BS in Biology, Minor in Fine Arts, 4 yrs. post Grad., Doctor of Chiropractic Degree June 1996.; [occ.] Doctor of Chiropractic, self employed.; [oth. writ.] Poetry has been an executing, new gift, my first was August 18, 1995, Inspired by a beautiful women named Margie. As of December 11 1995. I now have over 100 written in this period of time. All for her the spirit just keeps me coming.; [pers.] When the Glory of God shines down upon those that are called, we have a choice! Accept the challenge, or run and hide in the caves and forever be lost.; [a.] Westland, MI

KAYS, REED
[b.] October 28, 1952, Jacksonville, IL; [p.] C. M. and Anita Kays; [m.] Carol, July 20, 1996; [ch.] Brian Eric; [ed.] Bowling Green High (Missouri); [occ.] 3M Company; [memb.] Omaha Sports Club, Wellness Committee and work; [oth. writ.] Various short poems for loved ones and the occasional humorous article for the local county qazette.; [pers.] My life has been influenced most by my admiration for the hearts and souls of the hearts and souls of underdogs in life, in sports or wherever....whether they win or lose.; [a.] Ralston, NE

KEA, ANGELA WALKER
[b.] December 31, 1958, Wilmington, NC; [p.] Mr. and Mrs. Robert Murrill; [m.] Mr. Charles B. Kea Sr., July 25, 1992; [ch.] Jason, Ashley; [ed.] Miller - Motte Business College, Wilmington, NC Institute of Children's Literature West Redding, CT.; [occ.] Disabled; [memb.] The Southeast Writers Asso.; [oth. writ.] Several poems published in Chapbooks for Southeast Writers Asso., and Innerlife Magazine.; [pers.] I try to bring my work to life, using my imagination and life experiences I strive on up lifting all of my readers; [a.] Greensboro, NC

KECK, SUSAN RUTH
[pen.] Susan (Napier) Keck; [b.] October 21, 1953, Plymouth, IN; [p.] J.C. and Kay Napier, Will June Sirus; [m.] Rev. Robert E. Keck, May 15, 1993; [ed.] High School Graduate, Culver Comm., Jr. Senior School, Culver, IN 46511; [memb.] United Methodist Women, United Methodist Church, Current Opinion Club; [pers.] I endeavor to relate to others through poetry, the joys and griefs of humankind as we travel through lifes many ups and downs. And in so doing — hoping to lighten the load of another's burdens, or to share in their joy.; [a.] Sweetser, IN

KEEN, ALMA MARTHA
[b.] December 25, 1917, Lead, SD; [p.] Lawrence Wand, Ida T. McKenzie; [m.] Deceased Wm. Edgar Keen '63, November 30, 1933; [ch.] Nine 5 boys, 4

girls 28 grand children and 38 great grands!; [ed.] Elementary in S. Dakota No High School passed GED tests N.N.C. Nampa, Idaho (Northwest Nazarene College); [occ.] Retired Elem. School Teacher (BA in Education); [memb.] Member of church of the Nazarene and more importantly a member of the house gold of God Born Again Christians!; [hon.] Zeltarback Art Award taught Art and Home Ec. in Nampa Idaho Christian High School 2 yrs, also have sold several oil paintings acrilies, water colors also and chalk.; [oth. writ.] I self published my life story several yrs. age have written a children's story and had things published in the local newspapers, several times wrote political opinion was printed in newspaper here.; [pers.] I believe in the Lord Jesus Christ as my personal Saviour. I believe in the inspired word of God and try to live by the "Low of love" rather than by the O.T. regulations I love God and all people. Praises!; [a.] Kent, WA

KEHLER, DAVID
[b.] January 22, 1944, Winkler, MA; [p.] Rose and Cornelieus Kehler; [ed.] Grade 7; [occ.] Retired due to sickness; [hon.] Course at sickness Adult Learning Centre; [pers.] Treat other people the way I want to be treated; [a.] Winkler, MA

KELZ, JAMES W.
[b.] October 17, 1930, Honesdale, PA; [p.] Julius O. and Ruth W. Kelz; [m.] Margery J. Kelz, September 26, 1953; [ch.] Jim (35) Bill (34) Rues (31); [ed.] B.S. Penn State Univ. 1952 M.Ed. Penn State Univ. 1958 Ph.D Penn State Univ. 1961 Post Dn. 1 year Fellowship; [occ.] Harvard Medical School Community Psychiatry Retired professor Ememtus Penn State Univ.; [memb.] Am Psy Assoc, PA Psy Assoc. Am Eng Assoc, National Rehabilitation Assoc Phi Detta Kappa Pa Rehab Assoc. Penn State Alumni Assoc. and about 2D more; [hon.] Present Kappa Sigma Penn State President Phi Detta Kappa Penn State Pres. Nat'l Career Devel. Assoc Senator 6 yrs Am Eng Assoc and many more; [oth. writ.] Approximately 75 Professional Articles, Monographs, and book chapters plus innumerable budget requests and reports; [pers.] "Hold fast to dreams Langston Hughes; [a.] State College, PA

KENDALL, AMANDA
[b.] October 18, 1980, Joliet, IL; [p.] Bill and Linda Kendall; [ed.] K-9; [memb.] Math Club, FHA; [oth. writ.] "Confusion" in "Beyond The Stars"; [pers.] I was greatly influenced by the death of my idol, Kurt Cobain, and others greater musicians and writers such as Robert Frost and John Lennon; [a.] Manhattan, IL

KENNEDY, JOHN
[b.] August 28, 1929, Scotland; [p.] Elizabeth, Hamisk; [ed.] Post Secondary - Cambridge School of Business - New York - NY USA; [occ.] Retired Accountant; [pers.] I consider poetry the highest form of language and an influence by the English translation of Verijil's Epic poem Aenied; [a.] London Ontario, Canada

KERBY, F. T.
[pen.] February 11, 1929, Gravesend, Kent, England; [m.] Married in 1961, divorced in 1972; [ch.] Matthew and Lisa; [ed.] Graduate of University of Washington 1971 (after stint in Air Force 1948-1952

(Korean War), took a poetry course from Theodore Roethke; [occ.] Retired Boeing Editor/writer-with private business and working on new and revised poetry; [oth. writ.] Published Autumn, 1956 in the University of Washington Assay a critical essay on Franz Kafka's "A Country Doctor"; [pers.] Favorite poets, Dylan Thomas and Emily Dickinson, Carl Sagan, Haynes Johnson and Noam Chomsky reflect much of my personal philosophy; [a.] Kirkland, WA

KERLEY, SUSAN D.
[ed.] BA University of Central Florida, MA Indiana University; [occ.] College Instructor, Realtor; [memb.] MLA, Florida Assoc. of Realtors, AAUW; [hon.] Semi-finalist, world's shortest short story contest - 1986; [a.] Destin, FL

KERSEY, ROBERT E.
[pen.] Bob Kersey; [b.] February 4, 1927, Norfolk, VA; [p.] William O. Myrtle T. Kersey; [m.] Patsy B., April 3, 1955; [ch.] Kimberly, Pamela, Nancy; [ed.] Northview High, N. Georgia College Old Dominion Univ., St. Helena Ext., University of Virginia, Engineering; [occ.] Semi-retired construction firm president-consultant Artist; [memb.] Several Bible study Groups, Elder and Trustee Knox Presbyterian Church, Trustee Past Pres and YMCA or Greater Tidewater, Past Pres: Norfolk VA Beach Exec Club, Past Pres: Builders and Contractors Exchange, Past Pres: Associated Gen'l Contractors Or VA Artist at work gallery of VA beach D'Art Gallery or Norfolk; [hon.] Various Moderate Award in Art Exhibitions and Purchase Awards (Paintings); [pers.] I feel the gifts and talents I have discovered, introspectively, were given me to share, to make this world a better place, and also that others may be encouraged to recognize their own gifts and use them accordingly.; [a.] Norfolk, VA

KESSEL, CORINNE
[b.] January 2, 1977, Edmonton, Alberta, Canada; [p.] Alma and Dan Kessel; [ed.] McNally Composite High School, University of Alberta, 2nd year Bachelor of Music; [memb.] Toronto Conservatory Music Teacher's Association; [hon.] Dean's List, Max Wyman Leadership Scholarship, Kinsmen Achievement Award, Edmonton Southeast Youth Leadership Award, Rutherford Scholarship, NcNally All Round Musician Award; [oth. writ.] Local School Publications; [pers.] Escape life's often lonely emptiness by surrendering yourself to the inexpressible passion and longing found in your very soul.; [a.] Edmonton Alberta, Canada

KETCHUM, CLIFFORD W.
[pen.] Clifford W. Ketchum; [b.] February 23, 1921, Calgary, Alberta, Canada; [p.] Laura Belle Womacks, Clarence Wilbur Ketchum; [m.] Maretta Lois Embree Ketchum, August 23, 1950; [ch.] Keith Warren Ketchum, Kelvin Jory Ketchum.; [ed.] King Edward College, University of British Columbia (U.B.C.): Master of Education degree 3 years training and 2 years teaching (eve. courses) at a college of Theology.; [occ.] Retired (from a career of teaching mostly music and English courses); [memb.] King Edward College Choir Gloria Dei Chorale Reservist Band (Trombone/Euphonium) West Coast Amateur Musicians Society Bard on the Beach (Drama, mostly Shakespeare); [hon.] Doctor of Philosophy (St. Thomas more College, London) Honorary. Member Canadian College of Teachers

Director of several musical groups including our present 12 member Happy Gang (instrumental and vocal group) that averages 2 to 3 programs a week. Soloist (trombone, Euphonium). Perform wherever and whenever invited.; [oth. writ.] My interest in choral music has prompted me to set several of the Psalms of David to choral selections for Church choirs. In each case, both the world setting and the music (4 part) are mine. A friend of mine, and I, composed an entire Christmas canata.; [pers.] The older (and more experienced) I grow the more I feel that there's music in poetry, and vice versa. In both fields I am deeply devoted to the classics. The more I am able to persuade others to feel the same way, the more I will feel that all my efforts have been worth-while.; [a.] Vancouver British Columbia, Canada

KEYWORTH, HENRY
[b.] October 12, 1968, Bellshill, Scotland; [p.] Desmond Keyworth, Kathleen Keyworth; [ed.] Lord Selkirk High, Red River College; [occ.] Supervisor, Coordinator ARC Industries, Selkirk Manitoba, Canada; [oth. writ.] Numerous songs; [pers.] Listening to early British rhythm and blues music prompted me to a passion for writing songs. I wish to continue song writing and use it appropriately; [a.] Winnipeg Manitoba, Canada

KIANSTEN, MARKO MIKAEL
[b.] November 2, 1966, Lahti, Finland; [p.] Pirkko and Hanno Kiansten; [memb.] Guitar Orchestra - Victoria Conservatory of Music; [pers.] I am interested in Philosophy, classical guitar, sculpture, painting, and the humanities in general. I am grateful for the writings of William Blake, Krishnamurti, Rudolph Steiner, Lao Tau, Dostoeusky, and Plato, just to name a few.

KILLAM, MARK
[b.] November 27, 1965, Yarmouth, NS; [p.] Jean, Fred; [m.] Divorced; [ch.] Nicholas, Mark Frederick; [ed.] Nova Scotia Community College Burridge Campus; [occ.] Kitchen runner at a local restaurant.; [hon.] Volunteer of the year award (1991) Viking Cable (Cable Radio); [oth. writ.] Bubbles in the sky, slow down, brother wild in write on! produced by local school book.; [pers.] One of my goals in life has been to published so that my son con say, "This is what my father does." And now, he can say this. It's happened.; [a.] Yarmouth, NS

KIMBALL, PATTI
[b.] March 17, 1973, Peterborough, Ontario, Canada; [p.] Karen and Mel Kimball; [m.] Troy Ellis, October 5, 1996; [ed.] 6 OAC's and OSSD from Kenner Collegiate Vocational Institute and graduated from Sir Sandford Fleming College from the Social Service Worker Program.; [occ.] Product Consultant with M&M Meat Shops; [hon.] MVP Field Hockey, Ontario Scholar, Head Girl at Commencement for Kenner Collegiate, President of Girls Athletic Association, Co-Captain of Field Hockey Team made the Dean's List at Sir Sandford Fleming College.; [oth. writ.] This is my first published poem. I have written many other poems on various topics but haven't exposed them to the public.; [pers.] I am inspired by personal experiences and significant assurances in life. Everyone has a special talent, it's just a matter of finding it and believing it's special.; [a.] Peterborough Ontario, Canada

KIMBEL, STACY RENEE
[b.] January 5, 1964, San Jose, CA; [p.] Rosealie Kimbel, Delmar Kimbel; [ed.] Peter Burnett Jr. High, A. Lincoln High School; [occ.] Student; [hon.] Baseball, basketball MVP Most Valuable Player; [pers.] I love sports, music, dancing and writing poetry. Still water was inspired by a very special friend Tammy Elliott. My motivation and all my inspiration is due to my mother and my here my sister Pennae who has always told me since I was little I have talent all I have to do is use it, 1317 Palm St.; [a.] San Jose, CA

KING, MICHELLE
[b.] May 22, 1976, Edmonton, Alberta, Canada; [ch.] Ashley; [ed.] College; [occ.] Esthetician, Hair stylist; [oth. writ.] First publication; [a.] Edmonton Alberta, Canada

KINNE, MERLE W.
[b.] September 23, 1917, Minn; [p.] Alyce Henrietta Vandoenberg, Chester Kinne; [m.] Patricia A. Kinne, October 12, 1954; [ch.] Kevin; [ed.] Central H.S., Minneapolis, Dunwoody Inst. Minneapolis; [occ.] Retired; [memb.] Heritage Found, BPOE - Demit; [oth. writ.] Two articles published - international bow hunter Magazine. Forty Short stories, one novel of wild west, two of foreign intrigue. Western Poetry. Poem in "Beyond The Stars"!; [pers.] I've had to cram a lifetime of adventure into five years work. At seventy eight I hope to continue to do so, by the good graces of opens-minded publishers.; [a.] Long Beach, CA

KINSMAN, LISA-MARIE
[b.] January 14, 1963, Boston, MA; [p.] William and Beatrice Sullivan; [m.] Glen Milford Kinsman, October 2, 1993; [ch.] Katie and Ryan Kinsman (step-children); [ed.] High School Graduate of Lynn Vocational Technical Institute. Hoping to go onto Nursing School soon.; [occ.] Housewife, Stepmother and writer.; [memb.] Epilepsy Foundation of America, East Troy Baptist Church, International Society of Poets.; [oth. writ.] "My knight in shining armor", "An act of God," "Dr. Mark Smith", "Dr. Andrew Bragdon", "Lorraine," "Step-parenting", "Whatever happened to...?" and "Free at last".; [pers.] After suffering with epilepsy for 29 years, I hope to go on to nursing school. I want to help other epileptics and stomp out the fear and ignorance people have about epilepsy.; [a.] Sheshequin, PA

KIRCHMEIER, JUDY
[pen.] Jan McIrwrithe; [b.] November 21, 1946, Queens, NY; [p.] Lou Kirchmeier, Otto Kirchmeier; [ch.] RJ, Karie Both; [ed.] Univ. of Conn B. or Sci, Home Economics major, Ed. minor thinking of masters; [occ.] Home Ec. Teacher at Brand New Middle School, gr 5-8; [memb.] East West Dance Association; [hon.] GRS writing award for class trip to Washington, D.C. Gold Medal Amateur Dance Couple Cha Cha and Rumba; [oth. writ.] Working on my book, "You're moving where? "Growing, up is hard" (poetry) just brainstormed it!; [pers.] I have always been a writer and record feelings events. Erica Jong "Fear of 50" Poetry helped with writing process, which is how I did the cat's poem; [a.] Calgary Alberta, Canada

KIRKHAM, BONNIE B.
[b.] July 26, 1913, Gardner, WV; [p.] Frank Agee and Fannie Radford; [m.] G. Wm. Kirkham,

February 26, 1968; [ch.] Six; [ed.] Eight Grade graduate Gardner Union School, Mercer Co, West Virginia attended Spanishburg HS Mercer Co, West Virginia; [occ.] Home maker - now recently deceased; [hon.] Spelling Bee winner - First Place several years at the Nursing Home de here she passed away. Carehaven of Raleigh Daniels, Western Virginia; [oth. writ.] Mother has other poems she had give to me through the years, none of which have been published.; [pers.] Mother's life centered around her children and her religious faith. Her artistic ability was strangled by her socio-economic restraints. She made the extremely hard work on the farm fun for all her children.; [a.] Milwaukee, OR

KIRKPATRICK, KATRINA LEVERT
[pen.] Katrina Kirkpatrick; [b.] February 5, 1947, Jacksonville, FL; [p.] James B. and Frances Levert; [m.] Scott Kirkpatrick, November 23, 1976; [ch.] Two; [ed.] Associate of Science Degree: The Art Institute of Ft. Lauderdale, FL, Major: Ad Design Highest Achievement Award Also: LSU - Music Major; [occ.] Graphic Artist/Designer and Musician and Fine Artist; [memb.] Contra Costa Coventy Graphic Artists Network; [hon.] Hollywood Dream Festival, Los Angeles CA (7 paintings) Nov. 1987 Award of Excellence and gold and silver medal winner, Western Music Festival Poster 1989 and 1990 (Hall of Fame), 1992 Pac Bell 6 month Art Show: 2nd Place People's Choice Award for "Sophie"; [oth. writ.] Poetry and Songs; [pers.] My Art and Poetry is an interpretation of everything I value, think, feel and find beautiful in my life's experiences. Basically, I am a dreamer, and a lover of fantasy, romance, adventure and nature, most of which, in one way or another, is reflected in my work. Sometimes I like to take a new look at an old subject...ie...The Carousel Metamorphosis, or visualize a verbal statement...ie..."She's finally coming out of her shell." Other inspiration comes from the songs I've been intimately involved with during my first 15 year career on stage as a singer and musician. I use a lot of mixed media including watercolor, acrylic, ink, pencil, pastel and oil, and experiment with combining textures with airbrush to express a mood or disposition. I would describe my images as short stories of evolution, harmony and freedom of spirit.; [a.] Walnut Creek, CA

KIRKPATRICK, KEVIN
[b.] July 7, 1963, Okarche, OK; [p.] Glenn Kirkpatrick, M. Vee Washam; [m.] Lovina M. Kirkpatrick, January 5, 1993; [ch.] Samantha, Cory, Nickolaus; [ed.] High School graduate taking courses with, The Institute of Children's Literature and The Long Ridge Writers Group; [occ.] Manager in the Walmart Corporations Sam's Clubs; [hon.] 1994-1995 Editors Choice Awards, Award of Merit with four seasons poetry club.; [oth. writ.] 4 Other poems published in National Library of Poetry's Anthologies. Several poems published in "Four seasons poetry club magazine"; [pers.] To have someone read your work, and it movies them emotionally or intellectually, that is the highest honor.

KIRKPATRICK, LAURA A.
[b.] October 31, 1985, Washington, DC; [ed.] Norwood School Bethesda, MD (5th grade student)

KLADSTRUP, DONALD M.
[pen.] Don Kladstrup; [b.] June 30, 1917, Newell, IA; [p.] Peter Kladstrup, Henrietta Madsen Kladstrup; [m.] Ruth Marjorie Coon, August 30, 1940; [ch.] Donald M. Kladstrup II, Richard Bruce Kladstrup, Peter Lynn Kladstrup, Steven Earl Kladstrup; [ed.] Newell High School, Newell, Iowa 1938 State University of Iowa (Bachelor of Science in Commerce) graduated with high distinction, 1939 State University of Iowa (Master of Arts), 1959 Graduate School of Credit and Financial Mgt (Executive Award); [occ.] Retired (Formerly an executive and business manager with Eastman Kodak Company.; [memb.] Beta Gamma Sigma (Honorary) Order of Artus (honorary), Oak Hill Country Club, Rochester, NY, St. Paul's Lutheran Church, Pittsburgh, NY; [hon.] Beta Gamma Sigma (Honorary), Order of Artus (honorary) Lieutenant Colonel, USAF Reserve Certified Public Accountant (CPA), Alumni Award for Outstanding Executive Leadership (given by graduate) School of Credit and Financial Mgt - Nat'l Assoc. of Creditmen, at Tuck School, Dartmouth College in 1959.; [oth. writ.] "The Crown Jewels of Oak Hill", "The Evolution of a Legacy", Numerous business dissertations (following in-depth research), Numerous poems and short stories, Travelogs and journals covering travels to all seven continents, Many miscellaneous reports and news stories; [pers.] Honest optimism and a bottomless well of curiosity are blessings. They seem to be part of me, and I am truly thankful. They carry me a long way in my efforts to make every day productive. Life should not be wasted!; [a.] Rochester, NY

KLASSEN, HELEN
[b.] July 13, 1975, Tillsonburg, Ontario, Canada; [p.] Bernard and Maria Klassen; [ed.] East Elgin Secondary School; [occ.] Not presently working; [hon.] Grade 9 Math Award; [oth. writ.] One other poem published by National Library of Poetry.; [pers.] Poetry was never my thing, but friend and family greatly encouraged me that my poems were good enough to be published.; [a.] Vienna Ontario, Canada

KLIMASH, DEBRA
[b.] November 9, 1978, Beloit, WI; [p.] David Klimash, Bernice Kirsch; [ed.] High School Junior; [memb.] Band, Outing Club, The school paper, the advocate, Art club; [hon.] Honor student; [oth. writ.] Articles in the local paper (The Lewiston Sun); [pers.] I would like to thank my Aunt Tina and the rest of my family for having so much faith in me. They taught me to be myself.; [a.] Lisbon Falls, ME

KNIPPSHILD, SONIA
[b.] October 21, 1966, Abbotsford, British Columbia, Canada; [p.] Susan Fussi, Helmut Glawischnig; [m.] Darrell Knippshild, August 21, 1993; [ch.] Constance Jeanine, Daniel James, Sara Amber, Joseph Helmut, Russell James, Samantha Anne; [ed.] Grade 12, Smattering of College courses; [occ.] Homemaker; [memb.] Adult Swim Club; [oth. writ.] I have any written a few poems for personal occasions. I have no published writings at this point.; [pers.] For me, the most beautiful poetry comes from deep felt emotions. I find that the words I seek come easily when I am personally involved and it makes my poetry flow.; [a.] Ladysmith British Columbia, Canada

KNOPP, ALLEN
[b.] August 13, 1957, Edmonton; [p.] Herb and Arlene Knopp; [m.] Sharon Knopp, October 6, 1991; [pers.] These words were inspired by a lady named Laurie holt, from Ponoka Alta, Canada, who has dedicated her life, to helping others. Thank you, Laurie.; [a.] Red Deer Alberta, Canada

KNOWLES, PAUL N.
[pen.] P. K. Rider; [b.] May 10, 1942, Ada, OK; [p.] Dorothea Grice; [ed.] GED Rio Salado Com Call Php Az; [occ.] Directory Assistance Operator, Albuquerque N.M.; [memb.] CWA Union Steward (Communication Workers of America); [hon.] Neighbor Assoc. Award; [pers.] Poetry is where I've always hid my most personal pain, it keeps going when the going gets tough; [a.] Albuquerque, NM

KNOWLES, RAYMOND W. O.
[pen.] Raymond W. O. Knowles; [b.] March 20, 1907, Wellington, KS; [p.] William B., Jennie O. (Waters) Knowles; [m.] Deceased, August 28, 1926; [ch.] Robert W. (Deceased) Margaret P. Jackson, Dr. Richard D. Knowles; [ed.] High School, College, 60 hrs. Theological Seminary; [occ.] Retired Minister; [memb.] Kansas West Conference of the United Methodist Church, A.A.R.P. Volunteer at Colorado, Springs Police Department, Gold Hill Division, American Center for Law and Justice, CBN $2500 Club.; [oth. writ.] Article for Christian advocate of the Methodist church. Article for "Guide Posts. Article for American Ericanible Society" Record. "Many unpublished sermons."; [pers.] I do not believe that life is in vain. Failure is never disastrous unless we allow it to be so. And physical death does not have the final word. I want to spend my life being spent in doing things for others. Old age is a bad habit you do not have time to form if you keep busy."; [a.] Canon City, CO

KOBER, FRANKIE
[b.] March 8, 1943, Washington, DC; [p.] Albert and Rosalie Furr; [m.] Donald Kober, March 18, 1962; [ch.] Deborah, Ronald, Joseph and Marijo; [occ.] I work for the federal government; [hon.] Several eight ribbons for landscapes, seascapes and pet portraits awarded by the Montgomery County fair; [pers.] If my work touches someone's innermost self, gets them to think, feel and grow, that is the ultimate accomplishment. "This poem is dedicated to my good friend Sherry."; [a.] Silver Spring, MD

KOH, ANGELA
[pen.] Nil; [b.] July 8, 1983, Singapore; [p.] Peter Koh, Lily Koh; [m.] Nil; [ed.] Grades 1 to 5, Nanyang Primary School (Singapore), Grade 6 and now, Collingwood School (Canada); [occ.] Pupil; [memb.] U.K. - Mensa; [hon.] U.K. - Mensa; [oth. writ.] Through My Eyes - An Anthology; [pers.] Respect your parents and teachers always; [a.] Vancouver British Columbia, Canada

KOHLER, MARGARET ANN
[b.] May 18, 1941, Ireland; [p.] John P. and Mary Ellen Ansbro; [m.] Larry Dea Kohler, August 18, 1962; [ch.] Colleen, Trisha, Brian; [ed.] Graduated St. Mary's Academy H.S. 1960; [memb.] Green peace National Wildlife Federation World wildlife fund nature conservancy National Geographic Society; [oth. writ.] Collection of 25 poems I have never submitted for publication.; [pers.] I believe we

all have our place on this planet, and I strive to treat every living thing with respect and dignity.; [a.] Milwaukie, OR

KOMENDO, SANDRA KAY
[b.] November 22, 1974, Greenfield, IN; [p.] Terry and Sharron Crossley; [m.] James Anthony Komendo, February 14, 1992; [ch.] Justin Lee Anthony Kamendo; [hon.] Editor's Choice Awards 1995; [oth. writ.] This will be my third publishing in books. I also have had poems published in newspapers.; [pers.] The purpose in my writing is to look at life from every angle. I hope it makes people aware of the good and bad. I also hope my poems make us aware of the world we are living in and what we need to do to to make it safe for others.; [a.] Carthage, IN

KORSCH, CANDICE LEANNE
[b.] September 18, 1983, Kelowna, British Columbia; [p.] Ron and Betty Korsch; [ed.] Springvalley Elmo Hollywood Rd Middle School; [hon.] Citizenship Academic; [pers.] I love writing poems.; [a.] Kelowna British Columbia, Canada

KOWALSKI, RICHARD J. P.
[pen.] R. J. P. Kowalski; [b.] July 2, 1964, Sacramento, CA; [p.] Edward F. Kowalski, Virginia Ann; [m.] Gwea C. Murray Crowley, December 5, 1992; [ed.] Johnsonburg Area High Alfred University.; [occ.] Lithographer.; [memb.] Zete Beta Tall; [oth. writ.] Personal Poetry, short stories and comments on life and culture we all live in today unpublished.; [pers.] I'll always March to the beat of a different drummer, and sometimes life catches the beat.; [a.] Glendale, AZ

KOWK, JEANNETTE
[pen.] Jenny; [b.] October 11, 1956, Vancouver, British Columbia, Canada; [p.] Norm and Shirley Lozon; [m.] Joe Skinner Common Law (Engaged); [ch.] Kristina, Michael, Lisa Kowk; [occ.] Run own day care, also taking landscaping course, I'm an extra in movie shoots, and I sing in my spare time.; [hon.] I've come in fourth in a Karaoke contest, and one day hope to become a singer.; [oth. writ.] I've wrote other poems to my children and my spouse, but never published them. I've even wrote a song, and one day I hope it may be used.; [pers.] I try to bring out my true feelings in my poetry and singing, and there's a lot of love and meaning behind it.; [a.] Maple Ridge British Columbia, Canada

KRAMER, CRYSTAL
[pen.] Crystal Kramer; [b.] October 20, 1965, Harbor City, CA; [p.] Jack and Sandra Graham; [m.] Michael Kramer, July 15, 1989; [ch.] Ryan Kramer, Morgan Kramer; [ed.] Mt. View High, Mesa Community College; [occ.] Service Runner; [memb.] MS Association; [oth. writ.] A few published in school newspaper.; [pers.] As a young teen, I wrote poetry and I was inspired by man spirit and soul, and as I wrote I wanted people to see what people were inside.; [a.] Renton, WA

KRAWCHUK, EVELYN
[b.] October 2, 1949, Smoky Lake, Alberta, Canada; [p.] John and Doris Dubetz; [m.] Lot Krawchuk, August 31, 1968; [ch.] Four; [ed.] H.A. Kostash School Business College Rural Library Training; [occ.] Library Technician; [oth. writ.] Several poems

written no others have been published thus far.; [pers.] Take time to cherish God's love for you and in turn share that love with others around you.

KREMP, JON C.
[pen.] Jack Mannion; [b.] September 13, 1972, Plattsburgh, NY; [p.] Robert Kremp, Maureen Kremp; [ed.] Sarasota High, Sarasota, FL. Hunter College, NY. Comm. College of Rhode Island; [hon.] Dean's List; [pers.] A number of my pomes and stories reflect personal experiences while in the U.S. Navy (Submarine Force), as well as my civilian life.; [a.] Manassas, VA

KRIEGER, ROSEMARY G.
[pen.] RGK; [b.] March 5, 1938, Cincinnati, OH; [p.] Thomas George, Helen George; [m.] Benjamin W. Krieger, April 12, 1958; [ch.] Gregory, Kenneth, Catherine; [ed.] Regina High, Cincinnati, Ohio Harvard Amp., Spouses Program, Jack Carew DPS Program, Various training and seminar programs; [occ.] President and owner, RGK enterprises Inc. dba/EBC 1200 Corporate place; [memb.] Boca Raton Chamber of Commerce, National Association Women Business Owners Executive Suite Association, Nafe, Sterling Who's Who'; [hon.] EBC presidents award 1993-1994, Boca Raton Chamber of Commerce Person of the year award 1995, Boca Chamber Outstanding Membership Development Award 1995; [oth. writ.] "Violated" (published); [pers.] "Don't do it unless you can give it your very best"; [a.] Boca Raton, FL

KROPP, ARLENE
[b.] June 13, 1936, Vancouver, BC; [p.] Philip and Mary Dill; [m.] Ted Kropp, May 28, 1958; [ch.] Douglas, Randy, Shari; [ed.] B. Ed (U.B.C.) M.P.S. (Vancouver School of Theology); [occ.] Pastoral Care Co-ordinator; [memb.] United Church of Canada, Hospice Society, Univ. Women's Club, Abbotsford Retired Teachers' Assoc.; [oth. writ.] Sermons, Eulogies, Poetry; [pers.] My poetry reflects the corporate journey of personal growth and spiritual reflections.; [a.] Abbotsford British Columbia, Canada

KUEHN, IRENE
[b.] September 18, 1950, Far Rockaway, NY; [p.] William and Gloria Schmeelk; [ch.] Laurissa and Brian; [ed.] Lehigh County Comm. College, Taylor Business Institute; [occ.] Manager, Foster wheeler; [memb.] St. Mary's Catholic Church Lector, Tiger Schulman's Karate; [hon.] Red Belt Karate; [oth. writ.] Other poems published in anthologies and newsletters, poetry reading at state theatre, luncheon speeches, retreats (part of a team giving retreats); [pers.] Through my writing, I try to emphasize living with a positive out look and encourage spiritual growth, healing, and personal peace; [a.] Phillipsburg, NJ

KUHN, BERNICE
[b.] December 2, 1914, Hustisford, WI; [p.] Fred and Marie Tornow; [m.] Jerry Kuhn (Deceased), December 25, 1939; [ch.] A daughter, son (Deceased); [ed.] Hustisford High School, Dodge County Normal, University of Wisconsin , White water, WI, Bachelor of Education; [occ.] Retired, Former Elementary Teacher; [memb.] Original Senior Songsters chorus of Waukesha, WI, Ladies Aid - Grace Ev Lutheran Church, Altar Committee

Lutheran Church; [oth. writ.] Several poems published in American Poetry Anthology, also in church Bulletin.; [pers.] I write about anything that inspires me. I feel that my life is in God's hands whether it be good or bad. Exercise and proper nutrition are important to me.; [a.] Waukesha, WI

KURULIAK, JOYCE
[b.] November 15, 1937, Edmonton; [p.] Carl and Wanda Klammer; [m.] Dr. Metro Kuruliak, August 29, 1959; [ch.] Gregory Vinton, Marla Marie; [ed.] Holden High Orthondontic Assistants Training; [occ.] Homemaker; [oth. writ.] Personal use only. First submission.; [pers.] I've always enjoyed poetry, both reading and writing and as I enter my senior years I wish to do more writing. I enjoy writing about things that have influenced, inspired, left a mark on my life on Earth, the around, the world we live in. This allows me to write from the heart and the belief in the scripture found in Eccl 9:10 "What so ever thy hand findeth to do, do it with thy might, for there is no work, nor device, nor knowledge, nor wisdom, in the grave, whither thou goest." This scripture is a way of life for me.; [a.] Spruce Grove Alberta, Canada

LAARI, KARINA MAE
[b.] June 17, 1980, Terrace Bay, Ontario, Canada; [p.] John and Christine Laari; [ed.] From grade one to grade five, I attended the Metro Toronto School for the deaf, and ever since grade six, I've attended the Robarts School for the Deaf in London Ontario. Presently I'm grade ten; [hon.] In June 1994, when I was in grade eight, I receive the "citizenship Award" from Robarts School for the deaf. A year later June 1995, when I was in grade nine, I received the "Academic Award," also from Robarts School For the deaf; [pers.] I became deaf at 12 months of age as the result of a serious meningitis illness. From the time I was very young, I have written my own stories and illustrated them in my home-made books. I continue to love to read as well as write and pen my thoughts and ideas in my journals; [a.] London Ontario, Canada

LAFFERTY-CARTER, ROBERTA CAROL
[pen.] LaVedi Lafferty; [b.] December 30, 1936, Cincinnati, OH; [p.] Ruth Cone and Robert Baird Lafferty; [m.] Divorced/widowed, 1955, 1962, 1972, 1991; [ch.] Roblyn Lafferty Dresser; [ed.] Grants Pass High (Oreg) University of the Americas (Mexico) University of Alaska-Fairbanks (BA Engl); [occ.] Writer/Consultant; [memb.] The Theosophical Society Assn. for Transpersonal Psychology Unity and Diversity Council Eastern Star, Order of (OES) Meditation Group for the New Age (MGNA); [hon.] Honor Society, Dean's List, Governor's Certificate of Appreciation (for service: Council for Handi- capped and Gifted) Volunteer Recognition Award, from Arctic Alliance for People Listed in: Who's Who in the West: American Women, in the World, Int'l Register of Profiles, Foremost Women of the 20th Cent.; [oth. writ.] "Reincarnation: Explained" 1977, "The Past-Life Memory Program" 1977, "The Sacrifical Tide" 1980, and book, "The Eternal Dance" 1984, inclusion in book, "Sacred Sites" 1992. Plus asundry short pieces.; [pers.] I am an esotericist, interested in social issues and the universal aspects of human evolution. I find poetry to be an excellent means of giving voice to the soul with resonating impact.; [a.] Fairbanks, AK

LAHTI, PHYLLIS HANSON
[b.] May 6, 1921, Rock Island, IL; [p.] Helen M. Hebble and Dewey D. Hanson; [m.] May 23, 1944; [ch.] Jon T. Lahti, Evansville, Wis.; [ed.] HS and Omro Wi., BS from Oshkosh Wi., La Crosse Wi., BTA Pasadena Playhouse, Summer classes at Layton Art, Milwaukee, Wi., and Port Clyde, Maine; [occ.] Retired - sort of I'm studying Greek. Long ago I taught school.; [memb.] A non-joiner! I believe in "good", but not sure it can travel as fast or as far as "Evil."; [oth. writ.] A few thousand words stashed in computer and files: "3 Roses and a Brass Stein" (a gay treatise on Ms. Stein), ideas for paintings, and cartoons, and a book and taste the salt, poems that I hope are "hand-grenades wrapped in pink silk.".; [pers.] I am a camera, haunted by a man haranguing, for 3 aisles, a sad-eyed babe in grocery cart, by a shopper's self-incriminating scream, "Come back here, you damn little farts!" I grieve children betrayed by those they need to love, who give, instead of acceptance and praise, word-wounds that in a lifetime will not heal!; [a.] Mesa, AZ

LAIRD, BETHANY SHEA
[pen.] Beth, Shea; [b.] August 22, 1979, Meridian, MS; [p.] James B. Laird Jr., Renee Laird; [ed.] High School Junior; [occ.] Student; [memb.] District Vice-President of Slam, Chorus, Drama, Mu Alpha Theta, Hebron Baptist Church, Youth Legislature; [hon.] 9th Grade Homecoming maid, 1994 HS most beautiful; [oth. writ.] Unlisted; [a.] Little Rock, MS

LAMBERT, JOHN
[b.] September 27, 1971; [pers.] To Susie: I am sorry (she understands); [a.] Pittsburgh, PA

LAMBERT, WILLIAM J.
[pen.] William J. Lambert; [b.] December 24, 1919, Camden East; [p.] The late Winnifred and John Lambert; [m.] Evelyn, September 21, 1977; [ch.] Three; [ed.] Very little 8th grade; [occ.] Propane Operator Gardener; [memb.] War Amps of Canada, Distinguished Member of National Poetry; [hon.] Poetry Elite 1985, Public Recognition Canadian Forces 1939-45, Editors Choice Awards National Library of Poetry 1993 and 1995; [oth. writ.] The poets corner in local paper 2 yrs. I have 3 books on the market "Treasured Thoughts" Vol. I, II, III; [pers.] My inspirations - as swift as the waters nature is my educator, the best teacher of man. I am a lover of birds, flowers and all nature around. Now retired look back on my childhood years and put life time thoughts into poems.; [a.] Lyndhurst Ontario, Canada

LAMERS, AMANDA
[b.] April 14, 1978, Oshawa, Ontario, Canada; [p.] Martin and Marian Lamers; [occ.] Gr. 12 Student/ Father Leo J. Austin C.S.S. Whitby, Ontario; [memb.] School Yearbook, Jazz Band, 3rd Owasco Venturers; [hon.] Honor roll student caley Math contest award, numerous piano awards and scholarships completed Gr 10 Conservatory Piano; [oth. writ.] Poem published in local newspaper. Catholic Women's league poetry award.; [pers.] I plan to attend University and hope one day to enter the field of broadcast journalism.; [a.] Whitby Ontario, Canada

LANGLEY, MELISSA
[b.] August 31, 1970, Indianapolis, IN; [p.] R. M. Wheeler, Victoria Patterson; [m.] Michael Langley,

January 10, 1987; [ed.] Laurens Dist. 55 High Greenville Technical College; [occ.] Medical Laboratory Technician, Jewish Hospital Kenwood; [memb.] American Society for Clinical Pathologists; [pers.] Although I'm known as a very open person my deepest feelings only come out in my writing.; [a.] Cincinnati, OH

LANGMAR, ITALA
[pen.] Itala; [b.] Italy; [m.] Imre Langmar; [ch.] Emery Peter; [ed.] Doctor degree in Architecture - Venice University Italy; [occ.] Artist, Painter Fiber Artist; [memb.] National Georgraphic Art Institute of Chicago Art Encounter Evanson, Evanson Art Center Illinois, Suburban Fine Arts Illinois; [hon.] All my awards since I was 6 years old have been given to me on my paintings and prints and drawings most recent on September 1995 for a work on beauty of "Bellezza"; [oth. writ.] On May 1995 I wrote my first poem and many more followed. I started combining them in my paintings with abstract symbols.; [pers.] I started writing poems to elucidate my sometimes mysterious little paintings and to make more clear what or whom inspired them. Now I have a series in progress: Women and flowers. The poem, Midnight Gladiolus (a self portrait) is the very first. Each woman is represented by a flower and a poem on two separate canvases, size 10" by 10". These women I either know personally or have heard of. What they have in common is a personal vision, and a strong charismatic presence and/or authority. I intend to write a minimum of 25 poems on women and follow with 25 poems on men, in a new series called Men and Trees.

LANK, DAVID L.
[b.] July 20, 1942, Nova Scotia, Canada; [p.] Elmer and Louise Lank; [m.] Anne Fraser Lank, 1966; [ch.] David, James, Heather; [ed.] Business Administra- tion; [occ.] Nursing Home Administrator; [oth. writ.] Short stories of Nova Scotia Interest; [a.] New Glasgow Nova Scotia, Canada

LARABEE, DENNIS W.
[b.] March 5, 1965, Timmins, Ontario, Canada; [p.] Shirley Naveau, Roy Larabee; [ed.] Malaspina University College, completing Bachelor Degree in Social Work; [oth. writ.] Currently, in the process of writing a novel.; [pers.] My inspiration stems from many influences in my life. Especially from David Muirhead, an English Instructor who taught me how to ride the wings of imagination and soar.

LAROSE, LINDA
[ch.] Robert Larose Jr., Tricia-Lynn Larose; [ed.] Marymount College, Cambrian College, Sudbury, Ontario; [occ.] Manager/Instructor Academy of learning; [oth. writ.] Created self-help handbook (contacts to various self help groups) while working for social services in Canada. Have written several poems for various friends and family.; [pers.] A spiritual person is a person who does what he/she can, when he/she can, the best he/she can! We are what we believe we are!; [a.] Espanola Ontario, Canada

LARSON, CLIFF
[pen.] C. J.; [b.] September 14, 1985, Morristown, NJ; [p.] Debbie Larson; [ed.] Fifth in St, Peter's The Apostle School, Parssipany; [occ.] Attendees St. Peter's The Apostle School

LASSITER, DARRYL D.
[b.] September 4, 1963, Birmingham, AL; [p.] Robert and Johnnye P. Lassiter; [ed.] Jess Lanier High, 1981 B.S. Alabama State University 1986, Major Communications, Minor Music; [occ.] Newspaper Editor, Publicist Inter-sound Records; [memb.] Black Film makers Foundation, Image Film and Video, ITVA, NAACP; [hon.] Listed in Who's Who in the World, Who's Who in Hollywood, all major awards in the music dept. of Alabama State Univ.; [oth. writ.] Black College Alumni, book "Pay The Price" Screenplay, "Dead End Street" Screenplay several stories published in local papers and magazines. Many TV scripts; [pers.] I've been given so many chances in life and I want to do all the right things. My goal is to produce a movie and own my video/TV production company.; [a.] Atlanta, GA

LAUCK, GREGORY J.
[b.] October 11, 1969, Kankakee, IL; [p.] Dr. Michael and Carole Lauck; [ed.] Oak Park River Forest High School, University of Iowa (1987-1989) B.A. in Communications from Loyola University Chicago; [occ.] Freelance writer, Actor, Poet; [memb.] Kappa Sigma Fraternity (At University of Iowa) Assistant grand scribe responsible for out-of-house newsletter, alumni relations chairman received national honor for "Best Alumni Publication" (The Bugle) writer for Loyola's paper "The Phoenix" (Editor of Cityscope section) writer for vox - a College newspaper in Chicago. Poetry slam performer at "The Green Mill" in Chicago - Winter slam finalist and national slam semi-finalist; [oth. writ.] Several poems published in school papers and literary magazines.

LAURILA, DEREK
[b.] February 25, 1984, Greenbrae, CA; [p.] Anssi and Dorothy Laurila; [ed.] 1989-91 Vallecito Elementary School (K-1st Grades) 1991-95 Mary E. Silveira Elementary School. Presently a 6th grader at Miller Creek Middle School. All schools located in San Rafael, California; [memb.] 1991- Present: has played soccer and baseball for Dixie-Terra Linda Little League. Plays roller Lockey for Marin Roller Hockey league. Purple Belt Karate at East West Martial Arts in Novato.; [pers.] My writing reflects the positive humor in situations people and things. One should always look at the brighter side of things.; [a.] San Rafael, CA

LAWRENCE, MARVIN A.
[b.] April 12, 1924, Montgomery Co., VA; [m.] Ramona Abbott Lawrence, August 6, 1948; [ch.] Three sons living, one daughter deceased; [ed.] High School, various banking courses; [occ.] Retired spent 47 years with the National Bank of Blacksburg; [oth. writ.] Only a few poems; [a.] Blacksburg, VA

LAWRENCE, TREVOR
[pen.] Brother Lawrence; [b.] April 3, 1961, Kingston, Jamaica; [p.] Phyllis Douse, Cyril Lawrence; [ed.] St. Annes High, University of Manitoba; [occ.] Teacher (Grade 4) King Edward Community School; [memb.] Jamaican Association of Manitoba, Black Educators Association of Manitoba, Berean Church of God; [hon.] Bachelors Degree in Education, Post Baccalaureate in Education; [oth. writ.] Several poems published in new letters and local community news papers; [pers.] I use poetry as a camera to capture very important

historical events expressed in the form of culture, politics, social events and human interactions; [a.] Winnipeg Manitoba, Canada

LAZARUS, BRANDY T.
[pen.] Black Lark; [b.] January 9, 1979, Rota, Spain; [p.] Linda and Harvey Lazarus; [ed.] Student 10th grade; [occ.] Student; [oth. writ.] Why, My Love, The Perfect Woman, One Last..., The Clowns Frown, sSe, Me I, What If, The Wind of Change, Dieing, The World is Ending, Mental Suicide and others. Not published yet.; [pers.] Dreams are wonderful things you can find love or hell, control your dreams and you control the world.; [a.] Beacon, NY

LEAKE, EDWARD
[pen.] Michael Vaughn; [b.] June 23, 1960, Washington, DC; [ed.] Ballou High, Hampton University; [hon.] Dean's List; [oth. writ.] Article in the Washington Post; [pers.] I believe in myself, follow my dreams. I accept everyday as an opportunity to grow, first as a person and second, as a professional.; [a.] Greenbelt, MD

LEAN, TAMMI
[b.] September 27, 1962, Cobourg, ON; [p.] PerryLean, Jim and Diane Shields; [ch.] Jessica Diane; [ed.] CDCI East High School, Cobourg Ont., Loyalist College Belleville, Ont, Canada; [occ.] Single Mother Of One; [memb.] Volunteer at my daughters School (Thomas Gillbard PS, Cobourg, Ont Canada); [hon.] Singing awards at the Public School Level; [oth. writ.] Written many poems but for personal viewing only; [pers.] I have been greatly influenced by the love of my family. All my poems are the reflections of my feelings; [a.] Cobourg Ontario, Canada

LEATH, MS. FARRIS
[pen.] Vern; [b.] October 11, 1956, Henderson, TX; [p.] Mr. and Mrs. J. M. Howard; [m.] Deceased, October 14, 1978; [ch.] Four children and three grandchildren; [ed.] Graduated from Lincoln High of Dallas and Graduate from Allstate Business College of Dallas; [occ.] Home care provider and summer day care provider; [memb.] Member of the Macedonia Baptist Church Pastor Wesley Boyd; [pers.] When you put God first and continue to study his word he will guide you through any situation with a peace that surpasses all understanding; [a.] Dallas, TX

LEATHERBERRY, AGNES O.
[pen.] Mary Ann; [b.] February 10, 1913, Kickapoo Valley, WI; [p.] John and Bessie Markley; [m.] Vaughn Leatherberry, September 29, 1929; [ch.] Bernadine Leatherberry Smith and Ronald Leatherberry; [occ.] Retired; [oth. writ] I have had a few published in two different papers, as well as some history writings.; [pers.] When I write poems I like to feel I'm writing something that touches on the lives of people to help them see there is a purpose inlife and to keep their spirits up. I like the longer poems, like those I read in rural schools, that tell a story. I'd like to dedicate my poem "You'll Never Be Alone" to my son Ronald Leatherberry, now deceased.

LEBLANC, JULIE
[b.] November 19, 1979, Orleans, Ontario, Canada; [p.] Lorraine and Andre Leblanc; [occ.] Student

(High School); [pers.] I try to reflect my feelings or others peoples feelings in my poems I also base my poems on peoples everyday lives. Poetry plays a every important role in our culture. God forbid it should perish; [a.] Metcalfe Ontario, Canada

LEDBETHE, VONCILE T.
[pen.] Voncile T. Ledbethe; [b.] March 2, 1926, Eclectic, AL; [p.] John and Shady Taunton; [m.] Joe Fred Ledbethe (Deceased), November 9, 1946; [ch.] Joel Ledbethe and Jan Ledbethe; [ed.] High School Graduate; [occ.] Owner and Operator of Voncile's Beauty shop; [memb.] United Methodist Church; [oth. writ.] Poem in local news papers, poem "The New Year" in Sparkles in the Sand; [a.] Tallahassee, AL

LEDREW, DEBORAH
[b.] May 30, 1969, Niagara Falls, Ontario, Canada; [p.] Janice Seager; [m.] Dennis LeDrew, August 26, 1988; [ch.] Denise, Jacquelyne, and Dyanah-Alysha; [ed.] Cameron Heights Collegiate, Kitchener, Ontario, Canada; [pers.] Deborah's passions are her writing, her children and other children, family life, soccer, ice skating, fishing, puppies and other animals; [a.] Kitchener Ontario, CA

LEE, DANTE
[b.] May 18, 1981, Riverdale, MD; [p.] Irvin and Beverly Lee; [ed.] Eleanor Roosevelt High School, Greenbelt, Maryland; [pers.] Think for yourself, believe in your self. Do everything for yourself. For in the end it is yourself that will benefit.; [a.] Riverdale, MD

LEEDOM, PRISCILLA
[b.] August 11, 1962, Sioux City, IA; [p.] Don Moorman, Pat Moorman; [m.] Don Leedom, February 12, 1994; [ch.] Cory Christopher, Megan Sue

LEISMAN, SHIRLEY HOLVICK
[pen.] Sal; [b.] February 23, 1932, Washburn, WI; [p.] Barbara and Adolph Holvick; [m.] M. "Ken" Leisman, September 8, 1951; [ch.] Scott, Karen, Kathy; [ed.] Ashland county normal Univ. of Wis. Oshkosh Wis; [occ.] Retired housewife (teacher Asst. sales in gift shop); [memb.] Americanism chairman V. F. W. Auxiliary; [hon.] This poem was in newspaper and wise veterans of foreign wars news plus other articles; [oth. writ.] This is my first poem I wrote, I have written one more, be an eagle in Aug. 1995; [pers.] To sum this up my one word would be freedom in all things thought and deeds so we can all have peace; [a.] Mesa, AZ

LEITCH, KATIE
[b.] August 9, 1980; [ed.] I'm in 8th grade Chestnut Ridge Middle School in Washington Township; [pers.] This poem influenced by an ex-boyfriend who I'm back with, because of this poem. I love to write!; [a.] Sewell, NJ

LEMLEY, CHARLES A.
[b.] September 22, 1958, Salisbury, NC; [p.] Charles R. Lemley, Lelia B. Lemley; [ed.] Mars Hill College, Garduer Webb University, Regents College; [occ.] Legal Assistant; [oth. writ.] A selection of poetry; [a.] Mebane, NC

LENCH, CAROLE
[b.] December 8, 1939, Winnipeg, Manitoba, Canada; [p.] George and Ellen Harding; [m.] Donald,

July 18, 1981; [ch.] 3 Daughter; [ed.] High School; [occ.] Wife, Mother, Grandmother we are retired; [pers.] I have written poetry for years for my own personal gratification seldom mentioning this fact to anyone. When my husband told my mother-in-law I wrote, she was determined to read my wrote. It is thanks to this very caring lady, Dollie Lench that I had the courage to submit my work to the National Library of Poetry; [a.] Winnipeg Manitoba, Canada

LENTER, DEBRA J.
[b.] May 27, 1950, Milwaukee, WI; [ed.] Univ. of Wisconsin - Platteville Pre-Veterinary Med. MATC - Madison, WI Veterinary Technology National Certification Agency - Med. Tech-Microbiology certified Image consultant; [occ.] Women's Retail - Sales Artist and Poet.; [oth. writ.] "Lessons in Love - The Journey Home" a non-published anthology of poetry; [pers.] Though experiences differ from one person to the next, the emotions we experience are the same for all. The poetry I write reflects the common issues and emotions and the process of healing, forgiveness and letting go which are facilitated by unconditional love. I feel and believe it is the only way we as humanity can move forward into a future of cooperation, respect, understanding and harmony.; [a.] Lincoln, NE

LESTER, HARVEY J.
[pen.] SGM (Rev) Harvey Lester; [b.] October 19, 1947, Bartow, FL; [p.] Jessie and Annie Luster; [m.] Judith, May 25, 1970; [ch.] Monica, Jon, Marcus; [ed.] (MA) Marriage and Family Counseling (BA) Human Resource Admin (AA) Business Admin, graduate United State Army sergeant major academy; [occ.] Sergeant Major of Quarter, Master Corps Regimental Office; [memb.] Association of Quartermasters corps, United American Freewill Baptist Inc., Association of the United State Army American Legion, Veterans of Foreign War P #27; [hon.] Combat infantry badge (4) Meritorious Service medals, Purple hearts, (2) Army commenda-tion medals, Army achievement medals, white house great American family award, Fort Lee most outstanding black male for 1986.; [oth. writ.] Published "Poetry From The Soul Of Man" and poems published in contemporary poets of America and the American poetry anthology.; [pers.] We American are United as a nation by our God, by our blood, by our sweat, by our tears and by our brothers and sisters who died for our nation freedom and our democracy.; [a.] Fort Lee, VA

LESUER, JOSHUA PAUL
[b.] April 2, 1980, Syracuse, NY; [p.] Leonard and Peggy; [ed.] Currently enrolled in Springhill High School for sophomore year.; [hon.] One award for minor participation in band solo.; [oth. writ.] Many poems and stories, none published; [pers.] O but our lives are but a brief dash, a mark inscribed in endless history. Our accomplishments, traits, ideas briefly effect our society, before they are swallowed up by the sands of time.; [a.] Springhill, TN

LEU, MELISSA
[pen.] Taylor Andrews; [b.] May 5, 1980, Kitchener, ON; [p.] Wayne Brenner, Wendy Brenner; [ed.] Waterlou Oxford of Baden; [oth. writ.] Poems published in Waterloo County Anthology; [pers.] I write on how I perceive the world and by personal happenings. Most poems were written for my friend Tyler, who died at age 15, Dec. 29, 1994; [a.] Baden, ON

LEVACK, SYLVIA MARGARET
[pen.] Sylvia Levack McLellan and Missy Do; [b.] September 15, 1949, Truro, Nova Scotia; [p.] John and Vivian McLellan; [m.] Richard Levack, December 27, 1973; [ch.] Devon Douglas, Cherie Angela, Sheila Vivian; [ed.] Colchester County High, Success Business College; [occ.] Homemaker; [memb.] Women's Ministries Club, Evangel Pentecostal Church; [hon.] Outstanding Lyric writing, Nashville, Tennessee, Music City Song crafters (award); [oth. writ.] Children's Sunday school choruses, Poems for banquets, poems for senior citizens gathering functions and puppet plays; [pers.] My poems are intended to move the hearts of people so they will respond in a positive fashion. Some inspired by God and real life experiences others for fun and enjoyment.; [a.] Oakville, ON

LEVY, HAGIT
[b.] April 8, 1982, Israel; [ed.] Elementary School Grade 8; [hon.] Two honor roll awards 1995, Conflict Manager awards 1996/95; [oth. writ.] I have written many poems (about 100) that I've organized in a booklet, none of my poems except for "war" have been published; [pers.] I write my poems about things that I have experience or heard of in my life. I believe that poem writing is a way of communicating and expressing ones feelings. I also believe that poems has many meanings to it, and it depends as how the reader relates to it; [a.] Thornhill Ontario, Canada

LEWIS, GRETCHEN
[pen.] G. C. Lewis; [b.] May 13, 1961, Alberta, Canada; [p.] Paul, Suzanne; [ch.] Nicholas and Tasha; [ed.] B. A. in English Univ. of Calgary; [occ.] Clerical; [oth. writ.] Book - The Tarnished Pearl - have agent but not published yet. Written several free- lance articles for local papers; [pers.] The truth as untarnished no possible has always been my priority. The kernel of truth.; [a.] Calgary Alberta, Canada

LEWIS, MICHAEL
[b.] August 20, 1974, Kingston, Ontario, Canada; [p.] Peter and Lana Lewis; [ed.] Kingston C. V. L. and St. Lawrence College; [occ.] Early Childhood Educator; [oth. writ.] 'Colour Blind' published in 'Kcul Newsletter'.; [pers.] "True bravery is by performing without witness what one might be cable of doing before all the world."; [a.] Kingston Ontario, Canada

LEWIS, TASHA R.
[b.] September 25, 1980, Medford, OR; [p.] Tricia and Gary Lewis; [ed.] Crook County High School; [hon.] Green hand president for FEA, Captain of my cheerleading Squad; [oth. writ.] Poems: The Man, Love, One Cold Winter Day, I Go, True Blue Friends The Stranger, Brian Special, The Secret, Why Boyfriend, Life, Some Special, The Secret, Why, What And Felt For Him, Someone Special Book: The Last Soul; [pers.] I would just like to say that this is a real honor. And I'd like to say thank you for choosing my poem.; [a.] Prineville, OR

LEWIS-CHASE, EVELYN
[pen.] Eve Lewis Chase; [b.] May 17, 1942, Columbus, OH; [p.] William T. Lewis and Doris Ramsey-Lewis, and Catherine Lewis; [m.] Harry L. Chase, May 16, 1992; [ed.] Ohio State University,

School of Journalism International Studies; [occ.] Law firm word processor and Word for Windows trainer; [memb.] Ohio Press Club from 1965-1973, San Francisco Press Club from 1975-1977, former member Arizona Press Women, current Distin-guished Member Society of Poets, Honorary Chairman Friday Night Irregulars; [hon.] Through ISP I have been honored most recently with third place in the anthology Beyond the Stars and the Editors' Choice award for Reflections of Light, and the Poet of Merit award at the 1995 Convention and, of course, having my work selected for inclusion in five of its publications in the last year; [oth. writ.] Various articles, wire and news stories in my 10-year (Piqua, Greenville and Delaware, Ohio, Parkersburg, West Virginia, Yuma, Arizona) Newspaper career as well as a weekly column "Eve's Dropping". "Being Sensible" published in Today's Best Poems by the World of Poetry in 1980, "History for Me" published in Reflections of Light and "Tribute to Imogen" which won Third Prize in Beyond the Stars. "Vignettes", "Terrorism" have been accepted by NLP for publication next spring; [pers.] Most of my work (as in "Vacation Flashback") reflects my feelings on events and situations. The tow highest compliments a poet can receive are, in my opinion, I knew myself in your work". Or "I learned to see differently". Therefore, I thank those who have read my work and hope that it provide them with some insight and enjoyment.; [a.] San Francisco, CA

LIARD, GORDON
[pen.] George G. Gates; [b.] March 9, 1958, Fort William, Ontario; [ed.] Lakehead University, McMaster University; [hon.] All Ontario Scholar, 1987; [oth. writ.] Previously published in Northwest-ern Ontario Anthology of Poetry (Circa 1975); [pers.] In 1988 I withdrew from the University and moved to the rain forest to write my Master's Thesis. The resulting project Therapeutic Philosophy: Struggling to Articulate Authentic Human Presence, is a gesture towards a kind of post modern spirituality and openness in human relationship. It explores truth, love, and solidarity in a philosophical context of honoring felt awareness. My poetry is a result of Robert Service meeting Maurice Merleau-Ponty, Gabriel Marcel and Russell the mature humanist. I can be contracted.; [a.] Gibson British Columbia, Canada

LIGHT, JOE LEWIS
[b.] September 5, 1934, Dyersburg, TN; [p.] Hiawatha Virgie, Mary Light; [m.] Rosie Lee Light, September 28, 1968; [ch.] Ten children; [ed.] 1- 4- 5 - 11 -12 - 12 - Col - Col 12 - 12 those are my children Education, I got a G - E - D; [occ.] Artist; [memb.] American Legion; [hon.] One honor in art and one award in art; [oth. writ.] Songs; [a.] Memphis, TN

LILLARD, LYNN
[b.] September 23, 1963, Columbia, TN; [p.] Edward Hatton and Mamie W. Baker; [m.] Divorced; [ed.] No formal Education in literary; [occ.] Claims approver health net Inc; [oth. writ.] I've written plenty poems non-published at date; [pers.] "God promised us" was inspired first of all by my love and devotion for God and all his gifts, and secondly by the very special man in my life and heart, who not only inspired this poem but other's Keith Ellsworth Talbert; [a.] Nashville, TN

LILLEHEI, TERESA
[b.] June 27, 1969, Brooks, Alta; [p.] Vern Lillehei, Charlotte Lillehei, (stepmother) Elvera Lillehei; [m.] Dale Hein; [ch.] Amanda Lillehei; [ed.] Lethbridge Collegiate Institute High School, Lethbridge Alberta Hairdressing School; [occ.] Hair stylist; [oth. writ.] I have written several poems but I've never publicized any of them.; [pers.] Writing poems and reading other poems have been a great interest to me for years. I write about everyday experiences that life can give us; [a.] Brooks Alberta, Canada

LINDBERG, JACQUELINE
[b.] September 28, 1943, Boston, MA; [p.] Rodney, Elizabeth Berube; [m.] John (Deceased), September 10, 1966; [occ.] Manager - New England Deaconess Hosp Boston, MA; [hon.] Published photographer; [oth. writ.] Have never written a poem before; [pers.] Dedicated to my recently deceased father and my loving mother. May every child be so fortunate.; [a.] Walpole, MA

LIPE, ROGER A.
[pen.] Rediron; [b.] February 22, 1948, Hillsboro, IL; [p.] Charles Lipe, Bonnie Cozart Lipe; [ed.] Hillsboro High School, Southern Illinois University Carbondale, Illinois, A.A. 1978 - University honors, BS-1979 University Honors; [occ.] Director Mercury Software Systems Inc., Data Processing Consultant; [memb.] Vietnam Veterans of America, a Deadhead Military served with USAF 1967-70 in Vietnam and Thailand; [hon.] University honors; [oth. writ.] "Minus signs" is one of a large body of 300 poems written between 1970 and the present; [pers.] Be: Honest in friendship, true in word, generous of heart free in thoughts and humble in spirit, bean individual and smile, smile, smile; [a.] Hillsboro, IL

LITTLE, GLADYS M.
[pen.] Gladys M. Little; [b.] July 31, 1903, Altoona, IA; [p.] Amanda and Leonard Rathbum; [m.] Oscar Little, November 25, 1924; [ch.] Donna, Carolyn, Duane; [occ.] Senior Citizen Home maker; [memb.] Seventh Day Adventist Church; [pers.] Would rather not have person a history printed.; [a.] Muskegon, MI

LITTLER, GORDON
[pen.] Gord; [b.] August 24, 1924, Warrington, England; [p.] Mr and Mrs Vic Littler; [m.] The late Pamela Littler, March 27, 1954; [ch.] Russell, Beverly, Barbara; [ed.] Public School Penketh Warrington England; [occ.] Owner of creative printing unit #5 Advance Blvd Brampton Ontario Canada; [memb.] Life membership in British Canadian Club. Member of Mayfield Golf Club; [hon.] Member Bird and Tree Society of Great Britain. A number of awards while a member of Nortel Safety Committee also the City of Brampton Safety Council was a Rugby League Referee in England served in the Royal Navy 1943 1947 received the Atlantic and Pacific Medals.; [oth. writ.] Wrote an eleven page essay on "The Adventures of a Penny" in Public School, and received special mention; [pers.] My three children are amazed at the many things I have accomplished in my life I consider myself very fortunate I think someone is looking out for me Gord Littler; [a.] Brampton Ontario, Canada

LIVINGSTON, MS. PATRICIA JEAN
[b.] September 16, 1946, Dryden, Ontario, Canada; [p.] Joseph Toth, Mrs. Jean Chew; [m.] Divorced;

[ch.] Edward, Wade, and Anthony Guest, Mrs. Sherry Hall; [ed.] Tisnale, Sask, High School University Classes Hinton Alta Canada; [occ.] Charter Bus Driver and Home maker; [memb.] Served on school board in Saskatchewan while my children were growing up.; [hon.] I have many artistic hobbies, such as crafting, crocheting, painting pottery and I'm taking music lessons (guitar) I also love to cook.; [oth. writ.] I have been writing poetry for many years I have never submitted anything for publication before.; [pers.] My poems and other writing are my own observation of life as I see it, influenced greatly by my father and the behavior and survival of mankind throughout history; [a.] Saint Albert Alberta, Canada

LIZYNESS, LAURA
[b.] December 23, 1976; [p.] William Lizyness, Genevieve Lizyness; [ed.] Carlson High School; [occ.] Child Care Provider; [pers.] "And we know that all things work together for good to those who love God." Romans 8:28; [a.] Rockwood, MI

LOCKE, PAMELA J.
[pen.] Pamela J. Locke; [b.] December 27, 1951, Chicago; [p.] Shirley and Herbert Hartjen; [m.] Wallace A. Locke; [occ.] Writer of Poetry, Vice President of the Kyle J. Hickey Foundation; [hon.] A Semi-Finalist to be published by The National Library of Poetry, in Mists of Enchantment Printed on T-shirts for the 1994 AIDS Walk Chicago known as the Kyle Hickey Team; [oth. writ.] Several poems written for and read at many other functions.; [pers.] This poem is dedicated to Kyle J. Hickey, my nephew who lost his life to this disease. He inspired me and is now known as the Kyle J. Hickey Foundation so he can live on to help others with AIDS.; [a.] Carol Stream, IL

LOCKNER, RYAN
[b.] December 16, 1975, Schuyler, NE; [p.] Joyce and Derry Houser; [ed.] Shuyler Central High School; [occ.] Chef. (formerly in county jail so not employed); [pers.] My poetry has never been meant to dazzle or romance, but rather to intrigue and inform. I simply write about what we make of ourselves in this violence ridden land we call the United State of America; [a.] Schuyler, NE

LOCKWOOD, MARJORIE H.
[pen.] Marjorie Hart Lockwood; [b.] June 30, 1907, Hartford, CT; [p.] Evelyn Hope and Frederic Lewis Hart; [m.] Frederic Norman Lockwood, November '74, June 23, 1933; [ch.] Malcolm, Lewis and Valerie Beth; [ed.] Art, Piano, Pipe Organ Became, Concert Organist and Pianist, 1924; [occ.] Retired; [memb.] Eagles, Aerie 1037; [oth. writ.] Poetry, Limericks, Childrens' Stories, currently, writing my Biography.; [pers.] My maternal grandmother and mother, wrote, both, serious and humorous, poetry. So, I assume, that is, where, I got my, desire, to do so.; [a.] Fairbanks, AK

LOCONTO, ANGELA JAYNE
[b.] October 8, 1981, Massachusetts; [p.] Michael and Sally Loconto; [ed.] Fort Clarke Middle School in Gainesville, Florida; [occ.] 8th grade, honor roll student; [hon.] Poem published in church bulletin, read poems in front of large groups; [oth. writ.] I'm planning on writing a complete book of poems; [pers.] I think expressing your self is very important

and I've found that when I write it all kind of flows and I can discover my inner feelings; [a.] Gainesville, FL

LOGAN, JIM E.
[b.] March 1, 1948, Columbus, OH; [pers.] I've always tried to hold on to memories of those who were a special part of my life. Elias was the most charitable person I've ever known. He died very young. He lived a simple and humble life as a trappist monk.; [a.] Aurora, CO

LOGSDON, H. BRUCE
[pen.] H. B. Longstone;,[b.] October 15, 1944, Litchfield, IL; [p.] H. E. Logsdon, A. Lucille Logsdon; [m.] Linda Marie Logsdon, June 27, 1981; [ch.] Shana Allyn, Jaime Marie, Michael Joel; [ed.] Litchfield High, B.S. Education from Southern Ill. University in Carbondale, working on Masters at SIU-E in Instructional Technology; [occ.] Instructor of English and Communication Technology, Litchfield High School, Litchfield, IL; [memb.] National Education Association, (NEA), Illinois Education Association (IEA), NCTE, Quarts Creek Property Owners Association, Faculty Co-Sponsor of the Purple Light Anthology; [oth. writ.] Journalistic articles for SIU-E's Alestle, several poems in The Purple Light Anthology.; [pers.] I am intrigued by the challenge that each piece of poetry presents, from the conception of an idea based on an emotion or experience to its final, chiseled, sculptured form. I try to look at all things with open eyes and mind.; [a.] Litchfield, IL

LOHNES, MARY JULIET
[b.] April 16, 1972, Denver, CO; [p.] Michael James and Sandra L. Eckstein; [m.] Jerry David Lohnes, May 15, 1991; [ch.] Nicholas, Jared; [ed.] Schuyler Central High School, Schuyler, Nebraska; [occ.] Waitress and Bartender, Mom; [pers.] My only goal in life is that my poetry affects someone's life, and makes them realize that they are not alone. I was greatly influence by Robert Frost, Rod McKuen and Oscar Wilele; [a.] Longmont, CO

LONG, CHRISTINA
[b.] October 2, 1978, Houston; [p.] Glen Long and Robyn Dempsey; [ed.] Westwood H.S., Austin, TX; [occ.] Student

LORT, MARGARET A.
[b.] July 3, 1939, Denver, CO; [p.] Charles and Clara Armstrong; [m.] Art Lort, July 24, 1959; [ch.] Becky Campbell, Matt Lort; [ed.] 3 Years toward B.A. at University of Northern CO.; [occ.] Administrative Assistant at Denver Seminary; [oth. writ.] One article and one poem printed in Focal Point Magazine, one poem in previous National Library of Poetry anthology; [pers.] Since my two grandchildren were born in the last three years, I've wanted to be a grandma - poem writer it will take lots of hands - on practice and many fun experiences.; [a.] Highlands Ranch, CO

LOUDIN, JAN
[b.] May 14, Elkins; [p.] Mr. and Mrs. Nick Loudin; [ed.] A junior at Alderson - Broaddus College majoring in Elementary and Special Education LD and MI; [memb.] National Education Association, International Reading Council, Baptist Campus Ministries; [hon.] Read your way to the Governor's

mansion essay contest, I'm proud to be an American essay contest, young writers week 1987, Young writers week 1988, Education writing award 1994 and High School honor's student, Dean's List 1993 and 1994 at A-B College; [oth. writ.] Why I want to be a teacher articles battler columns (College Newspaper) various essays, short stories, and poems; [pers.] My goal is to use the talent that God blessed me with to the best of my ability; [a.] Philippi, WV

LOUSBERG, GUY T.
[pen.] Guybo; [b.] January 13, 1964, Menomonee Falls, WI; [p.] Mavis and Hubert Lousberg (Deceased); [ed.] Certificate in Management for the American Management Association - Certificate in Powerful Personal Communication NLPS; [occ.] Maintenance person at Alexian Village of Milwaukee; [memb.] Gloria Dei Lutheran Church of Menomonee Falls; [oth. writ.] Several poems published in The Alexian Village voice; [pers.] I write because I have to, not because I want to, writing for me is like eating and breathing, I have to do it.; [a.] Menomonee Falls, WI

LOVE, JAYNE ALISSA
[b.] September 12, 1971, San Mateo, CA; [p.] William Love, Martha Love; [ed.] Carlmont High; [occ.] Dance Instructor, Hart Studio of dance; [memb.] International Tap Association; [oth. writ.] Several poems yet to be published; [pers.] My writing mirrors the challenges our hearts often endure. The disappointments we all face that make us stronger individuals.; [a.] Belmont, CA

LOVELL, BOBBIE FAY
[pen.] Bobbie Lovell; [b.] February 16, 1933, Cullman, AL; [p.] James Fred and Pansy May Rutledge; [m.] Keith Lovell, July 1, 1955; [ch.] Vickie Lynn and Steven Ray, Two Grand Daughters Conni Jo Irvin, Katelynn Fay Martin; [ed.] Pattingall High H and R Block — Income Taxes; [occ.] Keith and I are Retired Housewife; [memb.] Tenn. Valley Genealogical Society, North Alabama Genealogical Society, Morgan County Genealogical Society; [oth. writ.] I have a poem published in "Traces In The Sand", Which is a book on the Allison family, The poem was in memory of my mother Pansy (Allison) Rutledge, Title of poem is "Farewell To Mother"; [pers.] I haven't did any writing for publication in the past, I'm now doing genealogical research on my fathers family, I hope to have my worked published when I get all the information I can get together; [a.] Eva, AL

LUCCHETTI, ALAN
[b.] 1980, Malad, ID; [p.] James and DeLauna Lucchetti; [ed.] Sophomore at Brighton High School '95; [oth. writ.] This is my first publication.; [pers.] I mostly write on emotions or my views or world events. I hope to be a well published poet/author someday.; [a.] Salt Lake City, UT

LUFF, SUSAN
[b.] July 17, 1976, Grand Falls, NewFounland, Canada; [p.] Joan and Freeman Luff; [ed.] Leaf Rapids Education Center (from 1984 to 1994); [pers.] The road to the future may be rough and hard times, but follow your dreams and always listen to your heart; [a.] Leaf Rapids Manitoba, Canada

LUGARDO, DONNA
[pen.] DJ; [b.] September 26, 1960, Chester, PA; [p.] Brenda and Henry Mincy; [ch.] Jason Mincy; [ed.] St. Michael's, Notre Dame H.S., Delaware Community College, Va. Beach Commonwealth College; [occ.] Resource Nurse Counselor; [memb.] Resurrection Church, Resurrection Prayer Group, Women's Networking Group; [hon.] Dean's List, President's List, Special Act Award, Outstanding Performance Award; [oth. writ.] Unpublished writings which I call "Through My Eyes"; [pers.] Live each day as if it were your last, because no one's guaranteed tomorrow.; [a.] Ellicott City, MD

LUNN, REAGAN
[pen.] Reagan Lunn; [b.] September 21, 1982, Fort Worth, TX; [p.] Kyle Lunn and Kathy Prothro; [ed.] Student in 7th Grade; [occ.] Student; [hon.] Gifted classes; [oth. writ.] Anthology of poems; [a.] Coppell, TX

LUNSFORD, JUANITA
[b.] November 26, 1932, Rock Island, IL; [p.] John Jones, Rebecca Jones; [m.] Cecil Lunsford, December 4, 1951; [ch.] Wanda, Alan, Michael, Janice, Tenna, Tim; [ed.] Rocky High; [a.] Brazil, IN

LYNCH, MARJORIE M.
[b.] July 27, 1923, Ayton, Ontario, Canada; [ed.] Grade Ten also High School Equivalency Certification, Shaws Business College - Toronto Ont., Numerous Accessory Courses: Art, etc.; [occ.] Retired from Federal Government 1988; [memb.] Former member SOS Childrens Village Society, Eucharistic Minister visiting Committee (sick) Local Church, Volunteer Senior's Health Alert Program, Treasurer Horizons Social Group in Residential Complex.; [hon.] Federal Government - Suggestion Award pertaining to operational forms.; [oth. writ.] Only for occasional and recreational purposes - not for publication.; [pers.] My poems tend to lean towards recognition and appreciation of nature and its effect and relation to modern development, as reflected in my enclosed poem entitled "Nature".; [a.] Burnaby British Columbia, Canada

MACDONALD, ELEANOR E.
[pen.] Eleanor E. MacDonald; [b.] May 21, 1930, Glace Bay, Nova Scotia; [p.] Late John and Edith Moores; [m.] John A. MacDonald, July 5, 1956; [ch.] Keith - 1957, Bruce - 1963; [ed.] Grade XII Stenographer and Typist Course; [occ.] Retired after 45 years in the work force; [memb.] United Church of Canada; [hon.] None - except your National Library of Poetry.; [oth. writ.] Several poems published in local newspapers also several articles in Cape Breton Post, recently asked to recite on Channel X writings and poems about 42 in 18 months - therapy for me following the death of my mother.; [pers.] I like to write about my memories as many people relate to these memories and tell me how much they enjoy reading my poetry. Sometimes events move me, as the April 19th 1995 bombing.; [a.] Glace Bay Nova Scotia, Canada

MACH, SARAH E.
[b.] April 18, 1933, Carey, Manitoba, Canada; [p.] Nora and Frank Johnston; [m.] 1953; [ch.] Bonny Patricia Caroe Rich, Chris Bruce Wilfred; [ed.] Grade Nursing Assistant Cosmetology; [occ.] Hairstylest; [pers.] It's a good life if we enjoy each day and look forward to tomorrow I have enjoyed my surely two years and look forward to the neath sin or so.; [a.] Morres Manitoba, Canada

MACHADO, ORLANDO JOSEPH
[pen.] Joseph MacLane; [b.] September 9, 1954, Havana, Cuba; [p.] Orlando and Josefa Machado; [ed.] Hialeah High, Miami Dade Junior College; [occ.] Clerk; [oth. writ.] Collection of poems (unpublished); [pers.] Humanity has survived because of its artists, writers and poets.; [a.] Hialeah, FL

MACINNIS, ANGELA
[pen.] ADM or TM; [b.] March 1, 1976, Kitchener, Ontario, Canada; [p.] Rod and Pat MacInnis; [ed.] Forest Heights Collegiate Institute, Richmond Christian Secondary School, Kwantlen College; [occ.] Student, part-time employee at local restaurant; [hon.] Honours Diploma in the Humanities Program; [oth. writ.] Chapter in Nurtural Reverie - a collection of short stories and poems.; [pers.] My nature as a poet does not limit me to taking challenges in short story or novel writing at this time, I'm writing a novel entitled: Fertility of the Soil.; [a.] Delta British Columbia, Canada

MACINTYRE, RON MAE
[b.] February 2, 1930, Dominion, Cape Breton, NS; [p.] John Anthony and Georgina MacIntyre; [ed.] Master of Rel. Ed.; [occ.] Roman Catholic Priest; [memb.] Knights of Columbus, Capuchin Franciscan Order; [pers.] I really love to be out in nature. Nature is filled with the Foot-Prints of God; [a.] Mount Pearl Newfoundland, Canada

MACKENZIE, K. F.
[pen.] Emel Mack; [b.] january 4, 1926, Everett, MA; [p.] John and Margaret MacKenzie; [m.] Margaret L. MacKenzie, September 8, 1945; [ch.] Michael and Michele; [a.] McLain, MS

MACKOWETZICY, JILL
[pen.] J. M. Tamarynn; [b.] November 25, 1956, Oldenberg, Germany; [m.] Ken; [ch.] Tianna; [occ.] Freelance Artist, wife and mother; [pers.] I tend to write as the mood takes me or if I'm experiencing an especially strong emotion. But I've always had a soft spot for historical fantasy.; [a.] Edmonton Alberta, Canada

MACLEOD, SHIRL
[pen.] Shirley Charles; [b.] October 16, 1950, Port Arthur, Ontario, Canada; [p.] Mary and Joseph Charles (Deceased); [m.] Ken, September 12, 1970; [ch.] Sheila - 8, Stuart - 11, Shane - 6, Scott - 16; [occ.] Head Secretary, St. Margaret School, Lakehead District Roman Catholic Separate School Board; [memb.] Port Arthur Chapter 1212 Women of the Moose, Branch 5 Legion Ladies Auxiliary, Thunder Bay Museum; [hon.] College of Regents Degree in Chicago, Physiology College Certificate, Word Processing College Certificate; [oth. writ.] Poetry published in National Library of Poetry, "Best Poems of 1995, and words put to music 4 songs on cassette in Nashville completed written. Many poems and songs hopes to have them professionally published in book, disc and cassette (display case).; [pers.] The element and thoughts that express the inner feelings is rewarding and a gift that really shines within, a memory to cherish and lasts for all my children to enjoy and embrace.; [a.] Thunder Bay Ontario, Canada

MACMULLIN, CATHERINE
[pen.] Cathy Carey; [b.] December 13, 1957, Bras D'or, Cape Breton, North Scotia, Canada; [p.] Marie Carey, Theodore Carey; [m.] Bernard Lawrence MacMullin, August 23, 1980; [ch.] Melissa Marie; [ed.] Bras D'or High School; [occ.] Housewife, volunteer full time mother; [memb.] World Vision Sponsorship, St. Alfred's Church St. Catharines, Ontario; [hon.] Won Poetry contests at schools and at Library's and at festival of Arts!; [oth. writ.] Write own memoriams for family and friends, also poems.; [pers.] My writing has been inspired by my special brother Teddy who became my guardian angel 27 years ago! I dedicate my poem Angel's Here on Earth" in his memory!

MADDEN, KIMBERLY
[b.] October 30, 1967, Downey, CA; [p.] Jeanne Clarke, Robert Madden; [ch.] Mitchell Thomas Richmond; [ed.] Currently attending a junior college to obtain a career in accounting.; [occ.] Mostly just being a mom, part time flagger; [memb.] I belong to a Bate of Oregon, a Motorcycle Organization (A Brotherhood Against Totalitarian Enactment); [oth. writ.] My poem "Miss Brittney" was published by Waterbury publishers in the book "The otherwise of the Mirror".; [pers.] "Time is the key to knowledge as knowledge is the key to life, the two must work together to form balance."; [a.] Sutherlea, OR

MADDY, MARK D.
[b.] February 22, 1962, Greensburg, IN; [p.] Forest and Joan Maddy; [ed.] Tri-West Hendricks High School, Phillips University, University of Texas at Brownsville; [occ.] Adult Education Instructor; [memb.] Phi Theta Kappa, First United Methodist Church, Lions Club, Valley Association for Independent Living; [hon.] National Honor Society, Mu Phi Epsilon, Phi Theta Kappa; [oth. writ.] Unpublished poetry, musical lyrics, essays.; [pers.] The thirteen years since I was paralyzed in a hanging incident have taught me many lessons. The most important is to take what I have today and make the most of it and make tomorrow even better.; [a.] Brownsville, TX

MADER, WILLIAM J.
[pen.] "Duke" or "Karmen"; [b.] October 7, 1944, Fort Sill, OK; [p.] William P. Mader, Madaline T. Mader; [ch.] Yvonne Marie, William John, Christopher A.; [ed.] Florida State University; [occ.] Founder, better health through meditation.; [memb.] Mensa, World Assoc. of Document Examiners, American College of Forensic Examiners; [hon.] Humanitarian of the Year 1984; [oth. writ.] Management book, Romance Books, Weekly News Paper columnist 10 yrs.; [pers.] Prose is a result of sensory perception or experience, poetry is a result of intercourse with one's own soul.; [a.] Stevensville, MD

MADGE, CONNIE
[pen.] Connie Marie Madge; [b.] February 13, 1964, Vancouver, British Columbia, Canada; [p.] Betty Ann Englehart; [ch.] Daniel Arthur Madge; [ed.] Graduate Kelowna Senior Secondary 1982; [occ.] Licensed Security Alarm Monitor; [oth. writ.] Published in hard cover three times in past year. Also in Echoes from the Silence Quill.; [pers.] Special thank to my sister Stephanie Englehart Howell. For her kindness and support. I believe in sharing smiles.; [a.] New Westminster, Canada

MADHOSINGH, ROBERT
[pen.] Robert Madhosingh; [b.] September 23, 1941, Trinidad, West Indies; [p.] Iris Madhosingh (single parent); [m.] Divorced (Jeannette), August 1, 1978; [ch.] Robert Jr., Terrence, Anthony; [ed.] B.Sc University of Winnipeg, B.Ed. University of Manitoba; [occ.] Physics teacher Shaftesbury High School, Assiniboine South Sch. Div.; [memb.] Science Teachers Association of Manitoba. Manitoba Association of Physics teachers.; [hon.] Borough of san Fernando (Trinidad), Scholarship 1953, Dean's Honor List - 1967, Track and Field Official with Athletics Canada; [oth. writ.] Articles in Toronto Star, Winnipeg Free Press 2 poems: "The Indian Life Call", "The Homeless" published in "Heartland Voice" by Winnipeg Free Press Spring/ Summer Issue 1995.; [pers.] Inspiration from the heart is often accompanied by tears, and it is then that we feel the presence of the divine. I write with feelings for and from the oppressed in our society.; [a.] Winnipeg Manitoba, Canada

MADISON, SHARON
[pen.] Sharon Madison; [b.] November 4, 1952, Faribault, MN; [p.] Neil and Mariah Cloutier; [m.] Michael Madison, November 28, 1987; [ch.] Tabitha Wheeler; [ed.] Faribault H.S. Faribault Technical College, Center for a Balanced Life, Acupressure Institute - Berkeley, CA, Int'l Institute of Reflexology; [occ.] Nationally Certified Massage Therapist and Certified Acupressurist, and Registered Foot Reflexologist; [memb.] Nat'l Certif. Therapeutic Massage Board, Therapeutic Massage Network, Int'l Inst' of Reflexology, The loft Writers, Associated Bodyworkers and Massage Professionals; [hon.] The Int'l Poet Merit Award Int'l Society of Poets (1992), The Certificate of Achievement from the Amherst Society (1992), and a medallion from the Beverly Hills Poetry Academy (1993), Int'l Certified Body work therapist (ABMP); [oth. writ.] Several Anthologies: The Nat'l Library of Poetry, the Amherst Society, and Sparrow Grass Poetry Forum, Inc.; [pers.] My poetry reflects the mirror of my soul and the wholeness of humanity for "We Are All One".; [a.] Invergrove Heights, MN

MAGEE, KAYE E.
[b.] November 19, 1952, Simcoe; [p.] Mr. And Mrs. V. Magee; [ch.] One who was adopted 25 yrs. ago.; [ed.] Grade 8; [occ.] Disabled, I have a heart problem and other Medical problems.; [oth. writ.] I've been writing since I was very young about things that happened in my life. The poem "I wonder" is about my only daughter that was adopted 25 yrs. ago. Whom I am now searching for now.; [pers.] When life has it's ups and downs writing poems can help you cope and understand better. It seems that when thoughts and feelings are on paper it helps the soul a great deal to face reality.; [a.] Cambridge Ontario, Canada

MAHBUBANI, REEMA
[pen.] Ritaka; [b.] February 10, 1985, Bombay, India; [p.] Ramesh and Seema Mahbubani; [ed.] Elementary school, grade six; [occ.] Student; [hon.] Halifax City Regional Library Poetry Awards; [oth. writ.] One of my poems is going to be published in one of Halifax City Regional Library book.; [a.] Halifax Nova Scotia, Canada

MAISINE, BRANDY
[b.] January 9, 1977, East York, Ontario, Canada; [p.] Bonita and Brian Maisine; [ed.] 1st year of BA at St. Mary's University, Halifax, Nova Scotia; [occ.] Cashier at Sobeys, full-time student; [hon.] A poem printed in junior high yearbook, another poem published in Kimberlins (1992 edition), graduated 1st from high school, the Gov. General's Award, 2200 scholarship to SMU, 3d place, NRC award for Astrophysics, AECL award for Scientific Achievement all from National Science Fairs.; [oth. writ.] Several short stories, an extensive collection of poetry.; [pers.] Writing has always been an intrinsic form of self-expression for me. I believe in the power of words and I want to use my words to make people feel connected. To me and to each other.; [a.] Mouth Uniacke Nova Scotia, Canada

MAJERUS, SUE
[pen.] Susan Murray Majerus; [b.] September 8, 1946, Great Falls, MT; [p.] James L. Murray, Dorothy Lanning Murray; [m.] Robert A. Majerus, June 26, 1992; [ch.] Rodeny L. Lukasik, Shonda Majerus Cornell; [ed.] Great Falls Central High, currently studying through Institute of Children's Literature; [occ.] Director of Membership Services, Great Falls Chamber of Commerce; [memb.] St. Luke's Parish, Mt. State Ceramic Assn., Great Falls Positive Board of Directors, Stephens Ministries, Leadership Great Falls Alumni, Co-chair '95 LGF Community Garage Sale Project, Chamber Blue Coats, Chamber Ambassadors; [hon.] Best Supporting Actress, Grade 10, Peggy (highest achievement for professional Ceramics; [oth. writ.] (10th Grade) published in Anthology of High School Poetry, several articles and cover stories Ceramic Arts and Crafts Mag, several stories published in local newspaper, writer for Chamber newsletter.; [pers.] I strive to be open, sharing and positive and to write poetry and stories with an underlying lesson within them.; [a.] Great Falls, MT

MALABED, RONALD
[b.] February 10, 1970, Manila, Philippines; [p.] Luzviminda and Hermenegildo Malabed; [ed.] South Lake High S.C.S. MI. (88) 1992 Bachelor, Wayne State Univ., Detroit, MI, 1995 Masters, Wayne State Univ., Detroit, MI; [occ.] Instrumental Music Teacher, James B. Webber School, Detroit, MI; [memb.] Music Educators National Conference International Trumpet Guild, Shore Line Concert Band, Cross PTE MI. LAC St. Clair Symphony Orchestra, S.C.S., MI. Detroit Federation of teachers; [hon.] Awarded as 1986 and 1987 Best Musician, South Lake High, 1988 John Philips Sousa, National Band Award, 1988 Recipient of Music Talent Scholarship, Wayne State Univ. Detroit, MI; [oth. writ.] Several poems in other hard book publications.; [pers.] I wish to thank all the people who strive to make this world a better place, especially the ones who teach our children.

MANDELBAUM, ARTHUR
[b.] November 18, 1918, Brooklyn, NY; [p.] Deceased; [m.] Fannie Mandelbaum, September 19, 1945; [ch.] Ilene Mandelbaum-Baraber; [ed.] Bachelor's Degree - Brooklyn, NY, M.S.W. Degree University of Denver - Approved Supervisor Marriage and Family Therapy; [memb.] Doctor of Science - Honorary Degree, Kansas State Univ. December 1984; Saturday Night Literary Club - Topeka, Kansas, President of above club (2 years); [oth. writ.] Published articles in professional

journals, published letters in Topeka Capital Journal; [a.] Topeka, KS

MANI, RAGHAVA S.
[b.] November 24, 1937, Madras, India; [p.] T. S. Raghavan, Seetalakshmi Raghavan; [m.] Prema Mani, July 9, 1959; [ch.] Gowri, Anand, Aruna, Arvind; [ed.] BA (Litt.) Vikram University; [occ.] Fine Artist; [memb.] Visual Arts Ontario Gallery 2000 (Artists' Co-Op); [hon.] Dean's List, University Literary Award, Award in Fine Arts; [oth. writ.] Written and illustrated many books for children.; [pers.] I like writing suggestive poems which lend to philosophical interpretations.; [a.] Cambridge Ontario, Canada

MANICKAVASAGAM, CHANDRAN
[b.] June 9, 1968, India; [p.] S. Manickavasagam, Raja Kumari; [m.] Dana Jean Manickavasagam, January 12, 1995; [ed.] Pursuing Masters in Computer Science, Bachelors in Electrical Engg. (Emphasis on Industrial Electronics); [occ.] Software Engineer; [hon.] Dean Honor List, award for essay writing and poems; [oth. writ.] Poems published in local and college newspapers.; [pers.] Believe in the saying "Patience prevails, perseverance succeeds and success triumphs."; [a.] Kansas City, MO

MANKE, ELIZABETH
[b.] August 24, 1959, Augusta, PA; [p.] Gary Williams, June Dorn; [m.] Kenneth Manke, November 16, 1990; [ch.] Chad Phillip Scott; [ed.] Strom Thurmund High; [occ.] Housewife; [hon.] Betta Club in high school; [oth. writ.] I have written a number of other poems none published as of yet but there's always tomorrow; [pers.] I strive to reflect the inner peace and love within myself and use the gift God gave to me.; [a.] Trenton, SC

MANN, BONNIE
[b.] September 21, 1950, Kansas City, MO; [m.] Rolla, June 28, 1995; [ch.] Eddie, Brian, Cobr; [ed.] High School, 2 years college; [occ.] Nurse's Aide State Hospital; [memb.] Victory Fellowship Church, Fulton, MO; [hon.] President Future Home Makers of America 1967, Walmart Sidekick Award, Medicine Licence, for Medication Aide, Sunday School Teacher Award - Teenagers; [oth. writ.] My dad - The Veteran American, Thanksgiving, Math, Christmas Trees, Those That Mourn, Angels, Homeless, Prayer Changes Things, Rumors, My Pastor; [pers.] I have tried to do what is right and fair in the world. I work with mental patients. It was a hard job, I have always loved writings; [a.] Fulton, MO

MANUEL JR., EDDIE LEE
[b.] December 21, 1968, Denver, CO; [p.] Eddie and Audrea Manuel; [m.] Beverly Manuel, April 8, 1995; [ed.] B.S. Degree in Justice Studies, Minor in Political Science from Arizona State University. Working toward B.A. Business.; [occ.] Parts Manager at Whirlpool Corporation; [memb.] Boy's Club of Arizona, Nat'l honor Society; [hon.] Alpha Phi Alpha Book Scholarship Award. Regents, Arizona Scholarship for Research.; [oth. writ.] Several critical writings in High School weekly news publication. Writings also published in Arizona State Universities daily newspaper.; [pers.] I look for truth through writing and a respect that can't be denied. I base my writings on past experiences on my life and others close to me.; [a.] Phoenix, AZ

MANZ, JOSEPH D.
[pen.] J. D. Manz; [b.] November 4, 1978, Burbank, CA; [p.] Mr. and Mrs. James Manz; [ed.] Wilson Aba High School, 10th grade AB student; [occ.] None employed yet.; [hon.] Wrestling Medal Fastest Din 5 sec. Trophies for Wrestling and Football 1st in Cub Scouts in Boy Car Derby.; [oth. writ.] Wrote poems but I never really had any published until now.; [pers.] I believe that man should look back for a sec. and see the damage they have done to the world I have been greatly influenced By Edgar Allan Poe and my mother and father Mr. and Mrs. James Manz.; [a.] Easton, PA

MARANA, KATHERINE JUHANCE
[b.] January 10, 1920, Chisholm, MN; [p.] Matt, Mary Juhance; [m.] Albert J. Marana, November 8, 1941; [ch.] Jean, Douglas, Alberta; [ed.] High school graduate Jean - Surgical Nurse 34 years authored material on surgery Mayo Clinic Accepted it Coordinator of Nursing Douglas Manager of Thorp Loan, Vice President - of 2 Banks - Alberta - Cum Laude Grad. of Hamlin University Social worker - major, in Art - Artist and Teaches now; [occ.] Widow - home keeper; [memb.] Senior Citizen's Club 55 Club, Den Mother, Brownies and Girls Scout - Leader Catholic Church; [hon.] 3 College grads, 6 grandchildren grads or attending with some scholarship and fellowships mother's sis. Brother in law seven mules of Knutt Rockne's team of Notre Dame. My grand mother saved many lives in 1918 in the epidemic of Flue and delivered the senator John Blatnick and hundreds of babies (Blatnick Bridge) in Duluth, MN.; [oth. writ.] My great grandfather in Yugoslavia was a practicing doctor in Slovenia with grandmother with an ox drawn cart delivered, babies, set limbs gave remedies for coughs put on poultices for infections daughter nurse 34 years cousin city nurse 37 years Granddaughter-nurse 54 years.; [pers.] Our Country and people especially young, will have to stop with materialistic ideals and more honest and moral ideas and achievements of bettering this Country and environment.; [a.] Chisholm, MN

MARCENIUK, HEATHER
[b.] April 12, 1981, Vanderhoof, British Columbia, Canada; [p.] Ron Marceniuk, Debby Marceniuk; [ed.] College Heights Elem, College Heights Secondary; [occ.] Student - gr. 9; [memb.] Softball and Candy Striping; [hon.] Honor Roll student for 3 years.; [oth. writ.] Rainforest being published in future Anthology, "Thoughts as Time Passes". Plus semi-finalist in contest.; [pers.] I see poetry as a way of expressing thoughts and feelings in a way that words can't but poetry can.; [a.] Prince George British Columbia, Canada

MARIE, RAINA L.
[pen.] Reyna; [b.] August 21, Pittsburgh; [ed.] UW - Milwaukee B.A. Spanish Certification 6-12 Spanish K-12 ESL; [memb.] Black Student Unon Latino Student Union Multucultural Dell Club; [hon.] Certificate of Completion for the Ronald McNair Research program my subject: The dual nature of the identity of Black in Latin America as expressed in the litarature of Latin American Blacks.; [pers.] For me creativity is not only a way of life, it is life.; [a.] Glendale, WI

MARR, QUINCY THOMAS
[b.] March 8, 1980, Bloomington, IL; [p.] John W. Marr, Michele M. Marr; [ed.] Presently a sophomore attending Gridley High School, Gridley, IL; [occ.] Student; [memb.] Alumni member of the Singing Y'ers Boy Choir, Gridley High School Marching Band, Jazz Band, Concert band, Chorus and Chamber Choir, Gridley High scholastic Bowl; [hon.] IMEA—District Chorus and Band participant, 1994, Gridley Grade School Music Award, Gridley High School First Honor Roll, First-place ratings 1992-1995 at IESA and IHSA Solo/Ensemble Contents; [pers.] As you go through life, always follow your dreams and do what you love. My inspiration and encouragement have come from my parents as well as Mrs. Matthews, my Literature teacher.; [a.] Gridley, IL

MARSHALL, LINDA R.
[b.] September 7, 1954, Marion, IN; [p.] Markle and Charmaine DeMezza; [m.] Kenneth D. Marshall, January 6, 1976; [ch.] One "Puttie" dog; [occ.] Retired/disabled volunteer; [memb.] National Multiple Sclerosis Society, Womens Auxiliary at Wesley Medical Center, St. Margaret Mary Catholic Church Fund Raising Committee for MS; [hon.] 1995 M.S. person of the year, peer counselor, chapter service chairperson 1993-94, Board of Trustee M.S. Society 1994, Facilitator for newly diagnosis support group 1991-94 chapter service committee 1989-94; [pers.] Even though I'm physically limited I set myself free when I put my pen to paper and express my deepest emotions this cleanses my soul and I'm freer than most; [a.] Wichita, KS

MARSHALL, ROCKY ALLEN
[pen.] Rocky Allen Marshall; [b.] November 8, 1963, Blounstown, FL; [p.] Jimmy Marshall and Mary Elliott; [m.] Pamela Marshall, June 1, 1985; [ed.] A master degree in making mistakes.; [oth. writ.] Drifting Back, Nothing New, Mothers Day and many more in unpublished.; [pers.] When a person loses every thing he though he had, including pride, he soon apprehends the true value of family and friends. I thank GOD for mine, because through their love, I have learned how to smile again.; [a.] Tallahassee, FL

MARTIN, JOHN P.
[pen.] Jay Parts; [b.] March 28, 1961, Richmond; [p.] John E. Martin, Lorraine Martin; [oth. writ.] Song lyrics; [pers.] I love music I became deaf at 30. I was asked to star in a movie, within a week I was burned and disfigured. My best lyrics became a poem and I 6'4" am getting shorter. Never give up.; [a.] Richmond, VA

MARTIN, KATHLEEN
[b.] May 14, 1947, Shrereport, LA; [p.] John M. and Ellalie A. Martin; [ed.] High school diploma, Cooper High school, Abirlene, Texas; [occ.] Vehicle Inspection Technician-Texas Dept. of public safety; [memb.] Manuscript Club of El Paso; [a.] El Paso, TX

MARTIN, OLIVE
[pen.] Olive Burns/Martin; [b.] March 15, 1942, Ridgetown, Ontario, Canada; [p.] Olive and Jack Perrodou; [ch.] Gregory Bruce and Patricia Lynn; [pers.] I enjoy expressing life itself whether it be in

joy or in sorrow for there is always love to be found, God and Nature Provide Both.

MARTINEZ, BOB G.
[pen.] Bob G. Martinez; [b.] June 7, 1949, Las Vegas, NM; [p.] Mary Jane Martinez; [m.] Annette E. (Poopsie), February 10, 1973; [ch.] 19 year old College Gal (Lita); [ed.] 1968 Denver North High School; [occ.] (Security) Denver Merchandise Mart; [memb.] Distinguished Member of I.S.P — N.L.P.; [hon.] Unanimously voted "Best Denver Poet of 1995" by my dear wife, Annette, and precious daughter, Lita! I was so honored to receive. All two votes.; [oth. writ.] Personal competition of poems, "Side Tracks" and journal of my life from birth to becoming a grandfather (unbroken single poem of over 300 pages).; [pers.] When I was a boy, my life saw no end... Now saved, I'll enjoy forever to spend!; [a.] Denver, CO

MARTINEZ, JOAQUIN ANDRES
[pen.] Nil; [b.] November 30, 1942, Acjutla, El Salvador; [p.] Joaquin A. Guerrero and Maria Martinez; [m.] Maria E. Martinez, August 2, 1975; [ch.] Nestor, Joaquin, Xiomara, Flor, Roberto, Carmen, Diana, Maria and Monica; [ed.] Book Kepper Guadalupe College, Sonsonate, El Salvador; [occ.] Line Assembler, Ton Toys Factory, London, Ontario; [memb.] San Stephan Church Choir member; [hon.] Nil; [oth. writ.] Some poems published in the E.S.L. Wheable School, London, Ont. and others unpublished. In both English and Spanish.; [pers.] "Tomorrow's men are made today in the home's warmth."; [a.] London Ontario, Canada

MARTINEZ, SUSANA MATOS
[pen.] Susana Martinez; [b.] May 24, 1914, Toa-Baja, PR; [p.] Nicolas Matos - Marcia Fernandez; [m.] Carlos Bancroft Martinez (Deceased), February 27, 1950; [ch.] Maria Martinez - Eva Martinez; [ed.] BA in Bilingual Education; [occ.] Retired; [memb.] Eslabon Cultural Hispano Americano - Orden Estrella de Oriente (Masonic) Institute of Puerto Rico; [hon.] Project Sabe 7-21-81 East Harlem Council 12-19-87, The Municipal Adm. of Catano, P.R. 4-8-88, The Municipal Government of Catano 6-11-88, East Harlem for Human Services Inc, Nd. of Directors 1993, Hispanic Heritage Month 10-8-93, The Puerto Rican Cultural Heritage 5-11-95; [oth. writ.] Two books of poetry: Petalos in 1981, Cristalin 1971 Fiction novel, UNDER THE APPLE TREE Without publish. Dozens of poems in spanish plus a fiction novel in spanish title "The Unavoidable Fate Of Three Women."; [pers.] My poetry is influence in what I believe and the sufferings of my fellows. By reading Agatha Christie Mystery - Destiny means a lot for me.; [a.] New York, NY

MASEK, EVELYN
[b.] May 9, 1929, Columbus, OH; [m.] Lawrence Masek, May 7, 1949; [ch.] Sherry Guidetti, Joseph Masek, Carolyn Guidry; [occ.] Retired; [oth. writ.] Several poems and other written material have been published in school books, Fraternal Journals, and Church Publications.; [pers.] I take great pleasure in writing for my loved ones, especially my grandchildren, and for my church.; [a.] Kirtland, OH

MASON, NICOLE
[b.] May 16, 1979, Shreveport, LA; [p.] William and Angela Morris III; [ed.] Norview High School;

[memb.] Key Club, Black Achievers Club, F.E.A., Parent Committee subcommunity, Volunteering at DePaul Hospital and volunteering at learning while serving, Calvary Revival Teen Choir.; [hon.] District Chorus, All-City Chorus, over 200 hours in volunteer work at De Paul Hospital.; [oth. writ.] Working on a poem book and a realistic fiction book.; [pers.] I thank God for keeping me and protecting me in the world of today. I try to capture how people feel through my poems.; [a.] Norfolk, VI

MASON, ROY
[b.] June 29, 1955, Charlottetown, Prince Edward Island, Canada; [p.] Earl and Mona Mason; [m.] Valerie Smith, August 15, 1991; [ch.] Nathaniel Mason (February 14, 193), Amy Mason (July 29, 1994); [memb.] Sports; [hon.] Many Trophies in "Running one of the top Marathon Runner on P.E.I."; [oth. writ.] Many songs and poems my writing, was real before six or seven hundred people in church.; [pers.] To help people to know there is a God who cares and understands how to meet their need. Available to make of slogan for others.; [a.] Charlottetown Prince Edward Island, Canada

MATHENY, ALTON
[b.] November 23, 1957, Mobridge, SD; [p.] Joyce and Milton Matheny; [m.] Holly, July 6, 1981; [ch.] Falisha, Jason, Justin; [ed.] Associates in General Studies; [occ.] Soldier at 1st Special Warfare Center; [oth. writ.] Contributions to "A Family Affair".; [a.] Raeford, NC

MATHENY, E. JOYCE
[pen.] Joyce Ellen; [b.] September 27, 1927, Emmons Country, ND; [p.] George Backhaw and Vera Yeater; [m.] Jack Wheeler, December 6, 1946 (Divorced), Milton N. Matheny, March 10, 1951; [ch.] Dennis Pay Wheeler, Danny Lee, Vicki Kay Dunfee, Valerie Ann and Alton George Matheny; [ed.] High School - some College, lots of continuing Ed Hours for Certification as an A.I.M. (Associate in Ministry Elca); [occ.] Retired - but part time in Respite Care Work for SD Social Services; [memb.] Pres. Mobridge Garden Club Sec. LB Missouri River Branch 8745 Sec./Treas. Klein Youth Center Inc. Co-Chair Lutheran Social Services Benefit Dinner yrs. VP and 4 yrs. Pres. SP Church Staff Workers Sec. L.E.O. Lutheran/Episcopal Dialog group; [hon.] (I did not want a plaque) Many cards - gifts and money after 26 yrs. as Parish Secretary. Award for serving (As Secretary) an Executive Board for a Billy Graham Rally in our Area. Certificate when Commissioned as a Church Staff Worker in ALC; [oth. writ.] Much poetry - Funerals, Baptism for weddings, Confirmation, Graduates, and a yearly poem at Christmas for member of our two Congregations. Conf. and Grads also yearly till I retired. Still do the Christmas. 2 Chapbooks by Plowman Press.

MATHEWSON, HEATHER
[b.] February 20, 1972, Calgary Alberta, Canada; [p.] Donald Mathewson, Barbara Mathewson; [ed.] University of Calgary, Bachelor of Science (Zoology), 1994; [occ.] Administrative Assistant, Computer Retail, Calgary, Alberta; [hon.] Canada Scholarship for Science and Engineering, University of Calgary Matriculation Merit Award, Alexander Rutherford Scholarship.; [oth. writ.] Poem and short story published in High School Anthology, poem published in Anthology of writing for 1988 Winter

Olympic Games.; [pers.] I try to learn as much as I can in whatever I do because the knowledge I gain will only make me stronger.; [a.] Calgary Alberta, Canada

MATTHEWS, KATHERINE H.
[b.] July 14, 1919, Albemarle, NC; [p.] William and Iola Hatley; [m.] William H. Matthews (Deceased), May 14, 1949; [ch.] Barbara, Phillip and Benjamin; [ed.] High School Graduate, Albermarle High School, Albermarle, NC; [occ.] Retired-Rural Mail Carrier U.S. Postal Service; [memb.] Mayo United Methodist Church, Rural Letter Carriers Assoc., M.U.M. Quilters (coordination); [hon.] Had a poem published in "Between the Raindrops" - Salutatorian for 1937 graduating class.; [pers.] Poetry has always been my favorite type of reading, even back on the farm in North Carolina. Putting words together and quilting are my favorite hobbies today.; [a.] Edgewater, MD

MATUGA, JANIS L.
[b.] May 18, 1967, East Chicago, IN; [p.] Joseph Matuga, Virginia Matuga; [ed.] Highland High School, The University of Texas at San Antonio; [occ.] Writer, Substitute Teacher Grades Pre-K - 12; [memb.] The Council of Magical Arts, Psychology Club; [oth. writ.] Short story published in CMA Journal, one under consideration for spring publication; [pers.] My world view is understanding: Cooperation: Respect: Coexistence; [a.] San Antonio, TX

MATUK, IYAD
[b.] March 19, 1950, Jordan; [p.] Fawzi and Zainab Matuk; [m.] Lucia Ching King Yiu, September 9, 1975; [ch.] Tamara, Camillia, Tiffany; [ed.] Biomedical Engineering, University of Toronto; [occ.] Professor, St. Clair College, Windsor, ON; [a.] La Salle Ontario, Canada

MAUS, LESLIE A.
[pen.] Albert Suam; [b.] December 18, 1942, Wilhelmina, MO; [p.] Leslie R. and Dollie N.; [m.] Diana J., July 31, 1966; [ch.] Leslie A II, Heidi J. Kevin G. and Keith A.; [ed.] 12th was graduated from Derby Senior High School 1961 - Derby Kansas; [occ.] Production worker and a cannery in Woodburn OR; [memb.] IOOF, VFW; [pers.] These are the 1990's. Don't blame today's troubles that happened in century's past on people today.

MAXIMILIAN, WENDY C.
[b.] April 5, 1952, Winnipeg, Manitoba, Canada; [p.] Walter J. Loepp, Betty M. Loepp; [m.] Charles J. Maximilian, August 18, 1973; [ch.] Janessa, Justin; [ed.] St. Mary's Academy; [occ.] Flight Attendant, Canadian Airlines International; [oth. writ.] Several poems and articles on humanity and spirituality.; [pers.] This poem is dedicated to my father, Walter J. Loepp. It was written within minutes of his passing to ease him from this life.; [a.] Winnipeg Manitoba, Canada

MAYCRINK, ANTHONY W.
[b.] November 14, 1975, Alma, GA; [p.] Brenda Gail Juton Maycrink, Paul Wesley Maycrink; [ed.] 10th; [occ.] Prisoner; [oth. writ.] Has been writing poems for 5 years.; [pers.] Has been writing poems from my heart and with feeling of what I have been through in prison.

MAYER, THOMAS A.
[b.] February 15, 1962, OH; [m.] Debbie A. Mayer, April 7, 1983; [ch.] Three; [ed.] Grade 12 seven years USN, Sea Air Resquel; [occ.] Grocery; [memb.] Bowling League Veterans Member; [hon.] Good Conduct, USN, Good Samertin Award 1987; [oth. writ.] Gentle silence, Hidden Wisdom, Heart Music, Child Faith; [pers.] Try to take just one day at a time.

MAYNOR, BRENDA S.
[b.] June 19, 1945, Wilmington, NC; [p.] Mr. and Mrs. Wade Hamilton Bowen; [m.] Wilkie Jr. Maynor; [ch.] Beverly Jean, Rita Marie, Mark Anthony; [ed.] High School Graduate; [occ.] Data Conversion Operator - U.S. Postal Service; [pers.] I dedicate this poem to God who inspired me to write it. To all of my loved ones for their support. A special thanks to my sisters Faye, Judy and Debra for their encouragement.; [a.] Fayetteville, NC

MAYS, DERIL KENT
[m.] Doris Lee Mays; [ed.] Doctorate in Psychology; [occ.] Retired; [oth. writ.] Professional publications.; [pers.] Existential psychology.; [a.] Barbourville, KY

MAZZEI, EDMUND J.
[b.] April 12, 1938, Boston, MA; [p.] Frank and Edith Mazzei; [m.] Jeaneth, May 7, 1994; [ch.] Rosa Marie, Edmund Jr, Gina, Angela, Paul, Tanya, Mark; [ed.] South Boston High, Florida International University (BA and MBA); [occ.] Commercial Real Estate Broker; [memb.] Coral gables, Chamber of Commerce, Boma, Miami, Boma International, Washington, DC, IADC; [hon.] Member of year, Boma International, 1989-1990, Dean's List, Secretary Treasurer, Boma International 1995-1996; [oth. writ.] Several Real Estate and Business articles published in Boma Skylines, Office guide and Miami, Miami today.; [pers.] Having desire is the product of a difficult time in my life. Sincere thanks to Dee Ann for the inspiration and experience. Philosophy: Expect the best our unconditional commitment to service excellence.; [a.] Miami, AL

MAZZUCA, JOHN LOUIS
[b.] March 18, 1942, Denver, CO; [p.] Louis and Josephine Mazzuca; [ch.] Louis Randall, Mitchell Ray, Andrew Sherman; [ed.] St. Joseph's High, Mesa College, Colo. University; [occ.] Self-employed- Financial Services Business.; [hon.] Dean's list, Phi Beta Kappa; [oth. writ.] Several poems published in poetry journals and local newspaper, Philosophical article in academic journal, article in Nat'l magazine.; [pers.] I sound sound for sound is around, I sound mood for feelings abound, I sound sense for nothing is found.; [a.] Grand Junction, CO

MCALLISTER, MOIRA
[b.] May 21, 1947, Scotland; [p.] George and Mary McAllister; [m.] Steve Barabas; [ch.] Heather Benson, Andrew Benson; [occ.] Hospital Admitting Clerk; [oth. writ.] I have a collection of poems written over the years and until now, have never strived for publication.; [pers.] Poetry can reflect any or all emotions. Happiness, sadness, anger, disappointment, humor and awe etc. I used this method to express myself.; [a.] Oshawa Ontario, Canada

MCALLISTER, MOIRA
[b.] May 21, 1947, Scotland; [p.] George and Mary McAllister; [m.] Steve Barabas; [ch.] Heather Benson, Andrew Benson; [occ.] Hospital Admitting Clerk; [oth. writ.] I have a collection of poems written over the years and until now, have never strived for publication.; [pers.] Poetry can reflect any or all emotions: Happiness, sadness, anger, disappointment, humor and awe etc. I use this method to express myself.; [a.] Oshawa Ontario, Canada

MCALPINE, PEGGY
[pen.] Peg; [b.] June 20, 1962, Millinocket, ME; [p.] Alton Russell Jones, Evelyn Lenora Jones; [m.] Douglas Green, December 30, 1995; [ch.] Shelly Lenora, Robert Dewayne, Chad Everette; [pers.] I dedicate this poem in the memory of my father, Alton Russell Jones. There's so many things I could say about him. He was the kindest man I ever know and a wonderful father. I never had the chance to tell him how proud I was to be his daughter. This poem says everything he meant to me. I want to thank him for helping me put my feelings into words. I thank the heavens above for making him my father. I love you Dad.; [a.] Bristol, NH

MCCLAIN, WILLIAM GEORGE
[pen.] Nil; [b.] May 20, 1937, Outlook, Saskatchewan, Canada; [p.] Roand and Evelyn; [m.] Barbara Ann, June 3, 1961; [ch.] Douglas and Bruce; [ed.] Alberta Grade Eleven; [occ.] Security Guard; [memb.] NIL; [hon.] Only military awards.; [oth. writ.] 156 other poems none of which have been shown or published.; [pers.] All my poems are Christian based poems.; [a.] Beausejour Manitoba, Canada

MCCLIMAN, FLORENCE FAVA
[pen.] Florence M. Fava; [b.] July 31, 1917, San Jose, CA; [p.] William P. Horton and Mary Manning; [m.] George L. Fava, July 3, 1935; [ch.] Harold L. Fava and Cheryll Ann Fava; [ed.] High School San Jose High, San Jose; [occ.] Retired; [memb.] Los Altos Hills Historical Society (Founding President of the Society in November 1973.) Unofficial and Official Historian of Los Altos Hills, Calif, for 18 years.; [hon.] Among honorees at the First Annual Awards Luncheon for Distinguished Women on the Mid-Peninsula, in 1973. Nominated in 1974 for a San Jose Mercury and News Women of Achievement Award. I also participated in the 1976 Anza Reinactment March from the Pajaro River T. San Francisco in Costume (1776-1976); [oth. writ.] Published 1. Los Altos Hills, The Colorful Story," 1976. (Book) "The People," "First Inhabitants 2. Of our Land (Not yet published); [pers.] History has always been my "Labor of Love"; [a.] Santa Rosa, CA

MCCLINTOCK, SANDRA HANNUM STORA
[pen.] Sandy H. S. McClintock; [b.] October 31, 1956, Anchorage, AK; [p.] Robert R. Hannum and Clarice L. Hannum; [m.] Gregory James "Mac" McClintock, December 31, 1992; [ch.] Rachel-Michelle "Rami" Aurora; [oth. writ.] Short stories, Chidren's Books, Poetry; [pers.] Fear. Fear fuels my writing. Fear of forgetting the touched places, remarkable people and transforming moments I have known.

MCCLURE, BOHUN PAMELA
[pen.] Pamela Bohun; [b.] April 20, 1967, Vancouver, BC, Canada; [p.] James and Beverly Bohun; [ed.] Princeton Senior Secondary, Capilano College; [occ.] Early Childhood Educator, Program Supervisor North Vancouver B.C.; [oth. writ.] Many other poems and songs not submitted for publication as of yet.; [pers.] I enjoy writing poetry as I find inner peace within myself. Our world we live in today at times can be confusing and maybe through my poems I can touch a person heart to say "yes" that's how I feel, they realize they are not alone!; [a.] Vancouver British Columbia, Canada

MCCORMACK, BRIAN HYLAN
[b.] October 23, 1968, Howell, MI; [p.] Lee McCormack, Eva McCormack; [m.] Sheila Kaye McCormack, September 3, 1994; [ch.] Amanda Christine and a new born in August, '96; [ed.] Zion Benton Township High School, College of Lake County; [occ.] Automobile Technician, Towing and recovery operator; [oth. writ.] Poems published in High School Mosaics books.; [pers.] Life goes hand in hand with the ideas and dreams that you have planned.; [a.] Beach Park, IL

MCCORMACK, JOHN THOMAS
[b.] July 5, 1965, Ontario, Canada; [p.] Francis and Winifred; [m.] Marianne Teresa; [ed.] Ongoing Studies/School of Life; [occ.] Musician/Songwriter; [memb.] Society of Composers, Authors and Music Publishers of Canada (Socan); [oth. writ.] Collection of songs and poems currently unpublished.; [pers.] Half empty or half full, it's still just a glass of water.; [a.] Burlington Ontario, Canada

MCCOY, MURIEL
[b.] March 4, 1944, Newburgh, NY; [p.] Mitchell and Henriett Elliott; [m.] Alfonso McCoy Sr., August 29, 1964; [ch.] Darbin, Relma, Alfonso Jr.; [ed.] 12th Grade; [occ.] Homemaker, Writer of Poems, Lyrist, Published and unpub. creator of small crafts and ideas.; [oth. writ.] "Brother," Grand baby, First born," "Life Keys", Marriage, Steal away, and now, It's time to say good to Mother"; [pers.] I've never strove to be famous, just to be good at what ever I do. I hold no "college" degrees. My degree, is living, loving, and giving to others. Also accepting others for whom ever would have them be.; [a.] Phoenix, AZ

MCCOY, VIVIAN
[b.] September 9, 1941, Forrest City, AR; [p.] Mr. and Mrs. Ralph Thomas; [ch.] Andy, Rufus, Robert, Nancy; [ed.] Fruitport High, MCC Com. College Los. Ang. School of Nursing.; [occ.] Private Duty Nurse; [memb.] Church of God in Christ American Lung Association; [pers.] My 7th gr. teacher headed me into poem writing. She was my greatest influenced. My English teacher.; [a.] Loxahatchee, FL

MCCULLOGH, LILIAN
[pen.] Lilian McCullogh; [b.] August 3, 1903, Minnedosa, Manitoba, Canada; [p.] Mr. and Mrs. A. T. Harper; [m.] J. F. McCullogh (Deceased), July 11, 1934; [ch.] Enid and Lucille; [ed.] Completed high school, taught in public school for 10 years, substituted in Brandon Urban schools for 5 years.; [occ.] Retired but writing stories.; [memb.] Rebekah Lodge (life member); [hon.] Has diploma's for

completing courses in article writing and Institute of children's Literature. Won 1st prize in local contest and was able to visit Wisconsin Dells.; [oth. writ.] Has a book published 'On Wings of a Dove'. Was Brandon correspondent for Winnipeg Tree Press for 7 years.; [pers.] I try to inspire people to love each other and to glorify God.; [a.] Brandon Manitoba, Canada

MCCURDY, ROSE MARY
[b.] November 15, 1953, Battle Creek, MI; [p.] Wanda and Eli Buncich; [m.] William C. McCurdy III, November 4, 1981; [ch.] Steven, Kimberly, Michael, Karen; [ed.] Olivet High School; [occ.] Owner, McCurdy's Carpet Center, Robert Isdale, AL; [pers.] I have been writing poems to bring happiness to my Mom. Now she has died and it's extremely hard for me.; [a.] Robertsdale, AL

MCCURDY, THOMAS
[b.] June 26, 1951, Cleveland, OH; [m.] Nancy, November 31, 1971; [ch.] Dana, Carrie, Adam, Aaron; [ed.] B.S. University of Maryland, University College; [occ.] Crisis Specialist

MCDONALD, BARBARA
[b.] February 9, 1924, England; [p.] Mr. and Mrs. J. C. Brooks; [m.] Divorced; [ch.] Two; [ed.] Private School, England grade 12; [occ.] Retired; [oth. writ.] Have written many poems, also children' stories (have not entered any in any contests or publications).; [pers.] Barbara, a born again Christian. Teach the word of God. Work as a volunteer in street ministry. Served 4 yrs. in royal air force in 2nd world war.; [a.] England

MCDONALD, DEANA P.
[b.] August 18, 1983, Waukegan, IL; [p.] Renee C. Johnson; [ed.] 7th grade, attend Jefferson Middle School; [occ.] Student; [memb.] Student Council, Community Theatre; [oth. writ.] I have written numerous poems other than signs of love.; [pers.] The world is so full of pain and broken hearts, but it is also full of love and happiness, therefore, you should hold on to the "good" things in life and ignore what wouldn't help you soar high above the world.; [a.] Waukegan, IL

MCDORMAN JR., MARSHALL D.
[b.] December 13, 1943, Baltimore, MD; [p.] Marshall and Anneturnbull McDorman (Deceased); [ed.] Ridgewood High, Ridgewood, NJ. Duke Univ, Durham N.C. B.S. Psychology East Texas Univ, Commence, Tex M.S. Psychology Southern methodist Univ, Dallas, Tex PLD can didn't Louisiana State Univ, Baton Rouge, LA. in Psychology (Incomplete); [occ.] Free-lance Writer; [memb.] Baltimore Writers alliance, Phirappapsi Fraternity; [a.] Owings Mills, MD

MCELLEN, LAURA
[b.] April 19, 1962, La Grange, IL; [p.] Kenneth D. Vesely, Nancy K. Vesely; [m.] Michael P. McEllen, March 15, 1986; [ch.] Kristin, Michael Jr., Amy; [ed.] Buffalo Grove High, Northern Illinois University; [occ.] Programmer, Analyst; [memb.] PTA, Girl Scouts of America - Brownie Leader; [pers.] Enjoy each of your children every day for all too soon their youth will be gone and you will look back and wonder how it passed so fast.; [a.] Arlington Heights, IL

MCENDREE, STEPHEN
[b.] July 2, 1969, Fort Worth, TX; [p.] Jerry and Jane McEndree; [m.] Tonya, April 21, 1990; [ch.] Expecting in May of 1996; [ed.] Richland High Tarrant County Junior College, ATI; [occ.] Computer Support Staff; [hon.] Award for Computer System installation Nov. 1994, Employee of the month July 1995; [pers.] In my writings, I hope to influence people to seek out the Lord and to see all the good things he has in store for them if they will simply accept him into their life.; [a.] Hurst, TX

MCFADYEN, KATIE
[b.] March 5, 1986, Winston Salem, NC; [p.] Angela and David McFadyen; [ed.] 4th Grade Speas Elementary; [occ.] School, Karate, Soccer, Chorus, Girl Scouts; [oth. writ.] Homework

MCFARLAND SR., FRED G.
[pen.] Fred G. McFarland Sr.; [b.] October 18, 1955, Strasburg, VA; [p.] Ernest and Mildred McFarland; [ch.] Mildred, Fred Jr., Sherry, Bonnie; [ed.] High School Graduate, Strasbury High Strasbury, VA., Flight Engineers School - US Air Force Police Science,; [occ.] Tractor, Trailer, Driver for all freight Del. Systems, Winchester, VA; [memb.] Eagles, Moose, American Legion, AARP; [hon.] (2) 1 Million Mile Safety Wards; [oth. writ.] Children's Book All About Tobacco, Rummors, Christmas Dream, Songs - Yvonne, Shenandoar Express, Gona Build Myself A Bar. Stop at the Crossing; [pers.] A happy heart is one that beats for the enjoyment of others.; [a.] Stephen City, VA

MCGOUGH, RICHARD D.
[b.] March 13, 1957, MacDill AFB, Tampa, FL; [p.] Richard P. and Patricia C. McGough; [m.] Martha Anne McGough, June 21, 1980; [ch.] Jarrett - 12, Leighanne - 10; [ed.] Masters - Aeronautical Science BS - Engineering Technology Design; [occ.] Pilot-American Airlines; [hon.] A few academic and a few military.; [oth. writ.] Various poems written for certain events and occasions but none published.; [pers.] In the time line of existence - from the beginning of earth itself, man and the future to come, our time here is shorter than words can convey. Next time you're having a bad hair day. Try and find some perspective. Live long and wise.; [a.] Clearbrook, VA

MCGOWAN, MS. TRACEY
[b.] February 26, 1977, Sudbury, Ontario, Canada; [p.] Rita McGowan (Mother), Terry McGowan (Father); [ed.] Elementary - Sacred Heart School High School - St. Patrick's; [occ.] Medical Disability Pension; [memb.] Autism Society, Society for Creative Anachronism; [hon.] Outstanding Achievement in Reading and Language Arts Father Gerald Labelle School.; [oth. writ.] None published.; [pers.] I have Aspergers Syndrome (A rare variety of Autism).; [a.] Sarnia Ontario, Canada

MCGUINN, DORIS FAUST
[b.] January 8, 1924, Wilmington, DE; [p.] John Howard Faust, Viola O. Faust; [m.] Richard H. McGuinn, January 8, 1942; [ch.] Doris Marie, Dick, Carolie, John, Barbara, Fred, Charles, Otis; [ed.] High School Grad; [occ.] Retired; [memb.] The Institute of Children's Literature; [oth. writ.] Several poems printed in church bulletins. Am compiling booklet of family poetry. To submit for publication.;

[pers.] We must not hide our talents, but share them. Perhaps we can brighten someone's dark corner.; [a.] Partlow, VA

MCGUIRE, JAMES B.
[b.] August 14, 1952, Marshall, TX; [p.] C. T. "Pete" and Betty McGuire; [m.] Jennell Sue McGuire, May 18, 1974; [ch.] Audrey Beth and Meghan Laine McGuire; [ed.] Oklahoma City University; [occ.] Scientist; [pers.] My poetry is heart felt, running and full spectrum of emotions.; [a.] Oklahoma City, OK

MCHUGH, KERRIE A.
[pen.] Kerrie McHugh; [b.] October 13, 1962, Glasgow, Scotland; [p.] RoseAnne and Michael McHugh; [m.] Divorced; [ch.] Ryan, Cameron, Aaron and Eileen; [ed.] Gladstone High School G.12, B.C.R.P.A. registered Fitness Consultant. Fitness First Aid and C.P.R.; [occ.] Fitness consultant and Aerobic instructor; [memb.] B.C.R.P.A member; [hon.] Completed the 1995 Vancouver Marathon. Top Sales person 1995 at Dyna Fit Fitness Club.; [oth. writ.] Several other poems ie. My child, Self Rosebud, Passion, Eyes Tell Me, Watching and Dreams.; [pers.] As life's pupils, if wise, we may gain insight from its lessons. My lessons are in my words.; [a.] Surrey Bristish Columbia, Canada

MCILVAINE, ALICE L.
[b.] December 25, 1940, Washington, PA; [p.] Phillip and Dorothy Moses; [m.] John W. McIlvaine; [ch.] Cynthia Bergmann, Heather Filer; [ed.] Washington High School, Penn Commercial Business College, Sulkowski Academy of Fine Arts; [occ.] Bookkeeper, Church Organist, Artist, Wife, Mother, Home and Family Engineer; [oth. writ.] Several poems published in local books; [pers.] Without poetry music, art, and the love of my husband and family, my heart would have no rainbows.; [a.] Waynesburg, PA

MCINTOSH JR., JOHN A.
[b.] February 20, 1948, Orlando, FL; [p.] John A. and Eva M. McIntosh; [m.] Linda J. March 21, 1975; [ed.] Bachelor of Arts (Pol. Sci.) Univ. of Georgia (1978), Masters (Public Admin.) GA. College (1981); [occ.] Electronics Technician; [memb.] Proud member of Kathy Mattea Fan Club, Amer. Federation of Gov't Employees (AFGE); [hon.] H.S. Honor Graduate, National Honor Society (1966), Honors Program (U of GA.); [oth. writ.] 4 published songs (BMI); [pers.] My goal is to obtain peace of mind by prayer, meditation and interaction with others, the work of Kris Kristofferson has been a major influence; [a.] Warner Robins, GA

MCINTYRE, PETER
[b.] May 2, 1945, Montreal, Canada; [m.] Karen Bentley, October 26, 1995; [ch.] Tomas Peter; [ed.] B.A. (U.W.O) 1966, M.A. (Geulph) 1972, M. Div. (Trinity Toronto) 1980; [occ.] Self Employed; [hon.] Merit award - Huron College (U.W.O) 1966 Athletic letter Medway High, Huron College; [pers.] I want to assist people along a path to whomever they are to be using my journey as an example although I continue to search.; [a.] Guelph, Canada

MCINTYRE, TAMARA
[b.] May 12, 1973, Silver Spring, MD; [p.] Toni and Bob McIntyre; [m.] Fiance: Daniel Leach; [ed.]

South Lakes High School, Reston, VA on 6/91. George Mason University, Fairfax, VA, grad in May 1996.; [occ.] Student, majoring in Counseling Psychology.; [oth. writ.] This is my first published work.; [pers.] I feel extremely blessed to be able to express my perceptions through poetry.; [a.] Reston, VA

MCKINNEY JR., WILLIE
[pen.] Ken; [b.] October 8, 1945, TX; [p.] Willie and Martha M. McKinney; [ch.] Rochea A. B. Mckinney, Lawrence J. T. McKinney, and Qiana S. McKinney; [ed.] B.S., B.A. Degree, Suffolk Unive. Roxbury Community College, A.A. Degree, New England Conservatory of Music, Northeastern University Courses; [occ.] Engineering Payroll, MBTA, Boston; [memb.] Rapid Investment (RIP) Partners, We can N.I. Revelation Baptist Church, Father's Day, Mother's Day Message, Publicity Assoc. of MA, CDC Assoc., NAACP, Heart, Assoc., United Way; [hon.] Roxbury Community College, 2nd Place Trophy Body Building, Gerard Duchaney Road Race, Medal-1995, Member, Site Council, English High School (oldest public high school in America), National Society of Poets, Distinguished member, International Poet of Merit Award-1995, Tufts Health Plan, On My Own Time - Special Recognition for Help Us To Save The Children-1995. Office of Economic Opportunity, Outstanding Achievement Award for Community Service, Roxbury Community College-First Chairman Of College Screening Committee in the History Of Community college system and First President of Student Government Association, Senatorial Citation, Commonwealth of MA, Senate; [oth. writ.] From Behind The Shadow, Stop By And Get Some Inspiration, My God, All I Need Is Time, Reach Out For The Children, Why, When; [pers.] I love by the belief that God is my greatest inspiration. It is through him that I have gained my ability to write poetry, because of that strong bond, I feel that I have the strength to endure that which I can't cure. My goal is to inspire the nation and reach people of all ages and nationalities and create a lasting memory in their minds. I write about life, relationships and reality, which all too ofted reflect the pursuit of, Truth, Citizenship, Education and encouragement in all endeavors of life.

MCKINNON, CAROLYN
[pen.] Carnie Sky Sparrow; [b.] October 4, 1964, North York; [p.] Frances Mulligan; [ch.] Raye, Jackie, Dylan; [pers.] During my night-shaded vision, I became intimate with my shadow. A seductive, acquainted dance with the devil and behold the tale of my awakening.; [a.] Nepean Ontario, Canada

MCKINNON, IRENE E.
[b.] January 23, 1915, Thomasville, GA; [p.] Lucille McKinnon, Charles McKinnon; [ed.] Phillips High, Birmingham, Al. Joye's Business School, Thomasville, GA.; [occ.] Retired Secretary And Bookkeeper; [memb.] First Methodist, United, Church, Thomasville, GA.; [pers.] This quotation from shakespeare expresses my philosophy: "To find sermons in stones, books in the running brooks, and good in every thing.; [a.] Thomasville, GA

MCKINNON, TAMMY
[b.] December 2, 1970, Brandon, Manitoba, Canada;

[p.] Jack McKinnon, Marcella McKinnon; [m.] C/L Mike Baker; [ed.] Crocus Plains Regional Secondary School, First Year Fine Arts University of Manitoba; [occ.] Freelance Graphic Artist and Fine Artist; [memb.] Art Gallery of Southwestern Manitoba; [pers.] "I Don't Remember the War" was written for remembrance day when I was thirteen. I have always felt more comfortable using my drawing ability, however, I am extremely honoured that this poem which was submitted by my grandma Bubu was chosen for publication.; [a.] Brandon Manitoba, Canada

MCKITRIC, KAREN ALLEN
[pen.] Ren McKitric; [b.] January 25, 1945, Milford, OH; [p.] George D. Gans Sr., Mildred Gans; [m.] John D. McKitric Jr. (Second marriage) July 8, 1989; [ch.] Walter Allen, Kennen Allen, Christopher Allen and Charles Allen; [ed.] Milford and Indian Hill Elementary, Indian Hill High, Poro School of Beauty Art, University of Cincinnati; [occ.] Instructional Assistant Cincinnati Board of Education; [memb.] Women writing for a change Ebenezer Baptist Church; [oth. writ.] Black History Skits and Plays - Performed at Ebenezer Baptist Church, Article in local newspaper, poems and essays.; [pers.] I hope always to be a tool for God to use to accomplish His will.; [a.] Cincinnati, OH

MCKNIGHT, MARY LOU
[b.] October 4, 1939, Lindsay, Ontario, Canada; [p.] Father - Deceased, Mother - 90 yrs.; [ch.] Two daughters, married and children; [ed.] Finished High School I took courses at Community Colleges. Continued to write and won awards. I had an agent but he didn't make it.; [occ.] Early Retirement E.L.M. Technician for 31 years Dr's Hospital - Toronto, ON; [memb.] Canadian Authors Association (Impending); [hon.] N.C.A. Records Hit Parade One of Top ten awards 1992. Received positive responses, from Majestic Records. T.N.C.A. in Nashville. 2 Types made NCA. - My Dream "Girl Lynn Marie" Majestic Records - The Day Our Lives Shaped Up.; [oth. writ.] Quill Books published 3 or 4 poems.; [pers.] My flare for writing discovered at an early age, my poetry, essays and short stories. Growing up in a small town difficult to obtain proper training. I had 2 or 3 publishing contracts NCAT Majestic.; [a.] Toronto Ontario, Canada

MCLAIN, INEZ A.
[pen.] Inez McLain; [b.] March 14, 1919, Jenkins, KY; [p.] Etta and Rollie Painter; [m.] Gene McLain, June 25, 1935; [ch.] Tyler McLain, My great grandson; [ed.] 3rd grade, me - 10th grade but that never interfered with my work, Me - I guess you could say - God taught me police and social studies work; [occ.] Retired LA enforcement officer Widow 51/2 years; [hon.] I guess the only recognition was appointed to run a Juvenile Crime Prevention Bureau against Crimes that were committed against children (It was a great job and I guess I handled it for four years until my judge changed to another court, then that judge changed, and put me over country adoptions.; [oth. writ.] In my 30's I wrote sentential poems.

MCLAIN, JERMEY
[b.] June 29, 1973, Indiana; [p.] Gary McLain, Teresa Lynch; [ed.] High School; [occ.] Labor

MCLAUGHLIN SR., WAYNE R.
[b.] May 21, 1941, Sewickley, PA; [p.] Olivia Mae White and Norman Harper McLaughlin Sr.; [m.] Rose Ann (Thompson) McLaughlin, August 9, 1968; [ch.] Wayne Jr., Tamara Lee, Franklin Henry, Chandra Camilissa, Steven, Susan Lynn; [ed.] Kirkwood Community College Achieved Applied Associate of Science - Computer Programming; [occ.] Assembler-Operator; [oth. writ.] Various religious fictional ballad, fictional, historical and comedic.; [pers.] We are all assigned a purpose under heaven. As H. W. Longfellow said in the builders "Nothing useless is, or low, each thing in it's place is lost, and what seems like idle show strengthens and supports the rest".; [a.] Belle Plaine, IA

MCLEOD, JOHN I.
[b.] November 14, 1957, Canton, MA; [p.] Robert S. McLeod, Dorothy J. McLeod; [occ.] Painter; [oth. writ.] In the making.; [pers.] My poetry stems from a desire to communicate my thoughts and feelings to others and to a true and living good, who genuinely cares for his people.; [a.] Port Saint Lucie, FL

MCLEOD, LYLE
[b.] February 18, 1948, San Diego, CA; [p.] Harold (Deceased), Loretta McLeod; [ed.] Hoover High School (San Diego) "66". Grossmont College (El Cajon) San Diego State Univ.; [occ.] Saddle and Western Leather Gear Maker - ("Santa Fe Saddlery"); [memb.] International Federation of Leather Crafters Guild, International Society of poets, Distinguished Member, (Life), Vietnam veteran - (Infantry); [hon.] Gen' L.G.W. Gatchell Memorial Award - San Diego Historical Society, "Honorable mention", Several poetry awards, Ft. Guijarros Museum foundation - "Special Award for Military History", U.S. Army Commendation Medal, for Vietnam Service.; [oth. writ.] "History of the Militia and National Guard in San Diego from 1846 to 1918." Poems Published: "Common Soldier", "The Cutting Word", "Friends of Memory," "Face of War", For NL of P and "Sounds of Poetry." "Wishing Wells," - Famous Poets Society; [pers.] War brought out my savagery: My horses and dogs - Humanity, Politicians - Disgust, friends - love, nature - faith. Life is a wonderment of up and down. Am I balanced, or what? If a horse throws you - remount! Life is like that!; [a.] Ilfeld, NM

MCMILLAN, RUTH
[pen.] V. R. E. Taylor; [b.] October 9, 1949, Camphellford, Ontario, Canada; [p.] Harold and Orpah Taylor (Both Deceased); [m.] George McMillan, June 13, 1986; [ch.] Lorna, William, Catherine, Elizabeth; [ed.] Sir John A. Mac Donald, Secondary School, Hamilton Ontario received my Grade 12 diploma in 1984, June, went back for my O.A.C, Gr. 13; [occ.] Housewife, and grandmother; [memb.] No memberships, but served on a committee as President for the building in which I live.; [hon.] I never received any honors or awards for my writing; [oth. writ.] I am now in the process of writing a novel. A fiction for adult materials. No other poems sent to newspapers or magazines at yet.; [pers.] I believe that writing poetry helps mankind to strive for peace and long life. I was influenced by reading German poetry in German. Author who inspired me was Wolfgang Johann Van Geothe.; [a.] Hamilton Ontario, Canada

MCMULLAN, EDNA
[b.] November 26, 1976, Niagara Falls, Ontario, Canada; [ed.] Stamford CVI, Niagara Falls, Ontario, Brock University, St Chaterines, Ontario, BA degree in classics; [oth. writ.] This is my first published piece. I also write short fiction.; [a.] Calgary Alberta, Canada

MCMULLEN, BETTY D. J.
[pen.] Betty Mac; [b.] June 10, 1926, Minneapolis, MN; [p.] Casey H. and Hazel A. Jones; [m.] Arthur E. McMullen, October 25, 1947; [ch.] Michael Casey McMullen, Paula Maureen McMullen Dobbins, Darcy Belle McMullen Kreger, Casey Cecile McMullen Highland, Shawn Anne McMullen Kobs, Claudia Joyce Mcmullen, Judy M. Dunlop (a foster daughter). They are all teachers, music majors and/or minors. Our only son vanished in MN Boundary Waters Canoe Area Wilderness and we searched for 20 years before learning from a psychic when his spirit visited her, that he'd fallen over a deep precipice, hit his head and died instantly, a day and a half on the Kekekabic Trail.; [ed.] 3 yrs College of Pharmacy U of MN: member U of M Concert Band, Orchestra and Marching Band. Am organist, pianist, oboist, and play several other instruments.; [occ.] Retired Librarian/Teacher; [memb.] Theta Nu, Honorary Music Sorority U of M, MN VFW Post 955 Auxiliary, MN AM Legion Aux 0395, MN Sr Fed 7 Co Region, BCT Bloomington Civic Theatre Charter Member; [hon.] Selected Represent. on E.O.C. Board, Journalist for Day, Brainerd Daily Dispatch, Selected for Executive Board 7 Co. Region, MN Senior Federation - a great honor to be selected to Executive Board as they determine where and how money to be spent.; [oth. writ.] Many poems and articles published in newspapers and magazines. Myself and couple others published theatre magazine called 8:30 Theatre in early '50's and I reviewed plays and wrote other articles. Also stories locally published small books i.e. "Cattail Collection" (5 co. publication) Put together Sourdough Calendar. Sold extensively, mailed out everywhere. Wrote for Compas from beginning, Caol Bly edited.; [pers.] I am chronic sufferer of Lyme Disease and now confine my writing solely to dispensing correct information on Lyme virus. It is deadly, a killer, mimics every other disease, attacks every organ and system in the body. I lecture at schools and help everyone who calls or writes for information, my mission till last breath. Hides in brain, behind eyes, comes out at will and does its dirty work.; [a.] Kathio Township, Onamia, MN

MCMURTRY, RYAN
[b.] July 23, 1978, North Platte, NE; [p.] John and Janet McMurtry; [ed.] Presently a student at Okabosa Walton Community College.; [occ.] Student; [memb.] Singer in local band.; [hon.] Numerous down hill skiing awards.; [oth. writ.] Many poems and songs, none currently published.; [pers.] My writings typically reflect my own views and feelings on various issues. I have been greatly influenced by my own experiences and hardships in overcoming dyslexia.; [a.] Niceville, FL

MCNALLY, ELIZABETH M.
[b.] August 9, 1906, New York City, NY; [p.] Edward M. McHugh - Isabelle Mullen; [m.] Arthur R. McNally, September 1, 1929; [ch.] Edward, Ann, Elizabeth; [ed.] B.A. Hunter College N.Y.C.

Subsequent courses in Speech; [occ.] Retired; [memb.] Phi Sigma Gamma (non-sectarian sorority); [hon.] Recording for the Blind (1981, 1988); [pers.] When I was a teacher at the High School of Art and Design in N.Y.C., a student teacher I was supervising worked on poetry with my classes. She taught them a form called quatrain. I was fascinated and wrote "Blue"; [a.] Milwaukee, WI

MCNEEL, CAROLYN J.
[b.] August 21, 1941, Chicago, IL; [m.] J.F. McNeel, February 20, 1960; [ch.] LouAnn, Den Frederick, Linda Joy, Jon Timothy; [ed.] Registered Nurse, Training for Nsg. Home Adm., Christian Education/ Women's Ministries; [occ.] Hospice Nurse for Porter Care/Avista Hospice; [memb.] Foot Hills Bible Church Children's Literature Society, Speaker for banquets, Christian Women's Clubs, "His Heart Ministry.; [oth. writ.] Various poems and children's stories-unpublished - 2 poems published in newspapers article on Nursing - Provider magazine article on Ideas for Elderly - Eynman Pub.; [pers.] I write from experiences. Enjoy telling stories to people of all ages. Actual incidents spark my writings to teach value lessons. I write for my patients, their families, my own family and friends. My writings are inspirational, values teaching and humorous; [a.] Golden, CO

MCNEILL, MARILYN A.
[b.] September 28, 1943, Helena, MT; [ed.] Complete High School, 2 years Dental School; [occ.] Retired; [oth. writ.] Two books - self published, "Dancing with life" 1993, "Come Dance with me" 1994; [a.] Grass Valley, CA

MCNUTT, ANNIE
[b.] April 29, 1950, Brockville, Ontario, Canada; [p.] Jean White; [ch.] Kristian, Jasmine; [ed.] L.C.U.I St. Lawrence College Kingston, Ontario; [occ.] Teacher St. Lawrence College Foster Parent C.A.S.; [oth. writ.] Humor articles in newspapers, contest winner Whig-Waggery.; [pers.] I believe after fostering over 40 children and the love of my two children, have deeply motivated myself to be the best I can, inspired with warmth and love from my mother.; [a.] Kingston Ontario, Canada

MCWILLIAMS, JANE ANN
[b.] August 12, 1960, Portland, OR; [p.] Bertha Marie and Delmar McWilliams; [m.] Dan Holcombe; [ch.] Jacob Cody, Jonathan Ian and Jared Daniel; [occ.] Homemaker, Artist; [hon.] I am honored to have been awarded a motherhood of 3 beautiful sons.; [oth. writ.] I am the Ocean, and many others never shared.; [pers.] The need to be Caretakers of this magnificent planet has never been more important than now. Now is the time to care. Love is the answer, we are the ripples.; [a.] Oregon City, OR

MEADOWS, TIM
[pen.] Timothy Wayne Meadows; [b.] June 28, 1981, Morehead, KY; [p.] Gerald and Ruth Meadows; [ed.] 9th grade; [oth. writ.] I write to express feelings. I wrote other poems, but never published, until now.; [pers.] I express feelings. I also let people know how I feel about my God. I have been influenced by my sister, Rebecca Belcher, who also wrote poems. Also my supporting parents, Gerald and Ruth Meadows.; [a.] Frenchburg, KY

MEALER, CHARLA
[b.] November 29, 1958, Dallas, TX; [p.] Noel L. Mealer, Susie Lee Mealer; [m.] Single; [ch.] Brandon Joel Mealer; [ed.] Judson Preparatory School, North Lake College; [occ.] Sales; [oth. writ.] Published one other poem in College Arts Magazine, much of my collection of work is yet unpublished.; [pers.] My hope regarding my writing is to cut through superficial understanding and portray truth in a simple way that will touch both heart and soul. I have been influenced by many modern poets and lyricists.; [a.] Irving, TX

MEDINA, JASMINE
[b.] June 6, 1981, Philadelphia; [p.] Milagros L. Thompson; [m.] James Thompson, February 14, 1991; [ch.] Jasmine, Mervin, Amanda; [ed.] High School Graduate William Penn High School; [occ.] Devoted myself to my children; [hon.] Citizenship Award, Certificate of Scholarship, Certificate of Achievement; [pers.] "Trying to be the best you can be is the only way you will get by" I love poems that describe how people feel about others.; [a.] Philadelphia, PA

MEDLEY, KEITH SEKOU
[b.] May 23, 1971, New Orleans; [ed.] Loyola University, B.A. in History and Philosophy, Dec. 1995, Southern University of New Orleans, Education, expected date of Graduation: Summer, 1996; [memb.] Phi Alpha Theta, History Honor Society; [pers.] Vigorous poetry uses simple language to reveal extraordinary things.; [a.] New Orleans, LA

MEEKER, MARY NACOL
[b.] April 24, 1922, Clarksville, TX; [p.] William and Hall; [m.] Robert J. Meeker, July 4, 1957; [ch.] Three; [ed.] Ed. D. Psychology Education, Ph.D Neurological Psychology; [occ.] Psychologist Research into intelligence; [memb.] National Assoc. for Gifted, Amer. Neurological Psychologists, oregon Watercolor Society; [hon.] 2 "first" awards for the best papers written in education (Ed. Press), selected by office of Ed. as a Psy. whose work would lead the way for education in the next century (1980); [oth. writ.] Hard cover textbooks anthologies, fiction, children's stories, non-fiction, over 90 training books, K-12 series for gifted education for State of Calif.; [pers.] Adventures into learning ought to go far beyond curriculum.....into creativity, into art, into the "new." The more one learns, the more intelligence is developed.; [a.] Vida, OR

MELCHER, NANCY
[pen.] Nancy Churchill; [b.] August 9, 1958, Clarinda, IA; [p.] Bobby and Anna Churchill; [m.] Larry Melcher, September 9, 1990; [ch.] Brian; [occ.] Registered Nurse; [oth. writ.] Several short stories and numerous poems.; [a.] Glenwwod, IA

MELIA, JACQUELINE
[b.] December 11, 1962, Dublin, Ireland; [p.] Monica and Brian Martin; [m.] Cy Michaud (Still pending); [ch.] Kyle Michaud - 8; [ed.] Life; [occ.] Is looking for an occupation.; [a.] Kelowna British Columbia, Canada

MENDONCA, LORRIE-ANN L.
[pen.] Leolani; [b.] October 6, 1958, Honolulu, HI; [p.] John A. Mendonca and Christabel Medeiros;

[m.] Stan B. Akiona; [ch.] Farrah and Justin Pu; [ed.] Graduated Class of 76 Moanalua High School; [occ.] Head Baker at Hotel Hana Mani; [oth. writ.] Prisoner of Love, Printed in Spirit of the Age; [pers.] Live life to its fullest and always try your best at anything you do. Believe in others as well as yourself. Always take the chance when opportunity knocks!; [a.] Hana, HI

MERCER, RACHEAL
[b.] February 15, 1979, Moorestown, NJ; [p.] James and Norma Mercer; [ed.] Currently High School Junior; [occ.] Student; [memb.] California Scholarship Federation, Choir, Student council, Cross-Country, Track; [hon.] Honor roll, Spanish Award, Presidential Award for Grades; [oth. writ.] Many poems this is the first submission for publication; [pers.] I use poetry as an outlet for my emotions.; [a.] Poway, CA

MERK, ALEKSANDRA
[b.] June 29, 1979, Toronto, ON, Canada; [p.] Elko and Renata Merk; [ed.] Presently attending Notre Dame College School in Welland, Ontario, Grade eleven; [oth. writ.] First ever publishing of my work.; [a.] Fonthill Ontario, Canada

MESECK, RONALD R.
[b.] January 18, 1946, Champlain, NY; [p.] Louis (Noah), Rose Marie; [ch.] Jason Jay, Michael Louis, Natalie Lain; [occ.] US Customs House Broker; [a.] Champlain, NY

MESERVY, JAY A.
[b.] October 30, 1933, Logan, UT; [p.] Joseph Alonzo Meservy and Aletha Saunders; [m.] Rosa Lynn (Rosie) Meservy, August 14, 1964; [ch.] Rebecca, Jason, Melinda, Megan and Katie; [ed.] Box Elder H.S. Utah State University, Univ. of Connecticut, Storrs, Comm., (B.A.) Univ. of Colorado College of Law, Univ. of Utah College of Law; [occ.] Attorney; [memb.] Utah State Bar, Davis County Bar, Church of Jesus Christ of Latter Day Saints (mormons), Bountiful Lions Club; [hon.] Personally recognized by three different International Lions Presidents -2 International President awards - twice district 28 U Lions "Lions of The Year"; [oth. writ.] "Ripples on the pond-" (a book of poetry), "The Terrible Horrible, awful, deplorable, lovable, little troll (a children's book in rhyme-published by Little America Books - Beautiful America publications, Oregon); [pers.] Children should be read to at a very early age and should be encouraged to read early have books and stories which carry a moral; [a.] Centerville, UT

MESSNER, BRENDA L.
[pen.] Brenda L. Messner; [b.] October 30, 1962, Sunbury, PA; [p.] Judith and Richard Carter; [m.] Joseph W. Messner, October 15, 1994; [ed.] B.S. in Business Administration, Accounting from Bloomsburg University; [occ.] Senior Accountant, American Urban Radio Network Pittsburgh, PA 15219; [memb.] St Joseph Church Choir; [pers.] I believe that we all need to return to a more symbiotic relationship with Mother Nature.; [a.] Coraopolis, PA

METIKOS, DUNJA
[b.] November 3, 1979, Sarajevo, Bosnia; [p.] Vasilije Metikos, Habiba Metikos; [ed.] Grade 1-7

Elementary School in Sarajevo, grade 8 Elementary School in Zagreb, Croatia (a refugee), grade 9 - Zagreb High School, grade 10-LIsbon High School, Lisbon N-North Dakota, finished Music School for Piano in Sarajevo, Bosnia; [occ.] High School Student, attending Grant Park High School (Grade II) in Winnipeg, Manitoba; [hon.] Certificate of Outstanding Achievement in Recognition of Creative Scientific Endeavor in Aerospace Research, NASA; [oth. writ.] Several other poems, short stories.; [pers.] I try to show the horrors and absurdity of war in my poetry. I try to uncover the pain and fear it causes. I have been inspired by the war in former Yugoslavia, where I was born and used to live.; [a.] Winnipeg Manitoba, Canada

MICHELOUD, MADELEINE
[pen.] Mish a Loo; [b.] March 12, 1930, Lausanne, Switzerland; [p.] Elise Etjules Micheloud; [m.] Bad Marriage 1958, Divorce in Calvary; [ed.] Montessori style with no diplomas at the end but one, TN Photography in 1952. Practiced Portraits, Photo-Journalism. Liked to do photo - Montages and tricky compositions.; [occ.] Lived in English speaking places since 1958 forgot my french and do not speak english well. Trying now to master better both Languages.; [memb.] American Museum of Natural History; [oth. writ.] I write rhymes since about 1944 but always threw them away. Now that I need money and since this hobby is a constant since in my life, I keep essays of short stories, songs for cabaret and poetic rhymes trying to better them.; [pers.] No philosophy, do not like indoctrination of any kind, do not like extremists and puritans. I am an Agnostic and what I have is a way of life. It is based on the quintessence of the Christian Commandments revised and adapted by my parents....; [a.] Calgary, AB

MIDDLETON, LENA
[b.] May 24, 1945, Harlan Co., KY; [p.] Lloyd Smith, Sarah Smith; [m.] Stanley Middleton, January 30, 1993; [ch.] James Matthew, Christopher, Cheryl; [ed.] Tecumseh High, Jackson Community College; [occ.] Housewife; [memb.] Missionary Baptist Church; [oth. writ.] I have written many, but nothing published; [pers.] My writing reflect experiences in my life, and people around me. I was greatly influenced by my American Lit Teacher MacRenfro, and the way he made poetry sing.

MIGNONE, TRACY ANN
[pen.] Tracy Ann; [b.] January 19, 1963, Mineola, NY; [p.] Tom and Barbara Mangan; [m.] Pasquale J. Mignone, November 17, 1984; [ch.] Tanya Marie - 8, Olivia Nicole - 5; [ed.] Mineola High School, graduated June, 1981; [occ.] Corporate Travel Agent; [oth. writ.] Many - none published.; [pers.] The words I use all come from the feelings I have. My more recent poetry reflects on the pain and heartache over losing my mother to cancer. She was always and to this day still is my strength and inspiration. I dedicate everything I write to her.; [a.] Bayside, NY

MILES, VIRGINIA
[pen.] Virginia Null Miles; [b.] April 29, 1918, Bethany, OH; [p.] Charles W. Null, Blanche H. Null; [m.] February 24, 1951; [ch.] Eight; [ed.] Springboro High School, Springboro, Ohio, Dale Carnegie Course; [occ.] Registrar for Lee Miles School of

Real Estate; [memb.] Sough Park United Methodist Church, Dayton, OH., Toastmaster's International; [hon.] 10 years 4H Advisor Speech Contest winner, Best Bread baker in Montgomery County Fair; [oth. writ.] 6 Children stories, nearly 100 poems, feature articles, 3 song with lyrics; [pers.] I have been a psychic palmist for over 40 years, reading for charity, benefits and parties. I taught cooking classes at YWCA. I like to spread joy wherever I go.; [a.] Dayton, OH

MILLARD, JOAN BENNETT
[pen.] Joan Bennett Millard; [b.] April 5, 1933, Fruitland, TN; [p.] Mr. and Mrs. Charles D. Bennett; [m.] Charles K. Millard Jr., January 3, 1954; [ch.] Three; [ed.] High School - some college; [occ.] Retired; [memb.] Not a joiner; [oth. writ.] Two poems published in "Young America Sings" and one poem was published in "The Air Force Times"; [pers.] If you can't return a favor to someone, pass it along to someone else. Treat everyone as a valuable friend everyone and most will become one.; [a.] Pomfret, MD

MILLARD, VIVIAN
[b.] June 7, 1931, Berlin, NY; [p.] Delmar and Mildred Amidon; [m.] I am a widow, October 28, 1950; [ch.] I have 6 children and 4 grandchildren, 2 great grandchildren; [ed.] High School, graduated in 1970, after the birth of my first 4 children, at the age of 39; [occ.] Retired; [oth. writ.] I have dozens of unpublished poems long ones and short ones on many subjects. This being my first published poem has been a full filling experience.; [pers.] I feel life is only as good as you make it. I want mine to be a life of love, reality and beautiful poetry; [a.] Buskirk, NY

MILLER, ANGREW GEORGE
[b.] October 14, 1976; [p.] George Miller, Martica Thomas; [ed.] 5 yrs. Rosary Boys' R.C. School (Port-of-Spain, Trinidad), 6 yrs. St. Mary's College (POS, Trinidad), 1 yrs. Fr. Leo J. Austin (Whitby, Ont.), presently: 1st yr. Student of Modern Languages University of Ottawa; [occ.] Student at The University of Ottawa; [memb.] Trinidad and Tobago Karate Association, Amnesty International; [oth. writ.] Steel Beauty (For Fr. Leo J. Austin's Anthology for 1995, "Austintacious"); [pers.] I thank everyone with whom I have had any contact for shaping me, especially my parents and family. I dedicate the poem especially to my grandfather, Andres always remember your family Thomas.

MILLER, BARBARA ANN
[b.] November 26, 1945, Portland, IN; [p.] Warren and Ruth McMichael; [m.] James E. Miller, August 15, 1970; [ch.] Michael W. Miller; [ed.] Lebanon High School, University of Indianapolis, BS, Indiana University, MS; [occ.] Director of Resources, Otterbein Lebanon Retirement Community; [memb.] Genntown United Church of Christ, Lebanon Optimist Club, LHS Parents Assoc., Tres., National Executive Housekeepers Assoc., Society for Human Resource Managers; [a.] Lebanon, OH

MILLER, BILL W.
[b.] October 2, 1964, Anderson, IN; [p.] Billie Miller, Elsie Miller; [ed.] Blue River Valley High, in Mt. Summit, Indiana; [occ.] Janitor at Eastside Bowl and Banquets II, Watseka, Illinois; [memb.] None, though I do attend church and support local charities

when able.; [oth. writ.] Scripts for various Comic Book Publishers and related industry journals.; [pers.] "Tornado Warning" was based on a true incident. I thank God I am able to share it.; [a.] Watseka, IL

MILLER, KIMBERLY ANN
[pen.] Kimberly; [b.] May 14, 1972; [ed.] Educated by experience and a profound curiosity of the super and the natural.; [oth. writ.] 2 many 2 mention, working on a book, no publishing yet.; [pers.] Live, Love, Learn, follow your will - silence is a statement.; [a.] Richland Town, PA

MILLER, LINDA F.
[b.] April 26, 1939, Walloon Lake, Charlevoix City, MI; [p.] Raymond Ecker and Venetta Ecker; [m.] Divorced; [ch.] Mary Hansen, Patricia Dofflemyer, Robert O'Brien (Deceased), Stacy Miller, William Miller (Deceased); [ed.] Melrose Twp. Unite School-Elementary Walloon Lake MI, Boyne City High School - Boyne City MI, Oakland County Community College, Royal Oak. Mich (56 credit); [occ.] Disability - was a telephone adjustor for Travelers Insurance Company; [memb.] The Reorganized Church of Jesus Christ of Latter Day Saint, no other at present.; [hon.] Poetry awards and Honors, Poetry printed in OCC Newsletter, Poetry printed in World Book of Poetry 1984, and 1991, Poetry 1984 Nat'l Library of Poetry 1991; [oth. writ.] Articles printed in High School - newspaper (Boyne Citizen) by line, Articles printed in church newsletters and in short Term Writing Club Warren, MI; [pers.] I am going to try to published a book of poetry a novel, an autobiography and a documentary on Heart Disease from a patient point of view and I'd like to do an acrylei and an oil painting. I take each one at a time; [a.] Warren, MI

MILLER, MARY ANN
[b.] September 13, 1920, York, NE; [p.] Bert and Elva Derby; [m.] Floyd L. Miller, May 3, 1941; [ch.] Rocky, Melody, Murray and Vicki Pratt; [ed.] Master's Degree in Ed. and Reading; [occ.] Retired teacher now Postal Clerk; [memb.] None at present very active during my teaching days member church of the Nazarene Bozeman, MT; [hon.] Teacher of the year - CA, 1973; [oth. writ.] Children's Book "Troublesome Toby" Book of Poems "Flight to the Stars", Autobiography "That's My Mom" Lots of poetry and short stories and articles.; [pers.] I believe we need to have a good, caring relationship with others, but it cannot be accomplished without a good working relationship with God.; [a.] Bozeman, MT

MILLER, STEPHEN V.
[pen.] Stephen Vincent; [b.] April 21, 1951, Oceanside, CA; [p.] Vincent Miller, Glenna Miller; [m.] Teresa Cassidy-Miller, October 21, 1989; [ed.] James Madison High, Bluefield College; [occ.] Welder; [pers.] I observe and interpret feelings, Moods, and events, people fascinate me.; [a.] Alexandria, VA

MINGES, SARAH
[b.] June 20, 1982, Cincinnati, OH; [p.] G. Stephen and Lynn Minges; [ed.] 1st through 6th Grade - St. John the Baptist Elementary 7th through 8th - William Henry Harrison Jr. High School; [memb.] Girl Scouts, Jr. High Band, honor Society; [hon.] Girl Scouts - Silver Award, Band - Plaque commend-

ing me on an outstanding performance my 7th grade year, school high honor; [a.] Harrison, OH

MIRANDA, BONNIE L.
[b.] October 1, 1974, Baltimore, MD; [p.] Sherri Smith; [ch.] Colby Debra Vergalito; [ed.] Francis Scott Key High, Western Maryland College; [occ.] Full Time Mother; [memb.] Phi Mu Fraternity; [hon.] Carroll County Fine Arts Council Creative Writing Award, Prose Award from Western Maryland College Literary Publication; [oth. writ.] Poem published in local newspaper, prose and poetry published in Western Maryland College Literary Publication; [pers.] A very special thank you to those few who have touched or broken my heart, for without the extremes there would be no inspiration. All of my love and devotion to my beautiful, magical daughter.; [a.] Taneytown, MD

MITCHELL, ANDREW W.
[b.] April 19, 1963, Vermilion, Alberta, Canada; [p.] Earle H. Mitchell, Darlliene V. Mitchell; [m.] Jo-Anne F. Mitchell (Divorced, August 20, 1993), August 30, 1986; [ch.] Lyndon Mitchell Ashley Mitchell, Derrick Mitchell; [ed.] Completed grade 12 at Edgerton Public School in 1981; [occ.] Cook Trainee; [oth. writ.] This is the first publication I have ever been offered. Thank you for the privilege.; [pers.] All the poetry I write in my only way to say "I love you" to the one I care for.; [a.] Saint Paul Alberta, Canada

MITCHELL, STEVEN R.
[b.] June 2, 1948, Independence MO; [p.] Paul and Daisy Mitchell; [m.] Connie Mitchell, September 26, 1986; [ch.] Brian Steven Mitchell; [ed.] William Chrisman High School; [occ.] Letter Carrier; [memb.] American Legion National Assoc. of Letter Carriers; [hon.] National Thespian Honor Society Eagle Scout; [pers.] Most Admired poet: Robert frost; [a.] Independence, MO

MOJADO JR., MIGUEL L.
[pen.] Migs, Bong Mojado; [b.] July 29, 1969, Cotabato City, Philippines; [p.] Miguel Mojado Sr. and Lydia Laude Mojado; [m.] Marites Mojado, December 26, 1992; [ch.] Roentgen Mark and Rachelle Madeline; [ed.] Notre Dame University, Cotabato, Philippines, Systems Technology Institute, Philippines; [occ.] Psychiatric Nurse, RN. Sutter Center for Psychiatry, Sacramento, CA.; [memb.] Philippine Nurses' Association, PI Omicron Frat. and Sorority, Ship for Southeast Asian Youth Alumni Association, Sacramento Metro Church of Christ.; [hon.] Frendus Academic Scholarship, Japanese Grant as Philippine Youth Ambassador to the 1991 (SSEAYP) Ship for Southeast Asian Youth Program; [oth. writ.] Several essays, news articles and poems published in Philippines Local Newsletters, Youth Journals and Newspapers.; [pers.] Poetry tries to capture what is beautiful, simple, and pure. The greatest expression of poetry I know is Jesus Christ and His death on the cross for us...It is not only beautiful but awesome, not only simple but a basic form of love, not only pure but holy.; [a.] Sacramento, CA

MOLINA, ONELIA
[pen.] Brittainy Esquivel; [b.] April 12, 1953, Premont, TX; [p.] Alberto Esquivel Jr., Sylvia E.; [m.] Mr. Richard Molina, November 4, 1978; [ch.]

Irene Iris, Alfredo Ricardo; [ed.] Ingleside High, Del Mar College, Texas A and I - Corpus Christi; [occ.] Elementary Teacher - Salazar Elementary; [memb.] American Professional Teacher Association, Licensed Professional Counselors Association; [hon.] National Honor Society; [oth. writ.] Booklet to TEA, "Minorities in Health Science Programs"; [pers.] I strive to reflect the feelings of some youths in their generation with the pressures and confusion that involves their confusing world.; [a.] Corpus Christi, TX

MOLNAR, CHLOE POLLOCK
[pen.] Chloe Pollock Molnar; [b.] April 4, 1930, Kittanning, PA; [p.] David and Fannie Pollock; [m.] Ernest S. Molnar, May 17, 1992; [ed.] BFA in Drama - Carnegie - Mellow University -1952 - graduated Cum Laude, Kittanning High School; [occ.] Retired; [memb.] Women in Film (Former member, Bd. of Directors), Carnegie-Mellow University West coast drama clan (Former member Bd of Directors), Huntington Beach Art Center, L.A. and Santa Fe Opera Leagues; [hon.] Phi Kappa Phi, Mortar Board, Carnegie-Mellow University National Service Award - 1982; [oth. writ.] None published; [pers.] I have spent my life trying to make this a letter world in which to live and love.; [a.] Huntington Beach, CA

MOLNAR, JASEN
[pen.] National Pen, U.S.A.; [b.] February 21, 1974, Murrayville, British Columbia, Canada; [p.] Ernie Molnar, Sharon Molnar; [oth. writ.] Never before published short stories and poems, songs.; [pers.] I would like to dedicate this poem to Julia Molnar and Ava Moojelski, and Sharon Molnar.; [a.] Abbotsford British Columbia, Canada

MONDRAGON, CATHERINE CANDELARIA
[pen.] Catherine C. Valdez; [b.] January 25, 1955, Pueblo, CO; [p.] Rupert Joe Valdez and Rose Gloria Valdez; [m.] Mike G. Mondragon, February 14, 1987; [ch.] Rupert Leo and Nicholas Augustine; [ed.] Central High School 1972, University of Southern Colorado; [occ.] Domestic Engineer; [hon.] The World of Poetry, Silver Poet Award 1986, 1972 contestant Miss Colorado Teen-ager Pageant, 1995 Editor's Choice Award (ALIKE), 1995 Honorable Mention from Range Chapter (Carousel).; [oth. writ.] Published in the Anthology, ALIKE in BEYOND the STARS, AN ANGEL WALKS in THE BEST POEMS of 1996 MOTHER EARTH in BENEATH the HARVEST MOON; [pers.] In order to succeed in today's generation, one must know that they want out of life. For life itself has so much to offer.; [a.] Pueblo, CO

MONTANO, HECTOR
[b.] January 16, 1975, Tucson, AZ; [p.] Hector Montano, Stella Montano; [ed.] Sunnyside High, Pima College, Univ. of Arizona; [pers.] Poetry is a very powerful form of expression. It can make a negative into a positive. My poetry has been influenced by my bad experiences in life.; [a.] Tucson, AZ

MONTOYA, ARLENE
[b.] July 21, 1968, San Diego, CA; [p.] Jose and Mary Montoya; [ch.] Reina Montoya Lee; [pers.] "Love" can bring one such happiness and from time to time cause great pain. During these times we feel

alone as if no other would understand. I know, because I've been there. My writings reflect on what our heart and mind feels and goes through. Who'd ever guess that a simple four letter word as "Love" can have an enormous impact on our lives. Enjoy!; [a.] Oakland, CA

MOON, MARC
[b.] February 24, 1971, Chathan, Ontario, Canada; [ed.] The greatest education, and the hardest lessons learned came from life.; [occ.] Youth worker, at Chatham-Kent Transition House; [pers.] The sky is always blue. Sometimes we just have to get above the clouds.; [a.] Lighthouse Cove Ontario, Canada

MOONEY, KAREN W.
[pen.] Karen LaRue Mooney; [b.] January 3, 1939, Cabri, Sask.; [p.] Ulysses Alexander LaRue and Violet Laurentzen; [m.] October 13, 1962 - separated 5 years; [ch.] 9 children (grown up); [ed.] Alberta College of Art Diploma/4 Yr Program/'64, University of Toronto Honour Art Degree/Art Specialist Program/'94; [occ.] Artist/Self Employed at present; [memb.] Alumni U. of T.; [hon.] For paintings, not writing; [oth. writ.] Approx 30 unpublished poems - some exhibited as part of art installations; [pers.] I am atempting to find some kind of rebirth, beauty, hope, or a redemptive quality in the ashes and brokenness of life.; [a.] Toronto, Ontario, Canada

MOORE, CAROL R.
[pen.] Tweety; [b.] January 6, 1952, Uxbridge, Ontario, Canada; [p.] Owen Moore, Lyla Moore (Nee Lapp); [ch.] Donald Alan, adopted out.; [ed.] Uxbridge High School; [oth. writ.] Several poems, unpublished as of yet.; [pers.] I write poems in my spare time, in lieu of keeping a diary. My wish, someday, is to dedicate a poem to may son who was born on February 3, 1970.; [a.] Uxbridge Ontario, Canada

MOORE, GEORGE E.
[b.] November 14, 1945, North Vancouver; [p.] George and Elsie; [m.] Jackie, November 26, 1977; [ch.] George, Anita, Greg; [ed.] Power Engineer; [occ.] Heating, Ventilation, Air Conditioning Technician (H.V.A.C.); [a.] Port Coquitlam British Columbia, Canada

MOORE, JOYCE G.
[m.] Billy Moore; [ed.] B.S. Florida A. and M. University Graduate Work California State at Los Angeles; [occ.] Success and Stress Management Facilitator for Seminars and Workshops.; [memb.] Neighborhood Improvement Assoc., KAPPA Silhouettes, FAMU Alumni, Cobb County Network.; [oth. writ.] Stress Management Digest and Solving The Mystery Of Success.. A Common Sense Approach To Life Management. Also self published Three poetry books.; [pers.] I truly believe that life is a beautiful canvas upon which we can learn to create a series of successful masterpieces. The most powerful teachers in my life have been my parents, and they presented me with my canvas early in my life.; [a.] Marietta, GA

MOORE, MINITA E.
[pen.] Kandi Moore; [ed.] B.S - Zoology, Registered Medical Technologist; [oth. writ.] Collection of poetry.; [pers.] I believe in the Triune God Head -

God the Father, God the Son and God the Holy Spirit. My writings are influenced by my Christian up-bringing. I focus on the strength and determination of the human spirit and write to give encouragement to those who hear and read my works.; [a.] Beverly Hills, CA

MOORE, PHYLLIS J.
[b.] May 30, 1912, Bottrel, Alberta, Canada; [p.] George and Olive Reid; [m.] Gordon Curtis Moore, September 23, 1940; [ch.] Diana Faust, Linda Entwistle; [ed.] Teachers Degree, including KIndergarten High School Public School, Commercial Course many individual course (night) Courses at Calgary University in Literature; [occ.] Retired in 1978; [memb.] Home and School Anglican Church Eastern Star - Kerby Centre for Seniors took courses in writing of all kinds, Mt. pleasant dance seniors good Companions Sr. Club, Children's Hospital, Children Amateur Club, Bed Ridden at home, authors; [hon.] Beauty is forever in Senior Competition it was Repeated in church folio wrote prose accepted in Edmonton magazine. Re closing the zoo many poems in the book our literary group published.; [oth. writ.] Haiku-Prose-Tank also children's stories, "Vindication" published in Saskatoon, Saskatchewan. I often write eulogies for friends.; [pers.] I am impressed by many people and find a story in almost all, (true or fictional I also find much to enjoy in animals.; [a.] Calgary Alberta, Canada

MOORE, VICKI M.
[pen.] Taylor Creek; [b.] February 6, 1953, East Saint Louis, IL; [p.] Bonnie Taylor and Frank Creek; [ch.] Keeley Ann Moore - 10 year old daughter; [ed.] Bachelor's in Nursing at University of New Mexico, Master's of Science in Nursing from University of Portland, Portland, OR; [occ.] Health Promotion Specialist, NM Dept. of Health, Public Health Dept.; [memb.] Unitarian Universalist Fellowship Leadership San Juan; [pers.] My personal life and professional practice are based on caring. I hope to continue writing poetry and other words that exemplify the sacred in life.; [a.] Farmington, NM

MOORHOUSE, PEARL
[pen.] Either (E.P.) or Elizabeth Pearl; [b.] September 6, 1917, Wabamun, Alta; [p.] Olive and Louis Root; [m.] Widowed; [ed.] Standard Norman Rockwell School of Fine Arts, two scholarships from Inter-nation these are in art. Also graduated in Pottery. Also got a scholarship in Writing from Chicago; [occ.] Retired; [memb.] Federation of Canadian Artist; [oth. writ.] All writings have never been seen by anyone but me.

MORANO, JOAB SKOTT
[b.] May 16, 1955, New York, NY; [ed.] Monroe High School, LOs Angeles, CA, Community College, Theatre of the Arts; [occ.] Designer of Marble and Stone, aspiring Actor; [memb.] Taiost Tai Chi Society/Screen Actors Guild; [oth. writ.] Several other poems and children's stories completed, seeking a publisher at this time.; [pers.] All my children's stories and poems are written to reflect the beauty in the world, healthfulness of the children's minds and bodies and the protection of everything and everybody.; [a.] Palm Bay, FL

MOREAU, AMANDA ADRIENE
[b.] May 24, 1981, Pembroke, Ontario, Canada; [p.]

Sharon and Tony Moreau; [ed.] Cathedral School and Bishop Smith Catholic High (presently attending); [pers.] Never wish for tomorrow it will only bring you closer to your death - Amanda Moreau.; [a.] Pembroke Ontario, Canada

MORGAN, DAVID
[pen.] David De Vayie; [b.] April 12, 1970, Edmond OK; [p.] May and Geraldine Morgan; [m.] Teresa Morgan, June 5, 1995; [ch.] Avary Danielle, Jennie Leigh Tausha; [ed.] Edmond Central High; [occ.] Printer; [pers.] I try to reflect the darker side of reality in my writings. My main influences are taken from previous experiences in my life; [a.] Edmond, OK

MORRIS, OLIVE M.
[pen.] Seretha; [b.] June 10, 1956, Aurora; [p.] Bettie A. Moore; [m.] Lionel Morris, July 6, 1982; [ch.] Tyshaun, Marqueda, Kazia; [ed.] Aurora High, Fayetteville State University, Pamlico Tech. College; [occ.] Machine Operator Instructor; [memb.] St. Stephen's Missionary Baptist Church; [hon.] Emergency Team First Responder, Substitute Teacher-Volunteer Safety Talk Contest; [oth. writ.] Poems for children published in newspaper, plays for churches.; [pers.] I like to touch the hearts of others through my writing. I am inspired by my children who bring me joy every day of my life.; [a.] Lumberbridge, NC

MORRISON, DORA C.
[pen.] Charlene Morrison; [b.] December 5, 1947, Neodesha, KS; [p.] Betty and Joe Kesterson (foster parents); [m.] Billie L. Morrison, December 3, 1972; [ch.] Michael and Janice Gregg; [ed.] Texas A and M consolidated High School, College Station, TX; [occ.] Legal Secretary; [memb.] None presently; [hon.] First place in high school for vocal solos in 1963, and 1965. Typing awards and spelling awards; [oth. writ.] I have started a book based on my life. A poem published in a small Kansas newspaper and a small article in a Texas farming paper.; [pers.] I believe in living each day to the fullest and enjoying life to the best of my ability.; [a.] Sparks, NV

MORRISON, KIM A.
[ed.] Master of Business Administration MBA in healthcare Administration MBA in Marketing (in progress); [occ.] Sales; [memb.] Organization Design Network, Noetic Sciences, PADI Advanced Open Water Scuba; [pers.] Poetry is elusive to me, ethereal and mysterious. I do not know how words and phrases form in my head, sometimes at inopportune moments. I do know the inspiration for my poetry, and am forever grateful for the people and experience that spark the creativity.

MORROW, GWEN
[b.] March 28, 1958, Camrose, Alberta, Canada; [p.] John and Grace Rock; [m.] Cecil Morrow, July 16, 1983; [ed.] Bashaw School; [occ.] Work with the mentally handicapped.; [oth. writ.] I have a collection of 50 poems I've written which I call, "My Friends and Family".; [pers.] I wrote, "I love you, Grandma!" about one hour after learning of her death. It was my personal way of accepting and grieving her passing. Grandma Rock was always a very important part of my life!; [a.] Red Deer Alberta, Canada

MORTON, CAROL
[b.] October 12, 1944, Omaha, NE; [p.] Clayton Harding, Doris Harding; [m.] C. Dale Morton, March 21, 1969; [ch.] Jacinda Christine, Michael John; [ed.] High School; [occ.] Title I reading and Math para. OPS; [memb.] PTA, M.R.C.

MORTON, RICHARD JOHN
[b.] May 30, 1964, Invirk, NWT; [p.] Rev. and Mrs. A. G. Morton; [m.] Leanne Morton, October 8, 1994; [ed.] Educated in England, in the Roman City of Lincoln took training in Business and Photography, graduated in the latter from College in 1984.; [occ.] Photographic Sales and Technician at a professional Film Lab.; [oth. writ.] Collection of poems written over the last five years reflecting the world, and my life.; [a.] Kelowna British Columbia, Canada

MOSBRUCKER, JOACHIM C.
[pen.] 'JC', 'Yocum'; [b.] November 18, 1912, In Farm Home with Mid-Wife; [p.] Adolph and Pauline (Dietrick) Mosbrucker; [m.] Elizabeth (Betty) Bode, September 27, 1940 (married 55 years); [ch.] Ileine, Thomas, Mark, James, Robert; [ed.] Seven yrs. Elementary, Diploma, Taught by Nuns yrs. USAAF World War Two 4 yrs. from 1941 to 1945, had course in Morse Code, and Blinker then taught P38 Pilots on Photo Recon. which was photographing the Enemy at nite. Operation of radio, and Radio Navigation; [occ.] That is taking nite Photo's of the Enemy. Retired Age 83. Entertain at Nursing Home, Christ, the King Catholic Church AARP. Pres-3 yrs. American Legion-KofC - 65 yrs.; [memb.] Knights of Columbus - State Offices Active in Church activities Read Scriptures still active with young people's moral training. Talked in over fifty schools on Americanism North and South Dakota only. My topic "The home and the Family are the Foundation of every Nation - As goes the Home and the family so goes the Nation. I have many Patriotism poems. All over U.S.; [hon.] American-ism Award from Kofc Circulating Patriotism Award from Kofc Circulating Patriotism Poetry for 21 yrs. Serving as their Chairman for 23 yrs. Assisted with 4H Program for 4 years. In 1974 was awarded 24 Trophy from State of North Dakota for Patriotism Talks.; [oth. writ.] Wrote over twenty (My View) to Daily news papers Bismarck Tribune have written many Patriotic Poems, some all over U.S.A. That was done at National Kof C Conventions, starting in 1969 to 1991 then I retired. But now still write some 'views' today. Farmed over 50 years but never owned an acre of Land. Being oldest of thirteen Children in the Family. (Helped out at home too long).; [pers.] My favorite saying is "If you do not develop yourself to the level of your inherited talents, and use this ability to enhance the betterment of society, then you have let your Maker down." (Jc) At present Has a four piece orchestra. Play, Guitar, Drum, and Harmonica all 3 at one time come and see with singing also. Entertain old Folks also taught and called square dances for 7 years. Now retired in Mandan, North Dakota.; [a.] Glen Ullin, ND

MOSSMAN, DEBRA
[b.] October 6, 1951, RI; [ed.] ADN Assost. Degree in Nursing; [occ.] Registered Nurse Kent County Memorial Hospital; [oth. writ.] Poems - nonpublished; [pers.] Life is so precious many times we pass through life with blinders on. Never understanding the many blessings the Lord has given us; [a.] Warwick, RI

MOTTA, LISA
[pen.] Lisa DiPietrantonio; [b.] Italy, Pescara; [p.] Antonio DiPietrantonio; [m.] Anthony Motta, July 10, 1976; [ch.] Maria and Elizabeth

MOUNT, DIANNA
[pen.] Dee Wynne; [b.] April 15, 1945, Napa, CA; [p.] Darvin Mount, Joyce Mount; [m.] Divorced; [ch.] Kelly, Danny, Eliz, April, Deanna; [occ.] Special Packs Co-ordinator (22 yrs.) Robert Mondavi Winery - Napa, CA; [memb.] Napa - Solano WIBC (Bowling) Calif. State 600 Club (Bowling), National 600 Club (Bowling); [oth. writ.] Unpublished verses, children's story poems.; [pers.] I enjoy writing, and do so whenever the spirit moves me. I also do my own Birthday and Special Occasion cards for family and friends, and have a passion for reading. My favorite author, M. H. Clark, J. Daily, R. Cook among others too numerous to mention.

MOUNT, KRISTYN ALYSE
[b.] October 22, 1983, Morristown Memorial; [p.] Alice Jane and Eugene Ippolito; [ed.] St. Peter the Apostle School 189 Baldwin Road Parsippany, NJ; [occ.] Student; [memb.] Junior Member of the National Geographic Society St. Peter the Apostle School Girls' Basketball Team and Cheer Leading Squad. Mission Club (V.P.) of St. Peter's; [hon.] 2nd Honors, Basketball Trophies, Cheer Leading Trophies, Gymnastics Trophies, Physical Fitness Awards Walk-A-Thon Certificate, and Certificate of Excellence (for a cat drawing); [pers.] I love to write about poetry and because it makes me feel good and it is one way I can express my feelings. My favorite things to write about are love, friendship and nature all these things make me happy.; [a.] Lake Hiawatha, NJ

MOYERS, ERMELINDA MARIA NORIEGA
[pen.] Ermelinda Moyers Orlinda; [b.] March 2, 1945, Alamogondo, NM; [p.] Gavino and Maria Noriega; [m.] William R. Moyers, October 30, 1967; [ch.] Michael, Vincent, Elaine and Marcus; [ed.] Alamogondo High, Nursing School-Fort Walton Beach FL, I.B.C. Alamogondo, N.M.; [occ.] Retired and now a housewife; [oth. writ.] I have written poem for 17 years, but never showed them until now. Only been published in nursing home in Alamogondo, N.M.; [pers.] I have just like to write poem, because I see people as they are. I like to see them happy when I write about them or their love ones. My poem have been published in Nursing home; [a.] Alamogordo, NM

MULLINAX, MELISSA NICOLE
[b.] July 8, 1980, RT, Jones; [p.] Margaret, Johnny Mullinax; [ed.] Pickens High School; [occ.] Student; [hon.] 4-U.S.A.A (United States Achievement Academy), Who's who among American High School Students, Recognition from Barbara Bush.; [a.] Jasper, GA

MULTON, LORI
[b.] March 24, 1967, Moose Jaw, Saskatchewan, Canada; [p.] Ev Sanford, Vern Bell; [m.] Michael Multon, August 31, 1995; [ch.] Amanda Anne, Jasmine Kimberly Dawn, Jordan Michael, Mervin and one little angel Andrew Allen Metro; [pers.] Special thanks to my husband Michael. Without his support this poem would not have been published I

believe every poem holds a different special meaning for each individual. I hope my work gives others the joy it gives me.; [a.] Moose Jan Saskatchewan, Canada

MUNDEN, VICKIE
[b.] November 5, 1948, Fort Worth, TX; [p.] Barbara and Jackie Munden; [m.] Divorced, April 5, 1965 to June 21, 1987; [ch.] Bobby, Robin, Holly, Robin (Deceased); [ed.] H/S and 1 yr. non-credited college four years of schooling was at Elk City, Oklahoma. All the Rest: Fort Worth, TX.; [occ.] Working on fictional 'novel' manuscript.; [oth. writ.] None published manuscript (but still trying!); [pers.] You must live in your own ideal reality, keeping in mind the Lord's plan for mankind. Peace, mercy, forgiveness, Love, humility and faith. Dean Koontz is my favorite writer of fiction.; [a.] Crowley, TX

MURNI, MOHAMMAD SHARIZAN
[pen.] Izan; [b.] March 26, 1977, Singapore; [p.] Murni Jamil, Rose Murni; [ed.] Langara College; [occ.] Student; [oth. writ.] Some in my possession unpublished.; [a.] North Vancouver British Columbia, Canada

MURPHY, DAVID
[pen.] Sundance Murphy; [ed.] Camp Laboratory High School Western Carolina University, Central Piedmont Community College; [occ.] Nurse; [hon.] Mercy Nursing Scholarship, Dean's List, Public Speaking Award SDAC; [oth. writ.] Forbidden Dream of the Storm Dance - Manuscript, Storm Dancer - poem, Ride the Wind, Thunder and Lightening - poem (etc. poems short stories); [pers.] I attained to put love and the love of beauty into my words and writings. My words flow from my heart at any given moment.; [a.] Raleigh, NC

MURPHY II, THOMAS E.
[b.] October 31, 1973, Montgomery, AL; [p.] Dennis and Kathy Murphy; [ed.] Psychology degree from U.S. Air Force Academy (Bachelor of Science); [occ.] Air Force Officer, Research Scientist; [hon.] Dean's List; [pers.] I've been inspired by the works of Walt Whitman, striving to coordinate the simple with the diverse. All the while praying my expectations ne'er exceed my talents.; [a.] San Antonio, TX

MURPHY, MEGAN ANN
[b.] September 29, 1983, Calgary, Alberta, Canada; [p.] Darcy and Barb Murphy; [ed.] Presently attending Rothesay Junior High School, Grade 7, French Immersion Program.; [memb.] Kennebecasis Valley Figure Skating Club; [hon.] Won first prize in school science fair in grade 6. Won "Hardest Worker Award" on basketball Tournament in Dec 1994. Placed Second in piano class at the New Brunswick Music Festival.; [oth. writ.] Seashore, Away at War.; [pers.] I enjoy expressing my feelings in a poem. I wrote "My Grampie" because I wanted to write something special about my grandfather who had just passed away.; [a.] Saint John New Brunswick, Canada

MURPHY, SANDRA
[b.] July 31, 1972, Waterloo, IA; [p.] Michael Murphy, Mary Murphy; [occ.] Regis High School, Cedar Rapids, IA, University of Iowa, Iowa City, IA, BA English; [a.] Marion, IA

MURUGAN, LINDE
[pen.] Linde Murugan; [b.] May 22, 1985, Gainesville, FL; [p.] Ramiah and Sutha Murugan; [ed.] Baby Gator Child Care, (K-3) Lakeview Christian Academy, (K-4 and K-5), Sycamore School (Grade 1 - at present Grade 5); [memb.] WTTV4 Kid's Club; [hon.] Library Essay Contest, Hoosier State Spellbowl, many other honors from school; [oth. writ.] Library Essay Contest; [pers.] Find the feeling then find the meaning; [a.] Indianapolis, IN

MUSGRAVE, EVELYN A.
[pen.] Jem; [b.] February 20, 1950, Marigot Village, Dominica, West Indies; [p.] Balfour and Lucian James; [m.] Denrick Musgrave, May 2, 1970; [ch.] Shyanne, Denise, Debra, and Tanya; [ed.] Public School Marigot, Dominica WI, Canadian Grade 12. Mohawk College; [occ.] Taxi Driver, Housewife; [memb.] Dominica Association of Ontario, Sissenou Club of Brampton; [hon.] 3 Community Achievement awards, for working with our youths on cultural programs.; [oth. writ.] Plays, and sketch for Cultural Groups. Greeting Cards for family and friends, Nursery Rhymes. Short stories of Dominica writing of Racism.; [pers.] If through my writings peoples of all races can see some good, can realize that it is better-less stressful to live with more Love and Less Hate - my works would have served its purpose.; [a.] Hamilton Ontario, Canada

MYERS, JEAN B.
[b.] December 27, 1931, Dallas, TX; [p.] Deceased; [m.] Widowed; [ch.] Two; [ed.] High School 4 yrs, SMU School of Continuing Education; [occ.] Home Health Care; [memb.] National Honor Society Certificates in Science of Mind 4 yrs. study; [oth. writ.] Published in School Paper and Church Publications.; [pers.] I live in a perfect Universe. To the degree that I practice this, the Universe reflects it back to me. I am here to become a spiritually mature person, one who knows that we are spiritual beings living in a spiritual universe.; [a.] Dallas, TX

MYRMINGOS, DENOS
[b.] January 26, 1975, Cook County; [ed.] I am a junior at the University if Illinois, Chicago (UIC). Upon graduating I will have my degree in secondary education in teaching english; [pers.] "Where is the wise man? Where is the scribe? Where is the debater this age? has not God made foolish the wisdom of the world? For since in the wisdom of God the world through its wisdom did not come to know God, God was well-please through the foolishness of the message preached to save those who believe. "1 Corinthians 1:20,21"; [a.] Burr Ridge, IL

NABORS, SANDRA
[b.] May 19, 1975, Little Rock, AR; [p.] John and Norene Sumler; [m.] Ronald Nabors, July 10, 1993; [ed.] High school, Heritage Christian School; [occ.] Title Clerk at Little Rock Dodge Inc.; [memb.] Sardis Vol., Fire Department Ladies Aux.; [oth. writ.] A poem of mine was published in Famous Poets Anthology. The title of the poem was Spring.; [pers.] I want to thank my family and friends for all of there support.; [a.] Little Rock, AR

NACEY, BEA
[b.] Fort Frances, Ontario, Canada; [m.] Cam Nacey; [ch.] Kathleen, Sean; [pers.] I strive to reflect spirituality in my poetry and to make a statement I believe to be true.; [a.] Victoria British Columbia, Canada

NADIN JR., VAL
[b.] February 25, 1952, NJ; [m.] Marie D. Nadin, 1981; [ed.] University of Tampa - Senior; [occ.] Student - full time; [pers.] I wrote this poem after reflecting upon the endless stream on conspiracies that confront society. And the penalties that usually follow those individuals who decide to commit these horrendous acts.

NAGODA, CARMEN MAJA
[b.] April 19, 1963, Galt; [ed.] Honours - Humber College of A.A. and T. - 3 years law; [hon.] Modelling Award; [pers.] In this lifetime I have learned quite a bit and realize that I shall never stop learning more and most important thing I've learned is that you must have some sort of attitude philosophy to live by. Mine being - like a fine wine, I intend to improve with age.; [a.] East York Toronto Ontario, Canada

NAMBIAR, ANIL
[b.] July 13, 1983, Brampton, Canada; [p.] Prem Nambiar, Ceela Nambiar; [pers.] 'War is a murder, it brings death to all who pass by it', this poem brings passion towards even those with a cold heart, it lights out a path for all.; [a.] Cupertino, CA

NANGINI, MARY ANGELA
[b.] January 1, 1948, Italy; [p.] Amalia Belli, Achille Nangini; [ch.] Michael, Nadia, Robert; [ed.] BA (1971), York U., B.Ed. (1978) Unives. of Toronto, B.Ed. (1985) York U. M.A. (1988) U. of Connecticut - Storrs, Doctoral Studies Completed (1995), Ontario Institute for Studies in Education; [occ.] Artist and Poet and Teacher of the Gifted: Metro Separate School Board; [memb.] Consortium and Educators of the Gifted of Ontario, Visual Arts Brampton, League of Canadian Poets (Ass.), International Society of Poets (Dist.); [hon.] 1. "Juror's Choice" Award for Pastel Artwork, "Memories" by Visual Arts Brampton's 10th Annual Juried Art Show, 2. "Editor's Choice" Award and "Poet of Merit", 1995 for "Carousel Waltz" in Anthology Walk Through Paradise by the National Library of Poetry; [oth. writ.] Author of 2 poetry books 1) Woman in Exile, The Edwin Mellen Press., Lewin Hon. 1991, 2) My Ontario, Beautiful, Mellen Poetry Press 1995, 3) Developed a Unifying Theory (unpublished) on the Phenomenon of Abundance and its antithesis - entropy; [pers.] My poetry has helped me develop a strategy for the renewal of personal energy: from attribute listening to analogy to "Being Metaphor". It's usefulness is to develop human potential and harness the human shadow.; [a.] Brampton Ontario, Canada

NEBLETT, BARBARA
[pen.] Nevy; [b.] September 25, 1944, Joplin, MO; [p.] Archie Skelton, Betty Skelton; [m.] James Neblett, October 12, 1973; [ch.] Keith Brian, Craig Allen; [ed.] Joplin High, Jasper County Jr., College; [occ.] Research, Data Entry, Proof-Reader for Publishing Company; [memb.] Lourdes Prayer League, Swarovski Collectors Society, Patron-Saint Jude Children's Research Hospital; [hon.] Dean's List, Nat'l. Hon. Society, 1st Honor Student High School, 1st Honor Student College, Outstanding Achievement Award (Asay Publishing Co.); [oth. writ.] Songwriter; [pers.] People seldom realize the "power" of their words. Our "words" can affect others for a lifetime — be edifying.; [a.] Seneca, MO

NEELY, ALEXANDRIA N.
[b.] January 15, 1983, Fresno, CA; [p.] Donna and Jeffery Neely; [ed.] I am a seventh grade student at Alta Sierra Intermediate School; [oth. writ.] I have gotten two poems published in Anthology of poetry by Young Americans (1994, 1995); [pers.] I was inspired by my fifth grade teacher, Mrs. Molter to begin writing poetry.

NEELY, THOMAS LAWTON
[pen.] Thomas L. Neely; [b.] September 11, 1915, Greenville, NC; [p.] Kreswell E. and Mamie Neely; [m.] Audrey R. Neely, April 11, 1982; [ch.] Charles, Carole, Timothy; [ed.] N. Greenville College, SC - AA, Wofford College, SC - BA, Southwestern Theo. Sem. TX - Th. M, Central Univ. of Venezuela; [occ.] Teacher; [hon.] Doctor of Divinity degree from Furman University, Greenville, SC, SC Governor's Award for service to a new hospital district; [oth. writ.] Book: Christ is All, In God's Image, Perilous Times, New Testament Worship, Formation of a New Testament Church, Christmas Traditions; [pers.] My life's desire has been to extend the Kingdom of God.; [a.] Black Mountain, NC

NEESER, JEFFREY
[pen.] J.R.F. Neeser; [b.] December 8, 1977; [p.] Glen and Ellen Neeser; [ed.] Currently in Paul Kane High School with plans to continue my education; [occ.] Student with part time job; [memb.] Member of the Creative Writing Club at Paul Kane; [hon.] Award for Excellence in Art grade 8 1992-93; [oth. writ.] A few poems in the magazine in 2 print, a short story posted on the Internet; [pers.] I'm glad that I have found what I want to do with my life when others around me still must find their calling.; [a.] Saint Albert Alberta, Canada

NELSON, HOWARD R.
[b.] June 5, 1961, Edmonton, Alberta, Canada; [p.] Roland and Lorna Nelson; [m.] Georgie (Edgar), October 8, 1994; [ch.] Mikayla Georgie; [ed.] Graduated Mount Elizabeth Secondary, Kitimat, B.C., Basic Seamanship and Hall Technician CFB Esquimatt; [occ.] Aspiring novelist; [oth. writ.] The light in the night newspaper column. Currently working on book one of a three part series in fantasy fiction, entitled, "The Krandukla Creed."; [a.] Red Deer Alberta, Canada

NELSON, MIKE
[b.] October 30, 1979, Garland, TX; [p.] Don Nelson, Laura Lantrip; [ed.] Poteet High School; [memb.] International Thespian Society, National Honors Society, Young Life; [hon.] All-Star Cast Award in U.I.L. Drama Competition; [oth. writ.] Folder full of finished and unfinished poems, songs, etc. No previous publications; [pers.] I study, read, and absorb the work of countless poets and songwriters and strive for eloquence and free expression. I live for the day when I might be half as good as W. B. Yeats; [a.] Mesquite, TX

NELSON, SHIRLEY A.
[pen.] Shirley Moline; [b.] December 1, 1945, Edmonton, Alberta, Canada; [p.] Paul and Eva Moline; [ch.] Lennea, Todd, Terry, Michelle, grandchildren: R.J., Danny and Amanda; [ed.] Graduate Fairview High School, additional college courses in English, Psychology and Anthropology; [occ.] Manager of Tony Brighton, Musicians and

Singer Extrodinaire; [memb.] T.O.D.D. - director (Support Group), Women of the Moose, Past Jr. Regent, P.G. Regional Hospital Auxiliary; [hon.] Literary Essay Contest, Fairview 10 year Volunteer P.G. Hospital Award, Award for Thesis entitled "Discrimination and its many forms."; [oth. writ.] B.C.A.P.A.V.W.S. a story on T.O.D.D. a support group I founded. Various poems and short stories have been printed in various local newspapers.; [pers.] I find inspiration for my writings from within the vast treasure chest of life's experiences. We need to search, grow and develop constantly through out our lives. I hope "wondering" has given you pleasure and cause for thought. Be safe!; [a.] Sechelt British Columbia, Canada

NELSON, STEVEN
[b.] January 24, 1952, Denver, CO; [ch.] Hilary Joy; [ed.] BA University of Colorado, BS Colorado Christian University, MA Regis University; [occ.] Commodities Trader; [memb.] Colorado Counseling Association, Inter-Denominational Council for Families in Transition, Stephen Ministry; [hon.] CCU Distinguished Service Award, DCC Achievement Award; [pers.] Life is a journey we all share.; [a.] Longmont, CO

NERO, MAXCINE FULLER
[b.] July 31, 1940, Diboll, TX; [p.] Malissie Randolph and Paul Fred; [m.] Don Nero, July 20, 1976; [ch.] Tyrone, Anita, Beverly Crystal; [ed.] H.G. Temple High, Valrie Hurd Beauty and Business College; [occ.] Custodian DJH; [memb.] Perry Chaple CME Church, Member International Society of Poets; [hon.] Poet Merit Award, Editors Choice Award; [oth. writ.] Illegal Granny Angeles Whisper; [pers.] Achieve and Pursue Your Dreams; [a.] Diboll, TX

NESSA, CHRISTOPHER
[b.] April 18, 1968, Doylestown, PA; [ed.] Council Rock High School, History Student Bucks County, Community College; [a.] Tinicum, PA

NICHOLSON, LOREE
[pen.] Lenai Stevens; [b.] April 24, 1963, Stettler, Alberta, Canada; [p.] Raymond Fix, Janette Miller; [ch.] Theo, Triston, Ausha; [ed.] Viscount Bennett Center (Upgrading); [occ.] Business Administrator; [pers.] We as people should united together under one love of neighbors, and all mankind; [a.] Calgary Alberta, Canada

NICKELL, NATALIE MARIA
[b.] December 31, 1967, Augusta, GA; [p.] David and Maria Luisa Nickell; [ed.] Shawnee Mission West High, University of Kansas; [occ.] Entertainer, Dancer in production show in Las Vegas; [hon.] Who's Who Among American High School Students, All-American Pom-Pom Girl 1989, Honor Roll; [oth. writ.] None published! Just my own stories, poems and thoughts that I write in my journal.; [pers.] I believe that everyone has a special way of sharing themselves with the world. Almost as if to leave a piece of themselves when they are physically gone. Writing is my way of leaving my mark, whether it's good or bad matters not, only that it reflects me and proves that I lived here on this beautiful yet confusing place we call Earth!; [a.] Las Vegas, NV

NIEHAUS, RODNEY J.
[b.] December 29, 1965, Saint Rita's Hospital, Lima, OH; [p.] Bernie and Jean Niehaus; [m.] Brenda Niehaus, June 17, 1989; [ch.] Mike and Mark Niehaus; [ed.] Associate of Applied Science in Nursing, Associate of Liberal Arts Advanced Emergency Medical Technician; [occ.] Registered Nurse and Director of Nursing; [memb.] L.E.A.R.A. Lake Erie Amateur Radio Association; [pers.] This poem is dedicated to the best dad a son could ask for, Bernie Niehaus, died age 53. Remember this "It's not how long you lived, but how you lived that's truly important"; [a.] Stow, OH

NIELSEN, MISS DANA L.
[b.] February 2, 1982, Saskatoon, Saskatchewan, Canada; [p.] Lloyd Nielsen, Margaret Nielsen; [ed.] Grade 8 student, Twin Lakes School; [occ.] Student; [hon.] Academic Achievement Principals Honor Roll; [oth. writ.] Writing more poems; [pers.] Last April, I got the idea for the poem, when my brother William was born at the hospital in Prince Albert. I enjoy writing poetry in my spare time; [a.] Buffalo Narrows Saskatchewan, Canada

NIGHTINGALE, CHRISTINE
[b.] October 18, 1949, Austria; [p.] John and Christine Van Soeren; [m.] Brian Shultz; [ch.] Johnathan, David, Julie; [ed.] B.A. University of Toronto, Toronto Teacher's College; [occ.] Elementary Teacher, Fallingdale School; [memb.] Mensa, Zone Leader, Salvation Army (Annual Fund raising); [oth. writ.] Pub. in Today's Secretary, Quarry, Zioo Rap; [pers.] As a writer I try to encourage others to be aware of and honest about the moral implications of technological possibilities and changing values.; [a.] Brampton Ontario, Canada

NIKOLENKO, TONY
[b.] August 30, 1971, Newport Beach, CA; [m.] Jeanine; [pers.] Try not to expect from others that which we are not capable of ourselves.; [a.] Mission Viejo, CA

NINE, ROBIN
[b.] March 5, 1963, Adrian, MI; [p.] Rothy and Marilyn Randolph; [m.] Timothy Nine; [ch.] Jennifer, Justin, Katrenna, and Kyle; [a.] Adrian, MI

NIQUETTE, DONNA
[pen.] Donna Lewis; [b.] December 25, 1954, Maryville, TN; [p.] Richard G. Powers, Frances E. Powers; [ch.] Stephen Michael Harris, Karen Lynn Harris, Christopher Lucien Niquette, Brittney Rose Niquette, Elizabeth Ashley Niquette; [ed.] Murfreesboro Jr. College, Hillsborough Community College, Valencia Community College; [occ.] Interpreter for the Deaf; [memb.] International Honor Society, Phi Theta Kappa; [hon.] Outstanding Student; [oth. writ.] Poem published in Valencia Community College Magazine, The Iconoclast; [pers.] I believe that my relationship with my Father in Heaven is the most important relationship in my life. He loves us all "just because".; [a.] Kissimmee, FL

NOBLE, BILL
[b.] April 17, 1928, Macomb, IL; [p.] Jesse and Gladys Noble; [m.] Chris Wolf - fiancee; [occ.] Retiree; [memb.] Life Member of VFW - 1921, American Legion - 285, Eagles Club - 3698; [hon.]

U.S. Navy 4 years; [pers.] This poem was written for my fiancee Chris Wolf. I also enjoy oil painting, pen and ink sketching, and pencil sketching. I love to read Western stories. When I write poetry, I try to express my true inner feelings.; [a.] Good Hope, IL

NOLEN, RUSSELL D.
[pen.] Russell D. Nolen; [b.] October 20, 1959, Little Rock, AR; [p.] Loy Nolen, Joy Richards; [ed.] Bryant High School, Henderson College; [occ.] Disab/Vet; [memb.] Sharon Baptist Church, former member - Benton Poet Society; [hon.] Captain Varsity Squad, 1975, Member National Honor Society 1974, Semi-finalist National Library of Poetry 1995 (North American Open Poetry Contest); [oth. writ.] The Emerald River, A Winter Poem, The Journey..., The Peace of Prayer, The Wind Has Away; [pers.] What the mind see's, and what the heart believes, can set the spirit free!; [a.] Benton, AR

NOONE, KATE
[b.] February 24, 1948, Scranton, PA; [p.] William King, Helen Cannon King; [m.] Robert Noone, October 23, 1971; [ch.] Bob, Brian, Maury; [ed.] West Scranton High, attended Univ. of Scranton; [occ.] Data Entry, Emery C.F., Dunmore, Pa.; [pers.] This poem is dedicated to my children Bob, Brian and Maury and to my grandchildren, Gabrielle and Bobby III.; [a.] Scranton, PA

NORDMAN, LILLIAN
[b.] June 6, 1922, Adair, IA; [p.] Mike and Eleanor Griffin; [m.] Grover Nordman, March 1, 1949; [ed.] B.A. degree; [occ.] Retired; [memb.] St. Joseph's Rosary Society, American Legion, Teachers Assoc.; [hon.] Won County Spelling Contest, 8th grade; [oth. writ.] A little book entitled "The Poor Little Hog-O-Moose" written in poetry; [pers.] Rhyming poetry is as pleasant to my ears as good music.; [a.] Marion, IA

NORTH, MARGARET
[b.] November 16, 1918, Hoghenden; [p.] Erwin and Edith Adair; [m.] Ted North, March 30, 1939; [ch.] 3 girls; [occ.] Retired - live on farm; [hon.] Won a lot of ribbons at fairs; [oth. writ.] Have a lot, but never been sent in.; [a.] Erskine Alberta, Canada

NOVAK, ALICE
[b.] May 5, 1953, Toledo, OH; [p.] Walter and Ethelyn; [m.] Frank; [ch.] Shana and Frank Jr.; [ed.] B.A. in Elementary Education, Marycrest College - Davenport, IA, M.A. in Education - Univ. of IL; [occ.] Asst., Professor - Black Hawk College (in Child Development); [pers.] This poem was originally written for my mother, Ethelyn E. Ball (1915-1991). I dedicate it to her in loving memory of the warm place she always saved for me.; [a.] Moline, IL

NOVAK, AMY JO
[b.] July 2, 1979, Jamestown, ND; [p.] Peg and Nick Novak; [ed.] Park Rapids Elementary, Park Rapids Junior High, and Park Rapids Senior High School; [memb.] Who's Who Among American High School Student; [hon.] President of Junior Class at Park Rapids High, Honor Choir, Varsity Club in 3 sports, Letter Winners, Honor Student; [oth. writ.] Cash prize for poem at Park Rapids Junior High, several poetic/short story publications in local newspaper,

cash prizes for several poetry contests, many, many unpublished works; [pers.] I am only 16 years old and I have been writing about personal experiences and life for several years. My advice to the world, live your life so that you may never have to look back and say "Why not?"; [a.] Park Rapids, MN

NOWAK, KINGA
[b.] September 1, 1979, Poland; [p.] Mariusz and Anna Nowak; [ed.] Bishop Allan Academy; [hon.] Just this one; [oth. writ.] Personal collection; [pers.] Thanks to all who believed and a special thank you to Anne Rice and David Yu whom without them this would never have been possible.; [a.] Toronto Ontario, Canada

NOWLIN, CHARLES R.
[pen.] C. Raymond Nowlin; [b.] May 12, 1935, Covington, VA; [p.] Alex and Jennie Nowlin; [m.] Eula, September 3, 1994; [ch.] 11 (5 boys, 6 girls); [ed.] High School, Military, College (2 yrs), Assoc. Electrical Eng.; [occ.] Retired working part time Sutherland Lumber; [memb.] Boy Scouts, Church; [oth. writ.] Various religious flyers, pamphlets, several short stories, and a volume of poems, two songs; [pers.] If there is no failure in God and God lives in me, there can be no failure in me. What seems like failure is only my contribution toward completion.; [a.] Fort Wayne, IN

NUCKOLS, PEGGY LOIS
[pen.] Lois Palms; [b.] February 16, 1946, Charleston, SC; [p.] David and Marie Nuckols; [ed.] BS in Psychology at MSCW in Columbus, Ms.; [occ.] Bellsouth Employee; [hon.] Honor Roll, CWA; [pers.] In memory of my Mother.; [a.] Jacksonville, FL

NYERS, AMELIA
[pen.] Kathryn Raw, Molly Nyers; [b.] Benwood, WV; [p.] Stephen and Christina Nyers; [m.] World War II interfered; [ed.] Elementary, some high, 1944-1945 University of Pittsburgh Pa; [occ.] Retired; [hon.] Ballet Tap Instructor Feb 1946-1993, Author of Verse - Children's Stories; [pers.] Education a way for the betterment of humanity.; [a.] South Bend, IN

O'BRIEN, LISA THOMAS
[b.] January 23, 1967, Watertown, NY; [p.] Lewgene and Flora Thomas; [m.] James P. O'Brien Jr., July 7, 1990; [ed.] Watertown High School; [oth. writ.] Looking at Life Through Winter's Eyes, Soldier of Peace, How Young The Memory are among several poems published in local papers and in the anthology Beyond The Stars; [pers.] Everyone has the ability to make a positive difference in the world. To be kind and understanding not only brightens the world, it brightens your heart as well.; [a.] Adams Center, NY

O'FLAHERTY, JOHN
[pen.] Jake; [pers.] I wrote these words for all of us, who hide from the eyes of ourselves, I wrote these words for you to see into my soul.

O'HARA, ERIN
[b.] June 17, 1978, Winnipeg, Manitoba, Canada; [p.] Harry O'Hara, Marilyn O'Hara; [ed.] Beaver Brae Secondary School; [a.] Kenora Ontario, Canada

O'KEEFE, JOHN C.
[b.] February 28, 1963, Fort Monmouth, NJ; [p.]

Arlene F. and Tarrance M. O'Keefe; [m.] Brigitte, March 17; [ch.] Sean, Caitlin; [occ.] Computer Programmer; [a.] Woodbridge, VA

O'LEARY, THOMAS JOHN
[pen.] Jonathan Owens; [b.] July 29, 1963, Evanston, IL; [p.] Michael O'Leary, Cathy O'Leary; [m.] Valerie R. Valentino, September 21, 1996; [ed.] Downers Grove North High, College of Du Page; [occ.] Account Representative Stritzel Awning and Aurora Tent Plainfield, IL; [memb.] Trinity Lutheran Church, Roselle, IL, United States Army Reserve; [hon.] Department of the Army - Army Achievement Medal (Twice Awarded), Department of the Army - Army Commendation Medal; [oth. writ.] Collection of songs arranged for piano; [pers.] If it is our children, and their futures, for whom the books we write, may the poet here God's whisper. Pen to paper, shining light.; [a.] Clarendon Hills, IL

O'NEILL, KAITLYN
[b.] London, Ontario, Canada; [p.] Jeff and Linda O'Neill; [ed.] Attending school in Courtenay, B.C.; [occ.] Student Grade 3-Courtnay Elementary

O'QUIN, TRACIE W.
[pen.] Rheba Wadsworth; [b.] January 24, 1962, Endicott, NY; [ch.] Jason, Adrian and Tanner Yezno; [oth. writ.] "The Ride", The Mermaid Rest And Lounge"; [pers.] I have been writing poetry since about 9 years of age. Since I live near the beach now I have a lot of inspiration I have 3 children Jason, Adrian, Tanner Yezno (yes - Yezno) "The Ride was a reflection of my younger wilder days, to my maturity and family life. Born and raised in Endicott, New York. Then at the age of 14 moved to the beache's of North Carolina poetry writing is a favorite past time of mine. Bartending for the last 10 years at my own Club and Rest.

OBACZ, CATHERINE E.
[pen.] Catherine E. Gusse; [b.] August 3, 1973, Newfoundland, Canada; [m.] Derek W. Obacz, May 28, 1994; [ch.] Jessica Mary-Lynn Obacz; [ed.] Graduated in Newfoundland at "Roncolli Central High School" (Avondale); [hon.] "Second Class Honors" 1989-1990, "Certificate of Merit" from Avalon East Drama Association; [pers.] I wrote this poem when I was in high school. My teachers encouraged my writings. I was greatly influenced by Rudyard Kipling's writings. If you believe hard enough your dreams come true.; [a.] Spruce Grove Alberta, Canada

ODEGAARD, DOUGLAS F.
[pen.] Dovy; [b.] January 9, 1963, Moscow, ID; [p.] Del, Arlyss Odegaard; [m.] Cheri L. Odegaard, November 23, 1991; [ch.] Ryan and Jordyn Odegaard; [ed.] High, North Idaho College; [occ.] Truck Driver; [memb.] Teamsters; [oth. writ.] Several to my wife; [pers.] Imagine the hate, the weary, the mad. Imagine the happy, the joy, the glad. Imagine the uselessness, imagine the worthlessness. Imagine what I've had.; [a.] Post Falls, ID

ODUTAYO, LEKAN SOLA
[b.] September 16, 1962, Ibadan, Nigeria; [p.] Rasheed Odutayo, Shakirat Odutayo; [ed.] BSc. Microbiology; [occ.] Math Teacher, Taek Won Do Instructor; [memb.] Scarborough Arts Council,

United Taek Won Do International, Flying Fist Taek Won Do Association, Democratic Alliance for Nigeria in Canada; [hon.] Best Grade 12 Chemistry Student, Higher Marks Dedication to Teaching Award; [oth. writ.] Several poems published through Scarborough Arts Council, book of my poems titled One Face, many phases - reflections through the journey.; [pers.] "Poetry for me is a feeling and the sound of that feeling".; [a.] Markhan Ontario, Canada

OLIVIER, BRUCE
[b.] August 5, 1945, Winnipeg, Manitoba, Canada; [m.] Linda Olivier, August 29, 1969; [occ.] Self Emp. - specializing - Canadian Native Art; [a.] Surrey British Columbia, Canada

ORCHARD, DANA ELIZABETH
[pen.] Peg O; [b.] November 1, 1919, Flip, MO; [p.] Jessie and Powell Bales; [m.] Arthur Verne Orchard, June 25, 1937; [ch.] Noel Verne and Janis Alene; [ed.] Eminence High School, Kindergarten in Fullerton, CA, 1st and part of 2nd at Eminence, 2nd thru 10th in Augusta, KS; [occ.] Trying to be a valued member of my family; [memb.] West Eminence Christian Church; [oth. writ.] Column in local paper entitled "Peg's Palaver", poems and several articles on Turkey Hunting, also in local paper; [pers.] I, sometimes compose or rewrite poems to place on cards I send to several hundreds of people each year, reminding them on special days of God's love.; [a.] Eminence, MO

OSBORN, LOIS
[pen.] Lois Osborn; [b.] October 7, 1957, Bureau County; [p.] Oscar and Ruth Anderson; [m.] Dale Osborn, June 18, 1973; [ch.] Chris and Jenny; [ed.] Black Hawk College, East Campus - Kewanee, IL; [occ.] Student of NRI, Washington, DC; [memb.] Bureau County, Historical Society; [oth. writ.] Several editorials for local newspapers and an article for the "Times Past" column in the Peoria Journal Star; [pers.] I would like my writing to reflect the beauty and eloquence I find in my two great interests, nature and history.; [a.] Buda, IL

OSBORNE, BELINDA B.
[pen.] Linda Brown, Linda Jewett; [b.] October 20, 1956, Aberdeen, WA; [p.] Shariyne R. Blackwell; [m.] Edwin James Tuffree, May, 1994; [ch.] Rebecca Irene Brown, Dyan Marie Brown, Donald Matthew Brown; [ed.] Hoquiam High School, G.E.D. at Grays Harbor College; [occ.] Domestic Engineer; [memb.] Humptulips Grange; [oth. writ.] Poem "Life" published in "On The Threshold Of A Dream", poem "Reaching Out" to be published in "Spirit of the Age"; [pers.] Life is a learning process, to lose our ego's and find our Creator.; [a.] Aberdeen, WA

OSBORNE, JOSEPH D.
[b.] December 24, 1970, Wurzburg, Germany; [p.] David and Barbara Osborne; [ed.] Harrison High School, PIkes Peak Community College; [occ.] Maintenance man for your Valet Dry Cleaners, Student; [memb.] American Heart Association; [oth. writ.] This is the first time my work has been published; [pers.] My poems reflect my beliefs, and my emotions. They prove that there are still a few men who believe in romance.; [a.] Colorado Springs, CO

OTT, WILLIAM
[b.] June 18, 1920, California; [p.] Roy and Mirle Ott; [m.] Frances Ott, 1943; [ch.] William Gary, Kathryn Mirle; [ed.] Army Staff College, Army School of Physical Training, University of New Brunswick; [occ.] Retired; [memb.] International Society of Poets; [hon.] Two Editors Awards from The National Library of Poetry; [oth. writ.] Book - Poetic Musings, Book - More Poetic Musings, poems in local newspapers; [pers.] My poems reflect my inner thoughts at the time of writing. I try to keep them short with an easy, flowing cadence. I am best known for my political satire.; [a.] Ottawa Ontario, Canada

OVERTON, ROBERT HAROLD
[pen.] Rho; [b.] March 24, 1947, Knoxville, TN; [p.] A. L. Overton, Betty J. Overton; [m.] 1973; [ed.] Fulton High School, 1965, University of Tennessee, 1971, B.S. Political Science; [occ.] Freelance artist and musician; [oth. writ.] Various features and photo-essays in the Clinton (TN) Courier-News, 1974-75; [pers.] Most of my experience in verse writing has been in the form of song lyrics, this poem just burst forth one day as I was playing with my electric typewriter, inspired by the drawing which accompanied it.; [a.] Knoxville, TN

OWER, HEATHER NICOLE
[b.] September 4, 1979, Duarte; [p.] Robert and Donna Ower; [ed.] K-9th and still going; [occ.] School; [pers.] I think the only people who can write poetry are the people who have a strong feeling towards life, love, family, etc.; [a.] Glendora, CA

OWUSU-ADUENING, PAUL
[pen.] Derick Slave; [b.] July 26, 1954, Boni (Ashanti), Ghana; [p.] Kwasi Amoako-Ayaa, Mary Bronya; [ch.] Franklin - 15, Fred - 10, Fabian - 8; [ed.] St. Marys College (Takorandi) (1970-1974), Specialist Training College (Winneba) (1979-1981), University of Science and Technology (UST), College of Art (Kumasi) 1989-1992; [occ.] Sculptor, Art Teacher; [memb.] Voluntary Workzamps Assoc. of Ghanna, Road Safety Volunteer Corps (Ghana), Artists Assoc. of Ghana; [oth. writ.] Several poems published in national newspapers/magazines, The Mirror, The Pioneer and 'Step'. I've published several articles (themes: Educational/political.; [pers.] Poetry is an outburst of the pent-up feelings of the poet, his passionate feelings about situations, his view of life in its variant shades and postures and his rendition of the silent voice of nature. My idols or models poets, the romantic poets: Blake, Wordsworth, Shelley, African Poets: Dennis Brutus, Wole Soyinka, Maya Angelou.; [a.] Gaithersburg, MD

OXMAN, NANCY G.
[b.] February 8, 1951, Philadelphia, PA; [p.] Joan and Stanley Green; [m.] Stephen Oxman, November 26, 1981; [ch.] Pat, Jaimie and Kaitlin; [ed.] Springfield High, Penn State University and additional creative and non-fiction magazine writing courses; [occ.] I "Want-to-be" Poet; [pers.] My poems are of the "humankind" reaching out to the very deepest cranny of one's soul. I believe people should be open-minded to everything but particularly to each other. Loving peace.; [a.] Havertown, PA

PACK, JEREMY A.
[b.] July 27, 1978, Buffalo, NY; [p.] Donald and Jennie Pack; [ed.] Melbourne High School; [hon.]

Marching Band Superior Ratings 3 years. Jazz Band, Orchestra, Air Force, R.O.T.C.; [pers.] Life isn't about what if, it's about making it happen; [a.] Palm Bay, FL

PACK, VELMA SAMPSON
[b.] April 13, 1965, Brooklyn, NY; [p.] Henry J, and Nevater Sampson; [m.] Randy Fitzgerald Pack, June 30, 1990; [ch.] 2 daughters: Chelsea Noel and Alexandra Eliza; [ed.] Walbrook High School in Balto, MD, B.A. in Liberal Arts from College of Notre Dame of MD; [occ.] Admin Assistant; [hon.] AKA Outstanding Young Woman (1987), Outstanding Citizen Awards (1987) from Mayor and Governor Balto, MD; [pers.] Every dream should be shared, every path leading to good, taken. Leave no good deed undone. Have no undone. Have no undone deed mistaken for anything other than your intention - to do good.; [a.] Baltimore, MD

PALMER, CHARLOTTE
[b.] September 19, 1911, Iowa; [p.] Walter and Kathryn Skene; [m.] Allan Palmer M.D., February 14, 1949; [ch.] Allan Mathieu, John Shaben; [ed.] B.A., M.A. University of Michigan Dr. Speech Clinic, Bowling Green St. U. '42-'46 Bowling Green, Ohio Instr. of Speech, Univ. Michigan '46-'48 Dir. Alumni Affairs, UC San Francisco '68-'82; [occ.] Retired; [memb.] Chi Omega Sorority, U. of M. Meals on Wheels, San Francisco, UCSF Faculty Wives; [hon.] Two rewarding sons; [oth. writ.] To Carmen, My Flower Girl To Harold, The Candy Maker To Number One Cafe, House of Fat Gloria, Our Own Flowerette Parody on "Old Father William" by Lewis Carrol; [pers.] A wonderful, happy life.; [a.] San Francisco, CA

PALMER, MAUREEN ROSE
[pen.] Mo's Art; [b.] July 15, 1946, Prince Edward Island, Canada; [p.] Lloyd and Dorothy Wigmore; [m.] Harry Roy Palmer, July 27, 1963; [ch.] Nadine Michelle, Brian Rodger Annette Jenean, Brody Alexander and Cassie Roi; [ed.] High School 33 yrs. in the University of Life; [occ.] Home Business Floral. Design and full time Mom. Breeder of Purebred Ragdoll Cats.; [memb.] Calgary White Hatters Decorative Painters, Calgary Activettes, Member of Ragdoll Fancier Club International; [hon.] Floral Design: Calgary Activettes Awards: June Hollinrace for Honesty and Integrity, Club Spirit Awards; Creative Living Section, Calgary Exhibition and Stampede 1989, won a First in Section & Class in Porcelain Doll Class and a First in Section & Class in sculpting an original Camel from fur and using a wire frame; Ribbons from the African Violet Society (raised and sold African Violets for a time); My husband and I were Foster Parents; [oth. writ.] Other writings published to this date...Article in Ragdoll World magazine; [pers.] I love to celebrate life and endeavor to be creative. In all that I do. Favorite saying: Life is what happens to us while we are making other plans.; [a.] Calgary Alberta, Canada

PALMER, TINA
[pen.] Tina May Palmer; [p.] David Desjardins and Kathy Desjardins; [m.] Michael Palmer, May 14, 1993; [ch.] Kachine Amber May Palmer; [occ.] House wife, short story writer; [oth. writ.] Three short children stories, Two young adult stories a few poems and sayings. Not published, but looking for

my break.; [pers.] Never give up on your dreams and don't be afraid to try something different, you might be really good at it.; [a.] London Ontario, Canada

PAMIN, DIANA DOLHANCYK
[pen.] Diana Dolhancyk; [b.] December 13, Cleveland, OH; [p.] Peter Dolhancyk, Diana Dribus Dolhancyk; [m.] Leonard Pamin; [ch.] Diana Anne, Louis Peter; [ed.] West Tech High, Titus College of Cosmetology; hobbies, Interior Design, Art, Music, Books; [memb.] Arthritis Foundation, nominated into International Society of Poets. I've sponsored a young girl in India for the past 15 yrs.; [hon.] Awards for outstanding achievement in poetry for "The Parting" in Journey of the Mind, published by the NLP, for "Stormy" in Songs on the Wind, for "Shadow Side" in At Water's Edge. Received International Poet of Merit Award from the International Society of poets. Nominated for Poet of the Year 1995 by ISP. Accomplishment of Merit Award for Outstanding Literary Achievement, for the poem "Rain," in Journey to Our Dreams. Published by Creative Arts and Science. Honorable Mention for the poem "The View," in Treasured Poems of America, by Sparrowgrass Poetry. Chosen to be in Best Poems of 1996, the poem "Love No More." The poem, "The Parting," was in the Sun Star newspaper, along with a picture and write up on the front page.; [pers.] Always give someone a smile, you'll never know whose heart you might lighten.; [a.] North Royalton, OH

PAMPERIN, CARLA SUE
[pen.] Scarlet Carla; [b.] October 30, 1963, Rome, NY; [p.] Beverly Harms and Robert Gump; [m.] James Alan Pamperin, April 17, 1995; [ch.] Brandon Louis Pamperin (age 14), Terry James Pamperin (age 12); [ed.] Kindergarten in Sioux City, IA, 1st-6th Clarion, IA 50525, 7th-9th Clarion Jr. High, 10th-11th Clarion Senior High. G.E.D. in April of 1989 in ICCC in Eagle Grove. 1 year of college, majoring in Secretarial at ICC in Eagle Grove, IA 50533.; [occ.] I'm working towards a Journalism career! And writing short stories, and children's books and poems; [memb.] Church of the Nazerine, The Eagle Grove Fitness Center; [hon.] Through my school years, I won an Art Scholarship and all the Physical Fitness Awards; [oth. writ.] Poem titles: Impressions, A Mother's Request, What's Love, Dreams Will Conquer, The Night We Met, Twin Sister, Who Am I, Guess What I Am, No Time Is My Time, The Day Never Ends; [pers.] All of my poems I've wrote from my heart, living the moment. I express myself through writing, when I have time! My dream is to be a journalist!; [a.] Eagle Grove, IA

PANGELINAN, LYNN FRICA TUDELA
[b.] November 14, 1978, Saipan, CNMI; [p.] Maria T. Pangelinan, Joseph I. Pangelinan; [ed.] Grace Christian Academy, College of St. Benedict, Junior Statesmen of America at Georgetown and Yale; [occ.] College Student; [memb.] Saipan Youth Council, CNMI Drug-Free Club; [hon.] G.C.A. Eagle Award; [pers.] This is dedicated to my beloved aunt, Margarita P. Tudela, for David. Geraldine Tudela, David, and Frank Pangelinan, I love you my sister and brothers. Without the Lord, I am nothing.; [a.] Saint Joseph, MN

PANKIW, SUSANNA
[b.] September 16, 1969, Red Deer, Alberta, Canada; [p.] Wayne and Gail Walker; [m.] Darryl Pankiw,

July 20, 1991; [ed.] Elk Point Jr./Sr. High, Augustana University, University of Alberta; [occ.] Business Ed/Elementary Teacher; [memb.] Business Education Council; [hon.] Senior High Accounting Award; [oth. writ.] I have a collection of personal poems but until now none of them have been published. This was also the first poem I have ever sent away.; [pers.] Emerald Lake is a poem that is very close to my heart. It is about my marriage to my husband, beside Lake Louise, Alberta. A lifelong dream come true!; [a.] Edgerton Alberta, Canada

PANTOR, ANDREA I.
[pen.] None; [b.] June 24, 1981, Bucharest, Romania; [p.] Elena Ortansa Pantor & Dan M. Pantor; [m.] None (single); [ch.] None; [ed.] Kindergarten-6th: P.S. 139, The Rego Park School; 7th-8th: JHS 190 - Russell Sage (in Forest Hills, NY); Currently a 9th grader at the Bronx High School of Science; [occ.] Student; [memb.] The New York Junior Academy, League for Environmental and Animal Protection Union (at school), Unites States Tennis Association, Staff of Literary Publication (at school); [hon.] Valedictorian of graduating 8th grade class, Placed 1st in N.Y.C. for poetry in the Scolastic Art & Writing Awards (1993), Placed 3rd in United States for poetry in the Scholastic Art & Writing Awards (1993), Placed 2nd in N.Y.C. for poetry in the Scholastic Art & Writing Awards (1994), Placed #2 in the N.Y.C. regional Science Olympiad Group Championships (1995), Placed #6 (out of 28 competitors) in the N.Y.S. Science Olympiad Championships in Syracuse, NY (1995), Poem chosen to be published in the annual school literary publication named: "Dynamo," Age 10-11 ranked #9 in the N.E. Region of the U.S. in Tennis.; [oth. writ.] 7th grade: 3 articles published in school publication; 8th grade: Take-Your-Daughters-to-work-Day Money Magazine Publication: 1 article written on an editor; A poem will be published in the annual literary publication at school; [pers.] Inspiration, you ask? Each cranny has been derived from my INSURMOUNTABLE family and friends: dead and alive.; [a.] Rego Park, NY

PAPION, CONNIE MARIE
[b.] March 10, 1961, Charles Town, WV; [p.] Mr. and Mrs. Andrew Young; [m.] Christopher Papion, June 13, 1987; [ed.] Associates Degree; [occ.] US Army; [memb.] First Baptist of Merrifield, Merrifield, VA Church membership; [hon.] Letters and awards of Commendation for Military Service High School basketball records. M.V.P. and points scored in a game.; [oth. writ.] Poems read and published in church news letters and Women's Ministry group; [pers.] I strive to acknowledge the presence of God and up list mankind spiritually in my writings , also expose God's goodness, mercy, and grace through my writings.; [a.] Lorton, VA

PARENT, SYLVIA
[b.] Ottawa, Ontario, Canada; [p.] Archille Parent and Cecilia Virginia Smith; [m.] Randy Demmon; [ch.] Melanie, Micheline and Julien; [ed.] B.A. Honours Linguistics, B. Education; [occ.] Elementary School Teacher and Storyteller; [memb.] Director of TEMA Signature-Singers and of 'Pervenche' (Storytelling); [oth. writ.] Children stories and songs in French and English; [pers.] "The child in each of us is empowered by stimulating our sense of wonder at the beauty in the ordinary. Thus

we explore the extraordinary."; [a.] Gloucester Ontario, Canada

PARKER, MAXINE L.
[b.] December 27, 1929, Richland, IN; [p.] L. Herrell Parker and Ada Silvey Parker; [ed.] Luce Township High School, Tennessee Temple College; [occ.] Retired; [oth. writ.] Poetry in High School Anthologies "Young America Sings", "1945 Pageant of Poetry", and "Poetry Digest Anthology"; [pers.] I have a love for animals, music, and genealogy.; [a.] Richland, IN

PARKER, MAZELL
[pen.] Zetta; [b.] AK; [p.] Lilian and Willie H. Jones Jr.; [ch.] Gary A. Ridgle and Kenneth Parker; [ed.] B.A. degree Dominguez Hills, University, Carson, California; [occ.] Social worker, Department of Children and Family Services - Los Angeles, CA; [memb.] Bethel AME Church Los Angeles, CA; [hon.] ISP member; [oth. writ.] Several poems published numerous other writings not published poems; [pers.] I strive to inspire readers, evoke emotions, arouse the senses to help seek the higher self; [a.] Los Angeles, CA

PARKS, DONALD WAYNE
[b.] January 4, 1963, Danville, VA; [p.] Raymond Douglas Parks and Corinne Widener Parks; [m.] Sandra Hope Wade, December 20, 1981; [ch.] Jennifer Whitney Parks; [pers.] This poem was written in honor of my grandfather, Roby Preston (Pres) Widener, the week before his death. The title is in part a statement in his namesake, and my wish for him. The poem is a reflection of how he and his wife, Bonnie Roxie Dunn Widener, lived their lives and cared for their family. The greatest wisdom and the greatest peace comes from understanding the things that are simple. More information on the R. P. Widener family may be found in "The Families of Washington Country and Bristol, VA", printed in 1996.; [a.] Danville, VA

PASINI, JACQUELINE
[b.] February 21, 1962, Buffalo, NY; [p.] James and Olivia Miller; [m.] John Joseph Pasini, May 5, 1995; [ed.] Chucky Doak High School - Graduated East Tenn. STate University 6 months; [occ.] Flight attendant with a Major Airline; [pers.] I wish to live my life in such a way that is pleasing to God.; [a.] Boca Raton, FL

PATENAUDE, RENEE
[pen.] Renee Patenaude, Raven, Sister Sun; [b.] January 7, 1971, Toronto, Canada; [p.] Arthur and Sandra; [occ.] Student/Esthetics; [oth. writ.] Publications in The Toronto Sun; [pers.] I like to call myself a "second-generation" hippie, who pushes herself to reach my innermust emotions through my poetry/lyrics. I am drawn to may written styles in the music Industry, from John Lennon to Courtney Love. I have a special drawing to the female artist and/or writers for their inspiration and show of emotions, And I still believe in the possibility of Peace, Love and Happiness. If not just for-but within ourselves; [a.] Mississauga Ontario, Canada

PATRYK, KIMBERLY
[b.] February 25, 1979, Philadelphia; [p.] Susan Patryk and John Patryk; [ed.] Naples High School; [hon.] National Honor Society; [a.] Bonita Springs, FL

PATTERSON, DARRYL
[b.] February 24, 1964, Lindsay; [p.] Barry Patterson and Sharon Patterson; [m.] Bonnie Patterson, October 11, 1991; [ch.] Mitchell Patterson and Mason Patterson; [ed.] Lindsay Collegiate, University of Waterloo, Nipissing University; [occ.] Teacher, Fenelon Township Public School; [pers.] Twice blessed. I love being a Dad.; [a.] Woodville Ontario, Canada

PATTERSON JR., GORDON D.
[pen.] Gordon D. Patterson Jr.; [b.] May 6, 1923, Columbus, OH; [p.] Gordon and Ethel Patterson; [ed.] B.S. Allegheny College, Meadville PA, M.S., Ph.D., Purdue University Fraternity, Alpha Chi Rho.; [occ.] Retired Chemist; [memb.] Westmister Presbyterian Church, Wilmington DE; [oth. writ.] Only technical (chemistry) plus "Creative Writing" at the Lorelton Retirement Home, Wilmington.; [a.] Wilmington, DE

PATTERSON, LOUISE EDNA
[b.] August 27, 1928, Pecos, TX; [p.] Amber Ross, Abbot Ross; [ch.] Diane Varnado and Patricia Eley; [ed.] High School; [occ.] Communication Manager Ochsner Foundation Hospital; [pers.] This poem was written in honor of my brother, William H. Ross, who suffers with Alzheimer's disease.; [a.] River Ridge, LA

PEARSON, DEBRA K. SHAW
[pen.] D. Kays Inspirational; [b.] August 11, 1956, Wichita, KS; [p.] Cecil J. Sr. and Glady's Shaw; [m.] Robert J. Pearson; [oth. writ.] Over 200 poems C 1995 Copyright; [pers.] To God be the Glory...for the gift He works through me, to inspire and minister encouraging words to this people as we travel through this life. Lord give us strength.; [a.] Wichita, KS

PEEBLES, LAURA
[pen.] Ireland Smith; [b.] July 31, 1981, Savannah, GA; [p.] Paula Peebles and Gary Peebles; [ed.] St. James Catholic School, Thomas Heyward Academy; [occ.] Student; [hon.] The performance Evaluation Clinic Award 1st place for the Art In The Park Contest; [pers.] I think life is very fragile and you should take the time to realize all the little things that make, life wonderful.; [a.] Early Branch, SC

PELLETIER, JANICE VERGINA
[b.] March 1, 1966, Edmonton, Alberta, Canada; [p.] Rod Biolo, Verna Biolo; [m.] Darcy Pelletier, July 1, 1989; [ch.] Jessica Ashlie, Erin Marie; [ed.] G.H. Primeaw High School, Alberta College, N.A.I.T., Grant MacEwan Community College; [occ.] Shop Clerk, Town of Morinvilley Morinville, AB; [hon.] Honor of being a mom. Honor roles at Alberta College N.A.I.T.; [oth. writ.] Non-published personal writings; [pers.] With the greatest dignity and honor, this poem is dedicated to Cathy Clarks. Thank you for the words of life I will carry always and for the perspective of my reality.; [a.] Legal Alberta, Canada

PEMBERTON, DORA D.
[b.] January 8, 1949, Phoenix; [p.] Levon O. Cunningham; [ch.] Anna, Glenn, Marc; [ed.] Scholarship ASU for Violin, Piano - Maj.; [occ.] Nurse - in Home Health; [oth. writ.] The Working Nurse Blues Country Club Doctor - many more; [pers.] All my poems are true stories of my patients and myself.; [a.] Phoenix, AZ

PENLAND, PATRICK A.
[ed.] PhD and post-doctorals in survey research and information science; [occ.] Information Consultant; [pers.] Background: Long involved with movements leading to a new age of universal knowledge, Patrick R. Penland has had filed service in the information delivery systems of such states as Michigan, North Carolina, and provincial Ontario. In addition, he has been associated with various universities including Oklahoma, Southern Connecticut, Minnesota, Toronto and the University of Pittsburgh. As an educator, Professor Penland has gone to great lengths to train other consultants. Using diverse methods including innovative instructional television, he has lectured extensively instructional television, he has lectured extensively throughout the United States as well as for Fulbright assignments in India, Iraq, Jordan, Israel, Mexico, Thailand, Taiwan, Manila, several European countries and Canada. The vast of Patrick R. Penland's research has been published in several books and numerous trade magazines. His name has appeared in various biographical listings of consultance. He has served on the editorial boards of professional journals. Emerging Direction: In the field of creative literature, Patrick R. Penland is already a published novelist. However with this contribution to the present anthology, Beneath the Harvest Moon, he has found an outlet for extensive poetic endeavor.; [a.] Bellingham, WA

PENNEY, HELEN SILKA
[pen.] Cheryl- Jean Donovan and Helen Graeme; [b.] June 24, 1934, Sand East, Windsor, Ontario, Canada; [p.] John and Doris; [m.] Charles Armstrong Penney; [ch.] Aunt to Christopher Dale, Darlene and Alistair Burns; [ed.] B.A. (University of Windsor) Masters Courses (University of Windsor), Post-grad (University of Toronto); [occ.] Teacher; [memb.] Women Writers of Windsor, Can Authors Association, International Society of Poets, Royal Country Scottish Dancers, the SCOTTISH CLUB of Windsor, ON.T., Can. Am. Friendship Centre, Windsor Home and School Council; [hon.] From students and parents Toronto, Social Studies (W.D. Lowe- av. 100%) 1986 (University Teacher's Law Course) from Husband, (Top class marks) Distinguished Poet-of -Merit Award (International Society of Poets), Editor's choice Award 1995 (National Library of Poetry); [oth. writ.] Gems of Peace (all poetry) Devon, England, 5 plays in the past, in progress- "Wee Bobby of Greyfriars" short story England, India Catholic Journal (University of Chicago) short story, many general writings yet to be published.; [pers.] I try to instill in my readers, an appreciation for the aesthetic qualities found in creation and in all Creatures, human or otherwise. I also hope that readers will learn to appreciate the necessity of all cultures to practise the "Brotherhood of Man" idea.; [a.] Windsor Ontario, Canada

PENROD, DORIS ANNA
[b.] November 9, 1912, Toledo, OH; [p.] Jacob Edwin Penrod, Anna Catherine Spatz Penrod; [ed.] B.S. in Ed., M. Ed., University of Cincinnati, Ohio; [occ.] Retired teacher; [memb.] Christ Church Cathedral (Episcopal), Daughters of the American Revolution, Daughters of the American Colonists, Altar Guild of Cathedral, Retired Teacher Ohio, Retired Federal Employees, Women's Committee of Cincinnati Symphony, (soon member of Dames of 17th Century), Eastern Star; [hon.] Graduate Cum Laude U. C., Historian, Waldschmidt House, Honor Grad High School (Maumee), College Honor in Voice, Dean's List, Elegy, orchestral composition performed by Cincinnati Civic Orchestra; [oth. writ.] Currently working on a history of Waldschmidt House, a Daughters of the American Revolution museum located in Camp Dennison, Ohio, suburb of Cincinnati. Literary Editor to High School Annual; [pers.] I believe a life firmly grounded in the teachings of Jesus, the Christ, will sail serenely through all of the storms of life and doubly enjoy the peaceful, fulfilled times.; [a.] Cincinnati, OH

PENTECOST, COLANDRA
[b.] August 28, 1975, Gatesville, TX; [p.] Floyd and Pamela Pentecost; [ed.] West Deleware Senior High School, University of Dubuque; [occ.] Poet, writer; [hon.] High School Honor Roll; [pers.] My one wish is to touch the hearts of those who read my work. I wish to give hope to the lost and wealth of the soul to the poor.; [a.] Hamilton, TX

PENTECOST, EILEEN
[b.] April 24, 1918, Nashville, TN; [p.] Frank and Helen Pentecost; [ed.] Garfield High School (Akron OH) St. John College (Cleveland OH) Mercyhurst College (Erie PA); [occ.] Volunteer Tutor, Teaching adults to read ACCESS to Literacy dept, Triton College (River Grove IL); [memb.] St Edmund Parish (Oak IL) Sister of St. Dominic (Akron OH) Delta Kappa Gamma Society, Inc.; [hon.] Teacher of the Year 1995 Triton College, Access to Literacy Department; [pers.] There is a spark of creativity in person. Caring teachers must "fire" it. My most memorable moment - a child said to me, "Sister Eileen, you love all children."

PENUEL, DEBRA NELSON
[pen.] Debbie Penuel; [b.] August 5, 1955, Brooklyn, NY; [m.] Jim Penuel, October 20, 1978; [ch.] Evelyn, Christina, Alison; [ed.] Broome Community College, R.N. University of New Orleans, B.B.A.; [occ.] Registered Nurse, Artist, Poet; [pers.] My poetry and art reflect my passionate journey of self discovery. I am a student of Life's Great Mysteries.; [a.] Fort Myers, FL

PERRI, ANGELA M.
[b.] February 4, 1975, Loyola Hosp.; [p.] Barbra J. and Nicholas; [ed.] Proviso West High School, Triton College, and the School of the Art Institute of Chicago, at age 16 to study painting and sculpture; [occ.] Student, Poet, Artist; [memb.] American Heart Assoc., and American Red Cross; [hon.] Yearbook, Cultural Arts and Poetry Awards; [oth. writ.] Several other non-published poems and short stories; [pers.] I believe there are 3 things that make any form of artist. A little insanity, a lot of creativity, and an over flow of emotions.; [a.] Westchester, IL

PETERS, JACKIE
[pen.] Jackie Peters; [b.] December 16, 1940, Reading, MA; [p.] Alberta Ashworth and Raymond Ashworth; [m.] Dennis Coldwell, November 11, 1988; [ch.] Doug, Scott, Kim, Kellie; [ed.] Wilmington High College, NECC, Bradford College; [occ.] Graphic Designer, DRI McGraw Hill; [hon.] Dean's List, graduated Magna Cum Laude, Poetry Contest Semi-Finalist in St. Francis Institute Contest, Andover and 3 poems in Anthology "Lelivre: A Collection of Poems", Pen and Ink Artwork published in Textbook "The Surface Plane" by Boles/Newman; [oth. writ.] "Daring to Begin Again" (Book of personal poems and illustrations published at Bradford College); [pers.] I write to get a better perspective of circumstances that occur in my life and hope that my insights can help others.; [a.] Bradford, MA

PETERS, MELISSA
[b.] June 29, 1980, Phoenix, AZ; [p.] Dwain and Lois Peters; [ed.] Intelli Charter School; [occ.] School; [pers.] I write how I feel and see teenage lives today. I'm only 15 but I try to get teenagers to see that life is beautiful with out drugs, having sex and having children at such a young age.; [a.] Glendale, AZ

PETERSON, AMY
[b.] March 10, 1979, Alexandria, VA; [p.] James Peterson, Margaret Peterson; [ed.] Thomas A. Edison High School; [oth. writ.] Several poems. This particular one was the first one I ever wrote. It was also published in my high school Literary Magazine.; [a.] Alexandria, VA

PETERSON, DOROTHY
[b.] February 19, 1951, Spartanburg, SC; [p.] Jessie and Virginia Barke Humphries; [m.] Marcus Chandler, June 24, 1990; [ch.] Dorothy, Richard, Randall; [ed.] Jr., at Limestone College in Counselling and Human Services; [occ.] Student; [pers.] This poem was written in honor of my son Randall, he died December 19, 1994, and his book of poetry named "A Child's Reign Is Not Insane" was published December 1995. He is my baby boy, my love, my joy.; [a.] Gaffney, SC

PETERSON, HOWARD L.
[pen.] Peter Lee; [b.] April 12, 1931, Seattle, WA; [p.] Laura and Hjalmer Peterson, Deceased; [ed.] Wallance High School, Wallace Idaho, Courses from Famous Writers and Inst. of Children's Literature; [occ.] Retired Airline Sales Agent; [memb.] Elks Lodge, #1800, Lake City, Wa.; [hon.] This poem has also been accepted by Vintage Magazine for publication in their spring '96 issue.; [oth. writ.] On Audio - 'Deadly Revenge', 'Death of the Panther' and 'The Deadly Dark'. Murder mysteries written under my name. I use a pen name for children's stories.; [pers.] I merely want to entertain the reader. Fiction, non-fiction, poetry, serious, humorous or fanciful works, I seek to entertain.; [a.] Bothell, WA

PETERSON, JACLYN
[b.] July 7, 1977, Springfield, Mass; [p.] Roger and Cusha Peterson; [ed.] Freshman at Northern Arizona University; [memb.] Associated Students of Northern Arizona University (ASNAU); [hon.] Alpha Dotta Pi; [pers.] Finding someone is special treat that one looks forward to in life, and weather to meet them in a class of they meet you while standing on a table dancing. Hold on them, and enjoy them for they are truly special.; [a.] Flagstoff, AZ

PETERSON, LEE W.
[b.] May 1, 1941, Huntington Park, CA; [p.] Wayne and Blanche Peterson; [m.] Kathleen Fullmer, August 26, 1965; [ch.] Debra, Shawn, Preston, Sterling, Forrest, Heidi, Sheridan, Autumn; [ed.] Mesa High School, Arizona State U., Brigham Young University (B.S., M.S.); [occ.] Physical

Education Teacher-Dobson High School, Mesa, Ariz. - Football, Wrestling Coach; [memb.] Arizona Coaches Assoc., Nat'l. High School Coaches Assoc., Mesa Education Assoc., Ariz. Education Assoc., Nat'l. Education Assoc.; [hon.] Arizona Assistant Coach of the Year 1993, Dean's List BYV, Several Service Awards from American Red Cross; [oth. writ.] Several articles in "Arizona Youth" Magazine; [pers.] To achieve balance in our lives, we need to pause to enjoy the wonders around us. Through words, we can create lasting impressions of those pauses.; [a.] Mesa, AZ

PETERSON, LELA MELANIE
[pen.] Andrea Marcus; [b.] October 24, 1928, Deming, NM; [p.] Leonard and Leona Peterson; [m.] Louis T.; [ed.] Graduate - Juarez Stake Academy Colonia Juarez, Chih., Mexico Lamson Business College and Kinman Business University in Spokane, WA.; [occ.] Retire; [memb.] Arizona Authors Association; [hon.] Editor's Choice Award presented by the National Library of Poetry in 1994; [oth. writ.] Compiling Family History, Book of Poetry, entitled "A Whisper of a Dream" and another entitled "Winged Seeds in the Sun. A fiction novel Entitled "Angel Feathers" - Pseudonym - Andrea Marcus Poetry Society, Colorado and Modern Poetry Society in Florida.; [pers.] The poems I write are attic treasures of my mind to share with family and friends.; [a.] Phoenix, AZ

PETERSON, LISA A.
[b.] April 26, 1956, Altus, OK; [p.] Jerry Peterson Jolonda Peterson; [ed.] Laura Easter, M. Michelle Easter, University of maryland Baltimore County, University of Maryland School of Social Work; [occ.] Social Worker; [memb.] National Association of Social Work, U.M.A.B. Alumni Assoc.; [hon.] Master of Social Work, Phi Kappa Phi, Omicran Delta Kappa, Dean's List, Who's who Among Student's in American Universities 1994, Governor's Citation - 1991, Louis L. Kaplan Scholarship, Charlotte, L. Newcombe Scholarship, House of Delegates Scholarships; [oth. writ.] Poems published in A Sea of Treasures, by the Nat'l. Library of Poetry and the Horrisburg Chapter N.O.W. newsletters; [pers.] My desire is to infuse my poetry with humanity and the make it breathe, sweat, laugh and cry.; [a.] Columbia, MD

PETERSON, ROYAL F.
[pen.] Royal F. Peterson; [b.] August 2, 1910, Olsburg, KS; [p.] Oscar and Natalia Peterson; [m.] Hanna Helene (Nelson) Peterson, July 7, 1937; [ch.] James, Miriam and Lois; [ed.] Graduate of Bethany College, Lindsborg, KS. BA 1993. Graduate, Augustana Theol. Seminary, Rock Island Ill. Degree: Master of Divinity, 1937, Augustana Theol. Seminary now merged with LSTC...Luth. School of Theology at Chicago); [occ.] Now retired; [memb.] Ministerium of the ELCA (Ev. Lutheran Church in America, and the Nebraska Synod of the ELCA....First Ev. Luth. Church in Lincoln, Nebraska; [hon.] A dozen and a half diplomas and awards are hanging on the walls of my study, and visible from my chair as I type; [oth. writ.] Baptized Into Christ, Publ. by Augustana Book Concern, Rock Island. Revisionist for translation from Swedish of Rosinous' Daily Meditations by J. Elmer Dalgren...Condensing more than 700 pages to make published volume of 380 pages. Publ. 19973.

Translated two chapters of a Swedish published by another writer inviting a dozen translators to participate in this publication. Printed two volumes of my poems by mimeograph a number of years ago.; [pers.] I believe in the Apostles Creed dating from the 5th Century and earlier, setting forth a relationship with the Triune God in which there is hope of God's highest purposes for the believer to be realized.; [a.] Lincoln, NE

PHILIPP, TONIA
[b.] September 9, 1975, Cedar Rapids, IA; [p.] Timothy Philipp, Shirley Philipp; [ed.] LaSalle High School, Kirkwood Community College, Mount Mercy College; [occ.] Student; [hon.] Phi Theta Kappa, Dean's List; [pers.] Poetry is a reflection of the mind, heart and soul.; [a.] Solon, IA

PHILIPS, JUDITH M.
[pen.] Judy Philips; [b.] February 26, 1935, Grafton, WV; [p.] Grover White, Myrtle White; [ch.] Alesia, Donna and Danny; [ed.] Flemington High Salem College; [occ.] Behavioral Health, United Hospital Center Clarksburgville; [pers.] My poems reflects life experiences of my family friends and myself.; [a.] Mount Clare, WV

PHILIPS, TANYA VICKERS
[b.] May 9, 1970, Gainsville, GA; [p.] David and Sandra Vickers; [ed.] As in Business Management; [occ.] Business Management for a contrasting firm; [oth. writ.] I have a personal collection of short stories and poems that I have written over the years.; [pers.] Edgar Allen Poe is a favorite Author of mine. I feel that my writing style is similar to his and writing poetry when I am angry calms the anger. I believe anger is shown in my work.; [a.] Virginia Beach, VA

PHILLIPS, PAMELA KELLY
[b.] April 13, 1956, Cincinnati, OH; [p.] Early Kelly, Luere Kelly; [m.] Brent Phillips, June 23, 1979; [ch.] Kamillah Aisha, Brenton Stanford; [ed.] Walnut Hills High School University of Cincinnati Defense Information School; [occ.] Public Affairs Specialist; [memb.] Society of Environmental Journalists, National Association of Black Journalists, Society of Professional Journalists, Zeta Phi Beta Sorority; [hon.] Academic and Professional Achievement Awards; [oth. writ.] Inclusion on Anthology "Full Circle Sixteen"; [pers.] My best poetry captures a moment in time and preserves it for all eternity.; [a.] Tullahoma, TN

PHILLIPS, PAMELA
[pen.] Whirling Rainbow Woman; [b.] March 15, 1965, Emporia, KS; [p.] Ed Burris; [ch.] Shaun and Zachery Phillips; [ed.] Received my GED and I'm attending Highland Community College; [occ.] I own my Jewelry Store; [oth. writ.] I have many other poems that I have written which come straight from my heart. Of course all the credit goes to the Great Spirit.; [pers.] I owe all my influences to the Indian culture. I have studied long and hard on many different tribes, which have led me to my own Indian name, "Whirling Rainbow Woman." My greatest inspiration is my two sons, Shaun and Zachery.; [a.] Horton, KS

PHILLIPS, ROBIN
[b.] June 16, 1948, Long Beach, CA; [p.] Gene

Saxby and Mary Edwards; [m.] Divorced; [ch.] Katy, Sean, Andy, Becky; [ed.] BA, Psychology CA, State University, Long Beach, UC Irvine Certificate, Counseling Skills, currently Felden Krais Student; [occ.] Development Therapist and Minister; [memb.] Infant Development Association, Rigpa, Reiki Outreach International Saddleback Valley Educational Foundation, Felden Krais Guild; [hon.] Nominated to Phi Delta Kappa, Service Award, Phi Gamma Delta; [pers.] Motion, particularly human movement, is the work I do and permeates my poetry. Whether it's child rearing, meditation or financial planning change always happens.; [a.] Laguna Niguel, CA

PHILP, MOIRA S.
[b.] May 1, 1933, George Town, ON; [ch.] Bruce, Erica, Anne and Michael; [ed.] Diploma - Home Economics MacDonald Institute U. of Guelph; [occ.] Retired; [oth. writ.] Sometime columnist for today's senior newspaper; [pers.] My journey has been filled with adventure. I look forward to the next chapter.; [a.] London Ontario, Canada

PHILP, STACY ANN
[b.] April 29, 1975; [p.] Arlene and late Michael Philp; [ed.] Currently attending Northeast Missouri State University of Kirksville, Missouri; [pers.] My love and thanks to my mother and sister, Tammy, who love me unconditionally and to Jennifer Kooistra who stands by me with her friendship and spiritual guidance. Above all my thanks to God for showing me I cannot live my life alone for others I touch are either strengthened by mine or weakened just as much.

PHIPPEN, JUNE
[pen.] June Phippen; [b.] February 2, 1936, Rayleigh Essex, England; [p.] Elizabeth and John Harrison; [m.] James Phippen, October 10, 1963; [ch.] Melody and Todd; [ed.] Gordan School for Girls, Crooks Business College; [occ.] Homemayer; [oth. writ.] "Button" is my first poem to be recognized; [pers.] "Family" is my first inclination in the field of poetry. I lean toward their past and present.; [a.] Courtice Ontario, Canada

PHYLENE, MAX
[pen.] "C'mon Here"; [b.] July 4, 1980, Stoop, IL; [p.] Mr. Allunknown Cohen; [ed.] Dawes School & ETHS in Evanston; Awful Hardnox School in Stoop, IL; [occ.] Writer, Dreamer, Fetcher; [memb.] Featherly Writers Group; Association of Literature Evaluations; PTA; [hon.] 3rd Place in Paws & Reflect Competition in 1990; Honorable Mention in 1991 Symposium of Spritual Insights; [oth. writ.] "Scratch, It's Only Me," "Green Eyes Are Not Envy," Several adult training inciteful publications & CATalogs; [pers.] To go where no human has gone before; to leap space and time while seeking goodies; and to CAT-or-gize the animal with humane elements.; [a.] Evanston, IL

PIATEK, LISA
[pen.] Fox Friday; [b.] July 18, 1897; [p.] Christine Piatek; [ed.] Grade 11 Student; [hon.] The honor of being blessed with a merciful God; [pers.] May love be stronger than jealousy and wait among the throned meadows to caress a rose.

PICHACH, CANDACE
[b.] August 17, 1980, Edmonton, Alberta, Canada;
[p.] Barb and Bob Pichach; [ed.] Memorial
Composite High, Duffied Junior High/Elementary;
[occ.] Currently in grade 10 at Memorial High; [a.]
Duffield Alberta, Canada

PICHURSKI, THEA ALIX
[b.] June 15, 1971, Toronto, Ontario, Canada; [p.]
Edward and Joan Pichurski; [ed.] Carleton
University Major Women Studies and History
Seneca College Law Enforcement Degree Huron
Heights Secondary School; [occ.] Student full time
special events coordinator - Carleton U. Women
Centre; [oth. writ.] Silence death publish in
Hysteriae; [pers.] The dream never dies the dreamer.;
[a.] Ottawa Ontario, Canada

PIERCE, TONYA
[b.] January 18, 1982, Marreo, LA; [p.] Gary and
Barbara Pierce; [ed.] 8th grader; [pers.] I love writing
poems. I one day would like to sing. Yes, I would
love to write more poems. I am 13 and still want to
be a singer now.; [a.] Westwego, LA

PIESZCHALA, TERRY
[b.] November 18, 1948, Hammond, IN; [p.] Andrew
Pieszchala, Maxine Bussart Craig; [ed.] Hillsborough
High Graduate; [occ.] Genealogical Researcher, Ex-
Meatcutter Assistant, former Banker; [memb.]
Church of the Nazarene, History Book Club, "Lost
In Space" Fan Club (St. Louis MO); [hon.] Award of
Merit Certificate for the poem "Bicentennial
Review" written in 1976, from World of Poetry
1990, Golden Poet Award 1991 from World of
Poetry, Editor's Choice Award 1995, from The
National Library of Poetry; [oth. writ.] Several
poems including Ancestors of Long Ago (in the
anthology "Edge of Twilight"), Astor, John Jacob
4th, Chronicle of a Fast, Halloween Night, Hot and
Humid, Lizzie Borden (in the anthology "Best
Poems of 1996"), Molasses and Honeysuckle Time,
My Country Grandmother, Old Maid Washes Feet
(in the anthology" A Moment in Time"), and Star
Dust. Also compiled books "Lest They Be
Forgotten", The Brinkerhoff-Bussart Genealogy and
Custer's Last Stand.; [pers.] Good poetry is like a
cool breeze of fresh air. Poems abound, but good
ones are rare.; [a.] Tampa, FL

PIKE, SISTER MARY THERESE
[b.] April 14, 1914, Lynn, MA; [p.] Elmer Pike,
Pansy G. Pike; [ed.] BS in Education, MA in Art;
[occ.] Retired; [memb.] Notre Dame V. Alumni,
Precious Blood Society Immaculate Conception
Chapel; [hon.] First place in several art shows,
"Understanding Modern Art" published in P.B.
Society Paper, Chairman of Art Board for City
Catholic Schools in Cincinnati, Ohio; [oth. writ.] Art
history course for Mount Marty College, S. Dakota
creative writing course for St. Mary's Hi Sch., Phx.,
Arizona. Many unpublish poems, plays that mere
perform. Choreographies for ballets.; [pers.] The
only worthwhile life is the one spent in doing good
for others.

PIKINA, ANNA
[b.] December 13, 1978, Dubna, Russia; [p.]
Alexander Pikina, Lidia Didenko; [ed.] Quince
Orchard High School, 11 grade, student; [occ.]
Student; [a.] Gaithersburg, MD

PILGER, MARSHA
[b.] June 10, 1944, Council Bluffs, IA; [p.] Mr. and
Mrs. Marshall Lockerby; [m.] Ronald G. Pilger, July
17, 1965; [ch.] Timothy and Andrew; [ed.] Bellevue
University (one year); [occ.] First Bank of Iowa;
[memb.] Pres, Pottawattamie Co. Genealogical
Society, Life Mbr Beta Sigma Phi Sorority, Nat'l
May Power Soc, Nat'l Daughters of the American,
Rev. War. Nat'l Soc of Ancient and Honorable
Artillery Society; [hon.] Beta Sigma Phi "Woman of
the Year"; [oth. writ.] Historical Documents and
articles for various histories, Pub. "Pilger Newslet-
ter" annually, three family histories published, (The
Locker by Family, Pilger Heritage, Memories of
Grandma" also one limited vol. issue of poetry by
family members entitled, "Reflections"; [pers.]
"Leave your footsteps upon the land for others shall
follow."; [a.] Council Bluffs, IA

PINEDA, CATHLENE
[b.] March 1, 1984, Vancouver; [p.] Edgar Pineda,
Charlene Forsyth-Pineda; [ed.] 6th grade student. I
am 11, and attend Mounds Park Academy; [occ.]
Student and Pianist; [hon.] Piano Awards. Best
Piano Player 6th Grade under U. St. Paul; [oth. writ.]
Inspiring stories, I find wherever something dramatic
happens to me, I write it down.; [pers.] I write down
my emotions. Whatever I felt or feel, I put down. I
put it in my vision, the way I see the problem, and let
my fingers type.; [a.] Saint Paul, MN

PINGLETON, CRYSTAL FAYE
[pen.] Cameo; [b.] December 4, 1982, Fort Walton
Beach, FL; [p.] Craig W. and Cheryl F. Steward;
[ed.] 7th grade; [occ.] Student; [memb.] Image,
Youth of America, Jr. Honor Society, First Baptist
Church of Lemay, All American Scholar Organization; [hon.] President's Academic Excellence Award,
Honor Roll Attendance Award, Several Pageant
Awards, Karate Awards; [pers.] If your mind can
dream it, your heart believes it, let your hands
achieve it!; [a.] Saint Louis, MO

PIPER, JO
[b.] April 5, 1929, Lake City, IA; [p.] Wilber and
Ella Chase; [m.] Charles M. Piper, March 23, 1951;
[ch.] Steven, Kevin, Alan; [ed.] BA in Education,
Rebuilding Seminars, Volunteer Training, Writing
Seminars; [occ.] Poet, Homemaker, Volunteer;
[memb.] International Society of Poets, Pi Tau Phi
Sorority, Church of Christ, Advisory Council for
Senior Transportation; [hon.] Distinguished Member
of International Society of Poets, College Honor
Society, 10 Editor's Choice Award from NLP; [oth.
writ.] "The Eden of Age" Retirement Recipe, "The
Gift", "The Word", "Love Letter", publications in
local paper; [pers.] "Love the Now" is completely
about and for a man with the name of Bill. He has
enriched my life more than he will ever know.; [a.]
Loveland, CO

PLATT, RICHARD
[pen.] Robin Williams; [b.] March 29, 1951, Ottawa,
Ontario, Canada; [p.] Percy Platt, Elsie McCalg; [m.]
Rita Berger; [ch.] Wayne, Jeffrey, Melanie, Alison;
[ed.] Champlain High School, Carleton University;
[occ.] Police Sergeant Ottawa Carleton Regional
Police Ottawa, Ontario, Canada; [oth. writ.] Several
poems, and children's stories including: "The
Twinkling Street Light" and "The Christmas
Sleigh."; [pers.] Children's imagination is both

constant and endless. It is a magical possession of
every child. I attempt to capture this magic through
the eyes of children.; [a.] Nepean Ontario, Canada

PLUM, FRANCIS
[b.] September 10, 1965, Spirit River, Alberta,
Canada; [p.] Stanley and Bertha Plum; [ed.] High
School, College programs self-taught typist,
computer, art, writing, drafting, sculpturing, etc.;
[occ.] Laborer; [hon.] County fair 1st place ribbons
on art work and photography; [oth. writ.] None
published, but many good poetry and prose
selections, also novels and short stories; [pers.] I
believe that each person should be in tuned to their
surroundings, to beware of danger and treat every
person as a friend.; [a.] Grande Prairie Alberta,
Canada

POLLARD, VESTA L.
[b.] August 12, 1923, Antlers, OK; [p.] Noah
Jackson and Margie A. Pollard; [ch.] Michael,
Charles, Daina, Lisa; [ed.] Elementary School -
Wasco, CA., Wasco High School, College of Beauty
Cosmetology, Bakersfield, CA; [occ.] Poetry,
Singing, Art; [hon.] Poetry Books Published: Our
World's Most Beloved Poems, Our World's Most
Cherished Poems, Who's Who In Poetry, By World
of Poetry Press. Silver Poet Award, Golden Poet
Award, Five Honorable Mention Awards, World of
Poetry Press. Many others. Editors Choice Award,
by The National Library of Poetry. Anthologies
"Best of 1996" Poem Book by National Library of
Poetry, "Path's Not Taken" National Library of
Poetry.; [pers.] "Life is like a Rainbow... It
majestically appears... displays its magnificent colors
and escapes into Heaven."; [a.] Arroyo Grande, CA

POSTON, SONYA
[b.] June 3, 1958, Ware, MA; [p.] Ray and Frances
Myers; [m.] James E. Poston, June 28, 1986; [ch.]
Taylor, Megan, Jacob, Tiffany; [ed.] Davidson
County Community College; [occ.] Dietician at
Huntingtowne Farms Elem. School; [hon.] Was
chosen to sing for my senior assembly; [oth. writ.]
Wrote song for talent show, personal poems for my
much loved husband, story line for video; [pers.] My
poems reflect around the happenings of my life at the
time thy are written.; [a.] Charlotte, NC

POTASH, DAVID T.
[b.] October 25, 1969, Montreal Province of Quebec,
Canada; [p.] Sydney Potash and Sara Ungor; [ed.]
Graduated Bialik High School, Montreal, JUne 1987,
Graduated Vanier College, Montreal June 1989,
Graduated Concordia University (BSC) Montreal
June 1992, currently Nova Southern V. College of
Optometry, North Miami Beach Florida, Class of
1997; [oth. writ.] One poem published in High
School Anthology. The poem is written in French.;
[pers.] My writings aim to portray pertinent thoughts
and feelings associated with the endeavors of
mankind.; [a.] Hallandale, FL

POTTER, NORMAN F.
[pen.] Norman F. Potter; [b.] September 14, 1916;
[p.] William H., and Alma F. (Rohde) Potter; [m.]
Aris M. (Eggert) Potter, December 31, 1944; [ch.]
Dianne J. (Potter) Wood and Nancy Jo (Potter)
Linerud; [ed.] 8th grade; [occ.] Retired (Dairy
Farmer); [memb.] Trinity Lutheran Church, Fraternal
Order of Eagles, National Horseshoe Pitchers

Association, ABC American Bowling Congress, BPAA Senior Bowling Proprietors Association of America; [hon.] ND Horseshoe Hall of Fame Valley City, Bowlers Association Hall of Fame, State 4H Livestock Judging Champion, ND Pioneer 4H Leader, 4H Alumni Award; [oth. writ.] "Spring From Our Milbroom Dooe", "Dairymans Household", "A Feather In Your Hat"; [pers.] "Be the best you can be and yet be yourself"; [a.] Valley City, ND

POWERS, JEANNETTA
[b.] March 15, 1924, Dovis County; [p.] Margaret and Pogan; [m.] Chartes C. Powers, September 3, 1960; [ed.] 10th grade; [occ.] Was a GE worker; [a.] Owensboro, KY

PRANAUSK, ERIC
[b.] January 14, 1976, Fontana, CA; [p.] Richard Pranausk, Rhonda Pranausk; [pers.] Read God's Word the Bible daily (John 17:3), Share with others what you learn. (2 Timothy 3:16, 17, Psalms 83:18); [a.] Moreno Valley, CA

PRATER, WILLIAM J.
[b.] February 3, 1952, Clinton, SC; [p.] William N. Prater, Guynelle Payne; [m.] Linda I. Riddle (Divorced), June 29, 1973; [ch.] William Kristopher, Richard Joseph; [ed.] American High School (Diploma), N.A.C.S. (Diploma); [occ.] O.E. Technician Greenwood Mills; [memb.] V.I.P. National Park Service, (former) Member National Parks and Conservation; [hon.] Merit Award for Early Completion of wildlife and Forestry; [oth. writ.] None published, but presently working on Wildlife book with photographs; [pers.] Inspired by my sister who has done much writing from 1970, newspapers, magazines, as well as editing.; [a.] Ninety Six, SC

PRATT, JEANNE F.
[pen.] "Ollies Girl"; [b.] March 12, Boston, MA; [p.] Margaret and Tom Mahoney; [m.] Chris L. Pratt, November 10, 1991; [ch.] Rick Steve Kathy James and Aileen (Died); [ed.] 12 years High School Ed. Creative Writing-American River Jr. College-Soc. Co.; [occ.] Retired after accident at Macy's my employer; [hon.] 3 poems published in local newspaper "Sacramento Union"; [oth. writ.] Have book of poems nearly finished title "Gems"; [pers.] I have always been influenced by Emily Dickonson and Sara Teasdale I feel "Poetry is the heart speaking in print"; [a.] Sacramento, CA

PRATT, KYLE COLLEEN DERBY
[pen.] Kyle C. Pratt; [b.] November 30, 1964, Columbia City, IN; [p.] Gordon Derby Jr. and Kathy Applegate; [m.] Rick D. Pratt, June 1985; [ch.] Joshua Adam Pratt - 10 years; [ed.] High School and Tax School; [occ.] Housewife; [oth. writ.] The Scary Snowday (Children's Book); [pers.] I'm a very emotional person and I believe this comes through in my writing. Quiet, serene atmospheres inspires me. I try to write so the reader feels what I feel.; [a.] Kendallville, IN

PRATTE, LOIS A.
[b.] February 3, 1933, Calais, VT; [p.] J. Earle Pike and Addie Pike; [ed.] Graduated from Cabot High, Cabot, VT. Attended Midwestern Un., Wichita Falls, Tex., received B.S. Degree in Human Services from New Hampshire College of Human Services

Manchester N.H.; [occ.] Home Health Aide; [memb.] North Branford, Congregational Church, United Church of Christ; [oth. writ.] Summer-published in Dance on the Horizon - The Piano is Silent - published in Dark Side of The Moon: Utter Despair published in Best Poems of 1995. The Rascal Jack Frost published in East of the Sunrise and Going Home will published in Spirit of the Age.; [pers.] I like to write about the beauty of nature, family and feelings within my heart. My Christian faith and compassion is reflected in my writing.; [a.] East Haven, CT

PRENDIVILLE, BONNIE LEE
[b.] July 22, 1953, Upper Darby, PA; [m.] Frank Prendiville, September 6, 1980; [ch.] Nicole Prendiville; [ed.] Upper Darby High School; [occ.] Home based ward processing service, creator of bi and monthly newsletter - computer Rookie Gazette; [a.] Secane, PA

PRESCOTT, LINDA
[b.] November 30, 1964, Kelowna, British Columbia, Canada; [m.] John Prescott; [ch.] Younne, Christy, Rebekah, Jessica, Bradley; [ed.] Grade 12 G.E.D.; [occ.] Mother and wife past Carpenter; [memb.] I am a member of victory church in Three Hills. I am a volunteer in a literary program in Three Hills.; [hon.] I feel very honored to have my poem published in beneath the Harvest Moon.; [oth. writ.] Although this will be my first published poem, I have written many poems on different topics. This is the first time I've sent one to anybody. I enjoyed any kind of writing, including songs and short stories.; [pers.] I believe in preserving our families, and giving our children security, love, faith and hope. I believe in teaching, loyalty and how to love people and God. I believe in empathy. I believe in Jesus Christ.; [a.] Elnora Alberta, Canada

PRICE, HELEN FAYE
[b.] January 14, 1945, Anderson, SC; [m.] Joseph Harry Price, May 30, 1964; [ch.] Twin daughter 30 yrs. old Cindy Wells, Windy Smiddie; [ed.] Florence High School S.C., Univ. of Tenn. at Chattanooga (BSW); [occ.] Medical Social Worker (ACBSW) with Home bound Medical Care Chatt. TN; [memb.] NASW, Pawnbrokers Assoc. of TN; [hon.] Dean's List Highest GPA, Adults Scholars Program President of Social Worker Assoc., UTC. 1985-87; [pers.] Happiness is increasing my own personal inner growth, improvement, progress. Spiritually, intellectually and physically. And sharing it with others to enrich then lives. May I never stop. If I do. I am in jeopardy.; [a.] Chattanooga, TN

PRINCE, CLARENCE
[b.] April 10, 1958, Nova Scotia; [p.] Gerald and Mary Prince; [m.] Roberta, August 14, 1983; [ch.] Kristin (9), CJ (7); [ed.] High School graduate; [pers.] I would like some info. as to where I could send more poems for publication. I enjoy writing I read a great deal.

PRINCE, IRVIN E.
[pen.] Irvin E. Prince; [b.] March 24, 1940, Jamaica West Indies; [p.] James and Iona; [m.] Divorced; [ch.] Troy, Mark, and Christina; [ed.] Brooklyn College and Fashion Institute Technology; [occ.] Realtor, Financial Broker; [memb.] New York State Association of Realtors Inc., New York Association

of Montgage Brokers; [oth. writ.] Written but not published. "Clean As The Dawn" "Share The love" "Ten Plus Four" "No One Knows" "My Complete Oneness" "Misunderstood" "Total Woman" "Let The River Run" "She's My Mother" "Distant Between Us" (song); [pers.] I strive to reflect the beauty in the nature and my fellow men in my writing. I have been influence by many writers, Albert Camus, Franz Kafka, J.D. Salinger, Alice Walker, to name a few.; [a.] Jamaica Estates, NY

PROCTER, CLIFFORD O.
[pen.] Santana; [b.] January 10, 1960, Middletown, OH; [p.] Mary Corley Joseph Procter; [m.] Angelica Procter, April 1977; [ch.] Denisha Jo'ell, Cherryl Ann, Lashawnda Marie Procter; [ed.] Basic GED; [occ.] Temporary Services; [oth. writ.]"Our Father Which Art In Heaven" "Death Pusher" "Reflections" I have many more poems; [pers.] I have been greatly influenced by my own life. Which includes incarceration, I want to let my poetry make a difference in all lives that are troubled and have not found the way.

PROCTOR, MIA CHAPELLE
[pen.] Mia Chapelle Proctor; [b.] March 31, 1971, AH, GA; [p.] Mr. Greg and Janice Jones; [ed.] C.L. Harper High School, Savannah State College; [occ.] Sales Associate (retail) Rich's Department Store; [hon.] 1st and 2nd place National Poetry Expo, Who's who among American High School Students; [a.] Atlanta, GA

PULS, YVONNE
[b.] October 11, 1950, Corpus Christi, TX; [p.] George Puls, Jr., and Patsy Traxler Rogers; [ch.] Troy, Jason, Bret, and Kyle McGatlin; [ed.] Golden High School Metro State College (BA) University of Colorado at Denver (MA); [occ.] 5/6 Multi Age Elementary Teacher, Shelton Elementary, Golden, CO; [memb.] CCIRA, JCIRA, IRA; [hon.] Kappa Delta Pi, Pi Nu Chapter Vice President's Honor Roll; [pers.] This poem was inspired by a basket of flowers and a note attached to them that read, "for your first day of the rest of your life - you can do it. Love, Mom". The flowers were on my kitchen table when I returned from court after my divorce.; [a.] Lakewood, CO

PUTNEY, JEN
[b.] December 11, 1972, Wellesley, MA; [p.] Jesse Putney, Sue Putney; [ed.] Proctor Academy, University of New Hampshire; [occ.] Student; [memb.] National Association of Social Workers; [hon.] Golden Key National Honor Society, Phi Gamma Phi, Pi Gamma Mu; [pers.] My poetry is simply a reflection of my unfolding journey through struggles, joys, losses, and love.; [a.] Durham, NH

PYATT, JOEY
[pen.] Eric Fieldmen; [b.] September 19, 1978; [p.] Connie Pyatt; [ed.] I am in High School (Martin High School); [pers.] You will be seeing more of my work in the future. I promise.; [a.] Arlington, TX

QUADAY, RICHARD RALPH
[pen.] Richard Ralph Quaday; [b.] September 2, 1920, Blue Earth, MN; [p.] William and Lorena Quaday; [m.] Neva Teresa Quaday, January 19, 1943; [ch.] Nine; [ed.] H.S., one year college; [occ.] Retired Farmer (44 years); [memb.] Blue Earth

Chamber of Commerce, Blue Earth Knights of Columbus, Mn. St. Student Loan Board K.C., Sts. Peter and Paul Catholic Church of Blue Earth, MN; [oth. writ.] Seven years "Quaday's Quote" Weekly Column, Faribault County Register Blue Earth, MN., Briefly "Corn Talk" MN., Corn Growers Monthly, Eight Years Article - Knights of Columbus Knightly. News State Publication Monthly - Student Loan Board Letter; [pers.] "Life is Beautiful"; [a.] Blue Earth, MN

QUELLETTE, WANDA
[pen.] One; [b.] October 16, 1953, Buckingham, Province of Quebec, Canada; [p.] Stan and May Quellette; [m.] Yves Gauthier, August 3, 1995; [ch.] Mathew - 1987 - 7 years old (Deceased), Jessica - 1990; [ed.] Secondary 6 (Gr. 13); [occ.] Federal Government Language Test Administrator; [memb.] World Vision, Heart Foundation, Cancer Foundation, Snow Suit Foundation; [hon.] Award for Emergency Procedures, Catholic (Christian) see good in all; [oth. writ.] One poem publish in newspaper (for anniversary death of son (died of Cardiac arrest), June 13, 1994; [pers.] I feel from the heart when I write, I write always. It drains my soul. And gives me peace of mind.; [a.] Masson Angers Providence of Quebec, Canada

QUERY, DEANE
[pen.] Deane Query; [b.] October 16, 1920, Kansas; [p.] Mr. and Mrs. C. A. Zook; [m.] Ronald Query, September 6, 1947; [ch.] Janet, Diane and Debra, grandchildren: Sarah, Jeff and Eric; [ed.] High School Grad. 1938; [occ.] Homemaker and grandmother sitter; [memb.] Panorama Baptist Church, National Assn. of Grandmothers; [hon.] No awards, just pleasure in writing; [oth. writ.] Numerous poems — recently two new ones. New Shoes and Paradise.; [pers.] I like to tell a story in my poetry.; [a.] Panorama City, CA

QUINN, ROBERT C.
[b.] January 14, 1952, Amityville, NY; [p.] Robert J. Quinn and Mary M. Quinn; [m.] Mary Lou Fuelling; [ch.] Carrie Anne Quinn and Ryan Carroll Quinn; [ed.] Hicksville High School, NY; [occ.] Floral Designer and Owner of Levittown Florist; [pers.] My strength comes from within me. I strive to succeed in all my endeavors so I will hopefully teach and encourage others to do the same. Writing is only one way... reading is another.

QUINTERO, MARGARET M. ABEL
[pen.] Margaret M. Abel-Quintero; [b.] January 20, 1957, Anderson, SC; [p.] Mary Sayre Abel and Arthur M. Abel; [m.] Jose Luis Quintero, August 10, 1985; [ch.] 2 - Nicolas Andres (1989), Sebastian Abel (1991); [ed.] Ph.D. (MA), Hispanic Languages and Literatures, Univ. of California Santa Barbara, B.A. (Spanish) Univ. of Iowa; [occ.] Spanish Professor, Saint Mary's College of California, Moraga, CA; [memb.] M.L.A, ACTFL, Phi Beta Kappa, Sigma Delta Phi; [hon.] Teaching Assistant of the Year (UCSB), Multiple Recipient of Gulbenkian Award for Graduate Study in Portuguese, U.C. Regents Scholar; [oth. writ.] "Sobre Ausencia y Presencia en Trilce" Article published in Cuadernos Hispanoamericanos, Dissertation, ECA Beyond Realism, A study of the Language of Flowers in Os Maias, poem to be published in the Voice Within (Summer, 1996); [a.] Pittsburg, CA

QUISTBERG, ALEXIS
[pen.] Alex; [b.] May 11, 1982, Oakville, Ontario, Canada; [p.] Margot and Don Quistberg; [ed.] Grade 8, Balaclava Public School; [occ.] Student; [a.] Freelton Ontario, Canada

RACHEFORT, ASHLEY RAQUEL
[b.] December 9, 1982, Richmond Hill; [p.] Dorothy and Bernard Rachefort; [ed.] I'm in grade eight currently attending coldwater public school; [pers.] I write poetry as a way to express my feelings, but if it evokes feelings in others then it has brought my poetry to a higher level.; [a.] Coldwater Ontario, Canada

RAINEY, CHERYL LYNN
[b.] January 21, 1967, Symrna, GA; [p.] L.J. and Ann Rainey; [ed.] Kennesaw State College 85-87 90-92, Chattahoochee Technical Institute 88-89; [occ.] Customer Service, Coordinator; [memb.] Sportslife Health Club, Dancers Workshop, McEachem Methodist Church; [oth. writ.] Gone but not forgotten, my precious prince, a great sense of worth lies in a strong man, if, for the love of bud, and yet still another, friends forever, our lives together fulfilled, forever and always, the final call, homicide - a word for murder; [pers.] Hold onto life as if today were the end and never take another moment with strife or in a frivolous disagreement lose sight of what is to be cherished, with peace, tranquility, and love - We all know it as living each moment to the fullest.; [a.] Powder Springs, GA

RAINS, MIKE
[b.] October 28, 1947; [ed.] University of Maryland; [occ.] Analyst - US Gov't; [memb.] LAB, ABC,AROC, BMWCCA; [hon.] Phi Kappa Phi; [pers.] Writings come from the times, experiences and thoughts of life.; [a.] Davidsonville, MD

RAMANUJAM, RAM N.
[pen.] Mythyly Putcha; [b.] July 15, 1969, India; [p.] P.N. Ramanujam and Padmini Ramanujam; [ed.] B.S. Chemical Engineering, India, M.S. Chemical Engineering U of Texas, Austin; [occ.] Chemical Engineer; [memb.] AICHE, ASME; [hon.] Deans List, Texas Merit Scholarship; [oth. writ.] Contributed two short essays - reader's digest and New Yorkshire. To date 9 articles published in "The Hindu" in India.; [pers.] I strive to reflect "The Optimist In Dental". My greatest influences have been Frijjof Capra, Albert Gntsteen and the Dalai Lama.; [a.] Oak Park, IL

RAMER, JOYCE
[pen.] Joyce Ramer; [b.] April 21, 1941, Prince Edward Island, Canada; [p.] George and Hilda Dingwell; [m.] Divorced; [ch.] Jo-Anne Wemmers; [ed.] High School in Prince Edward Island, many business and sales courses, Real Estate Broker; [occ.] Real Estate Agent; [memb.] Toronto Real Estate Board, Canadian Assoc. of Retired Persons, Canadian Relocation Assoc., Parent Finder's Inc., Canadian Adoption Reform Coalition; [hon.] Various Real Estate Sales Awards, "Woman of Distinction Nomination", #2 Employment Consultant, General Employment Enterprises, in Canada and United States; [oth. writ.] Several poems published in local newspapers and articles for local newspaper on Real Estate; [pers.] Reunited birth mother and my recent writings reflect the joy and gratitude felt

regarding our reunion and the generous love and sharing adoptive Mom of our daughter.; [a.] Stouffville Ontario, Canada

RAMSDELL, WALTER DEAN
[pen.] "Rambo"; [b.] October 27, 1957, North Carolina; [p.] Ann Bennett and William Ramsdell; [m.] Deborah Ann Ramsdell, November 20, 1987; [ch.] Jeremy J. Hargraves, Christopher A. Hargraves, Amber Marie, Anjelika Marie and Alynn Mychael Ramsdell; [ed.] High School Grad. (Widefield H.S. Colorado Springs, Colorado); [occ.] Diesel Mechanic (U.S. Army); [memb.] N.C.U.A. (Non Commissioned Officer Association); [hon.] 6- Good conduct meal, 3- Army commendation medals, 4- Army Achievement Medals; [oth. writ.] Crystal lies the flight of the Unicorn (Epitaph) Free the game spirit (Widefield year book); [pers.] "Seed of life, Flower of hope, Roots of happiness, Together all grow".; [a.] Lawton, OK

RAPPOLT, SALLY JEAN
[pen.] Sally Jean; [b.] June 8, 1956, Mesa, AZ; [p.] Leonard and Ruby Scheppe; [m.] Dane F. Rappolt, May 21, 1977; [ch.] Brian Christopher; [ed.] Bourgade High; [occ.] Administrator, Graphics Corrugated products; [oth. writ.] I have always written for family, friends and personal satisfaction. I have written hundreds of poems over the years, but this is my first publication.; [pers.] The most powerful words that have influenced and encouraged my writing came from a song by Niel Diamond "Be, as a page that aches for award which speaks on a theme that is timeless to Niel, I am eternally Grateful.; [a.] Phoenix, AZ

RASOR, ELMA M.
[b.] November 6, 1911, Buffalo, WY; [p.] Edwin and Mae Ward; [m.] George L. Rasor (Deceased 8-4-92), June 1, 1933; [ch.] Eugene A. Rasor; [ed.] High school; [occ.] Retired since 1967; [memb.] Grass Valley Gem and Mineral Capital City #160 Rebekahs (IOOF) CA, Sacto Esther #9 Independent Order Odd Fellows Grass Valley, CA; [hon.] Haven't tried for any; [oth. writ.] A manuscript on the history of an area called, Georgetown Divide in the Sierra Nevadas, Calif. I have composed over 800 poems since my husband passed away in 1992. A few have been published in our Odd Fellow bulletin. I am in the process of writing a book about the early days of this century.; [pers.] I believe in the fatherhood of God, the brotherhood of man and the sisterhood of woman. I believe in the watch word of Odd Fellowship—Friendship, Love and Truth. I believe that my main concern should be my God should reach out to our community and the world, for in God's eyes we are all Brothers and Sisters.; [a.] Sacramento, CA

RAYETPARVAR, ANGELA
[pen.] Venise Steele; [b.] May 13, 1966, Arkansas; [p.] Joseph Ward Sr., Odessa Williams (Deceased); [ch.] Joseph, Trevor, Danielle; [ed.] Emerson High School, School of Health Care Sciences, USAF, Witchita Falls, Texas; [occ.] Operating Room Technician; [oth. writ.] Working on a part fact, part fiction novel; [pers.] I don't consider myself as a poet. I just write what I feel. Writing, I feel, takes me to a whole other level. My sister, Bettye, says I'm like a mad woman.; [a.] Dallas, TX

REDDELL, DEBORAH L.
[pen.] Little Flower; [b.] August 8, 1967, Hanford, CA; [p.] Danny and Charlene Reddell; [ed.] Kofa High School Graduate Two Years Arizona Western College; [occ.] Social Worker Assistant I; [oth. writ.] Two wild horses, the true Indian, the mighty chief, eagle feathers, fate and the beanstalker. Currently working on a novel entitled "Blue Angel".; [pers.] 1) True poetry comes from the heart and is inspired by a great spirit. 2) There is nothing better then climbing the highest mountain and getting in touch with the spirit that sings and dances inside your soul! 3) Every person has gift given freely by God above. I hope that every person learns what their true gift is and uses it to the good of God. 4) Trey, thank you for your inspiration, insight, wisdom, humor, and spiritual love. You and God above are my inspiration for writing. It is great spirit is such a wondrous gift.; [a.] Yuma, AZ

REDMAN, STEPHEN JOHN
[b.] May 16, 1960, Fremont, MI; [p.] Mr. Gustav and Patricia Redman; [ch.] Sean C. and Erick J. Redman; [ed.] High School, Trade School (Horseshoeing and Blacksmithing); [occ.] Reforestation, Wildlife Habitat improvement, Trout stream improvement; [oth. writ.] I have numerous writings that I have been stacking up for years. Some have been copy write but none published. This is the first time I have released any of my writing to the public. My ultimate goal is to paint and to write about freedom in its true Identity going from this world and on into forever.; [pers.] As in all my writing, if I can pass on into tomorrow my work and thoughts of yesterday, then I will have achieved my goal. An essence of that feelings is installed in (Please Teach Me!) a direct statement in the importance about how I feel in passing inner knowledge into our children, our only link into the future.; [a.] White Cloud, MI

REEVES, GAIL STEFANIE
[b.] May 1, 1961, Blackpool, England; [p.] John and Jennifer Reeves; [m.] Richard Bergevin, July 3, 1982; [ch.] John Gordon; [occ.] Product Manager/ Inventory Manager Dorfin Distribution, St. Laurent, QC; [oth. writ.] Several poems published during my High - School years currently writing a book; [pers.] Writing is a Catharis. It always to focus during emotionally bewildering moments, and it gives face reign to my hopes and dreams. I could not suffer a life where words have been silenced. P.S. I am still married.

REGINALDO, PRISCILA SALES PADRON
[pen.] Mabel; [b.] January 16, 1962, Bacarra, Philippines; [p.] Marcelo Padron, Ofelia Sales; [m.] Sixto G. Reginaldo, April 17, 1989; [ch.] Jason and Aileen Caroline; [ed.] BS in nutrition (Phil.) MA in Public Administration in the Philippines; [occ.] Food service worker; [memb.] Nutritionist Dietitian Association of the Phil; [pers.] I try and express my self (By means of writing) through the use of pen.; [a.] Honolulu, HI

REID, EDWARD G.
[b.] June 24, 1939, Chilliwack, British Columbia, Canada; [p.] W.J. (Mike) and Marjorie (Nee Lee) Reid; [m.] Divorced 1990, October 20, 1962; [ch.] Lisa, Carl, Lyle, Janice; [ed.] BSP (Bachelor of Science in Pharmacy 1962); [occ.] Pharmacist Business owner (Pharmacy and Photo Store);

[memb.] BC Pharmacy Assoc. Can. Pharm. Assoc.; [pers.] "Our greatest freedom is our self restraint".; [a.] White Rock British Columbia, Canada

REID, GLORIA
[b.] May 27, 1955, Newfoundland, Canada; [p.] Cyril Noseworthy, Helen Hillier; [m.] Lowell Reid, July 12, 1975; [pers.] For as long as I can remember, writing poems and short stories has been as natural to me as breathing. Until now, only a select few friends and family members have ever read my work. This particular poem (Death), written in March 1984, was to help me cope with my father's passing.; [a.] Port Hope, Canada

REMOLACIO, REY RANIDO
[b.] February 1, 1979, Manila, Philippines; [p.] Roger and Remy Remolacio; [ed.] Currently In High School Simi Valley High School; [occ.] Student; [memb.] 1) National High School Honor Society 2) High School Marching Band Plays Flute 3) Simi Valley Library Volunteer; [hon.] Presidential academic fitness awards program 1991, High School Honors Class; [oth. writ.] Poems and essays written for school homework; [pers.] Special thanks to my parents for seeing the potential within me when others remained blind including myself.; [a.] Simi Valley, CA

RENAUD, ANNE MARIE
[b.] January 2, 1956, Sault Ste Marie, Ontario, Canada; [p.] Stan and Lucy Schinners; [m.] Harv Renaud, May 22, 1982; [ch.] Marisa Harvey; [ed.] Bawating High School Sault Ste Marie Ont. Canada; [occ.] Financial Clerk; [memb.] St. John The Rapist Anglican Church Richmond Ont Superintendent Sunday School; [hon.] Canadian Military Service - 13yrs. Medal of Service "Canadian Declaration", Special Service Medal, Nato Service; [oth. writ.] Personal poems and prose, local paper and children's stories; [pers.] I dedicate this poem to my father, died June 1, 95 "He toiled the land, He loved the beauty of the land, He died amidst the earth "Holding it in his hand".; [a.] Richmond Ontario, Canada

RENAUD, AUDRA ANGELIQUE
[pen.] Audra Angelique Renaud; [b.] March 15, 1981, McAllen, TX; [p.] Robert Rocco Renaud, Rosette Yvonne Renaud; [ed.] Freshman in senior high school elementary school: St. Paul Lutheran School Jackson Elementary School, High school: Valley Christian Heritage School; [occ.] Student, and and I help out my parents at our family business; [memb.] Beta Club, Volleyball Team, School Choir, Softball Team, Faith Pleases God Church, Church Youth Group (Explosive Youth); [hon.] Fall festival favorite, sweetheart (Valentine), Junior High Salutatorian, good Samaritan Award

RENNICK, CLINT
[b.] July 11, 1977; [p.] Liz and Alan Rennick; [a.] Broomfield, CO

RESA, MELODIE LYNN SOUTHARD
[pen.] Mel L. Southard-Resa; [b.] January 4, 1963, Colorado Springs, CO; [p.] Fredrick and Francena Southard; [m.] Raymond Resa, July 17, 1987; [ch.] Sorjia, "Alex" Alejandro, Jashua; [ed.] College - Imperial Valley College Imperial, California; [occ.] Housewife, Mother, College Student, and Army National Guard; [memb.] Currently organizing

"Black Parents, Against Violence", in Imperial Country, El Centro Elementary School Dist; [oth. writ.] I have, but have not submitted for publication or otherwise.; [pers.] To be published as a writer has always been a dream of mine. I am greatly influenced by my children and their amusement of their generation.; [a.] El Centro, CA

REYES, ANNA MARIA
[b.] November 26, 1964, Edwards AFB, CA; [p.] Richard and Angelina Reyes; [ed.] Roseville High School, American River College - Associate of Arts, California State University, Sacramento - Bachelor of Arts - English, Deans List; [occ.] Kmart Associate; [memb.] Senior member in the United States Air Force, Auxiliary Civil Air Patrol; [oth. writ.] "A Memorable Christmas" not published; [pers.] People should have fun in every thing they do wherever they are; [a.] Antelope, CA

REYNOLDS, LORENA APRIL
[b.] April 3, 1981, Newport Beach, CA; [p.] John Reynolds, Mary Reynolds; [ed.] Yosemite High School, Oakhurst, CA; [occ.] 9th Grade Student, Yosemite High School; [memb.] Yosemite High School Yearbook, Yosemite Volleyball Club; [hon.] Honor Roll Student; [pers.] My life is very busy, sometimes crazy, but I love it.; [a.] Coarsegold, CA

RIBBECK, ANNA
[pen.] Anna; [b.] May 26, 1921, New Orleans; [p.] Carolyn Schiebert and Sebastian Roy; [m.] Phillip Bertram Ribbeck, January 18, 1943; [ch.] 8; [ed.] BFA degree from Tulane University; [occ.] Real Estate Consultant and Sales; [memb.] National Real Estate Association, Altar Society, National Preservation Asso. Petroleum Club, Chamber of Commerce, Newcomer Club; [hon.] Woman of the Year, Newcomers of Memphis, Million Dollar Club, United Fund Volunteer, Known as "The Plant Doctor" had a TV show in Memphis; [oth. writ.] Poems published in newspapers and magazines, wrote poem for cover page of St Tammnay Chamber of Commerce, stories and a booklet "Houseplants"; [pers.] I am a lecture on houseplants, and feel close to God when in my garden - I make "Housecalls" for sick plants and am always asked to give invocations and write poetry for many events.; [a.] Covington, LA

RICE, ASHLEY
[pen.] Ashley Rice; [b.] June 12, 1984, Gainesville, FL; [p.] Raymond and Virginia J. Rice; [ed.] Currently 6th grade student at William H. English Middle School; [occ.] Student; [a.] Scottsburg, IN

RICE, STEPHEN
[b.] June 1, 1960, Cumberland, MD; [p.] Ralph E. and Catherine (Taylor) Rice; [m.] April C. (Butts), Rice/Memphis TN June 4, 1983; [ch.] Brandon Scott (15); [ed.] Keyser High Keyser Wva., Belleville Area College, Rogers State College, TSAILE Community College, 6 years, US Air Force (Dental); [occ.] Dental Equipment Sales and Service/Territory Mgr.; [memb.] BMI/ASCAP; [oth. writ.] Song lyrics for numerous bands. Published lyrics for Island records and Unison Records many many unpublished works including works including books; [pers.] As long as writing serves my growth and is fun I will continue to do so.; [a.] Bartlesville, OK

RICHARDS, RACHELLE
[b.] August 31, 1970, Winnipeg, MB; [p.] jean and John Richards; [ed.] Glenlawn Collegiate Grant MacEwen College; [occ.] Actress and Theatre Manager; [oth. writ.] Two previously published poems with the Poetry Institute of Canada.; [pers.] My poetry, generally is influenced by those around me. I thank my friends for believing in me and in the angels.; [a.] Edmonton, Alberta, Canada

RICHBURG, ELIZABETH
[pen.] Sweetheart; [b.] June 8, 1948, Philadelphia; [p.] Elizabeth and Andrew Brewer; [m.] Cornelius Richburg, August 16, 1975; [ch.] Doretha Judy Richburg; [ed.] Over brook High Lincoln Prep. College, Computer Date Processing, Ins. U.S. Dol PWBA LAN Training; [memb.] Pinn Memorial Baptist Ch, Dir of our People Community Development Corp.; [hon.] U.S. Dept of Labor Secretary's exception Achievement Award, (PWBA LAN Administrator's); [oth. writ.] Several other poems: A Lover's Rose, Legacy, Heaven, and one short story, In Between the Lines; [pers.] In life (reflections) was written for my "Cornelius Richburg" and in death it is dedicated to him.; [a.] Philadelphia, PA

RICHEIMER, MARY JANE
[pen.] Ric and Majari; [b.] October 20, 1913, Massillon, OH; [p.] Nellie Bea and Thomas C. Richeimer; [ed.] B.A. Lake Erie College, Painesville, Ohio, MA Kent State Univ., Kent Ohio, Grad. Work Columbia Univ., NYC, NY Northwestern Univ., Evanston, Ill., Associateship in the Univ., of london Eng. Institute of Education; [occ.] Retired; [memb.] AAVW IATE NS Ret. Teachers Evanston Hospital Auxiliary, St. Augustine's Episcopal Church Vestry, Wilmette, Ill., Viewers for quality television, volunteer teacher schools and Sunday School; [hon.] In who's who of American Women (During my teaching career I was an national and state committees. Now I edit our retirement community's newsletter, the chimes; [oth. writ.] A Century of Education, Planning my Future, poetry printed in various periodicals and the Cleveland Plain Dealer; [pers.] I think love is the greatest thing in the world and I try to show that in poem about every day events.; [a.] Evanston, IL

RICHMEIER, DEBBIE
[pen.] D. P. Gudhart; [b.] June 5, 1960, Saint Catherine; [p.] Elmer Richmeier, Kathryn Richmeier; [ed.] Holcomb High School; [occ.] Brookover feed lot, central plains Aviation. Partner in livestock; [memb.] St. Dominic Church; [pers.] I strive to build people up give them positive input in their lives.; [a.] Garden City, KS

RIDDLE, WESLEY

RIDDLESPERGER, BILEY
[b.] November 1, 1962, Athens, TX; [p.] Carolyn Duncan; [occ.] Hairstylist/Tech; [pers.] In writing, I like to reflect upon the characteristics we sometimes hide and lock away deep within our souls.; [a.] Athens, TX

RIETH, SHAUN
[b.] May 17, 1978, Hampton, VA; [p.] John Rieth, Sandra Krick; [ed.] Senior in Fort Dorchester High School, N. Charleston, SC; [occ.] Student; [memb.] Big Brother, Big Sister; [hon.] 1) Air Force Retired

Officers Association Award, 2) Who's who among American High School Students, 3) Honor Roll, 4) Academic Letterman; [oth. writ.] "Encounter with Orca."; [a.] North Charleston, SC

RIETZ, FRANCEL
[pen.] Francel Rietz; [b.] March 15, 1921, Wyoming; [p.] Bessie and James Irvine; [m.] Philip Rietz, September 12, 1938; [ch.] Two; [ed.] High School Graduate; [occ.] Retired Ranch Hand and owner; [pers.] Born and raised on a Wyoming Ranch. Married a Racher and I still live on the Ranch. Homesteaded by Rietz, love the Ranch. And only went 3M, to Mary my Husband Phil.; [a.] Wheatland, WY

RIGNEY, TINA
[b.] February 11, 1972, Sonoma, CA; [p.] Esther Kearn-Frolich; [ed.] High school graduate/ Cosmetology Lisensce; [occ.] Cosmetologist, Hair we are Woodland CA; [memb.] Calvary Baptist Church Calvary Baptist Bible Study; [oth. writ.] This is the first poem contest I have ever entered, though I have hundreds of poems that have never been heard.; [pers.] I enjoy writing poetry about love. In a society where many people have seemed to lost that reality. I've always believed in a happily ever after and if my life should ever end without finding what I belive in. At least I will have believed in something.; [a.] Woodland, CA

RILEY, TERESA L.
[b.] August 12, 1971, Maple Ridge, British Columbia, Canada; [p.] Jim and Melanie; [m.] Jon Lutjen; [ed.] The basic 13 yrs in the public schooling system, some university, and the ongoing course of real life; [occ.] I'm just surviving, and learning who I am; [oth. writ.] I have written 50th other poems, for personal expression. "I want to be", is my first published poem.; [pers.] I'd like to tell the world that you are not alone. The desperation and greed is real. My inspiration is the pain, hopes, dreams, and fears that everyone feels. If I can touch a soul and sooth an ache, I can live.; [a.] Lee Creek British Columbia, Canada

RINTA, CATHARINA M.
[b.] February 21, 1921, Amsterdam, Holland; [p.] Willem and Jacoba A. Steenbergen; [ch.] Henry V. Rinta and Christine E. Rinta Air Force Lieutenant - Colonel; [ed.] School in Holland; [occ.] Retired; [hon.] Received several honorable mentions won the arbor day poetry contest, 2 years in a row. Received 2 resolutions from the board of lake country commissioners for my poetry, in Ohio; [oth. writ.] Am published in several books, and newsletters; [pers.] Poetry helps to bring out the beauty in many things. It can be reality or fantasy. Sometimes what life can't give us, imagination can. We can express those feelings in our poetry.; [a.] Walkersville, MD

RIOS, MARINA
[b.] March 3, 1975, Mexico, DF; [p.] Fortino Rios and Paula Rios; [ed.] Hunt High School; [oth. writ.] One poem published in poems of Today; [pers.] In this writing, I strive to show one persons solution to hiding secrets.; [a.] Angier, NC

RIPPEY, DWAYNE JOSEPH
[pen.] Rip; [b.] March 18, 1960, Berkley, MI; [p.] Anita Rippey; [m.] Rachel Rippey; [oth. writ.] "Just

A Few Kind Words" - poetry book unpublished; [pers.] Keep dreaming

RISAVY, DOROTHY W.
[b.] November 9, 1922, Atlanta, GA; [p.] Jesse Wright Wilhelm, Clara May Fowler Wilhelm; [m.] Raymond F. Risavy, March 28, 1942; [ch.] Two; [ed.] High School and Various College Courses no degree; [occ.] Housewife; [memb.] Heart of tampa, St Paul's Catholic Church Univ. of S. Florida - Senior Citizen Courses; [hon.] An occasional pat of the back; [oth. writ.] I have written many poems. I hope to publish a book of poems for friends and relatives. Some were published in church monthly book and recited in variety shows.; [pers.] Life is a seesaw. I find myself helping someone laugh or cry or they are helping me laugh of cry I need people and I love people we are all miracles of wonder.; [a.] Tampa, FL

ROADES, ROBERT A.
[b.] January 21, 1926, Evansville, IN; [p.] Arthur Roades (F) and Kathryn Roades (M); [m.] (Deceased), October 3, 1946; [ch.] Kathryn Anne, Stephen and Bradley; [ed.] B.A. Colorado College, M.A., Ed. S Univ. of Northern Colorado; [occ.] English Professor (retired); [memb.]1) National Educational Ass., 2) AARP, 3) Phi Beta Kappa, 4) Grace Episcopal Church; [hon.] 1) B.A. Cum Laude, 2) Various Military Citations, 3) Graduate Scholarship Awards; [oth. writ.] Some Education Articles, Contributing Author To The Write, advantage - published by McGraw Hill; [pers.] I hope to do my part in sustaining "La Belle Letters" in a society where the arts are fading like the winter sun.; [a.] Sun City, AZ

ROARK, JOHN D.
[pen.] Dave Roark; [b.] July 13, 1953, Jefferson City, MO; [p.] Bill W. Roark, Nancy A. Northcutt; [ch.] Shannon Roark, John D. Roark II; [ed.] GED Army Ed. Center, Baumholder, GER. Lincoln University, Jefferson City, MV; [occ.] Student, Security; [memb.] Phi Alpha Theta Motorcycle Riders Foundation Freedom of Road Riders, Inc. Abate of Georgia Student Government Association; [hon.] Student Leadership Award Deans List, Honorary Member Cole Co. Sleriff's Patrol Combat Infantry mans Badge Army Commendation Medal; [pers.] U.S. Army, 1970-73 Vietnam, 101st And. Div. 1971-1972 I strive to remember the words of Satyana, "Those Who Forget The Part Are Condemned To Repeat It."; [a.] Jefferson City, MO

ROARK, SHEILA B.
[b.] December 17, 1946, NYC; [p.] Harry and Mary Galvin; [m.] N. Gail Roark, February 10, 1988; [ed.] Graduated from Notre Dame School in NYC -1964. Read five books a week and have self-educated myself since my graduation.; [occ.] Writer; [memb.] Board Member of Irving Women's Bowling Association, Poets Guild, International Society of Poetry; [hon.] Editors Choice Award - 1995 - National Library of Poetry, Honorable Mention - Iliad Press - 1995, World of Poetry Awards 1983 - 1987; [oth. writ.] My poems have appeared in local periodicals in Long Island, NY. Two of my poems will appear in the September/October issue of "Oatmeal and Poetry". I am also fortunate to have my poems found in 25 anthologies.; [pers.] Poetry is pure magic. It is away of sharing inner thoughts and

feelings with others. It is my special way of opening my heart and sharing my love.; [a.] Euless, TX

ROBAR, JILL ARIANNE
[b.] April 20, 1977, Gillam, Manitoba, Canada; [p.] Lynda Robar-Glennie, Milton Robar; [ed.] Graduated From Crocus Plains Regional Secondary School, Brandon, Manitoba; [occ.] Student; [memb.] International order of job's daughters (IOJD); [hon.] Passed honored queen (IOJD), three merit awards (IOJD); [oth. writ.] No other published writings; [pers.] I strive to "Hold up to mirror to life" and show people its soul. I am and have been influenced by my religion, drama and music.; [a.] Brandon Manitoba, Canada

ROBBINS, MARJORIE
[pen.] Peggy Robbins, M.C. Robbins; [b.] Waverly, TN; [p.] Harris and Jessie Cowen; [m.] N. Vick Robbins; [ch.] one son: Dr. Vick Robbins; [ed.] Graduate of Waverly High School in Waverly, TN and Martin College in Pulaski, TN; [occ.] Writing for national publications; [hon.] I have won a number of awards for my historical articles but none for poetry. I am currently writing mostly for The World and I, the monthly book-magazine of the Washington Times Corp. in Washington, DC and for three Civil War Magazines.; [oth. writ.] For three decades I have been writing for a dozen different national magazines. Varying from Smithsonian and American Heritage to American Legion Magazine and the Bird dog Cazette. I have co-authored several school texts and several reference book, including Historical Times Encyclopedia of the Civil War. But my first poem will be published in 1996 "Fouding In The Mountains" in Beneath The Harvest Moon.

ROBERGE, DORIS DAFNEY RUSSELL
[pen.] Dafney; [b.] Moshers Corner, Nova Scotia, Canada; [p.] Oswald and Elizabeth Russell; [m.] Leopold Roberge, February 1, 1964; [ch.] Gordon and Mark; [ed.] Secondary plus several university courses master travel business and investment real estate marketing; [occ.] Real Estate Broken; [hon.] Masters and president gold awards for sales; [oth. writ.] Several poems and songs published presently concentrating on a book; [pers.] I feel that there is something very important waiting to be learned from the past and until we do the world will be in in turmoil. History really does repeat itself.; [a.] Ottawa Ontario, Canada

ROBERTS, MARY ELLEN
[b.] September 10, 1911, Lake View, IA; [p.] Victor E. and Lula E. Westron; [m.] John D. Roberts, March 18, 1940; [ch.] Walker E., Mary Lou, John P.; [ed.] Elementary and high school, Lake View, IA, Kahler School of Nursing, Rochester, MN; [occ.] Retired; [oth. writ.] "The Wisdom and Verse of Mary Ellen Roberts."; [pers.] Due to my training, I would wish to help others.; [a.] Nampa, ID

ROBILLER, VERINA L. S.
[pen.] Verina; [b.] January 19, 1984, South Paris, ME; [p.] Louise and Jochen Robiller; [ed.] St Paul Catholic School, 6th grade, Diane Desporte - Dance Academy, Fisher Karate Institute; [occ.] Student; [hon.] Placed 1st place 5 years Science Fair Local - overall winner, St Paul Science Fair/honorable mention Regional Science Fair - Competed in Academic Competition for Excellence; [oth. writ.]

Several published poems in local newspapers and school newspapers; [pers.] I am most inspired by nature and my parents, teachers, and my friend Erica Benvenertti that encourage me to be the best I can be; [a.] Cass Christian, MS

ROBINSON, BRENDA
[b.] January 15, 1953, Hybart, AL; [p.] Wilson and Marzetta Nettles; [m.] Charlie Robinson, December 1, 1979; [ch.] LaToya and Keldrick; [ed.] J.F. Shields, Alabama State University; [occ.] Teacher Elem. Ed. Union Springs Elem. Union Springs, AL; [memb.] Alabama Education Association, National Education Association, and Freedom Life Drama Team; [oth. writ.] Short stories and other poems; [pers.] I hope to give encouragement and touch the lives of others through my writing.; [a.] Montgomery, AL

ROBINSON, RENEE
[b.] December 13, 1959, Laurium, MI; [p.] (Mother) Zoe Ann Vicory, (Father) Jackie Rauch; [m.] Darnell Robinson, September 3, 1983; [ch.] Renell; [ed.] Graduated Calumet High School in "1978"; [occ.] Mother and Homemaker; [hon.] Nominated for "Who's Who in Rising Young Americans"; [oth. writ.] I enjoy writing poetry for my family and myself. Currently writing a children's book.; [pers.] "The gift of my life" I wrote for my wonderful mother through the eyes of my child. Having my precious baby, has blessed me with seeing the innocence and wondrous beauty of life-as God intended! She will forever be an inspiration to me!; [a.] Las Vegas, NV

ROBSON, BRENDA
[b.] May 27, 1961, Allison, Ontario, Canada; [p.] Melville Robson, Ethel Robson; [ed.] Banting Memorial High School Allison, Ontario St. Lawrence College, Kingston, Ontario; [occ.] Medical Laboratory Technician; [oth. writ.] Short stories, poems, as yet unpublished; [pers.] My writing is governed by my heart and soul. Most of my inspiration comes from my family, especially from my brother, Gordon Robson, to whom "A friend" is dedicated.

RODEN, SUSAN HOFFMAN
[b.] November 12, 1956, Towas City, MI; [p.] Bob Hoffman, Susan Chase; [m.] Dan Roden, May 14, 1994; [ed.] Buffalo State College, Buffalo, NY; [occ.] Artist (Metalsmith), Homemaker; [a.] Manarch Beach, CA

RODGERS, LORI ANN
[b.] June 26, 1960, Vis, CA; [p.] Sid, Betty Grant; [m.] Rodney Rodgers, November 17, 1979; [ch.] Jake, Garrett, and Jessica; [ed.] J.C. Grad Business College; [occ.] Housewife; [pers.] As most people, struggling with an eating disorder, I find it difficult to feel negative feelings. Through poetry, I am able to feel and express my feelings.; [a.] Kingsburg, CA

RODKEY, MARGARET L.
[b.] July 7, 1928, Flinton, PA; [p.] Ross C. Jadaline, Hucken Berry; [m.] Theodore C. Rodkey, July 31, 1958; [ch.] Senen, Judy, Cindy, Teddy, Eddie, Diane, Jean, Jane; [ed.] 10th Grade; [occ.] Taking care of people who are sick; [memb.] International society of poets. Lifetime member; [hon.] I have received 2 award plaques several award merits; [oth.

writ.] I have 2 books published. 2 more to be published: A tapestry of thoughts, Sea of the treasures, Beneath the harvest moon. Poems of 1994.; [pers.] I like to write poems to help others to get their feelings out in the opening, so people can relate others to them.; [a.] Altoona, PA

ROGERS, JOSEPHINE
[pen.] Josie Rogers; [b.] September 24, 1934, Coehoren, KY; [p.] Wm and Eliz Boulware; [m.] John T. Rogers, August 1972; [ch.] Peter, Judy, Bob and Tom; [ed.] RN, CPNP, BS in writing; [occ.] Reporter; [memb.] Augusta Bible Church; [hon.] "Tales from the Streets" - my interview pieces, won 2nd in National Editorial Awards; [oth. writ.] Interviews With Homeless, Men Women and Children/People Who Live In Inner City Project Housing, published monthly in St. Louis Post - Dispatch; [pers.] I try to represent people who otherwise have no voice in our society.; [a.] Saint Louis, MO

ROGERS, SANDRA L.
[pen.] Sandy; [b.] August 10, 1962, Fort Devens, MA; [p.] Paul and Beverly Rogers; [ed.] Winslow High School; [hon.] Editors Choice Award, for outstanding achievement in poetry 1995; [oth. writ.] "He Walks Alone" published in the book titled "Beyond The Stars" 1995. A Morning Sentinel write up about my publication. I wrote a song "My Sweet Darling" it is waiting for National Release through majestic records and Country Wine Publishing Co. I have demo tapes and sheet music.; [pers.] I write about anything that touches my heart and the heart of others.; [a.] Waterville, ME

ROMAN, GENEVA
[b.] September 1, 1984, New York; [p.] Roman and Lisette Roman; [occ.] 6th grade student; [memb.] Member of the "Odyssey Of The Mind Program"; [hon.] 1) 20th Annual Conference of Young Authors by Phyllis Reynolds Naylor, Nov. 19, 1994 2) Geography Award Nov. 9, 1994, 3) Academic Achievement June 11, 1992, The Academic Excellence Program June 20, 1990, Reading and Art, June 10, 1993; [a.] Minot AFB, ND

ROSENBERG, PHILIP
[b.] March 20, 1922, Poland, Europe; [p.] Ann and Samuel; [ed.] Formal: High school, Addicted to daily journal writing for most of my life, artistic potential activated early commendation on drawing and ooil ptg., a compulsive writer, love of words. A voracious reader; [occ.] retired age 73-4 numerous jobs; [memb.] None worth noting, A loner Introverted, Love of Outdoors; [hon.] Never published, no desire to do so, Ms Toni Taylor, Staff Editor of McCalls and Look magazines: Teacher at the New School for Social Research... "You do have talent (emphasis hers) not only for poetry, but for putting a poetic quality in prose quality in prose, also for expression" Ms Sylvia Horwitz, teacher and free landce writer "Most outstanding and best critic in class" Dr. Henry Greenbaum MD and Psycho analyst: "talented"; [oth. writ.] Short prose items submitted in class; [pers.] Faced with a crushing inabilit to verbalize in group, suffering the taunts of the group, in desperation I resorted to to writing. Greatly to my surprise I unexpectedly tapped a latent resource lain dormant all of my life. "Lost Love" was one of several poems born within the laboratory

of the psychoanalytic process. The new magic of discovery opened wide the smoldering volcano of repression and from it burst new hope and optimism and wit it ego gratification and self-esteem; [a.] New York, NY

ROSS, CLAIRE F.
[pen.] Claire Ross; [b.] December 30, 1908, Hermansville, MI; [p.] Flora and Harry Friday; [m.] Malcom K. Ross, April 4, 1935; [ch.] 3 sons, 5 grandchildren, 7 great-grandchildren; [ed.] High school graduate, Menominee Michigan - 1927; [occ.] Retired from Federal Gov.; [memb.] Church - Full Gospel Chapel Kingsland, TX, Women's Aglow Fellowship; [oth. writ.] I have not had any of my writing published for sale. But, since my Spiritual re-birth I have journalled and just recently have had some of writings put in printed form to give my children, grand-children and great-grandchildren, family and close friends. This poem "God's Music" is one of them.; [pers.] I am a widow, 87 years old. I have 3 sons, 5 grand- children and 7 great-grandchildren. I began to recognize my gift to write at the age 70 years and began "journalling". Just recently I have had some of the writings put in printed form to share with family and close friends. I have titled my journal "Following in His Footsteps"; [a.] Burnet, TX

ROSSI, JULIE MARIE
[b.] November 19, 1982, Redwood City, CA; [p.] Steve Rossi and Catherine Rossi; [ed.] Seventh Grade Student At Central Middle School, San Carlos, California; [occ.] Student; [a.] San Carlos, CA

ROUNDS, NANCY J.
[b.] October 10, 1951, Indiana; [p.] Russel and Helen Morrow; [m.] Gerald Rounds, March 18, 1995; [ch.] Jennifer and Scott; [ed.] Indiana University, RN; [occ.] Sales Representative

ROUNDY, TERESALEE HOPE
[b.] August 25, 1984, Twin Falls, ID; [p.] Joe Roundy and Vicki Kidd; [occ.] Student at central canyon grade school; [pers.] Grandfather ken roundy, Idaho mountain pilot lives at twin falls, Idaho.; [a.] Nampa, ID

ROUNDY, WILMA BOOTH
[pen.] Ray; [b.] November 15, 1912, Flasher N, Oak; [p.] Zelma (Dorman) and Edwin Walter Clapp; [m.] Elton Booth, Otho Roundy and Harold Ray, Sept. 7, 1935, Aug. 30, 1971, March 29, 1982; [ch.] 2 girls - 2 boys; [ed.] Linfield Coll. B.S. degree 1936, Brigham Young U. MS. degree; [occ.] Taught secondary Ed - and Special Ed., now retired; [memb.] D.A.R. University Women Church of Jesus Christ of Latter Day Saints (LDS); [oth. writ.] My own book of poetry Editor of church news 9 years wrote my autobiography wrote biography of Elton Booth wrote biography of Otho Roundy; [pers.] Mankind is basically good- We are born clean, innocent and teachable. We are taught by example, precept and through our environment. We become what we are by the combination of heritage and learning.; [a.] Provo, UT

ROWLAND, SUSAN
[occ.] I am an oncology ICU nurse with a Masters in Psychology. I provide counsel of a hospice nature to

cancer patients and their families facing their most ultimate challenge, realizing faith.; [pers.] Through a practice known as the Stillness, talking and listening to our first source, I have come to understand that faith is not just the decision that there is a God. It is the extent to which the Father can be experienced, both in living and in death. The challenge of faith is to experience in living what we are certain of in death. The Stillness is both the means and the place where this is done. I assure you, have nothing to fear but your lack of understanding. The comfort of the Stillness is at your command.

ROWLEE, CHRISTIANE E. LANGER
[b.] February 5, 1961, Fulda, Germany; [p.] Bernhard and Camilla Langer; [m.] LPT Elon K. Rowlee III, July 15, 1994; [ed.] 13 years and final examination at German Secondary School; [occ.] Housekeeper and loving wife; [oth. writ.] I have a collection of my own poetry, none has ever been published.; [pers.] I am a very sensitive and spiritual being. I love nature and all of it's life. Through my poetry I'm trying to express my feelings, impressions and thoughts during my walk through this world.; [a.] Clayton, NY

ROY, JOANIE
[pen.] Joanie Reilly; [b.] June 26, 1957, St Louis, MO; [p.] Thomas Reilly (D) and Virginia Reilly; [m.] Gregory Roy, August 29, 1980; [ch.] Tommy, Erin, Ryan and Kevin; [ed.] Nerinx Hall High, Meramec College, Fontbonne College; [occ.] Homemaker, Parttime Receptionist P. bodies gitness company; [memb.] St. Peters Wome's Guild, St. Peters Parish Council, Nerinx Hall Alumni Assoc.; [pers.] My writings reflect the soul and spirit of those who have touched my life. The creativity expressed is a gift which sets me free! I've been writing since childhood and I'm now working towards completion of my first novel.; [a.] Saint Louis, MO

RUCKER, CHYLA
[b.] January 18, 1978, Muskegee, OK; [p.] Cheryl Smith; [ed.] Guthrie High School, Meridian Technology Center, Stillwater Study Cosmetology; [occ.] Student, Wal-Mart Companies; [memb.] Member of Mt. Lion Baptist Church, Heritage Club, Student Council, School Yearbook, UICA, Yes (Youth Environment Strategies); [hon.] Organization Semi Finalist in 4th place VICA hair contest 4th place VICA opening and closing team; [oth. writ.] Poems and short stories none published; [pers.] Nature forms us for ourselves, not for others, to be, not to seem.; [a.] Guthrie, OK

RUE, NATASHA
[b.] August 14, 1978, Dalton, GA; [p.] Kandra and Rodney Smith; [m.] John P. Rue, December 4, 1994; [ch.] Damian Austin Rue; [occ.] Housewife; [hon.] Trophey's for basketball and softball in high school. I went to Southwest High School.; [pers.] I like most sports, I like to write poems, I like to keep a journal most of all I love to spend time with my son Damian.; [a.] Dalton, GA

RUFFIN, FRANKLIN GENEVA
[pen.] All work in Franklin's name; [b.] January 9, 1936, Norfolk, VA; [p.] Charles and Eunice Franklin; [m.] Predell A. Ruffin, September 22, 1951; [ch.] 5 grownups and 10 grands; [ed.] I attended Booker T. Washington High in Suffolk,

VA. I am attending tidewater Community College. Now for a A.A. degrees. I have a GPA 32; [occ.] Retired due to disability 38 yrs. Beautitian and 15 yrs. PN of Nursing; [memb.] New of Testament Church Rapidan St Ports, VA. Pastor Charles Bowens II; [hon.] 4 awards from NRI Writing School Home Corsponing Course; [oth. writ.] "A Christmas Memory". Front page of Seniors Directory Newspaper Annapolish, MD (monthly) "Glorious Throne". Published by National Library of Poetry in the Question of Balance.; [pers.] I want to leave my footprints in the sand for the future generations, so that they will know that I have past this way before.; [a.] Norfolk, VA

RUHLOFF, DEBORAH
[b.] December 27, 1968, Hamilton, Ontario, Canada; [p.] Udo and Madelyn Ruhloff; [ch.] Madelyn - 5, Nicolas - 3; [ed.] College certified Health Care Aid High School as well as Community College Computers Studies; [occ.] Student; [hon.] Won several singing and band awards; [oth. writ.] Have written several poems, songs; [pers.] Self discovery is a matter of looking at yourself from your own point of view and not relying on what other have led you to believe.; [a.] Burlington Ontario, Canada

RUIZ, RALPH L.
[b.] June 9, 1956, Santa Monica, CA; [p.] Ralph Ruiz and Leona June Aranez; [m.] Judy M. Ruiz, November 19, 1993; [ch.] Christopher R. Ruiz; [pers.] This poem is dedicated to my Brother Colin Sean Ruiz March 26, 1965 to July 3, 1994 we all miss you. God Bless; [a.] Lake Havasu City, AZ

RUNDQUIST, THOMAS O.
[b.] July 12, 1944, Norfolk, NE; [p.] Elwin and Marzella Rundquist; [m.] Shirley A. Rundquist, August 8, 1970; [ch.] Laura and Jill Rundquist; [ed.] BSEd MSED, University of Nebraska; [occ.] Math Teacher Millard Central Middle School; [memb.] National Education Association, National Council of Teachers of Mathematics, Board of Trustees of the 2nd Unitorian Church, National Audubon Society; [pers.] I feel the quality of a person's life is directly proportional to the time he spends enjoying the natural world. Most of my writing relates to nature.; [a.] Omaha, NE

RUNKLES, NAOMI B.
[b.] July 23, 1916, Myersville, MD; [p.] Mary and Melvin O. Gladhill; [m.] George E. Runkles (Deceased), January 3, 1938; [ch.] Gary Runkles, Gloria Keeney,2-grandsons, 1 great granddaughter; [ed.] 10th grade; [occ.] Vendor, Columbus Flea Market; [hon.] Certificate of Merit, Recipe Popouri of Cookery, Recipe For TV Facts For Tiffany's Bakeries, Frederick MD, 1979, 150 Ribbons at community Show, Thurmont, MD. one grand prize; [oth. writ.] Lover of, Animals Also Flowers, Have a cat named Elsie, Black and White like president Clintons he sent me 2-8 x 10 pictures of his cat, socks; [pers.] Wrote songs for country music artist was played on radio stations born and raised in Maryland live in Columbus, GA 15 years; [a.] Columbus, GA

RUSS, KAREN F.
[b.] December 31, 1962, San Pedro, CA; [p.] Ray N. Olsen and Barbara L. Olsen; [m.] Robin B. Russ, August 31, 1985; [ch.] Bethany Faye Russ, Bobby

Ray Russ; [ed.] Thiel College, Greenville, PA (BA - English), Aurora High School, Aurora, Ohio Study abroad-Norwegian Language studies, Sandane, Norway; [occ.] Employee Development Manager and Senior Consultant for TRW, Inc., Fairfax, LA; [memb.] National Association for Female Executives, Thespians; [hon.] Magna Cum Laude, Honors in English, Lambda Sigma Honorary Society, Dean's List, Elizabeth Steward Scholarship, Sons of Norway Academic Scholarship, Multiple Quality and TQM Awards; [oth. writ.] Poems, short stories, songs, for family and publication in High School Paper. Numerous Corporate Newletter Articles and Reports. Business Process Re engineering white paper.; [pers.] My family is my source of inspiration for living, writing, and loving. Thanks for encouraging creative sparks.; [a.] Manassas, VA

RUSSELL, BOB
[b.] Esthampton, MA; [ed.] Saint Peter's College, Oxford, GB, Springfield (MA) College; [occ.] Greenhouse Worker; [memb.] Academy of American Poets, Poetry Society of America; [hon.] Pulitzer Prize Nomination, In Journalism, Holyoke Transcript-Telegram, 1978. Associated Press Newswriting Award, Best Reporting from the New England News Executives Association (A.P); [oth. writ.] Instructional Essays, Perspectives Magazine and R.E Today Magazine, Chicago, IL., Theater Reviews; [a.] Easthampton, MA

RUSSELL, LOIS SMITH PAYTON
[pen.] "Lo", "Madam Lokie", "Butter Ball"; [b.] January 5, 1926, Savannah, GA; [p.] Roosevelt and Minnie Holland Smith; [m.] CSM Morris Ray Russell, US Army (Deceased), January 7, 1953, previous marriage August 7, 1947; [ch.] Rudolp, A. Payton, Victor E. Payton and Paul J. Russell; [ed.] St. Mary's Catholic Sch. and Beach-Cuyler High Sch., Savannah, Ga., South Carolina State Univ., Organgeburg, S.C., Bethune-Cookman College, Daytona Beach, FL, Savannah State College, Savannah, GA, Georgia Sou. College, Statesboro, GA, Peoples Law School, Savannah, GA; [occ.] Substitute Teacher, Chatham Co. Board of Education, Savannah, Ga., (Retired Office Manager-Secretary, T.J. Hopkins, Inc., Savannah, Ga. and obtained Leave of Absence for foreign duty with spouse.); [memb.] Savannah Chapter of Squaws, Inc., Sacred Heart Council of Catholic Women, Savannah Deanery Council of Catholic Women, Reading and Speech Communication Institute, Historian for Sacred Heart Parish all of Savannah, Ga; [hon.] Beach-Cuyler High Sch.-Sewing and Chorus Awards, Savannah, GA, Bethune-Cookman College, Daytona Beach, FA, Award/Outstanding Service in Business Office, St. Mary's CCW-Outstanding Leadership/Service, Savannah, GA, Silver Tray and Commendation for writing Constitution/Bylaws for Wives Club Approved by US Republic of Europe, Major David F. Winn, US Army, Heidleburg, Germany, Achievement Cert., Col. Leland F. Tigh, US Army, Hunter AAF, Savannah, GA, Several Bowling Trophies, Savannah, GA, and Germany, Gold Wrist Watch for Outstanding Employment Service, T.J. Hopkins, Inc. and Several Scouting Awards, Den Mother for 15 years, Savannah, GA; [oth. writ.] Several poems were written and presented to others as plaques in gold frames with photo.; [pers.] Appreciation to Nuns of St. Mary's Catholic School for Background

and writing encouragement, Mr. Joseph M Green, English Instructor, Beach-Cuyler High School, Mrs. Louise Lautier Owens English Instructor of Savannah State College, English Instructor who gave much inspiration, and Father Thomas J. Peyton of Sacred Heart Church all of Savannah, Ga. It was a pleasure to engage in writing personality poems of individuals who did outstanding deeds in the community and for our youth.; [a.] Savannah, GA

RUTH, RICHARD
[b.] July 2, 1933, Phoebus, VA; [p.] Richard and Helen; [m.] Barbara, December 29, 1954; [ch.] Deborah, Michael, Scott; [ed.] US Naval Academy 1995, BS Force Washington Univ 1971, MS; [occ.] Retired Military and Civil Service; [pers.] Do what is right written laws do not cover every action in life.; [a.] Smithmill, PA

RUTLAND, MITZI G.
[pen.] M. G. Rutland; [b.] Alabama; [ed.] B.A. Degree in English - Creative writing writers digest - fiction writing (taking their class row) Going back to school in the fall to get my Masters in English; [occ.] Title Abstracter with a title insurance company; [hon.] I writing awards in school; [oth. writ.] Was editor and poetry editor of "Early Spring" Literary magazine; [pers.] I desire to write about injustice and see it removed from someone is life one strong at a time. I long to touch hearts, one story at a time!; [a.] Columbia, SC

RYAN, TANIA C. D.
[b.] November 30, 1965, Edmonton, Alberta, Canada; [p.] Michael J. Ryan and Vera K. Ryan; [oth. writ.] Finalist for city of North York, 1980 poet Laureate Competition; [pers.] I'll follow my dreams, I'll follow my heart, I'll travel the distance and let your soul be my guiding light thank-you mom and dad (my light); [a.] West Vancouver British Columbia, Canada

RYLE JR., WILLIAM L.
[pen.] Wm L. Ryle, Jr.; [b.] January 18, 1944, Columbus, GA; [p.] Wm Sr. and Mary Louise Ryle; [m.] Rose Joyce Ryle, November 23, 1967; [ch.] Wm Peyton and Christopher Douglas; [ed.] B.B.A. Univeristy of Georgia '68; [occ.] Office Leasing and Management; [memb.] Building Owners and Management Asso., Thomas Road Baptist, Real Property Administrator, U.S. Army OCS Assn.; [hon.] President, BOMA/Tallahassee, Past Pres., Orlando CIVITAN; [oth. writ.] Reflections, On The Ground At Last, The Chair By The Door, The Forest, Imprints, The Light Of Living; [pers.] Writing opens a window through which hope can be projected, as the writers thoughts are reflected. Used properly, it leaves the mark of mans goodness.; [a.] Tallahassee, FL

SAAVEDRA, CONCEPCION ROMANA
[b.] December 7, 1952, Lucena City, Quezon Province, Philippines; [p.] Magno M. Romana, Anita V. Romana; [m.] Elpidio V. Saavedra, March 19, 1988; [ch.] Joseph John, Mary Josephine, Marianne Joyce; [ed.] Mary Knoll Academy, University of Santo Tomas, University of the Philippines; [memb.] Philippine Institute of Certified Public Accountants (PICPA); [hon.] 1968 High School Salutatorian, 1968 Rector's Award, 1972 Magna Cum Laude, Bachelor of Science in Commerce, 1988 Young

Lady Achiever Award of PICPA; [oth. writ.] Several poems/articles in school publications; [pers.] Always pray, trust in God and do your part.; [a.] Toronto Ontario, Canada

SABATULA, RUTH
[b.] Metropolitan, Toronto, Ontario, Canada; [p.] John Anthony Donovan and Mary Olive Merlin - (maiden name) they are deceased; [m.] Jim Sabatula; [ch.] Candice, Steve was killed in truck accident; [ed.] I took a creative writing course in high school. I also completed a course through the Institute of Children's Literature and graduated.; [occ.] Homemaker, and mother of Candice; [pers.] I have always had a love for writing stories and poems. I feel that poems come more naturally to me.; [a.] Town Lindsay Ontario, Canada

SADLER, LINDA
[b.] March 15, 1947, Welch, WV; [p.] Virginia Ayers Marshall; [m.] Douglas Sadler, September 18, 1992; [ed.] Albemarle Senior High School; [occ.] Transfer Clerk, US Postal Service; [memb.] Skyline Pentacostal Holiness Church-Meadows of Dan, VA; [oth. writ.] A poem published in "On The Threshold Of A Dream" and three poems published by the poetry press. (These were published under Linda K. Hester); [pers.] I write poetry from personal life feelings. All seem to be based on a true happening, that I have had published. This poem being published in the book "Beneath The Harvest Moon" is about the sudden death of my baby sister. She was 14 years old.; [a.] Winston Salem, NC

SALERNO, STEPHANIE JO
[b.] June 12, 1957, Norfolk, VA; [p.] Joseph A. and Theresa M. Vita; [m.] Jim Salerno, June 27, 1987; [ch.] Dana Jillian, 6yrs., Corey Bennett-4yrs.; [ed.] Norfolk Catholic High School, Ferrum College: Associate in Art, Radford University, VA Wesleyan College: BA in Sociology, Minor in Theatre, Old Dominion Univ. Graduate School: Counseling and Paralegal Studies; [occ.] Homemaker; [memb.] I was a member in a local writing group which met once a week. VA Marine Science Museum, a dance troupe: Ferrum College Children's Theatre Group; [hon.] I have received an Honorable Mention Award in Photography, Ferrum College Art Show. Certificate of Achievement in Creative Writing: Continuing Education, VA Beach Public Schools.; [oth. writ.] I have written poems as gifts for family members and friends. I wrote a poem for the cover of my marriage ceremony program.; [pers.] Write from your heart... As a rainbow, towards heaven you can reach...; [a.] Virginia Beach, VA

SALUZZI, THOMAS V.
[b.] June 10, 1958, Brooklyn, NY; [pers.] The secret ingredient of a great life is pookie.; [a.] Parkland, FL

SAMS JR., CHARLES THOMAS
[pen.] Sonny Sams; [b.] December 8, 1953, Jacksonville, FL; [ed.] Master of Arts Degree (Education) University of North FL, Bachelor of Arts Degree (Criminal/Justice), University of North FL. Associate of Arts Degree (Psychology), FL. Community, College of Jacksonville; [occ.] Police Officer with the Jacksonville Sheriffs Office (16 years); [memb.] F.O.P., P.B.A., Police Brotherhood Assn. Nat'l Police Anglers Assn. FL Council on Crime and Deliquency, Nat'l Rifle Assoc. North FL.

Writers Assoc. Virginia Country Civil War Society, Boy Scouts Alumni Assoc.; [hon.] Medal of Valor, Jax Sheriff Office, Silver Stars for Bravery American Police Hall of Fame. Life Saving Award, Jax Sheriff Office Distinguished Service Medal American Police Hall of Fame. Heroism Award, Law Enforcement Technology Magazine, Valor Award American Society for Industrial Security - Officer of the Quarter Westside Businessmans Assoc.; [oth. writ.] I have formally been writing for over 20 years mainly for family and friends.; [pers.] Writing to me is my way of inner expression. My purpose is to leave something to my children to show that I was indeed here on this earth, if only for a short time.; [a.] Jacksonville, FL

SANDERS, RUTH M.
[b.] December 5, 1930, Nokomis, IL; [p.] Hubert and Ruth Crabbe; [m.] James W. Sanders (Deceased), May 15, 1966; [ch.] Angela, Mark and Brenda; [ed.] Nokomis Twp. High, Illinois Community College, Comprehensive Cake Decorating, Ft. Wayne, Ind.; [occ.] Retired from many yrs. of office work mostly Accts. Payable also, as shop owner - "Ruth's Kandy and Kake Supply"; [memb.] Held several offices as member of Christian Women's Club, including Chairman; [oth. writ.] The only poem I recall being published was in a national church paper.; [pers.] I have always loved poetry. As a teenager, I wrote a few poems, mostly romantic in nature. Later, my writings took on a spiritual form. Now, at retirement age, my desire to write has returned, seemingly a mixture of romance, spirituals and natures.; [a.] Nokomis, IL

SANFORD, EMMA L.
[pen.] E.L. Sanford-Michaels; [b.] November 27, 1953, Oklahoma City; [ch.] Michael, John; [occ.] Medical Records Technician; [pers.] "You must do the think you think you cannot do"; [a.] Tulsa, OK

SANGHERA, AMARJIT
[b.] August 3, 1982, Birmingham, England; [p.] Ajair and Gurbaksh Sanghera; [ed.] Currently in grade 8; [memb.] Member of School Band, Choir, Art Club and I also work in the school store; [pers.] I would like to thank my parents for their encouragement and support of my writing.; [a.] Oakville Ontario, Canada

SANGIONE, DALBIR S.
[pen.] Singh; [b.] July 15, 1964, Punjab, India; [p.] Baldev Sangione, Surjit Sangione; [m.] Balwinder Sangione, February 8, 1992; [ch.] Sangam and Pirtham; [ed.] MSC. (Chem) B Ed, (Punjabi Uni Patiala) India., Chem Eng. Technology (diploma) Anticipated in April 1996 at Northern Alberta Institute Of Alberta; [occ.] Student; [memb.] Alberta Society of Engineering Technologists; [oth. writ.] Wrote poems in Punjabi and English, under publication; [pers.] I give much emphasis to emotions, human nature and compassion for nature, beauty and humanity. My inspiration is from within and my great fore to universe and God.; [a.] Edmonton, AB

SANTIAGO, JENNIE
[pen.] "La Rubia"; [b.] September 28, 1961, Brooklyn, NY; [p.] Antonia Santiago, Mike Delfino; [ed.] Brooklyn College, Prospect Heights High School, The New School; [occ.] Jewelry Exchange;

[memb.] Hispanic Society; [oth. writ.] Several poems published in High School and some poetry and books that are not published at this time.; [pers.] I've always enjoyed writing for myself - but I hope to write for others enjoyment also one day professionally.; [a.] Brooklyn, NY

SAUER, KERI
[b.] December 27, 1975, Terrace, BC; [p.] Bill Sauer and Eleanor Virtanen; [ed.] 2nd year Bachelor of Arts in Political Science, working on degree in Corporate Law; [occ.] Cashier at Real Canadian Superstore; [pers.] My poetry reflects my past relationships and my feelings during adolescence. My father's support has helped me immensely. "Never deprive someone of hope, it may be all they have".; [a.] Prince George British Columbia, Canada

SAULSGIVER, DWIGHT
[pen.] D. Slas; [b.] October 27, 1960, Westfield, NY; [p.] Gordon, Patricia Davenport Saulsgiver; [m.] Tina, January 1, 1996; [ch.] Brittany JoAnn - 6; [ed.] South Western Central HS, 1978 Jamestown Community College 1990, AAS Human Svcs. 210 Credit Hrs. Vocational Food Svcs Education; [occ.] Cook, Warren Co. Sheriffs Dept.; [memb.] Lions Int. Tri-city Medecors National Sheriffs Assn. IPMS fmr. Youth Pastor - Church of God - Prarie DuChein with Youth Worker/House parent Warren DHS; [hon.] Veteran US Army 1978-1986 2nd place - short stories - JCC 1990 "Homecoming" Award winning model builder and stamp collector; [pers.] I started writing at 13 to express the feelings I couldn't talk about, now I share with teens to help them find direction. Everything in life has a purpose. Yesterdays pain brings tomorrows understanding.; [a.] Warren, PA

SAUNDERS, LANNA S.
[b.] November 14, 1951, Modesto, CA; [p.] Johnny and Mabel Hamilton; [m.] Lloyd D. Saunders, July 3, 1971; [ch.] Mistie Charlene, Marcella Lanor and Stephanie Louise; [ed.] White River High, Buckley, WA, 1970; [occ.] House wife, Domestic Engineer; [oth. writ.] Several poems and some "small thoughts" as I call them - none published; [pers.] I love my family, my Lord, and life. My real needs are small but I want everyone around me to be happy and comfortable, even strangers.; [a.] Quesnel British Columbia, Canada

SAURS, MARK L.
[pen.] Mark L. Saurs; [ed.] B.A. English, minor Education University of Richmond, VA; [pers.] Life Events. The treadmill of material from which we create our Art. Words become the picture, the feelings, the message - unique to each person. The Harvest is each individual's bounty.; [a.] Manakin Sabot, VA

SAVOY, TERITA MARIA
[b.] Washington, DC; [ed.] University of Maryland; [occ.] Writer; [oth. writ.] Editor of Magazine, titled "Like Warring Tribes"; [a.] Washington, DC

SAXTON, CATHERINE
[b.] Ireland; [m.] Divorced; [pers.] I wrote this poem about seven years ago.; [a.] Hamilton Ontario, Canada

SCHAEFER, TERRI L.
[pen.] Terri L. Schaefer; [b.] September 26, 1961,

San Diego, CA; [p.] John and Sharon Armitage; [m.] Michael J. Schaefer, July 10, 1993; [ch.] Jessica and Nicole Schorr, Stephanie Schaefer; [ed.] High School graduate; [occ.] Senior Administrative Assistant, Community Network; [memb.] National Notary Association; [oth. writ.] Many unpublished poems; [pers.] Live life to it's fullest each day. Take time for the things we tend to take for granted. Always keep the lines of communication, honest and open.; [a.] Santee, CA

SCHILD JR., JOSEPH E.
[b.] August 29, 1938, Chattanooga, TN; [p.] Joseph E. Schild Sr, Leona Jordan Schild; [m.] LaShon Schild, May 26, 1962; [ch.] Sydonna Cambron, Joseph E, III, Roderick Clark; [ed.] Chattanooga High School, Tennessee Technical University; [occ.] Owner-Schild Azalea Gardens and Nursery; [memb.] Burk's United Methodist Church, Tennessee Nurserymen's Assoc., The American Rhododendron Society, Azalea Society of America; [hon.] Garden Feature-Chattanooga Free Press, WDEF-TV Garden Feature; [oth. writ.] Poem published in book, publish own mail order Catalog (Descriptive) now editing a book of short stories and essays.; [pers.] As a new writer, I find inspiration in Nature, family ties and history, and in spiritual reflection of God's work in me and family.; [a.] Hixson, TN

SCHLUNDT, GORDON DEAN
[b.] May 10, 1934, Mich City, IN; [p.] Linder, Christine Schlundt; [ch.] Cynthia; [ed.] Clinton TWP HS (La Porte Cty, Ind) '52 1 1/2 yrs Indiana Univ 53-54; [occ.] Retail Sales, Rural King Farm Sup. Mattoon, IL; [memb.] Book of Month Club, AARP, Amer. Bowling Congress; [hon.] La Porte Herald-Argus Journalism Plague for School News reporting, 1952; [oth. writ.] None published, I must have 75 poems in a box which I've kept thru. The years, each deals with events that affected people I have known, (and myself); [pers.] Reading poetry should be an enjoyable experience. In writing it, I attempt to pluck an emotional string with which the reader can identify - his own "plodding headlong against a raging snow storm.."; [a.] Mattoon, IL

SCHMIDT, BONNIE ALLEN
[pen.] Bonnie Allen Schmidt; [b.] September 27, 1917, Trinidad, Colorado; [p.] Fred and Ruth Allen; [m.] Marvin Otto Schmidt, May 30, 1942; [ch.] Marvin Allen and Frederick Paul; [ed.] B.A. Music Education, Missouri Baptist College St. Louis; [occ.] Housewife. Formerly, Music Teacher Covenant Christian School; Secretary; [memb.] Southwest Baptist Church, St. Louis; Americans United; American Bible Society; Republican National Committee; [hon.] (Too far back to remember.) President's List; Dean's List; Music Fellow; [oth. writ] Miscellaneous poetry and songs; [a.] Fenton, Missouri

SCHMIDT, MR. DARRELL M.
[pen.] DMS; [b.] February 16, 1949, Luverne, MN; [p.] Merlyn and Lavonne Schmidt; [ed.] B.S. Moorhead State University (English and German), M. Ed. University of Minnesota, Duluth Learning Disabilities Certification, Bemidji State University Spanish Certification, Mankato State University; [occ.] Educator, Falls High School, International Falls, Minnesota; [memb.] American Federation of Teachers, Communication and Theater Association of Minnesota, Minnesota Council on the Teaching of

Languages, Kappa Delta Pi, International Thomas Hardy Society; [hon.] 1995 Minnesota Teacher of the Year Finalist, $500 Action Research Grant, from Bread Loaf School of English, Independent Study from the Council of Basic Education, Twice recipient of the National Endowment of the Humanities Seminars for high school teachers; [oth. writ.] "Wanderlust in Wessex"-excerpt published Travel Review Magazine, 125-page report to the Council of Basic Education, comparing the narratives of James Fenimore Cooper and Minnesota Regional Author Frederic Manfred, "The Eagle Has Landed," published in the Falls Daily Journal (based on the interview with Frederick Manfred before his death), poems submitted and published in Loonfeather, a Northern Minnesota Publication; [pers.] "I have been fortunate that my vocation avocation have been one of the same. My twenty-five year teaching career has been rewarding and resourceful—one must continually change curricula and methods."; [a.] International Falls, MN

SCHMIDT, ROBERT C.
[pen.] Bobby; [b.] January 23, 1954, East Saint Louis, IL; [p.] Philip (Felix) Schmidt, Virginia; [ed.] St. Henry Seminary Alihoff High; [occ.] Employment Counsellor; [memb.] Knights of Columbus, U.S.G.A.; [oth. writ.] Several poems published in small tabloids; [pers.] Challenge is all around us in our life. Just as no two people are the same neither are the days in our lives.; [a.] Belleville, IL

SCHMITT, CHRISTOPHER KARL
[pen.] Christopher Karl, Christopher Schmitt; [b.] April 2, 1968, Montclair, NJ; [p.] Franz Karl, Judith E.; [ed.] Rutherford High School; [oth. writ.] Published poetry in Beneath The Raindrops The National Library of Poetry; [pers.] As my life and words grow I stop to notice the essence of my ways that are sweetened by no one but myself.; [a.] Rutherford, NJ

SCHOENBERGER, KATHLEEN ANN
[pen.] KT; [b.] December 7, 1952, Lafayette, IN; [p.] Robert L. and Hazel Y. Schoenberger; [ed.] New Trier East High School, Winnetka, IL, Wheaton North High School, Wheaton, IL, University of Wyoming, Laramie, WY; [hon.] Winner of National Humane Society 1993 Luckiest Pet Calendar photo/ poem contest for the month of "Pawgust"; [oth. writ.] Several poems and stories yet to be submitted for publication; [pers.] Writing became a matter of entertainment for my own amusement while sailing and eventually living several years in the Caribbean.; [a.] Pueblo, CO

SCHULTZ, JOYCE LAWHORN
[b.] February 19, 1942, Wagoner, OK; [p.] Grady and Elizabeth Lawhorn; [m.] Cleo Schultz, December 8, 1990; [ch.] Tami Collins, Terri Craig; [ed.] Wagoner High School; [occ.] Antique Collector (Retired) Patient Counselor at Wagoner Community Hospital Wagoner, OK; [hon.] 1st place winner in writing contest on employ appreciation at local hospital; [oth. writ.] Mother's Day essay for local newspaper; [pers.] This poem was inspired as I returned home from visiting my sister in the hospital a few weeks before her death.; [a.] Wagoner, OK

SCHWARTZ, JILL C.
[b.] May 27, 1982, New Haven, CT; [p.] Louis Schwartz, Dona Schwartz; [ed.] Ursuline Academy;

[occ.] Student; [hon.] First place in Fire Prevention Essay Contest (Wilmington), Honorable mention at Albert Einstein Regional Science Fair (Botany), Honor student; [oth. writ.] Personal writing Portfolio; [pers.] Learn from your mistakes and errors and don't get discouraged when you fail. Always remember your friends because they'll be there to lean on if you do not succeed; [A.] Newark, DE

SCHWARTZ, TANYA
[b.] March 4, 1979, Montreal, Canada; [ed.] Currently in Beaconsfield High School. Working towards a career in the fine arts.; [occ.] Student; [oth. writ.] Several unpublished poems and short stories both in French and English; [pers.] I write my feelings at the time. My writing is a part of my growth and I feel it represents a great part of me.; [a.] Beaconsfield Quebec, Canada

SCOTT, MERLE
[b.] February 15, 1908, Chariton, IA; [p.] Mr. and Mrs. Ward Carpenter; [m.] Milton Scott, June 8, 1938; [ch.] Two girls, one boy; [ed.] Public School Music (3 yrs.) Cedar Falls, Iowa BS in Music Drake University 6 yrs. Teaching plus music lessons; [occ.] Retired (for yrs.); [memb.] OES - Sac city 50 yrs. and United Methodist Church 50 and Federated Women's Clubs "Music Club" (Nemaha) 45 yrs. "Today's Home" Early Form Bureau 50 yrs.; [hon.] Trip to worlds fair in Chicago, trip to Milwaukee with Cecilian Glee Club to Convention, UMW - Pin, OES 50 yrs. Pin, Form Bureau 50 yrs. Pin; [oth. writ.] Some years ago when I directed Community singing I wrote other words to various composers songs. (Five songs etc.); [pers.] I loved children and wanted them to enjoy music as much as I always have. I have sung in church choirs most of my lie and directed children's choirs and adults.; [a.] Nemaha, IA

SCULLION, ELEANOR ANNE
[pen.] Ms. Ellie; [b.] August 27, 1960, Calgary, Alberta, Canada; [p.] Myrna and Arthur Scullion; [ch.] 14 yrs. old son; [ed.] Gr. 10 Diploma, and half of my Gr. 11, reason being, first teachers strike. Oct of '76. Started working; [occ.] Single mother P/T Bartender; [memb.] Y.E.S. Youth Employee Service; [hon.] Sports, City of Toronto Track and Field, Aquatic Swim Team, Three Canada Fitness Awards; [oth. writ.] Never published but, I've had nothing less then praise. I'm sending two more of my poems.; [pers.] Poetry to me, is my way of expressing my thoughts. Also to me poetry is communication.; [a.] Toronto Ontario, Canada

SEABOLT, YVETTE
[b.] May 25, 1966, Louisiana; [p.] Wyatt A. Rutledge Jr.; [ch.] Gina M. Seabolt and Alona T. Rich; [ed.] Paulding Co. High, Chattahoochee Tech.; [occ.] Admin. Asst.; [oth. writ.] Reality or The Dream?; [pers.] My writings are feelings from my heart. Influenced by God and my daughters, Gina and Alona.; [a.] Marietta, GA

SEARLES, JANE
[b.] May 27, 1967, Oakville, Ontario, Canada; [p.] Robert Searles, Brenda (Parker) Searles; [ed.] Simcoe Composite High School Mohawk College; [occ.] Civilian Dispatcher, Ontario Provincial Police - Chatham; [memb.] Songwriters Assoc. of Canada, Ontario Geneological Society, Order of the Eastern Star, Canadian Diabetes Assoc.; [pers.] I find writing

to be very therapeutic and the best way to express myself.; [a.] Chatham Ontario, Canada

SEAY, TRAVIS L.
[b.] January 17, 1975, Claxton, GA; [p.] Philip and Helga Seay; [m.] Tone Knudsen; [ed.] Williston High (Williston, FL) currently a junior at Florida State University; [occ.] Student of Social Sciences Education; [memb.] Golden Key National Honor Society; [hon.] Valedictorian of W.H.S. class of 1993, Dean's List; [pers.] There is something good at the helm.; [a.] Tallahassee, FL

SECHLER, BRENT J.
[pen.] Brendon James; [b.] May 4, 1967, Napa, CA; [ed.] BA Acctg, Catawba College; [occ.] Staff Accountant, Charlotte, NC; [oth. writ.] 1st submitted writing; [pers.] I am influenced by a person's thoughts dreams and all of the emotions of life and what from each we may learn. This writing is dedicated to Rebecca.; [a.] Charlotte, NC

SELVAKUMAR, SIVANNY
[b.] November 12, 1981, Madras, India; [p.] C.R. Selvakumar and Kumari Selvakumar; [ed.] Currently in grade 9; [oth. writ.] Articles for the Waterloo Collegiate Institute Newspaper "The Norsestar"; [a.] Waterloo Ontario, Canada

SENEVIRATNA, PETER
[b.] December 30, 1927, Colombo, Sri Lanka; [p.] Michael and Elizabeth Seneviratna; [m.] Saku Seneviratna, February 15, 1974; [ch.] Rohan and Gamini, Chitra and Manel; [ed.] Studied at Madras, London, and California Universities; [occ.] Retired academic; [memb.] Australian Veterinary Association and Australian Society of Parasitology; [hon.] Colombo plan scholarship and Fulbright-Hays Post Doctoral Research Award to study at the University of California (Davis Campus); [oth. writ.] Significant number of research publications on veterinary parasitology, a book on diseases of poultry and three poems by The National Library of Poetry, USA; [pers.] Though the future is not for us to see, the human species can record its thoughts and ideas for those of the future in writing. Poetry is the best way of doing this, succinctly and elegantly. [a.] Canberra, Australia

SENOUR, TRACY JEAN
[b.] July 8, 1974, Milw, WI; [p.] Richard Timm, Jacqueline Timm; [m.] Edgar Philip Senour, July 29, 1995; [ch.] Justin Philip Senour; [ed.] James Madison H.S. and Mount-Mary College; [oth. writ.] I wrote had many articles published in ARCHES, Mount Mary's newspapers. I also had a poem published in Mount Mary's creative writing magazine.; [pers.] I was inspired by my wonderful English professors at Mount Mary College. I was especially inspired by Dr. Catherine Malloy who persuaded me to become an English Major at Mount Mary.; [a.] Milwaukee, WI

SHAFFER, HAZEL FRANCES
[b.] March 4, 1907, West Virginia; [p.] Albert L. Courtney and Ophelia Williamson; [m.] Harold Shaffer (Deceased), August 25, 1925; [ch.] Rev. Mr. Harold F. Shaffer, Chatham Cape Cod.; [ed.] High School and one yr. Business School; [occ.] Housewife; [memb.] Takoma Park, MD Art Association, Historian of Md. Doll Club, Nat'l

Federation Of Doll Clubs, Miniature Club, Our Saviour Episcopal Church, Silver Spring, MD; [hon.] Honored by Md. Doll Club with gold plaque 1995; [oth. writ.] Poem published in Wash. D.C. newspaper at age 14.; [a.] Silver Spring, MD

SHAKIR, AMBER R.
[b.] April 13, 1969, Newark, NJ; [p.] Arnold Shakir, Gloria Shakir; [ch.] Yusuf Shakir Cooper; [ed.] Trenton State College, Bachelor of Arts in English; [occ.] Data Entry Processor; [hon.] Richard Wright Award for Written Excellence; [oth. writ.] Several poems featured in Utimme Umana, a college magazine; [pers.] The effect I try to bring to the reader is powerful emotion cloaked in subliminal message, assaulting the heart and the senses.; [a.] Roanoke, VA

SHARPE, BESSIE H.
[pen.] Hiawatha; [b.] January 27, 1951, Columbus, OH; [p.] O'Neil G. and Bessie L. Johnson; [ch.] Bryant E. C. Sharpe and Kori R. Sanders; [ed.] Bachelors and Masters Degrees - Public Administration, San Diego State University, San Diego, CA; [occ.] Internal Quality First! Consultant, US Postal Service; [memb.] National Association of Female Executives, League of Postmasters, Smithsonian Associate, Library of Congress, National Museum of the American Indian, Friends of the Library, and Penn State Alumni Association; [hon.] Dean's List in college and numerous work-related honors and awards; [oth. writ.] Unpublished poems and short stories, Masters Thesis, work related publications; [pers.] "Perception is reality in the mind of the beholder."; [a.] Oakton, VA

SHATWELL, JEFFERY L.
[b.] July 30, 1970, Oakland, CA; [p.] Mac and Doreen Shatwell; [m.] Kathleen Shatwell, December 9, 1995; [occ.] Carpenter

SHAW, DAVID BRIAN
[pen.] Jimmy; [b.] December 9, 1976, Dayton, OH; [p.] John and Linda Shaw; [ed.] Dayton Christian High School; [occ.] Delivery man-going to school to be a photographer; [hon.] "Superior" rating at 1995 Assembles of God Fine Arts Festival; [pers.] I write only what I think and feel, and my inspiration to write comes from those who have helped me. Mr. Greg Kurtz, my family, and most important God - thank you.; [a.] Dayton, OH

SHAW, JACKLYN LAUCHLAND
[b.] Lodi, CA; [p.] J. and C. Lauchland; [ed.] B.A., University of California, M.Ed. University of Nevada (1983), Ed.D. (Pend.), California Coast University, (Credentials, USPC); [occ.] Professor, Author, Consultant (Education Communications and Curriculum); [memb.] Choir, alum, other associations (for professional and civic services); [hon.] World Trade/Tourism Assn. Committees of Correspondence (O.C.). Research Advisory Boards (biography).; [oth. writ.] Program for communications, game manual, research article, text, newslog and poetry; [pers.] Writing is work and play.; [a.] Santa Ana, CA

SHAW, VIOLET
[b.] April 29, 1936, Wallington, Surrey, England; [p.] Violet and George Pethard; [ch.] Ken, Andrew and Kathryn; [ed.] Victoria High School, Douglas College; [occ.] City of Coquitlam Engineering Dept.

SHELDON, KAYE
[b.] March 6, 1924, Hammersmith, London, UK; [p.] Kate E. Don Sly; [m.] Stephen, October 1, 1945; [ch.] (4) Christopher, Phillip, (twins - Karen and Jacqui); [ed.] 5 years and 10 years Art Course (Fashion and Designer); [occ.] Retired; [memb.] 22 years Public School Secretary, 10 years Real Estate Agent, 5 years Handicapped Society of Alberta; [hon.] Art Scholarship London, UK (1935); [oth. writ.] Hoping for publication of short stories!!!; [pers.] Never give up! Give of everything you can of yourself - it will come back twentyfold!!!; [a.] Durham Ontario, Canada

SHIELDS, ANN P.
[b.] October 27, 1931, Queens, NY; [p.] John F. Riordan Anne M. Riordan; [m.] Francis J. Shields, October 11, 1952; [ch.] Bradley, Thomas, Lynn, Denise, Frank Jr., Ann, Philip, Geraldine Erica Jerome; [ed.] Valley Stream Central High, Kaupert Secretarial, attended Univ. Wis. Steverns Point, WI; [occ.] Retired; [memb.] GFWC - Stevens Points Women's Club, Hospice of Portage County - Volunteer Patients; [hon.] Human Interest Articles published - Sunshine Magazine, Mother's Manual many poems published in economical publications - Thursday People News - non copyrighted; [pers.] Faith in the Lord, in my fellow travelers on this planet my children's support and my husband's constant guidance. Parents suppported creativity - I tried to continue this in our children lives!; [a.] Plover, WI

SHIELDS, MICHELLE L.
[b.] April 8, 1974, Roseburg, OR; [p.] Floyd Polano, Carol Poland; [m.] Stephen L. Shields, July 1, 1995; [pers.] In my lifetime I searched for an explanation for that which is not understood. (I wish to dedicate this poem to my lost love, Marius Dumitru.; [a.] Roseburg, OR

SHILES, DONALD M.
[b.] August 23, 1936, Camden, NJ; [p.] Elmer and Grace Shiles; [m.] Gaylie Shiles, January 29, 1960; [ch.] Patricia, Judith, Rebecca, Don Jr., Eleanor, Robert; [ed.] B.S. - SoColo State College, MA - Univ of Northern Colo. graduate of the Wiesbaden Art Institute of Germany; [occ.] Teacher at US Army School and Anne Arundel Community College; [memb.] Chesapeake Art Guild, Assoc. Lock, Smiths of America, Safe and Vault technicians of America, Disabled American Veterans, Veterans of Foreign Wars; [hon.] Numerous awards/prizes in local, Nat'l and International Art Contests and shows; [oth. writ.] Poems published in Nat'l Anthology of High School Poetry, and in local publications, numerous articles in professional magazines or lock something and security; [pers.] I paint and write to depict beauty and instill feelings of joy and gratitude in myself and others.; [a.] Severn, MD

SHISKIN, MRS. MARGARET
[pen.] "Mashka"; [b.] April 13, 1928, Arran, Saskatchewan, Canada; [p.] Fred and Anna Poswikoff; [m.] Michael Shiskin, May 26, 1946; [ch.] James, David, Clifford, Susan, Bonnie, Robyn; [ed.] Grade 10; [occ.] Retired homemaker, grandmother, great grandmother; [memb.] Church (St. Pauls) "Christian Womens Society"; [hon.] None, except for being there for the family and friends and cooking and baking endless meals. And

still doing it and enjoying being useful.; [oth. writ.] "When I Was Just A Little Girl", "Old Seniors Dilema", "The Robin's Bidding" and many other nonsensical comedy ones; [pers.] I feel we need to take time to feel to see to help one another in any way we see fit care for your fellowman wealth does not prevent illness and kindness never goes out of style.; [a.] Kelowna British Columbia, Canada

SHOOK, OFELIA E. K.
[pen.] Ofelia Martinez; [b.] July 15, 1959, Havana, Cuba; [p.] Raudel Martinez and Ofelia Soto Martinez; [m.] Michael K. Shook/self-employed business professional, August 9, 1989; [ch.] Tomio and Tsuruko Kurosawa Shook and (expecting); [ed.] St. Lawrence Elementary, Tampa Catholic High/ Santa Fe Community College, Hillsborough Community College/Central Florida Community College, Manhattan Beauty School/Division of Vocational Education Horticulture; [occ.] Professional Cosmetologist; [memb.] American Quarter Horse Association, The Cat Fanciers Association/ American Kennel Club/The American Half Grade Quarter Horse Association; [hon.] Volunteer Red Cross Nurse/National Guild Of Piano Players and National/Piano Playing Auditions/Carmen Morales School of Ballet and Spanish Dance with the Castanets/Intern teacher Manhattan Beauty Spanish teacher at New Hope Elementary School Tampa; [oth. writ.] Personal collections; [pers.] I must give give credit to my parents for instilling in me to put God first in my life. The courage to face any adversity and stand for what I believe is right to push myself to the limit. Never settle for anything less than the best I can be. To hope and to dream. That I can do anything in life I desire as long as I work hard to reach that goal. Never give up. Be kind, thoughtful, and compassionate of others less fortunate.; [a.] Fort White, FL

SHOPTAW, DAVID W.
[b.] February 21, 1962, Orlando, FL; [p.] Richard and Dorothy Shoptaw; [ed.] North Montgomery High U.S. Army Helicopter Repair School (UM-1) (UH-60A); [occ.] Equipment operator for city of Waco; [pers.] Thank you for taking the time to read such poor words.; [a.] Waco, TX

SHORES, RUTH PATRICIA
[pen.] Ruth P. Shores; [b.] December 24, 1948, London, Ontario, Canada; [p.] Peggy Macdonald, Francis John James Barned (Deceased); [m.] Arthur E. Shores, August 23, 1969; [ch.] Steven Andrew; [ed.] H.B. Secondary School S.T.T. Art Major, Ivan R. Sales School of Cosmetology; [occ.] Housewife (Domestic Engineer); [oth. writ.] A collection of poems written over the years. None published. Till now.; [pers.] Poetry is and has been a source of mind and soul searching. A way of expressing life experiences and feelings. The wonder of or the knowledge of.; [a.] Saint Thomas Ontario, Canada

SHUFLITA, ROSEANN
[b.] November 3, 1975, Melville, SK; [p.] Martha Shuflita, late - Mike Shuflita; [ed.] Ituna High School, University of Saskatchewan 2nd year Psychology Major; [occ.] Student; [hon.] Invited to the International Society of Poets Gala Poetry Symosium to accept two awards, also I have poems in my high school year book; [oth. writ.] "So Far In" published in wind in the night sky; [pers.] Believing

n your self is half the battle, since this is what makes all things possible; [a.] Saskatoon Saskatchewan, Canada

SHULL, JASON DEAN
[b.] December 21, 1975, Key West, FL; [p.] Patricia Lakous and Michael Lakous; [ed.] High School Graduate currently in College; [occ.] Dept. Store Worker; [hon.] John Phillip Sousa Award - many awards for solos and duets in the performing arts; [oth. writ.] Many personal poems I've written and collected over the years; [pers.] I try to make my poems as meaningful and heartfelt as possible. I believe it can touch a persons heart.; [a.] Lemoore, CA

SHUMAKE, ANITA
[b.] December 29, 1958, Parkersburg, WV; [m.] Don, March 4, 1978; [ch.] Ryan; [ed.] Presently earning a Bachelor of Arts Degree; [occ.] Student at West Virginia University Parkersburg, Secretary for Carpenters Local Union #899; [hon.] Dean's List; [pers.] This poem was written for my seventeen-year-old son Ryan. Who kindles flames of Nostalgia.; [a.] Parkersburg, WV

SICA, NICHOLAS A.
[b.] May 21, 1921, Hartford, CT; [p.] Olga Perrucci Sica, Nicholas R. Sica; [m.] Divorced, October 26, 1954; [ch.] Nicholas D. Eric, Valdy, Andre; [ed.] BSEE Stanford '49, MSSE VPI '76; [occ.] Retired Civil Servant; [memb.] Armed Force Comm. Elect. Ass'n., Library of Congress Associates, Common Cause, U.S. English, The Nature Conservancy, The Southern Poverty Law Center; [oth. writ.] Column in local weekly newspaper for three years. Title: Foolosophy, Sub Title: Ruminations of a Retired Bureaucrat. Extensive writing in Dept. Of Def.-Not available.; [pers.] At 74 my thinking is mostly 20-20 hindsight instead of the 20-500 foresight of my youth.; [a.] Luray, VA

SIGETY, ROBERT
[b.] May 30, 1979, Huron, SD; [p.] Tammy Stymiest, Patrick Sigety; [ed.] 10th grade; [occ.] Student; [a.] Deadwood, SD

SIGNOR, JASON EARL
[b.] December 21, 1971, Cortland, NY; [p.] Gene D. and Sharon S. Signor; [ed.] Rensselaer Polytechnic Institute (one year of Architecture school, 1990-91), Ohio State U. (Liberal Arts, 1991-1992), Syracuse University (Music) 1992 - present; [occ.] Music major at Syracuse University; [memb.] Chi Alpha Christian Fellowship, (Syracuse University); [pers.] My poetry is mostly a reflection of the pain and joy of relationships, brokenness and the need for reconciliation, between God and mankind, between people, and between mankind and the rest of creation.; [a.] Syracuse, NY

SIKORA-CHOLEWA, EWA
[b.] April 19, 1956, Warsaw, Poalnd; [p.] Jerzy Bogdanski, Izabela Prokop; [m.] Robert Cholewa; [ch.] Marcin Sikora; [a.] Chicago, IL

SILEOCH, MAE
[b.] August 8, 1921, Glasgow, Scotland; [p.] Deceased; [ed.] Ruthegle Academy, Glasgow Lower Leaving; [occ.] Retired; [memb.] C.E.C.C., N.T.M.C.C., Toronto, Canada; [hon.] A.L.C.M. (In Drama, Poetry and English Literature); [oth. writ.]

An essay in "Are You Listening" (essays by Ontario Senior Citizens); [pers.] Wrote poetry as an "Exit" for my emotions. No one has ever seen my poetry. Studied poetry from "Beowulf" on.; [a.] Toronto Ontario, Canada

SILVA, ROBERT
[b.] July 18, 1973, Harlingen, TX; [p.] Oralia Silva; [ed.] Harlingen High School; [occ.] U.S. Navy (USS Nebraska SSBN 739 Blue, Trident II Nuclear Submarine); [memb.] Famous Poets Society; [hon.] Round Robin Grand Prize winner at First Annual Famous Poets Society Convention September, 1995; [oth. writ.] Articles for local military newspaper, Editor for ship's newspaper; [pers.] Let no one stand in the way of your dreams. I thank my mother, Oralia, for letting me know that I achieve any goal I set. If you can see, you can make it be.; [a.] Saint Marys, GA

SIMMONS SR., WILLIAM JEROME
[b.] November 24, 1963, Conway, SC; [p.] Leonard Simmons Sr. and Frances Simmons; [m.] Thomasina M. Simmons, September 1, 1995; [ch.] William Jerome Simmons, Jr.; [ed.] B.S.-Biology, University of South Carolina; [occ.] Chemistry Instructor, Accounts Mgr./Sales Rep., Owner of Simmons Enterprises & Services, Inventor; [memb.] Subscribing Life Member of Kappa Alpha Psi Fraternity, Inc., Choir member at Cumberland A.M.E., Member of Aiken Alumni Chapter of Kappa Alpha Psi, Inc.; [hon.] Aiken Alumni Chapter of Kappa Alpha Psi Brother of the Year (1992), Westing house - SRS QISS Awardee, "Extra Cast" in the Disney movie remake of "That Darn Cat" which was filmed in Edgefield, SC; [oth. writ.] Author of the book, "Operation Desert Shield/Storm Through The Eyes Of A Black Lieutenant" Published by: Dorrance Publishing Co., 1-800-788-7654; [pers.] Motto: "One must have faith in the power of the divine presence, believe, and you will achieve."; [a.] Aiken, SC

SIMMONS, WILLIAM A.
[pen.] W.A.S.; [b.] September 19, 1957, Toronto, Ontario, Canada; [p.] Juan Albert and Joan Simmons; [m.] Christina Simmons, September 13, 1980; [ch.] Emily Rose Simmons; [occ.] Ambulance EM7; [oth. writ.] An unpublished collection of 365 poems in a book entitled I Was, I Am and I Will Be, life poems of the naked three; [pers.] "God is life, in all its forms, great and small alike. And God exists, in everything that we know as life."; [a.] Missisauga Ontario, Canada

SIMONIAN, JEANNINE L.
[b.] October 23, 1947, Fresno, CA; [p.] Dorothy Moore-Robert Pinckney; [m.] Kenneth G. Simonian, March 12, 1980; [ch.] Monique Mays, Robert Paul Scrivner; [ed.] American Institute of Hypnotherapy, Various Community Colleges-Business Major; [occ.] American Medical and Dental Certified Hypnotherapist, Reiki II Practitioner; [memb.] Reverend Universal Life Church, Metahysical Research Society of Spokane Washington; [oth. writ.] I have written other poems however, none have been published; [pers.] My life is filled with joy. What more could I ask for!

SIMONSON, MARIA D.
[b.] October 15, 1919, Shanghai, China; [p.] Father CMDR. USN; [m.] Cot. Gorden Simonson, Febraury

5, 1949; [ch.] 6 Foster; [ed.] Academic Cholet, Amiens France, Catholic Convent-Lausanne Switzerland, Sacred Heart-Jamaica; [occ.] Retired from Med. Faculty - Johns Hopkins Med. Institutions (Prof. Emerita); [memb.] Am Soc. Bariatic Physician, International Cabim and Cochpit New Ass'n. Johns Hopkins Med. Faculty (Net.) Red Cross and Charitable Unnumerable Organizations; [hon.] 7 Awards by foreign youth and 5 domestic and foreign Organizations; [oth. writ.] Many scientific journals, many currents magazine, 5 books; [pers.] The greatest gift is to serve those that need your suffering re-assurance and kindness. To believe in God with all your hearts.; [a.] Westminster, MD

SINDELAR, JENNY
[pen.] J. S. Arnette; [b.] September 28, 1970, Cedar Rapids, IA; [p.] Arno and Joyce Sindelar; [ed.] Marion High School, University of Northern Iowa, University of Iowa; [occ.] Commercial Writer/ Producer; [memb.] Society of Professional Journalists, AD Fed; [oth. writ.] Several News Articles in U of I's local chapter of SPJ's Newsletter "News Hawk", opinion articles in local newspaper; [pers.] You're not going to last forever. But if you're published, your name will; [a.] Cedar Rapids, IA

SINGLETON, CLAY
[pen.] Spiderman; [b.] January 1, 1955, New Orleans; [ed.] Eight; [occ.] I am in jail; [oth. writ.] Romance A Dream, Star, Dark, Imagine, 5 Foot 7, Lady, Special Sandy, Dim, Appear, You, Mom's; [pers.] I Clay have no money I only write to keep my mind right. Now I am hand-d-cap so I do not write to good but I do the best I can. Now it all up to you if you will print my poem I only write them. I have more this is only a few.; [a.] Saint Gabriel, LA

SIPOS, MIKLOS
[b.] May 19, 1967, Bethlehem, PA; [ed.] B.A. in Archaeology, Rutgers University; [occ.] Graphic Artist; [oth. writ.] Children's story "The Adventures of Moko the Cat" copyright 1994, Carlton Press, NY, NY; [a.] Lebanon, NJ

SKELHORN, LINDA MARGARET
[b.] March 7, 1952, Windsor, Nova Scotia, Canada; [p.] Margaret (Dill) (Horne) Curry, Norman Horne; [m.] Wayne Skelhorn, December 21, 1977; [ch.] Kellie, Sean, Margot, Davan; [ed.] N.S. Teachers College, Mt. St. Vincent University B.Ed., M.Ed.; [occ.] Grade 1 teacher Three Mile Plains District School; [oth. writ.] Enjoy writing for school, family, and friends; [pers.] My father was killed when I was 15 months old and every year I visited his grave on Father's Day. I wrote this poem as I thought about him one evening.; [a.] Windsor Nova Scotia, Canada

SKINNER, ROBERT J.
[pen.] Robert J. Skinner; [b.] June 26, 1920, Harrisburg, PA; [p.] Alice I. and Charles W.; [m.] Elsie E. Skinner, July 2, 1945; [ch.] Janette A., John C. and Roberts Jr.; [ed.] High School - Stewart Tech. School of Aviation NY CIYY - and several other schools on Jet Engines and Helicopters; [occ.] Retired from federal Govt.; [memb.] Past member of post 2001 American Legion. Past Member of VFW post 1718; [hon.] Many awards from coaching little league - teener league and american legion baseball. Also several awards from the senior olympics held in Syracuse, NY. 6-28 to 7-3, 1991; [oth. writ.]

"Memories Of The Past And Those Yet To Come"; [pers.] I believe in living one day at a time. I also believe your only as old as you feel and your age is just a number. Keep active and free from bad habits.; [a.] Harrisburg, PA

SKOIER, ANTHONY
[b.] February 7, 1963, Juliet, IL; [ed.] Plainfielo High School, Western Illinois University; [occ.] Manager, Namco Cybertainment; [pers.] I look to nature that mankind has forgotten I look towards love for those who are looking for it. Chivalry, honor and other traits that all people may have forgotten existed.; [a.] Juliet, IL

SLUTSKY, JORDAN
[b.] August 13, 1980, Bronx, NY; [p.] David and Natalie Slutsky; [ed.] Ellenville High School, Academic Study Associates; [memb.] High School Activities: Staff Member of the Ellenville Echo (Creative writing Editor), Drama Club, Mock Trial team, Class Officer (Secretary), Varsity Tennis Team Member, and National Junior Honor Society Member; [oth. writ.] Numerous other poems; [pers.] I am a fifteen year old female currently attending Ellenville High School. My goals for the future include becoming a creative writing major and, ultimately, a successful poet. My poetry represents honesty, maturity can only develop from truth.; [a.] Ellenville, NY

SMALE, ERNEST F.
[b.] October 3, 1924, Tintagel, Cornwall, England; [p.] Frederick Smale, Etuel Smale; [m.] Gloria Smale, January 17, 1950; [ch.] Bernadette, Deborah, Beverley, Kathryn, John; [ed.] Sir James Smith Grammar School; [occ.] Retired (Safety/Security Manager); [hon.] Canadian Decoration (C.D.); [oth. writ.] Some poems published in local newspapers and articles in professional magazines; [pers.] Legendary Cornwall is an enchanted, fabled land. I should have been versifying long ago.; [a.] Calgary Alberta, Canada

SMALLWOOD, SUSIA
[b.] July 5, 1951, Lewiston, NC; [p.] Anderson Pugh, Eulah Mae Pugh; [m.] Royal Smallwood, September 23, 1968; [ch.] Arretha, Michell, La Royal, Chris-grandson; [ed.] BSN - Nurse RN, C Currently pursuing MSA-Central Michigan University (Health Care Admin). Certified in Psychiatry and mental health pioneer in nursing award 5/95 - Bowie State Univ. Bowie MD; [occ.] Registered Nurse - Case Mgr DHS-CMHC - Region 3 - Wash, D.C.; [memb.] DCNA, Bowie State University Alumni Assoc. Scripture Cathedral Church-Bishop C.L. Long Pastor - Wash, D.C.; [hon.] Pioneer in Nursing Award 5/19 - Bowie State Univ Bowie, M.D.; [oth. writ.] Secrets from the Past published in Beyond The Stars 1995; [pers.] I am inspired to continue to put my feelings into words in an effort to help others. A special thanks to my BSU instructors Dr. Walker, Ms. Soden and Dr. Eller. Most of all thanks to my sisters Flora, Julia, Alice and Maggie for their support.; [a.] Temple Hills, MD

SMIALEK, LISA P.
[b.] February 28, 1972, Blue Island, IL; [p.] Walter and Arlene Smialek; [ed.] St. Francis de Sales H.S., Roosevelt University; [occ.] Assistant Editor, Employee Communications, AMA; [oth. writ.] Am

working to publish my own book of poetry.; [pers.] I enjoy expressing my opinion through poetry, and am most inspired to write by controversial societal issues, matters of the heart and nature. I greatly admire Alice Walker's poetry and novels.; [a.] Chicago, IL

SMITH, ADELINA
[b.] Toronto, Ontario, Canada; [ed.] Attended York University and received honours B.A. degree, majoring in Sociology; [occ.] Circulation Application Analyst with Toronto Public Library; [pers.] My poetry becomes the guide through my own eyes, of what I see, what I experience, and what I can imagine.; [a.] Thornhill Ontario, Canada

SMITH, ARLO JACOB
[b.] November 20, 1982, Seattle, WA; [p.] Desiree Smith, Larry R. Smith; [occ.] Student at Whitman Middle School, Seattle, WA; [memb.] Boy Scouts of America, Kaleidoscope - Modern Dance Company of Young People; [hon.] 3rd Place - Boy's Life Magazine, essay contest (1993); [pers.] I guess, I write because it gives me a wonderful media to express my feelings. What also moves me to write is the belief that everytime someone reads something I've created and thinks about it after wards is that I've talked to that person is a strange but beautiful way.; [a.] Seattle, WA

SMITH, CHERYL L.
[b.] May 4, 1965, Washington, DC; [p.] Lorraine F. Smith; [ch.] Dominique Butler; [ed.] Woodrow Wilson High, Washington, DC; [occ.] Reimbursement Assoc. Medical; [oth. writ.] Several poems of personal writings; [a.] Laurel, MD

SMITH, DOUGLAS S.
[pen.] D. Sank Smith; [b.] October 23, 1951, Fort Worth, TX; [p.] James and Francis Smith; [ed.] Tarrant County Jr. College; [occ.] Advertising: Freelance Photography, Media Consulting; [oth. writ.] Various songs and poems none published; [pers.] Writing is generally an extension of my deeper feelings I have no formal education in writing and have been influenced primarily by song writers such as: Bob Dylan, Paul Simon, John Lennon, David Crosby...; [a.] Dallas, TX

SMITH, ELSIE JOYE KEIZER
[pen.] Joy Smith; [b.] October 17, 1900, Halls Harbor, Nova Scotia; [m.] Vernon Harold Smith, December 24, 1920; [ch.] Gweneth Eileen; [ed.] Finished school and became school teacher; [memb.] Song Writer's Protective Association; [oth. writ.] Many songs etc.; [pers.] "Love your neighbour", "Live by golden rule"

SMITH, FATIMA R.
[b.] December 19, 1955, Mansfield, OH; [p.] Muhammad Fareed, Aaliyah Fareed; [m.] Darrell T. Smith, September 21, 1981; [ch.] Darrell Jr. Lashanna, Lamon, Lameer, Lamar, Laquawn, G. C. Niesha; [ed.] Youngstown State University, Harding Business College, Writers Digest, Laural Business School; [occ.] Production Worker, Youngstown, OH; [hon.] Harding Business College, Dean's List, certificate for poem. "When I Grow Old"; [oth. writ.] Published poems in Quills Books, The Poetry Center; [pers.] The best way I can show my feeling is through my poems. My book "Momma Didn't Tell

Me This". When I find a publisher. When I'm finished writing is realization for me.; [a.] Youngstown, OH

SMITH, HILDA
[b.] November 21, 1950, Winnipeg, Manitoba, Canada; [p.] Rachel Bronfman Goszer, Mendel Wexler Sztemfeld; [m.] Leonard Smith, July 5, 1970; [ch.] Penny, Michelle, Mandy, Brooke; [ed.] University of Manitoba Education diploma University of Calgary, Family Life Educator Certification, Piano, voice studies; [occ.] School teacher, family life educator, artist multi-mediarts; [memb.] Beth Igedec Synagogue past Co-President of Sisterhood, ORT, Hadassah Wizo, World Community Assn.; [hon.] President of 1st Teen Fashion Council, Hudson's Bay Wpg, Gulf Canada Resources Art Show, Guest, Composer and Vocal, Soloist-Calgary Philharmonic Orchestra, Volunteer honor cert. for work commentator with seniors; [oth. writ.] Original works for International Reading Association, newspaper publication and T.V. dance narration children's affirmations, songs and poems created for specific pre school classes in French, English, Jewish; [pers.] I am a child of holocaust survivors. Creativity, strength commitment joy - above all love deepen our awareness to live more truthfully respecting our differences intellectually and emotionally "learning, growing, knowing"; [a.] Calgary Alberta, Canada

SMITH, LENORA
[b.] March 9, 1963, Lewisburg, PA; [p.] Chris and Naomi Peachey; [m.] Rodney P. Smith, September 19, 1981; [ch.] Jesse J., Leanne R.; [ed.] Mifflinburg Area High School; [occ.] Housewife; [a.] Loganton, PA

SMITH, LITICIA, M.
[b.] December 30, 1964, San Francisco, CA; [m.] Kirk R. Smith, June 25, 1983; [ch.] Tyler James, Tahni Rochelle, Hunter Christian; [oth. writ.] Several poems published in various forms; [pers.] This poem dedicated to my husband and family. Most important to Ken and Tamara Lynn, without them these words would not exist. Within death to prove the belief in the mystery of God is worth all things. Always to love you. Be free.; [a.] Oakhurst, CA

SMITH, LORI
[b.] May 2, 1964, Hamilton, ON, Canada; [p.] Stan and Joyce Smith; [m.] Joseph Castellano (to be), September '96; [ed.] Grade 12 and in second year of college for social services; [occ.] Part time bookkeeper and full-time student; [memb.] 1st year college - Dean's List; [oth. writ.] Poems published in an anthology of Hamilton Region Women called "Struck By Lightning"; [pers.] All of my work comes from deep within my soul, which I continue to uncover one layer at a time. This poem was written for is dedicated to my friend, Tracy Mirza whose 4 children were taken from her to Pakistan.; [a.] Hamilton Ontario, Canada

SMITH, LORI
[b.] December 8, 1961, Marshalltown, IA; [p.] James Brown, Barbara Brown; [m.] Jeff Smith, February 16, 1980; [ch.] Allison Rae, Christa Marie; [ed.] Fredrick High School, Hamilton Business; [occ.] Daycare; [a.] Des Moines, IA

SMITH, MARY
[b.] April 16, 1947, Windsor, Ont.; [p.] Helen and
Bill Smith; [m.] David Smith, October 19, 1968;
[ch.] Barbara, Kary Stuart; [ed.] R.N. Diploma from
Victoria Hospital - London, Ont, Nursing, Footcare-
Mitchener Institute in Toronto; [occ.] Self employed
- nursing, Footcare - company name - happy soles;
[memb.] R.N.A.O. NEFCA CANIP; [hon.] This is
my first serious attempt at writing poetry.; [pers.]
Most of my clients are seniors and my inspiration
came from them.

SMITH, OMEGA
[b.] April 9, 1922, Oklahoma; [p.] Henry and
Marinda Simpson (D); [m.] Jess Smith (Deceased),
October 7, 1939; [ch.] Jean, Ron, Van and Steven;
[ed.] High School; [occ.] Retired Medical Assistant;
[memb.] First Baptist Church, Visalia-Member of
Women's Council; [oth. writ.] Poems published in
"Paths Less Traveled" by the Poetry Center Orinda
Calif. and in "Warm Thoughts" by American Arts
Assoc. Gulfport, MS; [pers.] I have been writing
poetry since I was a young girl - most of it is to show
the love of God for all people.; [a.] Visalia, CA

SMITH, SANDRA L.
[b.] February 6, 1940, Union, MS; [p.] Eleanor and
William Buckwalter; [m.] Divorced; [ch.] Kevin S.
Smith and Melinda L. Stinson; [ed.] University High
School (Los Angeles), B.A. Elementary Education -
Univ. of Colorado, M.S.S.W. Social Work - Univ.
of Tennessee; [occ.] Social Worker; [memb.] Nat'l
Assoc. of Social Workers; [hon.] Phi Kappa Phi;
[oth. writ.] Several poems published in various
anthologies through the Nat'l Library of Poetry and
letters to the editor of The Commercial Appeal,
(local newspapers).; [pers.] My poetry is a way of
reflecting my observations on many aspects of life,
as well as expressing my feelings about these
aspects. It is my hope that my poems may strike a
chord within the reader and plant a seed for thought.;
[a.] Germantown, TN

SMYTH, MILDRED J.
[b.] March 9, 1913, Blytheville, AR; [p.] Mary Ella
and Wm Parker Judd; [m.] Ruel N. Cooper
(Deceased), 1934, Alvin Smyth Sr. (Deceased 1960),
1954; [ch.] Mildred Anne Pruett, Betty Jo Bertrand,
Ruel N. Cooper II; [ed.] High School Private Music
Lesson - 6 yrs Business College, Music-Organ Jones
Boro, Ark College Mo. state Tchrs. License; [occ.]
Retired - Volunteer Church Musician; [memb.] Pres,
Business and Professional Club Ark. and MO, Office
Mgr's Rating under Civil Service; [hon.] State PTA -
MO. For Starting Bloomfield, MO. PTA where I
taught H.S. music; [pers.] Tucson choir direction -
American Lutheran Ch-following 2nd husbands
death 3 choirs, have held every position in Bolway
Christian Church from treasurer to board chair -
represented BCC as only AZ delegate at a siliman -
UN Calif. the only AZ. delegate and appeared on
program.; [a.] Treeson, AZ

SNEATH, PATRICIA A.
[b.] March 24, 1946, Van., BC, Canada; [p.] James
O. Taylor and Eileen A. Taylor; [m.] R.K. Moi, Sr.,
(Divorced); [ch.] Michaele D. Carter and Sherri-
Lynn A. Lutz; [ed.] Northern Lights College; [occ.]
Long Term Care Aide; [memb.] Rolla Seniors Art
Society and Alzhiemers Association; [oth. writ.]
None - first attempt; [pers.] Enjoy family, and

grandchildren. Live in rural Hamlet, which I love.
Try to live by the motto "There but by the grace of
God go I" - we never know what lies ahead, or what
we will face in life around the comes.; [a.] Rolla
British Columbia, Canada

SNOW, MATTHEW
[b.] January 25, 1969; [p.] Luther and Mary Snow;
[ed.] Creighton Prep High School ('87) English
Major, BA Degree Rockhurst College ('91); [memb.]
International Society of Poets; [oth. writ.] Various
published (and unpublished) poems and short stories;
[pers.] I draw inspiration from many ideas and just
write what my imagination creates. I feel that
inspiration from within is as important as impressions from an external source. Always follow what
exists inside.; [a.] Houston, TX

SNOW, NANCY L.
[b.] April 9, 1948, Toledo, OH; [p.] Louis Fuhr,
Marjorie Furh; [m.] Vern Snow Jr., May 5, 1995;
[ch.] Shelli, Traci, Cindi, Chris, April; [ed.]
Woodward High - University of Toledo Be and ME;
[occ.] Teacher Grade 6 McGregor Elementary
Toledo, Ohio; [memb.] NEA, TAWLS; [hon.]
Dean's List, President's List; [oth. writ.] This is my
first to be published; [pers.] I hope, someday to write
a children's book. I receive much personal
gratification from my writing and hope this carries
over to my students.; [a.] Toledo, OH

SNYDER, HILARY
[pen.] Hilary Snyder; [b.] December 21, 1982, Fort
Wayne, IN; [p.] Lori Imel, Stephen Snyder; [ed.]
Roanoke Elementary School, Riverview Jr. High
School; [memb.] Riverview Singers, Church, The
Challenger Space Mission Committee; [hon.]
Roanoke 6th grade Honor Society; [oth. writ.]
Children's stories, a song; [a.] Roanoke, IN

SNYDER, MARION TERINE
[pen.] Marion Kerr-Snyder; [b.] June 2, 1944,
Portage, WI; [p.] Ben C. and Marion (Scofield) Kerr;
[m.] Ronald G. Snyder; [occ.] Secretary/Bookkeeper
and Genealogist; [memb.] 1) The National Archives,
2) The New England Historic Genealogical Society,
3) Waupaca Historical Society, 4) A - Docent at the
Hutchingson House-Museum in Waupuca, Wis.;
[hon.] My great-great grandmother, Miranda
(Lincoln) Farrington was a cousin to President
Abraham Lincoln; [oth. writ.] Have finished two
genealogies - in the process of compiling the
information for two more. Will have my poem
"Autumn Days" published by the National Library of
Poetry in the spring of 1996 in the book Sound of
Poetry - Windows of the Soul.; [pers.] I write poems
of my love of family, nature, history and tranquility.;
[a.] Waupaca, WI

SNYDER, SUSAN E.
[b.] May 1, 1952, Cleveland, OH; [p.] Barbara L. and
John O. Jones; [m.] Michael J. Snyder, May 26,
1973; [ch.] Joseph and Robert; [ed.] Severna Park
High School, Severna Pk Md., Anne Arundel
Community College, Arnold, Md; [occ.] Title I
Reading Tutor, Harbour View Elementary,
Summerfield FL; [oth. writ.] Several poems
published in local newspaper and school library
currently working on three children's books, which I
hope to get published.; [pers.] This poem was written
for a childhood friend who passed away in June,

1995. It was about a dream, she had, about "stars
falling like gold dust", (my way of immortalizing her
memory) In memory of Barbara Rossing LaClair;
[a.] Summerfield, FL

SOMERS, GERALD A.
[b.] December 4, 1921, Marshalltown, IA; [p.] Eben
Arthur Somers and Edna Mae Lieberum; [m.] Gloria
Ann Graeszel, November 25, 1955; [ch.] Scott
James, Steven Craig, Cynthia Ann (Judd); [ed.]
Knox College, Galesburg, IL 1946-1947, University
of Chicago 1948-'49 B.L.S.; [occ.] Library Director
(Retired 1987 Brown County Library Green Bay,
WI); [memb.] ALA, WLA, AARP; [hon.] President,
Wisconsin Library Association 1965-'66, ETO 1943-
'45 8th Air Force, Presidential Unit Citation; [oth.
writ.] 36 Short Stories 1 Novella (Many other
poems); [pers.] Fredd and Nietzsche influenced me
the most, Picasso and Cezanne taught me to paint-
(Former to draw, latter to color) Politically, a student
of Lincoln and FDR, Madison and Hamilton.; [a.]
Green Bay, WI

SOSA, DEBORAH A.
[b.] March 14, 1961, Waco, TX; [p.] Arnold and
Edna Fox; [m.] Alvaro Sosa, January 20, 1989; [ch.]
Elisa Sosa; [hon.] Won first place on a "Still Life"
painting in 1978 at the Hendricks County Art
League; [pers.] In order to care about others, you
must first care about yourself.; [a.] Indianapolis, IN

SOTO, BERNIE
[b.] September 19, 1977, Surprise, AZ; [occ.]
Cashier at Target; [oth. writ.] Several, all dealing
with the subjects of death, joy, sadness, confusion
and questions of why.; [pers.] I get my inspiration for
my poems by studying people, thinking of
everything I can think about and from dreams and
my environment.; [a.] Peoria, AZ

SPEARMAN, CELA K.
[pen.] Cela K. Spearman; [b.] March 1, 1937,
Royalton, PA; [p.] Mr. and Mrs. Joseph S. Beckey
Sr.; [m.] Geo M. Spearman, December 22, 1962;
[ch.] Evam and Cela Jo, (grandson) Steven; [ed.]
Middletown Area High School; [occ.] Custodian-
Retired Secy.; [memb.] Nat'l. Honor Society Women
of Moose-Mdtn. #0553, Wesley United Methodist
Church-American Heart; [hon.] Silver and Gold
Poetry Awards; [oth. writ.] 2 other reunion poems;
[pers.] Try to convey to each person they are valued
more as we age and how we all change our looks and
our values.; [a.] Middletown, PA

SPENCER, MARGIE ANN RICHARDSON
[pen.] Margie A. Spencer; [b.] August 27, 1916,
Marion, MI; [p.] Paul and Maude Richardson; [m.]
John C. Spencer, December 23, 1970; [ch.] One son
and one step-daughter; [ed.] High School; [occ.]
Retired; [memb.] Christ Methodist Church, Lansing,
MI, Bird Key Y.C. Sarasota, FL, Sara Bay Country
Club; [hon.] My only reward is that friends enjoy
getting a poem for a special occasion.; [oth. writ.]
Poems for people and events; [pers.] Since I was
very young I could write short poems, as well play
the piano just by hearing a tune. I believe this is a
gift. Not everyone has this talent.; [a.] Sarasota, FL

SPENCER, VIRGINIA
[pen.] Ginny Spencer; [b.] August 21, 1947,
England; [p.] Geoff and Queenie Sperceley; [m.]

Ron, June 19, 1976; [ch.] Geoff; [occ.] Realtor; [oth. writ.] Many years of writing poetry stashed in a drawer published twice.; [pers.] I want my poetry to touch the heart using few words to create emotion.; [a.] Midlothian, VA

SPOTZ, LYNDA L.
[b.] June 7, 1965, Elmhurst, IL; [p.] Richard and Kay Franzen; [m.] Kurt A. Spotz, June 21, 1986; [ch.] Kurt A. Jr.; [ed.] Ass. in Arts Degree; [occ.] Day Care Teacher; [pers.] This poem is dedicated to my father who passed away July 5, 1995.

SPRANGER, ANGELA M.
[b.] April 1, 1979, Wausau, WI; [p.] James and Susann Spranger; [ed.] D.C. Everest Senior High; [occ.] Student, Customer Service Specialist; [memb.] D.C. Everest Senior High Marching and Concert Bands, Concert Choir, Fall Pom Pon Squad; [hon.] Presidential Academic Fitness Award, Renaissance, (Honor Roll) Varsity Letter, Who's Who Among American High School Students, many 1st and 2nd place medals in Solo and Ensamble, Editor's Choice Award; [oth. writ.] Together Forever, You Said, The Truth, Tears, Two Times, Used, Friends, A Country Rainstorm, Childhood Is; [pers.] I would like to say thank you Ben.; [a.] Schofield, WI

SPRUNT, DONALD ROY
[b.] October 6, 1960, Scarborough, ON; [p.] Harold and Dorothy Sprunt; [m.] Barbara Sprunt, June 4, 1994; [ch.] Kimberly and Tracy; [ed.] Uxbridge Secondary; [memb.] Royal Canadian Legion, New Market Dart Ass.; [oth. writ.] Poem published in local legion newsletter; [pers.] My wife is my inspiration.

SQUIRES, JANE
[b.] February 20, 1935, Greensburg, KY; [p.] Thurman Squires and Christial Squires; [ed.] Greensburg H.S., Union College, Ohio U.; [occ.] (Retired music, English teacher) Director, chancel choir, handbells at Community UMC, Brookville, OH play violin, Miami Valley Symphony Orch., Dayton, OH, Private Violin Inst.; [pers.] I have an urge to look closely at "small" things and acknowledge their significance.; [a.] Brookville, OH

STACKPOLE, SHARON K.
[pen.] Sharon Reed; [b.] January 4, 1942, Decatur, IL; [p.] Charles Reed and Vivian Reed; [m.] Charles G. Stackpole Jr., April 22, 1966; [ch.] Debby, Cindy and Scott; [ed.] High school, Creative Writing Classes; [occ.] Insurance Broker, Commercial Lines; [memb.] Miacomet Golf Club; [oth. writ.] Working on a mystery novel; [pers.] My Father, daughter and son all write poetry. We each have a completely different style. I feel we all contribute in our own way.; [a.] Nantucket, MA

STAFFORD, BETTY THOMPSON
[b.] August 20, 1925, Greeme Co, MO; [p.] William Joseph Thompson, Dorothula Emaline Gray Thompson; [m.] Thomas B. Stafford, October 5, 1946; [ch.] Sondra L. Stafford; [ed.] Sparta High School, Sparta, MO Draughon's Business College, Springfield, MO SMSU - Springfield, MO Beta Sigma Phi Sorority; [occ.] Part-time secretary; [memb.] American Cancer Society; [hon.] President's Annual Award Delta Materials Handling- Clark Equipment Joseph G. Costa, President; [oth.

writ.] Poems published in The Ozarks Mountaineer Bi-Monthly Magazine Kirbyville, MO; [pers.] "Back in 1513" is one of thirty-four poems I wrote as a school assignment in the 1942/43 school year. As World War II raged. I expressed in this poem a wish the Pacific had never been discovered. I write today to express my feelings (for others to share) of joys, pleasant memories, sorrows, frustrations, and the wonders that fulfill my life.; [a.] Memphis, TN

STAMM, ANN M.
[pen.] Annie; [b.] October 9, 1995, Hillman, MI; [p.] Louis and Margaret Stamm; [m.] August 15, 1958; [ed.] Hillman H.S. B.A.-Madonna College, MA (History) Univ. of Detroit, MA (Theology) Univ. of Detroit, D. Min. graduate Theological Foundation; [occ.] Professor - Religious Studies - Madonna University; [memb.] Felician Sisters, Alumni - Madonna U, GTF, Livonia PD Chaplain, Livonia FD Chaplain; [hon.] H.S. - Outstanding Teacher of the year, Washington Workshops Award, Faculty Outstanding Professor, Award - Madonna U, Dale Carnegie; [oth. writ.] Post-Doctoral Work: How Dead Is Dead, Anthologies: In The West Of Ireland '92, '94, Lydia Sigourney, Celia Thaxter, Ann Eliza Bleecker, at '91 Madonna Mind I-II-III-IV, "Bereavement, Loss and New Beginnings" Alzheimers and Parkinsons Diseases, Dissertation: Spirituality of Grief, books of prayers, Noses in Kneecaps, Books poems Give Me Your Hand; [pers.] Poetry is the music of the soul! Ever since I was a child, I breathed, recited, prayed, wrote poetry thanks to my Irish Mom who taught me its magic.; [a.] Livonia, MI

STARCHER, AMY RAE
[b.] November 29, 1980, Steubenville, OH; [p.] Robert and Kimberly Waddell; [ed.] Freshmen; [occ.] Student; [memb.] Dance Company, Band, Choir, Flag Corp., School Dance Line, D.A.R.E.; [hon.] Editor's Choice Award by the National Library of Poetry 1995, Dance Awards and Band 1995 Snow Queen Honor Roll; [oth. writ.] (A Better School) in anthology of poetry by Young Americans in 1994 edition (Alone) in at Water's Edge in 1995 edition; [pers.] To do my best at whatever I try, and never say I can't to reach for the stars.; [a.] Wintersville, OH

STEFFES, PATRICIA
[b.] June 14, 1958, Alexandria, VA; [p.] Major General (Ret.) E.Q. and Lucille Steffes; [ed.] Bachelor of Arts, Loretto Heights College, MSW Candidate Denver University March, 1996; [occ.] Social Worker/Executive Director of the Program, Inc.; [oth. writ.] Poetry in 1978 Peagasus, National Collegiate Poetry Press; [pers.] Today I get to be my Mother's Poetess.

STEINERT, KARYN
[pen.] Karebear; [b.] November 29, 1978, Keflavik, Ireland; [p.] Thomas (Deceased), Diane; [a.] Littleton, CO

STEWART, JOYCE TINA
[b.] February 12, 1944, Fort Vermilion, Alberta, Canada; [p.] Dan and Rose Cardinal; [m.] Divorced; [ch.] One daughter; [ed.] Grade 12, Accounting Courses at two different colleges; [occ.] Accounts payable clerk, West Coast Drugs; [oth. writ.] First time entry for any publication. I have been writing

poetry for twenty years for personal satisfaction and stress relief.; [pers.] I am a romantisist and hope my writing will bring reflection to the reader. Most of my poetry was written when I was sad, depressed, lonely and melancholy.

STEWART, MARK K.
[pen.] Polo Bob; [b.] April 11, 1953, Houston, TX; [p.] Raymond A. Stewart, Margaret I. Stewart; [ed.] Tarkington High School Harry Lundeberg School of Seamanship; [occ.] U.S. Merchant Mariner; [oth. writ.] Christian poems unpublished; [pers.] I write poems for God's glory. There is none greater to glorify.; [a.] Austin, TX

STEWART, TARYM
[b.] July 17, 1978, Little Rock, AR; [p.] Charles and Eula Stewart; [ed.] Little Rock Central High School (still presently attending - senior year); [occ.] Student; [memb.] National Beta Club, Interact Club (Associated with Rotary International); [hon.] Who's Who Among American High School Students, National Leadership and Service Award, National Art Achievement Award; [oth. writ.] Nothing previously published; [pers.] I'd like to thank Mr. Terry Wright for the inspiration for this poem. I hope that this publication will lead to future success in writing; [a.] Little Rock, AR

STIGALL, BETTY RUTH
[pen.] Betty Stigall; [b.] April 13, 1951, Hughes- Forest City, AR; [p.] Ruth McKinney and Eddie McKinney Jr.; [m.] Robert Lee Gilford Stigall, August 17, 1969; [ch.] Tracy Michelle and Robert Stigall Jr.; [ed.] High School; [occ.] School Bus Driver; [memb.] Pentecostal Church Of God Org.; [hon.] 26 Yrs. Childrens Church Director and Organizer. Award by local Church. Talent contest- singing-local; [oth. writ.] Several poems, Gospel songs country western type songs. I also play and sing. We have a Gospel Singing Group made up of myself, husband, daughter and son.; [pers.] I love all types of poetry. I speak and share a little of what's in my heart when I feel moved upon to write a poem or song. I feel good when someone tells me they have been blessed or ministered to by my writings.; [a.] Gosnell, AR

STOKES, ANNE
[b.] July 6, 1948, Mayfield, KY; [p.] Harry Barrett Stokes and Susan; [m.] Robert M. Krusen, April 17, 1992; [ed.] Mayfield High School - Mayfield, KY., Fashion Institute of America - Atlanta, GA; [occ.] Songwriter; [memb.] BMI; [oth. writ.] Wrote lyric for "In The Night" song which appeared in ABC movie of the week -Rivierra" Co-wrote lyric to "Can't Stop A Dreamer" with Cyril Neville and Barry Coffing on soon to be released Neville Brothers Album; [pers.] My philosophy - "Life Ain't for Sissys" (melody to "Holy Part" co-written by Mark T. Jordan and the late Ken Vassy); [a.] Nashville, TN

STOKES, TARA
[b.] January 24, Lancaster; [p.] Cheryl Zabawsky; [ed.] Presently in 9th grade; [hon.] Won and award for writing "The Saddest Summer", a story when my dad died 1991; [oth. writ.] "The Saddest Summer." "My Special Friend"; [pers.] The death of my father inspired me to write poems, and stories.; [a.] Lancaster, PA

STOUDT, KITTY C.
[b.] November 26, 1926, Queensland, Australia; [p.] Beryl Green, H. Hoffman (Deceased); [m.] Deceased, February 11, 1945; [ch.] One; [ed.] Australian Educated equivalent to 4 yrs. High School; [occ.] Tailor; [oth. writ.] None published; [pers.] I am dedicated to writing poetry I am usually inspired by. Natures wonders and aspects of human life. I have been writing poetry and lyrics for songs about 30 yrs.; [a.] Portland, OR

STOWELL, JAY LEROY
[pen.] WA4HVS, Mayor of Clingman's Peak; [b.] November 29, 1940, Spokane, WA; [p.] David Jay Stowell, R. Grace (Edson) Stowell; [m.] Martha (Spurlin) Stowell, June 30, 1973; [ch.] Still trying; [ed.] Bachelor of Arts in Speech for Radio and TV, Eastern Washington State University Cheney, Washington. Television Station Operation, John O'Connell School San Francisco, CA, June, 1973; [occ.] Unemployed! (I lost my job with NASA, December, 1994); [memb.] Calvary Baptist Church, Redwood City, CA. I am also a member of the human race; [hon.] Graduated from Eastern Washington State University with honors December, 1963. Honorable discharge from the Army Security Agency, December, 1967.; [oth. writ.] Infiltration Course Blues; [pers.] Space is the place for the human race! A space plank in every political platform will put real space platforms in our sky.; [a.] Redwood City, CA

STRADLEY, HENRY WARD
[pen.] Henry Ward Stradley; [b.] April 26, 1918, Wilmington, DE; [p.] Oakley Stradley - Emma Stradley; [m.] Kathryn E. Stradley, December 5, 1942; [ch.] Michael, Gary, Mark; [ed.] High School - Wilm, Del- Business College - Wilm Del-; [occ.] Retired Region Sales Manager - Hershey Chocolate Co.; [memb.] Masonic - Blue Lodge - HBG Consistory - Zembo Shrine Penbrook Lutheran Church; [hon.] Bronze Star (Military) WW #2 - Hershey Chocolate Co Presidents Cup Sales Award 1972; [pers.] Life is so great when you enter it with love and the respect for all things.; [a.] Harrisburg, PA

STRAIN, TERI
[pen.] Pinches Nelson; [b.] March 18, 1966, Victoria, British Columbia, Canada; [p.] Darlene Strain and the late George Nelson Strain; [ed.] Honours B.A. (English), Trent University Bachelor of Education, Queen's University; [occ.] Elementary teacher, Queen Elizabeth Public School, Peterborough, ON; [memb.] Peterborough Author's Association, P.O.E.T.'s Club, F.W.T.A.O. (Federation of Women Teacher's Association of Ontario); [hon.] Ontario Scholar, Dean's List (Trent University); [oth. writ.] Several poems shared with friends and family, Winnie-the-Pooh discovers fall (short story), untitled short stories; [pers.] I have been writing poems and short stories for as long as I can remember. Writing is a therapeutic process which helps me to deal with and express personal experiences, and to clarify and thoughts and beliefs.; [a.] Omemee Ontario, Canada

STRAWSER, MARSHA E.
[pen.] Marsha Scholes; [b.] March 3, 1950, Denver, CO; [p.] Regina Huseman, Marshall J. Strawser; [ch.] Jennifer, Joseph, Sarah, Zechariah, John; [ed.] Chofu High, Tokyo, Japan, B.C. Rain H.S., Mobile, ALA., U. of Wash., Seattle, Sierra College, Rocklin,

Ca., National Education Center, Sacramento, CA; [occ.] Medical Assistant/Office Mgr. Bruce D. Gorlick, D.P.M., FACFAS, Sacramento; [memb.] SARTA., American Heart Association; [hon.] 1st place award, Dramatic Interpretation, Tuscaloosa University, '68; [oth. writ.] Many other poems as yet unpublished. Am also working on a children's book, and I also am an artist, so will be dong my own illustrations. I also write songs and short stories for children. I am working on a book of my poems for publication.; [pers.] My own life's experiences and perceptions greatly influence my poetic endeavors, as well as my observations of other people's dealings with their own experiences and influences.; [a.] Sacramento, CA

STRUPP, JANET KAYE
[pen.] Jesse Ryan; [b.] April 19, 1947, Bryan, Ohio; [p.] Henry and Doris Strupp; [m.] James; [ch.] James, Erik, Jared; [ed.] B.A. in Sociology and Environ-mental Studies, Psy.D. in Clinical Psychology; [occ.] Clinical Psychologist and Art Gallery Director; [memb.] Various psychological associations; local, national, and international animal groups; [hon.] Scholarships, articles and poetry published in newspaper, doctoral dissertation published in "American Psychologist," poetry published by The National Library of Poetry; [oth. writ.] Working on writing more poems, children's books, and an autobiography.; [pers.] A passage from <u>The Tao of Pooh</u> -- "Within each of us there is an Owl, a Rabbit, an Eeyore, and a Pooh. For too long, we have chosen the way of Owl and Rabbit. Now, like Eeyore, we complain about the results. But that accomplishes nothing. If we are smart, we will choose the way of Pooh. As if from far away, it calls to Us with the voice of a child's mind. It may be hard to hear at times, but it is important just the same, because without it, we will never find our way through the Forest."; [a.] Dayton, Ohio

SUCKLING, PAULA J.
[b.] June 14, 1958, London, England; [p.] Peter J. and Shirley Suckling; [m.] Engaged to George T. Stewart; [occ.] Fire Dept. Communications Technician; [pers.] Poetic influences are Robert Frost, Elizabeth Barrett Browing and Sir John Suckling (1609-1641) - Philosophical influence is chief Seattle.; [a.] Georgetown Ontario, Canada

SUDA, JUDIE
[b.] 1948, Manitoba, Canada; [p.] Neely and Betty Moore; [m.] Tokue Suda; [ch.] Ian Maki, Kimiko Elizabeth; [ed.] High School, 3 years Nursing School various careers: R.N., Bible Teacher; [occ.] Part-time Secretary, Own publishing company "Victory Publishers"; [memb.] RNABC; [oth. writ.] Poems published in: "The Path Not Taken" (NLP), Christian INFO Newspaper and several self-published. Presently working on poetry "manu-script", "Be Strong and Courageous".; [pers.] As a christian, my inspirations are an outflow of my personal relationship with God. I strive to lead others to His love and healing through my poetry.; [a.] Abbotsford British Columbia, Canada

SUE, SHANE MARILYN
[b.] July 1, 1951, Granite City, IL; [p.] Owen Shane, Esther Shane; [m.] Divorced; [ed.] Jeromie Rushing, Carolyn Rushing, Ranae Harsh; [occ.] Granite City Senior High, Vanderschmidt School; [memb.]

Billing Clerk-Memorial Hospital Belleville, IL; [pers.] This poem was an actual event that happened to my son, Jeromie. He is no longer in a coma and did indeed get to spend Christmas at home and will be home to stay in March of this year after being in a rehabilitation hospital for 9 months. This poem was actually written due to a prayer, love, and a lot of hope from a broken mother's heart.; [a.] Madison, IL

SULLIVAN, DANIEL P.
[b.] April 15, 1933, New York City; [p.] William Sullivan, Mary Quinn; [m.] Kathleen E. Sullivan, December 15, 1967; [ch.] Howard, Scott, Kim, Michael and our son Matthew (murdered 3/23/91); [occ.] Retired; [memb.] Parents of Murdered Children Victims of Violence, Doris Tate Crime Victims Bureau, Nicole Brown Simpson Foundation; [pers.] I am working hard to change our judicial system to protect the victims of violent crime and to make our streets safe for all mankind.; [a.] Oceanside, CA

SULLIVAN, RALPH E.
[pen.] Bud Sullivan; [b.] September 7, 1929, Toronto, ON; [p.] Anne and Charles Sullivan; [m.] Marie Sullivan, September 10, 1954; [ed.] In-Toronto - Charles G. Fraser Public School and Central High School of Commerce; [occ.] Retired; [memb.] Worked 26 years Toronto Telegram - newspaper Toronto Sun Newspaper 22 years in the Business Office; [oth. writ.] Several poems published in local newspapers; [pers.] The old sages philoso-phy of "Do not unto others you would not have others do unto to you"; [a.] Toronto Ontario, Canada

SUMNER, ALFRED COOPER
[pen.] A. C. (Pat) Sumner; [b.] March 29, 1920, Rocky Mount, NC; [p.] A. C. and Mildred Sumner; [m.] Vera C. Sumner, July 11, 1970; [ch.] Vickie Wilburn and Joe Sumner; [ed.] Durham High School; [occ.] Retired; [hon.] 1st and 2nd place in Senior Citizens Arts, several poems published in Times News Alamance Magazine; [pers.] In my writings I have been greatly influenced by the Lord, all of nature and the mountains. When the inspiration comes, I get my pen.; [a.] Haw River, NC

SUTTON, RALF
[b.] August 24, 1955, W. Germany; [p.] Edwin Sutton, Aloha Sutton, Christa Winkler; [ch.] Alisha Sutton, Tara Sutton; [ed.] San Gorgonio High, Chaffey College; [occ.] Installer-Repairman, Genera Telephone of California; [oth. writ.] Everything I have written I keep in a box. Nobody else has read them.; [pers.] I am a positive person as for as my views on life are but when I write it tends to be towards the pessimistic or dark side of life.; [a.] Redlands, CA

SVEINSON, DENISE
[b.] June 19, 1953, San Diego, CA; [p.] Harry and Bernie Merrill; [ch.] Jason Vara and Dustin Sveinson; [ed.] Graduated from Mtn. View High school in Calif. in June 1971; [pers.] I show my feelings through my poetry. This was written for my ex-husband when his dad passed away in Aug. 1994.; [a.] San Jose, CA

SWANN, DIANA ELIZABETH BEHRENS
[pen.] Diana Behrens Swann; [b.] September 22, 1923, Norfolk, VA; [p.] Admr. Charles F. and Emma

Spencer Behrens; [m.] Melvin Julius Swann, March 17 (St Patrick's Day) (not my first marriage); [ch.] 1 daughter and 3 sons; [ed.] High school graduate - then Corcoran School of fine arts (D.C) One Business Institute (for typing course); [occ.] I was retired from Kent Sussex Industrial - by jealous woman when I did a portrait of a co-worker.; [memb.] Christ, Episcopal Church (choir member); [hon.] Scholarships offered at Corcoran School of Fine Arts - Dad got transferred - I went with family. My first husband left me - jealous if a good looking man looked at me-I had to be flirting, they still looked at me! (And I am 72 years old); [oth. writ.] Mostly poems! Some other works upon request by former employers, once a brief-re life with Admr and Mrs. Behrens (Dad used to be air-lifted to White House to aid Pres. Roosevelt, (Foremost authority on roentgenology in America and most foreign countries.); [pers.] I used my retirement"$" from ARC HGTRS, to get special schooling for Mel's children (so neglected by their mothers) (once I talked him out of shooting her when she was "making out" with mailman in a truck in front of his house, I gave him name of a good lawyer.; [a.] Washington, DC

SWINT, WANDA HOLLAND
[b.] July 18, 1939, Frenchburg, KY; [p.] Clyde and Gertrude Holland; [m.] Kenneth Ray Swint, May 31, 1963; [ch.] David Ray, Brian Keith; [ed.] Frenchburg High School, Morehead State University; [occ.] Retired elementary teacher; [memb.] First Baptist Church KEA, GCEA; [hon.] Who's Who Among American's Teachers Kentucky Colonel; [oth. writ.] Song "My Last Letter"; [pers.] Live for today, hope for tomorrow.

SWOBODA, MATT
[b.] February 9, 1978, Krakow, Poland; [p.] Ewa Swoboda and Witold Swoboda; [ed.] Crestwood Secondary School, gr. 10 Cello, gr. 10 Piano; [occ.] Student; [hon.] Excellence in Education Award; [oth. writ.] Little Red: A modern musical interpretation of an old tale, sketches; [a.] Peterborough Ontario, Canada

SWORD, DANITA LORENA
[b.] September 17, 1973, Tazewell, VA; [p.] Barbara and Daniel C. Bowling; [m.] Donald A. Sword, July 11, 1992; [ed.] High School graduate, from Tazewell High School, 1991 Sophomore in College at Southwest VA Community College; [occ.] Teacher's Aide; [memb.] International Society of Poets; [hon.] Talent Contests, (for singing) skating trophy; [oth. writ.] "Hungry Dances", "Without You", "Elvis", "Hillbilly King", "Illusions", "Just A Chance", "Mississippi Boy"; [pers.] I'm striving for a career in songwriting and many poetry publications. My influences are Shakespeare, Emily Dickenson, and Marthy Stuart.; [a.] Tazewell, VA

SYAL, HARSHI
[b.] June 16, 1950, Nairobi, Kenya; [p.] Dharan Pall and Samitra Devi Syal; [ed.] B.A. (Eng.), Masters (Eng.), Univ. of East Africa; [occ.] Medical Administrator; [oth. writ.] Poetry in Several Magazines, Several Short plays, one full length play "God minus - the life of Buddha"; [pers.] There is something new to be learnt from life every step of the way.; [a.] Northridge, CA

SYPUTA, LINDA
[b.] February 24, Chicago, IL; [p.] Mrs. Dorothy Gurtz, Frank Gurtz (Deceased); [m.] Stephen; [ch.] Trevor Gurtz; [ed.] McHnery College-Computer Literacy, Oakton College-Associate in Applied Science, Registered Nursing: Yuba College Associate in Science, Vocational Nursing Bay City College, Respiratory Therapy; [occ.] Registered Nurse, Respiratory Care Practitioner, ACLS (Advanced Cardiac Life Support); [memb.] Association of Nursing Students, American National Red Cross, Better Breathers Club, Sunshine Club, American Nursing Association; [hon.] Scholastic All-American, President's Scholar Award, Phi Theta Kappa, Dean's List, National Honor Society; [oth. writ.] Sunshine Club Cookbook; [pers.] We must not take the faults of our youth into our old age, for old age brings with it its own defects.

SZYPULA, STEPHEN J.
[b.] December 12, 1965, Malone, NY; [p.] Thomas Szypula, Theresa Szypula; [m.] Cheryl I. Szypula, April 22, 1995; [ed.] Little Falls Jr. Sr. High, Herkimer County Community College, Utica College of Syracuse University; [occ.] Financial Examiner/Analyst Supervisor, Florida Department of Insurance; [memb.] Society of Financial Examiners, Florida Society of Certified Public Managers; [oth. writ.] None published, this was my first publicly recognized work; [pers.] I could not have written this poem, if it were not for my endless love for and the overwhelming inspiration of my beautiful wife, Cheryl.; [a.] Tallahassee, FL

TACE, NOELLE
[b.] March 30, 1973, San Diego, CA; [p.] Col. Stephen A. Tace (Deceased), Heather J. Tace; [ed.] First Colonial High School, Radford University; [occ.] Subscriptions Director, Canyon State Publishers Inc.; [memb.] Sigma Kappa Sorority, Muscular Dystrophy Association; [oth. writ.] Selected poetry published in local newspapers, monthly column published in cardinals coverage magazine; [pers.] "I desire to uncover the confusion between actuality and imagination through my work".; [a.] Virginia Beach, VA

TAIZ, SIDNEY
[pen.] Sidney Taiz; [b.] March 29, 1907, Philadelphia, PA; [p.] Jacob and Elizabeth; [m.] Georgianna, December 20, 1955; [ch.] Jonathan, Lisa and Joshua; [ed.] S. Philadelphia High School, Philadelphia College of Pharmacy 1926; [occ.] Retired for Health reasons; [pers.] I look on every day as a learning day...there is so much to learn and too little time in an average life span..also one must be flexible to adjust to changes...many beyond our control.; [a.] Tucson, AZ

TANKSLEY, MATTHEW A.
[b.] February 13, 1980, Granada Hills, CA; [p.] Robert L. Tanksley, D. Kathleen Tanksley; [ed.] ABC Secondary School Independent Study Senior High; [occ.] Student; [memb.] 78's Arc (Ham Radio Club); [oth. writ.] No published poem but I have written many poems that remain unpublished; [pers.] The human mind has abused reality with his own fantasies that the only way to cope is to wrap yourself in your own fantasy. To walk the line between sanity and insanity.; [a.] Cerritos, CA

TATAR, SANTINA ARIGONI
[pen.] Santina Arigoni; [b.] January 7, 1918, Cremona, Italy; [p.] Alessandro Arigoni, Regina Delle-Donne; [m.] Peter Tatar, June 2, 1945; [ch.] Peter, Anthony, Klara, Van A.; [ed.] Teacher Elementary School (Cremona - Italy In New York City, Teacher Italian Language, French, Mathematic, Algebra; [occ.] Retired; [memb.] Diploma Gim Commercial School Steno type Collography nurse of Red-Cross, Religion Music Composer Teacher Institute in the Kindergarden School; [hon.] Diploma of meritt by the Board Education- New York - Write poems for Younger Children in Italian and English, First prize for the poem; [oth. writ.] "Hello Cadents" in Rome (Italy) - Winner in the contest and statue by the Ltohaw Consolate in N. York - Member in Cremma (Italy) of "El Fach" Club of dialetted; [pers.] Poets published poems in the Italo-Americano news frefers it progress Italo -Americano in New York, "Americo Ogyi" - "L' Italco" - "La Follis" - "Il Ponte" In Cremona, in the news paper, La Posvincis; [a.] New York, NY

TAYLOR, JAMES E.
[b.] November 17, 1944, Kentville, Nova Scotia, Canada; [p.] Reginald and Helen; [m.] Peggy (Sherman), June 1, 1968; [ch.] Britt Andrew and Jana Lyn; [ed.] Cornwalls District High School, B.A. Dalhousie University Halifax, N.S.; [occ.] Teacher; [memb.] Royal Canadian Legion Fieldwood Heritage Society N.S. Teachers union Canadian Geographic Society; [hon.] FEESA fellow some teaching awards; [oth. writ.] Personal poetry editorials; [pers.] I am concerned about the environment, present direction of values/moral decay in North America, the growing rift between rich and poor, the plight of the common person I appreciate the outdoors, personal contact and rural life styles.; [a.] Sheffield Mills Nova Scotia, Canada

TAYLOR, ROSS
[b.] March 31, 1969, Morgantown, WV; [p.] Ross C. Taylor Jr., Rebecca Taylor; [m.] Lori Taylor, June 6, 1992; [ch.] Caitlin Marie; [ed.] George Washington, University, University of San Francisco School of Law; [pers.] I wrote this poem for my daughter before I even knew I would have one. Since she has come into my life, I have learned even ore than I dreamed of.; [a.] Leesburg, VA

TEALEY, TERESA KOSTER
[pen.] Teresa Tealey; [b.] October 7, 1932, Washington, DC; [p.] Charles and Mabel Huppmann; [m.] Widowed twice. First, William Koster, Second Ernest Tealey; [ch.] Kevin and Heidi Koster; [ed.] B.A. George Washington Univ. 1950 M.B.A., F.I.T., Melbourne, Folorida 1981 C.T.C. Feb. 1985; [occ.] Certified Travel Counselor Past Pres. and Owner/Koster Film Facilities Washington, D.C. (1977 - sold co.); [memb.] Listed in Who's Who in Florida Women in 1990 (not sure of exact date); [oth. writ.] First poems published in the Children's Corner of the Washington Star; [pers.] Challenge is a crisis to meet or disaster to survive my life's a sad play I didn't write but, I play the Hero every day.; [a.] Stuart, FL

TEETERS, LANA F.
[b.] June 1, 1944, Long Beach, CA; [p.] L. Robert Nelson, Ardyne Nelson; [m.] I. L. "Skip" Teeters, June 24, 1967; [ch.] Brandon Teeters, Jeremy

Teeters; [ed.] East High -Duluth, Minnesota Univ. of Minnesota - Duluth, Minnesota; [occ.] Teacher (retired) and Homemaker Elementary; [memb.] Univ. of Minn. Alumni Assoc., International Yours Friendship Organization; [hon.] Woman of year welcome wagon award Atlanta, GA. East Cobb Welcome Wagon (1991-1992); [pers.] I love humor in poetry and Dorothy-Parker had a lot to do with it. My family always writes poems to each other just for the pure pleasure of it.; [a.] Charlotte, NC

TENEYCKE, TAMMY LEE
[b.] May 18, 1964, Raymond, Alberta, Canada; [p.] Dave and Waltraud Jensen; [m.] Erle Dean Teneycke, July 10, 1993; [ch.] Hans Lucas and Kayla Nichole; [ed.] Lethbridge Community College, Student of the Institute of Childrens Literature; [occ.] Homemaker; [memb.] Board of Parent Preschool Program; [oth. writ.] In progress: teen novel, poetry volume featuring the 'girl child' venturing into non-fiction articles.; [pers.] I believe that words powerful and enduring tool given to mankind. They can lift the spirit, sooth the soul and enlighten the mind.; [a.] Turin Alberta, Canada

TENNISON, COREY
[pen.] Corey Tennison; [b.] February 15, 1969, Nanaimo, British Columbia, Canada; [p.] Anni and Brian Tennison; [m.] Tina Bursey; [ch.] Danny Bursey (Tina's Son); [ed.] Grade 12 at Nanaimo District Secondary School; [occ.] Security; [oth. writ.] Various other poems and short stories; [pers.] I have just began writing poems and stories since my high school years. The poem that will be published was my, first in 8 years. I strive to learn from my writings; [a.] Nanaimo British Columbia, Canada

TETRAULT, GEORGE C.
[b.] January 2, Nalcam, Saskatchewan, Canada; [p.] Oscar and Carolyn Tetrault; [m.] Linda R. Tetrault, May 16, 1964; [ch.] David, Joel, Jon, Daniel and Nicole; [ed.] High School - St. Marys, College - Notre Dame and North Dakota State; [occ.] Architect; [memb.] VFW, KOFC; [oth. writ.] Annual Christmas poems

TEWS, ERIQ
[pen.] S. Dawson; [b.] April 12, 1980, Greendale, WI; [p.] Tim Tews Katy Tews; [ed.] Greendale High School; [occ.] Communications Distribution Engineer; [pers.] My personal thanks to the messiah whose music opened my eyes to a wonderful world of love and hate, joy and sadness, laughter and tears. Tori Amos, I wouldn't be me without you.; [a.] Greendale, WI

THOMAS, FREDA K.
[b.] March 9, 1915, Wales; [ed.] Reached Brock University did not graduate; [occ.] Retired; [memb.] Taoist Tui Chi Society-Master Moy Based in Orange Ville, Ontario took Calligraphy lessons; [oth. writ.] Japanese Haiku poems, song lyrics. Comic Poems (The British Spud, The Ant) Xmas Card thoughts short stories.; [pers.] I am a private person. Do not delve in my life. I am not a racist or a religious bigot. I hope I am kind and thoughtful, and decent minded.; [a.] Saint Catharines Ontario, Canada

THOMAS, JACOB
[b.] July 14, 1977, Greensboro, NC; [p.] Jack and Jerry Thomas; [ed.] North Cobb High School Georgia Institute of Technology (freshman); [occ.]

Student; [memb.] International Gospel Outreach; [hon.] Governor's Scholar, Georgia Scholar, Deans List; [a.] Acworth, GA

THOMAS, SARAH PRISCILLA
[pen.] Sarah Priscilla Thomas; [b.] October 7, 1977, Waukegan, IL; [p.] Leslie "Pat" Thomas and Marjie Thomas; [ed.] Homeschooled in Virginia Beach, Virginia where I grew up; [occ.] Customer service personnel; [hon.] Senator for Associated Student Government at Lake Washington Tech., Kirkland, WA; [oth. writ.] Other poems previously published in small school collections. In Virginia; [pers.] I would like to dedicate "Untitled" to Robert Gates. And many thanks go to my cousin Melanie, who fired my poetic ambitions again.; [a.] Bothell, WA

THOMPSON, DONNA JOAN
[pen.] D. Joan Thompson; [b.] March 5, 1951, Chilliwack, British Columbia, Canada; [p.] Alexander and Constance MacKenzie; [m.] Mark Twain Thompson, April 21, 1990; [ch.] James, Samantha and Barbara; [ed.] Grade 11, CHWK Sr. Sec. Also have upgraded myself in the use of computer skills and programming.; [occ.] Resident manager; [memb.] Child Abuse Awareness Society Co-Founder of Chilliwack Chapter; [hon.] The only awards I have ever received are for my personal efforts in bowling and billiards. In 1988 I won the Sr. Fraser Valley's Women's Single's with a record 279.4 for four games (5 Pin).; [oth. writ.] (Under Preston) Heaven Sent - December 20, 1981; [pers.] After 26 1/2 yrs of being apart, I finally married my teenage love, Mark. We had met when I was 2 1/2 yrs. old, and dated when I was 13. We had both married and had 3 children by the time we found each other again.; [a.] New Westminster British Columbia, Canada

THOMPSON, DOROTHY ANN
[b.] November 14, 1931, Far Rockaway, NY; [p.] Charles R. Fulton, Suzanna Cecelia O'Tool; [m.] Thomas F. Thompson, November 25, 1954; [ch.] Bonnie Lynn, Geraldine Marie, Deborah Ann, Michael Lee, Sandra Louise; [ed.] Modern School of Fashion and Design, Boston, MA; [occ.] Housewife, "Grandmother"; [memb.] Christ The King Lutheran Church: Sunday School Teacher, Now chairperson of Education Committee, Choir Member, Write and produce Sunday School Christmas plays; [pers.] Most of the activities I am involved in are connected to our church. My faith influences my writings. Other interests are music, arts and crafts, and photography; [a.] Keller, TX

THOMPSON, LOIS MARIE
[b.] May 31, 1928, Dayton, OH; [p.] Dr John C. Coldiron, Anna Evelyn, Coldiron; [m.] Philip Douglas Thompson, Sr., September 10, 1949; [ch.] Julia-Anna, Philip Douglas Jr.; [ed.] Hazard High School Christian College, Columbia, Missouri University of Kentucky; [occ.] Artist; [memb.] Warrenton Presbyterian Church, Antiquarian Society, Blue Ridge Flower Club Scottish Heritage Society and Scandinavian Society; [hon.] Phi Delta Delta Art Club, Kentucky Colonel; [oth. writ.] 'Whim', 'Spring' and 'Seeking' (poems); [pers.] I would like to depict, in a very honest way, my thoughts on subjects that reveal a nobility of spirit and feelings and scenes that amuse and inspire me.; [a.] Marshall, VA

THOMPSON, PAUL DOUGLAS
[b.] June 13, 1963, Kitimat, British Columbia, Canada; [p.] James Ronald, Margarie Elma Thompson; [ed.] Have Grade 11 in process of completed Grade 12, then on the university for Bachelor of Arts Child and Youth Care eventually being a drug/alcohol counselor; [occ.] Carpenter, Student; [hon.] This the first acknowledgement of my writing, giving me encouragement to expose more of my language of the heart; [pers.] In people we find encouragement in God we trust and love of all is our greatest healer gentleness opens doors my friends; [a.] Duncan, Canada

THOMPSON, RITA J.
[b.] December 24, 1923, Stranorlar, Co Donegal, Ireland; [p.] Wm. and M. Roulston; [m.] Thompson - Archie, August 17, 1955; [ch.] Barbara, Margaret, Peter-Suzanne; [ed.] Nursing and Midwifery Certificates Music (piano) Certificates; [occ.] Retired Housewife; [memb.] Mission G and CC Maple Ridge St. Andrew's United Church; [oth. writ.] Nothing Substantial; [pers.] Have always been interested in choirs and I liked getting people to study and compete in part singing.; [a.] Maple Ridge British Columbia, Canada

THOMPSON-STAFFORD, BETTY
[b.] August 20, 1925, Greene Co, MO; [p.] William Joseph Thompson, Dorothula Emaline Gray Thompson; [m.] Thomas B. Stafford, October 5, 1946; [ch.] Sondra L. Stafford; [ed.] Sparta high School, Sparta, MO; Draughon's Business College, - Springfield, MO; SMSU - Springfield, MO; Beta Sigma Phi Sorority; [occ.] Part-time Secretary; [memb.] American Cancer Society, National Secretary's Assn.; [hon.] President's Annual Award, Delta Material Handling-Clark Equipment Joseph G. Costa, President; [oth. writ.] Poems published in The Ozarks Mountaineer Bi-Monthly Magazine Kirbyville, MO; [pers.] "Back in 1513" is one of thirty-four poems I wrote as a school assignment in the 1942/43 school year, as World War II raged. I expressed a wish the Pacific had never been discovered. One great influence to me has been my niece Norma Stewart Maples. I write today to express my feelings (for others to share) of joys, pleasant memories, sorrows, frustrations, and the wonders that fulfill my life.; [a.] Memphis, TN

THOMSON, DAVID
[b.] July 8, 1943, Warren, PA; [p.] Mr. and Mrs. David A. Thomson; [ch.] Three daughter and three granddaughters; [ed.] 2 yrs at Edinboro Warren Campus; [occ.] Non-receiving SSI; [memb.] American Association of Artist and Authors, Glade Township Volunteer Fire Department, Trinity Memorial Episcopal Church; [hon.] Editor's Choice Award from National Library of Poetry; [oth. writ.] In the process of having my first collection, "In search of a Shrine" published. Have had three other poems published recently.; [pers.] I try to give an "emotional picture" of what I am describing in each of my poems; [a.] Warren, PA

THRASHER, GRADY
[b.] October 20, 1942, Toccoa, GA; [p.] H. Grady (Deceased) and Mildred G. Thrasher; [m.] Connie Thrasher, June 21, 1981; [ch.] Grady IV, Kelly, James Lord and Andy Lord; [ed.] BS Georgia Tech (1964) Doctor of Law Emory Univ. (1968); [occ.]

Attorney, Thrasher, Whitley, Hampton and Morgan (Law firm - Atlanta, GA); [memb.] Georgia and Atlanta Bar Associations; [oth. writ.] "The Awakenings", a short story published (Sept '94) in Poet, Artists and Madmen, an Atlanta literary monthly magazine; [a.] Atlanta, GA

TIBBITTS, JOSIE
[b.] August 16, 1979, Alexandria, VA; [p.] Thomas and Linda Tibbitts; [ed.] Currently enrolled at Hemet High School; [pers.] My goal is to reflect my observations about society, nature and the individual i na way that is artistic, yet decisive.; [a.] Hemet, CA

TIMBERS, KEITH A.
[pen.] Keith A. Timbers; [b.] May 2, 1959, Milton, Ontario, Canada; [p.] Gerald Timbers, Eileen Frank; [m.] Lorie Lee Timbers (Nee) Ryder, February 13, 1982; [ch.] Jenny Lee Timbers; [ed.] Grade 10 Milton District High School; [occ.] Roll Thread Operator; [oth. writ.] I have written several other poems currently unpublished; [pers.] My writings are influenced by nature and mankind. Mostly the way is slowly destroying the earth.; [a.] Milton Ontario, Canada

TITUS, RON
[b.] February 16, 1968, Covina, CA; [ed.] B.S. Business Admin, Calif, St. Polytechnic Univ., Pomona; [occ.] Bookkeeper, MT, San Antonio College; [memb.] National Wildlife Federation Defenders of wildlife; [oth. writ.] Several other poems published in anthologies; [pers.] A hope is for my writing to evoke images that stir the mind and touch the heart.; [a.] Pomona, CA

TOCZKO, KEVIN JOHN
[b.] December 13, 1967, Manchester, CT; [p.] Thomas John, Patricia Ann; [ch.] Joshua James, Jacqueline Jael; [ed.] G.E.D. Commonwealth of Virginia four year graduate of Virginia plumbing apprenticeship, 3 years U.S. Army; [occ.] Facilities maintenance specialist; [hon.] Apprentice of the year; [oth. writ.] Several unpublished poems on encouragement in your walk with God, the son, and the holy spirit, several about love, honesty, and our day by day walks of life.; [pers.] "Only you" is dedicated to Sheri Lynn Jones my inspiration, my close and dearest friend, and my only true and honest love, I will always appreciate, respect, and love you for just being you. I'll never forget you Sheri!; [a.] Herndon, VA

TOFFLEMIRE, JOANNE
[b.] July 29, 1974, Guelph, Ontario, Canada; [p.] John and Mary Tofflemire; [ed.] Working on a Bachelor of Arts Degree in Philosophy (Major) with Music, Spanish Minors; [occ.] University of Guelph Student; [memb.] In process of joining British Mensa Ltd; [pers.] The Sanest people are ironically found behind the walls of sanitariums.; [a.] Guelph Ontario, Canada

TOLLIS, LORETTA
[pen.] Loretta Tollis, Mickey Tollis; [b.] October 31, 1939, Canon City, CO; [m.] Gene, November 17, 1962; [ch.] Gena and Stephen; [ed.] High School 16 Credit Library Science Certification; [occ.] Elementary School Librarian (21 years); [memb.] ALA; [hon.] Poem "Charlie the Tuna" printed in National Society of Poets hard cover anthology.

Songs written to two poems, "Yes, I Think I'm An American" and "For There Must Be Love"; [oth. writ.] Articles in "Army" mag., "Quilter's" mag. and "Supercycle" mag. also in "The Woman" mag.; [pers.] Most of my poetry has been written for the students at my school. Some are used in classrooms to help the students with rhyming. Words. I've also written some for my family.; [a.] Canon City, CO

TOMPKINS, LUCILLE
[b.] July 16, 1925, Canton, NC; [p.] Loretta McClure and Charles Brown; [m.] James H. Tompkins, July 16, 1955; [ch.] Two; [ed.] High School 3 yr. College I am very busy taking care of the elderly and the sick. I enjoy my job very much.; [occ.] R.N. (Elderly Home Care); [oth. writ.] I have written several poems for my own pleasure. I hope to continue writing poems. I think poetry is the first way of self expression.

TOREN, MARTIN A.
[b.] September 12, 1952, Chicago, IL; [p.] Warren and Mary Jane Toren; [m.] Andrea Carol Toren, July 1, 1978; [ch.] Kaari Lynn; [ed.] Degree in Religion (B.A.) 1979 from University of Puget Sound Tacoma, Washington. Also Associates Degree in Medical Laboratory Technology, Shore live Community College, Seattle 1983; [occ.] Medical Laboratory Technician; [memb.] American Society of Clinical Pathologists (ASCP) Registry for work Mensa member; [oth. writ.] Several unpublished poems and songs; [pers.] Most of my poetry and song writing is developed through struggles of spirituality the progression of occasional hopeless-ness in life to the joy of eternal life and victory over earthly existence.; [a.] Seattle, WA

TOSTADO, PATRICIA
[pen.] Patricia Montano; [b.] March 25, 1962, Los Angeles, CA; [p.] Fred and Carmen Montano; [m.] Robert Tostado, March 7, 1982; [ch.] Adrianna, Priscilla, Samantha, Franchesca, Alexandria, Adam; [ed.] San Gabriel Mission High; [pers.] My writing is the legacy I leave my children.; [a.] Fontana, CA

TOUEIQ, SIKANDER
[b.] September 14, 1930, Aurangabad, India; [p.] Sardar Mirza, Armarum-Nisa; [m.] Prof. Dr. Sameena Srankat, February 18, 1965; [ch.] 3 daughters, 3 sons; [ed.] M.A. Dip in Linguistics Did M.A. in English Language and Literature form Osmania Univ. Hyderabad; [occ.] Retired Lecturer in English; [memb.] Lecturer in English, Anwar-ul Woom College, Hyd. do, Osmania College Kurnool. Loaned to the University of Kabul, Afghanistan by Asia Foundation, Afghanistan worked in Collabo. Columbia Univ. Team. at Kabul; [hon.] Essay in English won 1st prize "Astrology - Islamic View". World Asso. for Muslim Writers Abu Dhabi in 1994. 2nd prize for Urdu Radio - play in a national competition for script writers; [oth. writ.] Conducted by all India radio, in 1994. Invented a genre called it "Jabayee" in Urdu poetry. It is a seven-line composition like a sonnet but of its length. Articles in English and Urdu and poems in Indian and Pakistan Urdu Magazines.; [pers.] Unless man becomes a real human being, he can't achieve salvation. Its direct -path in Islam, which teaches man to be an ideal man.; [a.] Scarborough Ontario, Canada

TRAVIS, JEREMY WILLIAM
[b.] March 9, 1970, Brampton, Ontario, Canada; [p.] William Travis, Margaret Ewles; [m.] Andrea Victoria Galloway, December 17, 1993; [ed.] J.A. Turner S.S. (O.S.S.D.), York University (Honors B.A. in Music) George Brown College (Cert. In Labour Studies) Sheridan College (Certificate in Human Resource MGT.); [occ.] Composer, Private Teacher of music theory and piano; [oth. writ.] Several poems, essays, song lyrics, commission works, etc.; [pers.] Emotion communicated effectively through any medium is perhaps the highest achievement of man.; [a.] Brampton Ontario, Canada

TREMMEL, WILLIAM CALLOLEY
[b.] June 11, 1918, Englewood, CO; [m.] Opal Laverne Mitchell, 1943; [ch.] William Michael, James Harold, Susan Beth Young, John Mark Tremmel; [ed.] University of Denver, History/Music, Bachelor of Arts, 1940, Iliff School of Theology, Philosophy of Religion, Th. M., 1945, Iliff School of Theology, Philosophy of Religion, Th.D., 1950, University of Colorado, of Colorado, graduate study, 1947-48, University of Southern California, postdoctoral study, 1951, University of Chicago, postdoctoral study, 1954-55; [occ.] Associate Minister, Christ (United) Methodist Church, Denver, Colorado, 1943; [hon.] Scholarship: University of Denver, 1936-40, Kappa Kappa Psi: Honorary Music Fraternity, Pi Gama Mu: Honorary History Fraternity, Fellowship: Iliff School of Theology, 1942-46, Deacons's Orders, The Methodist Church, 1944, Elder's Orders, the Methodist Church, 1945, Fellowship: The Divinity School University of Chicago, 1954-55, Elected Fellow of the Committee of Social Thought, University of Chicago, 1955; [oth. writ.] Handbook of Worship for Ministers, Williams and Tremmel, (Denver: Iliff School of Theology Press, 1944, 1950). The social Concepts of George Herbert Mead (Emporia, Kansas: Emporia State Research Studies, 1957). A Different Drum (National Conference of Christians and Jews, 1964). Religion. What is it? (New York: Holt, Rinehart and Winston, 1978). Man's Religious Expressions, editor (Tampa, Florida: University of South Florida Publication, 1978). The Twenty-Seven Books That Changed The World (New York: Holt, Rinehart and Winston, 1981). Religion. What is it?, second edition, 1984, third edition, (Harcourt Brace, Inc., 1996)l. Dark Side - the Satan story, (St. Louis, Missouri: CBP, 1987). The Jesus Story-in the Twenty-Seven Books, (New York: Peter Lang, 1989), "Bernhardt's Analysis of the Function of Religion", chapter published in God, Values and Empiricism (Macon, Georgia: Mercer University Press, 1989). Running on the Bias (Tampa Florida: Tumbleweed Press, 1989). The Functional Phisology of William H. Bernhardt, Wm. C. Tremmel, editor, publisher, author (Tampa, Florida: Tumbleweed Press, 1990). "Bernhardt's Analysis of the Function of Religion", God, Values and Empiricism (Macon, Georgia: Mercer University Press, 1989). "Humankind and the Religious Dimension" in Empirical Theology (Birmingham, Ala.: Religious Education Press, 1992).; [a.] Tampa, FL

TREVINO, DARLENE
[b.] July 18, 1947, Monroe, WA; [p.] Harley and Marcels Johnsen; [m.] Jose Trevino, Jr., August 12,

1989; [ch.] Tiffany Hubbard, Tom Taggart; [ed.]
Graduated from Oregon City High School '1965';
[occ.] Clerk/Typist for Oregon Cutting Systems
Division of Blount, Inc.; [pers.] My favorite poet is
Henry Wadsworth Longfellow, whose writings have
been my greatest inspiration.; [a.] Oregon City, OR

TREWORGY, TONI
[pen.] "Toni" and "Lady Fox"; [b.] Ridgefield, NJ;
[p.] William Teseny and Marie A. Messina; [m.]
Mark Treworgy, 1993; [ed.] College Majors were in
the fields of Psychology and Marketing; [occ.] Runs
a custom metal Boat building Business with
husband; [memb.] American Society of Marine,
Artists; [hon.] First place - Regional Winner of the
"1982 Original song festival" for original tune
"Remember", aired over several major country music
stations across the U.S.; [oth. writ.] Nemerous press
releases, essays and articles published in several
local newspapers. Current projects Inc. book of
poetry and Art and a series of "travel", and
"Ecological awareness" books for children.; [pers.]
Through the gifts of creativity given to me, hope to
give back the gifts of love, peace and joy to others.;
[a.] Palm Coast, FL

TRIPP, MARGUERITE H.
[pen.] Meg or Rete; [b.] April 23, 1922, Dodge
County; [p.] W. C. and Eva Belle Holland; [m.]
Wilton Tripp, December 7, 1941; [ch.] Erwin -
Deceased, Joan Carter, and Derwin Tripp; [ed.] 2
years College at Middle GA College in Cochran GA,
Medical Technology Training at Grady Hospital in
Atlanta GA; [occ.] Retired Medical Technologist
Registered (mt-ASCP); [memb.] Gresston B. Church,
Gresston, GA. National Library of Poetry; [hon.]
Won Scholarship for Medical Technologist did not
take it (was too far from home.) My training was in
Grady Hospital in Atlanta GA; [oth. writ.] Several
poems I like the rhythm; [pers.] I strive to do unto
others as I would like them to do unto me. I strive
for peace, love and contentment, for mankind.; [a.]
Eastman, GA

TRUXAL, NELLIE LUCHSINGER
[b.] October 16, 1906, Blairsville, PA; [p.] Joseph
Knox and Emma Park Luchsinger; [m.] Karl M.
Truxal - Deceased, July 6, 1926; [ch.] Dorothy
Truxal Skoyec; [ed.] Master of Education - Indiana
University of PA. Additional post graduate work.
University of Pittsburgh and University of Dayton
(OH).; [occ.] Retired teacher - experience from 1
room school to head of math Dept. Jr. High;
[memb.] National Education Assoc., Pa. State
Education Assoc., Hernando Heritage Museum
Assoc., Historical Society of the Blairsville Area
(Pa.) Pioneer Club Indiana Univ. Of Pa., Interna-
tional Society of Poets, United Presbyterian Church
Blairsville Pa. for 70 years.; [hon.] Certificate of
appreciation for work as a volunteer at hernando Co
Florida Museum. Editor's Choice Award - National
Library of Poetry 1995 (Beyond Stars); [oth. writ.]
Contributed to 2 books of memories published by the
Hist. Soc. of the Blairsville Area. Researched and
wrote a study of early schools in West Central
Florida for the Hernando Co. Museum, 3 articles
pub. by the Tampa Tribune on growing up in the
early part of the century in "I Remember it Well".;
[pers.] I have traveled extensively and spent 5
winters in Spain. Now that age has forced me to
limit my travels somewhat, I have the time to write.

I strive to translate memories of a lifetime as well as
contemporary situations into poetry.; [a.] Tampa, FL

TUCKER, LAURA REVIN
[pen.] Lara Tucker; [b.] November 26, 1965, Oak
Ridge, TN; [p.] Landrum and Elennor Tucker; [ed.]
AB from Sarah Lawrence College, Bronxville, NY;
[occ.] Graduate Student in MFA program in Creative
writing; [memb.] Univ. New Orleans Who's Who in
American High School 1983, '84; [hon.] Featured on
New Orleans Radio Show - 1992; [oth. writ.] Poems
published in New Orleans and in Chapel Hill, North
Carolina in Newspapers and Literary Magazines; [a.]
Chapel Hill, NC

TUMA, MELISSA ANN
[pen.] Melissa Tuma; [b.] July, 27, 1913, Central
City, NE; [p.] Ronald and Georgia Francis; [m.]
Lowell K. Tuma, July 29, 1995; [ed.] 1992 -
Nebraska Christian H.S. two years at Central
Community College; [occ.] 1st Asst Mgr. of Fashion
Bug; [oth. writ.] I spend a great deal of my spare
time writing. I have never had anything published
before. I have just recently became interested in
publishing.; [pers.] I fell in love with writing while I
was in high school. It was a way for me to express
the dreams and emotions that God had pressed
against my heart to express within the dancing of my
pen on paper.; [a.] Grand Island, NE

TURCOTTE, LAURA
[b.] July 29, 1962, Maine; [m.] Kenneth Turcotte,
April 18, 1993; [ch.] Leonore (Previous Marriage);
[ed.] Graduated High School in 1980 - Special
Studies - Vocational Agriculture and Dog Grooming;
[occ.] Housewife; [oth. writ.] I have been writing
poetry since I was 16 yrs old. I hope to someday
have them all published.; [pers.] My poetry has been
great strength for me. It has given me peace of mind
through some difficult times in my life. Writing
poetry has given me a direct avenue to connect with
my innermost feeling it also has given me the ability to
look at life with a much more open minded perspective.
After all life is full of Angels; [a.] Phoenix, AZ

TURNBULL, M. MICKEY
[b.] Ottawa, Canada; [m.] Larry; [ch.] Cathy, Carol
and Jean, Grandchildren, Wesley, Melanie, Joel,
Jessica, Mark, Erica and Mitchell; [ed.] St. Clair
County Community College, Michigan, Dean's List,
Magna Cum Laude graduate, Member: Phi Theta
Kappa, Lambda Mu. Additional Credits from The
University of Western Ontario and York University.;
[occ.] Business Management field, Project
Procurement Manager, and Real Estate, I retired after
an automobile accident. I act as a Group Leader in
the chronic pain management field as to enhance my
ongoing recovery.; [memb.] St. James Cathedral
Welcoming Committee, Variety Club, Royal Ontario
Museum, Art Gallery of Ontario, Ontario Science
Centre, St. Christopher House Literary Program
shared by Seniors and children. Lifetime member of
The International society of poets. Member
Canadian Authors Association, Associate Member:
The League of Canadian Poets; [hon.] Three drama
scholarships, Certificates of Honour from The
Ontario Ministry of Citizenship and Culture and
Scarborough Support Services for The Elderly,
Honours Certificates from the Ministry for
Community Service Work.; [oth. writ.] Publications
in Patterns, Pegasus, National Poetry Press, Reporter

with multiple by lines for the Local, a weekly
newspaper published in Aruba. Public Relations
writing for St. Christopher House and "The Nacpac
Track" - (North American Chronic Pain Association), Anthologies: Dance On The Horizon, Echoes
Of Yesterday, Sparkles In The Sand, Best Poets Of
1995, Best Poets of 1996, The Path Not Taken,
Wordscape 2, Reflections By Moonlight, Beneath
The Harvest Moon; [pers.] Our lives are composed
of sorrows and joys. Through inner struggle we find
the capacity to reach for the ultimate within
ourselves, to explore the hopes and dreams within
the heart in order to enrich and ennoble our quality
of life. Poetry is the music of the soul... so sing!
Sing like a nightingale and cast the sweet notes
before all ears...make a celebration of the magic of
words...enchant one another with the beauty and the
wisdom of our hearts. A poem unheard is a poem
cold and waiting to be born. Economic times may be
a burden and grants may disappear but our culture
will always have a soul! The artist will paint the
masterpiece, the musician will write the symphonies
and the writers and poets will record their words
because that is what they do and that is what their
hearts command!!! Place your eloquent stamp on the
tapestry of our times for those to enjoy through
antiquity. I draw from my experiences and try to
translate the ideas, perceptions and thoughts into
pieces of work which can be shared by others. The
more that I write, the more I'm drawn to write, to
capture the fleeting experiences around me, for if
they are not recorded in that moment, they are lost
forever. The "POEM" is the writer's child...
Gratefully, I realize that my child can be less than
perfect and I offer up the very best of nurture so that
my POEM-CHILD will grow to adulthood with
confidence and balance. May my "Child" go forth
with curiosity, enthusiasm, compassion and love, all
subjects are interesting. Every topic compliments
the creative process...and there is no greater joy than
sharing ideas and the music of poetry with my
colleagues and peer!! My sincer thanks and
appreciation to The National Library of Poetry for
their support. Through them, I have re-activated a
love of words and poetry and I have returned to the
writing field. It is a joy to be writing again!!!

TURNER, WILSON M.
[pen.] W. Turner; [b.] November 19, 1940, Orange,
CA; [p.] Wilson and Betty Turner; [m.] Sandra
Ashdown-Turner, October 31, 1992; [ch.] Wilson
Turner, Robert Ashdown, Scott Ashdown; [ed.] UC
Berkley; [occ.] Graphic Artist; [oth. writ.] Quake of
87 - book several poems Three Windows And A
Poor - Play; [pers.] W. Turner passed away August
1995 of cancer; [a.] Santa Fe Springs, CA

TYLER, V.
[b.] Indiana; [occ.] Sales Person and etc; [memb.]
One a writer's Club, and by the way the author is
looking for a producer to make a play of a happy
Luke, thank you and look to address in a happy Luke
to get a hold oft the author, thanks.; [oth. writ.] A
happy Luke book! for those 13 yrs to senior citizen.
It is in your bookstores like wardenbooks. If any one
wants to buy this poem for a song or the one in a
happy get to V. Tyler. Thanks; [pers.] Keep hope
and faith a live and well you will sure need it over
the whole long trials of living. By the way Ms Maya
Angelo and early poets I like besides my works by.;
[a.] Kokomo, IN

UNROE, MARY YVONNE JONES
[pen.] Yvonne Unroe; [b.] May 10, 1948, Clinton, CO; [p.] Kenneth Burton Jones Sr., Nellie Lucille King Jones; [m.] Victor Dirk Unroe, October 25, 1968; [ch.] Victor Corbin Unroe; [ed.] High School; [occ.] Paraprofessional in Sp. Ed. at the Frankfort Middle School; [memb.] Woodside Christian Church; [pers.] I owe my talent to Marple Lawson who I was Secretary for at the Woodside Christian Church, and the Lord for giving me each word. Without the Lord I couldn't have written a single word. I also want to thank Karen Thompson for encouraging me to enter the contest which enabled this poem to be published.; [a.] Frankfort, IN

URBAN, KATHLEEN
[b.] Pittsburgh, PA; [p.] Frank Hartle and Betty Hartle; [m.] Allen D. Urban; [ch.] Nicole, Ashley and Travis; [sib.] Hamptom High, Butler County Community College; [oth. writ.] This is my first published writing; [pers.] I strive to give hope, inspiration, and humor in my writing. I have enjoyed the writings of Helen Steiner rice and the humor of Erma Bombeck; [a.] Freedom, PA

VALADEZ JR., FEDERICO
[b.] July 28, 1968, Fort Polk, LA; [p.] Federico Sr. and Heidi-Ingrid Valadez; [ed.] Bachelor of Arts in Psychology/Sociology December 1990 University of, Texas at San Antonio Master's in Education Guidance and Counseling, Currently enrolled, Sulross State University; [occ.] Social Worker; [memb.] Texas State Licensed Social Worker; [pers.] My writing reflects my passion and compassion for human beings to give the ultimate gift to one another - that of love, caring, and giving. This particular poem is dedicated to my family and all family and children from blended races ethnics groups.; [a.] Midland, TX

VALENZIO, LARRY J.
[b.] September 27, 1920, Toronto, Canada; [p.] Amadeo Valenzio, Edith Valenzio; [ed.] De La Salle, Christian Brothers High School, Chicago; [occ.] Retired Operations Mgr. Barton Brands Ltd. (Distillery); [memb.] American Legion; [hon.] WWII Veteran Normandy Invasion (Utah Beach), Croix de Guerre with the Bronze Star Decision No. 154 Certified by Le Chef de Bataillion Lemoine Awarded by French Government. Recorded in U.S. War Dept. Records by Major General Edward F. Witsell; [oth. writ.] Music, poetry, letters; [pers.] Sister: Grace J. Valenzio, brother Amedeo (Val) Valenzio. The use of GOD given gifts.; [a.] Chicago, IL

VALIQUETTE, BLANCHE
[pen.] Blanche Gerard; [b.] April 6, 1930, Mimico, Ontario, Canada:; [p.] Edmund Gerard and Nellie Gerard; [ch.] All adults now; [occ.] Retired certified nanny; [pers.] I strive for a lesson in my poems, and to make them more personal by including names places where possible.; [a.] Victoria British Columbia, Canada

VALLESE, PAMON
[pen.] Ziggy Pop; [b.] December 1, 1974, Somers Point; [p.] Kristine and Charles; [occ.] Student and Catholic University of America; [memb.] Covenant Life Christian Youth group; [hon.] Hoby Ambassador, Valedictorian and Wildwood Catholic H. S. Dean's List; [oth. writ.] Article "What it Adam and

Eve did drugs" and other anti-drug related articles along with valedictorian speech published in newspapers; [pers.] Writing poetry, although it began as a release, has shown me many ways that I can change for the better of all mankind; [a.] Washington, DC

VAN DEEST, KIMBERLY W.
[b.] March 28, 1971, Miami, FL; [p.] Larry and Faye Van Deest; [ed.] High School Grundy Center High School BS, Physical Education - Iowa State University, MS, Adult Fitness - Indiana State University; [occ.] Full Time graduate student; [memb.] American Heart Assoc. American College of Sports Medicine; [hon.] High School Salutatorian Academic First Team - Big 8 Conference (College) Dean's List; [oth. writ.] None Published; [pers.] Live for the day; [a.] Grundy Center, IA

VANDERVENT, LARRY
[b.] December 28, 1938, Spokane, WA; [p.] Curtis and Edythe Vandervent; [m.] Betty Jean, January 21, 1967; [ch.] Kim and Bryce; [ed.] Ph. D. Psychology Washington State University Pollman, WA; [occ.] College Teacher; [memb.] Amer. Psychological Association (APA); [hon.] APA National Teaching Award 1989, Fellow APA, 1991; [oth. writ.] Developed several (published papers on a neuroepistemology called neurological Positivism 1988-1995. The positive of knowledge is the algorithmic organization of the brain-1988.; [pers.] How strange the trembling of the leaves would seem to be, if we too could not feel the breeze - poetry science thereby?; [a.] Spokane, WA

VANLEUSDEN, SHERRELL
[b.] March 3, 1963, Meredian, MS; [p.] Bill and Shirley Crocker; [m.] Franz H. VanLeusden, January 29, 1994; [pers.] This poem is being published in memory of and with reverence for my grandparents, Elmo and Sally Tew and Joe and Violet Crocker. I miss them all very much.; [a.] Stonewall, MS

VANNI, KAREN JEAN
[b.] November 1, 1952, Duluth, MN; [p.] Betty Denzler and Raymond Foucault; [ch.] Chrissie; [ed.] Miami Coral Park Senior High School; [occ.] City of Miami Beach Parking Dept.; [hon.] Runner up Valor Award, City of Miami Beach 1985; [oth. writ.] Aspiring to published a compilation of 50 poems; [pers.] I truly love life, enjoy laughter, and write what I feel in my heart. I am influenced from personal experiences and my circle of friends; [a.] Miami, FL

VARSHNEY, MRS. MADHU
[b.] August 8, 1945, Kazimabad, India; [p.] Shyam and Priya Varshney; [m.] Hari Varshney, February 18, 1963; [ch.] Praveen, Peeyush and Vandana; [ed.] M.A., Agra University Agra, India; [occ.] Administrator; [memb.] India Club, Vishva Hindu Parishad; [hon.] Multi-Cultural Service Awards; [oth. writ.] Several poems and essays published in magazines several religious books published; [pers.] I believe in service to community and passing my heritage to younger generation; [a.] Vancouver British Columbia, Canada

VATON, DIANA
[b.] March 18, 1968, Comox, British Columbia, Canada; [p.] Karen Henrich and Jim Vaton; [m.]

Perry Klit, December 5, 1992; [ch.] Taylor; [occ.] Regional Co-ordinator, Ministry of Health, Alcohol and Drug Services; [memb.] Board of Directors for crimestoppers, membership in CFSA (Canadian Figure Skating Association; [a.] Campbell River British Columbia, Canada

VAUGHN, SHAWN D.
[pen.] Shawnie; [b.] September 7, 1962, Greer, SC; [p.] Sylvia and Christian; [m.] Timothy E. Vaughn, March 18, 1981; [ch.] Summer and Michael; [ed.] Greer High School Greenville Tech College; [occ.] Purchasing Associate; [memb.] S.C. Youth Sports Association, Business Education partnership; [hon.] Honor Society, Hosa Historian top Achievement Award; [oth. writ.] Several poems, no publications; [pers.] I write from the heart on experiences in my life. This one is for Charles and Beau.; [a.] Greer, SC

VELEZ, IANNETTE
[b.] September 30, 1981, Puerto Rico; [p.] Jeannette Irizarry and Danilo Garcia; [ed.] Last year of junior high school; [occ.] Student; [hon.] I have one of my poems published in Anthology of young poets. I have won awards on my writing; [oth. writ.] I have written 2 plays and I've written many short stories and stories and lots of my work have been published in my school newspaper.; [pers.] People told me that I have a very special gift of knowing how to write. I've given up in my writing but one person told me that I shouldn't stop doing something that I'm good at because that one person who told me that is a smart women for two things one for the words she said to me and two for giving birth to me. I now believe that if you good at something you should never ever give up on it; [a.] New York, NY

VENTURINI, DINA EMMA
[pen.] Ame Ventin; [b.] April, 26, 1936, Flume Veneto, Italy; [p.] Amalia and Vittorio Colussi; [m.] Walter, May 7, 1957; [ch.] Victoria and Mike; [ed.] High School - W.D. Lowe University - University of windsor, (Bachelor of Arts Degree in Sociology), St. Clair College (Secretarial Certificate); [occ.] Part-Time Demonstrator for price club, but am early retire; [memb.] Canadian Association of retired persons, University of Windsor Alumni membership Catholic women's league of Canada; [hon.] Secretarial Certificate from St. Clair College, Bachelor of Arts Degree in Sociology from University of windsor. Eucaristic minister — St. Gabrial's Church windsor police victim services volunteer hospice—volunteer; [oth. writ.] Several poems entered in contests which won awards; [pers.] What may seem impossible to achieve can be possible, if a person really wants to pursue it.; [a.] Windsor Ontario, Canada

VETTER, JANET DINGES
[pen.] J. Rose Vetter; [p.] Anna and Wm Henry Dinges; [m.] Floyd D. Vetter Sr.; [ch.] Floyd D. Better Jr.; [ed.] Elem. and H.S. Graduate (VA) Business Education (Wash. and Lee) Freelance certificate writing (ICS); [occ.] Retired; [memb.] 'Century Travel Club 1981-1993, Methodist Church, Council of Cultural relations (Bryan World 1972-1973); [hon.] Travel to 167 Nations and Independencies - (Silver Award) and 7 Continents; [oth. writ.] Travel articles - (News Local), Information file (Travel Club News Letters), Contest Honorable

Mention; [pers.] I am influenced by Almighty given awesomeness world wide; [a.] Manassas, VA

VIAU, SYLVIE
[b.] April 10, 1976, Noelville; [p.] Alice and Normand Viau; [ed.] I went to French River High School but I'm now going to College Boreal for their sign Language program; [occ.] Student; [pers.] Poetry is my way to express myself. My pen naturally knows what to do that's why it comes easily to me.; [a.] Sudbury Ontario, Canada

VINCENT, CHRISTINE
[b.] April 18, 1983, North Bay, Ontario; [p.] Gerry and Gloria Vincent; [ed.] Elementary School grade 7 French Canadian Language spoken French

VORMELKER, JOI M.
[b.] March 18, 1966, Metairie, LA; [p.] Nancy M. Vormelker and Richard S. Vormelker; [ed.] James Madison High School, 1984, San Antonio College, National Institute of Technology, National Education Center, October 1992; [occ.] Teacher; [memb.] Lamb's Book of Life Who's who's in High School, Who's Who's Honor Society, 1984; [oth. writ.] Other poems which at this time are unpublished; [pers.] God's grace, which is a gift, is shown through the death of his son Jesus on the cross. God gives me the words to show how much he loves us through his Son; [a.] San Antonio, TX

VURTURE, FRANK G.
[b.] January 20, 1928, Staten Island, NY; [p.] Edward Vurture and Sarah Vurture; [m.] Barbara Vurture, April 10, 1990; [ch.] David Alan, Steven Thomas, Gary Frederick and Richard William; [ed.] Newdorp H.S., New York University B.A., M.A.; [occ.] Retired Supervisor of Special Ed. N.Y.C. Board of Education; [memb.] American Legion, A.A.R.P. Ducks Unlimited, Retired School Supervisors and Administrators; [pers.] My poetry is strongly influenced by personal experiences, as they relate to the great outdoors and the common bond of similarity that Flora and Fauna have with mankind.

WADDELL, STEPHANIE
[b.] May 8, 1977, Saint John, New Brunswick, Canada; [p.] David Waddell, Janet Waddell; [ed.] Kennebecasis Valley High School; [memb.] St. Augustine's Church Member, Junior Church Leader; [oth. writ.] Articles and poetry for local high school magazine, 'The Crusader Chronicle', and articles for local church newspaper, 'News From The Pews'; [pers.] I hope to use my writing as a mirror on the world and on the lives within it. My greatest influences have been those around me with uncompromising integrity. I wish for my writing to hold the same integrity.; [a.] Quispamsis New Brunswick, Canada

WAGNER, RUTH PERRY
[p.] Alvin Lee and Mande Jane Perry; [m.] Joseph E. Wagner; [ch.] Sandra Jo Wagner, Edward Wagner, Leslie Ann Trent; [a.] Corpus Christi, TX

WAITES, MARQUEL
[b.] May 23, 1977, Long Beach, CA; [p.] Sheila Hayes; [ed.] David Starr Jordan High School, David Starr Jordan High School, JROTC; [occ.] Military Career; [memb.] JROTC, World Literary Crusade, Church of Scientology, New Morning Starr Baptist

Church; [hon.] TROA - Retired Officers Ass. Medal, JROTC Citizenship Award, Whose Who Among American Students Award, Medal of Merit Nominee, JROTC, Completion of JROTC; [oth. writ.] Catts Purr Newspaper (School Newspaper) Staff writer; [pers.] I live towards a positive life and my mind focus on achievable goals with God on my side.; [a.] Long Beach, CA

WALDSCHMIDT, ALLISON NICHOLE
[b.] February 9, 1983, Kankakee, IL; [p.] Dale and Brenda Waldschmidt; [ed.] South Wilmington Grade School; [a.] South Wilmington, IL

WALKER, DON S.
[pen.] Blax-Ink; [b.] March 24, 1958, Waco, TX; [p.] Sylvia M. Walker; [m.] Widowed; [ch.] Ashley Walker; [ed.] Richfield High School, East Texas State University; [occ.] Collection Officer and Author; [oth. writ.] Book: Just Us written about African American male single parents. Voted Man of the Week after first 2 weeks of publication by Dallas Post Tribune Newspaper Article.; [pers.] My God given burden is for single parents and the forgotten I am driven by my own tragedy of losing a first child and a wife with a 4 1/2 weeks old newborn to take care of now it's just us.; [a.] Dallas, TX

WALKER, ELIZABETH MEGAN
[b.] August 4, 1978, Cleveland, OH; [p.] Bruce Walker and Marcia Glasby; [ed.] I am a Junior at Keys Academy; [memb.] The National Authors Registry, Treasure Hills Presbyterian Church Choir; [hon.] I am in three other poetry books. Including this poem I have a total of six poems published.; [oth. writ.] Rose The Five Senses, Death, Me, Past, and Mother, all in other poetry books; [pers.] Everything I write comes from my heart. When you feel happy or sad or anything else, just get a pen and write down what comes to mind. In my poems are my most true feelings.; [a.] Harlingen, TX

WALKER, MARTHA WAID
[b.] February 18, 1936, Sunflower City, MS; [p.] Polly and Roscoe Waid; [m.] Clifton "Henry" Walker, September 19, 1975; [ch.] Stacy, Kim, Jimmy; [ed.] High School graduate; [occ.] Home maker; [memb.] Southsid Baptist Church; [oth. writ.] Other poems none published; [pers.] I write about what I know about and receive lots of encouragement from my friends and family.; [a.] Vicksburg, MS

WALLACE, BETT
[b.] November 14, 1942; [p.] Elizabeth Sybeldon, Lawrence Petersen; [m.] William M. Wallace, September 5, 1964; [ch.] Anne, Laurelei; [occ.] Artist, writer; [memb.] Duluth Art Institute, Tweed Museum of Art, Minnesota Alliance for Art in Education; [pers.] We are created with our own special gifts. Discover them, use them well.; [a.] Duluth, MN

WALTER, THOMAS MICHAEL
[pen.] Mike; [b.] May 28, 1958, MD; [p.] Kay L. Walter; [m.] Deceased, April 1979; [ch.] Christina; [ed.] High School; [occ.] Book Binder; [oth. writ.] Forever and ever gone; [pers.] Life is short enjoy it; [a.] Baltimore, MD

WALTERS, JESSICA
[ed.] The University of Texas at El Paso, Texas (1996); [occ.] College Student; [hon.] Special

Diploma: The Institute of Children's Literature; [oth. writ.] Portfolio of poems, essays, short stories, and songs, and a book for children; [pers.] "Do unto others as you would have them do unto you"; [a.] El Paso, TX

WALTHAM, SHERRY
[b.] August 22, 1958, Dunnville, Ontario, Canada; [p.] Betty O'Neill, (the late) Jack O'Neill; [m.] Larry Bowden (Common Law); [ed.] Dunnville Secondary; [occ.] Property Manager; [oth. writ.] I have written several poems over the past 23 years and have never attempted to have any of them published.; [pers.] My family has always been a great source of inspiration to me. Some of my poems have been written about them, some have been written for them and all of my poetry is because of them. I am eternally grateful for their love and support.; [a.] Hamilton Ontario, Canada

WALTON, PAMELA E.
[pen.] Pam Walton; [b.] June 9, 1950, Fort Campbell, KY; [p.] Mr. Charles J. Piecek and Juanita Marie Piecek (Deceased); [m.] Greg Walton, April 29, 1989; [ch.] Eric Sean Henson, Katie Walton; [ed.] Brownsville High, Tarrant County Jr. College; [occ.] Teacher Asst., Meadow Creek Elementary, Bedford, Texas; [memb.] Kindergarden Sunday School Teacher, Martin Methodist Church; [oth. writ.] Currently working on children's stories; [pers.] Never give up on your dreams, you are never too old to short college and always give thanks to your God

WALTON, RICHARD L.
[b.] July 12, 1953, Tucson, AZ; [p.] Clem and Opal Walton (Deceased); [ed.] Catalina High School; [hon.] Editor's Choice Award 1995 by the National Library of Poetry; [oth. writ.] The National Library of Poetry. Beyond The Stars-Joni; [pers.] Sometimes in life we are fortunate enough to meet someone very special. They help us to discover more about ourselves than we ever thought possible. Motivate us to express, inspires us to create and dream greater than we would other wise dare. To Jennifer, one such special person.; [a.] Tucson, AZ

WAMSLEY, CHAD
[pen.] C. Huston Wamsley; [b.] January 18, 1969, Bethesda, MD; [p.] Raymond and Barbara Wamsley; [m.] Carrie Calimer; [ed.] Damascus High School, Salisbury State University, BA Psychology; [occ.] Security Assistant, Redland Middle School; [memb.] International Society of Poets, Distinguished member, Tau Kappa Epsilon Fraternity; [hon.] Semi-finalist, The National Library of Poetry, Spare A Dime, Semi-finalist, The National Library of Poetry, My Reflection; [oth. writ.] Spare A Dime, My Solemn Prayer, That Old Rose, The Green Leaf Falls, Dreams And Tears, Windows To The Soul, You're An Oak, I Will Show You The Way; [pers.] There is always a little something in everyone just waiting to come out and shine; [a.] Germantown, MD

WARD, SANDRA LEE
[b.] August 7, 1957, St. Cath., Ontario, Canada; [p.] George Ward, and Willena Ward; [ch.] Cory, Matthew, Jessica; [occ.] Home maker; [oth. writ.] Several other poems for family and friends; [pers.] I like to write from the heart. To let people know. That I appreciate who they are and what they mean to me. Especially Mrs. Alma Bergie Matthew's grade One teacher; [a.] Saint Catharines Ontario, Canada

WARK, BRENDA LEE
[b.] February 17, 1959, Chester, PA; [p.] Nola Boggs and Jim Trader; [m.] Lee A. Wark, January 14, 1978; [ch.] Jason Wark; [ed.] Graduated from Chichester High 1977, Graduate of Chester - Upland Practical - Nursing Program - 1 year; [occ.] Licensed Practical Nurse at Fair Acres Geriatric Center; [hon.] Chester-Upland Practical Nursing Program - Perfect Attendance March 8, 1991, Academic Achievement Award March 8, 1991; [oth. writ.] Heaven Help Me, The Way Ward Heart, Somewhere in Time, Lightening and Rain, Broken Wings, Secret Silence Crossroads, You Give Me Love, My Dream Lover, The Drowning Sea, Take This Rain, Purple Shadows; [pers.] I write my poetry as a means of therapy when something bothers me or gets me down. My poems are about life, heartache, sadness and death. I write about the death of my patients which is the hardest feeling to cope with.; [a.] Linwood, PA

WARKE, MARY-ESTHER BEAN
[pen.] Mary-Esther Bean Warke; [b.] Alberta, Canada; [p.] Rev. Olive and Harry Bean B.A. M.A. and E.E.; [m.] John Warke, 1971; [ch.] Ardith Mary Storey; [ed.] Educated in Music, business, Religion; [occ.] Preparing a book of my poems and prose, Church work; [memb.] First Church of the Nazarene Edmonton, AB, Member of Liberal Party of Canada Canadian Council of Women; [hon.] Trophy for security sales A Song Evangelist Commission from the Church of the Nazarene. Have been musical programmer for both Church and Home and School Association...and Church pianist; [oth. writ.] The Gospel Herald The National Research Bureau's Magazine "The American Salesman" Our Family (Catholic publication) Methodist Publication, "The Word became Flesh." Correspondent for several newspapers ever the years Ferintosh History Book contributor.; [pers.] I love to write both poetry and prose. It is a great emotional release and has been reported to have helped many a soul going thru' adversity.; [a.] Sherwood Park Alberta, Canada

WARNER, ANGELIFAE ANNE
[b.] June 21, 1978, Stower, OH; [p.] Thomas and Pamela Warner; [ed.] Home schooled all through High School. I am currently a senior enrolled in a satellite program.; [occ.] High School Student; [memb.] The International Library of Poetry; [hon.] Editor's choice award from the Nationa Library of Poetry; [oth. writ.] Several poems published by the National Library of Poetry, one poem published by the Amherso Society, a novel and a book of poems being considered for publication.; [pers.] In the past there were great men of valor. We admire those people. However, we seldom look to see for what love they fought for, even died for. They died for the sake of freedom, in action, word and thought.; [a.] South Euclid, OH

WARNER, BONNNIE L.
[b.] September 17, 1952, Cleveland, OH; [p.] John and Betty Gregore; [m.] Rob H. Warner, September 14, 1985; [ch.] Jessica A. Menendez, Cheryl Warner, Jeffrey Warner; [ed.] New Smyrna Beach High School, Daytona Beach Community College; [occ.] Computer Programmer/analyst, Hawaiian Tropic, Ormond Beach, Florida; [memb.] Florida Real Estate License, Bella Vista Baptist Church; [hon.] High School Hall of Fame, Dean's List, Multiple Awards

for top listing and sales agent in Real Estate; [oth. writ.] Began writing my first romance novel in 1995; [pers.] Shower one's self with positive thoughts and be blessed with a healthy mind and a happy spirit. Share this gift with others by spreading love and compassion wherever you go. May my writings reflect what I believe.; [a.] Edgewater, FL

WARREN, PHILIP
[b.] October 8, 1971, Hamilton, OH; [p.] Steve Sr. and Mary Warren; [ed.] B.S. at Texas A and M University; [occ.] USDA Federal Investigator/ Marketing Specialist; [oth. writ.] An Inward Look: Rebirth as published in Mists of Enchantment; [pers.] I do most of my writing or at least find it easier to write while in a deep or depressed state of mind.; [a.] Conroe, TX

WASHINGTON, WILLENE
[pen.] Spice Washington; [b.] March 9, 1960, Mobile, AL; [p.] Cleveland and Willene E. Washington; [ch.] Lavette R. and Jerrod C.; [ed.] Mattie T. Blount High S.D. Bishop State Jr. College; [occ.] Mail Processor; [a.] Eight Mile, AL

WATKINS, SUSAN
[b.] November 6, 1968, Darby, PA; [p.] Michele and William Kauffman; [ch.] Charles Watkins IV; [ed.] Graduated Perry High School 1986; [occ.] Secretary at Liberty Publishing; [pers.] I dedicate this poem to Daniel Watkins, son of Chuck and Linda Watkins. He was only 8 years old and hit by a truck while riding his bike. "Daniel, I know you are with God, and are safe. Your family misses you very much.";
[a.] Pittsburgh, PA

WATSON, KAREN S.
[b.] January 12, 1951; [p.] Robt. E. and Mary K. McCrate; [m.] Gerald S. Watson; [pers.] When God has blessed us in so many ways, I feel an obligation to be thankful for not just what I have, but what I have learned. Our eyes should be opened so that we can see what the love of family and understanding of faith is all about. We should be grateful for not only the ability to love, but sharing in life's commitment to love one another as well. Our contribution to it all may not be perfection, but we need to at least acknowledge that there are many wonderful people who touch our lives everyday and bring both enrichment and joy into our lives. These people may be family or just friends...perhaps they influence us now or are a treasured memory of those who've lived before... Regardless, we need to remind ourselves daily of our obligation to share in God's love and keep the commitment alive.

WATTS, DALLAS MILLER
[b.] August 18, 1956, Kingston, Ontario, Canada; [pers.] I write from personal experiences.

WEAR, SARA BRADFORD
[pen.] Sara B. Ware; [b.] September 30, 1940, Colbert Co, AL; [p.] Walter Brandford; [ch.] Dr. Kelley Dianne Wear, Robert Bradford and Sarah Wear, Maury Vincent Wear, and Carmen Gogus, Jessica Erin Tritschler; [occ.] Freelance writer and contract Asst Johnny Cash, Pam Tillis Bob Dipero, Carlene Carter Country Music Association, Several Civic Organizations, B.M.I. affiliate; [hon.] Gavin Report recommended new release of "Hello Trouble" several "Pick Hits of the Week" recordings

recognition from Am. Heart Association for Fund Raiser Keys to cities, Achievement awards, numerous leadership awards "write-ups" in many publications - newspapers.; [oth. writ.] Acceptance Speech for Marty Robbins (Inductee Cowboy Hall of Fame, '82), Publicist for Country Music Artists, Jingles; [pers.] If one can feel what he cannot touch and has the insight of the blind, the wisdom of the deaf and dumb and can savor the aroma of a dried flower, he is a kindred spirit to the elements, a born poet. Personally, I just hang-out with live memories of great friends past; [a.] Nashville, TN

WEATHERS, JENNIFER LYNN
[b.] April 29, 1982, Cleveland, TX; [p.] Jane Weathers; [ed.] 8th grade Burleson Middle School; [oth. writ.] I have written lots of other poems one entitled "Friends" for my family's pleasure and my own.; [pers.] I am 13, the oldest of my identical twin sister, Jessica, and the oldest of 3 girls.; [a.] Cleburne, TX

WEAVER, JILLIAN FAITH
[b.] September 5, 1983, Aurora, CO; [p.] Harold and Carla Weaver; [ed.] Clinton Middle School Clinton, TN; [occ.] Student; [memb.] Girl Scouts of America, Optimist Club Competitive Basketball Team, Optimist Club Traveling Team, Band, East Tennessee Invitational Band; [hon.] A Honor Roll, Science Fair winner, 3 time champion Spelling, Math Counts, Duke Talent Identification Program, Energy Bowl, Scholars Bowl; [oth. writ.] Noises From The Cave, The Ghost Of Mystery Creek; [a.] Clinton, TN

WEBB, GLADYS
[occ.] Widowed (House Keeper); [memb.] Nazarene Church, Secretary of Sunday School Class, Sunday and Church Culler; [hon.] Mother of the Year Plaque in Honor from Elkhart Church of the Nazarene; [pers.] I believe in Christian values and am proud of my Christian heritage I try to, live it daily.; [a.] Elkhart, KS

WEBB, SILAS T.
[b.] March 17, 1976, ME; [p.] William L. Webb; [m.] Renee Peters (Fiance); [ed.] Currently a student of Delmar College; [pers.] Only tomorrow will you truly understand how much you didn't know yesterday.; [a.] Robstown, TX

WEBSTER, BRET
[b.] April 18, 1958, Pueblo, CO; [p.] Merle E. Webster and Mary F. Webster; [ed.] H. S. Pueblo East High 1976, University of Southern Colorado, 1984, obtained B.S. in Political Science; [occ.] Credit Analyst with Denver Publishing Co DBA: Rocky Mtn News; [hon.] Dean's List University of Southern Colorado Fall 1984, certified Paralegal, 1989; [pers.] My late father's unique common sense approach to life has had an immeasurable influence on my writing, May Angelus great commitment to humanity and my mother's unfailing love and support all my inspirations.; [a.] Denver, CO

WEBSTER, CHRISTINE
[pen.] Whoopi, Peanuts Crissy; [b.] July 6, 1956, Louisville, KY; [p.] Sarah Webster and Walter Stone; [ch.] Erica Doughs, Rashida Thomas, Lanisha Webster; [ed.] GED, 1 year Early Childhood Educ. at Jefferson Comm. College, present at School of

Banking and Business Major Computer Application; [occ.] Distributions on job 4 years; [memb.] AAA; [hon.] Elem. Music pins, certificates, Dean's List at JCC and School of Business and Banking; [oth. writ.] Time - I sent in 1980's to one other competition; [pers.] Before one can know someone else, one must get to know one's self first...; [a.] Louisville, KY

WEEKS JR., BLISS EUGENE
[b.] October 20, 1963, Kansas City, MO; [p.] Bliss Eugene, Mary Agnes Weeks; [m.] Diana Lyn DeLaTorre Weeks, September 26, 1985; [ch.] Travis Shane Stepson; [ed.] Northeast High School, K.C. MO. Platt College (Now-Northwest MO. Community College); [memb.] Toastmasters International Charter Member Club Omega Current Member Club Talu - Moberly Correctional Center, Moberly, MO; [hon.] Competent Toastmaster Recognition (CTM) and Able Toastmaster Recognition (ATM); [oth. writ.] "Midnights Love Flight" poem published in sparrowgrass poetry Forum Inc. treasured poems of America (Summer 1994 Edition); [pers.] Being human and imperfect we tend to make many mistakes in life. Those mistakes we have to learn from in order to grow, in romance, friendships and family relationships, in order to grow as a person.

WEEKS, MARY CAROL
[b.] July 10, 1936, Roanoke, VA; [p.] Herbert and Tula Thornburg; [m.] Corbin L. Weeks, December 24, 1954; [ch.] Jean Martin, Barry Weeks and Lisa Freeborough; [ed.] Graduate of Jefferson H.S. class of 1954; [occ.] Housewife and mother; [oth. writ.] Articles published in the Roanoke Times, Roanoke, VA; [pers.] My lifelong love of poetry stems from the inspired teaching of my favorite High School English Teacher, Mrs. Drewery; [a.] Vinton, VA

WEI, WANG
[b.] May 30, 1954, Beijing, P. R. China; [ed.] B.A. in English, Jilin University, P. R. China, 1982, M.A. in English, Texas A and M University, 1990; [occ.] Accounting Dept., Clipper America, Inc.; [memb.] Distinguished Member, the International Society of Poets, Member of China Poetry Society, Houston, Texas; [hon.] Prose in Creative Writing Contest, Jilin University, China, 1982; [oth. writ.] B.A. thesis: Comparative Study of the Nature Poetry in the Works of Tao Yuan-Ming and William Wordsworth, M.A. thesis: Chinese Ideograms in Ezra Pound's Canto 85, Poetry, prose, news reports in local news papers, P.R. China; [pers.] The language of poetry should have no boundaries. I pursue a harmony in the eastern and western cultures, languages, ideologies, poetics, and poetical forms.; [a.] Houston, TX

WEILHEIMER, NEIL
[pen.] Neil West; [p.] Doris and Ernest Weilheimer; [m.] Kelly - the most beautiful person I know, August 25, 1996; [ed.] BA - S.U.N.Y. Albany MA - New York University; [oth. writ.] Currently developing my first manuscript of poetry; [pers.] When the monsoon hits the heart of our village, always know that the desert's sun must rise so bright.; [a.] New York, NY

WEITZEL, SUSAN ROTH
[pen.] Susan Roth; [b.] April 19, 1948, Findlay, OH; [p.] Ellen and Vern Hart; [m.] Wm. Weitzel, September 5, 1987; [ch.] Stephanie; [ed.] Port Clinton High School and Nursing School of

Sandusky; [occ.] Nurse, Edison Health Care - have been a nurse for 27 years; [memb.] American Heart Assoc.; [oth. writ.] None published to date; [pers.] Started writing poems when my late husband developed cancer 1979, my daughter entered this poem written for her.; [a.] New London, OH

WELCH, CARMEN
[pen.] Carmen Welch; [b.] August 2, 1973, Niles, MI; [p.] Phil and Brenda Roggow; [ed.] Reed City High School and Big Rapids; [hon.] Carmen Welch Award (Most Improved Student); [oth. writ.] Editor of school newspaper. Written poems for the newspaper.; [a.] Glendale Heights, IL

WELCH, VELDA E.
[pen.] Max Welch; [b.] April 1, 1952, Florence, SC; [p.] Luvell and Katharine Welch; [m.] Rhonda Lynn Welch, July 19, 1991; [ch.] Kim Paul, Michael and Chris Davis; [ed.] 2 years college, El Paso Community College; [occ.] Director of an Extension Campus of a Community College Florence-Darlington Technical College; [memb.] American Lung Association, Non-commissioned Officer Association; [hon.] Command Sergeant Major (Retired) U.S. Army 1972-1994; [pers.] There was nothing like serving my country as a soldier.; [a.] Hartsville, SC

WELLS, BESSIE
[b.] January 18, 1928, Fort Smith, AR; [p.] Mr. Henry Jones and Mrs. Macy Jones; [m.] James Charles Wells (Deceased), March 11, 1947; [ch.] Two; [ed.] 12th Grade 1 year West Ark Community College; [occ.] Poetry; [hon.] Award of merit certificate from the World of Poetry Rank, Honorable mention January 1, 1991 of Sacramento, California

WELSCH, LORRAINE MARIE
[pen.] L. M. Welsch; [b.] September 18, 1961, Pittsburgh, PA; [p.] James R. Welsch and Rosemary M. Herrick; [ch.] Aubrey Louise; [ed.] Franklin Regional High School, Murrysville, PA; [occ.] Student; [memb.] U.S. Navy Chief Petty Officers Fraternity, Fleet Reserve Association; [oth. writ.] Private, unpublished works of poetry; [pers.] My writings have always been my "secret place". A place of refuge to hide and to express myself without fear of ridicule from my seven sisters and one brother, while growing up.; [a.] Jackson, NJ

WELSH, GEORGE W.
[b.] August 30, 1925, Chicago, IL; [p.] Wm. W. Welsh and Harriet Howel Welsh; [m.] Margaret Sinclair Welsh, February 16, 1980; [ch.] Wm. W. Welsh II; [ed.] Avery Coonley School, Hinsdale Township High School, B.S. in Wild Life Management from Colorado State University, '57; [occ.] Retired from Arizona Game and Fight Dept.; [memb.] Arizona Antelope Foundation, Arizona Desert Bighorn Sheep Society Rocky Mountain Elk Foundation, Mohave Sportsmans Club, N.R.A.; [hon.] Beta Beta Beta, Xi Sigma Pi, Desert Bighorn Council 1984, Outstanding Contributions Award; [pers.] Dedicated to my dog Schultz who was a large part of my life for 14 years!; [a.] Kingman, AZ

WEST, BERTHA A.
[b.] November 10, 1921, Sibley, IA; [p.] Charles and Albena Adreon; [m.] Glen, July 12, 1945; [ch.]

Marguerite, Adreonna; [ed.] Sibley High School-Sibley, IA Westmar College - Le Mars, IA, Univ. of Northern Colo., Greeley C.U. Boulder, Colo - Reality Seminars Methodist Church Member; [occ.] Retired: Taught Rural School for 6 years - (Grades P-8) in Iowa; [memb.] Arizona Porcelain Artists (Winter months); [hon.] Achievement Award for Service with the National Park Service - RMNP Retired from Rocky Mt. 1984; [oth. writ.] Poem - "Tundra Jewels" pub. by The Nature Assn. of Rocky Mt. National Park. My unpublished poems are for children and about nature's animals, etc.; [pers.] Open your eyes and ears to the wonderful sights and sounds of nature as they will radiate their beauty into your soul as strength for living - time is so precious; [a.] Estes Park, CO

WEST, FRANCES
[b.] 1918, Boise, ID; [p.] Emma Cleora and Daniel Simpson; [m.] William S. West (Deceased), April 9, 1938; [ch.] William A., David L., Nancy D., Mary A., Joleen R., Cleora M.; [ed.] High School; [occ.] Retired Sometimes I paint, and am trying to write my life story; [oth. writ.] The Door, Day and Night; [pers.] Book for the rainbow is based on the Bible account of the flood in Genesis 8:22 and 9:13.

WEST, JUDY ROGERS
[b.] August 16, 1949, Shelby, NC; [p.] Clyde and Carrie Rogers; [m.] Ron West, January 5, 1974; [ed.] Shelby High, Gardner Webb College; [occ.] Secretary-Textile Plant; [memb.] Dover Baptist Church; [oth. writ.] Poems published in local newspaper, poem written about church was put in corner stone in new building; [pers.] My inspiration for my poems have come from growing up in a simple, close-knit textile mill community and being raised in a christian home by loving christian parents.; [a.] Shelby, NC

WEST, MARIA
[pen.] Running Dawn, Mary Elite; [b.] August 14, 1977, Hillsboro, WI; [p.] James and Donna West; [ed.] I am attending Durand High School and am in my senior year and hope to go on to school; [occ.] High School Student; [memb.] I am a youth group member at my local church and I am also very involved in my High School choir; [hon.] Being published by The National Library of Poetry; [oth. writ.] Dream and Disaster, Final Farewell and Mine; [pers.] During my short life I have seen hate, war, and death. I hope that my poem will cause people to stop and think.; [a.] Durand, WI

WEST, SARAH
[b.] October 18, 1964, Shreveport, LA; [p.] Booker T. and Katherine West; [ch.] Decovin (Deceased), Darryl, D'Kemaan; [ed.] Lincoln High, Lamar University; [occ.] Sales Associate; [pers.] This poem was written after the death of my eleven year old son Decovin, because he was one of the precious gifts that the Lord gave to me.; [a.] Port Arthur, TX

WESTERN, JACK J. P.
[b.] July 20, 1923, England; [m.] Barbara Sylvia Western, September 9, 1944; [ch.] Three Seven Grandchildren; [ed.] Primary School, Secondary School - Police Colleges (3), Pastor Christian Church, Church of Christ many courses in many subjects/areas, O. P. S. Business Administration courses, 8 years, O. P. S. Practical Writing Courses,

O. P. S. Book Keeping Course, O. P. S. Adminstrators Hiring Course, O. P. S. Employee Evaluation Courses; [occ.] Entreprenuer, Bluewater Weddings Service Canadian Section, Part time Justice of the Peace; [memb.] International Police Association, Bomber Command Assoc. Canada Masonic - Lodge - Chapter Perceptory - Shrine - Et-Al Committee Canon Davis Church (Angelica) Director Sarnia Disaster Relief Organization, current 3 years Director (Founder) Bomber Comman association Canada Inc. 8 years current, Past President CSAO, Past Director Civil Service Ass'n Ontario 3 years. Past Director Ontario Public Service Employees Union, 3 Years, Past Executive officer International Police Association, (Offices Regional and National) 2nd V/P/ 1st VP, Treasurer, Secretary, President, 1960 to 1976. Region 1, 3rd V/P 2nd V/P and 1st V/P for National (9 years), International Police Association Canada, Region 1 and National, Member of Ontario Wide Justice of the Peace Association, Addendum 1st February 1995, Pastor Christian Church Church of Christ, President, Bluewater Weddings; [hon.] War medals WW II Canadian 125 Commemorative Medal, Royal Life Saving Society Medals and St Johns Ambulance medals; [oth. writ.] 6 not published books, (as yet) (Editor Lambton Shrine Club News) (Editor Gaggle and Stream 1992-1995 Bomber Command Ass'n Canada; [pers.] R.A.F. WW II 1942 - 1947 (WO-1) Police Service 1947-1967 Last Bank Chief of Police Family Court 1967-1995 (Title Court Admin. CLK of Court Justice of Peace Province of Ontario; [a.] Sarnia Ontario, Canada

WHALEN, FRANCES LESLIE
[pen.] Leslie Whalen; [b.] October 31, 1928, Baltimore, MD; [p.] Thomas Harrow and Margaret Harrow; [m.] Bill Whalen (Deceased), January 14, 1947; [ch.] Sherry Evans, Bill Whalen, Tara Jordan, Kim Whalen; [ed.] Edgar Allen Poe High, Baltimore School, St. Pete High; [occ.] Coating Inspector Essilor of America; [memb.] Valleyball Assoc. I.F.W. Animals, H.S.U.S. Humane Society of U.S. - A.S.P.C.A. American Society, prevention cruelty to animals; [pers.] I try to express deep feelings inside, toward nature and episodes that affected my life.; [a.] Saint Petersburg, FL

WHALEN, ROSALIND M.
[pen.] Chelsey Josephine; [b.] May 25, 1948, Saint John's, Newfoundland, Canada; [p.] John and Alfreda Dawe; [m.] Clarence Whalen, June 30, 1966; [ch.] Three boys; [ed.] Grade 10 (Elementary) Springfield Street School also IJ. Samson High School; [occ.] Housewife; [oth. writ.] Several poems I have not had any published. My poems are religious and inspirational; [pers.] I would like to write more about My Creator. And have a deeper understanding off Him.; [a.] Pefferlaw Ontario, Canada

WHALEY, ARTHUR H.
[b.] July 11, 1911, Patchogue LI, NY; [p.] Daniel Whaley, Charlotte Whaley; [m.] Mildred Whaley, March 12, 1937; [ch.] Daniel Claude, Susan Ann; [ed.] Patchogue High, Alfred Univ., B.S. Columbia Univ., M.A.; [occ.] Retired School Superintendent; [memb.] 32 F.A.M., R.A.M., KT, Shrine, B.R.O.E American Assoc. School Administrators, National Secondary School Administrators, Rotary International; [hon.] Phi Delta Kappa, Rotary International

Paul Harris Fellow; [oth. writ.] Editorial in Central N.Y. Study Council Mag. and several other poems; [pers.] I like to compose poems concerning family and friends. I endeavor to point out various characteristics of my subjects.; [a.] Middleville, NY

WHALEY, COREY W.
[b.] August 18, 1973, Oklahoma City; [p.] Benny R. Whaley and Margaret A. Whaley; [ed.] Edmond Memorial High School, Oklahoma Christian University of Science and Arts; [occ.] Student; [pers.] I am still quite young, but I still strive to share what I have learned and experienced. I do so not only through poetry, but also through photography, acting, and singing. I still have much to experience, as I will enter medical school next fall.; [a.] Edmond, OK

WHEELER, DENNIS R.
[pen.] Dennis Wheeler; [b.] January 1, 1948, North Bend, OR; [p.] E. Joyce Matheny; [m.] Dorothy J. (Beverle) Wheeler, March 13, 1971; [ch.] Ryan Todd, Chad Allen; [ed.] Associate of Arts degree in Administration of Criminal Justice - San Bernardino Valley College, San Bernardino, California; [occ.] Law Enforcement Officer Sergeant and Rialto Police Department Rialto, Calif. 92376; [memb.] Evangeli-cal Lutheran Church of America - California Peace Officers Association - California Association of Hostage Negotiators (Charter member); [hon.] Vietnam Veteran - Bronze Star W/V Device - Purple Heart - Air Medal with number 3 - Army Commen-dation medal; [oth. writ.] In 1995 2 Chapbooks published by "The Plowman Printing House", Box 414, Whitby Ontario Canada, L1N 5S4. Published with mother, brothers and sisters and other family members. Titled: A Family Affair "modern day poems by a family of modern day poets", A Family Affair II with same subtitle. Have a large manu-scripts of (A Family Affair with family poems) being reviewed for publishing by a family of South Dakota Poets. By Northwest Publishing in Salt Lake City, Utah. In case you haven't noticed, my mother E. Joyce Matheny, my brother Danny and Alton Matheny and my sister Valerie Matheny will all be published in your printing of Jensath The Harvest Moon. Poems published in a few local newspapers. Take what you will from this. Thanks; [a.] California, CA

WHEELER, KELLEY-ANN
[pen.] Polly; [b.] July 12, 1980, Riverview; [p.] Lorraine Wheeler and Stephen Wheeler; [ed.] Keypart High School; [oth. writ.] Other poems published in Crossings - another poetry contest; [pers.] Most of my writings come from my feelings and my thoughts. I really don't know what influenced me to write. I just express my thoughts and feelings better in poems than trying to explain them.; [a.] Keyport, NJ

WHITE, DAVID MICHAEL
[pen.] Davis Blanco; [b.] January 8, 1959, Muskogee, OK; [p.] Mary Wilma Marlow; [ed.] University of Oklahoma, Muskogee High School; [occ.] Membership Counselor at Southern Athletic Fitness Club (OKC); [memb.] New life Bible Church Oklahoma, wildlife federation, O.O Rugby football club, Dallas Hailegwins Old Boy RFC; [hon.] '86 Gold Medal Sooner State Games (Rugby) '87 Fred Irving Award (OU Rugby) '85 Mr. Rugby (OU);

[oth. writ.] Article on Golf in Sports Pulse Mag June 93, Dallas Texas; [pers.] I want people to relax when they read my poetry. I've had a fairly though life is good.; [a.] Norman, OK

WHITE, KIMBERLY ANN
[pen.] Kimberly Ann White; [b.] May 3, 1969, Danville, IL; [p.] Robert and Sandy Knight; [m.] Michael Brian White, July 27, 1991; [ed.] Heritage Hills High School, Danville Area Community College, Eastern Illinois University; [occ.] Child Care Director, YWCA Bloomington, IL; [memb.] School Age Child Care Network; [hon.] Honors and Presidents List; [pers.] I let my heart guide my writing in poetry and stories.; [a.] Bloomington, IL

WHITE, LAURA S.
[pen.] Bunki; [b.] November 30, 1968, Boynton Beach, FL; [p.] Vernice White; [ch.] Rebecka V. Maignan; [ed.] Boca Raton Community High South Technical Education Center; [occ.] Nursing Assistant; [memb.] West side Baptist Church Boynton Beach; [hon.] Drama Club in H.S. Junior Achievement H.S. American Red Cross Middle School Vocal Ensemble H.S. Agriculture H.S. (entitled Future Farmers of America); [oth. writ.] Write for the fun of it; [pers.] There are many things happening in our world today so I just focus on one specific thing and apply on paper, and the outcome is terrific.; [a.] Delray Beach, FL

WHITE, LISA
[b.] July 1, 1975, Philadelphia, PA; [p.] Edith White and John White; [ed.] John W. Hallhan High School, Rowan College of New Jersey; [pers.] Close the hate in your eyes and open the love in your heart, this is the key to a better tomorrow. The future starts with us, we can make the difference today. Life your life the way that brings happiness to others.; [a.] Philadelphia, PA

WHITE, ROBERTA KIMBERLY
[b.] March 2, 1972, Halifax, Nova Scotia, Canada; [p.] Clarence White, Judy Gaudet; [ed.] Diploma in registered nursing (Canadore College, North Bay, ON, Canada); [occ.] Registered Nurse - North Bay Psychiatric Hospital; [oth. writ.] Many poems of varying lengths and short and long stories; [pers.] Writing has always held a special place in my heart and I am over-joyed to be able to share that part of myself with many more.; [a.] North Bay Ontario, Canada

WHITEHEAD, TERRANCE TYREE
[pen.] Terrance Tyree Whitehead; [b.] January 19, 1977, Baltimore, MD; [p.] Ronald Harris and Jacqueline Whitehead; [ed.] High School, Gilman School College, University of Pennsylvania; [memb.] NAACP, varsity Track and Field; [hon.] Oxford Poetry Award; [oth. writ.] Several poems published in local magazines; [pers.] When a man is born a poet, the law says he must die a poet.; [a.] Baltimore, MD

WHITNEY, PATRICIA J.
[b.] March 15, 1942, Chicago, IL; [ed.] BA - Mundelein College - Chgo, IL. MBA - Rosary College - (Health Care Admin) MA - Concordia College (Gerontology); [occ.] Hospice Coordinator; [memb.] International Federation on Ageing; [oth. writ.] "The Spiritual Dimension in Hospice Care

with the Elderly" (Presented at the Second Global Conference on Ageing - International Federation on Ageing - Jerusalem September 1995); [pers.] The Spirit which enters our bodies nurtures us from the moment of birth until the moment of death. The length of one's life is irrelevant.; [a.] Forest Park, IL

WHITTIER, JASON R.
[b.] September 12, 1970, Saint Croix Falls, WI; [p.] David and Roberta Whittier; [m.] Tiffany L. Whittier, April 20, 1991; [ch.] Brittany; [ed.] Taylors Falls High, MN, Lakewood Community College MN; [occ.] Environmental Services; [memb.] Ducks Unlimited; [pers.] Writing poetry for me is a release. A way to make something intangible into something tangible. Such as thoughts, feelings and emotions. With poetry I can finally touch these things; [a.] Saint Croix Falls, WI

WHITTINGTON, ALLEN M.
[b.] August 28, 1968, Chicago, IL; [p.] Allen M. Whittington, Patricia Whittington; [m.] Yolanda Whittington, November 24, 1971; [ch.] Leon Nathaniel; [ed.] Victor Lawson Elementary School, Richard T. Crane High School; [occ.] Artist, Writer; [memb.] New Rising Sun M.B. Church; [oth. writ.] Several poems, articles for the Pontiac Newsletter; [pers.] My poetry is greatly influenced by my love for my family and my devotion to God.; [a.] Chicago, IL

WHYTE, WILLIAM J. H.
[b.] January 29, 1958, Toronto, Ontario, Canada; [p.] Gilbert Whyte, Lahja Whyte; [m.] Kathleen Whyte, July 5, 1986; [ch.] Natasha Elaine, Krystyn Leigh, and Jesse William; [ed.] Danforth Tech., Ryerson University; [occ.] Owner/Operator of a Maintenance Company; [memb.] County Town Singers Whitby Ont. I sing 1st Tenor; [hon.] Thomas Foster Memorial Award for service to others Elementary School and also the French Award in Junior High; [oth. writ.] Various songs and poems all unpublished at this time; [pers.] I use writing as a way of venting my frustrations and emotions! I am greatly influenced by world events ranging from Hunger to Happiness!; [a.] Whitby Ontario, Canada

WIGGINS, CYNTHIA
[b.] June 13, 1926, Graves County, KY; [p.] Brown and Pearl Mc Pherson; [m.] James Harold Wiggins, August 16, 1941; [ch.] James Richard and Gary Paul Wiggins; [ed.] High School Graduate and some college; [occ.] Songwriter, music producer for Janice and Jenson Gream (Country Singers); [memb.] Gospel Music Association in Nashville, Tennessee and member of Christian Country music in Nashville. Member of church of Christ in Mayfield, Kentucky; [hon.] The pleasure of hearing and seeing my songs being sung; [oth. writ.] Former columnist for three newspapers and two magazines; [pers.] I continue to write articles, stories, songs, videos and to make the world a more gentle place because I have been given the talents to use the written word for people to read and enjoy.; [a.] Mayfield, KY

WIGGLESWORTH, DENYSE P.
[b.] February 7, 1965, Toronto, Canada; [p.] Charles Wigglesworth, Eileen Rix; [ed.] West Hill Colle-giate, R.H. King, Centennial College; [occ.] Child and Youth Worker; [oth. writ.] First submission, first publication, have a collection of over 30 unpublished

poems and several short stories; [pers.] I put pen to paper and a whole other world opens up to me. A world of wonder, passion and fulfillment. It's like no other place I have ever been, its a place you never want to leave.; [a.] Whitby Ontario, Canada

WIGNARAJAH, PUSHPAM
[b.] Sri Lanka; [p.] Abraham and Alexandria Sebastian; [m.] Benjamin Wignarajah, May 31, 1961; [ch.] Roy, Roshnie and Roshan; [ed.] Higher Education Holy Family Convent Ilavalai, Jaffna Sri Lanka; [occ.] House wife; [memb.] Women's Welfare Association, Jaffna 1960-1964; [hon.] Recipient of several awards for English Literature in High School; [oth. writ.] Several poetries and two short stories published in local newspapers in Sri Lanka; [pers.] Witnessing certain events made me write the first story 'Dual Tomb' which brought fame especially from ladies. This made me to continue to put out feelings and emotions of human in writing.; [a.] Scarborough Ontario, Canada

WILBANKS, JAMES PATRICK
[b.] July 25, 1968, Ottumwa, IA; [p.] Austin D. and Patricia A. Wilbanks; [ed.] Ottumwa High School, Ottumwa, IA, Diploma, West Valley College, Saratoga, CA, Associate of Arts, U.C. Riverside, Riverside, CA, University of Northern Iowa, Cedar Falls, IA, Bachelor of Arts; [occ.] I am a Sales Banker at Firstar Bank Iowa, N.A. (Des Moines); [memb.] St. Augustin's Church in Des Moines, Iowa; [hon.] Certificate of Achievement, Nick Bollettieri Tennis Academy, 1993, University of Northern Iowa Dean's List, Spring 1991, University of Northern Iowa Panther Academic Award, Spring 1990, #2 National Doubles ranking, Division II, 1989, All-American Collegiate Tennis Honors, 1988 and 1989, West Valley College Honor's Graduate Spring 1988, California Junior College State Team Champion, 1987, California Junior College State Single's Champion 1987, Ottumwa High School State Single's Champion, 1985, All-American High School Tennis honors, 1986, All-American High School Tennis honors (Honorable Mention), 1985; [oth. writ.] "Precious Moments" is my first work to be published; [pers.] I like to remember the special people of my life.; [a.] West Des Moines, IA

WILBORN, ELLA L.
[pen.] Elli; [b.] December 29, 1957, Kankakee, IL; [p.] Huly and Delma Wilborn; [m.] Deceased; [ch.] Christopher D. Sheldon; [ed.] GED, CNA; [occ.] CNA; [oth. writ.] Poems in the American Poetry Anthology; [pers.] I listen a lot to what people are saying and the expressions on their faces. To tell the stories of love and or sorrow they have faced; [a.] Port Richey, FL

WILEY, K.
[pen.] Kathryn; [b.] August 26, 1949, Renfrewshire, Scotland; [p.] George and Nancy Harper; [ch.] Leah; [ed.] Churchill High School Winnipeg, Manitoba Canada; [occ.] Tutor (Adults) Mother and Home Maker; [memb.] Post Polio Network Manitoba, Inc. (Media Representative), Waverley Fellowship Baptist Church, Literary Partners of Manitoba, Winnipeg Volunteer Reading Aides; [oth. writ.] Poems and articles published in local newspapers, periodicals and monthly professional publications. Poems also read on local radio station. Poems date back to 1966! Work complete but unpublished: 1

(Fiction) Novel 2 short stories 1 Biography 36 Romance Card Verses; [pers.] My greatest joy in life is encouraging others, making them laugh, and leaving them with hope of a greater future.; [a.] Winnipeg Manitoba, Canada

WILEY, LEAH KAREN
[b.] April 11, 1959, Atlanta; [p.] Ronald and Jean Johnson; [ch.] Tony Michael and Kevin Blake; [ed.] H.S. Diploma - College - Atl. Tech; [occ.] Writer; [hon.] Nat'l Library if Poetry; [oth. writ.] Published Believing, You'll Never Even Notice, Winner Take All, Wings of Restoration; [pers.] May your days be poetry and chance your nights forever enhanced!; [a.] Riverdale, GA

WILLIAMS JR., BENTLEY N.
[pen.] Willie B. (Army); [b.] April 23, 1970, Kingston, Jamaica; [p.] Mr. and Mrs. Bentley H. Williams; [ed.] Plantation High, Plantation, FL. Broward community College, current, McFatter Vocational Technical School, Studying Nursing; [occ.] Customer Service/Sales at Luria's US Army Reservist; [memb.] Christian Life Center, Church, International Club, Veteran of Operation Desert Shield/Storm; [hon.] Army Achievement Medal, Army Commendation Medal, Meritorious Service During Operation Desert Shield/Storm; [oth. writ.] A Soldier's Eyes, End of An Era. Published in P'an Ku, The Literary Magazine at Broward Community College enclosed is a copy of A Soldier's Eyes for your reading pleasure; [pers.] Life is a paradox and its answers intriguing, yet among the many pathways to choose, one stands out. It's plain and rugged, but its end is fulfilling, and the rewards worth the journey. There's an invisible hand in all things, and its source is obvious, something beyond ourselves, our emotions, feelings, intellect, philosophies or religions. It's the hand of love, in the face of colors, cultures, and all things, it's the hand of God and there's but one.; [a.] Lauderhill, FL

WILLIAMS, DAWN M.
[b.] December 13, 1963, Troy, NY; [p.] Luisa Smith; [m.] Ken Williams, February 25, 1992; [ch.] Meagan Jane Williams; [ed.] Hillsborough High, Tampa College; [occ.] Artist/Housewife; [pers.] I am grateful for being blessed with this opportunity, and dedicate this poem to my mother. I love you mom!; [a.] Atlanta, GA

WILLIAMS III, HARRY E.
[b.] May 29, 1974, Oakland, CA; [ed.] Dauphin County Technical School Harrisburg Area Community College Computer Learning Network; [occ.] Weis Markets Hummelstown PA, Fourth Man (in charge of the store); [hon.] 1993 senior of the year award for the Scientific Data Processing Shop; [pers.] I want to say thank you to all my friends at Weis and CLN.; [a.] Middletown, PA

WILLIAMS, HECTOR J.
[b.] June 24, 1960, Lafayette; [p.] Rene Williams Sr., Thelma Sam Williams; [m.] Sarah L. Bernard Williams, June 27, 1987; [ch.] Toni Andrea Williams, Trent R. Williams; [ed.] Lafayette Senior High North Western University (Nacitoche); [occ.] Fire Fighter Lafayette Fire Dept. Fire Engineer; [memb.] LA Senate Campaign Committee Art Council Emmitte; [hon.] National Literary Award Outstanding Young Writer; [oth. writ.] Article

published in local newspaper. Poems published in monthly publications, series of children books due for publication in Spring 97; [pers.] The true essence of writing is the ability to transform life as we know it, onto paper and into the minds of all who read the words for true gratification; [a.] Lafayette, LA

WILLIAMS, JACQULIN D.
[pen.] Jacque'leen Delorey; [b.] December 6, 1959, Montgomery, AL; [p.] Willie Paul Williams and Mary Williams; [m.] George Williams II, August 7, 1982; [ch.] Aaron, Anjanae, Amanda Williams; [ed.] Wayne County College; [occ.] Medical Biller; [memb.] Golden Gate Baptist Church; [hon.] Dean's List; [oth. writ.] Poetic Manuscript and other writings; [pers.] I write straight from the heart, intensely inspired by life experiences and the effects of daily surroundings.; [a.] Detroit, MI

WILLIAMS, JASON ALAN
[b.] December 5, 1981, Morganton, NC; [p.] Darrell and Susan Williams; [ed.] Liberty Middle School 8th Grade; [occ.] Student; [memb.] Missionary Ridge Baptist Church; [pers.] No matter what happens strive to do your best, and never give up.; [a.] Morganton, NC

WILLIAMS, KELLY
[b.] May 24, 1976, Seattle; [p.] Daniel and Hollyann Williams; [ed.] 94 High School Graduate 2 year AA at High Tech Institute for CAD Drafting; [occ.] Drafter at an Architectural Firm in Seattle; [hon.] 1st entry of any work, wrote this poem when I was 17 year old; [pers.] Live life to the fullest for one day it will be your day to die.

WILLIAMS, MARY K.
[b.] April 25, 1953, Humboldt, TN; [p.] John Knox and Wilma Dixon Knox; [m.] Aubrey H. Williams Jr., March 30, 1972; [ch.] Virginia, Elaine, James, John; [ed.] Peabody High, Bethel College, University of Tennessee Jackson State Community College; [occ.] Retired; [memb.] Plateau writers Club of Clumberland county, Tennessee; [oth. writ.] A lifetime of essays, Poems, stories and other oddities; [pers.] Having grown up on a small farm in Tennessee during the great depression and World War II, my Philosophy is simple: Make the Best of it.; [a.] Fairfield Glade, TN

WILLIAMS, STEVEN R.
[b.] May 17, 1959, Lockney, TX; [p.] Dean and Jonell Williams; [m.] Cathy M. Williams, October 15, 1994; [ch.] Amanda Marie and Stephanie Anne Williams; [ed.] B.S. Electronic Engineering; [occ.] Sr. Design Engineer; [hon.] Dean's Honor List; [oth. writ.] Several writings not yet published. "Having You Near" published with The National Library of Poetry; [pers.] "Thoughts of You" is dedicated to Constance L. Jones, who was my inspiration for most of my writings.; [a.] Summerville, SC

WILLOUGHBY, DALE
[b.] May 14, 1917, So. Dixon, Dakota; [p.] Craig and Elizabeth Willoughby; [m.] Alberta Mae Reid, January 11, 1942; [ch.] Janet Marie, Nancy Lee; [ed.] Whittier Union H. S., CA, Long Beach State College CA; [occ.] Retired Captain, U.S. Marine Corps; [memb.] Academy of Model Aeronautics, Leader member, League of Silent Flight Founder, International Miniature Aircraft Assn. Founding

sponsor, American Air Museum Duxford England, Founding member; [hon.] World Record Holder FAI class F3B 33-R/C Glider - Speed in a straight line - Two occasions 1967 and 1969, meritorious service, A MA/Recomended for Ama Hall of Fame by Norwegian Aero Klubb Oslo Norway; [oth. writ.] Published "The Zephyr", 1965-68 Model Gliding Media, Business Editor, Real Estate/Construction Military Editor/Investigative Reporter Guam Tribune 1986-1990/Channel Chatter Editor, Flying Models Magazine; [pers.] The words to this poem are also lyrics to the instrumental The Home Coming by Hagood Hardy, given to me by inspiration of the Holy Spirit while on Guam in 1987; [a.] Anza, CA

WILLS, BETH SUDDUTH
[b.] Roxton, Lamar County, TX; [p.] Ernest abd Vola Sudduth; [m.] Raymond R. Wills; [ch.] Brenda and Marsha; [ed.] Southern Music School Baylor University; [occ.] Lancer, Lyricist, Poet; [memb.] Fine Arts Press, Nasco Writers International Society of Poets, Tyler Videos, First Baptist Church, Mt. Pleasant, Democratic National Committee; [hon.] Awards: Essays and poetry - Tyler High School and Baylor University Music videos - ABC - Tyler, Texas Golden Poet Award 1988 and 1990; [oth. writ.] Book-non-fiction-1968, Book of Poetry-published 1986, Essay published 1990, Poems and articles published in various magazines and newspapers; [pers.] When I sit at my faithful typewriter, I feel the presence of a silent partner, a Higher Power that tugs at my sleeve and guides me beyond my normal savvy. When I am apt to pause and stammer I am led into elegant speech.; [a.] Mount Pleasant, TX

WILSON, JANICE E.
[b.] April 18, 1956, York, PA; [p.] Mrs. Constance Smith, Mr. James Wilson (Deceased); [ch.] JaLayda L. Wilson; [ed.] William Penn Sr. High (York, PA), Washington School for Secretaries (Wash., DC); [memb.] Leadership York, York PA Crispus Attucks Community Center, York; [hon.] Certificate of Accomplishment - from Crispus Attucks Award - from Leadership York Program; [oth. writ.] Currently, no poems have ever been submitted. I write for a hobby; [pers.] Coming from within my heart, I see and feel the struggles and accomplishments as we, the children, men and women journey on this earth.; [a.] York, PA

WILSON, LOUISE PINION
[pen.] Louise Pinion Wilson; [b.] January 2, 1913, Berry Fayette Co, AL; [p.] James and Ruth Pinion; [m.] Deceased, October 29, 1972; [ch.] Dr Wm Lewis Wilson step son; [ed.] BS Degree in Elementary Education Jacksonville University, studied Art at Norton Art Gallery Palm Beach Fla., Birmingham Museum Art; [occ.] Retired teacher from Alabama and New Jersey; [memb.] Sovereign Colonial Society Americans of Royal Descent, DAR, National Society of Colonial Dames XVII Century, West Alabama Art Association, Magna Charta Damas, Ala. Council for the Arts and Humanities 1964-1968; [hon.] Creator of Forest Fantasy Hats, Contestant on To Tell The Truth December 6, 1965 Guest on The Ralph Enemy Show December 12, 1995 Art Gallery named for Louise Pinion Wilson Gallery Tuscaloosa; [oth. writ.] Family History "Pinion Pinyon Families Pains Perils and Pleasures", "Fashionable Forest Hat Designs", working on a new

book "Life Can Be Funny Without Money"; [pers.] Many people have urged me to write a story of my life, reared in a small, town creating hats was my delight for many years showing them to many convention group, even doing a hat showing on an Eastern Airline Plane in the Atlanta Airport owning forestland in North Alabama

WISECUP, STEPHANIE A.
[pen.] Stephanie Wisecup; [b.] May 5, 1971, Chattanooga, TN; [p.] Charles and Laurie Moore; [m.] James K. Wisecup, May 7, 1994; [ed.] High School graduate; [occ.] Operation Intern for Duport Chemicals; [oth. writ.] None yet in publication; [pers.] Look at life with an open mind, an honest heart and let the Lord lead wherever you go.; [a.] Harrison, TN

WOLFORD, LAURAL J.
[b.] October 28, 1926, Flint, MI; [p.] Rexford and Helen Youmans; [m.] Elmer A. Wolford, May 5, 1945; [ch.] Gary, Donnie, Lonnie, Kevin, Paul; [ed.] Northern High School, Flint, MI, studied "Writing for Children" and teaching the retarded. Attended various seminars and conferences in Christian Education SS Teacher/minister's wife.; [occ.] Homemaker; [memb.] College Park Church of God (affiliated Anderson, IN), Women of the Church of God (missions); [hon.] Betty Crocker Homemaker of the Week; [oth. writ.] Unpublished Childrens Booklets. A frequent speaker at banquets, prayer retreats, missionary meetings, and church meetings.; [pers.] Helping the unfortunate has a high priority with me. I try to live the best I can and not worry, because the world could end and I would have worried for nothing. In a nut shell, "Try to please God". That's what this life is all about!; [a.] Ocala, FL

WOLL, DAVID E.
[b.] May 1, 1944, Pana, IL; [p.] Earl and Blanche Woll; [m.] Margaret, July 23, 1933; [ch.] Rodney, Ryan, Theresa, Janet, Keri; [ed.] Edwardsville High School 1962; [occ.] HVAC Estimator; [memb.] National Rifle Association; [pers.] Life is a reflection of one's projections.; [a.] Edwardsville, IL

WONCH, DOUGLAS A.
[b.] February 1, 1946, Brantford, Ontario, Canada; [p.] Isabel, Les Wonch; [ch.] David, Robert, Russell; [ed.] Graham Bell School Brantford Collegiate Institute; [occ.] Unemployed; [oth. writ.] Plaques, memoriums, business cards etc.; [pers.] Like to write sentimental sayings that cope with people's feelings. I hope to lift peoples spirits in their times of sorrow or depending on the situation.; [a.] Brantford Ontario, Canada

WOOD JR., JOHN WELDON
[p.] October 30, 1943, New London, CT; [m.] John Wood and Rosalie; [ch.] Trisha Louise Wood, November 18, 1995; [occ.] Flagman; [pers.] My poems tell stories. They are a kin to folk tales, and in the oral tradition of that genre, they are meant to be read aloud.; [a.] Enumclaw, WA

WOOD JR., MORTON
[b.] February 20, 1923, Washington, DC; [p.] Morton Wood and Edith Hall Wood; [m.] Ella Boothe Wood, April 30, 1954; [ed.] B.S. Mechanical Engineering, Virginia Polytechnic Institute, Class of

1994; [occ.] (Retired) Consulting Engineer in private practice; [memb.] Tau Beta Pi (Engineering Honorary Scholarship Society), Phi Kappa Phi (Engineer Honorary scholarship Society), Retired Officers Ass., S.P.E.B.S.Q.S.A. (Barrershop Quartet Society), 66th Inf. Div. Vet. Assn, 1st Cav. Div. Vet. Ass., K.W.Y.A., Military order of the Purple Heart, Virginia Tech Alumni Assn.; [oth. writ.] Memories (mostly WW II and Korean War experiences as a rifle platoon leader), Limericks, Poems honoring (or roasting) Friend's retirements, Anniversaries, etc.; [pers.] I write poems just for the fun of rhyming and making light of events, occasionally to invent and tell a story.; [a.] Bethesda, MD

WOOD, WANDA L.
[b.] July 12, 1938, Dardanelle, AR; [p.] Wesley and Olean Stocks; [m.] Robert G. Wood, January 10, 1958; [ch.] Robert Gray Jr., Rhonda Sue Wood; [ed.] 11 years in Carden Bottom 1 year White Hall High School, Pine Bluffark, where I graduated I meet my spouse; [occ.] National Center, Toxicological, Research; [hon.] Nominated into International Society of Poets; [oth. writ.] I wrote my first poem about Dad. I also write, religious nature, two poems published; [pers.] I would like to thank you your staff, you made this year exciting for me - hope for further excitement thanks a lot; [a.] Pine Bluff, AR

WOODWARD, FRANCES WHITE
[pen.] Frances White Woodward; [b.] May 27, 1921, Winnipeg, Manitoba, Canada; [p.] Fred and Lilian Fox; [m.] Thomas B. Woodward, 1986; [ch.] John Frederick, Edward Wm, Frank Jr., Kay; [ed.] Salvation Army Seminary, Evenotti, Evans High, Mercer University; [occ.] Retired; [memb.] Bus and Proj. Women's Club, Auditor Society, member Salvation Army Auxiliary; [hon.] Certificate for completion of Mortgage Banking courses, winner of Church public speaking award for regional area, Music award in Sr. year of Memphis High School; [oth. writ.] Other poems, 50 in all are compiled in a book entitled "Diamonds In The Rough" (copy writes pending). None have been published or submitted to other publications.; [pers.] My joy is showing appreciation of family and friends thru' poetry. A few poems are on specific subjects such as "O Canada" regarding Hockey. Others relate to spiritual life.; [a.] Charlotte, NC

WOODWORTH, KIM CRAIG
[b.] October 5, 1957; [p.] John Craig and Geraldine Walden; [m.] Bill Woodworth, December 6, 1986; [ed.] Wichita State University Campus High School; [occ.] Area Advertising Sales Director, Comcast Cable; [oth. writ.] Numerous poems and children stories; [pers.] This poem was written for my sisters who are very special to me.

WOOTEN, ZELDIA MEGGS
[b.] August 15, 1945, Natchez, MS; [p.] Joseph and Zellie Middleton; [m.] Kenneth W. Meggs, March 23, 1978; [ch.] Luke, Joe, Bryan, John, Mark, Matt, Margerie, Chuck; [ed.] Buras High School, 7th grade '59 Marshall Ar. Received G.E.D. 1990; [occ.] Homemaker; [hon.] Got recognition from Pres. Regan for poem written for him. Wrote a lot of poems for influential friends and ladies for whom I have worked in their homes as professional maid.; [oth. writ.] Poems sent to Robert Frost, The Ark, Also 2 songs to my credit, "Crazy Heart" '83 "Night

Of Love" '93; [pers.] I try to treat people the way I wish to be treated. I have been greatly influenced by my teachers in my early years of school. Most especially Mrs. Browning, in 3rd grad.; [a.] Marshall, AR

WORD, ANN
[b.] April 12, 1942; [p.] Cleo Word and Rethel Word; [ch.] Denise Page; [ed.] Crispus Attucks High School undergraduate courses at Iupui and Butler Universities of Indianapolis, Indiana; [occ.] Computer Programmer Defense Finance and Analyst at Accounting Service Indianapolis Center; [memb.] Zion Tabernacle Apostolic Church, Metropolitan Opera Guild, Fine Arts Society of Indianapolis; [hon.] National Honor Society of Secondary Schools, was second in High School graduation class; [oth. writ.] Many poems, none published; [a.] Indianapolis, IN

WOZNIAK, TRICIA
[b.] August 3, 1977, Chicago, IL; [p.] Suzanne and Eugene (Father Deceased); [ed.] Queen of the Universe (Grammer School) Lourdes High School, Main study is Art; [memb.] Member of a theater group called Struggles Dinner Playhouse, High School - R.E.A.C.H (2 years) S.E.A. (Students Environmentally Aware) (1 year); [hon.] Honor Roll studen, Boulevard Art Center - Bronze (2nd year Art), Boulevard Art Center - Gold 3rd year Art); [pers.] Life is a test to see if we could handle the pressure. Treat others the way you would like to be treated.; [a.] Chicago, IL

WRIGHT, ALLEN
[pen.] Allen Wright; [b.] October 27, 1940, Toronto, Canada; [p.] Amie and Joseph Wright (Deceased); [m.] Sanoha, October 10, 1992; [ch.] Peter, Susan, Cheryl Nancy and Aaron; [ed.] New Toronto High School Humber College, Toronto Medical Institute; [occ.] Minister and Bishop Sanctuary of Prophets Interfatt Temple; [memb.] Martin Luther King Jr. Assn Gayati Parawar (Hindu) Brahma Kumaris Peace Organ. Apostolic Church of Canada; [hon.] Ordained as a Minister 1992 - raised to Bishop of the Apostolic Church 1995 - went to India 1994 - private audience with the Dali Lama; [oth. writ.] Publish newsletter Sage and Seer, was a columnist for a local newspaper for five years written articles about World Peace that have been published Worldwide including Trinidad and India; [pers.] As a minister of God, I try through the aid of meditation write messages that will inspire people to change their lives for the better. This world needs healing and I intend to help; [a.] Etobicoke Ontario, Canada

WRIGHT, DAVE L.
[b.] January 13, 1962, Regina; [p.] Irwin and Joyce Wright; [ed.] Third year University level classes majoring in Psychology and English; [occ.] Slipper and Receiver for Dutch Industries Ltd.; [oth. writ.] Several manuscripts of poetry. Nothing published; [pers.] All of my poetry comes from the heart, personal feelings and experience. It is my pleasure to finally share some of this with other people.; [a.] Regina Saskatchewan, Canada

WRIGHT, JACQUELINE
[b.] May 14, 1958, Groton, MA; [ed.] Littleton High School, MA Solari School of Hair Design, MA Henri School of Hair Design, MA, Fisher Junior College, Fitchburg State College, MA; [memb.] Fitchburg State College Alumni; [pers.] My poems consist

mostly of the understanding of both life and love.; [a.] Lenoir City, TN

WRIGHT, LOUISE
[b.] August 31, 1931, Morgantown, WV; [p.] George and Helen Wood; [ch.] William Kenneth Miller and Sherry Wright; [ed.] Morgantown High and two years of business college at the Stenotype Institute, Washington, D.C.; [occ.] Secretary (Retired from Capitol Hill after more than 39 years); [memb.] Charter member of the National Museum of Women in the Arts; [hon.] Editor's Choice Award, National Library of Poetry, 1994 and 1995. Semi-finalist winner of the 1995 International Society of Poets Symposium and Convention Poetry Contest; [oth. writ.] Five poems published or accepted for publication in various National Library of Poetry anthologies; [pers.] Enjoy writing about people and nature, creating "poetry pictures" and analogies I strive to inspire.; [a.] Alexandria, VA

WRIGHT, SUSAN
[b.] December 24, 1947, San Francisco, CA; [ch.] Stefani; [memb.] Fictioneers, Literacy Coalition; [pers.] Be Bold: Embrace your life!; [a.] Lynnwood, WA

WURTZ, MARIE B.
[b.] November 22, 1944, Newport News, VA; [p.] Alton Burns and Susie C. Burns; [m.] Richard R. Wurtz Jr., September 15, 1967; [ch.] Susan Marie, Trina Denise; [ed.] Newport News High School; [occ.] Administrative/ Engineering Assistant; [a.] Harvest, AL

WYMER, JENNIFER RENEE
[b.] June 30, 1980, Kansas City, KS; [p.] Melissa and Bob McKillip; [occ.] Sophomore in High School; [oth. writ.] About 130 other poems dealing with all types of emotions and feelings; [pers.] I began to write after my father passed away when I was 12. Since my mother already had died when I was 2 - my poems helped release a lot of pain and confusion. With the help of my aunt and uncle I have begun to live my life and come out of sadness and the darkness. I'd like to thank them for helping me through it all.; [a.] Hopewell, NJ

WYNN, M. CAROLYN KIGHT
[pen.] Carolyn Wynn; [b.] March 11, 1931, Warren, AR; [p.] Mildred Alice Abshire Kight and William Henry Kight; [ch.] Rebecca Gay Smith, Richard Scott Wynn; [ed.] To 10th grade of High School; [occ.] Retired from: Gen Corp polymer Corp. Xerox Assembly OP; [memb.] Ohio Vally Writers Guild; [hon.] National Library of Poetry (3rd Place winner - 95); [oth. writ.] Several poems and sonnets, unpublished. Poem "When I Was Ten" published in "National Library of Poetry" anthology, 3rd place, book, "Between The Raindrops"; [pers.] Most all of my poetry is centered on family, which has always meant the most to me. I'm an artists in acrylics, of which I've sold a number of but my work is mostly for family and pleasure.; [a.] Newburgh, IN

YANTIN, LINDA
[b.] June 9, 1951, Newark, NJ; [p.] John Wallace, Loretta Hartmann; [m.] Victor L. Yantin, May 21, 1977; [ch.] Victor T. Yantin Jr.; [ed.] West Orange High; [occ.] House wife, (Domestic Goddess); [memb.] Community united methodist Church; [oth. writ.] Currently a poem is in the process of being published, in a book by the community united

methodist churches.; [pers.] I write for the purpose of promoting Love, peace and Good-will in man kind. I have been in spired, and a devoted reader,of the poems by poet Helen Steiner Rice.; [a.] Kenilworth, NJ

YEMM, MR. TRICE D.
[b.] April 20, 1928, Carlinville, IL; [p.] Leon and Frances Yemm; [m.] Widowed; [ch.] Four; [ed.] After High School I took evening classes to pursue my special interests; [occ.] Retired from Government Service; [oth. writ.] I have had many poems published in newspapers and magazines and I have a book of poems published under the title "Sightings"; [pers.] I am primarily a seeker. My poems on the whole reflect a search into the Realm Of The Human Mystique.; [a.] Springfield, IL

YOHAM, STEPHEN
[b.] August 31, 1956, Miami, FL; [p.] Jerome Albert, Anne Mary; [m.] Judith Marie, August 30, 1986; [oth. writ.] Two fiction novels titled: "Three Weeks Under", and "The Taking Of Kate Weber"; [a.] Miami, FL

YOUNG, KENNETH DEAN
[b.] July 30, 1953, Bonham, TX; [p.] Charles C. and Johnie B. Young; [m.] Carolyn Gravely Young, March 1, 1978; [ch.] Mandy Lynn Young; [ed.] Titusville High, Brevard Jr Collge Santa Fe Community College; [occ.] Retired; [oth. writ.] Several Unpublished poems currently working of First Book; [pers.] When I write I try to do so with lots of feeling. If you can bring my poems to picture in your mind, then I feel I've accomplished more than just words.; [a.] Rocky Mount, VA

YOUNG, MARY
[pen.] Nil; [b.] October 31, 1940, Perth, Ontario, Canada; [p.] Harvey Babcock, Kathleen Babcock; [m.] Douglas, February 14, 1959; [ch.] Catherine, Barry, Sharon, David; [ed.] High School graduate; [occ.] Nanny to two children I have been a caregiver for many years; [oth. writ.] Other poems to numerous to mention one other was published in the Kingston Whig Standard - Kingston Ontario Canada in the 70's; [pers.] I owe my talent to the Glory of God and give Him all the thanks. My writings all have been about circumstances in people's lives. My Weddings - grandchildren, friends etc. They have touched the lives of many; [a.] Thurlow Ontario, Canada

YOUNG, MAURICE WELDON
[b.] September 20, 1948, Flint, MI; [p.] Ervin and Christeen Young; [ch.] Maurice Jr., Marisha, Amber Young; [ed.] Flint Northeastern High, St Paul Technical College, C.S. Mott College; [occ.] Machinist - 3M Minnesota, Minine and Manufactur-ing; [hon.] Honorable discharge - United States Air Force, 1994 Minnesota State Fair Talent Competi-tion Winner, The Bachelors Vocal Group; [pers.] I wish everyone A life filled with love, family and fun! I have been greatly influenced by the poetry of Walter Benton.; [a.] Eagan, MN

YOUNG, PAUL MARK
[pen.] Paul Mark Young; [b.] December 8, 1957, Washington, MO; [p.] William C. Young, Geneva E. Young; [m.] Renie Hoffman, June 2, 1996; [occ.] Ski Tech during the winter, live Sound Engineer in Summer; [pers.] I am influenced by my upbringing, and the people in my life, especially my parents, Grandparents and wish to thank Rennie for her patience, understanding, and love.; [a.] Thornton, CO

YOZT, ARTHUR KENNETH
[pen.] A. Kenneth and Ken Yozt; [b.] October 25, 1910, Punxsutawney, PA; [p.] Aaron Kingsley and Blande States Yozt; [m.] Widower; [ch.] Gertolen Anne and Allan Kinsley Yozt; [ed.] BA and MA, Carnegie Mellon Univ. Ed D, Columbia University; [occ.] Essentially, retired; [memb.] Society, for Italic Handwriting - Portland, Oregon, American Printing History Association, Geological Society of the Oregon Country, Portland Historical Stuetz, Portland Art Museum, American; [hon.] Rock Art Research, Association Callzeaphie Art in Portland Art Museum and private collections, Graduate Follow, Teaching College, Columbia University. Art number of Anrev. Amature, Printing Assoc, and National Amature Publishing Assoc.; [oth. writ.] Poems, Essays, Short Stories, Articles or Travel and Exploration Illustrated "Red Eagle And The Absaroka" cayteu, pub.1960; [pers.] Various Media in graphic expression has been my main operating field, plus teaching Art at College level.; [a.] Portland, OR

ZAKER, KIM
[b.] May 15, 1962, Wyandotte, MI; [p.] Ed and Irene Taylor; [m.] Tom Zaker, July 31, 1992; [ch.] Natalie Nicole; [ed.] Carlson High School DBI Down River - Medical Assisting; [occ.] Medical Assistant and Emergency Room Volunteer; [memb.] American Medical Technologists; [hon.] Certificate of proficiency for maintaining a 98% grade point average at DBI; [oth. writ.] To Grandma published in "Beyond The Stars"; [pers.] Live each day to the fullest, and never take life, love, or friends for granted; [a.] Rockwood, MI

ZALAR, GERTRUDE P.
[pen.] "A girl named Trude"; [b.] February 13, 1921, Juliet, IL; [p.] Matthias and Helen Pisut; [m.] Richard W. Zalar, September 16, 1944; [ch.] Richard W. and Barbara Judy; [ed.] 12 Years - In the Business World; [occ.] Retired - Home maker - Mother and Grandmother; [memb.] Hospital Auxiliaries, School board, Social Club Positions, Philatelist, Artist; [hon.] Commendation as Executive Secretary, Scholastic Recognition, Social Award as "Mother of the Year"; [pers.] Play, smile, think of me Pray for me—Let My name be enjoyed—that House-hold word that is always was. Let it be spoken without an effort without the easy way which you always use put no difference into your tone. Wear no forced air of solemnity or sorrow. Laugh as we always laughed at the little jokes that we enjoyed together.; [a.] Juliet, IL

ZAPPA, WILLIAM D.
[pen.] William D. Zappa; [b.] October 15, 1961, Maywood, CA; [p.] Karl and Geraldine Zappa; [m.] Aldrienne Marie Zappa, February 17, 1992; [ch.] William D. Zappa Jr.; [ed.] High School Grad., Voc. Auto Body and Paint, Also Certified through (C.D.F) as a tree sergeon and Topper; [occ.] Motorcycle Mechanic and Riding Instructor, For Quad Rentals; [hon.] Elementary Art Award's, Also 2 year Art College Scholarship was awarded to me for a free Hand Piece of Art I had drawn a few years ago; [oth. writ.] "At A Loss In Love", "A Chill In The Fall", "Before the Light", "Past Memory's Of A Special Love", "The Key"; [pers.] The Poem I've submitted, is a reflecting look into my Life and past. Being raised in Institution's can change a person's true

personality and way's till they are not even able find themselves again. Some never do I was fortunate rose above to find me!; [a.] Yucca Valley, CA

ZEBRUCK, SARAH
[b.] August 6, 1982, Dundas, Ontario, Canada; [p.] Jim and Kathy Zebruck; [ed.] Currently grade eight; [occ.] Student; [oth. writ.] Story on CANADA published in local newspaper; [pers.] My writing is greatly influenced by the past and I like to show the good and evil in Man, I like to reflect peace. I like to write about things that happen to me and the impact they had.; [a.] Dundas Ontario, Canada

ZEDALIS, JAMES E.
[b.] February 18, 1941, Nashua, NH; [ed.] Maine Maritime Academy; [occ.] Marine Engineer; [a.] Ozona, FL

ZEKUELD, KATHY
[b.] October, 25, 1959, Bowmanville; [p.] Carolyn Sturman, Reg Sturman; [m.] Simon Zekueld, March 14, 1981; [ch.] Michael, Lisa, Rebecca; [ed.] Bowmanville High and Life Experiences; [occ.] Head Cook for Meals on Wheels; [memb.] Kawartha Clover leafs; [oth. writ.] Letters to the editor of local newspaper; [pers.] I write out of a deep love for my family and friends. Music and everyday living greatly influence what I write.; [a.] Lindsay Ontario, Canada

ZIMMEL, VALERIE
[pen.] Valerie Lynn Marie Zimmel; [b.] August 31, 1970, Alberta, Canada; [p.] Terance & Cheryl Zimmel; [ed.] Strome School, Daysland High School and Academic Up-grading at Augustana University College; [occ.] Chambermaid, Meat Cutter, and Farm Hand; [memb.] International Society of Poets; [hon.] Numerous horse show ribbons, a Silver Medal in the 1987 Alberta Summer Games in Field Hockey, Editor's Choice Award and a Poet of Merit.; [oth. writ.] "To The One," in the anthology Journey of the Mind, "Best Friend," in the anthology Best Poems of 1996, "Heartbreak Of Someone So Special," in the anthology Reflections By Moonlight, and "Morning Wake Up Call," in the anthology The Path Not Taken.; [pers.] I believe in writing what comes from deep within. I like to write about things that happen within and around me.; [a.] Strome, Alberta, Canada

ZOFCIN, DENISE
[b.] April 26, 1950, Albany, NY; [p.] Judge John A. DeRonde and Kathleen Deronde; [m.] George Zofcin, December 1, 1973; [ch.] Christa Marie Zofcin; [occ.] Writer, Designer, Artist; [memb.] Carmel Presbyterian Church; [oth. writ.] There is a story, spring, Christa My Swan, The Gift, When I was ten, Grandma, Words, The Surgeon's Hands, Reward, Hope, Christmas, Eulogy For Jacob, Dear Father Whom I Never Knew; [pers.] To hope, To believe, To dream, to understand, to encourage, to give comfort, to seek wisdom, to right a wrong, to make another laugh, to look upon the internal, to look back with no regret, to forget oneself, to love.; [a.] Carmel, CA

ZOLADEK, MARGARET S. GREEN
[pen.] "Margo"; [b.] April 17, 1949, Chester, SC; [p.] Talton and Josephine Sanders; [m.] Stanley B. Zoladek, June 12, 1993; [ch.] Torrey Y. Green and Tanesha J. Green; [ed.] Chester Sr High - Chester,

South Carolina, Johnson Valley Technical Institute -
Hickory, North Carolina, Mitchell Community
College - Statesville, North Carolina, Mitchell
Community College - Statesville, North Carolina
Pennco Tech. - Bristol, Pennyslvania; [occ.] General
Office worker and Light Industrial laborer; [memb.]
Greater Works Ministries, Inc. in Philadelphia,
Pennyslvania, Dance Ministry, Livingwell Lady
Fitness Center and Bally's Fitness Center, St. John
Baptist Church in Statesville, NC; [hon.] A
leadership course certificate Awarded from Dept. of
Agriculture, Statesville, North Carolina; [oth. writ.]
Various other poems which I have not not released to
the public: some songs, a few children's stories and
short stories, and greeting card's verses. I had a
short article published in the journalistic paper at
Catawba Valley Tech in Hickory, North Carolina;
[pers.] I read to learn. I strive my writings to inspire.
I enjoy Maya Angelou's writings, Helen Steiner
Rice, Alice Walker and Norman Vincent Peale and
other various popular authors of novels, poetry and
autobiographies. I love to read the BIBLE also.; [a.]
Bensalem, PA

ZOSH, LILLIAN E.
[pen.] Emery Witt; [b.] February 26, 1924, Wilkes-
Barre, PA; [p.] Florence and John Witt; [m.] Joseph
Zosh (Deceased), December 27, 1942; [ch.] Four;
[ed.] Bachelor Of Science (Biology) Master Of
Education, Ph.D. Counseling Education; [occ.]
Retired; [memb.] National Board For Certified
Counselors, State Of Ohio Counselor - Social
Worker Board, American Counseling Association,
American Health Counseling, American Hypnosis
Board - in D.C.; [pers.] I've always wanted to write
but not sure of my ability. I hope I can improve over
time. This is a beginning!; [a.] Troy, OH

ZUBAIR, HAMEED MALIK
[pen.] Malik and Zuby; [b.] March 6, 1956, Lahore,
Pakistan; [p.] Abdul Hameed, Mumtaz Begum; [m.]
Uzma Zubair, December 12, 1985; [ch.] Zeeshan,
Ummaya, Sommaya; [ed.] Graduate Chemical
Engineer, Metallurgist, Specialization in Non
Destructive Testing from Cambridge (United
Kingdom), Almelo, (Holland); [occ.] CTFL LAB.
Dupont Kingston (Volunteer), Gas Bar Manager;
[memb.] Life Member, Pakistan Inst. Of Chem.
Engrs, Pakistan Inst. Of Metallurgical Engrs.,
Pakistan Institution Of Engrs., Professional Engineer
(Pakistan); [oth writ.] History of Pakistan, Chem.
Engr. In A Fix, Life At Gas Station Fishermen Of
Napanee, Napanee In Winter, A Canadian Forest
Beaver American Indians, Owl, A Piece Of Advice,
Lunch X-Mas, Resolution etc.,; [pers.] The pain,
agony, misery in the last few years has found an
outlet. My life as a poet is only two years. I am a
toddler, so much to do, to grow and grow fast, so
much to write; [a.] Napanee Ontario, Canada

ZUGASTI, ESTEBAN MARIO
[pen.] Mario; [b.] October 2, 1976, Los Angeles, CA;
[p.] Mario and Socorro Zugasti; [ed.] Chula Vista
High School, Freshman in College (Southwestern
Junior college); [occ.] Student; [hon.] Letterted in
tracknfield; [oth. writ.] Several other poems and
poems I've written in Spanish store in my computer
and in my notebook.; [pers.] I'm left handed so?!;
[a.] Chula Vista, CA

Index
of
Poets

Index

Egan, T. Joseph 491
Eichman, Richard 65
Eichor, James 130
Eidbo, Heather 563
Eigenhauser, Carol Ann 461
Eilenberger, Heidi M. 139
Eiler, Dorothea M. 457
Eiring, Karen Marie 587
Ek, Dawn A. 35
Elam, Amanda 157
Elder, Alma Elizabeth 211
Elder, Buck 571
Elek, Alice 648
Elkhalil, Kama! M. 395
Elliott, Brian C. 198
Elliott, Stacey 398
Ellis, Albert D. 286
Ellis, Lynn 171
Elmer, JoLene Joy 646
Elmi, Linda 304
Elmore, Katie 223
Elms, Deanne M. 116
Elpers, Louise 388
Elsbree, Michelle Pecora 315
Elwing 108
Elza, Stacey 82
Ember, Paul 98
Embro, Jimmy 97
Emile, Angelique L. 366
Emmett, Matthew 545
Emmons, Frances 575
Engdahl, April 137
Engebretsen, Amy 205
Englehart, Christina Marie 635
Ennis, Mark Edward 394
Enns, Kimberley 301
Eppler, Suzie 326
Epps, Alma Jean 152
Epps, Marganette 591
Epstein, Marissa 315
Erho, Darlene 101
Erickson, Janet 471
Erickson, Patricia J. 615
Erickson, Sarah Marie 255
Erstine, Emily Mae 191
Ertel, Scott 231
Ervin Jr., Robert C. 396
Esbjerg, Jennifer 264
Esho, Janet 570
Espedido, Joel T. 522
Esposito, Gina 193
Esser, Thomas M. 308
Essex, Derek Charles 432
Estareja, Romulo Habla 480
Etterle, Angie R. 158
Evans, Amber 175
Evans, Bernadine Ayers 576
Evans, Carol 213
Evans, Donald B. 351
Evans, Kristi G. 608
Evans, L. 514
Evans, Lilian 289
Evans, Sara Kirsten 418

Even, Susan E. 495
Everett, Bernadette 141
Evraire, Michael 424

F

Fabrizius, Joanne 268
Fagan, Benjamin P. 437
Fair, Mona 110
Fairhead, Claire 431
Fairman, Ray R. 69
Falcon, Mike 413
Falicki, Sandra 322
Fanucci, Mary 622
Fariss, Sallie T. 396
Farley, Frank F. 43
Farlow, Gary K. 191
Farmer, Inez 189
Farmer, Silas 13
Farnam, Melissa 330
Farnan, Maritza Blandino 481
Farnell, Duane S. 354
Farnsley, Bernice 142
Farr, Diane 273
Farr, Harlon 567
Farrar, R. Sarah 66
Farrell, Ronald P. 46
Faulconer, Julie Elizabeth 456
Fava-McCliman, Florence 121
Fazel, Robin F. 620
Fears, Brenda S. 4
Featheringill, Susan 501
Fechtelkotter, Jodi 212
Fecteau, Mary 240
Federico, Vivienne 328
Fediuk, Doris D. 529
Feece, Dianna 18
Feigelson, Marian 626
Felion, Brian A. 18
Felix, Analisa 29
Felix, Paul A. 508
Feltner, Mary Elaine 554
Felts, Loretta 492
Felty, Kathee M. 504
Fenchak, William J. 60
Fenimore, Russell 232
Fenn, Nathan 619
Fenner, Denise 24
Fenske, Doug 196
Fenter, Caleb 465
Ferguson, Greg 152
Ferguson, Kevin W. 510
Ferguson, Sharon 84
Fernandez, Abby 448
Feroce, Cynthia L. 45
Ferrier, June D. 25
Ferrin, Kevin K. 309
Ferris, Constance M. 141
Ferry, April 190
Fetta, Frank A. 372
Feucht, Eleanora 575
Fiebig, Thelma 522
Fielding, Aileen 144
Fielding, Carol 511

Fields, Geraldine 572
Figueroa, Desiree T. 561
Filip, Angel 472
Findlay, Sandy 513
Fink, Marlene "Molly" 67
Finnegan, Emmett Patrick 521
Fintel, Rhonda 597
Fiorido, Rob 181
Fischer, Joavan 559
Fisher, Abby Rae 92
Fisher, Arran 626
Fisher, Juanita 206
Fisher, Kristy 172
Fisher, Laura W. 180
Fisher, Shirley M. 183
Fister, John William 187
Fitzgerald, Donna Jean 200
FitzGerald, R. Alexander 86
FitzHugh, Emily 200
Fitzpatrick, Catherine Ann 263
Fitzpatrick, Mick 329
Fleetwood, Ina 44
Fleming, Emily 496
Fleming, James R. 162
Flenner III, Louis A. 588
Fletcher, Karen 536
Fletcher, Katie 619
Fletcher, Michele 334
Fletcher, Michelle 173
Fletcher, Ruth 545
Flinkert, Rita 105
Flinn, Kevin W. 655
Florio, Frank J. 131
Florio, Melissa 308
Flower, M. A. 114
Floyd, Barbara K. 124
Floyd, Theresa 256
Floyd-Greenidge, Phyllis 407
Fluker, Stephanie 241
Fodey, Sarah J. 101
Foehr, Sandra 174
Foisey, Russell 216
Follis, Linda 304
Fontenot, Rhonda 636
Foor, Iva L. 574
Forbes, Bryan 176
Force, Amber, Age 14 355
Ford, Andrea Shannon 15
Fordham, R. David 251
Foreman, Patricia 510
Forgacs, Joseph M. 468
Forrest, Dorothy 477
Forsythe, Brian 142
Forte, Marcel 651
Fortin, Renee 56
Fortinberry, Heather 208
Fortkamp, Marian 259
Foss, Marlo Dianne 106
Foster, C. E. 648
Foster, Geoff 174
Foster, Katie 318
Foster, Lisa 279
Foster, Michelle 640

Foston, Donald P. 175
Foucault, Mary 590
Fougere, Lilly R. 531
Fournier, Heather 571
Fowler, Kathryn Phelps 381
Fox, Joyce A. 24
Fox, Sara L. 505
Fox, Starla 64
Fox-Manning, Dee 143
Frady, Adam 202
Fraley, Megan 422
France, Tovah 494
Francis, Barb 266
Francis, Gloria 581
Francis, Marybeth 319
Francis, Phyllis 316
Francisco, Melanye L. 400
Frank, Barbara 190
Frank, Jenny 173
Franklin Jr., Howard E. 436
Franklin, Marcelle 63
Frantz, Rebekah C. 494
Franz, Paula 224
Franzke, Gregory P. 340
Fraser, Cindy 468
Fraser, Frances Gill 306
Frechette, Beth Ann 473
Frederick, Vera 506
Freeborn, Barbara 344
Freeman, John D. 472
French, Carole 564
Frenza, Christina M. 175
Fret, Jeff 430
Frewin, Barbara 521
Frey, Melissa A. 628
Friedel, Hannah 20
Friedlander Jr., Mark 654
Friedman, Dorothy 140
Frinier, Catherine 442
Frink, Jennifer 213
Frisco, Marie 481
Fritsch, Jaime 339
Fritz, Karen 61
Frizzell, Jennifer 441
Froelich, Nicole J. 319
Froystadvag, Gloria 282
Fruehwald, Linda A. 324
Fudge, Nancy D. 85
Fulcher, Mary T. 224
Fulda, Joseph S. 643
Fulkerson, Galena 197
Fuller, Betty N. 647
Fuller, Emma T. W. S. 16
Fuller, Maxcine 332
Fuller, Sara 239
Fulmer, Elizabeth J. 47
Fung, Kristin Ann 536
Funk, Herbert W. 475
Funk, Loraine O. 505
Fuqua, Ruth M. 505
Fur-tick, Mar-cia 393
Furco, Randy 67
Furner, Christopher 142

Niemann, Raymond E.   498
Nightingale, Christine   423
Nikolenko, Tony   597
Nine, Robin   67
Niquette, Donna   558
Noble, Bill   3
Noble, Hetty F.   454
Noblefranca Jr., Eusebio C.   341
Nolen, Russell D.   228
Noles, Ernest   36
Nolte, Marie   617
Nooft, Ginger Laurin   559
Noone, Kate   383
Nordli, Kurt   305
Nordman, Lillian   608
Norem, Caitlin   580
Norris, Debra E.   158
Norris, Elizabeth Pelaez   132
Norris, Felecia A.   42
North, Margaret   185
Norton, Bill   470
Norwood, Eileen Corey   558
Norwood, Gloria   200
Nouvion, Michele J.   293
Novak, Alice   452
Novak, Amy   655
Novak, Terry J.   593
Novielli-Moro, Josie   541
Novikova, Julia   305
Nowak, Kinga   275
Nowlin, Charles R.   205
Nuckols, Peggy L.   309
Nuzum, Jenifer   433
Nwoko, E. J.   513
Nyers, Amelia   211
Nystrom, Nicole Rosemary   266
Nzerue, Chike   467

O

Obacz, Catherine E.   105
O'Brien, Elizabeth   178
O'Brien, Lisa Thomas   618
Ochoa, Christina R.   438
O'Connor, Richard Scott   601
Odegaard, Doug   361
Odhiambo, Francis Peter   91
O'Donnell, John   573
O'Dowd, Allen W.   132
Odutayo, Lekan Sola   105
O'Flaherty, John V.   362
Ognibene, Maerushka Danko   380
O'Hara, Erin   552
Ohlhausen, Theo   290
Okamura, Jeannette   378
O'Keefe, John C.   37
Okell, Marietta   295
Okolo, Francis Anat   649
Okonkwo, Ifejika   567
O'Krafka, Mark   553
O'Latta, Joan   125
Oldham, William E.   498
O'Leary, Thomas J.   507
Oles, Florinda   636

Oley, Antoinette S.   651
Olive, Lisa   315
Oliver, Katrina   329
Oliver, Lorne   167
Oliver, Robin L.   408
Oliverius, Carol   436
Olivier, Bruce   529
Olmsted, Kathleen I.   178
Olp, Kathy   49
Olson, Erika   192
Olson, Melissa   229
Ondricek, Nadia   513
O'Neill, CoLetta M.   13
O'Neill, Kaitlyn   107
Ontman, Kevin   384
Orchard, Dana Elizabeth   472
O'Reilly-Baker, Celeste   540
Orem, Yvonne C.   399
Ortiz-Lamadrid, Ruben   229
Orvis, Sarah   47
Osborn, C. L.   83
Osborn, Lois   416
Osborne, Belinda B.   652
Osborne, Joseph D.   131
Osborne, Tami   309
Osenga, Raymond R.   415
Oster, Donald K.   202
Ostheimer, Helen Bazet   372
Ostrzycki, Becky   338
Oswald, Harold G.   555
Otoshi, Yoshiyuki   408
Ott, William C.   265
Otto, Opal   289
Ouellette, Lois A.   383
Ouellette, Wanda   535
Ousley, Susan   608
Overfield, Jack   190
Overholt, Lavonda G.   485
Overton, Randy   310
Overton, Robert Harold   219
Oveson, Oleta   244
Owen, Alisa Lynne   340
Owens, Danielle Rene   359
Owens, Gloria   448
Ower, Heather Nicole   434
Owings, Iva P.   129
Owles, Toby J.   175
Owusu-Aduening, Paul   502
Oxman, Nancy G.   230

P

Pack, Amanda   627
Pack, Jeremy A.   470
Pack, Velma S.   79
Page, Elaine   292
Pagel, Genevieve Hopf   464
Paget, Harry   439
Painter, Jennifer L.   201
Palazzo, Bernice H.   370
Pali   409
Pallante Berriman, Kimberly R.   504
Palm, Pat   83
Palmer, Charlotte   42

Palmer, Maureen   551
Palmer, Scott M.   626
Palmer, Tina Marie   653
Pampain, Carla S.   215
Pandolfo, Harriet S.   149
Pang, Elaina   270
Pangelinan, Lynn   395
Pankiw, Susanna   431
Pantano, Daniel   47
Pantor, Andrea   639
Paoli, John   456
Papp, Zoltan Alex   110
Parachuk, Tahnya   186
Parent, Sylvia   106
Park, Sarah   331
Parker, Cheryl M.   536
Parker, Christina   364
Parker, George C.   37
Parker, Kim   255
Parker, Maxine L.   89
Parker, Mazell   311
Parker, Richard L.   75
Parker, Thelma Jo   260
Parks, Donald W.   15
Paro, Carie L.   40
Parr, Dorothy J.   182
Parr, Eleanor   544
Parr, Katherine D.   386
Parrish, Melissa   80
Parrish, Niola   598
Parry, Marilyn H.   604
Parsons, Mary Lou   496
Parsons, Shirley D.   633
Pasha, Afsana L.   170
Pasini, Jacqueline   648
Patano, Bertie Currington   161
Pate, Joyce Kathleen   433
Patel, Ashwinbhai D.   121
Patenaude, Renee   99
Paterson, Frank T.   165
Patrick, LaWander D.   260
Patricoff, Henry S.   451
Patryk, Kimberly   627
Patterson, Carl   578
Patterson, Darryl   178
Patterson Jr., Gordon D.   363
Patterson, Louise   498
Patterson, Marsha   621
Patterson, Ronal   633
Pattison-Church, DeAnza   462
Paul, Anita   269
Paul, Jennifer   93
Paul, Josef   274
Paul, Mary-Frazier   413
Paulsen, Greg   101
Paulson, Diane   126
Payne, Maya   242
Payton, Angela   156
Peacock, Mary Rachael   585
Pearce, Ronnie   73
Pearl, Elizabeth   98
Pearllie, Rodger   426
Pearson, Debra K.   337

Pearson, Theresa M.   422
Peck, Carolyn F.   149
Peddell, Laura   291
Pedersen, Heidi L.   348
Pederson, Lynne   516
Peebles, Laura   45
Peeler, Keith D.   614
Peer, C. R.   619
Pelletier, Janice   511
Pellikka, Barbara A.   533
Peloquin, Ron   597
Pemberton, Dora D.   559
Pena, Annie   570
Pendleton, Anthony   33
Pendleton, Corrine   563
Peng, Alice   202
Penland, Patrick R.   323
Penn, Melissa   396
Penner, Shirley   519
Pennetta, Mario   278
Penney, Helen   428
Penney-Flynn, Sarah   423
Penrod, Doris   8
Penrod, MaryAnn   594
Penrose, Belle Harris   135
Pentecost, Colandra Lynn   451
Pentecost, Eileen   26
Penuel, Debbie   138
Perez, Hilda P.   467
Perez, Janet   7
Perez, Robert   249
Perkins, Jennifer L.   31
Perkins, Judith M.   371
Perla, Julia M.   459
Perri, Angela M.   355
Perron, Joslyn   194
Persaud, Maria   310
Person, Gwindale   559
Peter, Elizabeth   195
Peters, Douglas   268
Peters, Jackie   576
Peters, Margaret Herman   558
Peters, Melissa   224
Peterson, Amy   456
Peterson, Dorothy F.   468
Peterson, Fannie   210
Peterson, Howard L.   129
Peterson, Jaclyn E.   360
Peterson, Lee W.   254
Peterson, Lela Melanie   414
Peterson, Lisa A.   506
Peterson, Martin Edwin   487
Peterson, Roni Lyn   87
Peterson, Royal F.   333
Peterson, Samantha   509
Petrany, Clare   427
Petrunich, Carol Rose   373
Pettigrew, Constance C.   42
Pettus, Deborah Kirk   572
Phelps, Deborah   448
Phelyne, Max   628
Philipp, Tonia Ann   503
Philipsen, Heidi Elizabeth   563

Schonfeld, Worthy 420
Schott, Merle 652
Schrader, Penny M. 289
Schrammel, Sherry 500
Schreiber, Lana 385
Schroder, Jason Clay 38
Schroeder, LaVerne 317
Schuler, C. Scott 631
Schulman, Bruce R. 571
Schulte, Tanya D. 322
Schultz, Beverly K. 207
Schultz, Christine 159
Schultz, Diane Kay 348
Schultz, Joyce Lawhorn 361
Schultz, Melissa M. 479
Schumacher, Kris 406
Schummer, Paul M. 482
Schurter, Irene Gillard 111
Schussler, Lisa 274
Schutt, Barry 160
Schuttelhofer, Tania L. 620
Schutzenhofer, Mickey 75
Schwabe, Velma 268
Schwan, Shelly 97
Schwartz, Al 121
Schwartz, Jill 348
Schwartz, Manuel 505
Schwartz, Tanya Alicia 103
Schwartzbeck, Yvonne 242
Scialdone, Barbara Wicke 211
Scott, Beth 212
Scott, Melissa 218
Scott, Rise 219
Scott, Shilynda 503
Scoville, Diana L. 463
Scullion, E. 334
Scully, Lindsay 416
Seabolt, Yvette 493
Searcy, Cameron J. 134
Searles, Jane 99
Seay, Travis L. 77
Sebastian 387
Sebens, Mabel 231
Seese, Edward V. 123
Segedin, Elizabeth 368
Segerhammar, Brita 572
Seiders, Amy 346
Seifer, Dr. Henry H. 627
Seifert, Melissa 186
Sell, Margaret R. 548
Sellick, Silvana 120
Selvakumar, Sivanny 305
Seneviratna, Peter 270
Senour, Tracy 490
Serrano-Estrada, Jorge Luis 276
Serson, Judy 180
Setka, Cindy M. 634
Settle, Sherry 605
Severson, Sherry 248
Sewlal, Jo-Anne Nina 112
Shafer, Rosemarie 420
Shaffer, Hazel F. 343
Shah, Dhiraj 556

Shaikh, Nazima Z. 177
Shakir, Amber R. 643
Shane, Marilyn Sue 69
Shank, Opal Williams 492
Shank, Sara A. 55
Shanline, John 28
Shapiro, George J. 651
Sharp, David A. 148
Sharpe, Adonis V. 3
Sharpe, Bessie H. 131
Shatwell, Jeffery 362
Shaver, Jennifer 190
Shaw, Jacklyn L. 477
Shaw, David 580
Shaw, Krista 602
Shaw, Violet 300
Sheehan, Christy L. 351
Sheehan, Kerri 590
Sheerahamad, Sheharazade 491
Sheffield, Ami 36
Sheffler, Danielle 206
Sheldon, Kaye 301
Shelton, Jenny 367
Shelton Jr., Ivory 365
Shelton, Mary L. 326
Sherma, Arlene 376
Sherren, Sandra M. 108
Shields, Ann P. 568
Shields, Michelle L. 508
Shields, Nellie E. 248
Shields-Herzstein, Sandra L. 218
Shifler, Hubert I. 198
Shiles, Donald 581
Shimada, Junko 22
Shine, Juanita 555
Shireman, Ruth 86
Shirey, Kelly A. 484
Shiskin, Margaret 95
Shoemake, Thomas R. 610
Shoemaker, Andrew 573
Shoemaker, Anna K. 129
Shoemaker, Mary Rose 609
Shoptaw, David W. 126
Shores, Ruth P. 117
Shuda, Kristina 88
Shuflita, Roseann 512
Shull, Jason 155
Shultz, Libby 322
Shumake, Anita D. 339
Shun, Dave 473
Shupe, Robin 90
Shutts, Esha Lee 14
Sica, Nicholas A. 626
Siddoo, Kore 111
Siegel, Elise L. 443
Sigety, Robert 482
Sigl, Karen 608
Sigmon, Joy Renee 132
Signor, Jason 451
Sigurdson, G. Inga 269
Sikora, Ewa 656
Silberman, Sidney 53
Silva, Robert 490

Silverman, Danielle 456
Simmons, Renea A. 239
Simmons Sr., William J. 60
Simmons, William Albert 292
Simon, Mary Anne 69
Simoneau, Monique 650
Simonian, Jeannine 161
Simons, Ray 181
Simonson, Maria Day 392
Simpson, Don 100
Simpson, Gale 215
Simpson, J. Damien 484
Simpson, Jim 434
Sims, J. Boswell 633
Simulis, Roberta R. 310
Sinclair, Carolyn 283
Sinclair, Paula 184
Sinisi, James Patrick 209
Sinnaeve, Colleen A. 442
Sipos, Miklos 308
Sippel, Ruth S. 323
Siravo, Benjamin W. 214
Siska, Emily 213
Sisson, E. Frank 622
Skalski, Linda 623
Skeffington, Chanz 202
Skelhorn, Linda 304
Skinner, Gary L. 356
Skinner, Robert T. 89
Skjold, Annemarie 431
Sklenar, Linda 325
Skoien, Anthony 153
Slade, Evelyn 564
Slade, Heather 428
Slane, Liz 503
Slas, D. 343
Slaughter, Cheryl Ann 43
Slifka, Angela 530
Slobodin, Diane 157
Slobogian, Jenifer 121
Slobogian, Joyce 108
Slonaker, Jessica 357
Slone, Krietha L. 490
Slovick, Paula Lynn 312
Sluss, Connie 352
Slutsky, Jordan 36
Smale, Ernest 271
Small, John 285
Smallwood, Susia 592
Smaragdis, Nancy T. 620
Smeeks, Inez 581
Smialek, Lisa P. 318
Smiggart, Arlena 654
Smith, Adelina 430
Smith, Amber R. 154
Smith, Amy Lynn 25
Smith, Arlo J. 567
Smith, Audrey 111
Smith, Barbara Knight 337
Smith, Betty W. 555
Smith, Brenda G. 353
Smith, Cheryl L. 656
Smith, D. Sank 74

Smith, Diane 129
Smith, Dianne 101
Smith, Elsie Joye 164
Smith, Eveline 449
Smith, Fatima 450
Smith, Gail D. 290
Smith, Grace E. 357
Smith, Hilda C. S. 103
Smith, Ingrid 214
Smith, Ivan L. 441
Smith, Jaqueline E. 269
Smith, Joan R. 352
Smith, John D. 465
Smith, Larry N. 383
Smith, Lenora J. 628
Smith, Liticia M. 307
Smith, Lori 236
Smith, Mary 262
Smith, Mary L. 386
Smith, Maureen 113
Smith, Omega 384
Smith, Pat 601
Smith, Pearl E. 498
Smith, R. Dale 391
Smith, Sandra L. 644
Smith, Sandy 394
Smith, Sara 48
Smith, Selene 235
Smith, Sharon 385
Smith, Tara 649
Smith, Wayne A. 607
Smith, Wilfrid J. 53
Smithson, Jack 154
Smolski, Kim M. 287
Smyth, Mildred Judd 499
Sneath, Patricia 428
Snedden, Faithe C. 144
Sneed, Mary S. 506
Snell, Mattie A. 401
Snow, Matthew 496
Snukis, Stacy 611
Snyder, Doris 153
Snyder, Hilary 135
Snyder, Marie 312
Snyder, Susan E. 616
Solari, Andrea M. 568
Solivo, Erika 100
Solomon, Letitia M. 601
Somers, Gerald A. 162
Sommer, Susan L. W. 254
Sorrell, Christina C. 576
Sosa, Deborah A. 576
Soto, Bernie 345
Southard-Resa, Melodie L. 62
Southerland, Lisa 490
Sowards, Lisa 600
Spachner, Sharon 392
Spangler, Gerry 556
Spearman, Cela Beckey 462
Speicher, Kenneth 413
Spence-Thomas, Audrey 301
Spencer, Ginny 189
Spencer, Margie A. 622

Wells, Vicki L.   404
Welsch, Lorraine Marie   418
Welsh, George W.   562
Wemhoff, A.   218
Wendel, Cassandra N.   446
Wendel, Ronald   402
Wender, Naomi   610
Wentz, Lorraine   619
Wertz, Seth   187
Wesselink, Barbara   430
West, Bertha   572
West, Elaine D.   355
West, Frances   558
West, Heather   566
West, Judy Rogers   369
West, Marie   385
West, Mei   328
West, Neil   235
West, Rusty   256
West, Sarah   590
Weste, Kelly A.   166
Western, Jack   108
Western, Leonard J.   602
Wettlaufer, Helen M.   437
Wevers, Lisa   117
Weyrauch, Dorothy   162
Whalen, Leslie   229
Whalen, Rosalind   280
Whaley, A. H.   320
Whaley, Corey W.   358
Wharton-Ali, Mariam   56
Wheeler, Betty   571
Wheeler, Dawn   39
Wheeler, Dennis   558
Wheeler, Kari   248
Wheeler, Kelley-Ann   392
Whitacre, Gina A.   472
Whitbread, Jennifer   430
White, David Michael   462
White, Faline A.   449
White, Glenna S.   32
White, Gwynneth   21
White, Jessie H.   467
White, Kimberly   401
White, Laura S.   319
White, Lisa   499
White, Muriel   269
White, Roberta K.   522
Whitehead, Terrance Tyree   325
Whiting, William O.   504
Whitney, Danene   197
Whitney, Patricia J.   234
Whittaker, Thomas D.   234
Whittier, Jason   469
Whitworth, Warren N.   53
Whyte, William J.   546
Wickert, Susan   116
Wickman, Kim   603
Wicks, Andrew D.   563
Widawski, Eva   34
Wienecke, Melanie   638
Wiest, Sandy A.   490
Wiggins, Cynthia   444

Wigglesworth, Denyse   424
Wignarajah, Pushpam   545
Wilbanks, James Patrick   366
Wilborn, Ella L.   465
Wilcox, Debra   150
Wilcox Jr., Richard E.   330
Wilcox, Steven   202
Wilde, Keren   221
Wilder, Jean E.   528
Wiley, Branden   463
Wiley, Kathryn   116
Wiley, Leah Karen   404
Wilford, Noemey   504
Wilkerson, Patricia   626
Wilkie, Floris M.   179
Wilkins, Benjamin   151
Willard, Cindy   112
Williams, Amber Lynn   461
Williams, Bettie J.   446
Williams, Betty J.   201
Williams, Beverly J.   462
Williams, Charlotte M.   345
Williams, Dawn M.   194
Williams, Diane   208
Williams, Donna Leigh   445
Williams, Donna M.   476
Williams, Ethelene B.   44
Williams, Exie M.   440
Williams, Hector J.   138
Williams III, Harry E.   451
Williams, Jacqulin Deloris   458
Williams, Jason   562
Williams, Jeff   36
Williams Jr., Bentley N.   208
Williams Jr., Tracy L. C.   651
Williams, Karen   243
Williams, Kelly   87, 554
Williams, Lil   164
Williams, Mary Elizabeth   69
Williams, Mary K.   260
Williams, Shana   588
Williams, Sonja Lynn   617
Williams, Steven R.   313
Williamson, Bryce L.   152
Williamson, Omegia   58
Willis, Duke   201
Willman, Sandy   601
Willoughby, Dale   199
Wills, Beth Sudduth   347
Wilson, Amber   204
Wilson, Anna   40
Wilson, Audrey   436
Wilson, Beth Anne   638
Wilson, Betsy   440
Wilson, Debbie   435
Wilson, Dorothy G.   579
Wilson, Janice E.   441
Wilson, Louise Pinion   488
Wilson, Robert W.   615
Wilson, Ruth Ellen   287
Wilson, Tabitha   599
Wilson, Walter James   588
Wilson, Zak   397

Wilton, Sharon F.   651
Wiltse, Danielle   574
Wimer, Lisa   508
Winders, Shelley J.   381
Winkler, Paul Scott   491
Winland, Jennifer Pearl   196
Winnan, Anne   30
Winstanley, Sherrie   425
Winton, Ruby Anna   53
Wintz, Robin H.   605
Wintz, Roxie   240
Wiora, Jennie   363, 398
Wisdom, Etta   23
Wisecup, Stephanie   613
Withenack, Mary   242
Witt, Jody Anne   160
Wnek, Amber   564
Woeppel, Fred R.   511
Wolfinger-Brown, Jeanne   154
Wolford, Laural J.   387
Wolfram, Christine   294
Woll, David E.   335
Wonch, Doug A.   174
Wood, April   560
Wood, James   112
Wood Jr., John Weldon   475
Wood Jr., Morton   417
Wood, Pamela Ann   585
Wood, Robert Lee   88
Wood, Sharon Dianne   388
Wood, Wanda   57
Woode, Melanie   294
Woodley, Vivian I.   479
Woodmansee, Leann   419
Woodroffe, Sherryann   244
Woodruff, Jamey   205
Woods, J. Justin   409
Woods, Kellye   542
Woodward, Frances White   569
Woodworth, Dale A.   439
Word, Ann S.   575
Worth, Susanne C.   113
Wozniak, Lynn   69
Wozniak, Tricia   654
Wraye, Bronton   293
Wrenfro, Nikki   487
Wright, Allen   109
Wright, Amberley   365
Wright, Dave L.   107
Wright, Jacqueline Beth   561
Wright, Kim   656
Wright, Louise   222
Wright, Susan   499
Wright, Thurman   246
Wrisner, Shannon   307
Wurst, Barry W.   127
Wurtz, Marie B.   598
Wyatt, Sarah   479
Wykes, Annabel M.   429
Wymer, Jennifer   444
Wynn, Carolyn   335
Wynn, Randy   496

X

Xu, Andy   545

Y

Yacusiw, Billy M.   165
Yakichuk, Curtis   541
Yakichuk, Rhoda   108
Yantin, Linda   493
Yanuario, Walfrido   616
Yates, Tammi L.   618
Yemm, Trice D.   500
Yeo, Ruth-Anne   528
Yetman, Kerry   431
Yoham, Stephen   81
Yost, A. Kenneth   651
Young, Anthony Arthur   12
Young, Betty Henry   203
Young, Bill   32
Young, Dorothy W.   355
Young, Janet   91
Young, Juanita   148
Young, Kenneth Dean   484
Young, L. M.   525
Young, Linda M.   380
Young, Mark   505
Young, Mary   517
Young, Maurice Weldon   491
Young, Melissa Carol   419
Young, Paul M.   644
Young, Robert   588
Ypma, Ron   430

Z

Zabielinski, Barry   128
Zakem, Ken   424
Zaker, Kim   79
Zanoviak, William J.   602
Zappa, William D.   318
Zebruck, Sarah   541
Zedalis, J. E.   255
Zehren, John H.   557
Zeigler, Ralph   311
Zekveld, Kathy   185
Zell, H. Peter   582
Ziemer, Melissa M.   311
Ziga, Maryann   234
Zika, Susan Annette   397
Zilkie, Heidi   109
Zimmel,
    Valerie Lynn Marie   164
Zimmerer, John G.   446
Zimmerman, Mae M.   380
Zofcin, Denise   573
Zontanos, Manolis   539
Zornes, Theta J.   485
Zosh, Lillian   655
Zugasti, Mario E.   509
Zurba, Elizabeth   546
Zwahr, Carol Kleiber   568
Zwinkels, Hendricus P.   511